Readable.

Reliable.

Resourceful.

WORLD HISTORY

PERSPECTIVES ON THE PAST

The one to compare all others to.

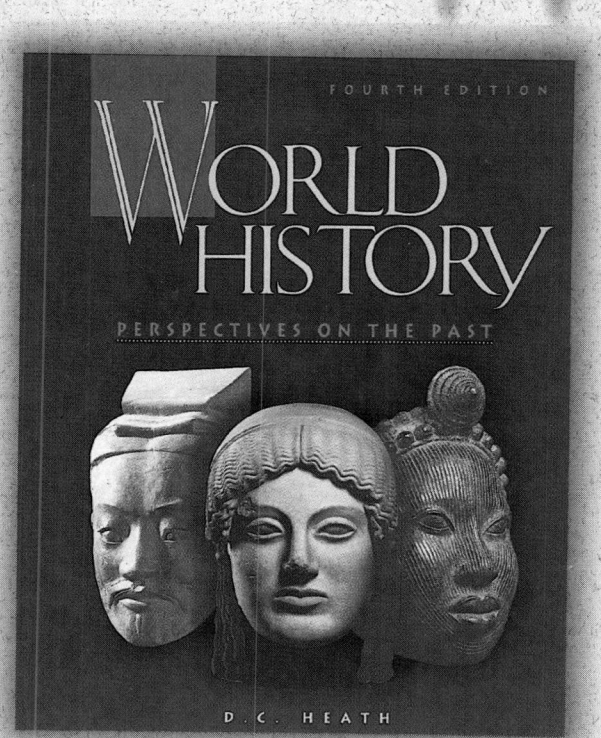

Larry S. Krieger

Kenneth Neill

Steven L. Jantzen

Jim R.L. Coulon
Contributing Writer,
Teacher's Edition

Copyright ©1994 by D.C. Heath and Company.
All rights reserved. No part of this publication may be reproduced by any means, electronic or mechanical, including photocopy, recording, or any information or storage retrieval system, without permission in writing from the publisher.

Published simultaneously in Canada
Printed in the United States of America
International Standard Book Number: 0-669-30852-8
1 2 3 4 5 6 7 8 9 – RRD – 99 98 97 96 95 94 93

Resourceful teaching options.

Teachers count on WORLD HISTORY: Perspectives on the Past not only for its interesting, accurate content and lively writing style—but also for its current geographic focus and teaching flexibility.

Readability.
Reliability.
Resourcefulness.

That's why more teachers choose WORLD HISTORY: Perspectives on the Past.

▶ **Teacher's Edition,** with a wraparound format and interleafed chapter planners, helps you organize lessons and address individual learning styles.

▶ **Teacher's Resource Package** contains reliable support in a convenient file case. Teaching resources are organized into four sections:

Geography
 Geography Skills Worksheets
 Outline Maps

Reinforcement
 Vocabulary Worksheets
 Independent Practice
  Worksheets
 Basic Skills Worksheets
 Reteaching Worksheets
 Making Connections
  Chapter Summaries

Enrichment
 Critical Thinking Worksheets
 Voices from the Past,
  Pupil Edition and
  Teacher's Annotated Edition
 History/Literature Readings/
  Worksheets
 Hot Off the Press Readings

Assessment
 Assessment Book with
  Section Quizzes
  Chapter/Unit Tests
  Alternate Chapter/Unit Tests

Geography

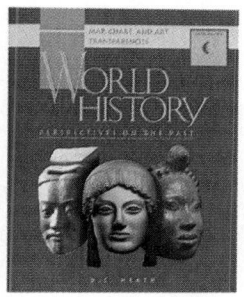

▶ **Map, Chart, and Art Overhead Transparencies** binder contains 150 full-color diagrams of maps, concept charts, and art from the text for group instruction.

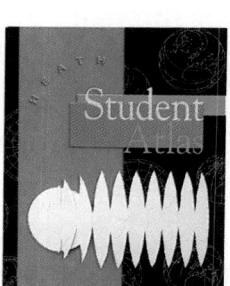

▶ **Student Atlas** includes updated maps to reflect recent world geopolitical changes. Along with new maps of the former Soviet Union and Eastern Europe, this valuable reference tool also includes physical and political maps, a gazetteer, and comparison charts on countries' area, cities, population, and language.

Reinforcement

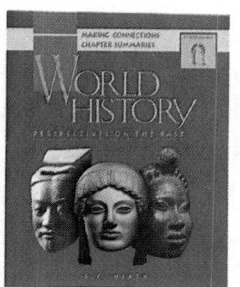

▶ **Making Connections**, a study guide, condenses each text chapter into mini-chapters, providing flexibility in topic coverage. Includes objectives, detailed chapter summaries, chapter questions, and a special feature, "Connecting Past and Present." Spanish edition available. (Included in Teacher's Resource Package.)

Enrichment

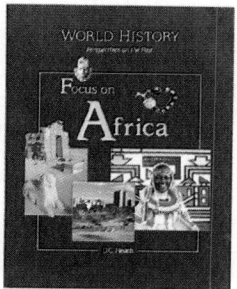

NEW! ▶ **Focus on Africa**, a 176-page companion volume, chronicles the history of Africa beginning with its ancient history and concluding with a discussion of modern-day Africa and the continent's struggle for democracy. Teacher's Edition available.

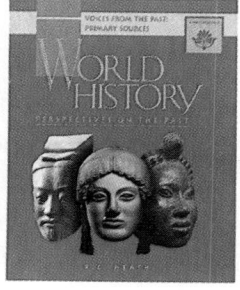

▶ **Voices from the Past Primary Sources** offers primary-source readings for every lesson. (Teacher's Annotated Edition is available. Also included in Teacher's Resource Package.)

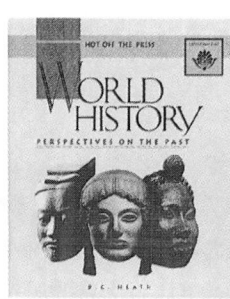

▶ **Hot Off the Press**—an annual supplement containing in-depth coverage of the major world events from the previous year—Earth Summit in Rio de Janeiro, events in the former Soviet Union, Yugoslavia, and the Middle East. (Automatically sent to adopters at no charge. Included in Teacher's Resource Package.)

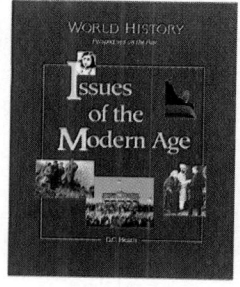

▶ **Issues of the Modern Age** extends the text with close examination of major turning points in world history that have shaped the world today.

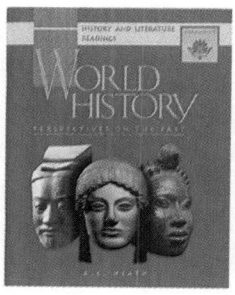

▶ **History and Literature** readings encourage students' study of history with powerful literary excerpts by famous authors such as George Bernard Shaw, William Shakespeare, Pearl Buck. (Included in Teacher's Resource Package.)

Assessment

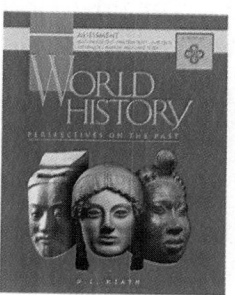

▶ **Assessment Book** provides Section Quizzes, Chapter/Unit Tests, and Alternate Chapter/Unit Tests for thorough evaluation of students' understanding of world history. (Included in Teacher's Resource Package.)

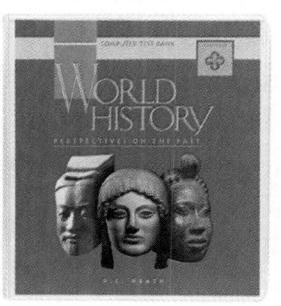

▶ **Computer Test Bank** with Teacher's Guide creates test questions and generates graphics such as maps, graphs, and time lines—helping you customize tests to meet individual needs. Available for use with Apple, Macintosh, and IBM compatible computers.

A note from the author— and fellow teacher.

On Monday, August 19, 1991, the people of Moscow awoke thinking that they were about to begin a routine day. But history had a surprise for them. When they turned on their televisions and radios, they heard shocking news: a "State Committee" had seized power and declared a state of emergency. The sound of tanks rumbling through the streets of Moscow confirmed that a coup was taking place.

History was tapping the citizens of Moscow on the shoulder, demanding that they make a fateful decision. Would the people obey authority? Or would they defy the coup and defend their newly won freedoms?

The citizens of Moscow are not alone in being tapped on the shoulder by history. Martin Luther was summoned to the Diet of Worms and asked to defend his revolutionary views on church doctrine. Winston Churchill was called upon to defend England during the darkest days of World War II. And history tapped Rosa Parks on the shoulder as she sat on a segregated bus in Montgomery, Alabama.

Martin Luther, Winston Churchill, and Rosa Parks all had courage—they defended their values. But historic challenges are not limited to past generations. Our students will soon graduate and face the challenge of living at the edge of the 21st Century. The questions for us as World History teachers are: Will our students be ready when history taps *them* on the shoulder? Will they have a keen sense of ethical literacy and the moral courage that goes with it? Will they have sound critical thinking skills to make informed decisions? And will they have a clear understanding of democratic values to put into practice as they become citizens in their local communities and states?

These questions are your goals as World History teachers. They were my goals as I wrote this text. **World History: Perspectives on the Past** is filled with stories of dramatic events and fascinating people. But it is more than a collection of good stories. It also gives your students the opportunity to gain a perspective on the past that will enable them to proudly and confidently answer the call when history taps them on the shoulder—when they need to think, weigh their options, and exercise their rights and responsibilities as citizens.

Larry S. Krieger

WORLD HISTORY

PERSPECTIVES ON THE PAST

AUTHORS

Larry S. Krieger

Social studies supervisor in Edison, New Jersey; coauthor of social studies textbooks and teaching materials; current world history teacher

Kenneth Neill

Author of textbooks on nineteenth- and twentieth-century world history; former history teacher; publisher/editor of *Memphis Magazine*, Memphis, Tennessee

Steven L. Jantzen

Author of works on history, government, and classroom-tested teaching strategies; editor of social studies texts; former high-school teacher of government and history

Senior Content Consultant

Dr. Lloyd Swenson
Professor of History
University of Houston
Houston, Texas

D.C. Heath and Company
Lexington, Massachusetts   Toronto, Ontario

Teacher Consultants

Candy Anderson
Willowridge High School
Fort Bend, South Dakota

Lolene Blake
Longmeadow High School
Longmeadow, Massachusetts

Spiro Cora
Wingfield High School
Jackson, Mississippi

John Dare
John Marshall Senior High School
Cleveland, Ohio

Sue Dillard
Shepton High School
Plano, Texas

Michael J. Harkins
Community Unit School,
District 300
Dundee, Illinois

James Lange
Bell High School
Los Angeles, California

Tasha Lohman
Bloomingdale Senior High School
Valrico, Florida

Eileen Murray
St. Edmunds School
Tonawanda, New York

John Petretich
Boardman High School
Boardman, Ohio

George Rislov
Shepton High School
Plano, Texas

Clint Rouse
Volusia County Schools
Daytona Beach, Florida

Ken Sacerdote
Manderin High School
Jacksonville, Florida

Content Consultants

Charmarie Jenkins Blaisdell Associate Professor of History, Northeastern University, Boston Massachusetts; specialist in European social and intellectual history; past president of the Sixteenth Century Studies Council

Joan Erdman Professor of Anthropology, Columbia College, Chicago, Illinois; Research Associate, Committee of Southern Asian Studies, University of Chicago

J. Rufus Fears Professor of Classics and Chair of the Department of Classical Studies, Boston University, Boston, Massachusetts

Dr. Eric Meikle Research Associate, Institute of Human Origins, Berkeley, California

Dr. Edward Reynolds Professor of History, University of California at San Diego; Faculty Director, Education Abroad Program, University of California at San Diego

Thomas Spear Professor of African History, Chair of African and Middle Eastern Studies, Williams College, Williamstown, Massachusetts

Leslie M. Swartz Specialist in Chinese studies and director of Harvard East Asian Outreach Program, Boston, Massachusetts

Dr. Lloyd Swenson Professor of History, University of Houston, Houston, Texas

Charles T. Wood Fellow, Medieval Academy of America; Daniel Webster Professor of History, Dartmouth College, Hanover, New Hampshire; former member of the executive committees of both the New Hampshire School Boards Association and the New Hampshire Joint Educational Council

Development Staff: Christopher R. Johnson, Marian Cain, Robin Herr, Bonnie Chayes Yousefian, Mary Hunter, Donna Lee Porter, Carole Frohlich

Cover Photographs: Terracotta head of a warrior (from the tomb of Shi Huang-ti; Chinese, 221–210 B.C.); marble head of the statue of a maiden (from the Acropolis; Greek, c. 500 B.C.); bronze head of an Oni (from Nigeria; Ife, c. 110–1400)

Copyright © 1994 by D.C. Heath and Company

All rights reserved. No part of this publication may be reproduced or transmitted in any form by any means, electronic or mechanical, including photocopy, recording, or any information storage or retrieval system, without permission in writing from the publisher.

Published simultaneously in Canada

Printed in the United States of America

International Standard Book Number 0-669-30850-1

1 2 3 4 5 6 7 8 9 10-RRD-99 98 97 96 95 94 93

Contents

South America

x

Concept Charts

Tables, Graphs, and Diagrams

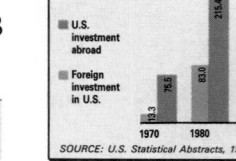

United States Investment Abroad/
Foreign Investment in United States
(in billions of dollars)
■ U.S. investment abroad
■ Foreign investment in U.S.
1970 1980 1983 1984 1985
SOURCE: U.S. Statistical Abstracts, 1987

oices from the Past

Voices from Our Time

DAILY LIFE and Economics in Daily Life

CITY TOURS

Focus on Geography

Skills Handbook

To the Teacher

Purpose of the Teacher's Edition
This Teacher's Edition is designed to help you create outstanding lessons. The writers—Larry Krieger, a social studies supervisor and the senior author of the text *World History: Perspectives on the Past,* and Jim Coulon, a curriculum writer and high school history teacher—have provided fresh ideas aimed at bringing a sense of discovery and joy to world history classes along with clear plans to integrate the wealth of materials that make up the complete package of *World History: Perspectives on the Past.*

In writing strategies and other teaching suggestions, the authors asked themselves, "How will this idea work in classrooms with today's students?" By focusing on this question, they developed a set of strategies for teaching world history that is both forward looking and practical. At the beginning of each chapter are interleaf pages containing teaching strategies that have been used, tested, or scrutinized by active professionals in classrooms much like your own.

You and your students will find *World History: Perspectives on the Past* rich in narrative content, reproductions of art and architecture, primary source excerpts and quotations, anecdotes, and good stories. The teaching strategies and the sidebar annotations enhance these abundant materials with background information and suggestions for discussion and student research that bring history to life. At the same time, Focus on Geography, Section Reviews, and Chapter Reviews provide basic reinforcement of learning.

Creating Outstanding Lessons Every component of the program is correlated and supported in the interleaf pages as well as in the sidebar margins around the reduced pupil pages. Detailed lesson plans for each section of the pupil text form the core of the interleaf pages—the six pages that immediately precede each chapter of the text. Lessons are developed using an effective teaching model. At the beginning of each chapter (in Chapter Focus) and each section (in Setting the Stage), there are suggestions for tapping prior knowledge, involving learners, and identifying for students the objectives of study.

For each section of a chapter, Teaching Strategies are correlated to the section objectives. These objectives and their corresponding teaching strategies are listed in the margin at the start of each section of the Teacher's Edition.

Ten different types of strategies provide a bank of resources for different teaching and learning styles and variations in curriculum focus and student interests.

The Teaching Strategies suggest ways to

- engage in critical thinking about lesson content
- integrate the study of geography and economics, the humanities, and scientific achievements into the study of world history
- reinforce instruction in the writing process
- use cooperative learning techniques

Following the section strategies, you will find suggestions for comprehension checks enabling you to monitor and adjust your teaching.

The sidebars—or annotations in the margin beside the text pages—provide further resources, such as additional suggestions for ways to use the illustrations that open each chapter. Ideas for cooperative learning activities are distributed throughout the text. Finally answers are provided on the appropriate pages for all caption questions, as well as the Voice from the Past, Map Study, and Focus on Geography features, and the Section and Unit Reviews. Answers to Chapter Reviews are found in the interleaf pages following the section-by-section strategies.

Planning Successfully *World History: Perspectives on the Past* presents options for varied needs of students and different teaching situations. One purpose of the Teacher's Edition is to provide support for optimizing the use of program components. The interleaf pages as well as the sidebars are excellent guides to all support materials and serve as convenient tools for planning how to use these materials.

At the beginning of each chapter of interleaf pages is an Advance Planner. By using this chart, you can see at a glance the ancillary materials and strategies used to teach the objectives listed for each section of the pupil text.

In addition, all worksheets, outline maps, transparencies, tests, and Voices from the Past are referenced at point of use in the chapter and section materials.

Meeting a Variety of Student Needs Materials for *World History: Perspectives on the Past* support students with differing learning styles and a wide range of ability levels. You will want to assign Independent Practice Worksheets, Geography Skills Worksheets, Vocabulary Worksheets, Basic Skills Worksheets, and Critical Thinking Worksheets to almost all of your students. The History and Literature Readings enhance interest and depth of learning for all students.

Higher ability students will profit especially from Voices from the Past and Critical Thinking Worksheets. Under the heading Enrichment Activities at the end of each section in the interleaf pages, there are suggestions for research, writing, and other projects that will work especially well with these students.

Students who need additional support will find Vocabulary Worksheets, Geography Skills Worksheets, and Basic Skills Worksheets particularly helpful. Suggestions for altering teaching strategies to help students achieve mastery of key objectives are found under the heading Reteaching Activities in the sidebar at the end of each chapter.

Finally three different formats—Chapter and Unit Tests, Alternate Chapter and Unit Tests, and Computer Test Bank Chapter Tests—are provided as resources for evaluation.

Student Guide to World History

Historians use themes to show patterns in history. 1

Summary

Relating past to present is like assembling a vast jigsaw puzzle. Historians look for common ideas or unifying themes which form patterns that add a richness, variety, and meaning to the human adventure. Ten such themes are identified to guide this study of world history: *Cooperation and Conflict, Impact of Ideas, Rise of Democratic Ideas, Economics and History, Technology and History, Human-Environment Interaction, Social Institutions, Cultural Development, Individuals and History,* and *Continuity and Change.* The historic event of German Unification in 1990 serves as a focus for this discussion of historical themes.

Setting the Stage

Discussing History: Conflicts (Objective 1) A major pattern studied in world history is the role of conflict, occurring when rival groups seek to coerce, harm, or even destroy each other. Ask students to identify conflicts that have occurred in history. Ask how conflicts have changed history.

Teaching Strategies

Relating Past to Present: The Impact of Ideas (Objective 2) Some ideas give rise to political, economic, and religious movements. These ideas often are expressed in words that end with the suffix *ism*, a doctrine or set of ideas. For example, nationalism refers to feelings of loyalty to and pride in one's country. Ask students to identify other *isms* and explain their meanings. (socialism, communism, conservatism, realism, impressionism, environmentalism)

Relating Past to Present: Technology's Role in History (Objective 3) Technology refers to the tools and skills people use to meet their basic needs. In prehistoric times, stone tools were a critical factor in promoting social change. Have students identify several technological tools that have had an impact on their lives.

Discussing History: The Individual's Role in History (Objective 4) Individuals play a decisive role in the course of history. Some perform great deeds, others contribute answers to difficult problems. Working in small groups, ask students to generate a list of individuals (perhaps 8 to 10) who have changed the course of history. Everyone in the group must agree on the names. Have a spokesperson from each group present the group's list. Compile a list of those names most often mentioned. Have students keep the list in their notebooks to refer to at the end of the year.

Enrichment Activities

1. **Making a Bulletin Board**
   Divide the class into groups. Groups should create a display, using pictures from magazines or their own artwork, showing one of the patterns of history mentioned in the summary.

2. **Writing a Report**
   Have advanced students report on an individual identified by the class as having changed the course of history.

3. **Researching for Bonus Points**
   Who invented the first digital mechanical calculator? (Pascal, 1642)

Summary

Calendars allow historians to measure the passage of time, to place events in sequence, and to determine accurate dates. In this text, years are labeled B.C. ("before Christ") and A.D. ("anno domini"). The text also uses the terms *decade* (10 years), *century* (100 years), and *millennium* (1,000 years). Broad zones of time are called ages and eras.

Setting the Stage

Discussing History: Calendars (Objective 1) Explain that people throughout history have invented different systems for measuring time. For example, the Jewish calendar measures time from the year in which the Jews believe God created the world. In contrast, the Muslim calendar begins with the year in which Muhammad founded their religion. Eratosthenes, a Greek geographer, devised a calendar based on the Olympic Games, called Olympiads, which occurred at regular four-year intervals. He numbered the Olympiads from the first held in 776 B.C. If we were using that system, 1992 would be the first year of Olympiad 693.

Teaching Strategies

Discussing History: Ways to Represent Time (Objective 2) Write the following list of objects on the board: coins, newspapers, birth certificates, diplomas, receipts, and grave stones. Ask students to determine the one characteristic all objects have in common. (each contains a date) Ask students why each listed item has a date. How does the absence of a date affect each item? Historians use dates to determine when events occurred and to place events into a correct sequence.

Discussing History: B.C. and A.D. (Objective 3) All calendars need some fixed point from which to count the passage of time. Modern historians use the birth of Jesus as a common fixed point. Use the information provided in the section "Historians label time in various ways" (page 5) to explain the distinction between B.C. and A.D.

Skill Building: Using Time Lines (Objective 4) Direct students' attention to the time line on page 5. Explain that this time line is a chart that measures time. Have students examine the time line to determine how much time each unit represents (100 years). Then ask them to find the dates that mark the beginning and end of this time line (400 B.C. and A.D. 2000). Explain that most time lines also include specific dates that mark important events. For example, the time line on page 5 locates the birth of Jesus in the year 1.

Enrichment Activities

1. **Making a Time Line**
   Ask students to make a time line entitled "My Life thus Far." Time lines should include specific units of time, particular dates, and several important events.

2. **Researching for Bonus Points**
   Who invented A.D.? (a monk, Dionysius Exiguus ["the little"] in A.D. 525)

Historians use themes from geography. 3

Summary

Place is important to historians and geographers, both of whom share many ideas about the world. Location, place, human-environment interaction, movement, and region are five themes that provide ways for thinking about the world of the past, as well as the world of the present.

Setting the Stage

Write the following five questions on the board:

1. Where is a place located?
2. What are the place's physical and human characteristics?
3. How have people interacted with the environment in that place?
4. How do people, goods, and ideas move from place to place?
5. What qualities does one place have that it shares with other places?

Ask students to explain why these questions are important to both geographers and historians. These questions serve as major themes or topics studied by modern geographers.

Teaching Strategies

Skill Building: Using Absolute and Relative Location (Objective 1) Emphasize the distinction between absolute and relative location. In order to reinforce these concepts, ask students to use a map to determine the absolute location of your state capital. Then ask them to describe your state capital's location relative to Washington, D.C.

Skill Building: Using the Five Themes (Objective 2) Use the text's discussion of the Rock of Gibraltar to illustrate each of the five themes. Then ask your students to identify the theme illustrated by each of the following statements:

1. The Rock of Gibraltar is not "solid as a rock." It now contains more than 30 miles of man-made tunnels. (interaction)
2. The Rock of Gibraltar is made out of limestone. (place)
3. During the mid-1960's, Spanish border authorities severely restricted the flow of traffic between Spain and Gibraltar. (movement)
4. The Spanish government insists that Gibraltar should be a part of Spain. (region)
5. The Rock of Gibraltar is near the entrance to the Mediterranean Sea. (location)

Enrichment Activities

1. **Applying Concepts**
   Divide your class into five groups and assign each group one of the five themes. Ask them to apply the theme to their hometown or city. Have each group report its findings to the class.

2. **Researching for Bonus Points**
   What is the absolute location of Washington, D.C.? (38°54′ N, 77°2′ W)

Historians use maps to represent place. 4

Summary

Historical events occur in physical settings. Historians use maps to depict these settings. The problem is to make an accurate map of a three-dimensional sphere on a flat two-dimensional surface without causing distortions of shape, distance, size, and direction. Mapmakers have designed a number of projections to help overcome these distortions; however, no single projection can eliminate all distortions.

Setting the Stage

Have students recall the last time they used a map and list their answers on the board. List reasons why historians use maps. Compare and contrast the two lists. This section views the history of mapmaking and then looks at ways mapmakers work out the problem of representing a round object—the globe—on a flat surface.

Teaching Strategies

Discussing History: Mapmaking (Objective 1) Review the contributions Eratosthenes, Hipparchus, Ptolemy, and European sea captains made to mapmaking. Students might be interested to learn that Ptolemy worked in the famous library in Alexandria between A.D. 127 and A.D. 150. He wrote a famous eight-volume study entitled *A Guide to Geography* that remained an authoritative source for more than 1,000 years. Unfortunately, Ptolemy's book included a number of errors. For example, he badly underestimated both the size of the Atlantic Ocean and the earth's circumference. Ptolemy's errors later misled Columbus in his attempt to reach the Indies by sailing west.

Skill Building: Using Different Projections (Objective 2) Explain that an accurate flat map would have the following four properties: 1) landforms would be drawn accurately; 2) the scale of distance would be the same for all parts of the map; 3) landforms would be depicted in the correct size; and 4) directions would be the same for all points on the map. Emphasize that no world map can have all four of these properties. Review the advantages and disadvantages of each of the projections discussed in the text.

Enrichment Activities

1. **Preparing a Report**
   Have students prepare reports on one of the following projections: Goode's Interrupted Equal-Area Projection, Robinson Projection, the Gall-Peters Projection. Students should include at least one illustration in their reports.

2. **Researching a Topic**
   Ask advanced students to report on the Landsat satellite program. Their reports should include descriptions of the program's history, an explanation of the types of equipment used by the Landsat satellites, a summary of the program's major discoveries, and an assessment of the program's impact on modern cartography.

3. **Researching for Bonus Points**
   How did Eratosthenes calculate the earth's circumference? (Eratosthenes began with two facts—he knew that the earth was a sphere and that a straight pole at Aswan casts no shadow on June 22, the date of the summer solstice. Eratosthenes began by measuring the angle of a shadow at Alexandria on June 22. The angle measured 7°12', or 1/50th of a circle. Eratosthenes correctly reasoned that the distance from Alexandria to Aswan must be 1/50th of the earth's circumference.)

Student Guide to World History

Throngs gathered in Berlin to celebrate the reunification of East and West Germany on October 3, 1990.

At the stroke of midnight on October 3, 1990, athletes from East and West Germany raised a 540-square-foot flag above the Reichstag building in what until that moment had been West Berlin. As the black, red, and gold flag slowly rose, thousands sang the West German national anthem. Fireworks suddenly illuminated the night sky with a dazzling display of light and color. As people cheered and wept for joy, the countries that had been East and West Germany became a single nation with a single capital.

The unification of Germany was a dramatic historical event. History, however, is more than a single event. It is the record of all the hopes, achievements, defeats, victories, discoveries, ideas, and beliefs of humans since they first appeared on Earth. History records the wars, disasters, plagues, and famines that have befallen humankind. It also shows that people are capable of acting with courage, kindness, and wisdom.

Every group of people has its own history. To forget that history would be as devastating to a group as loss of memory is to an individual. Knowing who you are includes remembering who you

Teaching with Pictures

Tell students that some historic events are times of happiness and celebration, while others are times of great sadness. Ask them what emotions are conveyed in the photograph on page 1. What clues in the photograph led to their answers? Ask students how photographs, pictures, and other artifacts can help them better understand world history. Does a painting of a bison on a cave wall (see page 16) tell them as much about prehistoric people as the photograph here reveals about the people of modern Germany?

DISCUSSION

Discuss the following views of history.

"History is . . . indeed little more than the register of the crimes, follies, and misfortunes of mankind."
—Edward Gibbon

"History is more or less bunk."
—Henry Ford

"Not to know what happened before one was born is always to be a child."
—Cicero

BACKGROUND

A German craftsman, born in the last decade of the fourteenth century, invented a method of printing from movable type. This new technology allowed for a much larger circulation of books and other printed material.

Air pollution is a major problem for several large metropolitan centers such as Mexico City, Los Angeles, and Tokyo. In Tokyo, air pollution is so serious that policemen are provided with oxygen masks as they direct traffic at busy intersections.

were yesterday and all the days before that. The history of a group of people—whether that group is a family, a religious group, or a nation—is part of that group's identity.

As different groups meet, trade, fight, and make alliances, their histories blend into a larger history. Taken together, the histories of all groups make up the history of the largest group of all—humankind.

The unification of Germany marked a turning point in world history. When historians described the ceremonies that occurred in Berlin, they also asked questions about what had happened and why it was important. This curiosity about events is an essential first step in thinking historically.

Thinking historically is a particular way of approaching records, ideas, and problems of the past. Historians also recognize, however, that the present is an extension of the past. When studying a recent event, they investigate the past in hopes of finding origins, causes, and relationships that can be linked to the present.

Historians use themes to show patterns in history. 1

Investigating the past and linking it to the present is like assembling a complex jigsaw puzzle. Instead of simply trying to fit individual pieces together, historians look for common ideas or unifying themes. These themes form patterns that add richness, variety, and meaning to the human adventure.

The authors of this text have identified ten broad themes to help guide your study of world history. The following description identifies and explains these themes.

Cooperation and Conflict The processes of cooperation and conflict have played a major role in shaping world history. Cooperation occurs when members of a group work together to achieve a common goal. In contrast, conflict occurs when rival groups seek to coerce, harm, or even destroy each other.

Since war and peace have always had an important impact on historical developments, historians have devoted a great deal of attention to

studying their causes and consequences. For example, wars have had a particularly important influence upon German history. The end of World War II left Germany defeated and divided. The United States, Great Britain, and France controlled 70 percent of Germany, and the Soviet Union occupied the rest. This division was one of the most important consequences of World War II.

The Impact of Ideas Some ideas provoke wars, while others inspire peace conferences. One historian has noted that ideas "are the threads which bind the minds of people together sufficiently for joint action to occur."

This text will examine a number of ideas that have given rise to political, economic, and religious movements. Many of these ideas are expressed in words that end with the suffix *ism*. An *ism* is a doctrine or set of ideas. For example, nationalism refers to feelings of loyalty to and pride in one's country. While France, England, and Spain became unified countries, Germany remained divided into hundreds of small kingdoms, duchies, and free cities. The rise of a spirit of nationalism there in the nineteenth century played a powerful role in the movement to unify Germany. Although Germany was again divided after World War II, the feeling of nationalism in time encouraged Germans to seek reunification.

The Rise of Democratic Ideas When you vote, run for office, or listen to a campaign speech, you are participating in a political process called democracy. Since democracy is a key idea in world history, this text devotes particular attention to describing its rise and development. As you will learn, the idea of democracy began in ancient Greek city-states more than 2,000 years ago. Today, as in ancient Greece, the cornerstone of democracy remains the belief that people have a right to make free political choices.

As you will see in Chapter 32, the Soviet Union after World War II refused to allow the people of Eastern Europe free elections to choose their own governments. The people of that region, however, never gave up their desire for democracy. In 1989, the nations of Eastern Europe successfully replaced or overthrew their communist governments. Free elections in East Germany showed that the people wanted a democratic system and possible reunification with West Germany.

Economics and History All societies must develop answers to three basic economic questions.

First, what goods and services should be produced? Second, how should these goods and services be produced? Finally, how should the goods and services be distributed? As you study world history, you will see that these questions have been answered in many different ways.

Historians devote careful attention to the different economic systems that have been developed. For example, during the years after World War II, capitalism and communism offered two competing ways of answering the three basic economic questions. In a capitalist system, private individuals and groups own property and attempt to earn profits. By contrast, in a communist economy, property is owned by the state, and central planners decide what will be produced. As you will see in Chapter 37, the failure of communism to provide an adequate standard of living helped spark the revolutions that occurred in East Germany and Eastern Europe in 1989.

Technology and History Technology refers to the tools and skills people use to meet their basic needs. From the first stone tools to modern supercomputers, technology has been a critical factor in promoting social change. For example, Communist rulers in East Germany built the Berlin Wall to prevent people from leaving East Germany (Chapter 32). Although the wall stopped the flow of people, it could not stop the movement of ideas. Television and radio successfully broadcast information over the wall. When the Berlin Wall finally came down in 1989, many East Germans reported that West German television programs had played a key role in undermining support for their government.

Human-Environment Interaction Since the dawn of civilization, people have been affected by their environments. At the same time, people have in turn modified their environments. **Human-environment interaction** is thus a major theme in world history. As you will see in Chapter 36, pollution is rapidly becoming a serious threat to the global environment. East Germany and the other nations of Eastern Europe suffered from severe environmental pollution. Shortly after reunification, the German government announced that it would launch a major campaign to clean up the East German environment.

Cultural Development The wisdom of philosophers and the masterpieces created by writers and artists are among the crowning achievements

As democratic revolutions swept Eastern Europe in late 1989, Romanians in Bucharest tore down the statue of Lenin as a symbol of communism.

of any civilization. This text devotes particular attention to the golden ages that have contributed greatly to our own civilization. The literature, art, and philosophy produced by these golden ages will be presented as an integral part of each civilization. Although no one can predict when a golden age will begin, the leaders of Germany hope that reunification will stimulate a period of cultural creativity.

Social Institutions Every society has certain basic needs that must be fulfilled if it is to endure. Among these needs are to raise new generations to replace the old, to train the young and instill in them the norms and values of the society, to explain the meaning of existence and reinforce moral values, to maintain order and security, and to provide food and shelter. The family, education, religion, government, and the economic system are five basic institutions that society has developed to meet these needs.

3

SECTION 1
Objectives and Teaching Strategies

OBJECTIVE 1. Identify the impact of conflict on history.

Teaching Strategy: *Discussing History: Conflicts* (page 1b)

OBJECTIVE 2. Discuss the impact of ideas on history.

Teaching Strategy: *Relating Past to Present: The Impact of Ideas* (page 1b)

OBJECTIVE 3. Explain the changes that technology brings to civilizations.

Teaching Strategy: *Relating Past to Present: Technology's Role in History* (page 1b)

OBJECTIVE 4. Identify the role of individuals in history.

Teaching Strategy: *Discussing History: The Individual's Role in History* (page 1b)

ANSWERS TO
Section Review 1

Define:
the relation of people to their environment

Answer:
1. (a) Cooperation occurs when people work together to achieve a common goal. Conflict, on the other hand, results when rival groups seek to coerce, harm, or destroy each other. (b) Ideas are "the threads which bind the minds of people to-

(continued)

ANSWERS TO (continued)

gether sufficiently for joint action to occur."

2. (a) more than 2,000 years ago in Greece **(b)** Every society must answer basic economic questions; how a society decides will determine, to a large extent, the success or failure of that society.

3. (a) Technology is a critical factor in promoting social change, e.g., mass communications has spread ideas to nations fighting progress. **(b)** people affected by their environment, people modifying their environment

4. (a) Cultural development reflects the ideas, art, literature, science, and technology of its society. **(b)** Each society must fulfill basic needs if it is to endure. The social institutions it creates determine the success or failure of societies to satisfy the basic needs of its people. Each society sets up institutions that vary in some degree. In the study of history, students are able to compare and contrast various social institutions.

5. (a) In the course of history, many individuals have had a great impact on history either by performing great deeds or by resolving difficult problems. **(b)** Even though a people may live only a short time, institutions, ideas, and problems live on. Although continuity is important, describing and analyzing changes is a challenging aspect of history.

6. Students' answers will vary, but answers should take into account such ideas as looking at a society from different viewpoints, comparing and contrasting ideas and institutions, examining issues from a historical perspective.

Each civilization that you study in this text developed a distinctive pattern of social institutions. As you examine these differences, you will be able to compare and contrast a variety of institutions. You will also be able to study the reasons why people have sometimes changed their institutions. For example, the unification of Germany offers a unique opportunity to study the integration of two different social systems.

Individuals and History Thus far, our themes have dealt with impersonal forces such as economics and geography. But individuals also play a decisive role in affecting the course of history. As you study the events described in this text, you will meet an extraordinary variety of men and women. Many of them will perform great deeds, while others resolve difficult problems. Their achievements and decisions form an enduring and often inspiring legacy.

While many of the individuals in this text lived in the past, a number are still alive. For example, in Chapter 37 you will meet United States President George Bush, Soviet President Mikhail Gorbachev, and German Chancellor Helmut Kohl. These three leaders made pivotal decisions that resulted in the surprising sequence of events that led to the unification of Germany.

Continuity and Change When students first approach world history, they often believe that the past has little relevance for the present. However, as you become more familiar with history, you will see that the past in reality is still very much alive. While individuals live only a relatively short time, institutions, ideas, and problems often endure for hundreds and even thousands of years.

While historians recognize the importance of continuity, they are also keenly aware that society is perpetually undergoing a process of change. Describing and analyzing social changes is one of the most fascinating and challenging aspects of studying world history.

Section REVIEW 1

Define: human-environment interaction
Answer:
1. (a) What is the role of cooperation and conflict in world history? (b) How may ideas influence history?

4

2. (a) When did democratic ideas first appear? (b) Why are economic ideas basic to world history?
3. (a) How has technology contributed to changes in history? (b) What are two aspects of human-environmental interaction?
4. (a) In what ways is cultural development central to world history? (b) How are social institutions related to history?
5. (a) To what extent is history the story of individuals? (b) How does history represent both continuity and change?

Critical Thinking
6. How will the ten themes described in this section help you to think historically?

Historians use many ways to represent time. 2

Historians work within the dimensions of time and place. Time tells *when* and place tells *where* people have lived and certain events have occurred. Together, time and place provide a frame for the human story that is history.

In the entire span of history, events happen on a particular date or during a certain period of time. Dates tell when some person lived, how long a war lasted, how many years passed between events. Dates allow historians to place events in correct sequence and to identify events that have happened at the same time.

People use different calendars.

How are specific dates assigned to the passing years? Different groups of people follow different customs. Take, for example, the year that people in the United States and Europe will call 2000. They use that number because the year will come approximately 2,000 years after the birth of Jesus. People call this system of dating "the Christian Era" or "the Common Era."

However, for many Jews, this same year will be called 5761 because, by Jewish tradition, God created the world 5,761 years before. That same year will be numbered 1421 by many Muslims because they began counting from the year Mu-

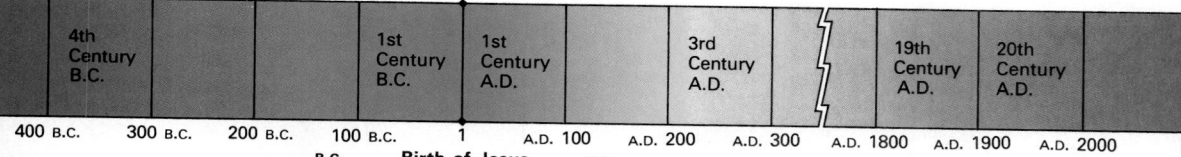

4th Century B.C.			1st Century B.C.	1st Century A.D.		3rd Century A.D.		19th Century A.D.	20th Century A.D.
400 B.C.	300 B.C.	200 B.C.	100 B.C.	1 A.D. 100	A.D. 200	A.D. 300	A.D. 1800	A.D. 1900	A.D. 2000

B.C.   Birth of Jesus   A.D.

This time line extends from 400 B.C. to A.D. 2000. It shows time in units of a century. The break on the right shows that a period of time has been omitted.

hammad founded their religion, the year that Europeans and Americans label 622.

In the past, people had even more ways of recording the passage of time. Some numbered their years only by the reigns of kings. Others counted forward or backward from great religious festivals. Historians must often do detective work to determine accurate dates from such sources.

Historians label time in various ways.

The dates given in this text are those of the Christian or Common Era. These dates fall into two groups, B.C. and A.D.

B.C. and A.D. In the early part of the book, many dates are followed by the letters B.C. These letters stand for "before Christ" and mean that the event took place a certain number of years before the birth of Jesus. Thus, the year 500 B.C. was 500 years before the birth of Jesus, or almost 2,500 years ago. As dates get closer to the birth of Jesus, the numbers get smaller. Thus, a person born in 378 B.C. might have lived until 318 B.C.

If a year is labeled A.D., it took place after the birth of Jesus. The letters stand for "*anno domini,*" a Latin phrase meaning "in the year of our Lord." These dates are usually written with the letters first: A.D. 939. If a year has no letters with it, you can assume it is A.D.

Other terms for time Besides numbering individual years, historians also group years into useful divisions:

A *decade* is 10 years.
A *century* is 100 years.
A *millenium* is 1,000 years.

We live in the twentieth century, but our years are labeled 19--. Why are these years called the *twentieth* century? Remember that years are numbered from the birth of Jesus. The years A.D.

1 to A.D. 100 were the first century. The years 101 to 200 were the second century, and so on. Thus, when you see *fifteenth century*, you should think of the years from 1401 to 1500.

The same division into centuries is used for the period of time before the birth of Jesus. The years from 100 B.C. to 1 B.C. are the first century B.C. The years from 500 B.C. to 401 B.C. are the fifth century B.C. Thus, an event in 735 B.C. took place in the eighth century B.C.

Broad time periods Sometimes historians talk about periods of time called *ages* or *eras*. An age or era is a broad zone of time. Historians use these terms to describe time periods when people shared certain patterns of life and thought. For example, certain times in history are known as the Bronze Age or the Middle Ages. The Stone Age is the period of time when people made many of their tools from stone.

It is impossible to give one exact date for the end of one era and the start of another. As age follows age, human ways of living change, but there is never a complete break. Every age has deep roots in the past.

Time lines show a certain period of time.

To represent a span of time, historians often use a time line such as the one shown above. A time line is like a graph, with each unit representing an equal amount of time. Together, these units show a period of historic time.

Time lines are based on particular dates that mark the start and end of the line. Between those dates, there usually are other dates to mark important events. Time lines may also serve to trace a historical sequence or the direction of change. By visually representing *when*, time lines are a useful tool for studying history.

5

OBJECTIVE 1. Identify different systems for measuring time.

Teaching Strategy: *Discussing History: Calendars* (page 1c)

OBJECTIVE 2. Identify various ways to represent time.

Teaching Strategy: *Discussing History: Ways to Represent Time* (page 1c)

OBJECTIVE 3. Distinguish between dates B.C. and A.D.

Teaching Strategy: *Discussing History: B.C. and A.D.* (page 1c)

OBJECTIVE 4. Interpret information presented on a time line.

Teaching Strategy: *Skill Building: Using Time Lines* (page 1c)

■ BACKGROUND

Point out that different groups of people have not only used different calendars but have also started their years on different dates.

■ DISCUSSION

Will the twenty-first century begin in 2000 or in 2001? (2001)

ANSWERS TO
Section Review 2

Answer:

1. (a) the "Common Era" or the "Christian Era" **(b)** Jews date calendars from the time they believe God created the earth. **(c)** Muslims date their calendar from the year Muhammad founded their religion.

2. (a) 736 B.C. **(b)** A.D. 12 **(c)** A.D. 1750

3. (a) seventh century B.C. **(b)** twenty-first century **(c)** fifteenth century

4. to trace a historical sequence or direction of change, show a period of historic time, to mark important events

5. There is never a complete break between the end of one era and the beginning of a new one; every new age has deep roots in the past.

6. (a) Students' answers will vary. **(b)** Responses will vary, but should include the idea of global interdependency.

Western Europe and North Africa

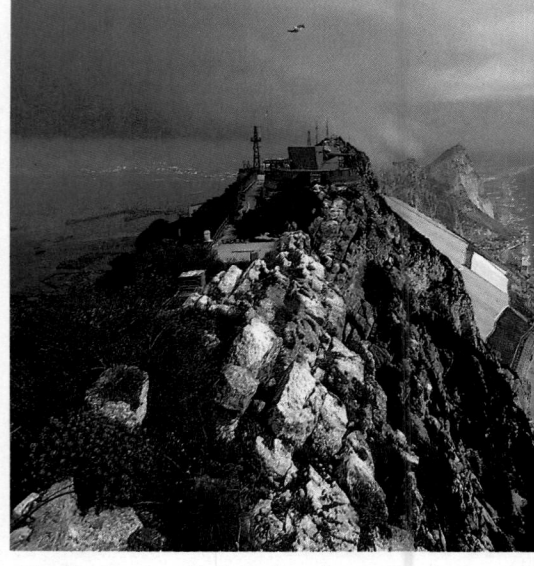

Gibraltar is a small place, just three miles long and three fourths of a mile wide. It is made up of a high limestone ridge. At the southern end, this ridge becomes a huge rock formation 1,396 feet high. Steep cliffs aid defense but limit people's living space.

Section REVIEW 2

Answer:

1. (a) What system do people in the United States use to number the passing years? (b) Why will the year A.D. 2000 be numbered 5761 by many Jews? (c) Why will Muslims number it 1421?
2. Which year in each of the following pairs is more recent? (a) 736 B.C. or 1288 B.C.? (b) A.D. 12 or 416 B.C.? (c) A.D. 1593 or A.D.1750
3. In what century is each of the following dates? (a) 697 B.C. (b) A.D. 2010 (c) A.D. 1435
4. What are three kinds of information found on a time line?

Critical Thinking

5. Why are the dates for the beginning and end of an age or era only approximate?
6. (a) What label would you choose to describe the present period of history? (b) Would this term apply to all parts of the world or only to certain regions?

6

Historians use themes from geography. 3

Because *place* is important to historians, they share with geographers many ideas about the world. Among these ideas are five basic themes: *location, place, human-environment interaction, movement,* and *region.* These five themes provide ways for thinking about the world of the past as well as of the present.

Location focuses on where a place is.

The theme of *location* answers the question of where in the world a certain place exists. For example, consider the problem of determining where the place called Gibraltar is located. On the immense sphere that is the planet Earth, how can you tell where this rocky fortress of only 2.3 square miles is found?

Absolute location The location of a place can be described in two different ways. One of these is absolute location, determined by latitude and longitude. A map will show you that Gibraltar is found at the point where the imaginary line of latitude at 36° north of the equator crosses the imaginary line of longitude at 5° west of the prime meridian. An absolute location thus is like an address. Gibraltar's address on Earth is latitude 36° North and longitude 5° West.

Relative location A second method for locating places—the one more often used by historians—is relative location. Where is Gibraltar in relation to other places? On what continent is it found? Near what seas does it lie?

Gibraltar is located in southwestern Europe. It lies at the western end of the Mediterranean where that sea meets the Atlantic Ocean. From Morocco in northern Africa, Gibraltar lies across a narrow strait from 8 to 23 miles wide. Describing Gibraltar in these ways shows its location relative to other bodies of land and water.

Place *deals with the characteristics of an area.*

Every place on Earth has its own special character. The Sahara is a desert, with a dry climate and little plant and animal life. The Amazon Basin is humid and teems with plants and wildlife. The physical characteristics of a place include its landforms, climate, vegetation, mineral and other resources, and nearness to a river, sea, or other body of water.

In addition to the physical characteristics of a place are its human and cultural characteristics. Is the place lightly or densely populated? What language do the people speak? What are their customs and religious beliefs? How do they earn their living? How are their society and government organized?

Physically, Gibraltar is dominated by the huge Rock of Gibraltar, 1,398 feet tall, from which the whole place takes its name. Culturally, the population of about 33,000 people comes from various countries, but they speak mainly English and Spanish.

Human-environment interaction *refers to the relation between people and land.*

Wherever people live, the physical character of that place affects their ways of living. People, in turn, change the character of their environment. They cut down forests, plow grasslands, build cities and roads for travel. Interaction between land and people is a central theme of both geography and history.

At Gibraltar, evidence of such interaction is found within the great Rock itself. Its cliffs are honeycombed with natural caves that, thousands of years ago, provided shelter for prehistoric people. The environment thus influenced the way

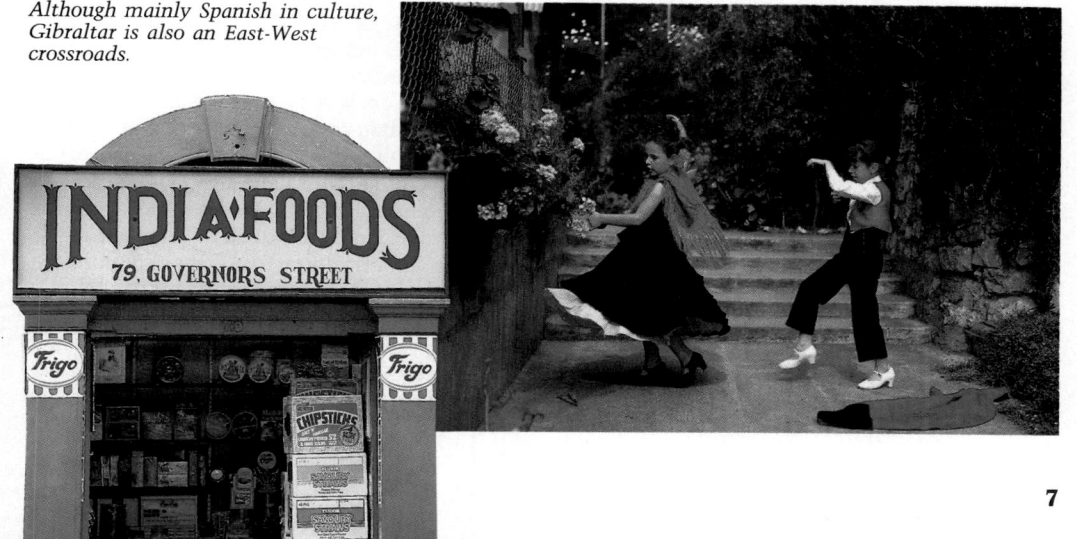

Although mainly Spanish in culture, Gibraltar is also an East-West crossroads.

7

SECTION 3
Objectives and Teaching Strategies

OBJECTIVE 1. Distinguish between and use the concepts of absolute and relative location.

Teaching Strategy: *Skill Building: Using Absolute and Relative Location* (page 1d)

OBJECTIVE 2. Identify five major themes or topics studied by modern geographers.

Teaching Strategy: *Skill Building: Using the Five Themes* (page 1d)

■ **BACKGROUND**

Ptolemy (A.D. 100–165) helped develop the geographic grids of longitude and latitude. He also constructed one of the first maps of the world.

James Michener, the noted American novelist, relies heavily on geographic works when researching his novels. He believes his novels (*Chesapeake, Centennial, Hawaii, Texas, The Covenant,* and *Alaska*) enjoy much success partly because he fixes them firmly within a regional geographic context.

ANSWERS TO
Section Review 3

Define:
the spread of ideas through trade, migration, and conquest
(continued)

ANSWERS TO (continued)

Answer:

1. **(a)** where in the world a certain place exists **(b)** absolute location, determined by latitude and longitude; relative location, determined by its relation to other places **(c)** Gibraltar—36° north of equator, 5° west of prime meridian; Gibraltar—located in southwestern Europe, at western end of Mediterranean Sea where it meets Atlantic Ocean

2. **(a)** physical, human, and cultural characteristics **(b)** physical—dominated by Rock of Gibraltar; human and cultural—people come from various countries but speak mainly English and Spanish

3. **(a)** Caves on Gibraltar provided homes. **(b)** British blasted tunnels within the rock to provide defensive positions

4. History provides numerous examples of the way movement has been used to change the course of society: armies attacking another nation, exploration of new worlds, or ideas spreading to new societies.

5. **(a)** physical, cultural **(b)** physical—climate, Gibraltar and lands surrounding the Mediterranean Sea share a Mediterranean climate; cultural—language, lands speaking the Spanish language

6. The five themes of geography provide historians with ways of thinking about the world of the past as well as the present.

7. **(a)** provide a framework for the human story that is history **(b)** dates allow historians to place events in correct sequence, place allows historians to locate an event

Because of Gibraltar's strategic location, Britain has fortified the Rock heavily. This enables Britain to control the passage of ships through the Strait. Britain has also taken advantage of the Rock's height to develop it as a communications center.

in which people lived. In modern times, British soldiers have blasted within the Rock a network of tunnels for military defense. They have altered their environment to meet a particular need.

Movement *concerns the interaction among people.*

The theme of *movement* deals with people's efforts to overcome the limits of *place.* History is the story of movement. Armies have marched across plains and over mountain passes. Ships have sailed across seas and oceans on expeditions of trade and war. At times, groups of people have migrated from one land to another in search of more favorable environments for living. Ideas, too, spread from culture to culture in **cultural diffusion,** thus opening new possibilities for people.

This theme of movement, combined with location, explains the importance of Gibraltar in history. Whoever controls Gibraltar also controls the movement of ships into and out of the Mediterranean Sea. In terms of military and naval power, few places have a more strategic location than Gibraltar.

Moors from North Africa invaded Spain by way of Gibraltar in 711. Spain held the fortress from 1462 to 1704, during the years when that nation was a major power. The capture of Gibraltar by Britain after a naval battle in 1704

marked the growth of British sea power. In time, Gibraltar became a base for protecting British trade with Egypt and India. It remains under British rule today, although Spain would like to take it back.

Regions *grow as units with some shared quality.*

A region is any area based on some one characteristic. This may be physical—as with landforms and climate—or cultural—as with language, religion, or ways of living. Regions vary greatly in size. They may be larger than some continents, as in the case of Siberia or the South Pacific, or as small as a single community or even your own neighborhood.

One place may be part of several different regions. Gibraltar, for example, is part of Western Europe (a political region). It also is part of the lands bordering the Atlantic Ocean (an oceanic region), lands sharing a Mediterranean climate (a climate region), lands ruled by Britain (a region based on a political unit), and lands speaking the Spanish language (a language region).

Regions change in the course of history. New patterns of interconnections appear and develop. Over time and across the spaces of land and sea, regions of the past have formed the world of today. Changes happening now will shape new regions of the world of tomorrow.

8

Define: (a) cultural diffusion
Answer:
1. (a) What question does *location* answer? (b) In what ways can the location of a place be described? (c) Give an example of each way.
2. (a) What are the main characteristics used in describing a place? (b) Give examples of each type.
3. (a) What are some ways that the environment affects people? (b) That people affect their environment?
4. Explain the meaning of the sentence "History is the story of movement."
5. (a) Identify two major bases for the development of regions. (b) Give an example of each, explaining how it helps to determine a region.

Critical Thinking
6. Why are the five themes described in this section important to historians?
7. (a) Why are the elements of time and place essential to the study of history? (b) Give examples to support your answer.

Historians use maps to represent place. 4

The events of history happen in a physical setting somewhere in the world. To show these settings, historians use maps, just as geographers do.

Mapmaking has a long history.

From the beginning of time, people have sought to show the world in which they live. If you have ever tried to map a large area, you know how difficult that is.

Early maps When did people first begin to make maps of their surroundings? The earliest known map was made for a Babylonian landowner about 2300 B.C. However, it was the Greeks of ancient times who first studied the world so as to present it in an accurate and systematic way. The word *geography* comes from the ancient Greek words for land (*geo*) and for writing or drawing (*graphien*).

As early as 350 B.C., Greek philosophers conceived of the earth as a sphere. Eratosthenes, a Greek mathematician and geographer, estimated the earth's circumference to be 24,662 miles. (The actual figure is 24,847 miles.) Another Greek geographer, Hipparachus, developed a system of grids, similar to today's lines of latitude and longitude, to locate places on the earth.

The most famous geographer of ancient times, Ptolemy, sought to map all the areas of the world. His map of the then-known world remained the best of its kind until the time of Columbus. Ptolemy also started the practice of putting north at the top of a map, south at the bottom, east at the right, and west at the left.

For more than 1,200 years after Ptolemy, the most complete and accurate maps were made by Arab ship captains and Chinese scholars. Major advances in European mapmaking began after A.D. 1300. As ship captains ventured farther on unknown waters, they charted coastlines and extended the known world. Columbus, for example, drew careful maps of the lands he explored. Gradually, maps became more accurate, detailed, and complete.

Modern maps In the almost 500 years since Columbus's first voyage, the whole world has been explored and mapped. Today, photos and images of the earth, taken from satellites, confirm the earlier knowledge. In addition, they provide new insights into the world in which we live.

An orbiting satellite provided the information for this Landsat image of Dallas, Texas.

9

SECTION 4
Objectives and Teaching Strategies

OBJECTIVE 1. Discuss the contributions of early mapmakers.

Teaching Strategy: *Discussing History: Mapmaking* (page 1d)

OBJECTIVE 2. Review the advantages and disadvantages of different map projections.

Teaching Strategy: *Skill Building: Using Different Projections* (page 1e)

■ BACKGROUND

It is logical to assume that mapmaking goes back to prehistory when people drew maps to show locations, hazards, or routes to villages or hunting areas. Originally, these maps were scraped on the ground, later on the bark of trees, and on animal skins.

The oldest specimen of maps found so far have been dated about 2300 B.C., when the Babylonians drew maps on clay tablets.

■ DISCUSSION

Why is it important for people to be familiar with geographical aspects of other countries around the world?

Why are maps so important to the study of history?

ANSWERS TO

Section Review 4

Define:

(a) set of lines on map that cross one another to form boxes, to identify the location of a place (b) grid lines that circle the globe from east to west (c) line of latitude midway between the north and south pole; line from which latitude is measured either north or south (d) imaginary grid lines that

(continued)

Robinson Projection

Azimuthal Equal-Area Projection

Mercator Projection

Azimuthal Equidistant Projection

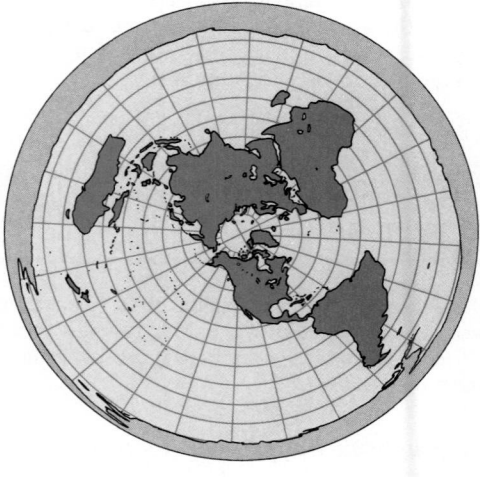

The Language of Geography
Geographers use certain terms in working with maps. Knowing these terms will help you use maps more effectively.
*1. Geographers use **grids,** or sets of lines that cross one another to form boxes, to identify the location of places.*
*2. Lines of **latitude** are the imaginary grid lines that circle the globe from east to west. They measure distances north and south.*
*3. The **equator** is the line of latitude midway between the north and south poles. It is the line from which latitude is measured, either north or south.*

*4. Lines of **longitude** are the imaginary grid lines that run north and south on a globe but measure distances east and west.*
*5. The **prime meridian,** which is the imaginary line running through Greenwich, England, is the line from which longitude is measured, either east or west.*
*6. Geographers often refer to a half of the globe, or **hemisphere.** This may be the hemisphere north or south of the equator or east or west of the prime meridian. Historians often speak of eastern and western hemispheres.*

10

Maps do not show the earth accurately.

The most accurate way to represent the earth is with a globe. Because the earth is a three-dimensional sphere, showing it on a two-dimensional map causes problems.

When a globe is transposed onto a flat surface, some areas are *distorted,* or shown inaccurately. For example, some maps may show the area of continents and oceans out of true proportion. Other maps may distort shapes, such as showing the polar regions as much larger than they actually are. Maps may also distort distance and direction.

The Robinson projection was developed to show the earth as accurately as possible. It seeks to reduce all types of distortion—in size, shape, direction, and distance.

Map projections can limit distortions.

Cartographers who design maps have developed a number of different **projections.** Each projection represents the globe in a particular way. As you will see, certain projections tend to meet particular needs. The map chosen for a given task, then should be the one most suitable for that purpose.

Equal-area projections To show the size of areas accurately, an *equal-area projection* is used. On this projection, the size of one body of land or water is true relative to that of others. One common projection of this type is the *azimuthal equal-area projection.* This projection is always circular. It is centered on a single point on the globe, such as the middle of a continent or one of the poles. An important characteristic of this projection is that a straight line from the center to any other point represents the shortest distance.

Projections to show true shape Maps that show the shapes of land areas like those on a globe are said to be *conformal.* On this projection, shapes are true only over small areas. Those of large areas may be greatly distorted.

One of the earliest projections of this type is the Mercator projection. It was originated by Gerhardus Mercator, a Dutch cartographer of the sixteenth century. He had the idea of forming a sheet of paper into a cylinder, wrapping it around a globe, and transferring the outlines of land from the globe onto the paper. The shapes of land thus shown are most accurate in low and middle latitudes and least accurate in high latitudes. The island of Greenland, for example, appears on a Mercator projection to be larger than the continent of South America. In reality, it is less than one-eighth the size of South America. Mercator maps were valuable to ship captains because a straight line on the map shows a true compass course.

Projections to show true direction The map best known for showing direction accurately is, again, the azimuthal projection. All straight lines drawn through the center of it show true compass direction. These lines, which are straight on the map, form great circles on a globe and show the shortest distance between two points. Great circles are thus the routes used by pilots of airplanes.

Projections to show distances accurately Projections that maintain distances accurately are said to be *equidistant.* However, distances can be kept accurate only over small areas or between two points. No projection can show true distances for the whole globe.

Distance is sometimes combined with other characteristics in a single projection such as the *azimuthal equidistant projection* to show both direction and distance correctly. On this projection a straight line from the center to another point forms a great circle, the shortest route by airplane.

Section REVIEW 4

Define: (a) grid, (b) latitude, (c) equator, (d) longitude, (e) prime meridian, (f) hemisphere, (g) projection
Identify: (a) Mercator
Answer:
1. Describe the contributions of the ancient Greeks to geography.
2. How did explorers like Columbus add to knowledge of the world?
3. Why is it difficult to show the earth correctly on a map?
4. What kinds of distortions are often found on maps?
5. What advantage does each of the major types of map projection have?

Critical Thinking
6. Why is it important to represent the world as accurately as possible?

11

ANSWERS TO *(continued)*

run north and south on the globe, but measure distances east and west **(e)** imaginary line running through Greenwich, England, line from which longitude is measured, either east or west **(f)** half the globe **(g)** used by cartographers to represent the globe in different ways

Identify:
Dutch cartographer of the sixteenth century who developed the *conformal* projection

Answer:
1. first studied the world in order to present it in accurate and systematic way; gave us the word *geography;* conceived of the earth as a sphere; estimated the circumference of the earth; developed a system of grids
2. charted coastlines, extended the known world, drew maps of lands he explored
3. Since earth is three-dimensional, it is difficult to represent on a two-dimensional plane.
4. areas of continents and oceans; shapes of landforms at poles; distances and direction
5. equal-area—shows size of areas accurately; conformal—shows shapes of small areas accurately; azimuthal—shows direction accurately; equidistant—maintains distance accurately
6. Answers will vary, but should include the idea that a full understanding of history must take into account the true nature of location, size, distance, populations, climate, topography of places studied.

Stonehenge on Salisbury Plain, England

	3500 B.C.	2900 B.C.	2300 B.C.
Political and Governmental Life		3100 B.C. Upper and Lower Egypt joined	2500–1500 B.C. ▶ Cities flourished in the Indus Valley
Economic and Technological Life		2800 B.C. Bronze Age begins	◀ 2000 B.C. Chinese work bronze and weave silk
Social and Cultural Life	▲ 3500 B.C. City-states rise in Sumer	2600 B.C. Great Pyramid built in Egypt	2000–1550 B.C. Babylonians build an empire

Unit I
The Beginnings of Civilization

Historical Themes

Human-Environment Interaction The geographic settings of ancient Southwest Asia, Egypt, India, and China varied. Within each country, people adapted to their environment and created a unique civilization.

The Impact of Ideas The first civilizations produced religions that had a profound impact on later civilizations. Monotheism, moral conduct, ethical behavior, and social order were among these contributions.

Economics and History The long transition from a nomadic life to permanent settlements aided the development of specialized labor, the production of surplus food and goods, and the start of trade.

1700 B.C.   **1100 B.C.**   **500 B.C.**

1500 B.C.
Shang dynasty begins in China

550 B.C.
Persian empire begins

322 B.C.
Mauryans rule India

1570–1075 B.C.
New Kingdom in Egypt builds wealthy empire

1000 B.C.
Israel becomes a kingdom

1500 B.C.
Hittites learn to use iron

1100–700 B.C.
Phoenicians trade around Mediterranean

130 B.C.
Great Silk Road opens from China to the West

1640 B.C. ▶
Hyksos invade in horse-drawn chariots

Great Wall of China

1700 B.C.
Hammurabi establishes code of laws

550 B.C. ▶
Start of Buddhism in India

1000 B.C.
The Temple is built in Jerusalem

13

The World about 1700 B.C.

KEY

- China under the Shang dynasty
- Babylonian empire under Hammurabi
- Indus Valley civilization
- Egypt during the Middle Kingdom
- Minoan and Mycenaean civilizations
- Fertile Crescent
- • City

ARCTIC HUNTERS
AND FISHERS

NORTH AMERICA

Missouri R.

Colorado R.

Rio Grande

Mississippi R.

ATLANTIC

OCEAN

FARMERS

PACIFIC

OCEAN

Orinoco R.

Amazon

River

HUNTERS AND
GATHERERS

**SOUTH
AMERICA**

FARMERS

R.

Paraguay R.

Parana

Clay figurine grinding corn

Historical Atlas

14

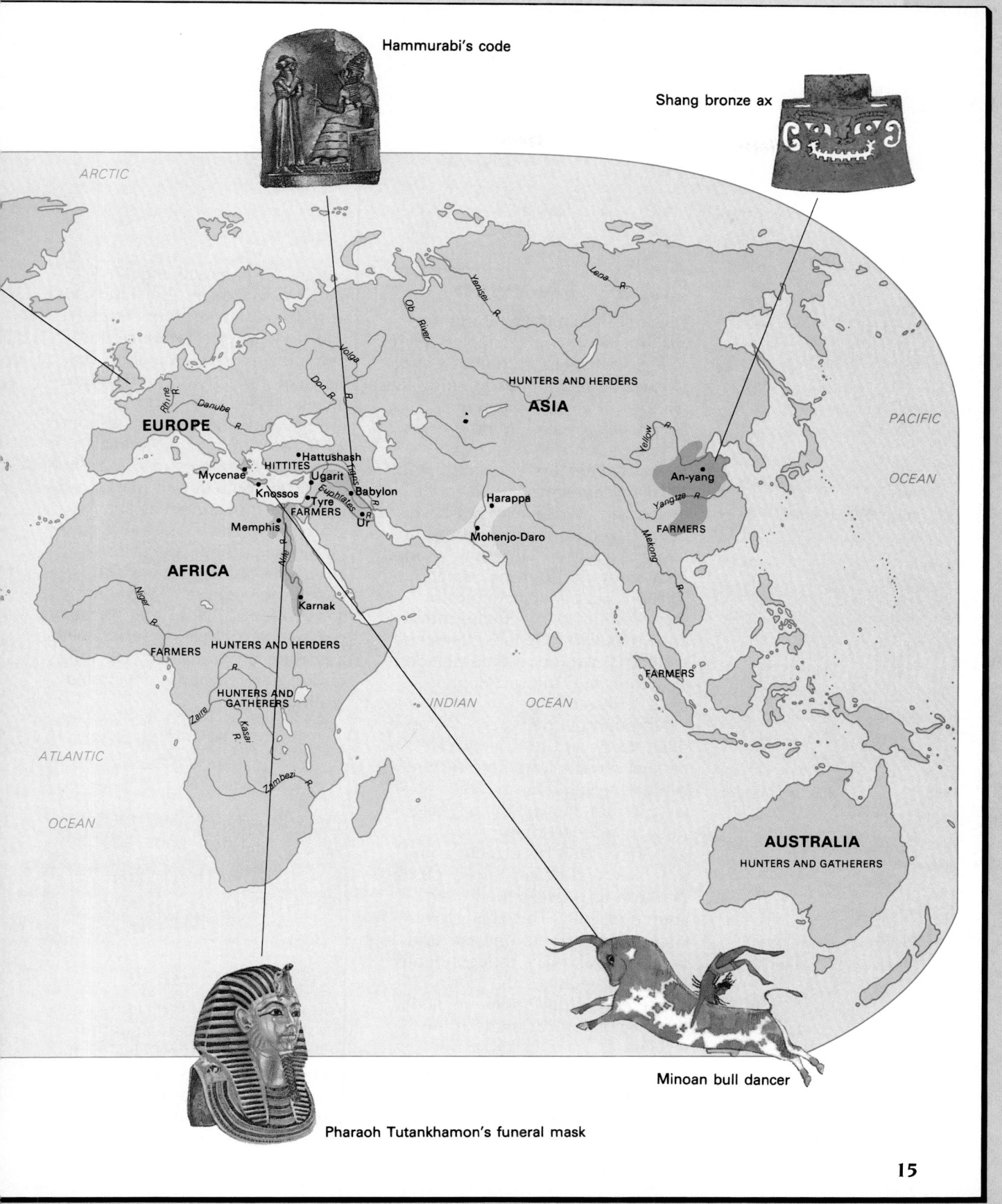

Hammurabi's code

Shang bronze ax

ARCTIC

EUROPE

Rhine R.

Danube R.

Don R.

Volga R.

Ob River

Yenisei R.

Lena R.

ASIA

HUNTERS AND HERDERS

PACIFIC

OCEAN

Mycenae

HITTITES

Hattushash

Ugarit

Euphrates R.

Tigris R.

Babylon

Knossos

Tyre

FARMERS

Ur

Memphis

Nile R.

AFRICA

Niger R.

Karnak

Yellow R.

An-yang

Yangtze R.

FARMERS

Mekong R.

Harappa

Mohenjo-Daro

FARMERS

FARMERS

HUNTERS AND HERDERS

HUNTERS AND GATHERERS

Zaire R.

Kasai R.

INDIAN

OCEAN

Zambezi R.

ATLANTIC

OCEAN

AUSTRALIA

HUNTERS AND GATHERERS

Minoan bull dancer

Pharaoh Tutankhamon's funeral mask

15

Prehistoric Times

Chapter Overview

The first hominids, or upright-walking creatures, originated in Africa. Scientists use a number of sophisticated techniques to study the remains of australopithecines, *Homo habilis*, and *Homo erectus*.

Many scientists believe that *Homo sapiens* first appeared about 200,000 years ago. The Neanderthals (who may or may not have been *Homo sapiens*) were the first beings known to bury their dead. They mysteriously vanished about 30,000 years ago. Anatomically modern humans, including those known as Cro-Magnons, launched a cultural revolution that included new tools and unprecedented artistic achievements.

Although people knew how to plant seeds and to domesticate certain animals long before they settled in permanent villages, it wasn't until about 8000 B.C. that they abandoned hunting and gathering, built permanent communities, and began to rely on agriculture to provide their main source of food. This changeover occurred first in Southwest Asia, but also took place independently in other regions of the world. These crucial developments laid the foundation for modern life.

Chapter Focus

You might begin by asking students to list physical traits that set humans apart from other animals. Answers include an upright skeleton, three-dimensional color vision, and a complex brain that enables us to create complex tools and plan for the future.

After compiling a list of traits, ask students to read the chapter opener on pages 16 and 17. Ask students to explain the significance of the Laetoli footprints. Stress that they provide evidence that hominids existed 3.6 million years ago. Point out that scientists now believe that upright walking was the first key feature that set hominids apart from other animals.

Now ask students to name the distinctive human trait Mary Leakey demonstrated as she searched for new clues about human origins. (intense curiosity about the human past, which is part of our unique capacity for self-awareness) Note that we begin our search for self-awareness with a chapter on prehistory, the long period before people developed writing.

Scientists search for human origins. 1

Setting the Stage

You might begin by dividing your class into groups containing four or five students. Then give each group a penny. Ask students to imagine themselves to be archaeologists who have just discovered this artifact in A.D. 3000. Have students make a careful list of the characteristics of this object. Then ask them to make deductions about how this object was used and what it tells us about the culture of the people who made it. For example, students could conclude that the artifact commemorates a trusted god named Liberty. Liberty's image is shown on one side of the artifact and his temple, E Pluribus Unum, is shown on the other side. If you look closely, you can see an image of Liberty inside his temple!

After going over each group's deductions, stress the problems archaeologists and anthropologists have in reconstructing prehistoric times. This section will describe what scientists have learned thus far. It is important to remember that there are still many unanswered questions and disputed interpretations of the evidence.

Teaching Strategies

Discussing Prehistory: Dating Prehistoric Objects (Objective 1) Ask students to explain why establishing accurate dates would be a particularly difficult problem during the prehistoric period. Students should note that prehistoric people did

Advance Planner

Unit I The Beginnings of Civilization
THEME The development of civilization from prehistoric times to early empires

Chapter 1 Prehistoric Times 4,000,000 B.C.–3500 B.C.
FOCUS Human origins

★ Advanced
● Basic

	SECTION 1	SECTION 2	SECTION 3
Objectives	1. Describe methods scientists use to determine prehistoric dates. 2. Identify Olduvai Gorge and explain why it is a significant prehistoric site. 3. Identify *Homo erectus* and explain why the species left Africa.	1. Make inferences about how the Neanderthals lived. 2. Compare and contrast Neanderthals and Cro-Magnons. 3. Speculate about why cave paintings were drawn.	1. Identify the factors that caused the agricultural revolution. 2. Make inferences from pictures of Stone Age art. 3. Describe aspects of daily life in a Neolithic village.
Setting the Stage	The difficulty of interpreting archaeological evidence	The beginnings of truly human behaviors	The transition from hunting and gathering to farming and herding
Teaching Strategies	Discussing Prehistory: Dating Prehistoric Objects Using Geographic Themes: Olduvai Gorge Discussing Prehistory: *Homo erectus* Check for Understanding	Skill Building: Making Inferences about Neanderthals Skill Building: Comparing and Contrasting Teaching with Pictures Check for Understanding	Relating Past to Present: Global Warming Teaching with Pictures: Mammoth-bone shelters Discussing Prehistory: Çatal Hüyük Check for Understanding
Guided Practice	Section Review 1	Section Review 2	Section Review 3
Independent Practice Worksheets	Independent Practice 1.1 Geography Skills 1 Vocabulary 1	Independent Practice 1.2 Basic Skills 1	Independent Practice 1.3 Critical Thinking 1
Enrichment	1. Primary Source: Voices 1.1 2. Preparing a Report: The Work of an Anthropologist or Archaeologist 3. Researching for Points	1. Primary Source: Voices 1.2 2. ★Speculating about Prehistory 3. Preparing a Report: Making Stone Age Tools 4. Researching for Points	1. Primary Source: Voices 1.3 2. Preparing a Report: A Farming Village 3. ★Interpreting a Quotation 4. Researching for Points
Chapter Closer	●**Reteaching Activities** Interpreting, Outlining, Listing		
	Chapter Review Summary, Reviewing the Facts, Basic Skills, Researching and Reporting Skills, Critical Thinking, Perspectives on Past and Present, Investigating History		
	Chapter Evaluation Chapter Test 1, Alternate Chapter Test 1, Computer Test Bank Chapter Test 1		

not keep a written record of their history. As a result, pinpointing dates for events that occurred thousands of years ago is very difficult.

Despite these problems, scientists have developed sophisticated techniques for determining prehistoric dates. As noted in the text, radiocarbon and potassium-argon dating are the two most widely used procedures. Explain that both methods are by-products of research in nuclear physics.

Radiocarbon dating measures the decay of radiocarbon substances. It allows scientists to date such commonly found substances as bone, shell, and charcoal. Although the method can be applied anywhere in the world, it is limited, since it can be only used on remains that are less than 50,000 years old.

Explain that the potassium-argon method is used to date volcanic materials. For a detailed explanation and concrete example of how the potassium-argon method works see *Lucy, The Beginnings of Humankind*, by Donald Johanson and Maitland Edey, pages 194–195.

Using Geographic Themes: Olduvai Gorge (Objective 2) Ask students to turn to the map of Africa on page 872. Point out that Olduvai Gorge is located in the Serengeti Plain in northern Tanzania. Olduvai, "the place of the wild sisal," is named for the spiky plants that grow in the region. Note that the gorge did not exist two million years ago. Rather, a shallow lake covered the region. Over time, ash from nearby volcanoes filled in the lake. The sediment covered and then preserved stone tools, animal fossils, and hominid remains.

The 300-foot-deep Olduvai Gorge was cut by an ancient river.

Walking through the gorge is like taking a trip through time. The brim contains sediment deposited just 17,000 years ago, while the bottom strata go back almost 2 million years. Explain that Mary and Louis Leakey discovered the remains of *Homo habilis* along the lowest strata of the gorge.

Discussing Prehistory: *Homo erectus* (Objective 3) Ask students to read the section "*Homo erectus* spread across Asia and Africa." Stress that *Homo erectus* was the first hominid to live in the temperate regions outside Africa. It is interesting to note that bands of *Homo erectus* could have covered the 8,700 miles between Nairobi, Kenya, and Beijing, China, in 20,000 years by moving just 12 miles per generation. While many *Homo erectus* settled across Eurasia, the majority remained in Africa. Richard Leakey (son of Louis and Mary) estimates that "until about 100,000 years ago, there were, perhaps, ten times as many people in Africa as there were in Eurasia. And during the periodic Ice Ages of the last million years, that figure may have been nearer to twenty times as many."

Check for Understanding Ask students to describe the advances associated with australopithecines, *Homo habilis*, and *Homo erectus*.

Enrichment Activities

1. **Reading a Primary Source** Assign Voices from the Past Resource Book 1.1.

2. **Preparing a Report** Ask students to prepare a report describing the life and work of one of the following scientists: Eugene Dubois; Raymond Dart; Mary, Louis, or Richard Leakey; or Donald Johanson.

3. **Researching for Bonus Points** When was carbon-14 dating discovered? Who discovered it? (1947; the United States chemist Frank Libby).

Modern humans spread across the world. 2

Setting the Stage

Ask students to recall their list of physical characteristics that set humans apart from other animals. Then ask students to name behaviors that set humans apart. Possible answers include elaborate burials, artwork, spiritual beliefs, and the creation of complex tools. Explain that these behaviors first appeared in the final 100,000 years of the Paleolithic Age. This section will focus on the achievements of humans (Neanderthals and Cro-Magnons and their contemporaries) who lived at that time. Taken together, their pioneering cultural contributions marked a momentous leap into truly human behavior.

Teaching Strategies

Skill Building: Making Inferences about Neanderthals (Objective 1) Divide your class into small groups. Then give each group a card containing the following questions:

1. What can we infer from a prehistoric grave containing skeletal remains surrounded by patches of flower pollen?

2. What can we infer from a prehistoric grave containing the skeleton of a 40-year-old man

who was blind in one eye, suffered from arthritis, and had a withered right arm?

3. What can we infer from a prehistoric cave containing 13 cave-bear skulls carefully packed inside a rough chest made of stones?

Ask each group to read its inferences. Then explain that each of these discoveries is associated with a group of people now known as Neanderthals (pages 21–22). Tell students that archaeologists have used these finds to infer that the Neanderthals believed in an afterlife, had a social structure capable of caring for the physically challenged, and had religious ceremonies that involved a belief in the spiritual power of the cave bear.

Skill Building: Comparing and Contrasting (Objective 2) Ask students to read pages 21–24 and complete the following chart (answers in italics) comparing and contrasting Neanderthals and Cro-Magnons.

	Neanderthals	Cro-Magnons
Scientific name	*Homo sapiens*	*Homo sapiens sapiens*
Life span	*up to 40 years*	*over 50 years*
Linguistic skills	*some speech*	*truly articulate speech*
Tools	*stone blades and scrapers*	*over 100 tools*
Art	*no examples yet found*	*necklaces, sculptures, and cave paintings*

Teaching with Pictures: Cave Paintings (Objective 3) Direct your students' attention to the cave painting on page 23. Explain that the bison shown in this picture was painted in the Altamira Cave about 15,000 years ago. Over the years, experts have carefully studied this and other paintings in the cave. Now ask your students to examine the painting and then answer each of the following statements either True, False, or

Don't Know. Point out that you will compare their answers with those of experts.

1. The painting was created for enjoyment and pleasure.

2. The bison is a sacred symbol designed to provide good luck in the next hunt.

3. The painting is part of an illustrated story about a successful hunt.

4. The painting was used during a secret ceremony in which young boys were initiated into their clan.

After eliciting student responses, announce that Don't Know is the correct answer for all four statements. Now ask your students to read the text's discussion on pages 23–24 to explain why experts still do not know why the paintings were drawn. Stress that without written records we can only guess what the artist had in mind when he or she painted the bison on page 23. You might conclude your discussion by asking students to speculate on reasons the cave paintings were drawn.

Check for Understanding Have students write a list giving their opinion of the three most important achievements during the late Paleolithic Age. Ask students to write a paragraph explaining which was the most significant.

Enrichment Activities

1. **Reading a Primary Source**
Assign Voices from the Past Resource Book 1.2.

2. **Speculating about Prehistory**
Explaining the cultural explosion associated with the arrival of *Homo sapiens sapiens* remains one of prehistory's most puzzling problems. Ask advanced students to write a paper speculating about possible causes.

For a discussion on this topic see pages 58–59 in the September 16, 1991 issue of *U.S. News and World Report*.

3. **Preparing a Report**
Although Stone Age tools appear to be simple, very few people today can make them. Ask students to prepare a report describing how Stone Age tools were created. The book *Cro-Magnon Man*, by Tom Prideaux contains a photo-essay (pages 83–91) showing a modern expert demonstrating how to make a scraper, perforator, and knife.

4. **Researching for Bonus Points**
Who is Jean Auel? (the author of best-selling novels about life in the late Stone Age)

Neolithic people began to farm.	3

Setting the Stage

You might begin by asking your students to consider the following problem: It is ten years from now and they are married and raising families. Both spouses in each family are self-employed. The women have to work an average of only 2 hours a day while the men work a maximum of 5 hours a day. This labor is sufficient to provide for their basic needs of food, clothing, and shelter. All their remaining time can be devoted to recreational, social, and religious affairs. Ask students whether they would exchange this situation for jobs requiring at least 10 hours of labor a day. Although the new jobs require more work, they have the potential to produce a higher standard of living.

After discussing student responses, explain that archaeologists now believe that Paleolithic hunter-gatherers did not have to work long hours to provide for their basic needs. Yet, about 10,000 years ago, they began to abandon their life-style for a new pattern based upon farming and herding. Explain that this was one of the most revolutionary changes in human history. Historians call the new era the New Stone Age, or the Neolithic Age.

Teaching Strategies

Relating Past to Present: Global Warming (Objective 1) Begin by explaining that climate is the prevailing or average weather conditions in a place or region. Then ask students to review the section, "Many factors caused the agricultural revolution" and describe how a change in climate 18,000 years ago may have helped cause the agricultural revolution.

Point out that many scientists now believe that the greenhouse effect (text page 837) could trigger another period of global warming. Ask students to speculate on the possible effects of a new global warming. For example, rising temperatures could speed desertification, while also shrinking polar ice caps and thus flooding low-lying regions around the world.

Teaching with Pictures: Mammoth-bone Shelters (Objective 2) Direct your students' attention to the picture of a mammoth-bone shelter on page 26. Explain that mammoths were gigantic woolly creatures that stood 14 feet high and

weighed 5 tons. A single mammoth tusk was 9 feet long and weighed 100 pounds. Archaeologists have uncovered evidence in Ukraine that Cro-Magnons used mammoth bones to construct groups of semipermanent dwellings. Researchers estimate that a shelter like the one pictured on page 26 required about 46,000 pounds of bones and took up to 10 people 5 days to build. Such an effort probably required some sort of social organization, which may have been the precursor to that of later villages and towns.

Explain that these semipermanent dwellings supported a more stable and varied way of life. For example, the Cro-Magnons created a variety of new tools and art objects. In the past, nomadic hunters would have been forced to limit the number of possessions they carried as they followed wandering herds. But these objects required a great deal of time to create. Anthropologists speculate that the Cro-Magnons may have been reluctant to give them up. Since hunting and gathering could no longer support their increasingly complex societies, Cro-Magnons may have turned to agriculture as a way of producing food.

Discussing Prehistory: Çatal Hüyük (Objective 3) You might begin your discussion by explaining that the site for this Neolithic town covers 32 acres. Thus far, archaeologists have uncovered just one acre, but that acre has revealed an enormous amount of useful and often intriguing information.

Tell students that the residents of Çatal Hüyük lived in homes built of sunbaked brick. Like the Pueblo dwellings in the southwestern United States, each house was set against its neighbor. The homes had no front or back doors. Instead, people entered their homes through wooden

doorways built into the roof. Connected by ladders, the terraced roofs served as the town's streets.

As explained in the text, Çatal Hüyük was a major center for the production of obsidian products. Çatal Hüyük was also an important religious center. One out of every three buildings excavated thus far was a religious shrine.

Physical anthropologists have learned a great deal about the residents of Çatal Hüyük from a study of 288 skeletons. You might ask students to guess the average life span in America today. (71 for men and 78 for women) Then tell students that in Çatal Hüyük men lived an average of 34 years while women averaged just 30 years. Ask students to speculate why women had a shorter life span. One possible reason is the large number of women aged 15–20 who apparently died during childbirth.

Check for Understanding Ask students to describe the causes and consequences of the agricultural revolution.

Enrichment Activities

1. **Reading a Primary Source**
   Assign Voices from the Past Resource Book 1.3.

2. **Preparing a Report**
   Ask students to report on one of the following farming villages: Jarmo, Jericho, Lepenski Vir, and Çatal Hüyük . (See *The World's Last Mysteries*, Reader's Digest, pages 141–152.)

3. **Interpreting a Quotation**
   Ask advanced students to interpret the following passage: "When those early agriculturists began to domesticate wild wheat and barley and the sheep and goats on the hillsides around them, they were, in a sense also domesticating themselves."

4. Researching for Bonus Points
What modern industry is based on a form of hunting? (fishing, whaling).

ANSWERS TO
Chapter Review 1

Reviewing the Facts

1. (a) human beings and other creatures that walk upright (b) period before people developed writing (c) scientists who study the physical features, development, and behavior of hominids (d) scientists who study the material remains of prehistoric and historic people (e) objects shaped by human hands (f) remnants, impressions, or traces of plants or animals that have been preserved in the earth's crust (g) way of life of a people (h) the part of a culture that includes tools and the skills to make and use them (i) Mexico and Central America (j) to tame for human use (k) smooth, dark volcanic glass

2. (a) famous scientists who discovered the Laetoli footprints and the first evidence of *Homo habilis* (b) first hominids to walk upright (c) anthropologist who discovered Lucy (d) first hominid believed to make tools (e) gorge in Tanzania where Leakeys discovered fossil remains of *Homo habilis* (f) Old Stone Age, dating from 2.5 million years ago to 15,000 years ago (g) New Stone Age, dating from 10,000 years ago to 3500 B.C. (h) first hominid to use fire and leave Africa (i) noted Kenyan fossil-hunter (j) cave in Iraq in which archaeologists first discovered evidence of Neanderthal burial customs (k) hominid, possibly *Homo sap-*

iens, who lived in Europe and Southwest Asia between 200,000 and 30,000 years ago (l) people who replaced Neanderthals (m) "doubly wise humans," anatomically modern humans (n) Spanish cave in which cave paintings were first discovered (o) archaeologist whose excavation at Jarmo proved that agriculture first began in the hill country of northeastern Iraq (p) Neolithic village in northeastern Iraq excavated by Robert Braidwood (q) arc of land stretching from the Persian Gulf to the Mediterranean (r) largest Neolithic village yet excavated

3. enabled them to travel more efficiently; or to spot threatening animals or prey; or to carry food, tools, and babies

4. (a) had a bigger brain and made tools (b) had a bigger brain, used fire, and left Africa

5. discovery of flower pollen at burial site, discovery of the remains of people whose disabilities would have prevented them from surviving on their own

6. multi-regional: Neanderthals and their contemporaries gradually evolved into anatomically modern humans at different times in several regions of the world. out-of-Africa: anatomically modern humans first emerged in Africa and then spread across Eurasia, replacing the Neanderthals and their contemporaries.

7. invented new tools such as the spear thrower and the sewing needle; were the first people known to produce art.

8. global warming and population pressure; if you have used the Teaching with Pictures on page 16e, students may include increasing social complexity.

9. Possible answers: Fertile Crescent, Africa, Southeast Asia, China, Mesoamerica, North America, Central Andes of Peru

Basic Skills

1. (a) 30,000 B.C.–Present
(b) 13,000–9000 B.C. (c) Jericho

2. (a) *Homo erectus* learned how to control and use fire. Increased brain size may have spurred intellectual curiosity. (b) Cro-Magnons and their contemporaries invented a wide variety of new tools. They also produced works of art.

3. Farming arose independently in a number of regions of the world.

Researching and Reporting Skills

1. (a) a long-lasting pattern of organization in a society (b) civilization includes cities, specialized workers, writing, advanced technology, and complex institutions (c) skilled workers who make goods by hand

2. (a) tools, fossilized bones, pollen grains (b) tools, pottery, artwork, remains of buildings

Critical Thinking

1. Both cultures had language, art, and religion and both hunted and gathered. The villagers of Jarmo were more settled and used agriculture to supply more of their food.

2. Answers will vary. Possibilities include upright walking, the use of fire, creation of cave paintings, and the use of agriculture.

Perspectives on Past and Present

1. Answers will vary.

2. Students might explain how Paleolithic leisure activities depended on imagination, whereas ours today often depend heavily on technology.

3. Help students think what some of these people's greatest needs were. Then identify what modern product or idea might be most useful to them.

Chapter 1

Teaching with Pictures

The picture on this page shows Mary Leakey studying one of the Laetoli footprints. Ask students to speculate on what scientists can learn from these 3.6-million-year-old clues.

Point out that Leakey and her team of experts were able to learn a great deal from the prints. For example, a footprint expert found a particularly well-preserved print showing the raised arch, rounded heel, pronounced ball, and forward-pointing big toe necessary for walking erect. Measurements revealed that the smaller prints are 7.28 inches long, while the largest are 8.46 inches long. Explain that the length of the foot represents about 15 percent of an individual's height. Ask students to use this rule of thumb to estimate the height of these two hominids. (The smaller one stood about 4 feet tall while the larger was about 4 feet 7 inches.)

For additional information on the Laetoli footprints, see "Footprints in the Ashes of Time," by Mary Leakey in the April 1979 issue of *National Geographic*. The article contains artistic recreations showing how the footprints were made and preserved.

4,000,000 B.C. - 3500 B.C.

Prehistoric Times

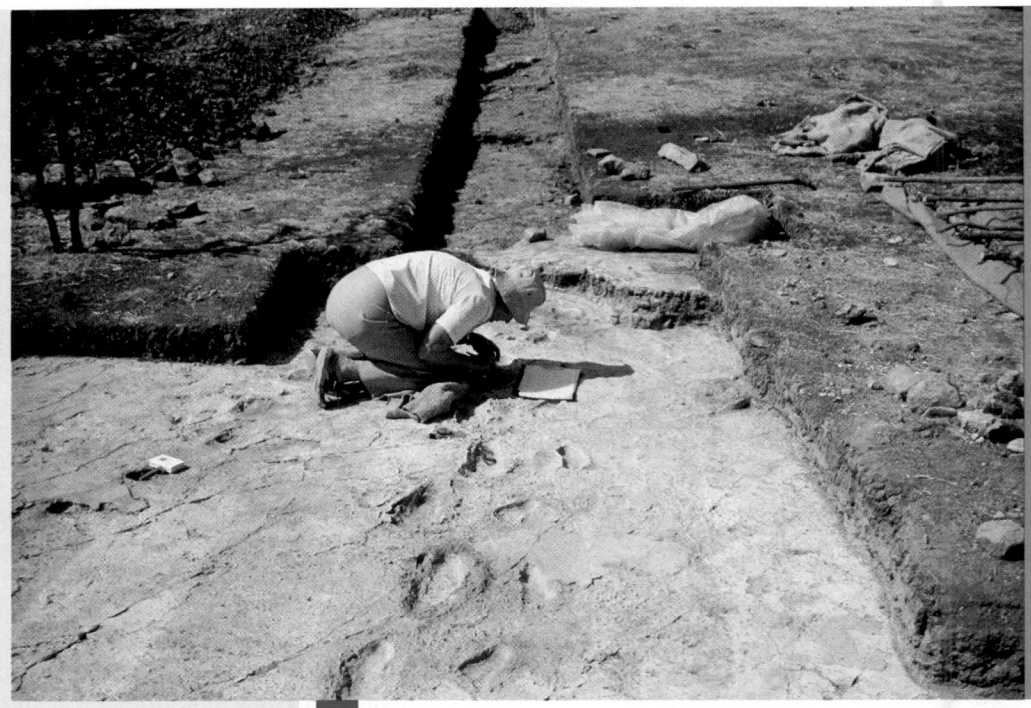

Mary Leakey with the 3.6-million-year-old hominid footprints at Laetoli, Tanzania

Key Terms

hominid
prehistory
anthropologist
archaeologist
artifact
fossil
culture
technology
Mesoamerica
domesticate
obsidian

Read and Understand

1. Scientists search for human origins.
2. Modern humans spread across the world.
3. Neolithic people began to farm.

Tanzania is a modern country located in eastern Africa. (see map page 872) Although Tanzania is a very young nation, its ancient geological sites contain some of the world's oldest human and humanlike fossils. A flat expanse known as Laetoli (lye-TOH-lee) is one such place. Located in a remote corner of northern Tanzania, Laetoli's rich fossil beds yielded no human or humanlike remains until 1974. In that year, Mary Leakey led a scientific expedition hoping to find new clues about human origins.

As a veteran of many expeditions, Leakey knew that finding the remains of human ancestors requires great patience, expert knowledge, and luck. Although Leakey's team found numerous animal fossils, two years of careful searching produced only a few jaw fragments and teeth from humanlike creatures. But lucky breaks often

16

Chapter 1 Resources

GEOGRAPHY
- Geography Skills 1
- Outline Map 1

REINFORCEMENT
- Vocabulary 1
- Basic Skills 1
- Reteaching 1
- Making Connections Study Guide 1

ENRICHMENT
- Critical Thinking 1

ASSESSMENT
- Chapter Test 1
- Alternate Chapter Test 1
- Computer Test Bank

come in unexpected ways. Letting off steam after a hard day of painstaking work, several scientists began throwing chunks of dried elephant dung at one another. As one scientist searched the ground for more ammunition, he noticed strange marks in an exposed layer of volcanic ash. A closer investigation revealed that the marks were footprints left by extinct species of animals.

The footprints had been created by an extraordinary set of circumstances. First, a nearby volcano erupted, covering the surrounding landscape with a fresh layer of soft ash. Then, a brief rain shower turned the ash into a surface like wet sand that recorded the trails left by wandering animals. Finally, the hot tropical sun dried and hardened the surface, thus preserving the footprints. Additional layers of ash and a thick covering of plant growth concealed them from view for the next 3.6 million years.

Even more dramatic revelations soon followed the discovery of the animal footprints. In 1977, two of Leakey's assistants uncovered footprints remarkably similar to those of modern human beings. Two more years of painstaking work uncovered 50 more prints.

After a careful analysis, scientists concluded that the trail had been made by three creatures now called australopithecines (aw-STRAY-low-PITH-uh-SYNES). Human beings and other creatures that walk upright, such as the australopithecines, are called **hominids.** The Laetoli footprints provide striking evidence that hominids existed at least 3.6 million years ago. Upright walking was the first key feature that set hominids apart from other animals.

The footprints (possibly made by a male, a female, and a juvenile) are more than just scientific evidence, however. They are also reminders from our long-buried past about the human condition. Mary Leakey wrote that studying the footprints produced "a kind of poignant time wrench. At one point, and you need not be an expert tracker to discern this, she stops, pauses, turns to the left to glance at some possible threat or irregularity, and then continues to the north. This motion, so intensely human, transcends time. . . ."

We have chosen to begin our study of world history with the Laetoli footprints for another reason. These footprints in time mark the beginning of a long and exciting journey. As human beings, we have the unique ability to reflect on our history and plan for our future. This self-awareness contributes to our intense curiosity about the human past. This chapter will examine **prehistory**—the long period of time before people developed writing. The next 36 chapters will describe world history since the invention of writing about 5,500 years ago.

Scientists search for human origins. 1

The earth contains many hidden traces from the prehistoric past. Finding these traces requires sharp eyes. Interpreting them requires even more skill. Anthropologists and archaeologists study and interpret prehistory. **Anthropologists** study the physical features, development, and behavior of hominids. **Archaeologists** study the material remains of prehistoric and historic people. These remains, or **artifacts,** include objects shaped by human hands as well as other evidence of human activity. Archaeologists are also interested in human ways of living.

For scientists studying human ancestors, **fossils** and tools and other artifacts are pieces from a 3- to 4-million-year-old jigsaw puzzle. Fossils are remnants (such as bones or teeth), impressions, or traces of plants or animals that have been preserved in the earth's crust. Anthropologists and archaeologists use these remains to reconstruct picture of the way of life, or **culture,** of prehistoric hominids.

Researchers today use sophisticated techniques in their investigations. For example, radiocarbon and potassium-argon dating are two widely used procedures. Radiocarbon dating uses the rate of decay of radioactive carbon atoms to date organic remains up to 50,000 years old. The potassium-argon method can date samples of rocks that are up to 3 billion years old.

This section will describe the findings of anthropologists and archaeologists who are using these and other techniques. During the past three decades, their discoveries have revolutionized our knowledge about the first hominids.

17

SECTION 1 Objectives and Teaching Strategies

OBJECTIVE 1. Describe methods scientists use to determine prehistoric dates.

Teaching Strategy: *Discussing Prehistory: Dating Prehistoric Objects* (page 16b)

OBJECTIVE 2. Identify Olduvai Gorge and explain why it is a significant prehistoric site.

Teaching Strategy: *Using Geographic Themes: Olduvai Gorge* (page 16c)

OBJECTIVE 3. Identify *Homo erectus* and explain why the species left Africa.

Teaching Strategy: *Discussing Prehistory: Homo erectus* (page 16c)

■ DISCUSSION

Point out that the radiocarbon and potassium-argon procedures enable scientists to accurately measure the actual, or absolute, age of an artifact. Prior to the discovery of these methods, researchers relied upon relative dating procedures. Using these methods, a scientist attempted to determine an artifact's age in relation to other objects at the site. For example, artifacts found in the bottom layer of a site were considered to be relatively older than artifacts found in layers closer to the surface. Ask students to describe possible problems with relative dating procedures.

SECTION 1 Resources

ASSESSMENT
- Section Quiz 1.1

REINFORCEMENT
- Independent Practice 1.1

ENRICHMENT
- Voices from the Past 1.1

The diagram on this page enables students to compare Lucy's skeleton with that of a modern human. Point out that although fully grown, Lucy stood only 3 1/2 feet tall. Johanson believes that she was between 25 and 30 years old when she died. He speculates that the absence of tooth marks on her bones suggests that she died quietly, possibly from an illness or accidental drowning. Since Lucy's body was not found by a scavenger, her skeleton remained covered for more than 3 million years, until rain or a flash flood exposed it. Lucy's skeleton can now be seen in the Cleveland Museum of Natural History.

However, it is important to remember that the picture of prehistory is still far from complete.

Australopithecines walked upright.

While Mary Leakey was beginning her work in Laetoli, an American anthropologist named Donald Johanson was searching for fossils in Ethiopia, a thousand miles to the north. As Johanson and a graduate student slowly walked through a parched gully, Johanson spotted a small bone from a hominid arm. The two star-

A comparison of Lucy (left) and a modern human. The darkened parts of Lucy's skeleton show the bones that were actually found. The skull should be darkened too but is left open for clarity.

tled anthropologists also found the back of a small skull, several ribs, and a thigh bone. Ignoring the 110-degree heat, they leapt up and down, exultant at their discovery.

Johanson had reason for his excitement. When pieced together, the bones formed 40 percent of the skeleton of an adult female hominid who lived 3 million years ago. Johanson and his colleagues nicknamed the skeleton Lucy after the Beatles song "Lucy in the Sky with Diamonds" that was popular in their camp. Johanson later summarized Lucy's significance when he explained that "she is the oldest, most complete, best preserved skeleton of any erect walking human ancestor that has ever been found."

Lucy and the hominids who left their footprints at Laetoli were australopithecines. Even with these dramatic finds, anthropologists still have few clues about how they lived. For example, anthropologists think it possible that at least some species of australopithecines used tools, but cannot prove that they did. Nonetheless, we do know that there were several species and that they lived between 4 million and 1 million years ago. Most australopithecines were small, ranging in height from 3 to 5 feet. Their brain size was only about one-third that of modern human brains.

As you have read, australopithecines were the first creatures to walk upright. Anthropologists have offered at least three theories to explain this revolutionary change. First, a change in global climate more than 4 million years ago caused Africa to become cooler and drier. As a result, open grasslands began to replace the tropical rain forests that were the australopithecines' habitat. Walking erect enabled early hominids to get from one forested area to another more efficiently than apes, who traveled across land on all fours. A second theory is that walking erect enabled early hominids to see over the grasslands in order to spot threatening animals or the small or young animals that they may have occasionally caught for food. Third, walking erect freed the australopithecines' hands so that they could carry food, tools, and babies.

Controversy still surrounds the australopithecines. For example, Johanson thinks Lucy and her kind were on the line that eventually led to the human genus, *Homo.* Others disagree, pointing to the huge gaps in the fossil record.

18

Homo habilis *may have used tools.*

The australopithecines eventually disappeared, but before they did, a new creature now known as *Homo habilis* first appeared in eastern Africa somewhere between 2.5 and 2.0 million years ago. (*Habilis* means "skillful," so scientists gave the creature the tongue-in-cheek name Handy Man.) *Homo habilis* remains were first discovered by Mary Leakey and her husband Louis at Olduvai (OHL-duh-WYE [or VYE]) Gorge in northern Tanzania. Carved by a river, the 25-mile-long gorge resembles a smaller version of the Grand Canyon. Its 300-foot-high walls expose so many layers of rich deposits that Louis Leakey called the gorge "a fossil hunter's dream."

Louis Leakey began searching for fossils in Olduvai Gorge in 1931, and Mary joined him in the mid-1930's. Three decades of pioneering work finally paid off in 1960, when they unearthed skull fragments 1.8 million years old. Reconstruction revealed that the skull housed a brain nearly 50 percent larger than that of the australopithecines. This large brain led the Leakeys to theorize that *Homo habilis* was the true remote ancestor of modern humans.

Their larger brains may have given *Homo habilis* a unique advantage over the larger and faster animals that competed with them for survival. Many scientists believe that they probably used their increased brain power to make stone tools. The Leakeys and other researchers have found tools made of lava rock that they believe *Homo habilis* used to cut meat and crack open bones. Modern archaeologists have shown that these razor-sharp stone blades could butcher 100 pounds of elephant meat in an hour.

This ability to make and use tools is one of the fundamental features of the modern human species. The appearance of stone tools marks the beginning of an era historians call the Stone Age. The Stone Age is often divided into three parts. The Paleolithic (PAY-lee-uh-LITH-ik), or Old Stone Age, began 2.5 million years ago with the first tools made by *Homo habilis*. The Mesolithic (MEZ-uh-LITH-ik), or Middle Stone Age, lasted from 15,000 to 10,000 years ago. Finally, the Neolithic (NEE-uh-LITH-ik), or New Stone Age, is usually dated from 10,000 years ago to 3500 B.C.

The bones of *Homo habilis* found by the Leakeys in 1960 at Olduvai. Louis is pictured at top left.

Homo erectus *spread across Asia and Europe.*

About 1.6 million years ago, before *Homo habilis* left the scene, a species now known as *Homo erectus*, or "upright man" appeared in eastern Africa. Fossilized remains show that it had a bigger body and brain than *Homo habilis*. For example, a skeleton discovered in 1984 by the noted Kenyan fossil-hunter Kamoya Kimeu (kah-MOY-yah kah-ME-OH) suggests that adult males stood as much as 6 feet tall. The average *Homo erectus* brain measured about three-fourths the size of a human brain today.

Some scientists believe *Homo erectus* was a more intelligent and adaptable species than *Homo habilis*. While *Homo habilis* stayed in

19

■ BACKGROUND

Archaeologists working in Olduvai Gorge have discovered clusters of stones that may have been part of a shelter built 1.8 million years ago. Researchers speculate that *Homo habilis* used the stones to anchor branches that formed a circular hut. This building method is still used by hunter-gatherers in parts of Africa.

ANSWERS TO
Section Review 1

Define:
(a) human beings and other creatures that walk upright (b) period before people developed writing (c) scientists who study the physical features, development, and behavior of hominids (d) scientists who study the material remains of prehistoric and historic people (e) objects shaped by human hands (f) remnants, impressions, or traces of plants or animals that have been preserved in the earth's crust (g) way of life of a people
Identify:
(a) famous scientists who discovered the Laetoli footprints and the first evidence of *Homo habilis* (b) first hominids (or first creatures to walk upright) (c) anthropologist who discovered Lucy (d) believed to be the first hominid to make tools (e) gorge in Tanzania where the Leakeys discovered the fossil remains of *Homo habilis* (f) Old Stone Age—2.5 million to 15,000 years ago (g) Middle Stone Age—15,000 to 10,000 years ago (h) New Stone Age—10,000

(continued)

ANSWERS TO *(continued)*

years ago to 3500 B.C. **(i)** first hominid to use fire and to leave Africa **(j)** noted Kenyan fossil-hunter

Answer:

1. They provided evidence that hominids existed at least 3.6 million years ago.

2. radiocarbon and potassium-argon dating

3. Walking erect enabled australopithecines to travel more efficiently or to spot threatening animals or prey or to carry food, tools, and babies.

4. (a) ability to make tools **(b)** ability to control and use fire and possibly, intellectual curiosity

5. Fire provided warmth and frightened away predators and may have been used in hunting.

6. Some anthropologists believe that the habitual use of hands, tools, and brain set in motion a complex feedback process that slowly produced hominids with larger and larger brains. The continued interaction between the human brain and complex tools may be continuing this long-term process.

Africa, *Homo erectus* became the first hominid known to leave the continent. Fossils and stone tools show that bands of *Homo erectus* hunters eventually settled in India, China, Southeast Asia, and Europe.

Anthropologists believe that fire played a crucial role in enabling *Homo erectus* to settle new lands. Unlike all previous hominids, *Homo erectus* learned how to control and use fire. Fire protected *Homo erectus* settlers from the freezing winters in northern latitudes, but it provided more than just warmth. Fire could be used to cook food and frighten away predators. Also, *Homo erectus* hunters may have used fire to drive frightened herds of animals into marshes or bogs where they could be slaughtered.

Fire helps explain how bands of *Homo erectus* were able to leave Africa, yet it does not tell why they left. Perhaps *Homo erectus*'s success as hunters sparked a rise in population. A growing population may then have created pressure to find new hunting grounds. But it is also possible that some *Homo erectus* may have chosen to explore new lands, to find out what was over the next hill. Increased brain size may have spurred intellectual curiosity. Like us, *Homo erectus* may have been curious to explore the unknown. At any rate, gradually, a few miles at a time, over thousands of years, *Homo erectus* spread across Asia and Europe.

Define: (a) hominid, (b) prehistory, (c) anthropologist, (d) archaeologist, (e) artifact, (f) fossil, (g) culture
Identify: (a) Louis and Mary Leakey, (b) australopithecines, (c) Donald Johanson, (d) *Homo habilis*, (e) Olduvai Gorge, (f) Paleolithic Age, (g) Mesolithic Age, (h) Neolithic Age, (i) *Homo erectus*, (j) Kamoya Kimeu

Answer:

1. Why are the Laetoli footprints significant?
2. Name two procedures that are widely used to date prehistoric remains.
3. Describe one theory that may explain why australopithecines walked upright.
4. What advantages may an increase in brain size have given (a) *Homo habilis*? (b) *Homo erectus*?
5. List three ways in which fire helped *Homo erectus*.

Critical Thinking

6. What factors may have caused the brain size of early hominids to increase? Do you think that human brain size will continue to increase? Explain.

Arlette Leroi-Gourhan (page 21) found evidence of burial ritual in the soil of Shanidar Cave in the Zagros Mountains of Iraq.

Modern humans spread across the world. 2

As a paleobotanist, Arlette Leroi-Gourhan specialized in studying prehistoric plant life. But what she found as she looked through her microscope was unprecedented. Peering into her lens, Leroi-Gourhan identified large clusters of ancient microscopic pollen grains from eight different types of flowers.

Finding ancient pollen grains was not unusual. But these specimens were different. They were contained in a soil sample drawn from the grave of a prehistoric man who had died 60,000 years ago. His grave had been unearthed at the back of Shanidar, a large cave in the Zagros Mountains of northeastern Iraq.

Archaeologists speculate that the man's family covered his body with flowers during a prehistoric funeral. The simple but profoundly human gesture of placing flowers in a loved one's grave marks a milestone in human history. Although we can never be certain, the prehistoric funeral held in that cave 60,000 years ago suggests a belief in a world beyond the grave.

Burial customs were one of many significant developments that took place during the final 100,000 years of the Paleolithic Age. In Europe and Southwest Asia, a people now known as Neanderthals (nee-AN-duhr-TALZ) dominated the first part of this era. Elsewhere, other early humans were prevalent. However, the Neanderthals and their contemporaries in Africa and eastern Asia had vanished by about 30,000 years ago. As you will see, they were replaced by anatomically modern humans, who colonized every continent except Antarctica. These prehistoric pioneers also invented complex new tools and painted the first artworks in world history. Taken together, these achievements mark a momentous leap into truly human behavior.

Neanderthals appear in Southwest Asia and Europe.

As you saw, *Homo erectus* first appeared about 1.6 million years ago. Many scientists believe that between 500,000 and 200,000 years ago, *Homo erectus* evolved into a new species—

Homo sapiens. Like humans today, the first *Homo sapiens* were almost indistinguishable from *Homo erectus* from the neck down. On the average, however, *Homo sapiens* had significantly larger brains. (The name *sapiens* comes from a Latin word meaning "wise.")

The first evidence of prehistoric *Homo sapiens* came from the Neander Valley in Germany. In 1856, quarry workers found a skullcap, ribs, and other fossilized bone fragments. These bones aroused intense curiosity. Although they clearly belonged to a human being of some sort, the bones were surprisingly thick and the skullcap's heavy slanted brow seemed unusual.

Some scholars refused to believe that prehistoric humans existed, so they were unwilling to acknowledge that the fossils were very old. Other scholars needed more evidence on which to base their judgments. This evidence came in the form of later discoveries of similar fossilized bones, which showed that the Neander bones were indeed ancient.

The people to whom the Neander bones (and other similar bones found elsewhere in Europe and Southwest Asia) belonged are called Neanderthals. (*Thal* is the German word for *valley*.) Scientists today are divided on whether the Neanderthals, who lived in Europe and Southwest Asia between 200,000 and 30,000 years ago, were a variety of *Homo sapiens* or a separate species (*Homo neanderthalensis*).

Anthropologists have thus far recovered the partial remains of about 400 Neanderthal skeletons. They show that Neanderthal men stood about 5 feet 6 inches tall while the women were about 5 feet tall. Although short, these people were powerfully built. Their well-developed muscles and thick bones were 10 to 20 percent heavier than those of people today.

Neanderthals successfully lived through harsh Ice Age winters. Caves provided an ideal source of protection from frigid winds. When caves were not available, the Neanderthals used wood and animal skins to build temporary shelters.

Although a large part of their diet must have come from wild plants, the Neanderthals seem to have been skillful hunters. Deer and other medium to large animals provided their most important source of meat. Occasionally, they may have hunted such larger animals as the gigantic 5-ton woolly mammoths. To cut up and

21

SECTION 2 Objectives and Teaching Strategies

OBJECTIVE 1. Make inferences about how the Neanderthals lived.

Teaching Strategy: *Skill Building: Making Inferences about Neanderthals* (page 16c)

OBJECTIVE 2. Compare and contrast Neanderthals and Cro-Magnons.

Teaching Strategy: *Skill Building: Comparing and Contrasting* (page 16d)

OBJECTIVE 3. Speculate about why cave paintings were drawn.

Teaching Strategy: *Teaching with Pictures* (page 16d)

■ BACKGROUND

Some nineteenth century scholars originally refused to recognize that the Neanderthal bones belonged to prehistoric people. For example, a German anatomist confidently explained that the primitive bones must have belonged to a Russian soldier who died in 1814 while chasing Napoleon out of Germany. To this day, the word *Neanderthal* carries connotations of clumsiness and stupidity based on that reaction to the Neanderthal bones.

SECTION 2 Resources

ASSESSMENT
■ Section Quiz 1.2

REINFORCEMENT
■ Independent Practice 1.2

ENRICHMENT
■ Voices from the Past 1.2

Point out that the Neanderthals occupied Europe and Southwest Asia for thousands of years. If the out-of-Africa theory is correct, the Cro-Magnons must have migrated into lands long occupied by the Neanderthals. These two groups may have had some interaction, as they shared the same lands.

Ask your students to speculate about what kind of interaction may have taken place between the Neanderthals and the Cro-Magnons. For example, would they have had cooperative or competitive relations? Would their physical and cultural differences have led to prejudice and discrimination?

Now divide your class into small cooperative learning groups. Ask each group to imagine a situation in which Neanderthals and Cro-Magnons had contact with each other. For example, what would have happened if Cro-Magnons arrived during a Neanderthal burial or if a band of Neanderthals wandered into a cave being painted by Cro-Magnons? (Not a real possibility, since most if not all cave painting was done after the Neanderthals died out.) Ask each group to write a dialogue describing the interaction between its Neanderthal and Cro-Magnon characters. Encourage your students to utilize information presented in their text.

skin their prey, Neanderthals fashioned stone blades, scrapers, and other tools.

To many people, the name Neanderthal conjures up the image of the club-carrying comic strip caveman. However, archaeological discoveries indicate that Neanderthals were probably caring people who attached importance to an individual's life and death. You have read, for example, about the evidence suggesting burial ritual. In addition, archaeologists have unearthed the fossil remains of people with physical disabilities that would have prevented them from surviving on their own. Rather than abandoning their handicapped members, the Neanderthals chose to protect and care for them.

While the Neanderthals lived in Europe and Southwest Asia, other *Homo sapiens* species populated Africa and central and eastern Asia. Their tools were similar to those of the Neanderthals. Less is known about these people since archaeologists in the past have focused mainly on Europe. That is changing as scientists learn more about the Neanderthals' contemporaries.

What happened to the Neanderthals?

The Neanderthals survived for more than 100,000 years and then vanished about 30,000 years ago. The causes of this disappearance remain one of prehistory's great mysteries.

At least two theories have been offered to explain what happened to the Neanderthals. The multi-regional theory argues that the Neanderthals gradually evolved into anatomically modern humans, and that contemporaries of the Neanderthals did so independently at different times in several regions of the world. These modern-looking humans were *Homo sapiens sapiens*, the "doubly wise humans." Those who lived in Europe are known as Cro-Magnons after the site in France where their fossil remains were first discovered in 1868.

An alternative to the multi-regional theory is supported by recent discoveries suggesting that *Homo sapiens sapiens* made their first appearance in southern Africa 100,000 (or possibly even 200,000) years ago. According to the out-of-Africa theory, anatomically modern humans emerged in Africa and then spread across Eurasia, eventually replacing the Neanderthals and their contemporaries.

22

Although the out-of-Africa theory explains where anatomically modern humans may have come from, it does not explain why the Neanderthals and their contemporaries disappeared. Scientists cite a number of advantages that gave Cro-Magnons an edge in the competition for food and shelter. While Neanderthals rarely lived past 40, bone studies reveal that some Cro-Magnons lived well into their 50's. This may have enabled Cro-Magnon populations to grow at a slightly faster rate and eventually replace the Neanderthals. In addition, Neanderthals may not have been capable of truly articulate speech. If so, the Cro-Magnons' advanced linguistic skills may have enabled them to plan complex cooperative projects that gave them an edge over the Neanderthals.

The origins of the Cro-Magnons and other early modern humans and the reasons for their success are still the subject of much debate. Additional discoveries will continue to help anthropologists sort out what happened. But what is certain is that the emergence of these people opened a new chapter in human history.

Modern Homo sapiens revolutionized human life.

Whatever gave early modern humans the edge, be it greater intelligence, better language skills, or some other factor, their emergence marks the beginning of a new era. This era saw revolutionary innovations in artistic expression and in **technology,** or tools and the skills to use them.

A new tool kit Cro-Magnon and other early modern humans launched a technological revolution by devising more efficient ways of making stone blades. In addition, the numbers and kinds of tools increased dramatically. These early people skillfully used stone, bone, and wood to fashion more than 100 different tools. Their tool kits included a variety of razor-sharp blades, fish hooks, and a chisel-like cutter used to cut bone and antler into other tools.

Early modern humans invented a number of new hunting weapons. For example, spear throwers enabled hunters to kill game at a distance of 30 to 50 feet. By increasing their range, hunters could capture more prey with less risk.

The sewing needle also played a key role in improving life. Archaeologists believe that the

Bison were a favorite subject of Paleolithic artists. No one today knows for sure the significance of the cave paintings.

The Lascaux Cave in France contains some of the finest examples of Stone Age art. Like the Altamira Cave, it was discovered by accident. After being opened to the public in 1948, the cave quickly became a popular tourist attraction. But the cave's popularity caused unforeseen problems. The hundreds of tourists who visited the cave each day increased the air temperature while also breathing carbon dioxide into the air. Within a short time, green spots composed of algae and bacteria appeared on the cave's walls. In order to protect the cave's fragile environment, authorities closed it to the public in 1963. However, tourists can see a carefully reconstructed model of the cave built nearby. Voices from the Past reading 1.2 provides a vivid description of a visit to the Lascaux Cave not long after it was opened.

first bone sewing needles were invented about 23,000 years ago. They enabled early modern humans to make close-fitting clothing sewn together with animal sinews. Their warm pants, hooded parkas, and snug boots protected them from the bitterly cold Ice Age winters.

Ice Age art The tools of early modern humans help us understand how they hunted for food and sewed clothing. But their world best springs to life through their artistic creations. Both sexes wore necklaces decorated with seashells, lion teeth, and bear claws. People spent long hours grinding mammoth tusks into polished beads, and they carved small but realistic sculptures of the animals that inhabited their world.

The best known Stone Age artistic achievements are painted on the narrow corridors and ceilings of European caves. These paintings were unknown to modern humans until 1879. In that year, Don Marcelino de Sautuola, Spanish nobleman and amateur archaeologist, explored a cave on his estate. The cave was located on a rocky hill known as Altamira, or "high lookout."

As De Sautuola searched the cave floor, his 12-year-old daughter María wandered into a low chamber barely 5 feet high. When she turned her lantern upward at the cave's ceiling, the flickering light revealed paintings of bison, horses, and deer that had been hidden from human eyes for thousands of years. Stunned by what she saw, María raced back to her father shouting "Toros pintados!" (Painted bulls)

De Sautuola immediately rushed to Madrid to report his amazing discovery. But experts refused to believe that prehistoric artists could paint such figures. Most scholars of the time thought prehistoric people lacked the ability to create works of art. As a result, De Sautuola was mocked and criticized.

Archaeologists now recognize that the lifelike paintings inside the Altamira Cave were drawn by skilled Cro-Magnon artists who lived between 12,000 and 25,000 years ago. More than 200 such caves have been discovered across Europe, mostly in France and Spain. In addition, rock art paintings have been found in Africa and Australia. (*Homo sapiens sapiens* probably arrived in Australia about 40,000 years ago, most likely by island hopping in small boats.) Since most African paintings are not in caves, they are

23

Define:
that part of a culture that includes tools and the skills to make and use them

Identify:
(a) People who lived in Europe and Southwest Asia between 200,000 and 30,000 years ago. Some scientists call them *Homo sapiens*; others call them *Homo neanderthalensis* (b) people (*Homo sapiens sapiens*) who replaced the Neanderthals (c) anatomically modern humans, including the Cro-Magnons and their contemporaries around the world, as well as people alive today ("doubly wise humans")

Answer:
1. Burial sites containing pollen grains, the remains of people with disabilities.
2. The multi-regional theory argues that Neanderthals and their contemporaries gradually evolved into anatomically modern humans at different times in several regions of the world. The out-of-Africa theory claims that anatomically modern humans first emerged in Africa and then spread across Eurasia, replacing the Neanderthals and their contemporaries.

3. The spear thrower enabled hunters to kill game at longer distances, thus helping them capture more prey with less risk. The sewing needle enabled people to make close-fitting clothing that protected them from the cold Ice Age winters.

4. (a) They may have had magical significance, been part of an initiation rite, or

(continued)

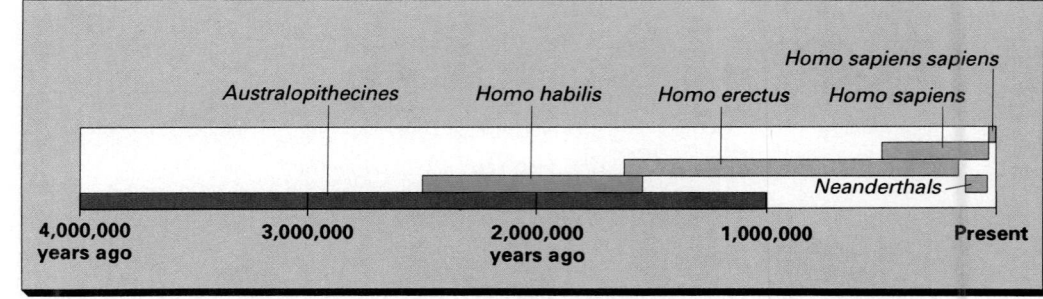

generally not as well preserved as the paintings in Europe.

While the authenticity of the cave paintings is no longer disputed, their purpose remains a mystery. Three major theories have been offered to explain why they were drawn. One theory is that the paintings had magical significance designed to give hunters power over their prey. A second theory sees the paintings as a pictorial textbook designed to help young hunters identify various animals. Finally, the paintings may have been part of an initiation rite during which children passed into adulthood.

Although their original purpose has been lost, the cave paintings remain vivid examples of the sudden burst of creativity that occurred during the late Paleolithic Age. But, as the great Ice Age glaciers slowly receded, a new era in world history began to dawn. As you will see, the way of life based on hunting and gathering changed forever when people began to live in permanent villages, growing crops and raising livestock.

Section REVIEW 2

Define: technology
Identify: (a) Neanderthals, (b) Cro-Magnons, (c) *Homo sapiens sapiens*
Answer:
1. What evidence is there that the Neanderthals cared for one another in life and in death?
2. Describe two theories that may explain how the Neanderthals disappeared.
3. Explain how the spear thrower and the sewing needle improved life.
4. (a) Describe three theories that may explain the purpose of cave art. (b) Which theory do you think offers the best explanation?

24

Critical Thinking
5. One archaeologist predicted that finding the origin of *Homo sapiens sapiens*—whether in Africa, Asia, or Europe—will promote worldwide unity. Do you agree? Why?

Neolithic people began to farm. 3

Today the rolling hill country in northeastern Iraq looks bare and desolate. Only a few trees dot the eroded foothills of the Zagros Mountains. On first glance, these isolated hills would appear to be an unlikely place to find the origins of agriculture. However, Robert Braidwood, an archaeologist at the University of Chicago, believed otherwise. He argued that the now barren hills were once the first birthplace of agriculture. "Nowhere else in the world," Braidwood pointed out, "were the wild wheats and barley, the wild sheep, goats, pigs, cattle, and horses to be found together in a single environment."

To test his theory, Braidwood chose to conduct a dig at Jarmo, a three-acre mound near the bend of a dry riverbed. After four years of painstaking work in the early 1950's, Braidwood uncovered 16 distinct layers, each representing a different settlement. Analyzing the deepest layer, Braidwood found that Jarmo had been first settled about 9,000 years ago. Its earliest residents lived in small mud-walled houses. They wore bone bracelets and fashioned elegant cups and bowls of ground stone.

Braidwood's most important finds, however, were the charred seeds of cultivated forms of wheat and barley. These long-buried seeds gave

In Africa, Saharan rock art (c. 6000–4000 B.C.) shows the transition from the hunting of wild animals (right) to the herding of cattle (left).

ANSWERS TO *(continued)*
served as pictorial textbooks for young hunters. **(b)** Answers will vary.

5. Answers will vary. Students who agree could argue that learning about our common origins will help people to understand that our similarities are greater than our differences. Students who disagree may argue that ethnic, racial, and religious conflicts have become too ingrained to be easily resolved.

convincing evidence that Jarmo's farmers had been growing crops as early as 7000 B.C.

Although they probably did not realize it, these farmers, and others like them elsewhere, were pioneering a new way of life. Until about 10,000 years ago, people lived by gathering plants and hunting game. Villages such as Jarmo marked the beginning of a new era. As you shall see in this section, the Neolithic Age witnessed the birth of agriculture and the beginnings of the first towns. These crucial developments laid the foundation for modern life.

Many factors caused the agricultural revolution.

Jarmo was at the eastern end of an area now called the Fertile Crescent. The Fertile Crescent (map, page 32) stretched in a large arc from the Persian Gulf to the Mediterranean Sea. The region is thought to be the first in the world in which agriculture replaced hunting and gathering. However, agriculture also arose independently in Africa, Southeast Asia, China, **Mesoamerica** (Mexico and Central America), North America, and the Peruvian Andes.

Braidwood's pioneering work helped establish the Fertile Crescent as a vital part of the agricultural revolution, but it did not explain why prehistoric hunter-gatherers gave up a way of life that they and their ancestors had followed for almost two million years. Over the years, anthropologists have proposed several explanations. However, as new discoveries are made and old ones reexamined, it seems clear that no one factor can account for the development of agriculture in each place in which it arose.

A *warmer world* The last Ice Age reached its peak 18,000 years ago. At that time, huge glaciers covered almost a quarter of the earth's land surface. However, global temperatures did not remain the same. During the next 7,000 years, they rose an average of 9° F.

This global warming had a dramatic impact on plant life around the world. For example, the Fertile Crescent had been a lush hill country filled with a wide variety of plants and animals. As the world became warmer, frequent droughts left the region more arid.

The drier environment supported grasses such as wheat, barley, and rye. Although gathering wild grain was backbreaking work, it was well worth the effort. In just three weeks, a family of four could harvest enough to last a year.

Population pressure The availability of grain helped support a small population boom. An estimated 10 million people inhabited the earth in 10,000 B.C. By today's standards, in a world whose population is fast approaching 6 billion, this may seem a very small population. However, hunter-gatherers needed a large territory to support a few people, possibly as much as 250 square miles of land for a band of 25 people. As populations slowly rose, hunter-gatherers felt

25

SECTION 3
Objectives and Teaching Strategies

OBJECTIVE 1. Identify the factors that caused the agricultural revolution.
Teaching Strategy: *Relating Past to Present: Global Warming* (page 16e)

OBJECTIVE 2. Make inferences from pictures of Stone Age art.
Teaching Strategy: *Teaching with Pictures: Mammothbone Shelters* (page 16e)

OBJECTIVE 3. Describe aspects of daily life in a Neolithic village.
Teaching Strategy: *Discussing Prehistory: Çatal Hüyük* (page 16e)

■ BACKGROUND

Although the last Ice Age ended 15,000 years ago, glaciers and ice sheets still cover about 10 percent of the earth's land area. If all the ice on the earth were to melt, so much water would be released that the global sea level would rise by more than 200 feet.

SECTION 3
Resources

ASSESSMENT
■ Section Quiz 1.3

REINFORCEMENT
■ Independent Practice 1.3

ENRICHMENT
■ Voices from the Past 1.3

BACKGROUND

With the agricultural revolution came a need for storing food for later use. People needed to protect their harvests from dampness, insects, and hungry hordes of rats and mice that quickly moved into the new farming villages.

The earliest farmers made containers of stone, wood, or basketry. Pottery bowls and jars, however, are easier and faster to make. Moreover, clay is available along the banks of many rivers and streams. At first, people simply molded their lumps of clay with their hands. Later, they learned to make smoother, rounder shapes using a potter's wheel.

Once people learned to harden the clay by firing it in ovens, clay pots and jars became an important part of everyday life. Broken pottery pieces are so common at ancient living sites that archaeologists often study the pottery to determine the date of the culture.

ANSWERS TO

Section Review 3

Define:
(a) Mexico and Central America (b) to tame for human use (c) smooth, dark volcanic glass

Identify:
(a) archaeologist who excavated Jarmo, proving that agriculture first began in the foothills of the Zagros Mountains (b) Neolithic village in northeastern Iraq ex-

(continued)

Reconstruction of a Ukrainian mammoth-bone dwelling (c. 28,000 B.C.). Patterns on a carving (c. 17,000–14,000 B.C.) suggest a halter as well as muscles. A dog skeleton in Illinois (c. 6500 B.C.).

pressure to find new food sources. Farming offered an attractive alternative, as it produced more food per acre than hunting and gathering.

Farming had deep roots.

Long before the first true villages, people had discovered that they could save seeds and plant them. People in Mesoamerica, for example, did that with the bottle gourd, which they used to carry water. If they traveled to an area in which the gourds didn't occur naturally, they simply planted the seeds they had saved. As people began settling in permanent villages, they planted food and other crops, such as flax from whose fibers linen is made. As people planted more and more crops, the size of villages could increase.

Just as early gatherers observed plants closely, early hunters were experts on animals. Gradually, some wild animals were **domesticated,** or tamed for human use. Fossil evidence indicates that as much as 30,000 years ago—long before the first true farmers—people living in what is now France had domesticated horses. So far, there is no evidence that people elsewhere used horses until about 4000 B.C. Somewhere along the line, possibly as early as 11,000 B.C., dogs descended from tamed wolves were assisting hunters as they drove wild animals into ravines for slaughter. By 7000 B.C., most farmers in

Southwest Asia had also domesticated sheep, goats, and pigs. These animals provided a valuable source of meat, milk, and wool.

The first farmers seem to have taken quite a while to learn the difficult task of training animals to serve as beasts of burden. Thus, oxen were not harnessed to a plow until about 4500 B.C. About 500 years later, people were using horses and camels to provide transportation.

Farming began in many places.

The changeover from hunting and gathering to farming took place not once, but many times. Neolithic people in many parts of the world independently developed agriculture.

Africa played a role in the agricultural revolution. The Nile Valley in Africa developed into an important agricultural center. As you will see in Chapter 3, the Nile's fertile fields supported the rapid growth of farming villages.

While agriculture was developing in Southwest Asia and northeast Africa, it also began in China. About 8,000 years ago, Chinese farmers along the middle stretches of the Yellow River learned to cultivate millet. A thousand years later, wild rice was first domesticated in the rich delta of the Yangtze River. (map, page 83.)

Mesoamerica and South America also became important centers of agriculture. Mexico and

26

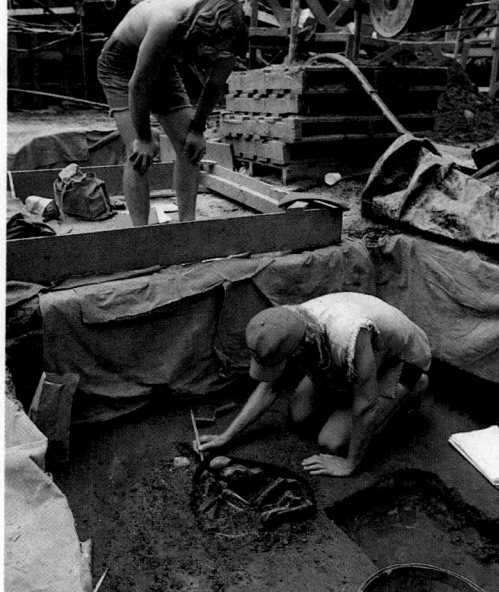

Central American farmers learned how to cultivate corn, beans, and squash. (See pages 326–327.) Taken together, these three foods provide all the proteins humans need. Meanwhile, farmers in the Central Andes of Peru were the first to grow tomatoes, lima beans, sweet potatoes, and white potatoes.

Villages grew and prospered.

Agriculture and the domestication of animals created a surplus of food that made permanent settlements possible. Many were farming villages, that grew up in areas with fertile soil. Others developed as centers of religion or trade. These settlements created a new way of life with distinctive advantages and new problems.

The village now known as Çatal Hüyük (chuh-**TUL** hoo-**YOOK**) illustrated the benefits of settled life. Çatal Hüyük (forked mound) was on a fertile plain in what is now south-central Turkey. The area's rich, well-watered soil produced large crops of wheat, barley, and peas.

Çatal Hüyük's agricultural surplus supported a number of highly skilled workers. Potters, for example, produced storage jars and cooking pots. But the village was best known for the **obsidian** products from its expert stonecutters. This smooth, dark volcanic glass was used to make highly prized mirrors, jewelry, and knives that were exchanged for seashells and flint.

At its peak 8,000 years ago, Çatal Hüyük was home to 6,000 people, the largest population of any Neolithic village yet excavated. Its prosperity supported a varied cultural life. Archaeologists have uncovered colorful wall paintings depicting animals and hunting scenes. Çatal Hüyük also boasted a number of religious shrines dedicated to a mother goddess who may have been thought to control the supply of grain.

The new settled way of life also had drawbacks—some of them the same ones that afflicted hunter-gatherer settlements. Natural disasters such as floods and fire could destroy a village, while a long drought could ruin its crops. Living close together, townspeople were particularly vulnerable to infectious diseases. Finally, a village's prosperity made it an inviting target for envious neighbors and roving nomad bands.

These problems did not keep resourceful villages from expanding. Permanent settlements provided their residents with opportunities for fulfillment—in work, in art, in leisure time—that the hunter-gatherer life-style could not match. Villages thus became cultural centers where new tools, arts, and crafts were created. As you will see, these villages soon became towns and cities. Within a short time, ambitious cities conquered and then led great empires.

Section REVIEW 3

Define: (a) Mesoamerica, (b) domesticate, (c) obsidian
Identify: (a) Robert Braidwood, (b) Jarmo, (c) Fertile Crescent, (d) Çatal Hüyük
Answer:
1. What three factors probably played a role in the origins of agriculture?
2. What evidence do you find in this section that people of the Neolithic Age wove cloth?
3. What were the first farm crops cultivated in (a) China? (b) Mesoamerica? (c) Peru?
4. (a) What were two benefits of village life? (b) What two drawbacks probably didn't affect hunter-gatherers as much as village dwellers?

Critical Thinking

5. Sir Mortimer Wheeler wrote that the most important benefit of agriculture was that it allowed people to "think between meals." What did he mean? Do you agree?

27

ANSWERS TO *(continued)*

cavated by Robert Braidwood **(c)** Fertile arc of land stretching from the Persian Gulf to the Mediterranean Sea **(d)** largest Neolithic village yet excavated
Answer:
1. global warming and population pressure
2. Farmers planted flax from whose fibers linen is made.
3. (a) millet and wild rice **(b)** corn, beans, and squash **(c)** tomatoes, lima beans, sweet potatoes, and white potatoes
4. (a) Agricultural surplus supported skilled workers and a varied cultural life. **(b)** Answers include infectious diseases, drought, and attacks by roving bands of nomads.
5. Encourage students to see that agriculture created a surplus that freed people to develop specialized skills and new cultural activities.

Concluding the Chapter

1. **Chapter Closer**
   Ask students to summarize the major prehistoric events. Challenge students to choose the single most important item he or she feels changed the course of human development.

2. **Reteaching Activities**
   a. Interpreting
   Have students refer to the time line on page 24 and write at least three general statements about the information they can get from the time line.
   b. Outlining Have students use the section title, heads and subheads to write an outline of Section 2.
   c. Listing Have students list four important changes that took place in the Neolithic Age.

Answers to Chapter Review appear on page 16f.

Summary

1. Hominid roots go back at least 4 million years. Scientists use a number of sophisticated techniques to study fossils and tools and other artifacts of prehistoric hominids. Originating in Africa, the earliest hominids (upright-walking creatures) are known as australopithecines. Most scientists agree that one or more species of australopithecines were the ancestors of the first known *Homo* species, *Homo habilis. Homo erectus,* the first species to use fire, was also the first hominid species to leave Africa.

2. Early humans appeared in several parts of the world. Many scientists believe that *Homo erectus* evolved into *Homo sapiens,* between 500,000 and 200,000 years ago. Remains of *Homo sapiens* have been found in Africa, eastern Asia, Southwest Asia, and Europe. They were the first beings known to bury their dead, and they may have had burial rituals. About 30,000 years ago, the last *Homo sapiens* vanished. Anatomically modern humans, such as Cro-Magnons (the *Homo sapiens sapiens* found in Europe) and their contemporaries elsewhere in the world, launched a revolution in toolmaking methods and in the number and kinds of tools they produced.

These people also produced impressive cave and rock art paintings.

3. The agricultural revolution began about 10,000 years ago. Although people knew how to plant seeds and to domesticate certain animals long before they settled in permanent villages, it wasn't until about 8000 B.C. that they abandoned hunting and gathering, built permanent communities, and began to rely on agriculture to provide their main source of food. This changeover occurred first in Southwest Asia, but took place independently in Africa, Southeast Asia, Mesoamerica, North America, and the Peruvian Andes. These crucial developments laid the foundation for modern life.

Reviewing the Facts

1. Define the following terms:
   a. hominid
   b. prehistory
   c. anthropologist
   d. archaeologist
   e. artifact
   f. fossil
   g. culture
   h. technology
   i. Mesoamerica
   j. domesticate
   k. obsidian

Neandertals disappear from fossil record

Cave paintings

Jericho

Domestication of animals well-established

Jarmo

Çatal Hüyük

30,000 B.C.   20,000 B.C.   10,000 B.C.   B.C. A.D.   Present

28

2. Explain the importance of each of the following:

a. Louis and
   Mary Leakey
b. australopithecines
c. Donald Johanson
d. *Homo habilis*
e. Olduvai Gorge
f. Paleolithic Age
g. Neolithic Age
h. *Homo erectus*
i. Kamoya Kimeu
j. Shanidar
k. Neanderthals
l. Cro-Magnons
m. *Homo sapiens
   sapiens*
n. Altamira Cave
o. Robert Braidwood
p. Jarmo
q. Fertile Crescent
r. Çatal Hüyük

3. Describe one theory that explains why australopithecines walked erect.

4. (a) How was *Homo habilis* different from the australopithecines? (b) How was *Homo erectus* different from *Homo habilis*?

5. What evidence shows that Neanderthals placed importance on an individual's life and death?

6. Describe two theories that explain what happened to the Neanderthals and their contemporaries.

7. What are two achievements that set Cro-Magnons and their contemporaries apart from earlier *Homo sapiens*?

8. What factors may help explain why people settled in permanent villages and began growing crops and raising livestock?

9. The agricultural revolution had several birthplaces. Name three of them.

Basic Skills

1. **Reading a time line** (a) On the time line on page 28, what are the starting and ending dates? (b) When were most prehistoric cave paintings done? (c) Which is older, Jarmo or Jericho?

2. **Identifying supporting details** Section headings in this text indicate main ideas, while paragraphs under each heading provide supporting details. For each of the following headings, give two supporting details: (a) "*Homo erectus* spread across Asia and Europe." (b) "Modern *Homo sapiens* revolutionized human life."

3. **Summarizing** In one or two sentences, summarize the section "Farming began in many places."

Researching and Reporting Skills

1. **Using a glossary** Use the Glossary in the Reference Section to find the meaning for the italicized words in the following sentences: (a) In Neolithic times, farming was already an *institution*.

(b) Though Jarmo's culture was relatively advanced, it was not yet a *civilization*. (c) Neolithic pottery was handcrafted by skillful *artisans*.

2. **Identifying primary sources** Anything that was used or created by people of the past is known as primary source evidence. Give two examples of primary sources for each of the following: (a) a prehistoric culture of 40,000 B.C., (b) a Neolithic culture of 6500 B.C.

Critical Thinking

1. **Comparing** Compare the way of life of the cave painters at Altamira with that at prehistoric Jarmo. What was similar about the two cultures? What was different?

2. **Synthesizing** From each section of the chapter, choose one event or development that you think is of particular significance in human history. Explain why you think each is of special importance.

Perspectives on Past and Present

1. Even today a few groups of people continue to live by hunting and gathering. Among them are the !Kung (Bushmen) of southern Africa, the Yanomama of Brazil, the Inuit of Alaska and Canada, and the Aborigines of Australia. (a) Research the culture of one of these groups. (b) How does this culture compare with that of ancient Paleolithic groups?

2. The hunting and gathering way of life left considerable time for leisure in early Paleolithic groups. How might the use of this leisure compare with your use of leisure time today?

3. If you were to travel back in time to Jarmo or Çatal Hüyük, what modern idea, tool, or invention would be most useful to take with you? Give reasons for your answer.

Investigating History

1. The most ancient city archaeologists have excavated so far is Jericho, which was founded about 8000 B.C. Find information on this extraordinary dig. (a) What environmental factors were key to the development of such a city? (b) What findings justify calling Jericho a city?

2. Examples of the cave art of Altamira and Lascaux have been published in many strikingly beautiful books. Look in your library for books on Paleolithic art. What do the paintings tell about the natural environment of the time?

29

CHAPTER
Evaluation

Chapter Test 1, Alternate Chapter Test 1, and Computer Test Bank Chapter Test 1 can be used to evaluate your students' understanding of this chapter.

Civilizations and Empires in Southwest Asia

Chapter Overview

Chapter 2 focuses on the civilizations and empires that flourished in and around the area known as the Fertile Crescent. Historians believe that the Sumerians built the world's first civilization. Five key traits that characterize a civilization are cities, specialized workers, writing, advanced technology, and complex institutions. All of these traits existed in Sumer.

Sumer overcame geographic problems only to succumb to political ones. Constant warfare among Sumer's independent city-states from 3000 B.C. to 2000 B.C. left them too weakened to withstand attacks from foreign enemies. New groups of conquerors adopted the Sumerians' way of life and contributed new ideas to civilization. The Babylonians' major achievement was the law code of King Hammurabi; the Phoenicians invented a simplified alphabet for writing; and the Jews developed a monotheistic religion.

Well equipped with iron weapons, the highly disciplined Assyrian army conquered Southwest Asia and parts of North Africa from 850 B.C. to 650 B.C. In 612 B.C., Assyria fell to the Chaldeans, and Babylon became the center of the last of the Mesopotamian empires. The next empire to rise in Southwest Asia was that of the Persians, who ruled over a vast area with tolerance and good government.

Chapter Focus

Direct students' attention to the story about the Sumerian school-boy on pages 30–31. The young boy's story was written about 4,000 years ago. Over the years, professional historians and their students have read and studied this story. Now help students examine the story to identify the following statements as true, false, or don't know. Point out that you will compare their answers with those reached by experts.

1. The young boy's mother prepared him a lunch to take to school.
2. School officials expected their students to arrive on time.
3. Students were expected to be respectful toward their teachers.
4. School officials punished students who broke school rules.

After reading these statements, announce that all of them are true. Experts did not know the answers to the four statements about the picture on page 16 (see page 16a). Ask students to explain why both experts and world history students can agree that the four statements about the young boy and his school are all true. Remind your students that the painting on page 16 was created *before* written records. In contrast, the young boy's story was written *after* the development of written records. The boy, unlike the prehistoric painter, can speak to us across time. This chapter presents the history of the various people who lived in Southwest Asia between 3500 B.C. and 331 B.C.

Chapter 2 Civilizations and Empires in Southwest Asia 3500 B.C.–331 B.C.

FOCUS A Sumerian student's day at school

★ **Advanced**

● **Basic**

	SECTION 1	SECTION 2	SECTION 3
Objectives	1. Locate the Fertile Crescent on a map. 2. List the five key traits of a civilization and explain how they apply to Sumer. 3. Explain how Sumer's civilization was shaped by solving three geographic problems. 4. Discuss various aspects of daily life among the Sumerians.	1. Explain the significance of Hammurabi's law code. 2. Describe some of the Phoenicians' achievements. 3. Compare and contrast the religious beliefs of the Jews with those of the Sumerians.	1. Discuss the rise and fall of the Assyrian empire. 2. Describe aspects of everyday life in Babylon. 3. Explain how the Persians ruled their empire.
Setting the Stage	Geography in History: The Fertile Crescent Transparency 2 Outline Map 17	Babylonian methods for solving problems Transparency 3	Peoples of the "cuneiform world" Transparency 4
Teaching Strategies	Discussing History: The Key Traits of a Civilization Using Geographic Themes: Human-Environment Interaction Teaching with Pictures: Daily Life in Ancient Ur Check for Understanding	Discussing History: Hammurabi's Code Discussing History: The Phoenician Alphabet Skill Building: Comparing and Contrasting Religious Beliefs Check for Understanding	Discussing History: Assurbanipal's Question Discussing History: The Wonders of Babylon Skill Building: Creative Writing Transparency 5 Check for Understanding
Guided Practice	Transparency 2 Q&A Section Review 1	Transparency 3 Q&A Section Review 2	Transparency 4 Q&A Transparency 5 Q&A Section Review 3
Independent Practice Worksheets	Independent Practice 2.1 Geography Skills 2 Vocabulary 2	Independent Practice 2.2 Basic Skills 2	Independent Practice 2.3 Critical Thinking 2
Enrichment	1. Primary Source: Voices 2.1 2. Discussing Sumerian Proverbs 3. Researching for Points	1. Primary Source: Voices 2.2 2. ★Solving a Puzzle 3. Preparing a Report: The Torah 4. Researching for Points	1. Primary Source: Voices 2.3 2. Researching for Points 3. Global Perspectives Transparency 1 4. Geography in History Outline Map 17

Chapter Closer	●**Reteaching Activities** Summarizing, Recalling Important Ideas, Recalling Important People
	Chapter Review Summary, Reviewing the Facts, Basic Skills, Researching and Reporting Skills, Critical Thinking, Perspectives on Past and Present, Investigating History
	Chapter Evaluation Chapter Test 2, Alternate Chapter Test 2, Computer Test Bank Chapter 2 Test

Civilization arose in the Fertile Crescent. 1

Setting the Stage

Explain that the young schoolboy lived and studied in an ancient region called the Fertile Crescent. Remind students that regions are geographic units that share a common quality. Ask students to examine the map on page 32. What quality makes the Fertile Crescent a region? Students should see that three rivers—the Jordan, Tigris, and Euphrates—provide this region with fertile soil and good supplies of water. This section examines the unique developments that occurred in the eastern end of the Fertile Crescent in a land known as Mesopotamia.

Teaching Strategies

Geography in History: The Fertile Crescent (Objective 1) Show Map Transparency 2, *The Fertile Crescent about 2500 B.C.,* and distribute Outline Map 17: The Fertile Crescent. Have students locate and label the Mediterranean Sea, Persian Gulf, Tigris and Euphrates rivers, and Mesopotamia, and also shade in the region of the Fertile Crescent.

Discussing History: The Key Traits of a Civilization (Objective 2) Review the concept of culture (page 18). Ask students to name traits they think would distinguish a civilization from the culture of Neolithic society, and list their responses on the board. Next to the list, write the traits most scholars agree are essential for civilization. Have students read pages 31–34 and then cite examples of the five traits that made Sumer a civilization.

Using Geographic Themes: Human-Environment Interaction (Objective 3) The Sumerians' response to geographic problems provides a case example of the theme of human-environment interactions. Ask students to read "Sumerians faced geographic problems" (page 34) and list the three geographic problems that the Sumerians confronted. Have students explain how the Sumerians solved these problems. Then ask students to evaluate the way in which the Sumerians responded to their environmental challenge.

Teaching with Pictures: Daily Life in Ancient Ur (Objective 4) Have students read the section on Sumerian life on pages 34–37. Then direct their attention to the artistic re-creation on page 35. The large building featured in this painting is a temple or ziggurat dedicated to the moon god Nanna and his wife Ningal. *Ziggurat* is a word meaning "mountain of god." Ziggurats were built high to represent a mountain where the gods could live and still be with their people. Perhaps the priests climbing the steps were chanting hymns to praise Nanna and scare off Wicked Udugs! Ask students to imagine that they are standing on top of this ziggurat. Their assignment is to write an imaginative paragraph describing the various sights in this painting. Encourage students to use concepts and ideas discussed in the chapter.

Check for Understanding Have students give examples from Sumerian society of a specialized worker, complex institution, and religious belief.

Enrichment Activities

1. **Reading a Primary Source**
   Assign Voices from the Past Resource Book 2.1.

2. **Discussing Sumerian Proverbs**
   Read these Sumerian proverbs to the students and ask if the proverbs hold true today.
   - A sweet word is everybody's friend.
   - Tell a lie; then if you tell me truth, it will be deemed a lie.
   - A loving heart builds the home; a hating heart destroys the home.
   - Into an open mouth, a fly enters.
   - Friendship lasts a day; kinship lasts forever.
   Now ask students to make a list of modern proverbs.

3. **Researching for Bonus Points**
   Who was the first person to decipher cuneiform? (Henry C. Rawlinson) What new river is formed by the meeting of the Tigris and Euphrates rivers? (Shatt al-Arab)

Newcomers contributed to civilization. 2

Setting the Stage

Describe the following problem: A builder built a house for a man. However, the builder failed to use sound construction techniques. As a result, the house collapsed, causing the owner's death. What action, if any, should be taken against the builder? Briefly discuss the students' answers. Then explain that this problem actually occurred 4,000 years ago in an ancient city called Babylon. A Babylonian king named Hammurabi solved this problem. Emphasize that Hammurabi and other people living in the Fertile Crescent faced problems that concern all civilizations. As students will see, the people's solutions to these problems still influence us. Use Map Transparency 3, *Peoples of Southwest Asia, 2000–1000 B.C.*, to show students the general location of the Babylonian Empire, the Phoenicians, Canaan, and the Hittites.

Teaching Strategies

Discussing History: Hammurabi's Code (Objective 1) Ask students to discuss reasons why societies develop laws, and list their reasons on the board. Then ask students to read "Hammurabi's Code." Hammurabi created his law code "to cause justice to prevail in the land, to destroy the wicked and the evil, to prevent the strong from oppressing the weak . . . and to further the welfare of the people." Discuss how these reasons compare with the students' list. Direct students' attention to the last paragraph on page 38. How do students feel about the differing punishments for rich and poor and for men and women? Can they think of another system that would be more equitable, or do they feel

that Hammurabi's system is fair? Ask students why they think Hammurabi's laws had such a lasting effect.

Discussing History: The Phoenician Alphabet (Objective 2) Have students read "Phoenicians invented the alphabet" (pages 39–40). Explain that, for practical reasons, the Phoenicians could not afford to take expensive scribes along on every voyage to keep records with the cumbersome cuneiform. They discovered a way to keep their records by using only 22 symbols. (Later the ancient Greeks and Romans changed the shapes of the 22 letters and added 4 others, making the alphabet we know today.) The new alphabet helped expand trade and literacy. The Phoenician city of Byblos soon specialized in the manufacture of writing materials. The Greeks took their word for book, *biblion*, from *Byblos*. Our own words *Bible* and *bibliography* are in turn derived from *biblion*.

Skill Building: Comparing and Contrasting Religious Beliefs (Objective 3) Ask students to complete the following chart (answers in *italics*) contrasting the religious beliefs of the Sumerians with those of the Jews.

	Sumerians	Jews
Number of gods	*3,000 gods*	*one God*
Where god(s) lived	*temples, homes, water, clouds, and stars*	*not limited to any geographic location*
Characteristics of god(s)	*immortal, all-powerful but also with human characteristics*	*not arbitrary; God was ruler of universe*
What was expected of god(s)	*protection during life*	*protection in return for honoring the commandments*

Check for Understanding Ask students to describe how the Babylonians, Phoenicians, and Hebrews solved some of the problems they faced.

Enrichment Activities

1. **Reading a Primary Source**
   Assign Voices from the Past Resource Book 2.2.

2. **Solving a Puzzle**
   The people living in the Fertile Crescent enjoyed playing a complex board game. The board has survived, but its rules have been lost. For a picture of the board, see *The Age of God-Kings* by the editors of Time-Life Books, pages 28–29. Ask advanced students to try inventing rules for playing the game.

3. **Preparing a Report**
   The Torah is the most sacred object in the Jewish religion. Ask interested students to report on the Torah's unique place in Judaism.

4. **Researching for Bonus Points**
   What was the name of the snail that the Phoenicians gathered to make purple dye? (murex snail)

Conquerors ruled ever larger empires. 3

Setting the Stage

Ask students to recall the geographic characteristic shared by the lands within the Fertile Crescent. Over time, this region also developed a shared culture. Modern scholars refer to it as "the cuneiform world." Explain that farming, irrigation, city life, and cuneiform writing were used throughout this cultural region. This section examines three powerful peoples—the Assyrians, Chaldeans, and Persians—who conquered and united the entire region. Show students Map Transparency 4, *The Assyrian Empire*, and ask them to name some of the peoples of the cuneiform world about 650 B.C.

Teaching Strategies

Discussing History: Assurbanipal's Question (Objective 1) Have students read "The Assyrian empire rose and fell" (page 44). Discuss the factors that caused Assyria's rise and fall. Conclude the discussion by explaining that Assurbanipal felt unappreciated. One of the tablets in his library bears this inscription: "I did well unto god and man, to dead and living. Why have sickness, ill-health, misery and misfortune befallen me? . . . Disturbing scandals oppress me always. Misery of mind and of flesh bow me down; with cries of woe I bring my eyes to an end." Read this passage to your students and ask how each of the following people might have answered Assurbanipal's question: a Hebrew prophet, the Sumerian wise man Utnapishtim (see Voices from the Past Resource Book 2.1), and a modern psychologist.

Discussing History: The Wonders of Babylon (Objective 2) Have students read "The Chaldeans rebuilt Babylon" (pages 44–46). Babylon was one of the greatest cities in the ancient world. A huge wall 65 feet high provided security against attack. More than 1,000 temples and shrines provided places to worship. The most important temple of all honored Babylon's chief god, Marduk. Marduk demanded constant attention. At one annual festival, worshippers offered Marduk more than two tons of frankincense. Priests attended to Marduk's golden image. When the priests were away, they left behind statues of hairdressers, a butler, and even a baker to attend to Marduk's every whim.

Skill Building: Creative Writing (Objective 3) First review "The Persians united a vast area" (pages 46–49). Show students Map Transparency 5, *The Persian Empire, 500 B.C.*, and ask them how the Royal Road helped unify the empire. Then have students imagine they are Darius' royal governors or satraps. Their assignment is to write Darius a letter describing the conditions in their province. Each student should examine the map on page 47 and select a specific area. The letter may include a discussion of local roads, customs, conquered peoples, and geography.

Check for Understanding Read the following descriptions aloud and have students identify the people described.

1. believed stars determine human destiny; conquered the Jews; rebuilt Babylon (Chaldeans)

2. ruled a vast area with tolerance and good government; used standardized coinage (Persians)

3. had a highly disciplined army; uprooted and enslaved conquered peoples (Assyrians)

Enrichment Activities

1. **Reading a Primary Source** Assign Voices from the Past Resource Book 2.3.

2. **Researching for Bonus Points** Riddle: What Babylonian beast had the head of a horned viper, the forelegs of a lion, the hind legs of a bird of prey, and a tail tipped with a scorpion sting? (the scaly-coated mushhushshu, or dragon of Marduk)

3. **Global Perspectives** Using Map Transparency 1, *The World about 1700 B.C.*, survey with students the various world cultures about 1700 B.C.

4. **Geography in History: The Persian and Assyrian Empires** Ask students to draw a key for Outline Map 17: The Fertile Crescent, indicating a symbol or color for the Assyrian empire and one for the Persian empire. Then, referring to the maps on pages 43 and 47, have students use the map key to designate areas over which the Assyrians and Persians ruled. What territories did the Persians rule that the Assyrians did not? (lands east of the Fertile Crescent, most of Asia Minor, Egypt, and India)

Reviewing the Facts

1. (a) complicated form of culture **(b)** skilled worker who makes goods by hand **(c)** way of writing that used wedge-shaped letters **(d)** long-lasting pattern of organization in a community **(e)** city and the surrounding countryside it controlled **(f)** exchanging goods for other goods **(g)** believer in many gods **(h)** state that has conquered other lands and now rules them **(i)** ability to read and write **(j)** believer in one god **(k)** religious teacher

2. (a) where first civilization developed **(b)** eastern end of Fertile Crescent between Tigris and Euphrates rivers **(c)** period during which people learned to use bronze **(d)** period during which people shifted from using bronze to iron **(e)** where the first civilization developed **(f)** developed and made public a law code **(g)** developed a 22-symbol alphabet **(h)** believed in one God **(i)** led enslaved Jews out of Egypt and received Ten Commandments from God **(j)** most powerful of Jewish kings and builder of a temple in Jerusalem **(k)** home of group who established a large empire in southwestern Asia **(l)** captured Jerusalem and rebuilt Babylon **(m)** established vast empire built on tolerance and good government **(n)** established policy of generosity toward conquered people **(o)** extended Persian empire and developed government of provinces ruled by satraps, an excellent road system, and standardized coinage **(p)** offered religious belief that one could control one's fate by electing to follow path of goodness

3. (a) cities, specialized workers, writing, advanced technology, complex institutions **(b)** Sumer was organized into city-states; had many specialized workers; developed cuneiform writing; used new technology; had organized religion.

4. (a) alphabet **(b)** monotheism **(c)** observations that formed the basis for astronomy and astrology

Basic Skills

1. (a) About 1,900 years, 2,100 years, 1,064 years **(b)** 238 years, 200 years

2. to the west, the Mediterranean Sea; to the north, the Taurus Mountains; to the east, the Zagros Mountains; to the south, the Syrian Desert and the Persian Gulf

3. Persian Government
   a. Darius divided empire into provinces.
      1. People kept their culture
      2. Satraps governed provinces
   b. Two important tools helped to unify the empire.
      1. An excellent road system
      2. Coins to facilitate trade

4. Possible examples: for *political history:* Sumerians created city-states, Babylonians wrote a code of law; for *economic history:* Sumerians had an irrigation system, Phoenicians traded dye and cedars for other goods; for *social history:* in Sumerian society there were many classes, women could join the priesthood; for *cultural history:* Jewish people adopted monotheism, Sumerians had a form of writing.

Researching and Reporting Skills

Students' answers will vary.

Critical Thinking

1. Surplus was used to pay taxes to support government, and to pay for specialized labor. Surplus food and manufactured goods became the objects of trade. Accumulation of surplus created personal wealth. Social classes resulted from accumulation of wealth and specialization of work.

2. (a) Hammurabi's code was based on existing practices; the Ten Commandments were religious in origin, believed to have been given by God to Moses. **(b)** Hammurabi's code established a principle of equal retribution for harm done to one of equal status; the Ten Commandments established a system of morality that condemned wrongdoing for all.

3. (a) The Assyrians established a rule of terror, including uprooting people; the Persians, a rule of tolerance **(b)** Tolerance makes acceptance by the conquered people more likely.

4. (a) Sailing vessels helped to carry traded items to distant countries; writing helped to keep business records for increasingly complex trading activity. **(b)** Sailing vessels made long-distance sea trade possible. Writing aided both record keeping and long-distance communication.

5. Monotheism, the belief in one supreme being, is the basis for most of the major world religions today.

6. The statement is supported: nobles are seated, their servants are not (page 30); King Gudea is seated (page 36); the god of justice is seated and the king stands (page 39).

Perspectives on Past and Present

Answers will vary. Students should point out that today's standards support the idea that all people are equal before the law.

Investigating History

Students' answers will vary.

Chapter 2

Teaching with Pictures

Tell students that this art illustrates two social classes of ancient Ur around 3500 B.C. The nobles, above, were part of the highest class, which was headed by the ruler and his family. It also included priests, army officers, and wealthy landowners. Below, the herders lived in small villages outside the city and were, along with the farmers, the common people. Traders and artisans in the city were also commoners. Ask students to describe what each group of people is doing and how the groups are typical of their class.

This panel from a wooden box comes from Ur, a city in Southwest Asia.

Key Terms

scribe	polytheist
civilization	empire
specialize	colony
artisan	literacy
surplus	monotheist
cuneiform	covenant
bronze	prophet
institution	ethical
irrigation	mono-
city-state	theism
barter	satrap
ziggurat	

Read and Understand

1. Civilization arose in the Fertile Crescent.
2. Newcomers contributed to civilization.
3. Conquerors ruled ever larger empires.

About 4,000 years ago, a boy sprinted down a city street, kicking up dust as he ran. The morning sun had just begun to rise above the walls of the city. Even so, the boy knew he was already late for school, which was called the *edubba*.

Historians know of this boy and his school from ancient clay tablets found in Southwest Asia, in what is now the country of Iraq. Part of one tablet tells of a student's typical day:

> When I awoke early in the morning, I faced my mother and said to her, "Give me my lunch. I want to go to school." My mother gave me two rolls and I set out. In school, the monitor in charge said to me, "Why are you late?" Afraid and with pounding heart, I entered before my teacher and made a respectful curtsy.

30

Chapter 2 Resources

GEOGRAPHY
- Geography Skills 2
- Outline Map 17
- Transparencies 1, 2, 3, 4, 5

REINFORCEMENT
- Vocabulary 2
- Basic Skills 2
- Reteaching 2
- Making Connections Study Guide 2

ENRICHMENT
- Critical Thinking 2
- History and Literature 2A, 2B

ASSESSMENT
- Chapter Test 2
- Alternate Chapter Test 2
- Computer Test Bank

The tablet goes on to tell of eight other offenses that the boy committed in school that day, including mistakes in his writing lesson and talking without permission. For each offense, a school official called "the man who holds the whip" lashed the boy across his bare back. In fact, the boy did so poorly in school that his father invited the schoolmaster home for dinner and gave him gifts to keep the boy from failing.

Civilization arose in the Fertile Crescent.

1

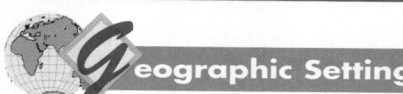 eographic Setting

The boy and his schoolmates were studying to be **scribes**—that is, professional writers—in an ancient region known to historians as the Fertile Crescent. On the map on page 32, you can see an arc of land with its eastern end touching the Persian Gulf and its western end lying along the Mediterranean Sea. Inside this arc is some of the best land for farming in Southwest Asia. The region's curved shape and the richness of its land led scholars to call it the Fertile Crescent. (Today this area lies within the nations of Israel, Jordan, Syria, Lebanon, and Iraq.)

In the western part of the ancient Fertile Crescent, the Jordan River watered grapevines, olive trees, and cedar trees. In the eastern part, ducks nested among the marshes created by the Tigris (**TY**-gris) and Euphrates (yoo-**FRAY**-teez) rivers. Along the northern curve of the Fertile Crescent, streams flowed down from the mountains. Wherever rivers and streams flowed, people built their villages. In ancient times, the settled life of farmers and villagers was possible only in lands with good supplies of water.

The land where the schoolboy made his home lay at the eastern end of the Fertile Crescent, between the Tigris and Euphrates rivers. This region is known as Mesopotamia (MEHS-uh-puh-**TAY**-mee-uh), which in Greek means "land between the rivers."

The schoolboy belonged to a group of people known as the Sumerians (soo-**MEHR**-ee-uhnz). Their homeland, Sumer (**SOO**-muhr), was in the southern part of Mesopotamia, in the marshes near the Persian Gulf. Sumer was neither a city nor a country. Rather, it was a collection of separate cities with a common way of life.

Although the cities fought and squabbled constantly, the Sumerian people shared a common culture. Historians believe the Sumerians built the world's first civilization. The next pages will describe what a civilization is and how Sumer differed from earlier settlements.

Key traits define a civilization.

Every group of people has its own culture—its own way of life including language, tools, customs, and rules. However, not all groups have a way of life that is considered a **civilization.** Civilization is one form of culture—a very complicated form.

The Sumerians stand out in history as the first group of people to become civilized. They developed a new way of life that set them apart from neighboring peoples.

Just what set the Sumerians apart from their neighbors? Historians and other social scientists have struggled with the problem of defining exactly what makes one group of people civilized and another group not. Most scholars agree that the following traits are essential for civilization.

The growth of cities One of the key traits for civilization is cities. (In fact, the word *civilization* comes from the Latin word for *city*.) By 3000 B.C., the Sumerians had built at least a dozen fair-sized cities. For example, Uruk may have had a population of 10,000, and it continued to grow to around 20,000 over the next 200 years. In Lagash, there were about 19,000 people and in Umma, about 16,000. People elsewhere in Asia, Europe, and Africa lived in farming villages, but none of those tiny communities could rightly be called a city.

A city is more than a large group of people living close together. Population size alone does not make a village into a city. One of the most important differences between a city and a village is that a city is a center of trade for a larger area.

Like their modern descendants, ancient city dwellers depended on trade. Farmers, merchants, and traders brought goods to market in the cities. The city dwellers themselves produced a variety

31

OBJECTIVE 1. Locate the Fertile Crescent on a map.
Teaching Strategy: *Geography in History: The Fertile Crescent* (page 30c)

OBJECTIVE 2. List the five key traits of a civilization and explain how they apply to Sumer.
Teaching Strategy: *Discussing History: The Key Traits of a Civilization* (page 30c)

OBJECTIVE 3. Explain how Sumer's civilization was shaped by solving three geographic problems.
Teaching Strategy: *Using Geographic Themes: Human-Environment Interaction* (page 30c)

OBJECTIVE 4. Discuss various aspects of daily life among the Sumerians.
Teaching Strategy: *Teaching with Pictures: Daily Life in Ancient Ur* (page 30c)

■ BACKGROUND

Stress that the ancient Sumerian cities were usually self-governing. Only in times of war with a common enemy did the cities unite under the leadership of a temporary king, called a *lugal*. Even he, however, did not preempt local administrators.

ENRICHMENT
■ Voices from the Past 2.1

ASSESSMENT
■ Section Quiz 2.1

GEOGRAPHY
■ Transparency 2

REINFORCEMENT
■ Independent Practice 2.1

1. to identify particular areas
2. Tigris and Euphrates rivers
3. Mesopotamia
4. good soil and access to mountains and desert
5. different physical characteristics, different ways of living.

Cooperative Learning

Have half of the class work in groups of four; the other half individually. Students working alone are to summarize the information in "Key traits define a civilization" (pages 31–34). Groups should divide the same section of text into four parts, according to the bold paragraph headings. Each group member is to summarize one of these smaller sections. Then have group members collaborate on a summary of the entire subsection. When summaries are complete, ask some individuals and some group members how they accomplished the task. Do they feel one method was more efficient than the other? Can they think of other jobs (at home or at school) that would benefit from specializing tasks in this manner?

The Fertile Crescent about 2500 B.C.

KEY

☐ Fertile Crescent

0   300 Miles

Focus on Geography

Geographic Skills
1. What is the purpose of the map key?
2. What major rivers flow through the Fertile Crescent?
3. What is the region between these rivers called?
4. What were two advantages of Sumer's location?

Geographic Theme: Region
5. This map actually shows three regions—the Fertile Crescent, Mesopotamia, and Sumer. In what ways is each one a region?

of goods for exchange, including pots, tools, and jewelry. Each person **specialized,** or did one kind of work, and exchanged goods with other people who were also specialists. The importance of trade thus led to another key trait of civilization—specialized workers.

Specialized workers Think back on the Sumerian schoolboy who was studying to be a scribe. Day after day, scribes in Sumer wrote letters for people, copied down laws, and kept business records for merchants. Scribes were specialists. They traded their services for food, clothing, and roofs over their heads. Some of the other specialists in Sumer were schoolmasters, merchants, priests, and even "the man who holds the whip." Still others were potters, metalworkers, and weavers. Such skilled workers who make goods by hand are called **artisans.** Artisans became an important social group as cities developed.

In early human societies, people spent much time in obtaining food. As people's skills improved

in hunting and gathering and in herding and raising crops, less time and fewer people were needed to provide food. In Sumer, farmers could produce a **surplus,** or more than was needed. They could trade that extra food to a potter for clay pots or to a scribe in payment for writing a letter. Farmers also paid some of their surplus in taxes to support the city government and the city temple with its priests.

Raising food was no longer a full-time job for everyone in the society. The ability to raise a surplus of food was the key that freed some people to do specialized jobs.

Writing Another essential trait of civilization also made its first appearance at Sumer—writing. Scholars call the Sumerians' way of writing **cuneiform** (kyoo-NEE-uh-fawrm) because of the letters' wedge-like shape. (In Latin, *cuneus* means "wedge.") The scribe's tool, called a stylus, was a sharpened reed with a wedge-shaped point. The scribe pressed the stylus into moist clay to create

32

symbols. Then he laid the clay tablet in the sun to dry and harden.

Sumerians invented writing as a necessity of city life. Priests needed some way to keep track of the grain and other merchandise that moved in and out of the temple storehouses. Merchants needed accounts of debts and payments. The first written symbols, therefore, stood for commonly traded objects—a donkey, an ox, a sack of grain. These signs were called pictographs because they pictured the things they stood for.

Eventually, ideas became associated with certain pictures. For example, a house might also stand for the idea of protection or safety. Such signs are known as ideograms.

Still later, signs came to stand for certain sounds. Cuneiform signs did not stand for single sounds, as letters in the alphabet do today. Instead, each cuneiform sign stood for a whole syllable. Thus, a sign might stand for the word *mouth*, which in Sumerian was pronounced *ka*. In that form, the sign was a pictograph. But the same sign also stood for the sound *ka* when that sound was used in other words. By putting groups of signs together, scribes could write full sentences and express many ideas. They could create everything from financial records to poems.

Sumerian writing grew more and more efficient. The earliest tablets used about 2,000 different signs. By 3000 B.C., that number had been reduced to 800. By 2500 B.C., the number had been cut down even further to about 600 written signs. However, this was still such a large number that only a few people learned to read or write.

Advanced technology To their list of civilization's hallmarks, historians usually add another important trait—advanced technology. The Sumerians were skilled in many fields of science and technology. Many of the basic inventions on which humans depend originated in Sumer.

The wheel, the plow, and the sailboat seem like simple devices today. In Sumerian times, however, they were revolutionary. With the plow, farmers could raise more crops, creating the food surplus that Sumer's cities needed to exist. The wheel and the sailboat together vastly improved human ability to move goods over long distances for trade. All these devices were probably in daily use in Sumer by 3000 B.C.

The Sumerians were also skilled in working metal, although they were not the first people

Sumerian skill in metalworking shows in this golden helmet, dagger, and sheath from about 2450 B.C. Gold is too soft for use in battle, so these items were ceremonial.

to make metal tools. People in Mesopotamia began using copper around 7000 B.C., at least 3,000 years before the Sumerians arrived. However, the Sumerians greatly increased the use of copper. They also used **bronze,** which is a mixture of copper and tin. Bronze is harder than pure copper and thus more useful for tools and weapons. After 2500 B.C., skilled metalworkers in Sumer's cities turned out bronze spearheads by the thousands. In fact, bronze eventually became so important in making tools of all kinds that the period of history beginning around 2800 B.C. at Sumer is often called the Bronze Age, just as earlier times were called the Stone Age.

Complex institutions As you might imagine, a bustling city required much more organization to run smoothly than did a tiny village or a group of wandering hunters. The long-lasting patterns of organization in a community are known as **institutions.** Complex institutions are another key trait of civilization.

Government is an example of an institution. For hunters and gatherers, family ties and group customs had supplied all the rules that were

33

Cuneiform needed many symbols because each one stood for a complete syllable rather than a single sound. Thus the syllables *ba-, da-, ad-, ab-, bad-,* and *dab-* required six symbols, whereas the English alphabet requires only three.

■ DISCUSSION

Ask students to think of examples to show how each of the five traits of Sumerian civilization are present in our own society.

■ BACKGROUND

Throughout history, cities have had an important role in the development of civilization. City tours, marked by a symbol, are used to introduce students to important cities at various times in history. This tour features the Mesopotamian city of Sumer.

necessary. In cities, a new kind of government took shape. The ancient Sumerians were the first people to set up formal governments with officials and laws.

Organized religion is another type of institution. Villagers and hunters and gatherers had worshiped local gods and spirits. With the growth of cities, however, religion was organized in a new way. Most cities had great temples where dozens of priests took charge of religious duties. Priests often kept track of the yearly calendar, managed grain storehouses, and organized important rituals.

Thus, there are five key traits that set Sumer apart from all the human societies that existed before it: (1) the rise of cities; (2) specialized workers; (3) the use of writing; (4) advanced tools; and (5) complex institutions. All the later peoples who lived in this region of the world built upon these key Sumerian traits.

Sumerians faced geographic problems.

Sumer's civilization was shaped in part by the land in which the Sumerians lived. The Sumerians came to Mesopotamia about 4000 B.C. No one knows for sure where they came from. They found that the Tigris and Euphrates rivers flooded their new homeland at least once a year. As the floodwater receded, it left a thick bed of mud. In this rich, new soil, farmers could plant and harvest enormous quantities of wheat and barley.

Good soil was the advantage of living on the flat, swampy land of Sumer. There were three disadvantages.

The water problem The flooding of the rivers was dangerous because nobody could predict when it would happen. Sometimes it came as early as April, sometimes as late as June. Moreover, after the flood receded, the mud quickly dried out. Little or no rain fell, and the land became almost a desert. How could Sumerian farmers get enough water from the rivers during the dry summer months to make their barley grow?

The defense problem Sumer was a small region, only about the size of Massachusetts. It was also as flat as a tabletop. The villages were little clusters of reed huts standing in the middle of an open plain. With no natural barriers for protection, a Sumerian village was almost defenseless. Time

and again, nomads from the mountains or desert swooped down and stole livestock and grain. How could the villagers protect themselves?

The resource problem The natural resources of Sumer were extremely limited. Besides the fertile soil, there were huge reeds ten feet tall that grew in dense masses along the river's edge. With bundles of these reeds, people could make primitive boats and one-room huts. But they could not make hammers or axes. Without a good supply of stone, wood, and metal, what were the Sumerians to use for tools or buildings?

The solutions Over a period of 500 years (about 3,500–3000 B.C.), the Sumerians found ways to handle these problems. To get water, Sumerians dug **irrigation** ditches that carried river water to their fields. For defense, they built city walls with mud bricks. Finally, Sumerians set up a broad trading network with the people of the mountains and the desert. Sumer's merchants traded grain, cloth, and tools for stone, wood, and metal. By dealing with their problems, the Sumerians cleared the way for their civilization's growth.

CITY TOUR

Sumerians created city-states.

Around each Sumerian city lay vast acres of barley and wheat. Each city and its surroundings formed a **city-state.** These city-states included Ur, Kish, Nippur, Lagash, Uruk, and others.

Picture yourself in a field of grain with the mud-brick walls of Ur in the distance. It is early in the morning, but already the summer sun is almost too hot to bear. (By noon, it will be nearly 100°F.) All around, people are working barefoot in the irrigation ditches that run between patches of green plants. With stone hoes, the workers widen the ditches, bringing life-giving water into their fields from the reservoir a mile away. Without this irrigation network, crops would die and the city-dwellers of Ur would starve.

Inside the city A broad dirt road leads from the fields up to the city's wall of mud bricks. Inside the city gate, the city dwellers go about their daily lives. A woman walks down a narrow lane with a jug of water balanced on her head.

34

Her dark hair is braided and coiled around her head. Her dress is a long, white cloth wrapped loosely around her, leaving her arms and one shoulder uncovered. Two men who pass wear skirtlike garments around their waists. Their hair falls down over their bare shoulders in wavy locks. Long, neatly trimmed beards hang low over their chests.

The dusty, unpaved streets are littered with garbage that people throw out their doorways. Most of the houses are small, windowless, one-story boxes packed tightly together along the street. However, a few wealthy families live in two-story houses with an inner courtyard. The courtyard allows some light and fresh air into these houses, but even rich people climb up to the flat roofs on summer nights to escape their stuffy rooms.

Trade The narrow streets finally open out onto a broad avenue where merchants squat under their awnings and trade a necklace for two or three sheep. This is the city's bazaar. People do not use coins to make purchases because money has not yet been invented. However, merchants and their customers know roughly how many pots of grain a farmer must give to buy a jug of wine. (This way of exchanging goods is called **barter**.) More complicated trades require the services of a scribe, who records on a clay tablet how much barley a certain farmer owes a certain merchant for a certain donkey.

The temple Farther down the main avenue stands Ur's tallest and most important building, the temple. Like a city within a city, the temple is surrounded by a heavy wall. Within the temple gate rises a massive, three-tiered structure known as a **ziggurat** (ZIHG-ur-aht), which means "mountain of god." Leading straight up the outside of the ziggurat is a flight of perhaps 100 mud-brick stairs. Every day, priests with shaved heads climb these stairs, often dragging a plump goat or sheep to sacrifice to Ur's gods.

■ DISCUSSION

Ask students what special buildings are likely to be found at the center of modern cities. Encourage them to see how architecture can express a society's values.

The ziggurat was central to Sumerian cities.

■ BACKGROUND

In the Sumerian creation story, humans were created for the sole purpose of working for the gods. This story in part explains the Sumerians' gloomy outlook.

ANSWERS TO

Section Review 1

Define:
(a) professional writer
(b) complex form of culture with the following key traits: cities, specialized workers, writing, advances in technology, complex institutions
(c) concentrate one's efforts in particular activity or field
(d) skilled worker who makes goods by hand
(e) amount remaining after need is satisfied
(f) Sumerian writing
(g) metal that is mixture of copper and tin (h) long-lasting pattern of organization in community (i) system of bringing water to crops
(j) self-governing, independent city and the surrounding countryside that it controlled

(continued)

Sumerians believed in many gods.

Like many peoples in the Fertile Crescent, the Sumerians were **polytheists** (PAHL-ee-THEE-ists), believers in many gods. Anu (the god of heaven), Enlil (the god of clouds and air), and Ea (the god of water and floods) were the most powerful of their gods. Ranking slightly lower were the gods of the sun, moon, and stars. Then came those gods who inhabited the temple of a particular city-state. Next came the gods who dwelled in every Sumerian home. Lowest of all were demons known as Wicked Udugs, who caused disease, misfortune, and every kind of human trouble. Altogether, the Sumerians believed in roughly 3,000 gods.

Sumerians described their gods as doing many of the same things humans do—falling in love, having children, quarreling, and so on. Yet the Sumerians also believed that their gods were both immortal and all-powerful. The power of the gods was absolute. Humans were nothing but their servants. At any moment, the anger of the gods might strike, sending a fire, a flood, or an enemy army to destroy a city. To placate the gods, the people of Sumer built ziggurats and made rich offerings.

Sumerians worked hard to earn the gods' protection in this life, but they expected little help from the gods after death. The Sumerians believed that the souls of the dead went to the "land of no return," a dismal, gloomy place between the earth's crust and the ancient sea. No joy awaited souls there. According to a Sumerian poem about dead souls, "Dust is their fare and clay their food."

Priests and kings ruled Sumer.

Historians believe that Sumer's earliest governments were controlled by the temple priests. Only the priests knew how to please the city gods and thus keep Ur safe. The ziggurat was far more than a place of worship. It was like a city hall from which priests managed all the major industries of Sumer. They managed the irrigation system and told farmers when to plant and when to harvest. They also demanded a portion of every farmer's crop as taxes. Part of the tax was an offering to the gods, and the rest was used to feed the hundreds of laborers employed at the temple.

In time of war, however, the priests did not lead the city. Instead, the men of the city chose a tough fighter who could command the city's soldiers. At first, a commander's power ended as soon as the war was over. However, as wars between cities became more and more frequent, the commander gradually became a full-time ruler, or king. This ruler usually passed his power on to his sons.

After 3000 B.C., every Sumerian city had both a powerful group of priests and a king. Most cities then had two great buildings, the priests' temple and the royal palace.

Sumerian society had many classes.

With civilization came greater differences between groups in society—between the rich and the poor, noble and peasant, free person and slave. A village farmer who visited Ur would have noticed at once that the priests and nobles were much wealthier than the village leaders back home. Priests and kings made up the highest level in Sumerian society. Wealthy merchants ranked next. The vast majority of ordinary Sumerian people worked with their hands in fields and workshops.

At the lowest level of Sumerian society were the slaves. Some slaves were foreigners who had been captured in war. Others were Sumerians who had been sold into slavery as children to

Gudea was king of the Sumerian city-state of Lagash about 2100 B.C. He was a pious king who built a great temple to the chief god of Lagash.

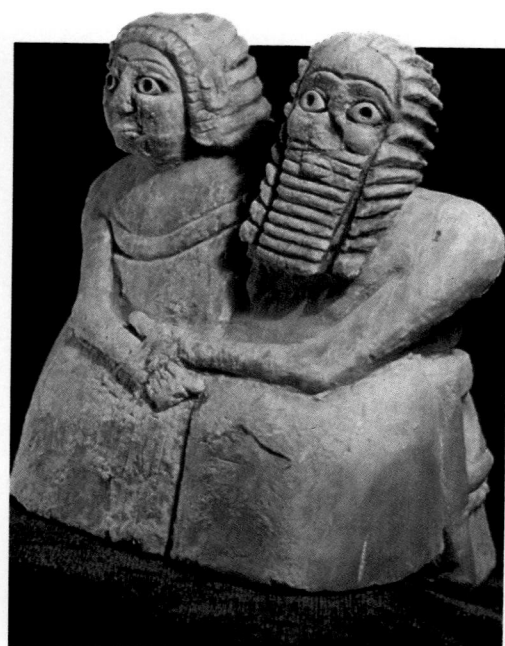

This small statue of a Sumerian husband and wife from Nippur suggests both affection and equality within marriage.

pay the debts of their impoverished parents. By working obediently day and night, Sumerian slaves could hope to earn their freedom.

Social class affected the lives of both men and women. On the whole, Sumerian women could engage in most of the occupations of city life, from merchant to farmer to artisan. Women could also join the lower ranks of the priesthood. However, none of Sumer's written records mentions a female scribe. Therefore, scholars have concluded that girls were not allowed to attend the schools where upper-class boys learned to read and write. In spite of these limitations, however, women in Sumer possessed more rights than women in many later civilizations.

Warfare brought Sumer's downfall.

For 1,000 years (from 3000 to 2000 B.C.), the city-states of Sumer were almost constantly at war with one another. For a time, the king of Kish was the mightiest ruler in Mesopotamia. But Kish's power gave way to that of the city-state Uruk and then of Lagash, Umma, and Ur.

All these city-states had their brief moments of glory.

Sumerian civilization ended because the constant warfare weakened all the city-states so much that they could no longer ward off attacks from a different enemy. Nomadic raiders from the deserts and the hills looked with envy on the riches of the cities. Around 2000 B.C., these warriors scaled the walls of Ur, swept through the streets, and burst through the gates of the temple. Ur was left in ruins. A grief-stricken scribe speaks for the goddess Ningal in this poem:

Woe is me, my house is a ruined stable,
I am a herdsman whose cows have been scattered,
I, Ningal, like an unworthy shepherd on whose flock the weapon has fallen!
Woe is me, I am an exile from the city that has found no rest;
I am a stranger dwelling in a strange city.

Section REVIEW 1

Define: (a) scribe, (b) civilization, (c) specialize, (d) artisan, (e) surplus, (f) cuneiform, (g) bronze, (h) institution, (i) irrigation, (j) city-state, (k) barter, (l) ziggurat, (m) polytheist
Identify: (a) Fertile Crescent, (b) Mesopotamia, (c) Sumer
Answer:
1. Explain how life in a Sumerian city differed from life in a small farming village in the same region.
2. (a) What were the advantages and disadvantages of Sumer's natural environment? (b) Explain how Sumerians overcame the disadvantages.
3. Give a brief description of daily life in Sumer, mentioning the activities of at least one member of each social class.
4. Why was this era called the Bronze Age?

Critical Thinking
5. (a) Writing was a key invention of the Sumerians. Do you think writing is still essential to modern civilization? Explain your answer. (b) Choose another of the Sumerians' inventions and explain how life today would have been different if that invention did not exist.

37

ANSWERS TO *(continued)*

(k) exchanging goods for other goods (l) tiered, towering temple (m) person who believes in many gods
Identify:
(a) fertile area between the Persian Gulf and the Mediterranean Sea (b) area at the eastern end of the Fertile Crescent between the Tigris and Euphrates rivers (c) city-states in southern Mesopotamia
Answer:
1. Answers should note larger population in city than in village; people farm in village, diversity of work is available in city; wealth and luxury as well as class distinctions apparent in city.
2. (a) Advantages: fertile land; ease of transportation; abundance of reeds. Disadvantages: no natural barriers for protection; no good supplies of stone, metal, and wood; irregular flooding pattern of the rivers.
(b) Sumerians built city walls with mud bricks to protect settlements, used reeds to build boats and huts, and dug irrigation ditches to bring water to crop fields.
3. Possible answer: Priests manage grain store-houses or keep track of the calendar; merchants bargain; artisans shape clay into vessels; farmers plant crops, tend to the irrigation system; slaves perform household duties for a family.
4. Bronze was very important in the making of tools and weapons.
5. (a) Students may consider the pervasiveness of electronic media and attempt to identify a role within these media for print. (b) Students may speculate on a world without wheels, plows.

ANSWER TO

Map Study

land along Tigris and Eu-
phrates rivers, including
Mesopotamia

Newcomers contributed to civilization. 2

Although the Sumerians never recovered from the attacks on their cities, their civilization did not die. Succeeding sets of rulers adapted the basic ideas of Sumerian culture to meet their own needs. As kingdoms grew larger, the Sumerian pattern of civilization spread more widely across Southwest Asia. At the same time, the newcomers made important contributions to civilization.

◢Turning Points in History

Hammurabi's Code In about 2000 B.C., a group of nomadic warriors known as Amorites invaded Mesopotamia. Within a short time, the Amorites overwhelmed the Sumerians and established Babylon as their capital. Amorite power reached its peak during the reign of a strong king named Hammurabi (1792–1750 B.C.). Hammurabi proved to be a highly successful general who conquered all of Mesopotamia. As a result, he created one

Map Study

Describe the geographic area covered by the Babylonian empire.

Peoples of Southwest Asia, 2000–1000 B.C.

KEY

Babylonian empire about 1750 B.C.

0   300 Miles

of the world's first **empires,** a state in which the ruler also controls other lands.

As the capital of a great empire, Babylon became a thriving commercial center. Soon its rapid growth caused problems. Babylon's merchants, farmers, and workers needed written laws to help them resolve disputes. Although individual Sumerian cities had developed codes of laws, Hammurabi recognized that a single, uniform code would help to unify the diverse groups within his empire. He therefore made a collection of laws known as Hammurabi's Code. Scribes carved these laws on a stone column, or stele. The eight-foot stele contained more than 3,500 lines of cuneiform characters.

A prologue explains the purpose of the code: "to cause justice to prevail in the land, to destroy the wicked and the evil, and to prevent the strong from oppressing the weak, . . . to enlighten the land and to further the welfare of the people." The code then lists 282 specific laws. These laws do not provide abstract theories of justice. Instead, they establish rules for dealing with everyday issues such as contracts, inheritances, leases, perjury, and debts and with theft and other crimes. The largest number of laws—88 in all—deals with marriage, family, and property.

Hammurabi's Code used three fundamental principles to deal with these different legal problems. First the code frequently invoked the principle of retaliation (an eye for an eye and a tooth for a tooth) to punish crimes. For example, if the ceiling of a house caved in and killed the occupant, retaliation demanded that the builder be executed.

Although the code applied to everyone, it set different punishments for rich and poor and for men and women. A common man who killed a member of the upper class would be executed. If the same man killed a poor farmer, however, he would only be required to pay a modest sum of money to the victim's family. Many of the laws applying to men and women also reflected a double standard. If a husband committed adultery, his spouse was permitted to leave him. An unfaithful wife, however, would be drowned. Although the code discriminated against women in some ways, it also gave them certain rights. Unlike women in other ancient societies, Babylonian women could divorce, own slaves, transact business, and bequeath property.

A carved relief on the stele shows the sun god Shamash giving the laws to Hammurabi.

Finally Hammurabi's Code established the principle that government had a responsibility for what occurred in a society. For example, if a man was robbed and the thief was not caught, the government was required to compensate the victim for his loss. The recording and public display of the laws showed the king's determination to promote public order with just laws.

Hammurabi's Code marked an important milestone in Mesopotamian civilization. It also became a standard that inspired future rulers. A thousand years later, Mesopotamian students still studied "the judgments of righteousness which Hammurabi, the great king, set up."

Two centuries after Hammurabi's reign, the Babylonian empire fell to nomadic warriors. During the next 700 years, the Fertile Crescent broke into small kingdoms as new peoples moved into the region. Some of these groups made important contributions to civilization. Among these groups were the Phoenicians (fuh-**NIH**-shuhnz) and the Jews.

Phoenicians invented the alphabet.

About 1100 B.C., the Phoenicians were the most powerful traders and merchants around the Mediterranean Sea. They did not rule a great empire, but they built a number of wealthy cities, something like the independent Sumerian city-states. The first Phoenician cities lay in what is now Lebanon. Later, however, the far-sailing Phoenicians settled widely around the Mediterranean Sea.

Wealth from trade The Phoenicians' wealth began in an unlikely way. Around their island city of Tyre (tire), millions of little snails washed up along the rocky shore. These snails were the resource from which the Phoenicians produced an intensely rich purple dye. To produce just one pound of dye, workers had to squeeze the drops from 60,000 smelly snail glands, a very costly process. All around the Mediterranean, the Phoenicians sold this rare dye at a fabulous price. Indeed, only a king's family could afford to wear "the royal purple" made at Tyre.

All in all, however, Phoenicia was poor in natural resources. Besides the snails, the only valuable item the land produced was fine, tall cedar trees that were in wide demand for building.

Thus, the Phoenicians turned to trade. In addition to purple dye and cedar, they traded goods they got from other lands, including wine, weapons, slaves, cloth, glass, precious metals, and ivory. Tyre competed fiercely with the other Phoenician city-states such as Byblos and Sidon for business that passed through Phoenician ports.

The Phoenicians' desire for trade made them excellent sailors. In narrow, single-sailed vessels equipped with long oars, they traveled all along the Mediterranean coasts of Europe and Africa. They even sailed past the Rock of Gibraltar into the stormy Atlantic Ocean. One Phoenician fleet may have circled the entire continent of Africa around 600 B.C. No other explorers are known to have attempted such a feat until 2,100 years later.

Between 1100 and 700 B.C., the Phoenicians founded trading **colonies,** or settlements controlled by them, on almost every Mediterranean island. Perhaps as many as 300 Phoenician cities dotted Africa's Mediterranean coast. The greatest was Carthage, on a natural harbor. (Later, Carthage rivaled Rome in power.)

39

SECTION 2 Objectives and Teaching Strategies

OBJECTIVE 1. Explain the significance of Hammurabi's law code.

Teaching Strategy: *Discussing History: Hammurabi's Code* (page 30d)

OBJECTIVE 2. Describe some of the Phoenicians' achievements.

Teaching Strategy: *Discussing History: The Phoenician Alphabet* (page 30d)

OBJECTIVE 3. Compare and contrast the religious beliefs of the Jews with those of the Sumerians.

Teaching Strategy: *Skill Building: Comparing and Contrasting Religious Beliefs* (page 30d)

■ BACKGROUND

Another example of Hammurabi's code: If a house falls in and kills the owner's son, the son of the architect shall be put to death, not the architect himself.

SECTION 2 Resources

GEOGRAPHY
■ Transparency 3

REINFORCEMENT
■ Independent Practice 2.2

ENRICHMENT
■ Voices from the Past 2.2

ASSESSMENT
■ Section Quiz 2.2

Phoenician	Greek	Modern

The alphabet On their travels, Phoenician merchants needed a simplified kind of writing to keep business records. Cuneiform, with its 600 symbols, was much too cumbersome. Consequently, the Phoenicians discovered a way to keep records using just 22 symbols.

The Phoenician writing system first appeared around 900 B.C. Soon it was carried to trading centers all over the Mediterranean world. Later, the Greeks and Romans changed the shapes of the 22 letters and added 4 others, making the alphabet we know today. The word *alphabet*, in fact, comes directly from the first two letters of the Phoenician alphabet, *aleph* and *beth*.

The invention of the alphabet was immensely important. Unlike cuneiform, the Phoenician way of writing was a simple system that many people could master fairly quickly. True, the majority

of the population still could not read or write. However, over the centuries, **literacy** (the ability to read and write) became more widespread. The growth of science and industry many years later would have been impossible without this spread of literacy.

Jews worshiped a single God.

Like the Phoenicians, the Jews were a small group of people in Southwest Asia. Also like the Phoenicians, their contribution to civilization was a large one.

Around 2000 B.C., a group of travelers left the Sumerian city-state of Ur. Among them, according to the Bible, was a man named Abraham and his wife, Sarah. Abraham, Sarah, and their family of nomadic herders gradually moved westward to the far end of the Fertile Crescent. After many years of travel, they came to a strip of land called Canaan (KAY-nuhn) near the Mediterranean Sea. This land was later known as Palestine. Such is the Biblical account of the beginnings of the Jewish people.

Monotheism The Jews were a small group who never wielded great political power in the ancient Fertile Crescent, but their influence on history was far-reaching. Unlike the other groups who dwelled around them, the Jews prayed only to one God. While other groups in the Fertile Crescent were polytheists, the Jewish people became **monotheists** (MAH-no-THEE-ists). This is a term that comes from the Greek words *mono* meaning "one" and *theist* meaning "god-worshiper."

According to Jewish tradition as recorded in the Bible, the one true God was the creator of all things and the ruler of the universe. The God that Abraham worshiped was not limited to any particular geographic place, as the city gods of Mesopotamia were. Thus, the Jews carried their worship of God into whatever lands they visited, rather than taking up the worship of local gods.

The leadership of Moses Around 1650 B.C., drought and famine brought hard times to Canaan. Many groups of people, including the Jews, migrated toward Egypt. Even in dry years, Egypt had water from its great river, the Nile. According to the Bible, at first the Jews had positions of honor in the Egyptian kingdom. Later, however, the Egyptians made the Jews their slaves.

40

Sometime between 1300 and 1200 B.C., the Jews fled from Egypt. The man who led them out of slavery to seek a land of their own was Moses. From that time on, Moses has been considered the greatest leader in Jewish history.

According to the Bible, while the Jews journeyed across the Sinai Peninsula, Moses climbed to the top of a mountain to pray. There he spoke with God. When Moses came down from Mount Sinai, he brought two tablets of stone on which were written ten laws, the Ten Commandments of the Bible.

These commandments and the other teachings from God that Moses delivered to his people became the basis for the religious laws of Judaism. The Jews believed that these laws formed a **covenant**, or promise, between God and the Jewish people. God promised to protect the Jews, and they, in turn, promised to honor God's commandments.

The covenant was based on the idea that God is just, not arbitrary as the gods of Mesopotamia were. Moreover, by the laws set forth to Moses, God demanded a high standard of moral conduct from human beings. This emphasis on justice, morality, and an individual relationship with God set Judaism apart. These ideas marked the birth of a set of religious traditions the impact of which has lasted thousands of years.

Building the kingdom of Israel On the far side of the Sinai Desert, the Jews came once more to Canaan, the land they believed God had promised them. The southern part of this land around the Dead Sea was brown and desertlike. The northern part, watered by the Jordan River, was green with olive trees and palms. The Canaanites, who already lived in the area, fiercely resisted the newcomers for centuries.

The Jews decided that they needed a king to lead them to victories. From about 1020 to 922 B.C., the Jews were united under three able kings in succession—first Saul, then David, and finally Solomon. Their kingdom was called Israel, and its capital was the city of Jerusalem. This short time period—less than 100 years—was the time of Israel's greatest power and independence.

DAILY LIFE ▸ The Ten Commandments and the Torah

The Ten Commandments created a permanent set of religious and moral laws. The first four commandments concerned the Jews' special relation with their God.

> *I am the Lord thy God . . . Thou shalt have no other gods before Me . . .*
> *Thou shalt not make unto thee a graven image . . .*
> *Thou shalt not take the name of the Lord thy God in vain . . .*
> *Remember the Sabbath day, to keep it holy . . .*

The last six commandments concerned the Jews' moral relationship with one another.

> *Honor thy father and thy mother . . .*
> *Thou shalt not murder.*
> *Thou shalt not commit adultery.*
> *Thou shalt not steal.*
> *Thou shalt not bear false witness . . .*
> *Thou shalt not covet . . .*

The Ten Commandments are contained in the Book of Exodus, one of the Five Books of Moses that make up the Torah. Each Sabbath, Jews around the world read aloud a portion of the Torah. The entire Torah is read each year.

41

■ BACKGROUND

Early Jewish scholars wondered why some people who obeyed the law suffered, while others who sinned seemed to go unpunished. The Book of Job offers this answer: God is unknowable; humans must trust God's justice.

ANSWERS TO

Section Review 2

Define:
(a) state that has conquered other lands and rules them **(b)** settlement controlled by founder **(c)** ability to read and write **(d)** person who believes in one God **(e)** promise (between God and the Jews) **(f)** religious teacher who was believed to be a messenger of God **(g)** belief in proper conduct in worship of one God

(continued)

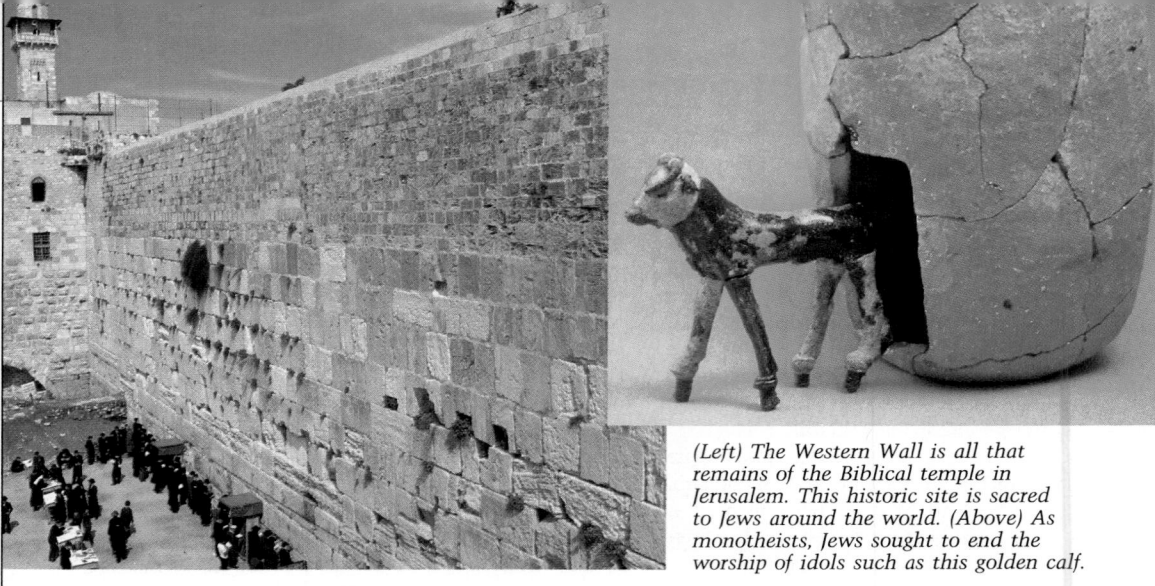

(Left) The Western Wall is all that remains of the Biblical temple in Jerusalem. This historic site is sacred to Jews around the world. (Above) As monotheists, Jews sought to end the worship of idols such as this golden calf.

ANSWERS TO (continued)

Identify:

(a) first conquerors of Sumer, from city of Babylon (b) Babylonian king and developer of law code (c) powerful traders and merchants around the Mediterranean in about 1100 B.C. (d) small group in Southwest Asia who became monotheists and settled in Palestine (e) according to the Bible, the man who led Jewish people into Canaan around 2000 B.C. (f) strip of land near the Mediterranean, later called Palestine (g) man who led the Jews out of slavery in Egypt and who, according to the Bible, climbed Mount Sinai and received the Ten Commandments (h) Jewish kingdom in Canaan (i) capital of the kingdom of Israel (j) most powerful of Jewish kings

Answer:

1. The basic ideas of Sumerian civilization were adapted by the newcomers.

2. The laws were published for all who could read to see; they also represented balance in the meting out of punishment.

3. It used many fewer symbols.

4. It stressed the worship of one God; it emphasized the ideas of justice, morality, and an individual relationship with God.

5. (a) Iron making is a more complicated process, requiring higher temperatures than are needed to make bronze. (b) It is harder, more common.

6. *writing:* facilitated the record-keeping necessary in the empire's administrative work; *law codes:* assured orderly treatment of different people.

The most powerful of the Jewish kings was Solomon. At the height of his rule, Solomon set about building a temple to glorify God. The temple was to be a permanent home for the Ark of the Covenant, which held the tablets of Moses' law. The temple that Solomon built was not large, but it gleamed like a precious gem. Bronze pillars stood at its door. The temple was stone on the outside, but its inner walls were made of Lebanese cedar covered in gold. The main hall was richly decorated with brass and gold. Solomon also built a palace for himself that was even more costly than the temple.

These building projects required high taxes and badly strained the little kingdom's economy. After Solomon's death, the Jews in the northern part of the kingdom revolted. In 922 B.C., the kingdom split in two, Israel in the north and Judah in the south. Thereafter, the Jewish people were swept up in the waves of conquest and migration that made Southwest Asia a battleground of empires for centuries.

The prophets Although the Jewish kingdom was broken, the Jewish religion continued to develop under religious teachers known as **prophets.** The prophets believed that they were messengers sent to reveal God's will to the Jews. Prophets such as Isaiah (eye-**ZAY**-uh) and Jeremiah sternly warned the Jews that God would punish greed, wickedness, or the worshiping of idols. Their emphasis upon proper conduct is called **ethical monotheism.**

Prophets taught that the Jews had a duty not only to worship God but also to live justly with one another. In the words of the prophet Micah, "It hath been shown to you, O man, what is good and what the Lord requires of you: Only to do justly, and to love mercy, and to walk humbly with thy God."

People learned to work with iron.

Although some of the important developments of civilization can be linked to particular groups, other changes cannot be pinned down to one group. The shift from bronze to iron as the chief metal for making tools is a change that cannot be linked to any single group. Like the earlier change from stone tools to bronze ones, the transition to iron had far-reaching effects.

From about 2800 to 1200 B.C., bronze was the basic metal used for tools and weapons. Bronze is a combination of copper and another metal, usually tin. Copper was not very hard to find in the Fertile Crescent and nearby lands, especially the island of Cyprus. Tin, however, must have come from a great distance, perhaps as far as western Britain or even Southeast Asia. Both copper and tin melt at lower temperatures than iron. Therefore, early metalworkers learned to make bronze long before they could build a fire that was hot enough to work with iron.

Between 1500 and 1200 B.C., the Hittites, a people living in Asia Minor, gradually learned

42

the complicated process of smelting iron. However, the skill of ironworking was so rare that a piece of iron was sometimes worth 40 times as much as the same weight of silver.

Iron has a number of advantages over bronze. It is harder than bronze, so that an iron sword or spear could cut through the bronze shield of an enemy warrior. The most important advantage, though, is that iron is a very common metal. It is found nearly everywhere. No longer did people have to depend on tin from distant lands. Once people had the skill to work with it, iron was much cheaper than bronze. Thus, people could use much more metal than could earlier people. Armies had more metal weapons, and artisans had more metal tools.

The shift from bronze to iron took hundreds of years. Gradually, from 1200 to around 700 B.C. in the Fertile Crescent, the Bronze Age came to an end and the Iron Age began. The use of iron gave urban civilizations a great advantage over less settled people who were not able to make metal weapons. In some ways, the use of iron paved the way for an age of empires.

Section REVIEW 2

Define: (a) empire, (b) colony, (c) literacy, (d) monotheist, (e) covenant, (f) prophet, (g) ethical monotheism
Identify: (a) Babylonians, (b) Hammurabi, (c) Phoenicians, (d) Jews, (e) Abraham, (f) Canaan, (g) Moses, (h) Israel, (i) Jerusalem, (j) Solomon
Answer:
1. How did Sumerian civilization remain important even after the fall of Sumer?
2. Explain why Hammurabi's Code was outstanding for its day.
3. What advantages did the Phoenician alphabet have over cuneiform?
4. How was the Jewish religion revolutionary in ancient times?
5. (a) Why did people learn to work with bronze before learning to work with iron? (b) What were the advantages of iron over bronze?

Critical Thinking
6. After 700 B.C., the Fertile Crescent entered a period when great empires arose in the region. The invention of a convenient writing system

and the use of law codes were two key elements that made large empires possible. Explain why each of those developments was essential to building an empire.

Conquerors ruled ever larger empires. 3

Although Southwest Asia in ancient times was a mixture of many peoples, the area was surprisingly united culturally. Modern scholars refer to it as "the cuneiform world." Empires came and went, but farming, irrigation, city life, and cuneiform writing remained. The culture that began in Sumer spread over a wide area, carried both by traders like the Phoenicians and by conquerors like the Babylonians.

In the years after 900 B.C., a series of empires united Southwest Asia. Each new empire seemed to rise out of the ashes of the old one. For a while, the new empire would grow larger and more powerful. Then it too would collapse and be replaced by another.

Map Study
Compare this map to the one on page 38. What territories did the Assyrians rule that the Babylonians did not?

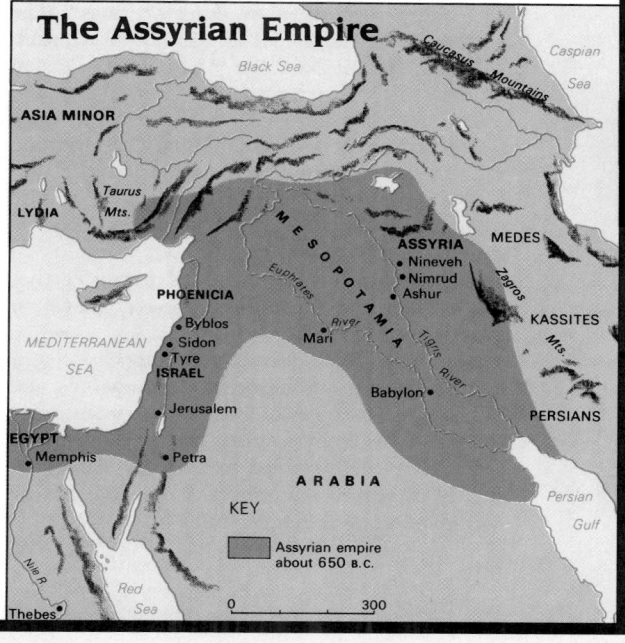

The Assyrian Empire

Compare this map to the one on page 38.

SECTION 3
Objectives and Teaching Strategies

OBJECTIVE 1. Discuss the rise and fall of the Assyrian empire.
Teaching Strategy: *Discussing History: Assurbanipal's Question* (page 30e)

OBJECTIVE 2. Describe aspects of everyday life in Babylon.
Teaching Strategy: *Discussing History: The Wonders of Babylon* (page 30e)

OBJECTIVE 3. Explain how the Persians ruled their empire.
Teaching Strategy: *Skill Building: Creative Writing* (page 30e)

ANSWER TO
Map Study

Assyria and eastern Mediterranean region, including Phoenicia, Israel, and Egypt

SECTION 3
Resources

ENRICHMENT
■ Voices from the Past 2.3

ASSESSMENT
■ Section Quiz 2.3

GEOGRAPHY
■ Transparencies 1, 4, 5

REINFORCEMENT
■ Independent Practice 2.3

■ BACKGROUND

Assurbanipal's library includes a long narrative poem called "The Epic of Gilgamesh." This story of the quest for immortality includes the Sumerian flood story.

This bas-relief shows the mighty king of Assyria, Assurbanipal, hunting lions. The carving adorns the wall of the king's palace at Nineveh, the capital of his empire.

The Assyrian empire rose and fell.

I am Assurbanipal, the Great King, the Mighty King, King of the Universe, King of Assyria, King of the World's Four Regions, King of Kings, Unrivaled Prince . . .

This was not just the idle boast of a vain king. When these words were carved in stone in 650 B.C., there was indeed a "king of kings." The empire of Assurbanipal (AH-soor-BAH-nee-pahl) spanned the Fertile Crescent from the Persian Gulf to the Mediterranean Sea.

The Assyrians (uh-SIHR-ee-uhnz) came from the northern part of Mesopotamia. Their farming villages in northern Mesopotamia had been attacked repeatedly by barbarians from the nearby mountains. Thus, over the centuries, the Assyrians learned to be tough fighters. Around 850 B.C., they began a campaign of conquest that made them, for a time, the greatest power in Southwest Asia.

Assyrian soldiers were well equipped for conquering an empire. They had iron swords and iron-pointed spears. Moreover, the Assyrians were the most disciplined army the world had yet seen. They were trained to march and fight in tightly organized columns and divisions led by commanders of different ranks.

With the precision of a machine, Assyrian soldiers marched shoulder to shoulder to within an arrow's shot of a city wall. At a signal from their commander, they stopped, strung their bows, and released a shower of arrows. Wave upon wave of arrows hissed over the walls of the besieged city. Meanwhile, other troops moved up to the city gates and hammered them with massive, iron-tipped battering rams. When at last the gates splintered, the Assyrians showed their victims no mercy. They tortured, killed, or enslaved the people of the city. To prevent later rebellions, the Assyrians uprooted conquered people from their homelands, sending great groups of captives to distant parts of the empire.

Between 850 and 650 B.C., the kings of Assyria conquered Syria, Palestine, and Babylonia. They extended their empire into North Africa by conquering Egypt. Cartloads of jewels and ivory, gold and silver rumbled into Nineveh (NIHN-uh-vuh), Assyria's capital city. Tribute from foreign kings was, after all, one of the great rewards of conquest.

Nineveh, on the Tigris River in Mesopotamia, was famous as the largest city of its day. It was about three miles long by one mile wide. In addition to the treasures of the empire, Nineveh also held the world's largest library. King Assurbanipal collected 25,000 clay tablets. Some were like foreign-language dictionaries, giving the same words in several languages. When archaeologists found the remains of the library, the tablets helped scholars decipher the cuneiform writing of ancient Mesopotamia.

The Assyrian army seemed invincible, and the Assyrian king was one of the most powerful rulers on earth. Yet Assurbanipal was almost the last of the mighty Assyrian kings. Assyrian power had spread too thin. Nineveh fell 21 years after Assurbanipal's death. In 612 B.C., the city's gates were rammed open by a combined army of Medes (meedz) and Chaldeans (kal-DEE-uhnz). The Assyrians' cruelty had made them many enemies who were pleased by their downfall. As the Jewish prophet Nahum wrote, "Nineveh is laid waste: who will bemoan her?"

The Chaldeans rebuilt Babylon.

Thus, around 600 B.C., Babylon again became the center of an empire, more than 1,000 years after Hammurabi had ruled there. After defeating

44

the Assyrians, the Chaldeans made Babylon their capital. From there, they began to build up their own empire.

The wonders of Babylon Many who beheld the new Babylon marveled at its beauty. The chief builder of Babylon was a remarkable Chaldean king, Nebuchadnezzar (NEB-yuh-kuhd-NEZ-uhr), who ruled from 605 to 562 B.C. The walls of his palace were covered with shiny tiles arranged in bright patterns of blue, yellow, red, and white.

The most impressive part of the palace was the famous hanging gardens of Babylon. According to legend, one of Nebuchadnezzar's wives missed the flowering shrubs of her mountain homeland. To please her, the king had sweet-smelling trees and shrubs from the mountains planted on terraces that rose 75 feet above the flat plain of Babylon. Slaves watered the plants daily from pumps hidden inside towering columns. These gardens won the admiration of Greek visitors, who listed the garden as one of the Seven Wonders of the World.

Indeed, the entire city was a wonder. Its walls were so thick that, according to one report, a four-horse chariot could wheel around on top of them. To ensure that the world knew who ruled Babylon, even the bricks were inscribed: "I am Nebuchadnezzar, King of Babylon."

The stargazers of Babylon The highest building in Babylon was a great, seven-tiered ziggurat more than 300 feet high and visible for miles. At night, priests observed the stars from the top of this ziggurat and others in the city. They kept detailed records of how the stars and planets seemed to change position in the night sky. The rise of each constellation, or group of stars, marked the beginning of a new month on the Chaldean calendar.

The Chaldeans believed that the stars determined human destiny. Thus, to foretell the future from day to day, Chaldean priests observed a belt of 12 constellations called a zodiac. Nebuchadnezzar consulted the temple's star charts carefully in governing his kingdom.

The priest-astrologers of Babylon also watched the four phases of the moon. They concluded that every month should be divided into four weeks—one week for each change from new moon to half, half to full, full to half, and half to new. Their calculations were accurate to within a few minutes.

The Chaldeans' observations formed the basis for both astronomy and astrology. Much of their knowledge was passed on to the Greeks, who used it to develop many theories about Earth, the planets, and the stars.

The Jews' Babylonian captivity Like other emperors before him, Nebuchadnezzar followed a policy of taking conquered groups from their homelands and sending them to another part of the empire. People who were cut off from their homeland were less likely to rebel against the empire.

Among the peoples that Nebuchadnezzar conquered were the Jews. After a long siege, his armies captured Jerusalem in 586 B.C. They pillaged the temple and burned the city. Thousands of Jews fled to surrounding lands. Nebuchadnezzar's soldiers captured about 15,000 Jews and sent them as slaves to Babylon.

This period of time was vitally important in the history of Jewish monotheism. While other people worshiped the god of whatever city they

This reconstruction of a city gate shows the grandeur of Nebuchadnezzar's Babylon. Above the gate rose the famous Hanging Gardens.

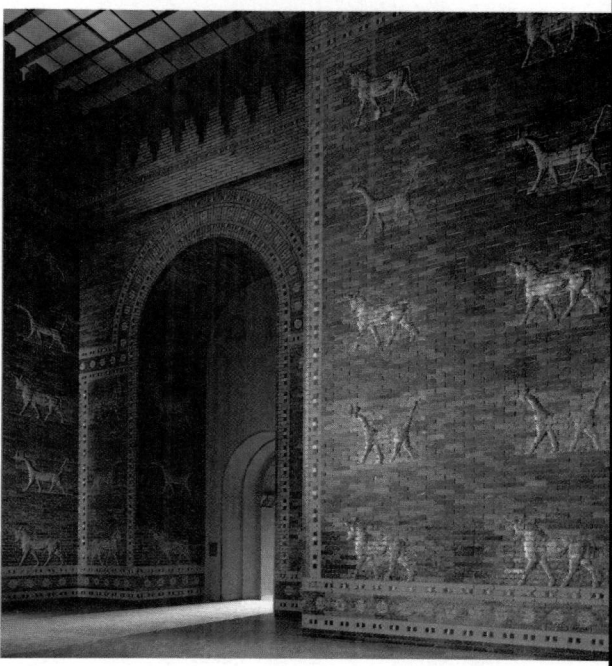

45

Cooperative Learning

Working in pairs, have students research one of the following: Babylon's hanging gardens, the city layout of Nebuchadnezzar's Babylon, or the Babylonians' knowledge of astronomy or astrology. Partners should share the research tasks, each taking notes. Then the recorder writes the report as his or her partner offers suggestions. Finally, pairs should join other pairs to form groups of six. Spokespersons then take turns presenting their reports to other groups in an informal manner. Encourage group members to question the spokespersons, and vice versa. It is the responsibility of the spokespersons to make sure that everyone understands what has been presented.

■ BACKGROUND

Some students may be familiar with the word *Diaspora,* referring to Jews who live outside of Palestine.

ANSWERS TO
Voice from the Past

1. sorrowful, resentful, bitter, vengeful

2. to sing of their homeland and be pleasant

3. to remember Jerusalem always

■ BACKGROUND

At its height, the Persian empire was approximately the same size as the continental United States.

V̲oice from the Past | *The Babylonian Captivity*

The Bible is a collection of writings that form the basis of both the Jewish and the Christian religions. Much of the material in the Bible is important for historic information as well as for religion. The following passage, Psalm 137, describes the feelings of the Jews after being taken captive to Babylon.

> *By the rivers of Babylon, there we sat down, yea, we wept, when we remembered Zion [their homeland].*
>
> *We hanged our harps upon the willows in the midst thereof.*
>
> *For there they that carried us away captive required of us a song; and they that wasted us required of us mirth, saying, Sing us one of the songs of Zion.*
>
> *How shall we sing the Lord's song in a strange land?*
>
> *If I forget thee, O Jerusalem, let my right hand forget her cunning.*
>
> *If I do not remember thee, let my tongue cleave to the roof of my mouth; if I prefer not Jerusalem to my chief joy.*
>
> *Remember, O Lord, the children of Edom [a people who joined forces with Nebuchadnezzar] in the day of Jerusalem; who said, Raze it [destroy it], raze it, even to the foundation thereof.*
>
> *O daughter of Babylon, who art to be destroyed; happy shall he be, that rewardeth thee as thou hast served us.*
>
> *Happy shall he be, that taketh and dasheth thy little ones against the stones.*

1. What are the feelings of the Jews in their exile?

2. What are their captors asking of them, according to the psalm?

3. What do the Jews vow to do concerning Jerusalem?

Jews being led into exile

lived in, the Jews held fast to their religion even apart from their homeland.

Nebuchadnezzar governed for 43 years. His empire fell shortly after his death. The fall of Babylon marked the end of the Mesopotamian empires. The empires that arose in the following centuries were much larger than Mesopotamia or even than the Fertile Crescent.

The Persians united a vast area.

The Assyrians had shown that it was possible to build an empire based on fear and harsh government. The giant empire that next arose in Southwest Asia showed that it was possible to build an empire based on tolerance and wise government. Beginning around 550 B.C., the Persians spread their rule from the Indus River to the Nile River and the Black Sea.

The rise of Persia The Persians' homeland lay east of the Fertile Crescent, among the mountains and plateaus of Iran. The rest of the world paid little heed to the Persians until 550 B.C. In that year, Cyrus (SYE-ruhs), king of the Persians, defeated several neighboring kingdoms. Suddenly, it was clear that a new power was arising in Southwest Asia.

In just 11 years, between 550 and 539 B.C., Cyrus conquered all of the Fertile Crescent and most of Asia Minor. His generosity toward conquered peoples was one reason for his astonishing success. When Cyrus's army marched into a city, there was no looting or burning. Instead of destroying the local temple, Cyrus was more likely to worship there himself. Cyrus believed that it was wise to let alone local customs and religions.

Knowing Cyrus's tolerance, Babylon peacefully opened its gates for him in 539 B.C. With great

46

The Persian Empire 500 B.C.

KEY
- The Persian empire
- The Royal Road

0 — 500 Miles

ANSWERS TO

Map Study

Indus River; Asia, Africa, Europe

■ **DISCUSSION**

Have students explain why the Persian approach to empire building may have resulted in a fragile hold over the conquered peoples.

Map Study

What river valley marked the easternmost end of the Persian empire? On what three continents did the empire hold land?

tact, Cyrus lifted up prayers of thanks for this bloodless victory to Babylon's chief god, Marduk. According to Persian accounts, "all the inhabitants of Babylon . . . princes and governors included, bowed to Cyrus and kissed his feet, jubilant and with shining faces."

As another act of generosity, Cyrus allowed the Jews to go back to Jerusalem in 538 B.C. and rebuild their city. The Jewish city flourished under Persian rule. It was during this period that many portions of the Bible were first put into writing.

In 530 B.C., Cyrus was killed in battle. His son, Cambyses (kam-**BYE**-seez), extended the Persian empire by conquering all of Egypt. After ruling only eight years, Cambyses died, probably from the infection of an accidental sword wound. Immediately, widespread rebellions broke out across the empire, showing how fragile Persian control really was.

Cambyses' successor, Darius (duh-**RYE**-uhs), had been a member of the king's bodyguard, an elite group of Persian soldiers known as the Ten Thousand Immortals. With their help, Darius won the throne and spent his first three years as king putting down revolts.

Darius extended Persian conquests in the east, leading armies up into the mountains of Afghanistan and down into the river valleys of India. The Persian empire was now immense. It embraced Egypt and Asia Minor in the west, part of India in the east, and the Fertile Crescent in the center.

Persian government How could this sprawling empire be governed? Darius's answer was to divide the empire into 20 provinces. The provinces were roughly equal to the homelands of the many groups of people within the Persian empire. Under Persian rule, the people of each province still practiced their own religion, spoke their own language, and to some extent followed their own laws. (This pattern of many groups—sometimes called "nationalities"—living by their own laws within one empire continued in Southwest Asia until the early 1900's.)

47

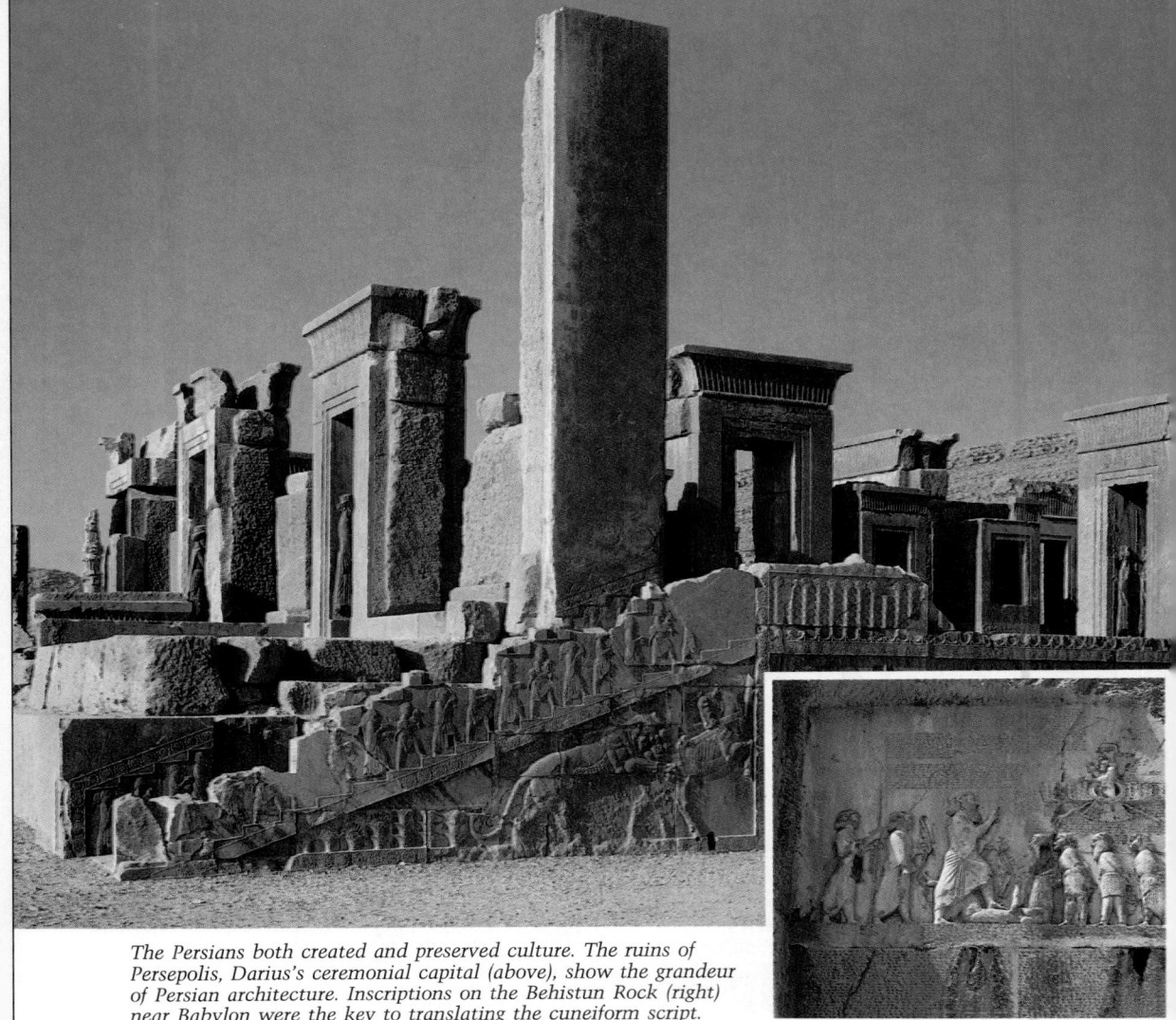

The Persians both created and preserved culture. The ruins of Persepolis, Darius's ceremonial capital (above), show the grandeur of Persian architecture. Inscriptions on the Behistun Rock (right) near Babylon were the key to translating the cuneiform script.

Although tolerant of the many groups within his empire, Darius ruled with absolute power as king of kings. In each province of the Persian empire was a governor called a **satrap** (SAY-trap). Darius also appointed an army leader and a tax collector for each province. To make sure his satraps did not rebel against him, Darius sent inspectors known as the "King's Eyes and Ears" to all parts of his kingdom.

The Persian king used two other important tools to hold his empire together. One was an excellent road system, and the other was standardized coinage.

The famous Royal Road of the Persian empire ran from Susa, the Persian capital, to Sardis in Asia Minor, a distance of 1,677 miles. An ordinary caravan took three months to travel this distance, but the king's messengers took only about a week. Royal riders dashed along the road. At 111 post stations spaced along the road, new riders on fresh horses took over for tired ones. With this system, royal commands reached all parts of the empire.

Darius's second idea, borrowed from the Lydians of Asia Minor, was to manufacture metal coins. For the first time, coins of a standard value

48

circulated throughout most of the civilized world. People no longer had to weigh and measure bits of gold or silver to pay for their purchases. Like the road system, the wider use of money made trade much easier. Trade, in turn, helped to hold the empire together.

The teachings of Zoroaster By Darius's time, about 2,500 years had passed since the first Sumerian city-states had been built. During those years, people of the Fertile Crescent had suffered often from war, conquest, and famine. Why was there so much evil in the world? A Persian prophet named Zoroaster (ZOH-roh-AS-tuhr) offered an inspirational answer.

Scholars know almost nothing about the life of Zoroaster except that he lived around 600 B.C. His ideas, however, are well-known. Zoroaster taught that two spiritual armies fight for possession of a person's soul. One army is led by Ahura-Mazda (AH-hoo-ruh-MAHZ-duh), god of truth and light. The other is commanded by Ahriman (AH-ree-muhn), god of evil and darkness. At the end of time, said Zoroaster, all souls would be judged according to the side they had chosen. Followers of Ahura-Mazda would be lifted into a paradise. Followers of Ahriman would suffer forever in a fiery pit.

This belief in a heaven and a hell was radically different from Sumer's gloomy vision of the afterlife. Zoroaster's religion was far more hopeful, because a person's own choice controlled his or her fate. Those who chose the side of goodness were not doomed to a dismal underworld.

The Persian empire lasted about 200 years. Through their tolerance and good government, the Persians brought political order to Southwest Asia. They preserved ideas from earlier civilizations and found new ways to live and rule. Their respect for other cultures helped to preserve those cultures for the future. At the same time, their own practical answers to problems—such as roads, coinage, and standardized weights and

measures—encouraged development within their empire.

During this long period of comparative peace, the region's great cities prospered. They were the meeting places of trade from India and the east, from Mediterranean lands and the west, and from the vast area of central Asia to the north. Commerce flourished, bringing rare goods from distant lands and untold wealth to the royal treasury. Learning and the arts also progressed as seen in the many languages and artistic styles that combined to form Persian culture.

The city that symbolized the Persian empire was Persepolis, the ceremonial capital that Darius built on the Iranian plateau. Persepolis was the source of the royal power that held the vast empire together. That same power sought to preserve the achievements of civilization. In particular, it preserved the written word—invented by Sumerians, simplified by Phoenicians—that recorded the history of the empires that rose and fell in Southwest Asia.

Section REVIEW 3

Define: (a) constellation, (b) astronomy, (c) satrap
Identify: (a) Assyria, (b) Assurbanipal, (c) Chaldeans, (d) Babylon, (e) Nebuchadnezzar, (f) Iran, (g) Persians, (h) Cyrus, (i) Darius, (j) Zoroaster

Answer:
1. Explain how the Assyrians succeeded in conquering a great empire.
2. What were the achievements of the Chaldeans in the time of Nebuchadnezzar?
3. What important religious stand did the Jews take during their captivity in Babylon?
4. How was the Persian king Cyrus's way of building an empire different from that of Assyrian kings?
5. How was Zoroaster's philosophy different from earlier religions of Southwest Asia?

Critical Thinking
6. Suppose you lived in a city in Mesopotamia. Would you rather have lived there in the period of the independent Sumerian city-states or in the time of the Persian empire? Explain your answer.

49

Footnote to History

Satraps lived in luxurious palaces. The Persian name for a satrap's private hunting park was *paradise* (from which comes our own word for a heavenly place).

ANSWERS TO

Section Review 3

Define:
(a) group of stars (b) study of the heavens (c) royal governor of each province of the Persian empire
Identify:
(a) empire builders from northern Mesopotamia (b) mighty kings of Assyria (c) conquerors of the Assyrians who rebuilt Babylon (d) resplendent capital of Chaldean kingdom (e) king of Chaldeans (f) homeland of Persians (g) people from Iran who conquered all of the Fertile Crescent and Asia Minor (h) Persian king who began rise of Persia (i) later Persian king responsible for building Royal Road (j) Persian prophet
Answer:
1. with skillful fighting, discipline, and brute force
2. rebuilding and beautifying Babylon; developing astronomical and astrological information
3. They continued to worship their one God.
4. Cyrus was tolerant and did not interfere with local customs; the Assyrians built their empire on fear.
5. It included the notion of a heaven attainable by all who followed Ahura-Mazda.
6. Answers should consider the strengths and weaknesses of the two: Sumer—greater independence than Persian empire but gloomier outlook; warfare among city-states; Persia—improvements in daily life; more hopeful religious outlook; good government.

Concluding the Chapter

1. **Chapter Closer**
   Ask students to explain the significance of written records for reconstructing the story of the past. Have students refer to the written records described in this chapter and the information these records disclose about life in ancient Southwest Asia.

2. **Reteaching Activities**
   a. Summarizing Have students write five statements describing the key traits of the Sumerian civilization.
   b. Recalling Important Ideas Have students identify the significance of each of the following: Hammurabi, Phoenicians, alphabet, Moses, Solomon, and the prophets.
   c. Recalling Important People Have students write a sentence to explain the importance of each of the following people: Assurbanipal, Nebuchadnezzar, and Cyrus.

Answers to Chapter Review appear on page 30f.

Summary

1. **Civilization arose in the Fertile Crescent.** About 5,000 years ago, many groups of people throughout the world were living in small farming villages. In the Fertile Crescent of Southwest Asia, however, the people of Sumer developed a more complex way of life. They built cities in which people worked at a variety of trades. For the first time in history, farmers were able to raise enough food to have a surplus. The ability to raise a surplus freed people to do specialized jobs. Sumerian government and religion were highly organized. Sumerians invented a system of writing, and their technology was advanced for its day. These traits made Sumer the first civilization.

2. **Newcomers contributed to civilization.** Beginning around 2000 B.C., waves of new peoples swept through the Fertile Crescent. Each new group adopted the ways of life begun in Sumer and added their own ideas. The Babylonians' most famous achievement was a code of law. The Phoenicians invented a system of writing that evolved into our present-day alphabet. The Jews developed a religion based on belief in one God. Between 1500 and 1000 B.C., the Bronze Age gave way to the Iron Age.

3. **Conquerors ruled ever larger empires.** Between 900 and 350 B.C., the Assyrians, the Chaldeans, and the Persians each took a turn at ruling Southwest Asia. Each group of people imposed its culture and ruling style on the area. Some of the important developments during this time were the increased use of iron, the beginnings of astronomy, the use of money for trade, and the belief in an afterlife.

Reviewing the Facts

1. Define the following terms:
   a. civilization
   b. artisan
   c. cuneiform
   d. institution
   e. city-state
   f. barter
   g. polytheist
   h. empire
   i. literacy
   j. monotheist
   k. prophet

2. Explain the importance of each of the following names, places, or terms:
   a. Fertile Crescent
   b. Mesopotamia
   c. Bronze Age
   d. Iron Age
   e. Sumer
   f. Hammurabi
   g. Phoenicians
   h. Jews
   i. Moses
   j. Solomon
   k. Assyria
   l. Nebuchadnezzar
   m. Persians
   n. Cyrus
   o. Darius
   p. Zoroaster

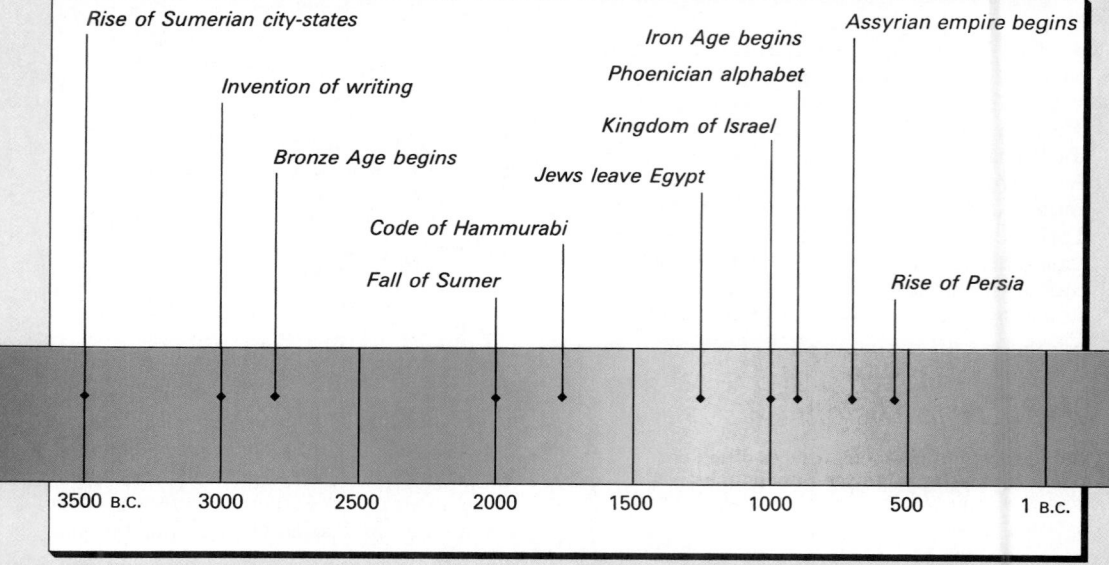

Rise of Sumerian city-states
Invention of writing
Bronze Age begins
Code of Hammurabi
Fall of Sumer
Jews leave Egypt
Kingdom of Israel
Phoenician alphabet
Iron Age begins
Assyrian empire begins
Rise of Persia

3500 B.C.   3000   2500   2000   1500   1000   500   1 B.C.

50

3. (a) What are the key traits of civilization? (b) Describe how each trait was present in Sumer.
4. What lasting contributions to civilization were made by each of the following groups? (a) the Phoenicians (b) the Jews (c) the Chaldeans

Basic Skills

1. **Reading a time line** Use the time line on page 50 and information from the chapter to answer these questions: (a) How many years were there between the beginning of the Bronze Age and that of the Iron Age? The invention of writing and of the alphabet? The Jews' exodus from Egypt and their captivity in Babylon? (b) How long did the Assyrian empire last? The Persian empire?
2. **Reading a map** Locate the Fertile Crescent on the map on page 32. Use geographic features such as deserts, mountains, seas, and rivers to define the boundaries of the Fertile Crescent.
3. **Outlining** Outline the content of the subsection entitled *Persian government* on pages 47 and 48. Your outline should show the main ideas and two or three details supporting each main idea.
4. **Using vocabulary** Historians often divide their subject into several categories. *Political history* deals with government, laws, and political leaders. *Economic history* sees how society employs labor, money, and tools to make, buy, and sell goods and services. *Social history* studies the way people live, how they relate to each other, how they view the world, and what values they teach their children. *Cultural history* refers to ideas, values, and beliefs and their expression through literature, the arts, and education. For each kind of history, give two examples of information from this chapter.

Researching and Reporting Skills

Of the political and religious leaders described in this chapter, whom do you think is greatest? To learn more about that person, do research in the library.
1. **Using the card catalog** Identify two books that refer to the person chosen. From each card, copy the book title, author's name, copyright date, and library call number.
2. **Acquiring information** In each book, read at least ten pages about your subject. Note why each author considers this person important as a leader.

3. **Summarizing** Write a summary of the historical importance of the leader you chose. Include information from both sources and your own ideas.

Critical Thinking

1. **Analyzing cause and effect** How did the production of surplus food affect the political, economic, and social life of Sumer?
2. **Comparing** (a) Compare the origins of Hammurabi's Code and the Ten Commandments. (b) How did their ideas for moral conduct differ?
3. **Evaluating** All conquerors face the problem of gaining obedience from conquered peoples. (a) How did the Assyrians and Persians each solve this problem? (b) Which solution do you consider more effective, and why?
4. **Synthesizing** (a) In both Sumer and Phoenicia, how did technological advances aid the expansion of trade? (b) Why were new inventions needed for trade to grow?
5. **Interpreting** What is the significance of the start of monotheism for history?
6. **Using visual evidence** It has been said that in Mesopotamian art, a seated or reclining figure has a higher social position than does a standing figure. Study the photos relating to Mesopotamia to see whether the statement is true. What conclusion do you draw? On what evidence is it based?

Perspectives on Past and Present

Reread the description of Hammurabi's Code on page 38. Do you agree or disagree with the statement, "Although this code was an outstanding example of justice for its day, it would fall short by today's standards"?

Investigating History

1. The Hanging Gardens of Babylon were one of the Seven Wonders of the Ancient World. Use reference books to find out what the others were, and choose one to research further. Write a brief description of that work, or make a drawing or model to show how it may have looked.
2. One monument enduring from the ancient world is the Behistun Rock in Iran. Do research to learn how this landmark aided the translation of early languages.

51

CHAPTER
Evaluation

Chapter Test 2, Alternate Chapter Test 2, and Computer Test Bank Chapter 2 Test can be used to evaluate your students' understanding of this chapter.

Ancient Egypt

Chapter **3**

Chapter Overview

The Nile River enabled Egyptian civilization to grow and prosper for more than 3,000 years. It provided a relatively predictable supply of fertile soil and an easy means of transportation. The Egyptians worshiped the Nile as a god who gave them life. Deserts on either side of the Nile shielded Egypt from attack. Egyptian farming villages were united first into agricultural districts called *nomes* and then into two kingdoms, Upper and Lower Egypt. A strong king named Menes united the two kingdoms in about 3100 B.C.

Egypt's rulers, or pharaohs, were considered divine and immortal. They ruled Egypt during three periods of peace and prosperity known as the Old, Middle, and New Kingdoms. Around 1200 B.C., invasions led to a decline from which ancient Egypt never recovered.

Egyptian society retained the same basic form for 3,000 years. Nobles lived in luxury, peasants worked in the fields, and slaves served their masters. Egyptian religion emphasized *maat*, or justice. Those who lived according to maat could expect eternal life in the afterworld. The Egyptians' achievements included a system of writing, methods for surveying land, a calendar, and sophisticated medical practices.

Chapter Focus

Ask students to write down at least two thoughts that come to mind when they think of Ancient Egypt. List volunteers' answers on the board. Typical student answers include King Tut, gold, the Nile River, pharaohs, and the pyramids. This chapter discusses each of these subjects. In addition, students will learn about the cultural achievements of one of history's oldest civilizations.

Direct students to the chapter opener on the discovery of Tutankhamon's tomb (pages 52–53). Carter's workers removed more than 200,000 tons of dirt and rubble before finding the tomb. Carter later wrote, "never before in the whole history of excavation had such an amazing sight been seen as the light of our torch revealed to us."

Carter was not exaggerating. During the next five years, he carefully removed more than 3,000 items from Tutankhamon's tomb. This fabulous treasure included more than two tons of gold. The picture on page 52 shows Tutankhamon's gold burial mask.

The Nile River shaped Egyptian life. **1**

Setting the Stage

Begin by asking students to name geographic features they believe would contribute to the development of a thriving civilization. List students' responses on the board. (fertile soil, natural resources, natural barriers, waterways, and access to an ocean or sea) Display Map Transparency 6, *Ancient Egypt/The Nile River,* and ask students to determine which of the geographic features they listed were

Chapter 3 Ancient Egypt 3100 B.C.–332 B.C.
  FOCUS The discovery of Tutankhamon's tomb

★ **Advanced**
● **Basic**

	SECTION 1	SECTION 2	SECTION 3
Objectives	1. Identify the location and physical characteristics of ancient Egypt. 2. Explain how the Nile influenced the development of Egyptian culture.	1. Explain the role of the pharaohs. 2. Discuss how and why the pyramids were constructed. 3. Compare and contrast Egypt's three kingdoms. 4. Identify and locate the empire built by the pharaohs of the New Kingdom.	1. Compare and contrast the lives of nobles and peasants in Egyptian society. 2. Define the concept of maat and explain its significance in Egyptian religion. 3. Identify Akhenaton and explain his religious reforms. 4. Describe some of the achievements of Egyptian culture.
Setting the Stage	Egypt's unique geography Transparency 6	Impressions of the pyramids	Traditional values and agents of change
Teaching Strategies	Using Geographic Themes: The Location and Physical Characteristics of a Place Transparency 1 Using Geographic Themes: Human-Environment Interaction Check for Understanding	Discussing History: Who Built the Pyramids? Discussing History: How Were the Pyramids Built? Skill Building: Comparing and Contrasting Egyptian Kingdoms Geography in History: Making a Map Outline Map 22 Check for Understanding	Discussing History: Egyptian Nobles and Peasants Discussing History: Analyzing Egyptian Religion Skill Building: Analyzing Effects Discussing History: Identifying Reasons for Egypt's Great Achievements Check for Understanding
Guided Practice	Transparency 6 Q&A Transparency 1 Q&A Section Review 1	Section Review 2	Section Review 3
Independent Practice Worksheets	Independent Practice 3.1 Geography Skills 3 Vocabulary 3	Independent Practice 3.2 Basic Skills 3	Independent Practice 3.3 Critical Thinking 3
Enrichment	1. Primary Source: Voices 3.1 2. Preparing a Report: Carter's Discovery 3. ★Researching the Aswan Dam 4. Researching for Points	1. Primary Source: Voices 3.2 2. Researching for Points	1. Primary Source: Voices 3.3 2. ★Analyzing a Primary Source: Hymn to Aton 3. Researching for Points

Chapter Closer	
●**Reteaching Activities**	Outlining, Summarizing, Organizing Information
Chapter Review	Summary, Reviewing the Facts, Basic Skills, Researching and Reporting Skills, Critical Thinking, Perspectives on Past and Present, Investigating History
Chapter Evaluation	Chapter Test 3, Alternate Chapter Test 3, Computer Test Bank Chapter 3 Test

present in ancient Egypt. Would they predict that Egypt would produce a successful or an unsuccessful civilization? This section examines Egypt's unique geography.

Teaching Strategies

Using Geographic Themes: The Location and Physical Characteristics of a Place (Objective 1) Ask students to turn to the map "The World about 1700 B.C." on pages 14–15, or use Map Transparency 1. Have students locate Egypt's position relative to Mesopotamia. Ask, "What was the closest nearby civilization at the time shown on this map?" (Babylonia) "What was the most distant civilization?" (China)

Now have students look at the map on page 55. Explain that ancient Egypt had a number of unusual physical characteristics. About 95 percent of Egypt was (and still is) a desert. The remaining 5 percent is oases watered by the Nile River. Emphasize that the Nile divides Egypt into two distinctive regions—the Nile valley (or Upper Egypt) and the Nile Delta (or Lower Egypt). The Nile valley is a very narrow strip of land, in places not more than a mile wide. In contrast, the delta is about 130 miles across. It contains some of the world's most fertile soil. This rich layer of soil was provided by the Nile's annual 100-day flood. (For a picture of the Nile flood, see *National Geographic's Peoples and Places of the Past,* page 49.)

Using Geographic Themes: Human-Environment Interaction (Objective 2) Review the discussion of the theme of human-environment interaction (page 7). Then write the following sentence on the board: Egypt was the "gift of the Nile," but every gift must be paid for.

Ask students to interpret this thought in terms of human-environment interaction. Encourage them to name the environmental "gifts" (transportation, water, fertile soil) that the Nile provided. Then point out that these gifts had no value until shaped by human culture. For example, the Egyptians developed a network of irrigation ditches to water their fields. To take full advantage of the Nile, they gave up local rule and united under the leadership of a single ruler.

Check for Understanding Write the following terms on the board and have students tell the significance of each to Egypt: Nile, deserts, Menes, delta.

Enrichment Activities

1. **Reading a Primary Source** Assign Voices from the Past Resource Book 3.1.
2. **Preparing a Report** Have interested students research Carter's discovery of Tutankhamon's tomb. (See *Gods, Graves and Scholars* by C.W. Ceram, pages 201–237.)
3. **Researching the Aswan Dam** The Aswan Dam provides a dramatic example of how culture can affect the environment. Ask advanced students to prepare a report examining the advantages and disadvantages of the Aswan Dam.
4. **Researching for Bonus Points** In what country does the Nile River originate? (on a hilltop in Burundi, four degrees south of the Equator)

Setting the Stage

Direct students' attention to the picture of the pyramids on page 59. Ask students to imagine that they are standing near the base of the Great Pyramid (note the group of people on the left side of the picture). Their assignment is to describe their impressions of the pyramids. Explain that many famous writers have recorded their impressions of the pyramids. For example, Julian Huxley wrote of his "pride in the magnitude of the human achievement involved . . . to produce an effect different from that of any other work of man." Now ask students to read their impressions. This section explains the purpose of the pyramids and how they were built.

Teaching Strategies

Discussing History: Who Built the Pyramids? (Objective 1) The Egyptians were convinced that each pharaoh had a spiritual double, or *ka,* that could live forever. As a result, they believed that a pharaoh could influence life even after his death. It seemed that if the soul of a man—like the seed of a plant—could be preserved through the human equivalent of a 'dry' season, he would be restored to life in another world when the time came for "rebirth." (This observation was made by historian Joseph Strayer.) The pyramid thus served to protect the pharaoh's *ka.* Ask students to summarize the role of the pharaoh in Egyptian society.

Discussing History: How Were the Pyramids Built? (Objective 2) The pyramids are a remarkable engineering feat. The Great Pyramid is the largest stone structure in the world. Ask students to speculate on how the Egyptians moved such huge masses of stone without the use of wheels. (The National Geographic book *Ancient Egypt* provides a photo-essay showing how modern researchers believe the pyramids were constructed.)

Skill Building: Comparing and Contrasting Egyptian Kingdoms (Objective 3) Using the text as a reference, have students complete a chart comparing and contrasting the Old, Middle, and New Kingdoms of Egypt. Suggested headings for the chart are *Dates, Pharaohs, Main Events, Cultural Achievements,* and *Causes of Decline.*

Geography in History: Making a Map (Objective 4) Distribute Outline Map 22: The Middle East. Ask students to label Lower and Upper Egypt, the Nile River, the Mediterranean and Red seas, Palestine, Syria, and the Sinai Peninsula. Have students determine the extent of the New Kingdom empire at its height and show that information on their maps.

Check for Understanding Write the following statements on the board:
1. The pyramids were public museums.
2. The history of ancient Egypt was marked by periods of prosperity and strong rule interspersed with periods of weakness.
3. The desert always protected Egypt from invasion.

Ask students to identify the sentence that is an accurate statement about Egypt (2) and to explain why the other statements are inaccurate.

Enrichment Activities

1. **Reading a Primary Source** Assign Voices from the Past Resource Book 3.2.

2. **Researching for Bonus Points** How did the Sphinx receive its name? (The Greeks named it after the Sphinx, a monster that spoke in riddles.)

Egypt's way of life endured 3,000 years. 3

Setting the Stage

Ask students to react to the following statement: "Social change is questionable and should in general be avoided. It is best to maintain traditional ways as much as possible." Point out that most Egyptians placed a high value on maintaining tradition. They believed that their gods created a beautifully balanced social system. Each generation had a responsibility to maintain the rituals and patterns of life that their parents had followed. This section examines various aspects of daily life in Ancient Egypt. It also examines one of Egypt's greatest agents of change—the pharaoh Akhenaton.

Teaching Strategies

Discussing History: Egyptian Nobles and Peasants (Objective 1) Review the text's discussion (pages 63–66) of the life styles of nobles and peasants. Point out that wealthy nobles built spacious villas in the country. They filled their homes with luxurious furniture made of ebony and cedar. The wealthy took great pride in their beds— while the poor slept on the ground, the rich reclined on mattresses cushioned with layers of sheets. Note that most wealthy Egyptians were born as nobles; however, it was possible for peasants to earn high positions in the army or in government.

Emphasize that most Egyptians were peasants. They plowed the fields, paid taxes, and mined the pharaoh's gold. Peasants normally accepted their lot; however, in about 1170 B.C., the government failed to pay a group of Theban workers for more than two months. The frustrated workers finally left their jobs, chanting: "We are hungry! We are hungry!" The government officials were forced to pay them, thus ending the first recorded strike in history.

Discussing History: Analyzing Egyptian Religion (Objective 2) Review the concept of maat (page 66). Emphasize that maat was an idea of goodness that included justice, right, truth, and order. The "negative confession" on page 66 provides a good example of maat. The following statements were also part of this confession: "I have not added weight to the scales; I have not held up the water in its season; I have not neglected offerings to the gods." Read these statements to students and ask them to explain why it was important for Egyptians to avoid these deeds.

Skill Building: Analyzing Effects (Objective 3) Review with students Amonhotep's decision to elevate the god Aton above all other gods. List on the board students' answers to the question, "What were all the effects of Amonhotep's decision?" (pages 67–68) Then ask students to study the list and distinguish immediate effects, short-term effects, and long-term effects. (Immediate—Amonhotep's name change to Akhenaton and his announcement to the priests and the people of the changes he wanted. Short-term—relocation of the capital, discrimination against the worshipers of other gods and the closing of their temples, decline in the power of priests, the driving of religious cults "underground." Long-term effects were negligible; ask students to suggest why.) Students should be able to note that all the changes ended with Akhenaton's death and made no lasting impression on Egyptian culture.

Discussing History: Identifying Reasons for Egypt's Great Achievements (Objective 4) On the board write, "Necessity is the mother of invention." Ask students to cite four examples from ancient Egyptian civilization that support this observation. (Out of a need for assessing and collecting taxes, Egyptians invented numbers; to survey and measure areas, geometry and surveying; to keep track of time between floods, a calendar; and to improve a crude writing system, hieroglyphics.)

Check for Understanding Ask volunteers to give an oral true or false response to each statement below and to correct each false statement.

1. Egyptian religion gave little power to priests. (F—Egyptians believed that priests would influence the gods with magic.)
2. Egyptians needed a knowledge of reading and writing to rise to the highest posts. (T)
3. Egyptian peasants were the lowest social class. (F—Slaves were the lowest class.)

Enrichment Activities

1. **Reading a Primary Source** Assign Voices from the Past Resource Book 3.3.
2. **Analyzing a Primary Source** Ask advanced students to prepare an analysis of Akhenaton's famous hymn to Aton. (See Will Durant's *Our Oriental Heritage*, pages 206–209.)
3. **Researching for Bonus Points** What does the name Nefertiti mean? ("The beautiful one is come") Who was Tutankhamon's wife? (Ankhasenaman)

ANSWERS TO
Chapter Review 3

Reviewing the Facts

1. **(a)** rapids of a river **(b)** region in which branches of a river fan out over a broad, marshy, triangular area of land **(c)** series of rulers from a single family **(d)** term for the ruler of Egypt **(e)** immense structure built as a tomb for the pharaoh **(f)** idea of justice, right, truth, and order **(g)** form of writing **(h)** paperlike material

2. **(a)** region of Egypt to the south of the First Cataract **(b)** region of Egypt to the north, beginning 100 miles before the Nile enters the Mediterranean **(c)** made possible the growth of Egyptian civilization **(d)** narrow corridor of land that invaders eventually crossed to reach Egypt **(e)** united Egypt **(f)** nomadic people who invaded and conquered Egypt **(g)** female pharaoh who encouraged trade instead of war **(h)** extended Egyptian empire to its greatest size **(i)** Egypt's last

great pharaoh **(j)** invaders who broke Egypt's power forever **(k)** Egyptian god of the dead **(l)** pharaoh who tried to convert Egyptians to a monotheistic religion **(m)** reestablished the religion of Amon **(n)** broke the code of the hieroglyphics in 1822

3. The flood cycle of the Nile gave Egyptians rich farmlands and an optimistic attitude.

4. **(a)** The pharaoh was regarded as a god with unlimited power. **(b)** The Mesopotamian king was considered a representative of the gods.

5. **(a)** pharaoh, nobles, artisans and shopkeepers, peasants, slaves **(b)** reading and writing, valor and service in pharaoh's army

6. belief in many gods, an afterlife for the just

7. system of numbers, geometry, surveying, calendar, medical knowledge and practice

Basic Skills

1. Possible answers: pyramids—Abu Rawash, Giza, Abusir, Saqqara, Maidum, el-Lahun; temples—Karnak, Luxor, Abu Simbel; mines—copper and turquoise in Sinai, gold east of Thebes and south of Abu Simbel; quarry—east of Akhetaton; cataracts—three on the Nile south of Syene

2. **(a)** north **(b)** south, north, west

3.

	Old Kingdom pyramids are built		Tutankhamon is buried		Assyrians conquer Egypt	
EGYPT						
2500 B.C.	2000		1500		1000	500 B.C.
MESOPOTAMIA		Sumerian era ends	Hammurabi rules		Babylonians conquer Jerusalem	

4. *Political:* the Nile valley provided geographic unity to Egypt. *Religious:* Egyptians worshiped the Nile as a god that gave them life. *Economic:* irrigation and flooding from the Nile shaped agricultural activity.

Researching and Reporting Skills

Students' research findings will vary.

Critical Thinking

1. The cataracts formed barriers to communication and travel.

2. Students may conclude that Egyptians thought makeup and jewelry beautified their appearance, or that they were vain.

3. (a) Students may use such words as stiff, stylized, flat, idealized. (b) Images of pharaohs are also stylized, images of the slave and of animals show more realism.

4. (a) Egypt was surrounded by deserts providing natural boundaries; Mesopotamia had no natural boundaries. The Nile in Egypt flooded in a more regular, predictable way than the Tigris and Euphrates in Mesopotamia (b) Egypt was well protected from invasions; agricultural activity was more predictable and regular in Egypt. Peace and regular crops contributed to stability.

5. (a) In Sumer, priests managed all industries, irrigation, time of planting and harvesting, and taxed people to support the ziggurat that functioned both as temple and city hall. In Egypt, priests controlled more land, slaves, and wealth than the pharaoh himself. In Sumer, they were feared and obeyed by all; in Egypt, by all except the pharaoh. (b) They were perceived in both Sumer and Egypt as knowing how to please the gods and keep the country safe. In Egypt they were hired to use their magic to protect individuals in the afterlife.

6. Answers may include: (a) Sumer: cities made of mudbricks, ziggurats, weaving, bronze tools, writing (cuneiform), use of numbers, measurement of angles, wheel, plow, sailboat; Egypt: canals, dykes, pyramids and temples, writing (hieroglyphics), papyrus, numbering system, beginnings of geometry, calendar, expertise in medicine. (b) Answers may vary; students may select Sumer's invention of the wheel, the plow, and the sailboat, and Egypt's surveying.

Perspectives on Past and Present

1. (a) Answers will vary. Students will probably conclude that Egyptian civilization valued continuity and that society today values change. In Egypt, age-long practices and beliefs were revered. They may note some elements of change in Egypt (building of a canal to improve navigation; geometry; discoveries of medicine). Modern society is characterized by a questioning of the existing state of things, efforts to bring about progress, adopting of new ideas, and new fashions. Elements of continuity might include respect for institutions of government, law, traditions. (b) Students might highlight the following differences between the two societies. Egyptian society existed for 3,000 years, whereas countries such as the United States have existed only a few hundred years. In Egypt, the predictable pattern of the Nile, the agricultural patterns, the stability of government, the belief in the pharaoh as god from whom all good things came, the near absence of invasions—all helped to create a positive attitude toward stability. In modern society, constant and rapid change in technology, life styles, ideas, technology, beliefs, and fashions is part of daily experience. Education and democracy encourage a search for progress.

2. (a) Egyptian women had the same rights as men. Priesthood and public office were open to them. Although the custom decreed that the Pharaoh should be male, a woman took the title and was one of Egypt's great rulers. (b) Students' answers might highlight the fact that today women have the same civil rights as men but that this does not always mean equality. For example, there is strong opposition in some churches to women priests; as yet no woman has been elected president; there is still a struggle to establish equal rights in the workplace.

Investigating History

1. (a) Champollion deciphered the hieroglyphics on the Rosetta Stone by first translating the Greek text and from that translating the Egyptian text. (b) By translating the inscription on the Rosetta Stone, Champollion provided a key to the language of ancient Egypt, written in hieroglyphics.

2. Students' answers will vary, but should include the gold coffin and throne, animal statues, jewels, and sacred objects.

3. (a) The rock paintings date from about 8000 B.C., a time when the climate of the Sahara was much more humid. (b) The paintings show scenes of hunting and herding. Thus, people lived by hunting and later by herding flocks. (c) The slow change to a desert climate began about 4000 B.C. The retreat of the glaciers in northern Europe was one major effect on climate.

Chapter 3

Teaching with Pictures

Ask students what a mummy is and why the ancient Egyptians mummified their leaders. Then ask what kinds of objects were likely to have been placed in their tombs. The burial mask of King Tut is full of symbolism. Ask students to examine the mask. Explain that the vulture and cobra represent the gods of Upper and Lower Egypt; Tutankhamon's beard likens him to an underworld god; and, finally, his eyes symbolize the sun and moon.

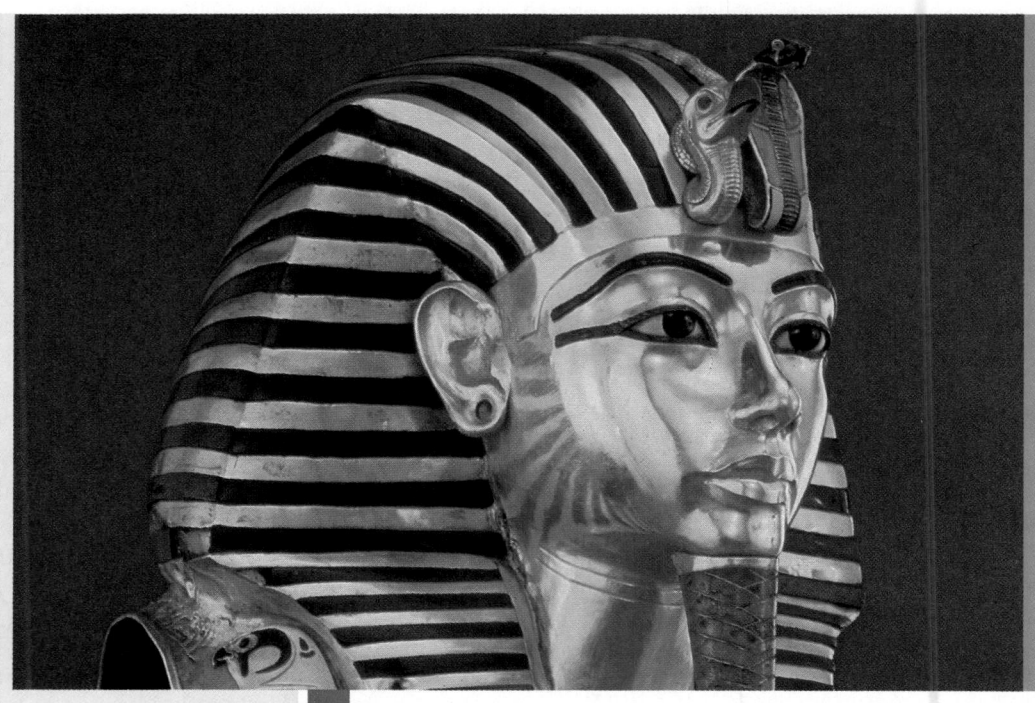

This golden mask covered the face of Tutankhamon's mummy. Its ears are pierced for earrings. The vulture and the cobra on the headdress represent two Egyptian gods.

Key Terms

cataract
delta
dynasty
pharaoh
pyramid
maat
hieroglyphics
papyrus

52

Read and Understand

1. The Nile River shaped Egyptian life.
2. Egypt's pharaohs ruled as gods.
3. Egypt's way of life endured 3,000 years.

It was late fall in 1922. In northeastern Africa, the sun blazed hot in the Valley of the Kings, which lies in Egypt near a sweeping curve in the Nile. British archaeologist Howard Carter had spent six years there moving tons of rock in search of tombs of ancient Egypt's last great rulers. More than 3,000 years had passed since these rulers had been laid to rest. Over the centuries, robbers had opened most of the tombs and taken their treasures. Still, Carter pressed on.

On November 26, 1992, Carter stood before a sealed door. If the wildest of Carter's dreams were true, behind the door lay the mummy and treasure of the ruler Tutankhamon (TOOT-ahngk-AH-mun). Carter made a small hole in the door and stuck a candle through. His report told what he saw.

Chapter 3 Resources

GEOGRAPHY
- Geography Skills 3
- Outline Map 22
- Transparencies 1, 6

REINFORCEMENT
- Vocabulary 3
- Basic Skills 3
- Reteaching 3
- Making Connections Study Guide 3

ENRICHMENT
- Critical Thinking 3

ASSESSMENT
- Chapter Test 3
- Alternate Chapter Test 3
- Computer Test Bank

At first I could see nothing . . . but presently as my eyes grew accustomed to the light, details of the room within emerged slowly from the mist, strange animals, statues, and gold—everywhere the glint of gold.

The wealth of gold within the tomb included four golden chariots, gilded couches, a golden throne with lions' heads carved in the arms, and much more. All these splendors had been created for Tutankhamon, who ruled Egypt for only a few short years. He became king at the age of 8 in about 1347 B.C. and died 9 years later in 1339 B.C., only 17 years old.

Carter had indeed found the tomb he sought, but where was the royal mummy? The young king's burial chamber lay behind yet another sealed door. When that door was opened, Carter's electric lamp revealed a breathtaking sight—a large, box-shaped shrine of gilded wood that filled the entire room. Nested within the large shrine were three smaller ones, and within the smallest shrine was a great stone coffin.

With a rope and tackle, Carter's crew of workers hoisted the heavy lid off the coffin. From inside, a golden face looked up at them through deep blue eyes of precious stones. Resting lightly on this gleaming mask was a fragile wreath of flowers, placed there by Tutankhamon's young widow. Carter later wrote,

Among all that regal splendour, that royal magnificence . . . there was nothing so beautiful as those few withered flowers . . . They told us what a short period 3,300 years really was.

The Nile River shaped Egyptian life. 1

Tutankhamon's reign was just a brief moment in ancient Egypt's long history. Egypt had already been a united kingdom for 1,700 years when young Tutankhamon came to the throne. The country he ruled was nearly as old as the city-states of Sumer.

Although Egypt existed at the same time as the cities of Sumer and the later empires of Southwest Asia, Egyptian civilization was very different from the ways of life that arose in the Fertile Crescent. Unlike Southwest Asia, Egypt was early united into a single country. That country survived, through good times and bad, for more than 3,000 years. At the center of Egypt's unity was the country's most important geographic feature, the Nile River. Indeed, the story of ancient Egypt begins with the story of the Nile.

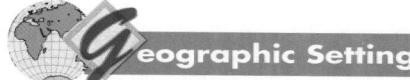
Geographic Setting

The Nile linked diverse lands.

From the highlands of eastern Africa to the Mediterranean Sea, the Nile River meanders over 4,100 miles, making it the longest river in the world. The map on page 55 shows how it winds through Egypt, a thin ribbon of water in a parched desert land. Egypt, however, has neither rainfall nor smaller streams to add to the Nile's waters. Instead, the great river brings its water to Egypt from the distant mountains, plateaus, and lakes of central Africa. So remote were these lands that people in ancient times called the mountains there the Mountains of the Moon. Only in the past two centuries have geographers learned the river's sources and its entire course.

The main source of the Nile is Lake Victoria, the world's third largest lake. It lies across the equator in eastern Africa. Fed by rain and melting snow from mountains to the west, the great lake overflows to form the Nile. After tumbling over several falls, the river passes through Lake Albert and begins its long journey to the sea. Rocky gorges and falls bring the river to the Sudd, a reed-choked swamp that stretches for hundreds of miles. After another 500 miles, the White Nile (the river's name after leaving the Sudd) mingles with the even greater flow of the Blue Nile to form the river that flows through Egypt.

The Blue Nile pours from a lake high on the plateau of Ethiopia. Rushing through canyons and gorges and fed by many streams, it leaves the plateau to cross the desert and merge with the White Nile. The Blue Nile held a special importance for Egypt. It bore the floods caused by spring rains in Ethiopia and the rich soil carried by the floods. Together, the floods and the new soil brought a yearly renewal of life to the river's lower valley in Egypt.

53

OBJECTIVE 1. Identify the location and physical characteristics of ancient Egypt.

Teaching Strategy: *Using Geographic Themes: The Location and Physical Characteristics of a Place* (page 52c)

OBJECTIVE 2. Explain how the Nile influenced the development of Egyptian culture.

Teaching Strategy: *Using Geographic Themes: Human-Environment Interaction* (page 52c)

■ BACKGROUND

In 1907, Carter had taken part in another expedition, during which seals with Tutankhamon's name were found. Carter became convinced that these seals were from the king's funeral and that the royal tomb was nearby.

SECTION 1
Resources

GEOGRAPHY
■ Transparencies 1, 6

REINFORCEMENT
■ Independent Practice 3.1

ENRICHMENT
■ Voices from the Past 3.1

ASSESSMENT
■ Section Quiz 3.1

■ BACKGROUND

Upper Egypt ranged from 4 to 20 miles wide along the Nile. Have students compare this distance to some local measurement to appreciate Upper Egypt's extreme narrowness.

■ DISCUSSION

How did the Egyptians make the Nile a "gift" by their own efforts, beyond merely enjoying it as a favorable part of the natural environment?

■ BACKGROUND

Stone stairs were used to measure the yearly flood and determine its strength or weakness compared to preceding floods.

The cataracts For most of their history, ancient Egyptians knew only the lower part of the Nile—the last 750 miles before it empties into the sea. Their domain ended in the south at Aswan, where jagged granite cliffs pinch inward. The narrowing cliffs and boulders that have fallen from them turn the river into churning rapids called a **cataract** (**KAT**-uh-rakt). Riverboats cannot pass this spot, known as the First Cataract. (Five other cataracts lie farther upstream to the south.)

Upper Egypt and Lower Egypt Between the First Cataract and the Mediterranean lay two very different regions. Upper Egypt (to the south) was a skinny strip of land from the First Cataract to the point where the river split into many branches. Lower Egypt (to the north, near the sea) began about 100 miles before the river entered the Mediterranean Sea. At that point, branches of the river fanned out over a broad, marshy, triangular area of land. Such a region is called a **delta** (map, page 55).

A transportation link The Nile provided an easy, reliable system of transportation between Upper and Lower Egypt. Going from one end of

Lake Nasser in Egypt and the Sudan was formed after the Aswan Dam was completed in 1968. The lake is 300 miles long.

54

Egypt to another required no more effort than climbing into a boat. The Nile flowed north, so northbound boats simply drifted with the current all the way from the First Cataract to the marshy flats of Lower Egypt. Southbound boats hoisted a wide sail. The prevailing winds of Egypt blew from north to south, carrying sailboats against the river current.

Farmers relied on the Nile's floods.

Every year in June, spring rains and melting snow from the mountains of central Africa caused the Nile River to rise and spill over its banks. This flood was not a menace to the Egyptians. Rather, they depended on it.

The gift of the Nile When the river receded in October, it left behind a rich, wet deposit of fertile black mud. Year after year, Egyptian peasants knew they could count on the flooding Nile to provide this rich layer of soil in time for their next planting.

Before the scorching sun could dry out the soil, the peasants would hitch their cattle to plows and prepare their fields for planting. All summer and fall, they tended the wheat and barley plants. They watered their crops from an intricate network of irrigation ditches. At last came the welcome harvest. This cycle repeated itself year after year—flood, plant, harvest; flood, plant, harvest. As an ancient Greek historian named Herodotus (huh-**RAHD**-uh-tuhs) remarked in the fifth century B.C., Egypt was the "gift of the Nile."

Worshiping the Nile Egyptian farmers were much more fortunate than the villagers of Mesopotamia. Compared to the rampaging, unpredictable Tigris River, the Nile was as regular as clockwork. The Egyptians worshiped it as a god who gave them life and seldom turned against them. They felt secure in their well-being. With nature so much in their favor, Egyptians tended to approach life more confidently and optimistically than their neighbors in the Fertile Crescent.

Even so, life in Egypt had its risks. If the Nile's floodwaters were just a few feet lower than normal, the amount of fresh soil and water for crops was greatly reduced. Thousands of people might starve. If the floodwaters were a few feet higher than usual, the water would spread beyond the

The Nile River

Ancient Egypt

Focus on Geography

Geographic Skills
1. Where on the African continent is Egypt located?
2. (a) Where does the main Nile begin? (b) Where does it end?
3. (a) Where does the Blue Nile begin? (b) Through what landforms does it flow?
4. In what different ways was life in ancient Egypt related to the Nile?
5. How did the cataracts affect contacts between Egypt and the lands farther south?

Geographic Theme: Interaction
6. From the map of Ancient Egypt, what conclusions can you draw about the importance of the Nile to the Egyptians?

ANSWERS TO

Focus on Geography

1. northeast corner
2. (a) Lake Victoria (b) Mediterranean Sea
3. (a) Ethiopia (b) plateau, desert
4. agriculture, transportation, religion
5. prohibited contact
6. The Nile is extremely important to the Egyptians; all of their communities are located along its banks.

---

fields to the mud-brick villages nearby. The unwanted water might destroy houses, granaries, and the precious seeds that farmers needed for planting.

Thus, the Egyptians were careful to observe all the religious rituals that were supposed to please the gods and keep Egypt safe. In a religious festival on the Nile's banks, they sang: "Hail to thee, O Nile, that issues from the earth and comes to keep Egypt alive."

Deserts shielded Egypt from attack.

All of Egypt's villages and cities were built along the Nile on a narrow strip of land made fertile by the river. Beyond that, on either side of the river, the land changed suddenly to desert. To the west stretched the sands of the Libyan Desert, a part of the Sahara. To the east along the Red Sea lay the Arabian Desert, which was even drier and more barren. The change from fertile land to desert was so abrupt that a person

■ BACKGROUND

In Egypt today, 99 percent of the population lives on about 3 percent of the land. The other 97 percent of the land is desert.

The Egyptians' own name for their country was *Kemet,* meaning "black earth." Black was the color of life, because it represented moisture in the soil.

ANSWERS TO
Voice from the Past

1. hunger, violence, lawlessness, unhappiness

2. (a) He was led by a dream vision to make an offering to a god and pray for the Nile's return. **(b)** One might look to other countries for immediate relief. To prevent future disasters, a system of dams could be built.

could stand with one foot in each. To the Egyptians, the desert stood for death and the river for life.

The vast and forbidding deserts forced Egyptians to stay close to their lifeline, the Nile. However, the deserts also shut out invaders. For much of its history, Egypt was spared the constant warfare that plagued the Fertile Crescent.

The main invasion route into Egypt lay across a narrow corridor called the Isthmus of Suez. In time, invaders would reach Egypt by way of this geographic link with Southwest Asia. However, for hundreds of years, the deserts kept Egypt secure from any serious attack.

Farm villages joined in nomes.

Egyptians lived in farming villages as far back as 6000 B.C., perhaps even earlier. During those times, they cleared and cultivated the land with stone tools. They domesticated cattle, goats, sheep, and donkeys. They worshiped the wild creatures that swam in the Nile such as the hippopotamus and the crocodile. They tried to preserve bodies of the dead by heaping up mounds of sand around them in the desert.

Eventually, the villages united into agricultural districts called *nomes* (nohmz). Each nome had its own rituals, gods, and chieftain. Often people of rival nomes raided one another's territory.

By 3200 B.C., Egyptians were coming into contact with the people of Mesopotamia. Caravans loaded with goods for trade were traveling between the two regions. Even more important, whole groups of people seem to have moved freely from one region to another in search of better land for farming or grazing.

At the same time, important changes were taking place in Egypt. The first kings arose, uniting the territories of many nomes. Egyptians also developed their own system of writing. These ideas may have been borrowed, at least in part, from Mesopotamia. The period of Mesopotamian influence was soon over, however. From then on, Egyptian culture followed its own path, which was very different from Mesopotamia's.

Voice from the Past | *Seven Lean Years in Egypt*

Although the Nile was a dependable, life-giving force in ancient Egypt, the river sometimes withdrew its gifts. In the following account, the ruler Djoser (JOH-suhr) describes one such crisis.

I was in distress on the Great Throne, and those who are in the palace were in heart's affliction from a very great evil, since the Nile had not come in my time for a space of seven years. Grain was scant, fruits were dried up, and everything which they eat was short. Every man robbed his companion . . . The infant was wailing; the youth was waiting; the heart of the old man was in sorrow . . . The courtiers were in need. The temples were shut up.

[The ruler then tells of a vision that came to him in his sleep.]

I discovered the god standing over me . . . I prayed to him in his presence . . . His words were:

"I am Khnum, thy maker . . . The Nile will pour forth for thee, without a year of cessation or laxness for any land. Plants will grow, bowing down under the fruit."

[Upon waking, the ruler went to the temple of Khnum. He made an offering to the god and prayed for the return of the Nile's floodwaters.]

1. Use the information here to describe what a drought meant for Egypt.

2. (a) How did the ruler handle the disaster? **(b)** How might a modern government handle a similar natural disaster today?

The god Khnum

Looking at economics This wall painting from an Egyptian tomb shows a tax assessor measuring a field of grain to decide how much tax the farmer must pay. Taxes sometimes amounted to 20 percent of the crop.

Menes united two kingdoms.

By 3200 B.C., the nomes of Egypt were divided into two groups under two kings. One king ruled Lower Egypt and wore a red crown. Another king ruled Upper Egypt and wore a tall white crown shaped like a bowling pin.

This carving shows the large figure of King Menes wearing the White Crown of Upper Egypt as he triumphs over his foes.

Then, about 3100 B.C., a strong-willed king of Upper Egypt named Menes (**MEE**-neez) united all of Egypt. As a symbol of his united kingdom, Menes created a double crown from the red and white crowns. Menes shrewdly established his capital near the spot where Upper and Lower Egypt met, about 100 miles from the Mediterranean Sea. The capital was called Memphis. Menes was the first of a long series of kings to rule over the united country of Egypt.

Section REVIEW 1

Define: (a) cataract, (b) delta, (c) irrigation, (d) nome
Identify: (a) Howard Carter, (b) Tutankhamon, (c) Nile River, (d) Upper Egypt, (e) Lower Egypt, (f) Menes
Answer:
1. Why was the Nile's yearly flood important to Egyptian farmers?
2. How did the surrounding desert affect life in ancient Egypt?
3. How did Menes alter Egypt's political organization?

Critical Thinking
4. Ancient Egyptians worshiped the forces of nature as gods. Why would they have regarded the Nile River as one of their most important gods?

57

■ **BACKGROUND**
The account of Menes is based on later Egyptian sources. No contemporaneous records of his reign remain. Some historians believe he was a legendary figure.

ANSWERS TO

Section Review 1

Define:
(a) churning rapid
(b) triangular region at the mouth of a river (c) system of supplying crops with water (d) agricultural district
Identify:
(a) archaeologist who discovered tomb of Tutankhamon (b) boy king who ruled Egypt 1347 B.C.-1338 B.C. (c) world's longest river; winds through Egypt
(d) narrow strip of land extending south from the First Cataract (e) northern part of Egypt (f) king who united all of Egypt
Answer:
1. When the flood waters receded, they left behind a rich layer of soil.

2. The deserts forced Egyptians to stay near the river and shielded Egypt from invaders.

3. He united Upper and Lower Egypt.

4. The Nile gave them life and security.

■ BACKGROUND

In earliest times, servants were sacrificed to accompany the pharaoh in afterlife. By the Third Dynasty, however, sculpted figures were used instead.

Cooperative Learning

Assign one of these roles to each pair of students: a housing developer, a member of Sayed Tawfik's staff (see Decisions in History, page 59). Each pair should prepare a statement advocating its position on the issue of development near the Egyptian monuments. Statements should take into consideration arguments the opposition is likely to bring up. Then group each pair with an opposing pair and have them present their statements to each other. Make sure that as discussions develop within the groups there is no negative feedback (i.e., students should criticize arguments, not the people making them). Remind students to acknowledge the valid points their opponents make.

Egypt's pharaohs ruled as gods.   2

The kingdom Menes created held together remarkably well, long after Menes died. Members of Menes's family passed the double crown of Upper and Lower Egypt from father to son to grandson. Such a series of rulers from a single family is called a **dynasty**. When one ruling family died out or lost control, another took its place. Eventually, the history of ancient Egypt would consist of an amazing 31 dynasties, spanning 2,800 years.

Like the Nile flooding and receding, the fortunes of Egyptian kings rose and fell. When strong kings held Egypt together, the region prospered. When the king's control weakened, in-fighting broke out among the nobles of the nomes. Outsiders might spot this sign of weakness and take the opportunity to invade. A century or two of war and misery would follow. Then a strong king would take control of Egypt again. Over and over, strength followed weakness; prosperity followed ruin.

Religion glorified pharaohs in the Old Kingdom.

The history of Egypt's first two dynasties is little known, but records improve with the Third Dynasty. Historians call the period that began with the Third Dynasty the Old Kingdom. This period lasted roughly from 2660 to 2180 B.C. The Old Kingdom set the pattern for Egypt's culture for nearly 3,000 years.

The power of the pharaohs The kings of Egypt are known as **pharaohs** (FAIR-ohz). It is useful to have a special term for Egypt's kings, because they were much more than political leaders to their people. In fact, the role of the king was one of the most striking differences between Egypt and Mesopotamia. In Mesopotamia, kings were considered to be representatives of the gods. But to the ancient Egyptians, pharaohs *were* gods, almost as splendid and powerful as the gods of the heavens.

The god-king stood at the center of Egypt's religion as well as its government and army. Egyptians believed that the pharaoh bore full

58

responsibility for the kingdom's well-being. It was the pharaoh who caused the sun to rise, the Nile to flood, and the crops to grow. It was the pharaoh's duty to foster truth and justice. All the good things of life came from the pharaoh. No wonder Egyptians obeyed the ruler's every word. Who would dare to disobey the commands of a god?

Immortality for the pharaoh Egyptians believed that their pharaoh ruled even after his death. He had an eternal spirit, or *ka* (kah), that continued to take part in the governing of Egypt.

In the Egyptian's mind, the ka remained much like a living pharaoh in its needs and pleasures. To provide for the pharaoh's eternal comfort, artists decorated the walls of his burial chamber with pictures of whatever he might need or like. A picture of many fat geese, for instance, would assure him of endless sumptuous meals. Images of loved ones and devoted servants would keep him company and see that his commands were carried out. The burial chamber was also stocked with such luxuries as fine jewelry, game boards covered with precious stones, and rich clothing. Inscriptions on the tomb walls recounted the pharaoh's achievements.

Even though the ka was a spiritual being, it needed to refresh itself occasionally by entering its human body. Thus, the Egyptians preserved the pharaoh's body by making it a mummy. Scholars still accept Herodotus's description of the process of mummification:

> First, they draw out the brains through the nostrils with an iron hook . . . Then with a sharp stone they make an incision in the side, and take out all the bowels . . . Then, having filled the belly with pure myrrh, cassia, and other perfumes, they sew it up again; and when they have done this they steep it in natron [a mineral salt], leaving it under for 70 days . . . At the end of 70 days, they wash the corpse, and wrap the whole body in bandages of waxen cloth.

The time of the pyramids Since pharaohs expected to reign forever, their tombs were even more important than their palaces. For the pharaohs of the Old Kingdom, home after death was an immense structure called a **pyramid**. The Old Kingdom was the great age of pyramid building in ancient Egypt.

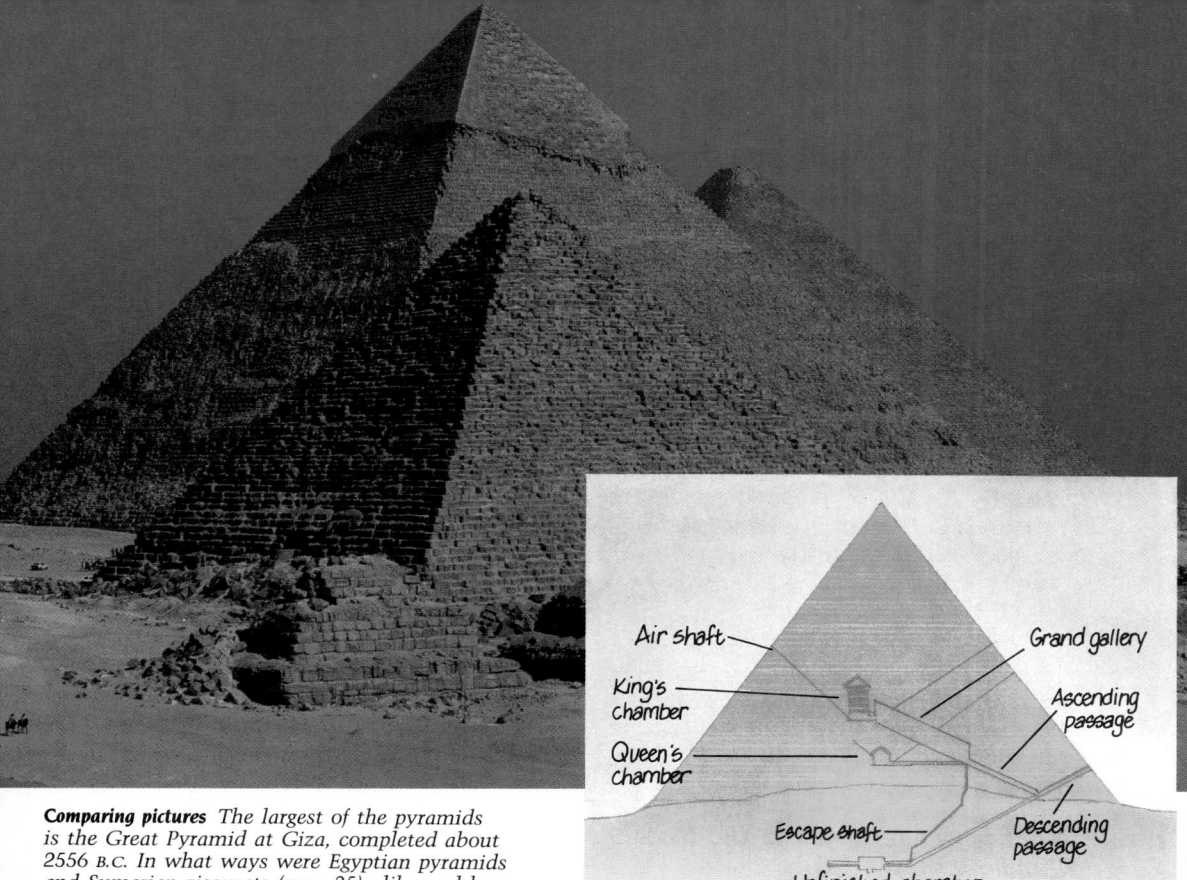

Comparing pictures *The largest of the pyramids is the Great Pyramid at Giza, completed about 2556 B.C. In what ways were Egyptian pyramids and Sumerian ziggurats (page 35) alike and how did they differ?*

Air shaft
King's chamber
Queen's chamber
Grand gallery
Ascending passage
Escape shaft
Descending passage
Unfinished chamber

Today, standing at the foot of the Great Pyramid at Giza, millions of stunned visitors have asked themselves: "How could this mountain of stone have been built by people who had not even begun to use the wheel?" Each perfectly cut stone block weighs at least 2½ tons. Some weigh 15 tons. More than 2 million of these blocks are stacked with precision to a height of 481 feet. The entire structure covers more than 13 acres.

Scholars today no longer believe the famous story told by Herodotus that 100,000 slaves were whipped and driven for 20 years before the last stone of the Great Pyramid was lugged into place. Modern historians think that peasants, not slaves, built the pyramids. Moreover, they did the work willingly for the glory of their god-king. In fact, they needed the work to keep busy and well-fed during the flood season. For cutting and hauling stones, they were probably paid with grain from the king's storehouses. Without work on the royal tombs, temples, and palaces, they would have gone hungry during the flood season.

About 80 pyramids still stand in the Egyptian desert. However, the bodies of the pharaohs no longer rest there. Robbers probably stole the mummies long ago, together with armloads of dazzling treasures.

Decisions in History

Thousands of Egyptian monuments are threatened by pollution and urban sprawl. Sayed Tawfik, in charge of preserving the monuments, faces a hard decision. Should he, as experts advise, declare the monuments off-limits and end development nearby? Or should he allow tourism, housing, and industry to expand as more important to the nation? What would you decide if you faced this choice? Why?

59

SECTION 2
Resources

ASSESSMENT
■ Section Quiz 3.2

REINFORCEMENT
■ Independent Practice 3.2

ENRICHMENT
■ Voices from the Past 3.2

SECTION 2
Objectives and Teaching Strategies

OBJECTIVE 1. Explain the role of the pharaohs.

Teaching Strategy: *Discussing History: Who Built the Pyramids?* (page 52c)

OBJECTIVE 2. Discuss how and why the pyramids were constructed.

Teaching Strategy: *Discussing History: How Were the Pyramids Built?* (page 52c)

OBJECTIVE 3. Compare and contrast Egypt's three kingdoms.

Teaching Strategy: *Skill Building: Comparing and Contrasting Egyptian Kingdoms* (page 52d)

OBJECTIVE 4. Identify and locate the empire built by the pharaohs of the New Kingdom.

Teaching Strategy: *Geography in History: Making a Map* (page 52d)

ANSWER TO
Comparing Pictures

Both pyramids and ziggurats were massive structures built up from the ground. They differed in that pyramids were not solid stone but contained chambers and passages, whereas ziggurats were pyramid-shaped towers culminating in a temple at the top.

■ **DISCUSSION**

Compare the quote from the Middle Kingdom to the quote from Djoser on page 56. How did pharaohs feel about their responsibilities for the well-being of their country?

The benefits and drawbacks of a strong central government are recurring issues in history. Discussion on that topic might begin here and be renewed in later chapters on the fall of Rome, feudal Europe, dynastic change in China, and dictatorships in modern times.

The First Illness brought ruin.

Toward the end of the Old Kingdom, the power of the pharaohs declined. More and more power fell into the hands of nobles and officials. Local rulers struggled among themselves for power. Civil war tore Egypt apart.

Some scholars think that these troubles began with a change in climate. Less rain fell in the African highlands, causing the Nile's floodwaters to be too low. Crops died, and the threat of starvation hung over Egypt. Because Egyptians looked to the pharaoh as a god, they expected him to control the forces of nature. When he failed, the people began to doubt his authority.

The Egyptians called this period of weakness and turmoil the First Illness. From 2180 to 2080 B.C., poor harvests, lawlessness, and warfare plagued the region. One Egyptian wrote of this unhappy time:

> . . . The desert is spread over the land. The provinces are destroyed. Barbarians are come into Egypt from without . . . Laughter has disappeared forever. It is wailing that fills the land . . .

Royal power returned in the Middle Kingdom.

Law and order returned to Egypt under the strong kings of the Middle Kingdom (2080–1640 B.C.). Farming revived, trade grew, and the arts flourished. The pharaohs moved the country's capital from Memphis to Thebes and built two massive temples there.

Projects for the public good Some of the prosperity of the Middle Kingdom was brought about by pharaohs who seemed to care about the welfare of the common people. They made trade and transportation easier by having a canal dug all the way from the Nile to the Red Sea. With the wealth that new trade brought in, the pharaohs undertook other public projects. To improve farming, they ordered the building of huge dikes to trap and channel the Nile's floodwaters for irrigation. They also created thousands of new acres of farmland by draining the swamps of Lower Egypt. Harvests were again plentiful; peasants could enjoy a daily diet of bread and beer. One king of this period boasted,

I was one who cultivated grain and loved the harvest god. The Nile greeted me and every valley. None was hungry in my years, none thirsted then. Men dwelt in peace through that which I wrought, and conversed of me.

Afterlife for commoners During this period, new religious beliefs also showed the increased importance of the common people. During the Old Kingdom, only the pharaoh had expected to live forever. During the Middle Kingdom, Egyptians came to believe that ordinary people had eternal souls as well. People of all classes planned for their burials, so that their place in the afterlife would be assured. This new belief took away some of the pharaoh's grandeur.

The Hyksos ruled during the Second Illness.

The prosperity of the Middle Kingdom did not last. A period known as the Second Illness ravaged the land for about 70 years. Civil war broke out again, leaving Egypt prey to enemies from outside the country. Invaders swept across the Isthmus of Suez into Egypt in horse-drawn chariots. The conquerors were Asian nomads known as the Hyksos (HIHK-sahs), which meant "the rulers of the uplands." They ruled much of Egypt from 1640 to 1570 B.C.

The proud Egyptians despised their less civilized rulers. However, the Egyptians learned several important new skills from the Hyksos. They learned how to make bronze, which was a harder metal than the copper they had used in the past for tools and weapons. They learned to wage war from horse-drawn chariots, shooting arrows from a powerful new kind of bow. And they learned new techniques in the gentler arts of spinning and weaving.

Around 1600 B.C., a series of warlike rulers began to restore Egypt's power. Among those who helped drive out the Hyksos was Queen Ahhotep (ah-HOH-tep), who took over when her husband died in battle. The inscriptions say of her, "She has pacified Upper Egypt and cast out its rebels."

The next pharaoh, Kamose (kah-MOH-suh), won a great victory over the hated Hyksos. Afterward, he described the battle this way:

60

When day broke I pounced on the foe like a falcon; at breakfast time I attacked him, I broke down his walls, I slew his people, I captured his women. My soldiers were as lions with the spoils of the enemy; slaves, flocks, fat and honey. They shared out their property with merry heart.

Kamose's successors drove the Hyksos completely out of Egypt and pursued them across the Sinai Peninsula into Palestine.

The New Kingdom was an age of empire.

Egypt now entered its third period of power and glory, the New Kingdom (1570–1075 B.C.). The kingdom was wealthier and more powerful than ever before. The buildings were larger and more lavishly decorated. (This was the period when Tutankhamon's tomb, with its wealth of gold, was built.) Showiness was the fashion throughout Egypt. Yet the art and architecture of the New Kingdom were not as creative nor as carefully crafted as in earlier periods.

The Egyptian empire The invasion of the Hyksos had shaken the Egyptians' confidence in the deserts as natural barriers for protecting the country. The pharaohs of the New Kingdom set out to strengthen Egypt by building an empire.

Equipped with bronze weapons and two-wheeled chariots, the Egyptians became conquerors themselves. The warlike pharaohs of the Eighteenth Dynasty (1570–1365 B.C.) set up a professional army including bowmen, charioteers, and infantry. The symbols of royal power had always been the red crown and the white crown. Now the pharaohs added a new piece of royal headgear—the blue crown, a war crown shaped like a battle helmet.

Rule by a queen Among the rulers of the New Kingdom, perhaps the most surprising was Hatshepsut (hat-SHEP-soot). This remarkable woman was one of Tutankhamon's ancestors. Although Egypt had several strong queens who wielded power through their fathers, sons, or husbands, custom decreed that the pharaoh be male. Nonetheless, Hatshepsut declared herself pharaoh around 1478 B.C., while her stepson, Thutmose (thoot-MOH-suh), was a mere child. On special occasions, she donned a man's kilt and attached

This statue of Hatshepsut shows her wearing the ceremonial beard of a pharaoh. Tutankhamon's golden mask has a similar beard.

the pharaoh's long, braided, ceremonial beard to her chin.

Hatshepsut ruled boldly for 22 years. Unlike most New Kingdom rulers, she was better known for encouraging trade than for waging war. Carved scenes on her great funeral temple show her officials on a trade expedition to the east African coast, buying myrrh, frankincense, ebony, ivory, and leopard skins.

Hatshepsut's death is still a mystery to historians. No one knows whether she died naturally or was murdered by her stepson, the impatient-to-rule Thutmose III.

A warrior pharaoh Thutmose III proved to be a more warlike ruler than his stepmother. Between the time he took power around 1450 B.C. and his death in 1425 B.C., he conducted 15 victorious invasions into Palestine and Syria. In addition, his armies pushed south as far as the Fourth Cataract and returned with thousands of slaves from Nubia on the upper Nile.

61

■ **BACKGROUND**
When Thutmose took power, he had Hatshepsut's name removed from all monuments.

■ **DISCUSSION**
The Jews were made slaves during the New Kingdom. The use of slaves drove down the value of free labor. For the first time, a wide gap divided rich and poor in Egypt. Help students understand the economic principle of supply and demand.

ANSWERS TO
Section
Review 2

Define:
(a) succession of rulers from a single family **(b)** king of Egypt considered to be a god **(c)** pharaoh's eternal spirit **(d)** huge tomb built for a pharaoh
(continued)

ANSWERS TO (continued)

Identify:

(a) Asian invaders who ruled Egypt from 1640 B.C. to 1570 B.C. (b) queen who helped expel Hyksos (c) pharaoh after Ahhotep; continued to fight Hyksos (d) female pharaoh who supported trade (e) warlike pharaoh who extended Egyptian empire (f) Egypt's last great pharaoh (g) invaders who conquered Egypt

Answer:

1. believed to be gods as well as temporal rulers

2. (a) residence of pharaohs after death (b) Pictures represented people and things he needed; jewels and fine clothes would supply luxuries.

3. The bounty of the Nile dried up, resulting in "diseases" that made life in Egypt difficult.

4. They undertook public works projects.

5. (a) period of 70 years in which civil war left Egypt open to Hyksos invaders (b) A series of warlike Egyptian rulers drove the Hyksos out.

6. (a) through trade (b) through conquest

7. competing civilizations; wave of invasions in Mediterranean area

8. regular flooding of Nile; law-abiding behavior; freedom from invasion; proper worshiping of gods and pharaohs

9. Herodotus lived in a society with a large slave population and may not have understood the willingness of Egyptians to work for the glory of the pharaoh and their need to find work during the flood season.

Egypt was now a mighty empire. It controlled regions far beyond the Nile River valley and drew boundless wealth from them. Egypt had never before—nor has it since—commanded such power and wealth as during the reign of the pharaoh Thutmose III.

Meeting their match By 1300 B.C., Egyptian armies had crossed the Sinai Peninsula and conquered parts of Syria and Palestine. This advance brought the Egyptians face to face with the Hittites, a group of people who had moved into Asia Minor around 1900 B.C. during the great migrations of that period. In later years, the Hittite kingdom expanded southward into Palestine. After a series of confrontations, the Egyptian and Hittite armies met at the battle of Kadesh in 1288 B.C. There they fought each other to a standstill.

Eventually, the pharaoh and the Hittite king made a treaty promising "peace and brotherhood between us forever." For the rest of the century, the two kingdoms were allies. However, the Egyptians could no longer think of themselves as the only powerful rulers in the world. From this time on, Egypt's rulers had to deal with other powers and even to recognize some as their equals.

An age of builders Like the Old Kingdom with its pyramids, the New Kingdom was an age of great buildings. Because the pyramids of the Old Kingdom were too visible and easily robbed, rulers of the New Kingdom built their tombs beneath desert cliffs. The site they chose was the remote Valley of the Kings near Thebes in which Carter found the tomb of Tutankhamon. Besides royal tombs, the pharaohs of this period also built great palaces and magnificent temples. (Indeed, the word *pharaoh* means "great house" and comes from this time period. The word became a royal title because the ruler's own name was too sacred to use.)

One of the greatest builders of the New Kingdom (and Egypt's last great pharaoh) was Ramses (RAM-seez) II, who reigned for 67 years (1279–1212 B.C.). He lived to the age of 99 and was the father of 150 children. Ramses created the giant temple to Amon (AH-muhn), Egypt's chief god, at Karnak. He also built a massive temple at Abu Simbel (AH-boo SIHM-buhl). Ramses decorated his temples with gigantic statues of himself (the ears more than three feet long). Although these

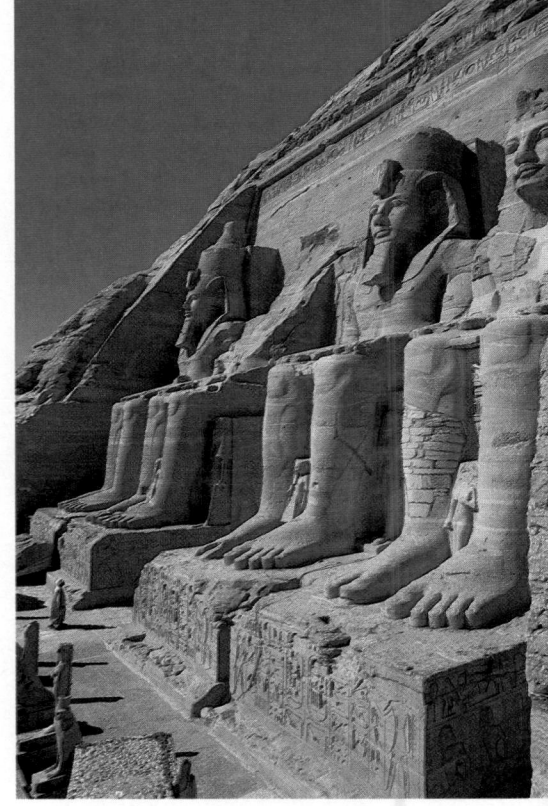

Ramses II's great temple of Abu Simbel was cut into red sandstone cliffs above the Nile River.

buildings are huge and impressive, they are not as skillfully built as those of the Old Kingdom.

Egypt's power waned.

After 1200 B.C., the empire built by Thutmose III and ruled by Ramses II slowly came apart. Other strong civilizations were now rising to challenge Egypt's power. The tribes of Palestine often rebelled against their Egyptian overlords. Even the vast western desert no longer stopped tribes of Libyans from raiding Egyptian villages.

Shortly after Ramses' death, a great wave of invasions took place all around the eastern Mediterranean. Like the earlier invasions of 2000 B.C. that destroyed the city-states of Sumer, the invasions of 1200 B.C. destroyed many kingdoms.

Egyptian records speak of attacks by "the Peoples of the Sea." Little is known of these invaders, but the destruction they left behind was vast.

Both the Egyptian empire and the Hittite kingdom fell to these mysterious enemies.

Egypt never recovered its power. The warlike Assyrians spoke of Egypt's pharaoh as "a broken reed." Taking advantage of the kingdom's weakness, the Assyrians invaded and conquered Egypt in 671 B.C. A century and a half later, the Persians took over Egypt. From then on, Egypt passed from one foreign conqueror to the next. Even the conquerors, however, were struck with the grandeur of Egypt's past.

Section REVIEW 2

Define: (a) dynasty, (b) pharaoh, (c) ka, (d) pyramid
Identify: (a) Hyksos, (b) Ahhotep, (c) Kamose, (d) Hatshepsut, (e) Thutmose III, (f) Ramses II, (g) Peoples of the Sea
Answer:
1. Explain why Egypt's pharaohs were unusually powerful rulers.
2. (a) Why were the pyramids even more important than palaces? (b) Describe the objects and paintings inside a pharaoh's burial chamber and explain what purposes they served.
3. Why did Egyptians give the name "First Illness" to the years around 2100 B.C.?
4. How did pharaohs of the Middle Kingdom help restore prosperity to Egypt?
5. (a) What was the "Second Illness" in Egypt? (b) How was it overcome?
6. (a) How was Egypt's wealth and power increased by Hatshepsut? (b) By Thutmose III?
7. What led to Egypt's downfall after the death of Ramses II?

Critical Thinking
8. When the Egyptians described times of suffering for their land, they called such times "illnesses." According to an Egyptian, what would have characterized a good or "healthy" time? You may wish to use some of the quotations from Egyptian sources in this section as examples.
9. Why might the Greek historian Herodotus have assumed that the pyramids had been built with slave labor, as mentioned on page 59? (Hint: Greeks in Herodotus' time had a democratic society.)

Egypt's way of life endured 3,000 years. 3

For 3,000 years, power passed from one pharaoh to another. Dynasties flourished and then died out. Invaders seized power and then lost it. Yet, in all that time, daily life for Egyptians changed very little. Each generation kept up the rituals and patterns of life that their parents had followed.

Nobles lived in luxury.

If you think of Egyptian society as a pyramid, the pharaoh stood at the top. Below the pharaoh and his family were the nobles. What was life like for the upper classes during Egypt's golden age?

Serving the pharaoh Nobles in Egypt did not lead an idle life. Many of the men spent busy days in the service of the pharaoh. They were governors, generals, tax collectors, and officials of all sorts. Others were priests, responsible for the upkeep and rituals of the great temples.

Women also served as government officials and priests. The Egyptians were better prepared for female leadership than were most ancient peoples, because women in Egypt held many of the same rights as men. For example, a wealthy or middle-class woman could own and trade property. She could propose marriage or seek divorce. If she were granted a divorce, she would be entitled to one third of the couple's property.

Home life At home, noble families enjoyed many luxuries. Imagine that you are going to a banquet at the home of a wealthy family. From the road you cannot see the single-story house. Only the mud-brick wall that surrounds it is

Footnote to History

By modern standards, many of the pharaoh's high officials and priests were very young. For example, a man named Bakenkhons became a priest at age 16, after spending several years as chief of the pharaoh's military stable. He soon rose to be a high priest. The Egyptians had good reason to appoint comparatively young people to high positions: The average life expectancy was only 36 years!

SECTION 3
Objectives and Teaching Strategies

OBJECTIVE 1. Compare and contrast the lives of nobles and peasants in Egyptian society.

Teaching Strategy: *Discussing History: Egyptian Nobles and Peasants* (page 52d)

OBJECTIVE 2. Define the concept of maat and explain its significance in Egyptian religion.

Teaching Strategy: *Discussing History: Analyzing Egyptian Religion* (page 52d)

OBJECTIVE 3. Identify Akhenaton and explain his religious reforms.

Teaching Strategy: *Skill Building: Analyzing Effects* (page 52d)

OBJECTIVE 4. Describe some of the achievements of Egyptian culture.

Teaching Strategy: *Discussing History: Identifying Reasons for Egypt's Great Achievements* (page 52e)

SECTION 3
Resources

ASSESSMENT
- Section Quiz 3.3

REINFORCEMENT
- Independent Practice 3.3

ENRICHMENT
- Voices from the Past 3.3

Egyptian houses were not lavish, even among upper classes, because the Egyptians considered their tombs to be more important than their homes.

Every upper-class Egyptian home included a garden with a pool. The bronze mirror, folding chair, and cat figurine were other common objects that might be found in the homes of the wealthy.

Both husband and wife wear their finest jewelry—golden earrings jiggling from their pierced ears and broad necklaces glittering with dozens of multicolored gems.

Servants bring in the food—bowls of figs, slabs of bread, platters of roasted duck and lamb. Everyone eats with his or her fingers and drinks wine from glass goblets. A harpist plays soft music in the background.

Social mobility Most of the wealthy Egyptians who led such pleasant lives had been born as nobles. Some, however, had been born to families of artisans or small shopkeepers. Still others had been born in families of peasant farmers or even slaves.

The way to rise in Egypt was through the pharaoh's service, especially through the army. A soldier who showed courage in battle might win a cash reward, called "the gold of valor." In

visible. You enter through the main gate and cross an open courtyard to the garden where the children are chasing one another around a rectangular pool. Since the children are all under 12 years old, they wear no clothing. Both boys and girls wear golden ornaments around their necks, and the girls wear strings of beads around their waists.

Inside the house, the host and hostess greet you. Their clothes are made of soft, sheer cotton.

64

time, he might become an officer. After a lifetime of service in the pharaoh's army, he would be rewarded with a small farm, livestock, and some peasants to work his land for him. His sons and grandsons could hold this land as their own, as long as one man in the family continued to serve in the army.

To win the highest posts, either in the army or in the government, people had to be able to read and write. Thus, most high positions went to people who had been born into families wealthy enough to send their children to school. But even humble village scribes taught their own children and perhaps some of their friends' children. In Egypt, unlike Sumer, girls as well as boys were permitted to study to become scribes. Once a person had the skill to read and write, many careers were open in the army, the royal treasury, the priesthood, and the pharaoh's court.

Peasants led a life of toil.

We know less about the peasants of Egypt than about the upper classes. Since the peasants' everyday lives were not considered very important, scribes recorded little about them. Most information about peasant life comes from wall paintings in tombs.

Those paintings show that peasants worked hard and had few comforts. Planting, cultivating, and harvesting in the hot sun were grueling work. Women worked beside men in the fields. Peasants did not even own the land they farmed. The land belonged to the pharaoh and was parceled out by royal officials. These officials hauled away a large share of the harvest as taxes.

Although farming was not possible during the flood season, this time of year rarely brought rest for the peasants. Instead, peasant men—and sometimes women—were called to work on the pharaoh's latest project. A tomb, dike, or canal required many workers.

Nonetheless, it seems that the peasants managed to enjoy life. They were usually left with enough to eat even after taxes. In this respect, they were better off than artisans such as toolmakers and jewelers, who might go hungry during hard times when no one needed their services. Peasants found time for music and games, and they sometimes joined their overseers in a great feast to celebrate the harvest. However, while the rich drank wine, peasants drank barley beer.

DAILY LIFE ▶ Egyptian Cosmetics

The dramatic, dark-lined eyes that look out at us from the artwork of ancient Egypt were the height of fashion 3,000 years ago. However, the dark lining was not just a beauty aid. It also softened the glare of the brilliant desert sun. The makeup, called *kohl,* was made from powdered stone—malachite for dark green and galena for black—mixed with water. Men and women applied it to their eyes with small sticks.

Oils were a key ingredient of many other cosmetics the Egyptians used. Some oils came from animal fats, and others were pressed from plant seeds. The Egyptians mixed oil with powdered red ocher (a kind of iron ore) to make lipstick, which they applied with a brush. They steeped flowers and fragrant woods in oil and rubbed the oil into their skin. Sometimes they decked their hairdos with cones of scented oil, which melted slowly in the heat. Like the eye makeup, these fragrant oils had a practical use. They protected skin, lips, and hair from the dry desert air. This glass fish at the right held sweet-smelling oil, and the other container held kohl.

65

■ BACKGROUND

The term *corvee* (kor-VAY) refers to the payment of taxes in labor instead of money. Throughout history, peasants have supported their rulers in this way.

■ DISCUSSION

Bring to class a book of Egyptian art. Have students speculate on the practical reasons for the Egyptians' appearance and home furnishings (e.g., style and color of clothing, importance of garden and pool, and so on).

■ **BACKGROUND**

Throughout the ancient world, mine slaves and galley slaves were the most unfortunate.

■ **DISCUSSION**

Have students compare the Egyptian views of good and bad, as expressed in the statement quoted on this page, with the Hebrew and Mesopotamian views of morality.

Slaves were the lowest class.

Until the time of the New Kingdom, peasants made up the lowest class in Egypt. Then, during the New Kingdom's wars of conquest, thousands of slaves were brought to Egypt from Asia and Nubia, a land to the south of Egypt.

The most fortunate slaves worked in the homes of the rich. They perfomed every kind of service for their wealthy masters—giving them baths, combing their hair, cooking meals, watching their children, feeding their cattle. Through loyal service to a priest or noble, house slaves could hope someday to be granted their freedom.

Other slaves were not so lucky. Whole families of slaves were sent into the mountains of Upper Egypt to work in the gold mines. Often they felt

During the New Kingdom, slavery became common in Egypt. Many slaves were war captives. This slave is carrying a heavy cauldron.

66

the stinging lash of the overseer's whip. Men, women, and children dropped from exhaustion. According to one account,

> *There is no forgiveness or relaxation at all for the sick, or the maimed, or the old . . . but all with blows are compelled to stick to their labor until, worn out, they die in their servitude.*

Religion taught fairness and hope.

Laws did not forbid Egyptians to mistreat their slaves. However, Egyptian religion taught that it was morally wrong to do so. The Egyptians used the word **maat** (muh-AHT) to speak of the virtues of a good life. Maat was the idea of justice, right, truth, and order. To live according to maat meant always trying to act rightly and justly. Everyone, including the pharaoh, was supposed to uphold this ideal. The idea of maat influenced even the god-king's behavior.

Judgment by Osiris Egyptians believed they would be judged for their deeds when they died. Osiris (oh-SY-rihs), the powerful god of the dead, would weigh each dead person's heart. To win eternal life, the heart could be no heavier than a feather. Each soul was required to come before the great judge, Osiris, and say something like this:

> *Hail to Thee, Great God, Lord of Truth and Justice . . . I have not committed inequity against men. I have not oppressed the poor . . . I have not laid labor upon any free man beyond that which he wrought for himself . . . I have not defaulted, I have not committed that which is an abomination to the gods. I have not caused the slave to be ill-treated of his master . . .*

If the heart tipped the scale, showing that the person was lying, a fierce beast known as the Devourer of Souls would pounce on the impure heart and gobble it up. But if the soul passed this demanding test for purity and truth, it could live forever.

Scenes painted on the walls of tombs showed how Egyptians imagined their future life. Souls journeyed by boat to a pleasant, fertile land, much like Egypt itself. Children in the underworld would still quarrel and pull one another's hair.

This statue of Khafre, a pharaoh of the Fourth Dynasty, shows the remote and godlike aspect of the pharaohs.

Peasants would still drive oxen over the fields. The rich would continue to enjoy banquets. Nothing would be changed.

The power of the priests What hope was there for those Egyptians who had committed just one mistake—perhaps stealing a jar of grain? How could their souls escape the snapping jaws of the Devourer? They believed their only hope was to employ the services of a priest. Egypt's priests specialized in magical charms and chants to protect both the living and the dead from troubles of all kinds. Many of these prayers were recorded in a text known as the *Book of the Dead*, which was placed in the dead person's coffin.

Because Egyptians believed that their priests could influence the gods with their magic, priests had enormous power and prestige. In fact, in the New Kingdom, the priests probably controlled more land, more slaves, and more wealth than the pharaoh himself.

A *challenge to tradition* Around 1375 B.C., one pharaoh dared to challenge Egypt's religious traditions and also the power of the priests. The name of this bold pharaoh was Akhenaton (AH-kuh-NAH-tuhn).

When the sun rose every morning in the Egyptian sky, Akhenaton worshiped it as a god. This was nothing new. The sun had always been worshiped by Egyptians as one of their many gods. However, Akhenaton made the new and shocking claim that this sun-god, Aton, was the only true god in all the universe. Perhaps the pharaoh truly believed this claim, or perhaps his goal was to lessen the priests' power.

Akhenaton did everything in his power to convert Egyptian religion from polytheism to monotheism. He ordered the religious cults that worshiped the cat-god, the crocodile-god, the baboon-god, and all the other gods to shut down their temples and worship only Aton.

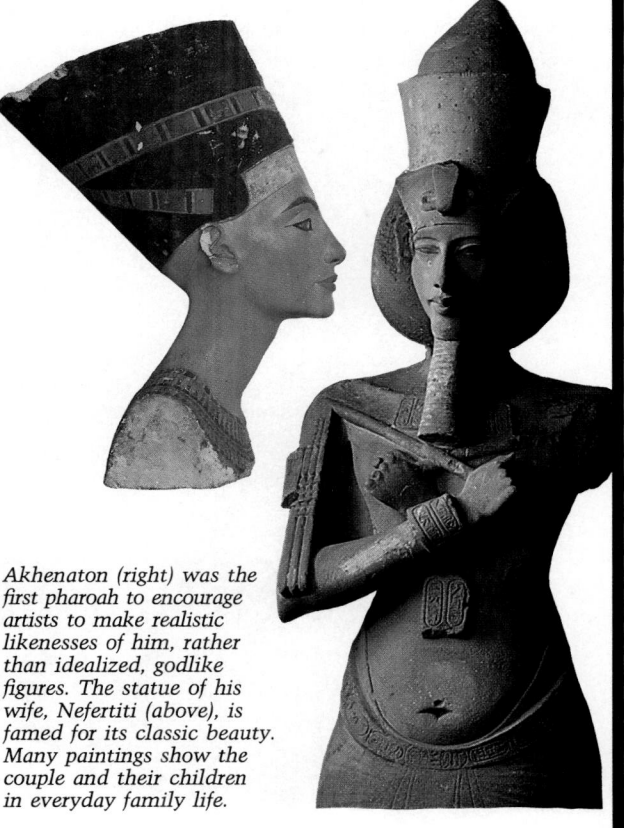

Akhenaton (right) was the first pharoah to encourage artists to make realistic likenesses of him, rather than idealized, godlike figures. The statue of his wife, Nefertiti (above), is famed for its classic beauty. Many paintings show the couple and their children in everyday family life.

67

■ BACKGROUND

Scholars have long debated whether Akhenaton was truly a religious idealist and monotheist or instead a shrewd politician whose move was designed to break the power of Amon's priests. Whatever his motives, his attempt to impose monotheism from above died with him. In contrast, where monotheism was a truly popular movement with widespread support, as among the Hebrews, it survived all attempts at suppression.

■ BACKGROUND

Like other ancients, Egyptians based their measuring system on body parts. A *cubit* was the distance from elbow to fingertips, with the pharaoh's arm as the standard. The royal *foot* was also a measure. The Romans adopted this system.

■ DISCUSSION

Why would a ruler want to establish a new capital? Encourage students to investigate capital relocations at St. Petersburg and Brasilia.

■ BACKGROUND

During the 1800's, a medicine called "mummy" was sold. Thought to be beneficial, it was the powdered remains of burial wrappings from Egypt's ancient graves.

Above all, people were commanded to stop worshiping Amon, god of air, wind, and the breath of life. The huge temples around Thebes were all dedicated to Amon. The high priests of Amon were the most powerful rulers in Egypt next to the pharaoh himself. Akhenaton ordered that all the offerings and taxes that had poured into Amon's temples now go to Aton's treasury. Naturally, the priests of Amon were furious.

Workers with chisels and hammers were sent all over Egypt to smash the name of Amon wherever it appeared. The pharaoh changed his own name, originally *Amon*hotep, to Akhen*aton*, meaning "He who serves Aton." Akhenaton then moved the royal capital from Thebes to a new city, which he named Akhet*aton*, "the Place of Aton's Power."

However, many Egyptians refused to abandon their old gods. They defied the pharaoh's laws by secretly worshiping Amon, Osiris, and their other favorites.

When Akhenaton died in 1362 B.C., the priests of Amon regained their power. The new pharaoh, who was only eight or nine years old, took the name Tutankh*amon*, moved the capital back to Thebes, and ordered the names and images of Aton to be destroyed. As a reward, when Tutankhamon died, the priests packed his tomb with the golden treasures that Howard Carter found nearly 3,300 years later.

Egyptians studied many subjects.

The breadth and richness of Egypt's culture impressed early visitors from Greece, Persia, and Mesopotamia. Even then, Egypt gave an impression of great age and secret wisdom that awed travelers from other lands. In many fields, Egypt richly deserved its reputation for knowledge.

Writing Crude pictographs had been the earliest form of writing in Egypt, but scribes quickly developed a better system. For most of ancient Egypt's history, scribes used a form of writing that we call **hieroglyphics** (HY-er-oh-GLIF-ihks). This term comes from the Greek words *hieros* and *glyphe*, meaning "sacred carving."

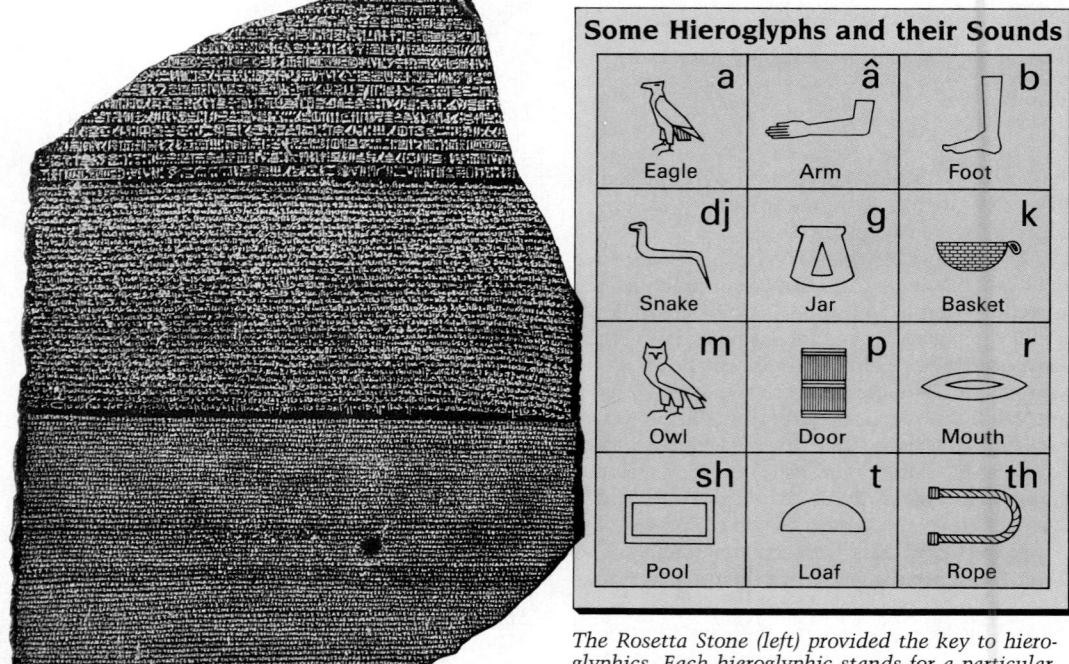

The Rosetta Stone (left) provided the key to hieroglyphics. Each hieroglyphic stands for a particular sound, as the examples above show.

68

Soon after Egypt's decline, the ability to read hieroglyphics was lost and remained so for 15 centuries. In 1799, near the delta village of Rosetta, some French soldiers found a polished black stone inscribed with a message in three languages. One version was written in hieroglyphics, another was in a simpler form of hieroglyphics, and the third was in Greek. Ancient Greek was a well-known language, yet deciphering the hieroglyphics on the Rosetta Stone still took many years of work. A young Frenchman named Jean François Champollion (shahm-pohl-YAWN) became fascinated by hieroglyphics when he was only a child. By the time he was 16, he had mastered 8 ancient languages. In 1822, at the age of 32, he finally broke the code of the hieroglyphics.

Although hieroglyphics were first written on stone and clay, the Egyptians soon invented a better writing surface. They used the tall stalks of **papyrus** (puh-PY-ruhs), a reed that grew in the marshy delta. The Egyptians split the reeds into narrow strips, soaked them, and then pressed them into sheets of paperlike material. (The English word *paper* comes from *papyrus*.) Egypt's dry climate preserved papyrus for centuries. Modern scholars can still read writings that are more than 5,000 years old.

Numbers The government of Egypt needed a way of doing arithmetic for the purpose of assessing and collecting taxes. Out of this need, Egyptians invented a system of written numbers for counting, adding, and subtracting. The system was fairly clumsy for numbers greater than 100. To express the figure 999, a scribe had to write 27 symbols. (On the other hand, to express 1 million required only one symbol—a picture of a man striking his hands above his head as if to say, "How in the world could there be such a big number?")

Geometry and surveying One job of the pharaoh's officials was to assign plots of land to peasant families. Because of the Nile's flooding, this job had to be redone every year. The floodwaters wiped out all previous boundaries, and the land had to be measured and marked again. To save time and expense, Egyptians invented an efficient mathematical system for surveying and measuring areas. This method was the origin of geometry.

A calendar To be sure of a good crop, peasants needed to plant at exactly the right time of year. Crops had to be ripe and harvested before the next flood. Therefore, the Egyptians developed a calendar to keep track of the time between floods. Officials had observed that a very bright star, now known as Sirius, began to appear above the eastern horizon just before the floods came. The time between one rising of Sirius and the next was 365 days. They divided this year into 12 months of 30 days each and added 5 days for holidays and feasting. This calendar was so accurate that it fell short of the true solar year by only six hours.

Medicine Egyptian doctors were the most famous in the ancient world. Their medical services were in demand at royal courts in many kingdoms around the Mediterranean Sea. Although Egyptian medical writings contain all sorts of magic charms and chants, Egyptian doctors also had much practical knowledge. They knew how to check a person's heart rate by feeling for a pulse in different parts of the body. They dealt with broken bones, wounds, and fevers. All in all, they approached their study of medicine in a remarkably scientific way.

Section REVIEW 3

Define: (a) maat, (b) hieroglyphics, (c) papyrus

Identify: (a) Osiris, (b) Akhenaton, (c) Aton, (d) Amon, (e) Tutankhamon, (f) Rosetta Stone, (g) Champollion

Answer:

1. (a) What kinds of work might a noble do in ancient Egypt? (b) A peasant?
2. What beliefs influenced the morals of people in ancient Egypt?
3. How was the ability to read hieroglyphics regained in modern times after having been lost for 15 centuries?
4. (a) What practical need led the Egyptians to invent a system of numbers? (b) A branch of mathematics that formed the basis for modern geometry? (c) A calendar?

Critical Thinking

5. As god-kings, Egypt's pharaohs might have ruled through terror, but generally they did not. What attitudes and beliefs in Egypt acted as a check on the pharaohs?

69

ANSWERS TO
Section Review 3

Define:
(a) idea of justice, right, truth, order (b) Egyptian form of writing (c) paper-like material

Identify:
(a) Egyptian god of the dead (b) monotheistic pharaoh (c) sun-god worshipped by Akhenaton (d) Egyptian god of air, wind, and breath of life (e) boy king who restored polytheism (f) stone inscribed in three languages, used to decipher hieroglyphics (g) Frenchman who broke the code of the Rosetta Stone

Answer:

1. (a) serve as governor, tax collector, general, official, priest (b) farm and work on public projects

2. belief in maat; belief that a righteous life would lead to eternal life

3. by studying Rosetta Stone and comparing hieroglyphics with ancient Greek language

4. (a) assessing and collecting taxes (b) redrawing of boundaries each year after the Nile's flooding (c) keeping track of time between floods to determine planting and harvesting times

5. Answer should stress idea of maat and idea that pharaohs felt responsible for well-being of subjects.

Concluding the Chapter

1. **Chapter Closer**
   Recall that the pyramids are the most commonly identified symbols of ancient Egypt. Ask students to write essays describing how the contents of pyramids reveal other important symbols of Egyptian civilization.

2. **Reteaching Activities**
   a. Outlining Have students use the headings to write a sentence outline of Section 1.
   b. Summarizing Have students write a paragraph summarizing the achievements of the Old Kingdom, the Middle Kingdom, and the New Kingdom.
   c. Organizing Information Have students compile three lists—one identifying the social classes in ancient Egypt, another identifying the characteristics of Egyptian religious beliefs, and the third identifying the cultural achievements of ancient Egypt.

Answers to Chapter Review appear on pages 52e–52f.

Chapter Review 3

Summary

1. The Nile River shaped Egyptian life. The Nile River flooded every year, leaving a blanket of rich soil on Egypt's land. The dependability of this pattern made Egypt an excellent farmland. Farming villages flourished as early as 6000 B.C., protected from invasion by the surrounding deserts. Eventually, groups of villages united to form small kingdoms. In 3100 B.C., all of Egypt was united under King Menes.

2. Egypt's pharaohs ruled as gods. Egypt's pharaohs were considered divine and immortal. Over the years, periods of weakness (known as "illnesses") alternated with periods of strength for Egypt. Around 1200 B.C., a wave of invasions began, leading to a decline from which ancient Egypt never recovered.

3. Egypt's way of life endured 3,000 years. Egyptian society was divided into social classes. Upper-class people generally held government jobs and lived in luxury. Peasants did the farming, and slaves served the rich. Egyptians of all classes were polytheists. Egyptian religion emphasized *maat*, or justice. Those who lived according to maat could expect eternal life in the afterworld. Among the Egyptians' cultural achievements were systems of writing and mathematics and a highly accurate calendar. They were also skilled in the field of medicine.

Reviewing the Facts

1. Define the following terms:
   a. cataract   e. pyramid
   b. delta   f. maat
   c. dynasty   g. hieroglyphics
   d. pharaoh   h. papyrus

2. Explain the importance of each of the following names, places, or terms:
   a. Upper Egypt   h. Thutmose III
   b. Lower Egypt   i. Ramses II
   c. Nile River   j. Peoples of the Sea
   d. Isthmus of Suez   k. Osiris
   e. Menes   l. Akhenaton
   f. Hyksos   m. Tutankhamon
   g. Hatshepsut   n. Champollion

3. How did the Nile's yearly cycle affect life in ancient Egypt?

4. (a) Describe the powers of the Egyptian pharaohs. (b) How was the pharaoh different from a Mesopotamian king?

5. (a) Describe the main groups that made up Egyptian society. (b) What skills were necessary for an Egyptian to move up in society?

6. What were some of the basic beliefs of Egyptian religion?

7. List some of the Egyptians' scientific achievements.

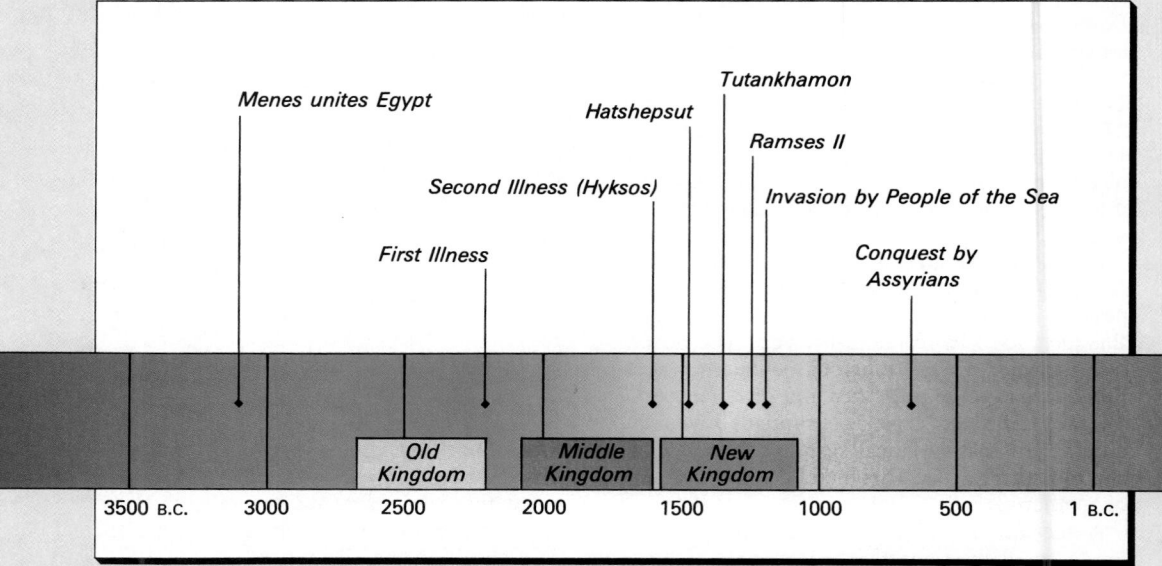

Basic Skills

1. **Using map symbols** On the map on page 55, locate a pyramid, temple, mine, stone quarry, and cataract.
2. **Identifying directions** (a) In what general direction does the Nile flow? (b) Where is the Valley of the Kings in relation to the Nile Delta? The Second Cataract? The temples of Karnak and Luxor?
3. **Creating a time line** Make a time line for ancient Egypt and Mesopotamia, starting with 2500 B.C. and ending with 500 B.C. Divide the line into five segments. Place these events above the time line, using a pointer to the correct date: Old Kingdom pyramids are built; Tutankhamon is buried; Assyrians conquer Egypt. Add these items below the line, using a pointer to the correct date: Sumerian era ends; Hammurabi rules; Babylonians conquer Jerusalem.
4. **Identifying supporting details** Give examples from the political, religious, and economic life of Egypt to support the idea that the Nile River shaped Egyptian life.

Researching and Reporting Skills

1. **Using the encyclopedia** Many historians question whether Akhenaton was sincere in his monotheistic beliefs or whether he had other reasons for wanting his subjects to give up their many gods. Look up articles about Akhenaton in two different encyclopedias. To what extent is the information in the articles similar or different?
2. **Summarizing** Summarize what each article says about Akhenaton's monotheism and the reasons behind it.
3. **Developing a bibliography** Locate three books that discuss the technology that made construction of the pyramids possible. List bibliographical information about these books—including author, title, publisher, date of publication, and the relevant page numbers.

Critical Thinking

1. **Inferring** What influence may the Nile cataracts have had on contacts between Egypt and the lands to the south?
2. **Drawing conclusions** What does the discussion of apparel and cosmetics in this chapter suggest about values in Egyptian society?
3. **Analyzing art** Study the paintings on pages 57 and 64. (a) Describe the way Egyptian artists painted human figures. (b) Compare the style of sculptures shown in this chapter to that of the paintings. What similarities and differences do you find?
4. **Interpreting** (a) Compare the relative location of Egypt and Mesopotamia. (b) How might that location have contributed to the stability of government in Egypt and to changes in Mesopotamia?
5. **Comparing** Priests held positions of power in both Sumer and Egypt. (a) Compare the extent of that power in those civilizations. (b) What were the reasons for that power in each case?
6. **Evaluating** Sumer and Egypt both made important contributions to civilization. (a) List the major contributions made by each. (b) Which contribution of each civilization do you consider most important? Give reasons for your answer.

Perspectives on Past and Present

1. Some cultures stress the importance of continuity, using words such as *tradition, time-honored,* and *customary.* Other cultures emphasize the value of change, using words such as *progress, modern,* and *up-to-date* to describe it. (a) Compare the attitudes of ancient Egyptian society toward change with those of society today. Give examples to illustrate your answer. (b) What factors might account for any differences?
2. (a) Describe the position of women in the society of ancient Egypt. (b) Compare this position with that of women in society today.

Investigating History

1. (a) Find out how Champollion succeeded in deciphering the hieroglyphics on the Rosetta Stone. (b) What was the significance of his work?
2. The opening of Tutankhamon's tomb revealed a great variety of treasures. In books on Egyptian art, find out what kinds of treasures were found.
3. Rock paintings in the Sahara indicate that at one time that region had rich grasslands. (a) Find out information about the rock paintings. (b) What can you conclude from them about people's way of life? (c) What climate changes occurred that caused the desert to form?

71

CHAPTER
Evaluation

Chapter Test 3, Alternate Chapter Test 3, and Computer Test Bank Chapter 3 Test can be used to evaluate your students' understanding of this chapter.

Ancient India and China

Chapter Overview

The first civilization on the sub-continent of India developed around 2500 B.C. in the valley of the Indus River. Around 1500 B.C., the Aryans, nomads from Central Asia, moved into the area, fusing their culture with that of the remaining Indus valley people to form a new civilization in which the Hindu religion and the caste system were dominant forces.

Although united culturally, northern India was not united politically until Chandragupta conquered the entire area in about 322 B.C. His grandson, Ashoka, converted to Buddhism, a religion that stressed enlightenment and righteous living.

Due to geographic factors, China developed in isolation. Respect for family and government were unifying cultural forces. Four separate dynasties provided long periods of political unity. Under the Han dynasty beginning in 202 B.C., civilization flowered in a long period of peace and prosperity. The teachings of Confucius, a philosopher who lived in the fourth century and taught the value of tradition and social order, won widespread influence. During the late years of the dynasty, Buddhism spread east to China.

Chapter Focus

Ask, "What does it mean to have wisdom?" Record several students' answers. Then direct students' attention to the chapter opener on pages 72–73. After students have read the opener, ask them to identify Buddha and Confucius. Ask, "How did these two thinkers an-swer the question, 'What does it mean to have wisdom?' " Have students compare their answers with those given by Buddha and Confucius. Explain that both men reflected and helped shape the cultures in which they lived. This chapter tells the story of two remarkable cultures that developed in ancient India and China.

A *new culture arose in northern India.* **1**

Setting the Stage

Geography in History: Making a Map Key (Objective 1) Use Map Transparency 7, *Ancient India*, to locate the major landforms in India. Explain that India makes up most of a vast subcontinent stretching almost 2,000 miles from north to south. It is 1,400 miles from the Bay of Bengal in the east to the Arabian Sea in the west. In area, the country is about half that of the continental United States. Point out that four distinctive regions—the northern mountains, Indus-Ganges plain, Deccan Plateau, and the coastal rim—contribute to India's great diversity of peoples and cultures.

Now distribute Outline Map 20: India. Ask students to draw a map key to designate types of landforms. Have students use the map on page 74 to locate and label the major landforms and rivers on the Indian subcontinent.

Chapter 4 Ancient India and China 2500 B.C.–A.D. 220
FOCUS The teachings of Buddha in India and of Confucius in China

★ **Advanced**
● **Basic**

	SECTION 1	SECTION 2	SECTION 3	SECTION 4
Objectives	1. Identify and locate the land-forms of the Indian subcontinent. 2. Identify and explain the basic ideas of Hinduism. 3. Explain the relationship between castes and the concepts of karma and dharma.	1. Describe the rise and spread of Buddhism. 2. Compare and contrast Hindu and Buddhist religions. 3. Identify Ashoka and explain how he contributed to the growth of Buddhism.	1. Identify the geographic features that isolated ancient China from other civilizations. 2. Explain how the family and royal government held Chinese society together. 3. Describe the cultural achievements of the Shang dynasty.	1. Describe the achievements of Emperor Shih Huang-ti. 2. Describe the achievements of Emperor Wu-ti. 3. Locate and compare the boundaries of the Ch'in and Han dynasties.
Setting the Stage	Geography in History: Making a Map Key Transparency 7 Outline Map 20	Discussing History: The Rise and Spread of Buddhism	Geography of China Geography in History: The Isolation of China Transparency 9 Outline Map 19	The Ch'in and Han dynasties Transparency 11
Teaching Strategies	Discussing History: Hindu Beliefs Discussing History: Castes Check for Understanding	Discussing History: Comparing Buddhism and Hinduism Discussing History: Ashoka's Rule Transparency 8 Check for Understanding	Discussing History: The Son of Heaven Teaching with Pictures: Bronze Treasures Transparency 10 Check for Understanding	Teaching with Pictures: Shih Huang-ti's "Burial City" Using Geographic Themes: Movement Geography in History: The Ch'in and Han Empires Outline Map 19 Check for Understanding
Guided Practice	Transparency 7 Q&A Section Review 1	Transparency 8 Q&A Section Review 2	Transparency 9 Q&A Transparency 10 Q&A Section Review 3	Transparency 11 Q&A Section Review 4
Independent Practice Worksheets	Independent Practice 4.1 Vocabulary 4	Independent Practice 4.2 Geography Skills 4 Basic Skills 4	Independent Practice 4.3 Critical Thinking 4	Independent Practice 4.4
Enrichment	1. Primary Source: Voices 4.1 2. Preparing a Report: Monsoons 3. Researching for Points	1. Primary Source: Voices 4.2 2. Preparing a Report 3. Comparing Leaders 4. Researching for Points	1. Primary Source: Voices 4.3 2. Creative Writing 3. ★Understanding Confucius 4. Researching for Points	1. Primary Source: Voices 4.4 2. Creative Writing 3. Researching for Points

Chapter Closer	●Reteaching Activities	Summarizing, Writing Identifications, Defending Opinions
	Chapter Review	Summary, Reviewing the Facts, Basic Skills, Researching and Reporting Skills, Critical Thinking, Perspectives on Past and Present, Investigating History
	Chapter Evaluation	Chapter Test 4, Alternate Chapter Test 4, Computer Test Bank Chapter 4 Test

Unit I Review	Geographic Theme	Location: Where did ancient cities develop?
	Historical Themes	Human-Environment Interaction, Impact of Ideas, Economics and History
	Unit Evaluation	Unit I Test, Alternate Unit I Test

Teaching Strategies

Discussing History: Hindu Beliefs (Objective 2) Explain that Hinduism is the world's third largest religion. Unlike Christianity or Islam, Hinduism has no central figure or single sacred book; nevertheless, the *Upanishads* (the name derived from two Sanskrit words, *upa*, meaning "near" and *shad,* "to sit") and the Vedas discuss the central ideas of the Hindu faith. Review the four key ideas discussed on page 77. The relationship between Brahman (the World Soul) and Atman (the Self) is particularly important.

Discussing History: Castes (Objective 3) A caste consisted of a group of people who shared the same or similar occupations, who ate together, and intermarried. Membership was hereditary. (Brahman privileges are discussed in *Our Oriental Heritage* by Will Durant, pages 484–487.) Ask students how the caste system is tied to the ideas of rebirth, karma (fate), and dharma (duty). Rebirth provided the only means of changing one's caste. Leading the best possible life and fulfilling one's dharma could positively influence one's karma, so that one would be reborn into a higher caste. Failing to observe the discipline of dharma could have the opposite effect. Ask students how these beliefs contrast with traditional American beliefs that people can achieve whatever they wish.

Check for Understanding Have students complete the following sentence fragments:

1. The region in which India is located is often called a subcontinent because . . . .
2. The Indus valley civilization was invaded by . . . .
3. Brahman is a . . . .
4. The social divisions within the Indian society are called . . . .

Enrichment Activities

1. **Reading a Primary Source** Assign Voices from the Past Resource Book 4.1.
2. **Preparing a Report** Monsoon rains have been called India's "breath of life." Predicting their arrival may be the world's most important weather forecast. Ask students to report on the monsoons. The December 1984 *National Geographic* is a good resource.
3. **Researching for Bonus Points** What is the name of the cape where the Bay of Bengal meets the Arabian Sea? (Cape Comorin)

Buddhism spread under Mauryan rulers.

2

Setting the Stage

Discussing History: The Rise and Spread of Buddhism (Objective 1) This section examines the wisdom Prince Siddhartha Gautama found and taught. It also discusses a dynasty that united India and helped spread a religion that became known as Buddhism. The religion spread throughout India and into present-day Sri Lanka, Afghanistan, Tibet, China, Mongolia, Korea, and Japan. Buddhism also spread southwest into Burma, Southeast Asia, Malaysia, and Indonesia. Have students use the map on pages 880–881 to trace this spread.

Teaching Strategies

Discussing History: Comparing Buddhism and Hinduism (Objective 2) After students have read "Buddhism taught nonviolence" (pages 79–80), discuss how it would feel to live in a society in which there was no hope of improving one's status. Hinduism teaches that each person has to repeat the cycle of life, death, and rebirth many times before achieving *moksha.* Buddha agreed with the Hindu goal of escaping from the pain of this world; however, his method of escape differed. Review Buddha's Four Noble Truths. Emphasize that Buddha believed that anyone who understood these Truths and followed the Eightfold Path could achieve *nirvana*. Direct your students' attention to the Voice from the Past on page 81.

Discussing History: Ashoka's Rule (Objective 3) After reading "The Mauryan dynasty built an empire" (pages 80–82), have students compare and contrast the reigns of Chandragupta and Ashoka. Ask students if a ruler should strive to be loved or feared. Use Map Transparency 8, *India under the*

Mauryan Dynasty, to show students the extent of the Mauryan Empire and the distribution of Ashoka's edicts. Emphasize Ashoka's role in the spread of Buddhism to the rest of Asia.

Check for Understanding Write the following names on the board: Ashoka, Chandragupta, and Buddha. Have students match each person with one of these quotations:

1. "Government is the science of punishment." (Chandragupta)
2. "The Enlightened One" (Buddha)
3. "officials of righteousness" (Ashoka)

Enrichment Activities

1. **Reading a Primary Source**
   Assign Voices from the Past Resource Book 4.2.

2. **Preparing a Report**
   Ask students to report on Buddha, Chandragupta, or Ashoka.

3. **Comparing Leaders**
   Ask advanced students to write an essay to compare and contrast the reigns and reforms of Akhenaton and Ashoka.

4. **Researching for Bonus Points**
   What were the names of Buddha's wife and son? (Princess Yasodhara and Rahula)

Setting the Stage

Geography in History: The Isolation of China (Objective 1) Use Map Transparency 9, *Ancient China*, to help students identify major geographic features, notably the Yellow and Yangtze rivers. Explain that the Yellow River was the most important river in ancient China. The river derives its name from yellow dust called *loess* deposited by northwest winds from the Gobi Desert. A layer of loess up to 450 feet thick that covers the North China Plain enabled the region to become China's fertile heartland. Ask your students to name the geographic barriers that permitted China to develop a unique cultural tradition.

Distribute Outline Map 19: China and Japan. Ask students to label the major rivers, mountains, and deserts as well as the major countries and seas that surround China.

Teaching Strategies

Discussing History: The Son of Heaven (Objective 2) Discuss the role the family played in Chinese society. Then explain that the Chinese believed in an all-powerful force called Heaven that regulated the universe. The Mandate of Heaven, or the right to rule, was granted to a family demonstrating unusual virtue. The ruler, known as the Son of Heaven, formed a crucial link between the human world and the forces governing the universe. The Son of Heaven held a demanding job. As the head of state, he commanded vast armies. As the Middle Kingdom's moral teacher, he had the responsibility of living a virtuous life. Emphasize that rulers who failed to fulfill their duties lost the Mandate of Heaven and could expect natural calamities and ultimately revo-

lution. The rise and fall of ruling families is called the dynastic cycle.

Teaching with Pictures: Bronze Treasures (Objective 3) Ask students to read "Civilization emerged in Shang times" (pages 84–85). Show Map Transparency 10, *China in Shang and Chou Times*, to trace the extent of the Shang empire and the succeeding Chou empire. Then review the cultural contributions of Shang artisans. Direct students' attention to the picture of the bronze ax on page 85. The Chinese used bronze to make tools, weapons, and ornamental containers that are considered by modern experts to be works of great skill and beauty. The ax blade on page 85 is 14 inches long. Archaeologists found it on the entrance ramp of a large tomb. Forty-eight decapitated skeletons were found nearby.

Check for Understanding Write the five traits of a civilization on the board (cities, specialized workers, writing, advanced technology, complex institutions). Call on students to give examples of each trait in ancient Chinese civilization.

Enrichment Activities

1. **Reading a Primary Source**
   Assign Voices from the Past Resource Book 4.3.

2. **Creative Writing**
   Ask students to imagine that they are Egyptian officials who have just returned to Thebes after visiting the Middle Kingdom. Have them write reports for the Pharaoh to compare and contrast everyday life in ancient Egypt and China.

3. **Understanding Confucius**
Ask advanced students to compile a list of five sayings of Confucius. The students should also prepare a brief explanation of what each saying means to them. (*Bartlett's Familiar Quotations* is a good source.)

4. **Researching for Bonus Points**
What was the ancient Chinese symbol for king and what do the different strokes mean? (The symbol was ‡. The three horizontal strokes stand for heaven, earth, and humanity. The vertical stroke stands for the king, who connects all three.)

Ch'in and Han emperors strengthened China. 4

Setting the Stage

Tell students they will be able to answer these questions as they read this section: Who built the Great Wall and why? What is inside the world's most incredible tomb? What was the Great Silk Road? Why would people have their bodies encased inside jade suits? Use Map Transparency 11, *China in Ch'in and Han Times*, to point out the locations of the Ch'in and Han empires, the Great Wall, and the Silk Road.

Teaching Strategies

Teaching with Pictures: Shih Huang-ti's "Burial City" (Objective 1) Identify Shih Huang-ti, review his achievements, and explain that he feared death. To find immortality, he commanded more than 700,000 workers to build a huge underground burial city. Local farmers discovered the site in 1974. The picture on page 91 shows part of an underground army made of clay that protected the eastern side of the burial city. So far, archaeologists have unearthed more than 7,000 life-sized warriors, 100 chariots, and 400 chariot horses. No two warriors are alike.

Using Geographic Themes: Movement (Objective 2) After students read "Civilization flowered under the Han dynasty" (pages 91–93), review the achievements of Wu-ti. Before the Great Silk Road was opened (map on page 92), China's trade was mainly coastal to Japan, Southeast Asia, Indonesia, and India. Indian traders brought Chinese goods to Persia and Arabia. Chinese goods reached the Roman empire through Arab traders. The Silk Road made it possible for western peoples to trade more directly for Chinese goods by land. The Chinese exported silk, cinnamon, and jade. In return, they received horses, gold, silver, and new foods such as pomegranates, broad beans, grapes, and clover. Emphasize that few, if any, caravans actually made the entire journey. Instead, the traders exchanged goods at established change-over points.

Geography in History: The Ch'in and Han Empires (Objective 3) Distribute Outline Map 19. Ask students to construct a key that includes symbols for the Ch'in and Han empires. Using the text and the map on page 92 as references,

have students designate the lands controlled by the Ch'in and Han dynasties. Ask students to draw the Great Wall using the map scale to ensure that the wall they have drawn extends about 1,400 miles.

Check for Understanding Ask students to write three achievements each of the Ch'in and Han dynasties.

Enrichment Activities

1. **Reading a Primary Source**
Assign Voices from the Past Resource Book 4.4.

2. **Creative Writing**
Ask students to write an eyewitness account of what they might have seen at a cross-over point on the Great Silk Road.

3. **Researching for Bonus Points**
The picture on page 93 shows the jade burial suit made for Han prince Liu Sheng. Who was Liu Sheng's wife and how was she buried? (His princess, Lady Dou Wan, was also buried inside a jade burial suit.)

ANSWERS TO Chapter Review 4

Reviewing the Facts

1. (a) large part of a continent separated from the rest of the continent by natural barriers (b) passing of the inner self from body to body (c) birth group in the Indian society, signifying social status (d) announcement of a ruler's policies

2. (a) mountain chain separating India from rest of Asia (b) site of first Indian civilization (c) one of

two largest cities in India's first civilization (d) nomadic people from central Asia whose culture blended with that of Indus valley people (e) collections of Aryan hymns (f) name for Siddhartha Gautama after he achieved enlightenment (g) united northern India, founded Mauryan dynasty (h) became an enlightened Buddhist ruler (i) site of China's first civilization (j) river in China flowing from Tibet (k) first historic Chinese dynasty (l) second historic Chinese dynasty (m) third historic Chinese dynasty (n) fourth historic Chinese dynasty (o) Chinese teacher and philosopher who urged social harmony (p) Chinese philosopher who believed in emulating order in nature (q) founder of lasting form of government; responsible for building the Great Wall (r) most powerful emperor of Han dynasty; responsible for start of silk trade

3. well-planned and regularly laid-out cities, public buildings, artifacts

4. (a) from the mingled beliefs of Aryans and Indus people **(b)** Hindu view supported caste system and defined role of each caste

5. (a) Ashoka converted to Buddhism and made Buddhism the official religion of the kingdom. **(b)** People can attain enlightenment and *nirvana* by following the Eightfold Path. They had to treat all living things with loving kindness.

6. (a) united northern India and founded a strong dynasty **(b)** adopted Buddhism and sent missionaries to neighboring lands

7. respect for family and for government

8. Confucianism, Taoism, and Legalism

9. restored internal order, built Great Wall

10. (a) a period of peace, unity, trade with new places **(b)** Buddhism spread through China.

Basic Skills

1. (a) Page 83, physical geography; page 92, political geography
(b) The Ch'in empire occupied the plains formed by the Yangtze and Yellow rivers, surrounded by sea, mountains, and desert. The Han empire extended beyond these natural boundaries.

2. *Geographic Features:* both isolated by natural boundaries and centered on fertile river plains. *Social Patterns:* India—Hinduism promoted caste system, Buddhism, a concern for all individuals; China—social classes, peasant revolts; close family ties and obedience to elders; greater importance to group than to individual; absolute authority of ruler. *Major Achievements:* India—city planning, cotton weaving and dyeing, many crafts; China—cities, writing, producing and weaving silk, Great Wall, network of highways. *Philosophies of Life:* India—Hinduism, Buddhism; China—Confucianism, Taoism, Buddhism, Legalism.

3. Bronze Age

4. (a) approximately 700 miles
(b) Located in a wide river plain, good for farming and supporting a growing population; on a waterway, and on major routes crossing the mountains between India and Asia Minor; good for trade. **(c)** entered India by Khyber and Bolan passes **(d)** would descend into the wide plain of the Indus past farmland, scattered villages, and cities; would then pass into the even broader, fertile valley of the Ganges, ending at the Bay of Bengal

Researching and Reporting Skills

1. In Gupta period, Chinese monks came to India to study Buddhism; in Rajput period, Buddhism declined. Buddha was worshipped in Hindu temples.

During Ming period, Chinese scholars turned to Confucianism, which later spread to Japan.

2. Answers will vary.

3. primary sources: b, d, and e; secondary sources: a and c

Critical Thinking

1. (a) *Indian caste system:* hereditary, based on religion and ritual purity; *Chinese social classes:* traditional, based on occupation
(b) In India, people were locked in by the caste system. In China, individuals were limited to their class, though revolts occurred and individuals occasionally improved their status.

2. (a) unfavorable **(b)** favorable
(c) favorable in later period

3. *agreed:* in India, Chandragupta, Ashoka in the early period; in China, Legalists, Ch'in Shih Huang-ti and his son; *disagreed:* in India, Buddha, Ashoka in later period; in China, Confucius, Lao-Tzu, Wu-ti

4. The Vedas provided the basis for a caste system in India. Confucius promoted traditional values and good morals as standards of wise government in China.

Perspectives on Past and Present

1. Have students use a world map of religions in an atlas such as Goode's *World Atlas* (Rand McNally).

2. Students should be aware of the official separation between church and state in many countries today. Yet many political issues involve religious or moral principles. Have students identify some of these issues.

Investigating History
Students' findings will vary.

Teaching with Pictures

After students study the photograph on page 72, have them describe the terrain in the valley and compare it to the terrain at higher elevations. Ask students why the monastery was built on rocky ground rather than in the valley. Interested students may do research to determine whether monasteries like this one are still in use today.

The Himalayas dwarf a Buddhist monastery

Key Terms

subcontinent
monsoon
reincarnation
moksha
caste
karma
dharma
nirvana
edict
Mandate of Heaven
dynastic cycle
loess
oracle bones
filial piety

72

Read and Understand

1. A new culture arose in northern India.
2. Buddhism spread under Mauryan rulers.
3. Imperial government united China.
4. Ch'in and Han emperors strengthened China.

The two wisest teachers of ancient India and China never heard of each other. The highest, most formidable mountain barrier in the world—the Himalayas (HIH-muh-LAY-uhz)—separated their two civilizations. Yet, by an odd coincidence, these two influential thinkers of ancient Asia were seeking the same goal at nearly the same time. Their common goal was to find wisdom and to know the truth about life. Born within a few years of each other, both wisdom seekers were probably in the prime of life about 525 B.C.

On the southern side of the Himalayas lived Siddhartha Guatama (sih-DAHR-tuh GAW-tuh-muh), later known as the Buddha. The Buddha preached his first sermon to five companions. They were so astonished

Chapter 4 Resources

GEOGRAPHY
- Geography Skills 4
- Outline Maps 19, 20
- Transparencies 7, 8, 9, 10, 11

REINFORCEMENT
- Vocabulary 4
- Basic Skills 4
- Reteaching 4
- Making Connections Study Guide 4

ENRICHMENT
- Critical Thinking 4
- History and Literature 4

ASSESSMENT
- Chapter Test 4
- Alternate Chapter Test 4
- Computer Test Bank

by his wise and gentle words that they exclaimed: "Truly, O Buddha, Our Lord, thou has found the truth!" Thousands of Indians agreed and became his devoted followers.

At the same time, in China, a teacher named Confucius (kuhn-FYOO-shuhs) wandered from village to village offering lessons in wisdom to any family that served him a meal. Young students began writing down his witty replies to their questions. Where, they asked, could you find a perfectly wise person? Confucius said: "I do not expect to find a saint today. But if I find a gentleman, I shall be quite satisfied."

What did it mean to have wisdom? To be wise, said Confucius, was to respect your elders and rulers so that families and kingdoms could live in harmony. The Buddha, on the other hand, said that wisdom lay in giving up all selfish desires so that your soul might escape the pain of life and death. Confucius and the Buddha followed different paths to wisdom in part because each man expressed the ideas of his own civilization. This chapter tells the story of the two remarkable cultures that grew up on either side of the world's highest mountains.

A *new culture arose in northern India.* 1

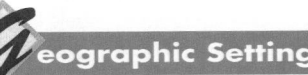

Geographic Setting

A great landmass lies between the Himalayas and the Indian Ocean. Today that region includes the countries of India, Pakistan, Nepal, and Bangladesh. When speaking of ancient times, however, historians generally refer to the entire region as India.

India's outline resembles a diamond-shaped kite. To the north (at the top of the imaginary kite), two mountain chains—the Hindu Kush on the west and the Himalayas on the east—meet at a point. This great wall of mountains separates India from the rest of Asia. As a result, India is sometimes called a **subcontinent** of Asia. Mountain passes like the 34-mile-long Khyber Pass have been used since prehistoric times by migrants and invaders coming into India.

South of the Himalayas lies an enormous flat and fertile plain formed by two rivers—the Indus River and the Ganges (GAN-jeez) River. These two rivers and the lands they water make up a large arc that stretches 2,000 miles across northern India. This arc is called the Indus-Ganges plain. Because the land is flat, easy to irrigate, and very fertile, this plain has always been the rich heartland of India.

The southern part of the Indian subcontinent (the bottom of the imaginary kite) is a peninsula that thrusts south into the Indian Ocean. The center of the peninsula is a high plateau cut by twisting rivers; this region is called the Deccan (DEK-uhn). Covered by dense forests or scrubby grasses, the Deccan is a harsh land.

A narrow border of lush, tropical land lies along the coasts of southern India. This coastal rim has a wet climate and rich soil. Valuable forests of teak and fragrant sandalwood grow there.

Throughout history, southern India often has been a land apart. Its culture remains very different from that of northern India, even though the two regions are united in one country today.

India's climate is dominated by seasonal winds called **monsoons.** From October to May, winter monsoons from the northeast blow dry air across the country. Then, in the middle of June, the winds shift. Spring monsoons blow from the southwest, carrying moisture from the ocean in great rain clouds. The people of India depend on these monsoons for rain to water their crops. If there is too little rain, plants wither in the fields and people go hungry. If there is too much rain, floods may sweep away whole villages. This climate pattern has shaped life for India's farmers since prehistoric times.

CITY TOUR
Cities flourished in the Indus valley.

India's first civilization developed on the rich plains of the northern subcontinent. The Indus River flows southwest from the Himalayas through what is now Pakistan. Like the Nile, the Tigris, and the Euphrates rivers, the Indus flooded each year. At each flood, the Indus spread

73

SECTION 1 Objectives and Teaching Strategies

OBJECTIVE 1. Identify and locate the landforms of the Indian subcontinent.

Teaching Strategy: *Geography in History: Making a Map Key* (page 72a)

OBJECTIVE 2. Identify and explain the basic ideas of Hinduism.

Teaching Strategy: *Discussing History: Hindu Beliefs* (page 72c)

OBJECTIVE 3. Explain the relationship between castes and the concepts of karma and dharma.

Teaching Strategy: *Discussing History: Castes* (page 72c)

■ BACKGROUND

This city tour features the ancient Indus cities of Harappa and Mohenjo-Daro. The symbol shows the brick steps leading into the public bath.

SECTION 1 Resources

GEOGRAPHY
■ Transparency 7

REINFORCEMENT
■ Independent Practice 4.1

ENRICHMENT
■ Voices from the Past 4.1

ASSESSMENT
■ Section Quiz 4.1

ANSWERS TO
Focus on Geography

1. Asia
2. the Indus-Ganges plain
3. between 25° and 35° N; The climate is probably warm year-round.
4. the Hindu Kush and the Himalayas
5. **(a)** The land is flat, easy to irrigate, and very fertile. **(b)** The river might flood and sweep away local villages.

■ BACKGROUND

Because the bricks were oven-fired (rather than sun-baked like those in the Fertile Crescent), the walls of these ancient cities have not crumbled, even though they have been buried in river mud for centuries.

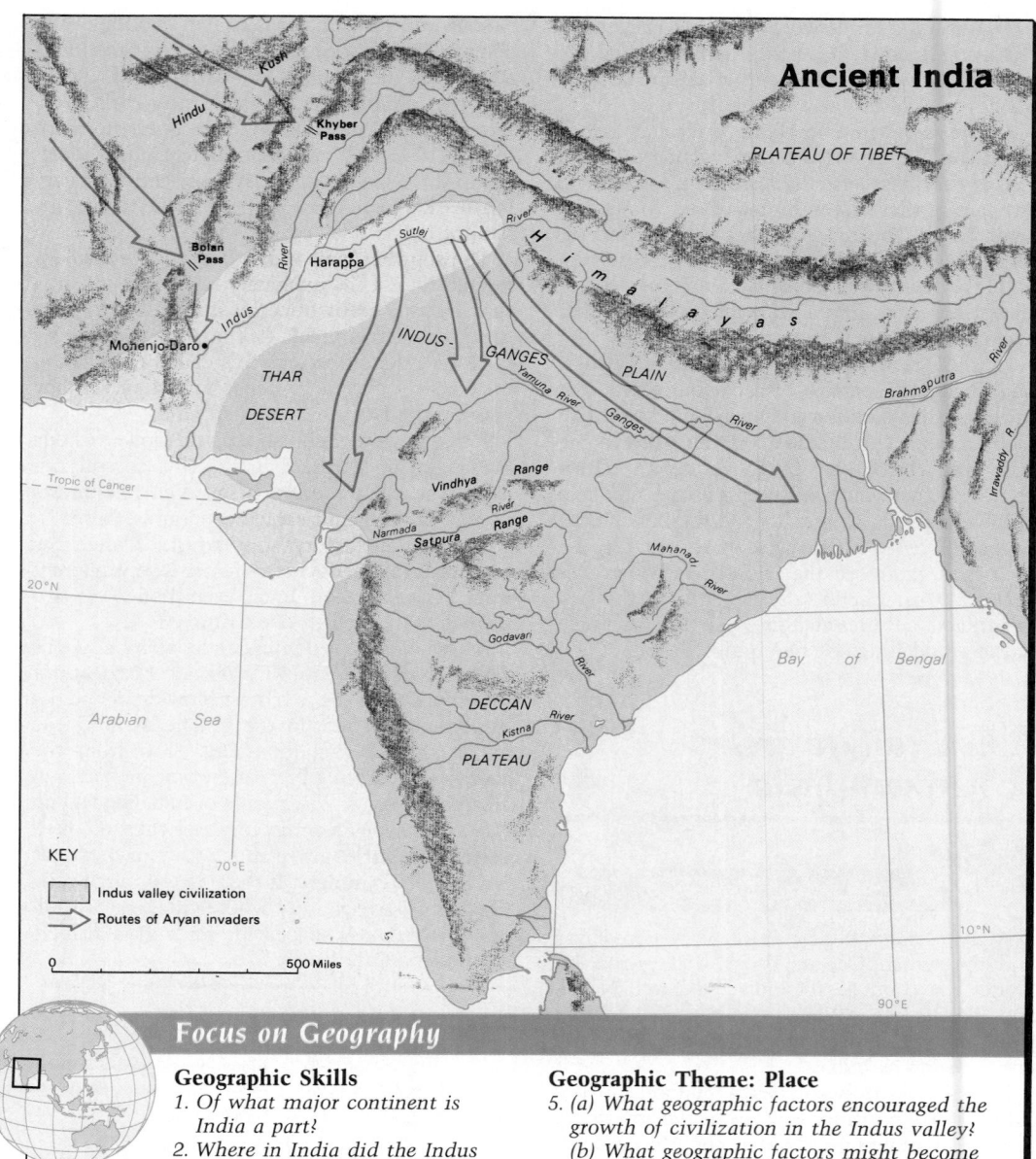

Ancient India

PLATEAU OF TIBET

Hindu Kush

Khyber Pass

Bolan Pass

Harappa

Mohenjo-Daro

Indus River

Sutlej

River

Himalayas

INDUS-GANGES PLAIN

Yamuna River

Ganges River

Brahmaputra River

THAR DESERT

Tropic of Cancer

20°N

Vindhya Range

Narmada River

Satpura Range

Godavari River

Mahanadi River

Irrawaddy R.

DECCAN PLATEAU

Kistna River

Arabian Sea

Bay of Bengal

70°E

KEY

☐ Indus valley civilization

⇨ Routes of Aryan invaders

0   500 Miles

10°N

90°E

Focus on Geography

Geographic Skills

1. Of what major continent is India a part?
2. Where in India did the Indus civilization develop?
3. Within what degrees of latitude was the Indus civilization located? What does this show about the climate there?
4. From what mountain ranges do the Indus River and its branches flow?

Geographic Theme: Place

5. (a) What geographic factors encouraged the growth of civilization in the Indus valley? (b) What geographic factors might become a threat?

74

a layer of rich silt across its valley, providing good soil for farming.

Well-planned cities Around 2500 B.C., while Egyptians were building the pyramids, people in the Indus valley were laying the bricks for India's first cities. Archaeologists have found the ruins of about 100 settlements along the Indus.

The largest cities were Harappa (huh-**RAP**-uh) and Mohenjo-Daro (moh-**HEHN**-joh-**DAHR**-oh). Each city had a population of roughly 30,000. Although these two cities were 350 miles apart, they were remarkably alike. Each was laid out neatly, with streets running north-south and east-west like a grid. Their walls were built with oven-fired bricks, all of a standard size. This regular pattern of building suggests careful planning by a strong central government.

Many kinds of specialized buildings lay within the two cities. Each had huge public storehouses for grain, an arrangement that suggests a well-organized government. One large building in Mohenjo-Daro was clearly a bathhouse, with a great brick tub about the size of a swimming pool. Shops lay along main streets.

Housing Dozens of tiny, branching alleys ran off the wide main streets. The doors to people's homes opened out onto these mazelike alleys. Few windows looked out on the street, however. For fresh air, families went to inner courtyards or up stairways to their rooftops. Houses might be two or even three stories high.

The cities of the Indus valley show more concern with cleanliness and sanitation than any other cities of their time. Many houses had brick-floored bathing rooms from which dirty water drained through clay pipes into gutters. Citizens of Mohenjo-Daro disposed of their garbage through narrow slits conveniently cut into the walls of their houses. The garbage fell into containers neatly lined up on the street below.

Everyday life Most people lived by farming. They raised wheat, barley, and perhaps rice for food. They also grew cotton to make cloth. The Indus valley settlers had domesticated cattle, sheep, goats, pigs, and fowl as well as cats and dogs. Some scholars think they may also have tamed elephants.

Next to agriculture, trade was the most important source of prosperity. The Indus valley city dwellers left hundreds of small clay seals that merchants probably used to mark shipments of goods. Some of these seals have also been found in the ruins of ancient Mesopotamia. Apparently the merchants of Mohenjo-Daro and the merchants of Ur exchanged goods. Perhaps they exchanged ideas as well.

The people of the Indus valley cities worked at a variety of crafts. Archaeologists have found kilns for pottery, vats for dyeing cloth, and many different kinds of metal, including gold, silver, copper, bronze, and lead.

Archaeologists have also turned up relics of everyday pleasures. Little cubes stamped with dots indicate that these early city dwellers enjoyed rolling dice. Children amused themselves with wheeled pull toys made of clay.

The fine brickwork of Mohenjo-Daro shows in a pool for ritual bathing (left). Cattle such as the one shown on the seal (above) are still common in India today.

75

■ DISCUSSION

Ask for reactions to this emphasis on cleanliness. Do students assume that cleanliness and sanitation are modern concepts?

Cooperative Learning

Divide the class into groups of three or four students. Have half of the groups prepare charts comparing Indus valley civilization with that of the Sumerians (Chapter 2). The other groups should prepare charts comparing the early inhabitants of India with the ancient Egyptians (Chapter 3). Students within each group should research city populations and layouts, types of housing and building materials, everyday life, and arts and crafts for civilizations they are assigned. Each group member must contribute to the group's chart. Then combine groups that have studied different civilizations and have group spokespersons present their information. A recorder in each group should add the new information to his or her group's chart.

If the land could no longer support the population or if there were no longer any flooding, why would invaders have been interested in the Indus valley?

■ BACKGROUND

Among the most important Aryan gods was Indra, god of the thunderbolt and a great warrior. In the hymns, Indra is called "destroyer of fortresses" and is said to have torn apart the defenses of a place called Hariyupia, which may have been Harappa.

The decline of the Indus valley civilization

Around 1750 B.C., the quality of building in the Indus valley cities became poorer. Mohenjo-Daro grew less and less prosperous. Gradually, the great cities fell into decay.

What happened? Some historians think that the Indus River changed course, as it has been known to do, so that its floods no longer fertilized the fields near the cities. Other scholars suggest that people wore out the valley's land. They overgrazed it, allowing their cattle and goats to eat the ground nearly bare. They overfarmed it, growing the same crops year after year. They overcut its trees, brush, and grass to build their houses and provide fuel for their cooking fires and kilns.

As the Indus valley civilization neared its end, around 1500 B.C., human enemies may have had a hand in the cities' downfall. A half-dozen groups of skeletons were found in the latest ruins of Mohenjo-Daro. Bones of men, women, and children lie together where they fell, seemingly never buried. Two skulls show injuries from a sword or axe. These signs of violence suggest that the city, already weakened by its slow decline, may have been abandoned after a devastating attack. Many historians believe the enemies were newcomers from the north side of the Himalayas.

Aryans moved in from the northwest.

Around 1500 B.C., nomads from central Asia trudged across the Khyber Pass and into the Indus valley. Some of the newcomers called themselves Aryans (AIR-ee-uhnz), which in their language meant "the nobles." Other central Asian groups, whose names and languages are unknown to us, probably drifted into India at the same time.

The newcomers were very different from the people they conquered. For one thing, the Indus valley people lived in cities and were chiefly farmers, artisans, and merchants. The Aryans were nomadic herders who counted their wealth in cattle. The Aryans did not move into the cities they conquered, but left them abandoned. It would be many years before the Aryans became city dwellers. Another major difference was that the Indus valley people were literate. The Aryans had no writing system. Instead, their priests preserved their culture from generation to generation by memorizing long hymns and poems. These poems were in the Aryan language, an early form of Sanskrit. Sanskrit remains a learned and sacred language in India today.

To escape the Aryans, some of the Indus valley people may have fled southward across the Vindhya (VIHN-dee-uh) Mountains to the Deccan. To this day, the people of southern India speak a different group of languages, known as the Dravidian language family.

Not all the Indus valley dwellers fled, however. Many remained as slaves to the newcomers. Although they were conquered, the people of the Indus valley had a lasting influence on Indian culture. Between 1500 and 500 B.C., a new society took shape in northern India. The cultures of the Indus valley dwellers and the Aryans blended into a uniquely Indian civilization. One product of that blending was the religion known today as Hinduism.

Hinduism shaped India's culture.

Hindu practices grew from the mingled beliefs of many groups in India. Figurines from the Indus valley seem to show early examples of some gods that were later important to Hindus. However, the earliest records of Hinduism—the long Sanskrit hymns that the priests memorized—are Aryan.

The Vedic Age When the Aryans migrated to India, they brought a rich collection of myths, or tales of their gods. They had gods of thunder, fire, earth, heaven, the moon, and the sun. Priests made offerings of food and drink to the gods. Everything in nature was believed to be in some way holy.

Footnote to History

Strange as it seems, English is distantly related to Sanskrit. Both are members of a large group of languages called the Indo-European language family. The relationship shows in the roots for some of the most basic words in any language—family terms.

English	Sanskrit
mother	matar
father	pitar
brother	bhratar
sister	svasar
daughter	duhitar
son	sunus

Aryan priests could sing from memory a great number of long and complicated hymns, each one suited to a different religious ritual. Some of these hymns may date back to 1500 B.C. Priests gathered the hymns into four collections called Vedas (VAY-duhz). The most ancient and important of these collections, the *Rig-Veda*, included 1,028 hymns of praise. It is probably the oldest set of scriptures still in active use. The Vedas were finally written down about A.D. 1400.

Millions of Indians today cherish the Vedas as sacred. Historians cherish them for a different reason. The Vedas are a most important clue to the history of India from 1500 to 500 B.C. This thousand-year period is called the Vedic Age.

The Upanishads Sometime around 400 B.C., the wisest Hindu teachers tried to interpret and explain the hidden meaning of the Vedic hymns. They discussed such questions as these: What is the nature of reality? What is morality? Is there eternal life? What is the soul? The teachers' comments were memorized by their students and later written down as a collection of essays known as the Upanishads (oo-PAN-ih-shadz). Most of our knowledge about Hindu beliefs comes from these writings. Here are the basic ideas expressed in the Upanishads.

1. The one true reality is Brahman, the mighty spirit that creates and destroys. Brahman reveals itself in millions of earthly shapes, from a mountain to a raindrop. Brahman is One, and yet expresses itself as Many.

Brahman is a unifying and all-powerful spirit. In European and American society, people tend to believe that human life is totally different from the life of a turtle or a butterfly. No, declares an ancient Hindu text, everything in nature is tied together by Brahman. The ancient text puts it poetically:

> Thou art woman. Thou art man. Thou art the dark-blue bee and the green [parrot] with red eyes. Thou hast the lightning as a child. Thou art the seasons and the seas. Thou dost abide with all pervadingness, wherefrom all things are born.

2. One aspect of Brahman is the Self, or Soul, called Atman. Atman can be compared to particles of salt dissolved in a glass of water. You cannot see the salt, yet it is everywhere in the water—just as Atman is everywhere.

Although this painting was done in the 1700's, it celebrates a battle from the Mahabharata, *a great Hindu poem based on events that took place before 1000 B.C.*

3. Nothing that lives ever dies entirely. When a living thing dies, its inner self is reborn in another form. This passing of the inner self from body to body is known as **reincarnation.** To be reincarnated, say the Upanishads, is much like being given a new coat to wear:

> Just as a man, having cast off old garments, puts on other, new ones, even so does the embodied one, having cast off old bodies, take on other, new ones.

4. All wise Hindus must seek to reach a state of perfect understanding called **moksha.** The inner self that attains moksha will never suffer another reincarnation. In moksha, the self disappears to merge with Brahman.

77

■ **BACKGROUND**

Point out that Hinduism is not the name of a religion in the same way that Christianity or Judaism is. Rather, it is a set of practices, rituals, and laws.

■ **DISCUSSION**

Why were these religious views readily adopted? (Answers should include the idea that other, more familiar gods were not rejected but were instead incorporated into the concept of Brahman.)

ANSWERS TO

Section Review 1

Define:
(a) large part of a continent separated by some natural barrier from the rest of the continent (b) seasonal wind (c) passing of inner self from body to body (d) state of perfect understanding (e) "birth group" (f) outcast (g) ethical law of cause and

(continued)

ANSWERS TO (continued)

effect **(h)** duties and obligations of each caste

Identify:

(a) mountains separating China and India **(b)** Its valley was the site of early civilizations. **(c)** largest ancient cities in the Indus valley **(d)** nomads from central Asia who arrived in the Indus valley around 1500 B.C. **(e)** set of beliefs and practices derived from the mingled traditions of the Indus valley dwellers and the Aryans **(f)** collections of Aryan hymns **(g)** essays seeking to explain the meaning of Vedic hymns **(h)** highest, priestly caste **(i)** second highest caste **(j)** third highest caste **(k)** fourth caste

Answer:

1. (a) regular pattern of city buildings **(b)** seals that merchants used to mark shipment of goods also found in ancient Mesopotamia **(c)** discovery of kilns, vats for dyeing cloth **(d)** quality of building became poorer, signs of violence

2. Aryans were nomadic herders; Indus valley people were farmers and city-dwellers with trades. Aryans were illiterate; Indus valley people had writing system.

3. (a) contain ancient, sacred hymns **(b)** contain insights into India during the Vedic Age

4. (a) A Hindu goal is the attainment of *moksha,* a merging of the self with *Brahman,* the universal spirit. Those not attaining this goal are locked in a cycle of reincarnation. **(b)** By the law of *karma,* proper behavior will guarantee rebirth into a higher caste and immoral acts will send a soul to a lower caste in the next reincarnation.

Castes structured Indian society.

During the Vedic Age, Indians began to develop a complicated set of divisions between groups of people. These social divisions were closely linked to the Hindu world view.

According to the *Rig-Veda,* four different groups of people had been created from the body of a Hindu god. First, the Brahmins were created from the god's mouth. They later became the priestly class and were the highest group in Indian society. (Note that a member of this class is a *Brahmin,* while the universal spirit is *Brahman.*) The second group, the Kshatriyas (kuh-**SHAHT**-ree-uhz), came from the god's arms. They were rulers and warriors. Third, the Vaishyas (**VYSH**-yuhz) were created from the god's legs. They were landowners, merchants, and artisans. The fourth group, the Shudras (**SHOO**-druhz), came from the god's feet. They were servants or slaves.

In reality, Hindu society was much more complicated than the myth suggested. There were hundreds of different groups, not just four. Over the years, these divisions in society became more and more defined. Eventually, each group had its own occupation, which was passed down from parent to child. People of each group ate only with each other and usually married only within their own group.

Hindus call these groups within their society *jatis,* a word that means "birth group." When Europeans came to India, they called the groups **castes** (kasts), from a Latin word that meant "pure."

Ritual purity was the basis for the ranking of castes. Hindus considered high castes purer than low castes. Priests were considered the purest group. Farmers were thought to be purer than people who make their living washing clothes. To share food or have any contact with a lower-ranking person was to risk contamination.

The very lowest group in society were those people outside the caste system—the outcastes or untouchables. Even lower than servants, untouchables could not so much as draw water from a caste well, lest their touch contaminate the water. They had to use separate wells or wait for a higher-ranking person to get water for them.

Why was one person born a Brahmin while another was born an untouchable? Hinduism

78

explained it by saying that Brahmins, in former lives, had committed no bad deeds. An untouchable, on the other hand, must have done bad deeds in an earlier incarnation.

Hindus believed in an ethical law of cause and effect called **karma.** It operated as automatically as the law of gravity. By the law of karma, moral behavior in one life guaranteed rebirth in a higher caste. Immoral behavior, on the other hand, automatically dropped a reborn soul to a lower caste. Says a Hindu scripture: "Just as he acts, just as he behaves, so he becomes."

To earn a good rebirth, according to Hindu teachings, a person had to be a good member of his or her caste. Each caste had its particular **dharma,** or duty. Dharma is the set of duties and obligations of each caste. For example, a boy born into the warrior caste had to be willing to fight, kill, and be killed. A woman's dharma was to obey her father while she was a child, her husband after she married, and her sons if she was widowed. The individual's own wishes or talents made no difference. According to an ancient Hindu text, it is better to do one's own duty badly than to do another's duty well.

Section REVIEW 1

Define: (a) subcontinent, (b) monsoon, (c) reincarnation, (d) moksha, (e) caste, (f) untouchable, (g) karma, (h) dharma

Identify: (a) Himalayas, (b) Indus River, (c) Harappa and Mohenjo-Daro, (d) Aryans, (e) Hinduism, (f) Vedas, (g) Upanishads, (h) Brahmins, (i) Kshatriyas, (j) Vaishyas, (k) Shudras

Answer:

1. What evidence has led historians to the following beliefs about India's first cities? (a) The cities were run by a strong central government. (b) People of the cities carried on trade with Sumer. (c) The people were skilled in a number of crafts. (d) The cities' downfall may have been caused by a slow decline, followed by an attack from outsiders.

2. How were the people of the Indus valley different from the Aryans who conquered them?

3. (a) Why are the Vedas of religious importance to many Indians? (b) Why are they important to historians?

Critical Thinking

4. (a) Explain how the ideas of Brahman, moksha, and reincarnation are all related in Hindu beliefs. (b) Explain how the ideas of reincarnation, karma, and caste are related.

Buddhism spread under Mauryan rulers. 2

Around 530 B.C., near the very end of the Vedic Age, a young man named Siddhartha Gautama challenged the ideas of the Brahmin priests. Even a lowborn person, he said, could gain enough wisdom in one lifetime to escape the cycle of death and rebirth.

The Buddha sought an answer to life's pain.

The date traditionally given for Gautama's birth is 563 B.C. The legends of his life are probably exaggerated. The stories say that Gautama was born into the warrior class and lived in luxury at his family's palaces near the foothills of the Himalayas. Pampered by his wealthy family, he never saw pain, suffering, or death. He married a beautiful woman who bore him a son.

Again according to legend, Gautama's comfortable life was shattered one day when he first saw proof of human suffering. While riding in his chariot, Gautama saw a man who was terribly sick, another who was old and feeble, and a third who had died. He realized that life was an endless cycle of pain and the only way to escape it was by seeking wisdom.

One night, when he was about 29, Gautama took a last look at his sleeping wife and son. Then he left his palace and joined a wandering, homeless band of five other wisdom seekers. For six years, Gautama tried to find wisdom through harsh discipline and suffering. For days at a time, he ate only a single grain of rice each day. His stomach became so empty that, by poking a finger into it, he could touch his backbone. Yet Gautama gained only pain, not wisdom. He decided, therefore, to seek wisdom in other ways.

At last, enlightenment came to him. After meditating deeply for many days in the shade

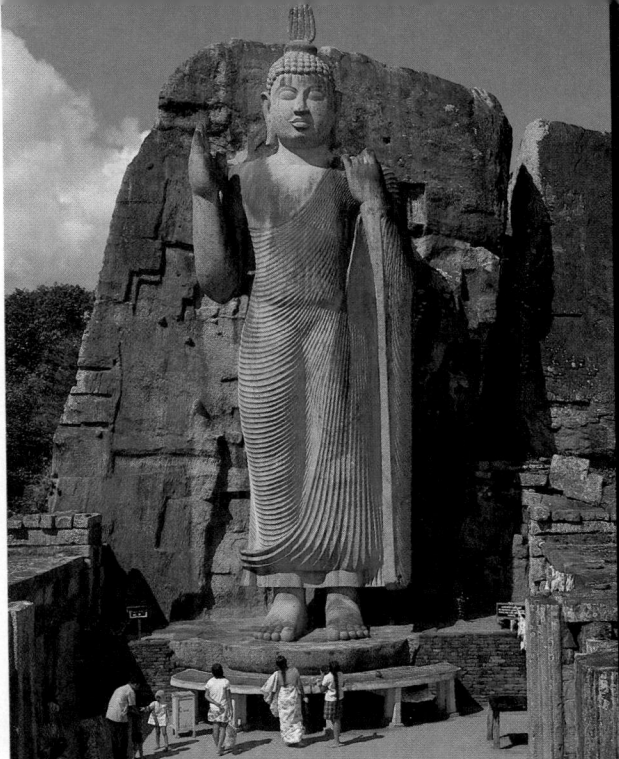

This Buddha on the island of Sri Lanka was cut from solid rock between A.D. 400 and 500.

of a tree, Gautama suddenly felt that the truth became clear to him. He rose and set out to teach others what he had learned. Thereafter, he was known as Buddha, a title meaning "the Enlightened One."

Buddhism taught nonviolence.

Buddha gave his first sermon to the five wisdom seekers who had been his companions. That sermon was a landmark in the history of world religions. Buddha taught the four main ideas that had come to him in his enlightenment, calling them the Four Noble Truths.

First Noble Truth Everything in life is suffering and sorrow.

Second Noble Truth The cause of all this pain is people's self-centered cravings and desires. People seek pleasure that cannot last and leads only to rebirth and more suffering.

Third Noble Truth The way to end all pain is to end all desires.

79

SECTION 2
Objectives and Teaching Strategies

OBJECTIVE 1. Describe the rise and spread of Buddhism.

Teaching Strategy: *Discussing History: The Rise and Spread of Buddhism* (page 72c)

OBJECTIVE 2. Compare and contrast Hindu and Buddhist religions.

Teaching Strategy: *Discussing History: Comparing Buddhism and Hinduism* (page 72c)

OBJECTIVE 3. Identify Ashoka and explain how he contributed to the growth of Buddhism.

Teaching Strategy: *Discussing History: Ashoka's Rule* (page 72c)

■ BACKGROUND

Also according to legend, Gautama's father had heard a prophecy that his son would lead a religion if he ever saw misery.

SECTION 2
Resources

GEOGRAPHY
■ Transparency 8

REINFORCEMENT
■ Independent Practice 4.2

ENRICHMENT
■ Voices from the Past 4.2

ASSESSMENT
■ Section Quiz 4.2

ANSWERS TO
Map Study

south and west of the Himalayas, across the subcontinent, and extending west and north into Afghanistan; the southernmost tip of India

■ BACKGROUND

Chandragupta loved pomp. For Hindu festivals, he dressed in a dazzling robe embroidered in purple and gold and was carried through the city streets on the shoulders of his attendants. Flapping close to his head was a flock of green and red parrots trained to fan the emperor with their wings.

India under the Mauryan Dynasty

Map Study

Describe the extent of Ashoka's empire. What part of India remained outside his control?

Fourth Noble Truth People can overcome their desires and attain enlightenment by following the Eightfold Path.

The Eightfold Path was like a staircase. According to Buddha, those who sought enlightenment had to master one step at a time. The steps of the Eightfold Path were right knowledge, right purpose, right speech, right action, right living, right effort, right mindfulness, and right meditation. By following the Eightfold Path, anyone could attain **nirvana** (nur-VAHN-uh), Buddha's word for release from pain and selfishness.

Buddha taught his followers to treat all living things (humans, animals, and even insects) with loving kindness. A devout Buddhist was not even supposed to swat a mosquito.

Buddhists and Hindus both sought to escape from the woes of this world, but their paths of escape were very different. Unlike traditional Hinduism, Buddhism did not require complex rituals. Moreover, Buddha taught in everyday language, not in the ancient Sanskrit language of the Vedas and the Upanishads, which most Indians in 500 B.C. could no longer understand. Buddha's religion was also unique in its concern for all human beings—women as well as men, lowborn as well as highborn.

80

The Mauryan dynasty built an empire.

Buddha lived near the end of the Vedic Age, around 500 B.C. More than 1,000 years had passed since the fall of the Indus valley cities and the arrival of the Aryans. In all those years, no single ruler had united India's many kingdoms. In Buddha's time, a dozen families had carved the Ganges River valley into little states that were often at war. However, a change was coming. Soon India was to experience a new type of government that brought together large territories under a single king.

In 512 B.C., the armies of the great Persian king Darius I came through the Khyber Pass and conquered northwestern India. For almost 200 years, the Indus valley was ruled by a Persian satrap, or governor. For the first time since the Aryan invasions, Indians felt both the benefits (unity and order) and burdens (heavy taxes) of centralized control.

Then, in 326 B.C., the Greek empire builder Alexander the Great led his armies over the mountain passes into India. The Indus valley passed into Greek hands, but only for five years. When Alexander died, his empire died with him. His ambition to unify all of northern India was finally achieved by another young conqueror—an Indian ruler named Chandragupta Maurya (chuhn-druh-GUP-tuh MOW-ree-uh).

The rise of Chandragupta Around 322 B.C., the young warrior Chandragupta stirred up a revolt against a weak king and thus made himself ruler of the largest kingdom on the Ganges. Over the next 24 years (322–298 B.C.), Chandragupta's army of 9,000 elephants and 700,000 soldiers trampled neighboring kingdoms. He united all of northern India (the Indus valley, the Ganges valley, and the southern Himalayas) under his rule. Chandragupta and his descendants who followed him as kings are known as the Mauryan dynasty.

Chandragupta ruled by force and fear. He planted government spies everywhere to prevent plots against him. He trusted nobody. To avoid being poisoned at a meal, he made servants taste all his food. To avoid being murdered in bed, he slept in a different room every night. People he suspected of plotting revolt were tortured to death. After all, said a political manual of the time, "Government is the science of punishment."

Chandragupta was succeeded on the throne by his son, about whom little is known. However, Chandragupta's grandson, Ashoka (uh-SHOH-kuh), became the most famous member of the Mauryan dynasty. Ashoka became the complete opposite of his cruel grandfather.

Ashoka's rule Ashoka inherited the throne in 273 B.C. At first, he was as warlike as Chandragupta. His victory against southern tribes ended in the slaying of perhaps 100,000 captives.

The later chronicles say that news of this massacre filled Ashoka with remorse. He decided henceforth to rule according to Buddha's teachings of "peace to all beings." (In fact, Ashoka's acceptance of Buddhism probably took place gradually.) He sent an apology to the southern tribes and promised kind treatment in the future.

Throughout his empire, Ashoka ordered huge stone pillars to be erected. Each pillar was inscribed with a public announcement, or **edict**, of his new policies. Some edicts guaranteed righteous treatment for all Ashoka's subjects. Others urged the people of his empire to live righteously themselves.

Instead of spies, Ashoka employed "officials of righteousness" to look out for the welfare of Indians of every caste. Was anyone imprisoned unjustly? Was a family suffering because of flood or drought? The emperor instructed his officials to furnish necessary aid.

Voice from the Past | The Teachings of Buddha

Buddha was first and foremost a great religious teacher. The following paired verses explain and illustrate many of his ideas.

All that we are is the result of what we have thought: it is founded on our thoughts, it is made up of our thoughts. If a man speaks or acts with an evil thought, pain follows him, as the wheel follows the foot of the ox that draws the carriage.

All that we are is the result of what we have thought: it is founded on our thoughts, it is made up of our thoughts. If a man speaks or acts with a pure thought, happiness follows him . . .

"He abused me, he beat me, he defeated me, he robbed me"—in those who harbor such thoughts, hatred will never cease.

"He abused me, he beat me, he defeated me, he robbed me"—in those who do not harbor such thoughts, hatred will cease.

For hatred does not cease by hatred at any time; hatred ceases by love—this is an eternal law . . .

As rain breaks through an ill-thatched house, passion will break through an unreflecting mind.

As rain does not break through a well-thatched house, passion will not break through a well-reflecting mind . . .

The thoughtless man, even if he can recite a large portion of the law, but is not a doer of it, has no share in the religious life . . .

The follower of the law, even if he can recite only a small portion of it, . . . possesses true knowledge and serenity of mind; he . . . has indeed shared in the religious life.

1. What basic contrast are the paired verses making?
2. Using the phrase "Thou shalt not," write commandments based on each of the paired verses.
3. What qualities does Buddha think people should seek in life? What phrases show that?

81

■ DISCUSSION

What problems might accompany winning control over large areas?

ANSWERS TO
Voice from the Past

1. The paired verses are making a basic contrast between a life of evil and a life of good—that is, a religious life.

2. Thou shalt not speak or act with an evil thought. Thou shalt not harbor thoughts of hatred. Thou shalt not let passion dominate thy mind. Thou shalt not fail to follow the law.

3. People should seek the qualities of pure thought, love for others, reflectiveness, lawfulness, true knowledge, and serenity of mind. The phrases are found in the second part of each verse.

ANSWERS TO
Section Review 2

Define:
(a) release from pain and selfishness (b) ruling family (c) public announcement of policy

Identify:
(a) wisdom-seeker who came to be called Buddha (b) religion that teaches the Four Noble Truths and the Eightfold Path (c) cruel leader who united northern India and founded Mauryan dynasty (d) last strong ruler of Mauryan dynasty

Answer:
1. (a) by following the Eightfold Path one step at a time (b) Buddhism required no rituals, recognized no castes or divisions of people.
2. 298 B.C. to 180 B.C.
3. (a) uniting India (b) spreading Buddhism
4. The suffering in Hinduism is a result of improper behavior (failure to respect *dharma*). In Buddhism, suffering is caused by self-centered cravings and can be avoided.

These lions stood atop a pillar set up by Ashoka about 250 B.C. The modern country of India has made this figure its badge.

Ashoka sent hundreds of Buddhist missionaries to neighboring lands such as Ceylon (the modern Sri Lanka) and even to kingdoms as far away as Syria. Thanks largely to his encouragement, Buddhism spread far beyond India and became a major world religion with millions of followers.

Ashoka was the last strong ruler of the Mauryan dynasty. In 180 B.C., only 50 years after Ashoka's death, the Mauryan empire was torn apart by rivalry among local princes. Again, India became a collection of small kingdoms. However, the basic form of Indian civilization—begun in the Indus valley and developed through Hinduism and Buddhism—was already established. This civilization proved strong enough to survive centuries of political disunity.

82

Section REVIEW 2

Define: (a) nirvana, (b) dynasty, (c) edict
Identify: (a) Siddhartha Gautama, (b) Buddhism, (c) Chandragupta Maurya, (d) Ashoka
Answer:
1. (a) How did Buddhists hope to achieve enlightenment? (b) How did the Buddhist path to enlightenment differ from the Hindu path?
2. During what years did the Mauryan dynasty rule India?
3. What were the great contributions of the following rulers? (a) Chandragupta (b) Ashoka

Critical Thinking
4. Both Hinduism and Buddhism accept that human life is filled with suffering. How do the two religions differ in their explanations of human suffering?

Imperial government united China. 3

The walls of China's first cities were built 1,500 years after the walls of Ur, 1,000 years after the great pyramids of Egypt, and 1,000 years after the tidy cities of the Indus valley. Though a late starter, the civilization begun on China's Yellow River 3,500 years ago outlasted all the others and continued into the twentieth century. The reason for this endurance lies partly in China's geography.

Geographic Setting

Geography isolated China.

Chinese civilization grew up in the valleys of two rivers, the Yellow River and the Yangtze River.* On the map, notice that both these long, twisting rivers flow out of the towering highlands of Tibet. The rivers flow east until they reach

* This book uses the traditional system for writing Chinese names, sometimes called the Wade-Giles system. This system is used in many standard reference books and in all books on China published before 1979. The new *pinyin* system appears in some current publications. For place-names, maps in this book show the pinyin form in parentheses after the traditional spelling.

Ancient China

MONGOLIA

GOBI DESERT

KOREA

JAPAN

Lake
Balkhash

Yellow
(Huang He)

Yellow
Sea

TAKLA MAKAN

Kunlun Mountains

NORTH CHINA
PLAIN

Wei River

of
Japan Sea

30°N

PLATEAU
OF TIBET

C H I N A

River

Chang Jiang

Yangzi

Tropic of Cancer

PACIFIC

20°N

H i m a l a y a s

Ganges River

Brahmaputra
River

West River
(Xi Jiang)

OCEAN

Red River

Irrawaddy

South
China Sea

PHILIPPINE
ISLANDS

INDIA

BURMA

ANNAM
(VIETNAM)

90°E

0   500 Miles

SIAM

Bay of Bengal

110°E

120°E

110°N

Focus on Geography

Geographic Skills

1. Within what degrees of longitude was ancient China located? What does this suggest about China's location compared to that of Europe? Compared to Southwest Asia?

2. (a) What geographic barriers lie to the north, west, southwest, and south of China? (b) How might these affect the development of China?

3. Describe the location of China's rivers in terms of where they rise and end.

4. What effect might the location, geographic barriers, and waterways of China have on the development of civilization there?

Geographic Theme: Location

5. What geographic factors of the North China Plain might encourage the growth of civilization there?

---

a broad, flat pocket of land near the Pacific Ocean. This rich plain is cupped on the north, west, and south by hills and mountains. About 90 percent of China's land that is suitable for farming lies within this comparatively small region. This plain was China's heartland.

Throughout China's long history, its political boundaries have expanded and contracted depending on the strength or weakness of its ruling families. Yet China remained a center of civi-

lization with cities, writing, organized government and religion, specialized crafts, and more. In the Chinese view, only barbarians (people who are not civilized) lived outside China's borders. Because the Chinese saw their country as the center of the civilized world, their own name for China was the Middle Kingdom.

Ancient China was isolated from all other civilizations. To its east lay the Pacific Ocean. To the west lay the forbidding desert, Takla Makan

83

SECTION 3
Objectives and Teaching Strategies

OBJECTIVE 1. Identify the geographic features that isolated ancient China from other civilizations.

Teaching Strategy: *Geography in History: The Isolation of China* (page 72d)

OBJECTIVE 2. Explain how the family and royal government held Chinese society together.

Teaching Strategy: *Discussing History: The Son of Heaven* (page 72d)

OBJECTIVE 3. Describe the cultural achievements of the Shang dynasty.

Teaching Strategy: *Teaching with Pictures: Bronze Treasures* (page 72d)

ANSWERS TO

Focus on Geography

1. between 75° and 125° E; China is east of Europe; China is east of Southwest Asia

2. **(a)** to the north, the Gobi Desert; to the west, the Takla Makan and the Plateau of Tibet; to the southwest, the Himalayas; and to the south, more rugged mountains **(b)** China developed in isolation from the rest of the world.

3. China's rivers flow eastward from the highlands of Tibet, passing through the

(continued)

SECTION 3
Resources

GEOGRAPHY
■ Transparencies 9, 10

REINFORCEMENT
■ Independent Practice 4.3

ENRICHMENT
■ Voices from the Past 4.3

ASSESSMENT
■ Section Quiz 4.3

ANSWERS TO (continued)

North China Plain and emptying into the Pacific Ocean.
4. An agricultural civilization developed in relative isolation.
5. Two rivers cross the plain providing fertile soil. The plain is surrounded by mountains and hills, isolating it.

■ BACKGROUND

Students researching the dynasties will want to know their *pinyin* names when they differ from those given in the text. *National Geographic* and the *New York Times* use the *pinyin* names (for example, Chou equals Xhou; Ch'in equals Qin).

■ DISCUSSION

The word for *wife* in China means "inside person." What does this use of language reveal about attitudes toward women?

and the icy 14,000-foot Plateau of Tibet. To the southwest were the Himalayas. And to the north lived the warlike nomads of Mongolia.

Strong bonds held Chinese society together.

The culture that grew up in China had strong bonds that made for unity. From earliest times, the group seems to have been more important than the individual. Above all, people's lives were governed by their duties to two important authorities—their family and their king or emperor.

The family In China, the family was central to society. Everyone's role in the family was fixed from birth to death. The elderly had privileges and power; the young had practically none. The oldest man was in charge of all the family's goods and possessions. He also had final approval of the marriages that the women of the family arranged for his children and grandchildren. The oldest woman—usually the grandmother—had authority over all the younger women. Children were expected to obey their elders without question. The most important virtue in Chinese society was respect for one's parents.

Women in Chinese society were treated as inferiors. They were expected to obey their fathers, their husbands, and later, their own sons. When a girl was between 13 and 16 years old, her marriage was arranged, and she moved permanently into the house of her husband. A young bride often entered her husband's household with fear, wondering how her mother-in-law would treat her. Only by bearing sons for her husband's family could a woman hope to improve her status. Eventually, of course, she might be able to rule over her own daughters-in-law.

In China, the family was closely linked to religion. The spirits of family ancestors were thought to have the power to bring good fortune or disaster to living members of the family. The Chinese did not regard these spirits as mighty gods. Rather, the spirits were more like troublesome or helpful neighbors who demanded attention and respect. Every family paid respect to its father's ancestors (the mother's family did not count) and made sacrifices in their honor. Only sons could carry on the traditional religious

duties, so sons were valued much more highly than daughters.

View of government In ancient China, a person's chief loyalty throughout life was to the family. Beyond this, people owed obedience and respect to the ruler of the Middle Kingdom, just as they did to their own grandfather. The ruler was like a super-grandfather who had supreme responsibility for the welfare of the Chinese people.

The Chinese believed that royal authority came from heaven. A just ruler had divine approval, known as the **Mandate of Heaven.** A wicked or foolish king could lose the Mandate of Heaven. The ancestral spirits might show their displeasure by causing a flood, riot, or other calamity. In that case, the Mandate of Heaven might pass to another noble family. This was the Chinese explanation for rebellion and civil war. The fall of one dynasty and the rise of another was never achieved without bloodshed.

Historians describe the rise and fall of dynasties as a cycle. Each dynasty rules vigorously for a while, then weakens and is replaced by a new ruling family. This pattern of strength, decline, and replacement is called the **dynastic cycle.**

Chinese history is marked by a succession of dynasties until dynastic rule was finally overthrown in the early 1900's. The first historic family to rule the Middle Kingdom (from about 1500 to 1027 B.C.) were the Shang (shahng) kings. The last Shang king was overthrown by the first Chou (jo) king. The Chou dynasty, the longest in Chinese history, lasted for eight centuries (from 1027 to 221 B.C.). It was followed by the shortest and cruelest dynasty, the Ch'in, which in turn was followed by the mighty Han dynasty. These four dynasties—Shang, Chou, Ch'in, and Han—span the first 1,900 years of China's history.

Civilization emerged in Shang times.

Archaeologists have found the remains of China's first civilization along the Yellow River. The river's color is indeed yellowish. From the western mountains, the water picks up a dusty, yellow soil called **loess** (les). The river spreads the loess over the peasants' fields. Winds from the west bring more rich loess to keep the farmlands of the Middle Kingdom fertile.

The Yellow River is fearfully unpredictable. Its floods can be generous or ruinous. At its

DYNASTIC CYCLE IN CHINA
Showing Role of Mandate of Heaven

Strong dynasty establishes peace and prosperity; it is considered to have Mandate of Heaven.

In time, dynasty declines and becomes corrupt; taxes are raised; power grows weaker.

Disasters such as floods, famines, peasant revolts, and invasions occur.

Old dynasty is seen as having lost Mandate of Heaven; rebellion is justified.

Dynasty is overthrown through rebellion and bloodshed; new dynasty emerges.

New dynasty gains power, restores peace and order, and claims to have Mandate of Heaven.

worst, when rains are unusually heavy, the river devours whole villages. (The great flood of 1887 killed nearly a million people.) Those who live near the Yellow River know well why it is nick-named "China's Sorrow." Yet the rich farmland constantly draws people back to the river valley.

Early cities China's first cities appeared near the Yellow River about 2000 B.C. Among the oldest and most important was Anyang (ahn-yahng). Anyang was one of the capitals of the Shang dynasty.

Unlike the cities of the Indus valley or the Fertile Crescent, Anyang was built mainly of wood. The city stood in a forest clearing. Nobles lived in large, rectangular wooden houses with thatched roofs. Average families lived in little cone-shaped huts or pit-houses.

Social classes Chinese society was sharply divided between nobles and peasants. Warrior-nobles owned the land. They served in the army and the government. They were skilled fighters with the horse, the chariot, and the bow and arrow. Noble families governed the scattered villages within the Shang lands, sending tribute to the Shang ruler in exchange for local control.

Meanwhile, peasants tilled the soil for their overlords. In Shang times, the farmers had no plows, only wooden digging sticks and hoes and sickles made of stone. The soil was so rich, though, that it yielded two crops a year of millet, rice, and wheat.

A separate class in Chinese society was made up of people who were skilled in special crafts. At Anyang, these artisans lived outside the city walls. Their houses were smaller than those of the nobles but much more spacious and comfortable than those of the peasants.

Crafts Bronzework was the leading craft in which Shang artisans excelled. Beautiful bronze objects were used in religious rituals and were also symbols of royal power. Some of these objects were small and graceful, such as bronze bells. Others were massive caldrons, weighing almost a ton. The skills of the Shang bronzesmiths, say modern admirers, have never been surpassed.

In earliest Shang times, the Chinese also learned how to draw the fine threads from a silkworm's cocoon and weave them into a light, beautiful fabric. Nobles prided themselves on their finely embroidered silk shoes, which they esteemed as a symbol of civilization. Barbarians, after all, were known to go barefoot.

Shang bronze ax, used for beheadings

85

■ BACKGROUND

The theory of divine right of kings will be studied in Chapter 18. In Tudor and Stuart England, that theory was interpreted to mean that rebellions were offenses against God as well as king. In China, by contrast, rebellions were seen as part of the dynastic cycle.

■ DISCUSSION

The need to build great dikes to control the Yellow River may be one reason why a strong central government was important to the people who lived in this region. Have students discuss this possibility.

After students have read the section "Confucius urged social harmony" (pages 87–88), divide the class into groups of three. Write the following three sayings of Confucius on the board: "The gentleman is easy of mind, while the small man is always full of anxiety"; "What the gentleman seeks, he seeks within himself; what the small man seeks, he seeks in others"; "In his errors a man is true to type. Observe the errors and you will know the man." The first group member chooses a saying, the second paraphrases it, and the third explains what he or she thinks it means. Then another saying is chosen, paraphrased, and so on, with students trading roles each time. Groups may discuss interpretations. Recorders should make note of their groups' agreed-upon interpretations. Have group spokespersons share their groups' interpretations with the class.

A writing system developed.

The earliest evidence of Chinese writing comes from Shang times. At Anyang and other Shang cities, archaeologists have found hundreds of animal bones and tortoise shells with written symbols scratched on them. These strange objects are known as **oracle bones** because priests used them to foretell the future. The writing on the oracle bones showed that people 3,500 years ago were part of the same cultural tradition that continues in China today. Some of the characters are very much like those in a modern Chinese newspaper.

In the Chinese method of writing, each character stands for an idea, not a sound. Recall that many of the Egyptian hieroglyphs stood for sounds in their spoken language. Sumerian cuneiform and the Phoenician alphabet also corresponded to spoken language. In contrast, there were practically no links between China's spoken language and its written language. One could read Chinese without being able to speak a word of it. (This seems less strange when you think of our own number system. Both a French person and an American can understand the written equation $2 + 2 = 4$, but an American may not understand the spoken statement, *"Deux et deux font quatre."*)

The Chinese system of writing had one great advantage. People in all parts of China could learn the same system of writing, even if their spoken languages were very different. Thus, the Chinese written language was very important in unifying a large and diverse land.

The disadvantage of the Chinese system was the enormous number of written characters to be memorized. To be barely literate, a person needed to know at least 1,000 characters. To be a true scholar, one needed to know between 5,000 and 10,000 characters. For centuries, this severely limited the number of literate, educated Chinese. As a general rule, a noble's children learned to write, but a peasant's children did not.

ECONOMICS IN DAILY LIFE ▶ *The Most Treasured Fabric*

According to legend, silk was discovered by the 14-year-old empress Hsi Ling-shi, who lived around 2500 B.C. Hsi Ling-shi was walking one day among the mulberry trees near the palace. A few days earlier, the trees had been covered with caterpillars eating the mulberry leaves. Now the caterpillars hung from the branches in mummylike cocoons.

Curious about the cocoons, Hsi Ling-shi plucked one from a branch and took it home. She dropped it in a pot of water and watched it soften into a loose, tangled web. When she picked up the web, she found she could unravel it like a skein of yarn to form a single long thread of silk.

The legend may or may not be true. The process of making silk became China's best-kept secret for the next 3,000 years. Foreign gold and silver poured into China from the silk trade. To pass on the secret of silk-making to the outside world was treason, punishable by death.

Silk was one of the first items carried in long-distance trade. During the Han dynasty, caravans loaded with silk began to travel the Silk Road, the long route between China and the Mediterranean area. The Chinese monopoly in silk production lasted until about A.D. 550, when Europeans smuggled mulberry seeds and silkworm eggs out of China. Silk still remained important in trade with the East.

The Chou dynasty ruled in troubled times.

In the long parade of dynasties that have ruled China, the Chou followed the Shang. No dramatic changes in civilization marked the change of dynasties. The Chou ruled much as the Shang had. The Chou ruled from around 1027 to 221 B.C. For the first 300 years of this long period, the Chou ruled a large empire including both eastern and western lands. The king's power was wielded locally by mighty lords, but final power still lay in the hands of the king.

Gradually, however, Chou rule weakened. In 771 B.C., the dynasty's weakness brought on a crisis. In this unhappy year, barbarians from the north and west sacked the city of Hao, the Chou capital. They murdered the Chou monarch, but a few members of the royal family escaped eastward to the city of Loyang (loh-yahng). Here in this new capital on the Yellow River, the Chou dynasty pretended to rule the Middle Kingdom for another 500 years.

In fact, the Chou kings at Loyang were almost powerless. Noble families, who supposedly owed allegiance to the king, could not be controlled. Trained as warriors, they sought every opportunity to pick fights with neighboring lords. As their power grew, these warlords claimed to be kings in their own territory. As a result, the later years of the Chou are often called "the time of the warring states."

In this time of bloodshed, traditional values collapsed. At the very heart of Chinese civilization was a love of order, harmony, and respect for authority. Now there was chaos, arrogance, and defiance. How could China be saved? Three solutions were offered by the Middle Kingdom's scholars and philosophers.

Confucius urged social harmony.

China's most influential scholar was K'ung Fu-tzu ("Master Kung"), better known as Confucius. Born in 551 B.C., Confucius was about 12 years younger than the Indian sage Gautama (Buddha). Confucius led a scholarly life, studying history, music, and moral character.

Confucius believed that social order and good government could be restored in China if society were organized around five basic relationships.

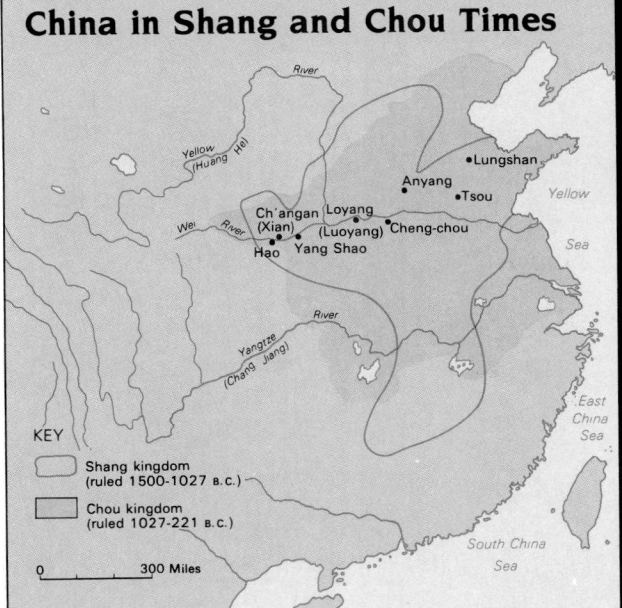

China in Shang and Chou Times

KEY

▢ Shang kingdom (ruled 1500-1027 B.C.)

▢ Chou kingdom (ruled 1027-221 B.C.)

0 ——— 300 Miles

Map Study

Which dynasty—the Shang or the Chou—controlled more land along China's coast? About how far is it from Loyang to Anyang? From Loyang to Tsou?

These were the relationship between ruler and subject, father and son, husband and wife, older brother and younger brother, and friend and friend.

A code of proper conduct regulated each of these relationships. For example, rulers should practice kindness and virtuous living. In return, subjects should be loyal and law-abiding. "If a ruler himself is upright, all will go well without orders. But if he himself is not upright, even though he gives orders, they will not be obeyed."

Three of Confucius's five relationships were based upon the family. Confucius stressed that children should practice what he called **filial piety,** or respect for their parents and elders. "In serving his parents, a filial son renders utmost respect to them at home; he supports them with joy; he gives them tender care in sickness; he grieves at their death; he sacrifices to them with solemnity . . ."

Confucius was not content to be merely a great teacher. He wanted to reform Chinese society by showing a prince or duke how to govern wisely. Impressed by Confucius's wisdom, the duke of Lu appointed him Minister of Crime. According to legend, Confucius so overwhelmed

87

ANSWERS TO
Map Study

Chou; about 150 miles; about 300 miles

ANSWERS TO
Section Review 3

Define:
(a) belief that royal authority came from heaven
(b) pattern of strength, decline, and replacement that characterizes dynasties
(c) fertile yellow soil carried by rivers **(d)** animal bones and tortoise shells with written symbols scratched on them; used by ancient Chinese priests to foretell the future **(e)** respect for parents and elders

(continued)

ANSWERS TO (continued)

Identify:
(a) one of two rivers that water China's heartland
(b) the other river
(c) mountainous region west of China (d) region north of China, inhabited by nomads
(e) first historic family to rule China (f) dynasty that followed the Shang
(g) scholar whose teachings later became basis for religion (h) Chinese thinker who stressed the natural order, or Tao

Answer:
1. (a) respect for and duties to the family and king or emperor (b) At the family level, religion revolved around the spirits of ancestors; at the government level, ancestral spirits authorized the power of a ruler.

2. (a) served in army and government (b) tilled the soil (c) created objects from bronze; wove silk

3. (a) People whose spoken languages were different could all read the written language. (b) The great number of characters in written Chinese required long years of study.

4. Nobles fought each other and chaos ruled.

5. (a) Social order can be maintained by upholding traditions. (b) Following the natural order is the way to achieve harmony. (c) A powerful leader can restore order by severely punishing misdeeds and greatly rewarding obedience.

6. (a) It suggests that virtuous behavior on the part of the ruler will spare him catastrophes. (b) Look for a discussion of specific contemporary leaders considered to be honorable and wise and those who are not.

There is no portrait of Confucius that was made during his own time. Like most later portraits, this one suggests his wisdom and kindness.

people by his kindly, courteous ways that almost overnight crime vanished from Lu. When the duke's ways changed, however, Confucius felt compelled to resign.

Confucius spent the remainder of his life teaching. The only record of his ideas are the writings of his students. Only later, 350 years after his death, did millions of Chinese begin to memorize his teachings.

88

Taoists sought harmony with nature.

For Confucius, the *social* order (family and government) was most important. For another Chinese thinker named Lao Tzu (low dzu), only the *natural* order was important. If you seek order and harmony, said Lao Tzu, go up into the hills, sit by a stream, and observe a drifting cloud or a soft breeze. Observe that nothing in nature strives for fame, power, or even wisdom. The cloud, the breeze, and the stream move without effort because they follow the Tao (dow), meaning "the Way" or the universal force that guides all things.

Of all the creatures of nature, only humans fail to follow the Tao. They argue about questions of right and wrong, good manners and bad. According to Lao Tzu, such arguments are futile. A simple creature like a turtle is naturally wise because it does not argue, does not strive for personal glory. The turtle simply follows the Tao of its nature. Humans should do likewise, said Lao Tzu. The philosophy of Lao Tzu came to be known as Taoism. Chinese who adopted the Taoist philosophy withdrew from society to live close to nature.

Legalists urged harsh government.

A third group, the Legalists, believed that a highly efficient and powerful government was the key to restoring order. The Legalists taught that a ruler should provide rich rewards for people who carried out their duties well. Likewise, the disobedient should be harshly punished.

In practice, the Legalists stressed punishment more than rewards. For example, anyone caught outside his own village without a travel permit should have his ears or nose chopped off, said the Legalists.

The Legalists believed in controlling ideas as well as actions. They suggested that a ruler should burn all writings that might encourage people to think critically about government. After all, it was for the prince to govern and the people to obey.

Eventually, Legalist ideas gained favor with a prince of a new dynasty that replaced the Chou. A powerful ruler soon put an end to China's long period of disorder, as you will read in the next section.

Define: (a) Mandate of Heaven, (b) dynastic cycle, (c) loess, (d) oracle bones, (e) filial piety

Identify: (a) Yellow River, (b) Yangtze River, (c) Tibet, (d) Mongolia, (e) Shang, (f) Chou, (g) Confucius, (h) Lao Tzu

Answer:

1. (a) What were the two important bonds that united early Chinese society? (b) What role did religion play in each of those bonds?
2. (a) In the Shang times, what kind of work was done by nobles? (b) By peasants? (c) By artisans?
3. (a) How did writing help to unite China? (b) Why was literacy in China long limited to the wealthy?
4. Why was the traditional way of life in China badly shaken during the late Chou years?
5. What were the basic ideas of the following? (a) Confucius (b) the Taoists (c) the Legalists

Critical Thinking

6. Reread the statement by Confucius on page 87 about the importance of a ruler's character. (a) How does that statement support the Chinese idea of the Mandate of Heaven? (b) In your opinion, how does that statement apply to leadership today?

Ch'in and Han emperors strengthened China. 4

The new dynasty that came to power was the Ch'in. It took its name from the small state of Ch'in, which was the family's home, in western China. In 256 B.C., the Ch'in armies destroyed the Chou forces. In 246 B.C., a new Ch'in king came to the throne. Though he was only a boy of 13 at the time, as he grew older he became as ruthless a ruler as any Legalist could wish.

The Ch'in dynasty built an empire.

This proud ruler was Ch'in Shih Huang-ti (chin shir hwahng-tee), whose name meant "First Emperor." *Huang-ti* was a title that this ruler took

for himself in 221 B.C. In earlier times, it had been used only for gods. Because the title means someone even greater than a king, it is translated *emperor*. From this time on, the ruler of China was known as an emperor.

Shih Huang-ti stopped the petty wars that had sapped China's strength. He conquered the barbarians to the south of his kingdom and protected the northern border by building the Great Wall. Most important, he gave China a form of government that lasted more than 2,000 years. His dynasty was even responsible for giving China its name. Nevertheless, Ch'in Shih Huang-ti was hated by one and all. A later Chinese scholar described Shih Huang-ti as having a "high pointed nose, slit eyes, pigeon breast, wolf voice, tiger heart." Furthermore, he was "stingy, cringing, graceless." Nonetheless, Shih Huang-ti was an effective ruler.

Stamping out opposition The First Emperor concentrated all his energies on two tasks: destroying outside rival armies and destroying resistance to his rule from within. His goals were extreme and so were his methods.

His armies struck out in every direction, attacking barbarians north of the Yellow River and south as far as what is now Vietnam. Because of his conquests, the China of the Ch'in dynasty was roughly double the size of China under the Chou dynasty.

At the same time, the Ch'in emperor crushed political opposition within China. To destroy the power of rival warlords, he commanded all the noble families to live at the capital city under his watchful eye. This edict, according to tradition, uprooted 120,000 noble families. To put a stop to wars between states, the First Emperor wiped out the ancient borders of Lu, Ch'u, Ch'in, and other states, and drew new boundaries. China was carved into 36 administrative districts, each of which was controlled by officials from Ch'in.

To prevent criticism of his rule, the emperor ordered the burning of all books that were judged to be either useless or harmful. This included all poetry of the Chou dynasty and all political writings—every book valued by Confucian scholars. Only practical books about medicine and farming were to be spared.

To unite his empire, Shih Huang-ti ordered a gigantic network of highways to be built by peasant work gangs. He also set uniform standards

89

OBJECTIVE 1. Describe the achievements of Emperor Shih Huang-ti.

Teaching Strategy: *Teaching with Pictures: Shih Huang-ti's "Burial City"* (page 72e)

OBJECTIVE 2. Describe the achievements of Emperor Wu-ti.

Teaching Strategy: *Using Geographic Themes: Movement* (page 72e)

OBJECTIVE 3. Locate and compare the boundaries of the Ch'in and Han dynasties.

Teaching Strategy: *Geography in History: The Ch'in and Han Empires* (page 72e)

ENRICHMENT
■ Voices from the Past 4.4

ASSESSMENT
■ Section Quiz 4.4

GEOGRAPHY
■ Transparency 11

REINFORCEMENT
■ Independent Practice 4.4

■ **DISCUSSION**

Have students compare the Great Wall to the Egyptian pyramids. Ask them to describe the attitude of the workers on both projects. Point out that in China, lawbreakers were sentenced to work on the wall.

The Great Wall of China is one of the few human-made features on Earth that is visible from space. Although Shih Huang-ti built the earliest unified wall, the wall as it exists today dates from the Ming dynasty (1368–1644).

for Chinese law, money, and weights and measures—even the length of cart axles. This last standard ensured that all vehicles fit the ruts of all Chinese main roads.

The Great Wall If scholars most hated Shih Huang-ti for his book burning, peasants most hated him for his Great Wall. This colossal wall, which still stands, was not entirely the idea of the First Emperor. Smaller walls had been built in Chou times to discourage attacks by northern barbarians. Mounted on tough war-horses, the barbarians could not ride through the walls, but of course they could and did ride around them. Shih Huang-ti decided to close the gaps and stretch a new wall so far to the west that an enemy would have to gallop halfway to Tibet to get around it.

Pushing wheelbarrows (a Chinese invention), about a million peasants collected, hauled, and dumped millions of tons of stone, dirt, and rubble. Slabs of cut stone on the outsides of the wall enclosed a heap of pebbles and rubble on the inside. Each section of wall rose to a height of 20 to 25 feet. From the Yellow Sea in the east to the edge of the Gobi Desert in the west, the Great Wall twisted like a dragon's tail for a total distance of roughly 1,400 miles.

The wall builders worked neither for wages nor for love of empire. They worked because it was the law, and to break Ch'in law was death.

Footnote to History

Before his death in 210 B.C., Shih Huang-ti ordered the building of a great tomb for himself. The whole site was as big as a city. Within the burial mound were more than 7,500 life-size clay statues of warriors, charioteers, archers, and spearmen. This royal bodyguard came to light in 1974, in one of the greatest archaeological finds of the century.

90

An army of clay soldiers was buried with Shih Huang-ti in a tomb that covered as much ground as a small city. Archaeologists have roofed over areas as large as two football fields to protect the figures as they are excavated.

■ **DISCUSSION**

In the discussion of the fall of Ch'in, remind students of the pattern of a ruler with strong control followed by a less able leader.

■ **BACKGROUND**

The Han dynasty was contemporaneous with the Roman Empire, but the Chinese leaders had many, many more subjects; in A.D. 2, China's population was 59,594,579.

Many died anyway from the crushing labor and the freezing winter winds. According to legend, thousands of human bones lie within the wall.

The fall of the Ch'in The Ch'in dynasty was short-lived. Shih Huang-ti's son, though just as cruel as his father, was less able. After three years under the rule of this second Ch'in emperor, the peasants rebelled. One of their leaders, a peasant from the land of Han, marched triumphantly into the capital city. Thus, in 202 B.C., the Ch'in dynasty ended and the Han dynasty began.

Civilization flowered under the Han dynasty.

The Chinese think of the Han years as a time of glory, unity, and peace. The Chinese even call themselves "the people of Han." There were several reasons for the high reputation of the Han. First, though the emperor still had great power, the hated laws of the Ch'in emperors were revoked. Legalist thinkers were expelled from the imperial palace. Second, the Han ruled during a time when barbarians rarely threatened the Chinese. Third, scholars spoke highly of the Han dynasty because these were the years when Confucius's teachings won widespread influence.

The most powerful of the Han emperors was Wu-ti, who ruled from 140 to 87 B.C. Wu-ti was known as the Martial Emperor because of his success in battle. Northern barbarians, the Huns, had earlier broken through the Great Wall and pitched their tents in one corner of the empire. But Wu-ti's armies drove them back beyond the wall. At the same time, the boundaries of the empire were extended westward to central Asia, south to Vietnam, and east into what is now Korea. The armies of the Han struck up to 2,000 miles from their emperor's palace.

Wu-ti and the Confucian scholars During Han rule, there was a renewal of learning. Scholars were again allowed to read the old Chinese classics, the poetry and history so loved by Confucius. Ch'in book burners had destroyed many ancient works, but a few scholars had hidden their classics. Others had memorized them. The most precious books were known as the "Five Classics" because, shortly before his death, Confucius was said to have collected the greatest writings of Chou times and organized them into five books. A sixth book, the *Analects*, contained Confucius's words of wisdom as recorded by his students.

91

Han; Vietnam, Takla Makan, to control the land along the Great Silk Road

■ BACKGROUND

Between the early and later Han rule, the rebel emperor Wang Mang took land away from nobles and ended slavery. His changes led only to more disorder and rebellion.

China in Ch'in and Han Times

KEY

- Ch'in empire (ruled 221-202 B.C.)
- Han empire (ruled 202 B.C.-A.D. 220)
- Great Wall
- Great Silk Road

0   500 Miles

Map Study

During which dynasty did part of Korea become subject to Chinese rule? What areas in the south and west did the Han dynasty add to its empire? What reason might Han emperors have had for wanting to rule the Takla Makan?

Wu-ti proclaimed Confucianism the official set of beliefs for his government. In 124 B.C., Wu-ti founded a national university to teach the Five Classics and other great writings of the past. Graduates who passed examinations on the Classics were chosen for high positions in Wu-ti's government. Soon the most powerful officials in China (outside the imperial family) were scholars who had mastered the Classics. In later years, these examinations were a key feature of Chinese government.

The Great Silk Road Wu-ti's conquests to the west of China encouraged the growth of overland trade. According to legend, Wu-ti sent a trusted Chinese official in search of a fresh supply of horses for his armies. Traveling far beyond the Great Wall, the official brought back reports that stunned Wu-ti. Far to the west, he had discovered foreigners (Persians) who were almost as civilized as the Chinese.

It was silk that first linked China with Persia and the rest of the civilized world. Camel caravans carried bundles of silk over a rocky, mountainous route that led past Tibet, across the Takla Makan, and into central Asia. This route was known as the Great Silk Road. After a journey of 4,000 miles, Chinese silk reached the great markets of Syria and Asia Minor at the eastern end of the Mediterranean Sea. By that time, the silk had changed hands many times, each time for a higher price.

Collapse of the Han dynasty In the years following Wu-ti's reign, China's prosperity declined. Chinese peasants suffered most in any time of troubles. They lived under a crushing burden of debts and taxes. In times of bad harvests or drought, many peasant families were forced to sell their children into slavery. Famine and plague stalked China's villages. Thousands of peasants fled into the mountains and became bandits.

92

This burial suit is made of 3,000 pieces of jade sewn together with gold thread. It belonged to Liu Sheng, a Han prince who died in 113 B.C. The jade suit was expected to preserve his body for eternal life.

They joined secret societies, each known by a colorful name: the Red Eyebrows, the Green Woodsmen, the Yellow Turbans. Led by these rebels, the peasants revolted.

Twice the Han dynasty was overthrown, partly because of peasant discontent and partly because of rebellious and ambitious warlords. There were therefore two periods of Han rule. The Early Han dynasty lasted from 206 B.C. to A.D. 8. The Later Han ruled from A.D. 25 to 220.

A period of peace followed the return of the Han to the throne, but soon the empire was in difficulties again. Cruel and corrupt officials gained power in the government. In the countryside, generals led armies in the emperor's name but, in fact, ruled for themselves. Peasants turned again to banditry. As disorder spread through China, the Han dynasty neared its end.

The spread of Buddhism During the late years of the Han dynasty, between 50 B.C. and A.D. 100, Buddhism became increasingly popular in China. Buddhism came to China with traders on the Great Silk Road or on trade vessels from the Indian Ocean.

In the villages of China, Buddhist monks taught that the Buddha had been a merciful god who came to earth to save human souls. Of course, Buddha himself, dead now for five centuries, had never claimed to be a god. Yet people in both India and China were carving statues of him and bowing before them. In the rocky hills of northern China, huge statues of Buddha were carved into sandstone cliffs and grottos. One such Buddha measured 50 feet from chin to topknot. (The topknot or bun of rolled hair was a Buddhist symbol for wisdom.)

In these bitter times for Chinese of all classes, the need for religious comfort was great. The worship of family ancestors continued, but people were also eager to embrace new beliefs. Millions of Chinese turned to the kindly Buddha. Thus, as the once glorious Han empire collapsed, the religion of Buddhism spread rapidly through the troubled land.

Section REVIEW 4

Define: emperor
Identify: (a) Ch'in, (b) Shih Huang-ti, (c) the Great Wall, (d) Han, (e) Wu-ti, (f) the Five Classics, (g) the Analects, (h) the Great Silk Road
Answer:
1. (a) What were Shih Huang-ti's achievements as a ruler? (b) What methods did he use to reach his goals?
2. (a) How did Wu-ti encourage learning during his reign? (b) How did he expand China's foreign trade?
3. What circumstances encouraged the spread of Buddhism into China?

Critical Thinking
4. Use the idea of the dynastic cycle to describe the rule of the Han dynasty. What characteristics marked each stage of the dynasty's development?

93

ANSWERS TO

Section Review 4

Define:
someone even greater than a king
Identify:
(a) dynasty that followed Chou (b) first emperor of China (c) protective wall that extended 1,400 miles (d) dynasty following Ch'in (e) most powerful Han emperor (f) greatest writings of Chou times, said to have been collected by Confucius (g) words of wisdom spoken by Confucius (h) trade route for silk

Answer:
1. (a) stopped internal wars, built wall, gave China lasting form of government
(b) Shih Huang-ti drew new boundary lines to take away nobles' power and set up administrative districts. He also burned books and used peasant labor.

2. (a) founded university to teach the Five Classics
(b) sent traders along Great Silk Road

3. contacts through trade; need for religious comfort in bitter times

4. *period of strength:* Wu-Ti's reign, including advancements in learning and trade; *period of decline:* civil war, rebellions, and decline in prosperity; *period of replacement:* collapse of Han dynasty

Concluding the Chapter

1. **Chapter Closer**
Ask students to recall the chapter focus discussion on Buddha and Confucius. Have each student write a chapter summary explaining how Indian and Chinese achievements reflected the goals of Buddha and Confucius.

2. **Reteaching Activities**
a. Summarizing Have students write one paragraph describing four important features of India's first civilization and a second paragraph explaining four basic beliefs of Hinduism.
b. Summarizing Have students use the headings and subheadings in this chapter to summarize the teachings of Buddha and the contributions of the Mauryan dynasty.
c. Writing Identifications Have students write a sentence about each of the following traits of early Chinese civilization: the family, the view of government, crafts, the teachings of Confucius, and Chinese writing.
d. Defending Opinions Have students write a paragraph stating in which dynasty, Ch'in or Han, they would have preferred to live and why.

Summary

1. **A new culture arose in northern India.** India's first cities grew up in the Indus valley. Around 1500 B.C., these cities were conquered by Aryans from central Asia. The blending of Indian and Aryan culture produced the religion known today as Hinduism and a caste system of society.

2. **Buddhism spread under Mauryan rulers.** Around 550 B.C., a new religion known as Buddhism developed in India. Around 300 B.C., the Mauryan dynasty united most of India. The greatest of the Mauryans was Ashoka, who adopted Buddhism and devoted much of his reign to humane causes.

3. **Imperial government united China.** Chinese civilization began over 3,000 years ago on a plain crossed by the Yellow and Yangtze rivers. A tradition of respect and obedience toward family and government helped the Chinese form a stable society. The teachings of the Chinese scholar Confucius greatly supported these values. Other major schools of thought were the Taoists and the Legalists.

4. **Ch'in and Han emperors strengthened China.** The harsh Ch'in dynasty strengthened China and paved the way for a period of prosperity under the Han. Near the end of Han rule, during a time of civil strife, Buddhism spread to China.

Reviewing the Facts

1. Define the following terms:
   a. subcontinent   c. caste
   b. reincarnation   d. edict

2. Explain the importance of each of the following names, places, or terms:
   a. Himalayas   j. Yangtze River
   b. Indus River   k. Shang
   c. Mohenjo-Daro   l. Chou
   d. Aryans   m. Ch'in
   e. Vedas   n. Han
   f. Buddha   o. Confucius
   g. Chandragupta Maurya   p. Lao Tzu
   h. Ashoka   q. Shih Huang-ti
   i. Yellow River   r. Wu-ti

3. What signs have archaeologists found indicating that life in India was highly civilized as early as 2500 B.C.?

4. (a) How did Hinduism develop in India? (b) How is Hinduism related to Indian society?

5. (a) How did Buddhism develop in India? (b) What are the main teachings of Buddhism?

6. (a) What important part did Chandragupta Maurya play in India's history? (b) How did Ashoka affect life in India and in countries beyond India?

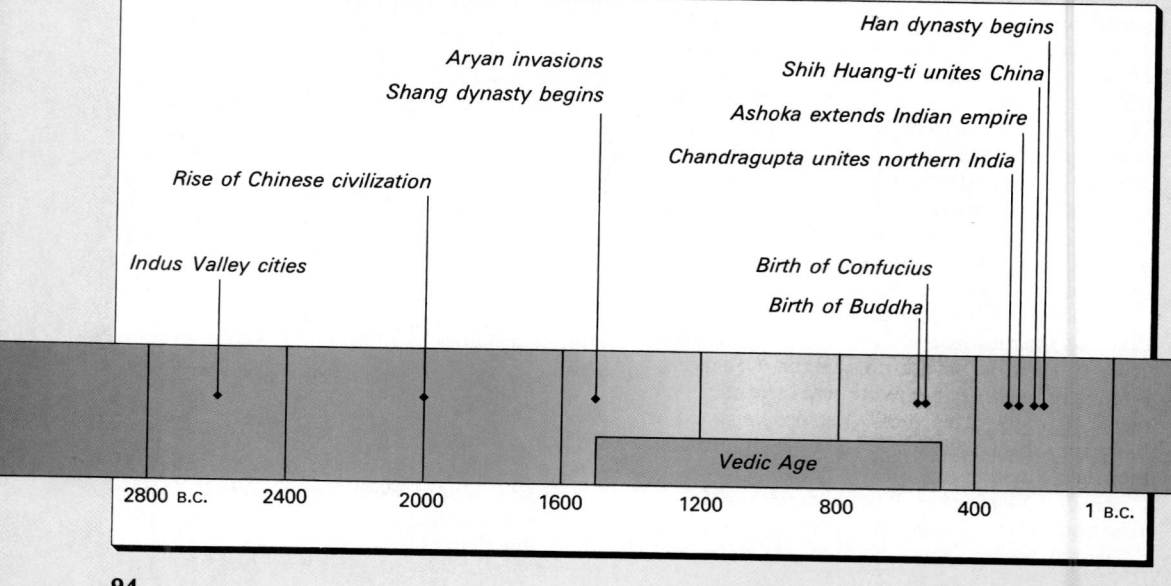

Aryan invasions
Shang dynasty begins
Rise of Chinese civilization
Indus Valley cities

Han dynasty begins
Shih Huang-ti unites China
Ashoka extends Indian empire
Chandragupta unites northern India
Birth of Confucius
Birth of Buddha

Vedic Age

2800 B.C.   2400   2000   1600   1200   800   400   1 B.C.

94

Answers to Chapter Review appear on pages 72e–72f.

7. What were the keys to unity in earliest Chinese society?
8. Describe three different philosophies that emerged in China during the troubled years of the Chou dynasty.
9. How did Shih Huang-ti restore order to China?
10. (a) Why are the early years of the Han dynasty considered a golden era in the history of China? (b) What religious change took place in China during the later years of the Han dynasty?

Basic Skills

1. **Comparing maps** (a) Compare the maps of China on pages 83 and 92. What kind of information is included on each map? (b) How may certain features of the first map have influenced the patterns of settlement and conquest shown on the second map?
2. **Charting information** Make a chart comparing ancient India and China. For the vertical rows, use the headings *Geographic Features, Social Patterns, Major Achievements,* and *Philosophies of Life.* Complete the chart by writing several phrases in each space.
3. **Comparing time lines** According to the time lines on pages 50 and 94 and information in the chapter, in what age—Neolithic, bronze, or iron—did cities begin to appear in China?
4. **Reading and interpreting a map** (a) Imagine that you are a citizen of Harappa in 2000 B.C. (a) According to the map on page 74, about how many miles would you travel if you journeyed by river from Harappa to the Arabian Sea? (b) What advantages does the location of your city have for the growth of a civilization? (c) By what routes did the Aryan invaders enter India? (d) As they traveled to the southeast, through what types of land would they be passing?

Researching and Reporting Skills

1. **Using an index** What happened to Buddhism in India and to Confucianism in China after A.D. 100? Find that information by using the Index at the back of this text.
2. **Using the *Readers' Guide*** (a) In the latest *Readers' Guide to Periodical Literature,* find an article about recent archaelogical discoveries in China. (b) After

reading the article, write three paragraphs summarizing the information.
3. **Distinguishing between primary and secondary sources** Rearrange the following book titles under the headings *Primary Sources* (written *by* people of the past) and *Secondary Sources* (written *about* people of the past):
   (a) *India: A Short Cultural History*
   (b) *The Analects of Confucius*
   (c) *Introduction to India*
   (d) *Poems of Ancient China: A Collection*
   (e) *Plays of Kalidasa*

Critical Thinking

1. **Comparing** Compare the social classes of ancient China with the caste system in India. (a) What were the underlying principles of each? (b) What were the consequences for the individual?
2. **Identifying viewpoints** Give the viewpoint of each of the following people concerning the topic noted: (a) Gautama toward human desires and passions, (b) Confucius toward traditional family values, (c) Ashoka toward the treatment of his subjects.
3. **Applying a concept** According to an Indian writer of Mauryan times, "Government is the science of punishment." (a) Which rulers and philosophers in both India and China would have agreed with him? (b) Which would have disagreed?
4. **Analyzing** What was the influence of the Vedas on India's civilization and the sayings of Confucius on China's civilization?

Perspectives on Past and Present

1. In what countries are Hinduism, Buddhism, and Confucianism important religions today? On an outline map of Asia, show these areas in color.
2. Religious and philosophical ideas had great influence on political life in ancient China. To what extent do they have an influence on politics today?

Investigating History

1. Writing was not only a form of communication in China but also an important art form. Look up in the library several books on Chinese calligraphy.
2. Why did Shih Huang-ti have an entire army of clay soldiers created for his tomb? An excellent article on this subject appears in the November 1979 issue of *Smithsonian.* Read the article and report on it in class.

95

CHAPTER
Evaluation

Chapter Test 4, Alternate Chapter Test 4, and Computer Test Bank Chapter 4 Test can be used to evaluate your students' understanding of this chapter.

ANSWERS TO
Geographic Theme

1. Memphis: on Nile near start of Delta; Thebes: on Nile in central Egypt; Babylon: on Euphrates River in central Mesopotamia; Uruk: on Euphrates in southern Mesopotamia; Çatal Hüyük: at northern edge of Taurus Mountains in Anatolia; Jericho: on oasis west of Jordan River and on north-south trade route; Jarmo: in foothills of Zagros Mountains east of Tigris River; Jerusalem: north and west of Dead Sea.

2. a good supply of water, a protected site, valuable resources nearby

3. Ninevah, capital of Assyria; Memphis, early capital of Egypt; Thebes, later capital of Egypt

Unit I Review

Geographic Theme: Location

Where did ancient cities develop?

The growth of ancient cities reflected the rise of civilization. At first a few cities, then many, showed that a new age had begun.

Geographers describe the location of cities in two ways. *Site* refers to the physical setting of a city. It may be on hills, as with Rome, or on an island, as with Paris and New York. *Situation* refers to a city's location in relation to other features. Is it on a river or harbor? Where a trade route crosses a river? Near mineral deposits or a source of water in the desert? Together, the site and situation of a city tell much about why it has developed and grown.

For ancient cities, the major concerns for *site* were safety and defense. Was the place safe from floods and other natural dangers? Did landforms there provide protection, perhaps through limited access to high places? Was this a favorable place for living?

Situation involved many concerns. Lacking the means for transportation, cities of ancient times were highly dependent upon their immediate environment.

Access to pure water and to food—whether hunted, raised, or harvested—was a basic requirement. If farming was to be the source of food, good soil was essential. Whatever its source, food had to be plentiful enough to support the population. Access to materials for clothing and shelter was another basic need. Although not essential to life, having materials such as obsidian for tools and precious stones for ornaments was an advantage, since these provided a basis for trade. From trade, cities obtained what they lacked. Trade also helped cities to grow.

1. Give a possible reason for the location of each city shown on the map below.
2. Until recently, archaeologists thought that early cities grew on rivers. Yet Çatal Huyuk, one of the earliest cities, rose in the highlands north of Mesopotamia. Give three possible reasons to account for its location there.
3. Using Unit I as a reference, find a reason other than site and situation for the location of one city shown below.

Cities of the Ancient Middle East

Historical Themes

Mesopotamia, Egypt, India, and China provide important examples of how human-environment interaction, key ideas, and economic developments shaped the development of civilization.

Human-Environment Interaction

Geography played a critical role in shaping the character of the first civilizations. The Nile River provided Egypt with fertile land and a reliable system of transportation. In addition, the surrounding deserts shielded Egypt from attack. As a result, Egypt developed a stable civilization that endured for centuries. By contrast, Mesopotamia had only limited resources and lacked natural barriers for protection. The Sumerians responded to these geographic challenges by developing trade and building fortified cities.

Geography also had a significant impact on civilizations in India and China. Warlike peoples invaded India by way of the Khyber Pass through the Hindu Kush. While agriculture in Mesopotamia and Egypt depended on annual floods, Indian farmers looked to the monsoon rains for moisture. Unlike India, China was isolated from the outside world. The Chinese viewed their country as a "Middle Kingdom" surrounded by barbarians.

Impact of Ideas

The first civilizations produced religious ideas that had a profound impact on world history. The Jews introduced the idea that there is one true God who created the universe and all living things. Jewish prophets warned that God demanded moral conduct and punished wrong behavior.

Like the prophets, Hindu religious leaders taught that all human conduct leads to ethical consequences. They emphasized an ethical law called karma, by which moral behavior in one life assures rebirth in a higher caste. Buddha accepted the idea of karma and also taught that anyone could attain nirvana—a release from the pain of rebirth—by following an Eightfold Path emphasizing nonviolence.

Unlike Hindus and Buddhists, Confucius focused on social order. He believed that all human

relationships should be governed by codes of proper conduct. For example, he taught that children should practice filial piety, or respect for their parents and elders.

Economics and History

When people lived as hunters and gatherers, they sought mainly to provide food, shelter, and clothing—the basic means for survival. The rise of farming and herding led to new ways of living. Food surpluses gave people more time for crafts, such as making pottery and tools. Surplus food and craft items led to trade as people exchanged surplus goods for scarce ones. Trade in turn led to the exchange of ideas.

As harvests and the production of goods increased, trade became more complex. Specialized labor developed, allowing some people to devote all their time to producing goods. The amount of trade was great enough to ensure that even large city populations would have enough food.

The first civilizations—those of Sumer, Egypt, India, and China—grew up near rivers. The rivers served as avenues of trade with surrounding regions and, in time, with distant lands. Civilizations were also linked by trade routes over land. Along with their goods, merchants and traders carried ideas. Buddhism entered China over the Great Silk Road, and the Phoenician alphabet spread literacy around the Mediterranean.

Analyzing Historical Themes

1. How did environment influence the development of early civilizations?
2. Compare and contrast the key ethical ideas of the Jews, Hindus, and folllowers of Confucius.
3. (a) What conditions were essential for trade to develop? (b) How did trade spread ideas?

97

ANSWERS TO
Analyzing Historical Themes

1. Geography determined whether civilizations were well protected, isolated, or vulnerable to attack; presence or absence of resources influenced growth of agriculture and trade.
2. Jews and Hindus focused on moral conduct, judged by one creator God (Jews) or by ethical law of karma (Hindus); Confucians focused on social order and proper conduct in relationships.
3. (a) surplus food, production of crafts (b) Merchants and traders carried ideas to other regions.

UNIT
Evaluation

Unit I Test and Alternate Unit I Test can be used to evaluate your students' understanding of this unit.

Fresco, Villa of Mysteries, Pompeii

850 B.C.	650 B.C.	450 B.C.

Political and Governmental Life

1100–700 B.C.
Phoenicians colonize
Mediterranean islands
▼

594 B.C.
Solon reforms Athenian
government

509 B.C.
Rome establishes a republic

336–323 B.C.
Alexander of
Macedon
builds empire

Economic and Technological Life

Greek phalanx

750–600 B.C.
Greek trading colonies
develop in Italy

264 B.C.
Punic Wars
begin

Social and Cultural Life

800's B.C.
Homer composes
Iliad and *Odyssey* ▶

477–432 B.C.
Parthenon built
in Athens

380 B.C.
Aristotle studies
with Plato

461–429 B.C.
Pericles leads Athens in Golden Age

Unit II
The Mediterranean World

Historical Themes

The Rise of Democratic Ideas Ancient Athens produced the idea of a democracy, with citizens taking part in governing. Rome formed a republic with legislative and executive branches and a code of laws.

Cultural Development The ancient Greek focus on ideas, spread by Alexander, inspired later civilizations. Rome's legacy of law and government influenced nations and empires that followed.

Individuals and History Different types of leaders arose in the Mediterranean world. Pericles and Augustus were great statesmen, while Alexander and Caesar used force to gain power. Socrates and Jesus used questions and parables to teach values.

250 B.C.	50 B.C.	A.D. 150

218 B.C.
Hannibal invades Italy in Second Punic War

59 B.C.
Caesar becomes consul

27 B.C.
Augustus becomes emperor of Rome

Fasces, symbol of Roman authority

27 B.C.–A.D. 180
Pax Romana prevails; Rome builds roads and aqueducts

A.D. 376–476
Barbarians overrun Roman empire

30 B.C.
Virgil writes *Aeneid*

A.D. 312
Roman Emperor Constantine becomes Christian

Hellenistic art: Nike of Samothrace

A.D. 79
Destruction of Pompeii

99

The World about 200 B.C.

KEY

- China under the Han dynasty
- Mauryan empire under Ashoka
- Roman republic
- Hopewell farming villages
- Olmec farming villages
- Kingdom of Kush
- • City

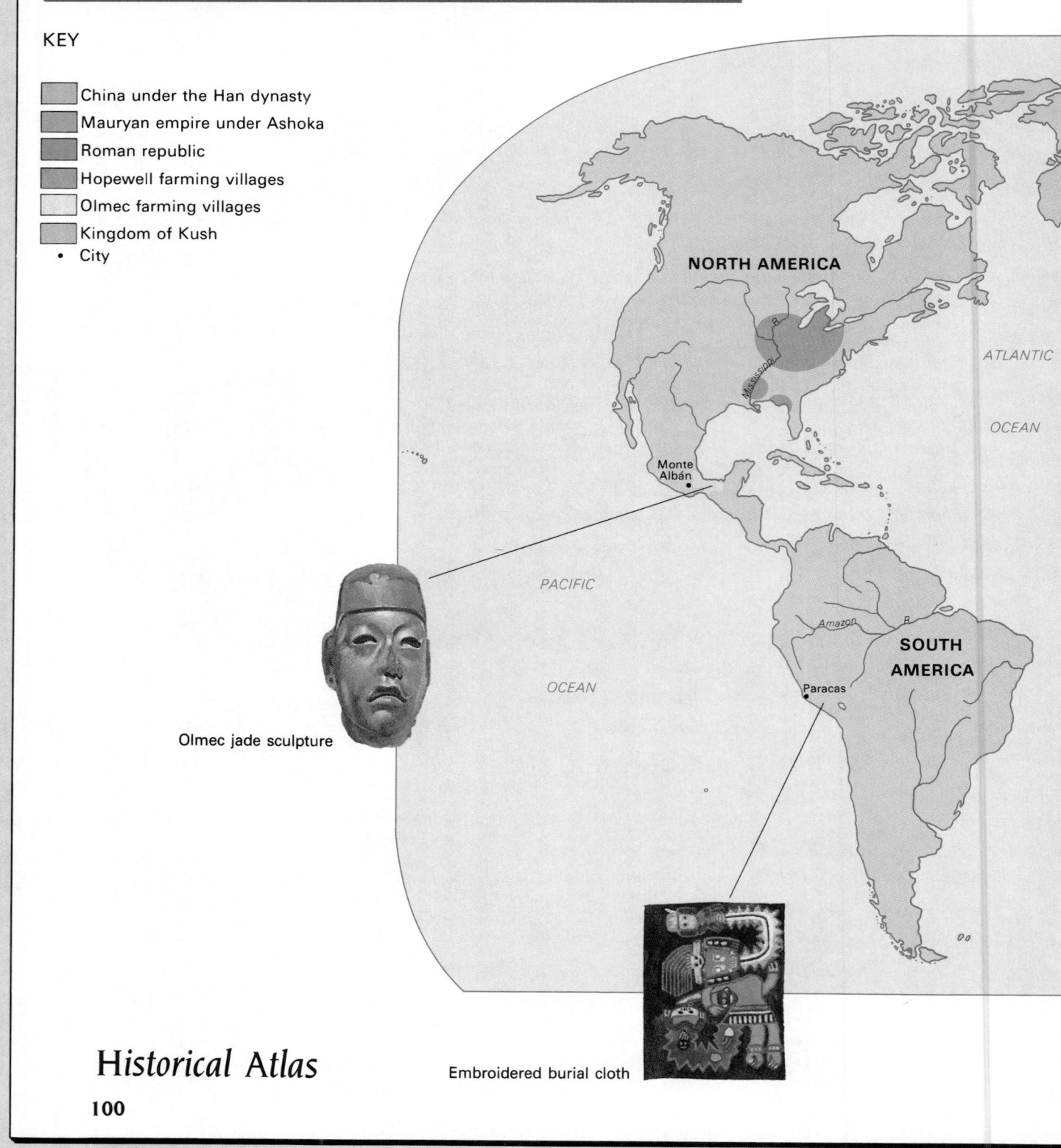

NORTH AMERICA

ATLANTIC

OCEAN

Monte
Albán

PACIFIC

Amazon

SOUTH
AMERICA

OCEAN

Paracas

Olmec jade sculpture

Embroidered burial cloth

Historical Atlas

100

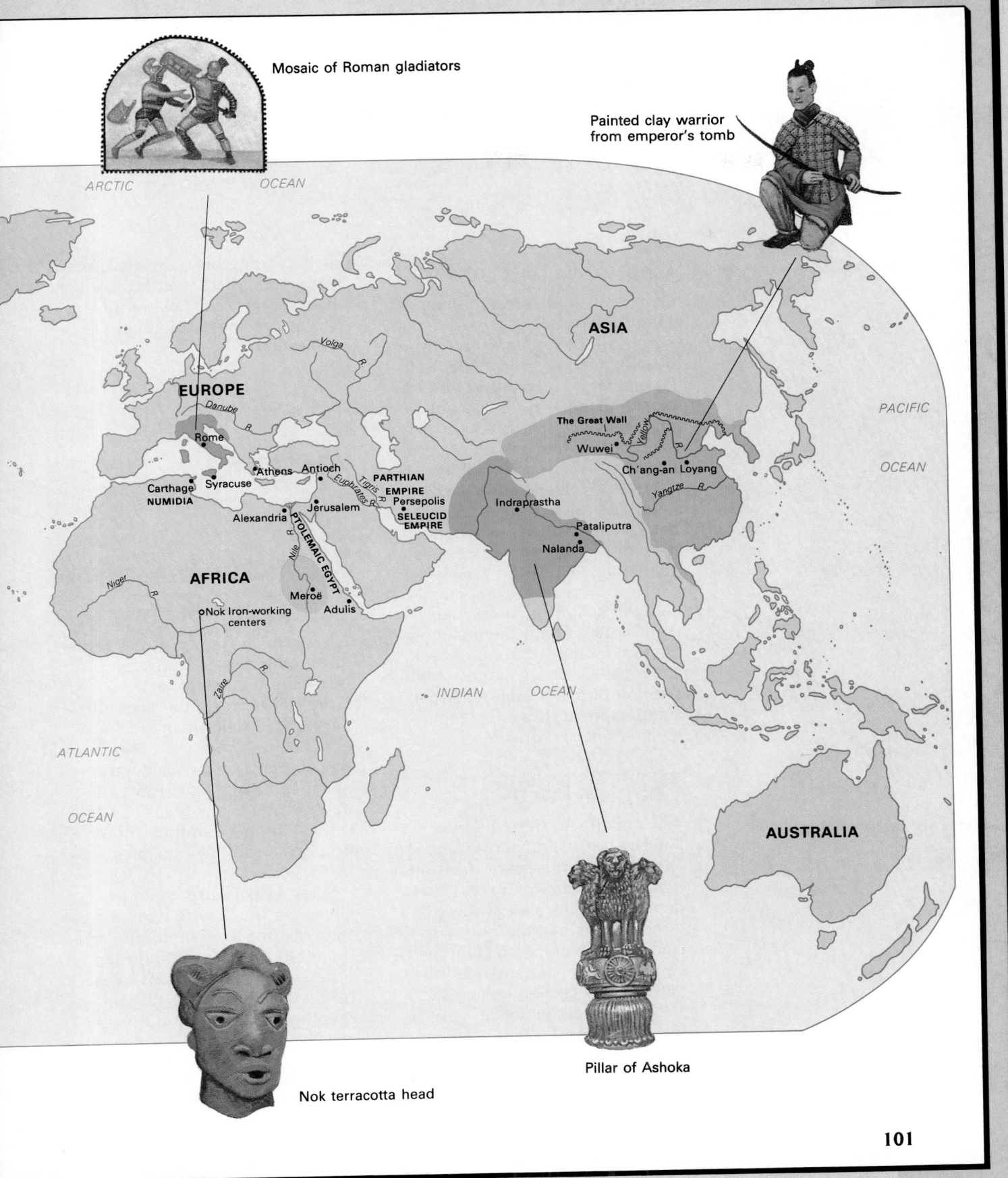

Mosaic of Roman gladiators

Painted clay warrior from emperor's tomb

ARCTIC OCEAN

ASIA

Volga R.

EUROPE

PACIFIC OCEAN

Danube R.

Rome

The Great Wall

Yellow R.

Wuwei

Ch'ang-an Loyang

Athens Antioch

Carthage Syracuse

NUMIDIA

PARTHIAN EMPIRE

Persepolis

SELEUCID EMPIRE

Tigris R.

Euphrates R.

Yangtze R.

Alexandria Jerusalem

Indraprastha

PTOLEMAIC EGYPT

Pataliputra

Nile R.

AFRICA

Nalanda

Niger R.

Meroë

oNok Iron-working centers

Adulis

Zaire R.

INDIAN OCEAN

ATLANTIC OCEAN

AUSTRALIA

Nok terracotta head

Pillar of Ashoka

101

Ancient Greece

Chapter Overview

Geography and climate influenced the development of Greek society. Mountainous terrain promoted the development of independent city-states that cooperated in times of outside danger but could not work together once the threat of war had ended. After the defeat of the Persians, Athens assumed leadership of a group of city-states known as the Delian League. Under Pericles, Athens experienced a flowering of the arts—Greece's golden age. However, rivalry between Athens and Sparta culminated in a war that weakened them both and left them vulnerable to conquest. Through Alexander the Great's conquest and creation of a vast empire, Greek culture spread throughout the Mediterranean world.

Chapter Focus

Ask students to describe how Ramses II, Chandragupta, and Shih Huang-ti reached major decisions that affected their empires. Students should recall that these three leaders had the power to decide on all matters affecting their empires. After students read the introductory section (pages 102–103), lead a discussion to answer these questions: What problem did the citizens of Athens face? What process did they use to solve this problem? How was this process different from the way decisions were reached in ancient Egypt, India, and China? In Greece, civic decisions were made through open debate. No other ancient society had such a keen awareness of individual worth or such a strong belief in what free people could achieve. Explain that this chapter examines the origins and achievements of Greek civilization.

Greek culture grew up around the Aegean Sea. 1

Setting the Stage

Geography in History: Greek Settlement (Objective 1) Duplicate and distribute Outline Map 18: Greece. Have students use the map on page 104 to help them label Athens, Sparta, Crete, Asia Minor, and the Aegean, Ionian, Mediterranean, and Black seas. Have students shade in the areas of Greek settlement in Asia Minor, make a key, and write titles for their maps.

Show Map Transparency 14, *Greece in the Bronze Age*, and ask students first to examine the area settled by the Greeks and then to compare it with the maps of the Fertile Crescent (page 32), Ancient Egypt (page 55), the Indus valley (page 74), and Ancient China (page 83). Ask, "How did the areas settled by the Greeks differ from these four regions?" Students should note that Greece was divided by mountains, lacked a major river valley, and included a long coastline with many inlets and bays. Explain that this combination of physical features had an important influence on Greek character and history.

Unit II The Mediterranean World
THEME The rise of the classical civilizations of Greece and Rome

Chapter 5 Ancient Greece 2000 B.C.–323 B.C.
FOCUS Decision making in Athens

★ Advanced
● Basic

	SECTION 1	SECTION 2	SECTION 3	SECTION 4
Objectives	1. Map areas of Greek settlement. 2. Describe the geography of Greece and explain its effects on the development of Greek civilization. 3. Discuss aspects of early Greek culture.	1. Describe a phalanx and its effect on the power of ordinary citizen-soldiers. 2. Compare and contrast Athens and Sparta. 3. Identify reasons the Greeks were able to defeat the Persians.	1. Describe Athenian achievements during the golden age. 2. Discuss the causes and consequences of the Peloponnesian War. 3. Recall the contributions of Socrates, Plato, and Aristotle.	1. Explain how Philip of Macedon gained control over Greece. 2. Describe and evaluate the achievements of Alexander the Great. 3. Explain how Greek culture spread during the Hellenistic Age.
Setting the Stage	Unit II time line Geography in History: Greek Settlement Transparency 14 Outline Map 18	Characteristics of Greek city-states Transparency 15	The golden age of Athens	The goals of Alexander the Great
Teaching Strategies	Skill Building: Identifying Cause and Effect Relationships Teaching with Pictures: The Olympic Games Check for Understanding	Teaching with Pictures: The Phalanx Discussing History: Sparta and Athens Analyzing a Quotation: Herodotus Explains the Athenian Victory Transparency 16 Check for Understanding	Teaching with Pictures: The Parthenon Discussing History: Causes and Effects of the Peloponnesian War Analyzing Quotations: Wisdom of the Greek Philosophers Check for Understanding	Discussing History: Philip of Macedon Discussing History: What Made Alexander "Great"? Transparency 17 Using Geographic Themes: Movement Check for Understanding
Guided Practice	Transparency 14 Q&A Section Review 1	Transparency 15 Q&A Transparency 16 Q&A Section Review 2	Section Review 3	Transparency 17 Q&A Section Review 4
Independent Practice Worksheets	Independent Practice 5.1 Vocabulary 5	Independent Practice 5.2 Geography Skills 5 Basic Skills 5	Independent Practice 5.3 Critical Thinking 5	Independent Practice 5.4
Enrichment	1. Primary Source: Voices 5.1 2. Creative Writing 3. ★Preparing a Book Report 4. Researching for Points	1. Primary Source: Voices 5.2 2. Preparing a Report: Sparta 3. Researching for Points	1. Primary Source: Voices 5.3 2. Creative Writing 3. ★The Trial of Socrates 4. Researching for Points	1. Primary Source: Voices 5.4 2. ★Solving a Puzzle 3. Preparing a Report: A Macedonian Tomb 4. Researching for Points

Chapter Closer	
●Reteaching Activities	Identifying Important Ideas, Writing Questions and Answers, Summarizing, Recalling Main Ideas
Chapter Review	Summary, Reviewing the Facts, Basic Skills, Researching and Reporting Skills, Critical Thinking, Perspectives on Past and Present, Investigating History
Chapter Evaluation	Chapter Test 5, Alternate Chapter Test 5, Computer Test Bank Chapter 5 Test

Teaching Strategies

Skill Building: Identifying Cause and Effect Relationships (Objective 2) Have students complete each statement below by writing an effect:

1. The Greek islands formed handy stepping-stones that encouraged the Greeks (to become sailors and trade with other lands).

2. Because the mountains made it difficult for the Greeks to unite their country under one government (the Greeks lived in a collection of independent communities).

3. Because of the absence of a large river valley, the Greeks (had no need for large-scale irrigation controlled by powerful priests and kings).

Teaching with Pictures: The Olympic Games (Objective 3) One important aspect of early Greek culture was the Olympic Games, held in honor of Zeus. As many as 45,000 spectators—all male—attended the five-day festival held at Olympia. The pictures on page 107 show two of the contests. The discus thrower is hurling a flat, circular bronze plate weighing about twelve pounds. The best throws are reported to have reached 100 feet. The chariot races began with a loud trumpet blast. As many as 40 chariots skidded and collided in bone-breaking accidents as they fought for position in a nine-mile race.

Check for Understanding Ask students to explain the role that geography, Homer's epic poems, and religion played in shaping Greek civilization.

Enrichment Activities

1. **Reading a Primary Source**
Assign Voices from the Past Resource Book 5.1.

2. **Creative Writing**
Ask students to pretend that they are reporters assigned to cover the ancient Olympic Games. Have each student write an imaginative report describing events at the games.

3. **Preparing a Book Report**
Ask advanced students to read and report on *In Search of the Trojan War* by Michael Wood.

4. **Researching for Bonus Points**
Who was Helen's Greek husband? (Menelaus) What two phrases were carved into the temple at Delphi? ("Know Thyself" and "Nothing Too Much")

Greek city-states competed for power. 2

Setting the Stage

The introductory section (page 108) provides a discussion of the characteristics of Greek city-states. Explain that the period after the Dark Ages was marked by the rise and development of the two most powerful city-states—Sparta and Athens. Use Map Transparency 15, *Greece and Its Colonies*, to show the rise of other Greek city-states around the Mediterranean.

Teaching Strategies

Teaching with Pictures: The Phalanx (Objective 1) Direct students' attention to the painting of the phalanx

(page 109). The phalanx was a disciplined body of heavily armed foot-soldiers arranged in formations 8 to 16 men deep and up to 200 men wide. The citizen-soldiers, or hoplites, wore bronze helmets, breastplates, and leg protectors called greaves. They carried spears 8 to 10 feet long. As shown in the picture, the spears formed hedges that broke up flights of enemy arrows. The phalanx increased the power of its citizen-soldiers while reducing the need for an aristocratic cavalry.

Discussing History: Sparta and Athens (Objective 2) Sparta was originally a center of Greek culture. It responded to the problem of overpopulation by conquering and annexing Messinia. As a result, Sparta controlled 3,200 square miles of territory where rebellious helots outnumbered the Spartans eight to one. To maintain control, the Spartans adopted a severe code of laws. Discuss the advantages and disadvantages of Spartan life.

After students read "Athens turned to democracy" (pages 111–112), have them identify the internal problem that confronted Athens during the sixth century. (a power struggle between rich and poor) Review how the reforms of Solon and Cleisthenes solved this problem while also creating a democratic government.

Analyzing a Quotation: Herodotus Explains the Athenian Victory (Objective 3) Review the story of how the Athenians repelled the Persian invasion. Use Map Transparency 16, *Greece in the Persian Wars*, to show the areas involved in the conflicts. Ask students to explain how the Greeks defeated this vast empire and then to evaluate this explanation by Herodotus.

Thus Athens . . . proved . . . how noble a thing freedom is, not in one respect only but in all: for while they were oppressed under a despotic government, they had no better success in war than any of their neighbors, yet, once the yoke was flung off, they proved the finest fighters in the world. This clearly shows that, so long as they were held down by authority, they deliberately shirked their duty in the field, as slaves shirk working for their masters: but when freedom was won, then every man amongst them longed to distinguish himself.

Check for Understanding Ask students to identify the importance of each of these: phalanx, Lycurgus, Solon, battle of Marathon, and Xerxes.

Enrichment Activities

1. **Reading a Primary Source**
   Assign Voices from the Past Resource Book 5.2.

2. **Preparing a Report**
   Ask students to report on what Sparta is like today.

3. **Researching for Bonus Points**
   How was the distance of a modern marathon determined? (Fixed at 26 miles, 385 yards during 1924 London Olympics. Length is distance from Windsor Castle to Royal Box in Olympic Stadium.)

Athens led Greece in its golden age. 3

Setting the Stage

Ask the class what the phrase "golden age" means and what types of achievements would characterize such an age. Then explain that during the fifth century B.C., Athens experienced the first and perhaps the most famous golden age in world history.

Teaching Strategies

Teaching with Pictures: The Parthenon (Objective 1) After students have read "Art flourished in Athens" (pages 115–116), direct their attention to the artistic re-creation of the Parthenon (page 116).

Constructing the Parthenon kept a small army of workers busy for 15 years. First, the marble was cut in huge blocks from quarries and dragged ten miles to the foot of the Acropolis. Then it was hoisted along the sloping side of the great hill. Some 22,000 tons of marble were chiseled with such precision that no mortar was needed to hold the stones together.

Discussing History: Causes and Effects of the Peloponnesian War (Objective 2) First review the section "Sparta defeated Athens in war" (pages 119–120). Then explain that when the Athenians surrendered, many of their enemies urged the Spartans to burn the city. Although the Spartans did tear down the Long Walls, they ordered that Athens be allowed to stand. Ask students to suggest the main cause of the Peloponnesian War and its effects on the Athenians.

Analyzing Quotations: Wisdom of the Greek Philosophers (Objective 3) Have students review "Philosophers searched for truth" (pages 120–122). Divide the class into three groups. Have each group analyze one quotation below and

report on the philosopher's contributions.

■ There is only one good, knowledge, and one evil, ignorance. (Socrates)

■ The life which is unexamined is not worth living. (Plato)

■ We make war that we may live in peace. (Aristotle)

Check for Understanding Have students identify the contributions of Pericles, Phidias, and Aeschylus to the golden age.

Enrichment Activities

1. **Reading a Primary Source**
   Assign Voices from the Past Resource Book 5.3.

2. **Creative Writing**
   Tell students to imagine that they have just spent a day in ancient Athens during the golden age. Ask them to write a diary entry about that day.

3. **The Trial of Socrates**
   Explain that a tragedy in Greek drama (page 117) had three elements. Ask advanced students to research the concepts of *ate* (blindness), *hubris* (false pride), and *nemesis* (punishment) and to apply them to Socrates. Was Socrates a Greek tragic hero? Why or why not?

4. **Researching for Bonus Points**
   What gift did the Athenians present to Athena at the Panathenaic festival? (A new robe, or peplos, woven by the women of the city, represented the battle of the gods and giants.)

Alexander's conquests spread Greek culture. 4

Setting the Stage

This section examines the ambitious goals of a Macedonian ruler known as Alexander the Great. As a youth, Alexander dreamed of performing a "great and brilliant deed to show the world." The deed he had in mind was to conquer and then unite the known world.

Teaching Strategies

Discussing History: Philip of Macedon (Objective 1) After students have read "Philip built Macedon's power" (pages 122–123), ask them to explain why Philip was able to conquer Greek city-states, which Persian emperors had failed to do.

Discussing History: What Made Alexander "Great"? (Objective 2) Show students Map Transparency 17, *The Empire of Alexander the Great*, and review the text's discussion of Alexander's conquests. Point out that Alexander was called "The Great" because of his impressive victories. Ask students to suggest criteria for evaluating the greatness of a leader. What qualities other than military success might be considered? Recall the long-term effects of Alexander's conquests, and suggest that greatness is often attributed to individuals whose actions have had lasting impact. Ask students in what ways Alexander's brief rule was a turning point.

Using Geographic Themes: Movement (Objective 3) The diffusion of Hellenistic culture illustrates the theme of movement. Ask students to list the various means by which Greek culture spread eastward.

Check for Understanding Have students describe the achievements of Philip of Macedon, Alexander the Great, and Archimedes.

Enrichment Activities

1. **Reading a Primary Source**
   Assign Voices from the Past Resource Book 5.4.

2. **Solving a Puzzle**
   Philip's death remains an unsolved puzzle. Ask advanced students to write a research report that attempts to explain who killed Philip and why.

3. **Preparing a Report**
   In 1977, archaeologists unearthed a spectacular Macedonian tomb in Vergina, Greece. Ask students to prepare a report on what archaeologists found and why they believe they located Philip's royal tomb. (One source is *National Geographic*, July 1978.)

4. **Researching for Bonus Points**
   What was the name of Alexander's famed horse? (Bucephalus)

ANSWERS TO
Chapter Review 5

Reviewing the Facts

1. **(a)** long, heroic poem
(b) heroic idea of excellence
(c) city-state **(d)** form of government run by noble families
(e) foot soldier **(f)** formation of foot soldiers forming solid wall of fighters **(g)** ruler who came to power through rebellion and usually stood for rights of small farmers and artisans **(h)** form of government in which citizens took part **(i)** type of drama involving men and women whose strong character led to their downfall **(j)** method of teaching by asking questions

2. **(a)** island near Greece where the Minoan civilization developed during the Bronze Age **(b)** leading city on mainland Greece; where Mycenaean civilization developed in the Bronze Age **(c)** last of the Bronze Age Greeks' triumphs before the Mycenaean civilization collapsed **(d)** poet who glorified the old heroes of Mycenae and Troy in the *Iliad* and the *Odyssey* **(e)** city-state that created a democracy through reforms and became cultural center of ancient Greece **(f)** city-state with the most powerful army in Greece **(g)** Athenian reformer who prevented civil war in Athens with his economic and political reforms **(h)** Athenian leader who introduced a series of laws that made Athens a full democracy **(i)** wrote *History of the Persian Wars* and was justly called the first true historian **(j)** year Athenians defeated the Persians on Marathon plain, preventing the destruction of Athens **(k)** 27-year war between Athens and Sparta that ruined Athens and weakened all of Greece **(l)** Athenian ruler who strengthened Athenian democracy, enlarged wealth and power of Athens, and made Athens the cultural center of Greece **(m)** the 27 years of war with Sparta, during which Athens lost its fleet, its empire, its power, and its wealth **(n)** writer of classic tragedy who helped invent drama **(o)** author of about 100 plays, including *Oedipus Rex* **(p)** Greek philosopher who taught that people must examine their ideas by standards of truth and reason **(q)** philosopher who wrote *The Republic*, which explained his idea of a perfectly gov-

erned society (r) philosopher who developed a set of logical statements known as a syllogism, which was important for developing rational and scientific thought (s) Macedonian king who united Greece under his leadership (t) king of Macedon who helped spread a common culture, Hellenism, throughout the many lands he conquered (u) year when Alexander died and his empire broke apart into three sections—Egypt, Asia Minor and the Fertile Crescent, and Macedon

3. Major changes include:
- 1200 B.C.—Bronze Age dominated by warrior kings.
- 750–110 B.C.—kings lost power; rise of aristocracy.
- Citizen-soldiers revolted against the nobles; tyrants came to power.
- 750 B.C.—city-states, such as Sparta and Athens, developed.
- 600–371 B.C.—Sparta built military state.
- 594 B.C.—Athens adopted political and economic reforms to create a democratic government.

4. excellence, courage, fame, and honor

5. Solon's contributions: reformed Athenian laws so that every male citizen participated in political debate and decision making; began legal system in which any citizen could bring charges against anyone who had committed a wrong. Cleisthenes' contributions: increased power of the Athenian assembly and created the Council of Five Hundred to propose laws and advise the assembly.

6. The arts of drama, sculpture, poetry, philosophy, architecture, and science reached new heights.

7. Philip used a combination of war, diplomacy, bribery, and trickery to defeat the Greek city-states one by one.

8. Everywhere Alexander conquered he established governments run by Greek administrators and had public buildings fashioned in the Greek style.

Basic Skills

1. Greek culture grew up around the Aegean Sea: the map shows Greek settlements clustered on the coastlines around the Aegean Sea.

2. *Title*: Greece in the Bronze Age; Greece and Its Colonies. *Historical period*: Bronze Age: 750–550 B.C. *Region included*: Greece and lands bordering the Aegean Sea; Europe, Asia Minor, North Africa. *Scale*: about 100 miles to an inch; about 400 miles to an inch.

3. Siege of Troy, Dark Ages, Solon's reforms, Persian Wars, Age of Pericles, death of Socrates, Alexander's conquests, Hellenistic Age

4. Greek philosophers
   A. Socrates
      1. questioned all accepted values.
      2. was condemned for his thinking.
   B. Plato
      1. founded a school.
      2. wrote *The Republic*.
   C. Aristotle
      1. studied with Plato.
      2. developed a system of logic.

Researching and Reporting Skills
Students' findings will vary.

Critical Thinking

1. For Sparta, students should mention the army, self-discipline, idealism, and endurance; for Athens, democratic principles, powerful fleet, and achievements in the arts, philosophy, and science. Reasons should support the opinions given.

2. (a) Both had the same democratic ideas of equal opportunity and justice for all citizens. Athenians gave more importance to the political responsibility of individuals. (b) In Athens, any citizen could speak to the assembly. In the United States, citizens speak through representatives. Athenian "citizens" comprised only one-fifth of the population. In the United States, citizenship and participation in the democratic process are open to all. (c) Answers will vary. The United States does not limit citizenship and participation. The "direct democracy" of the Athenians, however, permitted "one citizen, one vote," which is more strictly democratic than the electoral college system.

3. In Chinese society, the group was more important than the individual, and obedience to authority was more important than self-expression. The result was an authoritarian society with dynastic rule. In Greece, the rights of the individual were emphasized, resulting in a democratic society.

Perspectives on Past and Present

1. Pericles would say that nonvoters are not true citizens. Have students discuss reasons for the lack of citizen participation in government in the United States today.

2. Answers will vary. Refer students to "The First Olympics" in *Smithsonian*, June 1984.

Investigating History
Students' findings will vary.

Teaching with Pictures

Tell students that at the heart of each city-state (polis) was a hilly, fortified area called the acropolis. On each acropolis was a temple for the local god. On the acropolis in Athens, workers built the Parthenon, which housed the statue of Athena, the goddess of wisdom. Visitors to the Parthenon today see only a shell of its former grandeur. Athena's statue was carried away to Constantinople in about A.D. 400 and later disappeared. The Parthenons's roof was blown off in A.D. 1687 by a gunpowder explosion. Sculptural masterpieces tumbled to the ground. The best preserved figures were purchased and removed by the British Ambassador Lord Elgin. Known as the Elgin Marbles, they are on display in the British Museum in London.

Chapter

5

Ancient Greece

2000 B.C. - 323 B.C.

The acropolis of Athens is dominated by the ruins of the Parthenon at top right.

Key Terms

Western civilization
agora
epic
arete
myth
polis
citizen
acropolis
aristocracy
hoplite
phalanx
tyrant
helot
democracy

classical art
tragedy
comedy
philosopher
Socratic
*   method*
Hellenism

Read and Understand

1. Greek culture grew up around the Aegean Sea.
2. Greek city-states competed for power.
3. Athens led Greece in its golden age.
4. Alexander's conquests spread Greek culture.

On a June morning in 480 B.C., the male citizens of Athens hiked up a steep hill outside their city. Thousands—perhaps even 10,000—took their seats on rows of stone benches on the hillside. This was the day of decision for Athens. A colossal Persian army, rumored to number more than 2 million soldiers, was marching toward the city. At the same time, a fleet of 1,000 Persian ships was sailing along the coast of Greece.

In size, Athens was no match for the Persian empire. Athens was a Greek city-state of 250,000 people controlling a 117-square-mile plain. The Persian empire, on the other hand, stretched from the Indus River (in what is now Pakistan) to the shores of the Mediterranean and the Black seas. Should the people of Athens fight or run? The citizens on the hill had to decide.

102

Chapter 5
Resources

GEOGRAPHY
- Geography Skills 5
- Outline Map 18
- Transparencies 14, 15, 16, 17

REINFORCEMENT
- Vocabulary 5
- Basic Skills 5
- Reteaching 5
- Making Connections Study Guide 5

ENRICHMENT
- Critical Thinking 5
- History and Literature 5

ASSESSMENT
- Chapter Test 5
- Alternate Chapter Test 5
- Computer Test Bank

"Pray silence for Themistocles (thee-MIHS-toh-kleez), son of Neocles!" a voice shouted. From the speaker's platform, a stout, bullnecked man addressed the crowd. Themistocles argued that it would be foolish for Athenian soldiers to try to save their city from the Persians. If need be, let the Persians enter the city and burn it. Send the women, old men, and children to safety on a nearby island. Meanwhile, let all men of fighting age row out to meet the Persian fleet with the 200 new Athenian warships. Even though their ships might be outnumbered five to one, said Themistocles, this was the Greeks' only chance.

Naturally, there was strong opposition to this plan. Many Athenians could not bear the thought of allowing the Persians to destroy their city. In the end, though, Themistocles convinced a majority of the citizens to vote his way.

Almost three months later, Persian soldiers walked into a near-empty Athens and burned it to the ground. They destroyed the buildings of Athens, but they could not destroy its spirit. While their city lay in ruins, the Athenians won a complete victory at sea and forced the Persians to withdraw. (You will read the full story of this heroic encounter later in the chapter.) When the stunned Persians finally left Greece, the city of Athens rose from its ashes more glorious than ever before.

This story tells much about the Greek spirit. In Greece, unlike other societies you have studied, civic decisions were made through open debate. That was not the way in Egypt, where a pharaoh spoke with the authority of a god. Neither was it the way in China, where no peasant would dare to contradict the emperor. In Greece, people's freedom to express ideas and leaders' receptiveness to the will of the people did not come about by chance. That was the way the Greeks wanted to live.

In this chapter, you will see how the Greeks overcame a harsh environment to build a remarkable society. The history of ancient Greece is a story of individual thinkers, artists, writers, soldiers, and leaders who contributed to future civilizations. Although in time the Greeks were conquered, their culture spread to distant lands. Their ideas became part of **Western civilization,** the heritage of ideas that spread to Europe and America and remains a part of your culture.

Greek culture grew up around the Aegean Sea. 1

Geographic Setting

In ancient times, Greece was not a united country but a collection of lands and islands where Greek-speaking people lived. The mainland of the ancient Greeks was a rugged peninsula that jutted out into the part of the Mediterranean Sea known as the Aegean (ee-JEE-uhn) Sea. The rest of Greek territory consisted of lands on the coast of Asia Minor and hundreds of islands in the Aegean and Ionian (eye-OH-nee-uhn) seas.

Geography shaped Greek civilization.

Physically, Greece is a land of rough mountains, narrow valleys, and no navigable rivers. However, it has a long coastline with many inlets and bays. This combination of physical features had several effects on Greek character and history.

The sea The sea shaped Greek civilization just as rivers shaped the ancient civilizations of the Fertile Crescent, Egypt, India, and China. In one sense, the Greeks did not live *on* a land but *around* a sea. The Aegean Sea and the neighboring Ionian and Black seas united the Greek people. The "watery ways," as the Greek poet Homer called them, were the links between most parts of Greece.

Sea travel was also a link with other societies. Even in small ships and without compasses, Greek sailors could go from one island to another to reach the older, richer civilizations of Asia and Egypt. Sea travel and trade were important because Greece itself was poor in resources.

The land About three fourths of Greece is covered with mountains, the highest of which is Mount Olympus, the towering, snow-capped "home of the gods." These mountains divide Greece into a number of different regions. In ancient times, rugged terrain made transportation difficult. For example, the city-state of Sparta was only about 60 miles from Olympia, the site of the Olympic games. Yet it took Spartans nearly a week to travel that distance.

The mountains significantly influenced Greek political life. It was very difficult to unite the

103

SECTION 1 Objectives and Teaching Strategies

OBJECTIVE 1. Map areas of Greek settlement.

Teaching Strategy: *Geography in History: Greek Settlement* (page 102a)

OBJECTIVE 2. Describe the geography of Greece and explain its effects on the development of Greek civilization.

Teaching Strategy: *Skill Building: Identifying Cause and Effect Relationships* (page 102c)

OBJECTIVE 3. Discuss aspects of early Greek culture.

Teaching Strategy: *Teaching with Pictures: The Olympic Games* (page 102c)

■ DISCUSSION

Some authors have said that Greece's mild climate encouraged an open, democratic society. Did Egypt's mild climate have the same effect? (Students may be interested to know that the oldest continuous democracy is Iceland!)

SECTION 1 Resources

GEOGRAPHY
■ Transparency 14

REINFORCEMENT
■ Independent Practice 5.1

ENRICHMENT
■ Voices from the Past 5.1

ASSESSMENT
■ Section Quiz 5.1

ANSWERS TO
Focus on Geography

1. (a) Aegean Sea **(b)** about 250 miles

2. Sea travel linked the Greeks with each other and other societies and also promoted trade.

3. Greece is covered by rugged mountains, making it hard to unite the country under one government. Individual city-states arose.

4. Greece's mild climate allowed the Greeks to spend much time outdoors, at the marketplace, political meetings, theater, celebrations, and other events.

5. Living by the sea allowed a rich trade to be carried out.

Greece in the Bronze Age

KEY

☐ Areas of Greek settlement

0   100 Miles

Focus on Geography

Geographic Skills

1. (a) Around what sea did Greek civilization develop?
(b) How far is it from Mycenae to Troy?
2. How might nearness to the sea influence the development of Greece?
3. Describe the land surface of Greece and its effect on political development.

4. How might the climate of Greece affect people's ways of living?

Geographic Theme: Place

5. In spite of rough terrain and limited resources, what geographic factors might have contributed to the growth of rich cultures in Greece during the Bronze Age?

country under one government. Therefore, the Greeks were content to live in a collection of small independent communities. To most Greeks, home was their own valley and the mountains that enclosed it. Tiny but fertile valleys covered about one fourth of Greece. These valleys were watered by small streams, not large rivers suitable for large-scale irrigation and control.

Greece was never able to feed a large population. It is estimated that no more than 2 million people lived in ancient Greece at one time. Even this small population could not expect the land to support a life of luxury. Fruits and vegetables could grow in only a few places. Meat was rare because the country lacked grasslands to feed large herds of cattle or flocks of sheep. The three principal Greek crops were grains, grapes, and olives. As a result, the Greek diet was light and simple. For instance, a Greek soldier might march through the mountains all morning and fight a battle in the afternoon on a day's meal of a few olives and a small loaf of barley bread.

The climate Climate was the third important environmental influence on Greek civilization.

Greece has a Mediterranean climate. Temperatures are moderate, and rain falls only in winter. The Greek way of life, at least for men, was an outdoor life. Men spent almost all their leisure time at the **agora** (AG-uh-ruh), or marketplace, at the gymnasium, in political meetings, at the theater, and at civic and religious celebrations. All these public events took place outdoors.

The open gatherings, combined with the small settlements, meant that most people in a city-state knew one another. Citizens met often to discuss public issues and to exchange news. For the Greeks, taking an active part in civic life became both a duty and a virtue.

Rich cultures arose in the Bronze Age.

Across the southern end of the Aegean Sea lies the largest of the Greek islands, Crete. Here an elegant civilization flourished from about 2000 to 1400 B.C. Scholars call it Minoan (muh-NOH-uhn), after Minos, a legendary king of Crete.

Cretan civilization The Minoans were a seafaring people with great power in the Mediterranean world. They carried on a thriving trade with other Aegean lands. Safe on their island, they built beautiful palaces without fortified walls.

Life for the Minoans appears to have been very pleasant. Wall paintings in the king's palace-city at Knossos show a lively people with a zest for athletic contests, festivals, and stylish dress. Clad in ruffled gowns, women of the court wore delicate gold jewelry and styled their hair into long, graceful coils. They took part in activities ranging from dancing to strenuous sports. This evidence suggests that Minoan women enjoyed a level of social equality rarely found in the ancient world.

The many flowers, fish, and animals in Minoan paintings reveal that people delighted in the beauty of nature. Another remarkable aspect of Minoan life was its plumbing. At Knossos, pipes carried water for bathing, and even for a flush toilet.

The joys of Crete appear to have ended abruptly some time between 1400 and 1200 B.C. Historians do not know whether the cause was a natural disaster or human conquest. Did a nearby volcanic eruption, with an earthquake and tidal wave, destroy the Minoans' world? Were they overrun by invaders? Evidence shows that the Minoans attempted to rebuild but soon fell to invaders from mainland Greece.

Mainland Greece in the Bronze Age Around 2000 B.C., groups of Greek-speaking people moved into mainland Greece and began to settle there. They were part of the large wave of migrations that swept lands from India to the Fertile Crescent and beyond around that time. The mainland Greeks of the Bronze Age are often known as Mycenaeans (MY-suh-NEE-uhnz), from the name of their leading city, Mycenae (my-SEE-nee).

Mycenae was built to withstand almost any attack. It was located on a steep, rocky ridge and was surrounded by a protective wall up to 20 feet thick. From the citadel of Mycenae, a warrior-king ruled the surrounding villages and farms.

At the Minoan court, young men and women took part in the sport of dancing or leaping over bulls, as shown in this picture. Such rituals may have led to the legend that King Minos of Crete sacrificed young captives to the Minotaur, a monster that was half human and half bull.

105

■ **BACKGROUND**

Students may be interested in reading the myth of Jason and the minotaur.

■ **DISCUSSION**

Some scholars believe that the volcano that destroyed the island of Thera produced a giant tidal wave that destroyed Minoan shipping and harbors, putting an end to Minoan civilization. Can a single event destroy an entire civilization?

Cooperative Learning

In groups of three, have students do "investigative reports" on the mysterious disappearance of the Minoan civilization. One student can act as a researcher, another can write the script for an oral presentation, while the third student can act as a director, choosing the information to be presented and coordinating the report. Reports should include an overview of Minoan civilization and possible reasons for its disappearance. Then have each group present its report to the class.

Many countries have some sort of epic tradition—in France "The Song of Roland," in Spain "El Cid," in Sumer "Gilgamesh," in India the "Ramayana" and "Mahabharata." What is the importance of such epics to the people who preserve them?

■ BACKGROUND

In Greek mythology, Pelops was a powerful warrior who fought from a winged war chariot. Believing that they were Pelops' descendants, the royal family of Mycenae came to be known as the Pelopids. The name was also given to the peninsula on which Mycenae was located, the Peloponnesus.

Similar palace-forts dotted the southern part of Greece. In each lived a proud, warlike ruler. These kings dominated Greece from about 1600 to 1200 B.C.

Bronze Age society The nobles who lived within the fortresses enjoyed a life of surprising splendor. They feasted in great halls 35 feet wide and 50 feet long. In the center of the hall, a fire blazed on the circular hearth that was ten feet across. During banquets, the firelight glittered from a dazzling variety of gold and silver pitchers, bowls, and cups. When the royal Mycenaeans died, they were buried with their richest treasures. The body of one child was completely covered with a golden suit.

This enormous wealth was won by warrior-kings who led their armies in search of plunder. Trade was also a source of wealth, but Bronze Age trade often was close to piracy.

The warrior kings were only a tiny group at the top of Bronze Age society. The kings had weapons of bronze and jewelry of gold, but ordinary people still used tools of stone and wood. Most people lived as farmers, but there were also weavers, goatherds, shepherds, stonemasons, bakers, metalworkers, nurses, and more.

The Trojan War War was the main business of Greece's Bronze Age kings. Their most famous war was the siege of the great seaport of Troy in Asia Minor. Stories from this war were told hundreds of years later by the Greek poet Homer. According to Homer, a Greek army besieged and destroyed Troy because a Trojan youth had stolen Helen, the beautiful wife of a Greek king.

For many years, historians thought that Homer's stories were imaginary. However, a German archaeologist named Heinrich Schliemann (SHLEE-muhn) thought otherwise. As a boy, Schliemann read Homer's poems over and over. He became determined to find Troy. In 1871, using clues from Homer, Schliemann began to dig for Troy at a site in northwestern Asia Minor. He and his crew unearthed nine layers of city life as well as 8,700 pieces of gold jewelry.

Schliemann's discoveries at Troy, together with the ruins of Mycenae and other cities, showed that Homer's poems had some basis in fact. The Trojan War was probably a great Mycenaean raid against a rival trading city. It took place sometime around 1200 B.C., and it was the last of the Bronze Age Greeks' triumphs.

106

Dark Ages interrupted civilization.

Not long after the Trojan War, Mycenaean civilization collapsed. Around 1200 B.C., palace after palace was attacked and burned. At Mycenae, a layer of ashes covered the entire palace site, the silent remains of a terrible fire. These were the same years that the Egyptians and Hittites suffered under the attacks of the mysterious "Peoples of the Sea." A tablet from one Mycenaean citadel says, "The watchers are guarding the coast." But guards could not save Mycenaean civilization from destruction.

The Dorian migrations Into this war-torn countryside moved a new group of people, the Dorians (DAWR-ee-uhnz). The Dorians spoke a dialect of Greek and were distant relatives of the Bronze Age Greeks.

The Dorians were far less advanced than the Mycenaean Greeks. Dorian pottery and tools show little skill. The Dorians were not good traders either, and trade came to a standstill with their arrival. Most important to historians, the skill of writing was lost in this time of destruction. There is a 400-year gap in written Greek history from 1150 to 750 B.C. This period is known as Greece's Dark Ages. Without written records, little is known of the Dark Ages, but important events took place during these years.

The poems of Homer Lacking writing, the Greeks of the Dark Ages relied on the spoken word to pass on knowledge to their children. Bards (wandering poets) told stories that glorified the old heroes of Mycenae and Troy. A single tale might last many evenings around a hearth. Such long, heroic poems are called **epics**. The greatest of the bards, according to Greek tradition, was a blind old man named Homer.

We know almost nothing about Homer except his poems. He may have lived as early as 900 B.C. or as late as 750 B.C. His two great epic poems are the *Iliad* (IHL-ee-uhd) and the *Odyssey* (AHD-ih-see).

The *Iliad* is the story of heroes at war. All the action takes place outside the walls of Troy, at the very end of the Trojan War. However, Homer does not explain how the Greek army won the war. He was not interested in groups, only in individuals. Throughout the *Iliad*, the battles that matter are private duels between great heroes, not clashes between armies.

The Greeks' love of athletics showed in their art. The vase above features a chariot race, and the small picture at left shows a weight lifter working out. The "Discus Thrower" (far left) captures both grace and force.

Encourage students to read parts of Homer or the legends on which the poems are based. Discuss the characters of the Homeric heroes: Achilles, Odysseus, Agamemnon, Helen, and Andromache. What parts do the gods play in these stories?

Hector's decision to fight Achilles fulfilled Andromache's worst fears. In addition to slaying Hector, Achilles also killed Andromache's father and brothers. After the fall of Troy, the Greeks murdered her son Astyanax. Andromache was then taken to Greece and forced to serve as the slave of Achilles' son Neoptolemus. Following his death, Andromache married the Trojan warrior Helenus. Andromache and Helenus spent the rest of their lives in northern Greece.

■ DISCUSSION

Have students describe the qualities they associate with being heroic. Then ask students to construct a dialogue between Andromache and a modern-day Hector who has the traits of your students' ideal hero. Would the modern Hector's reply to Andromache's plea be the same as that of the ancient Hector?

Homer's second epic, the *Odyssey*, concerns the adventures of Odysseus (oh-**DIHS**-ee-uhs), a Greek hero. According to the *Odyssey*, Odysseus spends the ten years after the Trojan War in a series of adventures on his way home. Only through never-failing cunning is he able to survive.

The heroic ideal Listening to Homer's tales, the Greeks of the Dark Ages learned a powerful ideal called **arete** (**AR**-eh-tee). Simply stated, arete meant to strive for excellence, to show courage, and to win fame and honor.

Homer's heroes competed constantly for glory. The two most renowned heroes of the *Iliad* are Hector, Troy's greatest champion, and Achilles (uh-**KIHL**-eez), the Greek champion. In a dramatic

Footnote to History

According to later legends, it was Odysseus's clever scheme that finally brought down the walls of Troy. The Greeks built a gigantic, hollow wooden horse and left it outside Troy's gates. The Trojans convinced themselves the horse must be an offering to the gods and would protect Troy. They dragged the Greek "gift" into the city. Later that night, Greek warriors who had hidden inside the horse's belly leaped out and opened Troy's gates, letting in the Greek army.

scene, Andromache (an-**DRAHM**-uh-kee), Hector's wife, begs him not to fight Achilles:

"O Hector, your courage will be your destruction; and you have no pity on your little son or on me, who will soon be your widow. For soon all the Greeks will attack you and kill you; and if I lose you, it would be better for me to die . . ."

Then tall Hector of the shining helmet answered, "Wife, I too have thought upon all this. But I would feel deep shame if like a coward I stayed away from battle. All my life I have learned to be brave and to fight always in the front ranks of the Trojans, winning glory for myself . . ."

Hector's answer gives us an insight into the ideal of arete. Confronted with the likelihood of death and tragedy for his family, Hector chooses to live and die by the heroic code. In the following battle, the merciless Achilles slays Hector.

The Olympic games In war, Greek heroes sought glory in battle. In peace, they sought glory in athletic competitions. The most famous games, the Olympics, were held every four years beginning in 776 B.C. Young charioteers, boxers, wrestlers, runners, and javelin throwers came from all parts of Greece to compete on a grassy field at Olympia.

107

ANSWERS TO
Section Review 1

Define:
(a) heritage of Europe and America (b) marketplace (c) long, heroic poem (d) heroic ideal (e) athletic contest (f) story about gods

Identify:
(a) sea east of Greece (b) sea west of Greece (c) sea east of Thrace (d) civilization on Crete (e) mainland Greece civilization of the Bronze Age (f) legendary basis of Homer's *Iliad* (g) great epic poet (h) Greeks who lived during Greece's Dark Ages (i) period in Greek history during which skill of writing was lost (j) Homer's epic about end of Trojan War (k) Homer's epic about adventures of Odysseus (l) athletic competitions begun in 776 B.C.

Answer:
1. (a) served as link (b) made travel difficult, helped develop self-reliance (c) encouraged outdoor gatherings, civic life

2. farming kingdoms; also carried on trade; characterized by splendor of rulers

3. brought on the Dark Ages

4. glorified the heroes of old, thus uniting Greeks, and set up ideal standards

5. no powerful priestly class; religion linked to government, civic pride

6. (a) It was lost during the Dark Ages, so it could not have been too widespread. (b) Sample answer: computer technology; its loss would send day-to-day operations back to slower, less efficient techniques.

The games lasted five days. The most eagerly awaited event was known as the pentathlon (pehn-TATH-luhn). The pentathlon was considered the supreme contest of athletic skill. Contestants took part in five events—a broad jump, a discus hurl, a javelin throw, a stadium sprint (about 200 yards), and a wrestling match. The victor was crowned with the coveted Olympic prize, a wreath of olive leaves. As with the Homeric heroes, the true prize was honor and fame.

Greeks worshiped humanlike gods.

The Olympic games, like many other contests in ancient Greece, were held in part to honor the gods. The Greeks imagined their gods to be very much like humans in most ways. The Greek gods struggled with human passions and weaknesses—love, hate, anger, jealousy. They quarreled constantly with one another. However, unlike humans, the gods were immortal. The 12 most powerful gods and goddesses were believed to gather atop a snow-capped mountain in northern Greece, Mount Olympus. The Greeks also honored local gods and household spirits.

The Greeks developed a rich set of **myths** or stories about their gods. Through these myths, the Greeks sought to understand the mysteries of nature and the power of human passions.

The Greeks did not develop a powerful priestly class, as the Egyptians and Sumerians did. Instead, priests in Greece were ordinary officials. Serving as a priest was not a lifelong career. Rather, it was only one of many civic duties for a Greek citizen. Thus, religion in ancient Greece was closely linked to government and to civic pride.

Section REVIEW 1

Define: (a) Western civilization, (b) agora, (c) epic, (d) arete, (e) pentathlon, (f) myth
Identify: (a) Aegean Sea, (b) Ionian Sea, (c) Black Sea, (d) Minoan civilization, (e) Mycenaean civilization, (f) Trojan War, (g) Homer, (h) Dorians, (i) Dark Ages, (j) the *Iliad*, (k) the *Odyssey*, (l) the Olympics
Answer:
1. How was ancient Greek society influenced by each of the following geographic factors? (a) the sea (b) the land (c) the climate

108

2. Describe the society that existed in Greece and on nearby islands in the Bronze Age.
3. How did the Dorian migrations affect Greek civilization?
4. Why were Homer's poems important to Greek society?
5. How was the Greek religion different from the religions of Egypt and the Fertile Crescent?

Critical Thinking
6. (a) What evidence suggests that writing was a skill limited to a small group of specialists in Mycenaean society? (b) Suggest a comparable skill that might be lost today in a society destroyed by war, and explain the consequences of the loss.

Greek city-states competed for power. 2

After 750 B.C., the Greeks began to recover from the Dark Ages. This period was marked by the rise of the city-states, for which the Greek word was **polis** (PAHL-uhs). (This is the root of such words as *police, politics,* and *politician.*)

A polis included a city and its surrounding countryside. Most city-states controlled between 50 and 500 square miles of territory, although the largest, Sparta, controlled about 4,000 square miles.

The Greeks expected all **citizens** to share in the discussion of public matters. Only free adult men, however, were counted as citizens. Meetings were held in the agora or on a fortified hilltop called an **acropolis** (uh-KRAHP-uh-lihs). The Greeks knew that such general discussion was only possible with a fairly small population. Thus, the ideal polis, to Greek political thinkers, had between 5,000 and 10,000 citizens. (Women, children, slaves, and foreigners were not citizens but made the whole population of a polis much larger.)

The polis was the central force in Greek life. Citizenship was based on the ideal of human beings as free and rational individuals. Civic decisions were made by open debate, not by a pharaoh or an emperor. In Greece, the freedom to express ideas and the willingness of leaders to listen were not only acceptable but expected.

Power passed from kings to citizens.

Clearly, Greece in the time of the city-states was very different from Greece in the time of the warrior-kings that Homer described. During the Dark Ages, the kings had lost their power. In general, rule passed into the hands of a small group of noble families. Such a government is called an **aristocracy** (AR-uh-STAHK-ruh-see). Yet aristocratic rule soon proved oppressive and unjust. The nobles made laws to suit themselves and forced small farmers into slavery for debts.

A *new kind of army* Ordinary citizens became dissatisfied with aristocratic rule. The power of those small farmers and artisans was growing because of another change that had taken place in Greece. In the age of Homer, only kings and nobles were warriors. Only the rich could afford great bronze spears, shields, breastplates, and chariots. During the Dark Ages, however, iron became the most important metal for weapons and armor. Not only is iron harder than bronze, but it also is more common and therefore cheaper. Soon, even ordinary citizens could afford iron weapons and armor.

A whole new kind of army developed as a result of the use of iron. Now every citizen was expected to be a soldier for his polis. These soldiers, called **hoplites,** fought on foot. They stood side by side, each man with a spear in one hand and a shield in the other. As the hoplites faced their enemy, the shields formed a solid wall bristling with spears. This fearsome group of soldiers was known as a **phalanx** (FAY-lanks). In its day,

the Greek phalanx was the most powerful fighting machine in the world.

The rise of tyrants It was impossible for rulers to ignore the power of these citizen-soldiers. In many city-states, farmers who had lost their lands and debt-ridden artisans joined in revolt against the nobles. Often the rebels were led by a man from the nobility, perhaps someone who had lost out in a feud among the nobles themselves. With the support of the citizens, such men won power in many city-states.

The ambitious men who came to power through these rebellions were known as **tyrants.** Hated by the nobles, the tyrants usually worked to help the small farmers and artisans. Sometimes tyrants took lands from the defeated aristocrats and divided the property among the poor. To increase their popularity and impress their neighbors, tyrants were great builders. Many Greek cities gained forts, harbors, and temples under a tyrant's rule.

During the time of the tyrants, many Greek city-states also founded colonies. Groups of citizens moved abroad to islands and harbors around the Mediterranean. These new settlements were separate city-states, but they retained ties of loyalty to their home city. Colonies became an important source of trade and wealth for many Greek cities.

Some city-states passed from one tyrant to the next, as competing groups took power. Other cities, however, found new ways of governing. Among these city-states were two of the most powerful, Sparta and Athens.

The Greek phalanx used an 8-rank formation. The later Macedonian phalanx, shown here, had 16 ranks and longer spears.

109

SECTION 2 Objectives and Teaching Strategies

OBJECTIVE 1. Describe a phalanx and its effect on the power of ordinary citizen-soldiers.

Teaching Strategy: *Teaching with Pictures: The Phalanx* (page 102c)

OBJECTIVE 2. Compare and contrast Sparta and Athens.

Teaching Strategy: *Discussing History: Sparta and Athens* (page 102c)

OBJECTIVE 3: Identify reasons the Greeks were able to defeat the Persians.

Teaching Strategy: *Analyzing a Quotation: Herodotus Explains the Athenian Victory* (page 102c)

■ DISCUSSION

Ask: If you could live anywhere you wanted to, would you choose a city, a suburban area, a small town, or a farm?

After tabulating responses, explain that 37 percent of a representative sample of 16- to 17-year-olds preferred the suburbs. The remainder chose cities (29 percent), small towns (20 percent), and rural farms (29 percent).

Explain that if Greek teenagers had been asked this question, the vast majority would have preferred a small city-state, or polis. Review the characteristics of a polis and explain that the period after the Dark Ages was marked by the rise of two particularly important city-states—Athens and Sparta.

SECTION 2 Resources

GEOGRAPHY
■ Transparencies 15, 16

REINFORCEMENT
■ Independent Practice 5.2

ENRICHMENT
■ Voices from the Past 5.2

ASSESSMENT
■ Section Quiz 5.2

■ DISCUSSION

Could the Spartan military system have existed without the helots? Without their labor, what changes would the Spartans have been forced to make? (Consider that full-time soldiers depend on other workers for food, clothing, and weapons.)

■ BACKGROUND

Sparta was located in a region called Laconia. The Spartans, or Laconians, were known for their sparing use of words. For example, when King Philip of Macedonia invaded Greece, he asked the Spartans whether they wished him to come as friend or foe. The Spartans upheld their reputation for not wasting words when they returned a one-word answer, "Neither!" To this day the word *laconic* means "terse, concise, saying a lot with a few words."

The Spartans were more than just laconic. They also prided themselves on being tough warriors who avoided luxuries and led hardy lives. Spartan men lived in army barracks and ate meager servings of a coarse black porridge. The word *Spartan* (harsh and austere) is a lasting memorial to their disciplined lives.

Greece and Its Colonies

Map Study

Between 750 and 550 B.C., Greek colonies spread around the Mediterranean Sea. What settlement controlled the mouth of the Black Sea?

Sparta built an army state.

Sparta was located in the southern part of Greece, in the area known as the Peloponnesus (PEHL-uh-puh-NEE-sus). As the map on page 113 shows, this stretch of land is nearly cut off from the rest of Greece by the Gulf of Corinth.

While other city-states founded colonies abroad, Sparta looked no farther than the fertile fields of neighboring Messenia (muh-SEE-nee-uh). About 725 B.C., the Spartans conquered the Messenians and took over their land.

The Spartans treated the Messenians almost as slaves. Messenians became **helots** (HEL-uhts), peasants forced to stay on the land they worked. Each year, the Spartans demanded half of the Messenians' yearly crop. Around 600 B.C., the Messenians, who outnumbered the Spartans eight to one, revolted. The Spartans put down the revolt, but just barely. From then on, the Spartans lived in fear of a helot uprising. The Spartans concluded that the only way to survive was to make their

city-state overwhelmingly strong. They adopted a harsh set of laws known as the Code of Lycurgus (ly-KUR-gus). According to legend, Lycurgus gave Sparta its laws, then starved himself to death to save food for his polis.

Spartan babies were examined at birth to see if they were healthy. If not, they were left in the hills to die. All fit children stayed with their mothers until their seventh birthdays. Then the boys were sent to army barracks, and their training began. They wore one light tunic, winter or summer, and usually went barefoot. Their beds were hard benches. For food, they had meager servings of coarse black porridge. They were expected to get extra food by stealing from nearby farms, though they would be whipped if caught. Such schooling produced tough soldiers.

At the age of 20, a Spartan man was allowed to marry. He continued, though, to live in the barracks for another ten years. After completing full-time military service, men remained on active reserve for another 30 years.

110

Spartan girls also led hardy lives. They ran, wrestled, and played sports. As adults, they managed the family estates while their husbands served the polis. Spartan women had every right except the vote. As a result of their freedom, they scandalized other Greeks.

From around 600 until 371 B.C., the Spartans had the most powerful army in Greece, but they paid a high price for it. They created little literature, art, or architecture. The Spartans valued duty, strength, and discipline over individuality, beauty, and freedom of thought.

Athens turned to democracy.

In outlook and values, Athens stood in sharp contrast to Sparta. An ambassador from Corinth, a city halfway between the two rivals, once compared the Spartans to the Athenians as he spoke to the Spartan assembly. With typical Greek frankness, he told the Spartans that even though they had the strongest army in Greece, they were overly cautious and generally lacking in any excitement of the mind. Athenians, he said, were always eager to learn new ideas. They had been educated to think and act as free people.

Like other city-states, Athens went through a power struggle between rich and poor. However, Athenians avoided civil war by making timely reforms. Two of the leading reformers were Solon (SO-luhn) and Cleisthenes (KLYS-thuh-neez). These reforms created a **democracy,** a government in which all citizens took part.

Solon's reforms By 594 B.C., conflict between the rich aristocrats who ruled Athens and the poor farmers who made up most of its population had reached a boiling point. To prevent civil war, the aristocrats asked a middle-aged poet, philosopher, and merchant named Solon to head the government. Solon was well-known for his fairness, and the Athenians gave him full power to reform the laws. Solon's first acts were aimed at improving Athens's economy.

1. He canceled all debts and freed those who had been enslaved for debt.
2. He made farming profitable and encouraged farmers to grow more wine grapes and olives. These became the base of a rich trade for Athens.
3. He encouraged industry by requiring every father to teach his son a trade. Athenian pottery, for example, was sold all around the Mediterranean Sea.

Solon's political reforms were just as important as his economic ones.

1. He allowed every male citizen to attend the assembly. All important matters were debated there and decided by vote.
2. He began a new legal system in which any citizen could bring charges against anyone who had committed a wrong. Thus, if a citizen saw a crime committed against a slave, the citizen could bring a charge, even though the slave could not. The idea that all citizens were responsible for justice was revolutionary.

DISCUSSION

What does the choice of Solon as leader reveal about the values of the aristocrats who chose him?

BACKGROUND

Solon's code of laws was inspired by his respect for the rule of law. When asked what made an orderly and well-run state, he replied, "When the people obey the rulers, and the rulers obey the laws." Although Solon's code encouraged many enduring changes in Athenian society, it also included a number of provisions that did not stand the test of time. For example, Solon made it a crime to speak evil of the dead and forbade women to own more than three suits.

BACKGROUND

Draco was an Athenian lawgiver who preceded Solon. He wrote a strict code of laws that called for severe penalties for the smallest offense. His laws were said to be written not in ink, but in blood. To this day, *draconian* means "overly harsh and severe."

MILESTONES OF DEMOCRACY: ATHENS (509 B.C.)

	FORM OF GOVERNMENT	CITIZENSHIP	INDIVIDUAL RIGHTS
Benefits	Direct democracy: Polis was ruled by assembly of all citizens.	Citizens had right and duty to govern and were responsible for justice.	Citizens had equal rights under law and could claim justice for others.
Limitations	Only one fifth of the people were citizens.	Women, foreigners, and slaves were not citizens.	Noncitizens had few legal rights.

111

Ask students to read "Ode to a Grecian Urn" by Keats. Discuss the idea of timeless art presented by the poem. Would the Greeks have agreed?

■ BACKGROUND

Between 490 and 480 B.C., a rich deposit of silver was found in Athens. Themistocles persuaded the citizens to use the windfall for a fleet of warships rather than distribute it as a bonus to all citizens.

Leonidas and his men may have been outnumbered by 25 to 1. Despite these overwhelming odds, the Spartans were nonetheless able to successfully defend Thermopylae. Called the "Hot Gates" because of a nearby mineral spring, Thermopylae provided an ideal defensive position. A narrow path just 50 feet wide provided the only route through the pass. As a result, the Spartans were able to fight only a small portion of the Persian army at any given time.

The reforms of Cleisthenes About 60 years later, another Athenian leader, Cleisthenes, introduced further reforms. Beginning in 508 B.C., he convinced the Athenians to enact a series of laws that made Athens a full democracy.

Cleisthenes increased the power of the Athenian assembly. He also created the Council of Five Hundred to propose laws and advise the assembly. Members of this council were chosen by lot, so that every citizen had an equal chance of serving.

After all these reforms, Athenians enjoyed nearly a complete democracy. However, it is important to remember that only about one fifth of the people in Athens were citizens. The rest were slaves, foreigners, and women. Women in Athens had no part in government and very little part in its intellectual life.

The Greeks turned back the powerful Persians.

Danger of a helot revolt caused the Spartans to be inhumanly tough. Danger of revolution among poverty-stricken farmers caused Athens to become a democracy. The greatest danger of all—invasion by Persian armies—spurred Athens and Sparta alike to their greatest glory.

The full story of the Persian Wars is told by Herodotus (huh-**RAHD**-uh-tuhs), a Greek scholar, in his *History of the Persian Wars*. Because he tried to investigate the past, find out the truth, and report it, Herodotus is justly called the first true historian.

The first invasion The Persian Wars began in Ionia, a thin strip of coastland in what is now Turkey. Greeks had long been settled there, but around 520 B.C., the Persians conquered the area. The Greeks of Ionia submitted to Persian rule for a generation but then revolted. Athens sent ships and soldiers to the Ionians' aid. After the Persian king Darius defeated the rebels, he vowed to destroy Athens in revenge.

According to the legend, in 490 B.C., a Persian fleet carried 25,000 men across the Aegean Sea and landed northeast of Athens on a plain called Marathon. There, 10,000 Athenians, neatly bunched into phalanxes, were waiting for them. Shoulder to shoulder, singing as they ran, the Athenians charged. The casualties reportedly numbered 6,400 Persians and only 192 Athenians.

Though the Athenians were victorious, their city was now defenseless. Sailing along the coast, the Persian ships could reach Athens before the Greeks could march overland to defend it. Someone had to race back to Athens to tell people there how badly the Persians had been defeated. Otherwise, the citizens might surrender the city without a fight. A young runner named Pheidippides (fye-**DIP**-uh-deez) stripped off his clothes

DAILY LIFE ▶ Athenian Pottery

"We like beautiful things but don't spend a fortune on them," a leading Athenian remarked about the people of his city. Some of the loveliest objects in Greece, and throughout the Mediterranean for that matter, were easily affordable to almost every family in Athens. These objects were the graceful Athenian vases or pots.

The pottery was made and purchased for practical use as mixing bowls, pitchers, drinking cups, wine jars, and water jars. Different shapes were designed to serve different purposes. Often, Athenians bought new pottery for celebrations, and the scenes on the pottery showed the event they were celebrating—a marriage, an athletic contest, or a voyage.

Athenian potters were dedicated to high quality and beauty in their craft. They proudly signed their finest works. Their products have become a symbol for perfection in art.

112

Greece in the Persian Wars

MACEDON

Black Sea

Sea of Marmara

DARDANELLES

Mt. Olympus

Aegean Sea

GREECE

ASIA MINOR

Ionian Sea

Thermopylae

Delphi

Thebes

Plataea

Athens

Marathon

Salamis

Gulf of Corinth

Corinth

PELOPONNESUS

Olympia

Mantinea

Argos

MESSENIA

Sparta

Sardis

IONIA

MEDITERRANEAN SEA

CRETE

KEY
- ✿ Major battle
- Persian empire
- Greek city-states that opposed Persia
- → Darius' invasion, 490 B.C.
- ⇢ Xerxes' invasion, 480 B.C.

0 ———— 100 Miles

Map Study

Which Persian ruler took a direct sea route to invade Greece? Which ruler brought both a fleet and a land-based army? What two battles did his army fight? What battle did his fleet fight?

and ran 26 miles over the rocky ground from Marathon to Athens. With his last breath, he gasped, "Rejoice, we conquer." Then he collapsed and died. Persian ships arrived much later, saw the situation was hopeless, and sailed away.

The second invasion Ten years later, in 480 B.C., Darius the Great was dead. His son and successor, Xerxes (ZURK-seez), was determined to crush Greece. Xerxes assembled an enormous invasion force of ships and men.

Xerxes' army was like a marching exhibit of all the peoples of the Persian empire. There were Ethiopians in lion skins carrying spears tipped with gazelle horn. Arab soldiers followed him on camels. Scythians from Russia were known

by their pointed caps. The Persians sported leather jerkins and fish-scale armor. Xerxes' army was many times larger than any force the Greeks could muster.

The Greeks were badly divided. Some city-states decided to fight the Persians. Others thought it wiser to let Xerxes destroy Athens and return home. Some Greeks actually fought on the Persian side. Thus, Xerxes' army met no resistance as it marched down the eastern coast of Greece. Then, about 85 miles northeast of Athens, Xerxes came to a narrow mountain pass at Thermopylae (ther-MOP-ih-lee). Here he found 7,000 Greeks, including 300 Spartans, blocking his way.

113

ANSWERS TO
Map Study

Darius; Xerxes; Thermopylae, Plataea; Salamis

■ DISCUSSION

Many Greeks fought on the Persian side at Marathon, Thermopylae, and later battles. What does this fact show about Greek nationalism or its absence in this period?

ANSWERS TO
Section Review 2

Define:
(a) city-state (b) free adult men (c) fortified hilltop (d) government run by noble families (e) foot soldier (f) formation of foot soldiers forming solid wall (g) ruler who came to power through rebellion (h) peasant forced to stay on land (i) government in which all citizens take part

(continued)

ANSWERS TO (continued)

Identify:

(a) city-state in southern Greece, known for its army (b) neighboring land conquered by Sparta (c) Spartan lawgiver who supposedly starved himself (d) democratic city-state (e) economic and political reformer of Athens (f) made Athens a full democracy (g) Persian king set on defeating Athens (h) historian of the Persian Wars (i) site of victory in 490 B.C. for Athenians against Persians (j) citizen who convinced Athenians to give up their city but to fight Persians by sea (k) site of great Spartan bravery and sacrifice in Persian War (l) son and successor to Darius (m) site of Greek naval victory over Persians (n) site of Spartan victory over Persians (o) alliance of city-states, actually Athenian empire

Answer:

1. It was the central force in Greek life.

2. could now afford weapons and revolt

3. tended to favor interests of small farmers, artisans

4. (a) Helots greatly outnumbered Spartans. (b) They enforced harsh laws.

5. (a) There existed a power struggle between rich and poor. (b) Athenians turned to Solon to lead a reform.

6. It led to a golden age and formation of the Delian League with Athens as its leader.

7. Look for answers that show a need to make all classes more economically and politically equal.

8. Look for answers to stress the polis at the focus of Greek loyalty.

Xerxes expected to smash this small army with ease, but he underestimated the Spartans. For three days, the ground at Thermopylae ran red with Persian blood. Finally, a Greek traitor told the Persians about a secret path around the cliffs. Defeat for the Greeks was now inevitable.

The Spartan commander, Leonidas, told the Greeks from other city-states to retreat to safety. He and his Spartans would hold the pass as long as possible and die with honor at Thermopylae. The Persians killed them all. The Spartans' valiant sacrifice made a great impression on all Greeks.

In Athens, the citizens began to plan for the city's defense. It was then that Themistocles convinced Athenians to evacuate their city and pin all their hopes on victory at sea (page 94).

Early one September morning, 310 Greek ships (more than half rowed by Athenians) headed out to sea to face the Persians. Straight ahead was the island of Salamis (SAL-uh-mihs). To the left and right, blocking both ends of the channel, were masses of Persian ships. The Greeks appeared to be trapped.

But Themistocles knew the waters around Salamis better than the foreigners. The channel was too narrow to permit the large Persian fleet to maneuver well. Suddenly, the huge size of the Persian fleet turned into a terrible disadvantage. With lusty shouts, Athenian oarsmen drove straight for the wooden hulls of the enemy. Battering rams protruded from Greek ships below the waterline. These rams punched holes in the Persian ships. The great Persian fleet sank, ship by ship, in the channel.

Xerxes watched it happen. He had set his golden throne upon a rocky height to enjoy seeing the Greeks crushed. Instead, he saw his own navy destroyed. After the battle, Xerxes left Greece hurriedly with about half his army. The remaining half of the Persian army was defeated by the Spartans at a third great battle, which took place on the plain of Plataea (pluh-TEE-uh). Thus ended the second Persian invasion of Greece.

Consequences of the Persian Wars Athens basked in the glory of the Persian defeat. Athens alone had challenged Persian power from the beginning. Athenian heroes had fallen first in Ionia, then at Marathon. Athenian ships had fought at Salamis. The city of Athens, burned to ashes, had suffered the most damage. The Athenians claimed to be the war's greatest heroes.

Their pride in themselves and their city soared to new heights.

After the war, Athens became the leader of an alliance of 140 city-states called the Delian (DEE-lee-uhn) League. The purpose of the league was to ward off further Persian attacks. Soon, though, Athens began to use its powerful navy to control the other members of the league. City-states were forced to join the league and pay yearly dues to Athens. The Delian League thus became just another name for an Athenian empire.

The prestige of victory and the wealth of empire set the stage for a dazzling outburst of creativity in Athens. The city was entering its brief, brilliant golden age.

Section REVIEW 2

Define: (a) polis, (b) citizen, (c) acropolis, (d) aristocracy, (e) hoplite, (f) phalanx, (g) tyrant, (h) helot, (i) democracy

Identify: (a) Sparta, (b) Messenia, (c) Lycurgus, (d) Athens, (e) Solon, (f) Cleisthenes, (g) Darius, (h) Herodotus, (i) Marathon, (j) Themistocles, (k) Thermopylae, (l) Xerxes, (m) Gulf of Salamis, (n) Plataea, (o) Delian League

Answer:

1. Why was the polis important to Greeks?
2. How did the Iron Age help ordinary citizens gain power in Greece?
3. How was the rule of tyrants generally different from that of aristocrats?
4. (a) Why was revolt a constant threat in Sparta? (b) How did the Spartans respond to this threat?
5. (a) Why was revolt a threat in early Athens? (b) How did the Athenians respond to this threat?
6. How did the end of the Persian Wars affect the people of Greece, especially the Athenians?

Critical Thinking

7. Choose one of Solon's reforms and explain why it was important to making Athens a democracy.
8. At several major battles in the Persian Wars, there were nearly as many Greeks fighting for the Persians as against them. From your reading, what reasons can you suggest for this division among the Greeks?

Athens led Greece in its golden age. 3

During Athens's golden age, the arts of drama, sculpture, poetry, philosophy, architecture, and science all reached new heights. For 50 years (from 480 to 430 B.C.), Athens set off sparks of genius in all directions.

Pericles sought glory for Athens.

Among those who evacuated Athens before the Persians arrived in 480 B.C. was a teenager named Pericles (PEHR-uh-kleez). His aristocratic father, a leader of the Athenian assembly, had fought in the Battle of Salamis. When the Persians were finally driven out, much of Athens had been burned. In this bleak, war-scarred city, Pericles prepared to become Athens's leader.

Pericles first attended assembly meetings at the age of 20. Soon, his talent for oratory won him fame. He did not try to excite his audiences but only to reason with them. He made sense to aristocrats, farmers, and artisans alike.

In 461 B.C., the assembly elected Pericles one of Athen's ten generals. He was reelected year after year and became, in effect, the leader of Athens. This one man so dominated the life of Athens for 32 years (461–429 B.C.) that the period often is called the Age of Pericles.

Pericles had three goals: (1) to strengthen Athenian democracy; (2) to build a commercial empire; and (3) to glorify Athens.

To strengthen democracy, Pericles increased the number of public officials who were paid salaries. Earlier, many public jobs were unpaid, and so only the wealthier citizens could afford to hold such offices. Now even the poorest could afford to serve if elected or chosen by lot.

Through the Delian League, Pericles tried to enlarge the wealth and power of Athens. He used money from the league's treasury to make Athens's navy the strongest in the Mediterranean. The navy safeguarded Athenian commerce and settled disputes between league members.

Pericles also used money from the empire to beautify Athens. He persuaded the Athenian assembly (without the league's approval) to vote huge sums of Delian League money to buy gold, ivory, and marble. Still more money went to a

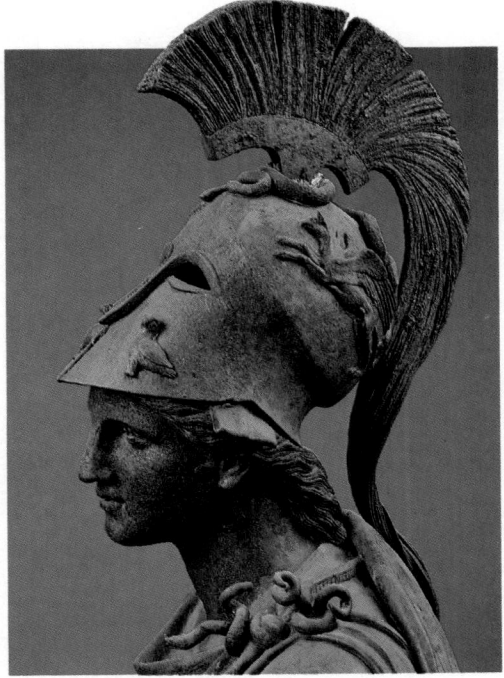

This marble statue of Athena is a Roman copy of the one placed in the Parthenon.

small army of artisans who worked for 15 years (447–432 B.C.) on building one of architecture's noblest works, the Parthenon (PAHR-thuh-nahn).

CITY TOUR

Art flourished in Athens.

The Parthenon was not novel in style. It was built in the traditional style that had been used in Greek temples for 200 years. Neither was it especially large—228 feet by 101 feet. What made it one of the masterpieces of all time was its excellent craftsmanship and design.

Within the temple stood a giant statue of Athena, goddess of wisdom and protector of Athens (which was named for her). Pericles had entrusted much work on the temple, including the statue of Athena, to his friend Phidias (FIHD-ee-us), a sculptor. The great statue of the goddess stood about 39 feet tall. A golden helmet crowned her head above her ivory face. A golden robe fell

115

SECTION 3
Objectives and Teaching Strategies

OBJECTIVE 1. Describe Athenian achievements during the golden age.
Teaching Strategy: *Teaching with Pictures: The Parthenon* (page 102d)

OBJECTIVE 2. Discuss the causes and consequences of the Peloponnesian War.
Teaching Strategy: *Discussing History: Causes and Effects of the Peloponnesian War* (page 102d)

OBJECTIVE 3. Recall the contributions of Socrates, Plato, Aristotle.
Teaching Strategy: *Analyzing Quotations: Wisdom of the Greek Philosophers* (page 102d)

■ BACKGROUND

This city tour features Athens in the time of Pericles. As the center of a polis, Athens was the scene of political, economic, social, and cultural activity. The Parthenon, standing high on the acropolis, dominated the city.

SECTION 3
Resources

ASSESSMENT
■ Section Quiz 5.3

REINFORCEMENT
■ Independent Practice 5.3

ENRICHMENT
■ Voices from the Past 5.3

ANSWER TO
Comparing Pictures

Greek temples like the Parthenon were set on the ground, not at the top of tiers. Columns, walls, and roof created a large interior.

■ BACKGROUND

The Parthenon was designed in a traditional rectangular shape. Its architects breathed life into the temple by playing a few subtle tricks on the eye. For example, the corner columns tilt very slightly inward so that their tops are a few inches closer together than their bottoms. This barely visible tilt helps give the Parthenon its upward thrust. In addition, each column bulges ever so slightly in the middle. This brings a sense of lightness to the whole building.

Once inside the temple, visitors could admire a band of carved stone, called a frieze, that told the story of the Great Panathenaic Festival the Athenians held every four years to honor Athena. Sculptors painted the frieze in rich colors so that the carved figures would stand out.

Comparing pictures *The Parthenon represented a new style of architecture, known for its proportion and symmetry, that developed in Greece. How does this style differ from that of the ziggurats in Sumer (page 35)?*

in great folds over her golden sandals. A graceful ivory hand rested on a huge shield. The morning sun rising over Athens briefly lit up her robe.

Phidias and the other sculptors of the golden age of Athens aimed to create figures that were graceful, strong, and perfectly formed. Their faces showed neither laughter nor anger, only serenity. Greek sculptors also tried to capture the grace of the human body in motion. Their values of order, balance, and proportion became the standards of what is called **classical art.**

Nearly all of the great sculpture and architecture of Periclean Athens was created for the polis.

They expressed the pride of Athenians in their city. Marble, bronze, and gold went into public temples, not into private homes. The many shrines and temples that the Persians destroyed were rebuilt and made more beautiful than ever.

The importance that Athenians gave to fine public architecture is shown by the temple of Athena Nike (*nike* meant "victory"). This temple was built while Athens was fighting for its life against Sparta. Money was short, and war casualties and plague carried off workers. Yet all through the 30 years of war, the Athenians struggled to complete the temple.

Pillars supported the roofs of the great Greek temples. The three classical styles for the tops (or capitals) of the columns were the Doric, the Ionic, and the Corinthian.

116

The Greeks invented drama.

Like the Parthenon, Athens's theatrical productions were both an expression of civic pride and a tribute to the gods. Writing plays to be performed on stage was a new form of art. Drama as we know it was a Greek invention.

Early in the spring, Athenians rose at dawn and walked to the city's outdoor theater to watch a festival honoring the god of wine, Dionysus. Just as athletes competed in the Olympic games, playwrights competed in this festival. A group of citizens judged the plays and awarded the winner a simple prize: a wreath of ivy.

In the Age of Pericles, two writers dominated these contests. First came Aeschylus (ES-kih-lus), who won the ivy wreath 13 times. Aeschylus shared deeply in Athens's glory; he himself had fought at Marathon and probably at Salamis. He probably wrote more than 80 plays, of which only 7 survive. The second great dramatist, Sophocles (SAHF-uh-kleez), won his first dramatic contest by beating the great Aeschylus in 468 B.C. All together, Sophocles wrote about 100 plays, including the most famous Greek drama of all, *Oedipus* (EHD-uh-puhs).

Greek plays were partly acted and partly chanted. A chorus of singers would comment on the action of the play, helping the plot along. The actors wore masks to identify their roles. The large protruding lips of each mask served as a megaphone to help carry the actor's voice to the back rows.

Both Sophocles and Aeschylus wrote the type of drama known as **tragedy**. To qualify as tragedy, a play had to portray men and women of strong character whose very strength led to their downfall. There was no such thing as a meek hero.

In classic tragedy, strength led the hero to pride, and pride inevitably led to an unforgivable sin. And always, in tragic drama, the gods punished the hero for sinning. The audience who saw these plays left the theater both saddened and uplifted— sad for the fate of mankind and uplifted by the nobility and courage the characters displayed.

Public drama was more than entertainment to the Athenians. It was a form of public education. The plays dealt with great issues that were important to the polis—the power of leaders, the power of the people, questions of justice and morality, questions of war and peace, and the duties owed to the gods, the family, and the city.

The Greek theater at Delphi was set on a hillside with nature as its backdrop. Actors wore masks such as the one at right to show their roles.

■ **BACKGROUND**

Although women's roles were often central to a play, all actors were men. This casting created another reason to wear masks. Point out that even in Shakespeare's time women's roles were played by male actors.

Only a tiny portion of the Greek plays have survived. Although we know of about 150 Greek tragedians, just 33 plays by Aeschylus, Sophocles, and Euripedes still exist. These three authors alone are known to have written at least 297 plays.

Cooperative Learning

Have students work in groups of five to create a skit that is a modern-day example of a Greek tragedy. Have students reread the section on Greek tragedy (page 117). Then have group members agree on a storyline, setting, and characters for their skit. With input from all group members, a recorder should write the dialogue for the skit. Finally, with one of the group members acting as a director, have the other group members perform the skit for the class.

For most Greek women, household chores were the main activity. However, Spartan women such as the runner above took part in athletic contests. Sappho, the woman shown on the vase, was considered one of the finest Greek poets.

Drama was so important to public life in Athens that citizens were sometimes paid to attend the plays, just as they were paid for holding public office. As part of their civic duty, wealthy citizens bore the cost for producing the plays.

Athens prospered in the golden age.

The Parthenon and the amphitheater were surrounded by a teeming city. How did it feel to live in such a place?

Athens reeked with the odor of the pigpens most familes kept in their backyards. Foul smells mingled with the raucous noise of the agora. Here merchants in outdoor stalls advertised their goods by shouting. The sound of clanging metal from nearby workshops added to the din. Athens was a city of small shopowners and artisans who specialized in every kind of craft: shoe making, sword making, pottery making, wine making, and so on. The shops were owned by foreigners as well as by Athenian citizens.

Free men and slaves worked side by side in a typical shop and might be given the same meager wages. There were perhaps 100,000 slaves in the city-state of Athens in the 400's, roughly one third the population. Most of them were non-Greeks captured in war. A rich family might own as many as 50 slaves. Even a poor citizen was likely to own one or two. Because poor citizens and slaves dressed much alike, however, it was almost impossible to distinguish them from one another.

The voices in the marketplace were mostly male. A woman's voice rarely was heard outside the home. Cooking meals, nursing babies, and weaving cloth were expected to consume all of a woman's time. If she stepped outside to buy fish at the market, her face was supposed to be veiled. She could not own or inherit land. She had very few legal rights and could not appeal to a jury in her own defense. Unlike her brothers, who started going to school at the age of six, she was educated at home. When she married, she lived in the part of her husband's house reserved for women. She was supposed to retreat there whenever her husband entertained male guests at home.

118

Most Athenian families lived in tiny, plain dwellings with thin, mud-brick walls. Typical furniture was a few tables and chairs. Often, a family's most valued possessions were the painted pieces of pottery in which they stored their wine and olive oil. The red and black vases made in Athenian workshops were famous throughout the Mediterranean world. In the Age of Pericles, they were Athens's chief export.

Despite its physical discomfort, Athens was in many ways a splendid city. Like the heroes in Sophocles' plays, however, the proud citizens of Athens were soon to suffer a tragic fate.

Sparta defeated Athens in war.

Tension between Athens and Sparta had been building for years. Many people in both cities thought war was inevitable. Instead of trying to avoid war, leaders began to press for a war to begin while they thought their own city had the advantage. Finally, in 431 B.C., the Spartans marched into Athenian territory. They swept over the countryside, burning the Athenians' local food supply.

Athens itself, however, seemed safe. Years before, Pericles had taken the precaution of building the Long Walls, two great ramparts that protected the roadway from Athens to the sea. Thus, Athens was safe from starvation as long as ships could sail into port with food from Athenian colonies as far away as the Black Sea.

Athens was the strongest sea power, but Sparta was the strongest land power. As the leading Athenian general, Pericles did not try to defeat the Spartans on land. Instead, his strategy was to avoid battles with the superior Spartan army and to use Athens's great navy to strike Sparta's territory from the sea.

From the earliest battles, an Athenian named Thucydides (thyoo-**SID**-ih-deez) wrote about the war in a journal. We still rely on his *History of*

Voice from the Past — Pericles' Funeral Oration

In the winter of 431 B.C., Athens honored its war dead with a public funeral. As part of the ceremony, Pericles spoke in praise of the dead and the city for which they had died. His speech is the best expression of the Athenians' pride in their polis.

Our constitution does not copy the laws of neighboring states. Instead, others copy what we do. Our plan of government favors the many instead of the few; that is why it is called a democracy. As for laws, we offer equal justice to everyone. As for social standing, advancement is open to everyone, according to ability. High position does not depend on wealth, nor does poverty bar the way . . .

We take pleasure in the arts, but without extravagance, and in knowledge, but without being soft . . . Our public leaders have their own businesses, as well as politics, to take care of. Our ordinary citizens see to their own livelihoods but are also capable of making political decisions. Unlike other nations, we Athenians do not call a man who takes no part in public life quiet or unambitious; we call such a man useless . . .

In short, our polis is the school of all Greece . . . This is the Athens for which these men nobly fought and died, because they could not bear the thought of losing such a city.

1. How does Pericles define a democracy?
2. In what aspects of life should a citizen take an interest to lead a full life?
3. (a) How does Pericles describe Athens's position in Greece? (b) What evidence does he offer of its leadership?

119

■ **DISCUSSION**

How does the Athens that Pericles describes differ from Sparta? Are Athenians generalists (with wide-ranging interests and abilities) or specialists? (generalists) Are Spartans generalists or specialists? (specialists: warriors)

■ **BACKGROUND**

Although Athens was famous for its beautiful marble temples, most of its citizens lived in simple mud-brick homes. Their walls were so fragile that burglars had no reason to break down the doors. Instead, they simply dug tunnels through the walls. As a result, burglars were called "wall-diggers."

ANSWERS TO
Voice from the Past

1. government favoring many over few
2. arts, business, politics
3. (a) "school" of Greece (b) Others copy Athens.

Where Herodotus stressed the splendor and pageantry of history, Thucydides accurately recorded the events of Athenian democracy. He wrote, "The lack of the fabulous may make my work dull. But I shall be satisfied if it be thought useful by those who wish to know the exact character of events now past which, human nature being what it is, will recur in similar or analogous forms. It has not been composed to court temporary applause but as a lasting impression."

■ DISCUSSION

Explain that the Greeks believed that a tragedy had three recognizable elements. First, the hero was stricken by *ate*, a blindness sent by the gods. Then the blindness led to *hubris*, a false sense of pride that led to an unforgivable sin. And finally, the gods punished the hero. The punishment was called *nemesis*. Ask advanced students to apply these concepts to the Peloponnesian War. Was the war a true example of a Greek tragedy? If so, who was guilty of hubris? What was the punishment?

---

the Peloponnesian War to understand how this war ruined Athens and weakened all of Greece.

Disaster for Athens Two events were particularly deadly to Athens—a plague and a disastrous military defeat in far-off Sicily. The plague struck in 430 B.C., in the second year of the war. While Spartan soldiers were again laying waste to Athens's farmland, Athenians sought safety behind the city walls. Overcrowding made Athens vulnerable to a frightful plague that killed roughly one third of the population, including Pericles. Thucydides himself fell sick and barely survived.

The second disaster took place in 415 B.C., after the war had gone on for 16 years. The Athenian assembly sent a huge fleet carrying 27,000 soldiers to the island of Sicily, near Italy. Their goal was to destroy the polis of Syracuse, one of Sparta's wealthiest allies. The expedition met overwhelming defeat in 413 B.C. Thucydides reported, "They were destroyed with a total destruction—their fleet, their army—there was nothing that was not destroyed, and few out of many returned home."

Somehow, a terribly weakened Athens managed to fend off Spartan attacks for another nine years. But in 404 B.C., Athens and its allies surrendered. The Spartans then forced the Athenians to join in tearing down the Long Walls, symbol of Athens's strength.

Cultural changes After 27 years of war, Athens had lost its fleet, its empire, its power, and its wealth. It had also lost its self-confidence. This loss of spirit was perhaps the most serious of all for the people of Athens.

Confidence in democratic government began to falter. One leader after another proved weak, corrupt, or traitorous. The assembly began to change its decisions with every shift of the political winds. Leaders and generals were in constant danger of exile if a new speaker persuaded the assembly to turn on them.

Oddly enough, the crisis in public confidence was accompanied by an artistic outburst. As people turned to their private lives, art began to reflect their joys and sorrows. For the first time, the faces of bronze and marble statues began to show emotion.

Drama also underwent a change. It was during the Peloponnesian War that a playwright named Aristophanes (AR-is-TAHF-uh-neez) wrote the first great **comedies** of the stage. In these plays, he

---

made fun of the politics, people, and ideas of his time. Athenians laughed at his biting jokes. The fact that Athenians could listen to such criticism of themselves, even in the midst of a great war, showed that the spirit of freedom and public discussion still lived.

Philosophers searched for truth.

In the years after the Peloponnesian War, yet another aspect of Greek culture reached new heights. In this time of questioning and uncertainty, several great thinkers were determined to seek for truth, no matter where the search led them. The name that the Greeks gave to such thinkers was **philosopher**—literally, "one who loves wisdom." The Greek philosophers questioned even the most basic and widely accepted ideas of their time.

Greek thinkers based their philosophy on two original assumptions. First, they assumed that the universe was put together in an orderly way. Land, sky, and sea were all subject to the same laws. These laws were absolute and unchanging. Second, the Greeks assumed that people could understand these laws through reason.

Socrates One of Greece's greatest philosophers fell victim to the frustrations aroused by Athens's defeat in the Peloponnesian War. He was an old Athenian soldier and stonecutter named Socrates (SAHK-ruh-teez). Socrates was not a handsome man, and his clothes and grooming left much to be desired. His agile mind, however, made up for his homely appearance.

Stopping a young man on the street, Socrates would ask if he knew where certain merchandise could be bought. After the youth answered easily, Socrates would ask if he knew where goodness and virtue could be found. No, the youth would reply, he did not know where one could find those. More questions would follow. Soon, Socrates and the young man would be deeply examining some idea like truth or goodness or beauty. This way of teaching by asking questions is still called the **Socratic method.**

Socrates questioned all the accepted values of Athens—democracy, patriotism, religion. He taught that people must examine their ideas by the demanding standards of truth and reason. Those who understood Socrates admired him deeply. The majority of citizens, however, could

This painting, "The Death of Socrates," was painted by the French artist Jacques Louis David in 1787, more than 2,000 years after Socrates died. What impression does the painting give of Socrates?

not understand this strange old man. The bitterness of a long war made them suspicious.

In 399 B.C., when Socrates was 70 years old, he was brought to trial. The father of one of his pupils accused him of "corrupting the youth of Athens" and failing to revere "the gods that the state recognizes." The 501 jurors at his trial listened to Socrates speak in his own defense. He said that his teachings were good for Athens because they forced people to think about their values and actions. In fact, he suggested that the city should give him a pension.

By a majority of 60 votes, the jury voted Socrates guilty as charged. The penalty was death. Friends visited Socrates in prison and pleaded with him to flee into exile. He calmly explained the flaws in their reasoning and drank the slow-acting poison made from hemlock. Athens thus lost one of its greatest citizens.

Plato Among those who had visited Socrates in prison was a brilliant, wealthy idealist named Plato (PLAY-toh). He was 28 years old when Socrates died, and the death convinced him that the average citizens of a democracy (who condemned Socrates) were unable to govern wisely.

Plato left Athens in bitterness after Socrates' death. He returned later, however, and established his own school. Plato's school, called the Academy, continued for 900 years.

Unlike Socrates, Plato was a writer as well as a teacher. In his early works, he wrote down the conversations of Socrates as he remembered them. Sometime between 385 and 380 B.C., Plato wrote his most famous work, *The Republic.* In it, he set forth his vision of a perfectly governed society. It was certainly no democracy.

In an ideal community, he wrote, all citizens would fall naturally into three groups. The most common type would be best suited for working as farmers and artisans. A more gifted type had minds and bodies fine enough to be trusted as warriors. Only the third and rarest type should belong to the ruling class. From this highest category, the person with the greatest insight and intellect ought to be chosen philosopher-king. This person might be either a woman or a man.

121

ANSWER TO
Caption Question

Socrates met death calmly and with self-control.

ANSWERS TO
Section Review 3

Define:
(a) style of art that includes standards of order, balance, and proportion (b) type of drama in which gods punish hero for sinning (c) plays that satirized the politics, people, and ideas of the time (d) one who loves wisdom (e) teaching by asking questions

Identify:
(a) leading statesman of Athens during golden age (b) Greek temple (c) goddess of wisdom and protector of Athens (d) sculptor (e) wrote Greek tragedies during age of Pericles (f) author of *Oedipus*

(continued)

ANSWERS TO (continued)

(g) war between Sparta and Athens **(h)** historian of Peloponnesian War **(i)** Greek playwright who wrote comedies **(j)** Greek philosopher condemned to death **(k)** wrote *The Republic* **(l)** school started by Plato **(m)** Plato's vision of a perfect society **(n)** developer of syllogism

Answer:

1. He used money from the Delian League for a navy and for works of art.

2. (a) reflected Greek standard of order, balance, proportion **(b)** form of public education that dealt with important issues

3. Females were rarely seen outside, lived in separate quarters, and could not own or inherit land or vote.

4. (a) attack on Athens by Sparta, weakening of Athens by plague and defeat in Sicily, surrender of Athens **(b)** Athens lost self-confidence.

5. (a) democracy, patriotism, religion **(b)** led to charges of "corrupting the youth of Athens"

6. (a) The death of Socrates convinced him that average citizens were unable to govern wisely. **(b)** He wanted to see a society led by a ruling class with a philosopher-king at its head.

7. He developed a system for organizing and testing ideas that was important for science.

8. (a) Look for *yes* answers to discuss artistic, political, and intellectual heights. Look for *no* answers to discuss inequality. **(b)** Answers may include political harmony, artistic greatness, social equality, intellectual stimulation.

What mattered most was that the state be ruled by its greatest philosopher.

Plato's writings dominated philosophic thought in Europe for nearly 1,500 years. His only rivals in importance were his own teacher, Socrates, and his own pupil, Aristotle (AR-ihs-tot'l).

Aristotle One of the brightest students at Plato's Academy was a physician's son named Aristotle. Few minds in history were as hungry for knowledge as his. He wanted to know about morals, music, mathematics, biology, botany, geology, medicine, politics, art, drama, language, geography, education, and law. He studied with Plato for 20 years.

Aristotle insisted that every truth followed logically from other truths. You could not miss a step, jumping from truth A to truth C. In the middle, you needed truth B to link the other truths. Aristotle developed a set of logical statements known as a syllogism (SIHL-uh-jihz-uhm). A syllogism consists of three logically related statements. Here is an example:

1. All people are mortal.
2. Socrates was a person.
3. Therefore, Socrates was mortal.

This system for organizing and testing ideas helped to develop rational, scientific thought.

Section REVIEW 3

Define: (a) classical art, (b) tragedy, (c) comedy, (d) philosopher, (e) Socratic method
Identify: (a) Pericles, (b) the Parthenon, (c) Athena, (d) Phidias, (e) Aeschylus, (f) Sophocles, (g) Peloponnesian War, (h) Thucydides, (i) Aristophanes, (j) Socrates, (k) Plato, (l) the Academy, (m) *The Republic*, (n) Aristotle
Answer:
1. How did Pericles strengthen Athens's position as a leader in Greece?
2. (a) How were the Parthenon and other works of art and architecture examples of Athenian values? (b) How was drama important to the polis?
3. How were the lives of Greek girls and women different from the lives of the boys and men?
4. (a) What were the key events of the Peloponnesian War? (b) What were its results?

122

5. (a) What topics did Socrates consider important for discussion? (b) How did his views lead to his condemnation and death?
6. (a) Why did Plato reject democracy? (b) What type of society did he advocate?
7. How did Aristotle aid the development of scientific thinking?

Critical Thinking
8. (a) Are historians justified in calling this period of Greek history a golden age? Give reasons for your answer. (b) Write a short definition of a golden age that would apply to other civilizations. (Save your definition for reference in later chapters.)

Alexander's conquests spread Greek culture. 4

Philip II, the king of Macedon, nodded his head in agreement as he pored over a long letter from the Athenian philosopher Isocrates. Isocrates pointed out that the Greek city-states had continued to fight one another in the half-century since Sparta defeated Athens. First one polis and then another rose to power, but none was able to bring peace or unity to Greece.

Isocrates called upon Philip to unite the Greeks and then take the offensive against Persia. The expedition would free the Greek cities in Asia Minor and seize Persia's vast wealth. As the leader who avenged the Persian invasion of Greece a century earlier, Philip would win everlasting fame.

Isocrates' ideas inspired both Philip and his son Alexander. In this section, you will see how Philip united Greece and how Alexander conquered Persia. You will also see how Alexander's conquests spread Greek culture into Asia.

Philip built Macedon's power.

While Athens and other city-states produced a cultural golden age, Macedon remained a little-known kingdom located north of the peninsula of Greece. The Macedonians were a tough, Greek-speaking people who lived in mountain villages rather than city-states. The Greeks looked down on the Macedonians as uncivilized, with no great philosophers, sculptors, or writers. They did, however, have an important resource in their shrewd and fearless kings.

In 359 B.C., the shrewdest of all the Macedonians, Philip II, became the country's new king. Though only twenty-three years old, Philip quickly proved to be a brilliant general and a ruthless politician. Realizing that the proud Macedonian nobles respected only power, Philip transformed the rugged peasants under his command into a well-trained professional army. His new army featured dense phalanxes 16 men across and 16 deep. Since the Macedonian phalanx was twice the size of the traditional Greek phalanx, it could easily burst through enemy lines. Philip then used fast-moving cavalry to crush his disorganized opponents.

Philip's powerful army proved to be unbeatable. Within a short time, he subdued the Macedonian nobles and prepared to invade Greece. As Philip gained in strength, an Athenian orator named Demosthenes (dih-MAHS-thuh-NEEZ) delivered eloquent speeches warning the Greeks that Philip was ruthless and had to be stopped. In one speech, Demosthenes bitterly reminded cautious Athenians, "For the sake of ruling and wielding power, he [Philip] has had an eye knocked out, his shoulder smashed, his leg and hand mutilated; he jettisons whatever part of his body fate wants to take away, just so long as he can live in honor and glory with what is left."

Demosthenes' warnings finally convinced the Athenians to take action. In 338 B.C., Athens and Thebes joined forces against Philip. By then, it was too late. The Macedonians soundly defeated the Athenians and Thebans at the decisive battle of Chaeronea (KAIR-uh-NEE-uh). Philip's eighteen-year-old son Alexander led a successful cavalry charge that helped win the battle.

Philip's victory made him the dominant power in Greece. Rather than occupy the conquered city-states, he called upon them to join an alliance called the League of Corinth. Philip then announced his plan to invade Persia.

Philip never got a chance to put his plan into action. In 337 B.C., he divorced Alexander's mother Olympias and married the daughter of a high-ranking Macedonian nobleman. The marriage infuriated Olympias and jeopardized Alexander's right to inherit the throne. These fears became a reality when Philip's second wife bore a son.

Despite mounting family tensions, Philip staged a huge festival to celebrate the marriage of his daughter. During a solemn procession, a former guardsman named Pausanias suddenly dashed forward and stabbed Philip. The dying king's bodyguard immediately killed Pausanias. With the support of the army, Alexander immediately proclaimed himself King of Macedon.

Turning Points in History

The Conquests of Alexander the Great
Alexander was only twenty years old when he became king in 336 B.C. Despite his youth, Alexander had been carefully trained for leadership. Philip had hired Aristotle as tutor to the young prince. The great philosopher encouraged Alexander's interest in science, geography, and literature. Alexander especially enjoyed Homer's description of the heroic deeds performed by Achilles during the Trojan War. Since his mother claimed to be descended from Achilles, Alexander also yearned to be a great hero.

Philip had also encouraged his son in the art of war. As a young boy, Alexander learned to ride a horse, use weapons, and command troops. Once he became king, Alexander promptly demonstrated that his military training had not been wasted. When Thebes rebelled, he destroyed the city and sold the survivors into slavery. Intimidated by this ruthless action, the other Greek cities quickly fell in line.

With Greece now secure, Alexander felt free to carry out Philip's plan to invade Persia. In 334 B.C., he crossed the Dardanelles with 30,000 infantry and 5,000 cavalry.

The fall of Persia Persian messengers raced along the Royal Road to spread the news of Alexander's invasion. Within a short time, a Persian army of about 40,000 men rushed to defend Asia Minor. Instead of waiting for the Persians to make the first move, Alexander ordered an elite cavalry unit known as the Companions to attack. Led by Alexander, the Companions galloped through a hail of arrows and smashed the Persian defenses.

Alexander's victory at Granicus (see map on page 124) alarmed the Persian king Darius III. Vowing to crush the Macedonians, he raised a

123

SECTION 4
Objectives and Teaching Strategies

OBJECTIVE 1. Explain how Philip of Macedon gained control over Greece.

Teaching Strategy: *Discussing History: Philip of Macedon* (page 102e)

OBJECTIVE 2. Describe and evaluate the achievements of Alexander the Great.

Teaching Strategy: *Discussing History: What Made Alexander "Great"?* (page 102e)

OBJECTIVE 3. Explain how Greek culture spread during the Hellenistic Age.

Teaching Strategy: *Using Geographic Themes: Movement* (page 102e)

■ DISCUSSION

Philip was a bold and determined leader. Ask students to react to this description of Philip by the Athenian orator Demosthenes: "For the sake of ruling and wielding power, he has had an eye knocked out, his shoulder smashed, his leg and hand mutilated; he jettisons whatever part of his body fate wants to take away so long as he can live in honor and glory with what is left." (see text on this page, column 1, paragraph 2)

SECTION 4
Resources

GEOGRAPHY
■ Transparency 17

REINFORCEMENT
■ Independent Practice 5.4

ENRICHMENT
■ Voices from the Past 5.4

ASSESSMENT
■ Section Quiz 5.4

123

The Empire of Alexander the Great

KEY

⭐ Battle

▨ Alexander's empire in 323 B.C.

→ Route of Alexander's army

0   300 Miles

ANSWERS TO
Map Study

Dardanelles; Egypt; near the Indus River

■ BACKGROUND

Even as a young boy, Alexander demonstrated great courage. When Alexander was twelve, Philip planned to purchase for him a great black stallion named Bucephalus. When Bucephalus seemed unmanageable, however, Philip changed his mind. Undaunted, Alexander ran forward and turned the powerful animal toward the sun so that it would not be frightened by its shadow. Bucephalus immediately calmed down and allowed Alexander to mount him. Henceforth, Alexander was the only person who could ride Bucephalus.

Although Alexander's conquests made him one of the world's richest men, his most treasured possession was a well-worn copy of Homer's *Iliad*, given to him by Aristotle. Alexander called it the "perfect portable treasure of all military virtue and knowledge." Alexander often read favorite passages about Achilles, and he slept with the book beside his dagger under his pillow.

Map Study

What narrow body of water did Alexander cross to reach Asia Minor? Where did he go after capturing Jerusalem? Where did Alexander build a city to honor Bucephalus, his favorite war horse?

huge army of at least 100,000 men to face the Macedonians in the Battle of Issus. Realizing that he was outnumbered, Alexander shrewdly ordered the Companions to charge straight at Darius. The frightened king fled, followed by his panicked army. The victory at Issus gave Alexander control over Asia Minor.

Shaken by his defeat, Darius tried to negotiate a peace settlement. He offered Alexander a huge sum of gold, his daughter's hand in marriage, and the western third of his empire. Alexander's advisers urged him to accept, pointing out that just one defeat would cancel all their victories. The rapid collapse of Persian resistance, however, fired Alexander's ambition. He rejected Darius' offer, confidently announcing that he now intended to conquer the entire Persian empire.

While Darius gathered another army, Alexander marched into Egypt in 332 B.C. The Egyptians welcomed Alexander as a liberator from Persian rule. During his stay, he founded the city of Alexandria at the mouth of the Nile.

After leaving Egypt, Alexander boldly marched into Mesopotamia to confront Darius. The des-

perate Persian king assembled a vast army that included 200,000 men and chariots armed with deadly rotating blades. The two armies collided at Gaugamela, a small village near the ruins of ancient Nineveh. With the outcome still in doubt, Alexander launched a cavalry charge, followed by a massive phalanx attack. As the Persian lines began to crumble, Darius panicked and fled.

Alexander's victory at Gaugamela ended Persia's power forever. The Macedonian army now advanced unopposed into Persia's wealthiest provinces. Within a short time, it occupied the ancient capitals of Babylon, Susa, and Persepolis. These cities yielded a huge treasure that Alexander distributed among his army.

The final conquests Although Alexander now reigned as the unchallenged ruler of Southwestern Asia, he was more interested in expanding his empire than in governing it. In 330 B.C., Alexander left the ruined Persepolis hoping to pursue Darius and conquer the empire's remote Asian provinces.

Darius' trail led Alexander to a deserted spot south of the Caspian Sea. When the Macedonians arrived, they found that the once all-powerful

124

ruler had been murdered by one of his satraps. Rather than return to Babylon, Alexander marched eastward, determined to explore new lands and reach the ocean that he believed marked the end of the world.

During the next three years, Alexander's army slowly fought its way across the desert wastes and mountains of Central Asia. In 327 B.C., it finally reached the Indus River and crossed into India. There a powerful Indian army that included 200 elephants blocked the path of Alexander and his army. After winning a fierce battle, Alexander's weary soldiers refused to advance.

The Macedonians had now fought for seven years while marching more than 11,000 miles. The exhausted soldiers yearned to go home. A respected veteran urged Alexander, "Lead us back now . . . A noble thing, O King, is to know when to stop." Bitterly disappointed, Alexander finally agreed to turn back.

After crossing one of the harshest deserts in the world, Alexander and his army finally reached Babylon in 324 B.C. Restless as always, Alexander soon announced plans to construct great roads and to explore Arabia. None of these plans were to be carried out. Alexander suddenly caught a fever that grew steadily worse. When it was clear that he was dying, his loyal Macedonian soldiers filed through the palace past his bedside to bid him farewell. Two days later, on June 10, 323 B.C., Alexander died. He was not yet thirty-three years old.

Alexander's legacy Although he ruled for only 12 years and 8 months, Alexander had a profound impact upon history. His conquests ended the era of independent Greek city-states. As he and his army marched through the Persian empire, thousands of Greek artists, merchants, and officials followed and settled there. They built new cities containing temples, gymnasiums, and theaters. As time passed, Greek settlers married Persian women and adopted Persian ways. A vibrant new culture called **Hellenism** emerged from the blend of Greek and eastern customs.

Although Alexander created a new empire, he died before he could rule it. Whether he would

This mosaic shows Alexander leading a charge against the Persian army. The mosaic is a Roman copy of a painting done soon after Alexander died.

125

Gordius, king of ancient Phrygia, tied a knot that could only be undone by the person who would rule Asia. Alexander cut rather than untied the rope. Ask what the story of the Gordian knot reveals about Alexander's character and methods?

Alexander's march westward from India across the Baluchistan desert (in today's southern Pakistan) was the most difficult in his career. When water became scarce, the thirsty soldiers butchered their horses and drank the blood. On one occasion, Alexander was offered a helmetful of water. Seeing that his men had none, he emptied it on the ground. After 60 days of wandering across the trackless desert, the Greeks finally staggered into the Persian royal residence at Pura.

125

■ BACKGROUND

A king asked Archimedes how he could be sure his crown was pure gold. A short time later, while taking a bath, Archimedes realized that gold would displace an amount of water equal to its weight. "Eureka," he shouted and absent-mindedly ran home naked to test his idea.

■ BACKGROUND

Pythagoras taught his secret doctrines to a select inner circle of students. Since the Greek word *esoterikos* means "inner," these doctrines were described as esoteric. To this day, *esoteric* refers to abstruse knowledge known only to a chosen few.

have been as great in peace as he was in war remains unknown. His heroic personality and the story of his unequaled skill as a military commander created a legend that still survives. "I set no limits of labors to a man of spirit," Alexander once told his troops. "It is a lovely thing to live with courage, and to die, leaving behind an everlasting renown."

The Hellenistic age produced many achievements.

Alexander's sudden death raised the question of who would inherit his empire. As he lay dying, Alexander correctly predicted that the empire would go to the strongest. That proved to be three ambitious generals. Antigonus (an-TIGH-uh-nus) controlled Macedon, while Ptolemy (TAH-luh-mee) seized Egypt and Seleucus (suh-LOO-kuhs) took Asia Minor and the Fertile Crescent.

Alexandria Although lacking political unity, the Hellenistic world produced a number of impressive scientific and cultural achievements. Alexandria in Egypt quickly became the foremost center of Hellenistic civilization.

Alexandria occupied a strategic site on the western edge of the Nile delta. Ships from all around the Mediterranean docked in its spacious harbor. Its warehouses bulged with wheat and other products from the Nile valley.

Alexandria's thriving commerce enabled it to grow and prosper. By the third century B.C., it boasted a diverse population that exceeded half a million people. Greek officials, Jewish merchants, and Egyptian priests mingled in crowded marketplaces with visitors from sub-Saharan Africa and even faraway India.

Both residents and visitors admired Alexandria's great beauty. Broad avenues lined with statues of Greek gods divided the city into blocks. The Ptolemies built magnificent royal palaces overlooking the harbor. A much visited tomb contained Alexander's coffin. Soaring 400 feet over the harbor stood an enormous stone lighthouse called the Pharos. It contained a polished bronze mirror that reflected the light from a blazing fire.

Alexandria's greatest attractions were its famous museum and library. The museum was a temple dedicated to the Muses, the Greek goddesses of arts and sciences. It contained art galleries, a zoo, botanical gardens, and even a dining

hall. Teachers and students were only a short distance from the nearby library. Its collection of half a million papyrus scrolls included all the masterpieces of ancient literature. As the first true research library in the world, it helped promote the work of a gifted group of scholars.

Astronomy and geography The museum contained a small observatory in which astronomers could study the planets and stars. Aristarchus (ar-uh-STAHR-huhs) of Samos reached two significant conclusions. First he estimated that the sun was at least 300 times larger than the earth. (Although he greatly underestimated the sun's true size, Aristarchus improved upon the belief that the sun was smaller than Greece!) Second Aristarchus advanced the theory that the earth and other planets revolve around the sun.

Unfortunately for science, other astronomers refused to support Aristarchus' theories. By the second century A.D., Alexandria's last great astronomer Ptolemy placed the earth at the center of the solar system. Astronomers accepted this view for the next 14 centuries.

While Hellenistic astronomers debated the earth's position in the solar system, a scholar named Eratosthenes (er-uh-TAHS-thuh-neez) correctly calculated the earth's true size. Eratosthenes was the director of the library and a highly regarded astronomer, poet, and mathematician. He skillfully used geometry to help him compute the earth's circumference at about 25,000 miles.

Mathematics and physics Both Eratosthenes and Aristarchus used a geometry text written by Euclid (YOO-klihd). Euclid was a highly regarded mathematician who opened a school of geometry in Alexandria. His best known book the *Elements* contained 465 carefully presented geometry propositions and proofs. Islamic and European universities used the *Elements* until well into the 1900's. Only the Bible has been more widely used and studied.

Another important Hellenistic scientist, Archimedes (AHR-kih-MEE-deez), studied at Alexandria. He calculated the value of pi (π)—the ratio of the circumference of a circle to its diameter. Archimedes also discovered that levers could be used to lift heavy objects. He once boasted, "Give me a place to stand and I can move the earth."

By building on the knowledge of Archimedes, Hellenistic scientists could have launched an

The oak leaf wreath from Philip II's tomb (left), the statue of the Winged Victory of Samothrace (right), and the model of Pergamum—the "Athens of the East" (above)—all show Hellenistic influence.

industrial revolution. They built a force pump, pneumatic machines, and even a steam engine. But they never seem to have considered producing large numbers of these machines. In an age when slaves were plentiful, labor-saving devices had little appeal.

Sculpture Sculpture, like science, flourished during the Hellenistic age. Rulers, wealthy merchants, and cities all purchased statues to honor the gods, commemorate heroes, and portray ordinary people in everyday situations. The largest known Hellenistic statue was created on the island of Rhodes. Known as the Colossus of Rhodes, the 105-foot high bronze statue may also have served as a lighthouse.

Although the Colossus of Rhodes was destroyed by an earthquake, another great Hellenistic statue was discovered by archaeologists in 1863. This was the famous Winged Victory of Samothrace. It commemorates a naval victory by the Greeks against foes who would have enslaved them. Although the body of the goddess appears still, her marble robes ripple as if blown by the wind. Her mighty wings are poised for flight.

By 150 B.C., Hellenism was in decline. A new city, Rome, was growing and gaining strength.

Through Rome, Greek-style drama, architecture, sculpture, religion, and philosophy were preserved. These ideas were to become the heart of Western civilization.

Section REVIEW 4

Define: Hellenism
Identify: Isocrates, Macedon, Philip II, Demosthenes, Companions, Darius III, Battle of Gaugamela, Alexandria, Aristarchus, Eratosthenes, Euclid, Archimedes
Answer:
1. Why was Philip's army so powerful?
2. What motive would Olympias and Darius III have had for killing Philip II?
3. What happened to Alexander's empire after his death?
4. Why didn't the Hellenistic scientists start an industrial revolution?

Critical Thinking
5. "Alexander's achievements, though brilliant, did not last long." (a) Give evidence to support this statement. (b) Give evidence to refute the statement.

127

ANSWERS TO
Section Review 4

Define:
Greek-Persian culture
Identify:
(a) Greek philosopher who urged Philip II to unite Greeks and attack Persia
(b) kingdom north of Greece (c) king of Macedon who conquered Greece
(d) Greek orator who warned that Philip was dangerous (e) elite calvary unit
(f) Persian king defeated by Alexander (g) Macedonian victory that ended Persian power (h) center of Hellenistic civilization
(i) Hellenistic astronomer
(j) astronomer who calculated Earth's true size
(k) Hellenistic mathematician
(l) Hellenistic scientist

Answer:
1. It was well trained and fought in large, powerful phalanxes.

2. Olympias wanted Alexander to inherit the throne. Darius III feared an invasion of Persia.

3. Three strong generals each seized part of the empire.

4. Labor-saving machines were not needed when slaves were plentiful.

5. (a) breakup of empire, decline of Hellenism, eventual takeover by Romans
(b) lasting influences of Hellenistic culture

Concluding the Chapter

1. **Chapter Closer**
   Ask students to summarize what they have learned by supporting the opinion that the spirit and ideas of Greek civilization long outlived ancient Greece.

2. **Reteaching Activities**
   a. Identifying Important Ideas Ask students to write a sentence explaining the significance of each of the following: Bronze Age, Crete, Trojan War, Homer, Olympic Games.
   b. Writing Questions and Answers Have students turn the headings in Section 2 into questions and then answer each question.
   c. Summarizing Have students write one paragraph summarizing the contributions of Pericles, Sophocles, Phidias, and Plato.
   d. Recalling Main Ideas Have students explain how each of the following individuals relates to the history of the Hellenistic Age: Philip of Macedon, Alexander the Great, Ptolemy, and Archimedes.

Answers to Chapter Review appear on pages 102e–102f.

Summary

1. Greek culture grew up around the Aegean Sea. Bronze Age cultures on Crete and mainland Greece laid the foundation for later Greek culture. Greek life was also shaped by the mountainous land, the mild climate, and the sea. Adventures of the heroes and gods of the early Greeks have come down to us in the form of epic poems.

2. Greek city-states competed for power. Two of the most powerful city states were Athens and Sparta. Spartans valued military strength above all, whereas Athenians encouraged individualism and creativity. Athens gradually developed a democratic government. After playing an important role in defeating the invading Persian army, Athens became the powerful leader of an alliance of Greek city-states called the Delian League.

3. Athens led Greece in its golden age. Pericles, leader of Greece for 32 years, helped Athens grow in military and economic strength. He glorified the city by supporting the work of architects, sculptors, and dramatists. Although Athens's confidence was much shaken by a war with Sparta, the struggle sparked great achievement in the area of philosophy.

4. Alexander's conquests spread Greek culture. Two kings of Macedon, Philip and Alexander, conquered Greece as well as a vast empire beyond. A combination of Greek culture with other cultures, called Hellenism, spread throughout this empire. The Hellenistic Age was marked by important advances in science as well as the arts.

Reviewing the Facts

1. Define the following terms:
   a. epic
   b. arete
   c. polis
   d. aristocracy
   e. hoplite
   f. phalanx
   g. tyrant
   h. democracy
   i. tragedy
   j. Socratic method

2. Explain the importance of each of the following names, dates, places, or terms:
   a. Crete
   b. Mycenae
   c. Trojan War
   d. Homer
   e. Athens
   f. Sparta
   g. Solon
   h. Cleisthenes
   i. Herodotus
   j. 490 B.C.
   k. Peloponnesian War
   l. Pericles
   m. 431–404 B.C.
   n. Aeschylus
   o. Sophocles
   p. Socrates
   q. Plato
   r. Aristotle
   s. Philip II
   t. Alexander the Great
   u. 323 B.C.

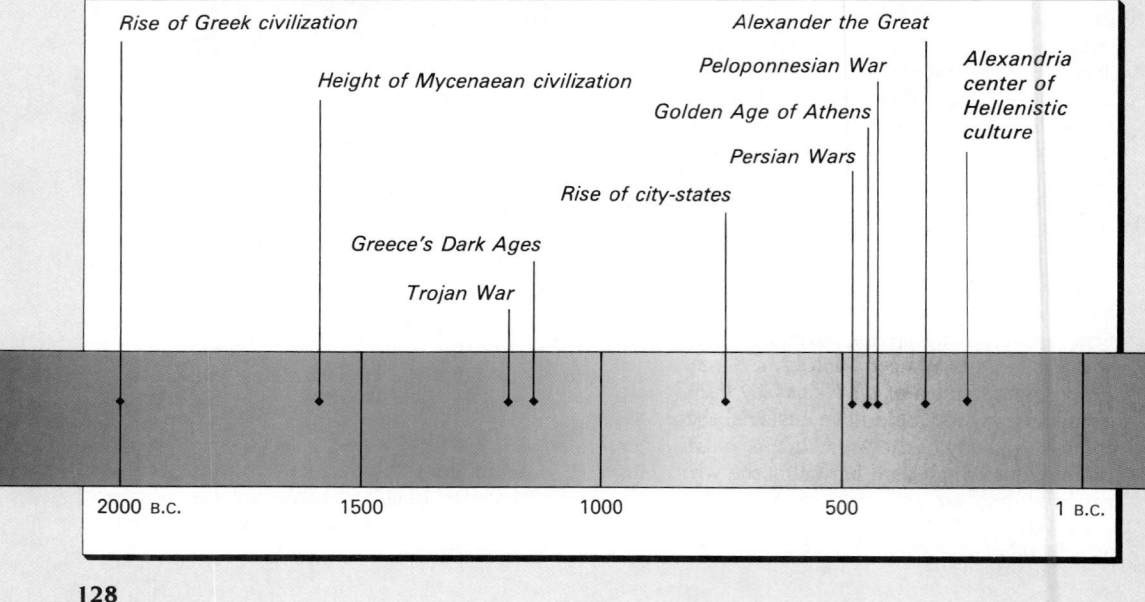

Rise of Greek civilization
Height of Mycenaean civilization
Alexander the Great
Peloponnesian War
Alexandria center of Hellenistic culture
Golden Age of Athens
Persian Wars
Rise of city-states
Greece's Dark Ages
Trojan War

2000 B.C. 1500 1000 500 1 B.C.

128

3. What major changes took place in Greek political organization between 1200 and 500 B.C.?
4. What Greek ideals were expressed both in Homer's poems and in the Olympic games?
5. How did Athens move from aristocratic rule to democracy?
6. Why is the period between 480 and 430 B.C. known as a golden age for Athens?
7. How did the disunity of the Greek city-states lead to their conquest by Philip?
8. How did Greek culture become influential across a broad area outside Greece?

Basic Skills

1. **Interpreting a map** Explain how the map on page 104 illustrates the main idea of that subsection.
2. **Comparing maps** Compare the maps on pages 104 and 110 in terms of title, historical period, region included, and scale.
3. **Sequencing** Arrange the following items in correct chronological order: Dark Ages in Greece, siege of Troy, age of Pericles, reforms of Solon, Persian Wars, death of Socrates, Hellenistic Age, Alexander's empire.
4. **Outlining** Outline the subsection of the text, "Philosophers search for truth," on pages 120–122. Use one heading and three subheadings. Under each subheading, give two items that summarize the major points.

Researching and Reporting Skills

1. **Using the card catalog** In the card catalog in your library, find one book that is a primary source and another that is a secondary source. Use the call numbers to locate the books. Quote a passage from each book to show which type of source it is.
2. **Researching the arts** Greece, together with its overseas settlements and colonies, contains varied examples of Greek architecture. Find information about one of these works. Prepare a report about it, either oral or written, or prepare sketches or diagrams to show the class. List the sources of your information, using proper citations.

Critical Thinking

1. **Giving an opinion** Although Athens and Sparta both had times of greatness, their values and form of government were very different. Which city-state do you think was greater? Give reasons to support your answer.
2. **Evaluating** (a) Compare the ideas of Athenian democracy with those of your country today. (b) In what ways are these ideas alike, and how do they differ? (c) Which do you think is more democratic? Why?
3. **Comparing** Compare the ancient Chinese and Athenian ideas about the role of the individual in society. (a) How are these philosophies alike, and how do they differ? (b) How did the differences affect the development of government in these societies?

Perspectives on Past and Present

1. Pericles said: "Unlike other nations, we Athenians do not call a man who takes no part in public life quiet or unambitious; we call such a man useless." How would Pericles evaluate the behavior of citizens who fail to vote in elections today?
2. If an Olympic athlete of today were to participate in some event of the Greek Olympics, what similarities and differences might that person find?

Investigating History

1. Use the library to find information about the excavations of Heinrich Schliemann at Troy in Asia Minor and Mycenae in Greece and of Sir Arthur Evans at Knossos on Crete. What did those digs show about Aegean civilization?
2. In the library, find books that describe the art of Minoan Crete, Athens at the time of Pericles, and Athens after the Peloponnesian War. (a) How were human and animal figures represented in each period? (b) To what extent might differences in the art of the three eras reflect what was taking place in the society at that time?
3. Find sources on Athenian drama that describe the setting, costumes, and masks that were used. (a) What was the role of song and dance in the theater of Greece? (b) Explain how the role of the audience in the Athenian theater differed from that of an audience today.

129

CHAPTER
Evaluation

Chapter Test 5, Alternate Chapter Test 5, and Computer Test Bank Chapter 5 Test can be used to evaluate your students' understanding of this chapter.

The Roman Republic

Chapter **6**

Chapter Overview

The earliest settlers of the Italian peninsula were the Latins, Greeks, and Etruscans. Early Roman culture was a blend of the traditions of these three groups. In its early years, Rome was ruled by kings. However, opposition to the rule of kings resulted in the establishment of the Roman republic in 509 B.C. and the determination among Romans never again to have a monarchy.

Within the republic of Rome, the plebeians succeeded in winning reforms from the patricians. By 275 B.C., Rome had set up a balanced government with a powerful patrician senate, a democratic assembly of citizen-soldiers, and two consuls in place of a king. The defeat of Carthage in the Punic Wars enabled Rome to dominate the Mediterranean Sea, but victory brought with it new problems that led to social unrest. Julius Caesar brought some political stability to the republic, but his actions threatened the powers of the senate and he was assassinated. When successive changes in leadership failed to bring peace, the Romans welcomed the strong leadership of Octavian, and in 27 B.C. the republic ended.

Chapter Focus

A myth is a traditional story that explains some practice or belief. Point out that myths can offer important insights into the ways people view themselves and their world. Have students read the story of Romulus and Remus on pages 130–131, and ask, "What belief does this myth express?" Lead students to see that the myth of

Romulus and Remus expressed the Romans' belief that Rome was destined to rule the world. Rome's founder, Romulus, was believed to be the son of the war god Mars, and a model Roman. This chapter examines the rise of the Roman republic.

The Romans built a great city. **1**

Setting the Stage

Using Geographic Themes: Location (Objective 1) Show Map Transparency 18, *Italy about 500 B.C.* Help students locate Italy, Rome, the Tiber River, and the Alps. Ask students to describe Rome's location on the Italian peninsula. Use Map Transparency 13, *The World about 200 B.C.*, to show the Italian peninsula's location near the midpoint of the Mediterranean region, and Rome's location relative to Ptolemaic Egypt and the Mauryan empire in India. Conclude by reading this quote by the famous Roman orator, Cicero:

> Romulus must at the very beginning have had a divine intimation that the city would one day be the seat and hearth of a mighty empire, for scarcely could a city placed on any other site in Italy have more easily maintained our present widespread domination.

Ask students to support or refute Cicero's statement. Can they find

***Chapter* 6** The Roman Republic 1000 B.C.–27 B.C.   ★ **Advanced**
FOCUS   The myth of Romulus and Remus   ● **Basic**

	SECTION 1	SECTION 2	SECTION 3
Objectives	1. Explain the role of geographic location in Rome's early growth. 2. Identify the contributions to Roman culture of the Latins, Greeks, and Etruscans. 3. Describe the character of an ideal citizen in the Roman republic. 4. Explain the system of social status in Roman society.	1. Identify the Twelve Tables and explain their significance in Roman law. 2. Compare and contrast the political institutions of the Roman republic and the United States. 3. Trace on a map the expansion of Rome.	1. Assess the impact of the Punic Wars on the republic. 2. Explain the main cause and long-term effects of changes in the Roman army. 3. Identify Julius Caesar and describe his rise to power.
Setting the Stage	The location of Rome Using Geographic Themes: Location Transparency 18 Transparency 13	Reasons for the historical probability of Rome's rise to power	Discussing History: The Impact of the Punic Wars on the Roman Republic Transparency 20
Teaching Strategies	Discussing History: Roman Borrowings Discussing History: *Gravitas* Relating Past to Present: The Toga Check for Understanding	Transferring Ideas: Law Codes and the Twelve Tables Relating Past to Present: The Governments of Rome and the United States Geography in History: The Expansion of Rome Outline Map 21 Check for Understanding	Skill Building: Identifying Cause and Effect Relationships Writing about History: Julius Caesar Check for Understanding
Guided Practice	Transparency 18 Q&A Section Review 1	Transparency 19 Q&A Section Review 2	Transparency 20 Q&A Section Review 3
Independent Practice Worksheets	Independent Practice 6.1 Vocabulary 6	Independent Practice 6.2 Basic Skills 6	Independent Practice 6.3 Geography Skills 6 Critical Thinking 6
Enrichment	1. Primary Source: Voices 6.1 2. ★Analyzing a Quotation 3. Researching for Points	1. Primary Source: Voices 6.2 2. ★Analyzing a Quotation 3. Creative Writing 4. Researching for Points	1. Primary Source: Voices 6.3 2. Preparing a Report 3. ★Solving a Puzzle 4. Researching for Points 5. Global Perspectives Transparency 13

Chapter Closer	●**Reteaching Activities**	Summarizing, Writing Questions and Answers, Giving an Explanation
	Chapter Review	Summary, Reviewing the Facts, Basic Skills, Researching and Reporting Skills, Critical Thinking, Perspectives on Past and Present, Investigating History
	Chapter Evaluation	Chapter Test 6, Alternate Chapter Test 6, Computer Test Bank Chapter 6 Test

another location on the Italian peninsula that would have been more advantageous than Rome's?

Teaching Strategies

Discussing History: Roman Borrowings (Objective 2) The Romans borrowed ideas from the Latins, Greeks, and Etruscans. After students have read pages 132–133, have them list in three columns the Latin, Greek, and Etruscan contributions to Roman culture.

Discussing History: *Gravitas* (Objective 3) The character of Rome's citizens was influenced by a set of values called *mos maiorum*, or "ways of the fathers." Roman values were rooted in their pioneer past and intensified by long, successful struggles against hostile foes. The Romans emphasized discipline, practicality, strength, tenacity, and loyalty. These values combined to produce a much admired trait called *gravitas*. Ask students to reread the passage about Andromache and Hector on page 107. How might a Roman Hector have replied to Andromache? How does the Roman ideal of *gravitas* differ from the Greek ideal of *arete*?

Relating Past to Present: The Toga (Objective 4) Ask students to identify the Roman social classes and the grounds for membership in each. After the students have read the Daily Life feature, "The Roman Toga" (page 134), have them explain the significance of this famous Roman garment. Then ask, "In what ways do clothes indicate social status in American society today? How are the Roman and American class systems similar? How are they different?"

Check for Understanding Ask students to explain the significance of the following concepts: republic, *gravitas*, patrician, and plebeian.

Enrichment Activities

1. **Reading a Primary Source**
   Assign Voices from the Past Resource Book 6.1.

2. **Analyzing a Quotation**
   The modern historian Michael Grant wrote, "Italy's central position in the Mediterranean is a call to self-assertion, suggesting many promising opportunities if and when its population is capable of grasping them." Ask advanced students to evaluate this statement in relation to early Roman history.

3. **Researching for Bonus Points**
   The Romans changed the names of 11 of the 12 Greek Olympians. Which god retained the same name? (Apollo)

Setting the Stage

Have the students suggest some strengths of the Roman republic, identified in the first section. Strengths might include Rome's central geographic location, stable political system, military power, and belief in a destiny to rule the world. Tell students that some historians have described Rome's rise to power as inevitable. Ask students what *inevitable* means. Help them to distinguish between the idea of inevitability and the concept of historical probability. Point out that patterns and trends in history can make some events more likely, but that historical developments are not necessarily inevitable. Explain that this section examines how the Romans unified the Mediterranean world.

Teaching Strategies

Transferring Ideas: Law Codes and the Twelve Tables (Objective 1) Ask students why they think the plebeians wanted a written code of laws. Recall that Babylon had a written code of laws under Hammurabi, and the Hebrews had the Ten Commandments. Have students compare and contrast the reasons for establishing the Babylonian, Hebrew, and Roman legal codes. Students should recognize that an important function of the Twelve Tables was to establish the idea that all free citizens had the right to be protected by the law. Ask students what effect this code had on Rome's social system.

Relating Past to Present: The Governments of Rome and the United States (Objective 2) Ask students to describe the executive, legislative, and judicial branches of American government. Have students compare the office of consul with the office of the President. Ask, "What might be some advantages and disadvantages of dividing the executive branch of government between two leaders?" Then have students compare the membership and functions of the Roman Senate and Assembly with those of the United States Congress. Ask, "What might be some advantages and disadvantages of dividing the legislative branch of government into two bodies?"

Geography in History: The Expansion of Rome (Objective 3) Distribute copies of Outline Map 21: The Roman Empire. Tell students that, for this activity, they will need to refer to the maps on pages 131, 139, and 140. Have students label the Mediterranean Sea, Italy, Gaul, Spain, Greece, Sicily, Macedon, Pergamum, Asia Minor, Africa, Egypt, and the cities of Rome and Carthage. Ask students to draw a map key and use the symbols in the key to show all areas controlled by the Etruscans or Latins in 500 B.C., the extent of Roman territory by 265 B.C., and the area controlled by Rome in 133 B.C. After students have completed their maps, have them write a map caption explaining how the Romans extended their power.

Check for Understanding Ask students to use the information presented in this section to answer this question: What factors contributed to the likelihood of Rome's rise to power?

Enrichment Activities

1. **Reading a Primary Source**
   Assign Voices from the Past Resource Book 6.2.

2. **Analyzing a Quotation**
   The famed historian Charles Gibbon wrote that Rome was "sometimes vanquished in battle, always victorious in war."

Ask advanced students to interpret and evaluate this statement, using facts to support their arguments.

3. **Creative Writing**
   Show students Map Transparency 19, *Rome and Carthage,* and have them trace the route of Hannibal's invasion of Rome. Ask students to imagine that they are accompanying Hannibal on his legendary march over the Alps. Their assignment is to write journal entries describing their experiences. (See the chapter, "Through the Alps to the Gates of Rome" in National Geographic's *Greece and Rome.*)

4. **Researching for Bonus Points**
   Where did Hannibal die and what were his last words? (Hannibal died in his house in Libyssa in the kingdom of Bithynia, now a part of modern Turkey. His final words were: "It's time now to end the great anxiety of the Romans who have grown weary of waiting for the death of a hated old man.")

Setting the Stage

Discussing History: The Impact of the Punic Wars on the Roman Republic (Objective 1) Use Map Transparency 20, *Roman Power in 133 B.C.,* to show students the extent of Rome's control after the Punic Wars. Ask students to speculate about the advantages for the Romans of conquering Carthage. List their ideas on the board. When the list is complete, point out that the text states, "Carthage was not the only loser of the Punic Wars. Rome was also hurt in many ways." Ask students why they think this was true. In this section students will learn how the Punic Wars created conditions that led to the end of the Roman republic.

Teaching Strategies

Skill Building: Identifying Cause and Effect Relationships (Objective 2) Ask students to identify the main cause and the long-term effects of Marius' decision to allow the Roman poor to enlist in the army. (Cause: Marius needed more soldiers to defend Rome, and there weren't enough landowners to fill the ranks of citizen-soldiers. Only landowners could serve in the army and the number of landowners had declined as farmers were forced to sell their lands. Effect: Marius' decision created armies of professional soldiers loyal to particular military leaders rather than to the republic. Military leaders could use their armies to advance their own political careers and, as a result, precipitate political instability and civil war.)

Writing about History: Julius Caesar (Objective 3) After students have read the sections on Julius Caesar (pages 144–146), tell them that the

Greek historian Herodotus wrote, "Circumstances rule men; men do not rule circumstances." Ask students to interpret the quotation and apply it to Julius Caesar's career. Draw two columns on the board. Have students find facts supporting Herodotus' proposition, and list their responses in the first column. Then ask students to find facts supporting the view that Caesar rose above circumstances in forging his career, and list students' responses in the second column. Conclude by asking students to take a point of view and write a letter to Herodotus agreeing or disagreeing with his statement, and including three pieces of evidence to support their arguments.

Check for Understanding Have students explain the roles of the following individuals in the collapse of republican government in Rome: Tiberius Gracchus, Gaius Gracchus, Marius, Sulla, Julius Caesar, Crassus, Pompey, and Octavian.

Enrichment Activities

1. **Reading a Primary Source**
   Assign Voices from the Past Resource Book 6.3.

2. **Preparing a Report**
   Caesar is often ranked among history's greatest military commanders. Ask students to report on Caesar's conquest of Gaul and Britannia.

3. **Solving a Puzzle**
   Caesar received numerous warnings to avoid the Senate on the fateful day of his assassination. Ask advanced students to research Caesar's death and propose a hypothesis answering this question: Why did Caesar

go unarmed to the Senate meeting?

4. **Researching for Bonus Points**
   Who was the son of Caesar and Cleopatra and what happened to him? (Caesarion; Octavian had him killed.)

5. **Global Perspectives**
   Have students perform the activities in Map Transparency 13, *The World about 200 B.C.*

ANSWERS TO Chapter Review 6

Reviewing the Facts

1. (a) government in which citizens have right to vote to choose their leaders (b) weightiness or seriousness (c) member of a privileged family who claimed descent from founders of Rome (d) person who was a free citizen but had less power than a patrician (e) one of two officials who took the place of king of Rome (f) power to overrule (g) aristocratic branch of Roman government (h) absolute ruler for six months chosen by consuls and elected by senate (i) soldier who fights in any country's army for pay (j) urban, landless poor (k) official who spoke on behalf of the plebeians (l) rule of three

2. (a) centrally located city where Roman republic began and from which it spread its power (b) peninsula near midpoint of Mediterranean (c) first settlers in Italy and Rome (d) third group of settlers in Italy who brought writing system and helped develop Rome's trade (e) when Roman republic was set up (f) father of the family, who had complete control

(g) Rome's strongest enemy, located near midpoint of Mediterranean coast (h) first written Roman laws that established idea that all free citizens had a right to protection of the law (i) decided which city, Rome or Carthage, would control Sicily and the western Mediterranean (j) Carthaginian military genius who defeated Roman armies twice (k) ended second Punic War when Scipio defeated Hannibal (l) date Carthage was destroyed (m) brothers who attempted reforms of Rome's government (n) consul of Rome, general, absolute ruler of Rome for ten years (o) date when Caesar defied senate's orders and marched against Pompey (p) date Caesar was murdered (q) Egypt's queen who married Caesar, wooed and won Antony, and caused third civil war in Rome (r) Caesar's friend who helped kill Caesar (s) Caesar's grandnephew and adopted son who became ruler of Rome for 41 years (t) Octavian's chief rival

3. (a) Rome was a central point within a central peninsula, making it an ideal position from which to send out ships and armies in all directions. (b) Latin settlers were simple farmers and shepherds and had little influence on the growth of Rome. Greek settlers established prosperous and commercially active cities and brought them into closer contact with Greek civilization. Etruscan settlers had great cultural influence on Romans and developed Rome's trade. (c) There was constant conflict between patricians who had all the authority to make laws for Rome and its people and plebeians. (d) It forced both patrician and plebeian men in Rome to lead double lives as farmers and soldiers.

4. (a) Patricians controlled Rome's government, plebeians were

barred from high office and military command. **(b)** The Twelve Tables gave plebeians more rights, including the protection of the law.

5. Consuls commanded Rome's army and directed its government, had power of life and death over citizens in wartime and great powers in peacetime as well; one consul could always veto others' decisions. Senate—members served for life; exercised enormous influence over both foreign and domestic policy. Assembly—democratic side of Roman government; little power in comparison to the consuls and the senate. Dictator—had absolute power to make laws and command the army, but power lasted for only six months.

6. Roman conquerors were willing to extend citizenship to people outside Rome itself.

7. **(a)** Rome took over Sicily, dominated and conquered the western and eastern halves of the Mediterranean Sea. At the end of the Third Punic War, Rome's Mediterranean empire stretched from Asia Minor to Spain. **(b)** Thousands of soldiers were killed and whole Roman armies destroyed, along with farms, homes, and villages.

8. They came to power through the use of their private armies.

Basic Skills

1. **(a)** about 200 miles **(b)** about 325 miles **(c)** Scale in the first map is about 1 inch to 100 miles; scale in the second map is about 1 inch to 300 miles, making areas seem smaller and distances seem shorter.

2.

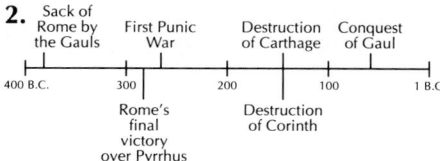

Sack of Rome by the Gauls | First Punic War | Destruction of Carthage | Conquest of Gaul

400 B.C. — 300 — 200 — 100 — 1 B.C.

Rome's final victory over Pyrrhus | Destruction of Corinth

3. Located at the midpoint of the Italian peninsula; located at the center of the Mediterranean, ideal for sending out troops and ships; located on the Tiber on convenient trade routes.

4.

	Rome	Carthage
Population	83,500	25,000
Army	500,000 loyal reserves	mercenaries
Navy	no fleet	500 ships
Resources	little wealth; war experience	wealth from trade

5. **(a)** Expected outcome: Roman defeat **(b)** The Romans copied a captured Carthaginian ship and improved on its design. Their new fleet was superior to Carthage's.

6. **(a)** Scipio Africanus **(b)** Tiberius Gracchus **(c)** Sulla **(d)** Julius Caesar

Researching and Reporting Skills

Students' findings will vary.

Critical Thinking

1. **(a)** *Gravitas* emphasized discipline, strength, and loyalty. *Arete* emphasized individual striving for excellence, courage, honor, and glory. **(b)** Roman civilization was concerned with strength, steadiness, duty to family and country, law, and the glory of Rome; Athenian society was concerned with individual achievement and self-expression.

2. **(a)** You might defeat your enemies and take control of the empire. **(b)** You will be a traitor and might be killed. **(c)** You would cross, because otherwise your army would be disbanded and you would be stripped of your power.

3. **(a)** The army gained needed manpower; members of the proletariat found needed employment; soldiers were better trained and more willing to fight. **(b)** Armies

were no longer loyal to Rome and became instruments of individual rivalries and civil war.

4. **(a)** Rome gained control of the western Mediterranean and of Sicily with its supply of wheat, slaves, and loot. **(b)** Among the social and economic costs were the destruction of many farmlands in Italy; small farmers dispossessed of lands as grain from Sicily flooded the market; large farmers acquired land for raising cattle (latifundia); cheap slave labor deprived citizens of work; poverty and unemployment created proletariat and caused riots; spoils from conquest flooded the markets; the rich became spoiled with luxuries; the growth of slavery undermined traditional values.

Perspectives on Past and Present

Sallust's viewpoint is that power and wealth corrupt people's moral standards. Sallust was probably referring to the violence, bloodshed, and political rivalries that followed the victories of the Punic Wars and to the excessive disparity of wealth among citizens. In present-day application, students might agree or disagree that money is the root of all evil and that ambition and greed can cause a society's decline.

Investigating History

Students' arguments will vary.

The Roman Republic

Chapter 6

Teaching with Pictures

Ask students to study the photograph of the frieze and to describe the action, weapons, and clothing of the warriors. Explain that as warfare was a way of life for many Romans, the military theme extended into Roman art and became part of the decoration on public buildings. This frieze is part of a column that depicts the Romans in battle with the Gauls.

Warfare was almost a way of life for many Romans.

Key Terms

republic	mercenary
gravitas	proletariat
patrician	tribune
plebeian	triumvirate
legion	civil war
monarchy	
consul	
veto	
senate	
dictator	

Read and Understand

1. The Romans built a great city.
2. The Roman republic spread its power.
3. Republican government collapsed in Rome.

According to an ancient Roman myth, the war god Mars fathered twin sons, Romulus and Remus. Their mother was a Latin princess, Rhea Silvia. A jealous Latin king feared that the twins might some day claim his throne, so he ordered them placed in a basket and set afloat on Italy's Tiber River. The king assumed they would drown. Miraculously, a she-wolf found the half-starved infants and fed them with her own milk. Soon after, a shepherd discovered the babies and brought them up as his sons.

As young men, Romulus and Remus decided to build a city near the spot where they had been abandoned as babies. In the rolling land near the Tiber, each brother chose a hilltop and claimed leadership of the new city. Soon they were quarreling bitterly over their rival

130

Chapter 6 Resources

GEOGRAPHY
- Geography Skills 6
- Outline Map 21
- Transparencies 13, 18, 19, 20

REINFORCEMENT
- Vocabulary 6
- Basic Skills 6
- Reteaching 6
- Making Connections Study Guide 6

ENRICHMENT
- Critical Thinking 6

ASSESSMENT
- Chapter Test 6
- Alternate Chapter Test 6
- Computer Test Bank

claims. In the heat of anger, Romulus struck his brother and killed him. The hilltop Romulus had chosen, the Palatine (PAL-uh-TYN), became the center of the new city. The city itself was called Rome, taking its name from the triumphant and murderous brother.

After a long reign, the myth continues, Romulus disappeared one day during a thunderstorm. A dark cloud enveloped him and lifted him up to heaven. Romulus, now a god, later came back to earth to speak to an old comrade. "Go tell the Romans," he said, "it is heaven's will that my Rome shall be capital of the world. Let them learn to be soldiers. Let them know and teach their children that no power on earth can stand against Roman arms."

Although this story is a myth, it has historic value (as many myths do). It tells how Romans in the days of Rome's greatness viewed themselves and their world. By 27 B.C., Rome had indeed become capital of the world—at least, of the world known to the people of Italy. Rome's ships controlled the entire Mediterranean Sea. Its armies exacted taxes and tribute from people on three continents—Africa, Asia, and Europe.

In the years of Rome's growth, Romans overcame the enemies who surrounded them. At the same time, they developed an effective government and an outstanding system of law. At last, however, disputes among groups of Romans gave way to civil war. The Roman government in which many men had a voice gave way to rule by a single man. This chapter will trace the development of Rome from a small village to "capital of the world."

The Romans built a great city. 1

The map on this page shows the long Italian peninsula. Shaped like a high-heeled boot, it seems ready to kick the nearby island of Sicily. To the east of Italy lies Greece. To the west stretch the southern coasts of modern-day France and Spain. To the south, only 80 miles from Sicily, lies the coast of Africa.

Geography was important to Rome's success. The Italian peninsula is near the midpoint of the

Italy about 500 B.C.

KEY
○ Etruscan settlement
○ Greek settlement
▨ Latium

0 _____ 200 Miles

Map Study
What mountains lie north of Italy? Where were most of the Greek settlements in Italy?

Mediterranean, dividing the sea into an eastern and a western half. Rome itself is located midway between the Alps and Italy's southern tip. Thus, the city is a central point within a central peninsula. Rome occupies an ideal position from which to send out ships and armies in all directions. Moreover, the city was built about 15 miles inland from the sea, at the first convenient place for crossing the Tiber River. Thus, many key trade routes between northern and southern Italy met at Rome.

Italy's land is mountainous but not as rugged as the land of Greece. The snow-capped peaks of the Alps sharply separate Italy from the rest of Europe. There are, however, passes through the Alps by which invaders and migrating groups could reach the peninsula. A lower mountain range, the Apennines (AP-uh-nynz), runs down the length of Italy. Especially on the western side of the Apennines, the country in ancient times was rolling, wooded, and fertile.

131

SECTION 1 Objectives and Teaching Strategies

OBJECTIVE 1. Explain the role of geographic location in Rome's early growth.
Teaching Strategy: Using Geographic Themes: Location (page 130a)

OBJECTIVE 2. Identify the contributions to Roman culture of the Latins, Greeks, and Etruscans.
Teaching Strategy: Discussing History: Roman Borrowings (page 130c)

OBJECTIVE 3. Describe the character of an ideal citizen in the Roman republic.
Teaching Strategy: Discussing History: Gravitas (page 130c)

OBJECTIVE 4. Explain the system of social status in Roman society.
Teaching Strategy: Relating Past to Present: The Toga (page 130c)

ANSWERS TO Map Study

Alps; along the coasts of Sicily and southern Italy

SECTION 1 Resources

GEOGRAPHY
■ Transparencies 13, 18

REINFORCEMENT
■ Independent Practice 6.1

ENRICHMENT
■ Voices from the Past 6.1

ASSESSMENT
■ Section Quiz 6.1

The Etruscans apparently loved music and dance as much as the sports of hunting, riding, and chariot racing. Their paintings show that even players of flutes and lyres went along on hunting trips.

Greeks, Latins, and Etruscans battled for Italy.

The earliest settlers of the Italian peninsula arrived in prehistoric times. Around 1000 B.C., Italy's prehistoric period drew to a close. Over the next 500 years, the region's culture was shaped by three dominant groups: the Latins, the Greeks, and the Etruscans.

The Latins The Latins wandered across the Alps into Italy around 1000 B.C. They settled on either side of the Tiber River, a region that they called Latium (LAY-shee-uhm). Rome began as a settlement of Latin shepherds, no more than a cluster of round wooden huts perched atop the 300-foot Palatine Hill.

According to the Roman myth, Romulus built his wall around this hill in 753 B.C. At that time, however, Rome barely deserved to be called a city. Its farmers and shepherds lived very simply and wore coarse, homespun clothing. Only a few trade goods from the outside world reached their village. The growth of Rome into a city would soon be influenced greatly by the other two groups that settled in Italy, the Greeks and the Etruscans (ih-TRUHS-kuhnz).

The Greeks Between 750 and 600 B.C., settlers from Greece established about 50 colonies on the coast of southern Italy and Sicily. The numerous Greek colonies prompted the Latins to call this area *Magna Graecia*, or Greater Greece. These prosperous and commercially active cities brought all of Italy, including Rome, into closer contact with Greek civilization.

The Etruscans A third group of settlers, the Etruscans, entered northern Italy between 1200

and 800 B.C. Historians have never been sure where the Etruscans originated, but evidence suggests they may have come from Asia Minor.

The Etruscans were much more civilized than their Latin neighbors. The Etruscans had a writing system, which the Latins did not. (Etruscan letters were adapted from the Greek alphabet, which the Greeks in turn had adapted from the Phoenicians.) However, linguists have not yet deciphered the Etruscan language, and so their writings remain unread.

The Etruscans had a great cultural influence on the Latins. Eventually, the Latin settlers of Rome adopted the Etruscan alphabet. Roman buildings show the influence of Etruscan architecture. Etruscans also helped to develop Rome's trade. Several of Rome's kings were of Etruscan background, having migrated to Rome from Etruscan cities.

Romans borrowed religious ideas.

Both the Greeks and the Etruscans had a great influence on the development of Roman religious ideas. Like the Greeks, the Romans were polytheists, believing in many gods and spirits. Unlike Greek gods, however, many early Roman gods had no names or personalities. Instead, they were spirits linked with daily cares such as guarding

Etruscan women had considerable freedom and equality, as suggested by this sculpture from the tomb of a married couple. Wives and husbands were partners, and children bore the names of both parents.

132

children's food, protecting the household, and keeping grain supplies safe.

From the Etruscans, Romans learned the practice of "taking the auspices," which literally meant "watching birds in flight." It was auspicious (a good sign) if, before a battle, a vulture or eagle soared overhead. There were also other ways of trying to interpret the will of the gods, including looking at the liver of a slaughtered animal.

Knowledge of Greek gods filtered into Rome through traders. The Romans gave their own names to these gods but kept the legends and personalities of the Greek divinities. The almighty Greek god Zeus became the almighty Roman god Jupiter. The Greek goddess Hera became the Roman goddess Juno.

Romans overthrew their kings and established a republic.

In its early years, Rome was ruled by kings. During the years of royal rule between about 600 and 509 B.C., Rome changed from a collection of hilltop villages to a city. Kings ordered the construction of many of Rome's first temples and public buildings. By royal order, the swampy valley below the Palatine Hill was drained, making a public meeting place. In later years, this valley, known as the Forum (FAWR-uhm), became the heart of Roman political life, as the agora was the heart of the Greek polis.

According to legend, the son of the last king of Rome attacked a Roman woman, Lucretia. The outraged Romans rose in revolt and overthrew the prince's father. Then, the Romans declared they would never again be ruled by a king. Henceforth, any Roman who plotted to make himself king could be killed without trial.

In 509 B.C., Rome set up a **republic,** a government in which citizens who have the right to vote choose their leaders. The word *republic* comes from a Latin phrase, *res publica,* which simply means "public affairs." For the Romans, a republic was not a democracy, because the right to vote and other political rights were not shared by all citizens. Rather, in the Roman republic, various groups struggled for power, sometimes resorting to violence. To understand how the Roman republic worked, we must look first at Rome's social organization.

Romans valued family ties.

Throughout Rome's history, the character of its citizens was influenced by a group of values called "the ways of the fathers." The Romans emphasized discipline, strength, and loyalty. A person with these qualities was said to have the important virtue of **gravitas** (weightiness or seriousness). The Romans honored strength more than beauty, power more than grace, usefulness more than elegance, and steadiness more than quickness of mind. The sober, weighty quality of gravitas left its mark on all aspects of Roman society, from its government to its art.

At the heart of Roman society was the family. By law and custom, power to rule the early Roman household belonged exclusively to one person—the eldest man, known as the *pater familias* (PAY-tur fuh-MIHL-yuhs), or "father of the family." The pater familias had complete power over his family. He controlled all family property. He could sell a family member into slavery or even kill any member of his household without penalty. Usually, of course, the pater familias acted as the protector of his family. It was he who spoke for the family in public assemblies or in the law courts. The pater familias in each household also acted as its chief priest.

Although the pater familias was the legal head of the family, Roman women were in charge of the daily running of the household. A woman in Rome had much greater freedom than in Athens. She was a citizen, with the right to own property and testify in court. She ate meals with her husband, even though he reclined on a couch while she sat upright on a chair. She often advised her husband on business and politics. She did not, however, have the key right, the right to vote. Officially, the Roman woman was expected to remain in the background.

Society was divided into classes.

Not all families were equal in Roman society. Although all male Roman citizens could take part in politics, the city was dominated by a small group of families. Romans of this upper class claimed that their ancestors had been *patres,* or "fathers," who founded Rome. These specially privileged families were known as the **patrician** (puh-TRIH-shuhn) class. They claimed that their

133

■ DISCUSSION

What activities could a Roman woman pursue that an Athenian woman could not?

■ BACKGROUND

Clans, clusters of families who share a common ancestor, were a key part of a Roman's identity. All males in Rome were given three names: a personal name, a clan name, and a family name. Anyone with the middle name Julius (as in Gaius Julius Caesar) was known to belong to one of the oldest, most powerful clans in Rome.

ANSWERS TO

Section Review 1

Define:
(a) government in which citizens vote to choose their leaders (b) virtue of weightiness or seriousness

(continued)

ANSWERS TO *(continued)*

(c) father of the family
(d) worn draped around the body **(e)** member of Roman privileged family
(f) common person
(g) massive military unit
(h) 1/60th of a legion

Identify:
(a) peninsula in Mediterranean **(b)** central city of Roman republic **(c)** mythical founder of Rome **(d)** hilltop center of Rome **(e)** mountain range separating Italy from rest of Europe **(f)** river flowing through Rome
(g) mountain range running down length of Italy
(h) group from across the Alps who settled near the Tiber River **(i)** civilized settlers who entered northern Italy between 1200 and 800 B.C.
(j) public meeting place

Answer:
1. central position helped military and trade
2. (a) earliest settlers
(b) introduced Greek culture and certain religious ideas
(c) influence on Roman writing, architecture, trade, and religious ideas
3. "the ways of the fathers," which emphasized discipline, strength, loyalty
4. (a) *pater familias* was head of household with complete power over his family **(b)** were citizens, could own property and testify in court, could eat with and advise husband
5. All male citizens had to serve in the army; no one could hold public office until he served ten years.
6. Look for answers to include a discussion of social, political, and religious values.

ancestry gave them the authority to make laws for Rome and its people.

The common farmers, artisans, and merchants were known as **plebeians** (plih-BEE-uhnz). The plebeians were free citizens with a number of rights, including the right to vote. However, they had far less power than the patricians, who held nearly all important political offices.

Birth alone (not merit or wealth) determined every Roman's social and political status. The line between the patrician and plebeian classes was extremely rigid. In the early years of the republic, for example, marriage between the two classes was forbidden by law.

Rome built a mighty army.

The constant threat of war forced both patrician and plebeian men in Rome to lead double lives as farmers and soldiers. All male citizens were required to serve in the army, and no one could hold public office until he had first served ten years as a soldier.

Learning to fight Roman-style meant being part of a massive military unit called a **legion.** The Roman legion was made up of 4,000 to 6,000 heavily armed foot soldiers (infantry). A group of soldiers on horseback (cavalry) cooperated with each legion. Every legion was divided into 60 smaller groups, each of which was known as a century.

In battle, the Roman legion proved superior to the Greek phalanx because the legion was more flexible. The wall-like phalanx could move effectively in only two directions—forward and backward. But each century in a legion could move independently. Under a skillful general, a Roman legion could surround and outflank its foes. The legions were the fighting force that spread Rome's power around the Mediterranean.

DAILY LIFE ▸ *The Roman Toga*

Practicality has never been a requirement of fashion. The Roman toga (TOH-guh) was an uncomfortable garment. It was hot in summer, cold in winter, and clumsy for just about any activity but standing still. The toga was, however, practical in one way: It was easy to make, since it involved no sewing. Not even a buttonhole was needed. An adult's toga was basically a large wool blanket, measuring about 18 by 7 feet. It was draped around the body in a variety of ways, without the use of buttons or pins.

In the early days of the Roman republic, both women and men wore togas. Women eventually wore more dresslike garments, called *stolas,* with separate shawls. For men, however, the toga remained in fashion with very little change.

Soon after the republic was formed, the toga became a symbol of Roman citizenship. Different styles of togas indicated a male citizen's place in society. For example, a young boy would wear a white toga with a narrow purple band along the border. When his family decided he was ready for adult responsibilities, he would don a pure white toga. On that day, usually when he was about 16, his family would take him to the Forum, where he would register as a full citizen. For the rest of his life, he would wear a toga at the theater, in court, for religious ceremonies, and on any formal occasion. At his funeral, his body would be wrapped in a toga to mark him, even in death, as a Roman citizen.

Define: (a) republic, (b) gravitas, (c) pater familias, (d) toga, (e) patrician, (f) plebeian, (g) legion, (h) century
Identify: (a) Italy, (b) Rome, (c) Romulus, (d) Palatine Hill, (e) Alps, (f) Tiber River, (g) Apennines, (h) Latins, (i) Etruscans, (j) Forum
Answer:
1. How did geography help Rome?
2. Why was each of the following groups important to Rome's development? (a) Latins (b) Greeks (c) Etruscans
3. What were the values of early Roman society?
4. (a) How was the Roman household organized? (b) What freedoms did women have in the family and in society?
5. How was the army linked to Roman society?

Critical Thinking
6. Compare the values of Roman society to those of another civilization.

The Roman republic spread its power. 2

For 500 years, the Romans governed their city and surrounding farmland as a republic. The history of these five centuries may be divided into two periods. In the first (509–265 B.C.), Roman troops battled for mastery of the Italian peninsula, and plebeians forced patricians to surrender some of their power. The second (265–44 B.C.) was marked by civil war, the rising power of army leaders, and the eventual triumph of Julius Caesar. Romans also extended their rule around the Mediterranean Sea.

Plebeians slowly won more power.

For centuries, Roman coins bore the letters *SPQR*, which stood for *Senatus Populusque Romanus*—the senate and the Roman people. Together, these two groups were the heart of Roman government. This simple phrase masked years of bitter struggle between patricians (who con-

trolled the Roman senate) and plebeians (who made up the majority of the population).

Conflict between patrician and plebeian After the Romans drove out their kings in 509 B.C., patricians controlled Rome's government. Plebeians were barred by law from holding most important positions in government—commanding armies, serving as high priests, or holding high offices.

In time, plebeians won a greater share of political power. Between 494 and 287 B.C., thousands of plebeians refused to fight in the Roman army unless patricians agreed to certain reforms. In this way, they gained access to many political offices and obtained more favorable laws. Enslavement for debt was ended, and marriage between patricians and plebeians was allowed.

Twelve Tables Among the first victories of the plebeians was the creation of a written law code. Roman law rested heavily on custom. When laws were unwritten, patrician officials often interpreted the law to suit themselves. Consequently, plebeians demanded that the laws of Rome be published.

In 451 B.C., a group of ten officials took on the task of writing down Rome's laws. The laws were carved on 12 great tablets, or tables, and hung in the Forum. They became the foundation

At Roman family meals, the husband reclined on a couch while the wife sat in a chair.

135

SECTION 2 Objectives and Teaching Strategies

OBJECTIVE 1. Identify the Twelve Tables and explain their significance in Roman law.

Teaching Strategy: *Transferring Ideas: Law Codes and the Twelve Tables* (page 130c)

OBJECTIVE 2. Compare and contrast the political institutions of the Roman republic and the United States.

Teaching Strategy: *Relating Past to Present: The Governments of Rome and the United States* (page 130c)

OBJECTIVE 3. Trace on a map the expansion of Rome.

Teaching Strategy: *Geography in History: The Expansion of Rome* (page 130d)

■ DISCUSSION

The dissatisfaction of plebeians came from an economic depression. Many demanded changes in laws that allowed enslavement for debt. **Debate:** Economic conditions, not idealist concerns, are the prime motivation for political change.

SECTION 2 Resources

GEOGRAPHY
■ Transparency 19

REINFORCEMENT
■ Independent Practice 6.2

ENRICHMENT
■ Voices from the Past 6.2

ASSESSMENT
■ Section Quiz 6.2

Divide the class into groups of four. Within each group, have each student write a short summary of two of the major subsections ("Plebeians slowly won more power," "Rome achieved a balanced government," etc.) in this section (pages 135–141). Make students responsible for assigning work within their own groups. When individual summaries are complete, each group member should orally present his or her work to the group. Group members should take notes on each presentation in order to have a complete section summary. Encourage students to ask each other questions if anything is unclear. Randomly choose one paper from each group to review for a group grade.

■ DISCUSSION

What are the pros and cons of limiting a consul's term to one year in every ten? (Pro: Power cannot remain with one person too long. Con: A consul had little chance to use experience acquired on the job.)

MILESTONES OF DEMOCRACY: ROME (275 B.C.)

	FORM OF GOVERNMENT	CITIZENSHIP	INDIVIDUAL RIGHTS
Benefits	Republic with representation: Two consuls were elected by assemblies of male citizens. A consul's power was limited by veto of other consul and by power of Senate.	Full or partial citizenship was granted to many conquered people.	Roman law protected rights of citizens and half-citizens. Allies had their own laws.
Limitations	At first, only patricians could hold higher office or be members of Senate. Women did not have right to vote.	Half-citizens had private rights and public duties of citizens but not right to vote.	Slaves had no rights.

for later Roman law. Although the laws were sometimes harsh, the Twelve Tables established the idea that all free citizens had a right to the protection of the law. Thus, the Twelve Tables helped to settle the conflict between patricians and plebeians.

Rome achieved a balanced government.

By about 275 B.C., Roman writers boasted that Rome had achieved a balanced government. They meant that their government was partly a **monarchy** (government by a king), partly an aristocracy (government by nobles), and partly a democracy (government by the people). The Romans believed that this mixture gave them the best features of all kinds of governments.

The office of consul In place of a king, Rome had two officials called **consuls.** Like kings, they commanded the army and directed the government. They had the power of life and death over citizens in wartime and great powers in peacetime as well.

The consuls' power was limited, however, by two rules. First, a consul's term was only one year long, and the same person could not be elected consul again for ten years. Second, one consul could always overrule, or **veto,** the other's decisions. (In Latin, *veto* means "I forbid.")

The powerful senate The **senate** was the aristocratic branch of Rome's government. Tradition said that Romulus had named 100 patricians to advise him, thus creating the first senate. Later, the number of senators increased, and plebeians could also be members. Membership was for life. Therefore, the senate provided continuity and stability in the government. It exercised enormous influence over both foreign and domestic policy.

The power of the people The democratic side of Roman government was the assembly. All citizen-soldiers were members of this branch of government. In the early days of the republic, the assembly had little power in comparison to the consuls and the senate. Over the years, however, the powers of the assembly increased. Eventually, its decisions gained the force of law.

The office of dictator In times of crisis, the republic could turn to another type of political leadership, a **dictator**—a leader who had absolute power to make laws and command the army. A dictator's power lasted for only six months. Dictators were chosen by the consuls and then elected by the senate.

136

The Roman ideal of a dictator is shown by the story of Cincinnatus (SIN-sih-NAY-tus). In 458 B.C., when Rome's armies were in peril, the senate named Cincinnatus dictator. Cincinnatus was plowing his four-acre farm when messengers brought him the news. He left his plow, defeated Rome's enemies, and stepped down as dictator within 15 days. Then he returned to his farm to finish his plowing.

Rome won control of Italy.

Political struggles between patricians and plebeians were remarkably bloodless during these years. Outside the city walls, however, the blood of both classes was spilled over Italian hills and fields as Rome's legions subdued Italy. City by city, the Romans defeated other Latin groups and the Etruscans. Roman power grew slowly but steadily. And then, Rome suffered a smashing defeat.

The sack of Rome by the Gauls In 390 B.C., Rome's walls were successfully stormed by marauding Gauls (gawlz), a people from the Po River valley, north of the Apennines. The Gauls sacked Rome, leaving it in ruins. Then, the Romans were forced to pay a humiliating bribe to persuade the Gauls to leave.

The Romans recovered rapidly, though. They built a stronger, larger wall around their city. The reconstructed Rome spanned 1,000 acres, making it the largest city in Italy. Foreign troops would not sack the city again for 800 years.

War with the Greeks Eventually, Romans controlled all of the Italian boot except its heel and toe. For centuries, those southern regions of Italy had been colonized by the Greeks.

The Greek cities watched the rise of Roman power with alarm. In 282 B.C., Greek colonists sought aid from Pyrrhus (PIHR-uhs), a king in western Greece. A brilliant general, Pyrrhus brought 20,000 soldiers to fight the Romans. Twice Pyrrhus's army slammed into the Roman legions and drove them from the field. In each battle, however, the Greek army suffered terrible losses. Pyrrhus learned a bitter lesson of warfare (and of life): You can win every battle and still lose the war. In 275 B.C., the Romans drove Pyrrhus's tired and decimated troops back to Greece. Ever since, a victory gained at too high a price has been known as a "Pyrrhic victory."

Rome governed Italy skillfully.

After 275 B.C., the Romans were masters of all Italy except the Po Valley in the north, which was still held by the Gauls. Different parts of the conquered territory were subject to different laws and treatment from Rome.

Latin neighbors on the Tiber were treated as full citizens of Rome. They could marry other Romans, vote in assemblies, and appeal for justice in a Roman court.

In territories farther from Rome, conquered peoples were given the status of half-citizens. They enjoyed all the rights of a Roman citizen except the privilege to vote.

All other conquered groups fell into a third category, allies of Rome. Allies were required to contribute troops to the Roman army. They were forbidden to make treaties of friendship with any state but Rome. An allied city was free, however, to govern its own people without any Roman interference.

Unlike the Athenians, the Romans were willing to extend their citizenship to people outside Rome itself. The new citizens became partners in Rome's growth. This policy helped Rome to succeed in building a long-lasting empire, where Athens had failed.

With most of Italy unified behind it, Rome was now ready to enter the second stage of its astonishing rise to power. In the 250 years after 275 B.C., Roman power spread far beyond Italy.

Rome fought with Carthage.

After the decline of Athens, trade in the Mediterranean region was dominated by two wealthy cities, both on the northern coast of Africa. One was Alexandria in Egypt, still ruled by the Ptolemies. The other was Carthage, the former Phoenician colony. Like Rome, Carthage had the advantage of a location near the midpoint of the Mediterranean coast.

In 264 B.C., Rome and Carthage went to war for control of Sicily and the western Mediterranean. Thus began the first of three periods of struggle known as the Punic (PYOO-nik) Wars. *Punic* comes from the Latin word for Phoenicia.

Let us compare the two cities and their capacity for making war. With a population of 250,000, Carthage was about three times the size of Rome.

137

■ **DISCUSSION**
Roman laws regarding citizenship were important in keeping the unity of Italy. Ask students to speculate what problems were avoided by this citizenship system.

■ **BACKGROUND**
Remind students that Carthage was one of the major colonies of the Phoenicians. Carthage had continued to prosper and controlled all of North Africa and parts of Spain and Italy.

■ **DISCUSSION**

Why did Rome's allies remain loyal to Rome even though Hannibal expected them to revolt and join him?

Carthage had a huge navy of 500 ships. Overseas trade had made Carthage an immensely wealthy city. Each year, it collected the equivalent of almost 1 million pounds of gold in tariffs and tribute. With this great wealth, Carthage employed the people of neighboring Numidia as **mercenaries**, soldiers who fight in any country's army for pay.

Rome's resources in ships and wealth seemed meager by comparison. In fact, at the beginning of the First Punic War, Rome had no navy whatsoever. Rome's power had always rested entirely on its armies. However, this great disadvantage was offset by three advantages. First, Rome could draw on a reserve of more than 500,000 troops made available through its conquests in Italy. Second, Rome's citizen troops were generally more loyal and reliable than the mercenaries employed by Carthage. Third, warfare was a Roman specialty. Over the centuries, Romans had directed much of their energy toward winning wars. All of Carthage's energies, on the other hand, had been aimed at winning wealth through trade.

Luck also seemed to favor the Romans. Toward the beginning of the first war, a Carthaginian warship washed up on the Italian shore. Needing a fleet in a hurry, the Romans hastily built 140 ships by copying the Carthaginian design. Unlike the Carthaginian model, however, each Roman warship was equipped with a long gangplank. When not in use, this gangplank was lashed upright to the mast. Attached to the bottom of the gangplank was an iron hook, shaped like a bird's beak and called a raven. When a Roman ship drew alongside a Carthaginian vessel, the gangplank crashed down between the two. Its beak stuck deep in the Carthaginian deck, binding the ships together. Roman soldiers then rushed over the gangplank.

By this means, the Romans won their first two naval battles against the African master of the Mediterranean. Carthage later avenged itself with several shattering victories of its own on land and sea.

The First Punic War dragged on for 23 punishing years before Carthage's last fleet was defeated and sunk in 241 B.C. The defeat marked the end of Carthage as a sea power. Rome took over the rich, grain-growing island of Sicily as the chief prize of victory.

138

Hannibal sought revenge on Rome.

From 241 to 218 B.C., Carthage and Rome each had other interests. Rome was bent on driving the Gauls out of northern Italy. Carthage set out to win much of southern Spain, which it then turned into a rich colony.

In 218 B.C., however, the uneasy peace between the two cities was broken. The mastermind behind this Second Punic War was a Carthaginian leader named Hannibal, one of the great military geniuses of all time. He was only a boy of nine when his father, a general, made him swear that he would always hate Rome and seek to destroy it. Hannibal grew to manhood on the southern coast of Spain. Here he observed his father's masterful tactics for fighting Spanish tribes and gained experience with troops of his own.

Hannibal's invasion of Italy When Hannibal was 29 years old, in 218 B.C., he assembled an army of 50,000 infantry, 9,000 calvary, and 60 elephants to try to capture Rome itself. He led his army on a long trek from Spain across France and up into the dizzying heights of the Alps. Desertions, battles with Gallic tribes, and blizzards in the mountains killed more than half his men and most of his elephants.

Rome assembled an army to fight this invader, but Hannibal destroyed it. A second Roman army, larger than the first, was also routed. In 216 B.C., a third army of 86,000 Romans found Hannibal's reinforced army of 50,000 men camped at Cannae on the eastern coast of Italy. By brilliant maneuvering, Hannibal drew the attacking army into a deadly trap. In this battle—Hannibal's greatest victory—between 40,000 and 70,000 Romans died.

For the next 13 years, Hannibal marched his armies at will up and down the Italian peninsula. The Romans did not dare to challenge him again in open battle. His soldiers lived off the land, seizing crops and cattle, pillaging farmhouses. However, they could not capture Rome itself. Its walls were too high and their own forces too small even to make the attempt. For years, Hannibal waited for Carthage to send him reinforcements. For years, he waited for Rome's allies to revolt and join his own armies. For years, Hannibal was disappointed.

The Battle of Zama Finally Rome found a general whose boldness and brilliance were nearly

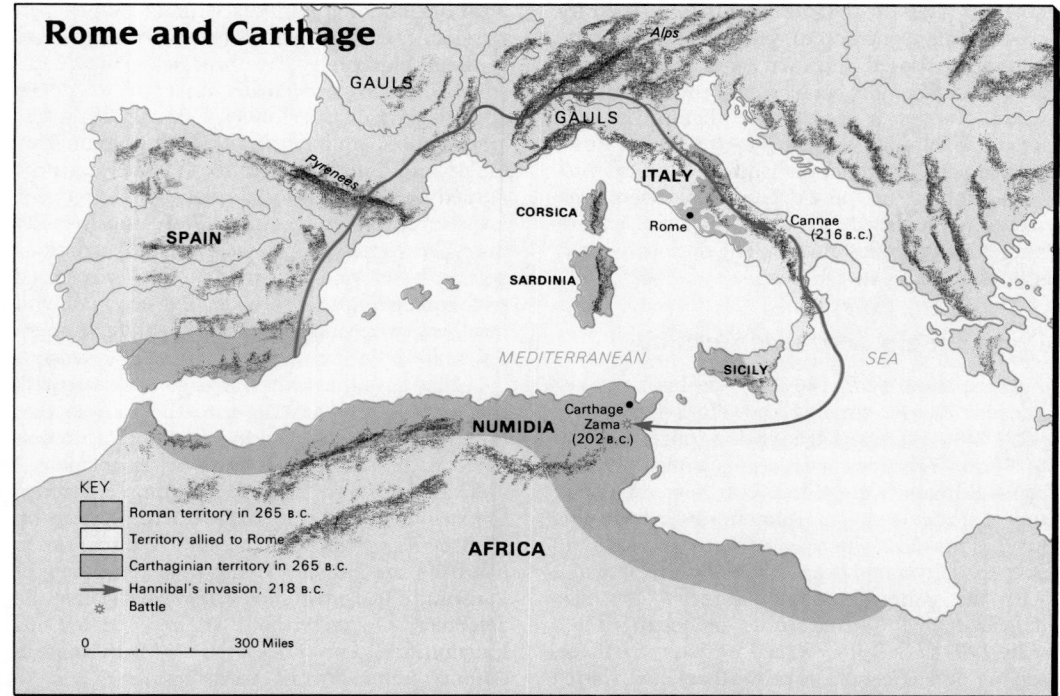

Rome and Carthage

GAULS
Alps
GAULS
Pyrenees
SPAIN
ITALY
CORSICA
Rome
Cannae
(216 B.C.)
SARDINIA
MEDITERRANEAN
SEA
SICILY
Carthage
NUMIDIA
Zama
(202 B.C.)
AFRICA

KEY
Roman territory in 265 B.C.
Territory allied to Rome
Carthaginian territory in 265 B.C.
Hannibal's invasion, 218 B.C.
Battle

0   300 Miles

Map Study

How far was Carthage from Rome? Where did Hannibal begin his march to invade Rome? What two mountain ranges did he cross on his way?

equal to Hannibal's. His name was Scipio (SIP-ee-oh). Scipio attacked Carthage itself, forcing Hannibal to rush home to the rescue. The great Carthaginian, unbeaten on European soil, was soundly thrashed by Scipio at the Battle of Zama in 202 B.C. (Hannibal survived and governed Carthage for seven years. He later killed himself to avoid capture by Rome.)

Thus ended the Second Punic War. Zama is one of the few battles that may truly have changed the course of history. Quite possibly, if Hannibal had been the victor, Carthage and not Rome would have become the greatest empire in the world. Because Rome was victorious, it was Rome that passed on its laws, its government, and its culture to Western civilization.

Scipio, in honor of his victory, was named *Africanus* (conqueror of Africa). In the terms of peace, Rome allowed Carthage to keep its lands in northern Africa but nothing more.

Rome made conquests to the east.

Rome now dominated the western half of the Mediterranean Sea. During the next 70 years, Romans also conquered the eastern half.

After the death of Alexander the Great in 323 B.C., his empire had been divided among his generals. Their descendants still ruled the lands around the eastern Mediterranean. The Antigonid dynasty ruled Macedon, the Ptolemaic dynasty ruled Egypt, and the Seleucid dynasty ruled most of what had been the Persian empire. These three—and a few other small kingdoms—were almost constantly at war with one another.

Greece lay nearest Rome, and it was the first to feel Rome's heavy hand. At first, Roman armies marching into Macedon looked like protectors of Greek freedom. The Greeks rejoiced when, in 197 B.C., the Romans freed them from the rule of Philip V of Macedon. Once settled in Greece,

139

Define:
(a) one of two rulers of Rome (b) power to overrule (c) aristocratic branch of Roman government (d) democratic side of Roman government (e) absolute ruler for six months (f) soldier who fights for pay

Identify:
(a) letters on Roman coins that stood for "the senate and the Roman people" (b) first written laws of Rome (c) dictator in 458 B.C. who represented the Roman ideal (d) people from Po valley who sacked Rome (e) Greek king and general who fought Romans, won every battle, but lost the war (f) trading center and former Phoenician colony (g) war between Rome and Carthage for control of Sicily and western Mediterranean (h) Carthaginian military leader who destroyed three Roman armies (i) site of Roman victory over Hannibal (j) Roman leader who defeated Hannibal (k) grandson of Scipio Africanus; led Roman army in destroying Carthage

(continued)

ANSWERS TO (continued)

Answer:

1. (a) barred from holding most important government positions, governed by severe laws (b) by refusing to fight in the Roman army (c) won rights for plebeians to hold some political offices, avoid enslavement for debt, marry patricians, and share in political power

2. part monarchy, part aristocracy, part democracy

3. granted certain citizenship rights, and treated conquered people as partners

4. (a) It had three times the population of Rome, was a wealthy trading center, had a huge navy, and employed mercenaries. (b) It had half a million troops in reserve; citizen-fighters were more loyal than mercenaries; warfare was specialty.

5. It set the stage for Rome, not Carthage, to be the transmitter of culture down through the ages.

6. (a) The Romans had freed them from the rule of Philip V of Macedon. (b) Romans interfered in Greek politics and crushed all opposition.

7. (a) Answers should include the roles of consuls, senate, and the assembly and their powers and membership. (b) right of all citizens to participate in government

8. (a) destruction of Corinth and sack of Carthage (b) no citizenship and outright destruction outside Italy

however, the Romans interfered in Greek politics, crushing all opposition to rulers favored by Rome.

As time passed, the exercise of Roman power in the east became increasingly ruthless. A few Greek city-states tried to free themselves from Rome's tightening grip, but the effort failed. Rome singled out Corinth for punishment as an example to the others. In 146 B.C., its people were massacred or enslaved, its walls wrecked, and its homes and temples burned. The once lovely city was reduced to an ash heap.

Rome finally destroyed Carthage.

In the same year, 146 B.C., Carthage was destroyed. By the time of the Third Punic War (149–146 B.C.), Carthage was no longer a threat to Rome. Yet it was still a prosperous city, and some Romans were filled with hate each time they thought of it. The Roman most responsible for this needless war was a senator named Cato (KAY-toh). Over and over, Cato ended his speeches with the same vindictive message: *"Carthago delenda est"* ("Carthage must be destroyed").

In 149 B.C., Rome forced war on Carthage, seizing on the excuse that Carthage had warred with neighboring Numidia without Rome's permission. The Carthaginians barricaded themselves in their beloved city. For three years, they withstood a Roman siege. Finally, under the leadership of Scipio Aemilianus (uh-MIHL-ee-AY-nuhs)—the grandson of Scipio Africanus—the Roman army broke into Carthage and set it afire. Carthage flamed and smoked for six days, while fighting raged from street to street. Watching the city burn, the Roman general wept. "This is a glorious moment," he said to a friend, "but I am seized with foreboding that someday the same fate will befall my own country." He was right, but Rome's downfall did not come for another 556 years.

Legend says that after Carthage was destroyed, the Romans plowed salt into the soil, so that not even crops would spring up again for Rome's hated rival. The legend, however, is untrue.

After the Third Punic War, Rome continued to expand eastward. In 133 B.C., the western tip of Asia Minor dropped peacefully into Roman hands as the gift of a dying king. This king of Pergamum had welcomed Roman aid against the Seleucids. Dying without an heir, he left his kingdom to Rome. Thus, Rome's Mediterranean empire stretched from Asia Minor to Spain.

Map Study

What territory had Rome gained by 133 B.C. in the region of Asia Minor? Name a city shown on this map that was not under Roman control.

ANSWERS TO

Map Study

Pergamum; Alexandria

140

Define: (a) consul, (b) veto, (c) senate, (d) assembly, (e) dictator, (f) mercenary
Identify: (a) SPQR, (b) Twelve Tables, (c) Cincinnatus, (d) Gauls, (e) Pyrrhus, (f) Carthage, (g) Punic Wars, (h) Hannibal, (i) Battle of Zama, (j) Scipio Africanus, (k) Scipio Aemilianus

Answer:

1. (a) Why were many plebeians dissatisfied with Rome's government in the early years of the republic? (b) How did they win reforms? (c) What changes did they bring about in Roman government?
2. Why did Romans consider that they had a balanced government?
3. Once Rome had conquered most of Italy, how did the Roman government win the support of the conquered people?
4. (a) At the start of the Punic Wars, why might Carthage have appeared the stronger power? (b) Why was Rome, in fact, the victor?
5. Why was the Battle of Zama a major turning point in history?
6. (a) Why did the Greeks at first welcome Roman armies? (b) Why did the Greek attitude change?

Critical Thinking

7. (a) How was the Roman republic different from a democracy? (b) What features of the republic were democratic?
8. (a) Give two examples of Rome's increasing ruthlessness as its empire grew. (b) How did Rome's treatment of conquered people outside Italy differ from that of the groups Rome conquered within Italy?

Republican government collapsed in Rome. 3

Carthage was not the only loser of the Punic Wars. Rome was also hurt in many ways. Thousands of men and boys who left their farms to fight in a Roman legion never came back. Those who did return found conditions in Italy drastically changed.

The gap between rich and poor grew.

Hannibal's armies had destroyed farms, homes, and villages. Returning soldiers could rarely afford to rebuild. Many small farmers sold their ruined acres to wealthy citizens. These new landowners treated farming strictly as a business. On their huge estates, known as *latifundia*, they found that raising cattle was more profitable than growing grain. (After the First Punic War, cheap wheat from Sicily had flooded Italian markets.) Labor for the latifundia was cheap because Rome's many wars brought thousands of chained captives to work as slaves.

Battle-scarred farmers could not return to their old way of life. Their land was gone, owned now by wealthy strangers, worked by slaves. Where could uprooted veterans go? Thousands of them sought new homes in or around Rome. They sought city jobs but seldom found them. Wealthy Romans preferred owning slaves to hiring free workers. This new class of urban, landless poor was called the **proletariat** (PROH-leh-**TAIR**-ee-uht). The people of this class were the poorest of Romans. Without work or hope, they became a dangerous and discontented mob within the city. From this time on, riots were a constant danger in Rome.

While poor farmers lost their land, the rich were corrupted by wealth. Winning a war always meant an opportunity for collecting loot. A victorious general might take a share of the spoils for himself and send the rest to the Roman treasury. After one year's victories, for example, Scipio Africanus displayed in the Roman Forum 123,000 pounds of silver that his army had brought back from Spain and Carthage.

Captured booty was proudly paraded through Roman streets during special holidays called "triumphs." The typical triumph consisted of a victorious general, dressed in purple-trimmed toga and golden crown, riding through a triumphal arch to the cheers of the crowd. He was followed by wagons of loot and bands of veterans.

The spoils of war brought dramatic changes in patrician life. Modest homes turned into ornately furnished mansions. There might be urns from Babylon, silk from China, gold from Carthage, and marble from Athens. While their dress remained rather simple, the rich learned to love exotic foods and lavish entertainment.

141

SECTION 3 Objectives and Teaching Strategies

OBJECTIVE 1. Assess the impact of the Punic Wars on the republic.

Teaching Strategy: *Discussing History: The Impact of the Punic Wars on the Roman Republic* (page 130d)

OBJECTIVE 2. Explain the main cause and long-term effects of changes in the Roman army.

Teaching Strategy: *Skill Building: Identifying Cause and Effect Relationships* (page 130d)

OBJECTIVE 3. Identify Julius Caesar and describe his rise to power.

Teaching Strategy: *Writing about History: Julius Caesar* (page 130d)

■ BACKGROUND

Hellenistic art and literature were adopted in Rome. How would the new emphasis on luxuries change the valued Roman characteristics exemplified by Cincinnatus?

SECTION 3 Resources

GEOGRAPHY
■ Transparency 20

REINFORCEMENT
■ Independent Practice 6.3

ENRICHMENT
■ Voices from the Past 6.3

ASSESSMENT
■ Section Quiz 6.3

Slaves were allowed to dress like free people. Dressed like all others, slaves would not realize their own numbers and hence their potential power.

The Romans had been exposed to the Etruscan practice of slave fights as part of funerals. Originally, gladiator spectacles were scheduled at the funerals of famous Romans.

Slavery became widespread.

The luxury of the rich depended on the labor of slaves. In Rome's slave market, a tablet around the neck of a foreign captive identified his or her special skills and place of origin. Every year, thousands of unhappy captives were inspected and sold. As a result of the First Punic War alone, 75,000 formerly free men and women became Roman slaves. By the year 100 B.C., slaves formed perhaps one third of Rome's total population.

Low-priced slaves, unskilled and uneducated, were assigned to heavy labor in Roman mines, on cattle farms, in vineyards, and in shipyards. The more expensive slaves, usually from Greece and Asia Minor, worked in Roman households as cooks, teachers, musicians, private secretaries, and messengers. In one mansion, a rich Roman kept 11 highly educated Greek slaves just to recite the poems of Homer at his banquets.

Romans lived with the ever-present danger of a massive slave uprising. As the Roman slogan went, "Every slave we own is an enemy we harbor." Three times between 138 and 70 B.C., thousands of slaves rebelled against their masters. The third uprising was by far the most threatening. It was led by the slave Spartacus, who had been trained as a gladiator (a person who fought other warriors or wild beasts as a form of public entertainment). Spartacus raised an army of 70,000 slaves and ravaged the Italian countryside from 73 to 71 B.C. They fought desperately for their freedom, beating the Roman army nine times before their revolt was crushed. About 6,000 of Spartacus's followers were crucified.

The Gracchi attempted reforms.

The worst threat to the Roman republic, however, came from the Roman citizens themselves. The richest families of the city, plebeian as well as patrician, competed for political power. It was a more violent kind of politics than the old struggle between patricians and plebeians. After the Punic Wars, political arguments and rivalries often were settled by bloodshed.

Two brothers, Tiberius and Gaius Gracchus (GRAK-us), attempted to reform Rome's government. The elder brother, Tiberius, was elected to the political office of **tribune** in 133 B.C. Tribunes were officials who spoke on behalf of the plebeians. They were elected by the assembly. Tiberius spoke eloquently about the plight of the landless, dispossessed farmers. "The wolves and the bears have dens to rest and sleep," said Tiberius. "But the men who fight their country's battles have nothing . . . You fight and die only for the wealth and luxury of others. You are called the masters of the world, but you do not have a single clod of earth to call your own." What could be done for these unfortunate citizens? Give them land, said Tiberius. Limit the size of large estates, and distribute lands to the poor people of Rome.

To a poor man, Tiberius's program seemed only fair. To a rich landowner, it seemed like robbery. Tiberius further alarmed the rich by seeking to be reelected as tribune, something never before attempted. On election day, some senators and their followers clubbed Tiberius to death and flung his body into the Tiber.

Gladiators fought to the death in Roman arenas. Political leaders used such games to entertain the proletariat and prevent rebellions.

Ten years later (123 B.C.), the murdered man's younger brother, Gaius Gracchus, was elected tribune. Gaius made the office of tribune the most powerful position in Rome. By his eloquence and political skill, he pushed through a series of laws designed to weaken the senate. He planned programs to deal with unemployment.

The senate's opposition to the younger Gracchus's reforms again led to open violence. Gaius was declared an enemy of the state. The senate offered a large reward for his head. Gaius and his supporters took refuge on one of Rome's hills, where they were attacked by a band of senators with their slaves and foreign mercenaries. Gaius died in the battle. Later, the senate executed 3,000 of his followers.

Army leaders took political power.

After the death of the Gracchi, two army leaders muscled their way to power. First came Marius, whose victories against German tribes made him immensely popular with the people. Then came Sulla, the strong-armed champion of the senate.

Marius and his army saved Rome from a frightening invasion of Germanic tribes in 105 B.C. As a result, he was elected consul five times in a row, breaking the tradition that a consul could not be reelected for ten years. Marius blamed the weakness of Rome's defenses on its dwindling number of citizen-soldiers. Only landowners could serve in the army, and too many farmers had been forced off the land. To make

■ DISCUSSION
Under Caesar, the government controlled the sale of wheat and gave wheat away to the needy. Have students speculate why the senate opposed this policy.

ANSWERS TO
Voice from the Past

1. lavish in offerings to gods, thrifty at home, loyal to friends, bold in warfare, just in peace
2. lust for money, lust for power
3. Look for an understanding of the temptations wealth and prosperity can bring.

Voice from the Past | The Perils of Success

The Roman historian Sallust lived between 86 and 35 B.C., when Rome was already the greatest power in the Mediterranean region. Sallust had strong views on the course of Roman history, especially on changes he believed had taken place in the character of the Romans.

[In Rome's early years,] good morals were cultivated at home and in the field; there was the greatest harmony and little or no greed; justice and integrity prevailed . . . [Citizens] were lavish in their offerings to the gods, thrifty at home, loyal to their friends. By boldness in warfare and justice in peace, they watched over themselves and their country . . .

But when our country had grown great . . . then Fortune began to grow cruel and to bring confusion into all our affairs. Those who had found it easy to bear hardship and dangers . . . found leisure and wealth, desirable under other circumstances, a burden and a curse. Hence, the lust for money first, then for power, grew upon [Romans]; these were, I may say, the root of all evils. For greed destroyed honor, integrity, and all other noble qualities; taught in their place insolence, cruelty, to neglect the gods, to set a price on everything. Ambition drove many men to become false; to have one thought locked in the breast, another ready on the tongue; to value friendships and enmities not on their merits but by the standard of self-interest, and to show a good front rather than a good heart. At first these vices grew slowly . . . Finally, when the disease had spread like a deadly plague, the state was changed and a government that had been second to none in equity and excellence became cruel and intolerable.

1. According to Sallust, how did Romans show their good moral character in early times?
2. What two evils caused Rome's later problems?
3. Do you agree with Sallust that hard times sometimes bring out people's better qualities? Explain your answer.

A Roman triumphal procession

143

■ DISCUSSION

What problems are inherent in a system in which the soldiers are indebted to the commander, not to the state?

■ BACKGROUND

Victorious Romans usually massacred the relatives of the defeated person. Caesar was one of the few relatives of Marius to escape death at Sulla's hands.

up for this loss of manpower, Marius allowed the city's poor to enlist in the army. The new recruits received weapons and armor from the state, unlike the self-equipped citizen-soldiers.

These new soldiers signed up for a period of 16 years—much of their adult lives. In other words, they became professional soldiers. As such, they were willing to fight for any army leader who rewarded them with land and gold. After Marius, Roman armies did not fight for the republic. They fought instead for the military leader who used his political power to give them weapons, food, and loot. More often than not, these leaders used their armies to advance their own political ambitions. It was now possible for rival politicians, each supported by his own army, to win power by force of arms.

In 88 B.C., Marius commanded one army while his rival, Sulla, commanded another. Over the next six years, both leaders used their armies to march against Rome. Each held power for a while and slaughtered the supporters of his opponent. Each forced his own laws on Rome. Sulla, who returned to power in 82 B.C., abolished the six-month limit to a dictator's term and had himself named dictator until he chose to step down. Both Sulla and Marius died peacefully in bed, somehow escaping the violent deaths they had dealt to others. But their pattern of using the army to gain political power outlived them both.

Julius Caesar rose to power.

Among those whom Sulla intended, but failed, to kill was a 20-year-old patrician named Gaius Julius Caesar (SEE-zuhr). Caesar escaped an early death because he understood the uses of money. He bribed Sulla's soldiers to spare his life.

Caesar had little money of his own, but like other ambitious Romans of his day, he knew that the quickest way to wealth was to govern one of Rome's provinces—Spain, Sicily, Gaul, Asia Minor, Macedon, or Africa. A provincial governor could amass a small fortune from just one year's collection of taxes, bribes, and war booty. The position of governor was seldom given to the best administrator. It went instead to the politician who won the goodwill of the senate and the Roman people.

For more than 20 years, Caesar played hard at the game of Roman politics. In the Forum, he

charmed crowds with his brilliant speeches. In his country villa, he threw lavish parties for influential politicians.

To support his extravagant life-style, Caesar borrowed huge sums from a man whose well-deserved nickname was Crassus the Rich. Crassus invested in Caesar's political career as a gambler might invest in a racehorse. The gamble paid off handsomely when Caesar was appointed governor of a province in Spain. Caesar collected enough booty there in one year to enrich himself, his soldiers, and Crassus.

The First Triumvirate In 60 B.C., Caesar and Crassus joined forces with Pompey, a popular general. To cement their alliance, Pompey married

Julius Caesar

Caesar's daughter, Julia. With the help of his two allies, Caesar was elected consul in 59 B.C. For the next ten years, the three men ruled Rome as a **triumvirate.** The senate and assembly were bribed and bullied into following their decisions.

The conquest of Gaul Abiding by ancient tradition, Caesar served only one year as consul. Then he assigned himself the governorship of Gaul. (See the map on page 140.) For eight years, he led his legions in a series of grueling but successful wars in western Europe. He pushed north into the dense woodlands and fertile valleys of central Gaul. He even crossed the English Channel and battled the barbaric tribes who lived in Britannia (present-day England). Back on the continent, he crossed the Rhine River to meet the onslaught of Germanic tribes. According to the historian Plutarch, Caesar's army killed a third of the people in the land it conquered.

Caesar was a tough and dauntless fighter. He drove himself and his troops relentlessly. Carrying 60-pound packs, Caesar's soldiers might march 50 miles in a day. At the day's end, each soldier pulled a shovel from his pack and dug his share of a trench to protect a camp more than one mile square. Inside, two legions (about 9,000 men) could eat and sleep safely before the next day's ordeal. Dinner in Caesar's army was meager: a few handfuls of grain and a cup of sour wine. Caesar himself ate no better. Because he shared fully in the hardships of the march, he won his men's enduring loyalty and devotion.

Never forgetting politics, Caesar sent back regular dispatches to Rome, telling of his victories. Collected into six books, these writings became one of the classics of Latin literature, Caesar's *Commentaries on the Gallic Wars.*

Caesar made himself ruler of Rome.

News from Gaul caused two reactions in Rome. The poorer citizens, who generally adored Caesar, loved him all the more for his conquests. But senators, alarmed at his immense popularity, feared for their own power. By 50 B.C., the triumvirate of Caesar, Crassus, and Pompey had come apart. Crassus was dead, killed in battle while commanding Roman troops in Asia. Pompey had become Caesar's rival rather than his ally. With Pompey's approval, the senate ordered Caesar to disband his legions and return to Rome.

Crossing the Rubicon Caesar's next move led inevitably to **civil war,** or to conflict between political groups. On the night of January 10, 49 B.C., he rode south across the Rubicon River in Italy, the southern limit of his military command. His troops followed loyally behind. Thus, Caesar defied the senate's order and directly challenged Pompey. To this day, "crossing the Rubicon" means making a decision from which there is no return.

Caesar's army marched swiftly through northern Italy and occupied Rome. Pompey barely managed to escape, fleeing eastward to rally his own armies. A year later (48 B.C.), Caesar's troops defeated Pompey's at Pharsalus in Greece. Pompey sailed to Alexandria in Egypt, hoping to win support there for his next campaign against Caesar. Instead, the young pharaoh ordered Pompey to be greeted warmly—and then murdered. When Caesar arrived in Alexandria, he was presented with Pompey's head as a gift. Caesar grieved at the sight, remembering that Pompey had once been both his ally and his son-in-law.

Becoming absolute ruler When Caesar returned to Rome in 46 B.C., he commanded the support of both his armies and the masses. In 44 B.C., the senate appointed him dictator for ten years.

As absolute ruler, Caesar made several sweeping changes. He granted Roman citizenship to many people in provinces outside Italy. He expanded the senate to 900 men, adding loyal followers from other parts of Italy and from Gaul. Caesar had made the senate more representative of the empire, but the patricians were angry that Caesar controlled the senate.

Some of Caesar's other actions would have pleased the Gracchi. He ordered landowners who used slave laborers to substitute free men for at

ecisions in History

Caesar hesitated before making his fateful decision to cross the Rubicon. He knew that invading Italy would violate the law and start a bloody civil war. Yet if he obeyed the senate, he risked being banished from Rome forever. Caesar's supporters urged him to ignore the Senate. Opponents demanded that he obey the law. Moderates urged both Caesar and Pompey to give up their commands and avoid a civil war. What decision would you have made, and why?

145

■ **DISCUSSION**

Caesar's *Commentaries* were written in the third person. What effect would this style have had on the appearance of objectivity in the accounts?

Have students evaluate Caesar's actions as absolute ruler. Were they designed to improve conditions in Rome or to consolidate his power?

■ DISCUSSION

The senate had been reduced to a powerless body that approved all of Caesar's measures. Why did Caesar, who was virtually a king, avoid that title?

■ BACKGROUND

Popular opinion of Cleopatra held that she was a dangerous woman who tempted Antony away from his loyalty to Rome. Most of Antony's troops deserted him in the Battle of Actium when Cleopatra demanded to enter the battle herself.

least one third of their work force. He set up a public works program to create more jobs. He also founded 20 colonies in Spain, France, Switzerland, Africa, and elsewhere to provide land for Rome's landless poor. These programs cut by more than half the number of Romans who lived on government grain handouts.

The calendar Caesar's most lasting reform was to set up a new calendar. He replaced the old Roman calendar, linked to the phases of the moon, with a new solar calendar worked out by the scholars of Alexandria. The new calendar was called the Julian calendar. It counted 365 days in a year and 1 extra day every fourth year. Because the Romans thought February unlucky, they made it the shortest month. The seventh month, July, was named after Julius Caesar, because it included his birthday. The Julian calendar was used in most of Europe until 1582, when slight changes were made for even greater accuracy.

Caesar's death On March 15, 44 B.C., Caesar walked to the Theater of Pompey, where the senate was meeting. Waiting for him were a number of senators with knives hidden beneath their togas.

The chief conspirators, Brutus and Cassius, had been generously pardoned by Caesar for their earlier support of Pompey. Brutus, especially, had been Caesar's friend since then. Even so, both men were still troubled by Caesar's ambitions and his disregard for the old constitution of the republic. They feared that he would make himself king. (According to the ancient laws, you may recall, anyone who plotted to become king could be killed without trial.)

As Caesar approached, the conspirators pressed up against him, pretending to discuss urgent business. Suddenly they struck. Stabbed countless times, Caesar groaned his last words to his old friend Brutus, *"Et tu, Brute!"* ("And you, also, Brutus!") Thus died one of history's most remarkable men.

Civil war followed Caesar's death.

Caesar's assassins thought they had saved the Roman republic. By that time, however, the republic was almost as dead as Caesar himself. Two civil wars (Marius against Sulla and Caesar against Pompey) had crippled the former power of the patricians. Soon after Caesar's death, a

146

third civil war broke out. The final victor of this conflict proved to be an even more astute politician than Julius Caesar. His name was Octavian (ahk-**TAY**-vee-uhn).

The Second Triumvirate Octavian was Caesar's grandnephew and adopted son. When Caesar was murdered in 44 B.C., Octavian was a frail, sickly youth of 18. Octavian's chief rival, Mark Antony, had been Caesar's trusted comrade. Compared to the young Octavian, Antony was a robust, mature leader and an experienced general.

There was little trust between the two men. For a time, however, they agreed to cooperate in destroying Caesar's enemies. Teaming up with Lepidus, a powerful politician, Antony and Octavian led armies into Rome and forced the assembly to grant them power to rule the state. For ten years (43–33 B.C.), Caesar's three avengers acted together as the Second Triumvirate.

Their vengeance was indeed cruel. A list was drawn up of more than 100 senators and 2,000 businessmen to be killed. One of those murdered was Cicero (**SIHS**-uh-roh), the senate's greatest orator. Although Cicero had not plotted to kill Caesar, he often had spoken in defense of the republic and against absolute rule. As for Caesar's chief murderers, Brutus and Cassius, they both committed suicide by falling on their own swords after their armies were routed by Antony in 42 B.C. at the Battle of Philippi in Greece.

War between Octavian and Antony The Second Triumvirate ended like the first, in jealousy and violence. Octavian defeated Lepidus and forced him to retire, but Antony's position still seemed secure.

Antony had married Octavian's sister as a political gesture. But while commanding Roman troops in Asia Minor, Antony met the bewitching Cleopatra. (She came to greet him on a barge rowed with silver oars and adorned with purple sails.) Egypt's queen wooed and won Antony as she had won Caesar. Antony sent back word to Rome that he was divorcing Octavian's sister and marrying Cleopatra. In the senate, Octavian accused Antony of plotting to rule Rome from the foreign city of Alexandria. Rome braced itself for a third civil war, this one between Antony and Octavian.

The two forces clashed in a naval battle off the west coast of Greece. In the Battle of Actium (31 B.C.), the fleet commanded by Antony and

Define:
(a) urban, landless poor
(b) person trained to fight for entertainment (c) official
(continued)

This cameo shows Octavian (Augustus) after he was well established as Rome's sole ruler.

Cleopatra was defeated by Octavian's navy. The couple later committed suicide. To make his triumph even sweeter, Octavian made Egypt another province of Rome.

Octavian became sole ruler.

Like Caesar before him, Octavian was now the sole ruler of Rome. The powers in his hands were as great as a king's or emperor's. However, Octavian remembered what happened to his grand-uncle, Caesar. As a politician, Octavian was more cautious than Caesar, and therefore he lived longer. Instead of seeking a crown, Octavian took only the title of "first citizen."

In 27 B.C., the senate begged Octavian to accept the title of Augustus (aw-GUS-tus). The word means "exalted one" and was normally reserved for the gods. Octavian offered token resistance and then graciously accepted the honor. Afterward, he was known by his honorary title, Augustus, rather than Octavian.

The Roman state under Augustus was no longer ruled by the senate and the assembly as a republic. It was ruled by one man as an empire. However, the senate and the assembly continued to meet and transact business in the old ways. Augustus continued to address the senate as if, at any time, it could strip him of his power and titles.

The senators were not fools. They understood that Augustus held the real power while they held almost none, yet they played along. After all, only by flattering and supporting Augustus could they hope to win appointment to a rich government post in the provinces. Besides, what could they hope to achieve by plotting to overthrow him? Nothing but another civil war, perhaps ending in their own deaths. Thus, Roman politicians found it convenient to let the ancient republic die while pretending that it still lived.

Octavian was to rule Rome for 41 years. His reign marked the beginning of the longest period of peace and prosperity that Rome ever knew.

Section REVIEW 3

Define: (a) proletariat, (b) gladiator, (c) tribune, (d) triumvirate, (e) civil war
Identify: (a) Spartacus, (b) the Gracchi, (c) Marius, (d) Sulla, (e) Julius Caesar, (f) First Triumvirate, (g) Cleopatra, (h) Brutus, (i) Octavian, (j) Second Triumvirate, (k) Mark Antony, (l) Cicero
Answer:
1. How did victory in the Punic Wars change Roman society?
2. How did slavery undermine Roman society?
3. What reforms did the Gracchi try to make?
4. How were military leaders able to gain political power in Rome?
5. (a) What tactics did Julius Caesar use in his rise to power? (b) What groups supported Caesar? (c) What groups opposed him?
6. (a) Why did Octavian and Mark Antony join forces? (b) How did Rome come under the rule of one man?

Critical Thinking
7. (a) What event do you think was the turning point in Rome's change from a republic to one-man rule? (b) Give two reasons to support your answer.

147

ANSWERS TO (continued)

who spoke for the plebeians (d) rule of three (e) conflict between political groups
Identify:
(a) leader of a slave revolt who was crucified
(b) brothers who attempted to reform Rome's government (c) army leader who saved Rome from Germanic invasion (d) foe of Marius who ruled as dictator in 82 B.C. (e) provincial governor who became dictator
(f) Caesar, Crassus, Pompey
(g) Egyptian queen who wooed Caesar and Antony
(h) conspirator in death of Julius Caesar (i) Caesar's grandnephew and adopted son; ruled Rome for 41 years (j) Antony, Octavian, and Lepidus (k) Octavian's chief rival (l) senate's greatest orator, killed for having spoken out against absolute rule

Answer:
1. created proletariat and immense wealth; increased number of slaves
2. Slave revolt was always a threat.
3. land reforms to benefit the poor, weaken senate, and deal with unemployment
4. could pay for armies to win power
5. (a) game of Roman politics, including bribery (b) soldiers, poorer citizens (c) senators, republicans
6. (a) to destroy Caesar's enemies (b) Octavian defeated Lepidus and Antony.
7. Many students might choose Caesar's crossing of the Rubicon, giving the following reasons: it defied the senate's order and challenged Pompey; it led to Caesar's appointment as dictator.

Concluding the Chapter

1. **Chapter Closer**
   Ask students to recall the myth of Romulus and Remus. Have students write evaluations of the extent to which Romulus' prophecy for Rome was fulfilled.

2. **Reteaching Activities**
   a. Summarizing Have students write a paragraph summarizing how geography and military organization helped Rome expand.

   b. Writing Questions and Answers Have students turn each of the headings in Section 2 into a question and then answer each question.

   c. Giving an Explanation Have students explain how each of the following items contributed to the collapse of the Roman republic: the rise of the proletariat class; the formation of armies loyal to military leaders; and the failure of the triumvirates.

Answers to Chapter Review appear on pages 130e–130f.

Summary

1. The Romans built a great city. Rome grew up at a location with many geographic advantages. Its early culture was influenced by Latins, Greeks, and Etruscans. At first, Rome was ruled by kings, but in 509 B.C. it became a republic. Roman society was divided into two classes, patricians and plebeians. Over the years, plebeians gradually won more and more rights. By about 275 B.C., Rome claimed to have achieved a balanced form of government.

2. The Roman republic spread its power. Between 509 and 265 B.C., plebeians won increasing political power, leading to a government that blended elements of monarchy, aristocracy, and democracy. Also by 265 B.C., Rome had won control of Italy. At that point, Rome began to expand around the Mediterranean, starting with the defeat of Carthage and extending eastward to Greece and Asia Minor.

3. Republican government collapsed in Rome. The Punic Wars and the spread of slavery brought great changes to Rome. Many Romans became landless and jobless. Political struggles became increasingly violent, and army leaders won control of the government. In 44 B.C., Julius Caesar became sole ruler of the Roman empire. After Caesar's assassination, Octavian held power, becoming king in all but name.

Reviewing the Facts

1. Define the following terms:
   a. republic
   b. gravitas
   c. patrician
   d. plebeian
   e. consul
   f. veto
   g. senate
   h. dictator
   i. mercenary
   j. proletariat
   k. tribune
   l. triumvirate

2. Explain the importance of each of the following names, dates, places, or terms:
   a. Rome
   b. Italy
   c. Latins
   d. Etruscans
   e. 509 B.C.
   f. pater familias
   g. Carthage
   h. Twelve Tables
   i. Punic Wars
   j. Hannibal
   k. Battle of Zama
   l. 146 B.C.
   m. the Gracchi
   n. Julius Caesar
   o. 49 B.C.
   p. 44 B.C.
   q. Cleopatra
   r. Brutus
   s. Octavian (Augustus)
   t. Mark Antony

3. Explain how each of the following factors influenced life in early Rome.
   a. the geography of Italy
   b. Latin, Greek, and Etruscan settlers
   c. the existence of social classes
   d. the constant threat of war

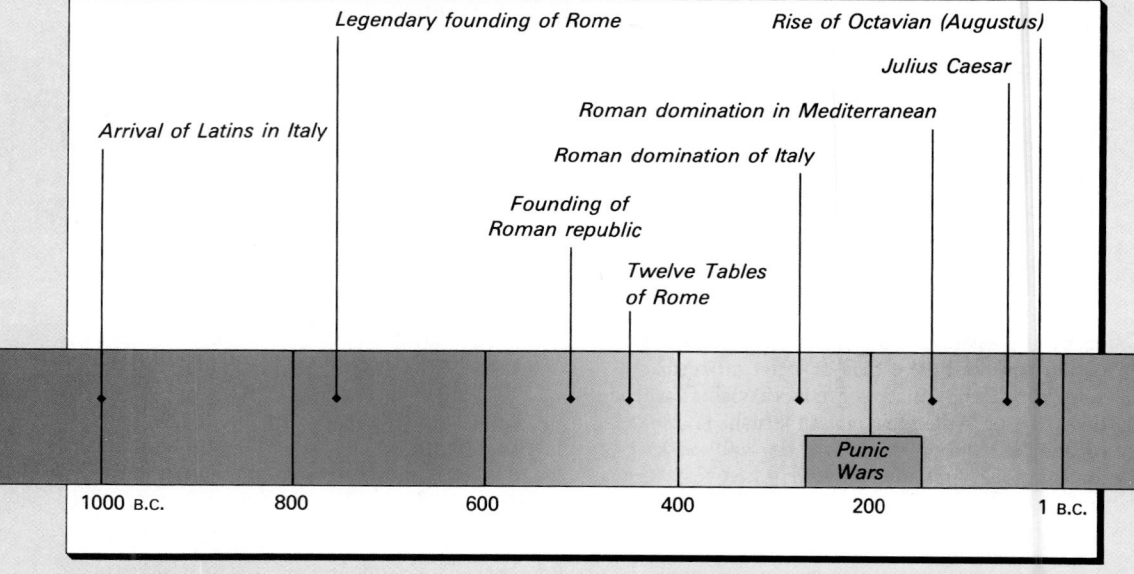

148

4. (a) What was the conflict between patricians and plebeians in the earliest days of the Roman republic? (b) How was the conflict reduced?
5. Describe the structure of Rome's government during the republic. In your discussion, include both the powers and the limitations of each part of the government.
6. How did Rome use its idea of citizenship to unify the lands it won in Italy?
7. (a) How was Rome strengthened by the Punic Wars? (b) How was the Roman republic weakened by the Punic Wars?
8. How was the rise of rulers such as Marius, Sulla, and Julius Caesar different from that of early leaders of the republic?

Basic Skills

1. **Comparing map scales** (a) On the map on page 104, what is the distance from Mount Olympus to Sparta? (b) On the map on page 139, what is the distance from Rome to Carthage? (c) Compare the scale of miles on the two maps. What illusion does the difference in scale create?
2. **Making a time line** Draw a time line for the period from 400 B.C. to 1 B.C., dividing it into eight 50-year segments. On the time line, place the following events in the correct location: first Punic War, destruction of Corinth, sack of Rome by the Gauls, destruction of Carthage, conquest of Gaul, Rome's final victory over Phyrrus.
3. **Identifying supporting details** Give three facts that support the general statement, "The geographic location of Rome offered many advantages for growth."
4. **Making a chart** Make a chart comparing Rome and Carthage at the start of the Punic Wars. For the vertical rows, use the headings *Population, Army, Navy,* and *Resources.* Complete the chart by filling in the information.
5. **Predicting outcomes** (a) On the basis of the information in the previous chart, what would you expect to be the outcome of the Punic Wars? (b) What factors changed the course of events?
6. **Using historical terms** Contemporaries are people who live at the same time, such as Cicero and Julius Caesar. Name a contemporary of each of the following people: (a) Hannibal, (b) Gaius Gracchus, (c) Marius, (d) Sallust.

Researching and Reporting Skills

1. **Using a historical atlas** A historical atlas is an atlas containing maps of places or regions at different times in the past. In a historical atlas, find a map of some period of Roman history and photocopy it. Explain to the class what the map shows.
2. **Reporting on history** Write a news story about the assassination of Julius Caesar. Start with the dateline "Rome, March 15, 44 B.C." In the lead paragraph, tell *who, what, when, where, why,* and *how* in relation to the event. In later paragraphs, give more details about the identity and motives of the assassins and the expected consequences for Rome. Finish by creating a headline for the story.

Critical Thinking

1. **Comparing** (a) Compare the Roman ideal of *gravitas* with the Athenian ideal of *arete*. (b) What do the differences in these ideals tell about the civilization they represent?
2. **Analyzing outcomes** Imagine that you are Julius Caesar deciding whether to cross the Rubicon. (a) What may you achieve if you cross it? (b) What might you lose by crossing it? (c) If you were Caesar, which decision would you make? Why?
3. **Analyzing** (a) Marius changed the Roman army from a body of citizen-soldiers to one of professional soldiers. What advantages did this change have for Rome? (b) What disadvantages?
4. **Analyzing** Rome was the victor in the Punic Wars, but at great cost. (a) What did Rome gain? (b) What were the social and economic costs for Rome?

Perspectives on Past and Present

Reread the quotation from Sallust on page 143. From your knowledge of this period of the Roman empire, evaluate how accurate his assessment is. To what extent might the quotation be applied to society today?

Investigating History

Read the murder scene in Shakespeare's play *Julius Caesar.* Then act out a trial in class to judge whether Brutus and Cassius should be pardoned for acting in defense of the Roman republic or be punished as murderers. Select a prosecuter, a defender, witnesses, and a jury to hold the trial.

149

CHAPTER
Evaluation

Chapter Test 6, Alternate Chapter Test 6, and Computer Test Bank Chapter 6 Test can be used to evaluate your students' understanding of this chapter.

The Roman Empire

Chapter Overview

The rule of Augustus ushered in Rome's greatest period of peace and prosperity—the Pax Romana. Augustus established economic programs and a stable government that allowed Rome to survive a series of untalented emperors. The Romans extended Greek ideals in art, literature, and philosophy, while making unique and enduring contributions in law, architecture, and engineering. Within the empire, great differences between classes developed. Jews and Christians challenged Roman traditions. Both groups were persecuted by many Roman emperors. Beginning in the third century, economic, military, and political problems weakened the empire, making possible the barbarian invasions that led to the empire's fall in A.D. 476.

Chapter Focus

A symbol is something that stands for or represents another thing. Point out that all famous buildings have some symbolic significance. For example, ask students to select a famous building (or monument) in the United States. Ask what the building symbolizes. Then direct students' attention to the photograph of the Colosseum on page 150. Ask why the Colosseum is a symbol of the Roman empire. What political purposes did the gladiator contests serve? The Colosseum is a symbol of the Roman empire at the peak of its power.

Augustus's rule began the Pax Romana. 1

Setting the Stage

Discussing History: Octavian's Rule (Objective 1) Recall that in Chapter 6 students learned that Octavian (Augustus) ruled Rome for 41 years. Write the titles *Princeps, Augustus,* and *Imperator* on the board. These titles mean "First citizen," "Revered and Exalted One," and "Commander," respectively. Although Augustus held all three titles and had absolute power, he gave the impression of working with the senate and avoided humiliating the senators. At the same time, he maintained control of government by setting up a civil service system.

Teaching Strategies

Teaching with Pictures: Aqueducts (Objective 2) Have students read the sections on Roman roads and public buildings (pages 151–152). Then direct their attention to the picture of the aqueduct on page 152. This aqueduct still delivers water to Segovia by gravity from a mountain spring 10 miles away. The aqueduct is 93 feet high. Roman engineers used a block and tackle to raise granite blocks weighing up to 6 tons. Ask why a secure supply of water was essential to the growth of cities.

Geography in History: The Roman Empire (Objective 3) Distribute copies of Outline Map 21: The Roman Empire. Have students create a

Chapter 7 The Roman Empire 29 B.C.–AD. 476

FOCUS The Colosseum as a symbol of the Roman empire

★ Advanced
● Basic

	SECTION 1	SECTION 2	SECTION 3	SECTION 4
Objectives	1. Assess the political skills of Augustus. 2. Describe Roman achievements in constructing public works, such as roads and aqueducts. 3. Show on a map the Roman empire at its height. 4. Define the problem of succession and explain its impact on Roman politics.	1. Identify and discuss the ideas of Roman philosophers and writers. 2. Describe the Roman Forum. 3. List important principles of Roman law.	1. Explain the origins of Chanukah. 2. Discuss the main teachings of Jesus. 3. Describe how Christianity spread through the Roman empire. 4. Explain why the Romans warred against the Jews and persecuted the Christians.	1. Identify problems that led to Rome's decline. 2. Evaluate the solutions offered by Diocletian and Constantine to solve Rome's problems. 3. Explain how the Germanic tribes overran and destroyed the western half of the empire.
Setting the Stage	Discussing History: Octavian's Rule	The diffusion of Greco-Roman culture	Sources of religious persecution	Multiple causes of the decline and fall of Rome
Teaching Strategies	Teaching with Pictures: Aqueducts Geography in History: The Roman Empire Outline Map 21 Transparency 21 Relating Past to Present: The Problem of Succession Check for Understanding	Identifying Quotations: Roman Philosophy and Literature Teaching with Pictures: The Roman Forum Discussing History: Roman Law Check for Understanding	Discussing History: The Origins of Chanukah Analyzing a Quotation: The Sermon on the Mount Using Geographic Themes: Movement Transparency 22 Discussing History: Religious Persecution Check for Understanding	Discussing History: Why Did Rome Fall? Transparency 23 Skill Building: Identifying Cause and Effect Relationships Using Geographic Themes: Movement Transparency 24 Check for Understanding
Guided Practice	Transparency 21 Q&A Section Review 1	Section Review 2	Transparency 22 Q&A Section Review 3	Transparency 23 Q&A Transparency 24 Q&A Section Review 4
Independent Practice Worksheets	Independent Practice 7.1 Vocabulary 7	Independent Practice 7.2 Basic Skills 7	Independent Practice 7.3 Critical Thinking	Independent Practice 7.4 Geography Skills 7
Enrichment	1. Primary Source: Voices 7.1 2. ★Augustus's Last Question 3. Researching for Points	1. Primary Source: Voices 7.2 2. ★Analyzing a Quotation 3. Researching for Points	1. Primary Source: Voices 7.3 2. Preparing a Report: The Siege of Masada 3. Researching for Points	1. Primary Source: Voices 7.4 2. Creative Writing 3. Researching for Points

Chapter Closer	●**Reteaching Activities**	Writing an Essay, Outlining, Explaining, Recalling Information
	Chapter Review	Summary, Reviewing the Facts, Basic Skills, Researching and Reporting Skills, Critical Thinking, Perspectives on Past and Present, Investigating History
	Chapter Evaluation	Chapter Test 7, Alternate Chapter Test 7, Computer Test Bank Chapter 7 Test
Unit II Review	**Geographic Theme**	Region: How did Rome unify the Mediterranean world?
	Historical Themes	Rise of Democratic Ideas, Cultural Development, Individuals and History
	Unit Evaluation	Unit II Test, Alternate Unit II Test

map comparing the Roman republic by 133 B.C. and the Roman empire at its height. (See the maps on pages 140 and 154 for reference, or use Map Transparency 21, *The Roman Empire at Its Height*.)

Relating Past to Present: The Problem of Succession (Objective 4) Ask students to identify the various methods the Romans used to try to resolve the problem of succession. Why was the lack of a fixed rule for succession a serious problem? Then ask students to describe the procedures established by the United States Constitution to handle succession. (You might wish to review Article 2, Amendment 22, and Amendment 25.) Ask, "Does this procedure work? Why, or why not?"

Check for Understanding Have students cite evidence to support the following statement from page 153: "The system of government set up by Augustus proved to be more stable and effective than its individual leaders."

1. **Reading a Primary Source** Assign Voices from the Past Resource Book 7.1.
2. **Augustus's Last Question** Just before he died, Augustus asked family members gathered around him this question: "Have I played my part in the farce of life creditably enough?" Ask advanced students to write an answer to Augustus's question.
3. **Researching for Bonus Points** When the gladiators marched into the Colosseum, with what phrase did they salute the emperor? ("Hail, Caesar; we who are about to die salute you.")

Romans extended Greek culture. 2

Setting the Stage

Cultural diffusion occurs when ideas and goods spread from one culture to another. Ask students to identify examples of cultural diffusion that they have already studied. (Silk Road, conquests of Alexander the Great) Now ask students to identify Roman achievements that would stimulate cultural diffusion. (Pax Romana, in general; road system, in specific) The blend of the Greek and Roman cultures is called *Greco-Roman*.

Teaching Strategies

Identifying Quotations: Roman Philosophy and Literature (Objective 1) Review the sections on philosophy and Latin literature (pages 155–157). Then read or distribute each of the following quotations. Have students identify the philosopher or writer they would most associate with each quotation. Ask students to explain the reasons for their choices.

- Death is nothing to us, since when we are, death has not come, and when death has come, we are not. (Epicurus)
- One universe, made up of all that is; and one God in it all, and one principle of being, and one law, the reason, shared by all thinking creatures, and one truth. (Marcus Aurelius; the Stoics)
- All the doings of mankind, their wishes, fears, anger, pleasure, joys, and varied pursuits, form the motley subject of my book. (Juvenal)
- The great cycle of the ages is renewal. Now justice returns, returns the Golden Age; a new generation now descends from on high. (Virgil)

Teaching with Pictures: The Roman Forum (Objective 2) After students read the section on Rome (pages 157–158), direct their attention to the artistic rendering of the Roman Forum (page 158). Ask them to imagine that they are part of the crowd standing in the foreground of the painting. They are touring one of the ancient world's most famous public squares. A guide explains that the Forum was the political, religious, and commercial center of the empire. The column on the right was known as the Rostra. Crowds often gathered around it to listen to orators give stirring speeches. (The word *rostrum*, today, refers to any platform for public speaking.) The Arch of Tiberius stands just behind the Rostra. Roman justices administered the law in the great Basilica Julia to the left. Temples to Saturn and Vespasian tower in the background. Statues of heroes, gods, and goddesses decorate all of the buildings. Conclude by asking students to write postcards home describing the sights they have just seen.

Discussing History: Roman Law (Objective 3) Explain that a great Roman jurist named Ulpian defined justice as "a constant and perpetual will to give every man his due." Have students explain this definition in their own words. Then review the basic principles of Roman law (page 159). Ask students to explain how these principles illustrate Ulpian's definition of justice.

Check for Understanding Have students cite examples of Greek influence on Roman culture and give examples of distinctly Roman cultural achievements.

Enrichment Activities

1. **Reading a Primary Source**
   Assign Voices from the Past Resource Book 7.2.

2. **Analyzing a Quotation**
   The famed historian Edward Gibbon wrote, "If a man were called upon to fix the period in the history of the world during which the condition of the human race was most happy and prosperous, he would without hesitation name that which elapsed from the accession of Nerva to the death of Aurelius." Ask advanced students to cite evidence supporting or refuting this statement.

3. **Researching for Bonus Points**
   What name did Romans give to the cold water room in their baths? (the frigidarium)

Christianity spread through the empire. 3

Setting the Stage

Review the definitions of *polytheism* and *monotheism*. Ask students why a polytheist might tolerate a monotheist, but a monotheist might not tolerate a polytheist. What conditions might lead to the persecution of religious minorities?

Teaching Strategies

Discussing History: The Origins of Chanukah (Objective 1) The eight-day Chanukah celebration, also known as the "Festival of Lights," dates to events described in this section. The holiday of Chanukah commemorates the struggle of Jews led by Judas Maccabee to recapture the Jewish temple in Jerusalem. The Hebrew word *Chanukah* means "rededication" and refers to the purification of the temple in 165 B.C. When the temple was rededicated, only enough oil was found to burn for one day. Miraculously, the sacramental oil lasted for eight days. In present-day practice, Jews light a candle on each of the eight nights of Chanukah.

Analyzing a Quotation: The Sermon on the Mount (Objective 2) Jesus won many followers because he taught that God's kingdom was open to everyone. Ask students to read the excerpt on page 161 and identify the qualities Jesus emphasized and to contrast them with qualities admired by the Romans.

Using Geographic Themes: Movement (Objective 3) First, review the section "Paul influenced the growth of Christianity" (page 162). Then display Map Transparency 22, *The Spread of Christianity in Roman Times*. Point out Paul's role in spreading the new faith to key cities in the eastern half of the Roman empire. Also note Christianity's rapid expansion between A.D. 300 and A.D. 450.

Discussing History: Religious Persecution (Objective 4) A scapegoat is a person or a group blamed for the errors of others. Roman emperors found it convenient to use Christians as scapegoats. As the third century Christian writer Tertullian explained, the Romans "take the Christians to be the cause of every disaster to the state, of every misfortune to the people. If . . . there is a famine, or if there is a plague, the cry is at once, 'the Christians to the lions.' " Suggest that the persecutions of the Christians showed the empire's growing weakness.

Check for Understanding Have students explain why the Romans persecuted Jews and Christians. How did these persecutions affect both religions?

Enrichment Activities

1. **Reading a Primary Source**
   Assign Voices from the Past Resource Book 7.3.

2. **Preparing a Report**
   Ask interested students to report on the siege of Masada. Reports should cover why Masada has become an important symbol for modern Israel.

3. **Researching for Bonus Points**
   What was the name of the apostle who replaced Judas? (Matthias)

Rome's empire declined and fell. 4

Setting the Stage

Ask students to recall a contest or game in which the side they were rooting for lost. Have students list reasons why their side lost. Ask, "How many listed only one reason? How many listed two or more reasons?" Note that events can rarely be explained by a single cause. Historians look for multiple causes to explain why an event occurred. A number of forces have been identified that worked together over an extended period of time to cause the fall of Rome.

Teaching Strategies

Discussing History: Why Did Rome Fall? (Objective 1) Begin by having students list Rome's problems. (succession, gap between rich and poor, rise of professional armies, declining faith in old gods, struggles against Jews and Christians) These problems worsened during the third century. Have students read the section "Crises weakened the empire" (pages 164–165). Ask which problem students think posed the gravest threat to Rome's security. Use Map Transparency 23, *Trade in the Roman Empire*, to link Rome's economic problems with its networks of trade.

Skill Building: Identifying Cause and Effect Relationships (Objective 2) The Romans tried to solve their problems. Have students read the sections on the reforms of Diocletian and Constantine (pages 166–167). Then draw a three-column chart on the board. Label the columns *Problems, Solutions,* and *Consequences.* In the first column, have students list problems that plagued the empire during the third century. Then ask the class to review the reforms initiated by Diocletian and Constantine and to link each reform with one or more of the problems on the chart. Enter this information in the second column. Have students complete the chart by assessing the success or failure of each reform and entering this information in the third column.

Using Geographic Themes: Movement (Objective 3) The Germanic invasions illustrate the theme of movement. Have students read the sections on how the Germanic tribes overran the western half of the empire (pages 167–168). Then use Map Transparency 24, *The Bar-barian Invasions*, to trace the movement of each tribe.

Check for Understanding Have students identify three main causes for the decline of the Roman empire.

Enrichment Activities

1. **Reading a Primary Source**
Assign Voices from the Past Resource Book 7.4.

2. **Creative Writing**
The fall of Rome might seem the inevitable result of crisis and decline; however, this was not necessarily the perception of the Romans, who proudly recalled their tradition of overcoming adversity. Divide the class into groups representing members of a family living in Rome. Assign family statuses (patrician, plebeian, slave). Have each group write a family diary containing entries for each of the following years: 192, 260, 290, 313, 330, 410, 452, and 476. Entries should describe key events in those years and their impact on family life.

3. **Researching for Bonus Points**
What were the names of Constantine's three sons? (Constantius, Constantinus, and Constans)

Reviewing the Facts

1. **(a)** salaried people of all ranks who performed work to run the empire **(b)** writing that mocked society for its foolishness and wickedness **(c)** country estate owned by wealthy city dweller, used as an escape from city life **(d)** church official who set moral standards and supervised finances of several local churches **(e)** father and leading bishop of Christian Church **(f)** increase in prices

2. **(a)** 207 years of Roman peace between 27 B.C. and A.D. 180 **(b)** Roman emperor who built foundation for Pax Romana **(c)** Roman emperor who wrote *Meditations;* Pax Romana ended with his death **(d)** year Pax Romana ended **(e)** Greek philosopher whose ideas about happiness influenced Romans **(f)** Greek philosopher who developed Stoicism **(g)** patriotic historian whose works were sponsored by Augustus **(h)** epic poet and author of *Aeneid* **(i)** founder of Christianity **(j)** apostle who dedicated his life to spreading teachings of Jesus **(k)** disciple of Jesus who was Rome's first bishop **(l)** Jewish revolutionaries who tried to overthrow Roman rule **(m)** emperor who tried to restore order in the empire and increase its strength **(n)** emperor who ended Christian persecution and moved capital from Rome to Byzantium **(o)** new name for Byzantium **(p)** law that changed Christianity from outlawed sect to religion approved by emperor **(q)** year when last Roman emperor was overthrown

3. The Roman empire was largely free of war. Trade and transportation improved. Public building program was initiated. Civil service began. Roman law developed.

4. **(a)** kingdom of God for believers; people should follow a

"golden rule" **(b)** With the exception of Nero, emperors during the first century did not actively persecute Christians. Toward the end of the second century, Christians were cruelly persecuted. In the fourth century, Constantine gave state approval to Christianity.

5. (a) Trade was disrupted on both land and sea; Rome's gold and silver were drained away to buy luxuries from other lands; harvests became increasingly meager. **(b)** At one time, Romans were willing to sacrifice their lives for their republic. In later centuries, citizens were not actively disloyal but were indifferent. It was no longer considered an honor to hold political office. Recruitment of barbarians into the army made the loyalty of troops suspect. **(c)** Germanic invasions destroyed the western half of the Roman empire.

Basic Skills

1. (a) 1,000 years; 600 years **(b)** 100 B.C. to 1 B.C. **(c)** about 100 years to one-half inch; about 100 years to one inch **(d)** the Pax Romana

2.

	Europe	Africa	Asia
Minerals	lead, gold, tin, copper, iron, silver	copper	silver
Foods	wine, olive oil, dried fish	grain, olive oil, spices, palm oil	spices, pepper, wine
Building Materials		marble	marble, timber
Clothing	wool, furs		silks, wool
Jewelry	amber	ivory, tortoise-shell	jade, pearls, ivory
Manufactured Goods	glass, pottery, bronzeware	glass, incense, papyrus	glass, incense
Other	slaves, horses, hunting dogs	slaves	purple dye

3. Summaries should include governing ability; encouragement of trade through coinage, elimination of border taxes, and building of roads; glorification of Rome through public building program; efficient civil service made up of salaried, experienced workers.

Researching and Reporting Skills

1. Group projects will vary.

2. Primary sources: St. Paul's Epistle, Constantine's triumphal arch, Marcus Aurelius's *Meditations*. These were works of contemporaries of the period. Secondary sources: Livy's description of the early heroes of Rome. Livy was a historian writing about the past.

Critical Thinking

1. (a) During the republic only Romans could be citizens. Citizenship gave males the right to participate in the assembly and gave equal access to public office (287 B.C.). Citizenship was later extended to non-Romans and conquered peoples. In Greece, citizenship was not extended to foreigners, women, or slaves. In Rome, Athens, and Sparta citizens had military and political duties to the state. **(b)** In the United States, citizenship extends to all persons born in United States territory or to an American parent, and to naturalized immigrants.

2. Buddhism also appealed to the poor. Both religions taught concern for all human beings and belief in a merciful God.

3. Students should provide examples from Roman history proving or disproving the characteristics listed in the quotation.

4. (a) Students might note that Roman law is practiced in many countries today. **(b)** Students might mention Roman roads, architecture, and political institutions as enduring achievements.

5. (a) a general increase in prices **(b)** too many expensive luxuries imported from abroad; little to export in exchange; paid for imports with large quantities of silver and gold; as these were in short supply, the Roman government minted coins with less and less silver content; these coins lost their value and more were needed to pay for goods, thus increasing prices dramatically **(c)** All people were poorer since their money was worth less. The poor in particular suffered greatly from the high prices for necessities. Imports became unaffordable and trade slowed down.

Perspectives on Past and Present

1. Students might point out the use of Roman columns, arches, and the dome in monumental architecture.

2. Answers will vary, but students should point out that Rome had no established procedure for the transition of power. As a result, such times often caused crises. In the United States, the president is elected every four years. In some countries there is no established procedure; often there is a period of shared power with a struggle between leaders until one takes control. In many countries, constitutional monarchies are hereditary, with power held by a parliament. In countries with dictatorships, there may also be a president; often, the army controls or decides the outcome of elections. Succession also may occur by a coup, or abrupt seizure of power often involving military action.

Investigating History
Students' findings will vary.

The Colosseum in Rome was a center for gladiatorial combats.

Teaching with Pictures

Explain to students that the Colosseum in Rome in A.D. 80 was an outstanding example of architecture and engineering, although it is in ruins today. The Colosseum was 160 feet (49 meters) high, 620 feet (189 meters) long, and 510 feet (155 meters) wide. The wooden floor of the arena, now missing, was the site of mock naval battles, duels between gladiators, and battles between men and animals. The ruins of the Colosseum do not reflect the color and splendor the Romans saw. Ask students to imagine awnings of brilliant scarlet, blue, and yellow stretching across the top. Ask volunteers to describe what it would be like to be among the 50,000 spectators at the Colosseum for a spectacle. Encourage them to look beyond the ruins in the photo to the latent magnificence of the place.

Key Terms

gladiator
policy
aqueduct
civil service
succession
Epicureanism
Stoicism
satire
villa
apostle
messiah
martyr
bishop
pope
inflation

150

Read and Understand

1. Augustus's rule began the Pax Romana.
2. Romans extended Greek culture.
3. Christianity spread through the empire.
4. Rome's empire declined and fell.

In A.D. 80, tens of thousands of spectators poured into Rome's new sports arena, the Colosseum (KAHL-uh-SEE-uhm). To celebrate its opening, spectacles were held every day for 100 days. The Colosseum was the largest building of its kind in the ancient world. A tribute to Roman engineering, it was built so tightly that its arena could be filled with water for mock naval battles.

From the outside, the Colosseum looked truly colossal. Its 160-foot-high walls had 4 tiers of windows, columns, and arches. The Colosseum's 80 entrances were set in the bottom row of arches. As many as 50,000 spectators with numbered tickets used 76 entrances, Emperor Titus and his party used two entrances, and the last two were reserved for the **gladiators,** the men fighting in the arena.

Chapter 7 Resources

GEOGRAPHY
- Geography Skills 7
- Outline Map 21
- Transparencies 21, 22, 23, 24

REINFORCEMENT
- Vocabulary 7
- Basic Skills 7
- Reteaching 7
- Making Connections Study Guide 7

ENRICHMENT
- Critical Thinking 7
- History and Literature 7

ASSESSMENT
- Chapter Test 7
- Alternate Chapter Test 7
- Computer Test Bank

Once inside, spectators climbed sloping ramps to their seats. The bottom tier featured boxes for the emperor, state priests, and senators. Above them, in rows of marble seats, sat distinguished citizens, members of the middle class, favored slaves, and foreigners, in that order. In the fourth tier, on wooden benches sat women and the poor. No matter where people sat, however, there was a clear view of the arena below. Overhead was a tremendous colored awning that could be rolled out on cables to shield the audience against sun and rain.

The show started early in the morning and lasted all day. Sometimes it opened with a contest between comics, but it soon became bloody. Mornings were devoted to animal shows. Tigers, lions, bears, elephants, and giraffes from distant parts of the empire were released into the arena to fight to the death. In the afternoon, professional gladiators fought animals or one another. Most gladiators were slaves, prisoners of war, or condemned criminals. But others, including a few women, were free Romans who chose to gamble their lives for a short span of glory and public adoration.

The Romans had adopted gladiator contests from the Etruscans. For the Etruscans, such contests had had religious importance. For the Roman government, however, the bloody entertainments in the Colosseum served a political purpose. They were one way to entertain the thousands of unemployed—and potentially dangerous—people who flocked to the city of Rome.

In many ways, the Colosseum is symbolic of the entire Roman empire. From the outside, both were awesome in their size and strength. Within, both combined bravery, honor, and glory with cruelty, sensationalism, and violence.

Rome was at the peak of its power from the time of Augustus's rule to A.D. 180. Then it began a long and uneven decline to the collapse of the western empire in A.D. 476. In the first part of this 500-year period, Rome advanced in architecture, law, philosophy, and literature. At the same time, faith in a new religion, Christianity, spread widely through the empire. Gradually, however, the Roman empire lost the strength to fight off its enemies. In the end, a barbarian king ruled in Rome, and Rome's culture was transferred to a new capital city in the east, Constantinople.

Augustus's rule began the Pax Romana. 1

Pax (pahks) is the Latin word for "peace." For 207 years (27 B.C.–A.D. 180), peace was the chief gift that Rome gave the people it ruled. Though legions still fought on the borders of the empire, the immense territory within those borders was largely free of war. This period of peace and prosperity is known as the *Pax Romana.*

The borders of the empire during the Pax Romana measured 10,000 miles and enclosed an area of more than 3 million square miles, about the size of the United States today. The empire extended north to Scotland in the British Isles, south to the Sahara in Africa, east to Mesopotamia in Asia, and west to the Atlantic Ocean. The population of the empire during this period was between 70 and 90 million people. The city of Rome itself was home to about 1 million people.

Augustus set up sound government.

Augustus was perhaps Rome's ablest emperor. He built the foundation for the Pax Romana through far-sighted **policies,** or plans for governing. He encouraged trade, glorified Rome with splendid buildings, and created a system of government that survived for centuries.

Just as important, Augustus set the tone for the empire by extolling the old values of simplicity, sober conduct, and patriotism. Augustus dressed in homemade white togas and lived in a small house on the Palatine Hill.

Trade and transportation In Augustus's time, a silver coin called a denarius (dih-**NAIR**-ee-uhs) circulated throughout the empire. (It looked very much like an American quarter.) Having a common coinage made trade between different parts of the empire much easier.

Footnote to History

As the adopted son of Julius Caesar, Augustus used *Caesar* as one of his titles. Over the years, the word came to mean "an emperor or ruler." So powerful did the word become that nearly 2,000 years later the ruler of Germany was called kaiser, and the ruler of Russia czar.

151

SECTION 1 Objectives and Teaching Strategies

OBJECTIVE 1. Assess the political skills of Augustus.

Teaching Strategy: *Discussing History: Octavian's Rule* (page 150a)

OBJECTIVE 2. Describe Roman achievements in constructing public works, such as roads and aqueducts.

Teaching Strategy: *Teaching with Pictures: Aqueducts* (page 150a)

OBJECTIVE 3. Show on a map the Roman empire at its height.

Teaching Strategy: *Geography in History: The Roman Empire* (page 150a)

OBJECTIVE 4. Define the problem of succession and explain its impact on Roman politics.

Teaching Strategy: *Relating Past to Present: The Problem of Succession* (page 150c)

■ **BACKGROUND**

Students should note that Greeks also enjoyed contests—the Olympics, for example—but their contests did not involve weapons or a fight to the death.

SECTION 1 Resources

GEOGRAPHY
■ Transparency 21

REINFORCEMENT
■ Independent Practice 7.1

ENRICHMENT
■ Voices from the Past 7.1

ASSESSMENT
■ Section Quiz 7.1

151

Have students look at the photo on this page. It shows one way the Romans devised to provide an adequate water supply to all citizens. Ask students to name as many uses as they can that people have for water in their daily lives. List the responses on the board. Then divide the class into groups of four or five students. Each group should generate a list of problems now facing our society in obtaining adequate water supplies. All group members must agree on the final list of four or five items. Students should then brainstorm to come up with solutions for those problems. One person should act as recorder, noting the various problems and solutions. Groups should present their ideas to the entire class. As a class, have students create a plan to conserve water during their own daily activities.

■ BACKGROUND

Augustus was also a shrewd politician. Although he held all the power, Augustus paid homage to the once-powerful senators, always rising in their presence.

Augustus also realized that it hurt trade to tax goods as they moved across each province's border. Therefore, he eliminated all such taxes, making Roman lands one large economic empire.

To improve transportation and to bind his empire together more tightly, Augustus began a program of highway construction. Continuing his work, later emperors turned Roman highways into one of the most lasting monuments of their civilization. Roman roads were as impressive in their own way as the pyramids of Egypt. The Romans also built **aqueducts,** or long, bridgelike structures that carried water from nearby hills to centers of population.

A *public building program* Marvels such as Rome's roads and bridges were possible through the use of an amazing new building material: concrete. The Romans had learned to mix lime mortar, pour it into a wooden mold, and wait for it to become as hard as stone. Concrete formed the backbone of Rome's bold architecture. The Romans used concrete and decorated its surface with more costly materials, such as marble.

Augustus, however, never bragged about his use of cement. He liked to boast that he had turned Rome from a city of brick into a city of marble. He commissioned Greek artists and architects to build temples similar to the Parthenon throughout the city. During Augustus's reign, Rome began to look like a world capital.

The civil service Under Augustus, Rome became the center of an efficient imperial government. Augustus left the senators their titles and money-making positions in the provinces, but he gave much of the real work of running the empire to plebeians and even slaves.

Augustus set up a **civil service**, with salaried, experienced workers to take care of Rome's grain supply, road repairs, the postal system, and all the other work of running an empire. People of all ranks served in this civil service. Hardworking, loyal freedmen (former slaves) won many of the highest and most influential positions. Because these men had a rare opportunity to improve their lot, they served Augustus well.

Peace continued after Augustus died.

Because Augustus had been a sickly youth, his enemies had hoped he would not rule long. But Augustus was more durable than he had looked. He died at the age of 76 in A.D. 14.

When Augustus died, the senate promptly hailed his adopted son and chosen successor, Tiberius (tye-**BIHR**-ee-uhs), as the new ruler. Tiberius and the three emperors after him are known as the Julian emperors because they were descended from the family of Julius Caesar. None of them, however, matched Augustus or Julius Caesar in boldness or skill.

Looking at economics *Aqueducts like this one at Segovia, Spain, carried water to many Roman cities. An adequate supply of water was essential to urban growth and economic development.*

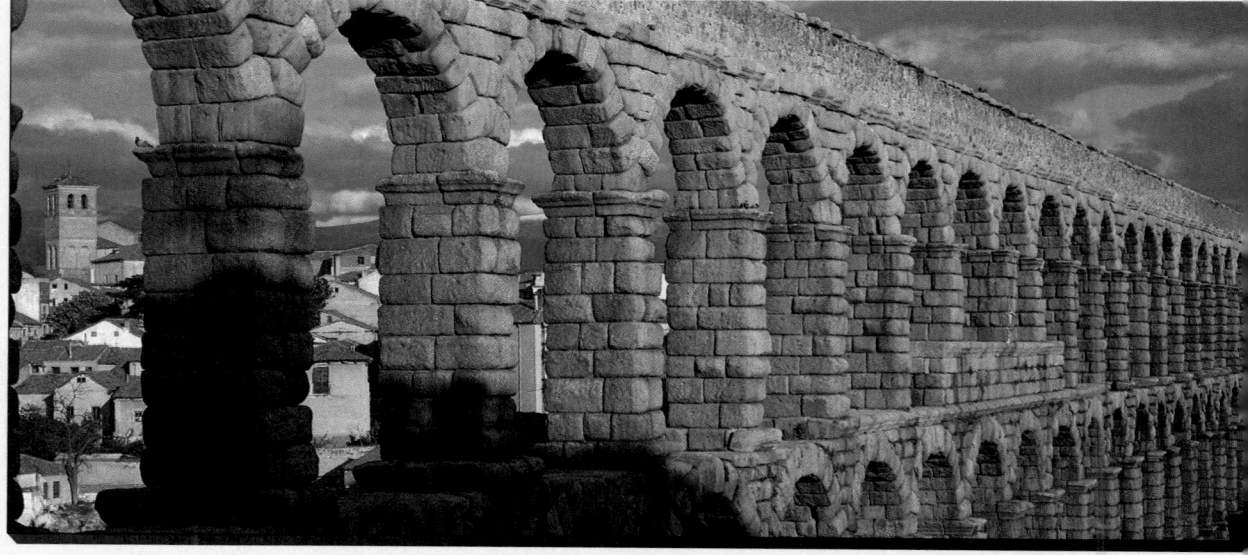

In the years of the Pax Romana, some of Rome's emperors were conscientious, intelligent, and able. Some were corrupt, cruel, or incompetent. One or two were probably insane. (Caligula, for example, appointed his horse consul and talked to statues in the Forum.) Yet the senate and the Roman people put up with each of them and even worshiped them. The system of government set up by Augustus proved to be more stable and effective than its individual leaders.

The problem of succession Rome's emperors never solved the problem of **succession,** or the transfer of authority after the death of an emperor. Was the new emperor to be a person selected by the senate or by the dying emperor himself? Should the favorite candidate of a provincial army be appointed? Or should the Praetorian (pree-**TOH**-ree-uhn) Guard—the army of 9,000 men stationed in Rome—impose its choice on the empire by force?

At one time or another, each of these methods was tried. Since there was no fixed rule of succession, every time an emperor died there was a potential crisis. When the emperor Nero committed suicide, for example, provincial armies and the Praetorian Guard took turns proclaiming a new emperor, then promptly murdering him, and installing another. In 18 months (A.D. 68–69), Rome had 4 emperors.

The Good Emperors The succession problem was temporarily solved by the men known to history as the Five Good Emperors, or the Adoptive Emperors. When Domitian (doh-**MEE**-shuhn) was assassinated in A.D. 96, the senate chose Nerva emperor. Nerva made only one vital contribution to the Pax Romana. He adopted as his heir a respected army leader, Trajan (**TRAY**-juhn). When Nerva died in 98, Trajan was peacefully accepted by armies and senate alike as emperor. Trajan then adopted a distant relative, Hadrian (**HAY**-dree-uhn), as his successor. Hadrian adopted Antoninus Pius, and Antoninus, in turn, adopted Marcus Aurelius (aw-**REE**-lee-us), who ruled until the year A.D. 180.

Voice from the Past | A Roman Citizen

"*Civis Romanus sum*" (I am a Roman citizen). Aside from being a proud boast, this statement guaranteed a person the protection of Roman law and important privileges in traveling and doing business within the empire. Around A.D. 150, a Greek writer named Aelius Aristides described Roman citizenship.

Most wonderful of all is your noble idea of citizenship. There is nothing on earth like it. For you have divided all the people of the empire . . . into two groups. The more cultured, better born, and more influential everywhere you have declared Roman citizens. . . . All others are mere subjects. No barrier of sea or land cuts one off from citizenship . . . Everything lies open to everybody, and no one who is worthy to be trusted with public office is considered a foreigner . . .

You have not made Rome a target of envy by letting no one else share in it . . . You have made the word "Roman" apply not to a city but to a universal people . . . As a result, there are many people in each city who are . . . fellow citizens of yours . . . You have no need to keep troops in those cities; the greatest and most influential men everywhere keep watch over their own native places for you. You have a double hold on those cities—from here [Rome] and through the Roman citizens in each.

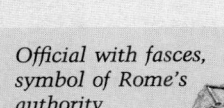

1. Within the empire, who could be a Roman citizen?
2. How might a city benefit from being ruled by local people who were Roman citizens?
3. Do you think this was a wise and fair policy for Rome to follow? Explain.

Official with fasces, symbol of Rome's authority

■ **DISCUSSION**

A short time before his death, Nerva said, "I have done nothing in my life which prevents me from retiring and living in safety the life of a private citizen." Refer students to the chart on page 156. Which other emperors could have said the same?

ANSWERS TO
Voice from the Past

1. the more cultured, better born, and more influential people
2. no need for Roman troops to be stationed there
3. Answers should consider benefits and drawbacks to Rome and to the conquered.

ANSWER TO
Map Study

Britain

ANSWERS TO
Section Review 1

Define:
(a) men who fought in Roman arenas (b) plan for governing (c) long, bridgelike structures that carried water (d) salaried, experienced workers (e) order of taking over power

Identify:
(a) sports arena (b) 207 years of Roman peace between 27 B.C. and A.D. 180 (c) Roman emperor who built foundation for Pax Romana (d) descended from family of Julius Caesar (e) succeeded one another peacefully

Answer:
1. expanded trade and transportation, developed public building program, instituted civil service

2. (a) no method of succession (b) adopted or named their successors during their reigns

3. the spread of disease, defeat of Roman legions on the northern frontier by Germanic tribes

4. Necessary government work would continue no matter who the ruler was.

The Roman Empire at Its Height

KEY

Roman empire in A.D. 120

Gades - Roman name
(Cadiz) - Modern name

0   500 Miles

Map Study

Rome's empire reached its greatest size under Emperor Trajan in A.D. 117. His successor, Hadrian, strengthened its borders. He ordered the building of the wall shown below to keep out barbarians. Where was it located?

Thus, for 85 years, 5 emperors succeeded one another without bloodshed. Although historians call the whole group the Good Emperors, three were perhaps better than good. Trajan, Hadrian, and Marcus Aurelius came close to greatness.

Even during Marcus Aurelius's lifetime, the Pax Romana was severely tested and strained. A dreadful disease—possibly the plague—swept across the eastern provinces into Rome itself, where it killed 2,000 people in a single day. German tribes overwhelmed Roman legions along the Danube River. After Marcus Aurelius's death in A.D. 180, the Pax Romana collapsed, marking the end of Rome's golden age.

Section REVIEW 1

Define: (a) gladiator, (b) policy, (c) aqueduct, (d) civil service, (e) succession
Identify: (a) Colosseum, (b) Pax Romana, (c) Augustus, (d) the Julian emperors, (e) the Good Emperors

154

Answer:
1. Describe three ways in which Augustus contributed to Rome's success as the center of a great empire.
2. (a) Why was the death of an emperor often followed by violence of some kind? (b) How did the five Good Emperors temporarily solve this problem?
3. Name two events that weakened the empire during the last years of the Pax Romana.

Critical Thinking
4. How might the growth of a civil service make the individual character of a ruler less important to the empire?

Romans extended Greek culture. 2

Under the Roman empire, hundreds of territories were knitted into a single political state. Cities grew in lands where cities had never been known before. Those cities looked very much alike because they had the same model: Rome. Governing lands as different as Britannia and Judaea, Gaul and northern Africa, was in itself a great achievement. The government in one province was set up much like that in another. Goods moved untaxed over Roman roads. Those goods were paid for with Roman coinage. Latin, the language of Rome, could be understood throughout the empire. People who could read shared in a growing body of Latin literature.

The Romans were proud of their ability to rule, but they acknowledged Greek leadership in the fields of art, architecture, literature, and philosophy. Educated Romans learned the Greek language. Emperors and wealthy citizens copied Greek architecture and hired Greek sculptors. The Pax Romana spread Greek as well as Roman achievements. The blend of these two cultures sometimes is called "Greco-Roman" culture.

New schools of philosophy arose.

The tradition of Greek philosophy had continued since the days of Socrates, Plato, and Aristotle. Meanwhile, over the years, traditional Roman religion had lost its meaning for many Romans. In the later years of the Roman republic and the early years of the empire, the Romans turned increasingly to two philosophies.

Epicureanism Epicurus (ep-ih-**KYU**-rus) lived in Athens between 342 and 270 B.C. He taught that the way to gain happiness was to free the body from pain and free the mind from fear. To avoid pain, Epicurus said that people should avoid all excesses, including those of pleasure. Next, people should accept death as the end of existence. There was no life after death and, therefore, nothing to fear. By the time this philosophy, **Epicureanism,** reached imperial Rome, the part about avoiding excess had been forgotten. Instead, wealthy Romans used the philosophy to justify pursuing pleasures.

Stoicism A Greek philosopher named Zeno (**ZEE**-noh) developed a philosophy that had even more influence on Romans than Epicureanism. Zeno gathered his followers on the porch (or *stoa*) near the marketplace in Athens. Hence, his philosophy became known as **Stoicism** (**STOH**-ih-**SIHZ**-uhm). This philosophy was popular in Rome because it encouraged virtue, duty, and endurance.

Zeno (336–263 B.C.) taught that the universe was controlled by a superhuman power, sometimes called the Universal Law, Divine Reason, or simply Supreme Power. The Stoics taught the virtues of duty, reason, and courage. Pain and pleasure were considered unimportant. Stoic ideas supported traditional Roman values. Wealthy families hired Stoic scholars as tutors for their sons. Many of these young men rose to political power as adults, giving the Stoics great influence in politics.

One of the most noted Stoics was the emperor Marcus Aurelius. During the seven hard and lonely years he spent with his armies on the Danube frontier, Marcus Aurelius wrote in the evenings to console himself. His words show his sadness but also his steadfastness.

> *Ants, loaded and labouring, mice, scared and scampering; puppets jerking on their strings—that is life. In the midst of it all, you must take your stand, good-temperedly and without disdain, yet always aware that a man's worth is no greater than the worth of his ambitions.*

Marcus Aurelius's daily jottings were collected into a book called the *Meditations*. This work

155

OBJECTIVE 1. Identify and discuss the ideas of Roman philosophers and writers.

Teaching Strategy: *Identifying Quotations: Roman Philosophy and Literature* (page 150c)

OBJECTIVE 2. Describe the Roman Forum.

Teaching Strategy: *Teaching with Pictures: The Roman Forum* (page 150c)

OBJECTIVE 3. List important principles of Roman law.

Teaching Strategy: *Discussing History: Roman Law* (page 150c)

■ BACKGROUND

Stoics said that all people everywhere share the divine spark and belong to a "world-state." This philosophy was used to bolster Roman imperialism: If there is going to be a world-state, who better to rule than the Romans?

SECTION 2
Resources

ASSESSMENT
- Section Quiz 7.2

REINFORCEMENT
- Independent Practice 7.2

ENRICHMENT
- Voices from the Past 7.2

Emperors of the Pax Romana

Name	Dates of Rule (A.D.)	Summary of Reign
Julian dynasty—related to family of Julius Caesar		
Tiberius	14–37	A good administrator; improved provincial government and the empire's tax system; later years marked by wholesale treason trials and executions
Caligula	37–41	Mentally disturbed; assassinated after short, brutal reign
Claudius	41–54	Considered slow-witted as a child but became an able, intelligent emperor; added Britannia to empire; set up government departments for accounts, correspondence, and justice
Nero	54–68	Became emperor at 16; devoted to the arts; a good administrator but increasingly vicious in his use of power; responsible for many murders, including that of his own mother; rebuilt Rome after the great fire of A.D. 64; began persecution of Christians; committed suicide
Army emperors		
Galba, Otho, Vitellus	68–69	Succession crisis; three emperors chosen by various factions in the armies
Flavian dynasty		
Vespasian	69–79	Ended civil war of A.D. 69; restored empire's finances; reformed army
Titus	79–81	Opened Colosseum; reign marked by the eruption of Vesuvius that destroyed Pompeii and Herculaneum
Domitian	81–96	Ruled dictatorially but efficiently; later feared treason everywhere and executed many; was assassinated
The Five Good Emperors, or the Adoptive Emperors		
Nerva	96–98	Senator, appointed emperor by senate; began custom of adopting heir
Trajan	98–117	Spanish-born (first emperor from provinces); conquered Dacia (Romania); empire reached its greatest extent during his rule
Hadrian	117–138	Consolidated earlier conquests rather than adding new lands; reorganized bureaucracy and set up postal service; traveled throughout empire
Antoninus Pius	138–161	Uneventful reign marked by public works and expanded programs for education and child welfare; army declined
Marcus Aurelius	161–180	Faced widespread barbarian invasions on Syrian and Danube frontiers; wrote philosophic work, *Meditations;* Pax Romana ended with his death

established his place in literature as one of Rome's great Stoic philosophers.

Stoics believed that human laws, like the Supreme Power itself, should be reasonable and just. Several social reforms during Rome's golden age show Stoic influence. For example, according to a law passed under Hadrian, the pater familias no longer had the power of life and death within the family. New laws also prohibited masters from killing or injuring their slaves.

Latin literature took many forms.

In literature, as in religion, the Romans first looked to the Greeks for inspiration. By the middle years of the republic, however, the Romans had begun to develop an important body of learning of their own. By Augustus's time, there was a group of writers who were able to record the emperor's deeds in glowing and lasting words. As far as Augustus was concerned, however, the skill of the writer was not as important as his patriotism. With patriotic writers, the emperor was generous.

Livy's history One of the most patriotic works sponsored by Augustus was Livy's history of Rome. It covered the years from Rome's founding to the rule of Augustus in 142 Roman-style books.

Livy had a bias typical of many historians. He liked the past better than the present. He thought the heroes of old—Romulus, Scipio, Cato—were more patriotic than Romans of his own time. The old heroes, he said, had been men of honor, courage, discipline, and moral strength. They did their duty toward family, gods, and state. Because of those virtues, Livy explained, they could conquer every foe.

Virgil's epic poem Patriotic virtue was also the theme of the most famous work of Latin literature, the *Aeneid* (uh-NEE-ihd). The poet Virgil devoted ten years of labor to this masterpiece. Often he was unable to write more than a few lines a day. Even then, he was so worried about the poem's flaws that he wanted it destroyed. Luckily, it was saved by Augustus himself.

The *Aeneid* is an epic consciously modeled after the Greek masterpieces of Homer. It traces Roman origins far back before Romulus and Remus to Aeneas, one of the Trojan warriors in Homer's *Iliad*. Reading the *Aeneid*, Augustus perhaps nodded approvingly at these verses:

Remember, Roman, these are your talents:
To rule people by law, and to establish the
ways of peace,
To spare the conquered, and to crush the
haughty.

The silver age of literature Roman literature kept growing and changing during the empire. Historians refer to the 124 years between the deaths of Augustus and Hadrian as the "silver age" of literature. Rome's best writers were still poets and historians, but their work took on a new tone. Criticism replaced patriotism. Praise was replaced by **satire**, writing that mocked society for its foolishness and wickedness. Imagine what Augustus might have thought about these lines from the poet Juvenal:

What should I do in Rome? I am no good
at lying.
If a book's bad, I can't praise it, or go
around ordering copies.
I don't know the stars [astrology]; I can't
hire out as an assassin.

While Juvenal wrote about the morals of private citizens, the historian Tacitus (TAS-ih-tus) directed his scorn at government. In his major work, the *Annals*, he portrays every emperor from Tiberius to Nero as cruel and corrupt. What were the blessings of the Roman peace? "They make a desert and call it peace," accused Tacitus.

Although many of the writers of the silver age made fun of Rome (or worse), they were not banned or sent into exile. By this time, Rome was so secure as capital of the world that it could tolerate criticism. There were moral and spiritual grounds for the writers' charges, but outwardly Rome was thriving.

CITY TOUR
Fine buildings adorned Rome.

Of the estimated 10,000 cities in the Roman empire, Rome was the most spectacular. The passion for beautifying the capital did not die with Augustus or Nero. Each emperor sought to make his mark on the city. According to one scholar, Rome became "the most spectacular

157

Remind students of the myth of Rome's beginning (page 130). Then share the following brief quote from Livy for discussion. "If any country is entitled to sanctify its beginnings by attributing them to divine action, that is true of the Romans. So tremendous is their military glory that when they claim their Father, their Founder's Father, to be none other than Mars, the nations of the earth must need endure it patiently—as they endure Roman rule."

■ BACKGROUND

The symbol for the city tour of Rome represents the Pantheon, located in the Forum. The Forum was built on marshes that had been filled early in the city's history.

ANSWER TO
Comparing Pictures

The Forum was Rome's center of government, including the *Curia* (Senate House) and *Tabularium* (Hall of Records). Although the Forum, like the Athenian acropolis, contained temples, it had less religious significance than the acropolis.

Comparing pictures *The Roman Forum became the showplace of the empire, filled with statues and buildings designed to impress the people Rome ruled. How did the Roman Forum differ from the Athenian acropolis (page 102)?*

tourist attraction in the ancient world." Visitors came from the provinces to see its 10,000 statues, 700 public pools and basins, 500 fountains, 37 monumental gates, and 36 marble arches.

After seeing Rome, visitors from Gaul and Spain went home and imitated its splendor. They too surrounded themselves with Roman buildings and gardens. Soon, new cities in western Europe looked like miniature Romes. Roman governors gladly supported the construction of Roman-style buildings. They saw it as a way of building allegiance to Rome itself. Unlike the Greeks who used architecture to glorify their gods, the Romans used it to glorify their rule.

The crowning achievement of Roman architecture was the dome. Once the Romans had learned to use concrete, they were able to mold on the ground rounded tops for their buildings. Then, when the walls and columns of a building were in place, the dome could be hoisted into place on top.

This is just how one of the most impressive buildings in Rome, the Pantheon (PAN-thee-ahn), was built. The Pantheon was dedicated to all the gods. Its domed roof rested on a drumlike structure called a rotunda. Light streamed into the Pantheon through a small opening or "eye" in the top of the dome.

158

Roman law united the empire.

Rome's most lasting contribution to later civilizations was its law. Early Roman law, such as the Twelve Tables, was concerned mostly with the rights of Roman citizens themselves. As the empire grew, however, the Romans came to believe that law should apply to all people.

Slowly, Roman judges began to recognize certain standards of justice. These standards were based largely on the teachings of Stoic philosophers. Here are some of the most important principles of Roman law:

- No person could be judged guilty of a crime until after the facts of the case were examined.
- All persons accused of crimes had a right to face their accusers and defend themselves before a judge.
- If there was doubt about a person's guilt, he or she should be judged innocent.
- Any law that seemed unreasonable or grossly unfair could be set aside.

Long after Rome fell to barbarian rule, the principles of Roman law endured. Those principles became the basis for law in many European countries and, later, for places that fell under European influence. The Roman empire spread far, but its legal ideas have spread farther.

Contrasts marked Roman society.

Most Roman citizens probably were far more concerned with the pains and pleasures of daily living than with literature, philosophy, or law. To many Romans, spending a day at the Colosseum was the chief benefit of Roman civilization. By A.D. 250, there were 150 holidays celebrating emperors' birthdays, gods' feast days, and other special occasions. On many of these days, the government provided games, races, or gladiator shows at public expense.

These public pleasures were enjoyed by rich and poor alike. In most other ways, however, the rich and the poor had little in common.

Life at the top At home, wealthy Romans lived extravagantly. They spent large sums of money on fancy houses, statues for their gardens, high-priced slaves, and especially banquets. A food's taste was less important than its rarity and cost. These were some of the dishes placed on the tables of wealthy Romans: as appetizers, tree fungi in fish-fat sauce, jellyfish and eggs; as main course, dormouse with pine kernels, boiled ostrich; and for dessert, fricassee of roses with pastry, parrot-tongue pie.

Guests normally arrived for a banquet in the late afternoon and did not stop eating until midnight. They had knives and spoons but no forks, and they picked up most foods with their hands. After each course, a slave stationed behind each guest provided a bowl of scented water for washing sticky fingers.

The eruption of Mt. Vesuvius in A.D. 79 buried the city of Pompeii in ash, killing hundreds. Everyday items —including frescoes, jewelry, and even a loaf of bread—were preserved intact for archaeologists.

159

■ **DISCUSSION**

Ask students to discuss the following quote from Cicero on law: "We are servants of the law in order that we may be free."

Define:
(a) belief that the way to happiness was to free body from pain and mind from fear (b) philosophy espousing virtues of duty, reason, and courage under Universal Law (c) writing that mocks society (d) country estate

Identify:
(a) Greek philosopher whose ideas about happiness influenced Romans (b) Greek philosopher who developed Stoicism (c) journal kept by Marcus Aurelius (d) patriotic historian (e) author of *Aeneid* (f) Virgil's epic poem about Roman origins (g) writer of satire (h) historian who criticized Roman government (i) domed building dedicated to all the gods

Answer:
1. (a) upheld the traditional Roman virtues (b) stressed human laws should be reasonable and just
2. Criticism, satire replaced patriotism, praise.
3. (a) rich: fancy houses, costly foods, leisurely, indulgent life; poor: inadequate food, crowded tenements, unemployment (b) Roman government provided food and housing.
4. (a) Answers should include ideas of innocent until proved guilty, rights of the accused, and unjust laws. (b) part of Western legal system

---

Life at the bottom Most families in Rome never tasted parrot-tongue pie. They were lucky to eat porridge at daybreak, cold sausage at noon, and porridge again for supper. During Rome's golden age, a large share of the city's population was unemployed most of the time. The imperial government supported these people with daily rations of grain, doled out free or far below market cost.

Only a short distance from Rome's elegant temples were the dingy, run-down, rat-infested homes of the poor. Poor families lived in crowded wooden tenements up to seven stories high. Tens of thousands of such buildings filled Rome's slums. The tenements were so poorly built that roofs and ceilings sometimes collapsed, killing those inside. Worst of all, a poor family faced the ever-present danger of fire touched off by a stray ember from someone's little charcoal stove.

Despite these conditions, the poor of Rome were better off than people without work in other ancient cities. The Roman poor had food and housing. After the collapse of the empire, almost no government took such care of its poorest citizens for nearly 1,500 years.

Villas in the countryside Most wealthy city dwellers also had country estates, called **villas.** Italian villas had libraries, art galleries, swimming pools, and athletic courts. Fountains sparkled in formal gardens, and Greek statues posed on lawns and terraces.

In provinces such as Gaul, North Africa, and Britannia, villas were the great estates that grew much of the empire's food supply. Peasant farmers lived on the villas and tilled the soil or tended the owner's livestock. The noble owners managed the villa, served as local officials, and amused themselves by hunting.

In later times, villas became increasingly self-sufficient. The people on a villa raised all their own food and made most of the other goods they needed. Many villas were fortified as protection against bandits (or tax collectors).

Section REVIEW 2

Define: (a) Epicureanism, (b) Stoicism, (c) satire, (d) villa
Identify: (a) Epicurus, (b) Zeno, (c) *Meditations*, (d) Livy, (e) Virgil, (f) *Aeneid*, (g) Juvenal, (h) Tacitus, (i) the Pantheon

160

Answer:
1. (a) How were the basic ideas of Stoicism well-suited to Roman traditions? (b) How did Stoicism influence Roman law to become more humane?
2. How did Roman literature change from the time of Augustus to the silver age?
3. (a) Describe some of the differences between the lives of the rich and the poor during the Roman empire. (b) What evidence shows that the Roman government took relatively good care of the poor?

Critical Thinking
4. (a) Restate in your own words the ideas of Roman law given on page 159. (b) Explain why each of these four principles is important to justice today.

Christianity spread through the empire. 3

By the time of Augustus, Rome's traditional gods—Jupitor, Juno, Mars, and others—had no strong appeal to most Romans. Nonetheless these gods were still important as symbols of loyalty to the Roman state. Roman rulers tolerated many religions, but they also expected Roman subjects to respect traditional Roman gods and the divine spirit of the emperor. The Roman attitude was no problem for the empire's many polytheists, but it was a very great problem indeed for monotheists such as Jews and Christians.

Jews came under Roman rule.

Most Jews probably saw the Romans as one of a string of pagan conquerors. After their return to Palestine from Babylon (page 47), the Jews had been ruled by Alexander the Great, by the Ptolemies of Egypt, and by the Seleucids of Persia. In general, the Jews tolerated and were tolerated by these rulers. However, in 168 B.C., the Seleucid king decided to build an altar to the Greek god Zeus in the Jewish temple in Jerusalem. The Jews would not stand for that. Led by Judas Maccabee (MAK-uh-bee), they recaptured and purified the temple in 165 B.C. In 142 B.C., the Jews won their independence.

The entire area of Syria and Palestine fell under Roman influence around 65 B.C. At first the Jewish kingdom remained independent, at least in name. Jewish kings ruled as representatives of Rome. Some Jews became friendly with the Romans and even went along with their plans to "romanize" Jerusalem. The ruler Herod, for example, was a romanized Jew. His loyalties were divided between Rome and his own people. He was also tolerant of polytheistic faiths. These divided loyalties angered many Jews. Rome finally took over the Jewish kingdom and made it the Roman province of Judaea in A.D. 6.

◢ Turning Points in History

The Life and Teachings of Jesus It was about the time of Rome's takeover of the Jewish kingdom that Jesus was born, although the exact year is not known. Jesus was both a Jew and a Roman subject. Historical records of the time mention very little about Jesus. Thus, the story of Jesus' life comes primarily from Christian sources, the four Gospels of the New Testament. (*Gospel* is the Greek word for "good news.")

According to the Gospels, Jesus was born in the town of Bethlehem near Jerusalem. He grew up in the village of Nazareth in northern Palestine. Each year he went with his parents to Jerusalem to celebrate Passover, the holiday in memory of the Jewish exodus from slavery in Egypt. There, his knowledge of religious matters impressed Jewish scholars.

Jesus' ministry Jesus began his ministry when he was about thirty years old. At that time, a religious leader named John the Baptist was warning his followers to repent their sins in preparation for the coming of the kingdom of God. John was known as the Baptist because, in a rite called baptism, he immersed his followers in the Jordan River as a symbol of their cleansing from sin. Jesus asked John to baptize him. Shortly afterward Jesus returned to Galilee in northern Palestine to begin his own preaching.

During the next three years, Jesus became a wandering prophet and teacher. As he traveled from village to village, he touched people with his gentleness and challenged them with his message. His teachings contained many ideas from Jewish tradition, such as the principles of the Ten Commandments. He also taught that God would end wickedness in the world and establish a kingdom of God for people who sincerely repented. From among his followers, Jesus chose 12 **apostles,** or special messengers who accepted his message and helped to spread his teachings.

To explain his message, Jesus often used everyday situations and told short stories called parables that contained moral lessons. The parable of the prodigal son told about a young man who had left home and wasted his father's money. After living an extravagant and degrading life, the young man came to his senses. He begged his father's forgiveness and was received at home again with open arms. This parable showed how God's love could overcome sin.

Jesus also emphasized the fatherhood of God as a personal relationship to each human being. He stressed the importance of people's love for God, their neighbors, their enemies, and even themselves. People should treat others as they themselves wished to be treated—a teaching that has come to be known as the Golden Rule. In his own life, Jesus provided an example of compassion for others.

Because he was not impressed with wealth, titles, or status, Jesus won many followers among the poor and dispossessed. His most famous sermon, recorded by the apostle Matthew (5: 3–7), was the Sermon on the Mount. In it, Jesus explained the ethical qualities he valued most.

> Blessed are the poor in spirit: for theirs is the kingdom of heaven.
> Blessed are they that mourn: for they shall be comforted.
> Blessed are the meek: for they shall inherit the earth.
> Blessed are they which do hunger and thirst after righteousness: for they shall be filled.
> Blessed are the merciful: for they shall obtain mercy.
> Blessed are the pure in heart: for they shall see God.
> Blessed are the peacemakers: for they shall be called the children of God.
> Blessed are they which are persecuted for righteousness's sake: for theirs is the kingdom of heaven.

161

SECTION 3
Objectives and Teaching Strategies

OBJECTIVE 1. Explain the origins of Chanukah.

Teaching Strategy: *Discussing History: The Origins of Chanukah* (page 150d)

OBJECTIVE 2. Discuss the main teachings of Jesus.

Teaching Strategy: *Analyzing a Quotation: The Sermon on the Mount* (page 150d)

OBJECTIVE 3. Describe how Christianity spread through the Roman empire.

Teaching Strategy: *Using Geographic Themes: Movement* (page 150d)

OBJECTIVE 4. Explain why the Romans warred against the Jews and persecuted the Christians.

Teaching Strategy: *Discussing History: Religious Persecution* (page 150d)

■ BACKGROUND

Herod died in 4 B.C., so many scholars believe that was the year Jesus was born. On the other hand, the Gospel of Luke links the event to the first census in Judaea, which probably took place in A.D. 6.

SECTION 3
Resources

GEOGRAPHY
■ Transparency 22

REINFORCEMENT
■ Independent Practice 7.3

ENRICHMENT
■ Voices from the Past 7.3

ASSESSMENT
■ Section Quiz 7.3

Jesus' death and resurrection The growing popularity of Jesus and his teachings worried Roman officials and Jewish leaders. Their concern increased when Jesus visited Jerusalem in about A.D. 30. Enthusiastic crowds welcomed Jesus, hailing him as the **Messiah,** or savior chosen by God. Many people believed that as the Messiah, Jesus would end Roman rule and bring a new age of peace and prosperity. (The word *Christ* comes from *christos*, the Greek word for messiah.)

The chief priests denied that Jesus was the Messiah. They thought that his teachings were blasphemy, or contempt for God. The Roman governor Pontius Pilate was concerned that Jesus' teachings about a kingdom of God challenged the authority of Rome. Pilate therefore sentenced Jesus to be crucified. (In Roman times, crucifixion—death by hanging on a cross—was often used to execute criminals.)

According to the Gospels, Jesus' follower Mary Magdalene visited Jesus' tomb two days later and found his body gone. The Gospels and other writings of the apostles also tell that Jesus appeared to his followers several times in the next 40 days. He encouraged them to spread his teachings. Then, one day as he stood among them, he blessed them and parted from them, rising up to heaven.

The apostles and other followers of Jesus were at first stunned and upset by his death. Their belief in Jesus' resurrection, or rising from the dead, revitalized their faith. Led by Peter, the apostles spread the teachings of Jesus throughout Palestine and Syria. As they spread the Gospel about the meaning of Jesus' life and death, the cross became a symbol of hope for the new Christian faith.

Paul influenced the growth of Christianity.

The apostle who most profoundly influenced the new Christian religion never knew Jesus in person. This man was known by two names— his Jewish name Saul and his Christian name Paul. At first, Saul thought Christianity should be stamped out. One day while traveling to Damascus in Syria, however, he had a powerful religious experience. He told of seeing a blinding burst of light and hearing the voice of Jesus. From that moment, Saul the Jew became Paul the Christian. The apostle Paul dedicated the rest of his life to spreading the teachings of Jesus.

The peace and cultural unity of the Pax Romana provided an ideal opportunity for the spread of the new religion. As a Roman citizen, Paul traveled freely within the empire. For 13 years (A.D. 45–58), he went from city to city around the eastern Mediterranean.

Paul had an enormous influence on Christianity. His letters, written to churches with which he worked, form an important part of the New Testament. Known as Epistles, these letters stressed that Jesus was the son of God who died for people's sins. Paul taught that believers would be saved by faith in and the grace of Christ as the redeeming son of God.

Paul also declared that Christianity was open equally to anyone, Jew or non-Jew. Without this openness, Christianity might have remained a small Jewish sect rather than becoming a world religion. Finally, through Paul's work, Christian churches were established in every major city in the eastern empire, from Jerusalem to Rome.

Christianity grew slowly but steadily. Christian teachings had strong appeal among the poor and powerless. Women, who were barred from some popular Roman cults, had great influence among Christian groups. The beliefs of Christianity also appealed to people who sought a philosophy of hope and to those who turned away from the extravagances of imperial Rome. From these humble beginnings, Christianity went on to become the world's most widespread religion.

Rome struggled with Judaism and Christianity.

As monotheistic religions, both Christianity and Judaism posed a problem for the Roman empire. Neither Jews nor Christians were willing to worship the emperor as a god.

War against the Jews The Romans went far in trying to keep peace with the Jews. The Roman government promised Jews freedom of worship and excused them from worshiping the emperor.

Despite Roman tolerance of Judaism, however, many Jews remained fiercely opposed to Roman rule. In A.D. 66, a band of Jewish revolutionaries called the Zealots (ZEL-uhts) tried to throw off the Roman yoke. When Roman troops finally put down the rebellion four years later, they

The Spread of Christianity in Roman Times

KEY
— Boundaries of the Roman empire
▓ Christian areas around 300
☐ Christian areas around 450
----- Paul's journeys
• Most important bishoprics

0   500 Miles

ANSWERS TO

Focus on Geography

1. spread Christianity throughout much of the eastern Mediterranean

2. mostly areas along coasts and some isolated inland regions

3. Asia Minor

4. By 450, Christianity had spread inland through much of Western Europe.

5. Christianity was spread by citizens throughout the Roman empire.

Focus on Geography

Geographic Skills

1. What effect did the travels and teachings of Paul have on the spread of Christianity?

2. To what types of locations had Christianity spread by A.D. 300?

3. Where was the largest Christian area in A.D. 300?

4. How did the spread of Christianity change between A.D. 300 and 450?

Geographic Theme: Movement

5. Compare the extent of the Roman empire and Christianity about 450. What conclusion about the spread of Christianity can you draw from this comparison?

---

burned the Jewish temple. All that remained was a western portion of the wall, which is today the holiest of Jewish shrines. The last stronghold, a fortress near the Dead Sea called Masada (muh-SAH-duh), held out until A.D. 73. Half a million Jews died in that war.

The tiny nation made one more attempt to break free of the Romans. In A.D. 130, the emperor Hadrian ordered that Jerusalem be rebuilt as a Roman colony and that a shrine to Jupiter be built in place of the Jewish temple. The Jews rose in rebellion. In three years of fighting, another half a million Jews died. This war ended the Jewish political state for almost 2,000 years, yet the Jewish religion survived.

Persecution of the Christians As a new religion, Christianity did not win the same respect from

Roman rulers as did Judaism. In A.D. 64, Nero ordered the first persecution of Christians. According to Christian tradition, the apostles Peter and Paul were killed in Rome on the same day during Nero's rule.

Except for Nero, however, the emperors of the first century did not actively persecute Christians. Later, however, as the Pax Romana began to crumble, the Romans became harsher toward those who would not worship the emperor. Toward the end of the second century, Christians were cruelly persecuted. With Marcus Aurelius's approval, many Christians were brought before Roman magistrates for trial. Those who gave up their religion and accepted the Roman gods were set free without punishment. Those who held to their faith were tortured and executed in the

163

ANSWERS TO
Section Review 3

Define:
(a) follower (b) disciple who spread the word of Jesus (c) savior (d) person who sacrifices his or her life for a cause or belief (e) church official (f) father of the Christian Church

Identify:
(a) the town where the Jewish temple was located and where Jesus was sentenced to death (b) a ruler who was a romanized Jew (c) founder of Christianity (d) books of the New Testament that tell the story of Jesus' life (e) Roman governor who sentenced Jesus to death (f) Jew who dedicated his life to spreading the teachings of Jesus (g) Jewish revolutionaries who tried to overthrow Roman rule (h) Jewish fortress near the Dead Sea (i) doctrine that Roman bishops outranked others

Answer:
1. (a) tolerant (b) Followers were monotheistic, did not worship other (Roman) gods.

2. kingdom of God in which all who accepted Jesus as their savior would find eternal life; love

3. spread Christianity throughout the Roman empire and wrote a large part of the New Testament

4. (a) Peace and cultural unity provided an ideal opportunity for the spread of Christianity. (b) Christians were persecuted, tried, and executed.

5. Students may see the attempt to create a scapegoat in these actions.

arena. They were regarded by other Christians as **martyrs,** people who sacrifice their lives for the sake of a cause or belief.

Religious persecutions showed only the growing weakness of the empire, not its strength. Christianity became a formidable religious force at the very time that Roman power was declining. By A.D. 200, around 10 percent of the people in the Roman empire were Christians.

The Petrine doctrine According to many Christians, Jesus had singled out the disciple Peter as the "rock" on which the Christian church would be built. After preaching in Jerusalem, Peter had traveled to Rome where he had acted as Rome's first **bishop.** A bishop was a church official who set moral standards and supervised the finances of several local churches. Peter died in Rome, a fact that became important to later Christians.

Eventually, every major city in the empire would have its own bishop. However, later bishops in Rome claimed to outrank all other bishops because Peter had been the leading apostle. Roman bishops argued that Peter was the first **pope**—the father of the Christian Church. This argument, known as the Petrine (PEE-TRYN) doctrine, was accepted by Christians in the western part of the empire but rejected in the eastern part.

Section REVIEW 3

Define: (a) disciple, (b) apostle, (c) messiah, (d) martyr, (e) bishop, (f) pope
Identify: (a) Jerusalem, (b) Herod, (c) Jesus, (d) Gospels, (e) Pontius Pilate, (f) Paul (Saul), (g) Zealots, (h) Masada, (i) Petrine doctrine
Answer:
1. (a) What attitude did the Roman government take toward most religions? (b) Why did Judaism and Christianity not fit into the empire?
2. What religious ideas did Jesus teach?
3. What was Paul's importance for the development of Christianity?
4. (a) How did the existence of the Roman empire help the spread of Christianity? (b) How did the Roman government attack Christianity?

Critical Thinking
5. Rome often persecuted Christians after disasters such as the great fire in Nero's reign. Why might a government take such action?

Rome's empire declined and fell. 4

Historians generally agree that the Roman empire began its decline with the rule of Marcus Aurelius's son, Commodus. Instead of adopting an able successor, Marcus Aurelius made the fateful mistake of choosing his own son to succeed him as emperor. Facing a time of troubles, Rome needed a strong, dedicated leader. Instead, it got the vain, irresponsible Commodus. He became a cruel ruler and, in A.D. 192, he was strangled in his bath. The decline of the empire, however, continued for almost 300 years. In A.D. 476, a barbarian king took over the rule of Rome.

The process of decline took place in three stages. First, there was a long time of turmoil known by historians as the "crisis of the third century." During these years, the empire was beset by economic, military, and political problems. Second, there was a time of revival, during which the empire was divided into two parts, an eastern half and a western half. As you will see, this change strengthened the Greek-speaking east but weakened the Latin-speaking west. Third, the western half of the empire fell to invaders.

Crises weakened the empire.

During the third century (A.D. 200–300), a host of problems confronted the Roman empire. These problems left the empire gravely weakened.

Economic decay During the Pax Romana, trade flowed over routes patrolled by Roman navies and armies. Rome's treasuries were enriched by gold and silver collected as plunder. Most important of all, the empire's farms grew enough grain to feed the population of the cities. During the crisis of the third century, all three sources of prosperity dried up.

Trade was disrupted by barbarian raids and by bands of pirates on Mediterranean sea lanes. Rome's gold and silver were drained away to buy luxuries from China, India, and Arabia, including spices, perfumes, rubies, pearls, and silk. Rome's small industries produced only wine, cheese, and glass. China, India, and Arabia had little interest in buying such plain goods. Romans paid out a fortune in gold and silver every year for the imported luxuries they craved.

Trade in the Roman Empire

tin
wool
gold
slaves
lead
hunting
dogs

BRITAIN
London

ATLANTIC
OCEAN

SCANDINAVIA

amber
furs
slaves
dried fish

EUROPE

Baltic
Sea

Black Sea

Caspian
Sea

From CHINA
silks
spices
jade

ASIA

From INDIA
ivory
incense
pearls
pepper

GAUL
pottery
glass
wine
copper
wool
bronzeware

Marseilles

slaves
silver
gold

ILLYRIA

Byzantium

ASIA MINOR
timber
silver
marble
wool

Antioch

SYRIA

purple dye
timber
glass
wool
wine

Damascus

Rome
Ostia

SPAIN
olive oil
wine
iron
tin
lead
horses

9 days

4 days

20 days

Carthage

marble
olive oil
grain
copper
slaves

Cadiz

NUMIDIA

MEDITERRANEAN SEA

Cyrene

Alexandria

grain
glass
incense
spices
papyrus

Gaza

EGYPT

Red Sea

KEY

Roman empire about A.D. 200

Major trade route

SAHARA

0   300 Miles

Thebes

From ETHIOPIA
ivory
palm oil
tortoise shell
slaves

Map Study

*Trade was crucial to Rome's economy. What goods reached Rome from China?
From Scandinavia? How long did a voyage from Alexandria to Rome take?*

Desperate to pay its mounting expenses, the Roman government started minting coins that contained less and less silver. Eventually, Roman coins lost 98 percent of their silver content. As a result, prices shot sky-high. For example, in the second century, a peck of wheat sold for half a denarius. By the end of the third century, the price had risen to 100 denarii. Such an increase in prices is called **inflation.**

Agriculture faced an equally serious crisis. Harvests in Italy and western Europe became increasingly meager. Scholars think that the overworked soil had probably lost much of its earlier fertility.

Military decay The empire's economic troubles were worsened by its growing military troubles. Throughout the third century, tribes of northern barbarians called Goths repeatedly overran the legions guarding the Danube frontier. At the same time, Syria and Asia Minor were threatened by Persia. The Persians' proudest victory (and Rome's

most humiliating defeat) occurred in A.D. 260 when the Roman emperor Valerian was captured in battle. For the rest of his life, Valerian was forced to crouch down and allow the Persian king to step on him while mounting a horse.

Roman soldiers now fought strictly for money, not for patriotism. To attract recruits into the army, the government promised ever higher cash awards. Partly to keep costs down, emperors began to recruit barbarians, who would accept lower pay. However, the loyalty of barbarian troops to the empire could hardly be trusted.

Political decay Loyalty was in fact a key problem, perhaps the most serious of all. At one time, Romans cared so deeply about their republic that they willingly sacrificed their lives for it. In the later centuries of the empire, citizens were not actively disloyal, but they were indifferent.

To hold political office had once been considered an honor (as well as an invitation to profit). But times had changed. By the 200's, local officials

165

**SECTION 4
Objectives
and Teaching
Strategies**

OBJECTIVE 1. Identify problems that led to Rome's decline.

Teaching Strategy: *Discussing History: Why Did Rome Fall?* (page 150e)

OBJECTIVE 2. Evaluate the solutions offered by Diocletian and Constantine to solve Rome's problems.

Teaching Strategy: *Skill Building: Identifying Cause and Effect Relationships* (page 150e)

OBJECTIVE 3. Explain how the Germanic tribes overran and destroyed the western half of the empire.

Teaching Strategy: *Using Geographic Themes: Movement* (page 150e)

**ANSWERS TO
Map Study**

silk, spices, jade; amber, furs, slaves, dried fish; 20 days

**SECTION 4
Resources**

GEOGRAPHY
■ Transparencies 23, 24

REINFORCEMENT
■ Independent Practice 7.4

ENRICHMENT
■ Voices from the Past 7.4

ASSESSMENT
■ Section Quiz 7.4

■ BACKGROUND

Because of their dependence on the military, rulers during the 50 year period A.D. 218–268 are often called the "Barrack Emperors."

■ DISCUSSION

Topic for debate: Diocletian's persecution of Christianity may actually have strengthened the religion and helped it gain converts.

Cooperative Learning

Divide the class into groups of four students. Each group member should assume one of the following roles: a Roman soldier, the son of a poor Roman farmer, a Roman shopkeeper, and a recently converted Christian. Each group member should prepare a statement describing how his or her character was affected by Diocletian's reforms. Descriptions should include the characters' reactions and feelings, as well. Have students share statements within their groups. Groups should prepare statements for the class that reflect their characters' attitudes. Statements might also include ideas for other reforms. Encourage group spokespersons to make their presentations in their chosen Roman roles.

usually lost money because they were required to pay for costly circuses and baths out of their own pockets. As the empire's prosperity faded, less and less money came in as taxes. However, the government in Rome continued to require each tax district to send in a certain amount. If the local tax collector could not gather up that much, he had to pay the difference himself. Naturally, few people were willing to serve the government under those conditions.

The only groups actively interested in politics were the armies. In a 50-year period (A.D. 218–268), provincial armies and the Praetorian Guard proclaimed 50 generals emperors of Rome. Of these, 27 briefly won the approval of the Roman senate. Seventeen of these men were murdered. Two others were forced to commit suicide.

Remarkably the empire survived for another 200 years. It was saved by two men who rank among Rome's greatest emperors, Diocletian (DY-oh-**KLEE**-shuhn) and Constantine (**KAHN**-stuhn-tyn).

Diocletian reformed the empire.

In A.D. 284, Diocletian, a strong-willed army leader and son of a slave, became the new emperor. With amazing boldness, he tried to restore order in the empire and increase its strength. These were Diocletian's reforms:

1. To secure the boundaries of the empire, Diocletian doubled the size of the Roman armies.
2. To beat inflation, he used price and wage controls. Costs were fixed for everything from a haircut to a bottle of wine.
3. To restore faith in the ancient gods of Rome, Diocletian ordered a general persecution of the Christians.
4. To increase the prestige of the emperor, Diocletian assumed the manner and costume of a Persian ruler. He wore purple robes embroidered with gold, a crown encrusted with pearls, and scarlet boots. Anyone who approached his throne was required to kneel down and kiss the hem of his robe.
5. To improve administration, Diocletian divided the empire into the Greek-speaking east (Greece, Asia Minor, Syria, and Egypt) and the Latin-speaking west (Italy, Gaul, Britannia, and Spain). Because the empire had grown too large and too complex for one ruler, each half was to have its own emperor. The eastern half of

166

the empire included most of the great cities and trade centers of the empire. As a result, the east was far wealthier than the more rural west. Diocletian took the eastern half for himself and named another ruler for the west.

These reforms were not totally successful. Wages for the new troops added to the already crushing load of taxes. Price controls failed. Christianity continued its rapid growth. Yet during his 21-year reign (A.D. 284–305), Diocletian did stop the decline of the empire. The borders were safe again, and the emperor was once more considered an exalted person. Diocletian retired in 305. He spent his last years peacefully tending his garden. But even while he lived, his plans for the succession failed.

Constantine accepted Christianity.

Civil war broke out immediately after Diocletian retired. By A.D. 311, four rivals were competing for power. Among them was a dashing young commander named Constantine. One of the most critical moments in history occurred in A.D. 312 when Constantine marched to the Tiber River to fight his chief rival. On the day before the battle, Constantine prayed for divine help. What happened next was reported by a Christian bishop, Eusebius (yoo-**SEE**-bee-uhs):

> *And while [Constantine] was thus praying, a most marvelous sign appeared to him from heaven. He said that about noon he saw with his own eyes a cross of light in the heavens, above the sun, and bearing the inscription, "In this sign, conquer."*

The next morning, Constantine ordered artisans to put a Christian symbol on his soldiers' shields. Then came the clash between the armies of Constantine and his rival. Near the Milvian Bridge, two miles outside Rome, Constantine scored an overwhelming victory. He marched into Rome and became emperor of the western half of the empire. He attributed his victory to the power of the Christian God.

The next year, A.D. 313, Constantine announced an end to the persecution of Christians. From Milan, he granted "both to the Christians and to all men freedom to follow the religion that they choose." By this famous Edict of Milan, Christianity became a religion approved by the

MULTIPLE CAUSES : FALL OF THE ROMAN EMPIRE

CONTRIBUTING FACTORS

Political	Social	Economic	Military
Political office seen as burden, not reward	Lack of interest in public affairs	Poor harvests	Threat from Persians and barbarians
Military interference in politics	Low confidence in empire	Disruption of trade	Low funds for defense
Civil war and unrest	Disloyalty, lack of patriotism, corruption	No more plunder from wars	Problems recruiting Roman citizens; recruiting of barbarians
Division of empire	Contrast between rich and poor	Gold and silver drain	Decline of patriotism and loyalty among soldiers
Moving of capital to Byzantium		Inflation	
		Crushing tax burden	

IMMEDIATE CAUSES

Pressure from Huns
Invasion by Germanic tribes and by Huns

FALL OF ROMAN EMPIRE

Conquest by barbarians
Sack of Rome

Like his conversion, Constantine's decision to choose Byzantium as his capital came about through a vision.

emperor. In 395, the emperor Theodosius made Christianity the empire's official religion.

Constantine founded a new capital.

Eventually, Constantine won control of the eastern as well as the western empire. In A.D. 330, he took the momentous step of moving the capital from Rome to the Greek city of Byzantium (bih-ZANT-ee-uhm) in what is now Turkey.

The new capital had four advantages over Rome. First, it stood at a crossroad for trade. Located on a narrow water passageway called the Bosporus (BAHS-puhr-uhs), Byzantium controlled all shipping between the Black Sea and the Mediterranean Sea. The city also dominated the east-west overland trade between Asia Minor and Greece. Second, the city was easy to defend against attack, as it was nearly surrounded by water. Third, the old Rome was a pagan city dedicated to pagan gods. Byzantium was strongly

Christian. Finally, Byzantium was located in the more prosperous half of the empire, the east.

Thus, the center of empire shifted from west to east. Soon the new capital was protected by massive walls and gleamed with stately buildings. The city even had a new name—Constantinople (KAHN-STANT-uhn-OH-puhl), city of Constantine.

Because of the policies of Diocletian and Constantine, there were now two empires, not one. Because of Constantine's victory at the Milvian Bridge, both empires were Christian.

Barbarians overran the empire.

The third phase of Rome's decline was a century of destruction beginning in A.D. 376 and ending in 476. Many different groups took part in Rome's destruction: Ostrogoths, Visigoths, Franks, Angles, Saxons, Burgundians, Lombards, Vandals. All these groups were semibarbaric peoples who spoke Germanic languages.

167

Germanic men wore their hair down to their shoulders. They loved to gamble, drink, and fight. They assigned most of the drudgery of farmwork to their sisters, wives, and mothers. The historian Tacitus said they had "blue eyes and reddish hair; great bodies, especially powerful for attack, but not equally patient of hard work." Though the different Germanic groups shared similar ways of life, they hated one another and were frequently at war. Rome often took advantage of this hatred.

When Rome was still strong, the Germanic tribes generally respected its borders. These stretched across Europe from the Black Sea to the North Sea. The longest section of the Roman border followed the Danube River. For many years, the Danube marked the dividing line between the barbaric north and the civilized south.

Though fearless fighters, the Germanic tribes were terrified of the Huns, a nomadic people from central Asia. The following exaggerated description by a Germanic historian, Jordanes, shows how the Huns were feared:

> They made their foes flee in horror because their swarthy aspect was fearful, and they had . . . a shapeless lump instead of a head, with pinholes rather than eyes. They are cruel to their children on the very day of their birth. For they cut the cheeks of the males with a sword, so that before they receive the nourishment of milk, they must learn to endure wounds.

When the Huns began to move west, they began the massive movement of Germanic peoples that eventually destroyed the western half of the Roman empire. The Huns kept raiding westward, destroying as they went. Germanic people near the Rhine River—Burgundians, Franks, and Vandals—began to feel the pressure and to move westward also. The Rhine River froze during an especially cold winter in A.D. 406. Bundled in furs, Vandal warriors and their families swarmed across the river ice. They met practically no resistance and so they kept moving westward through the Roman province of Gaul. There were no more than 15,000 Vandal warriors, but the empire of the west was now so disorganized that it could not muster even a medium-sized army to stop the barbarians.

Map Study

This map shows the routes of some barbarian groups that invaded the Roman empire. Which group eventually reached North Africa?

Define:
increase in prices as a result of devaluing money

Identify:
(a) weak emperor whose rule began the decline of Rome (b) emperor who instituted reforms to restore order and build economic stability (c) emperor who brought an end to Christian

(continued)

Barbarians sacked Rome.

During the first half of the fifth century, Rome was sacked twice by Germanic armies: first by the Visigoths in A.D. 410, next by the Vandals in A.D. 455.

In 410, Alaric (AL-uh-rik), king of the Visigoths, marched across the Alps toward Rome. Rome still was widely regarded as the center of civilization. The news that Alaric and his army stood outside its walls was shocking. A traitor opened Rome's gates, and thousands of Germans stormed in. They plundered the city for three days.

Rome remained rich enough to act as bait for other looters. In 455, the king of the Vandals from North Africa sailed to Rome in pursuit of more treasure. This ruthless leader, known as Gaiseric (GY-zuh-rik) the Lame, sacked Rome more thoroughly than Alaric had. Thousands of Romans were taken captive and shipped back to North Africa as slaves.

Attila the Hun Meanwhile, the Huns, who indirectly began this mayhem, were still on the rampage. In fact, the Huns seemed more dangerous than ever under their new leader, Attila (AT-uhl-uh). The Germanic writer Jordanes described this terrifying chieftain as a short man with a flat nose and thin, graying beard. "He was haughty in his walk, rolling his eyes hither and thither, so that the power of his proud spirit appeared in the movement of his body."

With his 100,000 soldiers, Attila threatened to conquer the entire empire. In the east, his armies sacked 70 cities. (The Huns failed, however, to scale the high walls of Constantinople.)

In A.D. 452, Attila advanced against Rome. But then the barbarian king was stopped in his tracks by a Christian bishop. The first truly powerful pope of Rome, Leo I, journeyed to Attila's camp near the Po River. No record survives of Leo's words to Attila. Perhaps Leo frightened the Hun by telling of the plague that was then ravishing Italy. Perhaps Attila was simply awed by Leo. Whatever the reason, Attila withdrew his forces.

The last emperor of the west By A.D. 455, the Roman emperor in the west was practically powerless. Germanic tribes now fought one another for possession of the western provinces. Spain belonged to the Visigoths, North Africa to the Vandals. Gaul was overrun by competing tribes: Franks, Burgundians, and Visigoths. Britannia was being invaded by Angles and Saxons. Italy was falling victim to raids by the Ostrogoths.

The last Roman emperor was a 14-year-old boy whose name, Romulus Augustulus, recalled 1,000 years of past glory. In A.D. 476, he lost his throne to a barbarian general named Odoacer (oh-doh-AY-sur). Odoacer sent Romulus Augustulus into exile. After 476, no emperor even pretended to rule Rome and its western provinces. Roman power in the western half of the empire had disappeared.

The eastern half, which came to be called the Byzantine empire, not only survived but flourished for another 1,000 years. Its emperors ruled from Constantinople.

Even though Rome's political power ended in the west, its cultural influence was felt for centuries afterward. Latin remained the language of learning in the west. The Christian Church, governed from Rome by a succession of popes, became the chief civilizing force of western Europe. Civilization, though shaken to its roots by the barbarian terror, did not perish.

Section REVIEW 4

Define: inflation
Identify: (a) Commodus, (b) Diocletian, (c) Constantine, (d) eastern empire, (e) western empire, (f) Battle of Milvian Bridge, (g) Edict of Milan, (h) Constantinople, (i) Germanic peoples, (j) Huns, (k) Alaric, (l) Gaiseric, (m) Attila, (n) Leo I, (o) Romulus Augustulus, (p) Odoacer
Answer:
1. What economic problems did the empire face in the third century?
2. By the third century, how had Rome's army changed since the days of the republic?
3. (a) What important religious change did Constantine bring about in the empire? (b) What political change did he bring about?
4. (a) Why did Germanic tribes invade the empire in the 400's? (b) Why was the empire unable to drive the invaders out?

Critical Thinking
5. (a) List three reasons why Diocletian should be considered a successful emperor. (b) List three reasons why he might be considered a failure.

169

ANSWERS TO (continued)

persecution and moved capital to Byzantium **(d)** part of Roman empire that included the Greek-speaking east **(e)** part of Roman empire that included Italy, Gaul, Britannia, and Spain **(f)** where Constantine won the victory that made him emperor of western empire **(g)** law that changed Christianity from outlawed sect to approved religion **(h)** name for Byzantium **(i)** semibarbaric people who spoke Germanic languages **(j)** nomadic people from central Asia **(k)** king of Visigoths who sacked Rome **(l)** Vandal king who led a second attack on Rome **(m)** Hun chieftain who led raids against much of Roman empire **(n)** first powerful pope of Rome **(o)** last Roman emperor, a 14-year old boy **(p)** barbarian general who overthrew Romulus Augustus

Answer:
1. disruption of trade routes, inflation, agricultural crisis
2. repeatedly defeated; soldiers fought strictly for money
3. (a) He enacted Edict of Milan, which gave Christianity legal status. **(b)** He moved the center of the Roman empire to Byzantium.
4. (a) because of pressure from the attacking Huns **(b)** too disorganized
5. (a) Possible answers: secured Rome's boundaries, stabilized economy and rule, restored faith in Roman gods and prestige of the emperor **(b)** Possible answers: Gains in almost all areas were only temporary; persecution of Christians may have made "problem" worse; dividing empire contributed to the fall of Rome.

169

Concluding the Chapter

1. **Chapter Closer**
   Recall that the Colosseum is a symbol of Roman power. Challenge students to use the information and pictures in this chapter to choose and explain another symbol of Rome's greatness and a symbol of Rome's decline.

2. **Reteaching Activities**
   a. Writing an Essay Have students write a short essay supporting the following statement: "Without the rule of Augustus, there would not have been a Pax Romana."
   b. Outlining Ask students to use the headings in Section 2 to construct an outline of the section content.
   c. Explaining Ask students to explain how early Christianity became organized as the Christian Church.
   d. Recalling Information Ask students to explain how Alaric, Attila, and Odoacer contributed to the fall of Rome.

Answers to Chapter Review appear on pages 150e–150f.

Summary

1. **Augustus's rule began the Pax Romana.** Augustus's wise policies began a period of peace that lasted from 27 B.C. to A.D. 180. Despite some unwise or cruel rulers, Roman government worked well under its civil service. The greatest problem was the lack of a clear way of choosing an emperor.

2. **Romans extended Greek culture.** Romans continued Greek traditions in philosophy, art, and literature. Epicureanism and Stoicism became influential philosophies. Literature moved from patriotic themes, such as Virgil's *Aeneid,* to criticism of Rome. Roman law established basic principles of justice. Although great contrasts in wealth marked Roman society, the poor at least had some care.

3. **Christianity spread through the empire.** While Judaea was under Roman rule, Jesus began a new religion known as Christianity. Despite early persecution of its followers, Christianity won acceptance.

4. **Rome's empire declined and fell.** Rome faced many problems in the 200's but partly recovered under Diocletian, who set up reforms and divided the empire into eastern and western halves. Constantine legalized Christianity and moved the capital to Constantinople. During the 400's, barbarians swept into the empire, sacked Rome, and deposed Rome's last emperor.

Reviewing the Facts

1. Define the following terms:
   a. civil service   d. bishop
   b. satire   e. pope
   c. villa   f. inflation

2. Explain the importance of each of the following names, dates, places, or terms:
   a. Pax Romana   j. Paul
   b. Augustus   k. Peter
   c. Marcus Aurelius   l. Zealots
   d. A.D. 180   m. Diocletian
   e. Epicurus   n. Constantine
   f. Zeno   o. Constantinople
   g. Livy   p. Edict of Milan
   h. Virgil   q. A.D. 476
   i. Jesus

3. List four major achievements of Roman civilization during the Pax Romana.

4. (a) What were the main teachings of Christianity? (b) How did the position of Christianity within the Roman empire change between the first and fourth centuries A.D.?

5. How did each of the following factors contribute to the decline of the Roman empire? (a) economic problems (b) the issue of loyalty (c) Germanic invasions

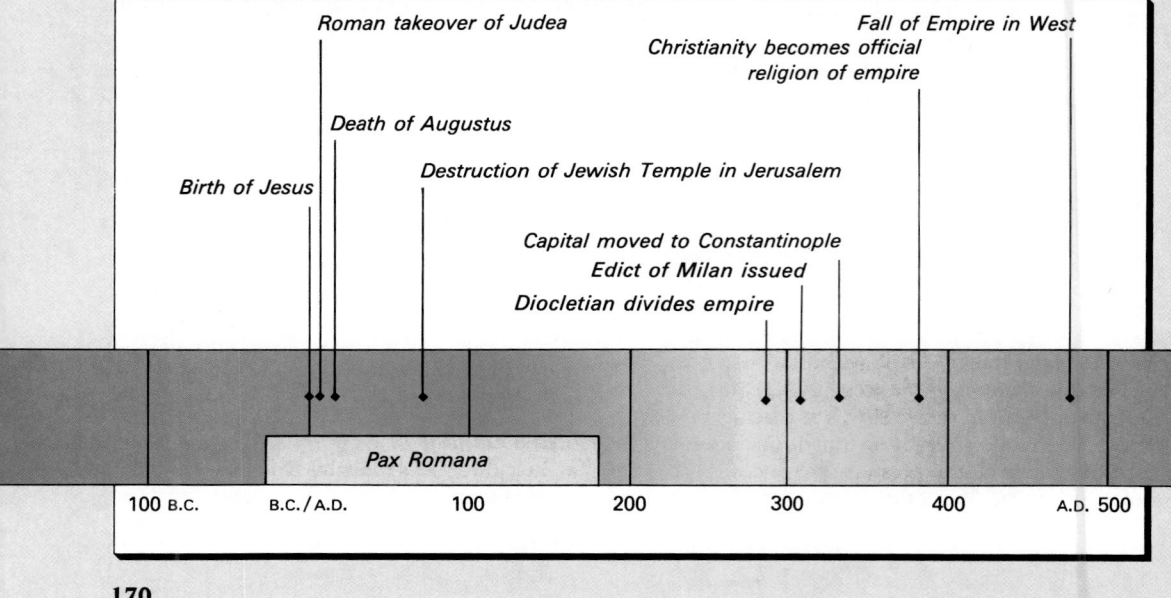

Roman takeover of Judea
Christianity becomes official religion of empire
Fall of Empire in West
Death of Augustus
Destruction of Jewish Temple in Jerusalem
Birth of Jesus
Capital moved to Constantinople
Edict of Milan issued
Diocletian divides empire

Pax Romana

100 B.C.   B.C./A.D.   100   200   300   400   A.D. 500

170

Basic Skills

1. **Comparing time lines** (a) How many years do the time lines on pages 148 and 170 each cover? (b) For what years do the two overlap? (c) How do the scales of the two time lines differ? (d) Which lasted longer, the Pax Romana or the Punic Wars?

2. **Classifying information** Using the map on page 155, make a chart to classify the goods that reached the market in Rome. Make three columns with the headings *Europe, Africa,* and *Asia.* For the vertical rows, use the headings *Minerals, Foods, Building Materials, Clothing/Jewelry, Manufactured Goods,* and *Other.* List items from the map in the appropriate spaces.

3. **Summarizing** Summarize the subsection entitled "Augustus set up sound government" on pages 151–152. Be sure to include all the main ideas and the most important supporting details for each.

Researching and Reporting Skills

1. **Organizing a group project** The chart "Emperors of the Pax Romana" provides the basis for a group research activity. Divide your class into three groups, one to report on the Julian emperors, one to report on the Army and Flavian emperors, and one to report on the Adoptive emperors. Each group should prepare the following: (a) a poster-sized bar graph showing the relative length of each emperor's rule; (b) photocopies of pictures of the emperors; and (c) a summary of each emperor's successes and failures. Groups will then present their materials and findings to the class.

2. **Recognizing primary and secondary sources** Identify each of the following as either a primary or secondary source: St. Paul's Epistle to the Ephesians, Livy's description of the early heroes of Rome, Constantine's triumphal arch, and Marcus Aurelius's *Meditations.* Give reasons for your answers.

Critical Thinking

1. **Comparing** (a) How did the Roman concept of citizenship differ from that in Athens and Sparta? (b) How does it differ from the concept of citizenship today?

2. **Analyzing** One of the characteristics of early Christianity was its appeal to the poor. What other world religion studied earlier also appealed to poor people? How would the teachings of each religion have this effect?

3. **Evaluating** On page 151, the text states that the Colosseum is symbolic of the entire Roman empire. "Both were awesome in their size and strength. Within, both combined bravery, honor, and glory with cruelty, sensationalism, and violence." (a) Do you think the Colosseum is an appropriate symbol of the Roman empire? (b) To what extent do you agree with the comparison? Why?

4. **Giving an opinion** Page 159 of the text states, "Rome's most lasting contribution to later civilizations was its law." (a) To what extent do you agree with this statement? Why? (b) What other achievements of Roman civilization are enduring?

5. **Applying a concept** At the end of the Roman empire, inflation added to the general economic crisis. (a) Define the term *inflation.* (b) What were its causes? (c) How might it affect society and trade?

Perspectives on Past and Present

1. Elements of Roman architecture have influenced many later styles. Find pictures of the government buildings and monuments in Washington, D.C., and analyze what elements of their style are Roman.

2. The transition of power from one leader to another is a time of crisis for many governments. How was this issue a problem for Rome? How is the problem handled in the United States today? How is it handled elsewhere? Use newspapers or news magazines to find accounts of ways in which new leaders come to power in at least three different countries.

Investigating History

1. In A.D. 79, a volcanic eruption destroyed the two Roman towns of Pompeii and Herculaneum. When archaeologists uncovered the towns, they found many details of Roman life perfectly preserved. Find information about these towns and the buildings, activities, and ways of life that existed there.

2. One apparently original feature of Rome's building program was the public bath. (a) Find out how the idea of the Roman bath originated. (b) Why did the baths become a feature of Roman life for both rich and poor?

171

CHAPTER
Evaluation

Chapter Test 7, Alternate Chapter Test 7, and Computer Test Bank Chapter 7 Test can be used to evaluate your students' understanding of this chapter.

ANSWERS TO
Geographic Theme

1. Rome's location was a major factor in its political expansion. Its central location in the Italian peninsula permitted expansion both northward and southward. Its central location in the Mediterranean region permitted expansion both eastward and westward.

2. (a) By 133 B.C. Rome had expanded to include Italy, Spain, Carthage, Greece, Macedon, and Pergamum. Between 133 B.C. and A.D. 117, Rome added Numidia, Mauretania, Gaul, Britain, Dacia, Thrace, Phrygia, Asia Minor, Syria, Judea, Egypt, and Libya. **(b)** The pattern in the first stage was to take over lands bordering the north shore of the Mediterranean and Carthage on the south shore. The second stage pattern was to expand farther into Mediterranean coastal regions and then to move inland, even crossing the Channel to Britain.

3. In order to expand into distant coastal areas, Rome had to control the Mediterranean Sea. Carthage stood in the way.

4. Roman political expansion resulted in the spread of Roman law, ideas of government, economic life, construction, and cultural characteristics to the whole Mediterranean area.

Geographic Theme: Region

How did Rome unify the Mediterranean world?

The events you have read about in this unit took place within one area, vast yet contained. This was the Mediterranean world, made up of the sea itself and the lands around it. Here, the sea and its bordering lands form a region, an area in which certain similar traits prevail. One type of climate so pervades this region that it is known as *Mediterranean*. In terms of land, many peninsulas reach into the sea, providing a close tie between land and water. Everywhere, the sea provides the unifying element that binds the region together. To the people of ancient times, it became the route to a wider world.

The earliest settlement of the Mediterranean moved from east to west. Using the islands as stepping-stones, the Phoenicians ventured into the western Mediterranean, founding Carthage in 813 B.C. and building an empire based on trade. In time, the seafaring Greeks also expanded westward. Their colonies were the start of many cities that have survived to modern times.

It was Rome, however, that united the Mediterranean world in a single political entity. Rome expanded steadily, first in Italy and then throughout the region. The defeat of Carthage left Rome unchallenged. Romans could truly call the Mediterranean *mare nostrum,* "our sea."

Rome continued to expand, reaching its greatest extent under Emperor Trajan, who died in A.D. 117. That expansion, however, was not only political. Roman law, architecture, customs, and institutions followed the Roman legions. Thus, Roman civilization came to unite the Mediterranean world.

1. Evaluate the importance of Rome's location to its political expansion.
2. (a) List the lands added by Rome during each stage of its expansion. (b) Describe the pattern of expansion at each stage.
3. Why was the defeat of Carthage's sea power essential to Roman expansion?
4. What was the effect of Roman political expansion on Mediterranean civilization?

The Expansion of Roman Rule

KEY
- Rome about 500 B.C.
- Roman lands in 133 B.C.
- The Roman Empire in A.D. 117

0   300 Miles

Historical Themes

Ancient Greece and Rome were the birthplaces of important ideas about government. These civilizations also produced vibrant cultures and dynamic leaders who changed the course of history.

Rise of Democratic Ideas

Ancient Athens was the first democracy, with direct participation by citizens in government. Nonetheless, only about one fifth of the residents of Athens were citizens with the right to vote and participate in government. In spite of that limitation, the Athenian idea of making policy through public debate and voting was the beginning of a democratic process.

The Roman republic was not a democracy, because the voting there was even more restricted than in Athens. Nonetheless, Rome's system of government—with power shared among a senate, two consuls, and an assembly—was clearly the basis for the United States' two houses of Congress and executive branch. Roman ideas on law and justice later influenced legal systems in many countries.

Cultural Development

Philosophy, the arts, mathematics, science, literature, and other ideas of the Greeks had a profound effect on later civilizations. Through his conquests from Egypt to India, Alexander spread Greek culture. After his death, that culture blended with others of the empire to produce a brilliant new culture called Hellenism. Rome too built a widespread empire that included many peoples and cultures. Those cultures continued and in time blended with the Greco-Roman heritage. Rome's legacy of law and government spread throughout the Mediterranean world.

Greek and Roman achievements later influenced the Byzantine and Islamic empires. Scholars there translated the works of Aristotle, Plato, and other classical philosophers. Classical culture reappeared in Europe in the late 1300's. Its rediscovery inspired the Renaissance, a rebirth of learning and artistic achievement. Greco-Roman culture exerted a strong influence again in the late eighteenth and early nineteenth centuries. Because that revival coincided with the founding of the United States, it had a profound impact on our

system of government and state architecture.

Individuals and History

Both Greece and Rome produced a number of individuals whose actions and ideas had a significant influence on Western civilization. Pericles and Augustus were great statesmen who presided over cultural golden ages. Pericles glorified Athens by building the Parthenon and supporting drama. Augustus rebuilt Rome and encouraged writers such as Livy and Virgil.

Pericles and Augustus were both men of action and political leaders. By contrast, Socrates and Jesus were teachers who touched people with thought-provoking questions and parables. Socrates questioned many accepted values, urging his students above all to "know thyself." Jesus used parables to show how God's love could overcome sin. He urged his followers to repent, since God would put an end to wickedness on Earth.

While Socrates and Jesus tried to persuade people to reexamine their lives, Alexander and Caesar used force to conquer empires and gain power. Alexander dreamed of winning glory by destroying the Persian empire. His conquests ended the era of independent Greek city-states and opened the Hellenistic age. Caesar too was a brilliant general whose conquests launched a new era. After returning to Rome, Caesar ended the Republic and became an absolute ruler.

Analyzing Historical Themes

1. What were the main advantages and limitations of Greek democracy?
2. What factors explain the recurring appeal of Greco-Roman thought and ideals?
3. Why were Socrates and Jesus effective teachers?

173

ANSWERS TO
Analyzing Historical Themes

1. advantages—direct citizen participation in government, policy made through debate and voting; limitations—only one fifth of residents could participate and vote

2. As Greek and Roman empires covered vast areas of Asia and the Mediterranean world, their cultures blended with many native cultures. The resulting Greco-Roman heritage was rediscovered several times by later European and Middle Eastern peoples.

3. Socrates asked thought-provoking questions about accepted values. Jesus used parables to show how God's love could overcome sin.

UNIT
Evaluation

Unit II Test and Alternate Unit II Test can be used to evaluate your students' understanding of this unit.

Chapters

From The Book of Hours of the Duc de Berry

	400	600	800
Political and Governmental Life	**528** Justinian makes code of laws	**632–750** Islamic conquests create an empire	**800** Charlemagne is crowned emperor
Economic and Technological Life		**750–1050** Trade and learning flourish in Islamic empire	**800's** Vikings raid Europe
Social and Cultural Life	**400's** Missionaries preach Christianity in northwest Europe	**600–700's** Monasteries are islands of culture and stability	**800's** Cyril creates Slavic alphabet **800–900's** Feudalism develops

Constantinople

Saint Benedict

Unit **III**

The Middle Ages

Historical Themes

Continuity and Change The decline of Rome left a vacuum that was in time filled by the Byzantine and Islamic empires and new states in western Europe. Roman ideas influenced all three cultures.

Social Institutions As Rome waned, the institution of feudalism became the basis of medieval society in Europe. Based on personal loyalty, it sought to provide social, political, and economic order.

The Rise of Democratic Ideas The Magna Carta and creation of Parliament were significant developments in England's government. Both limited royal power and aided due process of law.

1000	1200	1400

1066
Normans invade and conquer England

1215
King John of England signs Magna Carta

1453
Constantinople falls to Turks

1096
Crusades begin

1337–1451
France and England wage Hundred Years' War

1000's–1200's
Fairs develop as centers of trade

1000's–1100's
Towns and cities grow in western Europe

1492
Ferdinand and Isabella drive Muslims from Spain; Columbus reaches America

1200's
Gothic architecture spreads through Europe

Stained glass window, Canterbury Cathedral

The Alhambra at Granada

175

The World about 800

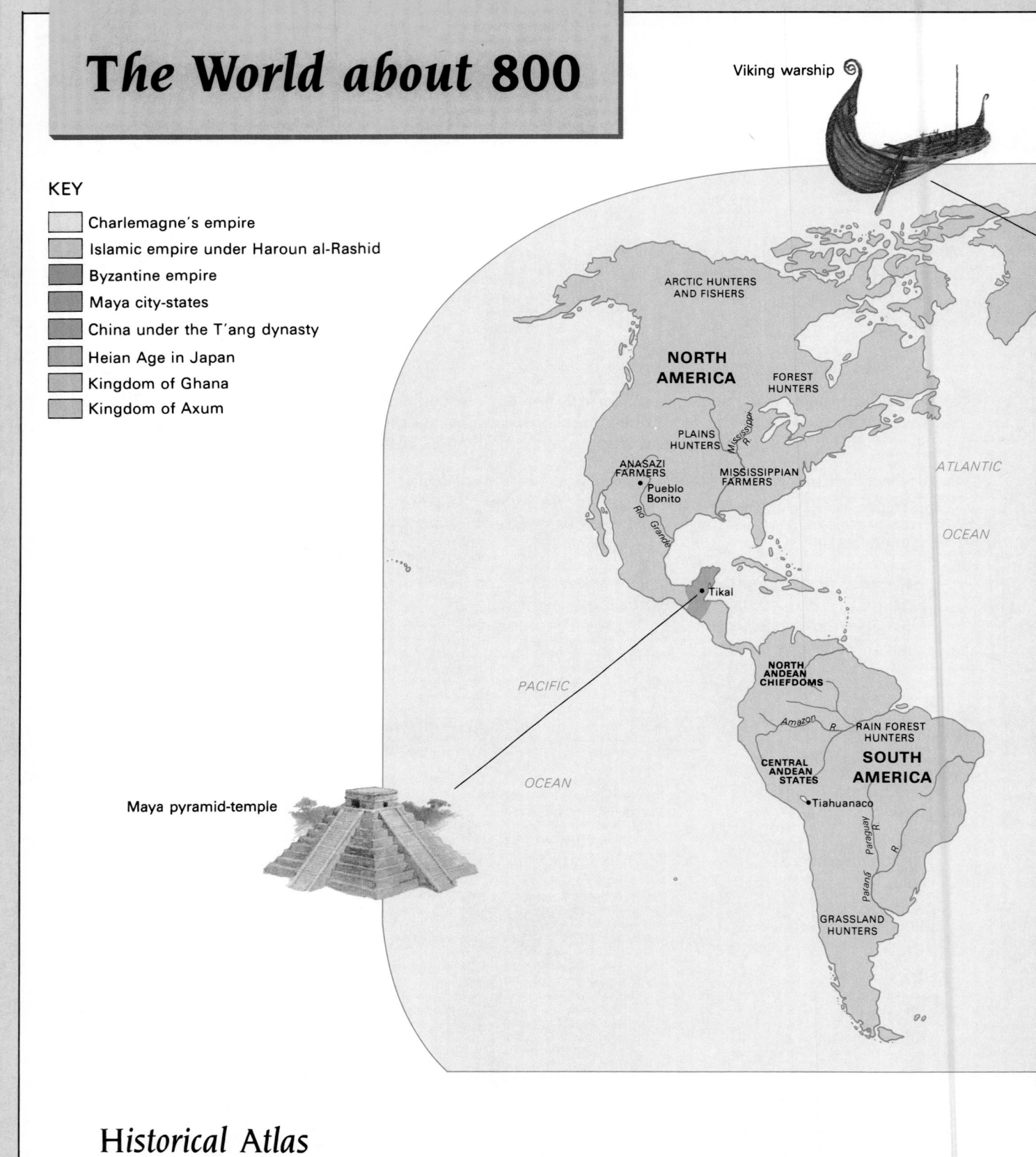

Viking warship

KEY

- Charlemagne's empire
- Islamic empire under Haroun al-Rashid
- Byzantine empire
- Maya city-states
- China under the T'ang dynasty
- Heian Age in Japan
- Kingdom of Ghana
- Kingdom of Axum

ARCTIC HUNTERS AND FISHERS

NORTH AMERICA

FOREST HUNTERS

PLAINS HUNTERS

Mississippi R.

ANASAZI FARMERS

MISSISSIPPIAN FARMERS

Pueblo Bonito

Rio Grande

Tikal

ATLANTIC

OCEAN

PACIFIC

OCEAN

NORTH ANDEAN CHIEFDOMS

Amazon R.

RAIN FOREST HUNTERS

CENTRAL ANDEAN STATES

SOUTH AMERICA

Tiahuanaco

Paraguay R.

Paraná R.

GRASSLAND HUNTERS

Maya pyramid-temple

Historical Atlas

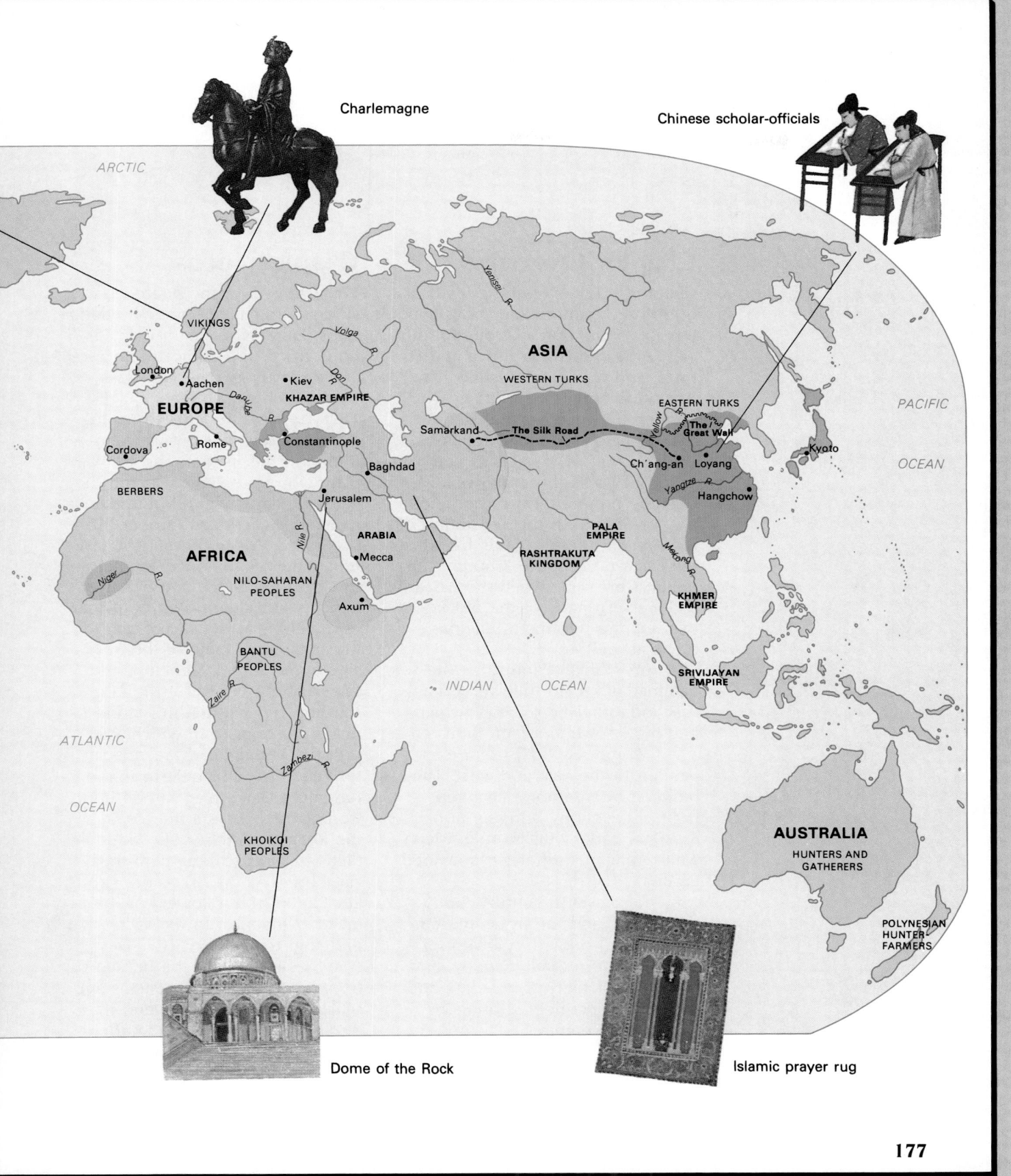

Charlemagne

Chinese scholar-officials

ARCTIC

VIKINGS

London
•Kiev
•Aachen
Volga R.
KHAZAR EMPIRE
Don R.
EUROPE
Danube R.
Rome
Constantinople
Samarkand
The Silk Road
Cordova
Baghdad
BERBERS
Jerusalem
Nile R.
ARABIA
AFRICA
•Mecca
NILO-SAHARAN
PEOPLES
Niger R.
Axum
BANTU
PEOPLES
Zaire R.

ATLANTIC

OCEAN

Zambezi R.

INDIAN   OCEAN

ASIA

WESTERN TURKS

EASTERN TURKS

Yenisei R.
Yellow R.
The Great Wall
Ch'ang-an   Loyang
Kyoto
Yangtze R.
Hangchow
PALA EMPIRE
RASHTRAKUTA KINGDOM
Mekong R.
KHMER EMPIRE
SRIVIJAYAN EMPIRE

PACIFIC

OCEAN

KHOIKOI PEOPLES

AUSTRALIA
HUNTERS AND GATHERERS

POLYNESIAN HUNTER-FARMERS

Dome of the Rock

Islamic prayer rug

177

The Byzantine Empire and the Rise of Islam

Chapter Overview

Chapter 8 discusses the growth of both the Byzantine and the Islamic empires, their spread from Southwest Asia into North Africa and Europe, and their final decline. The Byzantine emperor Justinian, who reigned between A.D. 527 and A.D. 565, tried to reconquer Roman lands to the west, oversaw codification of laws, and undertook a building program in Constantinople. In 1054, with the separation of the Roman Catholic Church and the Eastern Orthodox Church, the political break between the eastern and western parts of the old Roman empire became a religious break as well.

In the Arabian Peninsula, Muhammad attracted followers to a new monotheistic religion, which became known as Islam. Between A.D. 630 and A.D. 732, Islam expanded to the east and west. The building of an empire changed Islamic society by bringing non-Muslims under Muslim rule. Meanwhile, religious differences divided Islam.

By the eleventh century, both the Islamic and the Byzantine empires were troubled by invasions, problems of internal disunity, and political instability. The Seljuk and Ottoman Turks helped bring an end to both empires.

Chapter Focus

Write *sacred* on the board. Ask students to suggest possible definitions. Emphasize that sacred, or holy, places are dedicated to religious use. Now have the class read the chapter opener (pages 178–179). Ask students to name the three religious groups mentioned in this section and to explain why Jerusalem is sacred to each. Students should note that Jerusalem is sacred to Jews as the site of the Western Wall (the last remnant of Solomon's Temple) and to Christians as the site of Christ's ministry and death. Point out that Jerusalem is also a sacred city to Muslims. The Dome of the Rock shown on page 178 encloses the sacred stone of Mount Moriah. Muslims believe that this stone marks the spot from which the prophet Muhammad ascended to heaven. They also believe that on Judgment Day scales will be hung from arches outside the Dome of the Rock to weigh souls. The conflicting claims to Jerusalem today can be traced in part to the strong attachment the followers of three major faiths have to the sacred places in this ancient city. This chapter begins with the first confrontation between Christians and Muslims over Jerusalem and then discusses the growth and continued rivalry of the Byzantine and Islamic empires.

Advance Planner

Unit III The Middle Ages
THEME The Middle Ages was a period of reintegration of European societies after the fall of Rome

Chapter 8 The Byzantine Empire and the Rise of Islam 450–1453
FOCUS The sacred places of Christians, Jews, and Muslims

★ Advanced
● Basic

	SECTION 1	SECTION 2	SECTION 3
Objectives	1. Explain the geographic advantages of Constantinople's location. 2. Identify the boundaries of the Byzantine empire. 3. Identify evidence to support main ideas about the Byzantine empire. 4. Discuss Constantinople's role as the religious center of the first Christian empire.	1. Describe the career of the prophet Muhammad. 2. Identify the Five Pillars of Islam, and explain the significance of the Kaaba. 3. Trace the spread of Islam.	1. Describe how the Slavs became Christians. 2. Make a time line of the decline and fall of the Islamic and Byzantine empires.
Setting the Stage	Unit III time line Using Geographic Themes: Location and Place Transparency 28 Transparency 27	The rise and spread of Islam	The diffusion of Byzantine culture to Slavs and Islamic culture to Turks Transparency 30 Transparency 31
Teaching Strategies	Geography in History: Byzantine Empire Outline Map 21 Skill Building: Supporting Main Ideas Discussing History: A City Tour Check for Understanding	Discussing History: The Prophet Muhammad Teaching with Pictures: The Kaaba Geography in History: The Spread of Islam Transparency 29 Transparency 26 Check for Understanding	Discussing History: The Slavs Became Christians Skill Building: Making a Time Line Check for Understanding
Guided Practice	Transparency 28 Q&A Transparency 27 Q&A Section Review 1	Transparency 29 Q&A Section Review 2	Transparency 30 Q&A Transparency 31 Q&A Section Review 3
Independent Practice Worksheets	Independent Practice 8.1 Geography Skills 8 Vocabulary 8	Independent Practice 8.2 Basic Skills 8	Independent Practice 8.3 Critical Thinking 8
Enrichment	1. Primary Source: Voices 8.1 2. Researching for Points	1. Primary Source: Voices 8.2 2. ★Preparing a Report: Pilgrimage to Mecca 3. Researching for Points	1. Primary Source: Voices 8.3 2. Preparing a Report: Russia's Greek Orthodox Church 3. Creative Writing 4. Researching for Points

Chapter Closer	
●**Reteaching Activities**	Summarizing, Answering Questions, Outlining
Chapter Review	Summary, Reviewing the Facts, Basic Skills, Researching and Reporting Skills, Critical Thinking, Perspectives on Past and Present, Investigating History
Chapter Evaluation	Chapter Test 8, Alternate Chapter Test 8, Computer Test Bank Chapter 8 Test

Constantinople ruled an eastern empire. 1

Setting the Stage

Using Geographic Themes: Location and Place (Objective 1) Display Map Transparency 28, *Constantinople about 550*. First explain that Constantinople is located on a peninsula bordered by the Golden Horn, Bosporus Strait, and the Sea of Marmara. The Golden Horn provides Constantinople with a spacious harbor. The peninsula's land side is only 5 miles long and could easily be fortified with a wall. Now explain that a traveler once said that Constantinople's location provided a key that could unlock two worlds and two seas. Ask students to examine Map Transparency 27, *Constantinople/The Byzantine Empire under Justinian*, and to explain what the traveler meant. Point out that Constantinople is located at a point where the land routes from Asia and Eastern Europe meet. It is the only city in the world that straddles two continents. In addition, Constantinople also dominates the north-south sea route linking the Black Sea to the Mediterranean Sea. This section examines how a ruler named Justinian used Constantinople's natural defenses and commercial advantages to turn the city into the capital of a powerful Christian empire.

Teaching Strategies

Geography in History: Byzantine Empire (Objective 2) Explain that Justinian considered himself the rightful heir to the lands once controlled by the Roman empire. He ordered Belisarius to reconquer these lands. Distribute Outline Map 21: Roman Empire. Using the map on page 181 as a guide, have students use one color to shade in the area showing the Byzantine

empire before Justinian and another color to show the area conquered by Justinian. Students should label North Africa, Italy, Greece, Spain, Asia Minor, Egypt, and Palestine; the Mediterranean Sea, Black Sea, Red Sea, and Atlantic Ocean. Remind students to provide keys and titles.

Skill Building: Supporting Main Ideas (Objective 3) Write the following statements on the board. Have students write two facts to support each statement.

1. Legal reforms were Justinian's most important contribution. (He ordered the codification of all Roman laws and legal opinions of the preceding 400 years. Justinian's Code became the basis of Byzantine law for the next 900 years and later of western European laws.)
2. Constantinople was a well-protected city. (Sea walls guarded it from hostile navies. To the west, a moat and three walls blocked the only land route to the city.)
3. Differences developed between Byzantine Christians and Christians of western Europe. (Byzantine priests conducted services in local languages, whereas western European priests used Latin. Byzantine priests could marry, whereas Roman priests could not. The pope in Rome claimed leadership of all Christians and independence from emperors. Byzantine patriarchs accepted the authority of their emperor and refused to accept the pope in Rome as their superior.)

Discussing History: A City Tour (Objective 4) Emphasize that Constantinople was the first Christian capital of the first Christian empire. Pilgrims journeyed great distances to see such holy relics as the Crown

of Thorns, parts of the True Cross, and the Virgin Mary's robe. However, all of these relics were overshadowed by the immense presence of Hagia Sophia—the Church of the Holy Wisdom. When the first church of Hagia Sophia burned down, Justinian immediately commissioned a new one. More than 10,000 workers labored for almost 6 years. When he first saw the completed church, Justinian extended his arms toward heaven and cried, "Glory to God, who deemed me worthy of fulfilling such a work. O Solomon, I have surpassed thee!" (See *Hagia Sophia* by Lord Kinross.) Point out that Hagia Sophia, like the Parthenon and the Colosseum, was a symbol of the civilization that created it. Noting that the church was illuminated each night by thousands of candles, one Byzantine described Hagia Sophia as a "sacred light" that guided sailors into the city's safe harbor. The church thus symbolized a spiritual lighthouse for the world's first Christian capital.

Check for Understanding Have students explain the importance of Bosporus, Code of Justinian, Patriarch of Constantinople, Hagia Sophia.

Enrichment Activities

1. **Reading a Primary Source** Assign Voices from the Past Resource Book 8.1.
2. **Researching for Bonus Points** What happened to the Holy Table inside Hagia Sophia? (It was stolen by the Venetians in 1204; however, the ship carrying it sank and the Holy Table is now on the bottom of the Sea of Marmara.)

Setting the Stage

Ask students to imagine that it is A.D. 600. As military advisers to the Byzantine emperor, their duty is to report on any threats to the empire's borders. Have students examine the map on page 181 and make a list of the peoples who surrounded the Byzantine empire. Lists should include the Persians, Huns, Slavs, Gepids, Lombards, Franks, Visigoths, Berbers, and Arabs. Ask, "Which groups might pose a threat to Constantinople?" Point out that the Byzantine military advisers recognized the Persian empire and the Germanic tribes as powerful long-term rivals. They did not give much thought to the scattered Arab tribes then living in the Arabian desert. However, within 30 years a new religion called Islam burst forth from the Arabian desert, and its followers conquered a huge new empire stretching from Spain to the Indus River. This section introduces the prophet Muhammad and explains the basic beliefs of Islam. It also discusses the cultural achievements of the Islamic golden age.

Teaching Strategies

Discussing History: The Prophet Muhammad (Objective 1) Have the class list the problems Muhammad faced when he first announced that he was Allah's prophet. Students should note that Muhammad faced a formidable challenge—he was an illiterate merchant living in a polytheistic society. Explain that Muhammad successfully overcame these disadvantages. Illiteracy was not a severe handicap in the desert culture of Arabia. The Bedouins admired the spoken word and believed that particularly eloquent speakers were possessed by a supernatural force. Gabriel's visits filled Muhammad with confidence, and his passionate sermons convinced people that he was indeed Allah's prophet. Muhammad's experience with his wife's caravan business also proved to be an advantage. On his journeys, he met Byzantine Christians and Jews who told him about their monotheistic religions. Muhammad's message about a stern but compassionate god called Allah, his emphasis on charity to the poor, and his promise of an eternal reward for the faithful soon won many converts.

Teaching with Pictures: The Kaaba (Objective 2) Have students read the section on the Five Pillars of Islam (page 188) and direct students' attention to the picture of the Kaaba on page 187. Explain that more than two million Muslim pilgrims visit the Kaaba each year. Men dress in a white garment called an *ihram*. Women also dress simply and keep their faces unveiled. The Kaaba is 50 feet high. Muslims believe that it was originally built by Abraham and his son Ishmael. The eastern corner of the Kaaba contains a black meteor encased in silver. Muslims believe that the Black Stone represents the right hand of Allah. Pilgrims circle the Kaaba seven times hoping to touch or kiss the Black Stone. The Kaaba itself is empty. It is covered with an embroidered black cloth called a *kiswa*. More than 100 artisans work full time to produce a new kiswa each year. The finished kiswa contains 2,500 square feet of cloth and weighs 2 tons.

Geography in History: The Spread of Islam (Objective 3) Have students read "Islam expanded east and west" (pages 188–190). Then show Map Transparency 29, *The Spread of Islam*. Point out that the Muslim armies successfully conquered more territory than the Romans— all in one century. Have students locate Mecca and trace the boundaries of eastward and westward Islamic expansion. Note that the Muslim armies were finally stopped by the Franks at the Battle of Tours and by the Byzantine navy outside the gates of Constantinople. Conclude by showing Map Transparency 26, *The World about 800*. Have students identify the three empires that bordered the Islamic empire. Note Baghdad's central location in the Eurasian world.

Check for Understanding Have students define or identify the following items: Bedouin, Muhammad, Koran, Kaaba, Hegira, Mecca, and Baghdad.

Enrichment Activities

1. **Reading a Primary Source** Assign Voices from the Past Resource Book 8.2.

2. **Preparing a Report** Ask advanced students to report on the rituals associated with a pilgrimage to Mecca. (See *National Geographic*, November 1978.)

3. **Researching for Bonus Points** What does the phrase, "La ilaha illa Allah, Muhammad rasul Allah," mean? ("There is no god but Allah, and Muhammad is His Prophet.")

Setting the Stage

Recall the definition of *cultural diffusion*. Remind students that cultural diffusion is a process in which ideas and goods are transmitted from one society to another. This section describes how Byzantine culture influenced the early Russians. Use Map Transparency 30, *Russia about 1100*, to introduce the geography of Russia. This section also discusses how the Turks converted to Islam following their contact with the Islamic empire. The dramatic story of how Constantinople fell to the Ottoman Turks is highlighted in the Turning Points in History feature. Use Map Transparency 31 to trace the decline of the Byzantine empire.

Teaching Strategies

Discussing History: The Slavs Became Christians (Objective 1) To help students realize the significance of eastern culture to the Slavs, ask, "What was the importance of the Cyrillic alphabet?" (separated Slavs from peoples using Roman alphabet) For what reasons did the early Russians convert to Byzantine rather than to Roman Christianity, and why was this a significant decision? (beauty of Hagia Sophia; decision isolated Russia from western ideas)

Skill Building: Making a Time Line (Objective 2) Ask each student to use the information in the section to prepare a time line that shows the events leading to the breakup of the Islamic and Byzantine empires. The time line should cover the years 750–1453.

Check for Understanding Have students write a paragraph explaining the influence of Byzantine culture on the Slavs, and a paragraph explaining the influence of Islamic civilization on the Seljuk Turks.

Enrichment Activities

1. **Reading a Primary Source**
   Assign Voices from the Past Resource Book 8.3.
2. **Preparing a Report**
   Have students report on the role the Greek Orthodox Church plays in the Soviet Union today.
3. **Creative Writing**
   The fall of Constantinople shocked both Muslims and Christians. Ask some students to take a Muslim point of view and others a Christian point of view. The assignment is to write a newspaper article describing the fall of Constantinople. Compare and contrast the two sets of articles.
4. **Researching for Bonus Points**
   What did the Ottomans call Constantinople? (They called it *eis ten Polin*—Greek for "to the city." Istanbul did not become the city's official name until after World War I.)

Reviewing the Facts

1. (a) to place outside the church, cut off from Christians (b) person whose ideas are incorrect in the opinion of a church (c) bishop of Constantinople (d) holy war (e) leader with religious power (f) Persian ruler with political power

2. (a) eastern capital of the Roman empire (b) Byzantine emperor who codified law and built splendid buildings in Constantinople (c) served as a basis for Byzantine law for 900 years and guide to western Europe for legal questions (d) desert nomads in Arabia (e) important religious center, birthplace of Muhammad (f) founder of Islam (g) year of Hegira (h) holy book of Islam (i) center of Muslim civilization during its golden age (j) nomads who migrated into eastern Europe from plains of Asia (k) second capital of early Russia (l) ruler of Kiev who set Russia on path of Eastern Orthodox religion (m) year when the break between Roman and Byzantine churches became final (n) nomads from Central Asia who conquered Baghdad, all of Asia Minor (o) conquered the rest of the Byzantine empire (p) year when Constantinople fell to the Ottoman Turks

3. disagreements over use of icons, language in which services were conducted, behavior of priests, superiority of the pope

4. (a) marked first year of Islamic era (b) Islam's holy book that helped spread Arabic language in Middle East and North Africa (c) set out the duties for believers (d) group that split from the orthodox Muslims

5. (a) Umayyads considered Persians second-class citizens; Abbasids promised to return to Islamic idea of equality among believers (b) Umayyad: conquered North Africa and Spain, pushed the borders

of the empire to the Indus River valley; were able rulers and administrators. Abbasid: built the city of Baghdad, which became the center of Muslim civilization where arts and sciences flourished during its golden age.

6. (a) converted to Christianity; imitated Byzantine art and architecture **(b)** converted to Islam

Basic Skills

1. The conflict between the Byzantine empire and Islam was not only military but also religious.

2. This time of crisis justifies a woman's speaking up. Ordinary men might flee, but an emperor cannot endure without his empire.

3. Notes will vary. For example, *People* might include population size, language, religion, and occupations.

4. Spain, North Africa, Palestine, Sicily, Corsica, Crete, Sardinia, parts of Asia Minor and Persia

5. Slavic invasions began (700); Seljuk Turk invasions began (1050); Battle of Manzikert (1071); Ottoman Turk invasions began (1300); sieges of Constantinople (1397, 1422, 1453)

6. It took about 130 years from Hegira to height of empire.

Researching and Reporting Skills

Students' research findings will vary.

Critical Thinking

1. *Similarities:* Both were believed to have been received by prophets as the word of God; affirmed belief in one God; established customs, moral laws, special days of worship, rules against worship of idols. *Differences:* The Ten Commandments and the Koran specify different moral duties and religious practices. For example, the Koran mentions requirements of prayer, alms, fasting, and pilgrimage.

2. (a) Students' opinions will vary. **(b)** Under Augustus, a Gaul—if a citizen—would have the same rights as the Romans, including access to public office. The protection of Roman law would follow him wherever he went. There would be no limitations to trading activity throughout the empire. Under the Abbasids, a Greek would be considered a second-class citizen, would have to convert to Islam or pay taxes; would be free to trade or do business; would benefit from the advanced state of Islamic arts and sciences.

3. Arts, sciences, and trade flourish; public building programs beautify the cities; education is encouraged; government is efficient and stable.

4. *Political:* Islam's rule spread more widely than Byzantium's; Justinian's Code established a common system of law in his empire. Islam was weakened by political divisions. *Economic:* Constantinople controlled major land and sea routes between Mediterranean and Asia. Baghdad controlled caravan routes to India and China; its harbor on the Tigris was visited by ships from India and Arabia; set up first banks with "saak" (checks) to facilitate trade. *Religious:* Eastern Orthodox religion spread to Byzantine empire and was adopted by Russia. Islam spread through military conquests to Africa, Spain, and many other lands; became one of the world's major religions. *Cultural:* Constantinople and Baghdad were rivals in splendor; Hagia Sophia rivaled in beauty with the Dome of the Rock in Jerusalem. The University of Constantinople kept alive the works of ancient writers. Greek was the language of scholarship. In Islam, Arabic was the language used by scholars throughout the empire; ancient Greek manuscripts were translated into Arabic; literature, medicine, mathematics, and science flourished. Baghdad, the Abbasid capital, had great works of architecture and was a center of learning.

Perspectives on Past and Present

1. The writings preserved Greek and Roman culture, Roman law, the histories and philosophies of the ancient world, and Islamic literature and science.

2. Countries of today that were part of the Islamic empire in 755 include Iran, Iraq, Syria, eastern Turkey, Lebanon, Israel, Jordan, Egypt, Saudi Arabia, the Yemen Arab Republic, the People's Democratic Republic of Yemen, Oman, Kuwait, Bahrain, Qatar, and United Arab Emirates.

Investigating History

Students' findings will vary.

Chapter 8

Teaching with Pictures

Explain to students that the Dome of the Rock stands on the spot where the prophet Muhammad, founder of Islam, is believed to have ascended to heaven in the seventh century. Note that the golden dome, made of wood, and the octagonal-shaped building, covered with marble and mosaics, make the structure one of the most beautiful in Jerusalem. Point out that it is also the oldest and holiest Moslem shrine, completed in 691. Ask students to contrast the splendor of the shrine with the dwellings in the background.

The Dome of the Rock stands where Muslims believe Muhammad rose to heaven.

Key Terms

absolute
icon
iconoclast
excommunicate
heretic
patriarch
Hegira
mosque
jihad

caliph
astrolabe
sultan

Read and Understand

1. Constantinople ruled an eastern empire.
2. A new faith spread from Arabia.
3. The empires influenced Slavs and Turks.

Inside the gates of Jerusalem, a tall, muscular Arab climbed down from the hump of a white camel. From the camel's back, he took down a dusty prayer rug and carried it up the steps of a magnificent, high-domed church, the Church of the Holy Sepulchre. The Arab's name was Omar. The year was 637.

For about 300 years, Jerusalem had been a Christian city, part of the Byzantine empire. Christians considered the ground enclosed by the Church of the Holy Sepulchre to be the most sacred place on earth. According to tradition, the spot where Jesus had been crucified and the tomb in which he had been buried lay beneath the dome of this church.

178

Chapter 8 Resources

GEOGRAPHY
- Geography Skills 8
- Outline Map 21
- Transparencies 26, 27, 28, 29, 30, 31

REINFORCEMENT
- Vocabulary 8
- Basic Skills 8
- Reteaching 8
- Making Connections Study Guide 8

ENRICHMENT
- Critical Thinking 8
- History and Literature 8

ASSESSMENT
- Chapter Test 8
- Alternate Chapter Test 8
- Computer Test Bank

Omar, however, was not a Christian. He was a Muslim, one of the first converts to a new religion called Islam (ihs-LAHM). He had been a personal friend of Islam's founder, an Arab prophet named Muhammad (moo-HAM-uhd).

Omar did not enter the church. Instead, he reverently turned his gaze southeast toward Mecca, the Arab city from which he had come. He knelt on his prayer rug, touching his head to the ground as he prayed toward Mecca. *"Allahu akhbar!"* he cried aloud, meaning "God is most great."

On this day in 637, Omar entered Jerusalem as a conqueror. Some 60,000 Muslim warriors had invaded Palestine to win converts for God —or *Allah*, in the Arabic language. They had defeated the defending Christian armies from Constantinople.

Rising from his prayer rug, Omar asked a Christian priest to show him to the flat stretch of rock where the temple built by the Jewish king Solomon had stood. To Muslims, this plain gray rock was holier than anything else in Jerusalem. Muslims believed that their prophet Muhammad had ascended from this rock into paradise on a golden ladder of light. Omar eagerly followed his guide to the sacred rock, but he found it buried under a mound of garbage and dung. The pious Omar flew into a rage. "Oh, ye men of Greece," he shouted at the Greek-speaking Christians, "ye are the people who shall be slain on this dung-heap."

In the centuries that followed, thousands of Christians and Muslims spilled their blood in wars of religion and conquest. Religious belief can be an immensely powerful force in human affairs. It can inspire great acts of goodness and stunning works of art. It can also drive people to terrible acts against those who hold other beliefs. Both Christians and Muslims claimed theirs was the only true religion. Neither group would allow the other to live in peace.

In this chapter, you will follow the fortunes of two empires, one Christian and the other Muslim. You will see how the Byzantine Christians used their riches to create an artistic masterpiece, the dazzling church of Hagia Sophia in Constantinople. In Jerusalem, the Muslim Arabs erected another architectural masterpiece, the Dome of the Rock, over the very rock on which Christians had dumped garbage. You will see

how Christianity spread from Constantinople into Russia and how Islam spread from Arabia as far west as Spain and as far east as India.

Constantinople ruled an eastern empire. 1

Geographic Setting

Constantinople was founded by Rome's first Christian emperor, Constantine, in 330. He built the city on the site of a Greek seaport known as Byzantium. It was situated at a point where many major trade routes between Asia and Europe came together, as the map on this page shows.

Between the Black Sea and the Aegean Sea lies a much smaller body of water, the Sea of Marmara. Two narrow straits, like natural gateways, control the shipping routes from sea to sea. The gateway between the Aegean Sea and the Sea of Marmara is the Dardanelles. The gateway between the Sea of Marmara and the Black Sea is called the Bosporus. Whoever controls those

Map Study

What narrow waterway did Constantinople control? Name five routes by which goods reached the city.

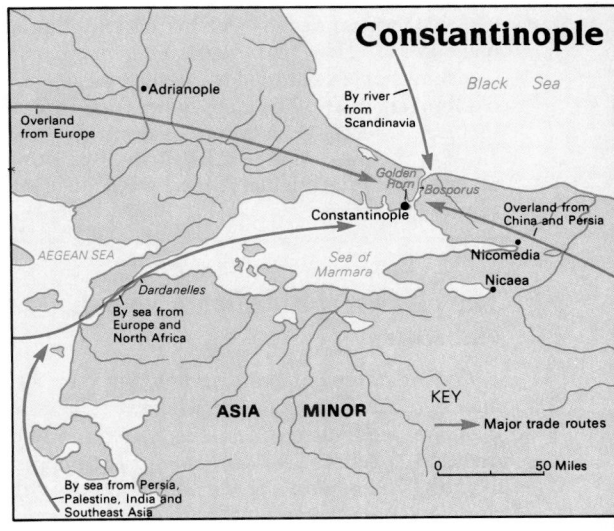

Constantinople

179

179

SECTION 1
Resources

GEOGRAPHY
■ Transparencies 27, 28

REINFORCEMENT
■ Independent Practice 8.1

ENRICHMENT
■ Voices from the Past 8.1

ASSESSMENT
■ Section Quiz 8.1

SECTION 1
Objectives and Teaching Strategies

OBJECTIVE 1. Explain the geographic advantages of Constantinople's location.
Teaching Strategy: *Using Geographic Themes: Location and Place* (page 178c)

OBJECTIVE 2. Identify the boundaries of the Byzantine empire.
Teaching Strategy: *Geography in History: Byzantine Empire* (page 178c)

OBJECTIVE 3. Identify evidence to support main ideas about the Byzantine empire.
Teaching Strategy: *Skill Building: Supporting Main Ideas* (page 178c)

OBJECTIVE 4. Discuss Constantinople's role as the religious center of the first Christian empire.
Teaching Strategy: *Discussing History: A City Tour* (page 178c)

ANSWERS TO
Map Study

The Bosporus; overland from Europe, by river from Scandinavia, by sea from Europe and North Africa, overland from China and Persia, by sea from Persia, Palestine, India, and Southeast Asia

Mosaics were a common Byzantine artform. This one shows Emperor Justinian.

gates also controls the shipping from much of Asia to the Mediterranean region.

Constantine built his great capital on a peninsula at the southern end of the Bosporus. The city was blessed with a spacious harbor known as the Golden Horn (*horn* because it was shaped like an ox's horn, *golden* because of the wealthy cargoes that floated on its waters).

Constantine liked to call his eastern capital New Rome. Two centuries later, emperors in Constantinople still ruled the eastern part of the old Roman empire. The lands under their control included Greece, Asia Minor, Palestine, Syria, and Egypt. This empire is called the Byzantine empire after the original Greek town on Constantinople's site.

The emperor headed both church and state.

The Byzantine emperors never forgot their Roman heritage. They saw themselves as heirs to the power of Augustus Caesar. To keep up ancient tradition, a senate still met in Constantinople. In truth, the emperor's power was **absolute,** with complete, unrestrained authority to rule. In spite

of these close ties with Roman tradition, the eastern empire developed its own political and cultural identity.

Religion was closely linked to politics in Constantinople. Even before Justinian, the eastern branch of the Christian church had refused to accept the Bishop of Rome as the sole leader of the Christian faith. Emperors claimed to rule in Jesus' name and acted both as religious and political leaders of the eastern empire. The emperor was thought to be divinely inspired so that his actions could not be questioned.

The Byzantine emperors also considered themselves rightful rulers of all the lands Rome had once held. Even in the 530's and 540's, a hundred years after the plunderings of Visigoths, Vandals, and Huns, one Byzantine emperor tried to reconquer all the western lands that Rome had lost to the barbarians. The name of this ambitious and controversial Byzantine ruler was Justinian (juhs-**TIHN**-ee-uhn).

Justinian reconquered Roman lands.

Justinian became emperor in 527 and ruled until 565. According to the official court historian, Procopius (proh-**KOH**-pee-uhs), Justinian was a ruddy-cheeked man of medium height and weight. He never lost his temper and never drank too much wine. He was a conscientious ruler, working from dawn to midnight.

Procopius flattered the emperor in the official histories, but in a *Secret History,* published after Justinian's death, Procopius gave vent to other feelings. Justinian, he wrote, was "deceitful, devious, false, hypocritical, two-faced, cruel, skilled in dissembling his thought, never moved to tears by either joy or pain . . . a liar always."

Whatever the truth may be about Justinian's character, he proved to be an able ruler. He launched three ambitious projects. First, he tried to reconquer Roman lands to the west. Second, he ordered a team of Greek and Latin scholars to compile and simplify the laws. Third, he undertook a massive building program in Constantinople. His works on the city and the laws were of lasting value to civilization. His wars, however, proved to be a waste of men and money.

The campaign to reconquer the Roman empire began successfully. In 533, Justinian sent his best

180

The Byzantine Empire under Justinian

KEY
- The Byzantine empire in 528
- Areas reconquered by Justinian

0 _____ 500 Miles

Map Study

Name three major areas that Justinian reconquered. For each area, tell what group or groups his armies had to fight.

ANSWERS TO
Map Study

north central African coast; Vandals; southern Spain; Visigoths; Italy; Ostrogoths

■ BACKGROUND

Despite his short-term victories, Justinian did, in the opinion of historian Joseph Strayer, reconquer the West "not through his armies but through his law."

general, Belisarius (BEL-uh-SAIR-ee-uhs), to win back the Vandal kingdom of North Africa. Belisarius broke down the Vandal defenses and rode triumphantly into Carthage. In only a few days, the entire northern coast of Africa beyond Egypt fell under Byzantine rule.

Belisarius's next assignment was to fight the Ostrogoths in Italy. With a tiny army of only 8,000 men, the Byzantine general outmaneuvered his barbarian foes. Entering Rome in 536, he received a hero's welcome as the city's liberator. For the first time in 60 years, wrote Procopius, "Rome was again brought under the Romans."

The rejoicing, however, quickly turned to sorrow. The Ostrogoths returned and drove out the Byzantines. The Byzantines struck back. In 18 years of siege and countersiege (535–553), Rome changed hands six times.

When the Byzantines finally won control of the city in 553, the triumph was an empty one. Rome lay in ruins. Fallen statues littered its streets. No water flowed in its magnificent baths. Once home to a million people, Rome's population had dropped to a mere 40,000, nearly half of whom roamed the streets as beggars or looters. The Byzantines, who had come to save Rome, ended by destroying it.

To North Africa and Italy, Justinian added part of Spain as his final conquest. His dream to reunite Roman lands seemed to have succeeded brilliantly. After his death, however, all the conquered territory quickly passed back into barbarian hands. Lombards overran Italy. Muslim Arabs swept through North Africa and Spain. Ironically, the destruction of Rome was the one lasting result of Justinian's costly wars.

Justinian ordered a code of laws.

In the long run, Justinian's legal reforms were far more important than his conquests. Between 528 and 534, he assigned a group of legal scholars

181

■ **BACKGROUND**

The tour of Constantinople shows a city remarkable not only for its architecture but also for its dramatic location above the Golden Horn, an arm of the Bosporus.

ANSWERS TO
Map Study

Constantinople was situated where many trade routes came together, had an excellent harbor; control of the Bosporus gave it political power; city was easy to defend because nearly surrounded by water; city was a major crossroads, thus important in the spread of culture.

to an incredible task. They were to codify all Roman laws and legal opinions since the time of Hadrian 400 years earlier! If a law made in Athens in the year 220 contradicted a law made in Alexandria in 350, which law should be followed in Constantinople in 530? This was the kind of perplexing question for which Justinian sought an answer.

The result of his commission's labors was the *Corpus Juris Civilis* (Body of Civil Law), known to later ages as the Code of Justinian. It consisted of four works.

1. *The Codex Justinian* presented nearly 5,000 laws from the Roman empire that Justinian's scholars thought were still useful for Byzantium. The laws were arranged by topic.
2. *The Digest* quoted and summarized the opinions of Rome's greatest legal writers. This massive work had 50 volumes.
3. *The Institutes* was a textbook telling law students how to use the new code.
4. *The Novellae* contained laws made after 534.

Justinian died in 565, but his code lived after him. It was the basis for Byzantine law for the next 900 years. Many centuries later, France and other countries in western Europe turned to Justinian's code as a guide on legal questions concerning justice, property, marriage, and divorce. Through Justinian's code, western Europe came to know again the benefits of Roman law.

CITY T O U R
Constantinople flourished.

While the code was being compiled, Justinian undertook a city building program larger than that of any Roman emperor, including Augustus. When he finished, Constantinople was the wonder of its age. It was known throughout the Eurasian world simply as "The City."

Some 300,000 people made their permanent homes in Constantinople. There were two requirements for citizenship: membership in the Christian church and the ability to speak Greek. The streets, however, were crowded with people from all over the world.

Constantinople was as well protected as any city could be in those dangerous times. Sea walls guarded it from hostile navies. To the west, a moat and three walls blocked the only land route to the city. The outermost wall was just high enough to shield Byzantine archers. The second wall was 27 feet high, and the third was 70 feet high. It is not surprising that Constantinople withstood many foes for more than 1,000 years.

The marketplace The city's main street was the *Mesê* (MEE-zuh), or Middle Way. The tables of merchants lined the Mesê on either side. Some tables were shaded by colorful awnings. Others were set back within colonnaded walkways.

Goods from all over the world found their way here, mostly by ship. Constantinople was noted for its luxury items: spices from India; ivory and gold from Africa; honey, timber, and furs from Russia. Cork came from Spain, tin and iron from England, wine from France, and grain and wool from north of the Alps. Chinese silk reached the Mesê by camel caravan, a journey of 230 days if all went well. Encouraged by Justinian, two missionaries to China smuggled out a few silkworms and mulberry-tree seeds. The secret of silk making, guarded by the Chinese for centuries, now belonged to the Byzantines.

Map Study

What were the advantages of Constantinople's location in terms of trade, political power, defense, and the spread of culture?

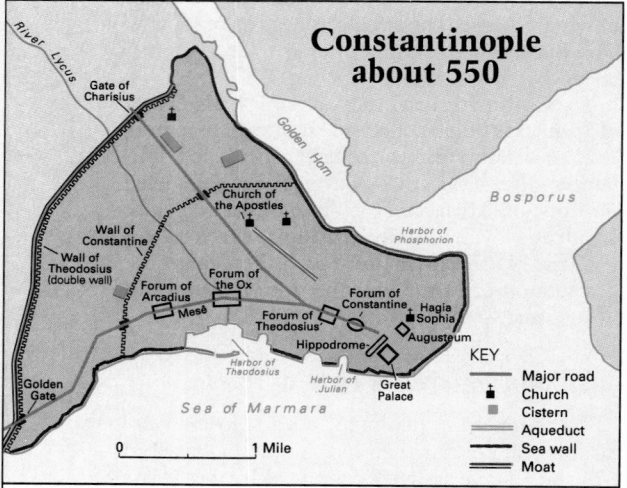

Constantinople about 550

River Lycus
Gate of Charisius
Church of the Apostles
Golden Horn
Bosporus
Harbor of Phosphorion
Wall of Constantine
Wall of Theodosius (double wall)
Forum of Arcadius
Forum of the Ox
Mesê
Forum of Theodosius
Forum of Constantine
Hagia Sophia
Augusteum
Hippodrome
Harbor of Theodosius
Harbor of Julian
Great Palace
Golden Gate
Sea of Marmara

KEY
— Major road
■ Church
▪ Cistern
═ Aqueduct
— Sea wall
═══ Moat

0   1 Mile

182

The imperial palace The palace was the center of government. Some 20,000 people worked there in the service of the emperor.

In the gardens, peacocks strutted around bubbling fountains. The most impressive fountain was made of gold in the shape of a pineapple. Wine gushed from it into a silver basin filled with pistachio nuts on which a visitor could snack.

In the throne room, a long gold path led from the entrance to the golden throne. Above the throne was a gilded tree with mechanical birds twittering on its branches. Two golden lions stood on either side of the throne, rigged to let forth mock roars. The throne itself was wide enough to seat two persons, a symbol of the emperor's partnership with Jesus. Anyone who approached the throne had to follow certain procedures. Each person was expected to lie prone three times, nose down and hands forward. Guests were allowed to kiss the emperor's toes or fingertips. The emperor, however, stared ahead, too lordly to speak.

Hagia Sophia Across from the imperial palace stood one of the architectural wonders of the world—the great cathedral called Hagia Sophia (HAY-ee-uh soh-FEE-uh). It was the greatest monument of Byzantine Christianity, a symbol of the Christian city.

Empress Theodora

Voice from the Past | A Question of Courage

In 532, early in Justinian's reign, a great riot broke out in Constantinople. It began as a fight between the Blues and the Greens, rival teams in the city's popular chariot races. It quickly became a full-scale revolt. The crowd burned much of the city and proclaimed a new emperor. Justinian hid in the palace. With him was his beautiful wife, Theodora, a former actress who had spent her girlhood in the circus. Procopius tells of the debate that went on within the palace while the mob raged through the city:

Now the emperor and his court were deliberating whether it would be better to remain or to flee in the ships. And many opinions were expressed on both sides. And the Empress Theodora also spoke as follows: "As to the belief that a woman should not be daring among men or assert herself boldly, I consider the present crisis does not allow us to debate that. My opinion is that now is a poor time for flight, even though it bring safety. For any man who has seen the light of day will also die, but one who has been an emperor cannot endure to be a fugitive. If now you wish to go, Emperor, nothing prevents you. There is the sea, there are the steps to the boats. But take care that after you are safe, you do not find that you would gladly exchange that safety for death. For my part, I like the old saying that the empire is a fine burial cloth." When the queen had spoken thus, all were filled with boldness and began to consider how they might defend themselves from their enemies.

[Made brave by Theodora's speech, Justinian remained in the city, gave orders for his troops to crush the mob, and restored order.]

1. What two courses of action were the emperor and his court considering?
2. (a) What does Theodora say about whether or not a woman should speak out? (b) What does this statement suggest was the usual opinion about women at the time?
3. (a) What course of action does Theodora support? (b) What does she say about the risk of death? (c) What does she warn the emperor might happen if he flees?
4. How do you interpret the proverb, "The empire is a fine burial cloth"?

183

■ BACKGROUND
The palace had a purple bedchamber where all children of the imperial family were born. In their first days of life, everything they saw—walls, carpets, ceilings—was colored purple. "Born to the purple" is still a phrase meaning royal birth.

ANSWERS TO
Voice from the Past

1. to remain or flee in ships
2. (a) usually not considered appropriate, but under the circumstances, not worth debating (b) not highly valued
3. (a) to stay and fight back (b) It is preferable to becoming a fugitive. (c) He might want to trade his safety as a fugitive for death.
4. To die while defending the empire is reward enough to suffer the pain of death.

■ **BACKGROUND**

In 529, Justinian closed the Academy in Athens, which had been founded originally by Plato.

■ **DISCUSSION**

Many monks earned their livings by making icons for sale. Some of the loudest and strongest protest to the iconoclasts came from the monasteries. Why do students think this came about?

The great dome of Hagia Sophia was a marvel of engineering. The building has been a Christian church, a Muslim mosque, and a museum.

Hagia Sophia's giant dome rose 180 feet from the floor, an amazing engineering feat. Four acres of gold mosaic tiles covered the dome and the surrounding vaults and arches. The floors, walls, and columns gleamed with every imaginable shade of polished marble—red, white, purple, blue, green, and black. Sunlight poured in the dome's 40 windows by day. At night, light blazed from huge silver candelabra hanging on long chains.

184

One of the greatest wonders of Hagia Sophia was a magnificent table for preparing the Christian ceremony of Communion. For the making of this table, Justinian ordered pearls and sapphires ground into a rich powder and mixed with molten gold and silver. This extravagant mixture was then poured into a mold for the table.

The university Like several other cities in the Roman empire, Constantinople had a university. Its teachers emphasized the arts of writing and speaking well. The professors included ten Latin grammarians, ten Greek grammarians, three orators, two law professors, and several philosophers. (In later years, Latin fell out of use in Constantinople, and only Greek was spoken at the university.) The university served as a training ground for civil servants and imperial administrators.

Scholars in Constantinople copied the greatest works of the ancient writers—Homer, Plato, Archimedes, Euclid, Livy, Virgil, and others. Had the Byzantines not preserved these works, many would have been lost forever.

Education for both men and women was widespread among the upper classes in the Byzantine empire. Only a few women attended the university, but both boys and girls studied at home with tutors. The learned women of Constantinople included writers, philosophers, and at least one doctor.

The Hippodrome Like Rome's Colosseum, the Hippodrome in Constantinople was the site of extravagant and often bloody scenes for public view. The most important sports events were the chariot races, for which the Hippodrome's 60,000 seats were usually filled.

The Church split into two branches.

Just as the Greeks of Athens spent hours debating politics, the Greeks of Constantinople discussed religion. A shoemaker or a rug seller might argue over the nature of God and Jesus. In the marketplace, **icons** were sold beside fruit and vegetables. Icons are small art objects that depict Jesus, Mary, or a Christian saint.

At one point, conflict over icons had weakened and almost destroyed the Byzantine empire. In the 700's, several emperors tried to end the use of icons in churches. The emperors charged that many people prayed to the icons as if they were idols. Riots and bloody fights broke out between

ANSWERS TO
Section Review 1

Define:
(a) complete, unrestrained
(b) small art objects that depict Christian figures
(c) icon smasher (d) to place outside the church
(e) person whose ideas are incorrect in the opinion of a church (f) bishop of Constantinople

Identify:
(a) Rome's first Christian emperor and founder of Constantinople (b) eastern capital of Roman empire built at Byzantium (c) gateway between Sea of Mar-

(continued)

⌊184

people who wanted to keep the icons in churches and the icon smashers, or **iconoclasts.**

The pope in Rome took the side of those who supported the icons. He **excommunicated** the Byzantine emperor. (That is, the pope declared that the emperor was outside the church, cut off from all Christians.)

Eventually, the Byzantine church again accepted icons, and the iconoclasts were labeled **heretics.** (A heretic is a person whose ideas are incorrect, in the opinion of the Church.)

The most lasting result of the controversy was an increase in bad feeling between Christians in Rome and Constantinople. Over the centuries, differences had developed between Byzantine Christians and the Christians of western Europe. For example, priests in the eastern empire conducted services in the local languages of their members—Greek, Coptic, Ethiopian, or Russian. Priests in western Europe conducted services only in Latin. Byzantine priests were allowed to marry, but Roman priests could not do so by church law.

Most important, the pope in Rome claimed to be supreme head of the Christian church, independent of any king or emperor. The bishop of Constantinople was known as the **patriarch** (PAY-tree-ARK). He accepted the authority of the Byzantine emperor. The pope in Rome claimed to be the leader of all Christians everywhere. The patriarchs, however, refused to accept the pope as their superior.

The break between Rome and Constantinople became final in 1054. That year, the pope and the patriarch excommunicated each other. The western branch of the Christian Church became known as the Roman Catholic Church. (*Catholic* comes from a Latin word meaning "universal.") The eastern branch became known as the Eastern Orthodox Church. (*Orthodox* comes from two Greek words meaning "correct belief.") Thus, the political break between the eastern and western parts of the old Roman empire became a religious break as well.

Byzantium faced many enemies.

Although Constantinople remained a rich and powerful city for hundreds of years, the Byzantine empire suffered many setbacks and dangers. The history of the empire after 565 was marked by a bewildering series of street riots, religious quarrels, palace intrigues, and foreign dangers. Many times, the empire appeared to be on the verge of collapse. Each time, it fought off its enemies and sprang back to renewed life only to be threatened by another crisis.

The first long crisis began with Justinian's death in 565. Plague swept through the empire, weakening its armies. Meanwhile, the Lombards moved into Italy and won much of the land Justinian had reconquered there. The Avars, a Hun-like people, invaded the Balkan peninsula (Greece and Macedon). To the east, the Persians threatened to pounce on their ancient foes, the Greeks. Then armies of Arabs, inspired by the prophet Muhammad, burst forth from the Arabian desert and threatened the Byzantine empire's very survival.

Section REVIEW 1

Define: (a) absolute, (b) icon, (c) iconoclast, (d) excommunicate, (e) heretic, (f) patriarch
Identify: (a) Constantine, (b) Constantinople, (c) Bosporus, (d) Justinian, (e) Procopius, (f) Belisarius, (g) Theodora, (h) Hagia Sophia, (i) Balkan peninsula, (j) Eastern Orthodox Church, (k) Roman Catholic Church
Answer:
1. (a) Why was Constantinople's harbor called the Golden Horn? (b) How did activities on the Mesê support this name?
2. What two sources did Byzantine emperors claim for their power to rule?
3. (a) What were Justinian's military goals? (b) Did he succeed? Explain.
4. (a) What was the original value of Justinian's Code? (b) What was its lasting value to Western civilization?
5. (a) What disagreements arose between the Christian Church of Rome and that of Constantinople? (b) What was the result of those disagreements?

Critical Thinking
6. What factors made Constantinople a great city? (Consider geographic, historic, and cultural influences.)
7. If you were writing a history of the Byzantine empire, how would you rate Justinian as an emperor?

185

ANSWERS TO (continued)
mara and the Black Sea
(d) Roman emperor who codified laws and undertook a massive building program in Constantinople (e) court historian under Justinian (f) general who temporarily recaptured Roman lands (g) wife of Justinian (h) cathedral in Constantinople (i) where Greece and Macedon are located (j) eastern branch of Christian Church (k) western branch of Christian Church
Answer:
1. (a) horn because of its shape; golden because of the wealthy cargoes that floated on its waters (b) Merchants' tables lined it on both sides.
2. political powers of Roman ruler and religious power as new apostles of Jesus
3. (a) reconquer Roman lands to the west (b) only temporarily, because after his death lands were soon lost again to barbarians
4. (a) codified laws and settled contradictions; basis of Byzantine law for 900 years (b) Western Europe came to know again benefits of Roman law.
5. (a) disagreements over use of icons, language in which services were conducted, behavior of priests, superiority of pope (b) east and west split into two hostile branches
6. geographic: favorable location for trade; historic: shift from west gave opportunity for new vitality; cultural: blending of Greek and Roman traditions with the added feature of Christianity
7. Answers should include consideration of his immediate achievements as well as his long-term impact.

■ **BACKGROUND**

Muhammad is said to have spent one month each year meditating in the desert. The Black Stone is said to have fallen from heaven. There is some speculation that it was, in fact, a meteorite.

A new faith spread from Arabia. 2

In the mid-600's, Arab victories swept away enormous chunks of the Byzantine empire, including Palestine, Syria, Egypt, North Africa, and Spain. By 650, only Greece and Asia Minor remained to the Byzantines.

The Arabs threatened to take even Constantinople itself. Every year from 673 to 678, their warships lay outside the great sea wall around Constantinople. What saved the Byzantines was a terrifying weapon that no one else possessed—"Greek fire." Greek fire was a mixture of chemicals (probably naphtha, sulphur, and saltpeter) that the Byzantines squirted through copper tubes at enemy ships. The mixture burst into flames on contact with the Arab ships, turning them into deathtraps. It even burned on the surface of the water.

Who were these Arabs who appeared so suddenly and threatened Constantinople so fiercely? Their story begins in the late 500's. The century in which Justinian lived was also the century in which the prophet Muhammad was born in Arabia.

Arab culture arose in the desert.

The Arabian peninsula stretches 1,400 miles north to south along the Red Sea, the sea that separates Arabia from Africa. The peninsula measures 1,250 miles from east to west at its southern edge. To the traveler, its deserts seem to stretch on forever under a blue sky and merciless sun.

The nomads who lived on this desert were called Bedouin (**BEHD**-oo-ihn). They slept in tents made from camels' hide and drank camel milk. Mounted on camels, Bedouin traveled between widely scattered oases and trading centers. During much of the year, Bedouin routinely raided one another's camps and caravans. However, certain times were considered holy, for making pilgrimages to a sacred shrine in Mecca.

Mecca was the largest of several towns near the western coast of Arabia. A few generations earlier, these town dwellers had themselves been Bedouin, but by the late 500's, they had left the Bedouin life behind. The leading Meccans were wealthy merchants. Travelers to Mecca brought both goods and ideas from the surrounding Roman, Byzantine, and Persian empires.

Before Muhammad, the Bedouins and the townspeople worshiped hundreds of gods and spirits. Spirits called *jinn* were thought to reside in rocks and other natural objects. Mecca was the home of the most sacred of these rocks. The Black Stone of Mecca was (and still is) embedded within the wall of a shrine called the Kaaba (**KAH**-uh-buh), which in Arabic means "cube." Besides the Black Stone, the Kaaba contained idols representing 360 gods, including one deity called Allah.

This shrine made Mecca an important religious center. Pilgrims flocked to it during the holy months. In this city, around the year 570, Muhammad was born.

Muhammad taught monotheism.

Muhammad was born into a minor branch of a powerful Meccan family. Orphaned at the age of six, the boy was raised by his grandfather and uncle. He received little schooling and probably never learned to read or write. (Even in well-to-do Arabian families, literacy was unusual.) Muhammad became a trader and business manager for Khadya (**KAHD**-yuh), a wealthy businesswoman 15 years older than he. When Muhammad was 25, he and Khadya married. It was both a good marriage and a good business partnership.

Muhammad had traveled to Syria as Khadya's business agent. There he may have talked with Byzantine Christians and learned about their religion. Communities of Jews were settled in the Arab towns. Both groups were monotheists. A few Arab holy men, known as *hanifs*, had already turned to the worship of one god.

Muhammad took great interest in religion and often spent time alone in prayer and meditation. At the age of 40, Muhammad's life was changed overnight by a vision that came to him while he meditated in a cave outside Mecca. His description was recorded by a follower:

While I was asleep, with a coverlet of silk brocade whereon was some writing, the angel Gabriel appeared to me and said, "Read!" I said, "I do not read." He pressed me with the coverlets so tightly that I thought it was death. Then he let me go, and said, "Read!" ... So I read aloud, and he departed from me at last ... I went forth until, when I was midway on the mountain, I heard a voice from heaven saying, "O Muhammad! Thou art the messenger of God, and I am Gabriel."

Muhammad had other visions in which the angel Gabriel again appeared with messages from Allah (the Arabic word for *God*). Who was Allah? Muhammad believed the messages came from the same God worshiped by Christians and Jews. After much soul searching, Muhammad finally became convinced that he was indeed the last and greatest of the prophets. Khadya and several close friends and relatives were his first followers.

By 613, Muhammad began to preach publicly in Mecca. At first, he had little success. Many Meccans thought his revolutionary ideas were bad for business. They feared that Mecca would lose its position as a pilgrimage center if people accepted Muhammad's beliefs. Some of his followers were stoned in the streets.

The Hegira marked a turning point.

Facing such hostility, Muhammad decided to leave Mecca. In 622, he fled to the town of Medina (muh-DEE-nuh), taking a little band of followers with him. This escape became known as the **Hegira** (hih-JYE-ruh), Arabic for "flight."

The Hegira marked a turning point for Muhammad. In Medina, he attracted many devoted followers. He also won great political influence. Muhammad's new religion became known as *Islam*, which means "surrender to God." Believers became known as *Muslims*, "the surrendering ones." On the Muslim calendar, the year of the Hegira became the year 1, the first year of the Islamic era.

From Medina, Muhammad led raids against Meccan caravans. Later, his armies completely defeated the Meccans. Such victories increased the prestige of Islam. Within ten years, almost all Bedouin had accepted Islam as their faith. In 630, the prophet and 10,000 followers entered Mecca in triumph. Muhammad went to the Kaaba and exultantly declared, "Truth has come and falsehood has vanished." Then, he destroyed the idols in the Kaaba, allowing only the Black Stone to remain. Muhammad died only two years later at the age of 62.

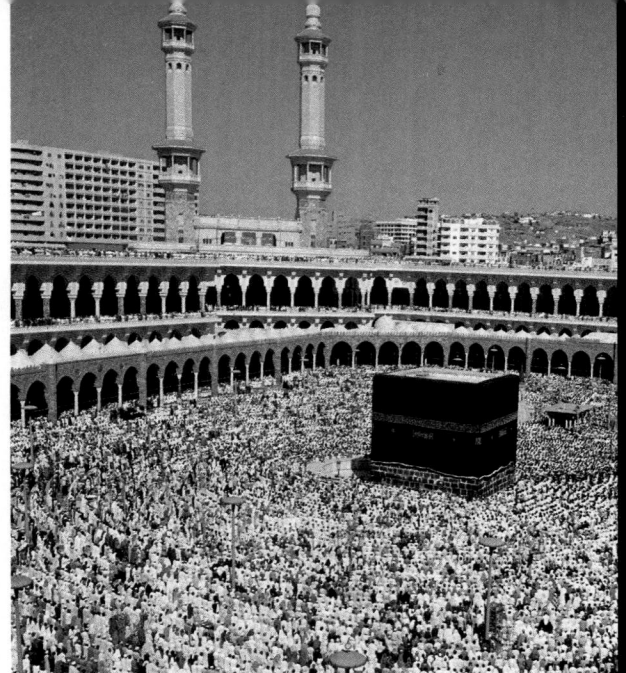

Pilgrims surround the Kaaba in Mecca. The towers in the background are minarets from which muezzins call Muslims to prayer.

The Koran is Islam's holy book.

While Muhammad lived, his followers had listened to his prayers and teachings. The Arabs had a long tradition of oral poetry, and they memorized and recited his words over and over. Muslims who were literate wrote them on scraps of parchment and even on palm leaves. Soon after the prophet's death, a new leader named Abu-Bakr ordered all the words of Muhammad to be gathered into a book. This book is the Koran (koh-RAHN), the holy book of Islam.

The Koran is about the same length as the Christians' New Testament. Its 114 *suras* (chapters) are arranged according to length, not subject. The longest sura comes first, and the shortest comes last.

The Koran was written in Arabic, and only the Arabic version was considered by Muslims to be the true word of God. Only Arabic could be used in worship. Because of this rule, the Arabic language spread widely in the Middle East and North Africa. Wherever Islamic conquerors carried the Koran, Arabic became the language of scholars and poets.

187

SECTION 2 Objectives and Teaching Strategies

OBJECTIVE 1. Describe the career of the prophet Muhammad.

Teaching Strategy: *Discussing History: The Prophet Muhammad* (page 178d)

OBJECTIVE 2. Identify the Five Pillars of Islam, and explain the significance of the Kaaba.

Teaching Strategy: *Teaching with Pictures: The Kaaba* (page 178d)

OBJECTIVE 3. Trace the spread of Islam.

Teaching Strategy: *Geography in History: The Spread of Islam* (page 178d)

■ DISCUSSION

Why might it be difficult for a self-proclaimed prophet to win converts in his own city? (Familiarity might make faith and belief impossible.)

SECTION 2 Resources

GEOGRAPHY
■ Transparencies 26, 29

REINFORCEMENT
■ Independent Practice 8.2

ENRICHMENT
■ Voices from the Past 8.2

ASSESSMENT
■ Section Quiz 8.2

■ DISCUSSION

Even today, women are rarely seen in mosques. Ask students what benefits, if any, Islam offers women.

■ BACKGROUND

The Arabs were masters of desert warfare, bewildering the enemy with their swift maneuvers, wheeling their camels and horses this way and that. Some historians have compared Arab mastery of the desert to British mastery of the sea.

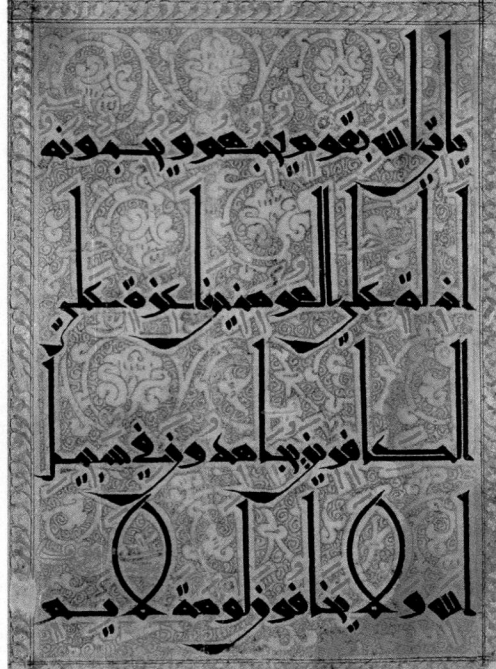

Because their religious art could show no figures of people or animals, Muslims decorated copies of the Koran with fine calligraphy.

The rules of Islam regulated life.

To be a Muslim was both simple and demanding. Muhammad's teachings set forth strict guidelines for right living. Every believer was expected to carry out five duties. These duties were known as the Five Pillars of Islam.

1. *Faith* To become a Muslim, a person had to make a statement of faith: "I testify there is no god but God, and Muhammad is His Prophet."
2. *Prayer* Every day, sleeping Muslims awoke at dawn to the sound of a *muezzin* (myoo-EZ-uhn), or crier, calling them to prayer. Their first morning chore was to purify themselves for prayer. They washed their hands and arms up to the elbow, their feet up to the ankles. They used water if it was available, but the Bedouin of the desert washed themselves with sand. Muslims were required to pray five times daily. Each time, they removed their shoes, turned to face the holy city of Mecca, lay flat on the ground, and recited a formal prayer either silently or in a low voice.

188

3. *Alms* Muhammad strictly commanded the faithful to give a portion of their wealth as alms to help the needy.
4. *Fasting* For one full month—the holy month of Ramadan (RAM-uh-DAHN)—Muslims were to eat nothing and drink nothing between sunrise and sunset. Only after sunset could families joyfully sit down together for a meal.
5. *Pilgrimage* Once in a lifetime, any Muslim who could afford the journey was expected to make a pilgrimage to Mecca. For many, this involved a grueling journey across mountains, deserts, and seas.

Along with the Five Pillars, the Koran also established other customs, morals, and laws for Islamic society. Believers were not to eat ham or pork. Believers were forbidden to drink wine or other intoxicating beverages. A man was allowed to marry as many as four wives, but only if he could support them all equally well. Marriage with unbelievers was forbidden.

Friday afternoon was set aside for communal worship and prayer. Muslims gathered in the local **mosque,** or Muslim temple, and prayed in unison, facing Mecca. One person led the prayers in the mosque, but he was not a priest in the Christian sense. Unlike many other religions, Islam had no formal priesthood. Women were sometimes prayer leaders for other women, but few women attended services in a mosque. In Islamic society, women and men led very separate lives.

Muhammad taught that there would be a Day of Judgment, at which time those who followed Islam's law would be rewarded. They would be welcomed into paradise, described by the Koran as a fabulous garden. There believers would bask forever, dressed in silk and drinking from rivers of milk and honey. Unbelievers and Muslims who shirked their religious duties faced eternal punishment. On the Day of Judgment, said the Koran, they would be cast into hell to wear shoes of fire, eat filth, and drink boiling water forever.

Islam expanded east and west.

In 732, exactly 100 years after Muhammad's death, Muslim armies from Spain crossed the Pyrenees into southwestern France. There, at the Battle of Tours, they were defeated by a Christian army commanded by the Frankish leader, Charles

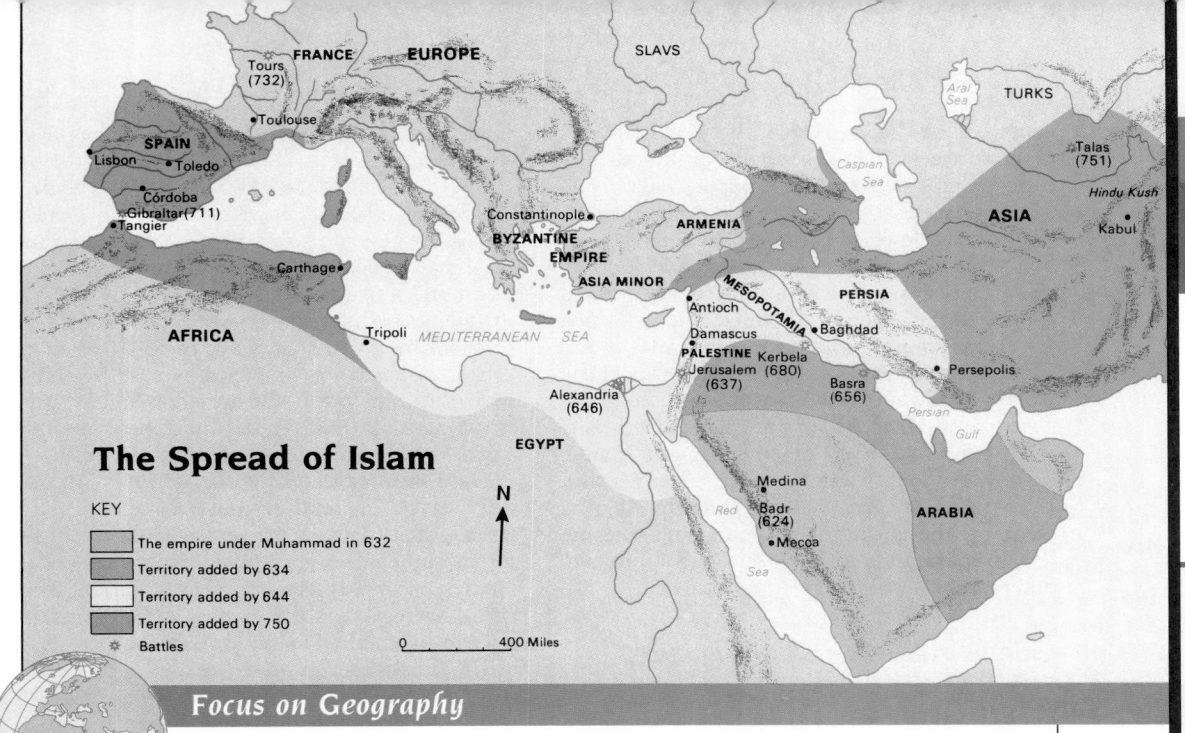

The Spread of Islam

KEY

	The empire under Muhammad in 632
	Territory added by 634
	Territory added by 644
	Territory added by 750
✵	Battles

N

0   400 Miles

Focus on Geography

Geographic Skills

1. By about how many miles had Islam spread west from Jerusalem by 644? By 711?
2. By what year had the Muslims won control of each of the following cities? (a) Mecca (b) Alexandria (c) Jerusalem (d) Gibraltar (e) Talas
3. Where was the advance of Muslim armies stopped in western Europe?
4. What prevented the Muslim conquest of Asia Minor at this time?

Geographic Theme: Movement

5. What geographic factors may have hastened the Muslim conquest of the lands shown?

ANSWERS TO
Focus on Geography

1. 1,200 miles; 2,200 miles
2. (a) 632 (b) 646 (c) 637 (d) 711 (e) 751
3. Tours
4. the Byzantine empire
5. The area is relatively flat and open.

Martel. As the crow flies, the Muslims were then 2,500 miles from Mecca. Their advance into Europe was stopped at Tours.

By 732, Muslim Arabs controlled the Iberian peninsula (Spain and Portugal), the land of the Carthaginians (North Africa), the land of the ancient pharaohs (Egypt), the holy land of the Jews and Christians (Palestine), the land of the ancient Babylonians (Mesopotamia), the land of the once great Persian empire, the land of northwestern India, and of course their own vast land, Arabia.

Reasons for conquest How did they do it, and why? Several factors help explain the blinding speed with which Muslim armies cut down their foes and spread their faith from India to Spain.

First, the Arabs were passionate in their new faith. The Koran taught that wars fought for God were just. A warrior killed in a **jihad** (jih-HAHD),

or holy war, was promised immediate entry into paradise. With this belief, Muslims rushed fearlessly into battle.

Second, the arid Arabian peninsula was badly overpopulated in the 600's. Arab armies were filled with warriors eager to move into more bountiful lands. As new converts accepted Islam, they swelled its armies still more.

Third, resistance was weak. The Byzantine and Persian empires had been fighting each other for centuries. Now they were both exhausted.

Results of conquest The Arabs proved tolerant rulers. They offered their subjects three choices: convert to Islam, pay a reasonable tax, or die. The first two choices were by far the most popular.

As Islam spread, Muslim society changed. Muhammad had taught that all Muslims were equal in the eyes of God. However, as Arab armies

189

■ **BACKGROUND**

In the year-long unsuccessful siege of Constantinople, some 150,000 of 180,000 Arabs lost their lives.

■ **DISCUSSION**

According to tradition, the Arab general who led the invasion of Spain ordered his captains to burn the boats in which the army had come. Then he told his troops that their only hope for life lay in victory. Why might the troops have been prepared to die? (honor in dying for *jihad*)

conquered new lands, people who were not Arabs began to accept Islam. Gradually, Islamic society came to have two classes: an upper class of Arab Muslims and a second class of non-Arab Muslims.

Christians, Jews, and Zoroastrians ranked below both Muslim groups. These groups paid a tax to avoid converting to Islam. (Indeed, their taxes supported the empire.) All three groups formed important communities within the cities of the Islamic empire. At least in the early years of the empire, Muslims treated both Jews and Christians with respect because they were also monotheists.

The building of an empire changed Islamic society. No longer was everyone under Muslim rule an Arab or even a believer in Islam. As time went by, the lands under Islamic rule became less a community of believers and more like other empires of history.

Caliphs ruled the Islamic empire.

In Muhammad's last years, he had been a political ruler as well as a religious leader. The leaders who followed him were called **caliphs** (KAY-lihfs), meaning "successors to the prophet." They too had both political and religious power.

The orthodox caliphate (632–661) The first four caliphs were men who had known Muhammad personally, either as friends or relatives.

Under their leadership, Islam's wars of conquest were launched.

The first caliph was Abu-Bakr, who ordered the writing of the Koran. The second was Omar, Islam's greatest conqueror. In 636, Syria fell before his fierce Bedouin warriors. Omar also gained Egypt and most of Persia.

Violence plagued the caliphs. Omar was stabbed to death by a Christian slave in 644. The next caliph, Uthman, was murdered by rebel Muslims in 656. Ali, the last of the orthodox caliphs, was assassinated in 661. These murders sowed the seeds for civil war and splits within Islam.

The Umayyad caliphate (661–750) With the death of Ali, the office of caliph passed to a new family, the Umayyads (oo-MYE-yads). In their rise to power, however, the Umayyads killed a rival, Husayn, who was Muhammad's grandson. The sin of having killed the prophet's grandson was later to haunt the Umayyad rulers.

The Umayyads continued the wars of conquest. It was under their rule that Arab fleets attacked Constantinople, but their hopes were thwarted by Greek fire. The Umayyad caliphs had much greater success elsewhere. Their armies conquered North Africa and converted the Berber tribes there to Islam. The fierce Berbers then helped the Arabs invade Spain in 711. By 718, Muslim armies had conquered Spain. From Spain, the forces of Islam

DAILY LIFE ▶ *Prayer Rugs*

The one piece of art that every Muslim owned was a small, wonderfully patterned carpet called a prayer rug. On this rug the worshiper knelt five times a day to pray. For Persians and Turks, carpet making was both an industry and an art form. A skilled weaver could tie knots at the rate of 900 per hour. Even so, the finest rugs were so densely knotted that an hour's work produced less than three square inches of rug. Ordinary rugs came in many elaborate designs, but prayer rugs followed a particular pattern. Each had a pointed arch in the middle, representing the prayer niche in a mosque. Woven into the border of each rug was a design of flowers, leaves, and vines. Early Muslims never created pictures of Muhammad or any other human or animal form in their religious art. Such pictures were thought to be an offense to God, who alone can create a living creature. Therefore, weavers used only abstract patterns.

190

swept into France but were turned back at Tours in 732. To the east, meanwhile, other Arab armies pushed the borders of the empire out to the Indus River valley. From Asia across Africa into Europe, the Islamic empire stretched over 5,000 miles—about 2,000 miles farther than the distance across the continental United States.

The Umayyads were able rulers and administered their vast empire carefully. However, many Muslims never forgave the death of Husayn. Other Muslims called the luxury of the Umayyad royal court sinful. A rebellion broke out against the Umayyads. In 750, the last Umayyad caliph was killed, and so were 80 other members of the family. The only survivor of the Umayyad family escaped to Spain. There he established his own separate Islamic kingdom that was to become the center of a rich civilization.

The Abbasid caliphate (750–1055) The leader of the revolt against the Umayyads was descended from Abbas, an uncle of Muhammad. The new rulers called themselves the Abbasid (uh-BAS-ihd) dynasty, emphasizing the link to the prophet.

The greatest support for the Abbasids came from Persia. Most Persians had accepted Islam. As converts, however, they were still second-class citizens under the Umayyads. With Persia's own proud history of empire, Persians resented the Arab ruling class. The Abbasids promised a return to the early Islamic idea of equality among believers. Yet going back to the past was impossible. Islam and its followers had changed irrevocably in the years since Muhammad's death.

Religious differences split Islam.

By the time of the Abbasids, Islam was no longer a united religion. The killing of Husayn, which helped cause the fall of the Umayyads, also had religious consequences. Muslims who believed that Husayn had been the rightful caliph became known as Shi'ites (SHEE-ytes). The movement began as a political split, but it became a religious one as well. The Shi'ites were especially strong in what is now Iraq.

Shi'ites denied the authority of the Umayyad caliphs and helped the Abbasids win power. The Abbasids, however, refused to tolerate the Shi'ites and sometimes persecuted them. Over the years, hostility increased between the Shi'ites and the Sunni (or orthodox) Muslims.

CITY TOUR

Baghdad was a wealthy city.

Because Persia was the base of Abbasid strength, the Abbasids moved their capital eastward, closer to the heart of the old Persian empire. On the western bank of the Tigris River, they built the city of Baghdad (BAG-dad), as opulent and glittering as Constantinople. Baghdad became the center of Muslim civilization during its golden age.

The Round city Picture three round walls, one inside the other, encircling a perfectly round city. This was Baghdad. At the very center of the inner circle was the famous Green Dome of the caliph's palace. Four broad avenues thrust into the heart of Baghdad, carving the city into four equal quarters. Everything in the city revolved around the caliph's palace.

Under the Green Dome was a grand throne room. There the caliph awaited his visitors behind an ornate curtain, which was drawn with a flourish. Standing behind the caliph's throne was a grim-faced soldier with a sword always drawn and sharpened. Thus, a visitor who displeased the caliph could be beheaded on the spot.

Wealth from trade Between the middle wall and the palace wall lay Baghdad's main business district. Along the four major avenues, merchants tempted passersby with Arabian perfumes, Syrian glassware, Chinese silks, and Indian silver and rubies. There were also swords from Russia, leather goods from Spain, and slaves from Africa and Scandinavia.

By the year 1000, perhaps 100,000 people lived in Baghdad. Their wealth was the result of their city's location. The chief caravan routes from India and China passed through Baghdad. Ships from Arabia, India, and Africa came to the city too. They sailed from the Persian Gulf up the Tigris River to Baghdad's wharves.

To encourage the flow of trade, Muslim money changers set up banks in cities throughout their far-flung empire. Banks offered letters of credit to merchants. Such a letter of credit was called a *sakk*. A merchant with a sakk from a bank in Baghdad could exchange it for cash at a bank in Mecca or in any other major city within the empire. In Europe, the word *sakk* was pronounced "check." Thus the practice of using checks dates back to the Islamic empire.

191

■ BACKGROUND

Founded in 762, Baghdad became the greatest Muslim city and possibly the largest in the world. Established as a capital, Baghdad also became a center of learning and trade. Located on the Tigris River, it was for a time the western end of the Great Silk Road linking the Middle East and China.

■ **BACKGROUND**

Many of the names we use for Arabs are Europeanized corruptions. The Arab form for Rhazes, for example, is ar-Razi; for Avicenna, Ibn Sina.

Muslim astronomers studied the stars at the royal observatory.

Arts and sciences flourished.

Under the Abbasids, the Islamic empire enjoyed a brief but brilliant golden age in arts and sciences. The Islamic empire reached the height of its power and prosperity in the reign of Harun al-Rashid (hah-**ROON** ul-rah-**SHEED**), who ruled from 786 to 809.

Like Hellenistic civilization, Islamic culture was enriched by many groups. The empire included a rich blend of cultures. Christians, Jews, and Zoroastrians played a large part in the empire's intellectual achievements. Yet the Islamic faith and the Arabic language were the bonds that held the empire together. Arabic became the language of scholarship for all who lived within the empire, much as Latin had been for the Romans and as Greek was for the Byzantines.

Islamic science Science thrived in the Islamic empire as it had in Hellenistic times. Scholars were inspired by ancient Greek sources—the ideas of Aristotle and Plato, the geometry of Euclid, and the medical knowledge of Galen. Manuscripts from many lands were brought back to Baghdad's House of Wisdom, a huge library where scholars translated Greek texts into Arabic. After mastering the Greek sources, Muslim scientists went on to make their own discoveries and inventions. These were some of their most notable works:

First chemical laboratories The first chemists to work in laboratories were Islamic alchemists (**AL**-kuh-mihsts), who tried to turn ordinary metals into gold. It was an impossible task, but as they worked, alchemists found ways to separate one chemical compound from another.

Treatment of disease The greatest names in Islamic medicine were Rhazes (rah-**ZEES**), and Avicenna (**AV**-ih-**SEN**-uh). Rhazes (850–923) wrote more than 100 treatises on medicine. The most famous of these told doctors how to diagnose smallpox and treat it before the patient's condition became hopeless. Avicenna (980–1037) wrote a five-volume encyclopedia that guided doctors of Europe and Southwest Asia for six centuries. Islamic doctors also excelled in the preparation of medicines.

Use of the astrolabe First used by ancient Greeks, the **astrolabe** was rediscovered and improved by Islamic astronomers. A sea captain or caravan leader adjusted the pointer on its brass disk to chart the position of a star, which is the most reliable way to find one's position on Earth.

Mathematics One of Islam's many mathematical wizards was named Al-Khwarizmi (al-**KWAH**-rihz-**MEE**). He wrote a textbook in the 800's explaining "the art of bringing together unknowns to match a known quantity." He called this technique *al-jabr*. We call it algebra.

Without the concept of zero, higher mathematics is almost impossible. Neither the Greeks nor Romans had a zero in their number system. The Hindus of India first used a number system based on sets of ten and a symbol for zero. The Muslims adopted the system, and from them it spread to western Europe. We therefore speak today of using Arabic numerals.

Islamic literature The science and mathematics of Islam can be appreciated by people of any culture. However, only people who understand Arabic can fully appreciate its literature. The Arabs considered poetry their greatest art. The thousands of poems created during Islam's golden age were meant to be sung and recited aloud in Arabic. Most often, poets sang of war or of romantic love. The goal of the Arab poets was to compress as much meaning and eloquence as possible into very few words.

Footnote to History

The alchemists' name for any distilled substance was *alkuhl,* from which comes our word *alcohol.*

192

ANSWERS TO

Section Review 2

Define:

(a) Muhammad's flight from Mecca (b) Muslim temple (c) holy war (d) political and religious leader who followed Muhammad (e) person who tried to turn ordinary metals into gold (f) device used to chart the positions of a star

Identify:

(a) peninsula along the Red Sea (b) desert nomads (c) capital of Islam (d) shrine housing the Black

(continued)

Cause and Effect
EXPANSION OF ISLAM

Causes

Religious zeal and belief in jihad
Overpopulation of Arabian Peninsula
Desire for new lands and wealth
Weakness of Byzantine and
Persian empires

EXPANSION OF ISLAM

Conquests by Islamic empire
Spread of Islamic beliefs

Effects

Arabic spoken throughout empire
Spread of Islamic civilization
Preservation of ancient knowledge
by Islamic scholars
Arab control of trade routes
Split between Shi'ite and Sunni Muslims

Among the Islamic writers was the Persian poet and astronomer, Omar Khayyám (kye-**AHM**). He lived and wrote around 1100, as Islam's golden age was beginning to fade. Omar Khayyám is best known for a collection of four-line poems called the *Rubáiyát* (**ROO**-be-aht). This famous stanza shows how the poet celebrated the fleeting pleasures of life:

A Book of Verses underneath the Bough,
A Jug of Wine, a Loaf of Bread—and Thou
Beside me singing in the Wilderness—
Oh, Wilderness were Paradise enow!

Islamic writers produced a great variety of literature. Arabs had a strong tradition of storytelling. For example, the work known in English as *The Arabian Nights* is a collection of folktales that includes the tale of Aladdin's magic lamp and the stories of Sinbad the Sailor. Islamic

scholars also filled volumes on history, geography, law, philosophy, and religion. To devout Muslims, of course, the Koran remains the supreme achievement of Islamic literature.

Islamic architecture Throughout their empire, the Muslims built beautiful mosques. The greatest of these buildings stood in Jerusalem. In 691, a caliph ordered a mosque built over the rock from which Muhammad was believed to have ascended into paradise—the rock that Byzantines had once used for a garbage dump. This mosque became known as the Dome of the Rock because its golden dome was its most striking and beautiful feature. The dome stands 70 feet above the sacred rock. Circling around the dome are bands of black inscribed with a swirling golden script. It is the Arabic script with verses from the Koran.

Below the dome, framed by a circle of marble columns, is the sacred rock itself. Muslim worshipers cannot walk on it—not until the Day of Judgment, when they expect saved souls to be brought to this spot and lifted to paradise. Worshipers spread their prayer rugs at the very edge of the walled-off rock and lie down to pray facing, as always, toward Mecca.

Section REVIEW 2

Define: (a) Hegira, (b) mosque, (c) jihad, (d) caliph, (e) alchemist, (e) astrolabe
Identify: (a) Arabia, (b) Bedouin, (c) Mecca, (d) Kaaba, (e) Muhammad, (f) Allah, (g) Khadya, (h) Medina, (i) Muslims, (j) Islam, (k) Koran, (l) Hegira, (m) Ramadan
Answer:
1. Briefly describe how Muhammad became a religious teacher.
2. Why is the Hegira important to Islam?
3. What are the Five Pillars of Islam?
4. (a) What lands did the Islamic empire control by 732? (b) Give three reasons for the rapid spread of the empire.
5. Name the three groups of leaders who ruled the Islamic empire between 632 and 1055, and briefly describe each period.
6. How did Islam split into Shi'ites and Sunnis?

Critical Thinking
7. How did the Byzantine and Islamic empires both combine political and religious power?

193

ANSWERS TO (continued)

Stone (**e**) prophet and founder of Islam (**f**) Muslims' name for God (**g**) wife of Muhammad (**h**) city in which Muhammad first began to attract many converts (**i**) followers of Muhammad (**j**) name of religion founded by Muhammad (**k**) holy book of Islam (**l**) Muhammad's escape to Medina (**m**) Muslim holy month
Answer:
1. During a life of meditation, Muhammad had a vision that the angel Gabriel revealed that he was the chosen prophet of God.
2. marked the turning point for Muhammad
3. strict guidelines for Muslims to follow in matters of faith, prayer, alms, fasting, pilgrimage
4. (**a**) Spain and Portugal, North Africa, Egypt, Palestine, Mesopotamia, Persia, northwest India, and Arabia (**b**) passionate faith, overpopulation on Arabian peninsula, weak resistance
5. orthodox caliphate: period of wars of conquest and assassinations; Umayyad caliphate; time of able rulers who conquered many lands but were brought down by revenge for Husayn's death; Abbasid caliphate: period marked by split among Muslims and conflicts with Shi'ites
6. Shi'ites believed Husayn had been the rightful caliph and split from the Sunni Muslims.
7. Byzantine emperors claimed they held the political powers of a Roman ruler and ruled in Jesus' name as new apostles. Islamic empires used ties with Muhammad as their authority.

Vladimir wanted a new religion to replace worship of Scandinavian gods. He rejected Judaism because the Jews could not explain to his satisfaction why they had lost Jerusalem. He rejected Islam because it forbade the drinking of wine.

The empires influenced Slavs and Turks. 3

Around the year 800, both the Islamic and the Byzantine empires were strong and stable. The Byzantines had lost much land to the Muslims, but Constantinople still ruled Asia Minor, Greece, and Sicily. At the same time, the giant empire of the Abbasids stretched from Gibraltar to the Indus River valley.

Within both the Byzantine and Islamic empires, the seeds of future trouble had already been sown. Internal divisions weakened the two empires. Enemy attacks eventually destroyed them.

In the meanwhile, the two empires profoundly influenced two groups of invaders—the Slavs and the Turks. The aging Byzantine empire had a powerful cultural impact on the Slavs. Eventually, several Slavic peoples, especially the Russians, adopted the Byzantine form of Christianity. The Turks, on the other hand, became Muslims even while they fought the armies of the Islamic empire.

Byzantine culture influenced the Slavic peoples.

In the 700's, while the Arabs threatened Constantinople from the south, the Slavs struck from the north. The Slavic people were groups of nomads who had migrated into eastern Europe from the plains of Asia. Each group had its own culture, but all spoke related languages. In the 700's and 800's, these groups were perpetually at war with the Byzantines, fighting for possession of the Balkan peninsula and land around the Black Sea.

Conversion of the Slavs While the Slavic rulers coveted Constantinople's wealth and territory, they also admired its civilization. Unlike the Arabs, the Slavs were persuaded to become Christian. Between 850 and 900, Byzantine missionaries began to win Slavic converts. Among the wisest and most statesmanlike of these missionaries was a monk named Cyril (SIHR-uhl). He and other missionaries invented an alphabet for the Slavic languages, so that Slavs could read the Bible in their own tongue. In honor of Cyril, this system of writing is known as the Cyrillic

194

(suh-RIHL-ik) alphabet. It is still used in some Slavic countries.

The Russian kingdom To the north of the Black Sea, a group of Slavs known as Russians lived in the forests south of the Baltic Sea. The story of Russia's origins comes from the *Primary Chronicle,* an account written around 1050 by an anonymous group of Russian monks who included in their story as much legend as fact.

According to this chronicle, the first Russians were a band of hardy hunters from Scandinavia. They migrated south into forestlands occupied by bands of Slavs. The Slavs called these Scandinavians *Rus* (roos). In 862, says the *Primary Chronicle,* the Slavs invited the Rus to become their protectors and rulers. Thus, 862 is the traditional date for the founding of Russia.

The first Russian prince had a decidedly Scandinavian name: Rurik. His capital city, Novgorod (NAHV-guh-rahd), lay far to the north near the border of present-day Finland. Soon, however, Russian princes moved south to Kiev (KEE-yef), a city better placed for shipping furs, amber, slaves, and honey downriver to Constantinople.

From the *Primary Chronicle* comes a charming—and perhaps true—story of how Kievan Russia was converted to Christianity. Princess Olga, who ruled Kiev from 945 to 955, was the first Russian ruler to become a Christian. However, she did not make Christianity the official religion of her kingdom. In 989, the ruler of Kiev was Vladimir (VLAHD-uh-meer), Olga's grandson. He sent envoys to investigate both Roman and Byzantine Christianity. They found the churches of barbaric Germany drab. Soon afterwards, in Constantinople, the envoys visited Hagia Sophia, the magnificent cathedral built by Justinian (page 184). Stunned by the beauty of its golden mosaics, they reported:

> Then we went on to Greece [Byzantium], and the Greeks led us to the buildings where they worship their God, and we knew not whether we were in heaven or on earth. For on earth there is no such splendor or such beauty, and we are at a loss how to describe it. We only know that God dwells there among men.

Vladimir therefore chose to be a Christian in the Byzantine manner, not in the Roman manner. In 989, he commanded his subjects to go to the

Dnieper River for baptism. Thus, Russians looked to Constantinople, not Rome, for religious leadership. This choice would have profound consequences for Russia in years to come, as it cut off the kingdom from western Europe.

The Russian kingdom prospered from its ties to Byzantium. By the year 1000, Kiev had a population of 8,000, making it the equal of Paris, the largest city of western Europe at that time. Kiev's gold-domed churches imitated those of Constantinople. Its mosaics too were much like those found in "The City." The pattern of Russian culture—Slavic in language, Byzantine in style—was established for centuries to come.

The Turks struck from the east.

Between the years 1000 and 1100, both the Byzantine empire and the Islamic empire faced new dangers. Chief among them were the ferocious attacks of a nomadic people from central Asia, the Turks.

The breakup of the Islamic empire The Islamic empire had already lost much of its territory. Spain broke away from the Islamic empire in 756, when the Abbasids came to power. After moving their capital east to Baghdad, the Abbasids lost other parts of their empire in the west—Morocco in 788 and Tunisia in 800. After the death of Harun al-Rashid in 809, parts of Persia also broke away. Then, in 868, the Abbasids lost control of Egypt.

In 945, a local Persian ruler took over Baghdad and ended the caliph's political power. Although the caliph was still the religious leader of Islam, a **sultan** now held all political power. The power of the Abbasids was broken.

Seljuk Turks In this time of weakness and division, a formidable enemy swept out of Asia. On the semiarid grasslands east of the Caspian Sea, nomadic Turks grazed their horses and practiced the art of war. Just as Roman emperors had used barbarians in their armies, caliphs in the 800's used the Turks. Finally, just as Rome fell to the barbarians, Baghdad fell to the Turks.

Large numbers of Turks moved into the Islamic empire around 970. This first group of migrating Turks is known as the Seljuk (SEL-jook) Turks, after the family that led them. By 1000, they had converted to Islam, joining the Sunni branch. Conversion did not stop them, however, from

Russia about 1100

KEY
Russian territory about 1100

BYZANTINE EMPIRE

0   300 Miles

Map Study

By what water route would travelers and traders from Kiev have reached Constantinople?

warring with other Muslims. In 1055, they captured Baghdad. Throughout the empire, Turks now replaced Arabs as the ruling class.

Twenty years later, the Seljuk sultans spearheaded a mighty drive against the Byzantine empire. In 1071, at the Battle of Manzikert, the Turks overwhelmed the Byzantines. Within ten years, the Seljuk Turks occupied all of Asia Minor, the eastern heartland of Byzantium. It was a staggering blow to the Byzantines, for even the mighty armies of the Arabs had never come so close to Constantinople by land.

The Ottomans posed a new threat.

While the Byzantine empire grew weaker, a new group of Turks—the Ottomans—suddenly appeared on its borders. The origins of the Ottoman Turks are obscure. At the start of the fourteenth century, they occupied a small principality in the rugged mountains of western Asia Minor. The Ottomans derived their name from an early leader named Osman (1290–1326), or

195

SECTION 3 Objectives and Teaching Strategies

OBJECTIVE 1. Describe how the Slavs became Christians.

Teaching Strategy: *Discussing History: The Slavs Became Christians* (page 178e)

OBJECTIVE 2. Make a time line of the decline and fall of the Islamic and Byzantine empires.

Teaching Strategy: *Skill Building: Making a Time Line* (page 178e)

ANSWER TO
Map Study

Dnieper River to the Black Sea

SECTION 3
Resources

GEOGRAPHY
- Transparencies 30, 31

REINFORCEMENT
- Independent Practice 8.3

ENRICHMENT
- Voices from the Past 8.3

ASSESSMENT
- Section Quiz 8.3

Cooperative Learning

Ask students to think of questions they would have liked to have asked the opponents at the fall of Constantinople. Working in groups of four, have half the class develop interview questions for Muhammad II. The other half should develop questions for Constantine XI. Students might ask questions about the opponents' reasons for fighting, the tactics being used, and the historical significance of the fall of Constantinople. Group members should take turns, offering one interview question at a time until the group has 12 to 15 questions. A recorder should write down all the questions. Then, using what they already know, outside resources, and their imaginations, have group members work in a similar manner to come up with answers for their interview questions. Group recorders should write down final answers.

The Decline of the Byzantine Empire

Map Study

Where was the westernmost boundary of the empire in the year 1000? What territory did the empire control by 1400?

Uthman in Arabic. Osman was the first in a succession of 36 Ottoman sultans who ruled for almost 600 years.

Osman and his successors built a powerful military machine. The Ottoman soldiers saw themselves as *ghazis*, fierce Islamic warriors dedicated to fighting a holy war against unbelievers. After taking over the leadership held by the Seljuk Turks, the Ottomans began to invade the decaying Byzantine empire. By 1350, they controlled most of western Asia Minor.

The next half century witnessed an even greater expansion of Ottoman power. In 1354, the Ottomans successfully crossed the Dardanelles and invaded the Balkans. Within a short time, they captured large areas of southeastern Europe and overwhelmed a Serbian army that tried to stop them. Only Constantinople—the real gateway to an empire in Europe—remained unconquered.

The Ottoman armies promptly encircled Constantinople. However, the city was saved for the

moment when the Mongol conqueror Tamurlane advanced from central Asia into Ottoman lands. His awesome army inflicted a crushing defeat on the Ottomans at the Battle of Argora in 1402. Only Tamurlane's death a short time later saved the Ottomans from destruction. Defeated but not destroyed, the Ottomans again turned their attention to conquering Constantinople.

Turning Points in History

The Fall of Constantinople Although the lands around Constantinople were all that remained of the Byzantine empire, the great city still remained a valuable prize. As long as the city remained under Byzantine rule, however, it hindered the movement of Ottoman ships and troops to conquered lands in Europe. The new Ottoman sultan Muhammad II vowed to capture

196

Constantinople. Shortly after becoming sultan in 1451, he grimly announced, "I want only one thing. Give me Constantinople!" Could it be captured now? As you have seen, Constantinople's thick walls had withstood repeated Muslim sieges for more than 750 years.

Muhammad spent the next 2 years assembling an army of 100,000 men and building a fleet of 125 ships. In addition, he commissioned a Hungarian engineer named Urban to construct a number of cannons that would be used to shatter Constantinople's famed triple line of walls. Urban's most formidable weapon was a cannon 26 feet long and 8 inches in diameter. Known as the Royal One, it could fire 1,200-pound stone cannonballs for a distance of one mile.

On the morning of April 5, 1453, Muhammad's force of men, ships, and cannons assumed their positions around Constantinople. The city they surrounded was only a shadow of its former greatness. Its population had shrunk from more than 1 million to just 50,000. Its once proud armed forces had been reduced to 7,000 men and 25 ships. Nonetheless the city was led by a brave emperor named Constantine XI and protected by 14 miles of walls that had withstood 22 sieges in over 1,000 years.

The great siege of Constantinople began on April 6, 1453. For the next two weeks, fighting raged on both land and sea. While the Ottoman cannons pounded away at the city's ancient walls, wave after wave of Turks attempted to scale them. The valiant Byzantine defenders hurled back every attack. Meanwhile, the Ottoman navy was unsuccessful in its attempt to break through a strong chain boom that protected the city's harbor on the Golden Horn.

Unable to break through either the land walls or the chain boom, Muhammad devised an ingenious plan to gain control of the harbor. His strategy called for the construction of a timber causeway that would connect the Bosporus Strait with the Golden Horn and bypass the chain boom. On Saturday, April 22, Muhammad's exultant soldiers pulled 70 ships over a 200-foot ridge and into the Golden Horn. This spectacular feat enabled the Ottomans to blockade Constantinople and attack its vulnerable sea walls.

Despite this severe setback, the Byzantines' desperate courage enabled them to hold back the Turks for another five weeks. Finally, on May 28, the citizens of Constantinople, Greek and Latin, gathered together for a final mass at Hagia Sophia. The next day the Ottomans broke through a small gate that had been accidentally left unlocked. Seeing the breach, Constantine XI gallantly led a final attempt to save his city. He died a hero's death at the side of his troops. With his death, the 1,123-year-old Byzantine empire also perished.

Muhammad II, henceforth called the Conqueror, triumphantly entered Hagia Sophia and humbly thanked Allah for his victory. He then ordered Constantinople's name changed to Istanbul (a Greek word meaning "into the city") and had Hagia Sophia transformed into a mosque. Within days, a huge crescent—symbol of the new Islamic empire—replaced the Christian cross atop the dome of Hagia Sophia.

The fall of Constantinople sent shock waves across the Christian world. While Greeks mourned the end of the Byzantine empire, Turks celebrated the emergence of the Ottoman state as a great imperial power. That empire went on to extend its power across the Balkan Peninsula, up the Danube valley, and into Hungary. Not until 1529 was its advance halted at the gates of another city—Vienna—in the heart of central Europe.

Section REVIEW 3

Define: sultan
Identify: (a) Slavs, (b) Cyril, (c) Rus, (d) Kiev, (e) Vladimir, (f) Turks
Answer:
1. How did the invention of the Cyrillic alphabet help convert the Slavs to Christianity?
2. How did the Russian kingdom begin?
3. What were the long-lasting results of Vladimir's choice of Orthodox Christianity?
4. (a) What conquests did the Seljuk Turks make? (b) The Ottoman Turks?

Critical Thinking
5. The Seljuk Turks and the Ottoman Turks came from central Asia, where they had lived as nomads. (a) What advantages might nomads have in fighting against the Byzantine and Islamic empires? (b) What advantages might the empires have had? (c) Why were the nomads successful?

197

ANSWERS TO

Section Review 3

Define:
Persian ruler who ended the caliph's political power
Identify:
(a) nomads who migrated into eastern Europe
(b) monk who invented Slavic alphabet (c) hunters from Scandinavia, the first Russians (d) second capital of early Russia (e) ruler of Kiev, an early Russian Christian (f) nomadic peoples from central Asia
Answer:
1. Slavs could read the Bible in their own language.
2. Slavs invited the Rus to be their rulers in 862.
3. Russia kept ties with the east and was cut off from western Europe.
4. (a) Baghdad, all of Asia Minor (b) all the rest of the Byzantine empire, including Constantinople
5. (a) They had nothing to lose; they were mobile, could strike anywhere.
(b) money, weapons
(c) internal weakness and division in empire

Concluding the Chapter

1. Chapter Closer
Have students relate present-day conflicting claims to the Holy Land to the events described in this chapter.

2. Reteaching Activities
a. Summarizing Ask students to name the three major projects undertaken by Justinian and to tell the outcome of each.

b. Answering Questions Have students turn each of the headings in Section 2 into a question and to write the answer to the question.

c. Outlining Have students use the headings in Section 3 to write a sentence outline.

Answers to Chapter Review appear on pages 178e–178f.

Summary

1. Constantinople ruled an eastern empire. Byzantine emperors claimed both political and religious authority. The most outstanding ruler was Justinian, who tried to restore the glories of the Roman past. He is most noted for his code of laws. After his death, the empire was threatened by revolts, religious quarrels, and invasions. The Roman and Byzantine branches of the Christian Church grew apart and eventually split.

2. A new faith spread from Arabia. Late in the 500's, Muhammad proclaimed the faith of Islam. Gradually, he gained many followers. After his death, Muslim warriors created an empire that spread from Spain in the west to the Indus River valley in the east. Throughout the empire, Muslims followed the same religious duties, which included prayer, fasting, almsgiving, and pilgrimage.

3. The empires influenced Slavs and Turks. By the year 800, both the Byzantine and Islamic empires faced internal and external dangers. The Byzantine empire came under frequent attack from the Slavs, who converted to Christianity, and the Muslims. The Islamic empire was weakened by religious conflict. Baghdad fell to the Seljuk Turks in 1055. Constantinople fell to the Ottoman Turks in 1453.

Reviewing the Facts

1. Define the following terms:
   a. excommunicate   d. jihad
   b. heretic   e. caliph
   c. patriarch   f. sultan
2. Explain the importance of each of the following names, dates, places, or terms:
   a. Constantinople   i. Baghdad
   b. Justinian   j. Slavs
   c. Code of Justinian   k. Kiev
   d. Bedouin   l. Vladimir
   e. Mecca   m. 1054
   f. Muhammad   n. Seljuk Turks
   g. 622   o. Ottoman Turks
   h. Koran   p. 1453
3. Name at least three issues that led to the break between the Roman and Byzantine churches in the year 1054.
4. Explain the importance of each of the following to the development of Islam. (a) Hegira (b) Koran (c) Five Pillars of Islam (d) Shi'ites
5. (a) How did the Umayyad and Abbasid caliphates differ? (b) What were the achievements of each caliphate?
6. (a) How did Byzantine culture influence Slavs? (b) How did the Islamic empire influence Turks?

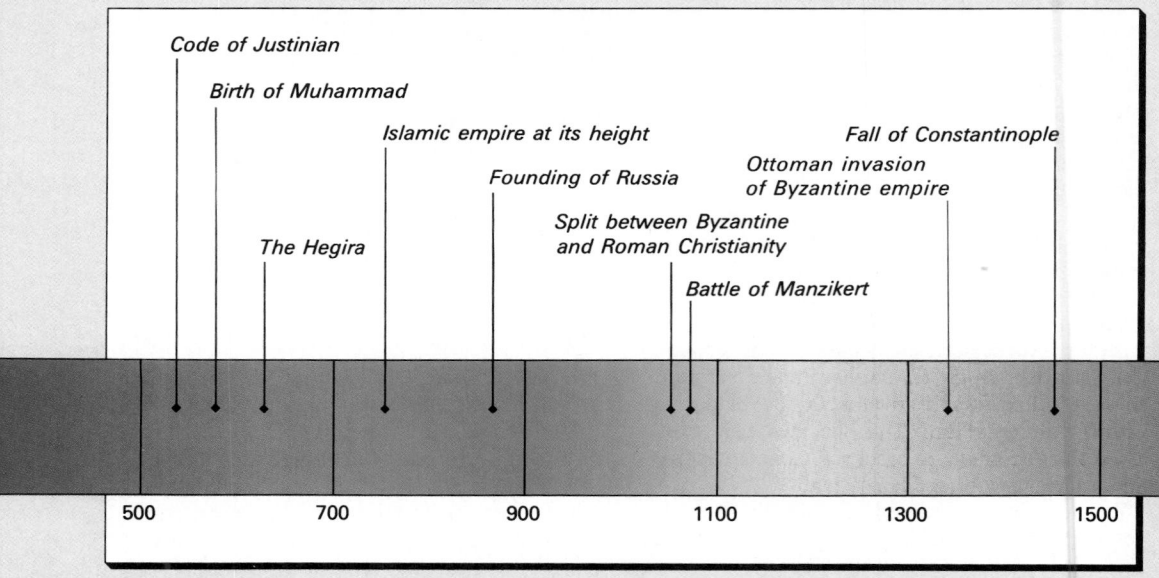

Code of Justinian

Birth of Muhammad

Islamic empire at its height

Founding of Russia

The Hegira

Fall of Constantinople

Ottoman invasion of Byzantine empire

Split between Byzantine and Roman Christianity

Battle of Manzikert

500   700   900   1100   1300   1500

198

Basic Skills

1. **Explaining a main idea** How does the story about Omar's entering Jerusalem and finding the sacred rock littered with garbage illustrate a main idea of this chapter?
2. **Summarizing** Using the "Voice from the Past" on page 183, write a paragraph summarizing the Empress Theodora's arguments against fleeing Constantinople.
3. **Taking notes** The city tour of Constantinople on pages 182–184 tells much about life in Byzantium. Taking notes will help to clarify that information. Divide a sheet of paper into five equal parts. Label them *People, Defenses, Trade, Public Buildings,* and *Education.* Under each heading, note information about that topic.
4. **Interpreting maps** What parts of the Byzantine empire under Justinian (shown on page 181) had become part of the Islamic empire in 750 (shown on page 189)?
5. **Sequencing** Using the map on page 196, list in chronological order seven events shown on the map. Include both battles and invasions. The completed list summarizes the conquest of the Byzantine empire by Muslim rulers.
6. **Reading a time line** Use the time line on page 198 to calculate how many years it took for the Islamic empire to expand to its fullest extent.

Researching and Reporting Skills

1. **Acquiring information** Islam drew some of its ideas from existing Jewish and Christian beliefs. (a) Do research to find out what aspects of the earlier religions Islam included. (b) What new ideas did Islam add?
2. **Preparing an interview** Imagine that you had the opportunity to interview either Justinian or Harun al-Rashid. Prepare a list of five questions you would ask Justinian about his Code of Laws or a list of five questions you would ask Harun al-Rashid about his hopes for the growth of learning in the Islamic empire.
3. **Organizing information** This chapter contains pictures that could be used to illustrate an oral report on the Byzantine or Islamic civilizations. (a) How could you use these pictures to make an oral report on one of these civilizations? (b) Find illustrations pertaining to either civilization and explain how you would use them in a report.

Critical Thinking

1. **Comparing and contrasting** Compare and contrast the teachings of the Jews' Ten Commandments with the rules established for Islamic life by the Muslims' Koran.
2. **Analyzing** (a) Which would you rather have been, a subject of Rome living in Gaul at the time of Augustus or a Greek subject living in the Islamic empire at the time of the Abbasids? (b) What would be the advantages and disadvantages of each?
3. **Synthesizing** In this chapter, you have read about the golden age in arts and sciences under the Abbasid rulers. You have also read about two other golden ages, those of Athens under Pericles and of Rome under Augustus. What are the main characteristics of a golden age?
4. **Evaluating** The Byzantine and Islamic empires were rivals. Which of the two had the greater impact on the world of that time? Evaluate them in terms of their political, economic, religious, and cultural influence.

Perspectives on Past and Present

1. In both the Byzantine and Islamic empires, scholars worked to preserve writings from the past. Why is the perservation of these writings important to people today?
2. Using a world map as a reference, draw in and label the present countries of the Middle East on an outline map of the region. Compare your map to the one of the Islamic empire on page 189. Which countries in the Middle East today were part of the Islamic empire in 750?

Investigating History

1. Sports and politics made an explosive combination in Justinian's Constantinople. Read about the violent rivalry between the Greens and the Blues at the Hippodrome stadium. (A chapter in Edward Gibbon's *The Decline and Fall of the Roman Empire* provides a vivid account.)
2. Using a current traveler's guide from the library, plan a visit to one of the cities mentioned in this chapter. Write a brief description of the places in the city that you want to see. If possible, include a map of the city and your plan for touring it.

199

CHAPTER
Evaluation

Chapter Test 8, Alternate Chapter Test 8, and Computer Test Bank Chapter 8 Test can be used to evaluate your students' understanding of this chapter.

Chapter 9

The Early Middle Ages

Chapter Overview

With the end of the Roman empire, life in western Europe changed in many ways. Towns declined, trade collapsed, and people returned to rural ways of life. The Roman Catholic Church acted as the strongest civilizing force in western Europe. Monasteries remained the only institution upholding learning and an orderly way of life.

Under the leadership of Charlemagne, the Franks created an empire. During his rule, Charlemagne spread Christianity and encouraged learning. However, after the death of Charlemagne's son, the unified empire was greatly weakened by its division among his three grandsons.

From the ninth to the eleventh centuries, Viking, Slav, and Magyar invaders further disrupted life in the monasteries and towns of western Europe. Between A.D. 850 and A.D. 950, feudalism developed in response to disorder and political instability. Under this system, lords and vassals provided land and protection for the people who served them, and peasants on manors supplied the goods and services.

Chapter Focus

Review the principles of Roman law. Then have students read pages 200–201. Ask them to describe how a Roman legal expert might have reacted to the trial. Emphasize that Roman law was based on the application of reason and human justice. Thus, people accused of crimes had a right to face their accusers and to defend themselves before a judge. If there was doubt about a person's guilt, he or she would be judged innocent. In contrast, the trial by ordeal was based on an appeal to divine justice. The Germanic peoples believed that God would protect the innocent and expose the guilty. He would therefore heal a burned hand, if the hand was innocent. Lake water, blessed by a priest, would "accept" an innocent soul by allowing it to sink, but "reject" a guilty soul by forcing it to float.

The trial by ordeal provides a vivid example of the decline of civilization following the fall of the Roman empire. This chapter examines a new period of history known as the Early Middle Ages.

New ways of life developed in Europe.

1

Setting the Stage

Transferring Ideas: The Decline of Civilization (Objective 1) Review the five key characteristics of civilization (pages 31–34). Then have students read "Roman civilization collapsed" and "Personal ties replaced citizenship" (pages 201–203). Have students describe the various ways in which civilization changed. Use Map Transparency 32, *The Barbarian Kingdoms about 500*, to locate areas occupied by Germanic tribes. Ask students which institution best survived the

Chapter 9 The Early Middle Ages 450–1000
FOCUS The contrast between Roman laws and the Germanic trial by ordeal

★ Advanced
● Basic

	SECTION 1	SECTION 2	SECTION 3	SECTION 4
Objectives	1. Describe how civilization declined following the collapse of the Roman empire. 2. Identify St. Benedict and explain the importance of the Benedictine rule.	1. Explain the importance of the Battle of Tours for western Europe. 2. Explain how Charlemagne expanded the Frankish empire and revived learning. 3. Explain how central authority broke down in the years following Charlemagne's death.	1. Describe a Viking ship and explain its importance. 2. Trace Viking routes on a map. 3. Explain why the Viking age ended.	1. State reasons for the development of feudalism. 2. Support general statements about feudalism. 3. Contrast the feudal economic system with the economic system of a modern industrial society. 4. Chart the duties and benefits of nobles, vassals, knights, peasants, and serfs in the feudal system.
Setting the Stage	Transferring Ideas: The Decline of Civilization Transparency 32	Discussing History: The Battle of Tours	The Viking invaders of Europe	Discussing History: Feudalism
Teaching Strategies	Discussing History: The Rule of St. Benedict Check for Understanding	Discussing History: The Revival of Learning Transparency 33 Transferring Ideas: The Problem of Succession Transparency 34 Check for Understanding	Teaching with Pictures: A Viking Ship Using Geographic Themes: Movement Transparency 35 Outline Map 9 Discussing History: The End of the Viking Age Check for Understanding	Skill Building: Supporting Generalizations Economics and History: Contrasting Economic Systems Discussing History: Analyzing the Feudal System Check for Understanding
Guided Practice	Transparency 32 Q&A Section Review 1	Transparency 33 Q&A Transparency 34 Q&A Section Review 2	Transparency 35 Q&A Section Review 3	Section Review 4
Independent Practice Worksheets	Independent Practice 9.1 Geography Skills 9 Vocabulary 9	Independent Practice 9.2 Basic Skills 3	Independent Practice 9.3 Critical Thinking 9	Independent Practice 9.4
Enrichment	1. Primary Source: Voices 9.1 2. Solving a Puzzle 3. ★Analyzing a Quotation 4. Researching for Points	1. Primary Source: Voices 9.2 2. Preparing a Report: Life of Charlemagne 3. Researching for Points 4. Global Perspectives: Transparency 26	1. Primary Source: Voices 9.3 2. Preparing a Report: Viking Life 3. ★Creative Writing 4. Researching for Points	1. Primary Source: Voices 9.4 2. Creative Writing: Manor Life 3. Researching for Points

Chapter Closer

●Reteaching Activities   Supporting a Generalization, Explaining Political Changes, Answering Questions, Explaining Key Phrases

Chapter Review   Summary, Reviewing the Facts, Basic Skills, Researching and Reporting Skills, Critical Thinking, Perspectives on Past and Present, Investigating History

Chapter Evaluation   Chapter Test 9, Alternate Chapter Test 9, Computer Test Bank Chapter 9 Test

fall of Rome. Students should identify the Church as the strongest remaining civilizing force in western Europe.

Teaching Strategies

Discussing History: The Rule of St. Benedict (Objective 2) Note that monasteries were self-sufficient communities. Both men and women were expected to follow the threefold rule of poverty, chastity, and obedience. Benedict's rules created a disciplined schedule that enabled monks and nuns to serve God and perform charitable services. Read the following rules aloud and ask students to discuss why Benedict included them:

■ Let him (the abbot) make no distinction of persons in the monastery. Let not one be loved more than another, save such as be found to excel in obedience or good works.

■ Whenever any weighty matters have to be transacted in the monastery, let the abbot call together all the community . . . . After hearing the advice of the brethren let him consider it in his own mind and then do what he shall judge most expedient.

■ All guests who come shall be received as though they were Christ.

Check for Understanding Have students name two examples to support each of these statements: **(a)** Civilization in western Europe declined after the fall of Rome. **(b)** The Roman Catholic Church became increasingly powerful.

Enrichment Activities

1. **Reading a Primary Source**
   Assign Voices from the Past Resource Book 9.1.

2. **Solving a Puzzle**
   In 1939, archaeologists discovered an Anglo-Saxon ship buried on the northeast English coast at a site now known as Sutton Hoo. The ship contained a fortune in gold, silver, and jewelry, but no human remains. Ask students to prepare a report speculating on what king, if any, was buried at Sutton Hoo. (See *The Barbarian Kings* by Lionel Casson.)

3. **Analyzing a Quotation**
   The historian Will Durant wrote that Gregory the Great "dominated the end of the sixth century as Justinian had dominated its beginning; and his effect on religion was exceeded in this epoch only by that of Mohammed." Ask advanced students to give evidence supporting or contradicting this statement.

4. **Researching for Bonus Points**
   Benedictine monks pray eight times a day. What are the names of the eight canonical hours? (nocturns, matins or lauds, prime, tierce, sext, none, vespers, and at bedtime, compline—the completion)

Charlemagne revived the idea of empire.   2

Setting the Stage

Discussing History: The Battle of Tours (Objective 1) Ask students to find information in Chapter 8 about the Battle of Tours (pages 189–191). Then ask why this battle was significant for western Europe. Point out that if the Muslims had won, western Europe might have become a part of the Islamic empire. Martel's dramatic victory at the Battle of Tours stopped the Muslim invasion and made Charles a Christian hero.

Discussing History: The Revival of Learning (Objective 2) Display Map Transparency 33, *The Empire of Charlemagne in 814*. Explain that Charlemagne's conquests carved out an impressive but short-lived empire. In contrast, his role as a leader in the revival of learning had significant long-term consequences. Ask students to identify these consequences.

Transferring Ideas: The Problem of Succession (Objective 3) Ask students to recall that the problem of succession contributed to the fall of Rome, and that the Carolingian rulers also had a serious problem. Frankish law and custom required the ruler to divide his empire among his sons. What problems did this system create? Direct students' attention to "Charlemagne's heirs ruled weakly" (pages 210–211). Louis the Pious divided his empire into three parts as shown on the map on page 210. Louis's three sons promptly fought a bitter civil war that ended with the Treaty of Verdun. The provisions of this treaty are shown on Map Transparency 34, *The Division of the Carolingian Empire, 843*.

Check for Understanding Have students explain why Charlemagne is an important historical figure in French history.

Enrichment Activities

1. **Reading a Primary Source**
   Assign Voices from the Past Resource Book 9.2.

2. **Preparing a Book Report**
   Einhard's *Life of Charlemagne* provides interesting insights into the life of this remarkable ruler. Ask interested students to report on this book.

3. **Researching for Bonus Points**
   Charlemagne and other members of the official family at Aachen sometimes addressed each other by classical or Biblical names. What was Charlemagne called? (David)

4. **Global Perspectives**
   Have students study Map Transparency 26, *The World about 800,* which also appears on text pages 176–177. Ask students to relate Charlemagne's empire to contemporary developments in other parts of the world.

Vikings terrorized Europe. 3

Setting the Stage

Ask students to recall previous examples of how barbarian peoples invaded civilized areas. Then have students read the introduction (page 211), which describes one of the first Viking raids on Charlemagne's empire. To capture the impact of this raid, have students suggest news headlines that might have appeared in the *Norse News* and the *Lindisfarne Ledger.* Emphasize that the sudden Viking raids stunned the peoples of western Europe.

Teaching Strategies

Teaching with Pictures: A Viking Ship (Objective 1) Although Vikings were ferocious, their minds were as keen as their swords. The ships (or "steeds of the waves") that carried them on journeys of piracy and commerce were technologically advanced. Archaeologists discovered the ship illustrated on page 212 in a trench near Oseberg, Norway, in 1904. Blue clay covered the ship and helped preserve its thousands of fragments. Archaeologists painstakingly marked and numbered each fragment before reconstructing the ship. The reassembled vessel is 71 feet long. Its prow rises 16 feet above the deck.

Using Geographic Themes: Movement (Objective 2) The Vikings were also wily traders and brave explorers. Use Map Transparency 35, *The Age of Invasions, 800–1000,* to show the range of Viking explorations, which stretched from the edge of North America to the Dnieper River in Russia. Now distribute Outline Map 9: Physical Europe. Have students label the following places: Scandinavia, England, Normandy, Ireland, Spain, Iceland; and the North Sea, Baltic Sea, Atlantic Ocean, Mediterranean Sea, and Black Sea. Using the map on page 213 as a reference, ask students to draw the routes the Vikings followed to England, Ireland, Iceland, Spain, and Russia.

Discussing History: The End of the Viking Age (Objective 3) After students read "The Viking Age ended about 1000" (page 214), discuss the reasons for the demise. Note that although Viking terror disappeared, the Viking influence remained. For example, English-speaking people use Viking names for several days of the week. On the Old English Calendar, each of these days honored a different Norse god: Wednesday was originally Odin's (Woden's) day; Thursday was Thor's day; and Friday was Frey's day.

Check for Understanding Have students name three achievements of the Vikings and explain their significance in European history.

Enrichment Activities

1. **Reading a Primary Source**
   Assign Voices from the Past Resource Book 9.3.

2. **Preparing a Report**
   Have students report on one aspect of Viking life. Possible topics include Viking religion, Viking traders in Russia, and the construction of Viking warships.

3. **Creative Writing**
   Viking poets called *skalds* recorded the heroic deeds of their warrior leaders. Ask advanced students to be skalds and to research and write about a Viking adventure.

4. **Researching for Bonus Points**
   At what site in North America did archaeologists confirm Viking settlement? (L'Anse aux Meadows in Newfoundland)

Feudalism became the basis for government. 4

Setting the Stage

Discussing History: Feudalism (Objective 1) After students read the introduction on page 214, ask them to suggest why there was a need for new political and military arrangements in western Europe. Recall that, in the years following the collapse of the Roman empire, personal loyalties replaced the Roman sense of civic responsibility toward the state. Ask students how they think this shift toward personal loyalties might have related to the increasing emphasis on local government and local self-sufficiency.

Teaching Strategies

Skill Building: Supporting Generalizations (Objective 2) Write the following statements on the board. Have students cite details to support each (see pages 214–217).

1. The control of land was the key to feudalism.
2. Feudalism was a system in which public power became private power.
3. Feudalism provided a system of local defense.
4. In theory, feudal society was a pyramid.

Economics and History: Contrasting Economic Systems (Objective 3) Refer students to the illustration on page 218 to familiarize them with a typical medieval manor. Ask students how the basic needs for food, clothing, and shelter were met under the manorial system and how these needs are met in a modern industrial society. Discuss the advantages of economic self-sufficiency in the Early Middle Ages. Ask students to name factors that discouraged economic inter-

dependence. Poor roads, outlaws, and frequent warfare made transportation and trade perilous. Ask students whether they think feudalism could work in an industrialized nation; have them give reasons for their answers.

Discussing History: Analyzing the Feudal System (Objective 4) Help students draw a five-column chart on the board. The chart should describe the duties and benefits of feudalism from the perspectives of lords, vassals, knights, peasants, and serfs. Ask students who received the greatest benefits from this system and who had the greatest responsibilities. Then ask why peasants may have felt that the right to stay on the manor was more important than the freedom to leave.

Check for Understanding Have students explain the economic role of the manor in feudal society.

Enrichment Activities

1. **Reading a Primary Source** Assign Voices from the Past Resource Book 9.4.

2. **Creative Writing** Using the illustration on page 218 as a guide, ask students to imagine living as peasants on the manor shown. Their assignment is to write a report describing daily life on the manor.

3. **Researching for Bonus Points** What privilege gave a lord the right to travel to one of his vassal's fiefs and be entertained for several days? (the right of purveyance)

ANSWERS TO
Chapter Review 9

Reviewing the Facts

1. **(a)** belonging to the Middle Ages **(b)** community in which Christians live in poverty and worship God **(c)** armored horseman **(d)** powerful landowner who ruled a county **(e)** Charlemagne's agents, sent out to monitor the governing counts **(f)** political and military system based on holding of land **(g)** person who could transfer control of a piece of land **(h)** person who received land from a lord **(i)** symbolic gesture representing granting of land **(j)** piece of land given to a vassal **(k)** small estate from which a lord's family gained its livelihood **(l)** peasant who was bound to the land

2. **(a)** established Christianity in Ireland **(b)** Frankish king who converted to Christianity **(c)** set of rules for monastic life **(d)** pope who established idea of Christendom **(e)** spiritual kingdom on earth **(f)** Clovis and his successors **(g)** father of Charlemagne who seized the Frankish throne with pope's blessing **(h)** Frankish king who expanded empire **(i)** royal agents sent out to see that counts governed justly **(j)** Charlemagne's capital **(k)** year Charlemagne was crowned emperor by pope **(l)** Charlemagne's descendants **(m)** divided Charlemagne's empire among his three grandsons **(n)** seafaring raiders from Scandinavia **(o)** Viking explorer who sailed to what is now Newfoundland

3. **(a)** recruited scholars, opened schools at palace, and ordered monasteries to open schools **(b)** trained future monks and priests, maintained libraries, developed a readable style of lettering

4. Christian missionaries traveled among the Germanic and Celtic groups to spread their beliefs. Pagan kings, such as Clovis, converted and helped the church to fight other Germanic groups who in turn were converted.

5. Kingdom was divided into counties, each ruled in the king's name by a count; counts administered justice and raised armies; king sent out royal agents to see that counts governed justly.

6. In return for an oath of loyalty, the lord transferred a piece of land called a fief to his vassal with a symbolic gesture (investiture). In turn, the vassal subdivided the land and gave to warriors smaller fiefs in return for support of armies. In cases of financial emergencies, lords could ask for aids, grants of money, from their vassals.

7. (a) emperor of the Romans and pope (b) The pope gained a protector and power because he named the emperor. The emperor became the protector of all Christendom, with spiritual and political authority.

8. (a) basic economic unit of feudalism (b) cleared for growing grain, as pasture, forest

9. (a) two or three days' labor every week on lord's land; giving a certain portion of the grain grown on the serf's own land to the lord; paying taxes (b) food, protection, a place to live

Basic Skills

1. (a) Charlemagne was crowned emperor (b) Leif Ericson's voyage to America

2.

Spain	France
Basques	Franks
Suevi	Bretons
Visigoths	Burgundians
	Visigoths

Germany	Britain
Franks	Picts
Saxons	Celts
Thuringians	British
Frisians	Angles
	Saxons
	Jutes

3. The diagram would link the third white knight with both Richard and William. The knight's shield might reflect the alliances by being divided in half, one part white and the other part blue.

4. Charlemagne maintained a centralized government by personally supervising the counts as well as by sending out his emissaries, the *missi dominici*. His successors did not keep such close control over the counts.

5. The church was the only institution to survive the fall of the Roman empire. Its monasteries were centers of order, stability, and learning; their libraries copied and preserved ancient manuscripts. Monasteries and cathedrals opened schools. Monks were the educators, secretaries, biographers of kings. Missionaries spread Christianity to the barbarians, converting and educating some of their leaders. Pope Gregory I became the spiritual and political leader of Rome. He promoted a vision of a united Christendom in western Europe.

Researching and Reporting Skills

1. "Feudalism in Western Europe," "The Life of Charlemagne" too broad; "Lindisfarne Island during the Roman Empire" too narrow.

2. Students' findings will vary.

3. The ceremony should convey the transferring of land use in exchange for oath of loyalty.

Critical Thinking

1. (a) Warfare brought an end to trade and a return to the land. The end of the empire also meant less need of administrative centers. (b) The decay of cities meant the end of specialized work activity, of government institutions, and of many cultural activities.

2. (a) Each feudal lord had a loyal following ready to take up his cause against other feudal lords or even against the king. It meant endless "feuds." (b) Negative. Constant warfare; people had no recourse against their lords, had no higher system of justice to defend them.

3. (a) Both events implied that the pope was legitimizing the king or emperor's political authority, as well as giving him spiritual authority over his subjects. It implied an alliance between these rulers and the pope, whose spiritual and temporal authority they now defended. The crowning of Charlemagne also revived the idea of a western Christian empire. (b) Likely to lead to confusion of temporal and spiritual powers; set the scene for future conflicts between popes and temporal rulers, who will try to control church matters and to limit the power of the pope in their territories. Since royal authority is legitimated by the Church, popes will claim some control over kings. Popes will also become dependent on the support of the Frankish kings or Holy Roman Emperor for their authority.

Perspectives on Past and Present

(a) Political and religious authority overlapped. (b) The pope ruled over the papal estates and crowned kings. The kings fought the enemies of the Church, imposed their religious beliefs on their subjects, and appointed bishops. (c) In the United States, the Bill of Rights forbids Congress to make laws on establishing a religious practice or preventing the exercise of religious freedom. It thereby affirms the principle of separation between church and state.

Investigating History

Students' findings will vary.

Teaching with Pictures

Refer to the chapter overview on page 200a to set the scene for life in the Early Middle Ages. When students look at the photo on this page, they should note that the chessmen are in battle garb and armed for war. Explain to students that both civilization and trade declined during this period, which is characterized by political instability, decentralized rule, and war.

The Early Middle Ages

Early medieval chessmen portrayed a warlike tone.

Key Terms

medieval	fief
Dark Ages	manor
monastery	serf
abbot	
knight	
count	
missi dominici	
feudalism	
lord	
vassal	
investiture	

Read and Understand

1. New ways of life developed in Europe.
2. Charlemagne revived the idea of empire.
3. Vikings terrorized Europe.
4. Feudalism became the basis for government.

A huge cauldron of boiling water steamed and bubbled over an outdoor hearth. Two Christian priests stood near it, preparing themselves for a terrible test. The priests had disagreed over a religious issue. They proposed to settle their quarrel by using the ordeal of boiling water. Each priest was expected to plunge his arm into the cauldron and pick up a small ring at the bottom. Afterward, their arms would be inspected, and the one whose burns healed cleanly would be declared the winner.

As a large group of spectators watched in excitement, the first priest boldly thrust his arm into the water and retrieved the ring. His hand and arm were unharmed. When the second priest tried to do the same,

Chapter 9 Resources

GEOGRAPHY
- Geography Skills 9
- Outline Map 9
- Transparencies 32, 33, 34, 35

REINFORCEMENT
- Vocabulary 9
- Basic Skills 9
- Reteaching 9
- Making Connections Study Guide 9

ENRICHMENT
- Critical Thinking 9

ASSESSMENT
- Chapter Test 9
- Alternate Chapter Test 9
- Computer Test Bank

he was badly scalded. The first priest was immediately hailed as the victor, even without the usual three-day waiting period to see how the burns healed.

Thousands of trials like this one took place all over western Europe between the years 500 and 1000. These were the years after the German-speaking barbarians destroyed the western half of the Roman empire. Throughout western Europe, Germanic customs replaced the reasoned logic of Roman laws. Trials like the one the priests used were known as trials by ordeal.

There were other kinds of ordeals besides that of boiling water. A person accused of a crime might, for example, be tried by the ordeal of cold water. In this ordeal, the accused person was bound hand and foot with a rope and then thrown into a pond. If the person's body bobbed quickly to the surface, the verdict was guilty. But if the person sank for a count of several seconds, he or she was fished out and pronounced innocent. Another method, called trial by combat, consisted of an armed fight between accuser and accused. If the accuser or the accused was a woman, she could name a warrior to fight for her. The winner was assumed to be telling the truth.

These practices were based on a simple idea. People believed that God would protect the innocent and expose the guilty. Such customs were nothing like the justice of the Romans and the Byzantines, who relied on trained judges and written laws. Trial by ordeal or combat was the rough justice of people who could neither read nor write.

This brutal era in western Europe began with the fall of the Roman empire. It is called the Early Middle Ages or the Early **Medieval** (meed-ee-**EE**-vuhl) period. For Europeans during these years between 500 and 1000, life was a struggle for survival. There were no great cities like Constantinople or Baghdad—Europe was too poor and disorganized for such grandeur.

People sometimes call these centuries the **Dark Ages,** because learning and civilization declined. Yet *Dark Ages* is a negative name and depends on one's point of view. While these times were dark ones for scholars who loved Latin learning, the Early Middle Ages were a glorious time for Germanic kings and warriors.

Civilization did indeed decline, but it did not disappear. During the grim centuries from 500 to 1000, a new kind of society gradually took shape in Europe. It had three roots: (1) the classical heritage from Rome; (2) the beliefs of the Roman Catholic Church; and (3) the customs of the various Germanic tribes. The blending of these elements eventually produced a strong, vital civilization. Before Europe became strong, however, it passed through a long period of weakness, division, poverty, and pain.

New ways of life developed in Europe. 1

By the end of the fifth century, the western half of the Roman empire had fallen to barbarians. The Visigoths held Spain, the Ostrogoths ruled Italy, the Franks controlled Gaul, and the Vandals governed North Africa. Rome's most distant province, Britannia, faced a double peril. Three fierce Germanic tribes—Angles, Saxons, and Jutes—attacked Britannia's eastern shores. At the same time, Celtic peoples—the Picts and Scots—raided Britannia from Ireland and Scotland.

Roman civilization collapsed.

Everywhere Roman civilization was under attack. This account of barbarian attacks was written in Britain around 545 by a chronicler named Gildas the Wise, but it could have been written almost anywhere in Europe:

> No sooner have they [the citizens] gone back to their land than the foul hosts of the Picts and Scots land promptly from their coracles [fishing boats] . . . They seize all the northern and outlying part of the country as far as to the wall [a Roman fortification]. Upon this wall stands a timid and unwarlike garrison. The wretched citizens are pulled down from the wall and dashed to the ground by the hooked weapons of their naked foes. What shall I add? The citizens desert the high wall and their towns, and take to a flight more desperate than any before. Again the enemy pursues them, and there is a slaughter more cruel than ever.

201

SECTION 1
Objectives and Teaching Strategies

OBJECTIVE 1. Describe how civilization declined following the collapse of the Roman empire.

Teaching Strategy: *Transferring Ideas: The Decline of Civilization* (page 200a)

OBJECTIVE 2. Identify St. Benedict and explain the importance of the Benedictine rule.

Teaching Strategy: *Discussing History: The Rule of St. Benedict* (page 200c)

■ BACKGROUND

Celtic languages survive today in parts of Wales, Scotland, and Ireland. Pressure from Angles and Saxons pushed the Celts farther and farther westward, where they remained for centuries outside the mainstream of life in Britain.

SECTION 1
Resources

GEOGRAPHY
■ Transparency 32

REINFORCEMENT
■ Independent Practice 9.1

ENRICHMENT
■ Voices from the Past 9.1

ASSESSMENT
■ Section Quiz 9.1

ANSWERS TO
Map Study

Burgundians, Franks, Bretons; Celts, Angles, Saxons, Jutes, Picts, British; Swedes, Finns, Balts, Slavs, Danes, Saxons

■ BACKGROUND

In 1939, Henri Pirenne published his famous thesis on the emergence of Europe and the breakup of the Roman empire. Noting continuities in trading patterns until 700, Pirenne argues that the Islamic invasions mark the real turning point from antiquity to the rise of modern Europe. Without Muhammad, Charlemagne could not have risen to or achieved such power.

Map Study

Compare this map with the one on page 154. What groups of people moved into the former Roman province of Gaul? What groups lived in the British Isles at this time? What groups bordered the Baltic Sea?

The collapse of trade and towns Constant warfare disrupted trade. Merchants feared pirates on sea and outlaws on land. The collapse of trade was a deathblow to cities in much of Europe.

Towns declined as Roman rule came to an end. Without the empire, there was no need for cities as centers of administration. With little trade, towns were no longer centers for business. Impoverished city dwellers left their decaying cities and drifted out into the countryside to grow their own food. The population of western Europe became overwhelmingly rural.

Loss of literacy and a common language At the same time, learning fell into a decline. The barbarians who invaded the Roman empire could not read or write. Among Roman subjects themselves, the level of learning sank sharply as more and more families left the cities for rural areas. By the year 600, priests were the only Europeans who were literate. Even their Latin was poor by classical standards.

At the height of the Roman empire, scholars from far-off Britannia had spoken the same language as Julius Caesar and Virgil. However, as German-speaking peoples joined the population, Latin began to change. Different dialects developed as new words and phrases became part of everyday speech. By the 800's, French, Spanish, Italian, and other so-called Romance (Roman-based) languages had evolved from Latin.

202

Personal ties replaced citizenship.

In the years of upheaval between 400 and 600, Germanic kingdoms replaced Roman provinces. The borders of those kingdoms changed constantly with the fortunes of war. The map on page 202 can give only an approximate idea of which group controlled which lands.

More important than shifting boundaries was that the whole idea of government changed. Family ties and personal loyalty, not public government or public law, bound Germanic society together. The Germanic people did not think of themselves as citizens of a state but as members of a family and followers of a particular leader.

Every Frankish, Saxon, or Visigothic chief had a band of warriors who had pledged their loyalty to him. In peacetime, these followers lived in their lord's hall. He gave them food, weapons, and treasure. In battle, warriors fought to the death at their lord's side. It was the greatest disgrace to outlive one's lord.

Although Germanic warriors would willingly die for a leader they knew, they felt no obligation to obey a king who was a stranger to them. And they certainly would not obey some official sent to collect taxes or administer justice in the name of an emperor they had never seen. This stress on personal ties made orderly government for large territories impossible.

Christianity won new followers.

While Roman roads and Roman law crumbled, there was one institution from Roman times that did not break down: the Roman Catholic Church. Throughout the Early Middle Ages, the Church acted as the strongest civilizing force in western Europe.

The work of missionaries Beginning in the 300's and 400's, many Christian missionaries traveled among the Germanic and Celtic groups that bordered the Roman empire. These missionaries risked their lives to spread their beliefs.

Among the most famous and successful was Patrick of Ireland. Patrick was born of Christian parents in Roman Britannia around 400, shortly before the Anglo-Saxon invasions. When he was 16, his village was raided by pagan Celts from Ireland, and he was captured and taken to be a slave. After six years, Patrick escaped from Ireland to northern Gaul, where he eventually became a bishop. His greatest goal was to convert the Irish to Christianity. In 432, he returned to Ireland as a missionary. Although he was often imprisoned and threatened with death, he established Christian churches throughout the island.

The Franks under Clovis Politics often played an important part in spreading Christianity. In the late 400's, a ruthless Frankish king named Clovis (KLOH-vihs) ruled much of northern Gaul. The Franks were pagans, but Clovis's wife was a Christian who urged her husband to convert.

In 496, Clovis led his warriors into battle against another Germanic army. When the battle began going badly for Clovis, he appealed to the Christian God. "For I have called on my gods," he cried, "but I find they are far from my aid . . . Now I call on Thee. I long to believe in Thee. Only, please deliver me from my enemies." The tide of battle shifted, and the Franks triumphed. Clovis and 3,000 of his warriors asked a bishop to baptize them.

Clovis's conversion was especially welcome to the Roman Church because Catholic bishops wanted his help against other Germanic peoples. The Ostrogoths, Visigoths, and Burgundians were all Christians (and most of them were more civilized than the Franks). However, they were not Catholic Christians. Instead, many Germanic groups had chosen a branch of Christianity known as Arianism (AIR-ee-uh-NIHZ-uhm). The Roman Catholic Church considered Arians heretics. Thus, Clovis's conversion marked the beginning of a special partnership between the Frankish kingdom and the Catholic Church.

By 600, the Roman Catholic Church had succeeded in winning over many of the Germanic peoples who had moved into Rome's former lands. In many places, however, the changeover to Christianity was only on the surface. Some kings even kept two altars, one Christian and one to their earlier pagan gods. Missionaries continued to go out among pagan groups into lands that Rome had never controlled.

Benedict set rules for monasteries.

In the days of the Roman empire, bishops were the most powerful leaders of the Church. Each leading city of the empire had its own bishop. As the population in western Europe shifted away

203

■ **BACKGROUND**
An Anglo-Saxon poet on the loss of a lord: "So have I wandered often in wretchedness/ Fettered my feelings far from my kin/ Homeless and hapless since days of old/ When the dark earth covered my dear lord's face."

At monasteries, monks and nuns grew crops and made wine, furniture, clothing, and religious artworks using the most advanced methods of their day.

Monasteries were also the wealthiest communities. Though individual monks and nuns could own nothing, the community as a whole received generous gifts of land and money from Christians.

from the cities, however, the Church had to adapt to increasingly rural conditions. One effect was the growth of **monasteries**.

Monasteries were communities in which groups of Christian men or women gave up all their private possessions and lived very simply. They devoted their lives to worship and prayer. Women who followed this way of life were called nuns; they lived in nunneries or convents. Men were called monks and lived in monasteries. Like priests, monks and nuns were expected to live according to the threefold rule of poverty, chastity, and obedience.

The Benedictine Rule A monk named Benedict set a pattern for monastic living. Born about 480 in Italy, Benedict went to school in a ravaged Rome. At the age of 15, he left school and hiked up into the Sabine Hills, seeking solitude. He lived as a hermit in a cave for several years. Hearing of his holiness, a group of monks came to him and persuaded him to be their **abbot** or head of the monastery.

Around 540, Benedict wrote a book describing a strict yet practical set of rules for monastic life. These were some of Benedict's rules:

- Once a monk enters a monastery, he is to remain there for life. Monks should not wander from one monastic house to another.
- Daily life in the monastery should follow a strict schedule. Eight times a day are set aside for prayer and worship.
- Monks should spend seven hours a day at manual labor in kitchen, field, or workshop.
- Two hours a day are reserved for reading the Bible and other Christian books.
- Monks should eat one or two meals daily, depending on the season. They may have a little wine, but no red meat.

Benedict's sister Scholastica (skuh-LAS-tik-uh) became head of a convent in which the same rules were adapted for women. Soon almost all Italian, English, and Frankish monks and nuns were living according to the Benedictine Rule.

Benedict's rules were strict but made some allowance for human frailty. Above all, they provided monks and nuns with a workable system for disciplining their lives.

The achievements of the monasteries In the Early Middle Ages, monastic communities were like islands of stability in a sea of chaos. They

Monte Cassino, the monastery founded by Benedict, was rebuilt after its destruction during World War II.

were the best-governed communities anywhere in Europe because they followed an orderly, written body of rules.

Monasteries were also the most educated communities. They operated schools, maintained libraries, and copied books. In the 600's and 700's, the monasteries of Ireland and England were the leading scholarly centers of the day. Above all, the monks of these lands excelled in making beautiful copies of religious writings, decorated with ornate letters and brilliant pictures. Through the work of the monks, at least part of Rome's intellectual heritage was preserved.

Gregory I expanded papal power.

Scattered throughout western Europe, monasteries and convents showed the spreading influence of the Catholic Church. At the head of the Church stood the pope in Rome, at first a bishop like other bishops but gradually becoming the strongest single figure in the Church.

One man who greatly increased the power of the popes was Gregory I. As pope, he wore only a rough monk's robe and humbly called himself "the servant of the servants of God." Yet while Gregory was meek on his own behalf, he was mighty on behalf of the papacy.

204

ANSWERS TO

Section Review 1

Define:
(a) task to determine guilt or innocence (b) belonging to the Middle Ages (c) A.D. 500–1000 when learning and civilization declined
(continued)

Skilled monks at Lindisfarne, England, made this beautiful gospel about the year 700.

Born in 540, Gregory grew up during the awful days when Justinian's Byzantine armies were driving the Ostrogoths from Rome and, in the process, wrecking the city. In 568, a new group of invaders struck at northern Italy. These were the Lombards, a fierce Germanic people. Conditions in Rome had never been worse. Starving Romans foraged for clumps of grass to eat.

Gregory became pope in 590 and soon made the papacy an office of political as well as spiritual power. The Byzantine emperor was too weak to protect Rome, so Gregory dealt directly with the menacing Lombards. In 599, he persuaded them to sign a peace treaty. At the same time, Gregory's palace became the center of Roman government. He used Church revenues to raise armies, repair roads, and relieve the poor. The pope was now acting as the mayor of Rome.

Gregory worked tirelessly to bring new groups into the Church. He sent missionaries to England under the leadership of a monk named Augustine in 596. This mission spread Christianity among the Anglo-Saxon kingdoms there. Gregory also wrote two influential books. One was the *Dialogues*, a collection of simply told religious stories, full of miraculous happenings. Most new Christians in this age could not grasp abstract religious ideas, but they understood Gregory's adventurous accounts of saintly lives. The second book, *Pastoral Care*, advised bishops on carrying out their spiritual duties, especially among new converts.

All that Gregory did as pope—writing books, sending out missionaries, governing Rome—expressed a new view of the world. He ignored the political divisions between kingdoms. In his view, the entire region from Italy to England, from Spain to western Germany was his responsibility as pope. Gregory had a vision of Christendom (**KRIS**-uhn-duhm), a spiritual kingdom fanning out from Rome to the most distant churches. This idea of a churchly kingdom, ruled by a pope, became a central part of the Middle Ages.

Section REVIEW 1

Define: (a) ordeal, (b) medieval, (c) Dark Ages, (d) literacy, (e) monastery, (f) abbot
Identify: (a) Patrick, (b) Clovis, (c) Arianism, (d) Benedict, (e) Scholastica, (f) Gregory I, (g) Lombards, (h) Christendom
Answer:
1. What were the three roots of medieval culture in western Europe?
2. Give two examples of ways civilization in western Europe declined after the fall of Rome.
3. (a) How did Christianity spread during the Early Middle Ages? (b) Why was Clovis's conversion to Christianity important?
4. (a) Describe the way of life followed in a monastery. (b) What part did Benedict play in the development of monasteries? (c) How were monasteries important to the preservation of civilization in this period?
5. What were the achievements of Gregory I?

Critical Thinking
6. (a) How did the Germanic ideas of government differ from the Roman ideas? (b) Which set of ideas is closer to those of our own time? Explain your answer.
7. Would it be correct to say that the idea of Christendom was a replacement for the Roman empire? Why or why not?

205

ANSWERS TO (continued)

(d) ability to read and write
(e) community of Christians who lived simple lives
(f) monastic leader
Identify:
(a) established Christianity in Ireland (b) Frankish king who converted to Roman Catholicism (c) branch of Christianity followed by Germanic groups (d) monk who set a pattern for monastic life (e) Benedict's sister and head of a convent (f) pope who established idea of Christendom (g) fierce Germanic people who invaded northern Italy (h) spiritual kingdom

Answer:
1. classical Roman heritage, beliefs of the Roman Catholic Church, customs of Germanic tribes
2. collapse of trade and towns, loss of literacy
3. (a) through missionaries and conversion (b) Clovis could help against other Germanic peoples.
4. (a) life of poverty, chastity, and prayer
(b) established rules for monastic life (c) operated schools, maintained libraries, and copied books
5. wrote books, sent out missionaries, established Rome as spiritual center of Christendom
6. (a) Family ties and personal loyalty bound Germanic society. Public government and law bound Romans. (b) Roman ideas are closer. Citizens are loyal to nation and bound by public laws.
7. Look for answer to recognize the unifying influence of both with the distinction that Christianity was concerned only with the spiritual.

Charlemagne revived the idea of empire. 2

After the breakup of the Roman empire, petty kingdoms sprang up all over Europe. For example, England was divided into seven tiny kingdoms, some no larger than the state of Connecticut. By far the largest and strongest of Europe's kingdoms was that of the Franks in what had been the Roman province of Gaul. The foundations for this kingdom were laid by the Franks' first Christian king, Clovis. (As you have probably guessed, the modern name *France* comes from the people of the Franks. *Louis*, the name of 16 later French kings, is a softer-sounding form of Clovis.)

Clovis's descendants lost power.

In 481, when the 15-year-old Clovis became king, the Franks controlled only a small area of flat, marshy land (the present-day Netherlands) on either side of the Rhine River. By the time Clovis died in 511, he ruled most of what is now France.

The Merovingian kings Clovis and his successors are known as the Merovingian (MAIR-oh-VIHN-jee-uhn) dynasty, after a legendary ancestor, Merovech. They were also called "the long-haired kings" because long hair was a symbol of power and authority among the Franks. The Merovingians ruled for about 275 years, but those were not peaceful years.

When a Merovingian king died, his sons treated the kingdom as private property to be divided among themselves. Such divisions weakened the kingdom and often led to civil war as each son tried to seize the whole kingdom. Yet the Merovingians succeeded in keeping the idea of kingship alive.

Mayors of the palace By the year 700, the power of Merovingian kings had dwindled to almost nothing. The most powerful person in the kingdom was not the king but an official known as the *major domo* or mayor of the palace. Officially, a mayor of the palace was in charge of the royal household and estates. Unofficially, he was the power behind the throne. He commanded armies and made policy. In effect, he governed the kingdom in the king's name.

In 714, the position of mayor of the palace was held by Charles, known as *Martel* (the Hammer). Charles Martel was king in all but name. He extended the power of the Franks to the north, south, and east. He even defeated a Muslim raiding party from Spain at the Battle of Tours in 732. (This battle marked the height of Muslim conquests in Europe.) Finally, at his death, Charles Martel passed his power on to his son, Pepin the Short.

DAILY LIFE ▶ Stirrups and Warfare

In Merovingian times, most Frankish warriors were foot soldiers, but during the 700's, warfare changed. The stirrup came into use in Europe. (It may have been invented in India.) As a result, the technology of war changed.

More and more warriors fought on horseback. Without stirrups to brace him, a charging warrior was likely to topple off his own horse. Mounted warriors with stirrups could use heavier armor and weapons. These armored horsemen were known as **knights**. Galloping full tilt at the enemy, a Frankish knight could knock a foot soldier off his feet or an enemy rider off his horse. The horse became essential to a noble warrior. Without a horse, a man was considered a peasant. Gradually, the most important part of an army came to be its mounted knights.

The pope named Pepin king.

Pepin was not content to be the power behind the throne. He wanted to be king in his own right. Pepin wrote a shrewd letter to the pope. Pepin asked, Who should be the rightful ruler of the Franks? Should it be the man who had the title of king but no power? Or should it be the man with the power but no title? The pope answered, "It is better that he who possesses power be called king than he who has none." Thus did Pepin the Short obtain the Church's blessing for seizing the throne.

The pope and the new Frankish king needed each other. Only the Church could give legitimacy to the rule of Pepin and his heirs. At the same time, only a strong king like Pepin could protect the pope from the Lombards, who again threatened Rome. In desperation, Pope Stephen II crossed the Alps in 754 to plead for help. Pepin agreed to fight the Lombards on the pope's behalf. Then occurred an event of immense historic importance. In a dimly lighted chapel, the pope anointed Pepin's head with holy oil and declared him "king by the grace of God."

Pepin was the first king ever to be anointed by a pope. Afterward, it became common for kings in western Europe to be crowned "by the grace of God" in a church ceremony. No longer were kings simply political rulers. They now had some spiritual authority as well.

Pepin soon led an army into Italy and defeated the Lombards in one city after another. In 756, he collected the keys to all the cities he had conquered and gave them to the pope. Thus, the popes became political rulers of scattered Italian lands known as the Papal States.

The Frankish kings and the Roman popes had entered into an informal alliance. It was an unstable alliance, however. Much of the later history of the Middle Ages, as we shall see, was the story of popes struggling to control kings, and vice versa.

Charlemagne extended Frankish power.

Pepin the Short died in 768 and left a greatly strengthened Frankish kingdom to his son, Charles. Charles was in his mid-twenties when he became king and in his early seventies at his death. He was king of the Franks for 46 years (768–814), longer than Augustus Caesar had been emperor of the Romans.

In fact, Charles's reign was a glorious time in the Frankish kingdom, just as Augustus's reign had been for Rome. In Latin, Charles was called *Carolus Magnus*, or Charles the Great. In French, his name became Charlemagne (SHAHR-luh-MAYN). His descendants were known as the Carolingian (KAIR-uh-LIN-jee-uhn) dynasty.

Charlemagne's personality Though his father was Pepin the Short, Charlemagne was gigantic, six feet four inches tall. Charlemagne followed the Frankish custom of wearing a mustache but no beard. His secretary and biographer, a monk named Einhard, wrote this description of him:

The upper part of his head was round, his eyes were large and lively, nose a little long, hair fair, and face laughing and merry. Thus his appearance was always stately and dignified, whether he was standing or sitting; although his neck was thick and somewhat short, and his belly rather prominent; but the symmetry of the rest of his body concealed these defects.

Charlemagne was a great sportsman. He especially liked to hunt deer on horseback or to plunge into a river and swim great distances. A king in the Middle Ages needed all Charlemagne's great physical strength and energy.

Charlemagne the conqueror In war, the king himself commanded the armies and fought in the front line. Every spring, Charlemagne called together all the great landowners of the kingdom, both nobles and bishops. They met at Charlemagne's capital, Aachen (AH-kuhn), or at another royal residence. Each noble brought his own followers, equipped for battle. This, for example, was one of Charlemagne's orders to his nobles:

Each horseman is expected to have a shield, lance, sword, dagger, bow, quiver with arrows, and in your carts shall be . . . axes, planes, augers, boards, spades, iron shovels, and other utensils that are necessary in any army. In the wagons shall be supplies for three months, together with arms and clothing for six months.

Summer after summer, Charlemagne led these armies against the enemies that surrounded his

207

SECTION 2 Objectives and Teaching Strategies

OBJECTIVE 1. Explain the importance of the Battle of Tours for western Europe.

Teaching Strategy: *Discovering History: The Battle of Tours* (page 200c)

OBJECTIVE 2. Explain how Charlemagne expanded the Frankish empire and revived learning.

Teaching Strategy: *Discussing History: The Revival of Learning* (page 200c)

OBJECTIVE 3. Explain how central authority broke down in the years following Charlemagne's death.

Teaching Strategy: *Transferring Ideas: The Problem of Succession* (page 200c)

■ BACKGROUND

Aachen is the German form of the French name *Aix-la-Chapelle*. Both names are used for Charlemagne's capital, and show the growing divergence of language within the Frankish kingdom.

SECTION 2 Resources

GEOGRAPHY
■ Transparencies 33, 34

REINFORCEMENT
■ Independent Practice 9.2

ENRICHMENT
■ Voices from the Past 9.2

ASSESSMENT
■ Section Quiz 9.2

Cooperative Learning

Tell students that they are going to identify the characteristics that made Charlemagne a great ruler. Working individually, have each student review Section 2 and make a list of the personal characteristics and actions that contributed to Charlemagne's greatness as a ruler. When the lists are complete, have groups of four discuss students' lists. Then, have each group compile a list of just six characteristics or qualities that group members feel contributed the most to Charlemagne's success. Everyone must agree on all six items. Recorders should write down the groups' choices and the reasons for those choices. Other group members should each present and explain two of their choices to the class.

The Empire of Charlemagne in 814

Map Study
Charlemagne, shown at the right, carries an orb as a symbol of imperial power. What enemies threatened his northeastern border?

kingdom. He conquered new lands to both the south and the east.

When a frightened pope again asked for protection against the Lombards, Charlemagne responded. He defeated the Lombards, captured their king, and took over northern Italy in 773.

Five years later, in 778, Charlemagne crossed the Pyrenees Mountains and marched into Muslim Spain. He hoped to win control of northern Spain, but the expedition failed. As the Franks retreated through the mountains, ambushers caught the Frankish rear guard by surprise and slaughtered it. Among the Franks to die was the leader of the guard, Count Roland. This massacre became a Frankish legend, retold in a great epic poem called the Song of Roland.

It was the Franks' eastern frontier, however, where Charlemagne fought his greatest wars. In what is now Yugoslavia and Hungary, an Asian people called the Avars ruled the Slavs. After seven years of brutal warfare, Charlemagne destroyed the Avar kingdom. The Saxons of Ger-

many were even more troublesome. Charlemagne fought them for nearly 30 years before they submitted to his rule and his Christian religion.

Charles did more than encourage missionaries to work among the Saxons and other pagans. He sometimes resorted to baptism by the sword, offering his defeated enemies the choice of becoming Christian or dying on the spot. Not for nothing did Christian chroniclers call him "iron Charles" and "the strong right arm of God."

By the year 800, the Frankish kingdom included two thirds of Italy, all of present-day France, a small part of Spain, and all of German Saxony. It had grown larger than the Byzantine empire. Only a ruler of Charlemagne's energy and ability could hope to govern such an empire.

Charlemagne strengthened his rule.

Like kings both before and after him, Charlemagne needed the help of powerful nobles to govern his kingdom. However, also like other

208

kings, he needed a way to limit the power of those nobles.

Royal officials All of Francia, as the Frankish kingdom was called, was divided into counties. Each county was ruled in the king's name by a powerful landholder called a **count**.

The counts administered justice and raised armies. In theory, the king could dismiss a count at any time. In practice, however, the same count might rule an area for as long as 30 years. Unless the counts were constantly reminded of the loyalty they owed the king, they might quickly become independent rulers.

Wisely, Charlemagne did not trust his counts. He sent out royal agents called **missi dominici** (MIHS-ee doh-MIHN-uh-kee), or "emissaries of the master," to see that counts governed justly and did not abuse their power. Charlemagne also regularly visited every part of his kingdom to judge cases, settle disputes, reward faithful followers, and keep the less loyal in line. By constant watchfulness, he managed to keep his powerful counts under control. (His sons and grandsons, however, were less successful at controlling their nobles.)

The royal estates Much of Charlemagne's power rested on his position as a great landowner. The Carolingian family owned huge estates scattered throughout Francia. Charlemagne and his sons kept a close eye on the management of their lands. This letter, for example, is part of a set of instructions to the overseer of a royal estate.

The greatest care must be taken that whatever is prepared by hand—bacon, smoked meat, sausage, partially salted meat, wine, vinegar, mulberry wine, cooked wine, mustard, cheese, butter, malt, beer, mead, honey, wax, flour, all should be prepared with the greatest cleanliness.

In each of our estates, the chambers shall be provided with counterpanes, cushions, pillows, bedclothes, coverings for tables and benches.

Most of a king's wealth came not from taxes but from goods like those listed in that letter—goods produced on the royal estates. These estates supported the royal court and also paid for the daily working of government. A king who allowed his estates to decline would quickly lose his political power too.

Charlemagne revived learning.

Charlemagne's court became the center for a revival in learning. Earlier Germanic kings had shown little interest in learning. Yet Charlemagne understood some Latin and even perhaps a little Greek. He learned to read, and he struggled to learn to write. According to Einhard, he "used to keep tablets and blanks in bed under his pillow that he might accustom his hand to form the letters; however, as he did not begin his efforts [until] late in life, they met with ill success." He was never able to write more than a word or two.

For his court at Aachen, the king recruited the leading European scholars of his day. There was a music teacher from Italy, a poet from Spain, and many others. By far the most influential of these imported scholars was an Englishman named Alcuin (AL-kwihn) of York. Charlemagne also invited Jews to settle in his kingdom because they were literate and could help with administrative work.

For his own numerous sons and daughters and for other children at the court, Charlemagne began a palace school. There students learned to read, write, and do a little arithmetic. Charlemagne himself visited the classes. On at least one occasion, the king's famous temper was aroused, and he pummeled a lazy student for mistakes in grammar.

By Charlemagne's order, monasteries and cathedrals were expected to open schools to train future monks and priests. (Since only boys could enter the priesthood, only boys attended these schools.)

Monasteries increased their libraries. Monks labored to make handwritten copies of rare Latin books. Each copy took many months of toil. As they worked, the monks developed a new style of lettering. Roman books had all been written in capital letters, and there was no spacing between words. To save time, monks began substituting small letters for the Roman capitals. To make the books easier to read, the monks added spaces between the words. Gradually, writers in monasteries perfected a beautiful and readable style of lettering known as Carolingian miniscule (MIHN-ih-skyool). Most of these small letters look almost exactly like the letters printed in a modern book.

209

■ **DISCUSSION**

The *missi dominici* were sent out in pairs. One was always a member of the clergy, the other was always a lay person. How did they symbolize the power Charlemagne claimed?

■ **BACKGROUND**

Charlemagne feared that "as the skill in writing was less, so also the wisdom for understanding the Holy Scriptures might be much less than it rightly ought to be," and so he ordered the monasteries to open schools for reading and writing.

ANSWERS TO

Section Review 2

Define:
(a) armored horseman
(b) landowner who ruled a county (c) agents sent to see that counts governed justly (d) lettering developed in monasteries

Identify:
(a) inhabitants of Europe's strongest kingdom (b) Clovis and his successors (c) real power behind the Merovingian throne (d) defeated Muslims at Battle of Tours (e) son of Charles Martel anointed by pope (f) Italian lands over which pope had political rule (g) Pepin's son who extended Frankish empire (h) Charlemagne's descendants (i) divided Charlemagne's empire

Answer:
1. (a) letting the surviving sons divide the kingdom at
(continued)

ANSWERS TO *(continued)*

the death of the king **(b)** the major domo's

2. (a) King needed credibility afforded by pope; pope needed military protection for Roman lands. **(b)** by being crowned by the pope **(c)** Pepin defeated the Lombards and gave the pope control of the Papal States.

3. (a) with the use of counts and *missi dominici* **(b)** supported royal court and government

4. recruited scholars, opened school at palace, ordered monasteries to open schools

5. (a) emperor of Rome **(b)** widened split between eastern and western Catholics

6. divided it into three kingdoms and weakened it

7. Muslims, Magyars, Vikings

8. Answers might stress the revival of learning, the spread of Christianity, his political and military achievements, or reviving the idea of empire.

■ **DECISIONS**

Charlemagne considered the marriage because it would strengthen his position as emperor in the eyes of the Byzantines. Irene reigned as a Byzantine emperor [sic] from 797 to 802, when she was deposed and exiled.

ANSWER TO

Map Study

Aachen

The pope made Charlemagne emperor.

By the year 800, Charlemagne was the most powerful king in western Europe. Then he traveled to Rome to help Pope Leo III, who had been attacked by a Roman mob. On Christmas Day in St. Peter's Cathedral, the pope placed a jeweled crown on Charlemagne's head and declared him emperor. The crowd of people in the church (probably coached in advance) shouted, "Hail to Charles the Augustus, crowned by God to be the great and peace-giving emperor of the Romans, life and victory."

What did the title of emperor mean? According to one argument, the title gave Charlemagne new prestige. He could deal as an equal with the Byzantine emperor. The counterargument says Charlemagne gained nothing but trouble from the crowning. The new title added nothing to his power. Moreover, news of the crowning angered the Byzantines and made another enemy on Charlemagne's troubled eastern frontier. After all, in the Byzantine view, the true Roman emperor ruled from Constantinople.

Another theory says that the crowning was the work of the pope and did not please Charlemagne at all. Why would the pope want to make Charlemagne emperor? Perhaps Pope Leo wanted an emperor who would stay in Rome and help govern the unruly city. Perhaps it was a shrewd political move, establishing the pope's power to name an emperor.

Probably Charlemagne's coronation meant different things to different people. Charlemagne and Pope Leo III each had his own motives, which we may never know. However, we do know the long-term consequences of the crowning.

First, the coronation marked another stage in the growing split between the Church of Constantinople and the Church of Rome. After 800, there were two Christian empires, Greek Orthodox in the east and Roman Catholic in the west. Each viewed the other with growing suspicion.

Second, there arose in western Europe a new idea of empire. Later popes repeatedly gave the title "Roman emperor" to one European king or another. In theory, the person entrusted with this title became the protector of all Christendom. The title meant little when held by a weak ruler, but in strong hands it could be a powerful tool.

210

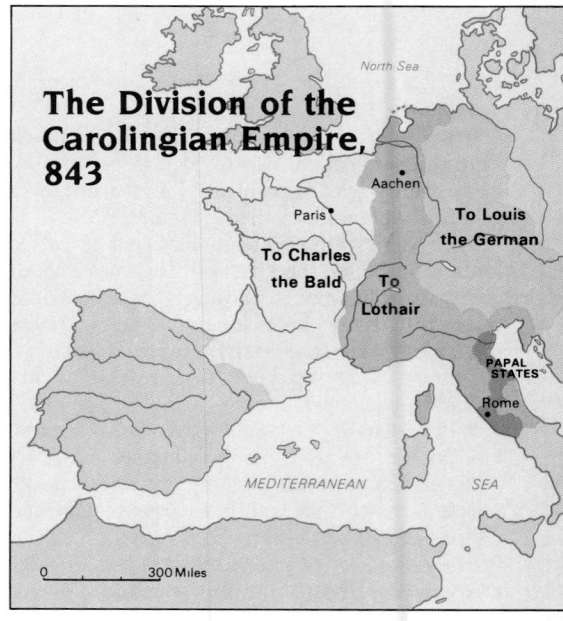

The Division of the Carolingian Empire, 843

Map Study

The Treaty of Verdun divided Charlemagne's empire among his three grandsons. Which important city lay in Lothair's territory?

Charlemagne's heirs ruled weakly.

When Charlemagne died at his palace in 814, his only surviving son, Louis the Pious, succeeded him as king and emperor. A devoutly religious man, Louis would have made a better monk than a king. As a ruler, he was ineffective. He died in 840.

Louis left three sons: Lothair (loh-**THAIR**), Charles the Bald, and Louis the German. Like the Merovingian princes, Louis's sons fought one another for the empire. The civil war ended in 843 when the brothers signed a pact called the Treaty of Verdun (vur-**DUHN**). This document divided Charlemagne's empire into three kingdoms, one for each brother.

Decisions in **H**istory

As Holy Roman Emperor, Charlemagne had a unique opportunity. The ruler of the Byzantine empire was a woman, the Empress Irene. Should he marry the empress and reunite the Roman empire? Or should he concentrate on his empire in Western Europe? What would you have done, and why?

Charles the Bald's kingdom would eventually become France. Louis the German's kingdom would become Germany. Lothair, the eldest son, kept the title of emperor and took the land between his brothers' kingdoms, including the imperial capitals of Rome and Aachen. His land became a battleground for the future kings of France and Germany.

After the Treaty of Verdun, Carolingian kings became almost as powerless as the long-haired Merovingians had been. Once again, central authority broke down.

At the same time, all of Europe from Ireland to Italy was repeatedly assaulted and plundered by terrible new invasions. From the south, Muslim pirates seized Sicily and raided Italy, even sacking Rome in 846. From the east struck the Magyars, barbarians from central Asia. Like the earlier Huns and Avars, the Magyar warriors terrorized Germany and Italy. And from the north came the most dreaded attackers of all, the Vikings (VY-kingz). Even before Charlemagne's death, the earliest Viking raids struck Europe.

Section REVIEW 2

Define: (a) knight, (b) count, (c) missi dominici, (d) Carolingian miniscule
Identify: (a) Franks, (b) Merovingians, (c) mayor of the palace, (d) Charles Martel, (e) Pepin the Short, (f) Papal States, (g) Charlemagne, (h) Carolingians, (i) Treaty of Verdun
Answer:
1. (a) What practice weakened the power of the Merovingian kings? (b) Into whose hands did their power pass?
2. (a) Explain how the Frankish king and the pope depended on each other. (b) How did kings gain some spiritual authority? (c) How did the pope become a political ruler?
3. (a) Describe how Charlemagne ruled his widespread lands. (b) Why were his own estates important to his government?
4. How did Charlemagne promote learning?
5. (a) What new title did Charlemagne receive from the pope in the year 800? (b) What were the consequences of this event?
6. How did the Treaty of Verdun affect the Frankish kingdom?

7. What groups invaded Europe in the 800's?
Critical Thinking
8. What do you think was Charlemagne's greatest achievement? Give reasons for your answer.

Vikings terrorized Europe. 3

To the monks on Lindisfarne Island near the northeast coast of England, it seemed to be just another peaceful morning when they awoke to perform their daily rituals. But on this morning in 793, a large sailing vessel lay near the shore, barely visible in the mist. Its square sail was striped red and white. Its prow swept upward in a graceful curve like a swan's neck, but at the top was a dragon's head.

As dawn broke, burly warriors jumped from the ship to the island shore, clutching swords and heavy wooden shields. The monks had no weapons. Some were killed at the altar even as they prayed. Others were dragged to the sea and drowned. The monastery was thoroughly ransacked. Golden crucifixes, silver chalices, ivory boxes, and silk and linen tapestries were all piled in the boat. Laughing and shouting, the attackers heaved on their oars. Soon their striped sail disappeared over the horizon.

News of this outrage soon reached the court of Charlemagne. "Never before," wrote Alcuin, "has such a terror appeared in Britain as this that we have just suffered from a pagan race." In 793, the terror was just beginning. From about 800 until the year 1000, the Vikings raided from Ireland to Russia. In many churches, a new prayer became part of the daily worship: "Save us, O God, from the fury of the Northmen."

Footnote to History

In the heat of battle, some Viking warriors lunged against the enemy howling, snarling, and biting their wooden shields in rage. In this state of hyperexcitement, they felt neither fear nor pain. Such warriors, feared even by other Vikings, were known as *berserkrs,* from which comes the modern word for someone in a violent frenzy, *berserk.*

SECTION 3
Objectives and Teaching Strategies

OBJECTIVE 1. Describe a Viking ship and explain its importance.

Teaching Strategy: *Teaching with Pictures: A Viking Ship* (page 200d)

OBJECTIVE 2. Trace Viking routes on a map.

Teaching Strategy: *Using Geographic Themes: Movement* (page 200d)

OBJECTIVE 3. Explain why the Viking age ended.

Teaching Strategy: *Discussing History: The End of the Viking Age* (page 200d)

■ BACKGROUND

An Irish chronicler on the Vikings: "If 100 heads of hardened iron could grow on one neck, and if each head possessed 100 . . . tongues of tempered metal, and if each tongue cried out incessantly . . . they would never be able to enumerate the griefs which the people of Ireland . . . have suffered at the hands of these . . . pagans."

SECTION 3
Resources

GEOGRAPHY
■ Transparency 35

REINFORCEMENT
■ Independent Practice 9.3

ENRICHMENT
■ Voices from the Past 9.3

ASSESSMENT
■ Section Quiz 9.3

By 930, fully 20,000 Norse were raising crops and grazing sheep on the remote island of Iceland.

Vikings were skilled seafarers.

The raiders were known by several names: Northmen, Norsemen, and Vikings. Their home lay far to the north in a wintry, rocky, forested region called Scandinavia (SKAN-duh-NAY-vee-uh). Today, this region consists of Norway, Sweden, and Denmark.

The people of Scandinavia were Germanic with customs and language similar to those of the Franks, Saxons, and Goths who had earlier invaded Europe. The Scandinavians, however, had had almost no contact with Rome. They were still pagans, worshiping warlike gods. Viking leaders took pride in nicknames like Eric Bloodaxe and Thorfinn Skullsplitter.

The Vikings carried out their raids with terrifying swiftness. They would beach their ships, strike, then quickly shove out to sea again. By the time local troops arrived, the Vikings were long gone.

The Viking warships were the technological marvel of their age. Long, lean, and light, the largest of these ships could hold 300 warriors, who took turns rowing its 72 oars. Most ships were smaller, with crews of 30 to 50 fighters. The prow of each ship swept grandly upward, often ending with the carved head of a sea monster or dragon. Although a ship might weigh 20 tons when fully loaded, it could sail in 3 feet of water. Thus, the Vikings could strike villages and monasteries far inland by rowing up shallow rivers and creeks.

Scandinavians settled far and wide.

Despite their fearsome reputation, it is wrong to think of the Vikings merely as ferocious brutes. They were also wily traders and careful farmers. As explorers, they were unsurpassed. They traveled far beyond western Europe, down rivers into the heart of Russia, to Constantinople, and across the icy waters of the northern Atlantic Ocean.

By the year 900, hundreds of Scandinavian families had made the perilous voyage to the distant island of Iceland. There they built a prosperous settlement.

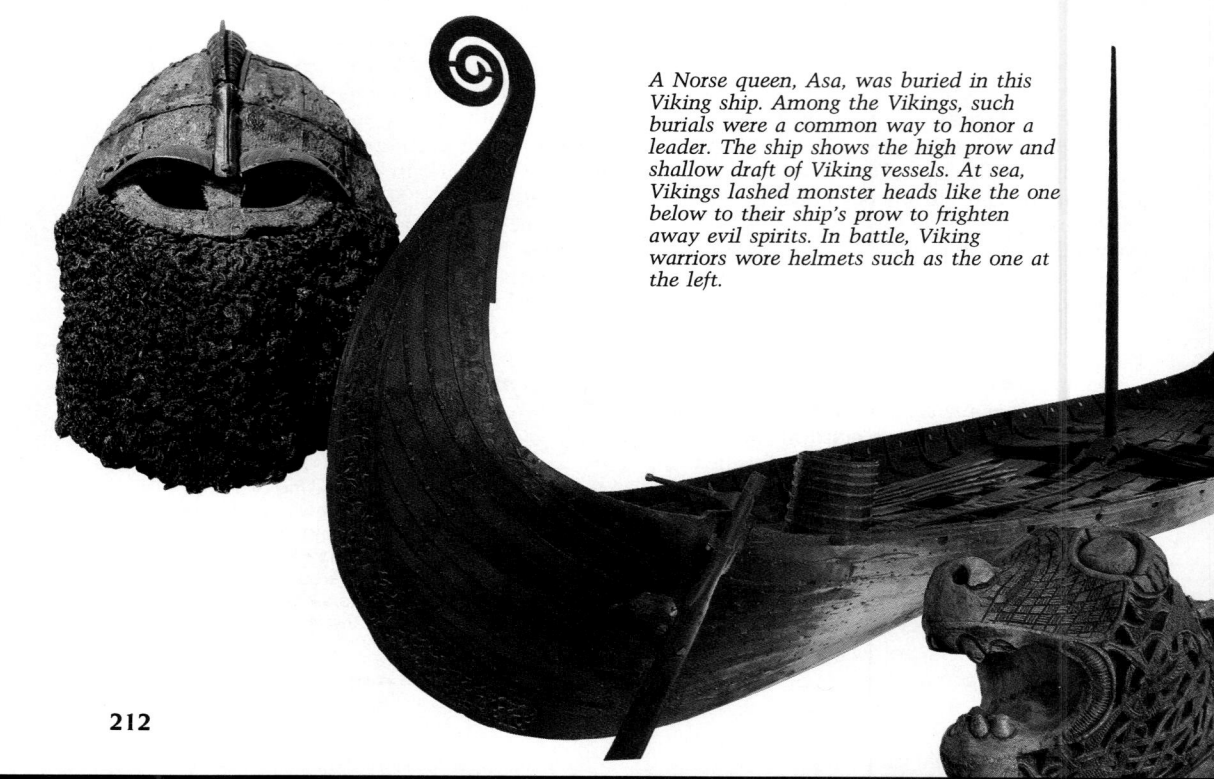

A Norse queen, Asa, was buried in this Viking ship. Among the Vikings, such burials were a common way to honor a leader. The ship shows the high prow and shallow draft of Viking vessels. At sea, Vikings lashed monster heads like the one below to their ship's prow to frighten away evil spirits. In battle, Viking warriors wore helmets such as the one at the left.

212

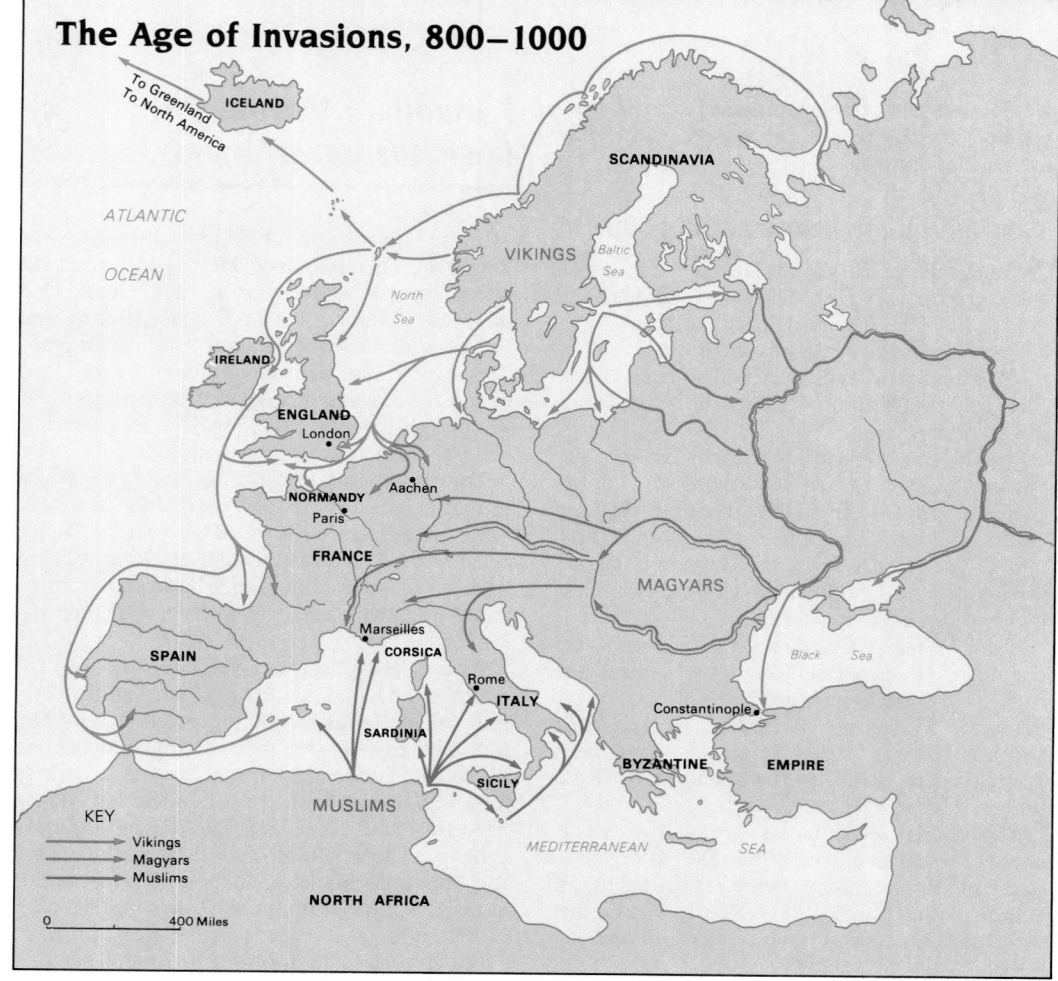

The Age of Invasions, 800–1000

ANSWERS TO
Map Study

Baltic Sea, North Sea, Atlantic Ocean, Black Sea, Mediterranean Sea; Magyars

Map Study

Of the three great groups of invaders that struck Europe, the Vikings ranged most widely. Name the seas and oceans that they reached. Which group of invaders came overland?

In 982, a red-bearded outlaw named Eric the Red sailed west from Iceland into uncharted Atlantic waters. He came upon an island that was largely buried under a massive sheet of ice. He misnamed the place Greenland. For a while, Norse settlers managed to eke out a living even in that harsh environment. Eventually, however, the settlement was abandoned.

About the year 1000, Eric the Red's son, Leif (leef) Ericson, sailed from Greenland to another unexplored land. This probably was the Canadian island now known as Newfoundland. The Vikings called it Vinland. There is no question that Leif Ericson reached the Americas before Columbus.

Meanwhile, the Vikings were also settling widely in western Europe. They established their own kingdoms in parts of Ireland and nearly conquered all of England. Only the courage and leadership of the English hero-king, Alfred the Great, finally halted their advance in 886. In northern France, Viking leaders won a rich territory that became known as Normandy.

In all these regions, Viking warriors were the forerunners of Scandinavian settlers. The raiders

213

ANSWERS TO
Section Review 3

Identify:
(a) sea-faring raiders from Scandinavia (b) today, Norway, Sweden, and Denmark (c) Arctic island settled by Vikings in 900's (d) Viking who sailed to Greenland (e) island discovered and misnamed by Eric the Red (f) Eric's son who sailed to what is now Newfoundland (g) island Vikings discovered

Answer:
1. (a) Scandinavia (b) They came in ships and were still pagan.
2. Greenland and Newfoundland (the Americas)
3. better defenses on part of Europeans, conversion of Vikings to Christianity, warmer climate
4. Kings had little power and few resources. The Vikings raided with such swiftness that the Europeans did not have time to muster troops.

were followed by whole families of farmers, traders, and artisans whose influence spread widely in much of Europe.

The Viking age ended about 1000.

Around the year 1000, the Viking terror, which had raged for two centuries, slowly receded and died. Why? Three facts help to explain it.

First, Europeans finally worked out a way to respond quickly to raids and small-scale invasions. (The way this system worked will be explained in the next section.)

Second, like so many barbarians before them (including Goths, Franks, and Saxons), the Vikings gradually adopted Christianity. For example, King Guthrum of the Danes agreed to become a Christian as part of his peace treaty with England's King Alfred. As Christians, the Vikings were less inclined to raid monasteries.

Third, after 1000, Europe's climate went through a warming trend that lasted several centuries. That trend explains why Viking settlements on Iceland and Greenland prospered. As farming became easier in Scandinavia, fewer Scandinavians turned to the seafaring life of Viking warriors.

The Vikings were the last great raiders to descend on western Europe. While the eastern lands of the old Roman empire were devastated by the Seljuk Turks, the Ottoman Turks, and other warriors from central Asia, western Europe was at last free of invasions.

Section REVIEW 3

Identify: (a) Vikings, (b) Scandinavia, (c) Iceland, (d) Eric the Red, (e) Greenland, (f) Leif Ericson, (g) Newfoundland

Answer:
1. (a) Where did the Vikings come from? (b) How were they different from the earlier Germanic groups who had invaded Europe?
2. What new lands to the west did the Vikings reach?
3. What factors helped to end the Viking terror?

Critical Thinking
4. Why was it very difficult for kings to defend their territory against Viking raids?

Feudalism became the basis for government. 4

In the late summer of 911, two men who had long been enemies stood face to face near the Seine (sayn) River in what is now France. One man was Rollo, the leader of a Viking army that had been plundering the rich river valley for years. The second man was the almost powerless king of France, known to history as Charles the Simple. Though he bore the title *king*, Charles controlled little of the land that is France today.

The two men had come to make peace. In a formal ceremony, Charles granted Rollo a huge piece of French territory. This part of France became the Northmen's land, or *Normandy*. In return, Rollo placed his hands between the king's hands and swore never to make war against the king again.

As part of the ceremony, Rollo was expected to kneel and kiss the king's foot, but this was more than the proud Viking could stand. "No, by God!" he bellowed. Instead, Rollo ordered one of his henchmen to perform the rite. Charles's foot was hoisted into the air so the tall Viking need not bend his knees. The Viking promptly showed his low opinion of royal dignity by tipping the king onto his back in the dirt. Yet Charles grimly swallowed his pride to win Rollo's oath of loyalty.

Other rulers and warriors in many parts of Europe were making similar agreements. The worst years of the invasions (about 850 to 950) were also the years when a new pattern of life emerged in western Europe. No king or pope dictated this pattern. No brilliant thinker proposed the new system. Instead of one solution, there were hundreds, each depending on local circumstances. Villagers in England responded in one way; villagers in northern Italy responded in another.

Yet overall, the pattern was similar. Everywhere, there was an increasing emphasis on local protection, local government, and local self-sufficiency. This new political system is known as **feudalism** (FYOO-duhl-ihz-uhm). Feudalism was a political and military system based on the holding of land. The control of land was the key to feudalism.

Lords and vassals exchanged vows.

At the heart of the feudal system was an agreement between a **lord** and a **vassal**. When Charles the Simple gave Normandy to Rollo the Viking, Charles became Rollo's lord. When Rollo placed his hands in Charles's and swore loyalty, Rollo became Charles's vassal (a person who receives land from a lord).

The bond between lord and vassal The personal bonds of loyalty that tied a vassal to a lord were the key to the feudal system. The oath sworn between them was the equivalent of today's written contract.

Kneeling, bareheaded, and without his sword, the vassal placed his hands in the hands of his lord. In this humble position, he swore to be the lord's man all the days of his life and to defend the lord against "all men who may live or die." The lord then raised him up and kissed him.

Next came **investiture** (ihn-VEST-ih-choor), a symbolic act through which the lord presented the vassal with a stick, small rod, or clod of earth. The lord thus transferred into the vassal's hands control of a piece of land. Such a piece of land was known as a **fief** (feef).

Redividing a fief By accepting a fief from Charles the Simple, Rollo became a royal vassal—the vassal of a king. But that grant was not the end of the feudal process. Like other royal fiefs, Normandy was huge. To protect such a fief, the vassal needed a private army.

Since the royal vassal had little money but plenty of land, he could afford to divide his fief into, let us say, 70 smaller estates. Keeping the best land for himself, he would give the other 69 estates as fiefs to 69 warriors who agreed to be his vassals. Thus, the royal vassal himself became the lord of other vassals.

These smaller vassals in turn divided their lands and granted fiefs to warriors of their own. Each local lord used grants of land to attract a personal band of warriors. At the bottom of the scale were the knights, men whose parcels of land were too small to be easily subdivided.

The advantages of this system for defense were clear. Every local lord had a force of knights ready to defend the land against all comers—Vikings, Magyars, Muslims, outlaws, or a neighboring lord. Moreover, lords usually fortified their lands, building strongholds at key places.

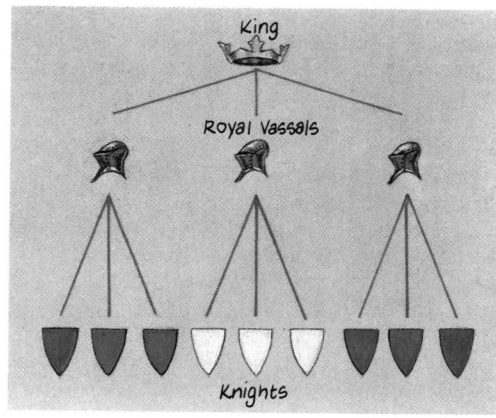

This diagram shows how the feudal system worked in theory. In real life, however, the system became a tangle of conflicting loyalties.

The feudal pyramid In theory, feudal society was a pyramid. At the bottom were many knights, each with a small fief. Above them were their lords, who held larger fiefs. And over all was the king.

In practice, however, the feudal system never worked so clearly. For one thing, an ambitious knight could collect fiefs from several lords by pledging to serve them all. In doing so, he ran a risk. Suppose, as often happened, two of his lords warred with each other. Then the knight would have to choose for whom to fight. His very life might depend on picking the winner. The feudal pyramid often became a complex tangle of conflicting loyalties that both lords and vassals tried to use to their own advantage.

Vassals served in war and peace.

Vassals were required to fight in the lord's army when called. From each of his knights, a lord could demand about 40 days of combat on horseback every year. Weapons, armor, and warhorses were expensive. A vassal needed a certain amount of land so he could afford such gear. Moreover, the skill to use the weapons took training and practice. Gone were the days of citizen-soldiers such as the Greek hoplites or the early Roman legions. Knights in the Middle Ages were specialists in war. Supported by wealth from their fiefs, knights devoted their lives to war.

215

SECTION 4
Resources

ASSESSMENT
- Section Quiz 9.4

REINFORCEMENT
- Independent Practice 9.4

ENRICHMENT
- Voices from the Past 9.4

SECTION 4
Objectives and Teaching Strategies

OBJECTIVE 1. State reasons for the development of feudalism.

Teaching Strategy: *Discussing History: Feudalism* (page 200e)

OBJECTIVE 2. Support general statements about feudalism.

Teaching Strategy: *Skill Building: Supporting Generalizations* (page 200e)

OBJECTIVE 3. Contrast the feudal economic system with the economic system of a modern industrial society.

Teaching Strategy: *Economics and History: Contrasting Economic Systems* (page 200e)

OBJECTIVE 4. Chart the duties and benefits of nobles, vassals, knights, peasants, and serfs in the feudal system.

Teaching Strategy: *Discussing History: Analyzing the Feudal System* (page 200e)

■ DISCUSSION

Why would the gestures of kneeling and placing one's hands in the hands of the lord have been important in an age when few people could read and write? (allowed witnesses to understand the verbal agreement)

■ BACKGROUND

Local violence among nobles was a problem. The Church would issue proclamations called *Peace of God* or *Truce of God* outlawing theft, injury, and other crimes and detailing the punishment, including excommunication, for committing them.

ANSWERS TO
Voice from the Past

1. landholdings of her husband
2. inheritance of husband's land
3. to inherit half of her grandfather's lands and to marry as she pleases

Women and church leaders as vassals Feudalism was both a military system and a landholding system. Noblewomen and church leaders often held great estates. Thus, these groups were part of feudalism even though they usually were not warriors.

A noblewoman might inherit a fief from her parents or her husband, or she might control land in the name of her young son. In such cases, a woman fulfilled the feudal duties that went with the land. She sent her vassal knights to war when the lord called. She might also command and defend her castle if her husband was away.

Church leaders too were part of the feudal system. They owed military service just as other vassals did. In the Early Middle Ages, being a churchman was no bar to being a warrior. Fighting bishops such as Turpin of Reims and Odo of Bayeux were famed for their might in battle. In later times, bishops were more likely to send their vassal knights than to go to war themselves.

Peacetime duties Vassals also owed their lords duties in time of peace. When Rollo was given Normandy, he received not only the land with whatever its farms produced but also the right to rule that land. He was expected to hold courts of justice, to charge tolls on the bridges, to collect taxes, and much more. Justice was the lord's largest peacetime responsibility.

From vassals who were bishops or abbots, a lord was likely to demand governmental and legal services. Being literate, a bishop or abbot could act as the lord's secretary. He could give learned council, keep written records, and write letters for the lord.

In case of financial emergency, lords could ask their vassals for a grant of money. Such a grant was called an aid. Traditionally, a lord could call

Voice from the Past | *Feudalism and Marriage*

Lords controlled the marriages of their vassals, both men and women. In the Middle Ages, marriages were an important part of politics. Marriages cemented alliances between families. When a woman married, her husband usually took over her property. Marriage to a wealthy woman might make a vassal even more powerful than his lord. The documents below come from the royal accounting office in England between 1140 and 1282.

- *Ralph son of William owes 100 marks as a fine, to be allowed to marry Margery who was wife of Nicholas Corbet who [held land of the king], and that the same Margery may be allowed to marry him.*
- *Walter de Cancy renders account of £15 to be allowed to marry a wife as he shall choose.*
- *Emma de Normanville and Roheisa and Margaret and Juliana, her sisters, render account of 10 marks for license to marry where they wish.*
- *Roheisa de Doura renders account of £450 to have half of all the lands which belonged to Richard de Lucy, her grandfather . . . and for license to marry where she wishes so long as she does not marry herself to any of the king's enemies.*
- *Alice, countess of Warwick, renders account of £1,000 and 10 palfreys [women's saddle horses] to be allowed to remain a widow as long as she pleases, and not to be forced to marry by the king . . . and to have the custody of her sons.*

1. What fact suggests that Margery may have been a wealthy woman?
2. What was the probable source of her wealth?
3. What two rights is Roheisa de Doura buying from the king?

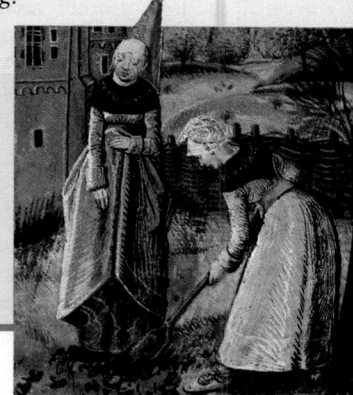

for aids at three times: (1) when the lord's oldest son was knighted; (2) when the lord's oldest daughter was married; and (3) if the lord was captured in a war and held for ransom. The lord could also travel to a vassal's fief and expect to be housed, wined, and dined for several days.

Historians often describe feudalism as a system in which public power became private. The Roman and Greek idea of public affairs had disappeared. Justice, military power, and political power had all become private possessions. They could be traded among lords or passed down to one's heirs. The duties a person owed were not to a polis or to an empire but to a personal lord.

Manors were the economic side of feudalism.

The great majority of people in the Middle Ages were neither lords nor vassals. Medieval writers said that there were three groups of people: those who fought (the nobles), those who prayed (the men and women of the Church), and those who worked (the peasants). Nobles and church leaders were part of the feudal system. The peasants—horseless, weaponless, and powerless—were outside the political system of feudalism. However, their daily toil lay at the heart of the economic system in the Middle Ages.

The basic economic unit was the **manor**. A manor was a small estate from which a lord's family gained its livelihood. Sometimes a manor was the whole of a fief, sometimes only one part of a fief. If a lord held more than one manor, as was often the case, stewards managed each manor when the lord was absent.

A manor usually covered only a few square miles of land, perhaps with a stream meandering through it. (Fish from streams and ponds were an important source of food.) About one third of the land was cleared for growing grain. Another patch of land was pasture for the peasants' oxen and the lord's horses. The rest was forest.

Self-sufficiency From these meager resources, the laborers on the manor—the peasants—had to produce everything they and the lord needed. Nothing was purchased from outside except salt, iron, and a few unusual objects such as millstones. Everything else—food, fuel, cloth, leather goods, lumber—was produced on the manor. The manor was thus a world unto itself.

Serfs on the land Most peasants were **serfs**. Serfs were not free, but they were not quite slaves either. Unlike slaves, serfs could not be bought, sold, or traded to another lord. Yet serfs could not lawfully leave the manor on which they were born. They were bound to the land. From a different viewpoint, serfs had the right to live on the same manor from birth to death. Although it is hard to understand today, a serf in the Middle Ages may have felt that the right to stay was more important than the freedom to leave.

Free peasants A few peasants enjoyed greater freedom than serfs. They could leave the manor if they wished. These free peasants were not required to do as much work for the lord as the serfs were. Still, one bad harvest or flood could force free peasants to become serfs in exchange for bread and protection. For example, a poor Frankish peasant named William became a serf at the monastery at St. Martin. A monastic document of the eleventh century reads:

> *Be it known to all who come after us that a certain man in our service, William, brother of Reginald, born of free parents . . . gave himself up as a serf to St. Martin of Marmoutiers, and he gave not only himself but all his descendants, so that they should forever serve the abbot and monks . . . And in order that this gift might be made more certain and apparent, he put the bell rope round his neck and placed four pennies from his own hand on the altar of St. Martin in recognition of serfdom.*

Peasants owed duties on the manor.

All peasants, whether free or serf, were tenants on the lord's manor. They paid dearly for the right to live and grow crops on the lord's land. A typical serf owed the lord the following duties:

- Two or three days' labor every week plowing, planting, and harvesting the lord's own land. (Every sack of grain harvested from this land went to the lord's family.)
- A certain portion of the grain grown on the serf's own land.
- One pig out of every ten pigs raised on the manor, plus the service of slaughtering it.
- As a "gift" at Christmas and Easter, delivery to the lord of so many eggs and chickens.

217

■ **DISCUSSION**
What is the relationship between feudalism and manorialism? (One is a political and military system and the other an economic system. Nonetheless, they were inextricably linked for centuries in many regions.)

Despite its egalitarian origins, the Church viewed peasants as those whose birth relegated them to a life of back-breaking testing for the future reward of life in heaven.

Tell students to imagine they have gone back in time to the Early Middle Ages. In groups of four, they set out to explore a feudal manor and stop to chat with a serf working in a field. He is grateful for a chance to rest and proves quite talkative. Now, back in the twentieth century, the groups wish to write letters to friends about their adventures and the serf they met. Group members should first discuss the general contents of the letter, which might include the serf's surroundings, situation, and the events of a typical day. Then have students take turns writing, with each group member writing for about two minutes while the others offer suggestions. The writer should read aloud as he or she is writing. The letter should be passed around the group until complete. Encourage students to include the thoughts and feelings the medieval serf might have expressed as they write their letters. Allow groups to share their letters with the class.

A medieval manor was largely self-sufficient. Its residents raised or made nearly everything they needed for daily life.

- A tax on all grain ground in the lord's mill and all bread baked in the lord's oven. (Any attempt to dodge these charges by baking bread elsewhere was punished as a crime.)
- A tax when the serf married. (No marriage could take place without the lord's consent.)

After all these payments to the lord, each peasant's family still owed to the village priest a tithe (church tax), representing one tenth of their income. Together, lord and priest typically collected from each serf six sacks of grain for every ten sacks produced.

Life on a manor was harsh.

Peasant men and women rarely traveled far from their own manor. They could see their entire world at a glance by standing in the center of a plowed field and looking around.

On some manors, the tallest structure on the landscape was a wooden tower set high on a hill and surrounded on four sides by a ditch and a wall. This was the manor's castle, a place of safety for lord and peasant alike whenever Vikings raided or a neighboring lord attacked. (Gigantic stone castles with moats and drawbridges did not exist until later in the Middle Ages.) Not far away was a plain two-story house of rough-hewn timber where the lord's family lived in times of peace.

Across the fields in another direction, one could see the thatch roofs of the peasants' one-room huts in the manor's village. Close by, facing the village well, stood a plain church.

By the stream, the waterwheel of the lord's mill turned slowly and ground the manor's grain into flour. The millwright who built and repaired mills was one of several skilled workers in the

218

Looking at economics *This drawing from the mid-1300's shows peasants stacking grain. Farming was the chief medieval economic activity.*

village. Another was the blacksmith, who forged the few metal items used on the manor.

For peasant men and women, probably the most familiar sight was the swishing tails of the oxen that they walked behind as they plowed a field. Since few peasants could afford a whole team of oxen, villagers shared their animals. The same team plowed everyone's fields. Land was shared too. Fields were laid out in long, thin strips because the plow was hard to turn. A peasant family might use strips of land scattered in fields all around the village.

Peasants raised wheat, barley, oats, and rye. Coarse, black bread made from these grains was the main course of many meals. In garden patches, families grew cabbages, onions, beans, and other vegetables. Hens scratched in the dooryards of the houses, more valuable for their eggs than for meat. Half-wild pigs nosed the ground for fallen acorns near the edge of the village woodlands. One slaughtered pig per year might be a peasant family's only source of meat. Honey was used for sweetener. Fruit trees grew apples, pears, cherries, and peaches. Yet after a bad harvest, peasant families lived on the edge of starvation.

In addition to hunger, there was the misery of being chilled to the bone when the winter winds blew. The cold seeped into a peasant's hut through cracks in the log walls. There were no floorboards, only the bare dirt ground. In one corner of the room, in a wooden frame, was a pile of straw crawling with vermin. This was the bed in which the whole family slept, parents and children together. Farm animals (geese, sheep, pigs) were commonly admitted into the hut to increase the general body heat. Though smelly, warming a hut with pig heat was safer than

burning a fire in the center of the room and risking that a spark would fly toward the family's straw bed.

Nobles had more to eat and warmer clothing than peasants did. Yet even nobles had little comfort and no protection from sickness or injury.

The years from 500 to 1000 were harsh for Europeans. Change came slowly. When one bad harvest could spell death, people were reluctant to try new ways. Yet, even by 800, changes were taking place that would improve life on the manor. By 1000, Europe was poised for a revival in farming, trade, government, and learning.

Section REVIEW 4

Define: (a) feudalism, (b) lord, (c) vassal, (d) investiture, (e) fief, (f) aid, (g) manor, (h) serf

Answer:
1. (a) What oath did a vassal swear to his or her lord? (b) What did the lord give in return? (c) How did a vassal become the lord of others?
2. (a) What services could a lord demand of vassals in time of war? (b) In peacetime?
3. (a) How did women become lords or vassals? (b) What part did church leaders have in the feudal system?
4. (a) What duties did a serf owe on a manor? (b) How might a free peasant become a serf?

Critical Thinking
5. (a) How was a local community self-sufficient both militarily and economically in the Early Middle Ages? (b) Why was self-sufficiency important in this age?

219

ANSWERS TO
Section Review 4

Define:
(a) political and military system based on holding land (b) person who transfers control of a fief (c) person who received land from lord (d) symbolic gesture representing the granting of the land (e) piece of land given to a vassal (f) grant of money lord could ask from his vassals (g) small estate from which a lord's family gained its livelihood (h) peasant who was bound to the land

Answer:
1. (a) oath of loyalty (b) fief (c) by dividing his fief and giving parts away to warriors who agreed to be his vassals
2. (a) 40 days of fighting, good equipment, good fighting skill (b) handling matters of justice, tax collection
3. (a) through inheritance or in the name of a young son (b) same as others
4. (a) 2–3 days' farming labor per week; paying tax on grain ground in lord's mill (b) Hard times might force trade of freedom for food and shelter.
5. (a) Except for salt, iron, and a few other items, everything was produced on the manor. (b) With decline of cities and public law, goods were not available in markets and trade routes were unsafe.

Concluding the Chapter

1. Chapter Closer
Ask students to give three examples of how Roman and Germanic cultures blended to create a new civilization in the Early Middle Ages.

2. Reteaching Activities
a. Supporting a Generalization Write the following on the board: "Throughout the Early Middle Ages, the Church acted as the strongest civilizing force in western Europe." Have students explain this statement and give evidence from the text to support it.

b. Explaining Political Changes Have students write a paragraph explaining the decline of the Merovingian dynasty and one describing the contributions to the Carolingian empire of Charles Martel, Pepin the Short, and Charlemagne.

c. Answering Questions Have students rewrite each heading in this section as a question and answer the question.

d. Explaining Key Phrases Have students explain how each of the following phrases related to feudalism: military system, political system, and landholding system.

Answers to Chapter Review appear on pages 200e–200f.

Summary
1. New ways of life developed in Europe. By the end of the 400's, the Roman empire had been broken into many Germanic kingdoms. Trade collapsed, towns declined, and the level of learning sank. Germanic leaders and customs replaced Roman government and law. Monasteries stood out as centers of orderly life, where learning was kept alive.

2. Charlemagne revived the idea of empire. The Franks had the largest of the Germanic kingdoms. The greatest of the Frankish rulers was Charlemagne, who conquered pagan lands, set up an effective administration, and encouraged learning. After his death, Europe suffered a new wave of invasions.

3. The Vikings terrorized Europe. From 800 to 1000, raiders from Scandinavia threatened much of Europe. They also explored and settled widely. After 1000, the Viking menace declined.

4. Feudalism became the basis for government. Feudalism developed as a form of local protection and government. Vassals pledged loyalty to a lord; in return, the lord gave each vassal a grant of land. Lords and vassals spent most of their lives training for battle and fighting wars. Peasants worked on manors to supply the goods needed to support themselves and the lords.

Reviewing the Facts
1. Define the following terms:
   a. medieval   g. lord
   b. monastery   h. vassal
   c. knight   i. investiture
   d. count   j. fief
   e. missi dominici   k. manor
   f. feudalism   l. serf

2. Explain the importance of each of the following names, dates, places, or terms:
   a. Patrick   i. missi dominici
   b. Clovis   j. Aachen
   c. Benedictine Rule   k. A.D. 800
   d. Gregory I   l. Carolingians
   e. Christendom   m. Treaty of Verdun
   f. Merovingians   n. Vikings
   g. Pepin the Short   o. Leif Ericson
   h. Charlemagne

3. (a) How was learning promoted by Charlemagne? (b) By monasteries?

4. What different methods were used to spread Christianity during the Early Middle Ages?

5. How was Germanic society organized?

6. Explain how the feudal system linked lords and vassals. Include information on investiture, fiefs, and aids.

Pepin annointed by pope

Charlemagne crowned emperor

Battle of Tours

Conversion of Clovis

Leif Ericson's voyage to North America

Benedictine Rule

Treaty of Verdun

Pope Gregory I

Rise of feudalism

Viking invasions

500   600   700   800   900   1000

220

7. (a) After 800, what were the titles of the two men who could claim leadership of all Christian Europe? (b) How did leaders depend on each other?
8. (a) What part did the manor play in medieval life? (b) Describe the ways land was used on a manor.
9. (a) What obligations did serfs have? (b) What did they get in return?

Basic Skills

1. **Reading a time line**   (a) Using the time line on page 220, tell what event happened at the same time as the start of the Viking invasions. (b) What event happened as the invasions ended?
2. **Classifying**   Using the map on page 202, make a chart to classify the peoples who settled in different areas of western Europe. Make four columns with the headings *Spain, France, Germany,* and *Britain.* Under each heading, list the names of the peoples who had settled there by 500. (See Chapter 32 for a map of Europe today.
3. **Interpreting a diagram**   On the diagram on page 215, assume that the royal vassals are named (from left to right) John, Richard, and William. If one of the white knights owed allegiance to both Richard and William, how would you change the diagram to reflect that relationship? (Draw six shields and two helmets.)
4. **Using historical terms**   Political power is *centralized* if it is exercised by a single strong government and *decentralized* if it is divided among many local governments. Illustrate the term *centralized* by describing the rule of Charlemagne and *decentralized* by describing the rule of his successors.
5. **Identifying supporting details**   Find details supporting the statement on page 203 of the text, "Throughout the Early Middle Ages, the Church acted as the strongest civilizing influence in western Europe."

Researching and Reporting Skills

1. **Selecting a topic for research**   Of the following research topics, which ones would you eliminate as either too broad or too narrow: *The Conversion of Clovis, Feudalism in Western Europe, The Life of Charlemagne, Life in a Benedictine Monastery,* and *Lindisfarne Island during the Roman Empire*? Give reasons for your choices.
2. **Organizing a group project**   Feudalism was a complex system organizing many aspects of life. Divide the class into five groups to research and report on the following areas as they are affected by feudalism: distribution of land, military organization, administration of justice, economic activity, and personal relationships.
3. **Role-playing**   As a class project, research and role-play the ceremony of investiture between a lord and his vassal. Discuss the significance of this ceremony to the structure of feudal obligations.

Critical Thinking

1. **Analyzing cause and effect**   One key to the collapse of Roman civilization was the disappearance of the cities. (a) What were the causes of this disappearance? (b) What were the effects on civilization?
2. **Analyzing**   The text stresses the fact that in the Early Middle Ages, ties of personal loyalty replaced citizenship. (a) What would be some of the consequences of this shift for the peace and prosperity of the times? (b) Was this change positive or negative? Why?
3. **Predicting outcomes**   In 800, Charlemagne was crowned emperor by the pope. (a) What was the significance of this event? (b) How might it influence future relationships between Church and state?

Perspectives on Past and Present

(a) What generalizations could you make about the relationship between politics and religion in the Middle Ages? (b) Give facts to support your statement. (c) Contrast this generalization about the Early Middle Ages with the principles governing the relationship between church and state in the United States today.

Investigating History

Look up information on Viking ships and sea travel. In what ways did their ships represent technological progress? What other factors enabled the Vikings to become explorers who succeeded in crossing the Atlantic?

221

CHAPTER
Evaluation

Chapter Test 9, Alternate Chapter Test 9, and Computer Test Bank Chapter 9 Test can be used to evaluate your students' understanding of this chapter.

The High Middle Ages

Chapter Overview

In the High Middle Ages, improved farming technology and increased food production stimulated population growth, which led to a revival of town life. Merchant and craft guilds formed to control trade, and a growing middle class won new liberties. The power and prestige of the Roman Catholic Church also increased during the High Middle Ages and royal governments in England and France grew stronger.

By the late 1100's, a revival of learning had begun. The first universities were established in western Europe and scholars took a new interest in the works of the ancient Greeks. As the ideals of society changed, a code of chivalry developed.

The High Middle Ages were also the Age of Faith. In 1095, Pope Urban II appealed to that faith and called on all knights in Christendom to rescue Jerusalem from the Muslim Turks. Thus began the first of the eight Crusades.

Chapter Focus

Begin by asking students to read the chapter opener (pages 222–223). Then direct their attention to the question asked by the abbot on page 223. The people of Chartres (and indeed all of Christendom) believed that the Virgin Mary had chosen Chartres as her special residence on earth. This belief was based on the fact that Chartres Cathedral possessed a sacred relic—the red tunic (or Virgin's Veil)—which Mary was said to have worn at the birth of Christ. The tunic was given to

Charlemagne. His grandson, Charles the Bald, then gave it to Chartres in A.D. 876. When the tunic miraculously survived a fire in 1194, the townspeople interpreted this as a sign that Mary required a new and even grander church.

Emphasize that like other great monuments, Chartres is an expression of the civilization that created it. The imagination, energy, and faith needed to construct Chartres reflect a revival of Europe's spirit after the long Dark Ages.

Farming improved and trade revived. 1

Setting the Stage

The collapse of the Carolingian empire was followed by a period of destructive Viking raids. In addition, most Europeans lived as impoverished serfs on feudal manors. Survival was a daily worry. Then something unexpected happened. European society started to show signs of strength. By the twelfth century, the society was capable of erecting monumental works like Chartres Cathedral. Ask students to speculate on the causes of this surprising burst of energy.

Teaching Strategies

Economics and History: Technology and the Revival of Agriculture (Objective 1) Ask students to list three new techniques that

Advance Planner

	SECTION 1
Objectives	1. Explain how new ways of farming helped to revive European agriculture. 2. Compare and contrast life in the towns with life on the manor.
Setting the Stage	Signs of strength in medieval society
Teaching Strategies	Economics and History: Technology and the Revival of Agriculture Discussing History: Comparing Towns and Manors Check for Understanding
Guided Practice	Section Review 1
Independent Practice Worksheets	Independent Practice 10.1 Geography Skills 10 Vocabulary 10
Enrichment	1. Primary Source: Voices 10.1 2. ★Preparing a Report: Guilds and Unions 3. Researching for Points
Chapter Closer	

SECTION 2	SECTION 3	SECTION 4	SECTION 5
1. Identify three abuses of power that Church reformers wanted to end. 2. Describe gothic architecture and explain its significance.	1. Discuss the consequences of the Norman conquest of England. 2. Draw a map of Europe in 1160.	1. Describe aspects of life in a medieval castle. 2. Compare the status of medieval women with that of women in ancient Egypt, Greece, and Rome.	1. Describe aspects of warfare in the Holy Land. 2. List and evaluate the consequences of the Crusades.
The role of reformers	European monarchs	The importance of literacy	Pope Urban II's speech at Clermont calling for a crusade
Discussing History: Reforming the Church Teaching with Pictures: Gothic Cathedrals Check for Understanding	Discussing History: The Norman Conquest Geography in History: Making a Map Transparency 36 Outline Map 9 Check for Understanding	Teaching with Pictures: Life in a Medieval Castle Skill Building: Comparing and Contrasting Women's Status Check for Understanding	Teaching with Pictures: The Mighty Krak Transparency 37 Discussing History: Consequences of the Crusades Check for Understanding
Section Review 2 Independent Practice 10.2	Transparency 36 Q&A Section Review 3 Independent Practice 10.3	Section Review 4 Independent Practice 10.4 Basic Skills 10	Transparency 37 Q&A Section Review 5 Independent Practice 10.5 Critical Thinking 10
1. Primary Source: Voices 10.2 2. Researching for Points	1. Primary Source: Voices 10.3 2. Researching for Points	1. Primary Source: Voices 10.4 2. ★Preparing a Report: Abelard and St. Bernard 3. Researching for Points	1. Primary Source: Voices 10.5 2. ★Analyzing a Quotation: Will Durant 3. Researching for Points

●**Reteaching Activities**   Recalling Main Ideas, Organizing Information, Summarizing

Chapter Review   Summary, Reviewing the Facts, Basic Skills, Researching and Reporting Skills, Critical Thinking, Perspectives on Past and Present, Investigating History

Chapter Evaluation   Chapter Test 10, Alternate Chapter Test 10, Computer Test Bank Chapter 10 Test

improved farming in the Middle Ages and to explain why they represented improvements. (heavier plows, new harness, three-field system)

These new agricultural techniques helped medieval farmers produce a surplus. Greater amounts of food meant greater numbers of people could be fed. As the population increased, pioneers gradually cut down the dense forests that covered four fifths of Europe. This "great age of clearing" further stimulated agricultural production. Changes in agricultural practices continue to play an important role in modern economies. For example, pesticides, machinery, and hybrid seeds enable a few farmers to feed a large population.

Discussing History: Comparing Towns and Manors (Objective 2) Have students read the sections on guilds and towns (pages 224–227) and Voice from the Past (page 227). Town life was strikingly different from life on the manor. Note these fundamental differences in outlook:

■ For merchants, wealth was based on the possession of money. For lords, wealth was based on the possession of land.

■ For merchants, a person's status in society was achieved by labor and bargaining. For lords, a person's status was inherited as a fact of birth.

Feudal barons frequently treated burghers with contempt. Fortunately for the towns, a burgher's money could be very persuasive. In exchange for a bag of money, lords consented to grant towns written charters. Towns became more independent and attracted people seeking greater personal freedoms.

Check for Understanding Have students complete the following equation: $x + y + z =$ growth of towns. Variables should include increased farm production, population growth, and increase in trade.

Enrichment Activities

1. **Reading a Primary Source** Assign Voices from the Past Resource Book 10.1.

2. **Preparing a Report** Ask advanced students to compare the role of a medieval guild with the role of a modern worker's union.

3. **Researching for Bonus Points** Where were the four Champagne Fairs held? (at Troyes, Bar, Lagny, and Provins)

Religious leaders wielded great power. **2**

Setting the Stage

Ask students to define *reformer*. Reformers want to improve society by correcting a problem or abuse. What reformers have students already studied? (Hebrew prophets, Confucius, Solon, and the Gracchi) The troubles that plagued Europe during the Early Middle Ages also affected the Church.

Teaching Strategies

Discussing History: Reforming the Church (Objective 1) Have students identify the three practices Church reformers wanted to correct. (clerical marriages, simony, lay investiture) Why did reformers see lay investiture as a major threat to the Church? (German emperors frequently selected popes who cared more about wealth than about serving the Church.)

Teaching with Pictures: Gothic Cathedrals (Objective 2) Refer students to the upper illustration on page 232. Point out the pointed arches, flying buttresses, and ribbed vaults. These techniques enabled Gothic architects to achieve height and light. Now direct students' attention to the picture of Bourges Cathedral at the lower right. Ask them to describe how it would feel to stand inside this cathedral. Call attention to the picture of the rose window from Chartres Cathedral. Stained-glass windows used symbols to illustrate stories from the Bible. For example, the outer ring of this window shows 12 minor prophets. The next ring contains 12 *fleur-de-lis*—symbols of the French royal family. Then a circle of 12 kings of Judah is followed by a ring of 4 doves, 4 angels, and 4 horses. Finally, all eyes focus upon the image of a crowned Mary, the Queen of Heaven, holding the Christ Child.

Check for Understanding Have students explain the roles of Pope Gregory VII, Francis of Assisi, and Abbot Suger in Church reforms of the High Middle Ages.

Enrichment Activities

1. **Reading a Primary Source** Assign Voices from the Past Resource Book 10.2.

2. **Researching for Bonus Points** What were the names of the architects who designed Chartres Cathedral? (Their names are unknown. Chartres was designed to glorify God and not individuals.)

Royal governments grew stronger. 3

Setting the Stage

Ask students to write three qualities that they feel a present-day national leader should possess. List these qualities on the board. Then explain that the leadership of kings played an important role in the political revival of Europe.

Teaching Strategies

Discussing History: The Norman Conquest (Objective 1) Have students read the sections on the Norman conquest and William the Conqueror (pages 233–234). Ask students to suggest three significant consequences of the Norman conquest. England emerged as the first centralized feudal kingdom in Europe. Some 200,000 Normans settled in England by 1087 bringing with them their French language and culture. As a result, about one fourth of the words in modern English are of French origin. Finally, the Duke of Normandy became both the King of England and the vassal of the French kings. Ask why this was a source of conflict. (William's conquest of England led to rivalry between the kings of England and France.)

Geography in History: Making a Map (Objective 2) The consolidation of territory is one result of centralized power. Show students Map Transparency 36, *The Kingdoms of Europe in 1160*, and have them locate the territories held by the Norman kings (England), Capetian kings (France), and the German emperors (Holy Roman Empire). Then distribute copies of Outline Map 9: Physical Europe. Using the map on page 235 as a guide, have students label the Mediterranean Sea, Atlantic Ocean, and North Sea. Then have them compare their work to a map of present-day Europe.

Check for Understanding Have students explain why English kings were successful and German kings less successful in building royal power.

Enrichment Activities

1. **Reading a Primary Source** Assign Voices from the Past Resource Book 10.3.
2. **Researching for Bonus Points** Harold and William were two of the three contenders for Edward's throne. Who was the third? (The Norwegian king Harold Hardrada—defeated in battle by Harold Godwinson.)

Learning revived and spread. 4

Setting the Stage

Have students discuss the importance of literacy and education in today's world. Ask, "Does education give someone in our society power? Money? Prestige? Happiness?" Literacy gave the medieval clergy great influence. Only the literate could read contracts, laws, and the most important document of the time—the Bible.

Teaching Strategies

Teaching with Pictures: Life in a Medieval Castle (Objective 1) Medieval castles were sources of protection as well as places of commerce for nearby farmers. Ask students to study the photo on page 239. Have them list the features that were essential to the security and produc-tivity of the castle and its residents. What role do students think knights played in daily life at the castle?

Skill Building: Comparing and Contrasting Women's Status (Objective 2) Ask students to compare and contrast the social status of Egyptian women (page 63), Greek women (pages 111–112), Roman women (page 133), and medieval European women (page 216). Ask, "In which societies did women enjoy higher status and more rights?" Ask advanced students to assess the effects of the code of chivalry on the perception and treatment of women during the Middle Ages. What was the role of noblewomen in the feudal political system? How did women's arts, such as tapestries, reflect the realities of daily life for ladies of the castle?

Check for Understanding Ask students to write a paragraph describing the life-styles of medieval students, nobles, and women.

Enrichment Activities

1. **Reading a Primary Source** Assign Voices from the Past Resource Book 10.4.
2. **Preparing a Report** Ask advanced students to report on the great debate between Abelard and St. Bernard. (See *The Age of Faith* by Will Durant.)
3. **Researching for Bonus Points** What were Roland's last words as he lay dying on the field of battle? ("O God the Father who has never lied, who called the holy Lazarus back to life, and Daniel from the lion's jaw preserved, Protect my soul, and pardon all my sins.")

Crusaders marched against Islam. 5

Setting the Stage

Begin by locating Clermont on the map on page 243. Then ask students to imagine that they are among thousands of people in a field outside Clermont on a cold November day in the year 1095. They have come to hear their fellow Frenchman, Pope Urban II. Urban implores them to free the Holy Land from the Muslims. Now read the following excerpts from Urban's speech, and ask students to write a brief reaction to each:

1. "On whom, then, rests the labor of avenging these wrongs, and of recovering this territory, if not upon you—you upon whom, above all others, God has conferred remarkable glory in arms, great bravery, and strength to humble the heads of those who resist you?"

2. "Jerusalem is a land fruitful above all others, a paradise of delights. That royal city, situated at the center of the earth, implores you to come to her aid. Undertake this journey eagerly for the remission of your sins, and be assured of the reward of imperishable glory in the Kingdom of Heaven."

Sample students' reactions. Explain that after hearing the Pope's speech, the excited crowd roared, "God wills it!" Within minutes, nobles, knights, monks, and serfs pledged to go on a crusade to free the Holy Land.

Teaching Strategies

Teaching with Pictures: The Mighty Krak (Objective 1) Review the sections on the Crusades (pages 241–245). Have students trace the routes of the Crusades on Map Transparency 37, *The Crusades*, and locate Syria on the map. The

crusaders defended their conquests in the Holy Land by building great castles, such as Krak des Chevaliers ("Castle of the Knights") in Syria. Direct students' attention to the picture of Krak on page 244. Construction of Krak began in 1110. The Muslims were never able to successfully storm the mighty Krak. Instead, a clever Sultan used a forged surrender order to trick a small garrison of knights into surrendering. The mighty Krak fell in 1271.

Discussing History: Consequences of the Crusades (Objective 2) Have students relate the goals of the Crusades with the actual results. Although the Crusades failed to regain the Holy Land, they had a number of other consequences that were not expected. First, they stimulated trade with Asia, thus strengthening the merchant class. Second, they enhanced the status of noble women, who managed the castles and manors while their husbands were away at war. Third, the Crusades weakened the nobility because many knights and lords were killed, captured, or lost. Finally, western Europe acquired the inventions of Asia, such as gunpowder, the crossbow, the compass, and Arabic numerals. The failure of the Crusades also contributed to the decline of Church power.

Check for Understanding Have students write short paragraphs explaining why the Crusades were a "sign of the times" in the High Middle Ages. Ask them to explain how the Crusades reflected the growing importance of the Church and expressed the concepts of knighthood and chivalry.

Enrichment Activities

1. **Reading a Primary Source** Assign Voices from the Past Resource Book 10.5.

2. **Analyzing a Quotation** The modern historian Will Durant wrote: "All medieval development, all the expansion of commerce and Christendom, all the fervor of religious belief, all the power of feudalism and glamour of chivalry came to a climax in a Two Hundred Years' War for the soul of man and the profits of trade." Ask advanced students to interpret and evaluate this statement.

3. **Researching for Bonus Points** What happened to Richard the Lionheart as he traveled across Europe on his way home from the Third Crusade? (He was captured and held for ransom.)

ANSWERS TO Chapter Review 10

Reviewing the Facts

1. (a) town dwellers (b) collective names for burgh dwellers (c) association of people who worked at the same occupation (d) worker in training (e) worker who had completed training but was not yet a master (f) list of a town's special privileges and tax exemptions (g) leading bishop (h) punishment by which no Church ceremonies could be performed in an offending ruler's lands (i) law of the Church (j) wandering monk who lived by begging (k) 12 people who answered facts about a case for a

royal judge (l) rulings of England's royal judges that formed a unified body of law (m) code of behavior governing knights (n) military expedition

2. (a) system in which two out of three fields were planted while one lay fallow (b) site of monastery that led way in Church reforms (c) Italian town to which Henry IV traveled to beg forgiveness from Gregory VII and thereby save his throne (d) agreement that settled disputes about investiture (e) experts sent by the Church to find and judge heretics (f) architectural style emphasizing light and height (g) defeated Harold at Battle of Hastings (h) the year of Battle of Hastings (i) William's great-grandson and strong ruler of England (j) founder of Capetian dynasty (k) strongest ruler of medieval Germany (l) first ruler to call his lands the Holy Roman Empire (m) lands under the control of Frederick Barbarossa (n) great Christian scholar who linked faith and reason (o) capital of Byzantine empire sacked in 1204, ending the Fourth Crusade (p) holy city won from Muslims in First Crusade (q) Muslim leader with whom Richard the Lionheart reached agreement in 1192

3. resulted in better harvests and, subsequently, a population increase, revival of towns, and increased trade

4. enforced standards of quality, fixed the price of goods, provided insurance for members and their families, arranged business details, trained new workers

5. Bishops were powerful nobles and kings wanted to control them. Popes believed that bishops should not be controlled by a king.

6. Unlike England and France, Germany did not become a united country.

7. (a) built ribs from the roof to the columns to help support the roof's weight (b) allowed walls to become frames for huge stained-glass windows

8. (a) Jewish scholars working in Muslim libraries translated Arabic copies of Greek works into Latin. (b) Byzantine scholars made Latin translations of Justinian's code. (c) Monks copied the writings.

9. (a) The Crusades won wide support in Europe at first because of the pope's promise of forgiveness of sins; the prospects of glory, adventure, and increased later trade replaced religious fervor. (b) little

Basic Skills

1. (a) masons, stonecutters, bricklayers, farmers, shepherds, shoemakers, shopkeepers (b) picks, cement mixing, trowels, T-squares, horse-drawn plough, earthenware, pewter or silver-smithing, boot making, jewelry making, woven goods

2. Students should mention the growing power of popes and of kings, the development of rule by law, the Crusades, the rise of independent towns, improvements in food production, the role of trade fairs and of guilds, the revival of learning, rise of chivalry, and changing roles of women.

3. First: from Lyons and Ratisbon by land and sea to Constantinople, then to Syria and Jerusalem; Second: from Metz to Constantinople, then by land and sea to Antioch and Palestine; Third: from northern France and Paris to Marseilles by land and sea, then by sea to Palestine; also from Ratisbon to Constantinople; Fourth: from Venice to Constantinople

Researching and Reporting Skills

1. Students' work will vary.

2. (b), (d), (f) These sources pertain to the topic and refer to the correct time period.

Critical Thinking

1. (a) Chivalry helped regulate feudal relationships and expressed Christian ideals. (b) Chivalry affected the conduct of warfare and the status of women and found expression in romantic love, literature, and song.

2. Noblewomen inherited fiefs and managed estates. Townswomen worked in craft guilds and in trade. Mostly, women were confined to home or convent, lacked political rights, and had little say in choosing marriage partners.

3. Although German kings headed the Holy Roman Empire, they failed to consolidate their power. Most land remained in the hands of powerful princes who elected the king.

4. Students might suggest that (a) guilds often supported the king against the nobles; (b) guilds often obtained town charters, winning independence from the feudal system.

5. (a) The Church governed from a central capital through curia and legates. Its bishops operated courts of law. It collected taxes. (b) absolving allegiances to the king, excommunicating the king, using the interdict

Perspectives on Past and Present

1. Burghers' sons studied for jobs in government or in the church; no women were allowed; classrooms and books had to be rented; exams were oral and in Latin.

2. Students' responses will vary.

Investigating History

Students' findings will vary.

Chapter 10

Teaching with Pictures

Before students read the chapter opener (pages 222–223), have them study the picture and speculate who these laborers might be. Tell students that the workers are nobles who are rebuilding the Chartres Cathedral in the year 1144. In 1134, for the fourth time in its history, Chartres Cathedral had been destroyed by fire. In 1144, a new and grander cathedral was rising slowly over the flat countryside. Point out to students that the window in the upper left corner is Gothic and shaped like those on page 232. Ask students why rebuilding the Cathedral took so many years.

The High Middle Ages

Building a cathedral

Key Terms

middle class	friar
burgher	flying
bourgeoisie	buttress
guild	jury
apprentice	common
journeyman	law
charter	chivalry
cardinal	troubadour
simony	crusade
lay investiture	
interdict	
canon law	
tithe	
heresy	

Read and Understand

1. Farming improved and trade revived.
2. Religious leaders wielded great power.
3. Royal governments grew stronger.
4. Learning revived and spread.
5. Crusaders marched against Islam.

What was this coming slowly down the dirt road through the fields? Who were these people pulling two-wheeled wagons laden down with stone blocks? A French abbot watching them knew from their rich robes that these haulers of stone were not peasants but nobles. In 1144, the abbot wrote an account of what he saw outside the town of Chartres (shahrt), southwest of Paris:

Who has ever seen! Who has ever heard tell, in times past, that powerful princes of the world, that men brought up in honor and

222

Chapter 10 Resources

GEOGRAPHY
- Geography Skills 10
- Outline Map 9
- Transparencies 36, 37

REINFORCEMENT
- Vocabulary 10
- Basic Skills 10
- Reteaching 10
- Making Connections Study Guide 10

ENRICHMENT
- Critical Thinking 10

ASSESSMENT
- Chapter Test 10
- Alternate Chapter Test 10
- Computer Test Bank

wealth, that nobles, men and women, have bent their proud and haughty necks to the harness of carts and that, like beasts of burden, they have dragged to the abode of Christ these wagons? . . .

From the stone quarry where the laborers picked up their load, it was a seven-mile trek to the massive structure they were helping to build, the Cathedral of Our Lady of Chartres. The pious workers who dragged the first stones to Chartres never saw the cathedral finished. Few Europeans in the 1100's lived beyond the age of 50. Normally, it took 40 to 60 years to build a cathedral.

In 1180, after two generations of back-breaking labor, the townspeople of Chartres celebrated the dedication of their new cathedral with feasting and bell ringing. Just 14 years later, in 1194, the roof of the great cathedral burst into flame. The work of two generations came tumbling down. Amazingly, the undaunted citizens of Chartres set to work and in just 25 years raised an even more magnificent cathedral, which still stands.

Chartres Cathedral is the symbol of an era. In western Europe, the period from 1000 to 1300 often is known as the Age of Faith. It was an age when hundreds of towering cathedrals were built throughout Europe. Church leaders exerted enormous political and economic influence in Europe. Yet it was not faith alone that built the great cathedrals. The Age of Faith was also a time of increasing material prosperity. In all spheres of life, the High Middle Ages were a time of vigorous growth for European civilization.

Farming improved and trade revived.

1

In the years between 1000 and 1300, dramatic changes were occurring at every level of European society. At the top, new royal families were coming to power. Church leaders were reforming and strengthening the Church. Nobles were creating a glittering society with mock battles and poetry contests. Perhaps the most important changes had begun much earlier at the lowest level of society, with the peasants who worked on the land.

New ways of farming increased food.

A civilization cannot exist without food. Europe's great revival would have been impossible without better ways of farming.

One of the first great improvements in farming had begun in Charlemagne's time. A new, heavier plow slowly came into use. This heavy plow cut deep into the dirt and turned it over. Very gradually, this plow replaced the earlier, lightweight plow that only scratched the top of the ground. With the new plow, farmers could plant crops in the rich, deep soil of Europe's river valleys. This soil produced better harvests, helping peasants get a step ahead in the race with hunger.

Using horsepower For hundreds of years, peasants depended on oxen to pull their plows. Oxen lived on the poorest straw and stubble, so they were easy to keep. However, oxen moved very slowly. Horses needed better food, but a team of horses could plow twice as much land in a day as a team of oxen.

The horse collar and the heavy plow were the newest technology for farming in the Middle Ages.

223

SECTION 1 Objectives and Teaching Strategies

OBJECTIVE 1. Explain how new ways of farming helped to revive European agriculture.

Teaching Strategy: *Economics and History: Technology and the Revival of Agriculture* (page 222a)

OBJECTIVE 2. Compare and contrast life in the towns with life on the manor.

Teaching Strategy: *Discussing History: Comparing Towns and Manors* (page 222c)

■ BACKGROUND

Horses' hooves were more delicate than oxen's and needed extra protection for the hard work of plowing. The horseshoe appeared in Europe about this time, probably from the plains of central Asia.

SECTION 1 Resources

ASSESSMENT
■ Section Quiz 10.1

REINFORCEMENT
■ Independent Practice 10.1

ENRICHMENT
■ Voices from the Past 10.1

■ BACKGROUND

In the year 1000, four fifths of Germany and France were covered by forest. Along the coast of modern-day Belgium, millions of acres of lowlands were flooded under tides.

ANSWERS TO Caption Questions

300; 400

■ BACKGROUND

In medieval England, people came from miles around to attend the St. Audrey's fair. The fair was particularly noted for the fine silk necklaces worn by the young ladies. At first, the necklaces were known as St. Audrey's laces. But soon the clipped speech of the people turned *St. Audrey's* laces into *tawdry* laces. Over time, cheap and showy imitations of the fine tawdry laces found their way into fairs all across England. Hence today's meaning: "cheap and gaudy."

The problem was that farmers in the Early Middle Ages did not have the right kind of harness to use on horses. Their harness went around the horse's neck. When the horse pulled against its harness, the poor animal was nearly strangled. Sometime before 900, farmers in Europe began using a harness with a collar that fitted across the horse's chest, taking pressure off its neck and windpipe. Over the next two centuries, the new harness was adopted widely in western Europe. As a result, horses gradually replaced oxen for plowing and pulling wagons.

With horses, a farmer could plow more land in a day. As a result, many farmers cleared new fields from the forests. All over England, France, and Germany, axes rang as the great forests that had covered the land began to fall. Along the marshy coastlands of present-day Belgium, peasants built huge seawalls to drain yet more new land. These new fields supplied enough grain to feed a growing population.

The three-field system At the same time, villagers began to organize their land differently. As you have read, peasants in a village shared the land. Each family had a few strips of land scattered around the village fields.

In the Early Middle Ages, peasants usually divided the village's land into two great fields. One field they planted with crops. The other they left to lie fallow for a year. Fallow land was not planted. It was plowed once or twice to keep down weeds, but otherwise it was let alone. Thus, if a village had 600 acres, each year farmers used 300 for raising food. The following year, farmers would plant the land that had been fallow and leave the other field to rest. This way of dividing a village's land was the two-field system.

Around 800, some villages began to organize their land into three great fields instead of two. With the same 600 acres, they used 200 acres for a winter crop of wheat or rye. In spring, they planted another 200 acres with oats, barley, peas, or beans. The remaining 200 acres lay fallow.

Under this new three-field system, farmers could grow crops on two thirds of their land each year, not just on half of it. The result was an immediate increase in food for the village. Moreover, this change gave peasants a healthier diet because peas, beans, and lentils were good sources of vegetable protein.

Like other farming changes, this one spread slowly. Three or four centuries went by before it was in wide use.

Towns grew larger and richer.

Greater amounts of food meant greater numbers of people. Scholars estimate that between 1000 and 1150, the population of western Europe rose by 40 percent, from around 30 million to about 42 million.

As Europe's population increased, people left the countryside to settle in towns. Compared to great cities like Constantinople or Baghdad, European towns were still primitive and tiny. Europe's largest city, Paris, probably had no more than 30,000 people by the year 1200. A typical town in medieval Europe had only about 1,500 to 2,500 people.

Nevertheless, these small communities became a powerful force for change. Townspeople did not fit into the traditional groups of nobles (those who fight), priests (those who pray), and peasants (those who work the land). In effect, townspeople formed a new social class called the **middle class**. A walled town was known as a burgh, and the people who made their homes in such towns gradually became known as **burghers**. In France, burgh dwellers became known collectively as the **bourgeoisie** (BOOR-zhwah-ZEE).

Many of Europe's Jews lived in the growing towns. Because Jews were forbidden to hold land,

In the diagram below, how many acres a year could peasants use to raise crops with the two-field system? With the three-field system?

Planted 300 Acres	Fallow 300 Acres

Two-field System · 600 Acres

Wheat or rye 200 Acres	Barley, peas, oats, beans 200 Acres	Fallow 200 Acres

Three-field System · 600 Acres

Medieval shops were often family businesses in which both husbands and wives worked. Here boots, jewelry, and tableware are for sale.

they had never been part of the feudal system. Jews were also barred from many businesses, and so they often did work that Christians could not or would not do. Being literate, Jews sometimes worked as business managers for large landholders. The Church forbade Christians to lend money at interest, yet many people still needed to borrow money. As a result, some Jews became money lenders. From there, it was a short step to all types of banking. When trade began to revive in the later Middle Ages, Jews often were active in long-distance trade. Jewish communities in different cities had the links necessary to arrange credit and transfers of money.

By the High Middle Ages, trade was the very lifeblood of the new towns. Trade and towns grew together. Neither could thrive without the other.

Fairs were centers of trade.

Chartres is a good example of a medieval town. As with any cathedral town, many residents had ties to the Church. Some were priests, monks, or nuns. Others worked for the Church, administering its lands and money. People from the countryside came to town to celebrate religious festivals. Travelers came to the city as pilgrims to honor the holy relics at the cathedral. (A relic was something that people believed had once belonged to Jesus or one of the Christian saints.)

Artisans appeared in the town to meet the needs of all those groups of people. Shoemakers, wheelwrights, candle makers, and others did a lively business in Chartres. At first, these people did not have permanent shops. Instead, they brought their goods to gatherings known as fairs.

The local fair Peasants from nearby manors would travel to Chartres on weekly fair days, hauling wagonloads of grain and baskets of hens. Business might take place in the very shadow of the cathedral. Cloth was the most common item offered for sale, but there were also foodstuffs—fish, meat, bacon, salt, honey, oil, butter, cheese, fruit, and wine. Customers could find leather, fur, iron, steel, dyes, knives, sickles, and ropes. Such local fairs met all the needs of daily life for a small community.

No longer was everything produced on a self-sufficient manor. This was a revolutionary change in the economic life of Europe.

The great fairs Four times a year—during religious festivals, when the most pilgrims would be in town—Chartres held great fairs. People

225

■ BACKGROUND

The regional markets—northern and Mediterranean—were linked by land routes that crisscrossed Europe. Many of them converged in Champagne, southeast of Paris. Fairs in Champagne continued from early spring to late fall without a break.

Cooperative Learning

Tell students they are going to produce a newspaper for an imaginary medieval town. Divide the class into groups of three students. Within each group, have students assume these roles: editor, proofreader, recorder. Have each group pick a topic for a newspaper feature. Topics might include the following: the three-field system; an upcoming fair; guild activities, including a list of new journeymen and masters and their crafts; or taxation. Have group members develop outlines for their articles. All group members must contribute as the article takes shape. The recorder should read aloud as he or she writes, while the other group members offer suggestions. Once the articles are written, editors should check for organization and grammatical and spelling errors. Proofreaders should then recheck for any other errors. All group members' names should be included in bylines, indicating that all contributed to the article and agree with its content. Collect all the articles when finished and post the "newspaper" in the classroom.

came to these fairs from far and wide. Besides buying the wares of local artisans, they could also visit the stalls set up by merchants from as far away as England or Italy.

At great fairs, townsfolk and peasants could taste Russian honey, sample Spanish wine, purchase Flemish cloth, sniff Byzantine perfumes sold by a Venetian, and inspect the handiwork of a local wheelwright. For amusement, people thronged around a pair of jugglers, a strumming minstrel, an acrobat or an animal trainer with a dancing bear.

Guilds controlled crafts and trade.

In a medieval town, even if there were a dozen shoemakers, they all made their shoes the same way and sold them for the same price. Competition was forbidden by the rules of the shoemakers' **guild**. A guild was an association of people who worked at the same occupation.

Merchant guilds The first guilds were formed by merchants. In their hometowns, they erected guild halls where they met to make rules and arrange the details of their business. Members of the merchant guild controlled all the trade in their town. For example, nobody could sell Flemish wool in Chartres except a member of the local merchants' guild.

Craft guilds As towns grew, skilled artisans started another kind of guild, the craft guild. Shoemakers, wheelwrights, glassmakers, wine makers, tailors, grocers, druggists, and others began to meet in their own guild halls. In most crafts, both husbands and wives worked at the family trade. In some guilds, especially cloth making, women were in the majority.

Guild functions Guilds enforced standards of quality. Bakers, for example, were required to sell loaves of bread of a standard size and weight. If a baker cheated a customer with an undersized loaf, his guild might punish him by hanging the loaf around his neck and parading him through the town.

Guilds also fixed the price of everything their members sold. The Church demanded that it be a just price, based on the cost of labor and materials plus a reasonable profit. To make a large profit was thought sinful.

Paying dues to one's guild was a form of insurance. When a member died, the guild paid

funeral expenses and also gave some money to support the member's family.

Training new workers The doors of the guild hall were open only to proved masters of the trade. How did someone master a trade? Usually, parents paid a fee to a master to take their child as an **apprentice**. An apprentice lived in the master's home and worked in the shop, which might well be in the same building.

The apprentice worked for the master for 3 to 12 years without pay except for room and board. At the end of this training period, an apprentice went to work for wages as a **journeyman** in the craft. As the final step, a journeyman made an item—whether it was a shoe, a barrel, or a sword—that qualified as a "master piece." Journeymen whose product met guild standards were welcomed into the guild as masters.

Town dwellers won new liberties.

Even a proud master artisan might have begun life as a serf on a manor. Many serfs ran away to town. By the 1100's, according to custom, a serf could become free by living within a town for a year and a day. As the saying went, "Town air makes you free."

At first, feudal lords treated the upstart burghers with contempt. Lords ruthlessly taxed the towns on their lands. Nobles charged fees for everything—the right to hold a fair, the right to use a bridge, or the right to hold a law court.

As time went by, however, burghers worked together to free themselves from the lord or bishop on whose land the town stood. Sometimes they fought for their independence against armies of knights. The greatest weapon the burghers had,

Footnote to History

Many people can trace their last names, or surnames, back to a medieval occupation. Sometimes the name even indicates whether the original worker was a man or a woman. For example, a man who made bread might be surnamed Baker; a woman who did the same job, Baxter. A man who wove cloth was Weaver or Weber; a woman, Webster. Spinning thread was a common job for unmarried women, as the modern use of the word *spinster* implies.

ANSWERS TO
Section Review 1

Define:
(a) unplanted (b) two out of three fields were planted while one lay fallow (c) new social class made up of townspeople (d) town dweller (e) burgh dwellers (f) gathering at which goods were traded (g) association of people who worked at the same occupation (h) worker in training (i) worker who completed training but is not yet a master

(continued)

Voice from the Past | A Town Charter

The growth of towns in the later Middle Ages opened the way for the transition from a rural and feudal society to a more urban and mobile one. Because many townspeople were merchants and artisans, they were outside the rigid class structure of feudalism. Thus they sought new forms of community that involved new traditions of membership. In the towns, members of the merchant guilds often led in creating new approaches to government. With wealth from trade, they were able to bargain with kings for political rights that were granted in the form of charters. The passage that follows is from the charter granted by King Henry II of England to the merchants of the town of Lincoln about 1150. Although granted to the merchants, the charter applied to all the citizens of the town.

Henry, by the grace of God, etc., ... Know that I have granted to my citizens of Lincoln all their liberties and customs and laws which they had in the time of Edward and William and Henry, kings of England ... And I have granted them their gild-merchant, comprising men of the city and other merchants of the shire ... I also confirm to them that if anyone has lived in Lincoln for a year and a day without dispute of any claimant, and has paid the customs, and if the citizens can show by the laws and customs of the city that the claimant has remained in England during that period and has made no claim, then let the defendant remain in peace in my city of Lincoln as my citizen, without [having to defend his] right.

1. What was the importance of a charter?
2. What does the term *citizen* mean as used in the charter?
3. How does this idea of citizenship differ from feudal relationships?
4. What is the significance of the passage about "a year and a day"?

however, was cash. In exchange for a bag of coins, many lords grudgingly granted towns written **charters.** Such charters listed the towns' special privileges and tax exemptions. In effect, a town charter bearing the lord's seal was a declaration of independence from the feudal system.

Section REVIEW 1

Define: (a) fallow, (b) three-field system, (c) middle class, (d) burgher, (e) bourgeoisie, (f) fair, (g) guild, (h) apprentice, (i) journeyman, (j) charter
Identify: (a) Chartres, (b) Age of Faith
Answer:
1. (a) Describe three improvements in farming that took place in the Middle Ages. (b) Explain how each helped to increase the food supply.

2. (a) Why did townspeople make up a new social class? (b) What important tasks did Jews perform in the Middle Ages?
3. (a) Why was it no longer necessary for manors to be self-sufficient? (b) How did people get the daily goods they needed? (c) How did they obtain luxury products such as silk?
4. (a) What was the difference between a merchant guild and a craft guild? (b) What regulations did guilds make?
5. How did townspeople become independent of the feudal system?

Critical Thinking
6. Write a series of cause-and-effect statements for the changes described in this chapter. Try to include as many specific changes as possible. Here is an example: "The heavy plow led to farming rich valley soils. Farming rich valley soils led to increased food production."

227

ANSWERS TO
Voice from the Past

1. formalized agreement between king and townspeople
2. refers to people of town, who are party to the agreement
3. feudal relationships based on personal loyalty; citizenship based on membership in community
4. phrase applies to newcomers who have left feudal lands and ties to live in town

ANSWERS TO (continued)

Identify:
(a) town southwest of Paris
(b) years 1000–1300
Answer:
1. (a) heavier plow, use of horsepower, three-field system (b) plow: opened up new lands to plant; horsepower: speeded up plowing; three-field system: allowed more land to be sown each year
2. (a) They did not fit into the traditional groups. (b) business managers, lenders, bankers, traders
3. (a) Trade increased. (b) bought at fairs (c) at great fairs
4. (a) merchant guilds—traders; craft guilds—skilled artisans (b) set and enforced standards, prices
5. fought or bought charters with money
6. Example: Increased food production supported a larger population. A larger population led to settlement of towns. Towns became centers of trade.

227

Religious leaders wielded great power. 2

During the Early Middle Ages, the Church had acted as the preserver of civilization in many ways. Yet the Church had also suffered in the years between 500 and 1000. Vikings had plundered many monasteries. As a result, the level of learning sank. Many priests could barely read their prayers. Church leaders were sometimes corrupt. Italian nobles controlled the election of popes and sometimes chose men whose morals were questionable. Many bishops and abbots cared more about their position as feudal lords than about their duties as spiritual leaders.

During the years between 1000 and 1300, the state of the Church improved dramatically. Religion spread more widely and deeply in society than before. Thousands of men and women became monks and nuns. At the head of the Church, strong popes challenged the power of emperors and kings.

Monks adopted stricter rules.

One of the first signs of reform in the Church was the founding in 910 of a new French monastery at Cluny (KLOO-nee). Cluny was founded by a nobleman, the Duke of Aquitaine. Unlike many lords, the duke did not try to make Cluny a source of personal wealth and power. Instead, he arranged that the monastery be subject only to the pope, not to any nearby lord or bishop.

The abbots of Cluny held strictly to the Benedictine rule. Soon Cluny's reputation for purity inspired the founding of similar monasteries throughout western Europe. By the year 1000, there were 300 houses under Cluny's leadership. Cluny acted as a headquarters for Church reform.

For many men and women, the Benedictine rule no longer seemed strict enough for a holy life. After the year 1000, new groups of monks and nuns chose to live by even stricter rules. For example, the members of the Cistercian (sihs-TUHR-shuhn) order, founded in 1098, vowed to build their monasteries only in the wilderness. The Cistercians often took the lead in the great movement to clear new farmlands. Their life of hardship won many followers.

228

Reformers ended abuses.

Reformers hoped to purify the Church by freeing it from control by lords and kings. The first step was to free the papacy from the control of Italian nobles. In 1059, a Church decree declared that all future popes would be chosen at a meeting of leading bishops known as **cardinals**. No longer could the Roman mob, the local nobles, or even the emperor choose a pope.

Reformers were also eager to abolish three conditions that were widespread in the Church of the early Middle Ages. First, they wanted to put an end to the *marriage of priests*. Many village priests married and had families, even though such marriages were against Church rulings.

Second, reformers wanted to stop the buying and selling of Church offices, called **simony** (SYE-muh-nee). Many bishops expected to make a profit from their high position. Every Church office brought with it land and a good income. One greedy bishop wrote: "I have gold and I received the [office of bishop] . . . I ordain a priest and I receive gold. I make a deacon and I receive a heap of silver . . ." Like marriage for priests, simony was against Church law but still was widely practiced.

Lay investiture was the third practice Church reformers wanted to end. Just as vassals received their fiefs in a feudal ceremony, bishops and abbots went through a ceremony to receive their Church offices. In both cases, the ceremony was known as investiture. Who should perform this ceremony for Church officials, a layman (feudal lord or king) or a Church leader? If the ceremony was performed by a layman, it was called lay investiture.

Whoever controlled the ceremony held the real power in naming a bishop. Naturally, kings favored lay investiture. Bishops were powerful nobles, and kings wanted to control them. Naturally too, Church reformers frowned on lay investiture. They said that a bishop should not be the political pawn of any king.

Gregory VII clashed with Henry IV.

In 1073, the foremost leader of the reformers became pope. He took the name of Gregory VII. The new pope quickly carried out the aims of the reform movement. He first ordered all married priests to abandon their wives and children. Then, in 1075, he banned lay investiture.

The young German ruler, Henry IV, flew into a rage. Henry held the title of emperor, passed down since the time of Charlemagne. Henry called a meeting of German bishops, who had all been invested by himself. With their approval, the emperor sent a vicious letter calling Gregory "not pope, but false monk" and ordering him to step down from the papacy.

Gregory replied in the same temper, sending this letter to the German bishops:

> I take from King Henry . . . the government of the whole kingdom of the Germans and the Italians, and I free all Christian people from any oath they have made or shall make to him, and I forbid any to serve the king.

Furthermore, the pope excommunicated Henry.

In this showdown, who would prove the stronger, pope or emperor? Everything hinged on the loyalties of the German bishops and princes. Would they side with their earthly lord or their spiritual lord? They decided to support Pope Gregory. Deserted by his bishops and threatened by rebellious German princes, Henry's position seemed hopeless. The only way to save his throne was to win the pope's forgiveness.

In the middle of winter, 1077, Henry journeyed over the snowy Alps to the Italian town of Canossa (kuh-NAHS-uh). He approached the castle where Pope Gregory was a guest. In Gregory's own words, "He [Henry] presented himself at the gate of the castle, barefoot and clad only in a wretched woolen garment, beseeching us with tears to grant him . . . forgiveness." As pope, Gregory had no choice but to forgive any sinner who came humbly to him. Still, he kept Henry waiting in the snow for three days before ending his excommunication.

This meeting in Canossa was one of the most dramatic confrontations of the Middle Ages, but it solved nothing. It was a master political stroke for Henry, who was free to go home and punish the nobles who had rebelled against him. Yet it was an even greater victory for the pope. He had humiliated the proudest ruler in Europe. The question of investiture was still undecided.

Gregory died in 1085, Henry in 1106. Their successors continued to fight over investiture until 1122. In that year, representatives of the Church and the emperor met in the German city of Worms (vohrms). They reached a compromise known as the *Concordat of Worms*. By its terms, the Church alone would grant a bishop his ring and staff, symbols of Church office. However, the emperor kept the power to grant that bishop the lands that went with his office. Thus, the emperor still had much control over the bishops. (The kings of France and England had reached the same sort of compromise earlier.)

Popes ruled a spiritual empire.

In many ways, the popes who followed Gregory VII exercised greater power than any king or prince. As with Henry IV, a king who quarreled with the pope faced excommunication, which freed all his vassals from their duties to him.

If an excommunicated king or duke continued to disobey, the pope had another weapon—the **interdict**. No Church ceremonies could be performed in the offending ruler's lands. There could be no marriages, no baptisms, no religious services of any sort. In the Age of Faith, fear of the interdict put great pressure on a king to bow to a pope's demands.

Church law and government In the 1100's and 1200's, the Church resembled a kingdom. It was governed by a single ruler (the pope) from a central capital (Rome). A group of advisers, called the papal *Curia*, served as the pope's staff. The Curia supplied him with information, offered advice, and carried out decisions. The pope also had his own diplomats, known as *legates*, who traveled through Europe dealing with bishops and kings.

Outside Rome, the power of the Church was in the hands of bishops. Bishops operated courts of law that rivaled the feudal courts of lords and kings. Bishops' courts ruled on such matters as marriage, divorce, and wills. Thus, all Christians were partly governed by **canon law**, the law of the Church.

The Church was like a kingdom in yet another sense. It collected taxes. Every Christian family was required to give to the Church one tenth of its yearly income as a **tithe.**

Social services According to canon law, bishops were to use at least one fourth of all tithes to care for the sick and the poor. Orphans, lepers, and beggars received care from Church funds.

229

SECTION 2
Objectives and Teaching Strategies

OBJECTIVE 1. Identify three abuses of power the Church reformers wanted to end.

Teaching Strategy: *Discussing History: Reforming the Church* (page 222c)

OBJECTIVE 2. Describe Gothic architecture and explain its significance.

Teaching Strategy: *Teaching with Pictures: Gothic Cathedrals* (page 222c)

■ BACKGROUND

In essence, the Concordat of Worms gave the pope and emperor veto powers over one another's appointments.

■ DISCUSSION

Christians of the Middle Ages felt a great burden of sin. Only the sacraments, they believed, could save them from the devil's clutches. For this reason, excommunication and the interdict were greatly feared punishments that meant eternal torture. Ask students how they feel about this.

SECTION 2
Resources

ASSESSMENT
■ Section Quiz 10.2

REINFORCEMENT
■ Independent Practice 10.2

ENRICHMENT
■ Voices from the Past 10.2

229

■ BACKGROUND

St. Francis to the birds:
" . . . Always and in every
place ye ought to praise
God . . . He giveth you the
mountains and the valleys
for your refuge, and the
tall trees wherein to build
your nests; and for as
much as ye can neither
spin nor sew, God clotheth
you and your children . . .
Therefore beware, little sisters of mine, of the sin of
ingratitude, but ever strive
to praise God."

Most hospitals in medieval Europe were operated by the Church. Around the year 1200, there were 400 hospitals in England and 12 in Paris alone. No needy person could be turned away.

War against heresy Like other rulers in the Middle Ages, popes thought of themselves as warriors. Time and time again, they urged Christians to go to war against Muslims. The Church also went to war against heretics.

With the widespread interest in religion of the 1100's and 1200's, people seriously pondered religious matters. As a result, many **heresies** sprang up in Europe in the 1200's when some people reached answers and held beliefs that differed from the Church's teachings. The Church struck back with all its might. In some cases, whole villages of suspected heretics were slaughtered.

The Inquisition (IN-kwuh-ZISH-uhn) was the leading arm of the Church in the war against heresy. The Inquisition was an organization of experts whose job was to find and judge heretics. Beginning around 1225, popes sent many such experts throughout Europe. These men left no stone unturned in their search for heresy, even accepting rumors and gossip. A person who was suspected of heresy might be questioned for weeks and even tortured. It was almost impossible for a suspect to prove his or her innocence.

Friars preached to the poor.

The Church had another weapon in its fight against heresy. In the early 1200's, wandering **friars** traveled from place to place. By preaching, friars tried to carry the Church's ideas more widely and win heretics back to the Church. Like monks, friars took vows of chastity, poverty, and obedience. Unlike monks, however, friars did not live apart from the world in monasteries. Instead, friars preached to the poor, especially in Europe's rapidly growing towns. Friars owned nothing and lived by begging.

The earliest order of friars were the Dominicans. They took their name from Dominic, a Spanish priest who walked barefoot through southern France preaching against heresy. Because Dominic emphasized the importance of study, many Dominicans were formidable scholars.

A second order of friars was founded by an Italian known as Francis of Assisi (uh-SEE-see). The son of a rich merchant, Francis gave up his wealth and turned to preaching when he was about 20 years old. Francis treated all creatures as if they were his spiritual brothers and sisters. Most famous is the episode in which, according to popular legend, he stopped along the road to preach to a flock of birds. Francis placed much less importance on scholarship than did Dominic.

Caring for the sick and needy was the responsibility of the Church in the Middle Ages. These nuns are treating patients in a French hospital of the 1400's.

230

ANSWERS TO

Section
Review 2

Define:
(a) leading bishop **(b)** buying and selling of church offices **(c)** practice in which feudal lord or king granted Church offices **(d)** papal punishment
(continued)

Women joined both the Franciscans and the Dominicans, although the Church did not allow them to travel from place to place as preachers. Like the men, these women lived in poverty and worked selflessly to help the poor and sick.

Soon white-robed Dominicans and brown-robed Franciscans were a common sight on the roads of Europe. In this age of reform, friars won wide respect for their poverty and their devout way of life.

Churches rose in a new style.

Although the friars chose to live in poverty, evidence of the Church's wealth could be seen everywhere in the Middle Ages. Between 1000 and 1100, towns in Europe began to build massive stone churches. The huge doors were framed by round arches like the arches on buildings in ancient Rome. The heavy roof pressed down on the thick walls and on two rows of thick pillars within the church. Walls were painted in brilliant colors. This style of architecture was called *Romanesque* (ROH-muh-NEHSK).

Romanesque churches were certainly impressive, but at least one man was not satisfied with them. That man was Suger (soo-ZHAY), abbot of the monastery of Saint Denis (sahn duh-NEE) near Paris. To Suger's eye, Romanesque churches had two great faults. First, they looked heavy and earthbound. Second, their tiny windows set in thick walls let in little light.

In 1137, Suger began to direct the rebuilding of the church at Saint Denis. He wanted the new building to thrust upward as if reaching toward heaven. He wanted light to stream in from all sides, reminding worshipers that God was the light of the world.

Suger's goals—more height and more light—seemed to defy the laws of medieval architecture. To lift a heavy roof higher and higher meant that you had to make the walls supporting it thicker and thicker. But thicker walls meant smaller and fewer windows, hence less light.

For several decades, master builders in France had been experimenting with new techniques. Under Suger's guidance, these ideas came together at Saint Denis. The result was a new style of architecture known as the *Gothic* style. Three new building techniques were the key to Gothic architecture:

1. *Pointed, ribbed vaults* In the new Gothic churches, narrow bands of stone called ribs ran from the roof to the columns below and helped support the roof's weight. The sections of walls between the pillars carried no weight at all. These walls became frames for huge stained-glass windows.
2. *Flying buttresses* Stone roofs pushed not only downward but outward. To support this outward pressure, Gothic builders made braces of beautifully carved stone. These braces slanted up against the outside walls of the cathedral. They were called **flying buttresses**.
3. *Pointed arches* To emphasize the height of a Gothic church, all the arches rose to points. The highest arch was the vaulted ceiling, where all lines joined as if pointing to heaven.

Soon Gothic cathedrals were rising in many towns of northern France. In 1163, the people of Paris set out to build the tallest church in Christendom. The vaulted ceiling of the Cathedral of Notre Dame (NOH-truh DAHM) eventually rose to 114 feet. Then Chartres, Reims, Amiens, and Beauvais built even higher cathedrals.

The Gothic style spread to other parts of Europe. In all, nearly 500 Gothic churches were built between 1170 and 1270. All were beautiful, but none had windows quite as beautiful as those of Chartres. The stained-glass windows at Chartres illustrated stories from the Bible. As illiterate peasants walked past the 176 windows, they could "read" those stories. The thousands of stone carvings that framed every door in the cathedral showed more Bible stories. Scholars called Chartres "a Bible for the poor."

Section REVIEW 2

Define: (a) cardinal, (b) simony, (c) lay investiture, (d) interdict, (e) canon law, (f) tithe, (g) heresy, (h) friar, (i) Romanesque, (j) Gothic, (k) flying buttress
Identify: (a) Cluny, (b) Cistercian order, (c) Henry IV, (d) Gregory VII, (e) Canossa, (f) Concordat of Worms, (g) Curia, (h) Inquisition, (i) Dominic, (j) Francis of Assisi, (k) Suger, (l) Romanesque, (m) Gothic
Answer:
1. What were the major changes that Church reformers tried to achieve?

231

ANSWERS TO (continued)
(e) Church law (f) Church tax (g) belief different from Church teaching (h) wandering preacher (i) architecture characterized by round arches, thick walls, and small windows (j) architecture characterized by flying buttresses and pointed arches (k) outside wall braces on a cathedral
Identify:
(a) site of monastery
(b) monastic order
(c) clashed with Gregory VII
(d) church reformer who became pope (e) Italian town where Henry IV met with Gregory VII (f) compromise reached by Church and emperor regarding investiture (g) pope's advisors (h) Church experts delegated to find heretics (i) founded Dominicans (j) founded Franciscans (k) abbot of Saint Denis
Answer:
1. abolish marriage of priests, simony, and lay investiture
2. (a) It gave him power. (b) Henry challenged the pope's ban; the pope excommunicated Henry; Henry was forgiven by Gregory.
3. governed by single ruler, had system of law, collected taxes, performed social services
4. (a) to find and judge heretics (b) to win heretics back
5. more height and more light
6. Both emperor and pope retained powers.
7. Examples: church as center of town, wandering friars, presence of monks and nuns, inquisitors questioning people

ANSWER TO
Comparing Pictures

The cathedrals at Chartres and Bourges represent the Gothic style of architecture. The focus on height and light gave a sense of soaring space. Although the vault came from Roman architecture, both Roman and Byzantine architecture were better known for the dome, and Byzantine for its interior decoration.

■ BACKGROUND

In their pride, builders sometimes built too high. The Gothic cathedral of Beauvais, begun in 1247, collapsed from its own weight in 1284.

Pointed arch

Flying buttress

Ribbed vault

Comparing pictures One of the glories of the Chartres cathedral is its rose window (below left). The Bourges cathedral (below right) clearly achieves the goals of Gothic architecture, height and light. What features set these cathedrals apart from Roman and Byzantine architecture (pages 158 and 184)?

232

2. (a) Why did Henry IV favor lay investiture? (b) Describe the main events in the conflict between Henry IV and Gregory VII.
3. How was the Church similar to a kingdom?
4. (a) In its fight against heresy, how did the Church use the Inquisition? (b) The work of the friars?
5. How was Gothic architecture different from Romanesque architecture?

Critical Thinking

6. Why was the Concordat of Worms a compromise settlement?
7. Suppose you visited a medium-sized town in France around 1250. What evidence might you see in daily life that this was the Age of Faith? List as many examples as you can.

Royal governments grew stronger. 3

In part, Europe owed its prosperity to the coming of more peaceful times. By 1000, the great invasions of Vikings, Magyars, and Muslims had come to an end. Law, order, and peace were slowly gaining ground. By the 1050's, kings, dukes, and counts were winning greater control over their lands, ending petty wars between vassals, driving out nests of bandits, and in general, keeping the peace.

Kings had little more power than other great lords. In the words of the time, the king was "first among equals." Yet, like other lords, kings began to strengthen their control over their own lands. In doing so, they laid the groundwork for the growth of royal power.

Norman conquerors ruled England.

Surprisingly, the king who laid the foundations for royal power in England was not English at all. He was William, Duke of Normandy. Although William was a descendant of Rollo the Viking, by 1050 the Normans were French in language and culture.

The Norman Conquest How did a French duke become king of England? The story began when England's aged King Edward the Confessor died

without an heir in January 1066. As Edward's second cousin, William claimed the English crown. William was ambitious, tough, and brave. Yet so was his rival, the English nobleman Harold Godwinson. Harold had been named king by a council of English lords. In the end, perhaps what helped William most was plain luck.

By the summer of 1066, William had gathered an army to invade England. The story of William's invasion is vividly recorded on the famous Bayeux (by-**YOO**) Tapestry, woven soon after the event. On this piece of linen 231 feet long, the drama unfolds scene by scene. The Norman knights and their horses crowded onto ships. They disembarked on English shores. Then came the battle that changed the course of English history—the Battle of Hastings.

On October 14, 1066, King Harold's English foot soldiers grouped themselves on the top of a small hill. The Norman knights on horseback charged. At the front of the Norman army went Taillefer, the Norman bard, spinning his sword in the air and singing the Song of Roland.

The battle raged from morning till dusk. Several times, the English seemed on the edge of victory. Then, luck stepped in for William. Late in the day, Harold fell dead with an arrow in his eye. The Normans broke through the English lines, and the Battle of Hastings ended in a decisive Norman victory.

William the Conqueror (1066–1087) After his victory, William (now called "the Conqueror") declared all England his personal property. The English lords who had supported Harold lost their lands. William then granted fiefs to about 200 Norman lords who swore oaths of loyalty to him. He also granted lands to the Church, appointing Norman bishops who were his loyal

Decisions in History

Henry II reformed the royal courts with the aid of his chancellor and friend Thomas à Becket. In 1162, Henry asked Becket to become the new archbishop of Canterbury. The two men could then work together to reform the church courts. Becket surprised the king by warning, "You will soon hate me . . . as much as you love me now." What conflict did Becket foresee? How might Henry II solve it? What would you have done?

233

SECTION 3
Objectives and Teaching Strategies

OBJECTIVE 1. Discuss the consequences of the Norman conquest of England.

Teaching Strategy: *Discussing History: The Norman Conquest* (page 222d)

OBJECTIVE 2. Draw a map of Europe in 1160.

Teaching Strategy: *Geography in History: Making a Map* (page 222d)

■ **DECISIONS**

Becket foresaw that Henry would also want to control the church courts, which Becket as archbishop was bound to defend. Four of Henry's knights, thinking they were following the king's wishes, murdered Becket in Canterbury Cathedral.

SECTION 3
Resources

GEOGRAPHY
■ Transparency 36

REINFORCEMENT
■ Independent Practice 10.3

ENRICHMENT
■ Voices from the Past 10.3

ASSESSMENT
■ Section Quiz 10.3

Soon juries were used to try violent crimes as well as property disputes. Since these criminal juries were often twice as large as others, they were called "grand juries."

Henry II was brilliant in the role of king, but he failed as father, husband, and French duke. His French wife, Eleanor of Aquitaine, plotted revenge against him for his ill treatment of her, and all four of his sons led armies of rebellion against him.

■ DISCUSSION

Philip II Augustus became king at the age of 15. He was called the "maker of Paris" because he paved the streets, walled the city, and began building the Louvre. Can students think of present-day rulers who might deserve such titles?

This scene from the Bayeux Tapestry shows Harold's English foot soldiers forming a shield wall against the mounted Norman knights at Hastings.

vassals. England suddenly had a new ruling class of French-speaking nobles. William kept about one fifth of England for himself, a powerful base for any king. Thus William made England the most centralized feudal kingdom in Europe.

Henry II (1154–1189) Thanks to William's harsh but efficient rule, later kings of England had a strong base on which to build. William's great-grandson, Henry II, became king in 1154 and further increased royal power.

Henry's greatest achievement lay in strengthening the royal courts of justice. He sent royal judges to visit every part of England at least once a year. These judges collected taxes, settled lawsuits, and punished crimes. Henry also introduced the use of the **jury** in English courts. A jury in medieval England was a group of loyal people—usually 12 neighbors—who answered questions about the facts of a case for a royal judge.

Suppose Knight X and Knight Y both claimed a certain piece of land. In earlier times, such a case might have been settled in trial by combat at a lord's court. In Henry's royal court, the judge would call together 12 nearby landholders who were the knights' social equals, or peers. The 12 were sworn to tell the judge what they believed to be true in the case. (The word *jury* comes from the French *juree,* meaning "oath.") Then the judge would decide which knight was in the right. Jury trials became a popular way of settling disputes. Only the king's courts were allowed

234

to conduct them. As the king's courts gained in importance, the power of the lords' feudal courts declined.

Over the centuries, case by case, the rulings of England's royal judges formed a unified body of law. Because this law was common to the whole kingdom, it was known as **common law.** Today, the principles of English common law are the basis for law in many English-speaking countries, including the United States.

The Capetian dynasty ruled France.

The kings of France, too, looked for ways of increasing their power. In theory, all French lords were vassals of the French king. In fact, however, after the breakup of Charlemagne's empire, French counts and dukes ruled their lands as if they were independent. By the year 1000, France was divided into about 30 feudal territories.

In 987, the last member of the Carolingian family—Louis the Sluggard—died. To succeed him, France's most powerful nobles chose Hugh Capet (KAP-uht), an undistinguished duke from the middle of France. The Capet family ruled only a small territory, but at its heart stood Paris, on a well-protected island in the Seine River. Hugh Capet ruled from 987 to 996. He began the Capetian (kuh-PEE-shuhn) dynasty of French kings.

When the French lords chose Hugh Capet, they assumed he would be a weak king. (They had no national loyalties to the region we call France. Such feelings did not exist until centuries later.) What they wanted was someone they could control. Hugh Capet did not disappoint them; neither did his son and grandson. The first three Capetian kings were little more than petty feudal lords.

Though weak rulers, the Capetians survived. The first six Capetians ruled for nearly 200 years (987–1180), an average of 32 years per reign. For many generations, Capetian queens bore healthy sons. Thus, bloody civil wars over the succession were avoided.

Time and geography were on the side of the Capetian kings. Their territory, though small, sat astride important trade routes in northern France. For 200 years, Capetian kings tightened their grip on this strategic area. The power of the French king gradually spread outward from Paris. Eventually, the growth of royal power would unite France.

The Kingdoms of Europe in 1160

KEY

Lands held directly by the Capetian family

✿ Battle

0   300 Miles

Focus on Geography

Geographic Skills

1. European kings in the 1100's sought to unite their domains. What problem did the French king face in uniting his lands?

2. (a) What lands did the Kingdom of England include? (b) How did the role of England's king differ at home and in France?

3. On the map, the Holy Roman Empire appears to be a unified geographic region. In political terms, how united was it?

4. (a) What various political divisions existed in the Iberian Peninsula (Spain and Portugal)? (b) What religious divisions also existed there?

Geographic Theme: Region

5. What steps would it take for France and the Iberian Peninsula to become unified political regions, or states?

ANSWERS TO
Focus on Geography

1. many feudal territories, no national loyalty

2. (a) parts of England, Ireland, France (b) In England, power was centralized under the king. France still had many feudal territories.

3. little unity, as German princes held much of the power

4. (a) Kingdom of Leon, Kingdom of Castile, Kingdom of Navarre, Kingdom of Aragon, Portugal (b) divided between Muslim and Christian

5. need strong kings to unite the separate territories, kingdoms

German kings failed to unite their lands.

After the death of Charlemagne, Germany was the strongest of the kingdoms that arose from the ruins of his empire. Yet in building royal power, the rulers of Germany faced a different set of problems than did the kings of England and France. When the last Carolingian died in 911, the German nobles claimed the right to elect the next king.

Otto the Great (936–973) In 919, the Duke of Saxony, known as Henry the Fowler, was elected king. He ruled until 936, winning several important victories over the Slavs and the Magyars. (One of Henry's distant descendants was the emperor Henry IV, who begged the pope's forgiveness at Canossa.)

235

236

ANSWERS TO
Section Review 3

Define:
(a) local people who answered questions about a case (b) body of law shared by whole kingdom

Identify:
(a) Norman who became king of England (b) English king defeated by William (c) battle at which Normans defeated English (d) strong ruler of England (e) founder of Capetian dynasty (f) strongest ruler of medieval German (g) lands controlled by Barbarossa (h) Holy Roman Emperor (i) battle at which foot soldiers defeated knights

Answer:
1. gave some land to Norman lords, kept one fifth

2. The royal courts settled all disputes.

3. Twelve peers would tell what they believed to be true and a judge would decide the outcome.

4. no succession problems; favorable geographic location on important trade routes

5. election by nobles

6. (a) gained support of Church officials
(b) maintaining lands and power won in italy

7. There might be two main countries: England, including France; and Germany, including Italy.

The strongest ruler of medieval Germany was Henry's son Otto I, known as Otto the Great. Otto, who became king in 936, consciously copied the policies of his boyhood hero, Charlemagne. He even chose to be crowned king at Charlemagne's old capital, Aachen.

Otto ended the threat of Magyar raids by crushing the Magyars at the Battle of Lechfield in 955. He also set about building up his own power within Germany.

Like other medieval kings, Otto's greatest problem was the power of the nobles within his kingdom. To limit that power, Otto turned for support to the bishops and abbots of the Church. These churchmen were themselves feudal lords with armies of knights at their command.

Otto was able to dominate the Church in Germany by granting fiefs only to loyal bishops and abbots. He made his brother archbishop of Cologne and his son archbishop of Mainz. With armies drawn from Church lands, Otto overpowered the great princes of Germany.

Despite this success, Otto still yearned to be crowned emperor as Charlemagne had been in 800. In 951 and again in 962, he invaded Italy. Italian towns such as Genoa, Pisa, and Venice had grown wealthy from trade with Asia, and they were a powerful bait for the German emperor. During his second invasion, Otto entered Rome to defend the pope from an Italian duke. This time, the pope rewarded Otto with the imperial crown he coveted.

The German-Italian empire created by Otto was known first as the Roman Empire of the German Nation and later as the Holy Roman Empire. It remained the strongest state in Europe until about 1100. In the long run, though, Otto's attempt to revive Charlemagne's empire caused trouble for later German kings. Italian nobles resented German rule. Popes too came to fear the political power of the German kings in Italy. As you have read, Henry IV of Germany nearly lost his crown in a long power struggle with the pope over lay investiture (page 229).

During that struggle, German princes regained much of the power they had lost under Otto. Thus, a later German ruler would have to begin again to build up royal authority. That ruler was Frederick Barbarossa.

Frederick Barbarossa (1152–1190) Seven German princes had the right to elect the German king. By 1152, even these princes realized that Germany needed a strong king to keep the peace. They chose Frederick I. A handsome, golden-haired man and a great warrior, Frederick was the ideal medieval king. His red beard earned him the nickname *Barbarossa* (Italian for "red beard").

Frederick was the first ruler to call his lands the Holy Roman Empire. Yet what he really ruled was not so much an empire as a patchwork of feudal territories. By his own forceful personality and his skill as a soldier, Frederick was able to control the German princes. But whenever he was out of the country, disorder returned.

Frederick did not concentrate on building royal power in Germany. Instead, like Otto the Great, he turned his attention south to the rich cities of Italy. Frederick invaded Italy repeatedly, spreading destruction wherever he went. His brutal tactics led Italian merchants to set aside their differences and unite against him. Also fearful of Frederick, the pope joined with the merchants. Together, Frederick's enemies formed an alliance called the Lombard League.

In 1176, the foot soldiers of the Lombard League faced Frederick's army of mounted knights at the Battle of Legnano (lay-**NYAHN**-oh). The German knights suffered a smashing defeat. For the first time, foot soldiers defeated feudal knights. The Battle of Legnano showed that towns could wield military as well as economic power. It was an omen for the future.

In 1179, Frederick made peace with the pope and returned to Germany. By that time, however, he had lost his chance to limit the power of the German princes. Their power continued to grow in spite of Frederick's efforts. After he drowned in 1190, his empire was torn to pieces.

Therefore, unlike England and France, Germany did not become a united country during the Middle Ages. There were several reasons why German kings failed to unite their country. First, the system of electing the king weakened Germany. It made the nobles more powerful than the king. Second, German rulers had fewer royal lands to use as a base of power than did the kings of France and England. Third, German kings continued to try to revive Charlemagne's empire by involving themselves in Italian politics. This policy led to wars not only with Italian cities but also with the pope.

Section REVIEW 3

Define: (a) jury, (b) common law
Identify: (a) William the Conqueror,
(b) Harold Godwinson, (c) Battle of Hastings,
(d) Henry II, (e) Hugh Capet, (f) Otto the
Great, (g) Holy Roman Empire, (h) Frederick
Barbarossa, (i) Battle of Legnano

Answer:

1. How did William the Conqueror lay the basis for strong central government in England?
2. How did Henry II's royal courts strengthen the king's power over the lords?
3. Describe a jury trial in medieval England.
4. What two factors aided the Capetians?
5. How did German rulers succeed to the throne?
6. How did Otto the Great make the crown stronger than the German nobles?

Critical Thinking

7. Look at a map of modern Europe. Suppose that the descendants of William the Conqueror and of Otto I had succeeded in holding the lands these two men ruled. How might the map of Europe be different today?

Learning revived and spread. 4

As kings grew more powerful, they needed officials trained in law and record keeping for their growing governments. At first, most royal officials came from the Church, because few others could read or write. By the late 1100's, however, literacy was spreading to people outside the Church. Just as Europe's material prosperity was growing, so was European interest in learning.

Scholars gathered at universities.

At the center of the new growth of learning stood an institution that was new to Europe—the university. Athens, Alexandria, Baghdad, and Constantinople had all had their universities, but never before had such a center of learning existed in western Europe. The first universities in Europe were not ivy-covered buildings on green campuses. The word *university* originally meant a group of scholars. People, not buildings, made up the medieval university.

DAILY LIFE ▶ Medieval Writing Materials

"Finished, thank God." Medieval students, who sometimes acquired books by renting and then copying them letter by letter, often added these words of relief to their last page. The process of copying a book was indeed a long and painstaking one. It began with the purchase of the paperlike material called parchment or vellum, made from the skin of lambs, calves, or kids. However, a student could not simply sit down with his sheets of vellum and begin to write. The vellum was usually rough when he bought it. The student had to scrape it with a knife or razor, sprinkle it with chalk, and rub it smooth and white with a rough stone. Then, with a ruler and a pointed tool, he drew grooves in the vellum to mark off lines and margins.

The student made his own ink from black soot, charcoal, or bark. His inkwell was a cow's horn set into a round hole in his writing board, and he wrote with the point of a goose feather. He would dip his pen into the ink, write a line, and then, if the weather was damp, dry the ink with the heat from a basin of coals. If he made a mistake, he would scrape it off with a knife and rub the area smooth again with a boar's tooth.

237

SECTION 4
Objectives and Teaching Strategies

OBJECTIVE 1. Describe aspects of life in a medieval castle.

Teaching Strategy: *Teaching with Pictures: Life in a Medieval Castle* (page 222d)

OBJECTIVE 2. Compare the status of medieval women with that of women in Egypt, Greece, and Rome.

Teaching Strategy: *Comparing and Contrasting Women's Status* (page 222d)

■ BACKGROUND

Henry I of England, who ruled from 1100 to 1135, was known as Beauclerc or "Good Scholar" because he could write his name. His great-grandson, Richard I, who ruled from 1189 to 1197, was a skilled poet. Thus, the progress of learning was apparent even in the royal family.

SECTION 4
Resources

ASSESSMENT
■ Section Quiz 10.4

REINFORCEMENT
■ Independent Practice 10.4

ENRICHMENT
■ Voices from the Past 10.4

Universities had arisen at Paris, France, and Bologna, Italy, by the end of the 1100's. (The exact dates are uncertain.) Others followed at Oxford, England, and Salerno, Italy.

Most students came from middle-class families, not from the nobility. They were the sons of burghers or well-to-do artisans. (Girls could not attend.) For most students, the goal was a job in government or the Church.

Since the university had no buildings, classes met in rented rooms or in the choir section of a church. Lucky students sat on a bench. Most squatted on the straw-covered floor as they tried to memorize the master's lecture. Because writing materials were scarce, all exams were oral.

As much as they might love books, few students could afford to own even one. Because all books were handwritten, a single book cost the equivalent of $600 or $700. Many students rented their textbooks, but even this was too costly for some. Often the only textbook for a course belonged to the teacher, who read it aloud, line by line, and offered his own comments.

To earn a bachelor's degree, students spent 3 to 5 years in school before taking a final exam. A master's degree required an additional 3 to 4 years (in Paris, as long as 15 years). With such a degree, however, a scholar could teach anywhere in Europe. There was no language barrier since scholars everywhere spoke Latin.

Scholars rediscovered Greek writings.

The revival of learning made Europeans more interested in the works of ancient scholars. At the same time, the growth of trade brought Europeans into contact with Muslims and Byzantines. In those empires, the writings of the old Greek philosophers had survived.

Christian scholars from Europe began visiting Muslim libraries in Toledo, Spain. There, Jewish scholars translated Arabic copies of Aristotle and other Greek writers into Latin. From Constantinople, Europeans brought home Latin translations of Justinian's code of laws. All at once, Europeans acquired a huge new body of knowledge on science, philosophy, law, and religion.

Christian scholars were excited by the Greek writings but also deeply troubled by them. After all, the ancient Greeks had been pagans. Their knowledge was not based on the Bible but on their own powers of reasoning. Could a Christian scholar use Aristotle's logical approach to truth and still keep faith with the Bible? This was the debate that shook scholars in the 1100's.

Aquinas linked faith and reason.

In the mid-1200's, the scholar Thomas Aquinas (uh-**KWYE**-nuhs) found no conflict between faith and reason. He believed that the most basic religious truths could be proved by logical argument.

Born in 1225 in Italy, Thomas Aquinas joined the Dominicans when he was about 18 years old. He then went to the University of Paris. After his studies, he stayed to teach there.

Between 1267 and 1273, Aquinas created a scholarly work of colossal scope called the *Summa Theologiae*. In its 21 volumes, he attempted to answer 631 philosophical questions about God and the universe. For each question, he used logic and reason to show the truth of the Church's answer. The *Summa Theologiae* was like a cathedral of scholarship. Its stones were reasoned arguments, but it rose from the same foundation as Chartres Cathedral—a foundation of faith.

Poems praised knightly heroes.

Learning was also reviving outside the Church. Most feudal lords cared little about the debate over reason and faith, but they enjoyed the heroic poems known as *chansons de geste* (songs of deeds). Sung to the accompaniment of a lute, each song celebrated a warrior-hero. Unlike learned writings, these poems were not in Latin but in the languages people spoke every day.

One of the earliest and most famous of the heroic poems was the Song of Roland. It praised the courage of the band of French soldiers led by Roland who perished in battle during Charlemagne's reign (page 208). Although the actual battle had been against bandits, the poem transformed it into a battle between a few French knights and an overwhelming army of Muslims from Spain. Many an evening, lords and knights heard the familiar tale. They applauded the valor of Roland's friend, Turpin, a warrior-bishop. Surrounded by enemies, Turpin fights on:

Turpin of Reims feels himself overcome,
His body pierced by four spears.
Yet he gets quickly to his feet,

Looks for Roland, runs to him,
And says one thing: "I am not beaten yet.
While life remains, no good knight gives
up."

The Song of Roland celebrated courage in battle, but later tales had wider scope. Stories about King Arthur and his knights dealt with battle but also with issues of pride, loyalty, and justice. The story of Tristan and Isolde, like many poems of the period, dealt with ill-fated love.

Poems show how the ideals of noble society were changing. In the early days, little was asked of a knight other than courage in battle and loyalty to his lord. By the High Middle Ages, however, knights were expected to live up to a complex set of ideals. These ideals became known as the code of **chivalry** (SHIH-vuhl-ree).

Knights lived by a code of chivalry.

The word *chivalry* comes from the French word *cheval* (horse) and *chevalier* (horse-riding lord).

The code demanded that a knight fight bravely in the defense of three masters: his earthly feudal lord, his heavenly Lord, and his chosen lady. Furthermore, a knight should aid the poor and defend the weak. Few knights actually met these standards. Even so, the ideals of chivalry helped raise European civilization to a new level.

A *knight's education* The education of a young nobleman began at age seven when his parents sent him off to the castle of another lord, possibly a relative. Here he acted as a page, waiting on his hosts and learning manners. In his free hours, he played with fellow pages at fencing, hunting, and chess. Before 1250, pages seldom were taught to read, since this skill was thought unmanly. (Girls learned music and weaving because these were judged to be feminine arts.)

At around the age of 14, the page was raised to the rank of squire. He now waited on a knight of the household, helping him with his armor and weapons. The squire also practiced his own skills with sword and lance on horseback. The

■ **BACKGROUND**

Castles were cold, uncomfortable places to live. Flies and mosquitoes swarmed into the open slits in walls that served as windows. Only a few rooms had fireplaces and beds. Most people in castles slept on mats in corners, halls, and courtyards.

■ **DISCUSSION**

How is castle-siege warfare different from the type of wars Europe suffered during the barbarian invasions of the late Roman empire? The Viking raids? Modern war? Focus attention on civilian involvement.

Medieval castles were often located on high hills for defense. As the local population grew, towns spread around the base of the hill or castle. From there, peasants went out to work the land. Knights were at hand to defend the castle, where people took refuge in case of attack.

■ **BACKGROUND**

In the joust, two mounted knights galloping at full speed attempted to knock each other to the ground with a mighty thrust of their long lances.

ANSWERS TO

Section Review 4

Define:
(a) group of scholars
(b) code of behavior governing knights (c) served a lord
(d) rank above page
(e) mock battle (f) poet who sang

Identify:
(a) Christian scholar who linked faith and reason
(b) Aquinas's great work
(c) heroic *chanson de geste*
(d) mother of Richard the Lionheart

Answer:
1. few books, uncomfortable classrooms, long duration of study
2. (a) through Muslim libraries (b) They were written by pagans. (c) It fused classical reasoning with Christian faith.
3. as page, learned manners; as squire, served a knight
4. increasingly limited to the home and convent
5. diverted energy from war

squire accompanied the knight on the hunt and in battle.

Becoming a knight A squire became a full-fledged knight when he was about 21 years old. First, to wash away impurities of soul and body, he had an elaborate bath. He spent a day fasting and a night praying in church. Then he knelt before the lord of the manor, who dubbed him a knight by slapping him on the shoulder with the flat of a sword. The new knight mounted his horse and galloped joyously around the church.

Mock battles for glory After being dubbed a knight, most young men traveled with companions for a year or two. They gained experience fighting in local wars or taking part in mock battles called tournaments.

In a tournament, two armies of knights charged each other, accompanied by the blare of trumpets and the cheers of lords and ladies. As in real war, prisoners captured in the tournament were held for ransom by their captor.

The idea of romantic love arose.

Before 1100, knights seemed interested only in winning the admiration of fellow men. In the Song of Roland and other heroic poems, women played a minor role. Then, in the 1100's, a whole new set of ideals evolved. Under the code of

These peasant women are breaking flax to get fibers to spin into thread and then weave into cloth.

240

chivalry, a knight's duty to his lady became fully as important as his duty to his lord. Indeed, in many poems, the hero's difficulty resulted from a conflict between the two duties.

Poets called **troubadours** (TROO-buh-DOHRZ) sang the praises of noble ladies and the knights who loved them. Sometimes troubadours sang their own verses in the castles of their lady. Other times they sent roving minstrels to carry their song to court.

Southern France was the homeland of the first troubadours. The most celebrated woman of the age was Eleanor of Aquitaine (1122–1204). Troubadours flocked to her court in the French duchy of Aquitaine. Later, as queen of England, Eleanor was the mother of Richard the Lionheart. Richard himself composed romantic songs and poems. Eleanor's daughter, Marie of Champagne, made love into a subject of study like logic or law. She presided at a famed Court of Love to which troubled lovers brought their grievances.

The role of women changed.

The idea of romantic love placed women on a pedestal where they could be worshiped. Yet women in the High Middle Ages probably had less real power than in earlier years. It is true that Eleanor of Aquitaine ruled England at times for her husband, Henry II, and later for her sons Richard and John. Few other women, however, had such opportunities.

As society became more peaceful and organized, women's roles were increasingly limited to the home and the convent. More and more often, lords passed down their fiefs only to their sons. Women held less property. As royal judges and officials gained power, queens shared less in ruling the land.

Girls from noble families were usually married around the age of 16, often to men in their 30's, 40's, or 50's. (Young men could not marry until they had property of their own, usually after their fathers died.) The girls themselves had little to say in the choice of a husband.

After marriage, a woman had her greatest power and independence while her husband was away at war. After 1100, as you will read in the next section, many knights left home for years to fight in the Crusades. In their absence, women often held power, but usually unofficially.

Define: (a) university, (b) chivalry, (c) page, (d) squire, (e) tournament, (f) troubadour
Identify: (a) Thomas Aquinas, (b) *Summa Theologiae*, (c) Song of Roland, (d) Eleanor of Aquitaine
Answer:
1. Why was learning difficult for students in a medieval university?
2. (a) How did scholars in western Europe become familiar with the writings of the ancient Greeks? (b) What problem did Christian scholars see in these writings? (c) What was the importance of the *Summa Theologiae*?
3. Describe the process by which a young nobleman learned to become a knight.
4. How did the role of women change during the Middle Ages?

Critical Thinking
5. Explain in what ways the ideas of chivalry and romantic love can be viewed as signs of a less warlike age.

Crusaders marched against Islam. 5

Near Clermont in southern France, a crowd of nobles and churchmen gazed upward at Pope Urban II as he addressed them from a wooden platform. His voice boomed forth:

From the confines of Jerusalem and from Constantinople, a grievous report has gone forth that an accursed race has violently invaded the lands of these Christians, and has depopulated them by pillage and fire.

The year was 1095. The "accursed race" was the Seljuk Turks who had recently stormed Baghdad, taken Jerusalem, and conquered all of Asia Minor from the Byzantine Greeks. The Byzantine emperor, Alexius Comnenus, appealed for assistance against the Turks. In response, the pope called on the knights of Christendom to join a **crusade**, or military expedition, to rescue Jerusalem and the Holy Land from the Muslim

Turks. Urban II's speech—one of the most influential in history—concluded:

Jerusalem is a land fruitful above all others, a paradise of delights. That royal city, situated at the center of the earth, implores you to come to her aid. Undertake this journey eagerly for the remission of your sins, and be assured of the reward of imperishable glory in the Kingdom of Heaven.

A feeling of intense excitement swept through the crowd. "God wills it!" someone shouted. Soon everyone was roaring, "God wills it! God wills it!" Thus began the First Crusade. Over the next two centuries, there were eight official Crusades and countless unofficial ones.

The Crusades had many causes.

In 1096, between 50,000 and 60,000 knights became crusaders. A crusader is someone who fights on behalf of a religious cause. The crusaders painted red crosses on their armor and marched eastward on a journey from which few would return. The ambitions of three groups fueled the Crusades.

The pope's goals Urban II, like Gregory VII before him, claimed to be the leader of all Christendom. What better way to show the pope's power than to send an army of knights from all Europe's kingdoms on a holy war?

Urban II also hoped to reunite Byzantine and Roman Christians. The Byzantine empire, though Christian, denied that the pope was the supreme head of the Church. Urban II still hoped to heal this breach. Perhaps a successful Crusade would persuade the Byzantines to unite with Roman Catholics under Urban's banner.

The knights' goals Most knights probably had mixed motives for joining the crusaders' army. Especially in the First Crusade, many were fired by religious zeal. If they died on the Crusade, the pope promised forgiveness for their sins. For other knights, the Crusades were a chance to win glory in battle. Earthly rewards were also tempting. Rich plunder awaited any army strong enough to conquer the cities of the Holy Land.

The merchants' goals Merchants played little part in the early Crusades, but after 1200 their influence grew. Some merchants supported the Crusades with gifts or loans of cash. Others used

241

SECTION 5 Objectives and Teaching Strategies

OBJECTIVE 1. Describe aspects of warfare in the Holy Land.

Teaching Strategy: *Teaching with Pictures: The Mighty Krak* (page 222e)

OBJECTIVE 2. List and evaluate the consequences of the Crusades.

Teaching Strategy: *Discussing History: Consequences of the Crusades* (page 222e)

SECTION 5 Resources

GEOGRAPHY
■ Transparency 37

REINFORCEMENT
■ Independent Practice 10.5

ENRICHMENT
■ Voices from the Past 10.5

ASSESSMENT
■ Section Quiz 10.5

their ships to transport armies over the sea, often for a hefty fee. The merchants of Pisa, Genoa, and Venice were eager to win control of key trade routes to India, Southeast Asia, and China. For centuries, Muslim traders had ruled the cities of Antioch, Damascus, and Jerusalem. If Christians held those trade centers, more wealth would flow to European merchants.

The First Crusade won Jerusalem.

By early 1097, three huge armies of knights had gathered outside the walls of Constantinople. Most of the crusaders came from France, but there were Germans, Englishmen, Scots, Italians, and Spaniards. They were led by French counts and bishops, not by kings. People of all classes also joined the Crusades.

The crusaders were well prepared for battle. However, they were woefully unprepared for the trek over the desert to Jerusalem. For two years, they suffered from heat, thirst, hunger, and fever. Yet they somehow mustered enough strength to capture several cities along their route. (Many of their victories were made possible by the fact that the Muslims were fighting among themselves, Arab against Turk.)

Finally, a bedraggled troop of about 12,000 knights (less than one fourth the original army) approached Jerusalem. They besieged the city for a month, sometimes praying and marching barefoot around its walls. Finally, on July 15, 1099, they captured the city.

A dreadful slaughter followed, as Muslim men and women were chased through the streets and murdered. The Jews of the city were rounded up, herded into a temple, and burned to death. One eyewitness reported:

> *Piles of heads, hands, and feet were to be seen in the streets of the city . . . But these were small matters compared to what happened at the Temple of Solomon [where] men rode in blood up to their knees and bridle reins.*

All in all, the crusaders had won a narrow strip of land stretching about 400 miles from Edessa in the north to Jerusalem in the south. Four feudal states were carved out of this territory, each ruled by a French duke or count.

242

Later Crusades accomplished little.

The crusaders' states were extremely vulnerable to Muslim counterattack. In 1144, Edessa was reconquered by the Turks. The Second Crusade was organized to recapture the city, but its armies straggled home in defeat.

In 1187, Europeans were shocked by the news that Jerusalem itself had fallen to a Muslim conqueror named Saladin (SAL-uh-dihn). This event touched off appeals by the Church for yet a third Crusade.

The Third Crusade was known as the Kings' Crusade because three of Europe's most powerful monarchs took the cross: the French king Philip Augustus, the German emperor Frederick I (Barbarossa), and the English king Richard I (the Lionheart). Of these three, only Richard won fame. Crossing a river, the 67-year-old Barbarossa fell from his horse and drowned. Philip Augustus caught a fever and went home.

King Richard fought valiantly to regain the Holy Land. In the process, he discovered that his foe, Saladin, could be as chivalrous as himself. Hearing that Richard was ill, Saladin sent his own personal physician and a refreshing gift of snow and peaches. The two leaders came to respect each other and in 1192 agreed to a three-year truce. Jerusalem remained under Muslim control, but Saladin promised that unarmed Christian pilgrims could freely visit the city's holy places.

Crusaders sacked Constantinople.

In 1202, a powerful pope named Innocent III appealed for still another Crusade to rescue Jerusalem from the Muslims. But the knights who took part in this Fourth Crusade never came close to Jerusalem. Instead, they became entangled in Byzantine and Italian politics.

The merchants of Venice were the main culprits in this disaster. They promised to furnish the crusaders with ships and money for their journey to the Holy Land. In exchange, the crusaders were to attack one of Venice's trading rivals—the island of Zara in the Adriatic Sea. The pope protested this diversion but was ignored. The crusaders took Zara. The pope struck back by excommunicating them.

Next, the crusaders moved against Constantinople and the unfriendly Byzantine emperor.

The Crusades

ATLANTIC
OCEAN

ENGLAND *North Sea*

HOLY ROMAN

Paris • Metz •

Ratisbon

FRANCE

Vienna

Clermont • Lyons

EMPIRE

Venice

Genoa

Zara

Frederick Barbarossa

Black Sea

Marseilles

PORTUGAL

SPAIN

Pisa

Rome

Richard the Lionheart

Adriatic Sea

Constantinople

ASIA MINOR

SELJUK TURKS

BYZANTINE

GREECE

EMPIRE

• Edessa

Antioch • SYRIA

THE HOLY LAND

Richard the Lionheart

NORTH AFRICA

Philip Augustus

Acre •

Tripoli

• Damascus

PALESTINE

MEDITERRANEAN SEA

Jerusalem •

KEY

Muslim lands

Kingdoms established by crusaders

→ First Crusade, 1096-1099

Second Crusade, 1147-1149

Third Crusade, 1189-1192

Fourth Crusade, 1202-1204

0   400 Miles

Map Study

Of the three great kings who set out on the Third Crusade, which one took an overland route? Which crusade never reached the Holy Land?

The city, split between rival leaders, could not defend itself well. When the crusaders entered the city, they went on a savage spree of looting. They stole the relics from Hagia Sophia and loaded the jewel-studded communion table onto a Venetian ship. (The ship sank and its priceless cargo was never recovered.) The looters set fires that burned much of the city, including libraries with priceless ancient manuscripts. The sack of Constantinople in 1204 ended the Fourth Crusade.

European crusaders controlled Constantinople for 57 years, until the Greeks drove them out in 1261 and restored the Byzantine empire. The breach between the Eastern Orthodox Church and the Roman Catholic Church widened into an ugly and permanent split.

The crusading spirit dwindled.

In the 1200's, Crusades became almost as common as medieval fairs and tournaments. In several later Crusades, armies marched not to the Holy Land but to North Africa. The Fifth

Crusade (1218–1221), the Seventh Crusade (1248–1254), and the Eighth Crusade (1270) were all aimed at Islamic cities in Egypt and North Africa. The French king who led the last two Crusades, Louis IX, won wide respect in Europe and was later declared a saint. None of these attempts accomplished much, however.

Of all the later Crusades, the Sixth Crusade (1228–1229) came nearest to success. The Holy

Footnote to History

In 1212, a German boy named Nicholas convinced many children that they could succeed where armies of knights had failed. Some 20,000 German children set out for Jerusalem believing that the Holy Land would fall to them without a fight. As they crossed the Alps into Italy, many died of hunger. Finally, a bishop persuaded some to go home. Others remained in Italy, where some fell into the hands of dishonest shipowners who sold the young crusaders into slavery in North Africa.

■ DISCUSSION

Compare Islamic *jihad* with the Christian attitude toward the Crusades.

243

243

Because the Krak was built into a hillside, its massive walls were in some places 80 feet thick. Protected inside were garrisons that included 2,000 knights and 400 horses. Huge storage rooms and cisterns held a five-year supply of food and water.

Cooperative Learning

Have students count off by fives. Then have them turn to the section of the chapter that matches the number they called off. Working independently, each student should write 10 review questions, with answers, for his or her section. Then have students assemble in groups; each group should have numbers 1 through 5 represented. Taking the sections in order, students read their questions to the other group members. These four should confer and attempt to answer questions without using their texts or notes. If they cannot answer, they should move on to the next question. Continue around the group until every member has read his or her questions. After answering as many questions as they can, all group members should look up and share answers for the unanswered questions so their chapter review is complete.

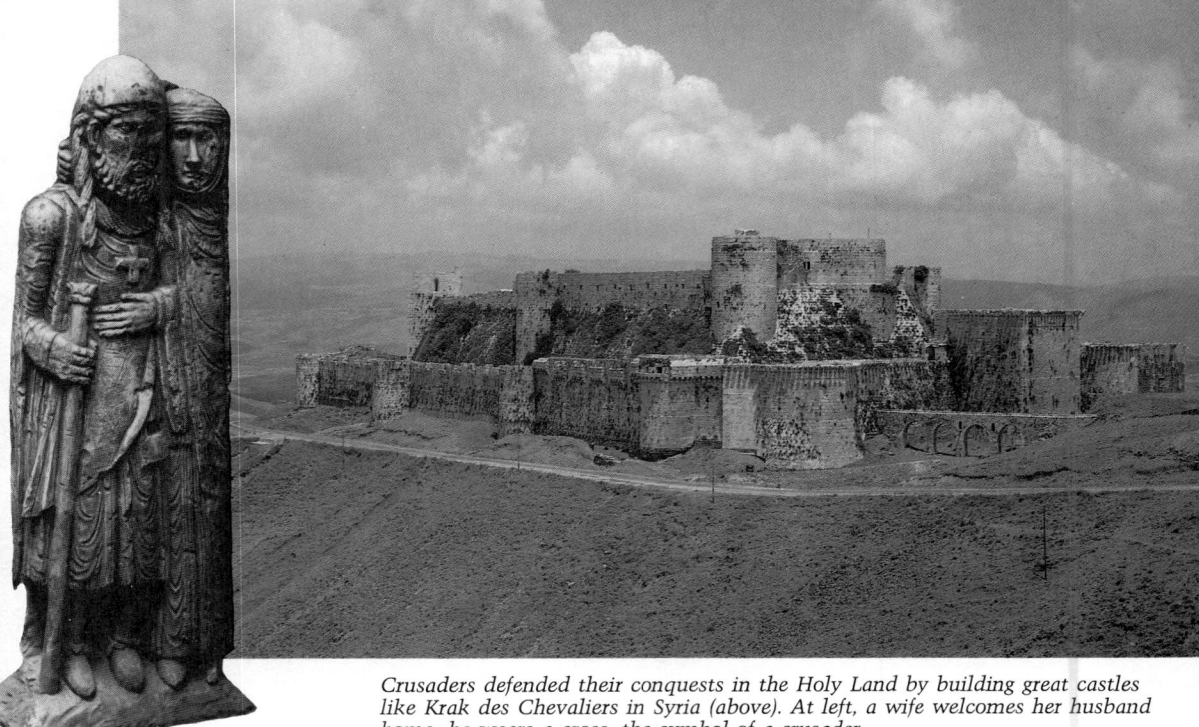

Crusaders defended their conquests in the Holy Land by building great castles like Krak des Chevaliers in Syria (above). At left, a wife welcomes her husband home; he wears a cross, the symbol of a crusader.

Roman emperor, Frederick II, led an army to the Holy Land. There Frederick met with Saladin's nephew and peacefully negotiated a treaty by which Jerusalem was returned to Christian rule. The pope, however, was not pleased. He called the treaty a pact with the devil and excommunicated Frederick.

The Christians' last stronghold in the Holy Land, the city of Acre, fell to the Muslims in 1291. By that time, many Europeans had become cynical about Crusades. Several popes had tried to use them against their religious or political enemies in Europe. For example, Innocent III declared a crusade against Frederick II, who threatened to control Italy.

The Crusades had important consequences.

As you have seen, the Crusades failed to accomplish their primary objective of conquering and holding the Holy Land. Like many great movements, however, the Crusades produced a number of additional and unexpected results.

244

1. *Decline of papal prestige* The success of the First Crusade strengthened papal prestige and power. However, the failure of later crusades lessened respect for the papacy.
2. *Decline in the power of nobles* The Crusades weakened the feudal nobility. Thousands of knights died in battle or lost their lives from disease. In addition, many knights had sold or mortgaged their properties to finance their expeditions. Led by France, European monarchs successfully took advantage of the nobles' misfortune by strengthening royal power.
3. *Decrease in Byzantine power* The Fourth Crusade dealt a serious blow to the Byzantine empire. Although Constantinople regained its independence, it never recovered its former power or prestige.
4. *Increase in religious intolerance* Two centuries of religious warfare not only promoted hostility between Christians and Muslims but also increased tensions between Christians and Jews. Angry mobs attacked Jewish communities that were often used as scapegoats for social problems.

Cause and Effect
THE CRUSADES

Contributing Factors

Feudalism
Chivalry
Religious idealism
Weakening of Byzantine empire

Immediate Causes

Conquests by Seljuk Turks
Byzantine emperor's call for help
Pope's ambition to reunite Christendom
Pope's appeal to Christian knights
Knights' religious zeal and earthly ambitions
Italian cities' desire for commercial power

CRUSADES

Immediate Effects

Temporary land gains in Palestine
Sack of Constantinople
Temporary gain in papal prestige

Long-Term Effects

Decline of papal prestige
Decline of feudal power
Increase in monarchs' power
Increased religious intolerance
Expansion of trade by Italian cities

5. *Increase in trade* The Crusades played a major role in stimulating trade between Europe and the Middle East. While living in the Holy Land, the crusaders acquired a taste for the new spices, foods, and clothes they purchased in Arab markets. Many crusaders brought home samples of these products.

The growing demand for luxury goods created economic opportunities for ambitious merchants from Venice, Genoa, and Pisa. Within a short time, these cities gained control over crucial Mediterranean trade routes. Italian merchants imported sugar, pepper, cinnamon, cloves, plums, watermelons, apricots, dates, pistachio nuts, and lemons, as well as Persian rugs and cotton cloth from trading centers in eastern Mediterranean lands. These goods created a demand that helped spark the age of exploration (see Chapter 15).

In the Crusades, all the forces of Europe's revival had come together with explosive energy. The Crusades grew from the forces of religion, feudalism, and chivalry. Yet by 1300, fewer and fewer people were answering the crusading call. Merchants did not want their flourishing trade interrupted by war. People's loyalty to the idea of Christendom lessened as new loyalties to their own lands of England, France, or Spain grew. The end of the Crusades signaled that the Middle Ages were drawing to a close.

Section REVIEW 5

Define: crusade
Identify: (a) Urban II, (b) Jerusalem, (c) Holy Land, (d) Byzantine empire, (e) Saladin, (f) Richard the Lionheart, (g) Constantinople, (h) Frederick II, (i) Innocent III
Answer:
1. What were the Crusades?
2. What reasons did each of the following have for supporting the Crusades? (a) the pope (b) knights (c) merchants
3. Based on the original goals of the crusaders, which Crusade was the most successful?
4. (a) Why was the Third Crusade called the Kings' Crusade? (b) What new view might it have given the crusaders of the Muslims?
5. What happened on the Fourth Crusade?
6. What caused interest in crusading to die down after 1200?

Critical Thinking
7. Which outcome of the Crusades do you think would in the long run be most important? Give reasons for your answer.

245

ANSWERS TO
Section Review 5

Define:
war fought to regain the Holy Land
Identify:
(a) pope who summoned fighters for the First Crusade (b) holy city won from the Muslims in First Crusade (c) land in which Jerusalem is located (d) eastern Christian empire centered at Constantinople (e) Muslim leader with whom Richard the Lionheart reached agreement in 1192 (f) king of England who took part in Third Crusade (g) capital of Byzantine empire (h) Holy Roman emperor who led Sixth Crusade (i) pope who called for the Fourth Crusade

Answer:
1. wars fought to regain Holy Land

2. (a) to show the pope's power, reunite Byzantine and Roman Christians (b) religious zeal, plunder, and glory (c) to win control of key trade routes

3. First Crusade

4. (a) Three of Europe's most powerful kings took part. (b) Muslims were chivalrous.

5. Crusaders took Zara, sacked Constantinople.

6. They became commonplace; people expected their kings to rule wisely at home; loyalty to idea of Christendom lessened.

7. Students' answers will vary.

Concluding the Chapter

1. **Chapter Closer**
   Have students explain how cathedral building symbolized the spirit of the High Middle Ages.

2. **Reteaching Activities**
   a. Recalling Main Ideas Remind students how the Chartres Cathedral represented the faith and optimism of the High Middle Ages. Challenge students to describe other achievements of the period that reflect this faith and optimism.

   b. Organizing Information Have students design a concept map for this chapter. With "The High Middle Ages" at the center, students draw and label radiating lines, naming events that, taken together, characterize the High Middle Ages.

   c. Summarizing Ask students to summarize the main points of this chapter by describing visits to the following places: a medieval fair, the monastery at Cluny, a royal court in England, a medieval university, and Jerusalem during the First Crusade.

Answers to Chapter Review appear on pages 222e–222f.

Summary

1. Farming improved and trade revived. Better farming methods made it possible for farmers to grow more food, which brought a population increase in the High Middle Ages. People began to move into towns. Trade expanded, and guilds formed for both merchants and artisans.

2. Religious leaders wielded great power. The great Gothic cathedrals that soared heavenward in many cities were symbols of the Church's power. Yet this power did not go unchallenged. For decades, kings and popes engaged in power struggles.

3. Royal governments grew stronger. England and France developed the basis for strong central governments. Despite the efforts of some strong German rulers, however, Germany did not become united.

4. Learning revived and spread. Europe's first universities developed in the High Middle Ages. Interest in learning grew in part as a result of the rediscovery of ancient Greek writings. Medieval society became more refined as chivalry and romantic love brought changes in knighthood and the view of women.

5. Crusaders marched against Islam. In 1095, the pope called for Christians to go to war to regain the Holy Land. Although the First Crusade captured Jerusalem, later ventures accomplished little.

Reviewing the Facts

1. Define the following terms:
   a. burghers
   b. bourgeoisie
   c. guild
   d. apprentice
   e. journeyman
   f. charter
   g. cardinal
   h. interdict
   i. canon law
   j. friar
   k. jury
   l. common law
   m. chivalry
   n. crusade

2. Explain the importance of each of the following names, dates, places, or terms:
   a. three-field system
   b. Cluny
   c. Canossa
   d. Concordat of Worms
   e. Inquisition
   f. Gothic
   g. William the Conqueror
   h. 1066
   i. Henry II
   j. Hugh Capet
   k. Otto the Great
   l. Frederick Barbarossa
   m. Holy Roman Empire
   n. Thomas Aquinas
   o. Constantinople
   p. Jerusalem
   q. Saladin

3. How did changes in farming lead to an overall change in medieval life?

4. What purposes did guilds serve?

5. Why did the appointment of bishops become the issue in a struggle between kings and popes?

First Crusade — Concordat of Worms

Gregory VII reforms the Church — Building of Chartres

Norman conquest of England — Rise of universities and revival of learning

Otto the Great becomes emperor of Germany — Thomas Aquinas

Capetian dynasty begins in France — Kings' Crusade

900 — 1000 — 1100 — 1200 — 1300

246

6. How did the development of Germany differ from that of England and France?
7. (a) Explain how medieval builders solved the problem of supporting the weight of a church roof without using thick walls. (b) What changes did this improvement allow?
8. What debt did universities owe to each of the following? (a) Jewish and Muslim scholars (b) Byzantine scholars (c) monks
9. (a) Why did the Crusades win wide support in Europe? (b) What did they achieve?

Basic Skills

1. **Acquiring information** Study the photos on pages 222, 223, and 225 to find information on medieval trades and occupations. (a) Identify as many of these as possible. (b) Describe the various tools and technologies shown.
2. **Summarizing** Summarize the changes in European civilization during the High Middle Ages by writing a paragraph on political changes, another on economic changes, and a third on social changes.
3. **Reading a map** Using the map on page 243, identify for each of the four Crusades the points of origin, the routes taken, and the destinations.

Researching and Reporting Skills

1. **Translating information** Write a 50-word advertisement or make a poster for a medieval fair to be held in Chartres on October 25, 1250.
2. **Identifying sources** If you were researching the Crusades, which of the following sources would you consult: (a) a history of Europe in the tenth century, (b) a history of Venice in the Middle Ages, (c) a biography of Peter Abelard, (d) an article on women in the twelfth century, (e) a history of the Church in English society from 1400 to 1600, (f) a history of medieval armament? Give reasons for your choices.

Critical Thinking

1. **Inferring** (a) What do you think caused the growth of chivalry in the Middle Ages? (b) What were some of the consequences?
2. **Synthesizing** Give a brief assessment of the role of women during the Middle Ages. Provide two examples of situations in which they could exercise power or rights and two examples of situations illustrating their lack of power or rights.
3. **Evaluating** The heading on page 235 states that German kings failed to unite their lands. Yet the map on the same page shows the Holy Roman Empire covering the Germanic kingdom as one unified block. How can you explain these apparent differences?
4. **Analyzing outcomes** The growth of cities and trade aided the development of guilds. (a) How might the growth of guilds affect the relationship between the king and the nobles? (b) How might it affect personal rights?
5. **Interpreting** According to your text, the medieval Church resembled a kingdom in many ways. (a) Identify three activities of the Church that resembled those of a government. (b) What powers did the pope have that could intervene between a king and his subjects?

Perspectives on Past and Present

1. If you were a student at a medieval university, how would your experience differ from that of a student today?
2. Two excellent movies, *The Lion in Winter* and *Becket*, depict the struggle for political power by Henry II of England. Watch the videotape of one film. What problems does Henry face? How does he deal with them?

Investigating History

1. Investigate the medieval past of London, Paris, Brussels, Antwerp, Cologne, or some other European city of your choice. For that city, locate a traveler's guidebook that identifies cathedrals, castles, guild halls, or other sites dating back to medieval times. Prepare an oral report or written description of your findings.
2. Two powerful leagues of cities were formed during the Middle Ages—the Hanseatic League and the Lombard League. Find information about one of these leagues. What were its objectives? What cities were members? Where did its members trade, and what products did they trade?
3. Look up the *Song of Roland* or the tales of King Arthur and his Knights of the Round Table. Write a short essay describing how that literary work expresses the ideal of chivalry.

247

CHAPTER
Evaluation

Chapter Test 10, Alternate Chapter Test 10, and Computer Test Bank Chapter 10 Test can be used to evaluate your students' understanding of this chapter.

The Origin of European Nations

Chapter **11**

Chapter Overview

Chapter 11 traces the growth of nation-states in Europe. In France, royal power increased when the king won control of land held by English kings. Later, central government was strengthened under Louis IX. In England, King John was forced to sign the Magna Carta, a document that limited royal power. Under Edward I, Parliament became part of English government.

As feudal loyalties were being replaced by national loyalties, the Church was weakened by the Great Schism. Plague reduced the population and a lack of workers doomed the manorial economy. New weapons put an end to feudal warfare.

In western Europe, new monarchs replaced feudal kings. To the northeast, the Russian empire began its rise to power.

Chapter Focus

Call attention to the quotation of Joan of Arc on page 249. Joan of Arc believed she was divinely inspired to fight for her country. This blend of religion and patriotism was a new phenomenon.

Help students define nationalism, which relates to the concepts of loyalty to country, patriotism, homeland, and allegiance. Point out that nationalism was a new phenomenon that paralleled the development of nation-states and governments.

England and France developed as nations. 1

Setting the Stage

Section 1 examines how the political boundaries and governments shaped during the thirteenth century formed the basis for modern England and France. Point out that earlier Norman kings of England had gained power by holding lands in England and France and by establishing royal courts of justice. Did similar strategies contribute to the rise of nation-states in England and France?

Teaching Strategies

Writing about History: The Conflict between France and England (Objective 1) The conflict between France and England actually helped to make both royal governments stronger, but in different ways. In England, the barons felt Henry III did not fully represent the country. Henry was also losing a great deal of money trying to retake territories in France. Under the strong leadership of French king Louis IX, who led the final crusades, French loyalty to the king blossomed.

■ Have students develop a "word bank" by listing at least ten words that pertain to the growth of national government in France and England.

■ Have students write short essays that explain how France and England developed into nations. Essays should contain the items in students' word banks.

Chapter 1 FOCUS

	SECTION 1
Objectives	1. Identify events that contributed to the political development of France and England. 2. Analyze the purposes and results of the Model Parliament and of the Estates General.
Setting the Stage	The centralization of political power in the hands of kings
Teaching Strategies	Writing about History: The Conflict between France and England Skill Building: Comparing and Contrasting Political Institutions Check for Understanding
Guided Practice	Section Review 1
Independent Practice Worksheets	Independent Practice 11.1 Vocabulary 11
Enrichment	1. Primary Source: Voices 11.1 2. ★Preparing a Report: Joan of Arc 3. Researching for Points
Chapter Closer	
Unit III Review	

Chapter 11 The Origin of European Nations 1150–1580
FOCUS Joan of Arc as a symbol of the growth of nationalism in Europe

★ Advanced
● Basic

SECTION 2	SECTION 3	SECTION 4	SECTION 5
1. Analyze changes in the relationship between the Church and secular governments. 2. Identify the main effects of the Great Schism on the power of the Church.	1. Explain the social and physical effects of the plague. 2. Analyze the warfare between France and England and its effects on nationalism.	1. Explain the phrase *new monarchs*. 2. Explain characteristics of Henry VII's reign.	1. Explain the influence of Mongol rule on the development of the Russian empire. 2. Describe the geography of Russia and its effects on Russia's development as a nation-state.
Changes in people's attitudes toward the Church in the late Middle Ages	How the plague and warfare damaged medieval life	Nation-states replacing the feudal system	Russia as a part of the Mongol Empire
Discussing History: Thomas Becket Skill Building: Drawing Conclusions Check for Understanding	Writing about History: The Plague Discussing History: The War between France and England Transparency 38 Check for Understanding	Discussing History: The New Monarchs Writing about History: The Reign of Henry VII Transparency 39 Check for Understanding	Discussing History: The Influence of the Mongols Geography in History: Russia Transparency 40 Check for Understanding
Section Review 2 Independent Practice 11.2	Transparency 38 Q&A Section Review 3 Independent Practice 11.3 Basic Skills 11	Transparency 39 Q&A Section Review 4 Independent Practice 11.4 Critical Thinking 11	Transparency 40 Q&A Section Review 5 Independent Practice 11.5 Geography Skills 11
1. Primary Source: Voices 11.2 2. Researching for Points	1. Primary Source: Voices 11.3 2. Preparing a Report: Changing Climates 3. Researching for Points	1. Primary Source: Voices 11.4 2. Researching for Points	1. Primary Source: Voices 11.5 2. Researching for Points 3. Global Perspectives Transparency 42

●**Reteaching Activities**	Outlining, Making a Time Line
Chapter Review	Summary, Reviewing the Facts, Basic Skills, Researching and Reporting Skills, Critical Thinking, Perspectives on Past and Present, Investigating History
Chapter Evaluation	Chapter Test 11, Alternate Chapter Test 11, Computer Test Bank Chapter 11 Test
Geographic Theme	Interaction: How did people use resources to develop trade?
Historical Themes	Continuity and Change, Social Institutions, Rise of Democratic Ideas
Unit Evaluation	Unit III Test, Alternate Unit III Test

Skill Building: Comparing and Contrasting Political Institutions (Objective 2) Why did the King of England include the English burghers in the first Model Parliament? Also, discuss the growing power of the king in France and his manipulation of the Estates General. Ask students to comment on the inclusion of the middle class in the French Assembly. What did the Estates General and the English Parliament have in common?

Assign students the title of *baron* or *burgher*. Direct them to write responses to the king's request for new taxes. Then have students compare responses to demonstrate the role of the constituency they represent.

Check for Understanding Have students demonstrate their comprehension of the term *nation-state* by completing the following sentence: Evidence that England was becoming a nation-state includes . . . . Have students complete a similar statement for France.

Enrichment Activities

1. **Reading a Primary Source**
   Assign Voices from the Past Resource Book 11.1.

2. **Preparing a Report**
   Have advanced students compare the historic Joan of Arc with the character depicted in *Saint Joan* by George Bernard Shaw.

3. **Researching for Bonus Points**
   What were Henry II's final words? ("Shame, shame, on a conquered king.")

Setting the Stage

Note that when the King of France made Pope Boniface VII a captive, there was little reaction from the French people, who accepted the king's actions. This section examines how people's attitudes toward the Church changed. Review the influence of the Church as discussed in Chapter 10 (pages 228–231). Ask how the development of the English and French monarchies might conflict with the power of the Church.

Teaching Strategies

Discussing History: Thomas Becket (Objective 1) Share with students the story of the relationship between Henry II and Thomas Becket. Before he was made Archbishop of Canterbury, Becket showed no traits of the single-minded, almost fanatical clergyman he eventually became. As Henry's chancellor and friend, he enjoyed a sumptuous royal lifestyle. Despite warnings, Henry appointed his friend Archbishop of Canterbury. Becket abandoned his former lifestyle for the austere trappings of a medieval monk. Henry's attempts to consolidate royal power often violated church jurisdictions, creating tensions between the former friends. In a fit of rage, Henry uttered words that he would later regret: "What cowards have I about me that no one will deliver me from this low born priest?" Eager to please their king, loyal knights carried out his inadvertent command and killed Becket in his own church.

Thomas Becket proved powerful even in death. Henry journeyed to Canterbury. There, in the cathedral of his slain friend, Henry knelt down before a long row of monks who obeyed the king's orders to beat him across his bare back.

Discuss how this episode illustrates the growing rivalry between the Church and developing monarchies.

Skill Building: Drawing Conclusions (Objective 2) Ask students to comment on the importance of stability for any institution. What is the effect of instability? Explain that the Avignon papacy and the Great Schism are important for what they show us about the declining power of the Church. To help students understand the chaotic nature of this crisis, have them write sentences about the papacy and the Church in 1380 from the points of view of a French cardinal, an Italian bishop, and a commoner married by a recently excommunicated priest.

Check for Understanding Refer to the Daily Life feature on religion and trade (page 255). Ask students to explain the concepts of just price and usury. What would be the effect of each one on trade? What does this feature show about the role of the Church in the Middle Ages?

Enrichment Activities

1. **Reading a Primary Source**
   Assign Voices from the Past Resource Book 11.2.

2. **Researching for Bonus Points**
   In what country was Avignon located in 1305? (in the Holy Roman Empire)

The 1300's brought plague and war.   3

Setting the Stage

Besides causing a great loss of life, the Black Death had emotional and economic repercussions throughout western Europe. Demoralized by the fear of death, people lost interest in their careers and ambitions. Section 3 examines how the plague and warfare led to a general disintegration of medieval life. Remind students that struggles between the Church and the emerging national governments had already created apprehension and instability.

Teaching Strategies

Writing about History: The Plague (Objective 1) Ask students to imagine they live in a medieval town during a plague outbreak. Have them brainstorm on the following questions:

■ What are the ramifications of the fact that half of the townspeople may have died or moved away?

■ How might the plague be affecting the economy?

■ How might the plague change one's life-style and one's expectations about the future?

Then have students write a first-person account from the perspective of a young person who has survived an outbreak of the plague.

Discussing History: The War between France and England (Objective 2) Review with students the technology and tactics of medieval warfare. New weapons resulted in a staggering loss of life during the Hundred Years' War. Archery had become the national sport in England. This gave young men practice with the longbow, which could pierce armor at 100 yards. Until this time, the use of cannons was limited. They had been as likely to destroy the person firing

them as the intended target. How did the longbow and cannon redefine military strategy and further diminish the role of traditional medieval knights? Display Map Transparency 38, *France in the Hundred Years' War,* and have students locate the great battle sites of the conflict. How did the period's battles contribute to the growing spirit of nationalism in France and England?

Check for Understanding Ask students how the Black Death, new weapons, and feelings of nationalism helped end feudalism.

Enrichment Activities

1. **Reading a Primary Source** Assign Voices from the Past Resource Book 11.3.

2. **Preparing a Report** Have students report on the phenomenon of changing climates, as mentioned on page 257, and how they affect people's lives. Interested students may want to research current global warming and draw parallels between climate changes of past and present.

3. **Researching for Bonus Points** What was the average weight of the cannons used in the 1300's? (6,000 to 8,000 pounds)

New monarchs ruled in western Europe.   4

Setting the Stage

Have volunteers list the attributes of a nation-state on the board. Then ask others to list the traits of the feudal system. Have students compare the lists and suggest why the feudal system was unworkable in an emerging nation-state.

Teaching Strategies

Discussing History: The New Monarchs (Objective 1) On the board list the three new sources of power available to the new monarchs: broad taxing power, a professional army, and professional officials. Explain that one reason Charles VII needed a professional army was to combat a growing number of bandits and outlaws, who were terrorizing the general population. The king's soldiers came from all classes and were paid from general taxes. The middle classes no longer depended on the nobles for protection. Ask students to explain how the new monarchies were different from feudal kingdoms.

Writing about History: The Reign of Henry VII (Objective 2) *Prewriting* Discuss with students the importance of stability in politics. After the War of the Roses, the desire for peace and order among English middle classes was very strong. The reign of Henry VII was a response to the desire for stability. Have students design a concept map to organize their writing. First have students write *stability* and list reasons it was needed. Next, they should draw lines from this central idea to statements describing the actions of Henry VII that contributed to stability. *Writing* Have students use their concept maps to write analyses of Henry's reign. Encourage them to include their own opinions.

Check for Understanding Ask students to explain how Louis XI, Henry Tudor, and Isabella and Ferdinand were *new monarchs*.

Enrichment Activities

1. **Reading a Primary Source**
Assign Voices from the Past Resource Book 11.4.

2. **Researching for Bonus Points**
Which religious order was responsible for implementing the Spanish Inquisition? (the Dominicans)

A *new empire arose in Russia.* 5

Setting the Stage

As feudalism was declining in western Europe, it was just developing in the Eurasian region that became Russia. The peoples there were under the control of the Mongols, fierce conquerors from central Russia, from 1240 to 1480. Events leading to the unification of Russia began during Mongol rule.

Teaching Strategies

Discussing History: The Influence of the Mongols (Objective 1) The Mongols did not actually govern Russia, but were content to collect revenues there. Russian princes were otherwise allowed to rule their principalities independently. Ask how this arrangement led to Moscow's emergence as a major principality. Point out that Russian princes ruled through terror, as had their Mongol overlords.

Geography in History: Russia (Objective 2) Ask what roles rivers played in Russian history. Show students Map Transparency 40, *Russia and Eastern Europe in 1480.* Have students describe Russia's geographical isolation. Ask them to hypothesize why Moscow became the place from which the Russian empire expanded.

Check for Understanding Ask why Russia did not develop as a nation-state to the same extent as France and England.

Enrichment Activities

1. **Reading a Primary Source**
Assign Voices from the Past Resource Book 11.5.

2. **Researching for Bonus Points**
Who were the late fifteenth-century designers of the Kremlin and why were they chosen? (In the Muscovites' rush to

claim international stature and to become the "third Rome," Italian architects were employed.)

3. **Global Perspectives**
Have students study Map Transparency 42, *The World about 1250,* or refer them to pages 274–275.

ANSWERS TO
Chapter Review 11

Reviewing the Facts
1. **(a)** people with definite territory, united under one government **(b)** feeling of loyalty to one's own land and people **(c)** Russian word for emperor **(d)** minor prince in Russia
2. **(a)** year Magna Carta was signed **(b)** gathering called by Edward I including commoners and lords **(c)** meeting of First, Second, and Third Estates **(d)** period when papacy was in Avignon **(e)** period when there were two popes **(f)** council that resolved Great Schism **(g)** plague during 1300's that weakened feudalism **(h)** war between France and England over English land in France **(i)** French heroine who defeated English at Battle of Orleans **(j)** English civil war between Houses of York and Lancaster **(k)** first Tudor king **(l)** French king who set French monarchy on road to recovery **(m)** Spanish king under whose rule Spain reached its modern borders **(n)** with Ferdinand, revived Inquisition, expelled Jews and Muslims **(o)** drive to expel Muslims out of Spain **(p)** year Columbus sailed on first voyage of discovery **(q)** capital of Russian empire **(r)** first czar of united Russian nation

3. (a) conflicts in France over English lands, John's need to raise taxes, the barons' demands **(b)** guarantees no taxation without representation and due process of law; limits power of monarchy

4. (a) included commoners as well as knights, bishops, and lords **(b)** 1295

5. (a) won back all King John's land in France **(b)** established Parliament of Paris which could overturn decisions of local courts **(c)** drove English out of France except for Calais; set up a royal council; set up the first permanent royal army **(d)** added dukedom of Burgundy to French state; ruled without needing to call Estates General

6. (a) People concluded that Avignon popes were hirelings of the French court; were shocked at extravagance of Avignon papacy. **(b)** Great Schism caused Christians to question the source of true religious authority: the pope—or which of several popes, a church council, or the Bible.

7. crop failures—caused famine; plague—killed millions of people; war—killed both French and English soldiers

8. Englishmen rejoiced at the news of their king's victories in France; Joan of Arc changed a prince into a king, led the French army to victory, awakened national spirit; in both countries, king was seen as a national leader fighting for glory of nation-state.

9. used new sources of power—control of taxes, a professional army, and officials

10. Mongols began work of uniting Russia; by the 1400's, Moscow was strongest Russian state. Ivan III, first czar, freed Moscow from Mongols and made it capital of a true empire.

Basic Skills

1.

1356 Battle of Poitiers					1429 Victory of Orleans	
1337	1357	1377	1397	1417	1437	1457
1346 Battle of Crécy				1415 Battle of Agincourt	1431 Joan's death at the stake	

2. (a)

	England	France
Taxes	Magna Carta: limited king's power to tax (1215); Edward I taxed towns	King's bailiffs collected taxes
Parliament/ Estates General	Burgesses part of Model Parliament (1295); powers over taxation	Third Estate part of General Estates (1302); no powers over taxation
Royal Courts	Right to jury trial (1215) Edward I strengthened royal courts	Bailiffs presided over king's courts Louis IX created Parlement of Paris

(b) Changes reflect growing importance of middle class and extension of civil rights.

3. All three countries neared present-day political boundaries. France acquired English territory within France. Spain and Portugal conquered Muslim territory. Italian, Polish, and Hungarian kingdoms acquired territory from the Holy Roman Empire.

4. Monarchs relied less on vassals for help; tax base and military enrollment broadened to all classes, with less dependence on feudal aid and on noble knights; administrative tasks given to new educated middle class.

Researching and Reporting Skills

1. Students' interviews will vary.

2. Students' surveys will vary.

3. Illustration on page 252 is a reproduction of a primary source for Edward I and the Model Parliament. Pictures of the Magna Carta (page 251) and St. Basil's Cathedral (page 267) are primary sources because they show physical remains.

Other pictures give valuable information about life in the Middle Ages, but might be primary or secondary sources depending on the dates they were produced. Primary source quotations appear on pages 249, 258, and 260.

Critical Thinking

1. (a) The statement is more like an opinion than a fact; it is a reasoned judgment based on evidence. **(b)** Losses of French territory helped English identify with England and limit royal power.

2. (a) Middle classes, prosperous from trade, bought freedom from the feudal system. King sought their political and financial support against nobles, which gave them power over the king. **(b)** In England middle class limited power of king. In France Third Estate took part in government but had less power.

3. Spain was left without tradespeople for thriving cities and healthy economy; without intellectuals to lead Spain into the modern era.

Perspectives on Past and Present

1. Examples include the Bill of Rights and the Nixon impeachment.

2. The existence of various denominations provides for wider range of beliefs. Principle of religious toleration gives acceptance to different beliefs. Within a given religious group, tolerance of dissent varies.

Investigating History

Students' answers will vary.

Chapter 11

The Origin of European Nations

Joan of Arc boldly led her army to defend France.

Teaching with Pictures

Have students read the chapter opener on pages 248–249. Explain that the English later captured Joan of Arc and convicted her of heresy and witchcraft because she claimed to be divinely inspired. They burned her at the stake on May 30, 1431. The French celebrate this day as a national holiday and consider Joan of Arc their greatest patriot. Ask students what impression they have of Joan as they view this statue. Does it suggest a seventeen-year-old maiden? What was the likely purpose of the sculptor? How does the statue differ from the text description of Joan of Arc? What event in her life might the statue portray?

■ BACKGROUND

Before accepting the aid of Joan of Arc, Charles VII, taken aback by the young girl who heard voices from heaven, had her questioned and found trustworthy by a committee of clergy.

Key Terms

due process of law
limited monarchy
burgess
parliament
representative
nation-state
schism
clergy
nationalism
Reconquista
czar
boyar

248

Read and Understand

1. England and France developed as nations.
2. The Church faced a crisis in the 1300's.
3. The 1300's brought plague and war.
4. New monarchs ruled in western Europe.
5. A new empire arose in Russia.

In April 1429, French peasants peered from their houses and fields as a small army of perhaps 4,000 soldiers moved across the war-torn countryside of northern France. Armies were no novelty to these peasants. France and England had been at war since 1337, and English armies had tramped all over France. This army, however, was something new. It was French. Its leader was not a hard-bitten captain but a black-haired, fair-faced peasant girl of 17 who called herself Joan the Maid. She is known to history as Joan of Arc.

Chapter 11 Resources

GEOGRAPHY
■ Geography Skills 11
■ Transparencies 38, 39, 40, 42

REINFORCEMENT
■ Vocabulary 11
■ Basic Skills 11
■ Reteaching 11
■ Making Connections Study Guide 11

ENRICHMENT
■ Critical Thinking 11
■ History and Literature 11

ASSESSMENT
■ Chapter Test 11
■ Alternate Chapter Test 11
■ Computer Test Bank

Joan had come to save the French city of Orleans, which the English had been besieging for the past six months. Without help, the city's defenders could not hold out much longer. When Joan reached the threatened city, she sent a message to the English:

You, men of England, who have no right in the kingdom of France, the King of Heaven sends the order through me, Joan the Maid, to return to your own country.

The arrival of this heroic young woman had an electrifying effect on the townspeople of Orleans. They hailed her as champion of all France against the English enemies.

Early in the morning of May 7, 1429, Joan buckled on her white armor. She took up her white linen banner decorated with angels and the lilies of France. The English had built forts blocking the roads into Orleans. Marching against these forts, following Joan's banner into battle, the French army attacked.

You will read later in the chapter whether Joan of Arc and her soldiers won or lost their fight for France. From a historical point of view, the outcome of the battle was less important than its cause. Joan and the men who followed her in 1429 were fighting for a cause that was new to Europe and the world. They were *not* fighting for one feudal lord against another. Unlike the crusaders of an earlier century, they were *not* fighting for Christianity against Muslim enemies. Instead, they were French people fighting in defense of their homeland, France, against a foreign enemy, England.

Joan of Arc had a feeling of loyalty to a nation—a feeling that we call nationalism. It was a new and powerful force in history. How that feeling of national loyalty arose in France and in England during the 1300's and 1400's is a major theme of this chapter.

In part, the growth of national feeling began with the power struggles of medieval kings from about 1200 to about 1500. These rulers fought against the Church, against powerful lords within their own realms, and against rival kings of other countries.

Slowly, these struggles shattered the power of two great medieval institutions—the Church and feudalism. In their place, we see the beginnings of a powerful new institution—the nation.

By 1500, for the first time, we can speak of nations in the modern sense of the word, not just of feudal kingdoms.

Such a fundamental change took a long time to develop. To see how France and England became separate nations—not just separate kingdoms—we must go back in time 300 years before Joan of Arc put on her white armor. The story begins with the feudal wars of England's King Henry II.

England and France developed as nations. 1

In the late 1100's, France and England were a mixture of interconnected feudal lands. In the early 1200's, however, the two countries began to follow separate paths.

England's king lost his French land.

Henry II, king of England from 1154 to 1189, was also feudal lord of more than half of France. From his great-grandfather, William the Conqueror, Henry had inherited Normandy and other lands in northern France. Henry added to his holdings by marrying Eleanor of Aquitaine, the richest heiress in Europe. She brought him fiefs in southern France. For his French lands, Henry was the vassal of France's Capetian king, Louis VII. However, Henry was a better soldier than Louis and often defeated him.

When Henry and Louis died, the story took a different turn. Henry was succeeded first by his son Richard I, the hero of the Third Crusade. A fearless fighter and skilled general, Richard the Lionheart was able to defend his French lands. When Richard died in 1199 after only ten years as king, he was followed by his younger brother, John, who ruled from 1199 to 1216. John was a complete failure as a military leader; indeed, he won the nickname John Softsword. He soon proved to be no match for the wily king who now wore the French crown, Philip II, known as Philip Augustus.

As a child, Philip had watched his father lose battle after battle to Henry II. When Philip became

249

SECTION 1 Objectives and Teaching Strategies

OBJECTIVE 1. Identify events that contributed to the political development of France and England.

Teaching Strategy: *Writing about History: The Conflict between France and England* (page 248a)

OBJECTIVE 2. Analyze the purposes and results of the Model Parliament and of the Estates General.

Teaching Strategy: *Skill Building: Comparing and Contrasting Political Institutions* (page 248c)

■ DISCUSSION

After one humiliating scene, the boy Philip warned Henry: "I can't hinder you, my lord, but I tell you now that when I am grown up, I will take back all of which you have deprived him." What purposes motivated other powerful leaders?

SECTION 1 Resources

ASSESSMENT
■ Section Quiz 11.1

REINFORCEMENT
■ Independent Practice 11.1

ENRICHMENT
■ Voices from the Past 11.1

John also lost a struggle with Pope Innocent III, who disagreed with John about who should be Archbishop of Canterbury. Innocent excommunicated John and put England under interdict. Pressure from English barons forced John to make peace with the Church in 1213 and become, through an oath of fealty, the pope's vassal.

king in 1180, at the age of 15, he set out to weaken the power of the English kings in France. His greatest triumphs came during John's reign. In 1204, Philip Augustus took Normandy from John. Within two years, he had also won the rest of John's lands in northern France. Only Aquitaine and Gascony in southern France remained loyal to John. By the end of his reign, Philip had tripled the lands under his own direct control. For the first time, a French king was more powerful than any of his vassals. Philip's victories set the stage for England and France to develop as two separate countries.

The barons rebelled against King John.

John's losses in France were just the beginning of his troubles. He soon faced another crisis in England. Some of John's problems stemmed from his own character. According to one historian, John was "selfish, cruel, shameless, cynical, lustful, dishonorable, and utterly false." These character flaws made John's subjects dislike him all the more after his defeats.

In some ways, John's defeats in France proved valuable to England. First, England was gaining an identity as a distinct nation. After John lost Normandy, many lords had to choose whether to hold lands in France or in England. Philip Augustus gave them a year to decide. For those who chose to keep their English lands, England became more important than before. No longer were their interests divided between lands in France and lands in England. Though their ancestors had been Norman, they grew more and more English in customs and loyalty.

John's losses were England's gain for another reason. His unsuccessful wars led directly to the most celebrated document in English history, the Magna Carta.

How did John's wars in France lead to a landmark in English liberty? Wars are always costly. In trying to win back his French lands, John raised taxes to an all-time high. He tried every possible way of squeezing money out of his barons. (The term *barons* includes all the nobles of England who were direct vassals of the king, regardless of their rank. Some were great lords, some were bishops, and a few were simple knights.)

▲ Turning Points in History

The Magna Carta In 1214, John tried again to recover his lands in France. Once again, Philip Augustus defeated him. Soon after John returned to England, his barons revolted. They demanded that John change his ways of governing.

John's situation was hopeless. To keep his crown, he was forced to agree to the barons' terms. Seething with anger, he rode to the appointed meeting place, a broad meadow called Runnymede on the Thames (tehms) River. The barons presented their demands. The date was June 15, 1215, a date that marks a milestone in English history. Four days later, the negotiations between the barons and the king were finished, and John affixed his seal to the document later known as the *Magna Carta* (Great Charter).

Original purpose The English barons were thinking mostly of themselves when they drew up the 63 clauses of the Magna Carta. They wanted to protect themselves from unjust taxes and to safeguard their own feudal rights and privileges. In later years, however, English people of all classes argued that certain clauses in the Magna Carta applied to every citizen.

In the Magna Carta, John made a variety of promises. For example, he agreed to respect the rights and privileges of the city of London. He promised merchants the right to travel freely in and out of England. The most important promises, however, guaranteed what are now considered basic legal rights, both in England and the United States.

Guarantee of basic rights Clause 12 of the Magna Carta declared that taxes "shall be levied in our kingdom only by the common consent of our kingdom." This clause meant that the king could not arbitrarily demand taxes. He had to have the agreement of his advisers, usually at a meeting of barons called the king's Great Council. In other words, said later generations of English men and women (and eventually, people in the United States), there shall be *no taxation without representation.*

Another important guarantee was stated in Clause 39: "No free man shall be arrested or imprisoned . . . except by the legal judgment of his peers or by the law of the land." In other words, people later claimed, a person had the right to a jury trial and to the protection of the law. (This right to have the law work in known, orderly ways came to be known as **due process of law.**)

The idea of limited monarchy The underlying idea of the Magna Carta was not stated in so many words. It is the idea of **limited monarchy.** The barons at Runnymede forced their king to recognize limits on his powers. They said that he must follow the established laws and customs of the land. As Winston Churchill, England's great leader of the twentieth century, wrote: "Throughout [Magna Carta] it is implied that here is a law which is above the King and which even he must not break. This [idea] of a supreme law . . . is the great work of Magna Carta; and this alone justifies the respect in which men have held it."

Parliament became part of English government.

John died in 1216, the year after he signed the Magna Carta. He left a young son, only nine years old, who became Henry III. Henry's long and unhappy reign (1216–1272) was marked by more losses in France and further conflicts with the barons.

For a time, it appeared that the strong foundations of England's royal government laid by William the Conqueror and Henry II would be washed away. Near the end of the 1200's, however, one of England's ablest kings restored royal power. Edward I, the son of Henry III and grandson of John, became king in 1272.

During Edward's long reign (1272–1307), he improved administration and strengthened the royal courts. His laws clarified the division of power between the king and the nobles, usually to the king's advantage.

Edward was able to limit the power of the troublesome barons. One reason for the barons' power had been the king's dependence on them for money. Now times were changing. Edward I was perhaps the first king to realize it. With the growth of towns and trade, it was easier to raise taxes from the middle-class burghers (or **burgesses** as the English called them) than from the upper-class barons.

In the past, people of the towns had been left out of the king's Great Council, the gathering that approved the royal plans for taxes. Only the great barons and bishops were ordinarily summoned to hear the king's requests for more money. Edward I was the first king to see the advantages of including townspeople in the meeting.

The Model Parliament In 1295, Edward I was planning another war to prevent his last remaining French lands from being conquered by the French king. To raise taxes for that war, Edward needed the support of all influential groups—not just the barons but the townspeople as well. Therefore, the king summoned two burgesses from every borough and two knights from every county to serve as a **parliament,** or legislative group. According to Edward's royal writ, the so-called

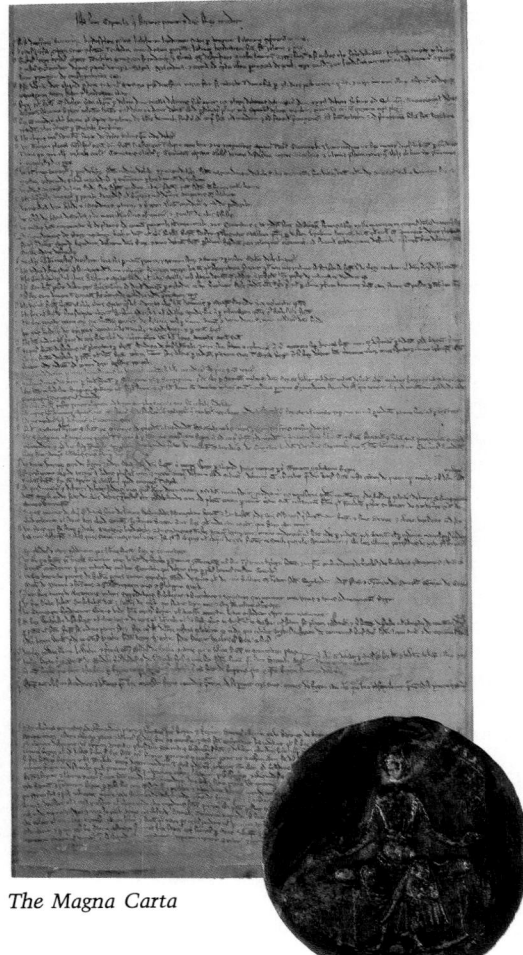

The Magna Carta

251

From the Magna Carta: "To no one will we sell, to no one will we refuse or delay, right or justice." Compare this to a modern quote: "Justice delayed is justice denied."

By 1300, England had three unique institutions: its court system, which relied on juries and the Common Law; its tax system, with townspeople and nobles in Parliament involved in the taxmaking process; and its monarchy, forced by the Magna Carta to respect subjects' rights.

Cooperative Learning

Arrange students in pairs. Assign each pair one of these viewpoints: ''With the adoption of a Parliament, England should do away with the monarchy,'' or ''Even with a Parliament, the English monarchy should be kept.'' Each pair should prepare a statement advocating its assigned position, keeping in mind any arguments that the opposition might present. Then group pairs with opposing pairs and have them present their statements to each other. Have the pairs debate their positions, acknowledging any valid points their opponents make. Students should offer constructive guidance by way of criticizing arguments, not the people who make them.

Edward I sits above the Model Parliament, with churchmen at the left, barons at the right, and burgesses seated on wool sacks in the center.

commoners of the kingdom were being summoned because ''what affects all should be approved by all.''

Thus, in November 1295, knights, burgesses, bishops, and lords met together at Westminster in London to consult with the king. Historians refer to this famous gathering as the *Model Parliament* because its new composition (commoners as well as lords) served as a model for later kings.

Over the next century, from 1300 to 1400, the king called the knights and burgesses whenever a new tax was needed. In Parliament, these two groups gradually formed an assembly of their own called the House of Commons. Nobles and bishops met separately as the House of Lords.

Footnote to History

Because the king's councils involved a lot of talk and discussion, they took their name from the French word *parler* (talk); the meetings became known as *parliaments*.

252

The strength of Parliament Under Edward I, Parliament was in part a royal tool that weakened the great lords. The knights and burgesses generally sided with the king even when the nobles opposed him. As time went by, however, Parliament became strong enough that, like the Magna Carta, it provided a check on royal power.

England was not the only country to develop something like a parliament. France, as you will read, had a similar group called the Estates General. Spain had an assembly called the Cortes. There were also assemblies in parts of Germany and Italy in the Late Middle Ages. However, England's Parliament proved stronger and longer-lasting than any of the others.

The English Parliament was truly a national assembly. Although its members came from different parts of England, they generally put their loyalty to England ahead of local ties. Their laws applied to the whole country.

Even so, England in 1300 was not yet a true nation. Its kings and barons were bound by the old feudal obligations of lord-to-vassal and vassal-to-lord. As we shall see, it would require 200 years of strife before the feudal order in England finally broke down.

French kings expanded their power.

While England was limiting the power of its kings by the Magna Carta and Parliament, French kings were increasing their power. Early in the 1200's, John's old enemy Philip Augustus did for France what Henry II had already done for England. He gave France a strong central government.

Royal officials called bailiffs (**BAY**-lifs) were sent out from Paris to every district in Philip's kingdom. These bailiffs presided over the king's courts and collected the king's taxes.

Louis IX France's central government was made even stronger during the reign of Philip's grandson, Louis IX. Louis ruled from 1226 to 1270. He came to the throne as a boy of 12, and in his early years, France was actually ruled by his mother, Blanche of Castile. Blanche carried on the work of Philip Augustus, putting down revolts by the nobles and defeating the English.

When Louis IX began to rule on his own, he showed that his mother had taught him well. Better known as Saint Louis, this immensely pious and popular king had a passion for justice.

So great was his reputation for honor and fairness that even the king of England, a traditional enemy, once appealed to him to settle a dispute.

Louis created a supreme court for France called the Parlement of Paris. This Parlement could overturn the decisions of local courts. The royal courts of France strengthened the monarchy while weakening feudal ties.

Philip IV and the Estates General In 1302, the king of France was involved in a quarrel with the pope. The French king was Philip IV, a handsome man whose nickname was Philip the Fair. As in England, the French king usually called a meeting of his lords and bishops when he needed support for his policies. To win wider support against the pope, Philip IV decided to include members of the middle class in the meeting.

In France, church leaders were known as the First Estate and great lords as the Second Estate.

The middle-class **representatives**, or delegates, that Philip invited to the council became known as the Third Estate. The whole meeting was called the Estates General.

The Estates showed the growing power of the townspeople and the middle class as a whole. Like Parliament in its early years, the Estates helped to increase royal power against the nobility. Unlike Parliament, however, the Estates never became an independent force that limited the king's power.

Nation-states began to arise.

By 1300, France and England were slowly taking new shapes, both geographically and politically. Geographically, each country was beginning to reach the borders that it would have, more or less, for the next 600 years. Politically, the kings

■ BACKGROUND
Louis died while on a Crusade in North Africa in 1270, which added the final touch to his popularity. He was declared a saint in 1297.

ANSWERS TO
Voice from the Past

1. A king's greatest duty was to govern justly and well.
2. Louis made himself accessible to people seeking justice. He also commanded officials to see that justice was done.
3. He would strengthen the popularity of the monarchy.

Voice from the Past | St. Louis, the Ideal Medieval King

Louis IX was a pious and popular king. In this reading, a French noble, Jean de Joinville, describes him.

This holy man loved God with all his heart, and imitated his works. For example, just as God died because He loved his people, so the king risked his life many times for the love of his people . . . He said once to his eldest son: ". . . I beg you that you make yourself loved by the people of your realm, for truly, I would rather that a Scot came from Scotland and governed the people of the kingdom justly and well than that you should govern them badly . . ." The holy king loved the truth so much that he kept his promises even to the Saracens.

A friar told the king . . . that he had never read that a kingdom was destroyed or changed rulers except through lack of justice . . . The king did not forget this lesson but governed his lands justly and well, according to the will of God . . . Often in summer he went to sit down under an oak-tree in the wood of Vincennes . . . and made us sit around him. And all those who had suits to bring him came up. And he would ask them: "Does anyone here have a suit?" And those who had requests would get up . . . And then he would call Lord Pierre de Fontaines and Lord Geoffroi de Villette and say to one of them: "Settle this affair for me." And if he saw anything to correct in what they said on his behalf, he would do so.

1. What did Louis consider a king's greatest duty to be?
2. Describe the way that Louis dispensed justice.
3. What effect would a ruler like Louis IX have on the monarchy in France?

253

ANSWERS TO
Section Review 1

Define:
(a) the right to have the law work in known, orderly ways **(b)** government in
(continued)

ANSWERS TO *(continued)*

which king is limited by law **(c)** middle-class burgher **(d)** legislative group **(e)** delegate **(f)** people who share territory, government, culture, loyalty

Identify:
(a) king of England from 1154 to 1189 **(b)** signed Magna Carta **(c)** king of France **(d)** English document limiting royal power **(e)** king of England 1272–1307 **(f)** first gathering of lords and commoners **(g)** parliamentary meeting in France **(h)** French king 1226–1270 **(i)** called Estates General

Answer:
1. feudal ties between French and English

2. **(a)** military weaknesses **(b)** His barons forced him to sign the Magna Carta.

3. **(a)** no taxation without representation; due process of law **(b)** limited it

4. **(a)** included commoners **(b)** House of Lords was made up of nobles and bishops; House of Commons was made up of burgesses and knights.

5. **(a)** gave France a strong central government **(b)** created Supreme Court for France **(c)** extended political power to middle class

6. It established the idea of a supreme law binding on everyone and guaranteed basic civil rights.

7. They were included in the ruling bodies.

8. geographic borders were established; kings became more powerful than feudal lords; middle classes gained political power

of each country were becoming more powerful than the feudal lords beneath them. In both countries, the middle classes—especially the townspeople—were winning a larger share of political power.

Between 1300 and 1500, France and England slowly became a new type of country—a **nation-state.** A nation-state is a group of people who occupy a definite territory and are united under one government. The people of a nation-state are culturally united as well. For example, they generally all speak the same language. Most important, they have a feeling of belonging together and a sense of loyalty to their country.

Section REVIEW 1

Define: (a) due process of law, (b) limited monarchy, (c) burgess, (d) parliament, (e) representative, (f) nation-state
Identify: (a) Henry II, (b) John, (c) Philip Augustus, (d) Magna Carta, (e) Edward I, (f) Model Parliament, (g) Estates General, (h) Louis IX, (i) Philip IV
Answer:
1. Explain why the histories of France and England were tightly interwoven during the Late Middle Ages.
2. (a) Why was John of England called John Softsword? (b) What happened when he tried to increase taxes?
3. (a) List two basic rights that the Magna Carta guaranteed. (b) How did the Magna Carta affect the king's power?
4. (a) How did Edward I change the makeup of England's Parliament? (b) How did the House of Lords and the House of Commons differ?
5. How did each of the following French kings increase royal power? (a) Philip Augustus (b) Louis IX (c) Philip IV

Critical Thinking
6. Why is the Magna Carta called a "landmark of English liberty"?
7. What evidence shows that the power of the middle classes was growing both in France and in England?
8. What factors contributed to the growth of England and France as nation-states during the 1300's?

254

The Church faced a crisis in the 1300's. 2

Feudalism and the Church were the two great forces that shaped society in the Middle Ages. As the Middle Ages drew to a close, feudal loyalties were being replaced by national loyalties. The Church too faced a crisis. At the beginning of the 1300's, the papacy seemed as strong as ever. Soon, however, both pope and Church were in desperate trouble.

Boniface VIII *overreached himself.*

The pope in 1300 was an able but stubborn Italian named Boniface VIII. Boniface well remembered the triumphs of past popes over kings and emperors. He did not realize, however, that these earlier power struggles had weakened the spiritual prestige of the pope. Boniface VIII tried to force the rulers of Europe to obey him as they had obeyed earlier popes.

Already, in 1296, Boniface had issued an official order stating that kings were not to tax the clergy. (Official statements by the pope were called *bulls.*) The bull of 1296 was aimed at the French king Philip IV, who was taxing Church property in France to pay for a war against England. Philip shrugged off the order and continued to tax the Church. Boniface was forced to back down.

A more cautious pope might have taken this setback as a warning. Boniface, however, still believed that the pope was stronger than any king. In 1302, he issued another bull known as *Unam Sanctam.* This bull declared that there were two powers on earth, the temporal (earthly) and the spiritual (heavenly). The spiritual power, he said, was always supreme over temporal power. In short, kings must always obey popes.

Philip merely sneered at this bull. Before Boniface could excommunicate him, the king sent a small army to Italy to kidnap the pope and bring him to France for trial. The pope was taken by surprise when, in September 1303, soldiers burst into his palace at Anagni (ah-NAHN-yee) outside Rome and took him captive. The townspeople of Anagni rescued the pope, but the shock was too much for the elderly Boniface. He died a month later.

Never again would a pope be able to force monarchs to obey him. For more than 100 years (1303–1417), the papacy suffered a serious decline.

The popes moved to Avignon.

Philip the Fair went on boldly to capture the papacy itself. In 1305, he persuaded the College of Cardinals to choose a French archbishop as the new pope, Clement V. In 1309, Clement announced that political violence in Rome threatened his life. Therefore, he was moving to the city of Avignon (AV-een-YOHN), right on the borders of France.

Avignon remained the home of the popes for the next 67 years. Yet could a pope rightly rule from any city except Rome? Throughout Europe, Christians were tormented by this question.

Many people concluded that the Avignon popes were mere hirelings of the French kings. The English, the Germans, and the Italians were especially unhappy. They complained that the Church was held captive in Avignon just as, centuries before, the Jews had been held captive in Babylon. Thus, this period in Church history came to be called the "Babylonian captivity."

Visitors to Avignon were shocked by papal extravagance. The pope served dinner on gold and silver plates to guests dressed in costly furs and brocades. He slept on pillows lined with ermine skins. A Spanish churchman wrote, "Whenever I entered the chambers of the churchmen of the papal court, I found brokers and clergy weighing and reckoning the money that lay in heaps before them."

A great schism divided the Church.

The move to Avignon had badly weakened the Church. When reformers finally tried to move the papacy back to Rome, however, the result was even worse.

In 1378, Pope Gregory XI died while visiting Rome. The College of Cardinals then met in Rome to choose a successor. As they deliberated, they could hear a mob outside screaming, "A Roman, a Roman, we want a Roman for a pope, or at least an Italian!" Finally, the cardinals announced to the crowd that an Italian had been chosen: Pope Urban VI. (By his very choice of name, Urban made it clear that he planned to keep the papacy in "the city"—that is, Rome.)

Many cardinals regretted their choice almost immediately. They had not counted on Urban VI's reforming zeal and overbearing personality. After a few months, 13 French cardinals decided to elect another pope. They chose Robert of Geneva, who spoke French. He took the name Clement VII.

Now there were two popes. Each declared the other to be a false pope. Each excommunicated his rival. The French pope moved back to Avignon while the Italian pope remained in Rome. Thus began the split in the Church known as the Great **Schism** (SIHZ-uhm), or division.

Which was the rightful pope? For political reasons, the French supported the pope in Avignon. On the same basis, the English, the Germans, and the Italians favored the Roman pope. In many parts of Europe, two bishops (one loyal to Clement, the other to Urban) claimed to represent the

---

ECONOMICS IN DAILY LIFE ▶ **Religion and Trade**

The beliefs of the medieval Church directly affected economic activity. Two of those beliefs concerned just price and the prohibition of usury. The concept of just price was stated by Thomas Aquinas: ". . . to sell dearer or to buy cheaper than a thing is worth is in itself unjust and unlawful . . ." Opposition to usury—that is, to interest (payment for the use of money)—was based on the idea that money was lifeless and so could not produce wealth. The Church's focus on real value and the need for charity reflected the insecurity of medieval life.

255

OBJECTIVE 1. Analyze changes in the relationship between the Church and secular governments.

Teaching Strategy: *Discussing History: Thomas Becket* (page 248c)

OBJECTIVE 2. Identify the main effects of the Great Schism on the power of the Church.

Teaching Strategy: *Skill Building: Drawing Conclusions* (page 248c)

■ BACKGROUND

During the Babylonian captivity, papal income was second only to the revenue of the French king, higher than any other European king's revenue.

SECTION 2 Resources

ASSESSMENT
■ Section Quiz 11.2

REINFORCEMENT
■ Independent Practice 11.2

ENRICHMENT
■ Voices from the Past 11.2

ANSWERS TO

Section Review 2

Define:
(a) official statement made by the pope (b) split

(continued)

ANSWERS TO (continued)

(c) Church officials
(d) person whose religious beliefs differed from those of the Church

Identify:
(a) pope taken captive at Anagni (b) French king against whom Boniface issued his *Unam Sanctam* (c) pope who moved to Avignon (d) home of the popes during the "Babylonian captivity" (e) Italian pope chosen after death of Gregory XI (f) split in the Church over rightful pope (g) wrote that the pope had more power than was his due (h) Bohemian who spoke for religious reform (i) meeting that ended Great Schism

Answer:
1. (a) that kings must obey popes (b) sent army to kidnap pope
2. Church was held captive at Avignon, just as the Jews had been held captive in Babylon.
3. (a) French cardinals elected a separate pope. (b) divided the Church (c) with resignation of three popes and election of one
4. Jesus was the true head of the Church; clergy should be poor; Bible was the final authority.
5. (a) preached in Czech rather than in Latin (b) tried as a heretic and burned at the stake
6. The Great Schism undermined confidence in the authority of the pope; conflicting opinions gained wider support; increasing nationalism weakened ties to Rome.

"true" Church. Churchmen at all levels excommunicated one another. People wondered if they had been baptized or married by a true priest.

After Urban and Clement died, rival groups of cardinals in Rome and Avignon continued to elect two popes. The Great Schism lasted from 1378 to 1417.

Two scholars challenged the Church.

Often, when an old source of authority collapses, new ideas arise. In the late 1300's and early 1400's, the most famous thinkers to respond to the crisis of the Church were two professors. One was an Englishman named John Wycliffe (WIHK-lihf), the other a Bohemian named John Huss.

"Christ was meek," wrote John Wycliffe in one of his many pamphlets. But "the pope sits on his throne and makes lords to kiss his feet." From 1360 to 1382, Wycliffe taught religion at the University of Oxford. His radical ideas were discussed widely throughout England. These were Wycliffe's major ideas:

1. The true head of the Church was Jesus Christ, not the pope.
2. Like Jesus and his disciples, the **clergy,** or Church officials, should own no land or wealth. Poverty was better for them than riches.
3. The Bible alone—not the pope—was the final authority for Christian life.

How could an English Christian be guided by the Bible when, as late as 1360, it could be read only in Latin or French? Wycliffe answered by translating the New Testament into English.

Because the popes since 1306 had been French and England was often at war with France, Wycliffe became a kind of English national hero by attacking the pope. When an English archbishop tried to charge him with heresy in 1377, there were riots in the London streets. The archbishop was forced to free Wycliffe. Instead of being burned at the stake, he died peacefully in 1384.

John Huss of Bohemia (now part of the Czech Republic) was not so lucky. Influenced by Wycliffe's writings, Huss taught that the authority of the Bible was higher than that of the pope. Huss became a spokesman for Czech national feeling as well as for religious reform. He preached his sermons in Czech rather than in Latin. In 1411, Huss was excommunicated.

256

In 1414, Sigismund, the newly elected emperor of Germany, arranged a Church council to end the Great Schism. He urged Huss to attend and even gave him safe conduct. When Huss arrived at the meeting, however, he was seized and tried as a heretic. In spite of the safe conduct, he was burned at the stake in 1415.

A Church council ended the schism.

The gathering that condemned John Huss was known as the Council of Constance (named for the German city where it met). The council's major task was to end the Great Schism by choosing a new pope.

In 1414, when the Council of Constance began its meetings, there were a total of *three* popes. There was the Avignon pope, the Roman pope, and a third pope elected by an earlier council. With the help of the Holy Roman Emperor, the council forced all three popes to resign. In 1417, the council chose a new pope, Martin V. He made good his claim to being the only pope, thus ending the Great Schism.

Where, Christians wondered, was true religious authority—with the pope, with a Church council, or in the Bible? In a later chapter, we shall see how this confusion led to a violent upheaval in the 1500's known as the Reformation.

Section REVIEW 2

Define: (a) papal bull, (b) schism, (c) clergy, (d) heretic

Identify: (a) Boniface VIII, (b) Philip IV, (c) Clement V, (d) Avignon, (e) Urban VI, (f) Great Schism, (g) John Wycliffe, (h) John Huss, (i) Council of Constance

Answer:
1. (a) What power did Boniface claim in *Unam Sanctam?* (b) What actions did Philip IV take in response?
2. Why was the period from 1309 to 1376 called the Babylonian captivity?
3. (a) How did the Great Schism begin? (b) What effects did it have? (c) How did it end?
4. What were Wycliffe's three major teachings?
5. (a) How did Huss inspire national feelings among the Czechs? (b) What happened to Huss?

Critical Thinking

6. During the earlier part of the Middle Ages, most European Christians had unquestioning faith in the authority of the Church. How did events in the 1300's change this outlook?

The 1300's brought plague and war. 3

A modern historian has called the 1300's "a violent, tormented, bewildered, suffering, and disintegrating age." During the 1300's, Europeans suffered from a series of disasters including crop failures, a terrifying new disease, and a war that dragged on for years.

Artists of the 1300's depicted death as the Grim Reaper, a skeleton on horseback whose scythe cut people down. It was an apt view. Consider what happened to the city of Barcelona in Spain. Famine struck in 1333; then came the plague in 1347, plague again in 1351, and two more years of famine in 1358 and 1359, followed shortly by another two years of plague in 1362 and 1363.

What brought on these catastrophes? Europe's population had been increasing steadily for more than 300 years. Using new methods such as the horse collar and the three-field system, Europeans had begun farming much new land. By 1300, however, almost all the great forests had been cleared and the swamps had been drained. The soil in many places was losing its fertility. Of course, medieval peasants knew nothing about chemical fertilizers. Year by year, the old fields produced smaller crops.

Moreover, a change was taking place in Europe's climate, though Europeans did not know it. From 1000 to 1300, Europe had enjoyed a time when temperatures were warmer than average. Around 1300, that period ended and temperatures dropped. During this "little ice age," as geologists call it, glaciers slowly advanced over Greenland and parts of Scandinavia. Fall frosts came early to the fields of Europe. The shorter growing season meant smaller harvests and a reduced food supply. Hunger paved the way for even grimmer events.

The great plague of 1348, called the Black Death, killed about a third of the people in Europe. In some cities, nine tenths of the population died. Here the people of Tournai (Belgium) bury their dead.

SECTION 3
Objectives and Teaching Strategies

OBJECTIVE 1. Explain the social and physical effects of the plague.

Teaching Strategy: *Writing about History: The Plague* (page 248d)

OBJECTIVE 2. Analyze the warfare between France and England and its effects on nationalism.

Teaching Strategy: *Discussing History: The War between France and England* (page 248d)

SECTION 3
Resources

GEOGRAPHY
■ Transparency 38

REINFORCEMENT
■ Independent Practice 11.3

ENRICHMENT
■ Voices from the Past 11.3

ASSESSMENT
■ Section Quiz 11.3

In 1347, about 3.7 million people lived in England. Only 30 years later—little more than a generation—the population had fallen by 1.5 million to 2.2 million.

■ DISCUSSION

Discuss the Grim Reaper as a creation of the medieval imagination. In what ways does the figure represent the interests and concerns of the medieval person?

The Black Death struck in 1347.

In 1347, four Genoese ships arrived in Sicily from the Black Sea. Besides trade goods from Asia, the ships brought a dread cargo—a disease that became known as the Black Death. Soon the illness was sweeping through Italy. From Italy, the outbreak followed trade routes to France, Germany, England, and other parts of Europe.

The victims of this terrible plague had a raging fever. Black swellings grew at their necks and joints. The name *Black Death* came from these swellings. Many victims died within 24 hours. No one had any idea what caused this terrifying outbreak, and medieval doctors were helpless against it. (Modern scholars know that fleas from infected rats spread one form of the plague. Thus, the terrible sanitary conditions in Europe's cities were an important cause of the high death rate.)

Death carts loaded with plague victims soon became a common sight in Europe. Whenever plague broke out, people fled in terror. Yet many were already infected and carried the disease with them to new places.

The death rate was appalling. A churchman visiting Avignon in 1348 wrote:

To put the matter shortly, one half, or more than a half, of the people of Avignon are already dead. Within the walls of the city there are now more than 7,000 houses shut up; in these no one is living, and all who inhabited them have left; the suburbs hardly contain any people at all.

This massive disaster tore medieval society apart. Whole villages disappeared as people either died or fled in fear. Even families were split. Fear of the plague was so great that some parents abandoned their sick children. The Church too failed. Priests were too few (and often too fearful) to give last rites to the dying.

Historians estimate that the plague killed 25 million people—about one third of Europe's population—in the 5 years between 1347 and 1352. The Black Death claimed more lives than any war until the twentieth century. Even more terrible, the plague came back again and again. New outbreaks occurred in 1361, 1369, 1374, 1390, and on into the 1600's. Though never again as severe as the first outbreak, plague became a constant danger.

258

Peasants rose in revolt.

The decline in population had far-reaching effects. Workers were scarce everywhere. Serfs could demand wages for their work. Thus, landlords could no longer collect their traditional rents and services. As a result, in many places serfdom began to disappear. The manor's economy, based on a fixed labor supply of workers who could not leave, was doomed.

The ruling class fought these changes. Nobles fiercely resisted peasant demands for higher wages. In 1381, peasants in England revolted, burning manors and killing local lords. Similar uprisings took place in France, Italy, and Belgium. In each case, nobles ruthlessly put down the revolts.

Although the peasants did not win the lower taxes or other reforms they wanted, the revolts were important nevertheless. The ideal society of the Middle Ages was gone. No longer was there peace among those who worked, those who prayed, and those who fought.

France and England fought the Hundred Years' War.

War added to the miseries of people in England and France. In 1337 (ten years before the first outbreak of the Black Death), war broke out once more over an English king's claims to land in France. The war lasted, off and on, for 116 years, not ending until 1453. It was called, somewhat inaccurately, the Hundred Years' War. Except for one futile French raid on English shores, the war was fought entirely on French soil.

The Hundred Years' War can be divided into four stages:

1. *1337–1360* Ably led by King Edward III, English forces invaded France. They captured the French king and gained control over much of France.
2. *1361–1396* The French reconquered almost everything the English had won.
3. *1397–1420* The English invaded France again. They conquered the northern half of the country. England's Henry V forced the French king to sign a humiliating treaty.
4. *1421–1453* The French rallied. In 1429, inspired by Joan of Arc, they began a drive that forced the English out of all France, except the western port city of Calais.

New weapons changed warfare.

The Hundred Years' War dealt a deathblow to feudal warfare. During the war, new weapons caused a revolution both in warfare and in society.

The longbow The weapon that gave England its early victories in the war was known as the longbow. Before battle, skilled English bowmen ranged themselves, side by side, along a wide arc. Into the ground they drove long, iron-tipped stakes that pointed outward to impale an enemy's charging horse. As the French attacked, the English bowmen drew their six-foot longbows. Then, as one French chronicler wrote, the sky became so thick with arrows that "it seemed as if it snowed." The arrows were dangerous at a range of 300 yards. They were absolutely fatal within 100 yards.

The result was disaster for the French. Slain and wounded horses tumbled over each other. Thrown on their backs, the French nobles in their heavy armor could not rise. They were as helpless as upside-down turtles. Foot soldiers killed them with long knives. Thus, the finest French cavalry was wiped out. The victors were English foot soldiers, mere commoners.

Such disasters befell the French knights at the Battle of Crécy (1346), the Battle of Poitiers (1356), and the Battle of Agincourt (1415). The age of feudalism, based on the power of warriors on horseback, could not survive long.

The cannon The second weapon that battered down the feudal system was the cannon. The sound of exploding gunpowder was first heard in Europe sometime after 1250. The English fired small cannons at the Battle of Crécy, but these did little more than scare the horses.

After 1400, however, European cannons grew huge and powerful. They could shoot stone balls 20 inches in diameter. In the last years of the Hundred Years' War, both sides used cannons to batter down the walls of each other's castles. Thus, the castle—like the knight's suit of shining armor—became an outdated relic.

National feeling grew in Europe.

Faith in feudalism and in the Church were both shaken by the upheavals of the 1300's. Among the peoples of Europe, they were replaced by a new feeling called **nationalism**.

During the Hundred Years' War, armies began to use cannons against the walls of enemy castles.

Nationalism is a feeling of loyalty to one's own land and people. It is a feeling that cuts across all class lines. During the Hundred Years' War, for example, English barons and peasants alike rejoiced at news of their king's great victories in France. After the Battle of Crécy, a jubilant throng greeted King Edward III when he returned to London. One proud Englishman wrote: "A new sun seemed to have arisen over the people in the perfect peace, in the plenty of all things, and in the glory of such victories."

No longer did people think of the king as simply a feudal lord. Instead, he was seen as a national leader fighting for the glory of the nation-state.

During the third stage of the war, English nationalistic feeling soared when people heard what had happened near the castle of Agincourt in France. In 1415, against 50,000 French troops, England's King Henry V urged his 8,000 soldiers into battle. "Hurrah! Hurrah! Saint George and Merrie England!" shouted the English as they strung their bows. The Battle of Agincourt ended in a stunning English victory.

Five years later, in 1420, Henry V forced the French king, Charles VI, to sign away his kingdom. (Henry was greatly aided by the fact that Charles suffered from periods of insanity.) By the Treaty of Troyes, Charles gave his daughter Katherine to Henry in marriage. Charles also agreed that Henry would inherit the French crown

259

Cooperative Learning

Working in groups of four students, have each group choose a recorder. Have students review the definition of *nationalism*. Then, ask group members to make lists of the positive and negative aspects of nationalism in the world today. All group members must agree on the positive or negative categorization of the items on their groups' lists. Finally, after completing the lists, each group should reach a consensus as to whether nationalism is a helpful or harmful concept in today's world. Have group spokespersons present conclusions to the class for discussion.

ANSWERS TO
Section Review 3

Define:
(a) feeling of loyalty to one's own land and people
(b) eldest son of a French king

Identify:
(a) great plague in 1347
(b) war over English king's claims to land in France

(continued)

ANSWERS TO
Map Study

Brittany, Normandy, Champagne, Aquitaine; Calais

ANSWERS TO (continued)

(c) forced Charles VI to sign away his kingdom (d) battle at which English defeated French (e) French warrior-saint (f) French city saved by Joan of Arc (g) French prince whom Joan of Arc helped restore to the throne

Answer:

1. (a) terrible plague (b) carried along trade routes from Italy to elsewhere in Europe (c) depleted population, thereby helping end serfdom and manorial system

2. English king's claims to land in France

3. (a) to drive the English out of France and give the French crown to Charles the Dauphin (b) the above (c) She was condemned by the English as a witch and heretic and burned at the stake.

4. (a) longbow and cannon (b) longbow: lessened effectiveness of knights in armor; cannon: battered down castle walls

5. The smaller population created a demand for workers and gave serfs new bargaining power.

6. It changed feudal warfare, making knights and castles obsolete.

7. (a) shouts of English during Battle of Agincourt for "Merrie England" (b) People from many sections of France united behind her.

France in the Hundred Years' War

Map Study

What regions of France did the English control in 1429? What land did they hold in 1453?

when Charles himself died. Thus, it seemed that France and England would become one kingdom.

However, Henry V died in 1422, just before Charles's death. Henry's son, Henry VI, was only nine months old. An English duke ruled northern France in the name of the baby king. Then, in 1429, a French girl felt moved by God to rescue France from its English conquerors. Her name, as you read on page 248, was Joan of Arc.

Joan of Arc turned the tide of war.

Perhaps no one in history accomplished so much in such a short time against such overwhelming odds as did Joan of Arc. In only six months, Joan changed a pathetic prince into a

king, led the French army to victory, and awakened the national spirit of a defeated people.

Yet Joan herself was not surprised by these events. She believed in miracles. She believed that several times, while she was tending her father's sheep, heavenly voices had spoken to her. Her mission, as dictated by those voices, was to drive the English army out of France and give the French crown to France's true king, Charles VI's son.

In February 1429, Joan made a hazardous journey to the court of the prince, Charles the Dauphin (DAW-fuhn). (*Dauphin* was the title given to the eldest son of a French king.) The Treaty of Troyes had robbed Charles of his kingdom. Though the Dauphin still pretended to be king, he lacked both spirit and confidence. He was dumbfounded when a crudely dressed peasant girl entered his court and said to him:

> *God send you long life, gentle Dauphin . . . I have been sent by God to take you to Reims to be anointed. Give me soldiers and I will raise the siege of Orleans, for it is God's will that the English shall leave France and return to their own country.*

As you read (page 249), on May 7, 1429, Joan led the French army into battle against the English forts that blocked the roads to Orleans. It was a hard-fought battle for both sides. The air was filled with arrows and the stinking smoke of cannon. Joan stayed always at the thick of the fighting. About noon, the French fought their way close to the main fort and threw up ladders to scale its walls. As Joan climbed swiftly up the first ladder, an English arrow tore into her shoulder. She pulled it out and urged her troops to fight on. The French threw up more ladders, but the English flung them down, throwing French fighters to their deaths. By sunset, the weary French had still not taken the fort. Despairing, their commanders sounded the retreat. The English looked out in victory from the safety of their walls.

Suddenly, Joan and a few soldiers charged back toward the fort. The entire French army stormed after her. This time, there was no stopping the French. They swarmed up their ladders and into the English fort. A mass of English soldiers tried to retreat across the nearby river, but the French set the bridge afire. When the bridge broke, the terrified English, weighed down by heavy armor, drowned in the river beneath.

Over the crackle of the flames and the cries of the dying, the bells of Orleans rang out in joy. The siege of Orleans was broken. Joan of Arc had guided the French onto the path of victory.

After that victory, Joan persuaded Charles to go with her to be crowned king. The route led through enemy territory, and Charles quaked with fear. Yet Joan brought him safely to Reims. At the cathedral on Sunday, July 17, 1429, he was crowned King Charles VII.

Joan had one year of triumph, 1429. Her last two years were years of betrayal and anguish. The English hated her and believed her to be a witch. In 1430, she was captured in battle and turned over to Church authorities to stand trial. Although Charles VII owed his crown to her, he did nothing to rescue her. Condemned as a witch and a heretic, Joan was tied to a stake and burned to death on May 30, 1431. One Englishman, wiser than the rest, cried out, "We are lost. We have burned a saint."

Joan's execution did the English no good. French nationalism did not die. Charles VII overcame his cowardice to become a strong king. By 1453, his troops had won back every part of France except Calais.

Joan of Arc is still revered by the French as their greatest patriot. In 1920, nearly 500 years after her death, the Church retracted its judgment of heresy and declared Joan a saint.

Section REVIEW 3

Define: (a) nationalism, (b) dauphin
Identify: (a) Black Death, (b) Hundred Years' War, (c) Henry V, (d) Battle of Agincourt, (e) Joan of Arc, (f) Orleans, (g) Charles VII
Answer:
1. (a) What was the Black Death? (b) How did trade encourage its spread? (c) What effects did it have on Europe?
2. What was the Hundred Years' War about?
3. (a) What did Joan of Arc believe to be her mission in life? (b) What did she accomplish? (c) How did her life end?
4. (a) What new weapons came into use during the Hundred Years' War? (b) How did each change warfare?

Critical Thinking
5. Why did the Black Death weaken the manorial economy?
6. How did the Hundred Years' War weaken the feudal system?
7. Give evidence that each of the following people was a *national* hero, not just a feudal leader. (a) Henry V (b) Joan of Arc

New monarchs ruled in western Europe. 4

Throughout this chapter, we have seen how the medieval world came apart in the 1300's. Out of that turmoil and pain, however, three strong nation-states of western Europe arose.

France was no longer a patchwork of lands, some attached to the French king, others to the English king. England, stripped of its holdings in France, was now a compact country surrounded by the sea. And, to the south of France, Spain had developed by 1500 as a third nation-state.

New monarchs replaced feudal kings.

Medieval kings had ruled according to feudal custom. To fight wars and govern their kingdoms, they had relied mainly on the support of their vassals. The strong rulers who arose between 1450 and 1500 did not base their power on feudalism (although they certainly used their rights as feudal lords when it suited them). Historians often call these rulers the "new monarchs." The new monarchs had three important new sources of power: control of taxes, a professional army, and professional officials.

Broad taxing power Feudal kings had received most of their income from their own estates and from the feudal aids of their vassals. (Remember that an aid was a grant of money for a specific purpose, such as ransoming the lord from captivity or fighting a war.) The new monarchs demanded every penny of those aids too, but they also received money from other groups. Every class in society—nobility, clergy, townspeople, and peasants—paid some kind of tax to the king.

Professional army Medieval rulers marched to war followed by an army of vassals, who owed

261

SECTION 4 Objectives and Teaching Strategies

OBJECTIVE 1. Explain the phrase *new monarchs.*
Teaching Strategy: *Discussing History: The New Monarchs* (page 248d)

OBJECTIVE 2. Explain characteristics of Henry VII's reign.
Teaching Strategy: *Writing about History: The Reign of Henry VII* (page 248d)

SECTION 4 Resources

GEOGRAPHY
■ Transparency 39

REINFORCEMENT
■ Independent Practice 11.4

ENRICHMENT
■ Voices from the Past 11.4

ASSESSMENT
■ Section Quiz 11.4

■ **BACKGROUND**

The horse of Richard III was slain in battle. Shakespeare had him exclaim, "A horse! A horse! My kingdom for a horse!"

military service in exchange for their land. The new monarchs hired soldiers from any class in society. No longer was fighting the specialized work of the nobility, although nobles still commanded most armies. Soldiering became a trade open to all, and professional soldiers were paid from the royal treasury.

Professional officials The new monarchs surrounded themselves with a new class of advisers and officials. Some were nobles, but many were middle-class townspeople. Educated officials from the middle class gave the king loyal service. They were the ruler's natural allies against the haughty and quarrelsome nobles.

Crafty kings strengthened France.

Charles VII, who had won the French throne with Joan of Arc's help, set the French monarchy on the road to recovery. By 1453, he had driven the English out of France, except for the single city of Calais. He set up a royal council, using middle-class men as his officials. He chose his advisers so wisely that he won the nickname "Charles the Well-Served." He also set up the first permanent royal army.

Charles found new sources of money in two taxes, the *taille* (TAH-yuh), a tax on land, and the *gabelle* (guh-BEL), a tax on salt. For more than 300 years, these two taxes on basic necessities of life were the main source of money for French kings.

Charles's son became king in 1461. Louis XI was known as "the Spider King." To achieve his ends, Louis resorted to trickery, intimidation, bribery, and espionage. He had spies in almost every noble's court in Europe. A cardinal who once betrayed him was locked up in a small cage for 11 painful years, unable either to stand up or lie down. Nobles who resisted Louis's rule usually were bribed or bullied into submission.

Like his father, Louis wanted to weaken the power of the great lords within France—above all the Duke of Burgundy. Burgundy had long been a thorn in France's side. This mighty dukedom included southeastern France, Flanders, Luxembourg, and other territories. During the Hundred Years' War, the Burgundians often had sided with the English. By 1482, Louis had added Burgundy to the French state.

Money flowed into Louis's treasury through the taille and the gabelle. Therefore, Louis needed

262

to call together the Estates General only once in his 22-year reign. He did not need its approval for his policies. Thus, Louis passed on to his heirs a monarchy of almost unlimited power. Unlike the kings and queens of England, French rulers after 1500 collected taxes without the consent of their subjects.

The Wars of the Roses split England.

While France was building its strength after the Hundred Years' War, England went through another time of turmoil. This was a civil war that began in 1455.

Two branches of the royal family claimed the English crown. One branch, headed by the dukes of York, took a white rose as their emblem. The other branch, descended from the dukes of Lancaster, had a red rose as their symbol. Thus, the civil war came to be called the Wars of the Roses. These battles were really a bloody family quarrel.

The wars disrupted the reign of three kings: Henry VI, Edward IV, and Richard III. Finally, Richard III was killed at the Battle of Bosworth Field in 1485. This battle marked the end of the Wars of the Roses and a turning point for England. Richard III often is called England's last medieval king. The man who defeated him set England on a new path.

Henry Tudor made peace in England.

The victor at Bosworth Field was another Henry. By marriage and inheritance, he was connected to both the Lancastrians and the Yorkists. His own family name was Tudor (TOO-duhr). Crowned Henry VII, he began the most renowned dynasty in English history: the Tudor dynasty. (His granddaughter, Elizabeth I, would later become England's greatest queen.)

Henry VII (1485–1509) ruled as a new monarch. His chief ministers were not great lords but members of the middle class. In every part of his kingdom, he used local landowners as officials called justices of the peace. In doing so, he continued a long tradition of local government.

Henry VII made himself as king the richest man in England. Much of his money came from feudal dues, which he collected with truly modern efficiency. Still more money came from "tonnage and poundage," taxes on imported goods. The

RISE OF THE MIDDLE CLASS

1000–1100
A new middle *class of burghers* emerges with growth of towns and trade.

1100's
Burghers form *guilds* to control trade and manufacture.
Burghers obtain *town charters* to end feudal obligations.

1295
In England, burghers and knights become members of *Model Parliament.*

1302
In France, middle class becomes *Third Estate* in Estates General.

1300's
Feudal lords lose power to kings and towns.
Longbow and cannon reduce lords' military power.

1400's
New monarchs in England and France choose officials from middle class to help them rule.

more trade grew, the more money flowed into Henry's hands. So Henry was eager to encourage trade, and business prospered during his reign. He made treaties with other rulers to open new markets for English merchants.

To safeguard the money he was piling up, Henry VII carefully avoided expensive wars. Thus, he did not need to keep—or pay—a standing army.

Many of England's great nobles had died or fled abroad during the Wars of the Roses. Henry completed the job of destroying their power. He limited their military might by having Parliament outlaw the private armies of paid fighters many lords had kept.

Henry also used the Court of Star Chamber to destroy over-mighty subjects. This court got its name from the starry ceiling in the room where its judges met. The Court of Star Chamber violated most ideas of fairness and justice. It met in secret. People accused of crimes had no right to know what evidence was being used against them. People were tortured so that they would confess. Yet most people in England accepted the Court of Star Chamber because Henry used it to keep peace after years of strife.

It is probably fair to say that Henry was respected but not loved. Unheroic and miserly, he was far from the Middle Ages' idea of a great king. Yet when he died in 1509, England was prosperous and peaceful.

Isabella and Ferdinand ruled Spain.

As far back as 1063, well before the First Crusade, the pope had urged Christian knights to drive the Muslims (or Moors) out of Spain. This drive became a centuries-long effort known as the **Reconquista** (ray-kahn-KEES-tuh), or reconquest. By the late 1400's, Muslims held only the tiny kingdom of Granada.

Four other kingdoms on the Iberian peninsula were ruled by Christians. The kingdom of Portugal faced the uncharted waters of the Atlantic Ocean. The small kingdom of Navarre sat astride the Pyrenees, bordering France. The large kingdoms of Castile (ka-STEEL) and Aragon (AR-uh-gahn) spanned the neck and midsection of the peninsula. (See the map on page 264.)

The heir to the throne of Castile was a capable and active princess named Isabella. Likewise, a determined and crafty prince named Ferdinand was heir to Aragon. Their marriage, in 1469, brought their kingdoms into close alliance.

The conquest of Granada Beginning in 1482, Ferdinand and Isabella set out to conquer the last Muslim kingdom, Granada. It took ten years, but in 1492, Granada fell to a Christian army. In the final battle, Isabella personally led her army, wearing the red cross of a crusader.

This crusading spirit linked religion closely with Spanish nationalism. To be a "true Spaniard"

263

■ **DISCUSSION**
With enough money in the king's treasury, of what use was the Parliament?

■ **BACKGROUND**
Ferdinand and Isabella expelled about 280,000 Jews from Spain, depleting the country of many of its skilled workers in trade, farming, and industry.

ANSWERS TO

Section Review 4

Define:
(a) ruler who did not base his power on feudalism
(b) tax on land (c) tax on salt (d) tax on imported goods (e) Christian effort to drive Muslims out of Spain
(continued)

ANSWER TO
Map Study

Castile

ANSWERS TO (continued)

Identify:
(a) French king who set monarchy on road to recovery (b) the "Spider King" (c) civil war in England between two branches of the royal family (d) new monarch who ruled a prosperous and peaceful England (e) drive to move the Muslims out of Spain (f) heir to Aragon; became king of Spain (g) heiress to Castile; became queen of Spain

Answer:
1. imposed taxes; set up professional armies, hired professional officials
2. set up a royal council and first permanent royal army, drove English out of France
3. (a) He used trickery. (b) could raise money from two well-established taxes whereas English needed to call Parliament to raise money
4. (a) served as chief ministers, justices of the peace (b) the Court of Star Chamber and having Parliament outlaw private armies
5. (a) heiress of Castile joined with heir of Aragon (b) Jews and Muslims were expelled.
6. (a) medieval rulers: land, plunder; new monarchs: taxes (b) medieval rulers: feudal system; new monarchs: paid soldiers from any class (c) medieval rulers: nobles; new monarchs: nobles plus middle-class townspeople

The Growth of Spain

Map Study
What Spanish kingdom nearly surrounded the Muslim territory on the Iberian Peninsula?

came also to mean being a "true Christian." The result was disastrous for Spaniards who were not Christian.

The Inquisition Spain had a long history of religious diversity and tolerance. Since the height of the Islamic empire in the 700's, Muslims, Jews, and Christians had all lived there. The three groups had often lived together in peace. Jews held high positions as bankers, merchants, scholars, physicians, and government officials. Under Ferdinand and Isabella, however, Spain's religious tolerance ended.

As a devout Roman Catholic, Isabella decreed that in a Christian state, there could be only "one king, one law, one faith." She and Ferdinand won permission from the pope to revive the Inquisition, the arm of the Church that had tracked down heretics in the Middle Ages (page 230).

All over Spain, boards of priests met to hear cases of suspected heresy. The primary suspects

were Jews and Muslims who had converted to Christianity. Assuming the suspects were guilty, the priests would demand that they confess. If the suspects refused, they often were tortured. Once they confessed, they were burned at the stake. A report by Isabella's secretary shows that 2,000 men and women were executed in this way between 1478 and 1490.

The expulsion of the Jews In the same year as the conquest of Granada (1492), Isabella and Ferdinand began a new campaign against the 200,000 Spanish Jews who openly practiced their religion. They were forced to become Christians or leave the country. The great majority, about 150,000, chose exile.

Jewish families, now homeless, set out from Spain to other lands. The departure of their ships was witnessed by another captain who recorded the event in his diary. That captain was Christopher Columbus, who sailed from the Spanish port of Palos in August 1492.

Columbus was just setting out on a voyage that he hoped would lead to Asia. In fact, his historic voyage took him to the Americas. Some exiled Jews sailed with him. Among them were the expedition's doctor and interpreter. Later, a few Jews became early settlers in the Americas. Most of the exiles, however, went to the Muslim countries of Southwest Asia, including lands that are now Iran, Syria, Israel, and Jordan.

Expelling the Jews and Muslims made Spain a religiously united nation, but it hurt the country economically. Many of Spain's leaders in business and trade had been Muslims or Jews.

After Isabella's death in 1504, Ferdinand seized the part of Navarre south of the Pyrenees. By his death in 1516, Spain had reached its modern borders.

Section REVIEW 4

Define: (a) new monarch, (b) taille, (c) gabelle, (d) tonnage and poundage
Identify: (a) Charles VII, (b) Louis XI, (c) Wars of the Roses, (d) Henry VII, (e) Reconquista, (f) Ferdinand, (g) Isabella
Answer:
1. In general, how did the new monarchs strengthen their powers?
2. List three accomplishments of Charles VII.

264

3. (a) How did Louis XI win the nickname "the Spider King"? (b) Why did Louis XI and his successors have more power than English rulers of the same period?
4. (a) What part did the middle classes play in Henry VII's government? (b) What methods did Henry use to keep the peace within his kingdom?
5. (a) How did a political marriage begin Spain's development as a nation? (b) How did the position of Spanish Muslims and Jews change in the late 1400's?

Critical Thinking

6. Compare the policies of medieval rulers with the policies of the new monarchs with regard to (a) sources of money, (b) the army, and (c) choosing officials. In each case, explain why the new policies increased royal power.

A *new empire arose* in Russia. 5

eographic Setting

At the eastern end of the European continent, in the land known as Russia, another country was taking shape in the 1400's. To understand how Russia developed, you must know something of its geography. The Ural (YOOR-uhl) Mountains divide Europe and Asia. Russians first settled on the European side of the mountains, and the European part of Russia remained its heartland. Later, Russians pushed eastward into the vast wilderness known as Siberia (sye-BIHR-ee-uh).

European Russia is mostly flat. The northern part, near the Baltic Sea, is covered with an immense forest of pine, spruce, and other cone-bearing trees. The southern part is a sweeping, grassy steppe with rich black soil.

The rivers of European Russia seem to twist and turn in every direction. Eventually, they empty into one of four bodies of water—the Caspian Sea, the Black Sea, the Baltic Sea, or the Arctic Ocean. In the warm months, barges floated easily over these broad and abundant rivers. In the freezing Russian winters, horse-drawn sleds glided safely over the river ice.

The Mongols conquered Russia.

During the 700's and the 800's, groups of people who spoke Slavic languages migrated from Asia into eastern Europe. They fought a series of bitter battles with the Byzantine empire. Yet these Slavs also accepted Eastern Orthodox Christianity along with other Byzantine influences (page 194). In the Early Middle Ages, the group of Slavs who became known as Russians built a rich trading kingdom centering on the city of Kiev.

In the middle 1200's, a fierce group of horsemen from central Asia slashed their way into Russia. These nomads were the Mongols. (You will read more of them in Chapter 12.) In 1240, they completely destroyed Kiev. Its churches were burned, its rich treasures were plundered, and even its tombs were broken open and the bones scattered. By 1241, the Mongols ruled all of Russia. From that time on, Russian history followed a new course.

In some ways, the Mongols actually began the work of uniting Russia. Kievan Russia had been a collection of small, independent kingdoms. The Mongols forced all the kingdoms of Russia to pay them tribute. In each kingdom, a Russian prince ruled under the Mongols and collected tribute for them. As long as a prince was obedient, the Mongols allowed him to rule as he wished. Russian historians call the period of Mongol rule from 1240 to 1480 "the Mongol yoke."

Moscow's princes united Russia.

Moscow, located in the northern forests, suffered less from Mongol raids than did the cities of the steppe such as Kiev. Moscow was first settled in the 1100's. By 1250, it was a primitive hamlet enclosed by a crude log wall. It took the princes of Moscow 240 years (1240–1480) to build a strong and independent state (map, page 266).

Note the location of Moscow near the headwaters of three great rivers: the Volga (VAHL-guh), the Dnieper (NEE-puhr), and the Don. If the ruler of Moscow could gain control of these rivers, he could control nearly all of European Russia.

Moscow began its rise to power under the Mongols. Its prince from 1328 to 1341 was Ivan I. As tax collector for the Mongols, he became known as Ivan Moneybags. He served the Mongols so well that they gave him the title of "Great

265

OBJECTIVE 1. Explain the influence of Mongol rule on the development of the Russian empire.

Teaching Strategy: *Discussing History: The Influence of the Mongols* (page 248e)

OBJECTIVE 2. Describe the geography of Russia and its effects on Russia's development as a nation-state.

Teaching Strategy: *Geography in History: Russia* (page 248e)

■ BACKGROUND

The Mongols lived in camps called *ordu*, from which comes the English word *horde*. One branch of the Mongols ruled the Khanate of the Golden Horde in Russia.

SECTION 5
Resources

GEOGRAPHY
- Transparencies 40, 42

REINFORCEMENT
- Independent Practice 11.5

ENRICHMENT
- Voices from the Past 11.5

ASSESSMENT
- Section Quiz 11.5

■ BACKGROUND

Ivan's marriage in 1472 to the niece of Constantinople's last emperor and the strict Orthodoxy of the Russian Church helped him build his claim to being the heir to Constantinople. Moscow as the seat of power became a "third Rome," and "Holy Russia" carried on the traditions of Byzantium.

Russia and Eastern Europe in 1480

Map Study

Mongol rulers were known as khans. What areas shown on the map were ruled by Mongols? What power bordered Moscow's lands on the southwest?

Prince." In 1328, the head of the Russian Orthodox Church made Moscow his residence. The Church became a major ally of Moscow's princes.

Ivan and his successors gradually enlarged their kingdom by purchase, war, trickery, and clever marriages. Generation after generation, they plotted to win control of the small states that encircled Moscow. By the 1400's, Moscow had become the strongest of the Russian states under the Mongols.

The prince of Moscow became czar.

The Russian state became a true empire during the 43-year reign of Ivan III (1462–1505). Born in 1440, Ivan was a boy of 13 when Constantinople fell to the Turks in 1453. In 1472, Ivan married the niece of the last Byzantine emperor. At that time, he began calling himself **czar**, the Russian word for *caesar* or *emperor*.

In 1480, Moscow finally freed itself from the Mongol yoke. Ivan III refused to pay the Mongol's their tribute. Rising to the challenge, the Mongol ruler led his army to the banks of the Ugra River. The Russian army stood on the opposite bank. The two armies glowered at each other, neither daring to cross the river. Finally, without shooting

a single arrow, the Russians and the Mongols turned around and marched back home. After this bloodless face-off, Moscow was free of Mongol control.

Ivan wanted to make Moscow a fitting capital for an emperor. The center of the city was a walled citadel or fortress known as the *Kremlin*. Ivan tore down the old triangular wall around the Kremlin and erected a massive new wall 60 feet high and 15 feet thick. Inside, he built a palace for himself, another palace for the head of the Russian Church, and three great churches.

Moscow became the capital of a new and aggressive empire. By the time of his death in 1505, Ivan had tripled the territory under Moscow's control. Ivan III was both the first czar and the first leader of a united Russian nation. Russians call him Ivan the Great.

Ivan IV ruled through terror.

The next important figure in Russian history also had a well-earned nickname: Ivan the Terrible. He came to the throne as Ivan IV in 1533, when he was only three years old. His youth was marked by struggles for power among Russia's nobles. These nobles, themselves often minor princes, were known as **boyars**. Like the feudal lords of western Europe, they held large estates. Just as the feudal lords struggled against the growing power of the kings in England and France, the boyars opposed the growing power of Russia's czars.

Ivan's mother, who acted as regent, died in 1538 when he was eight, probably poisoned by her boyar enemies. For the next eight years, the boyars kept Ivan a virtual prisoner, poorly fed and badly clothed. As a result, Ivan mistrusted and hated the boyars for the rest of his life.

In 1547, when he was 16, Ivan took power into his own hands, having himself crowned czar. He married the beautiful Anastasia, related to an old boyar family, the Romanovs. (You will hear more of this family later.)

The years from 1547 to 1560 are often called Ivan's "good period." He won great victories against the Mongols and destroyed the Mongol khanate on the Volga River. He also gave Russia a code of laws in 1550 and ruled justly. Hoping to increase Russia's trade with Europe, he began a long war to win access to the Baltic Sea.

Ivan IV is probably better remembered for his later "bad period," which began after his beloved Anastasia died in 1560. Little is known about these years because the records were lost in a great fire that swept Moscow. Some historians believe Ivan was insane part of the time. Others say his acts of cruelty were little different from those of other European rulers—for example, the use of the Inquisition by Ferdinand and Isabella in Spain.

Whatever the explanation, Ivan turned brutally against the boyars. He accused them of poisoning his wife. He organized his own police force whose chief duty was to hunt down "traitors" and murder them. The members of this police force were called *oprichniki* (oh-**PREECH**-nihk-ee), or "separate class." They dressed in black and rode black horses with dogs' heads on their saddles as symbols of terror. Thousands of boyars and ordinary people as well died in this reign of terror.

Ivan's uncontrollable rage at last led him to an act that was both the greatest personal tragedy and the greatest political disaster of his reign. In 1581, during a violent quarrel, he killed his older son and heir. Thus, when Ivan himself died in 1584, only his unintelligent younger son remained to succeed him as czar.

Ivan IV built St. Basil's Cathedral in Moscow to celebrate his victories over the Mongols.

Russia at the time of Ivan's death was an isolated and primitive empire. The story of how this empire became a major European power is left to a later chapter.

Section REVIEW 5

Define: (a) czar, (b) boyar, (c) oprichniki
Identify: (a) Ural Mountains, (b) Slavs, (c) Kiev, (d) Ivan I, (e) Kremlin, (f) Ivan IV
Answer:
1. Describe the geography of Russia.
2. (a) When did the Mongols conquer Russia? (b) How did they rule it?
3. (a) What geographic advantages helped Moscow's rise to power? (b) What other factors helped the city?
4. What achievements explain why Ivan III is known as Ivan the Great?
5. (a) What were the accomplishments of Ivan IV? (b) How did he come to be known as Ivan the Terrible?

Critical Thinking
6. (a) How was the czars' situation like that of the new monarchs? (b) How was it different?

267

ANSWERS TO
Section Review 5

Define:
(a) Russian word for caesar or emperor (b) Russian noble (c) Ivan IV's police force
Identify:
(a) divide Europe from Asia (b) migrants from Asia who settled in eastern Europe (c) trade center in early Russia (d) prince of Moscow under Mongols (e) walled citadel in Moscow (f) Ivan the Terrible
Answer:
1. Refer students to page 265.

2. (a) mid-1200's (b) united Russia under Mongol rule but allowed Russian princes local rule

3. (a) location in northern forests and nearness to rivers (b) trade, rise of Ivan I

4. expulsion of the Mongols, tripling of territory

5. (a) victories against Mongols; development of code of laws; expanded trade (b) turned against boyars, carried on a reign of terror

6. (a) conflict with nobles (b) no council like Parliament or Estates General to check power

Concluding the Chapter

1. **Chapter Closer**
   Ask students to explain why "The Origin of European Nations" is an appropriate title for this chapter.

2. **Reteaching Activities**
   a. **Outlining** Have students write a sentence outline of Sections 1 and 2, using the headings from the sections.
   b. **Making a Time Line** Have students prepare a time line covering events that took place between 1150 and 1580.

Answers to Chapter Review appear on pages 248e–248f.

Summary

1. England and France developed as nations. In England, the signing of the Magna Carta limited royal power. The middle class grew stronger when townspeople were included in Parliament. In France, Philip II won much English-held land and strengthened royal power. Later rulers set up royal courts and included the middle class in the Estates General.

2. The Church faced a crisis in the 1300's. The Babylonian captivity and the Great Schism weakened the authority of the Church. John Wycliffe, John Huss, and their supporters called for changes in the Church.

3. The 1300's brought plague and war. The Black Death killed millions and weakened the manorial economy. The Hundred Years' War further diminished feudal power, as the longbow and cannons doomed armored knights and castles. During the war, national loyalties increased in England and France.

4. New monarchs ruled in western Europe. Rulers in France, England, and Spain found new sources of tax money, hired professional soldiers, and chose middle-class officials. The Tudor dynasty came to power in England. French kings strengthened royal control. In Spain, the Reconquista linked Spanish nationalism with the crusading spirit, ending religious toleration for Jews and Muslims.

5. A new empire arose in Russia. The Mongol invasion destroyed Russia's old Kievan civilization. Beginning in the 1300's, Moscow became the new center of Russian power. Moscow's rulers eventually drove out the Mongols and added to their own territory.

Reviewing the Facts

1. Define the following terms:
   a. nation-state   c. czar
   b. nationalism   d. boyar
2. Explain the importance of each of the following names, dates, places, or terms:
   a. 1215   k. Henry VII
   b. Model Parliament   l. Charles VII
   c. Estates General   m. Ferdinand of
   d. Babylonian captivity   Aragon
   e. Great Schism   n. Isabella of
   f. Council of Constance   Castile
   g. Black Death   o. Reconquista
   h. Hundred Years' War   p. 1492
   i. Joan of Arc   q. Moscow
   j. Wars of the Roses   r. Ivan III
3. (a) How did the Magna Carta come to be signed?
   (b) Why is it important?
4. (a) What was new about the Model Parliament?
   (b) When did it first meet?

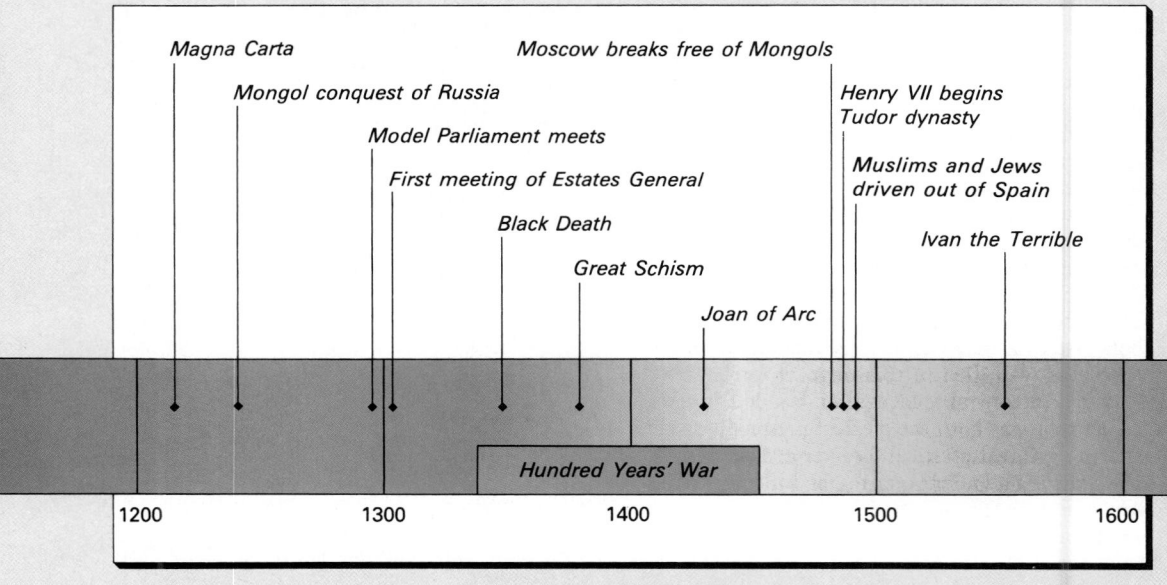

Magna Carta
Moscow breaks free of Mongols
Mongol conquest of Russia
Henry VII begins Tudor dynasty
Model Parliament meets
Muslims and Jews driven out of Spain
First meeting of Estates General
Black Death
Ivan the Terrible
Great Schism
Joan of Arc

Hundred Years' War

1200   1300   1400   1500   1600

5. Briefly describe how each of the following kings helped France become a strong nation-state. (a) Philip Augustus (b) Louis IX (c) Charles VII (d) Louis XI
6. (a) How was the Church's authority weakened by the Babylonian captivity? (b) How was the Church's authority weakened once again by the Great Schism?
7. Identify three factors that led to a population decline in the 1300's and explain the part each played in the decline.
8. How did the Hundred Years' War contribute to the rise of nationalism?
9. Briefly describe the new policies that were followed by the monarchs who came to power between 1450 and 1500.
10. How did Russia begin to become a unified empire?

Basic Skills

1. **Making a time line** (a) Using 20-year segments, make a time line of the Hundred Years' War. (b) Use shading or color to indicate the four stages described on page 258. (c) Include the following events: Battle of Crécy, Battle of Poitiers, Battle of Agincourt, Joan's victory at Orleans, and Joan's death at the stake.
2. **Making a chart** Between 1100 and the early 1300's, the kings of England and France faced many changes. (a) Make a chart to compare the changes in these countries. For the vertical headings, use *Taxes, Parliament/Estates General,* and *Royal Courts.* Fill in the appropriate information for each country. (b) What conclusions do you draw on the basis of the chart?
3. **Comparing maps** Between 1160 and the late 1400's, the boundaries of many European nations changed. Compare the maps on pages 260, 264, and 266 with that on page 235. What major change has occurred in each of the three countries?
4. **Summarizing** Summarize the section "New monarchs replaced feudal kings" on pages 261–262. For each paragraph, write a sentence describing the feudal customs and the new conditions that replaced them.

Researching and Reporting Skills

1. **Preparing an interview** If you could have interviewed Joan of Arc at the time of her trial, what three questions would you have asked?

2. **Surveying** Combine the questions about Joan asked by everyone in the class and analyze them. (a) What question was asked most frequently? (b) Into what different categories can the questions be divided?
3. **Interpreting primary sources** The primary sources in this chapter include both pictures and quotations. (a) Identify three visual sources and three quoted passages from the chapter that represent the times. (b) What does each source contribute to historical understanding?

Critical Thinking

1. **Distinguishing fact from opinion** Page 250 contains the statement, "John's losses were England's gain . . ." (a) Is this statement fact or opinion? Why? (b) Is there evidence to support the statement? If so, what?
2. **Analyzing cause and effect** (a) What factors caused the middle class to grow in power in England and France during the late Middle Ages? (b) What were the effects of this change in each country?
3. **Inferring** The Moors and Jews of Spain included many merchants and scholars. What effect might the policies of religious intolerance have had on Spain's economic and social development?

Perspectives on Past and Present

1. According to Winston Churchill, the great contribution of the Magna Carta was that it established the idea of a supreme law that even the king may not break. What are several examples of the use of this concept in the United States?
2. Religious dissenters like John Wycliffe and John Huss challenged a Church that considered itself the final authority in religious matters. To what extent have attitudes about religious dissent changed since that time? Give examples to support your answer.

Investigating History

Increased trade, which encouraged contacts among different peoples, helped spread the Black Death. Organize a debate on the following issue: A highly contagious disease such as the Black Death would or would not spread even more rapidly today than in the Middle Ages.

269

Chapter Evaluation

Chapter Test 11, Alternate Chapter Test 11, and Computer Test Bank Chapter 11 Test can be used to evaluate your students' understanding of this chapter.

ANSWERS TO
Geographic Theme

1. Italy: Venice, Florence, Genoa, Milan, Rome, Naples; northwestern Europe: Bruges, Amsterdam, Cologne, Paris, Hamburg, Bremen; Baltic area: Stockholm, Danzig, Copenhagen, Lübeck, Riga, Novgorod.

2. Flanders and northern France: fish, salt, flax, wine, wheat, paper, iron, textiles, manufactured goods; Spain: cork, cotton, fruit and foodstuffs, olives, wool, iron, copper, paper, metalware, leather; England: tin, lead, iron, fish, textiles, manufactured goods; Baltic region: grain, fish, flax, copper, hemp, wax, furs, honey

3. The Italian and Flemish cities had textiles and other manufactured goods; already had industry; other regions were mainly producers of food and raw materials. England did have some textiles and other manufactured goods.

4. Answers will vary, but main changes are expansion of trade and manufacturing within Europe and extension of trade to Americas and Asia.

Geographic Theme: Interaction

How did people use resources to develop trade?

The Pax Romana enabled a remarkably productive economy to develop, linked by the bonds of trade. That economy illustrates what geographers call *interaction*—the relation of people and their environment. From the resources around them, people of the empire produced goods to sell. Trade carried those goods to market and brought back what the local environment could not provide.

The collapse of the empire destroyed this network of production and trade. Roads fell into disrepair, routes became unprotected, and cities declined. As a result, economic units became local and self-sufficient. Long-distance trade and even regional exchange ceased.

Almost 500 years passed before an awakening of economic life began. Among the early signs of revival was the rise of towns in Italy and northwestern Europe. Venice, Genoa, and other cities grew through Mediterranean trade. In northern France and Flanders, towns such as Bruges and Antwerp became centers of cloth manufacture. Access to the sea gave both regions an advantage in sea-borne commerce.

For a time, the Mediterranean and northern European centers were separate. Eventually Venetian ships reached Flanders to start a new trade connection. Meanwhile, merchants rediscovered the Alpine routes leading to France and Germany. A third trading region, the Hanseatic League, grew to extend from Flanders across the Baltic Sea into Russia.

Once again, Europeans began to sell their natural resources and products. Using the means available in their environment, they made contact with the wider world. Whether from resources, manufacture, or trade, goods once again made the journey to distant markets. A new economic era had begun.

1. List four trading cities of Italy, four of northwestern Europe, and four of the Baltic area.

2. List the major products of the Italian cities, Flanders and northern France, Spain, England, and the Baltic region.

3. Compare the economic development of the Italian and Flemish cities with that of Spain, England, and the Baltic region.

4. What changes do you think would happen in the new era?

Trade and Manufacturing in Medieval Europe

COMMODITIES
copper, wool, fish, iron, cork, grain, lead, glass, honey, silver, hemp, olives, tin, paper, raisins, cotton, pitch, salt, flax, wax, wheat, furs, horses, wine, leather, currants, slave market, silk, timber, indigo, metal wares, fruits & foodstuffs

KEY
Textile and manufacturing areas
Northern sea routes
Venetian sea routes
Overland routes

0   300 Miles

Historical Themes

The Middle Ages provide an important example of how continuity and change helped shape new social institutions. They also made significant contributions to the rise of democratic ideas.

Continuity and Change

Western Europe, the Byzantine empire, and the Islamic empire all emerged from the ruins of the Roman empire. The processes of continuity and change played an important role in shaping the distinctive characteristics of each region.

The Byzantine empire consciously preserved Rome's political heritage. The emperors saw themselves as the rightful heirs to the power of Augustus. For example, Justinian's famous code drew upon the laws and opinions of Rome's greatest legal writers. While the Byzantines maintained Rome's political authority, they gradually developed a new branch of Christianity known as the Eastern Orthodox Church. The religious division between Rome and Constantinople became final when the pope and the Byzantine patriarch excommunicated each other in 1054.

The collapse of Rome had a devastating impact on western Europe. The barbarian invasions disrupted trade, destroyed towns, and dealt a serious blow to learning. By the year 600, priests were the only Europeans who were literate. While Rome's political authority vanished, the Roman Catholic Church survived and became the main civilizing force in western Europe.

The sudden emergence of Islam had a decisive impact upon the Mediterranean world. During the long years of Roman rule, the lands surrounding the Mediterranean had adopted Greco-Roman culture and the Christian religion. The Islamic conquests split the Mediterranean area into rival regions controlled by Christians and Muslims. The Islamic faith and Arab culture provided the Muslim world with strong bonds that still exist today.

Social Institutions

The decline of Rome stimulated the development of new social institutions. A new system known as feudalism became the basis for medieval society. Feudalism was

based on personal bonds of loyalty between lords and their vassals. The great majority of people in medieval Europe, however, were neither lords nor vassals. Most people were serfs, who lived on small, self-sufficient manors.

Feudalism and manorialism provided stable social and economic structures that enabled western Europe to revive. During the later Middle Ages, kings began to expand their power by slowly combining their lands into unified kingdoms. By the early 1500's, powerful nation-states were emerging in England, France, and Spain.

The Rise of Democratic Ideas

The Magna Carta and the creation of Parliament in England marked important milestones in the rise of democratic ideas. The Magna Carta established the principles of limited monarchy, due process of law, and the need for common consent to levy taxes. Since the Magna Carta required "the common consent" of the kingdom to raise taxes, Edward I called together the lords and representatives from the knights and burgesses. His Model Parliament further limited the monarchy and established the principle of representation of certain groups of the common people.

Analyzing Historial Themes

1. Give examples of how the processes of continuity and change affected western Europe, the Byzantine empire, and the Islamic empire.
2. Name two institutions that helped shape European life during the early Middle Ages.
3. What key democratic principles were established by the Magna Carta and the Model Parliament?

271

ANSWERS TO
Analyzing Historical Themes

1. western Europe—The collapse of Rome and barbarian invasions disrupted trade, destroyed towns, hindered learning, and increased the significance of the Roman Catholic Church. Byzantine empire—Rome's political and legal heritage was preserved while gradual change in religion led to division between Rome and Constantinople. Islamic—The sudden emergence of Islam ended continuity of Greco-Roman culture and Christianity in Mediterranean world by splitting it into rival regions ruled by Christians and Muslims.

2. feudalism, manorialism, monarchy, nation-states

3. Magna Carta—principles of limited monarchy, due process of law, need for common consent to levy taxes; Model Parliament—principles of limited monarchy, representation of certain groups of common people

UNIT
Evaluation

Unit III Test and Alternate Unit III Test can be used to evaluate your students' understanding of this unit.

Maya pyramid at Chíchén-Itzá

	100	400	700
Political and Governmental Life		**320–467** Gupta rulers bring golden age to India	**600's–700's** Ghana gains power in West Africa	**800's** Rajputs build new kingdoms in India

Yoruba pendant

Economic and Technological Life		**300's** Axum in Ethiopia trades from interior to Red Sea	**500's–1600's** Gold and salt trade thrives in West Africa	**794** In Heian, Japan, a golden age begins

Detail from The Tale of Genji

Mohica earspool

400's India uses decimal systems and concept of zero

Social and Cultural Life	**250–900** Maya civilization flourishes in Central America	**500's** Buddhism reaches Japan	**850–1250** Khmer empire peaks during Angkor period

Unit IV

An Age of Empires

Historical Themes

Human-Environment Interaction Japan, Africa, and the Americas provided unique settings for cultural development. While Japan was unified, Africa and the Americas produced a variety of cultures.

Continuity and Change Asian history was long marked by recurring cycles of conquest. In Africa and the Americas, the main pattern was one of tradition and continuity within many different environments.

Cultural Development In Asia, Africa, and the Americas, the arts were used as an expression of custom and tradition. Archaeological remains provide a record of those civilizations.

1000   **1300**   **1600**

◄1200's
Shogunate
established
in Japan

1400's
Incas build empire
in Andes

1600's
Japan bans foreigners

1644
Manchus set up Ch'ing
dynasty in China

1100's–1500's
East African coastal cities
centers of trade

Inca weaving from Peru

*Pueblo pottery:
glazed polychrome jar*

1275–1292
Marco Polo visits China

1433
Great Fleet sails from
China to Africa

1100's
Yorubas in Africa
are skilled
craftspeople

1300's
China develops public
elementary schools

1325
Aztecs build capital,
Tenochtitlán

1653
Shah Jahan builds
Taj Mahal in India

273

The World about 1250

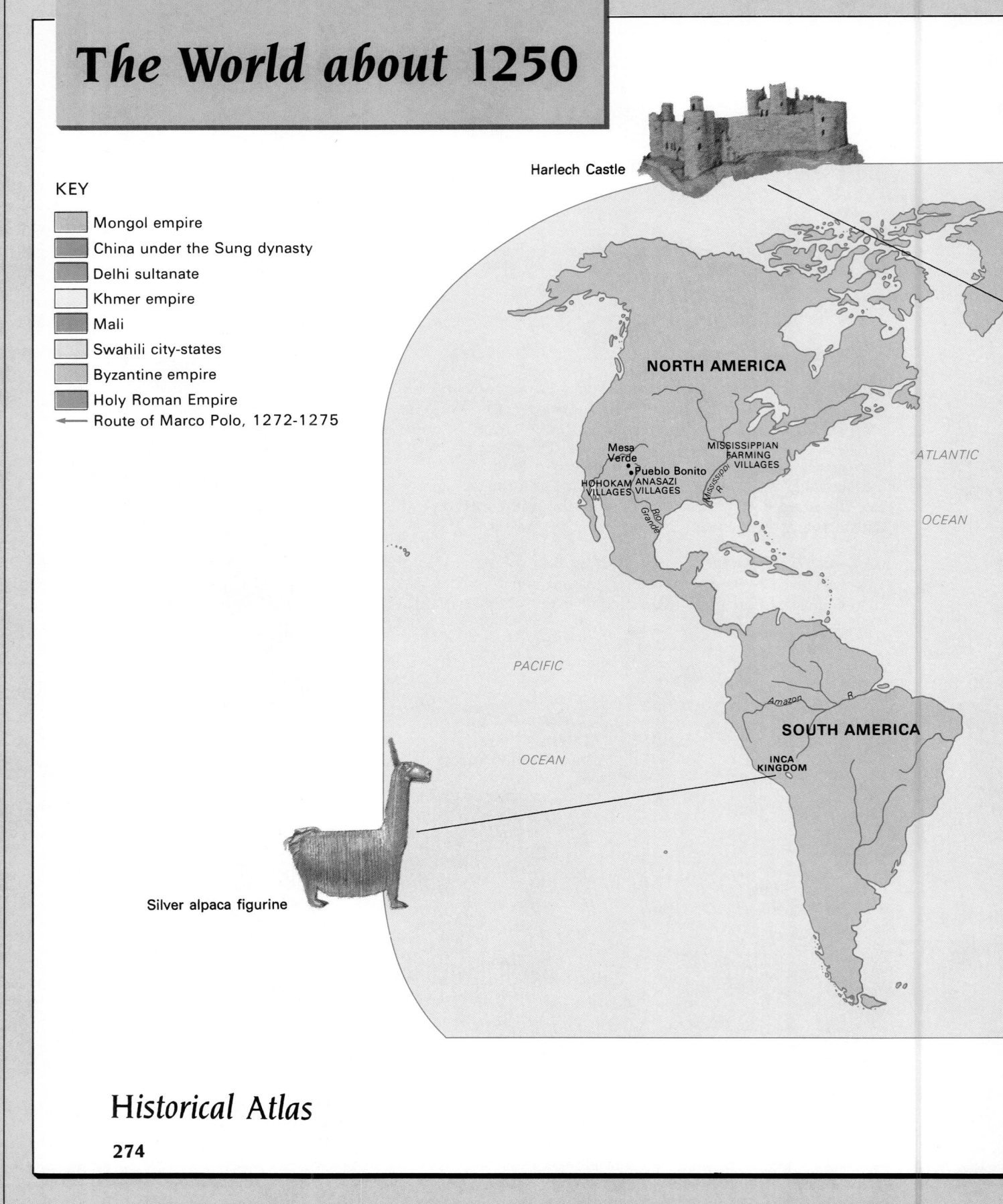

KEY

- Mongol empire
- China under the Sung dynasty
- Delhi sultanate
- Khmer empire
- Mali
- Swahili city-states
- Byzantine empire
- Holy Roman Empire
- ← Route of Marco Polo, 1272-1275

Harlech Castle

NORTH AMERICA

Mesa Verde
Pueblo Bonito
HOHOKAM VILLAGES
ANASAZI VILLAGES
MISSISSIPPIAN FARMING VILLAGES
Mississippi R.
Rio Grande

ATLANTIC OCEAN

PACIFIC OCEAN

Amazon R.

SOUTH AMERICA

INCA KINGDOM

Silver alpaca figurine

Historical Atlas

274

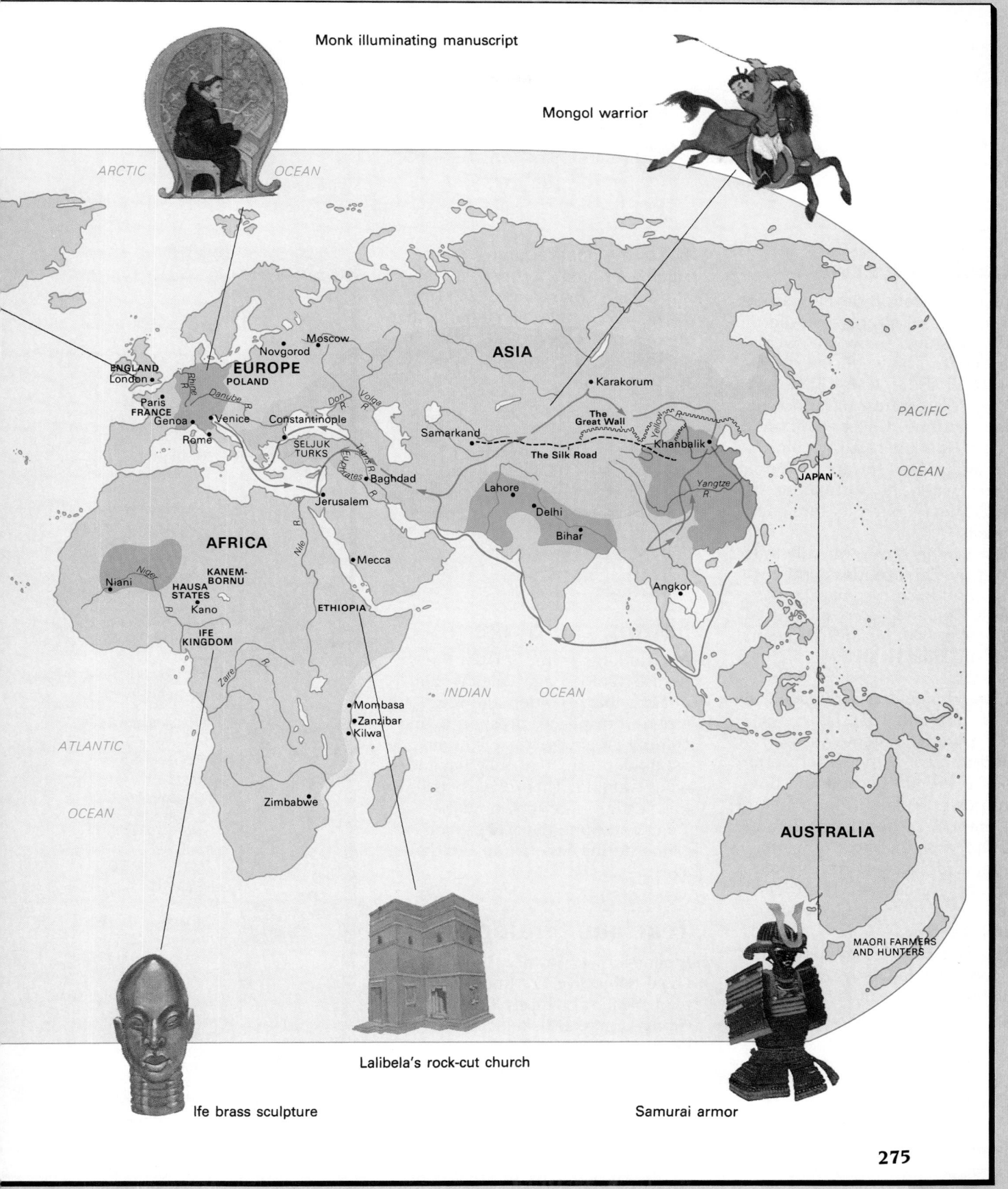

Monk illuminating manuscript

Mongol warrior

ARCTIC OCEAN

Moscow

Novgorod

ASIA

ENGLAND
London
EUROPE
POLAND

• Karakorum

PACIFIC

Paris
FRANCE
Genoa •
Rome
Rhone R.
Danube R.
Venice
Constantinople
Don R.
Volga R.
Samarkand
The Great Wall

OCEAN

SELJUK
TURKS

The Silk Road

Yellow R.

Khanbalik

Tigris R.
Euphrates R.
Baghdad
Jerusalem

Lahore

Delhi

Bihar

Yangtze R.

JAPAN

AFRICA

Nile R.

Mecca

ETHIOPIA

Angkor

INDIAN   OCEAN

Niger R.
Niani •
KANEM-
BORNU
HAUSA
STATES
Kano •

IFE
KINGDOM

Zaire R.

Mombasa
• Zanzibar
• Kilwa

ATLANTIC

OCEAN

Zimbabwe •

AUSTRALIA

MAORI FARMERS
AND HUNTERS

Lalibela's rock-cut church

Ife brass sculpture

Samurai armor

Golden Ages in China and Japan

Chapter Overview

China's civilization developed under a series of strong dynasties with occasional periods of weakened control between the dynasties. Until about 1450, China was the world's greatest naval power. After that time, China abandoned its navy, lost interest in exploration, and turned inward. Beginning in 1513, when the Portuguese arrived, China limited its foreign contacts.

The Japanese were greatly influenced by Chinese ideas and customs. Buddhism reached Japan from China and, from about A.D. 600 to A.D. 800, Japanese scholars went to China to study its civilization.

Clans dominated early Japan. Between 1000 and 1200, Japan developed a feudal system with warriors called *samurai*. A powerful warlord called a *shogun* became the dominant power, ruling in the name of the emperor. After the decline of the shoguns, the most powerful feudal lords became nearly independent; warfare and disorder ruled the country until the sixteenth century.

The first European ships were welcomed in Japan in 1543, but by 1638 most European merchants had been banned, and Japan remained closed to Europeans for 200 years.

Chapter Focus

After students read the chapter opener (pages 276–277), ask them to speculate why Chapter 12 begins with a description of Yang-ti's garden and artificial lake. Explain that the emperor's wealth is a symbol of the political unity won by rulers of China's Sui dynasty. Now show Map Transparency 26, *The World about 800*. Tell students that this chapter covers 1,300 years in the history of China and Japan.

Two great dynasties ruled China. 1

Setting the Stage

Ask students to recall what the phrase "golden age" means. Emphasize that a golden age refers to a period of peace, prosperity, and cultural creativity. Have students list golden ages that they have already studied. Then explain that this section describes how the T'ang and Sung dynasties ruled China during two famous golden ages.

Teaching Strategies

Economics and History: The Grand Canal (Objective 1) After students read "The Sui dynasty reunited China" (page 277), tell them that both the Yangtze and the Yellow rivers flow west to east. Use the map on page 278, or Map Transparency 43, *China in Sui and T'ang Times*, to show students how the Grand Canal provided a north-south artery linking the rice fields of the Yangtze delta to the northern provinces. A huge trading fleet of 40,000 ships carried rice and other supplies to the armies defending China's northern frontiers.

Advance Planner

	SECTION 1
Objectives	1. Identify the Grand Canal and explain how it helped unify China. 2. Describe how the Chinese used examinations to help choose government officials. 3. Draw a map of the T'ang and Sung empires.
Setting the Stage	The concept of a Golden Age Unit IV time line Transparency 26
Teaching Strategies	Economics and History: The Grand Canal Transparency 43 Relating Past to Present: Examinations Geography in History: Making a Map Transparency 44 Outline Map 19 Check for Understanding
Guided Practice	Transparency 26 Q&A Transparency 43 Q&A Transparency 44 Q&A Section Review 1
Independent Practice Worksheets	Independent Practice 12.1 Geography Skills 12 Vocabulary 12
Enrichment	1. Primary Source: Voices 12.1 2. Preparing a Report 3. Creative Writing 4. Researching for Points
Chapter Closer	

Unit IV An Age of Empires

THEME Golden ages and the rise and fall of kingdoms in 1300 years of change in China, Japan, India, Southeast Asia, Africa, and the Americas

Chapter 12 Golden Ages in China and Japan 300–1650

FOCUS Emperor Yang-ti's garden as a symbol of China's political unity under Sui rulers

★ Advanced
● Basic

SECTION 2	SECTION 3	SECTION 4	SECTION 5
1. Identify the Eurasian Steppe as a geographic region. 2. Identify Genghis Khan and list reasons the Mongols were successful conquerors. 3. Locate on a map the boundaries of the Mongol empire.	1. Locate the boundaries of the Ming empire. 2. Identify and describe the Forbidden City.	1. Describe Japan's geography and explain its influence on Japanese culture. 2. Explain how the Japanese adapted Chinese ideas. 3. Discuss aspects of daily life during the Heian age. 4. Identify the samurai and explain the code of bushido.	1. Describe the impact of the Portuguese on Japan. 2. Identify Oda Nobunaga, Toyotomi Hideyoshi, and Tokugawa Ieyasu and explain how they unified Japan. 3. Define Zen Buddhism and give examples of its influence on Japanese culture.
Using Geographic Themes: Region	Mongol leaders lose the Mandate of Heaven	Using Geographic Themes: Human-Environment Interaction Transparency 47	Causes of the collapse of the Kamakura shogunate and the Age of the Country at War
Discussing History: The Mongol Success Transparency 45 Geography in History: Mongol Conquests Outline Map 12 Check for Understanding	Geography in History: Using Map Symbols Transparency 46 Outline Map 19 Teaching with Pictures: The Forbidden City Check for Understanding	Using Geographic Themes: Movement Discussing History: Life in Heian Discussing History: The Samurai Warrior Check for Understanding	Using Geographic Themes: Movement Discussing History: The Three Unifiers Teaching with Pictures: Zen Gardens Check for Understanding
Transparency 45 Q&A Section Review 2 Independent Practice 12.2	Transparency 46 Q&A Section Review 3 Independent Practice 12.3 Critical Thinking 12	Transparency 47 Q&A Section Review 4 Independent Practice 12.4	Section Review 5 Independent Practice 12.5 Basic Skills 12
1. Primary Source: Voices 12.2 2. Relating Past to Present: Present-Day Mongolia 3. Researching for Points	1. Primary Source: Voices 12.3 2. ★Creative Writing 3. Researching for Points	1. Primary Source: Voices 12.4 2. Preparing a Report 3. Researching for Points	1. Primary Source: Voices 12.5 2. Preparing a Report 3. Researching for Points

●**Reteaching Activities** Making a Chart, Making a Time Line, Identifying Historical Figures

Chapter Review Summary, Reviewing the Facts, Basic Skills, Researching and Reporting Skills, Critical Thinking, Perspectives on Past and Present, Investigating History

Chapter Evaluation Chapter Test 12, Alternate Chapter Test 12, Computer Test Bank Chapter 12 Test

The canal also stimulated the development of the Yangtze region.

Relating Past to Present: Examinations (Objective 2) Ask students to describe how they feel before and after taking an important test. Then have them read "Scholar-officials governed China" (pages 278–279). Explain that thousands of Chinese students took a civil service examination each year. Fewer than 10 percent of the candidates passed. Recall the definition of civil service. Note that many government jobs in the present-day United States require qualifying exams. Read or distribute this poem:

I met someone who told me I
    had passed;
I was bowled over by this thun-
    derclap of joy and surprise,
I thought it was a mistake,
    . . . only a dream . . .
Parents, however much they
    love a child,
Have not the power to place
    him among the chosen few.
Only the examiner can bring the
    youth to notice.

Geography in History: Making a Map (Objective 3) Show students Map Transparency 44, *China in Sung Times*. Ask students how China's boundaries changed between the times of the Sui and the T'ang dynasties. Distribute Outline Map 19: China and Japan. Have students refer to the maps on pages 278 and 281, draw a map key, use map symbols to show the boundaries of each of the three dynasties, and label the three capitals. Tell students to save their maps to use again in Sections 3 and 4.

Check for Understanding List the three dynasties on the board and ask students to describe one significant development in each.

Enrichment Activities

1. **Reading a Primary Source** Assign Voices from the Past Resource Book 12.1.

2. **Preparing a Report** Have students report on one of the following topics: the Grand Canal, T'ai-tsung, Empress Wu, Ch'ang-an, Tu Fu, Li Po, Sung porcelain, the magnetic compass, the invention of gunpowder.

3. **Creative Writing** Ask students to select any picture of a landscape and write a poem about it using the three characteristics of T'ang poetry discussed in the text.

4. **Researching for Bonus Points** What was the name of the main avenue in Ch'ang-an? (Street of the Vermilion Sparrow)

The Mongols conquered a vast empire. 2

Setting the Stage

Using Geographic Themes: Region (Objective 1) Have students recall that a geographic region is an area that shares common characteristics. Now ask students to read "The Mongols came from the steppe" (pages 283–284) and to identify the geographic characteristics that made the steppe a region.

Teaching Strategies

Discussing History: The Mongol Success (Objective 2) First direct students' attention to the map of the Mongol Empire on page 285, or use Map Transparency 45, *The Mongol Empire*. Then ask, "How could groups of nomadic horsemen conquer such a huge empire?"

Geography in History: Mongol Conquests (Objective 3) Distribute Outline Map 12: Asia. Have students refer to the map on page 285 and then fill in the areas of the Mongol conquests. Ask, "What areas in addition to China did the Mongols conquer?" Point out that the Mongols achieved the only successful winter invasion of Russia in history. They invaded Russia in the winter so that their cavalry could use the frozen rivers as highways. Then have students add labels to their maps naming the regions on the frontiers of the Mongol Empire.

Check for Understanding Ask students to explain the significance of Genghis Khan, Kublai Khan, and Marco Polo to historical developments in China and Europe.

Enrichment Activities

1. **Reading a Primary Source** Assign Voices from the Past Resource Book 12.2.

2. **Relating Past to Present: Present-Day Mongolia** Ask interested students to prepare a report on life in modern Mongolia. (See *National Geographic*, February 1985.)

3. **Researching for Bonus Points** What was the name of Genghis Khan's capital and what is its only monumental remain? (Karakorum—a large stone tortoise)

China chose stability over change. 3

Setting the Stage

After students read the introduction (page 287), help them understand that from the Chinese point of view the Mongol leaders following Kublai Khan had clearly lost the Mandate of Heaven. Under such circumstances, the people had a right to rebel and to follow virtuous leaders who would establish a new dynasty. Tell students that this section describes how the Chinese overthrew the Mongols and established a new period of recovery and stability under the Ming dynasty.

Teaching Strategies

Geography in History: Using Map Symbols (Objective 1) Have students refer to the map on page 287, or show Map Transparency 46, *China in Ming Times*. Have students add a symbol to their map keys on Outline Map 19 and use the symbol to show China during the Ming dynasty. Ask, "In which empire—Sui, T'ang, or Ming—did China have the largest land area?"

Teaching with Pictures: The Forbidden City (Objective 2) First, have students read "The Ming dynasty brought peace" (pages 287–288). Then direct students' attention to the artistic rendition on page 288 of a courtyard in the Forbidden City. The painting on that page shows one of the Forbidden City's three great throne halls. Its yellow-tiled roof symbolizes both the sun and the emperor. The reddish-purple walls symbolize the North Star—the fixed point around which the heavens revolve. The Emperor's Honor Guard is shown standing at attention. Ask students how the Chinese view of their place in the world might affect their relations with other civilizations.

Check for Understanding Ask students to identify the main causes of the rise and fall of the Ming dynasty.

Enrichment Activities

1. **Reading a Primary Source** Assign Voices from the Past Resource Book 12.3.
2. **Creative Writing** Ask advanced students to hypothesize how history might have been different had China not abandoned its Grand Fleet.
3. **Researching for Bonus Points** How did court officials and guests show proper respect to the emperor? (They "kowtowed" by kneeling and touching their foreheads to the ground.)

Japan developed a unique civilization. 4

Setting the Stage

Using Geographic Themes: Human-Environment Interaction (Objective 1) Introduce this section by showing Map Transparency 47, *Japan, 1200–1600*. Point out that Japan is an archipelago that includes about 3,000 volcanic islands. Most Japanese have always lived on the four largest islands: Hokkaido, Honshu, Shikoku, and Kyushu. Now distribute Outline Map 19, and have students label these four islands.

Teaching Strategies

Using Geographic Themes: Movement (Objective 2) Explain that in A.D. 552 a Korean ruler sent ambassadors to Japan carrying gifts of Buddhist doctrine and a gold and copper image of the Buddha. During the next 200 years, the Japanese sent many scholars to study Chinese ways. Point out that the Japanese are the first people we know about in history who deliberately transformed their own culture.

Discussing History: Life in Heian (Objective 3) Have students read "Court society arose at Heian" (pages 292–293). The nobles at Heian enjoyed lives of luxury and elegance. Ask students what they think of the idea that one had to write poetry to be accepted. Explain that court poetry expressed the sentiment *mono no aware*—a sadness at the transience of things. For example, men and women wrote poems about the reflection of a cherry blossom on a pond's surface, or the setting of a pale moon in a garden thick with mist. Point out that these examples illustrate the love of nature and romantic search for beauty that characterized Heian culture. Conclude by asking students to write examples of beautiful or inspiring fleeting moments in nature.

Discussing History: The Samurai Warrior (Objective 4) Samurai warriors were the heroes of Japan's feudal age. They lived according to a harsh code called *bushido* that stressed the ideals of strength, courage, and physical hardship. Explain that dying an honorable death was deemed more important than living a long life. Ask students to compare and contrast the samurai and the knights of medieval Europe. Students should recognize that bushido and chivalry had similar elements as formal codes of conduct suitable to feudal relationships.

Check for Understanding Ask students to explain the roles of clans, nobles, samurai, and shoguns in Japan's history.

Enrichment Activities

1. **Reading a Primary Source**
   Assign Voices from the Past Resource Book 12.4.

2. **Preparing a Report**
   Have students report on one of the following topics: the training and equipment of samurai warriors, the art of women of the Heian Court, Shintoism, and the imperial cities of Nara and Kyoto.

3. **Researching for Bonus Points**
   Who was the legendary founder of the Japanese imperial family? (Emperor Jimmu)

Japan turned to isolation. 5

Setting the Stage

Ask students to recall that conditions in the Roman empire after Rome's victory over Carthage led to the collapse of the republic and to an era of civil wars. Then ask students to find an example in this section of a similar situation.

This section describes how a series of strong leaders restored order. It also discusses the effects of contact with Portuguese merchants and missionaries and Japan's decision to isolate itself from European culture.

Teaching Strategies

Using Geographic Themes: Movement (Objective 1) Have students read pages 295–296. Explain that the Portuguese contact with Japan is an example of the movement of cultural ideas and products.

Discussing History: The Three Unifiers (Objective 2) Ask students to make a chart on the board comparing the contributions of Nobunaga, Hideyoshi, and Ieyasu in unifying Japan.

Teaching with Pictures: Zen Gardens (Objective 3) Explain that Zen Buddhists sought spiritual enlightenment through self-discipline and meditation. Have students read "Zen Buddhism stressed meditation" and "Art suggested nature," (pages 296–297). Ask, "How did Zen influence Japanese culture?" Point out that the Zen emphasis on meditation strongly influenced painting, the tea ceremony, and gardening. Ask students how the garden's design (page 297) might promote a meditative calm. In addition to order and simplicity, Zen gardens have elements that are intended to be interpreted symbolically. The sand might represent water, and the rocks, mountains.

Check for Understanding What is the significance of each of the following: Francis Xavier, daimyos, Toyotomi Hideyoshi, and Zen Buddhism.

Enrichment Activities

1. **Reading a Primary Source**
   Assign Voices from the Past Resource Book 12.5.

2. **Preparing a Report**
   Have interested students report on Japanese castles, Zen gardens, the art of bonsai, or Japanese floral arrangements.

3. **Researching for Bonus Points**
   What was Toyotomi Hideyoshi's nickname? (Monkey-Face)

ANSWERS TO
Chapter Review 12

Reviewing the Facts

1. **(a)** large group of well-to-do people who rank below nobles but above common people **(b)** dry grassland region **(c)** Mongol leader **(d)** group of people who believed they were descended from the same ancestor **(e)** warriors who fought for lords **(f)** "the way of the warrior"—samurai code **(g)** military dictator **(h)** strong feudal lord

2. **(a)** dynasty that united China in the late 500's **(b)** dynasty in power during China's golden age (618–907) **(c)** capital of T'ang China **(d)** Chinese religion brought by Koreans to Japan **(e)** dynasty that marked beginning of Chinese military decline **(f)** trading route between China and Baghdad **(g)** homeland of the Mongols

(h) leader who united Mongols **(i)** conqueror of Sung China **(j)** Venetian official in the court of Kublai Khan **(k)** capital city of Kublai Khan **(l)** dynasty that followed Mongol rule **(m)** Yung-lo's northern capital, formerly Khanbalik **(n)** name of Manchu dynasty **(o)** chief religion of early Japan **(p)** old name for Kyoto and name of Japan's golden age **(q)** written by Lady Murasaki Shikibu; has been called the world's first novel **(r)** leader of first Christian mission to Japan **(s)** shogun who moved government to Edo (Tokyo)

3. (a) by passing 3 exams **(b)** freedom from paying taxes, serving in the army, performing manual labor; also, could gain land and fortune

4. printing, magnetic compass, gunpowder

5. (a) organizational skill, shrewdness, and cruelty **(b)** central steppes of Turkestan, Persia, Russia, China

6. (a) welcoming **(b)** isolation

Basic Skills

1. Approximate answers: **(a)** 4,400 and 1,800 miles; **(b)** 2,000 and 600 miles; **(c)** 8,800,000 and 1,080,000 square miles; Mongol empire approximately 8 times the size of Alexander's empire

2.

3. *Political*—T'ang: vast empire, scholar officials, capital Chang'an; Sung: smaller empire mostly in south, capital Hangchow; Ming: united China, capital Nanking in south, moved to Peking in north which enclosed Imperial City and Forbidden City, scholar officials. *Economic*—T'ang: lowered taxes, gave land to poor, expanded trade by land and sea; Sung: paid Tatars

for peace with silk, silver, and tea, had paper money, traded silk and porcelain; Ming: traded with Africa, abandoned Grand Fleet and sea trade, closed harbors to Europeans, opened trading post at Macao. *Cultural*—T'ang: drums regulate city, poetry, Confucianism, interest in foreign culture; Sung: gunpowder, printing, compass, poetry, golden age of painting; Ming: emphasis on education, elementary schools, high literacy, revival of Confucianism, encyclopedia, rejection of foreign influence

Researching and Reporting Skills

1. Students' research findings will vary.

2. Answers will vary. Students might select the T'ang for their scholarship, political and economic achievements, the Sung for their poetry and painting, or the Ming for their peace and prosperity, literacy, and preservation of the past.

3. Examples of research questions: How did Buddhism influence art or customs in China? In Japan? In what ways did the Japanese modify Buddhism?

Critical Thinking

1. Feudalism in both Europe and Japan was built on complex networks of personal loyalties among nobles—the king, vassals, and knights in Europe, and the emperor, shogun, daimyos, and samurai in Japan. The objects of relationships were land, power, protection, and prestige. The labor of peasants supported both feudal systems. Feudalism arose in Europe through the lack of strong, centralized governing authorities, and declined as kings consolidated their power and as an independent, urban middle class emerged. Feudalism arose in Japan through

competition between landowners and governing authorities and ended in civil war among the daimyos, leading to absolute rule by the victorious daimyo.

2. (a) as barbarians **(b)** despised them and their civilization **(c)** Students might say Mongols were great for their military skills, endurance, but cruel, destructive, and uncivilized.

3. (a) Patterns include growing internal problems, such as peasant rebellions due to excessive taxes and the decline of trade. **(b)** Advice might include treat your peasants well, keep trade flourishing, be prepared to defend your frontiers.

4. (a) simplicity of line, appreciation for beauty of the moment, of nature, landscapes, pagodas with winglike roofs **(b)** influence of China on Japan in early times: influence of Buddhism, Taoism, and Zen.

Perspectives on Past and Present

1. fear of influence of missionaries, invasion. Today, Japan limits imports. Advantages: protects Japanese goods from outstanding competition; prevents or lessens foreign debt. Disadvantages: isolates from new ideas and goods.

2. Long fingernails were a sign that a man did not perform manual labor. Women whose feet had been bound could do little household work. Modern status symbols include expensive homes, cars, or jewels.

Investigating History

Students' reports will vary.

Chapter 12

Teaching with Pictures

Have students study the picture and read the chapter opener on pages 276–277. Then ask them to explain how the art reflects an age of cultural vitality and richness. Students should note women's and men's costumes, activities, and deference to the emperor, as well as the setting of the painting.

Emperor Yang-ti rides through the imperial gardens with some attendants, while others care for his water lilies.

Key Terms

gentry
steppe
khan
clan
samurai
bushido
shogun
daimyo

Read and Understand

1. Two great dynasties ruled China.
2. The Mongols conquered a vast empire.
3. China chose stability over change.
4. Japan developed a unique civilization.
5. Japan turned to isolation.

Day after day, the golden leaves of autumn fluttered lazily to the ground outside the palace of the Chinese emperor Yang-ti. Yet the trees in Yang-ti's garden remained as green as in the summertime. How could this be?

Watchful peasants were seated in the branches of every tree. Each peasant held a basket filled with artificial leaves made of green silk. Whenever a natural leaf fell, a peasant instantly replaced it with a silken leaf.

At the same time, on Yang-ti's huge artificial lake, other peasants paddled boats among the thousands of floating lotus flowers. Blossoms that had withered overnight were plucked off and replaced by delicate petals of white and pink silk. Thus did the ambitious Yang-ti, who

Chapter 12 Resources

GEOGRAPHY
- Geography Skills 12
- Outline Maps 12, 19
- Transparencies 26, 43, 44, 45, 46, 47

REINFORCEMENT
- Vocabulary 12
- Basic Skills 12
- Reteaching 12
- Making Connections Study Guide 12

ENRICHMENT
- Critical Thinking 12
- History and Literature 12

ASSESSMENT
- Chapter Test 12
- Alternate Chapter Test 12
- Computer Test Bank

ruled China from 605 to 618, try to bring even the seasons under his control.

What was happening elsewhere in the world? In the year 618, the prophet Muhammad was just beginning to preach about Allah. The golden age of Islamic civilization lay 200 years in the future. The golden age of Rome lay 500 years in the past. Nowhere else in the world was there a monarch who could equal the power and wealth of Yang-ti. China in the 600's enjoyed a golden age of political unity and artistic splendor.

This chapter covers 1,300 years in the history of two Asian peoples, the Chinese and the Japanese. From 300 to 1650, both China and Japan passed through ages of extraordinary cultural vitality and richness.

Two great dynasties ruled China.   1

As you read in Chapter 4, the Han dynasty collapsed in A.D. 220. For 350 years, no emperor was strong enough to hold China together. More than 30 local dynasties rose and fell. A Chinese poet wrote, "The land was divided like a melon, or shared like beans."

Under the Shang, the Chou, and the Han, the center of China's civilization had been in the north, in the plains along the Yellow River. After 220, however, barbarians from beyond the Great Wall conquered much of northern China. Chinese nobles moved to the safer south, along the Yangtze River. During this long time of troubles, the south slowly became the new center of Chinese civilization.

The Sui dynasty reunited China.

In the late 500's, a new dynasty united China once again. In 581, Sui Wen-ti took over the north and then conquered the south. He brought China once again under the rule of a strong central government.

The new ruling family called themselves the Sui (sway) dynasty. (Recall the Chinese custom of giving the family name first and then the personal name.) There were only two Sui emperors, Wen-ti and his son, Yang-ti. Their dynasty was short (589–618), but it laid the foundation for the golden age that followed.

The Grand Canal The second Sui ruler, Yang-ti, completed the work of reuniting China. His greatest single accomplishment was the building of the Grand Canal. The canal cut across the center of China, tying together its two great rivers, the Yellow River in the north and the Yangtze River in the south.

The canal helped to unite northern and southern China both politically and economically. From his capital in the north, the emperor demanded obedience and tribute from the people of southern China. Barges carried tons of food from the rich rice fields of the south to the less fertile north.

The digging of this 1,000-mile waterway was a prodigious feat. Tens of thousands of peasant men and women toiled on the project for five years between 605 and 610. Perhaps as many as half the workers died on the job. (Yet more died on Yang-ti's project of rebuilding the Great Wall to keep out raiding Turks.)

The overthrow of the Sui The endless work of building canals, walls, and palaces turned people against the Sui dynasty. Yang-ti ranks as one of the most hated emperors in China's history. Overworked and overtaxed, the peasants rebelled. Rebel armies arose all over China. In 618, his own servants strangled Yang-ti.

T'ai-tsung founded the T'ang dynasty.

A young rebel general soon won the throne. He took the name T'ai-tsung (tye-dzoong), which meant "Grand Ancestor." The dynasty he founded was the T'ang. The T'ang dynasty ruled a united China from 618 to 907, nearly 300 years. T'ai-tsung's brilliant reign (627–649) ushered in a golden age when China was the richest, most powerful country in the world.

T'ai-tsung led armies northwest against the Turks of central Asia and northeast against the Koreans. His soldiers, clad in armor of rhinoceros hide, reconquered the northern and western lands that China had lost since the decline of the Han dynasty. Korea fought off T'ai-tsung's invasion, but it fell to his son in 660. For the next 90 years, Korea was forced to pay tribute to China.

T'ai-tsung remembered the Sui dynasty's mistake of overtaxing peasants. He lowered taxes.

277

SECTION 1
Objectives and Teaching Strategies

OBJECTIVE 1. Identify the Grand Canal and explain how it helped unify China.

Teaching Strategy: *Economics and History: The Grand Canal* (page 276a)

OBJECTIVE 2. Describe how the Chinese used examinations to help choose government officials.

Teaching Strategy: *Relating Past to Present: Examinations* (page 276c)

OBJECTIVE 3. Draw a map of the T'ang and Sung empires.

Teaching Strategy: *Geography in History: Making a Map* (page 276c)

■ DISCUSSION

Have students compare the Sui dynasty to the Ch'in (Chapter 4). (Both were short lived and harsh. Both overstrained the kingdom's resources and fell, but both paved the way for succeeding periods of strength and prosperity— the Han and the T'ang.)

SECTION 1
Resources

ENRICHMENT
■ Voices from the Past 12.1

ASSESSMENT
■ Section Quiz 12.1

GEOGRAPHY
■ Transparencies 26, 43, 44

REINFORCEMENT
■ Independent Practice 12.1

■ BACKGROUND

More than 3 million workers toiled for 5 years to dig a canal 20 feet deep, 60 feet wide, and 1,000 miles long. Yang-ti celebrated the Grand Canal's opening with a pleasure cruise on his royal barge, the Imperial Dragon Junk. This dragon-shaped riverboat was 200 feet long, 50 feet wide, and had 4 decks. Yang-ti sat on his gilded Dragon Throne on the top deck.

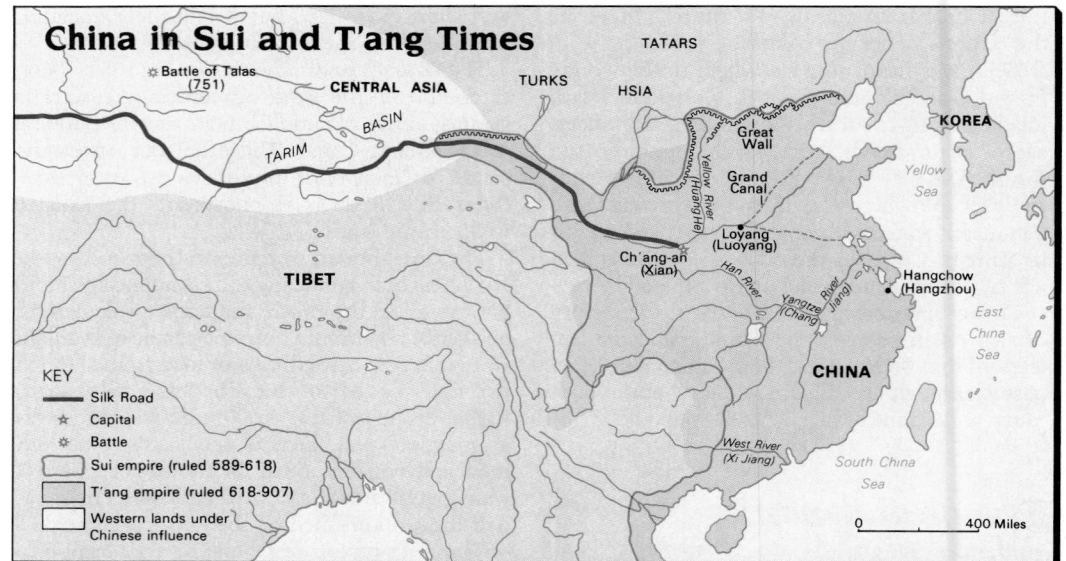

China in Sui and T'ang Times

KEY
- ▬ Silk Road
- ☆ Capital
- ✿ Battle
- Sui empire (ruled 589-618)
- T'ang empire (ruled 618-907)
- Western lands under Chinese influence

0   400 Miles

Map Study

Which dynasty controlled a larger area, the Sui or the T'ang? What region was under Chinese influence but was not part of China during this period? Name two regions shown here that were independent of China.

He also took lands from wealthy landlords and gave those lands to peasants.

Wu Chao strengthened T'ang rule.

Another able T'ang ruler was Empress Wu Chao (woo jaow). She became the only woman ever to rule China in her own name.

In 635, when she was 13, the beautiful Wu Chao left her family for T'ai-tsung's court. When T'ai-tsung died in 650, his son succeeded him. The new emperor made Wu Chao his chief wife and empress. After his death in 683, she ruled in her sons' names. Finally, in 690, Wu Chao took the throne herself.

China benefited from the empress's strong leadership. Her armies won victories in Korea. She lowered taxes. She also encouraged the spread of Buddhism in China.

Scholar-officials governed China.

The T'ang dynasty's most important reform was a system for choosing government officials. As early as the first century B.C., the Han emperor

Wu-ti had begun granting government jobs to scholars who passed an examination on the Five Classics of Confucius. Now, 700 years later, the system was revived and expanded.

Candidates for high office had to pass three grueling exams. Any man, from peasant to noble, could take the first exam. (Women could not compete except during Wu Chao's reign.) In theory, even a peasant could rise in government by doing well on the exams. In practice, however, the system favored wealthy men, because only they could afford an education.

The fortunate few who made it through the first test were known as Budding Scholars. They journeyed to their provincial capitals to take a second exam. If successful again, they traveled to the T'ang capital of Ch'ang-an. Here, locked in windowless cells, they spent days of mental torture taking the final exam.

The successful scholar became a member of China's elite class of scholar-officials. He might serve as a teacher or an administrator. In return, he was freed from paying taxes or serving in the army. He could adopt the fashion of growing his

278

fingernails long. (A two-inch fingernail showed clearly that its owner did no manual labor.) Finally, the scholar-official could use his special privileges to gain land and amass a fortune.

China continued to use the examination system for over 1,000 years. The system had its weaknesses. It did not weed out selfish or corrupt officials. Also, training in writing poetry and quoting Confucius was not always helpful in collecting taxes or supervising canal repairs.

With all its faults, however, the system gave China a remarkably intelligent governing class. No longer did a few ruling families control the country. Now talent was more important than high birth in winning power. As a result, many moderately wealthy families shared in China's government. Scholar-officials and their families formed a new class in Chinese society. This class is often described as the **gentry**, a large, well-to-do group of people who rank below nobles but above the common people.

Some scholars struggle with their exams, while others wait outside to learn if they passed.

CITY TOUR
Ch'ang-an: the T'ang capital.

The capital of T'ang China was Ch'ang-an, a city of about 2 million people. Ch'ang-an's layout showed the Chinese passion for order. Its walls, 18 feet high, formed a rectangle 6 miles long and 5 miles wide. The walls were carefully aligned with the cardinal points of the compass. In each wall were three evenly spaced gates. The streets within the city formed neat, rectangular blocks. The main avenue was almost 500 feet wide.

The imperial palace lay within a complex of palaces and beautifully landscaped parks. The stone-paved road that led to the main palace curved in the shape of a dragon's tail.

Booming drums regulated daily life in Ch'ang-an. At daybreak, the police who patrolled the streets beat on their drums to announce the opening of the city gates. At sunset, the markets closed and people scurried home to the beat of drums as the police locked the city gates. Anyone caught on the streets after the evening drums had sounded could be severely punished.

Within the city, more than 200 different trades and professions had their own sections. So did the various groups of foreigners—Jewish traders and shopkeepers, traders from India, musicians and dancers from Burma, Buddhist pilgrims from many lands, and caravan leaders from the deserts.

Shops in Ch'ang-an sold rugs from Persia, glassware from Syria, lapdogs from Samarkand (in central Asia), pine nuts from Korea, peacock feathers from Burma, and ivory and gems from Vietnam. Chinese women took up foreign fashions. Their silk gowns (tight bodice, plunging neckline, winglike shoulderpads) were modeled after Persian styles. Their hair was done up in the elaborate fashion begun by the princesses of Samarkand.

Once, China had been cut off from the rest of the world by oceans, mountains, and deserts. The T'ang emperors did not isolate themselves behind such barriers. Imperial armies guarded the Great Silk Road, which linked China to the west. Merchandise and travelers moved safely along it in both directions. Sea trade connected China to India and Southeast Asia. In fact, China was more open to foreign trade and influence during the T'ang years than at any other time.

279

■ BACKGROUND

Ch'ang-an (known today as Xian) reflected the highly structured and regulated life of T'ang China. Located at the eastern end of the Great Silk Road on the Wei River, Ch'ang-an was a center of trade and wealth that supported a sophisticated civilization.

Cooperative Learning

Divide the class into groups of four students. Each group should have two reporters, an editor, and a recorder. Have each group write an article that might have appeared in a Ch'ang-an newspaper in the mid 700's. Topics might include upcoming governmental exams, the layout or regulations of the city, the availability of many foreign products, or political events. Have group members discuss their topic, then the reporters should dictate the article to the recorder. The editor should then review the article, offering suggestions as needed. All four group members must be satisfied with the content of the article before they turn it in. Collect all the articles and share the newspaper with the entire class.

■ BACKGROUND

Review the dynastic cycle and the Mandate of Heaven (see Chapter 4).

■ DISCUSSION

Is a poetic interest in natural beauty more likely to arise in an urban or a rural society?

Drums such as this one regulated the lives of Chinese city dwellers. The booming of the drums announced daybreak and curfew.

Poets captured moments of beauty.

In earlier times, Chinese nobles had enjoyed rural pastimes such as horseback riding and hunting, much as the feudal lords of Europe did. In T'ang times, however, the gentry preferred living in the sophisticated atmosphere of cities. There the scholar-officials enjoyed the pleasures of literature and art.

During the golden years of T'ang China, every educated person was expected to write poems. For the gentry, it was almost a daily habit. "At this age," wrote a Chinese chronicler, "whoever was a gentleman was a poet." (Of course, educated people were still a tiny minority.)

Three qualities marked the Chinese poetry of this period. First, images from nature filled nearly all the poems. Mention of a butterfly's wing or a mountain stream subtly suggested the poet's mood. Second, each poem focused sharply on a single moment. Third, poems were brief, seldom longer than a dozen lines.

Li Po (lee boh) and Tu Fu were the most celebrated poets of the 700's. They were friends, but their poems were quite different. Li Po often wrote about the pleasures of life, whereas Tu Fu praised orderliness and the Confucian virtues.

280

Tu Fu's masterly touch shows in this poem titled "Welcome Rain One Spring Night":

> *A good rain knows its season*
> *And comes when spring is here;*
> *On the heels of the wind it slips secretly*
> *into the night;*
> *Silent and soft it moistens everything.*

The T'ang dynasty lost power.

By the early 700's, the T'ang dynasty was weakening. Crushing taxes brought hardship to the people but still failed to meet the rising costs of government. In times of famine, peasants fled their villages and ranged the countryside in bandit gangs.

Moreover, the T'ang could not control the vast empire they had built. In 751, Arabs soundly defeated the Chinese on China's western frontier at the Battle of Talas. Central Asia passed out of Chinese control and into Muslim hands.

To the Chinese, these troubles showed that the T'ang dynasty was losing the Mandate of Heaven. In 755, an army general led a revolt against the emperor. Although a new T'ang emperor regained the throne in 766, the T'ang dynasty never recovered its power and prestige. The government lost control over the more distant parts of China. At the same time, the Chinese began to turn away from foreign contacts, so trade declined. Finally in 905, Ch'ang-an was sacked and burned by rebels. In 907, the last T'ang emperor, a child, was murdered.

The Sung ruled a smaller empire.

After the end of the T'ang dynasty in 907, rival warlords divided China into unstable kingdoms. A poet summed up the chaos of these times: "States rose and fell as candles gutter out in the wind."

In 960, an able army leader proclaimed himself Emperor Sung T'ai-tsu (soong tye-dzoo). The Sung dynasty, like the T'ang, lasted about three centuries (960–1279).

Military decline The Sung dynasty was never as strong as either the Han or the T'ang. The Battle of Talas had marked the beginning of 500 years of military decline for China. Sung armies never regained the western lands lost at Talas in

751. More serious, they never regained the northern lands lost to the nomadic Hsia (shee-ah) and Tatars (TAHT-uhrz) during the T'ang decline.

Sung emperors tried to buy peace with their northern enemies. Beginning in 1004, they paid to the Tatar khan (chieftain) 6,250 pounds of silver and 200,000 bolts of silk each year. To appease the Hsia, they sent a yearly "gift" of 4,375 pounds of silver, 150,000 bolts of silk, and 30,000 pounds of tea. This policy worked for over 100 years.

Move to the south In the end, however, bribes failed to stop the barbarians. In 1126, the Tatars galloped as far as the Yellow River and captured the Sung capital of K'ai-feng (kye-fung).

The emperor was taken prisoner, but his family fled south across the Yangtze River to Hangchow (hahng-joh) in southern China. Thus the traditional center of Chinese civilization, the Yellow River valley, was lost to the Tatars. After 1126, the Sung emperors ruled only southern China.

Merchants thrived in Hangchow.

Despite its military troubles, the Sung dynasty was truly a golden age in southern China. Merchants prospered by selling rice, tea, fish, and other wares in the markets of Hangchow.

Unlike the orderly Ch'ang-an, Hangchow was a marvel of noise and confusion. There were no nightly curfews. Wine flowed all night in the city's restaurants. The canals that twisted through every section of Hangchow were choked with barges piled high with cargo. Mules laden with sacks clattered across the "rainbow bridges" that arched over the canals.

Paper money In the busy markets, two kinds of money passed from hand to hand. First, there were copper coins with square holes cut through the center. The standard unit for trading was "a thousand cash," a thousand coins fastened together on a long string. However, these strings of coins were clumsy and burdensome.

Therefore, between the years 1000 and 1100, the Sung government began to print paper money—the first such money in the world. The merchants of Hangchow could leave their strings of metal cash with bankers in exchange for paper bank notes. Each note carried the warning, "Counterfeiters will be beheaded."

Trade in silk and porcelain Merchants from Hangchow sent trade goods south to the Malay

China in Sung Times

TATARS
CENTRAL ASIA — TURKS
HSIA
Great Wall
KOREA
Grand Canal
Yellow Sea
Kai-feng (Kaifeng)
Yellow
Loyang (Luoyang)
Han
Yangtze River (Chang Jiang)
Hangchow (Hangzhou)
East China Sea
CHINA
West River (Xi Jiang)
South China Sea
KEY
★ Capital
0   500 Miles

Map Study

Compare this map with the one on page 278. What lands has China's emperor lost?

Peninsula and west to India, the Persian Gulf, and even the coast of Africa. Two luxury items were especially easy to trade for a profit in any Asian or African port. One, of course, was Chinese silk. The other was porcelain.

For hundreds of years, the Chinese were the only people who knew the secret formula for combining certain clays and minerals to produce the fine, bone-hard substance called porcelain. Even today, people call such fine cups and dishes "china." The porcelain of Sung times was famous for its delicacy and its subtle colors with such delightful names as plum-colored blue and crushed-strawberry red.

Artists painted beauties of nature.

Like the T'ang period, Sung times were an age of artistic brilliance. The T'ang dynasty was the golden age of the poet. The Sung dynasty was the golden age of painting.

Every well-to-do family had a cherished collection of silk scrolls tucked away in a cabinet. When a scholar wished to escape the hustle and bustle of court life, he could find peace and

281

ANSWER TO
Map Study

lands between Great Wall and Yellow River, lands along Silk Road

■ BACKGROUND

The Chinese called their paper money "flying money."

■ DISCUSSION

In Sung paintings, much of the silk canvas was untouched. The sky, for example, was usually an empty space. Ask students what sort of emotions such paintings would evoke.

ANSWERS TO
Section Review 1

Define:
(a) large group of well-to-do people who rank below nobles but above common people (b) fine, bone-hard substance used to make china

(continued)

ANSWERS TO (continued)

Identify:
(a) dynasty that reunited China under strong central government in the late 500's (b) canal built by Yang-ti to connect Yellow River in the north and Yangtze River in the south (c) founder of T'ang dynasty (d) dynasty in power during China's golden age (618–907) (e) only woman to rule China in her own name (f) capital of T'ang China (g) trading route between China and the West (h) battle at which Arabs defeated Chinese (i) army leader who founded the Sung dynasty (j) dynasty that marked beginning of military decline (k) market city in China

Answer:
1. (a) It reunited China and laid the foundation for the golden age that followed. (b) It overtaxed and over-worked the people, who revolted.

2. (a) by examination (b) gave China an intelligent ruling class, created gentry (c) did not weed out corruption or guarantee workers skilled in government or administration

3. (a) took control of China's northern lands and eventually captured Sung capital (b) paid bribes to appease them

4. T'ang—trade reached heights never matched again; Sung—busy trade centered on Hangchow

5. decline in military power and defeats by Arabs; decline in trade

6. printing, magnetic compass, gunpowder

7. Answers may stress similarities, particularly emphasis on nature, simplicity.

Graceful lines and subtle colors were characteristic of Chinese landscape painting during the Sung dynasty. In pottery, colors were soft but rich, as in this bowl for narcissus bulbs.

comfort by unrolling a scroll to view the beauties of nature. When he had sat long enough with trees, waterfalls, and mountain mists, he rolled up the scroll and returned it to the cabinet.

Sung artists did not use brightly colored paints. Black ink was their favorite paint. Said one Sung artist, "Black is ten colors." Grace of line was at the heart of Sung art.

China led the world in technology.

During the years of the T'ang and the Sung dynasties, no other area of the world was China's equal in skilled workers, science, and technology. Three Chinese inventions—printing, gunpowder, and the compass—were destined to have a revolutionary impact on the rest of the world. All three originated during the T'ang dynasty and were fully developed during the Sung.

Printing The Chinese began to print books around the year 600. Printers first cut a block of wood the size of two book pages. Over the block they pasted a sheet of thin paper on which the text was written. Using the writing on the paper as a guide, they carved around the characters so that they stood out in relief. By brushing ink onto the carved block and pressing it onto blank sheets of paper, a printer could produce a copy

of the original page. In one day, an expert printer could make 2,000 copies.

Sometime in the Sung dynasty, probably in the 1040's, an inventor named Pi Sheng (bee shung) took the next logical step—movable type. He arranged the individual characters on an iron plate coated with sticky resin and tar to hold them in place. Thus, the same characters could be used over and over, instead of carving a new set for each page. (Europeans did not discover how to print books until 1450.)

Magnetic compass The Chinese also learned that a magnetized needle floating in a bowl of water always points north-south. They first used

Footnote to History

Beginning in Sung times, the Chinese considered it beautiful for women to have very tiny feet. Upper-class parents would wrap their daughter's feet in tight bandages when she was about five years old. As the child grew, the wrappings forced her foot to curl painfully until the toes and heel came together. Women whose feet had been bound could hobble only a few steps. For a man, having such a wife was a sign of wealth because she could do little household work.

this device to make sure their houses faced south, as custom required. By 1119, traders from south China had discovered how useful the compass could be for finding directions at sea. Eventually, Arab traders carried the compass to the Mediterranean Sea.

Gunpowder As early as the 600's, fireworks lit up the evening sky over Ch'ang-an during festivals. The Chinese called their thrilling firecrackers "fire trees," "flame flowers," and "peach blossoms."

Sometime after the year 1000, the Chinese experimented with explosive weapons. They made a kind of hand-grenade and shot off small rockets. However, gunpowder remained a minor invention until Europeans learned of it, probably by way of the Arabs and Mongols.

Eventually, the Sung dynasty collapsed. It had already abandoned the northern half of China to the Tatars. In the 1200's, it lost the southern half as well to the Mongols, a warlike people akin to the Tatars. The destructive fury of the Mongols affected much of Asia and Europe. In China, the Mongols built a great empire.

Section REVIEW 1

Define: (a) gentry, (b) porcelain
Identify: (a) Sui dynasty, (b) Grand Canal, (c) T'ai-tsung, (d) T'ang dynasty, (e) Wu Chao, (f) Ch'ang-an, (g) Great Silk Road, (h) Battle of Talas, (i) Sung T'ai-tsu, (j) Sung dynasty, (k) Hangchow
Answer:
1. (a) What made the Sui dynasty important? (b) Why was it short-lived?
2. (a) How did Chinese officials earn their jobs? (b) What were the good points of this system? (c) The weaknesses?
3. (a) What part did the Tatars and the Hsia play in Chinese history? (b) What was the policy of the Sung toward them?
4. Describe the role of trade in China under the T'ang and Sung dynasties.
5. What political and military changes took place between T'ang and Sung times?
6. Describe three important inventions that the Chinese developed during the T'ang and Sung periods.

Critical Thinking
7. Explain why you agree or disagree with the following statement: "T'ang poetry and Sung painting share some basic values that were important in China."

The Mongols conquered a vast empire. 2

Who were the Mongols? To their enemies, they were "the devil's horsemen"—the ugliest, filthiest barbarians that ever lived. Of course, the Mongols saw themselves differently. In their own view, they were a noble people whose warlike, nomadic way of life was superior to the soft ways of city people. They felt nothing but contempt for the rich civilizations of India, China, and Persia.

Between 1200 and 1350, the Mongols conquered lands from the Pacific Ocean to the Adriatic Sea. Sweeping out of central Asia, they conquered much of the Islamic empire and destroyed Baghdad. They sent their armies westward to Russia, eastward to China, and south to the Himalayas. They ruled the largest unified land empire in history.

The Mongols came from the steppe.

The homeland of the Mongols was a vast grassland north of China's Great Wall. The hardy grasses there supported huge herds of horses, cattle, yaks, and sheep. Except for grass, the land was bare. One could travel for weeks without seeing a single tree. Savage winds swept the plain.

Mongolia lies at the eastern end of an enormous belt of **steppe**, or dry grassland, that stretches all across Asia and into eastern Europe. In this huge region lived a bewildering number of nomadic bands. You have already read some of their names—Huns, Avars, Turks, Tatars.

Whether called Hun, Tatar, or Mongol, the people of the eastern steppe followed basically the same way of life for centuries. They practically lived on horseback, following their huge herds of cattle, sheep, and horses over the steppe. They camped at night in great circular tents made of felt. Mare's milk was the one staple of their diet.

283

SECTION 2 Objectives and Teaching Strategies

OBJECTIVE 1. Identify the Eurasian Steppe as a geographic region.
Teaching Strategy: *Using Geographic Themes: Region* (page 276c)

OBJECTIVE 2. Identify Genghis Khan and list reasons the Mongols were successful conquerors.
Teaching Strategy: *Discussing History: The Mongol Success* (page 276c)

OBJECTIVE 3. Locate on a map the boundaries of the Mongol empire.
Teaching Strategy: *Geography in History: Mongol Conquests* (page 276c)

■ DISCUSSION

An Arab historian of the 1300's suggested the idea of cycles of warfare between the desert and the town. How were the early Arab armies examples of this conflict, first described in Chapter 2? The Turks? The Mongols?

SECTION 2 Resources

GEOGRAPHY
■ Transparency 45

REINFORCEMENT
■ Independent Practice 12.2

ENRICHMENT
■ Voices from the Past 12.2

ASSESSMENT
■ Section Quiz 12.2

■ BACKGROUND

Genghis Khan, orphaned in his teens, clawed his way to power by using bonds of personal loyalty. He chose key men and bound them to him as blood brothers.

As Mongol hordes swept westward over the central steppe, Genghis Khan expanded his army by forcing defeated Turks to fight for him.

The Mongols were fearsome warriors. Mounted on tough war ponies, their armies could cover great distances while living off the land. A Mongol warrior's most important weapon was his bow made of wood, horn, and sinew. Pulling the bow took over 100 pounds of force, and the Mongol archer pulled it while riding at a full gallop. He could hit an enemy over 200 yards away.

Genghis Khan united the Mongols.

For centuries, the Mongols had lived in loosely organized groups. Each group had its own leader, known as a **khan**. Around 1200, however, they suddenly united under the leadership of one of history's greatest conquerors. His name was Temujin (TEM-yoo-jin), but he is better known by his title, Genghis (JENG-gihs) Khan.

Temujin was born sometime around 1160. The first 20 years of his life were a struggle for survival. When he was 13, his father was murdered and Temujin nearly met the same fate at the hands of a rival Mongol family. However, he survived to become a minor chieftain.

Temujin spent the next 20 years fighting for power on the Mongolian steppe. He defeated his rivals one by one, showing no mercy. (After one victory, he slaughtered every person in the defeated group who was taller than a cart axle. Only the youngest children survived. They were brought up as his followers.)

In 1206, Temujin became the accepted ruler of all the steppe people. He took the title Genghis Khan, meaning "ruler of all between the oceans."

Between 1206 and his death in 1227, Genghis Khan conquered most of Asia.

Several traits lay behind Genghis Khan's stunning success as a conqueror. First, he was a brilliant organizer. He grouped his warriors in armies of 10,000, which in turn were organized into brigades of 1,000. Brigades were broken down into companies of 100, and companies were divided into 10-man platoons. Each group had its own commander. This organization meant that the army could carry out orders swiftly.

Second, Genghis Khan was shrewd as well as warlike. He never plunged recklessly into battle against an unknown enemy. He employed spies brilliantly to find out enemy weaknesses.

Finally, Genghis Khan used cruelty as a weapon. He believed in terrifying his enemies into surrender. If a city refused to open its gates to him, he might kill the entire population when he finally captured the place. The terror that the Mongols spread led many towns to surrender without a fight.

The Mongol empire divided.

Genghis Khan died in 1227, but the Mongol conquest continued. The sons and grandsons of Genghis Khan were responsible for the massacre of untold millions and the destruction of some of Asia's greatest cities. In about a 50-year period (1229–1279), they overthrew the Abbasid dynasty in Persia, burned Baghdad, conquered Kievan Russia, terrorized eastern Europe, and defeated China's Sung dynasty.

Mongol horsemen sharpened their riding skills in swift games of polo. Their small ponies were nimble enough for such games, but they were also hardy enough for long treks across the harsh lands of central Asia.

284

The Mongol Empire

ANSWERS TO

Map Study

Jerusalem, Baghdad; Khanate of the Golden Horde; Ilkhan empire; Empire of the Great Khan

Map Study

Name two cities that Marco Polo visited on his way to China. Which khanate controlled Russia? Persia? Korea?

Decisions in History

Japan's defeat of Kublai Khan left him with a hard decision. How could he increase his power? Should he concentrate on China? Attack Vietnam or Java? Invade Japan again? Expand westward? Which would you have advised, and why?

By 1259, there were four khans, each ruling a different part of the empire. One khan ruled the central steppes of Turkestan. A second held the lands of the fallen Islamic empire in Persia. A third ruled Russia. These three khans owed loyalty to the fourth khan, known as the Great Khan, who ruled China. As time went by, however, each khan became more and more independent.

Kublai Khan ruled China.

The conqueror of Sung China was Genghis Khan's grandson, Kublai (KOO-blye) Khan. He ruled China from 1260 to 1294, taking the Chinese name Yüan for his dynasty. Unlike his barbarian ancestors, Kublai Khan spent almost his entire life within China. Far from the Mongolian steppe, he did not share his ancestors' hatred for civilization. On the contrary, he rather enjoyed living in the luxurious manner of a Chinese emperor.

He ruled from a square capital in northern China that he called Khanbalik (City of the Great Khan). Today it is called Peking (Beijing).

Failure to conquer Japan Kublai Khan tried to extend his rule to Japan. In 1281, the Great Khan sent two fleets carrying a total of 150,000 warriors against Japan. It was the largest seaborne invasion force in history until World War II. The Japanese warriors fought the invaders to a standstill for 53 days. Suddenly, the sky darkened and a typhoon swept furiously across the Sea of Japan. Mongol ships were upended, swamped, and dashed to bits against the shore. Many Mongols drowned and others were quickly slain by the Japanese. For centuries afterward, the Japanese spoke reverently of the *kamikaze,* or "divine wind" that had saved Japan.

Marco Polo at the Mongol court Though warlike and cruel, the Mongols made the caravan routes across central Asia safe again for trade and travel. Ever since the decline of the T'ang dynasty, robbers and warring tribes had nearly shut down those routes. The Mongol empire put an end to such dangers. For about a century (1250–1350), Mongol armies kept peace across central Asia, just as Roman armies had once done around the Mediterranean Sea.

285

ANSWERS TO

Section Review 2

Define:
(a) dry grassland
(b) Mongol leader
(c) "divine wind"

(continued)

ANSWERS TO (continued)

Identify:
(a) ruled the largest unified land empire in history (b) leader who united Mongols (c) grandson of Genghis Khan and conqueror of Sung China (d) name of Kublai Khan's dynasty (e) served as an official in the court of Kublai Khan and spread information about China

Answer:

1. (a) nomadic (b) experienced in using bows while on horseback

2. organizational skill, shrewdness, cruelty

3. (a) most of Asia
(b) Persia, Baghdad, Kievan Russia, eastern Europe, China (c) central steppes of Turkestan, Persia, Russia, and China

4. made the caravan routes across Asia safe

5. Kublai Khan spent nearly his whole life in China and adopted many of its ways.

ANSWERS TO
Voice from the Past

1. square design, gates, street plan

2. Crowds and number of houses are greater than the mind can grasp, and suburbs have even more people than cities.

3. very important

4. laid out in squares, about the same size, same street plan; night curfew; both cities important trading centers

The most famous European to travel across Asia in these years was an Italian youth from Venice named Marco Polo. He was 17 when he set out from Venice with his father and uncle, who were on their second visit to Khanbalik. In 1275, after three years of travel, the Polos reached the court of Kublai Khan.

The shrewd khan made young Marco Polo a trusted official of the Mongol government. Nearly all the khan's highest officials were foreigners, because he distrusted the Chinese and kept them out of government. Polo served the Great Khan well for 17 years. He traveled across the Yellow and Yangtze rivers and returned with detailed reports of the empire. In 1292, two years before Kublai died, the Polos left China and made the long homeward journey to Venice by sea around Southeast Asia and India.

Captured in a war with the rival city of Genoa, Marco Polo had time in prison to tell the full story of his travels and adventures. To his awed listeners, he spoke of China's fabulous cities, its great armies, its fantastic wealth, and the strange things he had seen there. He mentioned the burning of "black stones" (coal) in Chinese homes. (Coal as a fuel was then unknown in Europe.) He told too of a new year's celebration in which the Great Khan received 100,000 white horses as a gift. He described a postal service in which 200,000 horses sped messages on paved roads between 10,000 relay stations. He told all these marvelous tales and more.

Voice from the Past | *The City of the Great Khan*

After Marco Polo was released from prison in Genoa, he spent the rest of his life quietly in Venice. He died in 1324 at the age of 70. According to legend, he was asked on his deathbed to take back the so-called tall tales in his book. He answered that he had told less than half the wonders he had seen on his travels. Here is his description of Khanbalik.

The new royal city is a perfect square, each of its sides being 6 miles long. The city wall has 12 gates, 3 on each side of the square. The whole city was laid out by line. The streets are so straight that if you stand at one gate, you can see the gate on the other side of the city.

The throngs of inhabitants and the number of houses in Khanbalik are greater than the mind can grasp. The suburbs have even more people than the city itself. Within each suburb, there are many hotels at which merchants can stay.

Everything that is most rare and valuable in the world finds its way to this city. This is particularly true for rich goods from India, such as precious gems, pearls, and spices. From other parts of Cathay [China] itself, at least 1,000 carriages and packhorses loaded with raw silk enter the city each day.

In the center of the city is a great bell, which is rung every night. After the third stroke, no one dares to be found on the streets, except for some emergency. In such necessary cases, the person is required to carry a light. Groups of 30 or 40 guards patrol the streets all night, looking for people who are out of their houses after the great bell has rung.

1. What features show that the city was carefully planned?
2. What evidence shows that Khanbalik was larger than cities in Europe?
3. How important was trade in Khanbalik's economy?
4. Compare this description to that of Ch'ang-an (page 279). How are the two cities alike?

Portrait of Kublai Khan

A fellow prisoner gathered Marco Polo's stories into a book. It was an instant success in Europe, but most readers did not believe a word of it. They thought Polo's account was a marvelous collection of tall tales. It was clear to Marco Polo, however, that the civilization he had visited was the greatest in the world.

Section REVIEW 2

Define: (a) steppe, (b) khan, (c) kamikaze
Identify: (a) Mongols, (b) Genghis Khan, (c) Kublai Khan, (d) Yüan, (e) Marco Polo
Answer:
1. (a) Describe the Mongols' way of life. (b) How did this way of life make them strong warriors?
2. List three factors that helped Genghis Khan conquer an empire.
3. (a) What conquests were made by Genghis Khan? (b) What did his descendants add to the empire? (c) Identify the four areas the khans ruled after 1259.
4. How did the spread of Mongol rule affect trade between Europe and Asia?

Critical Thinking
5. What evidence is there that the Chinese way of life influenced the Mongol conquerors?

China chose stability over change. 3

After Kublai Khan's death in 1295, Mongol rule weakened. Between 1295 and 1333, seven Mongols schemed and murdered their way to the Dragon Throne. China was beset by famines and revolts. The Yüan dynasty of the Mongols was near its end.

The Ming dynasty brought peace.

The bold leader who freed China from the Mongols was a commoner named Chu Yüan-chang (joo yoo-ahn-jang). Born into a peasant family in 1328, he was orphaned at the age of 16 and lived as a beggar. He entered a Buddhist monas-

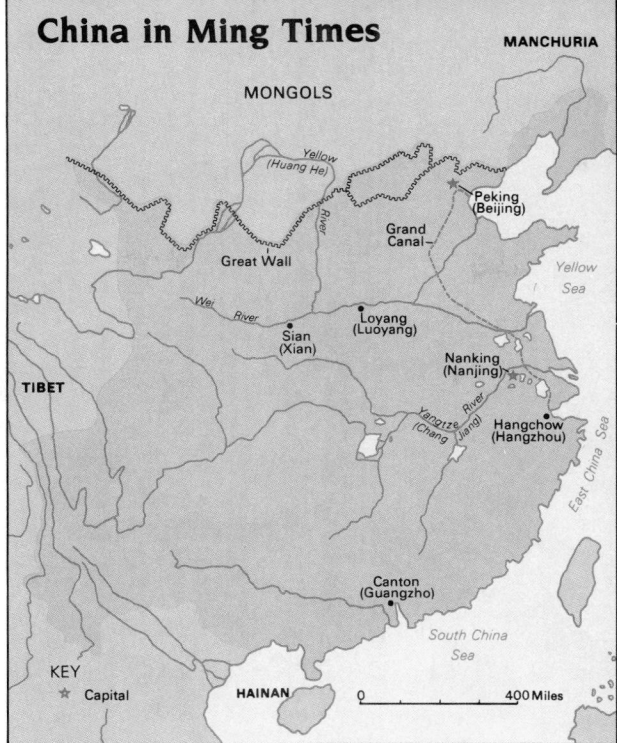

China in Ming Times

Map Study
What evidence shows that the Ming dynasty was more powerful than the Sung (map, page 281)?

tery where he learned to read and write. In 1352, Chu joined one of the secret groups resisting the Mongols. He proved to be a brilliant military leader. In 1368, Chu proclaimed himself the emperor of the new Ming (meaning "brilliant") dynasty. For himself, he took the name Ming T'ai-tsu, meaning "Grand Progenitor." By 1382, Ming T'ai-tsu had brought all of China under his rule.

China was divided into two major geographic zones. The southern, rice-growing zone followed the Yangtze River and centered on the seaports along the East China Sea. The northern zone was traditionally considered the true heartland of China. It had been the home of Confucius and of the Han and T'ang emperors. The first Ming emperor, Ming T'ai-tsu, was a southerner. He built his capital at Nanking (which meant "southern capital") on the Yangtze River and ruled there until his death in 1398.

Ming T'ai-tsu's son, Yung-lo, ruled from 1403 to 1424. He decided that he wished to rule from

287

SECTION 3
Objectives and Teaching Strategies

OBJECTIVE 1. Locate the boundaries of the Ming Empire.

Teaching Strategy: *Geography in History: Using Map Symbols* (page 276d)

OBJECTIVE 2. Identify and describe the Forbidden City.

Teaching Strategy: *Teaching with Pictures: The Forbidden City* (page 276d)

ANSWERS TO
Map Study

The Great Wall and the Grand Canal were longer; more cities had grown up.

SECTION 3
Resources

GEOGRAPHY
■ Transparency 46

REINFORCEMENT
■ Independent Practice 12.3

ENRICHMENT
■ Voices from the Past 12.3

ASSESSMENT
■ Section Quiz 12.3

Ming emperors such as Ch'eng-tsu (below) lived in the Forbidden City. The drawing above shows one of the city's hundreds of courtyards. Because the emperor stood for peace and harmony in China, the plan of the city emphasized balance, order, and symmetry.

the north, and he chose Kublai Khan's city of Khanbalik. Yung-lo gave Khanbalik a new name—Peking ("northern capital").

Peking was laid out in the traditional manner of a Chinese walled city. Gates facing north, south, east, and west pierced a high wall that enclosed the outer city. Broad avenues led from the outer gates to a smaller rectangular wall that surrounded the inner Imperial City. This city within a city was the center of routine government business.

Inside the Imperial City was yet another walled city with pagoda-like towers at its four corners. This was the Forbidden City—forbidden to everyone except the emperor and his court. Most residents of Peking lived and died without ever seeing what lay inside. The 250 acres of the Forbidden City held reception halls, private palaces, libraries, theaters, gardens, and athletic fields. More than 6,000 cooks prepared lavish meals for the 10,000 to 15,000 people who ate at the Court of Imperial Entertainments.

Ming scholars looked to the past.

From earliest times, the Chinese honored the ways of their ancestors. When a new dynasty came to power, its goal was not to bring new ways but to rule according to the good traditions of the past. Thus, China generally progressed by small adjustments, not by great changes.

The Ming emperors brought China's scholar-officials back to power. The Mongol emperors had deliberately excluded the scholar-officials (the gentry) from government. Ming T'ai-tsu restored the examination system (page 278).

Ming T'ai-tsu prized education so much that he opened public elementary schools in many cities. The use of printing made books easier to obtain in China than anywhere else in the world. Few rural children learned to read or write, but China's cities probably had a higher literacy rate than any other civilization in the 1300's.

To preserve the wisdom of the past, the second Ming emperor, Yung-lo, commissioned an encyclopedia of worthy Chinese writings from past ages. More than 2,000 scholars worked on the project for 4 years. When completed in 1408, the *Yung-lo Encyclopedia* filled 11,095 handwritten volumes. (The huge project was never printed.)

Turning Points in History

The Voyages of Cheng Ho Yung-lo's interests extended beyond the world of scholarship. He also supported a major program of naval expansion and exploration. During his reign, China became the greatest naval power in the world. Between 1405 and 1433, its great armada known as the Grand Fleet made seven voyages across the Indian Ocean.

The Grand Fleet must have inspired a sense of awe in everyone who saw it. The fleet included more than 100 ships, manned by 27,550 officers and men. The pride of the fleet was a group of ships known as treasure ships. The largest vessels in the world at that time, the treasure ships were more than 440 feet long and 180 feet wide. They weighed at least 1,500 tons—more than 15 times the weight of Portuguese ships. Armed with cannon and sailed by crews of almost 700 men, the treasure ships vividly symbolized China's power and ambition. That power reached its height in 1433, when the great admiral Cheng Ho led the fleet on its seventh voyage into the Indian Ocean.

Admiral Cheng Ho was pursuing diplomatic, commercial, and scientific objectives. As the emperor's personal ambassador, he met with the kings and sultans of southern Asia and East Africa and encouraged them to send tribute to the emperor. He also sought to expand China's trade. The immense hulls of the treasure ships were filled with highly prized porcelain, silks, lacquer ware, and art objects. These were exchanged for ivory, rhinoceros horns, pearls, and jewels. Finally Cheng Ho planned to survey new sea routes, collect rare animals, and search for new foods.

Cheng Ho must have felt a sense of great satisfaction when he ordered the Grand Fleet to turn eastward for its voyage home. More than 20 different realms and sultanates from the Indies to East Africa had established relations with the Chinese emperor. Merchants everywhere eagerly traded for Chinese goods. As a result, the ships brought back cargoes of rare treasures that would please the emperor and amuse the elegant ladies of the imperial court.

Despite this success, Cheng Ho's career was at an end. The Portuguese had begun to explore the African coast in hopes of reaching the Indies. Even if Cheng Ho had known of the Portuguese, he would have dismissed them with disdain. Portugal was a tiny country with only a million people. By Chinese standards, its export goods—wool, cloth, hats, strings of coral—were unimpressive. What could a mighty empire like that of China have to fear from a small country far on the western edge of Europe?

Nonetheless, 1433 marked a fateful turning point not only for China and Portugal but also for world history. In that year, when China's naval power reached its greatest height, it faced a sudden collapse. That decline began with Cheng Ho's death in 1434 and continued as new emperors opposed naval expeditions as wasteful extravagance. By 1500, it had become illegal to build large seagoing vessels. Even Cheng Ho's records were burned by a spiteful official who considered them "deceitful exaggerations of bizarre things far removed from the testimony of people's eyes and ears."

While China withdrew into isolation, Portugal advanced into a golden era of naval expansion and empire building. (See Chapter 15.) Just 64

289

(page 278). ... (See Chapter 15.)

■ BACKGROUND

The Ming exams were even more demanding than the T'ang and Sung. Those who passed the exams flaunted their success by flying red and gold silk banners from their homes.

In a poem celebrating Cheng-Ho's voyages, the poet tells of "barbarous" people in Java:
Strange the people are.
With unkempt heads and naked feet,
a barbarous tongue they speak;
dresses and hats they use not,
nor right nor virtue seek.

Cooperative Learning

Tell students that during the Ming dynasty, China lost its position as world leader in the fields of science and technology. Ask groups of three or four students to list measures the Chinese could have taken to prevent this loss of leadership. Then tell students that some people think the United States is in a similar position today. Ask group members to research this issue and list evidence that supports or refutes this opinion. Have them suggest measures the United States could take to maintain its leadership position in science and technology. Have spokespersons present their groups' conclusions for class discussion.

■ DISCUSSION

Remind students that the Chinese saw history as cyclical, not linear. What does this view of history imply about progress?

ANSWERS TO

Section Review 3

Define:
ability to read and write
Identify:
(a) freed China from the Mongols and became first Ming emperor (b) dynasty that followed Mongol rule (c) capital of Ming T'ai-tsu, on the Yangtze River (d) Yung-lo's northern capital (e) walled city inside Imperial City (f) commander of China's Grand Fleet (g) land to the north and east of China (h) name of Manchu dynasty
Answer:
1. (a) Ming T'ai-tsu's son, Yung-lo, wanted to rule from the north and chose Khanbalik, which he renamed. (b) Forbidden City was a walled city inside the Imperial City.

2. establishment of elementary schools, publication of an encyclopedia

3. abandonment of Grand Fleet

4. corrupt officials, lack of money, high taxes, hunger, peasant revolt, Manchu invasion

5. to be associated with splendor, to administer a huge domain

years after Cheng Ho's death, a Portuguese captain named Vasco da Gama circled Africa and entered the Indian Ocean. Already the memory of the Grand Fleet had faded there.

Sharp contrasts marked the outcomes of the Chinese and Portuguese naval programs. These outcomes symbolized the differences that divided western Europe and Asia at the beginning of the sixteenth century. Led by Portugal and Spain, western Europe turned outward in a vigorous program of scientific discovery and commercial growth. In contrast, China and other Asian civilizations turned inward in isolation. ▼

The Ming dynasty collapsed.

By 1600, the Ming had ruled for more than 200 years and the dynasty was weakening. Ming officials were corrupt. The government was out of money, despite crushing taxes. High taxes and bad harvests pushed millions of peasants toward starvation. Many were reduced to a homeless life of begging and banditry. As in the past, they joined secret societies and plotted revolt.

Dangers also threatened from outside China. To the north and east of China lay Manchuria (man-CHOOR-ee-uh). The people of that region were called the Manchus (MAN-chooz). Though the Chinese considered them barbarians, the Manchus had already adopted many Chinese ways. Indeed, they had set up a kingdom modeled after China. By the late 1500's, the Manchus were a threat on China's northern border.

Peasant revolt and Manchu invasion combined to bring down the Ming dynasty. As an army of peasant rebels approached Peking, the last Ming emperor despaired. "I have incurred the wrath of the gods on high," he wrote. "My ministers have deceived me. I am ashamed to meet my ancestors." Setting aside his brush, the emperor hanged himself from a locust tree. Thus, in 1644, the Ming dynasty ended.

A foreign dynasty took power.

Soon after the death of the last Ming emperor, Manchu armies entered China and took over Peking. The Manchu ruler was declared China's new emperor. As the Mongols had done, the Manchus took a Chinese name for their dynasty—the Ch'ing dynasty.

290

The Manchu conquerors tried to keep themselves separate from the Chinese people. Manchus could hold government positions without taking the civil service examinations. Marriage between Chinese and Manchus was barred. The Manchu rulers forced all Chinese men to braid their hair into a long pigtail as a sign of low status.

In most respects, however, life under the Ch'ing was much the same as life under the Ming. The Ch'ing dynasty ruled for more than two centuries (1644–1912). In Chapter 29, you will see how revolutionary changes began to transform Chinese society under the later Ch'ing rulers.

| Section **REVIEW** 3

Define: literacy
Identify: (a) Ming T'ai-tsu, (b) Ming dynasty, (c) Nanking, (d) Peking, (e) Forbidden City, (f) Cheng Ho, (g) Manchuria, (h) Ch'ing dynasty
Answer:
1. (a) How did Peking become the capital of China? (b) What was the difference between the Imperial City and the Forbidden City?
2. What factors encouraged learning in Ming China?
3. What evidence indicates that the Chinese lost interest in contacts abroad after 1433?
4. What factors, both within China and outside its borders, contributed to the downfall of the Ming dynasty?

Critical Thinking
5. Suggest some reasons why many Chinese rulers thought it important to build a grand capital city for their dynasty.

Japan developed a unique civilization. 4

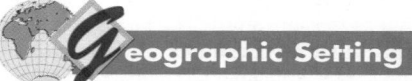

Geographic Setting

Japan lies east of China, in the direction of the sunrise. In fact, the name *Japan* comes from the Chinese words *jih pen,* which mean "origin of the sun." The islands of Japan are separated from China by 500 miles of ocean. The nearest part of the Asian mainland is Korea, across 100 miles of water. In their early history, the Japanese were close enough to feel the civilizing influence of China. Yet they were far enough away to be reasonably safe from invasion.

About 3,000 volcanic islands make up the Japanese island group, but many are very tiny. Most of Japan's people have always lived on the four largest islands: Hokkaido (hah-KYE-doh), Honshu (HAHN-shoo), Shikoku (shih-KOH-KOO), and Kyushu (kee-YOO-shoo).

Japan is about the size of California. The climate is temperate and the land is wooded. The islands are so mountainous, however, that only one fifth of the land is suitable for farming.

Clans dominated early Japan.

The first historic mention of Japan comes from Chinese writings of about A.D. 300. Archaeological evidence shows that people had lived in the Japanese islands for many centuries before that. However, because the early Japanese had no writing system, they left no historic records of their own.

Japan in the year 300 was not a united country. Instead, each **clan** controlled its own territory. A clan was a group of people who believed they were descended from the same ancestor.

The Yamato emperors The leading clan was the Yamato. The Yamato chiefs came to be called the emperors of Japan. Yet these emperors had no real power over the country as a whole. When rival clans fought for power, the winner gained control of the emperor and then ruled in the emperor's name.

The Shinto religion The Yamato rulers claimed the sun goddess as their ancestor. Other clans worshiped their own nature gods and goddesses. In different parts of Japan, people honored thousands of local gods and spirits. Their varied customs and beliefs eventually combined to form Japan's earliest religion. It was called Shinto (SHIHN-toh), meaning "the way of the gods."

The central idea of Shinto was the worship of nature. The sun goddess was the chief deity, but hundreds of lesser gods and spirits were thought to dwell in nature. Any unusual tree, rock, waterfall, or mountain was considered the home of a *kami*, or nature god.

The Japanese adapted Chinese ideas.

Around the year 500, the Japanese began to have more contact with mainland Asia. They were soon influenced by Chinese ideas and customs, about which they first learned from Korean travelers.

Buddhism in Japan For centuries, Korea had been in close touch with China. During the 500's, many Koreans migrated to Japan, bringing Chinese influences with them. One such group of Korean travelers brought with them a bronze statue of the Buddha. Within 50 years, the new religion had spread widely in Japan. For many centuries, the greatest Japanese scholars and sages lived as Buddhist monks.

The Japanese did not give up their Shinto faith. Shinto and Buddhism comfortably coexisted. Some Buddhist rituals became Shinto rituals, and some Shinto gods were worshiped in Buddhist temples.

Cultural borrowing The most influential convert to Buddhism was Prince Shotoku (shoh-toh-koo). In 607, Prince Shotoku sent a group of scholars to study Chinese civilization firsthand

Map Study

At the narrowest part of the sea, how far is Japan from Korea? From China? What sea lies east of Korea? West of Korea?

Japan, 1200–1600

291

SECTION 4 Objectives and Teaching Strategies

OBJECTIVE 1. Describe Japan's geography and explain its influence on Japanese culture.

Teaching Strategy: *Using Geographic Themes: Human-Environment Interaction* (page 276d)

OBJECTIVE 2. Explain how the Japanese adapted Chinese ideas.

Teaching Strategy: *Using Geographic Themes: Movement* (page 276d)

OBJECTIVE 3. Discuss aspects of daily life during the Heian age.

Teaching Strategy: *Discussing History: Life in Heian* (page 276d)

OBJECTIVE 4. Identify the samurai and explain the code of bushido.

Teaching Strategy: *Discussing History: The Samurai Warrior* (page 276d)

ANSWERS TO Map Study

about 200 miles; about 750 miles; Sea of Japan; Yellow Sea

SECTION 4 Resources

GEOGRAPHY
■ Transparency 47

REINFORCEMENT
■ Independent Practice 12.4

ENRICHMENT
■ Voices from the Past 12.4

ASSESSMENT
■ Section Quiz 12.4

■ BACKGROUND

The capital of Japan from 794 to 1868, Kyoto became a center of learning and the arts. A city of tradition, it is known for its Buddhist temples and Shinto shrines.

For a noble family in Japan, amusements included music, games, and writing poetry or love letters. The screen in the background, with its view of a landscape, shows the Chinese influence on Japanese art.

at Ch'ang-an. These scholars braved the dangers of shipwreck and storm without even a compass to guide them on the 500-mile voyage. Over the next 200 years, while the T'ang dynasty was at its height, the Japanese sent many such groups to learn more of Chinese ways.

The Japanese adopted the Chinese system of writing. Japanese artists painted landscapes in the Chinese manner. The gracefully curved, winglike roofs of Japan's Buddhist pagodas imitated Chinese roofs. The Japanese even followed Chinese styles in the simple arts of everyday living such as cooking, gardening, drinking tea, and hairdressing.

Imperial government For a time, Japan also modeled its government on China's. Prince Shotoku drew up a written plan of government based on the teachings of Confucius. Shotoku and his successors tried to build a strong central government like that of the T'ang rulers. Shotoku also tried to introduce China's examination system in Japan. However, the attempt failed. In Japan, noble birth remained the key to winning a powerful job. Unlike China, Japan continued to be a country where a few great families held power.

In imitation of Ch'ang-an, Japanese builders laid out a magnificent square city on the island of Honshu. This city, called Nara, was the first capital in Japanese history.

The Japanese adapted and changed Chinese ways to suit their own needs. While they learned much, they also retained their own traditions. Then, in the 800's, Japan's ruling family abruptly

broke contact with the T'ang court. Japanese leaders wanted nothing more from China. Japan's own culture was about to come into full flower.

CITY TOUR

Court society arose at Heian.

Nara was the Japanese capital from 710 to 784, less than a century. In 794, Emperor Kammu built a new capital called Heian (HAY-ahn), the modern Kyoto (kee-OHT-oh). Japan's golden age from 794 to 1185 is known as the Heian age.

"Dwellers among the clouds" In the year 800, most of Japan's 5 million people were farmers and fishers living in tiny villages. Heian itself had a population of about 100,000, of which only 3,000 belonged to the noble class. These families lived so far above the common people that they were called "dwellers among the clouds."

People of noble birth in Heian lived outdoors as much as possible. They gossiped and sipped tea around the fishponds in their gardens. A Japanese woman seated in her garden was as colorful as the surrounding cherry blossoms. She wore up to 12 silk gowns, one over the other. As breezes blew, the various colors flowed in shifting patterns. If one color was off by a mere shade, people at court might snicker about it.

Men and women alike used cosmetics heavily. They blackened their teeth because white teeth were considered ugly. They covered their faces

292

with white powder. Women plucked out their eyebrows and painted artificial brows high on their foreheads. Sometimes they gilded their lips. Men used perfumes as a mark of identification.

To be accepted in Heian society, one had to write poetry. To start a romance, a man or woman composed a short poem showing the writer's fine taste and artistry. The poem had to be written on a sheet of colored paper with a shade and texture that perfectly suited the feeling of the poem. The other person replied in the same way. If each person liked the other's poem, the man and woman went on with their flirtation. The slightest blunder with the brush might end the romance.

Leading women authors The best accounts of this elegant society come from the diaries, essays, and novels written by women of the court. The women writers of the Heian court were far more noteworthy than the male writers of the time.

Why? Two reasons have been suggested. First, Japanese women in the Heian Age were held in high esteem, unlike women in China or the Greco-Roman world. Men deferred to their artistic taste and their intellect. Second, Japanese men were bound by custom to use only Chinese characters when they wrote. Women wrote in a simpler script called *kana* that was better suited to the Japanese language. Thus, ideas flowed much more smoothly from a woman's brush.

The leading writer of this period was Lady Murasaki Shikibu (moo-rah-sah-kee shee-kee-boo). Around the year 1000, she wrote *The Tale of Genji,* which has been called the world's first true novel. It tells a long, involved story about the countless loves of its hero, Prince Genji, "the Shining Prince." A modern edition of it fills over 4,000 pages. Japanese scholars have so valued Lady Murasaki's masterpiece that their commentaries on it fill 10,000 volumes.

Feudal lords divided the land.

During the Heian Age, Japan's central government was strong. However, this strength was soon to be challenged by great landowners and clan chiefs who acted more and more as independent local rulers.

Between 1000 and 1200, Japan developed a feudal system much like the one in Europe during the Middle Ages. Each lord surrounded himself with a bodyguard of loyal warriors. Wars between rival lords became commonplace. Lesser lords pledged to fight for greater lords in exchange for protection. Peasants began to pay taxes to the lords, not to the central government.

The warriors who fought for the lords were called **samurai** (SAM-yuh-RYE), meaning "one who serves." The samurai lived according to a harsh code called **bushido,** which meant "the way of the warrior." A samurai's honor was constantly on the line. He had to prove his absolute courage in battle and absolute loyalty to his lord. Dying an honorable death was judged more important than living a long life.

A samurai's armor was one of the most elaborate costumes ever worn. It consisted of leather shinguards, billowing pantaloons, a kimono, broad thigh guards tied over the pantaloons, metal-cased shoulder guards, a chest protector, an iron collar, a cotton skullcap, an iron facemask, and a visored helmet. The samurai trained himself to get into this outfit in a minute. This armor weighed much less than the chain mail worn by European knights, and it provided good protection in battle.

Shoguns ruled puppet emperors.

By the 1100's, two clans, the Taira (tah-ee-rah) and the Minamoto (mee-nah-moh-toh), had gathered the largest armies of samurai. Up and down the island of Honshu, the armies of the two clans fought murderous battles. Heian was burned several times. After almost 30 years of fighting, the war ended in 1185 with a Minamoto victory.

In 1192, the emperor gave a Minamoto leader named Yoritomo the title of **shogun** (SHOH-guhn). The title meant "supreme general of the emperor's army." In effect, the shogun had the powers of a military dictator. Officials, judges, taxes, armies, roads—all were under his authority.

The emperor still lived in Kyoto, rebuilt on the ruins of Heian. Although the emperor enjoyed great prestige, the real center of power was at the shogun's military headquarters at Kamakura. The 1200's are known in Japanese history as the Kamakura shogunate. The system of central government led by the shoguns lasted in Japan until 1868, nearly 700 years.

Under the early shoguns, the local lords still held great power. Instead of trying to wipe out

293

■ **DISCUSSION**
Have students compare and contrast the samurai and the medieval knight.

ANSWERS TO

Section Review 4

Define:
(a) group of people who believed they were descended from the same ancestor **(b)** nature god **(c)** simple script used by Japanese women writers **(d)** warriors who fought for feudal lords **(e)** "the way of the warrior" **(f)** military dictator

Identify:
(a) leading clan of early Japan **(b)** chief religion of early Japan **(c)** convert to Buddhism, largely responsible for spreading Chinese influence in Japan

(continued)

ANSWERS TO (continued)

(d) Japanese capital from 710 to 784 **(e)** old name for Kyoto; name of Japan's golden age **(f)** modern city, formerly Heian **(g)** author of *The Tale of Genji* **(h)** name of clan whose leader was first to be named shogun **(i)** site of shogun's military headquarters

Answer:

1. (a) 500 miles east of China **(b)** mountainous islands about the size of California; temperate climate; wooded; only one fifth of land suitable for farming

2. (a) writing system, landscape painting, architecture, arts of everyday living, government **(b)** tried to introduce examination system and build a strong central government

3. (a) golden age when Heian was capital of Japan **(b)** Nobles lived an elegant life, outdoors as much as possible. They dressed in colorful clothes, used cosmetics heavily, and wrote poetry.

4. (a) Each lord had bodyguard of loyal warriors. Lesser lords fought for greater lords in exchange for protection. **(b)** lived by harsh code of honor, courage, and loyalty

5. (a) powers of a military dictator **(b)** Early shogunates built upon feudal system.

6. (a) Both were normally ruled by an emperor. **(b)** Differences: In Japan, the emperor had little real power. Japan was a country where noble birth was necessary to winning power, and only a few great families held power. Japan had long periods of rule by military dictators called shoguns.

In addition to this impressive suit of armor, a samurai wore two razor-sharp swords as symbols of his profession and high rank.

feudalism, the Kamakura shoguns chose to build upon it. They worked with the local lords. A lord who loyally served the shogun was given almost a free hand to rule his own province.

The Kamakura shoguns were strong enough to turn back the two naval invasions sent by the great Mongol ruler Kublai Khan in 1274 and 1281 (page 285). However, the Japanese victory over the Mongols drained the shogun's treasury. Loyal samurai were bitter when the government failed to pay them. The Kamakura shoguns lost prestige and power. Samurai attached themselves more closely to their local lords, who soon fought one another as fiercely as they had fought the Mongols. Civil war shook the land.

Define: (a) clan, (b) kami, (c) kana, (d) samurai, (e) bushido, (f) shogun
Identify: (a) Yamato, (b) Shinto, (c) Shotoku, (d) Nara, (e) Heian, (f) Kyoto (g) Murasaki Shikibu, (h) Minamoto, (i) Kamakura
Answer:

1. (a) Where is Japan located? (b) Give a brief geographic description of Japan.
2. (a) Name at least five things the Japanese borrowed from China. (b) What did Shotoku do to make Japan more like China?
3. (a) What was the Heian Age? (b) Briefly describe Heian society.
4. (a) How was Japan's feudal system organized? (b) What were the most important characteristics of the samurai?
5. (a) What powers did the shoguns have? (b) How did the shogunate affect feudalism in Japan?

Critical Thinking

6. Compare Japan's system of government to that of China. (a) Why might a casual observer think the two were similar? (b) What were the fundamental differences?

Japan turned to isolation. 5

A Japanese Buddhist once wrote, "The proud do not last long, but vanish like a spring night's dream. And the mighty ones too will perish, in the end, like dust before the wind." Japan's history from 1300 to 1600 was filled with the rise and fall of proud and mighty lords.

Feudal lords controlled Japan.

After the decline of the Kamakura shoguns, the most powerful of the feudal lords became nearly independent rulers in their own areas. They were known as **daimyo** (DYE-mee-OH), which means "great name." Each daimyo commanded his own army of sword-wielding soldiers. Peasants as well as samurai took up arms. Dangerous bands of lordless samurai roamed the land.

The years from 1467 to 1568 were known as the Age of the Country at War. Rival armies repeatedly attacked and burned Kyoto, the imperial capital. The powerless emperors lived in poverty amid the ruins of their city. (One emperor was so poor that, when he died, his burial was delayed for six weeks until money could be scraped up for a funeral.) Disorder spread through the country. At the same time, Japanese pirates terrorized both their own seacoast and the coastal cities of southern China.

Europeans reached Japan.

The first European ships arrived in Japan in 1543, during this time of fighting and disorder. As in China, these first Europeans were Portuguese. Unlike China, Japan had no strong central government to bar or limit contact with Europeans. Thus, some daimyo welcomed the first Portuguese merchants and missionaries. If one daimyo turned against the Europeans, they could always find another daimyo to help them.

The Japanese looked with amusement at the Portuguese sailors, who dressed in button-down jackets and baggy trousers, or pantaloons. The Japanese called the strange-looking newcomers *nampan*, meaning "southern barbarians." As other ships arrived on their coast, the Japanese received the visiting nampan (mainly Portuguese and some Dutch) with courtesy. Japanese merchants eagerly traded silks for guns. For a brief time (around 1600), rich daimyo thought it stylish to wear pantaloons, smoke tobacco, and play cards in the European manner.

From swords to guns The novelty that most intrigued the Japanese were the Europeans' guns. One Japanese writer described his experiment with a musket:

> Set up a small white target on a bank, grip the object [musket] in your hand, compose your body, and closing one eye, apply fire to the hole. The pellet hits the target squarely. The explosion is like lightning and the report like thunder. Bystanders must cover their ears.

Japanese craftsmen quickly learned how to make guns in their own workshops. Power-hungry daimyo began to equip their troops with muskets and bullets.

Catholic missionaries As in China, Catholic missionaries came to Japan close on the heels of European merchants. The leader of the first Christian mission to Japan later became one of the Church's most beloved saints, Francis Xavier (ZAY-vee-uhr). During Xavier's two years in Japan (1549–1551), he baptized hundreds of converts.

For almost 90 years, Catholic missionaries traveled freely in Japan. With amazement, they noted the Japanese habit of taking daily baths. (In Europe at this time, people rarely washed.) With some shame, the missionaries tried to change their own European table manners because these offended the Japanese. "They are much amazed," wrote one priest, "at our eating with the hands and wiping them on napkins, which then remain covered with food stains, and this causes them disgust."

Strong leaders restored order.

Soon after the Europeans arrived, a series of determined rulers strengthened Japan's central government. In the 1560's, a ruthless daimyo named Oda Nobunaga (oh-dah noh-boo-nah-gah) used firearms to defeat armies ten times larger than his own. He entered Kyoto in triumph in 1573. Nobunaga won and held the area around Kyoto, although he did not control all Japan.

After Nobunaga was assassinated by one of his own generals in 1582, two other ruthless but able men completed the process of uniting Japan. First Nobunaga's best general, Toyotomi Hideyoshi (toh-yoh-toh-mee hee-deh-yoh-shee), killed the assassin. Then Hideyoshi went on to win control over the shogunate at Kyoto. Many Japanese historians regard him as the greatest of their country's founding fathers. Although he never took the title of shogun, Hideyoshi was in fact the absolute ruler of Japan.

In 1588, Hideyoshi ordered a "sword hunt," in which he commanded all peasants to surrender their swords. Other decrees set up strict barriers between social classes. Hideyoshi himself had risen from common foot soldier to ruler of the country, but he did not intend for others to follow that path. Never again could a peasant or merchant hope to wear the armor of a samurai.

Hideyoshi's armies crushed any daimyo who defied him. He even had ambitions to conquer Ming China. However, his armies were defeated

295

SECTION 5
Objectives and Teaching Strategies

OBJECTIVE 1. Describe the impact of the Portuguese on Japan.

Teaching Strategy: *Using Geographic Themes: Movement* (page 276e)

OBJECTIVE 2. Identify Oda Nobunaga, Toyotomi Hideyoshi, and Tokugawa Ieyasu and explain how they unified Japan.

Teaching Strategy: *Discussing History: The Three Unifiers* (page 276e)

OBJECTIVE 3. Define Zen Buddhism and give examples of its influence on Japanese culture.

Teaching Strategy: *Teaching with Pictures: Zen Gardens* (page 276e)

■ BACKGROUND

Guns seemed so valuable to the Japanese that one metalsmith is said to have given his daughter in marriage to a Portuguese captain to get the secret of making guns.

Nobunaga's killer also burned down his palace. A European wrote, "Of this man, who made everyone tremble not only at the sound of his voice but even at the mention of his name, there did not remain even a small hair that was not reduced to ashes."

SECTION 5
Resources

ASSESSMENT
- Section Quiz 12.5

REINFORCEMENT
- Independent Practice 12.5

ENRICHMENT
- Voices from the Past 12.5

A favorite Japanese story: If a cuckoo failed to sing, Nobunaga would kill it. Hideyoshi would invite it to sing. Ieyasu would simply wait until the cuckoo did sing.

Cooperative Learning

Tell students they are going to be book reviewers. They have just read a biography of one of the three great rulers of Japan: Oda Nobunaga, Toyotomi Hideyoshi, or Tokugawa Ieyasu. Form groups of three or four students to write book reviews of the "biography" they have just read.

Groups must first choose the ruler they wish to study. Each group member should then choose one aspect of the ruler's life, reign, or legacy to research. After the research is completed, students should develop an article detailing the highlights, as if from a biography. You may wish to bring in some published book reviews so students can imitate their style. Every student in the group must participate in the project, either writing portions of the articles or compiling maps or pictures.

Groups should present their book reviews to the class. Remind students that the object of a book review is to interest others in reading the book.

in Korea in 1597. The great Hideyoshi died a year later of natural causes.

The last of Japan's three unifiers was Tokugawa Ieyasu (toh-koo-gah-wah ee-yeh-yah-soo), one of Hideyoshi's strongest supporters. In 1600, Ieyasu defeated his rivals at the Battle of Sekigahara. He assumed the title of shogun in 1603. He then moved Japan's administrative center east to the small town of Edo, later named Tokyo.

To keep the daimyo from rebelling, Ieyasu required that they spend at least half their time at his capital. Even when they returned to their lands, they had to leave their families in Edo.

Ieyasu founded the Tokugawa shogunate. On his deathbed in 1616, Ieyasu advised his son and successor, "Take care of the people. Strive to be virtuous. Never neglect to protect the country." For the most part, his advice was well followed. Tokugawa shoguns gave Japan stability until 1868.

Japan's door slammed shut.

By 1600, as many as 300,000 Japanese (out of a population of 20 million) had become Christian. The growing influence of the missionaries worried Japan's leaders. Hideyoshi threatened Christians with banishment. Ieyasu, the Tokugawa shogun, was alarmed by reports that the Spanish had conquered an island in the Philippines. Might these aggressive Europeans soon turn their guns against Japan? Might the missionaries plot with Japanese Christians to overthrow him?

In 1614, Ieyasu banned Christianity in Japan. Over the next 20 years, Tokugawa officials rounded up Christians and subjected them to torture and execution. In 1638, about 36,000 Japanese Christians made a final, desperate stand behind the walls of an old fortress. Their futile defense ended tragically. Only 105 of the Christians came out alive.

The Tokugawa shoguns also banned all European merchants except the Dutch. Earlier the Chinese had limited European traders to Macao. The Japanese now confined Dutch merchants to the port of Nagasaki. For the next 200 years, Japan remained closed to Europeans.

The Tokugawa policy of isolation from Europe had far-reaching effects on Japan. Gradually, Japan fell behind Europe in science, technology, and military power. On the other hand, isolation gave Japan a long period of peace and stability. During

296

Cause and Effect

JAPANESE ISOLATIONISM

Contributing Factors

Spread of Christianity
Growing influence of foreign missionaries
Spanish conquest in the Philippines

Immediate Causes

Rise to power of Tokugawa shogunate
Fear of European aggression

TOKUGAWA POLICY OF ISOLATION

Banning of Christianity
Banning of European merchants

Effects

Peace and stability
Growth of unique Japanese culture
Failure of Japan to keep up with scientific, technical, and military progress

the years of the Tokugawa shogunate, Japanese culture was rich and creative. Buddhist monks developed a unique religious outlook, and artists perfected an exquisite style of painting.

Zen Buddhism stressed meditation.

Buddhism in Japan followed a path of quiet contemplation. *Zen* was the Japanese word for meditation. Though there were other forms of Buddhism in Japan, Zen Buddhism had the greatest influence on Japanese culture.

Zen Buddhists seek spiritual enlightenment through meditation. Strict discipline of mind and body was the Zen path to wisdom. Young monks would sit rigidly for hours, staring straight ahead with unblinking eyes. If they fidgeted or showed signs of losing concentration, a Zen master might

Zen monks (left) seek enlightenment through meditation. In a Zen garden (right), sand patterns, carefully chosen rocks, and subtle blends of leaf color and texture provide a tranquil setting for meditation.

shout at them and beat them with a stick. Some Zen masters helped their disciples to free themselves from ordinary ways of thinking by asking unanswerable riddles. The master might say, for example, "When both hands are clapped, they make a sound. What is the sound of one hand clapping?"

Art suggested nature.

Japanese paintings, like tea, were made for meditation and spiritual enlightenment. Japanese artists followed the style of painting that arose in China under the Sung dynasty (page 281). Japan's greatest master of the Sung style was a Zen monk named Sesshu (sehs-shoo), who worked during the late 1400's. Sesshu's most famous surviving work is a silk scroll 55 feet long. It shows the four seasons in shades of black, white, and gray. To appreciate this great work, one must roll it open slowly and meditate on the differences between appearances and reality with each passing image of tree and rock.

Nature played a key role both in Japanese art and in Zen meditation. During the 1400's, a small garden of jagged rocks and clipped shrubs became a common feature of the Zen temple. These gardens had symbolic meaning. Instead of seeing merely a gray rock surrounded by raked white pebbles, a Zen meditator might see a lofty mountain peak towering above a vast sea. The garden was always starkly simple. As one gardener-artist of medieval Japan warned, "Take caution not to . . . overcrowd the scenery to make it more

interesting. Such an effect often results in a loss of dignity and a feeling of vulgarity."

The artistic traditions that developed during Japan's period of isolation had lasting importance for the country. For 200 years, Japan was able to continue on its own path, with little influence from the outside world.

Section REVIEW 5

Define: (a) daimyo, (b) nampan
Identify: (a) Francis Xavier, (b) Oda Nobunaga, (c) Toyotomi Hideyoshi, (d) Tokugawa Ieyasu, (e) Zen, (f) Sesshu
Answer:
1. Describe the political situation in Japan during the 1400's and 1500's.
2. (a) When did the first Europeans reach Japan? (b) How were they received?
3. What part did each of the following play in unifying Japan? (a) Oda Nobunaga (b) Toyotomi Hideyoshi (c) Tokugawa Ieyasu
4. (a) What was Tokugawa Ieyasu's policy toward the daimyo? (b) Toward Europeans?
5. (a) What policy did later Tokugawa shoguns adopt toward other countries? (b) How did this policy affect Japan?

Critical Thinking
6. (a) How did Japanese policy toward Christianity change between the 1550's and the early 1600's? (b) Give several reasons to explain this change.

297

ANSWERS TO
Section Review 5

Define:
(a) feudal lord who became a nearly independent ruler
(b) Japanese name for Portuguese sailors
Identify:
(a) leader of first Christian mission to Japan (b) ruthless daimyo who began the process of uniting Japan
(c) successor to Nobunaga, regarded as greatest of Japan's founders (d) last of Japan's unifiers (e) meditation
(f) Zen monk and artist
Answer:
1. Rival armies attacked and burned the capital; disorder spread through the country.
2. (a) 1543 (b) with amusement and courtesy
3. (a) conquered and ruled area around and including Kyoto (b) conquered daimyos who defied him, set up strict class divisions
(c) completed unification
4. (a) required them to spend half their time in Edo to keep them from rebelling
(b) banned Christianity and merchants except Dutch
5. (a) isolation from European countries (b) Japan had a long period of peace but fell behind Europe in science, technology, and military power.
6. (a) In early days, policy allowed Christians to travel about and make converts; later, policy banned Christianity. (b) feared Christians might side with Europeans in case of invasion, influence of missionaries

Concluding the Chapter

1. **Chapter Closer**
   Have students compare the development of China and Japan between the years 300 and 1650. Students should identify major similarities and differences.

2. **Reteaching Activities**
   a. Making a Chart Ask students to make a chart on the Chinese dynasties studied in this chapter. The chart should include these headings: *Name of Dynasty, Period of Rule, Major Contributions,* and *Causes of Decline.*
   b. Making a Time Line Have students make a time line showing the key events in Japanese history discussed in this chapter.
   c. Identifying Historical Figures List the following names on the board, and ask students to identify each: T'ai-tsung, Empress Wu, Genghis Khan, Marco Polo, T'ai-tsu, Cheng Ho, Prince Shotoku, Lady Murasaki, Francis Xavier, and Tokugawa Ieyasu.

Answers to Chapter Review appear on pages 276e–276f.

Chapter Review 12

Summary

1. Two great dynasties ruled China. After the Sui reunited China in the late 500's, the country experienced a golden age. The T'ang, noted for poetry, expanded the examination system. Printing, the compass, and gunpowder were invented. The Sung dynasty, noted for its art, moved the capital to southern China.

2. The Mongols conquered a vast empire. After Genghis Khan united the nomadic Mongols, they conquered most of Asia. China's ruler, Kublai Khan, encouraged trade and hired non-Chinese officials. Among them was Marco Polo, whose tales increased European interest in Asia.

3. China chose stability over change. The Ming dynasty at first encouraged trade but later limited foreign contacts. Under the Ming, traditional values were stressed. The Manchus, who succeeded the Ming, followed similar policies.

4. Japan developed a unique civilization. From the 500's to the 800's, Japan borrowed heavily from Chinese culture. Japan enjoyed a golden age, especially for literature, during the Heian period. Gradually, powerful landowners built up samurai armies in a feudal system. A shogun replaced the emperor as effective ruler.

5. Japan turned to isolation. Following the Kamakura shoguns, strong local lords called daimyo challenged the authority of the shogun. After a period of disorder, Japan was reunited. Under the Tokugawa shoguns, Japan cut off European contacts and banned Christianity. During this time, Japan fell behind Europe in science, technology, and military power.

Reviewing the Facts

1. Define the following terms:
   a. gentry
   b. steppe
   c. khan
   d. clan
   e. samurai
   f. bushido
   g. shogun
   h. daimyo

2. Explain the importance of each of the following names, places, or terms:
   a. Sui
   b. T'ang
   c. Ch'ang-an
   d. Buddhism
   e. Sung
   f. Great Silk Road
   g. Mongolia
   h. Genghis Khan
   i. Kublai Khan
   j. Marco Polo
   k. Khanbalik
   l. Ming
   m. Peking
   n. Ch'ing
   o. Shinto
   p. Heian
   q. *The Tale of Genji*
   r. Francis Xavier
   s. Tokugawa Ieyasu

Koreans bring Buddhism to Japan
Sui dynasty reunites China
Heian Age begins in Japan
Kamakura shoguns repel Mongol invasion
Kublai Khan rules China; Polos reach China
Genghis Khan conquers Asia
Manchus conquer China
Europeans reach East Asia
Daimyo control Japan
Last voyage of Cheng Ho

T'ang dynasty   Sung dynasty   Ming dynasty

500   700   900   1100   1300   1500   1700

298

3. (a) How did a person become a member of the gentry in China? (b) What benefits did that position bring?
4. What major T'ang inventions became important outside China?
5. (a) What methods did the Mongols use to build an empire? (b) What areas did they conquer?
6. (a) What was the Japanese attitude toward Europeans in the early 1500's? (b) After 1600?

Basic Skills

1. **Comparing maps** Compare the size of the Mongol Empire, shown on page 285 with that of Alexander the Great, shown on page 124. Use the scale of miles to estimate their length from east to west, their width in the center, and their area (length times width). How much larger was the Mongol empire?
2. **Making a time line** Make a time line to show Mongol expansion in Russia to the west and in China and Japan to the east. Indicate the dates of major expansion, consolidation of empire, and checks to Mongol expansion or control.
3. **Making a chart** Make a chart to show the various achievements of the T'ang, Sung, and Ming dynasties, using a column for each. For the vertical rows, use the following headings: *Political, Economic, Cultural,* and *Social.* Fill in the appropriate information.

Researching and Reporting Skills

1. **Using reference books** Locate in your library the reference work called *Books in Print.* Information is listed in separate volumes for book titles, authors, and subject. Using the "Subject" volume, look up books on the early history of Japan. Give the titles and authors of at least five books in which you might find information about Japanese shoguns and samurai.
2. **Writing an essay** Use the chart on the T'ang, Sung, and Ming dynasties to evaluate them. (a) Which civilization do you think was superior? (b) Write a brief essay expressing your opinion and providing supporting evidence.
3. **Formulating research questions** Buddhism had great influence in both Chinese and Japanese civ-

ilization. What questions would provide a framework for learning more about Buddhist influence on those societies?

Critical Thinking

1. **Comparing** (a) Compare the feudal system of medieval Europe with that in Japan between 1300 and 1600. (b) How did the two systems develop, and how did they end?
2. **Identifying viewpoints** (a) How did the Chinese look upon the Mongols? (b) How did the Mongols look upon the Chinese? (c) How would you characterize the Mongols?
3. **Drawing conclusions** This chapter describes the rise and fall of four Chinese dynasties. (a) What recurring patterns occur in the decline of these dynasties? (b) What advice might you give a Chinese emperor, based on these patterns?
4. **Synthesizing** (a) Identify and list some of the common characteristics found in Chinese and Japanese art through the ages. (b) Discuss what influences may have had this effect.

Perspectives on Past and Present

1. What reasons did Japan have for its policy of isolation? What countries today place strict limits on trade and foreign contact? What advantages and disadvantages do you see in such a policy?
2. In China, long fingernails and bound feet became fashionable. Why were these styles regarded as signs of wealth and status? What are some modern examples of status symbols?

Investigating History

1. One of the vital connections between East and West was the Great Silk Road. Look for information on this trade route in historical atlases, college texts, *National Geographic* magazine, or other sources available to you. Describe the cities and landscapes a traveler would encounter along this road. How did the road change over time? What other uses did it have besides trade?
2. Read Marco Polo's description of China in the time of Kublai Khan. Write a brief report explaining why his fellow Venetians would have trouble believing what he described.

299

CHAPTER
Evaluation

Chapter Test 12, Alternate Chapter Test 12, and Computer Test Bank Chapter 12 Test can be used to evaluate your students' understanding of this chapter.

Civilizations of India and Southeast Asia

Chapter Overview

After the Mauryan dynasty fell in 180 B.C., India was beset by 500 years of invasions until the Gupta dynasty ushered in a golden age in northern India. Science, learning, and the arts thrived. Under constant attack by the Huns, the dynasty disappeared during the 600's and six centuries of turmoil ensued. First, Rajput warrior-kings ruled in northern India. They became Hindu converts and built kingdoms and great temples. In the 700's, wars between Hindus and Muslims ended in Muslim rule by the Delhi sultans. Tamerlane, a Turkish-Mongol conqueror from central Asia, destroyed Delhi in 1398 but failed to build an empire that outlasted his life. Turkish sultans ruled from a rebuilt Delhi, but none was able to dominate India. In 1526, Babur, another Turkish-Mongol conqueror, ended the Delhi sultanate and established the Mughal dynasty. The Mughals were Muslim, although early Mughal rulers tolerated other religions. However, later Mughal rulers oppressed non-Muslims and left a heritage of bitter religious conflict. Europeans reached India in 1498 and began setting up strong bases along the major Asian sea lanes.

Except in Vietnam, where China's influence was strong, Indian culture was the main influence in Southeast Asia, the area that today includes Burma, Laos, Cambodia, Thailand, Vietnam, Malaysia, and Indonesia. In this region of diverse languages and cultures, control of harbors and trade routes was the key to power. The Khmers built the longest-lasting empire in this region where many kingdoms rose and fell. Between the 1200's and 1400's, Muslim traders introduced the religion of Islam, which soon became important along with Hinduism and Buddhism.

Chapter Focus

Ask students to name the most beautiful building they have ever seen. Then direct their attention to the picture of the Taj Mahal (page 300) and ask how the Taj Mahal compares with the building they have selected. Explain that the Taj Mahal was built by Shah Jahan to honor his wife Mumtaz Mahal's last request—to build a monument that expressed "the eternal wonder of the power of love." After students read the description of the Taj Mahal on pages 300–301, explain that the Taj Mahal is more than an expression of love. It is also a symbol of the two religions—Hinduism and Islam—that together shaped Indian history from 300 to 1700. This chapter begins with a discussion of a dynasty of Hindu rulers who created a golden age of Indian culture. It then describes how the Muslims conquered India and produced a golden age of their own. The chapter concludes with a discussion of the kingdoms that arose in Southeast Asia.

Advance Planner

Chapter 13 Civilizations of India and Southeast Asia 300–1700

FOCUS   The Taj Majal as a symbol of forces that shaped Indian history

★ **Advanced**
● **Basic**

	SECTION 1	SECTION 2	SECTION 3
Objectives	1. Identify scientific advances made by Gupta scholars. 2. Describe the Ajanta temples. 3. Explain how the Hindus and Muslims became fierce rivals.	1. Identify Akbar and describe his achievements. 2. Compare and contrast the extremes of wealth and poverty in the Mughal empire. 3. Locate strategic bases in the Indian Ocean trade and explain their significance to the Portuguese.	1. Label the major rivers, bodies of water, and countries of Southeast Asia. 2. Identify and describe Angkor Wat. 3. Describe the impact of Chinese influence on the Vietnamese.
Setting the Stage	Comparing the Mauryan and Gupta empires Transparency 8 Transparency 48	India as a land of contrasts Transparency 49	Stereotypes of Vietnam
Teaching Strategies	Discussing History: The Achievements of Indian Science Teaching with Pictures: The Ajanta Caves Relating Past and Present: Conflict between Hindus and Muslims Check for Understanding	Discussing History: Akbar, the "Very Great" Mughal Skill Building: Comparing and Contrasting Using Geographic Themes: Location Check for Understanding	Geography in History: Strategic Waterways of Southeast Asia Transparency 50 Outline Map 24 Teaching with Pictures: Angkor Wat Discussing History: China and Vietnam Check for Understanding
Guided Practice	Transparency 48 Q&A Section Review 1	Transparency 49 Q&A Section Review 2	Transparency 50 Q&A Section Review 3
Independent Practice Worksheets	Independent Practice 13.1 Vocabulary 13	Independent Practice 13.2 Basic Skills 13 Critical Thinking 13	Independent Practice 13.3
Enrichment	1. Primary Source: Voices 13.1 2. Reading a Play 3. Researching for Points	1. Primary Source: Voices 13.2 2. Preparing a Report: Mughal Rulers 3. ★Solving a Riddle 4. Researching for Points	1. Primary Source: Voices 13.3 2. Preparing a Report: Angkor Wat 3. Researching for Points

Chapter Closer	●**Reteaching Activities**	Summarizing, Making a Time Line, Finding Main Ideas
	Chapter Review	Summary, Reviewing the Facts, Basic Skills, Researching and Reporting Skills, Critical Thinking, Perspectives on Past and Present, Investigating History
	Chapter Evaluation	Chapter Test 13, Alternate Chapter Test 13, Computer Test Bank Chapter 13 Test

India flourished under the Guptas. 1

Setting the Stage

Display Map Transparency 8, *India under the Mauryan Dynasty,* and ask students to identify the Mauryans. Explain that 500 years of disunity followed the end of the Mauryan dynasty. Now show Map Transparency 48, *The Gupta Empire.* Describe how the Gupta dynasty conquered a mighty empire that ruled northern India during the fourth and fifth centuries. This section describes the achievements of the Gupta dynasty.

Teaching Strategies

Discussing History: The Achievements of Indian Science (Objective 1) Begin by writing "XXXIV + LIX = ?" and "34 + 59 = ?" on the board. Ask students which equation is easier to solve. Have students suggest advantages of Arabic numerals. (place value system, use of zero as a place holder) Explain that Europeans called the concepts zero to nine Arabic numerals because Arabs brought the symbols and the number system to Europe. Point out that, during the Gupta period, Hindu mathematicians were actually the first to use a system of numbers based on ten. Have students read "Science and learning advanced" (page 302) to find out what other intellectual advances were made. Students might be interested to learn that Indians discovered the process for twisting cotton fibers into a fine thread. Arabs called the light-weight Indian fabric *quittan*— hence our word *cotton*. The fabrics we call cashmere, calico, chintz, and dungaree were also first worn in India.

Teaching with Pictures: The Ajanta Caves (Objective 2) Direct students' attention to the picture of the Ajanta caves (page 303). Explain that the caves are actually 29 tunnels cut at regular intervals into a granite cliff. Each tunnel penetrates the rock to a depth of about 65 feet. The caves contain well-preserved murals illustrating Buddha's life and incarnations. Colonies of Buddhist monks once slept on stone pillows that lined a series of small chambers. Everything in the cave—statues, columns, living quarters—was chiselled from the cliff wall. Tell students that the last caves were created in the seventh century, just as India's golden age was coming to an end. The abandoned caves were not rediscovered until the nineteenth century.

Relating Past and Present: Conflict between Hindus and Muslims (Objective 3) Have students examine the map of modern South Asia (page 773). Explain that Pakistan and Bangladesh are Muslim nations; India is a Hindu nation. Point out that this modern division has its roots in the conflict between Hindus and Muslims that began during the 700's. Have students read "Hindus and Muslims met in war" and "Muslim sultans ruled from Delhi" (page 303). Ask students why Muslims and Hindus developed such a bitter conflict. Explain that religious differences were at the center of the conflict. Muslim conquerors such as Mahmud of Ghazni plundered Indian temples and destroyed centuries' worth of work.

Check for Understanding Have students explain the significance of each of the following in Indian history: the Gupta dynasty, Kalidasa, the Ajanta caves, the Rajputs, and Mahmud of Ghazni.

Enrichment Activities

1. **Reading a Primary Source** Assign Voices from the Past Resource Book 13.1.

2. **Reading a Play** Encourage interested students to read *Shakuntala* by Kalidasa. One source is *Masterpieces of the Orient*, edited by G.L. Anderson. Have students prepare an oral presentation for the class giving a synopsis of the plot and excerpts that reflect the love of nature characteristic of both Hinduism and Buddhism.

3. **Researching for Bonus Points** How does the play *Shakuntala* end? (The king finds a magic ring that he had given to Shakuntala. He then recovers his memory and the pair are reunited.)

Setting the Stage

Explain that many historians have described India as a land of contrasts. Ask students to provide examples justifying this claim. Students should identify the contrast between Muslims and Hindus, studied in Section 1. Explain that this section describes the contrast between the incredible wealth of India's Mughal rulers and the desperate poverty of India's people. It also introduces the first Europeans to reach India's coast and contrasts their rising strength with India's declining power.

Show Map Transparency 49, *India under Mughal Rule,* or refer to the map on page 305. Have students note the extent of the Mughal empire.

Teaching Strategies

Discussing History: Akbar, the "Very Great" Mughal (Objective 1) Ask students to list Akbar's achievements. Explain that Akbar was a successful commander who extended the Mughal empire to include almost all of northern India and much of the Deccan. Akbar was also an inventor who designed a crude machine gun that fired 14 rifles at once. He also created a huge cannon and built a portable war tent with two bedrooms. Finally, Akbar was a religious philosopher who created a new religion. Ask students to identify both his greatest achievement and failure.

Skill Building: Comparing and Contrasting (Objective 2) Direct students' attention to the painting of the Red Fort (page 307). Explain that the Red Fort was one of three royal residences. Shah Jahan's apartments gleamed with ruby-encrusted ornaments and ceilings of solid gold. As the emperor strode from room to room, he could listen to music performed by musicians stationed throughout the Red Fort. While Shah Jahan performed state duties, a team of kitchen slaves kept 15 complete meals ready to be served at a moment's notice.

Tell students that Shah Jahan's incredible wealth dazzled European visitors, but the same travelers were also shocked by the poverty and misery they saw throughout the Mughal empire. Have students read the two descriptions of poverty on pages 306–307 and identify the causes of the great extremes of wealth and poverty.

Using Geographic Themes: Location (Objective 3) Explain that some geographic locations are more strategic or advantageous than others. Ask students to recall why the locations of Rome and Constantinople were strategic. Then have the class read "Europeans reached India's coast" (page 308). Ask students which four bases the Portuguese used to dominate trade in the Indian Ocean. Use the maps on pages 305, 309, and 321 to locate these bases. Have students explain why these locations had such great strategic value. Note that in 1509 the Portuguese viceroy to India, Francisco d'Almeida, gained control of the Indian Ocean by defeating a large Egyptian and Arab fleet.

Check for Understanding Ask students to explain the significance of Mughal and Portuguese influence on Indian history.

Enrichment Activities

1. **Reading a Primary Source**
   Assign Voices from the Past Resource Book 13.2.

2. **Preparing a Report**
   The six Mughal rulers from Babur to Aurangzeb are known as the "Great Mughals." Ask students to report on one of these rulers. (See *National Geographic,* April 1985, and *The Taj Mahal* by David Carroll.)

3. **Solving a Riddle**
   Ask advanced students to report on Akbar's new religion, *Din Ilahi.* The report should also attempt to explain why the new religion failed to attract many followers. (See *The Taj Mahal* by David Carroll and *Our Oriental Heritage* by Will Durant.)

4. **Researching for Bonus Points**
   What inscription was carved on the ceiling of the emperor's throne room at the Red Fort? ("If anywhere on Earth there is paradise, It is Here! It is Here! It is Here!")

Kingdoms arose in Southeast Asia. 3

Setting the Stage

Introduce this section by writing *Southeast Asia* on the board. Then ask students to write down the first thought that comes to mind when they think of Southeast Asia. Call on a number of students and list their answers. Many students will associate Southeast Asia with the Vietnam War. Explain that the Vietnam War had a significant impact on the recent history of this region. Tell students that this section describes the major civilizations and cultural influences that shaped Southeast Asia between 500 and 1500.

Teaching Strategies

Geography in History: Strategic Waterways of Southeast Asia (Objective 1) Distribute Outline Map 24: Southeast Asia. Using the text, or Map Transparency 50, *The Kingdoms of Southeast Asia,* have students label the major rivers (Irrawaddy, Salween, Chao Phraya, Mekong, Red) and the bodies of water into which the rivers flow (Irrawaddy and Salween: Andaman Sea; Chao Phraya: Gulf of Siam; Mekong and Red: South China Sea). Then have students locate and label the Strait of Malacca, Sunda Strait, and Java Sea. Ask why these waterways are considered strategic. (These narrow straits pass through an area with few sea routes. As a result, they control most sea traffic between the Indian and Pacific oceans.) Conclude this map activity by having students refer to the map on page 776 to label the present-day countries in Southeast Asia.

Teaching with Pictures: Angkor Wat (Objective 2) Have students locate Angkor on the map on page 309. Explain that the city of Angkor covered 75 square miles—an area more than twice as large as Manhattan. Then refer students to the picture of Angkor Wat (page 311). Point out that Angkor Wat is one of 72 major stone temples and monuments that stood inside Angkor. Angkor Wat was built by Suryavarman II to honor the Hindu god Vishnu. The moat symbolizes the oceans; the outer wall stands for the mountains at the end of the world. The five central towers represent the peaks of Mount Meru, the Hindu home of the gods and the celestial center of the universe. The temple was damaged during the Cambodian civil war. However, restoration was undertaken in 1987.

Discussing History: China and Vietnam (Objective 3) Ask students to explain the consequences of the Chinese conquest of Vietnam. Point out that the Chinese built dikes and introduced Buddhism. While the Vietnamese were willing to learn from the Chinese, they resented outside rulers. Vietnamese soldiers used hit-and-run tactics to drive out the larger Chinese armies. Emphasize that the determination to be independent is an important theme in Vietnamese history.

Check for Understanding Ask students to name the two major influences on the cultures of Southeast Asia and to give examples of each influence.

Enrichment Activities

1. **Reading a Primary Source** Assign Voices from the Past Resource Book 13.3.

2. **Preparing a Report** Ask interested students to report on Angkor Wat. (See *National Geographic,* April 1960 and May 1982.)

3. **Researching for Bonus Points** What is a wat? (A wat is a Buddhist monastery.)

Reviewing the Facts

1. (a) slender tower (b) Muslim practice of keeping women in seclusion

2. (a) brought golden age to India (b) first of Gupta dynasty (c) great Indian poet and dramatist (d) destroyed Gupta empire (e) warrior-kings who ruled small kingdoms in northern India (f) important Hindu gods (g) Muslims who conquered India (h) city from which northern India was ruled by Turkish sultans (i) conqueror of Delhi (j) empire established by Babur (k) greatly expanded Mughal empire (l) followers of Nanak (m) Portuguese who reached India by sailing around Africa (n) built longest lasting empire of the region (o) Khmer temple to Vishnu

3. union of northern India under one ruler; inoculation, surgery, number system based on ten, great dramatic works

4. (a) Rajputs converted to Hinduism, built temples. (b) almost ceased to exist as separate faith (c) beginning of hatred between Muslims and Hindus

5. ruled fairly and expanded empire

6. (a) Indian jewels, spices, and cloth sold for high prices in Europe. (b) They set up bases along major Asian sea lanes.

7. The presence of many islands, rivers, hills, and mountains limited travel, communication, and the development of unity.

8. India, China, and, later, European countries

Basic Skills

1. (a) during Khmer Empire: first Muslim invasion of India, rise of Rajput kingdoms, building of Angkor Wat (b) 603 years

2. (a) Chandra Gupta, Samudra Gupta, Chandra Gupta II, Rajput warrior-kings, Mahmud of Ghazni, Muhammad Ghuri, Turkish sultans, Tamerlane, Babur, Akbar, Nur Jahan, Shah Jahan, Aurangzeb ordered destruction of Hindu temples. (b) Comments on each leader will vary.

3. Summary should mention location, splendor of Angkor period, Angkor Wat, aristocrats' life style, women's status, influence of Muslim traders, fall of empire.

4. Notes should mention conquest of Indus valley (712); Mahmud's troops sacking Indian cities, taking Hindus into slavery (917); Muhammad Ghuri's revenge and destruction of Nalanda (1191); Delhi sultans' treatment of Hindus; Akbar's tolerance and cooperation with Hindus (1156); his successors' intolerance and persecution of Hindus and Sikhs.

Researching and Reporting Skills

Students' findings will vary.

Critical Thinking

1. Japan: welcomed by some daimyos, considered amusing "southern barbarians," traded silk for guns; India: Mughals showed little interest, allowed spice trade to develop and Portuguese to set up trading bases.

2. (a) Rajputs: women respected, had property rights; highest virtue was devotion to husband demonstrated by suttee; Mughals: Hindu as well as Muslim women adopted purdah and veiled their faces. (b) In Southeast Asia women had higher status; lower class women could trade; women could be royal judges; all royal guards and servants were women.

3. (a) Similarities might include: onion domes in St. Basil, Taj Mahal, and Red Fort; pointed dome in Dome of the Rock; pointed arches in Dome of the Rock, Taj Mahal, Red Fort; ornate decorations with geometric patterns in stone work or mosaic in all four. (b) possible hypothesis: Mughal architecture was influenced by Russian, Byzantine, and Islamic styles of architecture as a result of Turkish conquests. (c) further research: trace styles found in Mughal architecture back to other examples of Byzantine and Islamic architecture along the routes of conquest by the Turks.

4. Possible answers include: (a) An all-inclusive religion might help unify Indians but might antagonize people from different faiths. (b) Students might adopt a policy of tolerance for all religions to foster respect, openness, and understanding.

5. Situated on sea routes linking Europe, India, and Africa with China and Japan; many ethnic groups with different languages passed through and settled; meeting place of Indian and Chinese cultures, and of three major religions.

Perspectives on Past and Present

Students might refer to the long history of extremes of wealth and poverty in India, institutionalized in the caste system and the Hindu belief in karma.

Investigating History

Students' answers will vary, but should include the information that the Ganges is sacred to Hindus. All three rivers are important as sources of water for irrigation. All are also prone to flooding because of seasonal rains and deforestation.

Chapter 13

Teaching with Pictures

Have students study the photograph of the Taj Mahal and its surrounding gardens and reflecting pool. Ask them to visualize the bright white marble in the sunlight against a blue sky. Then have students read the chapter opener on pages 300–301. They will be interested to know that the mausoleum itself is 186 feet (56.7 meters) square. The dome is 70 feet (21.3 meters) in diameter and 120 feet (36.6 meters) high. The outside of the dome features passages from the *Koran* and inlaid floral patterns. Each minaret is 130 feet (39.6 meters) high. Ask students what they think creates the majesty of the Taj Mahal.

Although the Taj Mahal was built by a conquering dynasty in the 1600's, it has become a symbol of India. The four outer towers are minarets, from which leaders call Muslims to prayer.

Key Terms

minaret
purdah

Read and Understand

1. India flourished under the Guptas.
2. Mughals ruled India in splendor.
3. Kingdoms arose in Southeast Asia.

Shah Jahan, the ruler of northern India, was one of the wealthiest kings in the world. He was also a heartbroken man. In 1631, after 19 years of marriage, his beloved wife, Mumtaz Mahal (moom-TAHZ- mah-HAHL), had died. She had given her husband 13 children but died giving birth to the fourteenth. The grieving monarch commanded that a tomb be built "as beautiful as she was beautiful."

Those events were the beginning of the romantic story of the Taj Mahal. Fine white marble and jewels were gathered from many parts of Asia and brought to a spot near Agra. For 22 years, 20,000 workers labored on Shah Jahan's last gift to his queen.

The ivory-white beauty of India's greatest monument is difficult to describe. Artists have praised it for its perfect proportions. Visitors

300

Chapter 13 Resources

GEOGRAPHY
- Geography Skills 13
- Outline Map 24
- Transparencies 8, 48, 49, 50

REINFORCEMENT
- Vocabulary 13
- Basic Skills 13
- Reteaching 13
- Making Connections Study Guide 13

ENRICHMENT
- Critical Thinking 13
- History and Literature 13

ASSESSMENT
- Chapter Test 13
- Alternate Chapter Test 13
- Computer Test Bank

have marveled at the way the towering dome and four **minarets,** or slender towers, seem to change colors as the sun moves across the sky. Inside are thousands of carved marble flowers inlaid with tiny sapphires, bloodstones, rubies, and lapis lazuli.

Shah Jahan dreamed of building an identical tomb of black marble for himself nearby. The two tombs were to be linked by a bridge of polished silver, a symbol of the royal couple's love. However, the black tomb was never built. One of Shah Jahan's sons revolted and imprisoned his aged father not far from the Taj Mahal. When the old emperor died in 1666, a mirror was found in his prison room. It was angled so that the dying man could gaze at the reflection of the Taj Mahal. When he died, Shah Jahan was buried in the Taj Mahal next to the bejeweled casket of Mumtaz Mahal.

During their lives, Shah Jahan and Mumtaz Mahal prayed to Allah, the Muslim name for God. In the 1600's, Islam was fairly new to India. The religion of ancient India had been Hinduism (pages 76–78), not Islam. At the point where Chapter 4 ended, in 180 B.C., the prophet Muhammad (founder of Islam) had not been born.

In this chapter, we must go a long way back in time to a dynasty of Hindu rulers called the Guptas. These powerful kings lived more than 1,000 years before the building of the Taj Mahal. We will see how Hinduism developed during this early period. Then we will see how Islamic Turks swept in from central Asia, slaughtering Hindus and destroying their temples. These conquerors brought the Muslim religion to India.

In the 1,400 years described in this chapter, there was much violence. However, there was also much splendor and beauty. The marble domes and minarets of the Taj Mahal stand as a monument to the achievements of these years.

India flourished under the Guptas. 1

In India, 500 years of disunity followed the end of the Mauryan dynasty (page 82) in 180 B.C. In northern India, waves of invaders continued to arrive from Persia, Afghanistan, and the plains

The Gupta Empire

KEY

- Empire of Chandra Gupta I
- Land added by Samudra Gupta
- Land added by Chandra Gupta II
- → Invaders

0   400 Miles

Map Study

What river valley formed the heartland of the early Gupta empire? Under what ruler did the empire reach its greatest size?

of central Asia. These newcomers set up many warring states and kingdoms. Southern India was not affected by those invasions. Politically, the south remained a land apart.

The Gupta dynasty ruled the north.

In A.D. 320, a Hindu prince named Chandra Gupta (CHUHN-druh GOOP-tuh) was crowned king of the upper Ganges valley. (He was no relation to the long-dead Chandragupta Maurya.) The new king was the first in a line of remarkable rulers who brought a golden age to India.

The Gupta dynasty ruled a mighty empire for nearly 150 years (320–467). After the founder of the line, Chandra Gupta I, came Samudra Gupta, called the Poet King. Samudra Gupta

301

301

SECTION 1 Objectives and Teaching Strategies

OBJECTIVE 1. Identify scientific advances made by Gupta scholars.

Teaching Strategy: *Discussing History: The Achievements of Indian Science* (page 300c)

OBJECTIVE 2. Describe the Ajanta temples.

Teaching Strategy: *Teaching with Pictures: The Ajanta Caves* (page 300c)

OBJECTIVE 3. Explain how the Hindus and Muslims became fierce rivals.

Teaching Strategy: *Relating Past and Present: Conflict between Hindus and Muslims* (page 300c)

■ BACKGROUND

The suffix *gupta* means "protector."

ANSWERS TO
Map Study

Ganges; Chandra Gupta II

SECTION 1
Resources

GEOGRAPHY
- Transparencies 8, 48

REINFORCEMENT
- Independent Practice 13.1

ENRICHMENT
- Voices from the Past 13.1

ASSESSMENT
- Section Quiz 13.1

301

■ DISCUSSION

Ask students what Fa-Hsien's China was like at the time of the Gupta empire in India. Then ask them what was happening in Rome.

■ BACKGROUND

The Gupta empire never extended into the rough, southern region called the Deccan. This region was, in a sense, like a separate country with its own distinct history. It too passed through an age of great creativity, which was recorded in stone monuments.

extended his kingdom to the mouth of the Ganges River, winning another nickname—"exterminator of all other kings."

The third Gupta ruler, Chandra Gupta II, was both a man of learning and a conqueror. During his reign, the Gupta empire stretched across northern India from sea to sea. For the first time in 500 years, northern India was united under one government.

Indian scholars in Gupta times left few written histories. To a Hindu, the passage of worldly time from past to present was unimportant. Therefore, few Indian scholars bothered to record current events. Instead, Indians celebrated their past in oral accounts called *itihas* (meaning "so it was told"). These oral records were very accurate, but they do not emphasize dates. Thus, modern historians have problems pinpointing when key events in Indian history took place.

Much of what we know about India comes from Chinese monks who traveled to India to study Buddhism in the land where it had begun. Around A.D. 405, the Chinese monk Fa-Hsien traveled widely in India and greatly marveled at the peace and prosperity he saw. He reported that the government supported free hospitals for the sick. He was especially impressed that as a stranger, he could travel freely and without fear.

Science and learning advanced.

Learning thrived during the Gupta period. Young Hindus of the priestly (Brahmin) castes attended school from the age of 9 to 30. The university at Nalanda on the Ganges River was famous throughout Asia and attracted students of philosophy from faraway kingdoms. Gupta scholars made many advances in science. The following list details only a few.

Inoculation Indian doctors were the first to give injections. Cowpox injections helped to stop epidemics of the deadly disease smallpox. In India's free hospitals, inoculation was widely used 1,000 years before Europeans first tried it.

Surgery Indian surgeons were remarkably advanced. They sterilized their cutting tools. They knew how to set broken bones. They repaired injured ears and noses by techniques of plastic surgery.

Number system Hindu mathematicians were the first to use a system of numbers based on

302

ten. (Muslims of Baghdad adopted the system and passed it along to Europe, so Europeans called these numbers Arabic numerals.) Hindu philosophers understood the concept of zero and wrote it as a number. They also had a symbol for infinity.

Kalidasa wrote great drama.

The greatest literature of India's golden age was drama. Imagine an Indian actor wearing a sparkling, richly embroidered costume and the jeweled crown of a king. Standing beside him is an actress in the plain cotton gown of a poor hermit's daughter. The actress is playing the title role in one of the most famous plays in world literature, *Shakuntala*. The plot involves an unfortunate accident by which the king, though married to Shakuntala, loses all memory of her.

Shakuntala was written by the poet and dramatist Kalidasa (**KAH**-lih-DAH-suh), whose genius has been compared to Shakespeare's. Unlike Shakespeare, however, Kalidasa wrote no tragedies. There might be moments of sorrow during the play, but all his plays ended happily.

Emotion is the key to Indian drama. Audiences at the Gupta court recognized eight pure emotions known as *rasas*. One scene might make them feel the emotion of laughter, another sadness, a third pride. The other five rasas were love, anger, fear, loathing, and wonder. Then the final scene of a drama swept the audience up in an overpowering emotion that combined all the others.

Huns destroyed the Gupta empire.

The last Gupta rulers faced the same frightening challenge as the last Roman emperors. During the 400's, the Huns rampaged across Asia and Europe. While Attila was terrifying Rome, other Hun chieftains crossed the rocky passes of the Hindu Kush into India. Under constant attack from the Huns, the Gupta empire shrank. The Gupta dynasty disappeared from history during the 600's.

For the people of northern India, the next six centuries (650–1250) were ones of turmoil. First, several proud, warlike tribes from central Asia crossed the Hindu Kush mountains and settled in northwestern India. The local Hindus called this new ruling group Rajputs, a name that meant "sons of kings."

The Rajputs built new kingdoms.

In the 800's and 900's, northern India once again became a land of small kingdoms, ruled by Rajput warrior-kings. Soon after coming to India in the 500's, the Rajputs converted to Hinduism as members of the Kshatriyas (warriors).

Like European knights and Japanese samurai, Rajput men lived by a code of honor and bravery. Women were respected and had some property rights as well. However, both poetry and drama stressed that a woman's highest virtue was devotion to her husband. If her husband died, a faithful wife could show her love by a Hindu rite known as *suttee*. As her husband's body burned on a funeral pyre, she would remain at his side and die honorably in the flames.

By the 800's, three gods had risen to new importance in Hinduism: Brahman the Creator, Shiva the Destroyer, and Vishnu the Preserver. Poems, tales, and songs honored these gods and told of their deeds. In the 800's and 900's, great temples were built where Hindus could worship.

During the Rajput centuries, Buddhism almost ceased to exist as a separate faith. Indians now worshiped Buddha in Hindu temples. Hindu priests taught that the gentle Buddha had come to earth as an incarnation of Vishnu. Thus, Indian Buddhism slipped quietly back into Hinduism.

Hindus and Muslims met in war.

In the 700's, Hinduism was one of the oldest religions in the world. Islam was the newest. The fierce conflict between Hindu and Muslim that began in this century has been called "probably the bloodiest story in history."

Arab Muslims conquered a major portion of the Indus River valley in 712, just as other Arab armies were conquering Spain. This first Muslim invasion, however, was mild compared to what followed.

In 997, a Turkish chieftain named Mahmud (muh-MOOD) became sultan of a little state in eastern Afghanistan called Ghazni. Mahmud of Ghazni was no barbarian. He loved Persian poetry and the Koran. He also loved gold and silver, and he made a solemn vow to plunder India every year. For 17 successive years, Mahmud's troops sacked India's cities and destroyed Hindu temples. They massacred and enslaved thousands.

The Buddhist temples at Ajanta were hollowed out of granite cliffs. Within the caves, the walls are covered with magnificent paintings.

The Rajputs resisted bravely, but their slow-moving war elephants were no match for the lightninglike attacks of the Turkish cavalry. Mahmud of Ghazni died in 1030, leaving behind a legacy of hatred between Hindu and Muslim.

Muslim sultans ruled from Delhi.

About 160 years later, in 1191, another Turkish sultan named Muhammad Ghuri (GOO-ree) rode into India bent on conquest. A desperate stand by the Rajputs defeated him. The next year he returned and took a terrible revenge. His armies conquered city after city. At Nalanda, he destroyed the famous university. Much of northern India was conquered by Turkish armies and ruled by Turkish generals from the city of Delhi.

Thus began what is called the Delhi sultanate. For over 300 years (1200–1526), northern India was ruled by Turkish sultans from their courts in Delhi. These Turkish rulers were Muslims, and they treated the Hindus as a conquered people. Hindu kingdoms survived as independent states only in the Deccan, to the south.

The conquest of the Muslim Turks, though cruel, may have saved India from the Mongols. Although the Mongols raided and threatened India, the Turkish rulers were strong enough to turn them back.

303

ANSWERS TO
Section Review 1

Define:
(a) slender tower (b) oral accounts of Indian history (c) social grouping in Indian society (d) injection to prevent disease (e) one of eight pure emotions that formed the basis of Indian drama (f) rite in which faithful Hindu wife dies honorably on her husband's funeral pyre (g) Turkish Muslim leader

Identify:
(a) builder of the Taj Mahal (b) wife in whose memory

(continued)

ANSWERS TO *(continued)*

Taj Mahal was built
(c) India's greatest monument **(d)** first of Gupta dynasty **(e)** rulers who brought golden age to India **(f)** number system based on ten, first used by Hindu mathematicians **(g)** great Indian poet and dramatist
(h) warlike tribes from Asia who attacked and destroyed Gupta empire **(i)** warrior-kings who ruled small kingdoms in northern India in the 800's and 900's
(j) Muslims from Afghanistan who conquered India and set up the Delhi sultanate

Answer:

1. (a) united the region and led it into a golden age
(b) inoculation, surgery, number system based on ten, great dramatic works

2. (a) honor and bravery
(b) devotion to her husband

3. (a) rule of northern India by Turkish sultans in Delhi
(b) Hindus treated as conquered peoples

4. (a) religion of people conquered by Turks, blended with Buddhism
(b) almost ceased to exist as separate faith **(c)** religion of Turkish rulers

ANSWERS TO
Voice from the Past

1. espionage and impoverishment
2. (a) Muslim **(b)** the Koran
3. reduction to poverty to make obedient, submissive
4. to prevent rebellion in which many would die

Section REVIEW 1

Define: (a) minaret, (b) itihas, (c) caste, (d) inoculation, (e) rasa, (f) suttee, (g) sultan
Identify: (a) Shah Jahan, (b) Mumtaz Mahal, (c) Taj Mahal, (d) Chandra Gupta, (e) Gupta dynasty, (f) Arabic numerals, (g) Kalidasa, (h) Huns (i) Rajputs, (j) Turks
Answer:
1. (a) How did Gupta rule affect northern India? (b) What were some of the key achievements in the arts and sciences under the Guptas?
2. (a) In the Rajput kingdoms, what virtues were expected of a man? (b) Of a woman?
3. (a) What was the Delhi sultanate? (b) What was its effect on the Hindu population?

Critical Thinking
4. Briefly summarize the status of each of these religions in northern India about the year 1200. (a) Hinduism (b) Buddhism (c) Islam

Mughals ruled India in splendor. 2

The greatest menace to the Delhi sultans came from their own homeland, the steppes of central Asia. Late in the 1300's, a fearsome conqueror rode out over the dusty steppe of Turkestan. He was Timur the Lame, or Tamerlane.

Tamerlane destroyed Delhi.

Tamerlane boasted descent from Genghis Khan, even though he was more Turk than Mongol. He led his forces westward into Persia, northward into Russia, and westward again into Mesopotamia and Asia Minor. From his capital in Samarkand, Tamerlane terrorized all of western Asia.

In 1398, Tamerlane led his armies south through the mountain passes into India. Within

Voice from the Past | *The Harshest of Sultans*

The most powerful of the Delhi sultans was the harsh Ala-ud-din (ah-**LAH**-ood-DEEN), who took the throne by murdering his uncle in 1296. A Muslim historian wrote the following account of Ala-ud-din's cruel measures.

The people were pressed and [taxed] and money was exacted from them on every kind of pretext ... The people became so absorbed in trying to keep themselves alive that rebellion was never mentioned. Next [Ala-ud-din] set up a system of espionage so minute that nothing done, good or bad, was hidden from him ... Nobles dared not speak aloud even in thousand-columned palaces, but had to communicate by signs. In their own houses, night and day, dread of spies made them tremble ...

The Hindu was to be [made so poor] as to be unable to keep a horse, wear fine clothes, or enjoy any of life's luxuries. No Hindu could hold up his head ... "I am an unlettered man," [Ala-ud-din] said, "but I have seen a great deal. Be assured that the Hindus will never become submissive and obedient till they are reduced to poverty. I have therefore given orders that just enough shall be left to them of [grain], milk, and curds, from year to year ... Although I have not studied the science or the Book, I am a Muslim of the Muslims. To prevent rebellion, in which many perish, I issue such ordinances as I consider to be for the good of the State and the benefit of the people."

1. What measures did the sultan use to prevent rebellion against him?
2. (a) What was the religion of the sultan? (b) What did he mean by "the Book"?
3. What was his policy toward Hindus?
4. What justification did the sultan give for his policies?

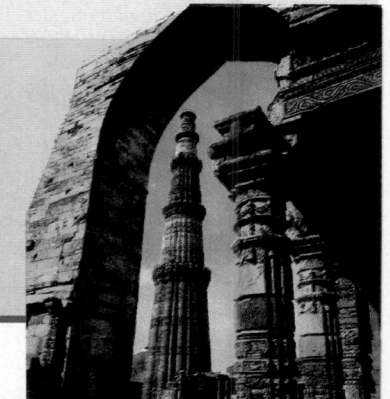

304

The Qutb Minar tower celebrates Turkish conquests in India.

India under Mughal Rule

KEY
- Empire in 1530
- Added by 1605
- Added by 1707

0   500 Miles

Map Study

Where were most of India's cities located? Why was the location of Hormuz strategic?

a few months, he had taken Delhi itself. Although he was a Muslim, he massacred Muslims and Hindus alike. About 100,000 people were sold into slavery. A witness wrote, "The city was utterly destroyed . . . for two whole months, not a bird moved in the city."

Unlike Genghis Khan, Tamerlane failed to build an empire that outlasted his own life. After his death in 1405, nothing remained of his conquests. Delhi was rebuilt, but the Turkish sultans who ruled there for the next century were weaker than their predecessors. To the west, Rajput princes strengthened their Hindu states. No single ruler was able to dominate India. Wars among the rival states and kingdoms were frequent.

Babur founded the Mughal dynasty.

In 1526, another Turkish-Mongol conqueror from central Asia ended the feeble Delhi sultanate for good. His name was Babur (**BAH**-buhr), which

meant "the tiger." He traced his descent from Genghis Khan on his father's side and from Tamerlane on his mother's side. Babur was a hulking, broad-shouldered, big-bellied man. As his son testified, "He never hit a man whom he did not knock down." He was also a wily politician, a skilled general, and an educated man who wrote an autobiography.

Babur conquered India with cannon and firepower. His troops carried a supply of gunpowder, muskets, and several hefty cannon across the mountain passes from Afghanistan into northern India. Soon Babur captured Delhi and Agra in north-central India. The Delhi sultanate was thus overthrown after 320 years (1206–1526).

The new empire established by Babur came to be known as the Mughal (**MOO**-gahl) empire. (*Mughal* was another form of the name *Mongol*.) Mughal monarchs became so rich and powerful that Mughal rule became a byword for wealth and imperial splendor.

305

SECTION 2 Objectives and Teaching Strategies

OBJECTIVE 1. Identify Akbar and describe his achievements.

Teaching Strategy: *Discussing History: Akbar, the "Very Great" Mughal* (page 300d)

OBJECTIVE 2. Compare and contrast the extremes of wealth and poverty in the Mughal empire.

Teaching Strategy: *Skill Building: Comparing and Contrasting* (page 300d)

OBJECTIVE 3. Locate strategic bases in the Indian Ocean trade and explain their significance to the Portuguese.

Teaching Strategy: *Using Geographic Themes: Location* (page 300d)

ANSWERS TO
Map Study

on coasts; controlled entry to Persian Gulf

SECTION 2
Resources

GEOGRAPHY
- Transparency 49

REINFORCEMENT
- Independent Practice 13.2

ENRICHMENT
- Voices from the Past 13.2

ASSESSMENT
- Section Quiz 13.2

305

■ BACKGROUND

The dates of Akbar's reign coincide almost exactly with those of England's Elizabeth I (1558–1603).

Akbar was an intelligent and cultured man who was eager for all kinds of knowledge, but he never learned to read or write. He mastered many fields of knowledge, from science to poetry, through conversation with scholars at his court. Some recent historians suspect he had the learning disability known today as dyslexia, which makes it difficult for a person to perceive letters and words.

Cooperative Learning

Working in pairs, have students teach a partner something by means of conversation only, as Akbar must have done. It could be a simple game or the procedure for a craft project. Do not allow any writing or drawing. Afterward, ask students if it was harder or easier to communicate in this way. Have them consider how dependent they were on their partners for providing accurate information.

Akbar enlarged the Mughal empire.

By far the greatest and most talented of India's Mughal monarchs was Babur's grandson. Though his Muslim name was Muhammad, he was known as Akbar, which means "most great." Akbar was 13 when his father (Babur's son) had a fatal fall down a flight of palace stairs. Akbar ruled the Mughal empire from 1556 to 1605.

Early in his reign, Akbar added new lands to the Mughal empire. Dressed in golden armor and mounted on an elephant, he fought countless battles against Rajput challengers. By the end of his reign, the empire covered almost all of northern India and much of the Deccan.

Like the Delhi sultans, the Mughal rulers were Muslims. However, Hindus in Mughal lands outnumbered Muslims by at least four to one. To unify his empire, Akbar decided that he needed Hindu support. Therefore, after defeating the Rajput princes, he did not seek revenge. Instead, he spared the Rajputs' lives and invited them to help rule. He married a Rajput princess and entrusted Hindus with high government offices. Akbar also removed the special taxes that Hindus had paid their Muslim rulers. His tax system stressed fairness. For example, in years of famine, taxes were dropped.

Akbar's wise policy toward Hindus was based on his personal religious tolerance. In his adult years, he ceased to believe that Islam was the only true faith. What Hindus taught might also be true, he thought. He was interested, too, in the teachings of Christian missionaries.

After learning about all these faiths, Akbar concluded that a new religion could embrace them all. He called his new religion *Din Ilahi* (Divine Faith) and made himself its leader. He made few converts, however, and his religion died with him in 1605.

Splendor disguised a weakening empire.

Under Akbar's successors, the strong empire he had built began to weaken. Later rulers were neither as tolerant nor as skilled in administration as Akbar had been.

A strong queen Akbar's son was named Jahangir (juh-HAHN-geer), meaning "world-grasper." He was sadly misnamed, however. Addicted to both wine and opium, he played little part in governing. His reign (1605–1627) might have been an even greater disaster for India if he had not married an able woman.

In 1611, Jahangir married a Persian princess whom he called Nur Jahan ("the light of the world"). Nur Jahan was probably the most powerful woman in India's history before modern times. For many years, she was the true ruler of the empire.

Religious intolerance You have already read about the next Mughal monarch—Shah Jahan, the builder of the Taj Mahal. In his 30-year rule (1628–1658), Shah Jahan was as cruel toward his enemies as he had been loving toward his wife. He was followed by his even more ruthless son, Aurangzeb (OH-rung-zeb), who imprisoned his aging father as you have read.

Shah Jahan and especially Aurangzeb turned away from Akbar's policy of treating Hindus and Muslims as equals. Aurangzeb tried to make his empire an Islamic state. In 1669, he ordered the destruction of Hindu temples. He also returned to the policy of taxing non-Muslims more heavily than Muslims. No longer did Hindus serve the empire in high positions. By his intolerance, Aurangzeb weakened his government.

Extremes of wealth and poverty During Shah Jahan's reign, the Mughal empire was at its peak. Its glittering treasures amazed European visitors. For example, at the Red Fort at Agra (one of three royal residences built of red sandstone) the Mughal treasury contained these items:

> 750 pounds of pearls, 275 pounds of emeralds, 5,000 gems from Cathay (China) . . . 200 daggers, 1,000 gold studded saddles with jewels, 2 golden thrones, 3 silver thrones, 100 silver chairs, 5 golden chairs, 200 most precious mirrors . . .

The list goes on and on. And it was said that the treasury at Lahore, the Mughals' third capital, was three times the size of Agra's.

India's poor, however, had few comforts. A European traveler left a description of a poor family's house that was not far from the great treasury of Agra:

> Their houses are built of mud with thatched roofs. Furniture there is little or none except some earthenware pots to hold water and for cooking and two beds . . . Their bed

The Red Fort at Delhi was one of three awe-inspiring Mughal capitals.

■ **BACKGROUND**
Interested students may wish to report on the relation of Sikhs to other sects in India today.

cloths are scanty, merely a sheet or perhaps two . . . This is sufficient in the hot weather, but the bitter cold nights are miserable indeed . . .

In 1630 (during Shah Jahan's reign), a Dutch merchant visited northern India during one of the region's frequent famines. He wrote, "As the famine increased, men abandoned towns and villages and wandered helplessly . . . wherever you went, you saw nothing but corpses."

Hinduism and Islam were rivals.

All India's earlier conquerors had eventually blended into the Hindu system, but the Muslims did not. Their strong monotheism kept them from being absorbed by the Hindu majority.

Yet Hinduism and Islam did affect each other. For example, Hindus began to dress in the same styles as Muslims. Hindu women in northern India began to veil their faces as Muslim women did. Northern Hindus also adopted the idea of **purdah**. Purdah was a Muslim practice of keeping women in seclusion. Women were not allowed to go out in public or meet socially with any man outside the family.

Some Hindus converted to Islam. Islam's idea of the equality of all believers had a strong appeal to lower-caste Hindus and to untouchables.

A few thinkers tried to blend the ideas of Hinduism and Islam. One such thinker was Nanak, who lived from 1469 to 1539. Nanak became the *guru* (religious teacher) of a new religion. His teachings combined the strict monotheism of Islam with the Hindu idea of a mystical union with God. Followers of Nanak became known as Sikhs (seeks), meaning "disciples."

The Mughal rulers persecuted the Sikhs and killed two of their gurus. As a result, the Sikhs became a community of soldiers, ready to defend themselves or to attack. Many Sikh men took the last name Singh, meaning "lion," while women took the name Kaur, meaning "lioness." When Mughal rule weakened, the Sikhs set up an independent military state in northern India.

307

ANSWERS TO

Section Review 2

Define:
(a) Muslim practice of keeping women in seclusion
(b) religious teacher

Identify:
(a) conqueror of Delhi
(b) Turkish-Mongol conqueror from central Asia who set up Mughal empire
(c) empire established by Babur (d) Babur's grandson who greatly expanded Mughal empire (e) son of Shah Jahan who tried to make empire an Islamic state (f) followers of Nanak who tried to blend Islam and Hinduism (g) Portuguese captain who reached India by sailing around Africa

Answer:

1. (a) gravely weakened
(b) undone entirely

2. expanded empire; treated Hindus with respect, invited them to help rule

3. royal: ornate, elaborate, splendid palaces such as the Taj Mahal; poor: mud-thatched roofs, little furniture, few bedclothes

4. clothing style, veiled women's faces, purdah

5. (a) Control of sea lanes around India passed to outsiders. (b) set up strong bases at strategic points all along the major Asian sea lanes

6. (a) Muslims—one God, equality of believers; Hindus—sought union with God, maintained a class system (b) Akbar—tolerant, promoted Hindus and Muslims equally; Aurangzeb and Shah Jahan—favored Muslims over Hindus politically and socially

Europeans reached India's coast.

While Shah Jahan concentrated on building lavish tombs and palaces, Europeans were increasing their influence in Asia. In 1498, a Portuguese captain and adventurer, Vasco da Gama, arrived in India after sailing all the way around Africa and north again to India. For the first time, powerful newcomers had arrived in India by sea rather than through the mountain passes of the Himalayas to the north.

Da Gama's voyage marked a great turning point in India's history. After 1500, control of the seas around India became the key to controlling India itself. The Mughal rulers, however, took little interest in building warships. In the end, the weakness of their navy proved fatal to both the Mughal empire and the smaller Hindu kingdoms to the south.

The spices Da Gama took back from his voyage sold in Europe for 27 times their cost in India. Obviously, there were fortunes to be made in the Indian Ocean. Portuguese merchants were quick to go after them.

The Portuguese did not try to conquer India or the spice-producing islands south of China (the East Indies). Instead, they set up strong bases at strategic points all along the major Asian sea lanes.

A Portuguese sea captain named Alfonso de Albuquerque (al-buh-KEHR-kay) seized the western Indian port of Goa in 1510. In 1511, his fleet sailed to the East Indies and occupied the strategic port of Malacca (muh-LAK-uh) on the Malay Peninsula. (See map on page 309). In 1515, he captured his last great prize, the Muslim city of Hormuz (hor-MOOZ). It lay at the entrance to the Persian Gulf. (See map on page 305.) From these three bases and the East African city of Zanzibar, the Portuguese dominated the Indian Ocean trade for the remainder of the 1500's. For the time being, however, the Europeans were not a serious threat to the Mughal emperors.

Section REVIEW 2

Define: (a) purdah, (b) guru
Identify: (a) Tamerlane, (b) Babur, (c) Mughal dynasty, (d) Akbar, (e) Aurangzeb, (f) Sikhs, (g) Da Gama
Answer:

1. (a) How was the Delhi sultanate affected by Tamerlane? (b) By Babur?
2. List two major achievements of Akbar.
3. Compare the home of a poor family with the royal residences of the Mughals.
4. What are some customs that Hindus adopted from Muslims?
5. (a) What important change was marked by Da Gama's arrival in India? (b) How did the Portuguese come to control trade in the Indian Ocean?

ECONOMICS IN DAILY LIFE ▶ Cloth from India

Indian farmers raised cotton to make cloth as early as 3000 B.C. By 300 B.C., Indian clothmakers were printing unique designs on their fabrics. Although European merchants at first were dazzled by India's jewels, they soon found that they could make even greater fortunes in the cloth trade. From Indian looms came cloth of many different weights and patterns. In Europe, each type of cloth came to be known by the name of the Indian city or region where it was woven. For example, the fabric madras takes its name from the Indian city Madras, calico from the city Calicut, cashmere from the region Kashmir. *Chintz* comes from a Hindi word whose root means "bright" or "many-colored." Even the word *dungaree* comes from the name of a section of Bombay where sturdy blue denim was woven.

The Brooklyn Museum

The Kingdoms of Southeast Asia

KEY

Khmer empire about 1200

Mongol invasions

0   400 Miles

Map Study

What geographic reason helps to explain why Vietnam was more heavily influenced by China than other countries in Southeast Asia?

Critical Thinking

6. (a) What were the critical differences between the beliefs of Hindus and Muslims? (b) What effect did the policies of Akbar, Aurangzeb, and Shah Jahan have on relations between Hindus and Muslims?

Kingdoms arose in Southeast Asia.   3

East of India, across the Bay of Bengal, lies Southeast Asia. It includes the modern countries of Burma, Laos, Cambodia, Vietnam, Malaysia, Indonesia, Thailand, Singapore, and Brunei.

Many groups settled Southeast Asia.

For thousands of years, many groups of people passed through Southeast Asia on routes linking Asia and the Pacific islands. As a result, the region has a great variety of languages and cultures. Burma alone includes more than 100 different language groups.

Southeast Asia has never been united either politically or culturally. Seas and straits separate the islands. On the mainland peninsula, five great rivers flow from the north and cut valleys to the sea. Between the valleys rise hills and mountains, making travel and communication difficult.

Southeast Asia lies on the most direct sea route between India and China. Throughout Southeast Asia's history, the key to political power has

309

SECTION 3
Objectives and Teaching Strategies

OBJECTIVE 1. Label the major rivers, bodies of water, and countries of Southeast Asia.

Teaching Strategy: *Geography in History: Strategic Waterways of Southeast Asia* (page 300e)

OBJECTIVE 2. Identify and describe Angkor Wat.

Teaching Strategy: *Teaching with Pictures: Angkor Wat* (page 300e)

OBJECTIVE 3. Describe the impact of Chinese influence on the Vietnamese.

Teaching Strategy: *Discussing History: China and Vietnam* (page 300e)

ANSWER TO
Map Study

It shares a border with China.

SECTION 3
Resources

GEOGRAPHY
■ Transparency 50

REINFORCEMENT
■ Independent Practice 13.3

ENRICHMENT
■ Voices from the Past 13.3

ASSESSMENT
■ Section Quiz 13.3

■ **DISCUSSION**

Compare the status of women in Southeast Asia with that of women in India (see page 307). Have students speculate on why there might be such a difference in attitude.

■ **BACKGROUND**

Although Angkor Wat and the cathedral at Chartres were both religious in purpose, their architecture is different. Angkor Wat, which is a group of temples, is larger in area. Its style is more ornate, with carved sandstone and a number of towers. The wide base, with a pyramidal form in the center, contrasts with the height of the cathedral at Chartres.

often been control of trade routes and harbors. Pirates frequently infested the seas, and powerful local kings used their fleets to protect merchants from piracy. In return, such kings charged merchants high fees to use their ports or pass through their waterways.

Traders and settlers carried India's culture.

Even before the rise of the Gupta dynasty, Indian traders were plying the seaways of Southeast Asia. Among the goods that attracted them were gold from the Malay Peninsula, fragrant woods such as sandalwood, precious jewels, and spices.

During Gupta times, Buddhist missionaries were active in Southeast Asia. Hinduism, too, spread widely in the region. The people of Southeast Asia adopted many Hindu myths and worshiped Hindu gods, especially Shiva and Vishnu. Yet some key ideas of Indian Hinduism were not accepted by Southeast Asians. For example, the caste system never became important in Southeast Asia.

Gradually, Indian influence spread to most areas of culture. Southeast Asian poets wrote long, elegant poems in India's ancient language of Sanskrit. Often the heroes of the poems were Hindu gods or warriors. Southeast Asian rulers built palaces and temples following Indian styles of architecture. They enjoyed Indian musicians and dancers. Some kings even encouraged Brahmins (members of India's highest caste) to come from India to serve as royal officials.

Trade furthered these cultural contacts. In some parts of Southeast Asia, Indian traders and merchants settled permanently. They intermarried with well-to-do local families. Thus, peacefully and without conquering armies, Indian ways of life became deeply rooted in Southeast Asia.

The Khmer empire ruled Cambodia.

Many kingdoms rose and fell in Southeast Asia's river valleys and deltas and on its islands. None was ever able to unite the entire region, but many of these kingdoms had moments of glory and left monuments of lasting beauty.

A people known as the Khmers (kuh-**MAIRZ**) built the longest-lasting empire of the region.

They came from the northern part of what is now Cambodia, moving southward along the Mekong River. They established a small kingdom in the late 500's and gradually expanded at the expense of neighboring kingdoms.

The Angkor period The greatest Khmer king was Jayavarman II (**JUH**-yah-**VAHR**-muhn), who came to the throne in 802. In his 50-year rule, this mighty conqueror greatly enlarged the Khmer kingdom. By 850, the Khmers' rule had reached the boundaries of modern Kampuchea.

The Khmer empire's time of greatest power is known as the Angkor period, after their capital city of Angkor. This capital was a splendid city with fine buildings of brick, stone, and wood. The Angkor period lasted from about 850 to about 1250.

The most famous and splendid of the Khmer buildings was Angkor Wat, a temple to the Hindu god Vishnu. Built in the early 1100's, the rectangular temple was more than half a mile long. The surrounding moat reflected its nine towers, their roofs shining with gold. The towers themselves were shaped like lotus blossoms, suggesting beauty, fragrance, and the power of life. The temple included a library and living quarters for its priests.

Khmer aristocrats lived in fine houses with tile roofs (not thatched with straw like the homes of commoners). They rode in gold or silver chair-cars or litters, carried on the shoulders of their servants. Other servants attended the nobles, shading them from the sun with golden-handled parasols.

Women had high status in the Khmer empire, as in most parts of Southeast Asia. Women from the lower classes ran market stalls. They sold ivory, feathers, oils, perfumes, and pearls. Upper-class women often were well educated and sometimes served as royal judges. All the king's guards and servants were women, for only women were allowed within the palace.

The decline of the Khmer empire After the splendors of the Angkor period, the Khmer empire began to decline around 1250. It was threatened by the Mongols, who sacked Vietnam's capital of Hanoi in 1257 and conquered Burma in 1287.

The Khmer empire itself never fell to the Mongols. With the Mongols, however, came another group of people—the Thais (tyes) from the borders of China. The Thais established their

310

Comparing pictures *Still magnificent even as ruins, the temple complex of Angkor Wat stands on the site of the ancient capital of the Khmer empire. Built in the 1100's, the temples have suffered damage in the many wars that have swept what is now Cambodia. What characteristics, if any, does Angkor Wat have in common with the cathedral of Chartres (page 232)? How does it differ?*

own kingdom, which grew stronger as the Khmer grew weaker. In 1430, a Thai army captured Angkor, ending the Khmer empire.

Muslim traders introduced Islam.

During the later years of the Khmer empire, a new influence reached Southeast Asia. Between the 1200's and the 1400's, Muslim traders from Arabia and India brought their religion to the area. Like the Hindu traders before them, the Muslim traders settled in towns and villages along the coasts. Islam became an important religion in the area, along with Hinduism and Buddhism.

Islam spread along the trade routes into the islands of what is now Indonesia. Parts of the Malay Peninsula and also such islands as Sumatra and Java became strongholds of Islam.

China dominated Vietnam.

Although China lies just north of Southeast Asia, the Chinese had surprisingly little influence on the region. Only Vietnam fell under China's rule. Vietnam lies on the eastern side of the Southeast Asian peninsula. Around 100 B.C., during the mighty Han dynasty, China took much of Vietnam. Vietnam remained under Chinese influence for 1,000 years.

Although the Vietnamese accepted many Chinese ways, they never thought of themselves

as Chinese. They kept their own language and customs, and they frequently rebelled against their Chinese rulers. When China's T'ang dynasty grew weaker, in the early 900's, Vietnam broke away. It became an independent kingdom in 939 and began a long, slow period of expansion.

Vietnam was unique in Southeast Asia, because it was the only country to be heavily influenced by China. All the other countries of Southeast Asia show much stronger links to India.

Section REVIEW 3

Identify: (a) Bay of Bengal, (b) Southeast Asia, (c) Malay Peninsula, (d) Khmers, (e) Angkor
Answer:
1. (a) Describe the location of Southeast Asia. (b) What are its major geographic features?
2. Describe the contacts between India and Southeast Asia.
3. (a) What territory was included in the Khmer empire? (b) When did it arise and what years marked its height? (c) What ended the empire?
4. How did Islam reach Southeast Asia?
5. What part did China play in Southeast Asia?

Critical Thinking
6. In Southeast Asia, how did geography influence each of the following? (a) political power (b) foreign contacts

311

ANSWERS TO
Section Review 3

Identify:
(a) body of water separating India and Southeast Asia
(b) area including modern-day countries of Burma, Thailand, Laos, Cambodia, Vietnam, Malaysia, and Indonesia
(c) peninsula off mainland whose gold attracted Indian traders
(d) people in Southeast Asia who built the longest-lasting empire in the region
(e) capital city of Khmer kingdom and name given to empire's greatest period

Answer:
1. (a) east of India across Bay of Bengal (b) islands separated by sea and straits, mountainous peninsula with many rivers
2. Indian traders and merchants and Buddhist missionaries helped to spread Indian culture.
3. (a) the area that is today Cambodia (b) late 500's; height 850–1250 (c) threats by Mongols, capture of Angkor Wat in 1430 by Thais
4. through Muslim traders from India and Arabia
5. dominated culture of Vietnam
6. (a) Key to political power was control of trade routes and harbors. Kings who protected merchants from pirates became powerful.
(b) allowed Vietnam to fall under China's rule and influence; parts of region more easily accessible from India became subject to Indian influences; resources attracted foreign traders and explorers

311

Concluding the Chapter

1. **Chapter Closer**
   Have students identify three significant shifts in power in India's history and their consequences.

2. **Reteaching Activities**
   a. Summarizing Have students write a paragraph summarizing the scientific and cultural achievements of the Gupta period.
   b. Making a Time Line Have students prepare time lines showing key people and events in Indian history from Tamurlane to the arrival of the Portuguese.
   c. Finding Main Ideas Ask students to turn each subheading in Section 3 into a question and then write two answers for each question.

Answers to Chapter Review appear on page 300f.

Summary

1. India flourished under the Guptas. India experienced 500 years of disunity and invasions before Chandra Gupta reunited the north in A.D. 300. Gupta rule marked a golden age for Hindu India. It was a time of advances in medicine, mathematics, and astronomy as well as outstanding artistic achievements. After the fall of the Gupta empire, small Rajput kingdoms arose. Invasions by Muslim Turks and the harsh rule of the Delhi sultans led to hatred between Hindus and Muslims.

2. Mughals ruled India in splendor. Late in the 1300's, Tamerlane—a fierce conquerer from central Asia—swept over northern India. Devastated by Tamerlane, northern India was next conquered by Babur, who set up the Mughal empire. The wise rule of Akbar kept peace between Hindus and Muslims, but his successors destroyed these gains. The arrival of Europeans further weakened the empire.

3. Kingdoms arose in Southeast Asia. Southeast Asia is noted for its geographic and ethnic diversity. Several kingdoms, among them the Khmer, developed there, but none united the region. Because of its location on key trade routes, Southeast Asia was influenced by both China and India and later attracted European interest.

Reviewing the Facts

1. Define the following terms:
   a. minaret   b. purdah
2. Explain the importance of each of the following names, places, or terms:
   a. Gupta dynasty   h. Delhi
   b. Chandra Gupta I   i. Tamerlane
   c. Kalidasa   j. Mughal
   d. Huns   k. Akbar
   e. Rajputs   l. Sikhs
   f. Brahman, Shiva,   m. Vasco da Gama
      Vishnu   n. Khmers
   g. Turks   o. Angkor Wat
3. What were the major achievements of the Gupta period, politically and culturally?
4. Between the time of the Rajput kingdoms and Mughal rule, what changes took place in each of the following religions in India? (a) Hinduism (b) Buddhism (c) Islam
5. Why is Akbar regarded as a great ruler?
6. (a) Why were Europeans eager to trade with India? (b) How did they gain control of trade without taking over India?
7. How did geography influence the development of Southeast Asia?
8. What foreign countries influenced Southeast Asia?

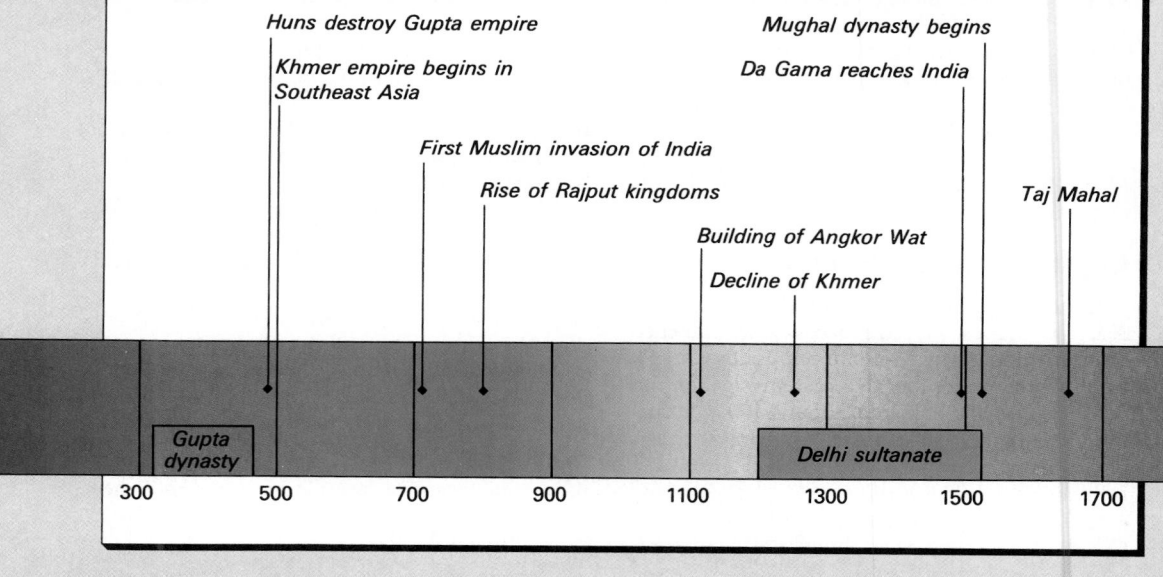

300   500   700   900   1100   1300   1500   1700

Basic Skills

1. **Interpreting a time line** Refer to the time line on page 312 to answer the following questions: (a) Which three events relate to an empire that once ruled the present-day country of Cambodia? (b) How much longer did that empire last than the Gupta dynasty in India?
2. **Sequencing** (a) List in chronological order the Indian and Turkish leaders mentioned in this chapter, beginning with Chandra Gupta. (b) Add a brief sentence describing some action of each leader.
3. **Summarizing** Write a summary of 150 to 200 words on the rise and fall of the Khmer empire.
4. **Taking notes** This chapter makes several references to the religious conflict between Hindus and Muslims. Locate these references; then take notes on them for future reference in relation to India.

Researching and Reporting Skills

1. **Using the *Readers' Guide*** Look through five volumes of the *Readers' Guide to Periodical Literature* for articles pertaining to either the Himalayas or Tibet. For each article you find, write a complete citation (author, title of the article, name of publication, date, and page numbers).
2. **Evaluating sources** Use the following criteria to evaluate each article as a source: (a) How informative is it in relation to your topic? (b) Is the publication in which it is found objective, reliable, and up-to-date? (c) What are the credentials of the author?
3. **Outlining** Make an outline of two of the articles you have identified.
4. **Making an oral presentation** Using your outline, make a brief presentation to the class of the main points of the articles you have read.

Critical Thinking

1. **Comparing** In the late 1400's and early 1500's, Portuguese merchants reached Japan and India. Compare the way people in each country reacted to the foreigners.
2. **Analyzing change** (a) How did the role of women in Indian society change from the time of the Rajput warriors in India to Mughal times? (b) How did the position of women in Southeast Asia differ from that of Indian women?
3. **Forming a hypothesis** A hypothesis is a tentative statement made to account for an observation. Its proof requires further evidence. Study the pictures of the Red Fort (page 307), the Taj Mahal (page 300), the Dome of the Rock (page 178), and St. Basil's Cathedral in Moscow (page 267). (a) Note any similarities in architecture and design. (b) Write a hypothesis to account for any resemblance among the buildings. (c) How would you go about finding further evidence to test your hypothesis?
4. **Evaluating** Assume that you are Emperor Akbar. You are thinking of establishing one state religion that would include ideas from India's major religions. (a) What would be the advantages and disadvantages of such a policy? (b) Decide what action you will take and explain your choice.
5. **Analyzing a concept** Writers sometimes call Southeast Asia the crossroads of Asia. Suggest at least three reasons why this is an appropriate name.

Perspectives on Past and Present

Americans and Europeans who travel in India today often note the contrast between the extremely rich and the very poor. What factors in the history you have read might account for these extremes of wealth and poverty in Indian society?

Investigating History

The rivers of India—in particular the Ganges, Yamuna, and Brahmaputra—are central to Indian religion and tradition. Find out about the role of one of these rivers in Indian life. What problems do these rivers sometimes cause? The *National Geographic* for November 1988 contains an article on the Brahmaputra.

CHAPTER
Evaluation

Chapter Test 13, Alternate Chapter Test 13, and Computer Test Bank Chapter 13 Test can be used to evaluate your students' understanding of this chapter.

Africa and the Americas

Chapter Overview

Geographically, Africa is divided into five regions—the northern and southern coasts, the deserts, the dry grasslands, the savannas, and the rain forest. Historically, the Sahara has been a dividing line in Africa. Among the great societies south of the Sahara were those of Meroë (the Kushite capital), Axum, the Swahili city-states, and Zimbabwe. Between A.D. 300 and 1600 three empires, Ghana, Mali, and Songhai, rose in western Africa. All the African empires were important trading centers.

In North America, there were many cultures and language groups. Archaeologists have found impressive remains of the Anasazi of the southwest, the Hopewell of the eastern woodlands, and the Mississippians of the midwest. In Mexico and Central and South America, many mighty empires developed. They included the Moche and Inca in Peru, the Olmec and Maya in Mexico and Central America, and the Aztec in central Mexico.

Chapter Focus

Begin by directing students' attention to the world map on page 880. Ask students whether they can locate a country where a major historic event could occur without the rest of the world finding out about it. Point out that modern communications make it virtually impossible for any country to exist in complete isolation from the rest of the world. Have students read the chapter introduction (pages 314–315). Ask which three continents had civilizations that were isolated from the rest of the world until the late 1400's. Note that the people living in sub-Saharan Africa, North America, and South America were isolated from the rest of the world.

Kingdoms and city-states arose in East Africa.

1

Setting the Stage

Using Geographic Themes: Place and Location (Objective 1) Direct students' attention to the map of Africa (page 316). Ask students what geographic factors affected Africa's contact with Europe and Asia. Northern Africa's proximity to the Mediterranean Sea fostered extensive contact with southern Europe and the Middle East. The Sahara discouraged contact between Europe and sub-Saharan Africa. Then point out that most of Africa's long coastline lacks natural harbors. Rivers fall steeply from the central African plateau, preventing oceangoing ships from traveling inland. In addition, the prevailing winds on Africa's Atlantic coast blow from north to south. European ships could therefore travel down the coast but would have found it harder to return against the wind.

Chapter 14 Africa and the Americas 1200 B.C.–A.D. 1500

FOCUS The rise and fall of isolated civilizations on three continents

★ Advanced
● Basic

	SECTION 1	SECTION 2	SECTION 3	SECTION 4
Objectives	1. Explain how geographic features affected Africa's contact with other regions. 2. Identify and describe the climate and geography of the five major regions of Africa. 3. Identify the kingdom of Axum and describe the rock churches of Lalibela. 4. Describe the economic importance of eastern Africa's Indian Ocean trade.	1. Explain the economic significance of the West African gold-salt trade. 2. Compare and contrast the Ghana, Mali, and Songhai empires. 3. Describe some of the similarities among early African cultures.	1. Explain how the first people came to North America. 2. Explain how the discovery of agriculture changed life in the Americas. 3. Describe how several cultures used geographic location to their own advantage.	1. Locate on a map and briefly describe the great American civilizations. 2. Describe and use the Mayan number system.
Setting the Stage	Using Geographic Themes: Place and Location	The role of trade in the growth of cities and empires	Asian hunters as the true discoverers of America	Civilizations without the wheel
Teaching Strategies	Using Geographic Themes: Desert Regions Transparency 51 Outline Map 13 Teaching with Pictures: The Rock Churches of Lalibela Transparency 52 Economics and History: Africa's Indian Ocean Trade Check for Understanding	Economics and History: The Gold-Salt Trade Skill Building: Comparing and Contrasting African Kingdoms Transparency 53 Discussing History: Traditional Culture of Africa Check for Understanding	Using Geographic Themes: Movement Transparency 54 Transferring Ideas: The Discovery of Agriculture Geography in History: Location Transparency 55 Check for Understanding	Geography in History: Central and South American Cultures Discussing History: Mayan Math Check for Understanding
Guided Practice	Transparency 51 Q&A Transparency 52 Q&A Section Review 1	Transparency 53 Q&A Section Review 2	Transparency 54 Q&A Transparency 55 Q&A Section Review 3	Section Review 4
Independent Practice Worksheets	Independent Practice 14.1 Vocabulary 14 Basic Skills 14	Independent Practice 14.2 Geography Skills 14 Critical Thinking 14	Independent Practice 14.3	Independent Practice 14.4
Enrichment	1. Primary Source: Voices 14.1 2. Preparing a Report: African Sculpture 3. Researching for Points	1. Primary Source: Voices 14.2 2. Preparing an Oral History 3. Researching for Points	1. Primary Source: Voices 14.3 2. Preparing a Report: Early Americans 3. ★Solving a Riddle 4. Researching for Points	1. Primary Source: Voices 14.4 2. Creative Writing 3. Researching for Points

Chapter Closer		
●Reteaching Activities	Making a Time Line, Making a Chart
Chapter Review	Summary, Reviewing the Facts, Basic Skills, Researching and Reporting Skills, Critical Thinking, Perspectives on Past and Present, Investigating History
Chapter Evaluation	Chapter Test 14, Alternate Chapter Test 14, Computer Test Bank Chapter 14 Test

Unit IV Review	
Geographic Theme	Place: What are the characteristics of three cities of the past?
Historical Themes	Human-Environment Interaction, Continuity and Change, Cultural Development
Unit Evaluation	Unit IV Test, Alternate Unit IV Test

Teaching Strategies

Using Geographic Themes: Desert Regions (Objective 2) Have students read "Africa has five major regions" (pages 315–317). Then direct their attention to the map on page 316, or use Map Transparency 51, *Regions of Africa.* Point out that the Sahara, the largest desert in the world, covers an area as large as the United States and contains half of the world's desert surface. Fossil evidence shows that the Sahara region experienced a series of wet and dry periods during the last 65 million years. The most recent wet period occurred within the past 10,000 years.

Since about 3000 B.C. the Sahara has been arid, and in recent times the desert has been expanding. During the past half century more than 400,000 square miles of once-productive land on the southern edge of the Sahara has become desert. What factors in human-environment interaction contribute to the spread of deserts? A combination of drought, deforestation, and overgrazing is currently causing the Sahara to expand at an alarming rate. Distribute Outline Map 13: Africa. Have students use the map on page 316 to label the five geographic regions and the major rivers. Remind students to include a map title and a map key.

Teaching with Pictures: The Rock Churches of Lalibela (Objective 3) Display Map Transparency 52, *The Kingdoms of Kush and Axum.* Ask students to locate the city of Lalibela. Direct students' attention to the picture of the Church of St. George (page 319). Ask, "Why is this church unusual?" Explain that workers first dug a trench 40 feet deep into a rocky hillside. Skilled craftsmen then carved the huge block of stone into a Greek cross. The interior of St. George contains beautiful mosaics and decorated columns.

Economics and History: Africa's Indian Ocean Trade (Objective 4) Have students read "Coastal cities traded with Asia" (page 319). Then ask them to use the map on page 321 to locate Kilwa. Trade made Kilwa one of the richest East African cities between the twelfth and fifteenth centuries. Archaeologists found evidence of great wealth at Kilwa when they uncovered ruins of a royal palace with more than 100 rooms, several inner courtyards, and a large octagonal swimming pool.

Check for Understanding Have students write a paragraph describing Africa's five regions. Then ask students to explain how the peoples of Kush, Axum, East Africa, and Zimbabwe took advantage of the geography and resources of their respective homelands.

Enrichment Activities

1. **Reading a Primary Source** Assign Voices from the Past Resource Book 14.1.

2. **Preparing a Report** Have students report on African sculpture. (See *The African Kings* by Mary Cable and *African Kingdoms* by Basil Davidson.) Alternatively, interested students might report on the impact of the expansion of desert on present-day Africa.

3. **Researching for Bonus Points** What are the names of four of the deserts located in Africa? (Sahara, Namib, Nubian, and Kalahari)

Setting the Stage

Ask students to use what they have learned about East Africa to explain how trade promotes the growth of cities and empires. Point out that the exchange of goods and services creates jobs, promotes urban development, stimulates cultural interaction, and produces the wealth that supports artistic expression.

Teaching Strategies

Economics and History: The Gold-Salt Trade (Objective 1) Ask students if they would exchange gold for salt. This unlikely exchange was the driving force behind the great trans-Saharan trade that brought enormous wealth to Ghana, Mali, and Songhai. Gold miners exchanged their treasure for horses, daggers, silks, jewelry, and fine clothing from North Africa. However, the product that they needed the most was salt, an essential ingredient in the human diet. Because salt was scarce in West Africa, the people of these regions were said to have a craving for it. In contrast, salt could be found in such great abundance in the western Sahara that great blocks of it were sometimes used to construct the walls of houses.

Muslim traders, eager to obtain West African gold, formed caravans loaded with huge quantities of salt. This gold-salt exchange stimulated the emergence of thriving commercial cities that became the centers of three great empires.

Skill Building: Comparing and Contrasting African Kingdoms (Objective 2) Review with students pages 321–324 and Map Transparency 53, *African Kingdoms, 1000–1500.* Then have students carry on a discussion of the following questions:

1. What role did trade play in the development of West African empires?
2. What were the most significant achievements of these empires?
3. What general statement can you make about the reasons these empires fell?

Discussing History: Traditional Culture of Africa (Objective 3) Have students read "Africans shared cultural patterns" and "The arts flourished in many forms" (pages 324–325). Then ask students to explain several general characteristics shared by many early West African cultures. The importance of family and lineage, women's active role in agriculture, and the blending of monotheistic and polytheistic religions are characteristic of many sub-Saharan cultures. Ask students to explain the significance and purpose of the various arts in Western African culture. Emphasize the link between the arts and religion, politics, and daily life.

Check for Understanding Ask students to explain the role that trade played in stimulating the growth of city-states and empires in Africa.

Enrichment Activities

1. **Reading a Primary Source**
   Assign Voices from the Past Resource Book 14.2.
2. **Preparing an Oral History**
   Have groups of students, as griots, prepare an oral history of some event discussed in this section. Each group can then present its story to the class.
3. **Researching for Bonus Points**
   What was the name of the Christian king Europeans hoped to find in Ethiopia? (Prester John)

Setting the Stage

Begin by asking, "Who discovered America?" List responses on the board. Then explain that historians believe nomadic hunters from Asia were the discoverers of America.

Teaching Strategies

Using Geographic Themes: Movement (Objective 1) Have students read "The Americas have many regions" and "The first Americans came from Asia" (page 326). Show Map Transparency 54, *Early Migration to the Americas*. Have a volunteer trace the westernmost route migrants used from Asia to South America. Ask students to describe the geographic features the migrants encountered along the way.

Transferring Ideas: The Discovery of Agriculture (Objective 2) Ask students to recall the Neolithic revolution and describe its importance. Then have them read "Farmers learned how to raise corn" (pages 326–327). What effect did learning to grow corn have on the way of life of early Americans?

Geography in History: Location (Objective 3) Display Map Transparency 55, *Some Early Cultures of the Americas*, or use the map on page 329. Point out to students that the Mississippi River and its many tributaries create a vast water network spanning much of North America. Have students list the general group names of cultures that lived near these rivers. How did the river network affect the way of life of the Hopewell and Mississippian cultures?

Check for Understanding Ask students to describe how the Anasazi, Hopewell, and Mississippian cultures adapted to their environment.

Enrichment Activities

1. **Reading a Primary Source**
   Assign Voices from the Past Resource Book 14.3.
2. **Preparing a Report**
   Have students report on one of the following topics: the Anasazi, the Hopewell, the Mississippians, or the Hohokam. (See *The First Americans* by Robert Claiborne.)
3. **Solving a Riddle**
   There is still a lively debate among scholars as to when the first nomadic hunters reached America. Some scientists believe that there is no evidence of humans in the Western Hemisphere earlier than 12,000 years ago. Others argue that the first people reached the Americas more than 30,000 years ago. Ask advanced students to report on this topic. (See *National Geographic*, September 1979, and *The First Americans*, by Brian Fagan.)
4. **Researching for Bonus Points**
   What is the name scientists have given to the land bridge that once connected Asia and North America? (Beringia)

Great civilizations arose in the Americas.

4

Setting the Stage

Discuss with students the advantages of wheeled vehicles pulled by beasts of burden, such as horses and oxen. Then point out that all of the civilizations they have studied thus far have had wheeled vehicles. Ask, "Is it possible for a civilization to develop without this advantage?"

Teaching Strategies

Geography in History: Central and South American Cultures (Objective 1) Direct students' attention to the map on page 329. Explain that most early Central and South American cultures developed in one of two regions, the coast of modern-day Peru or the area around modern-day Mexico City. Have students use the map on page 329 to locate the coast of Peru. Explain that the first civilization in South America began here as early as 3000 B.C. Little is known about this culture. Three later Peruvian civilizations, to be covered in this chapter, developed in the same region. Make a chart entitled "Peruvian Civilizations" on the board. Label three columns *Chavin, Moche,* and *Inca.* In the first row, fill in the approximate dates of each civilization: Chavin, ca. 800 B.C.–ca. 100 B.C.; Moche, ca. 100 B.C.–A.D. 700; Inca, ca. A.D. 1100–1530. Then have students locate the Valley of Mexico on the map on page 329. The southern end of the valley and the Gulf Coast rain forest to the east were home to the Olmec (ca. 1200 B.C.– ca. 400 B.C.), Maya (ca. 400 B.C.– ca. A.D. 900), and Aztec (ca. A.D. 900–1521). Make a chart entitled "Central American Civilizations" and fill in the names and dates provided. Save the charts and have

students fill in additional information, such as way of life and accomplishments, about each culture after they read Section 4.

Discussing History: Mayan Math (Objective 2) Have students read "The Maya built great cities" (pages 333–334). Point out that the Maya were skilled mathematicians who created an advanced system of numbers that used only three symbols—a dot, a bar, and a shell shape. Each dot stood for the numeral 1, each bar stood for the numeral 5, and the shell shape represented zero. As illustrated below, all numerals up to 19 were expressed by a combination of these three symbols.

0	1	2	3	4
5	6	7	8	9
10	11	12	13	14
15	16	17	18	19

Remind students that our number system is based on *10*'s. In contrast, the Maya counted in *20*'s and wrote large numerals in columns. In this system, the bottom row stood for numerals between 0 and 19, the second row stood for multiples of 20, the third row for multiples of 400, the fourth row for multiples of 8,000, and so on. For example, the numbers 267 and 2,953 are explained below.

(13 sets of 20, or 260)
(1 bar and 2 dots, or 7) } = 267

(7 sets of 400, or 2,800)
(7 sets of 20, or 140) } = 2,953
(2 bars and 3 dots, or 13)

After the students have practiced with this system, divide the class into groups and assign each group three numbers. Ask the groups to translate their numbers into Mayan symbols as rapidly and accurately as possible.

Check for Understanding Call on students to identify the Olmec, Tikal, Tenochtitlán, and the Inca.

Enrichment Activities

1. **Reading a Primary Source** Assign Voices from the Past Resource Book 14.4.

2. **Creative Writing** Ask students to pretend that they have been transported back in time to one of these three cities: Tikal, Tenochtitlán, or Cuzco. Have them write journal entries describing an aspect of daily life in one of these cities. (See *National Geographic,* December 1973, December 1975, and December 1980.)

3. **Researching for Bonus Points** What was the name of the Aztec Sun god? (Huitzilopochtili)

ANSWERS TO
Chapter Review 14

Reviewing the Facts

1. **(a)** place in desert where underground water comes to the surface in a spring or well **(b)** tallgrass plain **(c)** group in which all members believe they are descended from a common ancestor **(d)** record keeper who memorized and passed down history orally

2. **(a)** largest desert in the world **(b)** semiarid region just south of the Sahara **(c)** record keepers who memorized and passed on a community's history and laws **(d)** first people to form a major kingdom in sub-Saharan Africa **(e)** early Christian kingdom **(f)** Soninke title

for king and name of region he ruled **(g)** Sundiata's empire **(h)** ancient culture of present-day New Mexico **(i)** early civilization of Peruvian desert **(j)** people who built a culture based on trade in present-day Ohio **(k)** early civilization in Gulf Coast rain forest in Mexico **(l)** highly developed civilization of Guatemala and Mexico **(m)** people who established vast empire in Peru **(n)** people who developed powerful empire in the Valley of Mexico

3. northern and southern coasts—fertile land, moderate rainfall, warm temperatures, hot and dry summers; deserts—hot, dry, and with oases; dry grasslands—semi-arid region with short grass, few trees, suitable for grazing; savannas—tall-grass plains with alternating rainy and dry seasons; rain forests—almost daily rainfall, towering mahogany and teak trees, nearly bare ground

4. (a) In addition to living family members, a lineage included past generations (spirits) and future generations. **(b)** took the place of kings or other rulers; acted as a support group

5. Hopewell culture peaked around A.D. 400 in southern Ohio; depended on trade; skilled craftspeople; built burial mounds. Anasazi lived in North American southwest from A.D. 600 to 1200; depended on growing corn; skilled builders; built elaborate buildings of stone and mortar.

Basic Skills

1. All events occurred over a period of time.

2. (a) T'ang and Sung dynasties in China, Heian Age in Japan, first Muslim invasion and rise of Rajput kingdoms in India **(b)** Ming dynasty in China, daimyo control in Japan, Delhi sultanate and Da Gama's arrival in India

3. Examples of main ideas: **(a)** Kush civilization was heavily influenced by Egypt. **(b)** Christianity has been the religion of Axum and Ethiopia through the centuries. **(c)** In the coastal cities, a blending of races, religions, and languages resulted from trade and immigration. **(d)** Ghana flourished through control of the salt-gold trade. **(e)** In Mali, Muslim influence grew. **(f)** In Songhai, Timbuktu became a famous center of learning.

4.

	Aztecs	Incas
Location	Island on lake	High in mountains
Political organization	Empire taking tribute from conquered people	Empire taking tribute, strong administration
Religion	sun worship	sun worship
Major achievements	splendid city, canals, causeways, fountains, baths, zoo	stone masonry, highway network, messenger service, quipu, cities

Researching and Reporting Skills

1. Possible answers include: **(a)** Kushite writings **(b)** rock churches **(c)** remains of cities **(d)** Arab geographer al-Bakri **(e)** Ibn Battuta's accounts and reports of Mansa Musa's pilgrimage to Mecca **(f)** account by Muslim scholar **(g)** burial mounds **(h)** pottery **(i)** remains of cities; writing

2. Official writings and inscriptions, likely to be informative and objective about historical and political events; travelers' accounts, contemporary reports very informative about social and cultural aspects, but may be biased or exaggerated; burials, ruins, artifacts, informative but subject to interpretation.

3. Students' references will vary.

4. Students' titles will vary.

Critical Thinking

1. (a) location on trade routes; mineral resources **(b)** western kingdoms depended on trade in salt and gold; eastern kingdoms on iron and on trade from interior to the coast

2. (a) gold, salt, ivory, skins, iron, tortoise shells **(b)** jewelry, glass, cloth, porcelain, silk, and other luxuries from India, Arabia, and China

3. location on upper Nile and on land routes to Red Sea

4. Answers will vary, but as examples: The east-coast cities of Africa became places for the exchange of goods from the interior for goods from Asia. In North America, people of Hopewell culture lived by hunting and fishing in their forest environment.

5. (a) the wide variety of landforms and climates **(b)** Cultures in Central and South America were on a much larger scale.

6. Maya—surmounted by temple, used as place of worship; Egyptian—peaked, used as tombs of pharaohs

7. (a) *Maya:* cities, pyramids, calendar, concept of zero; *Aztec:* Tenochtitlán, architecture, city planning, political organization; *Inca:* agriculture, highways, stone-walled fortresses, political organization **(b)** Answers will vary, but the Mayas, for their early time, created a very sophisticated civilization.

Perspectives on Past and Present
Students' findings will vary.

Investigating History
Students' projects will vary.

Chapter 14

Teaching with Pictures

Ask students to study the map closely. How is the style of the map different from modern maps? Would students classify the map as physical or political? Explain that the man on camelback is a Berber trader, emerging from his tent village. The Atlas Mountains are shown as a wall across the upper portion of the map, while the River Niger flows beneath Mansa Musa's throne. Ask them why they think the European mapmaker included those items on the map. Finally, ask if the map shows a thorough understanding of the region.

The first European map of western Africa, drawn in 1375.

Key Terms

sub-Saharan
oasis
semiarid
desertification
savanna
Swahili
dhow
lineage
matrilineal
diviner
griot
pueblo
quipu
tribute

314

Read and Understand

1. Kingdoms and city-states arose in East Africa.
2. West African empires thrived on trade.
3. Early Americans had many ways of life.
4. Great civilizations arose in the Americas.

The people of Cairo were usually hard to impress. After all, the world-famous pyramids looked down upon their city from across the Nile. The sultan of Egypt, one of the most powerful and respected rulers in the Arab world, lived in a magnificent palace in Cairo. Nonetheless everyone from the sultan to the shopkeepers in the marketplace was dazzled by the incredible caravan that arrived in July 1324.

Five hundred slaves, each carrying a six-pound staff of gold, arrived first. They were followed by 100 camels, each of which carried a 300-pound load of gold dust. Hundreds of other camels brought enormous supplies of food and clothing. Thousands of servants and officials completed the procession.

Chapter 14 Resources

GEOGRAPHY
- Geography Skills 14
- Outline Map 13
- Transparencies 51, 52, 53, 54, 55

REINFORCEMENT
- Vocabulary 14
- Basic Skills 14
- Reteaching 14
- Making Connections Study Guide 14

ENRICHMENT
- Critical Thinking 14

- History and Literature 14

ASSESSMENT
- Chapter Test 14
- Alternate Chapter Test 14
- Computer Test Bank

Who, the people of Cairo wondered, led this caravan and what was its purpose? Their questions were soon answered. The caravan was led by Mansa Musa, the Muslim ruler of a fabulously wealthy West African empire called Mali. At that time, Mali covered an area about equal to all of western Europe. Only the vast Mongol empire was bigger.

The people of Cairo learned that Mansa Musa was a devout Muslim who was making a pilgrimage to the holy city of Mecca. His visit to Cairo created a sensation. One Egyptian later wrote that Mansa Musa gave away so much gold that the value of this precious metal declined for 12 years.

News of Mansa Musa's extraordinary wealth quickly spread across the Mediterranean Sea to Europe. In 1375, a Spanish mapmaker drew a map of an "unknown continent" that for the first time showed Europeans where western Africa was located. The map (see opposite page) also contained a drawing of Mansa Musa seated on a throne holding a gold nugget.

It is not surprising that a European mapmaker labeled West Africa an unknown continent. Until the late 1400's, Europeans had little contact with the people of Africa. Although ships from Arabia and China traded with cities on Africa's east coast, Asians knew little of the continent's interior. And the people on all three continents were unaware of the dynamic civilizations that thrived in North and South America.

Historians' knowledge of early civilizations in Africa and the Americas is still limited in certain ways. In some cases, linguists have not yet succeeded in deciphering the writings from those cultures. In other cases, conquest and war destroyed architectural and artistic wonders that can never be replaced.

Although knowledge of these early civilizations is incomplete, archaeologists and other scholars have made a number of remarkable discoveries. Their work has shown that many unique civilizations developed in Africa, North America, and South America. This chapter will describe the geographic conditions that tended to separate these civilizations from the European and Asian worlds. It will also trace their cycle of development and highlight their unique cultural contributions.

Kingdoms and city-states arose in East Africa. 1

Geography has played a major role in shaping African history. As you saw in Chapter 3, the Nile River strongly influenced life in ancient Egypt. While Egypt was an integral part of the Mediterranean world, the Nile cataracts limited contacts between Egypt and the lands south of the Sahara, or **sub-Saharan** Africa. This section will explain how geographic features tended to create a self-contained environment in sub-Saharan Africa. It will then describe the culture and achievements of the kingdoms and city-states that rose to power in eastern Africa.

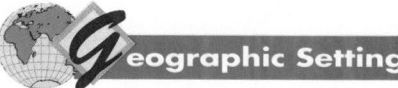
Geographic Setting

Africa has five major regions.

Africa is the second largest continent, exceeded in size only by Asia. It covers 11.7 million square miles, giving it about 20 percent of Earth's land surface. Africa stretches about 5,000 miles from north to south. Its greatest distance from east to west is 4,600 miles, about equal to the distance from New York City to Moscow. Geographers divide the continent into five distinct regions.

The northern and southern coasts Narrow strips of fertile land border the northern coast and the southern tip of Africa. Both areas have moderate rainfall and warm temperatures. Summers tend to be hot and dry. Though these coastal strips make up only a small part of the vast continent, they support dense populations.

The deserts The fertile coastal strips quickly yield to vast deserts. The Sahara in the north and the Kalahari in the south are Africa's two largest deserts. Altogether, deserts make up about one third of Africa's land.

The Sahara extends from the Atlantic Ocean to the Red Sea, covering an area roughly the size of the United States. *Sahara* comes from the Arabic word sahra, meaning "desert." It suggests the gasping sound made by parched travelers. Unlike many deserts, only a small part of the Sahara consists of sand dunes. The rest is a flat, gray wasteland of scattered rocks and pebbles with occasional rock outcrops and ridges.

315

SECTION 1
Objectives and Teaching Strategies

OBJECTIVE 1. Explain how geographic features affected Africa's contact with other regions.

Teaching Strategy: *Using Geographic Themes: Place and Location* (page 314a)

OBJECTIVE 2. Identify and describe the climate and geography of the five major regions of Africa.

Teaching Strategy: *Using Geographic Themes: Desert Regions* (page 314c)

OBJECTIVE 3. Identify the kingdom of Axum and describe the rock churches of Lalibela.

Teaching Strategy: *Teaching with Pictures: The Rock Churches of Lalibela* (page 314c)

OBJECTIVE 4. Describe the economic importance of eastern Africa's Indian Ocean trade.

Teaching Strategy: *Economics and History: Africa's Indian Ocean Trade* (page 314c)

■ BACKGROUND

Unlike Europeans, Arabs and North Africans had many contacts with Africa south of the Sahara. They were accustomed to desert travel and crossed the Sahara by camel caravan. Their ships sailed along the East African coast, trading silks and spices for ivory and gold.

SECTION 1
Resources

GEOGRAPHY
■ Transparencies 51, 52

REINFORCEMENT
■ Independent Practice 14.1

ENRICHMENT
■ Voices from the Past 14.1

ASSESSMENT
■ Section Quiz 14.1

ANSWERS TO

Focus on Geography

1. about four fifths; about three fourths
2. desert
3. altitude of plateau moderates the heat of the tropics
4. hindered trade and contact with overseas civilizations

■ BACKGROUND

Portuguese mariners discovered the Zaire River in 1483. A series of treacherous rapids a short distance upriver, however, prevented further exploration for nearly four centuries. The Zaire winds through one of the world's last great rain forests. In *Heart of Darkness*, Joseph Conrad said, "Going up that river was like traveling back to the earliest beginnings of the world, when vegetation rioted on the earth and the big trees were kings. An empty stream, a great silence, an impenetrable forest . . ."

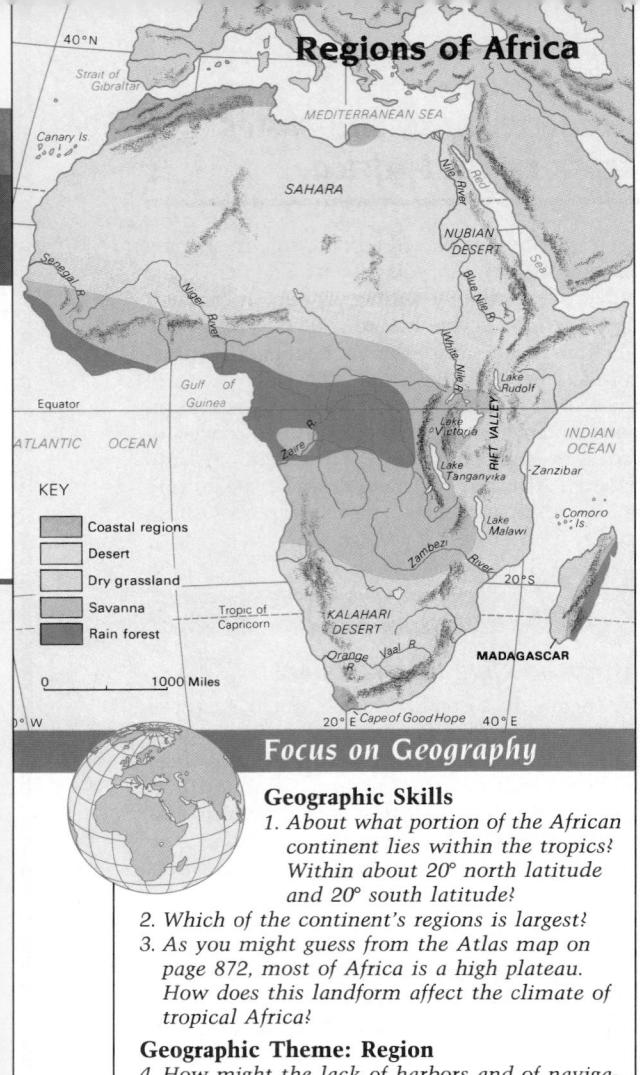

Regions of Africa

KEY

- Coastal regions
- Desert
- Dry grassland
- Savanna
- Rain forest

0   1000 Miles

Focus on Geography

Geographic Skills
1. *About what portion of the African continent lies within the tropics? Within about 20° north latitude and 20° south latitude?*
2. *Which of the continent's regions is largest?*
3. *As you might guess from the Atlas map on page 872, most of Africa is a high plateau. How does this landform affect the climate of tropical Africa?*

Geographic Theme: Region
4. *How might the lack of harbors and of navigable rivers affect Africa's development?*

Because of its vast size, the Sahara has been compared to a waterless ocean. Traders have used camels, the ships of the desert, to cross it since about A.D. 400. Nonetheless the Sahara is not totally arid. About 90 inhabited **oases** are found there. An oasis is a place where underground water comes to the surface in a spring or well. Caravans with as many as 10,000 camels followed fixed routes between oases. Caravans usually took about two months to cross the Sahara.

The dry grasslands Close to the deserts and inland from the east coast lies a border area of dry grassland. This region is too dry for farming but suitable for grazing. The **semiarid** climate, with less than 20 inches of rainfall a year, supports only short grass and a few trees. In this region, since prehistoric times, nomads have moved with their herds from one pasture to another.

The balance between animals and environment here is a delicate one. During cycles of drought, when even less rain falls and the grass dries up, both people and animals suffer. Overgrazing too is a threat to the environment, since it can even kill the grass. When that happens, the light soil dries out and begins to turn to desert. This process is known as **desertification.** The threat from desertification is greatest in the area called the Sahel, a semiarid region lying south of the Sahara and reaching from the Atlantic to Ethiopia.

The savannas As the average rainfall gradually increases, the dry grasslands give way to tall-grass plains called **savannas** (suh-VAN-uhz). Savannas cover about two fifths of the continent.

In the savannas, rainy seasons alternate with dry seasons. When the land is drenched with rain, tall grasses, wildflowers, and umbrella-shaped acacia trees come to life. However, farming is difficult on the savanna because heavy rains can strip minerals from the soil. Then, when the dry season comes, the ground turns almost as hard and dusty as the desert.

Despite their poor soil, the savannas have always supported the largest share of Africa's population. In most years, early farmers had enough rainfall to raise their crops of millet (a type of grain) and African rice.

The rain forest Inland from the Atlantic Ocean, straddling the equator, stretches a damp, densely wooded region known as the rain forest. Although rain forests cover less than one fifth of the continent, they are—like the desert—a barrier to travel. Africa's second longest river, the Zaire (zah-EER), twists slowly through the rain forest.

Although rain forests are often referred to as jungle, there is actually little undergrowth on the forest floor. This lack of vegetation is partly caused by huge mahogany and teak trees that grow up to 150 feet tall. Their leaves and branches form a dense ceiling, or canopy, that prevents up to 98 percent of the sunlight from reaching the forest floor.

316

The deadliest creature lurking in the forest gloom is not the Congo python or wild leopard but a small fly called the tsetse. Tsetse flies are hosts for tiny parasites called trypanosomes. These parasites carry a disease that is deadly to livestock and that may cause a fatal sleeping sickness in humans.

The tsetse fly has played a major role in African history. Historians believe that its presence forced Muslim missionaries and traders to avoid the rain forest in order to protect their horses and camels. In addition to keeping invaders out of the rain forest, the tsetse fly also prevented African farmers from using cattle, donkeys, and horses in areas near the rain forest.

Geography contained Africa.

Most of sub-Saharan Africa consists of a high plateau that drops sharply to a narrow coastal plain. In terms of climate, the plateau is an advantage because its altitude offsets the heat of the tropics. In terms of access to the continent, however, the plateau's edge is a barrier. Because Africa's major rivers surge over dangerous rapids and falls before reaching the sea, oceangoing ships cannot reach the interior. On the Zaire River, large vessels can travel inland for less than 100 miles before encountering rapids and falls.

Africa's shoreline also limited contact with the outside world. Unlike Europe, Africa has a very smooth coastline with few deep harbors or bays. In addition, dangerous sandbars, tricky currents, and difficult wind conditions combined to discourage outreach and trade. Within the continent, the vast distances combined with deserts and rain forests to limit travel and trade. Instead, life centered on the needs and traditions of family, kinship, and community.

Kush thrived on trade.

As you saw in Chapter 1, the earliest humans lived in eastern Africa. From there, they spread to other lands. During the long ages before the Sahara became a desert, it was the home of hunters and gatherers. In time, some people domesticated animals and became herders. Others— as in Mesopotamia, Egypt, India, and China— learned to grow crops.

The spread of the agricultural revolution quickened the pace of change as new societies and cultures developed. One early center of culture arose at Nok in what is now central Nigeria. There a group of people became skilled farmers. They learned to use iron to make tools and developed a unique style of art. Their culture, which thrived at the same time as the cultures of the Greeks and Persians, has become known only in the past half-century. It may be from this region that the early Bantu peoples began migrating to the southeast, bringing their language and culture to new areas of the continent.

The first major kingdom of sub-Saharan Africa arose in the middle region of the Nile valley. This was the kingdom of Kush. Egypt dominated Kush from about 2000 to 1000 B.C. During this time, Egyptian armies raided and even occupied Kush for a brief period. More important, the people of Kush learned about Egyptian civilization through trade. The Kushites adopted the Egyptian idea of a god-king, learned to write in hieroglyphics, and imitated the Egyptian style of pyramid building.

Although culturally indebted to the Egyptians, the Kushites were eager to assert their independence. In 751 B.C., a Kushite king named Piankhi (**PYANG**-kih) led an army down the Nile and conquered Egypt. Piankhi and his descendants became Egypt's Twenty-fifth Dynasty.

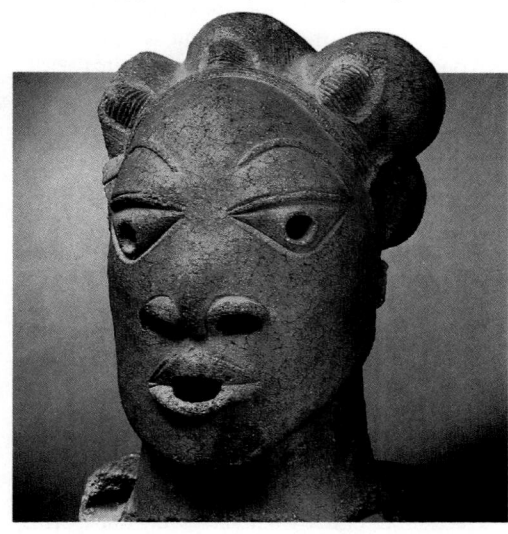

Nok terracotta sculpture from ancient Nigeria

317

■ **BACKGROUND**

At least 22 species of tsetse flies infest the savanna and forest regions south of the Sahara. Sleeping sickness is known to infect at least 20,000 Africans a year. In addition, the disease annually kills three million cattle. In recent years Zimbabwe, Malawi, Mozambique, and Zambia have spent millions of dollars trying to eradicate the tsetse fly. But many environmentalists question the wisdom of this campaign. "Eliminate the tsetse and cattle will invade," declared one environmentalist, "and cattle are the despoilers of Africa, bulldozing the continent into one big wasteland."

■ BACKGROUND

The Kushites also developed a writing system of their own. Unfortunately, it has not been deciphered. Thus, historians know less about Kush's golden age than about its earlier periods, when people used Egyptian writing.

The Egyptian pharaohs placed their tombs within their pyramids. In contrast, the Kushite kings placed their tombs under their pyramids. Archaeologists excavated most of the Kushite royal tombs during the early 1920's. Although thieves had long since plundered the tombs, the archaeologists did discover beautiful wall paintings, a few well-crafted ornaments, and a horse cemetery. The Kushites were noted for their superb horses, which were prized by nobles as far away as Assyria.

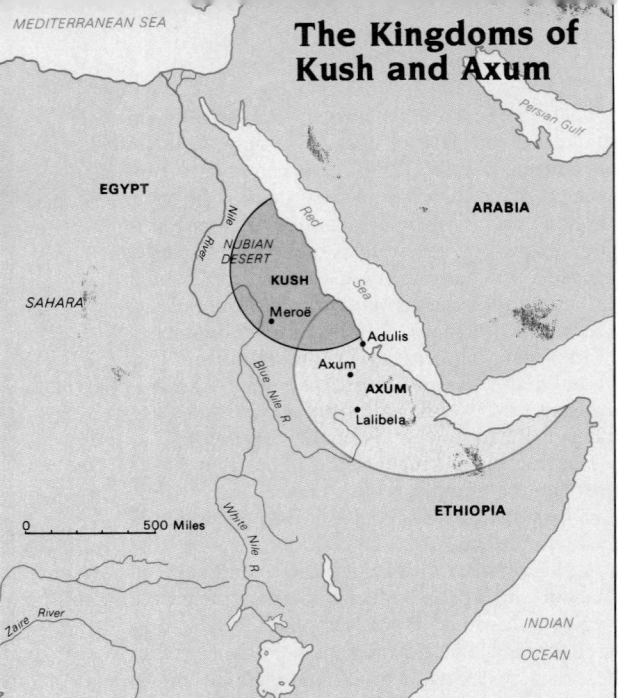

The Kingdoms of Kush and Axum

Map Study
On what sea did Axum's major port lie?

The Kushite dynasty proved to be short-lived. In 671 B.C., a Kushite king unwisely provoked the wrath of the Assyrian rulers who sought to conquer Egypt. Although the Kushites fought bravely, their bronze and stone weapons were no match for the iron spears and swords of the Assyrians. Within ten years, the Kushites withdrew from Egypt.

Despite the loss of Egypt, the Kushites demonstrated a remarkable ability to recover and build again. In about 550 B.C., the Kushite royal family moved to the city of Meroë near the Nile. Meroë was far enough away from Egypt to provide security and close enough to the Red Sea to take part in the growing trade among Africa, Arabia, and India.

The golden age of Meroë Meroë's energetic people exploited their favorable location and natural resources. Unlike Egypt, Meroë had abundant supplies of iron ore. By taking full advantage of this resource, Meroë became a major center for the manufacture of iron weapons and tools.

Ambitious merchants loaded iron ingots, tools, and spearheads onto their donkeys and transported the goods to the Red Sea. Here they exchanged

these goods for jewelry, fine cotton cloth, silver lamps, and glass bottles. Thus the mineral wealth of the central Nile valley flowed out from Meroë, and luxury goods from India and Arabia flowed in.

The Kushite kings ruled from beautiful palaces. Members of the royal family wore gold jewelry and collected pottery decorated with colorful animals, plants, and flowers. When Kushite kings died, they were buried with appropriate splendor inside stone-faced pyramids. Although much smaller than those in Egypt, the Kushite pyramids were nonetheless impressive.

The fall of Meroë After four centuries (from about 250 B.C. to about A.D. 150) of greatness, Meroë began to decline. Although some of the reasons for this collapse remain unknown, historians are certain that the rising power of Axum, a rival city located 400 miles southeast of Meroë, was the decisive cause. In about A.D. 350, King Ezana of Axum conquered Kush. The days of Meroë's glory were thus ended forever.

Historical knowledge about many aspects of life in Meroë remains limited. Scholars have thus far not been able to decipher the Kushite writing. Today Meroë is uninhabited and covered by drifting sands. Its ancient monuments lie in ruins, silent reminders of how fragile an achievement a civilization is.

Christian kings ruled in Axum.

In ancient times, Axum was the capital of a kingdom located in a rugged plateau region of eastern Africa called Ethiopia. By A.D. 300, Axum had grown rich and powerful by controlling trade between the African interior and the Red Sea. Persian and Arab merchants sailed to Axum's seaport of Adulis. Here they exchanged their wares for gold, ivory, and spices.

King Ezana became a Christian in A.D. 324, shortly before he conquered Meroë. Axum's rulers remained Christian through the centuries. When Islamic armies swept across Egypt and North Africa in the 600's, Ethiopia remained unconquered and unconverted. These Arab conquests, however, ended for centuries the contact between Ethiopia's kings and the Christian lands of western Europe and the Byzantine empire.

Finally, in 1520, a Portuguese explorer named Francisco Alvares journeyed into the Ethiopian Highlands. He was amazed to find Christians

318

worshiping in handsomely decorated churches. Built around 1200, many of the churches had been hollowed out of solid rock at the command of a devout king named Lalibela (LAH-lee-BAY-luh). Instead of towering skyward, each church was carved into bedrock below ground. Worshipers reached the church door by climbing down a flight of stairs about 30 to 40 feet deep. These stone churches symbolized the survival of Ethiopia's freedom and faith despite growing Muslim influence in East Africa.

Coastal cities traded with Asia.

At this time, trade was a vital factor in the growth of cities on the East African coast of present-day Kenya and Tanzania. From 1100 to 1500, more than 35 African city-states prospered along a thousand-mile strip of the East African coast. These cities bore such names as Malindi (muh-LIHN-dee), Mombasa (mahm-BAHS-uh), and Zanzibar (ZAN-suh-bahr).

The ancestors of the people who lived in these cities had migrated to the East African coast during the 700's. Most came from inland Africa and spoke languages from the Bantu language family. Other settlers on the coast were Arab Muslims who fled their homeland to escape political enemies.

Over the centuries, the two peoples—Bantu and Arab—intermarried. Their cultures blended and formed a new culture known as **Swahili** (swah-HEE-lee), from an Arabic term meaning "people of the coast." The Swahili language was at first mostly Bantu but later gained many Arabic words. In addition, Islam became the major religion of the coastal cities.

Most of the Swahili people lived by farming, fishing, and trading. They built small houses with walls of smoothed, sun-dried mud. Such houses clustered in villages all along the coast. At the best harbors, large towns grew up.

The Swahili ports welcomed trading vessels from Arabia, India, and even China. The most common ships in a Swahili harbor were triangular-sailed Arab vessels called **dhows** (dowz). More than 70 feet in length, a dhow was large enough to carry profitable cargo and sturdy enough to brave the monsoon winds of the Indian Ocean.

For centuries, the Arabs acted as middlemen in the Indian Ocean. They brought Asian luxuries

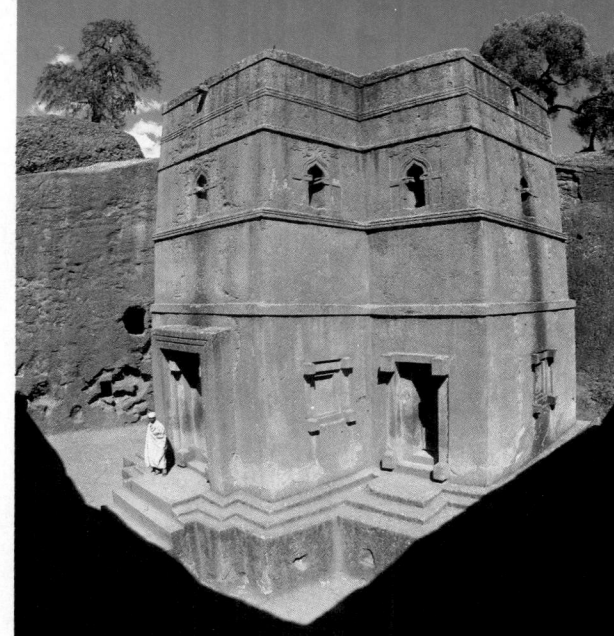

A rock church near the town of Lalibela

to Africa and African luxuries to Asia. In the busy markets of Kilwa, Mombasa, and Malindi, Arab sea captains displayed porcelain bowls and vases from China and jewels and cotton cloth from India. In return, they obtained African ivory, gold, tortoise shells, and rhinoceros horns. The 50-pound elephant tusks were carved into Indian chess pieces and the hilts for swords and daggers. Tortoise shells were made into decorative combs.

Zimbabwe became a kingdom.

Much of the gold and ivory traded in the Swahili markets came from the kingdom of Zimbabwe (zim-BAHB-way). This kingdom lay on a fertile plateau between the Zambezi and Limpopo rivers in southeastern Africa. Its inland location provided protection from Muslim influence.

As the kingdom's wealth increased, its rulers built an impressive residence known as Great Zimbabwe. The name *Zimbabwe* is derived from a Bantu phrase meaning either "stone enclosure" or "dwelling of the chief." Both of these meanings fit the stone structures that towered proudly over the surrounding savanna.

The kingdom of Zimbabwe reached the peak of its power in the early 1400's. Its power was

319

■ **BACKGROUND**
The Church of St. George shown on this page was constructed during the thirteenth century by King Lalibela. Workers began by digging a trench 40 feet deep into a hillside of volcanic rock. Skilled craftsmen then carved the huge block of stone into a Greek cross. The interior of St. George contains beautiful mosaics and finely decorated columns. According to legend, King Lalibela constructed this church when St. George galloped into town and demanded to know why no church had been built in his honor. Local residents still show visitors a rock that contains a curious hooflike mark.

ANSWERS TO

Section Review 1

Define:
(a) south of the Sahara
(b) place in desert where underground water
(continued)

ANSWERS TO *(continued)*

comes to the surface
(c) having less than 20
inches of rainfall a year
(d) the process by which
non-desert areas dry out and
turn to desert **(e)** tall-grass
plain **(f)** culture resulting
from the intermarriage of
Arab and Bantu people
(g) Arab vessel with triangular sail

Identify:
(a) largest desert in the
world **(b)** Africa's second-
longest river **(c)** semiarid region south of the Sahara
(d) site of early center of
culture located in central Nigeria **(e)** eastern African
kingdom whose economy
was based on iron
(f) Kushite capital and iron
manufacturing center
(g) Kushite king who conquered Egypt **(h)** capital of
ancient kingdom of Ethiopia
(i) residence of kings of
Zimbabwe

Answer:
1. northern and southern
coasts, deserts, dry grasslands, savannas, rain forest

2. presence of parasites prevented use of horses, camels, and other livestock

3. from conquered to
conquerors

4. (a) by controlling trade
between the African interior
and the Red Sea **(b)** its
Christianity

5. Arab middlemen took
Asian luxuries to Africa and
African luxuries to Asia.

6. Although northern Africa
was part of the Mediterranean world, the Sahara Desert and unfavorable
conditions for navigation
prevented contacts between
Europe and sub-Saharan
Africa.

Great Zimbabwe's 32-foot walls were 17 feet thick. The king lived in the high tower.

shattered, however, by the arrival of the Portuguese in the early 1500's. Today more than
300 huge stone ruins remain from the highly
organized society that prospered in Zimbabwe.

Section REVIEW 1

Define: (a) sub-Saharan, (b) oasis,
(c) semiarid, (d) desertification, (e) savanna,
(f) Swahili, (g) dhow
Identify: (a) Sahara, (b) Zaire River, (c) Sahel
(d) Nok, (e) Kush, (f) Meroë, (g) Piankhi,
(h) Axum (i) Great Zimbabwe
Answer:
1. Name the five geographic regions of Africa.
2. How have conditions in the rain forest affected
   human activity in that region?
3. How did Kush's relations with Egypt change
   over the years?
4. (a) How did Axum become a powerful city?
   (b) What set Ethiopia apart from other African
   kingdoms?
5. Describe the patterns of Swahili trade.

Critical Thinking
6. How did geographic conditions limit contacts
   between Africa and Europe?

320

West African empires thrived on trade. 2

While city-states were flourishing in eastern
Africa, powerful empires were developing in
western Africa. They arose in the savannas, the
sweeping grasslands between the Sahara and the
tropical rain forests. Three empires—Ghana, Mali,
and Songhai—rose to power there between A.D.
300 and 1600. This section will examine these
three empires and then describe several distinctive
patterns of daily life in Africa.

The gold-salt trade prospered.

The wealth of the savanna empires was based
on trade in two precious materials, gold and salt.
The gold came from a forest region south of the
savanna between the Niger (NYE-juhr) and Senegal
(SEHN-ih-GAHL) rivers (maps, pages 316 and 321).
Working in utmost secrecy, miners dug gold from
shafts as much as 100 feet deep or sifted it from
fast-moving streams. Until about 1350, at least
two thirds of the world's supply of gold came
from West Africa.

Although rich in gold, the savanna and forest
areas lacked salt, a material essential to human
life. In contrast, the Sahara contained abundant
deposits of salt. For example, salt was so plentiful
in the village of Taghaza that workers used slabs
of it to construct the walls of their homes.

Arab traders, eager to obtain West African gold,
carried salt from Taghaza across the Sahara by
camel caravan. After a long journey, they reached
the market towns of the savanna. Meanwhile,
other traders brought gold north from the forest
region. The two sets of merchants met in trading
centers such as Jenné (je-NAY) and Timbuktu
(TIM-buhk-TOO). There they exchanged goods under the watchful eye of the tax collector. Kings
taxed this trade heavily. In return, royal guards
kept peace in the markets. Royal officials made
sure that all traders weighed goods fairly and did
business according to law.

Some traders took part in a fascinating exchange
called the silent trade. At a spot near the Niger
River, Arab traders would pile their slabs of salt
in neat rows. Pounding on drums, they would
invite the gold merchants to trade. Then the
Arabs would mount their camels and ride off a

African Kingdoms, 1000–1500

KEY

- ▨ Swahili city-states
- ▢ Ghana about 1000
- ▢ Mali about 1400
- ▢ Songhai about 1600
- - - - - Trade routes

0 —————— 1000 Miles

Map Study

Which savanna empire reached Africa's west coast? What towns would a caravan go through on the shortest route from Tunis to Niani?

few miles. The gold merchants would arrive, look over the piles of salt, leave some of their gold, and withdraw into hiding. Next the Arabs would return and decide whether enough gold had been offered for their salt. If so, they would take the gold and leave the salt. If not, they would beat their drums, suggesting a second round of trading. Thus the traders swapped salt for gold without either group meeting the other.

Ghana taxed the gold-salt trade.

The trade routes lay across the savanna farmed by the Soninke (soh-NIHN-keh) people. The Soninke king demanded a heavy tax in both gold and salt from the Arab traders. The Soninke title for their king was *Ghana*. The Arabs applied this name to the entire territory. By the year 700, the empire of Ghana was well established.

321

SECTION 2
Objectives and Teaching Strategies

OBJECTIVE 1. Explain the economic significance of the West African gold-salt trade.

Teaching Strategy: *Economics and History: The Gold-Salt Trade* (page 314c)

OBJECTIVE 2. Compare and contrast the Ghana, Mali, and Songhai empires.

Teaching Strategy: *Skill Building: Comparing and Contrasting African Kingdoms* (page 314c)

OBJECTIVE 3. Describe some of the similarities among early African cultures.

Teaching Strategy: *Discussing History: Traditional Culture of Africa* (page 314d)

ANSWERS TO
Map Study

Mali; Timbuktu, Jenné

■ BACKGROUND

Scholars are debating whether the silent trade is legend or whether it actually took place.

SECTION 2
Resources

GEOGRAPHY
- Transparency 53

REINFORCEMENT
- Independent Practice 14.2

ENRICHMENT
- Voices from the Past 14.2

ASSESSMENT
- Section Quiz 14.2

■ **DISCUSSION**

How are the king and court of Ghana like the pharaoh and court of ancient Egypt? How are they different?

■ **BACKGROUND**

One gold nugget belonging to the ruler of Ghana weighed 30 pounds, and he tethered his horse to it.

ANSWERS TO

Voice from the Past

1. women treated with more respect than men
2. He admired it.
3. They lived apart from men, wore veils, and were not treated as equals to men.

■ **BACKGROUND**

Ibn Battuta has sometimes been called the Muslim Marco Polo.

Ghana's ruler demanded taxes and gifts from the chiefs of surrounding lands. As long as those chiefs made their payments, the king of Ghana left them in peace to rule their own people. When Ghana had a strong king, it controlled a wide territory. If the king was weak, Ghana's kingdom shrank. For much of its history, Ghana dominated a region about the size of Texas.

In 1076, an Arab geographer named al-Bakri wrote a description of Ghana's royal court:

> The king adorns himself like a woman, wearing necklaces and bracelets, and when he sits before the people he puts on a high cap decorated with gold and wrapped in turbans of fine cotton ... Behind the king stand ten pages holding shields and swords decorated with gold, and on his right are the sons of the vassal kings of his country wearing splendid garments and their hair plaited with gold.

Gold nuggets and slabs of salt (collected as taxes) were stashed away in the royal palace. Only the king had the right to own gold nuggets, although gold dust freely circulated in the marketplace. By this means, the king limited the supply of gold and kept its price from falling.

The Ghana acted as chief priest, judge, and military commander. In war, the Ghana could gather an army of 200,000 warriors. Nonetheless in 1076, Ghana's northern borders were overrun by zealous Muslim Berbers from the Almoravid (al-**MOHR**-uh-vihd) kingdom to the north. Although Ghana's armies eventually drove the Berbers out, the gold-salt trade was badly disrupted by the war. Ghana never regained its power.

Mali won control of trade.

As the supplies of gold gave out in the forest area, miners found new deposits farther east. As a result, the most important trade routes also

Voice from the Past | ***Ibn Battuta's Travel in Africa***

One of the greatest travelers in history was an Arab named Ibn Battuta (**IHB**-uhn bat-**TOO**-tah). Born in 1304 in Morocco, Ibn Battuta spent his entire adult life traveling through Muslim lands. He visited Mecca and Baghdad, Mombasa, and Kilwa. He traveled to India, Southeast Asia, and China. In 1352, this world traveler made the rugged trip across the Sahara to the savanna kingdoms. Here he found a number of things that surprised him.

> My stay in Walata lasted about 50 days ... It is an excessively hot place and has only a few small date palms ... The women are treated with more respect than the men, an amazing state of affairs. A man's heirs are his sister's sons, not his own sons. I have never seen such a custom anywhere else in the world except among the Indians of Malabar. But the Indians are heathens, while the people of Walata are Muslims, most careful about making their prayers, studying books of law, and memorizing the Koran. Yet their women show no shyness before men and do not veil themselves, though they go to prayers faithfully ...
>
> [Ibn Battuta then went on from Walata to Mali and described the people there.]
>
> They are seldom unjust and have a greater hatred of injustice than any other people ... There is complete security in their country. Neither the traveler nor the man who stays at home has anything to fear from robbers or men of violence.

1. What did Ibn Battuta find most surprising about the customs in Walata?
2. What did he think of people's practice of Islam?
3. From Ibn Battuta's reactions, what can you deduce about the way women lived in other Muslim countries?

shifted eastward. By 1200, a different group of people, the Mandingo, controlled the gold trade.

At first, a ruthless king named Sumanguru (su-MAN-gu-ru) ruled over the Mandingo. For years, the Mandingo submitted to Sumanguru's high taxes and cruel advisors. According to Mandingo legends, Sumanguru crushed any hope of rebellion by executing 11 out of 12 sons of a powerful rival. Sumanguru spared the twelfth son Sundiata (suhn-dee-AH-tuh) because he was badly crippled and seemed unlikely to survive.

Sumanguru, however, had made a mistake. As Sundiata grew to manhood, he gained strength and became a popular leader. Many Mandingo warriors joined Sundiata's ever-growing army. Although caught by surprise, Sumanguru vowed to destroy Sundiata. In 1235, their armies met in a bloody battle that ended with Sumanguru's death. In the words of a Mandingo storyteller, "the world knew no other master but Sundiata."

Sundiata proved to be as great a leader in peace as he had been in war. From his new capital at Niami, he promoted agriculture and reestablished the gold-salt trade. *Mali*, a Mandingo word meaning "where the king lives," became the name of his empire.

Mansa Musa Sundiata died in 1255. Influenced by Arab traders, some of Mali's next rulers became Muslims. The most famous of these was Mansa Musa, Sundiata's grandnephew. As you have seen, his glittering pilgrimage to Mecca captured the Arab world's attention.

Under Mansa Musa's leadership, Mali became a powerful empire that dominated West Africa. A 100,000-man army, which included 10,000 cavalry troops, maintained order and protected Mali from attack. Royal officials provided fair and efficient government.

Ibn Battuta In 1352, Mansa Musa's successor Sulayman prepared to receive an unusual guest named Ibn Battuta. Battuta had traveled for 27 years, visiting every country in the Islamic world except Mali. His visit to Mali provided him with a number of memorable experiences, including a reception at the royal court.

After leaving the royal palace, Battuta spent the next year traveling across Mali. He found that it was possible to travel safely without fear of crime. As a devout Muslim, Battuta praised the people of Mali for insisting that their children study the Koran.

Songhai conquered Mali.

Ibn Battuta left Mali in 1353. Within 50 years, the once-powerful empire began to weaken. Mansa Musa's successors lacked his ability. In addition, the trade routes again shifted eastward as existing mines gave out and new ones were discovered. By 1450, the Songhai (SONG-hye) people replaced the Mandingo as controllers of the all-important trade routes.

The Songhai had two extraordinary kings. One was a ruthless conqueror named Sunni Ali. The other was an excellent administrator whose name was Askia Muhammad. He set up an efficient tax system and chose able officials. Under his rule, the Songhai empire was prosperous and well governed.

Timbuktu was among the cities that flourished at this time. A famous university there attracted Muslim scholars from afar. One wrote:

Here are a great store of doctors, judges, priests, and other learned men that are bountifully maintained at the king's cost and charges. And hither are brought diverse manuscripts of written books out of Barbary (northern Africa), which are sold for more money than any other merchandise.

Timbuktu's mosque showed the influence of Islam.

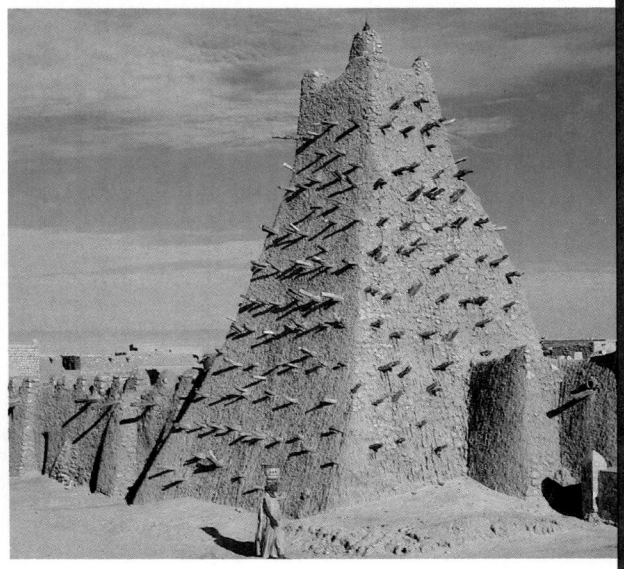

323

■ **BACKGROUND**

In Europe at the time of Mansa Musa's pilgrimage, Dante was writing *The Divine Comedy* and Giotto was painting frescoes.

Cooperative Learning

Ask students to imagine that they are pupils at the great university at Timbuktu sometime in the early 1500's. They have come from Arabia and are seeing the Songhai empire for the first time. Working in groups of four, have students write letters home from such a student describing what he or she is studying and other observations about Songhai. Group members should discuss the contents of the letter, then take turns writing, with each member writing for several minutes, then passing the paper on. The writer should read aloud as he or she writes; other group members should offer suggestions. Have group spokespersons share letters with the class.

■ **DISCUSSION**

Ask students to list the advantages of being a member of a lineage.

■ **BACKGROUND**

The work of Western artists—Picasso, for example—showed African influences. Have interested students find pictures of modern works that are influenced by African art.

The syncopated rhythms of modern ragtime are believed to have their roots in African music.

Despite its wealth and learning, however, the Songhai empire lacked gunpowder and cannon. In 1591, a Moroccan sultan named El Mansur led an army of about 4,000 men across the Sahara. Most of the invaders died as they hauled their heavy guns across the desert. The 1,000 survivors used their cannon to destroy 27,000 Songhai warriors armed only with swords and spears. Thus ended the great savanna empire of Songhai.

Africans shared cultural patterns.

The collapse of the Songhai empire brought an end to the 1,000-year period in which powerful savanna states ruled West Africa. During the sixteenth and seventeenth centuries, the center of political and economic influence shifted to the forest kingdoms, such as Benin, that developed along the Niger River delta. Whether they lived in savanna empires, forest kingdoms, or small tribal villages, the people of West Africa shared a distinctive traditional culture.

Family ties As in other parts of the world, family organization was central to African society. In many African societies, families were organized in groups called **lineages** (LIHN-ee-ihj-uhz). The members of a lineage believed they were descended from a common ancestor. Besides its living members, a lineage also included past generations (spirits of ancestors) and future generations (children not yet born).

In some African societies, lineage groups took the place of kings or other rulers. For example, a people called the Tiv in what is today Nigeria had no formal government. If a dispute arose among them, it was settled by respected elders from the lineages.

People in a lineage felt strong loyalties to one another. The lineage helped members in times of trouble, negotiated marriages for members, and supported members politically. Members of a lineage also had religious duties.

The status of women Women played an important role in African societies. As workers, they planted and harvested crops and occasionally took an active part in commerce and trade. Although men usually dominated the government, women could become the head of state in a few African kingdoms.

In some African societies, children traced their ancestors through their mothers rather than their

fathers. In this **matrilineal** system, young men inherited land or wealth from their mother's brothers rather than from their father. Ibn Battuta reported that this system was also used in Mali.

Religions African religions blended monotheism (belief in one supreme God) and polytheism (belief in many gods). Most African groups honored a large number of gods and spirits. Above these lesser gods was the principal creator of the universe. However, this High God, or Supreme Spirit, was thought to be too powerful and distant to listen to human appeals.

In daily life, the spirits of departed ancestors were especially important. As part of the lineage, they were the guardians of traditions, values, and laws. Most families believed that the spirits could either make trouble or bring good fortune, depending on how well their living relatives honored them. Thus the lineage was a religious group as well as a social and political unit.

At least one member of a village was trained in the magic art of communicating with both good and evil spirits. This important person, known as the **diviner,** called on the spirits for aid whenever there was an illness or a village crisis. The diviner also used religious rituals to cure sickness or deal with anger in the village.

After North Africa became part of the Islamic empire, traders brought the Muslim religion to many parts of Africa south of the Sahara. Even in places where Islam became strong, however, African religious traditions often survived too.

The arts flourished in many forms.

The arts linked religion, politics, and everyday life. Some types of art honored the king or the spirits of ancestors. Other forms of art included music for daily life or everyday objects made with fine craftsmanship.

Sculpture Artists in the rain-forest kingdoms used the beautifully grained woods that grew there to create works of art. The long tradition of metalworking in Africa likewise led to striking sculpture in gold and bronze. Most wooden sculptures from ancient times have crumbled to dust, victims of dampness or hungry insects.

Some of the most famous African sculptures were created by the Yoruba (YOR-uh-buh), a group of people in the rain forest of what is now Nigeria. Two successive groups of Yoruba people made

324

ANSWERS TO

Section
Review 2

Define:
(a) group in which all members believe they are descended from a common

(continued)

This copy of a bronze head and the crowned head in bronze are from Ife, a Yoruba city. The plaque shows the oba of Benin wearing a necklace, the symbol of royalty. Warriors shield him from the sun.

fine bronze sculptures between 1100 and 1600. One group governed a forest kingdom called Ife (EE-fay). The bronze heads of Ife were wonderfully natural and lifelike. As Ife in time declined, a second Yoruba group formed the state of Benin (buh-NEEN). Metalworkers in Benin made a series of bronze plaques that hung in the palace of the *oba* (king). The plaques showed people commonly seen at the royal court.

Music and dance Many kinds of African music had very complex rhythms. For example, several drummers might play together, each following a different rhythm. Such music is called polyrhythmic ("having many rhythms").

Music often accompanied dance. In many societies, dancers wore masks to honor spirits or family ancestors. Thus the art of the carved masks, the music of the drums, and the dancing of the villagers shared a common purpose. They bound a community together and enabled it to pass its heritage on through the centuries.

Oral history Most African languages had no writing systems. Instead, each group handed down its history and laws by word of mouth.

In many West African societies, specially trained people known as **griots** (GREE-ohz) were the record keepers. Griots memorized the great deeds of past kings, family histories, and important events in their village. Young griots studied with older ones so that knowledge of the past was handed down accurately. Even after Arab traders brought Arabic writing to sub-Saharan Africa, griots remained the historians of their people.

Section REVIEW 2

Define: (a) lineage, (b) matrilineal, (c) diviner, (d) griots
Identify: (a) Ghana, (b) Soninke, (c) Mali, (d) Sumanguru, (e) Sundiata, (f) Ibn Battuta, (g) Songhai, (h) Sunni Ali, (i) Timbuktu,
Answer:
1. Why was the gold-salt trade important to the development of West Africa?
2. What were Mansa Musa's most important achievements?
3. What caused the downfall of Songhai?
4. How did African religions embrace polytheism and monotheism?
5. What purposes did the arts serve in African society?
6. How did many West African societies keep records?

Critical Thinking
7. How did the lineage system ensure that society's values would be upheld?

325

ANSWERS TO (continued)

ancestor (b) tracing ancestry through mothers (c) village member trained in communicating with spirits (d) record keepers who memorized and passed down history orally
Identify:
(a) Soninke title for king and name of region he ruled (b) people of the Ghana empire (c) Sundiata's empire that controlled gold trade (d) ruthless king who ruled the Mandingo (e) defeated Sumanguru and founded Mali empire (f) Arab traveler who visited Muslim lands throughout Asia and Africa (g) group that replaced Mandingo as controllers of gold trade (h) ruthless Songhai king (i) savanna market town where gold and salt traders met; became prosperous center of learning under Songhai

Answer:
1. It encouraged the establishment of kingdoms and empires and gave them a source of wealth and power.

2. created powerful empire that dominated West Africa; amassed great wealth; went on pilgrimage to Mecca

3. lack of gunpowder and cannon

4. Most African groups honored many gods and spirits, but they believed in a principal creator.

5. to honor king, spirits, or ancestors; to enhance daily life; to preserve a community heritage

6. orally, through griots

7. The spirits of departed ancestors were the guardians of traditions, values, and laws. To bring good fortune, families believed they had to honor the traditions of lineage ancestors.

■ BACKGROUND

The wild corn the earliest farmers planted grew on cobs that were one inch long and about the same diameter as a pencil.

North America's first hunters lived in a dangerous world. Huge mammals roamed the lush grasslands that are now part of America's Great Plains. Giant bison with seven-foot horn spreads (a modern buffalo's is about two feet) thundered across the plains. Beavers as large as bears gnawed at trees with teeth eight inches long. The gigantic woolly mammoth was the largest animal of all. It stood 14 feet high and weighed 5 tons.

Early Americans had many ways of life. 3

As you have seen, Europeans in the Middle Ages were only dimly aware of sub-Saharan Africa. They were totally unaware that two huge continents lay beyond the Atlantic Ocean. The peoples of the Americas were likewise unaware that other civilizations existed. Protected by ocean barriers, they created a world of their own.

The people who settled North and South America had a long and fascinating history, much of which is still unknown. New findings continue to add to historical knowledge. Within recent years, archaeologists have discovered artifacts that provide further insights into the different ways of life the first Americans developed.

Geographic Setting

The Americas have many regions.

North America is the third largest continent. It stretches from the Arctic Ocean in the north to Panama's border with Colombia in the south. The continent includes the Aleutian Islands and the West Indies. Thousands of bays and inlets give North America a jagged 100,000-mile coastline—the longest of any continent.

North America's largest mountains, the Rockies, begin in Alaska and continue into Mexico. A vast, fertile plain reaches from the Rockies to the Appalachian Mountains. The Mississippi River and its tributaries drain this area and provide a transportation network.

South America is smaller and lies farther east than North America. It extends from a sunny Caribbean coastline in the north to the storm-tossed islands of Tierra del Fuego in the south—only about 700 miles from Antarctica.

The geography of South America is dominated by the Andes and the Amazon. The snowcapped Andes form a 4,500 mile mountain chain that runs the entire length of the continent. Of the world's mountains, they are second to the Himalayas in height. The huge Amazon contains more water than the next six largest rivers of the world combined.

The first Americans came from Asia.

Long periods of cold climate known as ice ages played a major role in shaping the landscape and history of North America. The most recent ice age peaked about 18,000 years ago. With temperatures about 18°F lower than today's averages, heavy snowfalls blanketed the Arctic. Huge sheets of moving ice called glaciers pressed southward at about 300 feet a year.

The buildup of glaciers absorbed great quantities of water, causing the level of the world's oceans to drop by about 400 feet. As a result, certain lands were exposed that had been at the bottom of the sea. For example, the Bering Strait is normally about 180 feet deep. As the sea level fell, a bridge of land called Beringia appeared there connecting Asia with North America.

Beringia was a treeless plain 55 miles long and about 1,000 miles wide. Its broad grasslands attracted herds of caribou and bison. Over a period of time, small bands of Siberian hunters followed the animals across the Beringian land bridge. These hunters, unaware of entering a new world, became the first Americans.

North and South America offered plenty of living space. As the hunters slowly migrated across the Americas, they adapted to the demands of each environment. By about 7000 B.C., a band of hunters had reached the most distant tip of South America. By then, rising seas had reclaimed Beringia and cut off contact with Asia.

Farmers learned how to raise corn.

The first Americans lived by hunting game and gathering wild plants. Their descendants, however, gradually began a new way of life. Like the peoples of ancient Egypt and Mesopotamia, they developed the methods for agriculture.

America's earliest farmers lived in the Tehaucán (TAY-wuh-KAHN) valley, 150 miles south of modern Mexico City. About 6,000 years ago, people living in this valley learned how to plant and harvest corn. Corn is a particularly productive crop. In the tropical climate of southern Mexico, a family of three could raise enough corn in four months to feed themselves for up to two years. The people of Mexico and Central America recognized corn's life-giving importance when they called it the food of the gods.

Corn was not the only crop grown by the early American farmers. Over the centuries, they also learned to cultivate potatoes, squash, avocados, pumpkins, tomatoes, peanuts, and a variety of beans. These crops provided a stable food supply, thus supporting the growth of permanent villages.

Many cultures developed in North America.

A wide variety of cultures developed in the lands of present-day United States and Canada. The Anasazi, Hopewell, and Mississippians have left particularly impressive remains. The map on page 329 shows the major groups and the regions where they lived in about 1500.

The Anasazi The Anasazi, or Ancient Ones, lived in the valleys and canyons of the American southwest. By A.D. 800, about 7,000 Anasazi lived in **pueblos,** or villages, that dotted the Chaco Canyon in northwestern New Mexico.

The most important of these pueblos is called Pueblo Bonito, meaning "beautiful village." At its peak, Pueblo Bonito was home to about 1,000 people. Its construction required a high degree of social organization and inventiveness. Like other people of the Americas, the Anasazi did not have horses, mules, or the wheel. Instead, they relied on human labor to quarry sandstone from the canyon walls and move it to the site. Skilled builders then used a mudlike mortar to construct walls up to five stories high. Windows were small to keep out the burning sun. When completed, Pueblo Bonito contained more than 800 rooms. In addition, a number of underground chambers called kivas were used for a variety of religious ceremonies.

The Anasazi created a way of life that thrived from about A.D. 600 to 1200. That way of life, however, depended on having enough rain to grow corn. When a prolonged drought struck in the late thirteenth century, the Anasazi abandoned their pueblos and mysteriously vanished.

The Hopewell Far to the east of the Anasazi, a people known as the Hopewell built a distinctive culture in what is today southern Ohio. The Ohio River provided the Hopewell with a central route for trade. Mica from the Appalachians, shells from the Gulf of Mexico, and even grizzly bear teeth from the Rockies all reached the Ohio valley over a complex network of trails and rivers.

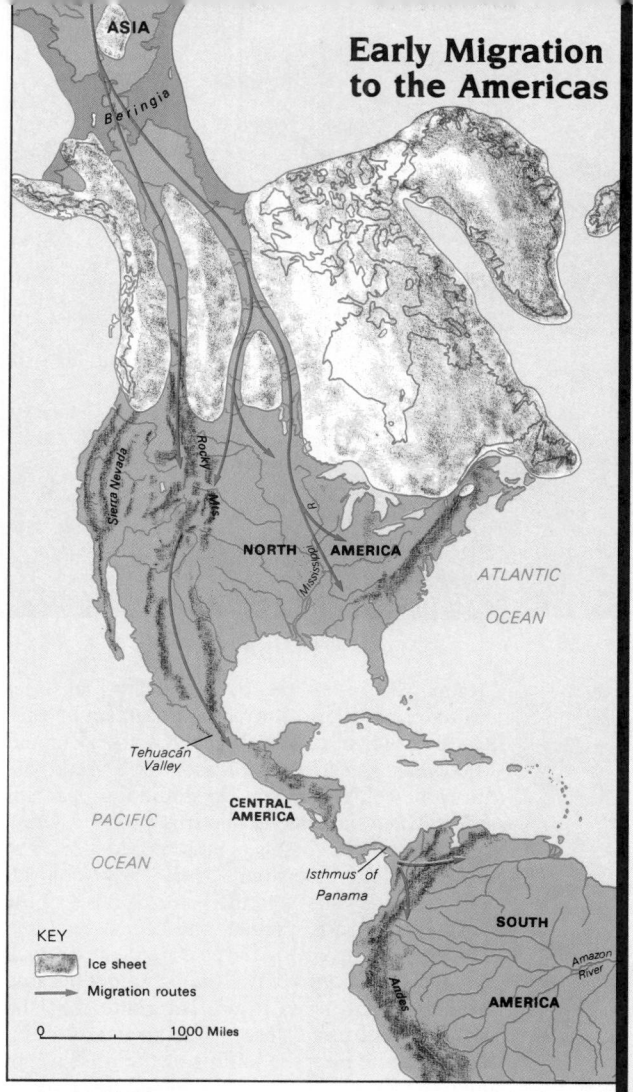

Early Migration to the Americas

Map Study

What narrow bridge of land links North and South America?

The Hopewell were skilled craftsmen as well as clever traders. Sculptors carved stones into pipes shaped like falcons, beavers, and wildcats. Other artists hammered sheets of copper into eagles and sliced mica into bird claws.

The Hopewell buried many of their finest products inside thousands of earthen mounds. Burial mounds found near present-day Chillicothe, Ohio, contained bear teeth necklaces, a 38-pound copper axe, and beautifully carved pipes.

327

SECTION 3
Objectives and Teaching Strategies

OBJECTIVE 1. Explain how the first people came to North America.

Teaching Strategy: *Using Geographic Themes: Movement* (page 314d)

OBJECTIVE 2. Explain how the discovery of agriculture changed life in the Americas.

Teaching Strategy: *Transferring Ideas: The Discovery of Agriculture* (page 314d)

OBJECTIVE 3. Describe how several cultures used geographic location to their own advantage.

Teaching Strategy: *Geography in History: Location* (page 314d)

ANSWER TO
Map Study

Isthmus of Panama

■ BACKGROUND

Note that agriculture here as elsewhere was based on local wild plants. Native Americans did not grow wheat or barley as did farmers in the Fertile Crescent.

SECTION 3
Resources

ENRICHMENT
■ Voices from the Past 14.3

ASSESSMENT
■ Section Quiz 14.3

GEOGRAPHY
■ Transparencies 54, 55

REINFORCEMENT
■ Independent Practice 14.3

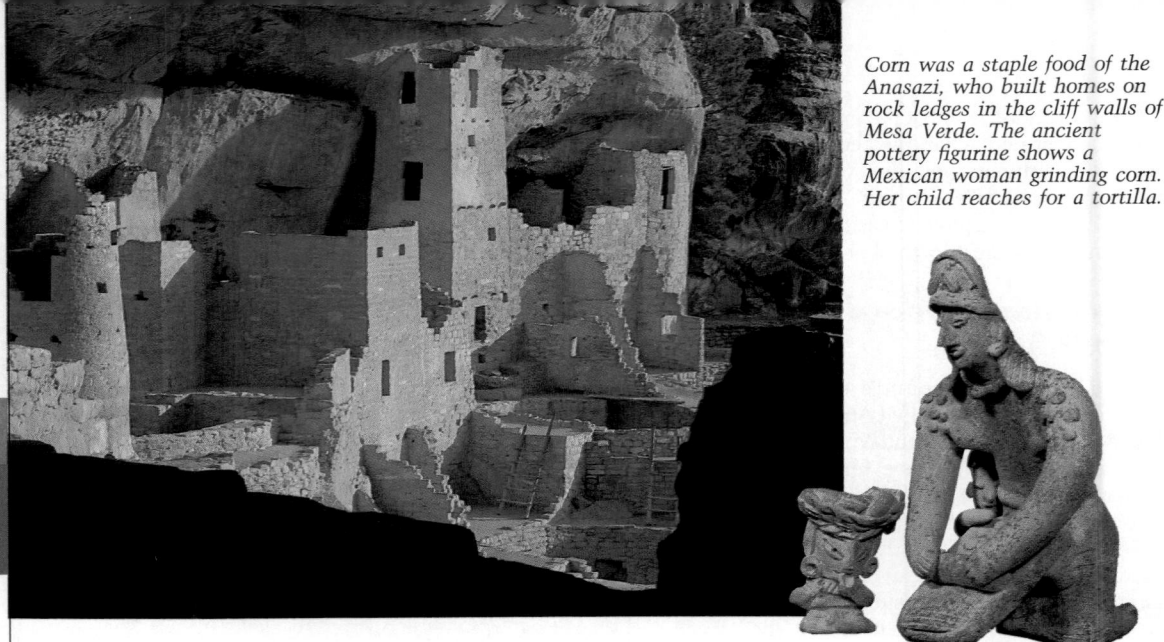

Corn was a staple food of the Anasazi, who built homes on rock ledges in the cliff walls of Mesa Verde. The ancient pottery figurine shows a Mexican woman grinding corn. Her child reaches for a tortilla.

ANSWERS TO

Section Review 3

Define:
(a) long period of cold climate during which glaciers built up (b) huge sheet of moving ice (c) Anasazi village (d) underground chamber used by Anasazi for religious ceremonies

Identify:
(a) land bridge connecting Asia with North America during ice age (b) valley in Mexico where earliest farmers lived (c) elaborate village constructed by Anasazi (d) ancient culture of American Southwest (e) culture in southern Ohio known for trade, crafts, and burial mounds (f) center of Mississippian culture

Answer:
1. Andes, Amazon River

2. by crossing land bridge between Asia and North America

3. in the Tehuacán Valley about 4000 B.C.

4. strong ruler with religious significance; highly organized society

5. permanent settlements; well-organized cooperative societies

Hopewell burial practices and artistic styles influenced people throughout eastern North America. Their culture reached its peak about 1,600 years ago. Then, for reasons still unknown, the Hopewell culture declined and disappeared.

The Mississippians In about A.D. 600, a group of people called Mississippians settled along the banks of the Mississippi River. They took advantage of the valley's fertile bottomlands to grow rich fields of corn, squash, and beans. By 1200, hundreds of thriving villages dotted the area.

The city of Cahokia in Illinois rapidly became the largest and most important center of Mississippian culture. Cahokia was strategically located at a site near the joining of the Mississippi and Ohio rivers. Traders crisscrossed these rivers in sleek canoes filled with highly prized flint and furs.

As many as 10,000 people may have lived in Cahokia during the twelfth century. A huge 100-foot-high earthen temple mound dominated the city. Its flat-topped peak contained a wooden temple that also served as the ruler's palace.

The ruler had absolute power over Cahokia, and many warriors to protect the city. The people of Cahokia expected their rulers to announce the proper time for planting and harvesting crops. They must have made wise decisions for a long time. The city's fields produced rich harvests, and its marketplace teemed with people. When

328

a ruler died, his grateful people buried him inside a mound with valuable treasures that included rolls of copper, choice arrowheads, and pearl necklaces.

Archaeologists believe that a combination of wars, disease, and overpopulation ended Cahokia's long period of prosperity. The city began to decline sometime after 1250. By 1500, only the abandoned mounds remained.

Section REVIEW 3

Define: (a) ice age, (b) glacier, (c) pueblo, (d) kiva

Identify: (a) Beringia, (b) Tehuacán, (c) Pueblo Bonito, (d) Anasazi, (e) Hopewell, (f) Cahokia

Answer:
1. What two geographic features dominate South America?
2. How do most scientists believe that the first people reached the Americas?
3. When and where did farming begin in the Americas?
4. What can be inferred about Mississippian society from the remains at Cahokia?

Critical Thinking
5. What characteristics did the Hopewell and Anasazi societies share?

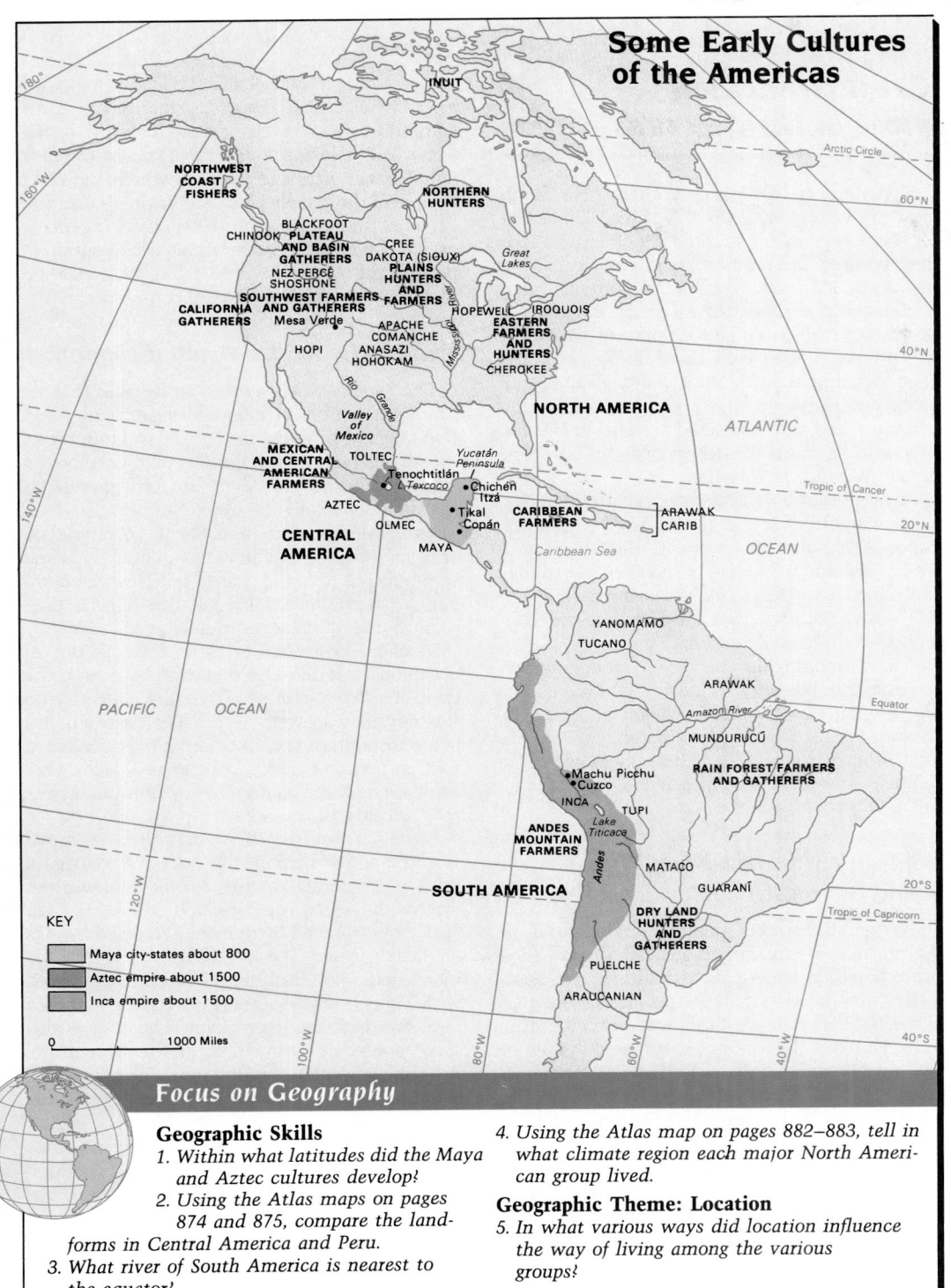

Some Early Cultures of the Americas

INUIT

NORTHWEST COAST FISHERS

NORTHERN HUNTERS

BLACKFOOT
CHINOOK PLATEAU
AND BASIN
GATHERERS
NEZ PERCÉ
SHOSHONE

CREE
DAKOTA (SIOUX)
PLAINS
HUNTERS
AND
FARMERS

Great Lakes

SOUTHWEST FARMERS AND GATHERERS

CALIFORNIA
GATHERERS Mesa Verde

HOPEWELL

IROQUOIS
EASTERN
FARMERS
AND
HUNTERS

APACHE
COMANCHE
ANASAZI
HOHOKAM

HOPI

CHEROKEE

NORTH AMERICA

ATLANTIC

Rio Grande

Valley of Mexico

MEXICAN
AND CENTRAL
AMERICAN
FARMERS

TOLTEC

Yucatán Peninsula

Tenochtitlán
Texcoco   Chichén Itzá

AZTEC

OLMEC

Tikal
Copán

Tropic of Cancer

CARIBBEAN
FARMERS

ARAWAK
CARIB

20°N

OCEAN

CENTRAL
AMERICA

MAYA

Caribbean Sea

YANOMAMO
TUCANO

PACIFIC   OCEAN

ARAWAK

Amazon River

Equator

MUNDURUCÚ

RAIN FOREST FARMERS
AND GATHERERS

Machu Picchu
Cuzco

INCA

TUPI

ANDES
MOUNTAIN
FARMERS

Lake Titicaca

Andes

MATACO

SOUTH AMERICA

GUARANÍ

20°S

Tropic of Capricorn

DRY LAND
HUNTERS
AND
GATHERERS

PUELCHE

ARAUCANIAN

40°S

KEY

Maya city-states about 800
Aztec empire about 1500
Inca empire about 1500

0   1000 Miles

Focus on Geography

Geographic Skills
1. Within what latitudes did the Maya and Aztec cultures develop?
2. Using the Atlas maps on pages 874 and 875, compare the landforms in Central America and Peru.
3. What river of South America is nearest to the equator?

4. Using the Atlas map on pages 882–883, tell in what climate region each major North American group lived.

Geographic Theme: Location
5. In what various ways did location influence the way of living among the various groups?

ANSWERS TO
Focus On Geography

1. between 12°N and 22°N latitudes

2. Central America had low mountain ranges, while Peru had the lofty Andes.

3. Amazon River

4. Northwest Coast—temperate marine; Plateau and Basin Gatherers—semiarid; California Gatherers—Mediterranean subtropical; Plains Hunters and Farmers—semiarid, humid continental; Northern Hunters—subpolar; Eastern Farmers and Hunters—humid continental, humid subtropical; Southwest Farmers and Gatherers—arid, semiarid

5. Location influenced diet and means of obtaining food, the development of agriculture, and the growth of permanent settlements and cities. Location also influenced the importance of trade and warfare to a culture's survival.

■ **BACKGROUND**

Walter Alva's vivid description of his discoveries can be found in the October 1988 and June 1990 issues of *National Geographic*. Both articles contain superb pictures, maps, and artistic recreations of the Moche tombs.

The remains of a large temple complex at Chavin include a three-story stone building complete with chambers, passages, stairs, ramps, and ventilation shafts. The walls were built of alternating layers of precisely cut large and small stones. Outside walls are decorated with carved stone heads of humans and cats.

Great civilizations arose in the Americas. 4

Peruvian archaeologist Walter Alva could scarcely believe his eyes: "A coffin! It's sealed. . . . Never opened!" After months of digging, Alva had become the first archaeologist to discover the unopened coffin of an ancient Peruvian ruler.

The coffin rewarded Alva's patience. Hundreds of priceless objects lay beside the body of a Moche warrior-priest who died about 1,700 years ago. The dazzling treasure included a gold peanut necklace, exquisite gold and turquoise ear ornaments, and a massive gold headdress. The collection represented the richest treasures yet found in the Western Hemisphere.

Alva's discovery captured world attention. Reporters described it as a "New World King Tut." Since Alva's first discovery in 1987, the mud-brick pyramid complex in northern Peru has continued to yield more astonishing finds. In 1990, Alva uncovered yet another tomb that contained even greater treasures.

These stunning discoveries are producing new insights into the early Peruvian civilizations. The excitement of Alva and his team is shared by archaeologists working in Guatemala, Mexico, and other parts of Peru. These areas were the home of five great ancient peoples—the Moche, Inca, Olmec, Maya, and Aztec.

Andean civilization began along the coast.

As you have seen, the first civilizations in Egypt, Mesopotamia, the Indus valley, and China were based on large-scale agriculture. Archaeologists now believe that the people who settled along the Peruvian coast followed a different pattern. Peru's long coastline is bordered by one of the world's driest deserts. Rather than trying to farm, the people there turned to fishing. The chilly waters of the Humboldt Current along the Peruvian coast are filled with tiny plankton that provide food for fish. These waters are among the richest fishing grounds in the world. Thus, the sea provided an assured supply of food.

The coastal civilization may have begun in Peru as early as 3000 B.C. After centuries of gradual progress, the rate of change suddenly increased after a new cult based upon a jaguar god appeared sometime after 800 B.C. Since the name of the jaguar god is lost, scholars have named the new cult Chavin after the town in which the chief temple to the god was found. Chavin civilization declined sometime after 100 B.C. However, it provided a foundation on which a new group of people, the Moche, would build a civilization that lasted from about A.D. 100 to 700.

The Moche built a wealthy empire.

The Moche rulers proved to be able leaders. The Peruvian desert is broken by several rivers that are fed by rainfall in the Andes. From these, the Moche built an extensive system of irrigation canals that turned the desert into fertile farmlands that produced corn, avocado, and peanuts.

As in Mesopotamia and Egypt, an elite class of warrior-priests rose to power. These lived and worshiped in pyramid-shaped temples that dominated river valleys. Most villagers lived in one-room houses built with mud-daubed reeds.

Moche warrior-priests must have possessed enormous wealth. The royal tombs now being excavated have yielded a dazzling collection of superbly crafted jewelry. For example, the remains of a warrior-priest excavated in 1990 were adorned with at least six gold and silver necklaces. One necklace featured gold spiders with human faces atop delicate golden webs.

Although the Moche were masters of metal working and irrigation, they never developed a written language. Despite the lack of written records, however, scholars have learned a great deal about Moche life from the detailed drawings on their pottery. These artifacts reveal that the Moche had a powerful army. Fierce soldiers armed with copper-headed axes are frequently shown with captured enemy prisoners. The designs also show a more peaceful side of Moche culture. Amazingly realistic portraits show doctors healing patients, women weaving cloth, and musicians playing pipes.

While Moche pottery offers important clues about their way of life, many questions remain unanswered. Researchers still do not fully understand Moche religious beliefs. Scholars cannot tell from the pottery why the Moche culture mysteriously declined sometime after 700 A.D.

Archaeologists excavate the tomb of a Moche warrior-priest. As they move the skeleton, a gold headdress is revealed. Other treasures include a necklace of gold peanuts that are larger than life-size.

The Inca unified the Andes.

Following the collapse of the Moche empire, a number of groups divided Peru into small states. Beginning in about 1100, a group called the Inca ruled over Cuzco, a small town set on a grassy plateau 11,000 feet above sea level.

In 1438, a remarkable leader named Pachacuti became the new Inca ruler. Pachacuti quickly lived up to the meaning of his name—"he who transforms the world." Inca armies under his command proved to be unbeatable. His son Topa Inca ("the unforgettable") was also a great general. By the late 1400's, the Inca conquered an empire that stretched for 2,500 miles along the western coast of South America.

Inca rulers were able to keep firm control over their vast empire. The emperors claimed to be descendants of the sun god. As the living Son of the Sun, they possessed absolute authority over their people. A large, well-organized bureaucracy carried out the emperors' commands.

A 10,000 mile network of stone highways helped to hold the Inca empire together. Teams of runners relayed official messages at a rate of about 150 miles a day. The runners often carried a series of knotted strings called a **quipu.** Since the Inca lacked a written language, they used the quipu to tally births, crops, herds, and deaths. Only highly-trained specialists could decipher the color-coded strings and knots.

To survive in their dry and mountainous land, the Inca developed special methods of farming. To prevent erosion on the steep slopes, they built terraces to hold the soil. Corn and potatoes were their two main crops. The potato is native to the Andes and is an especially nutritious food. An acre of potatoes yields almost twice as much food as an acre of grain. As a result, the Inca rarely experienced hunger.

CITY TOUR
Cuzco became the Inca capital.

All Inca roads led to the capital Cuzco. Pachacuti transformed the once sleepy village into a religious and political center. As part of his master plan, he redesigned Cuzco so that it took the shape of a gigantic crouching puma.

As an experienced military strategist, Pachacuti chose a rocky hill as the site for a huge fortress. As many as 20,000 workers labored for 30 years to construct the fortress. Its thick walls contained stones weighing up to 130 tons.

Like all Inca emperors, Pachacuti lived in a magnificent palace. Visitors entered through a silver gateway that led to an immense audience hall. Pachacuti surrounded himself with precious objects made specially for his enjoyment. Skilled

331

OBJECTIVE 1. Locate on a map and briefly describe the great American civilizations.

Teaching Strategy: *Geography in History: Central and South American Cultures* (page 314e)

OBJECTIVE 2. Describe and use the Mayan number system.

Teaching Strategy: *Discussing History: Mayan Math* (page 314e)

■ BACKGROUND

The Inca called their empire Tahuantinsuyo, meaning "The Four Quarters." Four main roads led from Cuzco to the four regions of the empire.

SECTION 4
Resources

ASSESSMENT
■ Section Quiz 14.4

REINFORCEMENT
■ Independent Practice 14.4

ENRICHMENT
■ Voices from the Past 14.4

Ask students to recall examples of royal status symbols they have previously studied. For example, Roman emperors wore purple robes.

An inner courtyard in the Temple of the Sun contained a garden with ears of corn made out of solid gold. Ask students what conclusion they can draw from this information.

■ BACKGROUND

A Mexican farmer discovered the first Olmec colossal head in 1862. Since then, archaeologists have found 12 more. Some of the huge stone sculptures weigh as much as 20 tons. As noted by one archaeologist, "The logistics of transporting these stones comprise one of the greatest puzzles of New World archaeology."

tailors wove royal robes made from bat fur and hummingbird feathers. The emperor also wore huge golden ear plugs that symbolized his power.

As in all great capital cities, Cuzco's busy streets buzzed with excitement. Proud nobles from across the empire rushed to meetings on litters carried by servants. Meanwhile, merchants exchanged goods in crowded marketplaces. Sharp-eyed bargain hunters could obtain rare sea shells from the coast, fine vicuna-wool clothing from the highlands, and exotic feathers from the Amazon rain forest.

Cuzco's most splendid building, the famous Temple of the Sun, was dedicated to the sun god Inti. The Inca believed that gold and silver were sacred objects that should be used to glorify their gods. They therefore covered the temple's walls with sheets of gold that reflected the sun's rays. A jewel-encrusted golden image of the sun stood inside the temple. Each day high priests carried the golden disk into the city's central square. Attendants then burned special offerings of food while a hushed crowd watched.

Another remarkable accomplishment was the building of a 20-foot-wide highway, carved through steep mountain walls. The road connected Cuzco with the important northern city of Quito. The emperor and the people of Cuzco believed that their city was the world's center, the "navel of the world." They had no idea that other people in the Western Hemisphere had also built great civilizations and splendid cities.

The Olmec built a civilization.

The rain forest of Mexico's Gulf Coast was an unlikely environment for a civilization to take root and thrive. Each year dark clouds drenched the area with up to 100 inches of rain. Giant ceiba, rubber, and mahogany trees formed a thick canopy that prevented most sunlight from reaching the ground. Jaguars silently stalked their prey along the banks of snake-infested rivers.

A people known as the Olmec settled in this demanding environment in about 1200 B.C. Olmec settlers planted crops in the rich soil left by flooding rivers. They slashed and burned trees to clear land for settlements. However, the rain forest was never far away. Late at night, the Olmec doubtless heard the howls of the wild jaguar. Olmec artists carved jade figures that were half jaguar and half human, suggesting that they worshiped the jaguar's spirit.

The Olmec built many ceremonial centers in which they performed rituals to please their gods. The centers contained large pyramids surrounded by altars. In addition, archaeologists have found 13 colossal stone heads weighing up to 20 tons each. The heads are believed to be portraits of actual rulers.

The Olmec civilization flourished for about 800 years before mysteriously collapsing around 400 B.C. Nonetheless Olmec cultural patterns continued to influence later civilizations in Mexico and Central America.

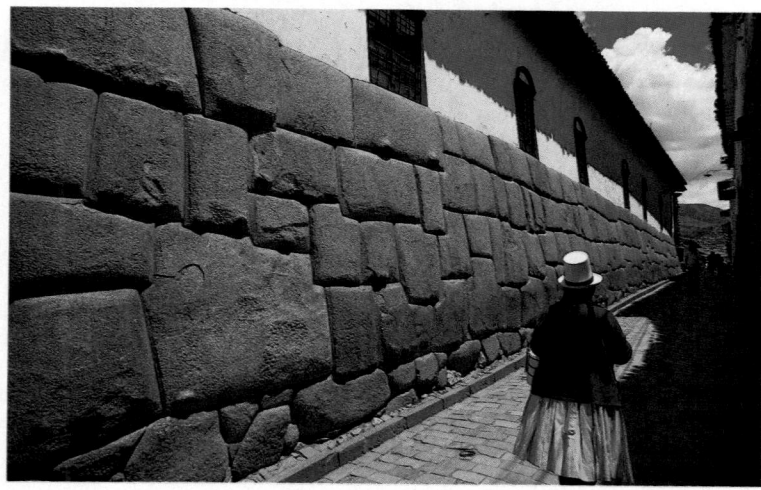

This skillfully-fitted stone wall was the base of an Inca temple. The Spanish destroyed the temple and built a church on the foundation. The wall and church still line the streets of Cuzco.

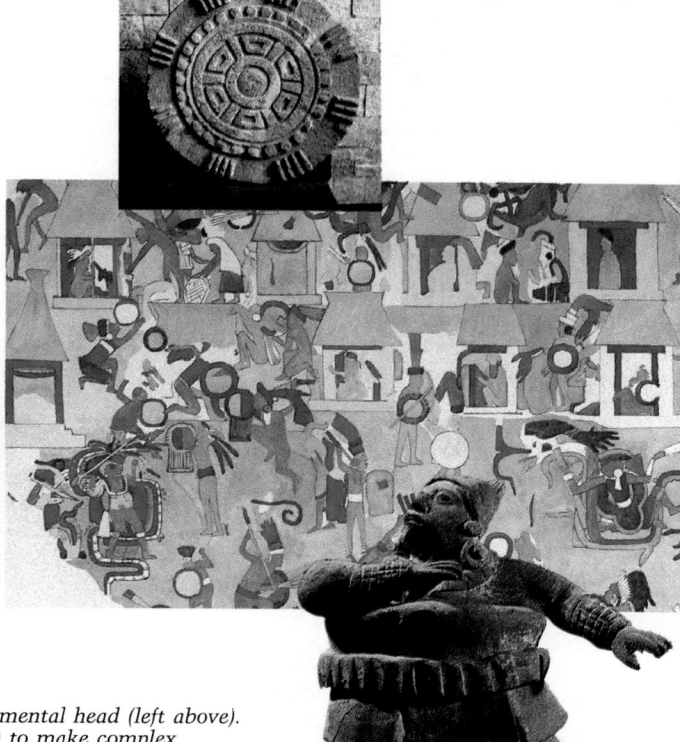

The Olmec used stone tools to carve this monumental head (left above). The Maya used this stone calendar (upper right) to make complex astronomical calculations. Paintings on the walls of the Temple of the Jaguar at Chichen Itza (center right) show scenes of battle and daily life. A Maya ballplayer (lower right) wore heavy gear for protection against a five-pound ball.

Cooperative Learning

In groups of four, have students do investigative reports on the "unsolved mystery" of the Maya civilization. Two group members can act as researchers, finding information and reporting back periodically to the other members. Another student can take the information from the researchers and transform it into a script for an oral "newscast." The fourth member can act as a director, choosing the information to be presented and coordinating the report. Reports should include an overview of Maya civilization and possible reasons for its disappearance. Then have one or two students from each group act as reporters and present their findings to the class.

The Maya built great cities.

As the Olmec civilization declined, a new group of people known as the Maya settled in the rain forests of Guatemala and Mexico's Yucatán Peninsula. After centuries of gradual growth, Maya civilization reached its peak between A.D. 300 and 900. During this time, the Maya built at least 80 independent cities.

These cities were the creative nerve centers of Maya civilization. They were built to uphold ritual and rule, rather than to provide homes for the common people. A powerful warlord and an aristocracy of priests and nobles governed each city. The rulers wore golden jaguar skins and headdresses topped with brilliant three-foot-long green feathers of the quetzal bird. After a successful battle, victorious warlords sometimes wore a belt containing a collection of enemy skulls.

The cities also served as important centers of trade. On market days, merchants displayed fine textiles, beeswax candles, flint tools, and precious jade ornaments. While the Maya did not have a uniform currency, cacao beans sometimes served as a medium of exchange. Wealthy nobles showed off their wealth by nibbling cacao beans as they shopped!

Religion played an important part in city life. Five towering pyramids dominated Tikal, the largest and most important Maya city. A glittering temple rose above each pyramid. Priests used these temples to perform elaborate rituals for their gods.

The Maya worshiped a number of gods. For example, they believed that each day was a living god whose behavior could be predicted with the help of an intricate system of calendars. Their 260-day religious calendar consisted of twenty 13-day months. A second 365-day solar calendar consisted of eighteen 20-day months, with a separate period of 5 days at the end. The two calendars were linked together like meshed gears

333

■ BACKGROUND

Today millions of descendants of the Maya live in Mexico, Guatemala, Belize, and Honduras. Many still speak Mayan languages, live in extended family groups, and follow ancient Mayan traditions.

■ DISCUSSION

Tenochtitlán's population was about five times larger than London's at the same time. Ask students if the size of a civilization's population center is indicative of the civilization's advancement.

■ BACKGROUND

The Aztecs also developed a calendar, based on the sun, as well as a system of writing and a system of numbers.

so that any given day could be identified in both cycles. The Maya used their calendars to help determine the best times to plant crops, attack enemies, or crown new rulers.

The precise calendars were based upon careful observation of the planets, sun, and moon. For example, Maya astronomers calculated that a year contained 365.2420 days. (Scientists now know that their year was .0002 of a day too short!) This exact calculation was made possible by a system of numbers that included a symbol for zero.

In addition to being sophisticated astronomers, the Maya were careful historians. They invented a complex system of writing to record the greatest events of their time. Maya writing consisted of about 800 signs called glyphs. Although scholars are beginning to make some progress in reading these glyphs, most of them still have not been translated.

The remarkable history of the Maya began and ended in a cloud of mystery. Archaeologists still wonder why the Maya suddenly abandoned their cities in the late eighth century. Although a deadly disease or a widespread peasant uprising may have been involved, no one knows for sure what happened. An unknown Maya once wrote, "All moons, all years, all days, all winds take their course and pass away." Perhaps this is the best explanation for the decline of their civilization.

Teotihuacán rose and fell.

The Maya did not live in complete isolation. They actively traded with merchants from Teotihuacán (tay-oh-tee-wah-KAHN), a thriving city located in the Valley of Mexico about 30 miles northeast of modern Mexico City.

The Valley of Mexico was a huge, oval-shaped basin about 7,500 feet above sea level. Mountain streams fed shallow lakes located in the center of the valley. Rich deposits of obsidian—a hard, black natural glass used to make weapons and tools—were located near Teotihuacán.

An unknown group settled in the valley in the second century. They used the natural resources there to transform Teotihuacán from a small village into the largest city in the Western Hemisphere. At its peak around A.D. 500, Teotihuacán had a population of about 200,000 people. Beautiful homes, busy workshops, and a pair of enormous temple-pyramids lined a broad central boulevard. The Pyramid of the Sun rose more than 20 stories high from a base as big as that of the Great Pyramid at Giza in Egypt.

After centuries of growth, Teotihuacán abruptly declined early in the eighth century. By 750, the city had become a ghost town. The vast ruins astonished later settlers in the area. They named the abandoned city Teotihuacán, meaning "the abode of the gods."

The Pyramid of the Sun overlooks the Avenue of the Dead in Teotihuacán.

Cuauhtémoc, who succeeded Montezuma, is a hero to Mexicans. His statue stands in Mexico City.

The Aztec rose to power.

Between 900 and 1300, waves of warlike invaders swept into the Valley of Mexico. One of these was a fierce and desperately poor group of people who called themselves Aztec. According to an Aztec legend, their war god Huitzilopochtili ordered them to build a city in the place where an eagle perched on a cactus with a snake in its mouth. In about 1325, the Aztec spotted such a sight on an island in Lake Texcoco. Within a short time, they began building there a great city called Tenochtitlán (tay-NOCH-tee-**TLAHN**)—the "place of the prickly-pear cactus."

After some 200 years of nearly constant war, the Aztec triumphed over all their neighbors. By the year 1500, the Aztec king was taking **tribute**—payment collected from conquered subjects—in gold, silver, cloth, cocoa beans, and furs. As many as 11 million people were subjects of the Aztec ruler.

Tenochtitlán As the empire of the Aztec grew, their capital city of Tenochtitlán also expanded. Viewed from the crest of a nearby mountain, Tenochtitlán was a breathtaking sight. The city was built on a number of small islands in Lake Texcoco. Several causeways connected them with the mainland. As many as 300,000 people may have lived in the city.

The central marketplace was the city's busiest spot. Nobles wearing brightly-colored cloaks searched for rare earrings and bracelets. The Aztec loved jewelry and used it to show their social status.

While anyone could shop in the central market, few people could enter the royal palace. For nobles and guests lucky enough to see it, the palace was a wondrous building. Skins of wild animals and beautifully dyed cotton decorated the walls. Skilled goldsmiths worked long hours to create magnificent works of art for decoration.

The Aztec king was both a political and a religious leader. The Aztec believed that the sun needed human blood to survive. Without this sacrifice, it would stop shining and all life would perish. The king and his high priests had the sacred task of preventing this disaster from occurring. Throughout the year, captives were led up the steps of the Great Temple to be sacrificed.

Year after year, the sun continued to rise and set. The Aztec continued their traditional ways unaware that other worlds lay on the other side of the oceans.

Section REVIEW 4

Define: (a) tribute, (b) quipu
Identify: (a) Walter Alva, (b) Moche, (c) Cuzco, (d) Pachacuti, (e) Olmec, (f) Maya, (g) Tikal, (h) Teotihuacán, (i) Aztec, (j) Tenochtitlán
Answer:
1. How did the origin of civilization in Peru differ from that in the river valley civilizations of Egypt and Mesopotamia?
2. How were the Inca rulers able to maintain control over their vast empire?
3. What were three major achievements of Maya civilization?
4. Why did the Aztec sacrifice human beings to their gods?

Critical Thinking
5. Both the Aztec and the Inca created formidable empires. What weaknesses, if any, did these empires have?

335

ANSWERS TO

Section Review 4

Define:
(a) payment collected from conquered subjects (b) Inca system of keeping records using knotted string
Identify:
(a) Peruvian archaeologist (b) wealthy, highly developed civilization in Peru between about 100 B.C. and A.D. 700 (c) Inca capital (d) ruler who expanded Inca empire (e) civilization that flourished in the rain forest of Mexico's Gulf Coast from about 1200 B.C. to 400 B.C. (f) advanced civilization that flourished in the rain forests of Guatemala and the Yucatan Peninsula from about 500 B.C. to A.D. 900 (g) largest, most important Maya city (h) largest city in the Western hemisphere around A.D. 500; located in Valley of Mexico (i) warlike people who developed empire in the Valley of Mexico (j) Aztec capital

Answer:
1. Peruvian civilization based on fishing; civilizations in Egypt and Mesopotamia based on large-scale agriculture
2. collected tribute from conquered subjects
3. pyramids, calendar, system of writing
4. They thought the sun needed human blood to survive.
5. They had to control a large area with many subjects. They were unaware of distant civilizations.

Concluding the Chapter

1. **Chapter Closer**
Discuss the achievements of the African and American cultures. Ask students how ways of life in these areas were different from those of European civilizations.

2. **Reteaching Activities**
a. Making a Time Line Have students create a time line to show the rise and fall of Ghana, Mali, and Songhai.
b. Making a Chart Have students prepare a chart with three columns labeled *Maya, Aztec,* and *Inca.* For each culture, have them give the dates when the empire flourished, where it was located, the name of its major city, and at least two achievements of the culture.

Answers to Chapter Review appear on pages 314e–314f.

Summary

1. **Early civilizations arose in Africa.** Africa has five geographic regions: the northern and southern coasts; the deserts; the Sahel; the savannas; and the rain forest. The Kushites built the first sub-Saharan kingdom. Meroë was conquered by Ethiopia, a Christian kingdom. The Swahili culture arose in cities on the east coast. Inland, Zimbabwe became a wealthy state.

2. **African empires thrived on trade.** In western Africa, the empires of Ghana, Mali, and Songhai developed on the savanna. They gained wealth and power from the gold-salt trade. In many of those societies, lineages were central to both family organization and religion. Art and music expressed the societies' traditional values.

3. **American peoples developed many ways of life.** Most scientists believe that the first Americans came from Asia by crossing a land-bridge about 20,000 to 40,000 years ago. Groups of people spread out over the Americas, creating different ways of life. Corn became the basic crop of many groups, while others continued to hunt and gather food.

4. **Empires flourished in the Americas.** The Moche and Inca of Peru, the Olmec and Maya of Central America, and the Aztec of Mexico each developed distinctive civilizations. New discoveries reveal their ways of living and accomplishments. The Aztec built an empire in the Valley of Mexico. The Inca ruled an empire in Peru, uniting it by skilled administration and good roads.

Reviewing the Facts

1. Define the following terms:
   a. oasis   c. lineage
   b. savanna   d. griot
2. Explain the importance of each of the following names, places, or terms:
   a. Sahara   h. Anasazi
   b. Sahel   i. Moche
   c. griots   j. Hopewell
   d. Kushites   k. Olmec
   e. Ethiopia   l. Maya
   f. Ghana   m. Inca
   g. Mali   n. Aztec
3. Describe the climate and vegetation of Africa's major geographic regions.
4. (a) Who were included in a lineage? (b) How did the lineage system help to organize society?
5. Compare the ways of life of the Hopewell and the Anasazi.

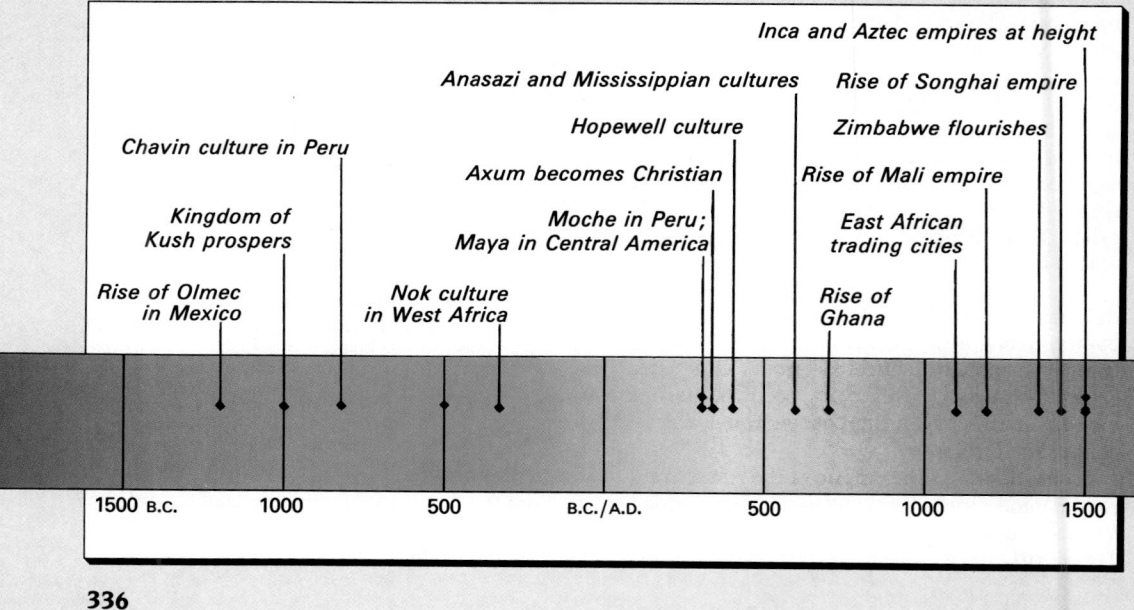

Inca and Aztec empires at height

Anasazi and Mississippian cultures   Rise of Songhai empire

Hopewell culture   Zimbabwe flourishes

Chavin culture in Peru   Axum becomes Christian   Rise of Mali empire

Kingdom of Kush prospers   Moche in Peru; Maya in Central America   East African trading cities

Rise of Olmec in Mexico   Nok culture in West Africa   Rise of Ghana

1500 B.C.   1000   500   B.C./A.D.   500   1000   1500

Basic Skills

1. **Interpreting time lines** Refer to the time line on page 336. For each event on the line, tell whether it occurred at the precise time shown or over a period of many years.
2. **Comparing time lines** Using the time lines on pages 298 and 312, find out what was happening in Asia during each of the following periods: (a) when Ghana was at its height in Western Africa; (b) when Aztec civilization was at its height in Mexico.
3. **Stating main ideas** Give one main idea (other than the section headings) on each of the following topics: (a) the kingdom of Kush, (b) the kingdom of Axum, (c) the coastal cities of East Africa, (d) the empire of Ghana, (e) the empire of Mali, (f) the empire of Songhai.
4. **Making a comparison chart** Make a chart comparing the Aztec and the Inca. For the vertical column, use the headings Location, Political Organization, Religion, and Major Achievements.

Researching and Reporting Skills

1. **Identifying primary sources** Identify from the text one primary source mentioned for each of the following: (a) Kush, (b) Axum, (c) coastal cities, (d) Ghana, (e) Mali, (f) Songhai, (g) the Hopewell, (h) the Moche, (i) the Maya.
2. **Evaluating sources** Discuss the value of the various types of sources in number 1 above, based on the following criteria: (a) objectivity, (b) type of information provided, (c) amount of interpretation needed.
3. **Finding and listing references** To prepare a report on one of the groups of people mentioned in this chapter, you might use a college textbook on world history to locate references. Find such a textbook in a library and look up in the index the name of the group you have chosen. Using the page references and end-of-chapter bibliographies, list three references that give information on your subject. For each reference, prepare a citation that includes author's name, title of reference, name and location of publisher, and date of publication.
4. **Choosing a title** Based on the sources you have identified, select one aspect of your subject's history as the topic for a possible report. Choose the title that will best convey what you intend your report to cover.

Critical Thinking

1. **Analyzing** (a) What geographic and environmental factors contributed most to the rise of the various African kingdoms? (b) Give examples to support your answer.
2. **Synthesizing** Trade was of major importance in the economy of the various African kingdoms. (a) What were the main resources and products exported from Africa? (b) What were the main kinds of imports and where did they come from?
3. **Inferring** What factors besides iron working aided the prosperity of Kush?
4. **Analyzing** Choose two of the societies described in this chapter and explain how each adapted to its geographic environment.
5. **Analyzing** (a) What factors might account for the wide variety of cultures that arose among the people of North America? (b) How did this pattern of cultures differ from that in Central and South America?
6. **Comparing** How did Maya pyramids differ in design and function from those of Egypt?
7. **Evaluating** The Maya, Aztec, and Inca developed distinctive civilizations. (a) List four major achievements of each civilization. (b) Which do you consider most advanced in terms of European civilization?

Perspectives on Past and Present

This chapter has highlighted certain characteristics of African civilization—such as the importance of family ties, religion honoring the spirits of ancestors, and music and dance that bound communities in a traditional heritage. Read about a contemporary African nation to find whether these characteristics still apply.

Investigating History

1. Alex Haley's book *Roots* gives an account of a present-day griot. Read that description and report to the class on the role of the griot in helping Haley to identify his ancestors.
2. The earliest known civilization in Peru was that of the Moche. Preceding the Inca by some 1,200 years, they rivaled their Maya contemporaries in art and technology. Read in the October 1988 *National Geographic* or news magazines of that date about the extraordinary discovery of a Moche ruler's tomb and what it tells of this early civilization.

337

CHAPTER
Evaluation

Chapter Test 14, Alternate Chapter Test 14, and Computer Test Bank Chapter 14 Test can be used to evaluate your students' understanding of this chapter.

ANSWERS TO
Geographic Theme

1. Díaz thought Tenochtitlán was a great city and that it compared favorably with Constantinople and Rome in terms of layout, size, and orderliness.

2. Tenochtitlán was situated on an island in a lake, with bridges connecting it to the mainland. The lake provided protection.

3. Answers will vary. However, Marco Polo's description of Khanbalik is the most precise in detail.

4. Marco Polo's description shows a very orderly city with great wealth and trade. The presence of the nighttime guards suggests that the city is orderly—perhaps in an autocratic way. Ibn Battuta's description is mainly about the role of women. The culture of Walata is strongly influenced by Islam. The people of Mali believe strongly in justice and security from crime. Díaz emphasized the size and beauty of Tenochtitlán and the planning shown by the aqueduct as evidence of culture. The orderliness among great crowds of people suggests a stable and disciplined society.

Geographic Theme: Place

What are the characteristics of three cities of the past?

Geographers are concerned with the special character of a place. Their interest includes both the nature of the land and the customs of the people. Historians share this interest when they study cities of the past.

In this unit, you have read accounts written by two of history's great travelers. Marco Polo described the "new royal city" of Khanbalik. The other traveler, the Arab Ibn Battuta, described the African city of Walata, then in the kingdom of Mali.

Another great city of the past is Tenochtitlán in Mexico. It is known today through the writings of a Spanish soldier, Bernal Díaz, who accompanied Cortés. Díaz had a chance to tour the city before it was destroyed. In his old age, Díaz recorded his recollections of the Aztec capital.

"We saw the fresh water which came from Chapultepec [by aqueduct] to supply the city, and the bridges that were constructed at intervals on the causeways so that the water could flow in and out from one part of the lake to another . . . We saw *cues* [temples] and shrines that looked like gleaming white towers and castles: a marvellous sight . . .

"Having examined and considered all that we had seen, we turned back to the great market and the swarm of people buying and selling. The mere murmur of their voices talking was loud enough to be heard more than three miles away. Some of our soldiers who had been in many parts of the world, in Constantinople, in Rome, and all over Italy, said that they had never seen a market so well laid out, so large, so orderly, and so full of people."

1. (a) What is Díaz's impression of Tenochtitlán? (b) What does his description tell about Aztec civilization?

2. What can you tell about the site and situation of Tenochtitlán?

3. Compare the accounts of Díaz with those of Polo and Battuta. Which description conveys the most vivid impression? In which city would you have preferred to live?

4. What does each description show about the culture and society of that city?

Tenochtitlán in about 1500

Historical Themes

Although they had little contact with each other, civilizations in Asia, Africa, and the Americas were all shaped by similar geographic and cultural themes.

Human-Environment Interaction

Geographic conditions played a pivotal role in shaping the early histories of Japan, Africa, and the Americas. Japan is separated from China by 500 miles of ocean. Its mild climate, mountain vistas, and jagged coastline make it one of the most beautiful countries on Earth. At the same time, Japan's earthquakes, typhoons, and volcanoes reveal nature in its most violent moods.

Many scholars believe that environmental influences had an important impact on Japanese culture. While emphasizing quiet reflection in the Shinto religion, the Japanese also glorified the violent ways of their samurai warriors.

Geographic conditions likewise influenced the development of civilization in Africa. As the Sahara changed from grassland to desert, it limited contacts between Europe and sub-Saharan regions. Africa's lack of natural harbors and navigable rivers hindered trade and communication.

While geography reduced Africa's contact with nearby lands, it completely isolated North and South America. By creating a temporary land bridge, the Ice Age enabled nomadic Asian hunters to reach North America. These migrants slowly spread across the Americas, adapting to a wide variety of environments.

Continuity and Change

China and India were repeatedly threatened by nomadic warriors from the Eurasian steppes. Between 1200 and 1350, the Mongols conquered a vast empire from eastern Asia to eastern Europe. Although the Mongols spared India, the subcontinent was later conquered by the Mughals. During the early 1600's, the Manchus overthrew China's Ming dynasty and became the new rulers.

Neither the Mongols nor the Manchus changed the basic patterns of Chinese culture. Despite their invasions, the cycle of dynasties' gaining and losing the Mandate of Heaven

continued. Confucian thought still dominated Chinese life.

Recurring cycles have also shaped Japanese history. Beginning in the seventh century, Japan launched an aggressive program to learn more about China. The Tokugawa shoguns ended this era of cultural borrowing, however, when they enforced a policy of cultural isolation. Although Japan avoided foreign conquest, periods of strong government alternated with periods of civil war.

While barbarian invasions and cultural isolation dominated China and Japan, recurring patterns of trade and culture shaped African life. Eastern Africa was long linked to Arabia and India by trade. In western Africa, the gold-salt trade brought wealth that enabled empires to thrive. African cultures all emphasized lineages and the worship of various gods and spirits. In the Americas, different ways of life developed in the various environments.

The cultural patterns that arose in Asia, Africa, and the Americas lasted for centuries. The sudden arrival of European explorers, however, changed the way of life in all three regions.

Cultural Development

Asia, Africa, and the Americas all produced impressive golden ages marked by achievements in the arts. Japan's Lady Murasaki wrote the world's first true novel, while India's Kalidasa wrote dramas that are still performed. People in Africa and the Americas created outstanding architecture, statues, and other works of art.

Analyzing Historical Themes

1. How did environmental conditions influence life in Japan, Africa, and the Americas?
2. What recurring patterns shaped African cultures?
3. What were important cultural achievements in Japan, Africa, and the Americas?

339

ANSWERS TO
Analyzing Historical Themes

1. Japan—quiet reflection of Shinto religion parallels natural beauty, glorification of violent samurai warriors parallels violence in nature; Africa—Sahara, lack of natural harbors and navigable rivers hindered trade and contact with nearby lands; Americas—isolated by geography, temporary land bridge allowed nomadic Asian hunters to reach Americas

2. trade, emphasis on lineages and the worship of various gods and spirits

3. Japan—world's first novel; Africa and Americas—architecture, statues, and other works of art

UNIT
Evaluation

Unit IV Test and Alternate Unit IV Test can be used to evaluate your students' understanding of this unit.

Painting of Lisbon Harbor by Gregorio Lopes

	1300	**1360**	**1420**
Political and Governmental Life	**1300's** Rise of independent cities in Northern Italy		**1434** Medici control Florence **1430's** Prince Henry the Navigator sponsors exploration
Economic and Technological Life	**1300's** Florence is financial center of Europe		**1400's** New technology opens way to exploration
Social and Cultural Life	**1300's** Renaissance begins in northern Italy **1321** Dante writes *The Divine Comedy*		**1455** Gutenberg prints Bible with movable type

Bronze doors of Baptistry in Florence

Detail from Giotto's The Crucifixion

Printing shop

Unit V

The Spread of New Ideas

Historical Themes

The Impact of Ideas New ideas produced by the Renaissance, the Reformation, exploration and discovery, and the Scientific Revolution marked the transition from the Middle Ages to a new era in Europe.

Individuals and History Strong individuals emerged as leaders in the arts, religious thought, political change, and exploration and discovery. Their work opened the door to a new age.

Technology and History New techniques and inventions—from the use of perspective in painting to the printing press, caravel, and telescope—changed people's perception of the world and of themselves.

1480	1540	1600

1485–1603
Tudor dynasty rules England

1519
Cortés conquers Mexico

Conquistador's helmet

1500's–1600's
Scientific Revolution brings new ideas

1490's
Explorations of Columbus and Da Gama

1566–1581
The Netherlands gains independence

1588
England defeats the Spanish Armada

Copernicus' sun-centered theory

1508–1512
Michelangelo paints in Sistine Chapel

1521
Luther begins religious revolt

1618–1648
Religious wars divide Germany

1600's
Dutch merchants develop capitalism

1600's
Amsterdam becomes a center of art

1605
Cervantes publishes *Don Quixote*

The World about 1500

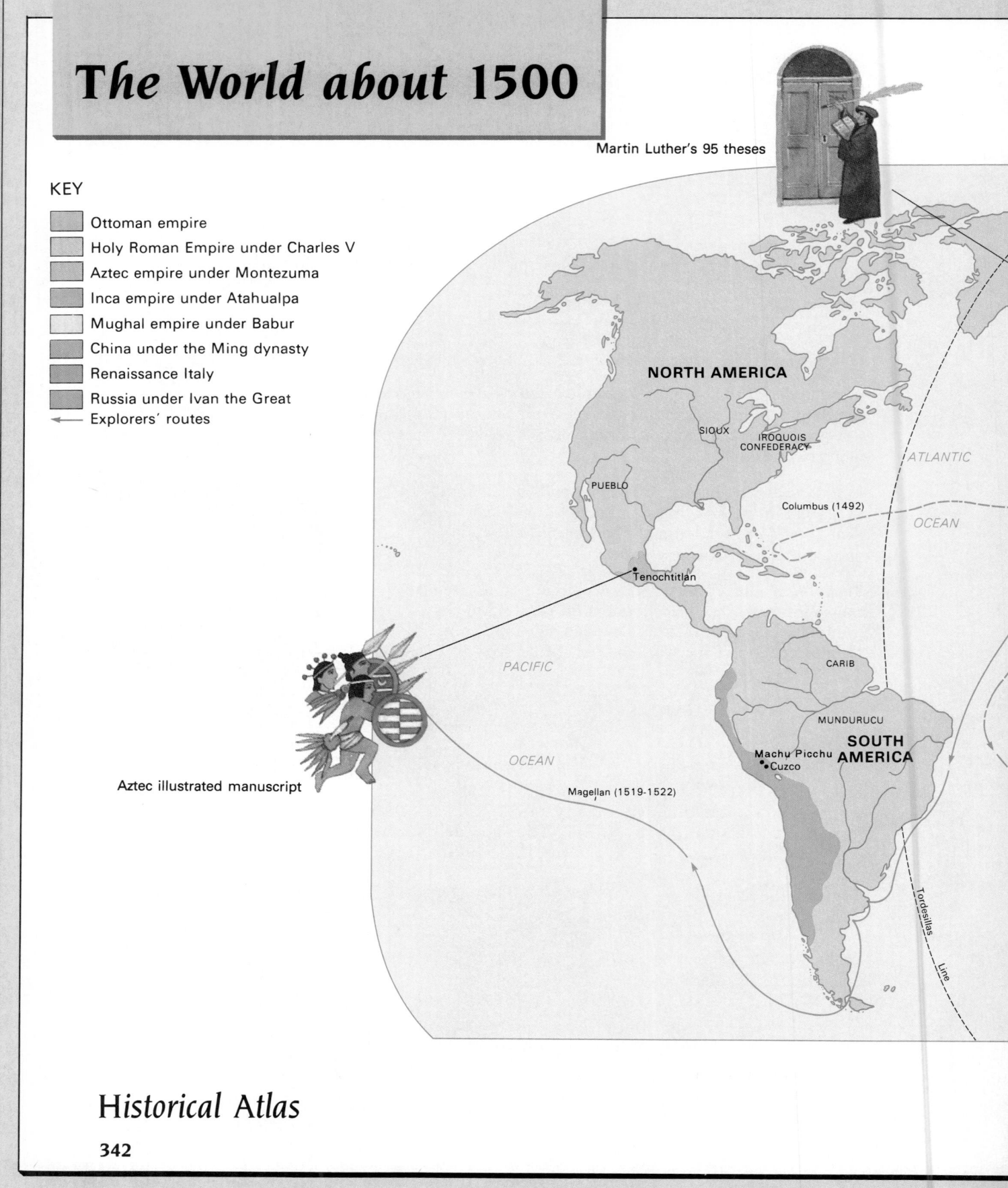

Martin Luther's 95 theses

KEY

- Ottoman empire
- Holy Roman Empire under Charles V
- Aztec empire under Montezuma
- Inca empire under Atahualpa
- Mughal empire under Babur
- China under the Ming dynasty
- Renaissance Italy
- Russia under Ivan the Great
- ← Explorers' routes

NORTH AMERICA

SIOUX

IROQUOIS CONFEDERACY

PUEBLO

ATLANTIC

Columbus (1492)

OCEAN

Tenochtitlán

PACIFIC

OCEAN

Aztec illustrated manuscript

Magellan (1519-1522)

CARIB

MUNDURUCU

SOUTH AMERICA

Machu Picchu

Cuzco

Tordesillas Line

Historical Atlas

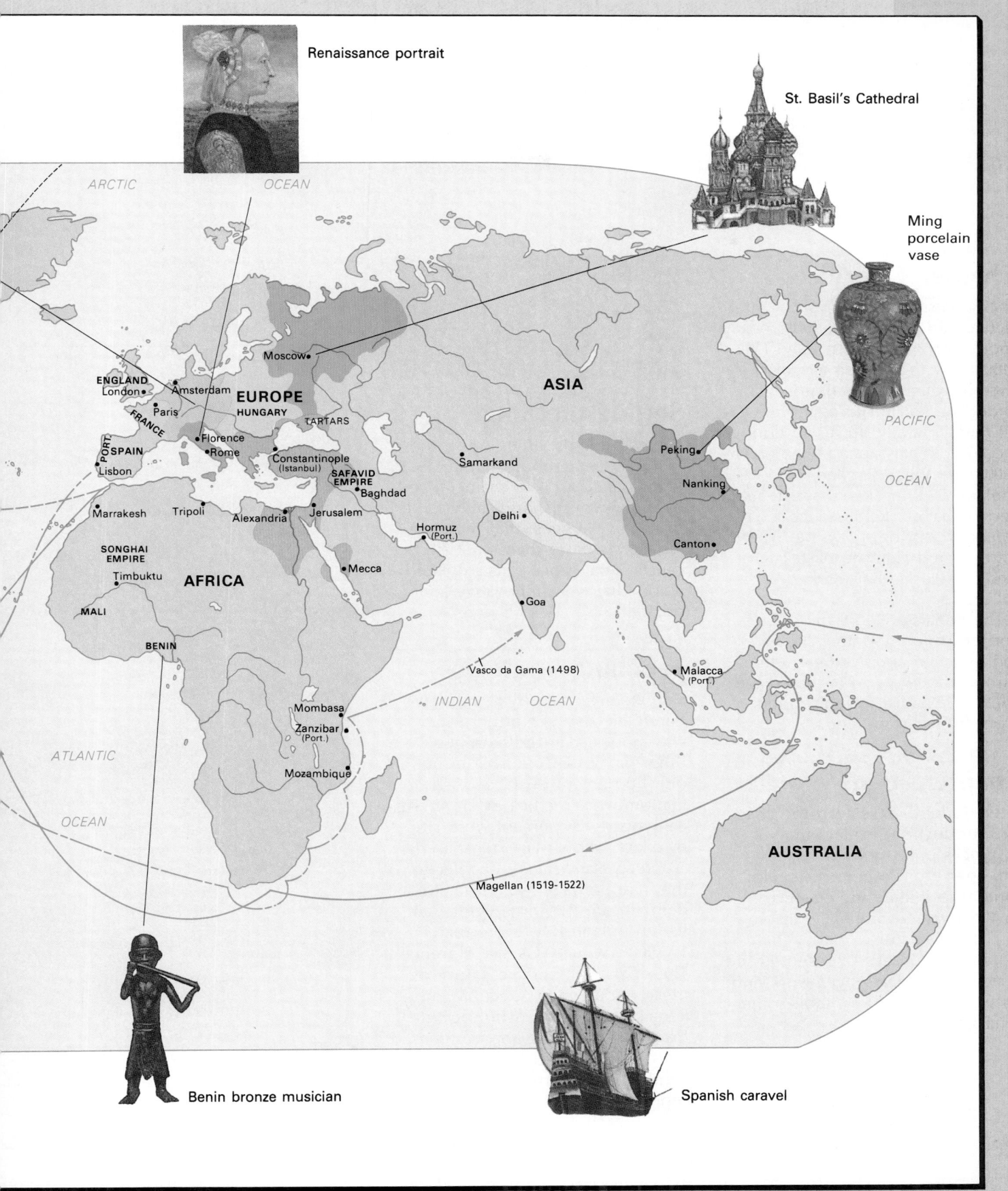

Renaissance portrait

St. Basil's Cathedral

Ming porcelain vase

ARCTIC OCEAN

ENGLAND
London•
Amsterdam•
EUROPE
HUNGARY
FRANCE
PORT.
SPAIN
Lisbon•
•Paris
•Florence
•Rome
•Moscow
TARTARS
ASIA
PACIFIC OCEAN
Constantinople (Istanbul)
SAFAVID EMPIRE
•Baghdad
•Samarkand
•Peking
•Nanking
Marrakesh•
Tripoli•
•Alexandria
•Jerusalem
Hormuz (Port.)
•Delhi
•Canton
SONGHAI EMPIRE
•Timbuktu
AFRICA
•Mecca
•Goa
MALI
BENIN
Vasco da Gama (1498)
•Malacca (Port.)
INDIAN OCEAN
•Mombasa
Zanzibar (Port.)
ATLANTIC
•Mozambique
AUSTRALIA
OCEAN
Magellan (1519-1522)

Benin bronze musician

Spanish caravel

The Renaissance and Exploration

Chapter **15**

Chapter Overview

The Renaissance, a period of intellectual and artistic creativity, began about 1300 in northern Italy. The 1400's saw the golden age of Florence in which artists flourished under the patronage of the powerful Medici family. In Rome during the High Renaissance of the early 1500's, da Vinci, Raphael, and Michelangelo lifted Renaissance art to new brilliance. Renaissance ideas spread to northern Europe, where German and Flemish masters created the works that marked its final phase.

The Renaissance was also a period of exploration and discovery. Led by Spain and Portugal, other European powers soon joined the quest to explore, colonize, and profit from distant lands.

Chapter Focus

After students have read the chapter introduction, explain that da Vinci's philosophy of art set him apart from other artists. Not content to imitate the classics, da Vinci valued originality above all. To him, nature—rather than the ancient Greeks—presented the perfect study. Da Vinci's work and his views about art symbolize the Renaissance spirit.

The Renaissance began in northern Italy. **1**

Setting the Stage

Direct students' attention to the pictures throughout Chapter 15. Renaissance art was characterized by individualism, originality, and discovery. Suggest that the Renaissance was more than a rebirth because Renaissance artists created works that were innovative and original.

Teaching Strategies

Skill Building: Classifying Information (Objective 1) Northern Italy was more urbanized than any other part of Europe. For example, only 10 percent of the English population lived in cities, while in Tuscany nearly 26 percent were city dwellers. Show Map Transparency 58, *Renaissance Italy*, or refer to the map on page 346. Have students locate the three cities that had populations of more than 100,000. (Venice, Genoa, Florence) The open, competitive nature of these trade centers encouraged Renaissance artists, who moved from city to city as opportunities arose. Ask students to identify conditions in northern Italy that supported the Renaissance and classify each as "economic," "political," or "social." (economic: prosperity through trade, powerful merchant class; political: well-defended, well-funded, independent city-states; social: secular, urban life-styles, competition among merchants to sponsor the arts)

Advance Planner

	SECTION 1
Objectives	1. Analyze the economic, political, and social conditions that gave rise to the Renaissance. 2. Describe how the works of Giotto, Dante, and Petrarch differed from the art of the Middle Ages.
Setting the Stage	The meaning of Renaissance
Teaching Strategies	Skill Building: Classifying Information Transparency 58 Writing about History: Comparing Medieval and Early Renaissance Thought Check for Understanding
Guided Practice	Transparency 58 Q&A Section Review 1
Independent Practice Worksheets	Independent Practice 15.1 Vocabulary Skills 15 Basic Skills 15
Enrichment	1. Primary Source: Voices 15.1 2. Writing a Report: *The Courtier* 3. Researching for Points
Chapter Closer	

Chapter 15 The Renaissance and Exploration 1300–1600
FOCUS Leonardo da Vinci's claim to genius

★ Advanced
● Basic

SECTION 2	SECTION 3	SECTION 4	SECTION 5
1. Explain the role of the Medici family in Florentine society. 2. Analyze the political philosophy of Machiavelli.	1. Describe the art of the High Renaissance. 2. Evaluate the qualities that distinguish great art.	1. Outline the causes and effects of the age of exploration. 2. Trace on a map the routes of the major European explorers.	1. Describe European settlements in North America. 2. Describe the development of the slave trade and identify its characteristics in the 1500's.
How the story of Ghiberti's doors reveals Renaissance priorities	Michelangelo's impact on his contemporaries	Voyages of discovery carried out the spirit of the Renaissance	Discoveries and opportunities
Relating Past to Present: Patrons of the Arts Discussing History: Machiavelli's Views Check for Understanding	Teaching with Pictures: Michelangelo's "Pieta" Writing about History: Evaluating Renaissance Art Check for Understanding	Skill Building: Relating Cause and Effect Using Geographic Themes: Movement Transparency 59 Outline Map 2 Check for Understanding	Economics and History: Indentured Servants Discussing History: The Slave Trade Check for Understanding
Section Review 2 Independent Practice 15.2	Section Review 3 Independent Practice 15.3 Critical Thinking 15	Transparency 59 Q&A Section Review 4 Independent Practice 15.4 Geography Skills 15	Section Review 5 Independent Practice 15.5
1. Primary Source: Voices 15.2 2. ★Creative Writing 3. Researching for Points	1. Primary Source: Voices 15.3 2. ★Preparing a Report: Michelangelo 3. Learning through Pictures 4. Researching for Points	1. Primary Source: Voices 15.4 2. Preparing a Report: Inventions 3. Researching for Points	1. Primary Source: Voices 15.5 2. Preparing a Report: The Slave Trade 3. Researching for Points 4. Global Perspectives Transparency 57

●**Reteaching Activities** Explaining, Recalling Information, Outlining, Summarizing Main Ideas

Chapter Review Summary, Reviewing the Facts, Basic Skills, Researching and Reporting Skills, Critical Thinking, Perspectives on Past and Present, Investigating History

Chapter Evaluation Chapter Test 15, Alternate Chapter Test 15, Computer Test Bank Chapter 15 Test

Writing about History: Comparing Medieval and Early Renaissance Thought (Objective 2) *Prewriting* After students have read pages 346–347, help them identify medieval influences in the work of Giotto (religious subjects), Dante (emphasis on religious faith, romantic love, and Roman poetry), and Petrarch (spiritual muse, use of Latin, love of classical writing). Then identify Renaissance influences. (Giotto: portrayal of depth and of real people in real situations; Dante: use of vernacular and portrayal of real people in true adventures; Petrarch: striving for classical simplicity) *Writing* Ask students to write essays explaining why these artists represent a transition from medieval to Renaissance thought.

Check for Understanding Have students explain how the pictures in this section illustrate Renaissance ideals and values.

Enrichment Activities

1. **Reading a Primary Source** Assign Voices from the Past Resource Book 15.1.
2. **Writing a Report** Have students read excerpts from *The Courtier* and explain how Castiglione's observations at the court of the Duke of Urbino related to his ideas on Renaissance values.
3. **Researching for Bonus Points** Who wrote, "Abandon all hope, ye who enter here"? (Dante Alighieri) To what do these words refer? ("the inferno")

Florence led the way in arts. 2

Setting the Stage

Have students read "Artists beautified Florence" (page 351). Tell students that Ghiberti included two self-portraits in the doors. What Renaissance priorities does this story reflect? (open competition, pride in achievement, individuality, and creativity) Point out that the creative use of perspective, realism, and detail is typical of Renaissance artists.

Teaching Strategies

Relating Past to Present: Patrons of the Arts (Objective 1) Ask students how artists earn a living in the United States today. (compete for commissions and grants, sell finished work, or receive support from collectors, philanthropists, corporations, and the government) To what extent does a society's support of the arts reflect its general prosperity and greatness?

Discussing History: Machiavelli's Views (Objective 2) Machiavelli studied the political motivations and actions of people in power, how they acquired power, and how they kept it. He based his writings on observations of Florentine political life. Explain that Florentines emphasized diplomatic skills. Surrounded by enemies, they skillfully used diplomacy to avoid disruptions.

Write the following quotations on the board:

"The end justifies the means."

"a prince . . . must if necessary be prepared to do evil."

"From this arises the question whether it is better to be loved rather than feared, or feared rather than loved. It might perhaps be answered that we should wish to be both: but since love and fear can hardly exist together, if we must choose between them, it is far safer to be feared than loved."

Have students describe political factors in northern Italy that led Machiavelli to these conclusions. Ask whether his analysis can be applied to present-day situations. Have students agree or disagree with each quotation and offer evidence to support their judgments.

Check for Understanding Have students explain the significance of Florentine politics and of the Medici in the development of Renaissance art and architecture.

Enrichment Activities

1. **Reading a Primary Source** Assign Voices from the Past Resource Book 15.2.
2. **Creative Writing** Have advanced students react to Machiavelli's conclusion that the end justifies the means.
3. **Researching for Bonus Points** Who was the model for the leader described in *The Prince*? (Cesare Borgia, Roman politician)

The Renaissance spread. 3

Setting the Stage

Michelangelo inspired and awed his contemporaries as he used classical styles and subjects to portray the personalities and struggles of his own time. Tell students that Michelangelo worked in a period known as the High Renaissance.

Teaching Strategies

Teaching with Pictures: Michelangelo's "Pieta" (Objective 1) Michelangelo's work challenged people's ideas about life and art and was a highlight of the High Renaissance. After students have read Section 3, have them identify characteristics of the High Renaissance. List responses on the board. Then direct students' attention to the works of Michelangelo (pages 354–355). Ask students what Michelangelo's "Pieta" conveys. While earlier representations of Christ's death stressed the brutal aspects, Michelangelo presented a vision of serenity, sad beauty, and peace. Explain that *pieta* in Italian means "pity." Ask students to speculate on Michelangelo's interpretation of Christ's death. Michelangelo believed the body should reflect what is in the soul. How does the "Pieta" express this belief?

Writing about History: Evaluating Renaissance Art (Objective 2) *Prewriting* Ask students what distinguishes great art. Write their responses on the board. Students should recognize that there are many standards and values used in evaluating works of art. "Great" works usually show technical skill and originality, and also portray great themes or communicate great ideas to viewers. *Writing* Have each student write an essay about a work of art described in this section. Students should include their own thoughts about the piece as well as an evaluation of it as as example of "great art."

Check for Understanding Ask students to explain how Renaissance artists and their works influenced Europeans who visited Italy.

Enrichment Activities

1. **Reading a Primary Source**
   Assign Voices from the Past Resource Book 15.3.
2. **Preparing a Report**
   Have students research whether Michelangelo was helped or hindered by Pope Julius II.
3. **Learning through Pictures**
   Ask interested students to prepare scrapbooks or collages of Renaissance art and architecture to share with the class. Students should caption or explain each selection.
4. **Researching for Bonus Points**
   What were Michelangelo's first works in stone? ("Madonna of the Stars," "Battle of the Centaurs")

Explorers discovered new lands. 4

Setting the Stage

Renaissance explorers shared the confidence, curiousity, ambition, and individualism that characterized Renaissance artists. This spirit, combined with economic, religious, and technological factors, launched the Age of Exploration.

Teaching Strategies

Skill Building: Relating Cause and Effect (Objective 1) Help the class generate a list of limitations that prohibited or discouraged exploration before 1400. Write this list on the board. (lack of knowledge about distant regions, lack of seafaring and navigation technology, high cost of expeditions with uncertain reward, fear of unknown, no perceived need to explore) Next to each item, have students indicate what events or attitudes during the Renaissance helped overcome each limitation. Then ask students to speculate which factors caused the most difficulty for Columbus as he tried to find a sponsor for his voyage.

Using Geographic Themes: Movement (Objective 2) Show Map Transparency 59, *Voyages of Discovery,* or refer to pages 362–363. Then distribute Outline Map 2: The World. Have students use the map and the information in Section 4 to label areas discovered by the European explorers. Have each student select four explorers, design a map symbol for each, and use the symbols to draw the routes of the four explorers on their outline maps.

Check for Understanding Have students explain in writing what conditions and events encouraged exploration.

Enrichment Activities

1. **Reading a Primary Source**
   Assign Voices from the Past Resource Book 15.4.
2. **Preparing a Report**
   Have students report on one of the following inventions: compass, astrolabe, caravel. Reports should include a description of the device, its history, and its significance to the European explorers.
3. **Researching for Bonus Points**
   Who explored the coast of Newfoundland for England in 1497? (John Cabot)

Other countries started colonies in America. 5

Setting the Stage

Once Magellan's voyage confirmed the existence of the new continents, explorers tried to find a shorter way around those continents to reach Asia. In the process, they discovered that the continents themselves offered great opportunities.

Teaching Strategies

Economics and History: Indentured Servants (Objective 1) Many of the Europeans who came to North America went into debt to finance their trips and their beginnings in the new settlement. Although some people could gather enough money by selling all their belongings and borrowing from family or friends, others had to exchange their own labor for passage to the colonies. Such people were known as indentured servants.

The servant and holder signed a contract that lasted for a specified period, such as five years. During this time the holder was obligated to provide food, clothing, and shelter for the servant. The servant performed whatever work the holder requested, such as field labor, domestic chores, or helping out in a shop or trade.

Various colonies had different laws concerning indenture. Some required that the holder provide the servant with clothing, tools, seeds, and a parcel of land upon completion of the contract. Other laws were not so generous.

Discussing History: The Slave Trade (Objective 2) The slave trade was part of a triangular route that began in a seaport in western Europe. Carrying rum, gunpowder, and trinkets, traders sailed to the "Slave Coast" in Africa. There they

bought slaves from African slave hunters who ruthlessly raided rival kingdoms to capture their victims. The slaves' voyage to the New World is called the "Middle Passage." Have students explain why so many slaves died during this trip. Ask why early colonial economic life in the Americas came to depend on slavery. (Mining and plantation agriculture were labor-intensive.)

Check for Understanding Have students explain the hazards and benefits for Europeans, Native Americans, and Africans that resulted from the colonization of North America.

Enrichment Activities

1. **Reading a Primary Source**
   Assign Voices from the Past Resource Book 15.5.

2. **Preparing a Report**
   Have students report on the slave trade in the 1500's. They should include information on how slaves were captured, sold, and transported to America.

3. **Researching for Bonus Points**
   Early expeditions down the African coast unsuccessfully sought to pass beyond a point of land just south of the Canary Islands. What was the name of this place, and why was it important? (Cape Bojador was a psychological barrier to sailors who feared its violent currents, dense fogs, strong winds, and shallow waters.)

4. **Global Perspectives**
   Assign students the activities in Map Transparency 57, *The World about 1500.*

ANSWERS TO Chapter Review 15

Reviewing the Facts

1. **(a)** everyday language of one's homeland **(b)** scholar who studied classical texts **(c)** sailing vessel designed for ocean travel **(d)** rapid spreading of disease

2. **(a)** Renaissance artist, engineer, architect **(b)** painter who revolutionized art by painting life-like figures **(c)** early Renaissance poet who wrote *The Divine Comedy* **(d)** poet whose writings reflected classical virtues of simplicity and purity **(e)** northern Italian city that led the way in the arts **(f)** leader of Florence who ruled with absolute power, held goodwill of people, and continued tradition of beautifying the city **(g)** painter who developed principles of perspective **(h)** book by Machiavelli that gave advice to rulers about political power **(i)** Michelangelo painted its ceiling with more than 300 massive human figures **(j)** great Renaissance sculptor of the "Pieta" and "David," painter of the Sistine Chapel **(k)** famous artist who painted walls of papal library **(l)** German engraver who helped spread the Renaissance to northern Europe **(m)** Flemish painter known for realistic detail and use of color **(n)** prince of Portugal and patron of explorers **(o)** explorer whose unexpected arrival in the Americas opened a new era of exploration and conquest **(p)** Spanish explorer whose expedition rounded the globe **(q)** French explorer who mapped eastern Canada and founded Quebec **(r)** English adventurer who founded Roanoke colony in 1585 **(s)** English explorer who claimed the Hudson River region for the Dutch

3. (a) golden age of creative and intellectual activity that began around 1300 (b) in northern Italy

4. (a) Portrait painting and autobiography developed because wealthy merchants wanted to be remembered beyond their lifetimes. (b) Artists and writers wanted to be known as individuals, and fame became the final reward for superior talent. (c) Explorers were confident, ambitious, and eager for individual glory.

5. (a) They wanted a share of the profitable Asian trade and routes they could control. (b) The Portuguese reached India by sailing around Africa, and Columbus reached the Americas while trying to sail to Asia across the Atlantic Ocean.

6. (a) introduction of new food crops (b) introduction of new food crops and diseases; conquest or political control (c) development of the slave trade to the Americas

Basic Skills

1. *Spain:* Columbus—West Indies, Central America; Balboa—Central America; Magellan—South America, East Indies, Spice Islands, Africa; Vespucci—South America, Central America. *Portugal:* Da Gama—Africa, India; Dias—Africa; Cabral—South America, Africa, India. *France:* Verrazano—New York Harbor; Cartier—eastern Canada; Joliet and Marquette, LaSalle—Mississippi River. *England:* Cabot—Newfoundland; Drake—South America, Central America, North America, Spice Islands, East Indies.

2. (a)
A. New values shaped the Renaissance.
   1. Celebration of the individual
      a. portrait painting
      b. autobiography
   2. Love of classical learning
      a. Greek and Roman art
      b. Greek and Roman writings
      c. rise of humanism
   3. Enjoyment of worldly pleasures
      a. display of fashion
      b. interest in earthly matters
(b) celebration of the individual—Leon Battista Alberti; love of classical learning—Petrarch; enjoyment of worldly pleasures—Lorenzo de Medici

Researching and Reporting Skills

1. Students' reports will vary.
2. Students' headlines will vary.

Critical Thinking

1. (a) Middle Ages: little interest in the individual; religious focus to most activities, asceticism, learning of theology; code of chivalry; women to inspire love and art, but to remain wives or nuns. Renaissance: individual achievement and glory; admiration for the ancient classics and their standards of beauty; competence in many fields; appreciation of worldly pleasures; women to be educated, to inspire and patronize the arts.
(b) Examples in *art*—medieval: anonymity of artists; subjects relating to religion or daily life; portrayal of religious or anonymous figures; Renaissance: artist often portrays self in picture; classical themes and codes of beauty; realistic portraits of individuals; *architecture*—medieval: Gothic reaching up to heaven in pointed arches and spires; Renaissance: classical columns, domes, rounded or horizontal lines; *literature*—medieval: anonymity of author; heroes religious, fictitious, or legendary; Renaissance: autobiographies, features real people

2. Artists such as Dürer visited Italy and carried Renaissance ideas back to northern Europe. Royal courts, such as that of Francis I, promoted Renaissance art and employed well-known artists.

3. (a) more interested in worldly matters, political and cultural, than in religion (b) Michelangelo was the most important artist of the Renaissance.

4. Thesis: (a) The Renaissance spirit of adventure and curiosity inspired the explorers. (b) Explorers showed the confidence, ambition, curiosity, and love of individual glory that was characteristic of the Renaissance artists.

5. (a) In both, women were expected to inspire the arts, act as good hostesses, but not take an active role themselves. Their influence or power was often through others or the result of belonging to a powerful family, not based on their own merit or competence.
(b) Answers will vary, but should include information about the era chosen.

6. Answers will vary.

7. (a) French: fur trade; English: tobacco; Dutch: fur trade
(b) geography, policy toward Indians, government support of settlement

Perspectives on Past and Present

Students should mention the shared ideal of achievement, personal glory, or fame. In the Renaissance this is expressed as "Man can do anything if he will." This ideal excluded women, and it took no account of individual differences. In the United States, individual achievement is a goal for both men and women. Society recognizes the need to compensate for economic and social limitations so that everyone has an opportunity.

Investigating History

Students' findings will vary.

Chapter 15

Teaching with Pictures

Have students examine the picture of Renaissance Florence. Ask them how big they think the city is. Then tell them that the population of the city was about 100,000. Encourage students to look for the various styles of architecture, particularly of the palaces and churches. Can they identify any of the styles? Ask students how this city differs from medieval towns of the twelfth and thirteenth centuries.

*Renaissance Florence
lay on the Arno River.*

Key Terms

*Renaissance
fresco
vernacular
humanist
perspective
monopoly
caravel
compass
dissenter
epidemic*

Read and Understand

1. The Renaissance began in northern Italy.
2. Florence led the way in arts.
3. The Renaissance spread.
4. Explorers discovered new lands.
5. Other countries started colonies in America.

An intriguing idea darted into the mind of Leonardo da Vinci (LAY-uh-NAHR-doh duh VEEN-chee). Eagerly he flipped open his notebook and wrote this message to himself: "Dissect the bat, study it carefully, and on this model construct the machine."

The machine that Leonardo imagined had huge, batlike wings measuring 80 feet from tip to tip. Below the wings, he imagined a person standing on a wooden framework and pedaling furiously. By ropes and pulleys, the pedals would make the wings flap. With this device, thought Leonardo, a person could fly.

344

Chapter 15 Resources

GEOGRAPHY
- Geography Skills 15
- Outline Map 2
- Transparencies 57, 58, 59

REINFORCEMENT
- Vocabulary 15
- Basic Skills 15
- Reteaching 15
- Making Connections Study Guide 15

ENRICHMENT
- Critical Thinking 15
- History and Literature 15

ASSESSMENT
- Chapter Test 15
- Alternate Chapter Test 15
- Computer Test Bank

The flying machine was only one idea among hundreds that excited Leonardo. Looking through his notebooks (5,700 pages of which have survived), we can track Leonardo's lifelong quest for knowledge. He wanted to know the physical universe inside and out—how it worked and how its hidden laws could be mastered by the human mind.

On one page are drawings of the muscles and tendons of a man's arm as it swings forward. On another page, Leonardo made a rough sketch of a falling man clinging to a tent-shaped cloth. A note next to it explains its purpose:

If a man has a tent made of linen of which the [openings] have all been stopped up . . . he will be able to throw himself down from any height without injury.

Here, in other words, is the first design for a parachute.

Leonardo knew he was a genius. In 1482, he wrote a letter offering his services to the duke of Milan in northern Italy. Leonardo assured the duke that there was no better weapons designer, military engineer, painter, or architect than he was. He concluded, "I commend myself to Your Excellency with all possible humility."

Another Italian of this time, Christopher Columbus, had fewer ideas than Leonardo. However, he believed in his one great idea as firmly as Leonardo believed in parachutes and flying machines. Columbus thought he could reach Asia by sailing west across the Atlantic Ocean. He

This sketch from one of the Leonardo da Vinci's notebooks shows an idea for a flying machine.

was looking for a patron to pay for his voyage at the very time that Leonardo was trying to interest the duke of Milan in new ideas for bridges and armored vehicles.

Columbus (born in 1451) and Leonardo (born in 1452) were only two of many individuals whose genius and daring made the years from 1300 to 1600 a golden age. They lived during the time we call the **Renaissance** (REN-uh-SAHNTS). The word means "rebirth."

What was being reborn? The educated men and women of Italy hoped to bring back to life the classical culture of Greece and Rome. Yet bringing back a past golden age is never possible. In striving to revive the past, the people of the Renaissance in fact created something new.

The Renaissance was a time of great intellectual and artistic creativity. Above all, people of the Renaissance had a new view of themselves and their world.

The Renaissance began in northern Italy. 1

Like other great changes in history, the Renaissance did not replace the Middle Ages overnight. Nor did the change take place at the same time everywhere in Europe. The Renaissance began in Italy around 1300. Later, its new styles of art, writing, and thought spread northward to the Netherlands, France, Germany, and England.

It is important to remember that early writers and artists of the Renaissance were creating their masterpieces in Italy while France and England were still locked in the Hundred Years' War. The bustling cities of northern Italy seem to be in a different world from the feudal villages of northern Europe, but both existed at the same time.

Italy offered new opportunities.

The Renaissance began in the city-states of northern Italy, especially Florence. The region of Italy that lies north of Rome and south of the Alps was different from the rest of Europe in two ways.

Urban centers First, northern Italy was a highly urban region. By 1350, three cities there had

345

OBJECTIVE 1. Analyze the economic, political, and social conditions that gave rise to the Renaissance.

Teaching Strategy: *Skill Building: Classifying Information* (page 344a)

OBJECTIVE 2. Describe how the works of Giotto, Dante, and Petrarch differed from the art of the Middle Ages.

Teaching Strategy: *Writing about History: Comparing Medieval and Early Renaissance Thought* (page 344a)

■ BACKGROUND

We know about Leonardo's ideas for flying machines from the many sketches he drew in his books. Unfortunately, the notebooks show only what he planned to do. They do not tell whether he ever tried to build his great bat machine.

■ DISCUSSION

Ask students to explain why a French historian described the Renaissance as a time for "the discovery of man" and "the discovery of the world."

ENRICHMENT
■ Voices from the Past 15.1

ASSESSMENT
■ Section Quiz 15.1

GEOGRAPHY
■ Transparency 58

REINFORCEMENT
■ Independent Practice 15.1

ANSWERS TO
Map Study

Adriatic; the Papal States;
Savoy, Milan, Modena

■ DISCUSSION

What characteristics made cities in northern Italy different from those in other parts of Europe?

■ BACKGROUND

One scene in the Arena Chapel, for example, shows a group of grief-stricken women whose children had been killed by Roman soldiers. Though Giotto painted for another 30 years, the frescoes in the Arena Chapel were his greatest achievement.

■ DISCUSSION

How is the celebration of the individual shown in Giotto's epitaph: "I am he through whose merit the lost art of painting was revived . . . But what need is there for words? I am Giotto, and my name alone tells more than a lengthy ode."

Renaissance Italy

Map Study

What sea did Venice control? Who ruled Rome and the surrounding territory? What states bordered Genoa?

populations of about 100,000, a huge figure by medieval standards. Two of those cities—Genoa in the west and Venice in the east—were major seaports whose merchants dominated the rich Mediterranean trade. The third city, Florence, was located inland on the Arno River. Its thriving economy was based on the making of fine woolens, leathers, and silks.

Aside from those three large cities, northern Italy had a number of other good-sized towns, as the map on this page shows. Thus, northern Italy was urban while the rest of Europe was still mostly rural. (The Black Death of 1348 struck Italy's cities hard, but they recovered quickly.)

The power of merchants Second, northern Italy was a merchant's region. In these cities, wealthy merchants dominated politics and society as well as business. You have read how the Lombard League defeated the Holy Roman Emperor, Frederick Barbarossa, in 1176 at the Battle of Legnano (page 236). After that defeat, the Holy Roman emperors had little control over Italy's cities.

The popes had left Rome for Avignon and were later weakened by the Great Schism. They could not dominate Italy's cities either.

Milan, Genoa, Florence, Venice, and the other independent city-states ran their own affairs. Each collected taxes and supported an army. Within these cities, merchants were the wealthiest and most powerful class.

Unlike feudal nobles, merchants did not inherit their social rank. Success in business depended mostly on the merchant's own wits. As a result, successful merchants took pride in their achievements. They believed they were great because of their merit as individuals. The theme of individual achievement is an important one in the Renaissance, as you will see.

Just as these merchants competed with one another in business, they also competed as patrons, or sponsors, of the arts. A Florentine merchant was as proud of spotting a promising young painter as of making a profitable deal in silks. Throughout northern Italy, wealthy families spent their money lavishly for the glory of helping artists create works of genius.

Such was the setting for the Renaissance. Like the blossoming of a flower, the Renaissance first showed itself as a lovely bud in the 1300's. Three of the earliest geniuses in this golden age were a painter, a poet, and a letter writer.

Giotto painted lifelike figures.

Giotto di Bondone (JOHT-oh dee bohn-DOH-nay) was 38 years old when, in 1304, he carried his paints and brushes into a small, empty building in Padua, Italy. The building, called the Arena Chapel, was owned by a wealthy merchant who had commissioned Giotto to decorate it with scenes from the Bible. Giotto dabbed his brush in pigment and applied his first masterly stroke to the wet plaster. The technique of painting on wet plaster was known as **fresco** painting.

Most painters of the time would have covered the walls with flat, stiff-looking figures like those painted throughout the Middle Ages. Giotto had a different style. He painted human figures that looked real and lifelike, with bodies and faces that seemed fully rounded. When Giotto painted on a flat wall, he created an illusion of depth. The people in his paintings all seemed to be interacting with one another. Their faces showed

346

realistic emotions. Giotto's acclaimed frescoes began a revolution in art.

Dante wrote The Divine Comedy.

Dante Alighieri (DAHN-tay AH-lee-GYAY-ree) was to the world of poetry what Giotto was to the world of painting. Dante was born in Florence in 1265, only a year before Giotto's birth. At the age of 9, Dante met an 8-year-old girl, Beatrice Portinari. Although he did not see her again for 10 years, she became his spiritual ideal. "From that time forward," he wrote later, "love quite governed my soul." He continued his spiritual love for her from afar, although he rarely saw or spoke to her. She died in 1290, at just 24 years old. Yet Dante worshiped her memory until his own death in 1321. For Dante, Beatrice was his muse—that is, the guiding genius of his writing. In his poems, he spoke of her as a kind of goddess.

Dante's most famous work was *The Divine Comedy*. (In this sense, *comedy* refers to a literary work with a joyous ending.) This long poem has three parts. In the first part, Dante imagines that the ancient Roman poet Virgil is guiding him on a tour of "the inferno" (hell). In the second part, Dante and Virgil visit a zone called purgatory, which lies between hell and heaven. Finally, in the third part, Dante is guided through paradise by the famous medieval monk, St. Bernard. Eventually, he meets Beatrice there.

Dante filled his poem with real people. He called dead friends and enemies by name and told of their earthly adventures. *The Divine Comedy* is full of comments on the political events of Dante's time. He showed a keen interest in human personalities.

Dante's masterpiece showed both the religious ideas of the Middle Ages and the worldly concerns of the Renaissance. *The Divine Comedy* was a kind of philosophic bridge between Europe's past and its future.

At a time when other serious poets wrote in Latin, Dante wrote *The Divine Comedy* in the **vernacular**, or everyday language of his homeland. By his work, Dante gave the Italian language new prestige, and he is sometimes called the creator of modern Italian. His example encouraged other poets to write in their own vernacular languages, as England's Geoffrey Chaucer did later in the 1300's.

Petrarch wrote poems and letters.

Another Italian poet, Francesco Petrarch (PEE-trahrk), was born in 1304, the year that Giotto began work on the Arena Chapel. Petrarch wrote both in Italian and in Latin. In Italian, he wrote beautiful sonnets in honor of a mysterious woman named Laura, who was his muse and spiritual ideal as Beatrice had been Dante's. (Little is known of Laura except that she died of the plague in 1348.) In classical Latin, he wrote letters to his many influential friends.

In Petrarch's letters, he imitated the graceful style of his favorite classical author, Cicero, the ancient Roman senator. Petrarch's writing showed a new idea of beauty. Instead of the complexity of medieval poetry, Petrarch strove for the classical virtues of simplicity and purity. If Dante's works were a bridge between the Middle Ages and the Renaissance, Petrarch had crossed that bridge and stood fully within the new age.

New values shaped the Renaissance.

No age or time breaks completely with the past. Yet the men and women of the Renaissance came to have a new outlook on life. Here are some of the characteristics that set the Renaissance apart from the Middle Ages.

Celebration of the individual Artists in the Middle Ages did their work skillfully. In general, however, they did not win fame as individuals. The glassmakers, stonecutters, and wood-carvers of the great cathedrals worked for the glory of God, not for personal glory. Even the author of the *Song of Roland* is unknown.

By the 1300's, however, artists and writers in northern Italy were eager to be known and remembered as individuals. From this time on, we know the names of people who created works of art. Fame was the final reward for superior talent.

Two new art forms show this interest in individual fame: portrait painting and autobiography. Wealthy patrons wanted their faces recorded for all time. Artists often painted self-portraits too. Autobiographies were the written equivalents of self-portraits. People believed that their own lives were interesting and important not just to themselves but to others. They wished to share their lives with the world.

347

The characters in medieval verses seemed shadowy and artificial. The chivalrous knight was always brave, and his lady always conformed to an ideal standard.

■ BACKGROUND

Young men and women of the upper classes in the Renaissance studied history, rhetoric, literature, and moral philosophy. These subjects were called the liberal arts because their purpose was to liberate the students' minds.

■ DISCUSSION

How might religious leaders have responded to the Renaissance emphasis on worldly pleasures? (Dominican monk Girolamo Savonarola's dramatic oratory often moved Italian audiences to burn wigs, makeup, and other trappings of Renaissance society in bonfires of protest.)

Cooperative Learning

Have students read "Ideals differed for men and women" (pages 348–349). Arrange students in pairs or small groups. Make several groups of all boys, several of all girls, and several that are evenly mixed. Have each group member make lists of the qualities he or she would expect to find in an ideal man and in an ideal woman today. Then have group members combine and edit their lists to produce two group lists. Each item on a group list must be approved by all group members.

Use groups' lists as the basis for class discussion. Compare today's ideals with those of the Renaissance. Note whether the composition of the groups affected their lists.

Admiration for the classical culture of Greece shows in this Renaissance painting, "The School of Athens." Under the central arch, Plato talks with his pupil Aristotle. They are surrounded by important figures from both ancient and Renaissance times. (This work is by Raphael, who is discussed on page 356.)

Love of classical learning Renaissance scholars despised the art and literature of the Middle Ages. Since the fall of Rome in 476, they said, the people of Europe had lived in darkness and ignorance. Even the beautiful Gothic cathedrals were dismissed as the work of barbarians. Admiring only Greek and Roman art, a Renaissance artist once cried, "Cursed be the man who invented this wretched Gothic architecture!" Petrarch summed up the Renaissance attitude by calling the medieval years "the Dark Ages."

Petrarch and other Renaissance scholars loved the writings of ancient Greece and Rome. Scholars who studied classical texts were called **humanists**, from the Latin word *humanitas*. According to Cicero, humanitas meant the learning that every educated, civilized person should have. Petrarch himself is considered the first humanist. He and his followers were the cultural leaders of the Renaissance. Under their influence, all painting, sculpture, and architecture carried on the traditions of ancient Greece and Rome.

Enjoyment of worldly pleasures In Renaissance Italy, almost everyone with money openly enjoyed material luxuries, fine music, tasty foods, and beautiful surroundings. For example, clothing itself became almost a work of art. Women's gowns were sometimes so encrusted with pearls or golden beads that the fabric underneath was nearly hidden. Men wore colorful stockings, fancy jackets called doublets, and plumed hats. Both men and women perfumed their clothing and hair.

348

This enjoyment of worldly goods showed a new attitude. In the Middle Ages, devoutly religious people had proved their piety by wearing poor, rough clothing and living on the plainest foods. Renaissance humanists suggested that a person might love and enjoy life without offending God. Most historians agree that Renaissance art and literature show a growing interest in earthly and human subjects.

Ideals differed for men and women.

For Renaissance thinkers, the ideal individual strove to master almost every art. Those who excelled in many fields were admiringly known as "universal men." Later ages called such people "Renaissance men."

A book called *The Courtier* became widely popular because it told young people how to become an accomplished person whom everyone would admire. Its author was Baldassare Castiglione (KAHS-teel-YOH-nay).

The ideal man A young man, said Castiglione, should be well educated in the Greek and Latin classics. He should be charming, polite, and witty. He should be able to dance, write poetry, sing, and play music. In addition, he should be physically graceful and strong, a skilled rider, wrestler, and swordsman.

Renaissance men tried to live up to this ideal. In his autobiography, Leon Battista Alberti (1404–1472) boasted of his many skills. Here, in the third person, is Alberti's description of his accomplishments and interests:

> He played ball, hurled the javelin, ran, leaped, wrestled, and above all delighted in climbing steep mountains . . . As a youth, he excelled in warlike games. With his feet together, he could leap over the shoulders of men standing by . . . He delighted in the organ and was considered an expert among the leading musicians.

In addition, Alberti designed and built several churches and made a scientific study of perspective. Alberti summed up the spirit of his times when he wrote, "Man can do anything if he will."

The ideal woman Upper-class women of the Renaissance were as well educated as the men. According to *The Courtier*, women too were expected to know the classics, to write well, to paint, to make music, to dance, and to be charming. Yet they were not expected to seek fame as men did. Like Beatrice and Laura, they were expected to inspire poetry and art but rarely to create it.

The most honored woman of the Renaissance in northern Italy was probably Isabella d'Este. Born into the ruling family of the city-state of Ferrara, she married the ruler of another city-state, Mantua. Her art collection was famous throughout Europe. She brought many of the greatest Renaissance artists, including Leonardo da Vinci, to the court of Mantua. She was also skilled in politics. She defended Mantua when her husband was taken captive in war and won his release.

Isabella d'Este and a few other women such as Caterina Sforza (who ruled Milan from about 1488 to 1500) exercised real political power. For the most part, however, women were expected to create a charming court and home but not to take part in public life. Although upper-class women of the Renaissance were far better educated than the women of the Middle Ages, most Renaissance women had less political, economic, and social influence than medieval women.

Renaissance individualism shows in these realistic portraits. The Duke of Urbino, who fought his way to a dukedom by his military skill, suffered a broken nose in battle. His wife, Battista Sforza, came from the ruling family of Milan. Behind them lies their duchy.

349

■ **BACKGROUND**

In the Middle Ages, courtly men learned fine manners to please their ladies. In the Renaissance, those roles were reversed. Women were now expected to please men.

■ **DISCUSSION**

What type of person would be described as a "Renaissance woman" or "Renaissance man" today?

■ **BACKGROUND**

By the mid-1400's, the city-states of Venice, Milan, and Florence dominated northern Italy. There, interest in culture was stimulated by the recovery of classical works, brought by refugees from Constantinople after that city fell to the Turks in 1453.

ANSWERS TO

Section Review 1

Define:
(a) period of rebirth of culture and artistic creativity beginning in about 1300 (b) painting done on wet plaster (c) everyday language of one's homeland (d) scholar who studied classical texts

Identify:
(a) artist, engineer, architect of Renaissance period

(continued)

ANSWERS TO (continued)

(b) painter who began revolution in art by painting realistic people **(c)** poet who wrote in the vernacular **(d)** Dante's masterpiece **(e)** poet and letter writer whose work reflected a modern, simple style **(f)** book by Castiglione outlining ideal accomplishments and behavior for men and women **(g)** outstanding Renaissance woman in northern Italy

Answer:

1. bustling urban centers dependent on trade, a merchant class that fostered a belief in individual achievement

2. painted lifelike figures and created an illusion of depth

3. **(a)** hell, purgatory, and paradise **(b)** included real people and political events, wrote in vernacular

4. imitated style of Cicero, used Latin in poems

5. portrait painting and autobiography

6. celebration of individual, love of classical learning, enjoyment of worldly pleasures

7. **(a)** well educated in Greek and Latin classics, charming and witty; able to dance, write poetry, sing, play music, wrestle, ride horses, be a swordsman **(b)** well educated in classics; could write well, paint, make music, dance, be charming, inspire poetry and art

8. Possible answer: the emphasis on humans rather than God as "the measure of all things"

Section REVIEW 1

Define: (a) Renaissance, (b) fresco, (c) vernacular, (d) humanist

Identify: (a) Leonardo da Vinci, (b) Giotto di Bondone, (c) Dante Alighieri, (d) *The Divine Comedy*, (e) Francesco Petrarch, (f) *The Courtier*, (g) Isabella d'Este

Answer:

1. What conditions in northern Italy encouraged the beginning of the Renaissance?
2. How did Giotto revolutionize painting?
3. (a) What are the topics of the three major parts of *The Divine Comedy?* (b) How did Dante change the writing of poetry?
4. How did Petrarch draw on the classics in his writings?
5. What new art forms showed the Renaissance interest in the individual?
6. List three characteristics of the Renaissance.
7. (a) What was the Renaissance ideal for a young man? (b) For a young woman?

Critical Thinking

8. Which of the characteristics of the Renaissance do you consider most revolutionary? Explain.

Florence led the way in arts. 2

The Renaissance burst into full flower in the 1400's. This century was called the *Quattrocento* (kwah-troh-**CHEN**-toh) in Italian. During the Quattrocento, dozens of the most talented painters, sculptors, and writers in history competed for fame in the thriving cities of northern Italy. In the forefront of artistic developments was Florence, the City of Flowers.

CITY TOUR
Business enriched Florence.

The golden age of Florence was based on the golden florins (the city's coin) of its merchants

and bankers. Florentines made their wealth chiefly through two industries—textiles and banking.

In 1338, one Florentine writer boasted that 200 workshops in Florence produced more than 70,000 pieces of cloth. Merchants in the various cloth guilds employed 30,000 Florentines, one third the city's population. As a result of the general prosperity, Florentines were well fed, consuming 110,000 sheep, goats, and pigs and 70,000 casks of wine in a year.

The riches gathered by the cloth guilds gave Florence a second major industry, banking. By 1300, wool merchants routinely deposited their gold coins in Florentine banking houses.

Florentine bankers grew rich loaning their depositers' money to borrowers. By the 1300's, Florence was the financial center of Europe. From London to Rome, merchants figured their losses or gains in terms of one coin: the florin. Kings, princes, nobles, and merchants throughout Europe depended on loans from Florence's banks. At times during the Hundred Years' War, both French and English armies were paid with loans from Florentine bankers.

Among Florence's leading merchants, the pursuit of wealth and the scramble for political power went hand in hand. Florentines boasted that they had a republican form of government like that of ancient Rome. In theory, any citizen who belonged to one of the city's 21 guilds could hold office. However, membership in the guilds was tightly restricted. As a result, only about 3,500 men were eligible to vote—about 3 percent of the total population. Among these citizens, the competition for office never ceased.

Although ruled by a wealthy elite, Florence had a democratic social atmosphere. Visitors in Florence were amazed to hear a lowly journeyman address a leading citizen by his first name.

The Medici ruled Florence.

As the golden age of the Quattrocento began, Florence came under the political rule of one powerful family, the Medici (**MEHD**-uh-chee). The Medici had made a fortune in trade and banking.

Cosimo (**KOH**-see-moh) de Medici was the wealthiest man of his time. In 1434, he won control of the government of Florence. He did not seek political office for himself, realizing that he could rule more effectively behind the

350

scenes. He made sure, however, that all eight members of the city council were loyal to him. The lower classes of the city loved him because he championed popular causes. For 30 years, Cosimo de Medici was virtually dictator of the city of Florence.

Like Pericles of ancient Athens, Cosimo took pleasure in beautifying the city he ruled. From his personal fortune, he spent 400,000 florins on artistic and scholarly projects. He paid off the staggering debts of a bankrupt friend and took in exchange the friend's collection of 800 books by classical authors. To house this rare collection, he built the first free public library in western Europe.

Cosimo de Medici died in 1464, but his family remained in control of Florence. After a brief rule by Cosimo's sickly son, power passed in 1469 to Cosimo's 21-year-old grandson, Lorenzo. He soon became known as Lorenzo the Magnificent. Lorenzo ruled with absolute power, yet he kept up the appearances of a republican government. He held the goodwill of the common people with balls, festivals, carnivals, and celebrations of all sorts. Like his grandfather, Lorenzo continued the tradition of beautifying his city.

Artists beautified Florence.

Florence entered its golden age through a set of gleaming metal doors. In 1401, the wool manufacturers' guild wanted an artist to create new doors for the Baptistry of the local cathedral, an old eight-sided building. The guild held a contest, inviting Florence's most promising artists to submit designs for the doors. With great fanfare, the judges announced the winner. The guild had bestowed the honor upon a 23-year-old goldsmith named Lorenzo Ghiberti (gee-BEHR-tee).

Ghiberti spent the next 50 years creating two pairs of bronze doors for the Baptistry. At a time

Decisions in History

In 1473, Pope Sixtus IV asked Lorenzo for a large loan to buy the town of Imola. The deal meant high profits for the Medici bank. However, Imola's strategic location could threaten the security of Florence. What should Lorenzo have decided about the loan, and why? What were the issues involved?

when 200 florins was a princely sum, the wool merchants and the city council spent 22,000 florins on the first pair alone. The new doors were so magnificent that the artist Michelangelo later likened them to the gates of paradise.

The finished doors were divided into panels, each showing a scene from the Bible. Each scene looked like a deep stage with the background trees and buildings far behind the people in the foreground. Yet the sculptured metal is only four inches deep at most. Ghiberti died in 1455, just three years after completing the doors.

Meanwhile, an architect named Brunelleschi (BROO-nuh-LAYS-kee) was working on the Cathedral of Florence, directly across the street from the Baptistry. Brunelleschi had been one of the losers in the contest to make the Baptistry doors. By 1420, however, his genius was recognized. Brunelleschi proposed to cap the cathedral with a gigantic dome. Such a dome had not been built in Europe since Roman times. Between 1420 and 1436, admiring Florentines watched his dome rise slowly. When it was completed, the cross at its top stood 370 feet above street level. It was twice as high as the famous dome of Constantinople's Hagia Sophia.

Donatello revolutionized sculpture.

Florence was also home to a host of younger artists. The most talented was a 17-year-old sculptor named Donatello (DAHN-uh-TEHL-oh). He came to work in Ghiberti's workshop just after 1400.

Donatello (1386–1466) left Ghiberti's workshop and journeyed to Rome to study its ancient ruins. When he returned to Florence, he was eager to make free-standing statues like those of the ancient Greeks and Romans. He rejected the style of medieval stonecutters, who usually carved only the front of their human figures. The back side merged into a cathedral's walls. Above everything else, Donatello wanted his figures to seem real and alive.

Like the ancient Greeks, Donatello wanted to show the strength and grace of the human form. In his statue "David," Donatello was the first European sculptor since ancient times to make a large, free-standing human figure in the nude. He was also famous for his heroic statues of men on horseback.

351

Teaching Strategy: Relating Past to Present: Patrons of the Arts (page 344c)

Teaching Strategy: Discussing History: Machiavelli's Views (page 344c)

SECTION 2
Objectives and Teaching Strategies

OBJECTIVE 1. Explain the role of the Medici family in Florentine society.

OBJECTIVE 2. Analyze the political philosophy of Machiavelli.

ANSWERS TO
Decisions in History

Lorenzo refused to make the loan, thus showing that he placed the interests of Florence first. Pope Sixtus IV chose Lorenzo's rival, Francesco de' Pazzi, as his new banker. When Pazzi tried to assassinate Lorenzo and Guiliano de Medici, Lorenzo escaped but his brother died.

■ BACKGROUND

In 1425, Donatello was putting the finishing touches on a statue of a biblical prophet. The prophet's expression seemed so thoroughly human that Donatello looked his creation in the eyes and shouted at it, "Speak! Speak or the plague take you!"

SECTION 2
Resources

ASSESSMENT
■ Section Quiz 15.2

REINFORCEMENT
■ Independent Practice 15.2

ENRICHMENT
■ Voices from the Past 15.2

■ **BACKGROUND**

During the golden age people began to think of artists as geniuses, not just artisans, and their status rose sharply.

Cooperative Learning

Arrange students in groups of four or five and assign each group one of the following people: Giotto di Bondone, Beatrice, Isabella d' Este, Cosimo de Medici, Lorenzo Ghiberti, or Machiavelli. Have group members assign these tasks: play the character, be an agent or translator, do research (one or two students), act as moderator. Researchers should gather information about the person's life and accomplishments and summarize it for the group. Students playing the character and agent/translator should study the information and learn how to say "yes" and "no" in Italian.

After the class has read Sections 1 and 2, have students close their books and play Twenty Questions to guess each group's identity. Moderators should conduct the flow of questions and keep score. Each student may ask only one question, and all questions must be answered "yes" or "no" in the correct language. Students may not ask whether the character is a man or woman.

A diagram shows how perspective works in this fresco by Masaccio. Lines come together at a vanishing point near the center. The horizontal line running through the vanishing point shows the eye level of the viewer.

Masaccio developed perspective.

To Ghiberti, Brunelleschi, and Donatello, we must add the name of a fourth genius of Florence's golden age: Masaccio (mah-ZAHT-choh). Last of the four to be born (1401), Masaccio was also the first to die (1428). Yet in his 27 years, he changed painting as profoundly as Donatello changed sculpture.

One hundred years earlier, Giotto had started a revolution in the arts by giving a sense of depth and roundness to his paintings. Masaccio carried the revolution further by using **perspective,** a technique developed by Brunelleschi that gave objects the appearance of distance.

Commissioned in 1425 to decorate a chapel in Florence, Masaccio used his new technique in a fresco called "The Healing of the Cripple and the Resurrection of Tabitha" (above). The picture shows two events in the life of the apostle Peter. Buildings stand at each side of the picture. Their upper stories slant downward, and the ground level slants up. People in the foreground look much larger than those in the distance. The

lines of the buildings and the relative sizes of human figures give the illusion of depth.

Masaccio realized that objects look smaller the farther they are from the viewer. He also realized that parallel lines, like the edges of a road, seem to come together in the distance. These are the principles of perspective. As a result of his new ideas, Masaccio has been called the "father of modern painting."

Machiavelli wrote about politics.

The golden age of Florence lasted nearly a century. Lorenzo the Magnificent died in 1492. Then, just two years later, a shocking event shattered the self-confidence of the Florentines. In 1494, King Charles VIII of France led an army across the Alps into northern Italy. His main goal was to claim Naples in the south, but his invasion route led past Florence, which he attacked.

Piero de Medici (son of Lorenzo) surrendered without a fight. Outraged by their ruler's weakness, a mob of Florentines stormed the Medici palace and drove Piero into exile.

352

For the next two generations, Florence and other Italian cities suffered from war and political upheavals. Spain's King Ferdinand of Aragon contested the French king's claim to Naples. In the early 1500's, French and Spanish armies attacked all along the Italian peninsula. All the great Italian cities—Florence, Milan, Venice, Rome—were forced to ally themselves with one foreign power or the other. Diplomacy and war became the keys to survival.

One result of the turmoil was a provocative book called *The Prince*. Its author, Niccolò Machiavelli (MAH-kyah-VEHL-ee), was bitter about the invasion of Italy by foreigners. Born in Florence in 1469, Machiavelli spent his youth under the rule of Lorenzo the Magnificent. As an adult, he saw the golden age begin to crumble. He served his city as a diplomat to many courts, where he observed dukes and kings. He tried to understand why one ruler succeeded while another failed.

In 1513, Machiavelli wrote a book of advice to rulers. *The Prince* is a book about power. How can a ruler gain power and keep it despite his enemies? asked Machiavelli. In answering this question, he began with the idea that most people are selfish, fickle, and corrupt. To succeed in such a wicked world, Machiavelli said, a prince must be strong as a lion and shrewd as a fox:

> . . . for the lion cannot protect himself from traps, and the fox cannot defend himself from wolves. One must therefore be a fox to recognize traps, and a lion to fight wolves.

Machiavelli said that a prince might have to trick his enemies and even his own people for the good of the state. His ideal ruler was the crafty Spanish king, Ferdinand of Aragon. When the king of France complained that Ferdinand had deceived him twice, Ferdinand boasted, "He lies, the drunkard. I have deceived him more than ten times!"

In *The Prince*, Machiavelli was not concerned with what was morally right but with what was politically effective. He believed that, in politics, the end justifies the means. According to *The Prince*, even immoral acts were justified if they served the interests of the state. Thus, although Machiavelli was himself an upright, honest, and religious man, his name has come to stand for trickery and double dealing.

Voice from the Past | *The Dangers of Flattery*

In *The Prince*, Machiavelli advised rulers that they must always *seem* to be honest, merciful, and true to their word, even if they were not always so. However, he warned princes that they must beware of people who tried to flatter them.

> *I must not leave out . . . a mistake that is hard for princes to avoid . . . And this is with regard to flatterers, of which courts are full . . . There is no other way of guarding oneself against flattery except by letting men understand that they will not offend you by speaking the truth. But when everyone can tell you the truth, you lose people's respect. A prudent prince must therefore take a third course, by choosing for his council wise men and by giving them alone full liberty to speak the truth to him. And they may speak the truth only of those things that he asks, so he must ask them about everything . . . A prince, therefore, should always take advice, but only when he wishes, not when others wish . . . He ought to be a great asker and a patient hearer of the truth . . . Indeed, if he finds out that anyone has hesitated to tell him the truth, he should be angry.*

1. (a) Why might a prince's court be full of flatterers? (b) Why would flatterers be dangerous to a prince?
2. How does Machiavelli say a prince can avoid being fooled by flatterers?

Ferdinand of Aragon

353

■ **DISCUSSION**

How might the emphasis on humanism (as opposed to the intense Christianity of the Middle Ages) in part explain the political theories of Machiavelli?

■ **BACKGROUND**

In their love of fine foods, fine wines, and fine arts, Renaissance popes were much like the Medici and other Italian princes of their time. Pope Nicholas V, for example, spent vast sums collecting classical texts for the Vatican library. Pope Leo X, son of Lorenzo de Medici, said, "Let us enjoy the papacy since God has given it to us."

ANSWERS TO
Voice from the Past

1. (a) to win the prince's favor **(b)** They would prevent him from knowing the truth.
2. by heeding the advice of wise men he has been given liberty to speak the truth

ANSWERS TO
Section Review 2

Define:
(a) the 1400's (b) technique that gave objects the appearance of distance

Identify:
(a) wealthy ruler of Florence for 30 years (b) Cosimo's grandson and leader of Florence (c) created bronze doors for Baptistry in Florence (d) architect who built dome on Cathedral of Florence (e) sculptor of lifelike statues (f) developed concept of perspective (g) author of treatise *The Prince*

Answer:
1. textiles and banking
2. (a) republican in name, allowing only about 3 percent of population to vote (b) as a virtual dictator, power behind the scenes
3. (a) wanted figures to seem real and alive (b) created free-standing figures
4. developed principles of perspective
5. (a) innately selfish, fickle, and corrupt (b) Hold power in whatever way you can in the interest of the state.
6. conflict between Spain and France, French and Spanish invasions of Italy
7. Florentine merchants and bankers embarked on a civic beautification program that led to the creation of brilliant works of art.

Define: (a) Quattrocento, (b) perspective
Identify: (a) Cosimo de Medici, (b) Lorenzo de Medici, (c) Ghiberti, (d) Brunelleschi, (e) Donatello, (f) Masaccio, (g) Machiavelli
Answer:
1. What were the main businesses of Renaissance Florence?
2. (a) Describe the government of Florence. (b) How did Cosimo de Medici control the city for 30 years?
3. (a) What were Donatello's goals in sculpture? (b) How did he accomplish these goals?
4. What contributions did Masaccio make to painting?
5. (a) What was Machiavelli's view of human nature? (b) Describe the advice he gave to rulers.
6. What political events threatened the Italian city-states in the 1500's?

Critical Thinking
7. In many ways, the achievements of the Renaissance were linked to civic pride. Explain how this statement applies to Florence.

The Renaissance spread. 3

In 1513, while Machiavelli was writing *The Prince*, Leonardo da Vinci was taking regular walks in the pope's garden in Rome. Leonardo was now an old man with a flowing white beard. Though raised in Florence, he had spent his most productive years as a painter in Milan. Now, in his last years, Leonardo sought the favor of a pope. After the death of Lorenzo de Medici, the popes had become the foremost patrons of art.

Renaissance art reached new grandeur in Rome during the early 1500's. In this period, known as the High Renaissance, three artists lifted Renaissance art to unsurpassed brilliance. The three were Leonardo, Raphael Santi (RAF-ay-el SAHN-tee), and Michelangelo Buonarroti (MI-kel-AN-juh-loh BWOH-nahr-ROH-tee).

At the same time that the Renaissance was bringing change to Florence, a revolution in

painting was occurring in northern Europe. This development is often called the Northern Renaissance. The Northern Renaissance produced a number of gifted artists.

Popes rebuilt Rome.

While the popes lived in Avignon during the 1300's, the once-great city of Rome began to decline. By the early 1400's, Rome had fallen into a shocking state of disrepair, with empty houses, roofless churches, and debris-strewn streets. Goats grazed among the ruins of ancient palaces. The Forum, in which great orators had once spoken, had become a pig market.

The revival of Rome began when Pope Martin V returned the papacy from Avignon in 1420. Martin and his successors are known as the Renaissance popes. They were determined to glorify the Church and make Rome the artistic capital of Europe.

One Renaissance pope in particular stands out. Julius II, who was pope from 1503 to 1513, loved art and power in equal measure. He longed for Rome to again become, in Livy's phrase, "the capital of the world." To achieve this goal, Julius boldly decided to tear down the old St. Peter's Basilica and build a magnificent new one. For this task, he enlisted Italy's greatest artists—including a young sculptor named Michelangelo.

Michelangelo's many-sided genius shows in his "Pietà" (far left), "David" (left), and the Sistine Chapel (above). Recently, 400 years of grime was cleaned from the chapel ceiling to reveal the original beauty of Michelangelo's colors.

SECTION 3
Objectives and Teaching Strategies

OBJECTIVE 1. Describe the art of the High Renaissance.

Teaching Strategy: *Teaching with Pictures: Michelangelo's "Pieta"* (page 344d)

OBJECTIVE 2. Evaluate the qualities that distinguish great art.

Teaching Strategy: *Writing about History: Evaluating Renaissance Art* (page 344d)

Michelangelo excelled in many arts.

Born in Caprese in 1475, Michelangelo was apprenticed at the age of thirteen to a painter. He soon turned from painting to sculpture, however. Lorenzo de Medici noticed Michelangelo's potential and invited the young sculptor to study at his home.

Michelangelo left Florence and moved to Rome in 1496. Two years later he received a commission from a Roman cardinal to create a statue of "a Virgin Mary clothed, with the dead Christ in her arms, of the size of a proper man, for the price of 450 golden ducats of the papal mint." Within a year, Michelangelo carved a marble sculpture known as the "Pietà" (pee-ay-TAH). Art critics immediately hailed the work as a masterpiece.

The "Pietà" features two eloquently simple figures carved out of a single block of marble. The Virgin Mary, still a young mother, tenderly cradles Jesus' limp body. The figures convey a feeling of sorrow and peace along with a sense of human worth and divine majesty.

"David" Now a famous sculptor, Michelangelo returned to Florence. In 1504, he completed yet another masterpiece. Astonished Florentines watched in awe as his white marble statue of David was hoisted onto a pedestal for public viewing. The Biblical warrior and king stands 16 feet tall. David's muscles ripple with power, while his face radiates strength and determination. Better than any other work of art, Michelangelo's heroic statue of David expresses the Renaissance belief in human dignity and greatness.

Sistine ceiling In 1508, Pope Julius II asked Michelangelo to paint the ceiling of the Sistine (sihs-TEEN) Chapel. The chapel had been built by Pope Sixtus IV in 1481 in the Vatican, the Pope's headquarters in Rome. Because the chapel measured 130 feet long and 44 feet wide—about the same size as Solomon's Temple—painting the ceiling was a major undertaking. To Pope Julius II, the Sistine Chapel was a particularly important artistic project, since it was the site in which cardinals met to elect a new pope.

Michelangelo worked on the Sistine ceiling from 1508 to 1511. Every day, for three years, he climbed the scaffolding in the chapel to his perch about 65 feet above the floor. To accomplish this huge task, he painstakingly painted more than 300 massive human figures onto the 5,800-square-foot ceiling. It was messy, tiring work. Michelangelo wrote the following poem vividly describing his daily agony.

355

SECTION 3
Resources

ASSESSMENT
■ Section Quiz 15.3

REINFORCEMENT
■ Independent Practice 15.3

ENRICHMENT
■ Voices from the Past 15.3

Although Michelangelo became rich, he gave most of his money to his unemployed relatives and to the servant who cared for him for 25 years. The artist himself was content with old clothes, simple food, and shared living quarters. Despite his artistic success, Michelangelo was extremely melancholy. He once wrote to his father that it had been 15 years since he had had "a single hour of well-being."

My stomach is thrust toward my chin,
My beard curls up, toward the sky,
My head leans right over onto my back,
My chest is like that of an old shrew,
The brush endlessly dripping onto my face
Has coated it with a multi-colored paving.

Yet even as the paint trickled into his eyes, Michelangelo never lost sight of his grand design. The ceiling contained nine paintings illustrating the Creation, the story of Adam, and the story of Noah. Toward the center, he painted the scene that was to command the viewer's attention. This scene shows God reaching out to infuse the spirit of life into Adam, the first man. One art historian pointed out, "An electric charge seemed to pass between their fingers."

Later work Julius II lived just long enough to see Michelangelo finish the Sistine ceiling. After the pope died in 1513, the artist—now in midlife—continued his creative activities as sculptor, painter, and architect. (His poetry did not come to light until after his death.)

During his later years, Michelangelo created several statues, the most famous of which depicts Moses. He returned to the Sistine Chapel in 1534 to begin painting the altarpiece "The Last Judgment." This powerful painting features a majestic Christ surrounded by saints. Judged souls rise on one side and fall on the other.

In his last years, Michelangelo designed a huge dome for the new St. Peter's church in Rome. He died in 1564, however, before the construction was finished. When finally completed, the dome soared 452 feet high. A young artist, awed by this mighty achievement, spoke of "the divine Michelangelo" and wrote, "The world has many kings, but only one Michelangelo."

Raphael perfected painting.

In 1508, the same year Michelangelo began painting the chapel ceiling, a young artist named Raphael started painting the walls of Julius II's private library. It was a short walk from library to chapel. Raphael, always eager to learn from older artists, often dropped in on Michelangelo.

The pope's library held both Christian and classical works. Raphael's assignment was to celebrate this knowledge and show its underlying unity.

Gradually, Raphael transformed the library into a kind of Renaissance hall of fame. On one wall, in a painting called "The School of Athens," were the white-bearded Plato and the black-bearded Aristotle in deep discussion. Around them were groups of listeners, including the greatest figures of both classical and Renaissance times. Among them, the pope certainly would have recognized the face of young Raphael and the brooding figure of Michelangelo. Another wall, dedicated to poetry and music, showed Homer and Dante.

Besides artistic genius, Raphael was blessed with a pleasant personality. His easy temper made him the favorite painter of Julius II's successor, Pope Leo X (a son of Lorenzo de Medici). For his patrons, Raphael painted dozens of lovely madonnas and flattering portraits. His death in 1520, when he was only 37, plunged the papal court into sadness.

Leonardo was both scientist and artist.

When Leonardo da Vinci came to Rome in 1513, he was sixty-one. The aging artist, curious as ever, continued to fill his notebooks with new inventions and observations. For example, while in Rome he invented a machine for making metal screws. His scientific explorations, however, were appreciated only by his kindly patron, the pope's brother, and virtually ignored by everyone else.

By then, Leonardo's best years and greatest achievements as a painter lay behind him. Those had occurred during the decade between 1496 and 1506. Even while experimenting with bicycles, hydraulics, masonry, and countless other things, Leonardo had found time to create two of the most famous paintings in history—"The Last Supper" and the "Mona Lisa."

Leonardo's fascination with human personality gives "The Last Supper" its power and originality. This great fresco, painted on the wall of a monastery in Milan, shows Jesus breaking bread with his twelve apostles the night before his betrayal. Only the central figure Jesus shows perfect composure after announcing, "One of you shall betray me." You can see the apostles on either side of Jesus leaning forward, throwing up their hands, pointing, falling back in dismay, searching each other's faces. Only one of the twelve remains

Leonardo da Vinci's "Mona Lisa"

frozen in his seat, unable to respond actively to Jesus' accusing words. This, of course, is the guilty one—Judas—transfixed by the truth.

Many lesser artists had attempted to depict the last supper. They had resorted to isolating Judas, making him sit across the table from the faithful disciples. Leonardo boldly departed from that tradition, revealing Judas only by the subtle expression of his face and body.

Leonardo's other great masterpiece, the "Mona Lisa," also reveals his interest in human psychology. The "Mona Lisa" was a portrait of a Florentine woman, probably Lisa del Giocondo. The painting fascinates viewers because the woman's face seems to change expression. Is she smiling in welcome or smirking in disdain? Are her eyes friendly or cold? One scholar has called this painting the first distinctly psychological portrait of the Renaissance.

Although Leonardo continued to maintain notebooks filled with new ideas, he did very little painting during his later years. In 1516, the French king Francis I invited Leonardo to be his honored guest. Leonardo spent the final years of his life in France. Years later, Francis recalled that "no other man had been born who knew as much as Leonardo."

The Renaissance spread to northern Europe.

The work of Michelangelo, Raphael, and Leonardo embodied the Renaissance spirit. All three artists showed an interest in classical culture, a curiosity about the world, and above all a belief in human potential. These ideals had a significant impact upon scholars and students who visited Italy. For example, the high social status of Italian artists astonished the German engraver Albrecht Dürer (**DYOO**-ruhr). "Here I am a lord," he wrote, "at home a parasite." Artists such as Dürer helped spread the Renaissance to northern Europe.

Royal courts Royal courts also played a major role in the spread of Renaissance styles. As you have seen, Francis I invited Leonardo to retire in France. Francis also promoted Renaissance art by purchasing numerous paintings by Italian artists and by employing many well-known artists. In 1528, Francis hired Italian artists, decorators, and architects to rebuild his castle at Fontainebleau. When completed, Fontainebleau became a centerpiece of the French Renaissance.

The German masters After returning to Germany, Dürer produced woodcuts and engravings that sold thousands of copies. The popularity of Dürer's work helped to spread Renaissance styles and inspired other German artists.

Dürer's emphasis upon realism influenced the work of another German artist, Hans Holbein the Younger. Holbein specialized in painting portraits that are almost photographic in detail. He enjoyed great success in England, where he painted portraits of Henry VIII and other members of the royal family.

Flanders At the time of the Renaissance, the region known as Flanders included parts of what is today northern France, Belgium, and the Netherlands. As in Italy, wealthy merchant families in Flanders were attracted to the Renaissance emphasis on individualism and worldly pleasures. Their patronage helped to make Flanders the artistic center of northern Europe.

Also as in Italy, the Renaissance in Flanders was marked by an interest in realism. The first great Renaissance painter in Flanders was Jan van Eyck. Born around 1380, he lived at about the same time as Ghiberti in Italy. Van Eyck used new oil-based paints that enabled him to create a variety of subtle colors in clothing and

357

■ BACKGROUND

The reason for Mona Lisa's smile may be mathematical: the smile is a segment of the same arc as the top of her forehead.

Students might be interested to learn that da Vinci's obsession with innovation resulted in the loss of many of his works. His constant experimentation with new pigments and dyes caused paintings to deteriorate prematurely.

Although Bruegel's paintings show crowds of peasants engaged in everyday activities, the people seem two dimensional, and nearly all the faces look alike. Bruegel's real focus is on the landscapes that surround people, making their actions seem small and insignificant. This was a significant departure from the practice of earlier Renaissance artists of treating the landscape as incidental background to the activities of people.

Section Review 3

Identify:

(a) pope who undertook beautification of Rome
(b) painter of Sistine chapel ceiling and creator of powerful sculpture **(c)** great painter whose paintings transformed the library of Julius II into a kind of Renaissance hall of fame
(d) painting of Jesus and 12 apostles by Leonardo da Vinci **(e)** popular German engraver who helped spread Renaissance styles to northern Europe **(f)** German realist painter **(g)** Flemish realist who used color to create perspective **(h)** Flemish painter of scenes from everyday life

Answer:

1. (a) disrepair **(b)** to glorify the Church and make Rome the artistic capital of Europe

2. "Pieta": moving depiction of Mary grieving over body of crucified son; "David": statue of the Biblical king which radiates strength and dignity; Sistine Chapel: many scenes including God reaching out to infuse spirit into Adam

3. to show unity between Christian and classical works

4. first psychological portrait

5. interest in realism, emphasis on individualism and worldly pleasures, patronage of wealthy merchants

6. Look for reasons that suggest qualities of genius and innovations in artistic style.

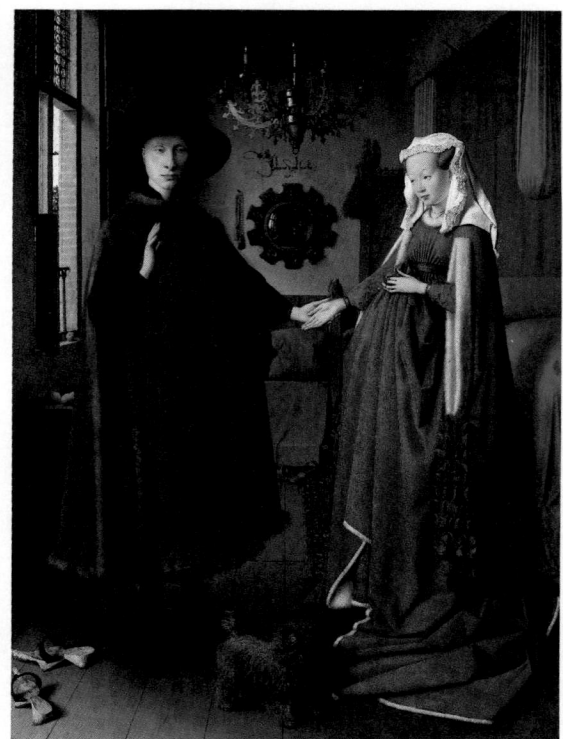

Van Eyck painted the "Wedding Portrait" for the Arnolfini family, Italian merchants who lived in Flanders.

jewels. Van Eyck's work is distinguished by his exceptional ability to paint realistic details. He also initiated a technique for creating perspective through the use of color. Intense color in the foreground gives way to soft, hazy colors in the background, thus creating a sense of distance. Van Eyck's work, like that of Italian painters, influenced later artists in northern Europe.

Flemish painting reached its peak after 1550 with the work of Pieter Bruegel the Elder (**BROI**-guhl). Bruegel captured scenes from everyday life such as weddings, dances, harvests, and the changing seasons. His rich colors, vivid details, and balanced use of space give a sense of life and feeling.

The end of the Renaissance In both Italy and Northern Europe, the Renaissance had stirred a burst of creative activity. The work of the later German and Flemish masters marked its final

phase. During the 1600's, new ideas and artistic styles appeared. Nonetheless Renaissance ideals continued to influence European life and thought. As you will see, the Renaissance belief in the worth and dignity of the individual played a key role in the rise of democratic ideas.

Section REVIEW 3

Identify: (a) Pope Julius II, (b) Michelangelo, (c) Raphael, (d) "The Last Supper," (e) Albrecht Dürer, (f) Hans Holbein, (g) Jan van Eyck, (h) Pieter Bruegel

Answer:

1. (a) What conditions prevailed in Rome in the early 1400's? (b) Why did the popes take on the task of beautifying the city?
2. Name three major works of Michelangelo and briefly describe each one.
3. What was Raphael's task in the work he did for the library of Julius II?
4. Why is the "Mona Lisa" a significant painting?
5. What were the main characteristics of the Northern Renaissance?

Critical Thinking

6. Which of the three High Renaissance artists discussed in this section do you consider the greatest? Explain your answer.

Explorers discovered new lands. 4

As you have seen, the Renaissance encouraged a new spirit of adventure and curiosity. While scholars and artists made new discoveries, ship captains were exploring unknown seas. During Leonardo's lifetime, Portuguese sailors charted the entire coast of Africa. Other explorers crossed the Atlantic Ocean and came upon two vast continents. In 1519, the year Leonardo died, a ship sailed from Spain that was to circle the entire world.

Historians believe that the Renaissance spirit played an important role in helping to launch the Age of Exploration. Like the artists, the explorers were confident, ambitious, curious, and eager for individual glory. Alberti's proud boast, "Man can do anything if he will," expressed a supreme confidence in the human ability to meet new challenges.

Many factors encouraged exploration.

As you have read (page 287), the stories of the Venetian Marco Polo's life at the court of Kublai Khan in China were gathered into a book. Two centuries later, an Italian sea captain, Christopher Columbus, read that book. He resolved to reach Cipangu (Polo's name for Japan) by sailing west across the Atlantic. During the 1400's, several factors both encouraged Europeans and enabled them to discover new routes to Asia.

The search for spices and profits As you have seen (page 245), the Crusades stimulated a growing demand for spices and other luxury goods. Since demand far exceeded supply, the spice trade was highly profitable. Italian merchants could charge high prices for these goods because they had a **monopoly,** or complete control of the trade. By the 1400's, the new monarchs of France, England, Spain, and Portugal wanted a share of this profitable trade. Since the Italian city-states controlled the trade with the eastern Mediterranean, European countries began to seek new routes to Asia. The fall of Constantinople to the Turks in 1453 added to their determination.

The desire to spread Christianity The Crusades left a legacy of hostility between Christians and Muslims. Led by Spain and Portugal, Europeans still hoped to reconquer northern Africa from the Muslims. Europeans also believed that they had a sacred duty to convert non-Christians.

The ability to use new technology In the 1200's, it would have been nearly impossible for a European sea captain to cross 3,000 miles of open water and find the way home again. In the 1400's, however, shipbuilders designed a new vessel—the **caravel.** The caravel had triangular sails for tacking into the wind. It had square sails for running before the wind. Its carefully designed hull could ride out an ocean storm.

Two other inventions, perfected earlier by Muslim mathematicians and instrument makers (page 192), were essential for crossing the Atlantic Ocean. These were the astrolabe and the **compass,** an instrument used to indicate direction. The astrolabe was a brass circle with carefully adjusted concentric rings marked off in degrees. Using these rings to sight the stars, a sea captain could tell how far north or south of the equator he was. Without the astrolabe, Columbus would almost certainly have been lost at sea.

The Portuguese explored Africa and reached India.

Cape Saint Vincent marks the southwestern tip of Portugal, the westernmost point of land in Europe. In about 1420, Portugal's Prince Henry opened a famous center for navigation at the town of Sagres nearby. Within the center's thick stone walls, geographers, astronomers, and navigators exchanged information about stars, winds, tides, and newly discovered lands.

Although Prince Henry himself never sailed unknown waters, he helped to launch the Age of Exploration. While others supported Renaissance artists, Henry organized and paid for voyages along the west coast of Africa. He hoped to discover new lands, to find gold, and to locate a legendary Christian kingdom thought to exist somewhere beyond the Muslim lands.

Prince Henry's first expeditions proved disappointing. Portuguese sailors were terrified that they would be lost in boiling seas filled with monsters. Prince Henry urged them on.

The first rewards proved to be new discoveries as Portuguese ships came upon the islands of Madeira, the Azores, and Cape Verde. The rewards of trade began in 1441 when a Portuguese ship brought home some gold and a number of Africans as slaves. Since the plague had caused a serious labor shortage, the slaves commanded a high price. During the next 60 years, the Portuguese enslaved almost 50,000 Africans.

By the time of Prince Henry's death in 1460, the Portuguese had established a series of trading posts along the West African coast. Those posts did a thriving business in gold, ivory, and slaves. In 1471, Portuguese explorers reached a new milestone with the discovery of the region that became known as the Gold Coast, or modern Ghana. Soon they controlled the West African trade in gold—one tenth of the world's production. With access to the riches of West Africa assured, the Portuguese dreamed of rounding Africa and finding a new route to the Indies.

359

SECTION 4
Objectives and Teaching Strategies

OBJECTIVE 1. Outline the causes and effects of the age of exploration.
Teaching Strategy: *Skill Building: Relating Cause and Effect* (page 344d)

OBJECTIVE 2. Trace on a map the routes of the major European explorers.
Teaching Strategy: *Using Geographic Themes: Movement* (page 344d)

■ DISCUSSION
Review the seafaring accomplishments of the Vikings (page 212) and discuss the nautical technology available to them.

SECTION 4
Resources

GEOGRAPHY
■ Transparency 59

REINFORCEMENT
■ Independent Practice 15.4

ENRICHMENT
■ Voices from the Past 15.4

ASSESSMENT
■ Section Quiz 15.4

■ BACKGROUND

Only 54 of the original 170 sailors on Da Gama's voyage returned to Portugal. The spices they brought back sold for 60 times the cost of the entire expedition.

In 1476, a red-headed Italian sailor was shipwrecked off the Portuguese coast. By this stroke of fortune, Christopher Columbus changed his home from Italy to Portugal.

Prince Henry the Navigator (left) created a center for navigation and sponsored many expeditions. The compass (left above) and the astrolabe (right above) helped explorers to sail unknown seas.

Bartholomeu Dias In 1488, a Portuguese captain named Bartholomeu Dias (DEE-ahsh) finally reached the southernmost tip of Africa. His ships were so battered by high winds that Dias named the spot the Cape of Storms. King John II of Portugal was so pleased with the voyage that he renamed that place the Cape of Good Hope.

Vasco da Gama During the next ten years, the Portuguese carefully planned for an expedition that would round the Cape of Good Hope and then reach India. Finally on July 8, 1497, a great crowd gathered in Lisbon to witness the beginning of Portugal's most ambitious voyage of discovery. Everyone present strained to catch a glimpse of the expedition's 37-year-old captain, Vasco da Gama. As the city's cannons thundered a farewell salute, Da Gama's fleet of four vessels and 170 men sailed away.

Ten months after leaving Portugal, Da Gama's ships arrived in Calicut, India. The city's shops were filled with rare silks, precious gems, and fragrant spices. After several months of hard bargaining, the Portuguese managed to fill their ships with sacks of cinnamon and pepper.

When he returned to Lisbon in August 1499, Da Gama received a hero's welcome. His remarkable voyage of 27,000 miles gave Portugal a direct sea route to India. Within a short time, the Portuguese won from the Arabs control of the Indian Ocean and the rich trade with China and the Spice Islands. And yet, even before Da Gama's historic voyage, Spain claimed to have found its own route to the East.

360

Turning Points in History

The Voyages of Columbus On May 1, 1486, a sea captain named Christopher Columbus came to Queen Isabella of Spain with a bold proposal. Like most educated people of the fifteenth century, Columbus believed that the earth was round. He confidently argued that he could reach the riches of the Indies by sailing west across the Atlantic. Columbus estimated that his voyage would be only about 2,000 miles long—far less than the trip around Africa.

Isabella listened carefully as Columbus presented his ideas. The thought of "attempting this great leap over the sea" intrigued her. She also realized that if Columbus was right, Spain would become a rich and powerful country. Isabella therefore referred Columbus's project, the "Enterprise of the Indies," to a special commission for further study. Four long years later, however, the commission rejected his plan.

Columbus was not discouraged. As a weaver's son growing up in the bustling Italian seaport of Genoa, he had long been fascinated by the sea. He had traveled extensively and become a sea captain and mapmaker.

Both his reading and his experiences at sea convinced Columbus that the Atlantic Ocean provided the shortest route to the Indies. Others, however, were not convinced. The Portuguese king had already rejected his idea, and the Spanish commission turned him down twice. Columbus had already packed his bags and started on the road to France when a messenger overtook him with good news. Queen Isabella and King Ferdinand had changed their minds. The "Enterprise of the Indies" would be given a chance.

The first voyage Once approved, the project moved swiftly. Within three months, Columbus commanded three ships—the *Niña*, the *Pinta*, and the *Santa María*. On August 3, 1492, the small fleet left Palos, Spain. After a brief stop in the Canary Islands, Columbus and his crew of about 90 sailors headed west into the uncharted waters of the Atlantic.

During the next few weeks, brisk winds drove the fleet westward at a pace of about 150 miles a day. With each passing day, Columbus's anxious crew became more and more nervous. After more than 30 days at sea, the terrified sailors plotted to throw Columbus overboard unless he would agree to turn back. At last the men suddenly spotted a branch covered with flowers—a sure sign that they were near land.

Hopes now soared as everyone eagerly scanned the horizon searching for land. Finally, at two o'clock on the morning of October 12, a lookout on the *Pinta* cried out the words everyone had been waiting to hear—"Tierra! Tierra!" Later that day, Columbus and his men landed and claimed the island for Spain. He named it San Salvador, meaning Holy Savior.

Within a short time, the island's astonished inhabitants came out to welcome the Spaniards. Since Columbus was convinced that he had found a shortcut to the Indies, he called the people Indians. In fact, the Indians were really Arawaks,

and Columbus was in the Bahamas some 9,000 miles east of the Indies.

Columbus remained on San Salvador for only two days. Although the Arawaks were friendly, they clearly had no spices and little gold. Nonetheless Columbus learned, by means of sign language, that lands farther south were ruled by a wealthy king who had much gold. Taking six Arawaks to help guide him, Columbus left San Salvador, certain that he would find the fabled land of Cipangu (Japan).

During the next few weeks, Columbus cruised near the northern coasts of what are today Cuba and Hispaniola. But instead of finding rich cities with spice-filled bazaars, he found only small villages with palm-thatched huts. Although Columbus failed to find spices and gold, he did make a number of important discoveries. He and his men were the first Europeans to taste pineapples, sweet potatoes, and corn. They were also the first to witness Indians smoking tobacco.

Columbus explored the Caribbean for almost three months. After the *Santa María* ran aground, however, he decided to return home. A difficult voyage brought him to Palos on March 15, 1493.

Columbus returned to a hero's welcome. Ferdinand and Isabella listened in awe as Columbus recounted his amazing adventures. The royal court marveled at the parrots and captive Arawaks Columbus had brought back. King Ferdinand promptly gave Columbus the title "Admiral of the Ocean Sea" and promised him a larger fleet for his next voyage.

Other voyages Columbus crossed the Atlantic three more times—in 1493, 1498, and 1502. He

■ BACKGROUND

In order to calm the fears of his crew, Columbus understated the distance he thought the ships covered each day. Since he unknowingly overestimated his speed, his statements turned out to be rather accurate.

■ DISCUSSION

How might history have been different if Columbus had agreed to his sailors' demands that he turn back?

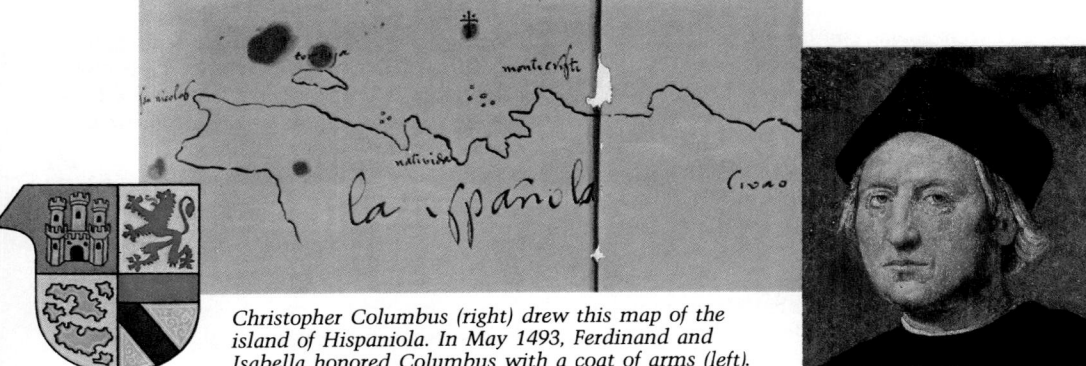

Christopher Columbus (right) drew this map of the island of Hispaniola. In May 1493, Ferdinand and Isabella honored Columbus with a coat of arms (left).

361

■ BACKGROUND

By 1499, even Queen Isabella of Spain, Columbus's chief supporter, had doubts that Columbus had really reached Asia.

Voyages of Discovery

KEY
Territories and routes

- Spanish
- Portuguese
- French
- English
- Dutch

Vasquo da gama

Map Study
Who led the first two voyages to sail around the world? What countries did they come from?

discovered the Virgin Islands, Puerto Rico, Trinidad, and Venezuela. On his fourth and final voyage, Columbus explored the coast of Central America. Nowhere did he find the fabulous civilization described by Marco Polo.

The hurricanes and hardships of his fourth voyage nearly killed Columbus. In 1504, he finally returned to Spain for the last time. Columbus died two years later, insisting that the lands he had explored were part of Asia.

Importance The disappointments of his later voyages do not lessen Columbus's importance. Although the Vikings had sailed to North America more than 500 years before Columbus (page 213), their exploration did not lead to lasting settlements. In contrast, Columbus opened a new era in which Europeans rushed to explore the Americas. Columbus's voyages helped to propel Spain into the forefront of European exploration, conquest, and settlement.

Other explorers reached the Americas.

Columbus's mistake was soon corrected. A Florentine merchant named Amerigo Vespucci (AHM-uh-REE-goh veh-SPYOO-chee) crossed the ocean in 1499 and 1501. In his letters, he described

He climbed over a hill and beheld a vast ocean. Dressed in full armor, Balboa plunged into the water up to his knees and claimed the entire ocean for Spain. Balboa had reached what is now called the Pacific Ocean.

Portugal claimed Brazil.

When Columbus first reached the Americas, it was not clear what lands he had found. Portugal suspected they might be lands that Portuguese sailors had reached first. Soon rivalry between Spain and Portugal reached a dangerous level.

In 1493, to keep peace, Pope Alexander VI ruled that Spain and Portugal might divide the so-called "Indies." He ordered a line drawn from north to south through the Atlantic Ocean. All newly discovered lands east of that line would be Portugal's. All such lands west of this Line of Demarcation would be Spain's.

In 1494, Spain and Portugal agreed in the Treaty of Tordesillas (tor-duh-SEE-yahs) to move the line a few degrees farther west. Explorers later found that the mouth of the Amazon River lay east of the line. Portugal then claimed that river and the lands around it.

In 1500, a second event strengthened Portugal's claims. A Portuguese sea captain named Pedro Alvares Cabral explored the forest along the mouth of the Amazon River. Cabral's men cut down a tree and found its wood was as red as a glowing coal from a charcoal brazier. They called it "brazil" wood from the Portuguese word for a brazier—hence the name of the country that Portugal later colonized.

Magellan's crew rounded the globe.

In 1519, a Portuguese nobleman named Ferdinand Magellan (muh-JEHL-uhn) decided he could reach Asia by sailing around the southern tip of the new continent. The king of Spain agreed to pay for the voyage. He gave Magellan five old ships that were barely seaworthy.

With 230 men aboard, Magellan's ships sailed in September 1519. For three years, nothing was heard from them, and they were given up for lost. Then, in September 1522, a lone ship with tattered sails limped into a harbor in Spain. The 18 men who staggered to shore were the only

the coastline of Brazil. This was not Asia, he wrote, but a newly discovered continent.

One of Vespucci's letters fell into the hands of a German publisher, Martin Waldseemüller (VAHLT-zay-MOO-luhr). In 1507, Waldseemüller published a new map of the world, showing a great blob of land west of the Atlantic. He labeled this land *America* to honor Amerigo Vespucci.

If this was indeed a new continent, how big was it? How far was it from Asia? Was there a way either through it or around it? For a Renaissance explorer, these were urgent questions.

In 1513, a Spaniard named Vasco Nuñez de Balboa slashed through the rain forests of Panama.

363

Cooperative Learning

Divide the class into small groups and have each group choose an explorer and an expedition from Section 4. Have group members assign the following tasks: biographer (reports on explorer's personal history), sponsor (outlines goals and procedures of impending voyage), recruiter (advertises voyage to recruit help), trip biographer (describes success/failure, results of voyage). After students have collected information and designed a "recruiting strategy," have the biographer, sponsor, and recruiter from each group present their information to the class. Class members should choose which voyage they would like to accompany. Then have trip biographers report on the outcome of each voyage. Have students vote on which voyage came closest to fulfilling the recruiter's and sponsor's descriptions.

ANSWERS TO

Section Review 4

Define:
(a) complete control of trade (b) new sailing vessel designed for ocean travel (c) instrument used to indicate direction

Identify:
(a) patron of explorers, member of Portugal's royal family (b) Portuguese captain who sailed to the southernmost tip of Africa (c) Portuguese captain who reached India by sailing around the Cape of Good Hope (d) explorer who reached the Americas by crossing Atlantic in 1492 (e) Florentine merchant who described Brazilian coastline (f) explorer who discovered Pacific Ocean (g) line dividing newly found lands between Spain and Portugal (h) explorer whose expedition rounded the globe

Answer:

1. Explorers were confident, ambitious, curious, and eager for individual glory.

2. search for spices and profits, desire to spread Christianity, and ability to use new technology

3. (a) to discover new lands, to find gold, and to locate a legendary Christian kingdom (b) Vasco da Gama

4. (a) to reach the Indies by sailing west (b) They opened a new era of European exploration and conquest.

5. Pope Alexander's ruling of Line of Demarcation and Cabral's exploration of Amazon River

6. proved Americas were continents and world was larger than thought

7. felt that the world was his to conquer

ECONOMICS IN DAILY LIFE ▶ *The Spices of Life*

"Take ginger, clove, and a little pepper, and crush together." So began a French recipe from 1393 for making a "black pudding." Indeed, without these spices, the pudding would have been little more than tasteless mush. Europeans craved spices partly because their food would have been so monotonous otherwise. In summer, most people depended on foods that were raised locally. In winter, they had only what could be dried or pickled for storage.

The poor flavored their foods with herbs from their own dooryard gardens: garlic, thyme, marjoram, bay leaf, and savory. The rich bought spices from distant lands: cinnamon, nutmeg, ginger, turmeric, cardamom, clove, mace, saffron, and—above all—pepper.

The start of Portugal's trade with the Indies in 1498 increased the supply of spices. In 1503, Portuguese ships brought back 1,300 tons of pepper. Although the price of pepper fell, the trade was so profitable that the Dutch took it away from Portugal in the 1600's.

survivors of Magellan's crew. All the others had died of hunger, cold, disease, or shipwreck.

As planned, Magellan had crossed the Atlantic and led his fleet south along the South American coast. One ship had capsized in a storm. The crew of another had mutinied. Three ships remained. In August 1520, Magellan reached a strait near the southern tip of South America. Vicious winds and jagged rocks made passage difficult. Somehow, after 38 days of struggling, the three ships reached the other side safely. This strait is now called the Strait of Magellan.

Magellan explored the western coast of South America. Then he headed out into the Pacific Ocean in search of Asia. Little did he realize that the Pacific was almost three times wider than the Atlantic. After three months, the sailors were so short of food that they ate rats, leather, and sawdust. Many died of hunger or of diseases brought on by malnutrition.

Finally, they reached the Philippines. Here was Asia at last. Unfortunately, Magellan joined in a war between local groups. He was killed by a poisoned arrow. One of the Spanish ships was destroyed there too.

The remaining crew members set out for home in the last two ships. One was captured by the Portuguese while sailing toward India. That left

364

only one ship and a sickly crew to sail home around Africa.

In 1522, as the survivors recounted their three-year adventure, it became clear what they had achieved. They had sailed around the world. They had proved that the Americas were separate continents that lay thousands of miles from Asia. Most of all, they had learned that the world was much larger than anyone had thought.

Section REVIEW 4

Define: (a) monopoly, (b) caravel, (c) compass
Identify: (a) Prince Henry the Navigator, (b) Dias, (c) Vasco da Gama, (d) Columbus, (e) Vespucci, (f) Balboa, (g) Line of Demarcation, (h) Magellan
Answer:
1. What role did the Renaissance spirit play in helping to launch the Age of Exploration?
2. What were three reasons why Europeans began to search for new trade routes to Asia?
3. (a) What was the goal of Prince Henry the Navigator? (b) Who achieved that goal?
4. (a) What was Columbus's goal in 1492? (b) Why were Columbus's voyages a turning point in world history?

5. What two events let Portugal claim Brazil?
6. Why was Magellan's voyage important?

Critical Thinking
7. How did Columbus demonstrate the spirit of the Renaissance?

Other countries started colonies in America. 5

Spain's dramatic discoveries opened a new world for ambitious European explorers. Although the Treaty of Tordesillas divided the newly discovered lands between Spain and Portugal, other European countries chose to ignore the treaty. During the seventeenth century, the French, English, and Dutch all founded colonies in North America.

France founded a vast empire.

Magellan's voyage proved that the East Indies could be reached by a long and difficult trip around the southern tip of South America. Because Spain claimed this route, other European explorers hoped to find an easier and more direct northern route to the Pacific. If it existed, a northwest passage through North America to Asia would become a highly profitable trade route.

In 1524, the French king Francis I sponsored a voyage by Giovanni de Verrazano to search for a new route to the Pacific. Although he failed to find a northwest passage, Verrazano did discover what is today New York Harbor. In 1534, another Frenchman, Jacques Cartier, discovered a broad river that he named the St. Lawrence. While sailing up the St. Lawrence, Cartier discovered a large island dominated by a hill. The island's inhabitants called their home Hochelaga. Cartier renamed it Mont Royal, later called Montreal. His voyage became the basis for France's claim to a vast interior region called New France.

Champlain In 1608, another French explorer, Samuel de Champlain, sailed up the St. Lawrence hoping to found a colony. He located a promising site below a high bluff overlooking the river. Champlain named his new colony Quebec, after a Native American word meaning "the narrow-

ing of the waters." The colony soon became the center for a thriving fur trade.

Champlain used Quebec as a base to explore more of the region. An expert cartographer, he drew an accurate map of eastern Canada. Champlain also was an accomplished navigator, making 23 voyages between France and New France. Champlain's policy of cooperating with Native Americans in the fur trade brought new wealth to France. Linked to the French by trade, the Huron and Algonquin also became allies in France's quest for land and trade.

Down the Mississippi As they pushed deeper into the wilderness, French fur traders learned from Native Americans about a great river to the west. In the summer of 1673, a fur trader named Louis Joliet and a priest named Jacques Marquette set out to discover if that river—the Mississippi—offered the long-sought northwest passage. After traveling more than 700 miles downstream, the two sadly concluded that the Mississippi flowed into the Gulf of Mexico.

Marquette and Joliet's disappointing news discouraged other explorers. A young French nobleman named Robert LaSalle, however, realized that the Mississippi offered a central highway for an inland empire. In 1682, LaSalle sailed down the Mississippi to the Gulf of Mexico. He triumphantly claimed the entire region for France and named it Louisiana in honor of King Louis XIV.

New France Both Champlain and LaSalle dreamed of building a great French empire in North America. While the French did claim a huge territory, it remained thinly settled. In addition, the French government insisted that only Catholics could settle in North America. New France had only about 80,000 settlers in 1750. Nonetheless the founding of New Orleans in 1718 and of forts along the Mississippi and Great Lakes established France's claim to a vast inland empire and a thriving trade in furs.

England founded thirteen colonies in America.

The explorations of the Spanish and French fired the imagination of an English adventurer named Sir Walter Raleigh. Raleigh knew that England already had interests in the Americas. In 1497, the English king Henry VII had aided the voyage of a merchant named John Cabot.

365

SECTION 5 Objectives and Teaching Strategies

OBJECTIVE 1. Describe European settlements in North America.

Teaching Strategy: *Economics and History: Indentured Servants* (page 344e)

OBJECTIVE 2. Describe the development of the slave trade and identify its characteristics in the 1500's.

Teaching Strategy: *Discussing History: The Slave Trade* (page 344e)

SECTION 5 Resources

ENRICHMENT
■ Voices from the Past 15.5

ASSESSMENT
■ Section Quiz 15.5

GEOGRAPHY
■ Transparency 57

REINFORCEMENT
■ Independent Practice 15.5

■ DISCUSSION

What might have happened to the colonists who disappeared on Roanoke Island?

The Roanoke colonists visited the Algonquin village of Pomeiock in 1585. The woman and her child lived in the village.

Cabot had reached Newfoundland and claimed it for England—the first English claim to lands in America.

Raleigh also knew that in 1577, a bold captain named Francis Drake had sailed from England to the Strait of Magellan, north along the Pacific coast, west across the Pacific, and around the world to England. Stopping at a bay on the California coast, Drake had claimed that region for England.

Raleigh dreamed of planting an English colony in North America. In 1585, he organized an expedition that landed on Roanoke Island, off the coast of present-day North Carolina. When food proved to be scarce, the settlers returned home the next year.

Undaunted by the colony's failure, Raleigh tried again in 1587. This time he convinced 117 people, including 17 women and 9 children, to return to Roanoke Island. When a relief party arrived three years later, they found Roanoke deserted.

Jamestown The tragedy at Roanoke showed that colonization was far too costly for one person. In 1606, a company of London investors obtained from King James a charter to found a colony between present-day North Carolina and New York. The following year a fleet of three ships reached the coast of Virginia. The colonists selected a site on a swampy peninsula about 30 miles from the mouth of the James River. They

named their settlement Jamestown in honor of King James I.

The Virginia area was home to many Native Americans, including the Tuscarora, Croatan, and Powhatan. At first, most of the them were friendly toward the colonists. In several severe winters, only their corn enabled the colonists to survive. As the colony grew, however, the Native Americans resisted the loss of their land.

The first few years of the colony proved to be a nightmare for the colonists. Seven out of ten people died of hunger, disease, or fighting with the Native Americans. Nonetheless the colonists did not give up. Despite untold sufferings, they gained a foothold in their new land. The outlook of the colony improved rapidly after farmers discovered that tobacco could be grown as a cash crop. In 1616, Jamestown shipped more than one ton of tobacco to England.

Raising tobacco required many workers. People from England had already begun coming to the colony as indentured servants. They agreed to work for a period of years to pay the cost of their voyage. In 1619, a Dutch ship brought from the Caribbean a number of Africans who also became indentured servants.

The early years of Jamestown were a financial disaster for the English company and its investors. Native American resistance was also a continuing threat to the colony. A major attack on

366

Jamestown in 1622—in which more than 300 colonists died—showed how real that danger was. In 1624, the London investors finally gave up and let King James take over the colony. As a royal colony, Virginia slowly grew and prospered. By the end of the century, it was annually shipping 11,000 tons of tobacco to England.

New England While the Jamestown colony struggled to survive, a group known as Pilgrims in 1620 founded a second colony, Plymouth in Massachusetts. Unlike the Virginia colonists, who had hoped to find gold, they were seeking freedom to practice their religious beliefs. In 1629, the Puritans, another group of religious **dissenters,** established a larger community at nearby Massachusetts Bay. The Puritans wanted to build a model community that would set an example for other Christians to follow. "We shall be as a city upon a Hill," said the Massachusetts Bay Colony's first governor John Winthrop. "The eyes of all people are upon us."

A land of freedom and opportunity After overcoming their initial difficulties, the English colonies in Virginia and New England began to grow and prosper. Their success encouraged others to settle in America. By 1750, about 1.2 million settlers lived in thirteen colonies stretching from Georgia to New Hampshire.

Although the colonies were settled for different reasons, they all shared a life-style that included at least three common elements. First, America's vast lands and growing economy provided opportunities for all those willing to work. Second, since the colonies were settled by a variety of religious groups, no one religion was strong enough to dominate the others. Finally, the colonial charters guaranteed that colonists would continue to enjoy English liberties such as the right to trial by jury and protection from unlawful imprisonment.

The Dutch founded New Netherlands.

In 1609, the Dutch tried to gain a foothold in America by hiring an English sea captain named Henry Hudson to search for a northwest passage. Later that year Hudson discovered and sailed up the great river now named for him. Although he failed to find a northwest passage, Hudson did discover the richest fur-bearing region south of Canada. The inhabitants of this region were the Algonquin and Iroquois. To those he met, Hudson offered beads, knives, and hatchets in exchange for beaver and otter skins. This was the start of a trade in furs that proved highly profitable for the Dutch.

The Dutch West India Company soon attempted to exploit Hudson's valuable discoveries. In 1624, the company built a trading post at Fort Orange, near where the Hudson joined the Mohawk River. (This site later became the city of Albany.) At the same time, the company also established a small settlement called New Amsterdam on Manhattan Island. The land between Fort Orange and New Amsterdam formed a Dutch colony known as New Netherland.

New Netherland quickly became a bustling center of trade. The Dutch who settled there lived in neat gabled homes, worshiped in a brick church, and even built a windmill. The town also attracted settlers from other countries. One visitor in the 1640's reported hearing 18 different languages spoken as he walked along New Amsterdam's winding streets. Many of these foreigners came because the Dutch allowed settlers to worship as they pleased.

Capture by England Despite its promising beginning, New Netherland lacked capable leaders. The men sent by the Dutch West India Company strictly enforced a number of petty rules. The small population and unpopular governor made the colony ripe for takeover by another country. As you have seen, the English had already colonized both Virginia and New England. The English king Charles II decided to take over the Dutch colony.

In 1664, four English warships sailed into New Amsterdam. The Dutch colonists surrendered without firing a shot. The English then renamed the colony New York in honor of the king's brother, the Duke of York. The English now controlled a solid stretch of territory from the Carolinas to New England.

Worldwide contact brought hazards and benefits.

As a result of the Age of Discovery, all of the continents around the Atlantic came in regular contact with one another. This development brought far-reaching changes on both sides of

■ **BACKGROUND**

The Pilgrims borrowed funds from a group of British businesspeople to establish their new colony. They planned to settle in Virginia, where they had received a land grant from Britain. When their ship, the *Mayflower*, landed instead on Cape Cod, the Pilgrims agreed to locate their colony there.

■ **DISCUSSION**

Why did many Europeans immigrate to North America? (reasons include search for religious freedom, job opportunities, land ownership, desire to better their futures, etc.)

■ BACKGROUND

Historians estimate that the total number of mainland Native Americans at the beginning of Spanish settlement was about 50 million. By the 1600's an estimated four million remained. In addition to disease, the Spanish mistreatment and exploitation of the Native Americans as slaves contributed to the decrease in numbers.

ANSWERS TO

Section Review 5

Define:
(a) easier, more direct route to the Pacific (b) people who sought freedom to practice their religious beliefs (c) rapid spreading of disease

Identify:
(a) French-sponsored explorer who discovered what is now New York Harbor (b) explorer who sailed St. Lawrence River and claimed region around Montreal for
(continued)

the Atlantic. In Europe, the changes were generally welcomed. For the peoples of the Americas and Africa, however, life was brutally disrupted.

Epidemics Before the Spanish came, the deadly germs of smallpox, measles, and influenza were unknown in the Americas. Native Americans did not have the immunities that Europeans had developed through long contact with those diseases. Columbus's crews exposed the Native Americans to germs carried by European explorers and colonizers.

Deadly **epidemics,** or rapid spreading of diseases, swept over the Caribbean islands. Smallpox wiped out whole villages in a matter of months. Hispaniola had an estimated population of 250,000 Native Americans in 1492. Twenty years later, the population had fallen to 60,000. Just 50 years after that, it was only 500. Smallpox spread to Mexico where it helped destroy the Aztec empire. In the first century of Spanish rule (1500–1600), Native Americans in Central and South America sickened and died by the millions. By 1650, the population of central Mexico had declined by 85 percent.

The impact of corn and potatoes European ships also carried a great number of beneficial goods across the Atlantic. Before Columbus's voyages, people in the Americas had never seen horses, cows, chickens, pigs, sheep, goats, donkeys, or oxen. In the 1500's, these farm animals came to the Americas with European settlers.

Spanish colonists also brought a wide variety of new plants to the Americas, including wheat, barley, rye, oats, rice, oranges, apples, bananas, apricots, peaches, pears, coffee, sugarcane, and olive trees.

Crossing the Atlantic in the other direction were plants that Europeans, Asians, and Africans had never before used. Among those plants were corn (or maize), manioc (or tapioca), potatoes, tomatoes, kidney beans, lima beans, squash, avocados, pineapples, melon, tobacco, quinine, and cacao (for chocolate).

In time, the potato—a staple of the Inca diet—was transported in European ships to almost every part of the Eastern Hemisphere. Both in Asia and in Africa, it became a tremendously important food. In Europe, crops of potatoes and corn yielded more calories per acre than the traditional crops of wheat, barley, or rye.

This revolution in the world's food supply eventually enriched the diets of people the world over. History books often dwell too much on the rise and fall of empires. The planting of the first white potato in Ireland and the first sweet potato in China probably changed more lives than the deeds of a hundred kings.

The slave trade began in the 1500's.

The settlement of the Americas affected Africa in an unexpected way. Ever since the time of Prince Henry the Navigator, trade between Europeans and Africans had been increasing. In western Africa, the powerful kings who ruled the forest kingdoms controlled trade with the Europeans for a time. The African rulers refused to allow Europeans to travel inland. Instead, the

Looking at economics *The West African slave trade was highly profitable. Control of that trade, known as the asiento, passed from Spain to Britain in 1713. To maximize their profits, slave traders loaded their ships with as many captives as possible. The diagram below shows how a ship was filled. Under such inhuman conditions, many people died during the voyage.*

368

Portuguese traders paid rent to the Africans for small posts near the coast.

Nonetheless, European influence had far-reaching effects. Some African rulers traded for guns, which they used to expand their power over their neighbors. In this way, kingdoms arose that depended on a steady supply of guns and gunpowder from Europe. In exchange, more European traders wanted slaves. The effects of slave trade were devastating to some African societies.

A letter from the Christian King Affonso I of Kongo to the king of Portugal in 1526 protested the taking of slaves.

> "And we cannot reckon how great the damage is, since the mentioned merchants are taking every day our natives, sons of the land and the sons of our noblemen and vassals and our relatives, because the thieves and men of bad conscience grab them . . . they grab them and get them to be sold; and so great, Sir, is the corruption . . . that our country is being completely depopulated, and Your Highness should not agree with this nor accept it as in your service. . . . it is our will that in these Kingdoms there should not be any trade of slaves nor outlet for them."

The growth of the slave trade was linked closely to the growth of European colonies in the Americas. Europeans began gold mines, silver mines, and plantations to raise sugar and other crops. Who was to work on these enterprises? European immigrants were too proud and too few to do the heavy work themselves. After the epidemics, there were not enough Native Americans either. Europeans then turned to captives from Africa.

Ships with chained men and women aboard were soon a regular sight in the harbors of Cuba, Hispaniola, and the Bahamas during the 1500's. By 1540, about 10,000 Africans each year became slaves in the Americas. The slave trade peaked in the 1700's. In that century, between 6 and 7 million Africans were shipped to the Americas as slaves. The transatlantic trade in African slaves continued for more than 350 years.

The human cost of the slave trade was terrible. Besides the approximately 10 million Africans who reached the slave markets, millions of others died in the hands of their captors.

Usually, a person captured for the slave trade was first made prisoner by other Africans. Some powerful African groups made a business of raiding inland villages and marching their captives to the coast for trade. The march was brutal, and many died along the way. At trading stations along the coast, the survivors were sold to European sea captains for rum, guns, and gunpowder. Many more captives died in the crowded, stinking holds of the slave ships. Modern historians estimate that for every two Africans sold in the Americas, at least one other died on the way.

Europe's power touched many lands.

The Age of Exploration marks the beginning of a period when Europe dominated much of the world. That period lasted more than 400 years, from the 1500's to the 1900's.

The people of Europe had gained political mastery over two huge continents, North and South America. Europeans were also the undisputed masters of the ocean routes across the Atlantic. Africa, the Americas, and Europe were now bound together by new economic and political ties. Until the mid-1900's, Europe controlled those ties for its own advantage.

Section REVIEW 5

Define: (a) Northwest Passage, (b) dissenter, (c) epidemic

Identify: (a) Verrazano, (b) Jacques Cartier, (c) Samuel de Champlain, (d) LaSalle, (e) Sir Walter Raleigh, (f) John Cabot, (g) Francis Drake, (h) Jamestown, (i) Henry Hudson

Answer:
1. (a) What territories made up New France? (b) Why was New France sparsely populated?
2. What were three elements that were part of the life-style in the thirteen English colonies?
3. (a) What were the major results of exploration and colonization for Europe? (b) What changes took place in the Americas as a result of European exploration and settlement?
4. (a) How did the African slave trade begin? (b) Why did the slave trade increase with the growth of European colonies in the Americas?

Critical Thinking
5. Compare and contrast the French and English colonies in North America.

369

ANSWERS TO (continued)
France (c) French explorer who founded Quebec, mapped eastern Canada, and cooperated with Native Americans in the fur trade (d) sailed down Mississippi River to Gulf of Mexico and claimed region for France (e) English adventurer who founded unsuccessful colonies on Roanoke Island (f) merchant who discovered Newfoundland and made first English claim in America (g) English sea captain who circled globe and claimed California (h) first successful English colony in America (i) discoverer of Hudson River who started Dutch fur trade

Answer:
1. (a) eastern Canada, Great Lakes area, and Louisiana territory along the Mississippi River (b) French government said only Catholics could settle there

2. opportunities for work, religious freedom, enjoyment of English liberties

3. (a) gained political mastery of two huge continents and won control of the seas (b) spread of epidemics decimated Native American population; growth of slave trade provided labor

4. (a) The need for workers in American mines and on plantations created a demand for slaves. (b) Workers became scarce as the native population was wiped out by epidemics.

5. New France was huge, but was sparsely settled; only Catholics could settle there, and fur trading was the economic mainstay. English colonies were more densely settled, open to followers of all religions, and centered on farming.

Concluding the Chapter

1. **Chapter Closer**
   Have students give four reasons why "Renaissance" is an apt name for the period described in this chapter.

2. **Reteaching Activities**
   a. Explaining Have students explain the significance of Northern Italian city-states and of the Medici in Europe's Renaissance.

   b. Recalling Information Have students explain how each of the following artists contributed to the Renaissance: Leonardo da Vinci, Michelangelo, and Raphael.

   c. Outlining Have students use the headings in Section 4 to outline the information about voyages of exploration.

   d. Summarizing Main Ideas Have students write statements summarizing the main hazards and benefits of worldwide contacts.

Answers to Chapter Review appear on pages 344e–344f.

Chapter Review 15

Summary

1. The Renaissance began in northern Italy. Northern Italy was a highly urban region. Merchants dominated the cities and competed as patrons of the arts. Painting and poetry changed greatly owing to the work of early Renaissance artists. Some of the characteristics of the Renaissance were a celebration of the individual, a love of classical learning, and an enjoyment of worldly pleasures.

2. Florence led the way in arts. During the 1400's, or Quattrocento, Florence was a wealthy city and a center for the arts under the leadership of the Medici. Such artists as Ghiberti, Brunelleschi, Donatello, and Masaccio adorned the city with their work. Machiavelli wrote *The Prince,* a book of advice to rulers.

3. The Renaissance spread to Rome and northern Europe. During the early 1500's, the Renaissance reached new grandeur in Rome under the sponsorship of the popes. Pope Julius II commissioned Michelangelo to paint the ceiling of the Sistine Chapel. Raphael and Leonardo too painted remarkable works. The Northern Renaissance produced a number of great painters and new styles of painting.

4. Explorers discovered new lands. Prince Henry led Portugal in the exploration of the West African coast. Vasco da Gama reached India, giving Portugal a monopoly of the spice trade and the routes around Africa. In 1492, Columbus—sailing for Spain—made the discoveries that opened the Americas to European exploration.

5. The French, Dutch, and English explored separate areas of North America and established colonies. The French built settlements and started the fur trade in Canada. The English started colonies at Jamestown, Plymouth, and Massachusetts Bay. Although the Dutch founded Albany and New Amsterdam, those colonies were taken over by England. The new worldwide contacts brought both benefits, such as the spread of crops and domesticated animals, and problems, such as the spread of diseases and the expansion of the slave trade.

Reviewing the Facts

1. Define the following terms:
   - a. vernacular
   - b. humanist
   - c. caravel
   - d. epidemic
2. Explain the importance of each of the following names, places, or terms:
   - a. Leonardo da Vinci
   - b. Giotto
   - c. Dante
   - d. Petrarch
   - e. Florence
   - f. Lorenzo de Medici

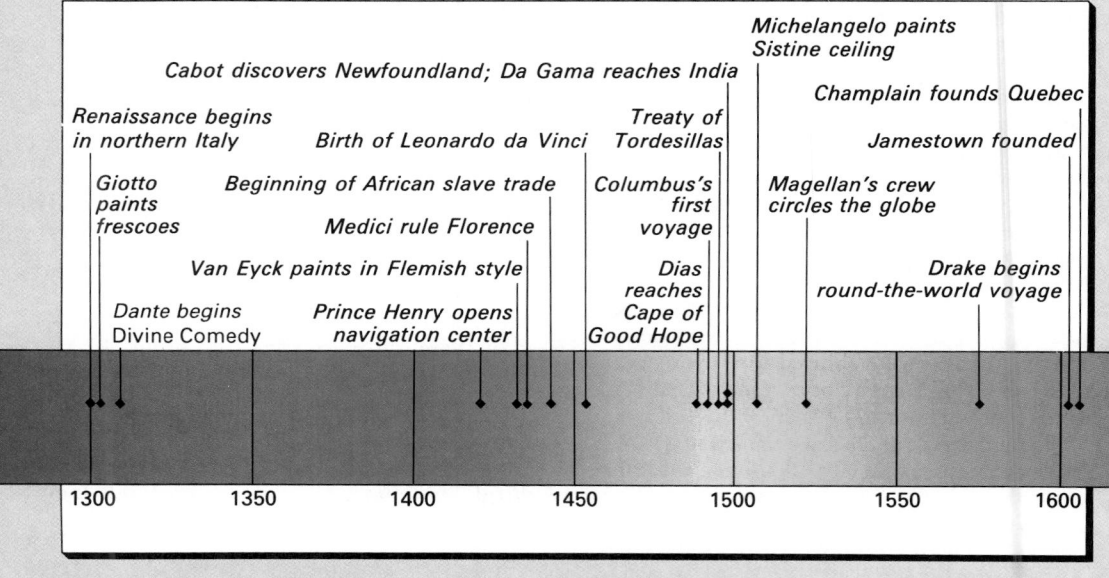

Timeline (1300–1600):
- Renaissance begins in northern Italy
- Giotto paints frescoes
- Dante begins Divine Comedy
- Birth of Leonardo da Vinci
- Beginning of African slave trade
- Medici rule Florence
- Van Eyck paints in Flemish style
- Prince Henry opens navigation center
- Cabot discovers Newfoundland; Da Gama reaches India
- Treaty of Tordesillas
- Columbus's first voyage
- Dias reaches Cape of Good Hope
- Michelangelo paints Sistine ceiling
- Champlain founds Quebec
- Jamestown founded
- Magellan's crew circles the globe
- Drake begins round-the-world voyage

370

g. Masaccio
h. *The Prince*
i. Sistine Chapel
j. Michelangelo
k. Raphael
l. Dürer
m. Van Eyck
n. Henry the Navigator
o. Columbus
p. Magellan
q. Champlain
r. Walter Raleigh
s. Henry Hudson

3. (a) What was the Renaissance? (b) Where did it begin?
4. How did the Renaissance emphasis on the individual affect each of the following groups? (a) Italian merchants (b) artists and writers (c) explorers
5. (a) Why were many European monarchs eager to find new trade routes to Asia in the 1400's? (b) Describe the two different routes explorers eventually found.
6. What changes did European exploration and settlement bring to each of the following continents? (a) Europe (b) the Americas (c) Africa

Basic Skills

1. **Classifying information** The map on pages 362–363 shows the major voyages of discovery made by European nations in the late 1400's and early 1500's. List the explorers for each nation, together with the places they explored.
2. **Outlining** (a) Make an outline of the subsection "New values shaped the Renaissance" on pages 347–348. (b) For each new value, give an example of a Renaissance person who illustrates that value.

Researching and Reporting Skills

1. **Making an oral report** Locate in the library a copy of the notebooks of Leonardo da Vinci. Study one invention that interests you and report on it to the class. Include the purpose and design of the invention, with visuals to illustrate it.
2. **Writing headlines** Write three different headlines announcing to the world Columbus's voyage to America. Take into account the knowledge and values of the time.

Critical Thinking

1. **Synthesizing** The ideals of humanism during the Renaissance were in strong contrast to the values of the Middle Ages. (a) Explain the main differences between the two periods. (b) How did these different ideals express themselves in the art, architecture, and life-styles of each period?
2. **Identifying causes** Identify and explain two causes of the Northern Renaissance and give an example of each.
3. **Inferring** (a) From the information about Julius II on page 354, what can you infer about his leadership in the Church? (b) From the information in this section, what can you infer about the importance of Michelangelo as an artist?
4. **Recognizing a thesis** (a) Identify the author's thesis on pages 358–359 concerning the explorers' relationship to the Renaissance. (b) What ideas and arguments support this thesis?
5. **Comparing** (a) How does the position of women in society during the Italian Renaissance compare to that during the age of chivalry? (b) In which era do you think women were better off? Give reasons for your answer.
6. **Identifying reasons** Of the reasons given for exploration, which do you think was most important to Columbus? Why?
7. **Comparing** (a) Compare the main types of economic activity in the French, English, and Dutch colonies. (b) What factors account for the differences among them?

Perspectives on Past and Present

Americans have a reputation for being a very individualistic people. They are expected to be self-reliant and, as one advertisement puts it, to "be all that you can be." How is the Renaissance ideal of individualism similar to or different from that of American individualism today?

Investigating History

Find information on the expeditions to America by the Vikings and Columbus. Compare the navigating and sailing technology used, including features of the ships, nautical instruments, and geographic knowledge that made their venture successful. Two fine sources are the volumes by Samuel E. Morison, *European Discovery of America: The Northern Voyages* and *The European Discovery of America: The Southern Voyages.* Present either a written or oral report with illustrations and captions.

CHAPTER
Evaluation

Chapter Test 15, Alternate Chapter Test 15, and Computer Test Bank Chapter 15 Test can be used to evaluate your students' understanding of this chapter.

The Reformation and the Scientific Revolution

Chapter Overview

The power and authority of the Catholic Church began to weaken by 1500 as the printing press made the works of Christian humanists and reformer Martin Luther more widely available. Luther's teachings spread within Germany, and his followers became known as Lutherans. The movement of Christians who turned away from the Catholic Church became known as the Protestant Reformation.

Protestantism spread to England when King Henry VIII broke with the Catholic Church after the pope would not set aside the king's first marriage. In Geneva, John Calvin systematized the Protestant philosophy and introduced the ideas of predestination and theocracy. To stop the spread of Protestantism, the Catholic Church initiated reforms to strengthen and purify itself.

Meanwhile, a scientific revolution was also changing old ways of thinking. Scholars challenged ancient scientific theories and developed tools that aided in making precise observations. Some of the new ideas were in direct conflict with the teachings of the Catholic Church.

Chapter Focus

Discuss with students the difficulties of presenting new ideas and of challenging old ones. This chapter examines the conflicts caused by new ideas, notably the ideas of the Protestant Reformation. Ask students to recall religious revolts studied previously, for example the Great Schism and the reforms of Cluny. Explain that Luther never meant to break away from the Church, only to reform it. Ask students to identify conditions that led to a climate of reform. For example, the invention of the printing press and widespread dissatisfaction with the Church helped spread Luther's teachings.

Martin Luther began a religious revolt. 1

Setting the Stage

Begin by asking students to imagine Luther's thoughts as he stood before the Imperial Diet. Tell them that Luther knew how John Huss (Chapter 11) had been executed 100 years earlier in a similar confrontation before the Council of Constance. Ask students to consider the courage that having strength of conviction requires.

Teaching Strategies

Discussing History: Causes of the Reformation (Objective 1) Share with students this phrase by Tetzel: "So soon as coin in coffer rings, the soul from purgatory springs." This slogan was used to raise money for St. Peter's Cathedral in Rome. However, Luther knew that money Tetzel raised was diverted to local bishops and banks. Martin Luther objected to Church corruption and to the sale of indulgences. Luther called monks like Tetzel "pardon merchants." Ask students what other complaints people had about the

Church and list students' responses on the board.

Challenge students to explain how humanist writers helped change public opinion. Critics of the Church such as Savonarola, Erasmus, and Thomas More felt that the Church was indifferent to Christ's teachings about humility, poverty, and piety. Their views reflected a new emphasis among Europeans on religious piety.

Discussing History: The 95 Theses of Martin Luther (Objective 2) Have a volunteer read the main ideas of Martin Luther (page 377). Ask students to explain Luther's ideas concerning "good works." How

Advance Planner

Chapter 16 The Reformation and the Scientific Revolution 1450–1650
FOCUS Conflicts caused by new ideas

★ Advanced
● Basic

	SECTION 1	SECTION 2	SECTION 3	SECTION 4
Objectives	1. Describe the conditions that led to a religious revolt. 2. Explain the main teachings of Martin Luther. 3. Assess the reactions to Luther's teachings and trace their spread.	1. Explain the effects of the Reformation in England. 2. Discuss significant traits of Calvinism. 3. Trace the distribution of religions in Europe in the 1500's.	1. Identify the goals of the Jesuits. 2. Describe reactions of the Church to Protestantism. 3. Explain how the Reformation contributed to disunity in the Holy Roman Empire.	1. Explain why the ideas of Copernicus and Galileo threatened the Church. 2. Explain the scientific method and describe scientific achievements of the sixteenth and seventeenth centuries.
Setting the Stage	Luther's courage	Henry VIII's reactions to Luther's teachings	The concept of "Counter-Reformation" Discussing History: The Jesuits	Acceptance of new ideas
Teaching Strategies	Discussing History: Causes of the Reformation Discussing History: The 95 Theses of Martin Luther Skill Building: Analyzing Effects Transparency 60 Check for Understanding	Discussing History: The Reformation in England Writing about History: Calvinism Geography in History: Protestant and Catholic Europe in the 1500's Transparency 61 Outline Map 10 Check for Understanding	Skill Building: Supporting Conclusions Skill Building: Comparing and Contrasting Reformation Monarchs Check for Understanding	Discussing History: Copernicus and Galileo Skill Building: Making Inferences Check for Understanding
Guided Practice	Transparency 60 Q&A Section Review 1	Transparency 61 Q&A Section Review 2	Section Review 3	Section Review 4
Independent Practice Worksheets	Independent Practice 16.1 Vocabulary 16 Geography Skills 16	Independent Practice 16.2 Basic Skills 16	Independent Practice 16.3 Critical Thinking 16	Independent Practice 16.4
Enrichment	1. Primary Source: Voices 16.1 2. Researching for Points	1. Primary Source: Voices 16.2 2. ★Preparing a Report: Women in the Reformation 3. Researching for Points	1. Primary Source: Voices 16.3 2. Preparing a Report: The Jesuits 3. Researching for Points	1. Primary Source: Voices 16.4 2. Researching for Points
Chapter Closer	●**Reteaching Activities** Summarizing, Outlining			
	Chapter Review Summary, Reviewing the Facts, Basic Skills, Researching and Reporting Skills, Critical Thinking, Perspectives on Past and Present, Investigating History			
	Chapter Evaluation Chapter Test 16, Alternate Chapter Test 16, Computer Test Bank Chapter 16 Test			

was Luther taking power away from priests? Why were these ideas threatening to the authority of the Catholic Church? Ask students to speculate on how the Catholic Church would react to Luther's ideas.

Skill Building: Analyzing Effects (Objective 3) Write the following headings on the board: *Immediate Effects, Short-Term Effects,* and *Long-Term Effects.* Have students supply information for each column on the effects of Luther's actions. Students should note that Luther was excommunicated by Pope Leo X and that Charles V issued the Edict of Worms, which branded Luther as an outlaw and a heretic. Short-term effects included the peasant revolt of 1524–1525 and conflict between princes of the Holy Roman Empire. Use Map Transparency 60, *Lands Ruled by Charles V,* to show the areas of conflict. Students should note that long-term effects (changes in language and clergy, rise of Lutheranism and Protestantism) continued to the present day, far outweighing immediate and short-term effects.

Check for Understanding Have students explain how the following people and events influenced the Protestant movement: need for Church reforms, humanist writers, teaching of Martin Luther, and the printing press.

Enrichment Activities

1. **Reading a Primary Source** Assign Voices from the Past Resource Book 16.1.
2. **Researching for Bonus Points** What was Thomas More's official title before he was beheaded? (Chancellor of England)

Protestantism spread in northern Europe. **2**

Setting the Stage

Before students read Section 2, share this quotation: (Henry VIII's criticism of Martin Luther).

> What serpent so venomous as he who calls the pope's authority tyrannous? . . . the whole Church is subject not only to Christ but . . . to Christ's only vicar, the pope of Rome.

Henry himself rejected the pope's authority, although he never changed his mind about Martin Luther. Henry repudiated the authority of Rome and dismantled the Catholic Church in England, leading to the spread of Protestantism.

Teaching Strategies

Discussing History: The Reformation in England (Objective 1) Ask students how England's monarchs responded to Protestantism. After they have read about Henry VIII's break with Rome, tell them the king decided to strike directly at the Church's main source of power—the monasteries and their wealth. Recall that the Catholic Church controlled one third of the land in England. Besides property, the clergy controlled 10 percent of England's wealth. By closing the monasteries and selling the property, Henry greatly increased his own wealth. The king's actions were carried out by royal agents— ominously known as "visitors"— who compiled itemized lists of the clerical treasures. Later they returned to take everything. Besides taking treasure, the king's agents destroyed relics that had been venerated for centuries. In all, nine tons of jewels and precious metal were taken from the ransacked monasteries. Discuss with students the impact Henry's actions had on the Catholic Church.

Conclude by asking if Henry's children continued his policies (page 381).

Writing about History: Calvinism (Objective 2) *Prewriting* Ask students to identify the traits of Calvinism (page 382). Ask students why the Calvinist belief in predestination emphasized religious and moral behavior. Have students recall Renaissance values (pages 347– 348). Explain that many Protestants were rebelling against these values. In Geneva, the followers of John Calvin founded a city based on their religious beliefs (theocracy). *Writing* Ask students to compare Calvinism to Renaissance values by writing a first-person narrative from the perspective of a Florentine citizen visiting Geneva. Narratives should include comparisons of religious beliefs, life-styles, and politics. Encourage creativity by having students contrast Florence and Geneva.

Geography in History: Protestant and Catholic Europe in the 1500's (Objective 3) Show students Map Transparency 61, *Protestantism and Catholicism in the 1500's.* Distribute Outline Map 10: Europe. Ask, "In what areas of Europe was Protestantism the strongest? What countries had strong Calvinist movements?" Have students use the map on page 383 as a reference while they label the countries of Europe, draw a map key, and use symbols in the key to designate areas of Europe that were Catholic or Protestant in the 1500's.

Enrichment Activities

1. **Reading a Primary Source** Assign Voices from the Past Resource Book 16.2.

2. **Preparing a Report**
Have students report on Marguerite of Navarre, Margaret More, or Catherine Parr. Ask students to explain how these women influenced the Protestant Reformation. Advanced students might wish to examine why opportunities for women were greater at the beginning of the Reformation, and how these opportunities later diminished.

3. **Researching for Bonus Points**
What was the name of the Archbishop of Canterbury who annulled Henry VIII's marriage to Catherine of Aragon? (Thomas Cranmer)

The Catholic Church made reforms. 3

Setting the Stage

Discussing History: The Jesuits (Objective 1) One result of the Protestant Reformation was a counter-reform movement by the Catholic Church. This counter-reformation was spearheaded by the Jesuits. Have students identify the Jesuits' goals. Explain that the Jesuits took a special vow to serve the pope and were trained to perform the most difficult and dangerous missions for the Church, including venturing into Protestant countries where their beliefs could be considered traitorous. The success of the Jesuits can be attributed to their strong mental discipline and the single-mindedness of their faith.

Teaching Strategies

Skill Building: Supporting Conclusions (Objective 2) Tell students to imagine that they are leaders of the Catholic Church during the Reformation. Have them explain the difficulties the Reformation posed for Church leaders. List students' responses on the board. Next, direct students' attention to the doctrines of the Council of Trent (page 384). Have students explain the four measures taken by the Church to counteract the Reformation. Ask how Pope Paul IV carried out the council's decrees. Discuss the effect of the Protestant Reformation on the Catholic Church. In light of these reforms, did the Protestant Reformation strengthen or weaken the Catholic Church? Have students use facts to support their conclusions.

Skill Building: Comparing and Contrasting Reformation Monarchs (Objective 3) Was the Peace of Augsburg a success or a failure for Charles V? Point out that it weakened the Holy Roman emperor's central rule. Have students recall the characteristics of the governments of England and of the Holy Roman Empire (see Chapter 10 and Chapter 11). Charles V's inability to unite his kingdom represented a continuation of historical trends in the Holy Roman Empire. Unlike Henry VIII in England, Charles had no unifying Parliament to legitimize his efforts to impose a state religion. Ask students to explain how Parliament helped Henry become head of the Anglican Church, in contrast to Charles' difficulties with the German princes.

Check for Understanding Have students complete the following sentence: As a response to the Protestant Reformation, the Catholic Church took the following actions: _____.

Enrichment Activities

1. **Reading a Primary Source**
Assign Voices from the Past Resource Book 16.3.

2. **Preparing a Report**
Have students report on the Jesuit Order. Reports should include information on the present-day work of the Jesuits.

3. **Researching for Bonus Points**
What did the vow taken by the Jesuits require? (obedience to the pope)

Scientists challenged old assumptions. 4

Setting the Stage

Social scientists in the present-day United States have found that an average of 15 years elapses between a discovery and its widespread acceptance. Ask students if they think future historians might identify television, computers, and medical technology as part of a scientific revolution. How have these scientific advances changed our world?

Teaching Strategies

Discussing History: Copernicus and Galileo (Objective 1) Ask students why Copernicus' discoveries might be referred to as the "Copernican Revolution." Then ask students to imagine Galileo's excitement over his observations with the telescope. He expected the heavenly bodies to be perfectly smooth spheres. Instead, he observed craters on the moon, rings around Saturn, and spots on the sun. Galileo was using a scientific method perfected by Renaissance artists: observation. Like the findings of Leonardo da Vinci and Michelangelo, Galileo's discoveries led him to challenge learning that was based on ancient writings. Like Martin Luther, Galileo professed ideas that threatened the Catholic Church. Discuss Galileo's decision to recant his beliefs. How did Galileo and Copernicus change the way people viewed their physical and spiritual worlds?

Skill Building: Making Inferences (Objective 2) A conclusion is the last step in the process of inductive reasoning, the basis of the scientific method. In inductive reasoning, conclusions are based on an accumulation of specific facts that are gathered through experiments and observations. Galileo and Kepler used this method. Ask students why the telescope, microscope, thermometer, and barometer are tools for inductive researchers. Ask, "How might the inductive method be better than the deductive method for scientific research?" (Facts can be verified; rules and principles might be wrong.)

Check for Understanding Ask students how perceptions about the universe were changed by scientific discoveries in the 1500's.

Enrichment Activities

1. **Reading a Primary Source** Assign Voices from the Past Resource Book 16.4.
2. **Researching for Bonus Points** What was the magnifying power of Galileo's first telescope? (power of 32)

ANSWERS TO
Chapter Review 16

Reviewing the Facts

1. (a) government controlled by church leaders **(b)** Earth-centered

2. (a) Italian friar who called for Church reform **(b)** Christian humanist who wrote *In Praise of Folly* **(c)** Christian humanist who wrote *Utopia* **(d)** More's book that describes a nearly perfect society **(e)** German printer who printed a Bible, the first full-size book with movable type **(f)** German artist whose drawings of biblical figures stirred religious feelings **(g)** German monk who challenged the Church and began Protestant Reformation **(h)** Holy Roman emperor who issued Edict of Worms declaring Luther heretic **(i)** meeting of German princes and bishops for trial of Luther **(j)** king of England who broke with pope **(k)** first wife of Henry VIII **(l)** parliament that approved the Act of Supremacy **(m)** returned English Church to the rule of the pope **(n)** set forth systematic Protestant philosophy that taught predestination **(o)** according to Calvin, the few people who will be saved by God's grace **(p)** Swiss city that became Calvinistic **(q)** brought Calvinism to Scotland **(r)** founder of Jesuits **(s)** list of books considered dangerous to the Catholic faith **(t)** agreement allowing German princes to choose either Catholicism or Lutheranism as official state religion and outlawing Calvinism and other forms of Protestantism **(u)** challenged Ptolemaic ideas with theory that Earth and other planets moved around the sun **(v)** confirmed Copernicus' ideas of planetary motion **(w)** observed surface of the moon through a telescope and was condemned by the Church for supporting Copernicus **(x)** studied human muscles, bones, and organs **(y)** studied human circulation; disproved Galen's theory

3. (a) Bands of angry German peasants demanding an end to economic and political bondage went about the countryside raiding monasteries, pillaging, and burning. **(b)** Luther wanted only peaceful reform and urged the German princes to crush the revolt. The lower classes felt betrayed by Luther.

4. (a) The Act made the English king, not the Roman pope, the official head of England's Church. **(b)** He closed all monasteries, seized their wealth and lands, and sold much of the land to nobles and members of the middle class, giving them reason to support Protestantism. **(c)** Edward VI was a staunch Protestant; Mary, a Catholic; and Elizabeth I, a Protestant.

5. (a) God has predestined who will be saved. **(b)** Protestant nobles led by John Knox overthrew the Catholic queen of Scotland, created a national church, and made Calvinism Scotland's official religion

Basic Skills

1. (a) Calvinists, Lutherans **(b)** Calvinism: Geneva, Netherlands, Scotland; Lutheranism: Brandenburg, Saxony, Denmark, Norway, Sweden **(c)** Catholicism: France, Spain, Austria, Italy

2. 1509, *In Praise of Folly*; 1516, *Utopia*; 1521, Diet of Worms; 1534, Act of Supremacy; 1555, *Peace of Augsburg*; 1559, *Index of Forbidden Books*

3. Role in Reformation: Luther sparked the Reformation by accusing Pope and Church of straying from the Bible; attacked "pardon merchants"; Calvin gave order to the new faith. Doctrine: Luther—salvation by faith alone, Bible the only authority, priesthood of all believers; Calvin—human nature sinful, only the elect will be saved, predestination. Political Ideas: Luther had support of peasants, then sided with princes against peasants; believed in obedience to earthly rulers, preached revolt against ungodly rulers. Calvin promoted ideal of theocracy; led a theocracy in Geneva. Writings—Luther: 95 Theses, translation of Bible into German; pamphlets, sermons. Calvin: *Institutes of the Christian Religion.*

Researching and Reporting Skills

1. Reaction against Renaissance: Reformation condemned luxuries, worldliness, immoral life, search for pleasure; preached sobriety and piety and return to virtues of the Bible. Reformation as result of humanistic thought: encouraged challenge of established ideas and authority; critical of uneducated priesthood; favored individualism by encouraging reading and personal interpretation of the Bible; asserted the priesthood of all believers, rejected pope's authority.

2. Pamphlet might make the following points: (1) Dangerous heresy; need to preach Christianity to the heathens; need for more educated clergy who will observe obedience and chastity. (2) Spiritual army is the answer. (3) Describes the Society of Jesus and its goals, showing how it is the answer. (4) Calls upon the reader to join.

Critical Thinking

1. Immediate causes: Henry VIII's wish to remarry and the pope's refusal to annul his marriage. Henry's hunger for Church wealth; Luther's denouncing the selling of indulgences; Calvin's leadership. Remote causes: nationalism conflicted with papal supremacy; people were indignant at luxurious living of Church authorities and at low moral and educational standards of priests; humanistic ideas challenged established thinking and encouraged individualism;

printing gave people the opportunity for individuals to read the Bible and helped to spread reformer's ideas.

2. Luther opposed certain teachings of the Church, role of priests, selling of indulgences; wanted salvation by faith, not by good works, with Bible as the only authority, and a direct relation of individuals to God.

3. (a) Eliminating abuses and improving moral, religious, and educational standards of clergy; fighting Protestantism by reaffirming authority of the Church and of tradition, and the doctrine that faith without good works will not save. **(b)** Coming to an agreement about the status of Protestantism in Germany in view of the failure of Charles V's efforts to crush the Protestant princes.

4. (a) Church lands that constituted one third of English lands were seized by Henry VIII and sold to nobles or wealthy middle class people. Luther's ideas resulted in peasant revolts against serfdom which Luther encouraged the princes to put down ruthlessly. German princes used the Reformation as a pretext to seize Church lands. **(b)** Landowners in possession of Church lands became staunch supporters of the Reformation in both England and Germany. Luther lost the support of the peasants and gained that of the princes.

5. (a) ideas of Aristotle and Ptolemy that the earth was center of the universe and that sun and stars circled around the earth; that earth was made of impure matter, whereas sun, moon, and stars were made of pure, eternal substances, smooth and perfect **(b)** The earth is not center of the universe. It circles around the sun and rotates on its own axis. Neither sun nor moon are made of

pure substance of heavenly light. The telescope showed mountains on the moon and dark spots on the sun. **(c)** Religious authorities were outraged, particularly if they took the Bible literally. It took science many years to develop the implications of these discoveries.

6. (a) Both were questioning authority and challenging established ideas. **(b)** The Reformation, because issues and conflicts of religion touched the daily lives of all people. The findings of the Scientific Revolution were condemned by the Church so that it took many years for them to have their full impact.

Perspectives on Past and Present

1. Evaluations will differ.

2. telescope: used today to explore deep space; microscope: today use electron microscope; thermometer: today can measure extremely high and low temperatures; barometer: used today in meteorology

Investigating History

Students' reports will vary.

Teaching with Pictures

Ask students if the painting shown here is supportive of Martin Luther. Ask what elements exhibit support for the reformer. Explain that the painting is based on the dream of Prince Frederick the Wise of Saxony on the night that Luther posted his 95 theses. The fire in the background represents the burning at the stake of several earlier reformers, including John Huss. In the foreground (below the fire), Luther is shown studying the Bible. At center right is the city of Rome with the pope and his cardinals. A lion represents Pope Leo X; *leo* is the Latin word for lion. At the left, Luther and his supporters write on the door of the castle church at Wittenberg with a giant pen whose other end reaches Rome and knocks off the pope's crown. Tell students that the painting is typical of the anti-papal feeling of the period.

This painting is a symbolic picture of Luther and his supporters. Using a giant quill, they are writing their demands for religious reform on the door of All Saints Church in Wittenberg, Germany.

Key Terms

Scientific Revolution
utopia
indulgence
Reformation
Protestant
predestination
theocracy
Huguenot
Counter-Reformation
geocentric theory
heliocentric theory
scientific method

372

Read and Understand

1. Martin Luther began a religious revolt.
2. Protestantism spread in northern Europe.
3. The Catholic Church made reforms.
4. Scientists challenged old assumptions.

Sweat glistened on the brow of a black-robed friar, Martin Luther. Torches lit the great hall in which he stood. Jammed together, craning their necks to see Luther, were the princes and bishops of Germany. They were members of the Imperial Diet (or assembly) of the Holy Roman Empire. At the head of the diet was the newly elected Emperor Charles V. The 21-year-old emperor stared grimly from his throne at the 37-year-old friar.

It was early evening on April 18, 1521. The setting was the town of Worms (vawrms) in Germany. Though they did not know it, the dignitaries who packed the hall were witnesses to a great turning point in European history.

About 20 books were stacked on a table near Luther. Europeans from London to Rome knew of the radical ideas these books contained. In them, Luther accused bishops, archbishops, and the pope of straying

Chapter 16 Resources

GEOGRAPHY
- Geography Skills 16
- Outline Map 10
- Transparencies 60, 61

REINFORCEMENT
- Vocabulary 16
- Basic Skills 16
- Reteaching 16
- Making Connections Study Guide 16

ENRICHMENT
- Critical Thinking 16

ASSESSMENT
- Chapter Test 16
- Alternate Chapter Test 16
- Computer Test Bank

dangerously far from the teachings of Jesus. Throughout Germany, Luther's books sold out as fast as they were printed. The German people regarded Luther as a national hero. The Church considered him a dangerous heretic.

At the Diet of Worms, Luther and his ideas were on trial. A Church official named Eck pointed at the stack of books. Were these Luther's work? he asked. "Yes," said Luther. Would Luther take back the heretical ideas in these books? Luther's reply rang through the hall:

> Unless I am convinced by Scripture and plain reason . . . my conscience is captive to the Word of God. I cannot and I will not recant [take back] anything, for to go against conscience is neither right nor safe. Here I stand. I cannot do otherwise. God help me. Amen.

Luther's defiant words led to a revolutionary change in the Christian religion. Many Europeans stopped accepting the pope as the head of a united Church. In this chapter, you will read about the split between the Catholic Church and a new group of Christians called Protestants.

Religious leaders such as Martin Luther were not the only ones to challenge the Catholic Church's authority in the 1500's and 1600's. Scientific thinkers too began to question traditional ideas. The challenge led to the **Scientific Revolution,** a radical change in the way of thinking.

Comparing these two revolutions, we could say that Protestantism changed the way many Christians thought of God, heaven, and the soul. The Scientific Revolution changed the way Europeans thought about Earth and the universe.

Martin Luther began a religious revolt.   1

Martin Luther's dramatic stand at Worms grew out of a long history of protest within the Church. Leaders such as Wycliffe (page 256) and Huss (page 256) were part of that history. By 1500, many forces had weakened the power of the Catholic Church. The most important of these forces were the new ideas of the Renaissance and the new technology of the printing press. The greatest

changes took place between 1517 and 1555. Thus, the new religious movement began during the last years of the High Renaissance in Italy.

The Catholic Church faced problems.

The Renaissance popes who ruled Rome from 1447 to 1534 patronized the arts, collected ancient manuscripts, and vigorously defended the Papal States from French and Italian armies. These worldly concerns left the popes little time for spiritual duties. It was a serious failing. One Renaissance pope, Pius II (1458–1464), wrote:

> People say that we live for pleasure, gather wealth, bear ourselves arrogantly, ride on fat mules and handsome palfreys [horses] . . . And there is some truth in their words: many among the cardinals and other officials of our court do lead this kind of life. If the truth be confessed, the luxury and pomp of our court is too great.

There were abuses among the lower clergy as well. Many priests and monks were so poorly educated that they could scarcely read. Some village priests had semi-official wives. How could such a pope as Alexander VI (1492–1503) condemn them? He publicly acknowledged his own five children, born before he became pope.

Many people were devoutly religious.

People had come to expect higher standards of conduct from priests and church leaders. During the 1400's and early 1500's, groups of Christians throughout Europe set increasingly strict standards for their own lives. In the Netherlands, for example, a group called the Brethren of the Common Life attracted many men and women. They lived very simply while helping the poor, the hungry, and the sick. Such groups spread to Germany, France, and Italy.

Likewise, Europeans in the 1500's expected a higher level of learning from priests. In the Middle Ages, when few people were literate, a priest who could read even a little was respected. During the Renaissance, however, learning spread more widely in society. By 1500, well-educated people sneered at the priest who was a poor reader.

Two groups of people led the demand for reform and for higher standards of religion. One group

373

OBJECTIVE 1. Describe the conditions that led to a religious revolt.

Teaching Strategy: *Discussing History: Causes of the Reformation* (page 372a)

OBJECTIVE 2. Explain the main teachings of Martin Luther.

Teaching Strategy: *Discussing History: The 95 Theses of Martin Luther* (page 372b)

OBJECTIVE 3. Assess the reactions to Luther's teachings and trace their spread.

Teaching Strategy: *Skill Building: Analyzing Effects* (page 372c)

■ DISCUSSION

How might a religious revolution and a scientific revolution go hand in hand?

SECTION 1
Resources

GEOGRAPHY
■ Transparency 60

REINFORCEMENT
■ Independent Practice 16.1

ENRICHMENT
■ Voices from the Past 16.1

ASSESSMENT
■ Section Quiz 16.1

■ BACKGROUND

Erasmus remained a loyal Catholic all his life. He refused to join Luther in revolt. His books, however, further weakened the prestige of both the pope and the priesthood.

ANSWERS TO

Voice from the Past

1. Iron is more useful.
2. by using gold and silver for common, everyday items, minimizing their rarity, associating them with criminals
3. the prizing of material possessions, especially those considered rare

included popular religious leaders who roused the people with fiery sermons. The other group consisted of Renaissance writers who became known as Christian humanists.

Savonarola An Italian friar named Girolamo Savonarola (jih-**ROHL**-uh-moh SAV-uh-nuh-**ROH**-luh) came to Florence to preach in 1490. In eloquent sermons, he called for reform of the Church. Florentines flocked to hear him. In 1494, he helped overthrow Florence's ruler, Piero de Medici. From 1494 until 1498, Savonarola virtually controlled Florence.

In 1497, Savonarola demanded that the people of Florence gather their personal "vanities" and burn them in a giant bonfire. People threw wigs, velvet gowns, and even rare manuscripts and paintings into the flames. Only a year later, however, Florentines turned against Savonarola. Before a jeering mob, a hangman executed him.

The case of Savonarola showed how easily a leader could turn people's religious passions in revolutionary directions. Yet more moderate voices also called for change. Popular books by humanist authors called attention to corruption in the Church and the need for reform.

Erasmus and More Around 1475, Renaissance ideas began to spread beyond Italy to northern Europe. This development is often called the Renaissance of the North. Scholars in northern Europe valued the Greek and Roman classics just as much as Italian humanists did. However, northern scholars showed more interest in religion. Thus, the leaders of the northern Renaissance are often called Christian humanists.

The best known of the Christian humanists were Thomas More of England and Desiderius Erasmus (DEZ-uh-**DAIR**-ee-uhs ih-**RAZ**-muhs) of Holland. The two were close friends.

Born in Rotterdam, Erasmus (1466–1536) was honored by princes, kings, and cardinals for his brilliant writings. In 1509, while he was a guest in More's house, Erasmus wrote his most famous work, *In Praise of Folly*. This short book poked fun at greedy merchants, heartsick lovers, quarrelsome scholars, and pompous priests. Erasmus's most stinging barbs were aimed at the clergy.

Voice from the Past | *Gold and Silver in Utopia*

In *Utopia*, Sir Thomas More described a society in which everyone had enough food, clothing, and possessions for a comfortable life. No one had more than necessary or sought wealth for its own sake.

Silver and gold get no more respect from anyone than their intrinsic value deserves—which is obviously far less than that of iron . . . [The author then describes the Utopians' way of making sure that people do not prize precious metals or jewels too much.] According to this system, plates and drinking vessels, though beautifully designed, are made of quite cheap stuff like glass or earthenware. But silver and gold are the normal materials . . . for the humblest items of household equipment, such as chamber-pots. They also use chains of solid gold to immobilize slaves. And anyone who commits a really shameful crime is forced to go about with gold rings on his ears and fingers, a gold necklace round his neck, and a crown of gold on his head . . .

It's much the same with jewels . . . If they happen to come across one, they pick it up and polish it for some toddler to wear. At first, children are terribly proud of such jewelry—until they are old enough to notice that it's only worn in the nursery. Then . . . they give it up.

1. Why might a Utopian value iron more than gold or silver?
2. How did Utopians keep people from valuing gold and jewels?
3. What forms of foolishness is More satirizing?

Sir Thomas More

This drawing of a printing shop in the 1500's shows the steps in the printing process. At the left, handwritten copy is taped to the wall. Workers take letters from type cases to make up a page. Another person (center, rear) inks a page of type that has been set. At the right, a man pulls the handle of the press that prints the sheets. A young apprentice (front) carries away the freshly printed pages to dry.

■ BACKGROUND

Durer studied in Italy, but his subjects and his style remained distinctly German. His woodcut, *The Knight, Death, and the Devil*, reminded German Christians that the Devil—evil personified—was constantly beckoning to them.

For example, he wrote, "One of their chief beliefs is that to be illiterate is to be of a high state of sanctity [holiness], and so they make sure they are not able to read."

How might a truly good society be organized? In 1516, Thomas More tried to answer this question in a book called *Utopia*. It told about a peace-loving people who lived in the imaginary land of Utopia, a name meaning "no place" in Greek. **Utopia** was a nearly perfect society based on reason and mercy. Greed, corruption, war, and crime had been weeded out.

Thousands of Europeans read the works of More and Erasmus. The reason that these authors could command such a wide audience was a remarkable technological breakthrough—the printing press.

The printing press spread new ideas.

The impact of the printing press on European society was revolutionary. It might be compared to the combined impact of television and the computer in recent times.

The first Europeans to use movable type were some printers in Mainz (mynts), Germany, between 1440 and 1450. The most famous of them was Johann Gutenberg (GOOT-uhn-burg), who printed a Bible around 1455. This Bible was the first full-size book printed with movable type.

Printing spread quickly to other cities in Europe. Print shops opened in Rome (1467), Venice (1469), and Paris (1470). By 1500, presses in about 250

cities had printed between 9 and 10 million books. For the first time, books were cheap enough that many Europeans could buy them.

How did printing prepare the way for a religious revolution? First, many writers criticized the corruption of the Renaissance popes. Erasmus, for example, wrote a savage satire about Pope Julius II.

Second, printed books on religion encouraged popular piety. Many printed books were illustrated with woodcuts and engravings. In Germany, the artist Albrecht Dürer (page 357) drew Jesus and other biblical figures as if they lived in a German town. His beautiful pictures deeply stirred people's religious feelings.

Third, the printing press made the Bible available to all who could read. When books were scarce, most Christians had depended completely on priests to interpret the Bible. After the Bible was printed, people could read it for themselves. Their interpretations, like Luther's, sometimes differed from those of the Church.

Footnote to History

Europeans had already learned from the Arabs how to make paper from old, shredded rags. Rag paper was much cheaper than parchment (made from sheepskin) or vellum (made from calfskin). Before the use of paper, a bookmaker had needed about 25 sheepskins to make a 200-page book.

375

Tetzel was quoted as saying: "How many mortal sins are committed in a day, how many in a week, how many in a month, how many in a year, how many in the whole course of life! They are well nigh numberless, and those that commit them must needs suffer endless punishment . . . Are you not willing, then, for the fourth part of a florin, to obtain these letters, by virtue of which you may bring . . . your divine and immortal soul safe and sound into the land of Paradise?"

Fourth, with the printing press, new ideas spread more quickly than ever before. Remember the stack of books for which Luther stood trial at the Diet of Worms. The ideas in them were similar to earlier writings of John Wycliffe and John Huss. Luther's books caused a revolution partly because so many people read them in a short time. With the printing press, the pen could indeed be mightier than the sword.

Luther challenged the Church.

All his life (1483–1546), Martin Luther wished only to be an obedient, God-fearing Christian. He did not set out to lead a religious revolution. What led this strongly religious man to defy the pope and Church traditions?

Luther's background The son of a copper miner, Luther was born in a tiny town in the German region of Saxony. As a child, he felt guilty and fearful much of the time. His father's bursts of anger terrified him. The stern teachings of local priests deeply impressed Luther.

When Luther was twenty-one, he narrowly escaped death. During a storm, lightning struck nearby, knocking him down. Afraid for his life, Luther cried, "Saint Anne, help me! I will become a monk." Luther's father, who wanted his son to be a lawyer, was furious.

As a monk, Luther tried desperately to win peace of mind. He confessed his sins at great length. He fasted regularly. He slept without a blanket until he nearly froze. Nevertheless, he still felt sinful, lost, and rejected by God.

Sometime between 1512 and 1515, Luther was alone in his study puzzling over a phrase in the Bible: "The just shall live by faith." In a flash, Luther thought he understood. Praying and fasting were not the keys to salvation. Instead, a strong faith in God was all that mattered. He wrote later, "Thereupon I felt myself to be reborn and to have gone through open doors into paradise."

The 95 theses Martin Luther might have lived quietly after finding peace. In 1517, however, something occurred that made him take a public stand. Like many other citizens of Wittenberg, he was offended by the deeds of a friar named Johann Tetzel. Tetzel was raising money in nearby towns to rebuild St. Peter's Cathedral in Rome. He did this by selling letters of **indulgence,** or pardons from the Church for certain sins.

This portrait of Martin Luther, drawn by one of his friends, shows him thoughtful and serious.

Strictly speaking, an indulgence could free a sinner only from the penance a priest had set, such as saying a certain number of prayers. The sinner would still have to pay the penalty set by God. Unfortunately, Tetzel was overeager to collect money. He gave people the impression that they could buy their way into heaven.

Luther was deeply troubled by Tetzel's tactics. On October 31, 1517, he took up his pen and wrote 95 theses (formal statements) attacking the "pardon-merchants." He posted his theses on the door of the castle church in Wittenberg and invited fellow scholars to debate him. Excited by the challenge, someone copied Luther's words and took them to a printer. Within six months, Luther's name was known all over Germany. The **Reformation,** or religious crisis in the Roman Catholic Church, had begun.

The pope tried to silence Luther.

Soon Luther went far beyond criticizing indulgences. He wanted a full reform of the Church. Luther's teachings rested on three main ideas:

1. *Salvation by faith alone* In Luther's view, people could not win salvation by their own efforts—what the Catholic Church called "good works." Faith in God was the only way to salvation.
2. *The Bible as the only authority for Christian life* All Church teachings, said Luther, should be clearly based on the words of the Bible. The pope, he said, was a false authority. (The Catholic Church accepted both the Bible and Church traditions as authorities.)
3. *The priesthood of all believers* According to Luther, each person had a relationship with God and all people with faith were equal. Therefore, people did not need priests to interpret the Bible.

On June 15, 1520, Pope Leo X issued a bull (an official statement) threatening Luther with excommunication unless he recanted. Luther did not take back a word. Instead, his students at Wittenberg gathered around a bonfire and cheered as he threw the bull into the flames. Leo answered by excommunicating Luther.

Charles V opposed Luther.

The pope seemed powerless to touch Luther. However, the young Holy Roman Emperor, Charles V, had greater authority in Germany. We have seen how Charles summoned Luther to Worms in 1521 to stand trial. Charles promised Luther safety from arrest while at Worms. Would Luther back down at last? As you have read, he did not.

Luther made his famous speech on Thursday, April 18. The next day, Charles replied: "A single friar who goes counter to all Christianity for a thousand years must be wrong . . . I will proceed against him as a notorious heretic." On May 26, Charles issued an imperial order, the Edict of Worms. It declared Luther an outlaw and heretic. According to this edict, no one in the empire was to give Luther food or shelter. All his books were to be burned. Legally, there was no place in Germany for Luther to hide.

However, Luther lived comfortably in Germany for almost 25 years after his trial at Worms. Charles V, the most powerful ruler in Europe, could neither capture Luther nor stamp out his ideas. What accounts for this extraordinary failure?

First, Charles's huge empire was simply too much for him to govern effectively. Charles belonged to a family called the Hapsburgs, who had risen to power in Austria. After the 1400's, most Holy Roman emperors were chosen from the Hapsburg family. By a series of careful marriages, the Hapsburgs won more and more lands. In 1521, their holdings included not only Austria and lands in Germany but also the Netherlands, parts of Italy, Spain, and Spain's empire in the Americas.

Charles had another problem. The German people, although divided politically, had a strong national spirit, and they resented sending German money to Rome. Luther's attacks on the pope's "greed" were popular with many Germans. An Italian churchman visiting Germany in 1521 wrote, "Nine tenths of the people are shouting 'Luther!' And the other tenth shouts 'Down with Rome!'"

Luther's ideas spread in Germany.

For almost a year after the Diet of Worms, Luther shut himself away in a castle owned by Prince Frederick the Wise of Saxony. While there, Luther translated the New Testament into German. Now even Germans who did not know Latin could read the Bible.

Luther returned to Wittenberg in 1522. There he discovered that many of his ideas were already being put into practice. Town priests had given up their colorful robes. They dressed in ordinary clothes and called themselves ministers. They led services in German instead of in Latin. Some ministers had married, because Luther taught that the clergy should be free to wed.

Luther and his followers had taken the long step from wanting reform within the Catholic Church to becoming a separate religious group. They became known as Lutherans.

The revolt against the papacy became much broader. In 1524, German peasants, excited by reformers' talk of Christian freedom, demanded an end to their economic and political bondage. Serfdom, they cried, must be abolished. Bands

377

ANSWERS TO

Section Review 1

Define:
(a) radical change in the way of thinking (b) a nearly perfect society (c) pardon from the Church (d) religious crisis in the Roman Catholic Church (e) Christians who turned away from the Catholic Church

Identify:
(a) German monk who challenged the Church and started Protestant Reformation (b) assembly at which Luther and his ideas were on trial (c) Italian friar who called for reform
(d) Christian humanist who wrote *In Praise of Folly*
(e) Christian humanist who wrote *Utopia* (f) book about a nearly perfect society
(g) German printer who used movable type to print Bible (h) Holy Roman emperor who condemned Luther as heretic (i) powerful Austrian family from which most Holy Roman emperors were chosen

Answer:
1. lived too extravagantly,

(continued)

were poorly educated, did
not keep their vows of
chastity

2. Printing press gave critics
of popes a vehicle for
spreading their views, encouraged popular piety,
made Bible available to all
Christians who could read,
and helped new ideas
spread quickly.

3. (a) Tetzel's selling of indulgences **(b)** Faith alone is
key to salvation; Bible is
only authority for Christian
life; all believers have a relationship with God and do
not need priests to interpret
the Bible.

4. (a) order issued by
Charles V declaring Luther
an outlaw and heretic
(b) size of empire and German nationalism

5. (a) princes who supported Luther **(b)** any Christian who turned away from
Catholic Church

6. (a) It was too big an empire to govern effectively
and suppress spread of Lutheranism. **(b)** Nationalistic
Germans resented sending
their money to Rome.
(c) Princes saw an economic
advantage—the seizure of
Church lands—in
Lutheranism.

7. Answers should include
discussion of Luther's break
with tradition, defiance of
authority, and role as cata-
lyst in launching a new era.

Lands Ruled by Charles V

KEY

▨ Hapsburg lands ruled directly by Charles V

☐ Lands ruled indirectly by Charles V as Holy Roman emperor

☐ Areas of German peasant revolt

0 ——— 300 Miles

Map Study

*On what three continents did Charles V control lands? Name three European
areas of which Charles was the ruler.*

of angry peasants went about the countryside
raiding monasteries, pillaging, and burning.

Luther was horrified by the peasants' revolt.
He insisted that he wanted only peaceful reform,
not violence and lawlessness. To the German
princes, he wrote a savage letter urging them to
show the peasants no mercy.

With brutal thoroughness, the princes' armies
crushed the peasant revolt of 1524–1525. Perhaps
100,000 people were massacred. The lower classes

felt betrayed by Luther, and many turned away
from his religious leadership.

After 1525, the success of Lutheranism depended increasingly on the support of German
princes. Some princes liked Luther's ideas for
selfish reasons. They saw his teachings as a good
excuse to seize Church property. Other princes,
however, genuinely shared Luther's beliefs.

In 1529, princes loyal to the pope agreed to
join forces against Luther's ideas. Princes who

supported Luther signed a protest against that agreement. From that time on, these protesting princes came to be known as Protestants.

Eventually, the term **Protestant** was used for many Christians who, seeking change, turned away from the papacy and the Catholic Church. Their movement was commonly known as the Protestant Reformation.

Section REVIEW 1

Define: (a) Scientific Revolution, (b) utopia, (c) indulgence, (d) Reformation, (e) Protestant
Identify: (a) Martin Luther, (b) Diet of Worms, (c) Savonarola, (d) Erasmus, (e) Thomas More, (f) *Utopia*, (g) Gutenberg (h) Charles V, (i) Hapsburg family
Answer:
1. What criticisms were made of many popes and lower clergy during the 1400's and 1500's?
2. Identify four ways in which the printing press prepared the way for the Reformation.
3. (a) What events led Luther to take a stand against the Church? (b) Summarize his three main ideas.
4. (a) What was the Edict of Worms? (b) Why was it unsuccessful?
5. (a) To whom was the term *Protestant* first applied? (b) What broader meaning did the term acquire?

Critical Thinking
6. Politics and religion were closely intertwined in the 1500's. How did each of the following political factors affect the spread of Luther's ideas? (a) the size of the Holy Roman Empire (b) German nationalism (c) the ambition of the German princes
7. Would you define Luther as a revolutionary? Why or why not?

Protestantism spread in northern Europe. 2

Martin Luther continued to write pamphlets and deliver sermons until his death in 1546. As time passed, however, the Protestant Reformation depended less and less on his leadership. Other reformers were also clamoring for change. Among them were John Calvin of France and John Knox of Scotland. Soon the Catholic Church was being challenged in many parts of Europe, especially in England.

Henry VIII *broke with the pope.*

When Henry VIII became king of England in 1509, he was 18 years old. He was the son of the "new monarch" Henry VII (page 262). Young Henry was handsome, strong, and intelligent. He loved tennis, classical literature, music, and food.

In religion, Henry VIII was a devout Catholic. He detested Luther. In 1521, Henry wrote a pamphlet calling Luther "a great limb of the Devil" and many other such names. Impressed by Henry's loyalty, the pope gave him a special title, "Defender of the Faith."

Yet political needs soon proved more important to Henry than religious loyalty. Henry was only the second king of the Tudor family, and he was anxious about the future of his line. Henry and his wife, Catherine of Aragon, had only one child—a daughter named Mary, born in 1516. Their five other babies, including three boys, had died in infancy. Henry feared that another civil war like the Wars of the Roses (page 262) would occur unless he had a male child to inherit his crown.

By 1527, Henry was convinced that Catherine would have no more children. He wanted a new queen to give him a son. He had already picked her out: a dark-eyed 20-year-old named Anne Boleyn (boo-**LIHN**).

How could Henry legally end his marriage to Catherine? Church law did not allow divorce, but the pope might set aside Henry's marriage by saying that it had never been legal in the first place. Such matters were often arranged.

In 1527, the king asked the pope to end the marriage. Unfortunately, 1527 was a very bad year to ask the pope for a favor. Pope Clement VII had taken the losing side in a war against Holy Roman Emperor Charles V. Charles's armies swept into Rome in 1527 and held the pope prisoner in the Vatican. Henry's unwanted wife, Catherine of Aragon, was the emperor's aunt. Charles would not allow his prisoner, the pope, to end his aunt's marriage. The pope turned down Henry's request.

379

SECTION 2
Objectives and Teaching Strategies

OBJECTIVE 1. Explain the effects of the Reformation in England.
Teaching Strategy: *Discussing History: The Reformation in England* (page 372c)

OBJECTIVE 2. Discuss significant traits of Calvinism.
Teaching Strategy: *Writing about History: Calvinism* (page 372c)

OBJECTIVE 3. Trace the distribution of religions in Europe in the 1500's.
Teaching Strategy: *Geography in History: Protestant and Catholic Europe in the 1500's* (page 372c)

■ BACKGROUND
Catherine of Aragon was the daughter of Spain's Isabella and Ferdinand. Their other daughter, Juana "The Mad," was the mother of Charles V.

SECTION 2
Resources

GEOGRAPHY
■ Transparency 61

REINFORCEMENT
■ Independent Practice 16.2

ENRICHMENT
■ Voices from the Past 16.2

ASSESSMENT
■ Section Quiz 16.2

The Church of England is also called the Anglican Church and, in the United States, the Episcopal Church.

The Protestant Archbishop of Canterbury, Thomas Cranmer, created a *Book of Common Prayer* to be read aloud in church by all English Christians. Soon English priests were being called "ministers" in the Protestant manner, and their approach to the bread-and-wine sacrament was more like Luther's than the pope's.

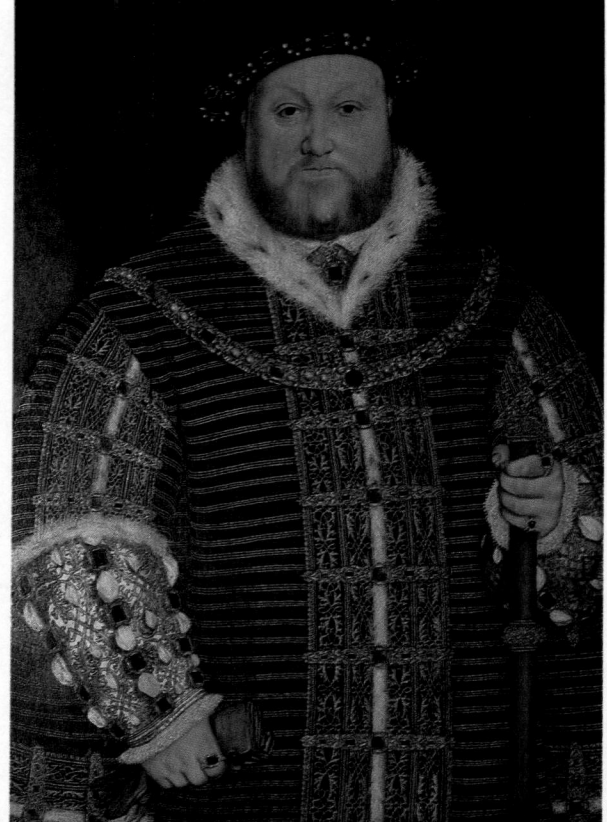

Henry VIII, the second Tudor king of England, broke with the Roman Catholic Church in 1534.

The king sought Parliament's help.

Henry soon looked for more radical answers to his marriage problem. In 1529, he called Parliament and asked it to pass a group of laws that stripped away the pope's power in England. This Parliament is known as the Reformation Parliament. It met whenever the king summoned it for seven years (1529–1536).

Parliament soon legalized Henry's divorce from Catherine. In January 1533, Henry married Anne. Parliament passed a law stating that the king was not responsible "to any foreign princes or potentates of the world." (In other words, the pope was not to interfere with the king's divorce and remarriage.)

After being crowned queen in May, Anne gave birth to Henry's child in September. Imagine the king's frustration when he learned that the child

was a girl. (Little did he realize that this daughter, Elizabeth, would be the greatest Tudor monarch of all.)

In 1534, Henry's break with the pope was made complete when Parliament voted to approve the Act of Supremacy. This act declared, "The king's majesty justly and rightly is and ought to be . . . the only supreme head in earth of the Church of England."

The English king, not the Roman pope, was now the official head of England's Church. Henceforth the king's agents collected all Church moneys. All priests and bishops were subject to the king's appointment and approval. Thus began the church that is called the Church of England.

The acts of the Reformation Parliament strengthened both the king and Parliament itself. The king won control of the Church of England. At the same time, Parliament gained power. Never before had a ruler asked Parliament to act on such fundamental questions.

Henry VIII *enforced his changes.*

Only a few people in England proved more loyal to the pope than to the king. The most famous of them was Thomas More. He refused to take an oath supporting the Act of Supremacy. For this refusal, Henry VIII ordered More beheaded. At his execution, More forgave his executioner and asked spectators to pray for the king. He said, "I die the king's good servant, but God's first." His death shocked people all over Europe.

The closing of the monasteries Soon after making himself supreme head of the Church of England, Henry made another sweeping change in religion. He closed all English monasteries and seized their wealth and lands. The monasteries had owned almost one third of the land in England, so this act vastly increased royal power and enriched Henry's treasury.

To raise money, Henry sold much of the land he had seized to nobles and to members of England's rising middle class. Suddenly there were many English landowners who stood to lose property if England returned to the Catholic Church. This group formed a solid base of support for the Protestant Reformation in England.

In most other ways, Henry remained more Catholic than Protestant. He insisted that English priests make no changes in Catholic rituals and doctrines.

Henry's later marriages Meanwhile, Anne Boleyn had fallen rapidly out of favor with the king. Henry ordered her imprisoned in the Tower of London and later beheaded in 1536.

Within a month of Anne's death, Henry VIII married a third time. His new wife, Jane Seymour, lived just long enough to fulfill his dearest wish. On October 12, 1537, she bore a son, Edward. Then she died 12 days later.

Henry VIII married three more times. To win an alliance with Germany's Lutheran princes, he arranged to marry Anne of Cleves, a German princess he had never met. After only a few months, he had that marriage set aside. The king's fifth wife, Catherine Howard, was young and beautiful but foolish. She was executed on charges of adultery after less than a year as queen. In 1543, he married Catherine Parr. A mature woman, she loyally cared for Henry, who was now so fat and ill that he could hardly move, until his death in 1547.

Henry's children After Henry's death, all three of his children eventually inherited the throne. Edward VI was the first to rule. As he was a staunch Protestant, the Protestants gained power during his reign. Edward's half-sister Mary ruled England next. She was a Catholic who returned the English Church to the rule of the pope. England's next ruler was Anne Boleyn's red-headed daughter, Elizabeth. Elizabeth I returned her kingdom to Protestantism.

Women influenced the Reformation.

Mary and Elizabeth Tudor could force their religious ideas on their subjects because they were queens. However, many other women also played prominent roles in the Reformation.

Some women of the nobility protected Protestant leaders who lived and taught within their lands. In France, one of the most influential Protestants was Marguerite of Navarre, the sister of King Francis I. Besides protecting several Protestant preachers, she passed her Protestant ideals on to her descendants. Her grandson, Henry of Navarre, later became Henry IV of France.

Educated women wrote treatises on religious issues that were widely read. Margaret More, daughter of Sir Thomas More, was a recognized

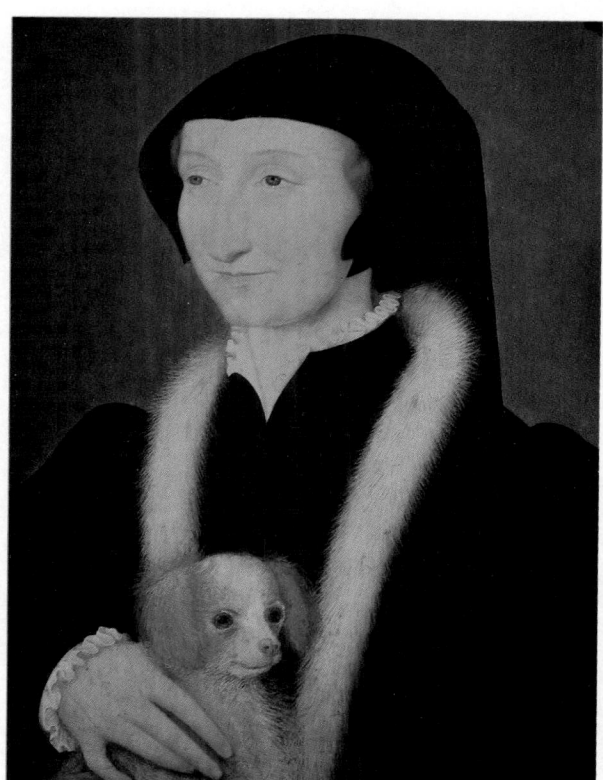

Marguerite of Navarre, sister of France's king, protected French Protestants.

scholar. Likewise, Catherine Parr, the last wife of Henry VIII, wrote a book that discussed such questions as justification by faith.

Protestant ideas also spread widely among middle-class women. Protestantism appealed to the middle classes—both men and women—partly because preachers spoke in the vernacular, not in Latin. In addition, nationalist feelings against Rome were as strong among women as among men in Germany, England, and the Netherlands.

Women, like men, often suffered for their religious views. In the bitter struggles over religion, many women died for their beliefs.

Women's influence on the Protestant movement was greatest in the early years, between 1519 and 1580. As the Protestant religion became more firmly established, its organization became more formal. There were fewer opportunities for women to act as leaders. Women once again found themselves in the background.

381

■ **BACKGROUND**
Catherine Parr proved herself a kind stepmother to Henry's three children by his other marriages. She saw to their educations and helped reconcile Henry to his two daughters.

Protestants agreed that faith alone was the key but they disagreed about the meaning of the Eucharist, the relation of the Protestant Church to the state, and the style of houses of worship.

The doctrines of the Anabaptists, founded in 1525 by Conrad Grebel, horrified Lutherans and Catholics alike. Anabaptists interpreted the Bible literally, saying that "Thou shalt not kill" commanded them to avoid weapons at all times, even in defense of their country.

Calvin formalized Protestant ideas.

The Church of England remained close to the Catholic Church in many of its doctrines and ceremonies. Meanwhile, other forms of Protestantism were developing elsewhere in Europe.

When Luther stood trial at Worms, John Calvin was a boy of 12 in Noyon (nwah-**YOH**), France. No one could have guessed that this shy, studious child would in some ways have even greater influence than Luther. Luther had sparked the religious revolution. A generation later, Calvin gave order to the new faith.

Calvin studied law and philosophy at the University of Paris. Early in the 1530's, he came under the influence of French followers of Luther. When King Francis I ordered these Protestants arrested, Calvin fled. Eventually, he made his way to Switzerland.

In 1536, Calvin published a book called the *Institutes of the Christian Religion.* This work set forth a systematic Protestant philosophy. The first edition of the *Institutes* was completely sold out in a year.

Calvin taught that men and women are by nature sinful. By God's grace, however, a very few people will be saved from sin. Calvin called these few the "elect." Because God is all-knowing, Calvin said, He has known since the beginning of time who will be saved. Calvin's doctrine is called **predestination.**

Calvin said that the duty of the elect is to rule society so as to glorify God. Therefore, he taught, the church should dominate the state. Calvin hoped for a **theocracy,** a government controlled by church leaders. This idea was a major difference between Calvinism and Lutheranism, for Luther preached obedience to earthly rulers. Calvin's ideas gave more support for revolt against an "ungodly" ruler, an idea that later influenced events in Scotland and several other countries.

Calvin did more than write about his ideas. He actually set up the kind of theocracy he had described in his book. In 1541, Protestants in the French-speaking city of Geneva, Switzerland, asked Calvin to lead their community. When Calvin arrived there in the 1540's, Geneva was a self-governing city of about 20,000 people.

To many Protestants, Geneva under Calvin's rule became a "city of saints." Calvin and his followers regulated the lives of everybody who lived in the city. Everyone in Geneva attended classes in religion. No one wore brightly colored clothing or played cards. No one could visit a public inn after nine o'clock at night. For breaking such rules, a person might be imprisoned, excommunicated, or banished from the city. Moreover, in Protestant Geneva as in Catholic Rome, anyone who preached a different set of doctrines might be burned at the stake.

Knox led the Scottish Reformation.

Protestants from everywhere in Europe came to Geneva to see how a sober, purified city was organized. Among the admiring visitors was a preacher from Scotland named John Knox. When he returned to Scotland in 1559, Knox put Calvin's ideas on church organization to work in Scottish towns. Each community church was governed by a small group of laymen called elders or presbyters (**PREHZ**-buh-tuhrs). From this organization, followers of Knox became known as Presbyterians.

In 1567, Protestant nobles led by Knox overthrew the Catholic queen of Scotland, Mary Stuart, in a nearly bloodless revolt. They put her one-year-old son, James VI, on the throne. Real power, however, was in the hands of the Protestant nobles. They created a national church and made Calvinism Scotland's official religion.

Protestant churches spread widely.

Elsewhere in Europe, the Calvinist form of church organization was widely adopted by Swiss, French, and Dutch reformers. Except for Scotland, no other kingdom officially converted to Calvinist belief. In France, the followers of Calvin became known as **Huguenots.** However, as the map on page 383 shows, communities of Calvinist Protestants were to be found from England to Italy.

In Sweden, Norway, and Denmark, Lutheranism became the official religion. Denmark had ruled both Sweden and Norway until 1523. In that year, Sweden revolted against the Danish king. The leader of the Swedish independence movement, Gustavus Vasa, became Sweden's new king. He soon ended papal power in Sweden and seized Church lands. Norway remained under Danish control and became Lutheran when Denmark made Lutheranism the official religion of the country in 1536.

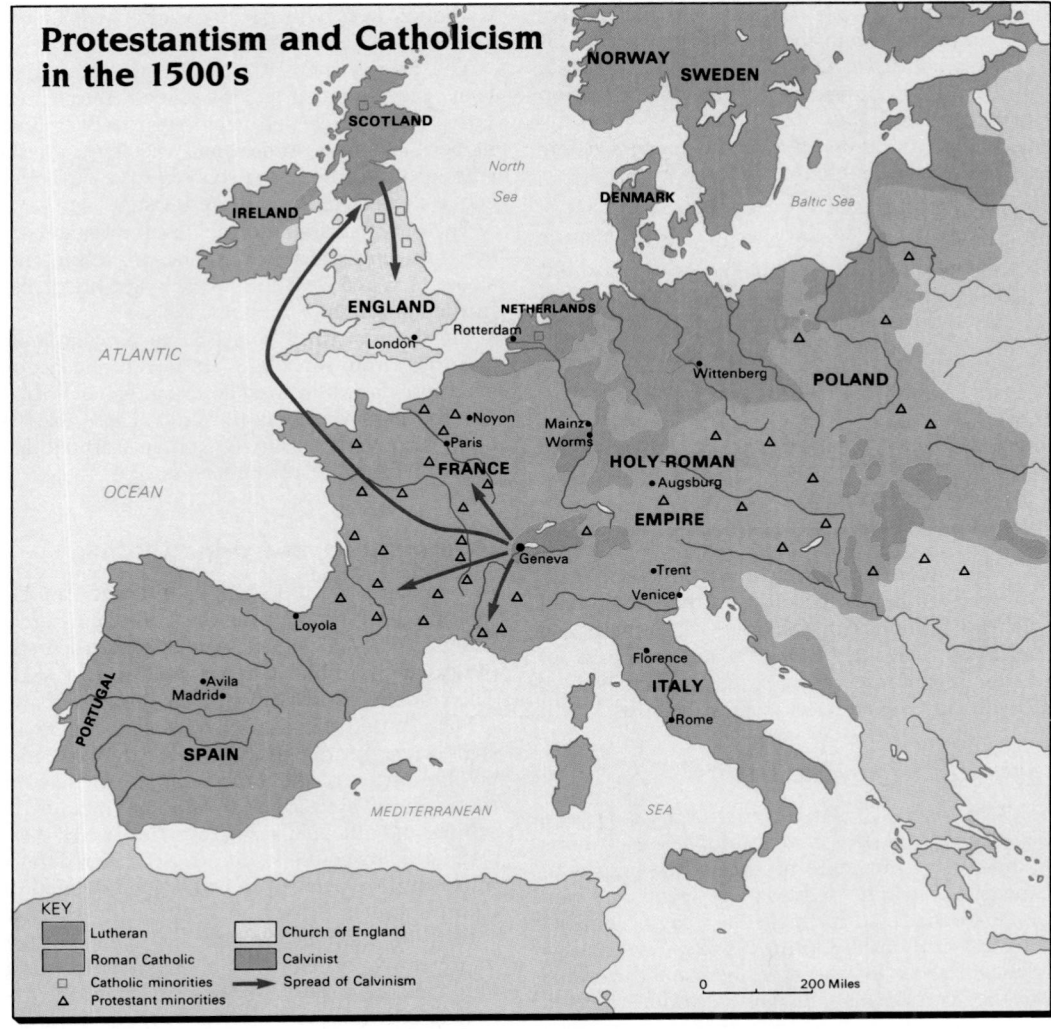

Protestantism and Catholicism in the 1500's

NORWAY
SWEDEN
SCOTLAND
North Sea
IRELAND
DENMARK
Baltic Sea
ENGLAND
NETHERLANDS
Rotterdam
London
ATLANTIC
Wittenberg
POLAND
Noyon
Mainz
Worms
Paris
FRANCE
HOLY ROMAN
Augsburg
OCEAN
EMPIRE
Geneva
Trent
Venice
Loyola
Florence
Avila
ITALY
Madrid
Rome
PORTUGAL
SPAIN
MEDITERRANEAN
SEA

KEY

Lutheran		Church of England	
Roman Catholic		Calvinist	
□ Catholic minorities		→ Spread of Calvinism	
△ Protestant minorities			

0   200 Miles

Map Study

Where was Protestantism stronger, in northern Europe or in southern Europe?
Where was the center of the Calvinist movement?

Section REVIEW 2

Define: (a) elect, (b) predestination, (c) theocracy, (d) presbyters, (e) Huguenot
Identify: (a) Henry VIII, (b) Catherine of Aragon, (c) Anne Boleyn, (d) Reformation Parliament, (e) Edward VI, (f) Mary Tudor, (g) Elizabeth I, (h) John Calvin, (i) John Knox

Answer:
1. Why did Henry VIII of England want to end his first marriage?
2. What part did Parliament play in the English Reformation?
3. (a) What changes did Henry make in the English Church? (b) What changes did each of his children make when they succeeded him?

383

ANSWERS TO
Map Study

northern Europe; Geneva

ANSWERS TO
Section Review 2

Define:
(a) according to Calvin, the few people who will be saved from sin by God's grace (b) Calvin's doctrine holding that God has known from the beginning of time who will be saved (c) government controlled by church leaders (d) laymen who governed community churches in Scotland (e) French Calvinist

Identify:
(a) Tudor king of England who began Church of England (b) first wife of Henry VIII (c) second wife of Henry (d) parliament that met at the king's summons from 1529-1536 (e) Henry's son and successor; staunch Protestant (f) Edward's half-sister and successor; Catholic who returned English Church to rule of pope (g) Queen of England who restored Protestantism (h) French religious reformer (i) preacher who spread Calvinism to Scotland

Answer:
1. feared his wife would not give birth to a boy and that there would be succession problems
2. superseded papal supremacy and greatly strengthened powers of king

(continued)

ANSWERS TO *(continued)*

3. **(a)** closed monasteries, seized their wealth, and sold their land **(b)** Edward VI— gave Protestants power; Mary—returned kingdom to Catholicism, Elizabeth— brought back Protestantism

4. **(a)** Elect are the few people who are chosen by the grace of God to be saved from sin and whose duty it is to rule society so as to glorify God. **(b)** Luther preached obedience to earthly rulers, but Calvin wanted a theocracy.

5. Knox and Protestant nobles overthrew Mary Stuart, put her infant son on throne, retained power themselves, and made Calvinism official religion.

6. Sweden, Norway, and Denmark

7. **(a)** duty to God greater than to king **(b)** Often rulers turned away from Catholicism and demanded that their subjects do the same or face punishment.

■ **DISCUSSION**

"Give me a child until he is five" said the Jesuit, "and I care not what you do with him afterwards." Have students discuss this viewpoint and note that at least one Protestant group, the Anabaptists, believed that baptism should be an adult rite.

4. (a) Briefly describe Calvin's idea of the elect and their place in society. (b) How were Calvin's political ideas different from Luther's?
5. How did Calvinism become the official religion of Scotland?
6. Where in Europe did Lutheranism become the official religion?

Critical Thinking

7. (a) What did Thomas More mean by his statement, "I die the king's good servant, but God's first"? (b) How does this statement show the dilemma that many people faced in the 1500's?

The Catholic Church made reforms. 3

While Protestants won many followers, millions of Catholics held fast to their traditional beliefs. Catholics in the 1500's had their own religious reformers. One great champion of Catholic reform was Ignatius (ig-**NAY**-shus) of Loyola, later canonized as Saint Ignatius.

Ignatius began the Jesuits.

Born in 1491, Ignatius grew up in his father's castle in Loyola in eastern Spain. The great turning point in his life came in 1521 when he was in the Spanish army fighting the French. A cannonball shattered his right leg, leaving him an invalid for months. During his recovery, Ignatius thought about his past sinfulness and the events of the life of Jesus. His daily devotions seemed to cleanse his soul. In 1522, he began writing a book. Titled *Spiritual Exercises*, his book laid out a day-by-day plan of meditation, prayer, and study.

Over the next 18 years, Ignatius gathered a band of followers. Eventually, he won the support of Pope Paul III. In 1540, the pope made Ignatius's company a new monastic order called the Society of Jesus. Those who later joined the order were commonly called Jesuits (**JEHZ**-uh-wuhts).

What made the Jesuits unique was their emphasis on absolute discipline and obedience. They were like a spiritual army. These disciplined

384

Catholics were willing to go anywhere in the world in the service of the pope.

The Jesuits concentrated on three activities. First, they founded superb schools throughout Europe. Jesuit teachers were rigorously trained in both classical studies and theology. Priests who attended the Jesuit schools were far better educated than many other priests.

The second mission of the Jesuits was to convert non-Christians to Catholicism. Jesuit missionaries risked their lives preaching Christianity in the Americas, Africa, and Asia.

The Jesuits' third goal was to prevent Protestantism from spreading. The zeal of the Jesuits overcame the drift toward Protestantism in Poland and southern Germany (Bavaria). These regions today are overwhelmingly Roman Catholic because of the work of the Jesuits.

Reforming popes led the Church.

Two popes of the 1500's, Paul III and Paul IV, took the lead in reforming the Catholic Church. They had two goals. One was to strengthen and purify the Catholic Church for its own sake. Their other goal was to combat Protestantism.

Pope Paul III (1534–1549) took three important steps in reforming the Catholic Church. First, he directed a council of cardinals to make a thorough investigation of simony, indulgence selling, and other abuses within the Church. Second, he approved the Jesuit order. Third and most important, he decided to call a great council of Church leaders.

In 1545, Catholic bishops and cardinals met in the town of Trent in northern Italy. After much heated discussion, they agreed on the following doctrines:

1. The pope's interpretation of the Bible was final. Any Christian who substituted his or her own interpretation was a heretic.
2. Christians were not saved by faith alone, as Luther argued. They were saved by faith *and* by good works.
3. The Bible and Church tradition shared equal authority for guiding a Christian's life.
4. Indulgences, pilgrimages, and venerations of holy relics were all valid expressions of Christian piety. (But the false selling of indulgences was banned.)

The picture above shows the interior of a Protestant church with the minister at the pulpit. At the right is a ceremony in a Roman Catholic church. Bishops are gathered in front of the pope. What differences do the pictures show between the two styles of worship?

Another reforming pope, Paul IV (1555–1559), vigorously carried out the council's decrees. In 1559, he drew up a list of books that he considered dangerous to the Catholic faith. This list was known as the *Index of Forbidden Books.* Catholic bishops throughout Europe were ordered to gather up the offensive books (including Protestant Bibles) and burn them in great bonfires. In Venice alone, 10,000 books were burned in one day.

Historians have given two different names to this wave of reform in the Catholic Church. Protestant historians have generally called it the **Counter-Reformation** because, they argued, its goal was to stamp out Protestantism. Catholic historians usually called this period the Catholic Reformation. They stressed the sincere desire of popes, cardinals, nuns, and monks to end Church corruption.

Religion divided Europe.

While the popes tried religious measures to strengthen the Church and crush Protestantism, Holy Roman Emperor Charles V turned to military measures. In 1544, Charles finally felt safe enough from his French and Turkish enemies to take up arms against the Protestant princes of Germany.

These Protestant rulers had joined together in a defensive group called the Schmalkaldic (shmahl-**KAHLD**-ik) League. In 1547, Charles's troops met the Schmalkaldic princes in battle and badly trounced them. However, the Catholic princes of Germany refused to join Charles in his war against Protestantism.

Weary of fighting, Charles ordered all German princes, both Protestant and Catholic, to assemble for an Imperial Diet in the city of Augsburg. At that meeting, the princes agreed that the religion of each German state was to be decided by its ruler. This famous religious settlement, signed in 1555, was known as the Peace of Augsburg.

By the terms of the Peace of Augsburg, German princes could choose either Lutheranism or Catholicism. Calvinism and other forms of Protestantism were outlawed.

From the point of view of Charles V, the Peace of Augsburg was not a happy settlement. After all, it led to religious division, not unity. All his life, Charles V had been deeply attached to the great institutions of the Middle Ages—feudalism, chivalry, and the Catholic Church. As Holy Roman emperor, he had hoped to preserve these

385

OBJECTIVE 1. Identify the goals of the Jesuits.
Teaching Strategy: *Discussing History: The Jesuits* (page 372d)

OBJECTIVE 2. Describe reactions of the Church to Protestantism.
Teaching Strategy: *Skill Building: Supporting Conclusions* (page 372d)

OBJECTIVE 3. Explain how the Reformation contributed to disunity in the Holy Roman Empire.
Teaching Strategy: *Skill Building: Comparing and Contrasting Reformation Monarchs* (page 372d)

SECTION 3
Resources

REINFORCEMENT
■ Independent Practice 16.3

ENRICHMENT
■ Voices from the Past 16.3

ASSESSMENT
■ Section Quiz 16.3

ANSWERS TO
Section Review 3

Define:
Protestant name for the period of Catholic Church reform
(continued)

ANSWERS TO *(continued)*

Identify:
(a) founder of Jesuits
(b) monastic order founded by Loyola **(c)** meeting at which Catholic leaders drew up doctrines reforming the Church **(d)** list of books Pope Paul IV considered dangerous to the Catholic faith **(e)** agreement allowing each German prince to choose Catholicism or Lutheranism

Answer:
1. (a) monastic order started by Ignatius Loyola
(b) founding good schools, converting non-Christians to Catholicism, and preventing Protestantism from spreading
2. (a) directed investigation of abuses in Church practices, approved Jesuit order, called a council of Church leaders **(b)** carried out council's decrees, drew up *Index of Forbidden Books*
3. Pope's word was final; good works as well as faith were necessary for salvation, the Bible and the Church were equal authorities for Christian conduct; indulgences, pilgrimages, veneration of holy relics were acceptable religious practices.
4. led to religious division
5. (a) Counter-Reformation; Catholic Reformation
(b) Counter—suggests that it is a defensive movement with a goal of preventing Protestantism from spreading, Catholic—stresses the desire of Catholics to end abuses and purify their own religion. **(c)** Writings of historians reflect their prejudices.

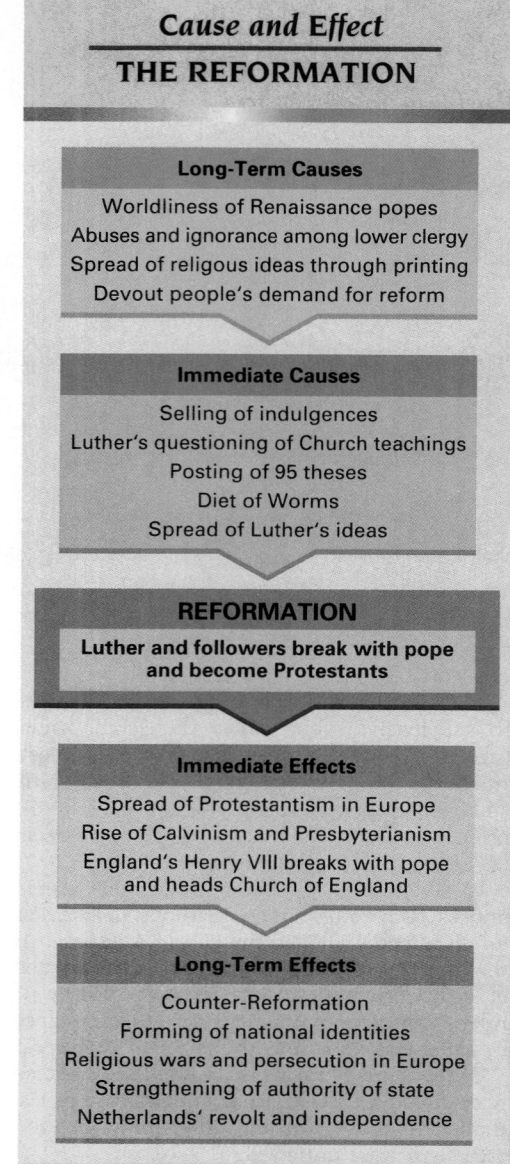

Cause and Effect
THE REFORMATION

Long-Term Causes

Worldliness of Renaissance popes
Abuses and ignorance among lower clergy
Spread of religous ideas through printing
Devout people's demand for reform

Immediate Causes

Selling of indulgences
Luther's questioning of Church teachings
Posting of 95 theses
Diet of Worms
Spread of Luther's ideas

REFORMATION
Luther and followers break with pope and become Protestants

Immediate Effects

Spread of Protestantism in Europe
Rise of Calvinism and Presbyterianism
England's Henry VIII breaks with pope and heads Church of England

Long-Term Effects

Counter-Reformation
Forming of national identities
Religious wars and persecution in Europe
Strengthening of authority of state
Netherlands' revolt and independence

institutions. However, the forces of historical change were too powerful for him to stop.

Charles was sick of troubles. He was eager to give up his crown, which had brought him little but grief. To his son, Philip II, he gave Spain,

parts of Italy, the Netherlands, and Spain's holdings in the Americas. He turned over the Holy Roman Empire to his brother, Ferdinand. Then Charles V, once ruler of the largest empire in the world, retired to a monastery in Spain. He died there in 1558.

Section REVIEW 3

Define: Counter-Reformation
Identify: (a) Ignatius Loyola, (b) Society of Jesus, (c) Council of Trent, (d) Index of Forbidden Books, (e) Peace of Augsburg
Answer:
1. (a) Who were the Jesuits? (b) What were their goals and achievements?
2. How did each of these popes strengthen the Catholic Church? (a) Paul III (b) Paul IV
3. What conclusions did the Council of Trent reach?
4. How did the Peace of Augsburg affect the states of Germany?

Critical Thinking
5. (a) What are the two names for this period of reform in the Catholic Church? (b) How do these two names show different attitudes on the part of historians? (c) Why might such differences arise?

Scientists challenged old assumptions. 4

Protestant leaders such as Luther and Calvin challenged accepted ways of thinking about God, salvation, and the soul. As you have seen, their ideas ignited a revolution in religious thought known as the Reformation. While the Reformation was taking place, another revolution in European thought was also occurring. It started when a small group of scholars began to question accepted ideas about Earth and the universe.

Before 1500, scholars generally decided what was true or false by quoting an ancient Greek or Roman author. Whatever Aristotle said about the material world was true unless the Bible said otherwise. Few European scholars tested Aristotle's ideas by looking at nature for themselves.

Beginning in the mid-1500's, however, a few scholars published works challenging the ideas of the ancient thinkers. As these scholars replaced old assumptions with new theories, they launched a profound change in European thought that historians call the Scientific Revolution. As you will see in this section, the Scientific Revolution was a way of thinking about the natural world based upon careful observation and a willingness to question accepted beliefs.

Copernicus and Kepler studied the universe.

During the Middle Ages, people believed that the earth was an unmoving object located at the center of the universe. According to that belief, the moon, Mercury, Venus, the sun, Mars, Jupiter, and Saturn all moved in a perfectly circular path around the earth. Beyond Saturn lay a sphere of fixed stars, with Heaven still farther beyond. Common sense seemed to support this view, since the sun appeared to be moving around the Earth as it rose in the morning and set in the evening.

The medieval view of the universe was supported by more than just common sense. Both Aristotle and the Alexandrian astronomer Ptolemy had written arguments defending this **geocentric,** or earth-centered, **theory.** In addition, the Church taught that God had deliberately placed Earth at the center of the universe. Earth was thus a special place on which the great drama of life took place.

Copernicus Although backed by authority and common sense, the geocentric theory did not accurately explain the movements of the sun, moon, and planets. This problem troubled a Polish churchman and astronomer named Nicolaus Copernicus (koh-**PUHR**-nih-kuhs). After studying planetary movements for more than 30 years, Copernicus concluded that the sun and not the earth was the center of the universe.

When scholars urged Copernicus to publish his new **heliocentric,** or sun-centered, **theory,** he refused, claiming that he was not yet ready. In 1543, one of his assistants finally persuaded Copernicus to release his report. Copernicus received a copy of his book *On the Revolutions of the Heavenly Bodies* just before he died.

The heliocentric theory represented the first new view of the universe in almost 2,000 years.

By encouraging other scholars to rethink old assumptions, Copernicus helped stimulate the Scientific Revolution. His work, however, angered both Protestant and Catholic leaders. They realized that the heliocentric theory would remove human beings from their special place in the universe. The impact of Copernicus's book was so far-reaching that its title gave rise to the use of the word *revolution* as meaning a radical change.

Kepler's laws Copernicus's bold but controversial ideas were based on logic, not on direct observation. Direct observation, however, soon became another approach to the study of science. During the late 1500's, a Danish astronomer named Tycho Brahe carefully recorded the movements of each planet and several hundred stars. When Brahe died in 1601, his assistant Johannes Kepler continued the work.

After carefully studying Brahe's data, Kepler proposed three laws of planetary motion. The first stated that the planets revolve around the sun in elliptical orbits. This law refuted the old belief that the planets moved in perfect circles. Kepler's second law held that planets move more rapidly as their orbits approach the sun. His third law stated that the time taken by planets to orbit the sun varies proportionately with their distance from the sun.

Kepler's three laws of planetary motion proved that the heliocentric theory was actually true. His work also used a new approach to the study of science called the **scientific method.** The scientific method uses a logical procedure for gathering and testing ideas. The procedure begins with a problem or question arising from an observation. Scientists next form a hypothesis, or unproven assumption. The hypothesis is then tested in an experiment or on the basis of data. In the final step, scientists analyze and interpret their data to reach a new conclusion confirming the hypothesis. As you will see, the scientific method provided a powerful tool for developing and applying knowledge.

Galileo analyzed the natural world.

In 1581, a seventeen-year-old medical student named Galileo Galilei (1564–1642) closely watched the movement of a cathedral's chandelier as it swung back and forth on its chain. Aristotle

387

SECTION 4 Objectives and Teaching Strategies

OBJECTIVE 1. Explain why the ideas of Copernicus and Galileo threatened the Church.

Teaching Strategy: *Discussing History: Copernicus and Galileo* (page 372d)

OBJECTIVE 2. Explain the scientific method and describe scientific achievements of the sixteenth and seventeenth centuries.

Teaching Strategy: *Skill Building: Making Inferences* (page 372e)

■ DISCUSSION

Luther on Copernicus: "The fool will overturn the whole art of astronomy. But as Holy Writ declares, Joshua commanded the sun to stand still and not the earth." Does a literal interpretation of the Bible conflict with scientific exploration?

SECTION 4 Resources

ASSESSMENT
■ Section Quiz 16.4

REINFORCEMENT
■ Independent Practice 16.4

ENRICHMENT
■ Voices from the Past 16.4

Cooperative Learning

Have groups of four students write letters to the great scientists of the period. Each group should choose a scientist from the following group: Nicolaus Copernicus, Johannes Kepler, Galileo Galilei, Andreas Vesalius, William Harvey, Zacharias Janssen, Gabriel Fahrenheit, and Evangelist Torricelli. One group member should write an introductory paragraph acknowledging the scientist's achievements. A second member should write a paragraph describing the immediate impact of the scientist's invention or discovery. The third student should bring the scientist up to date with developments in the field. The fourth group member should edit the letter and present it to the class.

ANSWERS TO
Section Review 4

Define:
(a) theory that Earth was the center of the universe
(b) theory that the sun was the center of the universe
(c) logical procedure for gathering and testing ideas

Identify:
(a) Polish scholar who theorized that Earth and other planets moved around the sun (b) Danish astronomer who recorded movements of planets and stars

(continued)

---

had said that a pendulum swings more slowly as it approaches its resting place. As he sat in the cathedral in Pisa, Galileo carefully tested Aristotle's idea and found it wrong. Feeling his pulse to keep time, he found that each swing of the pendulum took exactly the same amount of time, from the first sweep to the last.

Galileo had discovered the law of the pendulum. A short time later he designed a simple string pendulum that helped doctors take a patient's pulse. Galileo's curiosity about natural phenomena did not stop with this experiment. He soon gave up medicine to study mathematics. In 1589, at the age of twenty-five, he became a professor of mathematics at the University of Pisa.

While in Pisa, Galileo continued to study motion. For days, he patiently rolled balls down a slope and measured the speed at which they moved. His data led him to conclude that a falling object accelerates at a fixed and predictable rate. Galileo also tested Aristotle's theory that heavy objects fall faster than lighter ones. According to legend, he is said to have dropped stones of different weights from the Leaning Tower of Pisa. Contrary to what Aristotle had predicted, the objects fell at the same speed.

A *new vision* Later, at the University of Padua near Venice, Galileo continued his study of motion. He learned that a Dutch lens maker had built an instrument that could enlarge far-off objects. Without seeing this device, Galileo successfully built a telescope. He then astonished Venetian officials by demonstrating that a person using his telescope could see ships 50 miles away. The grateful Venetians promptly doubled Galileo's salary.

Instead of being content with his achievement, Galileo continued to build new and more powerful telescopes. Soon he had an instrument that made objects appear 30 times nearer and 1,000 times larger. Galileo began to use it to study the heavens in late 1609. Within a few months, he published a little book called *Starry Messenger*, describing his astonishing observations. Galileo announced that Jupiter had four moons, that the sun had dark spots, and that the moon had a rough and uneven surface.

As news of Galileo's discoveries swept across Europe, they created a sensation. His description of the moon's surface shattered Aristotle's theory that the earth was made of impure material,

388

Galileo used this telescope to observe the moon. His drawings showed that the moon's surface is rough, not smooth as others thought.

while the moon and stars were made of a pure, eternal substance that was smooth and perfect. Galileo's findings clearly supported the heliocentric theory. They also underscored the idea that the same physical laws operated throughout the universe. The laws of motion were thus the same in Venice as they were on the moon. A modern historian pointed out that Galileo "had found the key that was eventually to unlock the riddle of the universe."

Conflict with the Church New ideas are often treated at first with deep suspicion. Galileo's findings frightened both Catholic and Protestant leaders. In 1616, the Catholic Church banned Copernicus's ideas. Leading officials also warned Galileo to give up his new theories.

Although Galileo remained publicly silent, he continued his studies. Then, in 1632, he published a book presenting the ideas of both Copernicus and Ptolemy. Although he claimed to be neutral, Church officials saw clearly that he had given the strongest arguments to the Copernican theory.

The pope angrily accused Galileo of meddling "with the most important and dangerous subjects which can be stirred up in these days." Jesuit leaders charged that Galileo's ideas threatened to do the Church more harm "than Luther and Calvin put together." In 1633, the pope summoned Galileo to Rome to stand trial.

Under the threat of torture, Galileo knelt before the cardinals and read aloud a signed confession. In it, he called the ideas of Copernicus a false opinion. He said, "I abjure, curse, and detest the aforesaid errors and heresies." Galileo was never again a free man. He was allowed to return to his home near Florence, but he was kept under house arrest until he died in 1642. Nevertheless, the revolution in scientific thinking that Galileo helped to start could not be stopped.

Vesalius and Harvey studied the human body.

While astronomers used the scientific method to study the stars, other pioneering scientists asked questions about the human body. How, they wondered, was the human body put together? What were the functions of its various muscles, nerves, bones, and tissues?

During the Middle Ages, European doctors had accepted the answers of an ancient Greek physician named Galen. But Galen (A.D. 130–200) had never dissected the body of a human being. Instead, he had studied the anatomy of sheep, pigs, goats, and apes. Galen simply assumed that human anatomy was much the same.

Vesalius Galen's textbooks on medicine were generally unchallenged until 1543, the same year that Copernicus published his revolutionary book on astronomy. In that year, a Flemish doctor named Andreas Vesalius published a medical book called *On the Fabric of the Human Body*. It was illustrated with many beautiful drawings showing human muscles, bones, and organs in great detail. Both the text and drawings demonstrated that human anatomy was often distinctly different from animal anatomy.

Harvey The next major advance in biology was made by an English doctor named William Harvey. In a book published in 1628, he showed that the heart acted as a pump to circulate blood throughout the body. Galen's theory that blood came out of the liver was proved false.

Scientists used precise tools.

During the Scientific Revolution, scholars developed ways to make precise, reliable observations. Galileo's telescope was only one of the important instruments that aided science during the early 1600's. Other scientists and artisans developed more such tools.

Microscope The first microscope was invented by a Dutch maker of eyeglasses, Zacharias Janssen (YAHN-sen) in 1590. In the 1650's, Anton van Leeuwenhoek (LAY-vuhn-HOOK) used a microscope to observe bacteria swimming in his own saliva. He also described red blood cells.

Thermometer The first thermometer, made by Galileo in 1603, used alcohol. A German physicist named Gabriel Fahrenheit (FAHR-uhn-hyte) made a thermometer using mercury. Fahrenheit's thermometer showed water freezing at 32° and boiling at 212°. A Swedish astronomer, Anders Celsius (SEL-see-uhs), created another scale for the mercury thermometer. Celsius's scale showed freezing at 0° and boiling at 100°.

Barometer One of Galileo's students developed the first mercury barometer, a tool for measuring atmospheric pressure and predicting weather. Evangelista Torricelli (TOR-uh-CHEL-ee) made this advance in 1655.

Section REVIEW 4

Define: (a) geocentric theory, (b) heliocentric theory, (c) scientific method

Identify: (a) Copernicus, (b) Brahe, (c) Kepler, (d) *Starry Messenger*, (e) Vesalius, (f) Harvey, (g) Leeuwenhoek, (h) Fahrenheit, (i) Celsius, (j) Torricelli

Answer:

1. (a) According to Ptolemy, what was Earth's position in the universe? (b) How did Copernicus's view differ? (c) Which theory did Kepler's observations support?
2. What are four steps in the scientific method?
3. Why was Galileo's discovery that the moon had a rough and uneven surface important?
4. (a) How did Galileo answer the Church's anger? (b) What was the result?
5. (a) List four new instruments that came into use during the Scientific Revolution. (b) Identify the purpose of each one.

Critical Thinking

6. (a) Compare and contrast Luther's stand at the Diet of Worms with Galileo's behavior at his trial. (b) Why did Luther refuse to recant his views, while Galileo did recant his?

389

ANSWERS TO (continued)

(c) astronomer who confirmed Copernicus' ideas of planetary motion (d) book by Galileo describing his astronomical findings (e) Flemish doctor who studied human anatomy (f) English doctor who studied the circulation of human blood (g) used a microscope to observe bacteria (h) German physicist who created first mercury thermometer (i) Swedish astronomer who created another scale for the mercury thermometer (j) developed the first mercury barometer

Answer:

1. (a) center (b) Earth revolved around the sun (c) Copernicus' theory

2. Step 1. choose a problem; Step 2. form a hypothesis; Step 3. test hypothesis with an experiment; Step 4. analyze results and reach a conclusion

3. showed that the moon was not made of a pure, eternal substance

4. (a) by writing a book that appeared to support Copernican theory (b) He was forced to recant and was kept under house arrest until his death.

5. (a) telescope, microscope, thermometer, barometer (b) to enlarge far-off objects; to enlarge minute objects; to measure temperatures; to measure atmospheric pressure

6. (a) Luther defended his views, while Galileo offered no defense of his views. (b) Answers will vary. Students may suggest that since Luther's views were a matter of faith, he could not recant, while Galileo did recant in hopes of continuing his scientific studies.

Concluding the Chapter

1. **Chapter Closer**
   Ask students to choose two events described in this chapter that they think had the greatest impact on European history. Students should give evidence to support their choices.

2. **Reteaching Activities**
   a. Summarizing Ask students to summarize the teachings of Luther and Calvin.
   b. Outlining Have students use the headings in Section 1 to write a sentence outline.

Answers to Chapter Review appear on pages 372e–372f.

Summary

1. Martin Luther began a religious revolt. The early 1500's brought two kinds of revolution—one in religion, the other in science. The Protestant Reformation, which split Europe into Catholic and Protestant states, began with Martin Luther's criticism of the selling of indulgences. Luther was later excommunicated and outlawed for teaching ideas that conflicted with Church doctrine. He gained the support of many Germans, however, and the new technology of the printing press spread his ideas throughout Europe.

2. Protestantism spread in northern Europe. Several countries turned to Protestantism. Henry VIII of England broke with the Catholic Church when the pope would not set aside his first marriage. John Calvin set forth a systematic Protestant theology based on the doctrine of predestination. One of his followers, John Knox, led a revolt that made Calvinism the official religion of Scotland.

3. The Catholic Church made reforms. At the same time, the Catholic Church experienced reforms. Ignatius of Loyola formed the Society of Jesus to serve the pope. Pope Paul III called the Council of Trent, which reaffirmed Church doctrine. Paul IV enforced the new decrees and drew up a list of books believed dangerous to the Catholic faith.

4. Scientists challenged old assumptions. In the Scientific Revolution, scientists broke with the ancient teachings of Ptolemy. Knowledge of the universe increased. Copernicus proclaimed that Earth moved around the sun. The observations of Kepler and Galileo supported his theory.

Reviewing the Facts

1. Define the following terms:
   a. theocracy   b. geocentric theory
2. Explain the importance of each of the following names, places, or terms:

   a. Savonarola
   b. Erasmus
   c. More
   d. *Utopia*
   e. Gutenberg
   f. Dürer
   g. Luther
   h. Charles V
   i. Diet of Worms
   j. Henry VIII
   k. Catherine of Aragon
   l. Reformation Parliament
   m. Mary Tudor
   n. Calvin
   o. elect
   p. Geneva
   q. Knox
   r. Ignatius Loyola
   s. *Index of Forbidden Books*
   t. Peace of Augsburg
   u. Copernicus
   v. Kepler
   w. Galileo
   x. Vesalius
   y. Harvey

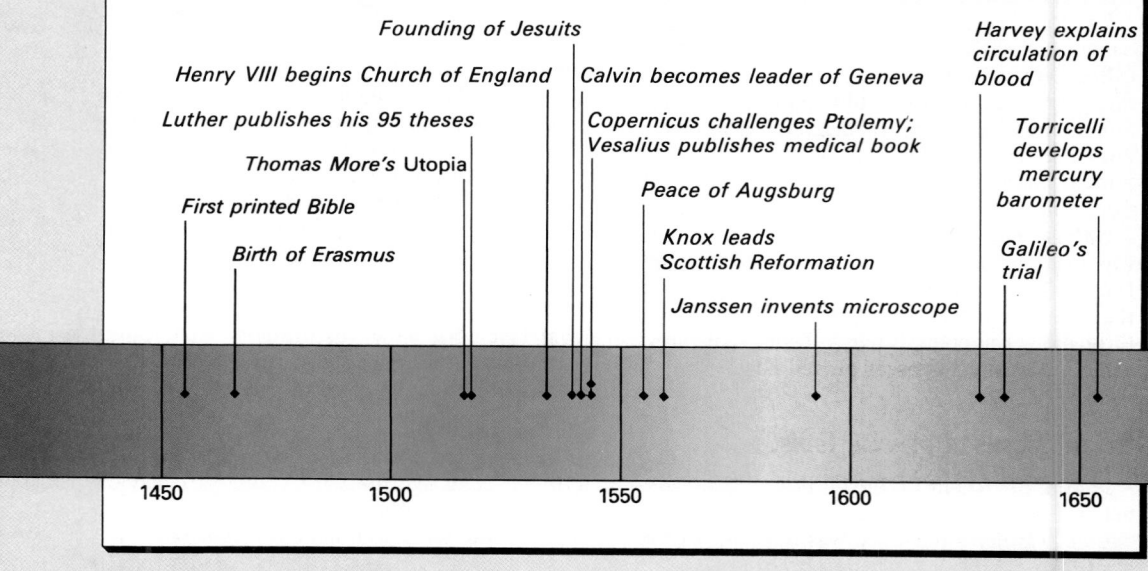

Founding of Jesuits

Henry VIII begins Church of England

Luther publishes his 95 theses

Thomas More's *Utopia*

First printed Bible

Birth of Erasmus

Calvin becomes leader of Geneva

Copernicus challenges Ptolemy; Vesalius publishes medical book

Peace of Augsburg

Knox leads Scottish Reformation

Janssen invents microscope

Harvey explains circulation of blood

Torricelli develops mercury barometer

Galileo's trial

1450   1500   1550   1600   1650

390

3. (a) What was the peasant revolt of 1524? (b) What were its results?
4. (a) How did Henry VIII strengthen Protestantism in England through the Act of Supremacy? (b) By his policy toward monasteries? (c) How did the religious outlooks of his children vary?
5. (a) What was Calvin's view on salvation? (b) How did Calvinism become established in Scotland in the 1500's?

Basic Skills

1. **Interpreting maps** Use the maps on pages 378 and 383 to answer the following questions: (a) What religious groups did Charles V have to contend with in the Holy Roman Empire? (b) What countries were the main centers of Calvinism, Lutheranism, and Catholicism in the 1500's?
2. **Sequencing** List the following events, together with their dates, in chronological order: Savanarola holds power in Florence, *In Praise of Folly,* Luther's 95 theses, *Utopia,* Edict of Worms, Act of Supremacy, Peace of Augsburg, *Index of Forbidden Books.*
3. **Making a comparison chart** Make a chart comparing Luther and Calvin. For the vertical column, use the following headings: Role in Reformation, Ideas about Religion, Political Ideas, and Writings.

Researching and Reporting Skills

1. **Having a roundtable discussion** Historians differ in their interpretation of the relation between the Renaissance and the Reformation. Some historians think the Reformation was a reaction against the Renaissance. Others think it was the result of the humanistic thinking of the Renaissance. Have a roundtable discussion to decide which thesis is more valid, based on the evidence.
2. **Writing a pamphlet** Imagine that Ignatius Loyola asked you to write a pamphlet to recruit people into the Society of Jesus. How would you present this organization and its goals so as to persuade people to join this spiritual army?

Critical Thinking

1. **Analyzing causes** (a) Identify the major causes of the Reformation. (b) Which were immediate causes and which were remote causes?
2. **Identifying arguments** (a) List the practices and beliefs of the Catholic Church that Luther opposed. (b) What argument did Luther use against each of them?
3. **Identifying issues** Identify and explain briefly the religious issues addressed (a) by the Council of Trent and (b) by the Peace of Augsburg.
4. **Analyzing economics** The Reformation was a religious movement, but its success in different countries was influenced by economic factors. (a) Identify three economic changes related to the Reformation. (b) How did those changes affect the establishment of Protestantism?
5. **Applying a concept** In the late 1500's, scientific thought underwent a revolution. (a) What old ideas and beliefs were challenged? (b) What new ideas and beliefs emerged to replace the old? (c) What impact did this change have on society?
6. **Relating** The Reformation and the Scientific Revolution occurred at the same time in Europe. (a) To what extent were they related and how? (b) Which had the greater impact on the lives of most Europeans in the seventeenth century? Give reasons for your answers.

Perspectives on Past and Present

1. The text suggests that the impact of printing in the 1500's was comparable to the modern-day invention of television and the computer combined. Evaluate this comparison, giving your own opinion about it.
2. The text on page 389 describes advances in technology that helped to make the Scientific Revolution possible. What is the state of each of these inventions today? That is, how has modern technology improved upon the original inventions?

Investigating History

For refusing to obey one of the Reformation laws of Henry VIII, Thomas More was executed. Read the award-winning play *A Man for All Seasons,* by Robert Bolt, or watch a videotape of the movie, which dramatizes More's defiance of his former friend, the king.

391

CHAPTER
Evaluation

Chapter Test 16, Alternate Chapter Test 16, and Computer Test Bank Chapter 16 Test can be used to evaluate your students' understanding of this chapter.

The Spanish Empire and Shifts in European Power

Chapter **17**

Chapter Overview

The 1500's and 1600's saw a major power struggle in Europe. Spain gained an enormous empire in the Americas. In 1581, the northern part of the Netherlands won independence from Spain. The Dutch developed a capitalist economic system and soon replaced the Italians as bankers.

During Germany's Thirty Years' War, in which Protestants fought Catholics, France entered on the side of the Protestants. When the war ended, Germany's political unity was destroyed, and its economy was in shambles. France was the strongest state in Europe.

The 1500's and 1600's were also a time of creativity. The paintings of El Greco and Velázquez in Spain and those of Rembrandt and Hals in Amsterdam reflected the values of their times. In France, the writings of Rabelais, Montaigne, and Descartes marked a sharp break with the ideas of the Middle Ages.

Chapter Focus

Understanding how different cultures interact is a part of studying the past. Cultural differences are potential sources of conflict. Note that many present-day conflicts center on divergent beliefs about economics and religion. The Spanish voyages of exploration became voyages of conquest. The wealth that flowed to Spain as a result of the conquests in the Americas enabled Spain to pursue its religious and political goals.

Spain built an overseas empire.

1

Setting the Stage

In 1545 the Spanish discovered rich gold and silver mines in Mexico and Peru. The precious metals were transported to Spain once a year in large convoys protected by warships. Spain relied on these shipments to maintain its vast empire and to finance the religious wars of Philip II.

Despite the Spaniards' disregard for the rights of Native Americans, many regarded the Aztec and Inca civilizations as highly advanced. They expressed astonishment that a non-Christian empire could be so well organized.

Teaching Strategies

Writing about History: Montezuma and Cortés (Objective 1) *Prewriting* Cortés was thirty-four years old when he met the forty-year-old Montezuma. Cortés was ambitious and determined to bring gold and glory to Spain and to himself. Equally ambitious, Montezuma had ruled a large empire successfully for 17 years, though he had been troubled by bad omens. *Writing* Divide the class into pairs. Have one student in each pair portray Montezuma, and the other, Cortés. Direct students to write from the point of view of Montezuma or Cortés, as follows: Montezuma's Diary—journal entries, interpreting the unfolding events of Spanish contact; Cortés's Letter—a letter from Cortés to

Advance Planner

	SECTION 1
Objectives	1. Contrast the Spanish and Aztec cultures. 2. Identify Spanish motivations for conquests in the Americas.
Setting the Stage	Spain's need for Indian wealth and labor
Teaching Strategies	Writing about History: Montezuma and Cortés Transferring Ideas: Crusading Conquistadors Check for Understanding
Guided Practice	Transparency 62 Q&A Section Review 1
Independent Practice Worksheets	Independent Practice 17.1 Basic Skills 17 Geography Skills 17 Vocabulary 17
Enrichment	1. Primary Source: Voices 17.1 2. ★Analyzing a Quotation: Cortés 3. Researching for Points
Chapter Closer	
Unit V Review	

Chapter 17 The Spanish Empire and Shifts in European Power 1500–1650
FOCUS The consequences of the meeting between Cortés

★ Advanced
● Basic

SECTION 2	SECTION 3	SECTION 4	SECTION 5
1. Explain why Cervantes's work is regarded as the first modern European novel. 2. Identify reasons for Spain's economic decline after 1600.	1. Contrast the economies of Spain and the Netherlands. 2. Describe elements of Rembrandt's art.	1. Explain the methods of Henry IV in uniting France and strengthening the monarchy. 2. Describe the political views and tactics of Cardinal Richelieu.	1. Identify the causes of the Thirty Years' War. 2. Explain how the provisions of the Treaty of Westphalia affected the nations of Europe.
Spain's economic decline	The importance of a leader's ability to communicate	Effects of religion and politics on nation-building	Discussing History: Causes of the Thirty Years' War
Skill Building: Analyzing a Quotation Economics and History: Inflation Check for Understanding	Economics and History: Capitalism Teaching with Pictures: *The Night Watch* Check for Understanding	Writing about History: Henry IV Discussing History: Cardinal Richelieu Check for Understanding	Skill Building: Recognizing Main Ideas Check for Understanding
Section Review 2 Independent Practice 17.2 Critical Thinking 17	Section Review 3 Independent Practice 17.3	Section Review 4 Independent Practice 17.4	Section Review 5 Independent Practice 17.5
1. Primary Source: Voices 17.2 2. ★Creative Writing 3. Researching for Points	1. Primary Source: Voices 17.3 2. Creative Writing 3. Researching for Points	1. Primary Source: Voices 17.4 2. ★Analyzing a Quotation: Descartes 3. Researching for Points	1. Primary Source: Voices 17.5 2. Preparing a Time Line 3. Researching for Points

●**Reteaching Activities**   Summarizing, Identifying Main Ideas, Recalling Information

Chapter Review   Summary, Reviewing the Facts, Basic Skills, Researching and Reporting Skills, Critical Thinking, Perspectives on Past and Present, Investigating History

Chapter Evaluation   Chapter Test 17, Alternate Chapter Test 17, Computer Test Bank Chapter 17 Test

Geographic Theme   Movement: How did European civilizations spread around the globe?

Historical Themes   Understanding History (Classifying, Identifying, Relating), Critical Thinking, Making Decisions, Continuity and Change

Unit Evaluation   Unit V Test, Alternate Unit V Test

Charles V. Conclude by having students read their journal entries and letters. What differences between Aztec and Spanish cultures do the writings reveal?

Transferring Ideas: Crusading Conquistadors (Objective 2) Spanish expeditions included priests whose job was to convert the Native Americans to Catholicism. The conquistadors were motivated by an intense Catholic faith as well as a desire for treasure. How was the Spaniards' belief in the superiority of Christianity demonstrated in their attitudes toward the Aztec and the Inca?

Check for Understanding Call on students to identify the main economic and cultural effects of the Spanish conquests on the following: conquistadors, Native Americans, Spanish government.

Enrichment Activities

1. **Reading a Primary Source** Assign Voices from the Past Resource Book 17.1.
2. **Analyzing a Quotation** Hernando Cortés wrote to Charles V: "It seems most credible that our Lord God has purposefully allowed these lands [Mexico] to be discovered . . . so that Your Majesties may be fruitful and deserving in His sight by causing these barbaric tribes to be enlightened and brought to the faith by Your Hand." Have advanced students analyze this quotation and explain its significance for understanding the Spanish conquests in the Americas.
3. **Researching for Bonus Points** Who discovered the lost Inca city of Machu Picchu in 1911? (Hiram Bingham)

Spain was a Catholic bulwark. 2

Setting the Stage

Review the definition of *empire* and the problems faced by rulers of the Roman and Byzantine empires. What makes ruling a large empire difficult? List students' responses on the board. Select a student to read the first paragraph of Section 2 (page 398). Then tell students that 50 years later, Spain was nearly bankrupt. Ask students to predict how a country with access to unlimited wealth could go bankrupt.

Teaching Strategies

Skill Building: Analyzing a Quotation (Objective 1) Read and discuss the excerpt from *Don Quixote* (page 401). Ask students why many critics regard *Don Quixote* as the first "modern" European novel. (It is a satire of medieval values.) Define a *satire* as a literary work that pokes fun at or mocks the manners and morals of a society. Have students find information in the text supporting the idea that Cervantes satirized the manners and morals of the Middle Ages. Conclude by asking students to speculate why *Don Quixote* is still widely read.

Economics and History: Inflation (Objective 2) Ask students to define *inflation* and to explain why it is an economic crisis. Point out that the conditions that ruined Spain's economy in the 1650's have caused economic problems in many countries throughout history. Inflation is a sharp and continuing rise in prices for goods and services. The rise in prices is caused by an oversupply of money in relation to the supply of goods. As a result, a given amount of money buys less than it did before. Ask students what caused Spain's inflation in the 1650's. (an oversupply

of silver and gold from Spain's American colonies)

Check for Understanding Have students list three reasons for Spain's rise to power and three reasons for Spain's economic decline.

Enrichment Activities

1. **Reading a Primary Source** Assign Voices from the Past Resource Book 17.2.
2. **Creative Writing** Have advanced students read excerpts from *Don Quixote* and write essays relating episodes from the novel to the present day. Share students' work with the class.
3. **Researching for Bonus Points** To what saint is the Escorial dedicated? (Saint Lawrence)

The Netherlands won independence. 3

Setting the Stage

Discuss the importance of communication and rapport between a leader and his or her country. The Spanish king Philip II did not share the same language, religion, political values, or economic policies as his Dutch subjects. The Netherlands had embraced new Renaissance and Reformation ideas, while Spain clung to medieval traditions. Ask students to trace these differences as they read.

Teaching Strategies

Economics and History: Capitalism (Objective 1) Have students compare the economies of Spain and the Netherlands. How was Dutch capitalism different from Spanish mercantilism? Spain's mercantilism depended on wealth from the American colonies. Define *capitalism* as the buying and selling of goods and services through the use of money and for the purpose of making a profit. How did the business class in Holland use trade and banking to earn profits? Have students write paragraphs summarizing how the Dutch East Indies Company practiced capitalism.

Teaching with Pictures: *The Night Watch* (Objective 2) The group portrait was a Dutch innovation and was perfected by Dutch and Flemish artists. Direct students' attention to the picture of Rembrandt's *The Night Watch* (page 405). This painting was commissioned by a military captain and 17 of his guardsmen. Each of the guardsmen paid an equal amount of money for the painting. Why might some guardsmen have felt slighted? Rembrandt is renowned for his ability to combine light, shadow, color, and movement. How does this picture utilize these four elements? Have students suggest how the painting portrays liveliness and motion.

Check for Understanding Ask students to explain the economic and religious differences between Spain and the Netherlands, and how these differences led to Dutch independence.

Enrichment Activities

1. **Reading a Primary Source**
Assign Voices from the Past Resource Book 17.3.

2. **Creative Writing**
Have students imagine they are journalists during the Dutch revolt. Have them write news accounts of the measures the Dutch took to drive out the Spanish.

3. **Researching for Bonus Points**
What was the formal name of Rembrandt's painting, *The Night Watch*? (The company of Captain Frans Banning Cocq and Lieutenant Willem van Ruytenburch)

France's crown changed hands. 4

Setting the Stage

Why do students think the framers of the United States Constitution separated religion from government? Why might religious struggles be more harmful to a country than strictly political conflicts? Do students think compromise is an effective tactic in solving religious disputes?

Teaching Strategies

Writing about History: Henry IV (Objective 1) *Prewriting* Ask students why Henry IV decided to become Catholic. Note that Henry needed the support of France's Catholic majority. He also knew that to rule France successfully he would need the support of the Huguenots. Henry solved his dilemma through compromise. The Edict of Nantes marked the first official recognition of the idea that two religions can co-exist in the same nation. *Writing* Have students write short essays contrasting the policies of Henry IV of France with those of Philip II of Spain in resolving religious conflicts and strengthening their monarchies.

Discussing History: Cardinal Richelieu (Objective 2) Have students recall Machiavelli's political ideas (page 353). According to Machiavelli, what qualities did a political leader need to be successful? Richelieu's political career reflected his belief in the Machiavellian principles of winning and maintaining power. Critics and admirers alike acknowledged that Richelieu was an outstanding statesman. Have students explain the significance of Richelieu's actions at La Rochelle (page 409).

Check for Understanding Have students explain the roles of the following people in the unification of France: Huguenots, Catherine de Medici, Henry IV, and Cardinal Richelieu.

Enrichment Activities

1. **Reading a Primary Source**
Assign Voices from the Past Resource Book 17.4.

2. **Analyzing a Quotation**
Have advanced students explain Descartes's claim, "I think, therefore I am." How did Descartes's philosophy reflect his faith in science and reason?

3. **Researching for Bonus Points**
Who was the founder of the French Academy? (Richelieu)

Religious wars split Germany. 5

Setting the Stage

Discussing History: Causes of the Thirty Years' War (Objective 1) Ask students to recall why the Peace of Augsburg was partly a failure for Charles V (page 385). The Thirty Years' War was a result of Charles's inability to unite his kingdom and to relieve tension between Protestant and Catholic princes. Religious disputes in the Holy Roman Empire were compounded by the intervention of France and Spain, and the war left the Holy Roman Empire weak and destitute.

Teaching Strategies

Skill Building: Recognizing Main Ideas (Objective 2) Peace negotiations for the Thirty Years' War were difficult and acrimonious. For example, Protestant Swedish delegates refused to sit in the same room with Papal representatives. Papal delegates refused to sit with the "heretics," and Pope Innocent X refused to sign the treaty. Furthermore, the French ambassador refused to negotiate unless he was addressed as "your highness." Have students list the major provisions of the Treaty of Westphalia. Ask why France was the "winner" of the Thirty Years' War. How did the treaty weaken the Hapsburgs? How was Sweden rewarded in the treaty? Why were Spain and Rome unhappy with the treaty? Did the Treaty of Westphalia solve religious disputes in the Holy Roman Empire?

Check for Understanding Ask students to explain how the Treaty of Westphalia attempted to resolve the political and religious conflicts that had caused the Thirty Years' War.

Enrichment Activities

1. **Reading a Primary Source** Assign Voices from the Past Resource Book 17.5.
2. **Preparing a Time Line** Have students prepare a time line covering events that took place in the Holy Roman Empire between 1618 and 1648.
3. **Researching for Bonus Points** What were Gustavus Adolphus's last words? ("I am the King of Sweden, who do seal the religion and liberty of the German nation with my blood.")

ANSWERS TO
Chapter Review 17

Reviewing the Facts
1. **(a)** Spanish fortune hunter **(b)** Spanish noble who acted as royal agent in Americas **(c)** privilege granted to settlers to become master of a particular area **(d)** economic system the goal of which is to make enough money to pay all the costs of a business venture plus profit

2. **(a)** Spanish conquistador who conquered the Aztec empire in Mexico **(b)** Spanish adventurer who conquered the Incas in Peru **(c)** privilege granted to certain settlers to become master of a particular area **(d)** king of Spain from 1556 to 1598 who built an empire that circled the globe **(e)** Greek seaport where, in 1571, Christendom triumphed over Muslim Ottoman Turks **(f)** fleet assembled by Philip II in attempt to defeat Protestant England **(g)** Spanish writer, author of *Don Quixote de la Man-* cha, the first modern European novel **(h)** Greek artist whose major works were painted in Spain **(i)** Dutch leader of revolt against Spain who hated foreigners ruling his country **(j)** greatest Dutch painter of the 1600's **(k)** French follower of Calvinism **(l)** power behind the throne of Catholic rulers of France, wife of Henry II **(m)** French Catholic leader who worked for peace, a strong monarchy, and religious toleration **(n)** first Bourbon king; brought peace and religious tolerance to France **(o)** declaration of religious tolerance **(p)** Catholic cardinal and virtual ruler of France during reign of Louis XIII **(q)** French government agent who collected taxes and administered justice **(r)** French monk, author of satires *Gargantua* and *Pantagruel* **(s)** French thinker who used a new form of literature, the essay, to write his thoughts **(t)** French mathematician and founder of modern philosophy **(u)** dates of the Thirty Years' War **(v)** royal German family **(w)** treaty that ended the Thirty Years' War

3. **(a)** defeat of the Ottoman navy, triumph of Christendom over Muslims **(b)** defeated by skilled English sea captains **(c)** Dutch revolt and declaration of seven provinces as independent from Spain

4. **(a)** capitalistic approach to trade and business and other economic changes of the late 1500's to 1600's

5. **(a)** In 1618, Ferdinand II sent an army into Bohemia to put down a Protestant revolt. Several German Protestant princes took this chance to challenge their Catholic emperor. **(b)** It left Germany ravaged and led to the decline of Hapsburg Spain and Austria.

Basic Skills
1. **(a)** silver $622.8 million; gold $291.8 million **(b)** costly wars against Netherlands in revolt, against England (the Armada);

costly imports of needed manufactured goods

2. (a) Value of gold dropped, prices went up. **(b)** Because Spain was heavily dependent on imports, gold and silver flooded Europe, and their value fell. Spain continued to import goods rather than developing its own industries; inflation raised prices for goods Spain needed.

3. (a) parts of Indonesia; Ceylon; southwest tip of Africa near Capetown **(b)** Indonesia gave them access to the spice trade; Capetown was an important stopping point on the trade route to India and the East Indies.

Researching and Reporting Skills

1. Editorials will vary. English editorial should reflect pride in English victory and skill of English seamen, together with admiration for Drake and relief that the Netherlands, England's ally, was saved from a Spanish invasion. A Spanish editorial should reflect dismay at loss of Spanish fleet, anger at England and the Netherlands, and sorrow for the loss of Spanish ships and sailors.

2. Cortés probably aroused his men's enthusiasm for conquest by promises of riches to be gained, opportunities to become landowners, and the chance to share in the new Spanish empire they would help to create.

Critical Thinking

1. (a) Philip II of Spain used wealth from Spain's colonies to build up his army and navy and to strengthen Catholicism and weaken Protestantism wherever possible—for example, in the Netherlands. Henry IV established religious toleration in France and sought to build up France's economy. **(b)** Philip II did not succeed: his Armada was destroyed and the

Netherlands remained Protestant. Henry IV did succeed: France became prosperous, and religious toleration contributed to peace within France. **(c)** Philip left a legacy of a nation in debt and an economy weakened by lack of investment in industry and trade. Henry left a legacy of a strong and prosperous nation.

2. (a) Although Spaniards claimed they were conquering new lands for Christendom, the true motive was acquiring gold and other wealth. **(b)** The description is accurate. Spaniards showed no concern for teaching Christian values, love, or human respect for the conquered. They exploited the conquered people without mercy and caused the destruction of their civilization.

3. (a) One hypothesis might deal with location, another with centralized government, and a third with competition with the Italian city-states. **(b)** For location, both Spain and Portugal have coasts and seaports on the Atlantic; therefore, it was natural for them to venture out on that ocean for exploration and trade. Both countries became unified nation-states relatively early and could organize their resources to support exploration and trade. Because the Italian city-states had a monopoly of trade with the eastern Mediterranean, Spain and Portugal were excluded and therefore sought other routes to the source of goods from the East.

4. (a) Capitalism was based on the idea of investing money for profit. This profit could be income from capital invested or interest on money lent over a period of time. **(b)** Medieval church was opposed to charging more than a "just price," thus prohibiting profit. It also opposed the idea that money could produce wealth; this was considered usury.

5. (a) *Causes:* The German princes electors were divided into two opposing groups, the Protestant's Union and the Catholic League. In 1618, a riot in Prague touched off a war between the two groups. Also, the Protestant Czechs hated their king, who was Austrian and Catholic. *Outcomes:* The war caused great destruction of property and loss of life in Germany. The war ended in defeat for the Hapsburgs. **(b)** Answers will vary, but the war actually changed little in terms of religious questions involved; therefore, it was relatively futile. **(c)** *Old problems solved:* German princes almost independent of Holy Roman Empire, Calvinism was recognized, and the independence of the Netherlands was recognized. *New problems created:* France obtained Alsace, and Sweden gained lands in northern Germany. France emerged as Europe's strongest nation.

Perspectives on Past and Present

1. (a) The treachery by which the Spanish defeated the Aztecs and Incas was accepted; so was enslavement of the Native Americans through the system of encomiendas which was approved by Spain. The Native Americans were despised as heathens and treated as less than human **(b)** would be considered violations of human rights and officially condemned

2. Centralizing of authority led to powerful monarchy; questioning led to a political and religious minority resisting royal power. Examples will vary.

Investigating History

Students' answers will vary.

The Spanish Empire and Shifts in European Power

1500 - 1650

Teaching with Pictures

Ask students to read the chapter opener on pages 392–393 to become familiar with Cortés and the Spanish invasion of Mexico in 1519. Then have them study the painting of Cortés's meeting with Montezuma and describe what is going on, how Montezuma is being treated by his people, and how the Indians and Spaniards are dressed. Point out to students that Mexico City was established on the site of Tenochtitlán.

■ BACKGROUND

In Nahua, the language of the Aztec's forebears, Quetzalcoatl meant a combination of a bird and a snake (*quetzal*, a bird; *coatl*, a snake), or a feathered serpent.

In royal splendor, the Aztec ruler Montezuma greeted the Spanish explorer Cortés and his translator, Doña Marina. In Aztec tradition, the ruler's feet could not touch ground, and his subjects could not look directly at his face.

Key Terms

conquistador
viceroy
encomienda
capitalism
capital
profit
Commercial Revolution

392

Read and Understand

1. Spain built an overseas empire.
2. Spain was a Catholic bulwark.
3. The Netherlands won independence.
4. France's crown changed hands.
5. Religious wars split Germany.

For several months, messengers had been bringing frightening reports to Montezuma, emperor of the Aztecs, in his capital city of Tenochtitlán in the Valley of Mexico. The reports told of white-skinned, bearded men arriving at the coast in winged towers. Were these strangers merely men from distant lands? Or was their leader, as Montezuma feared, the ancient Aztec ruler-god, Quetzalcoatl (ket-suhl-**KWAH**-tuhl), returning to claim the Aztec kingdom?

In fact, the strangers were a small force of Spaniards under the leadership of Hernán Cortés (air-**NAHN** kor-**TEHZ**). Cortés had sailed in March 1519 from the Spanish settlement on Cuba with about 600

Chapter 17 Resources

GEOGRAPHY
■ Geography Skills 17
■ Transparency 62

REINFORCEMENT
■ Vocabulary 17
■ Basic Skills 17
■ Reteaching 17
■ Making Connections Study Guide 17

ENRICHMENT
■ Critical Thinking 17
■ History and Literature 17

ASSESSMENT
■ Chapter Test 17
■ Alternate Chapter Test 17
■ Computer Test Bank

Spaniards, 11 ships, 16 horses, and a few brass cannon. His goal was to explore and colonize the North American mainland. Without knowing it, Cortés's little group of Spaniards was approaching the vast Aztec empire with its 11 million people (page 335).

Montezuma soon sent his own ambassadors to see these newcomers. Whether they were gods or men, he hoped rich gifts would persuade them to go away. Aztec ambassadors presented Cortés with ornaments of gold and turquoise. The most impressive presents, in the eyes of the gold-hungry Spaniards, were two discs as big as the wheels of a cart. One, made of gold, represented the sun. The other, of silver, represented the moon.

Far from persuading Cortés to leave, the sight of so much gold and silver only stiffened his determination to win more. So that none of his men could sail home with the treasure, he ordered all his ships sunk.

For the Spaniards, it was now conquer or die. If they failed, they might be carried up the steps of an Aztec temple and sacrificed to the sun god. Torn between hope and terror, Cortés's small force set off on the 250-mile march to Tenochtitlán. Never in history had so small an army planned to topple so great an empire.

As you will see in this chapter, Cortés's actions in the spring of 1519 had far-reaching results. His handful of Spaniards destroyed the Aztec empire, and this conquest laid the foundation for an empire that made Spain the richest power in Europe.

Spain quickly put its great wealth at the service of Catholicism in the religious wars that shook Europe throughout the 1500's and 1600's. There was little peace between Catholics and Protestants in those years. Armies from Catholic Spain fought for 80 years against Protestants in the Netherlands. France was torn apart by assassinations, massacres, and civil wars—often fueled by religious hatred. In Germany, Protestants and Catholics fought one of the most destructive wars in European history, the Thirty Years' War (1618–1648).

The period of time covered in this chapter was a time of violence. However, it was also a time of great creativity. Dutch and Spanish artists produced some of the greatest treasures of European art. Literature too flourished, especially in Spain and France.

Spain built an overseas empire. 1

In the 1490's, Christopher Columbus (page 360) founded the earliest Spanish settlements in the Americas on the islands of Hispaniola and Cuba. Within a generation, Spain's lands in the Americas grew to a great empire. Sailing out from the islands, daring Spanish fortune hunters called **conquistadors** (kohn-KEES-tuh-dohrs) searched the Americas for gold and precious gems. Hernán Cortés was one of the earliest, and most successful, of these conquistadors.

Cortés conquered the Aztecs.

After Cortés's fateful decision to sink his ships, he was committed to war against the Aztecs. The Spaniards were overwhelmingly outnumbered, but they did have several advantages. They were equipped with weapons the Aztecs had never seen. There were horses, steel swords and armor, crossbows, and light artillery.

Cortés also had another advantage. Traveling with him was a young Native American woman who had been given to him as a slave when his group first landed. Her name was Malinche, and she spoke the Aztec language and several others. She learned Spanish rapidly. The Spaniards gave her a Christian name, Marina.

Doña (Lady) Marina soon became Cortés's invaluable aide. She explained that the Aztecs were hated and feared by most of the peoples they ruled. She helped him win allies among these peoples. Later, she played on Montezuma's fears to keep him from taking a strong stand against the Spaniards.

On November 8, 1519, Cortés reached Tenochtitlán. Montezuma invited the Spaniards into the city as his honored guests. Much impressed with the place, Cortés would later call Tenochtitlán "the most beautiful city in the world."

Why did Montezuma let the Spaniards enter his capital? He still feared that Cortés might be Quetzalcoatl, a light-skinned god who had once ruled the lands around Lake Texcoco. One day he had vanished mysteriously, but he vowed to return and claim his kingdom. As fate would have it, Cortés arrived in exactly the same year

393

SECTION 1
Objectives and Teaching Strategies

OBJECTIVE 1. Contrast the Spanish and Aztec cultures.
Teaching Strategy: *Writing about History: Montezuma and Cortés* (page 392a)

OBJECTIVE 2. Identify Spanish motivations for conquests in the Americas.
Teaching Strategy: *Transferring Ideas: Crusading Conquistadors* (page 392c)

■ RESEARCH

Compare the religion, language, territory, and art of the Aztec and the Inca. How does their art reveal their views of the universe?

SECTION 1
Resources

GEOGRAPHY
■ Transparency 62

REINFORCEMENT
■ Independent Practice 17.1

ENRICHMENT
■ Voices from the Past 17.1

ASSESSMENT
■ Section Quiz 17.1

■ BACKGROUND

Smallpox can be spread through either direct or indirect contact with victims of the disease and their clothing or other articles.

Cooperative Learning

Have students work in groups of five to create skits about the first meeting of Cortés and Montezuma. Students should reread "Cortés conquered the Aztecs" (pages 393–394) and think about the concerns and plans of both leaders. Remind students that the translator, Marina, probably played a crucial role in the meeting. Have group members work together to develop a storyline, characters, and script for the skit. Finally, with one group member acting as a director, have the other group members perform the skit for the class.

ANSWERS TO

Voice from the Past

1. A battle has destroyed houses, and people are grieving.
2. (a) despair and destruction **(b)** adobe walls, quetzal feathers

---

Quetzalcoatl was expected to return. As the legend had foretold, Cortés came in "white-winged ships" from across the eastern sea. Thus, Montezuma feared Cortés as a god. His fear led to the fall of the Aztec empire.

After several days of sight-seeing in Tenochtitlán, the Spaniards boldly took Montezuma prisoner and kept him in their quarters. Despite his apparent success, however, Cortés was still in an explosive situation. While he was out of the city, one of his lieutenants interfered with an Aztec religious ceremony. An uprising broke out against the Spaniards.

When Cortés returned, he and Marina forced Montezuma to go out on the roof of the Spanish barracks to calm the crowd. The Aztecs flung stones at their former ruler, now the puppet of Cortés. Soon after, word came that Montezuma was dead. The Spaniards said he had been killed by a stone from the mob. Not surprisingly, the Aztecs believed the Spanish had killed him. The Spaniards were now surrounded by thousands of Aztecs demanding their blood.

On the night of June 30, 1520, the Spaniards tried to sneak out of the city, but a guard spotted them. The Aztecs swarmed out to attack the hated foreigners. Many Spaniards, slowed by the loot they carried, were either clubbed to death or carried away for sacrifice. Among those who escaped were Cortés and Doña Marina.

The Aztecs might have pursued Cortés and destroyed his small force, but another disaster befell the Aztecs just then. The morning after Cortés's flight, smallpox broke out in the city. This terrible disease, brought by the Spaniards, killed many Aztec leaders (page 368). Partly for that reason, the Aztecs failed to follow the fleeing Spaniards and wipe them out.

A year later, in 1521, Cortés returned. This time he had with him a huge army of Aztec-hating Native Americans. Trapped in their island city, the Aztecs refused to surrender. Cortés's army had to fight its way into the city, block by block. After an 85-day siege, Tenochtitlán lay in ruins. When it was rebuilt, it was as the capital of a Spanish colony.

Voice from the Past | *An Aztec Poem*

An anonymous Aztec poet voiced the grief that the Aztecs felt for the ruin of their once beautiful capital, Tenochtitlán.

Broken spears lie in the roads;
we have torn our hair in our grief.
The houses are roofless now, and their walls
are red with blood.

Worms are swarming in the streets and plazas,
and the walls are splattered with gore.
The water has turned red, as if it were dyed,
and when we drink it,
it has the taste of brine.

We have pounded our hands in despair
against the adobe walls,
for our inheritance, our city, is lost and dead.
The shields of our warriors were its defense,
but they could not save it.

We have chewed dry twigs and salt grasses . . .
we have eaten lizards, rats, and worms . . .
Gold, jade, rich clothes, quetzal feathers—
everything that once was precious
was now considered worthless.

1. The poet tells a whole story in the first stanza. What information can you deduce from reading just four lines?
2. (a) Which parts of this poem might apply to the fall of Troy, Carthage, or another great city? **(b)** What details are specific to Tenochtitlán?

394

High in the Andes lie the ruins of the great Inca city Machu Picchu. Though the Spaniards searched for it, no outsider found it until 1911.

■ **DISCUSSION**

Pizarro laid out the city of Lima and planned its cathedral, where his bones now rest. How do these actions demonstrate one role of the conquistador in settling the Americas?

Pizarro conquered the Incas.

Cortés was only one of many Spanish adventurers who hoped to win a large fortune in the Americas. Another was Francisco Pizarro (puh-**ZAHR**-oh). A gray-bearded man of 62, Pizarro landed on the coast of Peru in 1532 with about 200 soldiers. The Spaniards panted up the western slopes of the Andes and followed the Inca road to the city of Cajamarca (kah-huh-**MAHR**-kuh). They found the city deserted.

The Inca ruler, Atahualpa (AHT-uh-**WAHL**-puh), and his army were camped close by. Atahualpa had won the throne after a bitter war with his brother. The war between the two brothers severely weakened the Inca empire. Even so, Atahualpa had 30,000 men to fight Pizarro's small troop. Pizarro, on the other hand, had horses and superior weapons.

Through a messenger, Pizarro invited Atahualpa to Cajamarca for a friendly visit. The Inca ruler agreed. Meanwhile, the Spaniards hid themselves and their horses in the narrow alleys of the city. They waited in silence as Atahualpa was carried into the city on a gold litter. He was accompanied by a guard of between 5,000 and 6,000 men. The guards were not armed.

A Spanish priest greeted Atahualpa. Suddenly a shot rang out. From all directions, the Spaniards charged their startled visitors. Not one Spaniard died, but the slaughter of Inca guards was dreadful. Most important, Atahualpa was taken prisoner. Since only the emperor could lead the Inca army, no one could rescue him. The emperor's absolute power was his empire's fatal flaw.

Atahualpa offered a huge ransom for his release. He promised to fill a large room with gold and another with silver. Pizarro agreed to free the Inca when the ransom was paid. Soon the rooms were filled as promised. Pizarro melted down the finely crafted objects into gold and silver bricks. Then, breaking his promise, he ordered Atahualpa strangled to death.

A few months later in 1533, Pizarro's horses clattered down the streets of Cuzco (**KOOZ**-koh), the Inca capital. The Spaniards were now rulers of Peru, and Pizarro was rich beyond measure. However, the Spaniards began to fight among themselves. In 1541, a group of Pizarro's old comrades broke into his home and killed him.

395

Spaniards explored widely.

The conquests of Cortés and Pizarro filled Spaniards with pride. Both men had conquered rich empires and converted thousands of people to Christianity. Other conquistadors now looked to the lands north of Mexico for opportunities to find gold, spread Christianity, and win glory.

The discovery of Florida The gray-haired governor of Puerto Rico, Juan Ponce de Leon, listened with increasing interest to an incredible story. According to legend, a nearby land contained a wondrous fountain that restored youth to whoever bathed in it. Determined to find the fountain, the aging governor organized an expedition that sailed north in 1513.

De Leon first landed near present-day St. Augustine. He thus became the first European to set foot on what is now the United States. De Leon named the land Florida ("full of flowers") because of its many sweet-smelling azalea bushes and magnolia trees. He failed, however, to find the Fountain of Youth or a rich empire.

De Leon's failure did not dampen Spain's enthusiasm for exploring Florida. In 1528, a small fleet landed 300 well-equipped soldiers near what is now Tampa Bay. The Spaniards hoped to find

A plan of St. Augustine, founded by Spaniards in 1565. It was the first permanent European settlement on the North American mainland.

a great empire filled with treasures. Instead, they found only disaster and death.

The only survivors of the expedition included a resourceful officer named Cabeza de Vaca, a tall African named Estevanico, and two other soldiers. These four managed to reach an island near present-day Galveston, Texas. Although captured and enslaved by Native Americans, they eventually escaped. They finally reached Mexico eight years after landing in Florida.

Exploring the Southeast After recuperating from his long ordeal, Cabeza de Vaca returned to Spain. He soon attracted excited attention by repeating stories he claimed Native Americans had told him about the Seven Cities of Cibola. These fabulous cities were said to have emerald-studded walls and treasuries filled with gold.

The discovery of the Aztec and Inca empires encouraged many Spaniards to believe almost any report of riches in the Americas. Of all the conquistadors, none was more eager for adventure than Hernando de Soto. As one of Pizarro's chief officers, De Soto had returned home rich with Inca plunder. He now cast a greedy eye on Florida. After obtaining royal permission, De Soto used his new wealth to finance a well-equipped expedition to search for the cities of gold.

De Soto confidently landed on the western coast of Florida in May 1539 with 600 soldiers. During the next four years, the Spaniards explored the Southeast from the Atlantic to the Mississippi River and beyond.

Although De Soto and his men learned much about the geography of what is now the southeastern United States, they failed to find any gold. They also earned the hatred of Native Americans by stealing their food and making slaves of them. When De Soto died of a fever in the spring of 1542, his men cast his body into the Mississippi to keep it from being captured. In late 1543, only about 300 desperate survivors finally reached a Spanish settlement in Mexico.

Exploring the Southwest The reports of golden cities that excited De Soto also swept through Mexico City. The viceroy of New Spain chose a young captain, Francisco Vásquez de Coronado, to investigate the accuracy of these stories. Coronado quickly assembled an army of 300 men to head north looking for gold and glory.

Coronado's expedition began in February 1540. After traveling 1,500 miles across a harsh, barren

396

landscape, the conquistadors finally came upon one of the fabled seven cities near present-day Zuni, New Mexico. To their bitter disappointment, however, they found only a small village of adobe houses. Coronado refused to give up. He sent out two parties to explore the region. One party sighted the Grand Canyon. The other party worked eastward to the Great Plains.

These important discoveries failed to satisfy Coronado. Instead, he listened to Native American tales of wealthy cities far to the east where people ate from golden bowls and drank from golden jugs. Desperate for success, Coronado and his men pushed across the seemingly endless plains as far as present-day Kansas. Once again, a crushing disappointment awaited them. Instead of a great city, they found only grass huts.

Exploring Chile Meanwhile, far to the south, a man and a woman extended Spain's conquests in the Andes. In 1540, Pedro de Valdivia (vahl-**DEE**-vyah) and Ines Suarez (**IH**-nehz **SWAH**-rayth) led a small army south from Spain's strongholds in Peru. They marched along the coastal desert of what is now Chile. In 1541, they founded the city of Santiago, Chile's modern capital. Between 1540 and 1547, they conquered much of Chile for Spain.

By 1550, Spanish territory reached all the way from present-day Kansas to Chile. Spain's American lands were larger than the empires of Alexander the Great or Julius Caesar. This was also the first empire in history that was separated from its capital by an immense ocean. Its ruler was Spain's Charles I, who also held the title of Holy Roman Emperor as Charles V.

Colonists enslaved Native Americans.

The king of Spain claimed absolute power over his American lands. He entrusted the power to make laws for these lands to a group of officials called the Council of the Indies. The council met in Spain and sent its laws to two capitals in the Americas. One capital was Mexico City, which the Spaniards had built over the ruins of Tenochtitlán. The other capital was Lima, Peru. Pizarro founded Lima in 1535 and made it the capital of Peru because communication with Spain was easier from the coastal Lima than from the inland Cuzco.

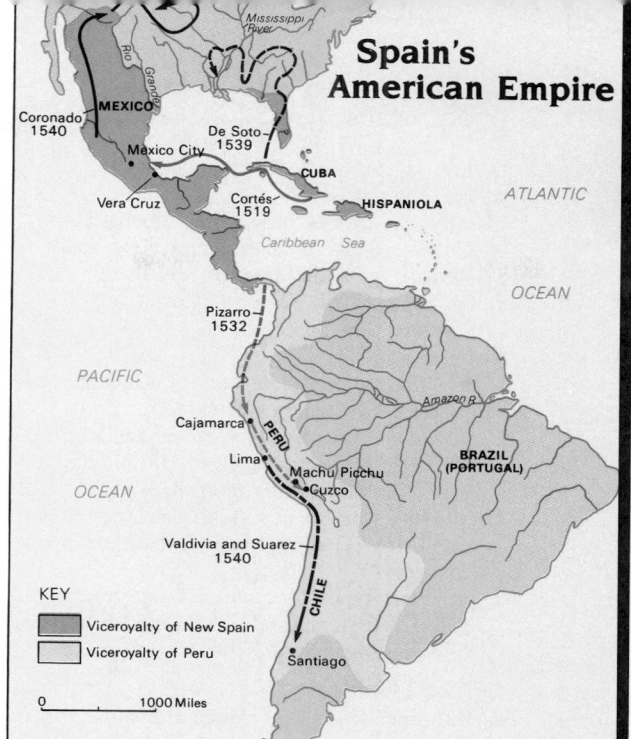

Spain's American Empire

KEY

▨ Viceroyalty of New Spain
☐ Viceroyalty of Peru

0   1000 Miles

Map Study

What viceroyalty included the former land of the Aztecs? Which Spanish explorer traveled farthest north? When did Pizarro go to Peru?

In both Mexico City and Lima was a royal agent called a **viceroy.** The viceroy in Mexico City ruled Spain's North American territory, called New Spain. The viceroy in Lima ruled Spain's South American lands, called Peru. Viceroys were noblemen born in Spain. No one born in America could reach such high office.

The viceroy's authority did not matter much to the average Aztec, Inca, or Maya. For the conquered people, the only rulers who mattered were the ruthless conquistadors who seized their villages. The Council of the Indies granted to certain settlers a privilege called an **encomienda** (EHN-koh-mee-EHN-duh). The holder of an encomienda became master of a particular area. He could force Native Americans in his lands to work long hours in his fields or silver mines. In effect, the Spaniards treated the Indians as slaves. Abuse in Spanish silver mines killed thousands of Native Americans.

397

ANSWERS TO
Map Study

New Spain; Coronado; 1532

■ BACKGROUND

Some Spaniards, especially missionaries, were deeply concerned about the Native Americans. One, Bartolome de las Casas, convinced the Spanish monarch to enact laws protecting them. The laws met with opposition from the *encomienderos* and were soon repealed.

ANSWERS TO

Section
Review 1

Define:
(a) Spanish fortune hunter
(b) Spanish nobleman who

(continued)

ANSWERS TO (continued)

acted as royal agent
(c) privilege granted to certain settlers

Identify:

(a) emperor of Aztec
(b) capital city of the Aztec
(c) conqueror of Aztec
(d) Native American woman who helped Cortés
(e) Spain's lands in North America **(f)** conqueror of Inca **(g)** Inca ruler killed by Pizarro **(h)** first European to set foot on what is now the United States **(i)** officer who reached Mexico, told stories in Spain about Seven Cities of Cibola **(j)** Spaniard who claimed the Mississippi River for Spain **(k)** Spaniard who explored as far north as Kansas **(l)** helped extend Spain's conquests in the Andes **(m)** woman who helped conquer Chile for Spain

Answer:

1. (a) He was the god who had once ruled the land around Lake Texcoco and had vowed to return to reclaim his kingdom. **(b)** The Aztec thought that Cortés was this god and let him enter the capital.

2. used an army of Aztec-hating Native Americans

3. There was no one to lead the Inca army.

4. (a) by the Council of the Indies, which met in Spain and sent its laws to viceroys in Mexico City and Lima **(b)** being born in Spain

5. (a) farming and mining **(b)** Native American slave labor

6. Possible answers: disease, attacks by Native Americans, vast expanse of land to be explored, difficulty of distinguishing between truth and fable about riches to be found.

Section REVIEW 1

Define: (a) conquistador, (b) viceroy, (c) encomienda

Identify: (a) Montezuma, (b) Tenochtitlán, (c) Cortés, (d) Doña Marina, (e) New Spain, (f) Pizarro, (g) Atahualpa, (h) De Leon, (i) De Vaca, (j) De Soto, (k) Coronado, (l) Valdivia, (m) Suarez

Answer:

1. (a) What was the legend of Quetzalcoatl? (b) How did it help Cortés?
2. How did Cortés finally conquer Tenochtitlán?
3. Why was the conquest of the Incas relatively easy after the capture of Atahualpa?
4. (a) How was Spain's American empire governed? (b) What qualified a person to become a viceroy?
5. (a) What types of economic enterprises did Spanish settlers establish in the Americas? (b) What workers did they use there?

Critical Thinking

6. List four factors that hindered Spanish exploration of the present southern United States and explain their effects.

Spain was a Catholic bulwark. 2

The riches of Spain's new empire were fabulous. By 1600, the amount of gold taken from American mines and shipped to Spain was estimated at 750,000 pounds. American silver mines yielded even greater treasure. Between 1550 and 1650, roughly 16,000 *tons* of silver bullion (metal bars) were unloaded from Spanish galleons and carted over Spanish roads. Between a fifth and a fourth of every shipload of treasure went to the king of Spain as his royal share. With the vast wealth of its American territories, Spain began to play a commanding role in Europe.

Philip II *ruled an empire.*

In 1556, Charles V divided his empire, giving Spain to his shy and serious son, Philip II, who ruled from 1556 to 1598. Under Philip's rule,

398

Spain became the staunchest supporter of Catholicism and the most dangerous enemy of Protestantism.

Europe was entering a time of violent conflict over religion. In 1559, Spain and France signed a treaty ending the long series of wars they had fought over lands in Italy. Thereafter, for nearly 100 years, most of the wars in Europe were fought over religion.

Philip's inheritance from Charles V included more than Spain and its American colonies. He also ruled the duchy of Milan in northern Italy, the kingdom of Naples in southern Italy, the territory called Franche-Comté on France's eastern border, and all 17 provinces that made up the Netherlands.

Toward the middle of Philip's reign, another great prize fell into his hands. In 1580, the king of Portugal died without an heir. Philip quickly seized the small but important Portuguese kingdom. Counting Portuguese strongholds in Africa, India, and the East Indies, he now had an empire that circled the globe.

Spain's wealth and its power grew together. Minted into coins, Spain's gold and silver supported an army of about 50,000 soldiers. Through the late 1500's, Spain had by far the largest and best-equipped army in Europe. Looking at Spain's awesome military machine, people said, "When Spain moves, the whole world trembles."

The nerve center of the Spanish empire was Philip's palace, the Escorial (es-**KOHR**-ee-uhl). All the roads and ship lanes in Spain's far-flung empire led ultimately to its massive, gray stone walls about 26 miles northwest of Madrid, the capital. The Escorial's outer gates were so huge that the keys to open them weighed half a ton. Within the gigantic walls, there were 86 staircases to climb, 1,200 doors to open, and 84 miles of corridors to explore.

In a small, candle-lit room within the Escorial, Philip II worked far into the night. The most powerful ruler in Europe, he was also the hardest working. He demanded reports, reports, and more reports from his chief advisers. Then, in his tiny office, he would agonize over decisions. Much of the time, he could not bring himself to choose one policy over another. At such times, the government of Spain ground nearly to a halt. Yet Philip would not allow anyone to help him. Deeply suspicious, he trusted no one for long.

Comparing pictures *The Spanish architects who planned the Escorial (above) were influenced by the buildings of Renaissance Italy. Yet they created a much plainer, sterner palace, well suited to the character of Spain's Philip II (right). How does the architecture of the Escorial differ from that of a Gothic cathedral (page 232)?*

As his own court historian wrote, "His smile and his dagger were very close."

The Escorial was more than a palace. It was also a monastery. From his bedroom, Philip II could slide open a hidden window that allowed him to watch the monks' church services. There, in private, he took part in their prayers.

The two functions of the Escorial—palace and monastery—show clearly the character of Philip II. Throughout his reign, he doggedly sought to strengthen both his monarchy and the Catholic Church.

Spain battled for Catholicism.

Philip II was eager to see Catholicism triumph over its religious rivals, the Muslim Ottoman Turks and the Protestants. Against the Ottomans, Philip achieved a stunning victory. However, Philip's struggles against Protestantism caused him only frustration.

War against the Ottoman Turks   In 1571, the pope called on all Catholic princes to take up arms against the mounting power of the Ottoman

empire. Philip responded like a true crusader. Huge Spanish galleons joined Venetian ships in the Mediterranean Sea and rowed toward the coast of Greece.

On October 7, 1571, near the Greek seaport of Lepanto (lih-**PAN**-toh), 200 Spanish-Venetian ships met the Ottoman fleet of 300 ships in a ferocious battle. Philip II's half-brother, Don John of Austria, commanded the Christian forces. His ships slammed into the Turkish galleys. Then the Spaniards and Venetians swarmed aboard and slaughtered the foe with sword and musket. The Battle of Lepanto crushed the Ottoman navy. It was a major victory for Christendom.

War against Protestant forces   As the champion of Catholicism, Philip wanted first and foremost to crush Protestantism in his own lands. He also worked constantly to weaken or overthrow Protestant rulers throughout Europe.

No other place on the map of Europe gave Philip as much trouble as a tiny corner of his own empire, the Netherlands. Later in this chapter, you will read how the Dutch rose in revolt against Philip (page 402). In his efforts to crush

399

OBJECTIVE 1. Explain why Cervantes's work is regarded as the first modern European novel.

Teaching Strategy: *Skill Building: Analyzing a Quotation* (page 392c)

OBJECTIVE 2. Identify reasons for Spain's economic decline after 1600.

Teaching Strategy: *Economics and History: Inflation* (page 392c)

ANSWER TO
Comparing Pictures

The Escorial served a worldly, political purpose rather than a religious one. The Escorial was divided into sections, many with courtyards. The dome, towers, classical columns, and decoration show the Renaissance influence.

■ DISCUSSION

To what extent might Philip's character have prevented his victory over Protestant forces? (Students may want to review page 398.)

ASSESSMENT
- Section Quiz 17.2

REINFORCEMENT
- Independent Practice 17.2

ENRICHMENT
- Voices from the Past 17.2

■ BACKGROUND

Don Quixote had a very vivid imagination. For example, he turned lowly inns into castles and windmills into fearsome giants. For that reason, the word *quixotic* came to refer to an unrealistic visionary, someone who is idealistic but impractical.

the revolt, Philip spent a fortune in Spanish gold to no avail.

After the Dutch, Philip's greatest Protestant enemy was Elizabeth I of England. Philip had once been married to Elizabeth's Catholic sister, Mary (page 381). After Mary's death in 1558, he hoped to keep England as an ally and a Catholic country. For a while, he even hoped to marry Elizabeth. Gradually, however, Elizabeth showed that she intended to keep England Protestant and that she did not intend to repeat her sister's mistake of marrying an unpopular foreign king. Later, Elizabeth openly assisted the Dutch rebels with money and troops. She also encouraged English sea captains to raid Spanish treasure ships for gold.

In 1588, Philip struck at England. He assembled a fleet of 130 ships with 31,000 men. This fleet was known as the Armada (ahr-MAHD-uh). Philip had high hopes for his mighty Armada, but the skilled English sea captains destroyed it. For England, the victory was the high point of the Elizabethan Age (Chapter 18).

Spain had a golden age in art and literature.

Despite these military setbacks, Spain remained a mighty nation. Philip's reign marked the beginning of a golden age for Spanish culture.

El Greco and Velázquez   The works of two great artists showed both the pride and the piety of Spain during its golden age. The first of these artists was El Greco (GREH-koh). The second was Diego Velázquez (vay-LAHTH-kayth).

El Greco (1541–1614) was not a Spaniard by birth but a Greek from the island of Crete. His real name was Kyriakos Theotokopoulos, but the Spanish gave him the name El Greco, which means "the Greek." His major works were all painted in Spain.

El Greco painted Catholic saints and martyrs as huge, long-limbed figures. The backgrounds of his paintings were usually a mass of swirling gray clouds. The use of deep, vibrant colors heightened the drama and religious intensity of El Greco's paintings.

El Greco's saintly figures showed the strength of the Catholic faith in Spain. The paintings of Velázquez (1599–1660) showed the pride of Spain's royal family. Velázquez was best known for his

The dramatic sky in this painting of Saint Bernardino is typical of El Greco's work.

portraits of Spanish kings and princes mounted on rearing stallions.

Cervantes   In 1605, an unsuccessful Spanish playwright named Miguel de Cervantes (suhr-VAN-teez) published a book that many critics call the first modern European novel. The book was named for its main character, Don Quixote (kee-HOH-tee) of La Mancha. In his own life, Cervantes had had his ups and downs. He had been wounded in the Battle of Lepanto and jailed for debt. He worked for a time as a tax collector. These varied experiences seem to have made Cervantes tolerant of humankind.

400

Don Quixote de la Mancha was a gentle satire of chivalry. Don Quixote was a Spaniard of noble birth and noble mind who went a little crazy after reading too many books about heroic knights. Hoping to "right every manner of wrong," he rode forth in a suit of rusty armor, mounted on a feeble nag. At his side, through all his adventures, was a stout and comical little squire named Sancho Panza.

Because of his romantic ideals, Don Quixote never saw things as they were. He saw a common tavern by the road as a grand castle. To him, a windmill became a hostile giant to be challenged and fought. Of course, Don Quixote's wild notions caused no end of trouble. Strangers laughed at his chivalric speeches, knocked him off his horse, and left him in the mud.

Sancho Panza, more sensible than his master, objected to everything the foolish knight proposed, but Don Quixote never listened. This bit of dialogue was typical:

> "What the devil kind of vengeance are we going to take," asked Sancho, "seeing there are more than twenty of them and not more than two of us, or maybe only one and a half?"
> "I," replied Don Quixote, "am worth a hundred."

So saying, the knight charged to the attack, only to receive another beating.

Don Quixote's misadventures made it clear that the age of knights in shining armor had passed. By 1600, chivalry seemed outdated and somewhat foolish to Cervantes's readers, even though its ideals still had some sentimental appeal, especially to kings and queens.

Spain's economy weakened.

With a prayer on his lips, Philip II died in his palace bed in 1598 after a reign of 42 years. His successors were weaker kings, notable mostly because Velázquez painted their portraits.

In the next 50 years, Spain's golden age gradually lost its glitter. By 1650, the Spanish economy was in a dreadful state. The king was hopelessly in debt to foreign creditors. In every Spanish town, prices soared wildly.

Strangely, Spain's great wealth in the 1500's was the direct cause of its poverty later. Boatloads of gold and silver from the Americas flooded Spain—and later the rest of Europe—with precious metals. As a result, the value of gold and silver dropped, and prices doubled and redoubled. Such an upward spiral of prices is called inflation.

Spain was most seriously affected by these skyrocketing prices. Spaniards found that they could neither eat gold nor hammer it into shoes.

Unlike many other parts of Europe, Spain never had a large middle class. The most powerful group in Spanish society was still the great feudal landholders. No class of burghers or bourgeoisie won political influence in Spain as such groups did in England and France.

Spain's methods of manufacturing were also old-fashioned. The guilds that had grown up in the Middle Ages still dominated business. These guilds did not produce enough manufactured goods for Spain's use. Instead, Spaniards imported much of what they needed from the Netherlands, France, and England. Thus, Spanish gold and silver tended to flow right out of Madrid into the pockets of Spain's worst enemies—the hard-working, hard-bargaining Dutch burghers of Amsterdam.

Section REVIEW 2

Identify: (a) Philip II, (b) Escorial, (c) Battle of Lepanto, (d) the Armada, (e) El Greco, (f) Velázquez, (g) Cervantes, (h) Don Quixote, (i) Sancho Panza

Answer:
1. (a) What lands did Philip II inherit? (b) What lands did he add to his empire?
2. What made Spain's government inefficient?
3. What were Philip's two goals?
4. (a) What action did Philip take toward the Ottoman empire? (b) What Protestant lands caused difficulties for Spain?
5. How did Spain's wealth from the Americas weaken its economy?

Critical Thinking
6. Cervantes, El Greco, and Velázquez present very different outlooks on life. What might Philip II have thought of the works of each man, if he had known of them? (Only El Greco's works were actually produced during Philip's lifetime.)

401

ANSWERS TO
Section Review 2

Identify:
(a) king of Spain from 1556 to 1598, who ruled an empire that circled the globe (b) Philip's palace (c) sea battle resulting in major victory for Christendom against the Muslims (d) Spanish fleet sent by Philip II to defeat Protestant England (e) Greek-born artist whose major works were painted in Spain (f) painter of Spain's royal family (g) Spanish author of *Don Quixote de la Mancha* (h) character in Cervantes's book (i) Don Quixote's squire

Answer:
1. (a) Spain, its American colonies, duchy of Milan, kingdom of Naples, Franche-Comté, and the Netherlands (b) Portugal and its strongholds in Africa, India, and the East Indies

2. Philip demanded many reports from his advisors, agonized over decisions, and trusted no one to help him.

3. to strengthen Catholic Church and his monarchy

4. (a) helped crush the Ottoman Turks in the Battle of Lepanto (b) the Netherlands and England

5. Gold and silver flooded Spain, causing the value of these metals to drop and prices to rise.

6. Philip would have approved of the contributions El Greco and Velázquez made to the strengthening of both the Catholic Church and the monarchy and probably would have disapproved of Cervantes's satire.

■ **BACKGROUND**

The city of Antwerp was completely destroyed by unpaid Spanish soldiers after their leader, the Duke of Alva, resigned.

■ **DISCUSSION**

Dividends paid by the Dutch East Indies Company were sometimes as high as 63 percent above a backer's initial investment. Compare this rate to current dividend rates to help students appreciate the lure of venture capitalism.

The Netherlands won independence. 3

Of Spain's many enemies in the late 1500's, the most stubborn (and successful) were the people who lived in the low marshlands between northern Germany and northern France. Today, this region is divided into two nations, Belgium to the south and the Netherlands to the north. In the 1500's, the whole region was known as the Netherlands, or the Low Countries. The northerners, known as the Dutch, took the lead in the battle with Spain.

It is not surprising that the Dutch rebelled against Spanish rule in the late 1500's. In culture, customs, and religion, the Dutch were strongly at odds with Spain and its ruler, Philip II. Broadly speaking, Spain still held to the great institutions of the Middle Ages: the Catholic Church, the feudal system of landholding, and the guild system for producing goods. The Netherlands, on the other hand, had many Protestant congregations. The feudal system had little influence on the busy towns of the Netherlands. Moreover, as Spain's economy faltered, the Dutch were taking the lead in new ways of doing business.

The Dutch revolted against Spain.

The Netherlands had long been part of the Holy Roman Empire. When Charles V divided his lands, he gave the Netherlands to Philip II along with Spain. Thus, the only link between the two lands was that they shared a ruler.

Spain, as you have read, was a thoroughly Catholic country. In the Netherlands, about one third of the people were Calvinists. Although they were a minority, the Calvinists were a strong, tightly knit group that included many powerful nobles and wealthy merchants.

In 1559, Philip II sent his sister Margaret to govern the Netherlands with the twin goals of stamping out Protestantism and raising taxes. These policies soon antagonized many Dutch.

In 1566, mobs of angry Calvinists rampaged through Catholic churches in many parts of the Netherlands. Calling themselves the Sea Beggars, they smashed windows, burned books, destroyed altars, and ruined all the rich ornaments.

402

In response, Philip II sent 20,000 soldiers under the Spanish Duke of Alva to destroy Protestantism in the Netherlands. The duke's troops broke into Dutch homes and carried off suspected heretics. On a single day in 1568, Alva executed 1,500 people. Between 1568 and 1578, the Netherlands flamed as war raged between Catholics and Protestants, Dutch and Spaniards.

The greatest leader of the revolt against Spain was Prince William of Orange. (He was also known as William the Silent for his remarkable ability to keep his plans secret.) Born a Lutheran but raised a Catholic, William's motives for fighting the Spaniards were political, not religious. He hated to see his country ruled by foreigners and wanted to free the Netherlands from Spain.

At first, William and the Dutch lost battle after battle, town after town to the Spaniards. Then, at the town of Alkmaar, the Dutch took a desperate step. Their lands were called the Low Countries because much of the land was actually below sea level. Only great dikes kept the seawater from flooding over the fields. To drive out the Spanish, the Dutch opened the floodgates, covering the land around Alkmaar with water. Thereafter, the Dutch took this terrible step several times, destroying their countryside to save their towns from Spain.

By 1579, the Dutch were in control of the northern part of the Netherlands. Seven provinces, led by the province of Holland, united and declared themselves independent of Spain in 1581. This country became the United Provinces of the Netherlands.

Meanwhile, the southern part of the Netherlands (which is modern-day Belgium) remained under Spanish control. The majority of people in this region were Catholics, and their language was closer to French than to German.

William the Silent hoped to establish a country where both Protestantism and Catholicism were tolerated. Few people, however, were ready to accept this idea. William himself was murdered in 1584 by a fanatic. Today, Dutch Catholics and Protestants alike honor him as the "father of his country."

Gradually, the idea of religious toleration did take root in the Netherlands. Somehow the Dutch managed to overcome the religious hatreds stirred up by their war for independence. In the 1600's, the United Provinces was the one country in

Europe that accepted people of almost all faiths. Jews, unable to practice their religion in most parts of Europe, found a haven in Amsterdam and other Dutch cities. Scholars from many parts of Europe also came to live in the United Provinces or sent their books there to be published. For the times, this kind of religious toleration was rare.

The Dutch established a republic.

Another distinctive feature of the United Provinces of the Netherlands was its government. Unlike most states of Europe, the United Provinces was not a kingdom but a republic. Each province had an elected governor called a *stadtholder*. The power of this official depended on the active support of the province's leading merchants and landholders.

Each of the seven provinces sent delegations to a legislative body called the States General. These lawmakers had few powers because each province jealously guarded its independence. Nevertheless, members of the States General were so proud of themselves that they insisted on being called "Their High Mightinesses."

The Dutch built a trading empire.

While Spain lived on the gold and silver from its colonies, a new economic system was thriving in the Netherlands. The Dutch took the lead in the development of a new way of organizing business, an economic system that later came to be called **capitalism.**

Capitalism and the Commercial Revolution

What were the features of this new economic system? Capitalists were people who invested large sums of money as **capital** in business ventures. Their goal was to gain enough money to pay all the costs of the venture as well as to make some additional money, or **profit.**

A capitalist who made a profit on a trading expedition did not spend all the money on luxury items. Instead, the successful capitalist reinvested the profit in another, probably larger, venture. Of course, there was always the risk of failure. Capitalists risked losing not only the chance for profit but all the capital they had accumulated as well. During the 1660's, however, the hope of profit kept the Dutch economy booming.

This painting by Vermeer shows the three-story houses that were common in Dutch towns. The top floor often served as the owner's warehouse.

The merchants of Amsterdam traded in many goods. They bought surplus grain in Poland and crammed it into their warehouses. Then, they waited for news of poor harvests in southern Europe so they could ship the grain south while prices were highest. Tons of smoked and pickled herring also found a ready market. Western Europe was short of timber, a fact that Dutch merchants were quick to exploit. They shipped great quantities of Scandinavian lumber to Spain, France, Italy, and England, all in ships owned by Dutch capitalists.

The Dutch had the largest fleet of ships in the entire world—10,000 ships in 1600. Even merchants of other countries often sent their cargoes in Dutch ships and, of course, paid dearly for it.

Banking As the trade routes of the Atlantic became more important than those of the Mediterranean, the Dutch replaced the Italians as the bankers of Europe. Soon after its founding in 1609, the Amsterdam Exchange Bank won a reputation as the safest, soundest bank in Europe.

403

SECTION 3 Objectives and Teaching Strategies

OBJECTIVE 1. Contrast the economies of Spain and the Netherlands.

Teaching Strategy: *Economics and History: Capitalism* (page 392d)

OBJECTIVE 2. Describe elements of Rembrandt's art.

Teaching Strategy: *Teaching with Pictures:* **The Night Watch** (page 392d)

Cooperative Learning

Have students work in teams of two. Make research materials available, or allow for time in the library. Each team should become "experts" on the shift from feudalism to capitalism, with one student focusing on feudalism and the other on capitalism. After team members have completed their research, they should collaboratively write a brief report or prepare a presentation for the class. Teams may wish to focus on similarities and differences between the two systems or the cause and effect of the shift from feudalism to capitalism.

SECTION 3 Resources

ASSESSMENT
- Section Quiz 17.3

REINFORCEMENT
- Independent Practice 17.3

ENRICHMENT
- Voices from the Past 17.3

■ BACKGROUND

At the peak of its power in 1669, the Dutch East Indies Company had 40 warships, 150 merchant ships, and 10,000 soldiers.

■ DISCUSSION

Every dwelling in the city of Amsterdam in 1663 could be reached by water. Discuss with students how this would affect everyday life.

Princes and merchants from many countries deposited money there. They also borrowed from the Dutch banks, and the interest on such loans enriched Amsterdam's bankers.

The Dutch East Indies Company Among the most prized luxury items in Europe were the spices imported from Asia. Ambitious Dutch merchants knew that the spice trade could bring enormous wealth to their country. They also knew that entering the spice trade was dangerous as long as Portugal controlled the routes around Africa and across the Indian Ocean.

In 1602, 17 of Amsterdam's wealthiest merchants pooled their money to form the Dutch East Indies Company. The firm had enough capital to outfit a heavily armed fleet far superior to Portugal's. Within 20 years, the Dutch had displaced the Portuguese in the East Indies, Ceylon, and the Cape of Good Hope. Shiploads of pepper, cloves, and nutmeg sold in Amsterdam brought huge profits to the company. The merchant owners used these profits as capital to invest in new trading ventures and in banks that financed other undertakings. Any Dutch citizen, however, could buy shares in the company, and those shares could be bought and sold.

Dutch merchants took the lead in their capitalist approach to trade, but merchants in other nations soon followed. English and French merchants in particular also invested in bold enterprises and expanded their markets. This system of trade, profit, and investment became so important to Europe that historians have called it the **Commercial Revolution.** It marked the beginning of the economic system later known as capitalism.

CITY TOUR
Amsterdam was a great city.

Holland was the wealthiest Dutch province, and Amsterdam was Holland's largest, most flourishing city. In fact, by 1650, it was Europe's financial and commercial center, far surpassing the Italian cities of Venice and Florence.

Amsterdam's growth through the early 1600's was spectacular. In 1610, there were 50,000 people living in Amsterdam. Only 10 years later, the population had doubled to 100,000. By 1660, the figure had swollen to 200,000. This phenomenal growth was due partly to Amsterdam's location on a sheltered bay, the Zuider (ZYE-duhr) Zee. However, human skill did far more than geography to account for Amsterdam's wealth.

Hoping to boost their city's commerce, a group of Dutch engineers designed a remarkable network of canals. The plan was approved in 1610 and completed in 1663. Three 80-foot-wide semicircular canals ran from the Zuider Zee into the heart of the fan-shaped city. A web of 600 smaller canals fed into the larger ones.

The Dutch merchants even designed their houses so that they could move merchandise efficiently. The top floor of each three-story house usually served as the owner's warehouse. It was equipped with a hoisting beam that jutted out over the water. When a barge tied up below, the merchant could lower a hook from the hoisting beam and thus quickly gather in a shipment of wheat, beer, or herring.

Imagine that it is a winter morning in the 1630's. Let us take an early stroll along a narrow

DAILY LIFE ▶ Tulips and Trade

Amsterdam in the 1600's was a hotbed of financial speculation. People bought and sold goods of all sorts in hopes of making a profit. In the mid-1630's, a new money-making craze swept the city—tulip bulbs. Everyone in Amsterdam, it seemed, had gone mad over exotic strains of tulips imported from Turkey. It was common for a single tulip bulb to be bought and sold ten times in one day, always for a profit. A wealthy Dutchman once traded his mansion for three tulip bulbs and considered it a bargain!

Rembrandt van Rijn's dramatic painting, "The Night Watch," shows the civic leaders of Amsterdam keeping guard over their city.

lane beside one of Amsterdam's canals. In the soft light of dawn, the milk pails of a milkman clank loudly. Moments later, the neighborhood baker drags a cart along the lane and calls out to the homeowners opening their shutters, "Hot white bread! Rye bread rolls! Barley biscuits!"

In the frosty air, as Dutch neighbors greet one another across the canal, their bodies seem oddly round and bulky. To keep warm, they bundle up in layer upon layer of woolen clothing. Men wear seven or eight waistcoats and pairs of trousers. Women pile on layer after layer of petticoats.

In one of the narrow houses, a family is taking the first meal of the day. The family members begin with a solemn Calvinist prayer before settling down to a standard Dutch breakfast: bread, cheese, butter, and beer. When finished, all stand to pray again. In the course of the long day, they look forward to three more meals. For the main feast at midday, a prosperous family will set out plates of herring, almonds, fruits, and a rice pudding dessert. The poor usually make do with four meals of cheese, bread, broth, and tankards of beer.

Dutch artists developed a new style.

During the 1600's, Amsterdam became what Florence had been during the 1400's. It boasted not only the best banks but also the best artists in Europe.

The greatest Dutch artist of the period was Rembrandt van Rijn (REHM-brant vahn ryne), who lived from 1606 to 1669. Rembrandt's paintings realistically captured moments of drama. In 1632, a wealthy physician commissioned Rembrandt to paint a group portrait. The artist showed the distinguished doctor standing over the corpse of an executed criminal, lecturing a group of fellow surgeons. Rembrandt's most famous group painting, "The Night Watch," showed his mastery of light and shadow.

Dozens of other artists worked in Amsterdam. The older master Franz Hals (1580–1666) painted brighter and less somber works than Rembrandt. His merry spirit showed itself in the vigorous faces of the people he painted.

The Dutch often chose domestic, indoor settings for their portraits. They apparently enjoyed

405

■ **BACKGROUND**
Wealthy merchants and bankers wanted portraits, landscapes, and scenes from day-to-day life in their homes both to offer tranquillity and to reflect their prosperity.

ANSWERS TO
Section Review 3

Define:
(a) elective system of government (b) economic system the goal of which is to make profits (c) money invested in business ventures (d) money remaining after all costs of a business are paid (e) economic changes toward capitalism

Identify:
(a) name given low marshland region between northern Germany and northern France (b) angry Calvinists who rampaged through Catholic churches (c) Dutch
(continued)

ANSWERS TO (continued)

leader of the revolt against Spain **(d)** elected governor of a province **(e)** trading firm with all the powers of a sovereign state **(f)** financial and commercial center of Europe by 1650 **(g)** greatest Dutch painter during the 1600's

Answer:

1. (a) It had many Protestant congregations, did not hold to the feudal and guild systems, and took the lead in new ways of doing business. **(b)** It had been part of the Holy Roman Empire and was given to Philip II by Charles V.

2. (a) policies aimed at stamping out Protestantism, raising taxes **(b)** antagonized many Dutch; led to rampages on Catholic churches

3. (a) to free the Netherlands from Spain **(b)** to establish a country where both Protestantism and Catholicism were tolerated **(c)** Seven provinces declared independence and became United Provinces of Netherlands in 1581; idea of religious toleration gradually took root.

4. by opening of floodgates

5. (a) 7 provinces **(b)** remained under Spanish control

6. (a) republic with each province having an elected governor **(b)** organized to make profits, reinvest profits

7. (a) to break Portugal's hold on the Indian Ocean spice trade; capital needed too much for investor **(b)** power to make war, coin money, and rule colonies

8. United Provinces was not a kingdom but a republic, and it permitted religious tolerance.

Both this painting and the one on page 403 are by Dutch artist Jan Vermeer. How are the two pictures similar in style and content?

seeing themselves doing chores in their homes and workshops. For example, the young artist Jan Vermeer (1632–1675) became famous for his paintings of middle-aged women doing such tasks as pouring milk and sewing. In his paintings, light from an open window seemed to flood the room.

Dutch art showed more interest in groups than in heroic individuals such as Michelangelo's "David" or Velázquez's Spanish monarchs. Frequently, Dutch artists painted group portraits of people—families, civic leaders, military units. As many as 40 people may appear in one painting. Taken as a whole, Dutch art revealed the prosperity, the civic spirit, and the values of a new age in Europe.

Section REVIEW 3

Define: (a) republic, (b) capitalism, (c) capital, (d) profit, (e) Commercial Revolution
Identify: (a) the Netherlands, (b) Sea Beggars,

406

(c) William of Orange (the Silent), (d) stadtholder, (e) Dutch East Indies Company, (f) Amsterdam, (g) Rembrandt
Answer:

1. (a) List three ways in which the Netherlands differed from Spain. (b) How did the Netherlands become a part of Spain?
2. (a) What policies did Philip's sister Margaret and the Duke of Alva follow in the Netherlands? (b) What were the results?
3. (a) What was William the Silent's political goal? (b) His religious goal? (c) What did he achieve?
4. How were the Dutch able to stop the Spaniards at Alkmaar?
5. (a) What part of the Netherlands declared itself independent of Spain in 1581? (b) What happened to the rest of the Netherlands?
6. (a) Describe the government of the Netherlands. (b) Briefly describe the way businesses in the Netherlands were organized.
7. (a) Why was the Dutch East Indies Company formed? (b) What help did the Dutch government give the company?

Critical Thinking

8. How was the United Provinces of the Netherlands unusual for its time in both politics and religion?

France's crown changed hands.   4

In 1559, France's future looked bleak. Its long series of wars with Spain for control of Italy had come to an end, with Spain the clear winner. France was exhausted by the wars. Moreover, the French king, Henry II, was severely injured in a jousting tournament and died from his wounds in 1559. Henry II had been a member of the Valois (va-LWAH) dynasty, the family that had ruled France since 1328.

Not content with defeating France, Philip II worked for the rest of the 1500's to weaken the French monarchy. His efforts helped bring about the downfall of the Valois. Yet, by destroying the Valois, Philip II unwittingly helped bring to power a strong new king, Henry IV.

Catherine de Medici ruled France.

Henry II left four young sons, all of whom were incompetent. All had short lives, so that three of Henry's boys briefly wore the French crown. Their strong-willed mother, Catherine de Medici, really ruled France in their name.

Catherine came to power at a time when France was deeply divided over religion. Calvinist ministers had made thousands of converts in France. French followers of Calvinism were a Protestant minority in Catholic France. By 1559, about one sixth of France's population was Calvinist.

Most of the major towns and cities in France were divided between Catholics and Huguenots. Intense hatred between the two groups frequently led to violence. Groups attacked each other's churches. Thousands of people were tortured, burned, or beaten to death for their beliefs.

Two ambitious French families further inflamed these religious hatreds. On one side was the House of Bourbon (BOOR-buhn), a family of French nobles who had become Protestants. On the other side was the House of Guise (geez), a noble family who staunchly championed Catholicism. The Bourbon and the Guise families hated each other, and each hoped to overthrow the Valois monarchy and start a dynasty of its own. Between 1562 and 1589, there were nine civil wars between Bourbons and Guises, Huguenots and Catholics.

The worst outbreak of fury began in Paris on August 24, 1572—the date known on the Catholic calendar as St. Bartholomew's Day. With the first light of dawn, Catholic mobs in Paris hunted for Protestant neighbors, dragged them from bed, and murdered them. The massacres spread to other cities and went on for over a month. About 12,000 Huguenots were killed.

The queen mother herself, Catherine de Medici, was largely to blame for the massacre. Catherine was Catholic, but her motives were not religious. Politics concerned her far more than religion. In 1572, she feared she was losing her influence over her weak son, King Charles IX. The Admiral de Coligny (koh-lee-NYEE), a Protestant noble, had become the king's closest adviser. To keep her position as the power behind the throne, she arranged for Coligny to be killed.

At first, the weak king objected to his mother's scheme. Finally, however, he yielded to her browbeating. He shouted in a fit of temper, "I consent. But then you must kill all the Huguenots in France so that none shall be left to reproach me. Kill them all! Kill them all." With Catherine's complete approval, the St. Bartholomew's Day massacre of the Huguenots began. On the same day, a hired killer assassinated Coligny.

The Valois dynasty ended.

After the St. Bartholomew's Day massacre, French politics became even more violent and confused. In 1574, Charles IX died of tuberculosis. His younger brother, Henry III, was destined to be the last Valois king of France. Though Henry reigned for 15 years, he did not rule. Nobody ruled France in these years of civil war.

Just as some German nobles supported Lutheranism to weaken the emperor, some French nobles became Protestants to weaken their Catholic king. Among the upper classes, religion and politics were closely linked.

For a while, it appeared that the Guise family might triumph and place their Catholic duke on the throne. Catholics both inside and outside France rallied around the Guise banner. Spain's Philip II supported the Catholic cause by sending Spanish armies into France. His French ally, the Duke of Guise, marched triumphantly into Paris.

Many French people—Catholics as well as Protestants—were outraged. Had France fought Spain for years only to have Spain handpick France's king? Nationalism began to outweigh religion for some French Catholic leaders. These leaders, known as the *politiques* (poh-lih-TEEKS), wanted peace for France. They wanted a king strong enough to stop the wars that were tearing France apart. The politiques worked for religious toleration and a strong monarchy.

In 1589, Catherine de Medici died. Shortly afterward, King Henry III ordered nine of his soldiers to murder the Catholic Duke of Guise. In revenge, a Dominican friar stabbed the king to death.

Henry IV brought peace.

The heir to the French throne was Prince Henry of Navarre. He was descended from the popular medieval king, Saint Louis (Louis IX). Henry was robust, athletic, and handsome. He soon showed

407

SECTION 4
Objectives and Teaching Strategies

OBJECTIVE 1. Explain the methods of Henry IV in uniting France and strengthening the monarchy.
Teaching Strategy: *Writing about History: Henry IV* (page 392d)

OBJECTIVE 2. Describe the political views and tactics of Cardinal Richelieu.
Teaching Strategy: *Discussing History: Cardinal Richelieu* (page 392d)

■ BACKGROUND
Catherine de Medici was a patroness of the arts. She initiated the building of a new wing on the Louvre, the construction of the Tuileries, and the building of the chateau at Monceau.

SECTION 4
Resources

ASSESSMENT
■ Section Quiz 17.4

REINFORCEMENT
■ Independent Practice 17.4

ENRICHMENT
■ Voices from the Past 17.4

■ BACKGROUND

By persuading the king to banish his own mother from the court, Richelieu demonstrated his control of the country. The king, however, always insisted that Richelieu seek his approval on state matters. Richelieu did, and he was never denied.

■ DISCUSSION

Gargantua and Pantagruel appealed to the masses and sold many more copies during Rabelais's lifetime than he ever imagined. His books, however, were placed on the Index of Forbidden Books and for many years could not be published in France. Ask students why they think the books were forbidden. Do things like this still happen?

himself to be decisive, fearless in battle, and a clever politician as well. He was the leader of the House of Bourbon and therefore a Huguenot. With the support of both the Protestants and the Catholic politiques, he became the first Bourbon king of France, Henry IV. Yet it took him nine more years of fighting to secure his crown.

Many Catholics, including the people of Paris, still opposed Henry. For the sake of his war-weary country, Henry chose to give up his religion. In 1593, he became a Catholic. Shortly afterward, the Catholics of Paris warmly welcomed him as their king. Explaining his religious turnabout, Henry IV is sometimes quoted as saying: "Paris is well worth a Mass."

In 1598, Henry took another giant step toward healing France's wounds. He declared that the Huguenots could henceforth worship in peace. In every district, Huguenots could set up at least one house of worship. Paris was the only large French city where Protestant worship was strictly banned. This declaration of religious toleration was known as the Edict of Nantes.

Henry devoted the rest of his reign to rebuilding France and restoring its prosperity. "I hope to make France so prosperous," he said, "that every peasant will have chicken in the pot on Sunday." Although chicken dinners remained beyond the reach of most peasants, no other French king had cared so much for the welfare of the common people. Aided by an able finance minister, the Duke of Sully, Henry restored the French monarchy to a strong position. Spanish armies no longer invaded French soil. After a generation of war, most French people welcomed Henry's peace.

Some people, however, hated the compromising spirit of their Bourbon king. In 1610, one such fanatic leaped into the royal carriage and stabbed Henry to death.

Cardinal Richelieu controlled France.

Henry's nine-year-old son, Louis XIII, became the second Bourbon monarch. Louis reigned from 1610 to 1643. Even after he became an adult, Louis XIII lacked the ability and strength of his father. However, he at least had the good sense to turn over the business of government to someone more gifted than himself.

In 1624, Louis appointed a Catholic cardinal named Richelieu (RISH-uh-loo) to be his chief

408

Richelieu was the power behind the French throne from 1624 to 1642. A shadowy figure, he was sometimes called "the gray eminence."

minister. Richelieu became virtual ruler of France. No statesman in Europe could match the iron will and cunning mind of this lean-faced, hawk-nosed cardinal.

The wily Richelieu devoted himself to two goals: increasing the power of the Bourbon monarchy and making France the strongest state in Europe. He saw three dangers to the French state: (1) the independence of the Huguenot cities, (2) the power of the French nobility, and (3) the

Footnote to History

Richelieu, plagued by ill health, often shunned the hectic social life of the royal court. He retreated to the peace and quiet of his own household and the companionship of his 14 cats.

encircling armies of the Hapsburgs. He fought relentlessly against all three.

First, Cardinal Richelieu feared a provision in the Edict of Nantes that gave Huguenots the right to fortify their cities. A walled city could defy the king. Indeed, several Huguenot cities had already rebelled, including the stronghold of La Rochelle. In 1627, royal troops besieged La Rochelle and starved it into submission. The loss of La Rochelle and other walled cities was a major setback for French Protestantism. Huguenots continued to worship freely while Richelieu lived, but later even this privilege was revoked.

The French nobles were the next group to lose their privileges under Richelieu. Many were ordered to take down their fortified castles. Richelieu's spies reported those who resisted or plotted against the king. In addition, Richelieu strengthened the powers of government agents to collect taxes and administer justice. These officials, called *intendants*, came from the ranks of the French middle class. They were staunchly loyal to the crown. Thus, the French ruler no longer needed the military and political services of the nobility. For the next 100 years, Bourbon kings would rule France as absolute monarchs, and no nobles would be strong enough to resist.

Richelieu triumphed over the Spanish and Austrian Hapsburgs as well. His successes formed part of the story of the Thirty Years' War (pages 410–411).

French thinkers questioned authority.

As France regained its political power, a new French intellectual movement began as well. The leading French thinkers of the 1500's witnessed France's religious wars with horror. What they saw turned some of them into skeptics (doubters) about the doctrines of all religions. To doubt old ideas, they thought, was the first step toward finding truth. The work of three French writers— François Rabelais (RAB-uh-LAY), Michel de Montaigne (mahn-TAYN), and René Descartes (day-KART)—marked another sharp break from the ideas of the Middle Ages.

Rabelais (1483–1553) François Rabelais was a monk who loved to laugh at human folly. He fled the monastery to pursue a career in medicine. Between 1532 and 1535, he published two satires on European society, *Gargantua* and *Pantagruel*. The comic heroes of these books were keen-witted giants with immense appetites for food and fun. Rabelais ridiculed everything that restricted the human spirit. People, he wrote, should live by one rule: "Do as you wish."

Montaigne (1533–1592) A later writer and thinker, Michel de Montaigne lived during the worst years of the French religious wars. Early in his life, the death of a dear friend caused him overwhelming grief. He shut himself away in his private library and thought deeply about life's meaning.

Montaigne set forth his thoughts in a new form of literature, the essay. An essay is a short written work on a single topic. It usually expresses the personal views of the writer. In his essays, Montaigne told about himself, his lost friend, the meaning of friendship, the books that he loved, the doctors that he shunned, and many other topics.

In the first edition of his *Essays* (published in 1580), Montaigne warned readers that his subject goes no deeper than himself:

> This is an honest book, reader . . . I want to be seen here in my simple, natural, ordinary fashion, without pose or artifice; for it is myself that I portray. My defects will here be read to the life . . .

In fact, Montaigne's essays showed him to have more virtues than defects. An admirer once called him "the wisest Frenchman that ever lived."

Descartes (1596–1650) The third important French writer and thinker of this age was René Descartes. Descartes was both a mathematician and a philosopher. In his mathematical writings, he developed the basic ideas of analytic geometry. He also studied optics, astronomy, and natural philosophy in its connections with what is now called psychology.

Descartes is considered the founder of modern philosophy. His most famous work was his *Discourse on Method*, which he wrote as a guide for "seeking truth in the sciences." Descartes believed nothing should be accepted on faith. Everything should be doubted until proved by reason. How could he prove his own existence? Descartes knew himself to be thinking, doubting. The one thing each person knows for certain, wrote Descartes, is, "I think, therefore I am."

409

ANSWERS TO
Section Review 4

Define:
(a) French Catholic leaders who wanted peace and worked for strong monarchy and religious toleration (b) French government agents (c) short written work on a single topic

Identify:
(a) family that ruled France from 1328 to about 1590 (b) power behind the throne of her sons (c) French followers of Calvinism (d) first Bourbon king of France (e) declaration of religious tolerance (f) virtual ruler of France during reign of Louis XIII (g) French monk, author of satires (h) French thinker who introduced the essay (i) founder of modern philosophy

Answer:
1. (a) wars with Spain for control of Italy, death of king (b) Hatred between Huguenots and Catholics led to violence.

2. (a) Bourbon and Guise (b) Protestant, Catholic

3. (a) She arranged for Coligny, a Protestant advisor to her son, to be killed in order to protect her position as power behind the throne. (b) Charles IX agreed to Coligny's assassination only if Huguenots would also be killed; Catherine approved of massacre.

4. religious toleration and a strong monarchy

5. (a) for the sake of his war-weary country (b) declared in the Edict of Nantes that Huguenots could worship in peace; set

(continued)

ANSWERS TO (continued)

up at least one house of worship in every district except Paris

6. (a) increase the power of the Bourbon monarchy and make France the strongest state in Europe

(b) Huguenots had right to fortify their cities, and a walled city could defy the king. (c) ordered many to take down their fortified castles and strengthened the powers of intendants to collect taxes and administer justice

7. Henry did not state that he believed in one specific religion.

8. He wanted peace for France and a strong monarchy and was more nationalistic than religious.

SECTION 5
Objectives and Teaching Strategies

OBJECTIVE 1. Identify the causes of the Thirty Years' War.

Teaching Strategy: *Discussing History: Causes of the Thirty Years' War* (page 392e)

OBJECTIVE 2. Explain how the provisions of the Treaty of Westphalia affected the nations of Europe.

Teaching Strategy: *Skill Building: Recognizing Main Ideas* (page 392e)

Define: (a) politiques, (b) intendants, (c) essay
Identify: (a) Valois, (b) Catherine de Medici, (c) Huguenots, (d) Henry IV, (e) Edict of Nantes, (f) Richelieu, (g) Rabelais, (h) Montaigne, (i) Descartes

Answer:

1. (a) What political problems did France face in 1559? (b) How did religion divide the French people?
2. (a) What two noble families wanted to overthrow the Valois? (b) What was the religion of each?
3. (a) How did Catherine de Medici use religious hatreds to maintain her political power? (b) What role did she play in the St. Bartholomew's Day massacre?
4. What were the goals of the politiques?
5. (a) Why did Henry IV change his religion? (b) What did he do to establish religious toleration in France?
6. (a) What were Richelieu's two goals? (b) Why did he fear the Huguenot cities? (c) How did he weaken the French nobles?

Critical Thinking

7. Henry IV defined his own religion this way: "Those who follow their consciences are of my religion, and I am of the religion of those who are brave and good." Why was this a wise political statement for him to make as France's king?
8. Explain why Richelieu is generally considered a politique, even though he was a cardinal in the Catholic Church.

Religious wars split Germany.   5

For a time, the German princes and electors had settled their religious differences by the Peace of Augsburg in 1555 (page 385). They had agreed that the churches in Germany could be either Lutheran or Catholic, but not Calvinist. Furthermore, the prince of every state was to decide the religion of that state.

410

The Catholic and Lutheran princes of Germany watched each other warily. As tension mounted, the Lutherans joined together in the Protestant Union in 1608. The next year, Catholic princes formed the Catholic League. It would take only a spark to start a war.

Germans fought the Thirty Years' War (1618–1648).

The spark came in 1618. A Protestant mob rioted in the streets of Prague in the Czech kingdom of Bohemia. These Czechs were angry that their king, Ferdinand II, was both a foreigner— a German-speaking Austrian—and an ardent Catholic. Ferdinand was also a leader of the Hapsburg family. (He was a nephew of Charles V, a cousin of Philip II.) In 1619, he became Holy Roman Emperor.

As an Austrian, Ferdinand II aroused the Czechs' national hatred. As a Catholic, he menaced the religious freedom of the Lutheran princes of Germany. As a Hapsburg, he posed a threat to the Bourbon kings of France. Ferdinand's many enemies soon united against him.

In 1618, Ferdinand sent an army into Bohemia to put down the Protestant revolt. Several German Protestant princes took this chance to challenge their Catholic emperor.

Thus began the struggle known as the Thirty Years' War. This war was as confusing as it was vicious. To simplify it, we can divide the Thirty Years' War into two major phases: the phase of Hapsburg triumphs and the phase of Hapsburg defeats.

Between 1618 and 1630, Hapsburg armies from Austria and Spain crushed the troops hired by the Protestant princes. The Czech uprising also failed, and its leaders were executed. In 1625, the king of Denmark entered the war on the Protestant side. On the Catholic side, Ferdinand II hired a ruthless soldier of fortune, Albrecht von Wallenstein. Wallenstein raised an army of 125,000 men. He paid them by allowing them to plunder German villages. Wallenstein's huge armies destroyed everything in their path. By 1629, the Protestant cause in Germany looked weak indeed.

Then the tide of war suddenly shifted as the Protestants found a new leader. In 1630, a tall Swedish king named Gustavus Adolphus landed

---

SECTION 5
Resources

ASSESSMENT
■ Section Quiz 17.5

REINFORCEMENT
■ Independent Practice 17.5

ENRICHMENT
■ Voices from the Past 17.5

on the north coast of Germany. With him was a tough, tightly disciplined army of 13,000 men. For two years (1630–1632), Protestant princes rallied around his banner. Gustavus Adolphus outmaneuvered the Hapsburg armies and drove them out of northern Germany. Then Gustavus Adolphus was killed in battle in November 1632. Wallenstein died soon after, murdered by his own officers.

The remaining years of the German war were dominated by Cardinal Richelieu, the power behind the French throne. Richelieu cared nothing that the Hapsburgs were Catholic as he was. He loved France and feared the Hapsburgs, so he brought France into the war on the Protestant side. In 1635, he sent French troops into Germany to join Swedish and German Protestants.

The war dragged on for 13 more years. It left Germany ravaged. The German population sank from 20 million to 13.5 million. Only a small share of these died in battle. Many died of hunger, as armies burned and destroyed the crops. Others died of such diseases as plague, dysentery, and typhus that spread from army camps to the people nearby. Still others simply fled. Whole villages disappeared. Many peasants were forced back into serfdom after marauding armies destroyed their homes. Both trade and agriculture were in a shambles. Germany's economy was ruined.

The Treaty of Westphalia ended the war.

Gradually, the French and their Protestant allies wore down the Austrian Hapsburgs and their Spanish allies. In 1648, Ferdinand II's son (the new Holy Roman Emperor) agreed to a peace treaty that heavily favored his Swedish, French, and Protestant enemies.

The Thirty Years' War ended with the Treaty of Westphalia. These were its major terms:

1. France took Alsace, a fertile strip of land along the west bank of the Rhine River.
2. Sweden took a piece of northern Germany on the North Sea and another piece on the Baltic Sea.
3. The princes of Germany won almost total independence from the Holy Roman Empire. Each German state could sign treaties and go to war without the approval of the emperor.

4. Calvinism gained equal privileges with Lutheranism and Catholicism. A Calvinist prince in Germany could now dictate the religion of his state.
5. The Dutch Republic (or United Provinces) won recognition as an independent state.

The long-term consequences of the treaty were more important than its terms. In effect, Germany lost what little unity it once had. Its 300 states became virtually independent. The Holy Roman Empire, which had earlier held the German princes together, survived only in name.

As the big losers of the Thirty Years' War, the Hapsburg states of Austria and Spain declined in power. As the major winner of the war, France emerged as Europe's strongest state.

Another European nation, England, was fortunate to stay out of the ruinous Thirty Years' War. However, England was going through serious religious and political troubles of its own. England's troubles as well as its growing strength will be described in the next chapter.

Section REVIEW 5

Identify: (a) Ferdinand II, (b) Bohemia, (c) Thirty Years' War, (d) Wallenstein, (e) Gustavus Adolphus, (f) Treaty of Westphalia
Answer:
1. (a) Why did the Protestants of Bohemia riot in 1618? (b) What happened when Ferdinand II tried to put down the revolt?
2. What was the turning point in the Thirty Years' War?
3. Why did France, a Catholic kingdom, join the Protestant side?
4. (a) What were the economic and social effects of the Thirty Years' War on Germany? (b) What was the political effect on German unity?
5. What did each of the following gain from the war? (a) France (b) Sweden (c) Dutch Republic (d) German Calvinists
6. (a) Which powers were the major losers in the war? (b) Which was the major winner?

Critical Thinking
7. Give evidence to support the following statement: The Thirty Years' War was more a political conflict than a religious one.

411

ANSWERS TO
Section Review 5

Identify:
(a) German-speaking Austrian Catholic king of Bohemia (b) Czech kingdom (c) religious war lasting almost 30 years (d) soldier of fortune hired to fight for the Catholics in Thirty Years' War (e) Swedish king who drove Hapsburg armies out of northern Germany (f) ended the Thirty Years' War

Answer:
1. (a) They were angry because their king was both a foreigner and an ardent Catholic. (b) Several German Protestant princes took this chance to challenge their Catholic emperor.
2. 1630, when the Swedish king, Gustavus Adolphus, landed on the north coast of Germany
3. Richelieu, the power behind the French throne, loved France and feared the Hapsburgs.
4. (a) War left Germany ravaged, its economy in shambles. The population dropped from 20 million to 13.5 million. (b) Germany lost what little unity it had.
5. (a) Alsace (b) parts of northern Germany (c) recognition as an independent state (d) equal privileges with Lutherans and Catholics
6. (a) Hapsburg states of Austria and Spain (b) France
7. Example: Richelieu, though Catholic, entered the war on the side of the Protestants.

411

Concluding the Chapter

1. **Chapter Closer**
   Have students write essays on the shift in power in Europe between 1500 and 1650. Encourage students to include the social, religious, and political changes that they feel were most significant in changing the balance of power in Europe.

2. **Reteaching Activities**
   a. Summarizing Have students identify reasons the Spanish economy was bankrupt in 1650.
   b. Identifying Main Ideas Have students discuss the ways in which Henry IV and Richelieu strengthened the French monarchy.
   c. Recalling Information Have students list the participants in the Thirty Years' War and the effects of the Treaty of Westphalia on each.

Answers to Chapter Review appear on pages 392e–392f.

Summary

1. Spain built an overseas empire. Early in the 1500's, Spain began building a vast empire in the Americas. Cortés conquered the Aztecs of Mexico, and Pizarro defeated the Incas of Peru. Explorations by others extended Spain's empire from what is now Kansas to Chile. Spain prospered, and its art and literature flourished.

2. Spain was a Catholic bulwark. At the center of Spain's empire was its emperor, Philip II, who ruled his lands absolutely. Determined to support Catholicism, Philip played a large part in the defeat of the Ottomans at Lepanto. His attempt to invade England with the Armada failed. He also failed to put down a revolt against Spanish rule in the Netherlands. Spain's prosperity, based only on gold and silver from its empire, soon collapsed.

3. The Netherlands won independence. Successful in their revolt against Spain, the Netherlands had a thriving trade and a capitalist economy. The Dutch established a republic in which many religious viewpoints were accepted. The artists of the Netherlands reflected its prosperity and civic spirit.

4. France's crown changed hands. After 1559, France was mired in a series of wars between Catholics and Huguenots as well as a power struggle between the reigning Valois kings and the competing houses of Bourbon and Guise. The civil war ended when Henry IV won the throne, changed his religion to Catholicism, and passed laws granting toleration to both Catholics and Huguenots. The skillful governing of Richelieu, minister to Louis XIII, made the French monarch an absolute ruler. During this era, French thinkers developed new literary forms and laid the basis for modern philosophy.

5. Religious wars split Germany. Germany became more disunited when conflicts between Catholics and Protestants led to the Thirty Years' War. The war caused great suffering in Germany, led to the decline of Hapsburg Spain and Austria, and left France the strongest state in Europe.

Reviewing the Facts

1. Define the following terms:
   a. conquistador   c. encomienda
   b. viceroy   d. capitalism
2. Explain the importance of each of the following names, dates, places, or terms:
   a. Cortés   e. Lepanto
   b. Pizarro   f. Armada
   c. encomienda   g. Cervantes
   d. Philip II   h. El Greco

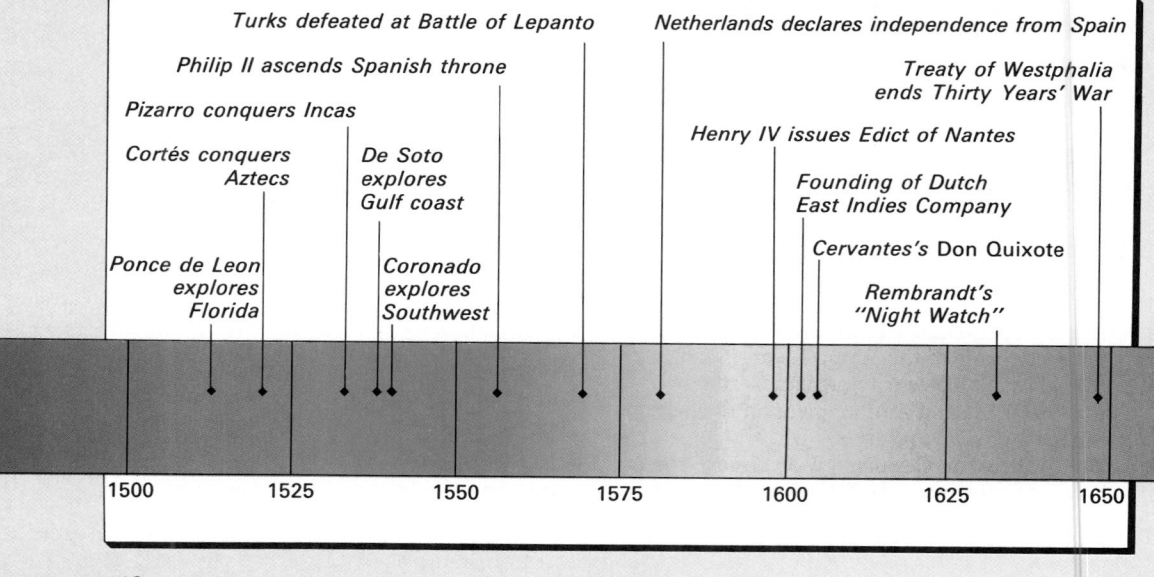

Turks defeated at Battle of Lepanto

Philip II ascends Spanish throne

Pizarro conquers Incas

Cortés conquers Aztecs

De Soto explores Gulf coast

Ponce de Leon explores Florida

Coronado explores Southwest

Netherlands declares independence from Spain

Treaty of Westphalia ends Thirty Years' War

Henry IV issues Edict of Nantes

Founding of Dutch East Indies Company

Cervantes's Don Quixote

Rembrandt's "Night Watch"

1500   1525   1550   1575   1600   1625   1650

412

i. William the Silent   q. intendant
j. Rembrandt   r. Rabelais
k. Huguenot   s. Montaigne
l. Catherine de Medici   t. Descartes
m. politique   u. 1618–1648
n. Henry IV   v. Hapsburg
o. Edict of Nantes   w. Treaty of
p. Richelieu   Westphalia

3. What was the outcome of (a) Spain's attack on the Ottoman empire? (b) The Spanish Armada's attack on the English? (c) Spain's war in the Netherlands?
4. What was the Commercial Revolution?
5. (a) How did the Thirty Years' War begin? (b) What were the results of the war?

Basic Skills

1. **Interpreting statistics** Shipments of gold and silver from America to Spain peaked between 1591 and 1600 to a total of 2,707,626,528 grams of silver and 19,451,420 grams of gold. (a) If the value of silver is currently $.23 per gram and the value of gold is $15.00 per gram, what was the value of those shipments of silver and gold by today's standards? (b) According to information in the chapter, how was most of this wealth used?
2. **Applying a concept** Review the concept of inflation on page 401. (a) As imports of silver and gold increased, what happened to prices in Spain? (b) How was the economy affected?
3. **Using maps** (a) Using the maps on pages 362–363 and 414, identify the parts of the Portuguese empire taken over by the Dutch. (b) What purposes did these territories serve for the Netherlands?

Researching and Reporting Skills

1. **Writing an editorial** Imagine that you are the editor of either an English or a Spanish newspaper at the time of the Spanish Armada. Write an appropriate editorial about the outcome of the battle.
2. **Writing a speech** After seeing examples of their wealth, Cortés was determined to conquer the Aztec, even to sinking his ships so there would be no turning back. Write a speech that Cortés might have made to his men before they attacked the Aztec, inspiring them to fight. What arguments might he have used to urge them to conquer?

Critical Thinking

1. **Comparing** Compare the leadership of Philip II of Spain and Henry IV of France. (a) What were the objectives of each? (b) How well did each succeed? (c) What legacy did each leave to his kingdom?
2. **Analyzing a quotation** A sixteenth-century diplomat summed up the motivation of the conquistadors with the words, "Religion supplies the pretext and gold the motive." (a) Explain the meaning of this quotation. (b) To what extent do you think it accurately describes Spanish conquests in the Americas?
3. **Forming a hypothesis** Spain and Portugal were the two countries that first explored the Americas and staked out empires there. Why were these two countries the leaders? (a) Form a hypothesis to answer this question. (b) Explain your reasoning.
4. **Analyzing economics** (a) What role did interest and profit have in the Commercial Revolution? (b) How did these ideas differ from those of the medieval Church?
5. **Evaluating** (a) List the causes and outcomes of the Thirty Years' War. (b) To what extent did the merit of the causes justify the outcomes? (c) What old problems did the Treaty of Westphalia solve and what new ones did it create?

Perspectives on Past and Present

1. People's values today differ greatly from those at the time of the Spanish conquest. (a) At that time, how was the conquistadors' treatment of the Native Americans judged? (b) How would it be judged today?
2. During the 1500's, political thinking in France developed in two different directions—one of centralizing authority and the other of questioning authority. What was the outcome for France? Can you think of countries today in which this has happened?

Investigating History

Read about the work of one of the artists of the period—such as Velázquez, El Greco, Hals, Vermeer, or Rembrandt. Choose one painting you particularly like. How does it relate to the society of its day and why does it appeal to you?

413

CHAPTER
Evaluation

Chapter Test 17, Alternate Chapter Test 17, and Computer Test Bank Chapter 17 Test can be used to evaluate your students' understanding of this chapter.

Geographic Theme: Movement

How did European civilization spread around the globe?

The age that began with the voyages of Dias, Columbus, Da Gama, and Magellan saw the spread of European influence around the world. Before 1450, European nations had no direct contact with the Americas, sub-Saharan Africa, and the Far East. Within less than a century, European influence would circle the globe.

The discovery of a sea route to the East and another to the newly discovered continents to the West caused a revolution in trade. Often political control became necessary to gain a monopoly of trade. Nations therefore staked out claims to strategic places and areas for trade.

European ships loaded with goods also carried an unseen export—the culture of their homelands. The governing of colonies was done in the language of the ruler. Colonial laws reflected those of the parent country. Religion too followed the flag. The efforts of French, Spanish, and Portuguese priests spread Catholicism worldwide.

Ideas know no boundaries. Their spread through trade, migration, and conquest is known as *cultural diffusion*. Thus, the expansion of European economic and political power after 1500 brought with it the diffusion of European culture. A Spanish cathedral rose where Tenochtitlán had stood, and Portuguese forts overlooked the trading cities of East Africa.

Often the spread of European thought and traditions overshadowed what was native to a place. Subject peoples everywhere faced the problem of adapting to foreign ways without losing their own culture and traditions.

1. List the overseas lands owned or held by the major European nations in 1700.
2. Using the maps on pages 768, 773, 776, 787, and 808, give the names of those places today.
3. From the information on the map, make a generalization about the influence of European civilization in the seventeenth century. Give examples to illustrate your answer.
4. What ways might subject peoples use to preserve their own culture and traditions?

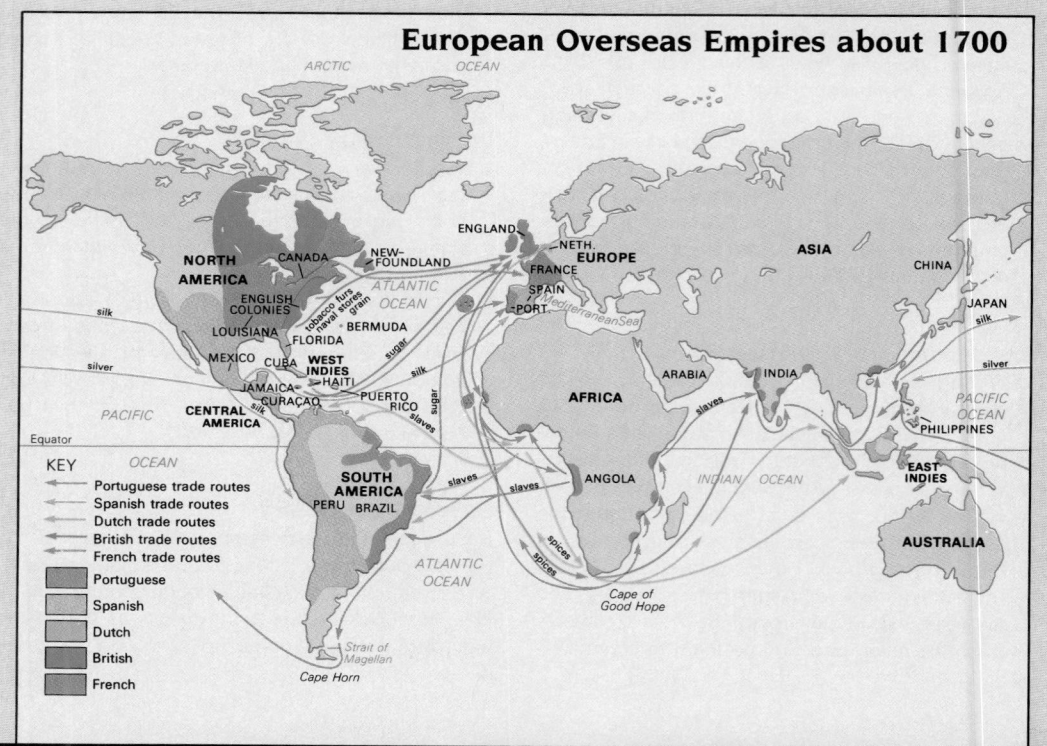

European Overseas Empires about 1700

KEY
- Portuguese trade routes
- Spanish trade routes
- Dutch trade routes
- British trade routes
- French trade routes
- Portuguese
- Spanish
- Dutch
- British
- French

ANSWERS TO
Geographic Theme

1. *Portugal:* Brazil, Mozambique, Zanzibar, Macao, Cape Verde, Gold Coast, Angola; *Spain:* Mexico, Cuba, Santo Domingo, Puerto Rico, Venezuela, Colombia, Peru, Chile, Philippines; *Netherlands:* Dutch Guiana, Cape of Good Hope, East Indies; *England:* Newfoundland, Atlantic Colonies, Hudson Bay, Jamaica, Bombay, Madras, Calicut, Calcutta; *France:* New France, Louisiana, Haiti, French Guiana

2. Brazil, Mozambique, Tanzania, India, Senegal, Ghana, Angola; Mexico, Cuba, Santo Domingo Puerto Rico, Venezuela, Colombia, Peru, Bolivia, Chile, Argentina, Philippines; Suriname, Union of South Africa, Indonesia; Newfoundland, United States, Canada, Jamaica, India; Canada, United States, Haiti, French Guiana

3. European civilization spread to all areas of the globe during the seventeenth century. Where Europeans held only trading posts, as in East Africa, India, and the Spice Islands, there was little cultural impact; where Europeans settled, as in Canada and the 13 colonies, the cultural impact was greater.

4. through oral and written traditions, arts and crafts, religion and festivals, and family life

Historical Themes

Key ideas, famous leaders, and new scientific discoveries and inventions played an important role in shaping events in Europe from 1300 to 1650.

Impact of Ideas

The Renaissance, Reformation, and Scientific Revolution introduced new ideas that had a far-reaching impact and marked a break from medieval life. The Renaissance celebrated individual achievement, the enjoyment of worldly pleasures, an interest in classical learning, and a renewed curiosity about the world. The impact of Renaissance ideas can be seen in the bold new statues, frescoes, and palaces created by Renaissance artists and architects. The hunger for knowledge and desire for wealth and fame motivated explorers like Columbus to sail uncharted waters and discover new lands.

In contrast to this focus on worldly concerns, Martin Luther and other religious reformers focused attention on the Catholic Church and its spiritual message. Luther challenged the Church by asserting that the Bible is the only authority for Christian life, that salvation can be achieved by faith alone, and that each person has a special relationship with God. Luther's ideas ignited a religious upheaval that split Europe into rival Catholic and Protestant states.

During the Reformation, another revolution in people's thinking also occurred. It started when a small group of scientists led by Kepler and Galileo began using the scientific method to study the natural world. Their studies led them to conclude that the same physical laws operated throughout the universe. This idea paved the way for the Scientific Revolution.

Individuals and History

The three centuries discussed in this unit produced many individuals whose deeds and works affected the policies of nations and the ways entire generations of people would look at and describe the world.

Artists such as Donatello, Masaccio, Michelangelo, Raphael, and Da Vinci drew on Classical ideas to produce new works that portrayed the world in fresh new ways. In writing, Dante's *Divine Comedy* mixed medieval concern for religion with a

Renaissance focus on worldly concerns, while Machiavelli's *The Prince* probed matters of practical politics. In science, Galileo's work opened the door to research that led to developments in physics in the twentieth century.

Martin Luther's challenge to the authority of the Church set off a religious crisis that would alter the course of European history. The Catholic Church responded to the Protestant challenge through reform efforts led by people such as Ignatius of Loyola.

The movement to create stronger nation-states continued. In England, Henry VIII—after a dispute with the pope—set up a new Church of England. He also gained the loyalty of the middle class by giving out property seized from the Church. Philip II of Spain used the gold and silver from his American colonies to build an army for use against Muslims and Protestants.

Technology and History

The leaders of the Renaissance, Reformation, and Scientific Revolution could not have translated their ideas into action without a small but vital group of new inventions. The caravel, compass, and astrolabe enabled Columbus and other explorers to sail great distances across uncharted waters. The printing press had a revolutionary impact by rapidly spreading new ideas and by making the Bible available to more people. Finally, the telescope enabled Galileo to study the planets and confirm the heliocentric theory.

Analyzing Historical Themes

1. How did Renaissance ideas and values differ from those of the Middle Ages?
2. Which of the individuals introduced in this unit do you think had the greatest impact on history? Explain.
3. Identify an important outcome of the invention of the caravel, printing press, and telescope.

415

ANSWERS TO
Analyzing Historical Themes

1. Renaissance focus on the individual, earthly matters, and learning marked a break from medieval life. Students may recall that the early Middle Ages were characterized by conformity, emphasis on the spiritual, and the decline of learning.
2. Answers will vary.
3. Caravel allowed explorers to sail great distances across uncharted waters; printing press made possible the rapid spread of new ideas; telescope enabled Galileo to study planets and confirm heliocentric theory.

UNIT
Evaluation

Unit V Test and Alternate Unit V Test can be used to evaluate your students' understanding of this unit.

Summer Palace near St. Petersburg

	1560	1600	1640
Political and Governmental Life	*Queen Elizabeth I*	**1603–1713** Stuart dynasty rules England	*Louis XIV*
Economic and Technological Life	**1577** Drake raids Spanish ships and sails around the world	**1607** England founds Virginia colony **1600** English East India Company founded	**1650's** Inflation ruins Spanish economy
Social and Cultural Life	**1576** First permanent theater is built in London	**1600's** Painting flourishes in Amsterdam	**1660's** France cultural center of Europe *Rubens'* Autoritratto con Isabella Brandt

Unit **VI**

The Transition to Modern Times

Historical Themes

Individuals and History Strong rulers wielded power in the era of absolutism. Enlightenment ideas, the abuse of absolute power, and the desire for freedom led to revolutions and new ways of governing.

Cultural Development Elizabethan England and the France of Louis XIV produced cultural golden ages marked by great works of literature and the arts. Versailles was a center of artistic and literary activity and the model for court life.

The Rise of Democractic Ideas The age of absolutism endured only briefly. Enlightenment ideas concerning the separation of powers, the consent of the governed, and political rights led to a new age based on the ideas of democracy.

1680   **1720**   **1760**

1689
Glorious Revolution
leads to Bill of Rights

1700's
Parliamentary rule
emerges in England

1799–1814
Napoleon rules France

1682
▼ Peter the Great modernizes Russia

◀**1776**
United States declares
its independence

1700's
Mercantilism brings
wealth to Europe

1768–1779
Cook explores the Pacific

1776
Adam Smith writes
The Wealth of Nations

1789 ▶
Parisian
women
march on
Versailles

1687
Newton discovers
law of gravity

1700's ▲
Age of Enlightenment
brings new ideas

The World about 1650

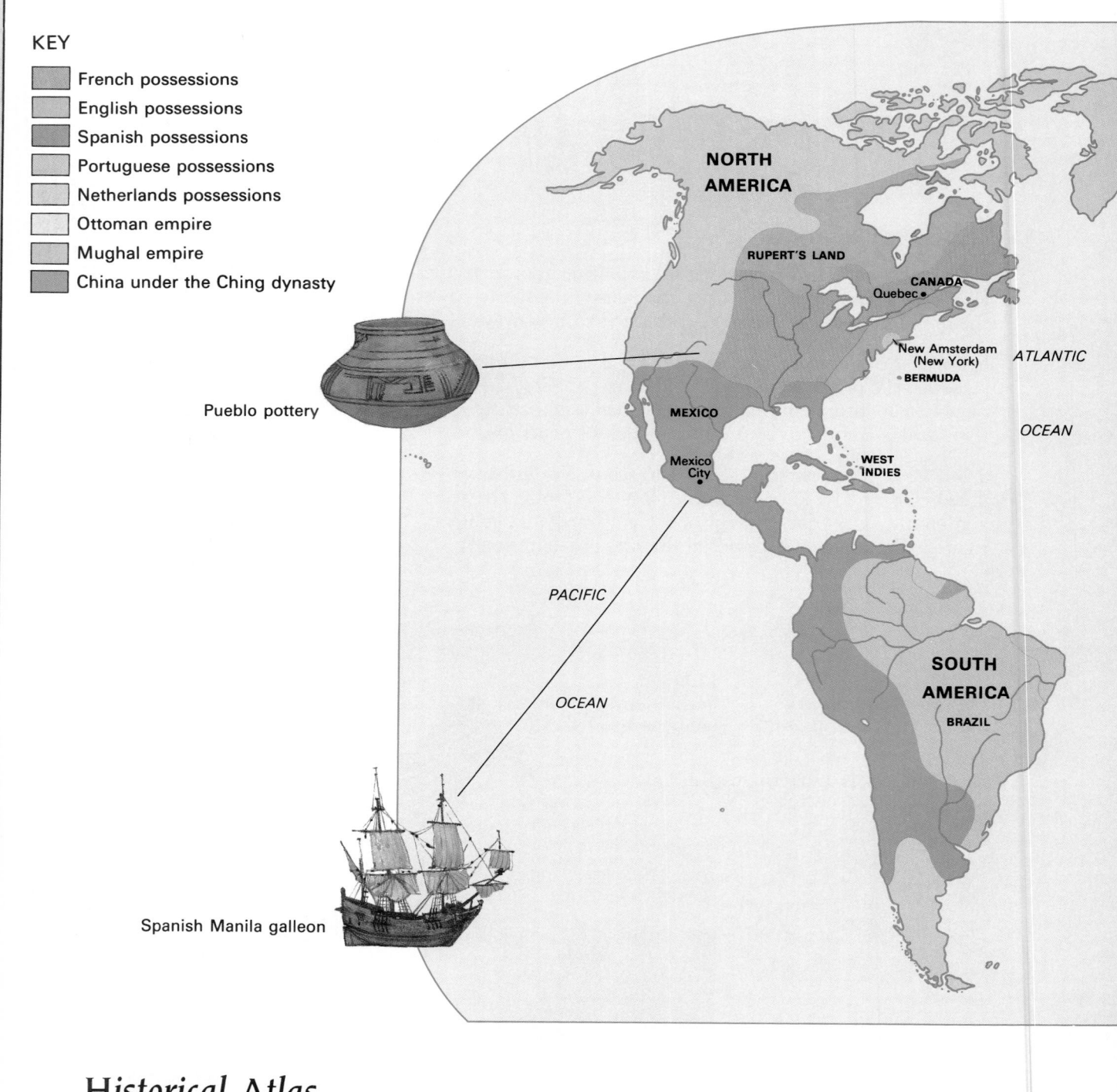

KEY

- French possessions
- English possessions
- Spanish possessions
- Portuguese possessions
- Netherlands possessions
- Ottoman empire
- Mughal empire
- China under the Ching dynasty

Pueblo pottery

Spanish Manila galleon

NORTH AMERICA

RUPERT'S LAND

CANADA
Quebec

New Amsterdam
(New York)

ATLANTIC

BERMUDA

MEXICO

Mexico City

WEST INDIES

OCEAN

PACIFIC

OCEAN

SOUTH AMERICA

BRAZIL

Historical Atlas

Louis XIV of France

Zen Buddhist priest

ARCTIC   OCEAN

ASIA

ENGLAND NETH.
London
Amsterdam
Paris HOLY Vienna
ROMAN
FRANCE EMPIRE AUSTRIA
EUROPE
PORTUGAL SPAIN
Lisbon Madrid Rome
Constantinople
Jerusalem

Moscow

RUSSIA

Peking
Ch'ang-an
Canton

JAPAN
Kyoto Edo

PACIFIC

OCEAN

AFRICA

Mecca

Delhi

Bombay
Goa
Calcutta

Pondicherry
CEYLON

PHILIPPINE IS.

ATLANTIC

OCEAN

INDIAN   OCEAN

EAST INDIES

NEW HOLLAND

Cape of
Good Hope

TASMANIA

NEW
ZEALAND

Bronze weight used
for measuring gold

Taj Mahal

419

England: Tudor Queen and Stuart Kings

Chapter Overview

Elizabeth I, the last and greatest of the Tudor dynasty, ruled England from 1558 to 1603. She faced many challenges: conflicts with Parliament over religious issues and monetary problems, a plot to overthrow her rule, and threats from Philip II of Spain. Despite political problems, Elizabethan England during the late 1500's enjoyed a golden age.

Elizabeth's successor, James I, inherited many of her unresolved problems. His belief in the divine right of kings led to heightened conflict with Parliament. However, James's reign was also marked by a notable achievement—the creation of the King James Bible. James's son, Charles I, faced even more serious problems with Parliament, leading to civil war.

In 1660, at the request of Parliament, Charles II restored the monarchy. During the Restoration, theater and the arts flourished, the Habeas Corpus Act was passed, and political parties took shape. The throne passed to James II, whose religious beliefs excited the fears of English Protestants and led to the Glorious Revolution. James lost his throne and Parliament invited James's Protestant daughter, Mary, and her Dutch husband, William, to rule England. During their joint rule, Parliament asserted its authority and passed the Bill of Rights, which made the monarchy conditional on the will of Parliament.

Chapter Focus

Ask students to imagine that they are the rulers of a country that faces imminent invasion by a powerful nation. Explain that a mixture of facts and rumors are pouring into the royal palace. Some reports suggest that the enemy fleet has been badly damaged. At the same time, their commanders are urgently requesting more supplies of gunpowder and cannon balls. Their advisers want them to leave the palace for a safer castle farther inland. Others say stay and fight. Ask students what they would do. How does Elizabeth's decision to personally defend England (pages 420–421) compare with the decisions reached by students? Ask students how they would have reacted to Elizabeth's speech. Explain that her speech electrified her tense army. Although the defiant Queen and her inspired army were not forced to defend their homeland, the speech marked a moment of supreme triumph for Elizabeth. Victorious, England was free to begin a period of extraordinary national development. This chapter describes Elizabeth's golden age and examines the great contest between Parliament and the Stuart kings.

Unit VI The Transition to Modern Times
THEME Conflicts between European monarchs and their subjects led to rebellion and an Age of Enlightenment

Chapter 18 England: Tudor Queen and Stuart Kings 1558–1688
FOCUS Queen Elizabeth's decision to participate in England's defense against the Spanish Armada

★ Advanced
● Basic

	SECTION 1	SECTION 2	SECTION 3	SECTION 4
Objectives	1. Explain how Elizabeth settled England's religious problems. 2. Identify the Spanish Armada and explain how England defeated it. 3. Explain the advantages of a joint-stock company.	1. Identify William Shakespeare and explain why he is considered a great playwright. 2. Describe the Globe Theater.	1. Explain the theory of the divine right of kings. 2. Describe how the civil war and Cromwell's rule affected England.	1. Explain why James II lost his throne. 2. Identify the Bill of Rights and explain its importance. 3. Compare and contrast the views of Thomas Hobbes and John Locke on the purpose of government.
Setting the Stage	Unit VI time line Elizabeth's strengths and weaknesses as Queen of England	The Elizabethan golden age	Conflict between the Stuart kings and Parliament	The Restoration
Teaching Strategies	Discussing History: The Art of Compromise Geography in History: The Spanish Armada Transparency 65 Economics and History: The Joint-Stock Company Check for Understanding	Analyzing a Quotation: Shakespeare Teaching with Pictures: The Globe Theater Check for Understanding	Analyzing a Quotation: Divine Right of Kings Writing about History: The Civil War and Protectorate Check for Understanding	Discussing History: Why James II Lost His Throne Transferring Ideas: Limiting the King's Power Skill Building: Comparing Views on Government Check for Understanding
Guided Practice	Transparency 65 Q&A Section Review 1	Section Review 2	Section Review 3	Section Review 4
Independent Practice Worksheets	Independent Practice 18.1 Vocabulary 18 Basic Skills 18	Independent Practice 18.2 Critical Thinking 18	Independent Practice 18.3 Geography Skills 18	Independent Practice 18.4
Enrichment	1. Primary Source: Voices 18.1 2. Creative Writing 3. Researching for Points	1. Primary Source: Voices 18.2 2. ★Preparing a Report: Shakespeare 3. Researching for Points	1. Primary Source: Voices 18.3 2. Researching for Points	1. Primary Source: Voices 18.4 2. ★Creative Writing 3. Researching for Points

Chapter Closer	●Reteaching Activities	Outlining, Recalling Information
	Chapter Review	Summary, Reviewing the Facts, Basic Skills, Researching and Reporting Skills, Critical Thinking, Perspectives on Past and Present, Investigating History
	Chapter Evaluation	Chapter Test 18, Alternate Chapter Test 18, Computer Test Bank Chapter 18 Test

Elizabeth I faced many challenges. 1

Setting the Stage

Have students read the introductory section about Elizabeth (page 421). Then ask students to pretend that they are writers for the *London Times*. Their assignment is to write an article assessing the new queen's strengths and weaknesses and predicting how she will handle England's religious conflicts, financial difficulties, and the threats posed by Mary Stuart and Philip II. Have several students read their articles to the class.

Teaching Strategies

Discussing History: The Art Of Compromise (Objective 1) Review the extraordinary religious changes that had occurred in England after the reign of Henry VIII. Recall that Henry VIII created a new Anglican Church. However, his son, Edward VI, allowed the Anglican Church to adopt many Protestant ideas and practices. Edward's half-sister, Queen Mary, suddenly reversed this trend when she reinstated the Catholic Church.

Elizabeth inherited a difficult and dangerous problem. About two thirds of the people supported the restored Catholic Church. However, the Protestant minority demanded that Elizabeth adopt Protestant ideas. Ask students to define *compromise*. Emphasize that in a compromise both sides have to give up something to reach an agreement. How did Elizabeth use compromise to resolve the religious issues that divided England?

Geography in History: The Spanish Armada (Objective 2) Show Map Transparency 65, *Europe in 1560*, or refer to page 424. Explain that the Spanish fleet maintained a

tight crescent formation as it slowly sailed through the English Channel. Although faster and more agile, the English fleet could not penetrate the Spanish formation. The two fleets fired more than 100,000 cannonballs at each other with little effect. Then the English sent eight fire ships to scatter the Armada, making it vulnerable to the English guns. The Spaniards lost 64 ships; the English did not lose any.

Economics and History: The Joint-Stock Company (Objective 3) The Portuguese and the Spanish dominated East Indian trade throughout the sixteenth century. English merchants recognized that small partnerships could not raise enough capital to finance the expensive fleets needed to compete with Spain and Portugal. The English solved this problem by forming an association of investors known as a joint-stock company. Anyone could invest in a joint-stock company. Individuals bought shares and then shared in the profits (and losses) in proportion to their investments. Ask students to pretend that they are organizers for the East India Company. Have them write brief advertisements urging people to invest in the company's first venture. Note that the East India Company's first fleet returned with one million pounds of pepper, the sale of which earned a 95 percent profit. Point out that there were risks. For example, the first fleet lost one ship and more than 25 percent of its original crew of 480 men. Neverless, in its first 21 years of business, the East India Company increased its capital 50 times over.

Check for Understanding Have students explain how Elizabeth solved each of the four problems discussed in this section.

Enrichment Activities

1. **Reading a Primary Source** Assign Voices from the Past Resource Book 18.1.
2. **Creative Writing** Ask students to write a paper speculating on what might have happened if the Armada had defeated the English fleet.
3. **Researching for Bonus Points** Who was the commander of the Spanish Armada? (Don Alonzo Perez De Guzman VII, Duke of Medina Sidonia)

The Elizabethan era was a golden age. 2

Setting the Stage

England's victory over the Spanish Armada released a surge of national confidence and energy. Ask students to identify other events that contributed to the "good times" that allowed England to flourish.

Teaching Strategies

Analyzing a Quotation: Shakespeare (Objective 1) Ask why Shakespeare is considered a great poet and playwright. Can students name some of his plays? Students might mention *Hamlet, Romeo and Juliet, Merchant of Venice, Othello, Macbeth, A Midsummer Night's Dream, Henry IV, Twelfth Night,* or others. Explain that Shakespeare was a skilled observer of human nature and a master of the English language. Write the following passage from *As You Like It* on the board:

> All the world's a stage,
> And all the men and women
>   merely players.
> They have their exits and their
>   entrances,
> And one man in his time plays
>   many parts.

Ask students to interpret this passage in their own words.

Teaching with Pictures: The Globe Theater (Objective 2) Direct students' attention to the drawing of the Globe Theater (page 429). The Globe was octagonal, shaped like a "wooden O." It probably had an outside diameter of 86 feet and was 33 feet high. Have students contrast the Globe with modern theaters. Note that no elaborate props were used and all the actors were men. Elizabethan audiences were expected to use their imagination. Modern scholars estimate that about one tenth of London's population attended a play each week.

Check for Understanding Have students describe places they could visit or events they could attend in Elizabethan London.

Enrichment Activities

1. **Reading a Primary Source**
   Assign Voices from the Past Resource Book 18.2.

2. **Preparing a Report**
   Ask advanced students to find and interpret three excerpts from Shakespeare's writings. *Bartlett's Familiar Quotations* contains a number of famous quotations.

3. **Researching for Bonus Points**
   What role did Shakespeare perform in his play *Hamlet?* (Hamlet's father's ghost)

3 England had a civil war.

Setting the Stage

Explain that James I and Charles I, the two kings who followed Elizabeth, were constantly in debt. For example, in 1617 James I owed 726,000 pounds, a huge sum at that time. Ask students to recall from whom the two kings had to request money. The class should recall that English kings had to ask Parliament for additional funds.

Teaching Strategies

Analyzing a Quotation: Divine Right of Kings (Objective 1) Have students explain the theory of divine right of kings. Then read or distribute the following excerpt from a speech given by James I to Parliament in 1610:

> The state of monarchy is the supremest thing upon earth: for kings are not only God's lieutenants upon earth, and sit upon God's throne, but even by God himself they are called gods. God has power to create or destroy, make or unmake, at his pleasure to give life or send death, to judge all and to be judged. And the like power have kings: they make and unmake their subjects, they have power of raising, and casting down; of life, and of death.

After students have read this passage, ask, "According to James I, what was the relationship between a king and God? How were kings and God alike? If you had been a member of Parliament, how would you have felt about the king's speech?"

Writing about History: The Civil War and Protectorate (Objective 2) Ask students to write diary entries from the point of view of a Royalist (Cavalier) or a Roundhead. Diaries should refer to the following events: Charles's flight to the north in 1642, his capture in 1648, his execution, and the rise and fall of Oliver Cromwell. Have students share their writings and summarize the differences in views between the Cavaliers and the Roundheads.

Check for Understanding Have students use the chart on page 433 to explain the events leading to civil war.

Enrichment Activities

1. **Reading a Primary Source**
   Assign Voices from the Past Resource Book 18.3.

2. **Researching for Bonus Points**
   Who was Praise-God Barebones? (a Puritan leader in the Barebones Parliament; Cromwell dissolved this Parliament and then was proclaimed Lord Protector)

Parliament won political power. 4

Setting the Stage

Ask students to review the problems that led to the conflict between Charles I and Parliament. What advice would students give to Charles II for dealing with Parliament, obtaining money, settling religious issues, and restoring entertainment?

Teaching Strategies

Discussing History: Why James II Lost His Throne (Objective 1) After students have read about James II, write this statement on the board: James II had none of the Stuarts' virtues and all of their vices. Ask students to agree or disagree with this statement, and identify Stuart "virtues" and "vices." Point out that James II was both a practicing Catholic and a strong believer in the divine right of kings. He lacked his father's tact in dealing with political and religious opponents. For example, he openly violated the Test Acts passed by Parliament, which prohibited a Catholic from holding any public office. Ask students how debate over James's succession led to the rise of political parties. Point out that while Whigs and Tories disagreed about the extent to which the monarchy ought to be limited, they agreed that the king would not be above the law. Ask students what groups were threatened by the birth of a male Catholic heir. Explain that while England's various Protestant sects disagreed with one another about doctrine, they were united against Roman Catholicism. Both Whigs and Tories therefore invited William and Mary to overthrow James II for the sake of Protestantism.

Transferring Ideas: Limiting the King's Power (Objective 2) Point out that the idea of placing limits on the monarch's power began with the Magna Carta. Have students recall the effects of the Magna Carta, Petition of Right, and Habeas Corpus Act in limiting the king's power. Ask students to explain the purpose of each provision in the Bill of Rights (page 437). Emphasize that the Bill of Rights marked a turning point in the history of democracy. It protected the principle of representative government while ensuring that citizens would be secure from arbitrary authority. Have students compare the English Bill of Rights with the First Amendment of the United States Constitution.

Skill Building: Comparing Views on Government (Objective 3) The rebellions against Charles I and James II raised troubling questions about the relationship between a people and their government. Was it lawful for subjects to overthrow their monarch? Were people capable of governing themselves? Tell students that the answers depended on one's view of human nature. Have students compare the views of the English philosophers Thomas Hobbes and John Locke. Allow students to debate the underlying philosophical question of whether people are by nature good or bad. Students should see that these opposing beliefs would naturally lead to different ideas about proper government.

Check for Understanding Have students explain the significance of the following concepts: divine right, habeas corpus, bill of rights.

Enrichment Activities

1. **Reading a Primary Source** Assign Voices from the Past Resource Book 18.4.
2. **Creative Writing** Plague and the Great Fire of London occurred during the mid-1660's. Ask advanced students to write a diary describing what it was like to live in London during this time. Encourage students to refer to Pepys's diary.
3. **Researching for Bonus Points** What was the name of the treaty that contained the secret agreement between Charles II and Louis XIV? (Treaty of Dover)

ANSWERS TO Chapter Review 18

Reviewing the Facts

1. (a) organization set up to attract capital (b) belief that royal power comes from God

2. (a) last and greatest ruler of the Tudor dynasty (b) person who wished to purify Church of England (c) Catholic queen of Scotland who plotted to overthrow Elizabeth (d) king of Spain who sent Armada to attack England (e) greatest English sea dog (f) fleet assembled by Philip II of Spain to invade England (g) great poet and dramatist (h) responsible for creating a new Bible (i) ruler whose policies led to civil war (j) document signed by Charles I granting concessions to Parliament

(k) person loyal to the king during the English civil war **(l)** Puritan who supported Parliament **(m)** dictator after civil war **(n)** restored the monarchy after the death of Cromwell **(o)** member of group that opposed James II **(p)** member of group that supported James II

3. (a) London was a bustling, heavily populated, commercial, culturally advanced city. **(b)** reveal human nature; literary achievement

4. Cromwell's protectorate—limited amusement and entertainment; Restoration—restored entertainment and social life

5. (a) He believed that governments protected people from their naturally evil ways. **(b)** He believed that rebellion was justified if governments abused rights.

Basic Skills

1. (a) 1626 Parliament dismissed; Charles demanded forced loans, quartered troops in private homes. 1628 Parliament presented Charles with Petition of Right; Charles dissolved Parliament. 1639 Archbishop Laud sought to impose Church of England on Scots. Needing money, Charles called Parliament. 1641 Parliament passed laws to limit king's power. 1642 Charles entered Parliament with armed men. Mob reaction forced Charles to leave London; raised army. Civil war began. 1646 Cromwell defeated king's forces, dismissed Parliament. 1648 king taken prisoner. 1649 tried for treason and executed. **(b)** 1685 James, a Catholic, asserted divine right to rule without Parliament's consent. Alienated Tory support by appointing Catholics to high office. When Parliament protested, James dismissed Parliament. 1687 King announced that Catholics could hold government posts; stationed soldiers outside London. When son (heir) was

born to James, Parliament planned to overthrow James; invited William and Mary to rule. **(c)** Similarities: Both kings tried to rule without Parliament; religious policies a major concern. Use or threat of armed force against Parliament and London brought resistance. Differences: Charles, Church of England; James, Catholic. Charles's quarrel with Parliament about taxes led to civil war, bloodshed, trial, and execution. James tried to rule without Parliament; led to peaceful revolution and new monarch.

2. established state church acceptable to moderate Catholic and Protestant groups; had Mary Stuart executed; delayed question of marrying Philip II, aided Dutch Protestants, defeated Spanish Armada; encouraged joint-stock company, obtained treasure from Spain

Researching and Reporting Skills

Students' answers will vary according to their research and the viewpoints assumed.

Critical Thinking

1. (a) treacherous enemy, cruel, heretic **(b)** good sport; winks at us when we raid Spanish ships **(c)** flirts with papist religion; loves luxury and power; disregards our concerns

2. Fact: "I am come amongst you . . . to live or die amongst you . . . think foul scorn." Opinion: "My loving people . . . I have placed my chiefest strength and safeguard in the loyal hearts and good will of my subjects . . . I know I have the body of a weak and feeble woman, but I have the heart . . . of a king."

3. Joint-stock companies helped to launch England into the Commercial Revolution and to expand its political and economic power

4. (a) Precedents included Magna Carta and Model Parliament, both limiting power of king. **(b)** Tudors mostly cooperated with Parliament, at least in appearance; found means of income without raising taxes. **(c)** Henry VIII sought Parliamentary support for Act of Supremacy; Elizabeth, for Act of Uniformity; she disagreed with Parliament but did not dissolve it.

5. (a) James I declared that he was not answerable to people or to Parliament, only to God. Charles I and James II both acted as if they were above the law. **(b)** Habeas Corpus limited monarch's power to jail or keep individuals in jail without trial. Bill of Rights affirmed limits to monarch's power, the authority of Parliament, and freedom of individuals; also forbade standing army in time of peace.

6. Elizabethan era a time of new ideas, great literature, a taste for adventure, a reaching out to the world.

Perspectives on Past and Present

(a) Freedom of speech and petition, no excessive bail; **(b)** United States Bill of Rights includes freedom of religion and assembly, which were not included in English Bill of Rights. Neither religious tolerance nor separation of Church and state were practiced in England at that time.

Investigating History

Students' answers will vary but should reflect knowledge of events and the ideas and actions of Cromwell.

Chapter 18

Teaching with Pictures

Have students study the painting "The Armada Portrait" by George Gower, circa 1588. Students will note the queen's elaborate gown and jewels. Ask them to explain the significance of the position of Queen Elizabeth's right hand. The ships on the left represent the Spanish Armada on its way to England. Those on the right represent the Armada after it was destroyed by the British navy.

Queen Elizabeth sits in triumph, her hand on the globe. The ships shown in the background symbolize the English victory over the Armada.

Key Terms

joint-stock company
divine right
habeas corpus
bill of rights
absolute monarchy

Read and Understand

1. Elizabeth I faced many challenges.
2. The Elizabethan era was a golden age.
3. England had a civil war.
4. Parliament won political power.

As she rode through the ranks of the cheering soldiers, Elizabeth Tudor planned her speech to stir their fighting spirit. As queen of England, she was their leader, and she bore the fearful responsibility for the crisis that threatened all England.

On this day in August 1588, the Spanish fleet that Philip II called his Invincible Armada was somewhere off the English coast. Everyone knew that the Armada was coming to invade England, but nobody knew when or where it would strike.

An English army of 10,000 men was camped along the Thames River 20 miles east of London to defend their country from the invaders.

420

Chapter 18 Resources

GEOGRAPHY
- Geography Skills 18
- Transparency 65

REINFORCEMENT
- Vocabulary 18
- Basic Skills 18
- Reteaching 18
- Making Connections Study Guide 18

ENRICHMENT
- Critical Thinking 18
- History and Literature 18

ASSESSMENT
- Chapter Test 18
- Alternate Chapter Test 18
- Computer Test Bank

Now the queen herself was in the camp, and the soldiers were wildly excited to see their high-spirited, beloved sovereign seated proudly on her white horse. For this special occasion, Elizabeth wore her brightest red wig adorned with two white plumes that were easy for all to see above the soldiers' long pikes.

From her horse, the queen called to her troops, "My loving people!" They stopped their shouts and listened to her words.

My loving people ... Let tyrants fear! I have always so behaved myself that, under God, I have placed my chiefest strength and safeguard in the loyal hearts and good will of my subjects. Therefore, I am come amongst you ... being resolved, in the midst and heat of battle, to live or die amongst you all—to lay down for my God, and for my kingdom, and for my people, my honor and my blood even in the dust! I know I have the body of a weak and feeble woman, but I have the heart and stomach of a king, and a king of England too, and think foul scorn that ... any prince of Europe should dare to invade the borders of my realm.

As you will read in this chapter, Elizabeth's navy had already destroyed the Spanish Armada, even as she spoke. This stirring victory raised English pride in their nation and their queen to new heights.

Elizabeth I was the last and greatest of the Tudor dynasty. She ruled England for 46 years, from 1558 to 1603. During her reign, daring English captains roamed the seas in search of treasure. English writers, scholars, and poets produced great works of art.

Yet, for all of its glory, the Elizabethan Age was not without troubles. In fact, political and religious conflicts raged frequently. By the end of Elizabeth's reign, England was on the brink of a great crisis. The central question was, Who would rule England—Parliament or the monarch? To answer that question, much English blood was spilled.

This chapter traces English history from Elizabeth's golden age through the troubled reigns of the Stuart kings. Finally, a revolution led to the beginning of a new era with a new philosophy of government.

Elizabeth I faced many challenges.   1

The 25-year-old Elizabeth came to the throne in 1558 at the death of her half-sister, Mary Tudor. Elizabeth was the third of Henry VIII's children to rule England. Like her father, Elizabeth had a fierce temper and a robust nature. Athletic as a girl, she showed amazing energy and strength into her old age.

One courtier who observed Elizabeth closely concluded that she was "more than a man, and (in truth) sometimes less than a woman." At times, she was quite crude. She would spit on the floor and swear in an astonishing manner. When her temper boiled over, she sometimes cuffed an offending courtier with a sharp blow to the head.

The other side of Elizabeth's character was graceful, witty, and refined. Her wardrobe included 2,000 velvet and jewel-encrusted gowns. She composed poetry and strummed a lute. She boasted of being as well-read in the classics as any prince in Europe. She had a scholar's command of Greek and Latin and spoke fluently in French, Italian, and Spanish. Her mind was remarkably quick, and nothing escaped her keen, penetrating eyes. One observer wrote of her:

All her faculties were in motion, and every motion seemed a well-guided action; her eyes were set upon one, her ears listened to another, her judgment ran upon a third, to a fourth she addressed her speech.

Elizabeth understood all too well the widespread prejudice against a woman ruler. All during her reign, Parliament urged her to marry a suitable man, either foreigner or Englishman. Yet she always resisted these pressures for the good of England and the preservation of her own power. Though she had many suitors, she remained unmarried until her death. She was nicknamed the "Virgin Queen."

This gifted queen needed all her intelligence and energy to guide England safely through the troubles of the late 1500's. These troubles came from four directions at once: religious conflicts, a rival queen, Spanish ambitions, and financial difficulties.

421

SECTION 1 Objectives and Teaching Strategies

OBJECTIVE 1. Explain how Elizabeth settled England's religious problems.

Teaching Strategy: *Discussing History: The Art of Compromise* (page 420c)

OBJECTIVE 2. Identify the Spanish Armada and explain how England defeated it.

Teaching Strategy: *Geography in History: The Spanish Armada* (page 420c)

OBJECTIVE 3. Explain the advantages of a joint-stock company.

Teaching Strategy: *Economics and History: The Joint-Stock Company* (page 420c)

■ BACKGROUND

During Mary Tudor's reign, Elizabeth became the target of complex plots. She was imprisoned in the Tower of London, accused of involvement in a rebellion. These early experiences taught Elizabeth to guard her thoughts and measure every word.

SECTION 1 Resources

GEOGRAPHY
■ Transparency 65

REINFORCEMENT
■ Independent Practice 18.1

ENRICHMENT
■ Voices from the Past 18.1

ASSESSMENT
■ Section Quiz 18.1

■ DISCUSSION

Ask students to speculate how Elizabeth felt about ordering Mary beheaded. (Time after time, Elizabeth looked for a way to avoid having Mary put to death. Even after reluctantly signing the death warrant, she postponed its delivery. Finally royal aides did what she could not and delivered the warrant for Mary's death.)

Religious issues divided England.

Elizabeth inherited the religious problem from her father, King Henry VIII. Since Henry's break with the papacy in 1534 (page 379), royal policy on religion had changed direction several times. Protestantism gained strength under Elizabeth's young half-brother, Edward VI (1547–1553). Then, her half-sister, Mary Tudor (1553–1558), made every effort to return the country to Catholicism. At first, no one knew which religion Elizabeth would choose. After all, she had been Protestant when Edward ruled and Catholic during Mary's reign.

When Elizabeth came to power, she knew she could not hope to satisfy either the extreme Catholics or the extreme Protestants. She decided, therefore, to establish a state church that moderate Catholics and moderate Protestants might both accept, however grudgingly.

In 1559, the first Parliament of Elizabeth's reign granted her request for two religious laws. The first, the Act of Uniformity, set up a national church much like the one under Henry VIII. This was to be the only legal church in England. People were required to attend its services or pay a fine. The second law, a new Act of Supremacy, declared Elizabeth the Supreme Governor of England's institutions, its church as well as its state.

As a concession to Protestants, priests in the Church of England were allowed to marry and to deliver sermons in English, not Latin. As a concession to Catholics, the Church of England kept all the trappings of a formal priesthood such as rich robes and golden crucifixes. To avoid controversy over doctrine, the wording of the queen's Book of Common Prayer was intentionally vague.

What mattered most to Elizabeth was not the religious beliefs of her subjects but their loyalty and obedience. She wanted no religious wars in England. It was not her intention, she said, "to pry windows into men's souls."

Mary Stuart plotted against Elizabeth.

Elizabeth's religious compromise did not please devout Catholics. They hoped that Elizabeth's Catholic cousin Mary Stuart, Queen of Scots, would someday become the queen of England.

Both the pope and the rulers of Spain actively supported Mary in her quest to unseat Elizabeth. Despite this outside support, Mary faced a revolt from Scottish subjects who were fast converting to the Presbyterian creed preached by John Knox. In 1567, Mary fled to England, where Queen Elizabeth provided protection. Mary, however, could not rid herself of the quest for power. In 1586, she was caught plotting to overthrow Elizabeth.

Early in 1587, Elizabeth ordered Mary beheaded. English Protestants lighted bonfires of celebration when they heard that the ax had fallen. Elizabeth, however, wept at the thought of having shed the blood of a cousin and fellow queen.

Philip of Spain threatened England.

When Mary Queen of Scots died, Philip II of Spain also grieved but for a different reason. He had been one of Mary's strongest supporters in her bid for the throne. With Mary's death, relations between England and Spain reached a low point.

The marriage question When Elizabeth first came to the throne in 1558, Philip II had seemed to be her ally. In those days, Philip had been more concerned with the power of Catholic France than with the threat of Protestant England. Moreover, he had been Elizabeth's brother-in-law, the husband of Mary Tudor. After Mary's death, Philip hoped to marry Elizabeth.

Elizabeth deliberately kept Philip (and dozens of other suitors) waiting. She used the hopes of

Decisions in History

Mary was brought to trial in October 1586. The court's ruling that she be sentenced to death for treason placed Elizabeth in a difficult position. Her chief advisers urged her to sign the death warrant. They argued that Elizabeth would never be safe while Mary was alive. They also pointed out that if Elizabeth died, Mary would become queen and bring the Catholics back into power. If this happened, England would face the possibility of a civil war between Catholics and Protestants.

Despite these arguments, Elizabeth hesitated. Some advisers pointed out that it was a dangerous precedent to put another monarch to death. In addition, the Catholic powers led by Spain might try to avenge Mary's death by invading England. What would you have done and why?

a marriage to win diplomatic advantages with many European countries. Eventually, it became clear to all that the strong-willed sovereign would not marry anyone.

Drake and the sea dogs While still pretending friendship for Philip, Elizabeth secretly encouraged English adventurers to attack Spanish treasure fleets. These fleets sailed from the Americas to Spain with rich cargoes of gold and silver. The bold English captains who raided them were known as "sea dogs."

The greatest of the sea dogs was Francis Drake. On his most daring expedition (1577–1580), Drake raided Spanish ships in the Caribbean and along the eastern coast of South America. Then he did what no English captain had done before. He sailed through the Strait of Magellan around the tip of South America and captured Spanish treasure along the coast of Chile and Peru as well. From there, Drake sailed as far north as San Francisco Bay, crossed the Pacific Ocean, and returned home with stolen prizes valued at 600,000 pounds. (This sum was more than twice the *yearly* revenue of the English crown.)

Drake thus became the first person since Magellan's crew to sail around the world. Instead of apologizing to Spain for his piracies, Queen Elizabeth knighted him aboard his ship, the *Golden Hind.*

Turning Points in History

The Defeat of the Spanish Armada By knighting Drake, Elizabeth recognized his achievements while also symbolically defying Philip II. During the next few years, Elizabeth further angered Philip by aiding Dutch Protestants in their revolt against Catholic Spain (page 402). Her decision to execute Mary placed England and Spain on a collision course. Within a month after Mary's death, Philip ordered his fleet to invade England.

By the spring of 1588, Philip had carefully assembled the largest invasion force that Europe had ever seen. This force—known as the Invincible Armada—included 130 ships, with 8,000 sailors and 20,000 soldiers. The Armada had orders to rendezvous with barges carrying the Duke of Parma's army from the Netherlands. The fleet would then carry the Duke's battle-hardened troops across the Channel to invade England. Dutch ships, however, prevented the rendezvous from taking place.

The battle The Spanish Armada was sighted off the southwestern coast of England on July 29. Lighted beacons along England's southern coast spread the news to London. An English fleet commanded by Lord Howard and Sir Francis Drake sailed to meet the Armada.

The first battle quickly showed that the two fleets had very different strategies. The Spaniards arranged their ships in a tight crescent-shaped formation. They hoped for a pitched battle so that their powerful short-range cannons could disable the English ships while Spanish soldiers boarded and captured the English vessels.

Knowing of the Spanish strategy, the English had developed fast, maneuverable ships that allowed them to keep out of range of the Armada. The English would then pound the Spanish with long-range cannons.

During the next week, the two fleets exchanged cannon fire in fierce but indecisive battles. The Spanish failed to sink any English ships. The English avoided coming too close to the Spanish and failed to inflict any serious damage. Thus, the Armada moved steadily up the English Channel, reaching Calais on August 6.

Worried English commanders realized that if the crescent could not be broken, the Spanish plan might succeed. The English then decided on a daring strategy—sending eight unmanned fire ships into the Spanish fleet.

The English plan worked. Shortly after midnight, favorable winds blew the burning ships toward the unsuspecting Armada. Panic-stricken Spanish captains cut their anchors and headed for open waters. The Spanish crescent formation had finally been broken.

The English swiftly closed in on the disorganized and now vulnerable Armada. English gunners blasted gaping holes in the giant Spanish ships. Although the Spaniards fought bravely, several of their ships suffered severe damage and 15 were captured. Defeat seemed certain when a sudden storm scattered the two fleets.

With supplies and ammunition running low, the Spanish commander reluctantly abandoned his mission. He ordered his battered fleet to return to Spain by crossing the North Sea and sailing around the British Isles. Fierce storms sank as

423

■ BACKGROUND

Marrying for love was uncommon. Fathers arranged marriages for their daughters. Widows had many suitors since their property went to their new husbands when they remarried.

In recent years, divers have located 6 of the 24 Spanish ships wrecked on the coast of Ireland. The divers recovered cannons, coins, silverware, and a wide variety of jewelry. Historians believe that the Spanish officers and noblemen planned to wear their gold chains and rings as they paraded in triumph through London.

1. Lisbon
2. to invade England
3. the Duke of Parma's army; because his troops were battle-hardened and would add to the strength of the Spanish forces
4. English ships prevented invasion; decline of Spain's political power, setback to Catholic Reformation, increase in England's international power and national pride
5. north across the North Sea, west around the British Isles, then south to Spain
6. allowed them to develop overseas trade and colonize North America

■ BACKGROUND

The more secular world of the English is reflected in the names of the ships they sent against the Armada: *Lion, Tiger, Dreadnought,* and *Revenge.* The Spanish, in contrast, were depending on the grace of God: *San Mateo, San Cristobal,* and so on.

ANSWERS TO

Section Review 1

Define:
organization set up to attract capital and invest in business
Identify:
(a) last and greatest Tudor ruler (b) religious law that

(continued)

Europe in 1560

KEY
- Spanish Hapsburgs
- Austrian Hapsburgs
- Boundary of the Holy Roman Empire
- Route of the Spanish Armada, 1588

Focus on Geography

Geographic Skills

1. From what port did the Invincible Armada sail for England?
2. What was the main objective of the Armada?
3. With whom did the Armada plan to rendezvous? Why?
4. What was the outcome of the fighting between English ships and the Armada?
5. By what route did the surviving ships of the Armada try to return to Spain?

Geographic Theme: Movement

6. How did the check on Spain's sea power affect England's opportunities for growth?

---

many as 42 Spanish ships. Only 67 ships safely returned to Spain.

The outcome The failure of the Armada marked a decisive turning point in European history. The defeat signaled the decline of Spain's political power. The defeat also held religious importance. Since all of Europe had viewed the battle as a contest between Catholics and Protestants, the Catholic Reformation suffered a serious setback.

As Spain's influence declined, England's power increased. Having humbled the mighty Armada, the English were now free to develop their overseas trade and to colonize North America. A great burst of national pride helped spark the Elizabethan Age. The victory over the Armada became a legend that helped to preserve England from foreign conquest.

Elizabeth had financial problems.

Another problem for Elizabeth was money. The yearly income of the English ruler was about 200,000 pounds. This was a meager sum indeed compared to the tons of gold collected by her rival, Philip II. The House of Commons always balked at a ruler's request for new taxes. How then was the queen to find enough money for the costly business of defending her country?

Elizabeth was, first of all, extremely tight-fisted. Soldiers in her army had cause to grumble about their poor wages and lack of supplies. The queen was always generous with her compliments but stingy with her cash.

Much of Spain's wealth came, as the English knew well, from its American colonies. England had played little part in the early voyages of exploration. In the late 1500's, however, the English began to think about building an American empire of their own.

Who had the funds to support such a venture? Certainly the queen did not, nor did a single merchant or even a partnership of merchants. Instead, English business leaders set up a special organization to attract capital from many people. It was known as the **joint-stock company.**

Investors in a joint-stock company bought shares of ownership. If the company went bankrupt, its owners lost the money they had invested. If the company prospered, the investors' shares of ownership entitled them to collect a proportional share of the profits. (Drake's voyage around the world in 1577 was a joint-stock enterprise that returned a 4,600 percent profit to its stockholders.) The joint-stock company was a sign that the Commercial Revolution (page 404) that began in the Netherlands had spread to England.

The most successful of England's joint-stock companies received its charter from the queen in 1600. Known as the English East India Company, its ambitious goal was to carve out a share of the rich East Indies spice trade.

Among the company's 101 owners were a London ironmonger, a vintner, and a leather seller, each of whom invested 200 pounds in the venture. They and their fellow owners waited through three suspenseful years before the company's four ships returned from the East Indies. As hoped, the ships carried tons of pepper, cloves, and other spices. Owners of the company became rich beyond their wildest imaginings.

While such ventures did not enrich the queen directly, they strengthened England economically. Moreover, the deeds of the sea dogs and the merchants weakened Spain at minimum cost to Elizabeth. Nonetheless, the queen's constant need for money would carry over into the next reign and lead to bitter conflict between the monarch and Parliament.

Parliament began to assert itself.

Toward the end of Elizabeth's reign, conflicts between Elizabeth and Parliament arose more and more often. Her religious compromise, which had kept peace for so many years, was no longer satisfactory. The people who objected most strongly were Puritans—men and women who wished to purify the Church of England of practices that they thought were too close to Catholicism. Puritans hated to see gold crucifixes at the altar and bishops dressed in rich robes.

The Puritans were a minority in the English population, but they were active in politics. When Parliament met, they formed a strong group in the lower house, the House of Commons. Puritan members of Parliament were outspoken in their demands for changes in the Church of England. Their bold speeches and petitions sent the queen into a towering rage. The rituals and organization of the church, she said, were her business.

Puritans were not the only outspoken members of Parliament. Others in Commons also wanted to be heard. Elizabeth, however, would have none of it. Instead, she left her successor, James I, a legacy of doubt and resentment.

Section REVIEW 1

Define: joint-stock company
Identify: (a) Elizabeth I, (b) Act of Uniformity, (c) Act of Supremacy, (d) Mary Stuart, (e) Philip II, (f) Francis Drake, (g) Armada, (h) Virginia, (i) English East India Company, (j) Puritan
Answer:
1. (a) Describe the religious problem that Elizabeth inherited from her father. (b) How did Elizabeth deal with the problem at the beginning of her reign?
2. (a) What threat did Mary Stuart pose to Elizabeth? (b) How did Elizabeth deal with it?
3. How did each of the following contribute to worsening relations between England and Spain? (a) English sea dogs (b) Dutch Protestants (c) Mary Stuart
4. What solution helped Elizabeth ease England's financial problems?
5. (a) Why did some members of Parliament begin demanding changes in policy? (b) How did Elizabeth respond?

Critical Thinking
6. Despite the advice of her councilors, Elizabeth chose never to marry. From a political point of view, do you think her decision strengthened or weakened her position as queen? Why?

425

ANSWERS TO (continued)
established national church in England (c) law declaring Elizabeth Supreme Governor of England's church and state (d) Elizabeth's Catholic cousin, beheaded for plotting to become queen (e) king of Spain, sent Armada to attack England (f) sailed around the world (g) Spanish fleet defeated by English in 1588 (h) area in North America named in honor of Virgin Queen (i) most successful English joint-stock company (j) person who wanted to purify Church of England
Answer:
1. (a) Henry had broken with pope and declared himself head of Church of England (b) decided to establish state church that moderates from both religions would accept
2. (a) She schemed to overthrow and murder Elizabeth. (b) Elizabeth ordered Mary beheaded.
3. (a) Elizabeth encouraged sea dogs to attack Spanish treasure ships. (b) Elizabeth aided Dutch Protestants in their revolt against Catholic Spain. (c) Elizabeth executed Mary Stuart, a Catholic, provoking Philip to wage war against England.
4. formation of joint-stock companies
5. (a) Puritans demanded changes in the Church of England. (b) claimed that ritual and organization of the Church were her business
6. Possible answer: Unmarried, Elizabeth was least likely to alienate factions and most likely to win diplomatic advantages.

425

Church spires formed the skyline of Elizabethan London. The grandest was St. Paul's, the large building at the top left. The Globe Theater and the Bear

■ BACKGROUND

■ BACKGROUND

The Elizabethan Age was a time of change for London. The growth of overseas trade brought new wealth to the city. During this time the first public theaters appeared, built in the suburbs to keep their noise outside the city.

St. Paul's (shown above) was the city's largest and most impressive church. Fashion-conscious Elizabethan men showed off their finest clothing as they proudly strolled up and down the church's central aisle, popularly known as Paul's Walk. Visiting tourists eagerly climbed to the top of the church tower for a panoramic view of the city.

The Elizabethan era was a golden age.

2

For England, the defeat of the Armada produced a burst of pride and self-confidence. The late 1500's became a golden age economically, politically, and culturally. The center of this age was England's greatest city, London.

CITY TOUR

London was a bustling city.

In 1588, London was Europe's most populous city. There were probably 200,000 Londoners to celebrate Sir Francis Drake's exploits. A center of trade, London hummed with activity. Its medieval walls enclosed a space of only one square mile. Houses were so close together that neighbors could reach out second-story windows and shake hands across the narrow streets.

Velvet-clad merchants led the commercial life of the city. However, they daily rubbed elbows with swarming masses of ragged poor. Standing in the doorways of their little shops, sellers of odds and ends would yell at a well-dressed pas-

serby, "What do you lack?" That was a standard cry heard by everyone throughout the city.

Another constant sound was the roar of the Thames River as it rushed through the great stone arches of London Bridge. This famous bridge spanned the river for 350 yards at one of its roughest parts. "The bridge at London," wrote one Englishman, "is worthily to be numbered among the miracles of the world."

The crowds passing over the bridge heard the water below but could not see it. Blocking their view were rows of shops and houses built right on top of the bridge. Like every other part of London, the bridge was a place of commerce.

The character of the city during its golden years was at once elegant and raw. We can best see this by observing a few of the many ways Londoners earned a living.

Boaters Because the streets of London were clogged with carts and crowds, the fastest way through the city was the Thames. Boaters waited along each bank of the Thames to offer rides, much as taxi drivers do today. Passengers in a hurry might order the boater to take a chance and shoot the rapids under London Bridge. More prudent souls heeded the old proverb: "London Bridge was made for wise men to walk over and fools to go under."

Water carriers In the days before pipes and plumbing, water carriers were a common sight

Garden, octagonal buildings, stood on the south side of the Thames. Above the gate to London Bridge, traitors' heads were displayed on pikes.

on city streets. Of course, only the well-to-do could afford to hire water carriers or "cogs" to bring fresh water to their homes. The poor went out to the city wells and the river to carry home their own water.

Because even the homes of the wealthy lacked plumbing, buckets were stashed in dark, closetlike rooms to collect human waste. Though there was a law against it, the buckets were usually emptied out the front door. A more sanitary contrivance, the flush toilet, was invented in 1596, but only the queen and a few others had such a luxury.

Cappers Those who followed the hat-making trade were popularly known as cappers. To keep cappers in business, the government of London passed a law in 1571 requiring that everyone over seven years of age wear a hat on Sundays and other holidays. The law was designed to prevent masses of idle cappers from rioting.

Barbers The barbers of London did a nice business catering to English gentlemen. The style of a Londoner's hair and beard received as much attention as his brightly colored doublets, stockings, hats, gloves, and knee-breeches. A writer of the period has left us this picture of the beard-trimmer's art:

> And therefore if a man have a lean and straight face, a Marquess Otto's cut will make it broad and large; if it be platterlike,

a long, slender beard will make it seem the narrower; if he be weaselbeaked, then much hair left on the cheeks will make the owner look big like a bowdled hen and so grim as a goose.

Rogues and vagabonds Lacking an honest trade, many young Londoners fell into a life of crime. Lurking everywhere on London's streets were the coneycatcher, the nip, the foist, the wild rogue, the ruffler, and the angler. These were just some of the nicknames for the city's horde of petty criminals. Each name indicated a special branch of thievery.

The angler, for example, literally fished for stolen goods. Attaching a hook to the end of a long pole, the thief would stick the pole through a victim's window and then pull out whatever it caught. One angler was said to have stripped the bedclothes right from under the nose of a snoring man.

Jailers and executioners The many criminals of London gave employment to jailers and executioners. Petty thieves, for example, were normally punished by painful mutilation. A judge might tell the jailer either to cut off the thief's right ear or to brand it with a red-hot iron. Executioners also had much to do, because there were 200 crimes in Elizabethan England that were punishable by death. Some 800 English citizens were hanged every year.

427

SECTION 2
Objectives and Teaching Strategies

OBJECTIVE 1. Identify William Shakespeare and explain why he is considered a great playwright.

Teaching Strategy: *Analyzing a Quotation: Shakespeare* (page 420c)

OBJECTIVE 2. Describe the Globe Theater.

Teaching Strategy: *Teaching with Pictures: The Globe Theater* (page 420d)

■ BACKGROUND

There may have been as many as 10,000 vagabonds in England during this period. What to do with this poor fraternity was a problem that plagued the cities. During Elizabeth's reign, the first law recognizing that the poor were a public responsibility was passed.

SECTION 2
Resources

ASSESSMENT
- Section Quiz 18.2

REINFORCEMENT
- Independent Practice 18.2

ENRICHMENT
- Voices from the Past 18.2

Arrange students in small groups and have each group choose one of Shakespeare's plays to discuss. Groups should appoint one member to research the characteristics of a tragedy, or comedy; one member to research the literary history of the chosen piece; and several members to research the theme, plot, characters, symbols, etc. Each group should choose one short scene to read aloud or act out for the class. Before performing the scene, groups should present the information they have gathered to provide context for their excerpt.

■ BACKGROUND

In 1613, a cannon was set off in the Globe during a play. A spark from it landed in the thatched roof of the gallery, setting the straw on fire. In less than an hour, the theater had burned to the ground. Although it was rebuilt within a year, the Globe was pulled down in 1644 when the Puritans closed all theaters.

Shakespeare wrote drama and poetry.

Nowhere in England could one see a greater variety of people—both high and low—than in London. Watching this pageant of human life was a man who became a master at revealing human nature in all its forms: the good and the evil, the wise and the foolish, the gentle and the terrible. No one better symbolizes England's golden age of literature than the poet and dramatist William Shakespeare. Many people regard him as the greatest writer of all time.

William Shakespeare was born in 1564 in Stratford-upon-Avon, a small town about 75 miles northwest of London. He spent an unremarkable childhood in this little town, attending grammar school with other boys and taking part in some of the town's lively fairs and pageants. At the age of 18, Will married Anne Hathaway. Records show that by 1592 he and Anne and their three children were living in London. It was in London that Shakespeare displayed his great genius both as a poet and a playwright.

It is difficult to define Shakespeare's genius. To some, it lies in his remarkable understanding of human nature. William Shakespeare revealed the souls of men and women brilliantly in scenes of dramatic conflict. However, Shakespeare was more than a skilled observer of human nature. He was also a poet who understood the sound and weight of every word. These lines from the tragedy *Macbeth* show Macbeth's despair:

Tomorrow and tomorrow and tomorrow
Creeps in this petty pace from day to day
To the last syllable of recorded time
And all our yesterdays have lighted fools
the way to dusty death.

The theater was popular in London.

English people enjoyed plays and drama long before William Shakespeare. As early as the Middle Ages, companies of actors traveled from town to town, performing in the courtyards of inns. The inn's guests watched from upper windows, either hooting or applauding the performance.

There were no fixed stages or theaters until 1576. In that year, an enterprising actor named James Burbage built the first permanent playhouse just outside the walls of London. He called it simply "The Theater." Londoners quickly got

428

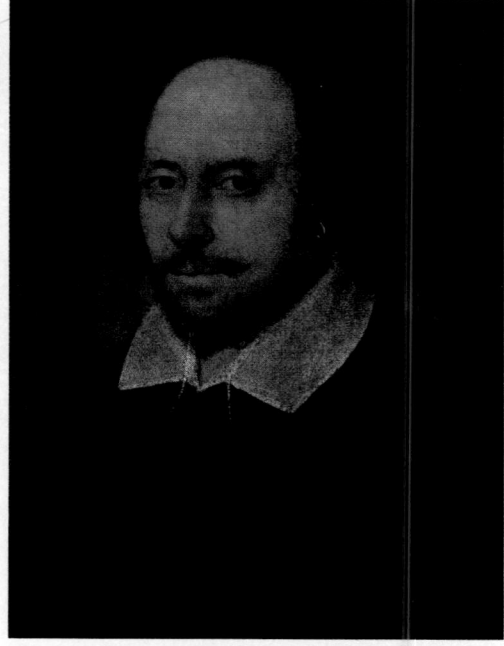

William Shakespeare (1564–1616) wrote 38 plays, including Hamlet, Othello, *and* Romeo and Juliet.

into the habit of packing the house every afternoon. (Evening shows were impossible because audiences could not see actors by moonlight.)

The number of theaters in England grew rapidly. In 1599, Richard and Cuthbert Burbage (sons of James) built the Globe Theater about half a mile from London Bridge. The Globe soon became home to a company of actors, one of whom was Shakespeare.

Shakespeare's most famous plays were first performed at the Globe. As in other theaters of the day, the audience sat around a central yard that was open to the sky. A wooden platform or stage jutted out into this yard, and a curtain

Footnote to History

Shakespeare invented new words and used old words in new ways. Among the more than 1,700 words that he was first to use are *bump, courtship, critic, dwindle, gnarled, hurry, lonely, majestic,* and *road.* It is hard to imagine English without them!

This drawing shows the stage areas and seating galleries of the Globe Theater. No picture exists of the original Globe, which burned in 1613.

was placed at the back of it (not in front as in modern theaters). Actors performed scenes in three places: on the main stage, in a space behind the drawn curtain, and on a balcony above the stage. Thus, as one scene ended on the balcony, the next could begin immediately on the main stage. There was no painted scenery, but actors used a great variety of props, including swords, cannon, cages, live animals, and artificial heads.

The Globe seated about 2,300 people. For a penny, one could sit or stand on the ground itself as a so-called groundling. For two or three pennies, one was admitted to the sheltered galleries three stories high that encircled the yard. Those who came to the theater to show off their fine clothes and good looks could be seated on the stage itself. Of course, such seats cost more.

Shakespeare's plays were written during the reigns of two English monarchs, Elizabeth I and her successor, James I. Shakespeare died in 1616. His friend and fellow playwright, Ben Jonson, said of him: "He was not of an age, but for all time."

Section REVIEW 2

Identify: (a) London, (b) William Shakespeare, (c) James Burbage, (d) Globe Theater

Answer:

1. How do do each of the following livelihoods reflect the character of London during the mid-1500's? (a) boater (b) water carrier (c) capper (d) barber (e) rogue (f) jailer

429

■ BACKGROUND

In addition to his greatness, Shakespeare had good circumstances for fame: by 1592, virtually all the other famous playwrights of the time—Marlowe, Greene, Kyd, Lodge, and Peele—had either died or given up writing for the stage.

ANSWERS TO

Section Review 2

Identify:
(a) England's commercial and cultural center (b) poet and dramatist (c) actor who built first permanent theater (d) theater in which Shakespeare's plays were first performed

Answer:

1. (a) reflected transportation via Thames (b) reflected lack of plumbing (c) reflected necessity to keep idle workers from rioting (d) reflected concern with personal appearance (e) reflected lack of trades available (f) reflected crime

2. insight into human nature and skill with words

3. no fixed stage; audience sat around a central yard open to the sky

4. Answers should consider which of Shakespeare's qualities would have been traits of a genius in any age or culture.

DISCUSSION

Ask students how they think Elizabeth would have reacted to James's ascension to the throne. (On her deathbed, Elizabeth confirmed James's succession: "Who should that be," she said, "but our cousin of Scotland?")

BACKGROUND

One historian said James I had "a genius for getting into difficulties, but was not without a certain shrewdness in stopping just short of catastrophe. If he steered the ship straight for the rocks, he left his son to wreck it."

2. Why do many scholars consider William Shakespeare the greatest English writer of all time?
3. Describe the stage and seating arrangements of an Elizabethan theater.

Critical Thinking
4. What did Ben Jonson mean when he wrote, "He [Shakespeare] was not of an age, but for all time"?

England had a civil war.   3

On a cold day in March 1603, the reign of Queen Elizabeth I quietly came to an end. Elizabeth was dead at the age of 69. Never having married, she left no child to inherit her throne. The Tudor dynasty died with her.

Elizabeth's nearest relative was her Scottish cousin, James Stuart. James was the only son of Mary Stuart, whom Elizabeth had executed for treason 16 years earlier. James Stuart was already King James VI of Scotland when Elizabeth died. In 1603, he became King James I of England as well. Although England and Scotland remained separate countries for another 100 years, they now shared the same king.

James I clashed with Parliament.

With the throne, James inherited all the unsettled problems of Elizabeth's reign. Key among these was the question of how much say Parliament would have in governing England.

As king, James believed he had absolute authority to govern England as he saw fit. Royal authority, James declared, came directly from God, and kings were answerable only to God, not to the people or Parliament. This theory that royal power came from God is called the **divine right** of kings.

Elizabeth too had believed in her divine right to rule, but Elizabeth had had more tact than James. Often, she flattered Parliament in an attempt to get her way. James had no such tact. In addition, Parliament was growing impatient. It was an explosive combination.

430

Quarrels with Parliament James's worst struggles with Parliament revolved around money. Despite Elizabeth's frugal habits, she had left a sizable debt. James needed money, and Parliament had no desire to give it to him. He felt it was beneath his dignity to bargain over money.

Puritan members of Parliament were especially offended by their new Stuart king. They complained that the Church of England was too Catholic. They urged James to make major changes in church rituals. The king angrily refused. Like Elizabeth, he insisted that the Church was strictly the ruler's business, not Parliament's.

The King James Bible Indeed, James was very interested in religion, and scholarship was his great strength. It bothered him that although there were many translations of the Bible, none was fully satisfying. Therefore, he gave to several committees of Bible scholars the task of creating a single authoritative text. The new version of the Bible was first printed in 1611. As befits a book produced in the age of Shakespeare, the King James Bible is noted for the elegance and power of its language. The King James Bible is still read by millions of English-speaking Protestants throughout the world.

The policies of Charles I led to war.

In 1625, James I died. His son, Charles I, became the second Stuart king to rule England. He inherited his father's problems with Parliament and made them even worse.

Charles was a firm believer in the divine right of kings. He had courage and intelligence. Like his father, however, he had too much pride and not enough common sense. Also like his father, he was always in need of money. As a result, the king and Parliament clashed constantly.

In 1626, a costly war with Spain forced Charles to go to Parliament for money. When Parliament refused to grant him the funds, Charles dismissed it. The following year, the country fought a war with France as well as Spain. To pay for it Charles demanded forced loans from knights and nobles. He promptly imprisoned those who refused to pay. He also quartered troops in private homes at the homeowners' expense.

By 1628, financial needs forced the king to call Parliament again. Parliament refused to grant Charles any money unless he signed a document

ECONOMICS IN DAILY LIFE ▶ *The Budget of James I*

Like many people today, King James I had a hard time balancing his budget. In 1617, he spent 726,000 pounds (a pound was worth about $5.00) more than he earned. In order to reduce his debts, James tried to cut costs and increase his income. The chart below shows his progress. In 1621, James had an income of 463,130 pounds, almost all of which came from rents and customs duties. His expenses totaled 336,708 pounds. Thus James had a small surplus.

Then, as now, warfare could be very expensive. In the year 1603 alone, Elizabeth had spent 380,618 pounds on her army and navy. Because the threat of war always existed, James repeatedly quarreled with Parliament about his budget and the need for taxes.

Royal Expenses in 1621

Privy purse	£ 5,000
Great wardrobe	20,016
Master of robes	4,000
Treasurer of the chamber	26,000
Running the court	54,081
Band of pensioners	6,000
Foreign ambassadors and agents	12,000
Office of the Works	10,000
Fees, pensions, and gifts	96,434
The prince's household	53,177
Army and navy	50,000
Total Spending (in pounds)	£336,708

that was known as the Petition of Right. In this document, the king made the following concessions:

1. He would not imprison subjects without due cause.
2. He would not force loans or levy taxes without the consent of Parliament.
3. He would not house soldiers in private homes without the owner's consent.
4. He would not impose martial law in peacetime.

The next year, weary of dealing with Parliament, Charles dissolved it. For the next 11 years, from 1629 to 1640, he refused to call Parliament at all. He resorted to all kinds of fees and fines on the English people to raise money. His unpopularity grew greater every year.

England reached the brink of war.

Although Charles's taxation policies enraged the English people, it was his religious policies that eventually cost him his head. During his reign, thousands of Puritans fled England to escape persecution. Worse still, Charles chose William Laud to be archbishop and lead the Church of England. In truth, Laud was a staunch Protestant. However, his love of ceremonies and rich robes was so great that many Puritans thought he might be a secret Catholic.

In 1639, Laud foolishly decided to force Charles's Presbyterian subjects in Scotland to follow the Church of England's style of worship. To defend their religion, the Scots gathered a huge army and threatened to invade England.

Charles needed money to meet this danger— money he could get only from Parliament. Between gritted teeth, he called a new Parliament. It turned out to be a mistake for the king.

Throughout the autumn of 1641, Parliament passed laws to limit the king's power. Charles was furious. In January 1642, he decided to take drastic action. Accompanied by 400 swordsmen, he strode into the House of Commons and demanded the arrest of five of its leaders. Alerted

431

SECTION 3
Objectives and Teaching Strategies

OBJECTIVE 1. Explain the theory of the divine right of kings.

Teaching Strategy: *Analyzing a Quotation: Divine Right of Kings* (page 420d)

OBJECTIVE 2. Describe how the civil war and Cromwell's rule affected England.

Teaching Strategy: *Writing about History: The Civil War and Protectorate* (page 420d)

■ DISCUSSION

Ask students to study the amounts listed for various expenditures in King James's budget. What areas would students recommend be cut, and by how much, if Parliament decided to reduce taxes?

SECTION 3
Resources

ASSESSMENT
■ Section Quiz 18.3

REINFORCEMENT
■ Independent Practice 18.3

ENRICHMENT
■ Voices from the Past 18.3

Divide the class in half. Assign one half the task of supporting the Cavaliers and Cromwell's policies. Assign the other half the task of supporting the Roundheads. Have students work in pairs to prepare statements supporting their positions. Match opposing pairs and have them present their arguments to each other. Pairs should summarize their opponents' statements, acknowledging valid arguments and avoiding negative feedback.

■ BACKGROUND

One view of the execution of Charles I (Maurice Ashley): "At four minutes past two the blow was struck. The citizens of London who watched the event were silent." Another view (Winston Churchill): "An incalculable multitude had streamed to the spot, swayed by intense though inarticulate emotions. When they saw the severed head 'there was such a groan by the thousands then present,' wrote a contemporary diarist, 'as I never heard before and desire I may never hear again.' "

ahead of time, the men had escaped and were hiding in London. "I see that the birds are flown," said the embarrassed king as he stomped from the House.

News of the king's action angered Londoners. A mob raged outside Charles's palace. The city was now too dangerous for the king. He abandoned it and raised an army in lands in the north where people were still loyal to him.

Cavaliers and Roundheads fought a civil war.

The king's flight to the north in 1642 marked the beginning of the English civil war. Two groups of English people squared off to fight.

Those who remained loyal to King Charles were known as Royalists or *Cavaliers.* (The term was an insult because it was linked to the Spanish *cavaliero,* suggesting that a person was a Spanish sympathizer.) In general, the Cavaliers included English nobles and church officials.

On the other side were the Puritan townspeople and merchants who supported Parliament. Puritans cropped their hair short over their ears, instead of wearing it long and curled as the fashionable Cavaliers did. For this reason, Cavaliers mockingly called the Puritans *Roundheads.*

A Roundhead soldier summed up the issues this way:

> *The question in dispute between the King's party and us was whether the King should govern as a god by his will, and the nation be governed by force like beasts; or whether the people should be governed by laws made by themselves and live under a Government derived from their own consent.*

At first, the Cavaliers held the advantage, controlling about three fourths of the country. They also had most of England's experienced military leaders. However, Parliament had great financial resources on which to draw. All the Puritans needed was a general who could win, and by 1644, they had found a military genius—Oliver Cromwell.

Cromwell was a country gentleman who had served in the House of Commons. Now he organized an army of zealous Protestants and inspired each soldier with the thought that God favored the Roundheads. "Truly," said Cromwell

to his troops, "I think he that prays best will fight best." His military machine was called the New Model Army.

At first, most English people went on with their lives, untouched by the civil war. As the war dragged on, however, more and more villages were destroyed, more crops were ruined, and more hatreds were aroused. By the end of the war, 100,000 people had died in battle. The hatreds and the sufferings of the war had made people on both sides much more radical in their ideas than they had been at the beginning.

In 1646, Cromwell's New Model Army defeated the king's forces. Charles himself was a prisoner in Scotland. It seemed that Parliament had won, but the fighting was not over.

In 1647, Parliament tried to dissolve the New Model Army considering its mission to be over, but the army refused to obey. The army and its leaders were much more strongly Puritan and much more radical politically than members of Parliament. The army did not intend to give up control of the country.

In desperation, some members of Parliament joined forces with the king. Cromwell defeated them and captured Charles in August 1648. Then, Cromwell and his army marched into London and surrounded Parliament. Army leaders ordered the expulsion of 143 members of the House of Commons.

In 1649, Cromwell and the Puritans brought Charles to trial for treason. The king listened as the sentence of death was read aloud. Parliament's makeshift court declared, "Charles Stuart, as tyrant, traitor, murderer, and public enemy to the good people of this nation, shall be put to death by the severing of his head from his body."

The execution was set for Sunday, January 30, 1649. It was a cold day. As Charles was dressing, he asked his attendant to bring him an extra shirt to wear. He did not wish to tremble from the cold, he said, and have people think he was afraid. He went calmly to the place of execution, laid his head on the block, and himself gave the signal to the headsman.

The execution of Charles was revolutionary. Kings had often been overthrown, killed in battle, assassinated, or put to death in secret. Never before, however, had a monarch faced a public trial and an official execution.

432

Cromwell ruled as military dictator.

With the king gone, Oliver Cromwell now held the reins of power. Of Parliament's original members, only a few remained. They had lost the respect of the nation and the army. In 1653, Cromwell announced to them, "You are no Parliament, I say you are no Parliament, and I will put an end to your sitting." His soldiers then drove the members out of the building.

To set up a new government, in 1653 Cromwell drafted a constitution, the first written constitution of a major European nation. This constitution set up a republic in which Cromwell ruled England as Lord Protector. In fact, his protectorate was little more than a military dictatorship, thinly disguised by talk of English liberty.

Now that the Puritans were in power, they set about reforming English society. They imposed their way of life and their beliefs. Puritan laws shut down theaters and forbade sporting events. Under Cromwell, merrymaking and amusement became illegal. Many English people bitterly resented the Puritan dictatorship.

The conquest of Ireland Harsh as Cromwell's policies were in England, they were far harsher in Ireland. The island of Ireland had fallen under English rule during the reign of Henry VIII, but the Irish rebelled frequently against their English overlords. Elizabeth, James, and Charles each faced the problem of putting down Irish revolts.

After Charles was beheaded, the Irish started rebelling again. In August 1649, Cromwell himself landed on Irish shores with a Protestant army. The English laid siege to the town of Drogheda. When it fell, Cromwell's army put all of its 9,000 inhabitants to the sword. They took special satisfaction in killing the town's Catholic priests and friars.

The Irish suffered more than a single massacre. Their lands and homes were taken from them and given to English soldiers as spoils of conquest. Several counties were set aside as strictly English property, and all Irish families who lived there were driven out. The general misery and homelessness took a frightful toll. One scholar estimates that 616,000 Irish, nearly half the island's population, perished from famine and plague between 1641 and 1652.

The death of Cromwell Oliver Cromwell ruled until his death in 1658. Next, his son Richard

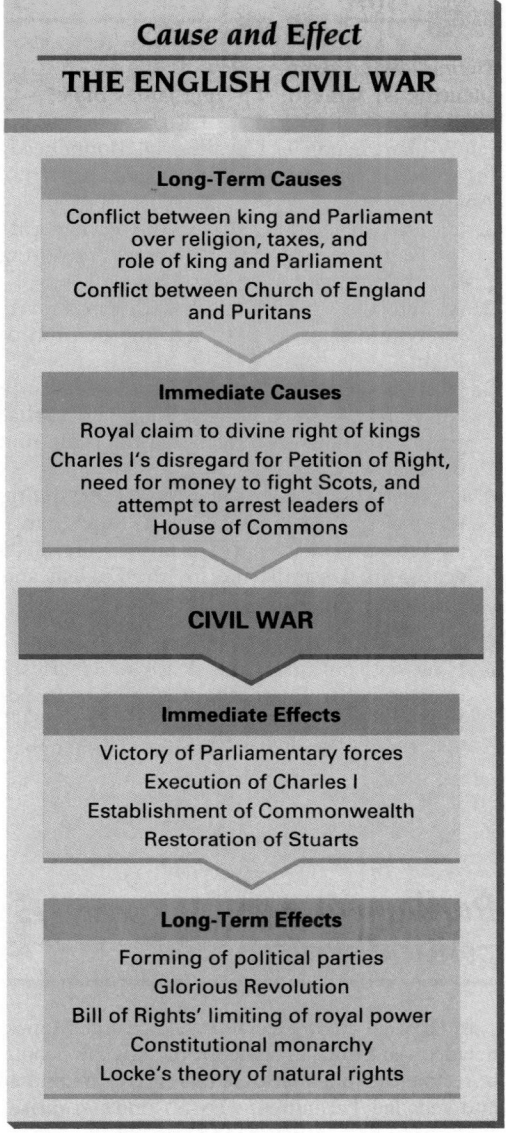

Cause and Effect
THE ENGLISH CIVIL WAR

Long-Term Causes

Conflict between king and Parliament over religion, taxes, and role of king and Parliament

Conflict between Church of England and Puritans

Immediate Causes

Royal claim to divine right of kings

Charles I's disregard for Petition of Right, need for money to fight Scots, and attempt to arrest leaders of House of Commons

CIVIL WAR

Immediate Effects

Victory of Parliamentary forces
Execution of Charles I
Establishment of Commonwealth
Restoration of Stuarts

Long-Term Effects

Forming of political parties
Glorious Revolution
Bill of Rights' limiting of royal power
Constitutional monarchy
Locke's theory of natural rights

briefly held the title of Lord Protector. However, Richard did not command the same respect as his father. His enemies laughed at him behind his back, calling him "Tumbledown Dick." The army deserted him. The English people, even many Puritans, yearned for the days when their government was headed by a king.

433

■ BACKGROUND
Cromwell's view on religious toleration is expressed in the following words: "Notions will hurt none but them that have them." Ask students to compare this view with the action the army took under Cromwell's direction.

■ DISCUSSION
Which long-term effects of the English civil war also affected the early history of the United States? How?

ANSWERS TO

Section Review 3

Define:
belief that royal power comes from God
Identify:
(a) first Stuart king (b) version of Bible commissioned by James I (c) son of and successor to James
(d) document signed by

ANSWERS TO (continued)

Charles I listing limitations on royal power **(e)** archbishop determined to force Presbyterian Scots to follow style of Church of England **(f)** person who remained loyal to King Charles **(g)** Puritan townsperson and merchant who supported Parliament **(h)** Roundhead leader, later Lord Protector of England **(i)** Cromwell's military machine

Answer:

1. (a) over how much say Parliament would have in governing England **(b)** King James Bible

2. (a) for same reasons as James and mainly over money **(b)** Parliament refused to grant Charles any money unless he signed the document.

3. (a) Laud decided to force Presbyterian Scots to follow style of Church of England **(b)** Charles's flight from London to north to raise army

4. (a) Cavaliers and Roundheads **(b)** whether people would be governed by an absolute monarch or a democratic system

5. (a) Cromwell **(b)** Merrymaking and amusement became illegal in England. In Ireland, the English seized Drogheda, killed priests and friars, and drove people from their homes and land.

6. Answers should note that the execution of Charles was revolutionary and represented a great threat to other monarchs. Most students will probably advise rulers to be more conciliatory.

Section REVIEW 3

Define: divine right

Identify: (a) James I, (b) King James Bible, (c) Charles I, (d) Petition of Right, (e) William Laud, (f) Cavalier, (g) Roundhead, (h) Oliver Cromwell, (i) New Model Army

Answer:

1. (a) Why did James I clash with Parliament? (b) Name one thing that he achieved during his reign despite such clashes.

2. (a) Why did Charles I clash with Parliament? (b) Why did he agree to sign the Petition of Right?

3. (a) What action of Archbishop Laud led to a confrontation between the king and Parliament? (b) What event marked the beginning of civil war?

4. (a) What two groups opposed each other during the war? (b) Over what issue did they fight?

5. (a) Who took control of England after the king's death? (b) Describe life for the English and Irish under his rule.

Critical Thinking

6. How do you think the death of Charles I affected other European monarchs who believed as he did in the divine right of kings? What advice would you give those monarchs?

Parliament won political power. 4

In 1659, an army general named George Monck decided the time had come for the English people to restore the monarchy. He marched into London and recalled Parliament. To no one's surprise, Parliament promptly voted to bring back a Stuart to rule England.

Charles II restored the monarchy.

Parliament invited Prince Charles Stuart, the elder son of Charles I, to return from exile. On a fine day in May 1660, Prince Charles sailed up the Thames. The crowds in London welcomed

434

him with joyous shouts. Church bells rang throughout the realm. On this jubilant note, the reign of King Charles II began. Because he restored the monarchy, the period of his rule (1660–1685) is known as the Restoration.

Charles restored more than the monarchy. He also restored the theater, sporting events, dancing, and merrymaking in general. Life at Charles's court was elegant, colorful, and scandalous. It was not long before people were calling their new king "the merry monarch."

Drama and poetry Theater and the arts flourished during the Restoration. Not surprisingly, comedy dominated the stage. High society flocked to see amusing plays that poked fun at the manners and morals of the times. For the first time, women appeared on the English stage to play female roles. (In Shakespeare's time, beardless boys had played women's parts.)

The greatest writer of the period, however, was not a dramatist but a poet. John Milton, aged and blind, was a devout Puritan. He had worn out his eyesight writing propaganda for Cromwell. He took no joy in the Restoration, but his greatest poem, *Paradise Lost*, was published under Charles II. It was a work of Christian philosophy, an attempt to explain why life's suffering and pain are justified in God.

A moderate ruler Although Charles restored the monarchy, he did not try to restore the idea of the divine right of kings. Unlike his father and grandfather, Charles II knew when to give in and had the good sense not to push himself or others too hard.

In religion, as in other things, Charles tried to steer a middle path. He wanted to give both Puritans and Roman Catholics some measure of religious freedom. In this, however, he met with firm opposition from Parliament. The Church of England remained the only legal religion.

The passage of habeas corpus Although England did not have religious freedom, the English people did win another important guarantee of freedom during Charles's reign. In 1679, Parliament passed a law known as **habeas corpus.** *Habeas corpus* is a Latin term that means "you have the body." This law gave every prisoner the right to obtain a writ or document ordering that the prisoner be brought before a judge. The judge could then decide whether the prisoner should be brought to trial or set free.

The Habeas Corpus Act meant it was no longer possible for the king or queen to put someone in jail simply for opposing the ruler. It also made it impossible for the monarch to hold someone in jail indefinitely without a trial. Today habeas corpus remains one of the most important guarantees of personal freedom in both the United States and England.

Problems over religion and money Although Charles had learned many lessons from his Stuart predecessors, in the end the very issues that ruined his father and grandfather returned to haunt him. Those issues were, of course, religion and money.

Charles had had Catholic leanings for many years. In addition, he was unable to live on the money that Parliament provided him. In secret, he turned to the Catholic and wealthy king of France, Louis XIV. Charles and Louis entered into a secret agreement. Louis promised to give Charles a lump sum of money every year. In return, Charles agreed to become a Catholic at some time in the future.

Although the people of England did not know of the agreement, they did know that their king was sympathetic to Catholicism. They also knew that he had no legitimate child to inherit the kingdom. Therefore, when Charles died, the throne of England would pass to his brother, James, who was openly Catholic. This concern led to the forming of political parties.

Voice from the Past · *The London Fire*

On the night of Sunday, September 2, 1666, a disastrous fire broke out in London. It began in a baker's shop and raged for 3 days, destroying more than 13,000 houses and leaving 100,000 Londoners homeless. The following account comes from the diary of Samuel Pepys (peeps), a royal official.

Jane [woke] us . . . about three in the morning to tell of a great fire they saw in the City . . . [Pepys soon goes down to see for himself.] Everybody endeavoring to remove their goods, and flinging into the river . . . poor people staying in their houses as long as till the very fire touched them, and then running into boats . . . Having stayed, and in an hour's time seen the fire rage every way, and nobody, to my sight, trying to quench it, but to remove their goods, and leave all to the fire . . . So I was called for and did tell the King . . . that unless his Majesty did command houses to be pulled down nothing could stop the fire . . . [Carrying the King's command, Pepys finds London's Lord Mayor.] At last met my Lord Mayor in Canning-Street, like a man spent, with a handkercher about his neck. To the King's command he cried, like a fainting woman, "Lord! What can I do? I am spent. People will not obey me. I have been pulling down houses, but the fire overtakes us faster than we can do it" . . .

As it grew darker, [the fire] appeared more and more, and in corners and upon steeples, and between churches and houses, as far as we could see up the hill of the City, in a most horrid malicious bloody flame . . . it made me weep to see it. The churches, houses, and all on fire and flaming at once; and a horrid noise the flames made, and the crackling of houses at their ruin.

1. How did Londoners try to save their possessions?
2. (a) What step did Pepys recommend for stopping the fire? (b) How would this step have halted the fire?
3. What two reasons did the Lord Mayor give for his inability to stop the fire?
4. How would such a fire be put out today?

435

SECTION 4
Objectives and Teaching Strategies

OBJECTIVE 1. Explain why James II lost his throne.

Teaching Strategy: *Discussing History: Why James II Lost His Throne* (page 420e)

OBJECTIVE 2. Identify the Bill of Rights and explain its importance.

Teaching Strategy: *Transferring Ideas: Limiting the King's Power* (page 420e)

OBJECTIVE 3. Compare and contrast the views of Thomas Hobbes and John Locke on the purpose of government.

Teaching Strategy: *Skill Building: Comparing Views on Government* (page 420e)

ANSWERS TO
Voice from the Past

1. by carrying their goods to the river
2. (a) that houses be pulled down (b) by providing no material to fuel the flames
3. Either people wouldn't obey him or the fire overtook them faster than they could work.
4. an equipped, on-call fire department

SECTION 4
Resources

ASSESSMENT
■ Section Quiz 18.4

REINFORCEMENT
■ Independent Practice 18.4

ENRICHMENT
■ Voices from the Past 18.4

435

■ BACKGROUND

The term "Whig" was used to refer to those who favored independence from Great Britain during the American Revolution. Around 1834 an American political party was formed to support manufacturing and financial interests and to oppose the Jacksonian Democrats. Its members were also known as Whigs. This party was succeeded in about 1854 by the Republican party.

ANSWERS TO

Section Review 4

Define:

(a) law that guarantees a prisoner's right to be brought before a judge
(b) document listing restrictions on ruler's power
(c) government with complete power

Identify:

(a) invited by Parliament to restore the monarchy after the death of Cromwell
(b) period of rule under Charles II (c) greatest writer of the Restoration
(d) member of Parliament who defended both the king and his Catholic brother

(continued)

MILESTONES OF DEMOCRACY: ENGLAND (1689)
Glorious Revolution and Bill of Rights

	FORM OF GOVERNMENT	INDIVIDUAL RIGHTS
Benefits	Limited monarchy; monarchs were subject to laws made by Parliament and could raise taxes only by vote of Parliament.	Individual rights were protected by due process of law.
Limitations	Only men with property could vote.	Freedom of worship was limited for Catholics, Jews, and Unitarians; individual rights were guaranteed only for upper classes.

Political parties developed.

The debate in Parliament over James's succession was fierce. Those who opposed James formed a group dedicated to keeping him off the throne. Those who defended both the king and his Catholic brother formed another group.

Each group invented a scornful label for the other. James's opponents were labeled "Whigs" (a Scottish word for assassins). His supporters were mockingly called "Tories" (the nickname for Irish bandits). These two groups were the ancestors of England's first political parties.

Long after the deaths of Charles and James, members of Parliament continued to identify with either Whigs or Tories. The two-party political system in both the United States and England today has its roots in this conflict.

James II lost his throne.

In 1685, Charles II died, and James II became king of England. Like his father, Charles I, James asserted his divine right to rule without Parliament's consent.

At first, the Tories supported James. Soon he antagonized even his firmest friends by appointing several Catholics to high office. This action openly violated the laws passed earlier by the Restoration Parliament. Tories as well as Whigs protested. James responded by dissolving his first Parliament and never calling another.

Three other events excited the fears of English Protestants. First, in 1687, James announced that government posts would be open to Catholics as well as Protestants. Second, James stationed 13,000 soldiers just outside London. Many Londoners feared that he was preparing to force England to accept Catholicism as the state religion. Third and most disturbing, James announced in 1688 that his second wife had given birth to a son. English Protestants were terrified at the prospect of a line of Catholic kings.

The infant prince was not James's only possible heir, however. James's first wife had been a Protestant. She had raised their eldest daughter, Mary, as a Protestant. Now an adult, Mary was the wife of William of Orange, a powerful Protestant prince of the Netherlands.

Whigs and Tories seized on a bold plan. They invited William and Mary to overthrow James II for the sake of Protestantism. William and Mary accepted the challenge.

William landed on English shores in November 1688 and led his army north to London. Nobody tried to stop him. The general of the English army, John Churchill, deserted James and joined William. Without any troops to fight for him, James sailed for France where he remained in exile until his death. Compared to Cromwell's civil war, this revolution was peaceful. The English still celebrate it as the Bloodless Revolution or the Glorious Revolution.

The English won a Bill of Rights.

In 1689, Parliament asked William and Mary to rule England as joint sovereigns. At their coronation, they solemnly vowed "to govern the people of this kingdom of England . . . according to the statutes in Parliament agreed on and the laws and customs of the same." This oath shows the significance of the Glorious Revolution. William and Mary recognized Parliament as the leading partner in ruling England.

To make clear the limits of royal power, in 1689 Parliament drafted a **Bill of Rights.** This document listed many things that a ruler could *not* do. These were the major prohibitions:

- No suspending of Parliament's laws
- No levying of taxes without a specific grant from Parliament
- No interfering with a member's freedom of speech in Parliament
- No penalty for a citizen who petitions the king about grievances
- No standing army to be kept in time of peace
- No posting of excessive bail in royal courts

William and Mary officially consented to these limits on their power.

Political ideas grew from conflict.

Did the English people have a right to rebel against Charles I in 1642 and against James II in 1688? Could a ruler lawfully be overthrown by his subjects? The revolutionary events of the 1600's challenged two English philosophers to think about these questions. No, said Thomas Hobbes, there was no such thing as a right to rebel. Yes, said John Locke, people oppressed by their government had every right to rebel.

Thomas Hobbes wrote his most famous work, *Leviathan* (lih-**VYE**-uh-thuhn), in 1651, two years after the beheading of Charles I. The horrors of civil war convinced him that all humans were naturally wicked. Left to themselves, he thought, people would give free rein to their evil ways. Governments were created, said Hobbes, to protect people from their own selfishness. The best government was one that had the awesome power of a leviathan (sea monster). Since the chief purpose of government was to stop society from falling into disorder, Hobbes reasoned, an **absolute monarchy,** having complete power, was best.

John Locke held a different, more positive, view of human nature. He believed that people had the gift of reason. As reasonable beings, they had the natural ability to govern their own affairs and to look after the welfare of society.

Governments were formed, said Locke, to protect three basic human rights: the right to life, the right to liberty, and the right to property. What was government? It was a contract in which the rulers promised to safeguard people's natural rights. If any government abused these rights, people were justified in rebelling.

Locke's ideas were published in 1690, only two years after the Glorious Revolution. His two *Treatises on Government* served to justify the overthrow of James II.

Locke's theories had immense importance for future revolutionaries. Less than 100 years later, on the other side of the Atlantic Ocean, a young lawyer named Thomas Jefferson would use Locke's ideas to justify the rebellion of 13 American colonies against their English king, as you will read in a later chapter.

Section REVIEW 4

Define: (a) habeas corpus, (b) bill of rights, (c) absolute monarchy
Identify: (a) Charles II, (b) Restoration, (c) John Milton, (d) Tory, (e) Whig, (f) James II, (g) William and Mary, (h) Glorious Revolution, (i) Thomas Hobbes, (j) John Locke
Answer:
1. What activities did the Restoration restore?
2. (a) In what way was Charles II a moderate leader? (b) How did religion and money cause problems for him toward the end of his reign?
3. How did the succession of James II lead to the development of political parties?
4. (a) Why did Parliament invite William and Mary to rule England in 1689? (b) Name three ways the Bill of Rights limited royal power.

Critical Thinking

5. Explain why habeas corpus was an important landmark for personal freedom.
6. Hobbe's *Leviathan* was written two years after Charles I was beheaded. Locke's *Treatises on Government* was written two years after the Glorious Revolution. How was each work influenced by events of the time?

437

ANSWERS TO (continued)

(e) member of Parliament who opposed James's succession (f) successor to Charles II who was overthrown for the sake of Protestantism (g) Protestant daughter of James and Protestant prince of Netherlands who agreed to rule England (h) bloodless overthrow of James II in which William and Mary came to power (i) English philosopher and author of *Leviathan* (j) English philosopher who asserted that governments are formed to protect life, liberty, and property
Answer:
1. theater, sporting events, dancing
2. (a) He did not restore divine right and, in religion, he tried to steer a middle course. (b) Charles turned to Louis XIV, wealthy Catholic king of France, for funds. People feared Charles's Catholic leanings and the fact that his successor would be his Catholic brother.
3. Parliament fiercely debated James II's succession.
4. (a) for the sake of Protestantism (b) It prohibited the sovereign from keeping a standing army in peacetime, levying taxes without a specific grant from Parliament, and suspending laws.
5. The fact that one could not be held indefinitely without being charged and tried limited the imprisonment of the ruler's opponents.
6. Events leading to Charles I's beheading convinced Hobbes that humans were naturally wicked. Influenced by the fact that James II was overthrown without bloodshed, Locke had a more positive view.

Concluding the Chapter

1. **Chapter Closer**
   Ask students to describe three characteristics of the Elizabethan golden age.
2. **Reteaching Activities**
   a. Outlining Have students write a sentence outline of Section 1 and Section 2, using section headings and sub-headings.
   b. Recalling Information Have students identify reasons that both James I and Charles I were unpopular with Parliament.

Answers to Chapter Review appear on pages 420e–420f.

Summary

1. **Elizabeth I faced many challenges.** The last of the Tudor rulers, Elizabeth I was a gifted queen who guided England through the troubles of the 1500's. These included religious conflicts between Catholics and Protestants; a plot against her life by her Scottish cousin, Mary Stuart; the threat of Philip II's Invincible Armada; and severe financial difficulties. Toward the end of her reign, Parliament began demanding rights that Elizabeth was not prepared to grant.

2. **The Elizabethan era was a golden age.** Under Elizabeth I, England had a golden age. The center of this golden age was London, the most populous city in Europe. Elizabethan London bustled with trade and was filled with people from every class, from the well-to-do to criminals. This human pageant was brilliantly captured by William Shakespeare, whom many regard as the greatest writer of all time.

3. **England had a civil war.** Elizabeth's cousin, James Stuart, King of Scotland, succeeded her at her death in 1603. His reign is remembered for the King James Bible, the establishment of the first English colony in the Americas, and bitter quarrels with Parliament over money and religion. His son, Charles I, had even more difficulty with Parliament. Eventually, those difficulties led to a civil war in which Puritan members of Parliament fought the king's supporters. Oliver Cromwell led the Puritans to victory. After the beheading of the king, Cromwell established a severe military dictatorship.

4. **Parliament won political power.** In 1660, Charles II, son of Charles I, was recalled from exile to restore the monarchy. Although Charles II followed moderate policies and saw the passage of habeas corpus, his death sparked hostilities over the Catholic religion of his successor, James II. Eventually, James's harsh policies and staunch Catholicism led to a Glorious Revolution, in which Parliament forced James II off the throne and invited James's Protestant daughter, Mary, and her Dutch husband, William, to rule England. In 1689, William and Mary signed the Bill of Rights, which limited royal power and recognized Parliament as the real ruler of England.

Reviewing the Facts

1. Define the following terms:
   a. joint-stock company   b. divine right
2. Explain the importance of each of the following names or terms:
   a. Elizabeth I   d. Philip II
   b. Puritan   e. Francis Drake
   c. Mary Stuart   f. Invincible Armada

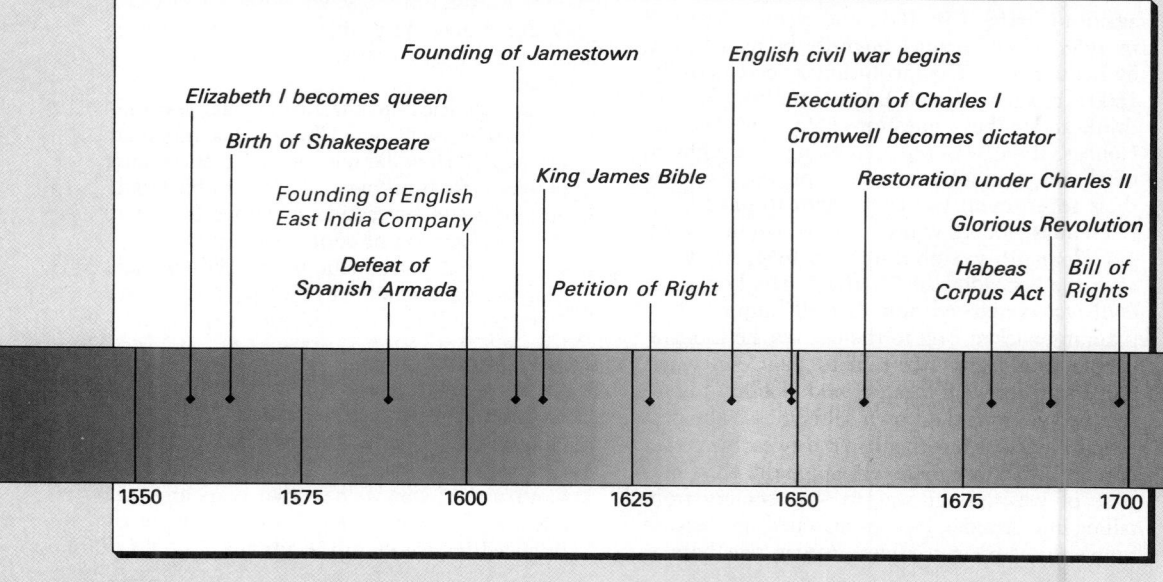

Founding of Jamestown

English civil war begins

Elizabeth I becomes queen

Execution of Charles I

Birth of Shakespeare

Cromwell becomes dictator

Founding of English East India Company

King James Bible

Restoration under Charles II

Glorious Revolution

Defeat of Spanish Armada

Petition of Right

Habeas Corpus Act

Bill of Rights

1550   1575   1600   1625   1650   1675   1700

438

g. William Shakespeare   l. Roundhead
h. James I   m. Oliver Cromwell
i. Charles I   n. Charles II
j. Petition of Right   o. Whig
k. Cavalier   p. Tory

3. (a) How was the vitality of Elizabeth's reign reflected in the city of London? (b) How do the writings of William Shakespeare symbolize the golden age of English literature?
4. What social changes took place in England during the protectorate of Oliver Cromwell and after the Restoration?
5. (a) Why did Hobbes oppose the civil war? (b) Why did Locke support the Glorious Revolution?

Basic Skills

1. **Sequencing** Certain parallels exist in the sequence of events of the two English revolutions. (a) List the main events from 1625 to the execution of Charles I. (b) List the main events from 1685 to the conclusion of the Glorious Revolution. (c) What similarities and differences do you observe in these two critical periods?
2. **Solving problems** The text on page 421 states that Queen Elizabeth faced four kinds of problems—"religious conflicts, a rival queen, Spanish ambitions, and financial difficulties." Explain how Queen Elizabeth dealt with each problem.

Researching and Reporting Skills

For a group research project on the English civil war, divide your class into two groups: Roundheads and Cavaliers.

1. **Finding primary and second sources** In your library's card catalog, find books relating to the period of the English civil war. Try to find both primary and secondary sources and to get several perspectives on the subject.
2. **Compiling a bibliography** From this research, prepare a group bibliography. References should be classified as primary or secondary sources and identified according to viewpoint on the conflict.
3. **Listing supporting arguments** From the complete bibliography, each group should select the materials pertaining to its side in the conflict. Each group should then divide the reading, take notes, and list arguments supporting its cause.

4. **Debating viewpoints** When the lists of arguments are complete, each group should prepare its full case. One or two members from each group may then be chosen to debate whether the civil war was essential to limiting royal power in England.

Critical Thinking

1. **Analyzing viewpoints** How might each of the following people have regarded the queen: (a) Mary Queen of Scots, (b) an English sea captain, (c) a Puritan member of parliament? Explain your answers.
2. **Identifying fact and opinion** From Elizabeth's speech to her troops on page 421, list the phrases that are fact and those that are opinion.
3. **Interpreting economics** What was the significance of the chartering of joint-stock companies in England?
4. **Synthesizing** (a) What precedents existed before the Tudors for limits on royal power? (b) To what extent did the Tudors respect those precedents? (c) Give examples from the reigns of Henry VIII and Elizabeth to illustrate your answer.
5. **Applying concepts** James I, Charles I, and James II believed in and acted according to the concept of the divine right of kings. (a) For each of these reigns, give an example of an act based on this principle. (b) Explain how the Habeas Corpus Act and the Bill of Rights limited this concept.
6. **Synthesizing** In what ways did the Elizabethan Era represent an English renaissance?

Perspectives on Past and Present

The Glorious Revolution in England ended with the adoption of the Bill of Rights. (a) Which of those rights are also included in the Bill of Rights of the United States Constitution? (b) What reasons might account for any differences?

Investigating History

From a historical perspective, is Oliver Cromwell a tyrant, a liberator, or both? (a) Read a selection about Cromwell and analyze what its author thinks of him. (b) To what extent do you agree or disagree with the author? (c) What is your own evaluation of Cromwell's leadership?

439

CHAPTER
Evaluation

Chapter Test 18, Alternate Chapter Test 18, and Computer Test Bank Chapter 18 Test can be used to evaluate your students' understanding of this chapter.

Europe in the Age of the Absolute Monarchs

Chapter Overview

Because Louis XIV was only five years old when he came to the French throne, the real power of the country remained with Cardinal Jules Mazarin, whose policies led to a series of revolts called the *Fronde*. After Mazarin died, Louis's minister of finance, Jean Baptiste Colbert, strengthened France's economy and industry following a policy of mercantilism. Unfortunately, Louis undid much of Colbert's work by persecuting the Huguenots, many of whom were skilled workers and business leaders.

Peter the Great of Russia was also an absolute monarch. When he became czar in 1682, Russia was an isolated and backward country. He gained access to a warm-water port, "modernized" Russian customs and institutions, and built a new capital city.

Austria, the most powerful state in the Holy Roman Empire, was ruled by the Hapsburgs. Prussia was created by the Hohenzollern rulers of Brandenburg. In 1740, Frederick the Great of Prussia invaded Silesia, an iron-rich territory held by the Austrian Hapsburgs. Maria Theresa, Austria's queen, opposed the Prussian attack. Other European countries, trying to keep the balance of power, became involved as well. As a result of the War of the Austrian Succession (1740–1748) and the Seven Years' War (1756–1763), alliances shifted in Europe and Britain's lands and power expanded overseas.

Chapter Focus

Have students read the opening section (pages 440–441). Point out that complex rules of etiquette regulated every detail of life at Versailles. Ask students why they think Louis enforced these rules. List student responses. Then explain that Louis once cautioned, "Those who imagine that these rules are merely matters of ceremony are gravely mistaken. The people over whom we reign, being unable to apprehend the basic reality of things, usually derive their opinions from what they see with their eyes." Ask students to describe how Louis would evaluate the answers listed on the board. Emphasize that in France, "the basic reality of things" was that Louis XIV ruled as an absolute monarch by divine right. Unlike the kings and queens of England, Louis exercised an undisputed monopoly over all the power of the French state. As a ruler with absolute or unchallenged power, Louis formulated foreign policy, commanded the army, regulated the economy, headed the church, and was the final judge of manners, fashion, and art.

The daily rituals at Versailles were thus a visual display of the power and grandeur of the French king. This chapter is about Louis XIV and the other absolute monarchs who dominated European history between 1648 and 1763.

Chapter 19 Europe in the Age of Absolute Monarchs 1648–1763

FOCUS Louis XIV's Versailles as a symbol of the power and grandeur of European monarchs

★ Advanced
● Basic

	SECTION 1	SECTION 2	SECTION 3
Objectives	1. Define mercantilism and explain how Colbert improved France's economy. 2. Explain the concept of balance of power.	1. Explain why Russia was isolated from western Europe. 2. Describe how Peter the Great modernized Russia.	1. Locate Hapsburg and Hohenzollern lands on a map. 2. Explain why Prussia and Austria fought over Silesia. 3. Describe the alliances that formed during the War of the Austrian Succession and during the Seven Years' War.
Setting the Stage	Louis XIV, the "Sun King"	Peter the Great's achievements	Competition between Austria and Prussia for control of eastern Europe
Teaching Strategies	Economics and History: Colbert and Mercantilism Writing about History: Balance of Power Check for Understanding	Using Geographic Themes: Movement Transparency 67 Discussing History: Westernizing Russia Check for Understanding	Geography in History: Hapsburg and Hohenzollern Lands Transparency 66 Outline Map 9 Discussing History: The Importance of Silesia Discussing History: Shifting Alliances Check for Understanding
Guided Practice	Section Review 1	Transparency 67 Q&A Section Review 2	Transparency 66 Q&A Section Review 3
Independent Practice Worksheets	Independent Practice 19.1 Vocabulary 19 Basic Skills 19 Critical Thinking 19	Independent Practice 19.2 Geography Skills 19	Independent Practice 19.3
Enrichment	1. Primary Source: Voices 19.1 2. Researching for Points	1. Primary Source: Voices 19.2 2. ★Analyzing a Quotation 3. Researching for Points	1. Primary Source: Voices 19.3 2. Creative Writing 3. Researching for Points

Chapter Closer	
●**Reteaching Activities**	Summarizing, Identifying Main Ideas, Outlining
Chapter Review	Summary, Reviewing the Facts, Basic Skills, Researching and Reporting Skills, Critical Thinking, Perspectives on Past and Present, Investigating History
Chapter Evaluation	Chapter Test 19, Alternate Chapter Test 19, Computer Test Bank Chapter 19 Test

The Sun King ruled France. 1

Setting the Stage

Have students write three adjectives or phrases that describe the sun. List student answers on the board. Possible choices include "brilliant," "dazzling," and "powerful." Ask students how they would feel if they were the sun. Discuss their responses. Now explain that the people of Europe called Louis XIV the "Sun King." Like the sun, Louis dazzled all who looked at him. And like the sun, Louis moved majestically and predictably through his day. This section describes the Sun King and discusses the achievements and failures of his long reign.

Teaching Strategies

Economics and History: Colbert and Mercantilism (Objective 1) Point out that Jean-Baptiste Colbert, the king's finance minister, faced a number of serious economic problems. France's domestic economy was disorganized. For example, a merchant attempting to transport goods from Paris to Calais had to pay tolls at 16 points. These tolls raised the price of French goods, making them less competitive in Europe's markets. As a result, France had an annual trade deficit of between 8 and 16 million dollars.

Explain that Colbert's approach to solving these problems was guided by his belief in the goals of an economic doctrine known as *mercantilism*. According to this doctrine, gold and silver constituted the most important form of national wealth. Because France lacked gold and silver mines, the country could obtain a surplus of these minerals only by achieving a favorable balance of trade. Colbert worked tirelessly to strengthen the

French economy. He recruited skilled weavers from Flanders, metal-workers from Germany, and mirror-workers from Venice to help develop new industries. (Competition for these workers was fierce. Italian agents poisoned the first two mirror-workers who left Venice.) At the same time, Colbert doubled the tariff on foreign imports.

These measures were only the beginning. Colbert eliminated many of the internal tolls. A new 162-mile Languedoc Canal promoted trade by connecting the Mediterranean Sea with the Bay of Biscay. Colbert and Louis chartered companies to trade with India, Morocco, and the East Indies. He also encouraged expansion in the fur trade in Canada. Finally, all able-bodied men were put to work. French workers toiled 12 hours for about 30 cents a day. Workers received only 90 days of rest a year.

Conclude your discussion by asking students to describe how Colbert might view America's current trade and budget deficits. What measures do they think Colbert would recommend to solve these problems?

Writing about History: Balance of Power (Objective 2) Have students read, "Louis fought costly wars" (pages 445–447). Explain the concept of balance of power. Reinforce this concept by having students write an imaginary dialogue among the rulers of England, Austria, the Dutch republic, and Portugal after they learn about Charles's decision to bequeath the Spanish throne to Louis's grandson. The dialogues should incorporate the political leaders' concern over maintaining a balance of power. Ask several students to read their dialogues to the class.

Check for Understanding Have students define and give examples of absolute monarchy, mercantilism, and balance of power.

Enrichment Activities

1. **Reading a Primary Source** Assign Voices from the Past Resource Book 19.1.

2. **Researching for Bonus Points** Louis rewarded one lucky noble at the end of each day by allowing him to hold a certain object. What was the object? (a candlestick)

Peter the Great changed Russia. 2

Setting the Stage

Introduce this section by asking students which rulers they have studied have had the greatest impact on their countries. List students' responses on the board. This section describes the achievements of an extraordinary Russian czar—Peter the Great. Students will examine how Peter successfully ended Russia's isolation from Europe, made the czar's power absolute, and built a new capital that gave Russia an outlet to the sea.

Teaching Strategies

Using Geographic Themes: Movement (Objective 1) Ask students to describe factors or conditions that promote the movement of goods and ideas. Students should recall the role of trade routes, military invasions, voyages of exploration, and new inventions such as the printing press in spreading ideas. Then explain that while the nations of Europe were benefiting from an unprecedented age of discovery and movement, Russia remained isolated from these developments.

Ask students to recall factors that they have previously studied that help explain Russia's isolation from western Europe. Point out that geographic barriers kept Russia closed in on itself. Travel by land was slow and expensive, and Russia's only seaport at Archangel was choked with ice much of the year. In addition, the Mongol conquest cut Russia off from the ideas of the Renaissance, Scientific Revolution, and Age of Exploration. While the Russians did expand eastward in Siberia, they lacked foreign colonies and thus did not benefit from trade with the New World. Tell students that religious differences also widened the gap between western Europeans and

Russians. Recall that the Russians adopted the Byzantine, or Eastern Orthodox, branch of Christianity. Russians thus shunned Roman Catholics and Protestants as heretics. Show Map Transparency 67, *The Growth of Russia, 1505–1796.* Ask students how the acquisition of land by Peter the Great made Russia less isolated.

Discussing History: Westernizing Russia (Objective 2) Explain that Peter was determined to end Russia's isolation from western Europe. During his dramatic 18-month tour, he visited Prussia, Hanover, Holland, England, Austria, and Poland. Peter's trip created a sensation throughout Europe. The czar worked in shipyards, visited workshops, studied microscopy with Leeuwenhoek, and even learned to pull teeth and to cobble shoes. He returned to Moscow with more than 700 European technicians, including naval captains, doctors, and mining engineers. He also brought back cases packed with guns, sail cloth, compasses, and anchors.

Most important, Peter brought back a desire to modernize Russia. Review the list of reforms (pages 449–450) and encourage students to explain their importance. In addition to these changes, Peter also reformed the Russian alphabet, opened mints to coin money, and built libraries, vocational schools, and a naval academy.

Stress that Peter's reforms marked a watershed in Russian history. They strengthened the czar's power while also ending Russia's isolation from Europe. From that time on, Russia began to play a leading role in European affairs. As noted by Will Durant, "Russia had discovered Europe, and Europe had discovered Russia."

Check for Understanding Ask students to cite three ways in which Peter the Great changed Russia.

Enrichment Activities

1. **Reading a Primary Source** Assign Voices from the Past Resource Book 19.2.

2. **Analyzing a Quotation** In his book, *The Rulers of Russia,* historian Peter Andrews wrote, "Peter's contemporary Louis XIV of France may have shone more brightly than any monarch in Europe, but it was Peter who cast the longer shadow." Ask advanced students to evaluate this statement.

3. **Researching for Bonus Points** What assumed name did Peter the Great use while he worked in a Dutch shipyard? (Peter Mikhailov)

Austria and Prussia rose to power.

3

Setting the Stage

Begin by writing the word *vacuum* on the board. Explain that a vacuum is a space with nothing in it. Ask what happens when a vacuum is exposed to air. Point out that the air will rush in to fill the vacuum. Then write the words *power vacuum* on the board. Ask students to recall that in politics a power vacuum occurs when a government lacks enough strength to defend its territorial boundaries. Explain that powerful nations have historically attempted to take advantage of power vacuums to control or conquer other countries. By the end of the seventeenth century, central Europe's power vacuum provided opportunities for aggressive new states. This section explains how Austria and Prussia competed to dominate central Europe.

Teaching Strategies

Geography in History: Hapsburg and Hohenzollern Lands (Objective 1) Distribute Outline Map 9: Europe. Ask students to locate and label the lands ruled by the Austrian Hapsburgs and those ruled by the Hohenzollerns. Display Map Transparency 66, *Europe in 1715*. Which part of Prussia was not within the Holy Roman Empire? Have students identify who controlled Berlin and Vienna.

Discussing History: The Importance of Silesia (Objective 2) Ask students to find Silesia on the map of Europe (page 453). Explain that Silesia had great strategic importance for both Prussia and Austria. It contained valuable iron and coal deposits that made it the most industrially advanced region in central Europe. Frederick the Great

recognized that the conquest of Silesia would almost double Prussia's population while more than doubling its resources. With Silesia, Prussia could become a great power; without it, Prussia would remain a small, vulnerable state. Point out that the Austrian Queen Maria Theresa recognized Silesia's strategic value and was determined to prevent Prussia from conquering it. One historian called Silesia the "keystone of Germany." Ask students to explain why this description was fitting.

Discussing History: Shifting Alliances (Objective 3) The War of the Austrian Succession and the Seven Years' War can be confusing. Use the following list of basic facts to help students sort out who fought whom in which war and for what reason:

- In both wars, Prussia fought Austria for possession of Silesia.
- In both wars, England fought France for possession of trading bases in India and colonial empires in North America.
- In the War of the Austrian Succession, Austria had England for an ally, while Prussia was supported by France.
- In the Seven Years' War, England and France remained enemies, but switched allies. Prussia became England's ally and Austria became France's.

Check for Understanding Ask students to explain why Prussia and Austria became bitter rivals.

Enrichment Activities

1. **Reading a Primary Source** Assign Voices from the Past Resource Book 19.3.
2. **Creative Writing** Ask students to choose an event discussed in this section that they would like to have

witnessed. Then ask them to write a paper entitled, "I Wish I'd Been There," explaining why they chose this event and what they wish to learn about it.

3. **Researching for Bonus Points** What was unusual about Frederick William's famed Potsdam Regiment? (All of the men were between six and seven feet tall.)

Reviewing the Facts

1. (a) rule by an absolute monarch **(b)** policy of favoring exports over imports **(c)** tax on goods arriving in a country **(d)** ratio of imports to exports **(e)** defensive strategy in which no one country or group of countries can dominate others

2. (a) absolute monarch known as Sun King **(b)** prime minister whose harsh policies led to riots **(c)** Louis's minister of finance who used mercantile policy to build France's economy **(d)** comic actor and playwright **(e)** ruler who modernized Russia **(f)** Swedish king whom Peter fought in the Great Northern War **(g)** ruling family of Prussia **(h)** Austrian ruling family **(i)** Hapsburg monarch who succeeded to the throne according to the terms of the Pragmatic Sanction **(j)** new state that rose to power in late 1600's

3. (a) backward society that knew little about western Europe **(b)** to modernize Russia; to acquire a warm-water port **(c)** To modernize Russia, he traveled to western Europe to learn western European customs. To gain a warm-water port, he modernized the army and won a large area of land on the Baltic Sea.

4. (a) Hapsburgs ruled over many lands; much territory had been won in the War of Spanish Succession. **(b)** The lands under the Hapsburg rule were widely scattered, with different peoples.

5. (a) Frederick William developed a strong standing army whose services he offered to any power that granted him territory. **(b)** Hohenzollern formula for success: build a good army and strike bargains for land and power.

Basic Skills

1. 1701–1713 War of Spanish Succession: cause—Louis XIV's grandson taking the throne of Spain; countries involved—France and Spain against England, Austria, Netherlands, Denmark, Portugal, several German states, Savoy; outcome—Louis's grandson remained king but thrones of France and Spain could never be united; France kept Alsace; Britain got Gibraltar, Nova Scotia, Newfoundland, Hudson Bay Territory; Austria got Belgium and Spain's Italian lands of Sardinia, Naples, Milan; Prussia and Savoy were recognized as kingdoms. 1740–1748 War of Austrian Succession: cause—Prussian invasion of Silesia; countries involved—Prussia, France, Spain, Bavaria, against Austria, Britain, Russia, Netherlands; outcome—Austria lost Silesia to Prussia. 1756–1763 Seven Years' War: cause—Austria's effort to regain Silesia; countries involved—Prussia, Britain, against Austria, France, Russia; outcome—Silesia remained with Prussia, France surrendered Canada to Britain.

2. three new powers: Russia, Prussia, Austria

Researching and Reporting Skills

Students' choices of topics and their development will vary.

Critical Thinking

1. (a) Possible answers: in France, etiquette of Versailles, building of Versailles, control over nobility, Edict of Nantes, decisions to make war, economic tariffs, patronizing of the arts. **(b)** Louis managed to rule without the Estates General; did not need their approval to levy taxes. In England, Parliament had already established the principle of representation and used this power to gain further limitations on royal authority.

2. (a) Aimed to have favorable balance of trade by increasing production and exports and limiting imports. They reduced debt and built country's wealth, particularly its gold supply. **(b)** Subsidized industry, established tariffs on imports, encouraged skilled workers to come to France, built navy to protect trade, built canals and roads to facilitate trade.

3. The Huguenots in France and the Jews and Muslims in Spain were the leaders in business and trade, representing the middle class. In both cases, religious unity was achieved but at considerable economic cost, although the cost was higher for Spain.

4. Russia was geographically cut off from trade by sea. Peter fought to gain harbors on the Baltic and Black seas. The winter cold of Russia helped Peter to defeat the Swedes.

5. Both built up their armies. Hohenzollerns used army and diplomacy to gain power and new lands. Peter the Great used social and economic reforms to modernize and strengthen Russia and make it a European power. He fought to obtain for Russia a window on the sea to improve trade and communication with Europe.

Perspectives on Past and Present

(a) Answers will vary. Consensus probably would be that France still leads in fashion but that cultural leadership is dispersed among many countries. **(b)** Profitable; prestige lent to the nation's products makes them highly desirable.

Investigating History

Students' reports will vary.

Chapter 19

Teaching with Pictures

Have students study the painting of Versailles. Ask them how big they think the palace is and how much land is attached. Then explain that the palace itself is one-fourth mile (0.4 kilometers) in length and contains 1,300 rooms. The gardens and park, including many fountains, pools, and two smaller palaces, cover 250 acres (101 hectares). Construction of the palace began in 1661 under Louis XIV and took more than 40 years to complete. Of the 20,000 people who were attached to the court, 5,000 lived in the palace itself. The palace at Versailles was the royal residence and seat of government for more than 100 years.

Make sure students note the orderliness of the palace and grounds. Ask them why having such a grand residence was important to Louis XIV. How does Versailles characterize his reign?

Louis XIV's grand palace at Versailles was a monument of beauty and splendor. It also stood at a safe distance from the dangerous mobs of Paris.

Key Terms

absolutism
mercantilism
export
import
subsidy
balance of trade
tariff
balance of power
junker

ead and Understand

1. The Sun King ruled France.
2. Peter the Great changed Russia.
3. Austria and Prussia rose to power.

"Sire, it is time."

In the privacy of his bedroom, the French king awoke, as he always did, to the whispered announcement of his chief valet. It was 7:30 A.M. at the royal palace of Versailles (vair-SYE), 11 miles southwest of Paris. From this moment until midnight, King Louis XIV understood that his every move would be watched and commented on a thousand times by the courtiers who lived at Versailles.

Louis had trained them all to depend on his little favors. A kingly nod to one courtier, a glance at another, a kind word to a third were treasured by the French nobles. Now, outside the curtains of his canopy bed, the 100 nobles on whom he had conferred his greatest favors were waiting. Every morning, these 100 privileged ones were permitted to enter the royal bedchamber and help the great king dress for the day.

440

Chapter 19 Resources

GEOGRAPHY
- Geography Skills 19
- Outline Map 9
- Transparencies 66, 67

REINFORCEMENT
- Vocabulary 19
- Basic Skills 19
- Reteaching 19
- Making Connections Study Guide 19

ENRICHMENT
- Critical Thinking 19
- History and Literature 19

ASSESSMENT
- Chapter Test 19
- Alternate Chapter Test 19
- Computer Test Bank

First, the four highest-ranking nobles would approach the bed. Only one of these four was judged worthy enough to draw the curtain of the king's bed. For the next two hours, different groups of honored courtiers would file into the room to aid the king as he dressed. One noble would receive the king's discarded nightcap from the royal hand. Another would present Louis with his royal slippers. A third and a fourth would hold the two sleeves of Louis's nightdress as he stepped out of it.

Meanwhile, outside the king's bedchamber, thousands of lesser nobles would station themselves in palace halls. They hoped the king might see them as he passed and perhaps favor them with a nod or a look.

At exactly 10:00 A.M., Louis would be carried in a sedan chair into his chapel to attend the Catholic mass. Hundreds of nobles stood ready to greet him there and bow toward him just as he bowed toward the holy altar. It was as if the king, not God, was the true object of their worship.

For French nobles, success or failure in life depended on winning Louis's favorable attentions. A single blunder at court might doom their hopes of advancement. Thus, they were careful to follow the intricate rules of etiquette laid down by their demanding king. For example, whenever they met a procession of servants carrying the king's dinner, they were required to doff their hats and bow low. Knocking on someone's door was considered rude. The proper way to announce one's presence was to scratch lightly at the door with the little finger of the left hand.

Louis XIV, who ruled France from 1643 to 1715, was the most powerful monarch in French history. He was an absolute monarch, a ruler with unlimited power. Unlike England's ruler, Louis did not share his power with a parliament. In Louis's view, he and the nation were one and the same. He reportedly boasted, "*L'état, c'est moi,*" meaning "I am the state."

Although Louis XIV was the most powerful monarch of his time, he was by no means the only absolute ruler. Of all the major nations of Europe, only England and the Dutch Netherlands resisted absolute rule. Elsewhere in Europe—France, Russia, Prussia, and Austria—powerful rulers dominated their lands. This chapter looks at Europe during the brief age (1648–1763) of **absolutism,** or rule by absolute monarchs.

The Sun King ruled France.   1

Just as the sun is the center of the solar system, Louis was the center of France's government. Just as the sun dazzles people's eyes, so Louis dazzled France (and indeed all of Europe). "The Sun King" was the flattering description Louis liked best.

Louis XIV was the third king of the Bourbon dynasty. His father, Louis XIII, had been a weak ruler who left government in the hands of the powerful Cardinal Richelieu (page 408). Richelieu died in 1642, followed six months later by Louis XIII in 1643.

The heir to the throne, little Louis XIV, was only five years old. Although technically he became king in 1643, real power rested in the hands of his mother, Anne, and her prime minister, the ruthless Cardinal Jules Mazarin (MA-za-RAN).

Violence marred Louis's childhood.

Like Richelieu, Mazarin worked steadily to increase France's power. Mazarin's greatest triumph came in 1648 when he represented France at the peace conference after the Thirty Years' War. The terms of the Treaty of Westphalia (page 411) made France the strongest nation in Europe.

Although France was at the peak of its power, its king was still a frightened, lonely ten-year-old boy. In fact, the young Louis XIV had much to fear. Many people in France hated Mazarin and his harsh policies. In 1648, this hatred broke out in a revolt led by nobles who feared that Mazarin was stripping away their powers and privileges. A series of terrifying riots began in Paris and spread to the countryside. These violent outbreaks were called the *Fronde.* (*Fronde* meant "slingshot" and was a scornful term suggesting that the rebels were naughty children.) The riots and revolts continued for five years.

During the years of rioting, Louis's life was often in danger. In 1651, a group of rebels broke into the royal palace in Paris and roughly demanded to see the 13-year-old king. The terrified queen mother led them to the chamber where they found Louis sleeping—or rather, pretending to sleep. Satisfied that the king had not escaped

441

441

SECTION 1
Objectives and Teaching Strategies

OBJECTIVE 1. Define mercantilism and explain how Colbert improved France's economy.

Teaching Strategy: *Economics and History: Colbert and Mercantilism* (page 440c)

OBJECTIVE 2. Explain the concept of balance of power.

Teaching Strategy: *Writing about History: Balance of Power* (page 440c)

■ BACKGROUND

Louis was the son of a loveless marriage. He claimed that his parents were so neglectful that once he almost drowned. The best friends of his youth were servants. They were the only common people he ever knew.

Louis had an all-absorbing concern to see that every noble idolized him. He was constantly checking to see who appeared regularly at court. Failure to appear meant certain disgrace.

SECTION 1
Resources

ASSESSMENT
■ Section Quiz 19.1

REINFORCEMENT
■ Independent Practice 19.1

ENRICHMENT
■ Voices from the Past 19.1

While Louis was growing up, Mazarin kept a tight hold on the purse strings, depriving Louis even of proper bedsheets and everyday clothing.

Government officials were exempt from taxation. For a fee, people could become employees of the Crown to evade paying their taxes. In 1664, 46,000 people were employed by the departments of justice and finance alone.

Paris, the rebels stomped out. Ever after, the king hated Paris. His later move to Versailles was partly caused by bitter memories of Paris.

In the end, the Fronde rebellion failed because its leaders distrusted one another even more than they distrusted Mazarin. Peasants and townspeople grew weary of disorder and fighting. For many years afterward, the people of France accepted the oppressive laws of an absolute king, because they were convinced that the alternative, rebellion, was even worse.

Louis ruled in grand style.

In 1661, Cardinal Mazarin died. Louis XIV, now 23, was glad to be rid of him. The king wished to rule France himself, to be king in fact as well as name. For the next 54 years, from 1661 to 1715, Louis dominated France.

Louis was indeed an impressive figure. Although he stood only 5 feet 5 inches tall, many people who saw him commented on his imposing height. His erect and dignified posture made him appear tall. (It also helped that he wore high-heeled shoes.)

Louis had very strong likes and dislikes. He hated cities but loved to travel through France's countryside. Because he hated delays, the people who traveled with him were at his mercy. Louis allowed no stopping except for his own comfort.

As king, Louis lived in a grand style. Eating was one of his chief pleasures. Nearly 500 cooks, waiters, and other servants worked day and night to satisfy his tastes. An observer claimed that the king once consumed four plates of soup, a whole pheasant, a partridge in garlic-flavored sauce, two thick slices of ham, a salad, a plate of pastries, fruit, and hard-boiled eggs in a single sitting!

The form of service was as important to Louis as the food itself. For example, three cupbearers busied themselves for eight minutes in the ritual of refilling the royal wineglass.

Colbert improved France's economy.

To Louis, all the pomp and ceremony of his court glorified France as well as himself. He wanted to make France the leader of Europe. As king, he devoted himself to helping France attain economic, political, and cultural brilliance.

Early in Louis's reign, France made impressive economic gains, thanks largely to the efforts of his dour, humorless minister of finance, Jean Baptiste Colbert (kohl-BAIR). Like other economists of his time, Colbert believed in the theory of **mercantilism** (MUHR-kuhn-TEE-lihz-uhm). According to this theory, a country's economic strength rested on certain conditions. These included acquiring gold and silver, expanding manufacturing, encouraging commerce, owning colonies, building up shipping and a navy, and **exporting,** or sending out, more goods than were **imported,** or brought into the country.

In 1665, when Colbert became Louis's minister of finance, the economy of France was weak. For the next 20 years, Colbert worked tirelessly to strengthen it. To expand manufacturing—for example, glassmaking, weaving, and silk production—he gave **subsidies,** or grants of money, and tax benefits to French companies. Colbert also sought to develop mining and agriculture. To obtain skilled workers, he encouraged those from other countries to settle in France.

Having more manufactured products enabled France to start exporting more than it imported. This gave it a favorable **balance of trade** that brought more gold and silver into France than went to other countries. To protect France's industries, Colbert placed a high **tariff,** or import tax, on goods coming into the country. The tariff too earned money for France.

Colbert also recognized the importance of colonies. They provided a source of raw materials for French industry and a market for manufactured goods. The government encouraged people to migrate to Canada, where the fur trade added to French commerce and brought more wealth to France.

Colbert knew that transportation was vital to trade. To improve travel within France, he encouraged the building of roads and canals. He added more than 100 warships to the French navy. Colbert's mercantilist measures were successful—so successful that by 1683 France had become the industrial leader of Europe. To Colbert, the purpose of this expanded economic activity was to serve the state.

Many of France's skilled workers and business leaders were Huguenots (French Protestants). They took a leading role in commerce, banking, and industry—the economic activities that Colbert

442

had encouraged. Both France and the Huguenots prospered from Colbert's policies.

Sadly, a single mistake by Louis undid much of Colbert's work soon after the minister's death in 1683. Louis, a devout Catholic, revoked the Edict of Nantes (page 408). For almost 100 years, the Edict of Nantes had protected the religious freedom of the Huguenots. Suddenly, Huguenots could no longer attend their own churches or schools. Instead, they could be imprisoned as enemies of the state.

Louis paid a high price for his religious intolerance. To escape persecution, 200,000 Huguenots fled France. Thus, the country lost many of its skilled workers and business leaders. The mercantilists of rival countries gloated over Louis's economic blunder.

CITY TOUR

Louis XIV *created Versailles.*

Louis was more successful in his cultural goals. Even after his death, the French set the standards for artistic taste and fashion. Every European ruler tried to imitate the way of life established by Louis at his grand palace at Versailles.

The tiny village of Versailles was located about 11 miles southwest of Paris. Prior to Louis XIV's reign, its only tie to royalty was the presence of a modest hunting lodge built by Louis XIII. The quiet village was to change forever, however, when Louis XIV decided to transform his father's lodge into a magnificent royal palace.

Beginning in 1668, Louis regularly rode out to Versailles to oversee the construction of his new palace and its gardens. An army of 36,000 workmen drained marshes, leveled hills, and labored on the scaffolding that surrounded the construction site. For years, thousands of marble blocks littered the grounds as Louis and his architects selected choice spots for ornamental trees and statues of Greek gods and goddesses. Although work continued until 1710, the impatient king officially moved into Versailles on May 6, 1682.

The splendors of Versailles The palace and grounds created by Louis were unique for their time. Unlike all previous royal residences, Versailles was completely unfortified. Instead of being

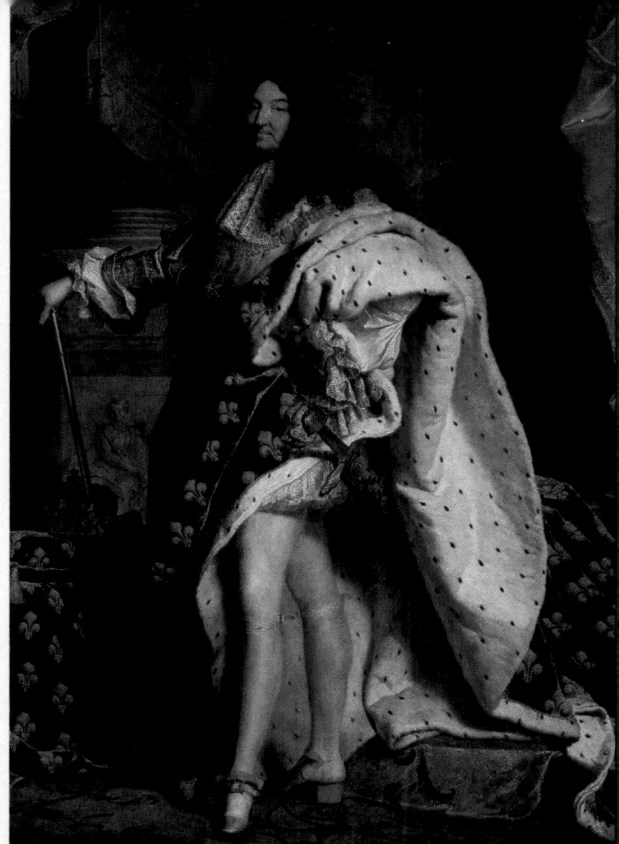

The gold fleurs-de-lis that adorn Louis XIV's cape in this portrait were the emblem of the Bourbon dynasty. The high heels on his shoes made him appear taller.

■ BACKGROUND
Moving the royal court from Paris to Versailles helped to consolidate the absolute power of Louis XIV.

surrounded by unsightly walls and a moat, it overlooked a magnificent garden.

Everything about the Versailles palace was immense. It faced a huge royal court dominated by a statue of Louis XIV. The palace itself stretched for a distance of about 700 yards. It was so long that food from the kitchens was often cold by the time servants reached Louis's chambers.

Because of its great size, Versailles was like a small royal city. The palace contained a chapel, theater, library, and numerous council chambers where the king's ministers met to discuss state business. In addition, about 1,000 nobles and their 4,000 servants crowded into the palace's 226 rooms. Another 5,000 servants were housed in nearby annexes.

While the nobles lived in relatively small rooms, Louis and his Austrian queen Maria

443

BACKGROUND

Just to decorate the gardens of Versailles, the following materials were needed: 1,400 fountains, 100 marble statues of Greek gods, 2 million flowerpots, and millions of tulips—half crimson, half yellow.

Parquet floors, marble walls, and gilded wood gleamed in the Hall of Mirrors where Louis XIV held his most lavish receptions.

Theresa enjoyed spacious royal suites. Louis's royal bedroom was located in the exact center of the palace. His bed was deliberately turned to the east so that it would face the rising sun—the symbol chosen by the king.

Although the king's bedchamber was impressive, the palace's most famous room was the Hall of Mirrors. This remarkable room was 246 feet long and 33 feet wide. Seventeen towering windows gave guests a splendid view of the palace gardens. Light from these windows flooded the room and reflected the gardens in 17 huge gold-framed mirrors on the opposite wall. So much solid silver furniture filled the red marble hall that it formed part of France's monetary reserves!

Louis used the Hall of Mirrors to hold state receptions and celebrate special occasions. Guests at the royal weddings of his daughters danced under the hall's 32 crystal chandeliers. The light from thousands of wax candles sparkled and reflected in the windows and mirrors.

Outside the Hall of Mirrors stretched Versailles' beautiful formal gardens covering almost 250 acres. There paths, flowers, and shrubs were arranged in precise geometric patterns. Four hundred

gardeners made sure that every plant was carefully clipped.

Louis loved his gardens and enjoyed taking special guests on private tours. The king especially looked forward to spring. At that time, more than a million yellow and crimson tulips burst into bloom. As Louis strolled through his garden, hundreds of fountains sprayed jets of water into the air. In one fountain, Apollo, the god of the sun (and the symbol of Louis XIV), rode a horse-drawn chariot as it rose from the surrounding pond.

Life at Versailles Although a courtier's life at Versailles was glamorous, it was far from comfortable. Even the best rooms were cramped and uncomfortable. Smells from the outdoor latrines seeped through the windows—in the few rooms that had windows. Many lower-ranking nobles settled for windowless, closetlike cubicles. In the summer, they roasted in those stifling quarters; in the winter, they froze.

Nonetheless thousands of French nobles gladly endured discomfort to share the glamour of Louis's court and its spectacular entertainments. One famous party in July 1689 lasted all day and night. After feasting and dancing to the music of the royal orchestra, awed onlookers watched as fireworks lighted the night sky. Some of the rockets twisted and turned to write the royal monogram—double L's—in fiery letters against the darkness.

Importance of Versailles Versailles held an almost irresistible attraction for the nobles of France and indeed of all of Europe. As the royal residence and center of French government, Versailles dominated French political and cultural life. And yet Versailles was also something more. Its gardens, royal suites, and elaborate daily rituals provided a visual display of Louis's absolute power. They surrounded him with a mystique of royalty while turning once-proud and rebellious nobles into willing servants. The elaborate ceremonies at Versailles impressed the king's subjects and excited the admiration and envy of other European monarchs.

France led Europe in the arts.

For his entertainment, Louis XIV demanded good music. At times, he could be heard humming the operas composed by the chief musician at his court, Jean Baptiste Lully (loo-**LEE**). Italian composers had written the first European operas around 1600. Now, thanks to Louis, operas became popular throughout Europe. They combined music, dance, and drama with the opportunity for spectacular costumes and special stage effects.

Comedies and tragedies Another of the king's favorite entertainers was comic actor and playwright Jean Baptiste Poquelin, better known by his stage name, Molière (moh-**LYAIR**). Molière lived from 1622 to 1673. This witty dramatist wrote some of the funniest and most popular plays in French literature: *Tartuffe, The Miser,*

Footnote to History

When Louis built the Hall of Mirrors, the only mirror-makers in Europe lived in Venice. The Venetian rulers jealously guarded this profitable business. For example, France imported 300,000 livres' worth of mirrors each year. In order to break this monopoly, Colbert used spies to lure 20 Venetian mirror-makers to France. Within a short time, the new royal workshop produced mirrors superior in quality to those of Venice.

The Misanthrope, The School for Wives. Each play is a biting satire on French society.

While comedy was Molière's specialty, tragedy was the specialty of his two friends and fellow dramatists, Pierre Corneille (cor-**NAY**) and Jean Baptiste Racine (rah-**SEEN**). These authors modeled their tragedies on the works of the ancient Greek playwrights Aeschylus and Sophocles (page 117), whom they greatly admired.

Like the classical Greek dramatists, the French playwrights always observed the "three unities" of classic drama. First, all action was related to a single plot; there were no subplots. Second, all the action took place in a single setting. Third, all the action took place in a single day. (These strict rules made French tragic dramas very different from the English tragedies of Shakespeare, whose work was not admired at the French court.)

Royal patronage Louis XIV was the principal patron of these artists. Not since Augustus of Rome had there been a monarch who aided the arts as much as Louis. He treated Racine, for example, as one of his favorite courtiers and gave him a generous pension for life. He brought hundreds of pieces of Renaissance sculpture from Italy to exhibit in his Versailles gardens. The "Mona Lisa" by Leonardo da Vinci was one of the smaller paintings that hung in his bedroom.

All of Versailles was a monument to the king's classical tastes in art. The buildings and grounds of the palace gave an impression of perfect balance, elegance, and classical grandeur. The chief purpose of art was no longer to glorify God, as it had been in the Age of Faith. Now the purpose of art was to glorify the king.

Louis fought costly wars.

By any measure, France was the most powerful country in Europe. In 1660, France had about 20 million people—4 times as many as Spain or England and 10 times as many as the Dutch republic. The French army, numbering 100,000 in peacetime and as many as 400,000 in wartime, was far ahead of other nations' armies in size, training, and weaponry.

By comparison, all of France's rivals were in decline or disorder. England was still recovering from its civil war. Spain continued its long decline. The Thirty Years' War had left most of Germany devastated.

445

■ BACKGROUND

Corneille and Racine often drew the plots of their plays from Greek mythology. One of Racine's masterpieces, for example, was *Andromaque*, based on the story of Andromache, the wife of the great Trojan hero Hector.

Louis persecuted the Huguenots, a Protestant group, causing almost 400,000 of them to leave the country. Among the Huguenots were many of France's best craftspeople.

ANSWERS TO Section Review 1

Define:
(a) rule by an absolute monarch (b) policy of favoring exports over imports (c) send a product out of a country (d) bring a product into a country (e) grant of money (f) ratio of imports to exports (g) tax on goods arriving in a country (h) defensive strategy in

(continued)

ANSWERS TO (continued)

which weaker nations combine to equal or exceed power of stronger nation

Identify:

(a) absolute monarch of France from 1643 to 1715 (b) power behind the throne during Louis XIV's childhood (c) minister of finance under Louis XIV (d) royal country house of Louis XIV (e) comic actor and playwright (f) French dramatist whose specialty was tragedy (g) French dramatist who modeled his works on the ancient Greek playwrights

Answer:

1. (a) revolt led by nobles (b) led to hatred of Paris and its mobs (c) It was better than the alternative, rebellion.

2. (a) encouraged skilled workers from abroad to settle in France (b) Louis revoked the Edict of Nantes.

3. (a) glorified France and Louis's absolute power (b) evoked awe and loyalty from courtiers

4. (a) by sponsoring opera, drama, and the fine arts (b) glorifying the king

5. (a) a costly war fought when Spain's King Charles II bequeathed his throne to Louis XIV's grandson, Philip (b) Philip V was allowed to remain King of Spain as long as France and Spain were not united; France kept Alsace; Great Britain gained Gibraltar from Spain and colonies in North America from France; Austrian Hapsburgs gained Netherlands, Sardinia, Naples, and Milan.

6. Look for answers to include the idea that other countries admired French styles and art but that admiration did not carry over into a willingness to accept political domination.

CHARACTERISTICS OF ABSOLUTISM

Basic Principle	Monarch rules by divine right and decides what is best for state.
Political	Ruler holds unlimited power; individuals are subjects owing loyalty and obedience.
Social	Ruler dominates upper classes, which in turn dominate lower classes. Ceremonies symbolize ruler's power.
Economic	Ruler encourages industry and trade to strengthen the economy.
Cultural	Ruler dominates cultural life either as patron of arts or by censorship.

Despite France's strength, however, Louis XIV failed in many of his military goals. Between 1667 and 1713, Louis fought a series of wars to expand France's boundaries to the Rhine River and to the Alps. Rather than bringing glory to France, these wars brought the country to the brink of bankruptcy.

Alone, no other country was a match for France. However, by joining together, weaker countries could equal or even exceed French power. This defensive strategy is known as a **balance of power.** In such a balance, no one country or group of countries can dominate others. Many smaller countries banded together to stop France's aggression.

Three times in 30 years (1667–1697), Louis sent French armies into the Netherlands to try to extend his borders to the Rhine River. Each time, he was stopped. At various times, England, Sweden, the Netherlands, Spain, Austria, and several German states joined forces against Louis. By the time the third war ended in stalemate in 1697, Louis had almost emptied the French treasury. His only important gain had been the German province of Alsace.

In 1700, the balance of power was once again threatened when the childless king of Spain, Charles II, died. On his deathbed, Charles bequeathed the Spanish throne and the huge Spanish empire to Louis's 17-year-old grandson, Philip. The two greatest powers in Europe, enemies for so long, were now linked by bonds of blood.

Smaller countries felt threatened by this sudden increase in the power of the Bourbon dynasty.

In 1701, England, Austria, the Dutch republic, Denmark, Portugal, several German states, and the Italian duchy of Savoy all joined together against France and Spain. They fought a long and painful struggle known as the War of the Spanish Succession.

The War of the Spanish Succession was a disaster for Louis. Several times he sued for peace. Each time, negotiations broke down because Louis insisted that his grandson must keep the Spanish throne. The costly war dragged on for 13 years.

At last, in 1713, a peace treaty was signed in the Dutch city of Utrecht. In the Treaty of Utrecht, France and Spain won only two points. First, Louis's grandson, Philip V, was allowed to remain king of Spain as long as the thrones of France and Spain were not united. Second, France kept the disputed territory of Alsace.

Great Britain,* on the other hand, was one of the victors in the war. From Spain, Britain took an important fortress at the southern tip of Spain known as the Rock of Gibraltar. This fortress gave Britain control of the strategic gateway to the Mediterranean Sea. (The British still hold Gibraltar today.) France gave to Great Britain any and all claims to the North American territories of Nova Scotia, Newfoundland, and Hudson Bay.

The Austrian Hapsburgs, also victors in the war, gained the Spanish Netherlands (what is

---

* In 1707, the kingdoms of England and Scotland were united by law. After that date, the kingdom was called Great Britain.

now Belgium). They also took over Spain's Italian lands, including Sardinia, Naples, and Milan.

Two smaller states on the winning side gained power and prestige. The German state of Prussia and the Italian duchy of Savoy were both recognized as kingdoms. These ambitious kingdoms later proved important in the development of Germany and Italy as nations.

The Treaty of Utrecht set up a new balance of power in Europe. On one side stood France and Spain, weakened but still imposing, both ruled by Bourbon kings. On the other side were the combined forces of Britain, Austria, and the Netherlands. The balance, however, was delicate. Any shift in power could tip Europe into a war.

Louis XIV's reign came to a sad end.

The War of the Spanish Succession left France near ruin, and Louis's last years were more sad than glorious. He still went through the same daily rituals at Versailles. In his old age, however, he was sorry for the great suffering his wars and high taxes had caused the people of France. Louis had suffered personal losses too. His only legitimate son died in 1711, and his favorite grandson died a year later.

In 1715, the saddened Sun King, now 77, developed gangrene in one leg. Gracious to the end, he said farewell to his wife, his courtiers, and his weeping servants. Then he called to his bed his five-year-old great-grandson, the future Louis XV. "My child," said the dying king, "do not imitate me in the taste that I have had for building or for war. Try, on the contrary, to be at peace with your neighbors ... Try to comfort your people, which unhappily I have not done."

Section REVIEW 1

Define: (a) absolutism, (b) mercantilism, (c) export, (d) import, (e) subsidy, (f) balance of trade, (g) tariff, (h) balance of power
Identify: (a) Louis XIV, (b) Jules Mazarin, (c) Jean Baptiste Colbert, (d) Versailles, (e) Molière, (f) Corneille, (g) Racine
Answer:
1. (a) What was the Fronde? (b) How did it affect Louis XIV? (c) How did it make the people of France feel about absolute rule?

2. (a) What did Colbert do to improve France's economy? (b) How were his achievements undermined by Louis XIV?
3. (a) What political purpose did Versailles serve? (b) What social purpose?
4. (a) How did Louis XIV promote culture in France? (b) What purpose did art serve during his reign?
5. (a) What was the War of the Spanish Succession? (b) How did the Treaty of Utrecht affect each of the countries involved in the war?

Critical Thinking
6. Under Louis XIV, France succeeded in dominating Europe culturally but was unable to dominate it militarily. Suggest some reasons for both its success and its failure.

Peter the Great changed Russia. 2

Like the king of France, the czar of Russia was an absolute ruler. In 1682, the year that Louis moved his court to Versailles, Peter Romanov became Czar Peter I. The log houses and onion-domed churches of Moscow, capital of Russia, were very different from the elegant corridors of Versailles. Yet in many ways, Peter I was like the Sun King.

Like Louis, Peter I came to the throne as a child. Also like Louis, Peter had a boyhood filled with violence, as older people used him in a struggle for power. Later, when Peter held power in his own hands, he avenged himself on his enemies, torturing them without mercy.

In some ways, Peter Romanov grew up to be a bullying brute. However, he was also a brilliant and able czar. His impact on Russian culture was probably even greater than the impact of Louis XIV on French culture. Peter I, called Peter the Great, made Russia a major European power.

Russia was isolated from Europe.

Peter I was neither the first czar to rule Russia nor the first to earn the title of "great." Both distinctions had gone in the 1400's to Ivan III (page 266). In 1480, Ivan had freed Moscow from

447

SECTION 2 Objectives and Teaching Strategies

OBJECTIVE 1. Explain why Russia was isolated from western Europe.

Teaching Strategy: *Using Geographic Themes: Movement* (page 440d)

OBJECTIVE 2. Describe how Peter the Great modernized Russia.

Teaching Strategy: *Discussing History: Westernizing Russia* (page 440d)

■ BACKGROUND

Russia grew eastward from 1500 to 1650. In the 1500's, Cossacks crossed the Urals following fur animals into the Siberian forests. They were eventually organized into a cavalry. By the 1640's, the boldest pioneers had reached the Pacific Coast.

SECTION 2 Resources

GEOGRAPHY
■ Transparency 67

REINFORCEMENT
■ Independent Practice 19.2

ENRICHMENT
■ Voices from the Past 19.2

ASSESSMENT
■ Section Quiz 19.2

The fine arts of western Europe did not interest Peter as much as the practical arts of shipbuilding and iron mining. Even so, he imported companies of German actors and formed an orchestra of foreign musicians.

■ DISCUSSION

What other examples of required uniformity of hair or dress—from history or from modern times—come to mind? Why might Peter have felt so strongly about this matter?

the Mongol overlords who ruled Russia. Ivan took the title of czar (emperor) and began to widen Moscow's rule.

The rise of the Romanovs Peter's family, the Romanovs, came to power in a time of troubles during the early 1600's. After the death of Ivan IV (Ivan the Terrible; page 267) in 1584, Russia was torn by power struggles among the nobles, or boyars.

In 1613, representatives from 50 Russian cities met to choose the next czar. Their choice was Michael Romanov, grandnephew of Ivan the Terrible. Thus began the Romanov dynasty, which was destined to rule the Russian empire for 300 years (1613–1917).

A land of boyars and serfs When the Romanov family came to power, Russian society was still dominated by the great, landowning families of the nobility, the boyars. Their vast estates were worked by serfs.

Serfdom in Russia lasted much longer than it did in western Europe. In France, England, and other parts of western Europe, serfdom developed in the late days of the Roman empire and began to weaken in the late 1300's and 1400's. In Russia, however, serfdom developed much later and continued to thrive into the late 1700's.

Serfdom in Russia was not much different from slavery. When a landowner sold a piece of land, the serfs were sold with it. Landowners could give serfs away as presents or to pay debts. It was against the law for serfs to run away from their owners.

An isolated land When Peter I came to the throne in 1682, most Russian boyars knew little of western Europe. In the Middle Ages, Russia had looked to Constantinople, not to Rome, for leadership. During most of the Renaissance, Russia was under the rule of the Mongols and remained cut off from western Europe. Thus, the ideas of the Renaissance, the Age of Exploration, and the Scientific Revolution had scarcely touched Russia.

Geographic barriers also kept Russia closed in on itself. Its only seaport was Archangel on the White Sea, which was choked with ice much of the year (see map, page 471).

Religious differences widened the gap between western Europeans and Russians. The Russians had adopted the Byzantine, or Eastern Orthodox, branch of Christianity. Western Europeans were

Peter the Great planned to make Russia a westernized nation and a naval power.

mostly Roman Catholics or Protestants, and the Russians shunned them as heretics. The few travelers from western Europe who reached Moscow were mostly Germans, and they stayed in the so-called German quarter of the city.

Peter dreamed of modernizing Russia.

In the 1670's and 1680's, people in the German quarter often saw the young Peter Romanov striding on long legs through their part of town. He was fascinated by the modern tools and machines in the foreigners' shops. Above all, he had a passion for ships and the sea.

Peter's love of ships was more than a boyhood fancy. The young czar believed that Russia's future depended on having a warm-water port. Only then could Russia compete with the more modern nations of western Europe.

After his troubled childhood, Peter I finally took full power in his own name in 1696, when he was 24 years old. He had the mind of a genius, the body of a giant, and the ferocious temper of a bear. One could not help but look up to Peter, who stood about 6 feet 8 inches tall.

Peter I came to the throne determined to modernize Russia. In 1698, at the age of 25, he went with 200 servants and 55 nobles on an overland journey to western Europe to learn about European customs. Never before had a czar traveled among western heretics.

On his journey, Peter insisted on keeping his identity a secret. He went to the Netherlands in the plain clothes of an ordinary worker. Pretending to be just another shipyard worker, he rose at dawn every morning and carried his own sack of carpenter's tools to the worksite. Nobody was fooled. A Russian giant in a Dutch seaport was a conspicuous sight. Yet if a fellow worker addressed him as "Your Majesty" or "Sire," he would not answer. No, he was just plain "Carpenter Peter," and for four months in Amsterdam, the czar insisted that everyone honor his disguise.

Traveling to England to see more ships, Peter presented himself to the king, toured London, and brushed off the gaping crowds that dogged his footsteps. An English gentleman who loaned Peter his house returned to find that the czar and his friends had played wild games with his property. Among other acts of destruction, they had thrown things at his paintings and flattened the hedges in his garden with a wheelbarrow.

Peter made many changes in Russia.

Peter admired everything that he saw in Europe—its ships, its industries, its cities, its elegant music, its fashions in clothing, even the way men shaved their faces. What would it take to make Moscow more like the countries of western Europe? Gentle persuasion would not do it. What was needed, in Peter's view, was to hammer Russia into a modern mold. "For you know yourself," said Peter to an official, "that, though a thing be good and necessary, our people will not do it unless forced to." Few rulers in history have attempted reforms as sweeping as Peter's.

The status of women Until 1700, Russian women followed the Byzantine custom of secluding themselves at home and veiling their faces in public. Peter set a new fashion by inviting noblewomen to social gatherings. Moreover, he demanded that they come without veils. The czar also decreed that parents could no longer marry off their daughters and sons unless the young people agreed to the match.

The Russian calendar Though Russian Orthodox priests opposed the change, Peter forced his people to give up their old calendar. No longer would Russians celebrate the new year on September 1. Henceforth, said Peter, Russians would follow the European custom of starting their year on January 1. In addition, Russians would date each year from the birth of Jesus, not from the

DAILY LIFE ▶ The Barber King

Surprisingly enough, the first thing Peter reformed when he returned to the Kremlin was not the army or industries but beards. To Peter, the Russian custom of wearing beards symbolized everything that was backward about his country. When his nobles fell on their knees to welcome him home, the czar raised them up, whipped out a long European razor, and commanded them to hold still while he shaved off their beards. The boyars were horrified. Russian men of the time treasured their beards as symbols of manhood and Christianity. Yet Peter decreed that all Russian nobles must shave off their beards. To make sure his decree was obeyed, he posted barbers at Moscow's gates. Noblemen who wished to keep their beards had to pay a beard tax every year and hang a metal tag from their necks to prove that they had indeed paid it.

449

Cooperative Learning

Peter the Great has just returned from his trip to Europe and is full of ideas. Changes are being made in all aspects of life—social, industrial, cultural—even including the way that years are counted. How does this affect the Russian people?

Working in pairs, have students write and then stage conversations between two Russians who are feeling the effects of Peter's reforms. Students should first decide on the roles they wish to play. They may choose from the following or think of one on their own: married women, boyars, farmers, factory workers, editors for Peter's new newspaper, soldiers, or teenagers. Students should then discuss the general tone of the conversation. They may choose to write out a script or simply improvise in front of the class. Encourage students to think about how Peter's changes affected everyday life for all different kinds of people.

Under Peter, all Russians were required by law to give service to the state. Such service included working in industries as well as serving in the army.

supposed time of the creation of the world as their old calendar had done. Thus, the czar's decree changed the Russian year 7208 into the European year of A.D. 1700.

Agriculture From Europe, Peter brought back specimens of potatoes and encouraged landowners to grow the new crop. Potatoes became a staple because they grew well in the cold climate.

Factories and mines To strengthen Russia's economy, Peter adopted the mercantilist ideas fashionable in Europe. He encouraged exports and discouraged imports. As a good mercantilist, Peter favored factories and subsidized their growth. Peter's factories were really more like centralized workshops, with perhaps a few machines run by hand. Still, when he came to the throne, Russia had only 13 such factories, and by the time of his death, there were about 200.

Peter also aided Russia's iron industry. With rich deposits of iron ore and large forests that supplied charcoal for smelting the ore, Russia soon was selling iron to other countries.

Newspapers Even literate Russians knew little of events outside their own country. To combat this ignorance, Peter started Russia's first newspaper and edited its first issue himself.

Peter I was an absolute ruler.

Like Louis XIV, Peter I of Russia was an absolute monarch. Many of the changes he made in his country were for the sake of increasing his own power.

For example, Patriarch Hadrian, the head of the Russian Orthodox Church, died in 1700. For more than 20 years, Peter neglected to appoint another patriarch. Then, in 1721, he abolished the office of patriarch altogether. In its place, he set up a group of high priests called the Holy Synod. At its head was Peter himself. The Russian church was now the czar's church, much as the English church had been made into the king's church by Henry VIII (page 379).

Peter also reduced the power of the great landowners, the boyars. He rarely gave high posts in government to the most powerful boyar families. Instead, Peter recruited able men from lower-ranking families, promoted them to positions of authority, and rewarded them with grants of land. Because these men owed everything to the czar, they were loyal to him.

When Peter first came to power, the Russian army was made up of cavalry (soldiers on horseback) who fought with sabers. They served only on a part-time basis. The armies of western Europe, on the other hand, were made up of highly trained infantry (foot soldiers) who marched forward while firing a constant barrage of bullets. These expert marksmen were full-time, professional soldiers.

To modernize his army, Peter hired European officers who drilled his soldiers in European tactics with European weapons. Russian soldiers no longer served on a part-time basis. Instead, as in western Europe, being a soldier became a lifetime job. By the time of Peter's death, the Russian army numbered 200,000 men. To pay for this huge army, Peter laid heavy taxes on nearly everyone in Russia.

Peter expanded Russia's empire.

Peter used his huge army to crush peasant revolts within Russia. He also turned it against neighboring countries to satisfy his greatest ambition—winning a warm-water seaport for Russia. He wanted, as he put it, a "window on the sea."

Peter believed that Russia needed a good navigable strip of coastline both on the Baltic Sea to the northwest and on the Black Sea to the south. The Swedes held the Baltic coast. The Ottoman Turks and their Tatar vassals held the Black Sea.

To win a warm-water port, Peter's first goal was to take Azov on the Black Sea from the Turks. His earliest campaign in 1695 failed badly. Undaunted, he saw that he needed warships. He helped build one with his own hands and besieged Azov again in 1696. This time the city fell to the Russians, though the Turks regained it several years later.

Peter then turned north to fight for a piece of the Baltic coast. His war against the Swedes, known as the Great Northern War, lasted 21 years (1700–1721).

At first, this war too went badly for the Russians. Early in the war, the Swedish King Charles XII scored a brilliant victory against the Russians. Then, in 1708, the Swedes suddenly invaded the Ukraine, a region on Russia's southwestern border. At first, Peter did not oppose the invaders. Instead, he left the Swedes to be starved and demoralized

450

Although St. Petersburg lay farther north than Moscow, the new city's location on the coast gave it a somewhat milder climate than the old capital.

■ **BACKGROUND**
So western a city was St. Petersburg that French— not Russian—was often the preferred language.

by Russia's most potent weapon, the winter cold. In the spring of 1709, Peter's army set upon the weakened, frostbitten Swedes and annihilated them at the Battle of Poltava.

The remaining 12 years of the Great Northern War went well for Peter. Sweden's Charles XII died in battle in 1719, and Peter successfully invaded both Finland and Sweden. The treaty of peace, signed in 1721, finally gave Russia a broad belt of land on the Baltic Sea.

Peter built a new capital.

Actually, Peter had secured his "window on the sea" many years before Sweden officially surrendered it. In 1703, he began building a new city on Swedish lands occupied by Russian troops.

The site for this city was a low-lying swamp at the mouth of the Neva River. The climate was damp and unhealthful, and the drinking water caused dozens of diseases. On the whole, the location was fine for wolves and wild ducks but terrible for people. To Peter, however, the location seemed ideal because ships could sail down the Neva into the Baltic and on to western Europe. Here at last, as Peter said, "a great window for Russia to look out at Europe" could be built. He called it St. Petersburg after his patron saint.

To build a city on this desolate swamp was no easy matter. Every summer, the czar's officials forced thousands of luckless serfs to leave home and trudge to the work camps on the Neva River. They had only the crudest tools and a few wheelbarrows. Workers lugged soil and stones across the swamp to make the city's foundations. Thousands of people perished from the terrible working conditions and rampant diseases. Estimates of the dead range from 25,000 to 100,000. St. Petersburg well deserved to be called "a city built on bones." Peter himself shared some of the hardships. He lived at the building site in a house that was little more than a log cabin.

In 1712, the czar proclaimed St. Petersburg his new capital. Russian nobles groaned when Peter ordered them to leave the comforts of Moscow and settle in St. Petersburg. Peter, however, was delighted with his new capital. "Truly," he wrote, "we live here in heaven."

451

ANSWERS TO

Section Review 2

Define:
(a) noble landowning family
(b) worker who was almost a slave

Identify:
(a) czar who made Russia a major European power
(b) Byzantine or Eastern Orthodox branch of Christianity (c) proclaimed capital by Peter

Answer:
1. (a) in 1613 (b) dominated by boyars; lands worked by serfs; isolated from western Europe

2. (a) religious differences, geographic barriers (b) to make it a modern nation

3. (a) westernized the calendar, strengthened the economy, introduced new crops, aided iron industry, started newspaper (b) abolished the office of patriarch in favor of the Holy Synod of which he was the head, promoted able men from lower ranking families to positions of power, and developed and trained a standing army

4. (a) for a piece of the Baltic coast (b) gave Russia a broad belt of land on the Baltic Sea

5. (a) ignorance of western Europe, feeling that western Europeans were heretics (b) While political and military changes can usually be forced or imposed on a people, social changes are adaptive and evolve.

In the fall of 1724, Peter was with his army along the Gulf of Finland. A ship ran aground, and the soldiers on it were about to drown. The 52-year-old czar plunged into the icy water to help, heedless of his own safety. He caught a cold that grew worse through the winter, and he died early in 1725. Near his death, he said, "I hope God will forgive me my many sins because of the good I have tried to do for my people."

For better or for worse, Peter the Great had tried to transform the culture and government of Russia. To an amazing extent, he had succeeded. By the time of his death, Russia was a power to be reckoned with in Europe.

Section REVIEW 2

Define: (a) boyar, (b) serf
Identify: (a) Peter the Great, (b) Russian Orthodox Church, (c) St. Petersburg
Answer:
1. (a) When did the Romanovs come to power? (b) Describe Russian society under the early Romanovs.
2. (a) Why had Russia been cut off from western Europe? (b) What was Peter's goal for his country?
3. (a) Describe three reforms that Peter made for the sake of modernizing Russia.
(b) Describe three reforms he made for the sake of his own power.
4. (a) Why was the Great Northern War fought? (b) What was its outcome?

Critical Thinking
5. (a) What cultural obstacles did Peter I face in his attempt to make Russia more like the countries of western Europe? (b) Why are rulers usually more successful in making political and military changes than social changes?

Austria and Prussia rose to power. 3

Between France in the west and Russia in the east lay the widespread lands of central Europe. The major powers of the region were the Holy Roman Empire, the kingdom of Poland, and the Ottoman empire. Unlike France and Russia, which were highly structured monarchies, the three powers of central Europe were not well organized.

Weak empires ruled central Europe.

Geographically, central Europe extends from the Elbe River in what is now Germany to the vast marshes of eastern Poland. Both the northern plain and the southern mountains lack clear natural frontiers, leaving the region open to warfare, migration, and shifting boundaries. Rulers thus had trouble gaining firm borders.

Socially, central Europe followed a different path of development from that of western Europe. During the late Middle Ages, serfs in western Europe slowly won freedom, and the middle-class townspeople gained power. In central Europe, the landowning aristocracy gained more and more control over their serfs. By 1700, Polish landowners could demand as much as five days' work a week from their serfs, leaving the serfs only two days to grow their own food. There was a great gap between the aristocracy and the serfs, with few middle-class merchants or free artisans between the two extremes.

Politically, central Europe fell under the rule of the Holy Roman emperor, the Ottoman emperor, and the king of Poland. Each of these rulers had more power in theory than in fact.

Poland On the map on page 453, the kingdom of Poland appears to be a large, united country. However, the king of Poland was elected by the Polish nobility, who allowed him practically no power. Poland's king had little income, no law courts, no officials, and no standing army. Usually, the nobles chose a foreigner as their king because they were too jealous of one another's power to choose someone from their own ranks.

The Ottoman empire The sultan of the Ottoman empire still exercised some power. He collected taxes and had a large standing army. The greatest of the sultans, Sulieman the Magnificent, had conquered Hungary and threatened Vienna. Since his death in 1566, however, the mighty empire had been steadily declining. The government in Istanbul (once Constantinople) was corrupt, and the large army was poorly equipped.

The Holy Roman Empire The Holy Roman Empire in the early 1700's was little more than

452

Europe in 1715

KEY
- Prussia
- Austrian Hapsburg lands
- Boundary of Holy Roman Empire

0 ——— 300 Miles

Map Study

What mainland regions of Italy did the Hapsburgs hold? What regions made up their largest single piece of territory? Why was Gibraltar a key point?

a name. In fact, after the Thirty Years' War, it consisted of about 300 states, each of which jealously guarded its rights and liberties.

In short, central Europe was a region of old, weakening empires and kingdoms. Historians call this situation a power vacuum. Such weakness tempts ambitious leaders to move into the area to fill the power vacuum. That was not long in happening.

In the late 1600's, two German-speaking families were eager to take advantage of central Europe's power vacuum. One was the Hohenzollern (HOH-ehn-TSAHL-uhrn) family of north Germany; the other was the Hapsburg family of Austria. Their ambitions threatened to upset Europe's delicate balance of power.

Austria regained power in the 1700's.

Even after the terrible losses in the Thirty Years' War, Austria still remained the most powerful and important state within the empire. Its ruling family, the Hapsburgs, was one of the oldest and most distinguished dynasties in Europe. As far back as the 1400's, most of the Holy Roman emperors were Hapsburgs.

The Hapsburg ruler in 1713 was Charles VI. Austria had just won much territory in the War of the Spanish Succession (page 446). Despite this victory, however, Charles's empire was not an easy one to rule. It had three main parts. First, there was the dukedom of Austria on the middle stretches of the Danube River. Second, to the

453

SECTION 3
Objectives and Teaching Strategies

OBJECTIVE 1. Locate Hapsburg and Hohenzollern lands on a map.

Teaching Strategy: *Geography in History: Hapsburg and Hohenzollern Lands* (page 440e)

OBJECTIVE 2. Explain why Prussia and Austria fought over Silesia.

Teaching Strategy: *Discussing History: The Importance of Silesia* (page 440e)

OBJECTIVE 3. Describe the alliances that formed during the War of the Austrian Succession and during the Seven Years' War.

Teaching Strategy: *Discussing History: Shifting Alliances* (page 440e)

ANSWERS TO
Map Study

All of Italy south of the Papal States; Austria, Bohemia, and Hungary; controlled access to the Mediterranean Sea

SECTION 3
Resources

GEOGRAPHY
- Transparency 66

REINFORCEMENT
- Independent Practice 19.3

ENRICHMENT
- Voices from the Past 19.3

ASSESSMENT
- Section Quiz 19.3

■ BACKGROUND

Poland's lawmaking body, called a *diet,* was virtually powerless. Rarely could it enact a law code since each member had the right to break up or "explode" the diet at any minute for any reason. From 1652 to 1764, 55 diets met and 48 were exploded.

The sprawling Holy Roman Empire founded by Charlemagne and Frederick Barbarossa was even less unified than Poland. The German-speaking part of this region was divided into a confusing host of petty states: duchies, principalities, and free cities.

Because of the foreign soldiers in this region, the German language had become corrupted. French, Italian, and Spanish were spoken in different circles, and Latin was still the language of the university.

Maria Theresa (1717–1780) (above) inherited the Hapsburg throne in 1740. At the Schönbrunn Palace (right), she was a patron of Vienna's rich culture. She also reformed the imperial government.

Voice from the Past | *A Call to Arms*

The year was 1741. Maria Theresa had lost Silesia. Prague, the capital of Bohemia, had also fallen. The future looked grim, as this letter from the queen to her chancellor, Prince Kinsky, reveals.

So Prague is lost, and perhaps even worse will follow unless we can secure three months' supplies. It is out of the question for Austria to supply them, and it is even doubtful if Hungary will be able to do so.

Here then, Kinsky, we find ourselves at the sticking point where only courage can save the country [Bohemia] and the Queen, for without the country I should indeed be a poor princess. My own resolve is taken: to stake everything, win or lose, on saving Bohemia; and it is with this in view that you should work and lay your plans. It may involve destruction and desolation that 20 years will be insufficient to restore, but I must hold the country and the soil, and for this all my armies, all the Hungarians shall die before I surrender an inch . . . You will say that I am cruel; that is true. But I know that all the cruelties I commit today to hold the country I shall one day be in a position to make good a hundred-fold. And this I shall do. But for the present I close my heart to pity . . .

454

1. The letter refers to Austria, Bohemia, and Hungary. How are these countries connected?
2. (a) What is Maria Theresa's resolve? (b) What alternative, if any, does she have?
3. How do Maria Theresa's sentiments compare with Elizabeth I's at the time of the Armada? (page 421)

Hapsburg imperial symbol

ANSWERS TO

Voice from the Past

1. ruled by Hapsburgs

2. (a) to stake everything on saving Bohemia (b) to give up Bohemia and concentrate on defending Austria and Hungary

3. Both show determination to defend their realms and both stress resolve to be amidst those in battle.

north, there was the kingdom of Bohemia. Third, to the east, lay the kingdom of Hungary. In addition, there were other German states and scattered lands in Italy.

Nothing about this patchwork empire was either natural or logical. Within its border existed a diverse assortment of peoples—Czechs, Hungarians, Croatians, Italians, and Germans. What held the empire together, generation after generation, was the fact that the Austrian, Hungarian, and Bohemian crowns were all worn by the same ruler, a Hapsburg.

How could the Hapsburgs make sure that they never lost claim to the lands that formed their empire? Charles VI spent his entire reign (1711–1740) working out an answer to this problem. By endless arm twisting, he persuaded the other rulers of Europe to sign an agreement known as the Pragmatic Sanction. By its terms, all the countries recognized Charles's only child as the heir to all his Hapsburg territories. That heir was a young woman named Maria Theresa.

In theory, the Pragmatic Sanction guaranteed Maria Theresa a peaceful reign. Instead, she faced years of war. Her main enemy was Prussia, a new state to the north of Austria. Like Austria, Prussia rose to power in the late 1600's. Soon Prussia's ruling family, the Hohenzollerns, challenged Maria Theresa and the Hapsburgs.

The Hohenzollerns ruled Prussia.

Like the Hapsburgs of Austria, the Hohenzollerns built up their state from a number of scattered holdings. At first, the small duchy of East Prussia in northern Poland was of little importance to the Hohenzollerns. Their most valued possession was a small state in the Holy Roman Empire called Brandenburg.

Brandenburg was never very powerful, but in the middle 1600's it enjoyed one distinction. Its ruling prince was one of the seven electors who chose the Holy Roman emperor.

In 1640, a 20-year-old Hohenzollern named Frederick William inherited the title Elector of Brandenburg. Frederick William, later called the Great Elector, had the unhappy experience of seeing Brandenburg overrun by rival armies during the Thirty Years' War. His capital, Berlin, was so badly devastated that its population fell from 14,000 to 6,000.

Frederick William, a tall and muscular man with piercing blue eyes, concluded that there was only one way to safety. Brandenburg, he decided, must have a strong standing army. At first, with his almost empty treasury, he could equip and feed only about 8,000 men. Yet even this small force gave him some leverage in dealing with other states.

With a keen eye for his own advantage, the Great Elector made alliances with the French, the Swedes, the Dutch, and the Poles. He offered the services of his army to any power that paid him well and granted him a little slice of territory. In some wars, he got money from Louis XIV, and in other wars, from Louis's enemies. So well did Frederick William play the diplomatic game that his armies rarely went into battle. Thus, he saved a great deal of money, which he used to build a larger army and strike better bargains.

The Prussian army grew in strength.

The three Hohenzollerns who followed the Great Elector were all named Frederick or Frederick William. They all followed his formula for success: Build a bigger and better army.

Frederick I The Great Elector's son was the first Hohenzollern to call himself a king. By the Treaty of Utrecht in 1713, his duchy of East Prussia (which lay outside the Holy Roman Empire) was recognized as a kingdom. Thereafter, all the Hohenzollern territories, including Brandenburg, were grouped under the name Prussia.

Frederick William I Frederick I's son and successor, Frederick William I, was a harsh and mentally unbalanced character who loved only his army. In his 27-year reign (1713–1740), he refused to spend money on anything but his soldiers and the development of military power.

Frederick William's obsession with his army had a lasting effect on Prussia. He more than doubled the size of the army, from 40,000 to 85,000 soldiers. He promoted his officers only from Prussia's landowning nobility, called the **junkers** (YUNK-uhrs). These army officers were far superior in social status and power to any civilian. Thus, more than any other country in Europe, Prussia became a military society. In fact, as a foreigner said, "Prussia is not a state that possesses an army, but an army that possesses a state."

455

■ **BACKGROUND**

Prussia became a kingdom of its own because of its army. The Hapsburg emperor needed to use it, and Prussia complied—for a price. The price: kingship for Frederick I.

■ **DISCUSSION**

In this first war between Prussia and Austria, Great Britain supported Austria and France supported Prussia. The Prussians and Austrians were fighting over possession of Silesia, while their allies were fighting for control of a worldwide trading empire. Discuss with students the other alliances these countries made, and for what reasons, in later decades.

■ **BACKGROUND**

In the mid-1700's, the French held parts of Canada and several islands in the Caribbean Sea. The British held several other Caribbean islands, Nova Scotia, Newfoundland, the Hudson Bay territory, and 13 colonies on the North American coast.

Frederick II (the Great) Frederick William worried that his son, another Frederick, might turn out badly because he enjoyed too many nonmilitary interests—music, philosophy, and literature. The scholarly young prince hated his father and tried to run away to France, but he and a companion were caught. As punishment, the furious father ordered Frederick, age 18, to witness the beheading of his friend. Despite such bitter quarrels, however, Frederick II followed many of his father's policies when he came to the throne in 1740.

Frederick II invaded Hapsburg lands.

In 1740, the same year that Frederick II became king of Prussia, Austria's Maria Theresa succeeded her father as the Hapsburg monarch. The newly crowned Prussian king scorned the Pragmatic Sanction, which his father had signed. Frederick wanted Austria's iron-rich land of Silesia. He assumed that, being a woman, Maria Theresa would lack the forcefulness to defend her lands.

The Prussian army invaded and occupied Silesia in December 1740. Thus began the War of the Austrian Succession. Following Prussia's lead,

The Mozarts—Leopold, Wolfgang, and Maria Ann—gave many concert tours. Wolfgang, when six, played for the empress at Schönbrunn.

456

other countries leaped to take advantage of Maria Theresa's supposed weakness. France, Spain, and the German state of Bavaria all sent armies across Austria's western border.

Austria's young queen reacted quickly. She had recently given birth to her first son, but nonetheless she made a dashing journey across Austria to her Hungarian lands. There, Maria Theresa appeared in person before an assembly of Hungarian nobles, who were not especially friendly to their Hapsburg rulers. Holding the infant prince, she delivered a stirring speech that instantly won over the assembly. The Hungarians pledged to give her an army of 100,000 men.

Maria Theresa also got help from Great Britain. Britain entered the war to fight its archrival France, which was allied with Prussia. With Great Britain, Russia, and the Dutch Netherlands on her side, Maria Theresa managed to stop Prussia and its allies from swallowing Austria and her other lands. She was not able, however, to turn the Prussians out of Silesia. In 1748, at the Treaty of Aix-la-Chapelle, Austria lost Silesia.

Maria Theresa resolved to regain Silesia. Her determination led to both a "diplomatic revolution" and a second Austrian-Prussian war.

Alliances shifted in Europe.

For more than 200 years, the Bourbon kings of France had been the chief enemies of the Austrian Hapsburgs. But was France still a threat to Austria? No, decided Maria Theresa's foreign minister, Count Kaunitz (KOW-nits). Austria's chief foe was now Prussia. Recognizing this, Kaunitz worked tirelessly to make France an ally. Aware of Austria's shrewd maneuvering, Britain decided its wisest move was to make an alliance with Prussia. After all, Britain had Europe's strongest navy and Prussia the strongest army. Together, they should be unbeatable.

By 1756, a so-called diplomatic revolution had taken place. Austria, France, and Russia were now allied against Britain and Prussia. Prussia's Frederick II decided to strike first.

Once again, Prussia and Austria were at war. This time, almost every country in Europe took part. In Europe, the war was known as the Seven Years' War (1756–1763). In North America, where France and Great Britain battled for colonies, it was known as the French and Indian War. Even

ANSWERS TO

Section Review 3

Define:
member of Prussia's land-owning nobility
(continued)

Berlin was the Hohenzollerns' capital—first of Brandenburg, then of Prussia. There Frederick II (1712–1786) reviewed his troops and listened to the music of Bach. The Brandenburg Gate was completed in 1791 as a triumphal arch.

Asia was involved, for there too France and Britain were rivals for colonies.

In 1763, the war on three continents ended with the signing of the Peace of Paris. Maria Theresa gained nothing from the war. Silesia remained in Prussian hands. France lost Canada and most of its lands in India to Britain.

Of the five major powers that fought the Seven Years' War, only one emerged with major prizes. This was Britain, the only country of the five whose king was *not* an absolute monarch. In the next chapter, we will see how new ideas began to replace absolutism in Europe.

Section REVIEW 3

Define: junker
Identify: (a) Holy Roman Empire, (b) Hapsburg, (c) Hohenzollern, (d) Pragmatic Sanction, (e) Great Elector, (f) Frederick I, (g) Frederick William I, (h) Frederick the Great, (i) Maria Theresa

Answer:
1. (a) Describe the geography of central Europe. (b) How did the region's geography make it difficult for strong states to develop there?
2. (a) Identify the three main parts of the Austrian Hapsburg empire in 1713. (b) How did Charles VI try to keep these lands for his daughter?
3. How did Frederick William build up the power of Brandenburg after the Thirty Years' War?
4. (a) What distinguished Frederick I from earlier Hohenzollern rulers? (b) What happened to the Hohenzollern territories during his reign?
5. (a) Why was the War of the Austrian Succession fought? (b) Describe the diplomatic revolution that took place after the war.
6. (a) Why was the Seven Years' War fought? (b) What country was the chief loser in the war? (c) Who emerged as the winner?

Critical Thinking
7. One observer of Prussia in the 1700's commented, "Prussia is not a state that possesses an army, but an army that possesses a state." Explain what this statement means.

457

ANSWERS TO (continued)

Identify:
(a) empire of about 300 geographically scattered holdings in central Europe
(b) Austrian ruling family
(c) Prussian ruling family
(d) agreement in which all participating countries agreed to recognize Maria Theresa as rightful heir to all Hapsburg territories
(e) Hohenzollern prince
(f) first Hohenzollern king
(g) unstable Hohenzollern king (h) Hohenzollern king who invaded and occupied Silesia (i) daughter of Charles VI; ruler of Hapsburg lands

Answer:
1. (a) rolling plains
(b) Absence of natural frontiers left area vulnerable to being conquered.
2. (a) dukedom of Austria, kingdom of Bohemia, kingdom of Hungary (b) by persuading other European rulers to sign the Pragmatic Sanction
3. by building a strong standing army
4. (a) first to call himself a king (b) grouped together under the name Prussia
5. (a) to claim Silesia's iron-rich land for Frederick II, king of Prussia (b) Prussia replaced France as Austria's chief foe; Austria, France, and Russia became allied against Britain and Prussia.
6. (a) because Prussia's Frederick II, with powerful enemies on three sides, decided to strike first
(b) France (c) Great Britain
7. Answers should consider economic, cultural, and philosophical effects of militarism on a society.

Concluding the Chapter

1. **Chapter Closer**
   Have students explain how powerful leaders influenced events in France, Austria, Russia, and Prussia. Ask students why "Europe in the Age of the Absolute Monarchs" is an appropriate title for this chapter.

2. **Reteaching Activities**
   a. Summarizing Have students list three positive aspects and three negative aspects of Louis XIV's reign.
   b. Identifying Main Ideas Have students discuss how Peter the Great changed each of the following in Russia: role of women, economy, army, calendar, capital, and boundaries.
   c. Outlining Have students use the heads and subheads to write an outline of Section 3.

Answers to Chapter Review appear on page 440f.

Summary

1. The Sun King ruled France. Louis XIV of France became king in 1643 at the age of five. For the next 17 years, real power rested in the hands of his minister, Cardinal Jules Mazarin. After Mazarin's death, Louis became the most powerful monarch in French history.

During his reign, Louis succeeded in some areas and failed in others. He wisely chose Jean Baptiste Colbert as his minister of finance but foolishly undid much of Colbert's work by forcing thousands of Huguenots out of France. As king, he patronized the arts and made France the cultural center of Europe. He also tried to expand France's power through wars but witnessed the defeat of his armies time and time again. Louis died regretting the costliness of his court and his wars.

2. Peter the Great changed Russia. Peter I of Russia came to the throne in 1682. At the time he came to power, Russia was a backward, isolated nation. Peter set out to win a warm-water port for Russia and modernize his country.

Like Louis XIV of France, Peter was an absolute ruler. During his reign, he made sweeping reforms that both modernized Russia and increased his own power. Peter also extended his country's borders. He won from Sweden a broad belt of coast on the Baltic Sea. There he built St. Petersburg, the new capital of Russia.

3. Austria and Prussia rose to power. Both Austria and Prussia lay in the strategic area of central Europe. Prussia was the creation of the Hohenzollern rulers of Brandenburg, who had extended their power by offering their armies' services in exchange for land. Austria, the most powerful state in the Holy Roman Empire, was ruled by the Hapsburgs. In 1740, the ruler of Prussia, Frederick the Great, invaded Silesia, a territory of Austria. One war followed another as the Hapsburg queen Maria Theresa tried to block Prussia's advances. The other countries of Europe, trying to protect the delicate balance of power, took part as well. In the end, a war was fought on three continents. Maria Theresa lost Silesia while her ally France surrendered much of its overseas empire to Prussia's ally, Great Britain.

Reviewing the Facts

1. Define the following terms:
   a. absolutism
   b. mercantilism
   c. tariff
   d. balance of trade
   e. balance of power

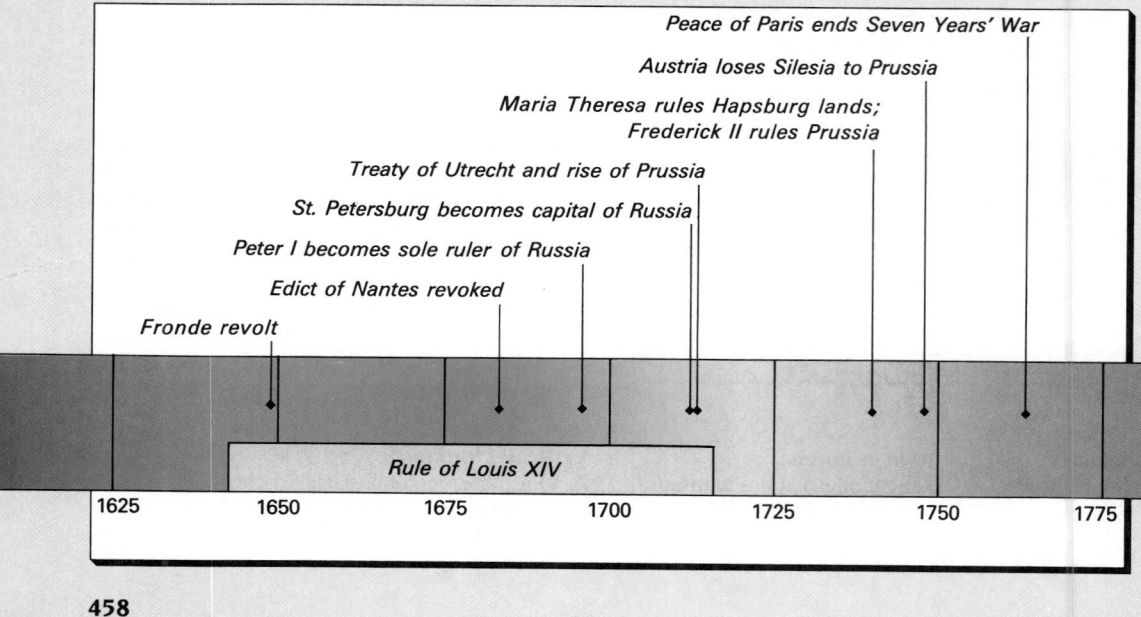

Peace of Paris ends Seven Years' War

Austria loses Silesia to Prussia

Maria Theresa rules Hapsburg lands; Frederick II rules Prussia

Treaty of Utrecht and rise of Prussia

St. Petersburg becomes capital of Russia

Peter I becomes sole ruler of Russia

Edict of Nantes revoked

Fronde revolt

Rule of Louis XIV

1625   1650   1675   1700   1725   1750   1775

2. Explain the importance of each of the following names, places, or terms:
   a. Louis XIV
   b. Cardinal Mazarin
   c. Jean Colbert
   d. Molière
   e. Peter I
   f. Charles XII
   g. Hohenzollern
   h. Hapsburg
   i. Maria Theresa
   j. Prussia
3. (a) Describe Russia when Peter I came to the throne. (b) What two goals did Peter have for Russia? (c) What did he do to accomplish each goal?
4. (a) Explain how Austria became a strong power. (b) Why were its lands difficult to rule?
5. (a) Explain how Prussia became a great power. (b) Why did it become a military state?

Basic Skills

1. **Organizing information** Make a chart of the wars fought by France, Prussia, Austria, and Britain from 1701 to 1763. For each war, include in the vertical column the headings Dates, Causes, Countries on Each Side, and Outcome.
2. **Interpreting a time line** Using the time line on page 458, identify the three new powers that were emerging as the reign of Louis XIV ended.

Researching and Reporting Skills
Writing a Historical Essay

In this chapter and the two that follow, you will be writing a historical essay. The purpose of a historical essay is to present a point of view, or thesis, on a historical subject.

Phase 1: Choosing a topic and developing a working thesis If possible, the topic should be a subject about which you can develop a point of view. Two examples might be "The role of individual X in the development of Y" or "The implications of C for D and E." The most interesting topics are those that highlight recurring patterns. After choosing a topic, you will analyze information in order to develop a viewpoint for a working thesis.

1. **Brainstorming about a topic** Look over Chapters 18 and 19, noting possible topics. Share your suggestions with others in a class discussion. Then make your final choice of topic.
2. **Organizing information under headings** Review sections of the text that pertain to your topic and take notes. Organize this information under headings.

3. **Developing a working thesis** Form an opinion that you believe is supported by your information. Write a sentence that expresses your opinion. This becomes the main idea of your essay.

Critical Thinking

1. **Applying a concept** In France, Louis XIV was the prime example of the absolute monarch. In England, the Stuarts asserted the divine right of kings but were unable to enforce that principle. (a) Give examples of Louis XIV's absolutism. (b) Explain what made absolutism possible in France and unacceptable in England.
2. **Analyzing an economic concept** Explain the concept of mercantilism. (a) What was its aim? (b) How did Colbert's policies apply the ideas of mercantilism?
3. **Synthesizing** In 1685, Louis XIV revoked the Edict of Nantes. Two centuries earlier Ferdinand and Isabella had expelled the Muslims and Jews from Spain. Compare the effect of these decisions on each country.
4. **Analyzing causes** Geographical factors had considerable impact on the history of Russia. Identify two ways in which they helped to shape events in the time of Peter the Great.
5. **Comparing** Both Peter the Great and the Hohenzollerns greatly increased the power of their countries. Compare the methods they used to achieve their goal.

Perspectives on Past and Present

In the time of Louis XIV, Europeans imitated the clothing styles and tastes of the court at Versailles. (a) To what extent is Paris still the fashion and cultural capital of the world? (b) What economic advantages does a nation derive from having a reputation for cultural leadership?

Investigating History

The age of the absolute monarchs was the era of baroque architecture—displayed in ornate castles—and of the music of Bach, Haydn, and Handel. Read about some aspect of the culture of the time and report on it or plan an audio presentation of music of the era.

CHAPTER
Evaluation

Chapter Test 19, Alternate Chapter Test 19, and Computer Test Bank Chapter 19 Test can be used to evaluate your students' understanding of this chapter.

Enlightenment in Europe, Revolution in America

Chapter **20**

Chapter Overview

The Age of Enlightenment in Europe brought together the ideas of the Renaissance and the Scientific Revolution. But the philosophical and intellectual ideals of the age were not consistently recognized in government.

Frederick II of Prussia and Catherine II of Russia paid only lip service to freedom and tolerance. Britain's government, a limited democracy, won the admiration of Enlightenment thinkers. The American colonies, however, overthrew British rule and established a republic.

Chapter Focus

Ask students to recall how it feels to be accused of something they didn't do. Then have them identify the injustice that is described in the chapter introduction (pages 460–461). Explain that French law discriminated against Huguenots by forbidding them to hold public office or to attend Protestant services. Donat Calas sought the help of the famous Enlightenment writer, Voltaire, because Voltaire had long fought injustice, prejudice, and intolerance. Voltaire wrote letters to arouse the conscience of Europe. The Queen of England, the Empress of Russia, and the King of Poland contributed to a legal defense fund. A special council reviewed the case and ruled that Jean Calas was innocent. Emphasize that in true Enlightenment fashion, Voltaire believed reason had triumphed over ignorance.

European thinkers expressed new ideas. 1

Setting the Stage

The Renaissance produced a new confidence in human intelligence and a curiosity about the world. The Scientific Revolution produced a new method of studying the physical world based on observation and experiment. The writers of the Enlightenment attempted to combine Renaissance curiosity with the scientific method to study and improve society.

Teaching Strategies

Discussing History: Sir Isaac Newton (Objective 1) Newton's use of the scientific method to discover the law of gravity had a profound impact on the leading thinkers of the eighteenth century. They hoped to use the scientific method to formulate laws of human behavior, enabling them to suggest reforms to help eliminate tyranny, ignorance, and intolerance.

Relating Past to Present: Progress (Objective 2) Begin by asking if it is possible to create better societies and better people. Challenge students to explain their answers. Explain that Enlightened thinkers, or philosophes, believed that progress was both possible and desirable. They thought that progress would lead to greater liberty and human happiness. Ask students to discuss the concept of progress in the United States today. How is progress defined? What benefits

Advance Planner

	SECTION 1
Objectives	1. Identify Isaac Newton and explain the impact of his ideas on the Enlightenment.
	2. Identify the philosophes and discuss five of their main ideas.
	3. Describe how scientific knowledge advanced during the 1700's
Setting the Stage	The roles of the Renaissance and the Scientific Revolution in the Age of Enlightenment
Teaching Strategies	Discussing History: Sir Isaac Newton
	Relating Past to Present: Progress
	Discussing History: Scientific Advances
	Check for Understanding
Guided Practice	Section Review 1
Independent Practice Worksheets	Independent Practice 20.1
	Vocabulary 20
	Critical Thinking 20
Enrichment	1. Primary Source: Voices 20.1
	2. Researching for Points
Chapter Closer	

★ **Advanced**
● **Basic**

	SECTION 2	SECTION 3	SECTION 4	SECTION 5
	1. Identify Adam Smith and discuss his three laws of economics. 2. Identify Baron de Montesquieu and explain the concept of separation of powers.	1. Compare and contrast Frederick II and Catherine the Great as enlightened despots. 2. Describe how Catherine the Great changed the political geography of eastern Europe.	1. Compare and contrast the role of the cabinet in the British and the American systems of government. 2. Identify and locate on a map parts of Britain's North American empire in 1763. 3. Explain the economic importance of the sugar trade.	1. Explain why the American colonists declared their independence from Great Britain. 2. Explain how the ideas of the Enlightenment influenced the United States Constitution.
	Contributions of the philosophes to ideals of good government	The characteristics of an enlightened ruler	Britain's constitutional monarchy	Are people ever justified in using force to change their government?
	Economics and History: Adam Smith Relating Past to Present: Separation of Powers Check for Understanding	Skill Building: Comparing and Contrasting Enlightenment Rulers Geography in History: The Partition of Poland Transparency 67 Check for Understanding	Skill Building: Comparing and Contrasting Systems of Government Geography in History: Britain's American Colonies Transparency 68 Outline Map 3 Economics and History: The Sugar Trade Check for Understanding	Analyzing a Quotation: Why Did the Colonists Rebel? Transferring Ideas: The United States Constitution Check for Understanding
	Section Review 2 Independent Practice 20.2	Transparency 67 Q&A Section Review 3 Independent Practice 20.3	Transparency 68 Q&A Section Review 4 Independent Practice 20.4 Basic Skills 20	Section Review 5 Independent Practice 20.5 Geography Skills 20
	1. Primary Source: Voices 20.2 2. Researching for Points	1. Primary Source: Voices 20.3 2. Analyzing a Quotation: Catherine the Great 3. Researching for Points	1. Primary Source: Voices 20.4 2. ★Creative Writing 3. Researching for Points	1. Primary Source: Voices 20.5 2. ★Creative Writing 3. Researching for Points

●**Reteaching Activities**   Writing a Paragraph, Identifying Main Ideas, Applying Main Ideas

Chapter Review   Summary, Reviewing the Facts, Basic Skills, Researching and Reporting Skills, Critical Thinking, Perspectives on Past and Present, Investigating History

Chapter Evaluation   Chapter Test 20, Alternate Chapter Test 20, Computer Test Bank Chapter 20 Test

might progress bring? Are there any limits to progress?

Discussing History: Scientific Advances (Objective 3) The German philosophe Immanuel Kant urged his readers, "Dare to know! Have the courage to use your own intelligence." Many eighteenth-century scientists followed Kant's advice. As students read "Scientific knowledge advanced" (pages 464–465), have them list the Enlightenment's scientific discoveries.

Check for Understanding Have students use the five key ideas of the Enlightenment to complete this sentence: Discover by (reason) and experience the (natural laws) that should operate in any situation; remove obstacles to their operation, and the result will be (progress) toward (happiness) and (freedom).

Enrichment Activities

1. **Reading a Primary Source** Assign Voices from the Past Resource Book 20.1.

2. **Researching for Bonus Points** What famous scientist died the same year that Newton was born? (Galileo)

Writers advocated liberty and reason. 2

Setting the Stage

Ask what the responsibilities of a good citizen are. List responses on the board. Then call attention to Diderot's definition of a good citizen (page 466). Diderot and other philosophes shared a concern for the welfare of society, the freedom of the individual, and the happiness of humanity. The philosophes believed that these ideals could be achieved in a society that allowed economic and political liberty.

Teaching Strategies

Economics and History: Adam Smith (Objective 1) Review the definition of mercantilism and its relationship to a favorable balance of trade. Students should recall Jean Colbert's economic advice to Louis XIV (pages 442–443). Ask students what advice Adam Smith would have given. Then divide the class into groups representing the interests of a monarchy, followers of Adam Smith, and followers of Jean Colbert. Suggest that the monarch impose a high tariff on foreign imports, and have students argue the point according to their group roles. Ask the students representing the monarchy's interests to state a decision and explain the reasons for their choice. Have students evaluate Smith's three natural laws of economics and give examples of self-interest, competition, and supply and demand in modern American economy.

Relating Past to Present: Separation of Powers (Objective 2) Ask students to name the three branches of government outlined in the United States Constitution. Explain that Montesquieu first discussed the concept of the separation of powers in his influential book, *On the Spirit of Laws.* Like other philosophes, Montesquieu opposed

tyranny and promoted liberty. He believed that a separation of powers would prevent the concentration of authority in one person. His ideas had a significant influence on the writers of the United States Constitution.

Check for Understanding Ask students to match each of the following names with the statement that best describes that individual's philosophy: (a) Rousseau (b) Smith (c) Montesquieu.

- Competition forces people to make a better product. (b)
- When the legislative and executive powers are united in the same person, there can be no liberty. (c)
- The only legitimate government is one that rules with the consent of its people. (a)

Enrichment Activities

1. **Reading a Primary Source** Assign Voices from the Past Resource Book 20.2.

2. **Researching for Bonus Points** In *The Wealth of Nations,* Adam Smith used the production of pins as an example of the advantages of the division of labor. How many pins could one person make in a day? How many pins could 10 people make? (1; 48,000)

Enlightened despots sought progress. 3

Setting the Stage

The philosophes were willing to consider a ruler enlightened if he or she favored religious tolerance, made economic and legal reforms, and enacted policies that were useful to society. Such rulers were known as enlightened despots.

Teaching Strategies

Skill Building: Comparing and Contrasting Enlightenment Rulers (Objective 1) Draw on the board a chart with two columns and four rows. Label the columns *Frederick II* and *Catherine the Great.* Label the rows *religious tolerance, economic reforms, legal reforms,* and *usefulness to society.* As a class activity, have students use information in the text to fill in the chart. Use the class chart as the basis of discussion: (a) What were the strengths and weaknesses of Frederick and Catherine as Enlightenment rulers? (b) Were Frederick and Catherine enlightened despots?

Geography in History: The Partition of Poland (Objective 2) Show students Map Transparency 67, *The Growth of Russia, 1505–1796.* Have students locate and describe Poland's boundaries before the First Partition in 1772. Between 1772 and 1795, Russia, Prussia, and Austria divided the entire Polish state among themselves. Ask how the partitions of Poland contributed to Catherine's goals for enlarging Russia. What effects did the partitions have on the balance of power among Austria, Prussia, and Russia.

Check for Understanding Have students define *enlightened despot* and name two enlightened rulers and the countries they ruled.

Enrichment Activities

1. **Reading a Primary Source** Assign Voices from the Past Resource Book 20.3.
2. **Analyzing a Quotation** The philosophe Denis Diderot visited Catherine in 1773. Catherine agreed with his theories but disagreed with his suggestions for specific political reforms. Years later she wrote:

   If I had believed him everything would have been turned upside down in my kingdom; legislation, administration, finance—all would have been turned topsy-turvy to make room for impractical theories. . . . Then, speaking openly to him, I said: Monsieur Diderot. . . . With all your high principles one would make fine books, but very bad business. . . . You work only upon paper, which endures all things; . . . but I, poor Empress as I am, work on the human skin, which is irritable and ticklish to a different degree.

   Read or distribute this passage and ask students these questions:

   - What does Catherine believe would happen if she tried to implement Diderot's ideas?
   - What did Catherine mean when she said, "but I, poor Empress as I am, work on the human skin, which is irritable and ticklish to a different degree"? Ask students what ideas of Diderot Catherine might have found impractical.

3. **Researching for Bonus Points** What gift did Count Orlov give Catherine in an unsuccessful attempt to win her love? (the 193-carat Orlov Diamond—the fourth largest in the world)

Britain developed new forms of leadership. 4

Setting the Stage

Britain, unlike Prussia and Russia, was never ruled by an enlightened despot. Ask how English politics differed from the politics of the other major states of Europe. Students should recall that the powers of the English monarchs were limited by law. Explain that historians call this type of government a constitutional monarchy.

Teaching Strategies

Skill Building: Comparing and Contrasting Systems of Government (Objective 1) A British cabinet is more powerful than its American counterpart because its members, including the prime minister, hold seats in the legislature—Parliament. As long as their party commands majority support, British cabinet ministers control both the legislative power of Parliament and the executive power of the king. In contrast, neither an American president nor any appointed cabinet members can vote in the United States Congress. Ask students to assess the advantages and disadvantages of the two systems in preserving democracy.

Geography in History: Britain's American Colonies (Objective 2) Distribute Outline Map 3: North America. Show Map Transparency 68, *British North America, 1763,* or refer to the map on page 474 to shade in and label the areas in North America that were part of the British empire by 1763. Ask what were Britain's colonies in the Caribbean. (Jamaica and Belize)

Economics and History: The Sugar Trade (Objective 3) The West Indies sugar trade played a vital role in the British economy. Between

1713 and 1792, Great Britain imported sugar from the West Indies valued at more than $800 million. During the same period, British imports from all of India and China were valued at only $500 million. The demand for sugar encouraged the development of the plantation system, which increased the slave trade. For example, between 1700 and 1786, Jamaican planters imported 610,000 African slaves. One modern historian estimates that by 1800 more Africans than Europeans had made the voyage to the Americas.

Check for Understanding Have students explain the role of the prime minister in the British government.

Enrichment Activities

1. **Reading a Primary Source**
   Assign Voices from the Past Resource Book 20.4.

2. **Creative Writing**
   Ask advanced students to write a paper predicting what might have happened if the British had allowed the colonists to send representatives to Parliament. The colonists would have been entitled to 112 representatives out of a total of 670.

3. **Researching for Bonus Points**
   How many colonies did the British have in North America and the Caribbean in 1775? (32)

Americans created a republic. 5

Setting the Stage

After the Stamp Act, many Americans began to question their relationship with Great Britain. Ask if people are ever justified in using force to change their government. Discuss student answers. Then ask how John Locke answered this question.

Teaching Strategies

Analyzing a Quotation: Why Did the Colonists Rebel? (Objective 1) Ask students what they think was the most important reason for which the colonists declared their independence from Great Britain. Explain that after the revolution, a prominent Massachusetts lawyer, Mellen Chamberlain, asked this question of Captain Levi Preston, a veteran of the battle of Concord.
Chamberlain: My histories tell me that you men of the Revolution took up arms against intolerable oppressions: What were they?
Preston: Oppressions? I didn't feel them.
Chamberlain: Why, were you not oppressed by the Stamp Act?
Preston: I never saw one of these stamps . . . I am certain I never paid a penny for one of them.
Chamberlain: Well, what then about the tea tax?
Preston: Tea tax! I never drank a drop of the stuff; the boys threw it all overboard.
Chamberlain: Well, then what was the matter? And what did you mean in going to the fight?
Preston: Young man, what we meant in going for the redcoats was this: We always had governed ourselves, and we always meant to. They didn't mean we should.
Read or distribute this passage and ask students these questions:

- How did the Stamp Act and the Tea Party affect Preston?
- According to Preston, why did the colonists declare their independence from Great Britain?
- Would Thomas Jefferson have agreed with the reason given by Captain Preston?

Transferring Ideas: The United States Constitution (Objective 2) Have students review the key ideas of the Enlightenment (page 462) and the theories of Montesquieu (pages 467–468). Which Enlightenment ideas are expressed in the preamble to the Constitution? Explain that the preamble expresses a commitment to reason and to a belief in liberty and human progress. Students should also note that Montesquieu's theories concerning separation of powers are found in the Constitution.

Check for Understanding Have students explain how Enlightenment ideas contributed to American independence and to the formation of the United States government.

Enrichment Activities

1. **Reading a Primary Source**
   Assign Voices from the Past Resource Book 20.5.

2. **Creative Writing**
   Voltaire died in 1778, nine years before the United States Constitution was written. However, what if Voltaire had lived to read the Constitution? Ask advanced students to write a letter from Voltaire to George Washington, reacting to the Constitution.

3. **Researching for Bonus Points**
   What song did Cornwallis's band play as he surrendered? ("The World Turn'd Upside Down")

Reviewing the Facts

1. **(a)** French thinker who believed in reason **(b)** power to carry out the laws **(c)** power to make laws **(d)** power to interpret laws **(e)** division of power into executive, legislative, and judicial branches **(f)** monarchy in which ruler is limited by law **(g)** executive committee that represented majority party of House of Commons **(h)** leader of majority party in Parliament **(i)** plan of government **(j)** government in which power is divided between national and state governments

2. **(a)** discovered law of gravity **(b)** exemplified Enlightenment thinking **(c)** editor of *Encyclopedia* **(d)** discovered lightning's connection with electricity **(e)** first European to explore South Pacific **(f)** argued in favor of free trade **(g)** believed political liberty hinged on separation of powers **(h)** argued that only legitimate government was one that ruled with consent of governed

3. **(a)** reason—divine force that applied to all aspects of life; nature—all that was good and reasonable; happiness—existed for all who lived by nature's laws; progress—used to perfect society; liberty—belief that society could be set free of restrictions **(b)** Salons publicized and spread Enlightenment ideas. **(c)** It brought together the most current thinking.

4. **(a)** Services are provided for the selfish motive of making money. **(b)** forces people to make a better product **(c)** ensures right amount of goods at lowest possible prices

Basic Skills

1. Political authority: absolute monarch held power by divine right; enlightened despot, by working for the good of the state. Both absolute in that they controlled all powers of government. Religion: absolute monarch wanted religious unity; enlightened despot, religious tolerance. Legal changes: absolute monarch oppressed individuals to control power; enlightened despot believed in granting legal rights and freedom to individuals. Cultural activities: absolute monarch patronized arts at his court; enlightened despot believed in progress based on education and scientific discovery, and supported learning.

2. Answers will vary.

Researching and Reporting Skills

Students' work will vary.

Critical Thinking

1. Renaissance focused thinking on worldly matters, interest in science; Reformation questioned authority, encouraged individual critical thinking, though focused on religious matters; Scientific Revolution developed belief in methods of natural science but did not perceive them in conflict with religion. Enlightenment integrated these different trends and took them a step further—to belief in scientific method, in ability to understand all aspects of life, including religion, laws of society, and principles of government.

2. Answers may include separation of executive, legislative and judicial branches; in economics, laissez faire; sovereignty of the people; religious tolerance; education of the people as liberation, and laissez faire in economics.

3. **(a)** To kings who considered themselves the ultimate authority, the idea of questioning authority and applying reason to it were very threatening. **(b)** The hostility of political authority increased the determination of Voltaire and Diderot to make their ideas known.

4. A free market means that competition will determine what goods are produced and establish the lowest price for goods sold. This provides what people want and eliminates those who produce inefficiently and cannot compete. In these days, the public good is served.

5. **(a)** Besides dividing power among the three branches of government, the Constitution also divided power between national and local governments. **(b)** the consent of the governed **(c)** to protect the rights of individual citizens against a powerful central government

Perspectives on Past and Present

(a) Cabinet ministers are official advisers chosen by the prime minister and who share the executive power with him or her. They also represent the majority party in the legislature. The prime minister is usually the head of the majority party. **(b)** In the United States, the president is head of the executive branch. The cabinet consists of advisers chosen by the president and having no involvement with Congress (the legislature). The executive power rests with the president, assisted by his advisers, and is separate from the legislative. In constitutional monarchies, the two overlap.

Investigating History

Answers will vary.

Chapter 20

Teaching with Pictures

Ask students to study the painting of the gathering of dignitaries in the palace of Frederick II. Tell students that Voltaire lived in Berlin, the capital of Prussia, for three years at the king's invitation. Although both men were scholarly and involved with music and literature, philosophical differences ultimately ended their friendship. Ask students why they think no women are present at this gathering.

Voltaire (in purple coat, leaning forward at left) dining at the Prussian palace with Frederick II.

Key Terms

philosophe	demand
salon	executive
baroque	legislative
physiocrat	judicial
free trade	cabinet
supply	federal
laissez-faire	
Enlightenment	
constitution	
prime minister	
market economy	
separation of powers	
enlightened despotism	
constitutional monarchy	

ead and Understand

1. European thinkers expressed new ideas.
2. Writers advocated liberty and reason.
3. Enlightened despots sought progress.
4. Britain developed new forms of leadership.
5. Americans created a republic.

It was a sad and shocking tale that the young man told, and the old Frenchman who listened to it was deeply moved. The young man was Donat Calas, a youth whose family had been forced to flee in poverty and disgrace from the French city of Toulouse. His hearer was Voltaire (vohl-**TAIR**), whose name was famous throughout Europe for his brilliant letters, pamphlets, plays, and satires.

Donat Calas told how, in 1761, his older brother Marc had been found hanged from the rafters of the family linen shop. Neighbors quickly accused the boy's father, Jean Calas, of killing his son.

The story of murder was all lies, said Donat Calas. He explained that Jean Calas was a Huguenot, hated as a heretic by the Catholic citizens of Toulouse. Because they thought his religion was evil, they

460

Chapter 20 Resources

GEOGRAPHY
- Geography Skills 20
- Outline Map 3
- Transparencies 67, 68

REINFORCEMENT
- Vocabulary 20
- Basic Skills 20
- Reteaching 20
- Making Connections Study Guide 20

ENRICHMENT
- Critical Thinking 20
- History and Literature 20

ASSESSMENT
- Chapter Test 20
- Alternate Chapter Test 20
- Computer Test Bank

believed he would act in evil ways. Young Marc had planned to become a Catholic, said the neighbors, and so his father killed him.

The neighbors told this story in court, and the judges of Toulouse believed them. Jean Calas was tortured and then executed. The judges ordered all his property to be confiscated. The surviving members of the Calas family, including Donat, were driven from their home and fled to Switzerland.

Donat Calas wept as he described the misfortunes of his family. Of course, he repeated, his father was innocent. What had really happened was obvious, Donat concluded. His moody and unhappy brother Marc had taken his own life. Jean Calas was executed only because of prejudice against the Huguenots.

Donat Calas had indeed found a sympathetic listener. Few people hated injustice and prejudice more than Voltaire. Now 68 years old, Voltaire had written thousands of letters and pamphlets denouncing intolerance and bigotry of all kinds.

Voltaire had hundreds of influential friends in Europe. From his country estate near Geneva, Voltaire sent forth a barrage of letters about the execution of Jean Calas. Friends rallied to the cause and wrote letters of their own.

French officials felt the sting of Voltaire's pen. In 1765, three years after the execution of Jean Calas, King Louis XV's council overruled the Toulouse judges and declared Calas innocent of murder. His family could return to Toulouse, reclaim their property, and collect a huge payment for the wrongs done to them.

Voltaire wept for joy at the news. In a long, happy letter to a friend, he exclaimed, "What great victories reason is winning among us!" Note that he did not take credit for the victory himself. No, the true victor in the struggle for justice was a higher power that he called reason.

Voltaire and his scholarly friends honored reason as if it were a kind of divine force. They hoped that, through the power of reason, society would make steady progress toward liberty and justice. In a society ruled by reason, they thought, injustice would disappear.

In this chapter, you will learn about the Age of **Enlightenment,** the period spanning the middle years of the eighteenth century (roughly 1720–1790), when scholars believed in the use of reason and in the scientific method.

In the English colonies of North America, the ideals of the Enlightenment played a large part in sparking a revolution against Great Britain. These ideals of liberty and reason helped to shape the government of the new country created by that revolution—the United States of America.

European thinkers expressed new ideas. 1

The Age of Enlightenment brought together the ideas of the Renaissance and the Scientific Revolution. Remember that Renaissance artists and writers adopted a secular outlook on life instead of the more spiritual outlook of the Middle Ages. They were also among the first Europeans to look critically at society in an effort to improve it. These new attitudes found their way into the Enlightenment.

Now recall the ideas of the Scientific Revolution. Copernicus, Kepler, and Galileo showed that the idea of an Earth-centered universe was wrong. Descartes had created a scientific philosophy for seeking truth. Everything had to be tested by the standard of reason. This idea too was basic to the Enlightenment.

Newton discovered the law of gravity.

In the history of ideas, as in other kinds of history, beginnings are seldom clearly marked. Isaac Newton may be called either the last and greatest figure of the Scientific Revolution or the first figure of the Enlightenment. Newton recognized what he owed to such earlier thinkers as Galileo and Kepler when he said, "If I have seen farther than others, it is because I have stood on the shoulders of giants."

Isaac Newton was born in England in 1642, while conflict was raging between the king and Parliament. Newton studied at Cambridge University and became a professor there. By the time he was 24 years old, he was certain that all physical objects (stones, birds, planets, stars) were affected equally by the same forces. However, he could not yet prove his ideas mathematically, and it was more than 20 years before he published these ideas.

461

SECTION 1 Objectives and Teaching Strategies

OBJECTIVE 1. Identify Isaac Newton and explain the impact of his ideas on the Enlightenment.

Teaching Strategy: *Discussing History: Sir Isaac Newton* (page 460a)

OBJECTIVE 2. Identify the philosophes and discuss five of their main ideas.

Teaching Strategy: *Relating Past to Present: Progress* (page 460a)

OBJECTIVE 3. Describe how scientific knowledge advanced during the 1700's.

Teaching Strategy: *Discussing History: Scientific Advances* (page 460c)

■ BACKGROUND

Newton created the first reflecting telescope, using mirrors. In addition, he analyzed light by shining it through prisms and discovering its separation into bands of color. He thus became one of the founders of the science of optics.

SECTION 1 Resources

ASSESSMENT
- Section Quiz 20.1

REINFORCEMENT
- Independent Practice 20.1

ENRICHMENT
- Voices from the Past 20.1

The remarkable Newton also made a breakthrough in mathematics known today as calculus. Alchemy, history, theology, and chemistry were among his other interests.

Alexander Pope, an English poet of the early 1700's, summarized Newton's achievement in two famous lines. "Nature and Nature's laws lay hid in night/ God said, Let Newton be: and all was light."

In 1609, the astronomer Kepler had worked out laws for a planet's motion around the sun (page 387). Galileo had studied the motion of pendulums and the acceleration of balls rolling down a slope (page 388). Newton's great achievement was to discover that the same force ruled the motions of the planets, the rolling balls, the pendulum, and all matter on Earth and in outer space. He disproved the idea that one set of physical laws governed Earth and another set governed the rest of the universe.

All objects attract one another, said Newton. He called this attraction "gravitation." The attraction varies both with the mass of the objects and with the distance between them. In 1687, Newton at last published his fully developed theories in a book titled *Mathematical Principles of Natural Philosophy*. In a single sentence, he summarized the workings of the universe:

Every particle of the universe attracts every other particle with a force varying inversely as the square of the distance between them and directly proportional to the square of their masses.

European scientists who read Newton's work were overwhelmed by its brilliance. Newton's laws became the starting point for investigating everything in nature.

The philosophes advocated reason.

In the early 1700's, a group of thinkers set forth the idea that people could apply reason to all aspects of life just as Newton had applied reason to science. These thinkers were known as **philosophes** (FEE-luh-sohfs). At the heart of their philosophy were five ideas:

1. *Reason* Enlightened thinkers such as Voltaire regarded reason as a sort of divine force, as we have seen. Reason, they said, was the absence of intolerance, bigotry, or prejudice in one's thinking.
2. *Nature* The philosophes referred to nature frequently. To them, what was natural was also good and reasonable. They believed that there were natural laws of economics and politics just as there were natural laws of motion.
3. *Happiness* A person who lived by nature's laws would find happiness, the philosophes

said. They were impatient with the medieval notion that people should accept misery in this world to find joy in the hereafter. The philosophes wanted well-being on Earth, and they believed it was possible.

4. *Progress* The philosophes were the first Europeans to believe in progress for society. Now that people used a scientific approach, they believed, society and humankind could be perfected.
5. *Liberty* The philosophes envied the liberties that the English people had won in their Glorious Revolution and Bill of Rights (page 436). In France, there were many restrictions on speech, religion, trade, and personal travel. Through reason, the philosophes believed, society could be set free.

Voltaire combated prejudice.

Thousands of Europeans in the 1700's shared these five ideas and thought of themselves as enlightened. None, however, was as widely admired (or as widely hated) as a Frenchman who called himself by an invented name, Voltaire.

Voltaire's real name was François Marie Arouet (AH-rweh). Born in Paris in 1694, he nearly died in infancy. He remained frail all his life and complained of almost every ailment: smallpox, fever, gout, a chronic itch, coughing fits, partial deafness and blindness, lost teeth, dropsy, paralysis, and grippe. He often ended his letters to friends by saying that he expected to die soon. Yet he did not put down his pen until death finally took him at the age of 84.

As a young writer, he adopted the name Voltaire, possibly because Arouet sounded too close to the French word for king. Voltaire's sharp tongue made him enemies at the French court, and twice King Louis XV had him jailed in a Parisian prison called the Bastille (ba-STEEL). All his life, therefore, Voltaire held a grudge against the French monarchy.

After one stay in prison, Voltaire was exiled to England for two years. While there, he read the works of John Locke, with their emphasis on reason and the natural rights of all human beings (page 437).

Voltaire came to admire the English government much more than his own. After he returned to Paris, much of his work mocked the laws and customs of France and even dared to raise doubts about the Christian religion. The French king and France's Catholic bishops were outraged. In 1734, fearing another unpleasant stay in the Bastille, Voltaire fled from Paris to a spot near the French border.

In his later years, Voltaire was less a French citizen than a citizen of the world. He moved to Switzerland, seeking freedom to write and publish his works. There, in 1758, Voltaire wrote his most famous work, *Candide*, a short, satiric novel that he dashed off in three days. Voltaire spent his last years living with his niece in the little Swiss village of Ferney.

From his study overlooking a lovely garden, Voltaire used his quill pen as if it were a deadly weapon in a thinkers' war against humanity's worst enemies—prejudice, superstition, and intolerance. Such attitudes were, he said, *l'infame*—infamous or shameful things. He often ended his letters with a fighting slogan, *"Écrasez l'infame!"* (ay-crah-zay lahn-fam). The phrase meant "Crush the infamous thing!" Soon it was the battle cry of every enlightened thinker in Europe.

Salons were intellectual centers.

In the 1700's, Paris was the cultural and intellectual capital of Europe. There, it was the fashion to have social gatherings known as **salons.** For these events, wealthy hostesses invited the best poets, the keenest wits, and the most charming conversationalists to their mansions for refined conversation.

One salon guest might be invited to read a poem or play a piece on the flute or harpsichord. The other guests would comment on the performance, showing off their good taste and broad understanding. The women who organized the salons were, in effect, the drama and music critics of their age.

The most influential of the salon hostesses in Voltaire's time was Marie Thérèse Geoffrin (zhoh-**FRAHN**). In her autobiography, Madame Geoffrin explained how her tastes and education were shaped early in life by her grandmother:

> She taught me to think, and made me reason; she taught me to know men, and made me say what I thought of them, and told

■ BACKGROUND

Voltaire's collected works fill 99 volumes. In addition to plays, poems, novels, and essays, he wrote at least 20,000 letters to the 1,700 men and women with whom he corresponded.

■ DISCUSSION

The royal court at Versailles had lost some of its prestige after the death of the Sun King, Louis XIV, so Louis XV's court did not attract the leading thinkers of the time. Ask students why thinkers would have been attracted to the court at Versailles.

Mme Geoffrin (third from right in front) hosts a salon at which an actor reads from a play. Enlightenment culture was limited to the wealthy class.

463

■ **DISCUSSION**

Diderot was also a play-wright whose so-called middle-class tragedies made common people—not just kings—the subjects of dramas and celebrated the ethic of honest hard work. Have students consider the leading characters in modern plays. Are they famous personalities or common people?

■ **BACKGROUND**

In 1781, William Herschel, builder of powerful tele-scopes, discovered a distant body beyond Saturn. It was Uranus. He also observed that the Milky Way was not a mass of stellar gas but a collection of stars.

me how she herself judged them . . . She could not endure the elegancies that dancing masters teach; she only desired me to have the grace that nature gives to a well-formed person.

Every Monday the great artists of Paris assembled in the Geoffrins' drawing room. Every Wednesday, the foremost writers and scientists dined at her elegant table. Her husband, a much older man, sat politely through these dinners and rarely spoke.

Diderot planned an encyclopedia.

Marie Thérèse Geoffrin also sponsored one of the most ambitious intellectual projects of the Enlightenment. The philosophe Denis Diderot (dee-**DROH**) imagined a set of large books to which all the leading scholars of Europe would contribute articles and essays. This *Encyclopedia,* as he called it, would bring together all the most current and enlightened thinking about technology, science, mathematics, music, art, medicine, government, law, geography, and more. Madame Geoffrin was so fond of the project that she contributed nearly half the total cost. Other hostesses also gave money to the effort. The first volume of the set was published in 1751 and distributed to 1,431 subscribers.

In a dingy attic room in Paris, Diderot labored for 20 years to complete the project. His seventh volume provoked the French king, Louis XV. Therefore, government censors banned further volumes. Fearing arrest, some leading philosophes withdrew from the project and urged Diderot to quit. Diderot pressed on, however, and found ways around the ban on publishing. The last volume under his editorship, number 28, was finally printed in 1772.

The popularity of the *Encyclopedia* soon spread to French-reading buyers all over Europe. It also inspired English and Scottish writers to produce their own *Encyclopedia Britannica* in the 1770's.

Scientific knowledge advanced.

In the 1700's, it was fashionable for wealthy families to display scientific instruments in their homes. They invited their guests to observe the planets through a telescope or an insect's wing under a microscope. Most educated men and women only dabbled at science. A few, however, pursued their observations and experiments seriously and made breakthroughs in every branch of scientific inquiry.

The discovery of oxygen Before the Enlightenment, no one knew that air was made up of a mixture of gases (mostly oxygen, nitrogen, and carbon dioxide). Then, in 1774, an English minister and scientist named Joseph Priestley separated one pure gas from air. He noticed how good he felt after breathing this special air and watched how alert two mice were while breathing it. Wrote Priestley, "Who can tell but that, in time, this pure air may become a fashionable article of luxury? Hitherto only two mice and I have had the privilege of breathing it."

Meanwhile, in France, during the 1770's, Antoine Lavoisier (lah-vwah-**ZYAY**) was performing similar experiments. In 1779, Lavoisier named the newly discovered gas oxygen.

Electricity Electricity mystified the scientific thinkers of the 1700's. Why, they wondered, did electric sparks sometimes jump between objects and give people a shock? In the British colony of Pennsylvania, a printer named Benjamin Franklin thought there might be a connection between a lightning bolt in a thunderstorm and the puzzling little electric sparks.

To test his theory, Franklin performed one of the most famous—and dangerous—experiments in the history of science. In 1752, he sent up a kite during a thunderstorm. At the end of the kite string was an iron key. A bolt of lightning struck the kite, and in a flash, the key emitted an electric spark. Wrote Franklin:

When the rain has wet the kite twine so that it can conduct the electric fire freely, you will find it stream out plentifully from the key at the approach of your knuckle.

Enthralled by Franklin's experiment, a number of Europeans tried to repeat it, and several were killed instantly by the shock.

Geography Two centuries after the voyages of Columbus and Magellan, vast stretches of the Pacific Ocean were still unknown to Europeans. In 1768, the English navigator and mapmaker James Cook set out on the first of three voyages to explore and chart the South Pacific.

Cook was not in search of gold, as Dias, Da Gama, and Columbus had been. Instead, Cook's

464

In the 1600's and 1700's, few words conjured up as much dread as smallpox. An infectious disease, it struck 60 of every 100 people. Of those 60, at least 20 died, and another 20 were horribly disfigured by scars.

Then, in the early 1700's, Lady Mary Wortley Montagu made an amazing observation. While traveling in Turkey, she saw that mothers there deliberately infected their young children with smallpox by breaking the skin and applying some liquid taken from the sore of a victim. (Such a process is called inoculation.) Children who were inoculated caught smallpox, but they had a good chance of getting only a mild case that protected them from ever having the disease again. Lady Montagu bravely had her son inoculated. She then returned to Britain and spread news of the procedure. By the middle 1700's, inoculation, although still dangerous, was being used all over Europe.

In 1796, British physician Edward Jenner discovered that an inoculation with the less dangerous disease cowpox (taken from a cow) gave permanent protection from smallpox for humans. Because cowpox was a much milder disease, the risks for this form of inoculation were much lower. Jenner used cowpox to produce the world's first vaccination.

■ **BACKGROUND**

Bach—considered by many to be the greatest composer of all time—had 20 children. Two of them, Johann Christian and Carl Philipp Emanuel, also became famous musicians.

Beethoven composed many of his best known works after he had lost his hearing. His hearing loss and a turbulent relationship with his nephew were sources of profound suffering for Beethoven.

voyages were scientific expeditions. They were sponsored by the Royal Society of London, a group founded in the mid-1600's to encourage the growth of scientific knowledge. Astronomers, artists, and a botanist went with Cook to gather information about distant parts of the world.

Captain Cook became the first European to reach and chart the east coast of Australia and the islands of Tahiti, New Zealand, and Hawaii. He died in 1779 during a fight with the Hawaiian islanders.

New forms dominated music.

Educated men and women of the Enlightenment were as interested in music as in literature and science. This age produced some of Europe's most brilliant musicians.

The baroque period Music of the late 1600's and early 1700's is called **baroque,** which in French means "odd." The term was first used for art that was more ornate than the art of the Renaissance. Baroque music is noted for its drama and complexity.

Two musical techniques, the fugue and counterpoint, reached their height in baroque music. In a fugue, the composer repeats a single melody, or two or three melodies, with slight variations on different musical instruments. We may hear the theme first on a horn, then on a violin, and later on a cello.

Counterpoint is the weaving of two or more melodies together. Probably the plainest example of counterpoint is a simple tune—"Three Blind Mice," for example—sung in rounds. Musicians in the 1700's created very intricate counterpoint.

Baroque music reached its height in the early 1700's. The greatest of the baroque composers were Johann Sebastian Bach (1685–1750) and George Frederick Handel (1685–1759).

The classical period By the time Bach and Handel died in the mid-1700's, the age of baroque music was passing. New composers wrote less ornate works. Unity, clarity, and balance became more important than the intricate patterns of baroque music. New forms, such as the symphony, the concerto, and the sonata, came to dominate music.

465

ANSWERS TO

Section Review 1

Define:
(a) period when scholars believed in the use of reason and in the scientific method (b) thinker who subscribed to the notion that reason could be applied to all aspects of life (c) place for refined conversation (d) term first used for ornate music
Identify:
(a) discoverer of laws of gravity (b) French writer and enlightened thinker (c) most influential salon hostess (d) author of *Encyclopedia* (e) compilation of most current and enlightened thinking (f) English scientist who
(continued)

ANSWERS TO (continued)

separated oxygen from air
(g) scientist who named oxygen **(h)** American printer who discovered lightning's connection with electricity **(i)** English navigator and mapmaker who explored the South Pacific **(j)** one of the two great baroque composers **(k)** one of the two great baroque composers **(l)** "Father of the Symphony" **(m)** child prodigy and composer of brilliant operas **(n)** considered by many to be greatest European composer

Answer:

1. reason, or the absence of intolerance, bigotry, and prejudice; nature, including natural laws governing economics and politics; happiness, or well-being on Earth; progress, or the notion that human beings and society could be perfected; liberty, to be obtained through reason

2. (a) Guests read a poem or played a piece of music, and other guests commented and engaged in refined conversation.
(b) drama and music critics

3. (a) to bring together all most current and enlightened thinking **(b)** *Encyclopedia Britannica*

4. (a) discovery of oxygen, use of inoculation, understanding electricity
(b) baroque—ornate music stressing counterpoint and fugue; classical—style stressing unity, clarity, balance

5. Look for answers to include Copernicus, Kepler, Galileo, and Descartes among the giants and to consider that discovery leads to further questions for investigation.

The period from 1750 to 1820 is known as the classical period in European music. Its most noted composers were Joseph Haydn (HYE-d'n), Wolfgang Amadeus Mozart (MOH-tsahrt), and Ludwig van Beethoven (BAY-TOH-vuhn).

Haydn, born in 1732, was not the first European to write full symphonies for strings and woodwinds. However, his compositions were so superior to earlier works that he is honored today as the "father of the symphony."

Mozart was a child prodigy who began composing music at the age of five and performed for Britain's King George III at the age of eight. At 12, he wrote his first opera. Mozart's operas baffled audiences with their originality and brilliance. His great operas—*The Marriage of Figaro, Don Giovanni,* and *The Magic Flute*—are widely performed today. In 1791, at the age of 35, Mozart died in poverty.

Beethoven (1770–1827) is considered by many to have been the greatest European composer of all time. While his earlier works were in the

A painting from Haydn's time shows the setting in which a chamber orchestra played. Note how the musician/composer is positioned in the center to direct from the harpsichord.

same classical style as Mozart's, the music of Beethoven's later years began new trends, which carried music on into the Age of Romanticism (Chapter 23).

Section REVIEW 1

Define: (a) Enlightenment, (b) philosophe, (c) salon, (d) baroque

Identify: (a) Newton, (b) Voltaire, (c) Marie Thérèse Geoffrin, (d) Diderot, (e) *Encyclopedia*, (f) Priestley, (g) Lavoisier, (h) Franklin, (i) Cook, (j) Bach, (k) Handel, (l) Haydn, (m) Mozart, (n) Beethoven

Answer:

1. Describe the five ideas that were at the heart of the Enlightenment.

2. (a) Describe an evening in a Parisian salon. (b) What role did French women play in these salons?

3. (a) What was the purpose of the *Encyclopedia*? (b) What British work did it inspire?

4. (a) Describe three scientific accomplishments of the Enlightenment. (b) Describe the two periods of music that flourished during the Enlightenment.

Critical Thinking

5. "If I have seen farther than others," said Newton, "it is because I have stood on the shoulders of giants." Who were the giants to whom Newton was referring? Could this be said of any scientific accomplishment? Explain.

Writers advocated liberty and reason. 2

Diderot once wrote, "I am a good citizen, and everything that concerns the welfare of society and the life of my fellow men is very interesting to me." The Age of Enlightenment was a time for thinking about the welfare of society, the freedom of the individual, and the happiness of humanity. In the opinion of the philosophes, these three ideals were almost identical. People could only be truly happy, they said, in a good society that allowed economic, religious, and political liberty.

The champion of economic liberty was a Scottish professor named Adam Smith. The champions of political liberty were a French aristocrat named Montesquieu (MOHN-tes-KYOO) and a Swiss commoner named Rousseau (roo-SOH). All three claimed to have discovered the "natural laws" by which society works.

Adam Smith supported free trade.

As a professor at the University of Edinburgh, Adam Smith (1723–1790) devoted almost every waking hour to philosophic questions. Often, he was so busy with his own thoughts that he dressed in rumpled, mismatched outfits.

In Diderot's *Encyclopedia*, Smith read the ideas of French economic theorists who called themselves "**physiocrats.**" The physiocrats argued that the old mercantilist ideas about wealth were wrong. Did nations become wealthier by placing heavy tariffs on foreign goods? No, said the physiocrats. All such governmental regulations actually interfered with the production of wealth. Instead, the government should allow **free trade**— the flow of commerce in the world market without government regulation. The economy would prosper by itself if the government left it alone. The French phrase for "leave alone" was **laissez faire** (LAY-zay FAIR).

Adam Smith defended the idea of a free economy in his book *The Wealth of Nations*, published in 1776. He argued that a free economy could produce far more wealth than an economy regulated by governmental laws. His arguments rested on three so-called natural laws of economics.

The law of self-interest People act for selfish reasons, said Smith. They work for their own good, not for their neighbor's good. For example, bakers do not bake bread out of concern for hunger. Bakers bake bread to make money. Their motives are selfish. In his second and third laws, Smith explained how both the buyer and the seller gain from the other's selfish motives.

The law of competition In a free market, every baker competes with other bakers. To stay in business, each baker must try to make bread more efficiently and sell it at a lower price than rival bakers can. In other words, competition forces people to make a better product. Thus, competition among selfish individuals leads naturally to economic progress for all.

The law of supply and demand What happens if bakers make more bread than people want to buy? In other words, what happens when the **supply,** or quantity available, exceeds the **demand,** or need, for bread? In that case, bakers would have to lower their prices to attract more customers. The low price would drive some bakers out of business. This process would continue until there would be just enough bakers to meet their customers' demand for bread.

According to Smith, in a **market economy** where natural laws were free to operate, plenty of goods would be produced at the lowest possible price. On the other hand, if the government interfered in the economy, none of the natural laws could operate. Economic liberty, said Smith, was essential to economic progress.

Montesquieu advocated separation of powers.

A French nobleman, the Baron de Montesquieu (1689–1755), devoted himself to the study of political liberty. For years, he studied the history of ancient Rome. He concluded that Rome's collapse was directly related to its loss of political liberties.

Montesquieu believed that Britain was the best-governed country of his own day. Here was a government, he thought, in which power was balanced among three groups of officials. The British king and his ministers held **executive** power. They carried out the laws of the state. The members of Parliament held **legislative** or law-making power. The judges of the English courts held **judicial** power. They interpreted the laws to see how each applied to a specific case. Montesquieu called this division of power into three branches **separation of powers**.

Although Montesquieu oversimplified the British system, it gave him the idea for his most famous book, *On the Spirit of Laws*. Published in 1748, it contained such maxims on government as these:

- When the legislative and executive powers are united in the same person . . . there can be no liberty.
- Again, there is no liberty if the judiciary power be not separated from the legislative and executive [power].
- Power should be a check to power.

467

SECTION 2
Objectives and Teaching Strategies

OBJECTIVE 1. Identify Adam Smith and discuss his three laws of economics.

Teaching Strategy: *Economics and History: Adam Smith* (page 460c)

OBJECTIVE 2. Identify Baron de Montesquieu and explain the concept of separation of powers.

Teaching Strategy: *Relating Past to Present: Separation of Powers* (page 460c)

Cooperative Learning

Divide the class into groups of four students. Have each group prepare a presentation on one of the following Enlightenment personalities: Newton, Voltaire, Adam Smith, Rousseau, Diderot, Montesquieu, or Marie Thérèse Geoffrin. One group member should briefly research the person's life. Two others should report on the subject's important writings or accomplishments. The last group member should prepare an outline for the presentation using the information from the other students. All group members should then participate in an oral presentation to the class.

SECTION 2
Resources

ASSESSMENT
- Section Quiz 20.2

REINFORCEMENT
- Independent Practice 20.2

ENRICHMENT
- Voices from the Past 20.2

ANSWERS TO

Section Review 2

Define:
(a) French economic theorist who believed that government regulations interfered with the production of wealth (b) flow of commerce without government regulation (c) French for "leave alone" (d) quantity available (e) need (f) economy in which natural laws are free to operate (g) carrying out laws (h) law-making power (i) interpreting laws (j) division of power into three branches

Identify:
(a) author of *The Wealth of Nations* (b) French noble who believed political liberty hinged on separation of powers (c) author of *The Social Contract*

Answer:
1. (a) believed people could be happy only in society that allowed freedom in these areas (b) Adam Smith (c) Montesquieu and Rousseau

2. self-interest, competition, supply and demand

3. (a) the loss of political liberties (b) separation of powers

4. (a) Legitimate government ruled with consent of people. (b) Rousseau believed in a broader democracy than did Locke.

5. (a) Each branch of government would limit the power of the other branches, and thus no branch could become a threat to liberty.
(b) Enlightened ideas held that happiness was possible on Earth and that political liberties were crucial to it.

(This last statement meant that each branch of government would limit the power of the other two branches. Thus, no branch could become a threat to liberty.)

Montesquieu's book was admired by political leaders in the British colonies of North America. His ideas about separation of powers became the basis for the United States Constitution.

Rousseau championed freedom.

The third great champion of liberty during the Enlightenment was a strange figure indeed. His name was Jean Jacques Rousseau.

Rousseau (1712–1778) was born in the Swiss city of Geneva, the son of a watchmaker. When he was 13 years old, he was apprenticed to an engraver, a harsh and unkind man. After three unpleasant years, Rousseau fled to Italy. Thereafter, he worked at many jobs, including music teacher, tutor, and secretary.

Eventually, Rousseau made his way to Paris and won recognition as a writer of essays. Diderot and other Enlightenment leaders tried to befriend him. Yet Rousseau felt out of place in the elegant salons of Paris. He much preferred walking in the woods. Sooner or later, Rousseau quarreled

Adam Smith saw the market as an invisible hand that guided the production of goods and services.

with almost everyone. At times in his later years, he was undoubtedly insane. Nonetheless, his ideas about government were brilliant.

Rousseau's best known book on government was *The Social Contract*, published in 1762. It states, "Man is born free, yet everywhere he is in chains," meaning that liberty was every person's natural birthright, yet many were oppressed.

How did this unnatural state of things come about? In brief, this was Rousseau's answer: In the earliest times, people had lived as free and equal individuals in a primitive "state of nature." As people became civilized, however, the strongest among them forced everyone else to obey unjust laws. Thus, freedom and equality were destroyed.

Like Locke, Rousseau argued that the only legitimate government was one that ruled with the consent of its people. However, Rousseau believed in a much broader democracy than Locke had advocated. The people, not monarchs or aristocrats, should be sovereign (dominant), said Rousseau. He believed that liberty and justice would thrive in a state where the "general will" of the people was all-powerful.

Section REVIEW 2

Define: (a) physiocrat, (b) free trade, (c) laissez-faire, (d) supply, (e) demand, (f) market economy, (g) executive, (h) legislative, (i) judicial, (j) separation of powers
Identify: (a) Smith, (b) Montesquieu, (c) Rousseau
Answer:
1. (a) How did the philosophes feel about economic, religious, and political liberty? (b) Who was the greatest champion of economic liberty? (c) Who were the leading champions of political liberty?
2. What were Adam Smith's three natural laws of economics?
3. (a) What did Montesquieu believe led to the fall of Rome? (b) What did he admire about the government of Great Britain?
4. (a) What was Rousseau's view on government? (b) How did it differ from Locke's?

Critical Thinking
5. (a) What did Montesquieu mean when he said, "Power should be a check to power?" (b) How did his viewpoint reflect enlightened ideas?

Enlightened despots sought progress. 3

What did the kings and queens of Europe think about the ideas of the philosophes? The French king, Louis XV (1715–1774), liked to be entertained but not enlightened. He was openly hostile to the philosophes and often ordered their writings censored.

Other monarchs, however, were enchanted by the new ideas about reason and progress. Several rulers conducted scientific experiments, played musical instruments, dabbled at poetry, read books of philosophy, and corresponded with Voltaire. They ruled according to the principles of **enlightened despotism**. These principles, the philosophes believed, included favoring religious tolerance, making economic and legal reforms, and justifying their rule by its usefulness to society rather than by divine right.

In the 1700's, Frederick II of Prussia and Catherine II of Russia were the foremost of Europe's enlightened despots. As despots, they were absolute rulers, in control of all the powers of government. As enlightened despots, they were absolute rulers who supposedly used their great power for the good of the people they ruled.

Frederick II made reforms in Prussia.

Frederick II was the young Prussian king who invaded Austria in 1740 and began the War of the Austrian Succession (page 456). Born in 1712, Frederick ruled Prussia from 1740 to 1786 during the Enlightenment. He is known as Frederick the Great.

Frederick was brilliant. He had a keen ear for music and a passion for witty conversation. He always carried his flute with him, even on military campaigns. He wrote long, flattering letters to his intellectual hero, Voltaire. Voltaire, who loved to be flattered, answered Frederick's letters with flowery phrases of his own.

Frederick invited Voltaire to come to Prussia so that they might talk of philosophy. Voltaire consented, and for three years (1750–1753) he lived in Frederick's palace at Potsdam. At first, the two men seemed like ideal companions. Both were witty. Both cared nothing for appearances and dressed in shabby, rumpled clothes. Each friend paid the other elegant compliments.

Before long, however, the king and the philosophe got on each other's nerves. Voltaire disliked editing Frederick's mediocre poetry. Frederick suspected Voltaire of some shady business dealings. Eventually, Voltaire tried to sneak out of Potsdam, but Prussian soldiers captured him and made him spend the night in jail. Both men were now thoroughly angry. Returning to France, Voltaire described the Prussian king as "a nasty monkey, perfidious friend, wretched poet." Frederick returned the abuse, calling Voltaire a "miser, dirty rogue, coward."

Was Frederick truly an enlightened ruler? His opinions were generally liberal and humane, but his deeds were not always so. He granted religious freedom to Catholics and Protestants, but he discriminated against Polish and Prussian Jews. He reduced but did not abolish the use of torture in his kingdom. He allowed freedom of the press. He admitted that serfdom was wrong. Yet he did nothing to end it because he needed the support of landowners.

Perhaps Frederick's most important contribution was his attitude toward being king. He called himself "the first servant of the state." From the beginning of his reign, he made it clear that his goal was to serve and strengthen his country. This attitude was clearly one that appealed to the philosophes.

Catherine the Great ruled Russia.

Catherine II of Russia was another monarch who wrote letters to Voltaire and claimed to rule by enlightened principles. Voltaire, in turn, flattered Catherine, calling her "the star of the north," "benefactress of Europe," "first person in the universe."

Catherine was born in 1729, the daughter of an unimportant German prince. At 15, she was sent to the distant Russian court at St. Petersburg to be married to the Grand Duke Peter, heir to the Russian throne.

Peter the Great's daughter, Elizabeth, was the ruler of Russia when Catherine arrived. The Grand Duke, whom Catherine was to wed, was her nephew. Peter was mentally unstable. His chief pleasures were playing with toy soldiers and torturing dogs and cats.

469

OBJECTIVE 1. Compare and contrast Frederick II and Catherine the Great as enlightened despots.

Teaching Strategy: *Skill Building: Comparing and Contrasting Enlightenment Rulers* (page 460d)

OBJECTIVE 2. Describe how Catherine the Great changed the political geography of eastern Europe.

Teaching Strategy: *Geography in History: The Partition of Poland* (page 460d)

■ BACKGROUND

Despite his reforms, "Old Fritz" (as Frederick came to be called) was not popular in Prussia by the end of his reign. He openly despised most people and showed real affection only for his pet dogs. His last wish was that he be buried beside his dogs.

SECTION 3 Resources

GEOGRAPHY
■ Transparency 67

REINFORCEMENT
■ Independent Practice 20.3

ENRICHMENT
■ Voices from the Past 20.3

ASSESSMENT
■ Section Quiz 20.3

■ BACKGROUND

In 1773, Diderot traveled to St. Petersburg to visit his benefactress. He became excited as he talked and gestured wildly—thumping on her knees and pounding on her shoulders—to make a point. Catherine finally put a table between them.

As wife of the heir to the throne, Catherine (shown here at nineteen) had the title "Grand Duchess."

Catherine soon saw that Peter's weakness and cruelty gave her an opportunity to seize power. She made important friends among Russia's army officers, and she became known as the most intelligent and best informed person at court. In 1762, only months after her husband became czar as Peter III, Catherine had him arrested and imprisoned. Soon afterward, Peter conveniently died in prison, probably by murder. In September 1762, Catherine was crowned Catherine II of Russia, beginning a reign that lasted 34 years.

Though Russia was not her native land, Catherine II dedicated herself totally to the country's welfare. In 1767, she called a large convention of nobles, free peasants, and townspeople to frame a constitution for Russia. To guide them, she wrote a brilliant essay suggesting many reforms. She wanted to stop capital punishment, end the use of torture, and abolish serfdom. Unfortunately, the delegates to the convention debated and quarreled for months. Finally, Catherine lost pa-

tience and dismissed them. Though they had accomplished nothing, Catherine had tried to listen to the wishes of the common people.

Catherine honored the great writers of the Enlightenment. (She herself wrote a large number of plays, fairy tales, and satiric essays.) Learning that Diderot desperately needed money, she wrote to him offering to buy his personal library for any price he named. He suggested a figure. She paid him twice what he asked and allowed him to keep the books during his lifetime.

In spite of her sympathy for enlightened ideas, however, Catherine did little to improve the life of the peasants in her empire. A great turning point in her plans for reform came in 1773. In that year, there was a massive uprising of Russian serfs, soldiers, and escaped prisoners. The leader of the rebellion was a soldier named Pugachev, who claimed to be the dead Peter III. As in the peasant revolts of western Europe in the 1300's, serfs burned manor houses and murdered landowners. When Pugachev promised to end serfdom, the revolt spread like wildfire. His mobs threatened Moscow itself.

With great brutality, Catherine's army crushed the rebellion. Her soldiers destroyed whole villages. Pugachev was brought in an iron cage to Moscow and was executed. After the revolt, Catherine saw that she could not keep her throne without the nobles' support. She dropped her plans for ending serfdom and gave the nobles absolute control over their serfs. Thus, Russian serfs lost their last traces of freedom. By the end of Catherine's reign, nearly 95 percent of Russia's people toiled as serfs for all-powerful landlords.

Catherine expanded Russia's lands.

Like Frederick II, Catherine ignored the philosophes' arguments against war. She waged war relentlessly against Russia's southern neighbor, the Ottoman Turks. Just as Peter the Great had fought for years to win a port on the Baltic Sea, Catherine sought access to the Black Sea. In 1783, her armies won the Crimean Peninsula on the Black Sea. Catherine's conquests of Turkish territory threatened the delicate balance of power in eastern Europe. Prussia's Frederick the Great and Austria's Maria Theresa both feared that Russia might grab the strategic straits leading to the Mediterranean Sea.

The Growth of Russia, 1505–1796

KEY

— Boundary of Poland in 1771

Russia in 1505 (at death of Ivan the Great)

Added by 1725 (at death of Peter the Great)

Added by 1796 (at death of Catherine the Great)

0   300 Miles

N

Focus on Geography

Geographic Skills

1. (a) What was Russia's only seaport in 1505? (b) Name two disadvantages in its location.
2. (a) What lands did Peter add to Russia? (b) What lands did Catherine add?
3. What seaport did Peter establish, and what were the advantages of its location?
4. About what distance is it from Moscow to St. Petersburg? From Moscow to Kiev? From St. Petersburg to Kiev?

Geographic Theme: Place

5. How might the additions of territory made by Peter and Catherine change Russia's role in eastern Europe?

ANSWERS TO

Focus on Geography

1. (a) Archangel (b) It is far north and far from other population centers.

2. (a) lands on the Baltic Sea, the Caspian Sea, and to the east (b) lands to the west and on the Black Sea

3. St. Petersburg; close to western Europe

4. 400 miles; 500 miles; 650 miles

5. By gaining ports and more territory, Russia could increase its trade, making it more powerful in the region.

ANSWERS TO

Section Review 3

Define:
absolute rule, based on enlightened ideas and the good of the people

Identify:
(a) Prussian king who called himself "the first servant of the state" (b) Russian monarch who claimed to rule by enlightened principles

Answer:

1. favor religious tolerance, make economic and legal reforms, justify his or her reign by its usefulness to society rather than by divine right

2. (a) Frederick II of Prussia and Catherine the Great of Russia (b) practiced some religious tolerance, reduced the use of torture, and accepted various enlightened ideas (c) Neither improved life of peasants.

3. (a) by waging war (b) threatened balance of power in eastern Europe (c) dividing Polish lands among Austria, Prussia, and Russia

4. His primary role was one of service to the people.

5. Answers should focus on the importance of liberty as an ideal of the Enlightenment and on the partitioning of Poland as counter to this ideal.

The partition of Poland It was a dangerous situation until Frederick suggested a scheme that satisfied all three countries—Austria, Prussia, and Russia. Frederick proposed that the three powerful countries should take chunks of territory from the weak kingdom of Poland, rather than fight a costly war over Turkish lands.

Catherine and Maria Theresa agreed to Frederick's plan. In 1772, Austria, Russia, and Prussia each took a generous slice of Poland and sent troops to occupy it. Poland's wishes in the matter were ignored. This flagrant land grab was known as the First Partition of Poland.

There were two later partitions, both suggested by Catherine. In 1793, Russia and Prussia took more of Poland's land. Two years later, in 1795, the three greedy neighbors took the rest. On a map of Europe, Poland no longer existed. It did not appear again as an independent country until after World War I.

Catherine's achievement Catherine was the only monarch who lived long enough to participate in all three partitions of Poland. By war and diplomacy, she had vastly enlarged the Russian empire, adding 200,000 square miles of Turkish and Polish lands.

At the end of her remarkable reign (1762–1796), Catherine the Great wrote the epitaph for her own tomb: "Enthroned in Russia, she desired nothing but the best for her country and tried to procure for her subjects happiness, liberty, and wealth. She forgave easily and hated no one." She exaggerated only a little.

Section REVIEW 3

Define: enlightened despotism
Identify: (a) Frederick II, (b) Catherine II
Answer:
1. According to the beliefs of the philosophes, what did a ruler have to do in order to earn the title *enlightened?*
2. (a) In the 1700's, what despots were the foremost of Europe's enlightened rulers? (b) In what respect did each try to be an enlightened ruler? (c) In what respect did each fail?
3. (a) How did Catherine the Great expand Russian lands? (b) Why did this concern Prussia and Austria? (c) What solution did Frederick II propose?

Critical Thinking
4. What did Frederick II mean when he called himself the "first servant of the state?" Was he? Explain.
5. Was the partition of Poland in accord with the principles of the Enlightenment? Why or why not?

Britain developed new forms of leadership. 4

The philosophes looked on England's government as the most progressive in Europe. England's ruler was no despot, not even an enlightened one. The Glorious Revolution of 1688 had given England a **constitutional monarchy.** The power of the ruler was limited by law.

Even while the English monarch's power was being limited at home, the power of the English nation was spreading overseas. During the 1600's and 1700's, England won colonies in many parts of the world, including North America and India. Indeed, after 1707 (when the kingdoms of England and Scotland were officially joined), the country even had an impressive new name—Great Britain. To rule this far-flung empire, Britain's monarch and Parliament developed new ways of working together.

Britain was a limited democracy.

After 1688, no British monarch could rule without the consent of Parliament. At the same time, Parliament could not rule without the consent of the monarch. Thus, there was danger of a stalemate if the crown and Parliament disagreed.

During the 1700's, that problem was gradually solved by the development of an executive committee called the **cabinet.** This committee acted in the ruler's name but in reality represented the majority party of Parliament. Only temporary and makeshift at first, the cabinet eventually became one of Britain's most durable institutions.

The development of the cabinet Under William and Mary, the cabinet was nothing more than a group of the monarchs' most influential ministers. Like earlier rulers, William III appointed and dismissed ministers at will.

BRITISH PARLIAMENTARY GOVERNMENT
After 1721

PARLIAMENT

HOUSE OF LORDS
(hereditary)

HOUSE OF COMMONS
(elected)

PRIME MINISTER
(head of majority party)

CABINET

MONARCH

chooses   answers to   confers with

However, because William needed Parliament's support, he decided that his cabinet ministers should belong to the majority party, which was Whig. Thus the king hoped to assure himself a majority vote in Parliament. For the first time, the cabinet ministers acted as links between the king and the majority in Parliament.

The rise of the prime minister Over the years, one minister began to dominate the cabinet. This trend became clear during the reign of a new dynasty, the Hanoverians (HAN-oh-**VAIR**-ee-uhnz).

In 1714, the last of the Stuart rulers, Queen Anne, died. The British crown passed to a distant relative from the little German state of Hanover. George I of England spoke no English and cared more about Hanover than about England. He ruled Britain from 1714 to 1727.

Partly because George I and his son George II knew as little of English politics as they did of the English language, they relied heavily on their ministers. In particular, both relied on the shrewd Sir Robert Walpole. In 1721, George I appointed him First Lord of the Treasury. For 20 years (1721–1741), Walpole was the unofficial ruler of Great Britain.

Walpole set the basic pattern of British politics in modern times. The king's cabinet became the center of power and policymaking. The leader of the majority party in Parliament headed the cabinet as the **prime minister.**

Limited democracy The British form of government was considered ideal by the thinkers of the Enlightenment, but it was far from a democracy. A small, wealthy group of citizens elected the members of the House of Commons.

In Walpole's time, only about 5 percent of the British population had the right to vote. Voting was limited to men who owned at least 40 shillings' worth of land. No women could vote. The upper classes—town merchants and country nobles—ran the government.

Britain built a worldwide empire.

Because wealthy merchants and aristocrats dominated the British government, British policies catered to their interests. To a British mercantilist, colonies were the key to prosperity. Thus, much of Britain's energy in the 1700's was directed toward winning and controlling colonies.

When the Seven Years' War (page 456) ended in 1763, Great Britain stood as the strongest colonial and naval power in Europe—indeed, in the world. In Asia, the French had been driven from the east coast of India, and Britain soon began extending its hold on the Indian subcontinent. In North America, Britain controlled all the territory east of the Mississippi River.

Most valuable to Britain's North American empire were some tiny islands in the Caribbean

473

SECTION 4
**Objectives
and Teaching
Strategies**

OBJECTIVE 1. Compare and contrast the role of the cabinet in the British and the American systems of government.

Teaching Strategy: *Skill Building: Comparing and Contrasting Systems of Government* (page 460d)

OBJECTIVE 2. Identify and locate on a map parts of Britain's North American empire in 1763.

Teaching Strategy: *Geography in History: Britain's American Colonies* (page 460d)

OBJECTIVE 3. Explain the economic importance of the sugar trade.

Teaching Strategy: *Economics and History: The Sugar Trade* (page 460d)

■ **BACKGROUND**

Queen Anne favored the Tory party because it was friendlier to royal power than were the Whigs. She packed the House of Lords with Tory peers (aristocrats).

ANSWERS TO

**Section
Review 4**

Define:
(a) monarchy in which the power of the ruler is limited by law (b) executive commit-
(continued)

SECTION 4
Resources

GEOGRAPHY
■ Transparency 68

REINFORCEMENT
■ Independent Practice 20.4

ENRICHMENT
■ Voices from the Past 20.4

ASSESSMENT
■ Section Quiz 20.4

ANSWERS TO
Map Study

Hudson's Bay Company lands in Canada; France

ANSWERS TO *(continued)*

tee that acts in ruler's name but represents majority party in House of Commons (c) leader of the majority party in Parliament

Identify:

(a) first Hanoverian king of Great Britain (b) first person to act as modern prime minister (c) British king at time American colonies declared independence (d) restrictions limiting colonial trade (e) law requiring colonists to pay a tax

Answer:

1. power of ruler limited by law

2. (a) Each had to have the consent of the other. (b) cabinet system

3. (a) worldwide, including territories in Asia and North America (b) imposed Navigation Acts and the Stamp Act

4. (a) Because the colonies had benefited from Britain's victory, the king and cabinet expected colonists to help pay costs of war. (b) with outrage and riots

5. Did the colonies exist to enrich Britain, or were they entitled to trade for their own profit?

6. Good answers would consider such factors as the natural rights of the governed, imposition by Britain of laws it was at a disadvantage to enforce, and the concepts of taxation without representation and of equality.

British North America, 1763

KEY
- British territory before 1763
- Acquired from France
- Acquired from Spain

0   800 Miles

Map Study

Where were Britain's largest holdings in North America before 1763? What country controlled the lands west of the Mississippi River?

Sea—Jamaica, St. Kitts, Barbados, and others. These formed the British West Indies. The sugar trade with these islands was a major source of British prosperity.

Far to the north of these islands lay Canada, the largest part of the British empire. Its riches in furs and timber attracted the interest of British mercantilists. However, most of Canada was a wilderness.

Between Canada and the Caribbean lay 13 British colonies along the Atlantic seaboard. Virginia, founded early in the 1600's (page 366), was the oldest of these colonies. By 1750, there were hundreds of small settlements strung along the Atlantic coast.

When George III became king of Great Britain in 1760, his Atlantic coastal colonies were growing

by leaps and bounds. Their combined population went from 275,000 in 1700 to 1,850,000 in 1765, a sevenfold increase.

Britain wanted profitable colonies.

According to the mercantilists, colonies existed for only one reason—to enrich the mother country. Britain therefore tried to keep tight control over colonial economic activities. It passed the Navigation Acts of 1660 and 1663 to carry out its mercantilist policies. Colonists could not sell their most valuable products to any country except Britain. Colonists could not buy French or Dutch goods without paying high taxes on them. Instead, colonists were expected to buy British manufactures. The result was that colonial merchants turned to smuggling. In practice, Britain found that enforcing the Navigation Acts was almost impossible.

Britain imposed new taxes.

After the Seven Years' War ended in 1763, George III and his ministers decided to deal firmly with the 13 colonies. Great Britain had run up a huge debt in the war against France. During the war, the British government had taxed people in Britain to pay the soldiers. Because American colonists benefited from Britain's victory, the king and his ministers expected the colonists to help pay the costs of the war.

American colonists had never paid taxes directly to the British government before. In 1765, Parliament passed the Stamp Act. According to this law, colonists had to pay a tax to have an official stamp put on wills, deeds, and other legal documents. Newspapers and other printed material had to be stamped too.

American colonists were outraged. Colonial lawyers argued that the stamp tax violated colonists' natural rights. In Britain, citizens consented to taxes through their representatives in Parliament. Because the colonists had no representatives in Parliament, Parliament could not tax them.

In Boston and other American cities, colonists rioted against the Stamp Act. "No taxation without representation!" became their battle cry. The protests became so fierce that Parliament gave up and repealed the Stamp Act in 1766.

Although the Stamp Act was dead, the basic conflicts between Britain and the 13 colonies remained. Did the colonies exist solely to enrich Britain? Did colonists have the same political rights as people in Britain? The colonists soon began to use arguments from Locke and other enlightened thinkers to prove that they did have such rights. Only ten years after the repeal of the Stamp Act, these issues led the colonies to declare their independence from Great Britain.

Section REVIEW 4

Define: (a) constitutional monarchy, (b) cabinet, (c) prime minister
Identify: (a) George I, (b) Robert Walpole, (c) George III, (d) the Navigation Acts, (e) the Stamp Act
Answer:
1. Why did the philosophes regard Britain's government as the most progressive in Europe?
2. (a) Why was there danger of stalemate in the British government if the Crown and Parliament did not agree? (b) What solution to this problem emerged over time?
3. (a) Describe the British empire in 1763. (b) What steps did Britain take to keep economic control over that empire?
4. (a) Why did the end of the Seven Years' War mark a shift in British policy toward the colonies? (b) How did the colonists react?
5. Describe the basic conflict between Great Britain and the colonies in 1766.

Critical Thinking
6. The British government felt that the Stamp Act was justifiable. The colonists strongly disagreed. In your opinion, who was correct? Support your point of view.

Americans created a republic. 5

In July 1776, a group of colonial Americans signed their names to a large piece of parchment titled *A Declaration*. Soon to be known as the Declaration of Independence, the document was firmly based on the ideas of John Locke and the Enlightenment. Locke had said clearly that people had the right to rebel against an unjust ruler, as the English had done in the Glorious Revolution of 1688 (page 437). In 1776, Americans justified their revolution by a long list of George III's abuses.

The prime author of the Declaration of Independence, Thomas Jefferson, summed up many of the ideas of the Enlightenment:

> We hold these truths to be self-evident, that all men are created equal, that they are endowed by their Creator with certain unalienable rights, that among these are life, liberty, and the pursuit of happiness.

The document ended by breaking the ties between the colonies and Britain. The colonies, said the Declaration of Independence, "are absolved from all allegiance to the British Crown."

From George III's point of view, the signers of this declaration were committing treason. From the American point of view, the colonists were justified in rebelling against a tyrant who had broken the social contract.

Growing hostility led to war.

In 1765, the year colonists rioted against the Stamp Act, most Americans still thought of themselves as loyal subjects of the British king. They had no thoughts either of revolution or of independence. Yet by 1776, many Americans were willing to risk their lives to break free of Britain.

Between 1765 and 1776, one event after another steadily led toward war. Colonial leaders who were eager for independence, such as Boston's Samuel Adams, encouraged conflict. At the same time, George III and his ministers antagonized many moderate colonists by their harsh stands.

In 1773, to protest an import tax on tea, Sam Adams organized a raid against three British ships in Boston Harbor. The American raiders dumped 342 chests of tea into the water. George III, infuriated by the Boston Tea Party, ordered the British navy to close the port of Boston. More British troops moved in to occupy the city.

In September 1774, representatives from every colony except Georgia gathered in Philadelphia. This First Continental Congress, as it was called, protested the treatment of Boston. The group

475

SECTION 5
Objectives and Teaching Strategies

OBJECTIVE 1. Explain why the American colonists declared their independence from Great Britain.

Teaching Strategy: *Analyzing a Quotation: Why Did the Colonists Rebel?* (page 460e)

OBJECTIVE 2. Explain how the ideas of the Enlightenment influenced the United States Constitution.

Teaching Strategy: *Transferring Ideas: The United States Constitution* (page 460e)

■ BACKGROUND

By 1770, the only tax remaining was the one on tea, retained to establish the taxing right over the colonists. The tea tax became a major issue.

■ DISCUSSION

Ironically, George III was a better king and better Englishman than either of his predecessors. He was the first king in 46 years who spoke English. Discuss with students how that fact might have affected the attitudes of George's subjects toward him.

SECTION 5
Resources

ASSESSMENT
■ Section Quiz 20.5

REINFORCEMENT
■ Independent Practice 20.5

ENRICHMENT
■ Voices from the Past 20.5

Cooperative Learning

Have the class examine the American Revolution from different points of view by writing newspaper editorials. Groups of four students should write editorials supporting or denouncing the war for either an English or a colonial newspaper. Students should discuss their chosen point of view and the contents of their editorials. Then, with one group member acting as a recorder, the other members should dictate the body of the editorial. Finally, have groups present their editorials for class discussion.

ANSWERS TO
Voice from the Past

1. unrestricted freedom in matters of religion
2. (a) They reflect the ideas of reason as the absence of intolerance or prejudice and of liberty as the absence of religious restriction.
(b) Such religious freedom had never before been granted.

decided to send a list of complaints to the king. When the king paid little attention to their demands, all 13 colonies sent delegates to a Second Continental Congress in 1775.

Early on April 19, 1775, British soldiers and American militiamen had an open confrontation on the village green in Lexington, Massachusetts. From there, the fighting spread to nearby Concord. By day's end, Americans had killed 73 British soldiers, and 49 American militiamen had been killed in return.

News of the fighting reached the Second Continental Congress meeting in Philadelphia. Its members voted to raise an army under the command of a Virginian named George Washington. The American Revolution had begun.

Americans won their independence.

At first, the odds seemed heavily weighted against Washington's ragtag, poorly trained army. The revolutionaries were challenging what was then the largest empire in the world. Opposing them were about 50,000 well-drilled, well-equipped professional soldiers. Added to these numbers were the 52,000 Americans who fought on the British side. (It is estimated that only one third of the American colonists actively supported the revolution while another third opposed it. The rest tried to remain uninvolved and waited to see which side would win.)

In the end, however, the Americans won their war for independence. Five factors help to explain their remarkable victory.

First, the Americans' motivation for fighting was much stronger than that of the British. The troops in Washington's army were defending their homeland. The British soldiers, on the other hand, were fighting mostly for money.

Second, Americans skillfully used hit-and-run tactics, shooting from behind trees and rocks. The British, trained to fight in closed ranks, were harassed and confused by the Indian-style tactics of American sharpshooters. The red British uniforms made clear targets.

Third, time itself was on the side of the Americans. The British could win battle after battle, as they did, and still lose the war. Fighting an overseas war, 3,000 miles from London, was terribly expensive. After a few years, tax-weary British citizens clamored for peace.

Fourth, the British generals were mediocre, whereas the American leader, Washington, was one of history's great men. When all seemed lost early in the war, he convinced his troops to stay with him through yet one more winter and to fight one more spring campaign. His tenacity and courage kept American hopes alive.

Fifth and possibly most important, the Americans did not fight alone. In 1778, their envoy in Paris, Benjamin Franklin, persuaded France to enter the war on the American side. As an

Voice from the Past | *Toleration in Virginia*

Few people expressed the ideals of the Enlightenment better than Thomas Jefferson—writer, legislator, diplomat, president, scientist, farmer, inventor, and fierce advocate of freedom. Below is an excerpt from his bill for religious freedom passed by the Virginia General Assembly in 1786.

Sect. II. We the General Assembly of Virginia do enact that no man shall be compelled to frequent or support any religious worship, place, or ministry whatsoever, nor shall be enforced, restrained, molested, or burdened in his body or goods, nor shall otherwise suffer, on account of his religious opinions or beliefs; but that all men shall be free to profess, and by argument to maintain, their opinions in matters of religion, and that the same shall in no wise diminish, enlarge, or affect their civil capabilities.

1. What does this bill propose?
2. (a) How do the proposals in the bill reflect enlightened thinking? **(b)** Why was the bill a landmark for religious freedom?

Th Jefferson

Besides writing the Declaration of Independence and serving as the third president of the United States, Thomas Jefferson was interested in literature, architecture, farming, and natural history. He designed his own home, Monticello (above), with classical proportions and balance.

■ **BACKGROUND**

Of the 11,000 men in Washington's army at Valley Forge in the winter of 1777–1778, Washington said that 2,873 were unfit for duty because they lacked shoes and proper clothes.

absolute monarch, Louis XVI of France had little sympathy for the ideals of the American Revolution. However, he was eager to weaken France's rival, Britain. Spain too declared war on Britain, as did several German states.

French entry into the war proved decisive. In 1781, a combined force of about 9,500 Americans and 7,800 French trapped a British army commanded by Lord Cornwallis near Yorktown, Virginia. Unable either to escape or to get supplies, Cornwallis surrendered. When this news reached London, George III's prime minister exclaimed, "It is all over!" Indeed it was.

In Paris in 1783, three American diplomats led by Benjamin Franklin signed a treaty with the British that ended the war. By this treaty, Great Britain agreed to recognize the United States as an independent nation. The treaty set the western boundary of the new nation at the Mississippi River. Britain kept Canada and gave back Florida to its earlier owner, Spain.

The Articles created a weak national government.

Shortly after declaring their independence, the 13 individual states had recognized the need for a national government. As victory became certain, all 13 states in 1781 ratified a **constitution,** or

plan of government, known as the Articles of Confederation. To protect their authority, the states created a loose confederation in which they held most of the power.

The Articles thus deliberately created a weak national government. There were no executive or judicial branches. Instead, the Articles established only one body of government, the Congress. Each state, regardless of size, had one vote in Congress. Congress could declare war, enter into treaties, and coin money. It had no power however to collect taxes or regulate trade. Passing new laws was difficult because the approval of nine states was needed.

These limits on the national government soon produced a host of problems. Although the new national government needed money in order to operate, it could only request contributions from the states. Angry Revolutionary War veterans bitterly complained that Congress still owed them back pay. Meanwhile, several states were issuing their own money and putting tariffs on goods from neighboring states.

The nation's growing financial problems sparked a violent protest in western Massachusetts. Falling prices for farm products and rising taxes forced many farmers into debt. Led by a Revolutionary War veteran named Daniel Shays, the farmers demanded that the state lower taxes

477

and issue paper money so that they could repay their debts. When the state legislature refused, Shays and his followers attacked several courthouses. Massachusetts authorities quickly raised an army and crushed Shays's Rebellion.

⬛ Turning Points in History

The Constitutional Convention Although Shays's Rebellion lasted only a short time, it sent shock waves across America. Concerned leaders such as George Washington and James Madison believed that the trouble in Massachusetts underscored the need for a strong national government. In February 1787, Congress officially approved a Constitutional Convention to revise the Articles of Confederation.

The Constitutional Convention held its first session on May 25, 1787. The delegates chose George Washington president of the convention. The 55 delegates were young (the average age was 42) but experienced statesmen. More than two thirds had served in the Continental Congress, and eight had signed the Declaration of Independence. In addition, the delegates were all familiar with the political theories of Locke and Montesquieu.

Problems and compromises Although the delegates shared basic ideas on government, they sometimes disagreed on how to put them into practice. For example, representatives from large states such as Virginia wanted a two-house legislature with representation determined by population. Their plan would have given the four most populous states a majority in both houses. In contrast, representatives from the small states wanted a single-chamber congress in which each state had one vote.

After weeks of heated debate, the convention reached a compromise. This plan, known as the Great Compromise, proposed a two-house legislature. Representation in the lower house would be according to population, while in the upper house, all states would have equal representation.

After accepting the Great Compromise, the convention turned to the controversial question of how to count slaves in determining the basis for representation. Since slaves comprised almost one third of their region's population, Southerners wanted to count them for purposes of Congressional representation. Northerners disagreed. Since slaves were considered property, Northerners wanted them counted for tax purposes but not for representation.

Once again, the convention used a compromise to resolve a disagreement. Under the terms of the Three Fifths Compromise, three fifths of the number of slaves would be counted for both tax purposes and for representation. Although the delegates resolved this issue, they avoided the larger problem of how slavery could exist in a society dedicated to liberty and equality.

Principles of government The delegates' deliberations produced not only compromises but also new approaches to governing. Using the political ideas of the Enlightenment, the delegates created a unique new system of government.

Like Montesquieu, the delegates distrusted a powerful central government controlled by one person or group. They therefore established three separate branches—legislative, executive, and judicial. This provided a built-in system of checks and balances, with each branch checking the actions of the other two.

Although the Constitution created a strong central government, it did not eliminate local governments. Instead, the Constitution set up a **federal** system in which power was divided between national and state governments.

The delegates agreed with Locke and Rousseau that governments draw their authority from the consent of the governed. Nothing sums up this principle and the Enlightenment belief in progress better than the Constitution's preamble:

> We the People of the United States, in order to form a more perfect Union, establish justice, insure domestic tranquillity, provide for the common defense, promote the general welfare, and secure the blessings of liberty to ourselves and our posterity, do ordain and establish this Constitution for the United States of America.

A Bill of Rights was added.

The delegates formally signed the new Constitution on September 17, 1787. In order to become law, however, the Constitution required approval by conventions in at least 9 of the 13 states.

MILESTONES OF DEMOCRACY: UNITED STATES (1791)
Constitution and Bill of Rights

	FORM OF GOVERNMENT	CITIZENSHIP	INDIVIDUAL RIGHTS
Benefits	Republic with representation; separation of powers provided checks and balances; federalism distributed power between central government and states.	Citizenship, including right to vote, could be acquired by birth or by naturalization.	Rights of individuals were protected by Bill of Rights. Most state constitutions also protected rights.
Limitations	Vote was limited mostly to white men with property.	Most non whites and women did not have right to vote.	Slaves had no rights.

The conventions were marked by sharp debate. Supporters of the Constitution, known as Federalists, argued that the new government would provide a better balance between national and state governments. Their opponents, known as Antifederalists, disagreed. The Antifederalists feared that the Constitution created a central government with too much power. They also pointed out that the Constitution lacked a bill of rights to protect the rights of individual citizens against a powerful central government.

In order to gain support, the Federalists promised to add a bill of rights to the Constitution. This promise cleared the way for approval. On June 21, 1788, New Hampshire became the ninth state to ratify the Constitution. Within three years, Congress formally added to the Constitution the ten amendments known as the Bill of Rights. These amendments protected such basic rights as freedom of speech, press, assembly, and religion.

The Constitution and Bill of Rights marked a turning point in people's ideas about government. The new government was a republic in form and a democracy in principle. Its leaders were chosen by the people and drew their authority from the people. The Constitution and Bill of Rights brought into being a government based on law rather than on royal power.

Section REVIEW 5

Define: (a) constitution, (b) federal
Identify: (a) Declaration of Independence, (b) Thomas Jefferson, (c) Continental Congress, (d) George Washington, (e) Articles of Confederation, (f) Great Compromise, (g) Bill of Rights
Answer:
1. (a) How did George III feel about the signers of the Declaration of Independence? (b) How did the signers of the Declaration feel about their actions?
2. Between 1765 and 1776, the attitude of Americans toward revolution changed dramatically. Describe three events that contributed to this change of feeling.
3. (a) Describe the five factors that contributed to American victory in their war for independence. (b) What help did Benjamin Franklin secure for the revolutionaries?
4. How did the writers of the United States Constitution adapt the political theories of the Enlightenment?

Critical Thinking
5. How does the opening statement from the Declaration of Independence (page 475) reflect enlightened thinking?

479

ANSWERS TO
Section Review 5

Define:
(a) plan of government
(b) form of government in which power is divided between national government and state governments
Identify:
(a) document justifying the American Revolution
(b) prime author of the Declaration of Independence
(c) gathering of representatives of all colonies except Georgia to protest treatment of Boston (d) commander of American army and first president of the U.S. (e) first national U.S. government
(f) plan that proposed a two-house legislature
(g) first ten amendments to the Constitution

Answer:
1. (a) They were committing treason. (b) justified in rebelling
2. Boston Tea Party; First Continental Congress's demands being little heeded by George III; open confrontation in Lexington
3. (a) motivated to defend homeland; hit-and-run tactics; British fighting long-distance war; relative mediocrity of British generals; alliance of France, Spain, and several German states against Britain
(b) persuaded France to enter the war
4. divided the government into branches to provide balance of power and ensure that laws of Congress would reflect "the consent of the governed"
5. by making a commitment to reason, liberty, and a belief in human progress

Concluding the Chapter

1. **Chapter Closer**
   Discuss with students how Enlightenment thinkers attempted to improve society. Have them explain how the ideas of the Enlightenment affected events in England, Prussia, and the United States in the eighteenth century.

2. **Reteaching Activities**
   a. Writing a Paragraph
   Have students write a short paragraph explaining how Newton and Voltaire personified the thinking and accomplishments of the Enlightenment.
   b. Identifying Main Ideas
   Have students write statements explaining the ideas of Adam Smith, Montesquieu, and Rousseau.
   c. Applying Main Ideas
   Have students explain how the ideas of the Enlightenment influenced the American revolution.

Answers to Chapter Review appear on page 460f.

Summary

1. European thinkers expressed new ideas. Much of the eighteenth century was governed by the spirit of the Enlightenment, a time when thinkers and writers, known as philosophes, valued reason above all else. Voltaire, a leading philosophe, dedicated his life to fighting prejudices. Scientific discoveries, exploration, and great music were all offshoots of the Enlightenment.

2. Writers advocated liberty and reason. Enlightened thinkers believed that their goals of social welfare, individual freedom, and the happiness of humanity could be reached through greater economic and political freedom. Adam Smith called for an economy free of government interference. Montesquieu urged that political abuses could be curbed by a separation of power in government. Rousseau went even further, calling for a state in which the people were sovereign.

3. Enlightened despots sought progress. Several eighteenth-century rulers were known as enlightened despots. They were absolute rulers who supposedly used their great power for the good of the people they ruled. Enlightened despots included Frederick II of Prussia and Catherine II of Russia. Although each had enlightened ideas, their deeds did not always reflect these.

4. Britain developed new forms of leadership. By the late 1600's, Great Britain was a constitutional monarchy in which the power of the ruler was limited by law. In the 1700's, a cabinet and prime minister developed, both of which helped prevent a stalemate between the monarch and Parliament. However, Britain was not a full democracy, as only male landowners could vote.

By 1763, Great Britain was the strongest colonial power in the world. Colonists in the Americas, however, were growing increasingly resentful of Britain's mercantilist policies.

5. Americans created a republic. Between 1765 and 1776, a series of hostile events led to the breaking of ties between Great Britain and its 13 American colonies. On July 4, 1776, a group of American colonists formally broke those ties with the signing of the Declaration of Independence. A war for independence followed in which the American colonists were victorious. A peace treaty signed in 1783 recognized the United States of America as a separate nation. Five years later, the United States Constitution, based on the ideas of Locke and Montesquieu, established a federal form of government. Its commitment to reason and its beliefs in human progress were clear statements of enlightened ideals.

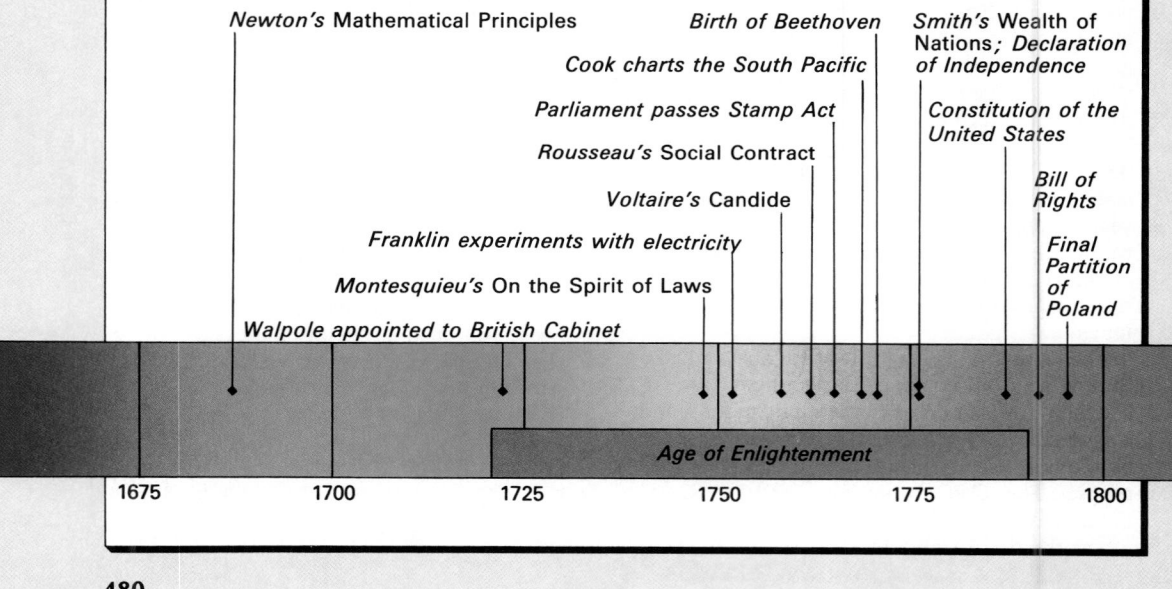

Newton's Mathematical Principles — Birth of Beethoven — Smith's Wealth of Nations; Declaration of Independence

Cook charts the South Pacific

Parliament passes Stamp Act — Constitution of the United States

Rousseau's Social Contract

Voltaire's Candide — Bill of Rights

Franklin experiments with electricity

Montesquieu's On the Spirit of Laws — Final Partition of Poland

Walpole appointed to British Cabinet

Age of Enlightenment

1675 1700 1725 1750 1775 1800

Reviewing the Facts

1. Define the following terms:
   - a. philosophe
   - b. executive
   - c. legislative
   - d. judicial
   - e. separation of powers
   - f. constitutional monarchy
   - g. cabinet
   - h. prime minister
   - i. constitution
   - j. federal

2. Explain the importance of each of the following:
   - a. Newton
   - b. Voltaire
   - c. Diderot
   - d. Franklin
   - e. Cook
   - f. Adam Smith
   - g. Montesquieu
   - h. Rousseau

3. (a) Briefly describe the ideas that characterized the Enlightenment. (b) How did salons promote these ideas? (c) How did Diderot's *Encyclopedia* reflect these ideas?

4. How did Adam Smith believe each of the following contributed to economic prosperity? (a) self-interest (b) competition (c) supply and demand

Basic Skills

1. **Making a chart** Make a chart comparing the typical absolute monarch with the typical enlightened despot. For the vertical column, use the headings Political Authority and Its Justification, Religious and Legal Changes, and Cultural Activities.

2. **Making a time line** Make a time line showing the main events of the Revolutionary War era from 1765 to 1790, using five-year increments.

Researching and Reporting Skills

Writing a Historical Essay

Phase 2: Consulting sources and refining the thesis In this phase, you will consult additional sources relevant to your topic in order to verify and refine your thesis.

1. **Locating primary and secondary sources** In your library, use the card catalog and the *Readers' Guide* to identify primary and secondary sources for your topic.

2. **Selecting and using resources** Choose at least one primary and one secondary source pertaining to your topic. Use indexes and headings to identify relevant information; study the text and illustrations useful to your essay. Take notes, including relevant quotations.

3. **Synthesizing information** Add this new information to your earlier notes. Check the chapter also for relevant materials. Modify your headings to include the new information.

4. **Refining your thesis** Check your information to see if it supports your working thesis. If necessary, revise your thesis to reflect any new relationship or viewpoint that emerges.

Critical Thinking

1. **Analyzing causes** To what extent did the ideas of the Renaissance, the Reformation, and the Scientific Revolution contribute to the Enlightenment? Give examples.

2. **Synthesizing** Enlightenment thinkers believed that progress would bring about liberty for all. What are three changes they proposed?

3. **Interpreting** (a) Why did the monarchy in France strongly oppose the ideas of the Enlightenment? (b) Why could the Enlightenment develop in the hostile political climate of France?

4. **Analyzing economics** Adam Smith believed that a free market would ensure the best product at the cheapest prices. Explain how this is possible.

5. **Synthesizing** (a) In what ways did the Constitution go beyond Enlightenment ideas? (b) What was the source of the Constitution's authority? (c) What was the purpose of the Bill of Rights?

Perspectives Past and Present

During the early 1700's, the cabinet became an established part of English government. (a) Investigate the role of the cabinet and of the prime minister in England and other constitutional monarchies. How does the prime minister relate to the executive and legislative branches of government? (b) How does the role of the cabinet in the United States differ from that in constitutional monarchies?

Investigating History

As the British left after surrendering at Yorktown, American bands played the popular song "Yankee Doodle." Research this song and other music of the period and make an audio presentation for the class. Include background information for each piece.

481

CHAPTER
Evaluation

Chapter Test 20, Alternate Chapter Test 20, and Computer Test Bank Chapter 20 Test can be used to evaluate your students' understanding of this chapter.

The French Revolution and Napoleon

Chapter Overview

In 1789, the bourgeoisie, workers, and peasants who made up France's Third Estate rebelled against the feudal and monarchical institutions of the Old Regime. The creation of a National Assembly was the first act of revolution, followed shortly by the fall of the Bastille. During the next two years, the National Assembly created a new constitution for France, and made sweeping religious and administrative changes. King Louis XVI discredited the plan for constitutional monarchy and increased the power of the radicals. It was 1795 before moderates regained control and drafted a new constitution.

In 1800, Napoleon seized control, eventually crowning himself emperor. He restored order and created Europe's greatest empire since Roman times. Eventually, Napoleon made some fatal errors. The weakened French empire crumbled under the attack of the Grand Alliance.

Chapter Focus

In the United States, July 4th marks the signing of the Declaration of Independence and is celebrated as a national holiday. Ask students if they know of any similar holidays in other countries. Explain that July 14th marks the fall of the Bastille and is celebrated as France's Independence Day with parades and music. Tell students that the storming of the Bastille became a great symbolic event in a historic upheaval known as the French Revolution.

The French monarchy faced a crisis. 1

Setting the Stage

A number of reasons have been offered to explain why the French people suddenly revolted against institutions that their ancestors had accepted for hundreds of years. Ask students to identify conditions that might lead to a revolution. Students might mention a tyrannical king who oppressed the people and jailed those writers and leaders who opposed his policies. Point out that Louis XVI was a relatively sensitive king who prohibited the use of torture on political prisoners. When it was attacked on July 14, 1789, the Bastille contained only seven prisoners.

Teaching Strategies

Analyzing a Quotation: Resentments of the Third Estate (Objective 1) Discuss the terms *Old Regime, estates,* and *bourgeoisie.* Why did the bourgeoisie, the sans-culottes, and the peasants all have reasons to hate the Old Regime? Note that the members of the Third Estate resented the unfair privileges of the clergy and the nobles. The French writer Beaumarchais voiced this resentment through a fictional character named Figaro. Outraged by Count Almaviva's pursuit of his bride-to-be, Figaro denounces the abuses of aristocratic society:

No, my Lord Count, you shan't have her, you shall not have her! Because you are a great nobleman you think you are a

Chapter 21 The French Revolution and Napoleon 1789–1815

FOCUS   Independence Day in France

★ **Advanced**
● **Basic**

	SECTION 1	SECTION 2	SECTION 3	SECTION 4
Objectives	1. Identify the three estates and explain why the Third Estate hated the Old Regime. 2. Describe the financial crisis that forced Louis XVI to call a meeting of the Estates General. 3. Identify the National Assembly and explain how it took power.	1. Describe the government created by the National Assembly and explain how it used the ideas of the philosophes. 2. Explain why the National Convention voted to execute Louis XVI.	1. List the reasons for Napoleon's victories. 2. Explain how Napoleon restored order to France.	1. Explain why the Spanish revolted against Napoleon. 2. Describe Napoleon's losses in the invasion of Russia. 3. Evaluate Napoleon's achievements and failures.
Setting the Stage	Causes of the French Revolution	Goals and achievements of the National Assembly	How Napoleon seized power	The roles of Great Britain, Spain, and Russia in Napoleon's downfall Transparency 69
Teaching Strategies	Analyzing a Quotation: Resentments of the Third Estate Economics and History: The French Financial Crisis Teaching with Pictures: The Tennis Court Oath Check for Understanding	Transferring Ideas: The Rights of Man Writing about History: Sentencing Louis XVI Check for Understanding	Discussing History: "The Little Corporal" Relating Past to Present: Napoleon's Enduring Reforms Check for Understanding	Teaching with Pictures: The Spanish Revolt Discussing History: The Invasion of Russia Writing about History: Napoleon's Place in History Check for Understanding
Guided Practice	Section Review 1	Section Review 2	Section Review 3	Transparency 69 Q&A Section Review 4
Independent Practice Worksheets	Independent Practice 21.1 Vocabulary Skills 21 Basic Skills 21	Independent Practice 21.2 Geography Skills 21 Critical Thinking 21	Independent Practice 21.3	Independent Practice 21.4
Enrichment	1. Primary Source: Voices 21.1 2. Researching for Points	1. Primary Source: Voices 21.2 2. Creative Writing 3. Researching for Points	1. Primary Source: Voices 21.3 2. Researching for Points	1. Primary Source: Voices 21.4 2. ★Solving a Mystery: Napoleon's Death 3. Researching for Points 4. Global Perspectives Transparency 71

Chapter Closer		
●Reteaching Activities	Preparing a Time Line, Summarizing, Identifying Main Ideas
Chapter Review	Summary, Reviewing the Facts, Basic Skills, Researching and Reporting Skills, Critical Thinking, Perspectives on Past and Present, Investigating History
Chapter Evaluation	Chapter Test 21, Alternate Chapter Test 21, Computer Test Bank Chapter 21 Test

Unit VI Review	
Geographic Theme	Place: How did planning change the growth of cities?
Historical Themes	Individuals and History, Cultural Development, Rise of Democratic Ideas
Unit Evaluation	Unit VI Test, Alternate Unit VI Test

great genius. . . . Nobility, fortune, rank, position! How proud they make a man feel! What have you done to deserve such advantages? Put yourself to the trouble of being born— nothing more! . . . Whereas I, lost among the obscure crowd, have had to deploy more knowledge, more calculation and skill merely to survive than has sufficed to rule all the provinces of Spain for a century!

Read or distribute this passage to your class, and ask them to answer these questions:

- According to Figaro, what has Count Almaviva done to deserve his advantages?
- What does Figaro mean in the last sentence?
- Why do you think Louis XVI forbade the presentation of these lines in the play, *The Barber of Seville?*

Economics and History: The French Financial Crisis (Objective 2) Although France itself was prosperous, the French government faced a grave financial crisis. A significant portion of the debt came from the cost of maintaining the royal family at Versailles. For example, Marie Antoinette spent 100,000 livres a year on clothing at a time when 50,000 livres would support a lavish lifestyle, and the average peasant earned 500 to 700 livres a year. By 1789, the government used 50 percent of its budget to pay interest on its debt and 13 percent to support the royal family's household staff of 15,000 people. Louis's ministers hoped to avoid bankruptcy by taxing the nobles. The nobles, however, refused to pay taxes unless the king called a meeting of the Estates General.

Teaching with Pictures: The Tennis Court Oath (Objective 3) Direct students' attention to the painting on page 485. It shows the president of the Assembly, Jean Sylvain Bailly, reading a motion known as the Tennis Court Oath. As the crowd outside shouted *"Vive l'Assemblé,"* the deputies pledged "never to separate but to meet in any place that circumstances may require, until the constitution of the kingdom is laid and established on firm foundations." The artist, Jacques Louis David, used the painting to portray several famous Revolutionary leaders. For example, the Abbé Sieyès is seated to the right of Bailly while Mirabeau strikes a dramatic pose in the right foreground.

Check for Understanding Have students explain how Louis XVI, the National Assembly, Abbé Sieyès, and the fall of the Bastille helped to bring about the French Revolution.

Enrichment Activities

1. **Reading a Primary Source**
   Assign Voices from the Past Resource Book 21.1.
2. **Researching for Bonus Points**
   Where are the keys to the Bastille located today? (in George Washington's home at Mount Vernon)

Setting the Stage

Have each student write a paragraph summarizing the goals and achievements of the National Assembly. Emphasize that the National Assembly had successfully defied the king and had pledged to enact constitutional reforms. However, serious problems still remained, such as the financial crisis and the Third Estate's demand for reforms.

Teaching Strategies

Transferring Ideas: The Rights of Man (Objective 1) Have students read, "The Assembly adopted many reforms" (pages 487–488). What Enlightenment ideas were contained in the *Declaration of the Rights of Man and of the Citizen?* Stress that the word *man* was used to designate all human beings. The Declaration used the philosophes' ideas of equality and natural law to justify the destruction of an unjust government based on absolutism and privilege. Instead, the new social order would be based on people's natural rights to "liberty, property, security, and resistance to oppression." Now ask, "How did the new government reflect the ideas of Montesquieu?" (The National Assembly created a limited constitutional monarchy that divided power between the king and an elected assembly.) Despite the new government, many difficult problems still remained.

Writing about History: Sentencing Louis XVI (Objective 2) The deputies to the National Convention unanimously agreed that Louis was guilty of treason. Then they had to decide on his sentence. Each deputy had to stand and explain his decision. Ask students to imagine that they are deputies to the National Convention and to write statements explaining their decisions on sentencing Louis. Compare students' decisions with these statements made by deputies at the National Convention:

Lacaze: From the depths of my conscience I vote for imprisonment until there is peace, and until such time as the foreign powers have recognized the republic; and then for exile.

Dartigoeyte: As a judge, I must avenge the blood of citizens spilt by the orders of the tyrant; as a statesman, I must do what seems in the best interests of the republic: I myself fear the return of tyranny if Louis lives. I vote for his immediate death.

Danton: One must never compromise with tyrants. One can only strike at kings through the head; nothing can be expected from European kings except by force of arms. I vote for the death of the tyrant.

Check for Understanding Have students explain the significance of the *Declaration of the Rights of Man and of the Citizen*, Robespierre, the Reign of Terror, and the Directory.

Enrichment Activities

1. **Reading a Primary Source**
   Assign Voices from the Past Resource Book 21.2.

2. **Creative Writing**
   Ask students to prepare a class newspaper on the events discussed in this section.

3. **Researching for Bonus Points**
   Both Louis XVI and Marie Antoinette were executed in the Place de la Révolution. What was the original name of the square, and what is its name today? (Place Louis XV and Place de la Concorde)

Napoleon conquered much of Europe. 3

Setting the Stage

The early disorder of the French Revolution left a power vacuum ready to be filled. Ask students to identify some of these events. Then write on the board, "In the weakness of authority . . . the person who really commands the army is your master." Ask students to interpret the statement and to recall military leaders who took over their countries during periods of disorder. Point out that the power of Julius Caesar and Yoritomo was based on their control over the Roman and Japanese armies. This section describes how Napoleon Bonaparte seized power in France and then dominated most of Europe.

Teaching Strategies

Discussing History: "The Little Corporal" (Objective 1) Explain that a number of factors contributed to Napoleon's victories. He often worked 20-hour days preparing for a battle. He carefully studied the battlefield terrain. While his opponents rested, Napoleon boldly marched at night and attacked an enemy in the rain or on a Sunday. Finally, Napoleon won the loyalty of his soldiers by sometimes fighting alongside them. His troops nicknamed Napoleon "the little corporal" because generals rarely fought with their armies.

Relating Past to Present: Napoleon's Enduring Reforms (Objective 2) List Napoleon's reforms on the board. Point out that many of his changes continue to influence France today. At least half of the 2,300 articles in the Napoleonic Code are still in effect. France still has a highly centralized government.

Check for Understanding Have students list three of Napoleon's achievements.

Enrichment Activities

1. **Reading a Primary Source**
   Assign Voices from the Past Resource Book 21.3.

2. **Researching for Bonus Points**
   Who was Napoleon's second wife? (Marie Louise, the daughter of the emperor of Austria)

Napoleon's empire collapsed. 4

Setting the Stage

Show Map Transparency 69, *The Empire of Napoleon, 1810,* or refer to the map on page 495. Explain that three of the countries shown on this map played leading roles in causing Napoleon's downfall. This section describes how Napoleon made disastrous mistakes with Great Britain, Spain, and Russia, which caused his empire's collapse.

Teaching Strategies

Teaching with Pictures: The Spanish Revolt (Objective 1) Napoleon planned to remove the Spanish royal family and make his brother Joseph king of Spain. On May 2, 1808, a large crowd gathered in Madrid to watch as French troops escorted the Spanish royal family out of Spain. The angry crowd suddenly attacked and massacred the French guard. The French commander promptly proclaimed martial law and ordered savage reprisals. Direct students' attention to Goya's painting (page 497) showing French troops executing Spanish rebels. Explain that the violence on May 2 sparked a nationwide uprising against Napoleon. The long struggle drained his strength and ended the myth of his invulnerability.

Discussing History: The Invasion of Russia (Objective 2) Have students read, "Napoleon invaded Russia" (pages 497–498). Then refer students to the diagram on page 498. Tell students that the Grand Army had 422,000 troops when it crossed the Niemen River into Russia. Ask, "How many troops did Napoleon have when he entered Moscow three months later?" (Napoleon

lost about 40,000 troops in battle. Epidemics and desertion claimed more than 250,000 men.) Ask, "How many soldiers did Napoleon have when the Grand Army returned to the Neimen River?" (Bitter cold and repeated Russian attacks caused the loss of about 90,000 more men. When Napoleon finally reached the Niemen, only about 10,000 exhausted survivors of the once proud Grand Army survived.)

Writing about History: Napoleon's Place in History (Objective 3) Historians still debate Napoleon's achievements and failures. Divide the class into four groups, and assign the following roles: middle-class leaders who supported the goals of the French Revolution, veterans of Napoleon's army, wealthy British aristocrats, and modern historians. Ask each group to write a brief report evaluating Napoleon's achievements and failures. Compare and contrast the different viewpoints.

Check for Understanding Call on students to identify the Continental System, Alexander I, Waterloo, and the Duke of Wellington.

Enrichment Activities

1. **Reading a Primary Source**
   Assign Voices from the Past Resource Book 21.4.
2. **Solving a Mystery**
   Ask advanced students to prepare a report answering these questions: How did Napoleon die? Was his death a murder? (Sources: See *Smithsonian,* April 1982, and *The Murder of Napoleon* by Ben Weider and David Hapgood.)
3. **Researching for Bonus Points**
   Where are Napoleon's remains now buried? (at the Invalides in Paris)

4. **Global Perspectives**
   Have students perform the activities on Map Transparency 71, *The World about 1800.*

ANSWERS TO Chapter Review 21

Reviewing the Facts

1. **(a)** desiring sweeping changes **(b)** temporary alliance between groups **(c)** seizure of power **(d)** yes/no vote on a matter of public policy **(e)** civilian fighting irregular war **(f)** banish
2. **(a)** fall of Bastille **(b)** overthrown by the revolution **(c)** monarchy and feudalism **(d)** social classes **(e)** urban workers **(f)** wife of Louis XVI **(g)** panic that swept France **(h)** nobles who fled France **(i)** most radical of political clubs **(j)** machine to behead people **(k)** leader during Revolution **(l)** Robespierre's period of power **(m)** French military genius who became emperor of France **(n)** unsuccessful blockade of British ships **(o)** Napoleon's last battle
3. moderate stage (1789–1792), radical stage (1793–1794), period of reaction (1794–1799), final stage (1799–1815)
4. Clergy formed the First Estate; nobles, the Second Estate; and commoners, the Third Estate.
5. **(a)** The nobles refused to pay taxes unless the estates met. **(b)** The Third Estate demanded that all three estates meet together.
6. limited, constitutional monarchy
7. **(a)** The Legislative Assembly was split into three general

groups, and the most radical had leaders who were successful in having the king removed.
(b) republic (c) Robespierre ruled as dictator and Committee of Public Safety executed many.

8. Napoleon began as a young military officer, became a public hero, led a conquering army, led a coup resulting in the consulate, became First Consul, and in 1804 made himself emperor.

Basic Skills

1. Summary should include: Were 98% of population. Composed of three groups. Bourgeoisie, made up of professionals and business people; wealthy, well educated, but no political power. Urban lower classes, made up of manual workers, tradespeople, and servants, most were poor. Peasants—the largest group—crushed by taxes from the king, the church, and nobility, and by the corvée.

2. (a) Belgium, Netherlands, northern and western Italy, Illyrian provinces (b) Spain, Confederation of the Rhine, Grand Duchy of Warsaw, eastern and southern Italy. These had only puppet governments, three of them headed by Napoleon's brothers, and were very unpopular. Spain responded with guerrilla warfare. In Germany and Italy, the people also turned against the French. (c) Norway, Denmark, Prussia, Austria, Russia were unwilling allies, ready to change sides at the first opportunity.

3. National Assembly: governing body formed by Third Estate; Storming of Bastille: reduced king's power, saved National Assembly; Legislative Assembly: governing body that deposed the king; National convention creates republic: ended all forms of monarchy; First coalition attacks France: Alliance of Britain, Spain, Portugal, Prussia, Austria against France; Reign of Terror begins: radical period in which Robespierre had aristocracy and others executed; Directory takes power: ended Reign of Terror, restored stability; Napoleon seizes power: start of conservative strongman rule; Napoleon becomes emperor: absolute rule replaced representative government; Napoleonic code issued: organized French system of laws, granted more equality, but placed Napoleon above laws; Napoleon's Continental System: sought to end Britain's trade access to continent but failed; Invasion of Russia: farthest extent of Napoleon's conquests, but ended in failure; Napoleon's exile to Elba: allowed Louis XVIII to take throne briefly, but did not lessen Napoleon's popularity with French people; Napoleon's defeat at Waterloo: final defeat, with exile to St. Helena

Researching and Reporting Skills

Students' writing of historical essays will vary but should follow sequence given.

Critical Thinking

1. National Assembly marked entry of Third Estate into French government, start of representative government, beginning of revolutionary change.

2. (a) bewildered, angry, fearful (b) mistrustful of other revolutionary leaders, determined to destroy enemies of Republic (c) fearful; angry at having sacrificed privileges, at loss of lands, at clergy appointed by election (d) angry, determined, wanting food

3. National debt leading to heavy taxes; taxes not equal but burdening Third Estate; poor harvests raising price of bread.

4. (a) Fall of Bastille was the taking over of power by the French people. The king, married to a foreign queen, defended by Swiss guards, supported by foreign powers, soon became identified with the foreign armies threatening the French. The people formed a citizen-army to defend their country. (b) Increased sense of pride and loyalty to Napoleon. When Napoleon provided leadership, his ideal of the greatness of France was eagerly adopted and followed by the people.

5. Answers will vary. Students may criticize Napoleon's opinion as exaggerating the good and ignoring the harm done during his reign. Students may agree with the concluding paragraph or criticize it for being too harsh on Napoleon. Conclusions will vary.

Perspectives on Past and Present

(a) During the reign of Peter the Great, Swedes had been defeated by the winter cold of Russia. Hitler's armies in World War II encountered a purposely devastated countryside as well as winter cold. (b) In all three cases, invading armies were greatly weakened or destroyed, leading to Russian victory.

Investigating History

Students' reports will vary.

Rebellious Parisians and soldiers dragged cannons toward the Bastille on July 14, 1789. The fall of the Bastille marked the beginning of the French Revolution.

Key Terms

estate
radical
coalition
coup
plebiscite
blockade
guerrilla
scorched-earth policy
exile

482

ead and Understand

1. The French monarchy faced a crisis.
2. Revolution brought reform and terror.
3. Napoleon conquered much of Europe.
4. Napoleon's empire collapsed.

eneath the towering gray walls of an old fortress, a shouting mob of Parisians brandished their stolen muskets. They had been rioting for several hours on this gray and misty day, July 14, 1789. The muskets in their hands and the ammunition in their pockets had been taken that morning from a military hospital on the other side of Paris. Now they were clamoring at the gates of the fortress called the Bastille.

Built in the Middle Ages, the Bastille served in the 1700's as a jail for political prisoners. It was guarded by 114 soldiers loyal to the French king. Their aristocratic commander, the Marquis de Launay (mahr-**KEE** duh loh-**NAY**), firmly refused to turn over the fortress and its 20,000 pounds of gunpowder to the mob. After several tense hours

---

Chapter 21
Resources

GEOGRAPHY
- Geography Skills 21
- Transparencies 69, 71

REINFORCEMENT
- Vocabulary 21
- Basic Skills 21
- Reteaching 21
- Making Connections Study Guide 21

ENRICHMENT
- Critical Thinking 21

ASSESSMENT
- Chapter Test 21
- Alternate Chapter Test 21
- Computer Test Bank

Chapter **21**

Teaching with Pictures

Tell students that the painting on page 482 is set outside the Bastille, with the Invalides hospital in the background. Ask students to comment on the appearance of the mob as it marches to the attack. Students should note that the people appear unruly, non-regimented, and are not in uniforms. Students should also mention the presence of women, children, and pets. Tell students that within several years, France developed one of the greatest citizen-soldier armies in history.

of waiting, he gave the order to fire. Cannons thundered from the battlements.

Some of the rioters were killed, and hundreds of others quickly took cover. They loaded their stolen weapons. It was a battle now between the soldiers' heavy cannons and the civilians' light muskets, and the civilians were taking a beating.

However, other soldiers in Paris sympathized with the mob. A few blocks from the Bastille, an ex-officer in the French Guard pleaded with his comrades:

> Brave guards, can't you hear the cannons? . . . That villain De Launay is murdering our brothers, our parents, our wives and children who are gathered unarmed around the Bastille. Will you allow them to be massacred? . . . Will you not march on the Bastille?

Tears streamed down the man's face as he spoke. Moved to fury by his speech, 60 soldiers followed him to the Bastille, dragging 4 cannons with them. Facing these heavy guns, the Marquis de Launay had no choice but to surrender.

It was a moment of triumph for the working people of Paris, a moment of stark terror for the marquis and his men. The mob dragged the captive soldiers through the narrow lanes of the city. "Stones were thrown at me," said one soldier, "and women gnashed their teeth and brandished their fists at me." That soldier survived the fury of the mob, but De Launay and others were hacked to death.

Meanwhile, in his palace at Versailles, France's King Louis XVI was peacefully asleep. Awakened by a duke, he heard the horrifying news of the fall of the Bastille. "Why, this is a revolt!" exclaimed the king. "No sire," the duke replied. "It is a revolution."

It was indeed a revolution that confronted Louis in the summer of 1789. Historians generally divide this revolution into four stages. First, there was a relatively moderate stage (1789–1792) in which the leaders wrote a constitution and a bill of human rights. Second came a radical and bloody stage (1793–1794) called the Reign of Terror. Third, there was a period of reaction against the violence of the revolution (1794–1799). In the fourth and final stage (1799–1815), an ambitious young general named Napoleon Bonaparte made himself France's dictator and later its emperor.

In this story of violent change and upheaval, the storming of the Bastille was only one episode. Yet it was a crucial one, as we shall see.

The French monarchy faced a crisis. 1

Why did millions of French people suddenly revolt against institutions that their ancestors had accepted for hundreds of years? Ways of life that once served people well can become rigid over time. New conditions change the way people see their world. What seems reasonable in one age may later seem hateful and unnecessary.

By the 1770's, the old institutions of monarchy and feudalism no longer worked for France. As a group, these institutions were known as the Old Regime.

The Old Regime had three estates.

Since the Middle Ages, the people of France had been divided into three large social classes, or **estates.** The Roman Catholic clergy formed the First Estate. The nobles made up the Second Estate. The commoners were the Third Estate. In the 1300's, these three groups had begun meeting as the Estates General (page 253), a French institution much like the early English Parliament.

The Old Regime worked well for the members of the First Estate and the Second Estate. They enjoyed wealth and special privileges under law. The Third Estate, however, had many reasons for dissatisfaction.

The First Estate The Catholic Church held about 10 percent of all the land in France. The highest officials of the French Church—the archbishops, bishops, and abbots—were enormously wealthy. Parish priests, on the other hand, were nearly as poor as the peasants to whom they preached.

French clergy paid no direct taxes to the royal government. Instead, they gave the government a "free gift" of about 2 percent of their income.

The Second Estate Although nobles made up less than 2 percent of France's population, they owned about 20 percent of the land. They also

483

483

SECTION 1 Objectives and Teaching Strategies

OBJECTIVE 1. Identify the three estates and explain why the Third Estate hated the Old Regime.

Teaching Strategy: *Analyzing a Quotation: Resentments of the Third Estate* (page 482a)

OBJECTIVE 2. Describe the financial crisis that forced Louis XVI to call a meeting of the Estates General.

Teaching Strategy: *Economics and History: The French Financial Crisis* (page 482c)

OBJECTIVE 3. Identify the National Assembly and explain how it took power.

Teaching Strategy: *Teaching with Pictures: The Tennis Court Oath* (page 482c)

■ BACKGROUND

The Bastille was located in a middle class neighborhood and its imposing presence was a daily reminder of the taking of political prisoners.

Someone stuck De Launay's head on a pitchfork, and with this grisly trophy, the jubilant crowd paraded through the streets of Paris.

SECTION 1 Resources

ASSESSMENT
■ Section Quiz 21.1

REINFORCEMENT
■ Independent Practice 21.1

ENRICHMENT
■ Voices from the Past 21.1

■ DISCUSSION

Louis XV—no doubt a worse ruler than his grandson, Louis XVI—accurately foretold the consequences of his negligence and extravagance, saying: "After me, the deluge." Have students discuss what form "the deluge" took.

■ BACKGROUND

The tennis court had been built for the amusement of the king's courtiers. When the members of the Third Estate found it empty, they entered noisily and ripped off one of its doors to make a table for their assembly leader.

held all the highest offices in the church, the army, the government, and the courts of law. For centuries, the people of this estate had enjoyed the privilege of paying no taxes. Their refusal to pay taxes was one cause for revolution.

The Third Estate About 98 percent of France's people belonged to the Third Estate. There were actually three groups in the Third Estate: (1) a city-dwelling middle class called the bourgeoisie, (2) urban lower classes, and (3) peasant farmers. Although these three groups belonged to the same political classification, they differed greatly in their economic conditions.

The bourgeoisie had been growing slowly in numbers and power since the Middle Ages. By profession, its members were lawyers, doctors, manufacturers, bankers, merchants, and shopkeepers. Many were well educated and believed strongly in the Enlightenment ideals of liberty and equality. Some of the bourgeoisie were as rich as nobles. Like nobles, wealthy middle-class men dressed in powdered wigs, fine waistcoats, and tight-fitting knee breeches called *culottes* with silk stockings below the knee. Yet the law treated them as peasants. Members of the bourgeoisie yearned for social status and political power equal to their wealth.

The workers of France's cities—butchers, brewers, weavers, tanners, peddlers, cooks, servants, and others—formed a second group within the Third Estate. They were poorer than the bourgeoisie, and their poverty showed in their clothing. Unlike the nobles and the bourgeoisie, poor men wore shirts and loose-fitting trousers that came down to their ankles. As a class, these urban workers were called *sans-culottes* (those who are without knee breeches).

The poor people of France's cities often went hungry. Most of Paris's poor people ate three pounds of bread a day and very little else. If the cost of bread rose, hungry mobs attacked carts of grain and bread to steal what they needed. In 1788, grain harvests were small. The price of bread doubled. Thus, the sans-culottes were in a dangerous mood in the spring of 1789.

The largest group within the Third Estate were the peasants. They made up more than four fifths of France's 26 million people. As a rule, French peasants in the 1700's lived better than peasants elsewhere in Europe. Even so, they lost about half their income in taxes. They paid feudal dues

to the nobles, tithes to the church, and royal taxes to the king's agent.

Besides taxes in money, peasants owed the *corvée*. The corvée was a form of tax that was paid with work rather than money. Every year, the law required the peasants to work without pay on government roads for a certain number of days.

Thus, the bourgeoisie, the sans-culottes of the cities, and the peasants of the countryside all had reasons to hate the Old Regime. The French Revolution was partly the outcome of these resentments from the lower classes. It was also the result of weak leadership at the top.

Louis XVI was a weak ruler.

Louis XVI, who became king in 1774, was good-hearted and generous. However, he was not a strong leader. He was indecisive and allowed matters to drift.

Louis and his wife, Marie Antoinette, were a devoted couple. They married when he was 15 years old and she was 14. Marie Antoinette was pretty, light-hearted, and charming. However, she was unpopular from the day she set foot in France because she came from the royal family of Austria, France's longtime enemy. The queen made herself even more unpopular by her habit of buying expensive gowns and jewels while the poor went hungry and the government treasury was empty.

Louis's government was deeply in debt. Part of the debt arose because Louis had borrowed heavily to help the American revolutionaries in their war against Great Britain. Britain was France's chief rival, and Louis had seized the chance to strike at the British.

Louis's ministers hoped to avoid bankruptcy by taxing the nobles. The nobles, however, refused to pay taxes unless the king called a meeting of the Estates General, which had not met since 1614. Reluctantly, Louis called a meeting of the estates at Versailles on May 1, 1789. As it proved, his order was nothing less than an invitation to revolution.

The National Assembly took power.

The First and Second estates (clergy and nobles) had dominated the Estates General in the Middle Ages. They still expected to do so in 1789. Under

484

On June 20, 1789, the king locked the Third Estate out of its meeting hall. Furious, members met at an indoor tennis court nearby, where they vowed to stand fast until a constitution was established.

the estates' medieval rules, each estate was to meet in its own hall and vote either for or against a given proposal. In the final decision, each estate was to have one vote. Thus, the First and Second estates could always outvote the Third Estate two to one.

In 1789, the Third Estate demanded that all three estates meet together. The votes of all members would count equally. The 610 members of the Third Estate would thus outnumber the 591 members of the combined First and Second estates.

Siding with the nobles, the king ordered the estates to follow the old rules. The representatives of the Third Estate, however, became more and more determined to wield power. The leading spokesman for their viewpoint was a clergyman sympathetic to their cause, the Abbé Sieyès (ah-**BAY** syay-**YAS**). In a bold pamphlet, he had written, "What is the Third Estate? Everything. What has it been up to now in the political order? Nothing. What does it demand? To become something herein."

On June 16, the Abbé Sieyès rose to address an excited gathering of bourgeois deputies. He suggested that the Third Estate change its name to the National Assembly. He called on the new assembly to pass laws and reforms in the name of the French people.

After a long night of excited debate, the deputies of the Third Estate agreed to Sieyès's idea by an overwhelming majority. The vote of June 17, 1789, created the National Assembly. In effect, the deputies proclaimed an end to absolute monarchy and the beginning of representative government. This vote was the first deliberate act of revolution.

Parisians stormed the Bastille.

In this crisis, Louis XVI acted indecisively. He tried to make peace with the Third Estate by yielding to their demands. He ordered the nobles and clergy to meet as one law-making body with the Third Estate (now the National Assembly). At the same time, the king sent orders for his mercenary army of Swiss guards to march toward Paris. He called on these Swiss troops because he could no longer trust the loyalty of French soldiers. The bourgeois deputies feared, with good

485

ANSWERS TO

Section Review 1

Define:
(a) French social classes
(b) city-dwelling middle class
(c) urban workers of Third Estate (d) form of tax paid with work

Identify:
(a) date of fall of Bastille
(b) fortress used in the 1700's as a jail for political prisoners (c) king of France at the time of the French Revolution (d) monarchy and feudalism (e) lawmaking body (f) King Louis XVI's wife (g) assembly that passed laws and reforms in the name of the French people (h) wave of panic

Answer:
1. (a) first—clergy; second—nobles; third—bourgeoisie, urban lower classes, and peasant farmers (b) first—held 10 percent of land; second—held high offices in church, army, government, and courts; third—supplied labor

2. (a) bourgeoisie, some of whom were well-educated professionals and prosperous merchants; manual laborers (b) Some of the bourgeoisie were as rich as nobles, yet the law treated them as peasants; poor peo-
(continued)

ANSWER TO
Comparing Pictures

As queen, Marie Antoinette had a ceremonial role. She had great influence in society, culture, and fashion of the court but no direct political rights. The Parisian woman—a member of the lower class—had neither rights nor influence. Parisian women in the Revolution, however, showed their concern for political matters and economic conditions.

ANSWERS TO (continued)

ple could not depend on a steady diet; and peasants had to pay high taxes.

3. Louis allowed matters to drift; Marie Antoinette bought expensive items.

4. The nobles refused to pay taxes unless he did.

5. (a) Each estate had one vote. (b) wanted the votes of all members to count equally and individually (c) He ordered the estates to follow the old rules. (d) creation of the National Assembly

6. (a) forced Louis to give up his plans of bringing foreign troops into the city (b) reduced king's power and saved the National Assembly (c) became a symbol of the revolution

7. Peasants banded together, broke into nobles' manor homes, tore legal papers binding them to pay feudal dues, and burned the houses.

8. Revolt suggests a short-term disruption; revolution suggests permanent change.

Comparing pictures *A Parisian woman (left) and Marie Antoinette symbolize two different classes. What role and rights did each have in French society?*

reason, that the troops were coming to break up the National Assembly.

In Paris, mobs were already rioting over the high price of bread. The riots reached their peak in the storming of the Bastille. What the mob wanted was the Bastille's supply of gunpowder to defend Paris and the National Assembly against the king's foreign troops.

The fall of the Bastille was important for several reasons. Militarily, it forced Louis to give up his plan of bringing his foreign troops into the city. Politically, it reduced the king's power and saved the National Assembly.

Perhaps most important, the fall of the Bastille became a great symbolic act of revolution in the minds of French people. Ever since 1789, they have celebrated July 14 as a national holiday similar to the United States' Fourth of July.

The Great Fear swept France.

Before long, rebellion was spreading from Paris into the countryside. From one village to the next, wild rumors circulated about a plot against

486

the common people. People said that nobles were hiring brigands to terrorize the peasants.

A wave of panic, called the Great Fear, swept France. Peasants banded together and hid in forests and caves. When they met no enemy brigands, they became brigands themselves. Waving pitchforks and torches, they broke into nobles' manor houses. Once inside, they tore up the old legal papers that bound them to pay feudal dues. Then they burned the manor houses as well.

In October 1789, thousands of Parisian women rioted over the rising price of bread. Their anger quickly turned against the king and queen. Why was the royal couple living in luxury at Versailles while the people starved? The women demanded that Louis and Marie Antoinette come to Paris.

Seizing knives and axes, the women marched on Versailles. They broke into the palace, ransacked the queen's apartments, and killed three guards. Finally, the king appeared on a balcony and told the angry mob below, "My friends, I will go to Paris with my wife and children." Never again would Louis and his family see the beautiful palace at Versailles.

Define: (a) estates, (b) bourgeoisie, (c) sans-culottes, (d) corvée

Identify: (a) July 14, 1789, (b) Bastille, (c) Louis XVI, (d) Old Regime, (e) Estates General, (f) Marie Antoinette, (g) National Assembly, (h) Great Fear

Answer:

1. (a) What were the three estates in France? (b) What part did each play in French society and government?
2. (a) Briefly describe each of the groups that made up the Third Estate. (b) Why was each dissatisfied with the Old Regime?
3. How did the characters of King Louis XVI and Queen Marie Antoinette add to the crisis that France faced?
4. Why did the king need to call a meeting of the Estates General?
5. (a) What was the voting system in the Estates General before 1789? (b) How did the Third Estate wish to change this system? (c) How did Louis react? (d) What was the result?
6. (a) Why was the fall of the Bastille important militarily? (b) Politically? (c) Symbolically?
7. What happened during the Great Fear?

Critical Thinking

8. At first, Louis XVI called the fall of the Bastille "a revolt," but he was told it was "a revolution." What is the difference?

Revolution brought reform and terror. 2

The night of August 4, 1789, was one of the most astonishing nights in the history of France. In a matter of hours, the National Assembly swept away the ancient privileges of the nobility and the clergy.

One by one, the nobles in the assembly gave impassioned speeches declaring their love of liberty and equality. The nobles who made these grand speeches were moved by fear as well as idealism. The Great Fear was at its height, and peasant bands were terrorizing the countryside.

The Assembly adopted many reforms.

The emotional speeches went on through the night. By morning, the National Assembly had voted to end feudalism, serfdom, church tithes, and the special privileges of nobles and clergy. The Old Regime was dead. "Liberty, Equality, Fraternity" became the slogan of the revolution.

The Rights of Man Three weeks later, on August 27, 1789, the National Assembly adopted a set of revolutionary ideas called *A Declaration of the Rights of Man and of the Citizen.* The first article of the document declared, "Men are born and remain free and equal in rights." The second article stated:

> The aim of all political association is the preservation of the natural ... rights of man. These rights are liberty, property, security, and resistance to oppression.

Other articles of the famous document guaranteed citizens equal justice, freedom of speech, and freedom of religion.

A limited monarchy For two years, the National Assembly argued over a new constitution for France. By 1791, they had made huge changes in France's government and society.

The National Assembly created a limited, constitutional monarchy somewhat like the British government. An elected assembly held the law-making power. Although the monarchy lost its absolute powers, the king and his ministers still held the executive power to enforce laws.

Departments The National Assembly abolished France's traditional provinces, which had existed since the Middle Ages. Instead, the assembly divided France into 83 districts called departments. A council of officials elected by the local citizens administered each department.

A state-controlled church The Catholic Church lost both its lands and its political independence. The government took over church lands. The assembly also ruled that church officials and priests were to be elected by property owners and paid as state officials. This law alarmed millions of devout French peasants, who rallied to the support of their parish priests.

These changes in the Catholic Church drove a wedge between the peasants and the bourgeoisie. From this time on, the peasants often opposed further revolutionary changes.

487

SECTION 2 Objectives and Teaching Strategies

OBJECTIVE 1. Describe the government created by the National Assembly and explain how it used the ideas of the philosophes.

Teaching Strategy: *Transferring Ideas: The Rights of Man* (page 482c)

OBJECTIVE 2. Explain why the National Convention voted to execute Louis XVI.

Teaching Strategy: *Writing about History: Sentencing Louis XVI* (page 482c)

■ DISCUSSION

Compare and contrast the events leading up to the French Revolution with those leading to the revolution in the American colonies.

SECTION 2 Resources

ASSESSMENT
■ Section Quiz 21.2

REINFORCEMENT
■ Independent Practice 21.2

ENRICHMENT
■ Voices from the Past 21.2

■ **BACKGROUND**

Some radicals were also known as Girondists because many of them came from the department of Gironde in southwestern France.

ANSWERS TO

Voice from the Past

1. same rights as those granted to men
2. all those suited to a particular woman's talents
3. the "right" to be executed

■ **BACKGROUND**

Olympe de Gouges was a playwright who turned her talents to political writing when the conflicts began. The work excerpted here was dedicated to Marie Antoinette.

The king reluctantly approved the constitution and the Declaration of the Rights of Man. Then, in June 1791, Louis and his family tried to escape from France to the Austrian Netherlands. Just as they neared the French border, however, a postmaster recognized the king from his portrait on some paper money. The royal family returned to Paris under guard. As a result of this attempted escape, Louis XVI discredited both himself and the plan for constitutional monarchy. His action increased the influence of his radical enemies and sealed his own doom.

In September 1791, having completed its new constitution, the National Assembly stepped down from power. It was followed by a newly elected group called the Legislative Assembly.

France was split by factions.

Despite the new government, the old problems remained. Angry cries for more liberty, more equality, and more bread soon caused the leaders of the revolution to turn against one another.

The Legislative Assembly split into three general groups. Each group tended to sit together in its own part of the meeting hall. On the benches to the right sat the conservatives, those who opposed more changes in government. In general, they trusted the king and upheld the idea of limited monarchy. On the left side of the hall sat the **radicals,** those who clamored for more sweeping changes. They hated the king and wanted to set up a republic in which the common people had full power. In the center sat the moderates. They wanted some further reforms but not as many as the radicals demanded.

To this day, radical politicians are commonly described as being "on the left," and conservative politicians are said to be "on the right." Moderates are called "centrists." These terms began with the French Revolution.

Outside the government, there were far more extreme groups, both on the right and on the left. People on the extreme right hoped to undo the revolution and restore the Old Regime. Among this group were the emigrés (EHM-uh-grayz) —nobles who had fled during the peasant uprisings. They lived abroad and plotted against the revolution. On the extreme left were the sans-culottes of Paris. Their radical leaders set

 Voice from the Past | *The Rights of Woman*

In 1791, a woman revolutionary named Olympe de Gouges (goozh) demanded the same rights for French women that French men were demanding for themselves. Here is part of her "Declaration of the Rights of Woman."

Woman is born free and lives equal to man in her rights. Social distinctions can be based only on the common utility . . .

The law must be the expression of the general will; all female and male citizens must contribute either personally or through their representatives to its formation; it must be the same for all: male and female citizens, being equal in the eyes of the law, must be equally admitted to all honors, positions, and public employment according to their capacity and without other distinctions besides those of their virtues and talents . . .

No one is to be [persecuted] for basic opinions; woman has the right to mount the scaffold; she must equally have the right to mount the rostrum [a public speaking platform].

1. What legal rights does De Gouges ask for women?
2. What political positions does she say should be open to women?
3. What is implied by "the right to mount the scaffold"?

The spirit of Liberty

up a new city government with representatives from each of Paris's 48 sections. This powerful city council, known as the Paris Commune, became a dominant force in the revolution.

France went to war with Austria.

France faced not only a revolution at home but also a disastrous foreign war. The ruler of Austria, Marie Antoinette's brother, threatened to attack France.

French radicals were delighted at the idea of war with Austria. They hoped that the war would give them a chance to spread their revolution to all the peoples of Europe. On April 20, 1792, the Legislative Assembly declared war on Austria. Soon Prussia joined Austria against France.

The war began badly for the poorly equipped French armies. By the summer of 1792, enemy armies were advancing toward Paris.

On July 25, the Prussian commander threatened to destroy Paris if the revolutionaries harmed any member of the royal family. This rash statement provoked the fury of the mob. On August 10, about 70,000 men and women surged into the palace in Paris where the royal couple was staying. The king's Swiss guard of 900 men fought desperately to defend Louis. The mob brutally massacred them and swarmed through the palace. Louis and Marie Antoinette were imprisoned in a stone tower.

Under the threat of the Parisian radicals, the Legislative Assembly gave up the idea of a limited monarchy. The lawmakers set aside the Constitution of 1791 and declared the king deposed. The assembly then ended its own existence by calling for the election of a new legislature.

The new governing body, elected in September, was called the National Convention. Just as the new government took office, France had a stroke of luck. A French army managed to defeat the Austrians and Prussians. For the moment, France was out of danger from abroad.

The radicals executed Louis XVI.

During the desperate summer of 1792, the leaders of the frenzied mobs on the streets had more real power than any governmental assembly. Although the mobs were poor, their leaders came from the bourgeoisie.

Both men and women of the middle class joined political clubs. The most radical of these clubs in 1792 was the Jacobin (JAK-uh-buhn) Club, where violent speechmaking was the order of the day. Its members wanted to remove the king and establish a republic.

One of the frequent speakers before the Jacobin Club was Georges Danton (dahn-TOHN), a leader of the Paris Commune. Fearless and devoted to the rights of Paris's poor, Danton used his talent for speechmaking to win political leadership.

Another prominent radical leader was Jean Paul Marat (muh-RAH). The very opposite of the strong, bull-like Danton, Marat was a thin, high-strung, sickly man who had hoped to win fame for his scientific research. After the revolution broke out, he edited a radical newspaper called *The Friend of the People*. His fiery editorials called for "five or six hundred heads cut off" to rid France of the enemies of the revolution.

By August 1792, Danton and Marat were two of the most powerful of the radical leaders. Together with the Paris mob, these men set the revolution on a new and more violent path.

The National Convention met in Paris on September 21. It quickly abolished the monarchy. Next, the assembly declared France a republic. Every adult male citizen had the right to vote and hold office. Women could not vote, however, despite the important part they had already played in the revolution.

Louis XVI was king no longer. Under the new republic, he was just a common citizen and prisoner. What was to be done with this dangerous citizen? The delegates to the National Convention tried him for treason and found him guilty.

The radicals demanded that Louis be condemned to death. They won by a single vote. On the morning of January 21, 1793, the ex-king walked with calm dignity up the steps of the scaffold to be beheaded by a machine called the guillotine (GIHL-uh-TEEN). Thousands died by the guillotine during the French Revolution.

France created a citizen-army.

The new republic's first problem was the hostile armies of Austria and Prussia. In the fall of 1792, Britain, Spain, and Portugal joined Prussia and Austria in an alliance known as the First Coalition. A **coalition** is a temporary alliance between

489

Cooperative Learning

Divide the class into groups of three students. Have students review the history of the Legislative Assembly in France in 1791–1792 (page 488). Assign a current controversial issue, perhaps one related to education or the environment, for the three group members to debate. Each group member should take on the role of a radical, conservative, or moderate. Have students prepare statements according to their roles' position on the issue, keeping in mind the opposition's point of view when preparing their arguments. Remind them that they will have not just one, but two opposing viewpoints to debate. When group members are finished, have them present their statements to one another and debate the issue.

■ BACKGROUND

Groups of national guardsmen from the provinces marched to defend Paris against the Prussians. Among them were men from the seaport of Marseilles who marched into Paris singing "La Marseillaise," which later became the French national anthem.

■ BACKGROUND

"Terror," said Robespierre, "is nothing but justice—swift, severe, and inflexible."

In the mid-1790's, many saw the Old Regime as the "good old days" and yearned for its return. Royalists pinned their hopes on Louis XVI's brother. The middle class wanted order restored but did not want to give up the power they had gained.

ANSWERS TO
Section Review 2

Define:
(a) desiring sweeping changes (b) nobles who had fled during the peasant uprising (c) machine used for beheading (d) temporary alliance between groups usually on different sides

Identify:
(a) document espousing liberty and other human rights
(b) elective group that suc-

(continued)

The guillotine was invented by a doctor as a more humane form of execution than the ax.

groups who are usually on different sides. In the face of so many enemies, France suffered a string of defeats.

The Jacobin leaders took extreme steps to meet the new danger. In February 1793, the convention drafted into the army 300,000 men between the ages of 18 and 40. By 1794, this number had grown to 800,000. Women too asked for the right to form regiments to defend France. The government never granted their request. However, a number of women fought beside men in France's armies during the revolution.

Most armies in Europe were made up of mercenaries, but the new French army was a people's army of loyal patriots. Led by dedicated officers, the French scored victory after victory.

Robespierre began the Terror.

Foreign armies were not the only enemies of the French Republic. The Jacobins had thousands of enemies within France itself—peasants who were horrified by the beheading of the king, priests who would not accept control by the government, and rival leaders who were stirring up rebellion in the provinces.

As dozens of leaders struggled for power, one man slowly gathered control into his own hands. His name was Maximilien Robespierre (ROHBZ-pihr).

Robespierre was one of the few members of the Jacobin Club who did not dress like a revolutionary. He wore a powdered wig in the old style, knee breeches, and stockings. Nicknamed "the Incorruptible," Robespierre never enriched himself at the public expense, unlike many of the men around him. In his fanaticism, however, Robespierre was merciless. His period in power is fittingly known as the Reign of Terror.

Robespierre and his supporters set out to build a Republic of Virtue. They tried to wipe out every trace of France's past monarchy and nobility. Many families named Leroy (king), for instance, changed their names to something less political. (Even if they did not support the monarchy, it was safer to take a new name.) Decks of cards no longer had kings, queens, and jacks. Instead, they had cards called liberties, equalities, and fraternities.

Firm believers in reason, the radicals wanted to make the calendar scientific. They divided the year into 12 months of 30 days and gave each month a new, "reasonable" name. October, for instance, was renamed Brumaire, or Fog Month. The new calendar had no Sundays because the radicals considered religion old-fashioned and dangerous. The Paris Commune closed all churches in the city. Towns all over France soon did the same.

In the summer of 1793, Robespierre formed the Committee of Public Safety. As head of the committee, Robespierre decided who should be judged an enemy of the republic. Those he accused were often tried in the morning and guillotined that very afternoon. From July 1793 to July 1794, he governed France nearly as a dictator.

The widowed queen, Marie Antoinette, was the most famous victim of the Terror. Calm and dignified, she rode in the death cart past jeering crowds. On the scaffold, she accidently stepped on her executioner's foot. "Monsieur," she apologized, "I beg your pardon. I did not do it on purpose." These were her last words.

However, the so-called enemies of the republic who most troubled Robespierre were not monarchists like Marie Antoinette. They were fellow revolutionaries who challenged his leadership. In October 1793, many of the leaders who had first helped set up the republic were executed. Their only crime was that they were less radical than Robespierre.

By the beginning of 1794, even Danton found himself in danger. (Marat had already been stabbed to death by a young woman from another political faction.) Danton's former friends in the National Assembly, afraid to defend him, joined in condemning him to death. On the scaffold, he told the executioner, "Don't forget to show my head to the people. It's well worth seeing."

Besides leading political figures, thousands of obscure people were sent to death on the flimsiest of charges. An 18-year-old youth was guillotined for sawing down a tree that had been planted as a symbol of liberty. A tavern keeper died because he had sold sour wine "to the defenders of the country."

During the Terror, at least 3,000 people were executed in Paris. Some historians believe as many as 40,000 were killed all together. Fully 80 percent were peasants, sans-culottes, or bourgeoisie—common people for whom the revolution had supposedly been fought.

Robespierre fell from power.

By July 1794, members of the National Convention knew that none of them was safe from Robespierre. To save themselves, they turned on him. A group of conspirators demanded his arrest, shouting "Down with the tyrant!" Robespierre tried to speak in his own defense, but delegates to both left and right shouted him down. Within two days, the revolution's last powerful leader went to the guillotine.

With Robespierre's execution, the radical phase of the French Revolution ended. Robespierre died on July 28, 1794. On the new revolutionary calendar, July was called *Thermidor* from the French word for "heat." Hence, the revolt against Robespierre is called the *Thermidorian reaction.*

Moderates ruled in the Directory.

Public opinion in France now shifted dramatically to the right. People of all classes were sick of the Terror. They were also sick of the skyrocketing prices for bread, salt, and other necessities of life.

In 1795, moderate leaders of the National Convention drafted a new constitution. This new plan of government put power firmly in the hands of the upper bourgeoisie. This constitution, the third since 1789, called for a two-house legislature and an executive body of five men known as the Directory.

The five directors were moderates, not revolutionary idealists. Some of them freely enriched themselves at the public's expense. Despite their corruption, however, they gave their troubled country a period of order.

The Directory also found the right general to command France's armies. With a string of astounding victories, this general crushed France's foes. The name of this supremely talented young man was Napoleon Bonaparte.

Section REVIEW 2

Define: (a) radical, (b) emigrés, (c) guillotine, (d) coalition
Identify: (a) *Declaration of the Rights of Man and of the Citizen*, (b) Legislative Assembly, (c) Paris Commune, (d) Jacobin Club, (e) Danton, (f) Marat, (g) Robespierre, (h) Committee of Public Safety, (i) Reign of Terror, (j) Directory
Answer:
1. What rights were proclaimed in *A Declaration of the Rights of Man?*
2. (a) What reforms did the National Assembly make in France's government? (b) In the Catholic Church?
3. What was the result of the royal family's attempt to escape France?
4. (a) What were the basic political divisions within the Legislative Assembly? (b) How did seating arrangements there affect the labels given to political groups?
5. (a) How did the limited monarchy come to an end? (b) What was the fate of Louis XVI?
6. After 1793, how did the French army differ from the armies of its enemies?
7. (a) Briefly describe the Reign of Terror. (b) How did it end?
8. What political outlook did the Directory represent?

Critical Thinking
9. There is a saying, "Revolutions devour their own children." (a) What evidence from the French Revolution supports that proverb? (b) Why might revolutions in general have such an effect?

491

ANSWERS TO (continued)
ceeded the National Assembly (c) radical city council (d) radical political club (e) leader of Paris Commune (f) prominent radical leader (g) leader who brought about Reign of Terror (h) committee that judged who was an enemy of the people (i) Robespierre's period of rule (j) executive body of five men
Answer:
1. liberty, property, security, and resistance to oppression
2. (a) created limited monarchy, created departments (b) took away church's lands and political independence
3. discredited royal family and plan for constitutional monarchy
4. (a) conservatives, radicals, and moderates (b) Even today radicals are seen as "on the left," moderates "in the middle," and conservatives "on the right."
5. (a) under threat of Parisian radicals (b) beheaded
6. It was a people's army of loyal patriots.
7. (a) period in which Robespierre had almost dictatorial powers, executing many (b) with members of the National Convention turning on Robespierre, sending him to the guillotine
8. moderate
9. (a) Robespierre, Marat, and many other revolutionary leaders were eventually executed in the name of revolution. (b) Answers should consider such characteristics of revolution as violence, a general climate of discontent and disorder, and the need for new leaders to take a more extreme position than their predecessors.

Like Alexander, Hannibal, and Julius Caesar, Napoleon overwhelmed his enemies by striking swiftly at their weakest point, whether on the battlefield or in government.

Napoleon conquered much of Europe. 3

Napoleon was a small man (five feet six inches tall) who cast a long shadow over the history of modern times. As a military genius, he ranks with Alexander the Great of Macedonia, Hannibal of Carthage, and Julius Caesar of Rome. In only four years (1795–1799), Napoleon rose from obscurity to mastery of France.

Napoleon rose through the army.

Napoleon Bonaparte was born in 1769 on the island of Corsica in the Mediterranean Sea. In that same year, French troops invaded Corsica and crushed a movement for Corsican independence. "I was born," wrote Bonaparte later, "when my country was dying."

When Bonaparte was ten years old, his parents sent him to a military school outside Paris where his French schoolmates snubbed him as a foreigner. Cut off from other students, Bonaparte devoted himself to mastering military tactics. In 1785, when he was 16, he finished school and became a lieutenant in the artillery. When the revolution broke out, he joined the army of the new government.

In October 1795, fate handed the young officer a chance for glory. An army of royalists threatened the palace where the National Convention was meeting, and a government official told Bonaparte to defend the palace. Bonaparte and his gunners greeted the thousands of royalists with a deadly cannonade. Within minutes, the attackers fled in panic and confusion. Napoleon Bonaparte was the hero of the hour. He was hailed throughout Paris as the savior of the French Republic.

In 1796, the Directory appointed Bonaparte to command a French army against Austria and the Kingdom of Sardinia. Crossing the Alps, the young general swept into Italy and won a series of remarkable victories. The French marched into Milan and made it the capital of a new Italian republic dominated by France.

Though Bonaparte posed as the liberator of northern Italy, he was in fact its conqueror. After a year of triumphant campaigning (1796–1797), Bonaparte was the most famous general in Europe.

Napoleon seized power in France.

Watching the early disorders of the French Revolution, a British statesman made this astute prediction:

In the weakness of authority . . . some popular general shall draw the eyes of all men upon himself. Armies will obey him on his personal account . . . The person who really commands the army is your master.

In 1799, the prediction came true.

By 1799, the Directory had lost the confidence of the French people. They were accused of corruption. In several elections, voters rejected the Directory's candidates. Only the directors' control of the army kept them in power.

Bonaparte decided that the time had come to seize political power. On November 9, 1799, he ordered 500 of his troops to occupy one chamber of the national legislature and drive out its elected members. The second chamber of the legislature, terrified by this show of force, voted to end the Directory. The chamber turned over power to three officials known as consuls. Bonaparte was one of the three.

Soon Bonaparte assumed dictatorial powers as the First Consul of the French Republic. Such a seizure of power is known as a **coup** from the French phrase *coup d'état* (koo day-TAH) or "stroke of state."

A Second Coalition attacked France.

At the time of Bonaparte's coup, France was still at war. Bonaparte's Italian campaign of 1796–1797 had forced Austria and Prussia to make peace, thus ending the First Coalition. The British navy, however, continued its damaging attacks against French shipping. In 1799, British diplomats arranged a Second Coalition of anti-French powers. The Second Coalition consisted chiefly of Britain, Austria, and Russia.

Once again, Napoleon rode out from Paris at the head of his troops. Once again, he led a huge French army over treacherous Alpine passes into northern Italy. Once again, he was victorious. The Austrians were forced to accept his peace terms. The Russians also made peace.

The British fought on, but in 1802, they agreed to Bonaparte's conciliatory peace terms. The

British and the French signed a peace treaty at Amiens (ahm-YAN) in March 1802. For the first time in ten years, Europe was at peace. Sadly, however, this peace did not last long.

Napoleon became emperor.

At first, Bonaparte pretended to be the constitutionally chosen leader of a free republic. In 1800, he and his two fellow consuls asked the French people to approve a new constitution, the fourth in eight years. They held a **plebiscite** (PLEHB-uh-syte), an election in which all citizens vote yes or no on an issue.

In the plebiscite of 1800, the French showed how desperate they were for strong leadership. They voted overwhelmingly for Bonaparte's constitution, which gave all real power to Bonaparte himself as the First Consul.

Bonaparte saw that he could take as much power as he wanted. In 1802, yet another plebiscite made him consul for life. French voters approved the change by a staggering majority (3,568,885 voting yes and only 8,374 voting no).

Two years later, in 1804, Bonaparte decided to make himself emperor. Again, the French voters agreed to his decision. Dressed in a splendid robe of purple velvet, Napoleon walked down the long aisle of Notre Dame Cathedral in Paris on December 2, 1804. The pope waited for him with a glittering crown. As thousands watched, the new emperor took the crown from the pope's hands and placed it on his own head.

Napoleon restored order.

At his coronation, Napoleon Bonaparte became Emperor Napoleon I. The French Republic was dead. In its place stood an absolute monarchy known as the French empire. Yet Napoleon did not try to return France to the days of Louis XIV. He kept many of the changes that had come with the revolution.

Economic order Napoleon managed to slow inflation by balancing the government's budget and setting up a national bank. The sans-culottes of Paris were finally able to buy bread.

Social order Noble emigrés returned to France by the thousands. Napoleon welcomed them as long as they behaved themselves politically. The bourgeoisie were also well pleased with Napoleon

Napoleon (1769–1821) rose through the army to become emperor of France. His loyal troops affectionately nicknamed him "the little corporal."

because he promoted officials according to merit, not according to noble family.

Religious order Both the clergy and the peasants wanted to restore the Catholic Church's position in France. In 1801, Napoleon signed a *concordat* (agreement) with Pope Pius VII. It spelled out a new relationship between church and state.

Napoleon agreed to recognize Catholicism as the faith of "the great majority of Frenchmen." The French government would appoint Catholic bishops, but those bishops could appoint parish priests without government interference. Everyone in France was free to worship as he or she wished.

For his part, the pope stopped trying to win back the lands that the revolutionary government

493

SECTION 3 Objectives and Teaching Strategies

OBJECTIVE 1. List the reasons for Napoleon's victories.

Teaching Strategy: *Discussing History: "The Little Corporal"* (page 482d)

OBJECTIVE 2. Explain how Napoleon restored order to France.

Teaching Strategy: *Relating Past to Present: Napoleon's Enduring Reforms* (page 482d)

■ DISCUSSION

Why did Napoleon choose not to have the pope bestow the crown?

■ BACKGROUND

After crowning himself, Napoleon also crowned his beloved Josephine, whom he had married in 1795 and to whom he wrote passionate love letters whenever his military duties separated them.

SECTION 3 Resources

ASSESSMENT
■ Section Quiz 21.3

REINFORCEMENT
■ Independent Practice 21.3

ENRICHMENT
■ Voices from the Past 21.3

During the period of empire, trial by jury was cut back and inhumane punishments such as branding and the cutting off of a hand were brought back into practice.

In preparation for the attack against Britain that never took place, Napoleon readied 170,000 soldiers and built more than 2,000 flat-bottomed boats.

had taken from the church. He also accepted Napoleon's policy of toleration for Protestants and Jews. This religious settlement of 1801 gave Catholics a favored position in France but not absolute dominance.

Legal order Napoleon thought his greatest work was his comprehensive code of laws known as the Napoleonic Code. Drafted by French jurists between 1801 and 1804, the new code gave the country a single set of laws.

In some ways, the Napoleonic Code grew out of the principles of liberty and equality of the French Revolution. It abolished the three estates of the Old Regime and granted equal rights before the law to people of all classes.

In other ways, the code limited liberty. Napoleon had even more power to censor newspapers than the king had had under the Old Regime. The code took away some rights that women had won during the revolution, such as the right to hold property. The new laws also restored slavery in the French colonies of the Caribbean, which had been abolished by the revolution.

The laws of the new code applied equally to all French citizens except one: Napoleon himself. He asserted his right, as emperor, to stand above the law. As he said, "If there are problems with a government that is too strong, there are many more with a government that is too weak. Things don't work unless you break the law every day."

Napoleon extended France's power.

Napoleon was not content to be simply master of France. Eager to extend his power, he took over part of Italy, set up a puppet government in Switzerland, and threatened Great Britain. In response, the British declared war in 1803. The Peace of Amiens had lasted only a year.

In 1805, Britain persuaded Russia, Austria, Sweden, and Prussia to join the Third Coalition against France. Napoleon met this challenge with his usual boldness. He believed that he was a "man of destiny" who could do no wrong. He wanted to "modernize" all Europe—that is, to force all of Europe to accept his idea of modernization. Between 1805 and 1807, in a series of brilliant battles, he nearly succeeded.

The Battle of Ulm (October 1805) Invading the Austrian empire, the French army caught 50,000 Austrians in a deadly trap and forced them

to surrender. Napoleon entered Vienna in triumph.

The Battle of Austerlitz (December 1805) On the first anniversary of his coronation as emperor, Napoleon won his greatest victory at Austerlitz (AW-stuhr-lits). Commanding 73,000 French troops, he smashed an army of 87,000 Russians and Austrians, took 20,000 prisoners, left 15,000 enemy dead on the field, and forced the Austrian emperor to make peace.

The Battle of Jena (October 1806) Moving north against Prussia, Napoleon and his troops won another devastating victory at Jena (YAY-nuh), wounding or killing 27,000 and taking 18,000 prisoners. As a result of this battle, French troops occupied Berlin.

The Battle of Friedland (June 1807) Advancing eastward into the Prussian part of Poland, Napoleon wiped out a large Russian army. Czar Alexander I, grandson of Catherine the Great, met with Napoleon on a raft moored in the middle of a Polish stream. Here the two rulers agreed to divide Europe between them. In this treaty, called the Peace of Tilsit, the czar agreed to allow France to dominate Europe as far east as Poland. In return, Napoleon gave Alexander a free hand to attack the Ottoman empire.

The Battle of Trafalgar (October 1805) In his war against the Third Coalition, Napoleon lost only one major battle, the Battle of Trafalgar (truh-FAL-guhr). However, this great sea battle was probably more important than all Napoleon's victories on land.

The Battle of Trafalgar took place in 1805 off the southern coast of Spain. The commander of the British fleet was Admiral Horatio Nelson, as brilliant in warfare at sea as Napoleon was on land. With 27 ships, Nelson attacked a 33-ship French fleet. In the middle of the furious battle, Nelson was struck in the back by a French shell. As he lay dying aboard his flagship, Nelson heard the welcome news of British victory. "Now I am satisfied," murmured the admiral. "Thank God, I have done my duty."

The destruction of the French fleet at Trafalgar forced Napoleon to give up his plan to invade Britain. Across the barrier of the English Channel, Great Britain remained a strong enemy able to challenge his power. Eventually, Napoleon's extravagant efforts to crush Britain led to his own undoing.

The Empire of Napoleon, 1810

KEY

- French empire
- Countries under Napoleon's control
- Countries allied with Napoleon
- Countries at war with Napoleon
- ✹ Battle

ATLANTIC OCEAN

GREAT BRITAIN

London

North Sea

KINGDOM OF NORWAY AND DENMARK

KINGDOM OF SWEDEN

Baltic Sea

Moscow

Friedland (1807) ✹

Berlin

Leipzig (1813)

PRUSSIA

Niemen R.

RUSSIAN EMPIRE

Elbe R.

Rhine River

Brussels

Amiens

Waterloo (1815)

Versailles

Paris

CONFEDERATION

Jena ✹ (1806)

GRAND DUCHY OF WARSAW

Kiev

Seine River

OF THE

Ulm (1805) ✹

RHINE

Austerlitz ✹ (1805)

Wagram (1809) ✹

FRENCH EMPIRE

Vienna

AUSTRIAN EMPIRE

Dniester River

Po River

Milan

Danube River

ILLYRIAN PROVINCES

Black Sea

PORTUGAL

Tagus R.

Ebro River

Madrid

KINGDOM OF ITALY

OTTOMAN

River

SPAIN

CORSICA

Rome

SARDINIA

Naples

KINGDOM OF NAPLES

Istanbul

EMPIRE

Trafalgar (1805) ✹

Gibraltar (Br.)

MEDITERRANEAN SEA

SICILY

0   300 Miles

Map Study

In 1810, what was the only country still fighting Napoleon? What countries were allied with him? What made Prussia's position dangerous?

Napoleon dominated Europe.

Through the first decade of the new century (1800–1810), Napoleon built Europe's greatest empire since Roman times. His victories over the Third Coalition gave him mastery over most of Europe. The only major European countries outside Napoleon's power were Britain, the Ottoman empire, Russia, and Sweden.

The map above shows the extent of Napoleon's power. The lands and kingdoms he dominated fell into three main categories.

First, there were the lands that Napoleon annexed directly to France. These territories included the Dutch republic and a number of Italian states.

Second, there were lands that remained independent in name but were in fact controlled by Napoleon. These included Spain, the Grand Duchy of Warsaw, and several German-speaking kingdoms in central Europe. (Napoleon ended the Holy Roman Empire once and for all by forcing the last emperor to step down.) This group of countries kept their traditional capitals rather than being governed from Paris. However, the rulers of these countries were merely Napoleon's puppets. Three of them were his own brothers.

In a third category, the powerful countries of Russia, Prussia, and Austria were loosely attached to Napoleon's empire through treaties of alliance.

The French empire was huge, but it was also unstable. At its largest, it held together for only five years (1807–1812). Then it quickly fell to pieces. Its sudden collapse was caused in part by Napoleon himself.

495

ANSWERS TO

Map Study

Great Britain; Norway and Denmark, Russia, Prussia, and Austria; Prussia, a small country surrounded by French-controlled land, was particularly vulnerable.

■ BACKGROUND

After the last Holy Roman emperor stepped down, the small German kingdoms within Napoleon's modern empire were loosely united in the Confederation of the Rhine.

495

496

Define:
(a) swift, unexpected seizure of power (b) election in which all citizens vote yes or no (c) agreement

Identify:
(a) military genius, emperor of France (b) code of laws (c) victory of Napoleon's forces over Russian and Austrian troops (d) commander of the British fleet who defeated Napoleon (e) sea battle that forced Napoleon to give up plans to invade Britain

Answer:

1. He defended the palace where National Convention was meeting; the Directory appointed him commander of the French army.

2. by ordering his troops to occupy one chamber of the national legislature; the second chamber then voted to turn its power over to three consuls, one of whom was Napoleon

3. by proposing laws that the people readily passed

4. (a) welcomed them as long as they behaved politically (b) his system of merit promotions (c) concordat, recognizing Catholicism as the faith of "the great majority of Frenchmen"

5. (a) by abolishing the three estates and granting equal rights (b) by censoring newspapers, abolishing right of women to hold property, and restoring slavery in the colonies

6. Austria, Prussia, and Russia

7. (a) held elections (b) True base of power was army.

Define: (a) coup, (b) plebiscite, (c) concordat
Identify: (a) Napoleon Bonaparte, (b) Napoleonic Code, (c) Austerlitz, (d) Horatio Nelson, (e) Trafalgar
Answer:
1. How did the National Convention and the Directory both help Napoleon rise to power?
2. How did Napoleon seize power?
3. How did Napoleon expand his power through plebiscites?
4. (a) What policy did Napoleon adopt toward the emigrés? (b) What actions won him the support of the bourgeoisie? (c) What agreement did he make with the Catholic Church?
5. (a) How did the Napoleonic Code carry out the ideas of the French Revolution? (b) How did it limit liberty?
6. What major powers did Napoleon defeat or force into alliance with France?

Critical Thinking
7. Napoleon claimed to be a freely elected leader. (a) What facts support his claim? (b) What facts do not?

Napoleon's empire collapsed.   4

"I love power," said Napoleon, "as a musician loves his violin." It was the drive for power that had raised Napoleon to great heights. Now that same love of power led to his doom. He made three disastrous misjudgments.

Napoleon set up the Continental System.

Napoleon's first misjudgment was to try to cut off all trade with Britain. In 1806, he declared that no state under his control could import British goods. In effect, Napoleon's navy set up a **blockade.** This policy meant that all ports on the European continent were closed to British shipping to keep British ships from Europe.

Napoleon called his policy the Continental System because it was supposed to make Europe

---

Cause and Effect
THE FRENCH REVOLUTION

Contributing Factors

Enlightenment philosophy
American Revolution
Social injustices of Old Regime
Economic crisis in France

Immediate Causes

Convening of Estates General
Indecision of Louis XVI
Fall of Bastille
The Great Fear

REVOLUTION

Immediate Effects

Declaration of Rights of Man
Abolishing of Old Regime
Execution of king and queen
Reign of Terror
War and forming of citizen-army

Long-Term Effects

Rise of Napoleon
Spread of revolutionary ideals
Growth of nationalism
Conservative reaction

---

more self-sufficient. His purpose was to destroy Britain's commercial and industrial economy.

Unfortunately for Napoleon, his blockade was not nearly tight enough. Smugglers managed to bring in cargo from Britain. British trade, though weakened, was not destroyed.

Indeed, Britain responded with its own blockade. The British navy stopped ships bound for

Spanish artist Francisco Goya (1746–1828) saw the horrors of his country's war against Napoleon. This scene shows French troops shooting Spanish rebels.

the continent and forced them to sail to a British port to be searched and taxed. Because the British had a stronger navy, they were better able than the French to make their blockade work.

The British navy regularly stopped the ships of neutral countries, including merchant vessels of the United States. Americans were so angered by these actions that the United States Congress declared war against Britain in 1812. The War of 1812, which ended in a draw, was only a minor inconvenience for Britain in its struggle with Napoleon.

The Continental System hurt Napoleon more than it hurt his enemies. It weakened the economies of France, Germany, and the other lands under Napoleon.

Guerrillas fought the French in Spain.

In 1808, Napoleon's ambition led to a second costly mistake. He planned to make his brother Joseph king of Spain. This move outraged the national feelings of the Spanish people.

For five years (1808–1813), bands of Spanish peasant fighters known as **guerrillas** struck at

French armies in Spain. (*Guerrilla* is a Spanish word meaning "little war.") The guerrillas were not a regular army that Napoleon could meet in battle. Instead, they were ordinary peasants who ambushed French troops and then fled into hiding. The British added to French troubles in Spain by sending troops to aid the rebels.

Napoleon lost about 300,000 men during this Peninsular War (so called because Spain lies on the Iberian Peninsula). These losses fatally weakened the French empire.

In Spain and elsewhere, nationalism was becoming a powerful weapon against Napoleon. People who at first had welcomed the French as their liberators now felt they were being abused by a foreign conqueror. Like the Spanish guerrillas, Germans and Italians and other conquered peoples turned against the French.

Napoleon invaded Russia.

In 1812, Napoleon's thirst for power led to his most disastrous mistake of all. Because Czar Alexander I refused to stop selling grain to Britain, Napoleon decided to invade Russia.

497

SECTION 4
Resources

GEOGRAPHY
- Transparencies 69, 71

REINFORCEMENT
- Independent Practice 21.4

ENRICHMENT
- Voices from the Past 21.4

ASSESSMENT
- Section Quiz 21.4

SECTION 4
Objectives and Teaching Strategies

OBJECTIVE 1. Explain why the Spanish revolted against Napoleon.

Teaching Strategy: *Teaching with Pictures: The Spanish Revolt* (page 482e)

OBJECTIVE 2. Describe Napoleon's losses in the invasion of Russia.

Teaching Strategy: *Discussing History: The Invasion of Russia* (page 482e)

OBJECTIVE 3. Evaluate Napoleon's achievements and failures.

Teaching Strategy: *Writing about History: Napoleon's Place in History* (page 482e)

Cooperative Learning

Divide the class into groups of four students. Ask students to review French involvement in Spain and the guerrilla war fought there (page 497). Tell them that wars against guerrillas are notoriously difficult to win as Napoleon (and the United States in Vietnam) found out. Have group members discuss ways that Napoleon might have handled the situation in Spain in order to have reduced his losses. Group members should consider both military and nonmilitary options. Have group members take notes on their discussions. Then reconvene the class and hold a class discussion on the subject.

ANSWERS TO

Reading a Diagram

about 422,000 men; about
10,000 men

■ BACKGROUND

The Battle of Borodino, the
only major battle Napoleon
fought in Russia, left 30,000
French soldiers and 50,000
Russian soldiers dead. Yet
it decided nothing. The
Russian army survived and
continued to retreat be-
yond Moscow.

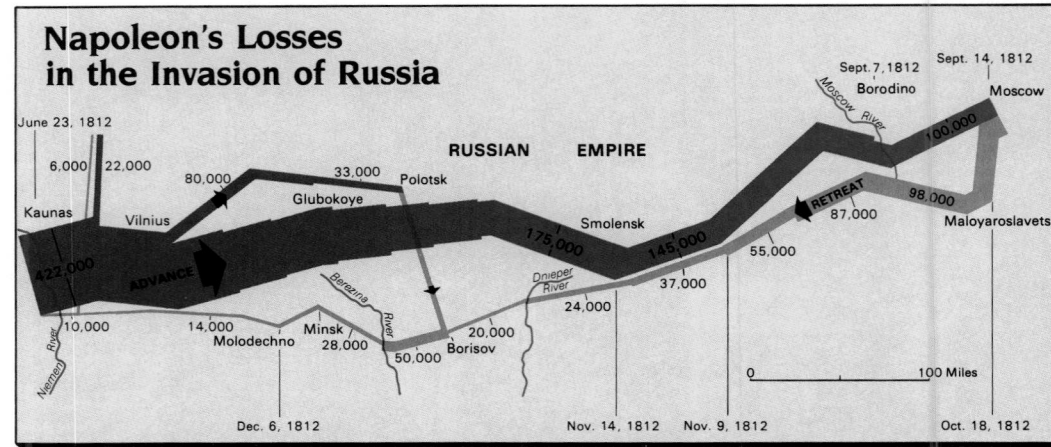

Napoleon's Losses in the Invasion of Russia

Reading a diagram *This diagram shows Napoleon's invasion of Russia. The Niemen River marked the Russian border. How many men did Napoleon have when he entered Russia in June 1812? When he left in December?*

In June 1812, Napoleon's army of more than 400,000 men took its first steps on the road to disaster. Many of these troops were not French. The emperor had drafted soldiers from all over Europe, and they felt little loyalty to Napoleon.

The Grand Army, as Napoleon called his forces, marched into Russia, but no Russian army came out to meet it. Instead, Czar Alexander pulled back his troops, refusing to be trapped in an uneven battle. As the Russians retreated toward Moscow, they burned grain fields and slaughtered livestock rather than leave them for the French. This **scorched-earth policy** of the Russians greatly weakened Napoleon's army. Desperate soldiers deserted the French army to search for scraps of food.

When Napoleon finally entered Moscow on September 14, he found the city in flames. Alexander destroyed Moscow rather than surrender it to the French. Napoleon stayed in the ruined city for five weeks, expecting the czar to make a peace offer, but that offer never came. By then, it was the middle of October, too late to advance farther and perhaps too late even to retreat.

Grimly, Napoleon ordered his starving army to turn back. As the snows began to fall in early November, Russian raiders mercilessly attacked Napoleon's ragged, retreating army. With freezing fingers, a French officer wrote a hurried message to his wife: "The Army marches covered in great

snowflakes . . . It is a mob without purpose, famished, fevered."

Soldiers staggered through the snow and dropped in their tracks from wounds, exhaustion, hunger, and cold. The temperature fell to 35° below zero. Finally, in the middle of December, the last survivors crossed the border out of Russia. Of his Grand Army, Napoleon had only 10,000 soldiers who were fit to fight.

A *coalition defeated* Napoleon.

Napoleon's enemies were quick to take advantage of his weakness. Britain, Russia, Prussia, Austria, and Sweden joined forces against him in the Grand Alliance.

In only a few months, Napoleon managed to raise another army. He faced his enemies outside the German city of Leipzig (LYPE-sihg) in October 1813. At this crucial point, Napoleon's brilliance failed him. He lost the Battle of Leipzig (also known as the Battle of Nations), and his army was cut to pieces.

Napoleon's empire crumbled quickly. By January 1814, armies of Austrians, Russians, and Prussians were pushing steadily toward Paris. In March, the Russian czar and the Prussian king led their troops in a triumphant parade through the French capital. Napoleon wanted to fight on, but his generals refused.

In April 1814, the defeated emperor gave up his throne and accepted the terms of surrender drawn up by Alexander I. The victors gave Napoleon a small pension and **exiled,** or banished, him to Elba, a tiny island off the Italian coast. The allies expected no further trouble from Napoleon. They were wrong. Napoleon had one last battle to fight, the Battle of Waterloo.

Napoleon returned briefly.

As Napoleon arrived in Elba, a Bourbon king arrived in Paris to rule France. It was Louis XVIII, brother of the guillotined king. (The young prince, Louis XVII, had died in prison.) However, the new king was chased from Paris only nine months after his return.

Napoleon escaped from Elba and, on March 1, 1815, landed in France. In a proclamation, he urged the French to rally to his cause. "Victory will march at full speed," he said. "You will be the liberators of your country."

Thousands of French people welcomed Napoleon back. The ranks of his army swelled with volunteers as it approached Paris. Within days, Napoleon was again emperor of France. Louis XVIII fled to the border.

The countries of the Grand Alliance quickly marshaled their armies. The British army, led by the Duke of Wellington, prepared for battle near the village of Waterloo in Belgium.

On June 18, 1815, Napoleon attacked. The British army defended its ground all day. Late in the afternoon, the Prussian army arrived. Together, the British and Prussians launched an attack against the French. Napoleon's exhausted troops gave way. The British and Prussians chased them from the field.

Thus ended Napoleon's last bid for power, called the Hundred Days. Taking no chances this time, the British shipped the prisoner Napoleon to St.

Decisions in History

After Napoleon's defeat at Waterloo, British leaders debated what to do with him. Should they give him passage to America? Asylum in England? Exile to St. Helena? Execution? Or some other alternative? If you were prime minister, which option would you choose, and why?

Helena, a remote island in the South Atlantic. Here Napoleon lived in lonely exile for six years, writing his memoirs. He died in 1821 of a stomach ailment, perhaps cancer. A short time before his death, he attempted to justify all he had done during his life:

Such work as mine is not done twice in a century. I have saved the Revolution as it lay dying. I have cleansed it of its crimes, and have held it up to the people shining with fame. I have inspired France and Europe with new ideas that will never be forgotten.

Without doubt, Napoleon was a military genius and a brilliant administrator. Yet all his victories must be measured against the millions of lives that were lost in his wars. Of his many achievements, only his law code and some of his reforms in France's government proved lasting—and they were not won on the battlefield. A later French statesman and writer, Alexis de Tocqueville, summed up Napoleon's character by saying, "He was as great as a man can be without virtue."

Section REVIEW 4

Define: (a) blockade, (b) guerrilla, (c) scorched-earth policy, (d) exile
Identify: (a) Continental System, (b) Peninsular War, (c) Grand Alliance, (d) the Hundred Days, (e) Waterloo
Answer:
1. List Napoleon's three misjudgments.
2. (a) How did Napoleon try to weaken Britain? (b) What were the results?
3. How did the Peninsular War weaken France?
4. Briefly describe Napoleon's invasion of Russia.
5. How did Napoleon fall from power in 1814?
6. (a) What was the reaction to Napoleon's return in France? (b) In the countries of the Grand Alliance?
7. (a) How was Napoleon finally defeated? (b) What happened to him afterward?

Critical Thinking
8. Reread the quotation from Napoleon above on this page. Evaluate his claims that he saved the French Revolution and inspired Europe with new ideas.

499

■ **BACKGROUND**
Some scholars have suggested that Napoleon was slowly poisoned with arsenic by his British guards.

ANSWERS TO
Section Review 4

Define:
(a) closing ports to shipping (b) civilian engaged in irregular warfare (c) destroying possible provisions (d) banish

Identify:
(a) Napoleon's policy intended to destroy British economy (b) French war fought with Spain (c) Britain, Russia, Austria, and Sweden (d) Napoleon's last bid for power after exile to Elba (e) where Napoleon was defeated

Answer:
1. trying to cut off trade with Britain; planning to make his brother king of Spain; invading Russia

2. (a) by imposing a blockade (b) weakened economies of own lands

3. wasted money and men

4. Refer students to page 498.

5. His enemies joined forces.

6. (a) Thousands welcomed him. (b) gathering of armies

7. (a) by the British and Prussians at Waterloo (b) exiled to St. Helena where he died

8. Look for answers to consider the extent to which Napoleon replaced one form of tyranny with another, Napoleon's administrative skills, and the lasting achievements of his rule.

Concluding the Chapter

1. **Chapter Closer**
Have students outline the four phases of the French revolution by identifying each phase and listing three significant events for each.

2. **Reteaching the Chapter**
   a. Preparing a Time Line
   Have students prepare a time line covering the main events between 1789 and 1815.
   b. Summarizing
   Have students write paragraphs summarizing Napoleon's rise to power and his acquisition of an empire.
   c. Identifying Main Ideas
   Have students identify Napoleon's three disastrous misjudgments.

Answers to Chapter Review appear on pages 482e–482f.

Summary

1. The French monarchy faced a crisis. Under the Old Regime, French society was divided into three estates. The First and Second estates had both political power and special privileges. The Third Estate—the majority of the people—had a wide variety of grievances against the Old Regime. When Louis XVI called a meeting of the Estates General in 1789, the Third Estate proclaimed a constitutional monarchy. The Paris mob stormed the Bastille.

2. Revolution brought reform and terror. By 1791, the National Assembly had proclaimed the equality of all men, reformed the government, and weakened the Church. In 1793, radicals won power, declared a republic, and executed Louis XVI. Their citizen-army defeated a coalition of enemies. Led by Robespierre, the radicals condemned thousands to death as enemies of the republic during the Reign of Terror. In 1795, the radicals were overthrown by the more moderate Directory.

3. Napoleon conquered much of Europe. General Napoleon Bonaparte overthrew the Directory in 1799. In 1804, he made himself emperor. He brought stability to France and set up a single legal system under the Napoleonic Code. Napoleon expanded his control over most of Europe.

4. Napoleon's empire collapsed. Napoleon's Continental System weakened European economies. A guerrilla war in Spain drained money and men from France's army. Napoleon's invasion of Russia ended in a disastrous retreat. In 1814, Napoleon was defeated by an alliance of powers. Although he returned briefly in 1815, he met his final defeat at Waterloo.

Reviewing the Facts

1. Define the following terms:
   a. radical
   b. coalition
   c. coup
   d. plebiscite
   e. guerrilla
   f. exile

2. Explain the importance of each of the following names, dates, places, or terms:
   a. July 14, 1789
   b. Louis XVI
   c. Old Regime
   d. estates
   e. sans-culottes
   f. Marie Antoinette
   g. Great Fear
   h. emigrés
   i. Jacobin Club
   j. guillotine
   k. Robespierre
   l. Reign of Terror
   m. Bonaparte
   n. Continental System
   o. Waterloo

3. What were the four stages of the French Revolution, from 1789 to 1815?

4. Describe French society under the Old Regime.

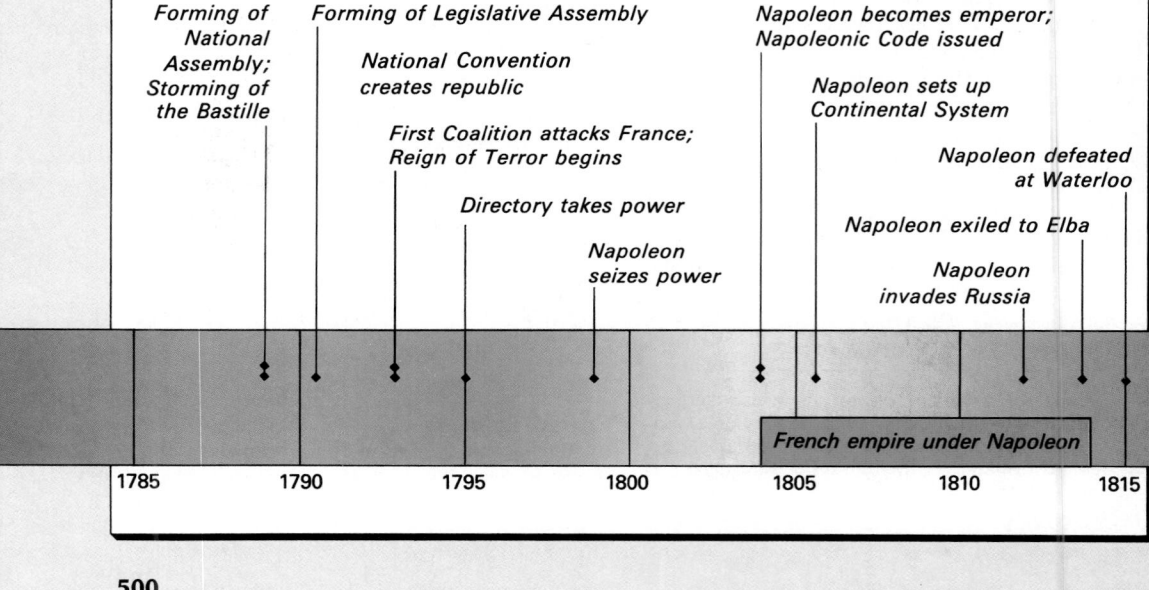

Forming of National Assembly; Storming of the Bastille

Forming of Legislative Assembly

National Convention creates republic

First Coalition attacks France; Reign of Terror begins

Directory takes power

Napoleon seizes power

Napoleon becomes emperor; Napoleonic Code issued

Napoleon sets up Continental System

Napoleon defeated at Waterloo

Napoleon exiled to Elba

Napoleon invades Russia

French empire under Napoleon

1785 1790 1795 1800 1805 1810 1815

500

5. (a) Why was Louis XVI forced to call a meeting of the Estates General in 1789? (b) What was the result?
6. What form of government did the National Assembly set up?
7. (a) Explain how the revolution steadily grew more violent. (b) What form of government did the Jacobin National Convention establish? (c) Briefly describe the Reign of Terror.
8. Trace the steps by which Napoleon rose to power.

Basic Skills

1. **Summarizing** Write a paragraph summarizing the information on page 484 on the makeup of the Third Estate.
2. **Interpreting a map** Answer the following questions, using the map on page 495 and your text for reference: (a) What countries were a basic part of Napoleon's empire? (b) What countries were under his control and how much support could he count on from them? (c) Which were the allied countries and to what extent could he depend on them?
3. **Interpreting a time line** Explain the significance of each of the items on the time line on page 500.

Researching and Reporting Skills

Writing a Historical Essay
Phase 3: Writing the Essay The essay should include a title, introductory paragraph, supporting paragraphs, and concluding paragraph. The tone should be persuasive.

1. **Selecting paragraph topics** Based on your notes, make an outline indicating the main idea of each paragraph and the details that will support your thesis.
2. **Writing an introductory paragraph** Write an introductory paragraph, stating your topic and your thesis.
3. **Writing expository paragraphs** Write supporting paragraphs as needed to present the points that support your thesis.
4. **Writing a concluding paragraph** Write a paragraph that will persuade the reader that the points presented support your thesis. Choose a title that will interest the reader in your topic. List your

bibliographical references, using standard citation form.

Critical Thinking

1. **Interpreting** The Abbé Siéyès suggested that the meeting of the Third Estate be renamed the National Assembly. What was the significance of this change?
2. **Identifying viewpoints** For each of the following people, write a sentence describing that person's point of view on the revolution: (a) Louis XVI, (b) Robespierre, (c) a highly placed member of the clergy, (d) the wife of a sans-culotte.
3. **Analyzing economics** Identify three economic factors that contributed to the revolution in France and describe their impact.
4. **Synthesizing** The revolution in France promoted a new sense of nationalism. (a) What examples of this can you find? (b) How did these events increase nationalistic feelings?
5. **Evaluating conflicting opinions** The last paragraph of the chapter comes to several conclusions about Napoleon's achievements. The quotation from Napoleon expresses a different opinion. (a) Write a paragraph discussing each opinion. (b) Write a third paragraph expressing your own conclusions.

Perspectives on Past and Present

Napoleon's invasion of Russia was neither the first nor the last that ended in defeat. (a) What invasions in the early eighteenth and mid-twentieth centuries met the same fate? (b) What similarities in purpose and outcome can you find among those invasions?

Investigating History

1. Dickens's novel *A Tale of Two Cities* is set in the context of the French Revolution. (a) Read a portion of the book to see how it presents events. (b) Write a brief report on its accuracy and particular point of view.
2. Select one of the important battles of the Napoleonic wars (Austerlitz, Trafalgar, Waterloo, or others). Study the battle thoroughly in a historical atlas and other sources. Describe the military strategy and tactics of the battle, using a diagram on the chalkboard to illustrate your talk.

501

CHAPTER
Evaluation

Chapter Test 21, Alternate Chapter Test 21, and Computer Test Bank Chapter 21 Test can be used to evaluate your students' understanding of this chapter.

ANSWERS TO
Geographic Theme

1. (a) Paris located on Seine River, Versailles in swampy area **(b)** Paris layout not precise; Versailles planned in regular layout of streets and avenues

2. Paris developed during Middle Ages when religion was central to peoples' lives. Versailles was built to glorify the king.

3. Versailles was a secular center, representing worldliness, and its planned streets and layout accommodated expansion; also recognized the need for planning.

Geographic Theme: Place

How did planning change the growth of cities?

Every city has its own unique character. Located in a particular kind of natural environment, it also has patterns of human use specific to that location. The physical and cultural characteristics that give a locale its identity are known to geographers as *place*.

The map of a city reveals much about its character. The maps of Paris and Versailles are a contrast in setting. To historians, they also show the difference between one historic era and another.

Paris began as a Gallic settlement on an island in the Seine River. Its location where roads join to cross the river made it a center of trade. When its feudal lord Hugh Capet was chosen king of France in 987, Paris became the royal capital. The construction and restoration of public buildings in the 1500's improved the central city, but most of it remained crowded and run-down. Even though Paris in 1789 was Europe's second largest city, its narrow and twisted streets reflected its medieval past rather than its future as a modern capital.

Eleven miles from Paris, the city of Versailles came into being after Louis XIV built his royal residence there. The site was not a favorable one. One courtier described it as "the saddest, the most unattractive of places, without views, any woods or streams, nothing but shifting sand and swamps." That was before Louis brought architects, designers, and landscape gardeners to transform the area into a new capital away from Paris. Swamps became gardens, and a landscape that improved upon nature provided a view. In the midst of this scene stood the great palace, with a planned town nearby. The gardens and orderly avenues of Versailles anticipated the modern city and the new age of urban planning.

1. (a) Compare the sites of Paris and Versailles. **(b)** How do the physical layouts of Paris and Versailles differ?
2. Paris is centered around the Cathedral of Notre Dame, whereas Versailles is centered around the palace. What do those facts show about the character of the cities?
3. In what ways does the town of Versailles represent the transition to a new age?

Paris in 1789

Champs Elysées · Palais des Tuileries · Louvre · Champs de Mars · Hôtel des Invalides · Palais de Justice · Hôtel de Ville · Faubourg · Notre Dame · Bastille · École Militaire · St. Antoine

0   3000 Feet

Versailles in 1789

Grand Trianon · Petit Trianon · Grand Canal · Fountain d'Apollo · Château · Place d'Armes · Aven

0   5000 Feet

Historical Themes

A number of influential leaders dominated European politics and thought during the period 1558 to 1815. This era also produced important cultural developments in England and France and major milestones in the rise of democratic ideas.

Individuals and History

The period between 1558 and 1815 produced a number of people who played a key role in shaping modern history. Elizabeth I, Peter the Great, Louis XIV, Voltaire, and Napoleon were individuals whose actions had far-reaching consequences.

Elizabeth I and Peter the Great were rulers who identified and dealt with the great issues facing them. Elizabeth found a compromise for England's religious conflicts, checked the power of Spain, and ruled in cooperation with Parliament. Peter ended Russia's isolation by importing ideas from western Europe and gaining an outlet to the sea.

Unlike Elizabeth and Peter, Louis XIV and Napoleon failed to achieve their objectives. Both rulers held enormous power and tried to use it to dominate Europe. Ultimately their ambitions exceeded their economic and military resources. Both Louis and Napoleon faced crushing defeats.

Voltaire commanded ideas rather than wealth or power. His writings about reason, justice, and liberty helped to end the Old Regime and inspired democratic revolutions in America and France.

Cultural Development

The early modern era saw the changes inspired by the Renaissance lead to cultural golden ages in England and France. England's victory over the Spanish Armada released a burst of confidence and pride. Prosperity from trade made London a vibrant setting for Shakespeare's work. His plays became masterpieces of world literature.

The golden age of France at Versailles owed its existence to the patronage of Louis XIV. The Sun King invited artists, playwrights, and composers to his palace. Royal courts throughout Europe imitated French styles of art and fashion.

Rise of Democratic Ideas

The two and a half centuries between the crowning of Elizabeth I and the fall of Napoleon mark an important era in the rise of democratic ideas. At the start of this era, most Europeans were subjects of absolute monarchs. When Louis XIV boasted, "I am the state," he expressed the prevailing view that placed the state above individuals and the ruler above the law.

The first major gains for democracy occurred in England. The long struggle between Stuart monarchs and Parliament ended in revolution and the execution of the king. The Habeas Corpus Act and Bill of Rights established certain rights for individuals and Parliament. The 1700's saw the rise of parliamentary rule, the cabinet system, and leadership by the prime minister, who was head of the majority party.

Britain's success in limiting royal power inspired political thinkers in the Enlightenment. Both Rousseau and Jefferson argued that government is based on the consent of the governed. Montesquieu emphasized that powers in a government should be separated to avoid any threat to liberty.

The American and French revolutions translated the new political ideas into reality. The American Declaration of Independence and the French Declaration of the Rights of Man identified individual liberties that governments must respect. The United States Constitution created a republic in which citizens had a voice in governing. Adding the Bill of Rights to the Constitution assured the protection of individual rights that are the basis of liberty.

Analyzing Historical Themes

1. (a) What individuals in this unit do you think had the greatest historical influence? (b) Does any of that influence still exist?
2. (a) What factors might account for the golden ages that developed in Elizabethan England and the France of Louis XIV? (b) Which age do you think was more enduring and why?
3. (a) What do you think were the main causes for the rise of democratic ideas as described in this unit? (b) What were the main effects?

503

ANSWERS TO
Analyzing Historical Themes

1. Answers will vary.

2. (a) England: victory over Spanish Armada increased national pride and confidence; London flourished from trade and served as setting for Shakespeare's plays; France: Louis XIV patronized artists, playwrights, and composers; royal courts throughout Europe copied French styles of art and fashion **(b)** Answers will vary.

3. (a) Answers will vary but may mention the focus on the individual inspired by Renaissance, Britain's success in limiting royal power, people's desire to have a voice in government, Voltaire's writings, economic prosperity. **(b)** Answers will vary but may include limitation of royal power, establishment of rights for individuals and their representatives in government, rise of parliamentary rule, cabinet system, and leadership by the prime minister.

UNIT Evaluation

Unit Test VI and Alternate Unit VI Test can be used to evaluate your students' understanding of this unit.

Chapters

"The Docks of Cardiff," by Lionel Walden

	1700	1740	1780

Political and Governmental Life

◄ **1740–1780**
Maria Theresa, ruler of the Hapsburg empire, queen of Hungary and Bohemia, and archduchess of Austria

◄ **1811–1824**
Bolívar leads Latin American struggle for freedom

Economic and Technological Life

1700's
Britain modernizes agriculture

1700's
Inventions mechanize the textile industry

1763
Britain wins India from France

1815
Congress of Vienna

Spinning jenny

Social and Cultural Life

1750's–1900's
Industrialism brings rise of middle class

1800's ►
Nationalism and romanticism prevail

Unit VII

The Age of European Dominance

Historical Themes

Technology and History New inventions and new forms of power led to a revolution in industry and transportation in Britain. The result was a vast increase in production of goods and world trade.

The Impact of Ideas The idea of nationalism led subject peoples in Latin America and the Austrian empire to seek independence. In Italy and Germany, nationalism led to unification.

Continuity and Change Periods of stability alternated with periods of change in the 1800's. Conservative leaders sought to restore the old regime, while others sought social and political reforms.

Economics and History The Industrial Revolution launched a new economic age based on mass production and trade and dominated by nations that became industrialized.

1820	1860	1900

1857
Sepoys rebel against British rule in India

1875–1900
Imperial powers divide Africa into colonies

1900–1914
Nationalist uprisings in Balkans

1871
Germany united as a nation

Chinese emperor's robe

1840's
Famine in Ireland causes emigration

1873
Japan begins to industrialize

The luxury liner Mauretania

1848
Marx views history as class struggle

1869
Suez Canal opens

1914
United States opens Panama Canal

Charles Dickens's Oliver Twist

Renoir's Lady with a Parasol

1865
Slavery ends in the United States

The World about 1800

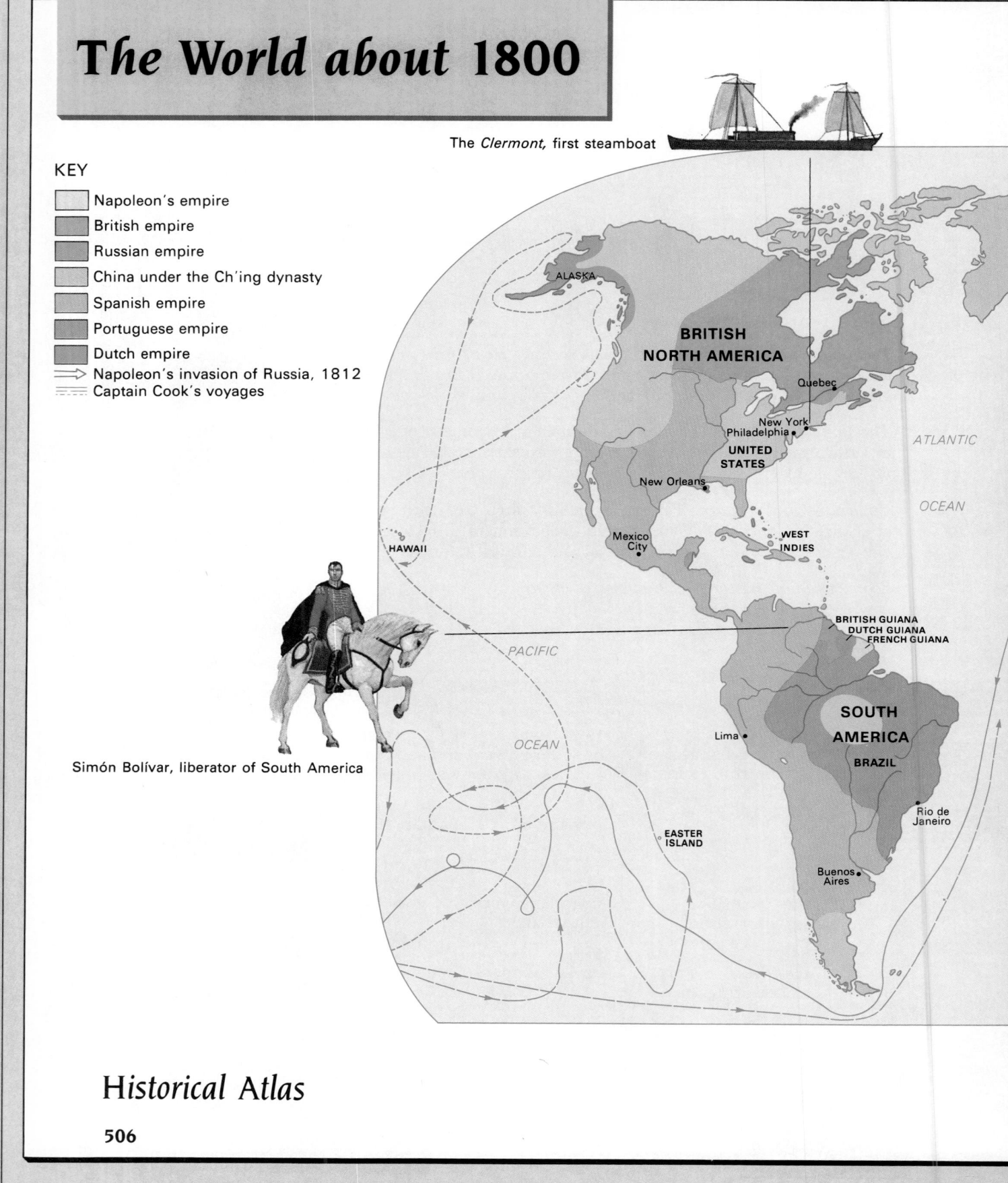

The *Clermont,* first steamboat

KEY

- Napoleon's empire
- British empire
- Russian empire
- China under the Ch'ing dynasty
- Spanish empire
- Portuguese empire
- Dutch empire
- ⟹ Napoleon's invasion of Russia, 1812
- Captain Cook's voyages

ALASKA

BRITISH NORTH AMERICA

Quebec

New York
Philadelphia

UNITED STATES

New Orleans

Mexico City

HAWAII

WEST INDIES

ATLANTIC

OCEAN

BRITISH GUIANA
DUTCH GUIANA
FRENCH GUIANA

PACIFIC

OCEAN

Lima

SOUTH AMERICA

BRAZIL

Rio de Janeiro

Simón Bolívar, liberator of South America

EASTER ISLAND

Buenos Aires

Historical Atlas

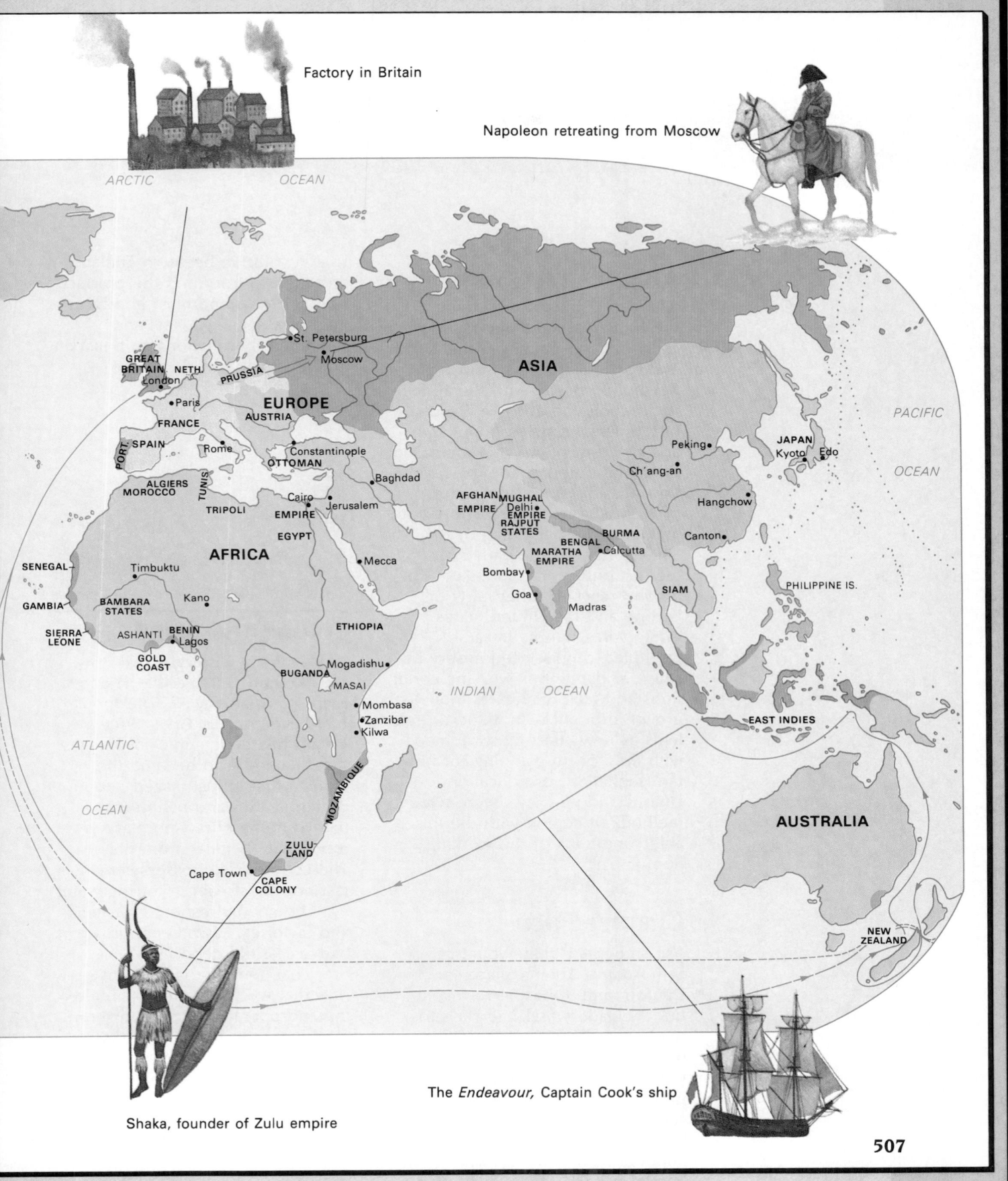

Factory in Britain

Napoleon retreating from Moscow

ARCTIC OCEAN

GREAT BRITAIN
London
NETH.
PRUSSIA
St. Petersburg
Moscow
ASIA
EUROPE
Paris
FRANCE
AUSTRIA
PORT.
SPAIN
Rome
Constantinople
OTTOMAN
ALGIERS
MOROCCO
TUNIS
TRIPOLI
EMPIRE
Baghdad
Cairo
Jerusalem
EGYPT
AFRICA
Mecca
SENEGAL
Timbuktu
GAMBIA
BAMBARA STATES
Kano
SIERRA LEONE
ASHANTI
BENIN
Lagos
GOLD COAST
ETHIOPIA
BUGANDA
Mogadishu
MASAI
Mombasa
Zanzibar
Kilwa
INDIAN OCEAN
AFGHAN EMPIRE
MUGHAL
Delhi
EMPIRE
RAJPUT STATES
BENGAL
MARATHA EMPIRE
Calcutta
Bombay
Goa
Madras
BURMA
SIAM
Peking
Ch'ang-an
JAPAN
Kyoto
Edo
Hangchow
Canton
PACIFIC OCEAN
PHILIPPINE IS.
EAST INDIES
ATLANTIC OCEAN
MOZAMBIQUE
ZULU-LAND
Cape Town
CAPE COLONY
AUSTRALIA
NEW ZEALAND

Shaka, founder of Zulu empire

The *Endeavour,* Captain Cook's ship

507

The Industrial Revolution

Chapter Overview

Chapter 22 traces the growth of the Industrial Revolution, especially in Great Britain in the 1700's and early 1800's. The Industrial Revolution began with the agricultural revolution and the enclosure of farmland. A rising population and new inventions that increased industrial output made the revolution possible. Industrialization brought changes in transportation, including the beginning of the Railway Age. In the early nineteenth century, the Industrial Revolution reached other parts of Europe and the United States. While some people became wealthier, others faced misery because of dangerous working conditions and factory abuses. Industrial growth brought with it social problems as new cities mushroomed with little or no planning for housing, sanitation, or education. Unions and new laws were two methods of coping with the miserable conditions of the working poor.

Chapter Focus

Ask students if they would call Sam Adams, Thomas Jefferson, Danton, and Robespierre revolutionary leaders. Ask the class to read pages 508–509. Would students call Joseph Pease a revolutionary leader? Pease would probably not have considered himself a leader in a historic revolution. Yet he was part of an important revolutionary change in human history—the substitution of power-driven machine tools for hand tools and animal power. This chapter describes how the Industrial Revolution began in England and then transformed the production and distribution of goods, created new social classes, and redefined the relationship between employers and workers.

Many factors aided industrial growth. 1

Setting the Stage

Geography in History: Great Britain's Resources (Objective 1) Show Map Transparency 72, *The Industrial Revolution in Great Britain.* Britain had geographic advantages that enabled it to become the world's first industrialized nation. Britain is an island nation with many fine harbors—no place is more than 90 miles from the sea. The country also possesses many fast-flowing streams. Flowing water was the energy resource for mills and factories. Also, Great Britain had accessible deposits of iron ore, coal, and limestone—materials that were essential for building and operating steam-powered machinery. By 1850, networks of canals and railways carried materials to cities, factories, and ports. Ask students to think of factors needed to begin an industrial revolution other than geographic advantages.

Unit VII The Age of European Dominance
THEME Economic and political changes in Europe between 1700 and 1914

Chapter 22 The Industrial Revolution 1700–1850
FOCUS The concept of a technological revolution

★ Advanced
● Basic

	SECTION 1	SECTION 2	SECTION 3	SECTION 4
Objectives	1. List the geographic advantages that helped Great Britain become the world's first industrialized nation. 2. Identify the enclosure movement and explain its importance. 3. Explain how a good banking system gave Britain an important economic advantage.	1. Identify the inventors and inventions that revolutionized the textile industry. 2. Identify cause and effect relationships among technological developments.	1. Describe how Britain's railroad age began. 2. Assess the impact of railroads on life in Great Britain. 3. Identify factors that slowed the spread of industrialization to America and Europe.	1. Link industrialization with urbanization. 2. Describe the living and working conditions of British factory workers during the early 1800's.
Setting the Stage	Unit VII time line Geography in History: Great Britain's Resources Transparency 72	Britain's textile industry	The impact of canals and railroads on Britain's industrial development	Manchester's transformation to an industrial city
Teaching Strategies	Discussing History: The Enclosure Movement Economics and History: British Banks Check for Understanding	Skill Building: Making a Chart Skill Building: Relating Cause and Effect Check for Understanding	Economics and History: The Liverpool-Manchester Railway Writing about History: The Impact of the Railroads Geography in History: The Spread of Industrialization Outline Map 9 Check for Understanding	Writing about History: Problems of Urbanization Economics and History: A Manchester Family's Weekly Budget Check for Understanding
Guided Practice	Transparency 72 Q&A Section Review 1	Section Review 2	Section Review 3	Section Review 4
Independent Practice Worksheets	Independent Practice 22.1 Vocabulary 22	Independent Practice 22.2	Independent Practice 22.3 Basic Skills 22	Independent Practice 22.4 Geography Skills 22 Critical Thinking 22
Enrichment	1. Primary Source: Voices 22.1 2. Researching for Points	1. Primary Source: Voices 22.2 2. Preparing a Report: Inventors and Inventions 3. Researching for Points	1. Primary Source: Voices 22.3 2. Researching for Points	1. Primary Source: Voices 22.4 2. ★Analyzing a Quotation: Alexis de Tocqueville 3. Researching for Points

Chapter Closer	
●**Reteaching Activities**	Outlining, Reading a Map
Chapter Review	Summary, Reviewing the Facts, Basic Skills, Researching and Reporting Skills, Critical Thinking, Perspectives on Past and Present, Investigating History
Chapter Evaluation	Chapter Test 22, Alternate Chapter Test 22, Computer Test Bank Chapter 22 Test

Teaching Strategies

Discussing History: The Enclosure Movement (Objective 2) The enclosure movement enabled landowners to consolidate small farms into large, efficient units. By the 1850's, about 500 families controlled half of the land in Great Britain. Another 1,300 families owned most of the remaining land. The consolidation of farm lands permitted large landowners such as Charles Townshend to try new agricultural techniques. Stress that the enclosure movement enabled Britain to produce more food. It also forced many small farmers off the land, which caused the rapid growth of cities and created a large supply of workers for the new industries.

Economics and History: British Banks (Objective 3) Britain had the most highly developed banking system in Europe. The Bank of England, founded in 1694, was the world's first modern bank. It accepted deposits and made loans on a national scale. In addition, it also printed bank notes that were widely accepted as substitutes for gold and silver. Between 1780 and 1815, the number of banks increased from 300 to more than 700. Britain's commercial prosperity enabled banks to make loans at low interest rates. Interest is a fee or charge for using money. Interest rates go down as the supply of money increases. Ask students how low interest rates for bank loans might stimulate an industrial revolution. During the eighteenth century, the interest rate on loans dropped from 10 to 3 percent. Inexpensive loans also enabled entrepreneurs to start new business enterprises.

Check for Understanding Have students explain how geography, the enclosure movement, and the banking system established a foundation for Britain's industrial growth.

Enrichment Activities

1. **Reading a Primary Source** Assign Voices from the Past Resource Book 22.1.
2. **Researching for Bonus Points** What was the Norfolk rotation? (the crop rotation invented by Charles Townshend to improve harvests on his Norfolk estate called for the successive planting of wheat, turnips, barley, and clover)

Britain led in the rise of industry. 2

Setting the Stage

In the textile industry, short fibers are spun into lengths of thread, which are then woven into cloth. The British textile industry produced only woolen cloth prior to the eighteenth century. Wool was important in British life. However, imported cotton from India steadily grew in popularity. Cotton offered a number of advantages. It was cheaper, lighter, and cooler than wool, and could be painted or printed with bright designs. British spinners and weavers could not produce enough cotton cloth to meet the rising demand for it. Enterprising merchants and inventors realized that they could make tremendous profits by finding a way to speed up the work of spinning and weaving.

Teaching Strategies

Skill Building: Making a Chart (Objective 1) Draw a chart with three columns and five rows. Label the columns *Invention/Date, Inventor,* and *What Invention Did.* Fill in the chart as a class activity. A completed chart is provided below.

Invention/ Date	Inventor	What Invention Did
flying shuttle 1733	John Kay	allowed a weaver to double weaving speed
spinning jenny 1764	James Hargreaves	allowed one spinner to work six or eight threads
water-frame 1768	Richard Arkwright	used water-power to drive spinning wheels
spinning mule 1779	Samuel Crompton	combined spinning jenny and water-frame, made strong thread
power loom 1785	Edmund Cartwright	speeded up weaving process

Skill Building: Relating Cause and Effect (Objective 2) Call on students to suggest one or more effects of the following technological developments:

1. Spinners and weavers could not keep up with the demand for cloth.
2. The flying shuttle allowed weavers to weave thread faster.
3. Machines became too large and expensive for home use.
4. Eli Whitney invented a machine to remove seeds from raw cotton.

Check for Understanding Have students give examples of how factories, inventions, and entrepreneurs contributed to a revolution in the textile industry.

Enrichment Activities

1. **Reading a Primary Source**
   Assign Voices from the Past Resource Book 22.2.
2. **Preparing a Report**
   Ask students to report on one of the inventors or inventions discussed in this section.
3. **Researching for Bonus Points**
   Where did Boulton and Watt manufacture their steam engines? (at the Soho Works in Birmingham)

Industry grew and spread to new lands.   3

Setting the Stage

Canals and railroads revolutionized transportation and industry during the nineteenth century. For example, before the railroad age began, horse-drawn wagons rarely traveled more than 20 miles in a day. In contrast, the first railroads carried passengers and freight at speeds of more than 30 miles an hour.

Teaching Strategies

Economics and History: The Liverpool-Manchester Railway (Objective 1) Ask students to recall the pioneering work of Richard Trevithick and George Stephenson (page 515). Have students locate the cities of Liverpool and Manchester on the map on page 518. Ask why merchants wanted a railway between these two cities. By the late 1820's, canals carried 1,300 tons of raw cotton and cotton goods from the port of Liverpool to factories in Manchester. The trip took two days. The high cost of transporting goods between Liverpool and Manchester prompted merchants and factory owners to connect the two cities with a railroad line. It took eight years to plan and construct the line. It was finally opened on September 15, 1830. A million spectators lined the roadbed to witness the historic event. When the first engine roared by at 24 miles an hour, spectators were amazed.

The Liverpool-Manchester line was a huge success. Within a short time, a dozen trains carried more than 1,000 passengers between the two cities each day. Freight trains were soon carrying more goods than the canals and road coaches combined. By the late 1840's, railways linked most of Britain's major industrial towns. Refer students to the graphs on page 515 to show the sharp rise in cotton, coal, and pig iron production during the railroad age. Coal and iron were needed for building railways and powering the steam engines.

Writing about History: The Impact of the Railroads (Objective 2) *Prewriting* Ask students what effects railroads had on life in Great Britain and write students' responses on the board. Discuss the four major effects described on page 516. *Writing* Ask each student to assume the role of a writer from the *Manchester Guardian* in 1840. The editor has asked for an article entitled "The Age of Railroads—Ten Years of Change." Suggest that students use "quotations" from imaginary interviews with a coal merchant, a textile factory owner, a canal operator, a farmer, a railroad engineer, and a family traveling to a seaside resort.

Geography in History: The Spread of Industrialization (Objective 3) Ask what factors slowed the spread of industrialization to Europe and America. (a combination of restrictive laws, the disruption caused by the Napoleonic wars, and the large supply of cheap British goods) Nevertheless, industrialized "islands" soon dotted the European and American landscapes. Distribute Outline Map 9: Physical Europe. Have students use atlases to locate and label the Ruhr Valley, Po Valley, Milan, Frankfort, and Lyons. Ask what geographic factors encouraged the development of industry in these areas. (harbors, rivers for water power, natural resources)

Check for Understanding Ask students to explain how canals and railroads helped promote industrial development.

Enrichment Activities

1. **Reading a Primary Source**
   Assign Voices from the Past Resource Book 22.3.
2. **Researching for Bonus Points**
   Who was the first person killed by a train? (William Huskisson; he was a Member of Parliament who was accidentally struck by a train during the opening ceremonies of the Liverpool-Manchester Railway.)

Industry changed ways of life. 4

Setting the Stage

Read this excerpt from *The Manchester Guardian*, November 17, 1832. "The manufacturing system as it exists in Great Britain, and the inconceivably rapid increase of immense towns under it, are without previous parallel in the history of the world." Ask what other new development was "without previous parallel."

The Industrial Revolution brought about a major transformation—urbanization. For centuries most Europeans had lived in rural areas. The factory system attracted workers to rapidly growing cities. For example, Manchester's population increased by 41 percent between 1821 and 1831. Ask students what possible problems rapid urbanization might cause.

Teaching Strategies

Writing about History: Problems of Urbanization (Objective 1) *Prewriting* Have students read, "Problems arose as cities grew" (pages 519–520). Use students' suggestions to develop concept extensions (clustering) on the board. Note the sharp contrasts between the technological marvels and wealth of cities and their environmental pollution and human poverty. Urban life made a vivid impression on the contemporary writers who flocked to see the big cities. *Writing* Divide the class into four groups. Assign each group one of the following roles: American business investors, southern England farmers, Oxford history professors, and French philosophers. Ask each group to write a report describing their impressions after visiting Manchester. Have students read their reports to the class and com-

pare and contrast the points of view.

Economics and History: A Manchester Family's Weekly Budget (Objective 2) The Factory Commission Report (Vol. XX, pages 39–40) of 1833 contains a wealth of information about living and working conditions in Britain's new industrial cities. For example, the "B" family included five children. They lived in a four-room home in Manchester. The father and his fourteen-year-old daughter worked in a cotton mill. Reprint and distribute the following "B" family budget. (Costs have been converted into dollar equivalents.)

"B" Family Weekly Budget

Item	Cost
Butter, 1½ lb.	.31
Tea, 1½ oz.	.09
Bread	1.12
Oatmeal	.13
Bacon, 1¼ lb.	.18
Potatoes	.33
Milk, one quart a day	.43
Meat on Sunday, 1 lb.	.14
Sugar, 1½ lb.	.18
Pepper, mustard, salt	.06
Soap and candles	.25
Coal	.38
Rent per week	.87
TOTAL	4.47
TOTAL INCOME	6.25
DEDUCT EXPENSES	4.47
Leaves for clothing, sickness of seven persons, schooling, etc., a surplus of	1.78

After students have examined this budget, have them answer the following questions: What item consumes the largest percent of the "B" family budget? Does the "B" family have a well-balanced diet? Does the "B" family income support an adequate standard of living?

Check for Understanding Ask students to list three ways in which the Industrial Revolution changed life in Great Britain.

Enrichment Activities

1. **Reading a Primary Source** Assign Voices from the Past Resource Book 22.4.

2. **Analyzing a Quotation** After visiting Manchester, Alexis de Tocqueville wrote: "From this foul drain the greatest stream of human industry flows out to fertilize the whole world. From this filthy sewer pure gold flows. Here humanity attains its most complete development and its most brutish, here civilization works its miracles and civilized man is turned into a savage." Ask advanced students to assess the validity of this statement.

3. **Researching for Bonus Points** What name was given to the riot that took place at St. Peter's field on August 16, 1819? For what battle was the riot named? (The Peterloo Massacre; the battle of Waterloo)

ANSWERS TO

Chapter Review 22

Reviewing the Facts

1. (a) period of increased output of machine-made goods (b) process by which landowners rented land to tenant farmers and fenced in their land (c) keeping a field fertile by planting different crops on it each year (d) person who organizes, manages, and takes on the risk of a business (e) group of workers speaking for all workers in a trade to bargain for better working conditions and higher wages (f) scientific approach to farming; improved production and released farm workers for manufacturing jobs (g) simple machine that allowed one spinner to work six or eight threads at one time (h) machine that used waterpower rather than human energy to drive spinning wheels (i) machine combining features of spinning jenny and water-frame; made improved thread (j) invention that speeded up weaving

2. (a) Fewer people went hungry, nutrition improved, and population increased, providing more workers. (b) forced many small farmers to move to cities and become part of industrial labor force (c) supplied extra workers that new factories and businesses needed; increased demand for goods (d) Fine harbors and navigable rivers gave Britain access to raw materials and markets. (e) Great Britain was rich in waterpower, coal, and iron ore, all important for industrialization.

3. From the flying shuttle came a need to produce a better spinning machine, the spinning jenny. Both the spinning jenny and the flying shuttle were hand-operated machines, so a water-frame was invented. Combining the features of the spinning jenny and the water-frame led to the spinning mule.

4. (a) increased production of raw cotton needed for British mills (b) made it possible for people to have a source of power that could be used anywhere

5. Businesses needed improved methods of transporting raw materials and finished products.

6. (a) As the middle class grew, conditions for workers seemed to decline. (b) *laissez-faire* (c) joined together in unions

Basic Skills

1. (a) sharp increase in production and consumption (b) Technological inventions were a factor in each trend; cotton gin increased consumption of cotton; steam engines needed coal; growth in industry created more demand for railroads, machinery, and buildings, and this in turn increased demand for iron.

2.

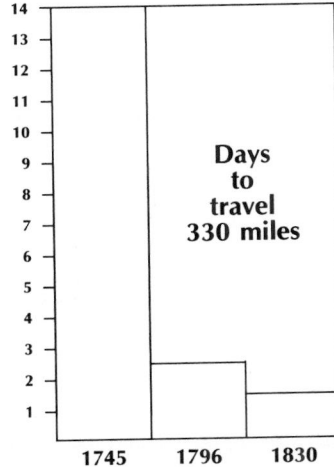

TRANSPORTATION REVOLUTION: London to Edinburgh

Days to travel 330 miles

3. (a) flying shuttle; spinning jenny; water-frame; spinning mule; cotton gin; power loom (b) Flying shuttle enabled weaver to go twice as fast; spinning jenny made up to 80 threads at once; water-frame used water power to drive spinning wheels; spinning mule produced better quality thread; cotton gin increased sup-

ply of raw cotton and thus enabled textile mills to work at capacity; increased weaver's production and factory work.

4. (a) Railroad and water routes available between London and other three cities. (b) All three cities near iron ore fields and accessible by water and rail.

Researching and Reporting Skills

Students' answers will vary.

Critical Thinking

1. Possible answers: (a) pride that inventions had spurred growth (b) happy over opportunity for enormous profits (c) though difficult conditions sometimes arose, it meant a comfortable and stable standard of living (d) some changes negative: forced into factory; poor working and living conditions; some changes positive: not subject to instability of farm life; possibility of regular wages.

2. (a) factory owners, shippers, merchants (b) landowners forced to share power in Parliament with factory owners, shippers, merchants, and other new members of the middle class

3. (a) *laissez-faire*: economic role of government should be hands-off (b) Entrepreneurs allowed to pursue profit and expansion without concern for resulting working conditions, social conditions, and deterioration of environment.

Perspectives on Past and Present

Students should point to technological advances in such things as computers, robotics, communications, CD's, and other changes spurred by electronics.

Investigating History

Students' answers will vary.

The Industrial Revolution

Chapter 22

Teaching with Pictures

As students look at the painting, explain that the Industrial Revolution began in Great Britain in the mid-1700's for a number of reasons they will learn about in this chapter. Ask students why they think this site was chosen for a city. Discuss with students the various pluses and minuses of industrialization as depicted here.

In many parts of Great Britain, industrial towns sprang up almost overnight around 1800. Smoke rising from the factories came to symbolize both plentiful jobs and unhealthy working conditions—some of the pluses and minuses of industrialism.

Key Terms

Industrial Revolution
industrialization
enclosure
crop rotation
factory
entrepreneur
union

Read and Understand

1. Many factors aided industrial growth.
2. Britain led in the rise of industry.
3. Industry grew and spread to new lands.
4. Industry changed ways of life.

One day in 1828, a British businessman named Joseph Pease stood clutching his hat and eyeing a windswept marshland near the mouth of the River Tees in northeastern England. The only other sign of human life was a scattering of farmhouses where fewer than 40 people lived. This was the small village of Middlesbrough.

Pease was one of a group of businessmen who planned to create a coal port and industrial city on the spot. That evening, he wrote in his diary that he could picture "a coming day when the bare fields . . . will be covered with a busy multitude, and numerous vessels crowding to these banks denote the busy seaport." That day was not long in coming.

By 1840, only 12 years later, Middlesbrough had been transformed from a sleepy farming village into a bustling seaport that exported 1.5 million tons of coal a year. Its population had mushroomed from

Chapter 22 Resources

GEOGRAPHY
- Geography Skills 22
- Outline Map 9
- Transparency 72

REINFORCEMENT
- Vocabulary 22
- Basic Skills 22
- Reteaching 22
- Making Connections Study Guide 22

ENRICHMENT
- Critical Thinking 22
- History and Literature 22

ASSESSMENT
- Chapter Test 22
- Alternate Chapter Test 22
- Computer Test Bank

40 to 4,000. Thirty years later, in 1870, the population had grown to 40,000.

Such transformations took place in many parts of England during the **Industrial Revolution,** a period of increased output of goods made by machines and new inventions. This revolution was different from the political revolutions that changed the governments of the United States and France. The Industrial Revolution was a series of dramatic changes not in the way a country was governed but in the way work was done.

Before the Industrial Revolution, most work was done by hand. People planted crops, wove cloth, and made shoes all by hand. Then, beginning in the middle 1700's, people began to use machines to do more and more jobs. No longer was muscle power the main way to get work done. Waterpower, once used only to run tiny grain mills, came into use for machinery. By 1800, steam power was replacing waterpower. In hundreds of factories, steam engines chugged away, turning wheels, pumping water, and driving the great forge hammers in iron mills.

In the 80 years between 1760 and 1840 in Great Britain, one invention led to another with a swiftness for which there is no parallel in history. The average British person born in 1760 saw more changes in his or her lifetime than ten generations of ancestors had seen in theirs.

Though the Industrial Revolution began in Britain, its effects soon spread outward. Eventually, it touched the lives of people worldwide.

Like all great changes, the Industrial Revolution had both good and bad results. Some of its changes led to a better quality of life for people. However, **industrialization,** the process of developing machine production of goods, also caused immense suffering. In this chapter, you will see that the Industrial Revolution was a mixed blessing in the land of its birth, Great Britain.

Many factors aided industrial growth. 1

The Industrial Revolution began in the middle 1700's in the lowland parts of eastern England and southern Scotland. Why industry arose in England at that particular time involves many factors—from England's geographic advantages to the resourcefulness of the British people. Let us look at some of these factors.

Changes in farming led the way.

The Industrial Revolution might not have taken place without the dramatic improvements in farming that began in the early 1700's. This agricultural revolution started sooner than the Industrial Revolution. Then, once industrialization began, the two revolutions went hand in hand.

The enclosure movement By 1700, small farms were disappearing in Great Britain. Wealthy landowners were buying up much of the land that village farmers had once worked. Then the landowners rented fields to families of tenant farmers who worked the land. This process was called **enclosure,** because the new owner sometimes put up a fence or hedge around his land.

The villagers who shared common fields generally kept on with traditional ways of farming. It was difficult to persuade everyone in the village to try a new method. A landowner with a large estate, however, was free to experiment.

In the 1700's, many of these wealthy landowners began to look for ways to increase the size of their harvests. Influenced by the ideas of the Scientific Revolution and the Enlightenment, they applied a scientific approach to their farms. They kept careful records of the methods they used on their land. With such records, they could compare one year's harvest with the next. They also exchanged ideas with one another about land use and crops.

Jethro Tull was one of the first of these scientific farmers. He saw that the usual way of sowing seed by scattering it across the ground was wasteful. Many of the seeds failed to take root. He solved this problem with an invention called the seed drill in 1721. The seed drill allowed farmers to sow seeds in well-spaced rows at specific depths. A larger share of the seed germinated, boosting crop yields.

Crop rotation The most revolutionary discovery of these scientific farmers was a new system of **crop rotation.** For centuries, the chief way to keep a field fertile had been to let it lie fallow every two or three years. This practice arose in the Middle Ages with the two-field and three-field systems on medieval manors (page 224). As

509

509

SECTION 1 Objectives and Teaching Strategies

OBJECTIVE 1. List the geographic advantages that helped Great Britain become the world's first industrialized nation.

Teaching Strategy: *Geography in History: Great Britain's Resources* (page 508a)

OBJECTIVE 2. Identify the enclosure movement and explain its importance.

Teaching Strategy: *Discussing History: The Enclosure Movement* (page 508c)

OBJECTIVE 3. Explain how a good banking system gave Britain an important economic advantage.

Teaching Strategy: *Economics and History: British Banks* (page 508c)

■ BACKGROUND

The Industrial Revolution, like the introduction of farming and the beginning of cities, is considered by most historians to be one of the few genuine turning points in world history.

ANSWERS TO Section Review 1

Define:
(a) period of increased output of goods made by machines and new inventions
(b) process of developing
(continued)

SECTION 1 Resources

GEOGRAPHY
■ Transparency 72

REINFORCEMENT
■ Independent Practice 22.1

ENRICHMENT
■ Voices from the Past 22.1

ASSESSMENT
■ Section Quiz 22.1

machine production of goods (c) process by which landowners bought up farm land and rented fields to tenant farmers; new owners often fenced in their land (d) process of keeping a field fertile by planting different crops each year

Identify:
(a) invented seed drill (b) allowed farmers to sow seeds in well-spaced rows at specific depths (c) found that crop rotation restored the soil (d) improved livestock by allowing only the best animals to breed (e) London club for the exchange of scientific ideas

Answer:
1. (a) middle 1700's (b) an economic, not political, revolution

2. (a) A landowner with a large estate was free to experiment with scientific farming methods. (b) forced small farmers off the land (c) supplied extra workers and created a demand for goods

3. abundant natural resources, especially waterpower and coal; favorable geography, an island nation with many harbors; favorable climate for new ideas; good banking system, with loans available at reasonable rates; political stability, with no wars on British soil

4. transformed from a sleepy farming village into a bustling seaport

5. Answers should consider scientific farming as necessary to feed the rapidly growing population and as a cause of the displacement of small farmers who became part of the industrial labor force.

These surveyors are measuring a field so that the landlord can enclose it. The drawing decorates a map of Bedfordshire in southeastern England.

a result, at least a third of the country in any one year was producing nothing but weeds.

After much experimenting, the gentleman farmer Viscount Charles Townshend found that it was not necessary to let the land lie fallow. The secret, he told people, was to rotate crops. One year, a farmer might plant a field with wheat or barley, which tended to wear out the soil. The next year, the farmer could plant turnips or clover, which restored the soil. Not surprisingly, the viscount was nicknamed Turnip Townshend in honor of his favorite crop.

Improved livestock Thanks to the efforts of other farmers, raising livestock also became more productive. For example, in the 1700's, Robert Bakewell began trying to raise larger sheep to provide more meat and wool. By allowing only the best animals to breed, he increased the weight of his sheep and also greatly improved the taste of the mutton.

As more and more farmers followed his lead, farm animals increased dramatically in size and quality. In 1700, the average weight of a steer sold for slaughter was 370 pounds. By 1786, that weight had more than doubled to 840 pounds. The average weight for sheep rose from 28 to 100 pounds over the same period.

Effects on population Scientific farming had a twofold effect. Better livestock and rising crop production meant more food. Fewer people went hungry, and nutrition improved.

510

On the other hand, the enclosure movement forced many small farmers off the land. Many lost fields that their families had worked for centuries. Some simply left Great Britain and moved to the British colonies in North America. Others crowded into British cities looking for work. They became the labor force for industry.

A rise in population helped industry.

Mystery still surrounds another change that played a part in the Industrial Revolution. During the 1700's, the population of Europe began to increase more rapidly than at any earlier time.

Since the great plagues of the Middle Ages (page 258), Europe's population had grown. That growth, however, was very slow.

In the 100 years from 1750 to 1850, the numbers increased at a phenomenal rate. It had taken 400 years from 1350 for the European population to double. Then it nearly doubled again in just a century.

Historians have long debated the causes of this population explosion. Some point to new farming methods that increased food supplies and improved health. Others point to medical advances such as Edward Jenner's discovery of a smallpox vaccine in 1796. Still others suggest that larger food supplies and better living conditions meant that people lived longer and married younger. These young couples soon had children, shortening the time span between generations.

Was the population explosion a direct cause of the Industrial Revolution? Probably not. After all, the population also rose rapidly in nearby Ireland, where little industrial development took place. Nevertheless, rapid population growth certainly helped quicken industrial progress. With more people, there was an increasing demand for food and other goods. At the same time, population growth supplied the extra workers that the new factories and businesses needed.

Great Britain had many advantages.

In 1700, Great Britain was neither the largest country in Europe nor the smallest. It was, however, rich in all the factors needed for industry.

Abundant natural resources The Industrial Revolution depended on three important natural resources. Two of these were waterpower and

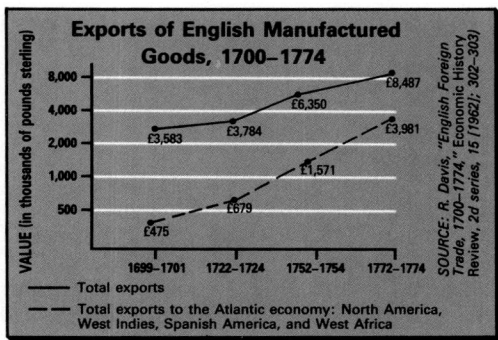

Exports of English Manufactured Goods, 1700–1774

VALUE (in thousands of pounds sterling)

8,000 — £8,487
4,000 — £6,350
2,000 — £3,583 £3,784 £3,981
1,000 — £1,571
500 — £679
— £475

1699–1701 1722–1724 1752–1754 1772–1774

— Total exports
--- Total exports to the Atlantic economy: North America, West Indies, Spanish America, and West Africa

SOURCE: R. Davis, "English Foreign Trade, 1700–1774," *Economic History Review, 2d series, 15 (1962); 302–303)*

Reading a Graph *How much did total exports increase between 1699–1701 and 1772–1774? To what regions did exports increase the most?*

coal, which supplied the energy for the new machines. The third was iron ore, used for machines, tools, and buildings. Great Britain was rich in all three.

A *favorable geography* Geography also gave Great Britain an advantage over other countries. An island nation with many fine harbors, its fleet of more than 6,000 merchant ships sailed to almost every part of the globe. This overseas trade gave Britain access to raw materials and markets. Both were essential to industrial growth. Trade also gave Britain a wealthy class of ship-owners and merchants who had money to spare for new projects at home.

A *favorable climate for new ideas* In the 1700's, British people in many walks of life were interested in science and technology. The Royal Society, founded in London in 1660, had become a world-famous "club" for the exchange of scientific ideas and practical inventions. Smaller clubs sprang up in other parts of the country. In Birmingham, for example, there was a scientific group known as the Lunar Society. Its members (who cheerfully called themselves Lunatics) met about once a month at the full moon.

New ideas were not only encouraged but also rewarded. Business people were willing to invest in the manufacture of new inventions. In fact, the business person and the inventor were often the same person.

A *good banking system* By the 1700's, Great Britain had the most highly developed banking system in Europe. Making loans was by far the most important service of British banks. By lending money at reasonable interest rates, banks encouraged business people to invest in better machinery, build new factories, and expand their operations.

Political stability Although Britain took part in many wars during the 1700's, none was fought on British soil. For ordinary people, it was a century of peace. This freedom from war and bloodshed gave Britain a tremendous advantage over its European neighbors. British business people did not have to worry about a hostile army destroying their property.

At the same time, the British government favored economic growth. Merchants and business people had considerable influence in Parliament. The government supported laws that encouraged new investment both at home and abroad.

Section REVIEW 1

Define: (a) Industrial Revolution, (b) industrialization, (c) enclosure, (d) crop rotation
Identify: (a) Tull, (b) seed drill, (c) Townshend, (d) Bakewell, (e) Royal Society
Answer:
1. (a) When was the Industrial Revolution? (b) How did it differ from other revolutions?
2. (a) How did enclosure help scientific farming? (b) How did scientific farming affect the labor force? (c) How did rising population help the Industrial Revolution?
3. Describe the five factors that contributed to industrialization in Great Britain.

Critical Thinking
4. In what way was Middlesbrough a symbol of the Industrial Revolution in England?
5. Was the revolution in agriculture necessary to the Industrial Revolution? Explain.

Britain led in the rise of industry. 2

In the middle 1700's, the situation in Britain was ripe for the development of industry. The country had a good food supply, a large work force, and plenty of people with money to invest.

511

SECTION 2 Objectives and Teaching Strategies

OBJECTIVE 1. Identify the inventors and inventions that revolutionized the textile industry.
Teaching Strategy: *Skill Building: Making a Chart* (page 508c)

OBJECTIVE 2. Identify cause and effect relationships among technological developments.
Teaching Strategy: *Skill Building: Relating Cause and Effect* (page 508c)

ANSWERS TO Reading a Graph

Exports increased by 4,904,000 pounds sterling. Exports increased the most to the Atlantic economy (North America, West Indies, Spanish America, and West Africa).

■ BACKGROUND

Great Britain also led the way because the feudal system, tying peasant workers to the land, had long since been abandoned. In France and Prussia, the feudal system clung longer and made the change to an industrial society slower.

SECTION 2 Resources

ASSESSMENT
■ Section Quiz 22.2

REINFORCEMENT
■ Independent Practice 22.2

ENRICHMENT
■ Voices from the Past 22.2

Between 1750 and 1769, Great Britain increased its cotton exports tenfold, exporting more cotton than it used at home. The exports brought in money for continued industrial expansion.

The money to be made in the cotton industry was so staggering that many small investors rushed in. In 1789, a draper named Robert Owen borrowed 100 pounds to start a mill. Twenty years later, he bought out his partners for 84,000 pounds.

Cooperative Learning

Have students work in groups of three to develop ideas for new inventions or improvements upon existing ones. Suggest to students that they consider ideas in the communications or transportation fields. Group members should discuss and agree on an idea for an invention. One group member should be responsible for presenting the idea to the class, another for drawing a sketch of the new invention, and the third member for developing a marketing program for the invention, perhaps creating an appropriate advertisement. When all the groups are finished, have them present their ideas to the class.

All the forces that had been slowly building suddenly came together in a giant burst of inventiveness. The changes appeared first in the textile industry.

Inventions revolutionized the textile industry.

Britain had long been one of the leading sheep-raising areas in the world. Raw wool and wool cloth had been Britain's major trade goods as far back as the Middle Ages. All this cloth was produced by hand. Spinners and weavers (mainly women) worked in their own homes, using spinning wheels and hand looms.

British clothmakers produced other fabrics as well as wool. Linen, a cloth woven from the fiber of the flax plant, was popular for lighter-weight clothing. Even more popular was cotton, which was also light but more durable and easier to care for than linen.

Working by hand at their wheels and looms, spinners and weavers could not keep up with the demand for cloth, especially cotton. Since they could not make as much cotton cloth as people wanted to buy, its cost remained relatively high. Cloth merchants saw that they could make greater profits if they found a way to speed up the work of spinning and weaving.

One invention led to another.

By 1800, six major inventions had totally transformed the cotton industry. The first invention came in 1733, when a watchmaker named John Kay made a shuttle that moved back and forth on wheels. The flying shuttle, as it was called, was little more than a boat-shaped piece of wood to which yarn was attached. Yet it allowed a weaver to work twice as fast.

Now weavers were working so quickly that spinners could not keep up. A prize was offered to anyone who could produce a better spinning machine. The prize went to a textile worker named James Hargreaves.

In 1764, Hargeaves invented a new spinning wheel. He called it the spinning jenny in honor of his wife. This simple machine allowed one spinner to work six or eight threads at a time. Later models could spin as many as 80 threads at once.

Both the flying shuttle and the spinning jenny were hand-operated machines. Richard Arkwright's water-frame, invented in 1769, brought a new breakthrough. The water-frame used the waterpower from fast-flowing streams to drive spinning wheels.

In 1779, Samuel Crompton combined features of the spinning jenny and the water-frame to produce the spinning mule. (It was so named because, just as a mule is the offspring of a horse and a donkey, this machine was the offspring of two inventions.) The mule made thread that was stronger, finer, and more even than earlier spinning machines.

The water-frame and the spinning mule were too large and expensive for people to use at home. Spinning and weaving slowly stopped being work that families did together in their homes. Instead, wealthy textile merchants set up several of the new machines in large buildings called **factories**. At first, the new factories needed waterpower, so they were built near a stream or waterfall.

With so many new machines for turning out thread, the weavers soon fell behind in their jobs. In 1785, a new invention promised to restore the balance by speeding up weaving. This was Edmund Cartwright's power loom, run by waterpower. Early power looms were inefficient, but steady improvements meant that by 1813 more than 2,000 were in use. By 1833, there were more than 100,000, most of them in large factories where they rattled away under the same roof as spinning machines. By the late 1700's, both spinners and weavers were working so fast that cotton growers could not keep up with them.

Much of England's cotton came from the southern part of the United States. In Virginia, Georgia, North Carolina, and South Carolina, farmers raised cotton on large plantations worked by slaves. One of the most time-consuming jobs on the plantation was removing the seeds from the raw cotton. In 1793, American educator Eli Whitney invented a machine to do this tedious chore. His cotton gin made it possible for slaves to pick and clean ten times as much cotton daily as they had before.

Whitney's invention spurred a dramatic increase in American cotton production: from 9,000 bales in 1791 to 987,000 in 1831. Now there was enough raw cotton to keep the factories of Britain humming.

Comparing pictures *During the Industrial Revolution, jobs such as spinning and weaving gradually moved out of home workshops (left) and into factories (right). How did the nature of the work and the working environment change?*

ANSWER TO
Comparing Pictures

The work changed from being a highly skilled craft, done within the familiar home environment, to being a less skilled tending of machines within the highly controlled, noisy, and polluted factory environment. In the factory, women could no longer carry on household activities or care for children while producing goods.

Thanks to continuous technological improvements in spinning and weaving, however, English merchants used all this cotton and still called for more. The output of cotton cloth from British factories rose from 40 million yards in 1785 to more than 2 billion yards in 1850—a staggering 5,000 percent increase.

Watt *improved the steam engine.*

The early power looms and spinning machines had one large drawback. They ran on waterpower, and so every factory that used them had to be near rushing water. Such places were often far from raw materials, workers, or markets. Therefore, many factory owners were eager for a new source of power. They found it in steam.

As early as 1705, coal miners were using steam-powered pumps to remove water from deep mine shafts. However, this early steam engine, called the Newcomen engine after its inventor, worked very slowly. It also took great quantities of fuel, making it expensive to run.

In 1763, the problem came to the attention of James Watt. Watt was a mathematical instrument maker at the University of Glasgow in Scotland. He helped science professors make the equipment they used in their experiments. Watt pondered the problem for two years. Then, one day in the spring of 1765, as he was strolling along the Glasgow Green, a solution suddenly came to him. Watt saw how to make the steam engine work much faster and more efficiently while burning less fuel.

In the 1770's, Watt went into partnership with a farsighted businessman named Matthew Boulton. Watt and Boulton were both **entrepreneurs** (AHN-truh-pruh-NUHRZ). An entrepreneur is a person who organizes, manages, and takes on the risks of a business.

With Boulton's financial backing, Watt continued to make better and better engines. By 1800, almost 500 steam engines were huffing and puffing in various British factories. James Watt, once a modestly paid craftsman, had become a millionaire.

513

ANSWERS TO
Section Review 2

Define:
(a) building where machines are set up to produce goods
(b) person who organizes, manages, and takes on risk of a business
Identify:
(a) inventor of flying shuttle
(b) inventor of spinning jenny (c) inventor of water-frame (d) creator of spinning mule (e) inventor of power loom (f) inventor of cotton gin (g) removed seeds from raw cotton (h) made the steam engine more efficient
Answer:
1. (a) textile (b) to keep up with the great demand
2. (a) flying shuttle, spinning jenny, water-frame, spinning mule, power loom, cotton gin (b) With the invention of the flying shuttle, spinners could not keep up with weavers. The spinning jenny solved that problem; the water-frame added power to drive the spinning wheels, and features of both were combined to form the spinning mule. Cotton gin increased production of raw cotton for factories. Power loom was developed to speed up weaving.
3. (a) ran on waterpower and needed to be located near streams (b) Steam as a source of power could be used anytime and anywhere.
4. Answers should consider that the steam engine provided power where people, resources, and markets were already in place.
5. Look for answers to consider the importance of both inventiveness and finances.

Watt's improvements made the steam engine much more practical for use in industry. For the first time in history, people had a source of power that could be used anywhere and anytime.

Section REVIEW 2

Define: (a) factory, (b) entrepreneur
Identify: (a) John Kay, (b) James Hargreaves, (c) Richard Arkwright, (d) Samuel Crompton, (e) Edmund Cartwright, (f) Eli Whitney, (g) cotton gin, (h) James Watt
Answer:
1. (a) What British industry did the first inventions of the Industrial Revolution affect? (b) Why were merchants in this industry looking for ways to speed up production?
2. (a) Name the six inventions that transformed the cotton industry. (b) How did each of these inventions lead to another?
3. (a) What drawback did early power looms and spinning machines have? (b) How did the invention of the steam engine solve this problem?

Critical Thinking
4. The steam engine has been called the greatest invention of the Industrial Revolution. Do you agree or disagree? Explain.
5. Could the Industrial Revolution have taken place without entrepreneurs? Why or why not? What role do entrepreneurs play in business today?

Industry grew and spread to new lands. 3

In 1800, a businessman could walk through his mill and look with pride at the latest model of the Watt steam engine. He could see the power looms and other machines to which it was connected by drive shafts and belts. Yet most of these mechanical wonders had been delivered to the factory by horse-drawn cart. When the businessman finished his inspection, he rode home in a horse-drawn carriage over mud-rutted roads that dated back to the Middle Ages. Great changes, however, were on the way.

Engineers built roads and canals.

Before the Industrial Revolution, the cheapest and most reliable way to travel in England was by water. Besides its good harbors, England also had many navigable rivers. Barges laden with coal, iron, bricks, and other goods floated up and down the rivers of England. Since a barge drawn by horse could carry a far greater load than a cart pulled by the same horse, water transportation was much cheaper than land transportation.

Yet water transportation had a major drawback. There was only one way to take goods across the stretches of land that lay between rivers. Workers had to unload the boats, put the goods into wagons, drive the wagons to the next river, and move the cargo again onto boats.

To solve this problem, the British built a network of canals. (A canal is a human-made waterway.) In the late 1700's and early 1800's, British workers built more than 4,000 miles of inland waterways. The new canals slashed the cost of transportation. Now coal and other raw materials could be carried by water to more places in Britain.

British roads also improved. John McAdam, a Scottish engineer, was largely responsible for the better roads. Working in the early 1800's, he built roadbeds with a layer of large stones for drainage. Over that bed, he put a carefully smoothed layer of crushed rock. Roads with the "macadam" surface were not nearly so muddy or dusty as the old ones. Heavy wagons could travel over them even in rainy weather without sinking to their axles in mud.

The Railway Age began.

The biggest change in transportation came with the use of steam power. Just as the steam engine itself was a key breakthrough in the late 1700's, the steam engine on wheels gave a tremendous boost to English industry after 1820. This invention is better known, of course, as the railroad locomotive. The railroad revolutionized transportation first in England and later in many parts of the world.

The idea of running wagons on iron tracks was not new. For centuries, horses had pulled carts of iron and coal along railway tracks in and around mines. Before 1800, however, no one succeeded in using steam power to run such a cart.

The Industrial Revolution in Cotton, Coal, and Pig Iron

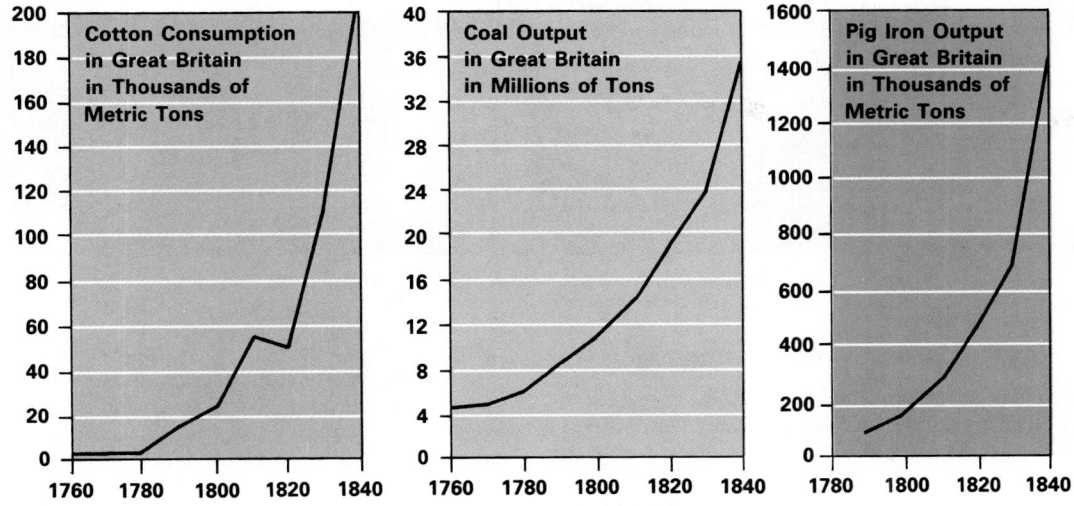

Reading graphs In what 20-year period did the use of cotton first show an increase? About how much pig iron did Britain produce in 1800? In 1820?

These vehicles needed smaller, more powerful engines than the ones that Watt was producing for factory use.

In 1804, an English engineer named Richard Trevithick made an engine that was both small and powerful. In fact, it ran at such high pressures that Watt and others expected it to blow up. Trevithick claimed his engine could pull a cart along a set of rails. A mine owner in Wales bet Trevithick the equivalent of several thousand dollars that such a feat was impossible. Trevithick won the bet by running his locomotive over ten miles of track, hauling ten tons of iron as well. "The public until now called me a scheming fellow," wrote Trevithick at the time, "but now their tone is much altered."

Other British engineers soon built improved versions of Trevithick's locomotive. By 1820, several hundred such vehicles were in operation in and around British mines. One of these early railroad engineers was George Stephenson, who gained a solid reputation by building some 20 engines for mine operators in northern England.

In 1821, Stephenson began work on the world's first railroad line. It was to run 27 miles from the Yorkshire coalfields to the port of Stockton on the North Sea. In 1825, the railroad opened,

using four locomotives that Stephenson had designed and built.

News of this success quickly spread throughout Britain. The entrepreneurs of northern England were especially interested. They wanted a railroad line to connect the port of Liverpool on the northwestern coast of England with the inland city of Manchester, the heart of the spinning and weaving industry. The track was laid, and in 1829, trials were held to choose the best locomotive for use on the new line.

Five engines entered the competition, but none could compare with the Rocket, designed by Stephenson and his son. With smoke pouring from its tall smokestack and its two pistons pumping to and fro as they drove the front wheels, the Rocket hauled a 13-ton load at an unheard-of speed—more than 24 miles per hour!

Footnote to History

In 1745, it took two weeks to travel from London to Edinburgh, a distance of 330 miles. By 1796, better roads cut the traveling time to two and a half days. In 1830, a passenger on a coach could make the trip in 36 hours.

515

SECTION 3
Objectives and Teaching Strategies

OBJECTIVE 1. Describe how Britain's railroad age began.
Teaching Strategy: *Economics and History: The Liverpool-Manchester Railway* (page 508d)

OBJECTIVE 2. Assess the impact of railroads on life in Great Britain.
Teaching Strategy: *Writing about History: The Impact of the Railroads* (page 508d)

OBJECTIVE 3. Identify factors that slowed the spread of industrialization to America and Europe.
Teaching Strategy: *Geography in History: The Spread of Industrialization* (page 508d)

ANSWERS TO
Reading Graphs

1780–1800; 200,000 metric tons; about 450,000 metric tons

■ BACKGROUND

Henry Cort's improved smelting methods (1784) moved the British iron industry away from small forges toward much larger, much more efficient blast furnaces, which boosted British iron production from 68,000 tons in 1790 to 677,000 tons in 1830.

SECTION 3
Resources

ASSESSMENT
■ Section Quiz 22.3

REINFORCEMENT
■ Independent Practice 22.3

ENRICHMENT
■ Voices from the Past 22.3

515

First-class passengers on the Liverpool-Manchester Railway rode in covered carriages (top). Second- and third-class passengers rode in open cars.

■ BACKGROUND

Railroads captured the imagination of people everywhere. In a very brief time, short lines were opened in the United States (1826), France (1828), Germany and Belgium (1835), and Russia (1837). Cross-country lines, of course, took a long time to complete.

Railroads boosted the coal and iron industries even more. From 1830 to 1850, Britain's iron output tripled, from 677,000 to 2,250,000 tons. Each mile of railroad track required 300 tons of iron. Coal output also tripled, leaping to 49 million tons.

■ DISCUSSION

How might the sudden surge of wealth and the growing middle class have weakened royal power?

Railroads spread across England.

The Liverpool-Manchester Railway opened officially in 1830. It was an immediate success. Thousands of passengers traveled between the two cities every day on a dozen separate trains. Freight trains soon carried more goods back and forth along this route than canals and road coaches combined.

Confident that there were great profits to be made in railroads, British business people began building new lines all over the country. Hundreds of different railroads opened during the 1830's and 1840's. Soon such lines linked nearly all the major cities and towns of Britain. In 1850, only 25 years after the first line had been built, Britain had nearly 6,100 miles of railroad track.

Perhaps the only business people who did not welcome the Railroad Age were the owners of canals and freight wagon lines. The "iron horse" soon drove many of them out of business.

Not everything went smoothly on these early railroads, of course. Breakdowns, accidents, and delays were frequent. At first, most passengers traveled in open cars where they were exposed to rain, wind, and the black clouds of soot that poured from the engine smokestack. Despite such drawbacks, however, railroads offered faster and more reliable transportation than anything known in earlier times.

Railroads had far-reaching effects.

No other industrial development had a greater effect on life in Great Britain than the railroads. In fact, the invention and perfection of the locomotive had at least four major effects.

First, railroads encouraged further industrial growth by giving manufacturers a fast, cheap way to transport both raw materials and finished products. Moreover, entrepreneurs could now build factories in many more locations. They no longer needed to be close to supplies of raw materials. Trains could deliver such supplies wherever there were tracks.

Second, the railroad boom provided millions of new jobs. Thousands of people did the backbreaking work of leveling hills, laying track, digging tunnels, and building bridges. Railroads used so much coal and iron that they boosted the demand for workers in those two industries as well. One mile of railroad track, for example, required 300 tons of iron.

Third, railroads gave a further boost to progress in agriculture. Now farmers could send milk and fruit to market in distant cities. In the same way, trains opened new markets for the fishing industry. Fresh fish could now be sold daily even in cities far from the sea.

Last but not least, railroads had enormous influence on the attitudes that ordinary people had about travel. Until this time, most people had thought of travel as something one did only when it was absolutely necessary. By offering quick and reasonably cheap transportation, railroads completely changed this view. Country people, for example, were now more willing to take jobs in distant cities, because they knew they could make regular visits home. At the same time, railroads began to open up a new world of travel for enjoyment. The spread of the railroads through Britain led directly to the growth of such popular seaside resorts as Brighton (south of London) and Blackpool (on the northwestern coast).

516

Industrialization spread to other countries.

For many years, the Industrial Revolution was limited mostly to the country of its birth, Great Britain. The reason was simple: Britain wanted to keep the secrets of industrialization to itself. Until 1825, it was against the law for engineers, mechanics, and toolmakers to leave the country.

The spread to the United States In 1789, a young British mill worker named Samuel Slater disguised himself as a farmer and boarded a ship headed for the United States. There he built a spinning machine from memory. The next year, a Rhode Island businessman named Moses Brown began work on a factory to house Slater's machines. In 1790, this factory—the first one in the United States—opened for business in Pawtucket, Rhode Island.

Early factories in the United States made only thread. The thread was then given to weavers who worked in their homes. Later, mills combined the spinning of thread with the weaving of cloth.

The number of mills grew slowly at first and then more rapidly. By 1850, they had spread over much of the northeastern United States.

The spread to Europe Industry made little headway on the European continent before 1815. The French Revolution and the Napoleonic wars disrupted business all over Europe. By the time peace returned, Britain had a commanding lead.

Goods from Britain's factories flooded European markets. British woolens and cottons were much cheaper than anything workers in Europe could make by hand. As a result, many European spinners and weavers found themselves out of work.

Belgium was one of the first countries in Europe to respond to the British challenge. Like Britain, Belgium had good supplies of coal and fine waterways for transportation. At first, the know-how to build industrial machines in Belgium came from British workers who left England illegally. In 1799, a British carpenter named William

Voice from the Past | A Girl in the Mills

In 1823, a New England businessman named Francis Lowell built a model factory town at Lowell, Massachusetts. His idea was to hire young women from farming villages. He offered safe, attractive living quarters and opportunities for education as well as jobs. At the age of 13, Lucy Larcom became a mill girl. Years later, she described her life at Lowell.

That children should be set to toil for their daily bread is always a pity; but in the case of my little workmates and myself there were imperative reasons, and we were not too young to understand them. And the regret with which those who loved us best consented to such an arrangement only made us more anxious to show that we really were capable of doing something for them and for ourselves. The novelty of trying to "earn our own living" took our childhood fancy; the work given us was light, and for a few weeks it seemed like beginning a new game with a new set of playmates. Replacing the full spools of bobbins with empty ones on spinning frames was the usual employment given to children. It was a process which required quickness but left unoccupied intervals . . . during which we were frequently allowed to run home.

1. (a) Why did Lucy and other mill girls probably go to work? (b) Why was the idea of young women earning their living a novel one for its time?
2. How did the mill girls feel about their work?
3. In time, Lowell followed the grim path of factory towns in Britain. Describe how Lucy's account differs from the one given by Samuel Coulson on page 521.

517

ANSWERS TO

Voice from the Past

1. (a) "to toil for their daily bread," earn their own living, and help their families **(b)** children—especially girls—had worked only at home

2. For a while it seemed like fun.

3. Lucy Larcom's work was light, often with free time that allowed her to run home; Coulson's daughters began work at 3 A.M. and ended at 10:30 P.M., with one hour off to eat and drink.

■ BACKGROUND

In 1813, Francis Cabot Lowell and Paul Moody developed a power loom, based on ones Lowell had seen in England, for use in United States factories.

ANSWERS TO

Section Review 3

Identify:
(a) inventor of "macadam" roads **(b)** made an engine that could pull a cart along a
(continued)

ANSWERS TO *(continued)*

set of rails **(c)** engine builder and designer of locomotive **(d)** brought British industrial secrets to the United States **(e)** built a factory to house Slater's spinning machines **(f)** built cotton-spinning machines in Belgium

Answer:

1. (a) barges; horse-drawn carts **(b)** A network of canals was built; Macadam improved roads by building roadbeds with drainage.

2. the railroad

3. (a) encouraged industry by giving manufacturers a fast, cheap way to transport raw materials and finished products **(b)** created millions of new jobs **(c)** boosted agriculture by opening markets

4. forbade engineers, mechanics, and tool makers to leave the country, or anyone in Britain to sell machines to other countries

5. cause: made possible the enlargement of markets necessary for continued expansion; effect: Railroad and canals grew out of industrial needs.

ANSWERS TO

Focus on Geography

1. iron ore, coal

2. cottons, woolens, metal goods, pottery, iron, coal

3. its location near iron ore and coal fields

4. coalmining

5. large city with large population of industrial workers; location along railroads, Thames River

The Industrial Revolution in Great Britain, 1850

KEY

- Major industrial areas
- Coal fields
- ⚒ Iron ore fields
- --- Major canals
- — Major railways

0   50 Miles

Focus on Geography

Geographic Skills

1. What two resources provided the basis for industry around Glasgow, Newcastle, Leeds, and Sheffield?
2. The industrial area in central England is known as the Midlands. What goods were produced there?
3. What contributed to the growth of Liverpool?
4. What was the major economic activity of Wales?

Geographic Theme: Interaction

5. What factors might account for the growth of London?

518

Cockerill began building cotton-spinning machines in Belgium while it was still under French rule. Later, Cockerill's sons opened factories that turned out steam engines, locomotives, and other machinery.

Soon, industrialized "islands" began to dot the European landscape. Among these areas were the coal-rich Ruhr Valley in northwestern Germany and the Po Valley in northern Italy. Cities such as Milan, Frankfurt, and Lyons expanded rapidly on the continent during the middle 1800's.

Britain led the world in industry.

Despite such growth, no other European country came close to rivaling Britain as an industrial power before 1850. In 1850, Britain still produced most of the world's iron and coal. British factories and mills accounted for 70 percent of Europe's cotton cloth production.

Yet another measure of British dominance was railroad development. With 6,084 miles of track in operation in 1850, Britain had more railroad lines than France, Russia, Austria, Belgium, and all the Italian states combined. With its highly developed industrial economy and splendid merchant fleet, Britain made foreign trade a major feature of its economy. During the 1840's, the value of British exports increased at an amazing rate. Little wonder that the country earned the title of "workshop of the world."

Section REVIEW 3

Identify: (a) John McAdam, (b) Richard Trevithick, (c) George Stephenson, (d) Samuel Slater, (e) Moses Brown, (f) William Cockerill

Answer:

1. (a) Name two ways goods were transported before the Industrial Revolution. (b) How was each method improved?
2. What invention changed transportation?
3. How did railroads affect each of the following? (a) the growth of industry (b) employment (c) agriculture
4. What did Britain do to prevent the spread of industrialization?

Critical Thinking

5. How was improved transportation both a cause and an effect of the Industrial Revolution?

Industry changed ways of life.

4

As the pace of industrialization quickened, life changed in many ways. By the 1800's, more people could afford to heat their homes with coal from Wales and to dine on Scottish beef. They had more clothing too, much of it from cloth made on power looms in Manchester or Liverpool. Industrialization affected every part of life.

More people lived in cities.

Perhaps the most obvious change brought about by the Industrial Revolution was in where people lived. For centuries, most Europeans had lived in rural areas. A much smaller share had lived in towns and cities. Now that balance began to shift toward the cities.

The growth of the factory system brought people flocking into cities and towns. Between 1800 and 1850, the number of European cities with more than 100,000 inhabitants rose from 22 to 47. Most of Europe's urban areas at least doubled in population during this period. Some, such as Glasgow and Berlin, tripled or even quadrupled in size.

Factories tended to develop in clusters because entrepreneurs built near sources of power. Major new industrial centers sprang up between the coal-rich area of southern Wales and the Clyde River valley in Scotland (map, page 518). The biggest of these centers developed in England, from the Midlands north along the Pennines and on the northwest and northeast coasts.

London, of course, remained the most important city in Great Britain. Among other things, it was Europe's largest city (twice as populous as Paris, its nearest rival) and was growing larger all the time. This population gave London a vast labor pool for industry. London thus shared in Britain's industrial growth.

However, new cities were challenging London's leadership. Perhaps the most famous of the new industrial cities was Manchester, which along with the port of Liverpool formed the hub of Britain's cotton industry. "What Manchester thinks today, London thinks tomorrow," declared the city's proud entrepreneurs.

CITY TOUR
Problems arose as cities grew.

The pride of Manchester's business leaders was typical of their go-ahead spirit. Yet Manchester was also typical of the new industrial cities in other ways. These cities grew so quickly that little thought or planning was given to housing, sanitation, or education for the people who poured in from the countryside to seek jobs. Let us look at life in Manchester in the early 1800's.

It is 5 A.M. on a chilly fall day in 1840. Men, women, and even small children are spilling out

Reading a table Which town was largest in 1685? In 1881? Use information in the text and on the map to explain what geographic feature helped the latter.

The Growth of Seven British Cities

	1685	1760	1881
Liverpool	4,000	35,000	555,425
Manchester	6,000	45,000	393,676
Birmingham	4,000	30,000	400,757
Leeds	7,000	(not known)	309,126
Sheffield	4,000	20,000	284,410
Bristol	29,000	100,000	206,503
Nottingham	8,000	17,000	111,631

Manchester

393,676

6,000   45,000

1665   1760   1881

519

SECTION 4
Objectives and Teaching Strategies

OBJECTIVE 1. Link industrialization with urbanization.

Teaching Strategy: *Writing about History: Problems of Urbanization* (page 508e)

OBJECTIVE 2. Describe the living and working conditions of British factory workers during the early 1800's.

Teaching Strategy: *Economics and History: A Manchester Family's Weekly Budget* (page 508e)

ANSWERS TO
Reading a Table

Bristol; Liverpool; its location as a port near the textile mills and its early railway connection

■ BACKGROUND

Manchester grew in the 1800's as a center for producing cotton textiles. Raw cotton came to Liverpool and from there was transported to Manchester by canal. This flow was reversed as the Manchester mills shipped cotton cloth to Liverpool and from there, to markets overseas. Note on page 614 the Geographic Theme based on the cotton trade.

SECTION 4
Resources

ASSESSMENT
■ Section Quiz 22.4

REINFORCEMENT
■ Independent Practice 22.4

ENRICHMENT
■ Voices from the Past 22.4

List the following on the board: air pollution, water pollution, inadequate waste removal, lack of housing, lack of green space (public parks), child labor/long work hours, poor medical care. These are all problems that existed in early industrial cities such as Manchester, England. Tell students to imagine that they are on the city council of an early industrial city and must decide how to appropriate funds to combat these problems. Have students, working individually, rank these problems, with those needing the most immediate attention ranked highest. Students should note reasons for their choices. Then, in groups of five, have students present their rankings to other group members. Then tell the class that only enough funds exist to work on four of the problems. Groups must work together to choose which four problems to address. Have a recorder write down the group's choices and reasons for those choices. Another group member should present the group's list to the entire class.

of the city's courtyards and alleys to make their way on foot to the cotton mills. Some have already had a cup of tea and a plate of oatmeal, but others will wait until the 8 A.M. break for tea and a piece of bread. The sky is dark, but gas lamps gleam along the alleys, where taverns are already open for business.

Although many of the brick buildings along the streets are new, they are blackened by the smoke and soot that hang over the city all the time. Manchester sprawls alongside the Pennine Hills, which are capped by bare, windswept moors. However, smoke from the clusters of cotton mills that ring the city blot out any glimpse of these open spaces.

Most of the streets are unpaved and have no drains. The larger streets are cleaned from time to time, but the alleys are not. These streets collect heaps of filth and excrement. In courtyards, some of the workers keep pigs that root as best as they can among the garbage. The stench that rises from these areas is almost unbearable.

The smell in other parts of the city is little better. Gasworks, bone works, breweries, and tanneries add their various odors to the smoky air. The city's main river, the Irwell, is filled with so much waste that, in the words of one visitor, it is "considerably less a river than a flood of liquid manure."

In 1760, Manchester had been a market town with a population of around 30,000. It became the center for the expanding British cotton industry for two reasons. First, Manchester was close to the port of Liverpool, where most of the raw cotton from the United States entered Great Britain. Second, the town had abundant sources of power. Streams tumbling down from the nearby Pennines supplied waterpower, and nearby coalfields offered fuel for steam power.

By 1800, there were more than 50 cotton mills in Manchester. By 1830, there were 130. By 1850, Manchester was home to some 300,000 people, 10 times the number of a century earlier.

This tremendous growth brought great wealth to Manchester—and also enormous social problems. The city was built almost overnight, without plans, without any kind of sanitary codes or building controls. Not until the 1830's did the city have a municipal government to keep order. Before then, Manchester was little more than "a huge overgrown village," as one observer said.

Not all quarters of the city were miserable, of course. Well-to-do merchants and factory owners made their homes in Alderley Edge, a pleasant suburb on the east of the city. For the working people of Manchester, Alderley Edge must have seemed light-years away. One person wrote:

The dwellings of the poor in the back streets and alleys are as woeful as they are degrading. The amount of room occupied by many families is miserably small; great numbers have only one bedroom for the whole family.

Not surprisingly, sickness was rampant. Cholera epidemics regularly swept through the slums of Manchester and other industrial cities. A British government study in 1842 showed that the average lifespan for working-class people in Manchester was 17 years, as compared to 38 years in a nearby rural area.

By the 1840's, changes were in sight. Streets were being paved and drains installed. The city's first three parks were created. Yet many of the grim conditions spawned by rapid industrial expansion would linger for a long time.

Manchester was a city of contrasts. "From this foul drain, the greatest stream of human industry flows out to fertilize the whole world," wrote the French journalist Alexis de Tocqueville after visiting Manchester in 1835.

The Industrial Revolution changed working conditions.

Faced with such living conditions, why did people continue to pour into Britain's cities? One reason was that country life was harsh too. The cities at least offered plenty of jobs. Moreover, a factory worker could hope for regular wages, rain or shine. In contrast, a spell of bad weather could wipe out a farmer's whole crop.

Families in the the country were used to working from dawn to dusk. Parents expected their children to work long and hard as well. The family worked as a unit, both at farm tasks and at home industries such as spinning and weaving. When such a family moved to town, however, they found that working conditions were different.

In the city, work hours depended on the factory bell or whistle, not on the season or the weather. Factory owners wanted to keep their machines

Child labor was one of the most shocking abuses of the early Industrial Revolution. Perhaps the worst conditions were in the mines, where boys and girls dragged cartloads of coal through dark, cramped passages.

■ **BACKGROUND**

Despite their long experience in the textile trade, women in textile factories were generally paid lower wages than men.

Most mill owners, according to Peter Gaskell in 1833, considered the workers no more than "so many accessories in his machinery, destined to produce a certain quantity of work at the lowest possible outlay of capital."

running for as many hours a day as possible. As a result, the average worker spent 14 hours a day at the job, 6 days a week. Instead of changing with the seasons, the work was the same week after week, year after year. Workers could not change their pace; they had to keep up with the machines.

Industry also posed new dangers in work. Factories were seldom well-lit or clean. Machines injured workers in countless different ways—a boiler might explode or a drive belt might catch an arm. The most dangerous conditions of all were found in the coal mines, where frequent accidents, damp conditions, and the constant breathing of coal dust combined to make the average miner's life span ten years shorter than that of other workers.

Children suffered in mills and mines.

In the factories as on the farms, whole families worked. Again, however, there were important differences. In the country, children worked side by side with their parents. In factories, family members often worked separately. In such cases, young children were at the mercy of impersonal overseers. During the early 1800's, children as young as six or seven years worked long hours in factories and mines.

Children were especially useful in the mines, where small size was a great advantage in moving about in narrow shafts and tunnels. Many were employed as "trappers," whose job was to keep the ventilation shafts in the mines clear. "It is a most painful thing to contemplate the dull, dungeon-like life these little creatures are doomed to spend," noted one mine visitor, "a life for the most part passed in solitude, damp, and darkness."

Orphan children faced the worst plight. Factory owners employed large numbers of these children in return for room and board. The child workers were seldom fed properly. Their lodgings might be nothing more than piles of straw beside the machines at which they worked 12 or 14 hours a day.

In 1831, Parliament set up a committee to investigate abuses of child labor. A worker named Samuel Coulson told the committee that in busy times, his small daughters started work at 3 A.M. and ended at 10:30 P.M. What rest periods did they have during those 19 hours? "Breakfast a quarter of an hour, and dinner half an hour, and drinking a quarter of an hour."

As a result of this committee's findings, Parliament passed the Factory Act of 1833. The new law made it illegal to hire children under 9 years old. Children from the ages of 9 to 13 were not to work more than 8 hours a day. Young people from 14 to 18 could not be required to work more than 12 hours. In 1842, the Mines Act placed similar limits on the work of children in mining.

While such acts limited the worst abuses, children continued to do exhausting work, often under unhealthy or dangerous conditions. They worked because the money they earned was essential to

521

■ **DISCUSSION**

How might the family conditions described here have affected population growth?

■ **BACKGROUND**

"Good" and "bad" neighborhoods developed in cities. The bad neighborhoods, many of them continuing into the present day, were home to the poor laborers.

their families. In 1825, a whole family—husband, wife, and three children—could earn about one British pound a week if they all worked in the mines. How much did the family need to live in any kind of comfort? One writer at the time estimated two pounds. Trapped by poverty, many parents could hardly consider allowing their children *not* to work.

The middle class expanded.

Although poverty gripped the lower class, wealth was spreading among other people in Britain. The Industrial Revolution brought enormous amounts of money into the country. Most of this wealth went into the pockets of factory owners, shippers, and merchants. These people made up a growing middle class.

This new middle class greatly changed the social structure of Great Britain. In the past, landowners and aristocrats occupied the top position in British society. They had the most wealth and the most power. Now, some factory owners and merchants were wealthier than the landowners and aristocrats. In an effort to be like the upper class, the newly rich families bought large estates and lived in high style.

Despite such attempts, there were still important social distinctions between the two classes. Landowners looked down on those who had made their fortunes in the "vulgar" business world. Not until late in the 1800's were rich entrepreneurs considered the social equals of the lords of the countryside.

Gradually, a middle class that was neither rich nor poor began to emerge. This group included an upper middle class of government employees, doctors, lawyers, and those who held management positions in factories, mines and shops. There was also a lower middle class made up of factory overseers and such skilled workers as toolmakers, mechanical drafters, and printers. These people earned incomes that gave them a comfortable standard of living.

Class tensions arose.

In the 1840's, a young German writer named Friedrich Engels went to Manchester, where his family owned a cotton business. Like many other visitors, Engels was appalled by the city's slums. One day, he discussed the subject with a middle-class gentleman as they walked the filthy streets. "I declared that I had never seen so badly built a town in my life," Engels later recalled. "He [the gentleman] listened patiently. At the corner of the street, as we parted company, he remarked: 'And yet there is a great deal of money made here. Good morning, sir!'"

Laissez-faire government Engel's companion cared little for the problems of Manchester's workers. Like many British business leaders of the 1800's, the gentleman believed that the gap between rich and poor was a natural one, an inevitable result of progress. The duties of government, as he saw them, were to wage war abroad and uphold law and order at home. He expected the government to take a hands-off attitude toward economic and social conditions.

This policy, known as laissez-faire, had been set forth by Adam Smith in the late 1700's (page 467). Now, in the 1800's, this idea was popular

---

ECONOMICS IN DAILY LIFE ▶ The Price of Bread

The political influence of the landed aristocracy in Britain can be seen in the Corn Laws (which applied to wheat). Parliament in 1815 passed a law forbidding the import of wheat if the price fell below a certain high level. Other similar laws followed. The result was high profits for landowners but an increased price for bread, a staple food for poor workers and the unemployed. In 1846, Parliament repealed the Corn Laws. This change marked a shift in power from the aristocracy to the middle class and to more of the common people.

PEEL'S CHEAP BREAD SHOP.
OPENED JANUARY 22, 1846.

522

among the upper and upper middle classes. These groups controlled the British Parliament. In the early 1800's, only men who owned a substantial amount of property could vote. Working people could neither vote nor hold office. Moreover, most members of Parliament came from rural parts of the country. Such bustling cities as Manchester, Leeds, Birmingham, and Sheffield had no representatives at all in Parliament.

Sometimes, workers turned violent in their demands for reform. Between 1815 and 1819, mob demonstrations and riots were common in Manchester and other industrial cities.

The government used violence as well. At one meeting in 1819, about 50,000 people gathered at St. Peter's Fields outside Manchester to hear speeches about reform. Although the gathering was peaceful, city officials panicked and ordered soldiers to break up the crowd. The troops charged with their sabers in hand, killing 11 and injuring hundreds. People all over Britain were shocked that these soldiers, who had last fought at Waterloo, were used against English people.

The beginning of unions Although workers could not vote, they found other ways of bringing pressure for reforms. Many workers joined together in groups called **unions**. A union spoke for all the workers in a particular trade. Unions bargained for better working conditions and higher wages. If factory owners refused these demands, union members could strike, or refuse to work.

The first workers to form unions were those whose special skills gave them extra bargaining power. Carpenters and spinners, for example, were in a far better position to strike than unskilled workers, who could easily be replaced. Thus, early unions helped the lower middle class more than the poorest workers.

The labor union movement was a slow and painful process. For many years, the British government denied the workers' right to form unions. Instead, union members were thrown in jail or fired. Although unions were not legally recognized for many years, they were tolerated after 1825.

Continuing tensions Because England was the first country to industrialize, social problems were the worst there. When the Industrial Revolution reached Belgium, Germany, and other parts of Europe, those countries learned from Britain's mistakes. By 1850, conditions for workers all over Europe gradually were improving.

Yet class tensions and factory abuses remained a major problem for every country that experienced the Industrial Revolution. Speaking in 1848, the French reformer and writer Alexis de Tocqueville gave a warning:

Consider what is happening among the working classes . . . Do you not see spreading among them, little by little, opinions and ideas that aim not to overturn such and such a ministry, or such laws, or such a government, but society itself, to shake it to the foundations upon which it now rests? Do you not see how, little by little, it comes to be said among them that all those placed above them are incapable and unworthy of governing them, that the division of wealth as it has happened in the world up to now is unjust?

De Tocqueville paused, then continued, "Gentlemen, I believe that at this very hour we are sleeping on a volcano." The years to come would prove how right De Tocqueville was.

Section REVIEW 4

Define: union
Identify: (a) Factory Act of 1833, (b) Mines Act of 1842, (c) laissez-faire government
Answer:
1. (a) Why did people flock into British cities and towns during the Industrial Revolution? (b) What problems arose as cities grew?
2. (a) Compare work in the country with city work. (b) What part did children play in factory work?
3. (a) What social class expanded as a result of industrialization? (b) How did landowners and aristocrats react to this growing class?
4. (a) Describe the class tensions that existed in industrialized nations by the mid-1800's. (b) How did laissez-faire governments contribute to this tension?
5. (a) Why did workers join together in unions? (b) How did the British government react?

Critical Thinking
6. The Industrial Revolution has been described as a mixed blessing. Do you agree or disagree? Support your answer with information from the chapter.

523

ANSWERS TO Section Review 4

Define:
an organization that bargains for better working conditions and higher wages
Identify:
(a) law that regulated child labor in factories (b) law that set limits on the work of children in mining
(c) adopted a hands-off attitude toward economic and social developments
Answer:
1. (a) to work in factories
(b) poor housing, sanitation, and education; unplanned growth of cities
2. (a) country—family worked as a unit, long hours from dawn to dusk, subject to weather; city—depended on factory bell, no seasonal change of pace, children at mercy of overseer (b) did exhausting, sometimes dangerous work, 12–14 hours daily for little pay
3. (a) middle class
(b) looked down on those who made fortunes in the "vulgar" business world
4. (a) great economic and social gaps between rich and poor (b) by not easing plight of poor and by using violence against workers in rebellions
5. (a) to bargain for better working conditions and higher wages (b) denied right to form unions
6. Answers should consider workers' control over their lives in terms of agricultural versus factory work, living standards, family relations, distribution of wealth, and the growing role of education, travel, and leisure.

Concluding the Chapter

1. **Chapter Closer**
   Have students review the industrial developments of the eighteenth century and choose one that they feel was most significant.

2. **Reteaching Activities**
   a. Outlining Have students write a sentence outline of Sections 1 and 2, using the headings and subheadings of the sections.
   b. Reading a Map Ask students to use the map on page 518 to explain the significance of each item in the map key for industrialization.

Answers to Chapter Review appear on page 508f.

Summary

1. **Many factors aided industrial growth.** Beginning in the late 1700's, the Industrial Revolution—a time of dramatic changes in the way work was done—transformed life in Great Britain. Many factors aided industrialization. These included new methods of farming that improved diets, a population explosion that created a large labor force, abundant mineral resources, a favorable geographic location for trade, a highly developed banking system, a favorable climate for new ideas, and political stability.

2. **Britain led in the rise of industry.** Industrialization occurred first in the British textile industry. New inventions speeded up weaving and spinning and led to the development of factories. The invention of a steam engine made it possible to locate factories near resources and markets.

3. **Industry grew and spread to new lands.** As industrialization sped up, businesses needed improved methods of transporting raw materials and finished products. Beginning in the late 1700's, Great Britain experienced a transportation revolution. Advances in transportation included a network of canals, improved roads, and the development of the railroad locomotive. Railroads spurred travel, promoted industry and agriculture, and provided jobs. Soon, despite British efforts to keep the secrets of industrialization to themselves, the Industrial Revolution spread to the United States and part of western Europe.

4. **Industry changed ways of life.** In the 1800's, industrialization affected every part of life in Great Britain. One of the most obvious changes was the growth of cities as people flocked to factories in search of work. Poor city planning, however, created inadequate housing and sanitation, pollution, frequent epidemics, and increased crime. Urban families had to adapt to new patterns of work, many of which threatened their health and the family unit. Working children suffered from abuses until Parliament passed laws to protect them. Some workers sought reforms by organizing unions, but laissez-faire attitudes and a lack of political power impeded progress. Industrialization also led to an expanded middle class that heightened tensions between rich and poor.

Reviewing the Facts

1. Define the following terms:
   a. Industrial Revolution   f. scientific farming
   b. enclosure   g. spinning jenny
   c. crop rotation   h. water frame
   d. entrepreneur   i. spinning mule
   e. union   j. power loom

Cartwright's power loom
Crompton's spinning mule
Arkwright's water frame
Watt's steam engine
Hargreaves's spinning jenny
Kay's flying shuttle
Tull's seed drill
Whitney's cotton gin
Beginning of Railway Age
Early unions form
First child labor law
Mines Act

1700   1725   1750   1775   1800   1825   1850

524

2. Explain how each of the following aided indus-trialization in Great Britain. (a) scientific farming (b) enclosure movement (c) population increase (d) geography (e) resources
3. Show how one invention led to another in the British cotton industry.
4. (a) What effect did the cotton gin have on British factories? (b) What effect did the steam engine have on industrialization?
5. Why did the Industrial Revolution require better methods of transportation?
6. (a) How did the expansion of the middle class affect class tensions? (b) What attitude toward the poor did the British government adopt? (c) How did workers try to bring about reform?

Basic Skills

1. **Interpreting graphs** Using your text and the graphs on page 515, answer the following ques-tions. (a) What general trend do all three graphs show? (b) What factors may account for the trend in each graph?
2. **Making a graph** Make a bar graph based on the transportation figures for 1745, 1796, and 1830 in the Footnote to History on page 515. Give your graph a title.
3. **Sequencing** (a) Arrange the following inventions in the order in which they were made: water-frame, cotton gin, spinning jenny, spinning mule, flying shuttle, power loom. (b) Explain what each invention contributed to the textile industry.
4. **Reading and interpreting maps** Answer the questions that follow, using the map on page 518 for reference. (a) What kinds of transportation were available between London and Bath, London and Wolverhampton, and London and Liverpool? (b) What were the advantages of Glasgow, Cardiff, and Leeds for industrial growth?

Researching and Reporting Skills

Writing a research paper In the preceding unit, you have written a historical essay. In this unit, you will write a research paper, bringing together ideas from various writers and ending with your conclusions. This project will be in five phases, over the chapters of this unit.

Phase I: Choosing and exploring a topic and iden-tifying sources
1. **Choosing a topic** In one of the chapters of this unit, find a subject you would like to know more about. Choose one aspect of it as your topic.
2. **Writing research questions** Write up to five questions identifying what you would like to know about the topic. These questions will guide you in finding the information you need.
3. **Identifying sources** (a) Consult a general reference work such as an encyclopedia or college text on your topic. This will give you an overview and provide you with a list of possible sources. (b) Consult the card catalog for books on your subject. (c) Use the *Readers' Guide* to identify articles on your subject. (d) Make a list of all the available sources on your subject.

Critical Thinking

1. **Comparing viewpoints** The impact of the In-dustrial Revolution varied according to social class. What might be the view of each of the following people toward the changes in industry: (a) an inventor, (b) an entrepreneur, (c) a skilled worker, (d) a hand weaver?
2. **Inferring** The Commercial Revolution of the sev-enteenth century had increased the wealth and power of the merchants. (a) What group would have been similarly affected by the Industrial Rev-olution? (b) How was the change reflected in po-litics?
3. **Applying economic concepts** Under mercantilism, governments had aided the growth of industry and trade. (a) What idea did Adam Smith introduce about the economic role of government? (b) How did this idea encourage the growth of industry and trade?

Perspectives on Past and Present

The Industrial Revolution was aided by the use of new technology. What changes in technology have led to a present-day revolution in industry?

Investigating History

To gain an understanding of conditions in an industrial city in the early nineteenth century, read selections from *Hard Times,* by Charles Dickens. What impres-sions do you get from this work?

525

CHAPTER
Evaluation

Chapter Test 22, Alternate Chapter Test 22, and Com-puter Test Bank Chapter 22 Test can be used to evalu-ate your students' under-standing of this chapter.

Restoration, Romanticism, and Revolution

Chapter Overview

The Congress of Vienna met in 1814 to settle European affairs after the defeat of Napoleon Bonaparte. Led by Metternich—Austria's chief minister—Austria, Great Britain, Prussia, and Russia took steps to encircle France, to restore a balance of power, and to return most rulers to their thrones. After 1815, conservatives once again controlled Europe. However, the political philosophies of liberals and radicals could not be stifled. New movements of nationalism and romanticism also developed. Nationalism was a force for change in Greece, Italy, and Germany. Romanticism, a reaction against the Enlightenment, influenced the arts and politics.

All these forces affected Latin America as well as Europe. Independence movements in the Americas resulted in Spain's loss through war of most of its American colonies, in Brazil's peaceful emergence as an independent country, and in the Monroe Doctrine in which the United States declared the Western Hemisphere closed to future colonization.

Reform and revolution also swept throughout Europe as France overthrew its Bourbon king, Britain broadened voting rights, and Napoleon III came to power in France. The year 1848 stands out as a year of European revolutions that eventually overthrew the agreements made at the Congress of Vienna.

Chapter Focus

Historians have noted that people often cling more strongly to the past during times of rapid social change. Have students speculate on reasons this might be so. Have students read the chapter introduction. Ask students why they think the Congress of Vienna wanted to "turn back the clock." Why were the delegates at the Congress of Vienna frightened by Napoleon Bonaparte? Explain that for the delegates in Vienna, the "good old days" existed when the rights and powers of the aristocracy were not challenged. As they read Chapter 23, have students speculate on the possibilites of returning to the past.

Chapter 23 Restoration, Romanticism, and Revolution 1815–1850

FOCUS Why did the Congress of Vienna want to bring back "the good old days"?

★ Advanced
● Basic

	SECTION 1	SECTION 2	SECTION 3	SECTION 4
Objectives	1. Explain the political and social ideals of Metternich. 2. Explain the concept of the balance of power as the main goal of the Congress of Vienna.	1. Relate the concept of nationalism to the outcomes of the Congress of Vienna. 2. Evaluate romantic themes in present-day cultures.	1. Name the contributions of Bolívar and San Martín to Latin American independence. 2. Explain how physical and cultural geography affected Latin American political boundaries. 3. Identify the basis of Mexico's nationalist movement.	1. Analyze the causes and effects of the revolutions of 1848. 2. Evaluate the results of the revolutions of 1848 and the failure of French radicals to maintain power.
Setting the Stage	Why political and social change is often met with resistance Transparency 73	The spread of nationalism in Europe	Causes of Latin American independence movements	Charles X's efforts to maintain his power
Teaching Strategies	Discussing History: Metternich Relating Past to Present: Balance of Power Check for Understanding	Writing about History: Nineteenth-Century Nationalism Relating Past to Present: Romanticism Check for Understanding	Writing about History: Bolívar and San Martín Using Geographic Themes: Region Transparency 74 Transferring Ideas: Mexican Nationalism Check for Understanding	Skill Building: Relating Causes and Effects Discussing History: The Revolutions of 1848 Check for Understanding
Guided Practice	Transparency 73 Q&A Section Review 1	Section Review 2	Transparency 74 Q&A Section Review 3	Section Review 4
Independent Practice Worksheets	Independent Practice 23.1 Vocabulary 23 Critical Thinking 23	Independent Practice 23.2 Geography Skills 23	Independent Practice 23.3	Independent Practice 23.4 Basic Skills 23
Enrichment	1. Primary Source: Voices 23.1 2. Researching for Points	1. Primary Source: Voices 23.2 2. Researching for Points	1. Primary Source: Voices 23.3 2. ★Preparing a Report: Brazil 3. Researching for Points	1. Primary Source: Voices 23.4 2. Researching for Points

Chapter Closer

●**Reteaching Activities** Summarizing, Recalling Information, Explaining

Chapter Review Summary, Reviewing the Facts, Basic Skills, Researching and Reporting Skills, Critical Thinking, Perspectives on Past and Present, Investigating History

Chapter Evaluation Chapter Test 23, Alternate Chapter Test 23, Computer Test Bank Chapter 23 Test

European leaders sought stability. 1

Setting the Stage

Ask students to imagine the excitement and satisfaction European aristocrats felt as they celebrated in Vienna. Since Napoleon Bonaparte's challenge to their world had been crushed, they expected a reinstatement of the old social order, headed by the aristocratic class. Ask students why political and social change is often met with resistance. Have students recall the changes caused by the Industrial Revolution and by the French Revolution. Tell students that the groups represented at the Congress of Vienna were frightened of revolutionary changes and wanted to reverse the trends that threatened their power. They hoped to restore what they perceived as order in European society. Show Map Transparency 73, *Europe in 1815,* to review the condition of the nations and empires of Europe.

Teaching Strategies

Discussing History: Metternich (Objective 1) Vienna was the perfect city to host a meeting that had the main goal of restoring old powers and ideas. The aristocratic palaces and offices of the monarchy in Vienna suggested stability and order. Suggest that Metternich's aristocratic manner and conservative ideas matched the setting of Vienna. Select a student to read Metternich's statement in the first paragraph of page 528. Why did Metternich fear democracy? Explain that Metternich offered Europe peace and stability, and believed that expanding the right to vote to all social classes would lead to chaos. Ask students to speculate on the observations Met-

ternich might make about democracy in the present-day United States.

Relating Past to Present: Balance of Power (Objective 2) Discuss the means by which present-day countries strive to maintain a balance of power. Ask students to explain why a balance is desirable and why it is difficult to maintain. List responses on the board. Ask what methods countries use to maintain a balance of power. (arms treaties and negotiation, trade agreements) Explain that the Congress of Vienna attempted to achieve an equilibrium between European powers so that none could become powerful enough to risk war or to conquer neighboring countries as Napoleon Bonaparte had done. Ask, "How did the Congress's treatment of France demonstrate attempts to achieve a balance of power in Europe?" Explain that after the negotiations in Vienna, Europe remained at peace for 30 years.

Check for Understanding Have students explain how the Congress of Vienna was a response to the French Revolution and how Metternich planned to achieve stability in Europe.

Enrichment Activities

1. **Reading a Primary Source** Assign Voices from the Past Resource Book 23.1.
2. **Researching for Bonus Points** Who was the French delegate to the Congress of Vienna? (Talleyrand)

New ideals affected politics and art. 2

Setting the Stage

Joan of Arc symbolized French nationalism in the fifteenth century (pages 248–249). Section 2 describes the spread of nationalism throughout Europe in the nineteenth century. The nationalist movements in the 1800's continued a centuries-old trend. Nationalist groups fought to establish independent nation-states in Italy, Greece, and Germany. National movements also sparked changes in literature and art that came to be known as the romantic movement.

Teaching Strategies

Writing about History: Nineteenth-Century Nationalism (Objective 1) *Prewriting* Discuss how the growing feelings of nationalism stimulated social unrest throughout Europe. Note that the Congress of Vienna was not interested in nationalist issues. Ask, "How did nationalist ambitions interfere with the Congress's goals of legitimacy and restoration?" Europe's aristocrats felt closer ties among themselves than with the middle and lower class members of their own countries. Metternich, for example, considered himself as much a citizen of Europe as of Austria. *Writing* Have students imagine they are members of Young Italy. Ask them to write a letter to Metternich explaining why the Congress of Vienna was wrong in restoring the old political divisions in Italy.

Relating Past to Present: Romanticism (Objective 2) Discuss the themes of nineteenth-century romanticism. Point out that the romantics championed individuality and nonconformity. Byron's personal life, for example, became the subject of gossip columns and public speculation. He willingly took the role of a social outcast, which made him a hero in the eyes of rebellious youths. Another romantic poet, Charles Baudelaire, delighted in shocking Parisian society by wearing outrageous costumes and by dyeing his hair green. Ask students how twentieth-century artists, writers, and musicians have expressed romantic themes such as nationalism, individualism, and idealism.

Check for Understanding Have students explain why nationalist movements found inspiration in romanticism, and why romantic themes supported nationalist movements.

Enrichment Activities

1. **Reading a Primary Source**
Assign Voices from the Past Resource Book 23.2.
2. **Researching for Bonus Points**
To whom did Beethoven dedicate his third symphony? (Napoleon Bonaparte)

Latin America won independence. 3

Setting the Stage

Call on students to name the present-day countries in Latin America. Ask students what countries in Latin America are in the news today and for what reasons. Explain that most of these countries gained their independence in the nineteenth century through revolutions. Latin Americans were influenced by the American and French

revolutions and viewed their own causes as part of the same struggle for liberty and justice.

Teaching Strategies

Writing about History: Bolívar and San Martín (Objective 1) *Prewriting* Have students compare the personalities and backgrounds of Bolívar and San Martín. Ask, "What was their common goal?" (Latin American independence) "Why had they arranged a meeting?" (to ally forces) Ask students to speculate why San Martín left his army with Bolívar and returned to Argentina. *Writing* Have students summarize the contributions of Bolívar and San Martín to Latin American independence and then offer an explanation of San Martín's departure. Students should review events leading up to the meeting, compare Bolívar's and San Martín's similar concerns about the Spanish army, and speculate on San Martín's reasons for leaving South America.

Using Geographic Themes: Region (Objective 2) Cultural geography is the study of geographic regions where people share common aspects of culture, such as language or customs. The landforms of Central America and South America encouraged a great diversity of regional cultures. At the same time, the physical and cultural geography of Latin America discouraged political unity. Explain that Simon Bolívar wanted to unite the newly independent countries of South America to create a system similar to the United States. However, Latin Americans set up independent, regional governments according to unifying geographic and cultural features. Show Map Transparency 74, *Latin America about 1830.* Ask what geographic features made unification difficult. (dis-

tances, mountains, cultural differences) Have students identify the countries that were established after independence.

Transferring Ideas: Mexican Nationalism (Objective 3) Select a student to read Father Hidalgo's words to the peasants (page 539). What did Hidalgo mean by "lands stolen from your forefathers 300 years ago"? (land taken by conquistadors) How did the actions of Spanish conquistadors in the 1500's establish a basis for Mexican nationalism in the 1800's? Explain that the basis of the Mexican revolution was conflict between wealthy landowners and landless peasants. Which groups most supported nationalism and why? Why did the creoles refuse to support Hidalgo's revolt?

Check for Understanding Ask students to identify the main causes and consequences of Latin America's independence movement.

Enrichment Activities

1. **Reading a Primary Source**
Assign Voices from the Past Resource Book 23.3.
2. **Preparing a Report**
Have advanced students report on present-day life in Brazil. They might include information on the native people of the Amazon and on the economic and political problems Brazil faces today. (See *National Geographic,* March 1987.)
3. **Researching for Bonus Points**
On what day do Mexicans celebrate their independence? (September 16, the day on which Father Hidalgo's revolt began)

Reform and revolution swept Europe.

4

Setting the Stage

Ask students how they think Americans would react if the President dissolved Congress, shut down newspapers, and limited voting rights. Explain to students that this is what the French king Charles X did in 1829. French citizens were outraged. Charles was counting on support from the representatives at the Congress of Vienna to suppress challenges to his power.

Teaching Strategies

Skill Building: Relating Causes and Effects (Objective 1) Review the political philosophies of conservatism, liberalism, and radicalism (page 529). Ask students to characterize the followers of each philosophy in 1848. Then ask whose interests were ignored at the Congress of Vienna. Explain that the revolutions in nineteenth-century Europe were fought mainly by peasants and workers, who had gained nothing at the Congress of Vienna. Their dissatisfactions were heightened by recurring economic depressions. Ask students how the French reacted to Charles X's policies. (They overthrew him and gave the crown to Louis Philippe.) Have students compare events in France with reform in England.

Discussing History: The Revolutions of 1848 (Objective 2) The revolutions of 1848 were violent responses to dissatisfaction with the resolutions of the Congress of Vienna. Ask students which revolts were most inspired by nationalist goals. The aristocrats at the Vienna Congress had ignored nationalistic feelings in their haste to restore old monarchies. The revolts attempted to shift power from aristocrats to the middle and lower classes. Which revolts succeeded in expanding rights for citizens? Point out that only in France was democracy the main goal of the revolutionaries. Why did the French become disillusioned with the radicals? (They were violent and quarrelsome.) Discuss how the election of Louis Napoleon was a reaction against French radicals.

Ask why Louis Napoleon and his philosophers appealed to French voters? (assurances of stability) Have students draw conclusions about the reasons for many of the failures for the revolutions of 1848.

Check for Understanding Have students summarize this section by completing the following sentence: Events in the 1830's and 1840's that undermined the power of conservatism in Europe included . . .

Enrichment Activities

1. **Reading a Primary Source** Assign Voices from the Past Resource Book 23.4.
2. **Researching for Bonus Points** What name was given to the reign of Louis Philippe? (the July monarchy)

ANSWERS TO
Chapter Review 23

Reviewing the Facts
1. **(a)** principle that rulers deposed by Napoleon be restored to their thrones **(b)** movement to give more power to elected parliaments **(c)** intellectual movement that emphasized feeling, individualism, love of nature, and love of the past **(d)** political strongman who ruled as a dictator
2. **(a)** settlement at this meeting preserved old political and social order and lasted about 40 years during which there were no wars **(b)** chief minister of Austria whose conservative goals were implemented at Congress of Vienna **(c)** one of Italy's early nationalists **(d)** ex-slave who drove French out of Haiti **(e)** brilliant general who led struggle for independence in northern South America **(f)** fighter for independence in southern South America **(g)** regent of Brazil who peacefully granted independence **(h)** priest who was a leader in Mexico's war for independence **(i)** farm worker turned priest who fought beside Hidalgo for Mexican independence **(j)** statement announcing that American continents could no longer be colonized by European powers **(k)** act that doubled the number of British voters **(l)** elected president of France who later declared himself emperor
3. **(a)** restore former monarchies, block France from expanding, and establish a balance of power **(b)** restoration of Bourbon rulers and many Hapsburg princes; creation of Kingdom of Netherlands and German Confederation; keeping France intact and awarding territories to winning power
4. Idea of nationalism won little support from the masses, and deep cultural differences divided northern and southern Italy. Metternich used censorship and arrests to stop the spread of nationalist ideas.
5. **(a)** Haiti **(b)** Slaves and free mulattoes led by Toussaint L'Ouverture revolted and drove the French forces from the island.
6. **(a)** Bolívar led his soldiers through the Andes to Colombia and defeated the Spanish army there, then freed Venezuela. In Ec-

uador, with the army of San Martín, he defeated the Spanish army. (b) San Martín freed Chile and preserved the freedom of Argentina.

7. (a) in 1810, Father Miguel Hidalgo led an army of peasants toward Mexico City where he was betrayed and executed. The next rebel leader, Morelos, ended up controlling most of Mexico. In 1813, a Mexican congress declared Mexico an independent republic. In 1820, Mexico's creoles, fearing that a new Spanish government would take away their privileges, united in support of independence. Iturbide, a creole officer who had executed Morelos, proclaimed Mexico independent in 1821. (b) It began in the countryside with Native Americans and mestizos playing an important role.

8. (a) American continent could not be colonized in the future by any European nation. (b) Both wanted to protect their economic interests in Latin America.

9. doubled the number of British male voters

10. Violence turned France against radicals and toward a more moderate, liberal government.

Basic Skills

1. Revolution in Latin America

Countries	European Colonial Power	Social Classes Involved	Leaders	Main Events
Haiti	France	Slaves, Free Mulattoes	Toussaint L'Ouverture	Revolt 1791
Venezuela	Spain	Creoles	Simon Bolívar	Independence declared 1811; Spain defeated Bogotá 1819; Free Venezuela 1821
Argentina	Spain	Creoles	José San Martín	Independence declared 1816; Victories in Chile 1817; Bolívar and San Martín 1821; Battle of Ayacucho safeguards independence 1824
Brazil	Portugal	Creoles	Dom Pedro	Napoleon invades Portugal 1807; Napoleon defeated; King leaves Dom Pedro regent; Dom Pedro declares independence of Brazil 1822
Mexico	Spain	Native Americans, Mestizos	Miguel Hidalgo, José Maria Morelos	Hidalgo and peasants march 1810; Morelos takes over most of Mexico but creoles oppose. He is executed 1815; Iturbide unites creoles in revolution. Mexican independence declared 1821

2. conservatism—supported the monarchy, rulers have total power to make laws and govern; liberalism—political power in the hands of landowners and educated, against complete democracy; radicalism—supported complete democracy, right of working class to vote, approved use of violence if necessary

3. (a) liberal—Louis Philippe, Bolívar; radical—Lamartine, Morelos, Louis Blanc; conservative—Charles X (b) Louis Philippe—shared power with Chamber of Deputies; Bolívar—represented creoles; Lamartine—wanted political power for French working class; Morelos—represented Mexico's Native Americans and mestizos in struggle against Spain; Louis Blanc—wanted political and economic reforms for French working class; Charles X—absolute monarch and tried to take power from Chamber of Deputies

Researching and Reporting Skills

Students' answers will vary.

Critical Thinking

1. Possible answers: degree of nationalistic feelings among people, responsiveness of monarch, strength and foresight of leaders

2. (a) opinion (b) yes; From the viewpoint of liberals and radicals it was a political failure. They lost reforms gained during period of French Revolution. The monarchists had strengthened themselves, as only landowners and royalty had any rights.

3. (a) to create republics; creole rule (b) Bolívar had only limited success; did lead to 16 independent countries and a few wealthy creoles captured power; but by 1830 all countries run by military dictators and people had few political freedoms.

Perspectives on Past and Present

Students' answers will vary.
(a) Nationalism is a significant factor in present-day Africa, Southeast Asia, and Latin America. (b) yes—In North America and much of Europe nationalism takes the form of patriotism and is most likely to surface around economic issues. It is not as much a motivational force as in newly emerging nations or where people are seeking independence from colonial powers, dictators, or dominating foreign nations. Note the Palestinian question in the Middle East, fighting in Nicaragua, political battles in Chile, and struggle in South Africa.

Investigating History

Students' answers will vary.

23 Restoration, Romanticism, and Revolution

1815 - 1850

Teaching with Pictures

Have students read the chapter introduction and direct their attention to the picture on page 526. Ask why the people who gathered in Vienna were celebrating, and which social classes were represented. Have students comment on the fashions, the setting, and the overall splendor of the scene. Tell students that it is estimated that the Austrian government spent the equivalent of $15 million entertaining its guests—at a time when the average working person earned scarcely the equivalent of $200 a year.

In the winter of 1814–1815, most of Europe's royalty came to Vienna. There, rulers and diplomats tried to undo the changes caused by the French Revolution and the Napoleonic wars.

Key Terms

diplomacy   mulatto
legitimacy   caudillo
conservatism
liberalism
radicalism
romanticism
peninsular
creole
mestizo

526

Read and Understand

1. European leaders sought stability.
2. New ideals affected politics and art.
3. Latin America won independence.
4. Reform and revolution swept Europe.

The first leaves were beginning to fall from the trees in Vienna, capital of the Austrian empire, as distinguished visitors began to arrive in September 1814. Never before had any city seen such a gathering of European royalty. They came from every corner of the continent—emperors and empresses, kings and queens, princes and princesses, grand dukes and grand duchesses, and hundreds of other lords and ladies. They came to attend a special meeting that promised to be the most glittering social event of their lifetime. With them came thousands of advisers and servants—foreign ministers, secretaries, ladies-in-waiting, and so on.

The Congress of Vienna had been called by four of the Great Powers—Austria, Great Britain, Prussia, and Russia—to celebrate and

Chapter 23 Resources

GEOGRAPHY
- Geography Skills 23
- Transparencies 73, 74

REINFORCEMENT
- Vocabulary 23

- Basic Skills 23
- Reteaching 23
- Making Connections Study Guide 23

ENRICHMENT
- Critical Thinking 23
- History and Literature 23

ASSESSMENT
- Chapter Test 23
- Alternate Chapter Test 23
- Computer Test Bank

confirm their victory over the fifth, France. (A Great Power was a country that could shape international events.) After nine years of almost constant war, the allied powers had finally defeated Napoleon, exiling him to the Mediterranean island of Elba. Now the victorious leaders gathered to restore the boundaries of Europe as they had existed before Napoleon's conquests.

Francis I, emperor of Austria, was host for the conference. He spared no expense in entertaining his guests. The royal visitors were treated to what seemed like a never-ending series of balls, parades, fireworks, horse shows, dances, theatrical performances, and concerts. On November 29, an enthusiastic crowd assembled to hear Vienna's most prominent composer, Ludwig von Beethoven (BAY-toh-vuhn) conduct his Seventh Symphony. Of course, there were always parties. "Nothing but visits and return visits," wrote one tired archduke. "Eating, fireworks, public illuminations. For eight or ten days, I haven't been able to work at all. What a life!"

In spite of appearances, some very important business took place in Vienna. The rulers and ministers who gathered there redrew the map of Europe. Their so-called Vienna Settlement lasted about 40 years. During that period (1815–1853), there were no wars among the Great Powers.

They also hoped through **diplomacy,** or the making of agreements by officials, to establish peace. In effect, they wanted to return to the time before the French Revolution. In this chapter, you will look at attempts to preserve the old political and social order and learn why it was impossible for such attempts to succeed.

European leaders sought stability. 1

While hundreds of aristocrats attended glittering parties, the real business of the Congress of Vienna went on behind closed doors. Most of the decisions made at Vienna during the winter of 1814–1815 were made in secret among representatives of the five Great Powers.

The rulers of three of these countries—King Frederick William III of Prussia, Czar Alexander I of Russia, and, of course, Emperor Francis I of Austria—were present at Vienna. However, none of these men was as influential as the suave and polished chief minister of Austria, Prince Klemens von Metternich (MEHT-uhr-nihk).

Metternich dominated the Congress.

Metternich (1773–1859) was a tall, handsome man whose charm worked equally well with his fellow diplomats and with the elegant ladies of Vienna. He was not Austrian by birth; his family had estates in what is now Germany. Like many European aristocrats, he considered French his first language, though he spoke four others fluently. Metternich thought of himself as a European, not as a citizen of any single country. "Europe has for a long time held for me the significance of a fatherland," he once said.

Early in his career, Metternich linked himself to the Hapsburgs, the rulers of Austria. He rose rapidly through the diplomatic ranks. In 1809, at the age of 36, he became Austria's foreign minister and held that office for the next 39 years, until 1848. Because of his immense influence on European politics, these years are often called the Age of Metternich.

Metternich dominated the Congress of Vienna.

527

SECTION 1
Objectives and Teaching Strategies

OBJECTIVE 1. Explain the political and social ideals of Metternich.

Teaching Strategy: *Discussing History: Metternich* (page 526c)

OBJECTIVE 2. Explain the concept of the balance of power as the main goal of the Congress of Vienna.

Teaching Strategy: *Relating Past to Present: Balance of Power* (page 526c)

■ DISCUSSION

Why was it to Metternich's advantage to feel the whole of Europe as his fatherland? (to discourage nationalist feelings that might disrupt Austria's control of loosely joined and disparate German states)

SECTION 1
Resources

GEOGRAPHY
■ Transparency 73

REINFORCEMENT
■ Independent Practice 23.1

ENRICHMENT
■ Voices from the Past 23.1

ASSESSMENT
■ Section Quiz 23.1

One reason for the restraint against France was the negotiating skill of Prince Talleyrand, France's representative at the Congress. He took advantage of the disagreements among the other powers to secure the best settlement for France.

Cooperative Learning

Review the viewpoints of the French conservatives, liberals, and radicals following the revolution. Tell students to imagine that their school has just had a nonviolent revolution. The senior class tried to take over control of the entire school. The junior and sophomore classes united to defeat the senior class. Now the students in this room must make some decisions about how to resume normal school operations. Should any concessions be made to the senior class? Should they be punished? Allow students to choose the roles of either conservatives, liberals, or radicals. Have groups of three students propose measures to resolve the issues of this imaginary revolution in the tradition of the Congress of Vienna. Group members should all agree to their groups' proposals. Combining groups to form a larger "Congress" might give students some idea of what the congress in 1815 was like. Do students feel that someone like Metternich would help or hinder the process?

Metternich disliked and distrusted the democratic ideals of the French Revolution. Like most other European aristocrats, he was convinced that Napoleon's warlike dictatorship was the natural result of experiments with democracy. Metternich believed in the value of keeping things as they were. "The first and greatest concern for the immense majority of every nation," he said, "is the stability of laws—never their change."

Metternich had three goals at the Congress of Vienna. First, he wanted to strengthen the countries that surrounded France to prevent future French aggression. Second, he wanted to restore a balance of power, so that no country was a threat to others. Third, he wanted to restore the royal families to the thrones they had held before Napoleon's conquests.

The Congress restored the old order.

Originally, the Congress of Vienna was scheduled to last for four weeks. Instead, it went on for nine months, until June 1815. One reason for the delay was Napoleon's escape from Elba in the spring of 1815. His last, desperate attempt to regain power in France ended in defeat at Waterloo in June 1815 (page 499). After this interruption, the Congress went on with its work. On the whole, the agreements that the diplomats made at Vienna followed Metternich's plans.

The encirclement of France To keep France from renewing its drive for power, the Congress made the countries around France stronger.

- The Austrian Netherlands was united with the Dutch Republic to form a single Kingdom of the Netherlands.
- A group of 39 German states were loosely joined into a newly created German Confederation, dominated by Austria.
- The Congress recognized Switzerland as an independent and neutral nation.
- The Kingdom of Sardinia in Italy was strengthened by the addition of Piedmont and Genoa.

The balance of power Although the leaders of Europe wanted to weaken France, they did not want to go too far. If they destroyed France, they would destroy the balance of power as well. Then a new country might become so strong that it threatened them all. Thus, the victorious powers were surprisingly easy on the defeated France.

France was required to give up all the territories Napoleon had taken. France itself, however, remained intact, keeping roughly the same boundaries it had had in 1790. France also kept most of its overseas possessions, its army, and an independent government. As a result, France remained a major European power.

The winning powers, however, took some prizes for themselves. Austria won the Italian territories of Venetia and Lombardy. Russia took over most of Poland. Prussia gained land in the Rhine valley of western Germany. Britain got a host of small but valuable territories for its overseas empire. Furthermore, the balance of power brought the peace and security needed for Britain's overseas trade to grow and flourish.

Legitimacy The Great Powers agreed that, as far as possible, those rulers whom Napoleon had driven from their thrones should be restored to power. This was the principle of **legitimacy.** In France, Louis XVIII returned as king. On the French flag, the Bourbon fleur-de-lis replaced the tricolor of the revolution.

The Congress also restored the Bourbon rulers in Spain and in the Italian Kingdom of the Two Sicilies. Hapsburg princes came back to rule several states in northern Italy. Many (though not all) of the former rulers of the German states of central Europe also regained their thrones.

The Congress of Vienna was a political triumph in many ways. Its settlements were fair enough that no country was left bearing a grudge. Thus, the Congress did not sow the seeds of future wars. In that sense, it was more successful than many other peace meetings in history. Not until 1853 were any of the five Great Powers involved in wars against one another. Not until 1914 did another major war occur.

New political philosophies arose.

Despite their efforts to undo the French Revolution, the leaders at the Congress of Vienna could not turn back the clock. That revolution had given Europe its first experiment in democratic government. Although the experiment failed, it set new political ideas in motion.

The major political divisions of the early 1800's had their roots in the French Revolution. The political labels of *conservative, liberal,* and *radical* grew from attitudes toward that revolution.

Europe in 1815

KINGDOM OF NORWAY AND SWEDEN

SCOTLAND

UNITED KINGDOM OF GREAT BRITAIN AND IRELAND

IRELAND

ENGLAND
London

DENMARK

North Sea

Baltic Sea

•St. Petersburg

•Moscow

RUSSIAN EMPIRE

Niemen River

PRUSSIA

•Warsaw

POLAND (to Russia)

Amsterdam HANOVER

K. OF THE NETHERLANDS

Berlin

Elbe River

Oder River

SAXONY

Prague

Dnieper River

Don River

Dniester River

ATLANTIC OCEAN

Paris•

Seine River

Loire River

K. OF THE KINGDOM

BAVARIA

Danube River

Rhine R.

AUSTRIAN

Vienna

River

Bug River

Prut River

FRANCE

SWITZ.

VENETIA

LOMBARDY

PARMA

MODENA

LUCCA

TUSCANY

PAPAL STATES

EMPIRE

Buda• •Pest

Danube R.

Black Sea

MONTENEGRO

Rhone River

PORTUGAL

Tagus River

Madrid

SPAIN

Gibraltar (Br.)

KINGDOM OF SARDINIA

CORSICA (Fr.)

Rome•

Naples•

KINGDOM OF THE TWO SICILIES

MEDITERRANEAN

MALTA (Br.)

CRETE

SEA

Athens•

OTTOMAN

Istanbul•

EMPIRE

CYPRUS

KEY
—— Boundary of the German Confederation

0   300 Miles

Map Study

Compare this map with the one on page 495. What parts of its empire did France lose? What replaced the Confederation of the Rhine?

Conservatism Conservatives argued that the revolution had accomplished nothing but harm. They believed in the principles of **conservatism**—protecting the existing traditional forms of government. Some moderate conservatives, mostly in Great Britain, believed in constitutional monarchy. More extreme conservatives believed in absolute monarchy. Metternich was a classic conservative, as were most of the other European leaders at the Congress. Conservatives drew their greatest support from wealthy landowners and nobles who had been satisfied with the old order and were happy to see it restored.

Liberalism Liberals approved of the early reforms of the French Revolution but hated the violence of the Reign of Terror. They supported **liberalism,** the movement to give more power

to elected parliaments. This meant limited parliaments for which only those who were educated and owned property could vote. Few liberals favored democracy. In fact, they feared the "mob" as much as conservatives did. Liberalism appealed mainly to the upper bourgeoisie, business leaders, and merchants. Such people were barred from politics in some countries because they were not of noble birth.

Radicalism Supporters of **radicalism** favored drastic and, if necessary, violent change. The word *radical* was used at this time to describe supporters of democratic government. Many radicals justified even the Reign of Terror as necessary to make France a true democracy. Radicals believed that governments everywhere should practice the ideals of the French Revolution.

529

ANSWERS TO
Map Study

The Netherlands, Hanover, parts of Italy, and the Illyrian Provinces; German Confederation

■ DISCUSSION

What do *conservative, liberal,* and *radical* mean today?

ANSWERS TO
Section Review 1

Define:
(a) the making of agreements by officials
(b) principle that rulers Napoleon had driven from their thrones should be restored (c) principle that advocated conserving traditional forms of government (d) principle that advocated more power for elected but limited parliaments (e) principle that supported democratic government and favored drastic change

Identify:
(a) meeting called by Austria, Great Britain, Prussia, and Russia (b) country that

(continued)

ANSWERS TO (continued)

could shape international events **(c)** minister who dominated Congress of Vienna **(d)** 39 loosely joined German states, dominated by Austria **(e)** agreement among rulers of Russia, Prussia, and Austria against liberalism **(f)** restored Bourbon king of France

Answer:

1. to restore boundaries of Europe as they had existed before Napoleon's conquests

2. Austria, Great Britain, Prussia, Russia, and France

3. strengthen countries surrounding France to prevent French aggression, restore a balance of power, and restore royal families to their thrones

4. **(a)** forced to give up all territories Napoleon had taken but allowed to keep most of its overseas possessions, its army, and an independent government **(b)** made stronger **(c)** loosely joined to form a newly created German Confederation

5. **(a)** belief in constitutional or even absolute monarchy **(b)** approval of early reforms of French Revolution and government by an elected, limited parliament **(c)** support of democratic government and idea of change

6. the only constitutional monarchy

7. Kings and princes were restored.

8. **(a)** settlement fair enough that no country leaves bearing a grudge and a balance of power remains intact **(b)** temporarily (Peace lasted about 40 years.) **(c)** political ideals of liberty, equality, and fraternity introduced by French Revolution

Radicals sometimes came from the working class. The Parisian sans-culottes are a good example. Radicalism also drew support from intellectuals and students. However, support for radicalism was not widespread.

Conservatives controlled Europe.

The Congress of Vienna was a victory for conservatives. Kings and princes were restored in country after country, in keeping with Metternich's goals. However, there were important differences from one country to another.

Britain's constitutional monarchy Britain was the only one of the Great Powers with a true constitutional monarchy. Parliament actually had far more power than the ruler. Yet Britain was far from a democracy. Most members of Parliament were wealthy landowners. They were elected by a tiny fraction of the population. Only men who owned a substantial amount of property were qualified to vote. Nevertheless, Britain's form of government was much more open than anything found in eastern Europe.

Absolute rulers in eastern Europe Generally speaking, governments were more conservative in eastern Europe than they were in western Europe. The rulers of Russia, Prussia, and Austria were absolute monarchs. Late in 1815, the rulers of those three countries drew up an agreement called the Holy Alliance. In this agreement against liberalism, Czar Alexander I, Emperor Francis I, and King Frederick William III promised to help one another if any of them were threatened by reformers or revolutionaries.

Tension in France Among the Great Powers, France's position was unique. The old Bourbon dynasty ruled once more, but an elected Chamber of Deputies shared some power with Louis XVIII. This parliament was even less democratic than Britain's. Only about one of every 300 French men (and no French women at all) had the right to vote.

France after 1815 was deeply divided politically. Conservatives were happy with the Bourbon restoration and determined to make it last. Liberals wanted the king to share more power with the Chamber of Deputies and to grant the middle class the right to vote. Many people in the lower class, especially in Paris, remained committed to the ideals of liberty, equality, and fraternity. They were determined to overthrow the Bourbons and make France a republic once again. It was an explosive mixture of ideas and factions that would contribute directly to revolutions in 1830 and again in 1848.

Section REVIEW 1

Define: (a) diplomacy, (b) legitimacy, (c) conservatism, (d) liberalism, (e) radicalism
Identify: (a) Congress of Vienna, (b) Great Power, (c) Metternich, (d) German Confederation, (e) Holy Alliance, (f) Louis XVIII
Answer:
1. What was the purpose for which the Congress of Vienna met?
2. Which countries were the Great Powers of Europe?

DAILY LIFE ▶ *City of Waltzes*

A princely visitor to Vienna in 1815 remarked, "The congress doesn't march—it dances." Indeed it did, to lilting tunes in three-quarter time, written for the new dance that was sweeping Vienna, the waltz. The aristocratic visitors found the waltz far more exciting than the formal minuet that they had danced for years. Adapted from a country dance, the waltz appealed to dancers of all social classes. The word *waltz* came from the German word for "revolving." Partners whirled across the floor with their arms wrapped around each other in a way that many people thought indecent for public view.

3. What were Metternich's three goals at the Congress of Vienna?
4. (a) What were the results of the congress for France? (b) For the small states around France? (c) For the German states?
5. (a) In general, what were the political ideas of conservatives? (b) Liberals? (c) Radicals?
6. How was the British government different from governments in the rest of Europe?
7. How was the Congress of Vienna a triumph for conservatism?

Critical Thinking
8. (a) What are the factors that make a peace conference successful? (b) By those standards, was the Congress of Vienna a success? (c) What trends or movements did the Congress fail to recognize?

New ideals affected politics and art. 2

Liberals, conservatives, and radicals debated the roles of kings, parliaments, and people in government. Meanwhile, two new movements were arising that blurred the lines between these political theories. One of the new movements was nationalism. The other was romanticism.

Nationalism was a force for change.

Nationalism is the belief that a person's greatest loyalty should be to a nation-state. In the years after 1800, this belief fired the hearts of millions of Europeans and reshaped the map of Europe.

To understand nationalism, let us review the meaning of the word *nation*. A group of people who share similar traditions, history, and language make up a nation. Usually, they live in the same geographic area as well. If such a group is united under its own government, it is known as a *nation-state*. For nationalists of all groups, forming such a nation-state became the goal of their lives.

In 1815, there were very few nation-states in Europe. A quick glance at the map shows no countries called Italy, Germany, Greece, Hungary, or Poland. Only France and Spain qualified as nation-states. England, like France, had developed as a nation during the late Middle Ages (pages 249–254). However, England was now part of Great Britain, along with Ireland and Scotland. Many Irish and Scots definitely did not think of themselves as part of an English nation.

Modern nationalism was born during the French Revolution. The leaders of the revolution stressed the equality of all French people. Overjoyed at the chance to govern themselves, the French felt a burst of national pride. "Our life, our goods, and our talents do not belong to us," cried one French army volunteer. "It is to the nation, to France, [that] everything belongs." This national pride was an important factor in Napoleon's remarkable victories.

Ironically, France's military success sowed the seeds of its own downfall, because nationalism grew quickly too among the people France conquered (page 497). Fired by national pride, Spaniards, Italians, and Germans rebelled against their French conquerors.

The downfall of Napoleon did not lead immediately to the creation of new nation-states in Europe. In 1815, many national groups were ruled by larger, more powerful states. Most Poles, for example, lived under Russian rule. Hungarians and many Slavs lived under Austrian rule.

As nationalism spread, such groups became more and more unhappy with their situation. They formed nationalist societies, often meeting in secret. These societies published books and newspapers that stressed each group's unique character and the glories of its past.

Greece won its independence.

The first new nation-state to win its freedom was Greece. For centuries, Greece had been part of the Ottoman empire, which controlled most of southeastern Europe. As nationalism spread across Europe, the Greeks were among the first to be affected. Greek nationalists demanded that Greece take its place among the nation-states of Europe. A major revolt against Ottoman rule broke out in 1821.

The Greek war for independence was a difficult struggle. However, the Greeks had two great advantages that other rebellious groups such as the Poles and the Irish did not. First, the Ottoman army was much weaker than the Russian or the British armies. Second, the cause of Greek

531

SECTION 2 Objectives and Teaching Strategies

OBJECTIVE 1. Relate the concept of nationalism to the outcomes of the Congress of Vienna.

Teaching Strategy: *Writing about History: Nineteenth-Century Nationalism* (page 526c)

OBJECTIVE 2. Evaluate romantic themes in present-day cultures.

Teaching Strategy: *Relating Past to Present: Romanticism* (page 526c)

■ BACKGROUND

Belgium also gained its independent status early, winning freedom in 1830, the same year as Greece.

SECTION 2 Resources

ASSESSMENT
■ Section Quiz 23.2

REINFORCEMENT
■ Independent Practice 23.2

ENRICHMENT
■ Voices from the Past 23.2

■ BACKGROUND

Like the Greeks, the Italian people could point to a glorious past. Ancient Rome had, of course, ruled a sweeping empire around the Mediterranean Sea. Latin was the ancestor of most languages in western Europe.

Lord Byron, a leading romantic poet, posed for this portrait dressed as a Greek nationalist.

independence was popular with many Europeans whose education had given them tremendous respect for ancient Greek culture. "Fair Greece! Sad relic of departed worth!" lamented Lord Byron, a British poet. "Immortal, though no more; though fallen, great!" Byron went to Greece as a volunteer soldier and died there in 1824.

Eventually, the Great Powers took the side of the Greeks. In 1827, a joint British, French, and Russian fleet destroyed an Ottoman fleet at the Battle of Navarino. In 1830, a treaty granted Greece full independence. This success encouraged other nationalities to seek independence.

Mazzini sparked Italian nationalism.

The situation in Italy was much more complicated than that in Greece. Italy was divided into many different states. Some parts were ruled by Austria. Others were fiercely independent, in the traditions of the Renaissance city-states. Part of Italy was ruled by the pope. Unity was the great ambition of Italian nationalists.

Modern Italian nationalism began with Napoleon. In 1805, he combined the many separate Italian states into a single French-controlled Kingdom of Italy. The Congress of Vienna restored most of the old divisions. Yet the idea of a united Italy survived.

Among Italy's early nationalists was Giuseppe Mazzini (maht-TSEE-nee). "A people destined to achieve great things," argued Mazzini, "must one day or other form a nation-state. Italy therefore will be one. Her geographical conditions, her language, her literature, and the desires of her people all point to this aim."

In 1831, the 26-year-old Mazzini formed a nationalist group called Young Italy, which no one older than 40 was allowed to join. At its peak during the 1830's, Young Italy claimed 60,000 members. Most were of middle-class backgrounds. Unfortunately for Mazzini, the idea of nationalism won little support from the Italian masses. Deep cultural differences divided northern and southern Italy. An urban worker in Milan had little in common with a peasant farmer in Sicily.

Austria proved an even bigger obstacle to Italian unity. The Austrian emperor ruled Lombardy and Venetia in northern Italy. Several of his Hapsburg relatives ruled other Italian states. Metternich saw Italian nationalism as a serious threat to Austria, so he made every effort to suppress such groups as Young Italy. Austrian officials arrested Mazzini many times.

In Italy, as in other European countries, nationalism was closely connected to liberalism. Both ideas appealed to people who were educated and eager to govern their countries. In most cases, both nationalists and liberals came from the middle class. Teachers, lawyers, and business people often led the struggle for more liberal government and the formation of nation-states.

Germany was disunited.

As in Italy, there was tremendous interest in nationalism in the German states during the early 1800's. However, unity seemed far away in 1815. The area where most Germans lived was divided into 39 separate countries. The Congress of Vienna had set up a loose union known as the German Confederation.

Every year, each German state sent representatives to Frankfurt to attend a Federal Diet. The diet was a kind of all-German parliament that discussed the problems of member states. The

532

German Federal Diet was almost powerless. It had no all-German army to enforce its decisions. It could make no laws unless all 39 states approved. Such agreement was almost impossible because the two largest states—Austria and Prussia—rarely agreed on anything.

Nevertheless, the German Confederation was an important first step toward a German nation. The Federal Diet became a rallying point for liberals and nationalists who wanted unity.

The largest and most powerful member of the German Confederation in 1815 was the Austrian empire. Its Hapsburg emperors ruled peoples of a dozen different nationalities.

The dominant national group within the empire was German. The Hapsburgs themselves were German. So were most of the empire's political and military leaders. Most Germans in the empire lived in and around the city of Vienna. Elsewhere in the empire, there were millions of Hungarians, Czechs, Serbs, Poles, Italians, Romanians, and other peoples.

Metternich was well aware that nationalism posed an enormous threat to the Austrian empire. Throughout his long tenure as Austrian foreign minister, he used censorship and arrests to stop the spread of nationalist ideas. While such tactics slowed nationalism, they did not wipe it out. The result was a constant buildup of pressure as the various peoples moved closer and closer to rebellion against the Hapsburgs.

Romanticism rejected reason.

Nationalism was strongly linked to a second great intellectual movement that began around 1800. That second movement was **romanticism,** which was a reaction against the Enlightenment. Romantics were in part rebelling against the orderly, rational approach of writers such as Voltaire and musicians such as Mozart. Romanticism affected politics as well as literature, art, and music. Many romantics were also nationalists. Lord Byron, who died fighting for Greek freedom, was a leading romantic poet.

Romanticism was marked by four distinctive characteristics. One was its heavy emphasis on emotion and passion. The romantics stressed feeling over thinking. As the German novelist Johann Wolfgang von Goethe wrote, "What I know, anyone can know, but my heart is my own, peculiar to itself."

Voice from the Past | *Poetry and Patriotism*

Britain's most popular romantic novelist and poet was Sir Walter Scott (1771–1832). Many of Scott's writings told heroic stories of the Middle Ages. This poem shows the link between romanticism and nationalism.

Breathes there a man with soul so dead,
Who never to himself hath said,
* 'This is my own, my native land!'*
Whose heart hath ne'er within him burn'd
As home his footsteps he hath turn'd
* From wandering on a foreign strand?*
If such there breathe, go, mark him well;
For him no Minstrel raptures swell;
High though his titles, proud his name,
Boundless his wealth as wish can claim;
Despite those titles, power, and pelf,
The wretch, concentred all in self,
Living, shall forfeit fair renown,
And, doubly dying, shall go down
To the vile dust from whence he sprung,
Unwept, unhonor'd, and unsung.

1. According to Scott, what sort of man is dead in his soul?
2. What do you think the phrase "concentred all in self" means?
3. (a) What is the fate of such a person in life? (b) In death?

533

■ BACKGROUND

Metternich convinced German rulers to enact the Carlsbad Decrees—measures abolishing the *Burschenschaft,* clubs of college students in which nationalism was becoming popular.

■ DISCUSSION

While Francis I suppressed literary creativity, Vienna did enjoy a golden age of music. Why might music have been encouraged but not literature?

ANSWERS TO
Voice from the Past

1. one who has never felt great joy when returning to his native land
2. thinking only of himself and not of his nation
3. (a) to forfeit renown
(b) to be unwept

ANSWERS TO
Section Review 2

Define:
(a) belief that a person's greatest loyalty is to a nation-state **(b)** group who share traditions, history, and language **(c)** reaction against Enlightenment
(continued)

ANSWERS TO *(continued)*

Identify:
(a) battle for Greek independence, 1827 **(b)** romantic poet who died fighting for Greek freedom **(c)** founder of Young Italy **(d)** nationalist group, all under age 40 **(e)** France's leading romantic novelist, a woman **(f)** Viennese composer of romantic music **(g)** British romantic novelist and poet

Answer:
1. **(a)** traditions, history, and language **(b)** France and Spain

2. stressed the equality of all French people and gave them opportunity for self-government

3. Greeks revolted against Ottoman rule, and, aided by the Great Powers, achieved independence.

4. little mass support; cultural differences between northern and southern Italy; Metternich's suppression of nationalistic groups

5. no all-German army to enforce decision; could make no laws without approval of 29 states

6. Austria consisted of many nationalities.

7. emotion and passion: Goethe; individualism: glorification of heroes; celebration of nature: Turner's landscape paintings; glorification of past: collections of old ballads and folktales

8. **(a)** geographical conditions, language, literature, and the desires of the people **(b)** Look for answers to consider the effect of geography on natural boundaries, the role of a common language and literature in uniting a people, and the effect of the French Revolution on the Italian people.

Romantic painters emphasized dramatic aspects of nature and the human soul (right). Among the leading figures of romanticism were George Sand (top), Beethoven (bottom), and Mary Shelley (center), author of Frankenstein.

A second characteristic of romanticism was its emphasis on the individual. Romantics celebrated individuals, especially heroic rebels. Romantic writers and artists glorified such legendary heroes as the English King Arthur and also such powerful historic figures as Napoleon. It mattered little whether the hero was a revolutionary or a king. It was heroic action that counted.

A third feature of romanticism was its celebration of nature. France's leading romantic novelist, Amandine Aurore Dupin, lovingly described the French countryside and rustic life. (To win a wider audience for her novels, Dupin took the male pen name George Sand.) British writer Emily Brontë made the windswept moors of northern England the setting for her powerful romantic novel, *Wuthering Heights.*

Last but not least, romanticism glorified the past. Romantics yearned for "the good old days," a past that seemed more noble than anything the modern age had to offer. They looked back longingly to a preindustrial age. The deeds of past kings, knights, and outlaws seemed more worthy of song and story than those of factory owners and railway engineers.

Romanticism touched many arts.

Similar ideas—the emphasis on emotion, individual expression, nature, and the glories of the past—affected all the arts. Painting and music as well as literature followed the romantic path.

Romanticism in music In music, Ludwig van Beethoven was a key figure. In his early years, he wrote music in the classical manner (page

Footnote to History

Beethoven never heard his Ninth Symphony. During his last years, he was completely deaf. When he finished conducting the first performance of the Ninth, the audience burst into thunderous applause. Beethoven, facing the orchestra, heard nothing. Only when a singer turned him around did he realize that he was being given a standing ovation.

466). In his later symphonies and concertos, however, Beethoven turned away from the tightly controlled compositions he had written in the 1700's. His ninth and last symphony is an overwhelmingly emotional celebration of freedom, dignity, and spiritual triumph. Later romantic composers such as Robert Schumann and Felix Mendelssohn similarly appealed to the hearts and souls of their listeners.

Romanticism in painting Emotion dominated the work of painters as well. Some painters, such as the English painter Joseph Turner and the German Caspar David Friedrich, used landscape scenes to convey moods. Other artists, including France's Eugene Delacroix, painted dramatic scenes from history to arouse the emotions of the viewer.

Romanticism fueled nationalism.

Many romantics were also whole-hearted nationalists. The celebration of past glories appealed to both romantics and nationalists. So did the strong emotions aroused by nationalism.

Writers collected the ballads and folktales of their national group. Such stories, said romantic nationalists, expressed the time-honored spirit of their people. In Germany, for example, the Grimm brothers gathered a collection of fairy tales, which they published in 1812.

In art, romantics often showed their country as a human figure. The French painter Delacroix, for example, portrayed France as a beautiful woman in such works as "Liberty Leading the People" and "Liberty on the Barricades."

Section REVIEW 2

Define: (a) nationalism, (b) nation-state, (c) romanticism
Identify: (a) Battle of Navarino, (b) Byron, (c) Mazzini, (d) Young Italy, (e) George Sand, (f) Beethoven, (g) Scott
Answer:
1. (a) What are the common characteristics of a nation? (b) Which countries in Europe were nation-states in 1815?
2. Explain how the French Revolution brought about the beginning of modern nationalism.
3. How did Greece become a nation?

4. What were some of the obstacles to Italian unification?
5. Why was the German Federal Diet weak?
6. Why was nationalism a threat to Austria?
7. Name four characteristics of romanticism and give an example of each.

Critical Thinking
8. Reread the quotation by Mazzini on page 532. (a) What four factors does he list as developing Italian nationalism? (b) How would each of those factors help Italy become a nation-state?

Latin America won independence. 3

Just as nationalism became a major force in Europe during the early 1800's, it also became important in the Western Hemisphere. As you know, 13 of Britain's North American colonies became independent in the late 1700's, forming the United States of America (page 476). Between 1800 and 1825, similar wars for independence were fought in the region called Latin America.

The term *Latin America* applies to the lands south of the United States where Spanish, Portuguese, and French are spoken. All these languages developed from Latin. The region includes Mexico, Central America, South America, and most of the islands of the Caribbean.

Several events outside Latin America helped to spark the drive for independence. The ideals of the Enlightenment spread to the educated people of Latin America. When the French Revolution broke out, many Latin Americans applauded its early reforms, if not its later violence. The American Revolution showed that determined rebels could defeat a European government. Finally, Napoleon's conquests in Europe set off a wave of nationalism that affected Latin Americans as well as Europeans.

Latin American society was divided.

On the surface, the Latin American revolutions of the early 1800's appear similar to the American Revolution. In every case, revolutionaries overthrew a government controlled by a European

535

SECTION 3 Objectives and Teaching Strategies

OBJECTIVE 1. Name the contributions of Bolívar and San Martín to Latin American independence.

Teaching Strategy: *Writing about History: Bolívar and San Martín* (page 526d)

OBJECTIVE 2. Explain how physical and cultural geography affected Latin American political boundaries.

Teaching Strategy: *Using Geographic Themes: Region* (page 526d)

OBJECTIVE 3. Identify the basis of Mexico's nationalist movement.

Teaching Strategy: *Transferring Ideas: Mexican Nationalism* (page 526d)

■ BACKGROUND

While royalty listened to Beethoven, the lieder (art songs) of Schubert had a smaller audience in the parlors of the bourgeoisie.

SECTION 3 Resources

GEOGRAPHY
■ Transparency 74

REINFORCEMENT
■ Independent Practice 23.3

ENRICHMENT
■ Voices from the Past 23.3

ASSESSMENT
■ Section Quiz 23.3

■ **DISCUSSION**

What effect did the American Revolution have on the revolutions of this period?

■ **BACKGROUND**

Napoleon's defeat in Haiti led to the Louisiana Purchase. Napoleon had hoped to use Louisiana for growing food for his West Indian colonies. When he lost the largest one, Haiti, he agreed to sell Louisiana to the United States for a mere $15 million.

country. The leaders of the revolution then set up a new national government.

However, there were important differences between conditions in Latin America and in the United States. In Latin America, colonial society was sharply divided into classes based on birth. Struggles among these classes played an important part in the revolutions.

At the top of Latin American society were the **peninsulars,** people who had been born in Spain or Portugal. They held the most important positions in colonial government and in the Roman Catholic Church.

Creoles (KREE-ohlz) ranked next after the peninsulars. Creoles were people who were born in Latin America but whose ancestors came from Europe. This class included many wealthy landowners and lesser government officials.

The peninsulars and the creoles formed an aristocracy in Latin America although they made up less than a fifth of the population. Below them ranked the common people, who had few political rights and little share in the wealth.

The common people included **mestizos, mulattoes,** African Americans, and Native Americans. Mestizos were people of mixed European and Native American ancestry. Mulattoes were of European and African ancestry. Some mestizos and mulattoes owned small farms or businesses. Most rented small farms from landlords. Most African Americans worked as slaves on large plantations, although there were free African Americans in many Latin American towns. Lowest ranking of all were the millions of Native Americans. Legally free, they were usually treated no better than slaves.

Slaves revolted in Haiti.

The first Latin American country to free itself from European rule was the French colony on the island of Hispaniola in the Caribbean Sea. Slaves and free mulattoes there rose in revolt against France in 1791.

In 1794, the revolutionaries found a skilled general in an ex-slave, Toussaint L'Ouverture (too-SAHN LOO-vuhr-TYOOR). Toussaint (1743–1803) drove the French forces from the island. Then, in 1802, he attended a peace meeting where he was treacherously taken prisoner. He was then sent to France, where he died in prison. However,

the French could not retake the island. Revolutionary leaders of African descent set up the independent country of Haiti in 1804.

Creoles wanted independence.

Elsewhere in Latin America, creoles took the lead in battles for independence. The creoles had a number of long-standing grievances against Spain. Peninsulars held almost all the high government offices in Spain's Latin American lands. Of the 170 viceroys who held office between 1492 and 1810, for example, only 4 were creoles.

Spain also kept tight control over the economy of its colonies. Merchants in Spanish colonies could trade only with Spain. They could send their goods only on Spanish ships. The valuable mines of Mexico and Peru were under direct Spanish control, which the creoles resented.

The direct cause of the Latin American revolts, however, was Napoleon's conquest of Spain in 1808. Napoleon made his brother Joseph king of Spain (page 497). Many creoles might have remained loyal to a Spanish king, but they felt no loyalty at all to a Frenchman placed on the Spanish throne by force.

Toussaint L'Ouverture

Fighting broke out in 1810 in several parts of Latin America. The wars for independence were complicated and confusing. Loyalties were divided. The viceroys and their armies remained loyal to Spain, as did some creoles. Native Americans and mestizos fought on both sides, often forced into armies against their will.

Bolívar and San Martín led the struggle.

The South American wars of independence produced two brilliant generals whose leadership was largely responsible for the success of the rebels. One was Simón Bolívar (see-**MOHN** buh-**LEE**-vahr). The other was the Argentinian José San Martín (hoh-**SAY** san mahr-**TEEN**).

Bolívar in the north Simón Bolívar (1783–1830) was a wealthy Venezuelan creole. He had traveled in Europe and read the works of Voltaire, Rousseau, and Montesquieu, even though they were banned in Latin America. Bolívar was both romantic and practical, a writer and a fighter, handsome and brilliant. He won admiration from friend and foe alike. Above all, he was tireless in the struggle for independence.

Bolívar's native Venezuela declared its independence from Spain in 1811. However, the struggle seesawed back and forth. The revolutionaries suffered many defeats, and Bolívar was twice forced into exile.

The turning point came in 1819. Bolívar built up an army from many sources. He promised to end slavery, winning many volunteers of African descent. Other volunteers came from Europe. In January 1819, Bolívar led his 2,500 soldiers on a daring march through the Andes into what is now Colombia. Coming from this unexpected direction, he took the Spanish army completely by surprise in Bogotá and defeated it.

Bolívar went on to free Venezuela in 1821. Next, he marched south into Ecuador. In the coastal city of Guayaquil, he met with the other great hero of the independence movement, San Martín.

San Martín in the south When the wars for independence broke out in Latin America, José San Martín (1778–1850) was in Spain fighting Napoleon. Hearing of the revolt in his homeland, Argentina, he returned at once. Soon he commanded a creole army there. While Bolívar was

Simón Bolívar

freeing the northern part of South America, San Martín freed the south.

Argentina declared its independence in 1816. However, the new country was not safe as long as Spanish forces had strongholds in nearby Chile and Peru. Thus, in 1817, San Martín led an army on a grueling march across the Andes to Chile. There he won several decisive victories and freed the country.

Next, San Martín took his army north by sea to Lima, Peru, in 1821. The Spanish army retreated into the mountains of Peru. To drive them out, San Martín needed a much larger force. Otherwise, the Spaniards would remain a threat to all of independent South America. This was the problem that faced San Martín and Bolívar when they met at Guayaquil.

The Spaniards were finally defeated.

Mystery has long surrounded the meeting between these two great generals. They differed in many ways. San Martín was a less dashing and romantic leader than Bolívar. San Martín wanted

537

■ **BACKGROUND**

When an earthquake thwarted a campaign, Bolívar responded: "If nature opposes our designs, we shall fight against her, and make her obey."

■ **DISCUSSION**

Bolívar had little time for the day-to-day business of government. He was always at the front. As soon as independence was secured for one country, he moved on to the next. He was honored everywhere. Ask students if they are aware of any modern-day leaders with similar reputations. What South American country is named for him?

ANSWERS TO
Focus on Geography

1. Spain and Portugal

2. most of South America and all of Central America and Mexico became independent

3. British Honduras in Central America and in Guiana on the northern coast of South America

4. Great Britain, Holland, and France

5. Most of Latin America was made up of independent countries; all still felt the effects and influences of their former colonial status.

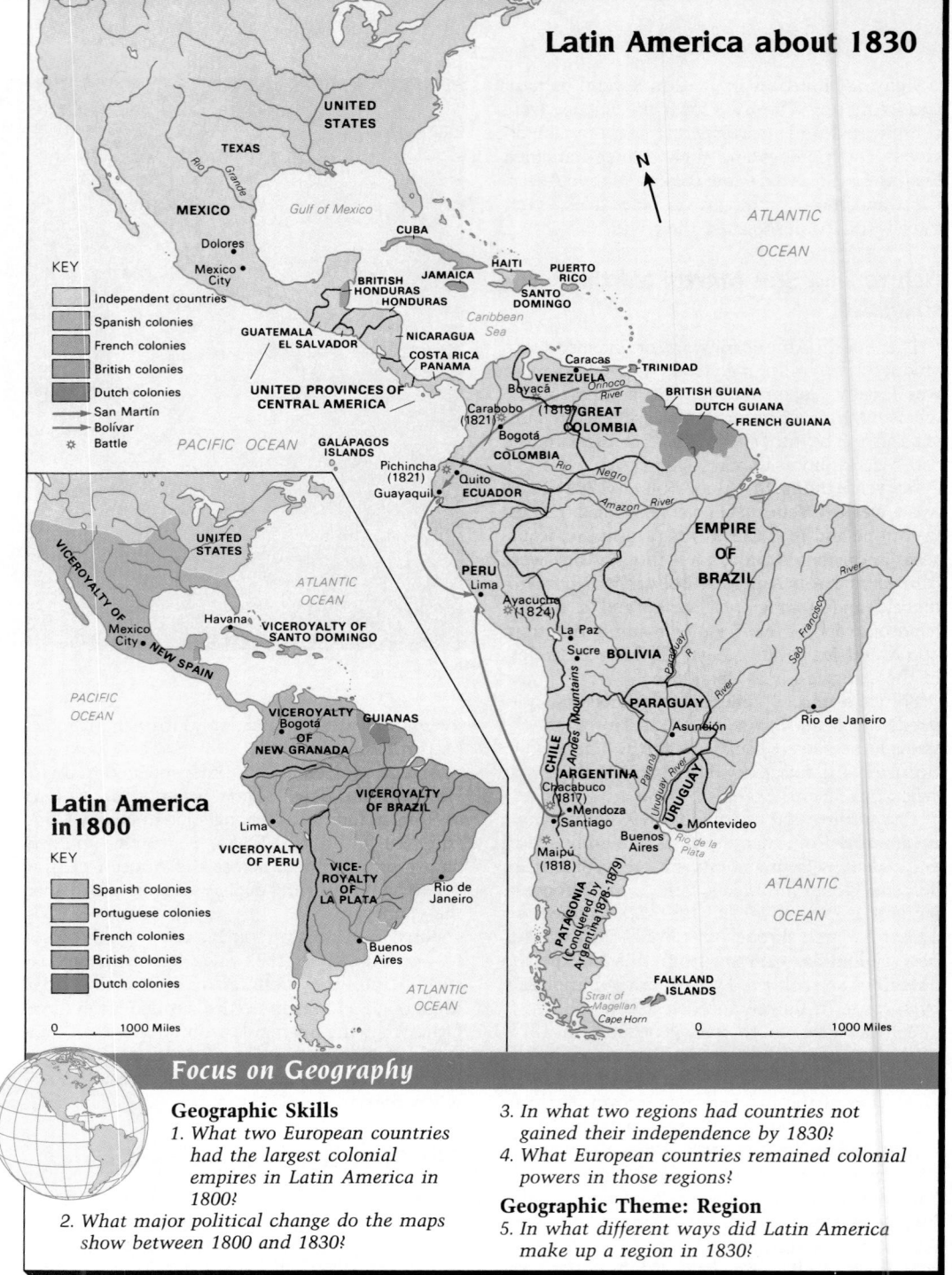

Latin America about 1830

KEY
- Independent countries
- Spanish colonies
- French colonies
- British colonies
- Dutch colonies
- San Martín
- Bolívar
- Battle

Latin America in 1800

KEY
- Spanish colonies
- Portuguese colonies
- French colonies
- British colonies
- Dutch colonies

0   1000 Miles

Focus on Geography

Geographic Skills

1. What two European countries had the largest colonial empires in Latin America in 1800?

2. What major political change do the maps show between 1800 and 1830?

3. In what two regions had countries not gained their independence by 1830?

4. What European countries remained colonial powers in those regions?

Geographic Theme: Region

5. In what different ways did Latin America make up a region in 1830?

538

the newly independent countries of South America governed as monarchies. In contrast, Bolívar hoped to establish republics that would be dominated by the creoles. Nonetheless, both knew that the first step was to defeat the Spaniards.

Although no one knows what the two leaders said to each other, the results were dramatic. San Martín left his army for Bolívar to command and returned to Argentina. Some historians think San Martín left in anger after a quarrel with Bolívar. Others say San Martín deliberately stepped aside in favor of Bolívar, so that the independence movement could unite behind a single leader. Whatever his reasons, San Martín soon sailed for Europe, where he died almost forgotten in 1850. Only later was he recognized as a true Argentinian hero.

Bolívar followed the Spaniards into the heights of the Andes. His forces defeated the Spanish army at the Battle of Ayacucho on December 9, 1824. This was the last major battle of the war for independence. South America was free of Spanish rule.

Brazil freed itself peacefully.

Meanwhile, Brazil won its independence peacefully. In 1807, Napoleon invaded Portugal. As his armies neared Lisbon, the Portuguese royal family fled to Brazil. After Napoleon's defeat, the king of Portugal returned to Europe. However, he left his son, Dom Pedro, as regent of Brazil.

When Brazilians demanded their independence in 1822, Dom Pedro agreed. He defied the Portuguese government's command to sail for Lisbon. On September 7, 1822, he issued the call, "Independence or death!" Brazilians celebrate this day as their national independence day.

In December 1822, Dom Pedro was named emperor. Brazil, South America's largest country, became South America's only monarchy.

Mexicans struggled for freedom.

In most Latin American countries, revolution began in the cities, but in Mexico, it began in the countryside. Only in Mexico did Native Americans and mestizos take a leading part in the struggle for independence.

The first outbreak of the Mexican revolution came in 1810. A group of creoles plotted a revolt, but the government learned of their plans. One of the leaders was Father Miguel Hidalgo (ee-THAHL-goh), a priest in the small mountain village of Dolores. Hidalgo was a poor but well-educated man, steeped in the ideals of the French Revolution. On September 16, 1810, he called on the peasants of his parish to rebel against their Spanish masters. "My children," he asked them, "will you be free? Will you make the effort to recover from the hated Spaniards the lands stolen from your forefathers 300 years ago?"

Hidalgo's peasants began a 200-mile march toward Mexico City. Armed with sickles, stones, and clubs, this unruly army moved southward, picking up thousands of new recruits and weapons along the way. Creole landlords fled for their lives. Soon Hidalgo had a force of 60,000 men behind him. He declared an end to slavery and called for other reforms.

At Mexico City, however, the main Spanish army and the creoles joined forces against Hidalgo's army. Hidalgo was betrayed by one of his officers, captured, and executed.

The rebels found another strong leader in José María Morelos (moh-RAY-lohs). Morelos was a farm worker turned priest who had fought beside Father Hidalgo. He proved a far better general than Hidalgo had been. By 1813, Morelos's army controlled all of Mexico except for the largest cities. A Mexican congress, called by Morelos, declared Mexico an independent republic in 1813. Morelos wanted to set up a democratic government, tax the wealthy, and distribute lands to the peasants.

Many creoles supported the idea of independence, but they were not willing to accept Morelos's social reforms. A creole officer, Augustín de Iturbide (EE-toor-BEE-thay), captured and executed Morelos in 1815. A few scattered groups of rebels fought on as guerrillas.

Suddenly, events took a new turn. In 1820, a revolution in Spain put a new group in power. Mexico's creoles feared that this Spanish government would take away their privileges. At once, the creoles united in support of independence. The very man who had killed Morelos, Iturbide, made peace with the last guerrilla leader. Then Iturbide proclaimed Mexico independent in 1821. Iturbide later made himself emperor, but he was soon ousted. When he tried to return to power in 1824, he was shot.

539

■ BACKGROUND

"More than anyone," wrote Bolívar, "I desire to see [Spanish] America fashioned into the greatest nation in the world." In this great hope he was disappointed. Venezuela, Colombia, and Ecuador were briefly united as Gran Colombia, but they soon divided.

ANSWERS TO
Section Review 3

Define:
(a) lands south of the United States where Spanish, Portuguese, and French are spoken (b) people born in Spain or Portugal (c) people born in Latin America whose ancestors came from Europe (d) people of mixed European and Native American ancestry (e) people of European and African ancestry (f) political strongman who ruled as dictator

Identify:
(a) ex-slave who drove French out of Haiti (b) general who led the struggle for independence in northern South America (c) fighter for independence in southern South America (d) last major battle of the war for independence against Spain (e) regent of Brazil who agreed to independence (f) priest who led

(continued)

539

ANSWERS TO (continued)

Mexico's war for independence **(g)** priest who fought beside Hidalgo for Mexican independence **(h)** creole officer who proclaimed Mexican independence **(i)** U.S. statement pronouncing Western Hemisphere closed to European colonization

Answer:

1. peninsulars at top; creoles; the common people, including mestizos, mulattoes, African Americans, and Native Americans, at the bottom

2. Revolutionary leaders defeated French forces with help of slaves.

3. (a) Peninsulars held all high offices; Spain kept tight control over economy, shipping, mining.
(b) Napoleon's conquest of Spain

4. through the military accomplishments of **(a)** Bolívar **(b)** San Martín

5. peacefully, when Don Pedro agreed to independence in 1822

6. It began in the countryside, with Native Americans and mestizos taking a leading role.

7. wealthy creole aristocrats and caudillos

8. to protect Latin American independence and American economic interests

9. (a) Answers should note the effects of the Enlightenment and the French Revolution on educated peoples in Latin America and the trend toward nationalism.
(b) Answers should consider the general trend toward independence and recognize that, in time, a leader probably would have emerged.

10. Possible answer: all the work can be undone.

Caudillos dominated governments.

By 1830, Latin America was home to 16 independent countries, but the citizens of these new countries had few political freedoms. All the countries were dominated by a small group of wealthy creole aristocrats. "Independence," said Bolívar shortly before his death in 1830, "is the sole benefit we have gained, at the sacrifice of all others . . . He who serves a revolution plows the sea."

Army leaders had come to power during the long struggle with Spain, and they continued to control Latin America after independence. By 1830, nearly all the countries of Latin America were run by **caudillos** (kow-THEE-yohs). Caudillos were political strongmen, usually army officers, who ruled as dictators. Many caudillos cared only for their own power and wealth. They did little to improve the lives of the common people. Changes of government most often took place at bayonet-point, as one caudillo was forced to give way to another.

Foreign interests dominated Latin America's economies.

In one way, Latin America was luckier than other nonindustrial parts of the world. Despite the political confusion, Latin America was never again carved into colonies as Africa and Asia were in the late 1800's. Having won independence, Latin America succeeded in keeping it.

The Monroe Doctrine Spain did not give up hope of winning back its former colonies. France too saw a chance to take over land in Latin America. Both Britain and the United States, however, were determined not to allow such a development.

In 1823, President James Monroe of the United States announced, "the American continents . . . are henceforth not to be considered as subjects for future colonization by any European powers." This statement is known as the Monroe Doctrine. Alone, the United States was not strong enough to enforce the Monroe Doctrine. However, Great Britain also wanted to protect Latin American independence.

British and American economic interests Britain had no political ambitions in Latin America, but it did have large economic interests. During the

wars for independence, many Latin American countries began trading with Britain rather than with Spain. British banks and businesses invested heavily in South America, especially in Argentina and Brazil.

Britain's only real economic rival in Latin America was the United States. However, most United States' exports in the early 1800's came from the farm rather than the factory. Thus, there was little direct competition between the United States and Great Britain. Both countries were happy with the economic advantages they gained by Latin American independence.

Section REVIEW 3

Define: (a) Latin America, (b) peninsulars, (c) creoles, (d) mestizos, (e) mulattoes, (f) caudillo
Identify: (a) Toussaint L'Ouverture, (b) Bolívar, (c) San Martín, (d) Battle of Ayacucho, (e) Dom Pedro, (f) Hidalgo, (g) Morelos, (h) Iturbide, (i) Monroe Doctrine
Answer:

1. Describe the divisions in Latin American society under Spanish rule.
2. How did Haiti gain independence?
3. (a) What economic and political grievances did the creoles have? (b) What was the direct cause of revolt in Latin America?
4. (a) How was independence achieved in northern South America? (b) In southern South America?
5. How did Brazil become independent?
6. How did the Mexican revolt differ from revolts in other Spanish colonies?
7. What groups dominated Latin America after independence?
8. Why was the Monroe Doctrine drawn up?

Critical Thinking

9. Historians have often debated the importance of individual leaders in history. (a) Would the Latin American revolts have taken place without Toussaint, Bolívar, San Martín, and Hidalgo? Explain your answer. (b) Which, if any, of the revolts would have succeeded without these leaders?
10. What did Bolívar mean when he said, "He who serves a revolution plows the sea"?

Reform and revolution swept Europe.

4

As we have seen, new ideas had widespread impact in Europe during the early 1800's. Nationalism and romanticism roused people's emotions. Liberalism gained ground with the growth of the middle class in western Europe. Members of this class were eager to have greater political power. They won large gains in Great Britain and France, but they failed, for the time being, in most other parts of Europe.

France overthrew its Bourbon king.

In 1830, a short and almost bloodless revolution ended the rule of France's Charles X. Charles, the last Bourbon king of France, brought on the revolution by his own stupidity. He ignored both middle-class liberals and Parisian radicals and tried to rule as an absolute monarch. He had nothing but contempt for the idea of a limited monarchy such as the one in Britain. "I would rather be a woodcutter," he once said, "than be the king of England."

Charles sparked the revolution by trying to take away what few powers France's Chamber of Deputies held. Riots broke out in Paris as liberals and radicals joined together to rid the country of this impossible king. Charles fled as an exile to Great Britain.

Within a few days, a group of liberal leaders offered the French crown to Charles's cousin, Louis Philippe, who was sympathetic to liberal reforms. Louis Philippe accepted, promising to rule as a "citizen king" who would share power with the Chamber of Deputies. France enjoyed almost two decades of peace and stability before another revolution broke out in 1848.

Britain's middle class won the vote.

Peaceful debate in the British Parliament, not armed revolution, won the most important liberal victory of these years. After a decade of pressure from factory owners and merchants, Parliament passed the Reform Bill of 1832.

The Reform Bill of 1832 set up new districts for electing members of Parliament. Many of the old districts had existed for hundreds of years. Some had been medieval villages but were now empty fields. Yet the owner of that field could elect a member of Parliament. In contrast, new cities such as Manchester and Sheffield had no representatives because those cities had grown up after the districts were formed. The reform bill put an end to such injustices. For the first time, the thriving new industrial cities had representation in Parliament.

The reform bill also gave more men the right to vote. Before 1832, only men who owned a substantial amount of property could vote. After 1832, men who paid a certain amount of rent could also vote. (Around the same time, Catholic men also won the right to vote.)

The Reform Bill of 1832 doubled the number of British voters. Nearly all middle-class men could now take part in elections. Still, this was less than 20 percent of the men in Great Britain.

The working class had little power.

Although Britain had the most liberal government in Europe, working class people still had no political influence. Daniel O'Connell, an Irish nationalist and liberal leader of this time, was asked to explain a political issue to some roadworkers. "Whatever happens," O'Connell told them, "you will still be breaking stones." Nevertheless, the working class was beginning to demand some say in politics.

As the Industrial Revolution progressed, working conditions improved a little. Workers' wages were rising, and ordinary people were better fed and better clothed. Life was no longer a grim struggle to survive. Workers began to organize.

By the 1840's, the Industrial Revolution was sweeping across the continent. It particularly affected the Ruhr and Rhine valleys in western Germany and the Po valley in northern Italy. Factories sprang up in cities such as Frankfurt, Cologne, and Milan. Radical political organizers in these cities were determined that the working-class voice would be heard.

1848 was a year of revolutions.

By 1848, working-class radicals and middle-class liberals in Europe were convinced that the Metternich system—the political agreements of

541

SECTION 4
Objectives and Teaching Strategies

OBJECTIVE 1. Analyze the causes and effects of the revolutions of 1848.

Teaching Strategy: *Skill Building: Relating Causes and Effects* (page 526e)

OBJECTIVE 2. Evaluate the results of the revolutions of 1848 and the failure of French radicals to maintain power.

Teaching Strategy: *Discussing History: The Revolutions of 1848* (page 526e)

■ BACKGROUND

The Industrial Revolution brought large numbers of workers together in the cities, where they could see how unfairly the fruits of their labors were divided. Slowly, but surely, they realized that if they united, they would become more powerful.

SECTION 4
Resources

ASSESSMENT
- Section Quiz 23.4

REINFORCEMENT
- Independent Practice 23.4

ENRICHMENT
- Voices from the Past 23.4

Ask students to think of questions they would like to have asked European rulers during the 1848 revolutions. Question topics might include the following: reasons for the revolutions, ways to stop the disturbances, or possible governmental changes. After students work on these questions for about 10 minutes, divide the class into six groups. Each group member should contribute one or two interview questions so that groups have a master list of 10 to 12 questions. Group recorders should assemble the final lists. Then randomly assign each group one of the following leaders: Louis Philippe, Alphonse de Lamartine, Louis Napoleon, Prince Klemens von Metternich, Czar Nicholas I of Russia, or King Frederick William IV of Prussia. Group members should work together to determine the answers their assigned leader might have given to the group's questions. Again, recorders should write down the answers. Then allow groups to share their "interviews" with the class. Or you may have pairs of students reenact the interviews, assuming roles as appropriate.

In 1848, revolts shook many European capitals. Here, troops fire on protestors in Vienna.

the Congress of Vienna—had long outlived its usefulness. Nationalists believed the time had come to sweep away old-fashioned empires and replace them with nation-states.

With such widespread discontent, it was only a matter of time before a violent outburst occurred. The explosion came in 1848. In January of that year, there was a revolution in the Kingdom of the Two Sicilies. Over the next 4 months, almost 50 similar revolts rocked Europe. "What remains standing in Europe?" asked Czar Nicholas I of Russia in April. His empire and Britain were the only major countries not touched by revolt.

The revolts meant different things in different places. In France, the revolutionaries planned to establish a democratic government. In Hungary, they wanted to throw off Austrian rule and set up a Hungarian nation-state. In the German states, rebels hoped for a united Germany.

At first, the revolutions caught Europe's rulers by surprise. Many monarchs granted concessions

542

to the rebels. Even Prussia's King Frederick William IV agreed to the election of a democratic parliament. He also agreed to support an all-German parliament that would meet in Frankfurt. Hungary and several states in northern Italy won temporary freedom from Austria.

The Austrian empire seemed to be falling apart. After 30 years as Europe's most powerful political figure, Metternich resigned. As he left Vienna for exile in Britain, he told a friend, "Everything is finished."

Everything was not finished, however. As spring turned to summer, the revolutionaries seemed to run out of steam. The rebels shared the common aim of overthrowing the conservative order, but they disagreed strongly over what to do next. Meanwhile, the rulers regained their courage. With the strength of their armies behind them, they began a counterrevolution. German princes called their representatives home from Frankfurt, and the all-German parliament vanished almost as suddenly as it had appeared. Elsewhere, Austrian armies crushed the rebels in northern Italy and put down the revolt in Hungary. By 1849, Europe had practically returned to its pre-1848 status.

On the surface, therefore, the revolutions of 1848 brought about little reform. However, the forces of change had not been destroyed, only contained. The demands for independence and an end to the old empires would be heard again and again.

France again overthrew its king.

Radicals were involved in many of the 1848 revolts, but only in France was the demand for democratic government the main point of revolution. Only in France—particularly in Paris—were radicals the moving force behind revolution.

During the late 1840's, King Louis Philippe turned a deaf ear to demands that the Chamber of Deputies be made more democratic. "Get rich by work, and you will have the vote," his chief minister scornfully told the working classes.

Paris rose up against the king in February 1848. Louis Philippe's government collapsed almost overnight. It was replaced by a temporary government led by Alphonse de Lamartine (lahm-ahr-TEEN), one of France's leading romantic poets. "Down with royalty!" shouted the Paris mob.

Define:
(a) revolution directed toward overthrowing a system
(continued)

Lamartine and his colleagues declared France a republic once more.

Things went sour for the new republican government almost from the start. A quarrel split the radicals into factions. One side, led by Lamartine, wanted only political reform. The other, led by Louis Blanc, wanted economic reform as well. Blanc's group demanded that the government set up national workshops to make jobs for the unemployed. Such workshops were indeed set up in Paris, but Lamartine's government soon closed them. This order led to bloody street battles in Paris. More than 10,000 workers were killed before the government subdued the rebels.

A *new Napoleon came to power.*

The violence turned France against the radicals toward a more moderate, liberal government. The new constitution drawn up later in 1848 called for a parliament and a strong president elected by the people.

France held a presidential election in December 1848, and the winner was none other than Louis Napoleon Bonaparte. Nephew of the great emperor, Louis Napoleon lacked his uncle's intelligence and strength of character. However, he had a name that French voters linked with past glories. "How could I help voting for this gentleman," said one old man in 1851, "I whose nose was frozen at Moscow?"

Louis Napoleon won widespread support from the peasants, who resented the dominance of Paris in French politics and wanted peace and order. Nationalists saw in him a man who could unite all of the country's political factions. Thus, a second Bonaparte came to power swearing to "remain faithful to the democratic Republic and to defend the Constitution."

Like his uncle, Louis Napoleon soon broke that oath. In December 1851, he dissolved the French parliament and declared himself sole ruler of France. Remarkably, an election held later that month (in which all French men had the right to vote) approved his deed by an overwhelming 92 percent. Adopting his uncle's constitution, Louis Napoleon then took the title Emperor Napoleon III.

Why did the French people accept this coup? Louis himself gave perhaps the best explanation: "The Empire means peace. It means peace because

France wishes it, and when France is satisfied, the world is quiescent [quiet]."

From his exile in London, the 78-year-old Metternich was puzzled by events in France. Louis Napoleon's success seemed to break all the political rules that Metternich knew. How could a conservative, absolutist monarch come to power in a democratic election? It seemed impossible. Said Metternich:

> He must choose between grasping the reins of government either as heir of Napoleon the First or as one elected by universal suffrage. He will destroy himself upon this contradiction.

Time proved Metternich wrong. Napoleon III governed France for the next 20 years.

The times had changed. The rules of politics were changing too. Over the next century, other absolute rulers would come to power through the ballot box. As we shall see, democracy proved to be a form of government that could destroy itself.

Section REVIEW 4

Define: (a) counterrevolution, (b) coup
Identify: (a) Charles X, (b) Louis Philippe, (c) Reform Bill of 1832, (d) 1848, (e) Lamartine, (f) Blanc, (g) Louis Napoleon
Answer:
1. (a) What brought on the French revolt of 1830? (b) What were its results?
2. Explain two ways that the Reform Bill of 1832 broadened the right to vote in Great Britain.
3. What goals did the revolutionaries of 1848 have in each of the following places? (a) France (b) Hungary (c) the German states
4. (a) What did the revolutions of 1848 achieve at first? (b) What happened in the counterrevolution?
5. (a) How did Louis Philippe fall from power? (b) What problems did the new French government face?
6. How did Louis Napoleon become emperor?

Critical Thinking

7. (a) What contradiction did Metternich think would lead to Napoleon III's downfall? (b) Could a leader follow such a path to power today? Explain your answer.

ANSWERS TO (continued)
established by a previous revolution (b) sudden overturn of government
Identify:
(a) last Bourbon king of France (b) cousin of Charles X who became citizen king (c) bill that gave almost all middle-class men in Britain right to vote (d) year of European revolutions (e) led temporary government that replaced Louis Philippe's government (f) leader of radical faction that wanted reform (g) took the title Emperor Napoleon III
Answer:
1. (a) actions of Charles X, who tried to rule as absolute monarch (b) riots; king fled to England
2. gave most middle-class men right to vote, industrial cities represented in Parliament
3. (a) to establish a democratic government (b) to throw off Austrian rule and set up a Hungarian nation-state (c) to unite Germany
4. (a) won many concessions from monarchs (b) Europe returned to its pre-1848 status.
5. (a) by turning a deaf ear to demands that the Chamber of Deputies be made more democratic (b) a split into factions that led to bloody battles
6. by dissolving the French parliament and declaring himself the sole ruler of France
7. (a) that a conservative, absolutist monarch could be elected democratically (b) Answers should note the nature of charismatic leadership, the role of an educated electorate, and the economic benefits of stability.

Concluding the Chapter

1. Chapter Closer
Have students write essays beginning with the following topic sentence: The Congress of Vienna failed to meet its objectives of restoring the old order and maintaining stability. Ask students to trace political development in Europe between 1815 and 1848.

2. Reteaching Activities
a. Summarizing Ask students to summarize the resolutions made by the Congress of Vienna.
b. Recalling Information Have students recall the contributions of Bolívar, San Martín, Mazzini, and Byron to nationalist movements.
c. Explaining Ask students to explain how nationalist movements were influenced by romantic ideals.

Answers to Chapter Review appear on pages 526e–526f.

Summary

1. European leaders sought stability. In 1815, representatives from Europe met in Vienna to make a peace settlement. Led by Metternich, they restored former monarchies, blocked France from expanding, and established a balance of power. Many parts of the settlement were opposed by middle-class liberals and by radicals.

2. New ideals affected politics and art. After 1815, European politics were heavily influenced by nationalism, particularly in countries that were divided or ruled by foreign powers. Nationalism was closely linked to romanticism, which glorified emotion, nature, heroic individuals, and the past.

3. Latin America won independence. The early 1800's saw a series of wars for independence throughout Latin America. In Haiti, slaves revolted against France and set up an independent country. Bolívar and San Martín led independence movements in South America. In Mexico, Native Americans and mestizos played a large part in the war for independence. Brazil won independence peacefully. Although free, Latin American countries were still dominated by a small wealthy class. Many countries fell under military rule.

4. Reform and revolution swept Europe. In Britain, reforms expanded voting rights. Elsewhere in Europe, however, nationalism and the desire for reform led to revolt. France overthrew one king in 1830 but remained a monarchy. In 1848, a wave of revolts swept Europe but were soon put down. Radical demands for reform in France led to the establishment of a republic, but violence soon turned people against the new government.

Reviewing the Facts

1. Define the following terms:
   a. legitimacy
   b. liberalism
   c. romanticism
   d. caudillo
2. Explain the importance of each of the following people or events:
   a. Congress of Vienna
   b. Metternich
   c. Mazzini
   d. Toussaint
   e. Bolívar
   f. San Martín
   g. Dom Pedro
   h. Hidalgo
   i. Morelos
   j. Monroe Doctrine
   k. Reform Bill of 1832
   l. Louis Napoleon
3. (a) What were Metternich's goals at the Congress of Vienna? (b) How was each met?
4. How were nationalist goals blocked in Italy and the German states?

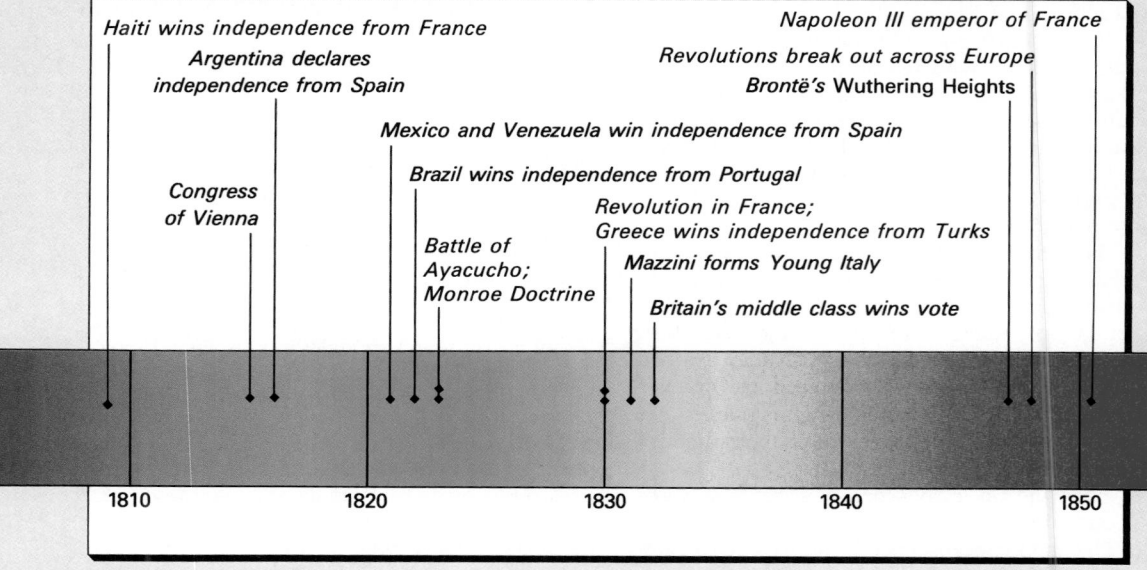

Haiti wins independence from France
Argentina declares independence from Spain
Napoleon III emperor of France
Revolutions break out across Europe
Brontë's Wuthering Heights
Mexico and Venezuela win independence from Spain
Brazil wins independence from Portugal
Congress of Vienna
Revolution in France; Greece wins independence from Turks
Battle of Ayacucho; Monroe Doctrine
Mazzini forms Young Italy
Britain's middle class wins vote

1810   1820   1830   1840   1850

544

5. (a) What was the first Latin American country to become independent? (b) How did it do so?
6. (a) Describe Bolívar's achievements in South America. (b) Describe San Martín's.
7. (a) Briefly describe the war for independence in Mexico. (b) How did it differ from revolts in South America?
8. (a) What stand did the United States take in the Monroe Doctrine? (b) Why did both the United States and Great Britain support this doctrine?
9. What were the effects of the Reform Bill of 1832 in Great Britain?
10. How did the events of 1848 help Louis Napoleon win power?

Basic Skills

1. **Making a chart**   Make a chart of the revolutions in Latin America. In the left-hand vertical column, list the main Latin American countries involved (Haiti, Venezuela, Argentina, Brazil, and Mexico). In the horizontal columns, use the headings European Colonial Power, Social Classes Involved, Leader(s), and Main Events.
2. **Paraphrasing**   Briefly explain the ideas and goals of conservatism, liberalism, and radicalism in Europe in the early 1800's.
3. **Classifying**   (a) Classify the following individuals according to the categories of liberal, radical, conservative: Bolívar, Lamartine, Louis Philippe, Morelos, Charles X, Louis Blanc. (b) Give a reason for each choice.

Researching and Reporting Skills
Writing a Research Paper
Phase 2: Consulting sources and writing a working thesis statement

1. **Taking notes**   Using the research questions you wrote in Phase 1, look for information in the sources you have located. Take notes on cards, identifying the subject of each note and the source and page number of the information. If other information unrelated to your questions seems important to your topic, frame a new question and record the information. Your notes should summarize the main ideas in your own words. You should also include quotations, graphs, and references to art or literature that may be useful in your report.

2. **Organizing notes**   Use the research questions to help in organizing your notes. Identify three or more categories of information. Group the cards in the appropriate categories. Save cards that do not fit for possible use later.
3. **Drafting a working thesis**   Based on your notes, establish what main idea emerges from your information. Write a sentence that states this thesis.
4. **Outlining**   Review your categories and decide in what order they should be presented to support your thesis. Then go back over your notes to identify and add subtopics and supporting points. Make an outline of the major topics and subtopics.

Critical Thinking

1. **Inferring**   Identify three factors that influenced the success or failure of the national uprisings in Europe in the 1800's.
2. **Identifying fact and opinion**   Reread on page 528 the paragraph beginning, "The Congress of Vienna was a political triumph . . . " (a) Does it express fact or opinion? (b) Would it be possible to come to different conclusions? If so, what are they?
3. **Evaluating**   (a) What were the goals of Bolívar for South America? (b) To what extent did he accomplish those goals? Support your answer with facts and examples.

Perspectives on Past and Present

Nationalism was a driving force in the political events of the 1800's. (a) How important is it in the world today? In what regions is it most active? (b) Is it more active in some regions than others? Give examples and explain how they illustrate the statement.

Investigating History

1. Using art history books for reference, identify three painters who belonged to the Romantic tradition. Choose a painting by each artist and explain how it characterizes that style.
2. Read about the revolution for independence in one Latin American country. How did the revolution begin? Who were the leaders? What were the main events? What new type of government was established?

545

CHAPTER
Evaluation

Chapter Test 23, Alternate Chapter Test 23, and Computer Test Bank Chapter 23 Test can be used to evaluate your students' understanding of this chapter.

Economic Expansion and Nationalism

Chapter **24**

Chapter Overview

By the middle of the nineteenth century, new inventions were spurring the process of industrialization in Europe and in North America and encouraging the development of global economic ties. Businesses were growing larger; many became corporations. Workers demanded more rights and protection. Realism in art and literature reflected these changes.

Italy and Germany continued the process of unification. By 1871, Italy was independent and united. Prussia defeated Austria and France and unified the German states into the new German nation. Great Britain and Germany emerged as the military and industrial leaders of Europe.

In the United States, the conflict over slavery between the industrial North and the agricultural South finally erupted in civil war. By its hundredth birthday, the United States had a rapidly expanding economy and was becoming a world leader in industrial production.

Chapter Focus

In the 1870's people in Europe and America read about the adventures of Phineas Fogg, the main character in Jules Verne's novel *Around the World in Eighty Days*. Verne's work was originally a newspaper serial and readers anxiously awaited each episode to see if Fogg would win his wager to circle the globe in 80 days. Verne was famous for writing stories with what were then curious inventions— submarines and spaceships. However, Phineas Fogg used the inven-

tions of the nineteenth century, such as the steamship, railroad, and hot-air balloon. Suggest to students that Verne might have gotten some of his story ideas from presentations at London's Great Exhibition of 1851.

Industrialism created a global economy.   **1**

Setting the Stage

Economics and History: Global Economy (Objective 1) Ask students to imagine their lives with no foreign products. How can events in the Middle East or in Japan affect economies worldwide? Interdependence among countries for resources and products has created a global economy. Before the technological advances of the nineteenth century, international economic activity was limited. Manufacturers waited months for materials and products to be shipped between continents. The invention of steamships and railroads dramatically reduced transportation times. As longer trade routes became more practical, merchants began to expand into foreign markets.

Teaching Strategies

Discussing History: Transportation and Communication in the Nineteenth Century (Objective 2) "The world is getting smaller." Ask students what this phrase means. Explain that before steamships, a

Chapter 24 Economic Expansion and Nationalism 1851–1876

FOCUS Nineteenth-century inventions made the world a smaller place

★ Advanced
● Basic

	SECTION 1	SECTION 2	SECTION 3	SECTION 4
Objectives	1. Explain the concept of "global economy." 2. Assess the impact of improved communication and transportation in the nineteenth century. 3. Identify the causes of immigration and emigration.	1. Discuss the main ideas of socialism. 2. Describe the views of Karl Marx and assess their impact on events in nineteenth-century Europe. 3. Contrast romanticism and realism.	1. Define *realpolitik* and identify its role in nineteenth-century politics. 2. Evaluate the contributions Cavour and Garibaldi made to the unification of Italy. 3. Explain how Bismarck helped to unify Germany.	1. Define the concept of westward expansion. 2. Identify the territorial gains made by the United States between 1783 and 1853 and assess the impact of expansion on economic development. 3. Explain how regional differences between the northern and southern United States affected the Civil War.
Setting the Stage	Economics and History: Global Economy	Workers' struggles to gain greater economic and political power	Discussing History: *Realpolitik*	Using Geographic Themes: Frontier Regions Transparency 77
Teaching Strategies	Discussing History: Transportation and Communication in the Nineteenth Century Using Geographic Themes: Movement Check for Understanding	Writing about History: Socialism Discussing History: Karl Marx Teaching with Pictures: Realism and Romanticism Check for Understanding	Discussing History: Italian Unification Transparency 75 Writing about History: Unification of Germany Transparency 76 Check for Understanding	Discussing History: American Expansionism Using Geographic Themes: Regions Check for Understanding
Guided Practice	Section Review 1	Section Review 2	Transparency 75 Q&A Transparency 76 Q&A Section Review 3	Transparency 77 Q&A Section Review 4
Independent Practice Worksheets	Independent Practice 24.1 Vocabulary Skills 24	Independent Practice 24.2	Independent Practice 24.3 Geography Skills 24 Basic Skills 24 Critical Thinking 24	Independent Practice 24.4
Enrichment	1. Primary Source: Voices 24.1 2. Creative Writing 3. Researching for Points	1. Primary Source: Voices 24.2 2. ★Preparing a Report: Realists 3. Researching for Points	1. Primary Source: Voices 24.3 2. ★Relating Past to Present 3. Researching for Points	1. Primary Source: Voices 24.4 2. Creative Writing 3. Researching for Points
Chapter Closer	●**Reteaching Activities**　Recalling Main Ideas, Outlining, Writing a Paragraph **Chapter Review**　Summary, Reviewing the Facts, Basic Skills, Researching and Reporting Skills, Critical Thinking, Perspectives on Past and Present, Investigating History **Chapter Evaluation**　Chapter Test 24, Alternate Chapter Test 24, Computer Test Bank Chapter 24 Test			

trip from New York to England took about four weeks. The steamship cut this time in half. Today, the same trip by aircraft takes less than five hours. Advances in railroad transportation were also dramatic. With the completion of the transcontinental railroad, the trip from New York to San Francisco was reduced from about three months to seven days. Before the use of the telegraph, the Pony Express was the fastest means of communication. In 1860, the Pony Express carried mail from St. Joseph, Missouri, to Sacramento, California, in about eight days. Ask students why the telegraph made the Pony Express obsolete. Before the completion of a trans-Atlantic telegraph cable, news from Europe reached the United States only as fast as ships could carry it. Ask how developments in transportation and communication made countries more interdependent.

Using Geographic Themes: Movement (Objective 3) Immigration to North America was often grueling and sometimes fatal. Steamship companies competing for profits overbooked passengers, resulting in overcrowding and unsanitary, unsafe conditions. Many passengers, crowded into airless lower decks, fell victim to deadly contagious diseases. Supplies of food and fresh water were short. However, these hardships did not discourage the flood of emigrants from Europe. Ask students to recall the effects of the Industrial Revolution and the revolutions of the mid-nineteenth century. (overpopulation, poverty, civil strife, political oppression) Ask students to speculate on the effects of nineteenth-century migrations on the development of the modern world.

Check for Understanding Have students write a paragraph explaining how advances in transportation and communication helped to foster a global economy. Students should mention some inventions that stimulated world trade.

Enrichment Activities

1. **Reading a Primary Source** Assign Voices from the Past Resource Book 24.1.

2. **Creative Writing** Have students write a first-person account of the decisions and experiences of a rural family seeking greater economic opportunities in the late nineteenth century.

3. **Researching for Bonus Points** What was the country of origin of the largest group of immigrants to the United States in 1854? (Germany)

Working people gained more influence. 2

Setting the Stage

Review the social problems caused by industrialization (pages 519–523) and the rise of reform movements (page 541). Tell students that in the nineteenth century, members of the working classes felt left out of Europe's economic expansion.

Teaching Strategies

Writing about History: Socialism (Objective 1) *Prewriting* Have students read "Socialists sought to re-

form society" (page 551). Discuss the ideas of Robert Owen. Ask, "Why did socialism appeal to many working class people in the nineteenth century?" (Workers gained greater economic and social equality.) Invite students to debate the advantages and disadvantages of living in a socialist society. Note that most present-day capitalist countries have some institutions that reflect socialist ideals, such as national health insurance, social security, and unemployment compensation. *Writing* Ask students to imagine they are employees of Robert Owen's cotton mill in New Lanark, Scotland. Have each student write a letter explaining the benefits of working for Owen.

Discussing History: Karl Marx (Objective 2) Have students read "Turning Points in History" (pages 551–552). Ask them to explain the terms *proletariat, bourgeoisie,* and *means of production.* Ask students why Marx felt that workers should own the means of production. Many revolutionaries were influenced by Marx's view that the Industrial Revolution favored capitalists who grew rich by exploiting workers. Recall, however, that the revolutions of 1848 brought few substantive economic reforms. As their standard of living rose, workers became more interested in benefiting from economic expansion than in staging revolts. Ask students what other changes in the mid-nineteenth century eased tensions between workers and employers. (unions and suffrage) How did labor unions and suffrage increase workers' influence?

Teaching with Pictures: Realism and Romanticism (Objective 3) Have students compare the paintings on pages 534 and 553 and identify the two movements in art these paintings represent. (romanticism and realism) Ask students how the pictures are different, and what they reveal about changing perceptions of society. (Realism emphasizes day-to-day struggle; romanticism emphasizes the extraordinary in nature and in human responses.) Have a volunteer read the quotation by Courbet (page 554). Ask students why Courbet mocked romantic writers. Then ask a student to read the excerpt from Dickens's *Hard Times* (page 554). How does the painting by Daumier illustrate Dickens's description? Invite students to identify realist and romantic themes in present-day art mediums such as music and cinema.

Check for Understanding Ask students to identify trends in the nineteenth century that increased the influence of workers. (interest in socialist labor reforms, growth of trade unions, extensions of suffrage)

Enrichment Activities

1. **Reading a Primary Source**
   Assign Voices from the Past Resource Book 24.2.

2. **Preparing a Report**
   Have advanced students report on the themes expressed by nineteenth-century realists such as Thomas Hardy, Gustave Flaubert, Anton Chekov, Leo Tolstoy, Henrik Ibsen, or George Bernard Shaw.

3. **Researching for Bonus Points**
   What was the Fabian Society, founded in Great Britain in 1884? (an organization to promote the gradual spread of socialism)

Italy and Germany formed nations. 3

Setting the Stage

Discussing History: *Realpolitik* (Objective 1) Ask students what they think the term *realpolitik* means. Help students infer that *realpolitik* echoed the new realism in literature and art. Nationalist leaders relied less on romantic ideals and more on practical realities. The new style of diplomacy was characterized by ruthlessness, shrewd manipulation, and effectiveness.

Teaching Strategies

Discussing History: Italian Unification (Objective 2) Show Map Transparency 75, *The Unification of Italy, 1850–1870,* or refer students to the map on page 556. Note Italy's many political divisions. Each region had its own plans for unification. The two leaders who unified Italy were contrasts in personality and in leadership style. Cavour was a purposeful, shrewd politician who practiced the rules of realpolitik. Ask why Cavour's Sardinian origins were an advantage. (Sardinia was the largest Italian state, and the only one ruled by an Italian dynasty.) Why did Cavour reject the methods of earlier nationalists? (too vague, impractical, and emotional) How did Cavour demonstrate realpolitik in his dealings with France and Austria?

The unification of southern Italy was accomplished in a different manner. Garibaldi was a romantic nationalist whose heroic style endeared him to local populations. Ask students why Garibaldi's success threatened Cavour. (Italy might unite under Garibaldi.) How did Cavour prevent Garibaldi from becoming too powerful? Why did Garibaldi step aside? Have students assess the merits of each leader's style and his importance to Italian unification.

Writing about History: Unification of Germany (Objective 3) *Prewriting* Display Map Transparency 76, *The Unification of Germany, 1865–1871.* Unification was effected under Otto von Bismarck, an advocate of realpolitik whose realistic assessment of Austrian strengths and weaknesses guided Prussian foreign policy. Invite students to interpret the quotation on page 557 from Bismarck's address to the Prussian parliament. What "great mistake of 1848" did Bismarck mean? How did Bismarck's words reflect the ideas of realpolitik? Bismarck's contempt for liberals in the German parliament stemmed from his observation that they endlessly discussed unification but never acted. *Writing* Have students write essays explaining how Bismarck united Prussia. Tell students to include the following information:

- Explain the rivalry between Austria and Prussia.
- Explain why Bismarck provoked wars with Austria and France.
- Evaluate Bismarck's leadership in terms of effectiveness and fairness.

Check for Understanding Ask students to explain how the unification of Germany and of Italy and conditions in France's Third Republic changed Europe's political boundaries and balance of power.

Enrichment Activities

1. **Reading a Primary Source**
   Assign Voices from the Past Resource Book 24.3.

2. **Relating Past to Present**
   Ask advanced students to assess the relevance of Count von Moltke's remarks (page 561) to the realpolitik of nineteenth-

century Europe and to the global politics of the present day.

3. **Researching for Bonus Points**
What Prussian general effectively used railroads and the telegraph to defeat Austria in the Seven Weeks' War? (Count Helmuth von Moltke)

The United States spread westward. 4

Setting the Stage

Using Geographic Themes: Frontier Regions (Objective 1) Explain that in Europe the borderlands separating countries were called frontiers. In America, *frontier* referred to borderlands separating settled regions from the "wilderness." Show Map Transparency 77, *The Growth of the United States, 1783–1853*. Have students identify the territories added to the United States in the nineteenth century.

Teaching Strategies

Discussing History: American Expansionism (Objective 2) Have students use the map on page 562 to identify the regions acquired in the Louisiana purchase. How did this land contribute to the economic development of the United States? (added vast farmlands, the Mississippi and Missouri river systems, and a port on Gulf of Mexico)

Next, have students identify the territories acquired from Mexico.

Call on students to name the present-day states that include land acquired as part of Texas in 1845 and from Mexico in 1848. Ask how these lands contributed to the economic development of the United States. (Texas—valuable ranges for grazing, rich oil deposits; California—ports on Pacific Ocean, rich gold deposits)

American expansionism was based on the concept of "Manifest Destiny"—the belief that Americans were destined to bring civilization to undeveloped lands. Some American expansionists wanted to annex Mexico and the Caribbean islands, but the American Civil War superseded such plans.

Using Geographic Themes: Regions (Objective 3) Read to students the following advice from William Sherman to a southern friend on why the South should not go to war against the North.

> The North can make a steam engine, locomotive, or railway car; hardly a yard of cloth can you make. You are rushing into war with one of the most powerful, ingeniously mechanical and determined people on earth right at your door. You are bound to fail.

Ask students to identify the main point of Sherman's advice.

On the board write *North* and *South*. Call on students to contrast the economies of the two regions in 1861. Students should consider the main resources, industries, and labor supply. Point out the economic significance of slavery and the fundamental differences between agricultural and industrial regional interests. Have students draw conclusions about the impact of regional differences on the United States' development as a federal union.

Check for Understanding Ask students to identify the four most significant developments marking the progress of the United States during its first 100 years. (westward expansion, preservation of the union, abolition of slavery, rapid industrialization)

Enrichment Activities

1. **Reading a Primary Source**
Assign Voices from the Past Resource Book 24.4.
2. **Creative Writing**
Have students draw conclusions about the status of American women in the nineteenth century based on the attractions of the United States Centennial Exposition, described on page 565.
3. **Researching for Bonus Points**
What was the formal name of the United States general nicknamed "Old Fuss and Feathers," who fought in the war against Mexico? Hint: He was also a Union general in the Civil War. (General Winfield Scott)

ANSWERS TO
Chapter Review 24

Reviewing the Facts
1. (a) share of ownership in a business (b) business organized by issuing shares of stock (c) movement of people from a place (d) movement of people to a place (e) belief that wealth of a country should be shared equally (f) right to vote

2. **(a)** Queen of Great Britain from 1837 to 1901 **(b)** socialist reformer who founded cooperative village of New Harmony, Indiana **(c)** co-author of *The Communist Manifesto* and *Das Kapital* **(d)** early moderate socialism **(e)** Marxist socialism **(f)** urban working class **(g)** Italian nationalist who united northern Italy **(h)** Italian nationalist leader of "Red Shirts" **(i)** French emperor who made alliance with Cavour **(j)** Prussian prime minister who united Germany

3. **(a)** Between 1850 and 1875, coal production in Germany increased from 6 million tons to 35 million tons per year, world output of iron increased fourfold, value of goods bought and sold among countries increased by 260 percent. **(b)** transcontinental railroad, steamships, Suez Canal **(c)** telegraph

4. **(a)** increased capital, limited liability **(b)** could share in the company's profits and profit from selling stocks

5. Possible answer: Shirt manufacturer in Britain could have 1,000 bales of cotton delivered from New Orleans to Manchester factory in 10 days; finished shirt might be on sale in shops in Vienna and St. Petersburg 3 weeks later

6. **(a)** Workers were slaves to the bourgeoisie. **(b)** Work was the true source of all value. **(c)** Factory-owning middle class took advantage of workers. **(d)** The proletariat were victims of the bourgeoisie.

7. **(a)** Prussia was the most industrial state and had the largest army in the loosely organized confederation. **(b)** Prussia went to war against Denmark to win these two border provinces. **(c)** Prussia defeated Austria to build national pride and crush its rival in the Confederation. **(d)** Defeating France gave Prussia Alsace and Lorraine, the final step in German unification.

8. Italy: lack of national leadership, frequent changes in government, economic problems which led to massive emigration; France: control of Paris by radicals, political divisions, frequent changes in government

9. In 1815, all the Great Powers were fairly equal in strength. By 1871, Britain and Germany were the strongest, both economically and militarily.

10. **(a)** North had a diversified economy with both farms and industry; South depended on a few cash crops, mainly cotton. **(b)** Southerners depended on slavery to protect their economy, while northerners considered slavery morally wrong.

Basic Skills

1. **(a)** East and West Germany correspond roughly to what was then Hanover and the Southern German States; parts of Prussia now Czechoslovakia, Poland, Hungary, and Russia. **(b)** Italy basically the same.

2. **(a)** Italy: 1858—war with Austria; 1859–1860—annexation of independent territories; 1866—war with Austria; 1870—takeover of Papal States from Church **(b)** Prussia: 1866—land in Germany from Austria; 1867—North German Confederation states joined Prussia; 1871—South German states join Prussia; 1871—Alsace and Lorraine conquered from France

Researching and Reporting Skills

Students' answers will vary.

Critical Thinking

1. Industrialization created more goods that could be traded and increased the market for these goods by making them more affordable; advances in transportation made it easier to ship goods to foreign markets.

2. **(a)** utopian socialism—Robert Owen, Charles Fourier; sought to protect workers; some central planning and state ownership of means of production; more equitable distribution of wealth; scientific socialism—Karl Marx and Friedrich Engels; inevitability of class struggle; only work has value; reacting to inequitable distribution of wealth **(b)** utopian socialism—peaceful reform; quarrels; scientific socialism—complete socialism; no large worker revolts; ignored importance of religion, nationalism, ethnic loyalties, and other ideals and concerns not directly related to economics.

3. **(a)** dealt with practicalities and power, not ideals **(b)** Cavour struck a deal with Napoleon III giving France Nice and Savoy for its help in driving Austria out of Italy; Bismarck deliberately deceived or provoked Denmark, Austria, and France into wars to acquire land for Prussia.

4. **(a)** Prussia's superior transportation system and ability to manufacture military equipment gave it a decisive advantage. **(b)** Prussia wanted the Alsace and Lorraine regions of France because of their rich coal and iron deposits.

5. Marx was enormously affected by squalor of living conditions and poverty of workers; saw sharp contrast with the wealthy few.

6. **(a)** Foreign trade by North expanded tremendously both in goods and farm products. **(b)** Industrial development, especially in the North, proceeded rapidly.

Perspectives on Past and Present

Students' answers will vary.

Investigating History

Students' answers will vary.

The Crystal Palace Exhibition displayed inventions and products from around the world.

Teaching with Pictures

Have students study the painting and read about London's Great Exhibition of 1851. Tell students that this first world's fair, whose theme was progress, showcased machinery, art, and crafts from many countries. Newly manufactured products on display included a steam engine, a reaper, the Colt revolver, and a high-speed printing press. The fair was housed in the Crystal Palace, a huge building made of iron and glass. Students might be interested to know that 5,000 iron girders and 30,000 panes of glass were used in its construction. Ask volunteers to comment on the grandeur of the architecture; the fountain, trees, and statuary; and the visitors themselves. Ask students to theorize about why Britain put on such an elaborate exhibition.

Key Terms

stock
corporation
emigration
immigration
socialism
utopian socialism
scientific socialism
bourgeoisie
proletariat
communism
suffrage
realism
realpolitik
kaiser

546

Read and Understand

1. Industrialism created a global economy.
2. Working people gained more influence.
3. Italy and Germany formed nations.
4. The United States spread westward.

It was May 1, 1851—a date thousands of Britons had been eagerly awaiting for months. By noon, more than 500,000 people had gathered in London's Hyde Park to witness the opening of the Great Exhibition. On display were arts, crafts, and inventions from all over the world. This exhibit was, in many ways, the first world's fair.

The 25,000 people lucky enough to have tickets for the opening ceremonies were crammed inside the Crystal Palace. This remarkable building had been designed especially for the exhibition. It looked like a gigantic greenhouse. More than 1 million square feet of glass on a framework of bare iron formed its walls and roof. The main hall was as long as six football fields and high enough to house several fully grown elm trees.

Chapter 24 Resources

GEOGRAPHY
- Geography Skills 24
- Transparencies 75, 76, 77

REINFORCEMENT
- Vocabulary 24
- Basic Skills 24
- Reteaching 24
- Making Connections Study Guide 24

ENRICHMENT
- Critical Thinking 24

ASSESSMENT
- Chapter Test 24
- Alternate Chapter Test 24
- Computer Test Bank

Promptly at noon, a flourish of trumpets announced the arrival of Queen Victoria and the royal family. Although the queen's political power was limited, her symbolic importance as head of the British empire was immense. During her long reign (1837–1901), Victoria skillfully used ceremonial occasions such as this exhibition to foster national spirit.

Prince Albert, Victoria's German-born husband, stood proudly by her side. He was an intelligent, energetic man who was fiercely devoted to his adopted country. The Great Exhibition had been his idea, a way of showing the world the awesome power of the British empire. It would also, Albert said, "give us a living picture of the point of development at which the whole of mankind has arrived."

Visitors to the Great Exhibition exclaimed over stuffed elephants from India, fine lace from Spain, diamonds from the Netherlands, cigars from Cuba, perfumes from Turkey, cannons from Germany, birchbark canoes from Canada, and porcelain from China and France.

Exhibit after exhibit showed the strength of British industry. Among the wonders on display were a printing press that could turn out 5,000 newspapers per hour and a locomotive engine that could pull a train at 60 miles per hour. While the Great Exhibition celebrated the height of civilization to which the "whole of mankind" had risen, it left no doubt as to which country was in the lead. More than half the exhibits came from Great Britain and its territories.

Many of the 6 million visitors felt that the Great Exhibition marked the dawn of a new age of progress. Indeed, the years after the Great Exhibition were a period of tremendous economic growth. Perhaps the most striking advances during this time were in travel and communications. Railroads, steamships, and the telegraph made the world seem smaller than ever before. News, goods, and people traveled faster.

People responded to the spread of industrialism in a variety of ways. Some groups demanded a new division of wealth, with equal shares for all. Others believed that the path to a better future lay in building strong nation-states. In Europe, nationalism led to the birth of two new nation-states, Germany and Italy. In North America, the United States added new lands and grew to be an industrial power.

Industrialism created a global economy. 1

The people who visited the Great Exhibition of 1851 lived in a world that their grandparents could not have imagined. It was a world of booming factories, speeding trains, and mile-long bridges. Above all, it was a world of change.

The pace of industrialization continued to quicken. In 1858, a German economist wrote, "Railroads and machine shops, coal mines and iron foundries, spinneries and rolling mills seem to spring up out of the ground, and smokestacks sprout from the earth like mushrooms." Between 1850 and 1875, coal production in Germany grew from 6 million tons to 35 million tons per year. During the same years, the total world output of coal nearly tripled. The world output of iron increased fourfold.

Because factory-made goods cost less than handmade items, mass-produced items found their way into every home. Thus, the demand for manufactured goods skyrocketed along with the supply of such goods.

Finally, the great boom brought a tremendous increase in world trade. Between 1850 and 1870, the value of goods bought and sold among countries increased by a staggering 260 percent. In other words, world trade more than tripled during these 20 years. Trade increased more rapidly during this period than at any other time in history.

Steam revolutionized transportation.

By 1850, the same changes that had swept Great Britain in the early 1800's were happening on a global scale. Leading the way were advances in transportation and communication.

The growth of railroads The late 1800's were a golden age for railroad builders. They laid thousands of miles of new track every year, spanning rivers with iron bridges and carving tunnels through mountains. Between 1850 and 1880, the length of railroad track in the world grew from 23,600 miles to 228,400 miles—almost the distance from Earth to the moon!

Although most railroad building took place in Europe and North America, the "iron horse" soon reached every inhabited continent. By 1875, even

547

OBJECTIVE 1. Explain the concept of "global economy."

Teaching Strategy: *Economics and History: Global Economy* (page 546a)

OBJECTIVE 2. Assess the impact of improved communication and transportation in the nineteenth century.

Teaching Strategy: *Discussing History: Transportation and Communication in the Nineteenth Century* (page 546a)

OBJECTIVE 3. Identify the causes of immigration and emigration.

Teaching Strategy: *Using Geographic Themes: Movement* (page 546c)

■ BACKGROUND

Steam engines were the driving forces of the great boom. In 1850, the steam engines of the world had a total capacity of some 4 million horsepower. By 1870, their combined horsepower had surged to more than 18 million.

SECTION 1
Resources

ASSESSMENT
■ Section Quiz 24.1

REINFORCEMENT
■ Independent Practice 24.1

ENRICHMENT
■ Voices from the Past 24.1

■ BACKGROUND

The first transcontinental railroad, completed at Promontory Point, Utah, was an achievement of technology and hard work. In one day work crews could build 10.6 miles of track, using 31,000 ties connected with 4,037 iron rails and 120,000 spikes.

■ DISCUSSION

A telegraph message carried the news of the railroad link at Promontory Point across the nation: "One, two, three—done!" Parades and fireworks greeted the news in cities and towns across the United States. Ask students why the entire country celebrated the event.

Looking at economics *The opening of the Suez Canal in 1869 provided a direct route between Europe and the East. In 1875, Britain purchased the Egyptian ruler's stock in the Suez Canal Company. As a shareholder, Britain could protect the shipments of Indian and Egyptian cotton bound for British mills.*

such nonindustrial countries as Brazil and Egypt had more than 1,000 miles of track. Swashbuckling railroad tycoons such as the Englishman Thomas Brassey became giants of industry. At one time, Brassey employed 80,000 workers and was building railroads on 5 continents.

Railroads boosted trade and industry wherever they spread. The iron and coal industries grew to meet the railroads' endless need for tracks, trains, and fuel. Other industries flourished as railroads brought them raw materials and carried their finished products to market.

Steamships Meanwhile, similar changes were taking place with water transportation. In 1807, an American named Robert Fulton designed the first practical steamboat. By the 1840's, more than 500 steamboats were chugging up and down the Mississippi River.

For ocean crossings, the changeover from wind power to steam power was slow. Early steamships needed to stop for fuel too often to make ocean travel practical. In 1850, only 5 percent of all oceangoing ships used steam power. By 1870, however, that figure had grown to 40 percent.

Breakthroughs in transportation Two celebrations in 1869 highlighted the dramatic advances in transportation. One took place in the United States and the other in Egypt.

On May 10, a crowd gathered in a lonely part of Utah to celebrate the opening of the first transcontinental railroad. At Promontory Point, a work crew laying track from the east met the crew laying track from the west. Amid cheers and brass bands, officials hammered a golden spike to mark the meeting place. On the new railroad, travelers could journey from Boston to San Francisco in less than a week.

Six months later, on November 17, a parade of 69 ships sailed out of the harbor of Port Said, Egypt. Led by the yacht of France's Empress Eugenie, the ships sailed southward through the just-completed Suez Canal. This 100-mile canal, planned by French businessman Ferdinand de

Footnote to History

In 1872, French writer Jules Verne published a novel called *Around the World in Eighty Days.* Just 20 years earlier, the journey would have taken about 11 months. Real-life travelers would not have shared all the adventures of Verne's hero, who fought off an Indian attack in the United States and rescued a princess in India. However, travelers *could* have made the trip in the same time. The novel was based on actual railroad and steamship schedules.

548

Lesseps, linked the Mediterranean and Red seas. No longer did ships from Europe have to go around Africa to reach Asia. The canal shortened the travel time between Europe and India by at least one month.

The telegraph speeded communication.

Trains and steamships carried letters, newspapers, and other kinds of information. However, by the mid-1800's, the field of communications was already far ahead of transportation in terms of speed. The telegraph could send information at the speed of electricity.

Electricity had fascinated the scientists in the Age of Enlightenment (page 464). During the 1840's, several inventors made telegraph systems using wires that carried low-voltage currents. The most successful telegraph was invented by an American artist, Samuel F.B. Morse. His system used a key (which looked something like a stapler) to make and break an electric circuit. Morse developed a code in which short bursts of current (dots) and longer bursts (dashes) stood for letters.

By 1850, all the major cities in the eastern United States were connected by telegraph lines. In 1851, a telegraph cable was laid under the English Channel to connect London and Paris. In 1866, the first successful transatlantic cable was completed, linking Newfoundland and Ireland. By 1875, it was possible to send messages around the world—from London to Calcutta, from New York to Melbourne, from Paris to Tokyo—in less than five minutes.

Business leaders formed corporations.

As world trade and industry expanded so did the size of businesses. Building transcontinental railroads and telegraph systems took a huge supply of money for investment, or capital. Many entrepreneurs needed help in raising the capital to start their businesses. To raise this money, an entrepreneur could sell shares of **stock** in the new company. Everyone who bought stock became a part-owner of the business.

By the mid-1800's, most major companies had thousands of owners. For example, Ferdinand de Lesseps set up a corporation to raise money to build the Suez Canal. He sold nearly 400,000 shares, which were purchased by several governments and more than 20,000 individuals.

If a company did well, stockholders stood to make money in two ways. First, each stockholder shared in the company's profits in proportion to the amount of stock he or she owned. Second, stockholders could often sell their shares of stock at a higher price than they had paid for them, because other people were eager to own a share of a thriving business. On the other hand, if the company did poorly, stockholders might lose the money they had invested. However, they could never lose more than they had originally paid for the stock.

Businesses organized in this new way were called **corporations**. They operated under charters obtained from the government. Countless businesses formed corporations and added the term *incorporated* (in the United States) or *limited liability* (in Great Britain) to their names.

Businesses were soon operating on a larger scale than ever before. These vast enterprises yielded correspondingly great profits. Investment banks, concentrated in London, specialized in channeling that income into new ventures all over the world.

Some corporations became so successful that they drove rivals out of business. For example, the American entrepreneur John D. Rockefeller began his rise to wealth by building an oil refinery in 1863. His business incorporated as the Standard Oil Company of Ohio in 1870. Soon Rockefeller owned not only oil refineries but also oil wells, oil pipelines, and oil sales agencies. He controlled every step of the business from the ground to the customer. By the 1880's, Standard Oil was the only major oil company in the United States. When a single company controls an entire industry, the situation is called a monopoly. In the late 1800's, monopolies arose in many industries, both in the United States and in Europe.

Economic ties circled the globe.

The transportation revolution, the growth of trade, and the huge increase in industrial production brought countries around the world into closer contact than ever before. A shirt manufacturer in Britain, for example, could have 1,000 bales of cotton delivered from New Orleans to his factory in Manchester in 10 days. The finished

549

■ DISCUSSION

What are the advantages of a corporation? (ability to amass capital, to buy raw materials in huge volumes at discount prices, to survive the sellout or death of a single owner)

■ BACKGROUND

In the 1890's, Standard Oil controlled 90 percent of the nation's oil refineries. It also enjoyed special favors from the railroads, which made large amounts of money from shipping Rockefeller's oil. Shortly after 1900, Rockefeller became a billionaire.

ANSWERS TO
Section Review 1

Define:
(a) share of ownership in a business (b) business organized by issuing shares of stock to raise capital (c) movement of people from a region (d) movement of people to an area
Identify:
(a) first world's fair (b) Queen of Great Britain from 1837 to 1901 (c) designer of first practical steamboat (d) canal linking Mediterranean and Red seas (e) inventor of telegraph
Answer:
1. Factory-made goods cost less than handmade items, and lower prices skyrocketed the demand.

2. (a) growth of railroads, invention of a practical steamship, and opening of the Suez Canal (b) helped them flourish by speeding

(continued)

ANSWERS TO (continued)

raw materials to factories and finished goods to markets

3. Trains, steamships, and telegraphs speeded communication worldwide.

4. (a) by selling shares of stock (b) by sharing profits and by selling stock at profit

5. (a) brought countries into closer contact (b) Failures had international impact.

6. from Europe to other continents; within Europe, from rural to urban areas

7. (a) Great Exhibition—demonstrated abundance of wares available around the world; Suez Canal—made it possible to obtain goods from Asia without going around Africa; Golden Spike—made possible distribution of goods across the United States in less than a week (b) Countries were economically prosperous and proud of their achievements.

ANSWER TO
Reading a Table

The United States' manufacturing had the largest relative increase.

ANSWER TO
Reading a Graph

Trade expanded most rapidly in the years 1840 to 1880 and 1900 to 1913. Point out the doubling of figures in the scale on the left.

shirts might be on sale in shops in Vienna and St. Petersburg three weeks after they left the factory.

Industrial countries depended on a steady stream of imports from many parts of the world. To keep their factories running, most industrial countries needed far more raw materials than they themselves could provide. As their cities swelled in size and population, most industrial countries also needed more food than they could grow. By 1875, for example, Britain imported more than 75 percent of the wheat its people consumed.

Much of this food and the resources for industry came from countries that had few factories of their own. In turn, those countries bought their manufactured goods from the industrial countries. The world was rapidly becoming interdependent.

The growth of a world economy brought risks along with benefits. In 1857, for example, the collapse of a major insurance company in the United States led to the failure of dozens of other businesses across the country. Within months, this financial crisis had shaken businesses in Britain, France, Argentina, and Australia. Such "crashes" took place repeatedly in the late 1800's. Crop failures or financial problems in one part of the world now had international impact.

Reading a table Which nation's manufacturing had the largest relative increase?

People relocated in search of work.

As we saw in Chapter 22, the Industrial Revolution was accompanied by a population explosion. In 1850, about 266 million people lived in Europe. By the end of the century, the population had risen above 400 million, an increase of more than 50 percent. That figure would have been even larger if many Europeans had not left the continent for other lands.

The 1800's were marked by great shifts in population. Some parts of the world had large-scale **emigration**—that is, many people left those places to settle elsewhere. In other places, there was large-scale **immigration**—that is, many people settled in that area. Between 1850 and 1900, an estimated 25 million people sought to escape poverty or oppression by emigrating to the United States, Canada, South Africa, Australia, New Zealand, and Latin America.

The migration within Europe, as rural people flocked to the cities, was even greater. For every seven children born in the rural areas of western Europe after 1850, one stayed at home, one emigrated to another country, and five moved to cities in their own country. These massive shifts in population played a large part in the development of the modern world.

Reading a graph During what two periods did trade increase most rapidly?

Relative Shares of World Manufacturing Output, 1750–1900

	1750	1800	1830	1860	1880	1900
United Kingdom (Britain)	1.9	4.3	9.5	19.9	22.9	18.5
France	4.0	4.2	5.2	7.9	7.8	6.8
German States/Germany	2.9	3.5	3.5	4.9	8.5	13.2
Russia	5.0	5.6	5.6	7.0	7.6	8.8
United States	0.1	0.8	2.4	7.2	14.7	23.6
Japan	3.8	3.5	2.8	2.6	2.4	2.4
China	32.8	33.3	29.8	19.7	12.5	6.2
India/Pakistan	24.5	19.7	17.6	8.6	2.8	1.7

SOURCE: *P. Kennedy,* The Rise and Fall of the Great Powers. *Random House, New York, 1987, p.149.*

The Growth of World Trade, 1750–1913 (in 1913 dollars)

NOTE: Data show total world exports and total world imports.

SOURCE: *W. Woodruff,* Impact of Western Man: A Study of Europe's Role in the World Economy. *St. Martin's Press, New York, 1967, p. 313 and references cited therein.*

550

Define: (a) stock, (b) corporation, (c) emigration, (d) immigration

Identify: (a) Great Exhibition, (b) Victoria, (c) Fulton, (d) Suez Canal, (e) Morse

Answer:

1. How did industrialization encourage the demand for goods?
2. (a) What changes occurred in transportation? (b) How did the growth of transportation affect other industries?
3. What changes took place in communications?
4. (a) How did entrepreneurs raise money for investment? (b) In what two ways could stockholders make money?
5. (a) What were the advantages of the increase in world trade? (b) What were the drawbacks of the world economy?
6. Briefly describe the major shifts in Europe's population in the late 1800's.

Critical Thinking

7. The text describes three ceremonial occasions—the Great Exhibition, the opening of the Suez Canal, and the driving of the golden spike at Promontory Point. (a) How did each affect trade? (b) What do these celebrations suggest about the spirit of the age?

Working people gained more influence. 2

By 1850, some of the worst abuses of the Industrial Revolution were slowly being corrected. From a modern point of view, however, workers still had many grievances. A number of people tried to solve these problems in new ways.

At first, many reformers had come from the middle and upper classes. For example, a few British aristocrats championed laws limiting child labor (page 521). Such upper-class reformers saw themselves as protecting the common people from the greed of the new entrepreneurs. In the late 1800's, however, working people themselves became more active in politics. Gradually they made their voices heard. As you will see in this section, demands for reform grew louder. Often, however, reformers disagreed on how to improve society.

Socialists sought to reform society.

The misery and poverty of the working class that resulted from the Industrial Revolution shocked a British reformer named Robert Owen. Although a factory owner himself, Owen criticized the new industrial society as "a miserly, selfish system. Under this system, to support life you must be tyrant or slave. It is all about individual wealth and power, with which the most successful are maintained with considerable hazard and gross injustice." Owen turned to cooperatives and unions to protect workers.

Owen sought to develop a model for improving conditions for workers. After years of serving as a shop clerk, Owen was by the age of thirty the owner of a cotton mill with 2,000 employees at New Lanark, Scotland. Owen treated his workers well. He built houses near the factory and rented them to his employees at low rates. He did away with child labor, giving his workers' children free schooling instead. Owen's most ambitious experiment was the founding of a cooperative village at New Harmony, Indiana, in 1825. After only four years, it broke up from constant quarrels.

Other reformers—such as the nobleman St. Simon and the philosopher Charles Fourier in France—wanted to offset the effects of industrialization with a new kind of economic system called **socialism.** It used government central planning to bring about reform. This approach involved state or community ownership of property such as factories, mines, railroads, and other key industries. Socialists hoped that this system would result in greater economic equality within society. Some socialists—such as Louis Blanc—advocated change through extension of the right to vote.

◢ Turning Points in History

The Communist Manifesto The moderation of early socialists was challenged in the 1840's by a more extreme form of socialism developed by Karl Marx (1818–1883). Marx believed that Owen, Fourier, and others like them were misguided dreamers or **utopian socialists.** As you may recall, the word *Utopia* means "nowhere" and was the title of a book describing an ideal

551

SECTION 2 Objectives and Teaching Strategies

OBJECTIVE 1. Discuss the main ideas of socialism.

Teaching Strategy: *Writing about History: Socialism* (page 546c)

OBJECTIVE 2. Describe the views of Karl Marx and assess their impact on events in nineteenth-century Europe.

Teaching Strategy: *Discussing History: Karl Marx* (page 546c)

OBJECTIVE 3. Contrast romanticism and realism.

Teaching Strategy: *Teaching with Pictures: Realism and Romanticism* (page 546c)

■ BACKGROUND

The gap between rich and poor is demonstrated in the following statistic: in the French manufacturing city of Lille, 9 percent of the population in 1875 controlled 90 percent of the community's wealth.

SECTION 2 Resources

ASSESSMENT
- Section Quiz 24.2

REINFORCEMENT
- Independent Practice 24.2

ENRICHMENT
- Voices from the Past 24.2

Another reason workers did not erupt in the way Marx predicted was that emigration gave millions of discontented workers a chance to improve their lives in new lands.

Cooperative Learning

Divide the class into groups of three students. Each group member should take on one of the following roles: Robert Owen, Karl Marx, or John D. Rockefeller. Each student should prepare a statement that presents his or her character's viewpoint on the need for reform in industrial society. The statement should also include the type of reform advocated by that particular person. Students should keep in mind the views of the other characters as they prepare their statements. Have each group member present his or her statement to the rest of the group. Then allow group members to debate the topic.

society. Marx described his own ideas as **scientific socialism** because he claimed that they were based on a scientific study of history.

Marx and Engels Marx was born in Germany in 1818. While a student, he became a radical activist and journalist. By 1848, Marx had been exiled from France, Belgium, and Germany. He finally found a haven in Great Britain, where he spent the rest of his life writing with a fellow radical, Friedrich Engels (page 522). Engels came from a well-to-do family that owned a textile mill in England. Marx and his family were often so poor that they depended on Engels for support.

Class struggle Marx outlined his ideas in a 23-page pamphlet entitled the *Communist Manifesto*. The manifesto set forth the theory that economic forces are key to understanding history.

Marx pointed out that there are never enough products available to satisfy people's needs or wants. As a result, human societies have always been divided into two classes—the haves and the have-nots. The haves control the means of producing goods and thus possess great wealth and power. The have-nots perform backbreaking labor but receive low wages while enduring poor working conditions.

The manifesto argued that the exploitation of the have-nots by the haves has caused a continuous class struggle. Thus the masters exploited their slaves in ancient Greece and Rome while powerful feudal nobles dominated their serfs during the Middle Ages.

Marx maintained that the Industrial Revolution had created a new struggle between social classes. He used the word **bourgeoisie** to describe the factory-owning middle class. These people were capitalists—people who invested money in business. Marx used the word **proletariat** to describe the working class. Although it is the workers' labor that gives value to a product, they get only wages, while the owners of the factories gain wealth and power.

A working-class revolution According to Marx, the Industrial Revolution made the rich richer and the poor poorer. He predicted that the workers would join together to overthrow the bourgeoisie. "Workers of the world, unite!" wrote Marx. "You have nothing to lose but your chains."

After overthrowing the bourgeoisie, the triumphant proletariat would create a new classless society based upon the principles of **communism.**

Marx described communism as a form of complete socialism in which the means of production—all land, mines, factories, railroads, and businesses—would be owned by the people. (In reality, these would be owned and controlled by the state. Private property would in effect cease to exist.) The result would be that all goods and services would be shared equally.

Importance of Marxism The *Communist Manifesto* was published in February 1848. At first, its passionate call for action seemed to produce results. As you have seen (page 542), widespread revolts shook Europe during the first four months of 1848. Although the revolts caught Europe's rulers by surpise, they were quickly put down. The *Communist Manifesto* thus produced few significant short-term results.

The consequences of the *Communist Manifesto* were felt mainly in the twentieth century. In the late nineteenth century, its vision inspired some new socialist parties. They were countered, however, by the renewal of moderate socialism, led by Beatrice and Sidney Webb in Great Britain. Their work aided the extension of voting rights and the founding of the Labour Party, which gave workers representation. In the twentieth century, Marxism revived to exert a powerful influence upon such revolutionaries as Lenin, Mao Tse-tung, Ho Chi Minh, and Fidel Castro.

Finally Marx believed that economic forces dominated society. Time would show, however, that economic forces—although important—are not the only factors that influence people's lives. As you have seen, religion, nationalism, ethnic loyalties, and a concern for democratic reforms are also powerful forces in history.

The failures of Marx's predictions Many of Marx's predictions proved to be wrong. The gap between the rich and the poor did not widen as he had expected. While the rich continued to prosper, the lives of the poor also improved. As you will see, the tremendous growth of trade and production brought benefits to almost everyone. The formation of labor unions also helped to raise wages and improve working conditions.

Marx also underestimated the ability of democratic governments to make peaceful reforms. As workers won the right to vote, they were eventually able to win the passage of reforms such as social security, minimum wages, and unemployment insurance.

Working men won the vote.

Although workers did not revolt, many did strive for changes in society. Brought together in factories, mines, and mills, workers soon saw that there was strength in numbers.

As you have read, workers began to form trade unions in the early 1800's (page 523). Trade unions did not try to remake society, as the socialists did. Instead, unions tried to raise wages and improve working conditions. By 1875, British trade unions had won the right to strike and picket peacefully and had built up a membership of 1 million people. In many other European countries, however, unions remained illegal.

The basis for workers' growing influence was the right to vote. The right to vote is often called **suffrage**. By the end of the 1800's, several industrial countries had universal manhood suffrage (the right of all adult men to vote). No country, however, allowed women to vote.

In the United States, nearly all adult white men had the right to vote by 1850. However, the great numbers of African Americans who were slaves had no voting rights. In some places, free African Americans had once had the right to vote, but it was taken from them. As you will see, African American men won the right to vote after the Civil War. It was many years, however, before women of any race could vote.

In Great Britain, as you have read, the Reform Bill of 1832 (page 541) gave the vote to most men in the middle class. In 1867 and 1884, further reform bills gave the vote to nearly all men.

In France, Napoleon III (page 543) broadened voting rights during the 1850's and 1860's. In 1871, France became the first European country to allow universal manhood suffrage.

Realism replaced romanticism in art.

Just as the working class was becoming more important in politics, it was also becoming more visible in the arts. Artists and writers turned away from romantic, idealized views of the past and of nature. Instead, novels and paintings began to reflect the lives of ordinary people and current social issues. This new artistic approach is called **realism.** Realists tried to observe and report what they saw in a precise, objective fashion.

Realism in painting In 1855, artists in Paris held a grand exhibit of French paintings. The works on display were mainly romantic landscapes, formal portraits, battle scenes, and figures from ancient myths.

Just outside the exhibit hall, an artist named Gustave Courbet (koor-BAY) set up a large wooden shack labeled the Pavilion of Realism. The paintings within were all by Courbet and included a huge, stark funeral scene that had been turned

The realist painters emphasized everyday life, especially among the lower classes. This painting by Daumier shows travelers in a third-class railroad carriage. Compare it with the romantic painting on page 534.

553

ANSWERS TO

Section Review 2

Define:
(a) belief that wealth of a country should be shared equally (b) moderate early socialism of Owen, Fourier, and others (c) Marxist socialism or communism (d) factory-owning middle class (e) wage-earning working class (f) complete socialism in which the means of production are owned by the people (g) right to vote (h) artistic approach that focuses on the ordinary and real

Identify:
(a) socialist reformer who founded cooperative village of New Harmony, Indiana (b) co-author of *Das Kapital* and *The Communist Manifesto*

Answer:
1. (a) Wealth of a country should be shared equally among citizens; society as a whole should own most factories and businesses.
(b) Owen preached cooperation between classes; Marx believed that the classes were doomed to conflict.
2. Without labor or raw ma-
(continued)

ANSWERS TO (continued)

terials, there would be no product and no value.

3. (a) by cheating them out of the wealth created through their efforts **(b)** Workers would overthrow the bourgeoisie, establish socialist society. **(c)** Gap between rich and poor failed to widen; everybody's life improved; formation of labor unions helped raise wages and improve working conditions.

4. by uniting workers to obtain higher wages and improved working conditions

5. (a) Middle class men were first given vote in Britain by the Reform Bill; a later bill extended voting rights to nearly all men. In 1871, France granted vote to all men. After Civil War, black men won vote in U.S. **(b)** women, slaves

6. lives of ordinary people and current social issues

7. (a) disagreed **(b)** agreed **(c)** probably disagreed **(d)** disagreed strongly

8. Change represented shift from idealism to real world, just as literature turned to realism.

ANSWERS TO
Voice from the Past

1. (a) red, unnatural red and black, painted, tall, black, purple, vast, large, small, same **(b)** rattling, trembling **(c)** ill-smelling

2. pollution, lack of sanitation, crowded living conditions, monotony

3. the city

down by the official exhibit. Realist painters such as Courbet scorned romantic art. Courbet called the romantics "painters of angels" and asked, "What do those look like? I've never had the luck to see one in the flesh."

Another outstanding artist of the realist school was Honoré Daumier (doh-**MYAY**). He became famous for his scathing pictures of what he saw as the pompous and self-satisfied middle class.

Realism in literature Realist authors turned to the novel as the form best suited to their goals. "The only reason for the existence of a novel," wrote American author Henry James, "is that it does attempt to represent life." Many European countries produced realist authors. France had Gustave Flaubert (floh-**BAIR**) and Honoré de Balzac (**BAHL**-zak). In Russia, there were Fyodor Dostoevsky (DAHS-tuh-**YEF**-skee) and Leo Tolstoy (tahl-**STOY**). William Thackeray, Charles Dickens, and Thomas Hardy wrote in Britain.

Define: (a) socialism, (b) utopian socialism, (c) scientific socialism, (d) bourgeoisie, (e) proletariat, (f) communism, (g) suffrage, (h) realism

Identify: (a) Robert Owen, (b) Karl Marx

Answer:

1. (a) What were the general beliefs of socialists? (b) How did Marx's and Owen's beliefs differ?
2. Marx stressed the importance of work as the source of value. Explain what he meant.
3. (a) According to Marx, how did bourgeois business owners take advantage of workers? (b) What did he predict would happen? (c) Why didn't these predicted events occur?
4. How did trade unions increase the power of working people?
5. (a) Briefly describe how the right to vote grew broader in Europe and the United States.

Voice from the Past | An Industrial City

Charles Dickens was the most widely read of the English realists, largely because he mixed his realism with plenty of sentiment and melodrama. At the same time, he vividly reminded his readers that they lived in a world where much was grim, ugly, and unjust. Here is how he describes an industrial town in his 1854 novel, *Hard Times.*

It was a town of red brick, or of brick that would have been red if the smoke and ashes had allowed it; but, as matters stood, it was a town of unnatural red and black, like the painted face of a savage. It was a town of machinery and tall chimneys, out of which interminable [endless] serpents of smoke trailed themselves for ever and ever, and never got uncoiled. It had a black canal in it, and a river that ran purple with ill-smelling dye, and vast piles of buildings full of windows where there was a rattling and a trembling all day long, and where the piston of the steam-engine worked monotonously up and down, like the head of an elephant in a state of melancholy madness. It contained several large streets all very like one another, and many small streets still more like one another, inhabited by people equally like one another, who all went in and out at the same hours, with the same sound upon the same pavements, to do the same work, and to whom every day was the same as yesterday and tomorrow, and every year the counterpart of the last and the next.

1. Dickens uses strong sensory words. What adjectives relate to each of these senses? (a) sight (b) hearing (c) smell
2. What real social problems does Dickens mention?
3. Which seems more alive and powerful, the city or the people in it?

554

(b) What groups were still denied the vote?

6. What new themes did art and literature begin to portray in the mid-1800's?

Critical Thinking

7. How might each of the following people have reacted to one socialist's statement, "Property is theft"? (a) Robert Owen (b) Karl Marx (c) a trade unionist (d) a stockholder in a business

8. How was the change in socialist ideas from Owen to Marx similar to the change in literary styles during this period?

Italy and Germany formed nations.

3

Many early nationalists had been romantics like Byron and Mazzini. In politics as in art, however, realism was replacing romanticism. During the late 1800's, a new group of national leaders practiced what they called **realpolitik.** This German term meant "the politics of reality." People used the word to describe tough, calculating politics in which idealism played no part.

As nationalism grew in strength, it destroyed the balance of power that Metternich had so carefully set up in 1815. In France, Napoleon III was bent on reviving French glory. In Germany and Italy, people were determined to form united nation-states. Austria wanted to preserve its empire. These conflicting goals touched off five wars among the Great Powers between 1854 and 1871.

Cavour united Italy.

The Congress of Vienna left Italy divided and almost entirely under foreign control. In the north, Austria ruled Venetia and Lombardy and also dominated the small states of Tuscany, Modena, Parma, and Lucca. In the south, Spain ruled the Kingdom of the Two Sicilies (map, page 556).

During the fateful year of 1848, revolts broke out in eight separate states on the Italian peninsula. Giuseppe Mazzini, the early leader of Italian nationalism (page 532), briefly headed a republican government at Rome. However, the 1848 rebellions failed in Italy just as they did elsewhere in Europe. Within months, the former rulers of the Italian states returned and drove Mazzini and other nationalist leaders into exile.

After 1848, Italian nationalists looked to the Kingdom of Sardinia for leadership. Sardinia was the only Italian state ruled by an Italian dynasty. This kingdom included the Piedmont, Nice, and Savoy as well as the island of Sardinia. It was the largest and most powerful of the Italian states and had the most liberal government.

In 1852, Sardinia's King Victor Emmanuel II named Count Camillo di Cavour (kuh-**VOOR**) his prime minister. Cavour (1810–1861) was a wealthy aristocrat and a moderate nationalist. He made uniting Italy his highest priority.

Cavour considered Mazzini and the earlier nationalists vague and impractical. He believed that careful diplomacy and well-chosen alliances were more useful than grand proclamations and romantic rebellions. In turn, nationalists such as Mazzini called Cavour a "pale ghost of Machiavelli." They feared his main goal was not to unite Italy but to broaden the power of Sardinia.

An alliance with Napoleon III The greatest roadblock to Italian unity was Austria. Cavour knew that Sardinia was going to need help from another Great Power to drive Austria out of northern Italy.

Cavour found an ally in France. Napoleon III hoped to make France Europe's greatest power, as it had been under his uncle, Napoleon I. However, Napoleon III lacked his uncle's brilliance, and most of his schemes backfired.

Napoleon III believed that France could dominate Italy if Austria were out of the way. In 1858, the French emperor and Cavour had a secret meeting at which Napoleon agreed to help drive Austria out of Lombardy and Venetia. In return, Cavour promised to give France the border regions of Nice and Savoy.

Cavour soon provoked a war with Austria. A combined French-Sardinian army won two quick victories against the Austrians. Meanwhile, Italian nationalists staged revolts against Austria all across northern Italy. They demanded that Sardinia take over their lands.

A strong, united Italy was not what Napoleon III had expected. For a time, he considered going to war against Sardinia. However, Cavour had been careful to maintain good relations with the other Great Powers so that France was isolated.

555

SECTION 3 Objectives and Teaching Strategies

OBJECTIVE 1. Define *realpolitik* and identify its role in nineteenth-century politics.

Teaching Strategy: *Discussing History:* **Realpolitik** (page 546d)

OBJECTIVE 2. Evaluate the contributions Cavour and Garibaldi made to the unification of Italy.

Teaching Strategy: *Discussing History: Italian Unification* (page 546d)

OBJECTIVE 3. Explain how Bismarck helped to unify Germany.

Teaching Strategy: *Writing about History: Unification of Germany* (page 546d)

■ BACKGROUND

Cavour published a newspaper called *Il Risorgimento* (The Resurgence), which eventually gave its name to the whole movement for Italian unity.

SECTION 3 Resources

GEOGRAPHY
■ Transparencies 75, 76

REINFORCEMENT
■ Independent Practice 24.3

ENRICHMENT
■ Voices from the Past 24.3

ASSESSMENT
■ Section Quiz 24.3

The Unification of Italy, 1850–1870

FRANCE
AUSTRIAN EMPIRE
SWITZERLAND
SAVOY
LOMBARDY
Turin Milan
VENETIA
Venice
To France, 1860
PIEDMONT
PARMA
MODENA
NICE
Genoa
Florence
Pisa
Arno R.
TUSCANY
PAPAL STATES
OTTOMAN EMPIRE
Po River
Drave
Save River
Adige R.
Danube River
Adriatic Sea
CORSICA (Fr.)
MEDITERRANEAN SEA
Tiber R.
Rome
SARDINIA
Tyrrhenian Sea
Naples
KINGDOM OF THE TWO SICILIES
Palermo
SICILY
MEDITERRANEAN SEA
AFRICA

0   100 Miles

KEY
- Kingdom of Sardinia, 1858
- Added to Sardinia, 1859-1860
- Added to Italy, 1866
- Added to Italy, 1870

Map Study

By skillful maneuvers, Cavour (above) led Italy to national unity. What border territories did he give up in 1860? What territory was the last to be added to Italy?

Napoleon backed down, accepting Nice and Savoy as Cavour had promised. In 1860, Sardinia annexed all of northern Italy except Venetia.

Garibaldi and the Red Shirts While Cavour was uniting the north, he was also secretly helping nationalist rebels in southern Italy. In May 1860, a small army of about 1,100 Italian nationalists sailed from Genoa to Sicily. They were led by a bold and romantic soldier, Giuseppe Garibaldi (GAR-uh-BAHL-dee). In battle, Garibaldi always wore a bright red shirt. Since his followers imitated him, they became known as the "Red Shirts."

Garibaldi was victorious in Sicily and began marching north. Volunteers flocked to his banner. Everywhere he was greeted as a liberator. Garibaldi spoke excitedly of freeing the rest of Italy, especially his beloved birthplace, Nice.

Now it was Cavour's turn to feel that his schemes had backfired. He had given Nice to France as a consolation prize, and he did not want to provoke Napoleon III again. "Garibaldi

556

has become intoxicated with success," Cavour complained to an adviser. "He is planning the wildest schemes."

Knowing that war against France would lead to disaster, Cavour arranged for King Victor Emmanuel II to meet Garibaldi in Naples. "The Red One" willingly agreed to step aside and let the Sardinian king rule the areas he conquered.

In March 1861, an Italian parliament met at Turin and declared Victor Emmanuel II king of Italy. The new nation thus had a government headed by a constitutional monarch and an elected parliament.

A *united* Italy faced problems.

Worn out by years of work, Cavour died shortly after Victor Emmanuel II became king. He never saw his country fully united. Venetia did not become part of the new nation until 1866. In 1871, Italy took over the Papal States. Rome became the national capital of a united Italy.

(According to a treaty called the Law of Guarantees, the pope kept the section of Rome known as Vatican City.)

The movement of the capital to Rome was a triumphant moment for Italian nationalists. However, unification did not cure all the country's problems. Many centuries had passed since the peninsula had last been united, and fierce rivalries flared between different provinces. The greatest tension arose between the industrialized north and the agricultural south. The people of these two regions had very different ways of living. They scarcely understood each other's versions of the Italian language.

After Cavour's death, Italy lacked strong national leadership. Garibaldi tried to head a government, but he lacked the political skill. Within the Italian parliament, there were no well-organized parties with clear-cut policies. As a result, prime ministers and cabinets changed frequently.

Italy also faced severe economic problems. There were bloody peasant revolts in the south and strikes and riots in the northern cities. One result of Italy's problems was massive emigration, particularly from the south. Between 1860 and 1910, 4 million Italians moved to the United States and another 1 million went to Argentina. "I had hoped to evoke the soul of Italy," wrote the old patriot Mazzini shortly before his death in 1872, "but all I can see is a corpse."

Austria and Prussia were rivals.

Like Italy, Germany finally achieved unity in the mid-1800's. Since 1815, 39 German states had formed a German Confederation. The two largest states, Austria and Prussia, dominated this loose grouping.

Austria, earlier the home of the Holy Roman emperor, was still considered the natural leader of Germany. Vienna, Austria's capital, was an important cultural center for German music, art, and literature. However, Austria faced serious problems. Most of the people in the Austrian empire were non-Germans who yearned to break away. Austria also lagged behind Prussia in industrial development.

Prussia, on the other hand, had everything to gain from nationalism. It had a mainly German population. As early as 1834, Prussia had taken the lead by forming the Zollverein (TSOHL-vur-eyn), a free-trade area that included all the major German states except Austria. Prussia was also the most industrial of the German states. Moreover, Prussia's army was by far the most powerful in central Europe.

Prussia was a conservative state. Although most adult men could vote, the Prussian parliament had little control over policies. The king, William I of the Hohenzollern family, had almost unlimited power. His ministers and army officers all came from Prussia's wealthy landlord class, the junkers. Prussia's middle class, although wealthy, had little political influence.

In 1862, William I chose as his prime minister a junker and a staunch conservative named Otto von Bismarck (1815–1898). A master of realpolitik, Bismarck set out to make Prussia the head of a united Germany. He saw Austria as Prussia's major rival. "Germany," he said, "is clearly too small for us both."

Bismarck had only contempt for the liberals who had led the movement for German unity in 1848. In his first speech as prime minister, he told the Prussian parliament, "The great questions of our day cannot be solved by speeches and majority votes—that was the great mistake of 1848 and 1849—but by blood and iron."

Bismarck united Germany by blood and iron.

In 1864, Bismarck took the first step toward increasing Prussian power. He led Prussia into war against Denmark to win two border provinces, Schleswig and Holstein. The quick victory increased national pride among Prussians and won Prussia new respect from other Germans.

The Seven Weeks' War In 1866, Bismarck purposely provoked Austria into declaring war on Prussia. This conflict was known was the Seven Weeks' War. As the name suggests, the war was quickly over. Thanks to Prussia's efficient railroad network, Prussian generals could move their troops to the battlefield more quickly than Austrian leaders could. Once there, the Prussians used their superior training and equipment to win one smashing victory after another.

Austria was humiliated. It lost some German lands to Prussia. It also lost Venetia to Italy, which had fought alongside Prussia. Worst of all,

Austria, afraid to sit idly by while Prussia grew in size and strength, joined the war on Prussia's side. It was the Prussian army, however, that defeated Denmark.

ANSWERS TO

Focus on Geography

1. Westphalia, Brandenburg, West Prussia, East Prussia, Silesia, Hohenzollern

2. (a) Hanover, Schleswig, Holstein, Mecklenburg **(b)** northern Germany

3. Lorraine, Alsace

4. Württemburg, Bavaria

5. Prussia expanded to link eastern and western parts of the kingdom in the north. The potential threat from France helped Prussia gain control of southern Germany.

The Unification of Germany, 1865–1871

KEY

- Prussia, 1865
- Annexed by Prussia, 1866
- Joined Prussia in North German Confederation, 1867
- South German States (joined Prussia to form German empire, 1871)
- Conquered from France, 1871
- German empire, 1871

0   100 Miles

Focus on Geography

Geographic Skills

1. *What six states made up Prussia in 1865?*
2. *(a) What four states did Prussia annex in 1866? (b) Describe their general location.*
3. *What states did Prussia win from France in 1871?*
4. *What two states joined Prussia in 1871?*

Geographic Theme: Location

5. *How did the idea of location influence Prussia's plan for expansion, 1865–1871?*

Chancellor Otto von Bismarck

558

Austria was forced to withdraw from the German Confederation.

Prussia now took control of northern Germany. For the first time, the eastern and western parts of the Prussian kingdom were joined. In 1867, the remaining states in the north joined the North German Confederation, which Prussia dominated completely.

Reeling from this defeat, the Austrian empire set out to rebuild its strength. The empire's biggest problem was the discontent of the many nationalities it ruled. The Hungarians, who had rebelled in 1848, were the largest of these groups. They wanted more independence.

In 1867, Austria agreed to a *dual monarchy.* Austria and Hungary became two independent and equal states with one ruler. Each state had its own parliament and officials. The two states still had a united army, however, and they acted as one in foreign policy. The new empire was known as Austria-Hungary.

The Franco-Prussian War By 1867, only a few southern German states remained independent of Prussia. Because most people in southern Germany were Catholics, they did not want to be dominated by Prussia, which was largely Protestant. However, Bismarck felt certain he could win their support if they faced a threat from outside Germany. He believed his best chance was to provoke a war with France.

Napoleon III of France, whose clumsy diplomacy had helped Cavour unite Italy, soon gave Bismarck a chance to win southern Germany. In 1868, Spanish revolutionaries overthrew Spain's Queen Isabella II and offered the throne to Leopold of Hohenzollern, a distant cousin of Prussia's William I. Napoleon III protested, as he did not want France surrounded by Hohenzollern rulers. The Prussian prince turned down the Spanish offer, but tensions remained high.

During this crisis, the French ambassador met with the Prussian king. Bismarck deliberately gave German newspapers a misleading account of the two men's conversation. Bismarck made it sound as if the king and the ambassador had insulted each other.

As Bismarck hoped, this news story caused an uproar. Soon public opinion in both countries demanded war. On July 19, 1870, France declared war on Prussia.

The Prussian army struck at once. Before most French soldiers had even left their hometowns, Prussian troops poured into northern France. In September 1870, the Prussian army surrounded the main French force at Sedan. Among the 100,000 French prisoners was Napoleon III himself, a beaten and broken man.

Only the city of Paris held out against the Germans. For four months, Parisians withstood a German siege. Finally, hunger forced them to surrender.

France was crushed. It had to pay Prussia the huge sum of 5 billion francs. As an even greater blow to French pride, France had to give Prussia the two border provinces of Alsace and Lorraine, which contained France's richest coal and iron deposits.

The Franco-Prussian War was the final step in German unification. Now people in southern Germany as well as those in the north were caught up in nationalistic fever. Despite their earlier doubts, they accepted Prussian leadership.

The Second Reich On January 18, 1871, at the conquered French palace of Versailles, King William I of Prussia was crowned **kaiser** (KYE-zuhr), or emperor, of the newly formed German empire. To Germans, the empire was known as the Second Reich (ryke). (They considered the Holy Roman Empire the First Reich.) Bismarck became the new nation's first prime minister.

The new German nation had a solid economic foundation. By 1870, Germany was the world's third biggest producer of manufactured goods, after Britain and the United States. After unification, German industry grew even faster. Soon it overtook Britain.

France formed the Third Republic.

In the aftermath of the Franco-Prussian War, France went through a series of crises. After being released by Prussia, Napoleon III spent his last years in exile in Britain. France's National Assembly met to decide on a new government.

559

Footnote to History

Food was so scarce in besieged Paris that people ate sawdust, leather, and rats. Even the animals in the Paris zoo were slaughtered for food by starving Parisians.

■ **BACKGROUND**

A French man called Bismarck "the craftiest of foxes, who had the art of making truth itself an instrument of falsehood; to whom gratitude and respect were as entirely unknown as all other noble sentiments save one: devotion to his country's ambition."

ANSWERS TO
Section Review 3

Define:
(a) politics of reality
(b) member of Prussia's wealthy landlord class
(c) system of government in which Austria and Hungary became two independent and equal states with one ruler (d) emperor

Identify:
(a) early leader of Italian nationalism (b) Italian nationalist; united northern Italy
(c) king of Sardinia, first king of Italy (d) emperor of France; made alliance with Cavour (e) Italian nationalist leader of "Red Shirts"
(f) Prussian prime minister, united Germany (g) free-trade area; all the major German states except Austria (h) war between Austria and Prussia (i) final step in German unification, in which

(continued)

ANSWERS TO (continued)

Prussia crushed France and won Alsace and Lorraine (j) newly formed German empire (k) republican government set up in France in 1875

Answer:

1. was largest and most powerful Italian state with most liberal government

2. (a) Sardinia needed help to drive Austria out of northern Italy. (b) Cavour promised to give France Nice and Savoy. (c) In 1860, Sardinia annexed most of northern Italy.

3. (a) by an Italian parliament which declared Victor Emmanuel II king (b) Venetia, Papal States

4. tensions between industrialized north and agricultural south; lack of strong leadership; lack of well-organized parties within parliament

5. had mainly German population, free-trade area, industry, powerful army, and Bismarck

6. led Prussia to war against Denmark to win Schleswig and Holstein, provoked France into declaring war on Prussia to gain a few southern states outside Germany

7. united French in hatred for Germany

8. great political divisions and frequent changes of government

9. Although five Great Powers had been equal in 1815, by 1871 Britain and Germany had become strongest, economically and politically.

10. (a) In both countries, a strong leader used nationalist sentiment and provoked war when it suited his political goals. (b) Germany was politically and economically stronger than Italy.

Meanwhile, in March 1871, a radical government called the Paris Commune took control of Paris. Once again, Paris faced war, this time a war against France's own National Assembly. When the assembly's troops marched into the city, Parisian workers threw up barricades in the streets and fought block by block. Thousands died, and much of the city burned. In May 1871, the National Assembly defeated the last Communards, as supporters of the Commune were called. The following week, more than 20,000 Parisians were executed.

Not until 1875 could the National Assembly agree on a new government. Eventually, the members voted to set up a republic. In the words of a leading French politician, it was "the system of government that divides us least." The Third Republic, as this new system was called, lasted nearly 60 years. However, France remained bitterly divided, with a dozen political parties jockeying for power. Between 1871 and 1914, France averaged a change of government every ten months.

Despite these divisions, the French were united in their hatred of Germany. Nearly all French people agreed that France must regain Alsace and Lorraine. As French political leader Léon Gambetta declared, "We shall demand each day before Europe our rights and our ravished provinces. France is at the mercy of Germany. We are in a state of latent war; neither peace or freedom nor progress is any longer possible in Europe."

The balance of power broke down.

For 40 years after the Congress of Vienna in 1815, the countries of Europe had remained at peace with one another. The first crack in the peace settlement had come with the Crimean (krye-MEE-uhn) War in 1853. That war pitted Britain and France against Russia. These three countries had competing interests in the Ottoman empire, now weak and crumbling. In a pointless struggle, British and French armies attacked the Crimea, a Russian peninsula in the Black Sea. Although the Crimean War cost the lives of 500,000 men, it was fought far from most European capitals. It did not lead to general warfare in Europe. Its most important result was to reveal the military weakness of the huge but backward Russian empire.

The first battles after 1815 to strike close to home were the wars of Italian and German unification. However, these wars were short, and many countries took no part in them. Europe had not known a major war since the fall of Napoleon.

Meanwhile, the political situation in Europe had changed greatly since 1815. At the Congress of Vienna, there had been five Great Powers—Britain, France, Austria, Prussia, and Russia. The wars of the late 1800's changed one Great Power, as Prussia became Germany, and added a sixth, Italy.

In 1815, all the Great Powers had been fairly equal in strength. By 1871, however, Britain and

DAILY LIFE ▶ *Balloons in War*

When Prussian troops surrounded Paris in 1870, French political leader Léon Gambetta was desperate to escape. If only he could get out of the city, he hoped to raise new armies to defend France. Gambetta took the only way not blocked by the Prussians—he left Paris by balloon. More than 160 other people did the same. During the four months of the siege, balloons also carried ten tons of mail in and out of Paris.

For a brief period, balloons were very important in war. During the United States Civil War, the North used its balloon corps to observe enemy troops and direct cannon fire. After the Franco-Prussian War, many countries added balloon corps to their armies.

Germany were clearly the strongest, both economically and militarily. Austria, Russia, and Italy lagged far behind. France struggled along somewhere in between. The balance of power had broken down, and the risk of a major war was increasing.

It is no coincidence that Britain and Germany, the two countries with the greatest military power, were also the industrial leaders. The Industrial Revolution had military as well as economic impact. In war, industrial countries had enormous advantages over nonindustrial countries. Victory usually went to the side with the most advanced weapons and the best transportation network.

As war became industrialized, it also became nationalized. France built a citizen-army during the French Revolution. By the end of the 1800's, all industrial countries relied on such armies.

Germany's military leader, Count Helmuth von Moltke, wrote:

> The days are gone by when, for dynastic ends, small professional armies went to war to conquer a city or a province. The wars of the present day call whole nations to arms. The entire financial resources of the state are appropriated to the purpose. In the interest of humanity, it is to be hoped that wars will become less frequent, as they have become more terrible.

Section REVIEW 3

Define: (a) realpolitik, (b) junker, (c) dual monarchy, (d) kaiser
Identify: (a) Mazzini, (b) Cavour, (c) Victor Emmanuel II, (d) Napoleon III, (e) Garibaldi, (f) Bismarck, (g) Zollverein, (h) Seven Weeks' War, (i) Franco-Prussian War, (j) Second Reich, (k) Third Republic
Answer:
1. What made Sardinia the leader in the Italian nationalist movement?
2. (a) Why did Cavour make an agreement with Napoleon III? (b) What were the terms? (c) What were the results?
3. (a) How was the kingdom of Italy established? (b) What additional territories were joined to it later?

4. What problems did the united Italy face?
5. Why did Prussia rather than Austria take the lead in uniting Germany?
6. Briefly describe the major steps that Bismarck took to unify Germany.
7. What lasting effect did the Franco-Prussian War have on relations between France and Germany?
8. What political problems did France face under the Third Republic?
9. How had the balance of power in Europe changed since 1815?

Critical Thinking
10. (a) In what ways were the unification of Italy and Germany alike? (b) How was the outcome different for the two countries? Explain.

The United States spread westward. 4

Across the Atlantic Ocean from Europe, another country was also establishing itself as a nation. When the United States declared its independence in 1776, all 13 states lay along the Atlantic coast. By the time the nation celebrated its hundredth birthday in 1876, its borders had reached the Pacific. To unite this territory, Americans fought bitter wars with Native Americans and with Mexico. The bloodiest war of all on the path to nationhood, however, was a war the people of the United States fought among themselves. It is known as the Civil War (1861–1865). Within ten years after the war, it was clear that the United States was on its way to becoming a world power to rival Britain and Germany.

Americans moved westward.

At the end of the Revolutionary War, the Mississippi River marked the western boundary of the United States. Surprisingly, it was Napoleon who gave the United States its first chance to expand west of this river.

The Louisiana Purchase Ever since 1763, when Great Britain drove France out of North America, Spain had held the lands west of the Mississippi. Then in 1800, Spain made a secret treaty with

561

SECTION 4 Objectives and Teaching Strategies

OBJECTIVE 1. Define the concept of westward expansion.

Teaching Strategy: *Using Geographic Themes: Frontier Regions* (page 546e)

OBJECTIVE 2. Identify the territorial gains made by the United States between 1783 and 1853 and assess the impact of expansion on economic development.

Teaching Strategy: *Discussing History: American Expansionism* (page 546e)

OBJECTIVE 3. Explain how regional differences between the northern and southern United States affected the Civil War.

Teaching Strategy: *Using Geographic Themes: Regions* (page 546e)

■ BACKGROUND

European settlers were lured to America by descriptions like these: "So at last I was going to America. Really, really going, at last! The arch of heaven soared. The winds rushed in from outer space, roaring in my ears, 'America! America!' "

SECTION 4 Resources

ENRICHMENT
■ Voices from the Past 24.4

ASSESSMENT
■ Section Quiz 24.4

GEOGRAPHY
■ Transparency 77

REINFORCEMENT
■ Independent Practice 24.4

561

■ BACKGROUND

Before Napoleon offered to sell the Louisiana Territory, the United States had been trying to purchase the city of New Orleans for its strategic trading location.

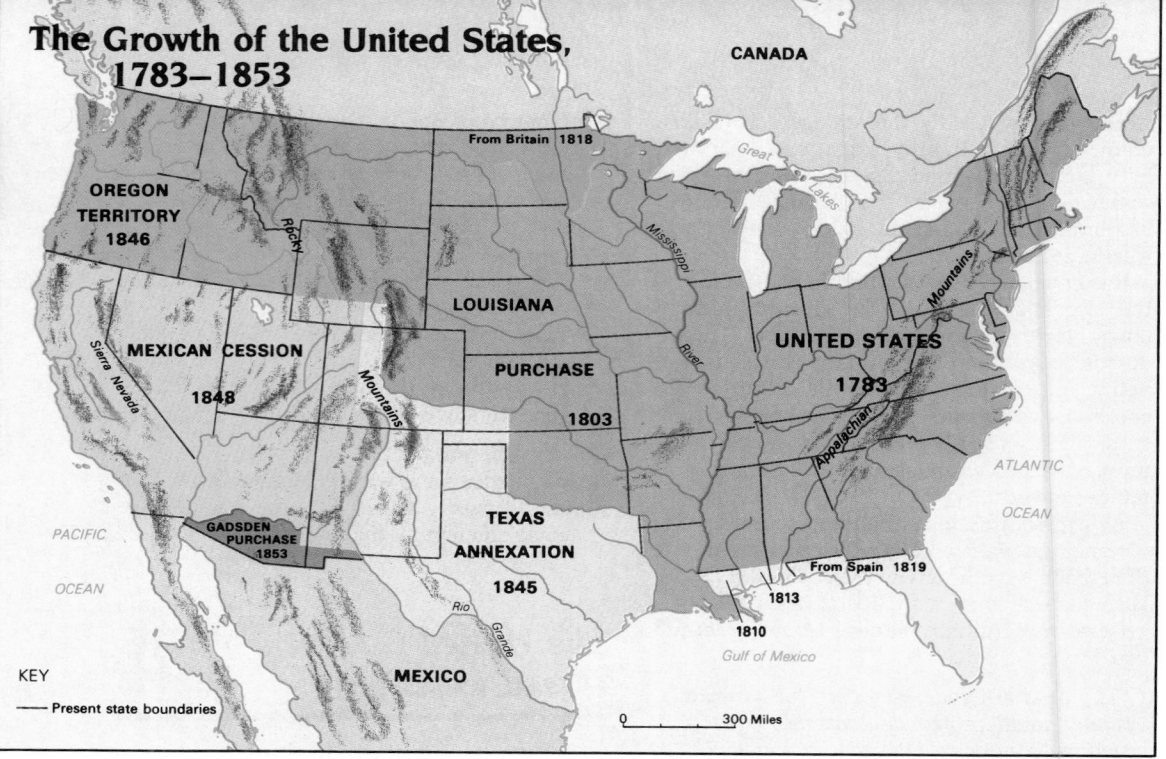

The Growth of the United States, 1783–1853

Map Study

What was the first territory to be added to the United States after 1783? What lands were added between 1805 and 1840? Between 1840 and 1860?

Napoleon, giving those lands to France. The region was known as the Louisiana Territory.

Napoleon dreamed of building a French empire in the Americas as well as in Europe. However, as you read in Chapter 23, Toussaint L'Ouverture led a revolt against French rule in Haiti. Toussaint's fighters and yellow fever all but wiped out a French army of 10,000 soldiers. Discouraged, Napoleon gave up the idea of an American empire and decided to sell the Louisiana Territory. The United States, under President Thomas Jefferson, was eager to buy.

In 1803, the United States bought the entire territory—828,000 square miles—at the bargain price of $15 million. The cost came to about three cents per acre.

The war with Mexico For the next 40 years, the Rocky Mountains were the western boundary of the United States. Then, during the 1840's, a new idea took hold. Some Americans began to argue that the Pacific Ocean was the country's natural boundary.

The lands west of the Louisiana Territory belonged to Mexico, which had won its independence from Spain in 1821 (page 539). However, a number of people from the United States had settled in the area, with Mexico's acceptance. Some settlers were unhappy with Mexican rule.

The largest number of American settlers were in Texas. In 1836, Texans revolted against Mexican rule. For nine years, Texas was an independent country. Then, in 1845, it joined the United States.

Mexico was angered by the United States' decision to annex Texas. The two countries soon quarreled over the new state's southern boundary. Both sides sent troops into the disputed area near the Rio Grande. In 1846, there was a skirmish between Mexican and American soldiers. Within a few days, the United States Congress declared war on Mexico.

The war lasted from May 1846 to September 1847. American troops invaded Mexico and advanced on Mexico City. In bitter fighting, they

562

captured the city and Mexico was forced to surrender. Just as the war began, people in California revolted and declared their independence.

In the Treaty of Guadalupe Hidalgo, the United States gained the land between Texas and the Pacific. The United States paid Mexico $15 million along with $3 million to settle claims of Americans against Mexicans.

Meanwhile, the United States had been negotiating with Great Britain over the Oregon Territory in the northwest. In 1846, the two countries agreed to set the northern boundary of the United States at 49° north latitude.

Conflict grew between North and South.

As people settled these western lands, questions arose over the laws and customs to be followed there. Ever since the nation's early days, the northern and southern parts of the United States had followed different ways of life. Each section wanted to extend its own way of life to the western lands.

The North had a diversified economy with both farms and industry. Northern farmers raised a variety of crops that fed the thriving northern cities. Mills and factories in the North competed with Britain in making cloth, shoes, iron, and machinery. For both its farms and factories, the North depended on free workers. Such workers could move from place to place to meet the needs of industry. They could also be laid off when business slumped.

The South depended on just a few cash crops, mainly cotton. To raise cotton, planters needed a large labor force year round. They relied on slave labor. Southerners traded their cotton for manufactured goods from Europe, especially Great Britain. The South had little industry of its own.

The economic differences between the two sections soon led to political conflicts. The bitterest of these conflicts arose over slavery. Many people in the North considered slavery morally wrong. They wanted laws that would outlaw slavery in the new western territories. Some wanted to abolish slavery altogether. Most white southerners believed slavery was necessary for their economy. They wanted laws to protect slavery in the west so that they could raise cotton on the fertile soil there.

Southerners feared the North's rising industrial power and growing population. Soon, they reasoned, the North would completely dominate the federal government. The election of 1860 seemed to confirm their worst fears. Abraham Lincoln, a northern candidate who opposed the spread of slavery, was elected president.

In the months after the election, 11 southern states made the fateful decision to withdraw from the United States. They established a separate nation called the Confederate States of America. On April 12, 1861, Confederate guns opened fire on Fort Sumter, a fort in South Carolina held by soldiers of the federal government.

The Civil War preserved the Union and ended slavery.

The Civil War lasted from 1861 to 1865. Counting losses on both sides, about 720,000 Americans died in the war. Many were killed in combat, but even more died of diseases such as yellow fever and dysentery that swept through army camps. No other war has taken so many American lives.

Clara Barton (1821–1912) helped the wounded in the American Civil War and the Franco-Prussian War. She founded the American Red Cross.

563

■ DISCUSSION

Which were the more compelling reasons for the conflict surrounding slavery: the economic considerations or the moral aspects?

563|

Ask students to imagine that they are recently arrived immigrants to the United States in 1876. One of the first sights they are taken to see is the Centennial Exposition in Philadelphia. Working in groups of four, have students write letters to family or friends in the old country. They should describe the exhibition and the impression of America that the exhibition created. Group members should discuss the contents of the letter, then write individually for about ten minutes. After writing, group members should share their letters. Have them discuss the different impressions that are apparent in the letters. Ask if it is possible to determine whose impression was most "correct." Then tell the groups to come up with a consensus as to how historians can or should evaluate first-person accounts such as letters and diaries.

ANSWERS TO

Section Review 4

Define:
(a) economy with both farms and industry (b) crop for which ready money is offered

Identify:
(a) land west of the Mississippi bought from France in

(continued)

In part, the North and the South fought over their different views of the Union (the country as a whole). The South believed that the states had formed the Union. Therefore, said southerners, states were free to leave the Union if they wished to do so. Northerners believed that the Constitution of the United States had established the Union once and for all.

To European observers, it was clear that the struggle between North and South was a war for the survival of the United States. It was as much a war of nationalism as the conflict between Prussia and Austria over the future of Germany.

From the beginning of the war, President Abraham Lincoln was determined to preserve the Union. In his inaugural speech, Lincoln reminded his hearers that he had taken an oath to "preserve, protect, and defend" the Union.

Although Lincoln was deeply opposed to slavery, he said repeatedly that the purpose of the war was to save the Union and not to end slavery. Yet many northerners believed that the war was a crusade against slavery. Lincoln eventually decided that ending slavery would help to save the Union. In late 1862, he issued the Emancipation Proclamation, declaring that all slaves in the Confederate states were free.

At first, the proclamation freed no slaves, because the Confederate states did not accept it as law. As Union armies advanced into the South, however, they freed slaves in the lands they conquered. The Emancipation Proclamation also made clear to people in Europe that the war was being fought against slavery. The proclamation made many Europeans, especially the British, less sympathetic to the South. They did not send the money and supplies that the South had hoped they would.

The longer the war went on, the more important the North's advantages in population and industry became. Its bigger population allowed it to raise larger armies. Its factories and railroads kept those armies supplied.

Worn down by lack of food and supplies, the major Confederate army surrendered on April 8, 1865. The Civil War was over.

The Union had been preserved at a tremendous cost. In the aftermath of the war, Congress passed

Lincoln visited the Union army near Antietam, soon after the bloodiest battle of the war. He had just decided to issue the Emancipation Proclamation.

the Thirteenth Amendment to the Constitution. That amendment forever abolished slavery in all parts of the United States.

Industry developed rapidly.

After the war, the American economy expanded at a rate never before seen in the history of the world. There were three main reasons for this rapid growth. First, the United States had a wealth of raw materials. Second, it had a rapidly growing population to provide workers. (During the 1870's, immigrants arrived at the rate of nearly 2,000 a day.) Third, the nation had a democratic political system that put few restraints on its business development.

As early as 1870, the United States had 53,000 miles of railroad track and 5.5 million horsepower in steam engines, more than any other country in the world. American factories led the world in the production of clocks, rifles, sewing machines, and copper wire. American farms led world production of corn, wheat, cotton, and cattle. Never before had so much real and potential wealth been concentrated within one country.

The nation celebrated its first century.

Americans were proud of their country and its achievements. They celebrated its hundredth birthday in 1876 with a magnificent Centennial Exposition in Philadelphia. Like the British exhibition of 1851, this celebration drew visitors from all over the world.

The exposition stood in an enormous 400-acre park on the outskirts of Philadelphia. The main exhibition hall—the United States' answer to the Crystal Palace—covered more than 21 acres. At the time, it was the largest building in the world. Another enormous building, the Machine Hall, held mechanical marvels from all over the world. Among them were several "automatic-writing machines" (the first typewriters) and an amazing new invention that could transmit a human voice by wire. Its inventor, Alexander Graham Bell, called it the telephone.

In the Agriculture Hall, visitors could watch self-rising flour in action and marvel at Gail Borden's new product, canned condensed milk. Other buildings included a Shoe and Leather Hall, a glassworks, a butter and cheese factory, an art gallery, and a Women's Building. In this last building, among exhibits of embroidery, knitted work, and other domestic arts, there were also machines invented by women. These included a machine for washing blankets, a steam iron, and an early dishwashing machine.

Between May and November 1876, more than 9 million people attended the Centennial Exposition—more than had visited any previous world's fair. Most were Americans, of course, but those who came from abroad undoubtedly went away impressed. The United States had made remarkable progress during the 100 years since its founding. Over the next 50 years, it would take its place as a major power in the world.

Section REVIEW 4

Define: (a) diversified economy, (b) cash crop
Identify: (a) Louisiana Purchase, (b) Abraham Lincoln, (c) Confederate States of America, (d) Civil War, (e) Emancipation Proclamation, (f) Thirteenth Amendment
Answer:
1. What part did Napoleon play in the expansion of the United States?
2. (a) How did Texas become part of the United States? (b) How did the annexation of Texas lead to war between the United States and Mexico? (c) What additional territories did the United States gain as a result?
3. How did the economies of the North and the South differ?
4. How was the issue of slavery related to the new western lands that the United States had gained?
5. How did the North and the South differ in their views of the Union?
6. (a) Briefly describe the political events that led to the outbreak of fighting. (b) What was the outcome of the war?
7. How was slavery ended in the United States?
8. What three factors promoted rapid industrial growth after the Civil War?

Critical Thinking
9. How might the Civil War be viewed as a conflict over nationalism?

565

ANSWERS TO (continued)
1803 (b) president during the Civil War (c) 11 Southern states that withdrew from the United States (d) war between North and South (e) declaration freeing all slaves in the Confederate states (f) constitutional amendment abolishing slavery
Answer:
1. sold Louisiana Territory to United States
2. (a) broke away from Mexico, was an independent country for nine years, and became state in 1845 (b) led to quarrel over southern boundary of Texas (c) all land between Texas annexation and Pacific Ocean
3. North—diversified economy; South—dependent on cash crops, mainly cotton
4. North wanted slavery outlawed in western territories, South wanted laws protecting slavery.
5. South believed states had right to leave; North believed that the Constitution had established a permanent Union.
6. (a) conflict over slavery in western territories, election of Abraham Lincoln in 1860, secession of Confederate states (b) preservation of union, ending of slavery
7. by the Thirteenth Amendment
8. raw materials, growing population, government that put few restraints on business
9. Look for answers to consider the conflicting views of southerners (whose primary commitment was to their state) and northerners (whose primary commitment was to the Union).

Concluding the Chapter

1. **Chapter Closer**
Have students summarize the effect of economic expansion and new ideas about nationalism on Europe and on the United States in the nineteenth century. Then ask students to give specific examples of the changes they have summarized.

2. **Reteaching Activities**
a. Recalling Main Ideas
Ask students to explain how Cavour and Bismarck demonstrated the political philosophy of realpolitik.
b. Outlining Have students outline the main ideas of this chapter by organizing important topics under the following headings: "Inventions," "Events," and "People." Tell students to use the section headings as a guide.
c. Writing a Paragraph
Have students write paragraphs on the impact of the invention of the steamship, the railroad or the telegraph on world history. Students should focus on the question, "How did these inventions make the world a smaller place?"

Answers to Chapter Review appear on pages 546e–546f.

Summary

1. Industrialism created a global economy. Industry boomed in the mid-1800's. Railroads, the Suez Canal, and the development of steamships speeded transportation. The telegraph made global communication possible. Many businesses became corporations to get new funds for investment. Production and the demand for raw materials soared, causing the growth of worldwide trade. Industrialization also brought about great shifts in population.

2. Working people gained more influence. As industry spread, socialists urged equal distribution of wealth. While Robert Owen tried to set up cooperative villages, Karl Marx called for a revolt against capitalists. Workers made gains through trade unions, and working men won the right to vote in some countries. The working class also became more visible culturally as realism replaced romanticism.

3. Italy and Germany formed nations. Under the leadership of Cavour, Italy formed a united kingdom. Problems plagued the new nation, however. Guided by Bismarck, Prussia became the center of a new German nation after winning wars against Austria and France. The rise of Germany signaled the collapse of the balance of power in Europe.

4. The United States spread westward. During the 1800's, the United States bought the Louisiana Territory, annexed Texas, obtained the Mexican Cession from Mexico, and negotiated with Britain for the Oregon Territory. Conflict between the industrial North and the agricultural South led to a Civil War. The North's victory ended slavery. After the war, the economy of the United States grew rapidly.

Reviewing the Facts

1. Define the following terms:
   a. stock
   b. corporation
   c. emigration
   d. immigration
   e. socialism
   f. suffrage
2. Explain the importance of each of the following names or terms:
   a. Victoria
   b. Owen
   c. Marx
   d. utopian socialism
   e. scientific socialism
   f. proletariat
   g. Cavour
   h. Garibaldi
   i. Napoleon III
   j. Bismarck
3. (a) Give examples of the way industry expanded after 1850. (b) What advances took place in transportation? (c) Communication?
4. (a) What was the advantage of incorporation for a business? (b) For stockholders?

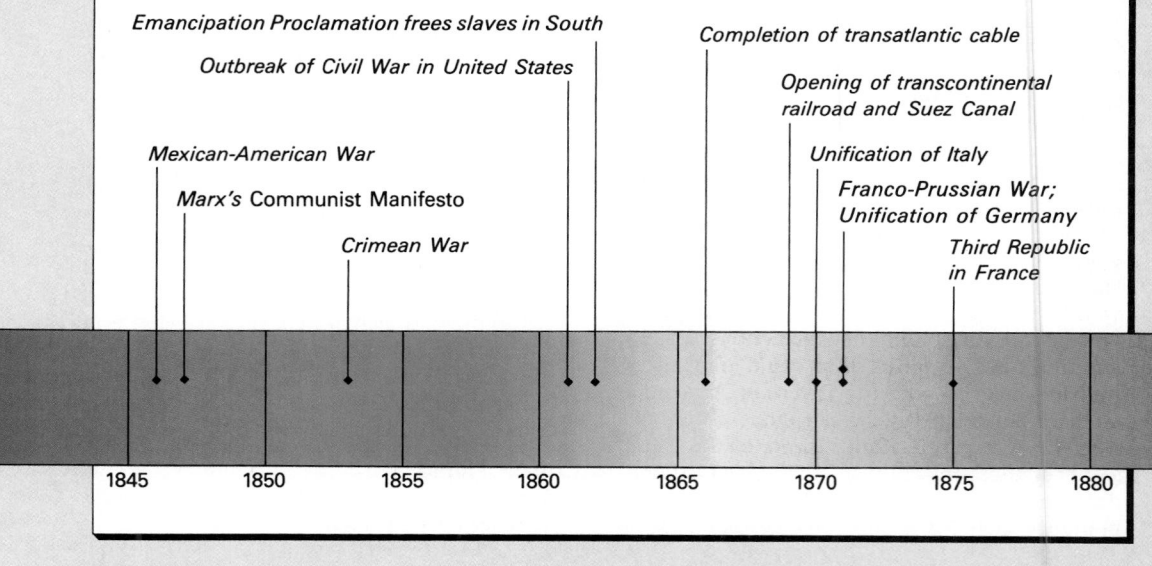

- Emancipation Proclamation frees slaves in South
- Outbreak of Civil War in United States
- Mexican-American War
- Marx's Communist Manifesto
- Crimean War
- Completion of transatlantic cable
- Opening of transcontinental railroad and Suez Canal
- Unification of Italy
- Franco-Prussian War; Unification of Germany
- Third Republic in France

1845 1850 1855 1860 1865 1870 1875 1880

566

5. Give specific examples to show that a world economy had developed by the late 1800's.

6. Briefly summarize Marx's ideas on the following topics. (a) relations between social classes (b) work and economic value (c) the bourgeoisie (d) the proletariat

7. Briefly describe the part each of the following played in the unification of Germany. (a) German Confederation (b) Schleswig-Holstein (c) Seven Weeks' War (d) Franco-Prussian War

8. Describe the problems that France and Italy faced after 1870.

9. How did the balance of power in Europe change between 1815 and 1875?

10. (a) How did the North and the South differ economically? (b) Why was the issue of slavery especially divisive?

Basic Skills

1. **Comparing maps** (a) Compare the size and location of Prussian territory in 1871 (page 558) with that of East and West Germany in 1945 (page 745). (b) Compare the size and location of Italian territory in 1870 (page 556) with that of Italy today (page 748). What differences do you note in each case?

2. **Translating information** Using the maps on pages 556 and 558, explain how (a) Italy and (b) Prussia acquired their territories by the dates specified by the keys. In each case, note from whom the different territories were acquired.

Researching and Reporting Skills
Writing a Research Paper
Phase 3: Drafting the paper

1. **Revising the thesis statement** Check your thesis statement to be sure that it states the main idea of the paper, covers the main topics of your outline, and is supported by your information.

2. **Choosing a title** Choose a title that suggests the subject of the paper.

3. **Writing an introduction** Your introduction should capture attention, provide brief background information, and contain your thesis statement.

4. **Writing the body of the paper** The body of your paper should support the thesis statement with information drawn from your research. Following your outline, write paragraphs that state a main idea and give supporting details. Paragraphs should be linked by transitions that support the flow of

your thinking. Your finished paper should be about five pages long. Make your draft longer by one or two pages so that it can be trimmed down in editing.

5. **Using and citing sources** As you cite information from different sources, paraphrase the information or use quotations. Cite each source in a footnote and in the bibliography.

6. **Using visuals** Insert visuals such as pictures, graphs, diagrams, or charts where they can enhance or clarify your meaning. Make sure that they are integrated in the paper by an introduction or comment and cite your sources.

7. **Writing a conclusion** Your conclusion should restate the thesis, emphasizing how earlier ideas support it.

Critical Thinking

1. **Synthesis** How did industrialization lead to the growth of a global economy?

2. **Summarizing** During the 1800's, improving conditions for workers became an important issue. (a) Summarize the major approaches, including people involved and the problems to be solved. (b) What were the advantages and limitations of each approach?

3. **Applying a concept** Cavour and Bismarck were representatives of realpolitik. (a) What is realpolitik? (b) How did each leader use this approach?

4. **Analyzing economics** (a) What economic factors were involved in Prussia's Seven Day War with Austria? (b) In the Franco-Prussian War?

5. **Analyzing** To what extent might the living and working conditions Marx saw around him account for his theory of revolution?

6. **Evaluating** (a) What were the effects of the Civil War on United States foreign trade? (b) On industrial development?

Perspectives on Past and Present

In the late 1800's, the right of all men to vote was a major issue. What political rights have become important issues in the late 1900's?

Investigating History

The Footnote to History on page 548 mentions Jules Verne's novel *Around the World in Eighty Days*. Either read the book or watch a videotape of the movie. Write a summary of the plot.

567

CHAPTER
Evaluation

Chapter Test 24, Alternate Chapter Test 24, and Computer Test Bank Chapter 24 Test can be used to evaluate your students' understanding of this chapter.

The Age of Imperialism

Chapter Overview

In the nineteenth century, European countries competed for overseas colonies. They met with success in Africa and India, but encountered difficulties in China and Japan.

The United States gained a few colonies in the Caribbean and Pacific after the Spanish-American War, and was successful in barring the establishment of new colonies in China and Latin America.

Chapter Focus

The British proclamation declaring Queen Victoria Empress of India symbolizes the general state of international affairs during the Age of Imperialism. This chapter describes how the industrialized nations used their enormous economic and military power to create vast empires.

Nations competed for overseas empires. 1

Setting the Stage

Direct students' attention to the definition of *imperialism* on page 569. This section describes how and why European nations built great empires.

Teaching Strategies

Economics and History: The Role of Colonies (Objective 1) The Industrial Revolution created a demand for raw materials and new markets. European powers prized colonies that provided such products as rubber, wool, jute, and coconuts.

In exchange, the industrialized countries exported machinery, steel, clothing, arms, railway equipment, and other manufactured goods to their colonies. The colonies also provided lucrative investment opportunities. By 1914, France and Germany had invested more than 20 percent of their industrial wealth abroad, while Great Britain had invested 25 percent.

Skill Building: Comparing and Contrasting Points of View (Objective 2) Many Europeans believed that they had a duty to spread Christianity and the benefits of technology to less-developed regions. However, many people did not share this view. Read or distribute the following statements on imperialism as a means of advancing civilization:

> We [the British] happen to be the best people in the world, with the highest ideals of decency and justice and liberty and peace, and the more of the world we inhabit, the better it is for humanity.
>
> Cecil Rhodes

> Our whole existence has been controlled by people with an alien attitude to life, people with different customs and beliefs. They have determined the form of government, the types of economic activity, and the schooling which our children

Advance Planner

		SECTION 1
Objectives		1. Explain why the European powers competed for overseas colonies. 2. Compare and contrast views on imperialism as a means of advancing civilization.
Setting the Stage		Definition of imperialism
Teaching Strategies		Economics and History: The Role of Colonies Skill Building: Comparing and Contrasting Points of View Check for Understanding
Guided Practice		Section Review 1
Independent Practice Worksheets		Independent Practice 25.1 Vocabulary 25 Critical Thinking 25
Enrichment		1. Primary Source: Voices 25.1 2. ★Creative Writing 3. Researching for Points
Chapter Closer		

Chapter 25 The Age of Imperialism 1875–1914

FOCUS   The relationship between Great Britain and India in the 1870's as an example of European empire-building

★ Advanced
● Basic

SECTION 2	SECTION 3	SECTION 4	SECTION 5	SECTION 6
1. Identify the Suez Canal and explain its geographic significance. 2. Identify the Kimberly diamond mine and explain its influence on the development of South Africa.	1. Describe the causes and consequences of the Sepoy Mutiny. 2. Compare a map of British India with maps of India in earlier times.	1. Explain how European merchants used opium to force open Chinese ports. 2. Locate territories China lost to other nations. 3. Cite reasons for United States endorsement of an Open Door Policy in China.	1. Describe the Japanese reaction to the arrival of Commodore Matthew Perry. 2. Identify changes that took place during the Meiji era.	1. Identify causes and consequences of the Spanish-American War. 2. Identify the Panama Canal and explain its significance.
The European division of Africa Transparency 78	Hindi words that were added to the English language during British rule of India	A Chinese emperor's letter to King George III of England rejecting commercial ties	Japan's isolation under the Tokugawa shoguns	Imperialism in Latin America and the basis of United States involvement in Latin American affairs
Geography in History: The Suez Canal Transparency 81 Economics and History: The "Big Hole" Check for Understanding	Skill Building: Relating Causes and Effects Geography in History: Comparing Maps Transparency 79 Check for Understanding	Analyzing a Quotation: The Opium Trade Geography in History: Imperialism in East Asia Transparency 80 Outline Map 19 Skill Building: Interpreting a Political Cartoon Check for Understanding	Writing about History: Perry's Arrival in Japan Discussing History: Industrialization of Japan Check for Understanding	Skill Building: Identifying Causes and Effects Teaching with Pictures: The Panama Canal Transparency 81 Check for Understanding
Transparency 78 Q&A Section Review 2 Independent Practice 25.2	Transparency 79 Q&A Section Review 3 Independent Practice 25.3 Basic Skills 25	Transparency 80 Q&A Section Review 4 Independent Practice 25.4	Section Review 5 Independent Practice 25.5	Section Review 6 Independent Practice 25.6 Geography Skills 25
1. Primary Source: Voices 25.2 2. Preparing a Report 3. Researching for Points	1. Primary Source: Voices 25.3 2. ★Creative Writing 3. Researching for Points	1. Primary Source: Voices 25.4 2. ★Preparing a Report: Open Door Policy 3. Researching for Points	1. Primary Source: Voices 25.5 2. Relating Past to Present 3. Researching for Points	1. Primary Source: Voices 25.6 2. Debating a Topic: The Spanish-American War 3. Researching for Points

●Reteaching Activities   Making a Time Line, Making Comparisons, Listing

Chapter Review   Summary, Reviewing the Facts, Basic Skills, Researching and Reporting Skills, Critical Thinking, Perspectives on Past and Present, Investigating History

Chapter Evaluation   Chapter Test 25, Alternate Chapter Test 25, Computer Test Bank Chapter 25 Test

have. . . . A man who tries to control the life of another does not destroy the other any the less because he does it, as he thinks, for the other's benefit. It is the principle which is wrong, the principle of one man governing another without his consent.

Julius Nyerere of Tanzania
What benefits did Rhodes believe Britain brought to its empire? (ideals of justice, liberty, and peace) What important principle did the European imperialists violate? (the right to self-determination) How might Cecil Rhodes have responded to Nyerere's statement? (imperialist nations have a responsibility to share their technology)

Check for Understanding Ask students to explain two factors that helped promote imperialism.

Enrichment Activities

1. **Reading a Primary Source**
   Assign Voices from the Past Resource Book 25.1.

2. **Creative Writing**
   Ask advanced students to imagine that they are the editors of a London newspaper. Have them write editorials defending or opposing imperialism.

3. **Researching for Bonus Points**
   In which village on Lake Tanganyika did Stanley find Livingstone? (Ujiji)

Imperialists divided Africa. 2

Setting the Stage

Show Map Transparency 78, *Imperialism in Africa, 1913*. Have students compare the map of Africa in 1913 with the inset of Africa in 1878. In 1878, Europeans controlled less than 10 percent of the continent. By 1913, 90 percent of Africa had been divided into colonies.

Teaching Strategies

Geography in History: The Suez Canal (Objective 1) Have students locate the Suez Canal on Map Transparency 81, *The World About 1900*. Ask how the canal affected international travel. (shortened distances between Europe and Asia)

In 1910, 4,533 ships and 234,000 passengers traveled through the canal. Ask students to hypothesize why knowledgeable travelers reserved north-facing cabins for their journeys. (North-facing cabins sheltered passengers from the hot equatorial sun. Travel agents named these popular but expensive accommodations "POSH"—"port outward, starboard home.")

Economics and History: The "Big Hole" (Objective 2) Until 1867, Cape Colony, Natal, and the two Boer republics were not very profitable for the British. Then a shepherd found an 85-carat diamond near the Orange River. Two years later, miners found a rich diamond field on a farm near Kimberly. Thousands of mines soon turned the field into the largest open pit mine ever dug. The "Big Hole" was more than 700 feet deep and nearly a mile in circumference. During the next 40 years, it produced 3 tons of diamonds. The Big Hole and other mines helped transform South Africa from a group of impoverished colonies into one of the richest prizes in the British Empire.

Check for Understanding Have students describe one consequence of the Suez Canal and of the Kimberly diamond mines.

Enrichment Activities

1. **Reading a Primary Source**
   Assign Voices from the Past Resource Book 25.2.

2. **Preparing a Report**
   Have students report on one of these topics: the explorations of David Livingstone or Henry Stanley, the Belgian Congo, the Suez Canal today, Cecil Rhodes, the Rand gold mines.

3. **Researching for Bonus Points**
   Who owned the farm on which the Kimberly diamond field was discovered? (Two Boer brothers, Johannes and Diedrich DeBeer)

The British dominated South Asia. 3

Setting the Stage

Write these words on the board: *pajamas, loot, thug, khaki*. Ask students to speculate which culture contributed these words to the English language. These Hindi words were adopted by the British during their rule in India.

Teaching Strategies

Skill Building: Relating Causes and Effects (Objective 1) Have students read "The Great Rebellion" (pages 578–579), and identify the immediate cause of the Sepoy Mutiny. Explain that the rumor about pig and beef fat on the sepoys' new rifle cartridges was part of a much larger problem. As its power over India increased, the East India Company tried to reform many aspects of Indian life. These reforms included abolishing slavery, making *suttee* (the self-immolation of Hindu widows) illegal, legalizing the remarriage of widows, banning female infanticide, making English the official language of education, and insisting that all castes receive equal treatments in the courts. The reforms angered many upper-caste Hindus who resented British interference in their culture. This anger helped fuel the Sepoy Mutiny.

Ask students to describe the consequences of the Sepoy Mutiny. (British government assumed direct command of India. British leaders continued to promote India's economic development, but refrained from demanding further social reforms.)

Geography in History: Comparing Maps (Objective 2) Show students Map Transparency 79, *Imperialism in India and Southeast Asia, 1900*, or refer to the map on page 579. Have them compare this map with maps of other Indian empires (pages 74, 80, 301, 305) to answer the following questions: Which empire covered the greatest area? (British India) Which areas in British India were not parts of the Maurya, Gupta, or Mughal empires? (southern India) Why was this region part of British India and not part of the other empires? (Previous invaders had entered India from the north while the British arrived by sea.)

Check for Understanding Have students describe how the Sepoy Mutiny affected India.

Enrichment Activities

1. **Reading a Primary Source** Assign Voices from the Past Resource Book 25.3.
2. **Creative Writing** Ask advanced students to imagine that they are founding members of the Indian National Congress. Have them write a list of grievances against British rule.
3. **Researching for Bonus Points** What does the title *Maharajah* mean? ("great ruler")

Imperialism threatened China. 4

Setting the Stage

Read aloud the Chinese emperor's response to British King George III's request to open trade.

> Our dynasty's majestic virtue has penetrated into every country under Heaven, and kings of all nations offer their costly tribute. . . . We possess all things. I set no value on objects strange or ingenious, and have no use for your country's manufactures. . . .

Ask students to describe the emperor's view of Chinese and of European culture. Was this view realistic?

Teaching Strategies

Analyzing a Quotation: The Opium Trade (Objective 1) Read this passage from a Chinese official's letter to Queen Victoria in 1839.

Of all that China exports to foreign countries, there is not a single thing which is not beneficial to people. . . . The goods from China carried away by your country not only supply your own consumption and use, but also can be divided up and sold to other countries, producing a triple profit. How can you bear to go further, selling [opium] in order to fulfill your insatiable (greedy) desire?

Have students explain Chinese and British views on the opium trade.

Geography in History: Imperialism in East Asia (Objective 2) Use Map Transparency 80, *Imperialism in East Asia, 1842–1912*, or the map on page 582 to identify European spheres of influence in China. On Outline Map 19: China and Japan, have students label areas China lost in the late 1800's, and to whom. Ask students why China could not resist foreign intrusion.

Skill Building: Interpreting a Political Cartoon (Objective 3) In the cartoon on page 583, what symbol represents China? Why? What seems to be the imperialist nations' attitude? How might an American official have responded to the cartoon? How did the United States respond to the partition of China? How did China's fate differ from Africa's?

Check for Understanding Ask how each event was a reaction against European intervention: Opium War, Taiping Rebellion, Boxer Rebellion.

Enrichment Activities

1. **Reading a Primary Source** Assign Voices from the Past Resource Book 25.4.

2. **Preparing a Report**
Have advanced students evaluate the effect of the Open Door Policy.

3. **Researching for Bonus Points**
Which U.S. Secretary of State issued the Open Door Policy? (John Hay)

Japan built a modern nation. 5

Setting the Stage
Recall Japan's isolation under the Tokugawa shoguns. This section explains how Japan changed from a feudal, isolated society to an industrialized world power.

Teaching Strategies
Writing about History: Perry's Arrival in Japan (Objective 1) *Prewriting* Have students study the picture on page 584. How did the artist depict the arrival of what the Japanese called the "black ship?" Explain that, in an elaborate ceremony, Perry presented the shogun's representative with a presidential letter calling for a treaty conference to open relations. Perry said he would return in the spring for an answer. *Writing* Have students write news articles about Perry's arrival from the point of view of the Japanese.

Discussing History: Industrialization of Japan (Objective 2) Provide students with the following key dates in Japanese industrialization.

- 1858, first steamship purchased
- 1859, first foreign loan negotiated with the British
- 1869, first telegraph
- 1872, first railroad completed
- 1872, first textile factories
- 1900, foreign trade totals $200 million a year (1854: $0)

Have students compare Japanese and Chinese responses to European contact. Ask whether the Japanese actually did "open the country to drive out the barbarians."

Check for Understanding Ask students to identify reasons for Japanese imperialism.

Enrichment Activities
1. **Reading Primary Source** Assign Voices from the Past Resource Book 25.5.
2. **Relating Past to Present** Have students research Japanese trade with the United States today.
3. **Researching for Bonus Points** What Gilbert and Sullivan musical popularized Japanese culture in 1885? (*The Mikado*)

Imperialism reached the Western Hemisphere. 6

Setting the Stage
Write these phrases on the board: *Monroe Doctrine, Sinking of the* Maine, *Panama Canal, Roosevelt Corollary.* Ask students to identify the world region with which these phrases are associated. Why was the United States interested in Latin America? (nearness, economic investment, tradition of supporting movements for independence)

Teaching Strategies
Skill Building: Identifying Causes and Effects (Objective 1) Ask students what caused the Spanish-American War. (U.S. economic interests in Cuba, reports of alleged Spanish atrocities against Cuban freedom-fighters, sinking of the *Maine*) What effect did the war have? (marked the emergence of the United States as an imperial power)

Teaching with Pictures: The Panama Canal (Objective 2) Help students locate the Panama Canal on Map Transparency 81, *The World About 1900.* The canal was an engineering triumph as well as a vital transportation link. More than 40,000 workers worked on the waterway for 10 years. Ask students to speculate on the functions of the railroad. (transported workers, machines; and excavated rock and dirt)

Check for Understanding Have students describe the effects of the Spanish-American War and the significance of the Panama Canal.

Enrichment Activities
1. **Reading a Primary Source** Assign Voices from the Past Resource Book 25.6.
2. **Debating a Topic** Ask students to debate this topic: Resolved—President McKinley could have avoided the Spanish-American War.
3. **Researching for Bonus Points** Name the first ship to travel the Panama Canal. (the *Ancon*)

Reviewing the Facts

1. (a) policy of conquering and ruling other lands **(b)** country outwardly independent but controlled by foreign power **(c)** country ruled jointly by two other countries **(d)** situation in which people living in a foreign country do not have to obey its laws **(e)** region in which foreign economic interests get priority

2. (a) ended slave trade in East Africa in 1880's **(b)** Belgian king who began colonization of Africa by claiming Congo River valley **(c)** Dutch settler in South Africa **(d)** British trading company that became leading power in India in 1757 **(e)** rebellion by Indian soldiers; led British government to take direct command in India **(f)** religious group that became mainstay of British army in India **(g)** nationalist group formed in 1885 to gain equal opportunities for Indians **(h)** Muslim group formed in 1906, similar in outlook to the Congress **(i)** war between Britain and China over opium trade in China **(j)** U.S. policy that protected American trade rights and protected China from colonization **(k)** Chinese secret society siege of European section of Peking **(l)** American commodore who opened Japan to foreign trade **(m)** era of industrialization and modernization in Japan **(n)** war between U.S. and Spain over Cuba **(o)** declaration of U.S. right to act as international police force in the Americas

3. (a) invaded Algeria, built the Suez Canal, took over Tunisia and Morocco **(b)** Britain took over Egypt to guard Suez Canal, made Egypt a protectorate, invaded Sudan with Egypt.

4. (a) South Africa had gold and diamonds **(b)** British sought gold and diamonds, tried to overthrow Boer government of the Transvaal **(c)** British won, allowed Boers to rule South Africa as a British colony

5. (a) Indian resentment of British rule **(b)** increasing control, improving the country

6. (a) prosperous agricultural country, nearly self-sufficient **(b)** to stop opium trade, weaken Chinese rulers

7. (a) Japan had little contact with industrialized nations, granted foreign trade rights for protection against conquest **(b)** Japan adopted some Western ways—industrialized, modernized its military, and defeated China and Russia to gain Korea and Manchuria.

8. (a) by lending capital for expansion, then taking ownership of factories and other businesses **(b)** built Panama Canal and announced Roosevelt Corollary

Basic Skills

1. (a) France and Britain **(b)** Britain and France were world's two dominant colonial powers.

2. (a) to keep foreign nations from recolonizing Latin America **(b)** negotiator in international disputes with Latin America; Roosevelt Corollary said U.S. could use military intervention to keep order; changes due to foreign investments, particularly British, and U.S. fear of foreign political influence in Latin America; U.S. wanted to protect its business interests in Latin America.

Researching and Reporting Skills

Students' answers will vary.

Critical Thinking

1. Economic competition, need for raw materials, new markets, and protection of shipping lanes led to race for colonies; colonies a sign of power. Examples: imperialists proudly displayed maps of possessions, U.S. and Germany cut into British trade; France, Spain, Portugal, Germany, and Belgium started colonization movements.

2. (a) Africa: many nations competed for colonies; different types of colonial rule apparent; no major market developed; most improvements benefited only Europeans; India and Southeast Asia: colonial competition primarily between British and French; Britain single power in India, where internal improvements benefited country. East Asia: China remained independent but divided into spheres of influence. **(b)** India and Southeast Asia valued more than Africa for bigger market, greater supplies of raw materials and resources.

3. European nations with the most colonies had economic and political influence. Those without colonies might align themselves with a particular country for economic reasons or to maintain balance of power.

4. (a) U.S. one of emerging economic powers that challenged Britain's economic leadership **(b)** East Asia and Latin America **(c)** U.S. followed example of Europe, though was less imperialist in China and recognized Cuba's independence.

Perspectives on Past and Present

(a) Africa was considered available to the European powers; African politics, culture were insignificant. **(b)** no—African countries are now independent; such actions would be strongly criticized in world organizations such as the U.N.

Investigating History

Students' answers will vary.

Chapter 25

Teaching with Pictures

Direct students' attention to the painting and explain that it shows the huge crowd of Indian rulers, British officials, and curious spectators who gathered outside Delhi to hear the British viceroy read a proclamation declaring Queen Victoria Empress of India. Then ask what this event reveals about the relationship between Great Britain and India in the 1870's. Explain that India had lost its independence and was a part of the British empire. Ask students how Great Britain could control a country that was 6,000 miles from Britain and had 10 times more people and 20 times more territory. Tell students that the Industrial Revolution gave Great Britain, France, Germany, and the United States enormous economic and military power.

Red-coated British soldiers stand at attention around a royal pavilion during a ceremony in India. Britain's Queen Victoria took the title Empress of India in 1876.

Key Terms

imperialism
strategic
protectorate
condominium
colonization
cash crop
sepoy
extraterritorial rights
sphere of influence
intervention

Read and Understand

1. Nations competed for overseas empires.
2. Imperialists divided Africa.
3. The British dominated South Asia.
4. Imperialism threatened China.
5. Japan built a modern nation.
6. Imperialism reached the Western Hemisphere.

On a warm November afternoon in 1875, the H.M.S. *Serapis* steamed into Bombay Harbor as British battleships formed two long lines to greet the vessel. On the bridge stood His Royal Highness Edward, Prince of Wales. As Queen Victoria's eldest son, he was heir to the British throne. Smiling, he waved to the cheering sailors and bowed to the captain of each ship as his own glided by.

When the *Serapis* finally docked, brass bands played and cannons fired salutes. Lord Northbrook, the queen's representative in India, welcomed the future king. Together they rode through streets crowded with cheering Indians. The *Times* of London reported, "The whole population of Bombay swarmed along the road," giving the Prince "a welcome such as an Indian city has seldom seen."

568

Chapter 25 Resources

GEOGRAPHY
- Geography Skills 25
- Outline Map 19
- Transparencies 78, 79, 80, 81

REINFORCEMENT
- Vocabulary 25
- Basic Skills 25
- Reteaching 25
- Making Connections Study Guide 25

ENRICHMENT
- Critical Thinking 25
- History and Literature 25

ASSESSMENT
- Chapter Test 25
- Alternate Chapter Test 25
- Computer Test Bank

The following day, his thirty-fourth birthday, Prince Edward officially greeted dozens of Indian princes who came to pay their respects. Seated on a silver throne, dressed in royal robes, and flanked by British officials in scarlet and gold uniforms, the prince received his guests one by one. Each was magnificently dressed for the occasion. One guest, the nine-year-old ruler of Baroda, wore so many jewels that he was compared to "a crystallized rainbow."

The prince spent four days in Bombay, attending state banquets, receiving visitors, and watching a spellbinding performance by magicians and snake charmers. Then he began a grand tour. Over the next three months, he visited Calcutta, Madras, and other major Indian cities. At each stop, he reviewed troops, inspected railway lines and stations, visited prisons, palaces, and sacred ruins, and attended countless balls, banquets, and fireworks displays.

Throughout his stay, the heir to the British throne was treated as if he were the next emperor of India. In many respects, he was. Shortly after his return home, Parliament would add *Empress of India* to his mother's long list of titles.

Only a century earlier, the British East India Company had been building a trading network based on forts in major Indian cities. Now this enormous country was part of the British empire. In the words of Prime Minister Benjamin Disraeli, India was "the brightest jewel in Her Majesty's Crown."

Disraeli had not always viewed British colonies as jewels. In 1852, he referred to India and other colonies as a "millstone round our neck." In this chapter, we will see why Disraeli and other Europeans changed their views of colonies in the late 1800's. The chapter will also explain how the empires Europeans built affected people around the world.

Nations competed for overseas empires. 1

In 1901, when Queen Victoria died and Edward became king, Britain and other industrialized nations controlled virtually the entire world. They ruled some lands directly; they governed others indirectly through treaties or trade agreements. As empires grew in size and number, people needed a word to describe this new policy of conquering and ruling other lands. The word they invented was **imperialism**.

Imperialists proudly displayed world maps with their nation's empire in bright colors. The British empire usually appeared in red. It was the largest empire the world had ever known, covering an area nearly 100 times larger than Britain, with a population of more than 400 million. Britain controlled territory on every continent but Antarctica. About one fourth of the world's land and people lived under British rule.

Britain's lead was challenged.

As late as 1870, many Britons believed that colonies were more trouble than they were worth. They noted that trade with their former colonies in North America had grown tremendously since the United States won its independence. Many Britons were eager to rid themselves of their remaining colonies.

Throughout the 1800's, Britain granted many of its colonies more freedom. By the 1840's, Canadians had a measure of self-rule. Soon after, Australians also won the right to govern themselves. Yet even as the British were granting some colonies more freedom, the British empire was adding more territory elsewhere. By the turn of the century, a majority of Britons had come to believe that colonies were essential to their nation's prosperity and prestige.

Britain's attitude toward empires changed as Britain's role in the world changed. In the mid-1800's, Britain was the most powerful nation in the world. Its factories produced more goods than those of any other country, and the British navy guarded the oceans so that those goods could be shipped safely to ports around the world. The British exported more than just goods. They also exported capital, the money needed to build factories, mines, railroads, and other businesses. Britain became the world's banker. The money its banks loaned came from the profits earned by manufacturers, merchants, and shippers.

By the late 1800's, however, Germany and the United States were challenging Britain's economic leadership. Although British factories continued to increase their output each year, Britain's share

569

569

SECTION 1 Objectives and Teaching Strategies

OBJECTIVE 1. Explain why the European powers competed for overseas colonies.

Teaching Strategy: *Economics and History: The Role of Colonies* (page 568a)

OBJECTIVE 2. Compare and contrast views on imperialism as a means of advancing civilization.

Teaching Strategy: *Skill Building: Comparing and Contrasting Points of View* (page 568a)

■ BACKGROUND

The crown of the Guicowar of Baroda alone was said to be worth more than $3 million, and he brought a gift of six heavy gold cannon. When the prince asked about his schooling, the boy replied that his favorite "studies" were hunting and cricket.

While in Bombay, the prince sampled all kinds of Indian foods and was so impressed that when the royal party returned to England, a cook, expert at making curry, went along.

SECTION 1 Resources

ASSESSMENT
■ Section Quiz 25.1

REINFORCEMENT
■ Independent Practice 25.1

ENRICHMENT
■ Voices from the Past 25.1

ANSWERS TO

Section Review 1

Define:
policy of conquering and ruling other lands

Identify:
(a) Queen Victoria's son, heir to British throne
(b) Englishman who became rich from South African diamond mines (c) ended slave trade in East Africa
(d) American reporter who found Livingstone (e) English writer who glorified imperialism

Answer:
1. (a) Germany and U.S.
(b) Britain had to find new markets for goods, protect existing markets, and safeguard sources of raw materials.
2. (a) Colonies provided new markets. (b) colonies needed for raw materials
(c) Race for colonies grew out of a strong sense of national pride.
3. (a) France, Netherlands, Spain, Portugal, Austria-Hungary, Russia, Belgium, Italy, Germany, U.S. and Japan (b) by fostering rivalries that could lead to war
4. a sense of duty to pass along what they saw as the progress of their civilization
5. (a) helped spread European values and technology (b) sent reporters to search the globe for stories of mystery, adventure, and excitement
6. (a) the mission to "civilize" non-Europeans (b) life in the colonies (c) that native populations were in effect prisoners of the Europeans

of the world's total production fell sharply. In 1870, it produced one third of the world's total. By 1900, British factories were turning out just one fifth.

At the same time, countries that had once welcomed British goods were now taxing those goods to protect their own factories. Increasingly, Britain had to find new markets for its goods or protect existing markets. It also had to safeguard sources of raw materials. The British Isles had only a few of the resources its factories needed. Most were imported.

Faced with economic decline, Britain looked to its colonies for markets and resources. In the late 1800's, the British government tightened its hold over India and other colonies. It also added new colonies in hopes of guarding critical trade routes and business interests.

Imperialism fostered rivalries.

Other countries followed Britain's lead. They too came to see colonies as necessary for their economic well-being. France, which had been a colonial power since the 1600's, greatly expanded its holdings in the late 1800's. By 1900, it had an empire second in size only to Britain's. The Dutch expanded too. Spain and Portugal, both of which had lost most of their original empires, tried to build new empires in Africa. At the same time, Austria-Hungary moved into the Balkans, and Russia expanded into the Caucasus, Central Asia, and eastern Siberia.

Countries that had no colonies set out to acquire them. Belgium, Italy, and Germany all took over lands in Africa. Germany also tried to control parts of East Asia and islands in the south Pacific. At the same time, German bankers made loans to governments in Latin America, and German capitalists were building a Berlin-to-Baghdad railway. Their hope was that where business went, the German flag would soon follow.

Two non-European countries, the United States and Japan, also became involved in overseas expansion during this period. Both were interested in East Asia. The United States was also deeply involved in Latin America.

Increasingly, Europeans viewed an empire as a measure of national stature. "There has never been a great power without great colonies," proclaimed one French writer. Thus the race for

colonies grew out of a strong sense of national pride as well as from economic competition. As the competition for colonies intensified, many countries claimed land that had little economic value. Pride, not profit, was their motive. Each country was determined to plant its flag on as much of the world as possible.

Europe believed in its own superiority.

Thanks to the Industrial Revolution, each European country had not only the weapons needed to win an empire but also the means to control it. Steamers, railroads, telegraph cables, and other inventions allowed nations to keep in close touch with even the most distant colony.

At the same time, the new technology encouraged Europeans to think that they had a right to conquer other countries. They regarded their steamships and factories as proof of their progress. They believed that they had the right and the duty to bring the results of that progress to other peoples.

Many Europeans went abroad with a strong sense of mission. One such European was Cecil Rhodes, a young Englishman who became rich in the diamond mines of South Africa. He boasted:

> I contend that we Britons are the first race in the world, and the more of the world we inhabit, the better it is for the human race. I believe it is my duty to God, my Queen, and my country to paint the whole map of Africa red [the color of the British empire on maps], red from the Cape of Good Hope to Cairo.

The push for expansion also came from missionaries who worked among the peoples of Asia, Africa, and the Pacific islands. Many missionaries believed that European rule was the best way to end evil practices such as the slave trade.

Perhaps the most famous of these missionaries was David Livingstone (1813–1873). A minister from Scotland, Livingstone went to Africa in 1841 to preach the Gospel and heal the sick. He grieved to see East Africans carried off to be sold as slaves in Arabian, Turkish, and Persian lands. Over the years, he became convinced that only the British government was strong enough to end the trade. As a result of his efforts and those of his followers, the slave trade was abolished in East Africa in the 1880's. At the same time, much of the region became part of the British empire.

Imperialism had mass appeal.

Stories of adventure in distant places have always appealed to people. In the late 1800's, Europeans and Americans were eager to read about soldiers who guarded the empire against fierce enemies in far-off lands, sailors who roamed the open sea, and merchants who traded for silks and spices in mysterious Asian ports. When David Livingstone wrote a book about his work in Africa, thousands of people in Europe and the United States bought copies.

Newspapers competed for readers by hiring reporters to search the globe for stories of adventure, mystery, or excitement. For example, in the late 1860's, David Livingstone and a group of Africans traveled deep into the heart of the continent in search of evidence against the slave trade. When several years passed with no word from him or his party, many people feared he was dead. An American newspaper hired reporter Henry Stanley to find Livingstone. Stanley arrived in Zanzibar in January 1871. Ten months later, he caught up with Livingstone on the shores of Lake Tanganyika.

Stanley's account of the meeting made headlines around the world. Stanley became a celebrity. Queen Victoria gave him a jeweled snuffbox. Cities across the United States held banquets in his honor.

Novels and poetry also glorified imperialism. The most popular writer of the day was Joseph Rudyard Kipling (1865–1936). Children and adults alike were fascinated by his poems and stories, many of which were set in India. Kipling appealed not only to his readers' spirit of adventure but

Footnote to History

When Stanley finally reached Livingstone's camp, he reported that his first impulse was to rush over and throw his arms around Livingstone. Then, perhaps remembering that he had come without an invitation and that the missionary was a reserved Scot, Stanley settled for a simpler greeting. He held out his hand and said, "Dr. Livingstone, I presume?"

also to their feelings of superiority. He saw imperialism as a mission to "civilize non-Europeans" and urged his readers to:

> Take up the White Man's Burden—
>   Send forth the best ye breed—
> Go bind your sons to exile
>   To serve your captives' need . . .

In answering the call of imperialism, Europeans altered life on every continent.

Section REVIEW 1

Define: imperialism
Identify: (a) Prince Edward, (b) Rhodes, (c) Livingstone, (d) Stanley, (e) Kipling
Answer:
1. (a) What countries challenged Britain's economic leadership? (b) How was the search for colonies a response to Britain's declining share in world trade?
2. What part did each of the following play in imperialism? (a) markets (b) raw materials (c) national pride
3. (a) What countries joined the competition for colonies? (b) How did this competition set up a potentially explosive situation?
4. What attitude did people in industrialized countries have toward other peoples?
5. (a) What part did missionaries play in imperialism? (b) How did newspapers and writers encourage imperialism?

Critical Thinking
6. Reread the lines from Kipling's poem on this page. (a) What did he mean by "the White Man's Burden"? (b) What was the exile of which he spoke? (c) What does the word *captives* indicate?

Imperialists divided Africa. 2

Nowhere was the competition for colonies more intense than in Africa. When the Age of Imperialism began in 1875, Europeans controlled less than 10 percent of the continent. By 1900, 90 percent of Africa was divided into colonies.

571

SECTION 2
Objectives and Teaching Strategies

OBJECTIVE 1. Identify the Suez Canal and explain its geographic significance.
Teaching Strategy: *Geography in History: The Suez Canal* (page 568c)

OBJECTIVE 2. Identify the Kimberly diamond mine and explain its influence on the development of South Africa.
Teaching Strategy: *Economics and History: The "Big Hole"* (page 568c)

■ DISCUSSION
How did the Industrial Revolution bring about a world culture?

SECTION 2
Resources

GEOGRAPHY
■ Transparencies 78, 81

REINFORCEMENT
■ Independent Practice 25.2

ENRICHMENT
■ Voices from the Past 25.2

ASSESSMENT
■ Section Quiz 25.2

■ BACKGROUND

The old voyage from London to Cape Town to Bombay was 10,667 nautical miles. The canal reduced this trip to 6,274 nautical miles—a savings of 41.2 percent.

Europeans explored Africa.

Until well into the 1800's, Africa was relatively unknown to Europeans. Although European ships had for centuries traded at ports along the coast, they brought back little knowledge of the continent's interior.

Beginning with the Scotsman Mungo Park's exploration of the Niger River in 1805 and 1806, European explorers slowly penetrated the African interior. The Frenchman René Caillié (kah-**YAY**) was the first European to cross the Sahara (1827–1828), while the German Heinrich Barth traveled widely in western Africa during the 1850's. Best-known of the explorers was David Livingstone, the Scottish missionary who spent 30 years in central Africa. These explorers gave Europeans their first detailed information about Africa and its peoples.

In the mid-1800's, Africa south of the Sahara contained more than 700 different ethnic groups, each with its own language and customs. Most were organized into communities based on ties of tradition and kinship. Occasionally, a powerful group formed a state that was strong enough to conquer neighboring groups and form an empire.

People in these states, who had traded with Europeans for centuries, had no reason to expect that relationship to change. Thus, they could neither foresee nor prevent the changes brought by the Industrial Revolution and imperialist rivalries that were to have such impact on their lives.

Europeans competed for colonies.

The scramble for African territory began after 1879. In that year, Henry Stanley, the reporter who found David Livingstone, returned to Africa and claimed most of the Congo River valley in the name of King Leopold II of Belgium. The Belgian Congo, as the colony later became known, was 80 times larger than Belgium.

Leopold's action alarmed France. The French responded in 1882 by taking the north bank of the Congo River. Soon Britain, Germany, Italy, Portugal, and Spain were also claiming parts of Africa.

The competition was so fierce that countries feared a war. To prevent fighting, representatives from European countries met in Berlin in 1884 and 1885 to lay down rules for this new competition. No African ruler attended this meeting, yet it sealed Africa's fate. Europeans agreed that any European country could claim land in Africa simply by sending troops to occupy **strategic** points, or locations that assured control of nearby areas. A map of Africa in 1913 shows how complete the European takeover had become.

North Africa Europeans had already moved into North Africa. There, the once-powerful Ottoman empire had become too weak to prevent local rulers from taking control in Morocco, Algeria, Tunisia, and Egypt. These local rulers were no match for the Europeans bent on conquest.

As early as 1830, France had invaded Algeria. Its aim was to build its prestige and to stop Algerian pirates who attacked French ships. Until 1869, no other European country paid much attention to North Africa. That year, a French company built a canal across the Isthmus of Suez. The canal linked the Mediterranean and Red Seas, providing a much shorter route from Europe to the Indian Ocean (page 548).

As the fastest route to India and Australia, the Suez Canal was crucial to Britain. It was so important that the British government bought stock in the company that owned the canal in 1875. Guarding the canal became a critical part of Britain's foreign policy. Therefore, when fighting broke out in Egypt in 1882, Britain took over the area. Egypt became a British **protectorate**—a country whose foreign policy is controlled by an outside government.

Next the British turned their attention to Sudan, which lay along the Nile River south of Egypt. Because water from the Nile was essential to the people of Egypt, the British believed that they had to control the headwaters of the Nile to guard Egypt and the canal. Many Britons also now shared Rhodes's dream of ruling all of Africa from Cairo to Cape Town. Thus, in 1896, Britain and Egypt invaded Sudan. The Sudanese defended their country fiercely, but in 1898, General Horatio Kitchener conquered the country. The following year, Britain and Egypt made Sudan a **condominium**—a country ruled jointly by two other countries.

France also dreamed of a great African empire. It would stretch from Dakar in the west to French Somaliland in the east. To fulfill that dream, the French gradually took over Tunisia and Morocco.

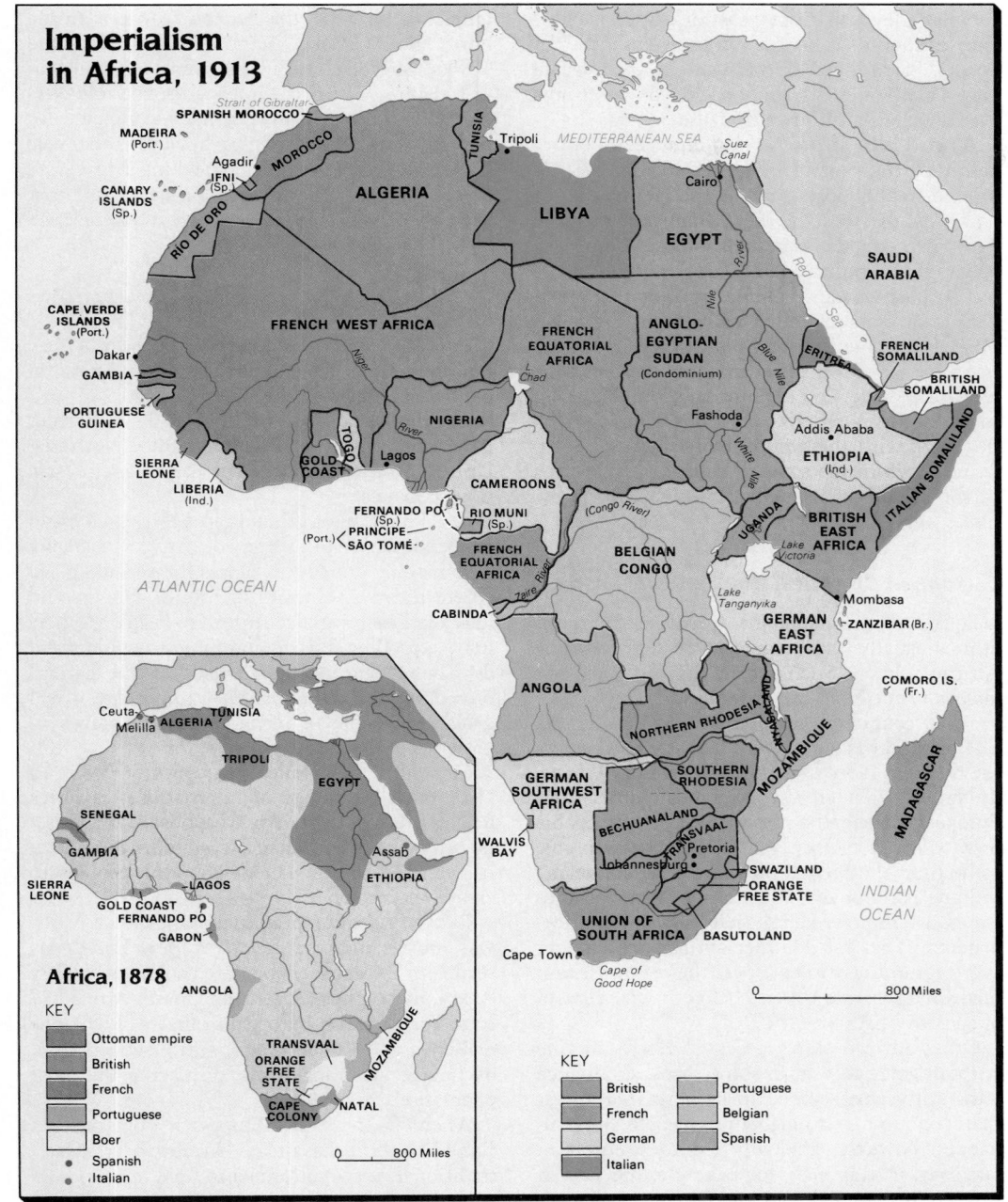

Imperialism in Africa, 1913

SPANISH MOROCCO
MADEIRA (Port.)
CANARY ISLANDS (Sp.)
Agadir
IFNI (Sp.)
MOROCCO
Strait of Gibraltar
ALGERIA
TUNISIA
Tripoli
MEDITERRANEAN SEA
LIBYA
Cairo
Suez Canal
EGYPT
RIO DE ORO
SAUDI ARABIA
Red Sea
CAPE VERDE ISLANDS (Port.)
Dakar
GAMBIA
PORTUGUESE GUINEA
FRENCH WEST AFRICA
Niger River
L. Chad
FRENCH EQUATORIAL AFRICA
ANGLO-EGYPTIAN SUDAN (Condominium)
Nile River
Blue Nile
White Nile
ERITREA
FRENCH SOMALILAND
BRITISH SOMALILAND
Fashoda
Addis Ababa
ETHIOPIA (Ind.)
ITALIAN SOMALILAND
SIERRA LEONE
LIBERIA (Ind.)
GOLD COAST
TOGO
Lagos
NIGERIA
CAMEROONS
FERNANDO PO (Sp.)
RIO MUNI (Sp.)
PRINCIPE (Port.)
SÃO TOMÉ
FRENCH EQUATORIAL AFRICA
(Congo River)
Zaire River
BELGIAN CONGO
UGANDA
BRITISH EAST AFRICA
Lake Victoria
Lake Tanganyika
GERMAN EAST AFRICA
Mombasa
ZANZIBAR (Br.)
ATLANTIC OCEAN
CABINDA
ANGOLA
COMORO IS. (Fr.)
NORTHERN RHODESIA
NYASALAND
MOZAMBIQUE
SOUTHERN RHODESIA
GERMAN SOUTHWEST AFRICA
BECHUANALAND
WALVIS BAY
TRANSVAAL
Pretoria
Johannesburg
SWAZILAND
ORANGE FREE STATE
MADAGASCAR
INDIAN OCEAN
UNION OF SOUTH AFRICA
BASUTOLAND
Cape Town
Cape of Good Hope
0   800 Miles

Africa, 1878

Ceuta
Melilla
ALGERIA
TUNISIA
TRIPOLI
EGYPT
SENEGAL
GAMBIA
SIERRA LEONE
GOLD COAST
FERNANDO PO
LAGOS
GABON
Assab
ETHIOPIA
ANGOLA
MOZAMBIQUE
TRANSVAAL
ORANGE FREE STATE
CAPE COLONY
NATAL
0   800 Miles

KEY
- Ottoman empire
- British
- French
- Portuguese
- Boer
- • Spanish
- • Italian

KEY
British	Portuguese
French	Belgian
German	Spanish
Italian	

ANSWERS TO
Map Study

Egypt, Anglo-Egyptian Sudan, Uganda, British East Africa, Rhodesia, Bechuanaland, Union of South Africa; Germany or Belgium

Map Study

Britain long planned a Cairo-to-Cape-Town railroad. In 1913, what British colonies could it have gone through? What other powers blocked its way?

573

Menelik said, "Ethiopia has need of no one. She stretches out her hands unto God."

The quality of European-run government in Africa varied. In French-controlled Senegal, the native population elected representatives to Paris. In the Congo, Leopold II ruthlessly exploited the rubber forests for his personal profit.

Cooperative Learning

Divide the class into groups of four or five students and have each group choose a recorder. Ask each group to list the benefits and disadvantages of colonialism from the point of view of the native Africans. Then have students do the same from the point of view of the Europeans. Tell students to compare the lists and write one general statement characterizing the relationship between European countries and African colonies. All group members must contribute to and agree upon the content of the statement. Then ask students to think of an alternate plan for the development of Africa that would have been more equitable. Have each group present its alternative to the class.

In 1898, they also pushed east into Sudan. There they encountered British troops at Fashoda. For weeks, Britain and France were at the edge of war. Then France suddenly backed down. It now turned its attention south of the Sahara.

Africa south of the Sahara European control south of the Sahara began in the mid-1800's around trading posts such as the French port of Dakar in the west or the British port of Cape Town in the south. From such outposts, Europeans spread their control inland.

The push toward **colonization,** or the establishing of colonies, often came from European officials and merchants. Many were tempted to use force whenever they came into conflict with an African state. Often, Europeans found it easier to shoot first and ask questions later than to negotiate with the group involved. As a result, home governments sometimes found themselves in the middle of wars about which they knew little.

European conquest took many forms.

Equipped with superior weapons, European armies usually had no great difficulty defeating African soldiers. Such defeats, however, did not always result in an easy conquest. It might take years to conquer a large empire. Samori Touré, a Mandingo, built an empire that stretched across the northern Ivory Coast into present-day Ghana. To protect that empire, he bought arms from Europeans along the coast. He also set up his own weapons factory. As a result, he was able to hold off the French for more than six years.

Some parts of Africa were not organized into states or empires. Here, each village was independent. Therefore, Europeans had to conquer every community to take over the region. Britain made 500 separate treaties before it won control of eastern Nigeria.

Other African states accepted European rule without going to war. In some cases, an alliance with Europeans seemed to be a smaller threat than conquest by a neighboring people. Such alliances, however, gradually led to a European takeover. In this way, for example, the British won control of Africa's Gold Coast.

Elsewhere, Europeans were sometimes invited into a region to protect a leader or a group against internal enemies. One of the best-known ex-

574

amples is Buganda, the African kingdom on the north shore of Lake Victoria. In the 1880's and 1890's, Buganda was in the midst of civil war as Muslims, Catholics, Protestants, and followers of the traditional Ganda religion competed for power. With British help, however, the two Christian groups removed the king and seized power. In 1900, they signed an agreement that gave them a privileged position in the British colony of Uganda.

Africa became a continent of colonies.

By 1900, Europeans controlled most of Africa. Only two countries remained free from European control, Liberia and Ethiopia.

Liberia, founded during the 1820's by former American slaves, was closely allied with the United States. This alliance kept Liberia safe from conquest.

The kingdom of Ethiopia in East Africa owed its independence to a variety of factors. Geography gave it some protection. It was located at a place where the rival empires of Britain, France, and Italy met. Each was determined to keep the others from expanding further, and Ethiopia could stand as a buffer state. Ethiopia also had the natural protection of mountains. Most important, it had a leader capable of using these advantages to protect his kingdom.

Menelik II, who ruled Ethiopia from 1889 to 1913, took advantage of international rivalries to get the most modern weapons. With these, he turned back an Italian invasion in 1896. Then he went on to conquer neighboring peoples to create an empire.

Colonial rule European rule of the rest of Africa was mostly indirect. Relatively few Europeans settled in the densely populated colonies of West Africa. By contrast, Algeria and South Africa had large numbers of Europeans. In the highlands of Kenya and Rhodesia too, white settlers took over large areas for farms, displacing the local populations.

Wherever possible, European governments turned to Africans already in authority. Many traditional rulers continued to hold office. However, this policy did not mean that life continued as usual for the people of Africa.

Europeans wanted African workers for mines and plantations. At first, Europeans simply used

People of the Congo gave artistic form to articles used in traditional rituals of family and community: slit drum (left), harp (right), and guardian figure (center).

■ **BACKGROUND**

When Europeans first arrived in South Africa, they encountered a native population of more than seven million, made up of dozens of different groups, including Bushmen who lived by hunting and gathering, the pastoral Bantus, and the warlike Zulus.

their superior weapons to force Africans into work crews. Later, however, most colonial governments used an economic weapon—taxes. Africans had long paid taxes to their rulers in goods and services. Now, however, they were required to pay taxes in money. The need for money forced many Africans to work on plantations or in mines, all owned by Europeans. Other Africans began to raise crops that Europeans wanted to buy rather than food crops for themselves. This shift to **cash crops** for export marked the beginning of a money economy.

Colonial governments used tax money to provide a range of services that led to better health care, improved farming methods, European-style education, and other changes. In a few cases, Africans benefited from these services. Usually, however, the new services were only for European settlers or traders.

The African people were now second-class citizens in their own lands. Many African leaders came to believe that only by borrowing from European cultures could they regain control over their own country. "The blacks had slept long; perhaps too long," observed Blaise Daigne, a Senegalese leader. "But beware! Those who have slept long and soundly, when once they wake up, will not easily fall back to sleep again."

Europeans were fearful of such an awakening. To guard against it, some colonial officials en-couraged rivalries among ethnic groups. As long as Africans were divided, Europeans could keep control. Many nations also kept education to a minimum in their colonies. Rather than train Africans, Europeans often brought in Indians, Chinese, and other Asians to handle jobs requiring special skills.

In setting up colonies, Europeans had two main goals. One was to keep order and avoid rebellions. The other was to gain a profit, or at least to make colonies pay their way.

Economic development When the scramble for Africa began, many believed that the African people would soon be buying European goods in great quantities. Shortly after his return from Africa in 1872, Henry Stanley, for example, told a group of Manchester business leaders, "There are 40 million people beyond the gateway of the Congo, and the cotton spinners of Manchester are waiting to clothe them." Stanley estimated that if each of these Africans bought just one Sunday dress or suit every year, the merchants of Manchester would enjoy a tremendous boost in sales.

Most of these sales, however, never came about. Poverty, custom, and climate limited the demand for European goods. Africa's tropical climate also made European-style farming impractical. Nonetheless businesses in time succeeded in developing commercial plantations based on peanuts, palm

575

ANSWERS TO

Section Review 2

Define:
(a) important (b) country whose foreign policy is controlled by outside government (c) country ruled jointly by two other countries (d) establishing of colonies (e) crop for export to Europe

Identify:
(a) linked Mediterranean and Red seas (b) British conqueror of Sudan (c) ruler of Ethiopian empire (d) British-controlled region of Cape of Good Hope (e) farmers and herders who built great empire in southern Africa (f) farmers and herders of Cape Colony region (g) Dutch settlers in South Africa (h) emigration of Boers from Cape Colony into African interior

Answer:
1. (a) Henry Stanley claimed most of Congo River valley

(continued)

ANSWERS TO *(continued)*

for Belgium. **(b)** to lay down rules for competition in Africa **(c)** European countries agreed to recognize claim based on effective occupation.

2. invaded Algeria in 1830 and gradually took over Tunisia and Morocco

3. (a) Britain took Egypt, making it a protectorate. **(b)** invaded by Egypt and Britain

4. (a) took France more than six years to conquer **(b)** independent villages with which Britain made 500 separate treaties **(c)** region in which Britain was invited to protect a leader or group

5. (a) Liberia and Ethiopia **(b)** Liberia was closely tied to the U.S.; Ethiopia had natural protection (mountains), a strong leader, and geographic position as a buffer state.

6. (a) Many traditional rulers continued to hold office. **(b)** shift to a money economy; made Africans second-class citizens

7. (a) Boers resented British rule; tensions mounted when diamonds and gold were discovered **(b)** Boers took up arms in 1899. **(c)** allowed Boers to keep their language in both schools and courts; helped them rebuild their farms

8. Politics—by denying Africans control of their own governments; taxation—by forcing them to pay taxes, thus requiring them to take low paying jobs in European-owned ventures; ethnic rivalry—by pitting group against group; education—by keeping Africans uneducated

oil, cocoa, and rubber. These products, used as cash crops for export, in part displaced the food crops grown for local consumption.

The major source of great wealth in Africa proved to be the continent's rich mineral resources. The Belgian Congo was found to contain untold wealth in its deposits of copper, gold, manganese, and tin. Even these riches seemed small compared to those in South Africa.

South Africa supplied great wealth.

The British first took control of the Cape of Good Hope in 1806, during the Napoleonic wars. They called the region Cape Colony. There the British found a number of African peoples. These included the Zulu and Xhosian groups, who were farmers and herders, and the Khoikhoi and !Kung, who were mainly hunter-gatherers. The British also found an established community of about 40,000 Dutch settlers. The Dutch called themselves *Boers* (from the Dutch word for farmer). Most Boers were strict Calvinists who believed that God had selected a small group, of which they were a part, for salvation. They used this belief to justify harsh treatment of the Africans.

The Boers disliked being ruled by Britain. They wanted their own government. Thousands migrated from Cape Colony during the 1830's into the African interior. This Great Trek brought the Boers into conflict with the Zulu people, who had built a great empire in southern Africa. After years of fighting, the Boers finally defeated the Zulu and set up three countries—Natal, Transvaal, and the Orange Free State.

At first, Britain accepted the independence of the three Boer states. At the time, Britain's main interest was the Cape Colony, which was an important stop on the route around Africa to India. In 1845, the British annexed Natal but let the other two states remain independent.

Then, in 1867, diamonds were discovered on a farm at Kimberley, on the border of the Orange Free State. Within weeks, Kimberley became a boom town. "Men who set out to work in the morning, not knowing where their dinner was to come from," noted one reporter, "became richer than any member of their family had ever been before it was time for an eleven o'clock snack."

Most of the miners were British. Among them was Cecil Rhodes, who gradually won control

of the entire Kimberley diamond field. By 1889, his company controlled 90 percent—a near monopoly—of the world's diamond output.

As British miners crowded onto Boer land, tension between the Boers and the British mounted. In 1886, gold was discovered in a ridge of mountains called the Rand in the heart of the Transvaal. Again British fortune-seekers stampeded into Boer territory. By 1895, the Boers were outnumbered by *uitlanders* (**AYT**-lahn-duhrz), the Boer term for foreign settlers.

When the Boers tried to keep their way of life by restricting uitlanders, the newcomers were outraged. They had the support of Cecil Rhodes. In 1895, one of his associates tried to overthrow the government of Transvaal. Although the attempt failed, the Boers blamed Britain for the uprising. As tensions mounted, the Boers took up arms against Britain in 1899.

On the surface, it appeared a hopelessly uneven match—100,000 Boers against the largest empire the world had ever known. The Boers, however, successfully used guerrilla tactics against the British army. Britain struck back by burning farms and destroying food supplies in the Boer regions. In 1902, the Boers were forced to make peace.

To prevent future trouble with the Boers, the British allowed the Dutch-speaking settlers to keep their language in both schools and courts. The British even helped Boers rebuild their farms. (On the other hand, the British did nothing to help Africans whose farms had been destroyed.)

Both the Transvaal and the Orange Free State became self-governing British colonies, much like Australia and Canada. In 1910, they were joined with Cape Colony and Natal. The new country had equal status with Canada and Australia within the British empire.

After the mining boom tapered off, the Boers were once more the majority of the Europeans in the new state. Two Boers, Louis Botha and Jan Christian Smuts, served as South Africa's first prime ministers.

In the end, the British bought peace with the Boers at the expense of the black African population. Blacks made up 75 percent of South Africa's people. Under Boer rule, they were reduced to a life little better than slavery. In 1912, a group of black South Africans formed the African National Congress to seek political rights and greater freedom.

Define: (a) strategic, (b) protectorate, (c) condominium, (d) colonization, (e) cash crop

Identify: (a) Suez Canal, (b) Kitchener, (c) Menelik II, (d) Cape Colony, (e) Zulu, (f) Xhosian, (g) Boers, (h) Great Trek

Answer:

1. (a) How did the scramble for colonies in Africa begin? (b) Why did representatives of European countries meet in Berlin? (c) What was the result of the meeting?

2. Briefly describe France's expansion in North Africa.

3. (a) What were the effects of the building of the Suez Canal on Egypt? (b) What were the effects on Sudan?

4. How did each of the following exhibit a different pattern of colonization? (a) the empire of Samori Touré (b) Nigeria (c) Buganda

5. (a) What two African countries remained free of European control? (b) Why?

6. (a) What did the policy of indirect rule mean for Africa? (b) What were some of the effects of colonial rule on African society?

7. (a) How did the Boers and the British come into conflict? (b) What were the results? (c) What concessions did the British make?

Critical Thinking

8. How did colonization make Africans second-class citizens in terms of role in politics, taxation, ethnic rivalry, and education?

The British dominated South Asia.   3

India was the cornerstone of the British empire. The Industrial Revolution had turned Britain into the world's workshop, and India was a major supplier of raw materials for that workshop. Its 300 million people were also a large potential market for British-made goods. It is not surprising, then, that the British valued India above their other colonies and that other nations envied Britain's control of that country.

British rulers in India built English-style homes where they lived surrounded by Indian servants.

Britain expanded control over India.

British economic interest in India began in the 1600's, when the British East India Company set up trading posts at Bombay, Madras, and Calcutta. At first, India's ruling Mughal dynasty kept European traders under control. By 1700, however, the Mughal empire was collapsing. Dozens of small states, each headed by a ruler or *maharajah*, broke away from Mughal control.

The growth of the East India Company The East India Company was quick to take advantage of the growing weakness of the Mughals. By 1757, the company was the leading power in India. It governed directly or indirectly an area that included modern Bangladesh, most of southern India, and nearly all the territory along the Ganges River in the north.

Officially, the British government regulated the company's efforts both in London and in India. In fact, the company ruled India with little interference from the British government. The company even had its own army, led by British officers and staffed by **sepoys** (SEE-poyz), or Indian soldiers. One early company official referred to this army as "a delicate and dangerous machine, which with a little mismanagement may easily turn against us."

577

SECTION 3
Objectives
and Teaching
Strategies

OBJECTIVE 1. Describe the causes and consequences of the Sepoy Mutiny.

Teaching Strategy: *Skill Building: Relating Causes and Effects* (page 568c)

OBJECTIVE 2. Compare a map of British India with maps of India in earlier times.

Teaching Strategy: *Geography in History: Comparing Maps* (page 568d)

■ **BACKGROUND**

British India was made up of dozens of different ethnic groups speaking more than 200 different languages. There were also a half-dozen major religions represented, of which Hinduism and Islam were dominant.

SECTION 3
Resources

ENRICHMENT
■ Voices from the Past 25.3

ASSESSMENT
■ Section Quiz 25.3

GEOGRAPHY
■ Transparency 79

REINFORCEMENT
■ Independent Practice 25.3

The Great Rebellion The army did indeed turn against the company in 1857. In that year, word spread among the sepoys that their British-made rifle cartridges were sealed with beef and pork fat. Soldiers had to bite off the seal to use the cartridges. Both Hindu and Muslim soldiers were outraged by the news. (Muslims are forbidden to eat pork, and Hindus are not allowed to eat beef.) Although the British quickly corrected the error, they could not quiet the soldiers' suspicions.

On May 10, 1857, the sepoys at Meerut rebelled. They marched to Delhi, where they were joined by Indian soldiers stationed there. Together, the soldiers captured the city. From Delhi, the rebellion spread in northern and central India.

The British called this outbreak the Sepoy Mutiny, but in fact it was a full-scale rebellion. Muslim rebels even tried to place a descendant of the last Mughal emperor on the throne.

. It took the East India Company more than a year to regain control of the country. The British government sent troops to help the company. The British were also helped by serious splits between Hindus and Muslims. Hindus did not want the Mughal empire restored. Indeed, many Hindus preferred British rule to Muslim rule.

At the same time, nearly all the princes and maharajahs who had made alliances with the East India Company remained loyal. Also loyal were the Sikhs, a religious group that had long been hostile to the Mughals (page 307). Indeed, from then on, the bearded and turbaned Sikhs became the mainstay of Britain's army in India.

India after 1857 The mutiny marked a turning point in Indian history. In 1858, the British government took direct command of India. A cabinet minister in London directed policy, and a British governor-general in India carried out the government's orders. (After 1877, this official held the title of viceroy.)

To reward the many princes who had remained loyal to Britain, the British promised to respect all treaties the East India Company had made with them. They also promised that the Indian states that were still free would remain independent. Unofficially, however, Britain won greater and greater control of those states.

The part of India that was under direct British rule was called the *Raj*. The Raj was divided into 10 provinces and some 250 districts. Sometimes a handful of officials were the only Britons among the million or so people in a district.

Convinced that they knew what was best for India, British officials built bridges, dams, canals, and European-style public buildings. Their irrigation projects opened millions of acres of land to farming. The British also created a network of telegraph lines and railroads that linked major Indian cities. By 1900, India had the third largest rail network in the world.

As in Europe, the development of railroads boosted trade, especially in inland areas that now were directly connected with seaports. The tea industry, for example, blossomed almost overnight in the hilly regions of the northeast. Other major export crops such as jute, cotton, and indigo also benefited from railway development.

The beginning of Indian nationalism The British were proud of the changes they brought to India. They boasted of the many improvements

DAILY LIFE ▶ **A New Look for the Army**

In 1850, a British soldier's uniform had a brilliant red coat, a shiny black hat, and white breeches. Such uniforms made a splendid sight on the parade ground—and a splendid target on the battlefield. During the sepoy revolt, British soldiers in India found that they were much safer after their bright uniforms were covered with a layer of yellow-brown dust (in the dry season) or mud (in the wet season). Dirt-colored uniforms made fine camouflage. Eventually, the British adopted this drab color as their official combat uniform. They called it *khaki*, from the Indian word for dust.

Imperialism in India and Southeast Asia, 1900

KEY

- United States territory
- British colonies
- British protectorates
- French colonies
- Dutch colonies
- Portuguese colonies

Focus on Geography

Geographic Skills
1. (a) What nations had major colonies in South and Southeast Asia in 1900? (b) What lands did each nation control?
2. What two areas did Portugal still hold?

3. (a) What is the absolute location of Calcutta? (b) The relative location?

Geographic Theme: Location
4. In what ways is the location of each of these places strategic? (a) Dutch East Indies, (b) Singapore, (c) Philippines, (d) Afghanistan

ANSWERS TO

Focus on Geography

1. (a) United States, Britain, France, Netherlands, **(b)** United States: Philippines; Britain: India, Burma, Ceylon, Malaya, Sarawak, N. Borneo; France: Indochina; Netherlands: Dutch East Indies

2. Goa, Timor

3. (a) about 22°N, 88°E **(b)** along the western mouths of the Ganges

4. (a) along route from Indian Ocean to the Pacific Ocean and China **(b)** controls strait **(c)** proximity to Chinese ports **(d)** on invasion route from Central Asia to India

they had made. Indians quietly noted, however, that money for the new roads, telegraph cables, and irrigation projects came from Indian taxpayers. Only the railroads were built by private British companies. Yet they too got help from taxpayers. Nor did the British do the work of digging roadbeds and laying track. Rather, they directed the projects and supplied the technical skills. Indians did the hard work.

Increasingly, Indians resented a system that made them second-class citizens in their own country. They resented the many signs that read, "For Europeans only." Even Indians with a European education faced discrimination. They were barred from top posts in the Indian Civil Service. Those who managed to get middle-level jobs were paid less than Europeans. A British engineer on the East India Railway, for example, made nearly

20 times as much money as his Indian counterpart.

A spirit of Indian nationalism slowly began to grow. This feeling led to the founding of the Indian National Congress in 1885 and the Muslim League in 1906. At first, such groups were mainly concerned with winning equal opportunities for Indians in the civil service. Gradually, however, their demands broadened. By the early 1900's, they were calling for self-government.

Britain protected the Raj.

Britain had no desire to give the Indians more control over their own country. Instead, as the competition for colonies in other parts of the world grew more fierce, the British tightened their control in South and Southeast Asia. The

579

ANSWERS TO
Section Review 3

Define:
(a) head of one of India's states (b) Indian soldier

Identify:
(a) Muslim empire in India (b) religious group members who became mainstay of Britain's army (c) part of India under direct British rule (d) nationalist group formed to gain equal opportunities for Hindus (e) group formed in 1906 to gain equal opportunities for Muslims

Answer:
1. by taking advantage of weakness of Mughals

2. (a) belief that the British-made rifle cartridges were sealed with pork and beef fat (b) princes and maharajahs who had alliances with East India Company and Sikhs (c) In 1858, British government took direct command of Indian affairs.

3. (a) India gained bridges, dams, canals, irrigation, telegraph lines, and railroads (b) economic exploitation, loss of self-determination

4. originally, to win equal opportunities for Indians in civil service; later, to gain self-government

5. moved into Burma, helped protect independence of Thailand, and invaded Afghanistan

6. (a) approved—protected raw materials and markets (b) approved—increased wealth, provided labor (c) resented—British rule discriminated against Indians in civil service (d) provided alternative to Muslim rule (e) Western education led to acceptance of British rule

British saw two threats to their control of India—France on the southeast and Russia on the northwest.

In the late 1800's, France took over French Indochina, including much of what is now Vietnam, Laos, and Cambodia. To keep the French from advancing farther west, the British moved into Burma. By 1885, Burma was a province of India. The British also helped protect the independence of Siam, now Thailand. Britain hoped Siam would be a buffer between French colonies in the east and British colonies in the west.

The British were also concerned about India's northern border. There they feared a Russian advance. As early as 1839, the East India Company had invaded Afghanistan in the hope of creating a buffer zone, but the invasion failed. In 1878, the British decided to try again. The Second Afghan War, which lasted three years, finally established India's northern border. It also checked Russian influence in the region.

Section REVIEW 3

Define: (a) maharajah, (b) sepoy
Identify: (a) Mughal, (b) Sikhs, (c) Raj, (d) Indian National Congress, (e) Muslim League
Answer:
1. How did the British East India Company win control of much of India?
2. (a) What caused the sepoys to revolt? (b) What groups supported the British during the revolt? (c) What were the results?
3. (a) From a British point of view, how did British rule benefit India? (b) From an Indian point of view, what were the drawbacks of British rule?
4. What were the goals of the Indian National Congress and the Muslim League?
5. What steps did Britain take to protect its control of India?

Critical Thinking
6. What point of view might each of the following people have taken on British rule of India? (a) a textile manufacturer in Britain (b) a British railroad executive in India (c) an Indian official in the civil service (d) a Sikh soldier (e) a maharajah educated in Britain

580

Imperialism threatened China. 4

To the east of India lay China. Here too Europeans were eager to win colonies. Indeed, at one time it seemed as if a scramble for China might follow the one for Africa.

Europeans forced treaties on China.

In the 1800's, the Manchus still ruled China as the Ch'ing dynasty (page 290). For many years, China had been a prosperous country, with a highly developed agricultural system. Farming was critical because, by 1800, China had some 300 million people—more than the entire population of Europe. China was not industrial, but workers in small workshops were able to produce most of the goods the Chinese needed.

Because China was practically self-sufficient, its emperors had little interest in trading with Europeans. For decades, Europeans could do business only at the port of Canton. Despite pleas from Britain and other nations, China refused to open other ports to foreigners. The Chinese regarded European goods as inferior to their own and bought few goods from the European merchants at Canton.

European merchants were determined to find a product the Chinese would buy in large quantities. Eventually, the British East India Company discovered such a product—opium. Opium is a habit-forming narcotic made from the poppy plant. The use of opium was strictly controlled in India, Europe, and China. Now, however, British merchants smuggled in so much opium that the weak Chinese government was powerless to control its flow.

In 1836, the Chinese government tried to stop the opium trade by appealing to Queen Victoria for help. A leading official wrote to her:

Suppose there were people from another country who carried opium for sale to England and seduced your people into buying and smoking it; certainly your honorable ruler would deeply hate it and be bitterly aroused.

When such pleas went unanswered, the quarrel over opium grew into a war. The Opium War

Canton was the first port where China granted foreigners trading rights. By 1800, flags of many countries flew over Canton's busy harbor. In the harbor were Chinese, European, and American vessels.

of 1839 was fought mostly at sea. Chinese fleets, armed with a type of cannon in use since the 1300's, proved to be no match for well-armed British gunboats. In 1842, the two sides signed a treaty at Nanking.

For China, the Treaty of Nanking marked the beginning of a century of humiliation. The treaty was a clear victory for Britain. The British won the right to trade at four Chinese ports besides Canton. In each of these ports, British citizens would enjoy **extraterritorial rights.** That is, Britons did not have to obey Chinese law. They were subject only to British law and to British courts. Furthermore, China was required to pay damages for the opium it had destroyed. The trade in the deadly drug continued.

The Treaty of Nanking was the first of many unequal treaties China would be forced to make as one European country after another established **spheres of influence**. These were regions in which the economic interests of a foreign nation came before those of China. In these regions, foreigners did much as they pleased.

A *revolt weakened southern China.*

By 1850, the Ch'ing dynasty was losing control of the country. The government was riddled with corruption. China was on the verge of bankruptcy as a result of the unequal treaties. Most serious of all, the population was increasing quickly while food production grew little. China's population reached about 430 million in 1850, nearly half again as large as 50 years before. The result was widespread hunger even in good years. In a bad year, such as 1852 when the Yellow River flooded, millions starved. As one Chinese official lamented:

Today there are law-breaking soldiers and greedy officials everywhere who encourage the bandits and indulge them. Whenever one thinks of it, one's heart goes cold. Right and wrong are turned upside down.

It was in this upside-down world that a man named Hung Hsiu-ch'uan (hoong sh'yoo-chwan) attracted a following. Hung, a teacher in a small village in southern China, claimed to have a divine mission to save the world. He told the peasants that with their help he would establish on Earth a "Heavenly Kingdom of Great Peace." Hung's revolt was called the Taiping Rebellion from the Chinese words for "great peace." By 1853, his ragtag army had about 1 million people.

Chinese officials were unable to keep the rebels from taking control of all of southern China. In Nanking, Hung established a government for his Heavenly Kingdom, but it did not stay in power long. With British help, the imperial army won back the south from the rebels in a 10-year war that took 20 million lives.

The rebellion convinced many Chinese officials that modernization was the country's only hope

581

SECTION 4 Objectives and Teaching Strategies

OBJECTIVE 1. Explain how European merchants used opium to force open Chinese ports.

Teaching Strategy: *Analyzing a Quotation: The Opium Trade* (page 568d)

OBJECTIVE 2. Locate territories China lost to other nations.

Teaching Strategy: *Geography in History: Imperialism in East Asia* (page 568d)

OBJECTIVE 3. Cite reasons for United States endorsement of an Open Door Policy in China.

Teaching Strategy: *Skill Building: Interpreting a Political Cartoon* (page 568d)

■ DISCUSSION

The following appears in a Chinese version of early European history: "In ancient times [the Europeans'] customs were barbaric. But during our Shang period, Greece and other countries came under the influence of the Orient. . . . Before long, writing and civilization began to flourish." Discuss cultural bias in telling history.

SECTION 4 Resources

GEOGRAPHY
■ Transparency 80

REINFORCEMENT
■ Independent Practice 25.4

ENRICHMENT
■ Voices from the Past 25.4

ASSESSMENT
■ Section Quiz 25.4

581

■ BACKGROUND

The most powerful figure in nineteenth-century China was Tzu Hsi, mother of one of several boy emperors. Out of touch with reality, she once used funds for naval construction to build a marble "ship" to adorn her Summer Palace.

Cooperative Learning

Divide the class into an even number of groups of three or four students. Half of the groups should take the viewpoint of those Chinese who wished to see their country modernize in order to prevent foreign takeover. The other half should take the viewpoint of those Chinese who wished to retain their traditional ways, ignoring Western influences. Each group should discuss the issue and prepare a statement advocating its assigned position. Then pair groups with opposing viewpoints and allow them to debate the course that China should have followed in the 1860's.

Map Study

What European power might rival Japan in northern China and Korea?

for survival. During the 1860's and 1870's, these officials tried to upgrade the army and navy, improve transportation and communication, and broaden China's educational system to include technical subjects and foreign languages.

Such efforts, however, met with strong opposition. A number of officials believed that China should borrow little if anything from the West. China's emperors seemed to agree. As a result, China continued to weaken.

582

Foreign influence expanded.

Outsiders were quick to take advantage of China's weakness. A second opium war with Britain and France from 1857 to 1860 gave foreigners even more trading rights. About the same time, the Russians forced China to give up the Ussuri territory, where the Russians built their major Pacific naval base of Vladivostok. In 1879, Japan annexed the Ryukyu Islands.

By 1885, much of China's empire was gone. The rest fell in the 1890's when Japan took over Formosa and the Liaotung Peninsula. Japan was able to keep only Formosa, as several European countries joined together to force Japan out of the peninsula. Once they did so, however, the Europeans demanded some Chinese territory for themselves. Russia took Port Arthur and the Liaotung Peninsula in 1896, and France took Kwangchow. By 1898, Germany controlled Kiaochow, and Britain held Weihaiwei.

The United States began to fear that China would be carved into colonies and American traders would be shut out. Therefore, in 1899, the United States declared the Open-Door Policy. This policy proposed an "open door" to China for merchants of all nations. A number of nations agreed to the policy. As a result, American trade rights were protected in China, and China was protected from colonization. Yet, though it was not carved into colonies, China remained at the mercy of outsiders.

In this French cartoon, Britain, Germany, Russia, France, and Japan carve up China.

Nationalism grew in China.

Although China kept its freedom, Europeans dominated most of China's largest cities. There, resentment simmered beneath the surface as some Chinese formed secret societies pledged to rid the country of the "foreign devils."

The most famous of these secret groups was the Society of Righteous and Harmonious Fists, better known simply as the Boxers. In 1900, the Boxers rebelled in Peking, shouting the slogan, "Death to the Foreign Devils." The Boxers surrounded the European section of the city and kept it under siege for several months. Eventually, an army made up of troops from eight nations (Britain, France, Germany, Austria, Italy, Russia, Japan, and the United States) arrived. It quickly defeated the Boxers.

Despite the failure of the Boxer uprising, a nationalist movement began to take shape in China. It drew its strength from the many humiliations the Chinese suffered at the hands of imperialists. Its goals were nationalism, republicanism, and land reform.

Section REVIEW 4

Define: (a) extraterritorial rights, (b) sphere of influence
Identify: (a) Opium War, (b) Hung Hsiu-ch'uan (c) Open-Door Policy, (d) Boxer Rebellion
Answer:
1. Why were China's emperors uninterested in trading with Europe?
2. (a) Why did the British import opium to China? (b) What was the Chinese response? (c) What did the British gain from the treaty ending the Opium War?
3. (a) What conditions led to the Taiping Rebellion? (b) What change in outlook did the revolt cause among China's leaders?
4. (a) What events caused the United States to announce the Open-Door Policy? (b) What did this policy protect?
5. What were the goals of Chinese nationalists?

Critical Thinking
6. Despite its losses in the 1800's, China remained an independent country. Why was China not carved into colonies as Africa was?

583

ANSWERS TO
Section Review 4

Define:
(a) rights of British citizens to be subject only to British law in China (b) regions in which economic interests of a foreign nation come before those of the home country
Identify:
(a) war Chinese fought against Britain to stop opium trade (b) rebel who took over southern China (c) protected American trade rights in China and protected China from colonization (d) Chinese secret society siege of European section of Peking
Answer:
1. China was practically self-sufficient.
2. (a) provide product Chinese would buy (b) protests, war (c) right to trade at Chinese ports, control over Hong Kong, and damages
3. (a) corruption in government, near bankruptcy, increase in population (b) Modernization was the country's only hope for survival.
4. (a) control of Chinese territory by foreign countries, U.S. fear that it would lose trade (b) American trade rights and China's independence
5. nationalism, republicanism, and land reform
6. Answers should consider China's history of unity and the role of the United States.

■ BACKGROUND

Europeans had little influence on most Chinese—those who lived in the countryside. A nineteenth-century proverb: ''The people fear the officials; the officials fear the foreign devils; the foreign devils fear the people.''

Japan built a modern nation.   5

When imperialists threated China, the Chinese fought to keep their traditional way of life. Japan chose a different course. It responded by becoming a powerful rival of European nations.

Americans ended Japanese isolation.

Japan in 1850 was almost as it had been in the 1600's when the Tokugawa family took control of the country and ushered in an era of peace. For 250 years, Tokugawa shoguns ruled over a remarkably stable society. During this period, the Japanese had almost no contact with the industrialized countries of the world. Japan continued to trade with China, but the only Europeans allowed in the country were Dutch traders who kept an outpost at Nagasaki.

Then, in 1853, four United States ships commanded by Commodore Matthew Perry steamed into what is now Tokyo Harbor. Perry came to ask the Japanese to open their country to foreign trade. The Japanese who lined the harbor were astounded by the foreigners' black ships made of iron and powered by steam. They were also shocked by the cannons and rifles that could have wiped out hundreds of the fiercest samurai in a matter of seconds.

The Japanese felt that they had no choice but to give in to Perry's demands and sign a treaty with the United States. They were not strong enough to force the foreigners to leave. The treaty the Japanese signed was the first of many with the Western powers. By 1860, Japan, like China, had granted permission to trade and extraterritorial rights to many foreign nations.

The Japanese feared that foreigners would take over Japan unless some changes took place. Therefore, in 1868, a new group of leaders overthrew the last of the Tokugawa shoguns. The new leaders ruled in the name of Emperor Mutsuhito, who was just 15 years old. Mutsuhito chose the name *Meiji* for his reign, meaning "enlightened rule."

Industrialization transformed Japan.

The Meiji era was a revolutionary time in Japan. During the 45 years of Mutsuhito's reign, one change followed another. Feudalism was ended,

Commodore Matthew Perry arrived in Japan in 1853. His huge warships dwarfed the Japanese boats that went out to meet them. With this show of strength, Perry forced Japan to open its ports to American merchants.

584

Japan responded to the threat from the West by developing its own industries.

and Japan adopted a constitution much like Germany's. As in Germany, real power was in the hands of a small group of men who were determined to build a powerful nation.

Industrialization in Japan "Open the country to drive out the barbarians" was the slogan of leaders such as Tomomi Iwakura (toh-moh-mee ee-wah-koo-rah). To do so, he vowed to seek knowledge throughout the world. In 1873, Iwakura led the first of many missions to Europe and North America. On these missions, the Japanese studied foreign ways of life and chose the best Western civilization had to offer. Observed one Japanese leader:

Are we to delay the using of steam machinery until we have discovered the principles of steam for ourselves? If we can select examples from them [Westerners] and adopt their contrivances, why should we not be successful in working them out?

Over the next 30 years, the Japanese economy became as modern as any in the world. The country's first railroad line was built in 1872, connecting Tokyo, the nation's capital, with the port of Yokohama some 20 miles away. By 1914, Japan had more than 7,000 miles of railroad track. Coal production grew from half a million tons in 1875 to more than 21 million tons in 1913. Meanwhile, large state-supported companies built thousands of factories. Japan's government took an active part in the development of industry.

Little help came from the outside. Fearful of economic dependence, the Japanese borrowed as little money as possible from European or American bankers. Any money they did borrow was quickly repaid. Japan earned most of the capital it needed to modernize by the sale of such traditional products as silk.

Japanese imperialism Economic development was only one part of Japan's plan to become a world power. Another part of the plan was military reform. Japan's new leaders believed that military strength was essential for a strong and independent nation. In modernizing its army and building a navy, the Japanese chose the best that Europe had to offer. Japanese leaders patterned their army after Germany's and their navy after

585

SECTION 5
Objectives and Teaching Strategies

OBJECTIVE 1. Describe the Japanese reaction to the arrival of Commodore Matthew Perry.

Teaching Strategy: *Writing about History: Perry's Arrival in Japan* (page 568e)

OBJECTIVE 2. Identify changes that took place during the Meiji era.

Teaching Strategy: *Discussing History: Industrialization of Japan* (page 568e)

■ BACKGROUND

Modernization brought many of the same problems to Japan that the Industrial Revolution had brought to other countries. Tokyo had wretched slums, and women and children in Japanese textile factories worked in deplorable conditions like those of early Manchester.

Mitsubishi and Mitsui are two of the large companies that are still in business today.

SECTION 5
Resources

REINFORCEMENT
■ Independent Practice 25.5

ENRICHMENT
■ Voices from the Past 25.5

ASSESSMENT
■ Section Quiz 25.5

ANSWERS TO
Section Review 5

Identify:
(a) American commodore who opened Japan to foreign trade (b) emperor after overthrow of the Tokugawa shoguns (c) "enlightened rule" of Mutsuhito (d) Russo-Japanese War battle (e) conflict between Japan and Russia for control of Manchuria

Answer:
1. (a) no contact with industrialized countries (b) fear that foreigners would take over Japan

2. overthrown by a new group of leaders in 1868

3. feudalism was abolished, Japan adopted a constitution like Germany's; the first railroad line was built; coal production increased

4. (a) won control of Korean peninsula and Manchuria (b) won Manchuria as well as recognition as a world power

5. Students should note that the leader believed in expediency and was confident the Japanese would make the most of Western technology.

Britain's. By 1890, Japan had several dozen warships and 500,000 soldiers.

Japan was now strong enough to renegotiate the unequal treaties it had signed in the 1850's. In 1899, the Japanese persuaded Western powers to give up their extraterritorial privileges in Japan.

As Japan became stronger, it also became more imperialistic. Like many European nations, Japan saw empire building as a way of meeting its economic needs. As in Europe, national pride also played a large part in Japan's imperialism. The Japanese were determined to show the world that theirs was a powerful nation.

From the start, Japan's leaders saw opportunities to expand at China's expense. In 1894, the two countries went to war. As a result of that war, China was forced to grant Korea independence. Soon, the Japanese began to take over Korea. They also moved into Manchuria, China's northeastern province, which was rich in iron and coal. Japan's growing interest in Manchuria alarmed the Russians, who were also eager to take over the province. In 1904, the conflict exploded in the Russo-Japanese War.

Most Europeans expected Russia to defeat Japan easily. To their surprise, the Japanese won victory after victory. At the Battle of Tsushima (soo-shee-muh), fought in the straits between Japan and Korea, the Japanese navy sank 38 of the 40 ships in the Russian Far Eastern Fleet.

With their victory in the war, the Japanese won control of all Russian business interests in southern Manchuria. Though still technically part of China, Manchuria was now a part of Japan's sphere of influence. More important, Japan won recognition as a great power. It was the only Asian country that was able to deal with the West as an equal.

Section REVIEW 5

Identify: (a) Matthew Perry, (b) Mutsuhito, (c) Meiji, (d) Battle of Tsushima, (e) Russo-Japanese War

Answer:
1. (a) What was the policy of the Tokugawa shoguns toward other nations? (b) What changed this policy?
2. How did the reign of the Tokugawa shoguns come to an end?

586

3. What changes took place in Japan during the Meiji era?
4. (a) How did Japan become an imperialist nation? (b) What was the importance of the Russo-Japanese War?

Critical Thinking
5. Reread the quotation on page 585. What attitude toward modernization did Japanese leaders take?

Imperialism reached the Western Hemisphere. 6

Europeans and Americans brought many changes to countries such as China and Japan. Contact with the West also changed life in places that once seemed very remote and isolated. In some of these places, Westerners took political control and started colonies. In others, they were interested only in economic power.

Outsiders dominated Latin America.

By 1870, a number of European nations were eyeing Latin America with new interest. It had many of the resources their factories needed. Suddenly there was a demand for tin from Bolivia and copper from Chile. There was also a market for Latin American food products. The revolution in land and sea transportation helped open those markets. For example, the development of refrigerated railroad cars and refrigerated ships enabled countries such as Argentina to ship huge quantities of refrigerated beef and mutton to Europe.

Latin Americans responded to the growing demand for raw materials and crops by increasing their output. In doing so, however, they needed capital to build railroads, docks, processing plants, and other facilities. Latin American governments borrowed money for improvements from banks in Europe and the United States. Latin American landowners and business people also borrowed money to expand their enterprises.

Gradually, however, outsiders took over ownership of plantations, mines, processing plants, and other key businesses in Latin America. By

1914, Britain had invested more than $5 billion in Latin America. The United States, which had only a very tiny investment in the region in 1870, had more than $1.6 billion invested by 1914. As outsiders became more involved in Latin America's economy, their political influence also increased.

The United States had the greatest stake in Latin America. Leaders in the United States believed that unrest in the region threatened the security not only of American businesses there but also the security of the United States itself. These leaders were especially fearful that Europeans might take over unstable governments in Latin America to protect their investments.

Since the 1820's, the United States had been using the Monroe Doctrine (page 540) to keep foreigners out of the Americas. In the 1890's, the United States began to use that doctrine in new ways. The United States government acted as a negotiator in disputes between Latin American nations and European powers. It was even willing to go to war to protect its interests in the region.

Spain and the United States fought a war.

Cuba was one of the last Spanish colonies in the Americas. The Cubans rose up against Spain in 1895. American newspapers printed daily reports of the conflict, shocking their readers with tales of Spanish brutality and Cuban heroism. While the Spanish efforts to put down the revolt were indeed brutal, many of the news accounts were exaggerated. As a result of these stories, the American public was prepared to accept war against Spain to free Cuba.

The United States had several reasons for watching the revolution closely. A number of Americans did business in Cuba. They had plantations, factories, and warehouses on the island. In fact, the United States bought most of its sugar from Cuba. Cuba had strategic importance as well. It guarded the entrance to the Gulf of Mexico.

Many people in the United States identified with the Cubans. They saw Cuba's fight for freedom as similar to their own war for independence.

United States' interest in Latin America increased after 1900 with the building of the Panama Canal. Here, workers dig the 8-mile-long Gaillard Cut.

587

SECTION 6
Objectives and Teaching Strategies

OBJECTIVE 1. Identify causes and consequences of the Spanish-American War.

Teaching Strategy: *Skill Building: Identifying Causes and Effects* (page 568e)

OBJECTIVE 2. Identify the Panama Canal and explain its significance.

Teaching Strategy: *Teaching with Pictures: The Panama Canal* (page 568e)

■ BACKGROUND

The United States had long had its eye on Cuba. In 1858, Senator Stephen A. Douglas said, "It is our destiny to have Cuba, and it is folly to debate the question."

■ DISCUSSION

The "yellow press" newspapers played a large part in this war. On February 9, about a week before the explosion of the battleship *Maine,* The New York *Journal* printed a letter stolen by a Cuban in which the Spanish insulted President McKinley. Ask students if they think the "yellow press" is in operation today.

SECTION 6
Resources

GEOGRAPHY
■ Transparency 81

REINFORCEMENT
■ Independent Practice 25.6

ENRICHMENT
■ Voices from the Past 25.6

ASSESSMENT
■ Section Quiz 25.6

Cooperative Learning

Have students, working in groups of four, write an editorial in the sensational-istic manner of the "yellow press" about the sinking of the battleship *Maine*. Two group members should act as researchers, providing information about the con-flict in Cuba and the rea-sons for U.S. involvement. Another group member should act as a recorder, writing the body of the ed-itorial, with input from all group members. The last member should act as an editor, correcting grammar, spelling, and the flow of the article. Remind stu-dents of the exaggerated tone of the "yellow press" and the reaction it was at-tempting to produce in the American people.

ANSWERS TO

Voice from the Past

1. The United States will be-come entangled in serious conflicts to protect its possessions.

2. Although we need mar-kets, we do not need to own the countries with which we trade.

Thus, when the United States battleship *Maine* mysteriously blew up in Havana Harbor on Feb-ruary 15, 1898, the United States was quick to blame Spain. On April 24, the two nations went to war.

The war lasted five months. When it was over, the United States had won Cuba, Puerto Rico, the Philippines, and Guam. Although Cuba was allowed its independence, the United States in-sisted on the right to intervene in Cuban affairs. The United States also claimed the right to build naval bases on the island.

The United States built a canal.

In the years after the Spanish-American War, the United States increased its involvement in Latin American affairs. The United States gov-ernment worked closely with investors to protect and expand trade in the region.

No president was more enthusiastic about ex-panding American interests abroad than Theodore Roosevelt, who led the nation from 1901 to 1909. He was especially eager to build a canal across the narrow Isthmus of Panama, which was then part of Colombia. Such a canal would shorten the sea route from New York to San Francisco by more than 5,000 miles. The United States Navy could move more quickly to defend either of the nation's coasts.

In 1903, the United States offered Colombia $10 million plus a yearly payment for the right to build a canal across Panama. The Colombian senate thought the price was ridiculously low for what would soon be an extremely valuable trade route. They demanded a higher price.

Roosevelt responded by encouraging a revo-lution in Panama. Panamanians had often tried to break away from Colombia. With help from the United States Navy, rebels in Panama quickly

Voice from the Past | A View of Imperialism

Carl Schurz came to the United States from Germany after fighting in the revolutions of 1848. He was elected to the United States Senate in 1869. The following excerpt is from a speech he gave in 1899, when the United States was preparing to take over the Philippines, Pacific islands that had belonged to Spain.

If we take those new regions, we shall be well entangled in that contest for territorial aggrandizement [expansion], which distracts other nations and drives them far beyond their original design. So it will be . . . with us. We shall want new conquests to protect that which we already possess. The greed of speculators, working upon our gov-ernment, will push us from one point to another, and we shall have new conflicts on our hands, almost without knowing how we got into them . . . We are told that our industries are gasping for breath; that we are suffering from over-production; that our products must have new outlets, and that we need colonies and dependencies the world over to give us more markets. More markets! Certainly. But do we, civilized beings, indulge in the absurd and barbarous notion that we must own the countries with which we wish to trade? Here are our official reports before us telling us that of late years our export trade has grown enormously . . . Trade is developed, not by the best guns, but by the best merchants.

1. What does Schurz predict will happen if the United States adopts imperialism?
2. How does he respond to economic arguments for im-perialism?

The patriot Emilio Aguinaldo fought for Philippine independence.

won their independence. They then leased the United States a ten-mile-wide zone in which to build a waterway.

For the next ten years, American engineers battled floods, heat, and mosquitos while building the canal. In 1914, the canal was finally opened. Ships from all nations began to use it. Latin America became a crossroads of world trade.

As interest in Latin America grew, Roosevelt issued a *corollary* to the Monroe Doctrine. (A corollary is an extension of an existing policy.) In 1823, the Monroe Doctrine had warned Europeans that the Americas were closed to further colonization. Now, Roosevelt's corollary said that as a result of that warning, the United States had the right to act as an international police officer in the Americas.

The Roosevelt Corollary was used to justify American **intervention,** or interference, in Latin America on several occasions. The United States sent troops to such countries as Haiti, Nicaragua, the Dominican Republic, and Cuba.

The situation in Latin America showed the link between political and economic independence. To be truly independent, a country needed to control both its own economy and its own government. The presence of foreign interests spurred a new growth of nationalism in Latin America.

Interest in Pacific islands grew.

Even before the Panama Canal opened, interest in the islands that dotted the Pacific was growing. By the late 1800's, Europeans and Americans were competing fiercely for control of the larger islands and island groups.

Rivalry grew for a variety of reasons. Some islands were rich in resources. Others were valued as coaling stations and naval bases. Steamships ran on large amounts of coal. Therefore, every trading nation needed places where its huge freighters could stop and refuel. Naval bases were also needed, where a ship could stop for repairs if necessary. The great engines that powered steamships required trained technicians with special equipment. Few nations were willing to rely on their rivals for coal or repairs. Each country wanted its own islands in the Pacific.

In 1876, Europeans and Americans controlled fewer than half the islands in the Pacific. By 1900, nearly all the islands had lost their independence. Britain was the leader here as elsewhere. It held Australia, New Zealand, Fiji, the southern Solomons, and many other islands in the Pacific. Germany took the northern Solomons and a number of islands once held by Spain. France controlled Tahiti.

The United States was mainly interested in Hawaii. By the 1880's, Americans dominated the islands and were eager for the United States to annex them. When Queen Liliuokalani refused to give up her country's freedom, she was overthrown. In 1898, Hawaii became part of the United States. The following year, as a result of the Spanish-American War, the United States also won control of Guam and the Philippines.

No part of the world was too remote for trade and colonization. The industrial nations were willing to compete for even the most distant island. By the early 1900's, explorers from several nations were racing to claim even the frozen wastes of Antarctica.

Section REVIEW 6

Define: intervention
Identify: (a) Latin America, (b) Spanish-American War, (c) Theodore Roosevelt, (d) Panama, (e) Roosevelt Corollary, (f) Liliuokalani
Answer:
1. (a) Why were European countries interested in Latin America? (b) How did European economic influence in Latin America increase?
2. Why was the United States concerned about events in Latin America?
3. (a) Give four reasons for the United States' interest in the Cuban revolt. (b) What was the result of the war between the United States and Spain?
4. How did the United States gain the right to build a canal in Panama?
5. Why were industrialized nations interested in Pacific islands?

Critical Thinking
6. (a) How are political and economic independence linked? (b) If two countries, such as Brazil and Great Britain, are trading, how can one trading partner be more dependent than the other?

589

ANSWERS TO
Section Review 6

Define:
interference
Identify:
(a) Western Hemisphere region where Latin-based languages are spoken (b) war between U.S. and Spain over Cuba (c) American president (1901–1909) who wanted to expand American interests abroad (d) site of Panama Canal (e) statement declaring right of the U.S. to act as an international police officer in the Americas (f) Queen of Hawaii
Answer:
1. (a) It had resources their factories needed.
(b) Foreigners took over ownership of businesses.
2. Unrest in the region threatened its security.
3. (a) Americans did business in Cuba; United States bought sugar from Cuba; Cuba had strategic value; and many Americans identified with Cuba's fight for freedom. (b) United States won many of Spain's Caribbean and Pacific holdings as well as right to build naval bases in Cuba.
4. by encouraging Panama to revolt against Colombia and then leasing the land for the canal from Panama
5. resources and strategic value as naval bases
6. (a) To be truly independent, a country needs to control both its economy and government. (b) One country may need the trade more.

Concluding the Chapter

1. Chapter Closer
Ask students to summarize the events that led historians to characterize the late nineteenth and early twentieth centuries as the "Age of Imperialism."

2. Reteaching Activities
a. Making a Time Line
Have students prepare a time line covering the events discussed in this chapter.

b. Making Comparisons
Have students compare and contrast European imperialism in Africa and China.

c. Listing Have students list the steps Japan took to modernize.

Answers to Chapter Review appear on page 568f.

Summary

1. Nations competed for overseas empires. The need for new markets, the desire to foster national pride and spread European values, and the lure of adventure all fostered imperialism. By 1900, European powers, the United States, and Japan had colonial empires in Africa, India, China, and the Pacific islands.

2. Imperialists divided Africa. Armed with superior weapons, European nations conquered all of Africa except Liberia and Ethiopia. Under colonial rule, Africans became second-class citizens.

3. The British dominated South Asia. By 1757, the British East India Company was the leading power in India. In 1857, following the Sepoy Mutiny, the British government forced the East India Company to turn over the rule of India to the British crown. Benefits of British rule were reaped mainly by Europeans. Discrimination against Indians caused the rise of nationalism in the late 1800's.

4. Imperialism threatened China. Defeat in the Opium War of 1839 forced China to open its ports to British traders. In the following years, one country after another established spheres of influence in China. By 1850, China was on the verge of bankruptcy. Corruption in the civil service, foreign control, and famine led to a rebellion against the Ch'ing dynasty.

In 1899, the United States proposed the Open-Door Policy to protect American trading rights in the country. Resentment of imperialism fostered secret societies and nationalism in China.

5. Japan built a modern nation. Japan's isolation ended when American Commodore Matthew Perry sailed into Tokyo Harbor in 1853. The Meiji era of modernization that followed gave Japan a strong economy. Military reforms fostered imperialism.

6. Imperialism reached the Western Hemisphere. Although Latin American countries maintained their independence, foreign investments tied Latin American economies to outside powers. United States control of Latin America increased after a war with Spain in the late 1800's. In 1904, the United States used the Roosevelt Corollary to justify intervention in Latin American affairs. Not long after, the United States began work on the Panama Canal. By the late 1800's, outsiders were also competing for control of Pacific islands.

Reviewing the Facts

1. Define the following terms:
   a. imperialism
   b. protectorate
   c. condominium
   d. extraterritorial rights
   e. sphere of influence

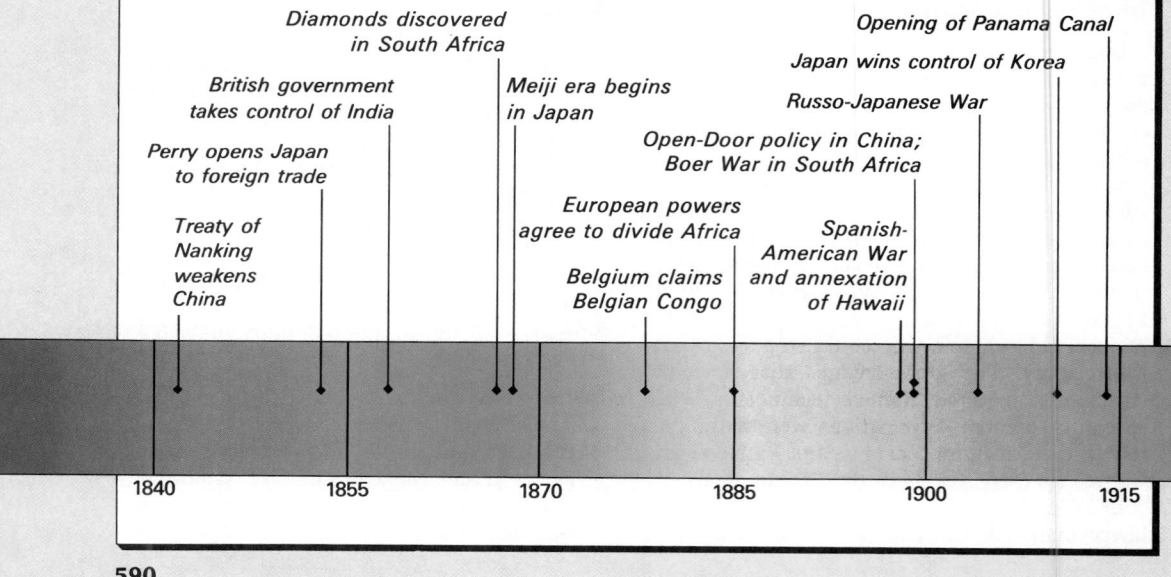

Diamonds discovered in South Africa

British government takes control of India

Perry opens Japan to foreign trade

Treaty of Nanking weakens China

Meiji era begins in Japan

European powers agree to divide Africa

Belgium claims Belgian Congo

Opening of Panama Canal

Japan wins control of Korea

Russo-Japanese War

Open-Door policy in China; Boer War in South Africa

Spanish-American War and annexation of Hawaii

1840   1855   1870   1885   1900   1915

2. Explain the importance of each of the following names or terms:
   a. Livingstone
   b. Leopold II
   c. Boer
   d. East India Company
   e. Sepoy Mutiny
   f. Sikh
   g. Indian National Congress
   h. Muslim League
   i. Opium War
   j. Open-Door Policy
   k. Boxer Rebellion
   l. Perry
   m. Meiji era
   n. Spanish-American War
   o. Roosevelt Corollary

3. (a) How did France gain control of parts of North Africa and West Africa? (b) How did Britain gain control of Egypt and the Sudan?
4. (a) Why did the history of South Africa differ from that of the rest of the continent? (b) What led to war between the British and the Boers? (c) What was the outcome?
5. (a) What led to the rise of nationalism in India? (b) How did the Raj respond?
6. (a) Describe China in 1800. (b) What were the goals of Chinese nationalists?
7. (a) How did Japan keep from becoming a colonized nation? (b) How did it become an imperialistic power?
8. (a) How did outsiders gain power in Latin America? (b) Name two ways the United States increased its power there.

Basic Skills

1. **Interpreting maps**   (a) Using the maps on pages 573, 579, and 582, tell what two major European powers dominated in Africa, India and Southeast Asia, and East Asia. (b) What would you conclude from these observations?
2. **Sequencing**   The Monroe Doctrine was formulated in 1823, and it was reinterpreted twice. (a) Explain its original provisions and intent. (b) Explain the two reinterpretations, including what led to the changes and their impact on the role of the United States.

Researching and Reporting Skills
Writing a Research Paper
Phase 4: Completing the research paper

1. **Revising**   Check your paper against the following questions: Does the introduction contain background information and a clear thesis statement? Does the body of the paper support the thesis statement? Are paragraphs introduced by a transition? Is the paper coherent? Does your conclusion provide a strong ending, focused on the thesis statement?
2. **Trimming for length**   Reducing the length of the paper to the required five pages by deleting unnecessary words and phrases will help to sharpen the focus.
3. **Writing a bibliography**   List your sources alphabetically. Entries for the bibliography do not have the first line indented, but the other lines are; the author's last name is listed first; periods are used in place of commas, and parentheses are deleted; no specific page reference is necessary. If many articles are used, you may want to make separate lists for books and articles. Place the bibliography at the end of your paper.
4. **Editing**   Check spelling, grammar, and punctuation. For quotations, check that you have used the exact words, that they are in quotation marks (or inset if longer than five lines), and that the author and source have been identified.

Critical Thinking

1. **Analyzing**   What political and economic factors led to the race for colonies in the late 1800's? Give examples.
2. **Comparing and contrasting**   (a) How did colonialism differ in Africa, India and Southeast Asia, and East Asia? (b) What factors may account for the differences?
3. **Inferring**   How might the race for colonies affect the balance of power in Europe?
4. **Synthesizing**   (a) What was the role of the United States during the age of imperialism? (b) In what parts of the world did it gain power? (c) What impact did it have on the spread of imperialism?

Perspectives on Past and Present
In 1884, representatives from European countries met in Berlin to determine how colonial powers could claim lands in Africa. (a) What attitudes did this approach imply? (b) Would this kind of decision making be possible today? Give reasons for your answer.

Investigating History
Make a study of one country in Africa, including its peoples, culture, precolonial history, and period of colonial rule. What modern nation emerged from that colony?

591

CHAPTER
Evaluation

Chapter Test 25, Alternate Chapter Test 25, and Computer Test Bank Chapter 25 Test can be used to evaluate your students' understanding of this chapter.

The Turn of the Century

Chapter Overview

The Industrial Revolution had changed the ways people worked. Now new inventions such as steel, the electric light bulb, the telephone, and the automobile began changing the ways people lived. New ideas in science also improved public health.

Women demanded voting rights, better jobs, equitable pay, and legal rights. Impressionism, post-impressionism, and expressionism replaced realism in art. Music was also influenced by new styles.

Europe faced rising tensions. In Germany, Kaiser William II took over the government and forced Bismarck to resign. Great Britain was split over Irish home rule and over the role of the House of Lords. Throughout Europe wide chasms existed between social classes. Nationalism also remained a strong force. Conflicts between European nations were barely diverted.

Chapter Focus

Ask students to pretend that they are professional photographers. Ask what scenes, inventions, or developments they would photograph to capture the spirit of our time. After the students have shared their ideas, have them read the chapter introduction (pages 592–593).

Tell students that Jacques Lartigue's snapshots captured the images of the era as developments in science and technology dramatically changed human history.

Inventions changed ways of life. 1

Setting the Stage

Ask students to explain the distinction between science and technology. (Science refers to the systematic methods by which knowledge of nature is sought. Technology refers to the practical application of this knowledge.) During the 1870's scientific knowledge was increasingly applied to technological problems. New inventions dramatically changed the way people lived, worked, and traveled.

Teaching Strategies

Discussing History: "The Wizard of Menlo Park" (Objective 1) Few inventions had more impact on the world than Thomas Edison's electric light bulb. Edison and his researchers worked up to 20 hours a day for more than a year to find a filament that could burn for a long period of time. They tried dozens of materials including gold, nickel, fishline—even coconut hair. Finally, in late 1879, Edison found that a charred cotton thread would glow for 13½ hours. On New Year's Eve, crowds of excited spectators gathered in Menlo Park, New Jersey, to see these remarkable new lights shining in Edison's laboratory. By 1900, 24 million bulbs provided what Edison described as "electric light so cheap that only the rich will be able to burn candles."

Advance Planner

	SECTION 1
Objectives	1. Identify Thomas Edison and describe how he developed the electric light bulb. 2. Identify Henry Ford and explain how he changed the automobile industry.
Setting the Stage	Defining "science" and "technology"
Teaching Strategies	Discussing History: "The Wizard of Menlo Park" Economics and History: The Model T Check for Understanding
Guided Practice	Section Review 1
Independent Practice Worksheets	Independent Practice 26.1 Basic Skills 26 Vocabulary 26
Enrichment	1. Primary Source: Voices 26.1 2. Researching for Points
Chapter Closer	
Unit VII Review	

SECTION 2	SECTION 3	SECTION 4	SECTION 5
1. Identify Joseph Lister and Louis Pasteur and explain how their medical discoveries saved lives. 2. Define and explain the concept of social Darwinism.	1. Describe economic and legal obstacles women faced in the late 1800's. 2. Explain the goals and strategies of the women's suffrage movement.	1. Describe the new styles of art that developed at the turn of the century. 2. Identify *The Great Train Robbery* and explain the role of movies in mass entertainment.	1. Evaluate the limits to democracy in the industrialized nations. 2. Explain how the issue of Irish home rule divided the British people. 3. Describe the social divisions in *la belle époque*.
Factors that contribute to increased life expectancy	Attitudes toward women in the late 1800's	Defining "mass culture"	Were promises of equality kept at the turn of the century?
Relating Past to Present: Antiseptic Surgery Analyzing a Quotation: Social Darwinism Check for Understanding	Skill Building: Comparing Points of View Discussing History: Women's Suffrage Check for Understanding	Teaching with Pictures: New Styles of Art Discussing History: *The Great Train Robbery* Check for Understanding	Analyzing a Quotation: Democracy in Germany Relating Past to Present: Irish Home Rule Discussing History: Social Divisions In *La Belle Epoque* Check for Understanding
Section Review 2 Independent Practice 26.2 Critical Thinking 26	Section Review 3 Independent Practice 26.3	Section Review 4 Independent Practice 26.4	Section Review 5 Independent Practice 26.5 Geography Skills 26
1. Primary Source: Voices 26.2 2. Preparing a Report: Scientists 3. Researching for Points	1. Primary Source: Voices 26.3 2. ★Relating Past to Present: The ERA 3. Researching for Points	1. Primary Source: Voices 26.4 2. Researching for Points	1. Primary Source: Voices 26.5 2. Researching for Points 3. Global Perspectives Transparency 81

●**Reteaching Activities**	Summarizing, Listing Goals
Chapter Review	Summary, Reviewing the Facts, Basic Skills, Researching and Reporting Skills, Critical Thinking, Perspectives on Past and Present, Investigating History
Chapter Evaluation	Chapter Test 26, Alternate Chapter Test 26, Computer Test Bank Chapter 26 Test
Geographic Theme	Movement: When did a global economy begin?
Historical Themes	Technology and History, Impact of Ideas, Continuity and Change, Economics and History
Unit Evaluation	Unit VII Test, Alternate Unit VII Test

Economics and History: The Model T (Objective 2) The first motor-cars were expensive to purchase, and even more expensive to operate and repair. Most cars cost more than $1,000, and half of them were priced above $2,000, well beyond an average worker's budget. In 1903, Henry Ford founded the Ford Motor Company in Detroit, Michigan. Five years later, after producing eight models including the Model A, Ford reached the revolutionary conclusion that he could produce a dependable, inexpensive car for "the great multitude" of people. Henry Ford became the first manufacturer to successfully mass-produce automobiles.

Ford's new automobile, the Model T, quickly became a success. In 1914, workers assembled 2,000 cars a day that cost an average of only $440. That year, Ford also raised his workers' salaries to the unprecedented amount of five dollars a day. He correctly realized that well-paid workers would be able to buy their own Model T's.

Check for Understanding Ask students to explain the contributions of these inventors: Henry Bessemer, Thomas Edison, Alexander Graham Bell, Henry Ford, and the Wright brothers.

Enrichment Activities

1. **Reading a Primary Source** Assign Voices from the Past Resource Book 26.1.

2. **Researching for Bonus Points** What was the winning speed in the first Indianapolis 500 race, held in 1911? (75 miles per hour)

Science presented new ideas. 2

Setting the Stage

Ask students how long they think they will live. Tell students that statistical data indicate the average American born in 1975 has a life expectancy of 72.6 years. [1976: 72.9; 1977: 73.3; 1978: 73.5; 1979: 73.9; 1980: 73.7] Tell students that in 1900 the average life expectancy for Americans was 47.3 years. Ask students why people live so much longer today. (advances in medicine and nutrition) Explain that many key medical discoveries were made around 1900.

Teaching Strategies

Relating Past to Present: Antiseptic Surgery (Objective 1) In the mid-1800's most doctors believed that a poisonous mist in the air caused disease. Unaware of bacteria, patients reasoned that the dirtier a surgeon's coat, the more operations he must have performed. Many patients asked for the most "experienced" (the dirtiest) doctors to operate on them.

Surgeon Joseph Lister objected to the unsanitary conditions in hospital operating rooms. Influenced by Pasteur's theory that disease was caused by bacteria, Lister insisted on cleanliness in his hospital ward. After many experiments, Lister discovered that carbolic acid could be used to clean bandages and medical instruments. He insisted that bandages be used only once and that surgeons regularly wash their hands. Since Lister's methods were designed to prevent sepsis, or blood poisoning, they became known as antiseptic surgery.

Analyzing a Quotation: Social Darwinism (Objective 2) Review the text's discussion of social Darwinism. Then explain that Spencer's ideas quickly spread to America.

The following exchange between Yale professor William Graham Sumner and his students illustrates social Darwinism:

Student: Professor, don't you believe in any government aid to industries?

Sumner: No! It's root, hog, or die.

Student: Yes, but hasn't the hog got a right to root?

Sumner: There are no rights. The world owes nobody a living.

Student: You believe, then, Professor, in only one system, the contract-competitive system?

Sumner: That's the only sound economic system. All others are fallacies.

Student: Well, suppose some professor of political economy came along and took your job away from you. Wouldn't you be sore?

Sumner: Any other professor is welcome to try. If he gets my job, it is my fault. My business is to teach the subject so well that no one can take the job away from me.

Read or distribute this passage, then ask students to answer these questions:

■ Did Sumner believe in government aid to industries? Why or why not? (No. He believed in free economic competition.)

■ How would Sumner have felt if another professor tried to take his job? (He believed the most competent person was entitled to the job.)

Ask students to explain how Sumner's ideas related to Darwin's theory of natural selection.

Check for Understanding Ask students to name one achievement in each field: medicine, chemistry, biology, and physics.

Enrichment Activities

1. **Reading a Primary Source**
   Assign Voices from the Past Resource Book 26.2.
2. **Preparing a Report**
   Have students report on one of the scientists discussed in this section.
3. **Researching for Bonus Points**
   Who discovered that chloroform was a better anesthetic than ether? (James Young Simpson)

Women sought rights and freedoms. 3

Setting the Stage

Read the following extract from John Stuart Mill's *Autobiography*:

> I saw no more reason why women should be held in legal subjugation [bondage] to other people than why men should be. I was certain that their interests required fully as much protection as those of men, and were quite as little likely to obtain it without an equal voice in making the laws.

Ask students to describe Mill's views on the issue of women's equality. For example, the role of women in making the laws. Then explain that Mill's views were not typical of the late 1800's.

Teaching Strategies

Skill Building: Comparing Points of View (Objective 1) Write the following statement by a member of the British Parliament on the board.

> "Women are creatures of impulse and emotion. They do not decide questions on the ground of reason as men do."

Have students compare this attitude toward women with Mill's. On what assumption is each view based? Then have students label two columns on a sheet of paper—*Obstacles Faced by Women* and *Gains Made by Women*. Tell students to complete this chart as they read and determine which view of women was predominant in the late 1800's.

Discussing History: Women's Suffrage (Objective 2) Read aloud George Dangerfield's description of Mrs. Emmeline Pankhurst, the fragile-looking widow of a Manchester barrister.

> It is known of Mrs. Pankhurst that she never proposed to spend her widowhood behind any scene, if there was the slightest chance of getting in front of it.

Ask students what Dangerfield might have meant by this remark. What evidence in the text supports their answers? Then have students review the tactics women used to win the vote. Ask students why women resorted to such drastic measures as hunger strikes or window smashing. Why do some believe that the most important battle fought by women was waged in the courts?

Check for Understanding Have students identify the economic and political advances made by women in the late 1800's and early 1900's.

Enrichment Activities

1. **Reading a Primary Source**
   Assign Voices from the Past Resource Book 26.3.
2. **Relating Past to Present**
   Since ratification of the Nineteenth Amendment in 1920, women in the United States have sought to extend their rights by adding an Equal Rights Amendment (ERA) to the Constitutution. Ask advanced students to investigate the history of the ERA and its place in the women's movement.
3. **Researching for Bonus Points**
   In what year did women in Great Britain win the right to vote? (1928)

Art and entertainment took new forms. 4

Setting the Stage

Ask students to estimate the number of movies, concerts, and sporting events they see—in person or on television—each month. Explain that these forms of entertainment are examples of *mass culture*. Point out that in earlier periods, art, music, and most theater were available mainly to the upper classes. By 1900, however, culture reached mass audiences.

Teaching Strategies

Teaching with Pictures: New Styles of Art (Objective 1) Ask students if they have ever seen a tree with blue leaves and a pink trunk. Then tell students that in 1905 French artist Henri Matisse unveiled a painting called *Landscape at Collioure* that included multicolored leaves and trees. Ask students to speculate why Matisse used such colors. Explain that Matisse sought to express how he felt about a landscape as opposed to what the landscape actually looked like. Refer students to Van Gogh's *Starry Night* (page 605). Van Gogh, like Matisse, distorted reality to express the ideas or moods suggested by an object or scene. Have students find other examples of the art styles described in this section.

Discussing History: *The Great Train Robbery* (Objective 2) Have students read "People flocked to see movies" on page 607. Explain that *The Great Train Robbery* marked the beginning of the modern film industry. Within a few years techniques such as fades, close-ups, and mobile cameras were used in full-length feature films, producing a string of box office hits. By 1916, 25 million Americans watched movies on any given day, making this the fifth largest industry in the United States.

Check for Understanding Have students cite two examples of mass culture and three reasons for its development.

Enrichment Activities

1. **Reading a Primary Source** Assign Voices from the Past Resource Book 26.4.
2. **Researching for Bonus Points** Who won the first World Series game? What was the score? (Boston over Pittsburgh, 5 to 3).

Europe faced rising tensions. 5

Setting the Stage

Write these promises of individual liberty on the board or on an overhead transparency:

Declaration of Independence: "We hold these truths to be self-evident, that all men are created equal . . . ."

Declaration of the Rights of Man and of the Citizen: "Men are born and remain free and equal in rights."

Ask students what situations gave rise to each of these promises. (the American and French revolutions) Challenge the class to consider the extent to which the promises of equality were kept during *la belle époque*, or the early 1900's.

Teaching Strategies

Analyzing a Quotation: Democracy in Germany (Objective 1) Tell students that, shortly after ascending the German throne at age twenty-nine, Kaiser William II declared: "I regard my whole position as given to me direct from heaven." What does this quote reveal about William's attitude toward the power of the king? What attitude would you expect him to take toward the prime minister and parliament? Have students check their answers by rereading "Germany had a hollow democracy" (page 608). Ask what factors limited democracy in other industrialized nations.

Relating Past to Present: Irish Home Rule (Objective 2) Assign students tasks in group research on "the Irish question" in Great Britain today. Have one group draw a map showing Northern Ireland and the Republic of Ireland. Have other groups use the *Readers' Guide to Periodical Literature* to find articles

on the tensions between Catholics and Protestants in Northern Ireland. Have students draw connections between the problems in Ireland today and Britain's failure to grant Ireland home rule in the late 1800's.

Discussing History: Social Divisions in *La Belle Epoque* (Objective 3) Write the following facts on the board:

- In 1900 nearly 41 million people lived in England. Of this number, 175,000 owned 90 percent of the land.
- At the turn of the century, one third of England's national income went to about 3 percent of the population.

Then read this statement, made by a member of the English working class: "They [the rich] don't have to think of tomorrow. They spend in an hour what would keep me and my little ones for a year."

Ask students to predict what effect this inequality eventually had. Then ask how England remained politically stable in light of such economic differences.

Check for Understanding Have students write two significant facts about each topic: the German Reichstag, "People's Budget," *la belle époque*.

Enrichment Activities

1. **Reading a Primary Source** Assign Voices from the Past Resource Book 26.5.
2. **Researching for Bonus Points** In what year did the Republic of Ireland win its independence from Great Britain? (1949)
3. **Global Perspectives** Have students complete the activities for Map Transparency 81, *The World about 1900*.

Reviewing the Facts

1. (a) process of change through natural selection **(b)** person who believes governments are evil and should be overthrown

2. (a) provides a cheap way to produce steel **(b)** used laboratory for research; made many inventions **(c)** invented telephone **(d)** invented wireless telegraph **(e)** built and flew first airplane **(f)** made surgery routine part of medical care **(g)** process of heating liquid to destroy bacteria **(h)** style of painting aimed at capturing an impression; replaced realism **(i)** style of painting expressing the artists' feelings; replaced realism **(j)** conservative chancellor who gave Germany first large-scale social welfare program in the world **(k)** Liberal party leader and champion of social welfare programs **(l)** mob attack on Jews in Russia, symbolic of tensions in eastern Europe

3. (a) steel **(b)** electricity

4. (a) excited scientific community but caused a controversy still debated today **(b)** natural selection or survival of the fittest; social Darwinism, superiority through power and belief in free economic competition

5. (a) periodic chart of elements **(b)** showed that each element contains only one kind of atom **(c)** discovered radioactivity and two new elements **(d)** suggested atoms were made up of smaller particles

6. organized campaigns, founded international councils, and organized demonstrations

7. (a) home rule for Ireland **(b)** World War I broke out one month before approval of a home rule bill, which Protestants were preparing to fight.

8. When House of Lords vetoed "People's Budget," the king threat- ened to appoint reform-minded lords. House of Lords voted to limit its powers rather than accept new members.

9. (a) nationalistic conflicts and persecutions of ethnic minorities **(b)** German and French hostility over Alsace and Lorraine, also Morocco

Basic Skills

(a) U.S., Germany **(b)** Britain, France **(c)** Russia, Austria-Hungary **(d)** Britain losing shares to rising industrial powers of U.S. and Germany; changes in Russian and Austrian production reflect political and social upheavals.

Researching and Reporting Skills

Students' presentations will vary.

Critical Thinking

1. (a) Problems: earned half of what men earned in wages; poor working conditions; confined to work as servants, in the garment or textile industries, or in professions such as teaching and nursing; no legal right to earn money when married. Progress: women formed own unions; gained laws limiting hours and setting health and safety standards in places where women worked; some women allowed into medical schools; jobs opened up in stores and offices (clerical work); laws allowed married women to earn money. **(b)** In terms of actual changes in conditions, relatively little progress was made.

2. prime minister in Germany appointed by kaiser; British prime minister leader of majority party in Parliament

3. (a) *Mass culture* refers to appeal of art, music, and theater to lower and upper classes. **(b)** new communications media and spread of public education **(c)** led to de- mocratization of culture, more interest in public issues

4. (a) accident and sickness insurance and old-age pensions **(b)** to gain wider support **(c)** Programs offset some negative effects of industrialization.

Perspectives on Past and Present

1. (a) creation of more democratic governments; to what extent governments should provide public services; social mobility; role of women in public life; living and working conditions for factory workers; rebuilding of cities; and what to do about the national aspirations of various peoples **(b)** All of the above are still controversial. It is unlikely that they will be resolved by the end of this century.

2. Possible answers: The impact of the Curies' discoveries can be seen in the development of atomic power and various medical and scientific advances.

Investigating History

Students' answers will vary.

Chapter 26

Teaching with Pictures

The poster art advertising the photography studio of P. Sescau was created by Henri de Toulouse-Lautrec. In the 1890's, the French artist became well known for the bold and beautiful posters he painted for Paris theaters, music halls, and other places of business. Tell students that Toulouse-Lautrec's technique was to portray people in an exaggerated pose that is characteristic of their work. Ask students how his technique was applied in this poster.

Photography (as shown in the poster above) was in vogue around 1900.

Key Terms

mass production
interchangeable parts
assembly line
evolution
social Darwinism
radioactivity
impressionism
mass culture
social insurance
home rule
anarchist
pogrom

592

Read and Understand

1. Inventions changed ways of life.
2. Science presented new ideas.
3. Women sought rights and freedoms.
4. Art and entertainment took new forms.
5. Europe faced rising tensions.

"Photography is a magic thing! A magic thing with all sorts of mysterious smells, a bit strange and frightening, but something you learn to love very quickly." So wrote seven-year-old Jacques Lartigue (lahr-**TEEG**) in his diary in 1901. His father, a wealthy Parisian banker, bought Jacques his first camera.

Photography had come a long way since Louis Daguerre (duh-**GARE**) had made the first hazy photographs in the 1830's. By the 1850's, homes all over the world were decorated with solemn, black-and-

Chapter 26 Resources

GEOGRAPHY
- Geography Skills 26
- Transparency 81

REINFORCEMENT
- Vocabulary 26
- Basic Skills 26
- Reteaching 26
- Making Connections Study Guide 26

ENRICHMENT
- Critical Thinking 26

ASSESSMENT
- Chapter Test 26
- Alternate Chapter Test 26
- Computer Test Bank

white family photographs. Known as daguerreo-types, such pictures cost as little as 25 cents each. By 1900, simple box cameras like the one Jacques owned could produce black-and-white photographs as good as those today.

Armed with his camera, young Jacques set out to capture the world around him. His pictures give a glimpse of life in a well-to-do family of the time.

By 1900, the upper classes in France and other industrialized countries had luxuries that earlier generations had never known. Electric lights or gaslights lit their houses at night. Coal furnaces or gas heaters warmed them in winter. Hot and cold running water, flush toilets, and bathtubs made their lives easier, cleaner, and more comfortable than ever before. The telephone kept them in touch with distant friends and relatives. Their servants—for even middle-class households had help—cooked meals on huge, iron stoves and washed clothes in machines.

Jacques's photos show not only his friends and relatives but also the new machines of the early 1900's. With his father, Jacques went to the military airfield outside Paris and saw France's first flimsy airplanes take to the sky. Most of all, however, Jacques loved automobiles. In 1912, his father bought a 35-horsepower Peugeot—"a big, open monster," Jacques called it. The Lartigue family, wearing goggles and rubber coats in case it rained, roared along the dirt roads at 30 miles per hour.

Sitting next to Yves, the family chauffeur, Jacques waited eagerly for the chance to pass another car.

> We see a car ahead of us. Yves accelerates. We are coming closer . . . We see the white cloud behind the wheels of the car, smell the dust . . . Oh, what a fantastic moment . . . There we go, past the other car! I feel cut off from the rest of the world, wonderfully superior to everybody else; I wish we would never stop!

Such an event, Jacques wrote sadly, "doesn't happen too often . . . there are still so few cars on the road."

In this chapter, we will see some of the new inventions and scientific developments that altered Jacques Lartigue's life in the early 1900's. We will also see how the writers and artists of this exciting age viewed their world. Finally, we will see how governments responded to the challenge of this new age.

■ BACKGROUND

Another Frenchman, Nicephore Neipce, had used light-sensitive silver compounds to create the world's first photographs during the 1820's. Daguerre's main contribution had been the discovery of a fixative that would keep the photographs from fading.

By the 1850's, more than 3 million daguerrotypes were being produced each year in the United States alone.

Jacques Lartigue (left) skillfully photographed scenes from daily life in the early 1900's. At right, the Lartigue's chauffeur changes a flat tire.

Edison's goal was to turn out "a minor invention every ten days and a big thing every six months or so." Partially deaf since the age of twelve, Edison believed his impairment helped him concentrate on his inventions.

Cooperative Learning

Arrange students in groups of five and have each group choose a recorder. Tell students to skim Section 1, "Inventions changed ways of life," and make a group list of all of the inventions discussed. Then have each group member write down the three most important inventions on the list and why they are important. Tell group members to compare lists, discuss the reasons for their choices, and reach a consensus on the three most important inventions. Emphasize that everyone must agree on the group list. Have group spokespersons present lists for class discussion.

Inventions changed ways of life.   1

Worldwide industrial production more than tripled between 1870 and 1914. The Industrial Revolution touched lands from Europe to Japan and Australia. Three countries dominated the world economy—Great Britain, Germany, and the United States. Together, these countries produced two thirds of all the world's manufactured goods in 1913. This economic growth was accompanied by rapid advances in technology.

Bessemer began an Age of Steel.

In the mid-1800's, despite all the advances of science and industry, iron was still the basic metal for tools and machines. In the 3,000 years since the Iron Age began (page 42), nothing had replaced iron. In the late 1800's, however, a new age began—the Age of Steel.

Steel is a mixture of purified iron and a small amount of carbon. It is tougher, lighter, and more flexible than iron. For hundreds of years, metalworkers made steel in small quantities for swords and knives. (Steel can hold a sharp edge, and iron cannot.) Purifying steel took weeks of steady heating, making the metal very expensive.

In the 1850's, an Englishman named Henry Bessemer developed a less costly way to make steel. He forced blasts of hot air through the molten iron to burn out impurities. Bessemer began using this new "blast furnace" in 1859 in his factories at Sheffield. Operating around the clock, the huge furnaces lit up the night sky with an eerie glare.

By the turn of the century, steel was widely used for machinery, ships, and railroad track. Steel rails lasted up to 15 times longer than iron ones. Steel girders replaced stone and iron as the supports for buildings. The first building with a steel frame was Chicago's ten-story Home Insurance Building, completed in 1884.

New sources of power came into use.

Before 1890, the tallest buildings stood about 20 stories high. With steel girders, architects could plan much taller buildings, but how would people reach the top floors? In 1889, the invention of the electric elevator made possible a new kind of building for crowded cities—the skyscraper. By 1913, New York City was a city of skyscrapers. Its 60-story Woolworth Building, completed that year, was the world's tallest building. It rose 792 feet above the shadowy streets.

Electricity was one of the new kinds of energy that were coming into use in the late 1800's. Just as iron was giving way to steel for some uses, coal and steam were giving way to electricity, oil, gasoline, and natural gas.

To many people, electricity seemed the most magical of the new kinds of energy. Early in the 1800's, Alessandro Volta and Michael Faraday had discovered ways to make small amounts of electricity. In 1872, the Belgian electrician Zenobe Gramme developed the first industrial dynamo. Dynamos generated electric power by using steam engines to spin electromagnets. With the invention of the dynamo, electricity moved out of the laboratory and into daily life.

Edison set up a research laboratory.

If electricity seemed like magic, without doubt its greatest magician was the American inventor, Thomas Alva Edison (1847–1931). Edison worked on everything from movie projectors to household irons, from phonographs to doorbells. Altogether, he patented more than 1,000 inventions.

As a 12-year-old boy in Michigan, Edison had sold newspapers and candy on commuter trains to and from Detroit. While the commuters were at work, he taught himself mathematics and science in the public library. He also set up a laboratory in one of the boxcars on the train.

By the time he was 20 years old, Edison was working as a telegrapher, but he regarded inventing as his real career. In 1870, he went from poverty to wealth in a single bound when he sold his invention of a stock ticker for $40,000.

The wizard of Menlo Park Edison used his money to start a laboratory in Menlo Park, New Jersey, where he worked full-time as an inventor. Indeed, the idea of a laboratory for industrial research and development was Edison's most important invention.

A steady stream of inventions flowed from Edison's laboratory. People began calling him "the wizard of Menlo Park." Actually, Edison was not

594

DAILY LIFE ▶ *Music for the Home*

"Mary had a little lamb," bellowed Thomas Edison into the mouthpiece of his newest invention. The device recorded the sound vibrations on a sheet of tin foil wrapped around a cylinder. When Edison turned the crank, a scratchy imitation of his own voice came back through the funnel-shaped speaker. It was the first phonograph.

Like Edison's prototype, the earliest record players needed no electricity. To hear a record, you simply wound up the phonograph with a crank. It played until it ran down. The earliest records were wax cylinders, later replaced by disks. On such recordings, people could hear all kinds of music, from music-hall entertainers to world-famous opera singers, in their own homes.

---

so much an inventor as a perfecter of already existing inventions. "The first thing," he said, "is to find out what everyone else knows and begin where they leave off."

The electric light In 1879, Edison developed the first practical electric light bulb. As early as 1808, an English scientist named Humphrey Davy had made a bulb in which a piece of thin metal would glow. The problem, which baffled inventors for years, was to find something that would glow but would not quickly burn itself out.

After months of trial and error, Edison discovered an answer—thin cotton thread coated with carbon. Making sure that a vacuum existed inside the bulb, Edison turned on the current.

It lit up . . . We sat and looked, and the lamp continued to burn. None of us could go to bed, and there was no sleep for any of us for 40 hours. We sat and just watched it, with anxiety growing into elation.

Within three years, Edison perfected light bulbs that would burn for 1,400 hours. He also designed and guided the construction of New York City's first electrical system. On September 4, 1882, as the sun set, New York's first electric streetlight glowed to life.

Telephones and radios carried voices.

Electricity had powered the first great advance in modern communications, the telegraph. In the late 1800's, it powered two more advances, the telephone and the radio.

Bell and the telephone Alexander Graham Bell (1847–1922) was a Scot who emigrated to the United States. He studied speech and sound to teach deaf students to talk. He was also interested in transmitting sound electrically. After several years of experimenting, he succeeded in changing the sound waves of the human voice into electric impulses, sending them through a wire and then changing them back to sound waves at the other end. Bell patented his invention, which he called a telephone, in 1876.

At the Philadelphia Exposition in 1876, Bell displayed his telephone to the astonished crowd. Among those watching was the emperor of Brazil, who used Bell's machine to speak with an aide in another room. "My word!" the emperor exclaimed when his aide answered, "It speaks Portuguese!"

The telephone quickly became an essential part of modern life. By 1900, there were nearly 2 million telephones in the United States, and by 1912, there were 8.7 million. The telephone also spread rapidly in the cities of western Europe, especially in Germany and Britain.

Marconi and the radio The next challenge was to send messages without using wires. Many people contributed to the invention of the radio. Physicists James C. Maxwell and Heinrich Hertz made the theoretical discoveries about electromagnetic waves, or radio waves. Then, in 1895, inventor Guglielmo Marconi used these waves to send telegraph signals directly through the air, without the use of wires. He used transmitters that sent out electromagnetic signals at certain

595

SECTION 1 Objectives and Teaching Strategies

OBJECTIVE 1. Identify Thomas Edison and describe how he developed the electric light bulb.

Teaching Strategy: *Discussing History: "The Wizard of Menlo Park"* (Page 592a)

OBJECTIVE 2. Identify Henry Ford and explain how he changed the automobile industry.

Teaching Strategy: *Economics and History: The Model T* (page 592c)

■ DISCUSSION

Ask students to explain the cause-effect relationship between the development of the phonograph and the development of superstars.

Did the harnessing of electricity have as great an impact on the way people live as did the ability to control fire?

SECTION 1 Resources

ASSESSMENT
■ Section Quiz 26.1

REINFORCEMENT
■ Independent Practice 26.1

ENRICHMENT
■ Voices from the Past 26.1

ANSWERS TO Section Review 1

Define:
(a) machine that generates large amounts of electric
(continued)

595

ANSWERS TO *(continued)*

power (b) the making of quantities of goods by machine (c) standardized, identical pieces (d) process in which a moving conveyer belt rolls parts past workers

Identify:

(a) developed blast furnace method to make steel (b) inventor of the light bulb, phonograph (c) inventor of the telephone (d) inventor of the radio (e) auto manufacturer who pioneered mass production (f) inventors of airplane

Answer:

1. Great Britain, Germany, and the United States

2. (a) Blast furnaces made it easier and cheaper to make. (b) machinery, ships, railroad tracks, buildings, skyscrapers

3. (a) coal and steam (b) electricity, oil, gasoline, and natural gas

4. invented electric light, record player, and developed the industrial laboratory for research and development

5. Telephone and radio communication became an essential part of life.

6. use of standardized, interchangeable parts and the assembly line method of production

7. (a) pride in a job done with the greatest efficiency in contrast to the pride of personal workmanship (b) advantages: steady job in thriving industry, lack of wasted time and energy, ability to specialize in one task; disadvantages: tedium of repetition, impersonality, and lack of pride in work

frequencies and receivers that could be "tuned in" to pick up the signals. In 1901, Marconi's wireless telegraph sent Morse code across the Atlantic. Primitive radios were soon standard equipment for ships at sea. Not until later could radios transmit human voices.

A *new engine burned gasoline.*

During the 1870's, many inventors experimented with an engine that would run on gasoline. Like the steam engine, the gasoline engine had a piston that moved inside a cylinder. Instead of steam pressure to move the piston, the gasoline engine used a series of small explosions inside the cylinder. Because the gasoline burned inside the cylinder, the new machine came to be called an *internal combustion engine.* It was much smaller than a steam-powered engine. Steam-powered vehicles were large because they had to carry coal, water, and a furnace in which the coal burned to heat the water. By contrast, the gasoline engine needed no furnace and no water, only a tank to hold the gasoline.

In 1885, German inventor Gottlieb Daimler mounted a gasoline engine on a bicycle to produce the world's first motorcycle. In 1890, he founded the Daimler Motor Company. He manufactured cars that he named for a friend's daughter, Mercedes.

Ford *built cars on an assembly line.*

By 1900, about 13,000 automobiles were sputtering and clattering along the roads of Europe and North America. Some of these vehicles could reach speeds of 10 to 15 miles per hour. Nearly all of them had been assembled by hand. Such cars were expensive to buy and to repair. As a result, they remained luxuries that the average worker never dreamed of buying.

One of the mechanics who built such cars was an American named Henry Ford. Ford decided to make cars that many people could buy. "The way to make automobiles is to make them all alike," he said, "just as one pin is like another pin when it comes from the pin factory, or one match is like another." Ford's solution was the Model T, a homely but reliable car. By 1913, it was selling for just $500, less than half the usual price of a car.

How did Ford lower prices? Part of the answer was **mass production,** or the making of quantities of goods by machine. Ford's Tin Lizzies were made from standardized, **interchangeable parts,** so that identical pieces could replace one another. Thus, the Tin Lizzies were easier to assemble and repair than other cars.

Ford's major innovation was to improve efficiency in his factory. He watched his workers and noticed that they spent much of their time carrying parts and tools to the car they were working on. To put an end to this wasted time and motion, Ford set up an **assembly line.**

The assembly line was a moving conveyer belt that rolled unfinished automobiles past the workers. Workers did their tasks one after the other while the chassis moved slowly past. By 1914, workers on Ford's assembly line could put a car together from start to finish in less than two hours. Soon, Ford's Detroit factory was producing 2,000 cars every hour.

By 1914, there were more than 600,000 cars in operation around the world. Of these, 75 percent were in the United States, where the Automobile Age had gotten off to a roaring start.

The Wrights *built an airplane.*

Meanwhile, in 1903, two brothers from Dayton, Ohio, had put the gasoline engine to a spectacular new use. At Kitty Hawk, North Carolina, on a cold, windy December morning, Wilbur and Orville Wright launched the age of powered flight. This first airplane flight lasted only 12 seconds and covered 120 feet. By 1905, the Wrights' third plane, *Flyer III,* could do all kinds of maneuvers and stay aloft for half an hour.

In 1908, Wilbur Wright went to Paris to demonstrate the airplane. The American pilot was greeted as a conquering hero. Crowds cheered as they watched him fly rings around the Eiffel Tower, staying aloft as long as two hours.

Unlike the automobile, the airplane developed slowly. Even in 1914, the total number of airplanes in the world was less than 1,000.

Inventions *became group efforts.*

The Wright brothers were among the last in a long line of independent inventors. Many early inventions of the Industrial Revolution were the

In the Wright Flyer, the pilot lay prone to minimize wind resistance. To take off, the plane rolled along a track made of two-by-four boards.

work of one or two people experimenting in their basements, backyards, or small workshops. After 1900, however, most major technical advances resulted from group effort. Technology had become too complex and too expensive for one person to undertake a project from start to finish.

Therefore, after 1900, it is seldom accurate to name one person as *the* inventor of a complex device such as the computer or the television. As the twentieth century progressed, most new inventions came from research laboratories such as the one that Edison founded at Menlo Park.

Section REVIEW 1

Define: (a) dynamo, (b) mass production, (c) interchangeable parts, (d) assembly line
Identify: (a) Henry Bessemer, (b) Thomas Edison, (c) Alexander Graham Bell, (d) Guglielmo Marconi, (e) Henry Ford, (f) Orville and Wilbur Wright
Answer:
1. What countries dominated industry in 1900?
2. (a) Why did steel become more common in the late 1800's? (b) What were some of its most important uses?
3. (a) What were the major sources of energy in the early Industrial Revolution? (b) In the later Industrial Revolution?
4. Briefly describe the contributions of Thomas Edison.
5. How did communications change in the late 1800's and early 1900's?
6. What changes did Henry Ford bring to the auto industry?

Critical Thinking
7. (a) Using the quotation from Ford on page 596, explain how his attitude on making goods differed from those of a traditional craftsperson. (b) From a worker's point of view, what would be the advantages and disadvantages of an assembly line?

Science presented new ideas. 2

Theoretical scientists such as Volta, Faraday, Maxwell, and Hertz laid the groundwork for Edison and Marconi. In a similar way, other scientists in the late 1800's and early 1900's were pushing the frontiers of knowledge forward.

597

SECTION 2 Objectives and Teaching Strategies

OBJECTIVE 1. Identify Joseph Lister and Louis Pasteur and explain how their medical discoveries saved lives.
Teaching Strategy: *Relating Past to Present: Antiseptic Surgery* (page 592c)

OBJECTIVE 2. Define and explain the concept of social Darwinism.
Teaching Strategy: *Analyzing a Quotation: Social Darwinism* (page 592c)

SECTION 2 Resources

ASSESSMENT
■ Section Quiz 26.2

REINFORCEMENT
■ Independent Practice 26.2

ENRICHMENT
■ Voices from the Past 26.2

■ BACKGROUND

Finally, in 1978, the last cases of smallpox were found in Somalia, East Africa. Health workers inoculated the people of the area, and no one else caught the disease.

In industrial areas of England, supporters of Darwin found evidence for the evolutionary process by observing moths. Originally white, these moths gradually mutated to gray and black as industrial soot changed the color of their habitat.

Medical discoveries saved lives.

At the beginning of the 1800's, doctors had few weapons in the fight against disease. Some of their "cures"—such as bloodletting—did more harm than good. Thanks to advances during the 1800's, more and more diseases could be cured or even prevented. By 1875, Europeans lived an average of 15 years longer than their grandparents.

As you have read, Edward Jenner discovered a way to prevent smallpox (page 465). By 1875, widespread inoculation had nearly wiped out smallpox in western Europe.

Another major discovery came in the 1840's. Several American doctors and dentists began using the gases ether and chloroform to "knock out" their patients during painful operations. With anesthesia, surgery became a routine part of medical care rather than a last-resort remedy.

Lister Although anesthesia made surgery less painful, nearly half of all surgical patients still died of infection. No one knew why. A Scottish surgeon, Joseph Lister (1827–1912), suggested that infection might be connected with the filthy conditions that were normal in hospitals. Patients were seldom bathed. Doctors worked in their street clothes and went from one patient to the next without even cleaning their instruments.

In 1865, Lister began a new program of cleanliness in his hospital ward. He insisted that his staff keep the place spotlessly clean. He began using carbolic acid to clean medical instruments. As a result, 85 percent of his patients survived. By 1890, other European and American hospitals were trying to live up to Lister's standard of cleanliness.

Pasteur Although Lister believed that tiny, invisible particles caused infection, he had no proof. Then, in 1865, Lister read about the work of the French scientist Louis Pasteur (pas-TUHR). (The two scientists later became friends.)

Pasteur (1822–1895) was experimenting to find out why milk soured and alcohol fermented. He discovered that the causes were microscopic organisms he called bacteria. He found that heat could destroy many harmful bacteria. The process of heating a liquid to kill the bacteria in it is now called *pasteurization*.

Pasteur also found ways to weaken the microorganisms that caused disease. Among other diseases, he worked with the virus that caused rabies,

which was always fatal. In 1885, grief-stricken parents brought him their nine-year-old son who had been bitten by a rabid dog. Pasteur hesitated to use his new methods on a person without more tests, but there was no other hope. He inoculated the boy, and the youngster recovered.

Armed with the new knowledge of bacteria, later scientists found the causes of many diseases. Slowly, they also began to find cures. Moreover, when people saw how closely disease and filth were connected, they began to be more careful with city water supplies and food products. As a result, such diseases as cholera and thyphus claimed fewer lives.

Darwin developed the theory of evolution.

No scientific idea of the 1800's caused a greater upheaval than the work of British biologist Charles Darwin (1809–1882). Darwin's research dated from the mid-1800's, but the controversy about his writings reached a peak in the latter part of the century. The cause of the controversy was Darwin's answer to the question that faced biologists: How can we explain the tremendous variety of plants and animals on Earth?

The most widely accepted answer in the 1800's was the idea of *special creation*. According to this view, every kind of plant and animal had been created by God at the beginning of the world and had remained the same since then.

Darwin challenged the idea of special creation. In 1859, he published a book titled *The Origin of Species by Means of Natural Selection*. Interest was so great that the book sold out immediately. Darwin put forward three major premises:

1. Within every species, more individuals are born than can survive. Therefore, every living thing takes part in a constant struggle for survival.
2. Variation means that no two individuals are exactly alike.
3. Those variants with some sort of advantage in current conditions are more likely to survive to reproduce. This differential reproduction is what Darwin meant by *natural selection*.

This process, Darwin reasoned, explains how species change over time and how new species gradually arise from old ones. Thus, over time, many different kinds of living things could have developed from a few early ones. Darwin's idea of change through natural selection came to be called the theory of **evolution.** (Darwin himself did not use the term evolution.)

The Origin of Species caused great excitement among scientists. Naturalist Thomas Henry Huxley wrote, "It is doubtful if any single book, except the *Principia* [of Sir Isaac Newton], ever worked so great and rapid a revolution in science." By 1900, nearly all biologists and botanists accepted the theory of evolution as the best explanation of variety among living things.

At the same time, Darwin's ideas roused a storm of debate outside the scientific community. Many people believed that the idea of evolution directly contradicted the account of creation in the Bible. The bishop of Oxford, for example, accused Darwin of "a tendency to limit God's glory in creation." In 1871, Darwin fueled the conflict when he published *The Descent of Man.* In this new book, he said that humans too had evolved from earlier forms of life.

The evolution controversy continued for decades. Even today, well over 100 years after *The Origin of Species* was first published, Darwin's ideas are not universally accepted.

Social Darwinists favored competition.

Darwin was a biologist, but a number of nineteenth-century thinkers incorrectly applied his ideas about plants and animals to economics and politics. The leader in this movement was Herbert Spencer, an English sociologist.

Free economic competition, Spencer argued, was natural selection in action. The best companies, for example, make profits, while inefficient ones go bankrupt. Spencer applied the same rules to individuals. Those who were fittest for survival enjoyed wealth and success, while the poor remained poor because they were unfit. This idea became known as **social Darwinism.** Social Darwinists believed that governments should not make laws that would upset the "natural" system of rich and poor.

Others carried Darwin's ideas even further. The German philosopher Friedrich Nietzsche (NEE-chuh) believed that some humans could and should evolve to a higher level by the use of willpower and courage. Such people would become *übermenschen* (supermen) above the common herd. "I am opposed," Nietzsche wrote, "to parliamentary government . . . because [it is] the means whereby cattle become masters."

■ BACKGROUND

Many other scientists in the 1700's and 1800's already accepted the general idea of evolution—it was not a new idea. Darwin's contribution was suggesting a mechanism—natural selection—to account for evolution.

In 1901, a London newspaper polled its readers, asking for lists of the ten most influential books of the past 100 years. Of the hundreds of different lists that the paper received, every one included *The Origin of the Species.*

DISCOVERIES AND INVENTIONS
Mid-1800's to early 1900's

TECHNOLOGICAL		MEDICAL		SCIENTIFIC	
1859	Bessemer steel process	1840's	Use of anesthesia in surgery	1859	Darwin's theory of evolution
1872	First industrial dynamo (electricity)	1864	Pasteur's discovery of bacteria, leading to pasteurization	1860	Mendel's discovery of hereditary genetic traits
1876	Telephone			1869	Mendeleev's chart on known elements (Periodic Table)
1879	Usable light bulb	1865	Lister's insistence on cleanliness to avoid infection		
1885	Internal combustion engine			1898	Curies' work on radioactivity, radium, and plutonium
1888	Kodak box camera	1875	Widespread use of inoculation for smallpox		
1901	Wireless telegraph and radio	1885	Pasteur's use of inoculation for rabies		
1903	First airplane				
1913	Model T Ford; assembly-line process				

Marie Curie

599

ANSWERS TO
Section Review 2

Define:
(a) substance that kills pain (b) microscopic organisms that cause disease (c) Darwin's premise that fittest individuals are most likely to survive (d) change through natural selection (e) natural selection applied to politics and economics (f) matter containing only one kind of atom (g) tiny particle (h) powerful form of energy
Identify:
(a) suggested relationship between infection and un-
(continued)

ANSWERS TO (continued)

sanitary conditions **(b)** discovered heat could destroy harmful bacteria **(c)** published *Origin of the Species by Means of Natural Selection* **(d)** idea that every kind of plant and animal was created by God at the beginning of the world and has remained the same ever since **(e)** idea of change through natural selection **(f)** idea that those who were fittest for survival enjoyed wealth and success **(g)** believed that some humans could and should become "supermen" **(h)** laid ground work for science of genetics **(i)** devised the Periodic Table **(j)** discovered radium and polonium

Answer:

1. inoculation, anesthesia, improved sanitation, control of bacteria

2. **(a)** Every kind of plant and animal was created by God at the beginning of the world. **(b)** Change took place through natural selection.

3. contradicted account of creation in the Bible

4. suggested natural selection is at work in survival of companies that prosper

5. Dalton theorized that all matter is made of atoms and that elements contain only one kind of atom; Mendeleev organized all the known elements and predicted new elements; the Curies discovered two elements for which Mendeleev had left room in his chart.

6. Look for answers to consider the nature of adaptation, the element of luck in entrepreneurship, the fact that wealth can be inherited, and the interdependency of the economic community.

Many nationalists and imperialists seized on both Darwin's and Nietzsche's ideas to support their own views. They argued that their own nation should prove its superiority through power, especially military power. As we will see in later chapters, several dictators used nationalism and scorn for democracy to justify their oppressive governments.

Science advanced in many fields.

Just as Copernicus and Galileo began a scientific revolution around 1600, Darwin was part of a new age of science that began in the late 1800's. Thanks to the work of many men and women, the foundations of modern biology, chemistry, and physics were established by 1914.

Biology Although Darwin said that living things passed on their variations from one generation to the next, he did not know how they did so. In the 1860's, Gregor Mendel discovered that there is a pattern to the way that certain traits are inherited. Although his work was not widely known until 1900, Mendel laid the groundwork for the science of genetics.

Other biologists took up the study of bacteria where Louis Pasteur left off. The German scientist Robert Koch, for example, discovered the organisms that caused tuberculosis and cholera.

Chemistry In chemistry, most of the major elements and compounds found in nature had been identified by the end of the 1800's. In 1803, the British chemist John Dalton had theorized that all matter is made of tiny particles called atoms. Dalton showed that elements contain only one kind of atom, which has a specific weight. Compounds, on the other hand, contain more than one kind of atom.

In 1869, Dmitri Mendeleev (MEN-duh-LAY-yef), a Russian chemist, organized a chart on which all the known elements were arranged in order of weight, from lightest to heaviest. He left gaps where he predicted that new elements would be discovered. Later, his predictions proved correct. Mendeleev's chart, called the Periodic Table, is still used by scientists today.

A husband and wife team working in Paris discovered two of the missing elements. Marie and Pierre Curie found that a mineral called pitchblende released a powerful form of energy. In 1898, Marie Curie gave this energy the name

---

radioactivity. The Curies discovered two new elements that they named radium and polonium. Both were highly radioactive. In 1903, the Curies shared the Nobel Prize for Physics for their work on radioactivity. In 1911, Marie won the Nobel Prize for Chemistry for the discovery of radium and polonium. The prizes awarded to the Curies show how closely the fields of chemistry and physics were linked.

Physics Physicists around 1900 were trying to unravel the secrets of the atom. Among the leaders in this field were two British physicists, Ernest Rutherford and J. J. Thomson. Earlier scientists believed that the atom was the smallest particle that existed. Rutherford suggested that atoms were made up of yet smaller particles. Each atom, he said, had a nucleus surrounded by one or more particles called electrons.

Soon other physicists such as Max Planck, Neils Bohr, and Albert Einstein were studying the forces that held atoms together. Their discoveries, as we shall see in Chapter 30, were fully as revolutionary as Darwin's ideas.

Section REVIEW 2

Define: (a) anesthesia, (b) bacteria, (c) natural selection, (d) evolution, (e) social Darwinism, (f) element, (g) atom, (h) radioactivity

Identify: (a) Joseph Lister, (b) Louis Pasteur, (c) Charles Darwin, (d) special creation, (e) theory of evolution, (f) social Darwinism, (g) Friedrich Nietzsche, (h) Gregor Mendel, (i) Dmitri Mendeleev, (j) Marie and Pierre Curie

Answer:

1. List four developments that improved health care during the 1800's.

2. (a) How did the theory of special creation explain the variety of living things? (b) How did the theory of evolution explain this variety?

3. Why did Darwin's ideas arouse controversy?

4. How did some thinkers apply Darwin's ideas to industrial society?

5. How were the contributions of Dalton, Mendeleev, and the Curies related?

Critical Thinking

6. Darwin did not fully agree with the social Darwinists. How do natural selection and economic competition differ?

Women sought rights and freedoms. 3

In 1906, Marie Curie became the first woman ever to teach at France's prestigious Sorbonne. She won two Nobel Prizes and was acknowledged as one of the foremost scientists of her time. Yet she could never become a member of the French Academy of Sciences because she was a woman. During the years when she was making her great discoveries, she could not even vote.

The massive changes that the 1800's brought to Europe and North America affected everyone's lives. By the late 1800's, however, it was clear that the Industrial Revolution and the social changes that went with it had had different results for women than for men.

Women faced economic problems.

In some ways, the Industrial Revolution opened economic opportunities to women. Factory work offered higher wages than work done at home. Women spinners in Manchester's cotton factories, for example, received much higher pay than women who spun cotton thread at home.

On the other hand, women factory workers usually earned only half as much as men. Employers claimed that women needed less money than men because women did not have to support families. This argument ignored the many women who worked because their husbands had died or deserted them or were too ill to work.

Trade unions began to win better wages for working men in the mid-1800's. However, these unions seldom accepted women as members. Unions fought to keep women out of skilled jobs that offered better pay. Men feared that if women worked at such jobs, employers would lower the wages for everyone doing the work. During the mid-1800's, women formed several unions of their own in the trades where they dominated. Still, by 1907, only 15 percent of the unions in Great Britain admitted women.

When reformers began demanding better conditions for workers, the laws often applied first to women and children. Lawmakers were more willing to protect women and children than men. Beginning in the 1830's, some laws limited the hours women and children could work. Other laws set health and safety standards in factories.

Sometimes, these laws backfired against women. If the law said that women could not work 16 hours a day, some employers simply fired women and hired men instead. Eventually, however, the reforms spread to all workers and benefited both men and women.

Women entered new fields.

The years around 1900 were a watershed for working women. A gradual shift took place in the kinds of jobs that were open to them. In the late 1800's, working women were clustered in three kinds of jobs. The largest share worked as servants in other people's homes. In industry, most women were either garment workers or textile workers.

Middle-class women with an education had other job possibilities. Some were teachers. There was a demand for teachers in the late 1800's because countries in western Europe were beginning to offer free public schooling. France began public education in the 1860's. The British government began to organize schools in 1870, although they were not free to all children until 1891.

Nursing was another career open to women. British nurse Florence Nightingale (1820–1910) took the lead in winning professional training

Florence Nightingale organized British army hospitals during the Crimean War.

601

OBJECTIVE 1. Describe economic and legal obstacles women faced in the late 1800's.

Teaching Strategy: *Skill Building: Comparing Points of View* (page 592d)

OBJECTIVE 2. Explain the goals and strategies of the women's suffrage movement.

Teaching Strategy: *Discussing History: Women's Suffrage* (page 592d)

■ BACKGROUND

By 1875, more than one third of France's primary schoolteachers were women.

■ DISCUSSION

Ask students to speculate on possible causes of the sexual imbalance in the teaching profession today.

■ BACKGROUND

Because working women were still expected to do the household chores, it is not surprising that in Britain the campaign for women's rights began in Manchester rather than in London.

ASSESSMENT
- Section Quiz 26.3

REINFORCEMENT
- Independent Practice 26.3

ENRICHMENT
- Voices from the Past 26.3

By 1900, under the Code Napoléon, the legal status of women in France was actually worse than it had been in the 1700's.

As early as 1848, Elizabeth Cady Stanton led a group of women reformers at a meeting in Seneca Falls, New York. There, supporters of women's rights drafted a declaration of independence, asserting that "All men and women are created equal."

Cooperative Learning

Arrange the class in small groups and have each group choose a recorder. Tell students to imagine they are going to interview a women's rights activist in the late 1800's. Have each group member think of two or more questions to ask the interview subject. Recorders should write down all the questions. Then direct the groups to collaborate on answering each question the way they think the interview subject would have answered. Have recorders write down the answers. Then have a volunteer from each group read the transcript of the imaginary interview to the class.

ANSWER TO

Caption Question

Men have the vote so it is smooth sailing for them, while women, handicapped by not having the vote, must struggle.

for women as nurses. In 1854, she went to Turkey and later Russia to help British soldiers in the Crimean War. Making her night rounds in the hospitals, she became known to hundreds of sick and wounded soldiers as "The Lady with the Lamp." When she returned to Britain, she used money that was donated in her honor to found the Nightingale School for Nurses. It was the first school of professional nursing in the world.

Teaching, nursing, library work, and social work were service professions in which many women worked. Opportunities for women in other professions were limited. In 1898, for example, there were only two women lawyers in all France.

In the late 1800's, a number of women's medical schools opened. Faced with this competition, several large medical schools for men began to admit women as well. By 1900, 10 percent of the medical students in the United States were women.

New jobs were also appearing for less educated women. After 1900, many women worked as shop clerks and office workers. (Before 1870, nearly all office clerks were men.)

While jobs in offices, stores, and schools were opening to women, jobs in industry were closing. The traditional women's industries—textiles and garment making—fell on hard times after 1900. Thus, the share of women in manufacturing jobs dropped sharply.

VOTES

HANDICAPPED!

602

Women had few legal rights.

Working women of the middle 1800's faced yet another problem. They had no legal right to the money they earned. An unmarried woman's wages legally belonged to her father. If she married, everything she owned or earned became her husband's property.

Women could not sue or make contracts. Often, if a woman's husband died, she could not even act as guardian of her children.

In 1900, no country in Europe allowed women to vote. Even in Britain, where Queen Victoria was perhaps the most popular monarch the country had ever had, women could not vote or serve in Parliament. "Women are creatures of impulse and emotion," declared one British member of Parliament in 1906. "They do not decide questions on the ground of reason as men do." Thousands of women (and men) throughout the developed world disagreed.

Women sought the right to vote.

In the United States, women such as Lucretia Mott and Susan B. Anthony organized a campaign for women's rights as early as 1848. By the 1880's, women were working internationally to win more rights. In 1888, women activists founded the International Council for Women. Delegates and

By 1900, women in many countries were organizing (right) to demand suffrage as a first step toward equality. Can you explain the symbolism of the poster (left)?

WOMEN'S SOCIAL AND POLITICAL UNION. VOTES FOR WOMEN

observers from 27 countries attended the council's 1899 meeting, coming from lands as far apart as the United States, New Zealand, Argentina, Iceland, Persia, and China.

Even among activist women, however, the question of suffrage (voting rights) for women remained controversial. Not all women were in favor of it; not all men were against it.

In Britain and the United States, there had been decades of peaceful efforts to win the right to vote for women. Around 1900, more militant organizations sprang up. In the United States, Carrie Chapman Catt headed the North American Woman Suffrage Association. In Britain, Emmeline Pankhurst formed the Women's Social and Political Union (WSPU) in 1903.

The WSPU became the most militant organization for women's rights. Besides peaceful demonstrations and parades, its members cut telegraph wires, heckled government speakers, chained themselves to railings at public buildings, and smashed windows. Their goal was to draw attention to the cause of woman's suffrage.

Emmeline Pankhurst and her daughters Christabel and Sylvia were arrested and imprisoned dozens of times. When she was jailed, Emmeline Pankhurst turned to hunger strikes to keep her cause before the public. British officials force-fed her to keep her alive.

The authorities could not stop another woman who was determined to become a martyr to the cause of woman's suffrage. In June 1913, the cream of European society was watching the English Derby at Epsom Downs. Suddenly, a young WSPU member, Emily Davison, threw herself in front of the king's horse and was killed.

Voice from the Past | *A Citizen's Right to Vote*

In 1872, Susan B. Anthony and 50 other women were arrested for trying to vote in the presidential election. After she was found guilty, Anthony made the following statement.

Of all my prosecutors, from the corner grocery politician who entered the complaint, to the United States marshal, commissioner, district-attorney, district-judge, your honor on the bench—not one is my peer, but each and all are my political superiors; and had your honor submitted my case to the jury . . . even then I should have had just cause of protest, for not one of those men was my peer but, native or foreign born, white or black, rich or poor, educated or ignorant, sober or drunk, each and every man of them was my political superior; hence in no sense my peer . . .

Precisely as no disfranchised person [person without the right to vote] is entitled to sit upon a jury, and no woman is entitled to the franchise, so none but a regularly admitted lawyer is allowed to practice in the courts, and no woman can gain admission to the bar—hence, jury, judge, counsel, all must be of the superior class.

[Here, the judge stated that the trial had been handled according to the established forms of law.]

Yes, your honor, but by forms of law all made by men, interpreted by men, administered by men, in favor of men and against women; and hence your honor's ordered verdict of guilty, against a United States citizen for the exercise of the "citizen's right to vote," simply because that citizen was a woman and not a man.

1. (a) According to Susan B. Anthony, why are none of the people who brought her to trial her peers? (b) What right do they have that she lacks?
2. What traditional right in American and British law does she imply she was denied?
3. What other opportunities and civic responsibilities were closed to women?

603

■ **BACKGROUND**

Harriet Martineau and Lydia Becker were other leaders of the suffrage movement in Britain.

ANSWERS TO
Voice from the Past

1. (a) Each was her political superior. (b) the right to vote
2. the right to trial by a jury of her peers
3. the right to sit on a jury, be admitted to the bar

ANSWERS TO

Section Review 3

Identify:
(a) founder of first school of professional nursing (b) organized campaign for women's rights (c) head of the North American Woman Suffrage Association (d) formed Women's Social and Political Union

Answer:

1. lower pay, exclusion from trade unions and skilled jobs

2. (a) domestic work, work in garment or textile factories (b) teaching, nursing, library work, and social work

3. no right to the money they earned; could not sue or make contracts; could not vote

4. by organizing, by demonstrating

5. (a) right to own property, to serve as safety inspectors in factories where women worked, to serve on local boards to oversee schools, poor-houses, and hospitals (b) right to vote

6. (a) Teaching demanded too much of women's intellects, while nursing might expose genteel women to overly harsh realities, and office work would require more "business sense" than women had. (b) Look for answers to cite stereotypes—women's nurturing capability and "capacity for detail."

At her funeral, thousands of women in white dresses carried banners supporting woman's suffrage. "Thoughts have gone forth whose power can sleep no more," read one banner. "Victory! Victory!"

In fact, victory was still many years away. Though the woman's suffrage movement commanded wide attention between 1880 and 1914, its successes were few. Women won the right to vote in New Zealand (1893) and Australia (1902). Only in two European territories—Finland (1906, then part of the Russian empire) and Norway (1913)—did women gain voting rights before World War I. Several western states in the United States also granted women the right to vote. Often, women won voting rights for local elections before they won statewide or national rights.

On other issues, women's rights made faster progress. Britain and most states in the United States enacted laws giving married women the right to own property. In Britain, women began to serve as safety inspectors in factories where women worked. Women also served on local boards to oversee schools and hospitals.

Section REVIEW 3

Identify: (a) Florence Nightingale, (b) Susan B. Anthony, (c) Carrie Chapman Catt, (d) Emmeline Pankhurst

Answer:

1. What were some of the economic problems that women faced?
2. (a) What fields of work employed most women in the late 1800's? (b) What new fields opened around 1900?
3. What were some of the restrictions on women's legal and political rights?
4. How did women try to secure their rights?
5. (a) In what areas did they achieve some success by 1914? (b) In what areas were they less successful?

Critical Thinking

6. In the 1850's, teaching, office work, and professional nursing were unusual jobs for women. (a) From the point of view of an employer of that time, explain why each of these jobs is "unsuitable" for women. (b) From the point of view of an employer in 1900, explain why each job is a "natural" one for women.

604

Art and entertainment took new forms. 4

The late 1800's and early 1900's saw great changes in the world of the arts. The period was also marked by new forms of art and entertainment for a mass audience.

New styles in art replaced realism.

Although France lagged behind Britain and Germany in economic and military power, its capital, Paris, still dominated European culture. Rebuilding carried out under Napoleon III had transformed central Paris from a maze of crumbling medieval streets into a magnificent urban center. Artists from Europe and America flocked to Paris. There they could enjoy unequaled cultural resources while exchanging ideas about a new style of painting, **impressionism.**

Impressionism Like other styles of art, impressionism involves a choice of subjects, an attitude toward these subjects, and techniques for presenting them. Impressionists concentrated on scenes from everyday life—crowded city streets, the arrival of a train at its station, or Sunday picnics on the Seine. Perhaps influenced by photography, they hoped to capture their impressions of a certain instant in the ever-changing world about them.

To convey their impressions of a scene, these painters adopted the new technique of painting thousands of dabs of pure color onto their canvas. As Edouard Manet explained, light could become "the principal personage of a painting." Impressionist works by Manet, Claude Monet, and Auguste Renoir do indeed seem to shimmer and sparkle.

Postimpressionism During the 1890's, a new group of painters, sometimes called the postimpressionists, carried this emphasis on light and color even further. Among these artists were Vincent van Gogh (van GOH) and Paul Gauguin (goh-GAN). Gauguin explained his colorful style this way:

By the combination of lines and colors, under the pretext of some motif taken from nature, I create symphonies and harmonies that represent nothing absolutely real in

Like many impressionists, Monet favored outdoor scenes for their natural light. A detail from his "Gladioli" (left), a tranquil garden scene, shows the impressionists' use of light and color. In "Starry Night" (right), the postimpressionist Van Gogh painted the sky as an overwhelming display of fireworks.

SECTION 4
Objectives and Teaching Strategies

OBJECTIVE 1. Describe the new styles of art that developed at the turn of the century.

Teaching Strategy: *Teaching with Pictures: New Styles of Art* (page 592d)

OBJECTIVE 2. Identify *The Great Train Robbery* and explain the role of movies in mass entertainment.

Teaching Strategy: *Discussing History:* **The Great Train Robbery** (page 592e)

■ BACKGROUND

While France lagged behind Britain and Germany in economic and military power, Paris still dominated European culture. It became a city of broad, tree-lined boulevards, opera houses, art museums, and galleries.

the ordinary sense of the word but are intended to give rise to thoughts as music does.

Expressionism Other early twentieth-century painters, such as the Norwegian Edvard Munch and the Russian Vasily Kandinsky, were mainly concerned with expressing the feelings that a scene aroused. They were therefore known as expressionists. Because the feelings they expressed were often grim and anguished, their paintings were unsettling and frightening.

New directions Even with wild colors and distortions, the paintings of Van Gogh and Munch could still be recognized as objects from the real world. Other artists, however, were beginning to change the shapes they painted beyond all recognition. One group of painters, for example, was nicknamed the cubists because their work featured geometric planes and angles. A picture of a person might look at first sight like an intricate stack of boxes.

One of the cubists was a young Spaniard working in Paris, Pablo Picasso. He explained why he rejected realism: "Nature and art, being two different things, cannot be the same thing, period. Through art, we express our concept of what nature is not."

Music often took nationalistic themes.

Romanticism was still the leading style of music in the late 1800's. These years were a golden age of opera. Composers such as Giuseppe Verdi (**VERD**-ee) and Giacomo Puccini (poo-**CHEE**-nee) wedded their emotional music to melodramatic plots.

Nationalism also played a strong role in music. The German composer Richard Wagner (**VAHG**-nuhr), for example, based many of his operas on old German legends. Nearly every European country had a composer whose work gave people a heightened sense of national identity.

Just as painters were branching out from tradition, some composers began to experiment with different kinds of music. The French composers Claude Debussy (deb-yoo-**SEE**) and Maurice Ravel (ruh-**VEL**) wrote loosely structured musical impressions such as *The Sea* (Debussy) and *The*

605

SECTION 4
Resources

ASSESSMENT
■ Section Quiz 26.4

REINFORCEMENT
■ Independent Practice 26.4

ENRICHMENT
■ Voices from the Past 26.4

ANSWERS TO

Section Review 4

Define:
(a) art form attempting to capture the impression of a scene **(b)** culture that appealed to large audience

Answer:

1. **(a)** impressionist: scenes from everyday life, emphasis on color and light; post-impressionist: greater emphasis on color and light; expressionist: express feelings, often unsettling or frightening **(b)** impressionism: Manet, Monet, Renoir; postimpressionism: Van Gogh, Gaugin; expressionism: Munch, Kandinsky

2. expressionism, cubism, postimpressionism

3. Compositions gave people sense of national identity. Wagner's operas took nationalistic themes.

4. **(a)** increased literacy, improvements in communications, reduction in working hours **(b)** sports, music halls, recorded sound, movies

5. **(a)** led to attempts to portray impression **(b)** Answers should consider commercial and the aesthetic.

6. **(a)** give rise to thoughts **(b)** defining culture, reflecting society, providing entertainment, exploring the human condition, and celebrating individualism

Waltz (Ravel). In fact, music critics compared them to the impressionist painters.

Other composers, such as the Russians Alexander Scriabin (skree-**AHB**-uhn) and Igor Stravinsky (struh-**VIHN**-skee), produced even more complex harmonies and rhythms. The Austrian Arnold Schönberg (**SHUHN**-buhrg) began to base his music on mathematical patterns rather than upon sounds that were pleasing to the ear.

Most of this experimental music did not appeal to a wide public. When Stravinsky's ballet *The Rite of Spring* was first performed in Paris in 1913, the audience rioted against what they thought was an insult to their ears.

The turn of the century also saw the beginnings of modern popular music. In Britain, singers with Cockney accents sang ballads at popular music halls. In the United States, ragtime—music based on a rapid melody and strong beat—was becoming very popular thanks to African American musicians such as Scott Joplin.

The arts reached new audiences.

In earlier periods, art, music, and most theater had been largely the concern of the upper classes. It was not until about 1900 that you could speak of **mass culture**—the appeal of artists, writers, and musicians to a much larger audience. There were at least three causes for the rise of mass culture around the turn of the century.

First, the spread of public education broadened literacy in both Europe and North America. The millions of new readers created an enormous market for newspapers, magazines, and books that were written in simple, colorful language.

Second, improvements in communication made it possible to meet this broad demand for information and entertainment. The new, high-speed presses and linotype machines could turn out thousands of pages in a few hours. The phonograph brought music directly into people's homes.

The third cause was a gradual reduction in working hours. By 1900, most industrial countries had limited the working day to ten hours. Most people worked Monday through Friday and half a day on Saturday. Thus, men and women of the lower and middle classes had more leisure time than ever before. They could take part in activities that their grandparents never had time to enjoy.

606

Sports entertained millions.

The five-and-a-half-day work week created the "weekend," a special time of relaxation and fun. All kinds of new leisure activities became popular. Millions flocked to beaches on summer weekends. Golf and tennis were a hit among the well-to-do, who could afford to join clubs with playing areas. People with less money took up soccer or baseball, which they could play with simple equipment on vacant lots.

For every person who played sports, there were 20 who enjoyed watching. In the United States, football and baseball skyrocketed in popularity. Teams from the rival American and National leagues played baseball's first World Series in 1903. Soccer became popular in Europe.

As a result of the growing interest in sports, the international Olympic Games began in 1896. They revived the Greek tradition of holding an athletic competition among states every four years. Fittingly, the first modern Olympics were held in Athens.

Baseball's popularity grew swiftly in the 1890's.

People flocked to see movies.

One of the most popular new leisure activities was an evening visit to the movie theater or the music hall. With names such as the Gaiety, the Grand, or the Orpheum, music halls offered a dozen or more different acts. Such variety shows often included singers, dancers, comedians, acrobats, and even trained parakeets.

During the 1880's, dozens of inventors worked on moving-picture cameras and projectors. One successful design came from France. Another came from Thomas Edison's laboratory.

The earliest films caused a sensation only because of their novelty. They were in black and white, lasted less than a minute, and had no plot. One, for example, showed a man sneezing— that was all!

In 1903, an American filmmaker named Edwin S. Porter offered the first feature film. As the lights dimmed, a fierce bandit appeared on the screen and fired his revolver directly at the audience. People shrieked with fear and delight. In the next eight minutes, they watched as a band of outlaws held up a train and fled, only to be hunted down by a white-hatted sheriff and his hard-riding posse. The film was *The Great Train Robbery*, and it packed theaters on both sides of the Atlantic.

Movies quickly became big business. By 1910, 5 million Americans attended some 10,000 theaters across the country each day. The European movie industry enjoyed similar growth.

The people who saw *The Great Train Robbery* were watching the beginnings of both a new industry and a new art form. Movies made possible a new kind of visual storytelling. Moving images, together with recorded sound, came to dominate mass culture in the twentieth century.

Section REVIEW 4

Define: (a) impressionism, (b) mass culture
Answer:
1. (a) What were the major characteristics of impressionist, postimpressionist, and expressionist painting? (b) Name the leading painters of these schools.
2. What trends in painting followed the impressionist period?

3. How did some music of the late 1800's reflect political trends of the time?
4. (a) What were the causes of the development of mass culture around 1900? (b) Give some examples of the new forms of art and entertainment for wide audiences.

Critical Thinking
5. (a) How did the development of photography change the function of painting? (b) What is the importance of each today?
6. Reread the statement by Gauguin on pages 604–605. (a) What purpose do painting and music share? (b) In your opinion, what is the importance of the arts in society?

Europe faced rising tensions. 5

More than ever before, the views of ordinary people were making an impact on society. By 1914, most industrialized countries allowed all adult men to vote. This development brought about two major changes in European politics.

First, political parties became more tightly organized than before. In earlier times, political parties had been loose-knit clubs. Now they were (or tried to be) well-oiled machines for winning elections. Major parties had branches in every election district. Those branches reported to a central committee. The central committee set party policies and made sure that party members in parliament supported those policies.

Second, the spread of democracy brought forward a new kind of political leader. Besides commanding the respect and support of fellow party leaders, a successful politician now had to appeal to large numbers of voters. As a result, politicians found they had to be part actors and part salespersons, able to win widespread support.

By itself, the right to vote did not guarantee democratic government. Much depended on the political system of each country. Even in the United States, for example, only the House of Representatives was elected directly by the voters. Senators were not directly elected. Until 1913, they were chosen by the state legislatures. France had a similar system with a Chamber of Deputies

607

SECTION 5 Objectives and Teaching Strategies

OBJECTIVE 1. Evaluate the limits to democracy in the industrialized nations.
Teaching Strategy: *Analyzing a Quotation: Democracy in Germany* (page 592e)

OBJECTIVE 2. Explain how the issue of Irish home rule divided the British people.
Teaching Strategy: *Relating Past to Present: Irish Home Rule* (page 592e)

OBJECTIVE 3. Describe the social divisions in *la belle époque*.
Teaching Strategy: *Discussing History: Social Divisions in* **La Belle Epoque** (page 592e)

SECTION 5 Resources

GEOGRAPHY
■ Transparency 81

REINFORCEMENT
■ Independent Practice 26.5

ENRICHMENT
■ Voices from the Past 26.5

ASSESSMENT
■ Section Quiz 26.5

■ **DISCUSSION**

Were Bismarck's policies comparable to those of the ancient Romans with their "bread and circuses?"

■ **DECISIONS**

Gladstone's support was not enough to save the Home Rule Bill. A combination of Conservatives, some Liberals, and Irish Protestants defeated the bill by 341 votes to 311.

and a Senate. In Britain, members of the House of Lords were not elected at all.

Such *upper houses* could reject bills passed by the *lower houses* and also frame bills of their own. In some other countries, the powers of elected legislatures were restricted both by an upper house and by a monarch who still made many major governmental decisions.

Germany had a hollow democracy.

Germany was a good example of the limits on democracy. The Reichstag (**RYKES**-tahg) was the lower house of the German parliament. It was elected by universal manhood suffrage. Members of the upper house, the Bundesrat (**BOON**-duhs-raht), were appointed by each of Germany's 25 states. Often, they were chosen by local princes and dukes.

Furthermore, the German kaiser (emperor) named his own chancellor (prime minister). Neither the Reichstag nor the Bundesrat had any control over the chancellor. Thus, if the Reichstag voted against raising the army budget, the chancellor might simply raise the budget anyway. "The Reichstag does not make history," said one German political leader, "but is merely playing a comedy."

Otto von Bismarck continued to govern Germany as chancellor until 1890. As we have seen, Bismarck was a staunch conservative who distrusted both democracy and socialism. However, he was shrewd enough to know that his government needed popular support. During the 1880's, therefore, Bismarck gave Germany the world's first large-scale **social insurance** program. His laws included insurance to help workers in case of accident or sickness. Soon he added old-age pensions for every German worker.

By passing these laws, Bismarck hoped to take support away from his enemies, the socialists. "Anybody who has before him the prospect of a pension, be it ever so small," Bismarck noted, "is much happier and more content with his lot, much more tractable and easy to manage, than he whose future is absolutely uncertain." Bismarck's goal was not so much to help the workers as to prevent revolution, and he succeeded.

Bismarck's political career ended abruptly. In 1888, Kaiser William II came to the throne. The young kaiser was headstrong, quarrelsome, and determined to rule Germany himself. Accordingly, he forced Bismarck to resign in 1890. However, Bismarck's system of state socialism, as he called his social programs, remained in effect. So did his military and nationalist policies. With their economic needs met, most Germans supported these policies even though Germany's government was basically undemocratic.

Britain faced two political crises.

Germany had half a dozen political parties, as did France and Italy. In Britain, two major parties dominated politics—the Liberals and the Conservatives. In the late 1800's, both parties produced prime ministers who were enormously popular, the Conservatives' Benjamin Disraeli and the Liberals' William Gladstone.

The Irish question The two parties differed little on questions of imperialism or reform. The issue on which the two parties were most seriously split was the Irish question. Ireland had been controlled by the British government for nearly 300 years. It had been ruled directly from London since 1801.

During the 1870's, nationalists in Ireland sought **home rule.** They organized an Irish Home Rule Party to work for a measure of independence for Ireland. In general, Conservatives opposed Irish Home Rule, while Liberals favored it. Liberal prime minister William Gladstone brought forward two home rule bills in Parliament, but both were defeated.

Meanwhile, in Ireland, a drop in the prices for farm products made it impossible for thousands of people to pay their rents. In just one year, landlords forced more than 2,000 families out of their homes. Some angry farmers and other nationalists turned to violence, burning barns and beating landlords' agents.

Decisions in History

Gladstone's First Home Rule Bill proposed granting Ireland a separate legislature, although keeping British control of the army and trade. Gladstone argued that home rule would strengthen Irish loyalty to Britain. Conservatives said the bill would weaken the empire by encouraging other demands for home rule. How would you have voted on this bill, and why?

During the 1870's and 1880's, both Protestants and Catholics in Ireland worked for home rule. By the 1900's, however, many Irish Protestants had turned against it. Most Irish Protestants lived in the northern part of Ireland, known as Ulster. They feared being a minority in a country dominated by Catholics.

In 1914, Parliament finally approved a home rule bill. By then, Irish Protestants were gathering weapons and holding military drills to fight against home rule.

Just one month before home rule was to take effect, World War I broke out in Europe. The problem of Irish independence was left to wait and to fester.

The issue of the House of Lords In 1909, Britain's Liberal finance minister was David Lloyd George. Orphaned as a child, he had been raised by his uncle, a shoemaker. Lloyd George became the champion of social welfare programs. Under his leadership, the Liberals put forward a program to provide old-age pensions, accident and illness insurance for workers, and even some unemployment benefits. To pay for these benefits, Lloyd George called for an income tax that would hit hardest at the wealthy. He called his program the "People's Budget."

The People's Budget easily passed in the House of Commons, but the House of Lords vetoed it. The House of Lords seldom opposed the Commons, but many lords were wealthy landowners who stood to lose money from Lloyd George's new taxes.

Lloyd George and the Liberals turned the budget issue into a question on the place of the House of Lords in British government. The Liberal party wanted to limit the powers of the House of Lords. Liberals won the next two elections, but still the lords refused to accept reforms. Finally, the king threatened to name enough new, reform-minded lords to pass the changes that the Commons demanded. The threat was enough. Rather than accept dozens of new members, the House of Lords voted to limit its own powers.

Henceforth, the House of Lords could only *delay* bills passed by the House of Commons. After two years, such bills became law whether or not the Lords approved of them. Britain had taken one more step toward a fully democratic form of government.

■ RESEARCH

Refer students to "Easter 1916" by William Butler Yeats and encourage them to research the meaning of the poem by studying the Easter Rebellion of 1916 in Ireland.

■ DISCUSSION

How did Lloyd George's program of social improvement differ from Bismarck's?

Queen Victoria (center front) was called "the grandmother of Europe." Her many children married into royal families all over the continent. Here she is surrounded by her royal relatives. At left are her grandson, Kaiser William II (seated), Britain's future George V (in black hat), and Victoria's son, soon to be Edward VII (in light coat).

609

■ BACKGROUND

In 1900, a person of the English upper class, for example, made 2,000 times as much money per year as an English coal miner. Help students understand this gap by having them research the average annual wage of a coal miner and multiply by 2,000.

In Vienna at the turn of the century, all the most fashionable people could be seen walking or driving along the Ringstrasse ("ring street").

Social divisions marked life in "the beautiful era."

Despite the growth of democracy in some countries, by 1900, both Europe and the United States had a tiny but fabulously wealthy upper class. Its members seemed, in the words of one French writer, "to live upon a golden cloud, spending their riches as indolently [lazily] and naturally as the leaves grow green."

For the wealthy, the years around 1900 were *la belle époque* (the beautiful era). Ladies and gentlemen of the upper class lived surrounded by servants. They maintained several homes, some in town and some in the country. All of Europe was their playground. In March, the wealthy went to the French seaside resort of Biarritz. In April, they visited the yearly exhibition of the French art society in Paris. In June, they flocked to the English Derby at Epsom Downs. The summer months found them at mountain spas such as Germany's Marienbad. In the fall, they went hunting at splendid country estates.

Only 1 or 2 percent of the European population belonged to the upper class. About 25 to 35 percent were members of the middle class. The middle class, as we have seen, had been growing since the Middle Ages and included a wide range of people—merchants, shopkeepers, doctors,

610

lawyers, teachers, and government employees. Industrialization created new middle-class positions—factory supervisors, sales representatives, and thousands of office workers. Middle-class families had enough money to buy such labor-saving gadgets as washing and sewing machines and to take summer vacations. Many middle-class families built comfortable houses in the fast-growing neighborhoods just outside the city. With the coming of electric streetcars, middle-class people began to live outside the city and commute to work each day. Some even bought Henry Ford's new Model T's.

The urban lower class, as well as the peasantry in eastern Europe, still lived on the edge of poverty. Despite major medical advances during the 1800's, tuberculosis and other deadly diseases were still a menace in slums and tenements from Moscow to Chicago.

As the representative of the workers, trade unions were growing stronger. Although strikes were not always successful, workers sometimes won higher wages and better working conditions. In 1889, for example, Ben Tillett led a walkout of 10,000 London dockworkers. For a month, no cargoes were loaded or unloaded. Then the shipowners agreed to pay the dockworkers higher wages and cut the work week from 55 to 48 hours.

ANSWERS TO

Section Review 5

Define:
(a) body of law-makers elected directly (b) accident and sickness insurance and old-age pensions (c) self-government (d) person who believes governments are
(continued)

Despite such gains, some radicals still believed that only a revolution would improve the lives of the working class. One group of revolutionaries called themselves **anarchists.** Anarchists believed that all governments were evil and should be overthrown. These radicals committed a number of assassinations around the turn of the century, including that of the czar of Russia in 1881, the French president in 1894, the king of Italy in 1900, and President William McKinley of the United States in 1901. However, the number of anarchists and revolutionary socialists remained very small in every country.

Crises shook Europe's fragile peace.

In different ways, Britain and Germany had both achieved stability by 1900. France too was fairly stable under the Third Republic (page 559). For the countries in the heartland of Europe, the age of nation building was over.

Around the edges of Europe, nationalism was still a deeply troubling issue. Ireland was one example. Norway was another. Norwegians finally won their independence from Sweden in 1905. The greatest conflicts over nationalism, however, were arising in eastern Europe.

Austria-Hungary, Russia, and the Ottoman empire were all multinational empires. All three lagged behind western Europe industrially and militarily. (The once powerful Ottoman empire was now so weak that it was known as "the sick man of Europe.") All three included peoples who wanted their own nations.

Ethnic minorities in these empires faced the risk of persecution. Bulgarians were massacred by their Ottoman rulers in the 1870's. In 1895, Ottoman ruler Abdul Hamid II turned on the Armenian minority in his empire, beginning a series of massacres that eventually took more than 1 million lives. Jews in Russia lived under the threat of **pogroms,** mob attacks in which many were killed and still more had their homes and businesses destroyed.

The most complex national conflicts arose on the Balkan Peninsula. There, Serbs, Bosnians, Montenegrins, Croats, Slovenes, Albanians, Bulgarians, and Romanians all hoped to build their own countries. Many of these groups spoke Slavic languages, but they maintained their separate identities.

Between 1900 and 1914, repeated uprisings and crises in the Balkans threatened both Austria-Hungary and the Ottoman empire. Russia saw itself as protector of all the Slavic peoples and often encouraged the nationalism of Slavic groups in the Balkans. In this role, Russia was a constant threat to Austria-Hungary.

Crises also arose in western Europe. France was still bitter about the loss of Alsace and Lorraine (page 559). In 1911, France and Germany came to the brink of war when a German gunboat threatened Morocco, a French colony in Africa.

War in the Balkans, hostility along the Rhine, saber rattling in North Africa—all made peace difficult to keep. Yet a strange optimism grew in Europe. As each crisis was solved without a general war, people began to think that war had been banished forever.

Section REVIEW 5

Define: (a) lower house, (b) social insurance, (c) home rule, (d) anarchist, (e) pogrom
Identify: (a) Reichstag, (b) Bundesrat, (c) William II, (d) David Lloyd George
Answer:
1. How did wider voting rights affect political parties and their leaders?
2. Why was Germany not a true democracy?
3. (a) What programs did Bismarck enact as his policy of state socialism? (b) What were his reasons for doing so?
4. (a) What was "the Irish question"? (b) How did the political situation in Ireland change between 1870 and 1900?
5. How did Britain's House of Lords lose its last political powers?
6. (a) What European countries were still multinational empires? (b) What groups were still frustrated in hopes for nations of their own?
7. How did each of the following create crises in this era? (a) Slavic nationalism (b) hostility between France and Germany (c) anarchists

Critical Thinking

8. Both Bismarck and Lloyd George passed social welfare programs. Did their actions reflect the same political philosophies? Explain.
9. (a) How is the phrase *la belle epoque* a good description of this era in Europe? (b) In what ways is the phrase a poor description?

611

ANSWERS TO (continued)
evil and should be overthrown (e) mob attack against Jews in Russia
Identify:
(a) lower house of German parliament (b) upper house of German parliament
(c) forced Bismarck to resign
(d) developed "People's Budget"
Answer:
1. Parties needed tighter organization; leaders had to "communicate" to appeal to voters.
2. Chancellor still had complete control.
3. (a) insurance to help workers in case of accident, old age pensions (b) to prevent revolution, to take support from socialists
4. (a) whether Great Britain or Ireland should rule Ireland (b) At first both Catholics and Protestants supported home rule, but later the Protestants opposed it.
5. House voted to limit own powers.
6. (a) Austria-Hungary, Russia, Ottoman empire (b) Serbs, Bosnians, Montenegrins, Croats, Slovenes, Albanians, Bulgarians, and Romanians
7. (a) uprisings supported by Russia against Austria-Hungary (b) German gunboat threatened French colony of Morocco. (c) assassinations
8. Bismarck's motives were to prevent revolution, so his actions reflected a political philosophy of near-dictatorship; Lloyd George seemed genuinely interested in expanding democracy.
9. (a) It accurately describes life-style of the few. (b) fails to describe widespread poverty

Concluding the Chapter

1. **Chapter Closer**
   Ask students to imagine that they are photographers at the turn of the century. The assignment is to create a photo-essay of the times. Have students describe five scenes or events they would photograph.

2. **Reteaching Activities**
   a. Summarizing Ask students to name five turn-of-the-century inventions and explain why each was important.
   b. Listing Goals Ask students to list three goals of the nineteenth-century women's rights movement.

Answers to Chapter Review appear on page 592f.

Summary

1. Inventions changed ways of life. Between 1870 and 1914, numerous practical inventions made people's lives more comfortable. Bessemer's blast furnace brought on the Age of Steel. Thomas Edison invented new uses for electricity. The telephone, radio, and combustion engine transformed transportation and communication. Ford's assembly line established the modern manufacturing process.

2. Science presented new ideas. New standards of cleanliness, the introduction of pasteurization, and the widespread use of inoculation decreased the number of deaths from disease. Darwin proposed the theory of evolution to explain the variety of living things. Later, a number of thinkers applied his ideas to economics and politics. The development of genetics and theories about the composition of elements led to advances in biology and chemistry.

3. Women sought rights and freedoms. Although by the late 1800's more women worked outside the home, they still faced economic and political restrictions. Many women in the United States and Britain believed that the right to vote would improve their status. Although women used a variety of tactics to call attention to their cause, they achieved only limited success by 1914.

4. Art and entertainment took new forms. The spread of public education, improved communications, and more leisure time helped create mass culture in the late 1800's. Sports and movies became especially popular. Painting styles shifted from realism to increasingly abstract forms, and composers experimented with new harmonies and rhythms.

5. Europe faced rising tensions. By 1900, the views of ordinary people were impacting society. Democratic rights expanded in Britain when the House of Lords lost its last political power. However, the controversy over Irish home rule divided British voters and produced rising tensions. In the early 1900's, democracy in Germany was severely limited, although Bismarck's state socialism recognized increasing public interests in politics. In eastern Europe, independence movements among persecuted minorities caused rising tensions.

Reviewing the Facts

1. Define the following terms:
   a. evolution   b. anarchist
2. Explain the importance of each of the following names or terms:
   a. blast furnace   c. Bell
   b. Edison   d. Marconi

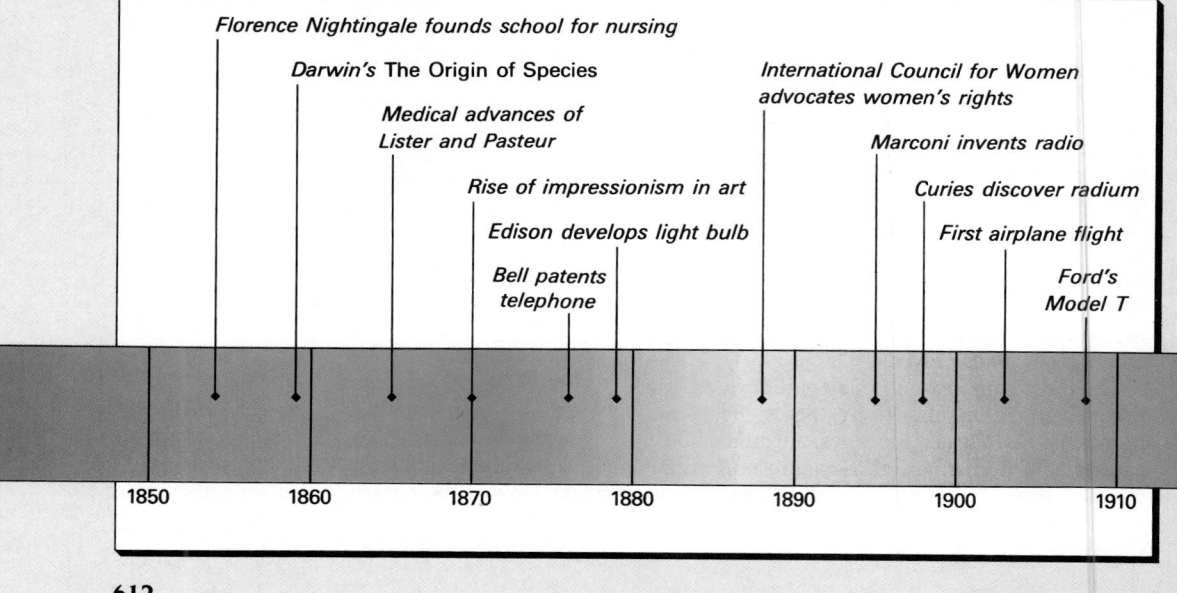

Florence Nightingale founds school for nursing

Darwin's The Origin of Species

Medical advances of Lister and Pasteur

Rise of impressionism in art

Edison develops light bulb

Bell patents telephone

International Council for Women advocates women's rights

Marconi invents radio

Curies discover radium

First airplane flight

Ford's Model T

| 1850 | 1860 | 1870 | 1880 | 1890 | 1900 | 1910 |

e. Wright brothers   i. expressionism
f. anesthesia   j. Bismarck
g. pasteurization   k. Lloyd George
h. impressionism   l. pogrom

3. (a) What metal largely replaced iron in the late 1800's? (b) What new source of energy came into use?
4. (a) How was Darwin's theory of evolution received? (b) Describe two ideas that were derived from it.
5. What contributions did each of the following scientists make? (a) Mendeleev (b) Dalton (c) Marie Curie (d) Rutherford
6. What steps did women take to win wider rights?
7. (a) What was the Irish question? (b) Describe the status of the Irish question in 1914.
8. How did the power of Britain's House of Lords decline?
9. (a) What issues threatened peace in eastern Europe? (b) What conflict threatened peace in western Europe?

Basic Skills

Reading and interpreting a table   Study the table below. Then answer the questions that follow. (a) Which of the countries shown steadily increased their relative share of world manufacturing output? (b) Which countries suffered a steady decline in relative share? (c) Which countries met both increase and decline in their relative shares? (d) What reasons can you find for the changes in each group of countries?

Relative Shares of World Manufacturing Output, 1880–1938 (percent)

	1880	1900	1913
Britain	22.9	18.5	13.6
United States	14.7	23.6	32.0
Germany	8.5	13.2	14.8
France	7.8	6.8	6.1
Russia	7.6	8.8	8.2
Austria-Hungary	4.4	4.7	4.4

Source: P. Kennedy, *The Rise and Fall of the Great Powers*, page 202.

Researching and Reporting Skills

The Research Paper

1. **Making an oral presentation**   In preparation for presenting your research paper orally to the class, review your paper and its outline. Use index cards to take notes on the main points and supporting ideas you wish to include. Assemble any visuals that may help your presentation. Practice making the presentation, using only the cards and visuals. Time yourself and trim your presentation to fit the time allotted. When you have made your presentation, invite discussion. Revise your paper to include suggestions from the discussion that may improve it.

2. **Giving feedback to others on their oral presentations**   As others take turns presenting their papers, listen and make constructive suggestions about their presentation, arguments, and thesis.

Critical Thinking

1. **Evaluating**   (a) Make two lists—one for the problems women faced at the turn of the century and another for the progress they made. (b) In terms of the problems, how much progress was actually made?
2. **Comparing and contrasting**   Both Britain and Germany had famous prime ministers in the late 1800's. How did the position of prime minister differ in Britain and Germany? Give examples to illustrate your answer.
3. **Applying a concept**   The 1900's saw the beginnings of mass culture. (a) Explain what this term means. (b) What technological and social changes favored it? (c) What effects did it have on social and political life?
4. **Inferring**   (a) What social welfare programs did Bismarck introduce in Germany? (b) What was his objective? (c) What difference did Bismarck's programs make to the people of Germany?

Perspectives on Past and Present

1. (a) What broad political, economic, and social issues remained unresolved at the turn of the last century? (b) What great issues are likely to remain unresolved at the turn of this century?
2. Fellow scientists were greatly impressed by the Curies' discoveries. What applications of those discoveries affect the world today?

Investigating History

Reference is made on page 611 to the persecution and massacre of certain ethnic groups. Read about one of those groups and write several paragraphs discussing whether the incidents might have been cases of genocide.

613

CHAPTER
Evaluation

Chapter Test 26, Alternate Chapter Test 26, and Computer Test Bank Chapter 26 Test can be used to evaluate your students' understanding of this chapter.

ANSWERS TO
Geographic Theme

1. by increasing need for resources and raw materials and amount of goods to be sold

2. the increased demand for cotton in the English textile mills

3. Spanish America, Europe, East Indies

4. The flow of resources and raw materials and of manufactured goods to and from all parts of the world is an example of movement. It illustrates the economic interaction between countries distant from each other.

Geographic Theme: Movement

When did a global economy begin?

The century after the voyages of Columbus and Da Gama brought enormous wealth to Spain and Portugal from their trade and colonies overseas. England lagged in exploration, although its development of the joint-stock company provided an economic resource for the future.

Under the mercantilist policies of the 1600's and 1700's, European nations competed for lands and trade. Out of a series of wars that ended with the defeat of France in 1763, Britain emerged with the lion's share. Not only the lands of Canada and India but also the oceans became spheres of British power. Although the American Revolution caused a brief setback, it was offset for Britain by the voyages of Captain James Cook, which opened the Pacific to British enterprise. In 1787, the first British settlers reached Australia.

While Britain's political power was expanding around the globe, the Industrial Revolution was taking place at home. The first breakthroughs in manufacturing came in the cotton textile industry. Hungry spindles and looms in Britain devoured huge quantities of raw cotton bought from the United States. That same cotton was shipped to markets around the world as cloth. By 1840, a world economy was in a sense being woven together out of cotton thread.

Three graphs demonstrate the enormous growth of the cotton trade in the early nineteenth century. The graph on page 515 in your text shows the rise in British consumption of cotton to 1840. The two graphs shown below indicate how much raw cotton was produced in the United States and how many British-made cotton goods were sold overseas. A global economy, led by Britain, had begun.

1. How did the Industrial Revolution hasten the growth of a global economy?

2. What do you think accounts for the great increase in cotton production in the United States between 1800 and 1840?

3. What three regions of the world bought the greatest amount of British exports of cotton goods in 1840?

4. How does the cotton trade illustrate the geographic theme of movement?

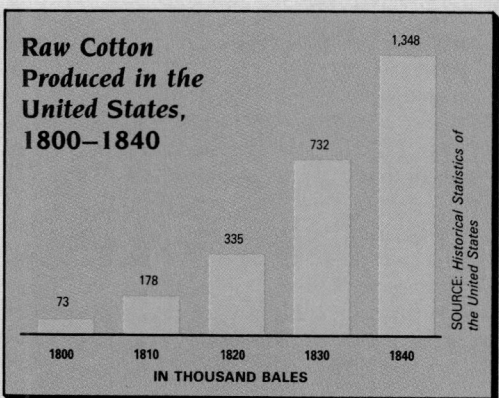

Raw Cotton Produced in the United States, 1800–1840

- 1800: 73
- 1810: 178
- 1820: 335
- 1830: 732
- 1840: 1,348

IN THOUSAND BALES

SOURCE: *Historical Statistics of the United States*

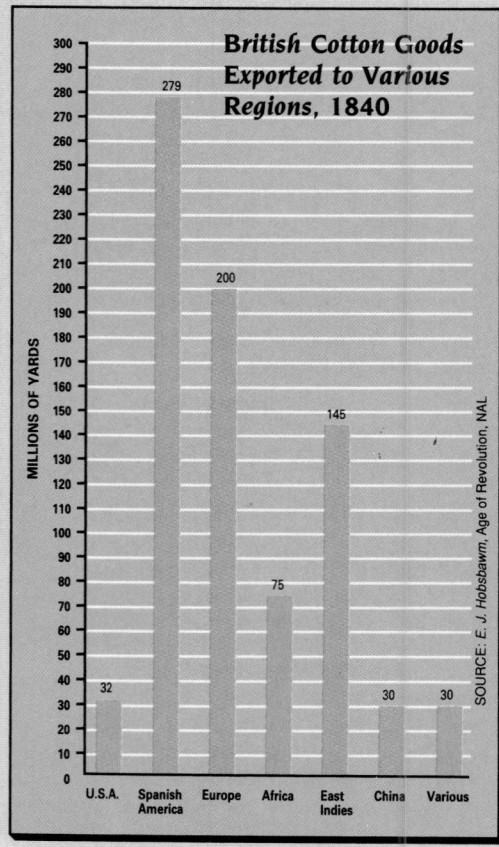

British Cotton Goods Exported to Various Regions, 1840

MILLIONS OF YARDS

- U.S.A.: 32
- Spanish America: 279
- Europe: 200
- Africa: 75
- East Indies: 145
- China: 30
- Various: 30

SOURCE: *E. J. Hobsbawm, Age of Revolution, NAL*

Historical Themes

New technologies, ideas, and economic developments caused a series of far-reaching changes in nineteenth-century Europe.

Technology and History

New inventions such as the spinning jenny, power loom, and steam engine created a revolution in manufacturing and transportation. The Industrial Revolution, which began in Britain, changed the way that people lived, worked, and thought. New cities sprang up as centers for manufacturing. Railroads quickly became a network providing the resources and markets on which the cities depended.

In the late 1800's, a second phase of the Industrial Revolution—this time with inventions based on electric power and the gasoline engine—set the stage for the twentieth century.

Impact of Ideas

The idea of nationalism found expression in a variety of ways. The subject peoples of Latin America and the Austro-Hungarian empire sought freedom under their own governments. In Italy and Germany, nationalism led to unification. In the hands of a political leader like Bismarck, nationalism became a tool for achieving political and military objectives. Overseas the idea of imperialism became an extension of nationalism, with nations competing for colonies.

Other ideas also affected life in the 1800's. The terms *liberal, conservative,* and *radical* showed the range of the political spectrum. Ideas of reform, rights, and suffrage set new goals for government and society. Realism portrayed the lives of ordinary people, while socialism sought ways to ease the plight of the poor. Marx's scientific socialism was an extreme answer to the problem of the distribution of wealth.

Continuity and Change

Throughout the 1800's, periods of political stability alternated with periods of change. The Congress of Vienna sought in 1815 to restore the Old Regime. In France, a period of conservative rule gave way in 1830 to a new king and more liberal policies. The revolution of 1848 led shortly to the start of an empire, while the end of the empire in 1871

led within a few years to a republic.

Britain underwent a series of reforms, starting with the Reform Act of 1832. From a very conservative government in 1815, it moved in a more liberal direction, which in the end set limits on the power of the House of Lords. Germany, by contrast, remained consistently conservative. Military power enabled it to achieve unification. Political authority was centralized in the kaiser and his chancellor rather than resting with the legislature, as in Britain.

Finally, the balance of power was a factor in continuity and change. Although it provided stability for most of the 1800's, the rise of Germany threatened to upset the balance after 1900.

Economics and History

The Industrial Revolution led to a new economic era. The mass production of goods created the need for resources and raw materials and for markets where goods could be sold. Advances in transportation and communication created vast networks that aided the growth of trade. For the first time, a truly global economy existed. Modern technology and improved transport enabled industrialized nations to dominate that economy.

Analyzing Historical Themes

1. (a) What were three major effects of the changes in technology in the 1800's? (b) Which do you think was most important and why?
2. Which do you think was more important to European politics in the 1800's, continuity or change? Why?
3. It has been said that nationalism in the 1800's was a two-edged sword. (a) What were its positive attainments? (b) Its negative effects?
4. (a) What were the main causes of economic growth in the 1800's? (b) Of political expansion overseas?

615

ANSWERS TO
Analyzing Historical Themes

1. **(a)** revolution in manufacturing and transportation; changes in way people lived, worked, and thought; growth of new cities as centers for manufacturing **(b)** Answers will vary.
2. Answers will vary but should take a point of view and support it with facts as evidence.
3. **(a)** encouraged people to seek freedom and unification, used as tool for political and military objectives **(b)** led to competition for power in Europe and rivalry for colonies overseas
4. **(a)** Industrial Revolution, mass production, advances in transportation and communication **(b)** Growth of large-scale businesses and corporations together with advances in transportation and communication fostered global economy.

UNIT
Evaluation

Unit VII Test and Alternate Unit VII Test can be used to evaluate your students' understanding of this unit.

Chapters

Nazi military parade in Berlin

	1880	**1893**	**1906**
Political and Governmental Life	**1880's–1914** Triple Alliance and Triple Entente divide Europe	**1890–1914** Kaiser William II seeks to expand German power	**1914** World War I begins in Europe **1910** Revolution rages in Mexico
Economic and Technological Life	*Age of steam and steel*	**1898** Marie Curie discovers radioactivity 	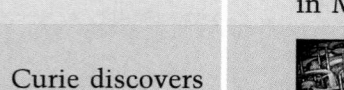 *Detail from mural by Siqueiros, Chapultepec Palace*
Social and Cultural Life	**1882** Electricity lights New York streets **1880's** Women organize for legal and political rights	*Nijinsky of the Russian Ballet*	**1914–1947** Gandhi protests against British rule in India

Unit VIII
Years of Crisis

Historical Themes

The Impact of Ideas Many new ideas arose to change the course of twentieth-century history. In Russia, Communist ideas led to revolution. In Italy and Germany, fascism led to totalitarianism.

Economics and History The Great Depression led to a worldwide economic crisis marked by unemployment, hunger, declines in business and trade, and terrible uncertainty.

Cooperation and Conflict Two world wars—one caused by a break in the balance of power and the other by fascist aggression—dominated this era. Nations sought ways to end aggression and resolve conflict.

Individuals and History Individuals who influenced this era included the dictators Stalin and Hitler and the democratic leaders Wilson, Churchill, and Roosevelt.

1919 **1932** **1945**

1917
Lenin leads Russian Revolution ▼

1933
Hitler comes to power

1936–1939
Civil war in Spain

1945
The war
is over ▶

1929
Stock market crash
begins depression

Battle of Britain

1945
Atom bombs destroy
Hiroshima and Nagasaki

1928
Stalin launches
Five-Year Plan

1939
World War II begins in Europe

*Flappers portray
the 1920's*

1935
Nuremberg Laws take
citizenship away from
German Jews

1945
United Nations
is founded ▼

617

The World about 1900

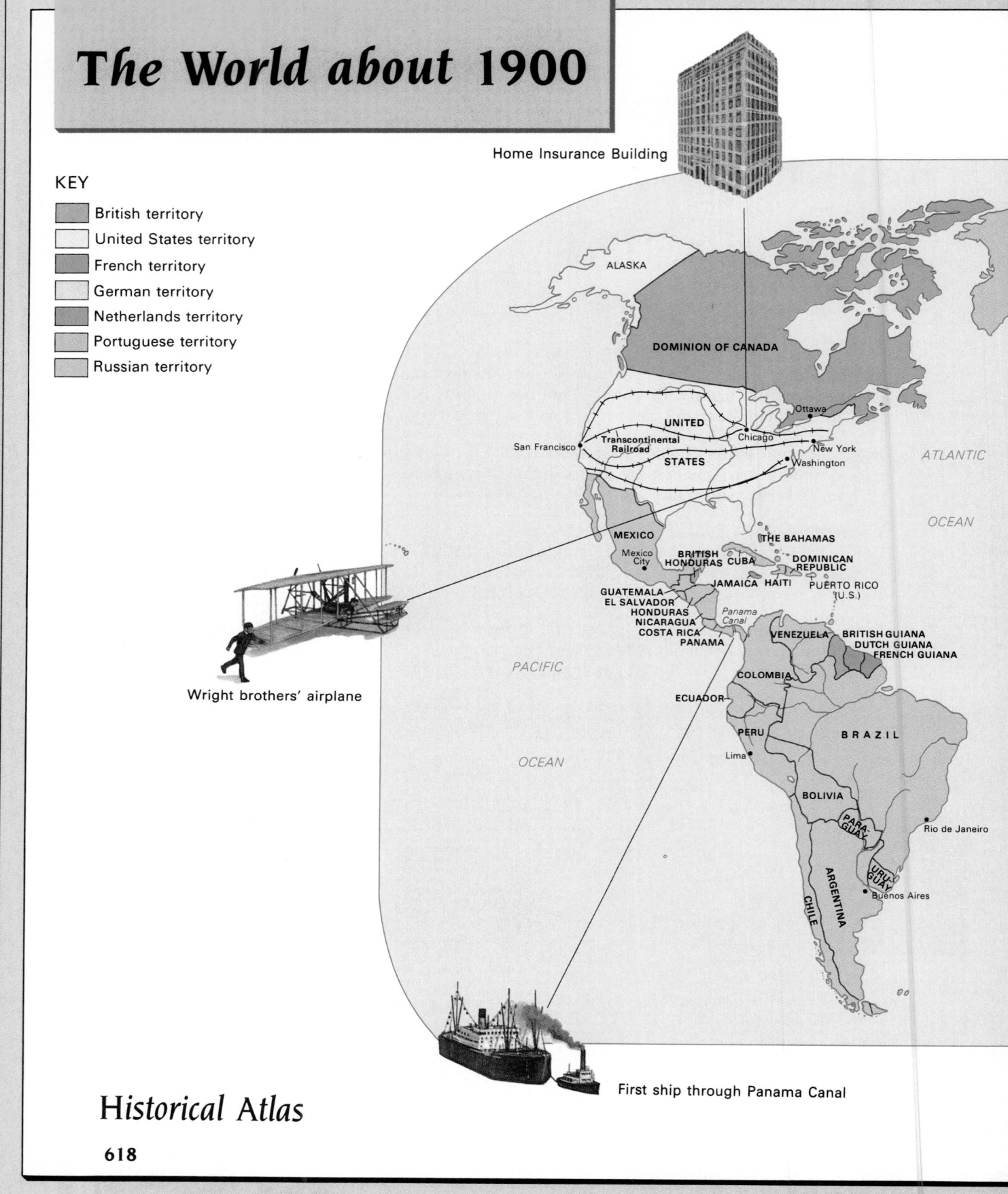

Home Insurance Building

Wright brothers' airplane

First ship through Panama Canal

KEY

- British territory
- United States territory
- French territory
- German territory
- Netherlands territory
- Portuguese territory
- Russian territory

ALASKA

DOMINION OF CANADA

Ottawa

UNITED

Transcontinental Railroad

San Francisco

Chicago

New York

STATES

Washington

ATLANTIC

OCEAN

MEXICO

Mexico City

THE BAHAMAS

BRITISH HONDURAS

CUBA

DOMINICAN REPUBLIC

JAMAICA HAITI

PUERTO RICO (U.S.)

GUATEMALA
EL SALVADOR
HONDURAS
NICARAGUA
COSTA RICA
PANAMA

Panama Canal

VENEZUELA

BRITISH GUIANA
DUTCH GUIANA
FRENCH GUIANA

COLOMBIA

ECUADOR

PACIFIC

PERU

Lima

BRAZIL

OCEAN

BOLIVIA

PARA-GUAY

Rio de Janeiro

ARGENTINA

URU-GUAY

CHILE

Buenos Aires

Historical Atlas

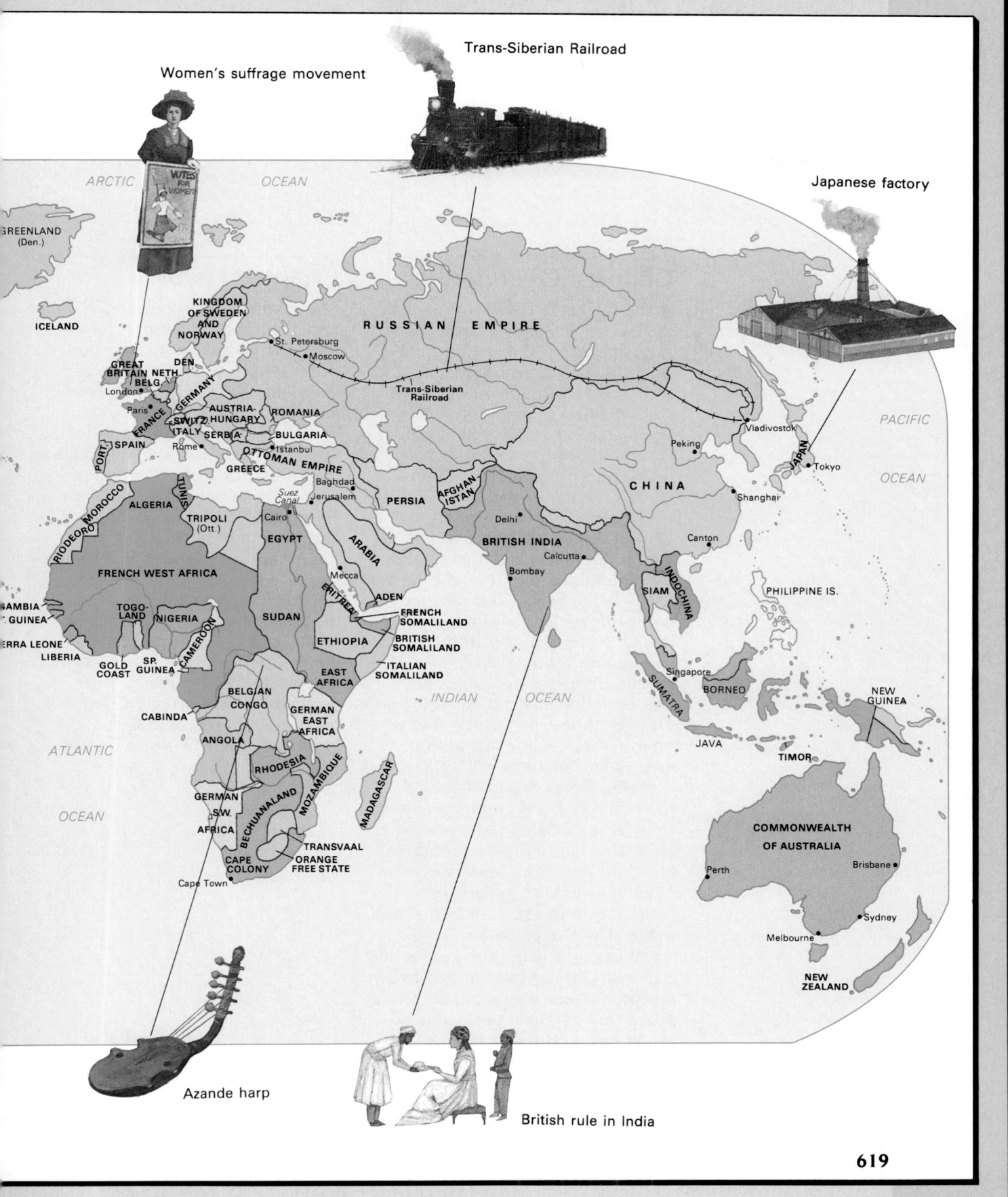

Women's suffrage movement

Trans-Siberian Railroad

Japanese factory

GREENLAND
(Den.)

ICELAND

ARCTIC   OCEAN

KINGDOM
OF SWEDEN
AND
NORWAY

RUSSIAN   EMPIRE

St. Petersburg

Moscow

GREAT
BRITAIN NETH.
BELG.
London

DEN.

Trans-Siberian
Railroad

FRANCE
GERMANY
SWITZ.

AUSTRIA-
HUNGARY

ROMANIA

ITALY

SERBIA

BULGARIA

PACIFIC

Vladivostok

Peking

JAPAN

PORT.

SPAIN

Rome

GREECE

OTTOMAN EMPIRE

Istanbul

Baghdad

CHINA

Shanghai

Tokyo

OCEAN

RIO DE ORO

MOROCCO

ALGERIA

TUNIS

TRIPOLI
(Ott.)

Suez
Canal

Jerusalem

Cairo

PERSIA

AFGHAN-
ISTAN

Delhi

Canton

EGYPT

ARABIA

BRITISH INDIA

FRENCH WEST AFRICA

Mecca

ERITREA

ADEN

FRENCH
SOMALILAND

Calcutta

Bombay

SIAM

INDOCHINA

PHILIPPINE IS.

GAMBIA
. GUINEA

TOGO-
LAND

NIGERIA

SUDAN

BRITISH
SOMALILAND

ERRA LEONE

LIBERIA

GOLD
COAST

SP.
GUINEA

CAMEROON

ETHIOPIA

ITALIAN
SOMALILAND

SUMATRA

Singapore

BORNEO

NEW
GUINEA

BELGIAN
CONGO

EAST
AFRICA

INDIAN   OCEAN

JAVA

TIMOR

CABINDA

GERMAN
EAST
AFRICA

ATLANTIC

ANGOLA

RHODESIA

MOZAMBIQUE

MADAGASCAR

COMMONWEALTH
OF AUSTRALIA

OCEAN

GERMAN
S.W.
AFRICA

BECHUANALAND

Perth

Brisbane

CAPE
COLONY

TRANSVAAL

ORANGE
FREE STATE

Cape Town

Sydney

Melbourne

NEW
ZEALAND

Azande harp

British rule in India

619

World War I

Chapter Overview

Archduke Franz Ferdinand, heir to the Austro-Hungarian throne, was assassinated in Sarajevo on June 28, 1914. About a month later, Austria declared war on Serbia. A web of alliances among the Great Powers quickly drew virtually all of Europe into the war. Russia backed Serbia and brought France into the conflict as one of the Allies. Germany joined Austria, forming the Central Powers. Britain and Italy joined the Allies, and Turkey and Bulgaria joined the Central Powers.

The belligerents used new technology in warfare, and the war moved to several new fronts. A revolution in Russia led to that nation's withdrawal from the war. The United States and Japan joined the war on the side of the Allies. An armistice ending World War I was signed November 9, 1918.

United States President Woodrow Wilson issued Fourteen Points to try to establish a lasting peace, but France and Britain were eager for vengeance. The leaders of the Allied Powers met in Paris in January 1919 to establish terms for peace. The United States Congress voted against joining the League of Nations. Germany was forced to accept harsh peace terms. The peace treaty's harsh terms for the losing side nurtured a lasting bitterness.

Chapter Focus

Ask students what they know about the assassination of John F. Kennedy in 1963. Why didn't this event lead to war? Remind students that Kennedy's assassin was an American and that, as far as anyone knew, no foreign power was involved. After students read pages 620–621, ask, "Where was Bosnia? Who was Archduke Franz Ferdinand? Who was Gavrilo Princip? Why did Princip assassinate the Archduke?" Explain that Princip, as a Bosnian Serb, was an Austro-Hungarian subject. Thus the assassination, like Kennedy's, might have been treated as a purely internal matter. Instead, it precipitated World War I. The deaths of Ferdinand and Princip set off one of the bloodiest and most catastrophic wars in history.

Conflicts divided Europe. 1

Setting the Stage

Have students imagine that they are advisers to the Austrian Emperor, Franz Josef. His nephew, Archduke Franz Ferdinand, has just been assassinated. The assassin, Princip, belonged to the Black Hand, a terrorist group based in Serbia. They suspect that the Black Hand is supported by leading members of the Serbian government and army. Ask, "What would you advise the Emperor to do?" After discussing student responses, conclude by explaining that Austria-Hungary decided to punish Serbia.

Teaching Strategies

Discussing History: The Naval Arms Race (Objective 1) Begin by pointing out that until 1904, Britain, unlike the other Great Powers, did not seek allies. Have the students look at the map of Europe on page 623 or show Map Transparency 82, *Europe before World War I.* Emphasize Britain's geographic isolation from the continent. For two centuries, the British navy was without any serious rival. Ask why sea power was considered so essential by this island nation. Note that Britain had only a small standing army and no conscription.

Point out that Kaiser William II began a massive warship-building program in 1898. Ask students what Britain's response would have been. You might write on the board the following figures for naval expenditures: Germany, 7 million pounds in 1900 and 23 million in 1914; Great Britain, 26 million pounds in 1900 and 45 million in 1914. In addition to increasing naval spending, Britain began to look for allies against the German threat.

Analyzing a Quotation: The Warlike Mood (Objective 2) Have students read "A warlike mood spread in Europe" (page 624). Then read or distribute the "Hymn of Hate," a poem that was chanted by the pre-war German navy as a toast to victory over Britain:

> We will never forgo our hate.
> Hate by water and hate by land.
> Hate of the head and hate of
>   the hand.
> Hate of the hammer and hate of
>   the Crown.
> Hate of the seventy millions
>   choking down.
> We love as one, we hate as
>   one.
> We have one foe and one
>   alone:
>   England!

After students have read the poem, ask why the German navy regarded England as its main enemy. If students were English, how would they feel about this poem?

Check for Understanding Ask students to name members of the Triple Alliance and Triple Entente.

Enrichment Activities

1. **Reading a Primary Source**
   Assign Voices from the Past
   Resource Book 27.1.

2. **Researching for Bonus Points**
   What was the name given to
   the 1904 treaty between France
   and Great Britain? (The Entente
   Cordiale)

Europe plunged into war. 2

Setting the Stage

Kaiser William II and his government took a big gamble in August 1914. After the assassination of Franz Ferdinand, Austria decided to attack Serbia; but before doing so, Austria asked Germany for a promise of support. The Kaiser gave his promise. He hoped that the war would be limited to Austria and Serbia, but he knew that there was a good chance Russia would come to Serbia's aid and that France would come to Russia's aid. It was an enormous risk.

Teaching Strategies

Skill Building: Analyzing Austria's Options (Objective 1) Review the time and place of the assassination of the Archduke Franz Ferdinand and the motive for the murder. Ask students what country they think Austria blamed.

Identify the following actions Austria could have taken, and ask students to suggest what reactions each could have provoked.

1. Austria could have ignored Serbia and said the murder was the work of independent terrorists.

2. Austria could have sent an army to wipe out the Serbian underground in Bosnia.

3. Austria could have demanded that Serbia find those who were in on the plot and try them.

4. Austria could have issued an ultimatum to Serbia with extreme terms that would have been difficult for Serbia to accept. This could have been used as an excuse for war against Serbia.

Ask the students which of these actions (or any others they can think of) would have been the best course for Austria to take. Then ask which action they think Austria took. (4)

Discussing History: England's Decision to Enter the War (Objective 2) Divide the class into groups of four or five students. Each group represents the British cabinet, meeting in early August 1914. Present the following information: Germany and Austria are at war with Russia and France. Britain has friendship treaties with Russia and France but has made no promise to help them in case of war with Germany. On the other hand, Germany has overrun Belgium, and if it goes on to defeat France, Germany will occupy almost the entire European coast facing England. Furthermore, if Germany defeats France, it will hurl its forces against Russia and will probably win on the Eastern Front as well. If that happened, Britain would have no allies in case of a future war with Germany. Ask, "What course of action would you recommend? Should Britain declare war on Germany and Austria, or should it take a neutral position, hoping for the victory of France and Russia?" Have each group discuss the issue and then come to a decision by vote. Conclude by noting that Germany was actually surprised by Britain's declaration of war. The British had assured the Germans of their neutrality during the whole July Crisis, and the Kaiser assumed they would stay out of the conflict. But after Germany went to war with France and invaded Belgium, Britain considered neutrality impossible.

Check for Understanding Ask students to explain why each of the Great Powers entered World War I.

Enrichment Activities

1. **Reading a Primary Source**
   Assign Voices from the Past
   Resource Book 27.2.

2. **Researching a Topic**
   Ask students to report on the events in Serbia after the Austrian declaration of war.

3. **Researching for Bonus Points**
   What was the name of France's secret military plan in case of war with Germany? (Plan XVII)

The war dragged on for four years. 3

Setting the Stage

Select a student to read aloud the excerpt from *All Quiet on the Western Front* (page 630). The conditions described in this passage were part of everyday life for soldiers on the Western Front, and this type of war dragged on for four years. In 1914, most Europeans expected the war to last for just a short time. Ask students how they would feel if they had marched off to war in 1914, with assurances of quick and glorious victory, only to find the reality of endless bombardments, mud, rats, and death.

Teaching Strategies

Economics and History: New Weapons (Objective 1) Review the importance of new technology in the Industrial Revolution. Remind students that industrial science was first used to invent and perfect machines that would produce more goods. Point out that in World War I, scientists were mobilized to perfect machines for killing people. The new mechanized tools of warfare were so powerful that the generals did not understand at first how effective they were. Have students read "World War I was an industrialized war" (pages 627–628). Ask them to name the new weapons, and list responses on the board. (machine guns, poison gas, tanks, airplanes, and submarines)

Discussing History: "Lafayette, We Are Here" (Objective 2) Have students read "The United States entered the war" and "The war came to an end" (pages 632–633). While the United States eventually helped the Allies win the war, America was at first unprepared for war. The United States army was only 200,000 strong and most of its weapons were obsolete. A small "expeditionary force" under General John J. Pershing was sent to France in June 1917, but its importance was more symbolic than real.

Describe the entrance of an American First Infantry battalion into Paris on July 4, 1917. The battalion marched up to the tomb of the Marquis de Lafayette, who had helped the Thirteen Colonies in North America to win their independence. Colonel Charles Stanton said "Lafayette, we are here." Ask students to imagine the effect this act had on French morale.

However, it was another year before the United States could mobilize an army of two million men, convert its massive industrial base to war production, and unleash its full might against the Germans. Use Map Transparency 83, *World War I in Europe*, to show troop movements and key battles of the war.

Check for Understanding Ask students to name five weapons first used in World War I and three changes in European life as a result of the war.

Enrichment Activities

1. **Reading a Primary Source**
   Assign Voices from the Past Resource Book 27.3.

2. **Researching for Bonus Points**
   What was the motto of the French troops at the Battle of Verdun? ("They shall not pass.")

Peace stood on shaky foundations. 4

Setting the Stage

Write "to the victor belong the spoils" on the board. Ask, "How many people agree with this statement? How many disagree?" Have students discuss the reasons for their answers.

Teaching Strategies

Discussing History: "Make Germany Pay" (Objective 1) Review Wilson's plans for world peace. Ask why his views were considered idealistic. Explain that both the French and the British had other plans. Clemenceau had two main objectives—to keep France strong and to keep Germany weak. France had been badly hurt in World War I. More than 300,000 houses had been destroyed, as well as thousands of bridges, factories, and schools; millions of farm animals; and 1.4 million French soldiers. In Clemenceau's view, France needed protection from Germany in case of another war.

Lloyd George favored treating Germany more leniently. However, in December 1918, British voters had returned his government to power with a mandate to "make Germany pay." Wrote young Winston Churchill at the time: "The Prime Minister and his colleagues were astonished by the passions they encountered. The brave people whom nothing had daunted had suffered too much. The crippled and mutilated soldiers darkened the streets. Every cottage had its empty chair. Hatred of the beaten foe, thirst for his just punishment, rushed up from the heart of deeply injured millions."

Discussing History: Decisions of the Big Three (Objective 2) The Big Three leaders faced a number of difficult problems. Divide the class into groups that include an American, British, and French delegate. Tell the groups that they must reach a decision on each of the following issues:

■ Should Germany admit full guilt for starting World War I?

■ What should be done with Germany's armed forces?

■ What should be done with Germany's overseas colonies?

■ What should happen in Alsace-Lorraine and the Rhineland?

■ Should Germany be forced to pay compensation for the cost of war? If so, how much?

Ask each group to prepare written answers to all five questions. Then have them share their decisions with the class. Compare the students' decisions with the decisions actually reached. Show Map Transparency 84, *Europe after World War I*. Have students identify changes created by the Treaty of Versailles

Check for Understanding Ask students to describe how the borders of Germany, Austria, Russia, and Italy changed after the war.

Enrichment Activities

1. **Reading a Primary Source** Assign Voices from the Past Resource Book 27.4.

2. **Researching a Topic** Ask advanced students to report on the effects of the war on Kaiser William II.

3. **Researching for Bonus Points** Who was the German Foreign Minister who signed the Treaty of Versailles? (Count Ulrich von Brockdorff-Rantzau)

ANSWERS TO Chapter Review 27

Reviewing the Facts

1. (a) glorification of armed strength (b) set of demands that, if not met, would end negotiations (c) to get an army positioned for war (d) policy of not supporting any side (e) system under which people could buy only small amounts of goods needed for the war effort (f) one-sided information that aims to convince people of a certain point of view (g) agreement to stop fighting (h) allowing people to decide for themselves under what government they wish to live (i) territory that was administered on behalf of the League of Nations (j) money to compensate for the costs of war

2. (a) Archduke of Austria-Hungary whose assassination set off World War I (b) German chancellor who attempted to protect German empire by isolating France (c) German kaiser who forced Bismarck to resign (d) weakened Turkish empire which Austria-Hungary saw as opportunity to extend its influence in the Balkans (e) plan whereby most of the German army would attack France in the west before Russia was mobilized in the east (f) first major clash on Western Front; stopped German advance and saved Paris (g) message that Germany would help Mexico regain United States land if Mexico would fight with Germany; brought United States into World War I (h) United States president whose Fourteen Points outlined a plan for lasting peace (i) Article 231 of Treaty of Versailles which placed sole blame for World War I on Germany

3. Europe was divided into two rival factions, and a dispute between any two powers would involve other countries. Slavic nationalism had kept Russia and Austria on the brink of war for years. The assassination of Archduke Ferdinand was the culmination of many years of tension and crises.

4. (a) great loss of life but not much gain by either side (b) more a war of movement, but stalemate was common

5. (a) Revolutionaries drove the czar from power. (b) Lacking supplies, the Russian army had felt betrayed by its leaders.

6. German U-boats sank three American ships, and Americans were angered over the contents of the Zimmermann telegram.

7. (a) restricted the size of the army, banned manufacturing of war material and submarines and airplanes, placement of troops in the Rhineland (b) Czechoslovakia

now included the border region formerly Germany's; 3 million Germans lived in the border region; anschluss (union) between Germany and Austria was forbidden.

8. (a) United States, Britain, France, Italy, and Japan were to be permanent members of the League of Nations Executive Council. There would also be a general assembly at which representatives of 42 Allied and neutral nations would meet. **(b)** Germany, Russia, and the United States **(c)** Germany and Russia were deliberately left out; United States Senate refused to join.

Basic Skills

1.

1878	1880	1890	1900	1910	1920
	Triple Alliance	Kaiser William II Leads Germany	British/French Treaty of Friendship	Triple Entente	
	Dual Alliance	Bismarck Treaty with Russia	Russian/French Alliance	Russia/Austria Conflict in Balkans	

2. (a)

Battles	Objectives	Main Events	Outcomes
Marne (1914)	Germany wanted to knock France out of war before Russia entered	Germany marching on Paris, Allies attack gap in German lines, Germans retreat	Schieffen Plan fails; quick victory in west impossible for Germany; two-front war
Verdun (1916)	Germans try to take Paris	300,000 die; British attack Germans at Somme	Stalemate; Germans advance four miles; British advance five miles
Marne (1918)	Defeat Allies before impact of American forces can be felt	German shock troops attack France; American troops begin to arrive	German army in disarray never to recover

(b) Possible answers: Students could say that 1914 Battle of Marne was turning point because it meant Germany would have to fight a two-front war. Students could point to 1918 Battle of Marne as collapse of German military.

Researching and Reporting Skills

Students' answers will vary.

Critical Thinking

1. Possible answer: World War I involved countries from all parts of the world. Outside of European nations the war also involved countries from North America (United States and Canada), Middle East (Ottoman Empire), Asia (Japan), and fighting in Africa (East Africa and Tanzania).

2. The Triple Alliance included Germany, Austria-Hungary, and Italy. The Triple Entente included Great Britain, France, and Russia. The Triple Alliance was formed by Germany as a way of isolating France, neutralizing it as a threat to Germany. Great Britain led in the formation of the Triple Entente to protect the three countries involved from German aggression.

3. (a) Bismarck's policies went through two very different stages. In the first he used the military and war as tools for unifying and strengthening Germany. It could be said that the Kaiser drew on that legacy when he rejected Bismarck's second-stage policy of peaceful coexistence. **(b)** Instead of keeping peaceful relations with Great Britain and Russia, the Kaiser let Bismarck's treaty with Russia lapse and directly challenged the dominance of the British navy and Britain's colonial empire. While Bismarck described Germany as a "satisifed power," Kaiser William was far from satisfied with Germany's status in the world community. He sought German dominance, while Bismarck was content with peaceful relations.

4. (a) ending secret treaties, freedom of seas, removing economic barriers to trade, reducing size of national armies and navies, and adjusting colonial claims with fairness toward the colonial peoples **(b)** For the most part, France's and Britain's goals were similar to Wilson's. The major difference was that France and Britain wanted Germany to pay reparations and demanded that Germany cede some of its lands and agree to sweeping military restrictions.

5. Possible answer: As an era of destruction and despair; as the era of a lost generation; as a time like the 1300's with terrible disasters.

6. (a) Possible answer: resolved problems—end secret treaties, freedom of seas, reducing size of military, League of Nations, and self-determination **(b)** war guilt clause, reparations, and sometimes self-determination. The positive factors tried to open the world to freedom of movement on the seas, an open market where one nation could not shut out others, and self-determination for nationalist groups. They also tried to reduce the threat of war by reducing the size of the military and by establishing the League of Nations. Finally the treaty helped ease tensions in some parts of the world by creating countries that represented the true desires of various minority groups. However, self-determination also had its negative impact. The treaty did not solve all minority problems and often created problems by the way it drew new national lines. Also the demand for reparations and the war guilt clause sowed the seeds of discontent that would eventually lead to the outbreak of World War II.

Perspectives on Past and Present

Students' answers will vary. Students should point to various organizations such as the United Nations, Organization of American States, International Court of Justice, etc.

Investigating History

Students' answers will vary.

Chapter 27

Teaching with Pictures

Ask students what is happening to the central characters in the picture. Encourage them to use vivid adjectives to describe the expressions on the characters' faces. Note that every single person in the picture is focused on the scene around the automobile. If this were a photo, how likely is it that *everyone* would have been watching the car? How does the attention of the crowd affect the impact of the picture on the reader?

Soon after the assassination at Sarajevo, readers of French newspapers saw this picture with a report of the event.

Key Terms

entente	propaganda
annex	convoy
militarism	abdicate
ultimatum	armistice
mobilize	mandate
neutrality	reparations
aggressor	
total war	
rationing	
self-determination	

620

Read and Understand

1. Conflicts divided Europe.
2. Europe plunged into war.
3. The war dragged on for four years.
4. Peace stood on shaky foundations.

June 28, 1914, was a hot, sultry day in Sarajevo (SAHR-uh-yeh-voh), capital of the Austrian province of Bosnia. Despite the heat, crowds had jammed the streets for hours. They were hoping to catch a glimpse of Archduke Franz Ferdinand, heir to the throne of Austria-Hungary. As nephew of the aged Emperor Franz Josef, Franz Ferdinand expected to rule Austria soon.

Not everyone in Sarajevo was pleased with this royal visit. Most Bosnians were Serbs, a Slavic people. Many wanted Bosnia to be part of Serbia, a neighboring Slavic country, instead of a province in the Austro-Hungarian empire. On this June morning, a handful of young

Chapter 27 Resources

GEOGRAPHY
- Geography Skills 27
- Transparencies 82, 83, 84

REINFORCEMENT
- Vocabulary 27
- Basic Skills 27
- Reteaching 27
- Making Connections Study Guide 27

ENRICHMENT
- Critical Thinking 27
- History and Literature 27

ASSESSMENT
- Chapter Test 27
- Alternate Chapter Test 27
- Computer Test Bank

Serbian nationalists were scattered among the crowds awaiting the archduke's arrival. They were determined to give Franz Ferdinand their own terrible greeting.

The royal train arrived in Sarajevo shortly before 10 A.M. An honor guard of Austrian troops stood at attention while the archduke and his wife, Sophie, got into the open car that would take them to the official welcoming ceremonies at the town hall. A six-car motorcade left the station, led by the mayor of Sarajevo. Franz Ferdinand and Sophie rode in the second car. The royal couple smiled and waved while people cheered and threw flowers to them.

One of the Serbian nationalists, however, threw something else—a bomb. As it hurtled through the air, Franz Ferdinand threw up his arm to protect himself and his wife. The bomb struck his upraised arm and bounced off, exploding in the street. The blast injured a dozen people and sent a dark cloud of smoke into the sky.

After a brief pause, the motorcade continued at top speed toward the town hall. Although unhurt, Franz Ferdinand was furious. "Mr. Mayor," barked the archduke after the party had arrived safely at the hall, "we come to visit you, and we are greeted with bombs! This is outrageous!"

Before any further ceremonies, Franz Ferdinand wanted to go to the hospital to visit those who had been hurt by the bomb blast. Sophie insisted on going with him.

It was just after 11:00 A.M. when the motorcade resumed. Once again, the archduke and his wife were in the second car, riding behind the mayor. Unfortunately, no one had told the mayor's chauffeur about the visit to the hospital. Holding to the original plan, he turned down a side street. "You've gone the wrong way!" screamed the mayor. The driver braked and began to back up. So did the archduke's chauffeur.

It was too late. Standing at this intersection, no more than two steps from the archduke, was Gavrilo Princip (**PREEN**-tseep). The slightly built young Serb was a member of the Black Hand, a secret society of Slavic extremists. Princip drew a small pistol and from point-blank range fired two shots. The first struck Sophie, and the second hit the archduke. Both died within minutes.

News of the assassination spread quickly across Europe. People everywhere were horrified, yet not really surprised. After all, there had been

Comparing pictures *The tone of this photo, taken before the assassination, contrasts with that of the engraving on page 620. How might photography as a medium change the reporting of events in the news?*

more than 40 assassinations of political leaders between 1900 and 1914.

Yet the assassination in Sarajevo was different from the others. It started a chain of events that, within five weeks, dragged almost all the countries of Europe into war. Two people died that June morning in Bosnia, but the terrible conflict that followed claimed the lives of more than 8 million soldiers and 6 million civilians.

In this chapter, we will look at both the immediate and the underlying causes of the war. Then we will see why neither side was able to win the quick victory that all leaders expected. Finally, we will see how the war left a bitter legacy for victors and vanquished alike.

Conflicts divided Europe.   1

How did the assassination of Franz Ferdinand trigger a world war? The answers are not simple. By itself, the murder of Franz Ferdinand could never have started such a vast conflict. However, tensions had been building in Europe for more than 50 years. Rivalry among the Great Powers—

621

SECTION 1
Resources

GEOGRAPHY
- Transparency 82

REINFORCEMENT
- Independent Practice 27.1

- Voices from the Past 27.1

ASSESSMENT
- Section Quiz 27.1

SECTION 1
Objectives and Teaching Strategies

OBJECTIVE 1. Analyze the arms race between the Great Powers.

Teaching Strategy: *Discussing History: The Naval Arms Race* (page 620b)

OBJECTIVE 2. Describe the growth of militarism in pre-war Europe.

Teaching Strategy: *Analyzing a Quotation: The Warlike Mood* (page 620c)

■ DISCUSSION

Photography resulted in a more realistic representation of the news than that shown in the overly sensational picture on page 620. Ask students if photography could, nonetheless, be used to bias a news report.

■ BACKGROUND

Princip was one of seven young men waiting to shoot the archduke in Sarajevo. All of them had tuberculosis. Princip died of the disease at 23 while in jail.

Emperor Franz Josef was admired throughout Austria-Hungary. Franz Ferdinand, however, was loved only by his wife and children. He was ill-tempered, miserly, and given to excess. For example, by the age of 46, he had shot 5,000 stags.

Kaiser William II is shown here in full regalia, with a crown, flags, and other symbols of his authority and power.

Austria-Hungary, Great Britain, Germany, France, Italy, and Russia—had led to crisis after crisis. The assassination at Sarajevo was merely the last step on the long road to war, a road down which Europe had been drifting for decades.

Bismarck shaped European alliances.

The conflict grew in part from a network of alliances going back to the 1870's. Ironically, these alliances had been designed to keep peace.

Between 1865 and 1871, Prussia's blood-and-iron chancellor, Otto von Bismarck, freely used war to unify Germany (page 557). After 1871, however, Bismarck turned to a policy of peace. Germany, he said, was a "satisfied power." Bismarck's new goal was to prevent war because war might shatter his newly created German empire. From 1871 to 1890, Bismarck worked to keep peace in Europe.

Bismarck saw France as the greatest threat to peace, because the French wanted revenge for their defeat in the Franco-Prussian War (page 559). Bismarck's first goal, therefore, was to isolate France. "As long as it is without allies," Bismarck stressed, "France poses no danger to us."

622

In 1879, Bismarck succeeded in partially isolating France by forming the Dual Alliance between Germany and Austria-Hungary. Three years later, these two countries were joined by Italy, making the Triple Alliance. In 1887, Bismarck took yet another possible ally away from France by making a treaty with Russia.

Bismarck's alliances were a fragile network. Germany had ties to both Austria-Hungary and Russia. Yet those two empires were locked in a struggle over the Balkans. Could Germany hold both its allies? And what part would Britain play? For the moment, the British seemed content to stand proudly alone. However, it was clear that a shift in the diplomatic winds might blow apart the web of treaties.

Shifting alliances threatened peace.

In 1890, Germany's foreign policy changed abruptly. In that year, Kaiser William II forced Bismarck to resign. Unlike his grandfather, who had let Bismarck rule Germany for more than 20 years, the new kaiser was determined to be his own master. A proud and stubborn man, William II was eager to show the world just how mighty Germany had become. The army was his greatest pride. "I and the army were born for each other," said William II at his coronation in 1888.

William II set Germany on a new course. Shortly after coming to power, he let the treaty of friendship between Russia and Germany lapse. The French were delighted. For years, France had been loaning Russia money for industrial development, hoping to earn the goodwill of the Russian government. The French reaped their reward in 1894 when Russia made an alliance with France.

According to the terms of the treaty, France and Russia promised to come to each other's aid if either was attacked by a third country. Such a treaty had been Bismarck's greatest fear. A war with either Russia or France would make Germany the enemy of both. Germany would then be forced to fight on both its eastern and western borders.

The impulsive kaiser made an even greater mistake in his dealings with Great Britain. Britain and Germany were economic rivals, but they had remained on fairly friendly terms during much of the 1800's. The kaiser himself was half English, as his mother was Queen Victoria's eldest daughter. Nevertheless, he held a lifelong grudge against Britain. He envied its worldwide empire and its mighty navy. The kaiser decided that Germany should challenge Britain. During the 1890's, Germany built its own small colonial empire, threatening British and French dominance. At the same time, William II started a tremendous ship-building program, planning to make the German navy equal to Britain's.

Alarmed, Great Britain began to enlarge its own fleet, joining Germany in a naval arms race. Moreover, the British government ended its policy of isolation and sought allies.

In 1904, Britain signed a treaty of friendship with France. In 1907, it signed a second treaty, this time with France and Russia. These treaties were **ententes,** or friendly understandings, rather than alliances. Although the Triple Entente did not bind Britain to fight alongside France and Russia, it did ensure that Britain would almost certainly not fight against them.

By 1907, two rival camps existed in Europe. On one side was the Triple Alliance—Germany, Austria-Hungary, and Italy. On the other side was the Triple Entente—Great Britain, France, and Russia. A dispute between any two powers could draw the entire continent into war.

The Balkans were a powder keg.

Nowhere was the situation more tense than on the Balkan Peninsula. With good reason, this area was called the powder keg of Europe. For nearly 100 years, many Balkan groups had been trying to free themselves from the Ottoman empire. As that empire weakened, several Balkan groups broke away. By the early 1900's, these breakaway groups had formed a half-dozen new nations—Albania, Bulgaria, Greece, Montenegro, Romania, and Serbia. Nationalism was a powerful force in all of these countries, each of which longed to extend its borders. For example, Serbia, which had a large Slavic population, hoped to absorb all the Slavs on the peninsula into its own nation.

Such nationalist movements threatened Austria-Hungary, which ruled many Slavic peoples. At the same time, Austria-Hungary saw the decline of the Ottoman empire as an opportunity to extend its own sphere of influence on the Balkan Peninsula.

Map Study

To which alliance system did Italy belong? France? Belgium?

While Austria felt threatened by nationalism in the Balkans, Russia was delighted. The Russians were Slavs, part of the same large language family as the Serbs, Bulgarians, and many other Balkan peoples. Russia encouraged these Slavic groups in their struggles for independence. By gaining influence in the region of the Balkans, Russia hoped to win access to the ports of the Mediterranean Sea.

Thus, Russia and Austria were on a collision course in the Balkans. The two countries almost went to war in 1908. In that year, Austria **annexed,** or took over, Bosnia and Herzegovina, two Balkan areas with large Slavic populations. Serbian officials, who had intended to take over the two provinces themselves, were outraged. Russia offered Serbia full support, but the Russian threat proved hollow. Russia was totally unprepared for war. When Germany stood firmly behind Austria, the Russians had no choice but to back down.

In the following years, one crisis after another broke out on the Balkan Peninsula. Each time, peace was maintained, but one nation or another felt humiliated. After 1913, no one was willing to yield again.

623

ANSWERS TO

Map Study

Triple Alliance; Triple Entente; neither

■ BACKGROUND

The German navy has been called William's toy. On every ship he had his own stateroom, decorated with pictures of his relatives and court favorites.

ANSWERS TO
Section Review 1

Define:
(a) treaty of friendship
(b) take over (c) glorification of armed strength

Identify:
(a) capital of Austrian province of Bosnia (b) heir to throne of Austria-Hungary assassinated in Sarajevo (c) alliance among Germany, Austria-Hungary, and Italy (d) forced Bismarck to resign (e) treaty among Great Britain, France, and Russia

Answer:

1. Most Bosnians were Serbs who wanted Bosnia to be part of Serbia. Archduke Ferdinand was assassinated by a Serbian extremist.

2. (a) prevent war in Europe; protect German empire; isolate France (b) Dual Alliance between Germany and Austria-Hungary; Triple Alliance (added Italy); treaty with Russia

3. When William II let the treaty of friendship between Germany and Russia lapse, Russia entered into an alliance with France. Great Britain signed a treaty with France and Russia following Germany's challenge to Britain's naval supremacy.

4. Nationalistic movements threatened Austria-Hungary, and Russia encouraged Slavic nationalists.

5. (a) thought war would settle international problems (b) yearned to put plans into practice (c) equated war with patriotism

6. Probable answer is *yes*. Students should recognize the factors in number 5.

A *warlike mood spread in Europe.*

By the summer of 1914, many Europeans believed that war was inevitable. There were some leaders in every country who thought that war was the best way to settle international problems. As a result, all the Great Powers except Britain kept large standing armies. With such an army, every government now felt it had the muscle to back up its demands in a crisis.

Generals in each country tried to perfect their plans for war. Many military leaders yearned for a chance to put their plans into practice. Most believed that their weapons were so advanced that no war could last longer than six months. A number of generals feared that if war did not begin soon, other countries might grow stronger. They urged political leaders not to delay.

Militarism, the glorification of armed strength, won support from ordinary civilians too. To many people, war seemed the purest kind of patriotism. "Happy are those who have died in great battles, lying on the ground before the face of God," wrote a French poet in the summer of 1914. Millions of Europeans appeared to share such feelings. In the 100 years since the Napoleonic wars, Europeans had forgotten the horrors of war and remembered only its glories.

Section REVIEW 1

Define: (a) entente, (b) annex, (c) militarism
Identify: (a) Sarajevo, (b) Franz Ferdinand, (c) Triple Alliance, (d) William II, (e) Triple Entente
Answer:
1. What factors led to the assassination of Archduke Franz Ferdinand?
2. (a) What were Bismarck's major goals after 1871? (b) What alliances did he make?
3. How was the Triple Entente formed?
4. How did Austria and Russia become rivals in the Balkans?
5. How did each of the following encourage the drift toward war in 1914? (a) political leaders (b) military leaders (c) popular opinion

Critical Thinking
6. Do you think World War I would have occurred if the archduke had not been assassinated? Explain your answer.

624

Europe plunged into war. 2

By 1914, rival alliances, nationalism, imperialism, and an arms race had brought Europe to the brink of war. All that was needed was a spark to light the fuse. The spark came with the killing of Franz Ferdinand on June 28, 1914, as you read at the beginning of this chapter.

Because the killer was a Serbian, Austria-Hungary decided to use the murder as an excuse to teach Serbia a lesson. "Serbia must learn to fear us again," one Austrian diplomat said bluntly.

Before acting, Austria consulted its main ally, Germany. Would the kaiser stand behind Austria if a war with Serbia involved other powers? Yes, came the kaiser's reply on July 5, and he set no limits on his support. The kaiser had given Austria-Hungary what amounted to a blank check. Germany would back its ally all the way.

Austria-Hungary made the first move.

On July 23, nearly a month after the assassination, Austria-Hungary sent Serbia an **ultimatum,** a set of demands that, if not met, would end negotiations and lead to war. The ultimatum was deliberately harsh. Serbia was to stop all anti-Austrian activity. In addition, the Serbian government would have to allow Austrian officials into Serbia to investigate the killing and judge those accused of the crime. Serbia had 48 hours to respond.

Serbian leaders knew that refusing the ultimatum would lead to war with Austria-Hungary, a more powerful country. The leaders therefore sought to meet Austria's demands. In effect, they accepted Austria's terms, though seeking arbitration of two items. Nonetheless, Austria—with Germany's support—wanted to punish Serbia. Four days later, on July 28, Austria declared war on Serbia.

Russia mobilized for war.

Serbia, although weaker than Austria-Hungary, had a powerful friend of its own. As protector of the Slavic peoples in southeastern Europe, the Russian government announced that it would stand behind the Serbs. This time, Russia would make up for backing down in 1908.

At this point, railroad timetables played a crucial part in turning the conflict between Austria and Serbia into a full-scale European war. Because armies were larger than ever before, moving soldiers into battle took days of travel in thousands of railroad cars. Russia faced special difficulties because it had few railroads and a large army. Russia needed many weeks to **mobilize**—that is, to get its army into position for war. The Russians felt they could not afford to wait.

By July 30, the Russian government had begun moving its army toward the Russian-Austrian border. Expecting Germany to join Austria, Russia also mobilized along the German border. At the same time, Czar Nicholas II of Russia told the kaiser (who was his cousin) that the army moves were just a precaution. Yet to German eyes, Russia's mobilization amounted to a declaration of war. On August 1, the German government declared war on Russia.

Russia looked to its ally, France, for help. Germany did not wait for France to act. Two days after declaring war on Russia, Germany also declared war on France.

The Great Powers took sides.

Germany now faced Bismarck's nightmare—a two-front war. It would have to fight France on its western border and Russia in the east. However, Germany's generals had long had plans for such a war. During the 1890's, General Alfred von Schlieffen (SHLEE-fuhn) drew up a master plan that called for a lightning-quick attack against France while Russia slowly mobilized. Under the Schlieffen Plan, almost the entire German army would race west to knock France out of action before the Russian army was ready to fight in the east.

Speed was vital to the German plan. The French had troops and forts all along their border with Germany, and the Germans knew that breaking through this border would be slow work. There was another route, however. France's northern border with Belgium was unprotected.

Germany demanded that its troops be allowed to cross through Belgium on the way to France. Belgium, whose **neutrality**—or policy of not supporting any side—had been guaranteed by the Great Powers since 1839, refused. The Germans ignored the refusal and marched into

Posters were important in the war effort. Britain used Lord Kitchener, hero of the Sudan, on a recruiting poster (left). A poster with the medieval knight Siegfried urged Germans to buy war bonds (right).

625

SECTION 2 Resources

REINFORCEMENT
■ Independent Practice 27.2

ENRICHMENT
■ Voices from the Past 27.2

ASSESSMENT
■ Section Quiz 27.2

SECTION 2
Objectives and Teaching Strategies

OBJECTIVE 1. Analyze Austria's options in response to the assassination of Franz Ferdinand.

Teaching Strategy: *Skill Building: Analyzing Austria's Options* (page 620c)

OBJECTIVE 2. Explain how the other Great Powers were drawn into the war.

Teaching Strategy: *Discussing History: England's Decision to Enter the War* (page 620c)

■ **BACKGROUND**

In the first three weeks of war, more than half a million men on each side were killed, wounded, or captured.

■ **DISCUSSION**

Could an event such as the assassination at Sarajevo trigger a war between the great powers today?

ANSWERS TO
Section Review 2

Define:
(a) set of demands that, if not met, would end negotiations (b) to get an army po-
(continued)

ANSWERS TO (continued)

sitioned for war **(c)** policy of not supporting any side **(d)** side that makes an unprovoked attack **(e)** spirit; enthusiasm

Identify:

(a) German army would attack France in west before Russia was mobilized in east **(b)** Germany, Austria-Hungary **(c)** Great Britain, France, Russia **(d)** German-French battle line **(e)** major clash on Western Front that saved Paris

Answer:

1. (a) to teach Serbia a lesson **(b)** would virtually accept Austria's demands **(c)** Austria declared war on Serbia.

2. (a) had few railroads **(b)** began to mobilize

3. (a) Russia's mobilization amounted to a declaration of war. **(b)** France was an ally of Russia; Germany declared war on France.

4. (a) by the Schlieffen Plan, which called for a quick attack against France while Russia was slowly mobilizing **(b)** Battle of the Marne, preventing quick German victory

5. After Germany marched into Belgium, Britain became concerned because of its closeness to Belgian ports.

6. After the Battle of the Marne, the Schlieffen Plan was in ruins and both sides dug in.

7. (a) Austria-Hungary was threatened by Serbian nationalists; Russia's great size and lack of railroads made mobilization difficult. **(b)** Weak powers knew stronger allies would support them.

Belgium on August 4. Britain was especially concerned, because of its closeness to Belgian ports. Outraged, Great Britain declared war on Germany.

By mid-August 1914, the battle lines were clearly drawn. On one side were Germany and Austria-Hungary, known as the Central Powers because of their geographic location in the heart of Europe. On the other side were Great Britain, France, and Russia. They were known as the Allied Powers or the Allies.

Other powers soon joined the war. In October, Turkey joined the Central Powers. A year later, Bulgaria did the same. In the beginning, Italy stayed neutral. The Italians said that the Triple Alliance was a defensive alliance and Germany had been the **aggressor,** making an unprovoked attack. However, nine months later, Italy joined the Allies against Germany and Austria.

In the late summer of 1914, millions of soldiers marched happily off to battle, convinced that the war would be short. Only a few people foresaw the horrors ahead. Staring out over London at nightfall, Britain's foreign minister, Sir Edward Grey, said sadly to a friend, "The lamps are going out all over Europe. We shall not see them lit again in our lifetime."

The German army invaded France.

Throughout August, 1.5 million German soldiers tramped over Belgium into northern France. There they encountered about the same number of French soldiers plus a small British force. (Britain did not keep a large peacetime army, so few British soldiers reached France until early 1915.) As summer turned to fall, these two sides formed a battle line that became known as the Western Front. (See map, page 631.)

At first, the French underestimated German strength. For years, French generals had stressed the importance of *élan* (ay-**LAHN**), or spirit, in battle. To attack the enemy boldly was all that counted. There was no need for defensive tactics, French army leaders reasoned, because victory would go to the army that attacked more vigorously.

Élan, however, was no match for the German fighting machine. All along the Western Front, German soldiers pushed back French forces. By September 2, German units were nearing the outskirts of Paris.

Germany now seemed within days of a victory on the Western Front. Problems quickly developed for Germany, however. The Germans had always feared Russia far more than France, and now Russia was mobilizing quickly. Therefore, the German high command decided to send thousands of men to the east. This move weakened the western army just at a time when the rapid advance into France had stretched German supply lines to the limit. Moreover, as the French retreated toward Paris, their lines of communication became shorter. As a result, the French and British were able to concentrate their forces.

The Allies struck back.

On September 6, the Allies attacked a gap in the German lines northeast of Paris in the valley of the Marne River. Every available soldier was hurled into the struggle. When the French army ran out of trucks, hundreds of taxicabs from Paris rushed more soldiers to the battlefield.

At the Marne, the German advance was stopped dead in its tracks. On September 12, German generals gave the order to retreat. The German army fell back to a new line about 40 miles north of the Marne. Paris was saved.

Although it was only the first major clash on the Western Front, the Battle of the Marne was perhaps its most important single event. The German retreat left the Schlieffen Plan in ruins. A quick victory in the west was no longer possible.

Germany had no hope of a quick victory in the east either. Although the Germans won several battles against the Russians in 1914, Russia was simply too big for overnight conquest. Germany's generals now faced the fearful prospect of a long war on two fronts.

Section REVIEW 2

Define: (a) ultimatum, (b) mobilize, (c) neutrality, (d) aggressor, (e) élan

Identify: (a) Schlieffen Plan, (b) Central Powers, (c) Allies, (d) Western Front, (e) Battle of the Marne

Answer:

1. (a) What was Austria-Hungary's goal in sending Serbia an ultimatum? (b) What was Serbia's reply? (c) What was the result?

2. (a) Why did Russia face particular difficulties in preparing for war? (b) What action did these difficulties lead Russia to take?
3. (a) What brought Germany into the war? (b) How did France become involved?
4. (a) How did Germany plan to solve the problem of a two-front war? (b) What development thwarted this plan?
5. Why did Great Britain enter the war?
6. How did the war become a stalemate?

Critical Thinking

7. It is sometimes said that in 1914 each side was pulled into war by its weakest member. (a) What were the weaknesses of Austria-Hungary and Russia? (b) How might the alliance system have encouraged them to act irresponsibly?

The war dragged on for four years. 3

After the Battle of the Marne, the war on the Western Front settled into a stalemate. Both sides dug in and held their existing positions. By early 1915, each army had built an elaborate system of tunnels, shelters, and trenches. These battle lines stretched more than 600 miles from the English Channel to the Swiss border. The space between the two sets of trenches won the grim name of "no-man's-land." As soldiers settled into the trenches for weeks and then months and then years, people began to realize that this war was unlike any other in history.

World War I was an industrialized war.

During World War I, countries on both sides used the technology of the Industrial Revolution to help their armies. They invented new weapons and made older ones more deadly.

New weapons on land One of these new weapons was the automatic machine gun. It fired so rapidly that a soldier's only protection was to take cover in the trenches. The machine gun played a major part in the deadlock and slaughter on the ground. Once the machine guns opened fire, neither side could advance.

In 1915, Germany turned to another new weapon, poison gas. It was a mixture that choked and blinded its victims. The Allies quickly began using gas too. Gas was an unpredictable weapon because winds blew it in random directions. In time, the invention of gas masks gave troops some protection from the burning clouds of mustard and chlorine gas.

In 1916, yet another invention, the tank, came into use. The British, who designed this armored motor vehicle, hoped it would smash through enemy lines. However, the first tanks had so many mechanical difficulties that they bogged down in mud or got stuck in shell holes. As a result, tanks were not used effectively until late in 1917.

New inventions in the air While millions of soldiers struggled on the ground, a handful of fighting men launched a new kind of battle in the air. Here, airplanes took part in war for the first time in history.

At first, planes were used mainly for scouting and taking photographs of enemy lines. Before

DAILY LIFE ▶ *Wartime Shortages*

During World War I, every country in Europe faced food shortages. For example, in Britain, milk, bread, tea, and bacon were very scarce; sugar and butter were almost unobtainable. To give everyone a fair chance at scarce goods, governments issued ration booklets. Each booklet held coupons for scarce items. The coupons were good until a certain date. Anyone who used all the coupons before that date had to wait until the next rationing period to receive more. The coupons at right belonged to King George V.

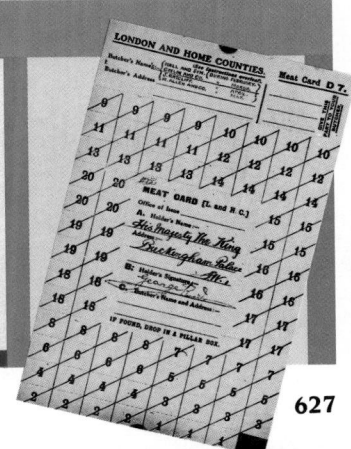

627

OBJECTIVE 1. Describe how new technology changed the nature of warfare.

Teaching Strategy: *Economics and History: New Weapons* (page 620d)

OBJECTIVE 2. Explain how the United States helped the Allies to win the war.

Teaching Strategy: *Discussing History: "Lafayette, We Are Here"* (page 620d)

■ BACKGROUND

Motor vehicles, invented in the nineteenth century, had never before been used in warfare.

SECTION 3 Resources

GEOGRAPHY
■ Transparency 83

REINFORCEMENT
■ Independent Practice 27.3

ENRICHMENT
■ Voices from the Past 27.3

ASSESSMENT
■ Section Quiz 27.3

■ **BACKGROUND**

Factories both in Germany and in Allied countries provided day care and canteens for workers' children.

Cooperative Learning

Assign groups of four students one of the following countries: Germany, Russia, France, or England. Group members should discuss the reasons for their country's entry into the war, and then write an editorial that might have appeared in a contemporary newspaper. The editorial should support the decision to go to war. Each group member should write for about two minutes, then pass the paper on to another student. Group members should offer suggestions during each writer's turn. Continue to pass the paper around the group until the editorial is complete. All group members must agree with the content of the editorial. Have groups share their editorials with the class.

long, both sides also used them to drop bombs. The Germans, for example, used a kind of blimp to bomb the city of London. In 1915, they devised a way of timing machine guns so that German pilots could fire forward through the spinning propellor. The Allies quickly did the same. The age of the dogfight, or aerial battle, began.

New inventions on the sea New weapons also changed the war at sea. Early in the war, Great Britain used its navy to blockade the North Sea coast. Britain hoped to keep food and war materials from reaching Germany. The Germans fought back with a new invention, the submarine or U-boat (*U* for *Untersee*, or "under the sea"). In September 1914, a German U-boat sank three armored British cruisers off the coast of the Netherlands. From then on, Germany used its large fleet of U-boats to attack ships carrying food and war supplies to Britain.

World War I *changed ways of life.*

World War I was a **total war**—that is, countries put all their resources into the war effort. Both human and industrial resources were turned to the demands of war.

Early in the war, each side dug one set of trenches. Later, soldiers added more trenches. Eventually, some armies boasted underground towns with kitchens, storage rooms, and sleeping quarters.

628

The roles of civilians In the past, most wars had been fought by professional soldiers. World War I was different. The long trench lines were manned by drafted civilians. As the war went on, governments called for more and more soldiers. In every country, the vast majority of men between 20 and 40 years of age were in military service for the duration of the war.

As more and more men went to war, millions of women replaced them in factories, offices, and shops. Women also plowed fields, paved streets, dug ditches, and kept the soldiers supplied with food, clothing, and weapons. Before the war, most people had believed that only men could handle certain jobs. For example, few people believed that a woman could build a tank or run a hospital. During the war, many people changed these views as they watched women tackle jobs that had once been considered men's work.

The role of government In each country, the wartime government took much greater control of the economy than ever before. Governments told companies what to produce and in what quantities. Workers were assigned to specific factories. People with special skills such as welding or engineering were ordered to use them. Many inefficient factories and those producing luxuries were closed. So many goods were in short supply that governments turned to **rationing.** Under this system, people could buy only small amounts of goods, that were needed for the war effort. Eventually, rationing covered a wide range of items from butter to shoe leather.

The role of propaganda Governments controlled the news. Leaders feared that honest reporting of battles might turn voters against the war. Governments also tried to keep up a fighting spirit by using all kinds of **propaganda.** Propaganda is one-sided information that aims to convince people of a certain point of view. All the warring countries used books, posters, and news reports to arouse hatred of the enemy.

The death toll mounted in the west.

Despite propaganda and news blackouts, the truth about the war could not be hidden forever. Casualty lists in the newspapers grew longer and longer. Wounded soldiers came home with tales of horror. Those still on the battlefield confirmed those stories in their letters.

Blinded by poison gas, British soldiers grope their way past fallen comrades.

"The men slept in mud, washed in mud, ate mud, and dreamed mud," wrote one soldier on the Western Front. The trenches swarmed with rats and insects. Fresh food was nonexistent. Soldiers lived on canned meat that was often spoiled, bread that was hard as rock, and limited supplies of drinking water. Between repairing the trenches by day and sentry duty at night, soldiers rarely slept more than an hour or two at a time.

Day and night, every man lived in fear. When their officers ordered an attack, the men went "over the top" of their trenches, usually into murderous machine-gun fire. One did not have to go over the top to die, however. A sniper's bullet or an artillery bombardment could bring death into the trenches. "Shells of all calibers kept raining on our sector," wrote one French soldier. "The trenches disappeared, filled with earth . . . The air was unbreathable. Our blinded, wounded, crawling, and shouting soldiers kept falling on top of us and died splashing us with blood. It was living hell."

The slaughter reached a peak in 1916. That February, the Germans launched a massive attack against the French near Verdun on the Meuse River. It lasted more than five months. Each side lost more than 300,000 men.

In July, the British army tried to relieve the pressure on the French by attacking the Germans northwest of Verdun in the valley of the Somme River. Thousands of tons of explosives rained from the sky, and the rat-tat-tat of machine guns echoed for hours at a time. In the first day of battle alone, more than 20,000 British soldiers were killed. Before the Battle of the Somme trailed off several months later, each side had suffered over half a million casualties.

What did each side gain from these two great battles? Near Verdun, the Germans advanced about four miles. In the Somme valley, the British advanced about five miles.

War raged on other fronts.

Even as war raged in the west, both sides were sending millions of men to fight on other fronts. These fronts played a crucial role in tipping the balance between the Allies and the Central Powers.

The Eastern Front The biggest of those other fronts was in the east, where Russians and Serbs battled Austrians, Turks, and Germans. The war in the east was more a war of movement than in the west, but here too stalemate was common.

At the outbreak of the war, Russian forces penetrated both Austria and Germany. In August 1914, the Germans crushed the invading Russians at the Battle of Tannenberg. Afterward, the Germans gradually pressed the Russians back into their own land.

Decisions in History

Near the end of 1916, the German government proposed a peace plan that could end the terrible loss of life. Under the terms of this plan, Germany would keep conquered territory in France and Russia. In addition, Belgium would come under German "influence." If you were an Allied leader, how would you have responded, and why?

629

■ **BACKGROUND**

Even war had its lighter moments. Soldiers organized their own fun—marathon card games, amateur shows, and Christmas parties with toys for French children.

■ **DECISIONS**

When a British minister argued for a negotiated settlement, Lord Lansdowne fiercely attacked "cranks, cowards, and philosophers who think we stand to gain more by losing the war than by winning it." The British soon joined the other Allies in rejecting the German plan.

■ BACKGROUND

The Germans did not release the news of the Tannenberg victory immediately. Instead they waited and announced it as an antidote to the bad news from the Marne.

ANSWERS TO

Voice from the Past

1. to kill and wear them down

2. difficult to bring in supplies during shelling

3. (a) fire caused by shelling **(b)** yelled, cursed, slaughtered rats

4. led to mental and emotional exhaustion

Russia never recovered from its defeat at Tannenberg. Short of food, guns, boots, and even blankets, the Russian army had only one asset—numbers. Russia's enormous population was used to refill the ranks of the army despite overwhelming casualties. For more than three years, that army tied up hundreds of thousands of German troops in the east. Thus, Germany could never hurl its full fighting force at the west.

The Ottoman front In October 1914, the Ottoman Turks entered the war on the side of the Central Powers, thus opening up a third front.

The following February, the British and French struck at the Ottoman nerve center, the straits linking the Black and Mediterranean seas. The Allies hoped to open the straits to send much-needed supplies to Russia. The Allied assault, known as the Gallipoli campaign, was a disaster. After almost a year of fighting, the Allies were forced to give up.

Later, the British mounted more indirect campaigns against the Ottomans by organizing Arab nationalists in the Middle East. These campaigns were more successful than the direct attack on

Voice from the Past | Bombardment in the Trenches

The novel *All Quiet on the Western Front* by Erich Maria Remarque tells of the war through the eyes of an 18-year-old German soldier. Here he waits in the trenches through days of artillery shelling, knowing that an attack will come afterward.

We wake up in the middle of the night. The earth booms. Heavy fire is falling on us. We crouch into corners . . .

The dug-out heaves, the night roars and flashes. We look at each other in the momentary flashes of light, and with pale faces and pressed lips shake our heads . . .

The attack does not come, but the bombardment continues. Slowly we become mute. Hardly a man speaks. We cannot make ourselves understood . . .

Our company commander scrambles in . . . He says that an attempt will be made to bring up food this evening . . .

We pull in our belts tighter and chew every mouthful three times as long. Still the food does not last out; we are damnably hungry. I take out a scrap of bread, eat the white and put the crust back in my knapsack; from time to time I nibble at it . . .

Towards morning, while it is still dark, there is some excitement. Through the entrance rushes in a swarm of fleeing rats that try to storm the walls. Torches [flashlights] light up the confusion. Everyone yells and curses and slaughters. The madness and despair of many hours unloads itself in this outburst. Faces are distorted, arms strike out, the beasts scream; we stop just in time to avoid attacking one another . . .

Night again. We are deadened by the strain—a deadly tension that scrapes along one's spine like a gapped knife. Our legs refuse to move, our hands tremble, our bodies are a thin skin stretched painfully over repressed madness . . . So we shut our teeth—it will end—it will end—perhaps we will come through.

1. Why would one army bombard the other for many hours before attacking?
2. How did the artillery shelling affect supplies for men in the trenches?
3. (a) What probably drove the rats into the trench?
(b) How did the soldiers react?
4. How did the days of shelling affect these soldiers mentally and emotionally?

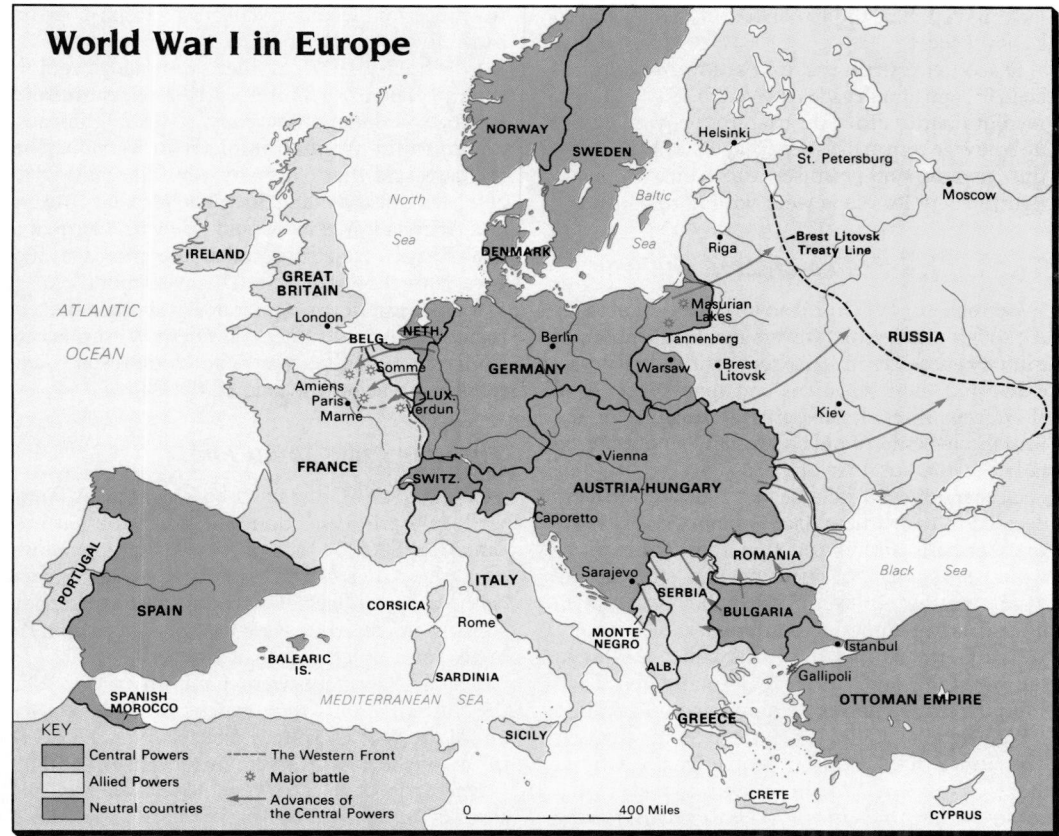

World War I in Europe

KEY

- Central Powers
- Allied Powers
- Neutral countries
- ----- The Western Front
- ✳ Major battle
- → Advances of the Central Powers

0 ——— 400 Miles

Map Study

Name two battles that took place along the Eastern Front.

Turkey had been. The Arabs were eager to revolt against their Turkish overlords. Gradually, Allied forces took control of Baghdad, Jerusalem, and Damascus.

The Italian front Another major front opened in May 1915 when Italy joined the war on the side of the Allies. Italy did not help the Allies as much as they had hoped. The Italian army lacked equipment, and public opinion in Italy was divided as to which side to support. However, fighting on the Italian front diverted some Austrian forces from the war in the east.

The war in Asia and Africa Far from the battlefields of Europe, places in Asia and Africa also saw fighting. Japan declared war against Germany within a few weeks after war had broken out in Europe. The Japanese quickly overran German possessions in China and captured most of Germany's Pacific island colonies. In Africa, the British and French conquered most of Germany's possessions. In German East Africa (modern Tanzania), however, Germany managed to hold out to the bitter end.

The Russian war effort weakened.

By 1917, Europe had lost more men in 3 years of fighting than in all the wars of the previous 300 years. Nowhere were the effects of war more sorely felt than in Russia. Russian soldiers facing the well-armed Germans lacked guns, ammunition, warm clothes, and food. Badly led and

631

Cooperative Learning

When the United States entered the war in 1917, there was a sizable minority of Americans who wanted the country to remain neutral. In fact, Wilson's campaign slogan of "He kept us out of war" had helped him win re-election in 1916. In groups of two or three, have half of the class prepare statements protesting American involvement in the war in 1917. The other half should prepare statements supporting the American declaration of war. Then pair opposing groups. Spokespersons should present their statements and engage in a debate over American participation in the war. Recorders should take notes to aid in class discussion when the debates are over.

lacking supplies, the Russian army felt betrayed by its leaders.

Discontent with the czar's government had been brewing for decades. In March 1917, Russian revolutionaries drove the czar from power and set up a new government. (See Chapter 28.) Although this government promised the Allies to go on fighting, few Russians were willing to continue.

The United States entered the war.

Germany in 1917 also had its share of problems. Although the Central Powers had won important military successes in 1916, those efforts had nearly exhausted their resources and manpower. Food shortages were already critical because of the British blockade. Worse, Germany's potato crop failed in the summer of 1916.

Desperate to strike a decisive blow, Germany decided to take a new risk. On January 31, 1917, the Germans announced that their submarines would sink without warning any ship in the waters around Britain. This policy was called unrestricted submarine warfare.

The Germans had tried this policy earlier in the war. On May 7, 1915, a German U-boat had sunk the British passenger ship *Lusitania*, killing 1,198 people including 139 United States citizens. The attack had outraged people in the United States. President Woodrow Wilson had sent a strong protest to Germany. The Germans, fearing that the United States would declare war, agreed to warn neutral ships before firing.

When the Germans returned to unrestricted submarine warfare in 1917, they knew their decision would lead to war with the United States. However, they hoped to starve Britain into defeat before the United States could mobilize. Ignoring warnings by President Wilson, German U-boats sank three American ships.

In February 1917, another event added fuel to the fire. The British intercepted a telegram from Germany's foreign secretary, Arthur Zimmermann, to the German minister in Mexico. The message said that Germany would help Mexico get back its lost land in New Mexico, Texas, and Arizona if Mexico would side with Germany. The British quickly decoded the message and gave it to the United States government.

Many Americans demanded war against Germany. On April 2, 1917, President Wilson asked Congress to declare war. The United States entered the war on the side of the Allies.

The war came to an end.

At first, the German U-boat campaign went well. In April 1917 alone, German submarines sank over 800,000 tons of Allied shipping. However, the Allies organized **convoys**—large, specially equipped fleets designed to guard merchant ships. The convoy system dashed Germany's hopes for a quick defeat of Britain.

Yet the Germans were far from beaten. On the Eastern Front, they sought to drive Russia out of the war. Despite the chaos after the overthrow of the czar, Russian armies struggled on.

One party of Russian revolutionaries, the Bolsheviks, had pledged to make peace. The leader of the Bolsheviks, a man known as Lenin, was living as an exile in Switzerland. In March 1917, the Germans arranged for a special train to carry Lenin secretly back to Russia. Just as the Germans had hoped, Lenin quickly led his party to power. In November 1917, the Bolsheviks took control of Russia. In March 1918, Germany and Russia

One of Britain's fearsome new tanks (left). A patriotic poster in praise of the tank (right).

signed the Treaty of Brest Litovsk (see page 652), which ended the war between them.

Victory in the east allowed Germany to send nearly all its forces to the Western Front. For the first time since 1914, Germany now had more soldiers in northern France than did the Allies. Soon, however, the arrival of American troops would again tip the balance in the Allies' favor. Thus, Germany needed to act quickly.

The Germans prepared one final attack on the Western Front. They formed crack units of "shock troops" by putting veterans from the east alongside those who had fought in the west. In March 1918, 6,000 German cannons opened the attack with the largest artillery barrage of the entire war. The combination of artillery, skilled troops, and dense fog helped the Germans win victory after victory. By early June, they had again reached the Marne. Paris was only 50 miles away.

Just as victory seemed within reach, the German drive stalled. The effort of reaching the Marne had exhausted supplies and men alike. Soldiers stopped advancing to loot shops for food. Germany had no more trained troops to replace those who had been killed or wounded. The only soldiers left were 15- and 16-year-old boys.

Meanwhile, American troops began arriving in France at a rate of about 250,000 a month. Marshal Ferdinand Foch (fawsh), the French general in command of the Allied forces, used the Americans to fill the gaps in his ranks. The "Yanks" were inexperienced but courageous and eager for action. With each passing day, the German army grew weaker while the Allied forces increased in strength.

In August 1918, the decisive battle of the war took place around Amiens. Leading the attack were some 300 Allied tanks that rumbled forward at a snail's pace, smashing through the German lines. The Germans continued to fight through September, but their resources were strained to the breaking point.

The other Central Powers were crumbling as well. First the Bulgarians and then the Ottoman Turks sued for peace. In November, a revolution in Austria-Hungary brought the empire to an end. Germany itself was on the very brink of revolution.

On November 9, 1918, Kaiser William II finally **abdicated,** or gave up his throne, and Germany became a republic. On the same day, a repre-

Cause and Effect
WORLD WAR I

Long-Term Causes

Forming of opposing alliances
Nationalist tensions in Balkans
Rivalry between Great Powers
Military buildup and militarism

Immediate Causes

Assassination of Franz Ferdinand
German support of Austrian aggression
Austria-Hungary's ultimatum to Serbia
Germany's invasion of Belgium

WORLD WAR I

Immediate Effects

Russian Revolution
Defeat of Central Powers
Destruction and loss of life
Treaty of Versailles
League of Nations
Breakup of Austro-Hungarian empire
Forming of mandates

Long-Term Effects

German and Italian resentment of treaty
U.S. policy of isolationism
Disillusionment of Lost Generation
Rise of fascism
World War II

sentative of the new government met with Marshal Foch. In a railway car in a forest not far from Paris, the two signed an **armistice,** an agreement to stop fighting. Two days later on November 11, World War I came to an end.

633

■ **BACKGROUND**

In 1916–17, young Americans began volunteering for the Red Cross and other relief organizations in Europe. Among them were John Dos Passos and Ernest Hemingway.

Trained airplane pilots were hard to find in World War I. After all, the Wright brothers first flew an airplane 120 feet in 1903. In fact, even experienced motor vehicle drivers were rare.

ANSWERS TO

Section Review 3

Define:
(a) space between two sets of trenches **(b)** submarine

(continued)

ANSWERS TO (continued)

(c) when countries put all resources into war effort (d) system under which people could buy only small amounts of goods (e) one-sided information that aims to convince (f) large, specially equipped fleet designed to guard merchant ships (g) give up rule (h) agreement to stop fighting

Identify:
(a) United States president during World War I (b) British passenger ship sunk by a German U-boat (c) ended the war between Germany and Russia

Answer:

1. machine gun, poison gas, tank, airplane, submarine

2. Countries put all resources into war effort.

3. As men went to war, women replaced them in factories, offices, and shops.

4. Government took greater control of economy.

5. (a) great loss of life but not much gain by either side (b) more movement than in the west, but stalemate common

6. (a) entered war on side of Central Powers (b) joined war on side of the Allies (c) entered war on side of Allies (d) joined Allied forces

7. While German supplies and men were exhausted, 250,000 American troops a month were arriving to supplement the Allied forces.

8. The loss of so many men is in itself a defeat. An entire generation of men had been killed.

The cost of the war was staggering.

World War I had shaken the economic and social foundations of European society. A whole generation of young men had been struck down. France lost 20 percent of its men between the ages of 20 and 44, and Germany lost 15 percent. Almost every family in Europe had a son, a husband, or a brother who had been killed or maimed.

The war also left deep scars in the memories of those who survived. Among them were writers, painters, and composers who passed on their experiences to others through their works. Their bitterness and pessimism ran through much of the art and literature of the 1920's and 1930's. Disillusioned and disheartened, these young people became known as the Lost Generation.

Although the war had ended, it was foolish to speak of winners, said Winston Churchill, Britain's under-secretary of the navy. Victory, he said, had been "bought so dear as to be indistinguishable from defeat."

Section REVIEW 3

Define: (a) no-man's-land, (b) U-boat, (c) total war, (d) rationing, (e) propaganda, (f) convoy, (g) abdicate, (h) armistice

Identify: (a) Woodrow Wilson, (b) *Lusitania*, (c) Treaty of Brest Litovsk

Answer:

1. What new weapons came into use in World War I?

2. Why is World War I called a total war?

3. How did the war affect the role of women in society?

4. What was the role of government during the war years?

5. (a) How did the war progress on the Western Front? (b) On the Eastern Front?

6. What part did each of the following countries play? (a) Ottoman empire (b) Italy (c) Japan (d) the United States

7. What factors led to Germany's defeat?

Critical Thinking

8. Restate Winston Churchill's evaluation of the Allies' victory in your own words. What evidence supports his statement?

634

Peace stood on shaky foundations. 4

The leaders of the victorious Allied Powers met in Paris in January 1919 to hammer out the peace treaties that would officially end World War I. People hoped that these treaties would mark the beginning of a lasting era of peace. Yet even before the treaties were ready to sign, those hopes were dashed.

Wilson proposed a plan for peace.

It was largely because of one man that hopes had risen so high. That man was President Woodrow Wilson of the United States. Americans had fought this war, said Wilson, not for their own selfish ends but "to make the world safe for democracy."

In January 1918, while the war was still raging, Wilson had drawn up a series of proposals. Known as the Fourteen Points, they outlined his goals for a just and lasting peace.

Of the Fourteen Points, the first five set general goals for the postwar world. They were these:
1. Ending secret treaties
2. Agreeing to freedom of the seas
3. Removing economic barriers to trade
4. Reducing the size of national armies and navies
5. Adjusting colonial claims with fairness toward the colonial peoples

The sixth through the thirteenth points were specific suggestions on changing national borders and creating new nations. Wilson's guiding idea in these points was **self-determination**—allowing people to decide for themselves under what government they wished to live.

Finally, the fourteenth point proposed a "general association of nations" that would protect "great and small states alike." To Wilson, this was the most important point. He hoped for an organization that would keep peace by encouraging its members to solve problems through negotiation. This proposal eventually led to the formation of the League of Nations.

The world hailed Wilson's Fourteen Points as a landmark in the quest for world peace. Both the Allies and the Germans accepted Wilson's proposal as the basis for peace negotiations.

Conflicting demands dominated the conference.

When Wilson arrived in France for the peace conference in December 1918, people greeted him as an angel of peace. "Here and there along the way," wrote a reporter who traveled on Wilson's train, "peasant families were seen kneeling beside the track to pray for him and his mission."

The task facing Wilson at Paris was not easy. Groups that had once been part of the Ottoman and Austro-Hungarian empires wanted the peacemakers to give them their own independent nations. However, many groups claimed the same lands. Not since Napoleon's defeat in 1815 had Europe faced such a task of rebuilding.

There were other problems as well. At first, both France and Britain had agreed with Wilson's ideas for a just peace. Now, however, both countries wanted to make the German people pay for the suffering the war had caused. Italy too had its own demands. In 1915, the Allies had lured Italy into the war by promising it parts of Austria-Hungary where many Italian-speaking people lived. Now Italy wanted its reward.

With so many conflicting ambitions, the peace talks at Paris were stormy. Although more than two dozen countries were represented, the major decisions were hammered out in private by France, Britain, and the United States. Italy played only a minor part. Russia, which had suffered perhaps the greatest loss of life, was in the midst of a civil war and was not invited to attend the conference.

The Allies dictated peace terms.

Spring came late to northern France in 1919. April was dreary, cold, and damp. May at last brought sunshine and warmth. The finches and nightingales began to return to the gardens and parks at Versailles, the magnificent estate built by Louis XIV.

On the afternoon of May 7, about 4 months after the conference had begun, some 70 delegates representing 27 countries gathered in an ornate conference room. In the front, on a raised platform, sat the Big Three, the men whose views had dominated the peace conference. These were Georges Clemenceau (kleh-mahn-SOH) of France, David Lloyd George of Britain, and Woodrow

Wilson, Clemenceau, and Lloyd George (center three seated) look on as the treaty is signed.

Wilson of the United States. None of the defeated countries had been allowed to take part in the discussions. Their representatives were present now only to hear the verdict.

The verdict was indeed harsh. Back in Germany, officials were horrified as they studied the Versailles treaty. Several resigned in protest. In the end, however, they had no choice but to sign.

The final signing ceremony took place in the Hall of Mirrors at Versailles, the same room in which the Germans had forced the French to sign a humiliating treaty in 1871 (page 559). The date was June 28, 1919—five years to the day after Franz Ferdinand's assassination at Sarajevo.

The treaty fell far short of a just and lasting peace. These were its terms:

Territorial losses Germany lost 13 percent of its land, where nearly 10 percent of its people lived. France, Poland, Belgium, and Denmark all received some of the territory.

France regained Alsace-Lorraine, which Germany had taken in 1871. France also won the right to work the rich mines of the Saar Basin

635

OBJECTIVE 1. Explain why France and Britain wanted to punish Germany.

Teaching Strategy: *Discussing History: Make Germany Pay* (page 620d)

OBJECTIVE 2. List and discuss the main terms of the Versailles treaty.

Teaching Strategy: *Discussing History: Decisions of the Big Three* (page 620e)

■ BACKGROUND

After the war, American troops remained cooped up in camps in France waiting for ships to carry them home. Meanwhile, the nearly empty ship, *George Washington*, lay at anchor waiting for President Wilson. This soured the soldiers' attitude toward their commander in chief.

ANSWERS TO
Section Review 4

Define:
(a) allowing people to decide for themselves under what government they wished to live **(b)** territory administered on behalf of the League of Nations **(c)** money to compensate for the costs of war

(continued)

GEOGRAPHY
■ Transparency 84

REINFORCEMENT
■ Independent Practice 27.4

ENRICHMENT
■ Voices from the Past 27.4

ASSESSMENT
■ Section Quiz 27.4

ANSWERS TO

Focus on Geography

1. Austria-Hungary, Germany

2. Polish corridor to Poland; Alsace-Lorraine to France

3. territory lost to form Hungary and Czechoslovakia, and to nearly double size of Romania and Yugoslavia; Trieste and southern Tyrol to Italy

4. Bessarabia to Romania; Finland, Estonia, Latvia, and Lithuania were formed; much territory to Poland

5. Albania, Bulgaria

6. The creation of new nations—such as Czechoslovakia—in central and eastern Europe recognized the nationalistic hopes of many minority groups, including those in Finland, Estonia, Latvia, and Lithuania. Other groups—Serbs in Yugoslavia, Bessarabians in Romania, and Sudeten Germans in Czechoslovakia—were still minorities within their new countries.

ANSWERS TO (continued)

Identify:

(a) Wilson's goals for the post-war world **(b)** Wilson's proposed organization to keep peace by encouraging members to solve problems through negotiation **(c)** Georges Clemenceau of France, David Lloyd George of Britain, and Woodrow Wilson of U.S.

(continued)

Europe after World War I

KEY

Territory lost by:
- Austria-Hungary
- Russia
- Germany
- Bulgaria

0   300 Miles

Focus on Geography

Geographic Skills

1. Which two Central Powers lost the most land?
2. What two regions did Germany lose and to what countries?
3. List the lands Austria lost and to what countries.
4. What new nations were formed from Russian territories?
5. List the other new nations formed in central and eastern Europe after the war.

Geographic Theme: Place

6. To what extent does this map reflect the nationalist hopes of minorities in central and eastern Europe? Give examples.

for 15 years. After that time, the people of the Saar region were to have the right to rejoin Germany if they so wished.

Poland, which had not appeared on a map of Europe since it was partitioned in the 1790's, once again became an independent nation. The new Poland received a large strip of German land called the Polish corridor. This strip cut off East Prussia from the rest of Germany and gave Poland access to the Baltic Sea.

All of Germany's territories in Africa and the Pacific were given as **mandates** to Britain, France,

636

and Japan. A mandate was a territory that was administered on behalf of the League of Nations. The Allies were to govern these lands until they were judged fit for independence.

Military restrictions The treaty had many clauses designed to keep Germany from ever again threatening the peace. The size of the German army was strictly limited. Germany could not manufacture war material. Submarines and airplanes were also banned. Furthermore, the Germans were forbidden to place any troops in the Rhineland, a strip of land in western Germany between the Rhine River and the French border.

War guilt The most severe part of the Treaty, however, was Article 231, the "war-guilt" clause. This clause placed sole blame for World War I on Germany's shoulders. As a result, the Germans were obliged to pay **reparations** to the Allies— that is, money to compensate for the enormous costs of the war. The final reparations bill came to $31 billion, which Germany was to pay over the next 30 years.

The League of Nations Although the peace conference dashed many of Wilson's hopes for a just and lasting peace, he did win one major victory. The Allies agreed to create a League of Nations. Five large nations—the United States, Britain, France, Italy, and Japan—were to be permanent members of its Executive Council. The League would also have a general assembly at which representatives of 42 Allied and neutral nations would meet. Germany was deliberately left out. So was Russia, which was still in the midst of civil war and revolution.

Other treaties created new nations.

The treaty with Germany was just one of five signed in Paris during 1919 and 1920. The other Central Powers also suffered losses in territory. However, out of the ashes of these old empires, Wilson's idea of national self-determination guided the creation of several new nations.

The Turkish treaty The treaty with the Ottoman Turks forced them to give up almost all of their old empire. Their territory was limited to what is now the country of Turkey.

The lands that the Ottomans lost in Southwest Asia were formed into several new territories— Iraq, Lebanon, Palestine, Transjordan, and Syria. Like the former German colonies, these areas became mandates. The League of Nations assigned control of Palestine, Iraq, and Transjordan to Great Britain. Syria and Lebanon went to France. Some Turkish territory went to Greece. The treaty also recognized the independence of Arabia.

The break-up of Austria-Hungary Several new countries were carved out of the Austro-Hungarian empire. Austria and Hungary were both recognized as independent nations. However, they lost some territory to the newly formed countries of Poland, Czechoslovakia, and Yugoslavia.* Trieste and southern Tyrol went to Italy. Finally, Romania received a large area, thus doubling its size.

The Bulgarian treaty By this treaty, the defeated Bulgaria gave up land to Romania, Yugoslavia, and Greece. Bulgaria had to pay almost a half-billion dollars in reparations.

Russian losses Even before the peace treaty was signed, Germany had to cancel the severe Treaty of Brest Litovsk in which Germany had taken about a fourth of Russia's European territory. Russia still lost more land than Germany.

The Allies, fearful of Russia's new revolutionary government, wanted to protect Russia's neighbors on the west. As a result, Russia lost the province of Bessarabia in the southwest to Romania. Poland also gained much Russian territory. Finland, Estonia, Latvia, and Lithuania, which had all declared their independence from Russia in 1918, were recognized as nations.

In several of these other treaties, the Allies added clauses aimed at further limiting Germany's size and power. The new country of Czechoslovakia, for example, included a region called the Sudetenland (soo-**DAYT**-uhn-LAND). Some 3 million Germans lived in this border region. Furthermore, the treaties forbade any *anschluss* (union) between Germany and the now tiny state of Austria, whose 6 million people were nearly all German speaking.

The United States rejected the treaty.

Across the Atlantic, many Americans objected to the Treaty of Versailles, especially to the League of Nations. Some believed that the United States' best hope for peace was to stay out of European affairs. Other Americans feared the League might undermine the powers of Congress in foreign

* Until 1929, Yugoslavia was called The Kingdom of Serbs, Croats, and Slovenes.

affairs. They wanted to be sure, for example, that no American soldiers could be ordered to fight without Congress's consent.

After a bitter debate, the United States Senate refused to join the League of Nations or accept the Treaty of Versailles. The United States worked out a separate treaty with Germany and its allies several years later.

In the end, the Treaty of Versailles did little to build a lasting peace. Instead, it left a legacy of bitterness and hatred in the hearts of the German people. Other countries felt cheated and betrayed by the peace settlements. Lacking the support of several world powers, the League of Nations was in no position to take action on these complaints. It was, as one observer described it, "a peace built on quicksand."

Section REVIEW 4

Define: (a) self-determination, (b) mandate, (c) reparations
Identify: (a) Fourteen Points, (b) League of Nations, (c) Big Three
Answer:
1. What were the general goals of the Fourteen Points?
2. What attitudes did Britain, France, and Italy take at the peace conference?
3. (a) Whom did the Treaty of Versailles blame for the war? (b) What role did the Central Powers play in the negotiations?
4. (a) What territory did Germany lose to France? (b) What new countries were created in eastern Europe from lands lost by Austria-Hungary and Russia?
5. What changes took place in Southwest Asia as a result of the war?
6. (a) Describe the organization of the League of Nations. (b) What powerful nations did not become members?
7. (a) Why did the United States reject the Treaty of Versailles? (b) How might the United States' refusal to join the League affect its work?

Critical Thinking
8. Review the proposals of the Fourteen Points (page 634). Which of these points, if they had been accepted around 1900, might have prevented war from beginning in 1914? Explain your answer.

637

ANSWERS TO (continued)

Answer:
1. ending secret treaties, agreeing to freedom of seas, removing trade barriers, reducing military, fairly adjusting colonial claims
2. France and Britain wanted Germany to pay for the suffering caused by the war; Italy wanted parts of Austria-Hungary.
3. (a) Germany (b) not allowed to negotiate
4. (a) Alsace-Lorraine (b) Poland, Czechoslovakia, Yugoslavia, Finland, Estonia, Latvia, and Lithuania
5. The lands the Ottomans lost were formed into the new territories of Iraq, Lebanon, Palestine, Transjordan, and Syria as mandates.
6. (a) Five large nations were to be permanent members of the Executive Council; 42 Allied and neutral nations would be represented in the General Assembly. (b) Germany and Russia initially, and ultimately the U.S.
7. (a) fear that membership would undermine Congress, involve U.S. in European affairs (b) League was weakened by absence of U.S., a major world power
8. An agreement on freedom of the seas would have prohibited attacks on passenger ships; reducing size of armies might have made countries less ready to fight; most important, the idea of self-determination would have brought independence to the nationalist groups within the Austro-Hungarian empire by peaceful means.

637

Concluding the Chapter

1. **Chapter Closer**
   Ask students to explain how the deaths of Ferdinand and Princip set off World War I.

2. **Reteaching Activities**
   a. Supporting a Main Idea
   Read aloud the sentence at the top of page 624: "By the summer of 1914, many Europeans believed that war was inevitable." Ask students to name three circumstances that made war seem "inevitable."
   b. Writing a Paragraph
   Ask students to write a paragraph explaining how a war that began between Austria and Serbia became a war that included most of Europe.

3. **Chapter Review Activities**
   Assign Chapter Review 27 activities.

Answers to Chapter Review appear on pages 620e–620f.

Summary

1. Conflicts divided Europe. By 1913, nationalism and the race for empires had divided Europe into two opposing camps. On one side was the Triple Alliance—Germany, Austria-Hungary, and Italy. On the other side was the Triple Entente—Great Britain, France, and Russia. Many Europeans felt that the only answer to the conflicts lay in armed might.

2. Europe plunged into war. The spark that set off the war was the assassination of Austrian Archduke Franz Ferdinand by a Serbian nationalist. When Austria declared war on Serbia, Russia leaped to Serbia's defense. The mobilization of Russian forces led to a German declaration of war. Defeat at the Battle of Marne dashed German hopes for a quick victory.

3. The war dragged on for four years. The war in the west turned into a stalemate that lasted for four years. During these years, new technologies of warfare and the total involvement of citizens and governments made World War I unlike any earlier war. In 1917, heavy Russian losses contributed to a revolution that overthrew the czar. The entrance into the war of the United States turned the tide for the Allies in 1917. On November 11, 1918, Germany surrendered.

4. Peace stood on shaky foundations. Even before the war ended, President Wilson proposed Fourteen Points for a just and lasting peace. In the end, however, the Allies dictated harsh peace terms to the defeated powers, causing extreme bitterness, especially among the Germans. However, Wilson's proposal to form a League of Nations was accepted. Strong isolationist sentiment led the United States to reject both the treaty and the League.

Reviewing the Facts

1. Define the following terms:
   a. militarism   f. propaganda
   b. ultimatum   g. armistice
   c. mobilize   h. self-determination
   d. neutrality   i. mandate
   e. rationing   j. reparations

2. Explain the importance of each of the following names, events, or terms:
   a. Franz Ferdinand   f. Battle of the Marne
   b. Bismarck   g. Zimmermann note
   c. William II   h. Woodrow Wilson
   d. Ottoman empire   i. war guilt
   e. Schlieffen Plan

3. Briefly describe the chain of events that resulted in the outbreak of World War I.

4. (a) Describe war along the Western Front. (b) How did it differ from war in the east?

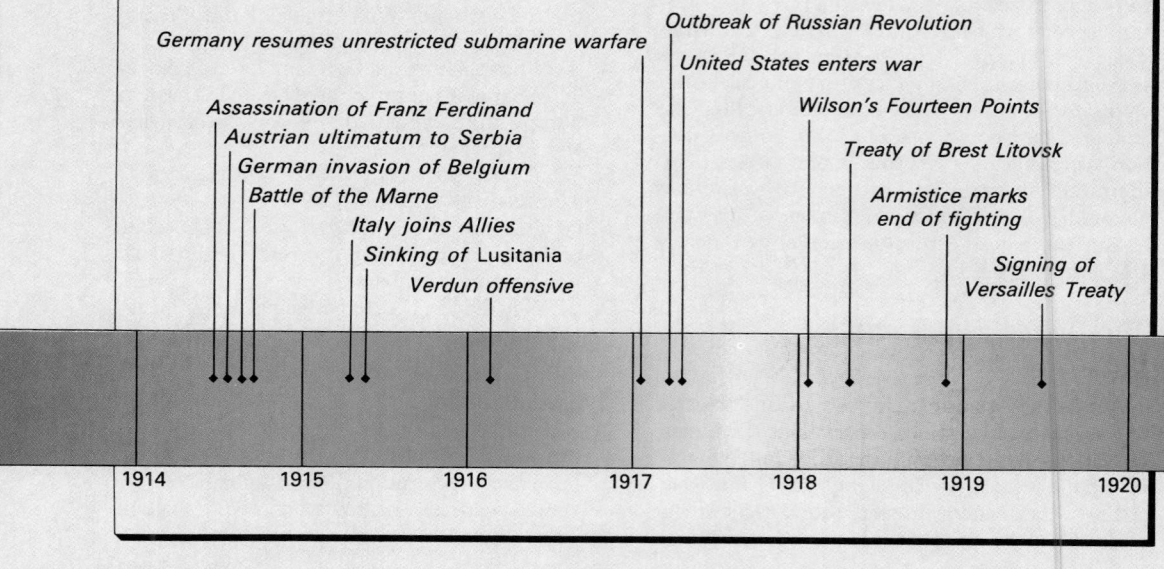

Germany resumes unrestricted submarine warfare

Outbreak of Russian Revolution

United States enters war

Assassination of Franz Ferdinand
Austrian ultimatum to Serbia
German invasion of Belgium
Battle of the Marne
Italy joins Allies
Sinking of Lusitania
Verdun offensive

Wilson's Fourteen Points

Treaty of Brest Litovsk

Armistice marks end of fighting

Signing of Versailles Treaty

1914   1915   1916   1917   1918   1919   1920

638

5. (a) What happened in Russia in 1917? (b) How had the war contributed to this event?
6. Why did the United States enter the war in 1917?
7. (a) What military restrictions were placed on Germany? (b) How did the Sudetenland and the prohibition of *anschluss* limit German power?
8. (a) Describe the League of Nations. (b) Which major powers did not belong? (c) Why?

Basic Skills
1. **Making a time line** Using information from pages 622 and 623, make a time line of events between 1875 and 1914 that led up to World War I.
2. **Making a Chart** Three major battles of World War I were the Marne (1914), Verdun (1916), and the Marne (1918). (a) Make a chart with the battles listed in a vertical column on the left. For the horizontal headings, use Objectives, Main Events, and Outcomes. (b) Which of these battles, if any, do you consider a turning point? Give reasons for your answer.

Researching and Reporting Skills
In this unit, you will be researching and reporting on history as viewed by contemporaries—the people who lived it and experienced it.
1. **Identifying primary sources** Using the subject catalog of your library, identify a number of primary sources, such as memoirs or contemporary accounts, about events during World War I. List the sources you find and select one to bring to class. Prepare a brief report on the book's content and point of view.
2. **Using biographies** Find a biography or biographical information about a political or military leader on either side in World War I. In what events did this person participate and what contribution did he or she make? Note that World War I marked the start of the air war, which had heroes such as Eddie Rickenbacker of the United States and Baron von Richthofen of Germany, as well as several famous squadrons.
3. **Using community resources** Try to find an individual in your community who remembers World War I or ask elderly members of your family or friends for recollections of the war. Does your community have a memorial to those who

died in the war? Look for information on someone named on the memorial. What military units are represented and where did they see action?

Critical Thinking
1. **Applying a concept** Why is World War I considered a world war? Support your answer with evidence from two continents besides Europe.
2. **Comparing** Compare the membership and the objectives of the Triple Alliance and the Triple Entente.
3. **Analyzing** (a) To what extent had Bismarck's policies contributed to Kaiser William II's desire to strengthen Germany? (b) In what ways did the Kaiser's policies differ from those of Bismarck?
4. **Evaluating** (a) List five general goals proposed by Wilson in his Fourteen Points. (b) How were the objectives of France and Britain similar to Wilson's goals and how did they differ?
5. **Predicting trends** The era of the late 1800's and early 1900's was known as the beautiful era, *la belle epoque*. In view of the destruction and loss of life in World War I, how might that era be described?
6. **Evaluating** (a) Which terms of the Treaty of Versailles do you think resolved problems and thus contributed to lasting peace? (b) Which terms do you think failed to resolve problems or created new problems? Give examples and reasons to support your answer.

Perspectives on Past and Present
The League of Nations was based on the idea of collective security—that nations would cooperate in maintaining peace. What examples exist today of international cooperation in keeping peace and resolving disputes?

Investigating History
1. The historian Barbara Tuchman has written two books about World War I, *The Guns of August* and *The Zimmerman Telegram.* Read selections from one of those books. How does the book help you to understand the war era?
2. Read or watch a film of the classic antiwar novel *All Quiet on the Western Front* by Erich Maria Remarque. What evidence does it use to support its viewpoint?

639

CHAPTER
Evaluation

Chapter Test 27, Alternate Chapter Test 27, and Computer Test Bank Chapter 27 Test can be used to evaluate your students' understanding of this chapter.

Russia in Revolution

Chapter Overview

During the 1800's, Russia lagged behind Europe. Revolutionary groups began developing after the Decembrists' revolt of 1825. The massacre of workers at the Winter Palace in 1905 provoked a wave of strikes that forced Czar Nicholas II to create a Duma (parliament), which he later dissolved. After the czar led Russia into two disastrous wars, he was forced to abdicate. A provisional government was overthrown by Lenin's Bolshevik party.

Once Lenin took power, he abolished the elected government, became a dictator, and withdrew from World War I. Lenin harshly put down a civil war and instituted new economic policies. After Lenin's death, Stalin took command of both the party and the government.

Stalin increased industrial production and replaced privately owned farms with collective farms. By the time Stalin died, the Soviet Union had made extraordinary progress as a modern power, but it had also become a totalitarian state.

Chapter Focus

Have students read the chapter introduction (pages 640–641). Ask what caused the protest. Point out that the protesters demanded bread, an end to war, and the czar's abdication.

In response, city authorities called out the Cossacks, who were among the czar's most loyal—and most brutal—troops. As Cossack officers gave their troops the order to charge, some of the strikers began to pray. The Cossacks, however, were as tired of the war as everyone else. They had no quarrel with these people. Instead of charging, they walked their horses carefully through the crowds, leaving their swords in their scabbards. "Some of them smiled," recalled one striker later, "and one of them gave the workers a good wink!"

Ask how the protests and the Cossacks' behavior symbolized the collapse of the czar's authority. Emphasize that the problems facing the czar had been building for almost 100 years. This chapter describes the causes and effects of the end of Russian autocracy.

Russia struggled to reform. 1

Setting the Stage

Ask students to identify two economic problems evident in the painting on page 642. (lack of industrialization, reliance on labor of serfs)

Teaching Strategies

Discussing History: The Autocracy (Objective 1) Explain that the Russian czars were autocrats with unlimited wealth. The czars owned railroads, industrial plants, and millions of acres of land. They used their wealth to build palaces and to lavishly entertain guests. The royal throne was encrusted with more than 870 diamonds and hundreds of other precious jewels.

Chapter 28 Russia in Revolution 1825–1939
FOCUS Causes of the Russian Revolution

★ **Advanced**
● **Basic**

	SECTION 1	SECTION 2	SECTION 3	SECTION 4
Objectives	1. Define *autocrat* and give examples of the czar's unlimited power. 2. Prepare a graph and chart showing the composition of Russian society and its problems. 3. Identify a Fabergé imperial Easter egg.	1. Identify the Social Revolutionaries, the Bolsheviks, and the Mensheviks and describe how they wanted to change Russia. 2. Identify and evaluate the mistakes of Nicholas II.	1. Explain how Lenin and the Bolsheviks came to power in 1917. 2. Locate lands Russia lost in World War I. 3. Explain how Stalin defeated Trotsky for control of the Communist party.	1. Contrast the policies of Lenin and Stalin. 2. Explain how Stalin transformed the Soviet economy. 3. Describe how the Soviet Union became a totalitarian state.
Setting the Stage	Russia's lack of industrialization and reliance on serf labor	Reformers vs. revolutionaries in imperial Russia	Observations on Lenin's character	The concept of totalitarianism
Teaching Strategies	Discussing History: The Autocracy Skill Building: Making Charts and Graphs Teaching with Pictures: The Imperial Easter Eggs Check for Understanding	Skill Building: Comparing Revolutionary Groups Writing about History: The Czar's Mistakes Check for Understanding	Writing about History: The Bolsheviks Seize Power Geography in History: Russia's Lost Lands Transparency 84 Outline Map 23 Transferring Ideas: Stalin as a Dictator Check for Understanding	Skill Building: Contrasting Points of View Economics and History: Transforming the Soviet Economy Discussing History: Totalitarianism as a Way of Life Check for Understanding
Guided Practice	Section Review 1	Section Review 2	Section Review 3	Section Review 4
Independent Practice Worksheets	Independent Practice 28.1 Geography Skills 28 Vocabulary 28	Independent Practice 28.2	Independent Practice 28.3 Basic Skills 28	Independent Practice 28.4 Critical Thinking 28
Enrichment	1. Primary Source: Voices 28.1 2. Creative Writing 3. Researching for Points	1. Primary Source: Voices 28.2 2. ★Creative Writing 3. Researching for Points	1. Primary Source: Voices 28.3 2. Researching for Points	1. Primary Source: Voices 28.4 2. Relating Past to Present 3. Researching for Points

Chapter Closer	
●**Reteaching Activities**	Making a Time Line, Identifying
Chapter Review	Summary, Reviewing the Facts, Basic Skills, Researching and Reporting Skills, Critical Thinking, Perspectives on Past and Present, Investigating History
Chapter Evaluation	Chapter Test 28, Alternate Chapter Test 28, Computer Test Bank Chapter 28 Test

The czars had absolute power. They controlled nearly half the peasant population. There was no parliament or court system to question their decisions. They could appoint and dismiss all government ministers. Finally, the czar commanded the army and headed the Russian Orthodox Church. In Nicholas I's words, "The czar is a father, his subjects are his children, and children ought never to question their parents." Ask students what problems might result from this way of thinking.

Skill Building: Making Charts and Graphs (Objective 2) Write this sentence on the board: In 1900, about 80 percent of the Russian people were peasants, 15 percent were urban or town dwellers, 3 percent were middle class professionals, and 2 percent were aristocrats. Ask students to make a graph illustrating the composition of Russian society. What conclusions can be drawn from the graph?

Distribute the following paragraph:

Russian peasants were discontented because they did not own enough land and frequently did not have enough food. Urban workers were discontented because they earned low wages and had poor working conditions. Middle class Russians were discontented because they wanted a share in the government. These discontents resulted in demonstrations, assassinations, and strikes.

Ask students to read this paragraph and then draw a chart to summarize its main points. Have students share their charts with the class.

Teaching with Pictures: The Imperial Easter Eggs (Objective 3) Russians of all classes celebrated Easter, the most important holy day in czarist Russia, by exchanging eggs. Nicholas II gave his wife and mother fabulous Easter eggs created by Carl Fabergé, a Russian goldsmith. Fabergé created 58 eggs for Nicholas II. Each egg contained a surprise. For example, the egg shown on page 645 contained a precise replica of the imperial coach, which required 15 months to create. Point out the imperial crown at the center of the roof surrounded by tiny gold eagles. Some of the other surprises included a model palace, portraits, and miniature animals.

Check for Understanding Have students describe Russian society and list two economic problems.

Enrichment Activities

1. **Reading a Primary Source** Assign Voices from the Past Resource Book 28.1.
2. **Creative Writing** Remind students that the United States Declaration of Independence listed grievances against Britain. Ask students to prepare a list of grievances and suggestions for reform that might have been written by a Russian revolutionary in 1900.
3. **Researching for Bonus Points** What revolutionary group took credit for assassinating Alexander II? (People's Will)

Setting the Stage

Ask whether Russia would benefit more from gradual reform or from revolutionary change. Arrange the students into pairs made up of one "reformer" and one "revolutionary." Have each student explain his or her point of view.

Teaching Strategies

Skill Building: Comparing Revolutionary Groups (Objective 1) Draw a chart with three columns and three rows on the board. Label columns *Social Revolutionaries*, *Bolsheviks*, and *Mensheviks*. Label rows *Followers*, *Economic Goals*, and *Political Goals*. After students read pages 646–647, have them fill in the chart as a class activity. Use it to discuss these questions: Which group appealed to the peasants? (Social Revolutionaries) Which groups appealed to the industrial workers? (Bolsheviks and Mensheviks) What was the Bolsheviks' political goal? (to establish a "dictatorship of the proletariat")

Writing about History: The Czar's Mistakes (Objective 2) *Prewriting* Have students read "The czar made serious mistakes" (pages 646–647). Have students identify the four mistakes. (involved Russia in disastrous war with Japan, refused to share power with the Duma, entered World War I, moved headquarters to the front) *Writing* The text states "Czar Nicholas made the fateful decision to go to war. It was this decision, more than any other single factor, that cost Nicholas his throne." Ask students to write essays agreeing or disagreeing with this conclusion.

Check for Understanding Ask students to identify the Bolsheviks, Alexander Kerensky, and the provisional government.

Enrichment Activities

1. **Reading a Primary Source**
   Assign Voices from the Past Resource Book 28.2.
2. **Creative Writing**
   Have advanced students speculate on what might have happened if Nicholas II had agreed to share power with the Duma.
3. **Researching for Bonus Points**
   What was Rasputin's full name? (Grigori Efimovitch Rasputin)

The Bolsheviks led a second revolution.   3

Setting the Stage

Read the following description of Lenin, written by M.J. Olgin in 1924 for the *New York Times*.

> There is nothing remarkable in the appearance of this man—a typical Russian with rather irregular features; a stern but not unkindly expression; something crude in manner and dress, recalling the artisan rather than the intellectual and the thinker. You would ordinarily pass by a man of this kind without noticing him at all. Yet, had you happened to look into his eyes or to hear his public speech, you would not be likely to forget him.

Ask students to list character traits Olgin mentions. How does Olgin's description compare with the material on Lenin in the text?

Teaching Strategies

Writing about History: The Bolsheviks Seize Power (Objective 1) Before beginning the section, write the following statement on the board: In a revolution, the people rise up spontaneously and take control of government. By a show of hands, determine how many students think this is an accurate statement about revolutions in general. How many think it is not accurate? Record the results next to the statement on the board. Then assign students to read "The Bolsheviks gained support" and "Lenin took control" (pages 651–652). Have students use what they have read to write paragraphs supporting or qualifying the statement. Call on volunteers to read their paragraphs aloud. Based on events in the Russian Revolution, how would students describe the concept of "revolution as a process"?

Geography in History: Russia's Lost Lands (Objective 2) Distribute copies of Outline Map 23: Russia. Show Map Transparency 84, *Europe after World War I*, or ask students to use the map on page 636 to label areas Russia lost at the end of World War I. What territories were recognized as independent nations? What geographic advantage did Russia lose? Ask why Lenin was unconcerned about the lost lands.

Transferring Ideas: Stalin as a Dictator (Objective 3) After students have read "Two men struggled to succeed Lenin" (page 653), reread aloud the following passage from the text: "Trotsky, however, had many enemies within the party. Some feared that he would become a dictator." Did Trotsky seem a likely candidate for dictator? Why or why not? How did Stalin manage to mask his own leanings toward dictatorship?

Check for Understanding Explain the importance of these phrases: "Peace, Land, and Bread" and "dictatorship of the proletariat."

Enrichment Activities

1. **Reading a Primary Source**
   Assign Voices from the Past Resource Book 28.3.
2. **Researching for Bonus Points**
   What was the fate of Leon Trotsky? (He moved from country to country before settling in Mexico. From there, Trotsky continued to oppose Stalinism until he was killed by an unknown assassin in 1940.)

Stalin became dictator.   4

Setting the Stage

Read the following definition of *totalitarianism*: "A political system in which government has total control over the lives of individual citizens." Ask students to compare this type of government to a democracy. Then list on the board or on a transparency the characteristics of totalitarian governments as described by American historian Louis L. Snyder.

- One leader becomes the symbol of government and state.
- All opposition is suppressed.

- Informers and secret police help ensure the power of the dominant party.
- Propaganda, controlled by the government, glorifies the party's leadership.
- Party leaders appeal to nationalism to preserve the party's power.

As students study Section 4, have them list aspects of Stalin's rule that relate to these characteristics.

Teaching Strategies

Skill Building: Contrasting Points of View (Objective 1) Have students analyze the following passages.

Of course, the socialist idea cannot be attained in one country alone. The workers and peasants who support the Soviet Government are only a fragment of [an] international army . . . struggling for the common cause of the . . . international socialist revolution . . . .

N. Lenin,
Report to the Third
Congress of the Soviets

And what do we mean by the possibility of the victory of socialism in one country? We mean the possibility . . . of the proletariat assuming power and using that power to build a complete socialist society in our country, . . . but without the victory of the proletarian revolution in other countries . . . For what else is our country . . . if it is incapable of achieving victory over the capitalist elements in its own economy . . . ?

J. Stalin,
Problems of Leninism

Ask what the main difference is between Lenin and Stalin on the question of a worldwide Communist revolution. What argument does Stalin use to support his view? Have students find information in the text (pages 654–655) describing Stalin's reasoning on this issue.

Economics and History: Transforming the Soviet Economy (Objective 2) To introduce Stalin's approach to developing the Soviet economy, read aloud two articles from the Soviet constitution of 1936, or "Stalin's Constitution."

ARTICLE 11. The economic life of the U.S.S.R. is defined and directed by the State plan of national economy in the interests of . . . strengthening . . . the independence of the U.S.S.R.

ARTICLE 12. Toil in the U.S.S.R. is an obligation and a matter of honor to each citizen who is fit for toil, according to the principle: "He who does not work does not eat." In the U.S.S.R. there is being realized the principle of socialism: "From each according to his ability, to each according to his toil."

Ask students to determine the purpose of Stalin's economic plans and his definition of work. Ask how such an economic system might affect individual freedoms.

Have students interpret the following chart to determine to what extent Stalin succeeded in modernizing the Soviet economy.

Industrial Output in the Soviet Union

Industry	1932	1938
Coal	64,000,000 tons	132,000,000 tons
Oil	22,000,000 tons	32,000,000 tons
Pig Iron	6,000,000 tons	14,000,000 tons
Steel	6,000,000 tons	18,000,000 tons
Automobiles	23,000 units	211,000 units
Tractors	50,000 units	176,000 units

Have students assess the human cost of Stalin's economic programs (pages 655–656). Ask, "By what means did Stalin implement his new economy? Why did Soviet peasants resist collectivization and state control of the land? How did Stalin deal with worker dissent?"

Discussing History: Totalitarianism as a Way of Life (Objective 3) Read the following report printed in a Soviet newspaper in Stalin's time: "Reactionary 'bourgeois tendencies' have been noted in Soviet circuses and persons responsible for it ought to be exposed." Explain that the reporter claimed to have seen what he called "ideologically empty . . . attractions." That is, he had observed circus performances offering pure entertainment similar to the "decayed circus art of capitalist countries." Ask students what Communist supporters believed circuses should do if not entertain people. Ask why control of all aspects of life, including circuses, was critical to the success of Stalin's regime.

Check for Understanding Have students explain and give examples of totalitarianism.

Enrichment Activities

1. **Reading a Primary Source** Assign Voices from the Past Resource Book 28.4.

2. **Relating Past to Present** Ask students to research and report on changes in the present-day Soviet Union that show a trend away from totalitarian government.

3. **Researching for Bonus Points** Who was the king of England when Stalin instituted his first Five-Year Plan? (King George V)

Reviewing the Facts

1. (a) resign as ruler (b) ruler with unlimited power (c) belief that everything must be destroyed so new society can be created (d) elected workers' council (e) economic system in which all economic decisions are made by government (f) government that controls citizens' lives

2. (a) rebellion by Russian officers to win a written constitution (b) believed revolutionary base would be peasants (c) believed revolutionary base would be urban working class (d) German philosopher who influenced Social Democrats (e) Bolshevik leader who gained control of the government (f) follower of Lenin (g) preferred to move slowly towards revolution (h) last czar to rule Russia (i) provoked a wave of strikes throughout the country (j) first Russian parliament (k) urged czarina to ignore demands for reform (l) dominant figure in provisional government (m) lost a power struggle to Stalin (n) staged by naval officers to demand free elections, free speech, and abolition of secret police (o) new name of Bolsheviks (p) ruler after Lenin's death

3. (a) swore not to reform (b) freed serfs (c) rejected reform (d) maintained autocracy

4. (a) middle class (b) The Social Revolutionaries wanted a democratically elected government. The Social Democrats wanted urban workers to revolt. (c) Bolsheviks and Mensheviks

5. (a) chose provisional government (b) allowed provisional government to rule (c) dominant figure in provisional government

6. (a) Opponents of Bolsheviks formed "White" armies to fight Red Army that won. (b) ruined economy

7. (a) Trotsky founded the Red Army. Stalin placed friends in important positions and was chosen Lenin's successor. (b) Trotsky believed in a world revolution. Stalin was only concerned with revolution inside Russia.

Basic Skills

1. (a) Decembrist revolt, freeing the serfs, Russo-Japanese War, revolution of 1905, St. Petersburg bread riots, abdication of Nicholas II (b) Decembrist revolt: reaction to lack of political rights of citizens; freeing of serfs: showed that protest could have impact on ruling family; Russo-Japanese War: led to more unrest, showed weakness of czar's government; 1905 revolution: demonstrated that demands of Russian people for more rights would not go away; bread riots: another sign of discontent and government's lack of concern for people; abdication: opened politics to a newly formed soviets and various socialist groups who would lead 1917 revolution

2. (a) Poland, Finland, Estonia, Latvia, Lithuania (b) Russia lost her window on the sea and lands closest to western Europe. One result was to isolate Russia.

Researching and Reporting Skills

Students' answers will vary.

Critical Thinking

1. Possible answer: War brought the fall of the czar, but conditions within the country were the most important factor in the breakdown. The people were disheartened by the war and felt no loyalty to the government.

2. (a) Lenin: provided strong leadership, consolidated Bolshevik power, organized Red Guard units, organized first Communist government, created New Economic Policy, and formed autonomous republics; Trotsky: organizer of 1917 takeover, founded Red Army (b) The work of both men was essential. Trotsky led Bolshevik takeover in 1917 when the party's popular support was still low, and defended the revolution against its opponents. Lenin, however, inspired the people. He organized the new government, forced out opposition, and was adept at adjusting economic and political policies to deal with realities.

3. (a) original goals: rural socialism, distribution of land among peasants, democratically elected government (b) Stalin was more concerned with industrial growth; abolished private farms and created collectives, established ruthless dictatorship instead of democracy.

4. (a) Lenin adapted from Marx the political and economic ideas of the dictatorship of the proletariat, the start of revolution among urban workers, class conflict, and state ownership of the means of production. (b) by leading the workers in revolt, making them the care of the new government, taking over factories, and giving the workers political control

5. (a) to develop USSR's economy (b) industrial growth, especially in Siberia; production targets; abolition of private farms (c) increased industry, energy production, farm production

6. powerful secret police, religious repression, execution of party members in disfavor, complete control of workers' lives, censorship

Perspectives on Past and Present

Students' answers will vary.

Investigating History

Students' answers will vary.

Chapter 28

Have students study the painting and read the introduction (pages 640–641). Then ask what problems angered the people of St. Petersburg. Point out that textile and steel workers, along with the women, demanded bread, an end to war, and the czar's abdication. Interested students may compare the winter food shortage of 1917 with that of 1990. In studying the painting, point out to students that the style of art, called socialist realism, embodies the principles of communism. The style is simple and direct and highlights the goals of Soviet life.

This Russian painting shows an uprising of the working people.

Key Terms

autocrat
nihilism
autocracy
soviet
command economy
collective farm
totalitarian

Read and Understand

1. Russia struggled to reform.
2. Russia moved towards revolution.
3. The Bolsheviks led a second revolution.
4. Stalin became dictator.

It was cold, bitterly cold, in St. Petersburg on the morning of February 25, 1917. As the sun rose over the frozen Neva River, thousands of women huddled in the doorways of the city's bakeries, waiting, as they waited almost every morning, for bread. By the time sleepy-eyed workers began to trudge through the snow to factories and offices, the lines to some bakeries were several blocks long.

Then came the news: There was no bread. The bakers could not bake without flour, and there were no trains to bring flour to the city. Russia had been at war for nearly three years, and the country's railroads were under enormous strain. Nearly every boxcar was needed to carry food and supplies to the army.

640

During past shortages, the women of St. Petersburg had quietly returned home without their bread. This time they refused to leave. Instead, they milled about the streets, shouting, "We want bread! We want bread!" They gathered on trolley tracks, stopping traffic. They forced passengers off streetcars and even turned over a few cars. Some women began throwing rocks through store windows.

The women did not consider themselves revolutionaries. They were just tired—tired of waiting for bread that never came, tired of watching their sons and husbands march off to die in war. They were tired of poverty—tired of seeing the carriages of the rich glide by while their own families huddled around grimy stoves in dark, crowded tenements.

Within hours, the women were joined by workers from several textile factories and the huge Putilov steelworks on the outskirts of the city. By early afternoon, great crowds had gathered along St. Petersburg's main street. The demonstrators shouted and sang. Many held up banners proclaiming "We want Bread!" or "End the War!" Others held a more menacing slogan—"Down with the Czar!"

Nicholas II, Russia's czar, did not pay much attention to the protesters. He was far more concerned with the war against Germany. On that same Thursday morning, Nicholas left St. Petersburg for his headquarters at the front. He felt certain that the police would easily handle the disturbances. Yet even as his train rumbled across the snowy Russian plains, unrest spread through the capital city.

By Monday, St. Petersburg was in the hands of rebellious workers and the many soldiers who had joined them. The czar soon realized that this was no ordinary disturbance, and he tried desperately to return to the capital. The uprising, however, had by then reached far beyond St. Petersburg. Railroad workers along the czar's route would not let his train pass. Meanwhile, at the front, soldiers refused to fight. Thousands deserted from the army daily. In this crisis, Nicholas called a meeting of his generals. They presented Nicholas with a bleak decision: He must abdicate (resign as ruler).

On March 2, 1917, Nicholas II gave up the throne that his family, the Romanovs, had held for more than three centuries. In this chapter, we will see that this revolution had been building for almost 100 years. We will also see why the czar's abdication did not bring peace or democracy to Russia.

Russia struggled to reform. 1

"Three centuries to build it up, and three days for it to vanish," wrote one observer in March 1917, speaking of the Russian monarchy. His comment was misleading. The old regime was not destroyed in a few days. The Russian Revolution was like a firecracker with a very long fuse. The explosion came in 1917, but the fuse had been burning for years.

To understand the revolution, it is necessary to go back in time at least to 1825. That year, Czar Alexander I, who had helped defeat Napoleon (page 498), died. With his death, Russia entered a period of turmoil that lasted nearly 100 years.

Most Russians lived as serfs.

In the early 1800's, while the Industrial Revolution was changing western Europe, Russia remained an agricultural country. More than 90 percent of all Russians depended on farming for their livelihood. A few owned large estates, but the vast majority—more than 80 percent of the people—were serfs. These men, women, and children worked for the owners of the large estates.

Serfdom had developed in Russia during the late Middle Ages (page 448). By the 1800's, serfs were permanently bound to the noble whose land they worked. Nobles had almost unlimited power over their serfs. They could buy and sell serfs in open markets like cattle. Landholders could beat their serfs or even exile them to Siberia. (Siberia is the bleak region of northeastern Russia that lies in Asia.)

By the 1820's, many Russians believed that serfdom must be ended. They argued that the system was morally wrong and also kept the empire economically backward. Serfs had no incentives to better themselves or learn new ways of farming. Why should they produce more food to fatten the landlords? Why should they learn

641

SECTION 1 Objectives and Teaching Strategies

OBJECTIVE 1. Define *autocrat* and give examples of the czar's unlimited power.
Teaching Strategy: *Discussing History: The Autocracy* (page 640a)

OBJECTIVE 2. Prepare a graph and chart showing the composition of Russian society and its problems.
Teaching Strategy: *Skill Building: Making Charts and Graphs* (page 640c)

OBJECTIVE 3. Identify a Fabergé imperial Easter egg.
Teaching Strategy: *Teaching with Pictures: The Imperial Easter Eggs* (page 640c)

■ BACKGROUND

With almost all of Russia's able–bodied men in the army, farming was done by women. They produced ample food, but the transportation system was unable to carry it both to the army and to the cities. As a result, the countryside had surplus food while the cities suffered shortages.

■ DISCUSSION

Why did serfdom continue in Russia long after its decline in western Europe?

SECTION 1 Resources

ASSESSMENT
■ Section Quiz 28.1

REINFORCEMENT
■ Independent Practice 28.1

ENRICHMENT
■ Voices from the Past 28.1

The Decembrists counted about 30 officers and 3,000 soldiers among their numbers. Some historians think that the revolutionaries' lack of organization was as responsible for their failure as Nicholas's troops.

The Decembrist revolt took place in St. Petersburg, the most Western of Russian cities. It would be the scene of much revolutionary activity in the years to come.

Harnessed like oxen, Russian serfs haul a barge up the Volga River. In more industrialized countries, steam engines did such work.

new skills or start new businesses? Educated Russians were convinced that freeing the serfs was the first and most necessary step toward modernizing Russia.

In Russia, all it would have taken to end serfdom was the command of the czar. The czar was an absolute ruler. He had complete control over the lives and property of his subjects. He was the sole source of all laws. The czar was an **autocrat**, a ruler with unlimited power. (The word comes from Greek words meaning "rule by oneself.")

For a time, Czar Alexander I toyed with the idea of freeing the serfs. He even took a few slight steps in that direction. Yet he did not do so. When he died suddenly of a fever in 1825, an important chance for peaceful reform died with him.

The Decembrists revolted.

Alexander's death brought on a revolt in December 1825. The army officers who led it became known to history as the Decembrists, after the month in which their revolt took place.

The officers were all veterans of the long wars against Napoleon. While fighting in western Europe, they had come into contact with such ideas

as bills of rights for citizens. When they returned to Russia, they found that the czar's government still ruled with unlimited powers. With no legal way to work for reform or even to express their ideas, a few young officers organized secret revolutionary societies. Their goal was to win a written constitution for Russia that allowed some of the rights of western Europe.

These secret groups were plotting an uprising when Alexander I died. No one was certain which of his several brothers would become the next czar. The oldest brother was Constantine, but he did not want to rule Russia.

Some young officers in St. Petersburg decided to take advantage of the confusion. They threw their support behind Constantine, even though he had already agreed to step aside for a younger brother, Nicholas. When it was time for the army to take the oath of loyalty to the new czar, the officers ordered their troops to shout "Constantine and Constitution." In their ignorance, many of the soldiers apparently believed that "Constitution" was Constantine's wife.

Troops loyal to Nicholas forcefully put down the Decembrists' revolt. Its leaders were executed or sent to forced labor in Siberia. Nicholas I never forgot the revolt. He ruled Russia with an iron hand for 30 years.

Nicholas I *resisted change.*

Nicholas I was determined to fight the "revolutionary spirit." He once said, "Revolution stands on the threshold of Russia, but I swear it will never enter Russia while my breath lasts."

When some educated Russians called for him to free the serfs, the czar refused. He agreed that serfdom was wrong, but he believed that he needed the support of the landlords to prevent peasant revolts. The czar explained, "The landlord is the most faithful, the unsleeping watchdog guarding the state; he is the natural police magistrate." Between 1825 and 1854, those faithful landlords and the czar crushed at least 500 peasant uprisings.

Nicholas also set out to combat any sign of political opposition among upper-class Russians. He did so by limiting education. After all, he argued, the government needed only a few educated officials. To end the demands for change, the czar's government strictly censored books, newspapers, and pamphlets. Nicholas also set up a secret police force to hunt out any person who dared to speak of change or reform.

Although Nicholas I succeeded in keeping revolution out of Russia, his foreign policy was less successful. In his efforts to take over parts of the Ottoman empire, he found himself at war not only with Turkey but also with Great Britain and France. The Crimean War (1853–1856) was a disaster for Russia. Russia's defeat on its own soil showed the weaknesses of the czar's autocratic government. The war also revealed that Russian technology was far behind that of Britain and France.

Alexander II *freed the serfs.*

In 1855, Nicholas I died, and his son Alexander II succeeded him. The new czar accepted the need for reforms. In fact, he commented that it was better to offer reforms from above than to have them forced on the government from below. Almost everyone agreed that the first step was the abolition of serfdom.

On March 3, 1861 (the day before Abraham Lincoln became president of the United States), Alexander issued a decree freeing the serfs. The new law left about half the farmable land in the hands of the nobles. The other half was parceled out to the serfs, who were required to pay the government for it. The government in turn paid the nobles for their lost lands.

The new law worked to the nobles' advantage. Most of them had heavily mortgaged their land. With the money the government gave them, they could pay off their debts. Moreover, they were also free of their old duties to feed, clothe, and house the serfs.

The newly freed peasants did not own their land outright as private property. Instead, the land became the property of the peasant community. Each peasant community was called a *mir* (meer). The mir as a whole owned the land, worked the land, and paid taxes to the government. It was almost impossible for a peasant to leave the mir, because then others would have to pay an extra share of taxes. Peasants remained tied to the mir much as serfs had been tied to their owners.

Freeing the serfs was only the first of Alexander's reforms. He also gave Russians a few more rights. For the first time, people charged with crimes could have public trials and a lawyer of their own choice. Alexander II also set up elected councils known as *zemstvos* to deal with local matters such as education and road maintenance. In addition, he expanded educational opportunities.

Reforms *encouraged unrest.*

Although some people were pleased with the reforms, many Russians believed that they fell far short of what was needed. In comparison with the people of western Europe, most Russians were still oppressed.

The peasants, for example, continued to bear many burdens. They alone paid a poll tax. They alone were subject to the death penalty if found guilty of a crime. They alone were bound to their mir by a system that kept them from moving freely from one place to another. To add to their discontent, few peasants had enough land to support their families. Russia's population was growing rapidly. Yet the amount of land available to peasants was limited. As a result, there were hundreds of peasant riots in the late 1800's.

Some educated Russians were also dissatisfied. Censorship still forced them to discuss their political ideas in secret. Their secret societies became

643

■ RESEARCH

The immediate cause of the Crimean War was a dispute among France, Russia, and Turkey over control of the Holy Places in Jerusalem. Conflict over these places continues to this day. Have students research this conflict.

■ BACKGROUND

A total of ten million serfs and their families were freed.

Alexander III was a man of giant physique, so strong that he could bend a horseshoe in one hand.

Despite progress on many fronts, countless Russians still lived on the verge of starvation. Rural schoolteachers, for example, often lived in huts with the peasants' cattle, were housed in unheated sheds, or slept in a corner of a one–room schoolhouse.

increasingly radical as the years went by. A few favored **nihilism** (from the Latin word *nihil* meaning "nothing"). Michael Bakunin, a nihilist leader, described their aims:

> Our first work must be destruction and annihilation of everything as it now exists. You must accustom yourself to destroying everything; the good with the bad; for if but an atom of this old world remains, the new will never be created.

Some idealistic students put their faith in the *narod*. (*Narod* means "people" in Russian.) Known as *narodniki*, these young students went among the peasants to teach them to read, to provide medical services, and to spread the idea of revolution. Hundreds of narodniki were arrested and shipped to Siberia. Those who remained grew more radical. Their goal soon became the assassination of the czar.

On March 13, 1881, as Alexander II rode in his carriage, a student threw a bomb at him. The bomb missed the czar but wounded several of his guards. As Alexander stepped down to help the injured, another radical threw a second bomb. His body shattered, Alexander could only whisper, "Home to the palace to die."

Alexander III *upheld the autocracy.*

Alexander III succeeded his father to the throne. He placed his faith in the "power and right of **autocracy**," a government in which he would have total power. He completely rejected reform. Alexander reduced the power of the zemstvos and put even stricter limits on what could be published. His secret police carefully watched both secondary schools and universities. Teachers had to send detailed reports on every student.

Alexander set out to strengthen "autocracy, orthodoxy, and nationality." Anyone who questioned the absolute power of the czar, who worshiped outside the Russian Orthodox Church, or who spoke a language other than Russian was regarded as dangerous. Other national groups within Russia were oppressed.

No group was treated more harshly than the Jews. They were forced to live in a special region in the southwestern part of the empire. Schools were closed to them. They were also subject to new laws that encouraged prejudice. As a result,

pogroms (riots against Jews) broke out in many parts of Russia. Police and soldiers stood by and watched as Jewish homes, stores, and synagogues were looted and destroyed.

Nicholas II *became czar.*

When Alexander III died in 1894, most Russians breathed a sigh of relief. They hoped the new czar, Nicholas II, would lead a new era of reform. Once again, they were disappointed. When a number of zemstvos demanded a constitution, Nicholas told them to forget "such foolish dreams." "I shall maintain the principle of autocracy," he announced at his coronation, "just as firmly and unflinchingly as it was preserved by my unfortunate dead father."

Cultural changes Nonetheless, Russia was changing despite Nicholas's attempts to hold it back. In universities, students argued over the ideas of foreign thinkers such as Charles Darwin, Karl Marx, and Louis Pasteur. At the same time, Russian artists, thinkers, and scientists were making their own unique contributions. Novelists such as Leo Tolstoy and Fyodor Dostoevsky became great literary figures. For the first time, Russian authors were widely read in translation outside their own country. Sergei Diaghilev (dee-AHG-uh-lehf) helped give Russian ballet its reputation as the finest in the world. Composer Peter Ilyich Tchaikovsky (chy-KAHF-skee) wrote music for the ballet (*The Nutcracker Suite*), as well as for the concert hall. His *1812 Overture* celebrated Napoleon's defeat at Moscow.

Economic developments Russia moved closer to the European mainstream in other ways as well. Although more than 85 percent of the population still lived in rural areas, Russian cities were growing rapidly. Between 1861 and 1870, the population of cities and towns had increased 45 percent.

The czar's government encouraged the growth of industries by investing national funds directly or by loaning money to local businesses. The czar also ordered tariffs to protect Russian products from foreign competition. Most of the new industries were concentrated in such cities as St. Petersburg, Moscow, Lodz, Baku, and various Black Sea ports.

The czar also encouraged foreign investment. With the help of British and French investors,

Inept as a ruler, Nicholas II was devoted to his wife and five children. Each Easter, the czar gave his wife a gem-encrusted egg such as the one above.

work began in 1891 on the Trans-Siberian Railway to connect European Russia with Russian ports on the Pacific. When it was completed in 1904, this railroad was the longest in the world.

Russia, however, was still far behind the West. In 1914, even after decades of expansion, the country's coal output was only one twentieth that of the United States. At the same time, the vast majority of the Russian people continued to live much as their ancestors had, tending small fields in the countryside. Those who did get jobs in the cities were not much better off. Working conditions in Russian factories were poor, and wages were miserably low. Trade unions were outlawed.

Russia was facing many of the same problems that Britain and other countries had faced in the early stages of the Industrial Revolution. The gap between rich and poor was enormous. As Leo Tolstoy wrote:

All our palaces, all our theaters, all these riches of ours, we owe to the effort of these same hungry people who make these things . . . The common people are hungry because we [lucky ones] are too full.

In the West, later stages of the Industrial Revolution brought a slow but steady improvement in the standard of living for all. Perhaps the same thing would have happened in Russia. We will never know. Events moved too swiftly toward a crisis.

Section REVIEW 1

Define: (a) czar, (b) autocrat, (c) mir, (d) zemstvo, (e) nihilism, (f) narodniki, (g) autocracy

Identify: (a) St. Petersburg, (b) Nicholas II, (c) Romanov, (d) Siberia, (e) Decembrists, (f) Nicholas I, (g) Alexander II, (h) Alexander III

Answer:
1. (a) What group made up the largest share of Russia's population in the 1800's? (b) Describe their social and economic position.
2. What were the goals of the Decembrists?
3. (a) What attitude did Nicholas I take toward reform? (b) Toward freeing the serfs?
4. What reforms did Alexander II make?

645

ANSWERS TO
Section Review 1

Define:
(a) king or emperor of Russia (b) ruler with unlimited power (c) peasant community (d) elected council (e) radical belief that everything existing must be destroyed (f) Russian students who went among the peasants to teach reading, provide medical services, and spread the idea of revolution (g) government in which ruler has total power

Identify:
(a) capital of Russia (b) czar who encouraged growth of industry and foreign investment (c) ruling Russian family for more than three centuries (d) northeastern Russia (e) led a revolt when Czar Alexander I died (f) czar of Russia for 30 years (g) freed serfs (h) set out to strengthen "autocracy, orthodoxy, and nationality"

Answer:
1. (a) serfs (b) had no rights; could be bought and sold, beaten or exiled by landholders

2. written constitution giving Russians some rights enjoyed by western Europeans

3. (a) determined to keep reform out of Russia (b) opposed it but needed support of landlords to prevent peasant revolts

4. freed serfs, gave people more rights, expanded educational opportunities

(continued)

ANSWERS TO *(continued)*

5. (a) Serfs were freed and given farmable land which became the property of the mir. **(b)** It was almost impossible for a peasant to leave a mir, because other peasants would have to do extra work and pay extra share of taxes.

6. Anyone who questioned the absolute power of the czar, worshipped outside the Russian Orthodox Church, or spoke a language other than Russian was regarded as dangerous.

7. (a) far behind the West **(b)** growth of industry, cities and foreign investment; completion of Trans-Siberian Railway

8. (a) preferred rights be guaranteed in a constitution **(b)** pleased with freedom, frustrated with mir **(c)** wanted destruction, not reforms, of existing institutions **(d)** approved expansion of educational opportunities

■ **BACKGROUND**

Also prominent were the anarchists, who believed in a society in which no person had control over another. However, to create such a society, they thought the existing system must first be completely destroyed.

5. (a) How did the position of the peasants change after they were freed? **(b)** How were their rights and freedom of movement still limited?
6. Describe Alexander III's policy of "autocracy, orthodoxy, and nationality."
7. (a) By 1900, how did Russia compare economically with western Europe? **(b)** What economic changes were taking place in Russia?

Critical Thinking

8. What opinion might each of the following people have expressed about Alexander II's reforms? **(a)** an old Decembrist **(b)** a serf in one of the new mirs **(c)** a nihilist **(d)** a narodnik

Russia moved toward revolution. 2

When the twentieth century began, Russia was still an autocracy. Yet a number of groups were trying to bring about change. Some were moderates, such as the Constitutional Democrats. This group hoped to limit the czar's power and create a constitutional monarchy like Britain's.

Other groups were interested not in reform but in revolution. Ever since the Decembrists of 1825, a handful of men and women in each generation had worked secretly for revolution. Only a few of these radicals were peasants or workers. Most were from middle-class backgrounds, sons and daughters of shopkeepers and teachers.

The revolutionaries were divided.

The radicals could be divided into two groups: those who appealed to the peasants and those who appealed to industrial workers. By the early 1900's, these two groups were known as the Social Revolutionaries (the SR's) and the Social Democrats (the SD's).

Social Revolutionaries The Social Revolutionaries believed the force to overthrow the czar's government would come from Russia's peasants. Unlike most European socialists, the SR's did not think that the revolution would begin with the urban working class. Instead, they considered

Russia a special case because of its enormous peasant class. The SR's believed that Russia could develop its own special kind of rural socialism. Their goal was a government that would distribute the land fairly among the peasants. The SR's also wanted to replace the czar with a democratically elected government.

Social Democrats The Social Democrats were Marxists. Karl Marx (page 551) was a German philosopher who argued that the workers of the world would one day overthrow the ruling classes and share equally in society's wealth. Like Marxists in other countries, the Social Democrats were convinced that future revolutions would be led by an urban working class.

Among the leaders of the SD's was a short, balding man in his early 30's who called himself Lenin. Lenin (1870–1924) not only planned to overthrow the czar but also hoped to spark a worldwide Marxist revolution. The son of a prosperous school inspector, Lenin was born Vladimir Ilyich Ulyanov (ool-YAH-nof). He took the name Lenin for his underground activities. Lenin became a revolutionary after his older brother was executed in 1887 for plotting to assassinate Alexander III.

Lenin worked tirelessly for revolution. He was arrested, sent to Siberia, and eventually forced to live in exile outside Russia. Yet his faith in Marxism never wavered. Speaking of Lenin, an early colleague wrote:

> There is no other man who is absorbed by the revolution 24 hours a day, who has no thoughts but thoughts of revolution, and even in his sleep dreams of nothing but revolution.

Bolsheviks and Mensheviks In 1903, Lenin's eagerness to act was the direct cause of a split in Social Democratic ranks. Most SD's thought that Russia would have to be industrialized before a Marxist revolution could take place.

Lenin believed the revolution could go forward at once. He admitted that Russia's working class was too small and too poorly educated to stage a revolution. Therefore, he argued, the workers needed a tiny, determined group of Marxists to show them the way. After overthrowing the czar, said Lenin, these radicals would establish a "dictatorship of the proletariat" until the people were able to take charge of society themselves.

Lenin presented these views at a stormy party conference in London, where many SD's gathered in exile. At that meeting, his policy was approved by a margin of one vote. From then on, Lenin and his followers called themselves Bolsheviks (BOHL-shuh-vihks), from the Russian word meaning "majority." Lenin's opponents who preferred to move more slowly were called Mensheviks (MEHN-shuh-vihks), from the word meaning "minority."

Actually, outside the convention the Mensheviks were by far the larger of the two groups within the Social Democrats. Most Russian SD's believed that Lenin's ideas contradicted those of Marx. Yet the names *Bolshevik* and *Menshevik* stuck with the two groups.

In 1903, such debates seemed academic—of interest to only a few political thinkers. None of the revolutionary parties posed a serious threat to the Russian government. Most of the radical leaders were either in prison or, like Lenin, in exile. None commanded wide popular support. These leaders were like officers in search of an army. They needed more than speeches and debates to enlist troops.

The czar made serious mistakes.

Between 1900 and 1914, Russia faced a series of crises that showed its weaknesses. Yet Czar Nicholas II still resisted change. Pressed by several moderate leaders, he grudgingly allowed some reforms. If World War I had not broken out, these changes might slowly have turned Russia into a constitutional monarchy. When the war came, however, time ran out for the Romanovs.

The Russo-Japanese War In 1904, Nicholas II decided that a victorious war would shift Russians' attention from problems within the country. Therefore, he declared war on Japan, Russia's neighbor in East Asia. Russia and Japan were both imperialist powers, and they were competing for control of Korea.

Russian soldiers and sailors marched off to war enthusiastically, but the result came as a complete surprise. They were soundly beaten. Defeat in war increased unrest at home and led to the revolution of 1905.

The revolution of 1905 On January 22, 1905, about 200,000 workers and their families approached the czar's Winter Palace with a petition.

They were asking for better working conditions, more personal freedom, and an elected national legislature. They were unarmed. Some carried pictures of the "Little Father," as they fondly called the czar. Nicholas was not at the palace, but his generals and police chiefs were. They ordered the soldiers to fire on the crowd. Between 500 and 1,000 people were killed. Russians called the day Bloody Sunday.

Bloody Sunday provoked a wave of strikes that spread across the country. By October 1905, the czar could no longer ignore the demands for change. He reluctantly promised more freedom. He also approved the creation of a Russian parliament, or *Duma* (DOO-muh).

The first Duma took office in May 1906. Its leaders were moderates who wanted Russia to become a constitutional monarchy more like Britain. The Constitutional Democrats, a middle-class party, held the largest number of seats. If Nicholas had chosen to work closely with the group, the history of Russia might have been different. The czar, however, hesitated to share his power with a parliament. Three months after the Duma opened, he dissolved it and sent its members home. There would be other Dumas, but none would have real power.

What were Nicholas's motives? He believed he was doing his duty to God and to the Russian

This commemorative painting shows a peasant striding over the old symbols of Russia.

647

OBJECTIVE 1. Identify the Social Revolutionaries, the Bolsheviks, and the Mensheviks and describe how they wanted to change Russia.

Teaching Strategy: *Skill Building: Comparing Revolutionary Groups* (page 640c)

OBJECTIVE 2. Identify and evaluate the mistakes of Nicholas II.

Teaching Strategy: *Writing about History: The Czar's Mistakes* (page 640c)

■ BACKGROUND

Britain proposed American mediation between Russia and Japan. President Theodore Roosevelt presided over the peace conference in Portsmouth, New Hampshire.

The first two Dumas were elected by universal male suffrage. The czar dissolved them as too liberal, suffrage was restricted, and a third Duma was elected. It supported imperial policies while the fourth Duma criticized the regime.

SECTION 2
Resources

ASSESSMENT
■ Section Quiz 28.2

REINFORCEMENT
■ Independent Practice 28.2

ENRICHMENT
■ Voices from the Past 28.2

647

■ BACKGROUND

Nicholas and Alexandra wrote a steady stream of letters to each other in English. He called her "Sunny"; she addressed him as "Dovey." They disdained the use of the telephone, considering it vulgar.

Hemophilia is a disease transmitted by women to their sons. Alexandra's grandmother, Queen Victoria, was a carrier. Because her daughters married into most of the royal houses of Europe, hemophilia came to be called "the royal disease."

---

people by "being firm." In this opinion, he had the complete support of his closest adviser—his wife, the Czarina Alexandra. The czar was devoted to his "Alix." A German princess by birth, the czarina passionately loved her adopted country. She was determined to protect the Romanov dynasty's autocratic power and pass it on in full to her son, Alexis.

World War I ended Romanov rule.

In 1914, the assassination of Archduke Franz Ferdinand touched off a crisis (page 621). The long-standing feud between Russia and Austria-Hungary over the Balkans came to a head. Czar Nicholas made the fateful decision to go to war. It was this decision, more than any other single factor, that cost Nicholas his throne.

Few Russians understood why their country went to war with Austria and Germany in 1914. Nonetheless, they answered the call for volunteers with patriotic fervor. Millions of soldiers marched west, singing "God Save the Czar!"

Before the year was over, however, the dreams of glory had turned into a nightmare. Although they fought bravely, the poorly equipped Russians were no match for the German army. Germany's advanced artillery destroyed whole Russian battalions. German machine guns mowed down advancing Russians by the thousands. Defeat followed defeat. Before 1914 was over, more than 4 million Russian soldiers were killed, wounded, or taken prisoner.

The czarina and Rasputin's influence When more defeats followed in 1915, the czar made another mistake. Nicholas moved his headquarters to the front so that he could inspire his troops to victory. He left the government of Russia in Alexandra's hands. The czarina, unfortunately, was strongly influenced by her friend, the mysterious Rasputin (ra-SPYOOT-uhn).

Rasputin was a Siberian peasant who claimed to be a holy man. Burly, uncouth, and commanding, he won the confidence of Nicholas and Alexandra by seeming to cure their only son of a dangerous blood disease, hemophilia. For ten years, Rasputin wielded great influence at the court, nearly all of it bad. He obtained powerful positions for dozens of his friends, even though they were unqualified for the jobs. He urged the czarina to ignore demands for reform.

Most Russian nobles resented the influence of this upstart peasant. In December 1916, three young aristocrats decided he must be killed. They lured Rasputin to a mansion and fed him poisoned cakes. The poison seemed to have no effect on his bull-like strength, so the conspirators shot him a dozen times. Thinking he was finally dead, they then threw him in the Neva River. When his body was found three days later, he had died of drowning. The murderers confessed their crime, but they had such widespread support in the capital that they were never punished.

A nation in chaos By the winter of 1916–1917, conditions in Russia were desperate. Food and fuel were in short supply, and prices were wildly inflated. Most of the best soldiers had long since died, and the ranks of the army were filled with unwilling men gathered up by the draft. In St. Petersburg, the first strikes had begun.

With Rasputin out of the way, people began to grumble about Alexandra. Rumors spread that the German-born empress was spying for the enemy. At the palace, the czarina mourned Rasputin. She ignored those who advised her to withdraw from politics and allow the czar to choose ministers and advisers who better understood the public mood.

Nicholas himself seemed unable to make any decisions. "Is it possible," he wearily asked an adviser, "that for 22 years I have tried to act for the best, and that for 22 years I have been wrong?" Perhaps Nicholas already knew the answer. Back at his headquarters at the front, he spent hours playing dominoes, as if he knew that the real game was already over.

A provisional government tried to rule.

In February 1917 came the bread riots and strikes that forced Nicholas from his throne (pages 640–641). After he abdicated, no one was certain who ruled St. Petersburg, let alone Russia. The czar had delivered his abdication to members of the Duma. Accordingly, the Duma chose several leaders to act as a provisional, or temporary, government.

The members of the Duma were mostly conservative or moderate men. Their main goal was to create a constitution for Russia. They had taken no part in the demonstrations and strikes

648

As in other countries, women in Russia held many crucial factory jobs during World War I. The inscription on the plate above is the Marxist slogan "Workers of the world unite!"

■ **BACKGROUND**

On February 27, an estimated 1.5 million people flooded the streets of St. Petersburg to protest Nicholas's policies, yet the czar seemed more concerned about an outbreak of measles among his children.

that led to the downfall of the czar. As a result, radicals in the capital ignored both the Duma and the provisional government.

The power of the soviets Gradually, another political organization began to develop. Workers and soldiers in the capital gathered to form **soviets.** A soviet (SOHV-ee-EHT) was an elected workers' council. Many such councils had been formed during the 1905 revolution. Throughout the turbulent winter of 1916–1917, workers set up more councils to organize protests and plan demonstrations.

Every factory and military barracks in the city sent representatives to the St. Petersburg Soviet. Most of those representatives were socialists. Many were revolutionaries recently released from prison or just back from exile. They belonged to the major radical groups—the Social Revolutionaries, the Mensheviks, and the Bolsheviks.

Because most workers and soldiers obeyed its commands, the St. Petersburg Soviet was more powerful locally than the provisional government. Yet its members were seriously divided on many issues. For the time being, therefore, the soviet let the provisional government try to run the country.

Kerensky as leader The dominant figure in the provisional government was Alexander Kerensky (KEHR-uhn-skee), a young lawyer born in the same town as Lenin. Their fathers had been friends. Kerensky, however, became a Social Revolutionary rather than a Bolshevik. He was the only Duma deputy who was also a member of the St. Petersburg Soviet. Because he commanded the respect of both groups, he led the provisional government.

The provisional government failed.

Almost immediately, Kerensky and the provisional government made a fateful mistake. They chose to continue the war against Germany. Many Duma leaders felt honor-bound by treaties Russia had made with the Allies. Others feared that the Germans might seize St. Petersburg and restore the czar to his throne. Thus, they made the foolhardy decision to keep on fighting.

The Russian army was no more willing to fight and die for the provisional government than for the czar. Desertions continued. Peasants were eager to return home and obtain a share of the lands from the great estates, which were being divided. They ignored Kerensky's plea to forget land distribution until the war was over. "Let the officers do the fighting for themselves," a ragged soldier was heard to say on a train near Moscow. "I don't care who wins the war. It's only for a lot of capitalists anyhow. My house is far from the front, and the Germans will never get to my village."

While the Russian army was falling apart, the Germans launched their own "secret weapon."

649

ANSWERS TO

Section Review 2

Define:
elected workers' council
Identify:
(a) German philosopher who argued that the workers of the world would overthrow ruling classes and share equally in society's wealth (b) planned to overthrow the czar and spark a worldwide Marxist revolution (c) Social Democrats who were followers of Lenin (d) Social Democrats who opposed Lenin (e) January 22, 1905, when soldiers killed 500–1,000 workers (f) Russian parliament (g) wife of Nicholas II (h) mysterious peasant who had great influence on the
(continued)

ANSWERS TO (continued)

czarina (i) dominant figure in the provisional government
Answer:
1. Social Revolutionaries believed the force to overthrow the czar's government would come from Russia's peasants; Social Democrats believed the urban workers would revolt.

2. (a) He believed a Marxist revolution should begin at once. (b) His policy split the party into Bolsheviks and Mensheviks.

3. (a) shift Russians' attention away from internal problems (b) Korea (c) Russian defeat increased unrest at home and led to the 1905 revolution.

4. (a) Bloody Sunday provoked a wave of strikes that spread across the country. (b) forced czar to promise more freedom and approve creation of a Russian parliament

5. Recurring defeats in battle, the death of many soldiers, and acute shortages led to bread riots and strikes that forced Nicholas to abdicate.

6. (a) chose leaders to act as provisional government (b) more powerful locally than provisional government (c) led provisional government

7. Russian army was no more willing to fight for provisional government than for the czar.

8. Russia was ripe for revolution. On the other hand, if Nicholas had not chosen to enter World War I and had worked closely with the Duma, he might have further split the revolutionaries and avoided being overthrown.

They helped Lenin return to Russia. He traveled through Germany in a sealed passenger car. On April 3, 1917, he arrived at the Finland Station in St. Petersburg. A wild and happy crowd gathered to welcome the Bolshevik leader back to Russia. Lenin was home after 17 years in exile.

Section REVIEW 2

Define: soviet
Identify: (a) Karl Marx, (b) Lenin, (c) Bolsheviks, (d) Mensheviks, (e) Bloody Sunday, (f) Duma, (g) Alexandra, (h) Rasputin, (i) Alexander Kerensky
Answer:
1. How did the ideas of the Social Revolutionaries differ from those of the Social Democrats?
2. (a) What course of action did Lenin support? (b) How did his proposal split the party?
3. (a) What was the czar's goal in the Russo-Japanese War? (b) What territory was in dispute? (c) What were the results of the war?
4. (a) Briefly describe the revolution of 1905. (b) What were its results?
5. How did World War I lead to the downfall of the czar?
6. After the czar's abdication, what part did the following play in government? (a) the Duma (b) St. Petersburg Soviet (c) Kerensky
7. Why was it a mistake for the provisional government to continue the war?

Critical Thinking
8. If Nicholas II had been a more competent ruler, could he have prevented the Russian Revolution? Or was it the result of events beyond his control? Present your viewpoint with evidence to support it.

The Bolsheviks led a second revolution. 3

Germany's strategy in helping Lenin return to Russia made sense. The Bolsheviks were strongly opposed to continuing the war. Lenin's return would certainly contribute to unrest in Russia, which in turn would help Germany's war effort.

Lenin, however, had bigger plans than simply pulling Russia out of the war. In a speech to the crowd that greeted him, he hurled abuse at the provisional government:

The people need peace, the people need bread . . . We must fight for the social revolution, fight to the end, till the complete victory of the proletariat. Long live the world social revolution!

The Bolsheviks gained support.

Later, Lenin met privately with his fellow Bolsheviks. The February revolution was only a modest beginning, he told them. It was now time to plan the Bolshevik takeover.

Lenin's plans seemed outrageous even to many of his followers. The Bolsheviks were not very popular. They had almost no support among the peasants. Even in St. Petersburg, most workers considered the Bolsheviks too narrow and undemocratic. There were only a few Bolsheviks among the St. Petersburg Soviet's deputies.

This detail of a painting shows Lenin speaking to a crowd of rebellious workers, soldiers, and sailors.

The very narrowness of their party proved to be the Bolsheviks' greatest advantage. Among the dozens of parties that sprang up after the czar was overthrown, only the Bolsheviks were tightly organized and well disciplined. They were more like a tiny army than a political party. As a result, in the chaos of 1917, the Bolsheviks were able to exert more influence than larger but less organized groups.

During the summer and fall of 1917, events played into the hands of the Bolsheviks. First, the war went from bad to worse, and the provisional government still insisted on fighting it. Second, in September, General Lavr Kornilov (kawr-NEE-luhf) tried to seize power. As commander-in-chief of the army, he was much admired by the upper and middle classes, who felt that the revolution had gone too far. Some people even said that Kornilov would restore the czar. Gathering troops loyal to his cause, the general led an army toward St. Petersburg.

The revolutionaries stopped Kornilov in the same way that they had stopped Nicholas's attempt to return to St. Petersburg in February. Marshaled by the Bolsheviks, railroad workers tore up tracks and diverted trains, making it impossible for Kornilov's troops to advance. The Bolsheviks also organized Red Guard units to defend the capital. Meanwhile, groups of workers and soldiers met with the general's troops, urging them to join the revolution. Within a few days, Kornilov had no army left.

The Bolsheviks had saved St. Petersburg. Throughout September, popular support swung suddenly to the Bolsheviks. Party membership increased rapidly. Public opinion was clear on two things: Russians did not want the czar to return, and they did not want the war to continue. Lenin's slogan of "Peace, Land, and Bread" captured the popular imagination. The Bolsheviks were the only party that seemed strong enough to protect the revolution against generals and czarists. They were the only party that seemed willing to end the war. They were the only party that promised land reform at once.

By late September, a majority of the deputies in the St. Petersburg Soviet supported the Bolsheviks. Leon Trotsky, second only to Lenin in popularity within the party, became the chairman of the soviet. Within days, soviets in Moscow and other cities also came under Bolshevik control.

Lenin took control.

Lenin decided that it was time to act. "History will not forgive us," he wrote, "if we do not seize power now." On the night of October 24, Bolshevik Red Guards took over government offices. The St. Petersburg Soviet ordered the arrest of the leaders of the provisional government.

The Bolshevik takeover was practically bloodless. The streetcars kept running, and the restaurants and theaters remained open. There were no loyal troops left to defend the provisional government. Kerensky and his colleagues disappeared as quickly and as completely as the czarist regime they had replaced.

The next evening, Lenin addressed the All-Russian Congress of Soviets, a group of representatives from soviets all over the country. They greeted him with thunderous cheers. After minutes of deafening applause, he told the crowd, "We shall now proceed to construct the socialist order!"

What was this new socialist order? The government ordered all farmland to be divided among the peasants. The Bolshevik government signed a truce with Germany, and peace talks began between the two countries. The new government also took over all major industries. From now on, workers' councils were to run the factories.

Lenin had long planned on a dictatorship of the proletariat, under which a small group would rule in the name of the people. He wanted Bolsheviks, and only Bolsheviks, to govern Russia. Yet other parties still had much popular support. When elections were held later in November 1917, the Social Revolutionary party won a majority in the new national assembly. In response, the Bolsheviks closed the assembly at once. The only democratically elected body in Russian history had a life span of a single day.

Footnote to History

Long before the rise of the Russian Bolsheviks, revolutionaries used the color red as their symbol. In one sense, it stood for the common blood of all people, regardless of social rank. In another sense, it stood for the bloodshed of violent revolution. The Bolsheviks' use of red has led many people to link it specifically with communism.

SECTION 3
Objectives and Teaching Strategies

OBJECTIVE 1. Explain how Lenin and the Bolsheviks came to power in 1917.

Teaching Strategy: *Writing about History: The Bolsheviks Seize Power* (page 640d)

OBJECTIVE 2. Locate lands Russia lost in World War I.

Teaching Strategy: *Geography in History: Russia's Lost Lands* (page 640d)

OBJECTIVE 3. Explain how Stalin defeated Trotsky for control of the Communist party.

Teaching Strategy: *Transferring Ideas: Stalin as a Dictator* (page 640d)

■ BACKGROUND

Red Square in Moscow was called that even before 1917. In Russian, the word *red* is closely related to the word meaning "beautiful." That was probably the original meaning of Red Square.

SECTION 3
Resources

ENRICHMENT
■ Voices from the Past 28.3

ASSESSMENT
■ Section Quiz 28.3

GEOGRAPHY
■ Transparency 84

REINFORCEMENT
■ Independent Practice 28.3

■ BACKGROUND

A legend persists that the youngest of Nicholas's and Alexandra's daughters, Anastasia, escaped to the West.

The Soviets use the term *comrade* much as the French used the term *citizen* at the time of their revolution.

Artists, according to Harrison E. Salisbury, sensed that what was happening was "no orderly, conspiratorial movement but an elemental force . . . impossible to tame, as pervasive as a flood and as devastating as a forest fire."

Lenin was pleased. "The dissolution of the Constituent Assembly," he bluntly told Trotsky, "means a complete and frank liquidation of the idea of democracy by the idea of dictatorship. It will serve as a good lesson."

Many Russians objected to the Bolsheviks and their policies. There was widespread unrest. Discontent increased when Russians learned about the Treaty of Brest Litovsk, which the Bolshevik government signed with Germany in March 1918. In the treaty, the Bolsheviks surrendered one fourth of Russia's European territory to Germany. They also gave up many of the country's mines and factories. Many patriotic Russians were outraged.

Lenin was unconcerned about the lost lands. He was certain that the socialist revolution soon would spread to Germany and the treaty would be set aside. (He was half right. Russia got most of its territory back later in 1918. However, the land was returned because the Allies defeated Germany, not because of a revolution.)

Civil war divided Russia.

By summer, the Bolsheviks' opponents formed several "White" armies, so-called to distinguish them from the Bolshevik Red Army. Several Western nations, including the United States, sent small armies to Russia to help the Whites, a fact that the Bolsheviks later recalled bitterly.

Russia's civil war between the Whites and the Reds proved more deadly than any of the earlier revolutions. It lasted from 1918 to 1920, leaving an estimated 15 million Russians dead. Many died of hunger. Others were killed in the fighting. Still others fell victim to a worldwide flu epidemic that began in 1918. Several thousand were shot by the Bolsheviks as suspected enemies of the new regime. Among the dead were the former czar, the czarina, and their five children. They were shot by the Bolsheviks in July 1918.

Victory eventually went to the Red Army, capably led and organized by Trotsky. The Whites might have won if they had not been deeply divided among themselves. They also lost support among peasants and workers because they threatened to restore farms and factories to their former owners.

In the aftermath of the civil war, Lenin and the Bolsheviks faced overwhelming problems.

War and revolution had left the Russian economy in ruins. Trade was at a standstill. In the upheaval, factories had been destroyed. Many of the people who knew how to run those factories had been killed or imprisoned. Other skilled workers returned to farming just to survive.

Lenin restored order.

The socialist order of Lenin's plans seemed to be coming apart. Unrest spread. The Cheka, the Bolshevik secret police, became more and more ruthless toward "enemies of the revolution." Even some former Bolshevik supporters now turned against the new government.

The Kronstadt revolt In March 1921, the sailors at Kronstadt, a major naval base on the outskirts of Petrograd, staged a revolt. In 1917, the sailors had been strong Bolshevik supporters. They had played a key role in overthrowing the czar. Now their complaints were almost the same as in 1917. They demanded free elections, freedom of speech, and the abolition of the secret police.

The Bolsheviks ignored the sailors' demands. Lenin and his colleagues brutally crushed the Kronstadt uprising. A former Lenin supporter was distressed. "What can I do now in this life?" he asked. "I cannot live outside this Russia of ours, and I cannot breathe within it."

The New Economic Policy Even Lenin realized that changes were needed. Late in 1921, he launched the New Economic Policy (NEP). It called for a temporary compromise with capitalism. Farmers were allowed to sell their surplus instead of having it taken by the government. Individuals were permitted to buy and sell goods for profit. The government even allowed private ownership of some small businesses. Lenin also tried to encourage foreign investment.

A *new name* and a *new party* Lenin began some political reforms as well. Acknowledging the many different national groups within the country, Lenin created a number of self-governing republics. In 1922, the Bolsheviks gave Russia a new name—the Union of Soviet Socialist Republics (USSR), or the Soviet Union.

By 1922, the USSR had a new capital as well. During the civil war, Lenin had moved the capital from Petrograd (today back to its original name, St. Petersburg) to Moscow, mainly because the inland city was safer from foreign invasion.

652

The Bolsheviks also gave their group a new name—the Communist party. The name came from the writings of Karl Marx. He used the word *communism* to describe the economic system based on centralized planning by the state that would exist after workers had seized power.

Thanks partly to the new policies and to the peace that followed the civil war, the USSR slowly recovered. By 1928, the country's farms and factories were producing as much as they had before World War I. After a decade of turmoil, life seemed to have returned to normal for most people in the Soviet Union.

Two men struggled to succeed Lenin.

Lenin did not live to see this recovery. He died in 1924 after spending the last two years of his life as a semi-invalid owing to a series of strokes. In the year before Lenin's death, a quiet struggle took place within the Communist party to determine who would succeed Lenin.

Trotsky The most obvious candidate was Lev Davidovich Bronstein (1879–1940). He was better known as Leon Trotsky, the name he had used in the Bolshevik underground. Trotsky had been an important figure in the revolutionary movement since the revolution of 1905. He was the organizer of the 1917 takeover, founder of the Red Army, and a capable, popular leader.

Trotsky, however, had many enemies within the party. Some feared that he would become a dictator. Therefore, more and more party members gave their support to Joseph Stalin, secretary of the Communist party.

Stalin Stalin was a quiet man who rarely received much public notice. He had been born in 1879 in Georgia, the mountainous region on the southern border of the Russian empire. During his early days as a Bolshevik, he changed his name from Djugashvili (joo-guhsh-VEE-lee) to Stalin. It was an appropriate choice, since *Stalin* means "man of steel" in Russian. Joseph Djugashvili was certainly that: cold, hard, and impersonal. One Communist who worked with him during this period described him as "just a gray blur, looming up now and then darkly."

Stalin worked behind the scenes. As party secretary, he was responsible for hundreds of important appointments. By 1924, he had placed many of his supporters in key positions.

Cause and Effect

THE RUSSIAN REVOLUTION

Long-Term Causes

Oppression of serfs
Class inequalities
Autocracy of czars
Defeat in Crimean War
Rise of Marxism

Immediate Causes

Defeat in Russo-Japanese War
Bloody Sunday
Losses in World War I
Indecision of Nicholas II
Strikes and riots

REVOLUTION

Abdication of Nicholas II
Failure of provisional government
Growing power of soviets
Return of Lenin to Russia
Bolshevik takeover under Lenin

Immediate Effects

Civil war
Peace with Germany under harsh treaty
Bolshevik control of government
Russian economy in ruins

Long-Term Effects

Establishment of Communist state
Victory of Red Army in civil war
New Economic Policy
Formation of USSR
Dictatorship under Communist party

653

■ **DISCUSSION**

Have students compare and contrast the long-term causes and effects of the Russian Revolution with those of the French Revolution.

Cooperative Learning

Divide the class into five groups and assign each group one of the boxes in *The Russian Revolution* chart. Have each group member select one point from the assigned box to outline. Students may use the textbook alone or in conjunction with library resources. Have group members present their outlines to each other for revision before combining them into a master outline of their topic. Have each group present its master outline to the class.

ANSWERS TO

Section Review 3

Define:
rule by a small group in the name of the people
Identify:
(a) commander-in-chief of Russian army who tried to seize power and was stopped by the Bolsheviks
(b) peace between Russia and Germany (c) opponents of the Bolsheviks (d) army of the Bolsheviks (e) revolt of sailors (f) Lenin's policy calling for temporary compro-
(continued)

ANSWERS TO (continued)

mise with capitalism
(g) name given to Russia by
Bolsheviks **(h)** new name for
Bolsheviks **(i)** founder of
Red Army **(j)** successor to
Lenin
Answer:
1. (a) not very popular with
the peasants or workers
(b) most tightly organized of
all the parties
2. The Bolsheviks prevented
Kornilov from taking over St.
Petersburg and returning the
czar. Party membership increased as the people
viewed the Bolsheviks as
protectors of the revolution.
3. Bolshevik Red Guards
took over government of-
fices. St. Petersburg Soviet
ordered the arrest of leaders
of the provisional
government.
4. (a) ordered all farmland
divided among the peasants
(b) took over all major industries and let workers'
councils run factories
(c) closed the national assembly **(d)** signed truce with
Germany
5. divided the country and
left the economy in ruins
6. (a) used secret police to
identify "enemies of the revolution" **(b)** began a New
Economic Policy (NEP)
7. As party secretary, he
placed many of his supporters in key positions. When
Lenin died, most of the
Communist leaders allied
themselves with Stalin
against Trotsky. Once Trotsky had been expelled, Stalin turned against the other
leaders one by one.
8. All Russians wanted the
war to stop, peasants
wanted the land to be di-
vided; and all citizens
wanted food to be more
plentiful.

As he lay dying, Lenin realized that Stalin, not Trotsky, was the more dangerous man. "Comrade Stalin has concentrated enormous power in his hands," wrote Lenin in a secret document that was not published until long after his death, "and I am not sure that he always knows how to use that power with sufficient caution."

Other Communist leaders did not see the danger. After Lenin's death, most allied themselves with Stalin against Trotsky. Indeed, Trotsky was expelled and forced to leave the USSR in 1929.

Having disposed of Trotsky, Stalin turned against his recent allies. He used his enormous power within the party to isolate them one by one. By 1928, Stalin stood alone, as totally in command of the party—and therefore the government—as Lenin had been.

Section REVIEW 3

Define: dictatorship of the proletariat
Identify: (a) Lavr Kornilov, (b) Treaty of Brest Litovsk, (c) White Army, (d) Red Army, (e) Kronstadt revolt, (f) New Economic Policy, (g) Union of Soviet Socialist Republics, (h) Communist party, (i) Leon Trotsky, (j) Joseph Stalin
Answer:
1. (a) What disadvantages did the Bolsheviks face in trying to take power in 1917? (b) What advantages did they have?
2. How did Kornilov's attempted coup help the Bolsheviks?
3. How did the Bolsheviks actually take control of the government?
4. What policies did the new government follow in each of these areas? (a) land, (b) industry, (c) democratic government, (d) the war against Germany
5. What were the results of Russia's civil war?
6. (a) How did Lenin deal with political discontent after the civil war? (b) How did he deal with the country's economic problems?
7. How did Stalin rise to power in the 1920's?

Critical Thinking
8. Why did Lenin's slogan of "Peace, Land, and Bread" win wide support? To what group or groups did each word appeal?

654

Stalin became dictator. 4

Although Trotsky and Stalin had much in common, their political views differed in one important way. Like Lenin, Trotsky was dedicated to the idea of *world* revolution. To him, the Russian Revolution was merely the first act in a worldwide uprising of the proletariat. Stalin, on the other hand, was not as concerned with developments outside the Soviet Union. He coined the phrase "socialism in one country" to describe his aims. To Stalin, the Soviet Union was the revolution, and it was up to the Soviet people to fashion a perfect Communist state. The rest of the world could wait. Stalin was, however, committed to centralized planning.

Stalin blended Marxism with old-fashioned Russian nationalism. He was convinced that someday foreign enemies would attack the Soviet Union. In the past, "Russia was ceaselessly beaten for her backwardness . . . because to beat her was profitable and went unpunished." Stalin was determined to keep history from repeating itself. Thus, he set out to make his country powerful enough to withstand an attack. "We are 50 or 100 years behind the advanced countries," he said. "We must make good this lag in 10 years. Either we do it, or they crush us."

Stalin launched two new revolutions.

In 1928, Stalin broke with the policies of Lenin to create what were in effect two new Soviet revolutions—in industry and in agriculture.

An industrial revolution In 1928, Stalin outlined a Five-Year Plan for the development of the USSR's economy. The plan called for a **command economy,** one in which all economic decisions were made by the government. It sought industrial growth throughout the country, especially in resource-rich Siberia. Stalin also set specific production targets for each industry. The rapid industrialization under Stalin's Five-Year Plans was achieved in part by limiting production of consumer goods. Instead, investment was made in state-owned mines, heavy industry, railroads, and energy resources.

The targets were deliberately set high. Many economists, including some in the USSR, were convinced that Stalin's goals were impossible to achieve. However, Stalin was determined to make the Soviet Union a great industrial power quickly.

From the start, the government decided who worked, where they worked, and for how long. It controlled every aspect of the worker's life. The secret police were ready to imprison or execute those who did not contribute.

Stalin's grim methods produced fantastic results. Although most of the targets of the first Five-Year Plan were not met, the Soviets made impressive gains. A second plan, launched in 1933, proved equally successful. Between 1928 and 1938, the electricity generated each year increased by nearly 800 percent, and steel production increased from 4 million tons to 18 million tons annually. By 1938, the USSR was becoming a major industrial power.

An agricultural revolution Stalin's agricultural revolution—also based on centralized planning—

Voice from the Past | *Applause for Comrade Stalin*

In the following source, Alexander Solzhenitsyn, exiled Soviet writer and Nobel prizewinner, retells this story of life in the Soviet Union during the Stalin years.

A district party conference was under way in Moscow Province. . . . At the conclusion of the conference, a tribute to Comrade Stalin was called for. Of course, everyone stood up. . . . The small hall echoed with "stormy applause, rising to an ovation." For three minutes, four minutes, five minutes, the . . . ovation . . . continued. But palms were getting sore and raised arms were already aching. And the older people were panting from exhaustion. It was becoming insufferably silly even to those who really adored Stalin. However, who would dare be the first to stop! The secretary of the District Party Committee could have done it. . . . [I]t was he who had called for the ovation. But he was a newcomer. He had taken the place of a man who'd been arrested. He was afraid! After all, NKVD men were standing in the hall applauding and watching to see who would quit first! . . . [T]he applause went on—six, seven, eight minutes! They were done for! . . . The director of the local paper factory, an independent and strong-minded man, stood with the presidium. Aware of all the falsity and all the impossibility of the situation, he still kept on applauding! Nine minutes! Ten! . . . Insanity! To the last man! . . . Then, after eleven minutes, the director of the paper factory assumed a businesslike expression and sat down in his seat. . . . To a man, everyone else stopped dead and sat down. They had been saved! . . .

That, however, was how they discovered who the independent people were. And that was how they went about eliminating them. That same night the factory director was arrested. They easily pasted ten years on him on the pretext of something quite different. But . . . his interrogator reminded him: "Don't ever be the first to stop applauding!"

1. (a) What was the original reason for the clapping? (b) What became the reason?
2. Why did the NKVD want to know who would stop first?
3. What does this selection show about totalitarianism?

Joseph Stalin

655

SECTION 4 Resources

REINFORCEMENT
- Independent Practice 28.4

ENRICHMENT
- Voices from the Past 28.4

ASSESSMENT
- Section Quiz 28.4

SECTION 4 Objectives and Teaching Strategies

OBJECTIVE 1. Contrast the policies of Lenin and Stalin.

Teaching Strategy: *Skill Building: Contrasting Points of View* (page 640e)

OBJECTIVE 2. Explain how Stalin transformed the Soviet economy.

Teaching Strategy: *Economics and History: Transforming the Soviet Economy* (page 640e)

OBJECTIVE 3. Describe how the Soviet Union became a totalitarian state.

Teaching Strategy: *Discussing History: Totalitarianism as a Way of Life* (page 640e)

■ BACKGROUND

Scholars say that Stalin was jealous, anti-Semitic, and chauvinistic, all the while demanding to be treated as a demigod.

ANSWERS TO Voice from the Past

1. (a) secretary had called for a tribute to Stalin (b) no one dared to be the first to stop
2. They wanted to find and eliminate independent people.
3. It demands conformity and unquestioning obedience.

During Stalin's agricultural revolution, droves of peasants—sometimes entire villages—were packed off to the mines, timber camps, and construction projects of the Arctic north.

Some scholars believe that Stalin, who decreed that "writers are the engineers of human souls," ordered the slow poisoning of the great Russian writer, Maxim Gorky.

Cooperative Learning

Arrange students in groups of four. Assign each member of a group one section of the chapter. Each student should write five questions about the material in the assigned section. Then have each group member present the five questions to the group for discussion. The group should reach agreement on the answer to each question. Have a group recorder write the questions and answers. Finally, ask each group to select several questions to present to the entire class for discussion. Compare the class answers to the group's answers.

was as complete and far more brutal than his industrial revolution. There were more than 25 million small farms in the USSR in 1928. That year, the government announced that these privately owned farms would be abolished. They would be replaced by **collective farms,** large units worked by hundreds of families. The government expected that these large farms, equipped with modern machinery, would produce more food with fewer workers.

The peasants, many of whom had only recently won their own land, resisted fiercely. For centuries, they had struggled against the nobles. Now they were being forced to submit to yet another landlord, the Soviet government.

Stalin showed no mercy. Between 5 million and 10 million peasants died. Millions more were shipped to Siberia. Many farmers destroyed their crops and livestock in protest against collectivization. The government confiscated what remained of the harvest to feed city workers. Thus, for the peasants, the winters of 1931 and 1932 brought terrible famines.

Eventually, Stalin got his way. By 1938, more than 90 percent of all peasants lived on collective farms. Agricultural production was recovering. That year the country produced about as much wheat as it had in 1928, before collectivization.

The human cost of these forced changes was enormous. A British writer traveling in the country during this period met a secret-police colonel who had taken part in forcing peasants onto collective farms. The colonel told him:

I am an old Bolshevik. I worked in the underground against the czar, and then I fought in the civil war. Did I do all that in order that I should now surround villages with machine guns and order my men to fire indiscriminately into crowds of peasants! Oh, no, no!

The USSR *became a totalitarian state.*

If Stalin's government was this brutal, how did he stay in power? Why was there no rebellion? One answer is that people were afraid to speak out. The Soviet Union in the 1930's had become a **totalitarian** state—a country in which a dictator or a small group controls every part of the lives of its citizens. Not even the slightest dissent was tolerated by the government.

Joseph Stalin was an absolute dictator, more powerful than the most autocratic czar. He crushed his enemies and anyone who he thought might become an enemy. The secret police arrested and executed millions of suspected traitors.

One of Stalin's first targets was religion. The Bolsheviks had tried but failed to repress religion in 1921. In 1929, the government again struck at religion. Many churches, synagogues, and mosques were closed or put to other uses. Schools, which had been ordered to ignore religion, were now required to teach lessons presenting religion as backward and harmful. Yet many people in the Soviet Union remained devoutly religious.

ECONOMICS IN DAILY LIFE ▸ *Tractors and Politics*

Tractors came to play both an economic and a political role in the USSR under Stalin. In 1928, there were only 7,000 tractors in the entire Soviet Union, even though most of the country's 150 million people were farmers. Tractors were far too expensive for individual peasant families. One of Stalin's goals in setting up large, state-run farms was to mechanize Soviet farming. By 1931, the need for tractors was even more serious. Angry peasants had killed about half the plow horses in the country as a desperate protest against Stalin's policy. During the 1930's, the government set up Machine-Tractor Stations throughout the countryside. They were more than equipment centers. They were also the rural political headquarters of the Communist party.

Much Soviet art in the Stalinist era celebrated the importance of working men and women. This poster urges, "Let's all get to work, comrades."

In 1934, Stalin even turned against members of the Communist party itself. During the late 1930's, thousands of old Bolsheviks were brought to trial and executed for "crimes against the Soviet state." Most of the accused had been longtime Communists who had fought in the revolution and the civil war. Indeed, many had helped Stalin become the party's leader. Among the accused were *all* the Bolsheviks who had held positions in Lenin's first government except Stalin himself.

People were arrested for having friends in foreign countries, for practicing their religion, for casual remarks overheard by police informers. Factory and farm managers who failed to meet their targets were in particular danger. Even the director of the Moscow Zoo was arrested because his monkeys got tuberculosis. The police themselves were not safe, especially if they didn't discover enough criminals.

Every family came to fear the knock on the door in the early hours of the morning. Such a visit might mean a son, father, mother, or daughter taken prisoner and not heard from again for months or years—or ever.

Only once during his long career did Stalin show any hesitancy. In 1932, after a bitter argument over the brutality of his campaign against the peasants, his wife Nadia killed herself. Grief-stricken, Stalin offered to resign. The party's leaders sat in shocked silence. No one wanted to be the first to agree that Stalin should step down. Finally, they asked him to stay in office. Never again did he offer to resign.

For almost 25 years, Joseph Stalin kept a firm grip on the USSR's destiny. More than any other individual, he was responsible for the Soviet Union's rise to a position as a great world power. Without his forced industrialization, the USSR might not have been able to stand up to Germany in World War II.

During Stalin's years in power, the Soviet Union became a modern state. Its people saw their standard of living rise. They became better educated and mastered the ever-changing world of science and technology.

The Soviet people paid a heavy price for the progress they made in the 1930's. In writing his autobiography, Soviet novelist Boris Pasternak refused to go any further than 1930. "To continue it would be immeasurably difficult," he said. "One would have to talk in a manner that would grip the heart and make the hair stand on end." In the end, the people of the USSR were less free in the 1930's than in the era of the czars.

Section REVIEW 4

Define: (a) command economy, (b) collective farm, (c) totalitarian
Identify: Five-Year Plan
Answer:
1. How did Stalin's ideas on communism differ from Trotsky's?
2. (a) How did Stalin revolutionize Soviet industry? (b) What were his policies to reorganize agriculture?
3. What are the features of a totalitarian state?
4. What steps did Stalin take in the 1930's to stamp out all possible dissent?

Critical Thinking
5. What features of Stalin's government were similar to czarist government?

657

■ **BACKGROUND**
Many of those condemned during the purge were suspected of sympathy with Trotsky. Trotsky himself was murdered in exile by Stalin's agents in 1940.

ANSWERS TO
Section Review 4

Define:
(a) economy in which all economic decisions are made by the government
(b) large farms worked by hundreds of families (c) dictator or small group controls every part of citizens' lives
Identify:
Stalin's economic development plan
Answer:
1. Trotsky advocated world revolution; Stalin was only concerned with revolution in Russia.
2. (a) set specific production targets for each industry with his Five-Year Plans
(b) replaced privately owned farms with collective farms
3. total control of citizens, repression of dissenters
4. repressed all forms of religion, executed members of Communist party, used secret police to find dissenters
5. Look for references to rule by absolute power and lack of personal freedoms in both.

Concluding the Chapter

1. **Chapter Closer**
   Ask students to identify three long-term causes of the decline of the czars' power and three immediate causes of the Bolshevik Revolution.

2. **Reteaching Activities**
   a. Making A Time Line Have students create a time line showing the major events covered in this chapter
   b. Identifying Have students identify the roles of Lenin, Kornilov, the New Economic Policy, the Communist Party, and Stalin in the Bolshevik revolution.

Answers to Chapter Review appear on page 640f.

Chapter Review 28

Summary

1. **Russia struggled to reform.** While the Industrial Revolution was transforming western Europe, Russia remained largely agricultural. Most Russian peasants were bound to the land as serfs. A series of uprisings in the early 1800's caused Nicholas I to increase controls. The freeing of serfs in 1861 by Alexander II failed to end discontent. Alexander III tightened controls once again. Limited industrialization under Nicholas II brought some changes, but Russia still lagged far behind.

2. **Russia moved toward revolution.** In the early 1900's, Russian radicals worked secretly for revolution. Social revolutionaries favored a peasants' revolt, whereas Social Democrats, or Marxists, favored the revolt of urban workers. Lenin's call for a dictatorship of the proletariat split Marxists into Bolsheviks (Lenin's supporters) and Mensheviks (his opponents). Russia's defeat in the Russo-Japanese War, Bloody Sunday, and World War I all added fuel to the fire. Riots and strikes in March 1917 forced the abdication of the czar. When Kerensky's provisional government continued to fight in World War I, Germany helped Lenin return to Russia.

3. **The Bolsheviks led a second revolution.** In November 1917, Lenin's Bolsheviks came to power. The new government ended the war, divided land among the peasants, and took control of major industries. The following summer, civil war broke out as Reds (Bolsheviks) battled Whites, who were opposed to Lenin's reforms. After the Reds emerged victorious, Lenin instituted a New Economic Policy that offered a compromise with capitalism. The new government also changed the name of Russia to the USSR. Lenin's death provoked an internal struggle between Trotsky and Stalin, which Stalin won.

4. **Stalin became a dictator.** Determined to make the Soviet Union a world power, Stalin forced rapid industrialization and collectivization of agriculture. Millions of peasants were killed when they offered fierce resistance to Stalin's agricultural reforms. Stalin instituted a totalitarian state.

Reviewing the Facts

1. Define the following terms:
   a. abdicate   d. soviet
   b. autocrat   e. command economy
   c. nihilism   f. totalitarian
2. Explain the importance of each of the following names or terms:
   a. Decembrist revolt   c. Social Democrat
   b. Social Revolutionary   d. Marx

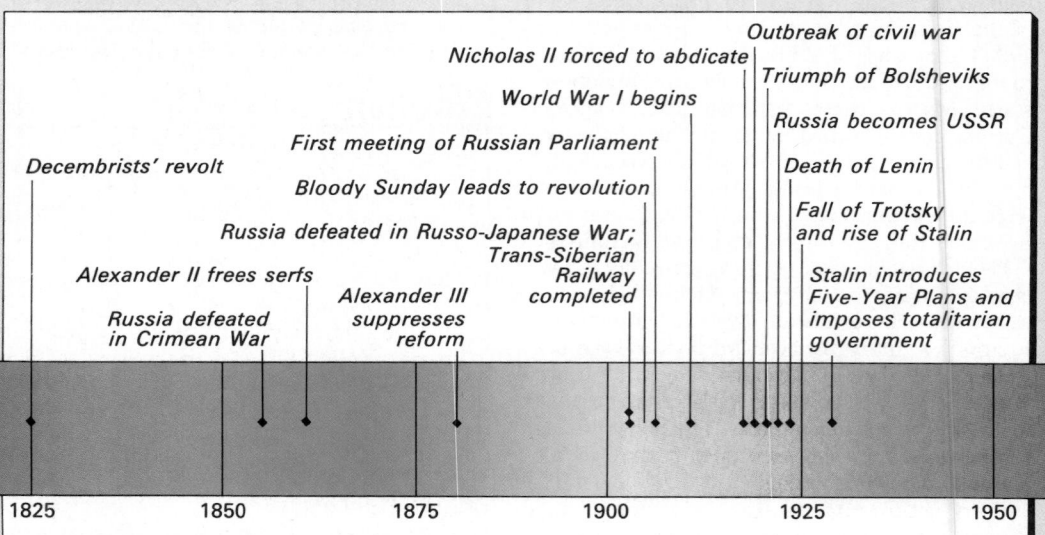

Outbreak of civil war
Nicholas II forced to abdicate
Triumph of Bolsheviks
World War I begins
Russia becomes USSR
First meeting of Russian Parliament
Death of Lenin
Decembrists' revolt
Bloody Sunday leads to revolution
Fall of Trotsky and rise of Stalin
Russia defeated in Russo-Japanese War; Trans-Siberian Railway completed
Alexander II frees serfs
Stalin introduces Five-Year Plans and imposes totalitarian government
Alexander III suppresses reform
Russia defeated in Crimean War

1825   1850   1875   1900   1925   1950

e. Lenin
f. Bolshevik
g. Menshevik
h. Nicholas II
i. Bloody Sunday
j. Duma
k. Rasputin
l. Kerensky
m. Trotsky
n. Kronstadt revolt
o. Communist party
p. Stalin

3. What was the attitude toward reform of each of the following czars? (a) Nicholas I (b) Alexander II (c) Alexander III (d) Nicholas II

4. (a) To what social class did Russia's radicals belong in the early 1900's? (b) Describe the goals of the two groups to which they belonged. (c) Into what two groups did the Social Democrats split?

5. Describe the role of each of the following in the provisional government of 1917. (a) Duma (b) Petrograd Soviet (c) Kerensky

6. (a) Briefly describe the Russian civil war that followed Lenin's takeover. (b) What was the result of the war?

7. (a) Describe the struggle between Trotsky and Stalin. (b) How did their views differ?

Basic Skills

1. **Sequencing** (a) List the following events in the order in which they happened: decree freeing the serfs, revolution of 1905, abdication of Nicholas II, Decembrist revolt, St. Petersburg bread riots, Russo-Japanese War. (b) Explain the importance of each event to the 1917 Russian Revolution.

2. **Reading a map** (a) Using the map on page 636, identify the European territories lost by Russia after World War I. (b) What was the effect of those losses?

Researching and Reporting Skills

1. **Using memoirs** Two memoirs from the time of the Russian Revolution provide first-hand accounts. During his exile in Mexico, Leon Trotsky wrote *A History of the Russian Revolution.* John Reed, a radical American journalist who traveled in Russia in 1917, wrote about his experiences in *Ten Days That Shook the World.* Read selections from one of these works. What impressions does it give of the times?

2. **Using literature** Find a book that discusses Russian literature. Identify some of the great Russian writers of the 1800's. Choose one and describe how that author's work anticipates the revolution.

3. **Using art or photographs** From history books, encyclopedias, or art books, find three pictures that illustrate events leading up to or during the Russian Revolution. Explain what information these works provide about the revolution.

Critical Thinking

1. **Evaluating causes** Conditions within the country and the effects of the war both contributed to the breakdown of government in Russia. Which factor do you consider to be more important as a cause of that breakdown? Give reasons for your answer.

2. **Comparing** Lenin and Trotsky both emerged as powerful leaders during the Russian Revolution. (a) What contributions did each make to the revolution? (b) How essential was the work of each leader to the success of the revolution? Give evidence to support your answer.

3. **Analyzing** (a) List the original goals of the Russian Revolution. (b) To what extent did Stalin implement them or undermine them?

4. **Applying ideas** (a) What political and economic ideas introduced by Marx did Lenin adopt? (b) How did Lenin apply these ideas through the Russian Revolution?

5. **Analyzing economics** (a) Why did Stalin introduce the Five-Year Plans? (b) What were the objectives? (c) What were the economic results?

6. **Applying a concept** Identify five ways by which Stalin established totalitarian rule.

Perspectives on Past and Present

Terrible persecutions were known to have occurred in the Soviet Union during the Stalin era. The Russian government has now permitted the release of information about some of these events. Use the *Readers' Guide* to locate news stories about the Stalin era. What events are mentioned and what is their significance?

Investigating History

1. Read selections from *Nicholas and Alexandra,* Robert K. Massie's history of the last czar and his family. Of special interest are the chapters "The Coronation," "Two Revolutionaries," "1905," and "Ekaterinberg." Write a brief report giving your impressions of the reading.

2. Watch one of the award-winning films of the Russian Revolution, *Dr. Zhivago* or *Reds.* What views about the revolution are expressed in each film?

659

CHAPTER
Evaluation

Chapter Test 28, Alternate Chapter Test 28, and Computer Test Bank Chapter 28 Test can be used to evaluate your students' understanding of this chapter.

Shifts in World Power

Chapter Overview

Chapter 29 discusses developments in India, Latin America, the Middle East, and China between 1900 and the outbreak of World War II. During that time, Indian nationalists in the Congress party and followers of Mohandas Gandhi began to challenge British rule. Turkey, Persia, Arabia, and Palestine sought self-rule. The new nations of Iran, Saudi Arabia, and the Republic of Turkey made different choices in entering the modern world. In Palestine, the conflict between Jews and Arabs over a homeland intensified. After ten years of revolution and civil war, Mexico developed a stable republic. Latin American nation building was slowed by factionalism, economic problems, and foreign intervention. Chinese nationalists overthrew the Ch'ing dynasty. Civil war erupted as the Nationalists and the Communists vied for control of China.

Chapter Focus

Ask students to define *nationalism* and to explain its role in independence movements and in wars of rebellion they have studied previously. Students might link nationalism with the rise of nations in Europe at the end of the Middle Ages; the American war of independence; the French Revolution; the unification of Italy, Greece, and Germany; and the Latin American independence movements of the nineteenth century.

Indians organized for independence. 1

Setting the Stage

Refer students to the map on page 579, "Imperialism in India and Southeast Asia, 1900." Point out the extent of British colonial rule. Ask students to recall the positive and negative effects of 300 years of British rule on the Indian people. Ask, "Why did the Indians resent the British? What were some signs of growing Indian nationalism?" Students should recall the founding of the Indian National Congress in 1885 and of the Muslim League in 1906. After World War I, Indian public protests increased.

Teaching Strategies

Skill Building: Identifying Causes (Objective 1) Write the following sentence fragment on the board: ". . . marked the beginning of the end of the British Raj." List on the board students' suggestions for completing the sentence. They might suggest the rise of Indian nationalism, Gandhi's leadership in the nationalist movement, the Amritsar massacre, the Rowlatt Act, and the Government of India acts. In each case, have students explain how the situation or event contributed to the erosion of British rule in India.

Discussing History: Gandhi and Nonviolence (Objective 2) Ask students why Gandhi was named *Mahatma* and what the poet Rabindranath Tagore meant by "great soul."

Chapter 29 Shifts in World Power 1900–1939
FOCUS The role of nationalism in independence movements and wars of rebellion

★ Advanced
● Basic

	SECTION 1	SECTION 2	SECTION 3	SECTION 4
Objectives	1. Identify the contributing causes of the Indian independence movement and trace its spread. 2. Describe and evaluate Gandhi's contributions to Indian independence. 3. Contrast the views of Hindu and Muslim nationalists.	1. Locate the Middle East on a map and describe the Middle East as a geographic and cultural region. 2. Explain the sources of Jewish nationalism and of the conflict between Arab nationalists and Zionists. 3. Identify foreign interests in the Middle East.	1. Describe the role of the United States in Latin American affairs during the early twentieth century. 2. Identify factors affecting the economies of Latin American countries.	1. Compare and contrast the aims and achievements of China's three great nationalist leaders. 2. Explain the outcomes of China's civil war in the 1930's.
Setting the Stage	Indian resentment of British rule	Using Geographic Themes: Region Transparency 85	Political traditions in Latin America	Reasons China rejected western models of government Transparency 86
Teaching Strategies	Skill Building: Identifying Causes Discussing History: Gandhi and Nonviolence Transferring Ideas: Hindu-Muslim Conflict Check for Understanding	Discussing History: Zionism Transparency 85 Writing about History: Foreign Interests in the Middle East Check for Understanding	Discussing History: The United States in Latin America Economics and History: What Weakens a Nation's Economy? Check for Understanding	Skill Building: Comparing and Contrasting Nationalist Leaders Skill Building: Making Predictions Check for Understanding
Guided Practice	Section Review 1	Transparency 85 Q&A Section Review 2	Section Review 3	Transparency 86 Q&A Section Review 4
Independent Practice Worksheets	Independent Practice 29.1 Vocabulary 29	Independent Practice 29.2	Independent Practice 29.3 Basic Skills 29	Independent Practice 29.4 Critical Thinking 29 Geography Skills 29
Enrichment	1. Primary Source: Voices 29.1 2. ★Relating Past and Present 3. Researching for Points	1. Primary Source: Voices 29.2 2. Preparing a Report: The Middle East 3. Researching for Points	1. Primary Source: Voices 29.3 2. Researching for Points	1. Primary Source: Voices 29.4 2. Researching for Points

Chapter Closer

●**Reteaching Activities** Summarizing, Comparing

Chapter Review Summary, Reviewing the Facts, Basic Skills, Researching and Reporting Skills, Critical Thinking, Perspectives on Past and Present, Investigating History

Chapter Evaluation Chapter Test 29, Alternate Chapter Test 29, Computer Test Bank Chapter 29 Test

Have students give examples of Gandhi's application of each of his philosophical principles to the way he conducted his life (page 662).

Point out that Gandhi's strategy for achieving *swaraj* emphasized economic self-reliance and nonviolence. Ask, "How could Indians become economically self-reliant?" (by meeting their own needs while refusing to participate in the British-run economy). "How could Indians gain power through nonviolence?" Point out that Gandhi's fasting and voluntary imprisonment were expressions of passive resistance. Gandhi defined passive resistance as a means of winning rights through personal suffering rather than through force of arms. Refusing to pay taxes, to observe segregation laws, or to attend courts were examples of civil disobedience. Gandhi referred to civil disobedience as the use of "soul-force" in refusing to act against one's conscience, regardless of the consequences. Invite students to express their opinions of Gandhi's views. Ask what made nonviolence a potent moral force. In what aspect of Indian politics were Gandhi's strategies least effective? (in uniting Hindus and Muslims)

Transferring Ideas: Hindu-Muslim Conflict (Objective 3) Review the historical precedents for Hindu-Muslim conflict. Students should be able to trace this conflict to Muslim invasions of India in the eighth, tenth, and twelfth centuries, and to the ensuing 400 years of Muslim domination (pages 303–306). Remind students of the charts they developed in Chapter 13 contrasting Hindu and Muslim beliefs. Students might extend the contrast by adding information in this section to their charts.

The British used the conflict between the Hindus and the Muslims to secure their control over India. In addition, the British contributed to the conflict by favoring Hindus and Sikhs for military and government posts and for social and economic privileges. Conclude by asking students to predict the possible outcomes of the conflict described in this section between Hindu and Muslim nationalists.

Check for Understanding Have students identify the main causes, leaders, strategies, and goals of the Indian independence movement.

Enrichment Activities

1. **Reading a Primary Source** Assign Voices from the Past Resource Book 29.1.
2. **Relating Past to Present** Ask advanced students to write essays linking the leaders, goals, and strategies of the Indian independence movement with those of the American civil rights movement of the 1950's and 1960's.
3. **Researching for Bonus Points** What was the Dandi Salt March? What was its purpose and its result? (Gandhi walked 241 miles from Ahmedabad to the sea at Dandi to protest the British salt tax. As a result, Indians practiced civil disobedience by distilling salt from sea water rather than paying the tax.)

Nationalism spread to the Middle East. 2

Setting the Stage

Using Geographic Themes: Region (Objective 1) Show students Map Transparency 85, *The Middle East in the 1920's.* Explain that the Middle East is a geographic and cultural region that includes the Anatolian peninsula, the lands bordering the eastern Mediterranean and the Tigris-Euphrates, the Arabian peninsula, and the Persian plateau. Ask why this region is named the Middle East. Students might note its central location on the Eurasian continent, but point out that Europeans gave the region its name, identifying its location in relation to Europe and to the "Far East."

Review the geographic themes of region and movement, and have students suggest reasons for the integrity of the Middle East as a region. Historically, it was a crossroads for cultural diffusion between Asia and both Africa and Europe. The map on page 189, *The Spread of Islam,* illustrates this point. Note that geographically and culturally, North Africa is part of the Middle East region.

Refer students to the map, *The World about 1900* (pages 618–619), and ask them to name the territories outside of North Africa that were part of the Middle East at that time. (Arabia, the Ottoman Empire, and Persia)

Teaching Strategies

Discussing History: Zionism (Objective 2) Ask students to explain the reasons for Jewish nationalism. (centuries of exile and persecution) Ask how the Dreyfus case and the Balfour Declaration stimulated the Jewish nationalist movement. Students should recognize that the Dreyfus case symbolized anti-Jewish prejudice and that the Balfour Declaration symbolized hopes for a Jewish homeland. Show Map Transparency 85, *The Middle East in the 1920's,* or refer to the map on page 668. Why were Arab nationalists opposed to Zionism? Clarify that Arab opposition was not the result of religious hatred. Muslims regarded Moses as a prophet of Allah and studied the Old Testament as well as the Koran.

Writing about History: Foreign Interests in the Middle East (Objective 3) Have students assess the role of the British in the Palestinian conflict. Ask why Britain was fearful of alienating the Arabs. Explain that the Arabs controlled a vital strategic resource—oil. The United States, the Soviet Union, and the nations of Europe had economic interests in the Middle East. Ask students to write essays using the information in this section to answer the following question: Why were foreign powers anxious to maintain political stability in the Middle East?

Check for Understanding Ask students to name five significant changes that occurred in the Middle East after World War I.

Enrichment Activities

1. **Reading a Primary Source**
   Assign Voices from the Past Resource Book 29.2.

2. **Preparing a Report**
   Ask interested students to report on one of the following topics: Ataturk's reforms, T. E. Lawrence and the unification of Arabia, *kibbutzim,* Theodor Herzl, and early oil exploration in the Middle East.

3. **Researching for Bonus Points**
   Who founded the first Jewish settlement, and when? (1882; Russian Jews)

Setting the Stage

Refer students to the map on page 538 and review the political problems Latin Americans faced after independence. Ask students to characterize Latin American governments. Suggest that Latin Americans lacked a tradition of democratic values and institutions. They looked to strong dictators, generals, or wealthy landowners to help them achieve unity and progress. Many dictators were reluctant to share power, to plan for succession, or to tolerate power in the hands of citizens. In many countries, rebellions and *coups* became a pattern of political change leading to political instability.

Teaching Strategies

Discussing History: The United States in Latin America (Objective 1) Recall the provisions of the Monroe Doctrine (page 540) and of the Roosevelt Corollary (page 589). Ask students to identify United States interests in Latin America. Emphasize that the defense of American property, businesses, and business investments was used to justify military intervention. American interests centered in Central America and the Caribbean. The United States intervened in Cuba's war of independence from Spain and in the Mexican Revolution. Between 1898 and 1933, the United States took possession of Cuba, Puerto Rico, and the Virgin Islands; ran the economies of Nicaragua, Haiti, and the Dominican Republic; and occupied the Canal Zone in Panama.

Ask students why the United States was anxious to control and protect the Panama Canal. Students should recall the strategic location of the Panama Canal (page 588) and its great commercial and military value. Conclude by asking how United States policies toward Latin America changed during the 1930's. Students should recall the aims of the Good Neighbor Policy.

Economics and History: What Weakens a Nation's Economy? (Objective 2) Ask students to identify economic indicators that show the strength or weakness of a nation's economy, and list their suggestions on the board. Then have students find information in the text describing economic conditions in Latin America in the early 1900's.

Help students to understand the basis for the poverty of many Latin American nations: foreign ownership of land and resources, resulting in a drain of profits; reliance on foreign investments, resulting in loss of control over economic policies; dependence on loans from foreign banks, resulting in increased national debt; and the lack of economic diversification, resulting in a dependence on foreign imports to meet basic needs and in a consequent drain of capital.

Countries relying on a single resource were vulnerable not only to changes in the demand for that resource on the world market, but also to competition from other countries that specialized in that resource. Latin American countries could not easily help each other to grow through trade because they were in competition with each other to export the same few products. Conclude by asking students to infer the characteristics of a strong economy.

Check for Understanding Ask students to name two results of the Mexican Revolution and two results of American intervention in Latin American affairs.

Enrichment Activities

1. **Reading a Primary Source**
Assign Voices from the Past Resource Book 29.3.

2. **Researching for Bonus Points**
Who were Pancho Villa and Francisco Madero and what were their roles in the Mexican Revolution? (a bandit cowboy and wayward revolutionary who stole from the rich to give to the poor; President of Mexico from 1911 to 1913 after Díaz's fall, whose weak leadership furthered the civil war)

China overthrew its emperor. 4

Setting the Stage

Ask students to recall reasons for the rise of nationalism in China (pages 582–583). Then tell students that the outcome of World War I gave the Chinese more compelling reasons to reject western models of government. Ask students to find out these reasons as they read. Show Map Transparency 86, *China, 1927–1938,* and have students compare the present-day People's Republic of China with colonial China in the early 1900's (page 582).

Teaching Strategies

Skill Building: Comparing and Contrasting Nationalist Leaders (Objective 1) Have students develop charts comparing and contrasting the roles and aims of Sun Yat-sen, Chiang Kai-shek, and Mao Tse-Tung. Charts should be organized in terms of the following categories: *Party, Main Goals, Main Achievements.* (Sun Yat-sen: Kuomintang; independence, nationalism, democracy, socialism; overthrew Ch'ing dynasty, established Republic of China, sided with the Allies in World War I. Chiang Kai-shek: Nationalist; defeat warlords and unite China, prevent Chinese Communist party from gaining power, modernize China; unification of China, defeat of Chinese Communists, establishment of the Nationalist Republic of China, improvement of urban economy. Mao Tse-tung: Communist; Communist revolution, economic reforms for workers and rural peasants; established Red Army, fought guerrilla war against Nationalists, survived the Long March)

Skill Building: Making Predictions (Objective 2) Ask students to describe the effects of China's civil war. Students might note that the Red Army was forced to retreat and that Japan exploited China's disunity by invading Manchuria. Point out that the outcome was inconclusive. Ask what events caused the Nationalists and the Communists to join forces during the course of their struggle. (warlords' opposition to nationalism, Japan's invasion of Manchuria) Have students give reasons supporting their predictions in answer to the following questions: What effect do you think World War II had on the civil war in China? On what side do you think China fought? Which party—Nationalist or Communist—do you think gained more followers during World War II? Which party do you think the United States supported?

Check for Understanding Have students write short essays beginning with the following topic sentence: During the early 1900's, China's nation-building efforts were torn by rival nationalist movements.

Enrichment Activities

1. **Reading a Primary Source**
Assign Voices from the Past Resource Book 29.4.

2. **Researching for Bonus Points**
What do the acronyms KMT and CCP stand for? (Kuomintang; Chinese Communist Party)

Reviewing the Facts

1. (a) passive resistance (b) to bring under government control

2. (a) primarily Hindu nationalist group which demanded self-rule (b) wanted a separate Muslim nation (c) founder of modern Turkey (d) leader who modernized Persia and changed its name to Iran (e) leader who kept Islamic traditions and united Saudi Arabia (f) belief that Israel is the Jewish homeland (g) British document that laid foundation for conflict between Arabs and Jews (h) strongman who ruled as a dictator in Latin America (i) Mexico's ruler who brought economic progress to Mexico (j) Mexican leader who instituted many reforms (k) policy affirming United States' respect for rights of Latin American countries (l) founder and leader of China's Nationalist People's party (m) Chinese Communist leader (n) leader of Chinese Nationalist party (o) retreat of Mao to escape Chiang's forces

3. (a) independence (b) separate Muslim nation

4. changed from military and political intervention to Good Neighbor Policy

5. (a) Nationalist party overthrew Ch'ing dynasty (b) civil war, famine, pillaging

6. (a) Because many Chinese felt humiliated by treatment at Versailles, they broke with the West and embraced communism. (b) distrusted the Communists

Basic Skills

1. (a) drastic decline (b) Policy kept industry in ruling nation; possessions provided raw materials and bought back finished goods. (c) Gandhi's focus on spinning and wearing homespun was a protest against British policy, since Britain couldn't keep people from spinning and weaving by hand.

2. mastery over themselves, trust for one another, abolishment of untouchable class, outlawing of alcoholic beverages, and use of homespun cloth instead of imported cloth

Researching and Reporting Skills

Students' answers will vary.

Critical Thinking

1. In general, India and the countries of the Middle East were seeking independence from the colonial rule of Britain or France. China and the Latin American countries had already achieved independence from colonial rule but were now faced with internal battles. Authoritarian governments ignored the needs of the people and continued to prevent the establishment of democratically elected governments.

2. (a) nonviolence, peaceful refusal to cooperate with British rule, boycotts of British goods, refusal to pay taxes, refusal to obey British laws or attend British courts (b) It was an effective approach because the Indian people did not have the resources to compete with British military might. Also, because the protest was nonviolent, Britain was at a loss as to how to deal with it.

3. (a) Both Turkey and Iran expanded public education, gave women more rights, and fostered economic growth. Turkey also broke connection between church and state and replaced Islamic law with secular law. Saudi Arabia was slower to modernize and tried to keep traditional ways. (b) Islam, lack of education; Saudi Arabia held to Islamic tradition; Ibn Saud ruled country like shaykhdom; laws of Islam were same as laws of state; women had few rights; government frowned on modern technology

4. (a) persecution in such places as Eastern Europe and Russia; anti-Jewish sentiment in many Western countries (b) Jews and Palestinian Arabs both felt that they had been promised their own country by the British.

5. (a) Peasants and factory workers had few rights and lived and worked in terrible conditions; lack of free elections; foreign ownership of businesses; wealth of Catholic church and its alliance with rich and powerful (b) Under Obregón, some reforms accomplished: villages took over lands from landlords; public schools were established; and free elections were held.

6. (a) Mao believed that revolution could start in a rural setting and be led by peasants. Marx and Lenin were convinced that revolution would be in the cities, led by workers. (b) by dividing land among local farmers, having soldiers help with harvest

Perspectives on Past and Present

Possible answers: (a) Castro, Nasser, Ortega, Nehru, Nyerere (b) land reform, control of foreign businesses and political influence, improved education, better living conditions

Investigating History

Students' answers will vary.

Chapter 29

Teaching with Pictures

Up to this point, all chapter opener illustrations of people have been paintings. Note that a painting is an artist's interpretation of a scene, whereas a photograph shows a scene exactly as it happened. Have students study the photograph and note the setting, the density of the crowd, and the people themselves. Students should see that people of all ages are participating in this protest. Ask students if this photo depicts violence or nonviolence. What clues in the photo helped them answer that question?

Chapter

29

Shifts in World Power

1900 - 1939

By 1930, massive demonstrations in support of independence were taking place all across India.

Key Terms

nonviolence
passive resistance
civil disobedience
boycott
shaykh
kibbutz
Zionist
nationalize

Read and Understand

1. Indians organized for independence.
2. Nationalism spread to the Middle East.
3. Latin America faced difficult changes.
4. China overthrew its emperor.

On March 30, 1919, and again on April 6, Hindus and Muslims came to the ancient city of Amritsar to fast and pray in protest against British rule in India. Amritsar was the capital city of Punjab, a province in north central India. The organizer of these protests was Mohandas Gandhi (GAHN-dee), leader of India's growing movement for *swaraj*, or self-rule.

Gandhi's appeal for self-rule won wide support in the Punjab. Most of the Indian soldiers who had fought for Great Britain in World War I had come from this province. Treated as valuable allies during the war, they had returned home only to find themselves once again second-class citizens.

660

Chapter 29 Resources

GEOGRAPHY
- Geography Skills 29
- Transparencies 85, 86

REINFORCEMENT
- Vocabulary 29
- Basic Skills 29
- Reteaching 29
- Making Connections Study Guide 29

ENRICHMENT
- Critical Thinking 29
- History and Literature 29A, 29B

ASSESSMENT
- Chapter Test 29
- Alternate Chapter Test 29
- Computer Test Bank

The British were alarmed by the protests in Amritsar, especially by the cooperation between Hindus and Muslims. Often, the two groups had been hostile to each other. On April 10, the British deputy commissioner decided to take a stand against the protests. He arrested two leaders of the protest movement—one Hindu, the other Muslim—and had them jailed without a trial. When their supporters petitioned for their release, British troops opened fire on them. As word of the British action spread, an enraged Indian mob took revenge by burning British banks and killing several British people.

To restore order, British officials called for army troops under General Reginald Dyer. Dyer had been born in India and had spent much of his military career there. Like many Britons, he thought that Indian nationalists needed to be taught a lesson. He got his chance on April 13, 1919.

That day, Indian peasants, dressed in their best holiday clothes, poured into the city for a Hindu festival. About 10,000 celebrators gathered in a walled park called Jillianbagh near the center of the city. A small group of nationalists was also meeting there, defying Dyer's ban on public gatherings.

Late in the afternoon, General Dyer arrived at the park with about 90 Indian soldiers. Some were armed with rifles, others with knives. Without a word of warning, Dyer ordered his men to open fire on the unarmed men, women, and children in the park. The terror-stricken crowd had no way to escape because Dyer's soldiers blocked the only exit.

The shooting, which lasted for ten minutes, was a slaughter. Nearly 400 Indians were killed. More than 1,200 lay wounded. Dyer ordered his troops to withdraw, leaving the injured on the ground without medical care.

News of the massacre spread quickly throughout India and to Britain. The British government ordered an inquiry. When questioned, Dyer expressed no regrets for his actions. He admitted that his men could have scattered the crowd simply by firing into the air. Instead, he had ordered them to shoot to kill. "I was going to punish them," he said. "My idea from the military point of view was to make a wide impression."

In this sense, Dyer's murderous behavior was completely successful. Never had a single British action made such a "wide impression" on the people of India. Almost overnight, millions of Indians changed from loyal British subjects into revolutionaries who demanded independence.

India was not the only country that set out to rid itself of foreign rule in the years after World War I. In this chapter, we will study the growing importance of nationalism not only in India but in the Middle East and China as well. We will also examine developments in Latin America, where countries faced intervention from outsiders as well as internal struggles.

Indians organized for independence. 1

By the early 1900's, British merchants, soldiers, and officials had been in India for more than 200 years. During those years, the British had gradually gained more and more control of India. By 1858, Great Britain ruled most of the country (page 578).

The British government boasted of the many improvements it had brought to India—bridges, canals, irrigation projects, and railroads. Many Indians, however, were not impressed. Their tax money had paid for most of those improvements. At the same time, many upper-class Indians were educated in British schools. There they discovered such European political ideas as nationalism, socialism, and democracy. Soon Western-educated Indian leaders began to apply these ideas to their own country.

In 1885, a group of Indian nationalists formed the Indian National Congress. Most but not all of its members were Hindus. In 1906, Muslims formed their own nationalist group, the Muslim League. Muslims made up a quarter of the Indian population and lived side by side with Hindus in many places.

The Congress party wanted self-rule.

At first, the Indian National Congress—later called the Congress party—spoke of "unswerving loyalty to the British Crown." The party was concerned mainly with winning equal opportunities for Indians in the civil service. Gradually, however, the demands of the Congress party

661

OBJECTIVE 1. Identify the contributing causes of the Indian independence movement and trace its spread.

Teaching Strategy: *Skill Building: Identifying Causes* (page 660a)

OBJECTIVE 2. Describe and evaluate Gandhi's contributions to Indian independence.

Teaching Strategy: *Discussing History: Gandhi and Nonviolence* (page 660a)

OBJECTIVE 3. Contrast the views of Hindu and Muslim nationalists.

Teaching Strategy: *Transferring Ideas: Hindu-Muslim Conflict* (page 660c)

■ BACKGROUND

Like the Congress party, the Muslim League remained an exclusive, upper-class group until well into the 1920's. Its founder, Muhammad Ali Jinnah, quit the Congress party because of its overwhelming Hindu membership.

SECTION 1
Resources

ASSESSMENT
■ Section Quiz 29.1

REINFORCEMENT
■ Independent Practice 29.1

ENRICHMENT
■ Voices from the Past 29.1

661

■ **BACKGROUND**

To protest the Amritsar massacre, Gandhi returned the British war medal that he had received for his brave service in the ambulance corps.

■ **DISCUSSION**

Archbishop Tutu of South Africa has said that one can use nonviolent resistance only against a moral people. Discuss this view with students.

Cooperative Learning

Divide the class into groups of four students. Imagining that it is 1935 in India, each group member should choose one of the following roles: a Muslim, a Hindu, a follower of Gandhi, or a British government official. Have students prepare statements describing their characters' views on the issue of Indian independence. Students should present their statements to their groups. Then have group members attempt to reach a consensus on a plan for India's independence, keeping in mind the concerns of each party.

broadened. Its supporters wanted Indians to have greater control of their own government.

After 1900, radicals within the Congress party called for an end to cooperation with Britain. "Every Englishman knows they are a mere handful in this country," a party leader told his colleagues in 1906, "and it is the business of every one of them to befool you into believing that you are weak and they are strong. [You must] realize that the future rests entirely in your own hands."

Yet, while the British may have been a mere handful in India, the number of Congress party supporters was not much larger. The vast majority of Indians were uneducated and uninterested in politics. In a country of 325 million people, there were only 8,000 university graduates. These educated lawyers, doctors, teachers, and journalists formed the nucleus of the Congress party. Often, they were as out of touch with ordinary villagers as were the British.

Gandhi led the independence movement.

The person who breathed life into Indian nationalism and brought it to the common people was Mohandas Karamchand Gandhi (1869–1948). As a young man, Gandhi studied law in Britain. Then he went to South Africa, where Indians filled many positions in the British colonial government. Like black Africans, Indians in South Africa suffered from the country's harsh racial laws (page 576). His sense of injustice aroused, Gandhi took a stand against these laws. In South Africa, he developed the religious and political ideas that made him one of the most influential leaders of the twentieth century.

While very conscious of his Hindu roots, Gandhi belonged to no specific religious group. He borrowed freely from all of the major world religions, including Christianity and Islam. His philosophy of action was based upon these four general principles:

1. Live simply, never seeking material rewards.
2. Be tolerant of the religious beliefs of others.
3. Spend life in the service of others.
4. Battle injustice in all its forms but never by resorting to violence.

Gandhi practiced what he preached. He lived an almost monastic existence, fasting regularly

and giving up all possessions. Yet he did not retreat from the world. In 1914, at the age of 45, Gandhi returned to India, where he became a leader in the Indian independence movement.

Gandhi did not limit his campaigns to fighting British injustice. He also worked to end the injustice of his fellow Indians toward the untouchables, the lowest group in Hindu society (page 78). Gandhi treated the untouchables as equals. He called them *harijans* (hahr-ih-JAHNS), meaning "people of God."

Gandhi built his philosophy around peace and love. Everywhere he went, "this great soul in a beggar's garb," as the poet Rabindranath Tagore called him, won the hearts of the Indian people. Soon they were calling him the *Mahatma* (muh-HAHT-muh), meaning "Great Soul."

When World War I broke out in 1914, Gandhi and millions of other Indians put aside their discontent with Britain. Indian soldiers helped Great Britain defeat Germany. Gandhi maintained his principles of **nonviolence,** refusing to resort to violence. He served as an ambulance driver and received a medal for bravery. In return for India's help, the British government promised to begin reforms in India that would eventually lead to self-government.

Tensions rose after World War I.

In 1918, Indian troops returned home from the war. They expected Britain to fulfill its promise. However, British reforms fell far short of Indian hopes. As a result, acts of anti-British terrorism erupted in parts of India. The British struck back with the Rowlatt Act, a law that gave the government the right to jail protesters without trial for as long as two years.

To protest the Rowlatt Act, Gandhi called for days of fasting and prayer in the spring of 1919, as you read at the beginning of this chapter. Then the Amritsar massacre took place, sparking an explosion of anger across India. After the massacre, Gandhi wrote, "Cooperation in any shape or form with this satanic government is sinful."

In December, Britain tried to soothe tensions by passing the Government of India Act. This law set up a dual system of administration in which the British governor-general shared power with an Indian legislature. Although the law gave Indians more voice in domestic affairs, the

662

British kept control over foreign policy and national security. Gandhi and many other nationalist leaders felt that the new law was a token offer. They rejected the British reforms.

Gandhi saw clearly that India could not defeat Britain by force of arms. Instead, he called on Indians to use nonviolent moral force. He called his policy *satyagraha*, meaning "hold fast to the truth." In English, it is called **passive resistance** or **civil disobedience.**

Gandhi argued that Indians did not need guns or weapons to bring the mighty British empire to its knees. He reasoned that Great Britain could not govern India if Indians peacefully refused to cooperate. Therefore, he urged Indians to **boycott,** or refuse to buy, British goods and to refuse to pay British taxes, obey British laws, or attend British courts.

For example, Gandhi urged all Indians to boycott British cloth and make their own. Gandhi himself devoted two hours each day to spinning his own yarn on a simple handwheel. He wore nothing but *khadi* (homespun cloth) and urged Indians to follow his example. As a result, the sale of British cloth in India fell sharply.

Civil disobedience took no money, no physical strength, no skill with weapons. It took only courage. Men and women, young and old, weak and strong—all could join in Gandhi's movement. Millions did so.

Throughout 1920, there were dozens of strikes, demonstrations, and protests. Thousands of Indians were arrested by the British, who struggled to keep trains running, factories open, and jails from bursting. Despite Gandhi's pleas to avoid violence, protests often led to riots. Sometimes, hundreds were killed or wounded. Alarmed by the violence, Gandhi called off civil disobedience in February, 1922. One month later, he was arrested and sentenced to six years in prison.

Hindus and Muslims drifted further apart.

Gandhi remained in prison for only two years. He was released in 1924 because his health was poor. What he found on his release horrified him. Unity between Hindus and Muslims, which he had worked so hard to achieve in 1920, had all but disappeared. Hatred between the two groups threatened to tear India apart.

Jawaharlal Nehru (left), head of the Congress Party, and Muhammad Ali Jinnah (right), head of the Muslim League, had different goals.

Conflict between Hindus and Muslims was not new in India. The two groups differed sharply both in their religious ideas and in their social traditions. Muslims believed in one God. Hindus believed that God was manifest in many forms. Muslims believed that all followers of Islam were equal before God. Hinduism accepted the division of society into castes that were not considered equal.

Besides such basic beliefs, each group had a number of customs and traditions that antagonized the other. Muslims, for example, ate beef, and Hindus considered the cow sacred. Some Hindus drank alcoholic beverages, a practice that was forbidden among Muslims. In towns where Hindu temples and Muslim mosques were close together, Muslims sometimes complained that Hindu music and processions disturbed their prayers. Hindus complained of hearing the Muslim calls to prayer five times a day.

663

■ **BACKGROUND**
About 70 percent of the Indian population was Hindu. Within its rigid social structure existed more than 2,000 castes.

ANSWERS TO
Section Review 1

Define:
(a) refusing to resort to violence (b) nonviolent moral force, or satyagraha (c) a form of passive resistance in which people refused to buy certain goods or pay taxes (d) refuse to buy

Identify:
(a) British slaughter of Indians (b) mostly Hindu national group (c) Muslim nationalist group (d) leader in Indian independence movement

Answer:
1. (a) original goal was to win equal opportunities for

(continued)

ANSWERS TO (continued)

Indians in the civil service; by 1935, was committed to gaining independence
(b) Most Indians were uninterested in politics.

2. live simply, be tolerant, serve others, battle injustice in nonviolent way

3. (a) Indians put aside nationalism and fought with Britain against Germans.
(b) made cooperation with Britain impossible

4. use civil disobedience

5. (a) Muslims: one God; all believers equal; Hindus: God manifest in many forms, castes not equal
(b) wanted the Hindus and Muslims to unite
(c) separate Muslim nation

6. (a) allowed home rule
(b) Congress party was committed to full independence; Muslim League would settle only for separate Muslim nation.

7. Possible answers: personal identification, ease of civil disobedience, appeal of belief in equality

ANSWERS TO
Voice from the Past

1. to acquire greater self-control and inner calm, trust one another, consider all as equals

2. stop serving and drinking alcoholic beverages; spin cloth at home; wear traditional khadi

3. division between Muslims and Hindus and among castes

Tensions increased as India became more urbanized during the early 1900's. Hindus and Muslims competed for jobs and housing in cities such as Calcutta and Delhi.

Hatred and distrust between the two groups erupted in riots. During the 1920's, there were more than 90 such outbursts, in which hundreds of Indians were killed and thousands wounded.

As early as 1906, some Muslims formed the Muslim League to ensure that their interests would be considered in discussions about India's future. The British encouraged the leaders of the Muslim League. They saw the Muslims as important allies in the British struggle to keep control of India.

Gandhi worked hard to heal the rift between Muslims and Hindus. He often spoke of the need for Indian unity. "There is no force in the cry of driving out the English if the substitute is to be Hindu domination," he said. "That will be no swaraj." Despite his urgings, however, by 1930 the Muslim League was calling for a separate Muslim nation.

Indians called for full independence.

During the 1920's and 1930's, British and Indian leaders held numerous conferences and round-table meetings. Meanwhile, both violent and nonviolent protests continued. Finally, in 1935, Britain passed a new Government of India Act. It called for a democratically elected national legislature to govern India. Each province was also to have its own assembly for local government.

The new act allowed Indians home rule—that is, complete control over domestic affairs. In 1918, Indians might have welcomed such a law. By 1935, however, home rule was no longer enough for most Indian nationalists. The Congress party was committed to full independence. "Between Indian nationalism, Indian freedom, and British imperialism there can be no common ground," said Jawaharlal Nehru, the leading figure in the Congress party in the 1930's.

The British reforms were not popular with Muslims either. The 1935 law provided safeguards for Muslim interests. However, the Muslim

Voice from the Past — Gandhi's Plan of Action

In 1920, Gandhi and the Congress party set a goal of winning swaraj within a year. Here were the steps Gandhi asked of all Indians.

Firstly, we must acquire greater mastery over ourselves and secure an atmosphere of perfect calm, peace, and good will . . .

Secondly, we must still further cleanse our hearts, and we Hindus and Muslims must cease to suspect one another's motives, and we should believe ourselves incapable of wronging one another.

Thirdly, we Hindus must call no one unclean or mean or inferior to ourselves, and must therefore cease to regard the "Pariah" class to be untouchable. We must consider it sinful to regard a fellow-being as untouchable.

These three things are matters of inward transformation, and the result will be seen in our daily dealings.

The fourth is the curse of drink . . . A supreme effort should be made . . . [to lead] liquor-sellers to give up their licenses, and the habitual visitors to these shops to give up the habit . . .

The fifth thing is the introduction of the spinning wheel in every home, larger production and use of khadi, and complete giving up of foreign cloth.

1. What inner changes of mind and spirit did Gandhi ask of Indians?
2. What outward changes in habits did he want?
3. What major social divisions did he think Indians had to heal to achieve swaraj?

League had decided to settle for nothing less than a separate Muslim nation. They had already chosen a possible name for their country—Pakistan (Land of the Pure).

Members of the league wanted Pakistan to be carved out of the parts of India where most Muslims lived. "It is a dream that the Hindus and Muslims can ever evolve a common nationality," said Muhammad Jinnah, leader of the Muslim League. Muslims, he said, were "a nation according to any definition of a nation, and they must have their homelands, their territory, and their state."

Thus, there was no easy answer for the British. To give in to either side would mean almost certain civil war. Meanwhile, Hindu-Muslim tensions continued to build. Riots became increasingly common. "We neither govern nor misgovern," wrote one British observer in the 1930's. "We're just hanging on."

Section REVIEW 1

Define: (a) nonviolence, (b) passive resistance, (c) civil disobedience, (d) boycott
Identify: (a) Amritsar massacre, (b) Indian National Congress, (c) Muslim League, (d) Mohandas Gandhi
Answer:
1. (a) How did the goals of the Congress party change from the time of its founding to 1935? (b) Why did the Congress party have little popular support in its early days?
2. What were Gandhi's four basic principles?
3. (a) How did World War I affect Indian nationalism? (b) What was the effect of the Amritsar massacre?
4. What course of action did Gandhi suggest against the British?
5. (a) What were some of the issues that divided Hindus and Muslims? (b) What course of action did Gandhi support? (c) What did the Muslims want?
6. (a) How did Britain try to solve the problem in 1935? (b) Why did their solution fail?

Critical Thinking
7. In your opinion, why was Gandhi able to win popular support for Indian independence when earlier nationalist leaders had not been able to do so?

Nationalism spread to the Middle East. 2

Nationalism was also on the rise in the region known today as the Middle East. The Middle East includes the part of Asia that stretches from Turkey to Afghanistan. When Europeans began trading with Asia, they called this region the Middle East because it lay between their homes and the more distant eastern lands of India, China, and Japan. Today, North Africa is also considered part of the Middle East because it has strong cultural ties to the Middle Eastern countries.

The Middle East is the birthplace of three great religions—Islam, Judaism, and Christianity. Islam is the youngest of the three and has by far the most followers in the region. During the 700's, warriors from the Arabian Peninsula turned much of the Middle East into a Muslim empire. Later, Seljuk Turks and then Ottoman Turks conquered the region and adopted the Muslim faith. By the 1400's, much of the Middle East was ruled by the Ottoman empire. Only Persia did not come under Ottoman control.

The Ottomans ruled the Middle East for about 500 years. After the 1500's, their empire began a long, slow decline that lasted into the twentieth century. The Scientific Revolution and the Industrial Revolution, which dramatically changed life in Europe, made little impact in Ottoman lands. The sultans, or rulers, of the empire were not interested in factories or new inventions. Thus, the Middle East fell behind Europe economically, but it preserved its traditional ways.

By the end of World War I, the Ottomans had lost control of all their lands outside present-day Turkey (page 636). Great Britain received the lands called Palestine, Transjordan, and Iraq as mandates (lands to be governed on behalf of the League of Nations). France received Syria and Lebanon as mandates.

Many people in the Middle East did not want to be ruled by France or Great Britain. Just as the people of India fought to have their own nation after World War I, the people of the Middle East also launched independence movements during this period. Each group in the Middle East chose a different path toward nation building.

665

SECTION 2
Objectives and Teaching Strategies

OBJECTIVE 1. Locate the Middle East on a map and describe the Middle East as a geographic and cultural region.

Teaching Strategy: *Using Geographic Themes: Region* (page 660c)

OBJECTIVE 2. Explain the sources of Jewish nationalism and of the conflict between Arab nationalists and Zionists.

Teaching Strategy: *Discussing History: Zionism* (page 660c)

OBJECTIVE 3. Identify foreign interests in the Middle East.

Teaching Strategy: *Writing about History: Foreign Interests in the Middle East* (page 660d)

■ BACKGROUND

During World War I, the Allies encouraged nationalist revolts within the Turkish empire. A number of British officers fought with Arab nationalist armies. Among them was T. E. Lawrence, "Lawrence of Arabia."

SECTION 2
Resources

GEOGRAPHY
■ Transparency 85

REINFORCEMENT
■ Independent Practice 29.2

ENRICHMENT
■ Voices from the Past 29.2

ASSESSMENT
■ Section Quiz 29.2

Because of its limited resources, Turkey remained primarily an agricultural country. Its ties to the West helped make Turkish culture considerably different from that of its neighbors.

Several countries chose modernization.

At the end of World War I, two countries in the Middle East chose to break with many of their Islamic traditions. Those countries were Turkey and Persia.

The Republic of Turkey In 1918, Turkey was all that remained of the Ottoman empire. It included the old Turkish homeland of Anatolia and a small strip of land around Istanbul.

In 1919, Greek soldiers invaded Turkey and threatened to conquer it. The Turkish sultan, weak and corrupt, was powerless to stop them. Many Turks believed that their country's only hope for survival lay in the overthrow of the sultan. In 1922, a group of Turkish nationalists overthrew the last Ottoman emperor. The leader of the revolution was an able army officer named Mustafa Kemal (1881–1938).

In 1923, Kemal and other nationalists established the Republic of Turkey, the first republic in the Middle East. As its president, Kemal set out to make Turkey a modern nation.

As a first step in modernization, Kemal broke the close connection between church and state that had existed under the sultans. He wanted to separate the laws of Islam from the laws of the nation. Kemal replaced Islamic laws with laws from various European nations. He replaced Islamic religious courts with secular ones.

Kemal also gave Turkish women equal legal and political rights, including the right to vote and to be elected to office. He had nothing but scorn for the Islamic custom that required women to wear veils in public. "What is the sense in this behavior?" Kemal asked. "Do the mothers and daughters of a civilized nation assume this barbarian posture? It makes the nation look ridiculous." Kemal himself made a point of dressing in European style.

Kemal believed that the future of his country lay in the education of its young people. He closed traditional Islamic religious schools and set up secular public ones. Students in the new schools learned to read and write the Roman alphabet, not the Arabic script.

Despite the limited natural resources of Turkey, Kemal also pushed for economic growth. He built railroads and factories in many parts of the country.

In this poster, the new Republic of Turkey is represented by an unveiled woman, leading Mustafa Kemal on horseback.

By the time of Kemal's death in 1938, Turkey had a firm sense of national identity. It was also committed to modernization in the pattern of Europe and the United States. Kemal's influence was so strong that the Turkish people gave him the name Atatürk, meaning "father of the Turks."

The change from Persia to Iran Unlike the rest of the Middle East, the ancient country of Persia never came under the control of the Ottoman Turks. However, both Great Britain and Russia established spheres of influence there in the 1800's. By the early 1900's, the two countries virtually controlled the Persian government.

In 1921, a Persian army officer named Reza Khan seized control of the weak Persian government. By 1925, he had deposed the ruling shah and taken the title for himself. He ruled as Reza Shah Pahlavi.

Reza Shah set out to modernize his country and free it from foreign rule. He was remarkably successful in both these goals. As Atatürk had done in Turkey, Reza Shah set up public schools, built roads and railroads, encouraged industrial growth, and gave women more rights. Unlike Atatürk, however, the shah kept all power in his own hands. In 1935, he changed the name of his country from Persia to Iran.

Saudi Arabia kept Islamic traditions.

While Turkey and Iran broke with many Islamic traditions, another new country held strictly to Islamic law. Soon after World War I, much of the Arabian peninsula was united under a single ruler who ruled in traditional fashion.

Arabia is a harsh desert land where water can be as precious as gold. For thousands of years, the Arabian desert was home to groups of nomads known as Bedouin (page 186).

The Bedouin lived in family groups. Members were related through their fathers and grandfathers. At the head of each group was a **shaykh**—a man usually chosen from one leading family within the group. The shaykh commanded tremendous respect from those he led.

In 1902, a shaykh named Abd al-Aziz Ibn Saud (sah-**OOD**) set out to extend his power. His early support came from a small sect of Islamic traditionalists. By military skill and well-planned marriages to the daughters of neighboring shaykhs, he gradually won control of eastern Arabia. After World War I, he began advancing westward. One by one, he overthrew the local ruling families.

In 1926, Ibn Saud proclaimed himself king of an Arab nation. Six years later, he renamed the country Saudi Arabia after his family.

Ibn Saud held firmly to Arab and Islamic traditions. He ran his country much like a Bedouin shaykhdom. Loyalty to the Saudi government was based on custom, religion, and family ties. Unlike Atatürk, who chose to separate church and state, Ibn Saud made the laws of Islam the laws of his kingdom. Women in Saudi Arabia had to wear veils in public as Islamic law required. Alcoholic drinks were banned. Legal penalties for crimes were set according to the Koran. For years, the Saudi government frowned on much modern technology, including telephones, automobiles, and even bicycles.

Jews and Arabs fought over Palestine.

After World War I, the British and the French held Lebanon, Syria, Transjordan, Iraq, and Palestine as mandates. The people of these lands faced a different problem from the people of Turkey or Saudi Arabia. Most people in the mandates mainly wanted freedom from European control.

Worn out from World War I, France and Britain could not halt the force of Arab nationalism. Iraq became independent of Britain in 1922, Transjordan in 1923. France signed treaties accepting the independence of Syria and Lebanon in 1936. Only Palestine was not yet free.

Until about 2,000 years ago, Palestine was the homeland of the Jewish people. Around 1000 B.C., Jewish kings ruled the country from Jerusalem (page 41). Twice the Jewish kingdom was

■ **BACKGROUND**
Ibn Saud named Mecca the religious capital and Riyadh the political capital of Saudi Arabia.

The banners of Ibn Saud's army proclaimed the basic beliefs of Islam: "There is no god but God, and Muhammad is his prophet."

■ BACKGROUND

Britain and France were willing to allow some home rule in their mandate territories. "My own ambition," said Balfour, "is that the Arabs should be our first brown dominion, and not our last colony."

Aided by international Jewish organizations, Jews bought land from absentee Arab landlords. Their kibbutzim were collective farms.

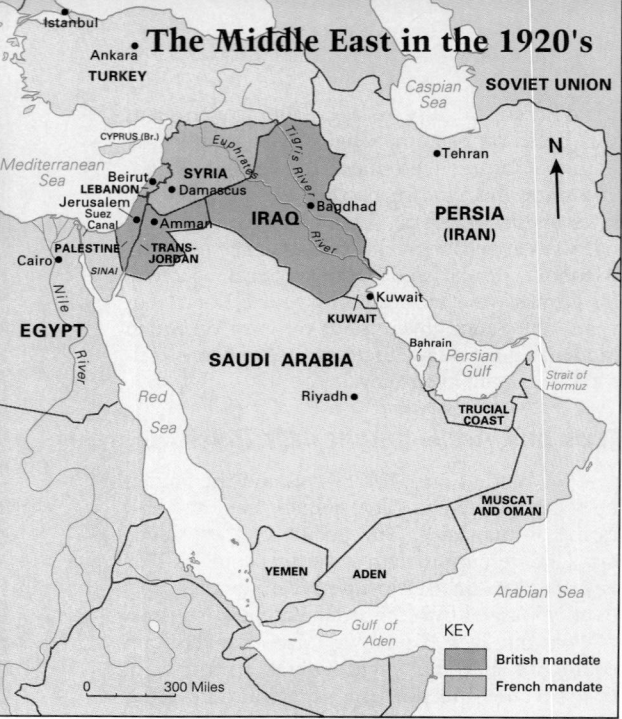

The Middle East in the 1920's

KEY

British mandate

French mandate

Map Study

In what country is the Suez Canal located? Into what body of water do the Tigris and Euphrates rivers flow?

destroyed, once by the Babylonians in 586 B.C. and again by the Romans in A.D. 70. Each time, many Jews fled Palestine and settled in other countries. Only a few managed to remain in their ancient homeland. Jews continued to live in Palestine even after the country came under Arab and later Ottoman rule.

Jewish nationalists The exiled Jews faced centuries of persecution and anguish. Still, they held on to their beliefs and traditions. For many Jews, these traditions were not enough. They wanted a homeland, a place where Jewish laws and traditions would also be the laws and traditions of their nation. Because of their ancient ties to Palestine, they now sought a homeland there.

During the 1800's, the desire for a homeland grew stronger among many Jews. Pogroms in eastern Europe and Russia forced thousands of Jews to escape to Great Britain, France, Germany, and the United States. Thousands also emigrated to Palestine. There they bought large parcels of land, which they organized into socialist farming

communities, called **kibbutzim** (kih-boo-TSEEM). (The singular form of *kibbutzim* is *kibbutz*.)

At first, most of the new Jewish settlers in Palestine came from eastern Europe. In the 1890's, however, a scandal in the French army fanned the flames of Jewish nationalism in western Europe as well.

In 1894, Captain Alfred Dreyfus, one of the few Jewish officers in the French army, was accused of selling secrets to Germany. The evidence against him was flimsy, but some other officers disliked him because he was Jewish. The army found Dreyfus guilty and sentenced him to life in prison. For 12 years, his family and friends worked to clear his name. The French army and its political supporters tried to hush up the issue. At last, another man was found to have been the spy. Dreyfus was declared innocent.

The Dreyfus case showed the strength of anti-Jewish feeling in France and other parts of western Europe. In response, western European Jews too began to work for a Jewish homeland in Palestine. Their leader was Theodor Herzl (1860–1904), a writer and journalist in Vienna. These Jewish nationalists were known as **Zionists**. (Zion is another name for Israel, the Jewish homeland.)

The Balfour Declaration Chaim Weizmann (VYTES-mahn), a Russian-born university professor, was the leader of the Zionist movement in Britain. Weizmann succeeded in winning the support of Britain's foreign secretary, Sir Arthur Balfour. In 1917, at the height of World War I, the secretary issued a document known as the Balfour Declaration. It stated:

His Majesty's Government views with favor the establishment in Palestine of a national home for the Jewish people, and will use their best endeavors to facilitate the achievement of that object, it being clearly understood that nothing shall be done which may prejudice the civil and religious rights of existing non-Jewish communities in Palestine or the rights and political status enjoyed by Jews in any other country.

Balfour worded his document carefully, fearing the loss of either Jewish or Arab support in the British war effort. According to the declaration, Britain favored a Jewish homeland but not at the expense of the Arabs in Palestine. The ambiguity of the Balfour Declaration laid the foundation

668

for conflicts that would dominate the Middle East for the next 30 years.

British rule Britain took control of Palestine in 1920 as a mandate. Immediately, both Arab nationalists and Jewish nationalists asked the British to fulfill the promises of the Balfour Declaration. Each group wanted its own country in Palestine. Each side believed it had the support of the British government.

While the British looked for an answer to the problem, Jews continued to immigrate to Palestine. Weizmann often spoke of creating a Palestine "just as Jewish as England is English." This trend alarmed Palestinian Arabs, who feared that Jews might become a majority. In 1929, a riot broke out between Jews and Arabs in Jerusalem. Over 100 people on each side were killed.

Jewish immigration increased during the 1930's. In 1933, Hitler came to power in Germany and began persecuting Jews (pages 695–696). Thousands of Jews fled Germany and settled in Palestine. By 1939, Jewish settlers had founded 200 kibbutzim in Palestine. The number of Jews living in the region had increased from 85,000 in 1914 to 445,000. Jews now made up about one fourth of Palestine's population.

Palestinian Arabs, alarmed at the growing number of Jews, staged violent demonstrations against the British. Britain, fearful of alienating the Arab community, tightened restrictions on Jewish immigration into Palestine. Thousands of Jews were left stranded in Germany. Jewish terrorism against the British became increasingly common. By the outbreak of World War II in 1939, many despaired of ever finding an answer to the Palestinian conflict.

Middle East oil attracted outsiders.

While nationalism simmered in many Middle Eastern countries, the region's economy was also taking a new direction. Even while traditional Islamic kingdoms such as Saudi Arabia and Iraq frowned on modern machines, they owned great deposits of oil to fuel those machines.

The knowledge that oil existed in the Middle East was not new. Since ancient times, people there had noticed places where petroleum seeped to the surface of the ground. In those days, however, people had little use for the sticky, foul-smelling liquid. That situation changed in the

Donations for the Jewish National Fund were collected in "Blue Boxes" like this one. The fund, established in 1901, is active in purchasing and developing land in Israel.

late 1800's and early 1900's when people found that oil could be used as fuel. Soon, oil was a valuable resource for industrialized countries.

The Middle Eastern countries themselves had little use for oil. They had few factories or machines to use it, nor did they have the technology to drill their own oil wells. Therefore, most Middle Eastern rulers were willing to rent drilling rights to foreign oil companies.

In the early 1900's, European and American companies began to drill for oil in the Middle East. In 1901, William Knox D'Arcy, a British speculator, made a deal with the shah of Persia, paying him a share of the profits in exchange for the right to drill oil wells in Persia. In 1908, D'Arcy made the first big oil strike in the Middle East. Soon his company, the Anglo-Iranian Oil Company, controlled the industry in Iran.

During the 1920's and 1930's, European and American companies found huge deposits of oil in Iran, Iraq, Saudi Arabia, and Kuwait. Geologists later learned that the land around the Persian Gulf has nearly two thirds of the world's known supply of oil.

Although foreign companies paid some money to the leaders of each country where oil was found, most of the profits went to the companies. The discovery of oil in the Middle East intensified old quarrels over boundaries and spheres of influence. It also, as you will see in later chapters, created new pressures on Middle Eastern society.

669

■ **DISCUSSION**

By the late 1920's, the major oil companies in Iraq were American. Why did American companies go into the Middle East when there were rich oil reserves at home?

ANSWERS TO
Section
Review 2

Define:
(a) Bedouin leader **(b)** Israeli socialist farm community **(c)** wanted a Jewish homeland in Palestine

Identify:
(a) region that stretches from Turkey to Afghanistan

(continued)

ANSWERS TO (continued)

(b) first president of Turkey
(c) modernized Persia and
changed its name to Iran
(d) proclaimed himself king
of nation he renamed Saudi
Arabia (e) Jewish nationalist
movement (f) ambiguous
document on issue of Jewish
homeland in Palestine
Answer:
1. (a) Scientific Revolution
and the Industrial Revolution
had made little impact.
(b) Ottomans lost control of
all their lands outside present-day Turkey; Great Britain
and France each received
some countries as mandates.
2. (a) Turkish nationalists
overthrew the Ottoman em-
peror. (b) wanted to mod-
ernize Turkey; examples:
gave women equal rights,
set up secular courts and
schools
3. (a) aimed to modernize
nation and give women
more rights (b) Shah kept all
power.
4. (a) nomadic herders,
lived in family groups with a
shaykh at head (b) over-
threw local ruling families,
united neighboring shaykhs
into Saudi Arabia, and
held to Islamic and Arab
traditions
5. (a) Palestine would be a
Jewish homeland. (b) in response to anti-Jewish feeling
in Europe
6. demands of Arabs and
Jews for own country, Arab-
Jewish conflict
7. Countries' drilling rights;
foreign countries soon controlled oil industry.
8. (a) probably Mustafa
Kemal, who tried to adopt
democratic, Western ways
(b) probably Ibn Saud, who
retained Muslim traditions

Section REVIEW 2

Define: (a) shaykh, (b) kibbutz, (c) Zionist
Identify: (a) Middle East, (b) Mustafa Kemal,
(c) Reza Shah Pahlavi, (d) Abd al-Aziz Ibn
Saud, (e) Zionism, (f) Balfour Declaration
Answer:
1. (a) Why did the Middle East lag behind Europe
economically? (b) What were the political results of World War I in the Middle East?
2. (a) How did Turkey become a republic?
(b) Describe Atatürk's general policy for Turkey and give two specific examples.
3. (a) How were Reza Shah Pahlavi's policies
like Atatürk's? (b) How were they different?
4. (a) Describe the Bedouin way of life. (b) How
did Ibn Saud combine nationalism and Islamic
tradition?
5. (a) What was the goal of the Zionist movement? (b) How did the movement begin?
6. What problems did the Balfour Declaration
create?
7. Why did the discovery of oil lead to the growth
of foreign influence in the Middle East?

Critical Thinking
8. Evaluate the leaders described in this section.
(a) Which probably was considered most successful by Europeans? Explain. (b) Which
probably was the most admired by traditional
Muslims? Explain.

Latin America faced difficult changes. 3

By 1900, most of Latin America had been free
of foreign rule for about 80 years. Although free,
Latin American countries still faced problems
that hindered their efforts at nation building.

Politically, Latin American countries remained
isolated. None of them played a large part in
World War I. Economically, on the other hand,
Latin America had many ties to other lands.
Latin American resources and products were sold
worldwide: beef from Argentina, coffee from Brazil
and Colombia, oil from Venezuela and Mexico,
tin from Bolivia, nitrates and copper from Chile,
and sugar from Cuba.

670

Few countries had democratic governments.

In many Latin American countries, political
strongmen called caudillos ruled as dictators (page
540). These men did little to help the common
people. Together with a small group of wealthy
aristocrats, they alone enjoyed the benefits of
independence.

To further their own interests, many caudillos
and their supporters encouraged foreigners to invest in Latin American mines, plantations, and
other businesses. The money from these investments lined the pockets of the caudillos and
the outsiders. The common people of Latin
America gained nothing.

There were, of course, exceptions. Reform-
minded presidents such as Uruguay's José Batlle
(BAHT-yay) and Hipólito Irigoyen (EE-reh-GOH-
yane) in Argentina tried to improve education
and welfare in their countries. Benito Juárez
brought an era of reform to Mexico in the 1860's.

However, such reformers made few lasting
changes. Sooner or later, the caudillos returned
to power. Usually, they had the support of the
upper classes, who felt threatened by programs
to give more power to ordinary people. One typical
caudillo was Juan Vicente Gómez, a ruthless man
who ruled Venezuela for nearly 30 years after
seizing power in 1908. "All Venezuela is my
cattle ranch," he once boasted.

Mexicans revolted in 1910.

Mexico suffered from the same problems as
other Latin American countries. In 1910, 800
wealthy aristocrats (in a country of 15 million
people) owned more than 90 percent of the rural
land. Peasants in rural villages lived at the mercy
of the landowners. Conditions in the cities were
not much better. Factory workers labored 12 to
15 hours a day for very low wages. No laws
protected their rights.

The rule of Díaz Mexico's ruler at the turn of
the century was Porfirio Díaz (1830–1915). Díaz
was an army officer who came to power in 1876.
Although he called for elections regularly between
1876 and 1910, they were not free elections. Díaz
controlled who could run, who could vote, and
how the votes were counted. He was reelected
seven times.

José Clemente Orozco, *Zapatistas.* (1931)

These Zapatistas (followers of Zapata) were peasant men and women who fought in the Mexican Revolution. Their strength and unity shows in this painting by one of Mexico's foremost artists, José Orozco. Orozco did many paintings in support of the revolution.

During his rule, Díaz brought Mexico economic progress. Under his leadership, railroads spread across the country and foreign business people set up new factories in many places. To many outsiders, Mexico seemed to be a stable, prospering country. They did not see the anger that seethed beneath the surface.

Revolution In 1910, that anger erupted as poor workers and farmers rose up against the government. Roving bands of fighters killed rich landowners and burned their houses.

The revolution had no single leader. In each part of Mexico, local leaders gathered their own armies. Often they fought with one another as well as with the government soldiers. One of the most famous fighters was Emiliano Zapata (sah-**PAH**-tah), a mestizo. "It is better to die on your feet than to live on your knees," Zapata told the peasants who joined him.

The rebels drew support in urban areas as well. There, protestors demanded better working conditions. Some leaders criticized foreign ownership of businesses in Mexico. Others attacked the wealth of the Catholic Church. Nearly all Mexicans were Catholics, but Church leaders were closely allied with the rich and powerful.

The government of Díaz toppled in 1911. Unfortunately, no single figure could command enough support to unite the country. The result was a bitter civil war that dragged on for nearly a decade.

Reform In 1917, a revolutionary leader named Venustiano Carranza took control in Mexico. He called for a convention to draft a new constitution for the country.

The constitution of 1917 was a revolutionary document. It provided for the breakup of large estates. It set up a labor code to protect the rights of workers. It set rules for foreign investments but did not eliminate them. It also limited the Catholic Church's role in politics and education and forced the Church to give up some of its property.

Although he had called for the constitution, Carranza failed to carry out its measures. Instead, he ruled oppressively. Peasant armies under Zapata and other rebel leaders continued their revolutionary struggle. In 1920, Carranza was overthrown.

In the fall of 1920, a moderate leader named Alvaro Obregón came to power. His presidency marked the end of civil war and the beginning of reform. Obregón put into effect many of the ideas of the 1917 constitution. Gradually, peasant villages took over lands from wealthy landlords. Public schools were established. Although poverty

671

SECTION 3 Resources

ASSESSMENT
- Section Quiz 29.3

REINFORCEMENT
- Independent Practice 29.3

ENRICHMENT
- Voices from the Past 29.3

SECTION 3 Objectives and Teaching Strategies

OBJECTIVE 1. Describe the role of the United States in Latin American affairs during the early twentieth century.

Teaching Strategy: *Discussing History: The United States in Latin America* (page 660d)

OBJECTIVE 2. Identify factors affecting the economies of Latin American countries.

Teaching Strategy: *Economics and History: What Weakens a Nation's Economy?* (page 660d)

■ BACKGROUND

The caudillos were usually military men. On a continent where there were few international conflicts, these generals used their armies to get and keep power at home.

■ DISCUSSION

The Mexican Constitution resembled the United States Constitution in some ways. It provided for election of government officials, a legislature with two houses, and a president who served one six-year term. It also contained more radical provisions: national ownership of mineral resources, restrictions on the Church's involvement in government, and guarantees of fair wages and working conditions. Why were such provisions necessary?

671

■ BACKGROUND

Nicaraguan poet Ruben Daris saw the United States as a "future invader." To the Yankees he wrote, "Beware! For Spanish America lives! The Spanish lion has a thousand cubs."

Cooperative Learning

In groups of four or five, have students research United States intervention in either Panama, Nicaragua, Haiti, Cuba, or the Dominican Republic in the early 1900's. After group members have determined the reasons behind and length of the intervention, ask them to discuss the reactions of that country's citizens to the United States presence. Have group members write an editorial that might have appeared in a Latin American newspaper regarding the situation. With one group member acting as a recorder, other members should dictate the body of the editorial. Another member might act as an editor, correcting spelling, grammar, and logic. Have groups share their editorials with the class.

and corruption continued to plague Mexico, the country remained stable politically. President succeeded president in an orderly way, without the coups that troubled other parts of Latin America.

The United States interfered in Latin America.

The Mexican Revolution drew the interest of many countries in the Western Hemisphere. None was more interested than Mexico's powerful neighbor to the north, the United States.

The United States' interest in Latin American affairs was not new. As early as 1823, its government had issued the Monroe Doctrine, warning European countries to keep hands off the newly formed Latin American countries (page 540). Many Latin Americans did not welcome the Monroe Doctrine. They believed that the United States itself was interfering in their countries by issuing such a declaration.

In the early 1900's, President Theodore Roosevelt aroused further fears in Latin America by his Roosevelt Corollary (page 589). This policy gave the United States the role of international police officer in the Americas.

By 1900, the United States was replacing Great Britain, Germany, and France as the major foreign investor in Latin America. Anxious about its economic interests, the United States used the Roosevelt Corollary to intervene in Latin American affairs time and time again.

The small republics in Central America and the Caribbean bore the brunt of United States intervention. These countries were Panama, Nicaragua, Haiti, Cuba, and the Dominican Republic.

For example, in the early 1900's, United States businesses owned large farms for growing tobacco, sugarcane, cotton, coffee, and bananas in Nicaragua. When rebels in Nicaragua took up arms against the government in 1912, the United States government sent marines to protect American business interests. The United States also wanted its troops to stop the fighting from spreading to nearby Panama, where the canal was being built. The marines stayed in Nicaragua until 1933.

Investments by United States businesses in Latin America grew rapidly between 1914 and 1929. At the outbreak of World War I, United States businesses jumped at the chance to buy British and German property in the region. By 1929, these businesses had invested nearly $5.4 billion in Latin America. This figure amounted to 35 percent of all United States investments in foreign lands.

Much of this money was invested in the oil business. In the early 1900's, deposits of petroleum were found in Mexico, Venezuela, Peru, and Colombia. United States companies channeled millions of dollars into Latin America. Other United States investments went into Chilean copper and nitrate, Argentinian beef and Cuban sugar.

Latin American nationalists resented the way in which the United States protected its interests

---

DAILY LIFE ▶ Art on Walls

Mexico's democratic revolution brought a revolution in art as well. No longer was art mainly for the rich. Instead, Obregón brought art to the people by offering the walls of public buildings for murals of Mexico's past. Mexican artists such as Diego Rivera, David Alfaro Siqueiros, and José Clement Orozco took up the offer and won worldwide fame for their powerful murals. Not only was this art in new places, but it had new subjects as well. Under Porfirio Díaz, Mexican artists had imitated Spanish and French painters. The new revolutionary artists turned instead to Mexico's Aztec heritage. Their murals glorified the long-ago battle of the Aztecs against Cortés and also the ongoing struggle of the peasants against the landowners.

in the region. Time and time again, they pointed out that the profits from United States businesses helped keep dictators in power. In Venezuela, for example, United States oil companies were on friendly terms with dictator Juan Vicente Gómez. When Gómez died in 1935, many Venezuelans hoped that the United States businesses would go as well.

Roosevelt announced the Good Neighbor Policy.

By 1935, however, the United States was taking steps to improve its relations with Latin America. In 1933, Franklin D. Roosevelt took office as president of the United States. (He was a cousin of the earlier president, Theodore Roosevelt.) The newly elected president announced a change of policy toward Latin America. The new plan was called the Good Neighbor Policy. Under this policy, the United States promised to respect the rights of Latin American countries.

True to his word, Roosevelt withdrew United States troops from Latin American countries where they had been posted. The last marines left Haiti in 1936. For the first time in 30 years, there were no United States armed forces anywhere in Latin America.

The damage to relations between Latin America and the United States, however, lasted after the troops went home. Latin Americans did not forget how the United States had treated them. Moreover, United States businesses still controlled millions of dollars' worth of property in the region. People in Latin America remained uneasy over the enormous power the United States had in their countries.

Latin American economies were weak.

Foreign ownership of Latin American businesses was only one part of a larger economic problem. In many Latin American countries, the entire national economy depended on a single export. For example, oil was the key to Venezuela's prosperity. Brazil and Colombia depended on coffee.

Countries that depend on a single resource have little control over their own economies. When the price of that resource falls on the world market, the economy of the country may collapse.

In the 1930's, many Latin American countries faced just such a crisis. During those years, the world economy slumped into a deep, long-lasting depression (Chapter 30). The crisis had widespread effects in Latin America.

Brazil is a good example. During the hard times of the 1930's, many people could no longer afford to drink coffee. World coffee consumption fell so sharply that more than 3 billion pounds of coffee sat in the warehouses of São Paulo, Brazil. Coffee workers lost their jobs. Unable to sell its coffee, Brazil had no money to buy the manufactured goods it needed from other countries.

Some Latin American governments reacted to the decline in foreign markets by encouraging the growth of national industries. Mexico went a step further. In 1938, it seized foreign oil properties and **nationalized** them—that is, it brought the oil industry under government control. Several other countries did the same. Later, Mexico compensated the foreign companies whose assets it had seized. Today, Mexicans celebrate March 18, the date of the oil takeover, as their declaration of economic independence.

Section REVIEW 3

Define: (a) caudillo, (b) nationalize
Identify: (a) Porfirio Díaz, (b) Alvaro Obregón, (c) Monroe Doctrine, (d) Roosevelt Corollary, (e) Good Neighbor Policy
Answer:
1. (a) What political problems did most Latin American countries face in the early 1900's? (b) What economic problems?
2. (a) Describe Porfirio Díaz's rule in Mexico. (b) How did he fall from power?
3. What changes were called for by Mexico's constitution of 1917?
4. How did Mexico regain political stability?
5. How did economic interests lead the United States to intervene in Latin America?
6. How did United States policy toward Latin America change during the 1930's?
7. What problems did reliance on a single resource create for many Latin American economies?

Critical Thinking
8. How is political independence related to economic independence? Use examples from Latin America in your answer.

673

ANSWERS TO
Section Review 3

Define:
(a) political strongman (b) to bring under government control
Identify:
(a) Mexico's ruler from 1876 to 1911 (b) Mexican leader who instituted many reforms (c) warning to Europe to keep hands off Latin America (d) policy that gave the U.S. the role of international police officer in the Americas (e) policy in which U.S. promised to respect rights of Latin America
Answer:
1. (a) political isolation, rule by corrupt caudillos (b) foreign ownership of businesses, dependence on exports
2. (a) economic progress, but no benefits to peasants and factory workers; controlled elections (b) as result of revolution
3. breakup of estates, protective labor code, rules for foreign investments, limits on Catholic Church
4. Obregón put into effect many ideas of 1917 constitution.
5. U.S. sent in marines or supported dictators to protect American business interests.
6. Good Neighbor Policy led to withdrawing troops.
7. When the price of that resource fell on the world market, the economy of the country collapsed.
8. Students should note that a nation cannot be politically independent unless it is economically independent.

Why has communism been more appealing in agricultural societies than in industrial ones, despite Marx's forecast that it would be factory workers who would rise in revolt against capitalism?

China overthrew its emperor. 4

In the early 1900's, China was independent in name only. Although the Chinese civilization was one of the oldest in the world, it had faced years of humiliation at the hands of outsiders (pages 580–583). Foreign countries had spheres of influence in China. Foreigners controlled China's trade and economic resources.

Many people in China believed that their country's only chance for survival lay in modernization and nationalism. They urged government officals to improve the army and navy, to build modern factories, and to reform education. Yet while some leaders wanted change, others feared it. They believed that China's greatness lay in its traditional ways.

Chinese nationalists overthrew the Ch'ing dynasty.

Among the groups pushing for modernization and nationalization was the Kuomintang, or Nationalist People's party. Its founder and leader was Sun Yat-sen. In 1911, the Nationalists succeeded in overthrowing the last emperor of the Ch'ing dynasty, which had ruled China since 1644. Sun Yat-sen became president of the new Republic of China.

Sun, a physician who had spent many years in the United States, hoped to establish a modern government based on what he called the Three Principles of the People. The three principles were (1) nationalism (meaning an end to foreign control); (2) people's rights (democracy); and (3) people's livelihood (meaning a form of non-Marxist socialism and land reform to benefit the peasant farmers).

Sun and his followers quickly discovered that it was easier to destroy an old government than to build a new one. The end of imperial rule, after 2,000 years, left China weak and disunited. Civil war broke out as one powerful group battled another. Provincial warlords ruled territories as large as their armies could conquer.

As always during times of unrest, the Chinese peasants suffered most. Warlord armies terrorized the countryside, pillaging and looting everywhere. Roads and bridges fell into disrepair, and crops were destroyed. Famine took the lives of millions. This was the situation in China when World War I broke out in 1914.

Sun Yat-sen's government, though practically powerless, sided with the Allies against Germany. Sun and other leaders hoped that the Allies, in gratitude, would return control of China to the Chinese.

On May 4, 1919, some 3,000 angry students—the first generation of young Chinese to receive a Western-style education—gathered in the center of Peking. They had just heard infuriating news of the Treaty of Versailles. The Allied leaders had refused to give up their territories and commercial interests in China. Even worse for China, Japan was to be allowed to keep the Chinese territory it had seized during the war. "Down with the European imperialists!" the students shouted. "Boycott Japan!"

The May Fourth protests spread to other cities and became a truly national movement. It was not a revolution as such—that would come later—but it showed how much China's young people wanted a strong, modern nation. "What should we fear?" asked Mao Tse-tung (MOW zuh-DUNG), a young schoolteacher from the countryside who supported the Peking students.

We should not fear the militarists. We should not fear the capitalists. What is the greatest force? The greatest force is the union of the popular masses.

As you will read, Mao later turned the masses into a powerful revolutionary army.

A Communist party arose in China.

China's humiliation at the hands of the Allied powers left a deep scar on many young Chinese intellectuals. Many turned away from Sun's belief in Western-style democracy. They turned instead to the ideals and beliefs of a powerful new leader. That leader was Lenin of the Soviet Union (Chapter 28).

Lenin was willing to help China's Nationalist government. He believed that the Soviet Union and China had common enemies—the European powers and the United States. Early in 1920, Lenin began sending military advisers and equipment to the Nationalists. Several of

674

the Chinese Nationalist leaders traveled to Moscow for military training.

In 1921, the Chinese set up their own Communist party. In the beginning, the Communist party was closely allied with the Nationalist (Kuomintang) party of Sun Yat-sen.

In 1925, Sun Yat-sen died, and leadership of the Nationalists passed to his brother-in-law, a Japanese-trained general named Chiang Kai-shek (jee-**AHNG** kye-shehk). Chiang set out to defeat the warlords and unite all of China under the Nationalists.

Although the Communists supported him, Chiang distrusted them. He believed that the Soviet Union was supporting the Nationalists only until the Communists grew strong enough to take over. Chiang, the son of a well-to-do landowner, did not agree with the Communists' goal of creating a socialist economy. Many of Chiang's supporters were bankers and business people in the coastal cities. They feared a revolution like the one that brought the Communists to power in the Soviet Union.

Together, Chiang's Nationalist forces and the Communists fought the warlords. Chiang led a successful march from Canton to Shanghai.

Then Chiang decided that time had come to strike at the Communists. At dawn on April 12, 1927, Nationalist troops and armed gangs moved into Shanghai. They killed many Communist leaders and trade union members in the streets of the city. Similar killings took place in other cities. The Chinese Communist party was nearly wiped out. Its few survivors went into hiding.

In 1928, Chiang became president of the Nationalist Republic of China. Great Britain and the United States both formally recognized the new government. The Soviet Union, as a result of the Shanghai massacre, did not.

Mao Tse-tung preached revolution.

The Nationalist government of Chiang promised democracy and political rights for all Chinese. As time went by, however, Chiang was not able to fulfill his promises. His government became less democratic and more corrupt. Those that disagreed with its policies were thrown into jail or killed.

In the cities, the Nationalist government set up new factories and businesses. It also built

Chiang Kai-shek (right) and Mao Tse-tung (left) were once allies but later became enemies.

railroads, updated China's laws, and opened new schools and hospitals. These improvements helped city people.

However, the Nationalists did nothing to improve life for China's rural peasants. Many peasants turned away from Chiang and the Nationalist government. They looked instead to the Chinese Communist party.

One of the leaders of the Communists in the late 1920's was Mao Tse-tung (1893–1976). Mao came from a prosperous peasant family. His father forced him to leave school to work when he was 13. Mao ran away and went to school whenever he could, finally finishing high school when he was 25. Afterward, he worked as a librarian and a teacher. He began his political activities in his student days and became a member of the Communist party.

When the Communists were nearly wiped out in 1927, Mao fled to the countryside. He had already begun to develop his own brand of communism. Karl Marx (pages 551–552) had written that the revolution would begin among urban workers. Lenin had already shown that a Marxist revolution could take place in a largely rural

675

SECTION 4
Objectives and Teaching Strategies

OBJECTIVE 1. Compare and contrast the aims and achievements of China's three great nationalist leaders.

Teaching Strategy: *Skill Building: Comparing and Contrasting Nationalist Leaders* (page 660e)

OBJECTIVE 2. Explain the outcomes of China's civil war in the 1930's.

Teaching Strategy: *Skill Building: Making Predictions* (page 660e)

SECTION 4
Resources

GEOGRAPHY
- Transparency 86

REINFORCEMENT
- Independent Practice 29.4

ENRICHMENT
- Voices from the Past 29.4

ASSESSMENT
- Section Quiz 29.4

1. (a) in Hunan, particularly near Juichin **(b)** Yenan

2. west from Juichin to the Yangtze River, north across Szechwan for about 450 miles, then northeast to Yenan

3. Manchuria, Jehol, lands west and south to the Yellow River, and the coastal provinces for 500 miles south from the Yellow River

4. It would force the Nationalists to retreat inland.

5. In the Long March, Mao and the Communist forces made a long, desperate journey to find a more secure stronghold. Japan's successful invasion allowed Japanese troops to take over the richest areas of China, while also forcing Nationalist armies to move farther inland. Both the Long March and Nationalist retreat were caused by outside pressures, while the movement of Japanese troops was motivated by aggression.

■ BACKGROUND

Words of a Chinese peasant song: ''Harvest every year; but yearly—nothing./ Borrow money yearly; yearly still in debt./Broken huts, small basins, crooked pots;/Half an acre of land; five graves.''

China, 1927-1938

KEY

- Areas under communist control before November, 1934.
- Area governed by Communists after 1935.
- → Route of the Long March, Oct. 1934 - Oct. 1935.
- Area occupied by Japan, 1933.
- Area held by Japan, 1938.

Focus on Geography

Geographic Skills

1. (a) Where were Communist strongholds located before 1934? (b) After 1935?

2. Describe the route of the Long March.

3. What part of China did Japan hold by 1938?

4. How might Japan's invasion affect the location of Nationalist strongholds?

Geographic Theme: Movement

5. How do the Long March, Japanese invasion, and Nationalist retreat illustrate the theme of movement?

In a very short time, several hundred million peasants will rise like a tornado or tempest, a force so swift and violent that no power, however great, will be able to suppress it. They will break all trammels [bonds] that now bind them and rush forward along the road to liberation. They will send all imperialists, warlords, corrupt officials, local bullies, and bad gentry to their graves.

Civil war broke out.

By 1930, civil war raged in China. The Communists set up strongholds in the southern Chingkang Mountains. The Nationalists attacked them repeatedly but failed to drive them out. From their mountain hideouts, the Communists waged a guerrilla war against Chiang's armies. Mao outlined his strategy:

1. Retreat when the enemy advances.
2. Harass when the enemy encamps.
3. Attack when the enemy hesitates.
4. Pursue when the enemy retreats.

Such tactics were only possible with the support of the peasants in the area where the guerrillas were fighting. "The people are the water, the soldiers are the fish," Mao observed. "The fish cannot live without water."

Mao ensured support for his army by dividing land the Communists won among local farmers. He also made sure that Communist soldiers respected peasant property by helping farmers with their harvest and protecting women and children. As a result, more and more Chinese farmers joined Mao's Red Army, as it came to be called.

The Red Army retreated.

In 1933, Chiang Kai-shek launched a huge campaign to destroy the Communists. He gathered an army of nearly a million men, surrounded the Communists' mountain stronghold, and began tightening the noose. Outnumbered nearly ten to one, Mao realized that battle was hopeless. In 1934, he and his followers fled the mountains.

This was the beginning of an epic journey called the Long March. Over the next year, the Communists covered about 6,000 miles, keeping one step ahead of Chiang's forces. They often traveled at night to escape being seen from Nationalist

country, but he had based his organization in Russia's cities. Mao went one step further. He believed he could bring Marxist revolution to a rural country and the peasants could be the true revolutionaries. Mao predicted:

676

airplanes. The chase lasted more than a year. About 100,000 Communists began the march. No more than 30,000—perhaps as few as 10,000—reached safety in northwestern China. There they were beyond the reach of Chiang's forces.

Mao and the other Communists who survived the march settled in caves in northwestern China. They quickly gained new followers. Meanwhile, as civil war between Nationalists and Communists continued, Japan invaded China.

Japan invaded Manchuria.

The Japanese had taken advantage of the fighting in China as early as 1931. In that year, Japanese forces invaded the northeast part of China, Manchuria. This attack marked the beginning of World War II in Asia.

In 1937, the Japanese attacked other parts of China. Thousands of Chinese lost their lives as cities and villages were bombed. Many more died of starvation because farms were destroyed. By 1938, Japan controlled a large part of China.

The Japanese invasion forced the Nationalists and the Communists to unite against this new enemy. Yet Chiang and Mao remained rivals with different goals for China. Chiang believed that the Communists were a greater threat than the Japanese. Although he received money and weapons from the United States to fight Japan, Chiang saved those resources to use against Mao.

On the other hand, Mao and his Red Army fought the Japanese in every way they knew how. More and more Chinese peasants joined Mao's army to help his fight. They looked to the Communists as heroes who were defending China from foreigners. As we shall see in Chapter 33, the loyalty Mao won from the peasants was a powerful weapon against the Nationalists.

Footnote to History

In the course of the Long March, members of the Red Army crossed at least 24 rivers. They climbed over 18 mountain ranges, some of them deep in snow. They fought 15 major battles and faced minor skirmishes almost every day. They crossed miles of swampland where they had to sleep sitting up, leaning back to back in pairs, to keep from sinking into the mud and drowning.

With the Red Army, Mao (on horseback) and his wife, Chiang Ch'ing (in round hat), made the grueling Long March to safety in western China.

Section REVIEW 4

Identify: (a) Sun Yat-sen, (b) Mao Tse-tung, (c) Nationalist party (Kuomintang), (d) Chiang Kai-shek, (e) Long March

Answer:
1. (a) What were the three principles of Sun Yat-sen's new goverment? (b) What problems did China face during his presidency?
2. Why were Chinese students angry over the terms of the Treaty of Versailles?
3. (a) Why did Chiang turn against his Communist allies? (b) What did he do?
4. (a) What improvements did Chiang's government bring to China? (b) What were the weaknesses of his government?
5. How was Mao's form of communism different from Marx's and Lenin's?
6. (a) What methods did Mao use to weaken the Nationalists? (b) What events led to the Long March? (c) What were its results?
7. (a) How did the Japanese react to the civil war in China? (b) Contrast Chiang's and Mao's policies toward the Japanese.

Critical Thinking
8. What did Mao mean by his statement, "The people are the water, the soldiers are the fish"?

677

ANSWERS TO
Section Review 4

Identify:
(a) founder and leader of Kuomintang (b) Communist leader (c) established Republic of China (d) wanted to unite China under Nationalists (e) journey Red Army made to escape Chiang's forces

Answer:
1. (a) nationalism, people's rights, livelihood (b) civil war, famine, breakdown of transportation
2. Allies did not give up territories and commercial interests; Japan kept territory seized during war.
3. (a) He feared they would take over government. (b) killed Communists
4. (a) In cities, it set up new factories and businesses, updated China's laws, and opened new schools and hospitals. (b) Government became less democratic and more corrupt and did nothing to improve life for peasants.
5. Mao felt that peasants, not urban workers, could be the true revolutionaries and the revolution could take place in rural country.
6. (a) guerrilla warfare (b) Mao fled with Red Army to escape Chiang's army. (c) Mao gained followers.
7. (a) by attacking Manchuria (b) Chiang used resources to fight Mao; Mao fought Japanese.
8. In guerrilla warfare, the army is dependent on people in the area for food, water, information. Without the people, soldiers would die.

Concluding the Chapter

1. **Chapter Closer**
   Ask students to compare and contrast the expressions of nationalism in India, the Middle East, Latin America, and China. In what ways were nationalist movements generally similar throughout the world, and in what ways were they different?

2. **Reteaching Activities**
   a. Summarizing Have students convert each heading in this section into a question and then answer each question by writing a summarizing sentence.
   b. Comparing Write *Nationalists* and *Communists* on the board. Have students find information in the text that explains the difference between the two parties.

Answers to Chapter Review appear on page 660f.

Summary

1. Indians organized for independence. Following World War I, Indian nationalists increased their demands for self-rule. When hundreds of Indians were killed at Amritsar, Gandhi led a program of civil disobedience and economic boycott. Although Gandhi hoped to unite Muslims and Hindus, Muslim leaders called for a separate state.

2. Nationalism spread to the Middle East. The collapse of the Ottoman empire in World War I led to independence movements in the Middle East. In 1923, Turkish nationalists, led by Kemal, established the Republic of Turkey. In 1921, Reza Khan seized control of what is now Iran and set out to modernize the country. Saudi Arabia, unified by Ibn Saud, was governed according to Islamic law. By 1936, only Palestine was not yet free of foreign rule. The Palestinian issue was complicated by conflict between Jews and Arabs, each of which wanted their own country.

3. Latin America faced difficult changes. Although politically independent, Latin American countries depended economically on foreign investors. Dictatorial governments did little to improve living conditions. In 1910, discontent led to a revolution in Mexico that turned into civil war. By 1920, Mexico had a stable government. Beginning in the early 1900's, the United States intervened in Latin American affairs to protect its investments. Although the Good Neighbor Policy of 1935 eased tensions, resentments remained.

4. China overthrew its emperor. In 1911, Chinese nationalists, led by Sun Yat-sen, overthrew the emperor and set up a republic. When the Nationalists were unable to maintain order, civil war broke out in the north. China's humiliation in the Treaty of Versailles convinced many Chinese to break with the West and embrace communism. In 1925, leadership of the Nationalists passed to Chiang Kai-shek, who came to mistrust the Communists. Led by Mao Tsetung, Communists won the suport of the people. In 1933, Chiang forced Mao's army into retreat. From their hiding places in the northern mountains, the Communists launched a campaign against invading Japanese, thus winning even more peasant support.

Reviewing the Facts

1. Define the following terms:
   a. civil disobedience   b. nationalize
2. Explain the importance of each of the following names or terms:
   a. Indian National   c. Kemal
       Congress   d. Reza Khan
   b. Muslim League

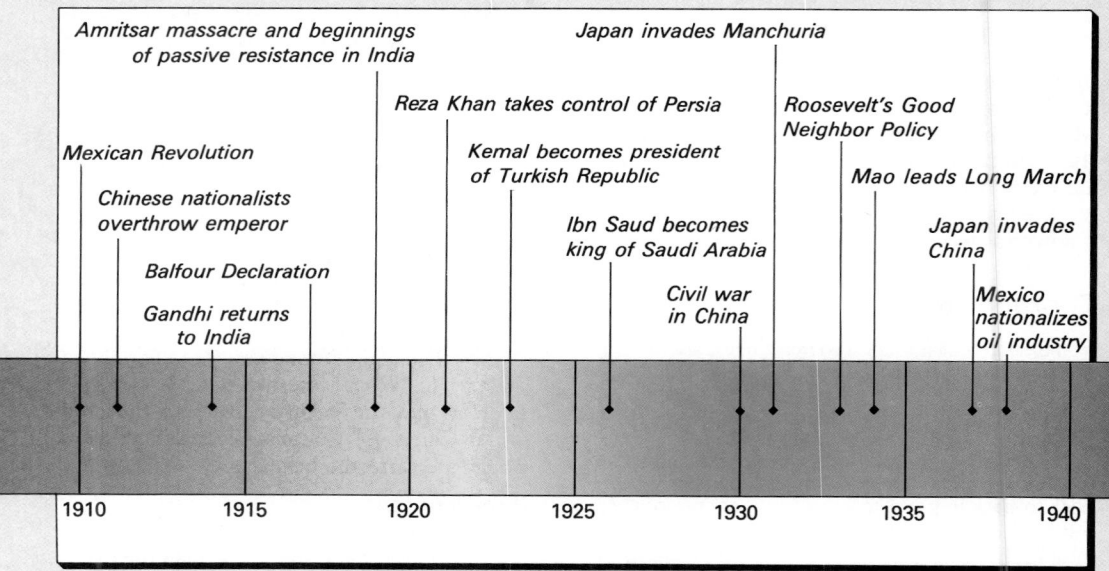

Amritsar massacre and beginnings of passive resistance in India

Japan invades Manchuria

Reza Khan takes control of Persia

Roosevelt's Good Neighbor Policy

Mexican Revolution

Kemal becomes president of Turkish Republic

Mao leads Long March

Chinese nationalists overthrow emperor

Ibn Saud becomes king of Saudi Arabia

Japan invades China

Balfour Declaration

Civil war in China

Mexico nationalizes oil industry

Gandhi returns to India

1910   1915   1920   1925   1930   1935   1940

678

e. Ibn Saud
f. Zionism
g. Balfour Declaration
h. caudillo
i. Díaz
j. Obregón
k. Good Neighbor Policy
l. Sun Yat-sen
m. Mao Tse-tung
n. Chiang Kai-shek
o. Long March

3. (a) What were the goals of Hindu nationalists in 1930? (b) Of Muslim nationalists?
4. How did United States policy toward Latin America change between 1900 and 1935?
5. (a) What happened in China in 1911? (b) What problems did the new government face?
6. (a) How did the Treaty of Versailles contribute to the Communist movement in China? (b) Why did Chiang break from the Communists?

Basic Skills

1. **Reading and interpreting a table**   (a) In the table on page 550, what trend exists in India and Pakistan's relative share of world manufacturing output between 1750 and 1900? (b) From what you know about British colonial policy, how can you account for this trend? (c) How is this trend related to Gandhi's focus on spinning and on wearing home-spun cloth?
2. **Summarizing**   Summarize briefly the main points in Gandhi's action plan (page 664).

Researching and Reporting Skills

1. **Using biographies**   Find biographical information about one of the nationalist leaders you have read about in this chapter. Choose an incident in the person's life that illustrates an important trait and report about it to the class.
2. **Identifying sources with opposing viewpoints** The history of Palestine between the two wars can be written from either a Jewish or an Arab point of view. Find two sources that will present these opposing viewpoints. Skim to find the arguments or interpretation of events on each side of the conflict.
3. **Using primary sources**   Gandhi and Mao were both popular leaders who communicated their convictions to thousands of the uneducated poor. Find a source that quotes their sayings. List five important sayings of each person and explain how these sayings would appeal to the masses.

Critical Thinking

1. **Synthesizing**   How did nationalist objectives in India and the Middle East differ from those in Latin America and China?
2. **Evaluating**   Gandhi used a new method of resistance to British rule. (a) What were the main features of this method? (b) Was this the most effective method or should he have used a different approach?
3. **Applying a concept**   Modernization as well as nationalism was an influence on many countries after World War I. (a) How did modernization affect countries in the Middle East? (b) What influences opposed modernization and where were they strongest?
4. **Analyzing**   (a) For what reasons did Jews begin returning to Palestine? (b) What conflict in nationalist ambitions developed in Palestine?
5. **Summarizing**   (a) List the various conditions that led to revolution in Mexico. (b) To what extent did the revolution change these conditions?
6. **Comparing**   (a) How did Mao's brand of communism differ from that of Marx and Lenin? (b) How did Mao gain the support of Chinese peasants?

Perspectives on Past and Present

Many of the newly emerging countries after World War I had dynamic nationalist leaders. (a) Who have been some of the comparable leaders since World War II? (b) What kinds of changes have they sought?

Investigating History

1. The first issue of *Time* magazine appeared in 1925 and of *Newsweek* in 1933. Find out if your library has microfilm for these magazines in their early years. If so, read and report on events related to one country of Asia, the Middle East, or Latin America.
2. The films *Gandhi,* depicting the struggle for independence in India, and *The Last Emperor,* depicting two revolutions in China, provide background for Asian history in the twentieth century. Watch the videotape of one of these films and report on it to the class.

679

CHAPTER
Evaluation

Chapter Test 29, Alternate Chapter Test 29, and Computer Test Bank Chapter 29 Test can be used to evaluate your students' understanding of this chapter.

The Years between the Wars

Chapter Overview

In the 1920's, Europe began to recover from the ravages of World War I. The decade of the 1920's saw great changes in technology, science, and the arts.

The Great Depression of the 1930's brought on new political crises. In Italy and Germany, the Fascist and Nazi parties gained control. In response to aggression by Mussolini and Hitler, Britain and France pursued a policy of appeasement, and the United States continued its policy of isolationism.

Chapter Focus

Begin by having students read the opening section, which describes the German inflation of 1923. That year was called the Year of Hunger in Germany. Many Germans longed for radical change. Some flocked to the Communist party. Others looked to Adolf Hitler and the Nazis. The Nazis promised to make Germany a great power once again.

In 1924, the mark regained its former value, ending the crisis. However, in 1929 the Great Depression struck, and more Germans looked to the Communists or to the Nazis for salvation. Tell students that this chapter explains how Europe achieved an unsteady recovery after World War I, but then collapsed under the impact of the Depression and began to move toward a second world war.

Europe recovered from World War I. 1

Setting the Stage

Remind students that the victory of 1918 had been won at a terrible price for the Allies in Europe. The cost was greatest for France. About 1,400,000 Frenchmen had been killed and about 750,000 had been wounded. France's richest agricultural, mining, and industrial areas were heavily damaged. France was never able to fully regain its former position in world affairs.

Teaching Strategies

Economics and History: Inflation (Objective 1) Review the definition of inflation. Inflation often occurs after a political or economic shock. The extreme inflation of 1923 in Germany came as a result of such a major shock. In that year Germany failed to keep up its reparation payments to France and the French seized control of the western part of Germany. The German government told the people who lived in this area not to go to work or to cooperate with the French in any way. To support them, the government printed and distributed massive quantities of paper money. With this huge increase in the volume of money, prices began to skyrocket. By the end of 1923, four trillion marks equaled the value of a United States dollar. In other words, the mark was essentially worthless.

Advance Planner

	SECTION 1
Objectives	1. Analyze Europe's political and economic difficulties in recovering from World War I. 2. Describe the steps taken to achieve permanent peace in Europe.
Setting the Stage	France's losses in World War I
Teaching Strategies	Economics and History: Inflation Discussing History: The "Spirit of Locarno" Check for Understanding
Guided Practice	Section Review 1
Independent Practice Worksheets	Independent Practice 30.1 Vocabulary 30
Enrichment	1. Primary Source: Voices 30.1 2. Researching for Points
Chapter Closer	

SECTION 2	SECTION 3	SECTION 4	SECTION 5
1. Identify Albert Einstein and explain his theory of relativity. 2. Write a generalization about the 1920's.	1. Identify weaknesses in the American economy that led to the Great Depression. 2. Compare and contrast the responses of the American, British, and French governments to the Great Depression.	1. Compare and contrast the careers of Mussolini and Hitler. 2. Identify *Kristallnacht* and trace its causes and consequences.	1. Locate the Axis powers on a map and identify the nations they invaded. 2. Evaluate the Munich Agreement.
Technological, social, and cultural changes in the United States after World War I	The effects of the stock market crash	The rise of new dictators in Europe	The philosophy of the League of Nations Transparency 87
Discussing History: Einstein's Theory of Relativity Skill Building: Making Generalizations Check for Understanding	Analyzing a Quotation: Overproduction and Unemployment Skill Building: Comparing Responses to the Depression Check for Understanding	Skill Building: Comparing Mussolini and Hitler Discussing History: The *Kristallnacht* Check for Understanding	Geography in History: Invasions of the Axis Powers Outline Map 2 Writing about History: The Munich Agreement Check for Understanding
Section Review 2 Independent Practice 30.2	Section Review 3 Independent Practice 30.3	Section Review 4 Independent Practice 30.4 Basic Skills 30	Section Review 5 Independent Practice 30.5 Geography Skills 30 Critical Thinking 30
1. Primary Source: Voices 30.2 2. ★Researching a Topic: Freud 3. Researching for Points	1. Primary Source: Voices 30.3 2. ★Creative Writing 3. Researching for Points	1. Primary Source: Voices 30.4 2. Preparing a Report 3. Researching for Points	1. Primary Source: Voices 30.5 2. Creative Writing 3. Researching for Points

●**Reteaching Activities**   Making a Time Line, Comparing and Contrasting, Identifying Main Ideas

Chapter Review   Summary, Reviewing the Facts, Basic Skills, Researching and Reporting Skills, Critical Thinking, Perspectives on Past and Present, Investigating History

Chapter Evaluation   Chapter Test 30, Alternate Chapter Test 30, Computer Test Bank Chapter 30 Test

Discussing History: The "Spirit of Locarno" (Objective 2) Have students read "Treaties raised hopes for peace" (page 682). In 1925 many Europeans fervently hoped that peace would be permanent; everyone dreaded the possibility of another world war. The Locarno Pact was an attempt to reduce tensions between Germany, France, and Britain.

French and British leaders hoped that Germany could be reconciled to the Treaty of Versailles if Germany was admitted to the League of Nations. Ask if this was a reasonable expectation.

Check for Understanding Ask students to identify the main cause and the main effect of Germany's inflation in the 1920's.

Enrichment Activities

1. **Reading a Primary Source**
   Assign Voices from the Past Resource Book 30.1.

2. **Researching for Bonus Points**
   Who was the President of the Weimar Republic from 1919 to 1925? (Friedrich Ebert)

Society faced rapid change. 2

Setting the Stage

Direct students' attention to the pictures on pages 683 and 685. Ask what kinds of changes the pictures suggest. The picture on page 683 shows the increasing importance of aircraft after World War I. The picture on page 685 shows the increasing prominence of women in politics. Note that World War I stimulated both technological and social changes.

Teaching Strategies

Discussing History: Einstein's Theory of Relativity (Objective 1) Begin by writing the formula "$E = mc^2$" on the board. Ask who devised the formula and what it means. Albert Einstein, a German physicist, wrote this famous formula. Scientists had carefully measured the speed of light and found that light travels at exactly the same speed no matter what direction it travels in relation to Earth. This made no sense, since Earth itself is moving through space.

Einstein put forward the idea that the speed of light is absolute, or unalterable. At the same time, things that seem absolute, such as space and time, are not. He explained that space and time for a spaceship crew are different from space and time for observers on Earth. Since relative motion is the key to Einstein's theory, it is known by the name of *theory of relativity*.

Einstein's theory had broad implications. According to the theory of relativity, an object increases both its mass and its energy as it approaches the speed of light. As a result, Einstein suggested, matter can be converted into energy according to the formula $E = mc^2$. (*E* stands for energy, *m* for mass, and *c* for the speed of light—the

constant—multiplied by itself). This meant that even a tiny atom contains an enormous amount of energy and became the basis for the development of the atom bomb in the 1940's.

Skill Building: Making Generalizations (Objective 2) Remind the class that the Middle Ages are sometimes called the "Age of Faith," and the late nineteenth century the "Age of Progress." Have students make up names for the decade of the 1920's. Then tell the class that the decade has been called the "Roaring Twenties," the "Golden Twenties," the "Jazz Age," and "Years of Hope." Ask why each name is appropriate.

Check for Understanding Have students give six examples of technological, scientific, cultural, and social changes that occurred during the 1920's.

Enrichment Activities

1. **Reading a Primary Source**
   Assign Voices from the Past Resource Book 30.2.

2. **Researching a Topic**
   Ask advanced students to prepare a report that explains this statement by Freud: "The poor ego has a still harder time of it; it has to serve three harsh masters, and has to do its best to reconcile the claims and demands of all three. . . . The three tyrants are the external world, the superego and the id."

3. **Researching for Bonus Points**
   Who were the three main characters in James Joyce's *Ulysses?* (Stephen Dedalus, Leopold Bloom, and Molly Bloom)

Setting the Stage

Have students read "The stock market fell in 1929" (pages 687–688). Explain that America's vast industrial and agricultural resources were physically undamaged and still capable of enormous productivity. Yet within a few months, unemployment rates began to rise at an alarming rate. Industrial production, prices, and wages fell sharply. A prolonged business slump known as the Great Depression had begun.

Teaching Strategies

Analyzing a Quotation: Overproduction and Unemployment (Objective 1) After traveling across the country during the Depression, Oscar Ameringer told the House Committee on Labor what he had seen:

A number of Montana citizens told me of thousands of bushels of wheat left in the fields uncut on account of its low price that hardly paid for the harvesting. . . . While I was in Oregon the *Portland Oregonian* bemoaned the fact that thousands of ewes were killed by the sheep raisers because they did not bring enough in the market to pay the freight on them. And while Oregon sheepraisers fed mutton to the buzzard, I saw men picking for meat scraps in the garbage cans of the cities of New York and Chicago. . . . the farmers are being pauperized by the poverty of industrial populations, and the industrial populations are being pauperized by the poverty of the farmers. Neither has the money to buy the product of the other; hence we have overproduction and underconsumption at the same time and in the same country.

Read or distribute the passage and then ask these questions:

- Why did sheep raisers in Oregon kill their ewes? (because the price of mutton was too low to pay for the cost of shipping)
- What did Ameringer see in New York and Chicago? (people picking for scraps in garbage cans)
- What conclusion did Ameringer reach about the causes of the Depression? (U.S. was suffering from both overproduction and underconsumption.)

Skill Building: Comparing Responses to the Depression (Objective 2) Draw a chart with three columns and three rows on the board. Label the columns *United States*, *Great Britain*, and *France*. Label the rows *Political Leadership*, *Programs*, and *Results*. Ask students to review pages 689–690. Then have them fill in the chart as a class activity. When the class chart has been completed, discuss the following: Which country had the most effective leadership? (United States) Did any of the programs successfully end the Depression? (no) How did the public respond to government measures in the United States? (Roosevelt's strong leadership helped preserve America's faith in the democratic political system.)

Check for Understanding Ask students to identify the causes and effects of the Great Depression.

Enrichment Activities

1. **Reading a Primary Source** Assign Voices from the Past Resource Book 30.3.
2. **Creative Writing** In 1933, a presidential advisor told Roosevelt, "Mr. President, if your program succeeds you will be the greatest President in American history." "If it fails," Roosevelt replied, "I shall be the last one." Ask advanced students to write essays speculating on what might have happened had the New Deal failed.
3. **Researching for Bonus Points** On what day did the stock market reach its lowest point? (July 8, 1932)

Setting the Stage

Write "Mussolini" and "Hitler" on the board. Ask students to write two questions asking what they would like to know about these two leaders. Explain that Mussolini and Hitler were two dictators who rose to power in the troubled years after World War I.

Teaching Strategies

Skill Building: Comparing Mussolini and Hitler (Objective 1) Draw a chart with two columns and six rows on the board. Label the columns *Mussolini* and *Hitler*. Label the rows *Attitude toward Versailles Treaty*, *Handling of Economic Crisis*, *Method of Taking Power*, *Style of Leadership*, *Goals*, and *Enemies*. Ask students to review pages 691–697. Then have them fill in the chart as a class activity. When the class chart has been completed, discuss the following: What role did the Depression play in the rise to power of Mussolini and Hitler?

(both took advantage of the social unrest in their countries) How did Hitler and Mussolini take power? (both were legally appointed to office) What goals did Mussolini and Hitler share? (both opposed democracy and began to create powerful dictatorships)

Discussing History: The *Kristallnacht* (Objective 2) Review the concept of scapegoating—blaming members of a minority for national problems. Can students recall an earlier example of scapegoating? (Roman emperors used the Christians as scapegoats.) The Nazis declared the Jews an inferior race. The Kristallnacht marked the first systematic action taken by the German government against the Jewish community. Within 24 hours, Nazi mobs destroyed 7,500 Jewish-owned businesses, burned 275 synagogues, and arrested more than 30,000 Jews. The Kristallnacht signaled the beginning of Hitler's "Final Solution"—the attempt to eliminate all Jews.

Check for Understanding Have students describe the role that the Depression played in the rise to power of Mussolini, Hitler, and the Japanese militarists.

Enrichment Activities

1. **Reading a Primary Source** Assign Voices from the Past Resource Book 30.4.
2. **Preparing a Report** Ask students to report on one of the following topics: the rise of Hitler, the rise of Mussolini, the Reichstag fire, the Kristallnacht, or Japanese aggression in Manchuria.
3. **Researching for Bonus Points** Who was convicted of setting the Reichstag Fire? (Marinus Van Der Lubbe)

The world drifted toward war. 5

Setting the Stage
Ask how the phrase, "all for one and one for all" reflects the philosophy of the League of Nations. The League was founded on the belief that the nations of the world acting together could stop aggression. Still the League failed to stop Japan, Germany, and Italy from breaking treaties and invading other nations.

Teaching Strategies
Geography in History: Invasions of the Axis Powers (Objective 1) Distribute copies of Outline Map 2: The World. Have students label Germany, Italy, Japan, Ethiopia, China, Austria, and Czechoslovakia. Tell students to devise a system of symbols to indicate the invasions of each Axis power on neighboring nations. Show Map Transparency 87, *Expansion of Nazi Germany, 1933–1939*, and have students note other areas of German expansion.

Writing about History: The Munich Agreement (Objective 2) *Prewriting* Hitler and Chamberlain signed a joint statement pledging that the two nations would not go to war. When he returned to England, Chamberlain told cheering crowds: "I believe it is peace in our time." British leader Winston Churchill disagreed and told the House of Commons: "We have been defeated without a war. And do not suppose this is the end. This is only the first taste of a bitter drink which will be forced on us year by year. Unless we arise again. And take our stand for freedom as in olden times." *Writing* Have students imagine that they are members of Parliament. They should write statements either supporting Chamberlain or agreeing with Churchill.

Check for Understanding Have students explain how Hitler violated the terms of the Treaty of Versailles.

Enrichment Activities
1. **Reading a Primary Source** Assign Voices from the Past Resource Book 30.5.
2. **Creative Writing** Ask students to choose an event discussed in this section that they would like to have witnessed. Then have them write essays explaining why they chose this event and what they hoped to learn about it.
3. **Researching for Bonus Points** What two leaders attended the Munich Conference other than Hitler and Chamberlain? (French Premier Daladier and Mussolini)

ANSWERS TO Chapter Review 30

Reviewing the Facts
1. (a) avoiding political ties to other countries (b) totalitarian form of government (c) making concessions to keep peace (d) trade-offs made at a conference
2. (a) Skyrocketing inflation can lead to weakened economy. (b) German government that faced severe economic problems after the war (c) provided loan to stabilize German currency (d) agreement to renounce war (e) developed theory of relativity (f) new art form that drew on the unconscious (g) gave black writers, artists, and composers worldwide

recognition (h) site of stock market crash of 1929 (i) business slump in the 1930's (j) Roosevelt's program for recovery from the Great Depression (k) established the first fascist government in Europe (l) right-wing political party in Germany (m) Nazi dictator of Germany (n) Hitler's plan for Germany (o) Hitler's secret police (p) name for Hitler's proposed German empire (q) urged a policy of appeasement (r) strengthened fascism in Europe (s) fascist dictator of Spain (t) conference at which Britain and France allowed Hitler to take Sudetenland

3. Locarno Agreement, Kellogg Briand Pact

4. won the right to vote, demanded wider career choices, became more independent

5. American loans were called back; many countries traded with the United States

6. (a) ended parliamentary democracy, abolished all political parties except Fascists, censored the press, controlled opposition (b) forced capitalists and workers to cooperate, set up state corporations to run economy

7. (a) conquered Ethiopia (b) invaded China (c) occupied Rhineland, forced Austria to become German province, took Sudetenland

8. (a) defeated elected government (b) showed how devastating the coming war would be

Basic Skills

1. (a) in 1926, 1928, 1930, 1932, 1934, and 1936 (b) in Germany, unemployment declined; in Britain, it remained high

2. Weimar Republic, burning of Reichstag, Enabling Act, Rhineland, Austria, Munich Conference, Kristallnacht, Czechoslovakia

Researching and Reporting Skills

Students' answers will vary.

Critical Thinking

1. Americans wanted to enjoy their prosperity by staying out of international politics.

2. (a) More goods were being produced than people wanted or could afford to buy. (b) There was a downward economic spiral. As people bought less, manufacturers cut back on production and on the number of people employed. Fewer employed people caused further cuts in buying, and this in turn reinforced the downward spiral. (c) Business activity declined, unemployment rose; many people were poor and hungry.

3. (a) loss of territory, including Alsace-Lorraine; France could work Saar mines for 15 years; loss of Polish Corridor, loss of overseas territories, size of army limited, weapons limited, troops forbidden in Rhineland, blame for war, payment of reparations (b) Loss of territory reduced economic strength; loss of Alsace-Lorraine and Saar mines limited industrial growth; loss of colonies took away source of resources and raw materials and the markets for German goods. Limitations on military preparations saved money but hurt national pride; blame for war was a psychological burden. Reparations drained away funds that could have been used for recovery and rebuilding. (c) social effects: lack of opportunity to recover from war; feelings of guilt and hopelessness; economic effects: loss of a major industrial region and large land areas limited ability to recover and become economically strong again; political effects: government's hand limited for rebuilding and leading Germany to a positive future

4. Germany's coalition president could have refused to name Hitler chancellor or prevented the elections that elected a majority of Nazis to power. It became difficult to stop Hitler once he was legally given dictatorial powers by the Enabling Act.

5. (a) deprived Jews of citizenship; did not allow them to write, publish, act, teach, work in hospitals or banks, or to sell books; Jews had to wear Star of David, endure violence, and were sent to concentration camps (b) individuals: loss of sense of security; continuing fear; group: sense of being the object of prejudice, with the future uncertain

6. (a) economic problems from Depression; social instability due in part to economic problems but also to rapid social change; lack of strong and positive political leadership (b) Possible hypothesis: Fascism is a response in times of social, economic, and political uncertainty. It offers strong leadership and simple answers that have popular appeal. Support for hypothesis: Hitler and Mussolini rose to power in countries that were experiencing severe economic problems. Both the Italians and Germans (particularly the latter) had felt seriously disadvantaged as peoples after World War I. Hitler and Mussolini offered quick solutions, easy explanations, and a sense of pride.

Perspectives on Past and Present

Students' answers will vary.

Investigating History

Students' answers will vary.

The Years between the Wars

Chapter 30

Teaching with Pictures

Have students study the painting and read the chapter opener (pages 680–681). Then ask them how the artist depicts anger, bitterness, and frustration in his characters. Runaway inflation, bitterness remaining from the First World War, and doubts about the future were reflected in the paintings of George Grosz in the 1920's. His works included satiric pictures condemning the wealthy, the military, and the overall moral collapse of society. Students may be interested to know that Grosz served in the German army in World War I, but he became so disillusioned that he moved to the United States in 1933.

The anger and discontent of German workers show in this picture of a Communist gathering of the 1920's by German artist George Grosz.

Key Terms

relativity
isolationism
depression
standard of
  living
free-enterprise
fascism
authoritarian
anti-Semitism
concentration camp
territorial integrity
armed aggression
puppet government
collective security

censor
nazism
appeasement
occupy
negotiation

Read and Understand

1. Europe recovered from World War I.
2. Society faced rapid change.
3. Wall Street's crash opened the Depression.
4. Fascist leaders became dictators.
5. The world drifted toward war.

In the summer of 1923, the printing presses at Germany's mints were rolling, and they were turning out money. Germans counted their currency in *marks*, and the presses printed 400 quadrillion (400,000,000,000,000,000) marks a day! Crushed by its huge war expenses and burdened with heavy payments to the Allies, Germany was in the midst of disastrous inflation. From 1918 to 1923, the value of the mark fell, slowly at first and then with terrifying speed.

What did inflation mean for the people of Germany? At the war's end, a loaf of bread cost two marks in Berlin. By December 1921, the price had risen to 40 marks, and just 1 year later a loaf cost more than 1,500 marks.

Bad as inflation already was, it went completely out of control in 1923. By summer, a glass of beer cost 2 million marks and a loaf of bread 4 million. Workers collected their pay twice a day so

680

Chapter 30 Resources

GEOGRAPHY
■ Geography Skills 30
■ Outline Map 2
■ Transparency 87

REINFORCEMENT
■ Vocabulary 30
■ Basic Skills 30
■ Reteaching 30
■ Making Connections Study Guide 30

ENRICHMENT
■ Critical Thinking 30
■ History and Literature 30

ASSESSMENT
■ Chapter Test 30
■ Alternate Chapter Test 30
■ Computer Test Bank

that they could rush out to buy the things they needed before prices rose even higher. People took cartons and wheelbarrows full of money to buy food for supper. By autumn, the mark was worthless. Bank notes for billions of marks lay in street gutters.

Upper-class Germans suffered least from inflation because their lands and factories rose in value, keeping up with rising prices. Ordinary people faced harder times. Prices rose faster than wages, so people could not buy as much food or clothing as before. The inflation was a great shock to Germany's middle class. Civil servants, professionals, and people with fixed incomes or pensions saw their life savings become worthless. People discovered that the money they had saved to buy a house now barely covered the cost of a table.

What was the good of saving or planning for the future? Germans asked one another. What was the good of Germany's new democratic government, asked many, if people lost everything they had worked for? Germany eventually strengthened the mark, but the confidence of the German people was harder to rebuild.

In Germany and throughout Europe, the 1920's were a time of doubts and uncertainties. Embittered by the past war, people also feared the future. Some artists and writers expressed this bitterness in their work. Many people hid their fears by living for the pleasure of the moment. Thus, a thin shell of gaiety covered dark doubts and unanswered questions.

Europe recovered from World War I. 1

In human suffering, the cost of World War I had been staggering. The economic losses were also immense. The Allied and Central Powers had spent about $200 billion fighting the war. By 1918, every major European country was nearly bankrupt.

Only two world powers came out of the Great War in better financial shape than they entered it—Japan and the United States. Neither country had suffered fighting on its own soil. Both had expanded their international trade during the war.

These economic changes showed one of the major effects of World War I—the decline of European dominance in world affairs. Much wealth and power was still concentrated in Europe, of course, but the war had drained the continent's resources. The European Allies and the Central Powers were like two boxers who had battered each other in a long and brutal fight.

A second effect of the war was the sudden rise of new democracies. Between 1914 and 1918, Europe's last absolute rulers—the Hohenzollerns in Germany, the Hapsburgs in Austria-Hungary, and the Romanovs in Russia—were all overthrown. In Russia, the new democratic government soon fell to a Communist dictatorship. Even so, for the first time in history, most European countries were ruled by democratic governments.

New democracies were unstable.

Many citizens of the new democracies had little experience with parliamentary government. Germany and the new countries formed from Austria-Hungary, for example, had been ruled by kings and emperors for generations. There were problems even in France and Italy, whose parliaments pre-dated World War I. There, the large number of political parties made effective government difficult.

Democratic government is based on the principle of majority rule. In countries where there are only two or three major parties, it is fairly easy for one party to win a working majority. In countries with a dozen or more political groups, however, it is difficult for one party to win enough support to govern effectively.

In such countries, the largest party usually forms a coalition government. A coalition is a temporary alliance of several parties to form a parliamentary majority. Because the parties disagree on so many policies, coalitions seldom last long. In France, for example, there were some 40 changes of government in the 20 years between 1919 and 1939.

Coalition governments have other problems as well. Because they are in office for short times and because their members do not agree on important issues, such governments find it hard to provide leadership toward any long-term goals. People may accept this weak leadership as long

681

SECTION 1
Objectives and Teaching Strategies

OBJECTIVE 1. Analyze Europe's political and economic difficulties in recovering from World War I.

Teaching Strategy: *Economics and History: Inflation* (page 680a)

OBJECTIVE 2. Describe the steps taken to achieve permanent peace in Europe.

Teaching Strategy: *Discussing History: The "Spirit of Locarno"* (page 680c)

■ BACKGROUND

Before the war, the mark had been worth about 25 American cents. In June 1921, its value had fallen to about 14 cents. During 1923, the mark continued to fall until it was so low that it took millions of marks to equal a single penny.

The United States lent more than $10 billion to its European allies. After the war, Britain and France were faced with loan repayment burdens that were almost as heavy as those of Germany.

SECTION 1
Resources

ASSESSMENT
- Section Quiz 30.1

REINFORCEMENT
- Independent Practice 30.1

ENRICHMENT
- Voices from the Past 30.1

ANSWERS TO
Section Review 1

Identify:
(a) postwar democratic government in Germany
(b) financial plan to strengthen Germany's economy (c) pledge to renounce war

Answer:
1. European nations were nearly bankrupt; Japan and the U.S., economically strong

2. (a) Democratic government replaced absolute rulers. (b) Citizens had little experience with parliamentary government; many political parties made effective government difficult; coalition governments did not provide leadership.

3. (a) lack of democratic traditions, too many political parties, new government bore the burden of defeat (b) skyrocketing inflation (c) Dawes Plan provided loan and rescheduled reparation payments.

4. (a) They signed a treaty promising not to make war against each other; Germany promised to respect the borders of France and Belgium. (b) Many countries signed the Kellogg-Briand peace pact and joined the League of Nations.

5. a cooperative spirit, which would encourage a lasting peace and economic cooperation

as a country faces no major problems. When difficulties arise, however, the weaknesses of a coalition government are magnified. People may then be willing to sacrifice democracy in exchange for strong leadership. Such a course of events is exactly what happened in Italy, Germany, and several other countries in the 1920's and 1930's.

The German republic was weak.

The new democratic government set up in Germany in 1919 was known as the Weimar (VYE-mahr) Republic after the city where the national assembly met. The Weimar Republic had serious weaknesses from the start. Under Bismarck and William II, few democratic traditions had had a chance to take root. Furthermore, postwar Germany had seven major political parties and many minor ones.

Worst of all, the democratic government bore the burden of defeat. It was not the Hohenzollerns who had signed the Treaty of Versailles but representatives of the new republic. As a result, millions of Germans always viewed the Weimar government and its supporters as traitors.

Germany also faced enormous economic problems that had begun during the war. Unlike Britain and France, Germany did not increase taxes greatly during the war. Thus, while Germany spent $37 billion fighting World War I, its government collected only $1.5 billion in taxes. To make up the difference, the Germans simply printed money when they needed it. This paper money began to collapse after Germany's defeat in 1918. The result was a time of skyrocketing inflation (page 680).

Most Germans blamed the Weimar government and its weak leaders for Germany's problems. They failed to see that the war had caused most of their difficulties. As far as many Germans were concerned, Germany had made only one wartime mistake: It had lost. Next time, they swore, the result would be different.

The Dawes Plan brought stability.

Germany recovered swiftly from the 1923 inflation, thanks largely to the work of an international committee headed by Charles Dawes, an American banker and statesman. The committee worked out a financial plan to strengthen

Germany's economy. The Dawes Plan provided for a $200 million loan from American banks to stabilize German currency. The plan also set a more realistic schedule for Germany's reparations payments.

Put into effect in 1924, the Dawes Plan worked extremely well. As the German economy began to recover, it attracted further loans and investments from the United States. By 1929, Germany's factories were producing as much as they had in 1913.

Treaties raised hopes for peace.

As prosperity returned, Germany began again to take an active part in European affairs. Germany's foreign minister, Gustav Stresemann (SHTRAY-zeh-mahn), tried to undo the worst features of the Versailles settlement through careful diplomacy. He was helped by France's foreign minister, Aristide Briand (bree-AHN), a moderate who favored better relations with Germany.

In 1925, Briand and Stresemann met in the Swiss town of Locarno, together with representatives from Belgium, Italy, and Great Britain. They signed a treaty promising that France and Germany would never again make war against each other. Germany also promised to respect the existing borders of France and Belgium. In return for this concession, Germany was admitted to the League of Nations.

In 1928, the "spirit of Locarno" led to the Kellogg-Briand peace pact. Frank Kellogg, the American secretary of state, arranged this agreement with France's Briand. Countries that signed the treaty pledged "to renounce war as an instrument of national policy." Almost every country in the world, including the Soviet Union, eventually signed.

Unfortunately, there was no realistic way to punish a country that broke its promise of peace. The League of Nations was the obvious choice to enforce the treaty, but it had no armed forces of its own.

Nonetheless, hopes were high in Europe in the late 1920's. Besides the peace treaties, Europeans were enjoying an economic boom. Industrial production rose to its pre–World War I level. However, much of the boom depended on massive American investment. As long as the American economy stayed healthy, the sun would shine on Europe.

Section REVIEW   1

Identify: (a) Weimar Republic, (b) Dawes Plan, (c) Kellogg-Briand pact
Answer:
1. How did World War I change the balance of economic power in the world?
2. (a) How did the war change forms of government in Europe? (b) Why were many of the new governments weak?
3. (a) What political problems did the Weimar Republic face? (b) What economic problems? (c) How were the economic problems solved?
4. (a) How did relations improve between France and Germany in the 1920's? (b) Among nations worldwide?

Critical Thinking
5. Explain what leaders in the 1920's meant by "the spirit of Locarno." What policies would such a spirit have encouraged?

Society faced rapid change.   2

Amid all the havoc World War I caused, it did have one positive result. It quickened the pace of invention. During the war, scientists developed new drugs and medical treatments that helped millions of people after the war. The principles of tank construction were put to use in building better automobiles, trucks, and tractors. The war's technological advances did not go to waste in the postwar years.

Technology made the world seem smaller.

During the war, millions of people communicated across battle zones and moved supplies thousands of miles. Therefore, many of the greatest improvements came in communication and transportation.

The spread of the automobile The automobile benefited from a host of wartime improvements—electric fuel pumps and starters, air-filled tires, and more powerful engines. "Check now what

The Pan-American China Clipper began passenger service across the Pacific in 1935.

the new, roomier Austin offers you! Dependability! Performance! Style! Comfort!" This British newspaper advertisement from the late 1920's showed how far the automobile industry had come since 1900. Cars no longer looked like buggies on wheels. They were sleek and brightly polished, complete with chrome-plated bumpers, headlights, and shock absorbers.

The beginnings of air travel The war also brought spectacular improvements in aircraft. By 1918, planes could fly several hundred miles.

During the 1920's, airplanes were put to many new uses. Daring pilots carried the first airmail letters. Wartime fliers became "barnstormers," visiting country fairs to perform aerial acrobatics and take people for their first airplane rides.

In 1919, two British pilots, John Alcock and Arthur Brown, made the first successful flight across the Atlantic Ocean, flying from Newfoundland to Ireland. The next major crossing came in 1927, when a young American pilot named Charles Lindbergh captured worldwide attention with his 33-hour solo flight from New York to Paris.

Most of the world's major passenger airlines were established during the 1930's, though air travel was too expensive for all but the rich. Still, everyone could enjoy the thrilling exploits of aviation pioneers such as Amelia Earhart, the first woman to fly across the Atlantic.

683

SECTION 2
Objectives and Teaching Strategies

OBJECTIVE 1. Identify Albert Einstein and explain his theory of relativity.
Teaching Strategy: *Discussing History: Einstein's Theory of Relativity* (page 680c)

OBJECTIVE 2. Write a generalization about the 1920's.
Teaching Strategy: *Skill Building: Making Generalizations* (page 680c)

■ BACKGROUND

In 1929, America produced 84 percent of the 6.3 million cars manufactured throughout the world. At that time, Europe produced a total of only 689,000 cars.

SECTION 2
Resources

ASSESSMENT
■ Section Quiz 30.2

REINFORCEMENT
■ Independent Practice 30.2

ENRICHMENT
■ Voices from the Past 30.2

Radio was a powerful medium. Whereas the flight of Alcock and Brown was reported in newspapers, Lindbergh's was broadcast to millions by radio. To this day, many believe Lindbergh made the first transatlantic flight.

Radio for millions Marconi's first successful experiments with radio were in 1895 (page 595). The first voice transmission took place in 1906. The real push for radio development, however, came during World War I. The advantages of wireless communication in battle were so great that all countries gave radio research a high priority. By the end of the war, armies had developed a wide range of radio equipment.

In 1920, the world's first commercial radio station, KDKA in Pittsburgh, began broadcasting. Almost overnight, radio mania swept the United States. Radio receivers were mass-produced, and by 1925 a family could buy one for as little as $25. Soon every major city had stations broadcasting news, plays, and music. In 1921, KDKA and several other stations carried live, play-by-play descriptions of the World Series.

Science challenged old ideas.

Just as studies of electricity had begun long before practical uses for it were known, scientific research in the early 1900's was far ahead of technology. The two most important thinkers of the era had begun their work at the turn of the century. However, their ideas became much more widely known during the 1920's and 1930's. These two thinkers were a German physicist named Albert Einstein and an Austrian physician named Sigmund Freud.

Taken together, Einstein and Freud challenged some of the most deeply rooted ideas that people held about themselves and the world in which they lived. They were part of a scientific revolution that was as profound as that of Copernicus and Galileo (pages 387–389).

Einstein's theory of relativity Einstein offered new and startling ideas on space, time, energy, and matter. He began by tackling a problem that baffled physicists at the turn of the century. The speed of light had been measured very carefully. Scientists found that the speed of light is constant; that is, it travels at exactly the same speed no matter what direction it moves in relation to Earth. Yet this finding seemed to break the laws of motion described by Sir Isaac Newton, because Earth itself moves through space. Why did Earth's movement have no effect on the speed at which light seemed to move?

In 1905, Einstein put forth the idea that while the speed of light is constant, other things that seem constant, such as space and time, are not. Space and time can change, said Einstein, when measured in relation to an object moving at high speeds. Such changes occur only near the speed of light—about 186,000 miles per second. Thus, we never notice such changes in our everyday world. Since relative motion is the key to Einstein's idea, it is called the theory of **relativity.**

Einstein's ideas had wide implications. For example, he said that matter could be changed into energy according to the formula $E = mc^2$. E stands for energy, m for mass, and c^2 for the speed of light multiplied by itself. Because the speed of light is such an enormous number, the formula shows that even a tiny atom contains an enormous amount of energy. This idea, which

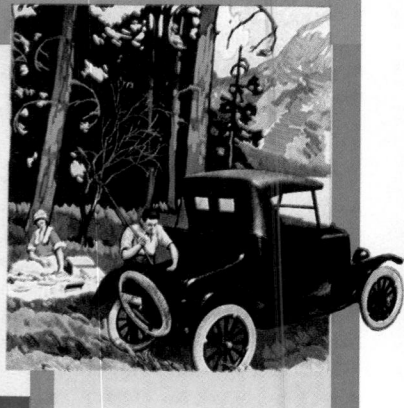

DAILY LIFE ▷ The Automobile

The humorist Will Rogers ended a tribute to Henry Ford by saying, "Good luck, Mr. Ford. It will take a hundred years to tell whether you have helped or hurt us, but you certainly didn't leave us as you found us." Rogers was right. The automobile was to change traditional patterns of life. By 1930, Americans owned three out of every four cars built. Owning a car enabled many people to move to the suburbs and commute to jobs in town. Others treasured their cars not only as means of travel but also as symbols of status. People also valued the convenience that cars gave them and the freedom that went with mobility. The automobile thus became a part of the life-style of the 1920's.

684

seemed fantastic in the early 1900's, became terrifyingly real when the atom bomb was developed in the 1940's.

Freud Freud's ideas were fully as revolutionary as Einstein's. Freud drew a new and, to some people, shocking picture of the workings of the human mind.

Freud began to develop his ideas while treating people with psychological problems. He found that some of these problems could be traced back to events in the patient's childhood. However, the patients had repressed (blocked) the happenings from their conscious memories. When a patient was able to uncover the repressed memory, the psychological problem was eased or cured.

From these experiences, Freud constructed a theory about the way the human mind worked. He called part of the mind the *unconscious*. In the unconscious, there were drives, especially sexual drives, of which the conscious mind was unaware.

Freud's theories ran into strong opposition. Many people were shocked by the idea that part of their mind was beyond their conscious control. Many were also shocked by the importance Freud gave to sex. All the same, his basic ideas had widespread influence.

Society became more open.

New ideas and new ways of life led to a new kind of individual freedom during the 1920's. Many people were willing to break with the past, to question traditional values, to consider new and different ideas.

This new spirit of independence was partly the result of World War I, which had disrupted customs and social patterns. Not surprisingly, young people were generally more willing to change than their elders. "What's the matter with kids today?" asked one popular song of the 1920's. The "matter" was that young people were experimenting with values that often differed from their parents'.

The new independent spirit showed clearly in the changes that women were making in their lives. Their work in the war effort was the decisive factor that won women the right to vote. After World War I, women's suffrage became law in the United States, Britain, Germany, Sweden, Austria, Hungary, Czechoslovakia, and elsewhere.

These French women are protesting that, if they become subject to the poll tax, they should have the right to vote.

Most women still followed traditional paths of marriage and family. However, growing numbers began to choose a different life-style. These women wanted greater freedom in their personal lives. Wives should not be second-class members of the family, feminists argued, but equal partners with their husbands. Margaret Sanger and Emma Goldman risked arrest by speaking in favor of birth control. As women sought new careers, the numbers of women in medicine, education, journalism, and other professions increased.

Art reflected society's doubts.

During the 1920's, new attitudes also appeared in art and literature.

'My nerves are bad to-night. Yes, bad. Stay with me.
'Speak to me. Why do you never speak? Speak.
'What are you thinking of? What thinking? What?
'I never know what you are thinking. Think.'

I think we are in rats' alley
Where the dead men lost their bones.

685

■ BACKGROUND

A French novel, *La Garçonne* (The Single Woman), became a best-seller in 1922. Its heroine attended college, got an interesting job, dressed stylishly, took part in sports, and drove her own car.

Cooperative Learning

Have students work in groups of four to develop slogans that women might have used when campaigning for the vote in the 1920's. Group members should first discuss the reasons women wanted the vote and the many changes that society had recently undergone. Students may wish to jot down ideas or take notes as they discuss these issues. Then group members should work together to devise three or four catchy slogans encouraging women's suffrage based on their earlier discussions. Recorders should write down the slogans and share them later with the class.

ANSWERS TO
Section Review 2

Define:
(a) name of Einstein's theory concerning space, time, energy, and matter (b) policy of avoiding political ties to other countries

(continued)

ANSWERS TO (continued)

Identify:

(a) German physicist who developed theory of relativity (b) Austrian physician who constructed theory about human mind (c) Czech writer who wrote eerie novels (d) Irish novelist who wrote *Ulysses* (e) writers and artists who tried to draw on the unconscious part of their minds (f) cultural movement of African American artists

Answer:

1. (a) passenger airlines, improved autos and trucks (b) Radio became widespread.

2. (a) Speed of light is constant, but space and time can change when measured in relation to an object moving at high speeds. (b) Matter can be changed into energy according to formula $E = mc^2$.

3. Although the emphasis on sex and the unconscious shocked some, the ideas were very influential.

4. Women won the right to vote and demanded wider career choices.

5. (a) Writers wrote of a world drained of hope and faith; artists tried to draw on the unconscious part of their minds. (b) jazz and movies

6. Though Americans refused to be politically tied to other countries, they still wanted to do business with them.

7. (a) People were willing to consider revolutionary ideas; women won greater rights; U.S. economy prospered. (b) Art expressed pessimism; U.S. turned to isolationism.

> What happens to a dream deferred?
> Does it dry up
> like a raisin in the sun?
>
> from "Harlem" by Langston Hughes

In his writings, Langston Hughes voiced both hope and despair for the future.

These lines come from poet T.S. Eliot's "The Waste Land" (1922). This long poem conjured up a picture of a world drained of hope and faith. The horror of World War I had made a deep impression on many artists and writers.

A Czech writer named Franz Kafka wrote eerie novels about people caught in threatening circumstances that they could neither understand nor escape. Kafka started writing before World War I, but much of his work was published after his death in 1922. It struck a chord among many readers in the uneasy postwar years.

Also in 1922, Irish-born novelist James Joyce caused a stir with *Ulysses*. This 1,500-page novel focused on a single day in the lives of three Dubliners. Joyce broke with normal sentence structure and vocabulary in an attempt to mirror the workings of the human mind.

One group of writers and artists was inspired directly by the ideas of Sigmund Freud. Calling themselves Surrealists, they tried to draw on the unconscious rather than the conscious part of their minds.

American cultural influences spread.

World War I showed that the United States was a world power both politically and economically. Soon it was clear that the United States had world influence culturally as well.

Perhaps the most distinctly American contribution to the 1920's was jazz. This music had

686

developed during the 1880's and 1890's in the southern United States, particularly among the African American musicians of New Orleans and Memphis. The development of the phonograph and radio helped bring jazz to other parts of the world. The lively, loose beat of jazz seemed to capture the new freedom of the age. Jazz swept the United States and Europe.

In New York, African American writers, artists, and composers were also achieving worldwide recognition. This cultural movement is known as the Harlem Renaissance. (Harlem was the major African American neighborhood of the city.) Among the best-known writers were poets Countee Cullen and Langston Hughes and novelist Claude McKay.

Another art form in which Americans took the lead was the motion picture. Movies began to draw large audiences before World War I (page 607). By the 1920's, the movies had become a major industry. Many countries around the world, from Cuba to Japan, produced movies. However, 90 percent of all films came from one place—the Los Angeles suburb of Hollywood.

Americans turned to isolationism.

Although proud of their country's achievements, many Americans were uncomfortable with their new position as world leaders. **Isolationism**—

Charlie Chaplin was a popular movie comedian.

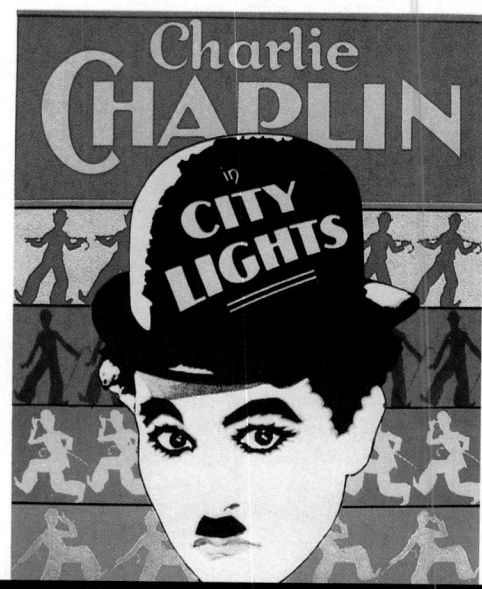

the idea that Americans should avoid political ties to other countries—won wide support. It was this feeling that led the United States to reject the Treaty of Versailles and remain outside the League of Nations.

Economically, however, the United States was not isolated at all. Under the Dawes Plan, loans from American banks helped Germany recover from the disastrous 1923 inflation. Other European countries had borrowed heavily from the United States during the war. In the 1920's, American businesses greatly expanded their overseas operations, especially in Latin America. The United States became a major trading partner for countries around the world. Foreign trade was closely tied to the nation's economy at home.

By 1929, the world economy was like a delicately balanced house of cards. The key card that held up all the rest was American economic prosperity. If something happened to the United States' economy, the whole card house might come tumbling down. In 1929, something did happen.

Section REVIEW 2

Define: (a) relativity, (b) isolationism
Identify: (a) Albert Einstein, (b) Sigmund Freud, (c) Franz Kafka, (d) James Joyce, (e) Surrealists, (f) Harlem Renaissance
Answer:
1. (a) What advances were made in transportation during the 1920's and the 1930's? (b) In communication?
2. (a) What generalization did Einstein set forth about light, space, and time? (b) About matter and energy?
3. Why were Freud's ideas revolutionary?
4. How did the changes of the postwar years affect women?
5. (a) What new trends appeared in art and literature during the 1920's? (b) Give examples of American contributions to world culture during this era.
6. How did the United States' return to political isolationism contradict its economic position?

Critical Thinking
7. (a) What features of life in the 1920's suggest a mood of optimism? (b) Of pessimism?

Wall Street's crash opened the Depression. 3

In 1929, a narrow street in New York City near the southern tip of Manhattan Island was the financial capital of the world. This was Wall Street. Coal merchants in Liverpool, factory owners in Berlin, wheat dealers in Winnipeg, and steel importers in Tokyo all paid close attention to events on Wall Street. Along its sidewalks were the offices of banks and investment companies that dominated the world economy.

The stock market fell in 1929.

The heart of Wall Street was an imposing gray building, the New York Stock Exchange. Here optimism about the United States' booming economy showed in soaring stock prices. Between January 1924 and September 1929, the *New York Times* average of stock prices rose from $110 to $455. Many people began to think stock prices would go up forever.

On Thursday, October 24, the New York Stock Exchange opened for what brokers hoped would be a profitable day of rising prices. Within an hour, their hopes were dashed. Everyone wanted to sell stocks, and no one wanted to buy them. Prices went down and down and down.

Overwhelmed by the record-breaking number of orders to sell, the stock ticker could not display the latest prices. By 1 P.M., the ticker had fallen 92 minutes behind transactions on the floor. Thus, frightened brokers could not get a true picture of what was happening. The wild shouting of the 1,000 brokers and their assistants became what one observer called a "weird roar." Great crowds gathered on the street outside the Stock Exchange. Rumors of business failures and attempted suicides swept through the crowd.

In the week following Black Thursday, as October 24 was soon called, stock prices continued to drop. Billions of dollars in paper wealth simply vanished.

At first, the crash appeared to have hurt only the million or so people who had gambled and lost on the stock market. The United States' vast industrial and agricultural resources were physically unhurt. There seemed to be no reason for

687

SECTION 3
Objectives and Teaching Strategies

OBJECTIVE 1. Identify weaknesses in the American economy that led to the Great Depression.

Teaching Strategy: *Analyzing a Quotation: Overproduction and Unemployment* (page 680d)

OBJECTIVE 2. Compare and contrast the responses of the American, British, and French governments to the Great Depression.

Teaching Strategy: *Skill Building: Comparing Responses to the Depression* (page 680d)

■ BACKGROUND

Stock prices were recorded on ticker tape, a paper ribbon on which a telegraphic ticker printed information. Brokerage firms generated miles of the tape each day.

SECTION 3
Resources

ASSESSMENT
■ Section Quiz 30.3

REINFORCEMENT
■ Independent Practice 30.3

ENRICHMENT
■ Voices from the Past 30.3

■ **DISCUSSION**

How do present-day pro-
duction and consumption
patterns compare to those
of the 1920's? Could we
have another Depression?
Students can find facts and
opinions about the econ-
omy in business
periodicals.

■ **BACKGROUND**

Shortly after the crash,
President Hoover pre-
dicted, "The crisis will be
over in 60 days." Mean-
while, newspapers and
magazines carried adver-
tisements optimistically declaring, "Wall Street may
sell stocks, but Main Street
is still buying goods." In
the immediate aftermath of
the crash, it was still possible to argue that America's
economy was fundamen-
tally sound. The crash appeared to be limited to the
million speculators who
had gambled on the stock
market. America's vast industrial and agricultural resources were physically
undamaged and still capa-
ble of enormous productivity. Looks, however, were
deceiving. The world economy was not fundamentally
sound.

prosperity to end. Yet, within a few months of
the crash, unemployment rates began to rise.
Meanwhile, industrial production, prices, and
wages declined. A long business slump, or
depression—the Great Depression—had begun.

The Great Depression touched every corner
of the American economy. By 1932, factory production had been cut in half. More than 86,000
businesses failed, and 9,000 banks closed. Around
9 million people lost their savings accounts. Unemployment soared from 3.2 percent in 1929 to
25 percent in 1933.

America—once the land of opportunity—now
had no help for its citizens. For millions of people,
the **standard of living,** or access to necessities
and comforts, drastically declined. One writer
recalled:

*The jobless were the most conspicuous fea-
ture of that dismal landscape. They clustered about poolrooms and taverns, sat in
the parks when the weather was fair, stood
in empty doorways to get out of the wind,
panhandled for nickels and dimes on the
streets, and sat for hours over a nickel cup
of coffee in dingy restaurants, staring out
the window.*

The world economy had weaknesses.

The Great Depression showed clearly that there
were serious economic weaknesses in the United
States and, indeed, throughout the world. Although the causes of the Great Depression are
complex, three weaknesses in the economy were
especially important.

Overproduction and underconsumption American industry became fabulously productive during
the 1920's. By 1929, American factories turned
out nearly half of the world's industrial goods.
Rising productivity led to enormous profits.

This new wealth, however, was not evenly
distributed. For example, the richest 5 percent
of the population earned 33 percent of all personal
income in 1929. Meanwhile, at the other end of
the scale, fully 60 percent of all American families
earned less than $2,000 a year. Thus, most families
were too poor to buy the goods being produced.

In short, there was both overproduction by
business and underconsumption by consumers.
As a result, store owners could not sell all the
goods they had on hand. They cut back their

orders from factories. Factories began to cut back
production and lay off workers. These actions
started a downward economic spiral. As more
workers lost their jobs, families bought even fewer
goods. In turn, factories made further cuts in
production and laid off more workers.

The plight of the farmer During the 1920's,
American farmers also became increasingly productive. Scientific farming methods and new farm
machinery dramatically increased the yield of
crops per acre. Farmers tried to maximize their
profits by raising just a few cash crops. Farming
became more and more like industry. Thus,
farmers became more dependent on the market
prices of wheat, corn, and pork.

At the same time, American farmers faced
new competition from abroad. For the first time,
countries such as Australia and Argentina were
exporting large amounts of grain. European farmers were increasing production too.

As a result, a worldwide surplus of agricultural
products drove prices and profits down. In 1930,
for example, the price of a bushel of wheat (in
terms of gold) fell to its lowest level in 400 years.

Unable to sell their crops at a profit, many
farmers could not pay off their loans. These bad
debts weakened banks and forced some to close.

Speculation in stocks The danger signs of
overproduction by factories and farms should have
warned people against speculating wildly in the
stock market. Yet no one heeded the warning.

The stock market crash dashed the hopes of
thousands of investors. Between September 1929
and July 1932, the *New York Times* industrial
average fell from $455 to an all-time low of $58.
Stockholders lost a staggering $74 billion.

The losses on Wall Street had both economic
and psychological consequences. Economically,
they swept away fortunes among the upper class.
Consumer spending dropped sharply. Psycholog-
ically, Americans' spirit of optimism was replaced
with a sense of doubt and fear.

The Depression spread worldwide.

When the American economy collapsed, the
shock waves were felt around the world. After
the stock market crash, worried American investors began to call back their loans abroad to cope
with the crisis at home. This withdrawal dealt
a hard blow to the economy of western Europe.

688

Smokeless Chimneys and—
ANXIOUS MOTHERS!

THE REMEDY

VOTE FOR THE **NATIONAL GOVERNMENT**

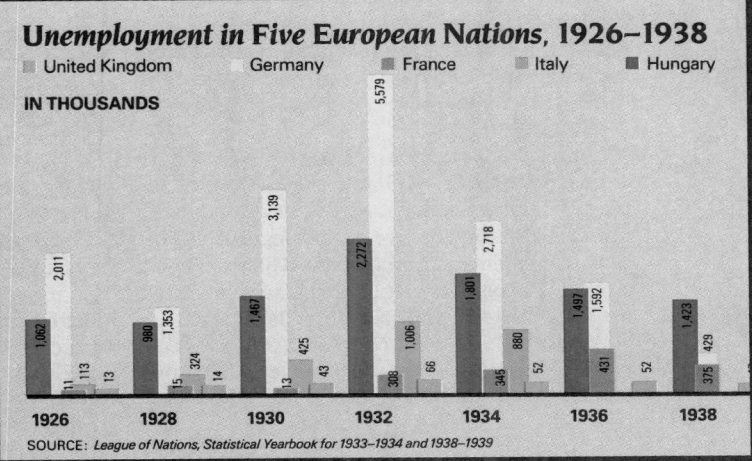

Unemployment in Five European Nations, 1926–1938

United Kingdom ▪ Germany ▪ France ▪ Italy ▪ Hungary

IN THOUSANDS

SOURCE: *League of Nations, Statistical Yearbook for 1933–1934 and 1938–1939*

Reading a graph Unemployment rose as economic activity declined during the Depression. In what year was unemployment highest in most countries? The poster shows the effects of unemployment.

Because of their war debts and dependence on American loans, Germany and Austria were particularly hard hit. A large Austrian bank, the Creditanstalt, failed, starting a financial panic in central Europe. As in the United States, this crisis began a downward spiral in the economy.

The effects of the Depression were felt throughout the world. Between 1929 and 1932, world manufacturing production fell by 38 percent. International trade dropped by an incredible 65 percent. Unemployment rates skyrocketed to record levels. In the United States, Great Britain, Germany, and Japan, more than 25 million angry, jobless people began to demand sweeping economic and political changes.

The Depression confronted democracies with a serious challenge to their economic and political systems. Each country tried to meet the crisis in its own way.

Roosevelt began the New Deal.

In the first presidential election after the Depression began, Americans elected Franklin Delano Roosevelt (1882–1945). At first glance, Roosevelt seemed an unlikely leader for such a grave crisis. Yet he proved to be a dynamic and effective president.

Born into a wealthy New York family, Roosevelt had held several positions in state and national government. In 1920, he ran unsuccessfully for vice president. Suddenly, in 1921, he was stricken with polio and paralyzed. After months of effort, he regained the use of his hands and arms. Next he struggled to walk. Eventually, wearing braces, he was able to take a few steps. Then he resumed his political career. In 1928, he was elected governor of New York.

Roosevelt's confident manner appealed to millions of Americans who felt bewildered and betrayed by the Depression. "If you have spent two years in bed trying to wiggle your big toe," he said, "everything else seems easy."

As president, Roosevelt immediately began a program of relief, recovery, and reform that he called the New Deal. Large public works projects helped to provide jobs for the unemployed. New government agencies gave financial help to businesses and farms. The Social Security Act of 1935 provided insurance for the elderly and the disabled. For the first time, the United States government spent large amounts of public money on welfare and relief programs.

Roosevelt and his advisers believed firmly in the capitalist **free-enterprise** system, based on a market economy. However, they also believed that government spending would create jobs and start an economic recovery. They were willing to spend more money than the government raised through taxes, creating a national debt.

689

ANSWER TO

Reading a Graph

Unemployment was highest in most countries in 1932.

Cooperative Learning

Tell students that to combat the Depression, Roosevelt's administration created a number of agencies intended to increase the number of jobs or regulate business. Most of these agencies were referred to by their initials. Divide the class into groups of six students. Each group member should choose one of the following agencies to research: CCC, PWA, WPA, TVA, AAA, NRA. Students should determine the name of the agency, its function, and how long it existed. Have students present their findings to other group members. Then have group members discuss the overall effect of the various agencies in helping end the Depression in the United States.

ANSWERS TO

Section Review 3

Define:
(a) long business slump
(b) access to necessities and comforts (c) capitalist economic system

(continued)

ANSWERS TO (continued)

Identify:
(a) financial center located in New York (b) financial slump of the 1930's (c) United States president who began New Deal (d) Roosevelt's program of relief, recovery, and reform (e) all-party coalition cabinet in Britain (f) coalition of moderates, Socialists, and Communists in French government

Answer:
1. (a) Everyone wanted to sell stocks and stock prices plummeted; rumors of business failures and suicides were widespread.
(b) Unemployment rates rose; industrial production, prices, and wages fell.

2. overproduction and underconsumption, bad farm debts, stock speculation

3. Supply raced ahead of demand; owners cut orders from factories; factories cut production.

4. American investors began calling back their loans; trade dropped; unemployment soared.

5. (a) large public works projects to provide jobs; new government agencies to give aid to businesses and farms; insurance for the elderly and the disabled
(b) The new Securities and Exchange Commission regulated stock market transactions; the federal government insured bank deposits.

6. (a) passed high protective tariffs, increased taxes, regulated currency, lowered interest rates (b) elected Popular Front coalition, passed reforms

7. wanted to show there would be changes, suggest that all would be new

The New Deal strategists also addressed some economic problems of the Depression. A new Securities Exchange Commission regulated the stock market. The banking system was reorganized, and the federal government insured bank deposits up to $5,000.

Roosevelt's policies were widely popular. He won reelection in 1936 and 1940. (He was the only American president to be elected to a third term.) Yet recovery from the Depression was slow. Unemployment in the late 1930's remained around 14 percent. National income, while on the rise, was still well below its 1929 level.

While the New Deal reformed America's economic system, Roosevelt's strong leadership preserved the country's faith in its democratic political system. Taking office at a time of grave national crisis, Roosevelt made a special point of explaining his policies to the American people. He became the first president to make frequent use of the radio, broadcasting informal speeches known as "fireside chats." His compassionate style, democratic values, and reform programs established Roosevelt as a leader of democracy in a world threatened by ruthless dictators.

Britain and France struggled to rebuild.

Coming less than a dozen years after World War I, the Depression struck hard at Europe. Despite hardship, however, Britain and France preserved democratic government.

"Muddling through" in Britain Because the British economy depended on foreign trade, the Depression hit Britain with great force. To meet the emergency, British voters in 1931 overwhelmingly elected an all-party coalition cabinet known as the National Government.

The National Government passed high protective tariffs, increased taxes, regulated the currency, and lowered interest rates to encourage industrial growth. These measures brought about a slow but steady recovery of the economy. By 1937, the unemployment rate had been cut in half, and production had risen above 1929 levels.

These gains, however, failed to lift Britain's mood of discouragement in the 1930's. Although its leaders lacked Roosevelt's dynamic style, the British government avoided political extremes and "muddled through" the Depression.

690

Weakness in France Unlike Britain, France in 1930 was still a heavily agricultural country. It was less dependent on foreign trade than was Britain. Thus, France was somewhat cushioned against the Depression. Nevertheless, by 1935, 1 million French people were out of work.

As we will see in the next section, the Depression brought anti-democratic groups to power in some European countries. In France too there were groups that wanted to end democracy and set up a dictatorship. This movement frightened both moderates and radicals. Therefore, moderates, Socialists, and Communists united to form a coalition. Known as the Popular Front, the coalition won power in the 1936 elections.

The Popular Front passed a series of reforms to help the workers. These reforms included pay increases, holidays with pay, and a 40-hour work week. Unfortunately, price increases quickly offset wage gains, and unemployment remained high.

Programs established by the National Government helped to improve Britain's economy.

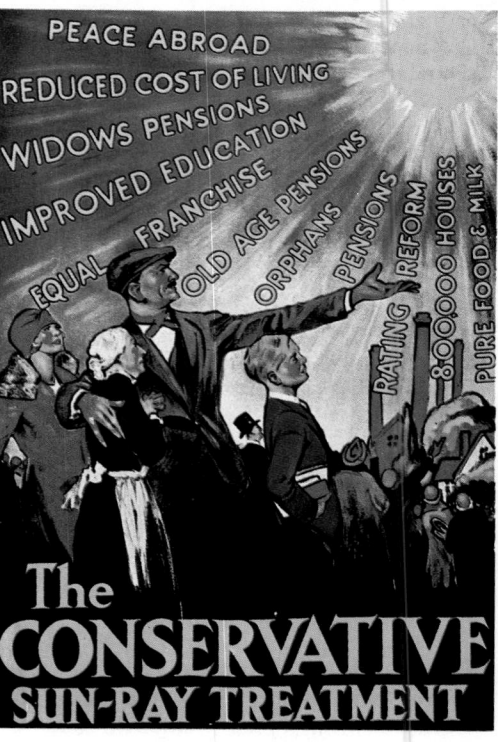

Define: (a) depression, (b) standard of living, (c) free-enterprise

Identify: (a) Wall Street, (b) Great Depression, (c) Franklin D. Roosevelt, (d) New Deal, (e) National Government, (f) Popular Front

Answer:

1. (a) Describe Black Thursday. (b) What other changes in the American economy showed that a major economic slump had begun?
2. What were the three major weaknesses in the economy that led to the Depression?
3. How did overproduction and underconsumption begin a downward economic spiral?
4. How did the crisis in the United States' economy lead to problems in other countries?
5. (a) What policies did Roosevelt begin to help the victims of the Depression? (b) To prevent similar crises in banking and stocks from occurring again?
6. (a) How did Britain respond to the Depression? (b) How did France?

Critical Thinking

7. Why do you think Roosevelt used the term *New Deal* for his policies?

Fascist leaders became dictators. 4

As the Depression spread across Europe, it created misery and suffering. Many families endured freezing winters for lack of money to heat their homes. Others lost their homes. Thousands of homeless people lived in shantytowns such as the Village of Misery outside Vienna, Austria.

The Depression dealt a particularly cruel blow to the youth. Teachers reported that many children could not go to school because they had no shoes. Teenagers frequently could not find jobs, while college graduates had to compete for low-paying work.

Parents were powerless to help their children. With nowhere to go and little to do, countless unemployed workers passed long hours standing on street corners. Their loss of self-respect created frustration and deep anger at society.

As a result of these conditions, millions of people lost faith in democratic government. In many countries, frightened and desperate people turned to extremist political groups. Some supported communism, hoping for a workers' revolution that would begin a new era. Still others turned to **fascism,** a new political movement that emphasized autocratic and nationalist policies. As you will see, fascist leaders in Italy, Germany, and Japan promised to revive economic growth, punish those responsible for hard times, and restore national pride.

Fascism glorified the state.

Unlike communism, fascism had no clearly defined theory or program. Fascists acted first and devised theories later. According to Benito Mussolini, the first of Europe's fascist dictators, "Fascism was not the nursling of a doctrine worked out beforehand with detailed elaboration: it was born of the need for action."

Nevertheless, most Fascists shared several ideas. They believed in an extreme form of nationalism. Unlike more peaceful nationalists, however, fascists were not content to serve their own nation and let others do the same. Fascists believed that nations must struggle. Peaceful states, they said, were doomed to be conquered.

Fascists looked to an authoritarian leader to guide the state and rally the people. Loyalty to the leader was part of loyalty to the state.

The trappings of fascism were also similar from country to country. Fascists wore uniforms or shirts of a certain color, used special salutes and war cries, and held mass rallies.

In some surprising ways, fascism was similar to its archenemy, communism. Both systems advocated dictatorial one-party rule. Both denied individual rights and insisted on the supremacy of the state. Both scorned democracy.

However, there were also differences between fascism and communism. Fascists, unlike communists, did not seek a classless society. Rather, they believed that each class had its distinct place and function. Communism claimed to be a dictatorship of the workers. Fascist parties allied themselves, in most cases, with aristocrats and industrialists. Many communists were internationalists, hoping to unite workers of all countries. Fascism was openly nationalistic.

691

SECTION 4
Objectives and Teaching Strategies

OBJECTIVE 1. Compare and contrast the careers of Mussolini and Hitler.

Teaching Strategy: *Skill Building: Comparing Mussolini and Hitler* (page 680d)

OBJECTIVE 2. Identify *Kristallnacht* and trace its causes and consequences.

Teaching Strategy: *Discussing History: The* **Kristallnacht** (page 680e)

SECTION 4
Resources

ASSESSMENT
- Section Quiz 30.4

REINFORCEMENT
- Independent Practice 30.4

ENRICHMENT
- Voices from the Past 30.4

■ BACKGROUND

Mussolini was an opportunist who changed his views with the times. For example, prior to World War I, he was a leading socialist editor who advocated international revolution, loathed militarism, opposed nationalism, and even referred to the Italian flag as ''a rag to be planted on a dunghill.'' However, when he saw that it was in his interest to do so, Mussolini repudiated those positions and advocated both nationalism and militarism.

Mussolini loved to display his skill in riding, fencing, and boxing. He grandly linked himself to the ''king of beasts'' by having his picture taken with lion cubs.

Mussolini launched a Fascist state.

Fascism began in Italy during the early 1920's. Italy had entered World War I in hopes of winning Austrian territory in the Alps and along the Adriatic Sea. The Treaty of Versailles, however, did not give Italy as much land as it had wanted. Angry veterans believed that Italy's sacrifice of 650,000 dead and 1 million wounded had been in vain. Millions of Italians felt betrayed.

Italy also faced a severe economic crisis. As the war drove up prices, the cost of living shot up 500 percent between 1914 and 1919. To make matters worse, unemployment was rising. As a result, there was widespread social unrest.

Italy's upper and middle classes feared that this unrest might lead to a communist revolution, as had just happened in Russia. To many Italians, their democratic government seemed helpless to deal with the country's problems. Growing numbers of people demanded action and waited impatiently for a strong leader.

The rise of Mussolini A newspaper editor named Benito Mussolini (1883–1944) boldly promised to rescue Italy. Unemployed veterans listened enthusiastically to Mussolini's speeches pledging to revive Italy's economy and rebuild its armed forces. Within a short time, Mussolini

Mussolini (left) and Hitler (center) lead a parade accompanied by some of their top military men.

692

and his followers organized the Fascist party. The term *fascism* was designed to recall memories of ancient Rome. In Latin, fasces meant a bundle of wooden rods tied around an ax handle. Roman officials carried such bundles as symbols of authority.

At first, the Fascists failed to win widespread support. As economic conditions worsened, however, Mussolini's popularity rapidly increased. While Mussolini publicly criticized Italy's government, groups of Fascists known as Blackshirts roamed the streets, beating up Communists and Socialists. As many as 3,000 people were killed between 1920 and 1922. This campaign of terror weakened Mussolini's opponents and won him support from the middle classes, the aristocracy, and industrial leaders.

By 1922, the Fascists were ready to take over Italy's government. On October 24, 1922, Mussolini told a cheering crowd of supporters, "Either they will give us the government or we shall take it by descending on Rome." Within 4 days, some 30,000 Fascists surrounded Rome. Although the government could have stopped Mussolini with a show of force, King Victor Emmanuel III gave in and named Mussolini prime minister. Mussolini soon gained emergency powers to restore order and make new laws.

Fascist policies The Fascist type of government proved to be **authoritarian,** requiring absolute loyalty and obedience to the state. The state's interest was more important than the individual's rights. Mussolini quickly abolished democracy and outlawed all political parties except the Fascists. The secret police filled Italy's jails with Mussolini's opponents. Government officials strictly **censored** all radio stations and publications, forcing them to accept the Fascist ideology.

Mussolini believed that capitalists and workers must be forced to cooperate for the good of the state. He therefore set up 22 state corporations to run all parts of Italy's economy. These corporations dealt with wages, prices, and working conditions. Strikes were against the law.

Il Duce Mussolini was now Il Duce (DOO-cheh), the leader of Italy. Il Duce was a dazzling orator. Although of modest height, he towered above the crowds as he addressed them from the balcony of his office in Rome. His black eyes ablaze, Mussolini would stand with his massive jaw thrust forward and his hands on his hips. His emotional delivery enthralled the crowd as he promised a great future for Italy.

Government propaganda encouraged Italians to accept Mussolini's leadership without question. Teachers were ordered to stress Mussolini's achievements by comparing him to Aristotle, Michelangelo, and Napoleon. Slogans such as "Mussolini Is Always Right" covered billboards across the country.

Under Mussolini's leadership, Italy became the model for the rise of fascism in other countries. Later fascist leaders, including Adolf Hitler in Germany and Francisco Franco in Spain, adopted Mussolini's methods. Many fascist governments came to power in eastern Europe in the late 1920's and early 1930's. All borrowed ideas and institutions from Italy.

Hitler led the Nazis.

Sometime in the late 1920's, the Italian embassy in Berlin received a letter from Adolf Hitler, asking for an autographed picture of Mussolini. The embassy sent the request to Rome. Il Duce's office thanked Hitler for his letter but refused to send him an autographed photo.

Like most other people at that time, Mussolini refused to take Hitler seriously. In the late 1920's, Hitler was still a little-known political leader whose life had been marked by failure.

Early life Hitler was born in a small town in Austria in 1889. As a young boy, he showed little ambition. After dropping out of high school, he moved to Vienna to study art or architecture.

At that time, Vienna was still the capital of the vast, multiethnic Austrian empire. Many Jews were among the city's intellectual and financial leaders. Hitler later claimed that his hatred of Jews and Slavs began there.

Hitler's dream of becoming a great artist was shattered when the Vienna Academy of Fine Arts rejected his application. During the next few years, Hitler lived in hostels, ate in charity kitchens, and made few friends. He disliked regular work. Much of the money he did earn came from painting postcards of views in Vienna.

When World War I broke out, Hitler suddenly found meaning for his life. He would fight to defend Germany and crush its opponents. Hitler volunteered for the German army and fought well enough to be awarded the Iron Cross twice.

This Nazi party rally, held in Nuremberg in 1935, used mass rituals to stir popular support.

The rise of the Nazis At the end of the war, Hitler settled in Munich. There he soon found a new cause. Hitler passionately believed that Germany had to overturn the Treaty of Versailles and combat communism. In early 1920, he joined a tiny right-wing political group that shared these views. The group later named itself the National Socialist German Workers' Party, called Nazi for short. Their policies, supported by people in the upper and middle classes, formed the German brand of fascism known as **nazism.** The party adopted the swastika, or bent cross, as its symbol. The Nazis also set up a private army called the Storm Troopers, or Brownshirts.

Within a short time, Hitler's success as an organizer and speaker helped to gain for him the title of *Führer,* or leader of the Nazi party. Although he was undistinguished in appearance, Hitler was a spellbinding speaker who could whip an audience into a frenzy. He typically began a speech in a normal voice. Suddenly, he would speak louder and louder as his anger at Germany's enemies swelled up. Finally he would seem to have lost all self-control. His face would puff

693

■ DISCUSSION

Begin your introduction to the rise of Hitler by reading aloud the following passage by the historian Quincy Howe: "This alleged war hero had never risen above the rank of lance corporal . . . This would-be leader of the blond, Protestant, beer-drinking, meat-eating, prolific Germans was a dark-haired, renegade Roman Catholic; a teetotaling, unmarried vegetarian of Austrian origin. As Hitler himself repeatedly emphasized, he counted on emotion to triumph over reason and on evil to overcome good."

After reading the passage, ask students to list reasons why many Germans underestimated Hitler. Then ask students to name the forces Hitler hoped to exploit. Explain that the Great Depression created economic conditions that enabled Hitler to appeal to people's fears and emotions.

Kurt Ludecke was a Nazi who befriended many prominent German leaders. In the following passage, he provides an eyewitness description of the climax of one of Hitler's campaign rallies. "Here in this vast stadium, so carefully and with such theatrical genius arranged for the occasion, the intensity of the long election campaign was compacted and brought into focus . . . Suddenly a wave surged over the crowd, it leaned forward; a word was tossed from man to man: 'Hitler is coming! Hitler is here!' A blare of trumpets rent the air and a hundred thousand people leaped to their feet in tense expectancy. All eyes were turned toward the stand, awaiting the approach of the Führer. There was a low rumble of excitement and then, releasing its pentup emotion, the crowd burst into a tremendous ovation, the 'Heils' swelling until they were like the roar of a mighty cataract . . ."

with fury, his voice rise to a screech, and his hands flail the air. Then he would suddenly stop, smooth his hair, and look quite calm again.

Mein Kampf Hitler's fiery oratory helped to build the Nazis into a growing political force. Inspired by Mussolini's successful march on Rome, Hitler plotted to seize power in Munich. In 1923, he led the Nazis in an attempted coup in Munich. The local authorities succeeded in putting down the coup and capturing Hitler.

Although his coup had failed, Hitler succeeded in using his trial to gain widespread attention. Sympathetic judges sentenced him to a five-year prison term of which he served only nine months. While in jail, Hitler spent most of his time writing *Mein Kampf* (My Struggle), a work that set forth his ideas and goals. He began by asserting that the Germans were a master race and that other "races"—such as Jews, Slavs, and gypsies—were inferior and should be destroyed.

Hitler went on to claim that, since the Germans were a master race, the Treaty of Versailles (page 635) was an intolerable outrage against Germany. He vowed to regain the lands taken from Germany after World War I. Hitler also declared that Germany was overcrowded and needed more Lebensraum, or living space. He promised to obtain new space by conquering eastern Europe and Russia.

Hitler became dictator.

After leaving prison in 1924, Hitler worked to rebuild the Nazi party. Nonetheless Nazi strength declined as Germany's economy began to recover from the war. Most Germans now chose to ignore Hitler and his message of hate. In 1928, membership in the Nazi party stood at 108,000 in a country of almost 60 million people.

The Great Depression ended the brief recovery. When American loans stopped, the German economy collapsed. Factories ground to a halt and banks closed. By 1932, nearly 40 percent of Germany's work force was unemployed. People roamed the streets shouting, "Give us bread."

Frightened and confused, Germans now listened intently to Hitler's angry speeches and simple solutions. By 1932, the Nazis became the country's largest political party. On January 30, 1933, Germany's president named Hitler the nation's new chancellor. That evening, thousands of Nazi supporters marched through Berlin.

Many people predicted that Hitler would become a responsible leader. Conservative leaders inside Germany believed that they could control Hitler and use him for their purposes. Time proved them wrong. While his opponents were divided and confused about their programs, Hitler knew exactly what he wanted—absolute power. Hitler's minister of propaganda, Joseph Goebbels, later wrote that the democratic authorities "could have suppressed us. This would not have been so difficult. But it was not done . . . we were allowed to cross the danger zone."

Shortly after becoming chancellor, Hitler called for new parliamentary elections. The Nazis hoped that the election would give them a parliamentary majority. Six days before the election, a spectacular fire destroyed the Reichstag, the German parliament building. The Nazis promptly blamed the Communists, although strong evidence suggested that the Nazis had set the fire themselves. By stirring fear of the Communists, the Nazis and their allies won a slim majority of seats in the election.

Now that he controlled a majority of the Reichstag, Hitler demanded passage of an enabling act that would give him absolute power for four years. In order to pass the act, the Nazis expelled the Communist deputies from the Reichstag. With the Communists gone, the Nazis easily won the two thirds vote needed to pass the Enabling Act. Only one deputy had the courage to speak out against the bill.

Germany became a totalitarian state.

Hitler used his absolute power ruthlessly to turn Germany into a totalitarian state. A series of laws banned all political parties except the Nazis. A special secret police called the Gestapo used sweeping powers to arrest anyone who opposed Nazi rule. Meanwhile, an elite black-coated unit known as the SS, or protection squad, became a security force loyal only to Hitler.

In 1934, Hitler ordered the SS to destroy his few remaining enemies. On June 30, 1934, the SS arrested and then murdered several hundred of Hitler's opponents. Known as the night of the long knives, this violent action shocked the German people into total obedience.

Economic control Like the Fascists in Italy, the Nazis quickly gained control over the economy.

694

CHARACTERISTICS OF TOTALITARIANISM

Dictatorship
One-party rule
Primacy of state over individual
Control by state of most aspects of life

	FASCISM/NAZISM	COMMUNISM
Basic Principles	Authoritarian; action-oriented; leader identified with state	Leninism, Marxism; dictatorship of proletariat
Political	Nationalist, militarist; racist (nazism)	Nationalist, internationalist
Social	Supported by industrialists and military	Supported by workers (USSR) and peasants (China)
Economic	Private property; control by state corporations or state	Collective ownership; centralized state planning
Cultural	Censorship, indoctrination, secret police	Censorship, indoctrination, secret police
Examples	Fascism in Italy and Spain; nazism in Germany	Communism in USSR and in China

The government supervised both labor and business. New laws banned strikes and dissolved independent labor unions. Workers had to join a National Labor Front, which included employers.

As you have seen, high rates of unemployment were a major factor in Hitler's rise to power. The Führer ended unemployment by putting millions of people to work constructing factories, building strategic highways, and manufacturing weapons. As a result, unemployment dropped from 6 million in 1932 to 1.5 million in 1936.

Cultural control Hitler wanted more than just political and economic control. He also wanted to mold German society in accordance with Nazi ideology. In order to achieve this goal, Hitler created a ministry of culture to supervise the press, broadcasting, literature, drama, music, painting, and film.

The Nazis skillfully used their control over the news to shape public opinion. Government-appointed radio wardens reported anyone failing to listen to Hitler's speeches and other important announcements. Special films such as *Triumph of the Will* glorified Hitler's leadership. Books that did not conform to Nazi ideology were destroyed in huge bonfires.

The art and music of Nazi Germany reflected Hitler's tastes. The Führer condemned almost all modern art, favoring classical and romantic styles. In music, Hitler had a passion for the operas of Richard Wagner, which were based on German myths.

German mythology found great favor among Nazis. Some Nazi leaders wanted to close Christian churches and return to the worship of the old Germanic gods. Hitler believed that persecuting Christians would only strengthen them. He simply forbade Christian clergy to criticize the Nazi party or the government. Parents were discouraged from sending their children to religious schools. The Nazis used the public schools to spread their own ideas. School children were required to join Hitler's youth movement. Boys learned to be ready to fight and die for the Führer. Girls prepared for motherhood so that Germany would have plenty of young soldiers.

The Nazis began to persecute Jews.

Hitler cleverly realized that people would believe a big lie if it was repeated often enough. Nazi propaganda loudly proclaimed that Germans were a superior race destined to rule the world.

695

Even when Hitler became Chancellor, his opponents continued to believe that they could control him. For example, Vice-Chancellor Papen told a friend, "In two months we shall put Hitler into such a tight spot that he will squeak." But, like others before him, Papen badly underestimated Hitler.

Historians focus upon three factors that enabled Hitler to seize absolute power so quickly. First, Hitler's opponents were divided and confused about their goals, while Hitler had the advantage of knowing exactly what he wanted. Second, Hitler ruthlessly used fear, force, and hatred to achieve his goals. And finally, as noted by Alan Bullock, "Hitler never abandoned the cloak of legality; instead he turned the law inside out and made illegality legal."

■ DISCUSSION

Why were the Germans under Hitler so intent on persecuting Jews, who made up such a small percent of the population? Were Germans afraid? Did they need a scapegoat? Can there be a rational explanation for prejudice?

■ BACKGROUND

Following World War I, Japan's democratic government was based upon a prosperous but fragile economic base. Just as today, Japan depended upon its export trade to pay for raw materials needed by its growing industries. For example, Japan imported 85 percent of its iron and steel, 79 percent of its oil, 74 percent of its tin and all of its rubber.

The global depression had a particularly devastating impact on Japan. In just one year, Japan's exports fell by almost one-third, while industrial unemployment rose by 25 percent.

At the same time, they preached that Jews, Poles, Americans, and other groups were inferior races.

Jews comprised less than 1 percent of Germany's total population. They included many distinguished people who had contributed to Germany's international renown. Among them were such leading scientists as Albert Einstein (page 684). Yet Hitler and the Nazis blamed the Jews for most of Germany's problems since World War I. Like the Roman leaders who blamed Christians for their problems, Hitler used the Jews as convenient scapegoats for Germany's troubles.

Nuremberg laws The result was that an ugly wave of **anti-Semitism,** or hostility toward Jews, soon swept across Germany. In 1933, the Nazis passed laws forbidding Jews to hold public office. Two years later, similar legislation—the Nuremberg laws—deprived Jews of German citizenship. Jews were not allowed to fly the German flag, to write or publish, to act on stage or in films, to teach, to work in hospitals or in banks, or to sell books. All Jews were required to wear a yellow Star of David as identification.

The Kristallnacht Nazi violence against Jews steadily mounted. On November 7, 1938, a seventeen-year-old Jewish youth tried to avenge the suffering of his family by assassinating a member of the German embassy in Paris. Nazi leaders used this tragedy as an excuse to launch a violent attack on the Jewish community.

On November 9 and 10, 1938, Nazi mobs carried out a "spontaneous" demonstration of anger against Jews. In 15 terrifying hours, the Nazis

Decisions in History

The 1936 Summer Olympic Games were scheduled to be held in Berlin. Many Americans, however, objected to the Nazis' racial policies directed against Jews, Slavs, Africans, and others. The passage of the Nuremberg Laws in September 1935 underscored the seriousness of Hitler's intentions. Three months later the American Athletic Union met to consider a resolution opposing United States participation in the Berlin Olympics. Supporters of the resolution argued that the United States had a moral duty to oppose Hitler's racial policies. Opponents argued that the AAU had no right because of a moral judgment against Germany to keep American athletes from taking part. Would you have voted for the resolution or against it? Why?

696

destroyed 7,500 Jewish-owned shops and businesses, burned 275 synagogues, and beat Jews on the streets and in their homes. The smashing of storefronts left streets littered with broken glass. As a result, the Nazis called their rampage the Kristallnacht, the crystal night.

The Kristallnacht represented more than broken windows and shattered glass. It signaled a significant escalation in the Nazi search for a final solution to the Jewish question. While the rest of the world ignored this catastrophe, thousands of Jews and other "inferior races" were sent to huge prisons called **concentration camps.**

Militarists ruled Japan.

As fascism spread in Europe, one of Asia's leading nations moved toward a similar system. Following a period of reform and progress in the 1920's, Japan fell under military rule.

During the 1920's, liberals were a majority in Japan's parliament. In 1922, Japan signed an international treaty agreeing to respect the **territorial integrity,** or territorial domains, of China. The Japanese also signed the Kellogg-Briand Pact renouncing war.

Japan's parliamentary government had several weaknesses, however. The constitution put strict limits on the powers of the prime minister and the cabinet. Most importantly, civilian leaders had little control over the armed forces. Army leaders were responsible only to the emperor.

As long as Japan remained prosperous, the civilian government kept power. However, when the Depression struck, military leaders soon won control of the country. Their plan for solving Japan's economic problems was to build a Pacific empire. Such an empire, they said, would give Japan raw materials, win markets for Japan's goods, and find space for its growing population.

Japanese businesses had already invested heavily in China's northeast province, Manchuria. Manchuria was rich in natural resources such as iron and coal. In 1931, the Japanese army seized Manchuria, despite objections from the parliamentary government. Japanese technicians and capital poured in to build mines and factories. Japan's new empire had begun.

The growing power of the military also had a great impact within Japan. Instead of a forceful leader like Mussolini or Hitler, the militarists

Voice from the Past | *Kristallnacht*

Kristallnacht—with its attacks against Jews throughout Germany—revealed to the world a totalitarian government in action. Fifty years after Kristallnacht, Francis H. Schott, the son of a doctor, remembered the events of that night in 1938 when his family was one of the many assaulted by Nazi mobs.

It is November 9, 1938, in Solingen, Germany . . . A jarring sound jolts us awake in the middle of the night. Glass and wood of the apartment door shatter. My little sister and I sit up in our beds, uncomprehending. The noise gets louder yet . . . My mother slips in from the adjacent bedroom and stations herself inside our closed door . . . The sound of destruction heightens as china and crystal are thrown into the corridor.

Suddenly I know. The Nazis have come to get us. They are smashing our things. My mother is trying to protect us . . . Then they are gone . . . No one is hurt, but the psychic shock is staggering . . .

Worse is to come, much worse. But on Kristallnacht, a twelve-year-old boy has absorbed a lesson. The orderly world . . . is gone. By fanning prejudice into hate, a Government can turn a populace into assault troops. Painful as it is, we must remember.

1. What was the young child's greatest fear?
2. What lesson did Francis Schott draw from the attack on his family?
3. What kind of future might German Jews have expected after Kristallnacht?
4. In what ways did Kristallnacht represent the actions of a totalitarian state?

encouraged the cult of the emperor. The Japanese considered their emperor divine. This cult helped to win popular support for the army leaders who ruled in the emperor's name.

Dictators promised easy answers.

By the mid-1930's, it was clear to everyone that Woodrow Wilson's dream of a world "made safe for democracy" had turned into a nightmare. In country after country across Europe, democracy had been destroyed. Only in those places with solid democratic traditions—Britain, France, and the Scandinavian countries—did democracy remain strong. Where such traditions were lacking, elections and political parties quickly gave way to dictators and secret police. By 1935, for example, only one democracy, Czechoslovakia, remained in eastern Europe.

Remarkably, most of these new dictators, including Hitler, were actually voted into power. People were willing to sacrifice their freedom

partly out of economic distress. During the Depression, many people lost faith in democratic government. The loss of freedom seemed a small price to pay for putting food on the table.

Hitler, Mussolini, and other dictators offered simple answers to complicated questions: Trust the leader. Think only of the glory of the nation. Believe in the superiority of one's own race above all others. The dictators appealed to the crudest of human emotions, hatred and fear.

In Italy, Germany, and Japan, the new dictators did solve some of their countries' economic problems. There was a catch, however. They boosted the economy with huge increases in military spending. In Germany, for example, the military budget grew from $8 million in 1933 to $135 million in 1939. The dictators were not spending these vast sums simply to provide jobs. Hitler and Mussolini intended to use their new might for **armed aggression,** or wars of conquest. "A minute on the battlefield," asserted Mussolini, "is worth a lifetime of peace."

697

ANSWERS TO

Voice from the Past

1. that the Nazis would take him and his family away
2. that he could not count on a safe and orderly world
3. at least, threats and intimidation, at worst, an unknown and possibly terrible fate
4. use of intimidation, lack of accountability on part of government; use of propaganda and prejudice against one group to strengthen the state's power

ANSWERS TO

Section Review 4

Define:
(a) form of government based on extreme nationalism and totalitarian dictatorship (b) holding all power (c) edit materials of objectionable matter (d) German fascism (e) hostility toward Jews (f) prisons for political prisoners (g) territorial domains (h) wars of conquest

Identify:
(a) Fascist dictator of Italy (b) German Fascist party (c) Nazi leader (d) guidebook of Nazism (e) living space (f) gave Hitler absolute power for four years (g) elite Nazi unit (h) laws that deprived Jews of German citizenship (i) crystal night

Answer:
1. (a) extreme nationalism; idea that peaceful states were doomed to be conquered by more warlike

(continued)

ANSWERS TO (continued)

(b) Both advocated dictatorial one-party rule, denied individual rights, insisted on the supremacy of the state. (c) Communists sought a classless society, but Fascists believed each class had its function. Communists claimed to be a dictatorship of workers, but Fascist parties allied with aristocrats and industrialists. Communists were internationalists; Fascists, nationalists.

2. (a) Italians felt betrayed by Versailles settlement, faced economic crisis and social unrest. (b) gathered veterans to combat communism; marched on Rome, took over the government

3. Germans were a master race; Versailles Treaty must be done away with; Germany needed living space

4. Many unemployed Germans began to support Hitler, leading to his appointment to office.

5. (a) deprived Jews of German citizenship, rights (b) escalation of Nazi persecution of Jews

6. Japan came under military rule.

7. (a) Economic problems led Germans and Italians to look toward strong leaders. (b) Hitler: blamed Treaty of Versailles for Germany's troubles, believed in military conquest; Mussolini: favored nationalism, militarism (c) Both were spellbinding speakers. (d) Both had troopers to eliminate opposition.

8. (a) trust the leader, think only of the glory of the nation, believe in the superiority of one's own race (b) seem to promise quick solutions to big problems (c) Students might suggest not believing in easy answers.

Section REVIEW 4

Define: (a) fascism, (b) authoritarian, (c) censor, (d) nazism, (e) anti-Semitism, (f) concentration camp, (g) territorial integrity, (h) armed aggression

Identify: (a) Benito Mussolini, (b) Nazi party, (c) Adolf Hitler, (d) *Mein Kampf*, (e) Lebensraum, (f) Enabling Act, (g) SS, (h) Nuremberg laws, (i) Kristallnacht

Answer:

1. (a) What ideas did fascists share? (b) How were fascism and communism alike? (c) How did they differ?
2. (a) What factors led to the rise of fascism in Italy? (b) How did Mussolini take control of the government?
3. What were the key ideas and goals that Hitler presented in *Mein Kampf*?
4. What impact did the Great Depression have on Hitler's rise to power?
5. (a) What were the Nuremberg laws? (b) What was the long-term importance of the Kristallnacht?
6. What change in political power occurred in Japan during the Depression?

Critical Thinking

7. Compare the rise of Hitler with that of Mussolini in terms of (a) economic conditions (b) political ideas (c) personal styles (d) private armies
8. (a) What "easy answers" did Hitler and Mussolini offer? (b) Why are such answers appealing in a time of crisis? (c) How can voters avoid being misled by such tactics?

The world drifted toward war. 5

By the mid-1930's, it was quite clear that the powerful countries of the world had split into two camps. On one side were dictatorships such as Germany and Italy whose leaders were bent on military conquest. On the other side were democracies such as Britain, France, and the United States whose leaders longed to keep peace.

One powerful nation—the Soviet Union—fit in neither category. During the 1930's, the Soviet Union took little part in world affairs while Stalin brutally forced the country through major economic changes (page 654). Nonetheless, the Soviet Union with its Communist government loomed large in the plans and fears of other countries.

The fear of a Communist revolution helped both Hitler and Mussolini in their rise to power. The Western democracies also deeply feared the Soviet Union. Indeed, many political leaders in Britain and the United States considered the Communist Soviet Union a greater threat than Nazi Germany. As the 1930's passed, however, it became obvious that fascism was a far more immediate danger. The democracies and the Soviet dictatorship temporarily set aside their differences to meet the fascist threat.

The League of Nations was weak.

Many people pinned their hopes for world peace on the League of Nations. The League enjoyed high prestige in the 1920's. France and Germany signed the Locarno pact (page 682) in 1925. In 1926, Germany joined the League. For a brief period, it seemed that the League was indeed helping to create a more peaceful world. Unfortunately, these hopes collapsed as dictatorships encouraged militarism in the 1930's.

Ironically, the three countries that posed the greatest threats to peace—Germany, Japan, and Italy—were all members of the League of Nations in 1933. At the same time, the two countries that were strong enough to stand up to the dictators—the United States and the Soviet Union—were not members. (The Soviet Union joined in 1934.) Thus, the burden of supporting the League fell mainly on Great Britain and France.

Britain and France had been the two leading world powers of the 1800's. However, World War I had weakened them both severely. The French were still determined to uphold the terms of the Versailles treaty, but France was not strong enough to stand up to Germany alone. Many British people, on the other hand, believed that the Versailles treaty had been unfair and that Germany was entitled to some geographic and military expansion. Above all, Britain's leaders wanted to avoid a war that would further weaken their economy.

During the 1930's, therefore, Britain and France did not take a firm stand against Fascist aggression. Instead, they followed a policy of **appeasement.** That is, they made concessions to the Fascists in hopes of keeping peace.

Japan invaded China.

The first direct challenge to the League of Nations came in 1931 when the Japanese army invaded the Chinese province of Manchuria (page 696). The Japanese set up a **puppet government**—that is, a government controlled by an outside power—in Manchuria.

Japan's attack on Manchuria clearly violated the Kellogg-Briand peace pact, which Japan had signed. Other members of the League protested vigorously, as did the United States. However, the League had no armed forces of its own. Thus, it could do little. Japan ignored the protests and withdrew from the League in March 1933.

In 1937, a border incident touched off a full-scale war between Japan and China. On July 7, the Japanese and the Chinese exchanged shots at a railroad bridge 20 miles from Peking. One Japanese soldier was found dead near the bridge. Given this excuse, Japanese forces swept into northern China. These events marked the beginning of World War II in Asia.

China's leader, Chiang Kai-shek, had an army of more than a million soldiers, but it was no match for the superior equipment and training of the Japanese. Peking and other northern cities fell to the Japanese in less than a week. The capital, Nanking, fell by the end of 1937. Between 100,000 and 200,000 people in Nanking were executed within 6 weeks.

Yet the Chinese did not surrender. Forced to retreat westward, Chiang Kai-shek set up a new capital at Szechwan (sech-wahn). At the same time, Chinese guerrillas continued to fight within the area conquered by the Japanese. Many of the guerrilla fighters were organized by China's Communist leader, Mao Tse-tung (page 675).

Mussolini attacked Ethiopia.

The League's failure to stop the Japanese encouraged Mussolini to plan aggressive actions of his own. Ever since coming to power in 1922, Mussolini had dreamed of building an Italian colonial empire in Africa. However, most of Africa had long since been carved into British and French territories. Mussolini bitterly complained that Britain and France had left Italy with "a collection of deserts" to choose from.

Mussolini's imperial ambitions required a victim. At that time, Ethiopia was Africa's only remaining independent nation. Since the Ethiopians had successfully resisted an earlier Italian attempt at conquest during the 1890's, Mussolini vowed that the time had come to avenge that defeat. In October 1935, Il Duce ordered a massive invasion of Ethiopia.

This time the Ethiopians were no match for the better-equipped Italians. Mussolini used airplanes, tanks, guns, and poison gas against the Ethiopian army, many of whose soldiers still fought with spears and swords. The Ethiopians fought courageously, but their situation was hopeless. In May 1936, Mussolini triumphantly told a cheering crowd that "Italy has at last her empire . . . a Fascist empire."

Like Chiang Kai-shek, the Ethiopian leader Haile Selassie urgently appealed to the League for help. The League was founded on the belief that peace could be maintained if the nations of the world acted together to stop aggression. Mussolini's invasion of Ethiopia represented a crucial test of this system of **collective security.**

At first, the League responded by overwhelmingly branding Italy an aggressor. Although the League condemned the attack, its members did nothing. The British government, for example, spoke out strongly against Italy's actions. Yet Britain continued to let Italian troops and supplies pass through the British-controlled Suez Canal on their way to Ethiopia.

The British and French hoped that appeasing Mussolini would help keep peace in Europe. But Haile Selassie knew better. When he spoke at a League of Nations meeting in Switzerland, he said, "It is us today. It will be you tomorrow."

Hitler defied the Versailles Treaty.

Selassie's warning proved to be all too accurate. In *Mein Kampf*, Hitler had written, "The whole of nature is a continuous struggle between strength and weakness, an eternal victory of the strong over the weak . . ." Hitler was determined that Germany be counted among the strong.

699

SECTION 5
Objectives and Teaching Strategies

OBJECTIVE 1. Locate the Axis powers on a map and identify the nations they invaded.

Teaching Strategy: *Geography in History: Invasions of the Axis Powers* (page 680e)

OBJECTIVE 2. Evaluate the Munich agreement.

Teaching Strategy: *Writing about History: The Munich Agreement* (page 680e)

■ BACKGROUND

On the road to Peking, the invaders forced the surrender of 20 truckloads of Chinese soldiers, then mowed down their defenseless prisoners with machine gun fire.

The Ethiopians had successfully resisted an earlier Italian attempt at conquest during the 1890's. It was partly to avenge that defeat that Mussolini chose them as his victims now.

SECTION 5
Resources

ASSESSMENT
■ Section Quiz 30.5

REINFORCEMENT
■ Independent Practice 30.5

ENRICHMENT
■ Voices from the Past 30.5

■ BACKGROUND

Hitler had long pledged to abrogate the Versailles treaty. In *Mein Kampf*, he wrote, "What a use could be made of the Treaty of Versailles! . . . How each one of the points of that treaty could be branded in the minds and hearts of the German people until sixty million men and women find their souls aflame with a feeling of rage and shame; and a torrent of fire bursts forth as from a furnace, and a will of steel is forged from it, with the common cry; 'Wir wollen wieder waffen! — We will have arms again!'"

■ DISCUSSION

Many historians believe that the British and French missed their best opportunity to stop Hitler when they failed to force him to withdraw from the Rhineland in 1936. Ask students to speculate on what would have happened if the French and British had enforced the Treaty of Versailles.

Hitler had long pledged to undo the Treaty of Versailles. As you have seen (page 636), this treaty severely limited the size of Germany's army. In March 1935, the Führer announced that Germany would no longer obey these restrictions. Led by Britain and France, the League issued a mild condemnation. Banners throughout Germany defiantly announced, "Today Germany! Tomorrow the World!"

Germany reoccupied the Rhineland.

The League's failure to enforce the Treaty of Versailles convinced Hitler that he could take even greater risks. The Treaty of Versailles had forbidden Germany's placing troops in a 30-mile-wide zone on either side of the Rhine River. Known as the Rhineland, this territory formed a strategic buffer between Germany and France.

On March 7, 1936, Hitler boldly ordered 35,000 German troops to march into the Rhineland and **occupy,** or control, it. Huge crowds of cheering citizens lined the roads to greet them. Meanwhile, Hitler and his generals nervously waited for the British and French to react.

Hitler's unexpected action stunned the British and French. Despite having the largest army in the world, the French were unwilling to risk a new war. The British urged appeasement.

Hitler later admitted that he would have been forced to back down if the French and British had challenged the reoccupation. "The forty-eight hours after the march into the Rhineland were the most nerve-wracking in my life," he confessed. "If the French had then marched into the Rhineland, we would have had to withdraw.

The German reoccupation of the Rhineland marked an important turning point for three reasons. First, Hitler's daring action strengthened his power and prestige within Germany. Cautious generals who had previously urged restraint now agreed to follow their Führer's leadership without question. Second, the reoccupation of the Rhineland changed the balance of power in Germany's favor. Both France and Belgium were now open to a surprise attack from German troops along their borders. Finally, the weak response by France and Britain encouraged Hitler to begin a program of military and territorial expansion.

The Rome-Berlin Axis Hitler's growing strength convinced Mussolini that he should seek an alliance with Germany. In October 1936, Italy and Germany reached an agreement that became known as the Rome-Berlin Axis. An axis is a

Map Study
What were Hitler's first and last gains before World War II?

Adolf Hitler

Pablo Picasso's Guernica *expressed his anguish at the wanton bombing of that village. The artist ordered that the painting should not go to Spain until democracy was restored there, as it was in the 1970's.*

straight line around which an object rotates. Hitler and Mussolini expected their alliance to become the axis around which Europe would rotate. A month later Germany also made an agreement with Japan. Thus Germany, Italy, and Japan were called the Axis Powers.

The democracies failed to act.

The growing power of the dictatorships in Germany, Italy, and Japan raised a number of troubling questions. Why did the nations of the world allow Japan and Italy to violate the Kellogg-Briand Pact (page 682)? Why did Britain and France allow Hitler to undermine the Treaty of Versailles? Finally why didn't the United States play a more important role in these events?

As world powers, both Britain and France could have been expected to take an active stand against aggression. The Depression, however, forced both nations to deal with serious economic problems at home. Helping unemployed workers in London and Paris find jobs seemed more important than aiding Ethiopia or China. In addition, the horrible suffering caused by World War I had created a deep desire for peace. Allowing Hitler to reoccupy the Rhineland seemed a small price to pay to avoid war.

As tensions in Europe and Asia increased, many Americans believed that the United States should avoid becoming involved in other nations' affairs.

These isolationists argued that America's entry into World War I had been a costly mistake. For example, a Congressional committee charged that American companies had secretly supported entering the war so that they could make enormous profits by selling military equipment.

The isolationists were determined to prevent a repeat of these mistakes. Beginning in 1935, Congress passed the first of three Neutrality Acts. These laws banned loans and the sale of arms to nations at war. They also warned Americans not to sail on ships of countries at war. The isolationists were convinced that these laws would keep the United States out of a new foreign war. As you will see in the next chapter, this belief proved to be tragically wrong.

Civil war broke out in Spain.

Hitler and Mussolini soon found another chance to test their strength against the democracies of Europe. In July 1936, civil war had broken out in Spain. The Fascist powers decided to support the Spanish general Francisco Franco.

Spain had been a monarchy until 1931. Between 1931 and 1936, a democratic government held office amid a series of crises. Many army leaders, however, favored a Fascist-style government. In July 1936, General Francisco Franco led a revolt against the elected government. Thus began a civil war that dragged on for three bloody years.

701

■ **DISCUSSION**

Explain that the small Spanish town of Guernica had little or no strategic value. The painting expresses Picasso's outrage and anguish over the senseless slaughter of innocent people. Point out that Picasso deliberately used only shades of black, gray, and white to highlight the agonized figures shown under a stark electric light. Since the painting was in New York City when World War II began, Picasso suggested that it remain in the United States until "the reestablishment of public liberties" in Spain. Following the restoration of democratic government, "Guernica" was returned to Spain in 1981. It can now be seen in the Prado museum in Madrid.

■ **BACKGROUND**

A Gallup Poll taken in September 1937 revealed that 73 percent of those surveyed believed that in order to declare war, Congress should first be required to obtain the approval of the people by means of a national vote. This idea was particularly popular among women, 79 percent of whom supported it.

Cooperative Learning

Divide the class into groups of five students. Each group member should choose one of the five chapter sections and write a short summary covering all major points. Then have students orally present their summaries, in order of sections, to the other group members. The other members should take notes so that they will eventually have a summary for the entire chapter. Students should ask questions if a group member's summary is unclear. In turn, each group member should quiz the others to ensure that they understand the material.

ANSWERS TO

Section Review 5

Define:
(a) policy of making concessions in hopes of keeping peace (b) government controlled by an outside power (c) belief that nations could stop aggression together (d) control (e) trade-offs

Identify:
(a) international organization that could not maintain a peaceful world (b) region along German-French border (c) British prime minister who advocated appeasement (d) Germany, Italy, Japan (e) Spain's Fascist dictator (f) western area of Czechoslovakia settled by Germans (g) conference at which Brit-

(continued)

Hitler and Mussolini sent tanks, cannons, and airplanes to Franco's forces, called the Nationalists. German and Italian troops even fought alongside Nationalist troops.

The Republican army, as supporters of Spain's elected government were called, received little help from abroad. The Soviet Union sent some aid. The Western democracies remained neutral. An International Brigade of volunteers fought with gallantry on the Republican side, but it could do little against a professional army.

Early in 1939, the Republicans collapsed. Franco became Spain's Fascist dictator and remained in power for more than 30 years.

In many ways, the Spanish civil war was a precursor of World War II. It showed what kind of war was soon to burst upon the world. In April 1937, a squadron of German planes appeared above the small village of Guernica (ger-NEE-kuh) in northern Spain. The planes dropped their load of bombs, killing hundreds of villagers, most of them women and children. There was no military reason for this attack. Several German pilots who took part later admitted that the bombing had been conducted as a "test." One of Franco's officers said of Guernica, "We bombed it, and bombed it, and bombed it, and *bueno*, why not?" Countless more bombs and immeasurably more agony lay in store for Europe and the world.

Germany took over Austria.

On November 5, 1937, Hitler held a secret meeting with his foreign minister and top military commanders. The Führer declared that Germany needed more living space in order to grow and prosper. He argued that Germany could obtain this space by absorbing Austria and Czechoslovakia into a Greater Germany. The Germans would then expand further by pushing eastward into Poland and Russia.

Hitler's first target was his native Austria. The Treaty of Versailles prohibited an Anschluss, (AHN-shloos), or union between Austria and Germany. However, the overwhelming majority of Austria's six million people strongly supported unity with Germany. In March 1938, Hitler ordered his army to restore order in Austria. When France and Britain ignored their pledge to protect Austrian independence, Hitler easily annexed it into Germany.

702

◢ Turning Points in History

The Munich Conference Hitler's campaign for German expansion focused next on Czechoslovakia. As you have seen (page 637), Czechoslovakia was carved out of the Austro-Hungarian empire at the end of World War I. During the postwar period, Czechoslovakia developed into a prosperous democracy. The nation had a strong army and a treaty of defense with France. In addition, the Soviet Union pledged to help defend Czechoslovakia if France acted first.

Although it had impressive strengths, Czechoslovakia also had a serious weakness. About three million German-speaking people lived in a mountainous region of western Czechoslovakia called the Sudetenland. This heavily fortified strategic region formed the Czechs' main defense against German attack.

The Anschluss stimulated pro-German sentiment in the Sudetenland. Hitler skillfully encouraged the Sudeten Germans to demand special political privileges. The Führer also ordered the leader of the Sudeten German party to stir up trouble. "We must always demand so much that we can never be satisfied," Hitler advised.

In September 1938, Hitler suddenly demanded that Czechoslovakia give up the Sudetenland. The Czechs indignantly refused and called upon France for help. Hitler threatened to invade the Sudetenland by October 1.

Hitler's threat pushed the world to the brink of war. As the October deadline approached, workmen feverishly dug air raid shelters in London. Thousands of panic-stricken people evacuated Paris, hoping to escape German bombers. Meanwhile, concerned families in the United States huddled around radios listening to the latest news from Europe.

News broadcasts announced that war seemed imminent. In a radio speech to the British people on September 27, Prime Minister Neville Chamberlain sadly confessed his despair: "How horrible, fantastic, incredible it is that we should be digging trenches . . . here because of a quarrel in a faraway country between people of whom we know nothing."

The next day Chamberlain addressed a packed session of Parliament. As the world nervously waited for him to declare war on Germany,

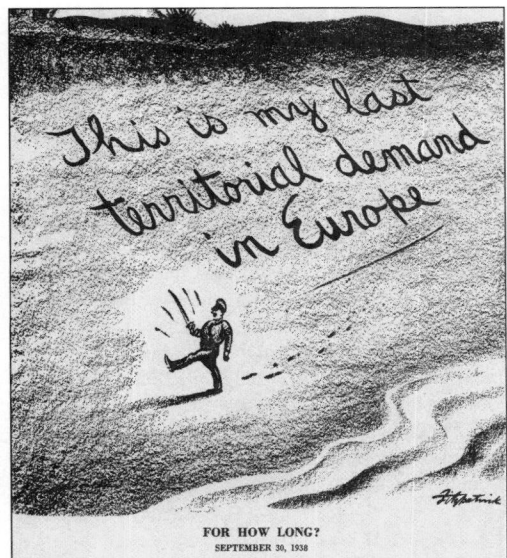

This is my last territorial demand in Europe

FOR HOW LONG?
SEPTEMBER 30, 1938

What was Hitler's next territorial demand?

Chamberlain unexpectedly received an urgent message from Hitler. A visibly relieved Chamberlain dramatically announced that Hitler had invited him, Mussolini, and the French premier to an emergency conference in Munich, Germany. The entire Parliament erupted with applause.

The meeting in Munich The Munich Conference began on September 29, 1938. Although most conferences involve **negotiation,** or trade-offs, this meeting dealt solely with the issue of Hitler's demand. Hitler solemnly promised that the Sudetenland was his last territorial claim. "I got the impression," Chamberlain later recalled, "that here was a man who could be relied on when he had given his word."

Chamberlain believed that he could preserve the peace by giving in to Hitler's demand. Early the next morning a tense world learned that the crisis was over. Britain and France agreed that Hitler could take the Sudetenland. In exchange, Hitler pledged to respect Czechoslovakia's new borders. He also signed a short declaration promising that Britain and Germany would "never go to war with one another again."

Chamberlain's policy of appeasement, or making concessions, seemed to be a success. When he returned to London, Chamberlain told cheering crowds, "I believe it is peace for our time." His prediction proved to be tragically wrong. Less than six months later Hitler's troops marched into Czechoslovakia. The Nazi dictator triumphantly announced, "Czechoslovakia has ceased to exist."

Importance of Munich The Munich Conference marked a turning point in world history. Chamberlain's failure to stand up to Hitler helped to make World War II inevitable. Filled with confidence, Hitler now made plans to attack Poland.

The Munich Conference also had important long-term psychological consequences. In the years following World War II, the Munich Conference became a symbol for surrender. Democratic leaders vowed that they would never again appease a ruthless dictator.

Section REVIEW 5

Define: (a) appeasement, (b) puppet government, (c) collective security, (d) occupy, (e) negotiation
Identify: (a) League of Nations, (b) Rhineland, (c) Neville Chamberlain, (d) Axis Powers, (e) Francisco Franco, (f) Sudetenland, (g) Munich Conference
Answer:
1. How did the attitude of the democracies toward the Soviet Union change during the 1930's?
2. What factors weakened the League of Nations?
3. Why did France and Britain fail to take a strong stand against Hitler time after time?
4. How did World War II begin in Asia?
5. How did Mussolini try to create an Italian colonial empire?
6. Give three reasons why the German reoccupation of the Rhineland marked a significant turning point.
7. (a) Why was the Spanish Civil War a test of strength between the Fascist powers and the democracies? (b) What was the outcome?
8. (a) What were the short-term outcomes of the Munich Conference? (b) The long-term psychological consequences?

Critical Thinking
9. (a) What is the difference between appeasement and compromise? (b) What were the results of appeasement in Asia, Africa, and Europe? (c) Do you think a peaceful compromise was possible? Explain your answer.

703

ANSWERS TO (continued)
ain and France allowed Germany to take Sudetenland
Answer:
1. At first, the democracies feared the Soviet Union. Later, democracies set aside differences with USSR to fight fascism.
2. United States and Soviet Union were not members; League had no army to enforce position.
3. Neither was strong enough to stand up against Hitler alone; British did not want to further weaken their economy.
4. Japanese forces invaded northern China in 1937.
5. He attacked independent Ethiopia.
6. Hitler's power was strengthened in Germany; balance of power changed in Germany's favor; weak response by France and Britain encouraged Hitler to further aggression
7. (a) Franco and the Nationalists were supported by Italians and Germans. The Western democracies remained neutral. **(b)** Franco became Fascist dictator of Spain.
8. (a) made Hitler confident, accelerated his plans for attack **(b)** became a symbol for surrender, later leaders vowed never to appease an aggressor again
9. (a) Appeasement—one gives in to another in order to keep peace; compromise—two agree on mutually beneficial terms **(b)** Ethiopia, Austria, Czechoslovakia, and part of China were lost to aggressors. **(c)** Possible answer: Hitler's master plan included conquering other nations, and he would not have agreed to a compromise.

Concluding the Chapter

1. **Chapter Closer**
   Ask students to explain why 1923 in Germany was called the Year of Hunger, and how the people responded to the events of that year.

2. **Reteaching Activities**
   a. Making a Time Line
   Ask students to prepare a time line covering the period from 1919 to 1938.

   b. Comparing and Contrasting Have students compare and contrast the ways in which the democracies and the dictatorships responded to the Depression.

   c. Identifying Main Ideas
   Ask students to identify and explain four events that helped bring Europe to the brink of war.

Answers to Chapter Review appear on pages 680e–680f.

Summary

1. Europe recovered from World War I. World War I brought an end to European dominance and saw the rise of new democracies. One of these, the Weimar Republic in Germany, faced severe economic problems as a result of the war. These problems were resolved in part by loans offered by the Dawes Plan of 1924. As prosperity returned, Germany improved its relations with France.

2. Society faced rapid change. During the 1920's, automobiles, commercial air travel, and radios widened social contacts. Albert Einstein's theory of relativity caused a revolution in scientific thought, while Sigmund Freud provided insights into the workings of the human mind. A growing spirit of independence was reflected in the women's movement. American jazz and movies spread American culture, although politically the United States turned to isolationism.

3. Wall Street's crash opened the Depression. Stock prices in the United States soared in the 1920's, until a crash on Wall Street brought on the Great Depression. The effects of the Depression spread worldwide. In the United States, President Franklin Roosevelt introduced the New Deal. In Britain, the government raised tariffs and lowered interest rates. France passed temporary reforms to help workers.

4. Fascist leaders formed dictatorships. The crisis of the Depression brought on political upheavals in many countries. In Italy, Mussolini established a Fascist government in 1922. In Germany, Hitler came to power in 1933 and instituted a Nazi revolution. Japanese military leaders began empire building.

5. The world drifted toward war. During the 1930's, a weak League of Nations and Anglo-French appeasement opened the way for Fascist aggression. Japan invaded Manchuria in 1931 and China in 1937. Italy invaded Ethiopia in 1935. In 1936, Hitler moved into the Rhineland and made a formal alliance with Italy. Their combined forces helped Franco form a Fascist dictatorship in Spain. In 1938, Hitler claimed Austria and the Sudetenland.

Reviewing the Facts

1. Define the following terms:
   a. isolationism   c. appeasement
   b. fascism   d. negotiation
2. Explain the importance of each of the following names, places, or terms:
   a. inflation   e. Einstein
   b. Weimar Republic   f. Surrealists
   c. Dawes Plan   g. Harlem
   d. Kellogg-Briand Pact   Renaissance

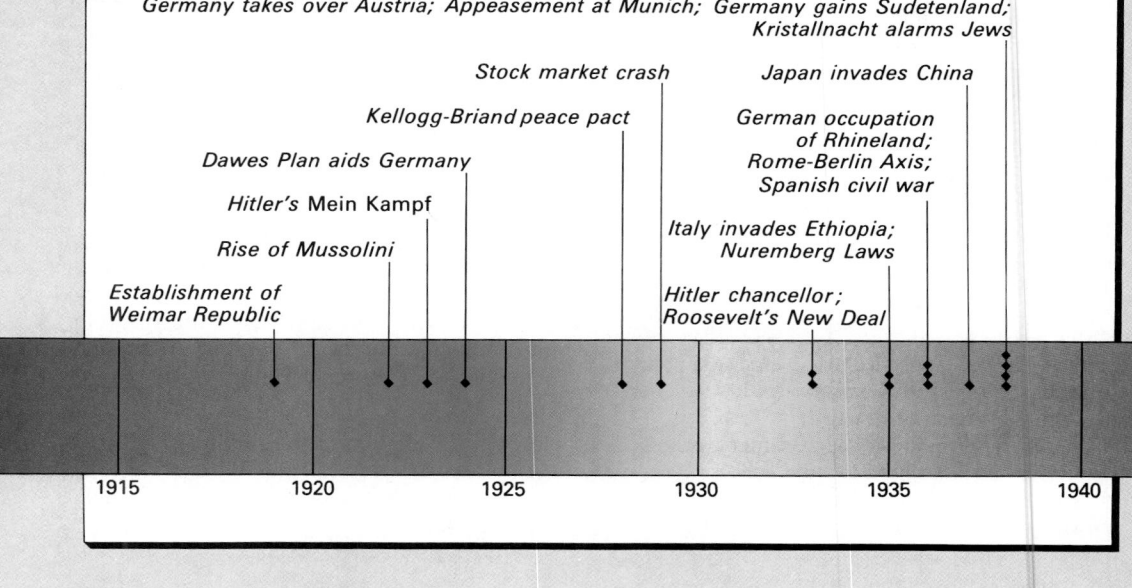

Germany takes over Austria; Appeasement at Munich; Germany gains Sudetenland; Kristallnacht alarms Jews

Stock market crash

Kellogg-Briand peace pact

Japan invades China

Dawes Plan aids Germany

German occupation of Rhineland; Rome-Berlin Axis; Spanish civil war

Hitler's Mein Kampf

Italy invades Ethiopia; Nuremberg Laws

Rise of Mussolini

Establishment of Weimar Republic

Hitler chancellor; Roosevelt's New Deal

1915   1920   1925   1930   1935   1940

704

h. Wall Street
i. Great Depression
j. New Deal
k. Mussolini
l. Nazi party
m. Hitler
n. *Mein Kampf*

o. Gestapo
p. Third Reich
q. Chamberlain
r. Rome-Berlin Axis
s. Franco
t. Munich conference

3. What steps were taken during the 1920's to assure future peace?
4. What changes occurred in the status of women in the postwar years?
5. Why did the economic crisis in the United States have a worldwide impact?
6. (a) What political changes did Mussolini institute? (b) What economic changes?
7. Describe the aggressions taken by each of the following countries between 1931 and 1938. (a) Italy (b) Japan (c) Germany
8. (a) How did Franco come to power in Spain? (b) In what way was the Spanish civil war a precursor of World War II?

Basic Skills

1. **Reading and interpreting a graph** (a) According to the graph on page 689, in what years was unemployment in Germany higher than in Britain? (b) How does the pattern of unemployment in Germany differ from that of Britain between 1936 and 1939?
2. **Sequencing** List the following events in the order in which they happened: Enabling Act, burning of the Reichstag, German troops in the Rhineland, Kristallnacht, the Munich Conference, Germany taking over Czechoslovakia, Germany taking over Austria, the establishment of the Weimar Republic.

Researching and Reporting Skills

1. **Interviewing** Find someone in your community who lived during the Depression. Make a list of questions you might ask about that person's experience. Tape or transcribe what is told you to share with the class.
2. **Using art and pictures** Divide your class into three groups to research (a) painting, (b) music, and (c) fashions and life-styles of the 1920's. Have each group make a presentation to the class using audio tapes and pictures.

Critical Thinking

1. **Analyzing inconsistencies** In the 1920's, American cultural influences and economic interests in Europe were growing. Why might political isolationism develop at the same time?
2. **Applying concepts** According to your text, overproduction and underconsumption were weaknesses in the economy. (a) Explain what is meant by *overproduction* and *underconsumption*. (b) What direct effects did these have on the economy? (c) What indirect effects?
3. **Analyzing** (a) Review and list the terms of the Treaty of Versailles (pages 635–637) that affected Germany. (b) For each item, describe its effect on conditions in Germany during the 1920's. (c) What were the social, economic, and political consequences of these effects?
4. **Evaluating** The steps taken by Hitler in his rise to power were all within the law. At what points and by what democratic process could Hitler have been stopped?
5. **Interpreting** (a) What actions did the Nazis take against Jews in Germany? (b) What was the effect upon Jews as individuals and as a group?
6. **Forming a hypothesis** (a) Identify the reasons for the rise of fascism in the early 1930's. (b) From this list, develop a hypothesis about the rise of fascism, with major facts to support it.

Perspectives on Past and Present

The League of Nations failed to act when China invaded Manchuria, Italy invaded Ethiopia, and German troops moved into the Rhineland. To what extent has that situation changed under United Nations leadership?

Investigating History

1. William Shirer, a United States reporter in Nazi Germany, wrote two books about the Nazi era. Read a chapter from either *Berlin Diary* or *The Rise and Fall of the Third Reich*. What impressions does the chapter give of that time?
2. As a class or group project, draw up a list of movie titles from the 1930's—such as Chaplin's *Modern Times* and Welles's *Citizen Kane*—that are available as either films or videos. View one or two of the titles in class, evaluating it on style, quality, and historical significance.

705

CHAPTER
Evaluation

Chapter Test 30, Alternate Chapter Test 30, and Computer Test Bank Chapter 30 Test can be used to evaluate your students' understanding of this chapter.

705

World War II

Chapter Overview

From 1939 to 1941, a string of German victories led to Axis domination of Europe. When Hitler invaded Poland, France and Britain declared war on Germany. Japanese aggression in the Pacific led to the development of an Asian empire that threatened American interests. On December 7, 1941, Japan attacked Pearl Harbor, and the United States entered the war on the side of the Allies. Important victories at Midway in the Pacific, Stalingrad in the Soviet Union, and El Alamein in North Africa turned the tide of the war. On June 6, 1944, Allied forces landed on the beaches of Normandy and began a march to Berlin. Facing British and American forces on the west, and the Soviet army on the east, the German Reich collapsed, and Germany surrendered. War in Asia ended with the dropping of atom bombs on Hiroshima and Nagasaki. The atom bomb, the Holocaust, and the massive loss of civilian life and property made World War II a war unlike any the world had ever experienced.

Chapter Focus

Have students read the chapter introduction on pages 706–707. Explain that Martin Gray witnessed the German attack on Warsaw. Ask, "What were Gray's most vivid memories of this attack?" List students' responses on the board. Between 1939 and 1945, people across Europe and Asia experienced the horrors of World War II. This chapter describes the Axis nations' attempt to conquer the world and their defeat by the Allies.

Germany overran much of Europe. 1

Setting the Stage

Begin by showing Map Transparency 88, *Axis Powers in Europe, 1939*. Identify the Axis powers and review the steps by which Hitler and Mussolini expanded their power. Then locate the Polish Corridor. Explain that the Treaty of Versailles created this strip of land to give Poland access to the Baltic Sea. Ask why Hitler would have opposed this arrangement. Point out that the Polish Corridor divided Germany and stripped it of the important seaport of Danzig. Then direct students' attention to the cartoon on page 709. According to the cartoonist, what did Hitler want? What impact would that have on Poland? Should Britain and France have offered to protect Poland?

Hitler's new demands convinced Britain and France to reevaluate their policies of appeasement. Meanwhile, Hitler secretly prepared for war.

Teaching Strategies

Discussing History: The *Blitzkrieg* (Objective 1) Military lessons can be learned from each war. Ask what lessons could be drawn from events on the Western Front. Explain that French generals concluded that their country could best be protected by strong defensive formations. They therefore constructed an elaborate set of fortifications known as the

Chapter 31 World War II 1939–1945
      FOCUS Martin Gray's account of the German attack on Warsaw

★ **Advanced**
● **Basic**

	SECTION 1	SECTION 2	SECTION 3	SECTION 4
Objectives	1. Define *blitzkrieg* and explain how Hitler used this new style of attack to defeat Poland, Norway, Belgium, and France. 2. Identify Dunkirk and explain how the British rescued the trapped Allied army. 3. Identify Winston Churchill and explain how he rallied his people to prepare for the Battle of Britain.	1. Evaluate Japan's decision to attack Pearl Harbor. 2. Explain the consequences of the Japanese attack on Pearl Harbor. 3. Identify the Battle of Midway and explain its significance.	1. Identify the Battle of Stalingrad and explain its importance. 2. Explain the importance of the D-Day invasion. 3. **Evaluate Truman's decision to use the atom bomb against Japan.**	1. Identify the Holocaust and explain how its victims are memorialized. 2. Explain and evaluate the reasons behind the internment of Japanese Americans during the war.
Setting the Stage	Hitler's goals Transparency 88	The threat of Japanese aggression in Asia Transparency 89	The significance of the United States' entry into the war	The concept of "total war"
Teaching Strategies	Discussing History: The *Blitzkrieg* Teaching with Pictures: The "Miracle of Dunkirk" Discussing History: "Their Finest Hour" Check for Understanding	Discussing History: Japan's Decision to Attack Pearl Harbor Discussing History: Was Pearl Harbor a Japanese Victory? Writing about History: The Battle of Midway Check for Understanding	Discussing History: The Battle of Stalingrad Transparency 90 Discussing History: The Importance of D-Day Writing about History: How to Defeat Japan Check for Understanding	Relating Past to Present: The Holocaust Discussing History: The Internment of Japanese Americans Check for Understanding
Guided Practice	Transparency 88 Q&A Section Review 1	Transparency 89 Q&A Section Review 2	Transparency 90 Q&A Section Review 3	Section Review 4
Independent Practice Worksheets	Independent Practice 31.1 Vocabulary 31	Independent Practice 31.2 Critical Thinking 31	Independent Practice 31.3 Geography Skills 31	Independent Practice 31.4 Basic Skills 31
Enrichment	1. Primary Source: Voices 31.1 2. Preparing a Report 3. Researching for Points	1. Primary Source: Voices 31.2 2. Creative Writing 3. Researching for Points	1. Primary Source: Voices 31.3 2. ★Preparing a Report: A Second Front 3. Researching for Points	1. Primary Source: Voices 31.4 2. Preparing a Report 3. Researching for Points

Chapter Closer	●**Reteaching Activities**	Making a Time Line, Analyzing
	Chapter Review	Summary, Reviewing the Facts, Basic Skills, Researching and Reporting Skills, Critical Thinking, Perspectives on Past and Present, Investigating History
	Chapter Evaluation	Chapter Test 31, Alternate Chapter Test 31, Computer Test Bank Chapter 31 Test
Unit VIII Review	**Geographic Theme**	Location: How did Soviet territory expand in the course of World War II?
	Historical Themes	Impact of Ideas, Economics and History, Cooperation and Conflict, Individuals and History
	Unit Evaluation	Unit VIII Test, Alternate Unit VIII Test

Maginot Line. In contrast, German generals concluded that tanks and airplanes gave new advantages to the offensive. Fast-moving tank formations could burst through weak spots or gaps in an enemy line. Meanwhile, fighter bombers and dive bombers could fly over fixed defenses to attack vital command posts and industrial centers. The leaderless enemy forces would then panic and ultimately would be forced to surrender. This highly mobile type of German warfare was called *blitzkrieg* or "lightning war." Have students read pages 708–711 and describe how Hitler used the blitzkrieg to defeat Poland, Norway, Belgium, and France.

Teaching with Pictures: The "Miracle of Dunkirk" (Objective 2) Refer students to the map on page 708. Note that the port of Dunkirk is located just south of the French-Belgian border. The German blitz krieg left about 400,000 British, French, and Belgian troops surrounded at Dunkirk. Then direct students' attention to the picture on page 710. The British organized a rescue fleet of more than 850 vessels that included Royal Navy destroyers, Channel ferries, fire-boats, whaleboats, fishing boats, and even private yachts. The fleet sailed through three narrow passageways that had been cleared of mines while German dive bombers attacked repeatedly. Point out the great columns of smoke in the background, which provided a protective camouflage for the rescue. Dunkirk's sandy beaches also helped in protecting the Allied soldiers. Heavy German bombs buried themselves in the sand before harmlessly exploding. The operation rescued 338,000 of the 400,000 trapped soldiers. The "Miracle at

Dunkirk" saved the Allied army and rescued commanders such as Brooke, Alexander, and Montgomery.

Discussing History: "Their Finest Hour" (Objective 3) The fall of France left Hitler in command of western Europe. Hitler then offered Churchill peace in exchange for British recognition of the German conquests. Ask, "What do you think Churchill's reply to Hitler's offer should be? What would be the advantages and disadvantages of accepting peace on Hitler's terms?" Discuss student answers. Then read to students Churchill's answer, which he gave in a radio broadcast to the British people: "We shall defend every village, every town, and every city. . . . Let us . . . brace ourselves to our duties, and so bear ourselves that if the British Empire and its Commonwealth last for a thousand years, men will still say: 'This was their finest hour.'" Ask students to imagine that they are British citizens who have just heard Churchill's speech. Divide the class into small groups and have them discuss their reactions to Churchill's leadership. Then have students read "Germany attacked Great Britain" (pages 711–712) to find out how the British responded.

Check for Understanding Have students explain the importance of Hitler's nonaggression pact with Stalin, the Nazi blitzkrieg tactics, the Battle of Britain, and the German invasion of the Soviet Union.

Enrichment Activities

1. **Reading a Primary Source**
   Assign Voices from the Past Resource Book 31.1.

2. **Preparing a Report**
   Ask students to report on one of the following topics: the Ma-

ginot Line, Dunkirk, the development and use of radar, the Royal Air Force, the "Ultra" secret, Winston Churchill, or the German siege of Leningrad.

3. **Researching for Bonus Points**
   What was the British code name for the rescue at Dunkirk? (Operation Dynamo)

Japan conquered an Asian empire. 2

Setting the Stage

Ask students to name the year that World War II began. Explain that European history books say World War II began when Germany invaded Poland in 1939. Chinese history books say that World War II began in 1931. What event occurred in 1931 to justify this date?

Show Map Transparency 89, *World War II in Asia and the Pacific, 1941–1945.* The Japanese invaded Manchuria in 1931. Six years later, Japanese armies pushed into China. Recall that the United States, Britain, and France had vital interests in Asia. At that time France controlled Indochina, Britain controlled Burma and Malaya, and the Philippines were United States territory.

Teaching Strategies

Discussing History: Japan's Decision to Attack Pearl Harbor (Objective 1) Divide the class into small groups. Tell each group that they are attending a secret meeting of the Japanese cabinet. Remind cabinet members that Japanese armies oc-

ANSWERS TO

Chapter Review 31

Reviewing the Facts
1. **(a)** sudden massive attack, lightning war **(b)** killing of an entire people
2. **(a)** land in western Poland taken over by Germany **(b)** German air force **(c)** British prime minister during World War II **(d)** French fortifications **(e)** port on English Channel **(f)** war-time government of France **(g)** French resistance organization **(h)** led the Free French **(i)** won the Battle of Britain **(j)** U.S. president who aided the Allies **(k)** law allowing U.S. to send war supplies to Britain **(l)** day Japan bombed Pearl Harbor **(m)** turning point of Pacific war **(n)** Hitler's destruction of the Jews **(o)** a genius in tank warfare **(p)** commander of British in North Africa **(q)** commanded Allies on D-Day **(r)** U.S. president who ordered use of atom bomb
3. **(a)** unprepared for blitzkrieg strike through Belgium **(b)** Vichy government cooperated with Nazis.
4. with Japanese invasion of Manchuria
5. **(a)** persuaded Congress to sell weapons, passed the Lend-Lease Act; gave Britain destroyers **(b)** Japan's attack on Pearl Harbor
6. **(a)** Europe's factories were destroyed in the war. **(b)** Many Americans began hating all Japanese.
7. **(a)** beginning of the Allied drive to seize North Africa **(b)** Germans were stopped by Soviets.
8. **(a)** Sicily fell to the Allies, Mussolini was forced to resign, and Italy sided with the Allies. **(b)** Allies landed in France on D-Day and advanced inland.
9. **(a)** Faced with Allies to the west and Soviets to the east, the German armies retreated. **(b)** Atom bombs were dropped on Hiro-

shima and Nagasaki, forcing Japan to surrender.

Basic Skills
1. **(a)** All events following the bombing of Pearl Harbor were Allied victories. **(b)** All events up to and including the bombing of Pearl Harbor were Axis victories. **(c)** Battle of Britain: failure to invade Britain made Hitler turn toward Russia, where German armies suffered major losses; Midway: stopped Japanese expansion; gave U.S. the offensive in naval war
2. **(a)** It gave Allies naval access to southern Europe from a variety of routes. **(b)** It shows how much more territory Germany would have to protect in a two-front war. It also points out how many enemies it would have to face simultaneously.

Researching and Reporting Skills
Students' answers will vary.

Critical Thinking
1. **(a)** Advantages: had fully prepared military, factories, and people for war; had elements of surprise; had time to make pact with Russia to prevent two-front war. Disadvantages: lack of access to raw materials; vulnerable to blockade and air attack; threat of sabotage from subject people such as Czechs; lengthening supply lines. **(b)** Advantages: access to raw materials; possibility of help (destroyers) from U.S.; help from overseas territories. Disadvantages: not prepared; military not in place; factories not geared to produce war equipment; no battle plans or coordination of resources with other friendly countries.
2. **(a)** war with United States seemed inevitable; advantage in striking first; eliminate U.S. as a Pacific power **(b)** destroy U.S. navy **(c)** temporarily harmed U.S. fleet; forced U.S. to declare war; and ul-

timately faced defeat at hands of rebuilt American navy
3. **(a)** All three battles were significant victories and turning points for the Allies in the European air war, the Pacific naval war, and the final defeat of Germany. **(b)** Each was strategic and critical in its own time.
4. **(a)** divided humankind into master race and everyone else, deprived Jews of property and political rights; sent Jews from all over Europe to concentration camps where they either worked at hard labor until they succumbed, or were put to death **(b)** Genocide is a crime against people, but no power exists to pass judgment on a people. This is why the United Nations drew up an international convention making genocide a crime. The U.S. ratified the convention in 1986.

Perspectives on Past and Present
World War II was a struggle to the end between two different political systems, democracy and totalitarianism. Germany—and the Axis powers—set out to conquer the whole world and take it over for their use. Local and regional wars tend to be over more limited and specific issues such as ownership of the Falkland Islands or control of disputed territories or resources.

Investigating History
Students' answers will vary.

Chapter 31 **706f**

Chapter 31

Teaching with Pictures

Tell students that while World War I had introduced the tank and airplane to warfare, World War II used them to their full potential. Tanks spearheaded large ground assaults. Bomber planes attacked enemy troops and civilian populations, destroying their war-making capabilities and morale. The German *Stuka* dive bombers shown here were greatly feared in the early part of the war because of their effective pinpoint bombing. Ask students how the style of the painting lends itself to the destruction being depicted.

In World War II, airplanes carried the war far from the battle front, bombing cities and towns and killing many civilians.

Key Terms

nonaggression pact
blitzkrieg
underground
embargo
genocide
Holocaust
internment camp

Read and Understand

1. Germany overran much of Europe.
2. Japan conquered an Asian empire.
3. The Allies launched a drive to victory.
4. World War II left a mixed legacy.

Only 21 years after the end of World War I, a second world war broke out in Europe. A Pole named Martin Gray was 14 years old in September 1939 when he heard the shuddering screams of German dive-bombers over Warsaw, the Polish capital. Years later, Gray recorded his grim memories of the beginning of World War II:

The sirens wailed, the bombers skimmed the rooftops, their shadows glided across the road, and in the streets the people were running, clutching their heads ... We went downstairs to the cellar, the walls were shaking and flakes of white plaster fell on our hair. My mother was deathly pale, my eyes stung, women screamed.

706

Chapter 31 Resources

GEOGRAPHY
- Geography Skills 31
- Transparencies 88, 89, 90

REINFORCEMENT
- Vocabulary 31
- Basic Skills 31
- Reteaching 31
- Making Connections Study Guide 31

ENRICHMENT
- Critical Thinking 31
- History and Literature 31A, 31B

ASSESSMENT
- Chapter Test 31
- Alternate Chapter Test 31
- Computer Test Bank

cupied French Indochina in July 1941. Great Britain, the Dutch East Indies, and the United States retaliated by cutting off all oil supplies to Japan. If nothing is done, Japan will run out of oil by the spring of 1942. Explain that the cabinet has three choices: 1. Give in to the American demands by withdrawing Japanese troops from Indochina. 2. Attack the American fleet at Pearl Harbor and then seize the Dutch East Indies. 3. Attack the Dutch East Indies while avoiding United States territories. Ask groups to make lists of the advantages and disadvantages of these three options and to explain their final decisions.

Discussing History: Was Pearl Harbor a Japanese Victory? (Objective 2) Begin by asking, "Was Pearl Harbor a Japanese victory?" Most people would answer *yes*. The Japanese attack handed the United States the worst naval defeat in its history. Of the 94 ships at Pearl Harbor, 19 were sunk or disabled. Suggest that despite their apparent success, the Japanese actually achieved only a limited victory. Japanese bombers failed to destroy Pearl Harbor's repair facilities and huge oil storage tanks. As a result, most of the damaged ships were repaired. In addition, the three aircraft carriers stationed at Pearl Harbor were not in port. Finally, the sneak attack united Americans against Japan and brought the United States into the war.

Writing about History: The Battle at Midway (Objective 3) Many historians believe that the Battle of Midway was an important turning point in World War II. Ask students to write essays explaining why this battle was a turning point and speculating on what might have happened if the Japanese had won. Have students share and discuss their essays.

Check for Understanding Have students explain the significance of the Lend-Lease Act, the Japanese attack on Pearl Harbor, and the Battle of Midway.

Enrichment Activities

1. **Reading a Primary Source**
   Assign Voices from the Past Resource Book 31.2.

2. **Creative Writing**
   Ask students to prepare a front page headline and news bulletin on one of the following events: passage of the Lend-Lease Act, the Japanese attack on Pearl Harbor, or United States victory in the Battle of Midway.

3. **Researching for Bonus Points**
   What were the names of the three United States aircraft carriers that were not at Pearl Harbor on December 7, 1941? (*Saratoga, Lexington,* and *Enterprise*)

> **The Allies launched a drive to victory.** **3**

Setting the Stage

Have students read the quote from Winston Churchill on page 718. Ask them why Churchill was certain that the Axis powers would be defeated. Explain that Churchill understood America's enormous industrial and military power. Despite initial setbacks, he believed that the Allies possessed overwhelming advantages that would ultimately lead to victory.

Teaching Strategies

Discussing History: The Battle of Stalingrad (Objective 1) Show Map Transparency 90, *World War II in Europe and North Africa, 1939–1945*. Help students locate the city of Stalingrad. Explain that Hitler hoped to conquer Stalingrad and then seize the vital Baku oil fields on the Caspian Sea. Artillery bombardments turned Stalingrad into a maze of ruined buildings. A Soviet army of one million troops surrounded the burning city. The battered German army finally surrendered on January 31, 1943. Twenty-four German generals and 100,000 soldiers became prisoners of war. Only 6,000 of these men are known to have survived. The Battle of Stalingrad marked a turning point in the war with Germany. From that time on, the German army began its long retreat to Berlin.

Discussing History: The Importance of D-Day (Objective 2) Hitler believed that an Allied invasion of France provided his best hope for victory. Ask, "Why would Hitler actually welcome an Allied attack?" Hitler believed that the Allied forces would be unable to breach his Atlantic Wall—a 2,400 mile barrier of fortresses and machine gun nests. He predicted that if the invasion failed, the United States and Britain would shift their attention to the Pacific. Hitler would then be free to transfer the 59 German divisions stationed in France to the Eastern Front for a decisive battle with the Soviet Union. Hitler also knew that his scientists were almost ready to unveil deadly new rockets and jet aircraft.

Writing about History: How to Defeat Japan (Objective 3)

Prewriting Explain that President Truman faced a difficult decision on how best to defeat Japan. As President, he had to choose one of these five options: (a) use a naval blockade to force the Japanese to starve or surrender; (b) invade Japan with five million American troops; (c) ask the Soviet Union to join the fighting against Japan; (d) demonstrate the power of the atom bomb by destroying a small unpopulated island; or (e) drop an atom bomb on a major Japanese city. *Writing* Ask students to assume the role of President Truman. Their assignment is to make a decision and then write an executive order explaining the reasons for their choices. Have students share and discuss executive orders. Compare students' choices with Truman's decision to use the atom bomb.

Check for Understanding Have students explain the significance of El Alamein, Stalingrad, and the D-Day invasion.

Enrichment Activities

1. **Reading a Primary Source**
   Assign Voices from the Past Resource Book 31.3.

2. **Preparing a Report**
   The United States, the Soviet Union, and Great Britain disagreed over the time and place to open a "second front" against Germany. Ask advanced students to report on the causes and consequences of the Allied decision to open a second front in 1944.

3. **Researching for Bonus Points**
   What was the nickname given to the atom bomb dropped on Nagasaki? ("Fat Boy")

World War II *left a mixed legacy.* 4

Setting the Stage

World War II is often referred to as a total war. What do students think is meant by the phrase "total war?" Explain that a total war involves the home fronts as well as the war zones. Unlike previous wars, more civilians than soldiers died in World War II.

Teaching Strategies

Relating Past to Present: The Holocaust (Objective 1) Have students read "The Holocaust claimed the lives of six million Jews" (pages 723–726). Then read the following passage by Elie Wiesel: "In all their chronicles and testaments, memoirs and prayers, litanies and poems, the victims stressed one single theme over and over again—remember, remember the horror, remember. Bear witness." Ask why the victims stressed this theme. Tell students that Congress established the United States Holocaust Memorial Council in 1980 to preserve awareness of this terrible tragedy and to provide an early warning against the threat of genocide anywhere in the world. The council opened a permanent memorial to the Holocaust victims in Washington, D.C. In addition, a Days of Remembrance observance is held annually throughout the United States, and similar observances are held throughout Europe.

Discussing History: The Internment of Japanese Americans (Objective 2) The bombing of Pearl Harbor produced near hysteria on the west coast of the United States. Residents feared a wave of sabotage followed by a Japanese invasion. The military held the same, unfounded fears. Ask students to comment on the following quote from the general in charge of the defense of the west coast: "The very fact that no sabotage has taken place to date is a disturbing and confirming indication that such action will be taken." Ask if such an attitude and its results— internment of an innocent people—are common during wartime. Why were German and Italian Americans not interned? Do students think such a scenario could occur again if the United States went to war today?

Check for Understanding Have students explain the importance of United States war production efforts and define the terms *genocide* and *Holocaust*.

Enrichment Activities

1. **Reading a Primary Source**
   Assign Voices from the Past Resource Book 31.4.

2. **Preparing a Report**
   Ask students to report on one of the following topics: Henry Kaiser—master shipbuilder, the impact of World War II on American women, the internment of Japanese Americans, and German concentration camps.

3. **Researching for Bonus Points**
   Which executive order authorized the United States Secretary of War to create internment camps for Japanese Americans? (Executive Order 9066)

Day after day, Warsaw's buildings crumbled and burned from the merciless hammering of German tanks and planes. Martin Gray's family huddled around their radio to find out what was happening in their city and elsewhere in Poland. Germans had taken over some of the Polish radio stations. As a Polish Jew, Martin Gray was shocked by their broadcasts:

> We listen to German broadcasts: they're announcing thousands of prisoners, to-morrow Hitler will be in Warsaw. "Poles," says the cheerful voice, "it's the Jews who are the cause of your troubles, the Jews who wanted the war, the Jews who are going to pay" . . . Then the bombers come back . . . the cellar shakes.

In two weeks, German tanks surrounded Warsaw and choked off all supplies. Civilians in the city could endure the bombing but not the lack of food. On September 27, 1939, the starving people of Warsaw surrendered to German troops. Martin Gray watched as the Germans took over the Polish capital:

> They marched slowly, their heels ringing on the cobbles of the narrow streets. I was walking along the pavement, behind the rows of curious bystanders. Their planes were skimming the rooftops above Jeru-salem Avenue. Patrols moved along the pavement; they didn't seem to notice the people, everyone drew aside. For a moment I followed three soldiers in ankle boots with long black bayonets. Yes, we were going to suffer.

The Poles suffered through six years of Nazi terror and oppression. Indeed, all of Europe suf-fered. Between 1939 and 1945, people in almost every major city of Europe heard what Martin Gray had heard—the sound of German bombers and tanks.

In Asia, the sounds were much the same. There the aggressor was not Germany but its ally in the east, Japan. Together the two countries hoped to dominate the world. They almost succeeded.

This chapter is the story of the drive by the so-called Axis countries—mainly Germany, Italy, and Japan—for world conquest. Opposing them were the Allies—Great Britain, France, the USSR, China, and the United States.

Germany overran much of Europe. 1

In the 1930's, the German dictator Adolf Hitler said over and over that Germany desired only peace and justice. Those who opposed Germany's reasonable desires, he said, were the enemies of peace. Yet all the while, he was preparing for war.

All during the 1930's, Britain and France fol-lowed a policy of appeasement. That is, they made concessions to Hitler in hopes of keeping peace. As a result, Hitler took the Sudetenland in 1938. One year later, German troops marched into western Czechoslovakia and seized it as well (page 703). The Italian dictator Mussolini, striving to keep up with his German ally, moved into the Balkans and took over Albania. Encour-aged by these victories, Hitler abandoned his talk of peace. He talked instead of war and conquest.

Hitler prepared for war.

On April 28, 1939, Hitler stood before the Reichstag (Germany's parliament) and announced his newest plan. This time, he wanted the Polish Corridor. This strip of land had been cut from Germany after World War I to give Poland access to the sea (page 636). Hitler demanded that the seaport of Danzig within the Polish Corridor be returned to Germany. Furthermore, he wanted a German railway and highway route through the corridor.

Hitler's demands convinced Britain and France that appeasement was no longer possible. The governments of both countries pledged to defend Poland if Hitler threatened its independence. At the same time, they asked the Soviet Union to join them in stopping Hitler's aggression.

The Soviets were still smarting from their ex-clusion at the Munich Conference (page 702). Soviet dictator Joseph Stalin was not eager to ally himself with the West. Furthermore, Hitler too was secretly seeking an agreement with Stalin.

In August 1939, Germany and the Soviet Union announced a ten-year **nonaggression pact,** pledging not to attack each other. This part of the pact was made public. In private, however, they agreed to divide eastern Europe. The Soviet Union was

707

OBJECTIVE 1. Define *blitz-krieg* and explain how Hit-ler used this new style of attack to defeat Poland, Norway, Belgium, and France.

Teaching Strategy: *Discuss-ing History: The Blitzkrieg* (page 706a)

OBJECTIVE 2. Identify Dun-kirk and explain how the British rescued the trapped Allied army.

Teaching Strategy: *Teaching with Pictures: The "Miracle of Dunkirk"* (page 706c)

OBJECTIVE 3. Identify Win-ston Churchill and explain how he rallied his people to prepare for the Battle of Britain.

Teaching Strategy: *Discuss-ing History: "Their Finest Hour"* (page 706c)

■ BACKGROUND

Martin Gray was eventually captured by the Germans and taken to a concentra-tion camp, but he escaped and joined the Russian re-sistance. After the war, he made his way to the United States. However, his family perished in the camps.

■ DISCUSSION

It has been written that out of the First World War came the seeds of the sec-ond. Ask students to re-view Chapter 30 to find examples to support this theory.

SECTION 1
Resources

GEOGRAPHY
■ Transparency 88

REINFORCEMENT
■ Independent Practice 31.1

ENRICHMENT
■ Voices from the Past 31.1

ASSESSMENT
■ Section Quiz 31.1

Map Study

Germany, Italy; Austria,
Sudetenland

■ BACKGROUND

On the morning of August 22, 1939, top Nazi generals filed into a conference room to meet their Führer, Adolf Hitler. "I have called you together," said Hitler, "to give you a picture of the political situation." Hitler then announced that he planned to order an invasion of Poland within 10 days. He confidently predicted that neither Britain nor France would dare to oppose him. "Our enemies are little worms," he boasted. "I saw them at Munich."

Having thus disposed of the Western democracies, Hitler turned to the Soviet Union. To everyone's astonishment, he triumphantly broke the news of a forthcoming nonaggression pact with Stalin. At the end of Hitler's speech, Hermann Göring jumped on the table and burst into cheers. Other Nazi generals then stood and joined the celebration.

to have the Baltic countries of Lithuania, Latvia, and Estonia. Germany and the USSR would each take over a part of Poland.

News of the agreement stunned the world. Hitler's Nazis had come to power by attacking communism and German Communists. Communist sympathizers around the world were shocked that Stalin would deal with Hitler. Even Hitler's Nazi supporters were taken aback. Hitler had written, "Never forget that the rulers of present-day Russia are common blood-stained criminals." Yet the advantage of the agreement for Hitler was clear. Germany need not fear a two-front war like the one it had faced in 1914.

In August 1939, Hitler ordered his generals to prepare to invade Poland in September. On the night of August 31, 1939—only hours before the planned attack—a small band of German soldiers disguised themselves in Polish uniforms. Then they pretended to seize a German radio station on the German-Polish border. They fired their pistols in the air and smeared blood over the face of a drugged prisoner. This phony raid was Hitler's excuse for attacking Poland. The Poles, he said, had violated Germany's borders.

Germany invaded Poland.

Early the next morning (September 1, 1939), wave upon wave of German planes roared over Poland. Swooping low over Polish airfields, squadrons of German dive-bombers strafed (raked

Map Study

Name the Axis Powers. What lands did Germany take over in 1938!

with gunfire) and bombed Polish planes, which were still on the ground. In less than 48 hours, the Germans wiped out the Polish air force. At the same time, German tanks and troop trucks crossed the Polish border, carrying an army of about 1,250,000 men. Long columns of German tanks rolled swiftly and easily over the flat Polish land, destroying everything in their path.

In a matter of days, the Poles lost their air force, their army, their railroads and telegraph centers, and their factories. They were demoralized, stunned, defeated.

The Germans called their sudden, massive attack **blitzkrieg** (BLITS-kreeg), meaning "lightning war." The fast-moving weapons of modern war—the armored tank and the airplane—were central to this new kind of warfare.

If Hitler thought that France and Britain would not honor their pledge to Poland, he was mistaken. Although not yet equipped to fight, they warned Hitler to stop his attack by 11 A.M. of September 3. The deadline passed, and Germany's armies rolled on. Britain and France declared war.

By the end of September 1939, Poland was conquered. Nazi armies occupied the western half. As agreed, the Soviet Union occupied the east. Warsaw held out until September 27 but finally surrendered. Meanwhile, Britain and France mobilized for war.

The Soviets made their move.

For six months after the fall of Poland, there was a strange lull in the fighting. Although German submarines began to attack British merchant and passenger ships, there was no fighting on land between the Allies (France and Britain) and Germany. Newspapers called it a "phony war."

The only aggression in Europe during this time took place in the north. Hitler had agreed that the three Baltic countries would be Soviet spheres of influence. One week after the fall of Poland, Stalin threatened to attack Estonia, Latvia, and Lithuania unless they yielded to his demands. Under pressure, all three signed treaties allowing Soviet military bases on their soil.

Next, Stalin demanded territory from Finland. The Finnish government promptly refused. In November 1939, nearly 1 million Soviet troops crossed the Finnish border. The Finns defended their country fiercely, attacking swiftly on skis

ALL I WANT OF HIM IS A THIN SLICE OF HIS NECK!

Hitler's demand for the Polish Corridor ended appeasement and led to the attack on Poland.

while Soviet troops struggled through the deep snow. In the end, however, the Soviets won through sheer force of numbers. In March 1940, Finland was forced to accept Stalin's terms.

Germany overwhelmed Scandinavia.

For Hitler, the winter of waiting was over. In the spring of 1940, he made his next move. Again he did the unexpected. Most people, including the French, thought Hitler would attack France. However, Hitler was not yet ready to do so. First, he wanted to control Denmark and Norway. There he planned to set up airfields and naval bases from which he could strike at Britain and British shipping.

On April 9, 1940, German tanks rolled into Denmark. German troops hidden on a merchant ship in Copenhagen's harbor now marched ashore. They captured the Danish king and his ministers. Denmark surrendered within 24 hours.

On the same day, bombers of the German *Luftwaffe* (air force) attacked Norway. A German invasion force scrambled onto Norway's rocky shores. The Norwegians were better prepared than

709

Poland's cavalry, mounted on horseback, was no match for the tanks of the German *Panzer* units. Horses and men went down in a slaughter that marked the last time mounted soldiers were used in a major war.

Soviet soldiers, expecting a quick victory, marched off to Finland wearing only light clothing. In the fighting, Finns lost 25,000 men while inflicting more than 100,000 casualties on the enemy.

German artillery pounded Dunkirk's docks and beaches while British rescue ships steered through the smoke to save Allied soldiers.

■ DISCUSSION

The Maginot Line was named after the French War Minister André Maginot. Begun in 1929, it stretched from Switzerland to Belgium. Its defenses included a chain of huge underground forts housing 1,000 men each. The forts contained their own power stations, water reserves, kitchens, telephones, and ammunition. Concrete roofs more than eight feet thick protected each fort. What does the building of the Maginot Line say about the lessons of history?

■ BACKGROUND

An amphibious evacuation under fire is considered the most difficult military operation to conduct. In addition to the bravery and skill of soldiers and sailors, the British evacuation of Dunkirk was helped by bad weather. Four straight days of heavy rains grounded the Luftwaffe and immobilized the German panzers. When the weather cleared, the Luftwaffe sank eight ships and damaged seven more in just one afternoon. Despite the success of the evacuation, Churchill somberly warned Parliament, "Wars are not won by evacuations."

the Danes had been. Even so, Norway's major seaports and its capital city, Oslo, fell to the Germans within two days.

German troops blitzed the west.

As war moved closer to Britain, a new leader came to power in Parliament. In May 1940, Neville Chamberlain, the leader of appeasement, was forced to resign as prime minister. His successor was Winston Churchill (1874–1965), who had long warned that Britain must make a stand against Hitler. In his first speech as prime minister, Churchill told the nation that there was no quick road to victory. "I have nothing to offer," he said, "but blood, toil, tears, and sweat." The next five years would prove how right he was.

In May 1940, a month after the Scandinavian attacks, Hitler prepared to strike at France. Along their border with Germany, the French had built an elaborate set of fortifications known as the Maginot (mah-jih-NOH) Line. The French expected this war to be a defensive one, as World War I had been, and the French army was well prepared for trench warfare. It was totally unprepared, however, for the German blitzkrieg.

France's 2 million soldiers stood ready to fight along the Maginot Line. Once more Hitler fooled

them. As in World War I, the German army swung west around the French defenses and struck through Belgium.

On the morning of May 10, 1940, German parachutists dropped from the skies over the Low Countries—the Netherlands, Luxembourg, and Belgium. Luxembourg collapsed in only a few hours. On May 14, Germany threatened to destroy all Dutch cities if the Netherlands did not surrender. As proof, the Luftwaffe pounded Rotterdam to rubble even as talks about surrender were in progress. One day later, Belgium fell.

Columns of German tanks moved into northern France, driving Allied troops back toward the port of Dunkirk on the English Channel. There the Allied troops were trapped with their backs to the sea. The Germans closed in for the kill.

The seafaring people of Britain set out to rescue their trapped army. The fleet that sailed for Dunkirk from British ports on May 26, 1940, was perhaps the strangest naval expedition in history. Bobbing on the choppy sea were private yachts, ferries, lifeboats, motorboats, paddle steamers, fishing boats, and dockyard tugs. At the helm of these 850 craft were civilian volunteers. Their task was to help the British navy carry stranded soldiers across the Channel.

For eight days, from May 28 to June 4, this hodgepodge fleet sailed back and forth between

710

Britain and the burning, bombed-out docks of Dunkirk. When the operation ended on June 4, an incredible 338,000 battle-weary soldiers had been carried safely to Britain.

France fell to the Nazis.

Even as the Nazi blitzkrieg swept through France, Italian armies were also on the march. At first, Italy's Fascist dictator, Benito Mussolini, had hesitated to take part in the war. Now, with France about to fall, Mussolini decided to grab for conquest and glory. On June 10, he declared war against both Britain and France. Italy then attacked France from the south.

France seemed doomed. As German forces neared Paris, masses of people fled the city. Cars, bicycles, carts, and taxis jammed the roads leading south from Paris. German planes screamed overhead, firing into the snarled traffic.

As the end approached, the French government asked Marshall Henri Pétain (pay-TAN), an aged hero from World War I, to become prime minister. On June 16, 1940, he told the French army, "We must cease to fight."

Hitler demanded that the French leaders surrender at Compiègne in the same railroad car where Germans had been forced to sign the armistice ending World War I. On June 22, 1940, the meeting took place. Hitler walked from the railroad car giddy with triumph.

According to the terms of surrender, France was divided into two parts. The Germans were to occupy the northern two thirds of France and control the coastline. Pétain's government was to hold the southern part.

Pétain and his ministers moved to the city of Vichy (VISH-ee) in southern France. Their government became known as the Vichy Regime. Many French people regarded Pétain as a traitor. Others believed he had acted to save France from destruction. As time went on, however, the Vichy government cooperated more and more closely with the Nazis.

In time, French freedom fighters found their own way to combat the Nazis. Led by General Charles de Gaulle, they formed an **underground**, or secret resistance movement, known as the Free French. Although capture meant certain death, French resistance fighters made heroic efforts to sabotage the Nazis for the rest of the war.

Germany attacked Great Britain.

In all of Europe, only one country still held out against Hitler. That country was Great Britain. In a speech after Dunkirk, Churchill had already made clear that the British would never give in to the Nazis. Foreseeing the grim possibility of a German invasion, Churchill said:

> . . . [W]e shall fight in the seas and oceans, we shall fight with growing confidence and growing strength in the air; we shall defend our Island, whatever the cost may be. We shall fight on the beaches, we shall fight on the landing grounds, we shall fight in the fields and in the streets, we shall fight in the hills; we shall never surrender.

■ **BACKGROUND**

The day after accepting the French surrender, Hitler made an unannounced visit to Paris. He began by touring the Opera House, which was specially lighted for his visit, and then drove along the Champs Elysées to the Arc de Triomphe. The next stop on his tour was the Invalides. There Hitler paused as he gazed at the magnificent Tomb of Napoleon. "This is the finest moment of my life," he whispered.

French resistance fighters used gadgets such as these to travel secretly behind German lines and communicate with others in the Free French. They hid a compass in a bootheel, a radio transmitter in a wine carrier, and news bulletins in a hollowed log.

711

■ BACKGROUND

Britain had to import many supplies by sea—oil from the Middle East, iron ore from South Africa, meat from New Zealand—for a total of a million tons of goods per week.

German intelligence chiefs believed that their secret code was unbreakable. They had not, however, counted on the work of Alan Mathison Turing, a brilliant British mathematician. Turing was an eccentric genius who had once melted all his money into silver ingots, buried them, and then forgotten their location. Nonetheless, he and a team of British cryptanalysts succeeded in deciphering the German code.

■ DISCUSSION

Ask students to speculate on reasons Hitler broke the Nonaggression Pact and invaded the Soviet Union. Explain that Hitler had four motives. First, he believed that the fertile steppes of the Ukraine would provide "living space" for the so-called German master race. Second, Hitler despised communism. Third, he believed that Britain would sue for peace once the Soviets were defeated. Finally, Hitler was convinced that his victorious armies could easily defeat the Soviets.

Ignoring the advice of his generals, Hitler decided to invade Britain. During the summer of 1940, the Germans prepared for Operation Sea Lion, a seaborne attack on Britain that would begin in mid-September. First, however, Hitler sent the Luftwaffe bombers to knock out Britain's defenses, particularly its Royal Air Force (RAF).

To face the Germans' 1,200 fighter planes and 1,300 bombers, the British had only 700 serviceable fighters. The fate of Britain rested on the skill and raw courage of its 1,400 pilots.

Although outnumbered, the British possessed two secret weapons. One was an electronic tracking system known as radar. A newly installed network of radar towers enabled the RAF to determine the number, direction, and speed of incoming German warplanes. Britain's second secret weapon was a decoding machine (page 719) called Ultra which enabled the British to crack German codes. Together these warnings gave RAF fliers the time they needed to scramble into their planes and rise to the attack.

The Battle of Britain began in July 1940. During the next six months, the British and German air forces collided in the largest air battles of World War II. Luftwaffe commanders repeatedly hurled more than 1,000 fighters and bombers at British air bases and cities. The RAF pilots defended their homeland with fierce courage. The young pilots flew three, four, and even five missions a day.

In late August, British bombers flew over Germany, hitting Berlin and other cities. Furious that Berlin had been bombed, Hitler ordered attacks against London and other British cities.

Decisions in History

Ultra provided British commanders with vital information about German battle plans. This information, however, sometimes forced Prime Minister Churchill to make agonizing decisions. For example, during the Battle of Britain, Ultra revealed that the Germans were preparing to launch an air attack on the city of Coventry in four to five hours. Some advisers urged Churchill to order an immediate evacuation of this historic city. Others pointed out that a sudden evacuation order might arouse German suspicions about the security of their top-secret code. If this happened, the Germans would change their code and the Ultra advantage would be lost. What would you have done if you were Prime Minister Churchill?

712

The piercing wail of air-raid sirens filled the air as bomb after bomb exploded in city streets, setting buildings ablaze. The cost to British civilians was terrible—300 to 600 lives lost per day and from 1,000 to 3,000 injured daily.

Despite the fire-filled days and nights, the people of Britain fought on, more determined than ever not to give in. By the end of 1940, Hitler knew he could neither wipe out the RAF nor break the spirit of the British people. As a result, he abandoned Operation Sea Lion. Churchill expressed the gratitude of the British people to the RAF pilots when he said, "Never was so much owed by so many to so few."

America aided the Allies.

During the Battle of Britain, 30 million Americans listened intently to radio broadcasts from London. A young American reporter named Edward R. Murrow vividly described how German bombing raids forced London families to huddle in subways. His open microphone enabled listeners to hear howling sirens as volunteers fought raging fires.

Murrow's dramatic eyewitness accounts helped bring the reality of war into American homes. They thus heightened the growing public debate about America's proper role in World War II. Many Americans wanted to keep their country out of war. Between 1935 and 1937, these isolationists succeeded in passing laws known as the neutrality acts. These laws made it illegal to sell arms or lend money to countries at war.

President Franklin Roosevelt recognized the strong feelings of the isolationists. He also knew that the Allies needed help. In 1939, Roosevelt persuaded Congress to allow the sale of weapons and other goods to fighting nations by a cash-and-carry policy. Thus, countries at war could buy such goods as long as they paid for them immediately and took them away on their ships. Because the British still controlled the sea routes, this act was a great help to them.

In September 1940, during the Battle of Britain, Roosevelt went a step further. He gave Britain 50 destroyers in return for 99-year leases on bases in Newfoundland, Bermuda, and Jamaica. That same year, Congress approved a Selective Service Act providing for the United States' first military draft during peacetime.

712

In the presidential election of 1940, Roosevelt tried to calm Americans' fears over the country's growing involvement in the war. He promised parents that their "boys were not going to be sent into any foreign wars." All he was doing, he argued, was helping the British defend themselves. Roosevelt stressed that the United States could serve as the "arsenal of democracy," supplying arms but not soldiers to the free countries of the world.

Soon after Roosevelt won reelection, Churchill told him that the British needed more help. By then, the entire northern coast of Europe was under Nazi control. Hitler's submarines were sinking British ships that carried food and war supplies to the island nation.

Roosevelt responded to Churchill's request by asking Congress to approve a new program to lend and lease supplies to all countries fighting against aggressors. A majority of the public agreed with Roosevelt that America should become the great arsenal of democracy. Congress passed the Lend-Lease Act in March 1941. The new law marked an important turning point. America's mighty industries now roared to life producing weapons to fight Hitler and Mussolini. Relieved Londoners celebrated the news by hoisting American flags over their homes and offices.

By the fall of 1941, the United States was arming merchant ships and using its navy to protect British ships across the Atlantic. In September, after a German submarine fired on an American ship, Roosevelt ordered navy commanders to shoot German submarines on sight. In effect, the United States was now engaged in an undeclared naval war against Hitler.

Hitler invaded the Soviet Union.

The failure to take Britain stunned Hitler. It did not, however, defeat him. His next step was to break the pact he had made with Stalin less than two years earlier. Like Napoleon 150 years earlier, Hitler decided to strike eastward before finishing off Great Britain. For Hitler, the Soviet Union was a tempting prize. There, Germans would find the living space, as well as valuable mineral resources.

Hitler's first step was to take over the Balkans. In April 1941, Germany attacked both Greece and Yugoslavia on the same day. Yugoslavia fell

Britain suffered terrible destruction and loss of life from German bombs and V-2 rockets.

in 11 days, Greece in 24. In Athens, the Nazis celebrated their victory by hanging swastikas on the Parthenon. By the end of the year, Bulgaria, Romania, and Hungary had all allied themselves with Germany.

With the Balkans in his power, Hitler was ready for war against the USSR. Early on Sunday morning, June 22, 1941, as the Soviet people slept, the roar of tanks and planes announced the beginning of the German blitzkrieg. In the first hours of the attack, Luftwaffe bombs destroyed 1,000 Soviet planes on the ground. Taken by surprise, the lines of the Red Army were smashed in a dozen places.

The invasion rolled on week after week. Like the pincers of a giant crab, two columns of the German army would crash through Russian defenses and surround whole divisions. In this way, the Germans moved steadily closer to their three goals—Leningrad in the north, Moscow in the center, and the oil-rich Ukraine in the south.

By mid-November 1941 (five months after the assault began), Leningrad was surrounded by German armies. Hitler then tried to starve the 3 million inhabitants of the city into submission. More than 500,000 Leningraders died during the winter of 1941–1942. Yet the city refused to surrender.

713

■ **BACKGROUND**

Roosevelt justifying Lend-Lease: "Suppose my neighbor's house catches fire and I have a length of garden hose . . . I don't say to him, 'Neighbor, you have to pay me for the hose.' No, I say I want it back after the fire is out."

President Roosevelt and Prime Minister Churchill had both warned a disbelieving Stalin that Hitler would turn on his ally and invade Russia. When the invasion came, however, Stalin was not ashamed to ask for help from Britain.

ANSWERS TO Section Review 1

Define:
(a) pledge that the signers will not attack each other
(b) lightning war (c) secret resistance movement
Identify:
(a) strip of land cut from Germany after World War I to give Poland access to the sea (b) German air force
(c) British prime minister during World War II

(continued)

ANSWERS TO (continued)

(d) French fortifications built as protection from a German invasion **(e)** port on English Channel from which Allied soldiers were rescued **(f)** France's Nazi-controlled government **(g)** underground resistance movement in wartime France **(h)** leader of French resistance **(i)** British air force

Answer:

1. (a) that Danzig, plus a German railway and highway route through the Polish Corridor, be returned to Germany **(b)** pledged to defend Poland if Hitler threatened its independence

2. Hitler wanted to avoid a two-front war. Stalin wanted to gain territory.

3. (a) The German army swung west around French defenses and struck through Belgium. **(b)** effectiveness of the German blitzkrieg

4. by a Nazi collaborator who headed the Vichy regime

5. (a) with a seaborne attack called Operation Sea Lion **(b)** Britain had radar, the ability to crack German codes, and a determined population.

6. (a) to obtain living space and valuable mineral resources **(b)** conquered the Balkans, destroyed 1,000 Soviet planes on the ground, smashed the lines of the Red Army **(c)** Hitler's troops were not prepared for the Soviet winter.

7. For: Hitler disliked Communists, wanted the space and valuable mineral resources of USSR. **Against:** Hitler had signed a ten-year nonagression pact with the USSR; Hitler could not handle a two-front war.

Meanwhile, other German armies reached the outskirts of Moscow. There they met stiff resistance from Soviet troops. They also faced the brutal cold of a Soviet winter. The Germans, clad only in summer uniforms, were not ready for the cold. Hitler had believed he would defeat the Soviet Union before winter set in.

Like Napoleon, Hitler faced a winter war near Moscow. Napoleon, however, had had the good sense to retreat when the snows started falling. Hitler instead sent a stunning order to his freezing generals: "No retreat!" The German troops dug in to face the long winter. The Soviets, on the other hand, were well trained for winter warfare. For both sides, it now appeared the war would be a long one.

Section REVIEW 1

Define: (a) nonaggression pact, (b) blitzkrieg, (c) underground
Identify: (a) Polish Corridor, (b) Luftwaffe, (c) Winston Churchill, (d) Maginot Line, (e) Dunkirk, (f) Vichy Regime, (g) Free French, (h) Charles de Gaulle, (i) RAF
Answer:

1. (a) What new demands did Hitler make in the spring of 1939? (b) How did Britain and France end their policy of appeasement?
2. Why did Hitler and Stalin sign a nonaggression pact?
3. (a) In what way was the German attack on France similar to the beginning of World War I? (b) What key difference between the two wars led to the French defeat?
4. How was France governed after its fall?
5. (a) How did Hitler plan to defeat Britain? (b) Why did he fail?
6. (a) What were Hitler's goals in attacking the Soviet Union? (b) What successes did the Germans achieve? (c) How did the campaign turn into a disaster for Germany?

Critical Thinking

7. Suppose you had been a news analyst in 1940. Write a short summary of the reasons why you expect Hitler to attack the USSR soon. Then take the opposite point of view and write a similar summary of the reasons why you would not expect him to do so.

714

Japan conquered an Asian empire. 2

While the German advance froze to a halt in the Soviet Union, the Japanese were making their plans. Just as Hitler envisioned Europe ruled by the master race, Japan had its own dreams of gaining its own sphere of influence. Japan called its planned empire the Greater East Asia Co-Prosperity Sphere. Stretching from Manchuria in the north to Australia in the south, this empire would serve the economic needs of Japan.

Japan's conquest of Asia began in 1931 when Japanese troops took over Manchuria, China's northeastern province. Six years later, in 1937, Japanese armies moved south into the ancient heartland of China. The Japanese believed that China would soon be theirs.

By 1939, the war between China and Japan had dragged on for three years. Japan's economy was strained to the breaking point. Japanese military leaders grew alarmed by their dwindling supplies of oil, iron, rubber, and tin. They began to eye the lands of Southeast Asia, where rich supplies of these resources lay.

Japan threatened American interests in Asia.

Relations between the United States and Japan were also moving toward a crisis. Roosevelt was determined to keep Japan from taking over China. In addition, Japan threatened the American-controlled Philippine islands, the British colonies of Singapore and Malaya, and the oil-rich Dutch colonies of the East Indies.

To put pressure on the Japanese, Roosevelt banned the shipment of American fuel, scrap iron, and steel to Japan. This loss of vital supplies made it difficult for Japan to continue its war in China. In effect, Japan's military rulers had two choices. One choice was to pull out of China and admit defeat. The other was to obtain more war materials by striking south against Indochina, Malaya, and the East Indies. The Japanese foresaw that the second choice would provoke war with the United States. In a fateful conference with Emperor Hirohito in September 1940, Japanese generals decided on the second choice—attack.

At the same time, Japan, Italy, and Germany signed the Axis pact (pages 700–701). Hitler now formally supported Japan's war plan.

Turning Points in History

The Japanese Attack Pearl Harbor The dramatic events of early 1941 in Europe overshadowed for most Americans the changes occurring in Asia. Few people recognized that Germany's swift victories in Europe created a new opportunity for Japan in the Pacific. Japan's military leaders saw their chance to move against the French, British, and Dutch colonies in Southeast Asia. Taking over the rice fields, rubber plantations, and tin mines of Indochina and Malaya and the rich oil fields of the Dutch East Indies would fuel Japan's war machine.

In July 1941, Japanese forces overran French Indochina. President Roosevelt retaliated by ordering a total **embargo**, or stoppage, on all trade with Japan. At that time, Japan imported almost 80 percent of its scrap iron and oil from the United States. The embargo angered Japanese

What do the samurai and the ships in this picture represent?

leaders. Military planners pointed out that Japan's armed forces were using up 12,000 tons of fuel a day. Their fuel reserves would last only a year.

Japanese leaders now faced a fateful decision. They could either give in to the United States demand that they withdraw from China and Indochina, or they could go to war with the United States. Japanese military commanders opposed withdrawal. They pointed out that the United States was unprepared for war. They also noted that the pact that Japan had signed with Germany and Italy in 1940 committed those two countries to aid their Axis partner. After weeks of debate, the Japanese decided that if they could not persuade Roosevelt to end the embargo, they would attack the United States Pacific Fleet and then seize the Dutch East Indies.

During the fall of 1941, Japanese and American diplomats held urgent negotiations in Washington. President Roosevelt was not surprised when the talks failed to produce an agreement. Unknown to the Japanese, the United States had broken their code by a secret process called Magic. While Magic clearly showed that the Japanese were preparing for war, it did not reveal when or where a possible attack might occur.

On November 27, officials in Washington warned all Pacific commanders to prepare for a surprise attack. Most officials predicted that the Japanese would attack the Philippines. No one foresaw that the Navy's huge base at Pearl Harbor would be a target. Experts believed that Pearl Harbor was too far from Japan and too well-defended.

In late November, a fleet of 31 ships secretly left Japan and headed into the vast and empty waters of the North Pacific. The fleet included 6 aircraft carriers equipped with more than 400 warplanes. The Japanese ships moved secretly, sending no radio signals that could be traced.

By early Sunday morning, December 7, 1941, the Japanese fleet lay 220 miles north of Hawaii. At 6:00 A.M., tense pilots climbed into the cockpits of their planes. Each pilot wore a scarf tied around his helmet bearing the word Hissho, or Certain Victory. Foam-tipped waves sprayed the flight decks as 185 planes hurtled skyward for the two-hour flight. As they approached Hawaii, the pilots easily spotted their targets—the main Pacific fleet at anchor in Pearl Harbor and dozens of planes lined up on nearby airfields.

715

SECTION 2 Objectives and Teaching Strategies

OBJECTIVE 1. Evaluate Japan's decision to attack Pearl Harbor.

Teaching Strategy: *Discussing History: Japan's Decision to Attack Pearl Harbor* (page 706c)

OBJECTIVE 2. Explain the consequences of the Japanese attack on Pearl Harbor.

Teaching Strategy: *Discussing History: Was Pearl Harbor a Japanese Victory?* (page 706d)

OBJECTIVE 3. Identify the Battle of Midway and explain its significance.

Teaching Strategy: *Writing about History: The Battle of Midway* (page 706d)

SECTION 2 Resources

GEOGRAPHY
■ Transparency 89

REINFORCEMENT
■ Independent Practice 31.2

ENRICHMENT
■ Voices from the Past 31.2

ASSESSMENT
■ Section Quiz 31.2

■ BACKGROUND

Americans considered the Battle of Midway revenge for Pearl Harbor since Admiral Nagumo, the commander of the Japanese fleet, had been Japan's hero in that battle.

Cooperative Learning

Have students, working in groups of four, produce articles that might have appeared in an American newspaper immediately following the attack on Pearl Harbor. Articles might include reports on the attack itself, a history of recent Japanese aggression in the Pacific, the simultaneous attack on the Philippines, plans for the war in the Pacific, plans for a war against Germany and Italy, or editorials urging enlistment and full support for the war. Each group should choose a topic. Then with one member acting as a recorder, the others should research and dictate the body of the article. Finally, one member may act as an editor and check the article for spelling and grammar. All group members must agree on the content of the article. Post the "newspaper" in the classroom.

At Pearl Harbor, a small boat picked up survivors from the burning USS West Virginia.

American sailors and pilots awoke to a deafening roar of explosives that suddenly shattered the morning calm. Bombs weighing almost a ton pierced the thick armor plates of the undefended warships. At the same time, specially designed torpedos sliced through the harbor's shallow waters and crashed into Battleship Row.

Although the desperate American forces tried to fight back, they could not stop the attack. Within two hours, the Japanese had sunk or damaged 18 ships, including 8 battleships. Twenty-four hundred and three Americans were killed and more than a thousand were wounded. The Japanese lost only 29 planes and 1 submarine.

News of the attack stunned the American people. The next day Congress declared war on Japan. Many Japanese leaders had predicted that the United States would lack the will to fight a prolonged war. They were wrong. An angry and now united America entered World War II determined to crush the Axis powers.

Japan overran the Pacific.

Only ten hours after the attack on Pearl Harbor, planes from a second Japanese fleet pounded American military bases in the Philippines. The Japanese marched into the city of Manila in Jan-

uary 1942 and overwhelmed the American and Filipino defenders at Bataan in April 1942 and Corregidor in May 1942.

Meanwhile, the Japanese had been striking out in other directions. During December 1941, they took Hong Kong from the British and added the American islands of Guam and Wake to their empire. More important for their drive to the south, they also attacked the Malay Peninsula.

By February 1942, the Japanese had hacked their way through Malayan rain forests to Singapore and forced the surrender of some 70,000 British defenders. Possession of both Malaya and the Philippines gave the Japanese an ideal base from which to launch attacks against the Dutch East Indies to the south. By March 1942, Japan had conquered the oil-rich Dutch islands of Java, Borneo, Sumatra, and Celebes. By May 1942, they had established full control of Burma, threatening both China and British India.

By mid-1942, Japan's red and white banner with its rising sun flew over most lands and islands of the western Pacific Ocean. Since the attack at Pearl Harbor, the Japanese had conquered a vast expanse of land and ocean. Their empire measured 5,000 miles from north to south and 6,000 miles from east to west. Now they hoped to push their conquests even farther, to Australia and perhaps Hawaii as well.

The Allies turned the tide of war.

The main Allied forces in the Pacific were the Americans and the Australians. In May 1942, they succeeded in stopping the Japanese drive toward Australia in the five-day Battle of the Coral Sea. During this battle, the fighting was done by airplanes that took off from enormous aircraft carriers. Not a single shot was fired by surface ships.

Japan's next thrust was toward Midway Island, which lies west of Hawaii. Here again, the Allies succeeded in stopping the Japanese. Americans had broken the Japanese code and learned that Midway was to be the target.

Admiral Chester W. Nimitz, commander in chief of the Pacific fleet, moved to defend the island. On June 3, 1942, his scout planes found the Japanese fleet. The Americans sent torpedo planes and dive-bombers to the attack. The Japanese were caught with their planes still on the

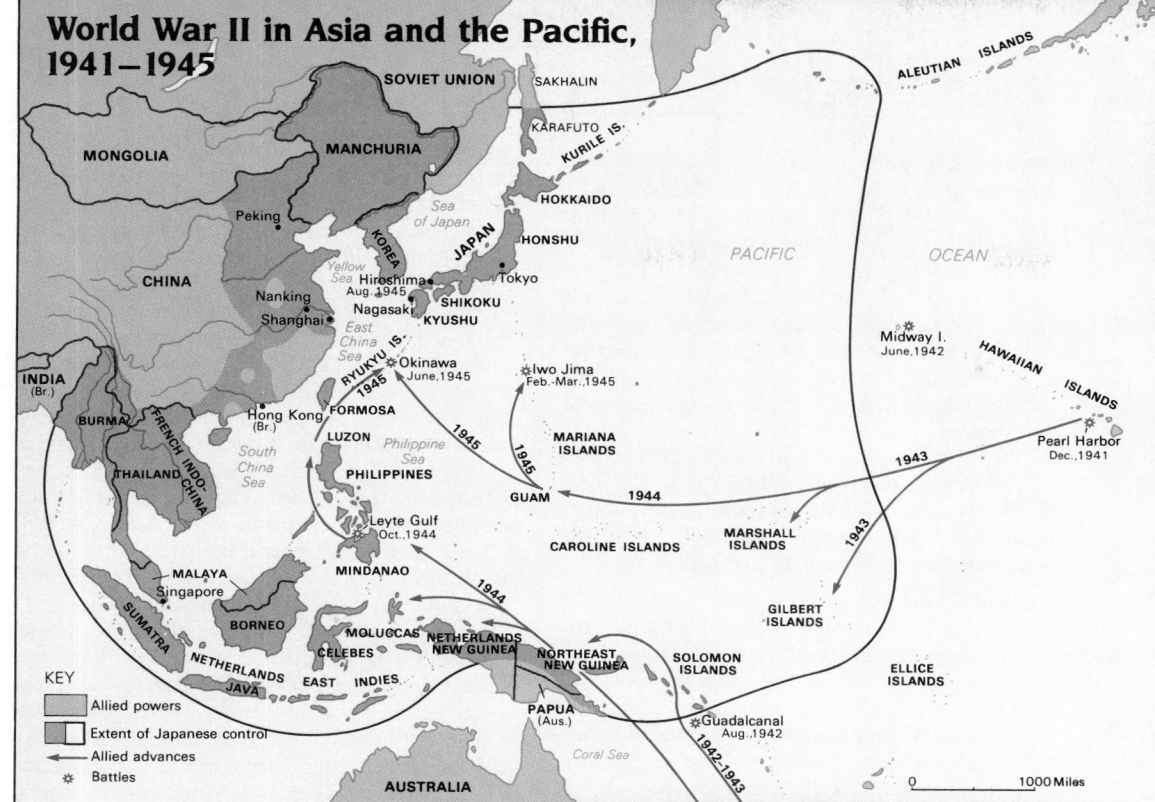

World War II in Asia and the Pacific, 1941–1945

KEY
- Allied powers
- Extent of Japanese control
- → Allied advances
- ✳ Battles

0   1000 Miles

ANSWERS TO
Map Study

Burma, Thailand, Malaya, French Indochina; Iwo Jima, Okinawa

■ BACKGROUND

Normally, training the flight crew for a bomber required one full year. At the start of the war, however, the need for crews was so great that the best candidates were trained in a concentrated six-months' course. When the crews of the 31st Bomber Squadron finished their training, they immediately flew their B-17's from Sacramento, California, to Hawaii. After a brief refueling stop in Hawaii, they rushed on to Midway to aid the naval forces defending that island.

Map Study

What countries on mainland Southeast Asia did Japan rule at the height of its power? What two islands did the Allies attack after the Marianas?

On December 7, 1941, the Navy's aircraft carriers were away at sea and thus survived.

decks of their carriers. American fliers destroyed 322 Japanese planes, 4 aircraft carriers, and several other ships. Stripped of its naval air power, the Japanese fleet was forced to withdraw. Hawaii was never again seriously threatened.

The Allies went on the offensive.

The Battle of Midway was a turning point in the Pacific war. Soon the Allies began "island hopping." Island by island, they won back territory from the Japanese. With each island, Allied forces moved closer to Japan.

The first Allied offensive was at Guadalcanal in the Solomon Islands. The savage struggle in the sweltering forests and tall grasses of Guadalcanal lasted from July 1942 to February 1943. Six times, United States cruisers and battleships

fought the Japanese navy to a stalemate. Finally, after losing thousands of men, Japan gave up the island.

The Japanese offensive in the Pacific had been halted. In the remaining years of the war, as we shall see, Japan was forced to yield all it had conquered to the relentless counterattack of the United States and other Allied powers.

717

ANSWERS TO
Section Review 2

Define:
a government order to stop trade

Identify:
(a) law authorizing president to send war supplies to any country whose defense was vital to the U.S. (b) first Allied offensive in the Pacific (c) American commander of the Pacific troops (d) turning point in the Pacific war

Answer:

1. with Japanese invasion of Manchuria

2. sold them weapons and other goods on a cash-and-carry basis; gave them 50 destroyers in return for leases on bases; passed Lend-Lease Act

3. (a) Roosevelt banned the shipment of American fuel, scrap iron, and steel to Japan, making Japan's war against China more difficult. (b) by striking south against Indochina, Malaya, and the East Indies

4. bombing of Pearl Harbor by Japanese

5. After the attack on Pearl Harbor the Japanese overran most of the Pacific before the Allies managed to stop them.

6. (a) stopping of the Japanese drive toward Australia (b) Americans stopped the Japanese by destroying their air force.

7. Yes, isolationists were a strong voice in Congress. No, unprovoked attacks on American fleets and conquest of democratic countries would have forced the U.S. into war.

Define: embargo

Identify: (a) Lend-Lease Act, (b) Guadalcanal, (c) Chester W. Nimitz, (d) Battle of Midway

Answer:

1. How did World War II begin in Asia?

2. What steps did the United States take to help the Allies before actually entering the war?

3. (a) What economic issues led to conflict between the United States and Japan? (b) How did Japan decide to solve its economic problems?

4. When and how did war break out between the United States and Japan?

5. Briefly describe the island war in the Pacific.

6. (a) What was the result of the Battle of the Coral Sea? (b) The Battle of Midway?

Critical Thinking

7. Isoroku Yamamoto, an admiral who had visited the United States, warned Japanese leaders against provoking war with that country. If Pearl Harbor had not been attacked, do you think the United States would have remained the arsenal of democracy without actually entering the war? Explain your answer.

The Allies launched a drive to victory. 3

On December 8, in his war message to Congress, President Roosevelt described December 7—the day on which Pearl Harbor had been bombed—as "a date which will live in infamy." To Prime Minister Winston Churchill of Great Britain, however, the date represented something quite different. It marked the beginning of an alliance between Great Britain and the United States that would in time, he believed, ensure the very survival of Britain. "No American," he later wrote, "will think it wrong of me if I proclaim that to have the United States at our side was to me the greatest joy . . . Hitler's fate was sealed. Mussolini's fate was sealed. As for the Japanese they would be ground to powder." Churchill knew that agony lay ahead, but he was now confident of an Allied victory.

Allied forces trapped the Desert Fox.

In October 1942, British and American forces began their first major campaign together, in North Africa. The stakes there were high. The Suez Canal—Britain's lifeline to India—and Mideast oil fields would go to the victor.

Since 1939, control of North Africa had seesawed back and forth between Germany and Great Britain. Then, early in 1942, German General Erwin Rommel had begun a massive offensive in the region. A genius in tank warfare, Rommel was known as the Desert Fox. He had slowly but surely pushed British forces east across Egypt. By summer, the British were holding on by a thread in the strategic city of El Alamein (el AHL-uh-MAYN), their backs to the Suez Canal.

In August 1942, General Bernard Montgomery arrived in the North African desert to command the British forces. Small, lean, and steely-eyed, Montgomery planned not to defend but to attack. He spent two months amassing artillery and tanks. Finally, in October, Montgomery was ready to strike. So swift and overwhelming was his attack that Rommel lost 60,000 men, 500 tanks, and 400 large artillery pieces in less than a week.

The Battle of El Alamein marked a turning point in North Africa and a major shift in the war as a whole. It was the beginning of the Allied drive to seize the North African coast.

American and British forces closed in on the staggering Axis army from two directions. From the west, American General Dwight D. Eisenhower led Allied troops through Morocco and Algeria. From the east, Montgomery continued to roll back the German army. In May 1943, the two pincers of the drive came together in Tunisia, trapping 250,000 Germans and Italians. The coast of North Africa was in Allied hands.

Soviet forces took the offensive.

For Hitler, the news from the North African desert was bad, but the news that had been coming from the Soviet Union was even worse. The Germans had been fighting in the Soviet Union for nearly two years, since June 1941. In November 1941, the bitter cold of winter had stopped them dead in their tracks outside Leningrad and Moscow (pages 713–714). When spring came, the German tanks were ready to roll again.

DAILY LIFE ▸ The Broken Code

All during the war, hundreds of British men and women lived with a carefully guarded secret. They could read the coded radio messages that the German army beamed back and forth. The Germans generated their codes with a complex electrical device like the one at the right. They thought these codes were unbreakable. However, early in the war, a few daring Poles smuggled a copy of the machine to Britain. The British name for this secret source of information was "Ultra."

Ultra was vital to Montgomery in North Africa. From it, he learned that Rommel was ill and the German army was desperately short of fuel. Without Ultra, Montgomery might not have been the victor at El Alamein.

In the spring of 1942, the Germans took the offensive in the southern Soviet Union. Hitler hoped to capture Soviet oil fields in the Caucasus. He also wanted to wipe out the city of Stalingrad.

The Battle of Stalingrad began in August 1942. From Stalin came the order to defend his namesake city at all costs. Soon the costs were appallingly high. Night after night and day after day, Soviet defenders holed up in bombed-out apartments and courtyards. From there, they fought the Germans with knives, guns, bayonets, and even clubs. Only death forced them to yield. Even so, after months of brutal house-to-house fighting, the Germans appeared to be in control. Then another winter set in.

Soviet commander Georgi Zhukov saw the cold as an opportunity to roll fresh tanks across the frozen landscape and begin a counterattack. Like a giant vise, Zhukov's army closed around Stalingrad, trapping the Germans in the city and cutting off their supplies. The Germans' situation was hopeless, but Hitler's order came: "Stay and fight! I am not leaving the Volga!"

The Germans did their best to follow the impossible order. When they finally surrendered on January 31, 1943, defying Hitler's orders even then, there were only 91,000 Germans left out of an original army of 280,000. Dazed and frostbitten, the German captives trudged through the snow to Soviet prison camps.

After Stalingrad, it was the Germans who were thrown on the defensive. Up and down the 1,800-mile front, Soviet tanks and artillery hammered Hitler's armies. By now, many German military leaders realized what Hitler refused to admit— that the Nazi empire was collapsing. The Third Reich's days were numbered.

Fascist rule crumbled in Italy.

By the spring of 1943, it was clear that the tide had turned in favor of the Allies. The question was where the Allied armies should attack next. Stalin urged the British and Americans to attack the Germans in western Europe, thus relieving pressure on the Soviet front. Churchill disagreed. Fearful of launching a full-scale invasion of western Europe too soon, he favored attacking Italy from the North African coast.

On July 9, 1943, an Allied invasion force of 160,000 soldiers and marines crossed the Mediterranean and approached the southern shore of Sicily. After a ferocious naval bombardment, they clambered into flat-bottomed landing craft, charged through knee-deep water, and won a beachhead on Sicily. Sicily fell to the Allies in August after a bloody but brief struggle lasting only 39 days.

Stunned by their army's collapse in Sicily, the Italian people forced the dictator Mussolini to resign. On July 25, 1943, he was placed under arrest. A new premier, Pietro Badoglio (bah-**DOHL**-yoh), took power. He renounced his country's pact with Hitler and urged the Italian people "to

719

SECTION 3 Objectives and Teaching Strategies

OBJECTIVE 1. Identify the Battle of Stalingrad and explain its importance.

Teaching Strategy: *Discussing History: The Battle of Stalingrad* (page 706d)

OBJECTIVE 2. Explain the importance of the D-Day invasion.

Teaching Strategy: *Discussing History: The Importance of D-Day* (page 706d)

OBJECTIVE 3. Evaluate Truman's decision to use the atom bomb against Japan.

Teaching Strategy: *Writing about History: How to Defeat Japan* (page 706e)

■ BACKGROUND

Germans bombed Stalingrad from the air but then could not move their tanks through the rubble-choked streets.

The Allied victories at El Alamein, Stalingrad, and Guadalcanal marked important turning points that prevented the Axis powers from reaching strategic objectives. The Axis never again won a major battle. Winston Churchill later wrote that in late 1942, the "hinge of fate," swung the war toward an eventual Allied victory.

SECTION 3 Resources

ENRICHMENT
■ Voices from the Past 31.3

ASSESSMENT
■ Section Quiz 31.3

GEOGRAPHY
■ Transparency 90

REINFORCEMENT
■ Independent Practice 31.3

719

Hitler began building the Atlantic Wall in 1942. During the next two years, a quarter of a million workers labored day and night to complete the project. The 2,400-mile-long barrier contained more than a million tons of steel and more than 20 million cubic yards of concrete. More than 300,000 German soldiers manned its network of observation towers, machine gun nests, and artillery stations. Nazi generals lined the beaches with antitank obstacles and more than 4 million land mines. When it was finally completed, Hitler confidently boasted, "No power on earth can drive us out of this region against our will."

fight the Germans in every way, everywhere, and all the time."

Italy's sudden change of loyalties did not save it from invasion. Hitler was determined to stop the Allies in Italy rather than fight on German soil. For almost two years, German armies occupied much of Italy, fiercely opposing Allied landings on Italy's western coast. The effort to free Italy did not succeed until 1945, when Germany itself was close to collapse.

The Allies invaded France.

Even as the Allies were battling for Italy in 1943, they began work on a daring plan to invade France and free western Europe from the Nazis. The enormous task of commanding the invasion fell to American General Dwight D. Eisenhower. Under his direction, the Allies gathered a force of 2 million British, American, and Canadian troops, together with mountains of military equipment and supplies. Another million stood ready to give sea and air support to the attack.

Hitler knew that such a force was being trained in Britain. The questions were when the invasion would take place and where on the French coast it would strike.

The Allies planned to attack Normandy in northern France. To keep their plans secret, the Allies set up a huge phantom army with its own headquarters and equipment. In radio messages they knew the Germans could read, Allied commanders sent orders to this make-believe army to attack the French port of Calais. Hitler was completely fooled and ordered his generals to keep a large army at Calais.

The Allied invasion, code-named D-Day, began on June 6, 1944. In the dead of night, an immense fleet of 5,300 ships set sail for their target, the beaches of Normandy. Shortly after midnight, 13,000 airborne troops parachuted into France.

Decisions in History

As Allied troops neared Paris in 1944, Hitler ordered General Choltiz to destroy the city. For the general, disobeying meant risking his own life and the lives of his family. Obeying meant destroying one of the world's most beautiful cities. What would you have done if you were General Choltiz? Why?

720

They were followed in the early morning hours by thousands upon thousands of seaborne soldiers—history's largest amphibious attack. After 5 days of fighting, the Allies held a strip of France 80 miles long. Less than 3 weeks later, 1 million men were ashore and moving steadily inland.

By the beginning of August 1944, German troops were pulling out of Paris to escape the Allied onslaught. Several units of the Free French movement led by Charles de Gaulle joined the Allies in their race toward Paris. Finally, on August 24, 1944, the Allies entered the city in triumph. Parisians were delirious with joy.

The German Reich collapsed.

Hitler now faced the old German nightmare—war on two fronts. The Soviet army, 5 million strong, advanced against Germany from the east. To the west, British and American forces were sweeping across the Rhine River into Germany itself. The German armies retreated.

The end was near for Hitler's Reich, but Hitler refused to recognize it. Germany must fight on, he said. "We shall never capitulate—never. We may be destroyed, but if we are, we shall drag a world with us—a world in flames." Yet, when Soviet tanks stood at the very gates of Berlin, the thought of falling into Soviet hands proved too much for him. On April 30, 1945, Hitler killed himself.

Mussolini, the overthrown Fascist dictator of Italy, was dead too. He had been assassinated on April 28.

The Allies too lost a leader in the same month. Franklin Roosevelt had just begun his fourth term as president. On April 12, 1945, an artist was drawing the president's portrait. Suddenly Roosevelt said, "I have a terrific headache." He never spoke again. A few hours later, Americans were stunned to learn that Roosevelt had died from a cerebral hemorrhage. Across the United States, people wept at the news. Wartime allies from Britain to China mourned.

Roosevelt's successor, Harry Truman, was president when the German Reich finally collapsed. On May 2, 1945, Berlin formally surrendered to the Soviet army. On May 7, the commanders of the German army and navy signed papers declaring the unconditional surrender of their forces. The war in Europe was over.

World War II in Europe and North Africa, 1939–1945

KEY
- Allies or under Allied control, Dec. 1941
- Major Axis powers
- Greatest extent of Axis control, Dec. 1941
- Neutral nations
- Allied advances
- Maginot line

ANSWERS TO Map Study

France, Belgium, Netherlands, Luxemburg, Denmark, Norway, Finland, Estonia, Latvia, Lithuania, Poland, Czechslovakia, Hungary, Romania, Bulgaria, Albania, Greece, Yugoslavia, part of USSR; from west through France, from south through Italy, and from east from USSR

Map Study

List the nations under Axis control in Europe in 1941. By what three major routes did the Allies close in on the Axis powers after 1943?

A *final horror ended the Pacific war.*

Meanwhile, Allied forces in the Pacific were closing in on Japan. By 1945, the Allies had reclaimed much of the Pacific, including the Philippines. From strategic bases such as Saipan in the Mariana Islands, the Allies launched long-range bombing missions against Japan.

In February, American marines landed on Iwo Jima, an island only 750 miles from Tokyo. The marines took the island after a month of bitter fighting and heavy losses. Then they moved on to the Ryukyu Islands just south of Japan. They captured Okinawa on April 1. The ordeal cost 45,000 American lives.

The taking of Iwo Jima and Okinawa opened the way for an invasion of Japan. However, Allied leaders knew that such an invasion would be a desperate struggle. Japan still had a large army that would defend every inch of its homeland. Moreover, thousands of Japanese pilots volunteered for suicide missions. These *kamikazes,* as they were called, crashed their explosive-filled planes into Allied ships, killing themselves at the same time.

President Truman saw only one way to avoid an invasion of Japan. He decided to use a powerful new weapon called the atom bomb.

By the 1930's, nuclear physicists had shown that the splitting of uranium atoms let loose tremendous energy. During the war, American scientists had urged President Roosevelt to develop a bomb using the energy of the atom before the Germans did so. Among the international team of scientists who urged the building of such a bomb were Albert Einstein and Lise Meitner,

■ BACKGROUND

In 1942, General Douglas MacArthur, commander of United States forces in the Pacific, fled the Philippines. When he arrived in Australia, MacArthur told reporters, "I came through and I shall return." Less than three years later, he returned to the Philippines. As he triumphantly waded ashore, MacArthur proclaimed, "People of the Philippines! I have returned. . . . Rally to me!"

721

Define:
Japanese pilot who volunteered for a suicide mission

Identify:
(a) German general, "Desert Fox" (b) commander of British forces in North Africa (c) commander of Allied forces in North Africa; commanded the Allied invasion of France (d) Soviet commander at the Battle of Stalingrad (e) code name for the day of the Allied invasion of Normandy (f) first city to be destroyed by atomic bomb

Answer:
1. (a) Whoever controlled North Africa controlled Suez Canal. (b) pushed British forces across North Africa to the Suez Canal (c) beginning of Allied drive to seize North African coast

2. Soviets trapped the Germans and cut off their supplies.

3. Mussolini was forced to resign, and Italians turned against the Germans.

4. In an all-out effort, Allies invaded Normandy.

5. The German Reich collapsed when German armies had to fight a war on two fronts.

6. (a) allowed them to avoid a costly invasion of Japan (b) August 6, on Hiroshima; August 9, on Nagasaki

7. One alternative might have been to demonstrate the power of the bomb to Japanese leaders on an uninhabited island.

This painting by a Japanese artist shows the aftermath of the atom bomb explosion at Hiroshima on August 6, 1945.

Jewish refugees from Nazi Germany, and a refugee from Fascist Italy named Enrico Fermi.

The first test of the new bomb took place on July 16, 1945, at Alamogordo in the New Mexican desert. The blinding burst of light and awesome roar of the first explosion was described by one witness as "magnificent, beautiful, stupendous, and terrifying."

Truman was delighted that the testing of this secret weapon had been successful. From the German city of Potsdam, where he was meeting with Churchill and Stalin, Truman issued a declaration on July 26, 1945. He warned the Japanese that they faced "prompt and utter destruction" unless they surrendered at once. The Japanese government did not reply.

On the morning of August 6, 1945, an American B-29 bomber released an atom bomb nicknamed "Little Boy" over Japan. The bomb drifted by parachute toward its target, Hiroshima, a city of 343,000 people. Two thirds of Hiroshima was instantly destroyed by the blast. About 80,000 people perished in the searing heat. Three days later, on August 9, a second atom bomb destroyed the city of Nagasaki and killed 40,000 people.

Aghast at these horrors, Japan's Emperor Hirohito urged his generals to surrender. He told them, "I cannot bear to see my innocent people suffer any longer." The formal surrender took place on

722

September 2, 1945, on the wide deck of the American battleship *Missouri* in Tokyo Bay. Representatives of the Allied powers watched as Japan's foreign minister signed the surrender.

Define: kamikaze
Identify: (a) Erwin Rommel, (b) Bernard Montgomery, (c) Dwight D. Eisenhower, (d) Georgi Zhukov, (e) D-Day, (f) Hiroshima
Answer:
1. (a) Why was North Africa vital to the British? (b) What did Rommel accomplish there? (c) Why was El Alamein a turning point?
2. How were the Germans defeated at Stalingrad?
3. What were the results of the Allied invasion of Sicily?
4. How was the invasion of France carried out?
5. How did the war in Europe draw to a close?
6. (a) How did the development of the atom bomb change Allied plans for the defeat of Japan? (b) When and where were atom bombs used?

Critical Thinking
7. Evaluate Truman's decision to use the atom bomb. What alternatives might have been considered?

World War II left a mixed legacy. 4

World War II generated waves of change that are still being felt in the world today. As you will see in this section, the war caused unprecedented destruction. At the same time, it also helped to create a new postwar age.

World War II caused massive destruction.

World War II caused more destruction than any other conflict in human history. Although no one knows how many people died, most experts estimate that the number of war dead reached at least 40 million.

Both the Allies and the Axis powers absorbed terrible losses. The Soviet Union alone suffered 20 million casualties, more losses than all the nations put together in World War I. At least 4.2 million Germans followed Hitler to their deaths. In addition, 4.3 million Poles, 2.2 million Chinese, and almost 2 million Japanese died in the conflict. Although the United States entered the war late, it suffered 291,000 killed and 670,000 wounded.

The cost in property damage was also devastating. Vast areas of Europe, China, and Japan were reduced to rubble. Historical cathedrals, homes, factories, and schools were all damaged. For example, one fifth of the dwellings in Poland were destroyed.

In some areas of Germany and Japan, the living envied the dead. Millions of displaced persons wandered across these shattered nations begging for help. Thousands of people starved to death during the first months after the war ended.

The Holocaust claimed the lives of six million Jews.

The Nazi nightmare did not stop on the battlefields of Europe. As you have seen (pages 694–696), Hitler divided humankind into two groups—a German master race and a lesser race composed of everyone else. Hitler hoped to enslave the non-Germanic peoples of Europe such as the Poles and Russians. He had other plans, however, for the group he hated most—the Jews.

Mass murder in eastern Europe Shortly after coming to power, Hitler deprived Jews of their political rights and property (page 696). The Kristallnacht signaled the beginning of a far more dangerous assault on the Jewish community.

The Jews' worst fears became a reality when Hitler conquered Poland and invaded Russia. Approximately 8 million Jews lived in the lands brought under Hitler's control. As Nazi armies swept across eastern Europe, they were followed by special SS units known as *Einsatzgruppen,* or mobile killing units.

The SS commander Heinrich Himmler ordered his troops to kill as many civilians as possible, especially Jews. In town after town, the SS methodically rounded up Jews and any other people who threatened Nazi rule. They then took their prisoners to isolated fields where no one would observe them. The killing units then brutally shot innocent men, women, and children and hid their bodies in mass graves. Historians now believe that the SS killing units murdered 1.4 million Jews.

The ghettos The killing squads were part of a program of mass murder that Nazi leaders began to call the final solution of the Jewish question. During the next stage of the final solution, Polish Jews were herded into confined areas of large cities called ghettos. The Nazis sealed each ghetto off from the rest of the city with barbed wire and stone walls. Jews caught outside the ghetto were usually killed.

By the end of 1941, most Polish Jews were confined inside badly overcrowded ghettos. The Warsaw ghetto, for example, contained half a million people squeezed into an area that usually housed 10,000. "The streets are so overpopulated," wrote one survivor, "it is difficult to push one's way through. Everyone is ragged, in tatters. Often they no longer even possess a shirt."

Despite these horrible conditions, the Jews valiantly struggled to maintain their traditions and keep their dignity. Ghetto theaters produced

Jews in Warsaw were forced to leave their homes and live in overcrowded ghettos.

723

SECTION 4 Objectives and Teaching Strategies

OBJECTIVE 1. Identify the Holocaust and explain how its victims are memorialized.

Teaching Strategy: *Relating Past to Present: The Holocaust* (page 706e)

OBJECTIVE 2. Explain and evaluate the reasons behind the internment of Japanese Americans during the war.

Teaching Strategy: *Discussing History: The Internment of Japanese Americans* (page 706e)

■ BACKGROUND

The Nazis portrayed their victims as subhuman. Britons and Americans were depicted as weak, decadent people who stood no chance against the strong, well-organized forces of Nazi Germany.

SECTION 4 Resources

ASSESSMENT
■ Section Quiz 31.4

REINFORCEMENT
■ Independent Practice 31.4

ENRICHMENT
■ Voices from the Past 31.4

ANSWERS TO
Voice from the Past

1. the Jews

2. because their families were in hiding, confined, or killed in the death camps; that friends and relatives did not know where the prisoners were

3. It was unexpected and symbolized their link with loved ones and with the outside world.

4. They had a strong will to survive and were determined to resist giving in to the Nazi system. Their ability to maintain hope was a triumph of the human spirit.

plays and concerts. Teachers taught lessons in secret schools. And writers kept records so that the rest of the world would find out the truth about what was happening.

The death camps The ghettos were only allowed to last a short time. In 1942 the Nazis began to replace the ghettos with death camps. On January 20, 1942, 16 top Nazi officials met in the Berlin suburb of Wannsee to coordinate the total destruction of the Jewish people. Such an attempt to kill an entire people is known as **genocide.**

During the remainder of the war, Jews and other victims of Nazi persecution were finally sent to more than 30 death camps located primarily in Germany and Poland. When the victims arrived, they were divided into two groups. In one group were those judged healthy enough to do heavy labor for the Nazi state. In the other were those who were to die at once. Always included in this second group were babies, young children, and aging grandparents. They might be shot, bayoneted, or gassed. Any who were merely wounded were buried alive.

At some camps, those selected for death were stripped of their clothes and herded into a chamber that their guards called a shower room. With chilling candor, the director of the Auschwitz (**OWSH**-vits) camp in Poland described his system for killing people.

Voice from the Past | *Moments of Reprieve*

Primo Levi, a young Italian Jew, was in Auschwitz, the largest of the Nazi death camps, from 1944 until the camp was freed in early 1945. Unlike the vast majority of Jews who were sent there and killed immediately, Primo Levi was set to work as a slave laborer in a nearby chemical factory.

At Auschwitz, the various categories of prisoners . . . were allowed to receive gifts, but not the Jews. Anyway, from whom could the Jews have received them? From their families, exterminated or confined in the surviving ghettos? From the very few who had escaped the roundups, hidden in cellars, in attics, terrified and penniless? And who knew our address? For all the world knew we were dead.

And yet a package did find its way to me, through a chain of friends, sent by my sister and my mother, who were hidden in Italy . . . The package contained ersatz chocolate, cookies, and powdered milk, but to describe its real value, the impact it had on me and my friend Alberto, is beyond the powers of ordinary language . . . That unexpected, improbable, impossible package was like a meteorite, a heavenly object, charged with symbols, immensely precious, and with an enormous momentum.

We were no longer alone: a link with the outside world had been established, and there were delicious things to eat for days and days. But there were also serious practical problems . . . Where to put the food? . . . How to protect it? . . . Our year-old hunger kept pushing us toward the worst possible solution: to eat everything right then and there . . . Our weakened stomachs could not have coped with the abuse; within an hour, it would have ended in indigestion or worse.

1. According to Primo Levi, which group of prisoners received the worst treatment?
2. Why was it almost impossible for Jewish prisoners in Auschwitz to hear from relatives or friends?
3. Why was the gift of a package of food so important?
4. Judging from what you have read about the Holocaust, how do you think people like Primo Levi maintained hope?

When they came for the Communists, I did not speak, because I was not a Communist.
When they came for the Jews, I did not speak, because I was not a Jew.
When they came for the Union Leaders, I did not speak, because I was not a Union Leader.
When they came for me, there was no one left to speak.

Martin Niemöller, German clergyman, after his release from Dachau

On April 10, 1945, American troops reached Buchenwald, a concentration camp with 20,000 prisoners. Many were too near death to be saved.

I used Zyklon B, which was a crystallized prussic acid, which we dropped into the death chamber from a small opening. It took 3 to 15 minutes to kill the people in the death chamber, depending upon climatic conditions. We knew when the people were dead because their screaming stopped. We usually waited about a half hour before we opened the doors and removed the bodies.

This cruel efficiency enabled Nazi officials at Auschwitz to slaughter up to 30,000 people a day. By the end of the war, 1.75 million people had been killed in Auschwitz alone. Altogether the Nazis murdered 6 million Poles, Russians, Czechs, and other civilians. This horrible destruction of human life is now known as the **Holocaust.**

Resistance The Holocaust claimed the lives of three out of every four Jews living in Europe. In many cases, the survivors owed their lives to the heroic deeds of their Christian neighbors. For example, many families in Amsterdam risked their lives by hiding Jews inside their homes. In Poland, Benedictine nuns concealed Jews in their convent. The Archbishop of Toulouse, France, defied the Nazi occupation authorities by stating, "There is a Christian morality . . . that confers rights and duties. These duties and these rights come from God . . . the Jews are our brethren . . . No Christian dare forget that."

A Swedish diplomat named Raoul Wallenberg courageously demonstrated his duty to help others. Backed by the Swedish government and the Catholic Church, he successfully protected thousands of Hungarian Jews from the Nazis.

Although unarmed and outnumbered, many Jews chose to resist the Nazis. The best-known uprising occurred in the Warsaw ghetto. A small number of Jews armed with homemade weapons repelled repeated Nazi assaults. When the ghetto fell, almost no one was left alive.

Almost 200,000 Jews managed to survive the horrors of the Nazi death camps. Many clung to life so that they could bear witness to what had happened. The survivors' efforts were not in vain.

725

■ BACKGROUND

German SS officers committed unimaginably brutal acts against individuals. The commander of a labor camp in Poland, for example, would stroll to his doorstep after breakfast and shoot a Jewish prisoner who was not working hard enough.

■ DISCUSSION

The German SS chief Adolph Eichmann was determined to destroy the Jewish community in Hungary. Raoul Wallenberg, a Swedish diplomat in Hungary, was equally determined to prevent that destruction. He had repeatedly thwarted Eichmann's efforts. In December 1944, Eichmann and Wallenberg finally confronted each other at the Swedish embassy in Budapest. Wallenberg fearlessly attacked Eichmann's Nazi racial doctrines. Seeing that he was losing the argument, Eichmann confessed, "I admit that you are right, Herr Wallenberg. I have never believed in nazism, as such, but it has given me power and wealth." Ask students to write a paragraph explaining how they would respond to Eichmann's statement. (Unfortunately, no record exists of what, if anything, Wallenberg said.)

Ask each student to write down the most important lesson he or she has learned from studying the Holocaust. Compile these lessons into a class list. Then read and discuss the following excerpt from a passage by Elie Wiesel describing his view on the Holocaust's most important lessons.

"The Holocaust, as we so poorly call the extermination of 6 million European Jews will remain a watershed in history. Are there lessons to be drawn from it? If so, they are simple ones, and they have a bearing on current affairs and crises.

"For instance, we may learn that both in good and evil the impossible is possible. And that hatred leads to murder and murder to more murder. And that whatever happens to one community affects all others. . . .

"In other words: When injustice occurs—and war is the greatest injustice of all—indifference is not only a sin but also a punishment. Thus intervention becomes a moral imperative. Everywhere? Yes everywhere. That is the duty of nations and individuals."

When an SS commander named Adolf Eichmann was asked about his hideous deeds, he replied, "I will obey, obey, obey." The Holocaust demonstrated that evil orders must never be obeyed and that the values of tolerance and respect for others must be preserved.

Cause and Effect
WORLD WAR II

Long-Term Causes

Discontent about Treaty of Versailles
Worldwide economic depression
Rise of totalitarian governments

Immediate Causes

Expansionism of Germany, Italy, and Japan
Failure of policy of appeasement
German invasion of Poland

WORLD WAR II

Immediate Effects

Devastation and loss of life in Europe and Asia
Recognition of Holocaust
Overthrow of fascism
Founding of United Nations
Demilitarization of Germany and Japan
Rise of U.S. and USSR as superpowers
Soviet control of Eastern Europe

Long-Term Effects

Cold War
Divided Germany
Formation of NATO and Warsaw Pact
Development of nuclear capability
Rise of nationalism in colonial territories

726

World War II *changed America.*

One week after the Japanese surrender, Winston Churchill told the House of Commons: "America stands at this moment at the summit of the world." Churchill's statement accurately reflected a new reality in global affairs. World War II had a lasting impact upon American life and the nation's place in the world.

The production miracle Early in 1942, President Roosevelt requested of American industry the immediate production of 60,000 warplanes. The President's request seemed impossible to meet. Nonetheless Ford Motor Company engineers believed they could design assembly lines capable of mass-producing B-24's. At the giant Willow Run factory near Detroit, 42,000 workers soon began to turn out a B-24 every hour. By the end of the war, American aircraft factories had produced more than 296,000 planes.

The United States also manufactured 102,000 tanks, 2.4 million trucks, and 87,600 warships. This equipment changed the course and outcome of the war. American Sherman tanks crashed through the German lines at El Alamein. Russian armies used American trucks to transport their troops. Joseph Stalin admitted, "This war would have been lost" without American production.

While expanded production helped to win the war, it also ended the Great Depression. From 1939 to 1945, the total value of goods and services produced by American workers more than doubled and unemployment virtually vanished.

Women and minorities World War II created new opportunities for American women. With more than 12 million men in the armed forces, the government urged women to take their places in the work force. Women responded by taking jobs in record numbers. By the end of the war, 36 percent of all women were in the work force. This experience changed the attitudes of many women about their traditional roles in society.

The war was also a turning point for African Americans. Thousands of them left the rural South for higher paying jobs in defense industries in the Northeast and Midwest. After fighting for freedom abroad, many African American soldiers returned home determined to end racial discrimination. This new attitude helped to spark the civil rights movement in the 1950's.

The imprisonment of Japanese Americans While World War II created new opportunities for women and African Americans, it produced tragic results for Japanese Americans. When the war began, 120,000 Japanese Americans lived in the United States. Most lived on the west coast.

As you have seen, the surprise attack on Pearl Harbor stunned the nation. Panic-stricken citizens feared that the Japanese would soon attack the west coast. False rumors spread that Japanese Americans were committing sabotage by mining coastal harbors and poisoning vegetables.

Fear and uncertainty created an ugly wave of prejudice against Japanese Americans. President Roosevelt felt he could no longer ignore the public's fears. On February 19, 1942, he authorized the establishment of military areas from which people posing a threat could be excluded.

One month later thousands of Japanese Americans were given only two days' notice of this move. Many were evacuated to **internment camps,** or prisonlike camps. No specific charges were ever filed against the Japanese Americans, and no evidence of subversion was ever found. Faced with expulsion, terrified families were forced to sell their homes and businesses for less than their true value.

The majority of internment camps were located in the desert. Each family was forced to live in a tiny apartment inside wooden barracks covered with tar paper. Barbed wire and army patrols restricted their freedom of movement.

Despite this mistreatment, Japanese Americans nevertheless demonstrated their patriotism by pledging allegiance to the American flag each day. Approximately 20,000 Japanese-American men voluntarily enlisted in the armed forces. Many won medals for their courage.

Four decades later, Americans acknowledged the terrible mistreatment of Japanese Americans during World War II. In 1988, Congress voted a taxfree payment of $20,000 to all those who had been sent to relocation camps. Congress also officially apologized to Japanese Americans for the grave injustice they had suffered.

A new role Just as the war produced vast social and economic changes, it also altered the United States role in the world. Americans could no longer isolate themselves from global affairs. As you will see in the next chapter, the United States soon entered a new era of world leadership.

This drawing by a Japanese American shows a young girl on her way to an internment camp.

Section REVIEW 4

Define: (a) genocide, (b) Holocaust, (c) internment camps
Identify: (a) *Einsatzgruppen,* (b) Zyklon B, (c) Auschwitz, (d) Raoul Wallenberg
Answer:
1. How did Jews cope with the trauma of being confined inside ghettos?
2. Give three examples of how Christians helped rescue Jews from the Holocaust.
3. What were two ways in which Jews resisted the Holocaust?
4. (a) How did American production help win the war? (b) What impact did the production miracle have upon life in the United States?
5. What new opportunities did World War II create for women and African Americans?
6. Why were Japanese Americans sent to internment camps?

Critical Thinking
7. Top Nazi officials defended their actions during the Holocaust by saying that they were only following orders. Do you agree with this defense? Explain your answer.

727

ANSWERS TO
Section Review 4

Define:
(a) killing of an entire people (b) systematic and deliberate destruction of the Jews by the Nazis (c) camps where Japanese Americans were relocated

Identify:
(a) German mobile killing units (b) chemical used in concentration camp gas chambers (c) concentration camp (d) Swedish diplomat who rescued Jews

Answer:
1. put on plays and concerts, ran secret schools, kept written records
2. Families in Amsterdam hid Jews in their homes. Nuns in Poland concealed Jews in their convent. Raoul Wallenberg and the Catholic Church protected Hungarian Jews.
3. staged ghetto uprisings, clung to life in the death camps
4. (a) supplied Allies with war equipment (b) ended the Depression, unemployment
5. Both women and African Americans entered the industrial workforce. African Americans came home from the war eager to win freedom in their own country.
6. fear of sabotage
7. Students' answers will vary.

Concluding the Chapter

1. **Chapter Closer**
   Ask students to choose six events described in this chapter that they regard as the most important benchmarks or turning points in the story of World War II. Students should use facts to defend their choices.

2. **Reteaching Activities**
   a. Making a Time Line
   Have each student make a time line of major World War II events between 1939 and 1945.
   b. Analyzing Have students develop a list of the major mistakes made by the leaders of Great Britain, Germany, Japan, the Soviet Union, and the United States during World War II. Ask students to evaluate the consequences of each mistake.

Answers to Chapter Review appear on page 706f.

Summary

1. Germany overran much of Europe. In the spring of 1939, Hitler announced his intention to take over the Polish Corridor. Britain and France responded by ending appeasement. Soon after, Hitler signed a nonaggression pact with Stalin. World War II in Europe began when Germany overran Poland. The Soviets followed by taking over the Baltic nations. By June 1940, Germany had overwhelmed Scandinavia and moved into France. On June 10, Italy joined the war on the side of Germany. After the fall of France, Germany began an unsuccessful air attack on Britain. Germany next invaded the Soviet Union but was halted by the severe Russian winter.

2. Japan conquered an Asian empire. Japan's conquests in Asia began in 1931 with the takeover of Manchuria. Six years later, Japan moved into China proper. The war in China was slowed by dwindling Japanese resources even as the United States was aiding the Allies with war supplies. When the United States cut off shipments of resources to Japan, Japan prepared to move into Southeast Asia. On December 7, 1941, Japan bombed Pearl Harbor in Hawaii and brought the United States into the war. Soon Japan held most of the western Pacific, but Allied victories at Midway and in the Coral Sea halted Japan.

3. The Allies launched a drive to victory. After defeating German forces in North Africa, Allied troops successfully invaded southern Europe, thus causing the collapse of Mussolini's government. To the east, defeat at Stalingrad gave rise to the threat of invasion of Germany on two fronts. A major Allied offensive began on D-Day, resulting in German surrender. The Allies ended the war in the Pacific by dropping atom bombs on Hiroshima and Nagasaki.

4. World War II left a mixed legacy. The war caused terrible loss of human life, with losses highest in the Soviet Union. More than 6 million Jews perished in the Holocaust, the Nazis' program of genocide. Wartime changes in the United States included increased output of weapons and new opportunities for women and minorities. Confinement to internment camps caused hardships for Japanese Americans.

Reviewing the Facts

1. Define the following terms:
   a. blitzkrieg   b. genocide
2. Explain the importance of each of the following names, dates, places, or terms:
   a. Polish Corridor   c. Churchill
   b. Luftwaffe   d. Maginot Line

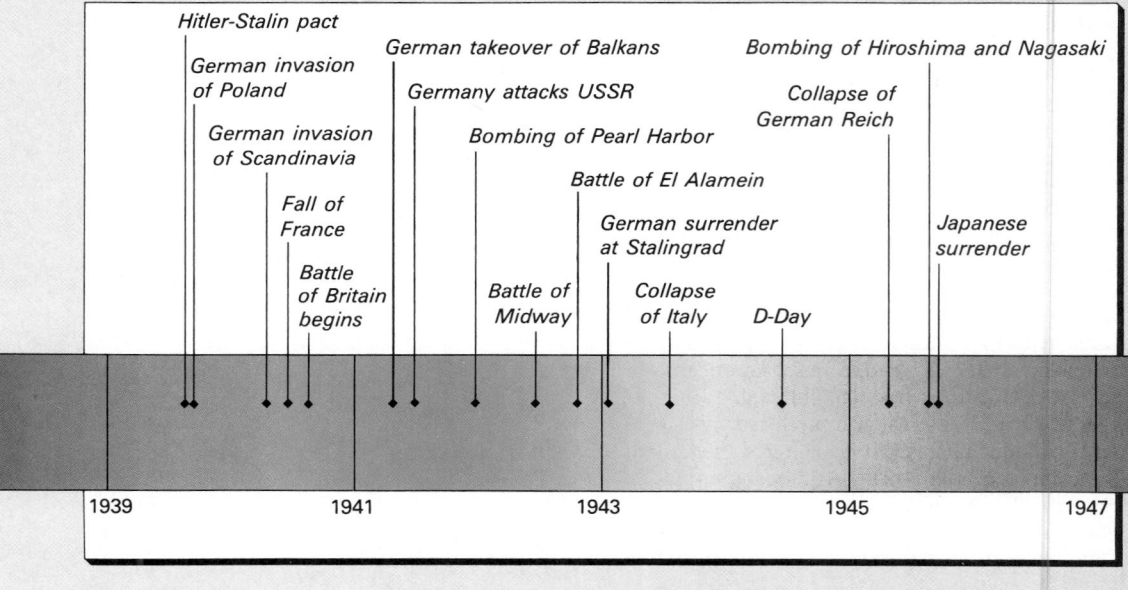

Timeline events: Hitler-Stalin pact; German invasion of Poland; German invasion of Scandinavia; Fall of France; Battle of Britain begins; German takeover of Balkans; Germany attacks USSR; Bombing of Pearl Harbor; Battle of Midway; Battle of El Alamein; German surrender at Stalingrad; Collapse of Italy; D-Day; Bombing of Hiroshima and Nagasaki; Collapse of German Reich; Japanese surrender. Timeline years: 1939, 1941, 1943, 1945, 1947.

728

e. Dunkirk
f. Vichy Regime
g. Free French
h. De Gaulle
i. RAF
j. Roosevelt
k. Lend-Lease Act

l. December 7, 1941
m. Battle of Midway
n. Holocaust
o. Rommel
p. Montgomery
q. Eisenhower
r. Truman

3. (a) What factors led to the fall of France? (b) How was France governed after its fall?
4. How did World War II in Asia begin?
5. (a) What did Roosevelt do to help the Allies between 1939 and 1941? (b) What brought the United States into the war?
6. (a) Why did the Allies look to the United States for supplies? (b) How did wartime propaganda harm Japanese Americans?
7. (a) What was the significance of El Alamein? (b) Of the Battle of Stalingrad?
8. (a) What were the results of the Allied invasion of southern Europe? (b) How was the invasion of western Europe carried out?
9. (a) Describe the end of the war in Europe. (b) Describe the end of the war in the Pacific.

Basic Skills

1. **Reading and interpreting a time line** (a) On the time line on page 728, which events were victories for the Allies? (b) For the Axis Powers? (c) Why are the Battle of Britain and the Battle of Midway considered turning points in the war?
2. **Interpreting a map** (a) Judging from the map on page 721, why was victory in North Africa essential to an invasion of southern Europe? (b) How does this map explain why Hitler feared a two-front war?

Researching and Reporting Skills

1. **Interviewing an eyewitness** Interview someone in your community who experienced World War II. Prepare a list of questions about the person's experiences in the war. Ask if the person would mind if you taped the interview; otherwise, take brief notes. Report on the interview to the class.
2. **Using memoirs** In the memoirs of a key figure in World War II, such as Churchill or De Gaulle, read a chapter that deals with some critical moment of the war. How does this information add to your understanding of the time?
3. **Creating a museum of artifacts and souvenirs** As

a class, search your home and community for objects and memorabilia of World War II, such as old photographs, newspapers, letters, or other materials. Display these objects as a class exhibit, making labels for the different objects with a brief explanation.

Critical Thinking

1. **Analyzing** (a) What were the advantages and disadvantages of the Axis powers at the start of the war? (b) Of the Allies?
2. **Analyzing** (a) Why did the Japanese government make the decision to attack Pearl Harbor? (b) What did Japan expect the result to be? (c) What in fact was the outcome?
3. **Evaluating** (a) Evaluate the importance to the Allied cause of the Battle of Britain, the Battle of Midway, and the invasion of Normandy. (b) Which do you think contributed most to Allied victory, and why?
4. **Analyzing ideas** Through the Holocaust, Hitler directed a program of genocide against the Jewish people. (a) What measures were used to carry out this program? (b) Why is genocide considered a crime against humanity?

Perspectives on Past and Present

World War II was truly a worldwide war. How does it differ from local or regional wars, such as the Vietnam War, Iran-Iraq War, Falklands War, and other similar conflicts?

Investigating History

1. Watch the videotape of such movies as *The Sands of Iwo Jima, From Here to Eternity,* and *The Longest Day,* which are focused on aspects of World War II. What impressions do you gain about the war and the people in it?
2. Make a study of one of the ghettos or death camps set up by the Nazis. Who were the Jews living in the ghetto or brought to the death camp? To what extent were there survivors?
3. Read selections from the writings or biography of one general of World War II, such as MacArthur, Eisenhower, Patton, Montgomery, or Rommel. Or read selections from Morison's *History of the United States Naval Operations in World War Two.* How do the impressions here differ from those in movies about the war?

729

CHAPTER
Evaluation

Chapter Test 31, Alternate Chapter Test 31, and Computer Test Bank Chapter 31 Test can be used to evaluate your students' understanding of this chapter.

ANSWERS TO
Geographic Theme

1. (a) part of eastern Finland, Estonia, Latvia, Lithuania, part of eastern Poland and Czechoslovakia, and Bessarabia **(b)** Soviet territory in Europe was substantially increased between 1941 and 1945.

2. pursued policy of expanding to the west to obtain warm-water ports and territories to serve as buffer against any invasion

3. (a) The Soviet Union emerged from World War II as a superpower due to success in war, military and industrial power, size of territory and population, and wealth of resources.
(b) New territories added to size, population, resources, industry, and warm-water ports for trade and naval bases.

Geographic Theme: Location

How did Soviet territory expand in the course of World War II?

Every nation views the world from its own perspective. The view from Moscow was unique because of the vastness of the lands ruled from there. The Soviet Union occupied one third of Asia and nearly half of Europe. Only the waters of the Bering Strait separate Siberia from a third continent, North America.

Being the world's largest nation had its problems. In the 1930's, the Soviet Union shared a common border with more than a dozen nations. Along most of those borders, high mountains give natural protection. To the west, however, the North European Plain stretches unprotected. Thus, the military build-up of Nazi Germany during the 1930's was of great concern to Soviet leaders.

The map on page 708 of your text shows the Soviet position in Europe at the start of 1939. That situation lasted only briefly. In August of 1941, people in Western Europe were stunned by word of a German-Soviet nonaggression pact. Each nation agreed to remain neutral if the other was at war. What people did not know was that a secret clause in the pact provided for the takeover of other countries by both nations. When German armies invaded Poland, Soviet armies took over the lands promised to them.

Almost two years after the start of World War II, the nonaggression pact ended abruptly when Hitler invaded the Soviet Union in June of 1941. German armies moved eastward, reaching as far as Moscow and Stalingrad (now Volgograd). Then invasion turned to retreat. Soviet armies surged west across the plain in pursuit of the retreating German army. At war's end, in 1945, they were at Berlin and the Elbe River, deep within Germany itself. The western Soviet Union and the lands it acquired as a result of the war are shown on the map below.

1. (a) What lands did the Soviets gain in the pact with Germany? (b) Compare the extent of Soviet territory in Europe in 1945 with that in January 1941.
2. What traditional policy of the czars did Stalin pursue in this seizure of territory?
3. (a) Describe the change in the Soviet role as a world power from 1941 to 1945. (b) How may the added territories have contributed to that change?

The Growth of the Soviet Union (Europe), 1939–1945

KEY
- Pre-war boundaries, 1939
- Soviet aggressions, 1939-1940
- National boundaries, 1945
- Soviet territorial gain, 1944

Historical Themes

The years between 1914 and 1945 provide important examples of the role that key ideas, economic forces, influential leaders, and the processes of cooperation and conflict played in shaping world events.

Impact of Ideas

A number of ideas had a significant impact on the early twentieth century. In Russia, the idea of communism—originated by Marx and developed by Lenin—became the basis of a new political and economic system. In Stalin's hands, it became the means to a totalitarian state. In Italy and Germany, the concept of fascism took hold through its appeal to people on the basis of political power and national glory. Combined with nationalism and imperialism, it provided Hitler and Mussolini with a philosophy for aggression and world conquest.

India's Mahatma Gandhi gave the world a more powerful and lasting idea—that of peaceful change through nonviolent resistance. In India, that idea became a means to gaining independence.

Economics and History

Rarely in history has a single economic event had the political and social impact that the Great Depression had on the world of the 1930's. Virtually every country on every continent was affected by the tremendous economic decline that began with the Wall Street crash of 1929. The extreme conditions of hunger, unemployment, and economic insecurity caused by the Depression created an environment in some countries where the political extreme of fascism could thrive. The Depression left a legacy of doubt and fear that would mark the generation that lived through it.

Cooperation and Conflict

Both of the great wars of the twentieth century grew out of military aggression and the desire for political expansion. There were, however, significant differences between the two conflicts. World War I resulted from a breakdown in the balance of power that had preserved peace in Europe for over a century. World War II, by contrast, resulted from the willingness of military powers—notably Germany, Italy, and Japan—to use aggression as a means for conquest.

Only through defensive wars could other nations—such as Britain, the United States, the Soviet Union, and China—survive.

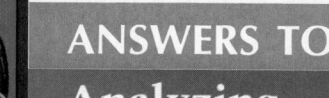

Although peace remained elusive in the decades after World War II, the principle of international cooperation, set forth in the charter of the United Nations, was firmly established. The destruction and horror of World War II would for generations symbolize the futility of war and the need for peaceful means to resolve conflicts.

Individuals and History

The ideas and actions of individuals continued to affect events and the direction of change in the twentieth century. Stalin and Hitler forged powerful totalitarian regimes that systematically violated human rights. By contrast, Wilson, Churchill, and Roosevelt championed the democratic ideas expressed in the Fourteen Points and the Atlantic Charter.* Eleanor Roosevelt led the United Nations commission that wrote the UN's Universal Declaration of Human Rights (page 739).

Analyzing Historical Themes

1. (a) Identify the main characteristics of fascism. (b) What factors account for the rise of fascism in the years between the wars?
2. (a) In what ways did the Depression contribute to the rise of fascism? (b) Why did the Depression leave a legacy of fear and uncertainty?
3. (a) How did the aims of Germany, Great Britain, Russia (the USSR), and the United States in World War I compare with those in World War II? (b) Compare the wars' outcomes for each country.
4. To what extent did Hitler represent the times in which he lived?

*This charter was a statement of goals for the postwar world drawn up by Franklin Roosevelt and Winston Churchill in August 1941. Among the goals was the restoration of sovereign rights and self-government to "those who had been forcibly deprived of them." The charter also included Roosevelt's Four Freedoms—freedom of speech and expression, freedom of worship, freedom from want, and freedom from fear.

731

ANSWERS TO

Analyzing Historical Themes

1. **(a)** appealed to desire for political power and national glory, provided philosophy for military aggression and conquest **(b)** appeal of nationalism and imperialism, rise of influential leaders, impact of Great Depression

2. **(a)** extreme conditions of hunger, unemployment, and economic insecurity created receptive environment for fascism **(b)** nearly everyone was affected, conditions were extreme, allowed fascism to thrive

3. **(a)** Germany was an aggressor in both WWI and WWII; Britain, Russia (USSR), and the U.S. were on the defensive in both wars. **(b)** In both wars, Germany was defeated and the Allies were successful.

4. representative in the sense of nationalism, quest for power; unrepresentative in extent of aggression, racism, and inhumanity to Jews

UNIT Evaluation

Unit VIII Test and Alternate Unit VIII test can be used to evaluate your students' understanding of this unit.

731

Chapters

Singapore, traditional and modern

	1946	1954	1962
Political and Governmental Life	**1947** India and Pakistan become independent **1948** Israel becomes a nation	**1950's–1970's** African nations gain independence	**1964–1975** Vietnam War *Kwame Nkrumah*
Economic and Technological Life	 *Marshall Plan aid to Europe*	**1957** European Common Market is organized **1960** OPEC is founded	
Social and Cultural Life	**1948** South Africa adopts apartheid **1949** China becomes Communist		▲ **1966–1976** Mao leads China in Cultural Revolution *Detail of painting by Haitian artist Joseph Jean-Gilles*

Unit IX

The Modern World

Historical Themes

Cooperation and Conflict The postwar era saw a new type of conflict, the Cold War, which was reflected in opposing alliances. Elsewhere, leaders sought ways to limit regional, ethnic, and religious conflict.

The Impact of Ideas The conflicting ideologies of communism and democracy were expressed in the Cold War. While nationalism inspired colonies to gain independence, fundamentalism emphasized traditional values.

Economics and History Aid from the United States speeded the postwar economic recovery of Western Europe and Japan, both of which prospered. Slow development in Africa and Latin America limited economic growth.

1970   1978   1986

1970's–1980's
Latin American nations make social and economic reforms

▼ **1979**
Margaret Thatcher becomes British prime minister

1988
Carlos Salinas de Gortari elected president of Mexico

1969
United States astronauts land on moon

1980's
Japan becomes world economic power

Tokyo stock exchange

1988
United States and Canada make trade agreement

◀ **1970's–1980's**
Drought brings famine to African Sahel

1984
Archbishop Desmond Tutu receives Nobel Peace Prize

1988
Benazir Bhutto leads Pakistan

733

The Modern World about 1985

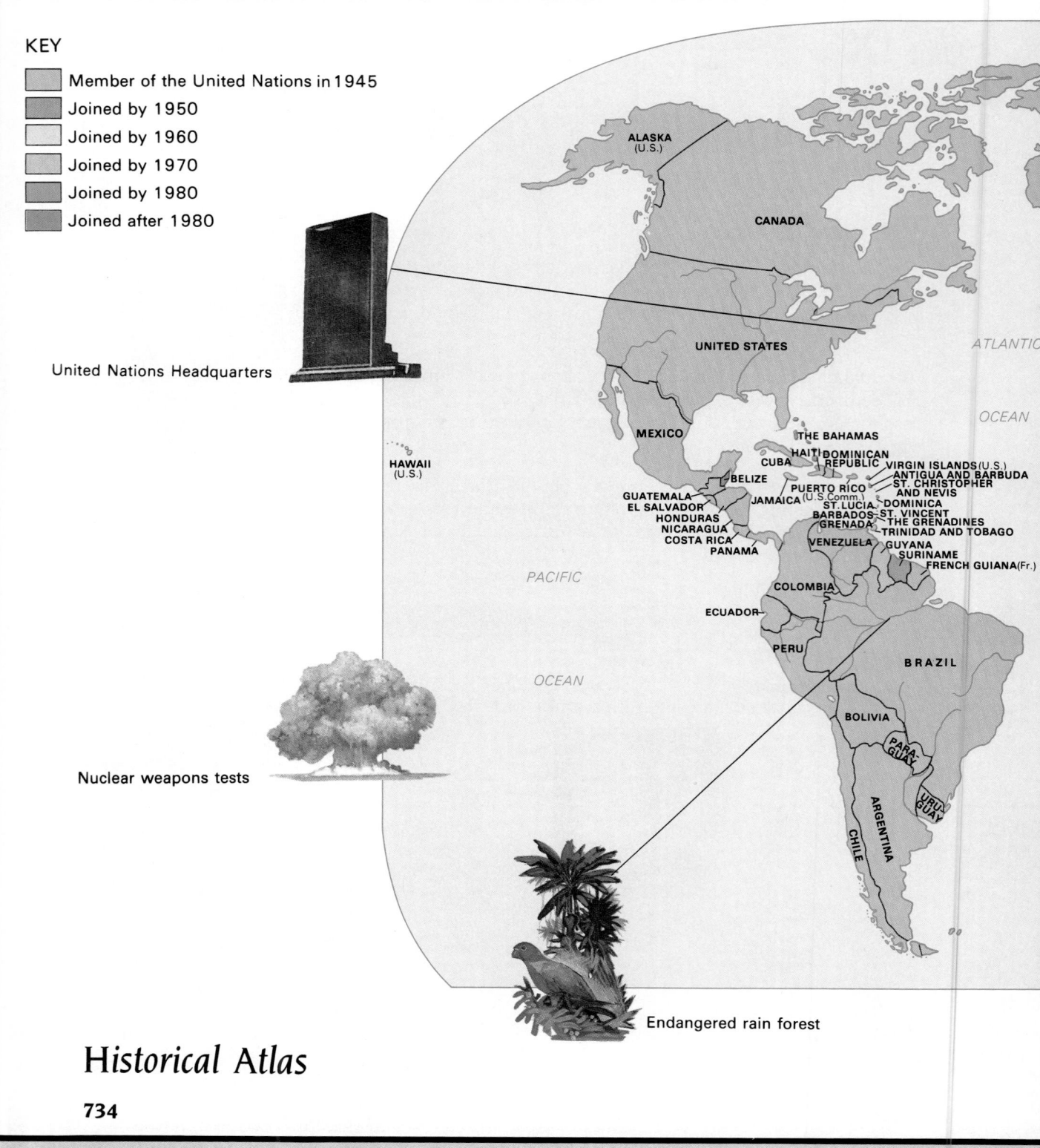

KEY

Member of the United Nations in 1945
Joined by 1950
Joined by 1960
Joined by 1970
Joined by 1980
Joined after 1980

United Nations Headquarters

Nuclear weapons tests

Endangered rain forest

ALASKA (U.S.)

CANADA

UNITED STATES

ATLANTIC

OCEAN

MEXICO

HAWAII (U.S.)

THE BAHAMAS
HAITI DOMINICAN
CUBA   REPUBLIC
          VIRGIN ISLANDS (U.S.)
BELIZE   ANTIGUA AND BARBUDA
          ST. CHRISTOPHER
PUERTO RICO   AND NEVIS
GUATEMALA (U.S.Comm.) DOMINICA
EL SALVADOR JAMAICA ST. LUCIA
HONDURAS BARBADOS ST. VINCENT
NICARAGUA GRENADA THE GRENADINES
COSTA RICA   TRINIDAD AND TOBAGO
PANAMA   VENEZUELA GUYANA
                   SURINAME
          COLOMBIA FRENCH GUIANA (Fr.)

ECUADOR

PERU

PACIFIC

OCEAN

BRAZIL

BOLIVIA

PARA-GUAY

URU-GUAY

ARGENTINA

CHILE

Historical Atlas

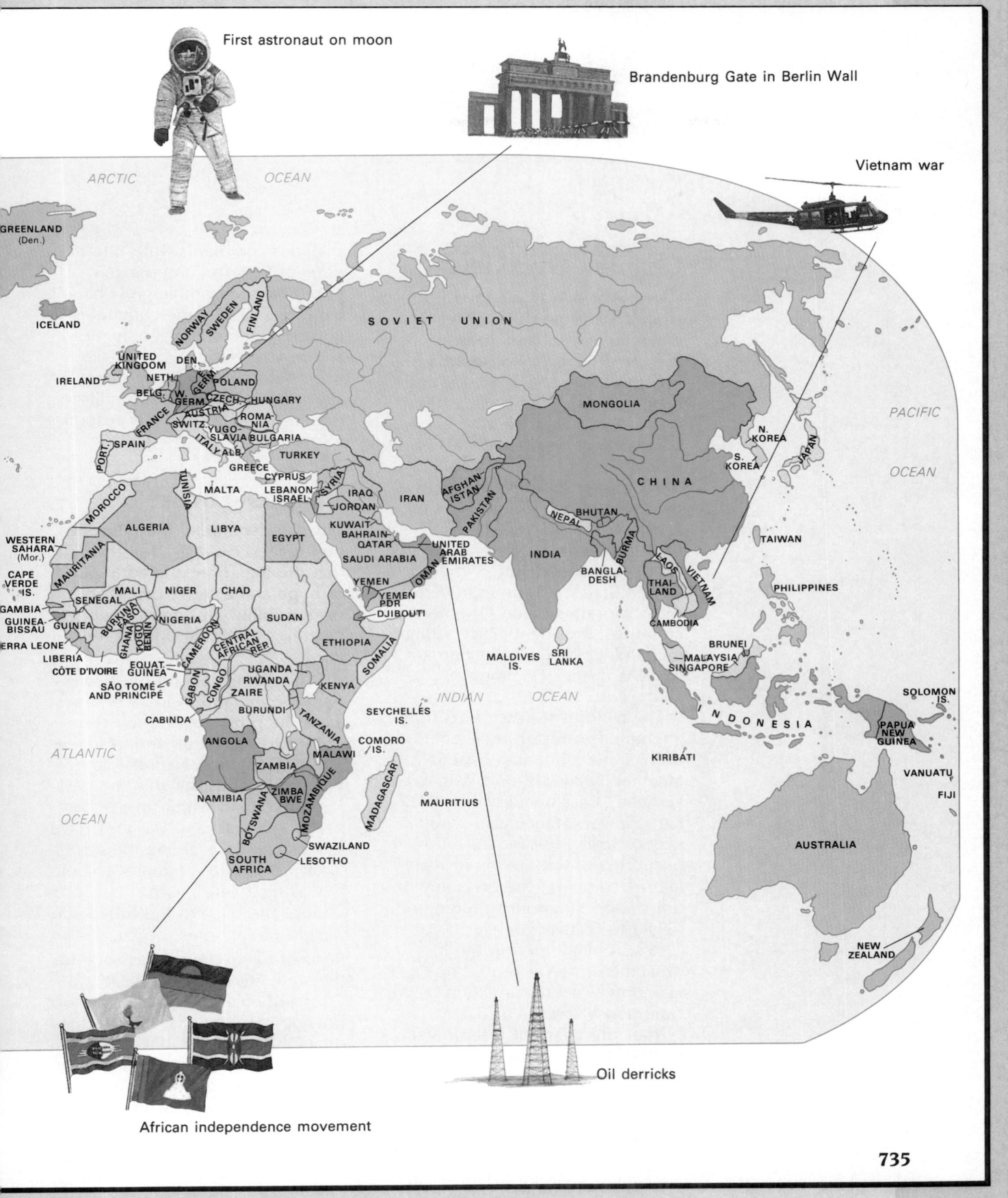

First astronaut on moon

Brandenburg Gate in Berlin Wall

Vietnam war

Oil derricks

African independence movement

735

Europe in the Cold War Era

Chapter **32**

Chapter Overview

When World War II ended, the United States and the Soviet Union emerged as rival superpowers. At President Franklin Roosevelt's urging, the United Nations, a worldwide peacekeeping organization, was founded. Yet the threats of nuclear arms and "cold wars" loomed.

Soon after the war, Europe was divided into two political camps separated by an "iron curtain." On the west were the generally democratic countries, allies of the United States. To the east were the Soviet-dominated Communist countries. President Harry Truman initiated a policy of containment to prevent further Communist takeovers.

The nations of Western Europe attempted to regain their political unity and economic prosperity after the Second World War. West Germany became an economic superpower. France also grew economically, but fought bitter, unsuccessful wars trying to maintain its colonies. The economy of the United Kingdom suffered and began to recover only in the 1980's. A major step in the improvement of Western Europe's economy was the formation of the Common Market in 1957.

After the death of Joseph Stalin in 1953, Nikita Khrushchev took control of the Soviet Union. However, even modest reforms, what Khrushchev called "de-Stalinization," cost him the support of party officials. After the loss of prestige abroad, Khrushchev fell from power.

Under communist rule, the nations of Eastern Europe experienced slow economic growth. Uprisings against the communist governments in Hungary in 1956, and in Czechoslovakia in 1968, were put down by Soviet invasions. Poland underwent military rule in the early 1980's in response to protests.

Chapter Focus

Have students read the introduction (pages 736–737). Tell them that the Big Three shared a mood of hope and a sense of historic responsibility. At one of their meetings Churchill offered this toast:

We see that we are on the crest of the hill and there is before us the prospect of open country. Do not let us underestimate the difficulties. Nations, comrades in arms, have in the past drifted apart within five or ten years of war. . . . We now have a chance of avoiding the errors of previous generations and of making a sure peace. . . . I propose the toast to the broad sunlight of victorious peace.

Read or distribute this passage to the students. Then ask what Churchill meant by the "errors of previous generations." Remind students that all three Allied leaders had seen the consequences of the punitive peace imposed on Germany by the Treaty of Versailles. Ask students if they think that the Allies had a chance of avoiding errors and "making a sure peace."

Unit IX The Modern World

THEME The development of rivalry between the United States and the Soviet
Union and the end of Europe's colonial empires

Chapter 32 Europe in the Cold War Era 1945–1990

FOCUS The meeting of the Big Three at Yalta as a turning point in history

★ Advanced
● Basic

	SECTION 1	SECTION 2	SECTION 3	SECTION 4
Objectives	1. Explain why the United States and the Soviet Union became rivals. 2. Identify the United Nations and describe its organization and goals. 3. Identify the arms race between the United States and the Soviet Union and discuss if it could have been avoided.	1. Explain why Truman issued the Truman Doctrine. 2. Identify and locate on a map the member nations of NATO and the Warsaw Pact in 1955.	1. Describe the influence of Charles De Gaulle on French government. 2. Explain steps Europeans are taking to strengthen economic unity. 3. Cite reasons for Southern Europe's rapid economic growth.	1. Describe the persecution suffered by Soviet dissidents. 2. Describe and evaluate the revolts of the Hungarians and the Czechoslovakians.
Setting the Stage	Changing goals and changing alliances after World War II Unit IX time line	Conditions in Europe at the end of World War II	Problems in implementing the Common Market Transparency 95	Changes in Soviet leadership
Teaching Strategies	Skill Building: Identifying Causes Relating Past to Present: The United Nations Discussing History: The Arms Race Check for Understanding	Evaluating Arguments: The Truman Doctrine Transparency 94 Geography in History: Political Alliances after World War II Transparency 93 Outline Map 10 Check for Understanding	Skill Building: Interpreting a Political Cartoon Economics and History: Competing for World Markets Discussing History: Southern Europe's Economic Growth Check for Understanding	Discussing History: Soviet Dissidents Skill Building: Comparing the Hungarian and Czechoslovakian Revolts Check for Understanding
Guided Practice	Section Review 1	Transparency 94 Q&A Transparency 93 Q&A Section Review 2	Transparency 95 Q&A Section Review 3	Section Review 4
Independent Practice Worksheets	Independent Practice 32.1 Vocabulary 32	Independent Practice 32.2 Geography Skills 32 Critical Thinking 32	Independent Practice 32.3 Basic Skills 32	Independent Practice 32.4
Enrichment	1. Primary Source: Voices 32.1 2. ★Preparing a Report: Bikini Atoll 3. Researching for Points	1. Primary Source: Voices 32.2 2. Researching for Points	1. Primary Source: Voices 32.3 2. Relating Past to Present 3. Researching for Points	1. Primary Source: Voices 32.4 2. Preparing a Report: Lech Walesa 3. Researching for Points

Chapter Closer

●**Reteaching Activities** Summarizing, Listing

Chapter Review Summary, Reviewing the Facts, Basic Skills, Researching and Reporting Skills, Critical Thinking, Perspectives on Past and Present, Investigating History

Chapter Evaluation Chapter Test 32, Alternate Chapter Test 32, Computer Test Bank Chapter 32 Test

Two superpowers arose after World War II. 1

Setting the Stage

Direct students' attention to the picture on page 738. Ask what goal united the Soviet and American forces during World War II. Emphasize that the common goal of defeating Germany united the two powers. Then ask if the two countries had any common goals after the defeat of Germany. Explain that the end of World War II marked the passing of one historic era and the dawning of a new one.

Teaching Strategies

Skill Building: Identifying Causes (Objective 1) Have students read pages 737–738. Then write the following sentence fragment on the board: "The relationship between the United States and the Soviet Union changed after the war because . . ." Students might suggest the relative losses the two nations suffered in World War II, the different goals that the two nations had for the future, the Soviet fear of American power, or the American fear of Soviet communism. Encourage students to explain how each of these factors contributed to the growing rivalry between the United States and the Soviet Union.

Relating Past to Present: The United Nations (Objective 2) Have students read the section on the United Nations (page 739). Then review the United Nations' goals and organization. Explain that the United Nations has not yet achieved its goal of ending "the scourge of war." Point out that it nevertheless does play a constructive role in global affairs. For example, the General Assembly provides a common forum for the United Nations' 159

member nations to discuss global and regional issues. The United Nations' 10,000 employees administer social, economic, and cultural programs throughout the world. (Many of the United Nations' cultural activities are described in the *UNESCO Courier*.) United Nations peacekeeping forces now play a significant role in patrolling global trouble spots. Tell students that the Nobel Committee recognized this valuable contribution when it awarded the 1988 Nobel Peace Prize to the United Nations soldiers.

Discussing History: The Arms Race (Objective 3) In 1946 the United States presented a plan to the United Nations to control nuclear weapons. The plan called for the creation of an international agency to control the use of atomic energy for peaceful purposes. The Truman administration pledged to give its nuclear secrets and weapons to this agency. In order to prevent cheating, the agency would have the authority to inspect atomic energy plants in all countries. Have students evaluate the plan's advantages and disadvantages.

The Soviet Union rejected the proposal. The Soviets insisted that international inspection was unacceptable. They then presented a plan calling for a total ban on the use of nuclear weapons as well as the destruction of all existing bombs. However, the Soviet plan failed to provide for inspections to prevent nations from secretly violating it. Because they disagreed on this important issue, the United States and the Soviet Union accelerated their nuclear programs, thus beginning the nuclear arms race.

Check for Understanding Have students compare and contrast the goals of the United States and the Soviet Union after World War II.

Enrichment Activities

1. **Reading a Primary Source**
   Assign Voices from the Past Resource Book 32.1.

2. **Preparing a Report**
   America conducted its first postwar atomic tests at the Bikini Atoll. Ask advanced students to report on these tests and the impact they had on the way of life of the people of Bikini. (See *National Geographic*, "Bikini— A Way of Life Lost," June 1986.)

3. **Researching for Bonus Points**
   Who was the first Secretary-General of the United Nations? (Trygve Lie of Norway)

The war left Europe divided. 2

Setting the Stage

World War II left Europe in ruins. Britain looked like a defeated country. More than half of its factories lay idle and millions of workers were unemployed. The situation in Germany was even worse. The few remaining factories produced only 29 percent of the nation's prewar output. Shoppers used cigarettes to buy scarce goods. Most Germans had to survive on less than 1550 calories a day—barely enough to survive. Meanwhile, economic conditions in France and Italy also declined. The Communist party gained strength in both countries and threatened to radically change their governments.

Describe these conditions to your students. Then ask how American policymakers of the 1920's would have responded to this situation. Explain that while the United States would have sent humanitarian aid, it would have tried to continue its policy of isolationism. Ask students if this policy could be continued in post-World War II Europe.

Teaching Strategies

Evaluating Arguments: The Truman Doctrine (Objective 1) Have students read "The Truman Doctrine blocked communism" (pages 743–744). Ask them to explain how the aid sent to Greece and Turkey represented the policy of containment in action. Tell students that not all Americans approved of the Truman Doctrine. Opponents criticized the Doctrine as "aid to reactionary governments," as an effort to "bail out the British Empire," and as a "bypassing of the United Nations." Ask students to evaluate these arguments. Ask what Truman's response to these oppositions might have been. Then show students

Map Transparency 94, *Division of Germany, 1945/Berlin,* and discuss the Berlin airlift. Emphasize the isolation of West Berlin within communist East Germany. Ask how the airlift was another example of the Truman Doctrine. Finally, ask students if the Truman Doctrine is still in effect today.

Geography in History: Political Alliances after World War II (Objective 2) Show students Map Transparency 93, *Postwar Europe,* and discuss the postwar political divisions. Distribute Outline Map 10: Political Europe. Have students refer to the transparency or to the map on page 745 to label the countries of Western Europe and Eastern Europe. Students should identify the NATO countries and the Warsaw Pact countries. Have students draw map keys and add titles to their maps.

Check for Understanding Have students identify the following postwar developments: Truman Doctrine, Marshall Plan, NATO, Warsaw Pact, and the Berlin Airlift.

Enrichment Activities

1. **Reading a Primary Source** Assign Voices from the Past Resource Book 32.2.
2. **Researching for Bonus Points** What is the present location of the headquarters of the NATO alliance? (Brussels, Belgium)

Western Europe moved toward cooperation. 3

Setting the Stage

To introduce students to the Common Market, write the names of the 12 member nations on the board: United Kingdom, Ireland, Portugal, Spain, France, Netherlands, Denmark, Belgium, West Germany, Luxembourg, Greece, and Italy. Show Map Transparency 95, *Europe Today,* and have students locate the Common Market countries. Then, explain that these nations lowered all trade barriers on December 31, 1992. The goal was to create a single market, or what supporters of the plan call "a Europe without frontiers."

Ask students to speculate about some of the practical problems that might arise with this plan. To stimulate discussion, tell students that a panel spent 5 years trying to get all 12 nations to agree on a definition of white bread. The panel finally gave up, declaring white bread to be anything so named by the country where it was baked.

Teaching Strategies

Skill Building: Interpreting a Political Cartoon (Objective 1) Louis XIV once said, "My dominant passion is certainly love of glory." Have the class turn to the political cartoon on page 749. According to the cartoonist, how would De Gaulle react to Louis's statement? What clues in the cartoon support students' answers?

Next, allow time for students to skim through the material on De Gaulle on page 749. Ask how De Gaulle changed the role of the president in French government. Suggest the following alternative caption for the cartoon, using another quote of Louis XIV: "*L'etat,* c'est moi"—"the state is me." Ask students to assess the appropriateness of this caption.

Economics and History: Competing for World Markets (Objective 2) To help students assess the economic clout that the European Community may hold now that internal trade barriers have come down, distribute copies of the following statistics.

■ In 1987, the European Community exported goods worth just under $400 billion—60 percent more than the United States and nearly 100 percent more than Japan.

■ In 1987, the European Community imported goods worth just under $400 billion—roughly equal to United States imports and nearly triple Japanese imports.

■ In 1987, the European Community's more than 320 million people made it the largest consumer group in the industrial world.

After students have examined these figures, ask why many Europeans believe that the plans for a single market without trade barriers will make Western Europe a world power. Suppose that the European Community should decide to raise high protective tariffs against foreign competition. What effect might this have on the economies of the United States and Japan? As a clue, point out the large number of imports consumed by the 12 member nations. Then challenge students to suggest why foreign critics of a "Euro-market" have nicknamed it "Fortress Europe."

Discussing History: Southern Europe's Economic Growth (Objective 3) A Spanish official recently declared, "We are Europe's Califor-

nia." A Portuguese spokesperson asked, "Could we be Europe's Florida?" To explore the meaning of these statements in terms of economics, ask students to compare the resources of California and Florida with those of Spain and Portugal. The most obvious similarities are climate—the almost year-round presence of the warm sun—and long coastlines with miles of beaches. Also point out the presence of "high-tech" industries in places such as California's "Silicon Valley" and Italy's Po Valley. If students have had an opportunity to travel in Southern Europe, call on them to describe the area's geographic resources. Ask students to summarize the reasons for Southern Europe's economic growth.

Check for Understanding Ask students to reconsider their predictions about the problems Europeans will face when the "single-market" plan goes into effect in 1992. (See Setting the Stage.) What do students think are the biggest obstacles for the Common Market to overcome?

Enrichment Activities

1. **Reading a Primary Source** Assign Voices from the Past Resource Book 32.3.

2. **Relating Past to Present** Call on volunteers to research life in Spain during the dictatorship of General Francisco Franco. Have students share their findings in oral reports to the class. Then ask the class why present-day Spain might shock someone who has not visited there since 1975, the year of Franco's death.

3. **Researching for Bonus Points** In what European city are Ferrari and Maserati sports cars manufactured? (Modena, Italy)

The USSR dominated Eastern Europe. 4

Setting the Stage

Ask students to recall how Stalin came to power in the Soviet Union (page 654). Remind them that a power struggle occurred after Lenin's death, which Stalin won by gaining party support. The same sort of power struggle occurred after Stalin's death in 1953. The new Soviet leader, Nikita Khrushchev, attacked Stalin's record and tried to set a new course for the Soviet Union and Eastern Europe.

Teaching Strategies

Discussing History: Soviet Dissidents (Objective 1) Following Khrushchev's denunciation of Stalin in 1956, Soviet writers began to tell of the injustices that the public had suffered under the former leader, a previously unheard of freedom. Khrushchev, in accordance with his policy of de-Stalinization, allowed such attacks. But following his ouster, the Soviets again began to repress dissident writers and artists. Stalin's regime had simply sent political dissenters off to labor camps. In the 1960's and 1970's, however, such brutal treatment attracted protests from abroad. The Soviets turned to intimidation of the dissidents and their families, or incarcerated the dissidents within psychiatric institutions. Eventually, the Soviet government began to expel the most popular dissidents, such as Alexander Solzhenitsyn, hoping to diminish their effectiveness by distance. Ask students if they think such a policy would be effective.

Skill Building: Comparing the Hungarian and Czechoslovakian Revolts (Objective 2) Have students read "The Hungarian revolt failed" and "Reforms were stamped out in Czechoslovakia" (pages 754–756). Ask students how the goals of the two protests differed. Emphasize that while the Hungarians called for a complete break with the Soviet Union, the Czechs wanted only to reform their communist government. Then ask what the Soviet response to both protests was. Tell students that while the Hungarians violently fought the Soviet invasion, the Czechs opposed the invasion in a nonviolent manner. The Czech army remained out of the conflict, and the civilian population responded in a number of nonviolent ways. They refused to collaborate with the invaders. They blockaded roads with human chains, took down or changed road signs, provided wrong information, and interfered with radio communications. Finally, Czech civilians attempted to undermine the morale of the invaders. They "attacked" invading tanks with white paint, surrounded and held conversations with the troops, and produced radio and poster propaganda. Ask students why they think the Czechs responded in such a manner. Ask which type of resistance, that exhibited in Hungary or in Czechoslovakia, was more effective. Why?

Check for Understanding Ask students to compare and contrast the protests in Hungary, Czechoslovakia, and Poland, including communist reactions.

Enrichment Activities

1. **Reading a Primary Source**
   Assign Voices from the Past Resource Book 32.4.

2. **Preparing a Report**
   Ask interested students to report on Lech Walesa's autobiography, *A Way of Hope*.

3. **Researching for Bonus Points**
   Who accepted Lech Walesa's Nobel Peace Prize for him in 1983? (his wife Danuta)

Reviewing the Facts
1. (a) area between rival countries (b) country controlled by another (c) form of socialism that involves government support for social insurance programs and ownership of major industries within a democratic system (d) military rule over civilian population

2. (a) planned for end of war (b) warfare without open conflict (c) trial of Nazis for war crimes (d) U.S. doctrine to control spread of communism (e) rebuilt Europe's economy (f) Western protective alliance (g) Eastern protective alliance (h) instituted policy of de-Stalinization (i) Western European economic unit (j) barrier between East and West Berlin

Basic Skills
1. (a) long Adriatic coastline and distance from USSR (b) These countries bordered the USSR and had no access to seas or harbors through which they could get supplies.

2. Students' answers may vary. Suggested responses follow. (a) By 1958, West Germany had twice as much production as all of Germany had in 1938; West Germans enjoy a high standard of living; West Germany quickly became a stable democracy; West Germany is internationally respected in technology, economics, and political alliances. (b) East German stores and markets had few goods or fresh food; many East German buildings were destroyed; many East Germans left for better conditions in West Germany.

Researching and Reporting Skills
Students' findings will vary.

Critical Thinking
1. (a) did everything short of war to prevent further Communist takeovers (b) 12 non-Communist

nations joined together to protect themselves against attack (c) helped Europe recover economically in order to be stronger and more cooperative with one another

2. Eastern Europe became a buffer zone as Communists won powerful posts in Eastern European countries and Soviet satellites were created. The Warsaw Pact strengthened Eastern Europe's unity under the USSR.

3. (a) aid from U.S., the Marshall Plan, cooperation among countries (b) Countries had stable currency, increased production, and expanded exports. (c) The countries were strong enough to withstand invasion and banded together against communism.

4. (a) spread of nuclear weapons, disagreements over economics and politics, division of Germany, split between Eastern and Western Europe, rival alliances (b) Students' answers will vary; encourage them to substantiate opinions.

5. (a) stop flood of people leaving East Germany, isolate East Germany from outside influences (b) dissatisfaction of citizens, distrust by other nations

6. Both showed citizens' dissatisfaction with Communist regime and their willingness to risk leaders' backlash to strive for changes.

7. Stalin feared that a free West Berlin might interfere with Soviet plans to dominate East Germany. The Western powers viewed any attempt at takeover as a test of their determination and the policy of containment.

Perspectives on Past and Present
Students' opinions will vary.

Investigating History
Students' findings will vary.

Chapter 32

Teaching with Pictures

Tell students that the photograph shows the "Big Three" leaders meeting at Yalta in February 1945. Explain that it was the last meeting between these three leaders, as Roosevelt died unexpectedly the following April, and Churchill was voted out of office in July. The last wartime meeting of the Big Three powers was held in July and August at Potsdam, Germany. In attendance were U.S. President Harry Truman, British Prime Minister Clement Attlee, and Soviet leader Joseph Stalin.

Churchill (left), Roosevelt (center), and Stalin (right) met at Yalta near the end of World War II.

Key Terms

superpower	satellite
Cold War	ideology
buffer zone	dissident
human rights	martial
nuclear weapon	law
free election	
iron curtain	
occupation zone	
containment	
gross national product	
Common Market	
moderate socialism	

Read and Understand

1. Two superpowers arose after World War II.
2. The war left Europe divided.
3. Western Europe moved toward cooperation.
4. The USSR dominated Eastern Europe.

Traces of pink were lighting the predawn sky when hundreds of Soviet soldiers heard the roar of planes approaching the airfield on the Crimean Peninsula along the north shore of the Black Sea. The planes bore the insignias of the Soviet Union's two major wartime allies, Great Britain and the United States. They carried about 700 passengers, including Winston Churchill, the British prime minister, and Franklin D. Roosevelt, the American president. The date was February 3, 1945.

At the airport, a Red Army band greeted the leaders, playing each country's national anthem. Soviet officials led their visitors to three nearby tents where they dined on smoked salmon and caviar. Then they set out on a six-hour automobile ride over winding mountain roads to the small Black Sea resort city of Yalta.

736

Chapter 32 Resources

GEOGRAPHY
- Geography Skills 32
- Outline Map 10
- Transparencies 93, 94, 95

REINFORCEMENT
- Vocabulary 32
- Basic Skills 32
- Reteaching 32
- Making Connections Study Guide 32

ENRICHMENT
- Critical Thinking 32

ASSESSMENT
- Chapter Test 32
- Alternate Chapter Test 32
- Computer Test Bank

At Yalta, Roosevelt and Churchill were greeted by their Soviet counterpart Joseph Stalin. Together the three Allied leaders toasted the defeat of Germany that now seemed certain. World War II was nearly over. Churchill spoke of "the broad sunlight of victorious peace."

Victorious peace, however, meant different things to each of the three leaders. For Churchill, it meant a free and democratic Europe that Britain would lead, thanks to its centuries-old parliamentary traditions and its mighty empire. For Stalin, victorious peace meant increased Soviet power and a chance to safeguard the USSR against any further invasions from the West. Finally, for Roosevelt, victorious peace meant a world in which democracy could thrive under the leadership of the United States.

These differences were reflected in the discussions of the three leaders at Yalta during eight fateful days. The question of Germany's future, for example, was hotly debated. Stalin—his country devastated by German armies in both world wars—favored a harsh approach. He wanted to keep Germany permanently divided into **occupation zones**—areas controlled by Allied military forces—so that it would never threaten the Soviet Union again. At the same time, he wanted to ensure that governments in neighboring countries such as Poland were friendly to the Soviet Union to provide even more security for the future.

Churchill disagreed strongly, but Roosevelt played the part of mediator. While the American president shared Churchill's desire for independent, democratic countries throughout Europe, he was prepared to make concessions to Stalin for two reasons. First, he hoped that the Soviet Union would quickly join the war against Japan in the Pacific. That struggle was expected to continue for another year or more. (The first test of the atom bomb was still five months away.) Second, Roosevelt wanted Stalin's support for a new world peacekeeping organization, the United Nations, that he felt would make war a thing of the past.

Like most such conferences, the historical meeting at Yalta produced a series of compromises. Churchill and Roosevelt agreed to a temporary division of Germany. Meanwhile Stalin agreed to join the war against Japan. He also agreed to participate in an international conference to take place in April in San Francisco. There, Roosevelt's dream of a United Nations would become a reality.

Sadly, just two weeks before that conference, President Roosevelt died suddenly. The millions who mourned his passing shared his hopes for the future. "We really believed in our hearts," one Roosevelt adviser later recalled, "that this was the dawn of the new day we had all been praying for and talking about for so many years."

Unfortunately such hopes were quickly dashed. Almost before the last Nazi guns were silenced in 1945, a great rift developed between the former Allies. As you will see, the United States and the Soviet Union became competing **superpowers,** or dominant world powers. Their bitter rivalry cast a dark shadow across Europe and the world.

This climate of icy tension between the superpowers, which people came to call the **Cold War,** lasted for several decades after World War II. This chapter deals first with the two great Cold War rivals, the United States and the Soviet Union. It then examines how the once-mighty continent of Europe became the major battleground in their struggle for supremacy.

Two superpowers arose after World War II. 1

In the spring of 1945, American troops rolled eastward across Germany. Soviet troops marched westward. On April 25, 1945, American and Soviet forces met at Torgau on the Elbe River in Germany. Nazi Germany had been crushed between the two great powers.

After months of fighting, the two armies were ready to celebrate. They saluted each other, drank toasts, danced jigs, sang, and shouted. "Today is the happiest day in all our lives," proclaimed a Soviet major to the Americans. "Long live your great leader! Long live our great leader!"

The United States and the Soviet Union now stood forth as the most powerful nations on Earth. Not only were they two of the world's largest countries, but also their abundant natural resources helped build strong economies. Their military strengths were similar as well. But the two countries had very different ambitions for

737

SECTION 1 Objectives and Teaching Strategies

OBJECTIVE 1. Explain why the United States and the Soviet Union became rivals.

Teaching Strategy: *Skill Building: Identifying Causes* (page 736c)

OBJECTIVE 2. Identify the United Nations and describe its organization and goals.

Teaching Strategy: *Relating Past to Present: The United Nations* (page 736c)

OBJECTIVE 3. Identify the arms race between the United States and the Soviet Union and discuss if it could have been avoided.

Teaching Strategy: *Discussing History: The Arms Race* (page 736c)

■ BACKGROUND

In all, 49 countries had declared war on Germany, but the Big Three had contributed most of the troops and war material.

SECTION 1 Resources

ASSESSMENT
■ Section Quiz 32.1

REINFORCEMENT
■ Independent Practice 32.1

ENRICHMENT
■ Voices from the Past 32.1

■ **RESEARCH**

Students may wish to research the assembly-line methods of home building that were developed after the war by William J. Levitt.

■ **BACKGROUND**

Remind students that the USSR (Russia) had suffered three devastating invasions between 1812 and 1945.

American soldiers (left) met their Soviet allies (right) on a ruined bridge over the Elbe River at Torgau in defeated Germany.

the future. These political differences contributed to the tensions that led to the Cold War.

At the war's end, the United States was both the most powerful and the most prosperous of all the countries in the world. Many Americans had suffered during the war. About 400,000 had died in battle, and many more were injured. However, no bombs had fallen on American cities. American factories were unscathed. Few other industrialized countries were as lucky.

In 1945, the United States had the biggest navy and the best-equipped army and air force in the world. The United States was also the only country to possess the war's most formidable weapon, the atom bomb. Militarily the United States was the unchallenged leader of the world.

Americans were eager to return to peace, however. Families wanted their sons, husbands, or fathers home from the army. Therefore, the United States demobilized as soon as the war was over.

"No nation in history," observed President Harry Truman (who took office when Roosevelt died), "had ever won so great a victory and asked for so little in return." It was also true that no country had ever emerged from a war so prosperous. In 1947, the United States produced half of the world's manufactured goods, 57 percent of its steel, 43 percent of its electricity, and 62

738

percent of its oil. Never before in history had so large a percentage of the world's wealth been concentrated in a single country.

After World War I, as you saw in Chapter 30, the United States had turned to political isolationism (page 686). After World War II, however, the American attitude was different. The United States even offered to make New York City the permanent headquarters of the new United Nations. Shortly before his death, Franklin Roosevelt had said, "We have learned that we cannot live alone, at peace; that our own well-being is dependent on the well-being of other nations."

The USSR demanded a buffer zone.

Like the United States, the Soviet Union emerged from the war as a nation of enormous economic and military strength. In fact, it was second in power only to the United States.

Unlike the United States the USSR had suffered heavy fighting on its own soil. Large areas of the Soviet Union had been occupied by Nazi armies. Many Soviet cities were destroyed. Fields around the cities were filled with mass graves. Soviet war losses have been estimated at 20 million, half of whom were civilians. For every American killed in the war, 50 Soviets died.

These losses help to explain why the United States and the Soviet Union acted differently after the war. While American leaders were most concerned about building a peaceful world, Soviet leaders were most concerned about protecting their country against future wars.

The best protection the USSR could have, Stalin reasoned, was a **buffer zone** along its western border. A buffer zone is a region that lies between two rivals, cutting down the threat of conflict. The area Stalin wanted as a buffer zone was eastern Europe. By dominating this region, Stalin hoped to ensure that the Soviets could stop any future invasion before the Soviet Union itself was hurt. Moreover, Soviet control of eastern Europe would bring about 100 million more people into the Communist system.

Stalin's plans ignored the wishes of the people who lived in eastern Europe. Like the USSR, most countries in eastern Europe lacked strong democratic traditions. Thus the Soviet Union could hope to push Communist governments into power without effective opposition.

The United Nations was founded.

Despite their different views of the world, both the United States and the Soviet Union participated in the San Francisco Conference. They were among the 50 countries who signed the United Nations charter in June 1945. Together these nations pledged "to save succeeding generations from the scourge of war."

The new peacekeeping organization was based in New York City, where a magnificent headquarters complex was completed in 1952. The UN charter provided for a main representative body called the General Assembly. Every member nation (the total would grow to over 150 in the years ahead) could cast a vote in the General Assembly. The General Assembly approved new members, discussed a broad range of issues, and made recommendations and agreements.

A second group, the Security Council, was in charge of investigating disputes, peacekeeping, and emergency action. Five countries—Britain, China, France, the United States, and the Soviet Union—were permanent members of the council. Six other members were chosen from the UN membership at large. These members served two-year terms on the council. (Later, the number of other members was increased to 10 so that the Security Council now has 15 members.)

Both the United States and the Soviet Union insisted on being permanent council members when the UN charter was written. The two countries also agreed that each permanent member would have veto power. In other words, the Security Council could take no action unless all five permanent members agreed.

Besides the General Assembly and the Security Council, the UN included many other organizations and agencies. For example, an International Court of Justice dealt with questions of international law. The Secretariat, headed by the Secretary-General, organized the daily business of the United Nations.

From the start, the United Nations enjoyed at least two advantages over the old League of Nations. First, no major powers refused to join. Second, the charter provided for a UN peacekeeping force, an armed group that could be drawn from the troops of member countries. The UN could use these troops to enforce its decisions or to separate warring groups.

Despite these advantages, the UN also faced a major stumbling block. Unless all five permanent members of the Security Council agreed on a course of action, the UN could do nothing. Time and again, one permanent member or another used its veto power to paralyze the United Nations.

The United Nations proved more effective on social and economic issues than in solving political crises. In 1948, it adopted the Universal Declaration of Human Rights, a document that supports **human rights** through the protection of individuals against oppression and the preservation of basic rights and freedoms. According to the preamble, the Declaration serves as "a common standard of achievement for all peoples and all nations." It also provides that all people are born free and equal in dignity and rights.

The UN also set up agencies such as UNESCO (United Nations Educational, Scientific, and Cultural Organization), FAO (Food and Agriculture Organization), WHO (World Health Organization), and UNICEF (United Nations International Children's Emergency Fund) to help coordinate worldwide efforts to battle disease, feed the hungry, and improve literacy.

Eleanor Roosevelt, widow of former President Franklin Roosevelt, served as a United States delegate to the UN from 1945 to 1951. She became chairman of the UN's Human Rights Commission.

739

Cooperative Learning

Ask students if they can think of a way to reorganize the United Nations to somehow make it more effective. Have them individually develop plans to increase the UN's effectiveness, or else defend its current organization. Then form groups of four or five students. Each group member should present his or her idea for reorganization. After all group members have presented their ideas, they must reach a consensus as to the best way to make the UN more effective. Group members should not "flip a coin" when choosing a plan, and the final decision must be unanimous. Have group spokespersons present their plans to the class.

ANSWERS TO
Section Review 1

Define:
(a) area controlled by military forces (b) dominant world power (c) era of tension between the superpowers (d) region between two nations that reduces the threat of conflict (e) basic rights and freedoms
(f) weapon getting its power from reactions involving the nucleus of an atom
Identify:
(a) meeting of Big Three focusing on ending the war
(continued)

ANSWERS TO (continued)

(b) succeeded Roosevelt as president (c) worldwide peacekeeping organization (d) main representative body of UN (e) UN group that investigates disputes, keeps peace, and takes emergency action (f) UN document supporting human rights (g) weapons competition between powerful nations

Answer:

1. (a) American factories and cities remained unscathed from bombings. (b) possessed biggest navy, best-equipped army and air force, atom bomb

2. favored international cooperation over political isolationism

3. (a) buffer zone along its western front (b) would give Soviets control of Eastern Europe

4. (a) All major powers joined, and the UN formed a joint peacekeeping force. (b) veto power of Security Council members

5. (a) The Soviet Union and the United States competed to see who could build larger and more powerful nuclear weapons. (b) Both sides were afraid to fall behind in the race.

6. The Soviet Union and the United States emerged from the war economically and militarily strong. The United States had not been occupied during the war, was anxious to disarm, and sought world democracy under its leadership. The USSR had been occupied, wanted world leadership as well as protection from further invasions. Competition for leadership, differing goals, and conflicting ideologies would make the countries rivals.

Nuclear weapons threatened modern civilization.

Overall the United Nations had a mixed record of successes and failures in the decades after World War II. The UN proved powerless, however, in dealing with the threat of nuclear war.

Of all the new weapons developed during the 1940's, none transformed warfare as dramatically as the atom bomb. At Hiroshima and Nagasaki, for example, just two of these murderous weapons killed 120,000 people. "The primary reaction of the populace to the bomb," as the official American report on its use noted, "was fear, uncontrolled terror, strengthened by the sheer horror of the destruction and suffering witnessed and experienced by the survivors."

The destructive power of the atom bomb was not limited to its tremendous blast. First came a heat flash that could burn, blind, and kill. Later, in the days and weeks after the blast, came radioactive fallout that spread sickness and slow death across a much broader area.

Once the United States had such a bomb, the Soviet Union was determined not to be left with weaker weapons. The Soviets began a crash program to develop their own atom bomb immediately after World War II. In 1949, they tested their first atom bomb in a remote part of Siberia. That test marked the end of the American monopoly on such bombs.

Now that both superpowers possessed such weapons, the world faced a new situation. Winston Churchill called it "a balance of terror." He meant that both countries would be so terrified of destruction that they would avoid war.

The atom bomb was the first example of a **nuclear weapon.** Weapons of this type get their power from reactions involving the center, or *nucleus,* of an atom.

In 1952, American scientists produced an even more destructive nuclear weapon, the hydrogen bomb. Soviet scientists quickly followed suit, testing their country's first hydrogen bomb in 1953. In a contest that came to be called the arms race, the two superpowers continued to compete in making more and larger nuclear weapons. Knowing that such a race might end in worldwide disaster, leaders in both countries also searched from time to time for ways to limit or slow this arms race.

740

Define: (a) occupation zone, (b) superpower, (c) Cold War, (d) buffer zone, (e) human rights, (f) nuclear weapon
Identify: (a) Yalta conference, (b) Harry Truman, (c) United Nations, (d) General Assembly, (e) Security Council, (f) Universal Declaration of Human Rights, (g) arms race
Answer:
1. (a) Why was the United States in a stronger economic position than other countries at the end of World War II? (b) Why was it in the strongest military position?
2. How was the United States attitude toward its world role in 1945 different from its attitude after World War I?
3. (a) What was the major Soviet goal in 1945? (b) Why was this important to the Soviets?
4. (a) What features made the UN stronger than the League of Nations had been? (b) What weakness sometimes kept the UN from taking effective action?
5. (a) How did the arms race develop? (b) Why was the UN powerless in dealing with the nuclear arms race?

Critical Thinking
6. Compare and contrast the situations of the United States and the Soviet Union in 1945. What factors help to explain why they became rivals instead of allies?

The war left Europe divided. 2

In 1945, Europe, which had once dominated the globe, was struggling to survive. "What is Europe now?" Winston Churchill asked at the end of World War II. "It is a rubble-heap, a charnel house, a breeding ground of pestilence and hate."

Europe faced dark days indeed. Hunger and want stalked the land from Bulgaria to Belgium. Tens of millions of Europeans were homeless, classified as "displaced persons." To make matters worse, the winter of 1946–1947 was the coldest in living memory, and fuel supplies were disastrously low.

Europe's overseas empires crumbled.

The countries of Europe were barely able to support themselves in 1945, let alone rule overseas colonies. At the same time, nationalist movements in Asia and later in Africa gained strength. Together these developments brought down the curtain on the age of European imperialism and changed the role of former imperial powers.

Great Britain made the most dramatic break from imperialism. This island nation once ruled a fourth of the world's land and 500 million of its people. In 1947, Britain gave up the brightest jewel of its empire, India. Britain also withdrew from the bitterly divided Middle Eastern state of Palestine (page 669). Thereafter Britain continued to divest itself of its colonies.

The shift away from imperialism was due to a sudden turnaround in British politics. In July 1945, British voters turned their great war leader Winston Churchill out of office. Churchill's Conservative party was replaced in power by the Labour party under Clement Attlee.

Why did the British vote against Churchill? Despite his inspired leadership, voters saw him as a symbol of the country's past, and many Britons believed that the country needed new directions. The Labour party leaders believed that imperial rule was wrong. They also thought that the government should spend its increasingly limited resources closer to home. They wanted better schools and hospitals as well as welfare benefits for those who needed them. Under the leadership of Attlee, Britain made fairly peaceful agreements for independence with many of its former colonies.

Like Britain, France faced the loss of its overseas lands. Unlike Britain, however, France struggled to hold on to its empire. As a result, the French found themselves trapped in long, bloody, expensive conflicts in Indochina and North Africa. Eventually, however, the French were forced to accept the end of the imperial era.

One by one, other European countries also lost their colonies. Yet Europe's influence survived in the places it had once ruled. Often former colonies kept English or French as their official language. Many newly independent countries kept close economic ties with their former rulers. As Europe recovered its prosperity, new trading partnerships replaced the old imperialism.

Amid the ruins of postwar Europe, homeless families struggled to stay together. Bombs destroyed these children's home in Alsace, France.

Germany was defeated and divided.

Hitler's policies left Germany in ruins. Some four million Germans had died in the war. Cities lay in rubble. Transportation was at a standstill. Every bridge across such major rivers as the Rhine and the Main had been destroyed in Allied bombing raids. So too had most of the country's businesses. In the Ruhr valley, only one factory in ten was still operating at the war's end.

East-West split As you have seen, Germany's postwar fate was determined in part at Yalta. Roosevelt and Churchill had gone along with Stalin's demand for a divided Germany, expecting that this division would be temporary. Four occupation zones were created in 1945: one each for the United States, Great Britain, France, and the Soviet Union.

The western Allies encouraged the growth of democratic government in their three occupation zones. In 1949, Britain, France, and the United States allowed their zones to join. The three zones became the Federal Republic of Germany. This self-governing democratic state became known as West Germany.

However, Stalin was not prepared to lose control over the Soviet zone. This was the easternmost section of Germany, including the capital Berlin. Under a Communist government, this section became the German Democratic Republic, known as East Germany. It remained under Soviet rule.

741

SECTION 2
Objectives and Teaching Strategies

OBJECTIVE 1. Explain why Truman issued the Truman Doctrine.

Teaching Strategy: *Evaluating Arguments: The Truman Doctrine* (page 736d)

OBJECTIVE 2. Identify and locate on a map the member nations of NATO and the Warsaw Pact in 1955.

Teaching Strategy: *Geography in History: Political Alliances after World War II* (page 736d)

■ BACKGROUND

Residential areas also suffered from the air war. Dresden and Essen had been almost completely demolished, while 75 percent of all the houses in Berlin had been destroyed or severely damaged.

SECTION 2
Resources

GEOGRAPHY
■ Transparencies 93, 94

REINFORCEMENT
■ Independent Practice 32.2

ENRICHMENT
■ Voices from the Past 32.2

ASSESSMENT
■ Section Quiz 32.2

■ **RESEARCH**

Investigations into Nazi war crimes continue to this day. Students can find out about current efforts to uncover these criminals.

■ **BACKGROUND**

During the Cold War, Soviet-Yugoslav relations were alternately friendly and hostile. Yugoslavia opposed Soviet repression in countries such as Hungary, Czechoslovakia, and Afghanistan.

The Nuremberg trials Besides geographic division, Germany had another price to pay for the war. The discovery of Hitler's death camps (pages 724–725) led the Allies to put 22 surviving Nazi leaders on trial for crimes against humanity. The trials were held in the southern German town of Nuremberg during 1946.

"The wrongs which we seek to condemn and punish," said one prosecutor about the Nazis, "have been so calculated, so malignant, and so devastating that civilization cannot tolerate their being ignored—because it cannot survive their being repeated." In the end, 12 Nazis were sentenced to death. Seven Nazi leaders received long prison sentences, and three were acquitted. The greatest war criminal of all, Adolf Hitler, had taken his own life during the last days of the war in Berlin.

Europe was split between East and West.

As Germany collapsed in defeat, armies from the Soviet Union had pushed the Nazis back across Eastern Europe. By the end of the war, Soviet troops occupied the countries of Bulgaria, Romania, Hungary, Poland, Czechoslovakia, and eastern Germany.

In most of these countries, local Communists had fought hard against the Nazis in resistance movements. Many of these Communists had spent at least part of the war in Moscow and were closely allied with the Soviets.

In 1945, with the support of the Soviet army, Communists gained powerful posts in Eastern European governments. As the Nazis had done earlier, they often gained control of the police, the newspapers, and the radio stations. Soon they took over completely.

Stalin had promised Roosevelt to allow **free elections**—that is, with vote by secret ballot in a multiparty system—in Poland and other parts of Eastern Europe "as soon as possible." By July 1945, however, it was clear he would not keep this promise. "A freely elected government in any of these East European countries would be anti-Soviet," Stalin said bluntly, "and that we cannot allow."

By 1948, Communist governments were in power in Albania, Bulgaria, Romania, Poland, Hungary, and Czechoslovakia. These countries

742

were sometimes called Soviet **satellites.** In this sense, a satellite is a country whose policies are dictated or heavily influenced by another country.

Tito and Yugoslavia As in the other countries of Eastern Europe, Communists came to power in Yugoslavia. However, Yugoslavia followed a somewhat different path from its neighbors and did not become a Soviet satellite.

The leader of Yugoslavia's Communists was Josip Broz, better known by his wartime name of Tito (TEE-toh). Tito had led Yugoslav partisans (guerrillas) against the Nazis. By the time the Red Army arrived in Yugoslavia in late 1944, much of the country had already been freed by Tito's fighters. Although he was a Communist, Tito was above all a fierce Yugoslav nationalist. He was determined that the Soviets should not dominate his country.

Geography gave Tito a strong position. Yugoslavia's rugged mountains offered protection against Soviet tanks. Likewise the country's long coastline on the Adriatic had plenty of harbors through which Tito could get supplies from the West if the need arose. With these advantages and his own army behind him, Tito refused to obey orders from Stalin. "We demand," said Tito, "that everyone shall be master in his own house."

"I will shake my little finger," Stalin boasted in 1948, "and there will be no more Tito." Yet Tito long outlasted Stalin. The Yugoslav leader remained in power until his death in 1980 and kept his country independent of the Soviet Union.

An iron curtain Europe was now divided into two political regions: a mostly democratic Western Europe and a Communist Eastern Europe. Winston Churchill described this new situation in 1946:

A shadow has fallen upon the scenes so lately lighted by the Allied victory. From Stettin in the Baltic to Trieste in the Adriatic, an iron curtain has descended across the continent. Behind that line lie all the capitals of the ancient states of Central and Eastern Europe . . . These famous cities and the populations around them lie in what I must call the Soviet sphere, and all are subject in one form or another, not only to Soviet influence but to a very high and, in many cases, increasing measure of control from Moscow.

The phrase **iron curtain** came to stand for the division of Europe. Stalin had achieved one of his long-term goals. Eastern Europe had become a buffer zone between the West and the USSR.

The Truman Doctrine blocked communism.

Churchill's "Iron Curtain" speech sparked a debate in the United States over how to respond to Soviet actions in Eastern Europe. Many Americans shared Churchill's view that Soviet expansion could only be halted by a strong alliance between the United States and Great Britain. However, others—led by Secretary of Commerce Henry Wallace—argued that the Soviet Union had a legitimate right to control the countries along its borders. "Getting tough," Wallace said, "never bought anything real and lasting—whether for schoolyard bullies or world powers. The tougher we get, the tougher the Russians will get."

George Kennan, a leading expert on Soviet affairs, offered a third view. Kennan believed that Soviet hostility would remain a constant factor in the years ahead. He pointed out that the Soviet leaders had an **ideology,** or system of beliefs, that led them to believe that "the outside world was hostile and that it was their duty eventually to overthrow the political forces beyond their borders." Given this antagonism, he recommended that the United States should adopt a policy of "long-term, patient but firm and vigilant containment." By **containment,** he meant taking

■ **BACKGROUND**
Churchill's "iron curtain" speech stirred debate in the United States, where leaders differed sharply in their attitudes toward Soviet actions in Eastern Europe.

THREE POLITICAL/ECONOMIC MODELS

	Democratic Capitalism	Democratic Socialism	Communism/Socialism
Political System	Representative democracy Individual rights protected by government. Free elections	Representative democracy Individual rights protected by government. Free elections	Totalitarian regime Rights of individuals not protected. No free elections
Economic System	Market economy Free market controls what will be produced, by whom, and for whom. Private property and enterprise encouraged by opportunity for profit.	Mixed economy Major means of production owned by government and operated for public good; people have voice through elections. Private property and free enterprise operate in many sectors.	Command or planned economy Economic planning by government; state owns means of production; people have no voice in planning. Little private property or enterprise: limited production of consumer goods
Social Policy	Little government intervention; limited social programs; low taxes	Government support for social insurance programs; high taxes affect distribution of wealth.	Party leaders act in interest of state; individual security without freedom of choice
Limitations of System	In free market economy government does not seek social justice.	Government control and high taxes limit incentives to enterprise and productivity.	System provides no incentive or reward for productivity; does not respect individual rights.

743

■ DISCUSSION

Fully half of Britain's merchant marine tonnage was sunk during the war. About 25 percent of the country's wealth was consumed by war losses. Have students speculate on how this might have affected the economy.

■ BACKGROUND

The poster reads, "Clear the road for the Marshall Plan."

measures to prevent any extension of Communist rule to other countries.

While the American government wavered between these positions, Communist pressure threatened the independence of both Turkey and Greece. In Turkey, the Soviets demanded a treaty that would give them control over the strategic Dardanelles Strait. In Greece, Communist rebels appeared to be on the verge of overthrowing a pro-Western government.

Since World War II, Greece and Turkey had depended upon Great Britain for support. As you have seen, Great Britain had been the strongest power in the eastern Mediterranean for more than a century. The British, however, now found themselves exhausted by World War II and unable to continue helping Turkey and Greece. On February 21, 1947, the British delivered two notes to the United States State Department acknowledging that they could no longer support these two countries. An American official later noted, "Great Britain had within the hour handed the job of world leadership with all its burden and all its glory to the United States."

President Truman accepted the challenge. On March 12, 1947, he asked Congress for $400 million for military and economic aid to Greece and Turkey. In a statement that became known as the Truman Doctrine he stated, "It must be the policy of the United States to support free peoples who are resisting attempted subjugation by armed minorities or by outside pressure." After a short debate, Congress overwhelmingly approved the request made by Truman. The aid proved vital in helping Greece and Turkey successfully confront the Communist threat.

The Truman Doctrine marked the first use of containment. Under this policy, the United States would not attempt to overthrow Communist governments where they already existed. It would, however, do everything short of war to prevent any further Communist takeovers. "The free peoples of the world look to us for support in maintaining their freedoms," said Truman. "If we falter in our leadership, we may endanger the peace of the world."

The Marshall Plan aided Western Europe.

Greece and Turkey were not the only countries to need aid. As you have seen, World War II left Western Europe in ruins. Secretary of State George Marshall argued that the United States had to act quickly. "The patient is sinking while the doctors deliberate," he warned. Marshall proposed a bold cure. Speaking at Harvard University in June 1947, he presented a plan to offer extensive economic aid to all the nations of Europe.

The Marshall Plan revived European hopes. Over the next 4 years, 16 Western European countries received almost $13 billion in economic aid. Although the countries of Eastern Europe—including the Soviet Union—were invited to participate, only Yugoslavia accepted.

DAILY LIFE ▶ Rebuilding Europe

Europeans used Marshall Plan aid in a variety of ways. For example, Greek farmers imported 7,500 American-bred mules to replace animals lost in the war. West Germans mixed cement from the United States with rubble to build badly needed apartments. And Austrian engineers used Marshall Plan dollars to construct a giant hydroelectric plant.

The Marshall Plan was a success. The combination of American aid and European initiative helped lay the groundwork for Europe's remarkable recovery. One British official summarized Europe's gratitude by describing the Marshall Plan as "a lifeline to a sinking man." The official then added, "We grabbed the lifeline with both hands."

The Marshall Plan proved to be a great success. Within four years, industrial production in the countries receiving aid was 41 percent higher than it had been on the eve of World War II. At the same time, currencies had been stabilized and exports were rising rapidly.

The Marshall Plan benefited the United States as well. As the American government bought food and goods to send to Europe, American farms and factories raised production to record levels. As a result, the American economy continued its wartime boom without faltering. Moreover Western Europeans soon became good customers for American exports.

Rival alliances arose.

Both the United States and the Soviet Union feared that the Cold War might suddenly turn hot. Both countries met the threat of war by organizing alliances.

The United States built up its armed forces in Western Europe. Meanwhile the draft was continued in the United States to keep the army and navy at record peacetime size. Likewise the Soviet Union kept a huge standing army and required its satellites to do the same.

The NATO alliance In 1949, the United States joined Canada and ten Western European countries to form the North Atlantic Treaty Organization (NATO). The European members were Great Britain, Belgium, Denmark, France, Iceland, Italy, Luxembourg, the Netherlands, Norway, and Portugal.

The 12 members of NATO pledged military support to one another in case any member was attacked. This alliance marked the United States first *peacetime* military commitment since the country's founding in 1776.

Greece and Turkey joined NATO in 1952, and West Germany joined in 1955. By then, NATO kept a standing military force of more than 500,000 troops as well as thousands of planes, tanks, and other equipment.

The Warsaw Pact The USSR, for its part, saw NATO as a threat. In 1955, the Soviets developed an alliance system of their own, known as the Warsaw Pact. The Warsaw Pact linked the USSR and seven Eastern European countries—Poland, East Germany, Czechoslovakia, Hungary, Romania, Bulgaria, and Albania.

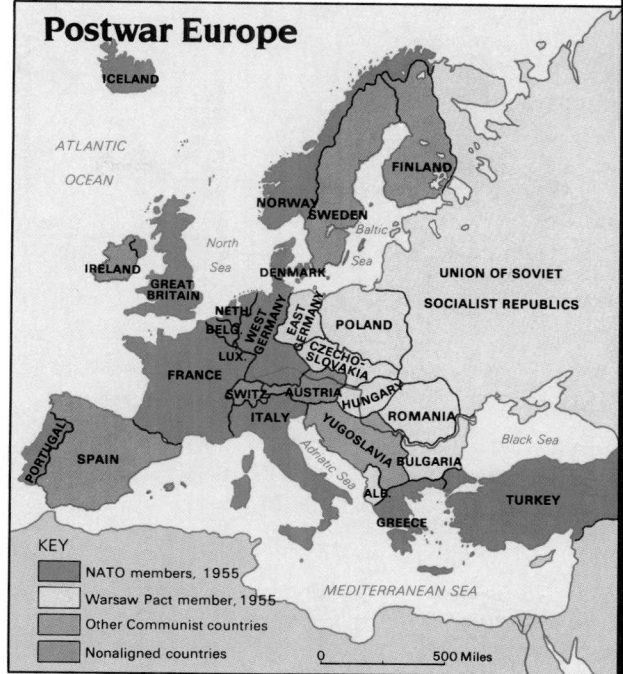

Postwar Europe

KEY

■ NATO members, 1955
□ Warsaw Pact member, 1955
▨ Other Communist countries
▨ Nonaligned countries

Map Study
What Communist country was not a member of the Warsaw Pact? What nations were neutral?

⊿Turning Points in History

The Berlin Airlift As Cold War tensions worsened, the city of Berlin became the focus of the first great test of wills between the United States and the Soviet Union. As Germany's largest city and former capital, Berlin had tremendous political and psychological significance. The Allies recognized this fact when they divided Berlin into four separate zones controlled by Britain, France, the United States, and the Soviet Union. The city itself, however, lay in East Germany, 110 miles within the Soviet occupation zone (see map page 746).

The Soviets increasingly came to view the presence of Western powers in Berlin as a check on their plans to dominate East Germany. These fears grew when the United States, Britain, and France announced plans to unite their occupation zones as one unit, West Berlin.

745

ANSWERS TO
Map Study

Yugoslavia; Spain, Sweden, Finland, Austria, Switzerland, Ireland

■ **BACKGROUND**

At a summit conference in 1955, the Soviets offered to disband the Warsaw Pact in return for the breakup of NATO and the withdrawal of all "foreign troops" from Europe.

ANSWERS TO
Section Review 2

Define:
(a) vote by secret ballot in a multiparty system
(b) country whose policies are dictated by another country (c) phrase that represents the division of Europe (d) system of beliefs
(e) Truman's policy to keep communism from spreading

Identify:
(a) trials of Nazi leaders for war crimes (b) Yugoslavian leader who kept his country

(continued)

ANSWERS TO
Map Study

Soviet; between the American, British, and French occupation zones, or West Berlin, and the Soviet occupation zone, East Berlin

Division of Germany, 1945

Map Study

In which occupation zone was Berlin located? Where was the Berlin Wall built?

ANSWERS TO (continued)

independent of the USSR **(c)** alliance of U.S., Canada, and 10 Western European countries **(d)** alliance of the USSR and 7 Eastern European countries

Answer:

1. **(a)** Colonial empires began to crumble. **(b)** British withdrew peacefully, while the French fought to keep their colonies.

2. Soviet troops occupied most of Eastern Europe. Local Communists were strong.

3. Yugoslavia remained independent of USSR.

4. **(a)** policy of containment **(b)** U.S. gave military and economic aid to defeat the Communist rebels in Greece.

5. In countries receiving aid, industrial production rose, currencies stabilized, and exports increased.

6. **(a)** military support if attacked **(b)** formed Warsaw Pact

7. **(a)** non-Communist island in East Germany **(b)** The Soviets blockaded West Berlin, but the Allies airlifted supplies to the city.

8. Answers might consider magnitude of the crimes, motives of the perpetrators, and methods used to carry out the crimes.

Although the three nations had a legal right to unify their zones, they had no written agreement with the Soviets guaranteeing free access to Berlin by road or rail. Stalin saw that this loophole provided an opportunity. If he moved quickly, he might be able to take over the part of Berlin held by the three Western powers. In June 1948, Stalin closed all highway and rail routes into West Berlin. As a result, no food or fuel could reach that part of the city. The 2.5 million residents of West Berlin had only enough food to last for 36 days.

The Soviet blockade of Berlin confronted President Truman with a difficult decision. If the Western powers gave up West Berlin, that meant leaving their sector to Soviet control. Truman also knew that such a move would be contrary to his policy of containment. On the other hand, the president knew that if he sent troops to reopen the closed roads, he might provoke a military showdown. Truman believed that the Berlin blockade represented a test of American determination. He therefore refused to withdraw, declaring, "We are going to stay, period."

Truman chose an unexpected and risky strategy to maintain a presence in West Berlin. On June

24, 1948, he ordered a massive airlift to supply the 4,500 tons of food, fuel, and supplies that the people of West Berlin needed every day. To guard against any Soviet attempt to interrupt the airlift, Truman transferred 60 bombers to bases in Britain. Each plane was capable of delivering atom bombs. Unknown to the Soviets, Truman was bluffing; the planes did not carry atom bombs.

For a few weeks, the world seemed close to war. Although Stalin did not make any serious attempt to disrupt the airlift, he refused to lift the blockade. Fearing the worst, Truman asked his advisers to brief him "on bases, bombs, Moscow, Leningrad, etc." Later he wrote in his diary, "I have a terrible feeling . . . that we are very close to war. I hope not."

During the winter of 1949, tensions slowly eased as the airlift—called Operation Vittles—became a success. During the critical winter months, the daily average of supplies delivered to West Berlin reached 5,000 tons. American pilots raised the spirits of West Berlin children by parachuting thousands of toys to them.

The success of the Berlin airlift showed the failure of the Berlin blockade. On May 12, 1949, Stalin reopened road and rail traffic between West Berlin and West Germany. The consequences of the airlift, however, proved to be long-term. The constant roar of the planes over Berlin provided a vivid demonstration of American power and will. Americans, in turn, came to admire the West Berliners' courage and determination. The crisis also changed the relationship between Germany and the Western Allies from that of occupiers and occupied to partners in a joint struggle to defend the free world. In the short term, the stalemate over the city continued. Soviet leaders still opposed a free West Berlin.

Section REVIEW 2

Define: (a) free election, (b) satellite, (c) iron curtain, (d) ideology, (e) containment
Identify: (a) Nuremberg trials, (b) Tito, (c) North Atlantic Treaty Organization, (d) Warsaw Pact
Answer:
1. (a) How did Europe's world influence change after 1945? (b) How did the British and the French differ in their reactions?

2. Give at least two reasons why Communists were in a strong position to take over governments in Eastern Europe.

3. How did the outcome of the Communist takeover in Yugoslavia differ from the outcome of takeovers elsewhere in Eastern Europe?

4. (a) What was the Truman Doctrine? (b) How was it applied in Greece?

5. What were three results of the Marshall Plan?

6. (a) What promise did NATO members make to one another? (b) How did the Communist countries respond?

7. (a) Why was Berlin a likely spot for trouble to develop in the Cold War? (b) What crisis arose there in 1948?

Critical Thinking

8. If you were asked to write a definition of "crimes against humanity," what important considerations would you want to include?

Western Europe moved toward cooperation. 3

In the decades after World War II, Europe was in effect not one but two continents. The countries of Western Europe were strongly influenced by the United States, which encouraged democratic institutions. Both the governments and economies in the countries of Eastern Europe, however, were dominated and controlled by the Soviet Union.

The iron curtain that divided postwar Europe was more than a political boundary. It also separated different economic systems. The countries of Eastern Europe had highly centralized economies. Here governments made nearly all major economic decisions and strictly controlled production and distribution. In Western Europe as in the United States, private enterprise and commerce flourished. In these countries, the pace of recovery from World War II was remarkably rapid.

West Germany prospered in peace.

The single most dramatic political and economic transformation in postwar Europe took place in West Germany. This new state—officially titled the Federal Republic of Germany—was created in 1949 by the combination of the British, French, and American zones of occupation. West Germany's government was headed by a chancellor who was responsible to a democratically elected legislature.

The economic miracle With three times the population of Soviet-dominated East Germany, West Germany in 1949 had a strong industrial base, abundant natural resources, and a highly skilled work force. Marshall Plan economic aid had already helped the country get back on its feet. Over the next decade, the people of West Germany created their own Wirtschaftswunder, or economic miracle.

The West German economy expanded rapidly during the 1950's. Thousands of modern, highly efficient factories were constructed. An excellent transportation system was built around the expanded Autobahn, or freeway, network. German companies soon dominated the European electrical, automobile, chemical, and steel industries. High-quality West German exports found markets all over the world and produced a steady flow of wealth that supported Germany's prosperity.

Booming West Germany became an economic superpower. Between 1950 and 1980, for example, the country's **gross national product** (GNP), or total value of goods and services produced, grew from $48 billion to an astounding $828 billion. And the country's highly democratic political structure helped ensure that the fruits of this prosperity were shared among the population. By 1980, the average West German earned more annually than the average American.

The Adenauer era West Germany's first chancellor was Konrad Adenauer. During his 14 years in office (1949–1963), the Old Man—as he was called affectionately by West Germans—ensured that his country developed strong democratic institutions as well as a healthy economy. Two major parties, Adenauer's Christian Democrats and the rival Social Democrats, dominated West German politics during this period.

Under Adenauer, West Germany allied itself strongly with the United States, joining NATO in 1955. NATO military bases soon dotted the country, and supply links with isolated West Berlin were maintained and strengthened. "Our country is the point of tension between two world blocs," Adenauer noted. "Long ago I made a great

747

SECTION 3 Objectives and Teaching Strategies

OBJECTIVE 1. Describe the influence of Charles De Gaulle on French government.

Teaching Strategy: *Skill Building: Interpreting a Political Cartoon* (page 736d)

OBJECTIVE 2. Explain steps Europeans are taking to strengthen economic unity.

Teaching Strategy: *Economics and History: Competing for World Markets* (page 736e)

OBJECTIVE 3. Cite reasons for Southern Europe's rapid economic growth.

Teaching Strategy: *Discussing History: Southern Europe's Economic Growth* (page 736e)

SECTION 3 Resources

GEOGRAPHY
- Transparency 95

REINFORCEMENT
- Independent Practice 32.3

ENRICHMENT
- Voices from the Past 32.3

ASSESSMENT
- Section Quiz 32.3

Germany lost territory; Poland's borders have shifted west, taking land from Germany and losing land to the USSR.

■ BACKGROUND

The Marshall Plan also provided an impetus to economic cooperation. All countries receiving aid under the plan had to work together and decide as a group how the money would be spent.

■ DISCUSSION

In Germany, a nation often characterized as warlike, pacifist sentiment is now stronger than in any other nation of Western Europe. Ask students why they think this is so.

Map Study

Compare this map with the one on page 708. How have Germany and Poland changed? (Note that the German Danzig has become the Polish Gdansk.)

decision: we belong to the West and not the East.''

Ostpolitik In 1969, Willy Brandt—like Adenauer, a wartime opponent of the Nazis—became West Germany's first Social Democratic chancellor. Brandt was very familiar with Cold War tensions; he had been mayor of West Berlin when the Berlin Wall was erected in 1961 (page 755). Nevertheless Brandt was determined to improve relations with the Soviet bloc through his Ostpolitik, or Eastern policy.

Breaking with the past, Brandt visited the Soviet Union and Poland in 1970 and signed treaties of friendship with both countries. Building upon

his concept of two German states within one German nation, Brandt also laid the foundation for better relations with East Germany. During the 1970's, Cold War tensions lessened in central Europe.

France took an independent course.

While much of France had been spared the devastation of World War II, the country was bitterly divided in 1945. Democratic government was restored as a fourth French Republic was created. But stability proved elusive. A dozen major political parties vied for voter support, and

748

weak coalition governments measured their life spans in months rather than years.

Like West Germany, France enjoyed an economic boom in the decades after World War II. Although the French economy remained less industrialized than that of its eastern neighbor, it continued to prosper. The major problem facing postwar France was its adjustment to a new role as a strictly European power.

Colonial wars France was one of several European nations that in 1945 faced the breakup of its colonial empire. Unlike most other nations, however, the French chose to resist independence movements in several of their colonies. In Southeast Asia, for example, France struggled against Vietnamese nationalists to maintain its control over Indochina. Only after a disastrous defeat at Dien Bien Phu in 1954 did French forces withdraw from the region.

Nowhere did the French fight more fiercely to maintain control than in Algeria, directly across the Mediterranean in North Africa. The French government had long regarded Algeria as part of France itself. More than a million French settlers lived in that country, far more than in any other overseas possession. Yet the French remained less than 10 percent of the total population, and in 1954, the Algerian majority began a war for independence.

This brutal guerrilla war between Algerian nationalists and the French dragged on for years. Thousands perished on each side. In 1958, the government began peace talks with the Algerian rebels. But the French army refused to stop fighting, instead seizing direct control of the government in Algeria.

De Gaulle took control Faced with civil war, the French National Assembly turned to General Charles de Gaulle, the one man who could command the respect of the rebellious military. De Gaulle had led the French government-in-exile during World War II, and he was a living symbol of France's resistance to the Nazis. A strong-willed and proud man, De Gaulle agreed to lead his country but only on the condition that the French constitution be changed so as to ensure more stability in government.

De Gaulle's great prestige as a military leader won back the loyalty of the French army in Algeria and the confidence of French settlers there as well. Peace talks were launched with the Algerian

General Charles de Gaulle had few doubts about his place in history.

nationalists. After years of negotiation, Algeria was finally granted full independence in 1962.

At home, De Gaulle had gotten his wish late in 1958, when French voters approved a new constitution giving much more power to the country's executive. De Gaulle thus took office as the first president of this Fifth Republic.

"France cannot be France without greatness," De Gaulle once remarked. During the 1960's, he charted an independent course for France, one that steered clear of both superpowers. France withdrew from NATO in 1966 and improved its relations with the Soviet bloc. France even exploded its own atom bomb. Although De Gaulle retired in 1969, these independent policies were continued by Georges Pompidou and Valery Giscard d'Estaing, his successors in the 1970's.

The Common Market was formed in Western Europe.

In 1981, the French people elected the Socialist leader François Mitterrand as president. The following year, Christian Democrat Helmut Kohl was elected chancellor of West Germany. During the 1980's, these two leaders built ever-stronger ties between their two nations and with their European neighbors. Both were staunch supporters of the European Economic Community (EC), or **Common Market**, an organization which encouraged free trade among its members.

The Common Market had its origins in the aftermath of World War II, when European statesmen like Jean Monnet of France determined

749

■ **BACKGROUND**

For more than 100 years, France had a low birthrate. The government's postwar decision to subsidize families with children led to a welcome population increase.

■ **DISCUSSION**

De Gaulle voiced the French sense of mission: "All my life I have had a certain idea of France . . . [I tend] to imagine France, like the princess in the fairy stories or the Madonna in the frescoes, as dedicated to an exalted and exceptional destiny." Has France lived up to De Gaulle's vision?

■ **BACKGROUND**

Student rebels in Paris hurled cobblestones from the streets at the police. Parisian authorities later paved over all the city's cobblestone streets to eliminate those weapons from future arsenals.

Cooperative Learning

Have students examine the poster concerning the Marshall Plan on page 744. Ask them what idea the poster is attempting to express. Also ask where the poster might have been displayed and for what audience it was intended. Then, working in groups of four, have students choose a country that does not currently belong to the Common Market and create a poster encouraging membership in that organization. Two group members can act as designers and artists. Another can write any text that appears on the poster. The fourth member can present and explain the poster to the class. Remind students to carefully consider the advantages of the Common Market, especially when the member countries fully integrate in 1992.

What Europe Bought

Petroleum products	$55.7
Office equipment	19.0
Apparel and accessories	16.7
Road vehicles, including cars	16.5
Electrical machinery and parts	16.1
Telecommunications equipment	12.8
Textiles, yarn, and fabrics	10.6
Paper and paperboard	10.5
Fruits and vegetables	9.5
Plastics and artificial resins	9.3

IN BILLIONS OF DOLLARS

SOURCE: European Commission of the European Community

Reading a table *This table shows the top 10 imports of the European Community (Common Market) in 1987. Which import is largest, and why?*

Who Sold to Europe

United States	$66.4
Japan	41.9
Soviet Union	15.0
Brazil	8.3
Canada	8.0
Taiwan	7.9
Hong Kong	7.4
South Korea	7.1
Saudi Arabia	6.6
Algeria	6.1
Yugoslavia	6.1
China	5.9
Libya	5.8
South Africa	5.6
Australia	4.8

IN BILLIONS OF U.S. DOLLARS

SOURCE: Organization for Economic Cooperation and Development

Reading a table *Imports from abroad by members of the European Community in 1987 totaled almost $400 billion. What two nations provided most of those imports?*

that economic cooperation was a key to the future peace and prosperity of their continent. As early as 1950, six European nations—Belgium, France, Italy, Luxembourg, the Netherlands, and West Germany—joined together to form the European Coal and Steel Community (ECSC). This provided for tariff-free trade in these products among member countries.

So successful was this experiment in economic cooperation that the same six nations in 1957 formed the European Economic Community. Its purpose was to gradually eliminate barriers to commerce within the group. Trade with countries outside the Common Market was subject to standard EC tariffs.

The Common Market became a cornerstone of the economic boom Western Europe enjoyed during the 1960's. Denmark, Great Britain, and Ireland joined the EEC in 1973. The total membership grew to 12 with the addition of Greece in 1981 and Portugal and Spain in 1986.

With the leadership provided by France under François Mitterand and West Germany under Helmut Kohl, the Common Market moved beyond economics during the 1980's. A European Parliament directly elected by citizens of member countries met regularly in the French city of Strasbourg. A permanent European civil service was headquartered in Brussels, Belgium, to handle administrative and economic functions.

The EC's quest for economic integration reached another milestone on January 1, 1993. On that date, its member nations dropped all internal trade barriers (see page 857). At the same time, the EC also considered a proposed Treaty on European Union that would create a common currency and establish a European Central Bank before 1999.

Democracy came to Southern Europe.

Three countries of the Mediterranean region—Greece, Spain, and Portugal—spent most of the postwar period under the control of dictators. During the 1970's, however, all three made the transition to democratic rule and were able to participate fully in the EC. At his death in 1975, for example, General Francisco Franco had controlled Spain for over four decades. King Juan Carlos, who had been a figurehead under Franco, courageously spearheaded a smooth transition to democratic rule.

Economically the countries of Southern Europe had lagged behind their northern neighbors.

750

Apart from northern Italy, which was heavily industrialized, these nations had the lowest per capita incomes in Europe outside the Soviet bloc.

During the 1970's and 1980's, however, the situation began to change. Northern Europeans discovered the Mediterranean Sun Belt as a vacation and retirement location. Economic development was also spurred by the EC as many industries began to relocate in the region.

The United Kingdom faced numerous difficulties.

Of all the former Great Powers of Europe, the United Kingdom faced the most difficult adjustment after World War II. Once the world's foremost imperial power, Britain now found itself economically weakened and politically divided.

Once the birthplace of the Industrial Revolution, Britain now found that time had passed it by. The nation's numerous factories were outdated and inefficient, while the loss of easy access to former colonial products and markets hampered British commerce. The country did enjoy an economic boom during the 1950's, but by 1965, the rate of growth had slowed considerably. By 1980, the United Kingdom's GNP was only half that of West Germany's and just slightly more than Italy's.

Political divisions During the decades after World War II, there were two major contenders for power in British politics: the Labour party and the Conservative party. Their ideas on how the country should develop differed completely.

The Labour party position was that **moderate socialism** was the answer to the United Kingdom's social and economic problems. This form of socialism involved government support for social insurance programs and ownership of major industries within a democratic system. When in power, therefore, Labour leaders increased taxes to pay for an ever-broader range of social services. Most medical services were provided free of charge, while unemployment and old-age benefits were increased dramatically. The Labour party felt that essential services should be run by the government to ensure fair distribution of costs and services. For example, the first postwar Labour government, in power from 1945 to 1951, nationalized railroads, banks, mines, and public utilities.

Leaders of the Conservative party, on the other hand, were convinced that what the country needed was more free enterprise, not more government control. Only by reducing taxes and supporting business, they argued, could the United Kingdom hope to regain its former prosperity.

Not surprisingly, the Labour party drew most of its support from the lower classes, particularly in the industrial cities. The Conservatives had stronger appeal to the middle and upper classes and to people in the suburbs and rural areas.

The Thatcher revolution For 30 years after World War II, Labour and Conservative governments alternated in power. In 1979, however, a new Conservative leader, Margaret Thatcher, won a landslide victory. Thatcher, the first woman to lead a major Western democracy, was determined to set Britain on a firm new course.

While she reduced income taxes, Thatcher also ruthlessly cut government spending and turned many nationalized industries back into private companies. The initial result was economic decline, with unemployment rates at their highest levels since the Depression.

Fortunately for the Conservatives, the development of newly discovered oil fields under the North Sea helped to generate jobs and revenue during the 1980's. At the same time, Conservative policies favored business development, and the economy improved as the decade progressed. The Iron Lady, as Thatcher was called by friend and foe alike, won reelection victories in 1983 and

Margaret Thatcher served as Britain's prime minister for 11 years, from 1979 to 1990.

751

■ BACKGROUND

By the 1970's, the poor performance of Britain's nationalized industries had discredited the idea of public ownership in that country.

ANSWERS TO
Section Review 3

Define:
(a) German for "economic miracle" (b) total value of goods and services produced by a nation (c) European organization which encourages free trade among its members (d) form of socialism that involves government support for social insurance programs and ownership of major industries within a democratic system

Identify:
(a) leader who rebuilt West Germany's economy (b) West German leader who improved relations with Eastern Europe (c) Willy Brandt's program to improve relations with USSR and Eastern Europe (d) French war hero and strong leader of the Fifth Republic (e) French Socialist president who strengthened ties with West Germany (f) West German chancellor, strong supporter of the Common Market (g) Spanish leader who led his country toward democracy (h) first woman prime minister of Britain

Answer:
1. (a) rebuilt West German economy, allied West Ger-
(continued)

ANSWERS TO (continued)

many with United States, NATO, and Common Market **(b)** improved relations with USSR and Eastern Europe

2. **(a)** lacked strong executive leadership **(b)** breakup of colonial empire

3. **(a)** National Assembly gave him full powers of government for six months. **(b)** Nationalist stand, independent of United States and NATO

4. **(a)** European Coal and Steel Community **(b)** 1957—Belgium, France, Italy, Luxembourg, the Netherlands, West Germany; 1973—Denmark, Great Britain, Ireland; 1981—Greece; 1986—Portugal, Spain **(c)** moved beyond economics

5. Southern European countries became democracies, economies improved.

6. **(a)** Labour Party advocated higher taxes to provide social services, government controls on business. Conservatives wanted less taxes, government control. **(b)** Thatcher cut taxes, government spending, turned nationalized industries back into private companies.

7. conflicts between Protestant majority and Catholic minority, presence of British troops

8. **(a)** Since Western Europe's countries were united militarily, economic unity was made easier. **(b)** Student's answers will vary. Possible answers: Yes—Would have organized to compete with U.S., Japanese economies; No—Countries would have concentrated on their own economies.

1987. But Thatcher's popularity did not last. A bitter fight over how to raise local taxes hurt her. Stung by the loss of support from Conservative party leaders, Thatcher stepped down in November 1990. John Major, a leading member of Thatcher's cabinet replaced her.

Northern Ireland In foreign affairs, Thatcher led her country to victory in a brief war with Argentina in 1982 over the status of the Falkland Islands. But neither she nor Major could find a solution to the problem in Northern Ireland.

Northern Ireland consists of the six northeastern counties of Ireland—all part of the province of Ulster. This small area had chosen to remain united with Great Britain when the rest of Ireland won its independence during the 1920's. A majority of the population in Northern Ireland was British in descent and Protestant in religion. A substantial minority of the people, however, was Catholic, with cultural ties to the rest of Ireland rather than to Britain.

For more than half a century, the Protestant majority controlled the government of Northern Ireland. Catholic protests against this monopoly of power began in the late 1960's and quickly turned violent. A radical militant group calling itself the Irish Republican Army (IRA) launched a terrorist campaign against British soldiers and police and Protestant civilians. Similar radical groups also surfaced among the Protestants.

In the years of senseless violence since that time, more than 2,500 people—many of them innocent civilians—have been killed in terrorist attacks. Compromise solutions involving power-sharing that have been proposed by both British and Irish leaders have so far been rejected.

Section REVIEW 3

Define: (a) Wirtschaftswunder, (b) gross national product, (c) Common Market, (d) moderate socialism

Identify: (a) Konrad Adenauer, (b) Willy Brandt, (c) Ostpolitik, (d) Charles de Gaulle, (e) François Mitterand, (f) Helmut Kohl, (g) King Juan Carlos, (h) Margaret Thatcher

Answer:

1. (a) What were Adenauer's major accomplishments? (b) How did German foreign policy change under Willy Brandt and his successors?

2. (a) What serious weakness undermined France's Fourth Republic? (b) What problems did France face abroad?

3. (a) How did Charles de Gaulle come to power in France in 1958? (b) What stand did he take in foreign policy?

4. (a) What was the first postwar effort at economic cooperation in Europe? (b) What European nations joined the Common Market and when? (c) How did the role of the Common Market change during the 1980's?

5. How did the political and economic situation of Southern Europe change after 1970?

6. (a) What issues divided the Labour and Conservative parties in the postwar United Kingdom? (b) How did Margaret Thatcher try to solve the country's economic problems during the 1980's?

7. Describe the issues that contributed to political tension in Northern Ireland.

Critical Thinking

8. (a) What role did Cold War tensions play in Western Europe's progress toward economic unity during this period? (b) Do you think organizations like the Common Market would have developed without the Cold War? Give reasons.

The USSR dominated Eastern Europe. 4

On March 5, 1953, Joseph Stalin died. For three decades, he had ruled the Soviet Union with an iron hand, using totalitarian methods to force an industrial revolution upon his undeveloped country.

After 1953, the Soviet economy continued to expand. The rate of economic growth during the 1950's was double that of the United States. But the fruits of this impressive development were not enjoyed by the Soviet masses. Government-owned factories churned out industrial and military products but precious few consumer goods. Politically the Soviet Union remained a police state, in which all decisions were made by the Communist party and in which no dissent was tolerated.

What nations are symbolized by the East Side Rockets being led by Khrushchev?

Khrushchev rose to power.

Stalin's death made clear a basic problem in the Soviet system: It lacked a legal, well-defined way for one leader to succeed another. Without public elections, leaders within the Communist party maneuvered for position, hoping to gain enough support to be named general secretary.

For the first few years after Stalin's death, a group of Soviet leaders shared power. As time went by, however, one man was able to gain more and more power. That man was Nikita Khrushchev (1894–1971). Few people would have predicted Khrushchev's rise. The son of a coal miner, he first worked as a metalworker and mechanic. Khrushchev had little formal education, but he was shrewd, tough, and at times ruthless. In 1939, he became a full member of the Politburo, an elite group of about 20 leaders that make policy decisions for the Communist party. By 1958, Khrushchev was both general secretary of the Communist party and premier.

De-Stalinization Khrushchev boldly demonstrated his power at a secret session of the Twentieth Communist Party Congress in Moscow in

1956. Before an astounded audience, he accused Stalin of jailing and killing loyal Soviet citizens.

Khrushchev's speech signaled the beginning of a policy called de-Stalinization. Workers destroyed monuments of the former dictator. Stalin's body was moved from its place of honor next to Lenin and buried outside the Kremlin wall. The city of Stalingrad was renamed Volgograd.

Khrushchev's overthrow Khrushchev called for a number of reforms that eventually led to his undoing. Many party leaders feared that changes in party organization would reduce their power. A final blow was Khrushchev's loss of prestige as a result of the Cuban Missile Crisis (page 816). In 1964, Soviet party leaders voted to remove Khrushchev from power.

Brezhnev opposed dissidents.

Within a short time, Leonid Brezhnev (1906–1982) replaced Khrushchev as the top Soviet leader. Brezhnev quickly adopted a policy designed to end domestic dissent. Government censors carefully controlled what writers could publish. The Communist party strictly enforced laws that limited such basic human rights as freedom of speech and worship.

Reading a graph *How did spending on research and development change in each country between 1961 and 1979? What factors might account for the increases? Why is such spending important?*

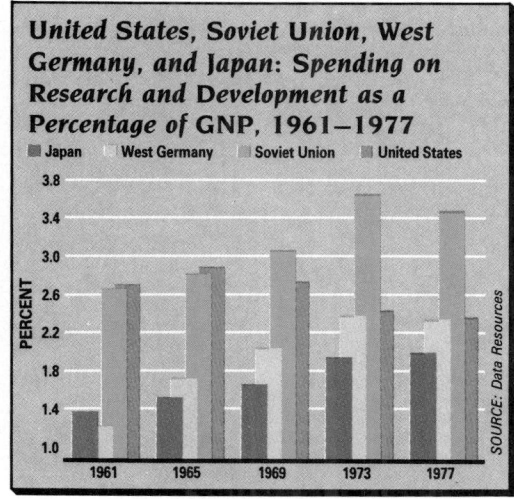

United States, Soviet Union, West Germany, and Japan: Spending on Research and Development as a Percentage of GNP, 1961–1977

SOURCE: Data Resources

753

SECTION 4 Objectives and Teaching Strategies

OBJECTIVE 1. Describe the persecution suffered by Soviet dissidents.

Teaching Strategy: *Discussing History: Soviet Dissidents* (page 736e)

OBJECTIVE 2. Describe and evaluate the revolts of the Hungarians and the Czechoslovakians.

Teaching Strategy: *Skill Building: Comparing the Hungarian and Czechoslovakian Revolts* (page 736f)

ANSWER TO Caption Question

Eastern European nations

ANSWERS TO Reading a Graph

Spending on research and development increased in the Soviet Union, West Germany, and Japan but decreased in the United States. The three nations were in part seeking to develop technology that already existed in the United States. Spending on research and development helps nations to compete in trade.

SECTION 4 Resources

ASSESSMENT
■ Section Quiz 32.4

REINFORCEMENT
■ Independent Practice 32.4

ENRICHMENT
■ Voices from the Past 32.4

753

Brezhnev clamped down on **dissidents** who dared to protest against government policies. The secret police arrested Alexander Solzhenitsyn, winner of the 1970 Nobel Prize in literature, and expelled him from the Soviet Union. When the physicist Andrei Sakharov criticized the government, he and his wife Yelena Bonner were exiled to the remote city of Gorky.

Brezhnev made it clear he would not tolerate dissent in Eastern Europe either. In 1968, for example, he ordered the armies of the Warsaw Pact nations to crush a reform government in Czechoslovakia. He justified this invasion by claiming that the Soviet Union had the right to use force to keep its Eastern European allies from turning away from communism. This policy became known as the Brezhnev Doctrine.

Eastern Europe was linked to the Soviet Union.

The Brezhnev Doctrine was merely a continuation of Stalin's policy toward the Soviet satellites in Eastern Europe. After World War II, for example, the Soviet Union did not allow these countries to accept Marshall Plan aid. However, the aid that the Soviets offered through Comecon (the Council for Mutual Economic Assistance) was far too little to repair the war's damages. Moreover, the USSR did not allow Eastern Europeans to choose their own economic priorities. Instead, the USSR insisted that they concentrate on developing industries that fit Soviet needs.

Such obstacles made Eastern Europe's economic recovery slower than Western Europe's. Gradually, however, industrialization spread more widely in Eastern Europe. East Germany and Czechoslovakia took the lead, with Albania remaining the least developed. By the 1970's, the standard of living in Eastern Europe had improved.

Most Eastern Europeans were loyal to their Communist governments. Yet there was a constant undercurrent of discontent with Soviet control that at times erupted in protests.

The Hungarian revolt failed.

As you have seen, Stalin's death in 1953 brought to power a new, more moderate group of Soviet leaders. The new leaders allowed the satellite countries a little more independence as long as they remained firmly Communist and wholeheartedly allied with the Soviet Union.

This small gain only whetted people's desire for more freedom in Eastern Europe. Beginning

In the Hungarian uprising of October 1956, protesters were successful at first. They even captured a Soviet tank in the main square of Budapest. A few weeks later, however, the Soviets returned and brutally suppressed the uprising.

754

in East Germany in 1953, a wave of strikes and protests swept across Czechoslovakia, Hungary, and Poland.

In Hungary, the protests grew to a major crisis. In October 1956, the Hungarian army joined with the protesters to oust Hungary's Soviet-controlled government. Angry mobs stormed through Budapest, waving Hungarian flags with the Communist hammer-and-sickle emblems cut out. The rioters beat and killed as many members of the Soviet-supported secret police as they could catch. "From the youngest child to the oldest man," said one Hungarian, "no one wants communism. We have had enough of it, enough of it forever."

Imre Nagy (nahj), the most popular and liberal Hungarian Communist leader, formed a new government. Nagy promised free elections, denounced the Warsaw Pact, and demanded that all Soviet troops leave Hungary.

Such reforms were far more than the USSR would allow. In early November, Soviet tanks rolled into Budapest, backed by crack infantry units of the Red Army. Armed only with pistols and bottles, thousands of Hungarian freedom fighters threw up barricades in the streets and fought the invaders but to no avail. The Soviets overthrew the Nagy government and replaced it with pro-Soviet leaders. Nagy himself was executed. Some 200,000 Hungarians fled west of the iron curtain.

The United States did nothing to help Hungary break free of Soviet control. Many Hungarians were bitterly disappointed. The American policy of containment did not extend to driving the Soviet Union out of its satellites.

No help came to Hungary from the United Nations either. Although the UN passed one resolution after another condemning the USSR, the Soviet veto in the Security Council stopped the UN from taking any action.

Decisions in History

President Kennedy was prepared to go to war to defend the freedom of West Berlin and maintain access to it. The building of the Berlin Wall, however, caught him by surprise. West Berlin Mayor Brandt urged the President to destroy the illegal barrier. White House advisers warned that doing so would provoke a grave East-West crisis. What would you have done and why?

Before East Germany built the Berlin Wall in 1961, only a barbed-wire barricade separated East and West Berlin. This East German soldier was one of many people who fled to the West.

East Germany led in industry.

Life in East Germany, as the German Democratic Republic is known, was bleak for many years after World War II. In East Berlin, whole blocks of bombed-out buildings stood as grim reminders of the war. East German stores and markets had few consumer goods. Meat and fresh vegetables were often in short supply. Meanwhile, in nearby West Berlin, new construction had replaced the ruins, and the standard of living was steadily rising.

Faced with this contrast, more than three million East Germans fled to West Germany between 1949 and 1961. Most of these refugees escaped by going from East Berlin to West Berlin. Suddenly, on August 13, 1961, the Communists built a barrier between the two halves of Berlin. Known as the Berlin Wall, the barrier eventually became a 28-mile wall of concrete and barbed wire. Escape to the West became much more difficult.

During the 1970's, the standard of living improved as East Germany developed the strongest

■ **BACKGROUND**
The Berlin Wall was the first barrier ever built to keep a population *in* rather than to keep enemies out.

755

ANSWERS TO
Voice from Our Time

1. The Communist government controlled the press.
2. to speak the truth
3. cannot suppress thought and the will to resist

■ DISCUSSION

General Wojciech Jaruzelski was the Polish leader who imposed martial law on December 13, 1981. Now retired and living in Warsaw, Jaruzelski strongly regrets his decision, but maintains that he had no other choice since he felt that the threat of Soviet intervention was real. Ask students what they would have done if they had been in Jaruzelski's position. Then ask how they think Poles should view Jaruzelski today. For example, should he be blamed for trying to suppress a mass movement for freedom and democracy? Or should he be praised for saving Poland from a bloody invasion like the ones in Hungary in 1956 and Czechoslovakia in 1968?

Voice from Our Time | A Czechoslovak Protest

During the occupation of Czechoslovakia in 1968, a group of Czechoslovakian scientists and writers living in Austria issued this *Manifesto against Aggression.*

. . . In the fateful hours of the occupation of . . . Czechoslovakia, we consider it necessary to proclaim certain basic convictions which we hold in common as intellectuals, as Czechs and Slovaks, as citizens of the Czechoslovak Socialist Republic.

1. We believe that as intellectuals we have one basic duty to our nation: to speak the truth . . .

2. We trust the strength of ideas, and we distrust power . . . We have no weapons but words and ideas, yet we are convinced that no force of oppression can withstand the thrust of thought. Today more than ever, we realize that an attack on ideas is an attack on man himself.

3. People may be deprived of all their civil rights, but they cannot be deprived of their freedom to think. Totalitarian dictatorships may rob people of everything except their will to resist. Tanks can occupy territory but not the minds of men . . .

7. The violent acts of recent days have demonstrated again that totalitarian dictatorship represents the greatest danger to mankind. It is a matter of indifference under what ideology the dictators send their tanks into peaceful countries and for what ostensible motives soldiers shoot unarmed citizens.

1. Why was this document not issued in Czechoslovakia?
2. What do the authors say is the basic duty of intellectuals to their country?
3. Why do the authors claim that dictatorships cannot totally defeat a people?

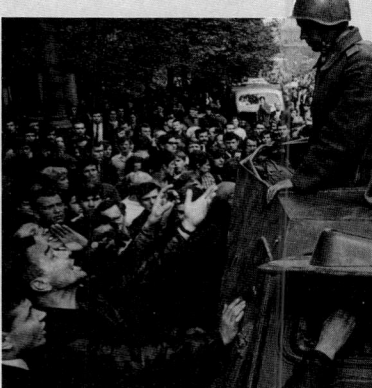

economy in Eastern Europe. Under longtime Communist ruler Erich Honecker, the East German secret police—the Stasi—spied upon millions of its own citizens. Dissent was not tolerated.

Reforms were stamped out in Czechoslovakia.

In 1968, students staged protests in many parts of Europe, both East and West. In Czechoslovakia, a new Communist leader, Alexander Dubcek (**DOOB**-chek), responded with a program of reforms. He loosened controls on writings and discussions. Dubcek said he wanted to create "socialism with a human face" but without giving up the basic ideas of communism. The time of Dubcek's reforms is often called Prague Spring, when new ideas bloomed in Czechoslovakia's capital.

Dubcek's new policies alarmed the Soviets. They called on the other Warsaw Pact countries to take action with them against Czechoslovakia. On August 20, armed forces from the USSR, Poland, East Germany, Hungary, and Bulgaria invaded Czechoslovakia over four frontiers. Dubcek remained in power briefly but was soon replaced by a leader more in tune with the USSR. For two decades after the Prague Spring, Czechoslovakia had one of the strictest governments in Eastern Europe.

Poland experienced dramatic changes.

Although the Soviets successfully crushed democratic reforms in Czechoslovakia, they could not prevent repeated protests from occurring in Poland. In 1956, discontented Poles demonstrated against harsh working conditions, food shortages, and plans to form collective farms. After restoring order, the Soviets installed Wladyslaw Gomulka to lead Poland. Gomulka stopped the move to collectives, gave more freedom to the Roman Catholic Church, and eased government control of industry. Discontent among the Polish people quieted but did not disappear.

Over the years, Gomulka's regime became more restrictive. Poles resented his government because it had been forced on them by the Soviets. His economic policies did not bring prosperity to Poland. Food prices were high, and meat was scarce. One Polish consumer complained,

> *Products appear and disappear, reappear . . . And then sometimes they just disappear for good. It used to be that our stores were stocked with many different kinds of cheese. I haven't seen cheese in six months.*

The Poles continued to hope for change. Their national spirit soared in 1979 when the Roman Catholic Church selected a Pole, John Paul II, as the new pope. In June 1979, when the popular pope visited his homeland, millions of Poles turned out to greet him and receive his blessing.

National pride soon led the Poles to defy Soviet dominance again. When the Polish Communist government announced another increase in meat prices, protests broke out in several cities.

Taking the lead, workers at the shipyard in Gdansk (guh-**DAHNSK**), declared a strike in August 1980. The workers shut themselves inside the shipyard and refused to work until the government recognized their union, called Solidarity. Both the union and the strike were illegal under Poland's Communist regime. Nonetheless Solidarity and its leader Lech Walesa (vah-**WEHN**-suh) received the fervent support of millions of Poles.

Eventually the government agreed to the most important of Walesa's demands. Solidarity won the right to exist as an independent trade union, and Polish workers won the right to strike. These were astonishing concessions for an Eastern European government.

For several months in 1981, Solidarity's workers moved aggressively to win even more reforms. By the end of the year, membership in the union reached more than 10 million. Watching and waiting from abroad, the Western democracies feared that Soviet tanks might crush the union. Instead, the Soviets urged Polish authorities to crack down on the protesters.

In 1981, the Polish government declared **martial law,** setting up military rule. Walesa and other Solidarity leaders were arrested and the union was declared illegal. In secret, however, Solidarity continued to oppose the government. In 1983, after two years in prison, Walesa was released. In the same year, he received the Nobel Peace Prize. That award brought worldwide attention to the plight of Polish workers.

The Communist party quickly discovered that military rule could not revive Poland's failing economy. During the 1980's, Poland's industrial production declined, and its foreign debt mushroomed. Public discontent deepened as the economic crisis worsened.

Section REVIEW 4

Define: (a) de-Stalinization, (b) dissident, (c) martial law
Identify: (a) Nikita Khrushchev, (b) Leonid Brezhnev, (c) Brezhnev Doctrine, (d) Imre Nagy, (e) Prague Spring, (f) Alexander Dubcek, (g) Berlin Wall, (h) Solidarity, (i) Lech Walesa
Answer:
1. What basic problem in the Soviet system became clear after Stalin's death?
2. How did the policies of Nikita Khrushchev and Leonid Brezhnev differ?
3. (a) What changes did Hungarians try to make in their government in 1956? (b) What were the results?
4. Why did the Berlin Wall become a major symbol of Cold War tensions?
5. (a) What changes did Alexander Dubcek seek to make in Czechoslovakia in 1968? (b) What was the Soviet reaction?
6. Why did Solidarity command such wide support among the Polish people during the early 1980's?

Critical Thinking
7. In view of Soviet policies toward Eastern Europe in the postwar era, what reasons did people in Eastern Europe have for resistance to those policies?

757

ANSWERS TO
Section Review 4

Define:
(a) attack on Stalin and his policies (b) person who protests Soviet policies
(c) military rule of a civilian population
Identify:
(a) Soviet leader who promoted de-Stalinization
(b) Soviet leader who repressed dissidents (c) Soviet Union has the right to forcibly prevent a nation from moving away from communism (d) led Hungarian revolt (e) time of Dubcek's reforms (f) Czechoslovakian leader (g) barrier that divided Berlin (h) Polish labor union (i) leader of Solidarity
Answer:
1. no legal, well-defined plan of succession
2. Khrushchev attacked Stalin, attempted reform. Brezhnev cracked down on dissenters, continued Stalinist policy.
3. (a) free themselves of Soviet control (b) Rebels were defeated by Soviet troops, tanks.
4. was a physical reminder of the separation of the two political systems
5. (a) attempted to create "socialism with a human face" (b) invaded Czechoslovakia
6. The people were dissatisfied with the government and the labor union called for basic changes.
7. absence of freedom, subordination to Communist control and Soviet interests

Concluding the Chapter

1. **Chapter Closer**
   Ask students to assess the extent to which the plans of the Big Three at Yalta were realized in the postwar world.

2. **Reteaching Activities**
   a. Summarizing Have students summarize the achievements and goals of the Common Market.
   b. Listing Have student list ways that the Soviet Union has exerted its control over Eastern Europe.

Answers to Chapter Review appear on page 736f.

Summary

1. **Two superpowers arose after the war.** After the war, the Western Allies hoped to spread democracy, whereas Stalin sought to increase Soviet power. The United States and the Soviet Union emerged from the war as rival superpowers engaged in a nuclear arms race. Although the founding of the United Nations symbolized a desire for peace, its efforts were hampered by the veto powers of the Security Council.

2. **The war left Europe divided.** World War II left Europe in ruins. A defeated Germany was divided into four occupied zones. The zones occupied by the Western Allies became a democratic state, or West Germany. East Germany remained under Communist control, and much of Eastern Europe also fell to the Soviets. The United States used containment to block the further spread of communism. The Soviet Union dominated Eastern Europe. Although the Soviets loosened controls after Stalin's death, they suppressed revolts in Hungary, Czechoslovakia, and Poland. A final outcome of the war was the loss of overseas empires for Europe.

3. **Western Europe moved toward cooperation.** After World War II, many countries in Western Europe joined the Common Market, which achieved economic unity by abolishing tariffs and import quotas. Postwar West Germany became a prosperous industrialized nation with a democratic government and strong ties to the West. France also faced political and economic problems after the war. Charles de Gaulle and succeeding presidents restored stability. Most countries in Southern Europe became more democratic and prosperous. Postwar Britain suffered major economic problems, which the Labour government tried to solve with a massive welfare program. In the 1980's, Prime Minister Margaret Thatcher introduced reforms to strengthen the economy.

4. **The Soviet Union dominated Eastern Europe.** Nikita Khrushchev, who replaced Stalin, began a policy of de-Stalinization. Foreign policy failures led to his downfall in 1964. Leonid Brezhnev cracked down on Soviet dissidents. Eastern Europe came under Soviet domination after World War II. The flight of East Germans to West Germany led to the building of the Berlin Wall. A revolt in Hungary was crushed in 1956. When Dubcek sought reforms in Czechoslovakia, the Soviets intervened. In Poland, economic crises led to the founding of Solidarity.

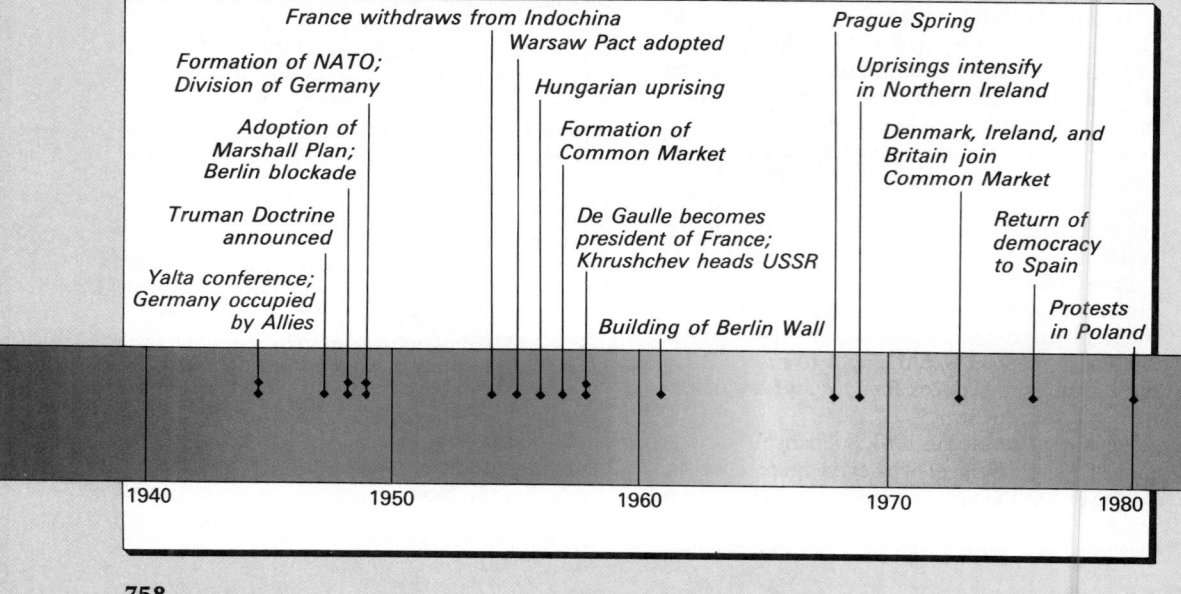

758

Reviewing the Facts

1. Define the following terms:
   - a. buffer zone
   - b. satellite
   - c. moderate socialism
   - d. martial law
2. Explain the importance of each of the following:
   - a. Yalta conference
   - b. Cold War
   - c. Nuremberg trials
   - d. Truman Doctrine
   - e. Marshall Plan
   - f. NATO
   - g. Warsaw Pact
   - h. Khrushchev
   - i. Common Market
   - j. Berlin Wall

Basic Skills

1. **Interpreting a map** (a) Judging from the map on page 745, what geographic advantages helped Yugoslavia avoid domination by the Soviets? (b) What geographic disadvantages did Romania, Hungary, and Czechoslovakia face?
2. **Supporting the main idea** Give two supporting details for each of the following generalizations: (a) "The single most dramatic political and economic transformation . . . took place in West Germany" (page 747). (b) "Life in East Germany . . . was bleak for many years after World War II" (page 755).

Researching and Reporting Skills

1. **Using biographical indexes** Biographical articles on leaders in all fields may be found in a multi-volume source, *Current Biography.* Use the cumulative index in the volume for 1950 to find articles about one of the following leaders or some other prominent leader of the time: George Marshall, Josip Broz (Tito), Joseph Stalin, Winston Churchill, Clement Attlee, Chiang Kai-shek, or Mao Tse-tung.
2. **Analyzing newspapers** For seven consecutive days, copy or clip articles from a daily newspaper that pertain to Europe. Classify the clippings into categories. Summarize the week's developments in a team report.
3. **Analyzing television news** For one week, watch the evening news on a selected television station. Determine (a) the percentage of time devoted to news events outside the United States and (b) the percentage of the news that deals with Europe. Take notes on the European events to report on to your class.

Critical Thinking

1. **Applying a concept** President Truman's policy of containment sought to limit Soviet expansion after World War II. Explain how each of the following served to implement that policy: (a) Truman Doctrine, (b) NATO, (c) Marshall Plan.
2. **Analyzing** Which of the postwar changes in Eastern Europe provided the security sought by the Soviet Union? Give examples.
3. **Analyzing economics** (a) What factors enabled the countries of Western Europe to recover economically after the war? (b) What were the economic outcomes of the recovery? (c) The political outcomes?
4. **Analyzing** (a) What factors and events accounted for the start of the Cold War? (b) What alternatives, if any, were there to the Cold War?
5. **Identifying viewpoints** (a) If you were a Soviet policymaker in 1961, what positive outcomes would you expect from the building of the Berlin Wall? (b) What negative outcomes?
6. **Interpreting** What was the significance of the Prague Spring and the organizing of Solidarity in Eastern Europe?
7. **Analyzing** Identify Stalin's various objectives for seeking to take over Berlin and the Western powers' objectives in resisting the takeover.

Perspectives on Past and Present

Notice that in the chapters of this unit, the "Voice from the Past" feature is retitled "Voice from Our Time." Why might the years after 1945 be called "our time"? Do you agree that 1945 marks the beginning of the era in which you live? Why or why not?

Investigating History

1. Read about the Cold War as recalled in Merle Miller's *Plain Speaking: An Oral Biography of Harry S. Truman.*
2. Make a study of one of the Eastern European countries that came under Communist control after World War II. What were the forces for resistance? Why did the Communists gain control? What was life like for people under Communist rule? Share the results of your findings with the class.
3. Investigate one agency of the United Nations. What was its purpose? In what places has it operated? What have been some of its achievements? What problems has it faced?

759

CHAPTER
Evaluation

Chapter Test 32, Alternate Chapter Test 32, and Computer Test Bank Chapter 32 Test can be used to evaluate your students' understanding of this chapter.

Change and Conflict in Asia

Chapter Overview

Enormous changes took place in Asia after World War II. During and after the American occupation, the Japanese economy recovered from the war. By 1970, Japan had become the world's third leading industrial nation.

At the end of World War II, China's Nationalists and Communists fought a civil war. By 1949, the Communists had won control of the country and established the People's Republic of China. Over the years, China broke with the USSR and gradually expanded its contacts with the United States and other non-Communist countries. In 1989, protests for democracy were violently put down.

In 1947, the former British colony of India was partitioned into two independent nations: India, predominantly Hindu, and Pakistan, predominantly Muslim. East Pakistan became a separate nation, Bangladesh, in 1971.

In Southeast Asia, former colonies became independent after the war. The country of Vietnam was finally unified in 1975 under a communist government after years of fighting. France and then the United States had attempted to prevent the communist takeover.

Chapter Focus

Have students review "Industrialization in Japan" (page 585). Then have students read about Expo 70 (pages 760–761) and evaluate the changes that had taken place in Japan since the 1870's. Share with students the following comment made by Hidetoshi Kato, one of

the organizers of the fair, "Expo 70 is a declaration of emancipation. Our people are now convinced that we can do most things without the support of the West." Use Map Transparency 97, *East Asia*, in conjunction with Sections 1, 2, and 3 on Japan and China.

Japan became an industrial giant. 1

Setting the Stage

Ask students to name Japanese products sold in the United States. (automobiles, computers, radios, televisions, and all appliances) In the 1950's and early 1960's, the label "Made in Japan" meant cheap or inferior goods in the minds of many Americans. However, by the late 1980's, the United States was Japan's biggest market. Japan has had tremendous success in producing "high tech" goods that are among the best in the world.

Teaching Strategies

Economics and History: A Productive Labor Force (Objective 1) Have students read "Japan's economy boomed" (pages 762–763). Discuss the importance of human resources to Japan's success.

Sarariman is the Japanese name for a salaried white-collar worker who looks forward to a lifelong job with a big company. In exchange for loyalty and hard work,

Advance Planner

	SECTION 1
Objectives	1. Cite reasons for Japan's economic success. 2. Identify problems brought about by Japan's rapid industrial growth.
Setting the Stage	Japanese products sold in the United States
Teaching Strategies	Economics and History: A Productive Labor Force Using Geographic Themes: Human-Environment Interaction Check for Understanding
Guided Practice	Section Review 1
Independent Practice Worksheets	Independent Practice 33.1 Vocabulary 33
Enrichment	1. Primary Source: Voices 33.1 2. Researching for Points
Chapter Closer	

★ Advanced
● Basic

SECTION 2	SECTION 3	SECTION 4	SECTION 5
1. List reasons the Chinese Nationalists lost power. 2. Locate the Korean peninsula and explain its strategic importance.	1. Describe the causes and effects of the Cultural Revolution. 2. Describe and interpret a picture that symbolizes the pro-democracy movement.	1. Identify the nations of South Asia. 2. Trace trends in conflict among the peoples of India.	1. Identify Corazón Aquino and explain how she became president of the Philippines. 2. Evaluate President Johnson's decision to escalate the Vietnam War.
Nationalist and Communist leaders in China Transparency 86	Changes resulting from the political and economic policies of Mao	Jinnah's demand for an Indian Muslim homeland	The break-up of European colonial empires in Southeast Asia after World War II Transparency 99
Discussing History: Why Did the Nationalists Lose? Using Geographic Themes: Location Transparency 92 Check for Understanding	Discussing History: The Cultural Revolution Teaching with Pictures: One Man and a Tank Check for Understanding	Geography in History: New Nations in South Asia Transparency 98 Outline Map 20 Skill Building: Making a Time Line Check for Understanding	Discussing History: Corazón Aquino Writing about History: Escalation or Withdrawal? Transparency 100 Check for Understanding
Section Review 2 Independent Practice 33.2 Basic Skills 33	Section Review 3 Independent Practice 33.3 Critical Thinking 33	Transparency 98 Q&A Section Review 4 Independent Practice 33.4	Transparency 99 Q&A Transparency 100 Q&A Section Review 5 Independent Practice 33.5 Geography Skills 33
1. Primary Source: Voices 33.2 2. Researching for Points	1. Primary Source: Voices 33.3 2. Researching for Points	1. Primary Source: Voices 33.4 2. Using Geographic Themes 3. Researching for Points	1. Primary Source: Voices 33.5 2. ★Preparing a Report 3. Researching for Points

●Reteaching Activities Summarizing, Writing a Paragraph

Chapter Review Summary, Reviewing the Facts, Basic Skills, Researching and Reporting Skills, Critical Thinking, Perspectives on Past and Present, Investigating History

Chapter Evaluation Chapter Test 33, Alternate Chapter Test 33, Computer Test Bank Chapter 33 Test

a *sarariman* can expect regular promotions and pay increases, job security, medical care, low-interest loans, company housing, and a retirement bonus. The job comes first, the family second. Ask students if they would prefer a secure position like a *sarariman's*.

Using Geographic Themes: Human-Environment Interaction (Objective 2) Discuss Japan's rapid industrialization in the 1950's and 1960's and the resulting environmental problems. The tragic mercury poisoning in the city of Minamata became known as Minamata Disease. Its symptoms include mental retardation, blindness, and severe birth defects. By the 1980's, almost 1,300 cases of the disease had been confirmed, with 305 deaths. Discuss the concept of *human ecology*— the interrelationships between people and their environments. Ask students to identify other positive and negative effects of rapid industrialization on human ecology.

Check for Understanding Ask students to describe three causes and three effects of Japan's "economic miracle."

Enrichment Activities

1. **Reading a Primary Source** Assign Voices from the Past Resource Book 33.1.

2. **Researching for Bonus Points** What is the name of the government department responsible for Japan's international trade? (The Ministry of International Trade and Industry, or MITI)

China became a Communist country. 2

Setting the Stage

Begin by writing the names *Mao Tse-tung* and *Chiang Kai-shek* on the board. Ask students to identify these two leaders. Remind students that Chiang was the leader of the Chinese Nationalists, while Mao was the leader of the Chinese Communists, and that the two forces had been fighting for control of the country since 1930.

Teaching Strategies

Discussing History: Why Did the Nationalists Lose? (Objective 1) Have students read the sections that discuss how China became a Communist country. Then ask why the Nationalists lost. Explain that historians now recognize five key reasons that help explain the collapse of Chiang's government. First, the Nationalist forces had to fight a long and exhausting war against the Japanese and against the Chinese Communists. Second, Chiang failed to carry out needed land reforms, thus losing the support of China's vast peasant population. Third, the Communists carried out land reforms while skillfully hiding their real economic goals. Fourth, the Soviet invasion of Manchuria denied Chiang that province's valuable industrial resources. Finally, Chiang's army misused America's economic and military aid.

Using Geographic Themes: Location (Objective 2) Show students Map Transparency 92, *The World in 1985*. Ask students to explain why the Korean peninsula represents a particularly sensitive strategic location. Help students recognize that the peninsula forms a partial land bridge linking the Chinese mainland and Japan. Historically, China and Japan have repeatedly used Korea as an invasion route to at-

tack each other. Both countries therefore wanted to make sure that a friendly government controlled the Korean peninsula. These strategic concerns played an important role in the Korean War.

Check for Understanding Ask students to name three reasons the Communists succeeded in China.

Enrichment Activities

1. **Reading a Primary Source** Assign Voices from the Past Resource Book 33.2.

2. **Researching for Bonus Points** What is the name of the square in Peking (Beijing) where Mao announced the formation of the People's Republic of China? (Tiananmen Square)

China changed under a Communist government. 3

Setting the Stage

Begin by writing the following Communist slogan on the board: "Let politics rule the farm and factory." Ask students to write a brief paragraph describing what they think this slogan means. Then tell the class that Mao wanted to change China into both a communist society and a modern industrial nation. He believed that these goals would be achieved by allowing the Communist party to dominate Chinese life.

Teaching Strategies

Discussing History: The Cultural Revolution (Objective 1) In her book *Life and Death in Shanghai*, Nien Cheng provides a vivid description of the injustices of the Cultural Revolution. Cheng, a former adviser to the Shell Oil Company in Shanghai, was falsely accused of espionage and put into solitary confinement for six and a half years. She endured physical abuse, constant interrogations, and a diet of watery rice porridge and pickled vegetables. Despite her long confinement, Cheng refused to "confess." She was finally released in 1973 and now lives in the United States.

Teaching with Pictures: One Man and a Tank (Objective 2) After students have read "Students called for democracy" (pages 770–772), direct their attention to the picture on page 772. Ask students to describe what this picture symbolizes. Explain that the confrontation between a defenseless man and a column of tanks symbolized the struggle between the Chinese people and their authoritarian government. Have students write a paragraph-length caption for this picture.

Check for Understanding Ask students to compare the methods and goals of Mao and Deng.

Enrichment Activities

1. **Reading a Primary Source** Assign Voices from the Past Resource Book 33.3.
2. **Researching for Bonus Points** Which Chinese dissident received sanctuary in the U.S. embassy in Beijing? (Fang Lizhi)

Setting the Stage

Begin by reading aloud the following quote by Muhammad Ali Jinnah of the Muslim League.

It is a dream that the Hindus and Muslims can ever evolve a common nationality. Muslims are a nation according to any definition of a nation, and they must have their homelands, their territory, and their state.

In 1947 the British agreed to turn over the government of India "into responsible Indian hands" no later than June 1948. Given past hostilities between Hindus and Muslims, ask students to speculate about some of the immediate consequences of independence. Into whose "responsible hands" would India fall?

Teaching Strategies

Geography in History: New Nations in South Asia (Objective 1) Show students Map Transparency 98, *South Asia*, and discuss India's border conflicts with China and Pakistan. Distribute copies of Outline Map 20 to the class. Then have students use the map on page 773 to label the following places on the outline map: India, Pakistan, Bangladesh, Nepal, Sri Lanka, Bhutan, Afghanistan, Indus River, Ganges River, Bay of Bengal, Arabian Sea. Point out that prior to 1972, Bangladesh was East Pakistan and present-day Pakistan was West Pakistan. Ask students why the divided country might have been difficult to govern. Have students compare their outline maps with the map on page 579. Ask them to identify nations that have been created since the start of the twentieth century.

Skill Building: Making a Time Line (Objective 2) Have students skim Section 4, writing down all important dates mentioned in the text. Next, divide the class into groups, and have each group arrange these dates along a time line for the period from 1945 to the present. Ask students to determine what interval of time is most appropriate for a time line of the period under study. When the groups have completed the project, post the time lines at the front of the classroom. What trends in Indian history can students identify on the basis of the time lines?

Check for Understanding Ask students to describe three problems India faced after independence and the steps taken to resolve those problems.

Enrichment Activities

1. **Reading a Primary Source** Assign Voices from the Past Resource Book 33.4.
2. **Using Geographic Themes: Human-Environment Interaction** Ask interested students to research the effect of monsoons on the poverty-stricken nation of Bangladesh. How has India responded to Bangladesh's pleas for help? Have students report their findings to the class.
3. **Researching for Bonus Points** What rock-and-roll star organized a concert in the 1970's to help starving people in Bangladesh? (former Beatle, George Harrison)

The Pacific Rim faced change and conflict. 5

Setting the Stage

Show students Map Transparency 99, *Southeast Asia*. Remind the class that foreign powers controlled all of Southeast Asia except Thailand during the early 1900's. Britain ruled Burma and Malaya. The United States controlled the Philippines. The Dutch held the East Indies. Finally, France ruled all of Indochina, a region including today's Laos, Cambodia, and Vietnam. Following World War II, however, the peoples of Southeast Asia demanded independence. Then show students Map Transparency 101, *The Pacific Rim*. Ask which Asian nations are part of this region. While some countries of the Pacific Rim, such as those in Indochina, are still experiencing conflict, others, such as South Korea and Taiwan, are becoming centers of world commerce.

Teaching Strategies

Discussing History: Corazón Aquino (Objective 1) Ask students if they would risk their lives to support a presidential candidate who had no previous political experience and who listed her occupation as housewife. Explain that Philippine president Ferdinand Marcos and his wife Imelda amassed a personal fortune that exceeded $5 billion, while 70 percent of the people lived below the poverty level. Marcos further enraged Filipinos by apparently ordering the assassination of the popular opposition leader, Benigno Aquino.

After the death of her husband, Corazón Aquino became the leader of the anti-Marcos forces. Despite her lack of experience, she proved to be a determined, shrewd, and courageous leader. On election day, millions of Filipi-

nos ignored Marcos's henchmen to vote for Aquino and democratic government. Unwilling to give up power, Marcos's men ripped up ballots and struck as many as three million names off the voters lists. Outraged Filipinos then staged a bloodless revolution that forced Marcos to flee the country and gave Aquino the presidency.

Writing about History: Escalation or Withdrawal? (Objective 2) *Prewriting* Use Map Transparency 100, *The War in Vietnam, 1957–1973*, to trace the main events of the Vietnam War. Despite more than 20,000 American advisers and billions of dollars in aid to South Vietnam, the Viet Cong controlled almost three fourths of South Vietnam's land and more than half of its people. South Vietnam faced imminent collapse. The President and his advisers considered these four plans of action. (a) The United States could withdraw and negotiate a peace settlement. (b) The United States could continue its policy of sending aid and advisers to help South Vietnam. (c) The President could escalate the level of American involvement. (d) The President could order an all-out attack on North Vietnam. *Writing* Ask students to assume the role of President Johnson's national security adviser. The assignment is to write a memo recommending a course of action in Vietnam. Have volunteers read their memos to the class. Compare and contrast student decisions.

Check for Understanding Ask students to explain how the United States became involved in the Vietnam War.

Enrichment Activities

1. **Reading a Primary Source** Assign Voices from the Past Resource Book 33.5.

2. **Preparing a Report** Ask advanced students to prepare reports describing what happened to the following people or groups: Ferdinand Marcos, Norodom Sihanouk, Pol Pot, and the "boat people."

3. **Researching for Bonus Points** What were the names of the two American destroyers supposedly attacked by the North Vietnamese in the Tonkin Gulf in August 1964? (the *Maddox* and the *C. Turner Joy*)

ANSWERS TO Chapter Review 33

Reviewing the Facts

1. **(a)** U.S. leader in Japan 1945–1952 **(b)** instituted the Five-Year Plan, the Great Leap Forward, and the Cultural Revolution **(c)** movement to establish proletarian culture, led to violence and near economic collapse **(d)** worked to restore order after Cultural Revolution **(e)** encouraged contacts with the West and private enterprise **(f)** prime minister after India became independent **(g)** helped India become an industrial nation **(h)** once part of Muslim Pakistan, world's poorest nation **(i)** defeated Marcos in election **(j)** Communist leader of North Vietnam **(k)** Communist guerrillas **(l)** incident that gave President Johnson authority to send American troops into Vietnam **(m)** Cambodian Communists

who won civil war (n) area that borders the Pacific Ocean

Basic Skills

1. Communists leaders made reforms
   A. Changes in government organization
      1. Model after Soviet Union
         a. Communist party sets policy
         b. National government carries out policy
      2. Mao Tse-tung authoritarian leader until 1959
   B. Changes in land ownership
      1. Agrarian Reform Law (1950)
         a. Government took land and divided it among peasants
         b. Violent reaction to law resulted in more than a million deaths
      2. Formation of collectives (1953–1957)
   C. Changes in industry
      1. Nationalization of all private industries and businesses
      2. Five-Year Plan (1953–1957)
         a. Set production targets
         b. Very successful
   D. Changes through the Great Leap Forward (1953–1961)
      1. Set up communes
      2. Failure of plan slowed growth and productivity and caused famine
2. Large number of nations formed partly because geographic features (seas, rivers, mountains, islands) prevented any unity while also bringing many different influences to the area.
3. These countries bordering seas and having harbors will play large role in trade.

Researching and Reporting Skills

Students' findings and reports will vary.

Critical Thinking

1. (a) Japan relied on itself after World War II—achieving high levels of productivity; instituting land reforms, and becoming economically strong to gain wide foreign trade. (b) Reliance on self and commitment to working toward a new Japan are long-lasting solutions not dependent upon military strength.

2. (a) losses suffered by China in war, aid Communists gave peasants, corruption among Nationalists (b) Students' answers will vary but might include economic difficulties, lack of support from urban workers, and international distrust.

3. (a) Japan—accepts and contributes to capitalistic world; China—although claims socialism, is starting to allow some capitalist ventures (b) Japan—Government does not control industries or economy but espouses success and contributes to it through few regulations and low taxes; China—government controls economy (c) Japan—economy based on free markets; China—very few free markets allowed

4. (a) Students' responses will vary; suggested responses include effective land use, technological knowledge, productivity of workers, government incentives for business. (b) Most students will find that China lacks the criteria they list.

5. As international interdependence increases, any emerging nations will have economic significance and be involved in political power struggles. The Third World nations will also impact the world as their cultural heritage gains exposure.

6. Although population growth contributes to a country's work force, it also means more food and housing are needed. In poor countries with limited resources, more people means always trying to stay even rather than modernizing and growing economically.

7. (a) imperialism—France did not want to lose colonies. (b) spread of communism—The U.S. constantly fought for containment. (c) Neither issue was widely accepted: Many French did not think keeping a colony was worth going to war; many U.S. citizens wanted U.S. to stay out of other countries' affairs.

8. (a) most countries had formerly been under colonial rule; poverty; rapid population growth (b) Colonial rule ended. Some countries, such as Japan, industrialized and prospered.

Perspectives on Past and Present

(a) Suddenly, these countries had a power vacuum and the hope for self-control. (b) Korea—U.S. fought possibility of communism by occupying South Korea right after war and joining UN forces as majority of troops; Vietnam—U.S. fought possibility of communism first by offering aid, then by direct involvement. (c) similar—Both conflicts became lengthy stalemates representing conflict between communism and the free world. different—Korea remained half Communist, half free; Vietnam fell to communism.

Investigating History

Students' findings will vary.

1945 - 1990's

Change and Conflict in Asia

Teaching with Pictures

Have students examine the photograph on page 760. Ask them what the photo implies about Japanese society and technology. Is the large screen an impressive development? Explain that in Japan, society and industry are closely linked. Japanese companies attempt to cultivate employee loyalty and trust in return for creativity and productivity. Such relations are one factor in Japan's continuing success in fields such as electronics.

A jumbo Sony screen dominates the Expo Plaza of the 1985 international exhibition north of Tokyo.

Key Terms

demilitarize   refugee
electronics   colonialism
pollution
limited war
cease-fire agreement
commune
partition
nonalignment
Third World
domino theory
boat people

Read and Understand

1. Japan became an industrial giant.
2. China became a Communist country.
3. China changed under a Communist government.
4. India and Pakistan became independent.
5. The Pacific Rim faced change and conflict.

For the people of Japan, March 14, 1970, was a long-awaited day of national pride. That day, Emperor Hirohito opened Expo 70 on the outskirts of the city of Osaka—the first World's Fair in Asia. For the emperor, the occasion marked a triumph in a reign that had seen both triumphs and tragedies. He had been his country's ruler for almost half a century, since 1926. He had reigned during Japan's expansion in East Asia in the 1930's, its early military successes during World War II, and its final defeat.

Now Japan had risen again to take its place among the world's richest and most powerful nations. This time, its power was based on economic, not military, strength. As Expo 70 showed the world,

760

Chapter 33 Resources

GEOGRAPHY
- Geography Skills 33
- Outline Map 20
- Transparencies 86, 92, 97, 98, 99, 100, 101

REINFORCEMENT
- Vocabulary 33
- Basic Skills 33
- Reteaching 33
- Making Connections Study Guide 33

ENRICHMENT
- Critical Thinking 33
- History and Literature 33

ASSESSMENT
- Chapter Test 33
- Alternate Chapter Test 33
- Computer Test Bank

Japan had become an industrial powerhouse. Out of defeat, the Japanese had created an economic miracle. The results of this miracle were on display at Expo 70. During the 6 months, more than 50 million visitors marveled at the exhibits. On display at the United States' pavilion were not only some moon rocks brought back to Earth by the *Apollo* astronauts in 1969 but also Babe Ruth's baseball uniform.

At the steel pavilion, 1,300 loudspeakers stunned visitors with a "Song of Steel." In 1970, Japan produced more steel than any other country except the United States and the USSR—despite having almost no iron ore deposits. In steel and many other industries, Japan had become the new "workshop of the world," as Britain had once been. The Japanese imported raw materials and exported quality finished goods to countries around the world.

The Japanese had achieved a workable blend between their own culture and the ways of the Western nations. Economically, Japan seemed poised to challenge the two great superpowers. One American futurologist (a specialist who estimates future developments) believed that this dream would become a reality. "It would not be surprising," he said, "if the twenty-first century turned out to be the Japanese century."

Emperor Hirohito did not live to see the fulfillment of that dream. He died on January 7, 1989, and was succeeded by his son Akihito.

In this chapter, you will see how Japan made this remarkable recovery from World War II. You will also see how China emerged from civil war as the world's second-largest Communist country and how new nations formed in Southern and Southeast Asia. Finally you will see how Asia began to play an ever greater role in world economic affairs.

Japan became an industrial giant. 1

In August 1945, Hirohito became the first Japanese emperor in centuries to speak publicly to his subjects. Atom bombs had just destroyed the cities of Hiroshima and Nagasaki. The whole country was on the brink of ruin. Over the radio,

Hirohito asked all loyal Japanese to "bear the unbearable"—defeat. On September 2, his country formally surrendered to the Allies.

The once prosperous Japanese economy was in ruins. Moreover, Japan itself was soon occupied by foreign forces. Most Japanese felt that their world had been turned upside down.

The United States occupied Japan.

From 1945 to 1952, about 30,000 American soldiers and civilians were based in Japan. General Douglas MacArthur, hero of the war in the Pacific, was in charge. MacArthur ran his army with an iron hand, and during the occupation he ran Japan the same way. The Japanese, devastated by the war, accepted the occupation as the price of defeat. In fact, many were pleased that the changes MacArthur ordered were not as harsh as those that had been forced on the losing countries after World War I.

The leaders of the United States had three goals for Japan. First, they planned to **demilitarize** the country—that is, to disband its armed forces and remove its military equipment. Second, they wanted to give Japan a stable, democratic government. Third, they hoped to revive the Japanese economy and make Japan a vital part of the capitalist world.

All three efforts succeeded. The armed forces were disbanded except for a small police force. In 1947, the Japanese adopted a new constitution that significantly changed the government. The emperor became a constitutional monarch like the monarch in Britain. Real political power now rested with the Diet (the Japanese parliament), led by a prime minister chosen by a majority of the Diet. All Japanese men and women over age twenty gained the right to vote.

One further change helped to strengthen the new government. Partly because of the pressures of the Cold War, a new status became essential for Japan. In September 1951, the United States and 47 other nations signed a formal peace treaty with Japan, officially restoring the independence of that nation. Six months later the last occupation troops were withdrawn. The two former enemies—the United States and Japan—now became allies. A new era had begun.

The revival of the Japanese economy after World War II was absolutely remarkable. Factories were

761

SECTION 1 Objectives and Teaching Strategies

OBJECTIVE 1. Cite reasons for Japan's economic success.

Teaching Strategy: *Economics and History: A Productive Labor Force* (page 760a)

OBJECTIVE 2. Identify problems brought about by Japan's rapid industrial growth.

Teaching Strategy: *Using Geographic Themes: Human-Environment Interaction* (page 760c)

■ BACKGROUND

The death of Emperor Hirohito on January 7, 1989, marked the end of an era. The emphasis on both tradition and modernization is likely to continue under the new emperor, Akihito.

To get around the prohibition of military forces, Japan has established "Self-Defense Forces." About two percent of the nation's GNP is spent on the military.

SECTION 1 Resources

GEOGRAPHY
■ Transparency 97

REINFORCEMENT
■ Independent Practice 33.1

ENRICHMENT
■ Voices from the Past 33.1

ASSESSMENT
■ Section Quiz 33.1

■ BACKGROUND

Tokyo replaced Kyoto as the capital of Japan in 1868. Today it is also a center of foreign trade and finance. The remarkable growth of Japan's domestic economy and international trade have given Japan new influence in the global economy.

In the late 1980's, production in Japan's steel industry began to falter owing to competition from countries such as Korea, where production costs were lower. Workers in these industries began to lose their so-called "lifetime" jobs.

Many Japanese companies offer daily exercise classes to help employees stay fit and alert.

rebuilt, new industries were launched, and agriculture flourished. Japan's factories could now benefit from having the latest equipment. Many of these new industries were oriented toward **electronics,** the growing technology that would lead to television, computers, automation, and a host of new consumer products. Land reform measures giving ordinary farmers title to the lands they worked proved an incentive to increase production. By 1953, the Japanese economy was performing at prewar levels.

Japan's economy boomed.

The progress made during the occupation period, however, was only the beginning. Through the 1950's and 1960's, Japan's economy expanded at the almost unheard-of rate of 10 percent a year. Japanese businessmen began to enter world markets in one new industry after another. Soon Japanese steel, ships, automobiles, cameras, bicycles, and even pianos were being sold around the world.

The rapid rise in exports brought prosperity at home. Between 1950 and 1970, for example, Japan's gross national product—the value of goods

762

and services produced by the country—soared from $10 billion to $200 billion a year. By the time of Expo 70, Japan had roared past Britain, France, and West Germany to become the world's third leading industrial nation.

What accounts for the remarkable success of Japanese industry and trade? At least four key factors were involved.

Effective use of imported technology In the Meiji Era (page 584), the Japanese began adopting the technology of Europe and the United States. After the war, they continued to borrow the best of Western technology. For example, the Sony Corporation bought the rights to manufacture transistors from an American company. Within 20 years, Sony had built a business empire based on the transistor. Sony sold radios, stereo equipment, and television sets worldwide.

A productive labor force Company loyalty was a key ingredient in Japan's economic success. In factories and offices across Japan, employees began their workday with songs such as this one:

> *For building a new Japan,*
> *Let's put our strength and minds together,*
> *Sending our goods to the people of the world,*
> *Endlessly and continuously*
> *Like water from a fountain.*
> *Grow, industry, grow, grow!*
> *Harmony and Sincerity!*
> *Matsushita Electric!*

Because workers felt a part of their company, they took pride in their work. Japanese companies set high standards for their products, and the workers tried hard to meet those standards.

Job security was one key to this strong loyalty. Japan's largest companies often guaranteed their most important workers lifetime jobs. Strikes were rare, and absentee rates were among the lowest in the world. With their jobs secure, Japanese workers also proved willing to change with the times. They eagerly adopted new technology.

High rates of saving and investment People in Japan saved a large part of their wages. In 1986 for example, Japanese workers saved 16.5 percent of their yearly incomes. (By contrast, American workers saved less than 6 percent.) Japanese banks used these deposits to lend businesses money for new equipment and projects.

The role of government The Japanese government actively supported business since the 1950's.

The government did not control industries, which were owned privately. However, the success of Japanese businesses was a major government goal. To encourage investments, the government set few regulations and kept taxes on business low.

Economic growth brought changes.

The tremendous expansion of the Japanese economy after 1950 brought dramatic changes in the way people lived.

Urban growth Between 1950 and 1970, the percentage of the Japanese population living in rural areas dropped from 60 percent to 8 percent. Millions moved into already overcrowded cities. Other people found that the sprawling cities spread out to absorb their homes and farms.

By 1970, more than half of Japan's 100 million people lived in the Tokaido Corridor. This narrow, 350-mile-long strip stretches along the Pacific coast of the island of Honshu from Tokyo to Kobe. It includes Japan's six largest cities.

Pollution Thousands of factories and millions of automobiles gave the Tokaido Corridor smog levels worse than those of any other urban area in the world. Sometimes Japanese schoolchildren had to wear face masks simply to play outdoors.

Water **pollution,** or contamination by harmful chemicals, was also a severe problem. In the 1960's, a number of people in the city of Minamata died of mercury poisoning. The poison came from the fish that make up a large part of the Japanese diet. Fish in Minamata Bay had absorbed high levels of mercury from chemical pollution. Japan's government and industry have made great strides in reducing pollution.

Roles for women Economic expansion brought new opportunities for Japanese women. Besides winning the right to vote in 1947, women gained the right to own property in their own name. During the 1970's, Japanese women became increasingly active in the work force. By 1990, more than 50 percent of them held jobs outside the home. Most top positions in Japanese government and business, however, remained in the hands of men. This was but one sign of the continuing strength of custom and tradition in Japanese society.

CITY T O U R

Tokyo became a megacity.

As Japan grew and prospered, so too did Tokyo, the nation's capital. More than 97 square miles of the central city had been destroyed by Allied fire bombing in 1945. Rising from the ashes, Tokyo was rebuilt and soon growing rapidly. By 1988, the Tokyo metropolitan area was home to more than 11 million people.

Modern Tokyo remained a place of contrasts, where fast-food restaurants like those in the United States stood beside ancient Buddhist

DAILY LIFE ▶ Preparing for Exams

February has a special meaning for high school seniors across Japan. At that time, they take a comprehensive college entrance exam. The tests are difficult. Only one third of those taking them get into college on their first try.

Everything in Japanese education is focused on preparing for the exams. Students attend school 240 days a year, with half days on Saturday. Homework assignments often keep students busy for five hours a night. The pressure to succeed is so great that many students also attend afternoon "cram" schools. Both parents and students know that top scores will open the way to good colleges and high-paying jobs.

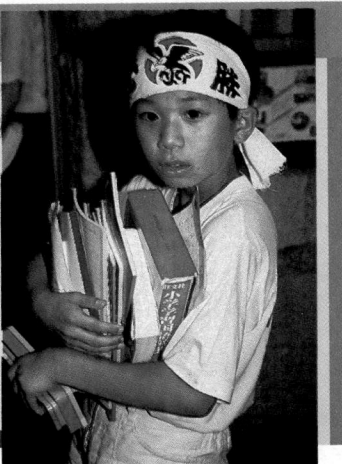

■ **BACKGROUND**

Because Japan is heavily dependent on imported oil, price fluctuations on the world oil market have a profound effect on the Japanese economy.

Cooperative Learning

Divide the class into groups of four students. Ask group members to list and discuss the factors that contributed to Japan's success in industry and trade. Tell them to be sure to discuss the role of education, as described in the Daily Life feature (page 763). Then ask group members to decide how each of these factors applies to trade and industry in the United States. Which of Japan's programs or policies are already in use in the United States? Which might be used to improve United States trade and industry? Have each group prepare a short presentation on its decisions for the entire class, with each group member participating.

■ **BACKGROUND**

Japan has a remarkably efficient railway system. *Bullet* trains carry passengers from Tokyo to Osaka at speeds up to 160 miles an hour.

ANSWERS TO

Section Review 1

Define:
(a) disband a country's armed forces **(b)** technology concerning television, computers, automation, etc. **(c)** contamination by harmful chemicals

Identify:
(a) former emperor of Japan **(b)** general in charge of Japanese occupation **(c)** Japanese parliament

Answer:

1. showed that Japan had become industrial giant

2. **(a)** demilitarize Japan, set up stable democratic government, revive economy **(b)** demilitarization—arms production halted, armed forces disbanded, war banned in constitution; democracy—constitutional monarchy with power in hands of Diet, universal suffrage; economy—land reforms

3. use of imported technology, productive workers, high rates of savings and investment, government support

4. urban overcrowding, pollution

5. won right to vote and own property, entered work force in large numbers

6. Students might consider such factors as economic power that includes control of large part of world's industrial production and marketplace, role in world affairs, and influences of culture on rest of world.

7. Great Britain lies off the coast of continental Europe, while Japan lies off the coast of continental Asia. Both are excellently located for trade.

temples. Visitors to Tokyo could choose to attend both the most popular new Broadway shows and the traditional Kabuki drama.

The heart of Tokyo was the city's financial district. During the 1980's, Tokyo wrested away from New York the honor of having the world's busiest stock exchange. The nearby Akihabara district was a shopping district that became known as the electronics capital of the world. There shoppers could select from a wide variety of cameras, stereos, and computers—all made in Japan, of course.

Despite the hustle and bustle, tradition remained strong in Tokyo. By Western standards, crime scarcely existed. And while the Japanese enjoyed such cultural imports as baseball and Mickey Mouse, they also flocked to traditional sumo wrestling matches. In quiet cobblestoned side streets, delicate wooden teahouses still served customers in age-old fashion—while jumbo jets roared overhead.

Section REVIEW 1

Define: (a) demilitarize, (b) electronics, (c) pollution

Identify: (a) Hirohito, (b) Douglas MacArthur, (c) Diet

Answer:

1. Why was Expo 70 significant for Japan?
2. (a) What goals did the United States set for Japan in 1945? (b) How was each achieved?
3. What factors help to account for Japan's economic miracle?
4. Briefly describe some of the changes rapid growth has brought to Japan.
5. How have the changes since 1945 affected the lives of women in Japan?

Critical Thinking

6. Some historians have called the 1800's the British century and the 1900's the American century. The futurologist quoted on page 761 said that the next century might be the Japanese century. What factors make a century "belong" to any given power? To what extent can such a statement be accurate?
7. Compare Japan and Great Britain in terms of their relation to nearby continents and their location for trade.

China became a Communist country. 2

In contrast to Japan, China in World War II had fought on the side of the victorious Allies. But the victory was a hollow one for China. Only the Soviet Union suffered higher casualties than China, most of whose cities had been occupied and devastated by Japanese armies. The civilian death toll alone topped 20 million.

China's war effort was not united.

As you saw in Chapter 29, a bitter civil war between the Nationalists (Kuomintang) and the Communists divided China on the eve of the 1937 Japanese invasion. During the world war, the Nationalists and the Communists claimed to be fighting the Japanese together, yet they continued to jockey for position within China.

Mao and the Communists Under their leader, Mao Tse-tung, the Communists had their stronghold in northwestern China. From there, they mobilized Chinese peasants for guerrilla war against the Japanese in the northeast. At the same time, Communist leaders set up political groups in villages throughout northern China.

In the areas they controlled, the Communists worked to win widespread peasant support. They encouraged peasants to learn to read, and they helped to improve food production. As a result, more and more recruits flocked to the Communists' Red Army. By 1945, much of northern China was under Communist control.

Chiang and the Nationalists Meanwhile, the Nationalist forces under Chiang Kai-shek had set up their stronghold in southwestern China. Here, protected from the Japanese by a series of formidable mountain ranges, Chiang gathered an army of 2.5 million men. Between 1942 and 1945, this army received $1.5 billion in aid from the United States.

American advisers, sent to help Chiang modernize his army, reported widespread corruption among the Nationalists. Supplies of food and medicine intended for the whole army often ended up in the hands of a few officers. Nationalist leaders were also out of touch with the peasants and refused to arm them.

Chiang's army fought occasional battles against the Japanese. In general, however, the Nationalist army saved its strength for the battle Chiang expected soon against the Communists.

China faced renewed civil war.

World War II in Asia ended suddenly with the flash of atom bombs at Hiroshima and Nagasaki. Japan's sudden surrender caught both Chiang and Mao by surprise. The United States urged Chiang and Mao to negotiate a political settlement of their differences. Yet even as the Japanese were surrendering, both the Nationalists and the Communists were preparing for civil war.

The civil war between Nationalist and Communist forces lasted from 1946 to 1949. At the beginning, the Nationalists appeared to have a huge advantage. Their army outnumbered the Communists' army three to one. The Nationalists were also better equipped. Chiang's forces received nearly $2 billion in aid from the United States between 1946 and 1949.

After Japan's surrender in 1945, Chiang's Nationalist troops moved back into southern and central China. However, they did little to win popular support. "They stole and looted freely," reported General Albert Wedemeyer, an American adviser. Famine still stalked the land, and China's economy was close to collapse.

As the Nationalists weakened, the Communists gained strength. They allowed Chiang to hold the cities while the Red Army spread through the countryside. As thousands of Nationalist soldiers deserted to the Communists, the two armies became roughly equal in size.

The Communists were victorious.

In the spring of 1949, China's major cities fell one by one to the Communists. What was left of Chiang's once enormous army fled south. By the fall of 1949, Chiang and other Nationalist leaders had fled to the island of Taiwan.

On October 1, 1949, Mao Tse-tung stood on the balcony of the ancient Imperial Palace in Peking. A crowd filled the immense square below. "Our nation will never again be an insulted nation," Mao told his listeners. "We have stood up." After more than 20 years of almost constant struggle, the Communists ruled all of mainland China. They established a new government, the People's Republic of China.

The United States refused to recognize Communist China.

For many years, the United States refused to accept the People's Republic of China as China's true government. After Chiang Kai-shek fled to Taiwan, the United States helped him set up a Nationalist government on that small island. Both Chiang and the United States called Taiwan the Republic of China. With American support, the Taiwan government continued to represent China in the United Nations until 1972.

Why did the United States continue to support Chiang despite Nationalist corruption and defeat? The answer lies in the Cold War. Mao was a Communist. Moreover, the Soviets soon sent massive aid to the People's Republic of China. To an American government already locked into a bitter struggle with the Soviet Union, Mao's victory in China seemed to be a giant step forward in a Communist campaign to conquer the world. This suspicion of Communist China was strengthened by the outbreak of the Korean War.

War split Korea into north and south.

Korea had been occupied by the Japanese since the early 1900's. After World War II, Japan was driven out. Soviet forces occupied the northern half of Korea, while American troops held the south. The dividing line was the thirty-eighth parallel of latitude. The Soviets set up a puppet government in the north. Then in the south, an American-supported government took control.

Soon after World War II, the United States cut back its armed forces in South Korea. By the beginning of 1949, there were only 500 American troops there. The Soviets concluded that the United States would not fight to defend South Korea. They prepared to back North Korea with tanks, airplanes, and money in an attempt to take over all of the peninsula.

On June 25, 1950, the North Koreans swept across the thirty-eighth parallel in a surprise attack on South Korea. Within a few days, North Korean troops had penetrated deep into South Korea. On June 27, President Truman ordered American troops stationed in Japan to support the South

OBJECTIVE 1. List reasons the Chinese Nationalists lost power.

Teaching Strategy: *Discussing History: Why Did the Nationalists Lose?* (page 760c)

OBJECTIVE 2. Locate the Korean peninsula and explain its strategic importance.

Teaching Strategy: *Using Geographic Themes: Location* (page 760c)

■ BACKGROUND

An American journalist reported, "The people permit, support, and wholeheartedly fight with [the Red Army]. The common people, for the first time, have been given something to fight for."

Chinese Communists soon retreated from a policy of inciting revolution in other Asian countries, preferring instead to cultivate the friendship of neutral nations.

SECTION 2
Resources

ENRICHMENT
■ Voices from the Past 33.2

ASSESSMENT
■ Section Quiz 33.2

GEOGRAPHY
■ Transparencies 86, 92, 97

REINFORCEMENT
■ Independent Practice 33.2

766

ANSWERS TO
Map Study

Pusan, Taegu; Chosan

ANSWERS TO
Section Review 2

Define:
(a) war in which one or both sides aim at less than all-out victory (b) truce

Identify:
(a) Chinese Communist leader (b) Nationalist leader of China (c) island site of Republic of China (d) war that ended in stalemate (e) commander of UN forces in Korea

Answer:
1. formed political groups in villages, gained support from peasants, recruited large army
2. took aid from U.S., fought occasional battles against Japanese
3. recognized only Nationalist China
4. North Korea attacked South Korea.
5. (a) sent troops to stop North Korean invasion (b) ordered its troops to support the South Koreans (c) joined war on North Korea's side
6. stalemate
7. (a) Nationalists had large, well-equipped army and aid from U.S. Communists had strong peasant support, Mao's military strategies. (b) possibly corruption and weakening of Nationalists

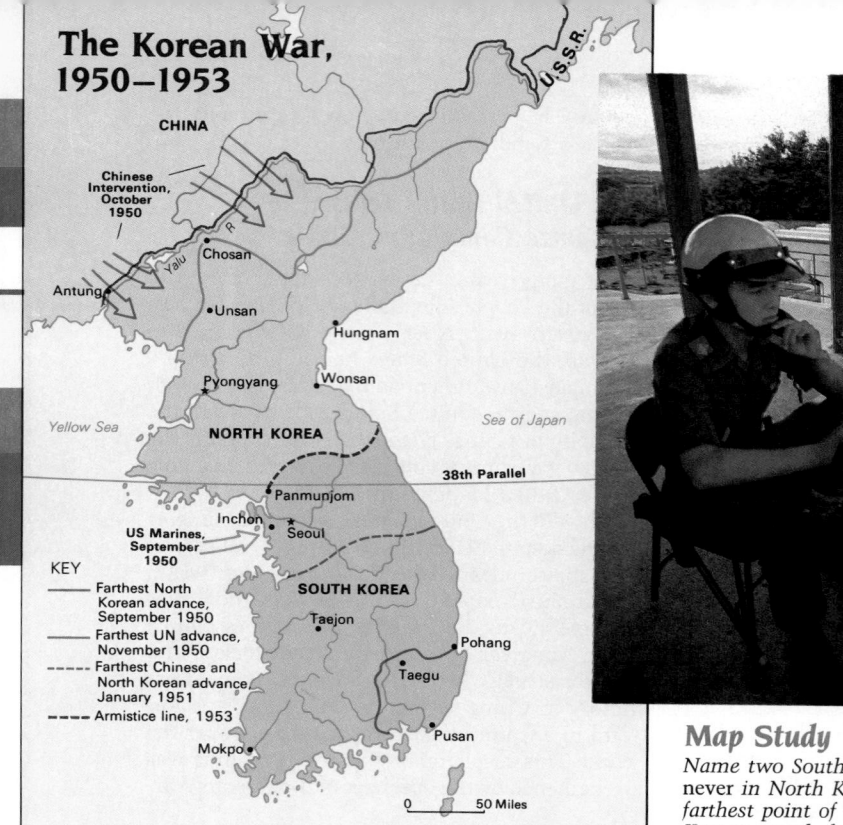

The Korean War, 1950–1953

KEY
— Farthest North Korean advance, September 1950
— Farthest UN advance, November 1950
- - - Farthest Chinese and North Korean advance, January 1951
-·-· Armistice line, 1953

0   50 Miles

Map Study
Name two South Korean cities in an area that was never in North Korean hands. Name a city at the farthest point of the UN advance. The South Korean guard above is at Panmunjom.

Koreans. He also sent an American fleet into the waters between Taiwan and China.

South Korea also called on the United Nations to stop the North Korean invasion. When the matter came to a vote in the Security Council, the USSR was not there. The Soviets were boycotting the council in protest over the presence of Nationalist China (Taiwan). Thus, the Soviets could not veto the UN's plan of action.

The United Nations voted to send an international force to Korea to stop the invasion. All together, 15 nations, including Britain and Canada, sent troops to Korea. Because the Security Council had approved this military action, the troops that supported South Korea fought under the UN flag. General Douglas MacArthur commanded the United Nations forces.

Meanwhile, the North Koreans continued their advance. By September 1950, they controlled the entire Korean peninsula except for a tiny area in the far southeast. In that month, however, MacArthur pulled a surprise attack of his own.

A small force of marines landed at the port of Inchon behind North Korean lines. As more and more UN troops followed, the North Koreans were driven back almost to their homeland.

The UN army chased the retreating North Korean troops across the thirty-eighth parallel into North Korea. In late November, UN troops approached the Yalu River, the border between North Korea and China. It seemed as if North and South Korea were about to become a single country again by force of arms.

Then, in October 1950, 300,000 Chinese troops joined the war on the side of North Korea. The Chinese wanted North Korea as a Communist buffer state to protect their northeastern province of Manchuria. They also felt threatened by the American fleet off their coast. The fight between North and South Korea had escalated into a war in which the main opponents were the Chinese and the Americans.

By sheer force of numbers, the Chinese drove the UN troops (most of which were Americans)

766

southward. At some points along the battlefront, the Chinese outnumbered them ten to one. By early January 1951, all UN and South Korean troops had been pushed out of North Korea. The Chinese advanced to the south, capturing the South Korean capital, Seoul.

"We face an entirely new war," declared General MacArthur. Convinced that Korea was the place "where the Communist conspirators have elected to make their play for global conquest," MacArthur called for the use of nuclear weapons against Chinese cities.

President Truman disagreed. He viewed MacArthur's proposals as reckless. "We are trying to prevent a world war, not start one," said Truman. He dismissed MacArthur.

Over the next two years, UN forces fought a **limited war.** In such a war, one or both sides aim at less than all-out victory over the enemy. The UN goal was to drive the North Koreans back to the thirty-eighth parallel. By 1952, UN troops had recaptured Seoul and were in firm control of South Korea.

Finally, in July 1953, North and South Korea signed a **cease-fire agreement** or truce. With minor changes, the border between the two Koreas remained the same. Counting civilians and soldiers, the war had cost an estimated 5 million lives.

Although the Korean War ended in a stalemate, it showed that Communist China was a great power. The Chinese had been able to match the military strength of the West, at least in a nonnuclear war fought in Asia.

| Section | REVIEW | 2 |

Define: (a) limited war, (b) cease-fire agreement
Identify: (a) Mao Tse-tung, (b) Chiang Kai-shek, (c) Taiwan, (d) Korean War, (e) Douglas MacArthur
Answer:
1. How did the Chinese Communists increase their power during World War II?
2. What course of action did the Nationalists follow during and after the war?
3. What policy did the United States follow toward China from 1949 to 1972?
4. How did the Korean War begin?
5. What part did each of the following play in

the war? (a) the UN (b) the United States (c) China
6. What was the outcome of the war?

Critical Thinking
7. (a) What advantages did each side have in China's civil war? (b) What factor do you think contributed most to Mao's victory?

China changed under a Communist government. 3

The triumph of the Red Army and Mao's Communist party in 1949 ended nearly half a century of revolution, civil war, and chaos in China. It also marked the start of a new era. Over the next 40 years, Mao and his successors strove to transform China into both a Communist society and a modern industrial nation.

Mao transformed China.

After taking power, Communist leaders set out to solidify their hold on the country. A small but highly disciplined group, the party's 4.5 million members (about 1 percent of the Chinese population) closely modeled their system on that of the Soviet Union. Like the Soviets, the Chinese set up two parallel and overlapping organizations, the Communist party and the national government. Until 1959, Mao was both head of state and chairman of the Communist party. Even today, the party sets policy and the government implements it.

Land reform The new government's most urgent task was to improve China's economy. Half a century of war and general chaos had left the country in ruin.

Mao was determined to reshape China's economy along the lines of Marxist socialism. Because 80 percent of the population still lived in rural areas, agriculture was the obvious place to start. Most Chinese farmers owned no land. Instead, 10 percent of the rural population owned 70 percent of the farmland. The Agrarian Reform Law of 1950 took the holdings of landlords and divided them among the peasants. More than a million landlords who resisted were killed.

767

SECTION 3
Objectives and Teaching Strategies

OBJECTIVE 1. Describe the causes and effects of the Cultural Revolution.

Teaching Strategy: *Discussing History: The Cultural Revolution* (page 760d)

OBJECTIVE 2. Describe and interpret a picture that symbolizes the pro-democracy movement.

Teaching Strategy: *Teaching with Pictures: One Man and a Tank* (page 760d)

■ **BACKGROUND**

Help students locate the 1953 armistice line. Explain that this line is now in a 2½-mile-wide buffer zone, called the Demilitarized Zone, that separates North Korea and South Korea. The zone remains one of the most heavily guarded boundaries in the world. Troops from each side occupy the zone, closely watching each other across the tense boundary. Each nation maintains a large army—about 800,000 troops in North Korea and 650,000 in South Korea. The South Korean forces are supported by about 40,000 American soldiers.

SECTION 3
Resources

GEOGRAPHY
■ Transparency 97

REINFORCEMENT
■ Independent Practice 33.3

ENRICHMENT
■ Voices from the Past 33.3

ASSESSMENT
■ Section Quiz 33.3

Mao never intended that peasants would keep the land as private property. He believed that small, privately owned farms were inefficient and contrary to socialist principles. Between 1953 and 1957, the government forced the peasants to join collective farms consisting of about 200 to 300 households.

Industry Mao's changes also affected industry and business. He wanted to set up centralized planning for the whole economy. Gradually, the government nationalized all private companies.

In 1953, Mao launched a Soviet-style five-year plan that set high production targets for industry. The plan was a striking success. By 1957, steel production had quadrupled and the output of coal, cement, and electricity had doubled.

The Great Leap Forward The success of the first five-year plan encouraged Chinese leaders to plan an even more ambitious program. Early in 1958, Mao proclaimed what he called "the Great Leap Forward." This plan called for still larger collective farms called **communes.** By the end of 1958, the government had created about 26,000 communes. The average commune contained 15,000 acres and more than 25,000 people.

Life on the communes was highly regimented. Peasants were organized into "production battalions" commanded by company and squad leaders. Workers ate in communal dining rooms, slept in communal dormitories, and raised children in communal nurseries.

The Great Leap Forward was a disaster for China. Peasants resented the vast, impersonal communes. Crop failures between 1958 and 1961 caused a famine that claimed more than 25 million lives. Poor planning hampered industrial growth. Faced with failure, the government officially gave up the Great Leap Forward in 1961.

Map Study

What are the two ways of spelling the name of China's capital city? Of what country is Taipei the capital?

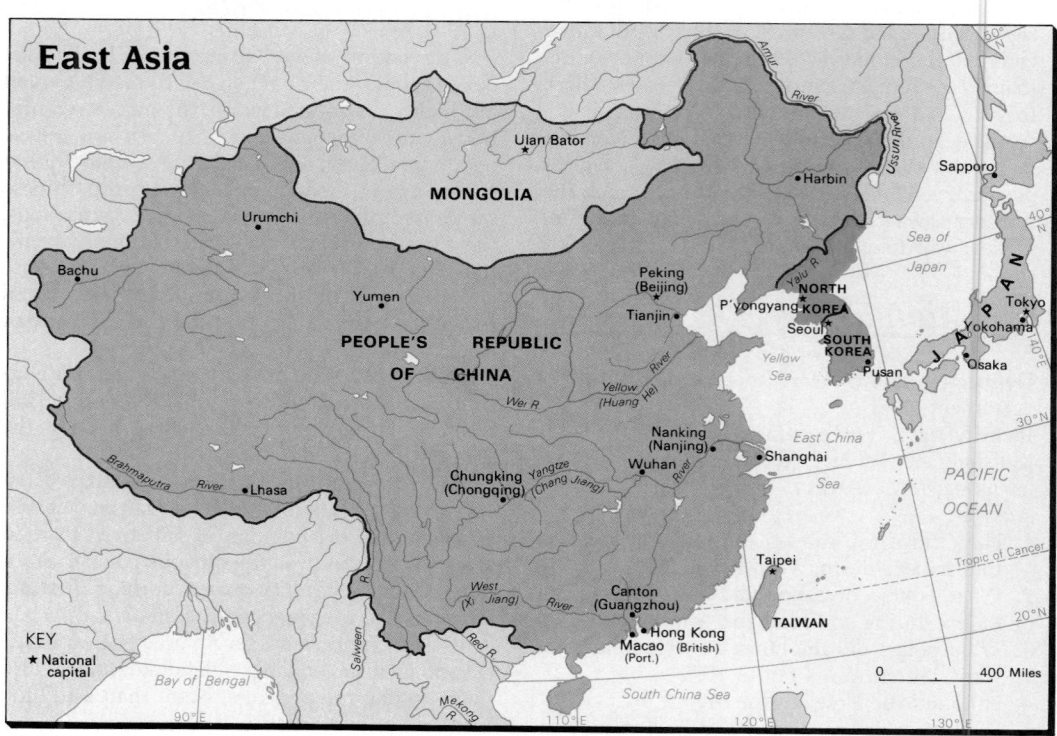

China and the USSR split.

China and the Soviet Union shared a firm belief in communism. In order to cement their close ties, Mao and Stalin signed a 30-year treaty of friendship in 1950. However, the spirit of cooperation did not last long.

The Soviets assumed that the Chinese would follow their leadership in world affairs. As the Chinese grew stronger and more confident, however, they resented their role as Moscow's junior partner. The independent foreign policy developed by Mao toward Africa and other parts of Asia especially angered the Soviets. In 1959, Khrushchev punished the Chinese by refusing to share nuclear secrets with them. The next year, the Russians ended economic aid to China and called home their advisers.

Rivalry for leadership of the worldwide communist movement was not the only cause of the Sino-Soviet split. The two countries share the longest border in the world. "What are you worried about?" one Soviet leader asked an American official in 1959. "You have the whole Pacific Ocean between you and China, while we have nothing but a line drawn on a map." In 1969, fighting broke out briefly along the Ussuri River in Manchuria. Although peace was quickly restored, the incident showed how wide the Sino-Soviet split had become.

A Cultural Revolution swept China.

After the failure of the Great Leap Forward and the split with the USSR, Mao took a less active role in government for a time. Other leaders continued his programs of modernization, though in less drastic ways.

The new leaders modified the highly organized communal system. Farm families could now live in their own homes and sell crops they grew on small private plots. Factory workers could earn wage increases, bonuses, and promotions. China also modernized its army. In 1964, China exploded its first atom bomb, a dramatic sign of the nation's development of modern technology.

Although the new policies brought economic progress, Mao disapproved of them. He believed that rewards such as higher wages weakened workers' revolutionary spirit. Such policies, he claimed, also created a privileged class and undercut the Communist goal of social equality.

Red Guards devotedly studied Mao's sayings, collected in a small red book. (Masks were protection from the dusty winds of the winter monsoon.)

Mao was determined to regain control of party policy and to revive the revolution. In 1966, he launched a new campaign, urging China's youth to "learn revolution by making revolution." The objective was to establish a proletarian society. Millions of high school and college students responded to Mao's call by leaving their classrooms and forming military-like units called Red Guards.

To achieve Mao's goals, the Red Guards spearheaded a major upheaval known as the Cultural Revolution. No individual or institution was safe from attack. The Red Guards shut down colleges and schools. They lashed out at professors, government officials, factory managers, even their own parents—anyone who seemed to have special privileges or who resisted the regime. Thousands of people were executed or died in jail.

As a result of the widespread disruption, factories closed and farm production declined. By 1967, even Mao had to admit that the Cultural Revolution had gone too far. With his approval, the army disbanded the Red Guards. Zhou Enlai* (joh ehn-lye), one of the founders of the Chinese

---

* In 1958, the Chinese adopted a new method of spelling Chinese words in the Roman alphabet. Under the new system, called Pinyin, *Mao Tse-tung* became *Mao Zedong*. *Peking* became *Beijing*. Because many newspapers in the United States have now adopted the new form, Pinyin spellings are used hereafter for the names of contemporary leaders.

769

■ **BACKGROUND**

Mao considered Stalin's successor, Nikita Khrushchev, a young upstart; Khrushchev thought of the aging Chinese leader as a relic of the past.

Mao became a father figure in China. According to Harold Hinton, the youth of the country were taught to worship him "to a degree that would have created envy in the hearts of previous emperors."

■ **BACKGROUND**

The greater acceptance of free markets became an important stimulus to economic and technological development in China.

Communist party, became the nation's new premier. Zhou restored order and promoted economic growth.

China opened its doors.

During the Cultural Revolution, China had played almost no role in world affairs. In addition to its tense relations with the Soviet Union, China displayed bitter enmity toward the United States. China's isolation worried Zhou. In 1971, he startled the world by inviting an American table tennis team to tour China. It became the first American group to visit China since 1949. Zhou greeted his guests in Peking's Great Hall of the People and declared, "We have opened a new page in the relations of the Chinese and American people."

Zhou's greeting signaled the start of a new era in Sino-American relations. In October 1971, the United States ended its opposition to admitting the People's Republic of China to the United Nations. Four months later, President Nixon made a state visit to China. Nixon met privately with Mao and held extensive talks with Zhou. The two leaders agreed to begin cultural exchanges and a limited amount of trade. Seven years later, the United States and China established formal diplomatic relations.

Deng introduced economic reforms.

Both Mao and Zhou Enlai died in 1976. The person who emerged as China's new leader was Deng Xiaoping (dung shah-oh-ping). Like Mao and Zhou, Deng was a veteran of the Long March and the last of the "old revolutionaries" who had ruled China since 1949.

Although a lifelong Communist, Deng boldly supported new economic policies. Unlike Mao, he was willing to use capitalist ideas to revitalize China's stagnant economy. Proclaiming "It is glorious to get rich," Deng launched an ambitious program of economic reforms called the "Second Revolution."

The Second Revolution began in the countryside. Deng eliminated Mao's unpopular communes and instead leased the land to individual farmers. They paid rent by delivering a fixed quota of food to the government. They could then grow any crops they wished and sell them

for a profit. This system produced more than twice as much food as the communes had in 1960, thus helping to prevent shortages.

The success of agricultural reform enabled Deng to extend his program to industry. The government permitted small private businesses to produce goods and services. At the same time, the managers of large state-owned industries were given more freedom to plan production. Finally, Deng welcomed foreign technology and investment.

Deng's economic policies produced striking changes in Chinese life. As incomes increased, people began to buy appliances and televisions. Chinese youth now wore stylish clothes and listened to Western music. Gleaming hotels filled with foreign tourists symbolized China's new policy of openness.

Students called for democracy.

Deng's economic reforms produced a number of unexpected problems. As living standards improved, the gap between the rich and poor widened. Increasingly, the public believed that corrupt party officials took advantage of their positions by accepting bribes and enjoying privileges denied to others. Further, the new Open Door policy admitted not only Western investments and tourists but also books, videocassettes, and new ideas. As Chinese students learned more about democracy, they began to question the lack of political freedom and rights in China.

In the spring of 1989, students sparked a popular uprising that shook China and stunned the rest of the world. Beginning in April, more than 100,000 students marched through Beijing to Tiananmen Square, the 100-acre plaza located in the heart of the city. There, the protesters began an ongoing demonstration to make their ideas known. Shocked officials stared in disbelief as students chanted, "Down with corruption!" "Down with dictatorship!" "Press freedom!" and "Long live democracy!"

The students' demands for less corruption and more democracy won widespread popular support. With each passing day, larger and larger crowds filled Tiananmen Square. In mid-May, about 3,000 students staged a hunger strike to demonstrate their willingness to sacrifice their lives for freedom. More than a million people poured into

770

Tiananmen Square to support the hunger strikers and the pro-democracy movement. Many students now boldly called for Deng Xiaoping to resign.

Deng and other top leaders held secret meetings. Deng realized that the Communist party faced a dangerous challenge to its authority. The Chinese have historically believed that when a dynasty lost the mandate of heaven, it also lost its moral right to govern (see page 84). To the Chinese, the demonstrations signaled that the Communist party was losing that mandate.

Deng ordered a crackdown.

The Chinese leaders recognized that they faced a fateful decision. Moderates such as General Secretary Zhao Ziyang argued for political reform. Deng and other hard-liners refused. Instead, they removed Zhao and declared martial law. More than 250,000 armed troops surrounded Beijing.

Although many students left Tiananmen Square after martial law was declared, about 10,000 chose to remain and continue their protest. Army units made repeated attempts to reach the square, but vast crowds of people blocked their path. The students revived their spirits by defiantly erecting a 30-foot statue that they named the "Goddess of Democracy." It resembled the American Statue of Liberty.

The standoff between the government and the students ended in tragedy. On June 4, 1989, thousands of heavily armed soldiers stormed Tiananmen Square. Tanks smashed through barricades and crushed the Goddess of Democracy. Soldiers sprayed gunfire into crowds of frightened students. The assault left hundreds dead and thousands wounded.

The attack on Tiananmen Square marked the beginning of a massive government crackdown. During the following weeks, police arrested an estimated 10,000 people. Using a propaganda technique known as "the big lie," state-controlled television and newspapers repeatedly told the Chinese people that reports of a massacre were

Students created the Goddess of Democracy to protest state power.

Voice from Our Time | A Student Speaks

The June 4 massacre of students in Tiananmen Square shocked the world. In the following excerpt, an anonymous Chinese student explains how he felt about what happened.

For most of the students, this was the greatest danger they had ever faced. It would be a lie to say that we were not afraid, but we were mentally prepared and determined. Some students could not believe that the army really would use deadly force. But most of all, we were motivated by a powerful sense of purpose. We believed that it would be worth sacrificing our lives for the sake of progress and democracy in China. . . .

At 4 A.M. Sunday the lights on the square were suddenly [put out]. Through the loudspeakers, we again heard orders to "clear out." A voice in my head said over and over, "The moment has come." [Moments later], machine guns erupted . . . [They] were shooting right at the chests and heads of the students . . . How many people died altogether? I don't really know. Am I pessimistic? No, I'm not at all pessimistic. Because I have seen the will of the people. I have seen the hope of China.

1. What goal motivated the students to stay in Tiananmen Square?
2. Why do you think the army turned off the lights in Tiananmen Square?
3. Why does the student say he is not pessimistic?
4. Why do you think the pro-democracy student chose to remain anonymous?

Cooperative Learning

Have students examine the picture on page 772. Divide the class into groups of five or six students. Group members should create a skit surrounding the scene in the photograph. Roles can include the man, the soldiers in the tanks, other demonstrators, and perhaps a government official. Group members should work together to devise a storyline and dialogue for the skit. Have a group recorder take notes and write down all the dialogue. Then with one group member acting as a director, have other members present their skit to the class.

ANSWERS TO
Voice from Our Time

1. achieving progress and democracy
2. to intimidate the students and prevent the press from recording what happened
3. He has seen the will of the people and their hope for the future.
4. Both he and his family could be punished.

On June 5, a man facing a column of tanks in Beijing symbolized resistance to state power. "Why are you here? . . . My city is in chaos because of you."

Define:
large collective farm

Identify:
(a) head of state and chairman of Chinese Communist party (b) industrial production targets (c) plan to build socialist society and stronger economy (d) revolution to establish a proletarian culture (e) leader who ended isolationist policy (f) encouraged contacts with the West and private enterprise, ordered crackdown on students

Answer:

1. (a) had two parallel and overlapping organizations, the Communist Party and the national government (b) head of state, Communist party chairman

2. (a) Most farmers owned no land. (b) Government distributed land, then formed collectives.

3. (a) Industry grew rapidly. (b) Poor planning slowed industrial growth.

4. (a) to restore purity of the revolution (b) Red Guards formed, colleges and schools closed, scientists and doctors were sent to work on farms, Chinese economy weakened.

5. (a) traded with industrial countries; sent students abroad; allowed some private enterprise (b) led to greater freedom and economic growth

6. more democracy and less corruption

7. No. As one writer noted, "Individuals told to think for themselves in order to boost production start wanting to boost their participation as well."

untrue. Government leaders claimed that "a certain small group" of criminals and thugs "plotted to arrest Communist party and state leaders." The government maintained that its troops showed heroic restraint but were "finally forced to fire on the rioters." Officials insisted that only 100 civilians died. Meanwhile, news reporters from around the world filmed and recorded what was actually taking place.

Although the crackdown succeeded in frightening the Chinese people into anxious silence, it failed to stop worldwide protest against the violence. President Bush canceled shipments of military parts to China and extended the visas of young Chinese studying in the United States. In Hong Kong, huge crowds demonstrated against the Chinese government. The massacre severely shook Hong Kong's confidence in an agreement calling for Britain to transfer political control of the colony to China in 1997.

The collapse of the pro-democracy movement left the future in China uncertain. Although the 85-year-old Deng remained firmly in control, no one could predict who would succeed him or determine policy. A student leader voiced the people's anger and despair when she told a reporter, "The government has won the battle here today. But they have lost the people's hearts."

772

Section REVIEW 3

Define: commune

Identify: (a) Mao Tse-tung, (b) Five-Year Plan, (c) Great Leap Forward, (d) Cultural Revolution, (e) Zhou Enlai, (f) Deng Xiaoping

Answer:

1. (a) How did China's government after 1949 resemble that of the Soviet Union? (b) What powerful positions did Mao hold?

2. (a) Why was land reform an important issue for China? (b) How did the ownership of land change under communism?

3. (a) What were the results of Mao's Five-Year Plan? (b) Of the Great Leap Forward?

4. (a) Why did Mao call for a Cultural Revolution? (b) Briefly describe what followed.

5. (a) What changes did Deng Xiaoping introduce? (b) What were their effects on China's economy and society?

6. What changes were the pro-democracy students seeking in their protests and demonstrations in June 1989?

Critical Thinking

7. Is it possible for an authoritarian government to make economic reforms without also making political reforms?

India and Pakistan became independent.

4

The people of India had been working since the early 1900's to win their independence from Great Britain (pages 660–665). Under their great leader, Mohandas Gandhi, many Indians had waged a peaceful struggle of marches, boycotts, and noncooperation against their British rulers. At the end of World War II, British public opinion turned against imperialism. It was clear that India would soon be free. It was not clear, however, whether independence could be achieved without bloodshed among Indians themselves.

Independence brought partition.

In February 1947, British Prime Minister Clement Attlee announced that Britain would turn over the government of India "into responsible Indian hands" no later than June 1948.

The Indian leaders who had been negotiating with Attlee included Jawaharlal Nehru of the Congress party and Muhammad Ali Jinnah of the Muslim League. As you have read in Chapter 29, India's Hindus and Muslims were bitterly divided. The Muslim League stated that it would never accept Indian independence if it meant rule by the Hindu-dominated Congress party. Jinnah said, "The only thing the Muslim has in common with the Hindu is his slavery to the British."

The Muslim League demanded **partition,** the division of British India into two countries, one Hindu and one Muslim. Muslims planned for an independent country to be called Pakistan.

At first, the British disagreed, insisting that a single Indian government take over when they withdrew. However, Hindus and Muslims were already clashing with each other. In August 1946, four days of rioting in Calcutta left more than 5,000 people dead and more than 15,000 hurt.

British leaders decided that partition was the best way to limit bloodshed. A boundary commission hastily drew the borders of the two new countries. Pakistan consisted of two Muslim regions 1,000 miles apart. One lay to the northeast of India, the other to the northwest. In the words of one historian, Pakistan "hung like elephant's ears from the body of India."

South Asia

Map Study

What nations have a border disagreement? Which South Asian nations are landlocked?

The new borders made little economic sense. East Pakistan included many jute-growing regions, for example. The jute mills were in Calcutta, which remained in India. Moreover, the boundaries left millions of Hindus in Pakistan and millions of Muslims in India.

On August 15, 1947, India and Pakistan became independent. Nehru became prime minister of India and Jinnah, prime minister of Pakistan.

As Gandhi and others had feared, a bloodbath followed. Millions of people struggled to cross the India-Pakistan border. Trainloads of **refugees,** or people fleeing their country, were massacred on both sides of the border. In all, more than 500,000 Hindus and Muslims died.

Gandhi himself fell victim to the violence of Hindu against Hindu. In January 1948, he was shot to death by a young Hindu who opposed Gandhi's efforts to win equal treatment for Harijans (untouchables). His death deprived India of its most honored leader.

Nehru sought to modernize India.

For the first 17 years after independence, India had one prime minister—Jawaharlal Nehru, who had been one of Gandhi's most devoted followers. Educated in Britain, Nehru described himself as

773

SECTION 4 Objectives and Teaching Strategies

OBJECTIVE 1. Identify the nations of South Asia.

Teaching Strategy: *Geography in History: New Nations in South Asia* (page 760d)

OBJECTIVE 2. Trace trends in conflict among the peoples of India.

Teaching Strategy: *Skill Building: Making a Time Line* (page 760d)

ANSWERS TO Map Study

India and Pakistan; Afghanistan, Nepal, Bhutan

SECTION 4 Resources

GEOGRAPHY
■ Transparency 98

REINFORCEMENT
■ Independent Practice 33.4

ENRICHMENT
■ Voices from the Past 33.4

ASSESSMENT
■ Section Quiz 33.4

India moved quickly to industrialize as a basis for economic development. Rapid population growth, however, limited the benefits from industrialization.

The diversity of religious, cultural, and language groups in India contributes to political unrest in the country. State boundaries within the country are redrawn almost annually to accommodate one group or another.

a "mixture of East and West, out of place everywhere, at home nowhere." Nehru won popularity among all groups in India. He emphasized democracy, unity, and economic modernization.

In foreign affairs, Nehru took a strong stand against **colonialism,** or the policy of retaining colonies. He also attempted to follow a policy of **nonalignment**—that is, taking neither side in the Cold War. India and other countries that chose to remain nonaligned came to be known as the **Third World.** Distinct from the First World—that of the democracies—and the Second World—that of communism—they would become a new influence in world politics.

Economic difficulties One major problem facing India was the lack of industry. Because Britain discouraged the growth of industry, India still depended heavily on agriculture. Almost 80 percent of the population lived in some 550,000 rural villages. The result was that most Indians lived in poverty, with average family income less than $1,000 a year.

Nehru and later leaders strove to modernize the country's economy. India began to adopt modern farming techniques in the 1960's. New strains of seed, for example, greatly increased crop yields. Likewise, India's industries grew slowly but steadily.

Despite great progress, major obstacles remained. One problem was the unequal distribution of land. More than 35 percent of India's farmland was owned by the wealthiest 5 percent of the rural population, while half the people owned no land at all.

Another obstacle was India's constantly growing population. The government set up birth control clinics around the country. Posters urged couples to have no more than two children. Such programs, however, had little success. Large families were a tradition in India, and poor couples counted on children for care in their old age. By 1985, India was home to approximately 768 million people, or 120 percent more than in 1947. That number was growing by 40,000 *every day!* "It's like a flood," one government official declared. "Every year we need an additional 2.5 million tons of grain—just to stay even."

Conflict with China and Pakistan Trouble on its borders distracted India from its domestic issues. India and China share a 1,500-mile border. In 1962, the two countries went to war briefly over a disputed area. China's forces surprised and overpowered those of India and occupied most of the land in question.

India's relations with neighboring Pakistan were almost always hostile. Indian leaders thought that partition had mutilated their country. The Pakistanis, for their part, were dismayed that their country did not include Kashmir, a large province in northern India where 75 percent of the people were Muslims. Clashes in Kashmir and other spots along the border led to full-scale war in 1965. After three weeks of fighting, India and Pakistan signed a truce that established an uneasy peace.

Indira Gandhi governed India.

Nehru's death in 1964 left the Congress party with no leader strong enough to hold together its many factions. Then in 1966, Nehru's daughter Indira Gandhi (no relation to the Mahatma) was chosen prime minister. Over the next ten years, she proved a forceful leader in her own right.

Under Indira Gandhi, India made economic progress. Both industrial and agricultural production grew during the 1970's. India became one of the world's top ten industrial nations. However, only some of this progress trickled down to the poor. Meanwhile, India's birthrate dropped slightly but remained among the highest in the world. By 1990, more than 15 percent of the total world population lived in India. That population was increasing rapidly.

Like Nehru, Indira Gandhi often pointed out that her country was the world's largest democracy. India also sought the status of a world power by exploding its first nuclear device in 1974.

Indira Gandhi was a controversial figure. In 1975, she was found guilty of illegal campaign practices, but she refused to step down as prime minister. Instead, she declared a state of emergency, arrested political opponents, and clamped down on the press. In 1977, her party's loss in parliamentary elections put her out of office. However, voters reelected her in 1980.

Gandhi soon faced a serious threat from Sikh extremists. The Sikhs are a religious group that blends elements of Hinduism and Islam (page 307). In 1984, Gandhi ordered government troops to crush a violent rebellion among Sikh extremists

774

seeking an independent state. Four months later, two of Gandhi's Sikh bodyguards assassinated her. Outraged Hindus retaliated by killing more than 2,500 Sikhs.

India's voters overwhelmingly chose Indira's son Rajiv to succeed her. He built up India's army and encouraged the growth of the electronics industry. Development, however, was limited by extreme poverty and a rapidly increasing population. In 1989, Rajiv Gandhi was defeated in an election. Two years later, he was assassinated while campaigning.

Religious strife rocked India.

Gandhi's death left the Congress party without its best-known leader. The party that had dominated Indian politics since 1947 now faced a serious challenge from the Bharatiya Janata party (BJP). The BJP received support from those who wanted India to become a Hindu nation.

Despite a strong showing by the BJP, the Congress party won a narrow victory in the 1991 elections. Party leaders named P.V. Narasimha Rao as India's new prime minister.

Rao soon faced a serious crisis between India's Hindu and Muslim communities. Egged on by BJP agitators, an enraged mob of 200,000 Hindus tore down a sixteenth century Muslim mosque in December 1992. Riots between Hindus and Muslims soon erupted all across India. The widespread violence threatened to undermine India's ability to remain a nonreligious state.

Pakistan became two countries.

Independence left Pakistan with two serious problems. A lack of leadership became acute after the death of Muhammad Ali Jinnah in 1948. The second problem was geographic. East and West Pakistan were separated by 1,000 miles of Indian territory. Although united by their Muslim faith, the two regions contained different ethnic groups. West Pakistan controlled the army and most of the nation's industry.

The people of East Pakistan resented their inferior position. "We have never been anything but a colony of the West," one leader asserted in 1970. Following widespread rioting in East Pakistan, full-scale civil war began in 1971. India's entry into the war forced Pakistan to surrender.

Prime Minister Indira Gandhi of India was assassinated by Sikh extremists in 1984.

East Pakistan became the independent nation of Bangladesh, "land of the Bengalis."

Independence did not solve Bangladesh's problems. The new nation struggled to deal with extreme poverty and rapid population increase. Severe floods slowed economic development.

The loss of Bangladesh disrupted the Pakistan economy, and measures begun by Prime Minister Zulfikar Ali Bhutto failed to revive it. In 1977, General Mohammad Zia-ul Haq overthrew Bhutto and established a military dictatorship. He died in a mysterious plane crash in 1988.

The death of Zia opened the door to free elections. In 1988, Pakistan's voters chose Benazir Bhutto, daughter of the former prime minister, as their leader. The first woman ruler of a Muslim nation, Bhutto failed to win wide support from the military. In 1990, military leaders charged her with corruption—charges that led to her removal from office. The elections that followed made Chandra Shekhar the new prime minister.

Section REVIEW 4

Define: (a) partition, (b) refugee, (c) colonialism, (d) nonalignment, (e) Third World
Identify: (a) Jawaharlal Nehru, (b) Kashmir, (c) Indira Gandhi, (d) Sikhs, (e) Rajiv Gandhi, (f) Bangladesh, (g) Benazir Bhutto

775

ANSWERS TO
Section Review 4

Define:
(a) division into two countries (b) person fleeing his or her own country (c) policy of retaining colonies (d) policy of not taking sides (e) nonaligned and less industrialized countries
Identify:
(a) first prime minister of India (b) large Muslim prov-
(continued)

ANSWERS TO (continued)

ince in northern India
(c) Nehru's daughter who became prime minister
(d) religious group blending Hinduism and Islam
(e) former prime minister of India, son of Indira Gandhi
(f) nation that was formerly East Pakistan (g) former prime minister of Bangladesh

Answer:

1. (a) emphasize democracy, unity, and economic modernization (b) nonalignment

2. (a) modernized economy (b) unequal distribution of land and constantly growing population

3. (a) Indian leaders thought that partition had mutilated their country; Pakistanis thought their country should include Kashmir. (b) war

4. (a) Their populations were mainly Muslim. (b) differences between ethnic groups; east poorer and more densely populated than west; west controlled army

5. as a result of war between Pakistan and India and resentments toward western Pakistan

6. Students may consider that ethnic and religious loyalties seem to outweigh nationalism or that changes since independence have fostered nationalism.

Map Study

Name Southeast Asia's island nations. Which of them is the largest in area? Which country has no coastline?

Answer:

1. (a) What were Nehru's goals within India? (b) In relations with other countries?
2. (a) What economic progress did India make under Nehru and Indira Gandhi? (b) What problems hindered progress?
3. (a) Why was there hostility between India and Pakistan? (b) What was the result?
4. (a) What did East and West Pakistan have in common? (b) What issues divided them?
5. How did East Pakistan become the independent country of Bangladesh?

Critical Thinking

6. Review the definition of *nationalism*. How strong is nationalism in South Asia?

The Pacific Rim faced change and conflict. 5

The defeat of Japan in 1945 created a power vacuum in eastern Asia. Besides Japan itself, the entire region of Asia that borders the Pacific Ocean—the Asian section of what geographers call the Pacific Rim—was dramatically transformed in the decades after World War II. From Korea to Indonesia, the nations that emerged from the ashes of the Japanese empire broke with the past and faced the challenges of the future. Today the Pacific Rim countries are a major center of world trade.

ANSWERS TO

Map Study

Philippines, Brunei, Malaysia, Indonesia; Indonesia; Laos

Former colonies became independent.

In Southeast Asia, the European nations that had controlled the region before the Japanese conquest attempted to regain power after the war. The force of nationalism, however, proved too powerful to resist.

In the Dutch East Indies, nationalists continued to fight against Dutch forces. In 1949, the East Indies became the newly independent nation of Indonesia with Sukarno as its first president.

As the fifth most populous country in the world, Indonesia faced many of the same economic problems as India. It also faced political problems. During the 1960's, a brutal civil war cost nearly half a million lives. Sukarno was succeeded in 1968 by Suharto, whose lengthy rule became a dictatorship. Nonetheless the country enjoyed considerable peace and prosperity, thanks largely to its valuable oil resources.

The Philippines also faced a difficult period of adjustment after declaring independence from the United States in 1946. Huge gaps existed between rich and poor, and rapid population growth put constant pressure on the economy.

The country began to slowly rebuild under Ferdinand Marcos, president from 1965 to 1986. Although he promised to "make democracy real," Marcos imposed strict authoritarian controls. Opposition to the Marcos regime grew as critics such as Benigno Aquino uncovered evidence of widespread government corruption.

Marcos's power began to decline following the assassination of Aquino in 1983. Although Marcos denied that his government was responsible, many Filipinos believed he ordered the killing. Three years later, Aquinos's widow, Corazón, ran against Marcos in a bitterly contested election. Marcos claimed victory, but public outrage over election fraud forced him to flee to Hawaii.

Corazón Aquino pledged to end corruption and restore constitutional democracy. She was succeeded in 1992 by Fidel Ramos in a peaceful transfer of power.

The French lost Indochina.

In French Indochina, independence was not won easily, nor did it bring peace. For 40 years after World War II, war haunted Laos, Cambodia, and Vietnam.

In her campaign to become president of the Philippines in 1986, Corazón Aquino used the letter L *(for* laban, *or "struggle") as her symbol.*

The richest part of French Indochina was Vietnam, the narrow coastal region that runs for nearly 1,000 miles beside the South China Sea. Vietnam had iron and coal mines in the north, and rubber plantations and rice fields in the south. This wealth, combined with French national pride, gave France strong reasons for wanting to hold the area after World War II.

However, a strong nationalist movement had grown up in Vietnam. Its foremost leader was Ho Chi Minh, a Communist guerrilla who had helped drive out the Japanese. Ho and other nationalists formed the Vietminh (Independence) League. The Vietminh was strongest in northern Vietnam.

War in Indochina, 1946–1954 When France tried to reassert its control over Vietnam, both nationalists and Communists fought the French armies. The French held most of the major cities, but French forces were nearly powerless in the countryside, where the Vietminh had the support of most peasants. The Vietminh used hit-and-run tactics to bottle up the French in the cities and a few strongholds. Ho called this way of fighting "the war of the flea."

777

SECTION 5
Objectives and Teaching Strategies

OBJECTIVE 1. Identify Corazón Aquino and explain how she became president of the Philippines.

Teaching Strategy: *Discussing History: Corazón Aquino* (page 760e)

OBJECTIVE 2. Evaluate President Johnson's decision to escalate the Vietnam War.

Teaching Strategy: *Writing about History: Escalation or Withdrawal?* (page 760e)

■ BACKGROUND

By the 1930's, Vietnam produced all of France's raw rubber and was one of the world's three leading exporters of rice. French colonists used their wealth to support a luxurious standard of living. The southern city of Saigon soon became the center of French culture in the colony. The city's tree-lined streets and fashionable shops earned it the title "Paris of the Orient." Visitors to Saigon dined in the famed Continental Hotel and then enjoyed a play in a magnificent new theater. Satisfied officials proudly called Vietnam "our marvelous balcony on the Pacific."

SECTION 5
Resources

GEOGRAPHY
■ Transparencies 99, 100, 101

REINFORCEMENT
■ Independent Practice 33.5

ENRICHMENT
■ Voices from the Past 33.5

ASSESSMENT
■ Section Quiz 33.5

■ BACKGROUND

Dien Bien Phu is located 170 miles west of Hanoi. In late 1953, the French built a heavily fortified base there, manned by 16,000 soldiers. The French generals hoped their new base would lure the Viet Minh into a set battle in which their firepower could inflict heavy losses on the Viet Minh. Convinced that this strategy would work, the French commander boasted, "A year ago none of us could see victory. There wasn't a prayer. Now we can see it clearly—like light at the end of a tunnel."

The commander's prediction proved to be wrong. The Viet Minh surrounded the French with a force of 50,000 men. Even worse, they shocked the French by hauling 200 powerful artillery pieces through 50 miles of mountainous jungle. Hidden on the hills around Dien Bien Phu, the Viet Minh artillery destroyed the French airfield.

Now desperate, the French turned to the United States for help. The Pentagon proposed a massive American air strike called Operation Vulture to end the siege. The plan included the possible use of three small atom bombs. Arguing that an air attack would lead to calls for American ground forces, President Eisenhower rejected Operation Vulture. He later

Meanwhile, the Indochina War was becoming increasingly unpopular with French voters. Many French people felt that Vietnam was not worth the lives and money it was costing. "For every ten men you kill," Ho Chi Minh had warned the French, "we will kill one of yours. And it is you who will have to give up in the end."

Ho proved to be right. In 1954, the French suffered a major defeat at Dien Bien Phu. After that loss, France agreed to a settlement. An international peace conference was held in Geneva to discuss the future of Indochina in general and of Vietnam in particular.

The role of the United States The United States government had sent arms and money to the French to help them defeat the Communists. The United States government saw Ho's victory as a threat to the rest of Asia. John Foster Dulles, American secretary of state, explained the government's viewpoint:

> If Indochina falls, Thailand and Burma would be in extreme danger; Malaya, Singapore, and even Indonesia would become vulnerable to the Communist power drive.

This belief that the fall of one Southeast Asian nation to communism would lead to the fall of its neighbors was known as the **domino theory.** This idea became a cornerstone of United States foreign policy during the Cold War era.

A divided Vietnam At the peace conference in Geneva, the United States tried to limit the Communist influence to the northern part of Vietnam. According to the peace terms, Vietnam was divided along the seventeenth parallel of latitude. North of that line, Ho Chi Minh's forces governed. To the south, the United States and France set up a separate government under Ngo Dinh Diem (noh dihn d'yem).

Unfortunately, Diem was neither popular nor capable. He did little to appeal to the people, unlike Ho Chi Minh, who began a program of land redistribution in the north. Instead, Diem ruled as a dictator.

Communist guerrillas, called Viet Cong, began to gain strength in the south. Some were trained soldiers from North Vietnam. Others were South Vietnamese who opposed Diem. Gradually, the Viet Cong won control of large areas of the countryside.

In 1963, a group of South Vietnamese generals— with the quiet backing of the United States— planned a coup. Meeting almost no resistance, they overthrew and killed Diem. The new leaders, however, had no more popular support than Diem. A Communist takeover seemed sure to follow.

The United States entered the Vietnam War.

Faced with this dilemma, the United States decided to step into the conflict directly. Americans had been serving as advisers to the South Vietnamese since the late 1950's. Now the number of those advisers steadily increased. The United States also sent more and more planes, tanks, and other military equipment to South Vietnam.

In August 1964, United States President Lyndon Johnson told Congress that North Vietnamese patrol boats had attacked two American destroyers in the Gulf of Tonkin. As a result, Congress gave the president authority to send American troops into Vietnam. By late 1965, more than 185,000 United States soldiers were on the ground in South Vietnam. Meanwhile, American planes bombed North Vietnam.

Escalation The war escalated—that is, the number of troops and the amount of fighting increased step by step. By 1968, more than half a million American soldiers had been thrown into the battle in Vietnam.

The United States had the best-equipped, most advanced army in the world. However, the Americans faced two major difficulties. First, they were not fighting an open battle but a guerrilla

▌ecisions in ⊞istory

The French base at Dien Bien Phu was held by 16,000 soldiers. They were surrounded, however, by a Vietminh force of 50,000 men. The French, desperate for help, turned to the United States for military assistance. To end the siege, the chairman of the American Joint Chiefs of Staff proposed a massive air strike called Operation Vulture. His plan included the possible use of three small atom bombs. The French supported Operation Vulture, arguing that it would save their army and help to defeat the Vietminh. Several influential American advisers opposed the plan. They argued that it would trigger a major confrontation with China. What would you have done and why?

war. Second, the Viet Cong had great popular support, while the South Vietnamese government became steadily more unpopular.

Unable to win a clear-cut victory on the ground, the United States turned more and more to air power. Trying to destroy enemy hideouts, American forces bombed millions of acres of farmland and forest. The bombing brought widespread misery to the peasants, turning them even more against the South Vietnamese government. Yet the American goal was to win support for that government. "It was as if we were trying to build a house with a bulldozer and wrecking crane," one American official later said.

The close of the war During the late 1960's, the war became increasingly unpopular in the United States. By 1969, a majority of Americans opposed the war. Bowing to intense pressure,

President Richard Nixon began withdrawing United States troops from Vietnam. However, he also authorized secret bombings in neighboring Cambodia to wipe out Viet Cong supply routes and hiding places.

To strengthen the South Vietnamese government, the United States sent South Vietnam the best equipment money could buy. However, equipment was not enough to save the corrupt and unpopular government in the south.

The North Vietnamese struck with a massive attack in the spring of 1975. Within six weeks, Communist troops took control of Saigon. All Vietnam came under a Communist government. Hanoi, once the capital of North Vietnam, became the capital of the whole country. Saigon, former capital of the south, was renamed Ho Chi Minh City in honor of the Communist leader.

wrote, "The jungles of Indochina . . . would have swallowed up division after division of U.S. troops." Unable to convince Eisenhower to change his position, the French surrendered Dien Bien Phu on May 7, 1954, after a bitter 55-day siege.

■ DISCUSSION

Eric Sevareid called the war in Indochina that lasted from 1945 to 1975 "the second Thirty Years' War." Why did the conflict last so long?

Map Study

By what route did North Vietnam move soldiers and supplies into South Vietnam? Through what countries did the route pass? What various purposes might helicopters (right) serve? In what kinds of terrain might ground forces like this soldier (lower right) be most active?

The War in Vietnam, 1957–1973

ANSWERS TO

Map Study

Ho Chi Minh Trail; Laos, Cambodia; Rugged terrain and thick vegetation made helicopters necessary for both moving troops and evacuating wounded; areas with thick vegetation.

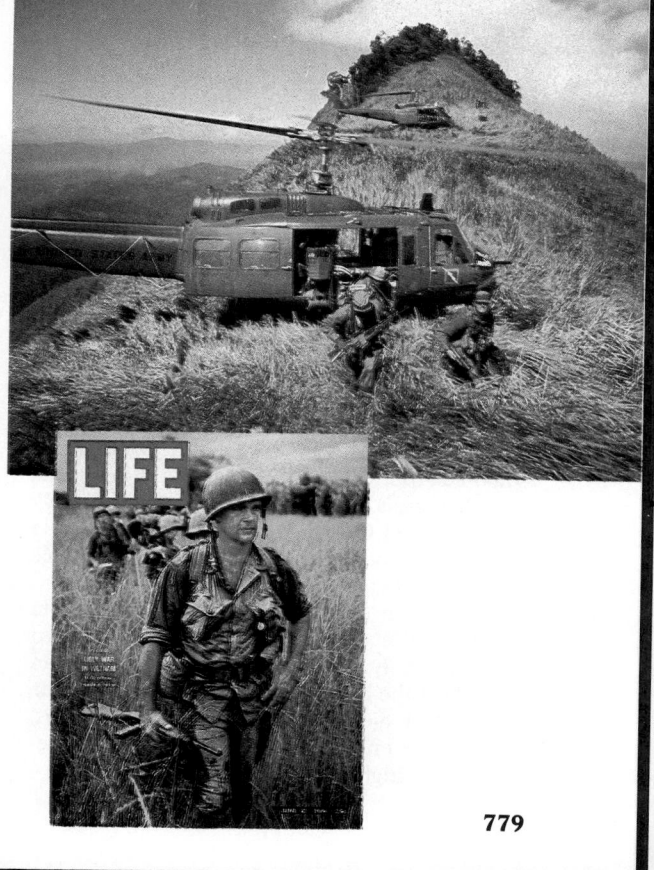

779

ANSWERS TO
Map Study

Trust Territory of the Pacific Islands, also Wake, Guam, Midway, the Hawaiian and the Aleutian Islands; The Pacific region remains vitally important and the U.S. maintains a strong influence there.

The Pacific Rim

Map Study

List the United States territories in the Pacific region. What do they show about United States interests and influence there?

Conflict continued in Southeast Asia.

After 1975, the victorious North Vietnamese imposed strict controls over the South. Officials sent thousands of people to "re-education camps" for training in Communist ideology. Hanoi also nationalized industries and placed strict controls on private businesses.

Communist oppression prompted 1.5 million people to flee Vietnam. Most refugees escaped in dangerously overcrowded ships. More than 200,000 of the **boat people,** as the refugees came to be called, died at sea—the victims of storms, disease, and cruel pirates. One refugee later described his frightening experience.

We left Cam Ranh Bay [in Vietnam] on . . . September 16, 1977, without any provisions. There were storms on the high seas. Without the navigation equipment, we could not manage the tiny boat. We threw off all five of our fuel-filled tanks and all our possessions to lighten the boat. We starved for fourteen days. My mother-in-law was the first one who died. Then all four of my children, and other children, too. Altogether, we lost eighteen children and two adults. . . . Several ships passed by. None responded to our cry for help.

The boat people who survived often spent long months in crowded refugee camps scattered

780

ANSWERS TO
Section Review 5

Define:
(a) region surrounding the Pacific Ocean **(b)** belief that the fall of one nation to communism would lead to the fall of its neighbors

(continued)

across Southeast Asia. About 700,000 Vietnamese refugees eventually settled in the United States. Many Vietnamese have also settled in Canada.

The tragedy of Cambodia The Vietnam War placed Cambodia in a precarious position. Its leader, Norodom Sihanouk (SEE-uh-nook), tried to remain neutral, but the North Vietnamese used Cambodia for supply routes and bases. In 1970, a pro-American group led by General Lon Nol overthrew Sihanouk.

The Lon Nol government faced a serious challenge from Communist rebels known as the Khmer Rouge, or Red Cambodians. After a bitter civil war, Lon Nol's army surrendered in April 1975. The Khmer Rouge promptly set up a Communist government led by Pol Pot. A ruthless tyrant, Pol Pot executed anyone linked to the Lon Nol regime.

Pol Pot launched a program to make Cambodia an agricultural society. Khmer Rouge soldiers forced people to evacuate all towns and cities. As the social structure collapsed, famine and disease swept across the country. Almost 2 million people—one quarter of the nation's population—died.

Pol Pot's brutal regime did not remain in power for long. Although Communist governments controlled both Cambodia and Vietnam, the two nations were traditional enemies. Pol Pot provoked a crisis by sending troops into Vietnamese territory. In December 1978, the Vietnamese retaliated by invading Cambodia and overthrowing the Khmer Rouge. They then installed a new regime that tried to rebuild the shattered country.

The Vietnamese withdrew their forces in September 1989. Two years later, Cambodia's warring factions signed a UN-sponsored agreement that ended the civil war. In 1992, the UN sent 20,000 soldiers to maintain peace and supervise elections scheduled for mid-1993.

The Pacific Rim experienced an economic boom.

Not all the nations of the Pacific Rim were confronted with problems of civil war and underdevelopment. As you have seen, Japan became an economic superpower during the 1970's and 1980's, while China also became more prosperous during this period.

Other Asian nations, following Japan's example, embarked upon programs of rapid industrialization designed to make their economies both modern and prosperous. South Korea, for example, developed rapidly after 1960, becoming a major exporter of automobiles and electronic goods. Similar expansion occurred in Taiwan and the modern city-states of Hong Kong and Singapore, which became thriving centers of international commerce.

These four newly-industrialized countries (NIC's) recorded such impressive growth that they became known as the Four Tigers. They also demonstrated how well Asian peoples could adapt to the economic changes that swept across the globe during the postwar period.

Section REVIEW 5

Define: (a) Pacific Rim, (b) domino theory, (c) boatpeople
Identify: (a) Sukarno, (b) Ferdinand Marcos, (c) Corazón Aquino, (d) Ho Chi Minh, (e) Ngo Dinh Diem, (f) Gulf of Tonkin incident, (g) Norodom Sihanouk, (h) Pol Pot, (i) Four Tigers
Answer:
1. What new nation replaced the former Dutch colony of the East Indies?
2. (a) How did the Philippines gain independence? (b) What problems did the country face?
3. (a) How did Marcos win control of the government? (b) How did he lose power?
4. How did Vietnam become divided?
5. (a) What part did the United States play in Vietnam before 1954? (b) Between 1954 and 1964? (c) From 1964 to 1973?
6. (a) How did the Khmer Rouge come to power in Cambodia? (b) What did they do? (c) What was their relationship to Vietnam?

Critical Thinking
7. Many countries in Southeast Asia have suffered guerrilla warfare. (a) How can guerrillas wage war successfully against larger, better-equipped government armies? (b) What underlying problems can make a government vulnerable to such a war?

781

ANSWERS TO (continued)

(c) refugees from Communist oppression who fled from Vietnam by boat
Identify:
(a) Indonesia's first president (b) corrupt Philippine leader (c) elected president of the Philippines (d) North Vietnamese guerrilla leader (e) unpopular and inept South Vietnamese leader (f) This attack by the North Vietnamese led Congress to give President Johnson the authority to send American troops into Vietnam. (g) Cambodian leader (h) leader of Khmer Rouge (i) South Korea, Taiwan, Hong Kong, Singapore
Answer:
1. Indonesia
2. (a) U.S. promised Philippines complete independence. (b) poverty, political corruption
3. (a) elected president (b) was corrupt
4. After the French defeat at Dien Bien Phu, the peace settlement divided Vietnam along the seventeenth parallel.
5. (a) sent American advisers (b) increased number of advisers, sent planes and military equipment (c) bombed North Vietnam, escalated war
6. (a) won control after a five-year civil war (b) attacked non-Communist enemies, made Cambodia an agricultural society (c) Although both were communist countries, they were traditional enemies; Vietnam invaded and overthrew the Khmer Rouge.
7. (a) highly motivated by nationalism, tactics more successful in jungle terrain (b) corruption, lack of effective leadership, poverty

Concluding the Chapter

1. **Chapter Closer**
   Ask students to compare and contrast economic developments in Japan, China, South Asia, and East Asia after World War II.

2. **Reteaching Activities**
   a. Summarizing Have students summarize the factors that contributed to Japan's economic revival.
   b. Writing a Paragraph Ask students to explain why colonial India became two independent countries in 1947. Have students write paragraphs telling whether partition did or did not settle most problems and giving reasons for their answers.

3. **Chapter Review Activities**
   Assign Chapter Review 33 activities.

Answers to Chapter Review appear on pages 760e–760f.

Summary

1. Japan became an industrial giant. Under United States occupation, Japan adopted a democratic form of government, pledged itself to disarmament, and instituted land reforms. Industrialization and postwar prosperity produced an economic miracle in the country. Yet rapid economic growth led to severe social problems, including pollution and crowding.

2. China became a Communist country. At the end of World War II, civil war once again broke out in China between Nationalists and Communists. Defeated Nationalists fled to Taiwan in 1949. Led by Mao Tse-tung, Communists set up the People's Republic of China, which the United States refused to recognize. After the war, Korea was occupied by Soviets in the north and United States troops in the south. In 1950, North Koreans, later aided by Chinese Communists, swept into South Korea. The United Nations sent a peacekeeping force to stop the invasion. The war ended in a stalemate in 1953.

3. China changed under a Communist government. In 1949, the Chinese Communist party reorganized the government, instituted massive land reforms, and centralized planning of industry and business. In 1958, Mao announced the Great Leap Forward, which established communes. Slowed industrialization led Mao to launch a purge called the Cultural Revolution that nearly destroyed China. Since 1976, Deng Xiaoping has encouraged contacts with the West and some private enterprise. However, in 1989 the government used force to suppress a student-led pro-democracy movement.

4. India and Pakistan became independent. In 1947, division between Muslims and Hindus led to the creation of two separate nations, India and Pakistan. Progress in India has been hampered by a rapidly expanding population and conflicts between Hindus and Muslims. Muslim Pakistan became two nations in 1971, Pakistan and Bangladesh.

5. The Pacific Rim faced conflict and change. Indonesia, the Philippines, and other colonies gained independence after World War II. The government of Ferdinand Marcos in the Philippines was ousted for misrule in 1985. Vietnam was divided into North and South Vietnam after the French defeat in 1954. In spite of United States aid the South Vietnamese could not defeat the Viet Cong. The United States withdrew from the war in 1973. The Viet Cong united the country and supported Communist takeovers in Cambodia and Laos.

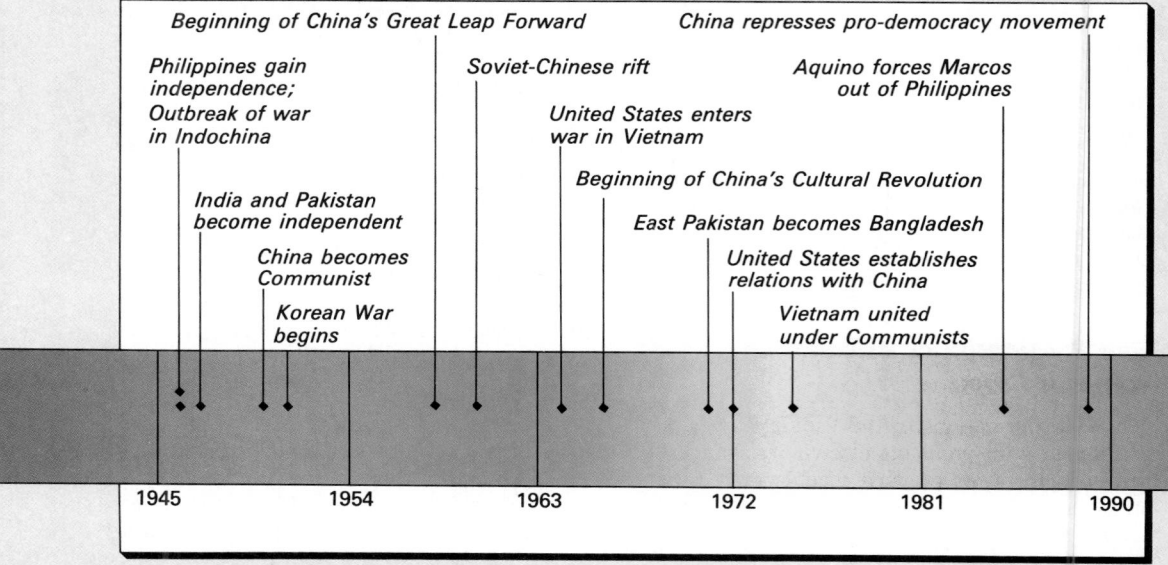

Beginning of China's Great Leap Forward — China represses pro-democracy movement
Philippines gain independence; Outbreak of war in Indochina
Soviet-Chinese rift
Aquino forces Marcos out of Philippines
United States enters war in Vietnam
India and Pakistan become independent
Beginning of China's Cultural Revolution
East Pakistan becomes Bangladesh
China becomes Communist
United States establishes relations with China
Korean War begins
Vietnam united under Communists

1945   1954   1963   1972   1981   1990

782

Reviewing the Facts

1. Explain the importance of each of the following names, places, or terms:
   a. MacArthur
   b. Mao Tse-tung
   c. Cultural Revolution
   d. Zhou Enlai
   e. Deng Xiaoping
   f. Nehru
   g. Indira Gandhi
   h. Bangladesh
   i. Aquino
   j. Ho Chi Minh
   k. Viet Cong
   l. Gulf of Tonkin
   m. Khmer Rouge
   n. Pacific Rim

Basic Skills

1. **Making an outline** Make an outline of the content under the heading "Communist leaders made reforms," using three levels—(**A** as the main heading, **1** as a subheading, and **a** and **b** as detail under the subheading).
2. **Applying geographic information** Using the index of your text for reference, review the earlier content on Southeast Asia. How might geography have influenced the forming of Southeast Asian nations, shown on the map on page 776?
3. **Interpreting maps** The nations of East and Southeast Asia that face the Pacific are part of an emerging trading region called the Pacific Rim. Judging from the map on page 780, how might the location of those nations affect their role in trade?

Researching and Reporting Skills

1. **Using statistical reports** (a) As a class project, use a variety of sources to obtain statistical information—for example, on population growth, manufacturing, and trade—about the nations of East, South, and Southeast Asia. Possible sources include UN publications, the *Statistical Abstract of the United States* or other U.S. government publications, *The Statesman's Yearbook, The Europa Yearbook*, and standard almanacs. (b) When all the information has been compiled, analyze it to determine the trends involved. (c) How may these trends affect future development?
2. **Using guides to television** Study the weekly guide to television programs to find a documentary presenting information on some aspect of modern Asia. View the documentary and write a brief report describing the source, type of information presented, and point of view.

Critical Thinking

1. **Solving problems** Before World War II, Japan had sought an empire as a source of resources and raw materials. (a) How did Japan solve this problem after World War II? (b) Compare the effectiveness of the two solutions.
2. **Inferring** (a) What factors enabled the Communists to take over China? (b) What problems might the Communist government have faced after it came into power?
3. **Comparing economic viewpoints** Compare the viewpoints of Japan and China toward each of the following: (a) capitalism, (b) government's economic role, (c) free markets.
4. **Evaluating** (a) What criteria would you use to evaluate China's potential for becoming an economic superpower? (b) How great is China's economic potential in terms of those criteria?
5. **Interpreting** The emergence of the Third World is a major development of this century. What is its international political, economic, and cultural significance?
6. **Analyzing** How does rapid population growth tend to affect modernization and economic development in Third World countries such as India?
7. **Identifying viewpoints** Two major causes leading to war in Vietnam were imperialism and the spread of communism. (a) Which cause do you think was more important to France? (b) to the United States? Give reasons to support your answers. (c) Why might public opinion in both nations be divided over fighting in Vietnam?
8. **Analyzing** (a) What factors hindered the growth of democracy in Southeast Asia? (b) What factors encouraged democracy? Give examples to support your answer.

Perspectives on Past and Present

Compare the Korean conflict with the war in Vietnam. (a) How did the end of World War II contribute to division in each country? (b) What was the role of the United States in each war? (c) How were the outcomes similar? How were they different?

Investigating History

During the postwar era, Communist China took over Tibet. Do research to find out what the objectives, main events, and outcomes of that involvement were.

783

CHAPTER
Evaluation

Chapter Test 33, Alternate Chapter Test 33, and Computer Test Bank Chapter 33 Test can be used to evaluate your students' understanding of this chapter.

Nationalism in Africa and the Middle East   Chapter 34

Chapter Overview

At the end of World War II, nations in Africa sought to free themselves from colonial bonds. Starting first in the Muslim nations of North Africa, a surge of nationalism spread throughout the African continent. By 1980 all of Africa, except Namibia, had won independence. Colonialism left a legacy of problems, including social instability, ethnic rivalries, and one-crop economies.

In meeting the challenges of independence, African nations adopted a variety of governments, including both democracies and dictatorships. Each nation, regardless of its political system, needed to industrialize. Overpopulation and indebtedness slowed progress. In South Africa, where the economy prospered, the issue of apartheid clouded the future. Independence based on white control led to black resistance within South Africa and criticism from other nations.

The fires of nationalism burned in the Middle East as well. In seeking their place among the more developed nations of the world, Arab countries formed the Organization of Petroleum Exporting Countries (OPEC). Oil, a valuable resource in the industrial world, suddenly became a political issue. Oil-rich Arab nations used it to undermine Western support of Israel, setting the stage for conflict in the 1970's. Access to oil, territorial disputes, ethnic and religious strife, and other sources of conflict continued to trouble the Middle East into the 1990's.

Chapter Focus

Note that Ghana was the first black African nation to gain independence in the twentieth century. Divide the class into two groups of reporters—British and Ghanian. Ask each group to write a paragraph that completes this topic sentence: "Ghana's independence ceremony marked . . ." Compare and contrast students' different points of view.

Teaching Strategies

Discussing History: Problems of Nation-Building (Objective 1) In 1960 Albert Luthuli became the first African to win the Nobel Peace

---

The age of imperialism ended in Africa.   1

Setting the Stage

Introduce the section by reading aloud the passage below. It is from Kwame Nkrumah's speech before the first session of Ghana's parliament in 1957.

> If we show ourselves disunited, inefficient or corrupt we shall have gravely harmed all those million in Africa who . . .
> looked to Ghana to prove that African people can build a state based on democracy . . . and racial equality.

Given the nature of colonial rule, why was democracy an experiment for most Africans? Show Map Transparency 102, *The Nations of Africa,* to review the African nations.

Advance Planner

	SECTION 1
Objectives	1. Analyze the factors that hindered nation-building in newly independent African countries. 2. Compare the political problems and solutions of newly independent nations.
Setting the Stage	For most African nations, democracy was an experiment Transparency 102
Teaching Strategies	Discussing History: Problems of Nation-Building Skill Building: Comparing and Contrasting Political Problems and Solutions Check for Understanding
Guided Practice	Transparency 102 Q&A Section Review 1
Independent Practice Worksheets	Independent Practice 34.1 Geography Skills 34 Vocabulary 34
Enrichment	1. Primary Source: Voices 34.1 2. Preparing a Report: African Nationalism 3. Researching for Points
Chapter Closer	

Prize. Luthuli, a Zulu chief, won the prize for his efforts to advance black self-determination in white-dominated South Africa. Read the following extract aloud.

> Our continent has been carved up by the great powers; alien governments have been forced upon the African people by military conquest . . . . Strivings for nationhood and national dignity have been beaten down by force; traditional economies and ancient customs have been disrupted . . . . But now . . . [o]ur people everywhere from north to south . . . are reclaiming their land, their right to participate in government, their dignity, . . . their nationhood . . .

Ask students what they think Luthuli meant by the disruption of traditional economies. What other economic problems did newly independent African nations face? Have students list the factors that hampered nation-building in Africa.

Chapter 34 Nationalism in Africa and the Middle East 1945–1990

★ Advanced

FOCUS Ghana's independence ceremony as a symbol of twentieth-century independence movements in Africa

● Basic

SECTION 2	SECTION 3	SECTION 4	SECTION 5
1. Identify the economic needs of newly independent African nations. 2. Assess some causes and effects of widespread famine in Africa in the 1980's.	1. Identify South Africa's neighboring countries and explain South Africa's interventions in their affairs. 2. Explain Nelson Mandela's views on majority rule in South Africa.	1. Identify the significance of the Suez Crisis. 2. Trace events leading to conflicts and conflict resolutions between Arab nations and Israel.	1. Explain the political effects of the discovery of oil in the Middle East. 2. Explain the significance of the rise of Islamic fundamentalism.
Economic and social challenges to new African nations	The issue of minority rule in history	Perceptions of Palestine Transparency 104	Continued conflict in the Middle East
Economics and History: Meeting Economic Needs Skill Building: Making Inferences Check for Understanding	Discussing History: South Africa and Its Neighbors Transparency 102 Analyzing a Quotation: Nelson Mandela Speaks to South Africa Check for Understanding	Discussing History: The Suez Crisis Discussing History: Peace-Keeping Efforts Transparency 103 Check for Understanding	Discussing History: Oil as a Force in the World Community Discussing History: Islamic Fundamentalism Check for Understanding
Section Review 2 Independent Practice 34.2 Basic Skills 34	Section Review 3 Independent Practice 34.3	Transparency 104 Q&A Transparency 103 Q&A Section Review 4 Independent Practice 34.4 Critical Thinking 34	Section Review 5 Independent Practice 34.5
1. Primary Source: Voices 34.2 2. ★Preparing a Report: African Unity 3. Researching for Points	1. Primary Source: Voices 34.3 2. ★Preparing a Report: Mandela 3. Researching for Points	1. Primary Source: Voices 34.4 2. ★Preparing a Report: Conflict and Conflict Resolution 3. Researching for Points	1. Primary Source: Voices 34.5 2. Preparing a Report: American Hostages 3. Researching for Points

●**Reteaching Activities** Summarizing, Identifying Leaders

Chapter Review Summary, Reviewing the Facts, Basic Skills, Researching and Reporting Skills, Critical Thinking, Perspectives on Past and Present, Investigating History

Chapter Evaluation Chapter Test 34, Alternate Chapter Test 34, Computer Test Bank Chapter 34 Test

Skill Building: Comparing and Contrasting Political Problems and Solutions (Objective 2) After students read "Independence brought political problems" (pages 787–788), have them note the differences between Uganda, Zaire, and Kenya and the leaders of those countries. Note that democratic governments developed in countries with stronger economies. Refer students to pages 670–673 on the political and economic challenges facing Latin American countries after independence. Have students compare the problems Latin American and African nations faced following independence. Based on this comparison, have students write conclusions about the challenges of nation-building for former colonies.

Check for Understanding Have students summarize the problems African nations faced as they became independent.

Enrichment Activities

1. **Reading a Primary Source**
   Assign Voices from the Past Resource Book 34.1.

2. **Preparing a Report**
   Have each student select a country in Africa and find out about the events leading to that country's independence.

3. **Researching for Bonus Points**
   Who is Chinua Achebe? (a Nigerian author of novels about the African experience in changing from colonialism to independence)

Africa faced social and economic challenges. 2

Setting the Stage

Write on the board *unity, stability,* and *economic development.* These were the chief problems that newly independent countries faced. Discuss why national unity was a problem. (ethnic rivalries) Ask students why they think social and economic issues can complicate political changes.

Teaching Strategies

Economics and History: Meeting Economic Needs (Objective 1) Read the following statement by Tom Mboya, a Kenyan diplomat.

> The leaders [of Kenya] must establish order to enable the Government to promote economic and social development. The responsibility for virtually all types of development becomes the concern of the Government; for the . . . people are poor and they still lack business and commercial skill. On its part, the Government finds itself with many projects in hand, but without the capital or technical know-how to sustain development.

According to Mboya, what is the main job of government? What factors make it difficult for the government to do its job? Point out that whatever type of government African nations adopted upon independence, their success depended on how well they met economic needs. Recall the importance of diversification for establishing a stable economic base. Discuss the roles of population growth, literacy, and entrepreneurship in economic development.

Skill Building: Making Inferences (Objective 2) In the 1980's the worst famine of the twentieth century engulfed much of Africa. To illustrate its causes and effects,

distribute copies of the following facts.

- Since independence, Africa's population has increased by 3 percent every year, while food production has increased by only about 1.5 percent.
- In the early 1980's, 22 African nations suffered famines; by 1990, 6 nations still needed famine relief.
- In 1983, drought spread across the continent. Some relief came in 1985 when the rains reappeared, but the drought resumed in 1987 and 1988.
- Throughout the 1980's, thousands of people died each day of malnutrition and disease.
- In 1986, locust swarms defoliated the land in vast areas of Africa, devouring as much as 80,000 tons of crops a day.
- By the late 1980's, efforts to import food increased the total indebtedness of all African nations to more than $100 billion.

Ask students to infer some of the causes and effects of famine. Then challenge them to suggest long-term solutions. What role do they think the United States should play in helping to implement long-term solutions, and why?

Check for Understanding Ask students to identify some of Africa's industrial and agricultural successes.

Enrichment Activities

1. **Reading a Primary Source**
   Assign Voices from the Past Resource Book 34.2.

2. **Preparing a Report**
   Have advanced students report on the efforts of African nations to achieve unity and cooperation for their mutual benefit. Have students share their findings and draw conclusions

about factors that encourage or discourage international cooperation.

3. **Researching for Bonus Points**
In what year did the Aswan High Dam in Egypt begin operation? (1968)

Setting the Stage

Refer students to the chart on page 795, "Racial Composition in South Africa, 1989." Point out that although whites constitute only 4.9 million out of a total population of 36.5 million, they completely dominate politics. Ask students how such an inequality can exist. Have students recall other situations with similar circumstances. (India, Latin America)

Teaching Strategies

Discussing History: South Africa and Its Neighbors (Objective 1) Have students locate Zimbabwe, Angola, Mozambique, and Namibia on Map Transparency 102, *The Nations of Africa*, or refer them to the map on page 787. Ask them where these countries are in relation to South Africa.

After students read "South Africa interfered in other countries" (pages 793–794), have them list South Africa's reactions to the events in those countries. Why did South Africa interfere in other countries? What did they hope to achieve?

Analyzing a Quotation: Nelson Mandela Speaks to South Africa (Objective 2) Write on the board the following quote from Mohandas Gandhi: "There is no force in the cry of driving out the English if the substitute is to be Hindu domination. That will be no *swaraj* [self-government]." Then have them read the Voice from Our Time feature on page 794. Ask students how Gandhi and Mandela approached the problem of governing their countries after the end of minority rule. Why does Gandhi warn against Hindu domination? Does Mandela seem to have the same concern for his country? Explain. Finally, ask students if they feel Mandela will have as great an impact on South African affairs as Gandhi did in Indian affairs.

Check for Understanding Have students explain how South Africa differs economically, politically, and culturally from other African nations.

Enrichment Activities

1. **Reading a Primary Source**
Assign Voices from the Past Resource Book 34.3.

2. **Preparing a Report**
Have advanced students report on Nelson Mandela.

3. **Researching for Bonus Points**
Which four South African homelands have been declared independent? (Transkei, Bophuthatswana, Venda, Ciskei)

Setting the Stage

Have students recall the start of the Zionist movement in the late 1800's (page 668). The movement called for settlement of Palestine and the founding of a Jewish state. Few European Jews had any knowledge of the Middle East. Zionist founder Theodor Herzl noted that most Jews imagined Palestine to be "a land without people waiting for a people without a land." Ask students why that notion was inaccurate. (Palestinian Arabs considered it their homeland as well.) Show Map Transparency 104, *The Middle East Today*, and have students identify the Arab nations that border Israel.

Discussing History: The Suez Crisis (Objective 1) Have students recall the United States' interest in building and maintaining control of the Panama Canal (pages 588–589). Ask them to compare American interests with British, French, and Egyptian interests in the Suez Canal. Explain that Egypt decided to nationalize the Suez Canal to finance the building of the Aswan High Dam with canal profits. Britain and France considered the canal vital to their economic interests, and did not want it controlled by a leader they thought unfriendly. Israel had been waiting for a chance to attack terrorist bases within Egypt and possibly overthrow Nasser. Following the Israeli, British, and French attack, Egypt sank ships in the canal to block it, and other Arabs destroyed oil pumping stations, forcing Europe to ration oil. Under international condemnation, the attackers were forced to withdraw. Although his army had been badly beaten, Nasser became an Arab hero.

Discuss with students Nasser's decision to "face down" Britain and France. Why was this a turning point in history?

Discussing History: Peace-Keeping Efforts (Objective 2) Show students Map Transparency 103, *Israel, 1967–1973*. Help students locate the following contested territories: Sinai Peninsula, Gaza Strip, West Bank, and Golan Heights. Point out the strategic value of these regions to Israel, Egypt, Syria, and Jordan. Tell the class that in 1967 the UN Security Council passed Resolution 242. Write on the board the following points endorsed by the resolution.

- withdrawal of Israeli armies from territories occupied during the Six-Day War
- political independence for every state in the Middle East
- the right of people to live within secure and recognized boundaries free from external threats
- settlement of the Palestinian refugee problem

Have students use the information on the map to assess the steps that have been taken since 1967 toward fulfilling the UN mandate.

Check for Understanding Have students identify the following: Gamal Abdel Nasser, David Ben-Gurion, Yom Kippur War, Suez Canal Crisis, Six-Day War.

Enrichment Activities

1. **Reading a Primary Source** Assign Voices from the Past Resource Book 34.4.

2. **Preparing a Report** Have advanced students report on conflict and conflict resolution in the Middle East during the 1980's.

3. **Researching for Bonus Points** What was Golda Meir's role in Israel's nation-building? (She was Israel's Prime Minister from 1969 to 1974.)

Cultural conflicts caused Middle East tensions. 5

Setting the Stage

The root of the continued conflicts between Arabs and Israelis can be traced to religious, cultural, and economic issues. Since 1980, conflict has been almost continual. The Persian Gulf Crisis of 1990–1991 marks another chapter in this conflict, although in the latest crisis, Arab nations fought each other.

Discussing History: Oil as a Force in the World Community (Objective 1) Have students read pages 799–800, detailing the discovery of oil in several Arab states. Have students complete the following sentence opener: If oil had been discovered in Israel instead of the Arab countries, _____. Encourage students to address the powerful role that oil has played in the region and the world. Then ask students if there might have been less conflict in the Middle East if no oil had been discovered there.

Discussing History: Islamic Fundamentalism (Objective 2) Clarify the concept of fundamentalism as any movement for religious reform that calls for strict adherence to the basic rules and principles of the religion as it was originally practiced. Have students recall the

basic rules and principles of Islam (page 188). In what ways might strict adherence to Islam conflict with the demands of living in a modern, westernized nation? In present-day Saudi Arabia—a conservative, mainly Sunni Muslim country—businesses and shops are required to close during each of the five daily prayers. Patrolling religious police enforce this rule. Ask what effects such closings would have on businesses in the United States.

Practical differences are only a part of this cultural conflict. Muslim conservatives and fundamentalists view many Western ideas and behaviors as immoral.

Have students use information in the text to assess the impact of Islamic fundamentalism. Did the Ayatollah Khomeini's regime correct the abuses of the deposed Shah's Western-style government?

Check for Understanding Call on students to explain how nationalism, terrorism, and Islamic fundamentalism relate to conflicts in the Middle East.

Enrichment Activities

1. **Reading a Primary Source** Assign Voices from the Past Resource Book 34.5.

2. **Preparing a Report** Have interested students report on the taking of American hostages by Iran under the direction of the Ayatollah Khomeini in 1979.

3. **Researching for Bonus Points** Who won the 1978 Nobel Peace Price? (Anwar Sadat, Menachem Begin)

Reviewing the Facts

1. (a) nation that is building industries **(b)** policy separating people of different ethnic groups **(c)** restrictions on trade **(d)** movement stressing strict obedience to basic rules of a religion as it was originally practiced **(e)** conservative Muslim leader **(f)** widespread campaign of civil disobedience

2. (a) first African nation to gain independence **(b)** first president of Ghana **(c)** first president of Egyptian republic **(d)** African nation that prospered as one-party democracy **(e)** first president of Côte d'Ivoire **(f)** authoritarian ruler of Zaire **(g)** African nation united as a federal republic **(h)** first president of Tanzania **(i)** black township in South Africa, scene of bitter riot in 1976 **(j)** Palestinian Arab group seeking to establish its own state in the region of Palestine **(k)** branch of Islam **(l)** Mideast nation that has become battleground for many factions

3. (a) Colonial powers did not encourage industry and weakened economies dependent on cash crops. **(b)** National borders drawn without regard for ethnic groups encouraged ethnic conflict.

4. (a) white minority **(b)** apartheid, banning, homelands

5. (a) by partition of Palestine according to UN plan **(b)** Many lost their homeland.

Basic Skills

1. (a) Nile—Egypt, Sudan, Ethiopia, Kenya; Niger—Guinea, Mali, Niger, Nigeria, Benin; Zaire—Angola, Zaire, Congo; Zambezi—Mozambique, Zimbabwe, Zambia, Angola; Limpopo—Mozambique, Zimbabwe, South Africa, Botswana **(b)** The African rivers flow in different directions and fragment the continent. The Mississippi River system unifies a huge area.

2. (a) colonialism—revolt by African colonies, terrorist tactics by some African nationalists, altered economy of colonies, colonial governments with no relation to African culture, lack of preparation for self-government, borders representing no regard for African groups; environment—drought, famine **(b)** revolt—Morocco, Tunisia, Algeria; terrorism—Kenya; altered economies—Kenya, Ghana; governments with no relation to culture—South Africa; lack of preparation for self-government—Zaire; borders—Nigeria; drought—Ghana; famine—Ethiopia, Somalia, Mozambique, Zambia, Kenya, the Sudan

3. (a) Mediterranean and Red seas: Suez Canal; Persian Gulf and Arabian Sea: Gulf of Oman/Strait of Hormuz **(b)** Red and Arabian seas (Gulf of Aden)

Researching and Reporting Skills

Students' findings will vary.

Critical Thinking

1. Islamic tradition, ties to Middle East and successes there in gaining nations

2. (a) Students' answers will vary but should include improvement of educational opportunities, to train workers and leaders; expansion of export products; development of various industries, develop natural resources **(b)** By importing food, a country does not develop its own industries and agricultural opportunities; lack of employment of native people, money leaves country rather than being used within the country.

3. (a) Students' answers will vary but might include lack of a middle class, political rivalries, ethnic conflict, poor conditions for agriculture, lack of advanced technology, and rapid population growth. **(b)** Students' opinions will vary.

4. (a) Israel—Jewish homeland; Palestinians—Arab nation-state, land of Palestine **(b)** Each group has a strong nationalistic vision regarding the same piece of land. **(c)** Students' answers will vary. **(d)** religion, respect for traditions, need for own land; accept other answers

5. (a) jihad, restrictions in role of women, Koran laws, etc. in contrast to Western ideas **(b)** Wealth from oil has led to use of modern technology; social and cultural traditions are retained; has also led to concentration of wealth in certain countries and particular groups within those countries.

Perspectives on Past and Present

Imperialism has been replaced with ideas such as isolationism, detached aid, and protectorate systems. Some factors accounting for this include the need to concentrate resources on bettering own country's conditions, dissatisfaction with warlike traits often necessary for imperialism, desire to spread democracy.

Investigating History

Students' findings will vary.

Teaching with Pictures

Have students study the photograph. Explain that the ceremony shown was held in 1957 to celebrate Ghana's independence. Ask students to describe the different types of clothing visible in the picture and identify the various groups that are present. Ask why, in a country just becoming independent and entering a new era in its history, so many participants are wearing traditional clothing. Ask students why tradition is important to a country, especially a new one.

34 Nationalism in Africa and the Middle East

1945 - 1990's

In the forefront of Ghana's independence ceremony in 1957 were Britain's Duchess of Kent and Ghana's new President Kwame Khrumah.

Key Terms

industrialized nation
developing nation
less developed country
subsistence farming
apartheid
segregate
bantustan
economic sanctions
terrorism
per capita income
fundamentalism
ayatollah
intifada

Read and Understand

1. The age of imperialism ended in Africa.
2. Africa faced social and economic challenges.
3. Southern Africa confronted change.
4. New nations arose in the Middle East.
5. Cultural conflicts caused Middle East tensions.

Church bells pealed joyously through the night air in the city of Accra. It was midnight, March 6, 1957. The bells marked the end of the British colony of Gold Coast and the birth of the nation of Ghana, named after the ninth-century African kingdom. As the red, green, and yellow flag of Ghana was hoisted atop the parliament building in Accra, 50,000 people cheered. The new country's president Kwame Khrumah (**KWAHM**-ee en-**KROO**-muh) wept for joy.

The next day a week-long celebration began. Accra was host to 2,000 foreign visitors. Among them was a Soviet delegation that presented Ghana with a jet plane and several automobiles. Vice President Richard Nixon headed the United States delegation. With him were UN representative Ralph Bunche and the Reverend Martin Luther King, Jr. They gave the new country a library of technical books.

Chapter 34 Resources

GEOGRAPHY
- Geography Skills 34
- Transparencies 102, 103, 104

REINFORCEMENT
- Vocabulary 34
- Basic Skills 34
- Reteaching 34
- Making Connections Study Guide 34

ENRICHMENT
- Critical Thinking 34
- History and Literature 34

ASSESSMENT
- Chapter Test 34
- Alternate Chapter Test 34
- Computer Test Bank

Ghana was one of the first African nations to gain independence. That independence was an important symbol for all Africans. In the 500 years since the ship captains sent by Prince Henry had explored Africa's west coast, the people of Africa had lived under European domination. The terrors of the slave trade had been followed by the unending burdens that came with colonialism. Now, at last, freedom was within reach. By 1970, virtually every country in Africa and the Middle East had cut its ties to its former European ruler.

In this chapter, you will study the independence movements in Africa and the Middle East and examine how the new governments tried to deal with the major political, economic, and social problems they encountered.

The age of imperialism ended in Africa. 1

In 1950, the political map of Africa showed only four independent countries—Egypt, Liberia, Ethiopia, and South Africa. The European powers still directly controlled all others. Appearances, however, were deceiving. "The wind of change is blowing through this continent," British Prime Minister Harold Macmillan observed when he visited Africa in 1960. "Whether we like it or not, this growth of national consciousness is a political fact."

Nationalism led to independence in Africa.

The years following World War II marked a turning point for Africa. Signs of this change had appeared earlier. Between World War I and World War II, an educated and westernized African middle class had appeared in cities throughout the continent. Those Africans had studied at schools run by missionaries and colonial governments. Often these Africans had attended college in Europe or the United States. From this educated elite came the first nationalist leaders who worked to end colonial rule.

After World War II, these leaders gained new support. About 200,000 African soldiers fought alongside British and French soldiers in North Africa, Asia, and Europe. They helped to free France, Burma, and Ethiopia. Fighting for the freedom of others made them determined to gain their own. The examples of new nations such as India and Pakistan inspired them to begin.

African countries sought independence.

The nationalist winds of change blew first across North Africa. Arab peoples of this region had been influenced by Middle East nationalist movements (pages 665–669) in the years after World War I. Libya, Tunisia, and Morocco gained their freedom relatively peacefully. Algeria, however, won its independence in 1962 only after a bitter seven-year civil war against French forces.

Nationalist ideas also spread across sub-Saharan Africa, where the postwar years brought the rise of a new generation of African leaders. After returning to the Gold Coast following ten years of study in the United States and Britain, Kwame Nkrumah founded the Convention People's Party in 1949. Leaders such as Houphouet-Boigny in the French colony of Ivory Coast (today's Côte d'Ivoire) and Jomo Kenyatta in Kenya established similar groups. These leaders were determined to gain independence for their people. As Nkrumah said, "There is a new African in the world, and that new African is ready to fight his own battles . . . We prefer self-government with danger to servitude in tranquillity."

European rulers did not welcome the independence movement in sub-Saharan Africa any more than they had in North Africa or India or Indonesia. Thus as independence movements gained in strength, European governments sought to check them. They arrested and imprisoned nationalist leaders like Nkrumah and executed extreme nationalists. At the same time, these powers now recognized that having colonies involved the costs of government, defense, and development. Rulers also realized that since the African population outnumbered Europeans 800 to 1, Europeans were too few in number to maintain control indefinitely.

In Britain, the Labour party accepted the idea of giving up African colonies. Even then Britain was more willing to grant freedom to West African lands with a mainly African population than to

785

OBJECTIVE 1. Analyze the factors that hindered nation-building in newly independent African countries.

Teaching Strategy: *Discussing History: Problems of Nation-Building* (page 784a)

OBJECTIVE 2. Compare the political problems and solutions of newly independent nations.

Teaching Strategy: *Skill Building: Comparing and Contrasting Political Problems and Solutions* (page 784c)

■ BACKGROUND

Libya, which had come under the control of Italy in 1912, became independent in 1951. The established monarchy was overthrown in 1969 by a military group led by the radical leader Colonel Muammar al-Qaddafi, who continues to rule. Libya is a member of OPEC and a major oil-producing nation.

SECTION 1
Resources

GEOGRAPHY
■ Transparency 102

REINFORCEMENT
■ Independent Practice 34.1

ENRICHMENT
■ Voices from the Past 34.1

ASSESSMENT
■ Section Quiz 34.1

■ **BACKGROUND**

The mines, factories, and railroads of Africa have been called "unassimilated" technology, because the majority of Africans are kept outside their use by social, political, and industrial discrimination.

areas such as Kenya and Southern Rhodesia where many Europeans had settled. Thus the first African country to gain independence was West Africa's Ghana, under the leadership of Kwame Nkrumah. East Africa's Kenya, by contrast, underwent a period of violence. There a radical nationalist group the Mau Mau used terrorist tactics to regain lands and to win independence.

The success of the nationalist movement in Ghana stirred other African colonies to action. Over the next few years, new African nations appeared almost regularly. In turn, the British and French governments—the major colonial powers—made an orderly but rapid withdrawal. By 1968, 38 independent nations had replaced European dominance of the continent.

Colonialism left a legacy of problems.

The joy that Africans felt over independence was soon overshadowed by the reality of the enormous problems facing them. Nationalist leaders had promised that independence would bring great benefits. In reality, that promise raised hopes that could not be fulfilled. The new nations actually entered an era filled with hardship. They needed to develop their institutions of government, achieve social stability, and build economies that would support the state and provide people with a decent standard of living.

Yet, like many new nations before them, those in Africa often lacked the knowledge and means to reach their goals. Years of oppression had destroyed old patterns of government and community life. Britain and France had done little to prepare their colonies for independence, and Belgium and Portugal had made no effort at all. In fact, colonialism had left a legacy of problems that the new nations would have to solve in order to survive.

Lack of unity Most of the new nations were based on the colonial units set up by the Europeans. The boundaries of those units, however, showed no regard for the people who lived there. As a result, boundaries often divided ethnic groups, enclosed rival groups, or contained so many different groups that a sense of unity was almost impossible to develop. Nigeria, for example, included groups that were traditional enemies. The result was civil war in which more

than a million people died. By contrast, Uganda had so many different groups that the government radio had to broadcast in 24 different languages.

Lack of adequate economic development As you have seen (Chapter 25), colonial rulers viewed their colonies as sources of wealth. Thus mines and plantations provided resources and raw materials for the rulers' factories, rather than crops and materials for the people of the colonies. Workers were paid low wages, while profits went to foreign businesses. Even after independence, much land and many resources were still foreign-owned. Even the best-off of the new nations were poor by world standards.

The colonial pattern of focus on cash crops and resources also created problems. Ghana, for example, depended mainly on the export of cocoa. Zambia depended on the export of copper, Uganda on coffee, and Chad on cotton. Income for these countries was related to the prices for their goods on world markets. To pay for imports of food and machines, nations had to continue exporting. This too left nations at the mercy of world markets and the high cost of manufactured goods. At the same time, it left little or no capital for developing the new industries or transportation systems needed to provide more jobs and income.

Decline of traditional ways In many countries, colonial practices had undermined community and family life. Thousands of men had been forced to work in the gold and copper mines of the Congo, Rhodesia, and South Africa. Often they were away from home for months or years at a time, unable to visit their families. Elsewhere forced migrations disrupted communities and weakened traditional ties and the customs of everyday life.

Lack of education Most ruling powers had done little to develop schools or to educate people as doctors, engineers, technicians, or government workers. Thus the new nations lacked both professional people as leaders and skilled workers to aid in economic development. In 1965, more than 80 percent of adults in Africa could neither read nor write. The low rate of literacy also made it difficult for nations to develop stable governments. Rulers had avoided developing democratic traditions, and there was only a small middle class. Nonetheless Tanzania's success in achieving an 80 percent literacy rate showed that support for education could bring progress.

786

Independence brought political problems.

The early years of independence were a time of stress and confusion for most of the new nations. They now faced problems similar to those of Latin American nations in the 1800's and the nations of Southeast Asia after World War II. In Africa, country after country fell prey to one-man rule, often by military leaders or strongmen who sought to gain control of resources and wealth.

Even advocates of democracy like Kwame Nkrumah often resorted to dictatorial methods. Nkrumah himself was overthrown and replaced by another strongman in 1966. This became a common pattern in sub-Saharan Africa, where there were more than 70 successful coups between

ANSWERS TO
Map Study

Ethiopia, Sudan, Uganda, Egypt

Map Study
Name the nations through which the Nile River flows from its sources.

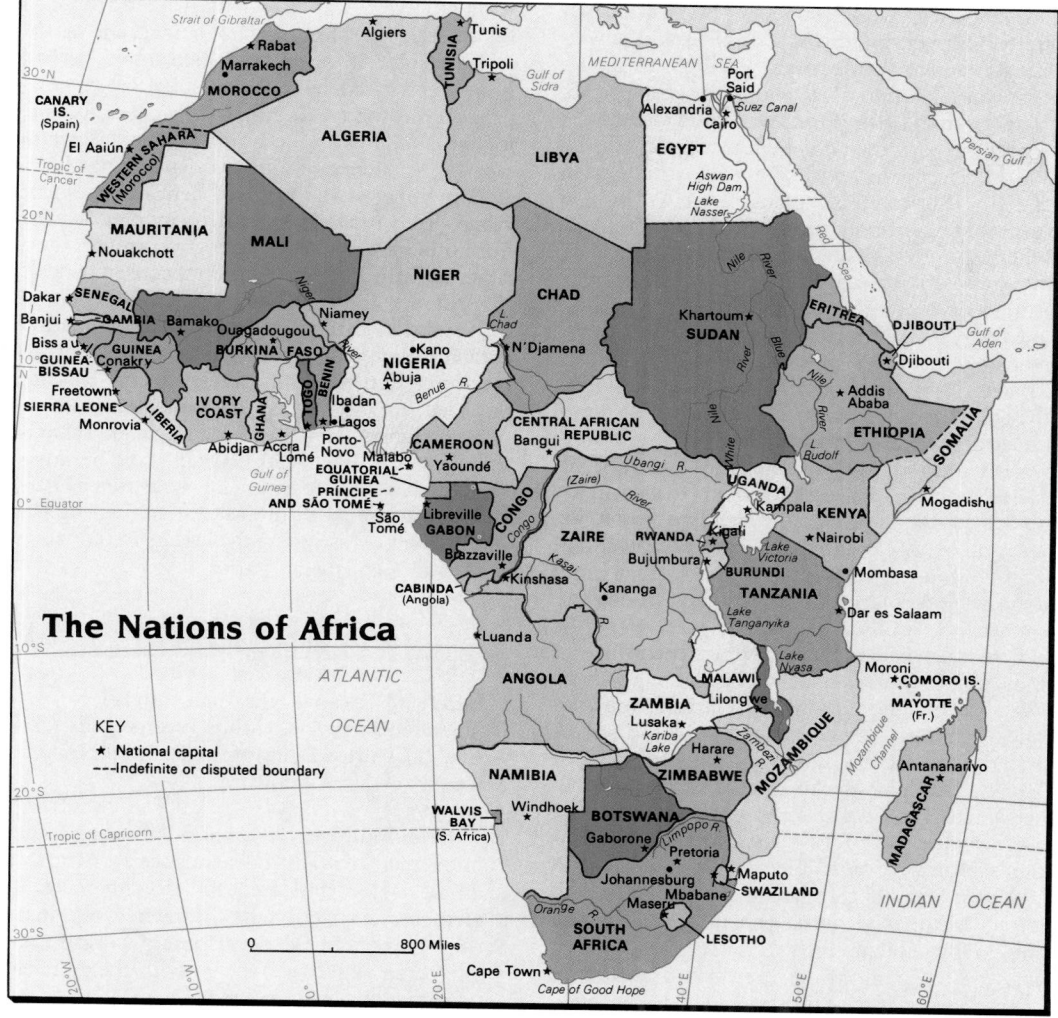

The Nations of Africa

787

ANSWERS TO

Section Review 1

Identify:

(a) first president of Ghana
(b) leader of the Ivory Coast
(c) leader of Tanzania
(d) cruel dictator of Uganda
(e) first prime minister of the Congo (f) dictator who changed the name of the Congo to Zaire (g) Kenya's first president

Answer:

1. could no longer burden the costs of government, defense, and development, realized they were too few in number to maintain control

2. lack of education, colonial rulers had not developed democratic traditions

3. Because of the difficulty of establishing democracies, one-man rule often developed.

4. rival ethnic groups competed for power, fought for independent nations

5. President Jomo Kenyatta involved all groups in the government, encouraged British settlers to remain, and transferred farmlands to African owners. Kenya had fertile tea and coffee plantations.

6. rival groups were enclosed within the same borders, colonial powers did not industrialize the colonies or educate the people, traditional life had been undermined

1957 and 1990. Even in those countries with some democratic institutions, not a single ruler during this period left office peacefully as a result of ballot-box defeat.

To a large extent, the progress made by Africa's new nations depended upon their leaders. Felix Houphouet-Boigny of the Côte d'Ivoire, for example, brought decades of peace and prosperity to his country. He encouraged modern agricultural techniques and built thousands of schools. In Tanzania, Julius Nyerere sought to achieve economic stability and encouraged education and community development.

Uganda For every Houphouet-Boigny and Nyerere, however, there was a ruthless and power-hungry dictator. An extreme example of such a ruler was Idi Amin of Uganda. After seizing power in 1971, Amin for the next seven years ran Uganda according to his own cruel whims. An estimated 300,000 Ugandans perished during Amin's reign of terror. Entire ethnic groups were killed, and suspected political opponents were murdered. When Amin was finally driven into exile in 1979, his successor massacred 200,000 members of Amin's own ethnic group in revenge.

Zaire Of all European possessions in Africa, probably the most mismanaged had been the Belgian Congo. Belgium had ruthlessly exploited the colony's rich resources of rubber and copper under a system of forced labor. While draining wealth from the colony, Belgium provided no social services such as education. It also made no attempt to prepare the Congolese people for independence. Nonetheless their desire for freedom led to independence in 1960. At that time, there were only 16 college graduates among the country's 16 million people.

Belgium's sudden granting of independence to the Congo resulted in chaos. Patrice Lumumba, who became the nation's first prime minister, ruled a bitterly divided country. In the southeastern province of Katanga, a local leader named Moise Tshombe declared that region's independence. This was a serious threat, especially since copper from Katanga's mines was the nation's primary export. Tshombe's action led to civil war. Fighting continued through 1965, when Joseph Mobutu, an army general, seized power and finally subdued the rebels. In 1971, Mobutu changed the name of his country to Zaire, the original name of the great river called the Congo

788

by Europeans. Over the next two decades, Mobutu ruled as an absolute dictator.

By 1990, economic pressures combined with political unrest to cause problems for Mobutu. Student demonstrations were violently suppressed. In April 1990, however, Mobutu announced that other political parties might organize in Zaire. This offered a glimmer of hope for improvement in the country's grim authoritarian rule.

Kenya Unlike Zaire, East Africa's Kenya enjoyed relative peace and prosperity after winning independence from Britain in 1963. One reason for this stability was the leadership of Jomo Kenyatta, Kenya's first president, who ruled until his death in 1978. Kenyatta had studied and taught in Britain for 15 years. Like Nkrumah, he had been imprisoned by the British prior to independence. Although Kenya, like Nigeria and Zaire, included competing ethnic groups, Kenyatta worked to overcome old rivalries among them. As a member of the Kikuyu, Kenya's dominant group, Kenyatta was careful to involve leaders from other groups in the new government. Over time, he built a Kenyan national consciousness.

Fertile tea and coffee plantations in its central highlands had made Kenya one of Africa's richest colonies. Kenyatta encouraged British settlers to stay after Kenya became independent. He also provided for the transfer of some farmlands to African owners. They formed a stable, prosperous middle class. By 1970, Nairobi—the nation's capital—had become the major center for business and commerce in all of East Africa. During the 1980's, Kenya was among the leaders in economic growth in sub-Saharan Africa.

Section REVIEW 1

Identify: (a) Kwame Nkrumah, (b) Felix Houphouet-Boigny, (c) Julius Nyerere, (d) Idi Amin, (e) Patrice Lumumba, (f) Joseph Mobutu, (g) Jomo Kenyatta

Answer:

1. Why did European powers finally accept the movement toward independence in Africa?

2. What factors hindered the development of democratic governments in the new nations?

3. Why was political development during this period so closely connected with the policies of individual African leaders?

4. Why did countries like Zaire and Nigeria experience civil war in their early years of independence?
5. What factors contributed to stability and growth in Kenya?

Critical Thinking
6. Why was Africa's colonial legacy a handicap to the development of nations?

Africa faced social and economic challenges. 2

The most pressing problems following independence in sub-Saharan Africa were actually not political. Many involved social and economic problems so difficult that even the best-governed countries found progress elusive.

Africa's population expanded rapidly.

As in Asia and Latin America, the population of Africa grew enormously in the period after World War II. Between 1950 and 1980, the continent's population doubled, increasing from about 215 million to nearly 500 million. It was expected to double again by the year 2000.

A population explosion As elsewhere in the Third World, this explosive growth was due more to falling death rates than to a rise in birthrates. (The term *Third World* is used for nations that are economically and industrially less developed, as well as for nations that remained nonaligned in the Cold War.) Thanks largely to the UN's World Health Organization, modern public health procedures were introduced in the years after World War II. In addition, hospitals were built and diseases that had formerly killed millions were checked. Between 1951 and 1966, deaths from smallpox and cholera declined 95 percent worldwide.

This progress in the battle against disease was a remarkable achievement. Because birthrates remained high, however, it also led to population growth. In many African countries, the birthrate exceeded 4 percent per year—the highest in the world. By 1990, fully half of Africa's population was under twenty years of age.

Migration to cities The high rate of population growth was complicated by another factor—the migration of people from rural areas to cities. This migration occurred in most Third World countries in the postwar era as millions moved from villages to cities in search of work.

The cities, such as Lagos in Nigeria, were unable to cope with such waves of migration. The population of Lagos grew from 500,000 in 1960 to nearly 10 million in 1990. Millions of people ended up living in shacks, scavenging for food, and surrounded by crime and disease. A related problem in some countries was that of refugees. War, ethnic conflict, drought, and political strife forced millions of people from their homes.

Some progress is being made toward solving such problems. Because most countries have established systems of education, literacy is increasing and future leaders are being educated. The traditionally important role of women in African society—as traders, producers of food, and keepers of the home—is expanding. New educational opportunities for women are a key to improving their position in society. One example of the changing status of women is Angie Brooks of Liberia, the first woman to become president of the UN General Assembly.

Population growth slowed economic development.

Rapid population growth had occurred previously in many parts of the world. Europe and North America had seen high rates of growth during the nineteenth century. That growth, however, had occurred during the Industrial Revolution, when countless new industries and businesses could provide jobs for the increased population. The situation was far more complex in Africa's newly independent nations.

Under colonialism, ruling nations obtained basic resources and raw materials from their possessions. Industries in those nations made the resources and raw materials into manufactured products to sell back to the colonies at a profit. Colonies were generally forbidden to carry on manufacturing. Thus the **industrialized nations**—those that had already developed industry—had an economic advantage.

As colonies became nations, they too sought to industrialize to gain a similar advantage.

789

SECTION 2 Objectives and Teaching Strategies

OBJECTIVE 1. Identify the economic needs of newly independent African nations.

Teaching Strategy: *Economics and History: Meeting Economic Needs* (page 784c)

OBJECTIVE 2. Assess some causes and effects of widespread famine in Africa in the 1980's.

Teaching Strategy: *Skill Building: Making Inferences* (page 784c)

SECTION 2 Resources

ASSESSMENT
- Section Quiz 34.2

REINFORCEMENT
- Independent Practice 34.2

ENRICHMENT
- Voices from the Past 34.2

■ **DISCUSSION**

As early as the 1970's, Ethiopians were starving due to disruptions caused by war, inefficient land reform, and an invasion of locusts. Ask students how these three phenomena work together to cause problems that seem much larger than the sum of the individual problems.

ANSWERS TO

Section Review 2

Define:
(a) country that has developed industry (b) country that is developing industry (c) country with limited resources and opportunities for growth (d) farming that yields just enough for the farmer to live on

Identify:
(a) cooperative village
(b) first African to win Nobel Prize for Literature
(c) Senegal's first president, also a poet

Answer:
1. fewer deaths, because of better medical care, birthrate remained high
2. hindered it; income must go to provide food, rather than to new economic development
3. old methods of agriculture; African soil too light for intensive cultivation; devastating drought
4. establishment of museums for regional art, Wole Soyinka's reception of the Nobel Prize for Literature
5. Students' answers will vary.

Building industries, however, requires large amounts of capital to invest in factories, equipment, railroads, and modern technology. Nations such as Nigeria, where income from oil was used to build industries, are called **developing nations**. Countries such as Rwanda that have limited resources and opportunities for growth are called **less developed countries** (LDC's).

After gaining independence, many countries sought to industrialize rapidly, often with the help of foreign loans. Huge government projects such as the Aswan Dam in Egypt were designed to provide jobs and build modern facilities that would aid the growth of industry. Nigeria's rich resources, particularly oil, enabled it to gain wealth from exports. Some of that wealth was invested in new industries such as oil refining and chemicals. Nigeria also plans to start selling liquefied natural gas to Europe by 1995. The gas production plant will be sub-Saharan Africa's largest construction project of the early 1990's.

In most countries of sub-Saharan Africa, however, the prospects for development remain limited. Without the resources of a highly skilled or educated population, modern businesses and industries have proved difficult to launch and maintain. As a result, most nations continue to rely on the export of such products and resources as coffee, cocoa, and minerals to gain income. As the population has increased, more of that

Famine victims in Ethiopia search for grain after sacks broke on being dropped from relief planes.

income has gone to provide food rather than to new economic development that would help to break the cycle of poverty.

African agriculture faced problems.

In agriculture as in industry, development has met serious problems. While foreign-owned plantations often use modern methods, much of Africa's agriculture consists of **subsistence farming.** This type of farming produces no surplus to sell and often yields only a poor living for those who work the land. Also most soil in Africa is light and unsuitable for intensive hand cultivation as in parts of Asia or machine cultivation as in Europe and the Americas. The result has been to limit production.

Zimbabwe today is providing a new model for agriculture. Farmers are changing from subsistence farming to producing larger harvests that provide a surplus to sell. Zimbabwe now is exporting food products to neighboring countries.

Agriculture has also suffered from the drought that devastated large areas of the continent during the late 1900's. Particularly hard hit have been the countries of the Sahel, the semiarid region that stretches across Africa just south of the Sahara. In 1990, the Sahara was 160 million acres larger than it was just 10 years earlier. This change has significantly reduced the amount of land available for herding and farming. The nations of Ethiopia and the Sudan have been particularly hard hit. The situation there is complicated by brutal civil wars that have hampered relief efforts of the UN and other agencies.

African culture adapted to a changing world.

Throughout sub-Saharan Africa, independence has brought new interest in the recovery and renewal of traditional aspects of African culture. Governments sought to encourage traditional crafts and industries, and new museums displayed examples of the continent's proud artistic heritage. In Tanzania, having a single national language aided President Julius Nyerere in creating a new model for development. He established ujamaa (cooperative) villages designed to provide a form of socialism for Tanzania. Although this program did not achieve financial success, it aided progress in education, medical care, and participation by citizens in decisions for local communities.

In many parts of Africa, as in India, the language of former colonial rulers continued to aid communication among people speaking hundreds of different local dialects. Political leaders in most African countries were fluent in either French or English. These languages were adopted officially by the Organization of African Unity (OAU), founded in 1963 to promote unity within Africa and its members' interests around the world. Many African authors achieved success by writing in English or French. In 1986, Wole Soyinka, a Nigerian poet and playwright, became the first African to win the Nobel Prize for Literature.

Perhaps the most remarkable African literary figure of the period was Senegal's Leopold Senghor. Educated in France, Senghor led the movement for independence among France's African colonies during the 1950's. In 1960, he became Senegal's first president. For 20 years, he led one of Africa's few real democracies, all the while writing and publishing poetry in French.

The widespread use of English and French served to link African countries to the rest of the world. Television and radio helped to build increased communication with Europe and the Americas. The result was a culture in transition— one that included both African and non-African elements along with traditional and modern ones. In this mix of cultures and eras, ox-drawn carts and motorcycles jostled for position on dusty village roads, soft drink cans littered refugee camps, and farmers listened to portable radios while harvesting millet by hand just as their ancestors had done centuries earlier.

In West African villages, generations of women preserve the ancient art of painting their mud houses in traditional yet innovative designs.

3. Identify three major causes of food shortages in Africa in the 1970's and 1980's.
4. What are two examples of the emergence of a distinct culture in the new nations?

Critical Thinking
5. It has been said that technology is not the answer to Africa's economic problems but that whole new solutions are required for the continent's unique needs. Do you agree with this statement? Why?

Southern Africa confronted change. 3

The winds of change that brought independence to most of Africa during the 1960's were slower to reach southern Africa. Angola and Mozambique—two of the larger countries there—were colonies of Portugal, whose government resisted giving up the nation's overseas possessions. In the British colony of Southern Rhodesia (now Zimbabwe), the white minority delayed surrendering power to the African majority. In South Africa, the white-controlled government continued to rule the continent's wealthiest country.

Section REVIEW 2

Define: (a) industrialized nation, (b) developing nation, (c) less developed country, (d) subsistence farming
Identify: (a) ujamaa village, (b) Wole Soyinka, (c) Leopold Senghor
Answer:
1. What changes led to rapid population growth in Africa after World War II?
2. How did population growth affect economic development in new African nations?

791

SECTION 3 Objectives and Teaching Strategies

OBJECTIVE 1. Identify South Africa's neighboring countries and explain South Africa's interventions in their affairs.

Teaching Strategy: *Discussing History: South Africa and Its Neighbors* (page 784d)

OBJECTIVE 2. Explain Nelson Mandela's views on majority rule in South Africa.

Teaching Strategy: *Analyzing a Quotation: Nelson Mandela Speaks to South Africa* (page 784d)

SECTION 3 Resources

GEOGRAPHY
■ Transparency 102

REINFORCEMENT
■ Independent Practice 34.3

ENRICHMENT
■ Voices from the Past 34.3

ASSESSMENT
■ Section Quiz 34.3

ANSWER TO

Comparing Pictures

Located near the world's largest gold field, Johannesburg gets its wealth from mining, industry, and banking. Blacks who work in Johannesburg must, by the system of apartheid, live outside the city in townships lacking security, adequate housing, and modern public services.

Afrikaners dominated South Africa.

None of the sub-Saharan nations matched South Africa in terms of resources. Its temperate climate and fertile soil gave it the continent's choicest farmlands. At the same time, its rich mineral resources made it the world's leading producer of gold and diamonds.

The benefits from these riches, however, were not shared equally among the nation's people. Almost all factories and mines, together with the most productive farmlands, were owned and operated by people of Dutch and British descent. A majority of this population were Boers (page 576), the descendants of Dutch settlers. Later they were known as Afrikaners.

The Afrikaners' vision for the nation proved to be based on continued control by the white minority. Black South Africans, who made up more than 75 percent of the population, had few rights and freedoms. They could not vote or hold seats in the parliament, and they lacked such basic rights as freedom of speech, assembly, and the press. In addition, they were denied equal treatment and opportunity in many spheres of South African life. Two other large population groups—Asians and people of mixed race—also endured discrimination.

A *segregated society* In 1948, the South African government began to limit the freedom of black Africans even more. It launched a system of **apartheid** (uh-PAHR-TATE) that called for a complete racial separation. Laws were passed banning all social contacts between whites and blacks. Schools, hospitals, and neighborhoods were to be separate. Blacks were excluded from high-level jobs and from attending the best universities. Parks, playgrounds, and beaches were also **segregated,** or set apart according to race.

The homelands policy In 1959, the parliament passed new laws extending racial segregation by creating separate **bantustans,** or homelands, for South Africa's major black groups. Afrikaners hoped that all blacks would in time be resettled in these homelands, which would be given semi-independent status.

The homelands policy was highly unfair. Although blacks made up three quarters of the population, only 13 percent of the country's land was set aside for them. The remaining 87 percent—including the best farmland and the fabulously rich gold and diamond mines—remained in the hands of whites, who made up only 15 percent of the population.

The government forced thousands of black families to move to the bantustans. Because the

Comparing pictures *Johannesburg, South Africa (left), is a center of wealth. Outside it lie black townships such as Crossroads (right). What factors might account for the economic differences?*

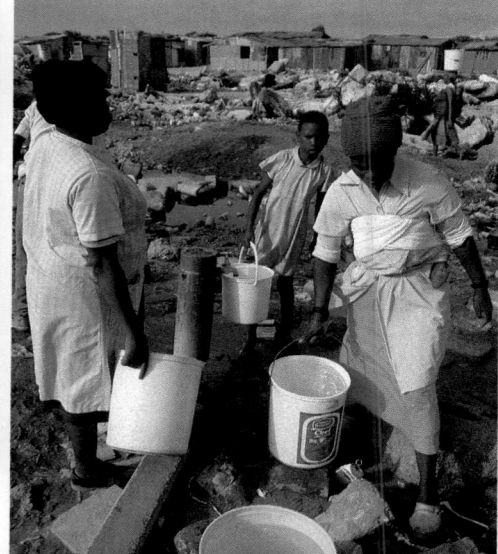

792

nation's economy depended heavily on underpaid black labor, however, millions of blacks continued to live in areas reserved for whites. Excluded from white residential areas, they began to build shanty towns around the major cities. One such town was Soweto, outside Johannesburg. Blacks living in such areas were required to carry registration passes. Because such passes were available only to people with jobs, families were often separated. Families that tried to stay together in spite of the law lived in constant fear of the police.

World opinion strongly condemned South Africa's racist policies. Because of apartheid, the country was expelled from the United Nations in 1974. Nonetheless the nation remained prosperous due to its exports of gold, diamonds, and other products. A powerful Afrikaner-led army discouraged foreign interference.

Black South Africans resisted apartheid.

Black South Africans resisted the control imposed by the Afrikaner minority. They had long sought to change the system that denied them true freedom and political rights. The African National Congress (ANC), founded in 1912 to seek political rights, was the oldest such organization on the continent. After 1931, when South Africa became independent, ANC leaders organized strikes and boycotts to protest the government's racist policies.

The Sharpeville Massacre The establishment of apartheid led to new resistance. Black protests reached a peak in 1960, when—in an incident called the Sharpeville Massacre—police killed 69 people demonstrating against the system of passes. The government then banned the ANC and imprisoned or exiled thousands of its members. The key ANC leader Nelson Mandela was sentenced to life imprisonment.

The Soweto demonstrations The cycle of protest, repression, and violence continued. Riots in black townships such as Soweto and Sharpeville became regular occurrences. In 1976, more than 600 students were killed in Soweto while protesting the use of the Afrikaner language in their classes. A ruthless government crackdown followed. In 1977, the leader of those protests Steve Biko died while in police custody.

Black leaders such as Anglican Archbishop Desmond Tutu increasingly sought to focus world attention on the lack of freedom and human rights in South Africa. "There is no peace in Southern Africa," Tutu said when he accepted the Nobel Peace Prize in 1984. "There is no peace because there is no justice."

South Africa interfered in other countries.

By 1980, South Africa had become an international outcast. The United Nations in 1974 had suspended South Africa's membership in the world organization and in 1977 had forbidden the sale of military equipment to that country. Many nations later imposed **economic sanctions**, or restrictions on trade, against South Africa. In 1986, the United States also announced measures to reduce American business involvement there unless apartheid was ended.

Afrikaners knew that the survival of apartheid depended on military strength. Government leaders therefore began to interfere in the affairs of neighboring countries to prevent any challenge to their power or racist policies.

Zimbabwe During most of the postwar era, South Africa had had an ally in Ian Smith, leader of the white settlers in the neighboring British colony of Southern Rhodesia. Despite being outnumbered 25 to 1 by blacks, Rhodesia's ruling whites refused Britain's orders to turn power over to the black majority. In 1965, Rhodesia gained its independence. Only whites were represented in the new government.

South Africa gave Smith's government full military and economic support. Other African nations, however, supported black patriots such as Robert Mugabe who resisted Smith's rule. Finally, in 1980, a compromise agreement was made by which Rhodesia became the new nation of Zimbabwe. Mugabe became president, with full representation of the black majority in the parliament and political life. Zimbabwe enjoyed political stability, while its resources helped to maintain a decent standard of living.

Angola and Mozambique Unlike Zimbabwe, the former Portuguese colonies of Angola and Mozambique endured a difficult transition to independence. The lack of preparation for that change was complicated by Communists' seizure

793

Define:
(a) system of complete separation of the races (b) set

(continued)

ANSWERS TO *(continued)*

apart according to race
(c) South African homeland
(d) restrictions on trade
Identify:
(a) South African of Dutch descent **(b)** shanty town outside Johannesburg **(c)** black South African organization seeking political rights
(d) killing of 69 black protesters by police **(e)** black leader of the ANC
(f) former leader of Rhodesia **(g)** president of Zimbabwe **(h)** black South African archbishop **(i)** South African prime minister who began reforms **(j)** black political group
Answer:
1. banned social contacts between blacks and whites, segregated most public places, set up black homelands
2. organized protests, strikes, boycotts
3. to prevent any challenge to their power or racist policies
4. (a) to aid in the ending of apartheid **(b)** peaceful majority rule
5. ethnic differences, interference by whites seeking to maintain power

---

ANSWERS TO

Voice from Our Time

1. the people
2. equal voting rights for all people, black and white
3. universal suffrage in a democratic and nonracial society

of power in both countries. South Africa moved quickly to arm and support rebel groups opposing the new governments. Communist Cuba sent thousands of troops to aid the Angolan government. By 1985, both Angola and Mozambique were embroiled in bitter civil wars. The real losers were the people of both countries, where fighting reduced economic activity to the lowest levels in all of Africa.

Namibia A civil war also developed in Namibia, a region once ruled by South Africa as a mandate and later held in defiance of UN demands for withdrawal. Namibian guerrillas seeking freedom for their country battled South African forces for more than a decade. A compromise agreement finally led to Namibia's independence in 1990. South Africa promised to withdraw from Namibia if Cuban forces would leave neighboring Angola. South Africa, however, retained Namibia's main seaport at Walvis Bay.

Change came to South Africa.

As changes swept across Zimbabwe and Namibia, South African leaders recognized that they could not maintain apartheid forever. The

pace of change quickened when F.W. de Klerk became president in 1989.

A new era De Klerk was determined to transform his country and end its isolation. On February 2, 1990, he lifted the ban outlawing the African National Congress. Just nine days later, he released Nelson Mandela from prison.

These dramatic actions marked the beginning of a new era in South Africa. Over the next 18 months, the parliament repealed apartheid laws that had segregated public facilities and restricted black land ownership. "The new South Africa is on the march," De Klerk triumphantly announced. "Nothing can stop it anymore."

World leaders welcomed the end of apartheid. On July 10, 1991, the International Olympic Committee lifted a 21-year ban barring south African athletes from the Olympic Games. The next day, President Bush issued an executive order ending American economic sanctions.

"I still cannot vote" While legal barriers were falling, serious economic inequalities remained. During the early 1990's, the average black worker earned just one-fifth as much as the average white worker. Although blacks could le-

---

Voice from Our Time | *Mandela Speaks to South Africa*

In February 1990, Nelson Mandela—longtime leader of the African National Congress—was released after 27 years in prison. His first public speech was at the central square in Cape Town.

I stand here before you not as a prophet, but as a humble servant of you, the people. Your tireless and heroic sacrifices have made it possible for me to be here today. I therefore place the remaining years of my life in your hands. . . .

Our struggle has reached a decisive moment . . . We have waited too long for our freedom. We can no longer wait . . . Universal suffrage on a common voters roll in a united democratic and nonracial South Africa is the only way to peace and racial harmony.

In conclusion, I wish to go to my own words during my trial in 1964. They are as true today as they were then. I wrote: I have fought against white domination, and I have fought against black domination. I have cherished the idea of a democratic and free society in which all persons live together in harmony and with equal opportunities.

1. Who does Mandela believe is responsible for his release from prison?
2. What is the "common voters roll" he refers to?
3. What does Mandela see as the only solution to South Africa's racial problems?

794

RACIAL COMPOSITION IN SOUTH AFRICA

Racial or Ethnic Group	Number
White	**4,900,000**
Boer	2,790,000
British	2,110,000
Mixed Race (Colored)	**3,200,000**
Asian	**900,000**
Black	**27,500,000**
Zulu	7,400,000
Xhosa	6,900,000
Sotho	5,400,000
Tswana	3,600,000
Other	4,200,000

South African society is made up of four main population groups and subgroups.

gally purchase homes in white neighborhoods, less than 1 percent could afford to do so.

Apartheid also left complex political problems. Mandela pointed out the need for a new constitution by reminding whites, "I still cannot vote in my own country." Forming a multiracial government was difficult. After lengthy negotiations, De Klerk agreed to hold the nation's first universal elections in early 1994. These elections would create a new government and pave the way for adopting a new constitution.

In addition, unexpected political problems arose in the nation's black community. The prospect of power led to rivalries among black political groups themselves. The most powerful of these was the Inkatha, supported mainly by the Zulus and their leader Chief Buthelezi. In the early 1990's, more than 6,000 people died in this tragic conflict. While ethnic differences accounted for some of this rivalry, many people feared that it was encouraged by white groups seeking to maintain control.

Section REVIEW 3

Define: (a) apartheid, (b) segregate, (c) bantustan, (d) economic sanctions

Identify: (a) Afrikaner, (b) Soweto, (c) African National Congress, (d) Sharpeville Massacre, (e) Nelson Mandela, (f) Ian Smith, (g) Robert Mugabe, (h) Desmond Tutu, (i) F.W. de Klerk, (j) Inkatha

Answer:
1. How did the South African government restrict black citizens in the postwar period?
2. How did black South Africans resist apartheid?
3. Why did South Africa become involved in neighboring countries?
4. (a) Why did De Klerk release Mandela? (b) What does Mandela want for South Africa?

Critical Thinking
5. What factors might account for the divisions within South Africa's black community?

New nations arose in the Middle East. 4

As you have seen, the countries of the Middle East won a large measure of independence before World War II. As in Africa, however, traditional cultures found it difficult to adapt to the rapidly changing postwar world. In addition, religious conflicts continued to threaten the peace in this troubled region.

The Middle East faced problems.

As you saw (pages 665–669), nationalism swept through the Middle East after World War I. As a result, most of the region's modern states were created in the 1920's (map, page 668). While older than the countries of Africa, these nations faced many of the same political problems.

Disputed borders As in Africa, the nations of the Middle East are the outgrowth of colonialism. Here too national boundaries correspond to those drawn by the Europeans, which has often led to problems. Millions of Kurds, for example, lost their homeland as Kurdistan was divided among Turkey, Iraq, Iran, and the Soviet Union.

Another example of border conflict existed between Syria and Lebanon. Both countries had once been controlled by France as mandated territories. French officials had created Lebanon

795

SECTION 4 Objectives and Teaching Strategies

OBJECTIVE 1. Identify the significance of the Suez Crisis.

Teaching Strategy: *Discussing History: The Suez Crisis* (page 784d)

OBJECTIVE 2. Trace events leading to conflicts and conflict resolutions between Arab nations and Israel.

Teaching Strategy: *Discussing History: Peace-Keeping Efforts* (page 784e)

SECTION 4 Resources

GEOGRAPHY
■ Transparencies 103, 104

REINFORCEMENT
■ Independent Practice 34.4

ENRICHMENT
■ Voices from the Past 34.4

ASSESSMENT
■ Section Quiz 34.4

largely to satisfy the Maronite Christians in and around the city of Beirut. This angered Muslims in the region, who considered Lebanon part of Greater Syria.

Lack of democratic traditions Almost all of the Middle East had been part of the Ottoman empire before World War I. As a result, there was no tradition of democracy in the region. Instead, most countries were ruled by hereditary princes or shaykhs. The king of Jordan, for example, traced his ancestry back to Biblical times.

In countries where monarchs were eventually overthrown, traditional rulers were usually replaced by military ones. In 1952, King Farouk of Egypt was overthrown by a group of army officers. A similar military revolt ousted the Iraqi monarch in 1958.

In the Middle East, as in Southeast Asia and Latin America, the military had enormous influence in politics. Middle East nations, however, were also often involved in actual fighting with their neighbors. At times, groups seeking greater power turned to **terrorism**, or the use of violence, to achieve their goals.

Israel became a Middle East power.

One Middle East country that had not gained its independence before World War II was Palestine. It still remained a British mandated territory. Thus the status of Palestine was by far the most difficult problem facing the Middle East after the war. Although in ancient times the location of the kingdom of Israel, Palestine had for centuries been mainly Arab. The Jewish population increased, however, as Jews began migrating to Palestine in the late 1800's. Britain's Balfour Declaration had recognized the interest of Jews in Palestine. Many Jews had hoped for a homeland there. Arabs, however, who still made up 70 percent of the population, wanted Palestine to be an Arab State.

The end of World War II—when the world learned that the Nazis had killed more than 6 million Jews—brought a tremendous outpouring of sympathy for the Jews. The result was strong support for the establishment of a Jewish homeland in the Middle East. Palestine's Arabs, however, saw no reason why they should be displaced. "Give them [the Jews] and their descendants the choicest lands and homes of the Germans who oppressed them," suggested King Ibn Saud of Saudi Arabia in 1945.

A troubled beginning After long efforts to hammer out a compromise between Arabs and Jews ended in failure, Britain decided to turn responsibility for Palestine over to the United Nations. On November 29, 1947, a special UN committee recommended the creation of not one but two Palestines, one Jewish and the other Arab. Jerusalem would be maintained as an international city under permanent UN trusteeship. The UN General Assembly accepted the compromise plan. On May 14, 1948, David Ben-Gurion, longtime leader of the Jews residing in Palestine, announced the creation of an independent Israel—a dream fulfilled—in the region where Jews were a majority.

Many groups in the Middle East did not welcome the creation of Israel. Arabs in particular were dissatisfied with the UN's decision. They were convinced that the Jews had been given the more valuable lands and cities of Palestine. Within hours of Ben-Gurion's announcement, six Arab states—Egypt, Iraq, Jordan, Lebanon, Saudi Arabia, and Syria—attacked Israel.

This first of many Arab-Israeli wars ended within months with complete victory for Israel. Despite their larger size, the Arab armies were no match for the well-trained Israeli forces. When the fighting stopped in 1949, the Jews controlled half of Arab Palestine.

In addition, the Palestinian state that had been part of the UN plan never came into being. Instead, Egypt gained control over the Gaza Strip while Jordan annexed a 30-mile-wide band of territory west of the Jordan River known as the West Bank. The Jordanians also gained control over the holy sites in East Jerusalem.

While war raged, thousands of Palestinian Arab families had begun migrating from the areas under Jewish control. Most of them settled nearby in UN-sponsored refugee camps that ringed the borders of their homeland. The seeds for decades of conflict had been sown.

Internal progress More than a million Jews, many of them highly skilled and educated, flocked to Israel from around the world. With their help, the new nation made remarkable economic progress during the 1950's and 1960's.

The new Jewish state adopted a democratic form of government. Although Israeli politics was marked by bitter rivalries among many political parties, Israel presented a united front against its Arab neighbors. Dealing with frequent border clashes and terrorist attacks made the Israeli army one of the world's best fighting forces.

Conflict between Israel and its neighbors continued.

The period after World War II was marked by a growing sense of unity among the Arab peoples of North Africa and the Middle East. In part, this unity rested on their shared opposition toward Israel. The 1948 war was only the first of many armed conflicts between the Jews and their Arab neighbors. Hardly a month went by without a military incident, and full-scale wars broke out in 1956, 1967, and 1973.

Turning Points in History

The 1956 Suez Crisis The second Arab-Israeli war had its roots in a conflict between Egypt and the region's former colonial powers, Britain and France. In 1952, King Farouk of Egypt—a corrupt monarch who had ruled since 1936—was overthrown by a group of army officers. Farouk had allowed European business leaders to dominate the country, much as they had since the 1870's.

Gamal Abdel Nasser, a young army colonel, emerged as Egypt's popular new leader. He introduced reforms designed to modernize Egypt and improve living conditions for the poor. As a nationalist, he was also determined that Egypt would shape its own future.

Nasser was particularly concerned about the major symbol of European influence in Egypt, the Suez Canal (see page 548). Although part of modern Egypt, it was still controlled by British and French business interests.

In July 1956, Britain and the United States angered Nasser by withdrawing their offer to finance the building of the Aswan High Dam across the Nile in Egypt. Nasser decided to nationalize the canal. "The canal belongs to us!" he told a frenzied crowd. "It will be run by Egyptians! Egyptians! Egyptians!" After finishing his

Israel, 1967–1973

KEY
- Israel before 1967
- Israeli conquests, 1967
- Israeli occupation, 1973 ceasefire
- ★ Capital city

Map Study

In the Six-Day War (page 798), Israeli soldiers crossed the desert of the Sinai Peninsula all the way to the Suez Canal. What other territory did Israel occupy as a result of that war? As a result of the October War of 1973? What countries border Israel?

speech, Nasser ordered the Egyptian army to seize the canal. By nightfall, Nasser's forces were in full control of the Suez area.

Britain and France reacted angrily. These European powers considered control of the canal essential for the flow of trade with the Middle East and with southern and eastern Asia. "The Egyptian has his thumb on our windpipe," said Anthony Eden, the British prime minister.

To regain control of the canal, British and French leaders made a secret agreement with Israel. The Israelis, who considered Nasser a dangerous enemy, welcomed the opportunity to join Britain and France. On October 29, 1956, the Israeli army marched toward Suez. With air support provided by their European allies, the Israelis quickly defeated the Egyptians. Within ten days, British and French forces reoccupied the canal.

That victory, however, proved hollow. Other world powers felt that Britain and France had

797

ANSWERS TO
Map Study

Gaza Strip, Sinai Peninsula, Golan Heights, West Bank; areas west of Suez Canal and north of Golan Heights; Egypt, Jordan, Syria, Lebanon

ANSWERS TO

Section Review 4

Define:
use of violence to achieve political goals

Identify:
(a) Middle Eastern people with divided homeland
(b) Jewish leader in founding of Israel (c) conflict sparked by Egypt's nationalization of the Suez Canal
(d) leader of Egypt after king was overthrown (e) 1967 Arab-Israeli conflict (f) 1973 Arab-Israeli conflict

Answer:

1. disrupted borders, lack of democratic traditions

2. Jews wanted to create a Jewish homeland there, Arabs wanted it to be an Arab state.

3. (a) War for Israeli independence (1948), Suez Crisis (1956), Six-Day War (1967), Yom Kippur War (1973)
(b) Israelis were victorious.

4. (a) Egyptian nationalization of the Suez Canal
(b) Britain and France began to give up their African empires.

5. The United States and the Soviet Union became more involved, causing an arms race and several conflicts in the region.

behaved like bullies. They believed that Egypt had the right to control the Suez Canal so long as that country's government kept the waterway open to ships of all nations. As a result, the United Nations condemned Britain and France for their actions in the Suez affair. Even the United States and the Soviet Union—in a rare moment of agreement—supported the UN action.

In the face of worldwide opposition, Britain, France, and Israel backed down. In November 1956, a United Nations peacekeeping force moved into the Suez region. Two months later the canal was reopened to shipping and the first steps were taken to put the canal under Egyptian control.

The Suez crisis of 1956 was a turning point in the history of the Middle East and modern Africa. Egypt had stood up to its former colonial masters and emerged victorious. In addition, historians agree that the incident convinced both Britain and France that the time had come to consider giving up their African empires. The colonies' move toward independence began in Ghana in 1957 and continued throughout the 1960's.

At the same time, the Suez crisis made Nasser a great Arab hero, much admired across the Middle East. A brilliant speaker and ambitious politician, Nasser dreamed of an Arab world under his leadership. Arab unity proved elusive, however. Tensions among Arab states kept Nasser's dream from becoming a reality.

The Cold War spread to the Middle East.

The Cold War too was to have an impact on Middle East conflicts. After 1956, both the United States and the Soviet Union became more deeply involved in the conflict. The United States—with a large and influential Jewish population—gave Israel economic and military support. The Soviet Union backed Arab states such as Syria, Iraq, and Egypt with loans and military equipment. Each superpower hoped to gain a strategic advantage in the region. The result was a miniature arms race and two major conflicts.

The Six-Day War Equipped with Soviet tanks and aircraft, Nasser and his Arab allies felt ready by early 1967 to confront Israel. Nasser announced, "We are eager for battle in order to force the enemy to awake from his dreams, and

meet Arab reality face to face." He moved to close off the Gulf of Aqaba, Israel's outlet to the Red Sea.

In June 1967, it was Nasser who was rudely awakened. Striking without warning, Israeli jets attacked airfields in Egypt, Iraq, Jordan, and Syria. Safe from air attack, Israeli ground forces struck like lightning on three fronts. The war was over in six days. Israel lost 800 troops in the fighting, while Arab losses exceeded 15,000.

Determined to protect itself from future Arab attacks, Israel kept a number of strategic areas. These included the Sinai Peninsula taken from Egypt, the Golan Heights taken from Syria, and the West Bank region taken from Jordan. It also occupied Jerusalem, which formerly had been divided between Israel and Jordan. "We have returned to our holiest of places," said Israeli General Moshe Dayan, "never to depart again."

The Yom Kippur War A fourth Arab-Israeli conflict erupted in October 1973. After Nasser's death, his successor Anwar Sadat plotted a joint Arab attack on the date of Yom Kippur, the holiest of Jewish holidays. This time the Israelis were caught by surprise as Arab forces inflicted heavy casualties and recaptured some of the territory lost in 1967. Soon the Israelis succeeded in launching a counterattack and recovering most of the lost territory. An uneasy truce was agreed to after several weeks of fighting.

Section REVIEW 4

Define: (a) terrorism
Identify: (a) Kurds, (b) David Ben-Gurion, (c) Suez Crisis, (d) Gamal Abdel Nasser, (e) Six-Day War, (f) Yom Kippur War
Answer:
1. Identify two major political problems in the Middle East after World War II.
2. Why was Palestine the focus of disagreement after World War II?
3. (a) What four Arab-Israeli wars were fought between 1948 and 1973? (b) What was the outcome of each?
4. (a) What were the causes of the Suez Crisis? (b) What were the effects?

Critical Thinking
5. How did the Cold War affect the politics of the Middle East between 1970 and 1980?

Arab technicians operate a Gulf refinery.

Cultural conflicts caused Middle East tensions.

5

No region of the world had experienced as much turmoil as the Middle East since World War II. These conflicts were deep-rooted and involved much more than simply political struggles for territory and influence.

Contributing to Middle East instability were three distinct cultural conflicts. The first was economic in nature, resulting from the rapid development in certain oil-rich countries after World War II. The second conflict was religious, involving the traditional values of the Islamic community and the extent of modernization permitted by that faith. The third clash, of course, was the age-old conflict between religions—Jewish and Muslim, Christian and Muslim, Sunni and Shi'ite. All three of these cultural clashes reflected the tension between modernism and traditionalism that marked Middle East life.

The Middle East Today

Black Sea
Istanbul
Adana ★Ankara
●Izmir **TURKEY**   ★Tabriz
Nicosia
CYPRUS ★ **SYRIA**   ★Tehran
Beirut **IRAQ**
LEBANON ●Damascus Baghdad **IRAN**
Jerusalem Amman   Abadán
Cairo Suez Canal **JORDAN** ★Al-Kuwait
ISRAEL   **KUWAIT**
Gulf of Suez   **BAHRAIN** Strait of Hormuz
EGYPT   Manama★ ★Doha
Medina Riyadh★ **QATAR** ●Abu Dhabi Gulf of Oman
SAUDI **UNITED** ●Muscat
Mecca● **ARABIA** **ARAB EMIRATES**
Red   **OMAN**
Sea
  Arabian Sea
  YEMEN
KEY ★San'aa
★ Capital city Gulf of Aden
0   500 Miles

Focus on Geography

Geographic Skills

1. (a) In what country is the Suez Canal located? (b) Why is the Suez Canal important?
2. What strait connects the Persian Gulf and the Arabian Sea?
3. (a) List the countries located on the Persian Gulf. (b) What two nations dominate the Persian Gulf?
4. What country lies between Iraq and the Persian Gulf?

Geographic Theme: Location

5. (a) What major resource is located in the Persian Gulf region? (b) Why do most nations of the world oppose a military buildup by any one nation in that area?

The oil boom transformed Middle East economies.

After World War II, countries such as Egypt and Syria faced economic problems complicated by rapid population growth. Several Arab nations, however, "grew" something much more valuable. As you have seen (page 669), huge deposits of oil were discovered in the Middle East around the Persian Gulf. The Gulf states—Iran, Iraq, Kuwait, Saudi Arabia, and the United Arab Emirates—enjoyed great prosperity as a result.

799

SECTION 5
Objectives and Teaching Strategies

OBJECTIVE 1. Explain the political effects of the discovery of oil in the Middle East.

Teaching Strategy: *Discussing History: Oil as a Force in the World Community* (page 784e)

OBJECTIVE 2. Explain the significance of the rise of Islamic fundamentalism.

Teaching Strategy: *Discussing History: Islamic Fundamentalism* (page 784e)

ANSWERS TO
Focus on Geography

1. **(a)** Egypt **(b)** is a shorter route between Europe and Asia
2. Strait of Hormuz
3. **(a)** Iran, Iraq, Kuwait, Saudi Arabia, Qatar, United Arab Emirates **(b)** Iran, Saudi Arabia
4. Kuwait
5. **(a)** oil **(b)** to prevent one country from controlling much of the world's oil supply

SECTION 5
Resources

ASSESSMENT
■ Section Quiz 34.5

REINFORCEMENT
■ Independent Practice 34.5

ENRICHMENT
■ Voices from the Past 34.5

■ BACKGROUND

The flow of oil from the Middle East is critical to the economies of many industrialized nations. The geography of the region, however, creates bottlenecks at the Suez Canal, Bab el Mandeb, and the Strait of Hormuz, where the movement of oil can be halted.

ANSWER TO
Reading a Graph

1981

The founding of OPEC The original drilling agreements made by the Gulf states with European and American oil companies were highly favorable to the foreign investors. After World War II, however, Middle East leaders began to demand a larger share of oil revenues. Countries such as Iran and Iraq nationalized their oil industries overnight. Others, like Saudi Arabia, gradually increased their percentage of ownership.

In 1960, Middle East states took the lead in founding the Organization of Petroleum Exporting Countries (OPEC). This group worked to monitor production and ensure that oil-producing nations received fair prices for their highly sought product.

By 1970, all of the Persian Gulf states had gained control of their own oil resources. Together they achieved a position of dominance within OPEC. At the same time, worldwide consumption of oil had reached record levels. The Middle East's share of total oil sales had risen dramatically, from just 5 percent in 1939 to more than 30 percent in 1970.

The oil crisis of 1973 During the Yom Kippur War with Israel, the Arab oil-producing states

Reading a graph The rise in oil prices caused a worldwide energy crisis. In what year did prices peak?

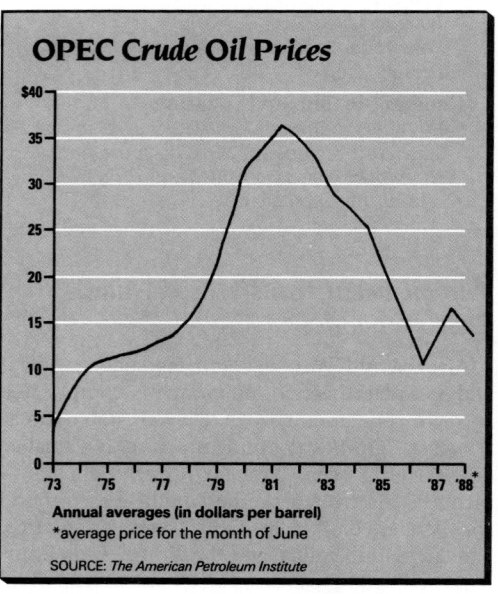

OPEC Crude Oil Prices

Annual averages (in dollars per barrel)
*average price for the month of June

SOURCE: *The American Petroleum Institute*

800

---

decided to show what impact they could have upon the world economy. OPEC announced that it was severely reducing oil production. It also cut off all oil shipments to countries, such as the United States, that supported Israel. The result was an energy crisis that brought shortages of gasoline, heating oil, and electricity to much of the Western world.

OPEC's action also produced other dramatic results. Oil prices shot up overnight, tripling and quadrupling their previous levels in Europe and North America. The high cost of oil affected industries and homes alike. In addition, inflation became a major problem in the developed world, which experienced serious economic problems as a result of OPEC's action.

Oil prices remained high for several years. Gradually, however, they began to decline. Over time, OPEC's strict production limits were abandoned by most individual countries. Meanwhile, conservation efforts reduced international demands. By 1986, world oil prices had fallen dramatically.

The price drop was destined to be only temporary, however. After all, the Gulf states held under their desert sands more than two thirds of the world's known oil reserves. This fact ensured that the Middle East would be critically important to the international economy in the decades ahead.

Cultures in transition The development of the oil industry in the Middle East brought internal tensions as well as conflict with the developed world. Several oil-producing states—including Saudi Arabia, Kuwait, and the United Arab Emirates—had long been among the poorest regions in the world. Oil exports and the high price of oil combined to give these states wealth beyond imagining. By 1975, the countries of the Persian Gulf region had the highest **per capita income**, or income per person, in the world.

Much of this money was reinvested at home, particularly in industry and in social services as shaykhs built hospitals, schools, roads, and magnificent public buildings. They also invested huge sums abroad, mainly in Western Europe and North America. Despite their wealth, most leaders of the Persian Gulf states maintained their strict Islamic traditions. Arab society in those wealthy nations became a curious mix of old and new— of humble prayer mats and Mercedes-Benzes, of luxurious modern homes and veiled women, of the latest computer technology and hand-lettered volumes of the Koran.

Islamic fundamentalism became a force.

While the contrast between traditional and modern ways was most evident in countries such as Saudi Arabia, every Muslim state in the Middle East faced a similar problem. Islamic culture had changed little in a thousand years. Now powerful outside forces created great pressure for change. In particular, the trend toward modern technology and life-styles caused people to question their traditional ways. To offset that pressure, a movement arose to resist Western influence. It was called Islamic **fundamentalism**, or obedience to the basic laws of that religion.

Modernization in Iran In no country was this clash between the values of past and present more dramatic than Iran, the modern name for the ancient country of Persia. Although Iran's huge oil reserves indicated untold wealth, Iranians were deeply divided about what kind of society that wealth should support.

An educated and well-traveled man, Shah Muhammad Reza Pahlavi (son of Reza Shah Pahlavi, page 666) wanted to use Iran's wealth to westernize his country and integrate its people into the modern world. Through his efforts, Tehran, Iran's capital, became a city of gleaming skyscrapers, foreign banks, and modern factories.

The revolution of the ayatollahs The Iranian people, however, were not all pleased with the shah's policies. Millions still lived in poverty, and the shah's secret police ruthlessly punished opponents of the regime. Even more important was the opposition of the country's conservative Muslim leaders known as **ayatollahs**. The ayatollahs opposed Western life-styles and bitterly resented the shah's concern with worldly matters. They wanted Iran to become an Islamic republic, ruled in strict accordance with the Koran.

The leader of the opposition to the shah was an elderly religious leader, Ayatollah Ruhollah Khomeini, whose tape-recorded messages sent from exile in France roused millions to frenzy. Shouting "Death to the shah!" and "Down with America!", Iranian workers went on strike and riots broke out in every major city late in 1978.

Ayatollah Khomeini led a fundamentalist revolution against the shah.

Faced with overwhelming opposition, the shah fled from Iran in January 1979. The Ayatollah Khomeini returned triumphantly from exile. He and his fellow religious leaders established an Islamic theocracy in Iran. Alcohol and Western-style music were banned, and women were again separated from men in schools and other public places. The Koran became the legal code for the country. Thieves, for example, had their right hands cut off as punishment, while thousands of Iranians were executed for not adhering strictly to Islamic law.

Not surprisingly, hatred of the United States was a cornerstone of Khomeini's policies. The United States had supported the shah for decades and had allowed Iran's deposed leader into the country for medical treatment. In 1979, with the Ayatollah's blessings, a group of young Islamic extremists seized the United States embassy in Tehran and took more than 60 Americans hostage, demanding the return of the shah to face trial.

801

■ **RESEARCH**

Students can investigate the current situation in Lebanon to see if a way has been found to reduce factional fighting there.

■ **BACKGROUND**

In 1986, the United States, using Israel as an intermediary, secretly sold arms to Iran in return for that country's help in securing the release of American hostages held by Lebanese factions.

Most of the hostages remained prisoners for 444 days before being released early in 1981.

The Iran-Iraq War The Iranian revolution was part of a broader Islamic religious revival that swept across the Middle East. From Iran, the Ayatollah Khomeini encouraged Muslim fundamentalists in other Middle East countries to overthrow their governments and replace them with more conservative leaders.

Tensions ran high between Iran and neighboring Iraq. For centuries, there had been tension between the Arabs of Iraq and the Persians of Iran. Each country's people belonged primarily to a different sect of Islam. And Saddam Hussein, Iraq's military ruler who had come to power in 1979, was exactly the kind of secular leader the Iranian ayatollahs despised.

War broke out between Iran and Iraq in 1980. For eight years, Muslim killed Muslim in the name of religious purity. Iraqi and Iranian planes bombed each other's cities. Saddam Hussein used chemical weapons against Iran, the first major use of such horrible tactics in battle since World War I. Altogether a million people perished before a UN ceasefire ended hostilities in 1988.

The Iran-Iraq War ended Khomeini's dream of an Islamic revolution that would sweep across North Africa and the Middle East. The aged ayatollah died in 1989. His successor Hashemi Rafsanjani tried to rebuild Iran and improve its relations with other countries. He could not, however, ignore the ayatollahs, who remained a powerful force in Iranian politics.

Lebanon Another Middle East nation torn apart by religious discord was the tiny country of Lebanon. After World War II, Lebanon enjoyed peace and prosperity, thanks to the National Covenant signed in 1943. This agreement divided political offices between the country's Muslim and Christian populations, which were roughly equal in size.

The National Covenant broke down during the 1970's. The Muslim population had grown substantially, and that community's leaders demanded more political power. The Maronite Christians refused and were backed by the United States and Israel. Civil war followed with Syria and other Arab states supporting the Lebanese Muslims.

In the years that followed, Beirut—Lebanon's capital and a city once described as "the Paris

802

of the Middle East"—was turned into rubble by warring factions. Terrorist attacks became an almost daily occurrence. Thousands perished, including 241 United States marines in a terrorist attack on the American embassy in Beirut in 1983. As a nation, Lebanon stood on the brink of destruction.

Egypt and Israel traded land for peace.

As you have seen, the Arab-Israeli conflict had repeatedly exploded into war. Since no peace treaty ended the Yom Kippur War, many people feared that another war could start at any time. Then, in November 1977, Anwar Sadat stunned the world by offering peace with Israel. In a dramatic gesture, he flew to Jerusalem and told Knesset, the Israeli parliament, "we used to reject you. . . . Yet, today we agree to live with you in permanent peace and justice." Sadat emphasized that in exchange for peace, Israel would have to recognize the rights of Palestinians and agree to withdraw from territory seized in 1967 from Egypt, Jordan, and Syria.

Sadat's dramatic gesture achieved his goal of knocking down the psychological wall between Egypt and Israel. Recognizing that Sadat had created a historic opportunity for peace, President Carter invited Sadat and Israeli prime minister Manachem Begin (BAY-gin) to Camp David, the presidential retreat in rural Maryland.

Isolated from the press and from their domestic political pressures, Sadat and Begin discussed the issues dividing their two countries. At times, both leaders threatened to leave without an agreement. Each time, Carter persuaded them to continue talking. After 13 days of negotiations, Carter triumphantly announced that Egypt agreed to recognize Israel's right to exist. In exchange, Israel agreed to return the Sinai Peninsula to Egypt. Known as the Camp David Accords, these agreements ended 30 years of hostilities between Egypt and Israel.

While world leaders praised Sadat, his peace initiative enraged many Arabs. In 1981, a fanatical group of Egyptians assassinated Sadat. Egypt's new leader, Hosni Mubarak maintained peace with Israel while also working to restore relations with other Arab countries.

The Palestinians demanded an independent state.

Israel and Egypt achieved a settlement by trading land for peace. But Israel and the Palestinians remained unable to reach a similar agreement. As you have seen (page 798), Israel won control over the West Bank and Gaza Strip during the Six-Day War. Unwilling to give up these strategic territories, the Israeli government began building settlements on them. By 1993, almost 100,000 Jews lived in the West Bank.

The Palestinians resented Israeli rule. As their anger mounted, many turned to a radical group called the Palestine Liberation Organization (PLO). Led by Yasir Arafat, the PLO vowed to eliminate Israel and create a Palestinian state. During the 1970's and 1980's, PLO guerrillas conducted a campaign of terrorism against Israel. PLO terrorists hijacked planes, assassinated diplomats, and blew up shops and buses. In one appalling attack, gunmen killed 11 Israeli athletes at the 1972 Munich Olympics.

Israel also turned to extreme measures. Israeli forces responded to PLO attacks by bombing suspected Palestinian bases. In 1982, the Israeli army invaded Lebanon in a costly attempt to destroy a number of Palestinian strongholds. The Israelis soon became involved in Lebanon's civil war and were forced to withdraw.

The Arab-Israeli conflict also claimed its share of foreign victims. In war-torn Beirut, for example, many American and European diplomats, businessmen, and scholars were kidnapped and held hostage, often for years at a time.

Intifada Despite the ongoing acts of violence, most Arab Palestinians living in the West Bank and Gaza Strip gave only passive support to the PLO. They went about their daily lives, respecting Israeli authorities, paying Israeli taxes, and obeying Israeli laws.

That situation abruptly changed in December 1987 when the Palestinians suddenly defied Israeli authorities by launching a widespread campaign of civil disobedience called the **intifada,** or "uprising." Pictures of unarmed teenagers throwing rocks at well-armed Israeli soldiers focused world attention on the Palestinian demand for an independent state.

The intifada signalled the beginning of a new Palestinian strategy. In November 1988, the PLO proclaimed an independent Palestinian state in Gaza and the West Bank. At a news conference a month later, Arafat renounced terrorism and accepted Israel's right to exist. He also called upon the United Nations to convene an international peace conference on the Middle East.

The Middle East Peace Conference Following an intensive diplomatic effort by the United States, Israel and its Arab neighbors finally agreed to hold a peace conference in Madrid, Spain, in October 1991.

As expected, the status of the territories proved to be a bitterly divisive issue. The Syrian foreign minister demanded that Israel return "every inch of Arab lands occupied . . . by war and force." Israel's hard-line prime minister Yitzhak Shamir (shah MEAR) insisted that "the issue is not territory but our existence."

Although additional talks were held in Washington, the negotiators failed to achieve a breakthrough. However, hopes for progress rose again when Yitzhak Rabin (rah BEAN) became Israel's new prime minister in June 1992. Unlike Shamir, Rabin was willing to suspend new Jewish settlements in the occupied territories and discuss trading land for peace.

Section REVIEW 5

Define: (a) per capita income, (b) fundamentalism, (c) ayatollah, (d) intifada
Identify: (a) OPEC, (b) Muhammad Reza Pahlavi, (c) Ruhollah Khomeini, (d) Iran-Iraq War, (e) Saddam Hussein, (f) Anwar Sadat, (g) Menachem Begin, (h) Camp David Accords, (i) Yasir Arafat
Answer:
1. What were three major sources of cultural conflict in the Middle East in the late 1900's?
2. What were the reasons for the international oil crisis of 1973?
3. What have been some of the effects of Arab fundamentalism?
4. What was the purpose of the Camp David Accords?
5. How was terrorism used as a political weapon?

Critical Thinking
6. Describe the intifada from the viewpoint of (a) a Palestinian, and (b) an Israeli.

803

ANSWERS TO
Section Review 5

Define:
(a) income per person
(b) obedience to the basic laws of a religion
(c) conservative Muslim leader (d) Palestinian campaign of civil disobedience
Identify:
(a) Organization of Petroleum Exporting Countries
(b) former leader of Iran
(c) ayatollah who led Iran after revolution (d) eight-year religious war (e) leader of Iraq (f) president of Egypt who promoted Mideast peace (g) prime minister of Israel who signed Camp David Accords (h) treaties signed by Egypt and Israel (i) leader of the PLO
Answer:
1. economic—oil found in some countries; religious—Islamic values; religious—conflict between Muslims, Jews, and Christians

2. Arab oil producers reduced oil production, cut off oil to countries that supported Israel.

3. Iranian government was overthrown; Iran and Iraq went to war.

4. to lessen tensions between Israel and Egypt

5. hostage-taking, random attacks used to force political actions

6. Students' answers will vary. Possible answers follow. (a) Palestinian viewpoint—demonstrate Israeli brutality, need for an independent Palestinian homeland (b) Israeli viewpoint—Palestinians as lawbreakers, using violence to achieve their goals

Concluding the Chapter

1. **Chapter Closer**
Ask students to summarize the main political and economic consequences of independence for African nations.

2. **Reteaching Activities**
a. Summarizing Have students write a paragraph summarizing three problems that confronted the new nations in Africa.

b. Identifying Leaders Have students identify each of the following leaders: Kwame Nkrumah, Gamal Abdel Nasser, Jomo Kenyatta, Desmond Tutu, P. W. Botha, David Ben-Gurion, Anwar Sadat, and Ayatollah Ruhollah Khomeini.

Answers to Chapter Review appear on page 784f.

Summary

1. The age of imperialism ended in Africa. In the 1920's, a westernized African middle class took the lead in independence movements. The struggle for independence began in North Africa, where it took many forms and spread south. African countries faced economic and political crises brought on by colonial rule.

2. Africans built new nations. After independence, African nations patterned their new countries after Western democracies. When the Western model failed, Africans experimented with a variety of political and economic systems, including one-party democracy in Ivory Coast, one-man rule in Zaire, and a federal republic in Nigeria. In Nigeria, a military coup in 1985 brought democracy to an end. Tanzania was led by Julius Nyerere, who worked hard to bring economic stability. South Africa remained under white rule after independence in 1931. In 1948, South Africa set up apartheid to segregate the black majority and keep power in the hands of the whites. In 1959, South Africa forced the black majority to settle in homelands. The white government used brute force to crush resistance.

3. Nationalism sparked Mideast conflicts. Although the partition of Israel in 1948 provided Jews with a homeland, it led to the loss of a homeland for Palestinian Arabs and sparked several Arab-Israeli wars. In 1979, Egypt and Israel signed a peace accord, but relations in the region remain tense. In Iran, a revolution ended modernization and brought Shi'ite Muslim religious leaders to power. Iran has tried to spread a Shi'ite revolution to neighboring Iraq. Division in Lebanon led to civil war in 1958. Fighting has intensified because of the presence of the PLO, which has launched attacks against Israel.

Reviewing the Facts

1. Define the following terms:
   a. developing nation
   b. apartheid
   c. economic sanctions
   d. fundamentalism
   e. ayatollah
   f. intifada

2. Explain the importance of each of the following names, places, or terms:
   a. Ghana
   b. Nkrumah
   c. Nasser
   d. Côte d'Ivoire
   e. Houphouet-Boigny
   f. Mobutu
   g. Nigeria
   h. Nyerere
   i. Soweto
   j. PLO
   k. Shi'ite
   l. Lebanon

3. (a) How did the effects of colonial rule weaken African countries economically? (b) What problems

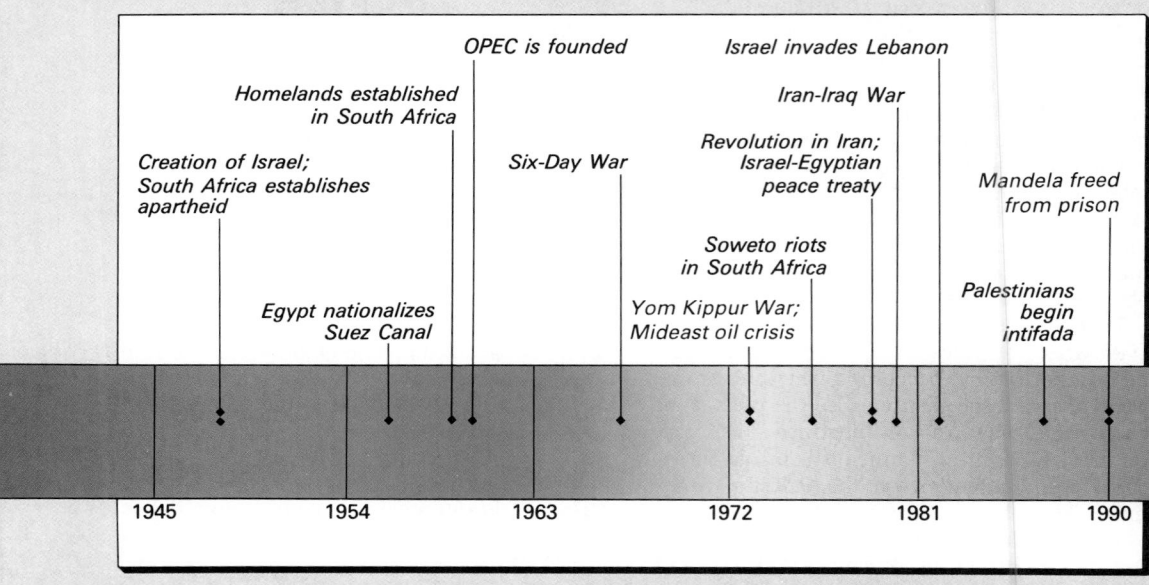

Homelands established in South Africa

OPEC is founded

Israel invades Lebanon

Iran-Iraq War

Creation of Israel; South Africa establishes apartheid

Six-Day War

Revolution in Iran; Israel-Egyptian peace treaty

Mandela freed from prison

Soweto riots in South Africa

Egypt nationalizes Suez Canal

Yom Kippur War; Mideast oil crisis

Palestinians begin intifada

1945   1954   1963   1972   1981   1990

did they face in nation-building?

4. (a) Who controls South Africa today? (b) What methods has the South African government used to keep control?

5. (a) How was the state of Israel created? (b) What was the result for Palestinian Arabs?

Basic Skills

1. **Reading and interpreting a map** (a) The five great rivers of Africa are the Nile, Niger, Zaire, Zambezi, and Limpopo. Using the map on page 787, list the countries that touch each river. (b) Compare the continental position of these rivers with that of the Mississippi River system in North America. What differences do you find?

2. **Classifying** Section 1 describes a number of problems caused by colonialism and the African environment. (a) List the problems described in each group. (b) For each problem, find examples of countries in the chapter that illustrate it.

3. **Locating** The water routes of the African-Middle East crossroads are important to world trade. Certain parts of these routes are critical because they are bottlenecks for shipping. (a) Using the maps on pages 797 and 799, identify the waterway between the Mediterranean and Red seas and between the Persian Gulf and the Arabian Sea. (b) There is also a third bottleneck. Where is it located?

Researching and Reporting Skills

1. **Using a newspaper index** The *New York Times Index* is a major resource for finding current information. Use a recent volume to locate articles about some aspect of life in one African or Mideast country.

2. **Using regional or national magazines** Using periodicals such as *Africa Report* or *Asia,* find information about cultural events in or pertaining to Africa or the Middle East. What similarities and contrasts are shown between traditional and modern aspects of that culture?

Critical Thinking

1. **Synthesizing** What various influences contributed to the growth of nationalism in North Africa?

2. **Inferring** (a) How might some African nations increase their economic development? (b) How does importing food tend to limit a country's development?

3. **Analyzing** (a) What conditions made it difficult for the new nations in sub-Saharan Africa to organize and launch new governments? (b) Which of these do you think was most important? Why?

4. **Resolving conflicts** One reason why conflict continues between Israel and the Palestinians is that the basic interests of both groups have been in opposition. (a) Identify the various basic interests of both groups. (b) In what ways are these opposed? (c) What range of alternatives exists for resolving these differences? (d) Which basic interests are vital to each group as a start for negotiations?

5. **Analyzing** The tension between tradition and modernization continues in the Middle East. (a) What are several current examples of this tension? (b) How has wealth from oil affected the balance in the OPEC nations of the Middle East?

Perspectives on Past and Present

Review the content in your text about nineteenth-century Western attitudes concerning imperialism (pages 570 and 586). To what extent have these attitudes changed at the end of the twentieth century? What factors account for that change as well as any lack of change?

Investigating History

The lack of protection for basic political rights in South Africa contrasts with the progress made in many countries of the world. As a class or group project, read about current political and social conditions in South Africa. Then, using the first eight amendments to the United States Constitution as criteria, evaluate the status of political rights among the different population groups in South Africa.

805

CHAPTER
Evaluation

Chapter Test 34, Alternate Chapter Test 34, and Computer Test Bank Chapter 34 Test can be used to evaluate your students' understanding of this chapter.

The Americas in the Modern World

Chapter 35

Chapter Overview

In the past 30 years, Latin American countries have struggled to achieve and maintain prosperity in the face of overpopulation and political instability. Rapid population growth and slow economic growth have contributed to urban poverty and to large foreign debts. Rapid industrialization in Brazil and Mexico has not solved the problems of competing in the world economy.

Progress toward greater democracy has been uneven. Brazil, Chile, and Argentina, for example, have undergone cycles of dictatorship and democracy. Some authoritarian leaders have improved economics at the expense of human and civil rights. In the 1980's Argentina, Mexico, and Chile moved toward more democratic government.

In the Caribbean, Puerto Rico became a commonwealth of the United States. Cuban revolutionaries overthrew a corrupt dictator and established a Communist government. The reactions of the United States and the Soviet Union to the Cuban Revolution led to confrontation in the 1960's. El Salvador, Guatemala, and Nicaragua were torn by civil war. In Nicaragua, fighting between the Sandinistas and the Contras finally ended in the late 1980's, and the first democratically elected president of Nicaragua took office in 1990.

Since 1945 nations in northern North America have prospered. In the United States the efforts of civil rights activists led to the passage of laws that ended many forms of racial discrimination. In foreign affairs, the Vietnam conflict led to changes in the United States' role as world leader. As European and Asian economies recovered from the effects of World War II, the dominance of the United States began to decline. Canada increased its international role in the 1980's and developed closer economic ties with the United States.

Chapter Focus

Political and economic events in the Americas affect the United States. For example, the United States sends hundreds of millions of dollars in aid to Latin American countries and American banks lend billions. Economists predict that Latin America's ability to repay their debts will increasingly affect the United States' economy. Some Latin American countries are able to compete with the United States and other nations in world markets. For example, Brazil, the fifth largest country in the world, produces computers, rockets, satellites, and surgical supplies, and contains the world's largest reserve of iron ore. It is second only to the United States as an exporter of food.

Chapter 35 The Americas in the Modern World 1945–1990
FOCUS The Pan-American Highway as a symbol of the links between the nations
of the Western Hemisphere

★ **Advanced**
● **Basic**

	SECTION 1	SECTION 2	SECTION 3	SECTION 4
Objectives	1. Describe Latin American efforts to overcome economic instability. 2. Describe the effects of rapid population growth in Latin America.	1. Evaluate recent progress in Latin America's struggle toward democracy. 2. Describe Latin America's efforts to achieve economic stability.	1. Identify the forces involved in the Nicaraguan conflict. 2. Describe the relationship between the United States and Puerto Rico.	1. Describe social changes in the United States and their link to postwar prosperity. 2. Evaluate the effects of the 1988 free trade agreement between the United States and Canada.
Setting the Stage	Prewar changes in countries of Latin America Transparency 105	Major countries of Latin America Transparency 105	Political geography of the Caribbean Basin Transparency 106	Signs of postwar prosperity in North America
Teaching Strategies	Economics and History: Latin American Foreign Debt Discussing History: Urban Overpopulation Check for Understanding	Discussing History: The Pace of Change Economics and History: "Enterprise for the Americas" Check for Understanding	Discussing History: The Nicaraguan Conflict Discussing History: Puerto Rico's Choices Check for Understanding	Skill Building: Making Generalizations Transparency 118 Economics and History: The Free Trade Accord Transparency 107 Outline Map 4 Check for Understanding
Guided Practice	Section Review 1	Transparency 105 Q&A Section Review 2	Transparency 106 Q&A Section Review 3	Transparency 107 Q&A Section Review 4
Independent Practice Worksheets	Independent Practice 35.1 Basic Skills 35	Independent Practice 35.2 Basic Skills 35	Independent Practice 35.3 Critical Thinking 35	Independent Practice 35.4 Vocabulary 35 Geography Skills 35
Enrichment	1. Primary Source: Voices 35.1 2. Researching for Points	1. Primary Source: Voices 35.2 2. Researching for Points	1. Primary Source: Voices 35.3 2. ★Researching a Topic 3. Researching for Points	1. Primary Source: Voices 35.4 2 Researching for Points

Chapter Closer

●**Reteaching Activities**   Summarizing, Explaining Main Ideas, Recalling Information

Chapter Review   Summary, Reviewing the Facts, Basic Skills, Researching and Reporting Skills, Critical Thinking, Perspectives on Past and Present, Investigating History

Chapter Evaluation   Chapter Test 35, Alternate Chapter Test 35, Computer Test Bank Chapter 35 Test

Key trends influenced Latin America. 1

Setting the Stage

Show students Map Transparency 105, *The Nations of Latin America*, or refer to the map on page 808. Have students locate Mexico, the Caribbean Basin countries, and the nations of South America. Ask students to characterize the economies and political systems of Latin American countries before World War II.

Teaching Strategies

Economics and History: Latin American Foreign Debt (Objective 1) Have students read "Economic problems caused instability" (pages 807–809). Ask them to explain the concepts of diversification and import substitution. Emphasize that enacting such programs requires large amounts of money. Help students to relate the concepts of principal and interest to the problem of national debt. Ask students how much money a country would have to pay a lender in a given year on a $50 million loan at 18 percent interest. ($9 million) Many developing countries have difficulty paying the interest on their loans and might never be able to repay the principal. Reasons for these difficulties include devalued currency, inflation, low market prices for the country's main product, domestic crises, and political corruption.

The inability of debtor countries to repay loans threatens the international economy. Large banks repaid interest to other governments and businesses. Bank failures caused by bad debts can therefore have a global impact. Explain that cities and countries, like banks and businesses, can go bankrupt. Aside from the human suffering that would result, bankrupt coun-

tries might face social and political upheaval, leaving them vulnerable to foreign intervention. This, in turn, might upset the relationships among world powers. The bankruptcy of a nation can therefore have an even greater global impact than its defaults on international loans. Ask students what steps they think might be taken to help developing countries reduce their foreign debts.

Discussing History: Urban Overpopulation (Objective 2) Ask students what services a city must provide its inhabitants. (transportation, sanitation, safety, employment) Discuss the difficulty of providing these services in a city where the population increases by nearly 800,000 people every year. This is the estimated rate of population growth in Mexico City, and by the year 2000 an estimated 28 million people will live there. This rapid increase in population has outpaced the ability of the city to provide sufficient jobs and adequate services. For example, in Mexico City 14,000 tons of garbage are produced daily, but the city can dispose of only 8,000 tons per day. Large above-ground dumps now exist where the city's homeless sift through the refuse for saleable items. Air and water pollution remain unchecked. Doctors estimate that chemical and biological pollutants kill 30,000 children every year. Conditions such as these exist in most major urban areas of Latin America. Discuss the problems of rapid population growth, and challenge students to suggest solutions. Tell them that many countries in Latin America are attempting to relocate populations by creating employment opportunities in rural areas. Ask students to find a specific example of this trend in the text. (Brasília)

Check for Understanding Have students write paragraphs describing the conditions in Latin American countries that have prevented economic prosperity.

Enrichment Activities

1. **Reading a Primary Source** Assign Voices from the Past Resource Book 35.1.
2. **Researching for Bonus Points** What is the Argentine name for the Falkland Islands? (Malvinas Islands)

Nations sought greater stability. 2

Setting the Stage

Show Map Transparency 105, *The Nations of Latin America*, or refer to the map on page 808. Have students locate Argentina, Brazil, Chile, and Mexico. These are the major countries of Latin America, and their histories, problems, and successes are similar to those of other Latin American nations.

Teaching Strategies

Discussing History: The Pace of Change (Objective 1) Remind students that history is an ongoing process of change. In developing areas such as Latin America, political and economic instability encourage more rapid change than commonly occurs in countries such as the United States or Japan.

Have students collect current articles and listen to news reports about Latin American countries. Ask them to note information about economic, social, or political affairs that updates what they have read in the text. Examples might include changes in political leadership, movement toward democracy or socialism, foreign relations, inflation and unemployment rates, and trade agreements. Discuss the implications of this information with the class.

Economics and History: "Enterprise for the Americas" (Objective 2) Several initiatives in the early 1990's focused on creating free trade zones in Latin America. United States President George Bush proposed the "Enterprise for the Americas" plan in June 1990. It included such measures as forgiving $7 billion in Latin American debt to the United States, contributing $100 million to encourage private investment in Latin America, and creating a free trade zone to include all nations of the Americas. Ask students how the removal of trade restrictions and tariffs on trade among Latin American countries would support their goal of economic stability.

Check for Understanding Ask students to describe what progress was made in the 1980's toward democracy and economic stability in Argentina, Brazil, Chile, and Mexico.

Enrichment Activities

1. **Reading a Primary Source** Assign Voices from the Past Resource Book 35.2.
2. **Researching for Bonus Points** Which political party in Puerto Rico supports statehood? (New Progressive Party)

The Caribbean Basin faced political turmoil. 3

Setting the Stage

Show Map Transparency 106, *The Caribbean Basin,* or refer to the map on page 815. Have students identify the countries of the Caribbean Basin and their capitals. Ask how the political geography of this region differs from that of Mexico and South America. (Countries are smaller and are confined by the sea.) Why are political developments in the countries of Central America and the Caribbean important to the United States? Students should recall the strategic and commercial importance of the region and the traditional role of the United States in Latin American affairs.

Teaching Strategies

Discussing History: The Nicaraguan Conflict (Objective 1) Draw a three-column chart on the board with the following headings: *Somozas, Sandinistas,* and *Contras.* Call on students to identify the membership, goals, policies, and alliances of the three groups and list students' responses in the chart. Then ask why the Sandinistas rebelled against the Somozas and why the Contras rebelled against the Sandinistas. Tell students that the United States supported the Somoza regimes in Nicaragua and the Reagan administration aided Nicaraguan Contras against the Sandinistas. Ask students to speculate why the United States government wanted to end Sandinista rule. (feared spread of communism through Nicaragua's dependence on Cuban and Soviet aid) Point out that many United States citizens as well as Latin Americans and others were critical of the United States' role in the Nicaraguan conflict.

Discussing History: Puerto Rico's Choices (Objective 2) The territory of Puerto Rico was a Spanish colony from 1493, when it was claimed by Christopher Columbus, until 1898, when Spain ceded it to the United States in the Treaty of Paris. The island was granted ever-greater autonomy between 1900 and 1949, when islanders were first permitted to elect their governor. On July 25, 1952, Puerto Rico became a commonwealth.

Residents of the Commonwealth elected or appointed most officials and determined their own budget and code of laws. Congress retained the right to pass laws concerning Puerto Rico. Puerto Ricans became United States citizens, but only those who moved to the mainland were allowed to vote in presidential elections. The island's delegate to Congress had no vote.

Growing interest in changing Puerto Rico's status led to passage of a House bill in 1990 requiring a referendum on the issue. The referendum would have allowed Puerto Ricans to choose among statehood, a modified commonwealth, independence, or continuation of commonwealth status. The bill died when the U.S. Senate failed to act on it.

Ask students to list advantages and disadvantages of statehood for Puerto Rico. (advantages: full rights of citizenship and representation, increased social service benefits; disadvantages: loss of income tax exemption and revenues from taxes on trade with mainland, companies losing tax incentives might leave island, causing higher unemployment)

Check for Understanding Ask students to list the causes of conflict in Caribbean Basin nations since World War II.

Enrichment Activities

1. **Reading a Primary Source**
   Assign Voices from the Past Resource Book 35.3.

2. **Researching a Topic**
   Ask advanced students to find out what roles drug trafficking, the Panama Canal, and Oliver North played in the United States policies toward Latin America in the 1980's.

3. **Researching for Bonus Points**
   On what day of the year do Cubans celebrate their national independence? (July 26)

The United States and Canada changed.   4

Setting the Stage

During the two decades after World War II, the United States and Canada experienced unprecedented prosperity. Rising wages enabled citizens to purchase consumer items, such as refrigerators, washing machines, automobiles, televisions, and radios, which flowed off assembly lines that had been converted to peacetime production. Throughout the 1950's and 1960's, however, there was an undercurrent of anxiety and discontent. African Americans felt left out of the economic boom. Americans continued to fear communism and went to war to prevent its spread.

Teaching Strategies

Skill Building: Making Generalizations (Objective 1) Ask students to identify social changes in the United States after 1945 and write students' generalizations on the board. The list should include references to the civil rights movement, the women's movement, and the anti-war movement. Other social changes might refer to efforts to protect the rights of children, senior citizens, Native Americans, immigrants, veterans, disabled citizens, and patients. Point out that new economic pressures and opportunities after the war were underlying themes in movements for social change.

Tell students that demographic changes included a "baby boom," suburban development, and population movement to southern and western regions. Use Map Transparency 118, *United States*, to identify the states in these regions. New economic pressures and opportunities changed patterns of family life and created needs for expanded family-support services. Ask students to express opinions on the effects of postwar social changes on Americans' expectations of personal life, family life, and work.

Economics and History: The Free Trade Accord (Objective 2) Show students Map Transparency 107, *The United States and Canada*, and ask them to determine the approximate length of the border between Canada and the United States. (about 3,000 miles) This is the longest undefended border in the world. Ask why this border is not defended. Then distribute Outline Map 4: Political North America. Have students refer to the transparency or to the map on page 823 to label the Canadian provinces and main bodies of water.

In 1989, goods valued at $167 billion flowed between Canada and the United States, making them the world's largest trading partnership. Explain that by 1999, goods that flow between the United States and Canada will not be subject to trade barriers such as tariffs or quotas. Ask students to evaluate the advantages and disadvantages of free trade for both countries. How might the free trade agreement benefit businesses in both the United States and Canada?

Some Canadians oppose the free trade agreement on the grounds that Canada's national and cultural identity might be overwhelmed or compromised by American influence. Ask students to discuss this issue from the point of view of the Canadians.

Check for Understanding Call on students to identify changes that have taken place in the United States and Canada during the postwar period.

Enrichment Activities

1. **Reading a Primary Source**
   Assign Voices from the Past Resource Book 35.4.

2. **Researching for Bonus Points**
   Who designed the Vietnam War Memorial? (Maya Yin Lin)

Reviewing the Facts

1. (a) growth of cities **(b)** full rights of citizens **(c)** movement aimed at making Quebec independent of Canada **(d)** general vote on a legislative act

2. (a) president of Argentina from 1946 to 1955 **(b)** islands over which Argentina lost a war to Britain **(c)** military dictator of Chile who lost public referendum in 1988 **(d)** Mexican president who narrowly won election in 1988 **(e)** dictator of Cuba from 1934 to 1959 **(f)** leader of Cuban revolution **(g)** corrupt president and dictator of Nicaragua **(h)** Nicaraguan rebels who overthrew Somoza government **(i)** Nicaraguan rebels who fought the Sandinistas with U.S. aid **(j)** Sandinista leader **(k)** first elected president of Nicaragua **(l)** corrupt dictator of Panama defeated in 1989 **(m)** African American civil rights leader

3. rapid population increase, urbanization

4. Economic development brought soaring national debt and continued unequal distribution of wealth.

5. More than ten million American citizens and millions of seasonal workers in the U.S. are of Mexican descent.

6. Platt Amendment gave U.S. the right to intervene in Cuban affairs.

7. (a) by overthrowing the Somoza government **(b)** distributed land, nationalized key industries, asked for military aid from Cuba and the Soviet Union, suspended elections, placed strict controls over the press **(c)** feared Nicaragua was being used for a Communist takeover of Central America

8. (a) Technological superiority and availability of capital helped U.S. dominate world trade by supplying goods to countries devastated by war. **(b)** Focus on social issues, including the civil rights movement and the women's movement, brought greater social equality. Society was divided over the Vietnam War.

Basic Skills

1. (a) Inside tropics: Mexico, Guatemala, Belize, Honduras, El Salvador, Nicaragua, Costa Rica, Cuba, Jamaica, Haiti, Dominican Republic, Panama, Colombia, Venezuela, Guyana, Suriname, French Guiana, Ecuador, Peru, Bolivia, Brazil, Paraguay. Outside tropics: Argentina, Chile, Uruguay. **(b)** Land in Latin America is tropical savannah, tropical rain forest, or a mixture of both; crops are varied and include grains, sugarcane, soy, and coffee; raw materials include large oil and iron ore deposits. Andes area is mountainous.

2. (a) *civil rights movement:* pro arguments—African Americans were not participating in economic prosperity, racial discrimination continued to exist; con arguments—white racists resisted civil rights movement; outcomes—end to racial discrimination, Civil Rights Act, Voting Act; *women's movement:* pro arguments—discrimination against women kept salaries low and job opportunities limited; con arguments—traditional view of women's roles; outcomes—women gain more access to elected positions, anti-discrimination laws passed, ERA amendment is not adopted; *Vietnam War:* pro arguments—fight against communism; con arguments—war was immoral and unwinnable; outcomes—U.S. withdraws from Vietnam, South Vietnam is taken over **(b)** Students' answers will vary.

Researching and Reporting Skills

1. Students' answers will vary. Suggested topics: Latin American debt payments, struggles between Communist and democratic regimes in Latin America, drug trade between Latin America and U.S.

2. Student's answers will vary but should include all Latin American countries and Native American ethnic groups.

Critical Thinking

1. (a) uneven distribution of wealth, rule by military leaders or dictators, frequent changes in leadership **(b)** democratic elections took place in Chile and Argentina, one-party domination in Mexico is diminishing

2. employment opportunities must be created to meet the demands of a rapidly expanding population

3. civil wars, population explosion, economic difficulties, government corruption

4. political oppression (Cuba, Haiti, Chile); lack of jobs (most Latin American countries)

5. (a) escaped WWII devastation, developed foreign trade, technological innovations **(b)** economic prosperity at home, economic dominance abroad led by multinational corporations

6. (a) imports exceed exports as foreign competitors are able to compete with U.S. companies **(b)** U.S. share of foreign markets is diminishing.

7. strong economy, increased nationalism

8. (a) encouraged trade, made U.S. and Canada more competitive in world markets **(b)** increased trade between U.S. and Canada

Perspectives on Past and Present

Students' answers will vary.

Investigating History

Students' answers will vary.

Chapter 35

Teaching with Pictures

The Pan-American Highway is a system of highways linking the capitals of 18 Latin American countries. Four routes fan out north of Mexico City to four different points on the United States border. Although highways continue north through the United States and Canada to Alaska, neither country has officially designated any roadways as part of the Pan-American Highway.

Construction of the system began in the late 1920's and was generally complete by the 1960's. The Pan-American Highway Congress oversees the development and progress of the highway system today. Ask students how the Pan-American Highway supports unity and cooperation among the Latin American countries. Point out that the system is a vital transportation route for agricultural and manufacturing products and supplies.

The Pan-American Highway crosses rugged terrain ranging from the rain forests of Brazil and Guatemala to the tundra of Canada. Here it descends from the Andes of Peru to a river valley.

Key Terms

diversification
import substitution
urbanization
liberation theology
multinational corporation
civil rights
deficit
recession
separatism
referendum

Read and Understand

1. Key trends influenced Latin America.
2. Nations sought greater stability.
3. The Caribbean Basin faced political turmoil.
4. The United States and Canada changed.

In August 1929, the Brazilian capital of Rio de Janeiro buzzed with excitement. The first International Highways Exposition ever held in the Americas had captured the imagination of the city. Featured in the exposition was the highway that would link the Americas from northern Alaska to the Straits of Magellan.

Thousands of Brazilians waited in long lines for hours to see exhibits highlighting the proposed Pan-American Highway. Displays showed the latest construction techniques and equipment, and films dramatized the efforts of workers carving roads through dense jungles and over lofty mountains. As part of the exposition, 200 delegates from countries all over the Western Hemisphere met in a spirit of international friendship to establish a timetable and raise funds for building the highway.

Chapter 35 Resources

GEOGRAPHY
- Geography Skills 35
- Outline Map 4
- Transparencies 105, 106, 107, 118

REINFORCEMENT
- Vocabulary 35
- Basic Skills 35
- Reteaching 35
- Making Connections Study Guide 35

ENRICHMENT
- Critical Thinking 35
- History and Literature 35

ASSESSMENT
- Chapter Test 35
- Alternate Chapter Test 35
- Computer Test Bank

The launching of the highway project was delayed by the Great Depression. Finally, in 1936, construction began. Over the next three decades, road builders in two dozen countries overcame obstacles of all kinds to complete 17,000 miles of highway. From Alaska, the road ran into Canada and through the United States, Mexico, and Central America. It ran the entire length of South America, with several east-west links across the continent. By 1990, only two short stretches of the highway remained incomplete.

The Pan-American Highway has helped to foster trade, tourism, and communication among all the countries along its route. In this chapter, you will see how the modern countries of South America, the Caribbean Basin, and northern North America have developed in recent times.

Key trends influenced Latin America. 1

The Rio Grande River, which defines the border between the United States and Mexico for 700 miles, is more than a political boundary. It also separates the cultural region known as Latin America from the cultural region formed by the United States and Canada.

Latin America is divided into 26 nations. Although they differ dramatically in size and resources, these nations are being influenced by common political, economic, and social trends.

Latin Americans sought democracy.

Most Latin American nations won their independence in the early 1800's. The new republics faced difficult problems. When civilian governments often could not solve these problems, they were replaced by military leaders supported by wealthy landowners. Repeated cycles of civilian governments being overthrown by military coups prevented Latin America from developing a tradition of stable democratic governments. Even though most nations of the region had democratic constitutions, real power was often in the hands of the military. In country after coun-

try, the army protected the interests of the upper classes.

Military leaders and dictators continued to dominate many Latin American countries after World War II. They used secret police to arrest and sometimes torture their opponents.

Despite this repression, most Latin American nations considered themselves democracies. Although their constitutions provided for universal suffrage, many countries lacked free elections, and their citizens still lacked basic political rights.

Economic problems caused instability.

In the postwar era, Latin American nations faced economic problems similar to those of many newly independent nations in Asia, Africa, and the Middle East. Although most countries of Latin America had been independent for more than a century, their economies still were focused on producing and exporting food, raw materials, and minerals. Most industries and railroads were foreign-owned, and the income from them went to the investing nations, such as the United States and Britain.

In terms of economic development, therefore, Latin American nations were still considered developing nations. Several—such as Bolivia and some Central American nations—were less-developed countries. Nonetheless, World War II had forced Latin American nations to become more self-reliant. After the war, they were eager to forge ahead in development.

Diversification Even in the postwar era, many countries still relied upon a single major export. Coffee accounted for 54 percent of Colombia's exports in 1980. Other examples included such exports as Venezuela's petroleum (90 percent), Chile's copper (48 percent), and Cuba's sugar (80 percent). Reliance upon a single major export meant risk. Loss of a coffee crop or a decline in the price of sugar or oil could cause disaster.

After World War II, many Latin American countries tried to reduce their dependence on single exports by **diversification,** or exporting a greater variety of products. Some sought more varied agricultural products. Others nationalized key industries, hoping that such control would enable them to keep a larger share of the profits.

Import substitution Other countries tried to encourage industrial development at home by

807

SECTION 1
Objectives and Teaching Strategies

OBJECTIVE 1. Describe Latin American efforts to overcome economic instability.

Teaching Strategy: *Economics and History: Latin American Foreign Debt* (page 806c)

OBJECTIVE 2. Describe the effects of rapid population growth in Latin America.

Teaching Strategy: *Discussing History: Urban Overpopulation* (page 806c)

■ BACKGROUND

Latin America includes Mexico, Central America, South America, and the Caribbean islands. This region is two and a half times the size of the United States.

SECTION 1
Resources

GEOGRAPHY
■ Transparency 105

REINFORCEMENT
■ Independent Practice 35.1

ENRICHMENT
■ Voices from the Past 35.1

ASSESSMENT
■ Section Quiz 35.1

The United States, Belize,
Guatemala; Cuba; Ecuador;
Brazil

Cooperative Learning

Arrange students in pairs
and have each pair select
one nation of Latin Amer-
ica. Students should find
out their country's major
exports and rank them in
order of importance. If
possible, students should
determine what percentage
of total exports each product comprises. (The annual
Britannica Book of the Year
contains this information
under individual country
listings in the "World
Data" section.) Ask each
pair of students to decide
whether their country has a
diversified economy or is
mainly dependent on a single major export. Then students should make a
poster or display to illustrate their findings.

The Nations of Latin America

KEY
★ Capital city

0   1000 Miles

Map Study

*What countries border Mexico? What is the largest island in the Caribbean?
What country's capital lies almost directly on the equator? What is the largest
country in Latin America?*

808

borrowing heavily from foreign banks to launch new industries and by putting high tariffs on manufactured goods imported from abroad. This policy of replacing foreign goods with locally manufactured ones was called **import substitution.**

Import substitution was most successful in the larger Latin American countries such as Argentina, Brazil, and Mexico. By 1990, Brazil, for example, had become the world's fourth-largest manufacturer of automobiles.

Foreign debt Prosperity remained elusive. These countries rarely generated enough revenue from exports to repay the sizable loans needed to launch import-substitution programs in the first place. Latin America's total foreign debt soared from $15 billion in 1970 to $420 billion in 1990. Brazil, Mexico, and Argentina owed almost two thirds of this amount.

Society remained divided.

As you have seen (page 536), Latin American society since the earliest European discovery had been composed of different ethnic groups. Often these ethnic differences were reflected in social and economic classes.

Distribution of wealth In most countries of Latin America, a handful of wealthy families owned huge estates and businesses, while the majority of families struggled to survive as tenant farmers or urban workers. Class distinctions remained important in postwar Latin America. In country after country, the business and political elite remained largely creole in origin, while the people at the bottom of the social pyramid were of African or Native American origin.

The lower classes, however, were not completely powerless. The trade union movement, for example, was extremely powerful in those Latin American cities with a large industrial base. In addition, the Catholic Church—in a region where the vast majority of the population was Catholic—came more and more to represent the interests of the urban and rural poor.

The population explosion Latin American society was marked after World War II by rapid population growth. The region's population surged from 166 million in 1950 to 450 million in 1990.

This tremendous population increase created severe social problems. As the population rose, millions of people migrated from rural villages to nearby cities. These cities were ill-prepared for the massive influx of people. They lacked the financial resources to provide the newcomers with adequate housing, utility service, and transportation. As a result, enormous slums, or shanty towns, sprawled around the edges of many cities. As you have seen, this trend toward **urbanization,** or the growth of cities, has occurred in developing nations around the world.

The drug trade In recent years, the international drug trade has become an increasing threat to the stability of Latin American society, as well as to society worldwide. By the early 1990's, for example, Latin America exported more than 80 percent of the cocaine and 90 percent of the marijuana entering the United States. Most of the cocaine was produced in Bolivia, Peru, and Colombia.

The $4-billion-a-year trade in cocaine made Colombia's drug lords the world's wealthiest criminals. The drug lords formed groups known as cartels, which have wielded enormous power. For example, Colombia's Medellin cartel used its vast wealth to bribe police officers, judges, and customs officials.

The cartels' willingness to use bribery, threats, and violence has made them an international problem. In February 1990, President Bush met with the leaders of Colombia, Bolivia, and Peru to discuss ways of fighting the drug traffickers.

Latin America and the United States became more interdependent.

The drug trade illustrates the changing relationship between the United States and Latin America. In the past, United States interaction with Latin America focused primarily on obtaining raw materials, protecting investments, and fighting the spread of communism. Within the last few years, these concerns have broadened to include shared problems such as the drug trade, debt crisis, and environment.

Immigration is also playing an important role in creating a new relationship between the United States and Latin America. During the past two decades, millions of people from Mexico, the Caribbean region, and Central America have immigrated to the United States. By the early 1990's, Hispanics became the United States fastest growing ethnic group.

809

■ **DISCUSSION**

What single factor is responsible for most of Latin America's population increase? (Improved medical care helped reduce death rates.)

■ **BACKGROUND**

Officials estimate that 1.5 million people in Bolivia, Peru, and Colombia are involved in growing, refining, and smuggling cocaine. Hundreds of thousands of families earn far more money farming coca than they could earn by raising a legitimate crop. In Bolivia the government began paying farmers to destroy their coca crops. In the first four months of 1990, farmers were paid to destroy 8,400 acres.

ANSWERS TO
Section Review 1

Define:
(a) exporting a greater variety of products (b) policy of replacing foreign goods with locally manufactured ones (c) growth of cities

Answer:
1. They were ruled by military leaders and dictators, the countries lacked free elections, and citizens lacked basic political rights.

2. Economies were focused on food, raw materials, and minerals. Industries and railroads were foreign-owned, so profits went abroad.

3. Causes: risks of reliance on single major export, heavy borrowing from foreign banks to launch new industries; consequences: rapidly increasing foreign debt

4. urbanization; growth of slums in cities ill-prepared to receive migrants

5. Wealthy cartels use bribery, threats, and violence to influence police, judges, and customs officials.

6. Many countries experienced repeated cycles of civilian governments being overthrown by military leaders or dictators who protected the interests of the upper class.

Section REVIEW 1

Define: (a) diversification, (b) import substitution, (c) urbanization

Answer:
1. In what ways were most postwar Latin American governments still undemocratic?
2. What factors limited industrialization in Latin America despite political independence?
3. What are the causes and consequences of the debt crisis in Latin America?
4. What impact has rapid population growth had on Latin America?
5. Why are the drug cartels a threat to the stability of countries such as Colombia?

Critical Thinking
6. Why has democracy proved difficult to achieve in Latin America?

Nations sought greater stability. 2

Each nation of Latin America is unique in its geographic setting, population, and political and economic development. This section takes a closer look at four of the region's major countries—Argentina, Brazil, Chile, and Mexico.

Perón shaped modern Argentina.

Argentina, which is South America's second-largest country, has always been one of its richest. Its fertile soil and highly developed agriculture made it one of the world's leading exporters of beef and grain. Argentina was also heavily industrialized, even before World War II. Its large urban work force was organized into trade unions.

The Perón era The urban working class in time grew in political influence. It found a hero in Juan Perón, a young Army colonel of modest origins who became president in 1946. Perón was among the first to recognize the potential political power of the urban poor—the *descamisados*, or "shirtless ones."

Further enhancing Perón's reputation with the masses was his wife Eva—"Evita," as she was known to the millions who idolized her. As Minister for Social Welfare, Evita portrayed herself as the champion of the poor.

Although the policies of Juan and Eva Perón had great appeal, they created problems. The welfare programs proved expensive, and corruption thrived at all levels of government. Evita died of cancer in 1952, and her husband sorely missed her influence with the masses. His policies had made many enemies, including wealthy businessmen, landowners, and most importantly his former colleagues in the military. When a group of officers combined against him, Perón was driven into exile in 1955.

Military rule Two decades of chaos and violence followed Perón's departure. Groups within the military battled for power and sought to prevent Perón's return from exile.

Finally, in 1973, Perón won back the office of president. A million *descamisados* turned out to welcome their hero back to Buenos Aires. But Perón was now an old man—almost eighty—and within a year he died. By 1976, the generals had again seized power.

What followed were six years of terror that Argentines called "the dirty war." The military rulers launched a vicious campaign against hundreds of thousands of "enemies of the state"— that is, anyone who opposed the government. Torture and murder became everyday events as more than 20,000 Argentines simply vanished.

The Falklands War The military leaders brought neither peace nor prosperity to troubled Argentina. In 1982, the generals sought to gain public support by seizing the Falkland Islands, an isolated group of British-owned islands in the stormy South Atlantic. The British government sent a major naval force. In a matter of weeks, Britain recaptured the Falklands.

Its defeat in the Falklands brought an end to the military government. Angry crowds demanded a civilian government. In 1983, Raul Alfonsin was elected president in the first truly free election Argentina had seen in 40 years.

The 1980's proved a time of healing for Argentina as Alfonsin worked to rebuild democratic institutions and control runaway inflation. Although Alfonsin made progress in restoring democracy, neither he nor his successor, Carlos Menem, elected in 1989, was able to stabilize the economy.

810

Brazil remained a land of contrasts.

Brazil is Latin America's largest and most populous country. It differs from its neighbors in one major respect: Its heritage and language are Portuguese rather than Spanish. Brazil has always been a land of contrasts. Its extremes range from massive industrial cities to primitive villages and from elegant resorts to cardboard slums.

After gaining its independence from Portugal in 1822, Brazil became America's only monarchy. The monarchy lasted until 1889, when Emperor Don Pedro II was forced to abdicate and a republican form of government was established. Although the new constitution paid lip service to democracy, the country was actually ruled by a wealthy elite.

Brazil's economic miracle Like Argentina, Brazil saw rapid industrial growth during and after World War II. Most industries were located in the south, around the city of São Paulo.

Under the leadership of Juscelino Kubitschek, president of Brazil from 1955 to 1960, the economy continued to expand. In 1957, work began on a new national capital, Brasília, in the wilderness some 800 miles northwest of Rio de Janeiro.

Kubitschek's dreams proved expensive. His chief successor, João Goulart, inherited massive foreign debts and runaway inflation. When Goulart began to consider land reform, the wealthy elite allowed the Brazilian army to seize power.

Military rule For the next two decades, Brazil was ruled by military leaders. The generals cut wages, stabilized prices, and encouraged foreign banks to invest in the country.

ecisions in History

The Yanomamo are a Stone Age group of people who have lived in isolation in the Amazon rain forest for thousands of years. In 1987, however, Brazilian prospectors discovered one of the world's richest deposits of gold on Yanomamo lands. Within a short time, 40,000 prospectors invaded the region. Since their arrival, more than 15 percent of the Yanomamo have died from contagious diseases. Miners now demand that the governments involved remove the Yanomamo and open the entire area to mining. Meanwhile, anthropologists and human rights groups urge the governments to close the Yanomamo's land to outsiders. If you were a government official, which decision would you favor and why?

The economic boom of the 1960's, however, had a dark side. Some of the world's worst pollution hung over Brazil's cities and seeped into its water. Moreover, prosperity was financed by keeping workers' wages low, limiting spending on social services, and borrowing heavily from abroad. The military government jailed and tortured people who spoke out against its repression.

By the early 1980's, the Brazilian economy was in chaos. Foreign debts exceeding $100 billion led to pressures for change. After the military leaders finally agreed to new elections, they were replaced by a civilian government in 1985.

Return to democracy Foreign debt was not the only cause of Brazil's economic problems. The nation's population and cities continued to grow uncontrollably. Also, the nation's distribution of wealth was such that by 1985, the top 10 percent of the population was receiving more than 50 percent of the nation's total income.

A dramatic effort for economic reforms was launched by President Fernando Collor de Mello (page 863), elected in 1989. Collor froze most of the nation's bank accounts, stabilized the currency, and reduced the amount of inflation.

Chile survived revolutions.

Chile in the past two decades has seen two revolutions, one radical and the other conservative. During the first half of the twentieth century, Chile had established a strong tradition of democratic rule. In the late 1960's, however, food shortages and declining copper prices produced rising social unrest. In 1970, Chile's frustrated voters elected a Marxist candidate named Salvador Allende (ah-YEN-day) as their president.

Allende: The radical Allende promptly implemented a radical economic plan designed to transform Chile into a socialist state. He began by freezing prices and increasing wages. The government then broke up large plantations and seized copper mines owned by American companies. Arguing that "the United States had already taken too much wealth out of Chile," Allende refused to compensate the copper companies for their losses. The United States and many foreign banks responded by cutting off all loans.

As economic conditions worsened, Allende faced growing opposition from the middle class, business leaders, and the military. On September

811

SECTION 2
Objectives
and Teaching
Strategies

OBJECTIVE 1. Evaluate recent progress in Latin America's struggle toward democracy.

Teaching Strategy: *Discussing History: The Pace of Change* (page 806c)

OBJECTIVE 2. Describe Latin America's efforts to achieve economic stability.

Teaching Strategy: *Economics and History: "Enterprise for the Americas"* (page 806d)

■ DISCUSSION

Why did Brazil's leaders choose to build a new capital in the midst of the tropical rain forest? (to encourage economic development in the region)

SECTION 2
Resources

GEOGRAPHY
■ Transparency 105

REINFORCEMENT
■ Independent Practice 35.2

ENRICHMENT
■ Voices from the Past 35.2

ASSESSMENT
■ Section Quiz 35.2

Define:

urban poor, or "shirtless ones," in Argentina

Identify:

(a) Argentine president from 1946 to 1955 and 1973 to 1976 (b) president of Argentina who was freely elected in 1989 (c) president of Brazil from 1955 to 1960 (d) new capital of Brazil begun in 1957 (e) Brazilian president elected in 1989 (f) Marxist president of Chile from 1970 to 1973 (g) military dictator of Chile from 1973 to 1988 (h) president of Chile elected in 1989

Answer:

1. Perón recognized potential power of the urban poor.

2. (a) first free elections in 40 years, progress toward rebuilding democratic institutions and controlling inflation (b) return to elected civilian government, efforts for economic reform

3. led by civilian presidents rather than army leaders; Native American and mestizo population participated in politics

4. All experienced rapid post-war industrial growth and, in the 1980's, economic instability.

5. Foreign borrowing helped fund industrialization and economic expansion, but the heavy burden of debt eventually caused economic instability.

11, 1973, General Augusto Pinochet (pee-noh-SHAY) led a military coup that overthrew the Allende government. Allende died during the brief but bloody battle for the presidential palace.

Pinochet: The conservative Once in power, Pinochet transformed Chile into a military dictatorship. He suspended the constitution, closed Congress, banned political parties, and censored news broadcasts. Security forces arrested thousands of Allende's supporters. Many were tortured and murdered.

Once his opponents had been silenced, Pinochet reversed Allende's socialist policies. He returned the copper mines to American businesses and also allowed wealthy landowners to regain their holdings. As foreign investments returned, inflation dropped to less than 10 percent.

Despite his economic success, Pinochet proved to be an unpopular ruler. His human rights violations touched off international protests and growing unrest within Chile. In October 1988, Pinochet permitted a plebiscite to determine if the people wanted him to remain in office for another eight years. The Chileans stunned Pinochet by voting to remove him from power. In December 1989, Patricio Aylwin defeated a presidential candidate backed by Pinochet. Aylwin's election signaled Chile's return to democratic government.

Mexico faced economic challenges.

Of all Latin American nations, Mexico has been affected the most by its relationship with the United States. Mexico, in turn, has influenced its neighbor. By 1990, people of Mexican descent formed the second-largest minority group in the United States. More than 10 million are American citizens, while millions more are seasonal workers.

Political stability In the 80 years after the Revolution of 1910, Mexico enjoyed relative political stability. One reason was that the army was less important politically than it was in other Latin American countries. In the 40 years after World War II, all of Mexico's presidents were civilians. The country's Native American and mestizo population—a majority of the total—participated fully in the country's political life.

Stability in governing did not mean that democracy prevailed. One political party—the Par-

tido Revolucionario Institucional (PRI)—won every election in the postwar era. The PRI provided stability, yet it took advantage of its power. Over time, PRI members became a privileged class. Dissatisfaction with the PRI was apparent in the presidential elections of 1988. Although the PRI candidate, Carlos Salinas de Gortari, won, it was by a narrow margin.

Economic challenges Mexico, like Argentina and Brazil, enjoyed rapid industrial growth after World War II. Steel production doubled in the 1960's; automobile manufacturing quadrupled. In the 1970's, a discovery of major oil reserves made Mexico a leading oil producer.

Short-sighted planning added to Mexico's economic problems. In spite of high earnings from oil, the nation continued to borrow heavily. Large sums went toward social programs to help the ever-growing ranks of the urban poor. Mexico's economic situation worsened after 1981, when world oil prices began to decline.

In the late 1980's, economic reforms began to stabilize the economy. At the same time, Mexico's mineral and fuel resources attracted new foreign businesses. Broader experience with technology is likely to lead in time to the growth of new industries such as electronics.

In the years ahead, the trade barriers between the United States and Mexico may be lowered. President Bush and President Salinas in November 1990 discussed a possible trade agreement.

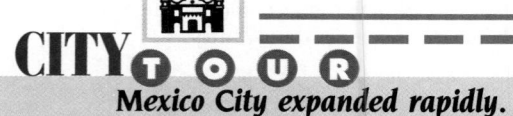

CITY TOUR
Mexico City expanded rapidly.

Mexico City is a scene of striking contrasts. The oldest major city in the Americas, it is the center of the nation's Aztec, Spanish, and Mexican cultural heritage. The city's main plaza, the Zócalo, reflects this heritage.

The huge Metropolitan Cathedral—with its ornate chapels, paintings, and sculptures—dominates the Zócalo. Nearby stand the ruins of the Great Temple of the Aztec. Across the plaza, the National Palace contains the offices of the president of Mexico.

Mexico City also displays wide boulevards lined with modern skyscrapers and some of the finest shops in Latin America. Chapultepec Park provides a green oasis where people can relax. To the west is the Palace of Fine Arts.

Despite its many attractions, Mexico City faces three critical problems—rapid population increase, poverty, and pollution. Between 1950 and 1990, its population soared from 3 million to 20 million. Today it is the world's fastest-growing city. About 1,000 jobless peasants migrate to the city each day. Most of them live in huge slums, or *barrios*, that surround the city.

As Mexico City has grown, its air pollution has increased to become the world's worst. Fumes from cars, buses, and trucks combine with industrial pollution to create a blanket of smog over the valley in which the city lies.

The people of Mexico City know that solving these problems will be difficult. However, a favorite bumper sticker reflects their optimism: "Mexico City, I believe in you."

Democracy grew in Latin America.

The strong progress toward greater democracy in many Latin American nations in the past five years marks a positive new trend. Despite poverty, social divisions, and foreign debt, the majority of the population sought change. In the 1980's, popularly elected governments replaced military rulers in such key countries as Brazil, Argentina, and Chile. By the early 1990's, more than 90 percent of the people in Latin America lived under democratically elected governments.

| Section **REVIEW** | 2 |

Define: *descamisados*
Identify: (a) Juan Perón, (b) Carlos Menem, (c) Juscelino Kubitschek, (d) Brasília, (e) Fernando Collor de Mello, (f) Salvador Allende, (g) Augusto Pinochet, (h) Patricio Aylwin
Answer:
1. How did Juan Perón differ from earlier military rulers in Latin America?
2. (a) What progress toward democracy took place during the 1980's in Argentina? (b) In Brazil?
3. In what two ways did political development in Mexico during this period differ from that of most of Latin America?

A celebration of Mexico's Revolution Day on November 20 in the Zócalo, or Constitution Plaza, in front of the National Cathedral

4. What was similar about the pattern of economic development in Argentina, Brazil, and Mexico during the postwar period?

Critical Thinking
5. How has foreign borrowing both helped and hurt Latin American economies?

The Caribbean Basin faced political turmoil. 3

In a Cuban courtroom in 1953, the young revolutionary Fidel Castro faced his accusers. As he began his defense, only three judges, an armed guard, and a few reporters were allowed to hear him. Castro freely admitted to leading an armed uprising against the government of Fulgencio Batista. He denounced Batista's corrupt rule and insisted that the Cuban people had a right to rebel against tyranny. "Cuba should be the bulwark of liberty," Castro declared. He called for free elections and a free press. Seeing that his judges were unmoved, Castro defiantly proclaimed, "Condemn me! It does not matter! History will absolve me!"

813

SECTION 3
Objectives and Teaching Strategies

OBJECTIVE 1. Describe the relationship between the United States and Puerto Rico.

Teaching Strategy: *Discussing History: Puerto Rico's Choices* (page 806d)

OBJECTIVE 2. Identify the forces involved in the Nicaraguan conflict.

Teaching Strategy: *Discussing History: The Nicaraguan Conflict* (page 806d)

■ BACKGROUND

The symbol for the city tour of Mexico City shows the Basilica of Our Lady of Guadalupe.

SECTION 3
Resources

GEOGRAPHY
■ Transparency 106

REINFORCEMENT
■ Independent Practice 35.3

ENRICHMENT
■ Voices from the Past 35.3

ASSESSMENT
■ Section Quiz 35.3

The Platt Amendment of March 1901 permitted United States intervention in Cuba "for the preservation of Cuban independence." It also limited Cuba's right to negotiate treaties, ceded rights to a naval base in Cuba to the United States, and outlawed the transfer of Cuban lands to any power other than the United States.

Cuba and other nations of the Caribbean Basin have much in common. They enjoy a tropical climate and share a heritage that includes a blend of Native American, African, Spanish, and other European cultures. They also share the burden of economies that have depended on a single cash crop and governments often controlled by corrupt rulers.

Revolutionary leaders in the Caribbean Basin attacked these evils and promised democratic reforms. Most failed to keep their promises and became ruthless dictators. As a result, the Caribbean Basin has been plagued by a cycle of political instability and violence.

Cuba struggled for independence.

Cuba is the largest and most strategically located island in the West Indies. Located close to the United States, it commands a network of vital sea-lanes. The island possesses many fine harbors, fertile soil, rich deposits of minerals, and rolling plains that can support large herds of cattle.

These natural advantages made Cuba a valuable colony in Spain's empire. While independence movements swept across Latin America, Spain stubbornly refused to give up Cuba. As many as 400,000 Cubans died in a bitter struggle for independence that lasted from 1868 to 1898. As you have seen (page 587), the United States helped to free Cuba during the Spanish-American War.

Although free from Spain, Cuba had to include a document called the Platt Amendment in its new constitution. The Platt Amendment gave the United States the right to use military force to intervene in Cuban affairs. Even though the amendment was cancelled in 1934, many Cubans viewed it as a national humiliation.

Although Cuba finally enjoyed a measure of political independence, its economy remained closely tied to the United States. By the late 1950's, United States companies controlled 90 percent of the island's electric and telephone service, 50 percent of the railroad service, and 40 percent of the sugar production. Havana, Cuba's capital, became a gathering place for American and European tourists.

While foreign tourists enjoyed Havana's attractions, most Cubans endured terrible living conditions. As many as three-fourths of the rural population lived in huts made from palm trees. The majority of these dwellings lacked toilets, running water, and electricity. A majority of Cuba's children did not attend school.

A long series of military and political leaders culminated in the dictatorship of Fulgencio Batista. A former Army sergeant, Batista dominated Cuba from 1934 to 1959. He eliminated free elections, dissolved the Cuban Congress, and used the secret police to intimidate his critics.

◢ Turning Points in History

The Cuban Revolution Resentment against Batista grew among Cubans during the early 1950's. One of his most vocal critics was a young lawyer named Fidel Castro. Although the son of a wealthy sugar planter, Castro vowed to distribute Cuba's wealth more evenly. He also promised to reduce United States influence in Cuban affairs.

Fidel Castro led a revolution in Cuba.

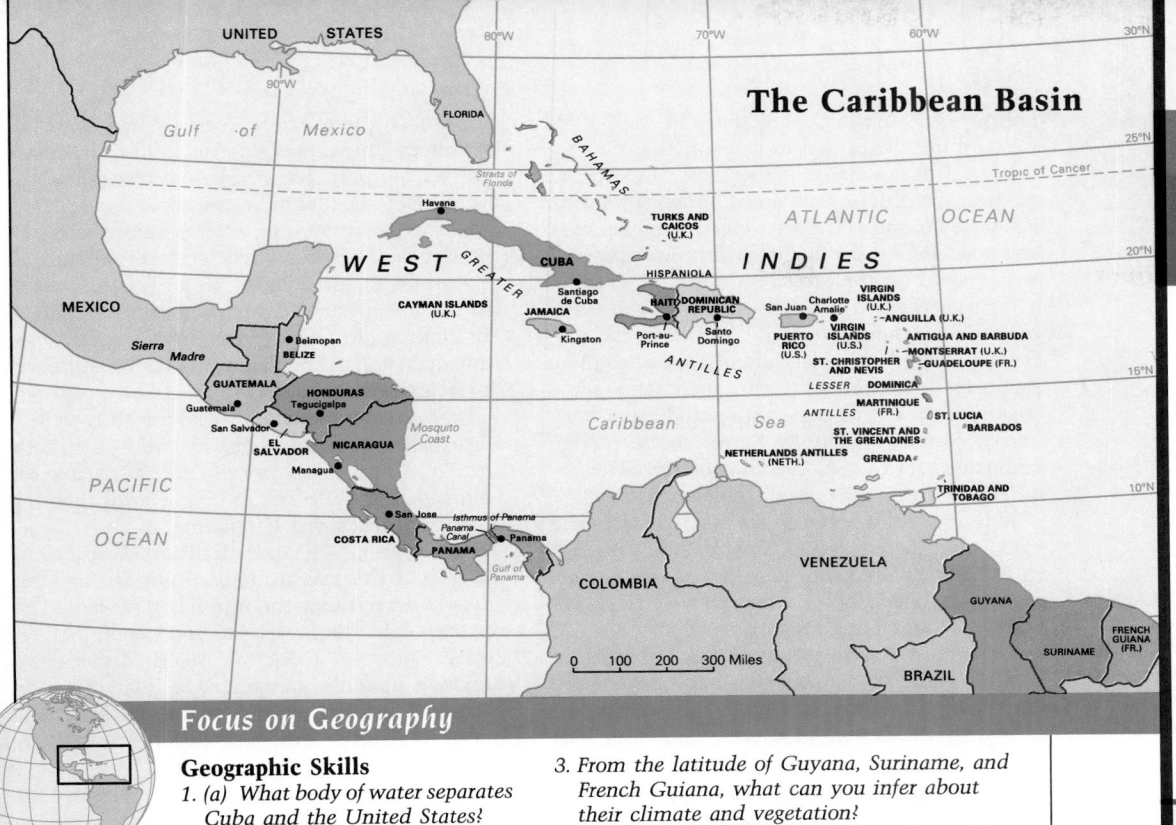

The Caribbean Basin

Focus on Geography

Geographic Skills

1. *(a)* *What body of water separates Cuba and the United States?*
   (b) *What is the approximate distance between them?*
2. *What two nations are located on the island of Hispaniola?*
3. *From the latitude of Guyana, Suriname, and French Guiana, what can you infer about their climate and vegetation?*
4. *What two countries share a boundary with Panama?*

Geographic Theme: Region

5. *Identify and explain three characteristics that make the Caribbean Basin a region.*

On July 26, 1953, Castro and about 165 followers launched a surprise attack on an army barracks. They hoped to seize weapons and ignite a popular uprising against Batista. The attack failed, however, and half of Castro's band of revolutionaries was killed, wounded, or arrested. The judges ignored Castro's passionate defense and sentenced him to 15 years in prison.

The failure of Castro's revolt convinced Batista that his power was secure. In May 1955, he confidently released Castro and other political prisoners. Still determined to overthrow Batista, Castro fled to Mexico, where he soon organized a new group of rebels.

In December 1956, Castro's revolutionaries returned to Cuba. His tiny army of 82 men landed on the southeastern tip of Cuba. All but

a dozen were soon killed or captured by Batista's forces. Castro and the survivors fled into the nearby Sierra Maestra. From a guerrilla base in the mountains, Castro persuaded the local peasants to support his cause. He promised to improve their lives by redistributing land and building more hospitals and schools.

Castro's guerrilla army gradually grew in size and strength. As his forces launched increasingly bold hit-and-run raids on government targets, Batista's support began to collapse. On January 1, 1959, the defeated dictator boarded a plane and fled to the Dominican Republic. One week later Castro triumphantly entered Havana.

Castro's shift to communism At first, many people throughout the Western Hemisphere praised Castro for bringing democracy to Cuba.

815

ANSWERS TO

Focus on Geography

1. **(a)** Straits of Florida
(b) about 100 miles
2. Haiti, Dominican Republic
3. hot, wet climate; tropical vegetation
4. Costa Rica, Colombia
5. The countries of the Caribbean Basin share a tropical climate, a heritage that includes a blend of Native American, African, Spanish, and other European cultures, and similar economies focusing on single cash crops.

■ BACKGROUND

When Castro's forces took control in January 1959 they were fewer than 1,000 in number.

Many supporters of Batista fled to Miami after the revolution. There they built a prosperous community.

Arrange students in small groups and assign each group one of the nations of the Caribbean Basin not covered in the text. Refer students to encyclopedias, almanacs, travel guides, or other references to find out the following information: location, size (area), population, literacy rate, population growth rate, geographic features, natural resources, major products, exports and imports, foreign debt, and type of government. Then have each group appoint members to serve as its country's cabinet. Cabinets may include ministers of trade, education, health, natural resources, finance, etc. Each minister should design a plan outlining one-year and five-year goals for his or her area of expertise. Plans should also include suggestions on how to achieve these goals. Cabinet members should present their plans to the group. Finally, the group as a whole should design a comprehensive plan for its country. Have each group present part or all of its plan to the class for discussion.

During a trip to the United States in April 1959, Castro himself seemed to confirm these hopes.

Instead of building a democracy, however, he suspended elections and named himself president. People who opposed him were jailed, executed, or forced into exile. Tight government controls were placed on the press.

Castro began to nationalize the Cuban economy. Under the Agrarian Reform Law, the government seized large plantations and turned them into peasant communes. Castro then nationalized sugar mills, oil refineries, mines and other businesses owned by United States or by foreign companies. President Eisenhower retaliated by ordering an embargo on all trade with Cuba.

While relations between the United States and Cuba were deteriorating, Castro boldly turned to the Soviet Union for assistance. The Soviets eagerly responded by agreeing to buy Cuban sugar while also supplying modern weapons.

Importance Castro's revolution marked a turning point by launching a radical program that changed Cuba's economy and society. Its link with the Soviet bloc also made Cuba an issue in the growing Cold War tensions.

Cuba reflected Cold War tensions.

Many Cubans believed that Castro had betrayed the revolution by refusing to hold elections and by embracing the Soviet Union. Throughout 1959 and 1960, thousands of people fled Cuba each month. Many settled in Miami, Florida.

Castro's policies angered President Eisenhower. In 1960, he approved a plan sponsored by the Central Intelligence Agency (CIA) to train and equip a small army of anti-Castro Cuban exiles. The plan called for them to invade Cuba, set up a rebel government, and overthrow Castro. Known as La Brigada, the anti-Castro army included about 1,400 men. Kennedy, who learned of the operation after becoming president, worried that this force was too large to remain a secret and too small to be successful. He reluctantly approved the plan.

The Bay of Pigs On April 17, 1961, La Brigada attempted to make a surprise landing at a remote beach on Cuba's southern coast called the Bay of Pigs. Their dream of overthrowing Castro soon turned into a nightmare. A Cuban army of 20,000 men, supported by tanks and aircraft, quickly

surrounded them. Since Kennedy had ruled out any direct United States participation, La Brigada received no help. Despite heroic resistance, the outnumbered exiles were forced to surrender.

Flushed with victory, Castro swiftly arrested thousands of suspected rebels, thus removing all opposition to his regime. While Castro consolidated his power, Kennedy's prestige declined. His failure to rescue La Brigada convinced Khrushchev that America would not resist further Soviet expansion.

The Cuban Missile Crisis In July 1962, Khrushchev secretly began to build 42 missile sites in Cuba. Each missile carried a nuclear warhead 20 to 30 times more powerful than the bomb that destroyed Hiroshima.

On October 14th, an American U-2 spy plane discovered the missile sites. Kennedy and his advisers agreed that the missiles represented an unacceptable threat to America's national security. After a week of secret discussions, Kennedy publicly announced a quarantine, or blockade, of Cuba to prevent the arrival of new missiles. He also demanded that the Soviets remove the missiles already in Cuba.

Kennedy's dramatic announcement alarmed the nation and the world. When Khrushchev denounced the blockade, the two superpowers seemed to be on a collision course. As tensions mounted, nearly a quarter-million troops assembled in Florida to invade Cuba.

The first break in the crisis occurred when Soviet ships suddenly halted to avoid a confrontation with United States warships at sea. A few days later Khrushchev offered to withdraw his missiles if the United States pledged it would not invade Cuba. Kennedy accepted the offer, thus ending the crisis.

Castro faced a bleak future.

The Cuban Missile Crisis left Castro heavily dependent upon Soviet support. Between 1961 and 1989, the Soviets provided Cuba with more than $60 billion in economic aid. By 1989, the Soviet Union supplied more than three-fourths of Cuba's imports and all of its oil.

Soviet aid came to an abrupt end following the August Coup in 1991 (pages 850–851). The loss dealt a crippling blow to the Cuban economy. Strict rationing limited motorists to just 15 gallons of gasoline a month. Shoppers waited in long lines for scarce rations of milk, bread, and eggs.

Faced with the threat of economic collapse, Castro defiantly refused to adopt economic reforms or give up any power. He instead turned to the police to stifle opposition. But this tactic can only delay his regime's inevitable collapse.

Puerto Rico became a commonwealth.

Puerto Rico lies east of Cuba in the Caribbean. It became a United States possession after the Spanish-American War. At first, the United States ruled Puerto Rico directly. In 1952, however, the United States Congress made the island a self-governing commonwealth.

Puerto Ricans are United States citizens. The island enjoys broad powers of self-government, although Congress holds final authority. Island residents cannot vote in presidential elections.

Puerto Rico's relationship with the United States remains controversial. Many Puerto Ricans want to improve their commonwealth status. Other views range from those who favor complete independence to those who support statehood.

Haiti's Jean-Bertrand Aristide was exiled by a military junta in 1991.

Haiti struggled to gain democracy.

Haiti is located on the western third of the island of Hispaniola. As you have read (page 536), in 1804 it became a republic by rebelling against Napoleon. From 1843 to 1915, a succession of 22 dictators ruled Haiti. United States Marines occupied Haiti from 1915 to 1934.

In 1957, François "Papa Doc" Duvalier seized power and began a new era of dictatorial rule. A secret police force known as the *Tontons Macoutes* used terror and torture to ensure obedience and silence critics. When Papa Doc died in 1971, his son Jean-Claude "Baby Doc" Duvalier became president. Baby Doc lived a life of luxury in the poorest country in the Western Hemisphere. Many Haitians fled to other Caribbean countries and to the United States.

Haiti's long-suffering citizens finally overthrew Baby Doc in early 1986. After almost five years of political turmoil, Haitians held their first truly democratic elections in December 1990. The voters elected as president a popular Roman Catholic priest named Jean-Bertrand Aristide.

Aristide was an outspoken supporter of a doctrine known as **liberation theology.** This doctrine stresses that the church has a moral obligation to improve the plight of the poor. Although Aristide enjoyed great popularity, his policies angered the wealthy and the army. On September 30, 1991, a military junta seized power and exiled Aristide. Although hard-hit by an American-led trade embargo, the junta refused to permit Aristide's return.

Changes swept Central America.

The seven nations in Central America share many common characteristics. Like other countries in the Caribbean Basin, they have been influenced by United States investment, trade, and military intervention. In addition, their economies have all been dominated by cash crops. The growth of huge coffee and banana plantations produced a small class of wealthy landowners and millions of poor and oppressed peasants. This situation has made the region a battleground.

Panama The United States has played a major role in Panama's affairs. As you have seen (pages 588–589), the United States helped Panama win its independence and then built the Panama

817

■ BACKGROUND
After Puerto Rico achieved commonwealth status, thousands of Puerto Ricans flocked to New York and other mainland cities. Since 1974, however, there has been a reverse migration, with many Puerto Ricans returning to their island.

■ BACKGROUND

The Somoza family fortune—one of the largest in Latin America—included almost 20 percent of Nicaragua's cultivable land.

Canal. A treaty signed in 1903 gave the United States virtual sovereignty over the 530-square-mile Canal Zone. Panamanians welcomed the Canal's economic benefits but resented foreign control.

A long dispute over the Canal dominated relations between the two countries. In 1964, after violent riots in the Canal Zone, Panama briefly broke off diplomatic relations with Washington. Four years later Panama's new strongman, General Omar Torrijos (toh-**REE**-hohs), pledged to negotiate a new Panama Canal treaty.

After a lengthy debate, the United States Senate in 1978 ratified two new Panama Canal treaties. The United States agreed to transfer full control over the Canal to Panama on December 31, 1999, but retained the right to defend the Canal against any threat.

The new relationship between the United States and Panama did not last long. A new strongman—General Manuel Noriega—seized power. Noriega proved to be a brutal and corrupt dictator. In February 1988, a federal grand jury in Miami indicted him on drug-trafficking charges. When Noriega refused to yield power to civilian authorities, the United States broke diplomatic relations with his regime and also imposed strict controls on trade.

Tensions between the two countries continued to mount throughout 1989. In May of that year, Noriega agreed to hold national elections. He annulled the results, however, when his democratic opponents, led by Guillermo Endara, won an overwhelming majority. Noriega then appointed himself Panama's "Maximum Leader" and on December 15 declared a state of war with the United States. The next day Panamanian soldiers killed an off-duty United States marine.

President Bush believed that these provocations created an intolerable situation. On December 20, 1989, he ordered more than 10,000 United States troops to invade Panama. The invasion was designed to protect American citizens, bring Noriega to justice, and assist in restoring a democratic government. The troops quickly crushed Noriega's forces.

Both Americans and Panamanians hoped that Noriega's defeat would pave the way for a new era of cooperation between their countries. The United States ended trade sanctions and recognized Endara as president.

Nicaragua Like Panama, Nicaragua has had a long history of United States involvement in its affairs. In 1912, President Taft ordered United States Marines to occupy Nicaragua as part of an effort to create a more stable government. When the Marines left in 1933, the leader of the American-trained National Guard, General Anastasio Somoza (soh-**MOH**-sah), gained power.

The Somozas ruled Nicaragua for the next 46 years. They rigged elections and assassinated political opponents. For example, in 1978 government assassins gunned down Pedro Joaquin Chamorro, a crusading newspaper publisher and leading critic of the Somoza regime.

The assassination of Chamorro sparked a popular revolution against the Somoza government.

DAILY LIFE ▸ *The Latin Beat*

Latin American music, which combines elements from the region's different cultures, has become a major influence around the world. As early as the 1920's, Argentina's tango swept the international scene. It was followed in the 1940's by Caribbean rumba and calypso music. The Brazilian form of jazz known as bossa nova became an international hit in the 1960's. Most recently, the Jamaican musical form known as reggae has gained worldwide attention. All of these musical styles share such characteristics as a primary tune, contrasting harmonies, syncopation, and strong rhythmic patterns. Most are played on instruments traditional in Latin culture—the guitar, flute, marimba, rhythm sticks, and many different kinds of drums.

On February 25, 1990, the Nicaraguan people elected Violeta Chamorro their nation's new president. In her victory speech, Chamorro explained her goals and ideals for Nicaragua.

I want to congratulate all Nicaraguans because today is everyone's triumph. We have shown the world an example of civic duty, demonstrating that we Nicaraguans want to live in democracy, want to live in peace, and above all, that we want to live in liberty.

We have obtained the first democratic election in the history of this country. . . . Now I will honor my commitment to achieve national reconciliation because this is the only way we will be able to have peace and economic well-being.

This is the first election in our history won by the opposition. . . . This is an election that will never have exiles or political prisoners or confiscations. . . . I want to say to you that today we must all congratulate each other with a fraternal embrace because Nicaragua will again be a republic.

1. What did the election demonstrate to the world?
2. Why was this election a turning point for Nicaragua?

The rebels formed a broad-based group known as the Sandinista National Liberation Front (FALN). The Sandinistas took their name from Augusto César Sandino, a popular rebel killed by the National Guard in 1934.

The Sandinistas in 1979 overthrew Anastasio Somoza Debayle (General Somoza's younger son) after a bloody civil war that claimed 50,000 lives. Once in power, the Sandinistas launched a program that included land distribution and the nationalization of key industries. Led by Daniel Ortega, the Sandinista government asked for military aid from Cuba and the Soviet Union.

As cricitism of his government grew, Ortega suspended elections and placed strict controls over the press. Rebel groups calling themselves Contras (from the Spanish word for against) began to fight the Sandinistas. The Contras included many Nicaraguans who had opposed Somoza but did not want him replaced by a new dictator. The Reagan administration sent aid to the Contras and imposed a strict embargo.

The long civil war and the trade embargo had a devastating impact on Nicaraguan life. As many as 30,000 people died in the fighting. The economy neared collapse as inflation reached 1,700 percent a year. In 1987, Costa Rican President Oscar Arias Sanchez persuaded Ortega to accept a peace plan calling for a cease-fire, an end to outside aid to the Contras, and democratic reforms.

Ortega agreed to hold free elections on February 25, 1990. An opposing group known as the National Opposition Union (UNO) supported Violeta Chamorro, widow of the publisher assassinated in 1978. Mrs. Chamorro pledged to support human rights and democratic reform. She stunned the world by easily defeating Ortega. Chamorro became president in the first democratic transfer of power in Nicaraguan history.

Section REVIEW 3

Define: liberation theology
Identify: (a) Platt Amendment, (b) Fulgencio Batista, (c) Fidel Castro, (d) La Brigada, (e) Jean-Claude Duvalier, (f) Jean-Bertrand Aristide, (g) Omar Torrijos, (h) Manuel Noriega, (i) Pedro Joaquin Chamorro, (j) Sandinistas, (k) Anastasio Somoza Debayle, (l) Daniel Ortega, (m) Contras, (n) Violeta Chamorro

819

ANSWERS TO

Voice from Our Time

1. that Nicaraguans wanted a democratic government
2. It was the first democratic election in Nicaragua's history.

ANSWERS TO

Section Review 3

Define:
doctrine that church has moral obligation to use political action to improve plight of the poor
Identify:
(a) document that gave the U.S. the right to use military force to intervene in Cuban affairs **(b)** dictator of Cuba from 1934 to 1959 **(c)** revolutionary leader who overthrew Batista **(d)** small army of anti-Castro Cuban exiles sponsored by the CIA **(e)** dictator of Haiti from 1971 to 1986 **(f)** first freely elected president of Haiti **(g)** strongman of Panama who died in 1981 **(h)** dictator of Panama from 1981 to 1989 **(i)** critic of Somoza regime who was assassinated in 1978 **(j)** rebels who overthrew Somozas and took over government **(k)** son of General Somoza, overthrown in 1979 **(l)** leader of Sandinista government **(m)** rebels who fought Sandinista government with help from U.S. **(n)** first democratically elected president of Nicaragua
(continued)

ANSWERS TO (continued)

Answer:

1. (a) nations of Central America, Caribbean islands, and Suriname, Guyana, and French Guiana (b) tropical climate; heritage that includes blend of Native American, African, Spanish, and other European cultures; single cash crop economies; governments often controlled by corrupt rulers

2. (a) to distribute Cuba's wealth more evenly and to reduce U.S. influence in Cuban affairs (b) named himself president, suspended elections, nationalized economy, joined Soviet bloc, made Cuba Communist

3. Castro arrested suspected opponents of his regime, and Kennedy's prestige declined. The Soviet Union became convinced that the U.S. would not resist further Soviet expansion.

4. Soviet Union withdrew missiles in exchange for U.S. pledge not to invade Cuba.

5. (a) to protect American citizens, bring Noriega to justice, restore democratic government (b) previously elected candidate Endara became president

6. first democratic election in Nicaraguan history; reform candidate won

7. (a) Cuba remained communist, heavily dependent on Soviet economic aid, while other Caribbean nations moved toward democracy and economic stability (b) Answers will vary.

ANSWERS TO
Reading a Graph

U.S. investment abroad; foreign investment in U.S.

Answer:
1. (a) What lands make up the Caribbean Basin? (b) What are three characteristics that these lands have in common?
2. (a) What objectives did Castro set for his revolution? (b) What did he actually do?
3. What were the outcomes of the Bay of Pigs invasion?
4. How was the Cuban Missile Crisis resolved?
5. (a) Why did Bush decide to invade Panama? (b) To what extent did he achieve these goals?
6. In what various ways was the Nicaragua election of February 1990 important?

Critical Thinking
7. (a) In what ways is Cuba isolated from key trends in the Caribbean? (b) Do you think the Castro government can survive? Explain.

The United States and Canada changed. 4

Only two nations—the United States and Canada—make up northern North America. The people of these countries are primarily English-speaking. Both countries were industrialized early. Both are rich in land and resources and have supported a very high standard of living. Finally, after World War II, both nations entered a period of rapid economic growth.

The United States enjoyed prosperity.

The United States emerged from World War II as the richest and most powerful nation in the world. It had escaped the devastation that World War II had brought to Great Britain, Germany, Russia, Japan, and other countries. By supplying goods to countries rebuilding after the war, the United States developed a huge foreign trade.

There was innovation as well as wealth in postwar America. Most of the major scientific breakthroughs of the 1950's and 1960's came out of United States laboratories and factories. This technological superiority—along with the billions of dollars of capital available through American banks—enabled American companies to play dominant roles in the world economy.

820

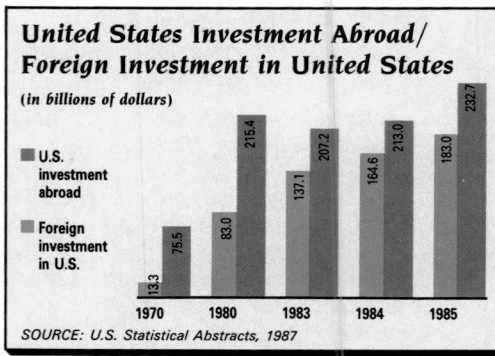

United States Investment Abroad / Foreign Investment in United States
(in billions of dollars)

- U.S. investment abroad
- Foreign investment in U.S.

	1970	1980	1983	1984	1985
U.S. investment abroad	75.5	215.4	207.2	213.0	232.7
Foreign investment in U.S.	13.3	83.0	137.1	164.6	183.0

SOURCE: U.S. Statistical Abstracts, 1987

Reading a graph Which investment was greater for the years 1970 to 1985? Which increased more from 1970 to 1985?

As communications and transportation methods improved, companies such as Ford, Coca Cola, and International Business Machines (IBM) became **multinational corporations,** operating in many countries. Often they had more resources and influence in international affairs than many small countries.

The postwar era brought changes.

American society changed in a variety of ways after the war. A baby boom brought very rapid population growth. The middle class—always larger than in Europe—continued to expand.

Even in this enormously rich country, however, there were still millions of people who did not share in the postwar prosperity. Appalachia, where the coal mines had given out, had no jobs and people lived in extreme poverty. People in the inner cities also faced hardships as businesses and jobs moved to the suburbs.

The civil rights movement Among those who did not share in the new prosperity were most African Americans. For them, prejudice limited the opportunities for education and jobs. In many parts of the country, they were treated as social inferiors and even denied the full rights of citizens, or **civil rights.**

A major change came in 1954, when the Supreme Court, in the case *Brown v. Board of Education of Topeka,* ruled that schools separated by race were illegal. Change was slow, however, and often there was resistance to it. The real pressure for change came from African

Americans themselves, under the leadership of Dr. Martin Luther King, Jr., an Atlanta minister. Dr. King followed the strategy of nonviolent protest used by Gandhi in India.

That method slowly became effective. The 1964 Civil Rights Act, which outlawed discrimination and supported equal opportunity, ended the old system of segregation.

Sometimes violence did occur. Dr. King himself was assassinated in April 1968. The passage of civil-rights laws did not completely end prejudice and racism. Nonetheless, by 1970, many minorities had taken significant steps toward full equality as citizens of the United States.

The movement for women's rights Closely related to the civil-rights movement was the quest for equal rights for women. During the 1960's and 1970's, many women sought to enter the work force. There they often encountered discrimination in employment and salary.

By the end of the 1980's, women could point to significant changes in law and the attitudes of society. Sandra Day O'Connor had become the first woman justice on the Supreme Court of the United States, and several states had had women governors. Setbacks too had occurred.

Dr. King emphasized traditional civic values to create a moral force against segregation.

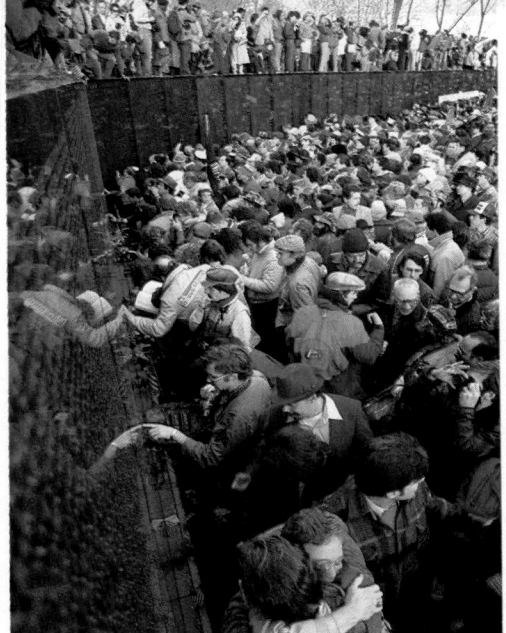

The Vietnam War Memorial lists all the soldiers who died in combat. At its dedication, people searched for the names of friends and relatives.

The Equal Rights Amendment (ERA), a proposed amendment to the constitution banning discrimination against women, was not approved by enough states to become law.

The Vietnam War Another issue of public concern during the 1960's was the Vietnam War (see Chaper 33). At first about 82 percent of the people in the United States approved intervention. By 1971, public opinion had reversed itself. Opposition to the war came to a head in 1969 when 200,000 protesters marched on Washington. At the same time, many other people considered the protesters unpatriotic. The raising of the Vietnam Memorial in Washington in 1982 symbolized the end of differences over the war.

The United States' role changed.

The Vietnam War marked a turning point for the United States. The war had raised questions about the role of the United States in world affairs. It also forced the nation to recognize that military strength would not always prevail.

The economic dominance of the United States also began to change after 1970. By then, the countries of Europe and Asia had recovered from the effects of World War II. Their own industrial

821

SECTION 4
Objectives and Teaching Strategies

OBJECTIVE 1. Describe social changes in the United States and their link to postwar prosperity.

Teaching Strategy: *Skill Building: Making Generalizations* (page 806e)

OBJECTIVE 2. Evaluate the effects of the 1988 free trade agreement between the United States and Canada.

Teaching Strategy: *Economics and History: The Free Trade Accord* (page 806e)

■ BACKGROUND

Despite many gains, the average woman's wage remained far below the average man's wage. In 1981, for example, wives who worked full time averaged $13,700 per year while their husbands averaged $23,800.

One measure of the wealth of the United States is its gross national product, which was $200 billion in 1945, $500 billion in 1960, and more than $5 trillion in 1989.

SECTION 4
Resources

GEOGRAPHY
■ Transparencies 107, 118

REINFORCEMENT
■ Independent Practice 35.4

ENRICHMENT
■ Voices from the Past 35.4

ASSESSMENT
■ Section Quiz 35.4

■ **BACKGROUND**

In 1950 the United States produced 70 percent of all the cars, trucks, and buses in the world. By 1985 its share of the world market had been cut in half.

■ **DISCUSSION**

What historical factors account for the strong French influence in Quebec?

■ **BACKGROUND**

The Official Languages Act of 1969 declares that the English and French languages are equal in status throughout Canada, thereby requiring all federal officials and institutions to be bilingual.

ANSWERS TO

Section Review 4

Define:
(a) company that operates in many countries (b) the full rights of citizens (c) shortfall in revenue (d) declining business activity and rising unemployment (e) separation of a province from the nation (f) general vote on the legislative act

Identify:
(a) black minister who used nonviolent protest to work for civil rights (b) 1954 Supreme Court ruling that educating blacks and whites in separate schools was illegal (c) fight for full citizens' rights for blacks (d) first woman justice on the Supreme Court (e) failed

(continued)

products could now compete favorably in world markets with those of the United States. Foreign companies even began to expand within the United States itself. One effect of these changes was an increasing **deficit,** or shortfall in revenue, in the United States balance of payments as imports exceeded exports. Another concern was a federal deficit that increased as government spending continued to exceed income. This deficit, along with the trade deficit, caused concern about the nation's economy.

Nonetheless, the nation's economy appeared to be strong. Employment levels remained high, and the economy enjoyed steady growth. Two factors—innovation and incentive—were important aspects of the economy. New advances in technology held out hope for increased productivity and future growth.

In 1990, concern about the economy increased as economic activity slowed. By January 1991, the government recognized that the nation was entering a period of **recession,** with declining business activity and rising unemployment.

Canada enjoyed peace and prosperity.

Since World War II, Canada has played an active role on the world stage. A founding member of the United Nations, it has several times sent troops to serve with UN peacekeeping forces. Although Canada changed from a dominion to an independent nation in 1982, it remains a member of Britain's Commonwealth of Nations.

Economic independence Canada's economy has long had close links with that of the United States. Its rich mineral and agricultural resources are now matched by growth in industry and trade,

Decisions in History

The question of Quebec separatism has long loomed as a threat to Canadian unity. In 1987, the Canadian government proposed a compromise plan, the Meech Lake Accord, giving the province of Quebec special status within Canada. The plan, however, required approval by the legislatures of all ten Canadian provinces. Many Canadians felt that any proposal giving special privileges to one province was unfair to other provinces. Those who supported the proposal felt that recognition of Quebec's important minority group was essential to preserve Canada's unity as a nation. If you were a provincial legislator, how would you vote on the Meech Lake Accord and why?

822

including its booming trade with other nations of the Pacific Rim. In 1988, Canada and the United States made a free trade agreement that links their economies even more closely. While encouraging trade, this agreement will also make the two nations more competitive with Europe's Common Market and the East Asian nations.

Separatism in Quebec In Canada, the national government holds only limited power over the various provinces. Thus, disputes between the national and provincial governments are common. After 1970, the status of the province of Quebec—whose citizens are primarily French in origin and culture—posed a particularly difficult problem. As a minority within the nation, the *Quebecois* felt discriminated against in terms of jobs, political power, and social status.

Many *Quebecois* believed in **separatism,** or separation from Canada. During the 1970's, more and more French-Canadians gave their support to Rene Levesque's Parti Quebecois (PQ). Levesque was elected prime minister of Quebec in 1976. Upon taking office, Levesque made French the sole official language of the province. He also planned a **referendum,** or general vote on a legislative act, concerning independence for Quebec.

Meanwhile the Canadian government tried to accommodate nationalist sentiment among French Canadians. These efforts at conciliation seemed to pay off. In a 1980 referendum on Quebec's future, 59 percent voted in favor of the province's remaining part of Canada.

The separatist movement revived again after 1987, when the federal government proposed the Meech Lake Accord. This accord provided constitutional protection for the special status of Quebec. In 1990, the accord ended when two provinces failed to approve it. A second effort, the Charlottetown Accord, was rejected by voters in October 1992.

Section REVIEW 4

Define: (a) multinational corporation, (b) civil rights, (c) deficit, (d) recession (e) separatism, (f) referendum
Identify: (a) Martin Luther King, Jr., (b) *Brown* v. *Board of Education,* (c) civil rights movement, (d) Sandra Day O'Connor, (e) Meech Lake and Charlottetown accords

The United States and Canada

KEY
- ⊛ National capital
- — National boundary
- ★ State or provincial capital
- — State or provincial boundary

0 —— 500 Miles

0 —— 100 Miles

PACIFIC OCEAN

HAWAII (U.S.)

Map Study

What Canadian provinces or territories do not border the United States?

Answer:

1. What factors explain the rapid growth of the American economy after World War II?
2. What social issues dominated American life in the postwar period?
3. How did the role of the United States in world affairs begin to change after 1970?

4. How did Canada's political relationship with Great Britain change during the postwar era?
5. Why was the status of Quebec as part of Canada a matter of debate during this period?

Critical Thinking

6. What problems did minorities face in the United States and Canada during this period?

823

Northwest Territories, Newfoundland, Nova Scotia, Prince Edward Island

ANSWERS TO *(continued)*

attempts to provide constitutional protection for the special status of Quebec

Answer:

1. lack of wartime destruction, supplying goods to rebuild, growth of foreign trade, technological superiority, availability of capital
2. civil rights movement, women's rights movement, Vietnam War
3. U.S. began to lose some of its political and economic power.
4. Canada became an independent nation in 1982, but it remains a member of Britain's Commonwealth of Nations.
5. people of Quebec felt discriminated against, wanted to separate from Canada to preserve French heritage
6. U.S.: prejudice, limited opportunities for education and jobs, denial of civil rights, segregation; Canada: discrimination in terms of jobs, political power, and social status

Concluding the Chapter

1. **Chapter Closer**
   Ask students to name the regions they would cross if they traveled the length of the Pan-American Highway, and to identify some political and economic characteristics of the countries they would see.

2. **Reteaching Activities**
   a. Explaining Main Ideas
   Ask students to explain how overpopulation and foreign debts have affected Latin American economies.
   b. Recalling Information
   Ask students to recall the causes and results of the Cuban Revolution and the Nicaraguan conflict.

Answers to Chapter Review appear on page 806f.

Summary

1. Key trends influenced Latin America. The postwar era brought problems of political, economic, and social instability to Latin America. Economic problems such as debt and explosive population growth confronted many countries. The United States and Latin America have cooperated in fighting the drug trade. Migration from Latin America to the United States has increased greatly in the past decade.

2. Nations sought greater stability. Dictators and military strongmen ruled Argentina in much of the postwar era. The Falklands War, in which Britain defeated Argentina, ended military oppression. Military rulers also dominated Brazil and sought prosperity through foreign loans for development. Although more stable, Mexico lived under one-party rule and foreign debt.

3. The Caribbean Basin experienced political turmoil. In 1959, Castro led a revolution against Batista. Castro promised a democratic revolution but became a dictator allied with the USSR. In the Cuban missile crisis, the United States forced the USSR to withdraw its missiles from Cuba. Puerto Rico is a stable self-governing commonwealth. Central America saw the end of Noriega's rule in Panama and greater democracy in Nicaragua.

4. Postwar changes affected the United States and Canada. Foreign trade and new technology aided postwar prosperity in the United States. Social issues included the civil rights and women's rights movements and concern over the Vietnam War. Reassessment began for the nation's foreign role, budget and trade deficits, and possible recession. Canada enjoyed prosperity and new independence but was threatened by separatism.

Reviewing the Facts

1. Define the following terms:
   a. urbanization
   b. civil rights
   c. separatism
   d. referendum

2. Explain the importance of each of the following names, places, or terms:
   a. Juan Perón
   b. Falkland Islands
   c. General Augusto Pinochet
   d. Carlos Salinas de Gortari
   e. Fulgencio Batista
   f. Fidel Castro
   g. Anastasio Somoza
   h. Sandinistas
   i. Contras
   j. Daniel Ortega
   k. Violeta Chamorro
   l. Manuel Noriega
   m. Dr. Martin Luther King, Jr.

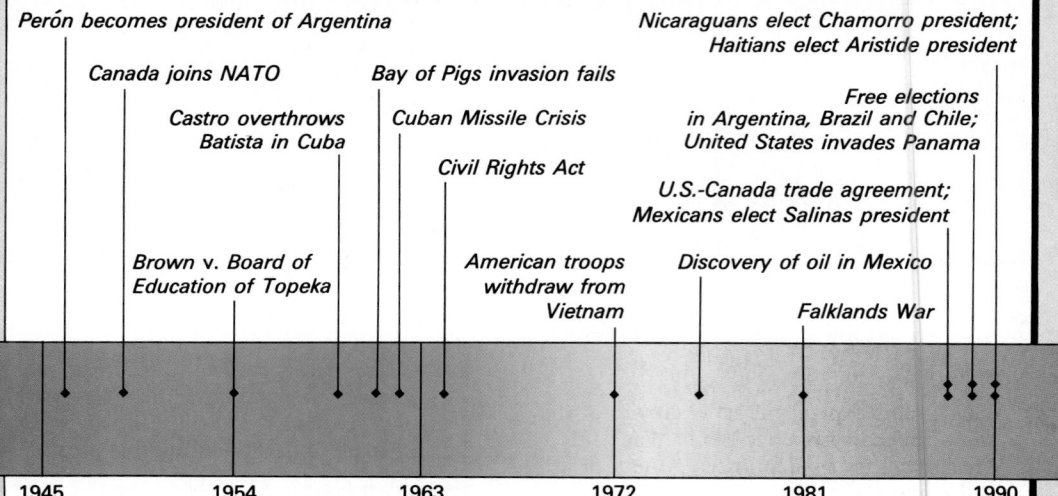

Perón becomes president of Argentina

Canada joins NATO

Castro overthrows Batista in Cuba

Brown v. Board of Education of Topeka

Bay of Pigs invasion fails

Cuban Missile Crisis

Civil Rights Act

American troops withdraw from Vietnam

Nicaraguans elect Chamorro president; Haitians elect Aristide president

Free elections in Argentina, Brazil and Chile; United States invades Panama

U.S.-Canada trade agreement; Mexicans elect Salinas president

Discovery of oil in Mexico

Falklands War

1945   1954   1963   1972   1981   1990

824

3. What are two current population trends in Latin America?
4. Why was economic development both a benefit and a problem in many Latin American nations?
5. How has rural poverty in Mexico affected relations with the United States?
6. How did the United States maintain control over Cuba after it gained its independence?
7. (a) How did the Sandinistas come to power in Nicaragua? (b) What changes did their government make? (c) Why did the United States support their opponents?
8. (a) After World War II, how did the economic role of the United States change? (b) How did society change?

Basic Skills

1. **Reading a map** (a) Using the map of Latin America on page 808, list the countries located mainly within the tropics and those located mainly outside the tropics. (b) What does this information tell you about the kinds of foods, crops, and raw materials produced in Latin America?
2. **Making a chart** (a) From the 1950's through the 1970's, three issues stirred controversy in United States society: the civil-rights movement, the women's movement, and the Vietnam War. Make a chart, using those topics for the horizontal headings. For the vertical column, use the headings *Issue, Arguments Pro, Arguments Con,* and *Outcomes.* (b) How did the outcomes of each issue affect society?

Researching and Reporting Skills

1. **Identifying sources with opposing viewpoints** Choose a current controversial issue relating to Central America and read about it in two different newspapers. If possible, also consult a magazine likely to present a Latin American viewpoint. To what extent do these three sources agree or disagree concerning the issue?
2. **Using regional publications** Skim several issues of *Americas,* the magazine about Latin America published by the Organization of American States. This publication often features information on Latin American writers or artists and their works. Note what different countries and ethnic groups are represented.

Critical Thinking

1. **Solving problems** Lack of representative and democratic governments is still a problem in Latin America. (a) What have been major reasons for this situation? (b) What recent progress have several countries made in solving this problem?
2. **Synthesizing** One of the advantages of industrialization is that it provides employment. Why then is the growth of industry so important to Latin America?
3. **Analyzing** What factors have contributed to instability in some countries of the Caribbean and Central America?
4. **Identifying cause and effect** What various conditions in Latin America have caused people to become refugees? Give examples.
5. **Analyzing economics** (a) What were the main reasons for the United States' becoming a global economic power after World War II? (b) What were the economic effects for the United States at home and abroad?
6. **Interpreting a concept** (a) What are the reasons for the deficit in the United States balance of payments? (b) What is the significance of the deficit in terms of United States foreign trade?
7. **Analyzing** Since World War II, Canada has assumed a more active and independent role in world affairs. What factors may have contributed to this new role?
8. **Inferring** (a) Why did the United States and Canada make such a strong trade agreement? (b) What changes may result?

Perspectives on Past and Present

The Monroe Doctrine marked the start of United States involvement in Latin America. What stages have occurred in that involvement? What are the current trends in United States policy toward that region?

Investigating History

In the past 50 years, Latin American writers have made a significant contribution to world literature. Among these writers are Gabriela Mistral, Pablo Neruda, Gabriel Márquez, Miguel Asturias, Carlos Fuentes, Octavio Paz, Mario Vargas Llosa, and Jorge Luis Borges. Read selections from the works of one or more of these authors. What viewpoints are expressed?

825

CHAPTER
Evaluation

Chapter Test 35, Alternate Chapter Test 35, and Computer Test Bank Chapter 35 Test can be used to evaluate your students' understanding of this chapter.

ANSWERS TO
Geographic Theme

1. (a) Australia, China, and Taiwan **(b)** U.S., Soviet Union, and Japan

2. (a) Singapore, South Korea, and Taiwan **(b)** China, Canada, and the U.S. **(c)** Singapore, South Korea, and Taiwan **(d)** China, U.S., and Soviet Union

3. That it was economically very active as a region, with a strongly rising GNP and per capita GNP. The nations of East Asia were doing particularly well.

Geographic Theme: Region

What dynamic new region became a major factor in the world economy during the late twentieth century?

The Pacific Rim—an area comprised of the nations that border the Pacific Ocean—became a major new trading area in the late 1900's. As the Mediterranean once united the ancient world, so the Pacific linked the lands around it. While Rome alone dominated the Mediterranean, a number of powerful and less-powerful nations interacted across the vast Pacific.

That interaction was heavily based on economic development and trade. Both of those were in a period of rapid change. The economic powers—such as Japan, China, the United States, and Canada—found new opportunities in the region's growth. The small nations, though lacking political power, were industrialized and capable of advanced technology. They were thus able to produce and export goods that bring a high return. That income, in turn, could be invested to produce more wealth.

Not only trade but also banking and finance became important activities throughout the region.

The chart below shows the economic growth of Pacific Rim nations. Note the relative amount of growth in GNP and per capita income in the various countries. Clearly, this was a time of rapid change for the smaller countries. It was also a period of transition for long-industrialized countries. They faced competition in special areas of industry and technology where they had previously held the lead. Thus, they had to seek to develop new specialties and take greater advantage of their resources in order to maintain their own economic growth.

1. (a) Which three nations had the highest rate of population growth? **(b)** Which three had the least?
2. (a) Which three countries had the highest rate of increase in GNP? **(b)** Which three had the lowest? **(c)** Which three had the highest rate of growth in per capita GNP? **(d)** Which three had the lowest?
3. What conclusions about the Pacific Rim can you draw on the basis of this chart?

Nations of the Pacific Rim: Population and Economic Growth

NATION	POPULATION		GROSS NATIONAL PRODUCT (Billions of US Dollars)		PER CAPITA INCOME (US Dollars)	
	1970	1987 (est.)	1969*	mid-1980's	1969*	mid-1980's
Australia	12,522,400	16,200,000	30.4	166.2 (1983)	1,861	9,960 (1983)
Canada	21,400,000	25,900,000	78.5	335 (1985)	2,313	13,541 (1985)
China	759,600,000	1,062,000,000	80.0 (1966)	343 (1985)	100 (1966)	330 (1985)
Japan	103,500,000	122,200,000	168.0	1,233 (1984)	1,300	10,200 (1984)
Singapore	2,100,000	2,600,000	1.3 (1968)	18.4 (1984)	672 (1968)	7,270 (1984)
South Korea	32,100,000	42,100,000	8.0	90.6 (1986)	170 (1968)	2,180 (1986)
Taiwan	14,000,000	19,600,000	4.8	60 (1985)	373	3,142 (1983)
United States	207,678,247	243,800,000	931.4	4,206.1 (1986)	3,687	14,461 (1986)
U.S.S.R.	241,748,000	284,000,000	400.0 (1968)	2,062 (1985)	1,678 (1968)	7,896 (1985)

SOURCE: D. Phillips and S. Levi, The Pacific Rim Region, Enslow Publishers, Inc., 1988.

*Except as noted

Historical Themes

The twin processes of cooperation and conflict played a major role in shaping the postwar world. In addition, economic forces and ideas such as nationalism and Islamic fundamentalism had a powerful impact on world events.

Cooperation and Conflict

The Cold War between the United States and the Soviet Union dominated world affairs during the postwar era. It also led to the division of Europe into two rival blocs. In 1949, the United States, Canada, and ten Western European nations formed the North Atlantic Treaty Organization. The 12 members of NATO pledged military support to one another in case any member was attacked. The Soviet Union countered by organizing its Eastern European satellites into an alliance known as the Warsaw Pact. Although the two alliances did not come to blows, they had many tense confrontations.

The Cold War was not limited to Europe. The United States and the Soviet Union competed in a rivalry that ignited wars in Korea, Vietnam, and Nicaragua. The most dangerous confrontation occurred when President Kennedy refused to allow the Soviet Union to place nuclear missiles in Cuba. The Cuban missile crisis brought the world to the brink of nuclear war.

Although the Cold War dominated global affairs, regional and ethnic rivalries still caused serious conflicts. Age-old ethnic and religious disputes sparked civil wars in Africa and Northern Ireland. In the Middle East, a series of four Arab-Israeli wars left a legacy of hatred and destruction. Nonetheless, the Camp David Accords between Israel and Egypt offered a model for the use of cooperation to break the cycle of violence.

Impact of Ideas

The struggle between communism and democracy centered around a contest between contrasting ideologies. The Soviet Union called for a worldwide communist revolution based on one-party rule, the suppression of individual rights, and state ownership of property. In contrast, the United States supported a multiparty system, free elections, individual liberties, and private enterprise.

While the contest between these ideologies overshadowed international relations, nationalism remained a potent source of change. In 1947, both India and Pakistan won their independence from Great Britain. Nationalism played an especially important role in Africa. Between 1950 and 1970, 38 nations gained their independence from colonial rulers.

Nationalism also played an important role in the Middle East. In 1948, David Ben-Gurion announced the creation of an independent Israel. The ensuing Arab-Israeli wars left the Palestinians without a homeland. During the 1970's, Islamic fundamentalism also became an influential idea in the Middle East. It sought to resist Western culture and protect traditional Muslim values.

Economics and History

World War II left much of the world in ruins. As the only great power undamaged by the war, the United States used its great wealth to help rebuild Europe. The Marshall Plan revived the economies of Western Europe. In 1957, six Western European nations formed the European Economic Community, or Common Market. Within a short time, the Common Market became a major economic unit.

American aid also helped Japan recover from World War II. Japan's productive labor force, effective use of technology, and high rate of investment fueled remarkable economic growth. By the early 1990's, Japan was an economic superpower.

While Western Europe and Japan surged ahead, Africa and Latin America failed to experience sustained economic growth. Rising populations and continued reliance upon one-crop economies thwarted ambitious plans to modernize traditional economies. As a result, both regions lacked sufficient development to provide their people with an adequate standard of living.

Analyzing Historical Themes

1. How did the Cold War illustrate both cooperation and conflict?
2. What role did nationalism play in shaping postwar events?
3. What factors account for the postwar economic recovery in Western Europe and Japan?

827

ANSWERS TO

Analyzing Historical Themes

1. The Cold War brought cooperation among members within each of the rival blocs, while rivalry and confrontation between the U.S. and the Soviet Union led to conflicts throughout the world.

2. encouraged movements for independence in India, Pakistan, Africa, and the Middle East

3. Western Europe: U.S. helped rebuild, Marshall Plan revived economies, formation of Common Market fostered economic growth; Japan: U.S. aid, Japan's labor force, effective use of technology, and heavy investment stimulated economic growth.

UNIT Evaluation

Unit IX Test and Alternate Unit IX Test can be used to evaluate your students' understanding of this unit.

Earth viewed from space

	1982	1984	1986
Political and Governmental Life		**1985** Gorbachev leads USSR ▼	**1986** ▶ Aquino elected Philippine president
Economic and Technological Life	**1980's** Microchips aid electronic revolution		**1986** Nuclear disaster at Chernobyl
Social and Cultural Life		**1980's** AIDS memorial quilt 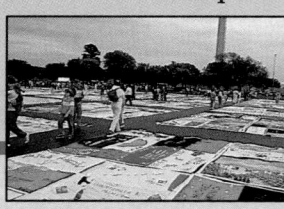	**1987** Intifada protests in Israel

Unit X

Perspectives on the Present

Historical Themes

Technology and History A new era in technology resulting from a revolution in electronics (television, computers, and telephone transmission of data) affected homes, businesses, and science.

Human-Environment Interaction Pollution caused by a population explosion and greatly increased use of fossil fuels threatens the global environment. Scientists seek ways to offset the damage done.

The Rise of Democratic Ideas The desire of people in Eastern Europe and the Soviet Union for greater freedom and rights caused a revolt against communism there as people turned to democracy.

Cooperation and Conflict As communism declined, people looked to a new era of peace and cooperation. Iraq's invasion of Kuwait in August 1990 led to a war in which Allied forces prevailed.

1988

1990

1992

1989
Eastern Europe
revolts

1989
China represses
democracy ▼

Saddam Hussein

1990
Germany is
unified

1990 ▶
Iraq invades
Kuwait

1990
Earth Day anniversary

1992–1993
Operation Restore
Hope in Somalia

1992
Common Market ends
internal trade barriers

1990 ▶
Mandela freed

1990
Nicaragua
holds free elections

1989
Baltic states
seek freedom

829

The Global Village

Chapter Overview

The Soviets launched the Space Age in 1957 when they orbited the first artificial satellite, *Sputnik*. Neil Armstrong's mission to the moon in 1969 was a dramatic technological and scientific achievement in the United States' space program. Since then the United States and the Soviet Union have launched space stations, unmanned probes to distant planets, and reusable space shuttles. Computers spread from research facilities to office and home use.

Technology changed patterns of work, but proved to be a double-edged sword. While it did improve the quality of everyday life, it also created long-term threats to the global environment. The greenhouse effect and ozone depletion pose serious problems that require international cooperation if people want the world to continue as a habitable place to live.

Science and technology have had an impact on the world community as a world culture has developed. Although science and technology have created a variety of problems in more industrialized societies, they have also increased people's awareness of problems associated with human rights.

Chapter Focus

Have students read the chapter introduction (pages 830–831), which discusses the celebration of Earth Day 1990. Ask students if they have ever participated in any of the Earth Day activities held in their city or neighborhood. New awareness of environmental issues has focused attention on global problems. Ask students to consider the many remarkable changes during the last 30 years that have led to this focus on globalism. Have them write down one or two words to complete this sentence: "We are living in an age of . . ." List students' answers on the board. Tell students that historians have suggested words such as "interdependence," "change," and "disruption" to describe this era. Ask students if they think these are appropriate names. This chapter discusses the major technological and scientific trends that have shaped our lives. It describes how the world has become more interdependent as people work together to find solutions for problems that now exist on a global level.

Chapter 36 The Global Village 1945–Present
FOCUS Global interdependence

★ **Advanced**
● **Basic**

	SECTION 1	SECTION 2	SECTION 3
Objectives	1. Identify major achievements of the Space Age and evaluate the impact of its technology on the world community. 2. Trace the development of super-computers and explain the significance of this new technology. 3. Describe recent developments in surgery.	1. Discuss the worldwide scope of modern business. 2. Identify the greenhouse effect and explain its consequences. 3. Identify the ozone layer and explain the consequences of ozone depletion.	1. Describe the impact of technology on culture. 2. Discuss the issue of human rights and describe worldwide attempts to address the issue.
Setting the Stage	Effects of technology on quality of life	The environmental impact of techno-logical change	The emergence of a global community
Teaching Strategies	Discussing History: The Space Age Relating Past to Present: Supercomputers Discussing History: Microsurgery Check for Understanding	Economics and History: Business on the International Stage Using Geographic Themes: Human-Environment Interaction Using Geographic Themes: Human-Environment Interaction Check for Understanding	Relating Past to Present: Technology and the Quality of Human Life Discussing History: Human Rights Check for Understanding
Guided Practice	Section Review 1	Section Review 2	Section Review 3
Independent Practice Worksheets	Independent Practice 36.1 Basic Skills 36 Vocabulary 36	Independent Practice 36.2	Independent Practice 36.3 Geography Skills 36 Critical Thinking 36
Enrichment	1. Primary Source: Voices 36.1 2. Preparing a Report 3. Researching for Points	1. Primary Source: Voices 36.2 2. Writing a Story 3. Researching for Points	1. Primary Source: Voices 36.3 2. ★Preparing a Report 3. Researching for Points

Chapter Closer ●**Reteaching Activities**	Making Lists, Writing an Essay
Chapter Review	Summary, Reviewing the Facts, Basic Skills, Researching and Reporting Skills, Critical Thinking, Perspectives on Past and Present, Investigating History
Chapter Evaluation	Chapter Test 36, Alternate Chapter Test 36, Computer Test Bank Chapter 36 Test

The postwar era changed science and technology.   1

Setting the Stage

Read or distribute the following list of scientific goals:

- send astronauts to Mars
- deploy a defense system that can destroy enemy missiles
- build personal computers that can talk and listen
- build supercomputers that will mimic the human decision-making process
- design improved medical procedures that will dramatically increase life expectancy
- find a cure for AIDS

Ask students to select one goal they would especially like to see achieved and explain their choices. New discoveries might enable scientists to achieve all these goals within the next half century.

Teaching Strategies

Discussing History: The Space Age (Objective 1) Have students identify some major achievements of the space program. Explain that the Apollo voyages to the moon, the *Skylab* research station, and the Space Shuttle program mark major achievements in the United States Space Program. Government and NASA officials are debating possible new goals for the United States manned-space program. Divide the class into small groups. Ask groups to prepare reports recommending one of the following:

- *Space station* The construction of a space station, which would serve as a laboratory and as a staging area for flights to the moon and to Mars.
- *Lunar base* The construction of a moon base, as a possible launching station for missions to Mars.

- *Mission to Mars* A mission to Mars as a joint project with the Soviets. Discuss with students the scientific and technological advances necessary to carry out this mission.

Relating Past to Present: Supercomputers (Objective 2) Ask students to solve the following mathematical problem as rapidly as they can without using a calculator: $37 \times 43 + 62 + 13 = x$. (1666) Before the invention of computers, complex mathematical problems required hours to solve. For example, during World War II, workers at the Army Ballistic Research Laboratory needed 40 hours to calculate artillery trajectories. When scientists at the University of Pennsylvania invented the world's first all-electronic digital computer—ENIAC (Electronic Numerical Integrator and Computer)—in 1964, the new machine calculated artillery trajectories in just 20 seconds.

Computer scientists have made rapid progress since then. By the late 1980's, supercomputers achieved a sustained speed of one billion calculations per second, and can simulate weather patterns, crack secret codes, design aerospace vehicles, and create special effects for Hollywood films.

Discussing History: Microsurgery (Objective 3) Ask students if they think it is possible for surgeons to successfully detach a patient's toe and then reattach it to the patient's hand to replace a lost finger or thumb. In recent years, advances in microsurgery have enabled surgeons to detach and reattach body parts. "In the past," said New York plastic surgeon William Shaw, "you could move tissue around, but you couldn't restore feeling or function. Microsurgery now allows us to reattach tiny veins, arteries, and nerves, and that changes everything." Shaw

and other surgeons believe that they will soon be able to "harvest" skin, ligaments, and bone from different body areas, reassemble them into a functioning joint, and attach the joint to the patient's body.

Check for Understanding Have students explain how the space program and supercomputers are important to science and society.

Enrichment Activities

1. **Reading a Primary Source** Assign Voices from the Past Resource Book 36.1.
2. **Preparing a Report** Have students report on one of the following topics: recent developments in personal computers, goals of the U.S. Space Agency, supercomputers.
3. **Researching for Bonus Points** What was the name of the Soviet space agency? (Glavkosmos)

Technology spurred global development. 2

Setting the Stage

Discuss the impact of the following events. Have students rate them in terms of their effect on the United States and on the planet Earth:

- Chinese leaders use coal as their nation's primary source of fuel.
- Fast-food restaurants in the United States use foam packaging for take-out orders.
- Brazilian settlers burn Amazon forests to clear land for new farms.

Explain that these economic activities contribute to environmental dangers such as the greenhouse effect and ozone depletion, which threaten to affect all life on this planet.

Teaching Strategies

Economics and History: Business on the International Stage (Objective 1) Tell students that since the end of World War II, business has become, to an even greater extent, an international venture. Ask students to research where some of their recent purchases were manufactured (clothes, compact discs and tapes, sports equipment, tape players, or stereos). Write the responses on the board. As a class activity, help students construct a chart (pie or bar graph) detailing the results.

Using Geographic Themes: Human-Environment Interaction (Objective 2) Many scientists predict that the greenhouse effect will raise global temperatures by three to nine degrees during the next century, having a dramatic impact on the global environment. As weather patterns change, parched areas in East Africa could receive more rain, while droughts in the American Midwest could worsen. The

warming trend could also lengthen the growing season in parts of Canada, the United States, the former Soviet Union, and Scandinavia. Rising temperatures would melt polar icecaps, causing sea levels to rise. Flooding could threaten low-lying areas and coastal resorts throughout the world. Experts warn that Manhattan Island will have to build a sea wall to protect itself from rising waters.

Ask students to suggest ways to reverse the greenhouse effect. Point out that reforms will be difficult. Experts warn that fossil-fuel emissions would have to be cut by 60 percent to stop the current warming trend of two-tenths of a degree Fahrenheit per decade.

Using Geographic Themes: Human-Environment Interaction (Objective 3) Explain to students that air-conditioned cars, aerosol sprays, and fast-food wrapped in foam packaging all release a chemical known as *chlorofluorocarbon* (CFC), which eventually reaches the ozone layer above the earth's surface. The ozone layer shields the earth from ultraviolet (UV) radiation. CFC's trigger a complex chemical reaction that destroys Earth's ozone layer. As the ozone layer diminishes, increasing amounts of UV radiation reach the earth. Scientists believe that increased exposure to this radiation causes higher rates of skin cancer and harms many crops. Some scientists fear that higher levels of UV radiation will also harm plankton, the tiny organisms that form the base of the marine food chain. Ask students how the issue of ozone depletion is being addressed. (biodegradable cartons, alternative sources of energy, banning of CFC's, tighter emission controls for automobiles)

Check for Understanding Have students list the consequences of the greenhouse effect and ozone depletion.

Enrichment Activities

1. **Reading a Primary Source** Assign Voices from the Past Resource Book 36.2.

2. **Writing Short Stories** Have interested students write creative stories describing what life would be like in the year 2050 if the greenhouse effect or ozone depletion continues unabated.

3. **Researching for Bonus Points** What is UV-B? (a form of ultraviolet light; each 1 percent drop in ozone allows 2 percent more UV-B to reach the ground.)

Technology had a human impact. 3

Setting the Stage

Ask students if they have ever watched live television coverage, perhaps a concert on MTV or a news event such as the Gulf War or the Tiananmen Square incident in China. Ask students if seeing events "live" changes the way they feel about events. Does such worldwide technology have the capability to change the course of history? For example, could Saddam Hussein have succeeded in conquering Kuwait in a less communicative world?

Teaching Strategies

Relating Past to Present: Technology and the Quality of Human Life (Objective 1) Ask students what they think life was like before the widespread use of automobiles, televisions, portable radios, computers, and other modern conveniences. Ask them if modern technology has brought people in their family and people around the world closer together. Have students interview a member of their family or community who remembers life before such modern technology, and then report back to the class. Did the older generation believe that all technology has been beneficial? Then have students, in groups of four or five, list scientific and technological innovations that have occurred in the last ten years. Have each group select one item and write a paragraph finishing this statement: _____ (their item) has had the greatest impact on the world because _____.

Discussing History: Human Rights (Objective 2) Every year Amnesty International provides information about governments that engage in activities contrary to the Helsinki

Accords of 1975. These agreements, signed by 35 European nations, Canada, and the United States, seek to ensure respect for human rights and freedoms. Ask students to name countries that have been cited for ignoring these accords. (Iraq, Israel, South Africa) Why is it important to publish this information yearly? Can they name a time when the information was used as a basis for action? (the Persian Gulf Crisis)

Check for Understanding Have students list ways science and technology have had an impact on the world during their lifetimes.

Enrichment Activities

1. **Reading a Primary Source** Assign Voices from the Past Resource Book 36.3.
2. **Preparing a Report** Have advanced students report on one of the following topics: Chernobyl, Three Mile Island, depletion of the ozone layer, greenhouse effect, Helsinki Accords, China syndrome.
3. **Researching for Bonus Points** What is the name of the nonprofit organization that serves as an environmental watchdog? (Greenpeace)

Reviewing the Facts

1. (a) spacecraft that can return to Earth under its own power (b) producing complex systems in microscopic form to reduce their weight (c) branch of physics dealing with tiny charges of electricity (d) tiny electronic device that can do the work of a hundred vacuum tubes (e) crystals making up electronic circuits (f) beam of light capable of performing extremely fine operations (g) drugs that attack bacteria (h) study of heredity in living organisms (i) global warming of Earth's atmosphere (j) thin layer of gas that protects Earth from the sun's harmful ultraviolet rays

2. (a) Soviet satellite launched in 1957 (b) U.S. space program that sent explorations to the moon (c) American mathematician who perfected binary number system (d) device that transmits data from one computer to another (e) General Agreement on Tariff and Trade, to promote world trade (f) moisture that destroys forests and life in lakes (g) CFC's that destroy Earth's ozone layer (h) energy source extracted from remains of prehistoric animals (i) Soviet nuclear power plant where an accident spread radioactivity over Europe (j) international agreement signed in 1975 seeking to ensure respect for human rights and freedoms

Basic Skills

1. (a) importers: others 26.8%, USA 18.6%, Germany FRG 9.2%, France 6.2%, U.K. 6.1%, Japan 6.1%, Italy 4.8%, Canada 4.1%, Netherlands 3.6%, Belg-Lux 3.3%, China PRC 2.1%, USSR 2.1%, Switzerland 2.0%, Hong Kong 1.7%, Spain 1.7%, Korea Rep 1.6%. exporters: all other 27%, Germany 12.2%, USA 10.9%, Japan 10.6%, France 6.3%, Italy 4.9%, Canada 4.5%, U.K. 5.4%, Netherlands 4.0%, Belg-Lux 3.5%, Sweden

1.9%, Switzerland 1.9%, Hong Kong 1.8%, Korea Rep 1.8%, USSR 1.7%, China PRC 1.6%, **(b)** USA, USSR, U.K., Switzerland, China PRC **(c)** Korea, Hong Kong, Netherlands, Italy, Belg-Lux, Germany FRG, France, Canada, Japan **(d)** All countries in answer **(b)** have negative trade balance, all countries in **(c)** have positive.

2. (a) Soviets launch *Sputnik 1*, first space vehicle to orbit Earth, 1957; Yuri Gagarin, Soviet who becomes first person to orbit Earth, 1961; Telstar, first communications satellite, 1962; Neil Armstrong and Buzz Aldrin walk on moon, 1969; *Challenger* explodes, killing seven American astronauts, 1986; *Voyager 2*, scientific spacecraft, reaches Neptune, 1989.
(b) Students should make a time line using the above information.

3. (a) communications, electronics, medicine **(b)** communications—answering machines, cordless phones, computerized calling, and television; electronics—transistor radios, computer, compact disc players, and navigational equipment; medicine—robotics, heart by-pass surgery, organ transplants, and the use of lasers
(c) Students should make charts, using the above information.

4. (a) Answers will vary, but should include ideas about materialism, the individual, the family, and drug abuse. **(b)** Answers will vary.

5. (a) microtechnology, superconductors, ultraviolet, and antibiotics **(b)** micro—small; super—over or beyond; ultra—extremely or excessively; anti—opposed to **(c)** micro—microtechnology refers to smaller units that allow a reduction in weight and size of products; super—superconductors go beyond the limits of our ability to transmit electricity; ultra—ultraviolet refers to rays in the extreme violet range; anti—antibiotics are drugs that fight disease.

Researching and Reporting Skills
Students' answers will vary.

Critical Thinking
1. (a) Answers will vary.
(b) Students' responses will vary.
2. (a) Students' answers will vary, but should include such ideas as changes in ways of life, family life, relations between nations, manufacturing processes. **(b)** Students' answers will vary, but should include electronics, space travel and technology, medical advances.
3. (a) Answers should include the idea that since more healthy babies are born and the number of elderly are growing, society will grow in those two sectors of the population. Therefore, programs must be enacted to care for these population groups. **(b)** People must plan more carefully for old age, saving more money for health care and longer retirement period. **(c)** The government will have to budget more money for Medicare, Medicaid, and social security benefits. More hospitals, nursing facilities, geriatric facilities, and recreation facilities must also be opened.
4. (a) burning of fossil fuels, industrial chemicals, garbage and trash **(b)** acid rain, the greenhouse effect, inability of the earth to absorb more waste
5. (a) global pollution, business and trade on an international level, nuclear energy **(b)** trade wars, pollution globally, trade barriers, nuclear accidents that affect other countries
6. (a) business, communication, industry, education, entertainment **(b)** business—human-computer interaction, storage of great amount of information; communication—photo-duplication,

facsimile machines, modem technology; industry—computer-aided design, robotics; education—research, teaching skills, simulation games, reinforcement activities; entertainment—high definition television, modular games

Perspectives on Past and Present
Sample answer: Both the Renaissance and the modern era involve the exploration of new worlds and the development of technology necessary to accomplish these tasks. These changes were enormous in both cases, although the world today seems to be moving away from Humanism as people are becoming more isolated. Culturally, the Renaissance was a time of greater artistic involvement. This is mainly because patronage of the arts was more widely practiced than it is today. The consequences today, as was true during the Renaissance, will be enormous, as new ethical, societal, and philosophical questions have to be tackled.

Investigating History
Students' answers will vary.

Teaching with Pictures

As students study the picture of the Earth Day celebration, have them consider why so many people gathered in Central Park that day. Tell them to look for clues in the photo to answer that question. Students might suggest that the people felt strongly about environmental concerns and gathered that day to let others know that these concerns are important. Ask students if they feel that being one in a crowd of so many thousands of people would constitute "taking a stand" about the issue of environmental awareness. Finally, ask students how they could show others in the school or community what their stand is on environmental concerns, whether they be local or global.

Chapter
36

The Global Village

(1945 - Present)

Celebration of Earth Day 1990 in New York City.

Key Terms

satellite	laser
space shuttle	robotics
electronics	antibiotics
transistor	genetics
silicon chip	fossil fuel
gigabit	acid rain
micro-technology	
greenhouse effect	
ozone layer	
super-conductor	
materialism	
extended family	
nuclear family	

Read and Understand

1. The postwar era changed science and technology.
2. Technology spurred global development.
3. Technology had a human impact.

April 22, 1990, was a beautiful spring Sunday in New York. Nearly three quarters of a million people gathered in Central Park in honor of Earth Day, the twentieth such celebration. "It's like the earth's birthday," said a construction worker in San Francisco. It was cold on the slopes of Mt. Everest, the world's highest mountain. There in Nepal, a small group of people gathered to pick up trash. Around the globe, some 200 million people in 140 nations paused to call attention to the environmental problems facing humanity.

They gathered in Antananarivo, the capital of the African island-nation of Madagascar, where 90 percent of the rain forests have already been destroyed. They gathered in Brazil's São Paulo, a smog-choked, overcrowded city where many residents suffer from pollution-related diseases. They formed a 500-mile long human chain across France. And in the Soviet Union, survivors of the Chernobyl

Chapter 36 Resources

GEOGRAPHY
- Geography Skills 36

REINFORCEMENT
- Vocabulary 36
- Basic Skills 36

- Reteaching 36
- Making Connections Study Guide 36

ENRICHMENT
- Critical Thinking 36

ASSESSMENT
- Chapter Test 36
- Alternate Chapter Test 36
- Computer Test Bank

nuclear disaster gathered in the nearby city of Kiev to call attention to the dangers presented by nuclear power.

Earth Day 1990 offered powerful evidence of just how interconnected the world has become. "This is one spaceship," observed a United Nations' official. "There are no passengers. We're all crew . . . . No one can sit it out. It's a matter of investing in our survival."

Among the thousands of events marking Earth Day 1990 was a simple ceremony at the United Nations headquarters in New York City. There 42 cosmonauts and astronauts—representing 14 different countries and more than two years of time in space—gathered to stress the unity of humankind. During the ceremonies, they contacted the two Soviet cosmonauts orbiting the earth in that country's Mir space station.

The astronauts who gathered in New York had seen firsthand the wonders that modern science and technology had been able to achieve. All had seen the earth from a different perspective—from space and even from the moon itself.

In their speeches, the astronauts reminded listeners of just how fragile Earth appeared from space. One of the speakers was Soviet space veteran Gherman Titov, who had been the second person to orbit the earth in 1961.

"We should remember that all of us in our Spaceship Earth are like cosmonauts," observed Titov. "The crews of real spaceships—many of whom are here today—worry about water supplies, fuel supplies, their cabin environment. So we on the earth must do the same. Upon us depends what we leave for future generations: a bright, blue planet, or a black one."

American astronaut Mary Cleave had this advice for the millions watching the ceremony on television. "We are married to this planet. We must love, honor, and cherish it."

This chapter will examine how a sense of global unity developed during the second half of the twentieth century. It was an era of phenomenal change, with breakthroughs in transportation and communications, in medicine and physics.

These new developments in science and technology made the world seem smaller—a "global village" where rapid communication spread the word of continuing changes. These changes brought fresh challenges that would affect the world and its people in the twenty-first century.

The postwar era changed science and technology. 1

The four decades after World War II produced a revolution in science and technology. As you have seen, the Industrial Revolution almost two centuries earlier had changed the ways goods were produced and people lived and worked. The second half of the twentieth century brought a different kind of revolution—one based on breakthroughs in such fields as physics, chemistry, engineering, and biology.

The world entered the Space Age.

The need for new technology during World War II had produced a number of discoveries and inventions. Among these were radar, jet engines, rockets, and the atom bomb. Competition between the United States and the Soviet Union during the Cold War era led to the development of satellites and missiles that operated in space.

The result of that competition was a space race. In October 1957, the Soviets launched *Sputnik I*, the world's first artificial **satellite,** or space vehicle orbiting the earth. The United States followed early in 1958 with *Explorer I.* In April 1961, a Soviet cosmonaut, Yuri Gagarin, became the first person to orbit the earth. The first orbital flight of an American astronaut, John Glenn, occurred in February 1962.

In July 1969, the first two humans—the American astronauts Neil Armstrong and Buzz Aldrin—landed on the moon. "That's one small step for a man," said Armstrong as he stepped on lunar soil, "but one giant leap for mankind." Altogether, twelve American astronauts visited the moon during the Apollo space program.

Over the next 20 years, American and Soviet space programs both concentrated on the development of **space shuttles,** spacecraft that could return to the earth under their own power. During the 1970's and 1980's, many such missions were sponsored by the Soviet and American governments. A chilling reminder, however, of just how dangerous such missions could still be came in January 1986, when seven American astronauts were killed in the explosion of the space shuttle *Challenger* shortly after takeoff.

831

OBJECTIVE 1. Identify major achievements of the Space Age and evaluate the impact of its technology on the world community.

Teaching Strategy: *Discussing History: The Space Program* (page 830c)

OBJECTIVE 2. Trace the development of super-computers and explain the significance of this new technology.

Teaching Strategy: *Relating Past to Present: Supercomputers* (page 830c)

OBJECTIVE 3. Describe recent developments in surgery.

Teaching Strategy: *Discussing History: Microsurgery* (page 830c)

■ BACKGROUND

The Soviets launched the first woman into space aboard *Vostok 6* on June 16, 1963.

Tales of fanciful flights to Earth's nearest neighbor, the moon, can be traced back to the second century A.D. when the Greek rhetorician Lucian wrote a satirical account of such a fantastic journey.

SECTION 1
Resources

ASSESSMENT
■ Section Quiz 36.1

REINFORCEMENT
■ Independent Practice 36.1

ENRICHMENT
■ Voices from the Past 36.1

831

Experimentation to create a workable television system began in the late nineteenth century. In 1884 Paul Nipkow, a German scientist, patented his idea for a complete television system, the key to which was a rotating disc with holes in a spiral pattern.

In 1926 in England, John L. Baird first demonstrated a true television system by electronically transmitting moving pictures.

Cooperative Learning

Divide the class into an equal number of groups of two or three students. Half of the groups should prepare a statement supporting the space program and its requisite costs. The other groups should prepare a statement arguing that the money spent on the space program would be better used on the world's social and ecological problems, such as hunger or pollution. All group members should participate in preparing the statement, with each member taking notes on the final product. Then pair groups with opposing viewpoints. Have groups present their statements, then allow time for students to debate the topic.

The successful flight of Discovery in 1988 gave new impetus to the space program.

Techniques and knowledge gained from the space program led to other scientific ventures in space. Among these were weather, navigation, and scientific satellites. The first communications satellite, Telstar, was lofted in 1962. Beaming television, radio, and telephone signals around the world in seconds, Telstar and its more advanced versions, such as INTELSAT (1967) and Comstar (1981), seemed to make the world smaller. The scientific space probe *Voyager 2* was launched by the United States in 1977. After sending back pictures of the planets Jupiter (1979), Saturn (1981), and Uranus (1986), *Voyager 2* reached Neptune in 1989. From there, it left the solar system and headed toward the stars.

Technology found new applications.

Carrying out the space missions had involved major breakthroughs in science and technology. In time, many of these advances were applied to developing new consumer products and to meeting human needs.

Travel One area to benefit from the space programs was earth-bound travel. Space research had made available new materials and approaches that found uses in autos and airplanes. In auto construction, aluminum and plastic helped to make cars lighter and more fuel-efficient.

Other forms of transportation also made significant improvements. Many cities developed rapid transport systems to move the growing numbers of commuters who daily traveled between large cities and the surrounding suburbs. For longer-distance travel, countries such as Japan and France have built high-speed rail systems.

Commercial jet travel across the Atlantic began in 1958, which was also the first year that more people crossed that ocean by air than by sea. By 1970, virtually all transcontinental travel was by air. By 1976, the supersonic *Concorde*, built by Britain and France, regularly flew between New York and Paris in less than four hours.

Communications Some of the most significant changes in the technology of consumer products occurred in communications. Telephones underwent a revolution, based on such innovations as answering machines, cordless phones, computerized calling, and cellular telephones. Automatic dialing systems made possible direct dialing to places around the world.

Perhaps the most dramatic breakthrough in mid-century communications was television. The concept of transmitting light dots (which could be combined to form images) first became practical after World War II. By 1951, there were more than ten million sets in the United States alone. By 1990, 98 percent of all American homes had television, with similar levels of use in Canada and Western Europe.

Within a short time, television had become the main recreational activity for billions of people. The launching of the United States Telstar Communications satellite led to the worldwide broadcast of the 1969 moon landing, various sports events, and the 1989 opening of the Berlin Wall. "'Time' has ceased, 'space' has vanished," wrote Canadian sociologist Marshall McLuhan in 1967. "We now live in a *global* village."

Microtechnology was a new frontier.

One of the major problems in space engineering had been how to provide space vehicles with enough power to break the bonds of Earth's gravity. One solution developed by American engineers was **microtechnology**—producing complex

832

systems in miniature or microscopic form to reduce their weight. This technique proved to have almost infinite uses in consumer products.

One area in which microtechnology found immediate application was **electronics,** a branch of physics that deals with tiny charges of electricity. In 1950, American engineer William Shockley produced the first **transistor,** a tiny electronic device that could do the work of a hundred vacuum tubes (the major components of radios and televisions at the time).

The invention of the transistor created an electronic revolution. One of its first applications was in the transistor radio. Transistors found countless other uses in instruments, communications systems, navigational equipment, and—most important of all—the computer.

The computer launched a new age.

Although people had long dreamed of machines that could perform complex calculations, the real breakthrough came with the work of the American mathematician John von Neumann in the 1940's. He perfected a binary number system through which any number could be expressed by combinations of just two digits. These digits could then be made to correspond with the on/off positions of an electric switch. The binary system opened the door for mathematic computation at speeds equal to that of electric currents.

Computers The basic principles developed by Von Neumann led to the development of generations of computers, each smaller yet more advanced than the preceding generation. The development of transistors and other advances in microtechnology in time enabled computer scientists to store millions of pieces of information on a single two-inch **silicon chip**—the crystals that make up electronic circuits.

The real impact of computers upon business and society came in the 1980's. In that decade, dramatic improvements in the production of transistors and silicon chips made possible the production of both new mainframe computers and inexpensive but powerful personal computers. Within a short time, most businesses organized their data bases around computers.

Meanwhile, a new generation of supercomputers was beginning to evolve. It was marked by two main characteristics. One of these was the use of parallel processing, in which the computer could perform various sets of operations at the same time, rather than solving a problem by a single sequence of steps. This capability would enable computers to perform such complex tasks as simulating the world's climate. The other characteristic was the use of high definition TV, or HDTV. This innovation focused on providing and storing higher-quality images and permitting far greater manipulation of images. The early 1990's brought a race between American and Japanese scientists to perfect this process.

Communications networks The effects of the computer revolution were increased by a number of additional inventions that speeded communications. One of the most important new developments was the photo-duplicating process. Machines using this process could copy letters and documents in seconds. A further refinement of the process came in the late 1980's with facsimile (fax) machines that could transmit copies over telephone lines. By 1990, businesses were able to transmit important written communications around the world in a matter of minutes.

These last innovations illustrate an emerging characteristic of the electronic revolution—that of one system linked to other systems in an entire network of communications. For example, a computer linked to a device called a modem could now transmit data directly to another computer via telephone.

As computer chips grow smaller, computers become more compact and complex.

833

ANSWERS TO

Section Review 1

Define:
(a) space vehicle orbiting Earth (b) spacecraft that can return to Earth under its

(continued)

ANSWERS TO *(continued)*

own power **(c)** tiny electronic device that can do the work of 100 vacuum tubes **(d)** producing complex systems in microscopic form to reduce their weight **(e)** branch of physics dealing with tiny charges of electricity **(f)** crystals making up electronic circuits **(g)** units equal to one billion bits of information **(h)** beam of light capable of performing extremely fine operations **(i)** technology of using robots **(j)** drugs that attack bacteria **(k)** study of heredity in living organisms

Identify:

(a) celebration of global environmentalism **(b)** first artificial satellite **(c)** U.S. space program that explored the moon **(d)** first man to walk on the moon **(e)** space shuttle that exploded shortly after take-off **(f)** space probe that reached Neptune in 1989 **(g)** creator of the first transistor **(h)** mathematician who perfected binary number system

Answer:

1. During the Cold War, the two countries competed in developing new technology.

2. People are able to see events and news stories as they occur.

3. They created an electronic revolution—the transistor radio, navigational equipment, and the development of the computer.

4. laser surgery, heart by-pass surgery, pacemakers, development of antibiotics

5. Students' answers will vary, but should include the ideas of global interdependency and the immediate nature of communication.

Computer-aided design and manufacturing became important new tools for industry. Human-computer interaction gave work a new dimension.

One network still in early stages of implementation is the replacement of copper telephone wiring with fiber-optic cables. Such cables can carry vast quantities of data and images as well as standard voice communication. When completed, this system will provide a huge communications network to speed exchanges of information. By linking television and computer networks, it will vastly expand the output of information. This system will be able to handle information in **gigabits,** or units equal to one billion bits of information.

Technology advanced medicine.

The postwar era was a time of major progress in medicine. Some advances were made possible by the new microtechnology. Others were the product of scientific research.

Surgery Before World War II, surgeons seldom performed operations in sensitive areas such as the inner ear, eye, and brain. More powerful microscopes and miniaturized equipment, however, enabled surgeons to develop techniques for such specialized work. Innovations such as the **laser**—a beam of light that can perform extremely fine operations—also provided a new tool for surgery. The use of **robotics**—the technology of using robots—will bring new advances in the future. Tiny robots with even tinier gears and controls will monitor blood pressure and aid the body's own natural systems.

Dramatic improvements were made in other types of surgery as well. The first successful heart by-pass operation was performed in 1954. By 1990,

this procedure had become routine. In 1960, the development of the first heart pacemaker—a transistorized device that could be implanted in a patient's chest to maintain a regular heartbeat—was another important development. Organ transplants—for example, of the kidneys—enabled thousands of patients not only to survive but also to lead more normal lives.

Antibiotics The wartime development of new drugs such as sulfanilamide, penicillin and streptomycin was a major breakthrough. Such drugs acted as **antibiotics,** attacking bacteria that caused infection or disease. They proved highly effective against such once-feared diseases as diphtheria and scarlet fever, as well as wartime wounds. The development of polio vaccines during the 1950's helped to eliminate that dread disease. Regulatory drugs such as insulin—used for controlling diabetes—were also discovered.

Genetic research In the 1980's, the study of **genetics,** or heredity in living organisms, became an important area of medical research. Scientists learned that genes acted like chemical road maps, setting the patterns for cell growth and development. This research had many applications. Biologists discovered, for example, that adding genes from other plants could make certain food plants more productive or resistant to disease.

Research into human genetic makeup proved more difficult and also more controversial. At the same time, it held the potential for treating certain inherited diseases. In 1986, American scientists launched a massive research project designed to identify the function of every single unit of DNA in human genes.

834

Controversy over genetic research developed because some people feared that scientists were tinkering with the nature of life itself. There were fears that genetically-altered bacteria might spread disease or that altered genes might affect development in both animals and humans. Debate continued over the extent of genetic experimentation that should be permitted.

Section REVIEW 1

Define: (a) satellite, (b) space shuttle, (c) microtechnology, (d) electronics, (e) transistor, (f) silicon chip, (g) gigabit, (h) laser, (i) robotics, (j) antibiotics, (k) genetics

Identify: (a) Earth Day, (b) *Sputnik I,* (c) *Explorer I,* (d) Neil Armstrong, (e) *Challenger,* (f) *Voyager 2,* (g) William Shockley, (h) John von Neumann

Answer:

1. How did the space race between the United States and the Soviet Union develop?
2. How did television contribute to bringing the world closer together?
3. What was the impact of new developments in microtechnology?
4. What were the major medical innovations in the postwar period?

Critical Thinking

5. What are likely to be the effects of the communications revolution on people's lives in the future?

Research scientists are seeking a cure or ways to limit the effects of the terrible disease AIDS (Acquired Immune Deficiency Syndrome).

Technology spurred global development. 2

As you have seen, science and technology brought about a revolution in travel, communications, business, and medicine in the postwar era. Just as the Industrial Revolution had led to worldwide trade, the innovations in technology changed the location and operation of business to a global scale.

Business became international.

The decades after World War II witnessed a vast growth in world trade. In part, this became possible through improved transportation and communications, which linked the businesses of the world more closely.

Dispersal of business and industry By 1990, few major businesses and industries limited their activities to a single country. Instead, the number of multinational corporations increased greatly. About a third of these were headquartered in the United States. Companies based in Western Europe, however, as well as those of the Pacific Rim, became increasingly important. By 1989, the world's seven largest banks were in Japan.

In the past two decades, multinational corporations have developed a new approach to producing goods. Improved transportation has enabled companies to manufacture components on different continents and assemble them into finished products on a third continent. Many industries were moved to the developing countries of Asia, Africa, and Latin America, to take advantage of labor and resources available there at lower cost than in the industrialized nations. As a result, industrial development has proceeded rapidly in many developing countries.

For the industrialized world, where most multinational companies have their headquarters, the past three decades have brought economic expansion. In Western Europe, Japan, and northern North America, this was an age of affluence. Prosperity, however, was not spread evenly around the globe. Developing and less developed countries continued to face enormous problems of poverty.

Although foreign businesses brought employment and the development of resources, profits

835

SECTION 2 Objectives and Teaching Strategies

OBJECTIVE 1. Describe the worldwide scope of modern business.

Teaching Strategy: *Economics and History: Business on the International Stage* (page 830d)

OBJECTIVE 2. Identify the greenhouse effect and explain its consequences.

Teaching Strategy: *Using Geographic Themes: Human-Environment Interaction* (page 830d)

OBJECTIVE 3. Identify the ozone layer and explain the consequences of ozone depletion.

Teaching Strategy: *Using Geographic Themes: Human-Environment Interaction* (page 830d)

■ BACKGROUND

In principle, one laser beam can carry as much information as all the existing radio channels. However, laser light can be blocked by fog, rain, or snow, so that, for reliable communication, the laser beam has to be enclosed in a protective pipe.

SECTION 2 Resources

ASSESSMENT
■ Section Quiz 36.2

REINFORCEMENT
■ Independent Practice 36.2

ENRICHMENT
■ Voices from the Past 36.2

■ BACKGROUND

The environmental watch-dog group, Greenpeace, was founded in Canada in 1969. Its early campaigns to save whales and prevent the killing of baby seals gained worldwide recognition for the group.

ANSWERS TO
Reading a Graph

The United States; a high standard of living and many different industries needing resources and raw materials; United States, Japan, and Germany (Federal Republic); United States, United Kingdom, Switzerland, USSR, and China (People's Republic).

■ DISCUSSION

The number of usable landfill sites in the United States has declined by 66 percent since 1980. One third of the remaining landfills will close by 1995. Challenge students to think of solutions to the waste disposal crisis.

■ BACKGROUND

Every year, 2.2 million tons of hazardous waste cross international borders, turning the world into a global dumping ground.

went to owners overseas. Countries strong enough to nationalize certain resources and industries had some protection. Weaker countries were often disadvantaged in dealing with powerful multinational corporations.

Free trade The rapid spread of business worldwide became possible only because trade barriers between countries were gradually reduced. As you have seen, trade agreements had existed among countries such as those of the European Community. A number of regional trade associations such as the Latin America Free Trade Agreement (LAFTA) had also been formed. In addition, worldwide trade agreements also existed, the main one being the General Agreement on Tariff and Trade (GATT). GATT was originally formed in 1947 to encourage the postwar revival of world trade. By 1990, 96 of the world's leading industrial nations were participants. GATT was designed to keep tariffs low and to insure that barriers to international commerce were reduced. GATT remains an active organization with ongoing negotiations and debate on matters pertaining to trade.

Environmental pollution increased.

The global spread of industry meant that highly developed technology also migrated around the world. To many developing nations, technology seemed a benefit because it brought capital investment and jobs. Economic growth, however—whether in industrialized or developing nations—proved to have a price. That price was pollution.

Technology and pollution How could technology become a threat to the environment? The answer lies in the fact that modern technology consumes huge quantities of energy that are obtained mainly from **fossil fuels** such as coal and oil. Scientists had long known that burning coal causes pollution. During the 1960's, industrialized nations began to pay a price for the cheap coal they had burned since the start of the Industrial Revolution. **Acid rain,** caused by sulfur combined with moisture in the air, fell over large areas of North America and Europe, destroying forests and killing life in lakes and ponds.

In addition to air pollution, water and soil pollution also became major problems. Even the

Reading a graph *Which nation imports the most merchandise? What are some reasons for that? Which three nations export the most merchandise? Which nations export less than they import, with an unfavorable balance of trade?*

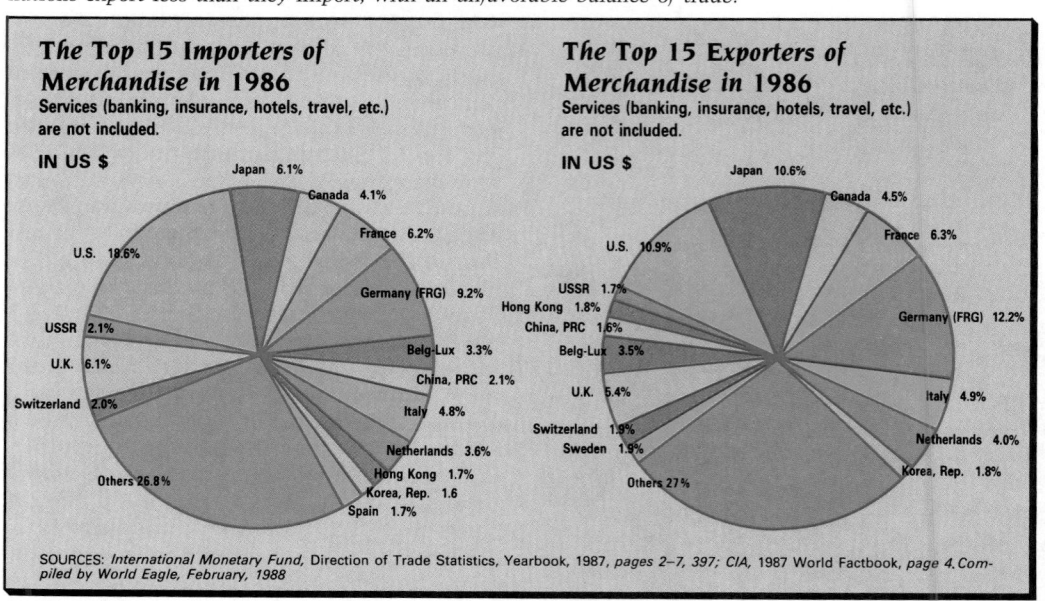

The Top 15 Importers of Merchandise in 1986 — Services (banking, insurance, hotels, travel, etc.) are not included. IN US $ — Japan 6.1%, Canada 4.1%, France 6.2%, Germany (FRG) 9.2%, Belg-Lux 3.3%, China, PRC 2.1%, Italy 4.8%, Netherlands 3.6%, Hong Kong 1.7%, Korea, Rep. 1.6, Spain 1.7%, Others 25.8%, Switzerland 2.0%, U.K. 6.1%, USSR 2.1%, U.S. 18.6%

The Top 15 Exporters of Merchandise in 1986 — Services (banking, insurance, hotels, travel, etc.) are not included. IN US $ — Japan 10.6%, Canada 4.5%, France 6.3%, Germany (FRG) 12.2%, Italy 4.9%, Netherlands 4.0%, Korea, Rep. 1.8%, Others 27%, Sweden 1.9%, Switzerland 1.9%, U.K. 5.4%, Belg-Lux 3.5%, China, PRC 1.6%, Hong Kong 1.8%, USSR 1.7%, U.S. 10.9%

SOURCES: *International Monetary Fund*, Direction of Trade Statistics, Yearbook, 1987, *pages 2–7, 397; CIA*, 1987 World Factbook, *page 4. Compiled by World Eagle, February, 1988* oceans were in danger from pollution caused by accumulated wastes, as in the Mediterranean, or by accidents, such as oil spills caused by tankers running aground. A special threat came from the use of chemicals common in modern technology—for example, in the production of plastics, insect sprays, and countless other products. In 1984, the accidental release of poisonous gas from an American-owned chemical plant at Bhopal, India, claimed more than 2,000 lives.

Population and pollution A second factor in the increase of pollution is the tremendous surge in world population. World population in 1900 was about 1.6 billion people. By 1990, it had passed 5 billion and was predicted to grow to at least 10 billion in the next century.

This huge increase affected the environment in a variety of ways. More food and resources were needed for human consumption, and this put a burden on the environment. A by-product of consumption was waste—garbage and trash. The higher the level of consumption—as in the affluent industrialized world—the greater the amount of waste. In time, the earth could no longer absorb the quantities of waste produced.

Pollution became a global problem.

Recognition of the dangers caused by environmental pollution was slow. Although the first international conference on the environment, sponsored by the UN, was held in Stockholm, Sweden, in 1972, little actual progress was made. Results from a second conference, held in 1991 in Rio de Janeiro, were disappointing as well.

To scientists' growing concern, evidence showed that the buildup of pollution in the earth's atmosphere was affecting the world's climate. If conditions were allowed to worsen, the effects on both human life and property could be immeasurable.

The greenhouse effect In the earth's atmosphere, a balance has always existed between the gases of oxygen and carbon dioxide. In recent centuries, however, the burning of large amounts of fossil fuels has upset that balance. The result has been to put billions of tons of excess carbon dioxide into the atmosphere every year. Between 1850 and 1990, the amount of carbon dioxide in the atmosphere rose by 25 percent—more than in the previous thousand years combined.

Urban Areas (ranked by population, 1991)	1970	1991	2000 (proj.)
Tokyo-Yokohama, Japan	14.9	27.2	30.0
Mexico City, Mexico	8.7	20.9	27.9
São Paulo, Brazil	8.1	18.7	25.4
Seoul, South Korea	5.3	16.8	22.0
New York City, U.S.	16.2	14.6	14.6
Osaka-Kobe-Kyoto, Japan	7.6	13.9	14.3
Bombay, India	5.8	12.1	15.4
Calcutta, India	6.9	11.9	14.1
Rio de Janeiro, Brazil	7.0	11.7	14.2
Buenos Aires, Argentina	8.3	11.7	12.9
Moscow, Russia	7.1	10.4	11.1
Manila, Philippines	3.5	10.2	12.8
Los Angeles, U.S.	8.4	10.1	10.7
Cairo, Egypt	5.3	10.1	12.5
Jakarta, Indonesia	4.3	9.9	12.8
Teheran, Iran	3.3	9.8	14.3

THE WORLD'S 16 LARGEST URBAN AREAS (in millions)

Source: U.S. Bureau of the Census, in The World Almanac, 1993, page 818.

What urban area is projected to be the largest in the year 2000? Where are the fastest-growing areas?

This excess carbon dioxide has trapped heat that would otherwise escape from the lower atmosphere. As a result, a global warming trend has developed, with average world temperatures rising by 1° Fahrenheit over the past century. This global warming, called the **greenhouse effect,** has accelerated as the atmosphere has become increasingly filled with carbon dioxide and other pollutants. Scientists disagree as to how fast global temperatures are rising. A scientific panel on climate change that met in Britain in May 1990, however, predicted a temperature rise worldwide between 3° and 7° Fahrenheit by the year 2100.

Experts agree, however, that the greenhouse effect, even at low levels, may have a profound impact upon world climate. Rising temperatures may speed the process of desertification (page 316) already underway in places such as the Sahel in Africa. Another effect will be the shrinking of polar ice caps, causing a rise in the

837

ANSWERS TO
Caption Questions

Tokyo-Yokohama; Latin America and Asia

Cooperative Learning

Ask students to think of ways that they can personally conserve resources or prevent pollution. Have each student make a list of eight to ten actions that they would be willing to take to achieve the above goal. Then divide the class into groups of four or five students. Have students present their personal lists to the group. Group members should then create a "Pledge to Preserve the Planet," consisting of ten mutually agreed-upon actions that all members would be willing to take. Have group members sign their final products and post the pledges in the classroom.

ANSWERS TO
Section Review 2

Define:
(a) coal and oil (b) global warming of Earth's atmosphere (c) harmful precipitation caused by air pollution (d) thin layer of gas that protects Earth from sun's ultraviolet rays (e) materials that transmit electricity very efficiently over long distances

Identify:
(a) site of accidental release of poisonous gas that killed more than 2,000 people (b) site of nuclear reactor accident

Answer:
1. increase in multinational corporations; manufacture of component parts on different continents; rapid industrial development in developing countries
2. allows the rapid spread of business worldwide
3. (a) consumption of energy pollutes the air; wastes and accidents cause air, water, and soil pollution (b) burdens environment with greater quantities of waste
4. conservation, development of nuclear energy, development and use of superconductors
5. Students' answers will vary. Answers should include the idea that the world is interdependent and one country's pollution affects the world's environment.

The cutting of rain forests in Brazil contributes to the greenhouse effect. Oil spills like that from the Exxon Valdez *harm both fisheries and wildlife such as this sea otter.*

level of the world's oceans. The effect will be to threaten low-lying coastal regions such as Bangladesh and the Netherlands, as well as harbors and beaches around the world.

A second factor contributing to the greenhouse effect has been the destruction of tropical rain forests. These forests are a major factor in regulating world climate. They act like a sponge, absorbing excess carbon dioxide in the atmosphere and converting it to oxygen. Thus, the forests help to control carbon dioxide levels and to limit the greenhouse effect.

Once covering 14 percent of the earth's land surface, these invaluable resources are being destroyed at a record rate. Most of the world's surviving rain forests are located in developing countries such as Brazil, Indonesia, and the nations of central Africa. There, the demand for land and resources became so great that an estimated 26 million acres of forest were being destroyed annually by 1990. If this trend continues, global warming will increase.

The ozone layer During the 1970's, scientists discovered another threat to the environment caused by human activity. This danger involved the **ozone layer** in the upper atmosphere. This thin layer of gas protects the earth from the sun's harmful ultraviolet radiation that might otherwise destroy plant life and cause cancer in animals and humans. Scientists became alarmed when in 1985 they discovered a hole in the ozone layer over Antarctica. A similar gap was found over the Arctic in 1988.

838

The decline in the ozone layer is caused by the use of certain chemicals called chlorofluorocarbons (CFC's), which are used in refrigerating systems and aerosol sprays. These have been found to react in the atmosphere with ozone, destroying the ozone shield. Fortunately, the countries of the developed world responded quickly to this challenge. In 1989, 13 industrialized countries agreed to halt all production of CFC's by the year 2000. The lingering effect of these chemicals, however—and the unknown dangers posed by the two existing ozone layer holes—will continue to pose a threat in the years ahead.

Nuclear energy One of the main hopes for limiting the use of fossil fuels was nuclear energy. During the 1950's, scientists developed nuclear power plants in which controlled reactions could occur. These reactions generated enormous amounts of energy. By 1988, there were 421 such reactors in operation around the world, including 108 in the United States.

Nuclear energy brought its own set of problems, however. In addition to energy, the reactors produced radioactive wastes that could endanger all living things. Safe disposal of nuclear wastes proved extremely difficult. In addition, the danger of on-site accidents always existed.

Just such an accident occurred in 1986 at the Chernobyl nuclear power plant near Kiev in the Soviet Union. While only 31 deaths occurred at the time of the meltdown, dangerous levels of radiation were released into surrounding areas.

The hundreds of thousands of people who were probably exposed are at risk in the years ahead. In fact, by the early 1990's, scientists had already noted a sharp increase in thyroid cancer in the region's children, and an estimated 6,000 to 8,000 people had died of radiation related illnesses.

Another environmental concern is the need to protect endangered plants and animals. As wildlife habitats are reduced, hundreds of species of animals and plants are threatened with extinction. Among them are the cheetah, tiger, and African elephant, whose total numbers were reduced by half during the 1980's. Scientists know that maintaining the diversity of plant and animal life helps to protect the biological gene pool by ensuring continued variety within species.

Scientists seek new sources of energy.

In a world that depends increasingly on technology, the demand for energy continues to grow. Scientists know that no simple solutions exist for this dilemma of enjoying the benefits of technology while still preserving the environment. Several approaches, however, offer promise. One is conservation, based on more efficient use of electricity, more efficient auto engines, improvements in heating and cooling technology, and reduction of industrial pollution.

In the long run, science and technology must contribute solutions. That progress is already underway. The 1980's saw the development of solar cells that used thin-film technology to produce electricity more cheaply and efficiently from sunlight. The new **superconductors**—materials that transmit electricity very efficiently over long distances—promise to provide an abundant and less expensive source of energy. A new kind of nuclear energy, based on fusion rather than the present fission, is expected to become practical within several decades. Although new and safer types of power plants using fission are already available, public acceptance is limited. The problem of disposing of nuclear wastes remains.

Section REVIEW 2

Define: (a) fossil fuel, (b) greenhouse effect, (c) acid rain, (d) ozone layer, (e) superconductor
Identify: (a) Bhopal, (b) Chernobyl

Answer:
1. What changes occurred in international business in the postwar era?
2. Why is free trade important to the global economy?
3. (a) In what ways are technology and economic development a threat to the environment? (b) How does population growth impact on the environment?
4. What are possible solutions to the need for energy?

Critical Thinking
5. Why is protection of the environment a worldwide problem requiring international cooperation?

Technology had a human impact. 3

The changes in communications technology that stimulated the global economy also had a profound effect upon societies and cultures worldwide. While people in countries around the world sought to maintain their own unique cultures, they became increasingly aware of a broader global culture in the emerging "global village."

Worldwide cultural patterns emerged.

As you have seen, the beginnings of mass culture had appeared early in the twentieth century, spurred by inventions such as the radio and movies. In the decades after World War II, television had an even greater effect, adding a visual dimension to global communications. The variety of its offerings—from sports events to comedies, soap opera, game shows, theater, concerts, and news broadcasts—appealed to different audiences worldwide. The development of VCR's during the 1980's led to a movie renaissance as new generations discovered the entertainments of the past.

The development of satellite communications technology further expanded television's global influence. For the first time in history, the reporting of world events was so immediate that it affected the outcome of those events. In June 1989, Chinese students in Tiananmen Square

839

SECTION 3 Objectives and Teaching Strategies

OBJECTIVE 1. Describe the impact of technology on culture.

Teaching Strategy: *Relating Past to Present: Technology and the Quality of Human Life* (page 830e)

OBJECTIVE 2. Discuss the issue of human rights and describe worldwide attempts to address the issue.

Teaching Strategy: *Discussing History: Human Rights* (page 830e)

SECTION 3 Resources

ASSESSMENT
■ Section Quiz 36.3

REINFORCEMENT
■ Independent Practice 36.3

ENRICHMENT
■ Voices from the Past 36.3

■ BACKGROUND

The concept of human rights can be traced back to the Greco-Roman natural-law doctrines of Stoicism, which held that a universal force pervades all creation and that human conduct should therefore be judged according to the law of nature.

ANSWERS TO

Section Review 3

Define:
(a) focus on possessions, constant entertainment, and immediate satisfaction
(b) many relatives within a household (c) family of parent(s) and children
Identify:
(a) document that established worldwide standards

(continued)

kept abreast of events by faxed reports transmitted by telephone from overseas. In December 1989, when a revolt against the government began in the Romanian city of Timisoara, other Romanians watched satellite transmissions of those events and decided to join the rebellion themselves.

Advances in technology in other types of communications besides television contributed to the rise of a worldwide culture. The development of the transistor radio, tape players, and such high tech equipment as compact disc players (CD's) helped to link audiences worldwide.

Mass culture became broader.

Traditional forms of artistic expression besides music also flourished in the postwar years. Variety was a major characteristic of the arts, rather than a single artistic style that marked the times. In literature, traditions that had once bound authors in terms of style and subject matter were broken. Non-Western works enriched world literature as the Nobel Prize for Literature was won by writers from all parts of the world.

The global community created by technology found an interest in the art of all nations. Art exhibits from many countries toured the world, and the ancient art of non-Western peoples received long-overdue recognition.

The Live Aid concert held in July 1985 was viewed by people all over the world. It raised about $70 million for famine relief in Africa.

840

Technology varied in its impact.

As you have seen, societies in the twentieth century differed widely. Traditional societies like those in the Islamic world sought to preserve their culture and traditions. Societies in industrialized nations, however, were more affected by the impact of technology and rapid change.

Materialism The growing affluence of many industrialized nations enabled people there to afford the latest innovations in technology. Many people rushed to buy the latest offerings promoted by enticing advertisements on television. The focus on **materialism**—on possessions, constant entertainment, and immediate satisfaction—at times created a sense of instability.

The individual Many people found a sense of fulfillment from acquiring material goods. At the same time, however, innovations such as television and computers could have the effect of isolating people from society. These were by nature impersonal, separating individuals from contact with others. The concerns and interactions of traditional society seemed less important.

The family As people became more mobile and more affluent, the traditional **extended family** of many relatives within a household gave way to a more **nuclear family** of parents—often a single parent—and children. The distraction of entertainment and the desire for recreation increasingly limited close personal contact among family members. The breakup of families through divorce or separation at times limited such contacts even further.

Drug abuse One characteristic of modern culture was the focus on self-fulfillment. This focus became one reason why, in recent decades, some people turned to the use of drugs. Other people had different reasons, whether peer pressure, the excitement of defying authority, or the desire for escape from the real world. Whatever the reason, the effect was destructive for the individual involved and a disaster for society.

Human rights became a worldwide concern.

The pressures felt by individuals in adjusting to rapid change was reflected in the concern of the world community for the value of individuals, groups, and societies worldwide.

840

On December 10, 1948, the United Nations General Assembly adopted the Universal Declaration of Human Rights. In its 30 articles, this document identifies the basic political, economic, and social rights of all people.

All human beings are born free and equal in dignity and rights. . . . Everyone is entitled to all the rights and freedoms set forth in this Declaration, without distinction of any kind, such as race, colour, sex, language, religion, political or other opinion, national or social origin, property, birth or other status. . . . Everyone has the right to life, liberty, and security of person.

1. Why is it important to have a document focused on human rights?

2. What is the origin of the terms used in the last sentence?

ANSWERS TO
Voice from Our Time

1. to set a worldwide standard
2. writings of John Locke

The UN Declaration of Human Rights Concern for humanity was expressed in the work of a commission of the United Nations in 1948. After long study and discussion, the commission prepared and the General Assembly adopted the Universal Declaration of Human Rights. This document sought to establish a worldwide standard for the value and dignity of individuals and groups that all countries would respect.

One aspect of world societies significantly affected by the UN Declaration is the status of women. Traditional societies have long limited women to subordinate roles and lesser rights. Even in so-called modern societies, women have often lacked equality as citizens, workers, and participants in the national community.

The UN Declaration, which focuses on the worth and dignity of the individual, makes clear that this is a single standard to be applied to all people. As such, it is consistent with the principles of democracy, which recognize and respect the equality and rights of all citizens.

The Helsinki Accords Further emphasis on the importance of human rights was provided by a later agreement among 35 European nations, together with the United States and Canada. This agreement was made at an international conference in Helsinki, Finland, in 1975, and is known as the Helsinki Accords. The agreement sought to ensure respect for human rights and freedoms, to grant exit visas permitting the reuniting of families, and to facilitate a freer exchange of people, publications, and information.

Although nonbinding, the Accords—like the Declaration of Human Rights—sought to establish an international standard for protecting human rights and freedoms. They were a major factor in the quest for democracy in Eastern Europe in recent years.

In the absence of means for enforcement of human rights provisions, a private organization known as Amnesty International, founded in London in 1961, provides information on actions by governments that are contrary to the Declaration and the Accords. Such actions include arbitrary arrest and imprisonment and violations of human rights in various countries.

Section REVIEW 3

Define: (a) materialism, (b) extended family, (c) nuclear family
Identify: (a) Universal Declaration of Human Rights, (b) Helsinki Accords, (c) Amnesty International
Answer:
1. How did new types of communication contribute to the rise of a global culture?
2. What were some new directions in mass culture in the age of the global village?
3. Why might advances in technology cause a sense of isolation and an impersonal quality in human contacts?
4. Why was the UN Declaration of Human Rights of special importance to women?

Critical Thinking
5. How did the growth of global communications aid in implementing the UN Declaration of Human Rights and the Helsinki Accords?

841

ANSWERS TO *(continued)*

for human rights **(b)** agreement that sought to ensure respect for human rights and freedoms **(c)** private organization that reports on human rights violations

Answer:

1. Television, transistor radios, fax machines, compact disc players, and tape players helped to link audiences worldwide.

2. Literature and the arts were characterized by variety, with non-Western styles receiving worldwide recognition.

3. Technology such as television and computers had the effect of isolating people from society, lessened the importance of traditional society.

4. Traditional societies limited women to subordinate roles and lesser rights. Elsewhere, women lacked equality as citizens, workers, and participants in the national community. The UN declaration recognizes and respects the equality and rights of all citizens.

5. The growth of global communication ensured that these two documents became known worldwide quickly and allowed violations to be reported quickly.

Concluding the Chapter

1. **Chapter Closer**
Ask students to explain how technology has made their lives different from that of their parents when they were teenagers.

2. **Reteaching Activities**
a. Making Lists Have students make two lists covering the advantages and disadvantages of modern technology.
b. Writing an Essay Have students write essays explaining how their lives are interrelated with the lives of teenagers on a distant continent.

Answers to Chapter Review appear on pages 830e–830f.

Summary

1. The postwar era revolutionized science and technology. The postwar era brought an explosion in new technology, beginning with the space program in which the United States and the Soviet Union competed for achievements in military and scientific projects. A high point was the moon landing by American astronauts in 1969. Advances in technology also affected travel and communications. Microtechnology made possible the development of electronic goods such as television, computers, and medical instruments. Future advances will include further progress in communications and information-related technology.

2. Technology spurred global economic development. The revolutions in worldwide transportation and communications encouraged the spread of business and industry around the world. Multinational companies operated around the world, often locating manufacturing operations in developing nations. Industrialization and rapid population growth led to increased pollution that threatened the global environment. The greenhouse effect and danger to the ozone layer threatened the global environment. Scientists sought new sources of energy that would cause less pollution.

3. Technology had a human impact. The spread of communications worldwide brought people of all countries into greater contact. It also led to the development of a mass culture shared by countries around the world. To some extent, the impact of technology on individuals led to increased isolation. These factors affected individuals, families, and communities. Worldwide concern for humanity was expressed in the UN Universal Declaration of Human Rights and the Helsinki Accords.

Reviewing the Facts

1. Define the following terms:
   a. space shuttle
   b. microtechnology
   c. electronics
   d. transistor
   e. silicon chip
   f. laser
   g. antibiotics
   h. genetics
   i. greenhouse effect
   j. ozone layer

2. Explain the importance or meaning of each of the following names, places, or terms:
   a. *Sputnik*
   b. *Explorer*
   c. John von Neumann
   d. modem
   e. GATT
   f. acid rain
   g. chlorofluoro-carbons
   h. fossil fuels
   i. Chernobyl
   j. Helsinki Accords

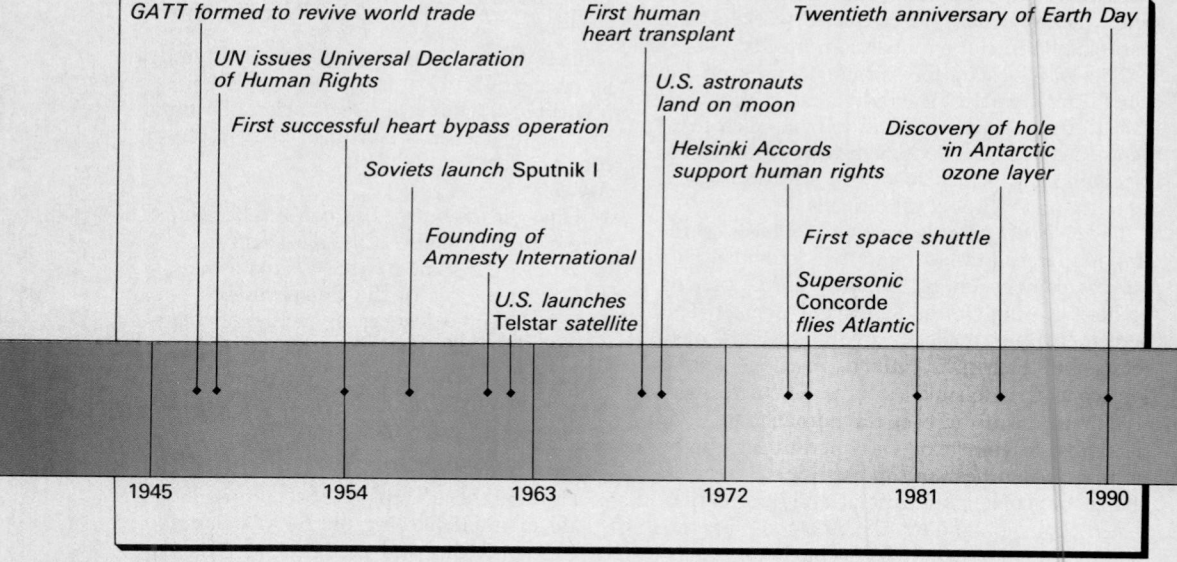

GATT formed to revive world trade

UN issues Universal Declaration of Human Rights

First successful heart bypass operation

Soviets launch Sputnik I

Founding of Amnesty International

U.S. launches Telstar satellite

First human heart transplant

U.S. astronauts land on moon

Helsinki Accords support human rights

Supersonic Concorde flies Atlantic

Twentieth anniversary of Earth Day

Discovery of hole in Antarctic ozone layer

First space shuttle

1945   1954   1963   1972   1981   1990

842

Basic Skills

1. **Reading graphs** Study the two circle graphs on page 836. (a) List the top importers and top exporters for 1986. Begin with the largest and include percentages. (b) Which nations export more than they import? (c) Which nations import more than they export? (d) What is the status of each nation's balance of trade?

2. **Making a time line** (a) List six major events that have marked the progress of space exploration. Note their dates. (b) Make a time line of the period from 1955 to 1990 and enter the events you have selected.

3. **Making a classification chart** Since World War II, the world has experienced a technological revolution. (a) Name three major fields in which this revolution has taken place. (b) Classify some discoveries or breakthroughs in each category. Find at least four for each category. (c) Present them in chart form, using your categories as heads of columns.

4. **Summarizing** Reread the section "Technology varied in its impact," page 840. (a) Identify the main ideas in this passage. (b) Summarize the passage, writing one sentence to express each main idea.

5. **Studying vocabulary** Understanding prefixes can help you remember the meaning of words. (a) Identify three key terms in this chapter that have prefixes. (b) Look up the prefixes' meaning in a dictionary. (c) Explain how each prefix contributes to the meaning of the term.

Researching and Reporting Skills

1. **Using an atlas** Your text states that tropical rain forests help to fight the greenhouse effect. (a) In an atlas, find a vegetation map of the world. Identify the main areas where tropical forests are found. (b) Which of these does your text say are endangered?

2. **Using community resources** Look up in a phone book businesses that sell alternative energy equipment. Call or write to them, asking them to send you pamphlets or catalogs of some of their equipment. Share and discuss your findings with fellow students.

3. **Using a newspaper index** Use a newspaper index to find articles concerning foreign ownership of businesses and real estate in your region. (a) What

foreign countries are represented? (b) What kinds of businesses are involved?

Critical Thinking Skills

1. **Evaluating** New inventions such as answering machines, fax machines, and cellular phones have expanded the use of telephones. (a) What impact do you think these new machines have on human relationships? (b) Give an example of this impact for each invention.

2. **Comparing** The new technological revolution has been compared to the Industrial Revolution. (a) In what ways are the two similar? (b) In what ways do they differ?

3. **Predicting outcomes** The continuous improvement in medical care is extending life expectancy. (a) How is this affecting the distribution among age groups in society? (b) What are some likely consequences for individuals planning their lives? (c) For government planning?

4. **Identifying cause and effect** (a) What are the causes of pollution in the world today? (b) What are the main effects?

5. **Analyzing** This chapter emphasizes the growing interdependence in the world. (a) What are the main factors contributing to this interdependence? (b) What conflicts is it likely to cause?

6. **Synthesizing** Computer technology has radically changed many fields of human endeavor. (a) List five major fields of human activity changed by computers. (b) What are some of the main contributions made by computers in these areas?

Perspectives on Past and Present

The past 30 years have been a time of exploration and discovery in some ways similar to the period following the Renaissance. Compare the two periods in terms of factors contributing to exploration and discovery, degree of change, and consequences for the world.

Investigating History

Environmental concerns are shared by industrialized countries as well as by Third World countries. Look for magazine articles that present the dilemma faced by a Third World country such as Brazil. What are the different positions taken by Brazilians confronted with environmental issues? What arguments do they present?

843

CHAPTER
Evaluation

Chapter Test 36, Alternate Chapter Test 36, and Computer Test Bank Chapter 36 Test can be used to evaluate your students' understanding of this chapter.

Changing Patterns of World Power

Chapter Overview

The Soviet Union entered a new era in 1985 with the ascension of Mikhail Gorbachev to power. Gorbachev launched a series of reforms designed to revitalize the Soviet Union. But the reforms had the unintended consequence of releasing long-suppressed ethnic tensions and triggering a hard-line coup against Gorbachev. When the coup failed, the Soviet Union collapsed and Gorbachev resigned.

The changes in the Soviet Union quickly spread throughout Eastern Europe. In 1989, demonstrations in East Germany led to the fall of the Berlin Wall. Within a short time, people throughout Eastern Europe overthrew their Communist governments.

The collapse of communism brought many changes to Europe. East and West Germany became a united Germany once again, as Poland applied shock therapy to its troubled economy. Ethnic differences in Czechoslovakia led to its split into Slovakia and the Czech Republic. Ethnic and religious differences shattered Yugoslavia and threw it into a bloody civil war.

With the collapse of the Soviet Union, the United States found itself as the last superpower. Aggression in the Middle East and famine in Africa created new challenges for American diplomacy. The spread of democracy and global economic integration were creating a new world order, but ancient hatreds and the global arms trade posed serious challenges to world peace.

Chapter Focus

Begin by asking students to recall the definition of *Cold War*. Remind students that the Cold War was a period of economic, political, and ideological competition between the United States and the Soviet Union. Then ask students to write down the first two words that they associate with the Soviet Union.

Explain that when Mikhail Gorbachev became general secretary of the Communist party in 1985, President Reagan referred to the Soviet Union as the "evil empire." Ask students what might have prompted Reagan to use that description. Explain that the Soviet Union had recently invaded Afghanistan, cracked down on Polish labor unrest, and deployed nuclear weapons near Western Europe. Point out that when Gorbachev resigned on December 25, 1991, the Cold War had ended and the Soviet Union had passed into history.

Tell students that this chapter will describe how the momentous events that took place while Gorbachev was in power helped end the Cold War. The chapter will also describe the characteristics of the new era of history we are now beginning to enter.

Gorbachev launched a new era. 1

Setting the Stage

Ask students whether they have ever had the experience of doing something they were sure would work, only to be completely surprised by the actual results. Explain that recent events in the former Soviet Union provide many examples of events that produced unexpected consequences.

Ask students to read the section introducing Mikhail Gorbachev on pages 845–846. Then ask students to describe the type of leader the members of the Politburo thought they were selecting. What clues in Gorbachev's past suggested that he might be a new type of Soviet leader? Tell students that this section will describe Gorbachev's reforms and the unexpected changes they unleashed.

Teaching Strategies

Discussing History: Gorbachev's Reforms (Objective 1) Begin by asking students to describe the conditions inside the Soviet Union that prompted Gorbachev to launch his program of reforms. Stress that the Communist party exercised complete control over all aspects of Soviet life. For example, the party prevented open communications by placing restrictions on who could own computers and telephones. When Gorbachev came to power in 1985, the Soviet Union's 278 million people owned only 36 million telephones. (By contrast, the United States, with a population of about 250 million, has more than 150 million telephones.) Ask students how such controls would hinder scientific and economic progress. Point out that Gorbachev recognized that the Soviet Union could not compete with the dynamic economies of the United States, Western Europe, and Japan.

Now discuss Gorbachev's reform program of *glasnost, perestroika,* and *demokratizatsiya.* Ask students to review the goals, achievements, and unanticipated consequences of each policy. For example, *glasnost* was designed to open Soviet society. The relaxation of controls produced greater freedom of press and religion. But *glasnost* also undermined the authority of the Communist party by exposing Soviet citizens to new ideas and by

Advance Planner

Chapter 37 Changing Patterns of World Power
FOCUS The beginning of the post-Cold War Era

★ Advanced
● Basic

	SECTION 1	SECTION 2	SECTION 3	SECTION 4
Objectives	1. Describe Gorbachev's reforms and discuss their consequences. 2. Discuss reasons why Gorbachev was caught off guard by the coup plotters. 3. Describe reasons the coup failed.	1. Discuss the reasons East Germany opened the Berlin Wall. 2. Explain the rise to power of Chechoslovakia's playwright-president Vaclav Havel.	1. Discuss the causes of neo-Nazi violence in Germany. 2. Discuss the advantages and disadvantages of shock therapy. 3. Discuss American foreign policy options in Bosnia and Russia.	1. Identify and describe four global trends. 2. Explain the role geography played in causing the Persian Gulf War. 3. Discuss America's foreign policy options for the post-Cold War era.
Setting the Stage	Unexpected consequences of Gorbachev's actions	Effect of Soviet reforms on Eastern Europe	Problems with the change to democracy	Naming the new era
Teaching Strategies	Discussing History: Gorbachev's Reforms Relating Past to Present: Leaders Who Ignored Warnings Writing about History: The August Coup Check for Understanding	Writing about History: What If? Discussing History: Vaclav Havel Check for Understanding	Transferring Ideas: Scapegoating Economics and History: Shock Therapy Writing about History: United States Policy in Bosnia and Russia Check for Understanding	Discussing History: Global Trends Using Geographic Themes: Location and the Persian Gulf War Discussing History: American Foreign Policy Check for Understanding
Guided Practice	Transparency 108 Q&A Section Review 1	Section Review 2	Transparency 109 Q&A Section Review 3	Transparency 110 Q&A Section Review 4
Independent Practice Worksheets	Independent Practice 37.1 Vocabulary 37	Independent Practice 37.2	Independent Practice 37.3 Geography Skills 37 Basic Skills 37	Independent Practice 37.4 Critical Thinking 37
Enrichment	1. Primary Source: Voices 37.1 2. ★Analyzing a Quotation 3. Researching for Points	1. Primary Source: Voices 37.2 2. ★Creative Writing 3. Researching for Points	1. Primary Source: Voices 37.3 2. ★Preparing a Report: Updating Eastern Europe or the former Soviet Union 3. Researching for Points	1. Primary Source: Voices 37.4 2. ★Creative Writing 3. Researching for Points

Chapter Closer	
●Reteaching Activities	Making a Bulletin Board, Listing
Chapter Review	Summary, Reviewing the Facts, Basic Skills, Researching and Reporting Skills, Critical Thinking, Perspectives on Past and Present, Investigating History
Chapter Evaluation	Chapter Test 37, Alternate Chapter Test 37, Computer Test Bank Chapter Test 37

Unit X Review	
Geographic Theme	Location: What will be Germany's future role in Europe?
Historical Themes	Technology and History, Human-Environment Interaction, Rise of Democratic Ideas, Cooperation and Conflict
Unit Evaluation	Unit X Test, Alternate Unit X Test

encouraging ethnic groups to express their discontent.

Relating Past to Present: Leaders Who Ignored Warnings (Objective 2) Ask students whether they have ever ignored a warning and later regretted doing so. Then ask whether they can name leaders they have previously studied who ignored warnings that turned out to be true. For example, Julius Caesar ignored repeated warnings that his life would be threatened if he attended the Senate on March 15 in 44 B.C.

Now ask what warnings Gorbachev received during the summer of 1991. Why did he receive those warnings? What groups opposed him and why? Conclude by asking students to speculate on reasons Gorbachev ignored warnings that turned out to be true. Possible reasons include his tendency to overestimate his ability while underestimating his opponents.

Writing about History: The August Coup (Objective 3) *Prewriting* Ask students to read the section on the August Coup on page 850. Then direct their attention to the picture on this page. Explain that thousands of citizens in Moscow and other Soviet cities risked their lives by nonviolently confronting the troops. Remind students that a similar strategy in China (pages 770–772) had resulted in the tragic Tiananmen Square massacre. *Writing* Divide the class into pairs and assign one student the role of a soldier and the other the role of a protestor. Ask each pair to write a realistic dialogue portraying the exchanges shown in the picture on page 850. Stress that the citizens are trying to persuade the soldiers to disobey orders. What arguments would they use? Encourage the

soldiers to ask questions. Conclude by having several of your teams read their dialogues to the class.

Check for Understanding Ask students to explain the causes and consequences of Gorbachev's reforms and of the August Coup.

Enrichment Activities

1. **Reading a Primary Source** Assign Voices from the Past Resource Book 37.1.

2. **Analyzing a Quotation** Read aloud to students the following observation by Alexis de Tocqueville on the French Revolution: "The most perilous moment for a bad government is when it seeks to mend its ways. Only consummate statecraft can enable a king to save his throne when, after a long spell of oppressive rule, he sets to improving the lot of his subjects." Ask advanced students to compare and contrast the situation in France before the French Revolution with the situation in the Soviet Union before the Second Revolution.

3. **Researching for Bonus Points** Where was Gorbachev's Black Sea vacation home located? (at Foros on the Crimea, not far from Yalta)

Communism collapsed in Eastern Europe 2

Setting the Stage

Begin by reminding students that most Eastern Europeans bitterly resented the Communist regimes imposed on them by Stalin after World War II. Ask students to recall examples of popular revolts against Soviet rule. Then ask students why the revolts in Poland, Hungary, and Czechoslovakia failed. Stress that in each case, the government, backed by Soviet power, suppressed the revolt. Ask students how Gorbachev's rule created new conditions. Explain that this section will describe how these new conditions triggered a series of revolutions that toppled Communist governments throughout Eastern Europe.

Teaching Strategies

Writing about History: What If? (Objective 1) *Prewriting* Ask students to read the sections describing how Poland elected a non-Communist prime minister and how Hungary opened the iron curtain (pages 853–854). Explain that those events placed Communist leaders in East Germany under increasing pressure to maintain order. *Writing* Ask students to write a short paper speculating on what would have happened if hardliners had overthrown Gorbachev on November 8, 1989, the day before Krenz decided to open the Berlin Wall. Would events have taken a different course, or was the momentum of change already too great to resist?

Discussing History: Vaclav Havel (Objective 2) The following remark was made about Vaclav Havel, "Beware! Here speaks a rebel, one of that dangerous breed, the soft and polite." Remind students that Havel was the Czechoslovakian playwright who came out of government-imposed isolation to lead his country's revolution. Ask how a person who is "soft and polite" can be dangerous.

Explain that since the 1968 Czechoslovakian revolution, Havel had remained "soft and polite" while courageously producing a wealth of anti-Communist literature. Havel's writings centered on "living in truth," an impossibility under a Communist regime. He was imprisoned several times, once for refusing deportation.

Before the 1989 revolution, Havel lived under intimidating government surveillance in a Prague apartment. It was there that revolutionary crowds sought him out and convinced him to take a leading role.

Ask students whether Havel seems a likely person to be a revolutionary leader. Would Havel have emerged as a leader if the revolution had been more violent?

Check for Understanding Ask students to discuss the causes and consequences of the fall of the Berlin Wall.

Enrichment Activities

1. **Reading a Primary Source**
   Assign Voices from the Past Resource Book 37.2.
2. **Creative Writing**
   Ask students to pretend that your local museum has just received a segment of the Berlin Wall. Their assignment is to write an inscription for a plaque to be placed on this segment.
3. **Researching for Bonus Points**
   Name the Bulgarian party boss who was overthrown in 1989. (Tudor Zhivkov)

Setting the Stage

Begin by asking students whether it is possible for a nation or region to achieve a long-desired goal only to have new problems arise. Explain that this situation is occurring in Europe today.

Students should recall that after World War II, the United States and Western Europe adopted the goals of forming a European common market, reuniting Germany, and liberating Eastern Europe from communism. Point out that all of those goals have now been achieved.

At the same time, new and unexpected problems have arisen. Ask students whether they can identify some of the new problems affecting Europe. (Answers should include the civil war in Yugoslavia, the breakup of Czechoslovakia, neo-Nazi violence, and continuing turmoil in the former Soviet Union.) Tell students that this section will discuss the forces and problems that are forming a new Europe.

Teaching Strategies

Transferring Ideas: Scapegoating (Objective 1) Ask students to name examples of scapegoating. Students should recall that the Roman leaders blamed the Christians for their problems and that Hitler used the Jews as scapegoats for Germany's troubles. Stress that in each instance individuals and groups whose needs were being blocked took out their frustration by discriminating against a minority group.

Now have students read the section "A new Germany emerged" on pages 857–858. Ask which group in Germany is being used as a scapegoat. What conditions are causing the outburst of violence against foreigners? Stress that unification has caused great hardship in the former East Germany. Unemployed workers and alienated youths feel threatened by the influx of refugees entering their country. Conclude by asking how the current unrest in Germany differs from the Nazi persecution of the Jews during the 1930's. (Germany is now a much stabler country, its leaders are speaking out against the neo-Nazis, and millions of Germans are participating in demonstrations against the violence.)

Economics and History: Shock Therapy (Objective 2) Ask students what might happen if every factory, farm, or service-provider in the United States was suddenly told how many people it should employ, what it should produce, and at what price to sell its product or service. Students should recognize that these changes would cause severe economic disruption.

Explain that Poland and other countries in Eastern Europe and the former Soviet Union are experiencing these types of problems, except in reverse. The change there is from a command economy to a free market. Tell students that economists call the rapid elimination of price controls and government subsidies shock therapy. Ask students to discuss some of the advantages and disadvantages of shock therapy.

A *new world order* began to emerge. 4

Writing about History: United States Policy in Bosnia and Russia (Objective 3) Have students read the sections on pages 860–862 on the collapse of Yugoslavia and the turmoil in Russia. Explain that the ongoing crises in these regions is presenting the United States with a number of difficult decisions. Ask students to pretend that they are editors of your local newspaper. Their assignment is to write an editorial taking a position on one of the following questions.

1. Is there anything the United States can do to end the fighting in Bosnia?
2. Should the United States provide large-scale aid to the Yeltsin government?

Have students read their editorials to the class. Compare and contrast their views.

Enrichment Activities

1. **Reading a Primary Source**
   Assign Voices from the Past Resource Book 37.3.

2. **Preparing a Report**
   Ask advanced students to prepare updated reports on the situation in one of the Eastern European countries or in Russia or in one of the other former Soviet republics.

3. **Researching for Bonus Points**
   What does the name Sarajevo mean? (*Sarajevo* is derived from a Turkish word meaning "square before the palace.")

Setting the Stage

Begin by asking students to recall the names given to historic eras they have previously studied. Possible answers include the Middle Ages, Reformation, Renaissance, Enlightenment, Industrial Revolution, and Cold War era. Then point out that we are leaving one era, the Cold War era, and entering a new and as yet unnamed era. Ask students to suggest possible names for this new period of history. Then explain that this section will begin by describing four trends that are shaping the post-Cold War world.

Teaching Strategies

Discussing History: Global Trends (Objective 1) Have students read the section "Four key trends shape a new era" on pages 863–865. After introducing and explaining each trend, divide the class into small cooperative learning groups. Ask the members of each group to determine which of the four trends they think is playing the most important role in shaping the post-Cold War world. Have each group present its conclusions.

Using Geographic Themes: Location and the Persian Gulf War (Objective 2) Direct your students' attention to the map of Kuwait and the Persian Gulf on page 862. Tell students that territorial disputes played an important role in aggravating relations between Iraq and Kuwait. Point out that Kuwait possessed a 120-mile-long shoreline as well as the best deepwater port on the Persian Gulf. In contrast, Iraq's narrow coastline extended for only 26 miles. Furthermore, Kuwait's Bubiyan and Warba islands blocked Iraq's access to the Gulf.

Explain that this distribution of strategic Gulf coastline infuriated

Iraqi leaders. In early 1989, Saddam Hussein offered to buy or lease Bubiyan and Warba islands. But the Kuwaitis refused, fearing that Iraq would eventually use the islands to threaten nearby Kuwait City.

Discussing History: American Foreign Policy (Objective 3) Begin by explaining that after World War II, most Americans agreed that the Soviet Union posed the greatest threat to American security. The United States responded by developing a Cold War policy based upon containing Communist expansion (pages 742–745).

Now ask students to name the greatest threat facing the United States today. Given this threat, what foreign policy do they think the United States should adopt? For example, if students feel that global problems such as the environment and poverty are the greatest threat, they might suggest a foreign policy based upon working with the United Nations to cooperatively solve global problems. In contrast, if they view regional conflicts as the greatest threat to world peace, they might favor a foreign policy based upon the need for a strong America as the world's only superpower.

Check for Understanding Have students identify and give an example of each of the four trends shaping the post-Cold War world.

Enrichment Activities

1. **Reading a Primary Source**
   Assign Voices from the Past Resource Book 37.4.

2. **Creative Writing**
   Ask advanced students to write a paper on what might have happened if the United States had not responded to Iraq's invasion of Kuwait.

3. Researching for Bonus Points
Which Security Council resolution authorized the use of force if Iraq failed to withdraw from Kuwait? (Resolution 678)

ANSWERS TO
Chapter Review 37

Reviewing the Facts
1. **(a)** period of reduced tensions **(b)** openness **(c)** economic restructuring **(d)** democratization **(e)** economic program calling for the rapid elimination of price controls and state subsidies **(f)** Serbian policy of driving out Bosnian Muslims **(g)** all financial interactions among people, businesses, and governments that cross international borders

2. **(a)** treaty by which the United States and Russia pledged to reduce their nuclear arsenals by two-thirds **(b)** Solidarity leader who became president of Poland in 1990 **(c)** dissident playwright who led the revolution against Czechoslovakia's Communist government and became president of Czechoslovakia **(d)** European economic organization **(e)** East African country suffering from famine **(f)** United States-led relief effort to help Somalia **(g)** country invaded by the Soviet Union in 1979 **(h)** banned nuclear missiles with ranges of 300 to 3,400 miles **(i)** Estonia, Latvia, and Lithuania **(j)** chancellor of reunited Germany **(k)** Persian Gulf nation invaded by Iraq **(l)** Intermediate Nuclear Forces **(m)** top decision-making group in the Communist party

Basic Skills
1. Causes of the Persian Gulf War

Long-Term Causes	Immediate Causes
Iraqi arms buildup Hussein's ambition to be the most powerful Arab leader	Failure of Kuwait to forgive a $10 billion loan made to Iraq
Lack of Iraqi access to the Persian Gulf	Refusal by Kuwait to sell or lease Bubiyan or Warba islands to Iraq

2. (1) the opening of the Berlin Wall
(2) the reunification of Germany
(3) the aborted coup against Gorbachev
(4) Gorbachev's resignation
(5) Czechoslovakia's split into two countries

3. lack of Iraqi coastline, Iraqi desire for Kuwaiti oil fields

Researching and Reporting Skills
Student's findings will vary.

Critical Thinking
1. **(a)** Gorbachev attempted to ease international tensions by reducing Soviet military forces, withdrawing Soviet troops from Afghanistan, and signing the INF Treaty **(b)** Brezhnev, although agreeing to some arms control, followed a much harder line

2. **(a)** Students should name three of the following: greater religious and artistic freedom, dissidents were freed, criticism of government officials allowed, creation of small private businesses, and decrease in power of Communist party. **(b)** greater freedom from controls but lowered living standards

3. **(a)** encouragement from Gorbachev to experiment with *glasnost* and *perestroika*, failing economies, oppressive governments **(b)** civilian demonstrations

or labor unrest, followed by elections in which the Communist party was voted out or taken over by reformers

4. **(a)** Although many countries still keep formidable arsenals, military might is less important today. **(b)** Economic power is becoming more important. Japan and the members of the EC are very powerful nations.

5. Created hatred that fueled the civil war

6. **(a)** removal of all trade barriers among EC members, global news services, formation of North American Free Trade Association **(b)** Goods, services, and information can now freely flow across international borders.

7. **(a)** Bush enforced restrictions against Iraq and sent troops to Somalia. **(b)** Bush set a precedent for using United States troops for humanitarian missions.

Perspectives on Past and Present
1. Students' answers will vary. Both Hussein and Hitler promised no further aggression if their conquest were allowed. Lessons of the past were useful, as appeasement might have urged Hussein to further aggression.

2. According to the United States, both were fought to stop aggression. However, the Gulf War was not part of a Cold War struggle against communism. The United States used overwhelming force to win a conventional war instead of using gradual escalation to fight a guerrilla war.

Investigating History
Student's answers will vary.

Teaching with Pictures

Explain that the picture on this page was taken just before midnight December 31, 1991. Then ask students to identify the two symbols shown in this picture. Explain that the time on the clock symbolizes the ending of one year and the beginning of a new one. Then ask students what flag had formerly flown over the Kremlin. Remind students that a red flag bearing a distinctive gold hammer-and-sickle emblem had flown over the Kremlin since 1917. The Russian flag in this picture symbolizes the dramatic political changes taking place in the former Soviet Union. Tell students that this chapter will begin by describing how the Soviet Union collapsed.

The Russian flag flew over the Kremlin after the Soviet Union collapsed.

Key Terms

détente
glasnost
perestroika
demokratizatsiya
shock therapy
ethnic cleansing
global economy

Read and Understand

1. Gorbachev launched a new era.
2. Communism collapsed in Eastern Europe.
3. The post-Cold War era brought changes.
4. A new world order began to emerge.

As he sat at his desk inside the Kremlin, Mikhail Gorbachev briefly paused to straighten his papers. In a few moments, he would deliver a major speech, and, as always, he wanted to be prepared. As president of the Soviet Union, Gorbachev had given many important speeches, but this address would be unlike any he or any other Soviet leader had ever given.

Gorbachev began by firmly declaring, "I hereby discontinue my activities at the post of president of the Union of Soviet Socialist Republics." Saying that this was his "last opportunity" to address the Soviet people, Gorbachev admitted that he had made mistakes during his six years as president. But then he proudly reviewed his achievements, declaring, "We're now living in a new world."

844

Chapter 37 Resources

GEOGRAPHY
- Geography Skills 37
- Transparencies 95, 102, 104, 108, 109, 110

REINFORCEMENT
- Vocabulary 37
- Basic Skills 37
- Reteaching 37
- Making Connections Study Guide 37

ENRICHMENT
- Critical Thinking 37

ASSESSMENT
- Chapter Test 37
- Alternate Chapter Test 37
- Computer Test Bank

Gorbachev was right. The world was vastly different from when he first took power in 1985. At that time, the Soviet Union was the world's most feared totalitarian dictatorship. But Gorbachev had quickly recognized that "something was wrong." Blaming poor living conditions on the country's rigid political and economic system, he had launched a bold program of reforms.

Gorbachev's sweeping changes had electrified his country and transformed the world. For the first time, Soviet citizens were encouraged to speak, write, and worship freely. Gorbachev's "new thinking" also had a revolutionary impact on Soviet foreign policy. He allowed the Berlin Wall to fall, and he freed Eastern Europe from Soviet domination. Gorbachev accepted German reunification and slowed the arms race. As a result of these dramatic changes, the Cold War thawed and then melted away.

These historic achievements earned Gorbachev world-wide praise. But they also raised expectations among the Soviet people that he could not meet. The Soviet Union had been put together by force. As controls eased, people increasingly criticized Gorbachev for failing to improve the economy. At the same time, the Soviet Union's increasingly restless republics demanded greater freedom from the central government in Moscow.

Gorbachev's resignation on December 25, 1991, did not come as a surprise. The Soviet Union was rapidly falling apart. By late 1991, all 15 of its republics had declared their independence. Gorbachev had become a leader without a country.

A few minutes after Gorbachev's resignation, Kremlin guards lowered the Soviet flag for the last time. The red flag bearing the distinctive gold hammer-and-sickle emblem had flown over the Kremlin since Lenin seized power in 1917. The guards then raised the white, red, and blue flag of the Russian Republic. Chimes from the Kremlin's tower rang for several minutes to mark the historic event. The Soviet Union passed into history, and a new era began.

Many chapters in this text have featured key turning points in history. Momentous events are not confined to the past. Great changes are transforming the world you are living in. This chapter begins by describing how Gorbachev's reforms changed the Soviet Union. It then explains how

his policies unintentionally helped cause the collapse of communism in Eastern Europe. Although the Cold War ended, global problems did not disappear. Conflicts in the Persian Gulf, Yugoslavia, and Somalia challenged world leaders. Global issues such as the plight of refugees and environmental pollution still remained.

Gorbachev launched a new era. 1

On March 10, 1985, members of the Politburo, the Communist party's top decision-making group, held a secret meeting inside the Kremlin. The two dozen leaders faced a difficult decision. Since Leonid Brezhnev's death in 1982, the party's aging leaders had tenaciously tried to maintain their power. Time and events, however, were against them. Brezhnev's successor, Yuri Andropov, had died after only 15 months in power. Just 13 months later, Andropov's successor Konstantin Chernenko had also died. Who would succeed him?

As the Politburo debated that question, its choice narrowed to two men. The party's old guard favored Viktor Grishin, the aging conservative Moscow party boss. Others, however, argued for a vigorous but little-known Politburo member named Mikhail Gorbachev.

Gorbachev's supporters praised his youth, energy, and political skills. Andrei Gromyko, the senior Politburo member, told his colleagues that Gorbachev "has a nice smile, but he's got iron teeth."

Gromyko's support helped Gorbachev become the party's new general secretary. The cautious officials who voted for Gorbachev knew that reforms were needed to revitalize the Soviet Union. However, they did not foresee that Gorbachev's rise to power marked the beginning of a Second Russian Revolution.

Gorbachev tried "new thinking."

Gorbachev was part of a new generation of Soviet leaders. At 54, he was the first general secretary born after the Bolshevik Revolution. He joined the Communist party in 1952 and was

845

SECTION 1
Resources

GEOGRAPHY
■ Transparencies 95, 108

REINFORCEMENT
■ Independent Practice 37.1

ENRICHMENT
■ Voices from the Past 37.1

ASSESSMENT
■ Section Quiz 37.1

SECTION 1
Objectives and Teaching Strategies

OBJECTIVE 1. Describe Gorbachev's reforms and discuss their consequences.
Teaching Strategy: *Discussing History: Gorbachev's Reforms* (page 844a)

OBJECTIVE 2. Discuss reasons why Gorbachev was caught off guard by the coup plotters.
Teaching Strategy: *Relating Past to Present: Leaders Who Ignore Warnings* (page 844c)

OBJECTIVE 3. Describe reasons the coup failed.
Teaching Strategy: *Writing about History: The August Coup* (page 844c)

■ BACKGROUND

The Politburo functioned as a board of directors for the Communist party. At the time Gorbachev was chosen to be general secretary, the Politburo included 10 full members and 11 candidate, or nonvoting, members. In addition, the five secretaries of the Central Committee could attend meetings. Accounts from those present indicate that the Politburo was originally evenly split between Grishen and Gorbachev. Ask students to speculate on how Soviet history would have been different if Gorbachev had lost.

■ BACKGROUND

When he took office in 1983, President Reagan viewed the Soviets with great suspicion. Calling the

Soviet Union an "evil empire," Reagan charged that its leaders "reserve unto themselves the right to commit any crime, to lie, and to cheat." Many Americans agreed with Reagan and supported his call for a massive military buildup. Between 1980 and 1985, United States defense budgets increased from $144 billion to $295 billion. This huge expansion included plans for a fleet of new bombers, an enlarged navy, and an antimissile defense system called the Strategic Defense Initiative (SDI). Known as Star Wars after a popular 1977 movie, SDI called for a vast system of space-based lasers and other high-tech defenses against nuclear missiles. Reagan's supporters argued that the Soviets' costly attempt to keep up with America's military buildup accelerated their economic collapse.

■ BACKGROUND

Mikhail and Raisa Gorbachev first met at a ballroom dancing class while they were students at Moscow State University. One of their friends later said, "I think for Gorbachev it was love at first sight. Just like in the movies." They were married in 1954. Raisa graduated with a degree in Marxist-Leninist philosophy and later earned the equivalent of a Ph.D in sociology. Raisa was the most visible wife of any Soviet leader. The wives of Stalin, Krushchev, Brezhnev, Andropov, and Chernenko rarely appeared in public. For example, it was not known for sure that Yuri Andropov even had a wife until she appeared to mourn him at his funeral in

President Gorbachev introduced the policy of glasnost in an effort to encourage Soviet citizens to discuss ways of revitalizing their society.

a law student in Moscow when Stalin died. Unlike other Soviet leaders, Gorbachev was too young to be directly affected by Stalin's ruthless purge of independent-minded party members (page 655).

After graduating from law school, Gorbachev steadily rose through the party ranks. When he became a full member of the Politburo in 1980, conservative members must have considered Gorbachev to be one of them. Subsequent events would show that he was not.

Once in office, Gorbachev discovered that he had inherited a number of difficult problems. He later admitted that he began by trying to make a series of gradual changes. Neither he nor anyone else knew where these changes would lead.

The arms race A costly arms race had dominated United States–Soviet relations since the end of World War II. Hopes for meaningful arms control had brightened momentarily when President Nixon visited Moscow in 1972. After lengthy negotiations, Nixon and Brezhnev signed the Strategic Arms Limitation Treaty (SALT), which froze for five years the number of offensive ballistic missiles held by the two superpower nations.

SALT seemed to signal the beginning of a new period of reduced tensions called **détente**. Despite high hopes, détente did not last long. In

December 1979, the Soviets suddenly invaded Afghanistan to support an unpopular Communist regime. Two years later, Brezhnev forced Polish leaders to abolish Solidarity (page 757).

The invasion of Afghanistan and the crackdown in Poland convinced President Reagan that the Soviet leaders could not be trusted. He rejected arms limitation talks with what he called the "evil empire."

"New thinking" Gorbachev recognized that the arms race placed a heavy burden on the Soviet economy. Military spending consumed 25 percent of the nation's budget, compared to 7 percent in the United States. With so much of its resources committed to the arms race, the Soviet economy was steadily falling behind the dynamic rates of growth in the United States, Japan, and Western Europe.

Gorbachev concluded that the troubled Soviet economy could no longer bear the costs of an accelerating arms race. Shortly after taking power, he announced his intent to pursue a foreign policy based on "new thinking," stressing diplomacy instead of force.

Gorbachev's new thinking lowered global tensions. In December 1987, he became the first Soviet leader in 14 years to visit the United States. Reagan and Gorbachev opened a new era in superpower relations by signing an Interme-

846

diate Nuclear Forces (INF) Treaty banning nuclear missiles with ranges of 300 to 3,400 miles.

The policy of new thinking also produced a surprising change in Soviet policy toward Afghanistan. After more than nine years of fighting, the last Soviet forces withdrew from Afghanistan in February 1989. They left behind a country devastated by a brutal war. Officials estimated that more than 1 million Afghans had died and that another 7 million had lost their homes.

Gorbachev began a policy of openness.

As international tensions eased, Gorbachev turned to problems within the Soviet Union. Soviet leaders from Lenin to Brezhnev had created a totalitarian state that controlled the mass media and restricted human rights. Soviet citizens lived in a climate of fear that rewarded silence and discouraged individual initiative. "Stalin did the thinking for everyone," wrote one novelist, "so everyone stopped thinking."

Soviet reformers warned Gorbachev that rigid government controls had created "an era of stagnation." They stressed that badly needed reforms could not occur without a free flow of ideas and information. In 1986, Gorbachev introduced a new policy known as **glasnost,** or openness, which encouraged Soviet citizens to discuss ways of revitalizing their society.

Within a short time, glasnost began to produce a number of remarkable changes. Although Soviet authorities still frowned on organized religion, more than 1,000 churches were allowed to open. At the same time, more Soviet Jews were permitted to leave the country. The government also released many dissidents including Andrei Sakharov, and Soviet youth began to enjoy live concerts by Billy Joel, Bon Jovi, Paul McCartney, and other rock stars.

The relaxation of controls also enabled people to read books by previously banned authors such as Alexander Solzhenitsyn. Freed from having to blindly follow the "party line," reporters actively investigated social problems and openly criticized government officials. "It's more exciting right now to read than to live!" marvelled one astonished reporter. "The oxygen of democracy is intoxicating and contagious."

The reporter was right. Glasnost opened Soviet society to the outside world in a way that even reformers such as Gorbachev could not have predicted. As fear subsided, Soviet citizens were exposed to a wide variety of new ideas. "Broader contacts with the outside world [gave] people an opportunity to compare, and consequently to choose," observed one reformer. "The Soviet system . . . suffered a crushing defeat in an open contest with the civilized world."

Gorbachev sought economic renewal.

The new openness gave Soviet citizens an opportunity to complain publicly about their economic problems. Angry consumers protested that they had to stand in long lines to buy food, soap, and other common household items. Buyers who could afford a car had to be even more patient. The average wait to purchase even the cheapest model was seven years.

Reform-minded economists blamed these problems on their country's inefficient system of central planning. As you have seen (pages 654–656), Stalin forcibly established an economic system based on state ownership of land, industry, and capital. Party officials set up plans for agriculture and industry. These plans told managers at every farm and factory how much to produce, what wages to pay their workers, and what prices to charge consumers.

The system of centralized planning created an enormous bureaucracy centered in Moscow. By the time Gorbachev became general secretary, 64 government ministries fixed production targets for more than 70,000 items, while also setting more than 200,000 prices each year.

Gorbachev recognized that this inefficient system had to be reformed. In 1986, he launched a new program called **perestroika,** or economic restructuring, to revitalize the Soviet economy. At first, Gorbachev concentrated on firing incompetent workers and trying to reduce the high rate of alcoholism among workers.

When these relatively modest reforms failed to make a difference, Gorbachev began to experiment with free-market principles. For example, local managers were given greater authority over their farms and factories. They were encouraged to rely on profits instead of government funding. In addition, new laws allowed people to open small private businesses.

847

1984. In contrast, Raisa accompanied Mikhail on most of his foreign trips.

■ BACKGROUND

Glasnost received its first major test when a reactor at the Chernobyl nuclear power plant exploded on April 26, 1986. The blast destroyed a thousand-ton lid protecting the reactor core and killed 31 people. A deadly radioactive cloud three miles long spread across the Soviet Union and into Europe. Meanwhile, firefighters worked feverishly to prevent the raging fire from spreading to another reactor.

Soviet officials at first refused to admit the extent of the disaster even to their own citizens. The official silence from the Soviet government suggested that *glasnost* might be an empty slogan. Stung by this criticism, Gorbachev permitted both Soviet and Western reporters to investigate the disaster. Four months later, the Soviets presented a detailed report on the accident to the International Atomic Energy Agency.

The tragic consequences of the Chernobyl disaster are still being felt. An area 12 miles in diameter around the site is expected to remain uninhabitable for years to come. Many of the thousands of emergency workers who put out the fire have been afflicted with serious illnesses caused by their exposure to the radiation. By early 1993, more than 500 of these workers had committed suicide rather than endure the painful effects of their illnesses.

Direct your students' attention to the picture on this page. Remind students that this was the first time that Communist party officials had to compete for votes in an election. Ask students to speculate on what Lenin would say to the woman shown casting her ballot.

■ BACKGROUND

The Congress of People's Deputies began its first session on May 25, 1989. The twelve-day session was televised live throughout the entire country. Millions of people watched spellbound as the deputies openly questioned Gorbachev and debated the pace of economic reform. The televised sessions marked an important turning point for the Soviet people. Yeltsin later wrote that the debates "gave the people more of a political education than seventy years of stereotyped Marxist-Leninist lectures . . . On the day the Congress opened, they were one sort of people; on the day that it closed, they were different people . . . Almost the entire population was awakened from its state of lethargy."

Perestroika raised hopes, but it failed to revive the Soviet economy. A disappointed Gorbachev admitted, "Changes are not coming as fast as we would like them to." As living standards continued to decline, popular unrest mounted.

Gorbachev promoted political reforms.

When the Politburo chose Gorbachev as its new general secretary, the Communist party had a monopoly on all economic and political power. The party used censorship, secret police, and political repression to maintain a tight grip over Soviet society. These practices deliberately restricted individual initiative and limited innovation. For example, the Soviet people were not allowed to take full advantage of computers, photocopiers, and fax machines. Although these machines would increase productivity, they would also promote a freer exchange of ideas.

Demokratizatsiya Gorbachev and his top advisers concluded that the Communist party had become the biggest obstacle to reform. In 1988, he introduced a third new policy called **demokratizatsiya,** or democratization, that would shift power from the party to the state.

Gorbachev believed that the Soviet Union could only solve its problems when the people felt they had a stake in governing their country. "A house can be put in order only by a person who feels he owns the house," Gorbachev explained.

The Congress of People's Deputies The plan for restructuring the government called for the election of a 2,250-member Congress of People's Deputies. In all previous elections, voters merely ratified candidates chosen by the Communist party. This election, however, would be different. Even though there was still only one political party, candidates would compete for office.

The election produced a number of unexpected results. Although the Communist party won the majority of seats, the voters rejected several powerful party bosses. They also elected a number of outspoken reformers such as Andrei Sakharov and Boris Yeltsin.

Like Gorbachev, Boris Yeltsin was a product of the Communist system he was now dedicated to changing. As the Moscow party boss and a member of the Politburo, Yeltsin gained national attention by denouncing the privileges enjoyed by the party elite. Yeltsin and Gorbachev became bitter rivals when Yeltsin strongly criticized Gorbachev for the slow pace of reform.

A Russian woman votes in the first Soviet election in which voters were given a choice of candidates.

848

Nationalism and ethnic unrest threatened the Soviet Union.

As a result of Gorbachev's reforms, many once unthinkable ideas suddenly became a reality. For the first time, Soviet citizens voted in free elections and publicly criticized their leaders. But glasnost also had unintended consequences that caught Gorbachev by surprise.

The Soviet Union was a vast multinational state that included more than 100 different ethnic groups. Russians had always been the largest and most powerful ethnic group. However, non-Russians formed a majority in the 14 republics surrounding the Russian Republic.

Although long-suppressed, ethnic tensions still existed beneath the surface of Soviet society. As central controls loosened, ethnic protests spread across the country. Nationalist groups in Georgia, Ukraine, and Moldavia demanded greater control over their internal affairs. Meanwhile, Muslims living in the five Central Asian republics demanded more religious freedom; and a long-festering feud between Muslims and Christians living in Azerbaijan and Armenia erupted into armed clashes.

Confrontation in Lithuania The greatest threat to Soviet stability occurred in Lithuania, Estonia, and Latvia. Known as the Baltic states, these three republics had been independent nations between the two world wars. The Nazi-Soviet pact of 1939 (pages 707–708) ended their freedom. Although they belonged to different ethnic groups, the Baltic peoples shared a common desire for independence.

Ignoring Gorbachev's pleas for restraint, the Lithuanian parliament declared the republic's independence from the Soviet Union on March 11, 1990. When economic sanctions failed to force Lithuania to back down, hard-liners in the Communist party urged Gorbachev to use force.

Although Gorbachev wanted to avoid violence, he feared that if Lithuania succeeded in defying Moscow's authority, the other republics would be encouraged to do the same. The confrontation suddenly turned violent on January 13, 1991. Firing bursts of gunfire, Soviet tanks plowed through a crowd of unarmed civilians guarding the main television and radio station in Vilnius, the Lithuanian capital. The assault left 14 people dead and over 150 wounded.

The bloody clash in Lithuania provoked a storm of protest. In Moscow, more than 100,000 people marched to the Kremlin in a demonstration against the crackdown. At the same time, other republics demanded greater autonomy.

A new Union Treaty Shaken by these events, Gorbachev abandoned the use of force to hold the nation together. In April 1991, he invited the leaders of nine republics to meet with him to discuss a new Union Treaty dividing power between the central government and the republics. The new agreement promised the republics a much larger role in governing the country.

Gorbachev loses popularity.

As the crisis deepened, Gorbachev's popularity plummeted. An opinion poll in March 1991 showed that only 14 percent of the people still supported him. In contrast, more than 70 percent named Yeltsin as the most popular leader. Just three months later, voters overwhelmingly chose Yeltsin to become the Russian Republic's first freely elected president.

While Yeltsin's popularity steadily increased, Gorbachev's problems rapidly multiplied. *Perestroika* raised public expectations far more than living standards. By the summer of 1991, industrial production dropped 20 percent while inflation skyrocketed. Long lines of angry shoppers waiting to buy scarce goods vividly underscored Gorbachev's failure to revive the economy.

The bleak economic news alarmed hard-liners in the party. They anxiously watched as Gorbachev negotiated the new Union Treaty. Outraged conservatives realized that the treaty would reduce the importance of the central government, thus undermining their power.

Faced with the threat of losing their power and privileges, top officials in the Communist party, Defense Ministry, and KGB vowed to block the Union Treaty. Their threats did not go unnoticed. Leading reformers repeatedly warned Gorbachev of plans to overthrow him.

These ominous events should have alerted Gorbachev to the imminent threat of a coup. However, like Julius Caesar in ancient Rome, he ignored the warnings and left himself unprotected. When Gorbachev left Moscow for his annual vacation at the Black Sea, his senior officials made final plans to overthrow him.

849

■ **DISCUSSION**

Gorbachev's unsuccessful attempt to restore Moscow's authority over the Baltics produced three unintended consequences. First, the crackdown instilled the Baltic people with an even greater determination to win their independence. Second, many reformers lost confidence in Gorbachev's leadership. They accused him of abandoning his vision of transforming the Soviet Union into a modern, democratic nation based on the rule of law. And finally, hard-liners in the Communist party, KGB, and army blamed Gorbachev for preventing them from crushing the Lithuanian government. More than ever they yearned for a strong leader who would save the Soviet Union from collapse by cracking down on the rebellious republics.

■ **DISCUSSION**

The March 1991 poll also revealed the public's mounting sense of despair. When asked, "What does the Soviet Union offer its citizens?" 65 percent replied, "Shortages, waiting in lines, and a miserable existence."

Review the Turning Points feature on this page. Note that the Alpha Group members faced a particularly difficult assignment. At the time, the White House was surrounded by a huge crowd. The assault plan called for the Alpha Group to use grenade launchers to blast away the barricades. They were then to storm their way to the fifth floor and arrest Boris Yeltsin. Meanwhile, a second Beta group would suppress any pockets of resistance.

Now divide your class into small cooperative learning groups. Tell each group that they are Alpha Group members. Their task is to prepare a statement explaining why they will or will not obey their orders to attack the White House. Point out that Alpha team members faced court-martial and even execution if they disobeyed orders. Ask each team to read its statement to the class.

■ BACKGROUND

At first, Gorbachev tried to curb the outcry against the party. In his first appearance after the coup, he argued that most party members were loyal citizens who should not be blamed for the coup. But Gorbachev's attempt to defend the party seriously damaged his credibility. Outraged delegates in the Russian Parliament heckled him during a speech two days after the coup. "If he had come here immediately, we would have carried him on our shoulders," said one dismayed delegate. "Instead,

▲ Turning Points in History

The August Coup On August 18, 1991, a group of hard-line Soviet leaders suddenly interrupted Gorbachev's vacation. Speaking for a State Committee, the group demanded that Gorbachev accept emergency rule or resign. When he refused, the plotters returned to Moscow, leaving Gorbachev's compound surrounded by troops and cut off from the rest of the country.

The next day, the Committee issued a statement declaring that Gorbachev's reforms had placed the Soviet Union in "mortal danger." The Committee then issued a second decree suspending political parties, banning strikes, and closing all independent newspapers. By mid-morning, hundreds of tanks and armored personnel carriers began rolling into Moscow.

The State Committee assumed that this show of force would ensure obedience. They were wrong. Under Gorbachev's reforms, people had lost their fear of the party, and they were willing to defend their freedoms.

By noon, many protestors began to gather at the Russian Parliament building just two miles from the Kremlin. Nicknamed the White House because of its marble facade, the 19-story building served as Boris Yeltsin's headquarters. "We are waiting for Yeltsin's response. We are ready to defend him," shouted one demonstrator.

The crowd outside the White House didn't have to wait long. Like everyone else, Yeltsin had been caught off guard by the coup. He narrowly avoided arrest by quickly leaving his home and dashing to his office inside the White House. Shortly after noon, he walked outside the White House and boldly climbed atop one of the nearby tanks. As his supporters cheered, Yeltsin defiantly urged his followers to disobey the State Committee's decrees.

Yeltsin's courageous action helped inspire others to step forward. Fearing an armed attack, thousands of volunteers worked feverishly building barricades around the White House.

Their fears were not misplaced. On August 20, the State Committee ordered an elite force of commandos known as Alpha Group to assault the White House. But the Alpha commanders and their men refused to obey. "They want to smear us in blood," one commander told his men. "I for one will not storm the White House."

Alpha Group's refusal to attack the White House helped doom the coup. On August 21, the military ordered its troops to leave Moscow. Later that night, Gorbachev and his family flew back to Moscow. As he approached the capital, he told his aides, "We are flying into a new era."

Crowds of citizens surround the tanks in Moscow during the coup attempt. The soldiers' refusal to fight doomed the coup.

850

Countries of the Former Soviet Union

KEY
★ National capital

0 — 600 Miles

Map Study
Describe the location of Estonia, Latvia, and Lithuania, the first three republics to declare independence.

The coup had far-reaching effects.

Gorbachev soon found that his country was changing far more rapidly than either he or anyone else could imagine. Within four months, both the Communist party and the Soviet Union collapsed. The end of the old order forced Gorbachev to resign, thus leaving Boris Yeltsin as the most powerful leader in Russia.

The collapse of the party The failure of the coup sparked joyous celebrations across the Soviet Union. At a victory rally in Moscow, a huge crowd roared its approval as Yeltsin condemned the Communist party for supporting the coup. His speech captured the mood of anticommunism sweeping the country. "We are all sick of the Communists," said one Yeltsin supporter. "They have been strangling us for 70 years."

At first Gorbachev tried to curb the outcry against the party. But when this failed, he resigned as general secretary. The Soviet Parliament voted to suspend all party activities. Having first seized power in 1917 in a coup that succeeded, the once all-powerful party now collapsed in the aftermath of a coup that failed.

The collapse of the Soviet Union The coup also played a decisive role in accelerating the breakup of the Soviet Union. As the coup began to unravel, both Estonia and Latvia declared their unconditional independence. On September 6, 1991, the Soviet government officially granted them independence.

Other republics soon followed the Baltic example. As the Soviet Union broke up, Gorbachev desperately pleaded for unity. "We should not break things down," he argued. "We do not have

851

he started saying that he is still a Communist. He missed a great opportunity." Ask students to speculate upon reasons Gorbachev misread public opinion so badly.

ANSWER TO
Map Study

They are west of Russia, on the Baltic Sea.

ANSWERS TO
Section Review 1

Define:
(a) period of reduced tensions (b) openness (c) economic restructuring (d) democratization

Identify:
(a) reformer and last leader of the Soviet Union (b) Strategic Arms Limitation Treaty. It froze for five years the number of offensive ballistic missiles. (c) treaty banning nuclear missiles with ranges of 300 to 3,400 miles (d) Soviet dissidents (e) supreme legislative body (f) first freely elected president of the Russian Republic (g) Lithuania, Estonia, and Latvia (h) loose federation of 11 former Soviet republics

Answer:
1. (a) The troubled Soviet economy could no longer bear the costs of an accelerating arms race. (b) INF Treaty and Soviet withdrawal from Afghanistan

(continued)

ANSWERS TO *(continued)*

2. Greater freedom of religion, press, and speech opened Soviet society and reduced the level of fear.

3. to shift power from the party to the state

4. (a) agreement redistributing power between the central government and the republics **(b)** It would reduce their power and privileges.

5. Yeltsin's leadership, Alpha Group's refusal to attack the White House, and opposition from the Soviet people

6. (a) lost power and resigned **(b)** became most popular and powerful leader in Russia **(c)** lost all power and collapsed **(d)** broke apart

7. Answers will vary. Students can argue that the Soviet Union was doomed to fall apart since it was held together by force. Others argue that Gorbachev would have held the Soviet Union together if he had tried to negotiate a new Union Treaty before ethnic unrest became unmanageable.

ANSWERS TO
Caption Questions

It is the hammer and sickle of the Soviet flag and symbolizes the Soviet Union. Gorbachev's actions set off a chain reaction, or domino effect, destroying the Soviet Union.

the right to make a mistake of this proportion." But no one was listening. By early December, all 15 republics had declared independence.

Recognizing that the Soviet Union was doomed, Yeltsin met with the leaders of other republics to determine a new course of action. They agreed to form a Commonwealth of Independent States (CIS), a loose federation of former Soviet territories. Only the Baltic republics and Georgia refused to join.

The end of an era The formation of the CIS meant the death of the Soviet Union. On Christmas Day 1991, Gorbachev announced his resignation as president of a country that by then had ceased to exist. "He tried to reform the unreformable," one former colleague observed sadly, referring to Gorbachev's devotion to the Communist party. But despite his failures, Gorbachev will always be remembered as the man who launched one of the most dramatic revolutions of the twentieth century.

Section REVIEW 1

Define: (a) détente, (b) *glasnost*, (c) *perestroika*, (d) *demokratizatsiya*
Identify: (a) Gorbachev, (b) SALT, (c) INF Treaty, (d) Andrei Sakharov, (e) Congress of People's Deputies, (f) Yeltsin, (g) Baltic states, (h) Commonwealth of Independent States

Answer:
1. (a) Why did Gorbachev decide to change foreign policy? (b) What were two consequences of his new thinking?
2. How did *glasnost* change Soviet life?
3. Why did Gorbachev launch his program of *demokratizatsiya*?
4. (a) What was the Union Treaty? (b) Why did hard liners oppose it?
5. What were three reasons the August Coup failed?
6. What impact did the coup have on (a) Gorbachev? (b) Yeltsin? (c) the Communist party? and (d) the Soviet Union?

Critical Thinking
7. Could Gorbachev have done anything to prevent the breakup of the Soviet Union?

852

ROBERT ARIAIL
Courtesy Columbia State (S.C.)

What is the significance of the shape in which the dominoes are arranged? What is the message of the cartoon?

Communism collapsed in Eastern Europe. 2

On May 2, 1989, squads of Hungarian soldiers rushed to the barbed-wire fence separating their country from Austria. These troops, however, were not defending their border. Instead of weapons, they were equipped with huge pliers. Photographers and television crews recorded the scene as the soldiers cut open the barbed-wire barrier.

That fence was part of the iron curtain that had divided Europe since the beginning of the Cold War. Hungary's decision to open its border marked the first break in this barrier in 40 years.

This section will examine the momentous events that occurred in Eastern Europe in 1989. It begins with the forces of change that were sweeping across the region. Those forces triggered a series of revolutions that toppled Communist governments in Eastern Europe.

Eastern Europe faced change.

As 1989 began, Eastern Europe seemed still firmly tied to the Soviet Union. With the exception of reform-minded Hungary, hard-line Communists remained in control. Aging leaders in East Germany, Czechoslovakia, and Romania rejected Gorbachev's calls for reform.

While these leaders vowed to resist change, powerful forces were steadily eroding their bases of support. Nationalists within each country in Eastern Europe bitterly resented the Communist regimes imposed on them by Stalin after World War II. Popular revolts had erupted in Poland in 1953, in Hungary in 1956, and in Czechoslovakia in 1968. In each case, the government, backed by Soviet power, suppressed the revolt.

Deteriorating economic conditions throughout Eastern Europe intensified people's discontent. Consumer goods and even basic foodstuffs were often in short supply. Rising national debts and declining living standards became convincing proof that the command economies were not working. The people of Eastern Europe thus found themselves caught between a failing economy and oppressive governments that prevented them from voicing their grievances or seeking change.

Popular discontent and the declining appeal of communism helped to prepare Eastern Europe for change. Although these forces had been present for some time, they had always been suppressed by the threat of Soviet intervention. That condition changed rapidly after Gorbachev took power in 1985. Instead of insisting on conformity, Gorbachev encouraged Eastern European governments to experiment with *glasnost* and *perestroika*.

At a Warsaw Pact meeting in 1989, Gorbachev rejected the Brezhnev Doctrine of the Soviets' right to intervene in support of communism. "Each people," he announced, "determines the future of its own country and chooses its own form of society. There must be no interference from outside, no matter what the pretext."

Poland tested Gorbachev's new policy.

The people of Poland were the first to test Gorbachev's new policy. As you have seen (page 757), in December 1981, the Polish government had banned Solidarity and declared martial law.

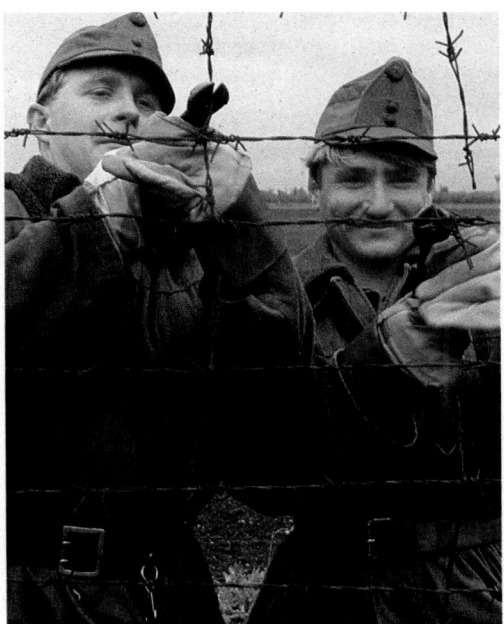

Hungarian soldiers smile gleefully as they cut the barbed wire fence at the border between their country and Austria.

The secret police had arrested Lech Walesa and thousands of other Solidarity members.

The Communist party quickly discovered, however, that military rule could not revive Poland's failing economy. In the 1980's, Poland's industrial production declined, while foreign debt rose to almost $40 billion. Frustrated consumers endured long lines, shortages, and rising prices. Young couples found that they had to work 2 years to buy a car and wait 20 years for an apartment.

Public discontent deepened as the economic crisis worsened. In August 1988, defiant workers walked off their jobs, demanding raises and the reinstatement of Solidarity. Faced with Poland's worst labor unrest since 1980, General Jaruzelski agreed to hold talks with Solidarity leaders.

These talks sparked a series of significant changes. In April 1989, Jaruzelski legalized Solidarity and agreed to hold Poland's first free elections since the Communists took power.

Polish voters promptly handed the Communists a stunning defeat as Solidarity candidates swept to victory. On August 25, 1989, the Polish

853

SECTION 2
Resources

GEOGRAPHY
- Transparency 95

REINFORCEMENT
- Independent Practice 37.2

ENRICHMENT
- Voices from the Past 37.2

ASSESSMENT
- Section Quiz 37.2

SECTION 2
Objectives and Teaching Strategies

OBJECTIVE 1. Discuss the reasons East Germany opened the Berlin Wall.

Teaching Strategy: *Writing about History: What If* (page 844c)

OBJECTIVE 2. Explain the rise to power of Czechoslovakia's playwright president Vaclav Havel.

Teaching Strategy: *Vaclav Havel* (page 844c)

■ BACKGROUND

General Jaruzelski declared martial law and banned Solidarity on December 13, 1981. Just six months later, President Reagan and Pope John Paul II held a private meeting in the Vatican library to discuss the Polish situation. Both leaders were convinced that a free non-Communist Poland would lead to the fall of communism throughout Eastern Europe. Reagan and the pope formed a secret alliance dedicated to keeping Solidarity alive by supplying it with money, equipment, and strategic advice.

Over the next few years, Solidarity received fax machines, printing presses, transmitters, telephones, shortwave radios, video cameras, photocopiers, and computers. Solidarity put the equipment to good use. Using broadcasting equipment supplied by the CIA, Solidarity regularly broke into government radio and television programs with the message, "Solidarity lives!"

853

Erich Honecker proudly boasted that East Germany was a socialist paradise in which workers enjoyed the highest standard of living in Eastern Europe. He strongly opposed Gorbachev's reforms and would not allow the words *perestroika* or *glasnost* to be spoken over the airwaves or printed in the East German press.

The exodus of East Germans to Hungary and Czechoslovakia deeply embarrassed Honecker. When massive demonstrations broke out across East Germany, Honecker vowed to use a "Chinese solution" to restore order. In early October, he issued live ammunition to a large force of soldiers, policemen, and secret police agents gathered in Leipzig. Honecker ordered his security forces to be prepared to open fire on demonstrators.

Although they shared Honecker's fear of change, many Politburo members opposed using force on their own people. Egon Krenz, the Politburo member in charge of security, argued that a violent crackdown would destroy the Communist party's standing at home and abroad.

Ask students to pretend that they are members of the East German Politburo. Would they support Krenz, or Honecker? Could the rising tide of public protest be stopped? Would a "Chinese solution" work? Explain that on October 9, Krenz flew to Leipzig and cancelled Honecker's order. Honecker resigned just nine days later.

parliament chose Solidarity leader Tadeusz Mazowiecki (tah-DAY-oosh mah-zoh-vee-ET-skee) as the nation's first non-Communist prime minister in more than 40 years. Mazowiecki's election was a historic milestone. For the first time since the Russian Revolution, a Communist regime had been turned out of office peacefully.

Hungary opened the iron curtain.

In Hungary as well as in Poland, economic problems led to political change. By the beginning of 1989, rising foreign debt and popular demand for better living conditions convinced leaders that it was time for a fresh approach.

During 1989, Communist reformers supported a series of far-reaching changes. As you have seen (page 852), the Hungarians removed the 160-mile barbed wire fence along their border with Austria. Another important sign of change was the recognition given to a former hero of freedom. In June, Hungarians solemnly reinterred the body of Imre Nagy, the prime minister during the 1956 uprising, who had been buried in an unmarked grave. More than 200,000 people filed through Heroes' Square in Budapest to pay tribute to Nagy. The huge demonstration underscored the popular opposition to communism and Soviet domination.

In the weeks following the funeral, Hungarian leaders launched significant economic and political changes. To stimulate economic growth, they encouraged private enterprise and allowed a small stock market to operate. A new constitution permitted a multiparty system with free parliamentary elections.

The changes continued when radical reformers took over a Communist party congress in October. Inspired by the collapse of communism in Poland, the radicals deposed the party's leaders and then dissolved the party itself. For the first time, a European Communist party had voted itself out of existence.

Communism fell in East Germany.

While Poland and Hungary turned rapidly to reform, hard-line leaders in East Germany stubbornly refused to accept change. East Germany's 77-year-old party boss Erich Honecker dismissed Gorbachev's program of reforms as unnecessary.

854

Most East Germans rejected Honecker's position. The nation's young professional workers were especially angry and frustrated. They resented Honecker's authoritarian government and demanded freedom to express their views. A schoolteacher summed up how many people felt when she said, "I feel buried alive."

Hungary's decision to open its border with Austria created a sudden opportunity for East Germans to escape. In the fall of 1989, more than 30,000 discontented East Germans traveled to Hungary and then crossed the border into Austria. When Honecker banned travel to Hungary, thousands of people fled instead to Czechoslovakia. By October, huge demonstrations occurred in cities throughout East Germany. Demands for freedom and democracy received thunderous applause.

Crowds of joyful Berliners climb atop the Berlin Wall in celebration of its fall. The Brandenburg Gate is behind them.

As the crisis deepened, Honecker tried to regain control by ordering the police to use force to break up a demonstration in Leipzig. But party leaders and the police refused to carry out his order. Stunned by the sudden loss of authority, Honecker resigned on October 18.

◢ Turning Points in History

The Fall of the Berlin Wall The new East German leader, Egon Krenz, promised to make sweeping changes. Krenz boldly gambled that he could restore stability by allowing people to leave East Germany. On November 9, 1989, he opened the Berlin Wall.

Thousands and then tens of thousands of East Germans soon poured through the Berlin Wall. As the incredible news spread that the wall had been opened, the long-divided city of Berlin erupted into a joyous celebration. Once-feared border guards smiled as huge crowds climbed on top of the wall to celebrate. The jubilant Berliners danced, sang, and chanted, "The wall is gone! The wall is gone!" Many slammed hammers into the wall, smashing the despised symbol of Communist oppression into small concrete souvenirs.

The celebration did not stop at the wall. During the night and for the next two days, a flood of East Germans roared across the border into West Berlin. Huge crowds of cheering West Berliners rushed to greet them. Many people handed out flowers and food. Church bells rang, long-separated friends were reunited, and people wept for joy.

Now that the unthinkable had occurred, curious East Germans began to explore the city they had only heard about. Because the East German currency was worthless in West Berlin, they formed long lines outside banks to obtain the 100 marks ($50) in "greeting money" given by the West German government to East Germans visiting West Berlin for the first time. They then headed for the Kurfurstendamm, the glittering shopping boulevard in the heart of West Berlin.

The sights along the Kurfurstendamm amazed the East Germans. People marveled at shops filled with modern appliances, fashionable clothes, and abundant supplies of groceries. Many people used their greeting money to buy fresh fruits and vegetables to take home.

Krenz's dramatic gamble did not work. When the public discovered evidence of widespread corruption among party leaders, Krenz and other top officials were forced to resign in disgrace. By the end of the year, the East German Communist party had virtually ceased to exist.

▲▲▲▲▲▲▲▲▲▲▲▲▲▲▲▲▲▲▲▲

Czechoslovakia ended communism.

While huge crowds were demanding change in East Germany, neighboring Czechoslovakia remained quiet. A hard-line government led by Milos Jakes resisted all change. Vivid memories of the violent crackdown against the reforms of 1968 (page 756) made the Czechs cautious.

■ **BACKGROUND**

While the dramatic events in East Germany and Czechoslovakia captured world attention, the winds of change also swept across Bulgaria. Although blessed with fertile lands, Bulgaria suffered from a stagnant economy and terrible pollution caused by the nation's mining and metal industries. In late October, a small environmental group organized a series of demonstrations to protest against pollution. Bulgaria's longtime party boss Tudor Zhivkov ordered the police to break up the demonstration.

Zhivkov's actions proved to be a fatal mistake. Following the pattern of protest used in East Germany, party reformers dismissed Zhivkov. The new government then promised to legalize opposition groups and hold free elections. Unlike the Polish, Hungarian, East German, and Czechoslovakian Communist parties, the Bulgarian party did not disintegrate. Instead, it changed its name to the Socialist party and tried to stay in power by making reforms.

Identify:

(a) Poland's non-Communist prime minister (b) Hungarian prime minister during the 1956 uprising (c) deposed East German leader (d) East German leader who opened the Berlin Wall (e) Czech playwright-president (f) reform leader of Czechoslovakia during the 1968 revolution (g) former Romanian leader (h) Romanian secret police

Answer:

1. nationalism, deteriorating economic conditions, Gorbachev's reforms

2. For the first time since the Russian Revolution, a Communist regime had been peacefully voted out.

3. Thousands of East Germans fled through Hungary and Austria to West Germany; those left behind demonstrated against the government.

4. By then the Czech people were frustrated with the Communist government, and the brutal crackdown angered them.

5. (a) massacre of demonstrators in Timisoara (b) because Ceauşescu's reign was unjust, brutal

6. Answers may vary.
(a) electing skilled, honest governments and developing strong economies (b) Hungary seems best prepared, since it began making economic changes before dissolving its Communist party.
(c) Romania, since the government was still dominated by Communists

Finally on October 28, 1989, a few thousand people gathered outside the building where the popular Czech playwright Vaclav Havel was being detained. An eloquent critic of the government, Havel had been repeatedly imprisoned for protests against the state. Now, as he looked out the window, Havel felt renewed hope: "For the first time, I felt that something was different, that something was going to change."

Havel's feeling proved to be right. Three weeks later, 25,000 students—inspired by the fall of the Berlin Wall—gathered in Prague to demand reform. Following orders from the government, the police brutally attacked the demonstrators, injuring hundreds. "They had arms," Havel recalled, "we had the truth."

The government's brutal crackdown aroused the Czech people to action. "Every door of every home seemed to open up, pouring 40 years of frustration into the streets," reported one journalist. During the next eight days, enormous crowds gathered each day in Wenceslas Square in the center of Prague to demand an end to Communist rule.

The demonstrations reached a climax on November 24, when 500,000 people crowded into downtown Prague. Alexander Dubcek, the reform leader ousted by the Soviets in 1968, addressed the people of Czechoslovakia for the first time in 21 years. He reminded people that the ideals of freedom and democracy were still alive: "An old wise man said, 'If there once was light, why should there be darkness again?' Let us act to bring the light back again."

Hours after Dubcek's speech, Milos Jakes and his entire Politburo resigned. One month later, a new Parliament elected Vaclav Havel president of Czechoslovakia.

Romanians overthrew their dictator.

By late 1989, only Romania had been left untouched by the rising tide of democratic revolutions in Eastern Europe. Romania's ruthless dictator Nicolae Ceauşescu (chow-SHES-koo) still seemed to have a firm grip on power. His secret police, the Securitate (suh-KOO-rih-TAH-tay), enforced his orders with brutal efficiency.

While other Eastern Europeans were gaining political rights and economic reforms, Romanians continued to live in fear and poverty. Ceauşescu used severe censorship to stifle ideas.

Crowds filled Wenceslas Square in Prague, Czechoslovakia, during what is known as the Velvet Revolution because it occurred without civil war.

Strict laws forbade Romanians to speak with foreigners. All typewriters and personal computers had to be registered with the police. When the Romanian economy declined, Ceauşescu tried to save fuel by forbidding people to heat their homes for more than four hours a day. He himself, however, lived in luxurious comfort.

Like all tyrants, Ceauşescu relied upon force to impose his will. On December 17, he ordered the army to fire upon demonstrators who were protesting in Timisoara (tee-mee-SHWAH-rah). The army killed and wounded scores of people.

The massacre in Timisoara ignited a popular uprising against Ceauşescu. Within days, the army joined the people as they fought to defeat the Securitate and overthrow Ceauşescu. Shocked by the sudden collapse of his power, Ceauşescu and his wife attempted to flee. They were, however, captured and then hastily tried and executed on Christmas Day.

The execution of Ceauşescu ended the revolt. A coalition of groups called the National Salvation Front took power. Although the Front promised to hold free elections, it was dominated by Communist officials.

The overthrow of Ceauşescu ended a year of stunning events that changed the course of Eastern Europe's history. Although Communist rule had ended, Eastern Europe's new democracies faced the difficult task of trying to revive their countries.

Section REVIEW 2

Identify: (a) Tadeusz Mazowiecki, (b) Imre Nagy, (c) Erich Honecker, (d) Egon Krenz, (e) Vaclav Havel, (f) Alexander Dubcek, (g) Nicolae Ceauşescu, (h) Securitate

Answer:
1. What were three forces that made people in Eastern Europe eager for change?
2. Why did the election of Tadeusz Mazowiecki mark a historic milestone?
3. What impact did Hungary's decision to open its Austrian border have upon East Germany?
4. Why did Milo Jakes's decision to use force fail to stop the protestors in Czechoslovakia?
5. (a) What action provoked a popular uprising in Romania? (b) Why did Romania have the most violent revolution in Eastern Europe?

Critical Thinking
6. (a) What do you think are the most important problems facing the new governments in Eastern Europe? (b) Which country seems best prepared to solve these problems? (c) Which country seems least prepared to solve them? Explain your answers.

The post-Cold War era brought changes. 3

The Goldene Bremm checkpoint had blocked the border between France and Germany for decades. On a normal day, long lines of traffic formed on both sides of the checkpoint as inspectors examined passports and collected customs duties. But on January 1, 1993, the long lines vanished and the once busy station was vacant. "We're making history!" exclaimed one happy motorist as she drove across the border.

The French motorist was participating in a historic event. On January 1, 1993, the 12 member nations of the European Economic Community eliminated tariff and customs barriers. For the first time, people and goods could all flow freely from one country to another. The European Community thus became more like the United States marketplace, where consumers and businesses operate freely from California to Maine.

The creation of a single market in Western Europe signalled the beginning of a new era in European history. Although filled with promise, the new period was also fraught with unexpected perils. As you will see in this section, the new Europe included a unified Germany, a peaceful division of Czechoslovakia, a bloody civil war in Yugoslavia, and continuing turmoil in the former Soviet Union.

A new Germany emerged.

The collapse of communism in Eastern Europe had a profound impact upon the two Germanys. As you have seen (pages 854–855), the desire for freedom and higher living standards ignited the protests that led to the fall of the Berlin Wall. At first, many East Germans hoped to rebuild

857

SECTION 3 Resources

GEOGRAPHY
■ Transparency 109

REINFORCEMENT
■ Independent Practice 37.3

ENRICHMENT
■ Voices from the Past 37.3

ASSESSMENT
■ Section Quiz 37.3

SECTION 3 Objectives and Teaching Strategies

OBJECTIVE 1. Discuss the causes of neo-Nazi violence in Germany.

Teaching Strategy: *Transferring Ideas: Scapegoating* (page 844d)

OBJECTIVE 2. Discuss the advantages and disadvantages of shock therapy.

Teaching Strategy: *Economics and History: Shock Therapy* (page 844d)

OBJECTIVE 3. Discuss American foreign policy options in Bosnia and Russia.

Teaching Strategy: *Writing about History: United States Policy in Bosnia and Russia* (page 844e)

■ BACKGROUND

The removal of tariff and customs barriers marked a major historic milestone. However, it did not end the EC's quest for greater integration. In December 1991, the heads of state and government of all 12 EC countries held a summit meeting in the medieval Dutch town of Maastricht. After two days of talks, they signed the Maastricht Unity Treaty calling for the creation of a single European currency by January 1, 1999. The new currency would be called the ECU, or European Currency Unit.

Germany's policy toward political refugees has been one of the most generous in the world. The law guaranteed asylum to anyone who said the word *asyl* (asylum) on German soil. In 1992 alone, 438,000 seekers of political asylum poured into Germany. Critics argued that only about 5 percent of those refugees were truly fleeing persecution. After a lengthy and often bitter debate, a German Parliament committee drafted constitutional changes that would drastically limit the eligibility of asylum-seekers. Ask students whether they would favor or oppose this change.

their country. But this goal soon disappeared as thousands of East Germans continued to pour into West Germany.

As East Germany collapsed, Germans became more and more determined to reunify their country. West German Chancellor Helmut Kohl argued that since East Germany was no longer a Communist state, there was no reason to have two Germanys.

The movement to reunify Germany raised a number of troubling issues. France, Poland, and the Soviet Union feared that a united Germany would once again try to dominate Europe. Recalling the horrors of the Holocaust, Jews and others urged caution. "The Germans want to think of the future," observed one historian, "but their neighbors are thinking of the past."

Reunification Kohl assured world leaders that Germans had learned from their tragic past. He stressed that West Germany had become a prosperous democracy committed to human rights. For the first time in its history, German unity would come peacefully and not at the expense of other countries. "We seek a European Germany," pledged Kohl, "not a German Europe."

Kohl's assurances helped persuade other European nations to accept German reunification. After a series of lengthy negotiations, the Soviet Union reluctantly agreed that the united Germany would remain in NATO. Forty-five years after its crushing defeat in World War II, Germany was officially reunited on October 3, 1990.

Rebuilding eastern Germany More than forty years of Communist rule had left eastern Germany in ruins. Its railroads, highways, and telephone system had not been modernized since World War II. Many industries produced poorly made goods that could not compete in the global market. The absence of strict environmental standards had produced serious air and water pollution. Most workers in eastern Germany lacked the financial and managerial skills needed to participate in a complex free-market economic system.

Rebuilding eastern Germany's bankrupt economy proved to be far more costly than Kohl had anticipated. During the early 1990's, the German government spent $100 billion a year modernizing outdated highways, railroads, and factories in the eastern part of the country. The soaring costs of unification forced Kohl to raise taxes.

While the German taxpayers tightened their belts, workers in eastern Germany faced a long, painful climb out of poverty. As inefficient factories closed, output shrank. Almost three million workers had lost their jobs by 1993, pushing the unemployment rate above 40 percent.

Neo-Nazi violence The economic collapse in eastern Germany was not Kohl's only problem. Despite its difficulties, Germany still remained a powerful magnet for refugees trying to escape war-torn Yugoslavia (pages 860–861) and other impoverished countries in Eastern Europe. The German constitution guarantees all refugees free housing, food, and clothing until their applications to live in Germany are approved or rejected. Since the fall of the iron curtain in 1989, about 1,000 refugees seeking political asylum have fled into Germany each day.

The growing influx of foreigners angered many Germans. Unemployed workers accused foreigners of stealing jobs by working for cheap wages. "Our country is hurting," complained one bitter construction worker. "Germany should be for Germans first."

The anger against foreigners was particularly great among alienated youths known as skinheads. During the early 1990's, thousands of skinheads joined neo-Nazi groups. Like Hitler's followers in the 1930's (pages 695–696), they used foreigners as convenient scapegoats. In 1991 and 1992, neo-Nazis instigated thousands of violent acts against foreigners.

These attacks jolted Germany by bringing back ugly memories of Nazi violence in the 1930's. Promising to crack down on the neo-Nazis, Kohl vowed, "This republic is not Weimar." Kohl was right. Unlike the Weimar Republic, the new Germany has deep democratic roots and citizens willing to speak out against racism. In late 1992, more than two million Germans participated in candle-light vigils protesting antiforeigner violence.

Eastern Europe faced new problems.

As you have seen (pages 852–857), reformers such as Vaclav Havel and Lech Walesa led a wave of "people power" that swept away the Communist regimes in Eastern Europe. Communism's sudden collapse created high hopes for equally swift changes to democracy and free

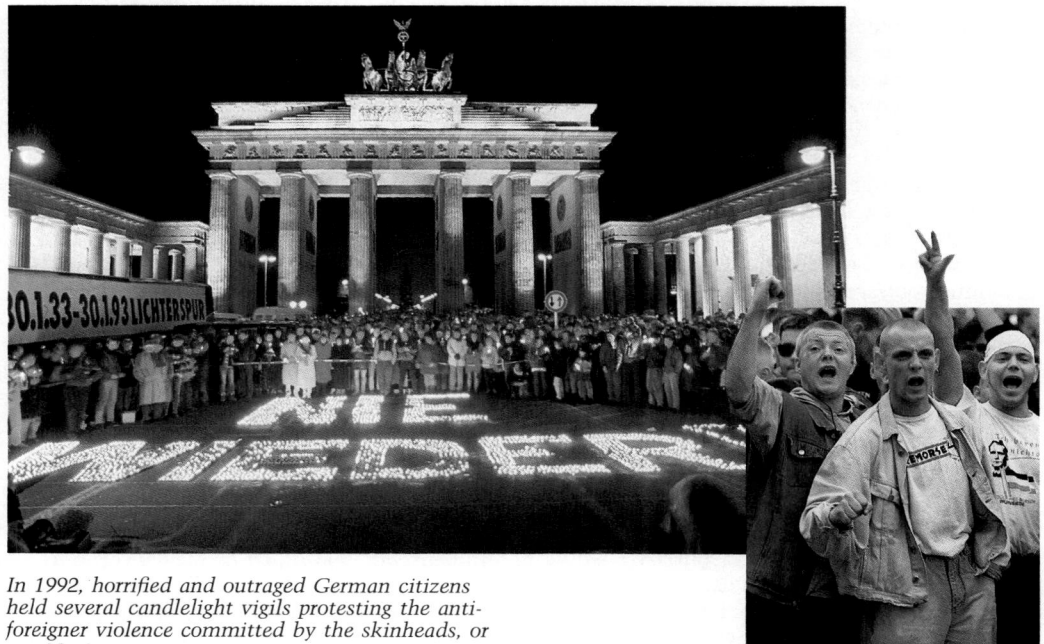

In 1992, horrified and outraged German citizens held several candlelight vigils protesting the anti-foreigner violence committed by the skinheads, or neo-Nazis.

Cooperative Learning

Begin by directing students' attention to the pictures of skinheads and antiviolence protestors on this page. Point out that both groups have strongly held views. The skinheads are frustrated by economic dislocation caused by reunification and the growing influx of foreigners competing for jobs. Like many other Germans, they have historically not thought of themselves as members of a multi-ethnic society. In contrast, the antiviolence protestors are proclaiming their commitment to preventing a repeat of the tragic events of the 1930's.

Now divide the class into small groups containing two to four students. Assign each group the task of writing a dialogue between skinheads and Germans protesting against antiforeign violence. Insist that the dialogues avoid inflammatory remarks and concentrate on the issues dividing the two groups. Ask several groups to read their dialogues to the class.

markets. These hopes soon faded, however, as people realized that they still faced difficult political, economic, and social challenges.

The pace of change in Eastern Europe varied from country to country. As the leading nations in the revolt against communism, Poland and Czechoslovakia continued to be in the forefront of change.

Poland's shock therapy In December 1990, Polish voters overwhelmingly chose Lech Walesa as their new president. Walesa pledged to revitalize Poland's bankrupt economy. This pledge proved difficult to fulfill. No country had ever successfully made the transition from a command economy to a free-enterprise system.

Following the advice of leading Western economists, the Polish government decided to adopt a bold but risky strategy called **shock therapy.** This drastic program called for the elimination of price controls and the removal of subsidies, or payments, for inefficient state-owned industries. Supporters of shock therapy argued that it offered the fastest possible way of creating a prosperous free-market economy.

At first, the program produced more shock than therapy. Ending price controls caused in-flation to soar above 600 percent. Halting subsidies to inefficient industries forced them to close, sending unemployment to 13 percent.

While shock therapy produced hardships, it also began the process of transforming the Polish economy. Rising prices provided farmers and businesses with an incentive to produce more goods, thus reducing shortages.

As Poland's economy slowly began to recover, industrial production rose and inflation dropped. However, almost three million workers remained unemployed. The stress of unemployment was particularly difficult for workers who had been taught that the state would always provide them with a job. Noting the high social cost of shock therapy, one Polish economist warned that his country would remain "perched on the edge of catastrophe for a long time."

Czechoslovakia split apart.

Following the collapse of Communist rule, Czech reformers promptly launched an economic program based on shock therapy. As in Poland, the therapy caused a sharp increase in unemployment.

859

■ BACKGROUND

Although their citizens speak similar languages, Slovakia and the Czech Republic are different in many important respects. With 10.4 million people, the Czech Republic is almost twice as populous as Slovakia. Ethnic Czechs comprise 81.3 percent of the population in the Czech Republic, while Slovaks comprise 85.6 percent of the population in Slovakia. Moravians (13.2) percent) are the largest minority in the Czech Republic, while Hungarians (10.8 percent) are the largest minority group in Slovakia.

■ BACKGROUND

The chart on page 861 shows the ethnic composition of the former Yugoslavia's six republics and two autonomous regions. For purposes of easy reference, the largest ethnic group in each region is as follows.

- Serbs comprise 85 percent of the population in Serbia and 54 percent in Vojvodina.
- Montenegrins comprise 62 percent of the population in Montenegro.
- Slovenes comprise 91 percent of the population in Slovenia.
- Croats comprise 78 percent of the population in Croatia.
- Slavic Muslims comprise 44 percent of the population in Bosnia.
- Macedonians comprise 65 percent of the population in Macedonia.

The economic hardship was particularly great in Slovakia, the republic occupying the eastern third of Czechoslovakia. The Slovak economy was heavily dependent upon military plants that employed more than 70,000 workers. As subsidies ended and weapons production dropped, unemployment soared above 12 percent, triple the rate in the Czech Republic in the western part of the country.

The disparity between the Czech and Slovak economies outraged many Slovaks. They urged the government to slow down the pace of reforms. However, economic policy was not the only issue dividing Czechs and Slovaks. Slovak nationalists resented the Czech-dominated federal government. Slovaks, led by Vladimir Meciar, demanded greater autonomy.

The growing tension between Czechs and Slovaks alarmed Vaclav Havel. As president, he was an important symbol of national unity and he warned that if Czechoslovakia split, "We would be cursed by future generations."

Separatist leaders in both republics ignored Havel's warning. In June 1992, Slovak voters elected Meciar as their republic's new prime minister. When Meciar and the Czech prime minister Vaclav Klaus could not decide on a common economic policy, they agreed to divide Czechoslovakia peacefully.

Czechoslovakia had been created as a multi-ethnic state after World War I (page 637). It endured Nazi occupation during World War II and more than four decades of Communist rule, but it could not survive the rising tide of ethnic separation sweeping across Eastern Europe in the 1990's. After just three years of freedom from Soviet domination, Czechoslovakia split in two at the stroke of midnight on January 1, 1993.

Yugoslavia disintegrated.

While the Czechs and Slovaks were peacefully dividing their country, nearby Yugoslavia was breaking apart in a bitter civil war. Yugoslavia also was created after World War I. The new nation included six major ethnic groups (Serbs, Croats, Muslims, Slovenes, Macedonians, and Montenegrins) and another half dozen smaller ethnic groups.

Yugoslavia was organized into six republics based on the historic homelands of its major

Slavic national groups. In addition, Serbia included the self-governing provinces of Kosovo and Vojvodina (map, page 861).

Although the Slavs shared a common country, they often had little else in common. Ethnic and religious differences that had existed for centuries created bitter disputes. For example, the Serbs practice the Greek Orthodox faith, and their written language uses the Cyrillic alphabet. In contrast, the Croats and Slovenes are Catholics who use the Roman alphabet. Both groups of Christians were suspicious of the Muslims.

The collapse of Yugoslavia As you have seen (page 742), Josip Tito successfully gained control over Yugoslavia after World War II. He held his diverse country together by keeping tight control over its hostile ethnic groups.

When Tito died in 1980, the long-simmering ethnic resentments boiled over once again. Croatia and Slovenia claimed that the national government gave too much of their income to the poorer republics in the south. Leaders in both republics demanded that Yugoslavia become a loose alliance of sovereign states.

Meanwhile, a new Serbian leader, Slobodan Milosevic, launched a determined program to reassert Serbian leadership over Yugoslavia. Milosevic skillfully fanned the flames of Serbian nationalism by ruthlessly seizing control of the previously self-governing province of Kosovo.

Milosevic's aggressive program of Serbian nationalism frightened Slovenia and Croatia. Refusing to agree to a Serb-dominated Yugoslavian government, both republics declared their independence on June 25, 1991. The Serbian-led Yugoslav army promptly invaded both republics.

The Slovenes repelled the Serbs in less than two weeks. But the civil war in Croatia proved to be far more bloody. Unlike Slovenia, Croatia had a large Serbian minority. Fearing that they would be persecuted by the Croats, the Serbs appealed to Milosevic for help.

Centuries of Serbo-Croatian hatred burst into an all-out civil war. The fighting claimed thousands of lives and left historic cities in ruins. By January 1992, Serbian forces occupied one-third of Croatia.

The Bosnian nightmare Once ignited, the frenzy of hatred in Yugoslavia could not easily be contained. In late February of 1992, Bosnia-Herzegovina joined Slovenia and Croatia in de-

Breakup of Yugoslavia

AUSTRIA · HUNGARY · ROMANIA
Drava R.
SLOVENIA ★Zagreb
Ljubljana ★
CROATIA · *Vojvodina*
Sava R.
BOSNIA AND HERZEGOVINA · Belgrade ⊛
Sarajevo ★ · *Serbia* · BULGARIA
Montenegro · *Kosovo* · Sofia ★
Podgorica ★ · Skopje ★
Adriatic Sea · MACEDONIA
★ Tiranë · GREECE
ALBANIA

National capital.
National boundaries.
Former republic boundary.
Autonomous province boundary.
Independent states (1992).
Non-recognized Independent state.
Federal Republic of Yugoslavia.
Border of Socialist Federal Republic of Yugoslavia (prior to 1992).
Capital of former republic.

Ethnic Groups of Yugoslavia

SERBIA · VOJVODINA
MONTENEGRO · KOSOVO
SLOVENIA · CROATIA
BOSNIA · MACEDONIA

Serbs
Hungarians
Slavic Muslims
Albanians
Montenegrins
Slovenes
Croats
Macedonians
Others

Map Study

Which nations now make up what was once Yugoslavia? What regions are still included in Yugoslavia? (Graphs) Where is the heaviest concentration of Serbs outside of Serbia?

claring independence. Bosnia's ethnically mixed population included Muslims (44 percent), Serbs (31 percent), and Croats (17 percent).

While Bosnia's Muslims and Croats overwhelmingly endorsed independence, the 1.3 million Serb community strongly opposed it. Faced with the threat of the Bosnian Serbs falling under "foreign" control, Milosevic ordered 100,000 troops to support the Serbian rebels.

The Bosnian powder keg exploded in March 1992. As many as 100,000 people died during the next 9 months. At the same time, more than 1.5 million people—one-third of Bosnia's entire population—were forced to flee their homes.

Those grim statistics do not fully describe the nightmare that engulfs Bosnia. Serbian forces are dug into the hills that surround Sarajevo, the capital of Bosnia. Serbian troops have fired thousands of artillery shells into the city's once beautiful streets. The random violence has destroyed hospitals, homes, and schools. No one is safe from the relentless shelling.

The fighting in Bosnia is more than just a brutal civil war. It is also a ruthless campaign by the Serbs to drive Bosnian Muslims out of their land. Called **ethnic cleansing,** this policy reminds many people of the Nazi program of genocide in World War II. Ignoring global pleas to stop the violence, the Serbs had gained control of 70 percent of Bosnia by early 1993.

Decisions in History

The crisis in what was once Yugoslavia presented President Clinton with a difficult decision. Some advisers urged the United States to use military force to prevent Serbian aggression from spreading. Others advocated strict economic sanctions to cripple Serbia's economy. And finally, many argued that the crisis could only be resolved by a diplomatic settlement that divided Bosnia into a number of autonomous regions. If you were President Clinton, which policy would you follow and why?

861

■ DISCUSSION
Ask students whether they would describe the situation in Yugoslavia as a civil war or as an example of genocide. Encourage students to clarify and refine their definitions of these two terms.
A civil war is a conflict between two political groups within the same nation. In contrast, the United Nations Genocide Convention defines genocide as acts such as murder and torture that are carried out with "a specific intent to destroy, in whole or in substantial part, a national, ethnic, racial, or religious group." Stress that this definition includes two specific standards. First, there must be specific intent. Second there must be large scale. Tell students that it makes a great deal of difference whether the crisis in Yugoslavia is defined as a civil war or as an example of genocide. Historically, the United States has been reluctant to intervene in a civil war. In contrast, the United States Senate formally ratified the United Nations Genocide Convention in 1988. As a result, the convention's definition of genocide is legally incorporated into the United States Criminal Code, which President Clinton is legally bound to enforce.

ANSWERS TO
Map Study

Slovenia, Croatia, Bosnia and Herzegovina, Yugoslavia, Macedonia; Vojvodina, Serbia, Kosovo, Montenegro; Vojvodina

ANSWERS TO
Section Review 3

Define:
economic program calling for the rapid elimination of price controls and state subsidies

Identify:
(a) chancellor of reunited Germany (b) alienated youths who have formed neo-Nazi groups to oppose foreigners living in Germany (c) former leader of Solidarity elected president of Poland in December 1990 (d) leader of Slovakia (e) nationalist leader of Serbia (f) Serbian policy of driving out Bosnian Muslims

Answer:

1. (a) rebuilding eastern Germany and neo-Nazi violence (b) The German government is spending $100 billion a year to modernize eastern Germany. At the same time, it is cracking down on the neo-Nazis.

2. (a) It offered the fastest way of creating a prosperous free-market economy. (b) At first, unemployment increased while inflation soared above 600 percent. However, as Poland's economy slowly recovered, industrial production rose and inflation dropped.

3. differences over economic policy combined with Slovak resentment of the Czech-dominated federal government

4. The Serbs practice the Greek Orthodox faith, while the Croats are Roman Catholics. The Croats claimed that the Yugoslav government gave too much of their income to the poorer republics.

(continued)

This haunting photograph is a reminder of the toll that the brutal civil war in Bosnia-Herzegovina takes on the nation's children.

Yeltsin led Russia into a new era.

The unification of Germany, the division of Czechoslovakia, and the disintegration of Yugoslavia would have been unthinkable during the Cold War. These dramatic events were made possible by the revolutionary changes that have taken place inside the former Soviet Union. This transformation began under Mikhail Gorbachev and is now continuing under Boris Yeltsin. But there are no guarantees that the changes in Russia will be permanent. Russia now faces a critical turning point in its struggle for democracy.

"The economy is sick" As you have seen (page 847), Yeltsin inherited a deepening economic crisis. After telling his country, "The economy is sick," Yeltsin boldly proposed a program of shock therapy as the cure. On January 2, 1992, he ended price controls and began to cut subsidies to state-run industries.

As in Poland, shock therapy produced mixed results. Higher prices did lure goods into shops, ending some shortages and reducing lines. But prices did not stabilize as Yeltsin had hoped. Instead, prices skyrocketed and inflation soared

above 1,000 percent. "We used to go shopping with one 10-ruble note," complained a Russian worker. "Now we need a suitcase full of them."

Inflation was not Yeltsin's only economic problem. As obsolete factories lost their subsidies, they cut production and laid off workers. In 1992, industrial production fell 20 percent. This catastrophic drop was greater than the decline experienced in the United States during any year of the Great Depression.

"A *very dangerous moment*" When he announced his decision to use shock therapy, Yeltsin explained that the hard times would be brief. "We're talking of six to eight months," he promised. Yeltsin clearly overestimated the ability of shock therapy to solve Russia's economic crisis quickly.

Yeltsin is painfully discovering that his impoverished government does not have the economic resources to make a rapid transition from communism to capitalism. It also may not have the time to make these changes. While Yeltsin has made major strides in making Russia a more open society, its democracy is still very fragile.

As Yeltsin's popularity begins to decline, Russia's increasingly angry and frustrated people may be tempted to turn to an authoritarian leader to restore order. In an interview with American journalists, Gorbachev's former Foreign Minister, Eduard Shevardnadze, pleaded for help, warning, "The dark forces are becoming stronger. It is a very dangerous moment."

Section REVIEW 3

Define: shock therapy
Identify: (a) Helmut Kohl, (b) skinheads, (c) Lech Walesa, (d) Vladimir Meciar, (e) Slobodan Milosevic, (f) ethnic cleansing
Answer:

1. (a) What are the two most pressing problems confronting reunified Germany? (b) How is Germany dealing with each problem?
2. (a) Why did Poland use shock therapy to stimulate its economy? (b) What were the consequences of the shock therapy?
3. What were two reasons why Czechoslovakia split apart?
4. What cultural differences and historic experiences have made Serbs and Croats enemies?

5. (a) What caused the civil war between Croatia and Serbia? (b) What have been the consequences of the fighting in Bosnia?
6. What did Shevardnadze mean when he said, "The dark forces are becoming stronger"?

Critical Thinking
7. According to one historian, "Europe now faces problems that are remarkably similar to the ones it faced in 1914." Do you agree? Cite examples to support your position.

A *new world order* began to emerge.   4

The moment William Jefferson Clinton had worked for since he was a teenager in Arkansas had finally arrived. At 11:58 A.M. on January 20, 1993, he faced Chief Justice William Rehnquist and promised to "preserve, protect, and defend the Constitution of the United States." America's new president then shook hands with George Bush, the outgoing president.

President Clinton took office in a world that was dramatically different from the one George Bush had confronted just four years before. On January 20, 1989, the Berlin Wall still stood, Germany was still divided, and the Soviet Union still existed. But now all of this had changed as the first post-Cold War president of the United States prepared to lead his nation into a new era.

Before his inauguration, Clinton expressed his excitement and uncertainty about entering into a new era when he told a group of diplomats, "While we cannot yet discern all the contours of the new age in which we are living, we know it is clearly an era of both peril and promise."

This section will describe four trends that are shaping the post-Cold War world the new president faces. It will also examine the Persian Gulf War and Operation Restore Hope in Somalia as tests of the new emerging world order.

Four key trends shape a new era.

As you have seen throughout this text, broad trends shape and define each period of history.

The spread of democratic ideas and global economic integration are binding our world together, making it freer and smaller. At the same time, religious and ethnic hatreds and the global arms trade are breaking the world apart, making it more divided and a more dangerous place to live.

The spread of democracy Democracy is now making remarkable gains across the world. Since the fall of the Berlin Wall, free elections have been held throughout Eastern Europe and the former Soviet Union. Multiparty elections are legal in all but six sub-Saharan countries. And more than 90 percent of Latin Americans live under democratically elected governments.

As free elections have spread, respect for the rule of law has also deepened. For example, in 1989, Fernando Collor de Mello became Brazil's first freely elected president since 1960 (page 811). Although Collor promised to clean up Brazil's notoriously corrupt government, he soon became involved in a 55 million-dollar influence peddling scheme. After a massive public outcry, the Brazilian congress voted to impeach Collor in October 1992. Rather than face a Senate trial, he resigned three months later. "We have proven that we have the strength and will to make democracy work," boasted a proud student leader.

This pride and conviction are important. Democracy's roots are still quite shallow in nations that experienced long periods of dictatorial rule. For example, Jean-Bertrand Aristide won Haiti's first democratic election in 1990 (page 817). However, powerful business leaders and top army officers felt threatened by Aristide's reforms. Refusing to accept majority rule, they overthrew Aristide in September 1991.

Although the Cold War has ended, Communist regimes continue to rule in China and in 11 other countries. Fidel Castro for example, still clings to power in Cuba (page 817). Faced with the loss of Soviet aid, Castro has tightened controls in a desperate attempt to hold power.

The global economy The spread of democracy coincided with a second key trend, the rise of a global economy. The **global economy** refers to all financial interactions among people, businesses, and governments that cross international borders. As world commerce has increased, trade barriers have fallen. As you have seen (page 857), on January 1, 1993, the European Community removed all barriers to the movement of goods

863

ANSWERS TO (continued)

5. (a) Milosevic's aggressive program of Serbian nationalism (b) More than 100,000 people have died and more than 1.5 million have fled their homes.
6. Russia's increasingly angry and frustrated people may be tempted to turn to an authoritarian leader to restore order.
7. Answers will vary.

SECTION 4 Objectives and Teaching Strategies

OBJECTIVE 1. Identify and describe four global trends.

Teaching Strategy: *Discussing History: Global Trends* (page 844e)

OBJECTIVE 2. Explain the role geography played in causing the Persian Gulf War.

Teaching Strategy: *Using Geographic Themes: Location and the Persian Gulf War* (page 844e)

OBJECTIVE 3. Discuss America's foreign policy options for the post-Cold War era.

Teaching Strategy: *Discussing History: American Foreign Policy* (page 844e)

■ BACKGROUND

Democracy is now making important gains in sub-Saharan Africa. According to Freedom House, a nonprofit monitoring organization in New York, the number of sub-Saharan African states that can be considered full democracies has risen from 3 in 1989 to

SECTION 4 Resources

GEOGRAPHY
■ Transparencies 102, 104, 110

REINFORCEMENT
■ Independent Practice 37.4

ENRICHMENT
■ Voices from the Past 37.4

ASSESSMENT
■ Section Quiz 37.4

9 in 1992. The states with full democracies include Gambia, Mali, Benin, Cape Verde, Namibia, Botswana, Zambia, and São Tomé and Príncipe. Another 21 states have limited political freedom, and 17 have almost none.

ANSWERS TO

Voice from Our Time

1. Can we make change our friend and not our enemy?

2. world economy, environment, AIDS crisis, arms race

3. The new world is more free because of communism's collapse, but it is less stable because that collapse has unleashed old ethnic animosities.

■ BACKGROUND

The data superhighway would be made up of hair-thin strands of glass. The glass is so pure that a person could see through a window of it 70 miles thick. Fiber-optic cables are the most perfect transmitter of information yet invented. A single hair-width strand of fiber-optic line can carry as much information as thousands of regular phone lines. For example, while a phone line can carry several pages of information per second, a fiber-optic cable could transmit the contents of the entire *Encyclopaedia Britannica* every second!

V̄oice from Our Time | *Can we make change our friend?*

In this excerpt from his inaugural address, President Clinton describes the challenges of living "at the edge of the twenty-first century."

Today a generation raised in the shadows of the Cold War assumes new responsibilities in a world warmed by the sunshine of freedom but threatened still by ancient hatreds and new plagues. . .

When George Washington first took the oath I have just sworn to uphold, news traveled slowly across the land by horseback and across the ocean by boat. Now the sights and sounds of this ceremony are broadcast instantaneously to billions around the world. Communications and commerce are global, investment is mobile, technology is almost magical, and ambition for a better life is now universal. We earn our livelihood in America today in peaceful competition with people all across the earth. Profound and powerful forces are shaking and remaking our world. And the urgent question of our time is whether we can make change our friend and not our enemy. . .

To renew America, we must meet challenges abroad as well as at home. There is no longer a clear division between what is foreign and what is domestic. The world economy, the world environment, the world AIDS crisis, the world arms race—they affect us all.

Today, as an old order passes, the new world is more free but less stable. Communism's collapse has called forth old animosities and new dangers. Clearly, America must continue to lead the world we did so much to make.

1. According to President Clinton, what is the "urgent question of our time"?
2. Name four global problems that now affect the entire world.
3. What does Clinton mean when he says, "the new world is more free but less stable"?

and people. At the same time, the United States, Canada, and Mexico prepared to form a North American Free Trade Association.

Led by Japan, the nations along the Pacific Rim also played an increasingly important role in the global economy. Japan's spectacular growth has transformed it into an economic superpower. In 1993, Japan boasted 15 of the world's 30 largest banks. Its export-driven economy recorded an annual trade balance of more than $100 billion.

The emerging global economy is characterized by more than just an increase in world trade. Advances in telecommunications are creating a worldwide information network. For example, global news services like CNN broadcast events to households throughout the world.

The information revolution has only just begun. President Clinton supports building a high-speed computer network linked by fiber optic cables (page 834). This "data superhighway" would accelerate the flow of information in the same way that the transcontinental railroads and interstate highways speeded the flow of goods. Thus, a high school student doing a research paper could tap into an enormous electronic library that included universities and museums throughout the world.

Ethnic and religious conflict While the global economy is bringing the world together, deep-seated ethnic and religious conflicts are splitting nations apart. As you have seen, the collapse of communism released long-suppressed ethnic tensions in the Soviet Union and Eastern Europe.

864

Ethnic and religious conflicts are not limited to Eastern Europe and the former Soviet Union. In Canada, the French-speaking province of Quebec has repeatedly threatened to secede if its demand for greater independence is not met (page 822). At the same time, Kurds in Iraq, Turkey, and Iran are demanding independent states for themselves.

Nationalism can be a powerful force for uniting different groups. However, it also can be a terrifying force that can tear nations apart. For example, India is a vast multinational state that includes 700 million Hindus and 110 million Muslims. The tensions between these two groups have roots that go back to the eleventh century (page 303).

Conflict erupted again in December 1992 when Hindu fanatics destroyed a 464-year-old Muslim mosque, claiming it was built over the birthplace of the Hindu god Rama. The destruction of the mosque ignited a riot that claimed 1,000 lives and left more than 4,000 injured.

Arms control The outbreak of ethnic and religious conflicts highlighted the need to control the spread of nuclear and conventional weapons.

During the Cold War, the United States and the Soviet Union built huge arsenals of nuclear weapons. Despite the restraints imposed by the INF Treaty (pages 846–847), there are still 24,000 nuclear warheads in the United States and in the nations of the former Soviet Union.

As the Cold War ended, so did the necessity for keeping all of these weapons. In 1991, the United States and the Soviet Union negotiated a second Strategic Arms Reduction Treaty, or SALT II, agreeing to sharply reduce the number of their long-range nuclear warheads. Just 18 months later, on January 3, 1993, Russian president Yeltsin and United States president George Bush signed the SALT II agreement, pledging to reduce their arsenals by two-thirds. By the year 2003, each country will be limited to just 3,000 to 3,500 nuclear warheads.

Although these treaties reduced the threat of nuclear war, they failed to halt the spread of nuclear weapons. Experts believe that India, Pakistan, Israel, and South Africa can produce nuclear weapons, while North Korea is close to making one. Iraq, Iran, and Libya have reportedly tried to make or buy nuclear bombs.

Hundreds of years of conflict erupted into violence in India when Hindus destroyed a centuries-old Muslim mosque.

865

■ **DISCUSSION**

The Treaty on Nuclear Nonproliferation represents an important curb on the nuclear arms race. More than 150 nations have signed the agreement. However, on March 13, 1993, the Communist government in North Korea announced that it would abandon the treaty. Experts believe this action indicates that North Korea is close to producing a nuclear weapon.

Remind students that the division of Korea remains one of the major unresolved issues left by the Cold War. Ask students whether the United States and its allies should take any action to prevent North Korea from building a nuclear weapon. For example, what are the advantages and disadvantages of bombing nuclear processing sites 56 miles north of Pyongyang?

■ DISCUSSION

Saddam Hussein began his political career by joining Iraq's Baath party in 1957 when he was 20 years old. Although small, this party was able to seize power in 1968 in a bloodless coup. Although an army general became Iraq's new president, Hussein actually made most decisions.

Hussein gained full power in 1979. Shortly after taking control, he executed more than 20 cabinet members, including some of his closest friends. This brutal action consolidated his power, while also inspiring fear and obedience.

After eliminating his rivals and silencing his critics, Hussein concentrated on transforming Iraq into the Arab world's most powerful nation. During the 1980's, he used more than $50 billion of Iraq's huge oil revenues to purchase military equipment—more than any other nation in the world. He also invested heavily in programs to produce chemical, biological, and nuclear weapons.

Iraq's growing military strength encouraged Hussein to believe he could attack Iran and capture the strategic Shatt al-Arab waterway. Although the Iran-Iraq War proved to be long and costly, it left Iraq with the most powerful military force in the Persian Gulf region. Proudly calling himself the Sword of the Arabs, Hussein once again prepared to achieve his goal of becoming the most powerful leader in the Arab world.

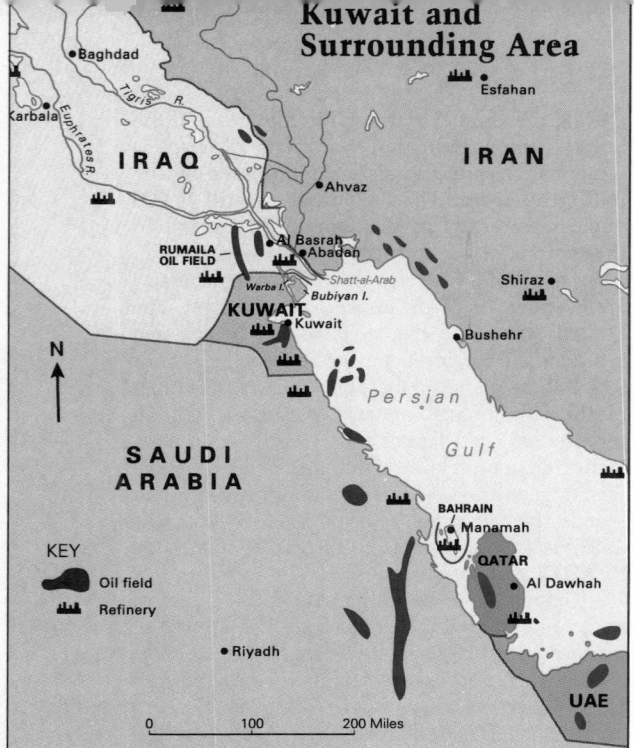

Kuwait and Surrounding Area

KEY

Oil field

Refinery

0   100   200 Miles

Map Study

What geographic and political factors limit Iraq's access to the Persian Gulf?

Crises in the Persian Gulf and Somalia tested the new world order.

During the Cold War, the United States followed a clear policy of containing Communist aggression (pages 743–744). Relations between Washington and Moscow were tense but stable. The Soviet Union's collapse left the United States as the world's only superpower. It also left America searching for a new foreign policy. President Bush wanted America to support a "new world order" based on international cooperation. Crises in the Persian Gulf and Somalia soon tested this goal, leaving difficult choices for the Clinton administration.

The Persian Gulf War On August 2, 1990, Iraqi president Saddam Hussein stunned the world by ordering his army to invade Kuwait. Catching the oil-rich emirate by surprise, Iraq's powerful army easily conquered it.

Conquering Kuwait was part of a much larger plan. Hussein dreamed of becoming the world's most powerful Arab leader. Kuwait owned al-

most 10 percent of the world's proven oil reserves. Since Iraq also had 10 percent, taking Kuwait would double its oil reserves. Hussein would then be in a position to intimidate Saudi Arabia and dominate the world oil market.

President Bush argued that Iraq had to be confronted. First, the United States would not allow any nation to dominate the Persian Gulf and thus control the world's oil supply. Second, Hussein's nuclear weapons program alarmed Israel and threatened to upset the Middle East's balance of power. Finally, Bush felt that standing up to Iraq would deter other would-be aggressors.

During the next few weeks, Bush forged an international coalition to stop Hussein. By January 1991, the United States had rushed more than 400,000 troops to defend Saudi Arabia. This force included soldiers from 27 other nations.

The UN Security Council passed a resolution demanding that Iraq withdraw its forces by January 15, 1991. When Hussein refused, Bush ordered a massive air offensive. Called Operation Desert Storm, the attack used high-tech bombs and bombers to destroy Iraq's air defense centers. Coalition warplanes then cut Iraq's supply lines and pounded its army.

On February 24, Bush ordered a ground assault to liberate Kuwait. In the largest land operation since World War II, coalition forces commanded by H. Norman Schwarzkopf pushed through Iraqi defenses and liberated Kuwait on February 27. The assault took only 100 hours.

Aftermath of war Although the Gulf War ended, Hussein's problems were far from over. Within weeks, Shi'ite Muslims in southern Iraq and Kurdish rebels in the north revolted. Defying predictions that he would soon be overthrown, Hussein suppressed both uprisings.

Hussein's survival posed a continuing threat to stability in the Gulf. In an effort to prevent him from rebuilding his military, teams of UN inspectors examined Iraq's chemical, biological, and nuclear weapons facilities. The UN also set up no-fly zones, banning Iraqi military flights over Kurdish and Shi'ite territories.

These restrictions did not stop Hussein from testing UN and American resolve. In January 1993, he violated UN restrictions by interfering with inspection teams and by deploying missile batteries in the no-fly zones. Bush retaliated by ordering the bombing of the missile sites and

866

the destruction of an industrial complex. The attacks took place two years after the Gulf War began and just days before Bush left office.

Operation Restore Hope Oil reserves gave Iraq and Kuwait global strategic importance. In contrast, Africa's Somalia lacked highly prized resources and seemed destined for a small role in the new world order.

Located on the eastern Horn of Africa, Somalia is a sickle-shaped country of 8.5 million people (map, page 872). During the early 1990's, a civil war between rival clans killed thousands and left the country with no organized government. As authority vanished, Somalia's fragile economy collapsed. That collapse, combined with a long drought, produced widespread famine. By late 1992, the famine claimed 1,000 lives a day.

Somalia's collapse posed no threat to world peace or to America's vital interests. Yet heart-wrenching pictures of the nation's starving children touched the world. Relief poured into Somalia in an attempt to avert further tragedy. However, warring clans stole desperately needed food and threatened relief workers' safety.

Faced with a terrible human tragedy, President Bush decided to act. With the support of the UN Security Council, Bush sent more than 25,000 United States troops into Somalia. Known as Operation Restore Hope, the mission was intended to protect relief workers so they could feed thousands of starving people. The mission marked the first use of American military power for a purely humanitarian cause.

We face new challenges.

The crises in the Persian Gulf and Somalia are examples of how the role of the United States is changing to meet the challenges of a new world order. Throughout history, each generation has faced new challenges. The burden of change is especially great for a generation leaving one historic era and beginning a new one.

As students living at what President Clinton calls "the edge of the twenty first century," you face exciting challenges. As citizens of the world's greatest democracy, you have the responsibility of leading the United States as it defines its new role in the world. As members of your school and local community, you have the opportunity to put your ideals into practice.

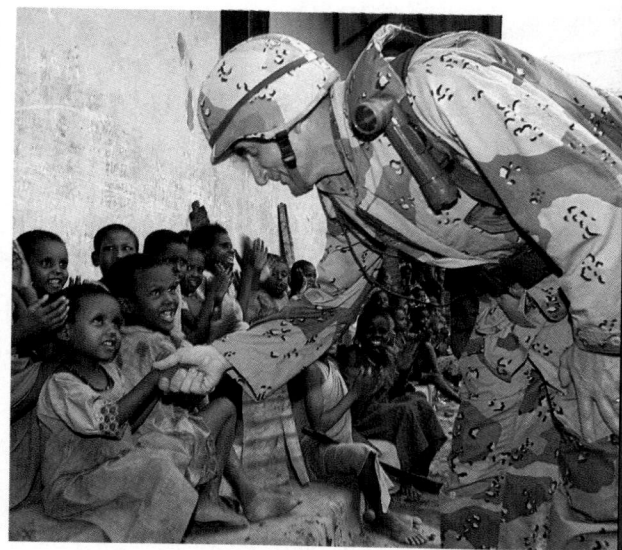

U.S. Marines were sent to Somalia in an effort to ensure that food reached the thousands of starving people for whom it was intended.

It is our hope that the people, ideas, and events you have studied in your journey through world history will provide you with a perspective on the past and a guide for the future.

Section REVIEW 4

Define: global economy
Identify: (a) Bill Clinton, (b) Fernando Collor de Mello, (c) Jean-Bertrand Aristide, (d) SALT II, (e) Saddam Hussein, (f) Operation Desert Storm, (g) Operation Restore Hope
Answer:
1. (a) Give three examples of the progress democracy is making. (b) What are two threats that democracy still faces?
2. (a) How is the global economy uniting the world? (b) Give examples of how ethnic and religious conflicts are splitting nations apart.
3. (a) Why did Saddam Hussein invade Kuwait? (b) Give three reasons why President Bush opposed Iraq's invasion of Kuwait.

Critical Thinking
4. Which current trends (a) contribute to world peace? (b) threaten world peace?

867

ANSWERS TO
Section Review 4

Define:
all financial interactions among people, businesses, and governments that cross international borders
Identify:
(a) man elected president of the United States in 1992
(b) Brazilian president who resigned because of his involvement in an influence peddling scheme (c) popular Haitian president overthrown in a September 1991 coup (d) agreement in which the United States and Russia pledged to reduce their nuclear arsenals by two-thirds (e) leader of Iraq whose invasion of Kuwait instigated the Persian Gulf War (f) United States-led military campaign to free Kuwait (g) United States-led relief effort to help famine victims in Somalia
Answer:
1. (a) Free elections have been held throughout Eastern Europe; multiparty elections are legal in most sub-Saharan nations; and more than 90 percent of Latin Americans live under democratically elected governments. (b) Communist regimes, corruption, and military coups
2. (a) The global economy is reducing trade barriers and creating a worldwide information network. (b) Examples include tensions in Quebec, Iraq, and India.
(continued)

ANSWERS TO (continued)

3. (a) to gain control of Kuwait's oil reserves, intimidate Saudi Arabia, and thus dominate the world's oil market (b) Bush wanted to maintain the Middle East balance of power, deter other aggressors, and prevent any one nation from dominating the Persian Gulf.
4. (a) The global economy and the spread of democracy contribute to world peace. (b) The arms race and ethnic and religious strife threaten world peace.

Concluding the Chapter

1. **Chapter Closer**
   Have students write essays answering the following question: What changes in world power do you expect to see within your lifetime?
2. **Reteaching Activities**
   a. Making a Bulletin Board Have students bring in recent articles and pictures on the following topics: events in the former Soviet Union and Eastern Europe, arms talks, the European Economic Community, Japan's economic power, and events in Iraq, North Korea, Haiti, and Somalia. Have students use these materials to create a current events bulletin board.
   b. Listing Have students list ways in which the world is interdependent.

Answers to Chapter Review appear on page 844f.

Summary

1. **Gorbachev launched a new era.** Mikhail Gorbachev launched a series of reforms that helped bring about the collapse of the Soviet Union as a political entity. His efforts to loosen political control caused an attempted coup against him. Opposition to the coup was led by the president of the Russian Republic, Boris Yeltsin. The coup failed, but discontent with Gorbachev's rule continued. Eventually all the republics that made up the Soviet Union declared independence. The Soviet Union passed into history, and Gorbachev resigned his position.

2. **Communism collapsed in Eastern Europe.** Popular discontent and the declining appeal of communism led to changes in Eastern Europe. Poland was the first Eastern European country to reject the Communist party. Hungary opened its borders and dissolved its Communist party. Demonstrations in East Germany led to the fall of the Berlin Wall. Communist governments also fell in Czechoslovakia and in other Eastern European nations.

3. **The post-Cold War era brought changes.** East and West Germany became a united Germany once again, as Poland applied shock therapy to its troubled economy. Ethnic differences in Czechoslovakia led to its split into Slovakia and the Czech Republic.

Ethnic and religious differences shattered Yugoslavia and threw it into a bloody civil war.

4. **A new world order began to emerge.** With the collapse of the Soviet Union, the United States found itself as the last superpower. Aggression in the Middle East and famine in Africa created new challenges for the United States. The spread of democracy and global economic integration were creating a new order, but peace was challenged by ancient hatreds and global arms trade.

Reviewing the Facts

1. Define the following terms:
   a. détente
   b. *glasnost*
   c. *perestroika*
   d. *demokratizatsiya*
   e. shock therapy
   f. ethnic cleansing
   g. global economy

2. Explain the importance or meaning of each of the following names, places, or terms.
   a. SALT II
   b. Lech Walesa
   c. Vaclav Havel
   d. Economic Community
   e. Somalia
   f. Operation Restore Hope
   g. Afghanistan
   h. INF Treaty
   i. Baltic states
   j. Helmut Kohl
   k. Kuwait
   l. INF
   m. Politburo

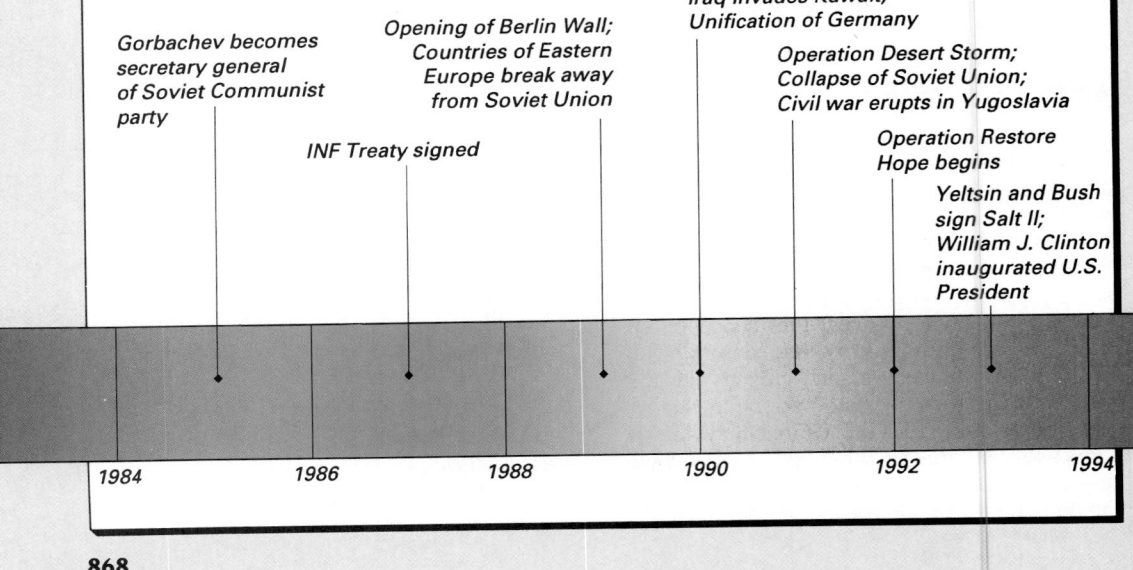

Gorbachev becomes secretary general of Soviet Communist party

INF Treaty signed

Opening of Berlin Wall; Countries of Eastern Europe break away from Soviet Union

Iraq invades Kuwait; Unification of Germany

Operation Desert Storm; Collapse of Soviet Union; Civil war erupts in Yugoslavia

Operation Restore Hope begins

Yeltsin and Bush sign Salt II; William J. Clinton inaugurated U.S. President

1984 1986 1988 1990 1992 1994

868

Basic Skills

1. **Making a chart** Make a chart showing the causes of the war in the Persian Gulf. Distinguish between long-term and immediate causes.
2. **Sequencing** Arrange the following events in correct chronological order: (a) the opening of the Berlin Wall; (b) Gorbachev's resignation; (c) Czechoslovakia's split into two countries; (d) the aborted coup against Gorbachev; (e) the reunification of Germany.
3. **Interpreting a map** Using the map on page 866 as a reference, identify two possible causes for the conflict between Kuwait and Iraq.

Researching and Reporting Skills

1. The role of the United States in the civil war in Bosnia has been discussed in Congress and in the media. Look in your library for articles in daily papers or weekly magazines expressing opposing points of view: (a) one in support of United States intervention and (b) one in opposition. List the points made by both sides in this debate. Then express your opinion in a short essay.
2. **Using the *Readers' Guide*.** In the *Readers' Guide to Periodical Literature*, identify three articles discussing the problems faced by the Clinton administration. Read one article and prepare a brief summary of the viewpoints presented.
3. **Using a newspaper index** Using the *New York Times Index* or that of any major newspaper, identify the main arguments presented by President Bush in support of Operation Restore Hope.

Critical Thinking

1. **Contrasting** (a) Describe Gorbachev's foreign policy from 1986 to 1990. (b) How did it contrast with that of Brezhnev?
2. **Evaluating outcomes** (a) Identify three major outcomes of Gorbachev's domestic policies. (b) How did these outcomes affect the quality of life in the Soviet Union?
3. **Synthesizing** (a) What were the main reasons for the revolts of the countries in Eastern Europe? (b) What common pattern can you identify in the sequence of events leading to these revolts?
4. **Making a generalization** (a) To what extent is the importance of nations today determined by their military might? (b) What other factors are of equal or greater importance today? Give examples to support your answers.

5. **Analyzing** What role did ethnic and religious differences play in the breakup of Yugoslavia?
6. **Applying a concept** (a) Identify three economic events that show the development of a global economy. (b) How do these events show the growing economic interdependence of all people?
7. **Evaluating** (a) How did the actions of President Bush in his last days in office affect the foreign policy of the incoming Clinton administration? (b) In what ways did Bush's action hinder or help the new president?

Perspectives on the Past and Present

1. One argument for the war on Saddam Hussein was that he was like a new Hitler. In the case of Hitler, policies of appeasement only led to more German aggression or demands. How were the two situations in Iraq and Germany alike or different? Was this a situation where the lessons of the past were useful? Explain.
2. The United States government promised the nation that the Gulf War would not be another Vietnam. In what ways did the Gulf War differ from Vietnam? How were the two wars similar?

Investigating History

1. Your text states that the spread of democracy is a major trend in creating a new world order. Choose a country in Eastern Europe and one in Latin America where this statement seems to be borne out. Identify for each country its successes or its limitations in becoming a democracy.
2. Ethnic unrest has long existed in many of the newly independent republics within what was once the Soviet Union. This ethnic unrest was kept in check for the most part by the authoritarian Soviet regime, but resumed with a vengeance after the Soviet Union collapsed. Investigate the current conflict in one of these republics to identify reasons for the unrest. Identify and evaluate possible solutions for ending the conflict.
3. In weekly magazines from January to June 1993, look up reports on the problems facing the early days of the Clinton administration that deal with the four trends identified as signs of the new world order. Pick one of these problems and in a short report show how President Clinton solved or failed to solve it. What steps would you have taken to solve the problem? Why?

869

CHAPTER
Evaluation

Chapter Test 37, Alternate Chapter Test 37, and Computer Test Bank Chapter Test 37 can be used to evaluate your students' understanding of this chapter.

ANSWERS TO
Geographic Theme

1. (a) After World War II, Germany was divided between the four Allied powers for occupation. **(b)** East Germany—Mecklenburg-Vorpommern, Brandenburg, Saxony-Anhalt, Thuringia, Saxony; West Germany—Schleswig-Holstein, Hamburg, Bremen, Lower Saxony, North Rhine-Westphalia, Hesse, Rhineland-Palatinate, Saarland, Baden-Wurttemberg, Bavaria

2. West Germany was aided economically by the Marshall Plan and developed a democratic government. East Germany became a Communist state under Soviet control.

3. located on the Great European Plain and in the heart of central Europe

Geographic Theme: Location

What will be Germany's future role in Europe?

The lack of a peace treaty after World War II left Germany's future undecided. Allied occupation and Stalin's desire for a buffer zone ended with the division into East and West Germany.

The two Germanys became a study in contrasts. The USSR sought reparations—resources, goods, rail lines, and whole factories. Already weakened by war, East Germany was forced to become communist. A Comecon and Warsaw Pact member, East Germany lived under Soviet control.

The three Allied occupation zones united in 1948 to form West Germany. The allies provided aid—such as the Marshall Plan—and encouraged the rebuilding of industry, new economic development, and democratic government. West Germany became a participating member of the Common Market and NATO. By 1990, West Germany was the world's fourth largest economic power.

The decline of communism in the USSR and Eastern Europe opened the door to German re-unification. On October 3, 1990, East and West Germany united under West Germany's democratic constitution.

Today Germany is emerging as a leading European state. Located on the Great European Plain and in the heart of central Europe, it has the potential to dominate that region. Europeans recognize the need for Germany to be united, but they wonder what kind of leadership it will offer. As a strong and prosperous democratic state, Germany could lead Europe into a new era of cooperation and growth.

1. (a) Why was Germany divided? (b) What states made up East Germany and West Germany?
2. How did the development of East and West Germany differ?
3. In what ways is Germany's location important?

The Reunification of Germany, 1990

KEY
— Border between East and West Germany

0   100 Miles

870

Historical Themes

Technology, human-environment interaction, the rise of democratic ideas, and cooperation and conflict are key themes shaping the world of today.

Technology and History

Dramatic breakthroughs in telecommunications, electronics, and transportation helped make the world a smaller place. Fax machines, computers, and overnight cargo service made it possible to send information and packages almost anywhere in the world. Television also played a central role in shaping culture and bringing the people of the world into closer contact.

Computers have had a particularly important effect on social change. Although computers have touched many aspects of everyday life, their greatest impact is being felt in the workplace. Millions of employees throughout the world use computers to do word processing, file reports, and calculate statistical data. Computers are also at the cutting edge of high technology—the application of electronics to industry, communications, and medicine. For example, new high-speed supercomputers are used to simulate weather patterns, crack secret codes, design aerospace vehicles, and create special effects for Hollywood films.

Human-Environment Interaction

As you have seen, human-environment interaction played a key role in influencing the growth of early civilizations. In recent years, however, human actions have for the first time begun to threaten the global environment. Each year billions of tons of excess carbon dioxide are poured into the atmosphere, causing a global warming trend known as the greenhouse effect. Experts warn that warmer temperatures could speed desertification and shrink polar ice caps.

Environmental pollution was not limited to the greenhouse effect. Chlorofluorocarbons (CFC's) released into the atmosphere have begun to damage the earth's protective ozone layer. Meanwhile the destruction of rain forests in Brazil, Central America, Africa, and Indonesia threatens the survival of countless species of plants and animals and adds to the greenhouse effect.

Rise of Democratic Ideas

The late 1980's and early 1990's opened a new era

in the rise of democratic ideas. Beginning in 1985, Mikhail Gorbachev launched a series of bold new policies designed to make the Soviet government more responsive to its people. As a result of *glasnost* and *demokratizatsiya,* Soviet citizens began to speak out on public issues and to vote in free elections involving several political parties.

Gorbachev's reforms helped to spark a series of revolutions in Eastern Europe. In 1989, all of the former Soviet satellites replaced their Communist regimes with more democratic governments. For the first time in modern history, every nation in Western Europe had a democratic government, and every nation in Eastern Europe was making progress toward that goal.

Cooperation and Conflict

The collapse of communism in Eastern Europe raised hopes that the triumph of democracy would usher in a new world order based on global cooperation. The hoped-for new world order received its first serious test when Iraq invaded Kuwait on August 2, 1990. The United Nations responded by passing resolutions demanding that Saddam Hussein withdraw his forces. President Bush organized an international coalition to enforce trade sanctions against Iraq and defend Saudi Arabia. When Saddam refused to comply with a UN resolution ordering him to withdraw, Bush launched Operation Desert Storm to liberate Kuwait.

Analyzing Historical Themes

1. (a) How have advances in telecommunications contributed to social change? (b) To economic change?
2. What major threats to the environment have appeared in recent years?
3. What recent gains have occurred in the rise of democratic ideas?
4. How do cooperation and conflict continue to influence world events? Give examples.

871

ANSWERS TO
Analyzing Historical Themes

1. (a) brought people into closer and more rapid contact, computers revolutionized workplace
(b) supported rapid growth of high technology in fields such as industry, communications, and medicine
2. global warming, damage to ozone layer, destruction of rain forests
3. The nations of the former Soviet Union, Eastern Europe, and many Latin American countries moved toward more democratic governments. South Africa showed signs of granting some political rights to its black majority.
4. The spread of democracy increased hopes for a new world order based on global cooperation; cooperation built an international coalition to liberate Kuwait and defend Saudi Arabia during the conflict with Iraq.

UNIT
Evaluation

Unit X Test and Alternate Unit X Test can be used to evaluate your students' understanding of this unit.

Africa

Elevation key

Feet	Meters
14,000	4,000
7,000	2,000
1,500	500
700	200
0	0
Below sea level	Below sea level

★ Capital city   • Other city

872

Asia

Elevation key

Feet	Meters
14,000	4,000
7,000	2,000
1,500	500
700	200
0	0
Below sea level	Below sea level

★ Capital city   • Other city

ARCTIC OCEAN

PACIFIC OCEAN

ATLANTIC OCEAN

RUSSIA

CENTRAL SIBERIAN PLATEAU

CHERSKIY RANGE

Lena R.

Yenisey R.

GOBI DESERT

MONGOLIA

Ulan Bator

KHANGAI MTS.

ALTAI MTS.

GREATER KHINGAN RANGE

JAPAN

Tokyo

SEA OF JAPAN

NORTH KOREA

SOUTH KOREA

Seoul

Beijing

Huang R.

CHINA

Shanghai

Taipei

TAIWAN

PHILIPPINES

Manila

PHILIPPINE SEA

SOUTH CHINA SEA

VIETNAM

LAOS

Hanoi

BURMA

THAILAND

CAMBODIA

Phnom Penh

Bangkok

Rangoon

ANNAMITE MTS.

Chang Jiang (Yangtze) R.

Xi Jiang R.

KUNLUN MTS.

TIBETAN HIGHLANDS

TAKLA MAKAN

TIEN SHAN

KAZAKHSTAN

KAZAKH UPLAND

Alma-Ata

Bishkek

KYRGYZSTAN

TAJIKISTAN

PAMIRS

HIMALAYAS

NEPAL

BHUTAN

Brahmaputra R.

Mt. Everest

Dhaka

BANGLADESH

Ganges R.

Calcutta

INDIA

DECCAN PLATEAU

Bombay

New Delhi

Islamabad

PAKISTAN

Indus R.

Kabul

AFGHANISTAN

HINDU KUSH

Dushanbe

TURKMENISTAN

Ashgabat

UZBEKISTAN

Tashkent

Surgut

Ob R.

Salekhard

URAL MOUNTAINS

Tyumen

TURAN PLATEAU

CASPIAN SEA

Moscow

EUROPE

Arctic Circle

Baku

AZER.

CAUCASUS

GEORGIA

ARM.

Tbilisi

Yerevan

BLACK SEA

TURKEY

ANATOLIAN PENINSULA

Ankara

Istanbul

CYPRUS

LEBANON

SYRIA

ISRAEL

Jerusalem

JORDAN

IRAQ

Baghdad

Tigris R.

Euphrates R.

IRAN

Tehran

ZAGROS MTS.

KUWAIT

SAUDI ARABIA

Riyadh

BAHRAIN

QATAR

U.A.E.

OMAN

Muscat

Persian Gulf

ARABIAN PENINSULA

YEMEN

Sana

Mecca

HIJAZ

ASIR

RED SEA

INDIAN OCEAN

Bay of Bengal

SRI LANKA

Colombo

MALAYSIA

SINGAPORE

BRUNEI

INDONESIA

Jakarta

MALAY PENINSULA

BARISAN MTS.

IRIAN MTS.

MAOKE MTS.

Equator

Tropic of Cancer

20°N

40°N

60°N

80°N

0°

20°E

40°E

60°E

80°E

100°E

120°E

140°E

160°E

180°

| 0 | 500 | 1000 Miles |
| 0 | 500 | 1000 Kilometers |

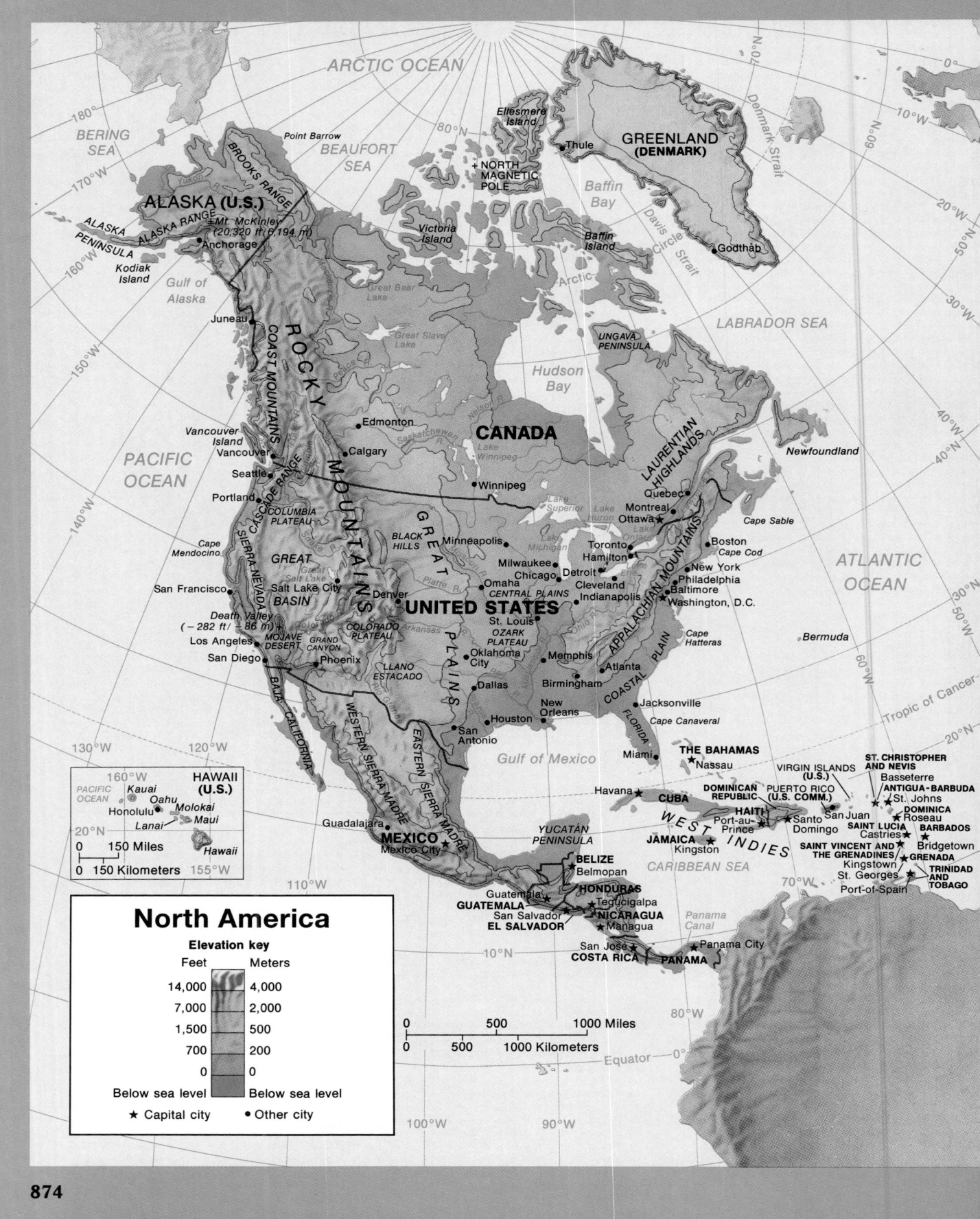

North America

Elevation key

Feet	Meters
14,000	4,000
7,000	2,000
1,500	500
700	200
0	0
Below sea level	Below sea level

★ Capital city   • Other city

ARCTIC OCEAN

BERING SEA

BEAUFORT SEA

Ellesmere Island

GREENLAND (DENMARK)

• Thule

+ NORTH MAGNETIC POLE

Baffin Bay

Denmark Strait

Point Barrow

ALASKA (U.S.)

BROOKS RANGE

Yukon R.

ALASKA RANGE
±Mt. McKinley
(20,320 ft/6,194 m)
Anchorage

ALASKA PENINSULA

Kodiak Island

Gulf of Alaska

Juneau

Victoria Island

Baffin Island

• Godthåb

Arctic Circle

Davis Strait

LABRADOR SEA

Great Bear Lake

Great Slave Lake

Hudson Bay

UNGAVA PENINSULA

PACIFIC OCEAN

Vancouver Island
Vancouver

Seattle

Portland

Cape Mendocino

COAST MOUNTAINS

CASCADE RANGE

COLUMBIA PLATEAU

Edmonton

Calgary

Saskatchewan R.

Peace R.

CANADA

Lake Winnipeg

Nelson R.

Winnipeg

Lake Superior

Newfoundland

LAURENTIAN HIGHLANDS

Quebec

Montreal
Ottawa

Cape Sable

ATLANTIC OCEAN

San Francisco

SIERRA NEVADA

GREAT BASIN

Great Salt Lake
Salt Lake City

Denver

BLACK HILLS

Minneapolis

Milwaukee
Chicago

Lake Michigan

Lake Huron

Lake Ontario

Lake Erie

Toronto
Hamilton
Detroit
Cleveland

Boston
Cape Cod

New York
Philadelphia
Baltimore
Washington, D.C.

APPALACHIAN MOUNTAINS

GREAT PLAINS

CENTRAL PLAINS

Omaha

Platte R.

Indianapolis

Ohio R.

Death Valley
(-282 ft/-86 m)

Los Angeles

San Diego

MOJAVE DESERT

GRAND CANYON

Phoenix

COLORADO PLATEAU

Colorado R.

Arkansas R.

OZARK PLATEAU

St. Louis

UNITED STATES

Oklahoma City

LLANO ESTACADO

Dallas

Memphis

Birmingham

Atlanta

Cape Hatteras

COASTAL PLAIN

Bermuda

BAJA CALIFORNIA

WESTERN SIERRA MADRE

EASTERN SIERRA MADRE

San Antonio

Houston

New Orleans

FLORIDA

Jacksonville

Cape Canaveral

Tropic of Cancer

Guadalajara

MEXICO
Mexico City

YUCATÁN PENINSULA

Miami

THE BAHAMAS
★ Nassau

Havana ★ CUBA

Gulf of Mexico

BELIZE
Belmopan

Guatemala ★
GUATEMALA
San Salvador
EL SALVADOR

HONDURAS
Tegucigalpa
NICARAGUA
★ Managua

San Jose ★
COSTA RICA

PANAMA
★ Panama City

Panama Canal

HAITI
Port-au-Prince

JAMAICA
Kingston

DOMINICAN REPUBLIC
Santo Domingo

PUERTO RICO (U.S. COMM.)
San Juan

VIRGIN ISLANDS (U.S.)

ST. CHRISTOPHER AND NEVIS
Basseterre
ANTIGUA-BARBUDA
★ St. Johns

DOMINICA
★ Roseau

SAINT LUCIA
★ Castries
BARBADOS
★ Bridgetown

SAINT VINCENT AND THE GRENADINES
Kingstown
★ GRENADA
St. Georges
TRINIDAD AND TOBAGO
Port-of-Spain

WEST INDIES

CARIBBEAN SEA

Equator

HAWAII (U.S.)

PACIFIC OCEAN

Kauai
Oahu
Honolulu
Molokai
Lanai
Maui
Hawaii

0   150 Miles
0   150 Kilometers

0   500   1000 Miles
0   500   1000 Kilometers

South America

Elevation key

Feet	Meters
14,000	4,000
7,000	2,000
1,500	500
700	200
0	0
Below sea level	Below sea level

★ Capital city   • Other city

ATLANTIC OCEAN

Tropic of Cancer — 30°N

20°N

Gulf of Mexico

CARIBBEAN SEA

10°N

PACIFIC OCEAN

Maracaibo •
Caracas ★
VENEZUELA
LLANOS
Georgetown
GUYANA ★ Paramaribo
Medellín • SURINAME • Cayenne
Bogotá ★ GUIANA HIGHLANDS FRENCH GUIANA (FR.)
Cali •
COLOMBIA

GALÁPAGOS ISLANDS
(ECUADOR)
Quito ★
ECUADOR Equator — 0°
Guayaquil •

AMAZON BASIN

PERU
Recife •
ANDES
Lima ★ — 10°S
BRAZIL
BOLIVIA Salvador •
La Paz ★
Arequipa •
Sucre ★ Brasília ★
São Francisco
BRAZILIAN HIGHLANDS
Tropic of Capricorn
Belo Horizonte •
GRAN CHACO
PARAGUAY — 20°S
Asunción ★ São Paulo • Rio de Janeiro •
Paraná
MOUNTAINS
Tucumán •
CHILE PAMPAS
Córdoba • URUGUAY
Santiago ★ Mt. Aconcagua
(22,834ft/6,960m) Buenos Aires ★ Montevideo ★ — 30°S
Concepción • Rio de la Plata
ARGENTINA
Bahía Blanca •

Salinas Grandes
(−131ft/−40m) — 40°S

PATAGONIA

0	500	1000 Miles
0	500	1000 Kilometers

FALKLAND ISLANDS (U.K.)
Tierra del • Stanley — 50°S
Fuego

Cape Horn SOUTH GEORGIA ISLANDS
(U.K.)

120°W 110°W 100°W 90°W 80°W 70°W 60°W 50°W 40°W 30°W 20°W

875

Southwestern Pacific

Elevation key

Feet	Meters
14,000	4,000
7,000	2,000
1,500	500
700	200
0	0
Below sea level	Below sea level

★ Capital city

◉ State/territory capital city

• Other city

0	500	1000 Miles
0	500	1000	1500 Kilometers

Scale correct at 20° south latitude

PACIFIC OCEAN

MICRONESIA

MELANESIA

INTERNATIONAL DATE LINE

KIRIBATI

AMERICAN SAMOA (U.S.)

PHOENIX ISLANDS

WESTERN SAMOA ★ Apia

TONGA ★ Nuku'alofa

COOK ISLANDS (N.Z.)

KERMADEC ISLANDS (N.Z.)

CHATHAM ISLANDS (N.Z.)

★ Tarawa

KIRIBATI

MARSHALL ISLANDS

Bikini

Eniwetok

Majuro ★

MARSHALL ISLANDS

TUVALU Funafuti ★

FIJI Suva ★

★ Yaren **NAURU**

Kolonia ★

PALAU ISLANDS (U.S.)

CAROLINE ISLANDS

FEDERATED STATES OF MICRONESIA

GUAM (U.S.)

SOLOMON ISLANDS Honiara ★

VANUATU Port-Vila ★

LOYALTY ISLANDS

NEW CALEDONIA (FR.)

Bismarck Archipelago

PAPUA NEW GUINEA

BISMARCK RANGE

Mt. Wilhelm (14,793 ft/4,509 m)

Port Moresby ★

Cape York

Torres Strait

CORAL SEA

GREAT BARRIER REEF

North Island

South Island

NEW ZEALAND

Auckland

Wellington ★

Christchurch

Dunedin

Stewart Island

TASMAN SEA

Brisbane

Gold Coast

Newcastle

Sydney ◉

Wollongong

Canberra ★

AUSTRALIAN CAPITAL TERRITORY

Mt. Kosciusko (7,310 ft/2,228m)

Cape Howe

QUEENSLAND

GREAT DIVIDING RANGE

GRAY RANGE

NEW SOUTH WALES

VICTORIA

Melbourne ◉

Geelong

SNOWY MTS/AUSTRALIAN ALPS

Bass Strait

TASMANIA Hobart ◉

TIMOR SEA

Darwin ◉

CAPE YORK PENINSULA

Gulf of Carpentaria

BARKLY TABLELAND

NORTHERN TERRITORY

TANAMI DESERT

MACDONNELL RANGES

Alice Springs

MUSGRAVE RANGES

SIMPSON DESERT

GREAT SANDY DESERT

KIMBERLEY PLATEAU

HAMERSLEY RANGE

Port Hedland

North West Cape

WESTERN AUSTRALIA

GIBSON DESERT

GREAT VICTORIA DESERT

AUSTRALIA

SOUTH AUSTRALIA

NULLARBOR PLAIN

Great Australian Bight

West Cape Howe

Perth ◉

DARLING RANGE

GREAT ARTESIAN BASIN

MURRAY RIVER BASIN

FLINDERS RANGE

Lake Eyre (−52 ft/−16m)

Whyalla

Adelaide ◉

INDIAN OCEAN

Europe

Elevation key

Feet	Meters
14,000	4,000
7,000	2,000
1,500	500
700	200
0	0

Below sea level

Below sea level

★ Capital city   • Other city

0   200   400   600 Miles

0   200   400   600 Kilometers

ICELAND

Reykjavik

ATLANTIC OCEAN

NORWEGIAN SEA

FAROE ISLANDS (DEN.)

SHETLAND ISLANDS (U.K.)

Orkney Islands

NORWAY

LONG MTS

Bergen

Trondheim

Oslo ★

KOLEN MTS.

SWEDEN

Göteborg

GÖTALAND PLATEAU

Stockholm ★

Lake Vänern

Lake Vättern

Gotland

BALTIC SEA

FINLAND

LAKE REGION

Lake Onega

Lake Ladoga

Helsinki ★

Turku

Gulf of Bothnia

Gulf of Finland

Tallinn ★

ESTONIA

LATVIA ★ Riga

LITHUANIA

Vilnius ★

VARANGER PENINSULA

Murmansk

Arkhangel'sk

WHITE SEA

KOLA PENINSULA

Pora R.

N. Dvina R.

W. Dvina R.

Arctic Circle

70°N

60°N

50°N

40°N

RUSSIA

URAL MOUNTAINS

UPPER KAMA UPLAND

Perm

Ufa

Samara

Kazan

Nizhniy Novgorod

VOLGA UPLAND

Volga R.

Moscow ★

St. Petersburg

CENTRAL RUSSIAN UPLAND

Don R.

Volgograd

KAZAKHSTAN

CASPIAN DEPRESSION

CASPIAN SEA

Ural R.

BELARUS

Minsk ★

DNEPR UPLAND

Kiev ★

UKRAINE

Khar'kov

Dnepr R.

Odessa

SEA OF AZOV

CRIMEA

BLACK SEA

Dnestr R.

MOLDOVA

Kishinev ★

ROMANIA

Bucharest ★

Danube R.

Constanta

CARPATHIAN MOUNTAINS

TRANSYLVANIAN ALPS

BULGARIA

Sofia ★

BALKAN MTS.

RHODOPE MTS.

Istanbul

TURKEY

Bosporus

Dardanelles

CAUCASUS MTS.

Mt. Elbrus 18,510 ft (5,642 m)

NETHERLANDS

POLAND

Gdansk

Gulf of Danzig

Vistula R.

Warsaw ★

Kraków

GREAT EUROPEAN PLAIN

Oder R.

(RUSSIA)

GERMANY

Berlin ★

Leipzig

Hamburg

Elbe R.

DENMARK

Copenhagen ★

Malmö

Kattegat

Skagerrak

NORTH SEA

UNITED KINGDOM

IRELAND

Dublin ★

Belfast

Glasgow

Edinburgh

HIGHLANDS

Manchester

Birmingham

CAMBRIAN MTS.

Cardiff

London ★

Thames R.

PENNINES

British Isles

IRISH SEA

CELTIC SEA

Land's End

English Channel

CHANNEL ISLANDS

NORMANDY HILLS

The Hague

Amsterdam ★

Brussels ★

BELGIUM

LUXEMBOURG ★

Luxembourg

Paris ★

Seine R.

Loire R.

FRANCE

Bordeaux

Bay of Biscay

MASSIF CENTRAL

Lyon

Rhône R.

Marseille

Bonn

Rhine R.

BLACK FOREST

SWITZERLAND

LIECHTENSTEIN

Bern ★

Lake Geneva

Mont Blanc 15,771 ft (4,807 m)

ALPS

Vienna ★

AUSTRIA

CZECH REPUBLIC

Prague ★

SLOVAKIA

Bratislava ★

HUNGARY

Budapest ★

Lake Balaton

GREAT HUNGARIAN PLAIN

SLOVENIA

Ljubljana ★

CROATIA

Zagreb ★

Venice

Po R.

ADRIATIC SEA

DINARIC ALPS

BOSNIA AND HERZEGOVINA

Sarajevo ★

YUGOSLAVIA

Belgrade ★

SERBIA

MONTENEGRO

Skopje ★

MACEDONIA

ALBANIA

Tirane ★

PINDUS MTS.

GREECE

Thessaloniki

Athens ★

PELOPONNESUS

AEGEAN SEA

IONIAN SEA

Crete

Rhodes

MONACO

ITALY

SAN MARINO

APENNINES

Rome ★

Naples

Tiber R.

TYRRHENIAN SEA

CORSICA (FR.)

SARDINIA (ITALY)

Palermo

SICILY (ITALY)

MALTA ★ Valletta

MEDITERRANEAN SEA

ANDORRA

PYRENEES

SPAIN

Barcelona

Valencia

Ebro R.

Bilbao

CANTABRIAN MTS.

M E S E T A

Madrid ★

Duero R.

Tagus R.

IBERIAN PENINSULA

Sevilla

GIBRALTAR (U.K.)

Strait of Gibraltar

BALEARIC ISLANDS (SP.)

Minorca

Majorca

Ibiza

PORTUGAL

Lisbon ★

Porto

877

Strait of Juan de Fuca
Cape Flattery
Puget Sound
130°W
Seattle
Olympia
45°N
WASHINGTON
RANGE
F.D. Roosevelt Lake
Pend Oreille Lake
Flathead Lake
LEWIS RANGE
ROCKY
Clark
Milk R.
Fort Peck Lake
Missouri R.
Lake Sakakawea
Portland
Columbia R.
CASCADE
BITTERROOT RANGE
Helena
MONTANA
NORTH DAKOTA
Bismarck
Salem
OREGON
COLUMBIA PLATEAU
Willamette R.
Boise
IDAHO
ABSAROKA RANGE
Yellowstone R.
G
Lake Oahe
SOUTH DAKOTA
Pierre
Klamath
40°N
Goose Lake
SNAKE RIVER PLAIN
Snake R.
BIGHORN MOUNTAINS
Bighorn
Powder R.
R
BLACK HILLS
BADLANDS
White R.
Cape Mendocino
COAST
RANGES
SIERRA
Pit R.
Sacramento R.
Pyramid Lake
Lake Tahoe
GREAT
Great Salt Lake
GREAT SALT LAKE DESERT
WYOMING
E
SAND HILLS
NEBRASKA
125°W
San Francisco Bay
San Francisco
San Jose
CENTRAL VALLEY
Sacramento
Carson City
NEVADA
BASIN
Salt Lake City
WASATCH RANGE
UINTA MOUNTAINS
Green R.
RANGE
Cheyenne
FRONT RANGE
South Platte R.
Denver
North Platte R.
A
T
Republican R.
Platte R.
Lincoln
35°N
Mt. Whitney (14,494 ft/4,418 m)
Death Valley (-282 ft/-89 m)
San Joaquin R.
UTAH
Lake Powell
COLORADO
SAN JUAN MOUNTAINS
M
O
U
SANGRE DE CRISTO MOUNTAINS
COLORADO
P
Smoky Hill R.
KANSAS
Point Conception
Lake Mead
PLATEAU
CALIFORNIA
GRAND CANYON
PAINTED DESERT
N
Arkansas R.
CHANNEL ISLANDS
Los Angeles
MOJAVE DESERT
Salton Sea
Colorado R.
ARIZONA
Santa Fe
T
Canadian R.
OKLAHOMA
Oklahoma City
PACIFIC
San Diego
Gila R.
Phoenix
NEW MEXICO
Rio Grande
A
Red R.
Lake Texoma
OCEAN
120°W
SONORA DESERT
SACRAMENTO MOUNTAINS
LLANO ESTACADO
I
N
Colorado R.
TEXAS
Dallas

El Paso
Pecos R.
EDWARDS PLATEAU
S
Brazos R.
Austin
160°W
Kauai
Honolulu
Oahu
Molokai
Lanai
Maui
155°W
HAWAII
PACIFIC OCEAN
Hawaii
Hilo
0   50   100 Miles
0 50 100 Kilometers
ARCTIC OCEAN
70°N
Point Barrow
BEAUFORT SEA
Arctic Circle
BROOKS RANGE
San Antonio
Padre
170°E
60°N
Bering Strait
St. Lawrence
ALASKA
Yukon R.
Tanana R.
Rio Grande
0   250   500 Miles
0   250   500 Kilometers
ALASKA RANGE
Mt. McKinley (20,320 ft/6,194 m)
Attu
BERING SEA
Anchorage
180°
170°W
50°N
ALEUTIAN ISLANDS
ALASKA PENINSULA
Kodiak
Gulf of Alaska
Juneau
COAST MOUNTAINS
PACIFIC OCEAN
160°W
150°W
140°W

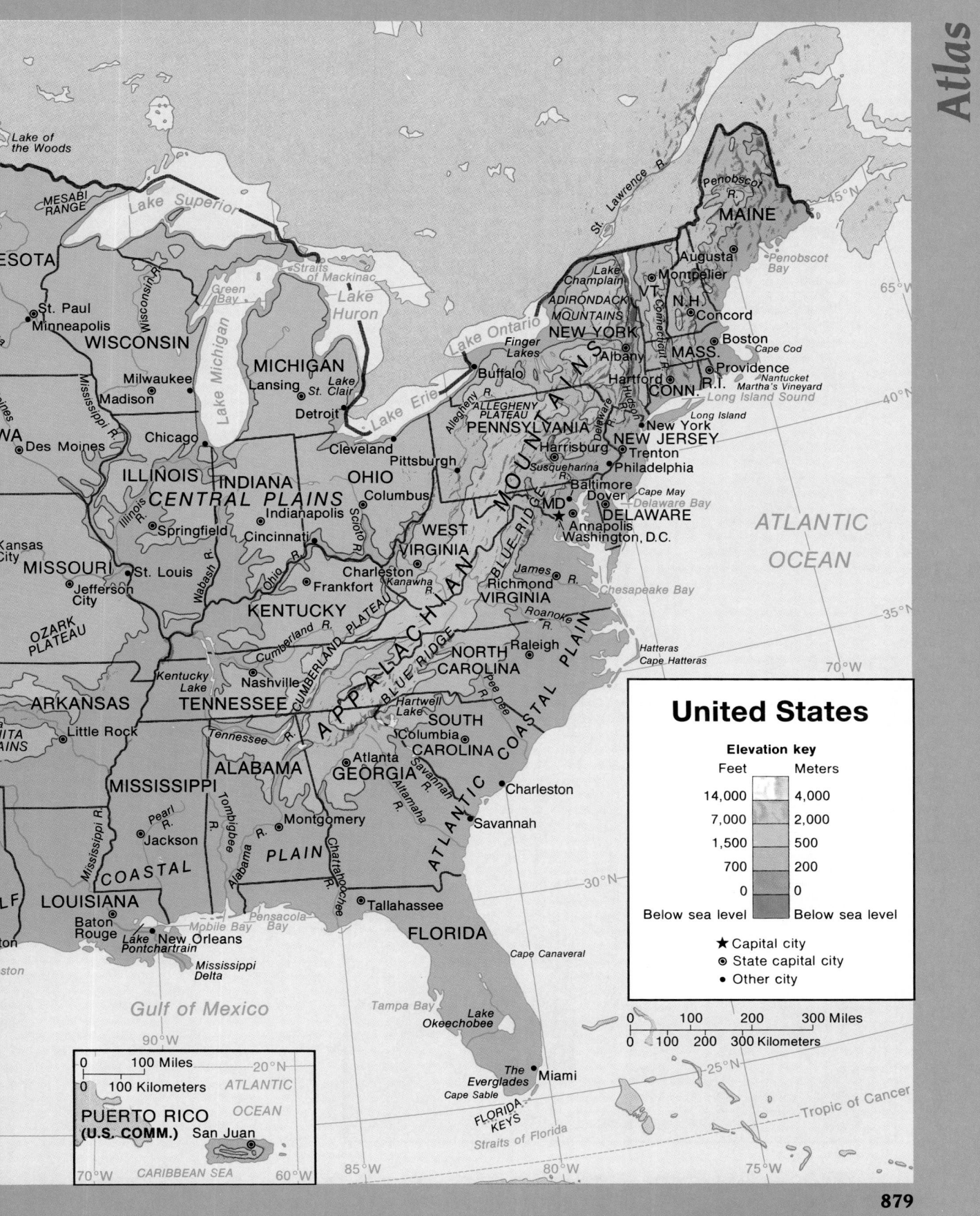

Lake of
the Woods

MESABI
RANGE

Lake Superior

-ESOTA

Straits
of Mackinac

St. Lawrence R.

Penobscot
R.

45°N

MAINE

Augusta

Penobscot
Bay

65°W

St. Paul
Minneapolis

Green
Bay

Lake
Huron

Lake
Champlain

Montpelier

VT.

N.H.

Concord

WISCONSIN

Wisconsin R.

MICHIGAN

Lake Michigan

Lake Ontario

ADIRONDACK
MOUNTAINS

Boston

Cape Cod

Milwaukee

Lansing

Lake
St. Clair

Finger
Lakes

NEW YORK

Albany

MASS.

Providence

Mississippi R.

Madison

Buffalo

Hartford

CONN.

R.I.

Nantucket

Martha's Vineyard

40°N

-WA

Des Moines

Chicago

Detroit

Lake Erie

Allegheny R.

ALLEGHENY
PLATEAU

Long Island Sound

Long Island

Cleveland

PENNSYLVANIA

New York

ILLINOIS

INDIANA

OHIO

Pittsburgh

Delaware R.

NEW JERSEY

Harrisburg

Trenton

CENTRAL PLAINS

Columbus

Susquehanna
R.

Philadelphia

Illinois R.

Springfield

Indianapolis

Scioto R.

Baltimore

Cape May

-Kansas
City

MISSOURI

St. Louis

Cincinnati

Frankfort

WEST

VIRGINIA

Charleston

Kanawha R.

MD.

Annapolis

Dover

DELAWARE

Delaware Bay

ATLANTIC

OCEAN

Wabash R.

Jefferson
City

Ohio R.

KENTUCKY

Cumberland R.

CUMBERLAND PLATEAU

James R.

Richmond

VIRGINIA

BLUE RIDGE

Washington, D.C.

Chesapeake Bay

OZARK
PLATEAU

Roanoke R.

35°N

ARKANSAS

Kentucky
Lake

Nashville

APPALACHIAN

BLUE RIDGE

NORTH

Raleigh

Hatteras

Cape Hatteras

70°W

-HITA
-AINS

Little Rock

Tennessee R.

CAROLINA

Pee Dee R.

Hartwell
Lake

SOUTH

ATLANTIC COASTAL PLAIN

TENNESSEE

ALABAMA

Columbia

CAROLINA

MISSISSIPPI

GEORGIA

Atlanta

Savannah R.

Charleston

Pearl
R.

Tombigbee R.

Montgomery

Altamaha
R.

Savannah

Jackson

Alabama R.

PLAIN

Chattahoochee R.

COASTAL

Tallahassee

-LF

LOUISIANA

Baton
Rouge

Pensacola
Bay

Mobile Bay

-ton

Lake
Pontchartrain

New Orleans

Mississippi
Delta

FLORIDA

Cape Canaveral

Gulf of Mexico

90°W

Tampa Bay

Lake
Okeechobee

United States

Elevation key

Feet		Meters
14,000		4,000
7,000		2,000
1,500		500
700		200
0		0
Below sea level		Below sea level

★ Capital city

◉ State capital city

• Other city

0	100	200	300 Miles
0	100	200	300 Kilometers

30°N

The
Everglades

Cape Sable

Miami

25°N

FLORIDA
KEYS

Tropic of Cancer

0	100 Miles
0	100 Kilometers

20°N

ATLANTIC

OCEAN

PUERTO RICO

(U.S. COMM.)

San Juan

70°W

CARIBBEAN SEA

60°W

Straits of Florida

85°W

80°W

75°W

879

The World: Political

----- Disputed or undefined boundaries

0   1000   2000   3000 Miles
0   1000   2000   3000 Kilometers

EUROPE

0   500   1000   1500 Miles
0   500   1000   1500 Kilometers

ARCTIC OCEAN

GREENLAND
(DEN.)

ICELAND

Arctic Circle

NORWAY

FINLAND

RUSSIA

SWEDEN

ESTONIA

UNITED DENMARK
KINGDOM

LATVIA

LITHUANIA

IRELAND

BELARUS

NETH.
BEL.

GER.

POLAND

UKRAINE

FRANCE

CZECH
REP.

SWIT.

SLOVAKIA

AUST. HUNG.

MOLDOVA

KAZAKHSTAN

SLOVENIA

ROMANIA

CROATIA

YUGOSLAVIA

MONGOLIA

BOSNIA AND HERZE.

ITALY

BUL.

ALB.

GEORGIA

PORTUGAL

SPAIN

GREECE

TURKEY

ARMENIA

AZERBAIJAN

TURKMENISTAN

UZBEKISTAN

KYRGYZSTAN

TAJIKISTAN

NORTH
KOREA

JAPAN

PEOPLE'S REPUBLIC OF
CHINA

SOUTH
KOREA

MALTA

CYPRUS
LEBANON
ISRAEL

SYRIA

IRAQ

AFGHANISTAN

MOROCCO

TUNISIA

JORDAN

IRAN

KUWAIT

QATAR

PAKISTAN

BHUTAN

TAIWAN

WESTERN
SAHARA
(MOR.)

ALGERIA

LIBYA

EGYPT

BAHRAIN

NEPAL

SAUDI ARABIA

INDIA

BURMA

PACIFIC OCEAN

UNITED ARAB
EMIRATES

BANGLADESH

MAURITANIA

OMAN

LAOS

CAPE
VERDE

SENEGAL

MALI

NIGER

CHAD

SUDAN

ERITREA

YEMEN

THAILAND

VIETNAM

GAMBIA

MARSHALL ISLANDS

GUINEA-
BISSAU

BURKINA
FASO

DJIBOUTI

CAMBODIA

GUINEA

BENIN

CÔTE
D'IVOIRE

SIERRA
LEONE

NIGERIA

CENTRAL AFRICAN
REPUBLIC

CAMEROON

ETHIOPIA

SRI LANKA

BRUNEI

FEDERATED STATES
OF MICRONESIA

LIBERIA

MALDIVES

GHANA

TOGO

MALAYSIA

EQUATORIAL GUINEA

SÃO TOMÉ AND PRÍNCIPE

UGANDA

SOMALIA

SINGAPORE

KIRIBATI

CONGO

KENYA

Equator

NAURU

GABON

RWANDA

INDONESIA

TUVALU

ZAIRE

BURUNDI

PAPUA
NEW
GUINEA

SOLOMON
ISLANDS

TANZANIA

SEYCHELLES

ANGOLA

COMOROS

MALAWI

INDIAN OCEAN

VANUATU

ZAMBIA

FIJI

MOZAMBIQUE

NAMIBIA

ZIMBABWE

BOTSWANA

MADAGASCAR

MAURITIUS

SWAZILAND

AUSTRALIA

SOUTH
AFRICA

LESOTHO

NEW ZEALAND

20°W   0°   20°E   40°E   60°E   80°E   100°E   120°E   140°E   160°E   180°

Antarctic Circle

ANTARCTICA

The World: Climates

Humid Tropical Climates

Wet Tropical
(Hot and very rainy all year)

Wet-and-Dry Tropical (Hot all year
with wet and dry seasons)

Subtropical Climates

Humid Subtropical (Hot, humid
summers and mild winters)

Mediterranean Subtropical (Hot, dry
summers and mild, rainy winters)

Dry Climates

Arid
(Desert climate with very little rain)

Semiarid
(Semidesert climate with some rain)

Midlatitude Climates

Temperate Marine
(Mild and rainy all year)

Humid Continental (Warm summers
and cold, snowy winters)

Subarctic (Short summers and long,
cold, snowy winters)

Cold Polar Climates

Subpolar (Always cold and dry with
short, cool summers)

Polar (Ice cap, with freezing
temperatures all year)

Highland Climates

(Temperature and precipitation vary
greatly with latitude and elevation)

Barrow

Anchorage

60°

NORTH

Edmonton

Regina

Seattle

AMERICA

Montreal

Chicago

Denver

New York

40°

ATLANTIC
OCEAN

Los Angeles

Phoenix

Houston

Jacksonville

New
Orleans

Miami

Tropic of Cancer

20°

Mexico City

PACIFIC OCEAN

0°

Equator

Quito

Manaus

Lima

SOUTH

Brasilia

20°

AMERICA

Tropic of Capricorn

Rio
Jan

40°

Buenos Aires

180° 160° 140° 120° 100° 80° 60°

60°

ARCTIC OCEAN

Hammerfest

Arctic Circle

Reykjavík

St. Petersburg

Copenhagen

Moscow

London

EUROPE

Zurich

Yakutsk

ASIA

Rome

Beijing

Lisbon

Seoul

Algiers

Baghdad

Tokyo

Cairo

Delhi

Shanghai

Riyadh

Calcutta

Mecca

Bombay

Khartoum

Madras Bangkok

Dakar

AFRICA

PACIFIC OCEAN

Lagos

Yaoundé

Singapore

Equator

Nairobi

Jakarta

Kinshasa

INDIAN OCEAN

Darwin

AUSTRALIA

Johannesburg

Perth

Cape Town

Sydney

Melbourne

0°   0°   20°   40°   60°   80°   100°   120°   140°   160°   180°

Antarctic Circle

ANTARCTICA

Amundsen-Scott
Station (South Pole)

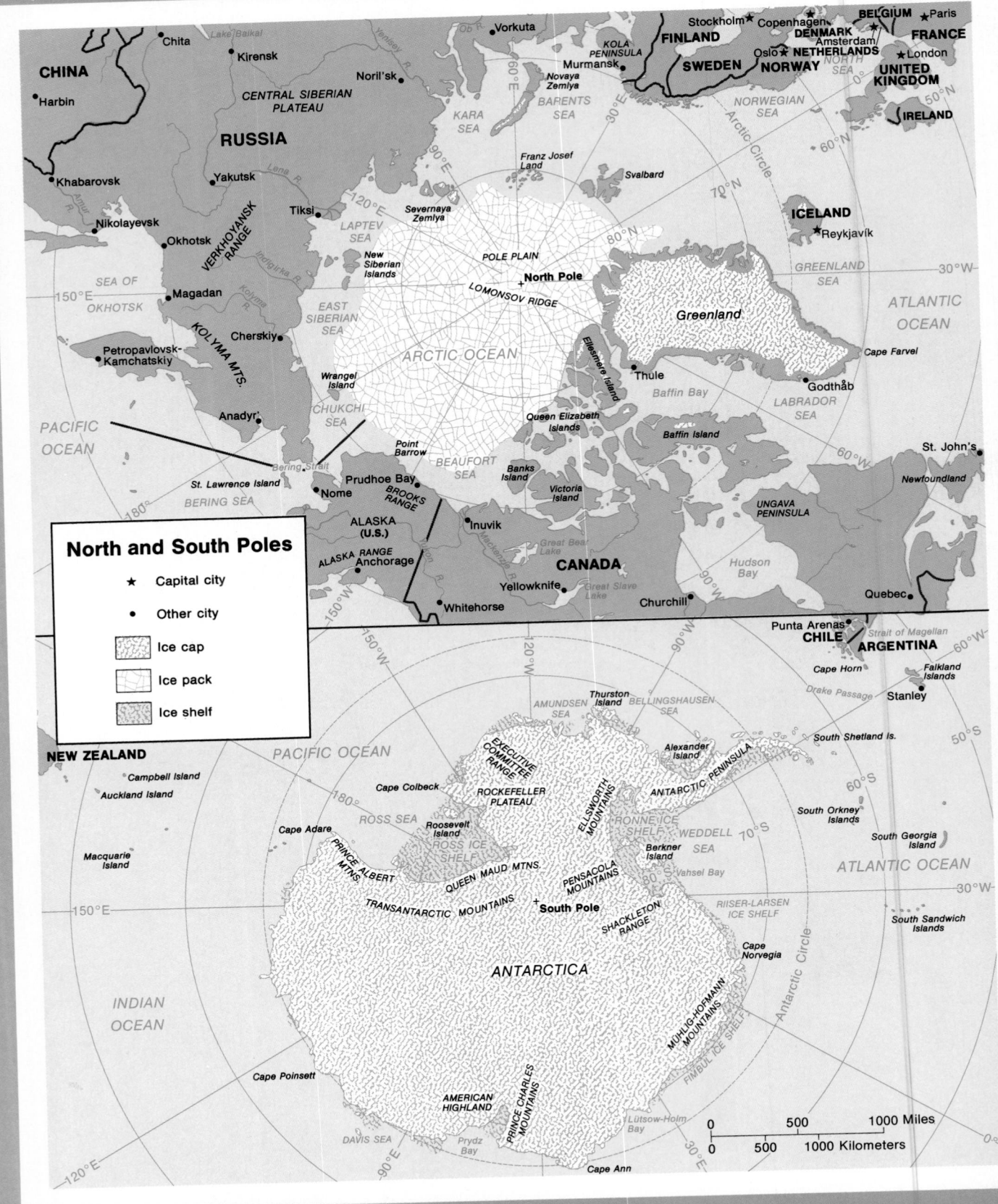

North and South Poles

★ Capital city
• Other city
Ice cap
Ice pack
Ice shelf

Skills Handbook

Skills for Studying History

Studying history involves much more than memorizing dates and names, as you would items on a shopping list. To study history is to learn about the beliefs, discoveries, and events that have shaped human life in the past, and to understand how these forces influence our lives today as we continue to make history. Specific skills needed in the study of history are described in this Skills Handbook.

Basic skills will help you locate the information, grasp the facts, and organize them in your mind. You need the facts as reference points when you talk and write about history.

Critical thinking skills will help you evaluate the information you discover, understand how ideas and events of the past are related, and use your knowledge to solve problems and make predictions. As you develop and use these skills, you begin to think as a historian does. You become a true student of history.

Basic Skills

1. Reading Strategically

A textbook is a kind of resource material. Although you may enjoy reading through your textbook sequentially as you would a story, you also are using the book to find the key facts and concepts you need to remember for class discussions, written assignments, and tests.

To facilitate this task, use these reading strategies:

A. Survey the chapter by skimming it. Skimming provides you with a preview of the main ideas in the chapter and a sense of the order in which things happened. To skim, read in sequence the chapter title, the title of the numbered sections within it, and the heads and subheads under these sections. Briefly study the pictures and other visual devices and the captions that accompany them. Read the list of **key terms** at the beginning of the chapter so that you will be alert to specific words and phrases you will need to understand and define. Complete the skimming strategy by reading the questions in the *Section Reviews* and in *Reviewing the Facts* in the Chapter Review. These questions provide you with further clues

about main ideas and details to look for as you read.

B. Write questions you want to find answers for in the chapter. The bases for these questions are in the statements under *Read and Understand* at the beginning of the chapter. Each statement refers to a section of the chapter. Rephrase the statements to make questions that begin with such words as *who, how, why, in what way,* and so on; for example, *What caused farming to improve and trade to revive? How did religious leaders wield great power?*

Read and Understand

1. Farming improved and trade revived.
2. Religious leaders wielded great power.
3. Royal governments grew stronger.
4. Learning revived and spread.
5. Crusaders marched against Islam.

C. Read to find the answers to your questions. The boldfaced heads that follow the section head provide the main ideas that will answer the question you have written about it. By reading each paragraph carefully, you can find the details that support and explain these main ideas.

D. When you finish reading a section, recite an answer to your question. If you feel that your answer if not complete, use the *scanning* strategy; that is, go back through the section to find the specific information you need to flesh out your answer, using the bold-faced heads and words as a guide. Then provide yourself with a study tool by writing your answer in the form of notes.

E. Review your grasp of the facts and ideas in the section. To review, try to answer your section question without looking at your notes. Check that you do not have any problem understanding the information. If you do, ask for help in clarifying your thoughts.

When you are able to do this successfully even after a few days have elapsed, you can be pretty sure that you have learned the main ideas and details.

2. Building Vocabulary

In your study of history, you need to learn the meanings of key words and terms used by historians and then build those words and terms into your vocabulary by using them correctly when you speak and write about history. Meanings of words can be discovered in various ways.

A. Look for a definition just before or after the word is used. In your textbook, the key terms for a chapter are listed on the first page and then shown in boldface where they first occur in the chapter. Usually the definition is given in the same paragraph.

> A walled town was known as a burgh, and the people who made their homes in such towns gradually became known as **burghers.** In France, burgh dwellers became known collectively as the **bourgeoisie** (BOOR-zhwah-ZEE).

Notice that the example paragraph also gives the definition of *burgh* (a walled town).

B. Use context clues to unlock the meaning of new words. Although the definition of a new word may not be directly given, you can often figure out its meaning from the context—the sentence or paragraph—in which it is used. The new word may not be a key term for historians; yet knowing the definition can make your understanding of an event more vivid and can enrich your general vocabulary.

- Meanings of new words and expressions can often be discovered from **similar** words in the context. For example, from the familiar word *earliest* in the following context, you can determine that *prototype* means an early or first form of something.

  > Like Edison's prototype, the earliest record players needed no electricity.

- A clue to meaning may be found in a **contrasting** word in the same context. For example, you can determine that in the following context *shrink* has the meaning "avoid" (rather than "grow smaller") to contrast with *welcome.*

  > "I do not shrink from this responsibility; I welcome it." (John Fitzgerald Kennedy)

- You can often determine the meaning of a new word simply by using **common sense.** For example, you can figure out from the context of the following sentence that *doff* means "take off," since that is what a person usually does with a hat when bowing.

  > Whenever they met a procession of servants carrying the king's dinner, they were required to *doff* their hats and bow low.

C. Use the Glossary and a dictionary to check your understanding of a word's meaning. The key terms for each section are defined in the glossary of this book. To delve more deeply into the meanings of these terms, and of words you have started to define from context clues, use a dictionary.

D. Keep a notebook of key terms and their definitions. You can use such a notebook as a study tool as you prepare for tests and as a research tool as you plan and draft essays and research papers. Various organizations are possible. Here are two possible ways to record key terms and their meanings.

- Organize the key terms by chapter. Copy the term and its definition from the glossary. Include the textbook page number (also given in the glossary) on which the word appears.

Then use the key term in an original sentence based on information in the section.

vernacular: The everyday language of a region or country. (p. 347) Dante wrote in Italian, which was the vernacular of his country.

■ Organize your notebook into groups of words that deal with central ideas, such as *Types of Government, Agriculture, Industry and Trade*. As you learn new terms, write them and their definitions under the appropriate central idea heading. Create new categories as they are needed. Here is the beginning of a central idea list from Chapters 1 and 2.

Industry and Trade

technology: The part of a culture that includes tools and the skills to make and use them. (p. 22)

artisan: A skilled worker who makes goods by hand. (p. 32)

Central idea lists are a handy tool when you are assigned to write a paper on a particular aspect of history.

E. Use the key terms as often as possible as you make notes, participate in class discussions, and answer history quizzes. By using the terms frequently, you make them part of your general vocabulary as well as of your "history vocabulary." Your familiarity with the terms will stand you in good stead when you take vocabulary tests and write answers to essay questions.

3. Using Reference Materials

As you study history, you will take on assignments that require research in a library. Some of these assignments send you searching for established knowledge about the past, while others involve you in tracking down the latest information about current events. In addition to using the encyclopedias, atlases, nonfiction books, newspapers, and news magazines with which you are familiar, learn to use the abundant other reference materials that most libraries offer.

A. To do research about the past, use specialized reference books that zero in on the topic you are researching. An atlas of the modern world shows you maps and gives you data about nations and regions as they are today; a *historical atlas* shows you how boundaries have changed through the centuries. Historical atlases also reproduce maps and descriptions that were made long ago, so that you can better understand ancient peoples' concepts of the world.

If you are researching specific cultures of the past, ask the librarian to help you find reference books like *Who Was Who in the Greek World*, the *Handbook of Classical Mythology*, *Festivals of Western Europe*, or *Latin American History: A Teaching Atlas*. Fascinating reference works like these are often tucked away on the shelves of your local library or are available through the interlibrary loan system. Such reference books have many more details about specific subjects than a general encyclopedia is likely to have. In specialized reference books, you can find data that bring the past to life for you and add interest and verve to your written and oral reports.

B. To do research about current events, begin with indexes to periodicals. Newspapers, magazines, and journals are called *periodicals* because they are published at regular times, or periods. The standard guide to them is a set of volumes, organized by year, called the *Readers' Guide to Periodical Literature*. It shows you where to find articles on your subject. Subjects are arranged alphabetically. Much of the information is given in abbreviations. (A key to the abbreviations is at the front of each volume of the Guide.)

ART, MEXICAN ←— subject

title of article → Mexican art dance.

author's name → C. Brown.

illustrated → il

name of magazine → *Forbes*

volume page → 146: 104–5

month, day, and year of publication → Ag 20 '90

Your library may also have the *National Newspaper Index,* which lists in alphabetical order subjects covered recently by five major newspapers. Based on your search through this index or through the *Readers' Guide,* jot down the names and issues of magazines and newspapers you need. Ask your librarian where you can find them.

C. For an overview of some recent articles and of the latest news about your subject, refer to volumes of summaries. *Readers' Guide Abstracts* are volumes with summaries of *some* of the thousands of articles listed in the *Readers' Guide* index. Summaries are arranged alphabetically according to subject.

> **KOREAN REUNIFICATION QUESTION**
> Same bed, different dreams. D. S. Jackson, il *Time* 136:39–40 Jl 2 '90
> Many of the reasons for the separation of North and South Korea have disappeared, but the two nations still have major differences. Since the Korean War, South Korea has become an economic powerhouse. Although the nation is capable of assuming much of its defense against a diminished threat from North Korea, U.S. troops remain in South Korea. North Korea is still dependent on Soviet military and economic support, but the Soviets are no longer eager or able to finance the extension of communism. The leaders of the Soviet Union and South Korea recently met, and trade between the two nations is expected to increase. Despite these changes and the desire of millions in North and South Korea for reunification, the two nations have gone in different directions for too long for reconciliation to come easily.

Facts on File is a weekly publication that summarizes recent news from around the world.

Each issue has a front-page list of all the summaries in that issue. Issues for the current year are kept in a looseleaf binder. At the back of the binder are two cumulative indexes: one for all the subjects covered since the beginning of the year and one for subjects covered in the last few weeks.

4. Using and Interpreting Visuals

Students of history study and make charts, graphs, tables, and diagrams as a way of organizing information in a simple, visual form. By studying visuals, you get both an overview and a summary of the material you have been reading.

A. Diagrams and charts use labeled pictures or symbols. Diagrams show how something is arranged or how it works. For example, the diagram on page 59 in this textbook shows the arrangement and location of features inside an Egyptian pyramid. The diagram helps you to envision the interior more concisely than words alone can.

Charts are used to show relationships between people or ideas. The chart below shows the relationship between a king, vassals, and knights. By noting their position on the chart and the vertical lines, you can see the chain of command among these feudal people. Your reading of the section will amplify and expand on the relationship summarized in the chart.

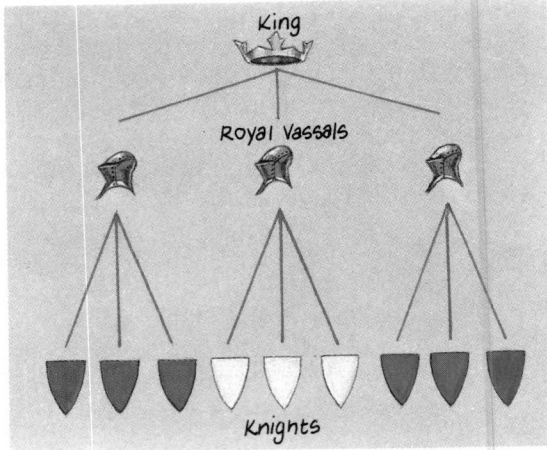

This diagram shows how the feudal system worked in theory. In real life, however, the system became a tangle of conflicting loyalties.

When studying a chart or diagram, first read the title or caption that explains its purpose. Then study the details and the labels and figure out how the details are related. A good way to check your understanding of a chart or diagram is to try to reproduce it from memory.

B. Graphs and tables present facts in the form of numbers, or statistics.

Graphs and tables help you to see trends or to do comparison and contrast studies. The title or caption tells what information is being presented.

- Because the numbers on these visuals often involve millions, or even billions, check the heading or the label at the bottom to see what the numbers stand for. On the table below, for example, the numbers stand for *billions* of dollars. That means that in the numbers given, you have to change the decimal point to a comma and add eight zeroes.

What Europe Bought

Petroleum products	$55.7
Office equipment	19.0
Apparel and accessories	16.7
Road vehicles, including cars	16.5
Electrical machinery and parts	16.1
Telecommunications equipment	12.8
Textiles, yarn, and fabrics	10.6
Paper and paperboard	10.5
Fruits and vegetables	9.5
Plastics and artificial resins	9.3

IN BILLIONS OF DOLLARS

SOURCE: European Commission of the European Community

- A line graph—and often a bar graph, too—has a horizontal axis and a vertical axis, which you must read in order to understand the graph. In the line graph to the right above, the horizontal axis names years (1973 through 1988) and the vertical axis names dollars per barrel of crude oil. By putting the two sets of information together, you can figure out that in the year 1982, crude oil cost about $37 a barrel.

  To build your skill in reading line graphs and bar graphs, pose questions for yourself based on the graph. On the basis of the line graph above, for example, you might ask and answer these questions: In what year shown on the graph was crude oil lowest? In what years did crude oil cost about $15 per barrel?

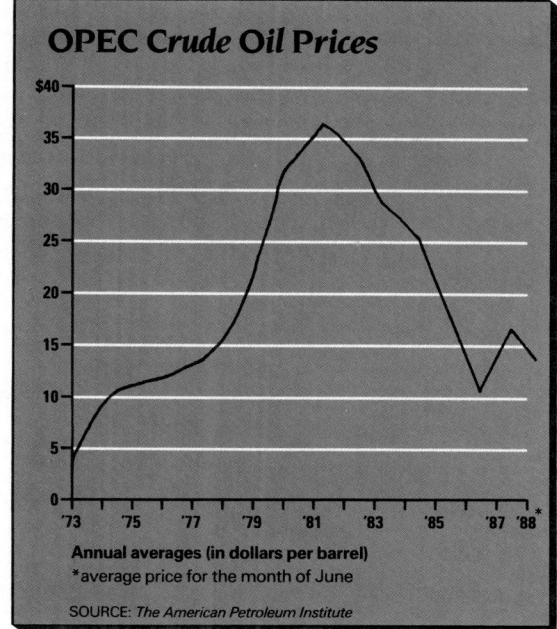

OPEC *Crude Oil Prices*

Annual averages (in dollars per barrel)
*average price for the month of June

SOURCE: *The American Petroleum Institute*

- A circle graph usually presents numbers in the form of percentages. The entire circle represents 100%. Each segment of the circle represents a part of that. For example, from the circle graphs on page 836 of this textbook you can see that in 1986 the United States imported more merchandise than any other nation did, and that the largest exporter of merchandise was Germany.

  Visuals rarely tell *why* or *how* things happen. It is up to you, as a history student, to figure out what forces make crude oil prices fluctuate, or why Europe buys more goods from the United States than it does from Japan. Use visuals as tools for presenting information and for posing provocative questions to answer through further study.

5. Organizing Information

As a student of history, you are exposed to a vast array of facts and ideas. If you organize these facts and ideas, they become easier to study and remember for tests and class discussions. You can also put organization strategies to work in the prewriting stage when you are preparing a written report on some aspect of history.

A. Classify information to put it into manageable groups. To classify is to group facts that share a common characteristic. As you read, look for similar bits of information, write them in lists, and give each list a heading. The result will be a chart that you can use as a learning and reference tool. For example, as you read the material on pages 327 and 328 of this textbook, you might develop a classification chart like this one:

EARLY PEOPLE OF NORTH AMERICA

Group	Anasazi	Hopewell	Mississippians
Location	American Southwest	southern Ohio	banks of Mississippi
Dwellings and structures	pueblos	burial mounds	villages, city of Cahokia
Activity	farming	trade	farming and trade
Products	corn	carved pipes, copper axes	corn, squash, beans

Notice that the entire chart is given a title when it is finished. The title tells the purpose for which you have made the chart: to organize some of the details about the lives of early people of North America.

B. Outline information as a way of showing main ideas and supporting details. Outlines organize data so that you can use it to develop a report. To outline, you organize your information into main ideas and supporting ideas. On the outline, main ideas are called main topics. Supporting ideas are called subtopics and details. The following is part of an outline that brings together main ideas and details about American Indian Art.

The Art of American Indians

I. Pottery and Basketry	**(main topic)**
A. Coil-Method Pottery	**(subtopic)**
1. Painted pots for use in ceremonies	**(detail)**
2. Pots in the shape of animals	**(detail)**
3. Pots for storing grain	**(detail)**
B. Woven Fibers	**(subtopic)**
1. Baskets for carrying food	**(detail)**
2. Hats and sandals	**(detail)**
3. Mats and wall coverings	**(detail)**
II. Metalwork	**(main topic)**
A. Gold jewelry of the Caribbean	**(subtopic)**
B. Metalwork in the Andes	**(subtopic)**
1. Making bronze	**(detail)**
2. Gilding metals	**(detail)**

Notice that if you have *one* subtopic, you must have at least one other, and if you have one detail, you must have at least one other.

Use this rule to help you organize your ideas. For example, if you can think of only one detail, combine it with the subtopic or reread your notes to find other details.

C. Summarize information to identify the main idea of a passage or section. To summarize, you must first make sense of what you have read and then analyze the passage to decide what the main point is. Then you state the main point in your own words. By using this strategy, you are more likely to remember the material and make it useful as you plan reports.

Usually, a paragraph can be summarized in a single sentence. Read the paragraph below and the one-sentence summary that follows it. Notice that the summary leaves out details.

> The remarkable history of the Maya began and ended in a cloud of mystery. Archaeologists still wonder why the Maya suddenly abandoned their cities in the late eighth century. Although a deadly disease or a widespread peasant uprising may have been involved, no one knows for sure what happened. An unknown Maya once wrote, "All moons, all years, all days, all winds take their course and pass away." Perhaps this is the best explanation for the decline of their civilization.
>
> *Summary:* The mysterious decline of the Maya civilization may have been caused by disease or a revolt.

To summarize an article or a longer section in your textbook, you would write a summary paragraph. An example of such a summary is shown on page 888. The paragraph briefly states each main idea from a two-page article. As practice in writing a summary paragraph, analyze the section "Louis XVI was a weak ruler" on page 484 in this textbook, then restate the main ideas in a paragraph of not more than four sentences.

6. Taking Tests

Study strategies help you to learn. Test-taking strategies help you to "show that you know." There are three basic kinds of test questions, and there is a special strategy you can use with each kind.

A. As soon as you get the test, familiarize yourself with it by skimming through it. Read the directions to find out what you will have to do in each section. Then decide how you will allot your time among the sections.

B. When reading true/false questions, look for qualifying words. Think hard about statements that have words like *never, always, all,* and *only*. Ask yourself, "Is this statement *always* true? Are there any exceptions?" If there are exceptions, the answer is *false*. On the other hand, statements with qualifying words like *sometimes* and *usually* often can be answered *true*.

C. When reading multiple-choice questions, try to answer the question first without looking at the answer choices. Then look through all the choices to find one that is similar to your answer. This answer is likely to be the correct one. However, if you can't answer the question on your own, look through the choices and eliminate those that you feel are definitely wrong. Then consider the remaining choices and pick the one that seems most likely to be correct.

D. When answering true/false and multiple choice questions, don't linger over questions that have you stumped. First use your time on answers you think you know. Then go back and make educated guesses to answer the "stumpers." In most cases, any answer is better than no answer at all. Your educated guess may just be right.

E. Essay questions require close reading, and the answers require some planning. The directions for essay questions usually contain key words that tell you exactly how to approach the answer:

- *Describe* or *discuss* indicates that your answer should contain main ideas and details about key events and persons.

Examples: Briefly describe the Reign of Terror. Discuss the rights proclaimed in *A Declaration of the Rights of Man*.

- *Contrast* indicates that your answer should point out differences.
Example: Contrast romanticism and realism in art.

- *Compare* means that you should concentrate on likenesses but include some differences too.
Example: Compare the nationalist movements in Austria and Italy.

- *Trace* usually indicates that your answer should show a sequence of events.
Example: Trace the development of Maya city-states.

- *Explain* and *relate* indicate that your answer should show a cause and effect relationship.
Examples: Explain how the French Revolution brought about the beginning of modern nationalism. How was the code of chivalry related to the idea of romantic love?

- *List, identify,* and *define* usually call for brief, succinct answers.
Examples: List the major causes of the French Revolution. Identify the two major trade routes to Asia used by European explorers. Define the term *humanist*.

After you have determined what an essay question requires you to do, use scratch paper to briefly note the points you want to make in your answer and in what order. By organizing your ideas first in this way, you will avoid a lot of erasing and backtracking. You will be able to concentrate on writing clear sentences.

Keep in mind that while essay questions are designed primarily to test your knowledge of a subject, your score is likely to be affected too by your spelling, punctuation, and grammar.

Allow yourself time to read through your answer to edit and proofread it.

Once basic skills have helped you to grasp and organize information, critical thinking skills take you one step further. First, they will help you evaluate if the information is correct. Second, they will give the information added meaning by identifying relationships to other established data. Finally, some critical thinking skills will help you use the information to solve problems and make decisions.

Critical Thinking Skills

1. Evaluating Sources

Basic skills enable you to collect a body of information on a subject. To decide how valuable the information is, you first have to determine its source and decide how accurate the information is.

A. Analyze data to decide whether it is a primary source or a secondary source. Primary sources are records made by people directly involved in an event. The record may be in the form of writing, as a letter or document of the time. The diary entry on page 435 of this textbook is an example of a written primary source. It is a vivid description of the disastrous London fire of 1666, as witnessed by a royal official.

Historians also consider paintings, drawings, maps, and artifacts such as sculpture and pottery as primary sources when they portray eyewitness scenes or events. Careful study of these things can reveal much about the past. The painting on page 222, for example, was made by an artist of the Middle Ages who had many opportunities to observe the building of a cathedral. From the painting you can learn how the workers dressed, how they divided their labor, what tools and materials they used, and the sequence in which they built various parts of the structure.

Secondary sources are written accounts or pictures made by people who did not actually witness the event. Most of the materials you use in your study of history are secondary sources, such as textbooks, encyclopedias, modern drawings showing a long-ago event, and biographies of famous people of the past. To determine whether a source is primary or secondary you have to find out when it was made, who probably made it, and whether the maker most likely participated in or actually saw the event.

B. Analyze data to see how reliable, or credible, it might be. When you study a primary source, keep in mind that not all eyewitness accounts are complete and factual in every detail. Eyewitnesses may forget details or have reasons for leaving out data or for adding things that are not entirely accurate. For example, portraits of kings and queens may make them look much handsomer than they really were because portrait painters were expected to make flattering pictures of their rulers. This does not mean the portraits are not valuable as sources of information. By studying the clothes, the props, and the background of the portrait you can learn much about the life of royal people at that time.

When you analyze a primary source, don't confuse the accuracy of the writing or drawing with the credibility or honesty of the person who made it. For example, an ancient map may not give an accurate picture of the world. But such a map *does* give an accurate picture of what a learned geographer of ancient times believed the world to be.

Reliable secondary sources have the following characteristics:

■ The author or authors are experts in the subject. You can check the qualifications of the authors by reading the brief notes about them at the front or back of the book or by looking in a biographical dictionary.

■ The author or authors have used many different sources. Historians refer to primary historical sources such as records, documents, and diaries. They refer to primary sources from art and archaeology such as drawings, murals, and structures remaining from ancient times. Historians also use secondary sources, such as the work of other historians who are considered reliable. Usually, a history book or article will note the major sources used by the writer. The sources may be given within the text itself or in footnotes or in a bibliography.

■ The material is as up-to-date as possible. Check the date of publication on the copyright page of a textbook or an encyclopedia or on the cover of a periodical. This is important even if you are studying an event of the distant past, for historians are constantly discovering new data about ancient times.

C. Contrast and compare different interpretations of the same event. Historians may have honest differences in the conclusions they reach. There are many aspects of the past that are still being disputed by reliable historians and many questions that remain to be answered. This is part of the challenge and excitement of the historian's work.

2. Distinguishing Fact from Opinion

As you evaluate primary and secondary sources, you will want to identify statements that are facts and statements that are opinions.

A. A fact is something that has actually happened or something that can be proved through evidence, observation, or testing. Since it is impossible for you or for anyone else to experience, test, and observe all the events of history, you count on experts to present the facts to you. Once you have checked the credibility of the authors, you can generally rely on the information presented.

B. An opinion is an expression of a belief or judgment. Some opinions are openly stated and labeled as such. On page 183 of this textbook is an example of an openly stated opinion. The Empress Theodora says that it is her opinion that the emperor and his court should not flee from a mob, and she tells exactly why she holds that opinion.

Although some stated opinions contain signal phrases like "I think that . . ." or "It seems to me that . . . ," other opinions are simply presented as if they were facts that everyone should acknowledge. Ghandi's ideas, presented on page 664 of this book, are an example. His statements are his opinions about how Hindus and Muslims could unite. The statements are not facts because they do not tell about things that have happened or things that can be proved. As you study history, learn to distinguish between the facts of reality and the opinions and beliefs of great men and women. It is often the latter that influence events and bring about change.

3. Identifying Point of View and Bias

Whereas *fact* and *opinion* refer to the content of words, *point of view* and *bias* refer to the speaker's state of mind. It is up to you, as a student of history, to detect these ways of presenting information.

A. A point of view is the particular focus one takes when considering a problem or a situation. It is possible for one person to take different points of view. For example, in looking at woodlands you might take the point of view of a developer who wishes to cut down the trees and build houses. Then you might take the point of view of an environmental expert who wishes to preserve the woods as an animal sanctuary.

Political cartoonists deliberately choose a point of view and then present it in an exaggerated way to emphasize their point. Other points of view are left out. In the cartoon on this page, the artist's point is that Americans are spending money even when they know they should be saving it.

THIS SAYS MOST AMERICANS DON'T PLAN FOR A RAINY DAY.

OF COURSE WE DO. WE JUST PLAN TO GET WET.

BUS STOP

FINANCE

NEW CARS

Mike Luckovich
Atlanta Constitution
Creators Syndicate

To detect point of view in historical documents and articles, look for the ideas and facts that the authors emphasize and think about what ideas and facts they might be leaving out or touching on only lightly. To get a balanced picture, try to find documents or articles that develop alternative points of view about the same situation.

B. A bias is a one-sided, unexamined view.
A person who is biased has made a judgment about an event, a person, or a group without really considering the many aspects of the situation. Biased speakers and writers can be detected in various ways.

- Their statements about certain people or groups are loaded with emotional words like *stupid*, *ignorant*, and *impossible*; or *great*, *wonderful*, and *right*.

- They tend to use words that allow no exceptions, like *always* and *never*.

- They usually exhibit an "us-and-them" approach to life. The "us" is the group to which the speaker or writer belongs. The "them" is everyone who does not conform to the ways of that group. People who are biased have difficulty seeing the likenesses that all groups share.

In historical documents written by explorers, you may often detect bias in the explorers' reactions to peoples and cultures that are new to them. When you study these documents, try to separate the facts from the writer's bias.

4. Identifying Cause and Effect

Each event in history is related in some way to events that precede or follow it. Students of history want to identify these relationships so that they can clearly understand the significance of the events.

A. A *cause* is an event that makes something else happen. An *effect* is the outcome or result of an event. Any human action usually has more than one cause and several effects. Historians attempt to point out these multiple causes and effects and classify them in the following way.

- An *immediate cause* is the one that directly precipitates an event. For example, two of the immediate causes of the Reformation were Martin Luther's denouncing of the selling of indulgences and questioning of the Church's teachings.

- A *long-term cause* or underlying cause is one that has existed for a long time. Two of the long-term causes of the Reformation were the worldliness of the Renaissance popes and the abuses and ignorance of the lower clergy.

- An *immediate effect* is one that takes place directly after an event occurs. For example, the immediate effect of a volcanic eruption is the burning and burying of the surrounding land.

- A *long-term effect* is one that can be determined only many years after the causative action has taken place. For example, one long-term effect of a volcanic eruption is the eventual enrichment of the soil.

B. To trace a cause and effect relationship, center on a focus point. You may select this point yourself, or it may be assigned to you by a teacher or in an essay question. An example is, What were the effects of the Peloponnesian War on the Athenians? The question focuses on events and situations that happened in Athens *after* the war. After determining your focus, you would follow these steps to construct your answer.

- Read or recall various events that took place in Athens after the war and write them in sequence in a list or on a time line.

- Determine which of the events were actually caused by the war. Keep in mind that events in a sequence are not always related.

- Use the labels **I** and **L** to identify immediate effects and long-term effects.

Effects of the Peloponnesian War	
loss of population to warfare and disease	I
loss of farmlands, fleet, Long Walls	I
loss of Athenian wealth and power	I
loss of confidence in democracy	I
decline of all Greek city-states	L
vulnerability of city-states to outside invasion	L

- Prepare a concluding statement that shows how and why the war had these effects. You can adapt the steps above to answering questions that focus your attention on *causes*, such as "What were the causes of the Peloponnesian War?" In that case, your time line or list would note events or situations that occurred *before* the war. You would label them **I** and **L** for immediate and long-term, and write a statement that explains how these events were related to the outbreak of war.

C. In reading historical documents and reference materials, evaluate the material to make sure that claims of cause and effect are substantiated. On page 606 of this textbook, the material headed *The arts reach a new audience* claims that mass culture was caused by the spread of literacy, improvements in communication, and a gradual reduction in working hours. Notice that the writer of the material does not simply list these causes but explains to the reader *how* these causes are related to mass culture. For example, literacy contributed to mass culture *because* millions of new readers created a demand for books and periodicals. Reduction in working hours contributed to mass culture *because* people had more leisure time to spend on entertainment.

When you write about cause and effect relationships, provide enough explanation to make the relationships clear and convincing.

5. Comparing and Contrasting

Another strategy for determining relationships is to compare and contrast events, situations, or people. To contrast means to point out and emphasize differences. To compare means to point out and emphasize similarities (though the term comparison is often used to include differences as well). You can use the contrast-compare strategy as a study tool to help you organize information you have read, and as a technique for organizing and writing research papers.

A. Decide on your main purpose for making contrasts or comparisons, then select the characteristics you wish to study. For example, after reading in Chapter 2 of this textbook about the religions of the Sumerians and the Jews, you may want to organize the information to show contrasts between religions.

- State your purpose in a brief topic phrase, for example, *Differences between the Beliefs of Sumerians and Jews.*

- Determine the main characteristics of the topic that you wish to compare or contrast. You might decide, for example, that you wish to contrast Sumerian and Jewish beliefs about the numbers of gods, where the gods lived, what the gods were like, and what they were expected to do.

- Set up a chart like the one below to organize your findings. Fill in the columns with details that compare or contrast, according to your purpose.

Differences Between Beliefs of Sumerians and Jews		
	Sumerians	Jews
Number of gods	(3,000 gods)	(one God)
Where god(s) lived		
Characteristics of god(s)		
What was expected of god(s)		

B. Use contrast and comparison to link past and present. As you study history, likenesses and differences between cultures through time and between the ancient world and our own constantly occur to you. For example, as you read about the ancient Greek ideals about heroism, you might consider which of these ideals we still hold today and also how Greek ideals and modern ideals about heroism are different. To organize your information and insights on this subject, you might set up a chart or list that allows you to both contrast and compare, using the following headings:

HEROIC IDEALS		
	Ancient Greece	Modern World
Alike		
Different		

As you become more adept at the strategy of comparing and contrasting, you will be able to include more than two cultures or periods in your analysis. For example, by studying the material on pages 63, 111–112, 133, and 216 of this textbook, you could set up a chart or outline comparing and contrasting the lives of women in Egypt, Greece, Rome, and medieval Europe. Details on your chart would show likenesses and differences among these women's political rights, social status, occupations, and daily life.

C. Make use of visual materials in your contrast and comparison studies. Tables and graphs are set up for the purpose of making numerical likenesses and differences clear and for showing historical trends. The table below, for example, allows you to contrast and compare the rate of population growth in certain cities. The figures for the city of Manchester are then translated into a bar graph. Such visual devices help you compare and contrast quickly and provide you with data to make your own graphs and tables when you are preparing a report on likenesses and differences through time.

Historical maps can also help you contrast and compare. By studying the maps on pages 110 and 124 of this textbook, for example, you can quickly see the difference in the amount of territory held by Greece in 550 B.C. and in 330 B.C.

The Growth of Seven British Cities

	1685	1760	1881
Liverpool	4,000	35,000	555,425
Manchester	6,000	45,000	393,676
Birmingham	4,000	30,000	400,757
Leeds	7,000	(not known)	309,126
Sheffield	4,000	20,000	284,410
Bristol	29,000	100,000	206,503
Nottingham	8,000	17,000	111,631

Manchester

1665	1760	1881
6,000	45,000	393,676

6. Making Decisions and Solving Problems

Historians, like scholars in other fields, use the facts they have collected and organized as the basis for making decisions and solving problems. There are specific strategies history students can use as they carry out these operations.

A. Conclusions are based on verifiable facts.

You can reach a conclusion in two ways: through *inductive reasoning*, or through *deductive reasoning*.

- Inductive reasoning is based on facts collected through observation and experiment. As you study the work of the scientists Galileo and Keppler, you will see how inductive reasoning operates. It is a process you use yourself as you draw conclusions. For example, if you have filled out a comparison chart to show known facts about the lives of women in Sumer and the lives of women in medieval Europe, you can make the valid conclusion that women in Sumer took a more active part in business and commerce than medieval women did.

- Deductive reasoning derives conclusions from a statement that has already been verified. It reasons that, if the statement is true, then further statements and conclusions may be drawn. The following paragraph from this textbook shows a conclusion reached through the deductive method. The fact on which the conclusion is based is underlined.

> On the whole, Sumerian women could engage in most of the occupations of city life, from merchant to farmer to artisan. Women could also join the lower ranks of the priesthood. However, none of Sumer's written records mentions a female scribe. Therefore, scholars have concluded that girls were not allowed to attend the schools where upper-class boys learned to read and write.

B. Inferences extend the information given.

Inferences are ideas and meanings not stated in the material. You discover them as you read between the lines. For example, on page 75, archaeologists at Mohenjo-Daro identified a bathhouse about the size of a swimming pool. You can infer that there was a supply of water nearby. There must also have been a piping system to bring water to the bathhouse and drains to empty the pool.

You can also make inferences based on certain aspects of a work of art that act as clues to information. They might reveal the intentions or feelings of the artist. For example, from Goya's painting on page 497 you can infer that his feelings favored the Spanish rebels. The events depicted and the concrete details shown in a painting also provide information about a period.

Your inferences, based on careful study of literal materials, will enrich and expand your understanding of history.

7. Making Generalizations

A generalization is a broad statement that attempts to summarize information about a topic or state a general principle that applies to similar situations. You often write generalizations to serve as topic sentences of paragraphs in research papers and essays. You often encounter generalizations as you read historical material. In writing them or reading them, check to make sure the generalizations are valid.

- **Make sure your generalization is true for all the examples that relate to it.** For example, in reading about the lives of women in ancient times you might make this preliminary generalization: In ancient times, women were oppressed and stifled in their ambitions. Further reading, however, would reveal to you that in many cultures women were active in scholarship, art, and business. Thus, your preliminary generalization would not be valid.

- **Revise your generalization so that it will apply to the new information by rewording it or use qualifying words and phrases.** The preliminary generalization above could be reworded in the following ways:

> In many cultures of ancient times, women were oppressed and stifled in their ambitions.
> In ancient times, women were sometimes oppressed and stifled in their ambitions.

The qualifying words, underlined above, make the generalization supportable. The revised generalization allows you to both make your point and include exceptions, too.

- **When doing research, test the generalizations that are made by others.** Look out for generalizations that the writer does not or cannot support with facts or for which you can think of important exceptions. This is particularly important to do when you are reading articles that express the author's opinion, such as a newspaper editorial or material written by people who are biased or who view situations from only one point of view.

8. Predicting Outcomes

Although history is a record of the past, it is often used to predict what might happen in the future. For predictions to be useful, however, they must be based on facts and on valid conclusions and generalizations. Historians make predictions by examining present trends, repeated patterns of events, comparisons between situations in the past and present or by finding general principles that seem to apply to cultures through time. Predictions can also be used as a component in solving current problems.

A. Use facts and conclusions to build a *hypothesis* about the future. A hypothesis is an educated guess about what happened in the past or what might happen in the future. A hypothesis takes available information, links it to previous experience and knowledge, and comes up with a possible explanation, conclusion, or prediction.

In studying the Maya civilization, for example, historians cannot yet determine exactly what caused that culture to decline because there are no adequate written records to provide this information. However, historians do know that other cultures have declined because of invasion, famine, natural disasters such as earthquakes, or a series of revolts that upset the political system. On the basis of this knowledge, historians hypothesize that one or more of those events caused Mayan civilization to collapse.

As a student of history, you can also build hypotheses based on (1) available information, (2) the detection of links and similarities, (3) your own knowledge and experience. You may wish to hypothesize, for example, about what will happen in developing nations if current methods of growing and supplying food are not adequate for a rapidly expanding population or about how the economic system of our country will change if the United States continues to import more than it exports.

B. Use similarities between past and present to predict the future. History can be helpful in predicting future events by providing examples of similar situations for which the outcome is known. These can help you to form hypotheses about what is likely to happen.

C. Keep in mind that even the most knowledgeable predictions and well-thought-out hypotheses may turn out to be wrong. Because no formulas can predict exactly what human beings will do, predictions and hypotheses sometimes have to be discarded. For example, knowing the facts about the economy and political systems of Eastern Europe, few experts predicted the sudden overthrow in 1989 and 1990 of established governments there.

Glossary

— a —

abbot: A man who is head of a monastery. (p. 204)

abdicate: To resign as a ruler. (p. 633)

absolute: Not limited by constitutional restraints. (p. 180)

absolute monarchy: A system of government in which the ruling monarch has unlimited power. (p. 437)

absolutism: A government in which the ruler's power is unlimited. (p. 441)

acid rain: Rainwater that is polluted with chemicals. (p. 836)

acropolis: A fortified hilltop in an ancient Greek city. (p. 108)

aggressor: A person or nation that initiates an unprovoked attack. (p. 626)

agora: In ancient Greece, the marketplace where people gathered. (p. 105)

anarchist: A person who believes that all governments are evil and therefore should be overthrown. (p. 611)

annex: To take over without permission. (p. 623)

anthropologist: A person who studies early human beings and the way societies and cultures originate and are organized (p. 17)

antibiotic: A chemical used to destroy or slow the growth of harmful bacteria. (p. 834)

anti-Semitism: Hostility or discrimination against the Jews. (p. 696)

apartheid: South Africa's legal system of complete, rigid separation between blacks and whites. (p. 792)

apostle: One of Jesus' followers who preached and spread the teachings of Jesus. (p. 161)

appeasement: A policy of making concessions to an aggressor in hopes of avoiding war. (p. 699)

apprentice: A person who is learning a trade or craft from a master and who works without pay except for room and board. (p. 226)

aqueduct: A long bridgelike structure that carries water to populated areas. (p. 152)

archaeologist: A person who studies the remains of ancient societies to learn about past ways of life. (p. 17)

arete: The ideal of striving for excellence, showing courage, and winning fame and honor. (p. 107)

aristocracy: In ancient Greece, a government dominated by a small group of noble families (p. 109); today, a small privileged group.

armed aggression: Military invasion; a war of conquest. (p. 697)

armistice: An agreement to stop fighting. (p. 633)

artifact: A human-made object like a tool, weapon, or ornament that represents a stage of human development. (p. 17)

artisan: A skilled worker who makes goods by hand. (p. 32)

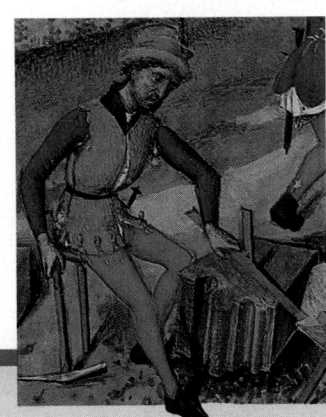

assembly line: A line of factory workers and machinery along which a product passes, with each worker doing a specialized task until the product is complete. (p. 596)

astrolabe: An instrument that is used to observe and calculate latitude by charting the position of the stars. (p. 192)

authoritarian: Requiring absolute loyalty and obedience to the state. (p. 692)

autocracy: A government in which the ruler has unlimited power and uses it in an arbitrary manner. (p. 644)

autocrat: A ruler with unlimited power; an absolute ruler. (p. 642)

ayatollah: A Shi'ite Muslim religious leader. (p. 801)

— b —

balance of power: A defensive strategy to maintain an equilibrium, in which weak countries join together to match or exceed the power of a stronger country. (p. 446)

balance of trade: The difference in value between a country's imports and its exports. (p. 442)

bantustan: In South Africa, the racially segregated areas set aside for blacks to live in. (p. 792)

baroque: In the late 1600's and early 1700's, a style of art, architecture, and music that was elaborate, ornate, dramatic, and complex. (p. 465)

barter: A form of trade in which people exchange goods not money. (p. 35)

bill of rights: A list of citizens' rights, freedoms, and privileges that the government guarantees to protect. (p. 437)

bishop: A church official who sets moral standards, supervises finances, and governs several churches. (p. 164)

blitzkrieg: A war conducted with a sudden, quick, massive offensive. (p. 709)

blockade: The closing off of a nation's port or ports by ships or troops to prevent passage in or out. (p. 496)

boat people: Refugees who fled Southeast Asia in crowded boats, 1975–1979. (p. 780)

bourgeoisie: In medieval France, people who lived in burghs, or towns, rather than in rural areas (p. 224); according to Marx, the factory-owning middle class. (p. 552)

boyar: A member of the Russian noble class. (p. 267)

boycott: To protest by refusing to buy a product or service. (p. 663)

bronze: A mixture of copper and tin. (p. 33)

buffer zone: A region that lies between two rivals, cutting down the threat of conflict. (p. 738)

burgess: In England, a citizen of a borough. (p. 251)

burgher: A person who lives in a town, or burgh. (p. 224)

bushido: The Japanese code of conduct for the samurai, stressing honor, courage, and loyalty. (p. 293)

C

cabinet: An executive committee chosen by the head of a country to help make government decisions. (p. 472)

caliph: An Islamic leader who holds both political and religious power. (p. 190)

canon law: The law of the Roman Catholic Church. (p. 229)

capital: Wealth such as money, machines, tools, or buildings that can be used to produce more wealth. (p. 403)

capitalism: An economic system characterized by the investment of money in business ventures with the goal of making a profit. (p. 403)

caravel: A small ship developed in the 1400's, with triangular sails for tacking into the wind and square sails for running before the wind. (p. 359)

cardinal: A leading bishop in the Roman Catholic Church. (p. 228)

cash crop: A crop that is raised for profit rather than for use by the producer. (p. 575)

caste: A rigid social group, membership in which is determined at birth and never changes during a person's life; in Hinduism, *caste* is linked to religious purity. (p. 78)

cataract: A set of rapids in a river, blocking the passage of boats. (p. 54)

caudillo: A dictator, usually an army officer, of a Latin American country. (p. 540)

cease-fire agreement: The suspension of hostilities; a truce. (p. 767)

censor: To examine printed materials, media broadcasts, and movies in order possibly to ban, alter, or delete information. (p. 692)

charter: In the Middle Ages, a written list of special privileges, tax exemptions, and rights granted to a town. (p. 227)

chivalry: A code of ideals demanding that a knight aid the poor, defend the weak, and fight bravely for his three masters: his earthly feudal lord, his heavenly Lord, and his chosen lady. (p. 239)

citizen: A freeman in Greece (p. 108); a native of a state or nation. (p. 133)

city-state: A political unit made up of a city and the surrounding countryside that is under the control of the city. (p. 34)

civil disobedience: The use of nonviolent moral force to gain a concession from the authorities; passive resistance. (p. 663)

civil rights: Rights guaranteed to citizens under the Constitution; nonpolitical rights of citizens. (p. 820)

civil service: Workers employed by a government to carry out functions such as repairing roads, delivering mail, collecting taxes, and so on. (p. 152)

civil war: Conflict between two political groups within the same nation. (p. 145)

civilization: A form of culture that includes cities, specialized workers, writing, advanced technology, and complex institutions. (p. 31)

clan: A group of people who are descended from the same ancestor. (p. 291)

classical art: Art based on ancient Greek and Roman principles of order, balance, proportion, and simplicity. (p. 116)

clergy: An official of a religious group. (p. 256)

coalition: A temporary alliance between groups who are usually on different sides. (p. 489)

Cold War: The climate of icy tension that existed between the superpowers for several decades after World War II. (p. 737)

collective farm: A large unit made up of land from many small farms and owned and operated jointly by a group. (p. 656)

collective security: A system in which nations act together to stop aggression. (p. 699)

colonialism: A policy of retaining colonies. (p. 774)

colonization: The establishing of colonies. (p. 574)

colony: A settlement in a new territory by a group of people who keep their ties to their home government; a region governed by a foreign power. (p. 39)

comedy: Drama that makes fun of politics, people, and ideas. (p. 120)

command economy: An economy with centralized planning by the state. (p. 654)

Commercial Revolution: A period in Europe, from the 1400's to the 1700's, when capitalism thrived with the expansion of trade, business, and investments. (p. 404)

common law: The unified body of law that developed, case by case, from the rulings of England's royal judges and became common to the whole kingdom. (p. 234)

Common Market: The European Economic Community, an organization, established in 1957, that encourages free trade among member nations. (p. 749)

commune: A large, collective farm where ownership, labor, and production are shared in common. (p. 768)

communism: A theory of government in which wealth and property are owned in common and production and labor are shared equally among the people. In reality, the means of production and distribution are owned and controlled by the state. (p. 552)

compass: An instrument that indicates direction by using a magnetic needle. (p. 359)

concentration camp: A prison camp in which political prisoners or prisoners of war are held by force. (p. 696)

condominium: A country ruled jointly by two other countries. (p. 572)

conquistador: A Spanish soldier and fortune hunter who took part in the conquest of the Americas. (p. 393)

conservatism: The philosophy of protecting or conserving the existing traditional forms of government. (p. 529)

constitution: A written plan of laws and principles to guide government or society. (p. 477)

constitutional monarchy: A government led by a ruler whose power is limited by law. (p. 472)

consul: A powerful official in the Roman republic who commanded the army and directed the government. (p. 136)

containment: Prevention of any extension of Communist rule to other countries. (p. 743)

convoy: A specially equipped fleet, or group, of vehicles designed to protect ships or troops. (p. 632)

corporation: A business owned by stockholders who share in its profits but are not personally responsible for its debts. (p. 549)

count: A powerful landowner who ruled a county in a king's name, administered justice, and raised armies. (p. 209)

Counter-Reformation: A movement in the 1500's to reform the Catholic Church and to work against Protestantism. (p. 385)

coup: A sudden takeover of a country's government. (p. 492)

covenant: A contract or pledge between two or more people. (p. 41)

creole: A person born in Latin America whose ancestors came from Europe. (p. 536)

crop rotation: The system of growing a different crop in a field each year to preserve the fertility of the land. (p. 509)

crusade: A military expedition to recover Jerusalem and the Holy Land from the Muslim Turks. (p. 241)

cultural diffusion: The spread of a people's way of life, such as its customs, beliefs, religions, language, government, and family structure. (p. 8)

culture: The way of life— language, tools, skills, beliefs, and traditions—that people develop and leave to their children. (p. 17)

cuneiform: An ancient form of writing that used wedge-shaped symbols. (p. 32)

czar: The Russian emperor. (p. 266)

— d —

daimyo: A feudal lord in Japan who commanded a private army of samurai. (p. 294)

Dark Ages: A period, in the Early Middle Ages, from about A.D. 500–1000, when learning and civilization declined. (p. 201)

deficit: A loss of money resulting from expenditures exceeding income. (p. 822)

delta: A broad, triangular, marshy region at the mouth of a river. (p. 54)

demand: Quantity of goods that buyers will purchase. (p. 467)

demilitarize: To disband the armed forces and remove military equipment from a region. (p. 761)

democracy: A government in which the citizens hold the final power. (p. 111)

demokratizatsiya: A Russian term for democratization, which encourages individual initiative. (p. 848)

depression: A long business slump when many people are out of work and many businesses close. (p. 688)

desertification: A process in which a semiarid region dries out and begins to turn to desert. (p. 316)

détente: A policy of reduced tension between the United States and the Soviet Union. (p. 846)

developing nation: A Third World country having slow economic growth and low per capita income. (p. 790)

dharma: In Hinduism, the set of duties and obligations required of each caste. (p. 78)

dhow: A triangular-sailed Arab vessel. (p. 319)

dictator: In Rome, a political leader elected for a limited time and given absolute power to make laws and command the army (p. 126); any political leader who takes on such powers, usually without legal basis. (p. 653)

diplomacy: The art of making agreements and settling differences by officials to establish peaceful relations. (p. 527)

dissenter: A person having an opinion different from that of the established church. (p. 367)

dissident: A person who expresses an opinion that differs from those held by the general society. (p. 754)

diversification: The policy of expanding business or product lines to increase the variety of items produced. (p. 807)

diviner: A person in African society who is trained in the art of communicating with spirits and making predictions. (p. 324)

divine right: The idea that rulers receive their authority from God and are answerable only to God. (p. 430)

domesticate: To tame wild animals for the use of humans. (p. 26)

domino theory: The belief that the fall of one country to communism would lead to the fall of its neighbors. (p. 778)

due process of law: Administration of the law by proceeding according to established legal principles that protect individual rights. (p. 251)

dynastic cycle: The pattern of the rise, decline, and replacement of a ruling dynasty. (p. 84)

dynasty: A series of rulers from a single family. (p. 58)

e

economic sanctions: Restrictions on trade imposed against a nation in order to force it to change its policy. (p. 793)

edict: A public order or announcement that has authority. (p. 81)

electronics: The technology leading to automation and televisions, computers, and other products. (p. 762)

embargo: A government order to prohibit the shipment of goods in or out of a port. (p. 715)

emigration: The departure from a country to live elsewhere. (p. 550)

empire: A state that conquers other territories and people and then rules them. (p. 38)

enclosure: The process by which wealthy landowners buy the open fields in a village, fence them, and then rent them to tenant farmers, who work the land. (p. 509)

encomienda: A privilege granted by Spain to certain settlers in the Americas, allowing them to control the land and people in a particular area. (p. 397)

enlightened despotism: An absolute ruler who uses his or her power for the good of the people being ruled. (p. 469)

Enlightenment: The period spanning the middle years of the eighteenth century, which was characterized by the use of reason and scientific method. (p. 461)

entente: A friendly understanding or agreement between nations. (p. 623)

entrepreneur: A person who organizes, manages, and takes on the risks of running a business. (p. 513)

epic: A long heroic poem that tells the story of a historical or legendary hero. (p. 106)

Epicureanism: A philosophy of life that justifies pursuing sensuous pleasure. (p. 155)

epidemic: The sudden, rapid spread of disease to a large number of people. (p. 368)

equator: An imaginary line of latitude midway between the North and South Poles. It is the line from which latitude is measured, either north or south. (p. 10)

estate: In the Middle Ages, one of the three large social classes: nobles, clergy, and commoners. (p. 483)

ethical monotheism: Belief that proper moral conduct involves the worship of one god. (p. 42)

ethnic cleansing: A ruthless campaign by Serbs to remove Bosnian Muslims from their land, by forcing them to leave or by killing them. (p. 861)

evolution: The theory—based on Darwin's theory of natural selection—of how species change over time and how new species gradually arise from old ones. (p. 599)

excommunicate: To cut off from the Church. (p. 185)

executive: Of the branch of government that carries out the laws. (p. 467)

exile: To banish or expel from one's country. (p. 499)

export: To send goods out of the country for sale. (p. 442)

extended family: A family group that includes a nuclear family and close relatives living in one household. (p. 840)

extraterritorial rights: Exemption from having to obey the laws of the local territory. (p. 581)

— f —

factory: A large building where goods are manufactured. (p. 512)

fascism: A political movement that believes in an extreme form of nationalism: denying individual rights, insisting upon the supremacy of the state, and advocating dictatorial one-party rule. (p. 691)

federal: A form of government in which power is shared between the national government and the governments of the separate states. (p. 478)

feudalism: A political and military system based on the holding of land, with an emphasis on local protection, local government, and local self-sufficiency. (p. 214)

fief: The piece of land given to a vassal by a lord. (p. 215)

filial piety: Respect shown by children for their parents and elders. (p. 87)

flying buttress: A carved, arched, stone structure that braces the outside wall of a building, especially a Gothic cathedral. (p. 231)

fossil: A trace or fragment of ancient plants and animals. (p. 17)

fossil fuels: Fuels—such as oil, coal, and natural gas—that come from the hardened remains of plants and animals. (p. 836)

free election: An election held in a multiparty system, with voting by secret ballot. (p. 742)

free-enterprise: A competitive economic system based on private ownership and the principles of supply and demand. (p. 689)

free trade: In the international market, the flow of commerce without regulation. (p. 467)

free-trade agreement: *See* free trade.

fresco: The technique of painting on wet plaster. (p. 346)

friar: A member of the Roman Catholic Church who takes the same vows as a monk but travels around preaching instead of living in a monastery. (p. 230)

fundamentalism: A movement within a religion, emphasizing obedience to the basic laws from which the religion developed. (p. 801)

— g —

genetics: Scientific study that deals with heredity in living organisms and involves research in genes and chromosomes. (p. 834)

genocide: The intentional killing of an entire people. (p. 724)

gentry: A social class ranking below nobles but above common people; in Chinese society, the class of scholar-officials. (p. 279)

geocentric theory: The theory that the earth is in the center of the universe. (p. 387)

gigabit: A unit of storage capacity equal to one billion bits of information. (p. 834)

gladiator: In ancient Rome, a person who fought an opponent to the death in a public arena. (p. 150)

glasnost: A Russian term for the policy of openness in the Soviet Union. (p. 847)

global economy: All the financial interactions—among people, businesses, and governments—that cross international borders. (p. 863)

gravitas: The Roman virtue of weightiness, or seriousness, which is related to the qualities of discipline, strength, and loyalty. (p. 133)

greenhouse effect: A worldwide warming trend caused by increased amounts of carbon dioxide trapped in the earth's atmosphere. (p. 837)

grid: A set of lines that cross one another to form squares, used to identify the location of places. (p. 10)

griot: A person in West African society who is trained as a record keeper. (p. 325)

gross national product: (GNP) The total value of goods and services produced by a country in a year. (p. 747)

guerrilla: A band of fighters—not part of a formal army—who attack suddenly and withdraw swiftly. (p. 497)

guild: An association of people who work at the same occupation. (p. 226)

— *h* —

habeas corpus: The right of a prisoner to obtain a writ or document ordering that the prisoner be brought before a court or judge. (p. 434)

Hegira: Muhammad's flight from Mecca to Medina in A.D. 622. (p. 187)

heliocentric theory: A theory that the sun is in the center of the universe. (p. 387)

Hellenism: A blend of Greek and Eastern cultures; Hellenistic culture. (p. 125)

helot: In ancient Sparta, a peasant forced to work the land. (p. 110)

hemisphere: One half of a sphere or globe. It can be the hemisphere north or south of the equator or east or west of the prime meridian. (p. 10)

heresy: Religious beliefs or opinions that differ from the dogma of the Church. (p. 230)

heretic: A person whose ideas are incorrect in the opinion of the Church. (p. 185)

hieroglyphics: A form of Egyptian writing based on pictorial characters for words and sounds. (p. 68)

history: A systematic record of past events that includes the development of peoples, cultures, and countries. (p. 1)

Holocaust: The systematic murder of the European Jews by the Nazis. (p. 725)

home rule: Self-government given to a country, territory, or political unit by a higher governing body. (p. 608)

hominid: A creature that walks upright rather than on all fours. (p. 17)

hoplite: A foot soldier of ancient Greece who fought with a shield and a spear. (p. 109)

Huguenot: In the 1500's and 1600's, a French Protestant who was a follower of Calvinism. (p. 382)

human-environment interaction: The effect of the environment on people's way of living, and the ways people modify their environment. (p. 3)

humanist: One who studies classical texts. (p. 348)

human rights: The protection of individuals against oppression; the preservation of basic rights and freedoms for individuals. (p. 739)

— *i* —

icon: A small piece of art that depicts a religious image. (p. 184)

iconoclast: A person who opposes the use of or belief in icons. (p. 185)

ideology: A set of beliefs that influences political, social, and economic actions. (p. 743)

immigration: Entering and settling in a country other than one's native country. (p. 550)

imperialism: The policy of extending one country's rule over many lands. (p. 569)

import: To bring goods into the country for sale. (p. 442)

import substitution: The policy of replacing foreign goods with locally-manufactured products. (p. 809)

impressionism: A style of painting that captures the light effects and the impression of scenes from everyday life. (p. 604)

indulgence: A pardon given by the Roman Catholic Church in return for repentance for sins. (p. 376)

industrialization: The process of developing machine-made goods. (p. 509)

industrialized nation: A nation that has developed industry. (p. 789)

Industrial Revolution: The period (1800's and 1900's) of greatly increased output of machine-made goods. (p. 509)

inflation: An overall rise in the prices of goods and services. (p. 165)

institution: A long-lasting pattern of organization in a society. Governments, families, education systems, and organized religions are examples of institutions. (p. 33)

interchangeable parts: Machine parts that are identically made so that they can replace each other. (p. 596)

interdict: An order from the pope prohibiting Church ceremonies in the lands of a ruler who is disobedient to the pope. (p. 229)

internment camp: A prisonlike camp for political prisoners, aliens, or prisoners of war. (p. 727)

intervention: The act of interfering in another country's domestic or foreign affairs. (p. 589)

intifada: The campaign of civil disobedience by the Palestinians to gain an independent Palestinian state. (p. 803)

investiture: A feudal ceremony in which a vassal receives land or a bishop takes office; an act that symbolically confirms an agreement through the exchange of objects. (p. 215)

iron curtain: The division of Europe into two political regions—communist and non-communist. (p. 743)

irrigation: The process of bringing water to crop fields by means of canals and ditches. (p. 34)

isolationism: The idea that a country should avoid political or military alliances with other countries. (p. 686)

— *j* —

jihad: In Islam, a holy war. (p. 189)

joint-stock company: A business arrangement in which many investors together raise money for a venture too large for any of them to undertake alone. They share the profits in proportion to the amount they invest. (p. 425)

journeyman: A person who, after completing an apprenticeship, works at a craft for wages under the supervision of a master. (p. 226)

judicial: Having to do with the branch of government that interprets the laws. (p. 467)

junker: A member of Prussia's landowning nobility. (p. 455)

jury: A group of people sworn to give a verdict based on evidence in a court of law; in medieval England, usually 12 neighbors who answered questions about the facts of a case for a royal judge. (p. 234)

— *k* —

kaiser: The German emperor. (p. 559)

karma: In Hinduism and Buddhism, the ethical laws of cause and effect determining a person's destiny; under karma, a person's behavior in this life will determine the person's fate in the next life. (p. 78)

khan: The leader of a group of Mongols. (p. 284)

kibbutz: In Israel, a communal farm or settlement where people live, work, and share profits in common. (p. 668)

knight: An armored warrior who fought on horseback. (p. 206)

— *l* —

laissez-faire: A belief in the absence of government regulation of business. (p. 467)

laser: A device that produces a beam of light, often used in extremely fine operations such as surgery, communications, and printing. (p. 834)

latitude: A set of imaginary grid lines, always the same distance apart, that encircle the globe from east to west. They measure distance north and south. (p. 10)

lay investiture: The feudal ceremony of investiture performed by a person who is not a member of the clergy. *See also* investiture. (p. 228)

legion: The massive military unit of the Roman army. It was made up of 4,000–6,000 infantry men and a group of cavalry men. (p. 134)

legislative: Having to do with the branch of government that makes the laws. (p. 467)

legitimacy: The principle that rulers who have been driven from their thrones should be restored to power. (p. 528)

less developed country: A nation that has limited resources and few opportunities for economic growth. (p. 790)

liberalism: A political philosophy of limited government and protection of individual rights and freedoms. (p. 529)

liberation theology: The doctrine that the Church has a moral obligation to use political action to improve the plight of the poor. (p. 817)

limited monarchy: A government headed by a king or queen whose powers are limited by laws. (p. 251)

limited war: A war in which one or both sides aim at less than an all-out victory by agreeing to limit the kinds of weapons used. (p. 767)

lineage: A group of families—including past generations and living members—descended from a common ancestor. (p. 324)

literacy: The ability to read and write. (p. 40)

loess: A dusty, yellow-brown, rich soil deposited by wind and floodwaters. (p. 84)

longitude: A set of imaginary grid lines that run from the North Pole to the South Pole. The lines measure distances east and west. (p. 10)

lord: In the feudal system, the person, a vassal, who makes a grant of land to another person. (p. 215)

— *m* —

maat: In ancient Egypt, the idea of goodness that included justice, right, truth, and order. (p. 66)

mandate: A territory that was administered on behalf of the League of Nations—or currently, on behalf of the United Nations—until it was judged ready for independence. (p. 636)

Mandate of Heaven: In ancient China, the belief that the royal authority to rule comes through divine approval. This authority is communicated by the gods to the ruler. (p. 84)

manor: A small estate from which a lord's family gained its livelihood. (p. 217)

market economy: An economy characterized by competition, supply and demand, and the absence of regulation. (p. 467)

martial law: Law that is enforced by military authorities over the civilian population of a country as if the country were in a state of war. (p. 757)

martyr: One who chooses to die rather than give up a principle or cause. (p. 164)

mass culture: The appeal of artists, writers, and musicians to an audience of all classes, not just the upper class. (p. 606)

mass production: Large quantities of goods made by machines. (p. 596)

materialism: The focus on possessions, comforts, and material things rather than on intellectual or spiritual matters. (p. 840)

matrilineal: A system in which a young man inherits land or wealth from his mother's brother rather than from his father. (p. 324)

medieval: Relating to the Middle Ages, or the period in Europe after the fall of the Roman empire. (p. 201)

mercantilism: An economic theory under which a country increases its wealth by exporting more goods than it imports. (p. 442)

mercenary: A soldier who is paid to fight in another country's army. (p. 138)

Mesoamerica: The lands (Mexico and Central America) between the United States and South America. (p. 25)

messiah: A savior chosen by God. (p. 162)

mestizo: A person in Latin America who is of mixed European and Indian ancestry. (p. 536)

microtechnology: The technology producing complex systems in miniature form to reduce their weight. (p. 832)

middle class: In the Middle Ages, the class of people positioned between the nobles and the peasant; today, the social class made up of professionals, skilled workers, business people, and wealthy farmers. (p. 224)

militarism: Glorification of armed strength. (p. 624)

minaret: A slender tower on a mosque that is used to call Muslims to prayer. (p. 301)

missi dominici: Royal agents of Charlemagne, who checked on the ruling counts. (p. 209)

mobilize: To position an army for war. (p. 625)

moderate socialism: Government support for social welfare programs and government ownership of major industries within a democratic system. (p. 751)

moksha: In Hinduism, the state of perfect understanding in which the inner self disappears to merge with the all-powerful spirit. (p. 77)

monarchy: Government headed by a king or queen. (p. 136)

monastery: A religious community of men or women who give up all their possessions, live in seclusion, and devote their lives to worship, prayer, and self-denial. (p. 204)

monopoly: Complete control over an industry, a product, or a service. (p. 359)

monotheist: A person who believes in one god. (p. 40).

monsoon: A seasonal wind that blows dry air part of the year, then shifts directions, bringing heavy rainfall the other part of the year. (p. 73)

mosque: A Muslim temple. (p. 188)

mulatto: A person in Latin America who is of European and African ancestry. (p. 536)

multinational corporation: A company that has branches in many countries. (p. 820)

myth: A story, often about gods and heroes, used to explain nature and the power of human passions. (p. 108).

— n —

nationalism: A feeling of loyalty for one's own land and people (p. 259); the belief that one's greatest loyalty should be to one's country.

nationalize: To bring an industry under government control. (p. 673)

nation-state: A group of people who occupy a definite territory and are united under one government. (p. 254)

Nazism: German fascism; the doctrine of the National Socialist German Workers' Party, based on totalitarianism, racial superiority, and state control of industry. (p. 693)

negotiation: The process of making trade-offs. (p. 703)

neutrality: A policy of refusing to support either side, especially in war. (p. 625)

nihilism: A belief that the existing society and government must be destroyed so that a better society can be created. (p. 644)

nirvana: In Buddhism, the condition of release from pain and selfishness achieved when the soul merges into the supreme being and reaches a perfect state of blessedness. (p. 80)

nonaggression pact: An agreement pledging not to attack another nation. (p. 707)

nonalignment: A policy of refusing to take sides in the Cold War. (p. 774)

nonviolence: A policy of refusing to resort to violence. (p. 662)

nuclear family: A family group that includes parents or a single parent and children. (p. 840)

nuclear weapon: A weapon that is powered by atomic energy. (p. 740)

— o —

oasis: A place in a desert where underground water comes to the surface in a spring or well. (p. 316)

obsidian: A smooth, dark-colored volcanic glass. (p. 27)

occupation zone: An area controlled by Allied military forces. (p. 737)

occupy: To seize or take over an area. (p. 700)

oracle bones: Animal bones and tortoise shells scratched with Chinese characters. They were used by Chinese priests to foretell the future during the Shang dynasty. (p. 86)

ozone layer: The upper level of the earth's atmosphere (about 8 to 30 miles above the earth). (p. 838)

— p —

papyrus: A reed that grows in a marshy delta, especially in the Nile River region. (p. 69)

parliament: A legislative body consisting of two houses (Lords and Commons) similar to that established in the eleventh century in England. (p. 251)

partition: The division of a country into two or more parts. (p. 773)

passive resistance: The use of nonviolent moral methods to resist authority; civil disobedience. (p. 663)

patriarch: The bishop of Constantinople, head of the Eastern Orthodox Church. (p. 185)

patrician: In ancient Rome, a member of the privileged upper class. (p. 133)

peninsular: A person in Latin America who was born in Spain or Portugal. (p. 536)

per capita income: The amount of money that a person would receive if the total income of the workers of a country were divided equally among all the men, women, and children in the country. (p. 800)

perestroika: A Russian term for economic restructuring and relaxing of government control in the Soviet Union. (p. 847)

perspective: A technique of giving objects in a picture the appearance of depth and distance. (p. 352)

phalanx: A Greek army unit made up of soldiers standing side by side, their shields and spears forming a solid wall. (p. 109)

pharaoh: A king of Egypt, who was considered a god. (p. 58)

philosophe: One of a group of thinkers in the early 1700's who believed in reason, liberty, natural law, progress, and human happiness. (p. 462)

philosopher: A person who seeks wisdom and truth. (p. 120)

physiocrat: An economic theorist who argued against government regulations and favored freedom of industry and trade. (p. 467)

plebeian: A common farmer, artisan, or merchant in ancient Rome. A plebeian was a free citizen with the right to vote. (p. 134)

plebiscite: An election in which all citizens vote yes or no on an issue. (p. 493)

pogrom: An organized, systematic, mass murder of a minority group, such as the Jews in Nazi Germany. (p. 611)

policy: A plan of action that guides an individual, group, or government. (p. 151)

polis: A Greek city-state. (p. 108)

pollution: Air or water contamination by harmful wastes or chemicals. (p. 763)

polytheist: A person who believes in more than one god. (p. 36)

pope: The bishop of Rome, head of the Roman Catholic Church. (p. 164)

predestination: The doctrine that God has known since the beginning of time who will be saved. (p. 382)

prehistory: The period of time before the beginning of written records. (p. 17)

prime meridian: The imaginary line that runs through Greenwich, England, and is the starting line from which longitude is measured, either east or west. (p. 10)

prime minister: The leader of the majority party in a country's parliament. The prime minister heads the cabinet. (p. 473)

profit: The money gained from the sale of goods after expenses have been paid. (p. 403)

projection: A way of drawing the earth's curved surface on a map. (p. 11)

proletariat: The poorest class in ancient Rome (p. 141); according to Marx, the urban working class. (p. 552)

propaganda: One-sided information designed to convince people of a certain point of view. (p. 628)

prophet: A messenger sent to reveal God's will. (p. 42)

protectorate: A country or state that is controlled by an outside government. (p. 572)

Protestant: A Christian who is a member of a Protestant church. (p. 379)

pueblo: A village of Native American dwellings in the Southwest. (p. 327)

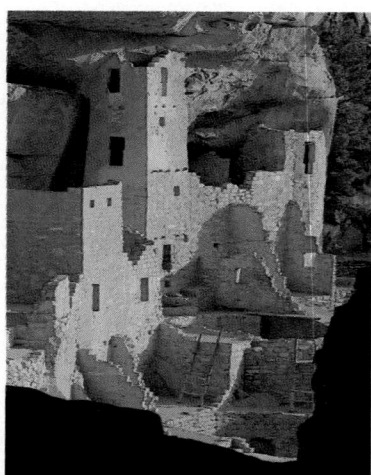

puppet government: A government controlled by an outside power. (p. 699)

purdah: The Muslim practice of keeping women in seclusion. (p. 307)

pyramid: An immense structure used as a tomb by the pharaohs. (p. 58)

q

quipu: A series of knotted strings used by the Incas to tally births, crops, herds, deaths, and other facts and events. (p. 331)

r

radical: A person favoring sweeping economic or social change. (p. 488)

radicalism: A political movement supporting drastic and, if necessary, violent change. (p. 529)

radioactivity: The energy released from an atom in elements such as uranium or radium. (p. 600)

rationing: A system limiting the amount of goods people can buy during a time of shortage. (p. 628)

realism: A philosophy characterized by the precise, accurate observation and report of real life. (p.553)

realpolitik: "The politics of reality"; used to describe the tough, practical politics in which idealism plays no part. (p. 555)

recession: A temporary economic slowdown involving increased unemployment and decreased production. (p. 822)

Reconquista: Over about 5 centuries, the reconquest, or recovery, of Christian lands from the Muslims. (p. 263)

referendum: A direct popular vote on a legislative act or some public issue. (p. 822)

Reformation: A religious crisis in the 1500's in the Roman Catholic Church that led to the establishment of Protestant churches. (p. 376)

refugee: A person who flees to a foreign country to escape danger. (p. 773)

reincarnation: The idea that the inner self is reborn in another form. (p. 77)

relativity: The principle of relative motion and the interrelation between time, space, and matter based on Einstein's theory. (p. 684)

Renaissance: A movement in Europe between the 1300's and 1600's, marked by a revival, or rebirth, of interest in classical Greek and Roman art, literature, and learning. (p. 345)

reparations: Monetary or material compensation paid after a war by a defeated nation for the damages it caused other nations. (p. 636)

representative: A delegate; a person who acts for a constituency and is a member of a legislative body. (p. 253)

republic: A government under which citizens with the right to vote choose their leaders. (p. 133)

robotics: The technology that uses computer-controlled robots. (p. 834)

romanticism: A movement in reaction to the orderly, rational approach of the Enlightenment. It emphasized imagination, emotion, and passion. (p. 533)

— S —

salon: A gathering, held by a prominent hostess, made up of distinguished writers, poets, artists, musicians, and political leaders. (p. 463)

samurai: A Japanese warrior who fought for his lord and lived according to the code of bushido. (p. 293)

satellite: A country whose policies are dictated or heavily influenced by another country (p. 742); an object that orbits the earth or another planet. (p. 831)

satire: Literature that mocks society for its foolishness and wickedness. (p. 157)

satrap: A royal governor of a province in the Persian empire. (p. 48)

savanna: A grassy plain with a few scattered trees. (p. 316)

schism: A division in a church or religious group. (p. 255)

scientific method: A logical procedure for gathering and testing ideas by forming a hypothesis and then testing it. (p. 387)

Scientific Revolution: In the 1500's and 1600's, a new and radical way of thinking about the natural world by using careful observation and questioning old theories. (p. 373)

scientific socialism: Marx's ideas of socialism, stating that scientific laws determine economic forces—such as class warfare—and will result in a true socialist society. (p. 552)

scorched-earth policy: Systematic burning of grain fields, killing of livestock, and destroying of other items to keep them from the enemy. (p. 498)

scribe: A professional writer who reads and copies manuscript. (p. 31)

segregate: To separate groups by race—for example, in workplaces, recreational areas, educational institutions, and housing. (p. 792)

self-determination: Free choice of people in a territory to decide under what government they wish to live. (p. 634)

semiarid: Having less than 20 inches of rainfall a year. (p. 316)

senate: In ancient Rome, the aristocratic branch of government. (p. 136)

separation of powers: The division of governmental power among three branches—executive, legislative, and judicial—so that no single branch can become a threat to liberty. (p. 467)

separatism: A movement for the creation of an independent state. (p. 822)

sepoy: A soldier in India, serving under the British. (p. 577)

serf: A peasant who was bound to a manor and owed duties to the lord of the manor. (p. 217)

shaykh: The spiritual leader of a group of Bedouin, including members of related families. (p.667)

shock therapy: The abrupt elimination of price controls and of subsidies to industries in an effort to quickly create a free-market economy. (p. 859)

shogun: The supreme general of Japan's army, who had the powers of a military dictator. (p. 293)

silicon chip: The crystals that make up electronic circuits and are capable of storing millions of pieces of information. (p. 833)

simony: The buying and selling of church offices. (p. 228)

social Darwinism: An extension of Darwin's ideas; the theory that those who are the fittest for survival enjoy wealth and success, while the poor remain poor because they are unfit. (p. 599)

social insurance: A plan for state-sponsored insurance for accident or sickness, and of old age benefits. (p. 608)

socialism: The belief that the wealth of a country should be shared equally among all its citizens. (p. 551)

Socratic method: A way of teaching that tries to arrive at the truth by asking questions. (p. 120)

soviet: A workers' council that has political powers and organizes political activities. (p. 649)

space shuttle: A reusable spacecraft that is designed to carry people and goods into space and then return to Earth. (p. 831)

specialize: To concentrate on one kind of work. (p. 32)

sphere of influence: A region dominated by, but not directly ruled by, a foreign nation. (p. 581)

standard of living: A measure of the necessities and comforts accessible to a person or group. (p. 688)

steppe: A vast stretch of dry grassland in Asia and eastern Europe. (p. 283)

stock: A share in the ownership of a business. (p. 549)

Stoicism: A philosophy of life that encourages virtue, duty, and endurance. (p. 155)

strategic: Crucially located to assure control of nearby areas. (p. 572)

subcontinent: A large region that is part of a continent, but is separated from the rest of the continent in some way. (p.73)

sub-Saharan Africa: The lands south of the Sahara. (p. 315)

subsidy: A grant of money, especially from the government. (p. 442)

subsistence farming: Farming that produces the amount of food necessary for a living, with no surplus to sell. (p. 790)

succession: The transfer of power or authority to another person or persons—for example, after the death of a ruler. (p. 153)

suffrage: The right to vote. (p. 553)

sultan: An Islamic ruler who has political power but not religious authority. (p. 195)

superconductor: A material that can transmit electricity efficiently over long distances and that has little or no resistance to the transmitting of electricity when cooled to temperatures near absolute zero. (p. 839)

superpower: A dominant world power. (p. 737)

supply: Quantity available for use or purchase. (p. 467)

surplus: Excess; more than is needed. (p. 32)

Swahili: A culture formed from the blending of the Arab and Bantu cultures. (p. 319)

— *t* —

tariff: A tax on goods imported from another country. (p. 442)

technology: The part of a culture that includes tools and the skills to make and use them. (p. 22)

territorial integrity: Territorial domain of a state. (p. 696)

terrorism: The use of violence in order to achieve a goal. (p. 796)

theocracy: A government controlled by church leaders. (p. 382)

Third World: The countries that remained nonaligned in the Cold War. (p. 774)

tithe: A contribution to the church of one tenth of a family's yearly income or produce. (p. 229)

totalitarian: A political system in which the government has total control over the lives of individual citizens. (p. 656)

total war: A war in which nations commit all their resources—human and industrial—to the war effort. (p. 628)

tragedy: A play that portrays men and women of heroic character, whose strength leads to their downfall. (p. 117)

transistor: A small electronic device that is a basic component in radios, televisions, and computers. (p. 833)

tribune: A Roman official elected by the assembly to speak on behalf of the plebeians. (p. 142)

tribute: Forced payment collected from a conquered people. (p. 335)

triumvirate: A group of three political leaders who ruled Rome. (p. 145)

troubadour: In the Middle Ages, a poet and musician who traveled around and entertained people with songs about chivalry and courtly love. (p. 240)

tyrant: In ancient Greece, a man who took over the government by force but usually supported the interest of the common people against the nobles. (p. 109)

U

ultimatum: A final demand that if not met will end negotiations and lead to war. (p. 624)

underground: Relating to a secret political resistance movement. (p. 711)

union: A group of workers in a trade or industry who join together to bargain for better working conditions and higher wages. (p. 523)

urbanization: The process of changing from a rural- to a city-dwelling population that results in densely populated areas and vast numbers of city buildings. (p. 809)

utopia: A nearly perfect society—without greed, corruption, war, and crime—based on peace, reason, and mercy. (p. 375)

utopian socialism: The philosophy of Robert Owen calling for a society in which all social classes cooperate and wealth and goods are owned and shared in common. (p. 551)

V

vassal: A person who receives land from a lord and pledges military service in return. (p. 215)

vernacular: The everyday language of a region or country. (p. 347)

veto: To overrule another's decision. (p. 136)

viceroy: A person who governs on behalf of a king; in Spain's empire, a noble who governed a part of Spain's territory in the Americas. (p. 397)

villa: A country estate. (p. 160)

W

Western civilization: The heritage of ideas that spread to Europe and America and remain part of that culture. (p. 103)

xyz

ziggurat: A Sumerian temple built in tiers. (p. 35)

Zionist: A person who favors a Jewish national homeland in Palestine. (p. 668)

Index

Aquitaine, Duke of, 228
Arabian Desert, 55
The Arabian Nights, 193
Arabian peninsula, 186
Arabic language, 187, 192
Arab-Israeli conflicts, 796–798
Arabs: trade in Indian Ocean, 319; nationalism among, 667–669; Palestinian, 667–669, 796, 802. *See also* Muslims
Arafat, Yasir, 803
Aragon, 263, m264
Araucanian people, m329
Arawaks, m329, 361
Archaeologists, 17, 52
Archangel, 448
Archbishop of Canterbury, 233
Archimedes, 126
Architecture: Persian, p48; Egyptian, 62, p62; Greek, 115–116, p116; Roman, 150–152, p150, 157–158, p158; Islamic, 193; medieval, 231; Gothic, 231, p232; Romanesque, 231, p232; Renaissance, 350–353; Spanish, p399; French, 443–445; skyscrapers, 594
Arena Chapel, 346
Arete, 107
Argentina, 537, 586, 670, 672, 688, 752, 809–810, 813
Argora, Battle of, 196
Arianism, 203
Aristarchus of Samos, 126
Aristide, Jean-Bertrand, 817, 863
Aristides, Aelius, 153
Aristocracy, 109
Aristophanes, 120
Aristotle, 122–123, 238, 386
Ark of the Covenant, 42
Arkwright, Richard, 512
Armada, Spanish, 400, 420–424, p420, m424
Armenians, 611, 849
Arms control, 846, 865
Arms race, 740, 845, 846
Armstrong, Neil, 831
Army. *See* Militarism
Arouet, François Marie. *See* Voltaire
Around the World in Eighty Days (Verne), 548
Art: prehistoric, 22–24, p23, p25, p26, 27; of Fertile Crescent, p30; Chinese, 85, 281–282, p282, 292; Minoan, 105, p105; of ancient Greece, p107, 112, p112, 115–116, p115, 120, 126; classical, 116; Byzantine, p180; Islamic, 190, p190, 192; of Middle Ages, p205; Japanese, 292–293, p292, 297; African, p317, 324–325, p325, p575; Renaissance, 346–347, 350–358; Spanish, 400–401, p497; Dutch, 405–406, p405, p406; Elizabethan, 428–429, p429; French, 443–445; romanticism in, 534–535, p534; realism in, 553–554, p553; impressionism, 604; of early 1900's, 604–607; mass culture, 606–607; Lost Generation, 634; Russian, 644, p657; between the World Wars, 685–686; German, 695; after World War II, 840
Articles of Confederation, 477

Artifact, 17
Artisans, 32, 85, 115, 225
Aryan language, 76
Aryans, 76
Asa, Norse queen, p212
Ashoka, 81–82
Asia: prehistoric, 20, 21–22, 24–27; trade with Africa, 319–321, m321; migrations across Beringia, 326; in World War I, 631; nationalism in, 665–670; World War II in, 699, 714–717, m717, 721–722, p722; after World War II, 760–781; today, 776–781, m776. *See also* names of countries and civilizations.
Asiento, p368
Askia Muhammad, 323
Assembly, Roman, 136, 147
Assembly line, 596, c599
Assurbanipal, Assyrian king, 44, p44
Assyrians, m43, 63, 318
Astrolabe, 192, 359, p360
Astronauts, 831
Astronomy: Babylonian, 45; Egyptian, 69; Hellenistic, 126; Islamic, 192; Maya, p333, 334; geocentric theory, 387; heliocentric theory, 387; Scientific Revolution and, 387–388, p388
Aswan High Dam, p54, 797
Atahualpa, 395
Atatürk. *See* Kemal, Mustafa
Athena (goddess), 115–116
Athens, 102–103, p102, 109–123, c111
Athletics: in ancient Greece, 107–108, p118; medieval tournaments, 240; Maya, p333; of early 1900's, 606
Atman (self or soul), 77
Atom bomb, 685, 721–722, p722, 738, 740, 746, 749, 769
Atomic theory, 600
Aton (god), 67–68
Attlee, Clement, 741, 773
Augsburg, Peace of, 385, 410
August Coup (Soviet Union), 850–852
Augustine (monk), 205
Augustus (Octavian), Roman emperor, 146–147, p147, 151–153, 157
Aurangzeb, 306
Auschwitz, 724–725
Austerlitz, Battle of, 494
Australia, 569, 589, 604, 688, 716
Australopithecines, 17, 18, p17
Austria: Thirty Years' War, 410–411; War of Spanish Succession, 453; in 1700's, 453–455, m453; Seven Years' War, 456; War of Austrian Succession, 456; war with France, 489–490; in Second Coalition, 492; in Third Coalition, 494; opposition to Napoleon, 498–499; Congress of Vienna, 526–528; rule of Italy, 532, 555; in German Confederation, 533; revolutions of 1848, 542, p542; German unification and, 557–559, m558; Seven Weeks' War, 557–559; in World War I, 629; independence of, 637; German takeover of, 702
Austria-Hungary: imperialism of, 570; decline of, 611, 637; in World War I, 622–626, m631, 633; after World War I, m636
Authoritarian government, 692

Authoritarian socialism, c743
Autobahn, 747
Autobiography, 347
Autocracy, 642, 644
Automobile, 593, 596, c599, 683–684, p684
Avars, 185, 208, 283
Avicenna, 192
Avignon popes, 255–256
Axis Powers, 700–701, 707, m708, m720
Axum, 318–319, m318
Ayacucho, Battle of, 539
Ayatollah, 801–802
Aylwin, Patricio, 812
Azerbaijan, 849
Azov, 450
Aztecs, m329, 335, 392–394, p392, 812

Babur, Mughal ruler, 305
Baby boom, 820
Babylon, 38–39, m38, 44–47, p45, 124–125
"Babylonian captivity", 255
Bach, Johann Sebastian, 465
Badoglio, Pietro, 719–720
Baghdad, 631; under caliphs, 191; under Turks, 195; Mongols in, 284–285, m285
Bahamas, 361, 369
Bahrain, m668
Bailiff, 252
Bakri, al-, 322
Bakunin, Michael, 644
Balance of power, 446–447, 528, 560–561
Balance of trade, 442
Balboa, Vasco Nuñez de, m362, 363
Balfour Declaration, 668, 796
Balkans: nationalism in, 611, 623; in World War I, 623; in World War II, 713
Baltic countries: in World War II, 708–709; independence of, 851, nationalism in, 849
Balzac, Honoré de, 554
Bangladesh, 73, 577, 775, 838
Banking: in Islamic empire, 191; in Middle Ages, 225; Dutch, 403–404; French, 493; industrialization and, 511; in U.S., 690; Japanese, 762. *See also* Coinage.
Bantu people, 317, 319
Bantustans, 792–793
Barbarians: invasion of Roman empire, 167–169, m168, 201–203, m202; defeat by Charlemagne, 208, m208; invasions of Europe, 211
Barbers, 427, 449, p449
Barcelona, 257
Barometer, 389
Barons, 250–251
Baroque music, 465
Barrios, 813
Barter, 35
Barth, Heinrich, 572
Barton, Clara, p563
Baseball, 606, p606, 684
Bastille, 462, 482, 485–486
Bataan, Battle of, 716

Bathhouse, 75, p75
Batista, Fulgencio, 813–815
Batlle, José, 670
Battle of Nations. See Leipzig, Battle of.
Bavaria, m202, 456
Bayeux Tapestry, 233, p234
Bay of Pigs, 816
Beard tax, 449, p449
Bear Garden, p426
Beauvais cathedral, 231
Becket, Thomas à, 233
Bedouins, 186–187, 667
Beethoven, Ludwig van, 466, 527, 534–535, p534
Begin, Menachem, 802
Beijing, 285–288, 583, 699, 765, 770–772, p771, p772, c837
Beirut, 802–803
Belgian Congo. See Zaire.
Belgium, 402; industrialization of, 517–518; imperialism of, 570; in Africa, 572, m573, 786, 788; in World War I, 625–626; after World War I, 635, 682; in World War II, 710; after World War II, 745, 750
Belisarius, 181
Bell, Alexander Graham, 565, 595
Benedict, 203–204, p204
Benedictine Rule, 204, 228
Ben-Gurion, David, 796
Benin, m321, 324, p325
Berbers, 190, 322
Beringia, 326, m327
Berlin, 455, p457, 519; in World War II, 712, 720; divided, 741, 745–746, 755; airlift, 745–746
Berlin Wall, 748, 755, p755, 845, 855, p854–855, 857
Berserkrs, 211
Bessarabia, 637
Bessemer, Henry, 594, c599
Bethlehem, 161
Bharatiya Janta party, 775
Bhopal disaster, 837
Bhutto, Benazir, 775
Bhutto, Zulfikar, 775
Bible, 40–41, 46–47, 256, 377, 384; Gutenberg, 375; King James, 430
Biko, Steve, 793
Bill of Rights: English, c436, 437; U.S., 478–479, c479; French, 483
Binary number system, 833
Birmingham, England, 523
Birth control, 685
Bishops, 164, 216, 228–229, 236
Bismarck, Otto von, 557–559, p558, 608, 622
Black Death, 257–258, p257. See also Plague.
Blackfoot, m329
Black Hand, 621
Blackpool, England, 516
Black Sea, 179
Blackshirts, 692
Black Stone of Mecca, 186–187
Black Thursday, 687–688
Blanc, Louis, 543, 551
Blanche of Castile, 252
Blast furnace, 594
Blitzkrieg, 708–710, 713, p713
Blockade, 496–497

Bloody Sunday, 647
Blue Nile, 53
Boater, 426
Boat people, 780
Boers, m573, 576, 792, c795
Bogotá, 537
Bohemia, 410, 454–455
Bohr, Neils, 600
Boleyn, Anne, 379–381
Bolívar, Simón, 537–539, p537, m538
Bolivia, 586, 807, 809
Bolsheviks, 632–633, 646–654, 657
Bombay, 568–569, 577, c837
Boniface VIII, pope, 254
Bonner, Yelena, 754
Book of the Dead, 67
Borden, Gail, 565
Borneo, 716
Bosnia, 611, 620–623, 860–861, c861, m861
Bosporus, 167, 179–180, 197
Bossa nova, 818
Boston Tea Party, 475
Bosworth, Battle of, 262
Botha, Louis, 576
Botha, P.W., 794
Bottle gourd, 20
Boulton, Matthew, 513
Bourbon, House of, 407–408, 441–447, 528
Bourgeoisie, 224, 484, 552
Bourges cathedral, p232
Boxers, 583
Boyars, 267, 448, 450
Boycott, 663
Brahe, Tycho, 387
Brahman (spirit), 77, 303
Brahmins (caste), 78
Braidwood, Robert, 24, 25
Brain size, 19, 20, 21
Brandenburg, 455, p457
Brandt, Willy, 748, 755
Brassey, Thomas, 548
Brazil, 539, 673, 809, 811, 813, 863
Brest Litovsk, Treaty of, 633, 637, 652
Brethren of the Common Life, 373
Bretons, m202
Brezhnev, Leonid, 753–754, 845, 846
Brezhnev Doctrine, 754
Briand, Aristide, 682
Brighton, England, 516
Britain. See Great Britain.
Britain, Battle of, 712
British East India Company, 577–578, 580
British West Indies, 474
Bronstein, Lev Davidovich. See Trotsky, Leon.
Brontë, Emily, 534
Bronze, 42–43, 60, 85, p85, 324–325, p325
Bronze Age, 33, m104, 105–106
Brooks, Angie, 789
Brown, Arthur, 683
Brown, Moses, 517
Brownshirts. See Storm Troopers.
Broz, Joseph. See Tito.
Bruegel, Pieter, 358
Brunei, 309
Brunelleschi, Filippo, 351
Brutus, Marcus, 146
Buchenwald, 725

Budapest, 755
Buddha (Gautama), 72–73, 79–80
Buddhism: in India, 72–73, p72, 79–82, p79, p81, 303; in China, 93; in Japan, 291, 296–297, p297; in southeast Asia, 310
Budding Scholars, 278
Buenos Aires, c837
Buffer zone, 738
Buganda, 574
Bulgaria, 623, 626; after World War I, m636; in World War II, 713; in Warsaw Pact, 745
Bulgarians, 611, 633, 637
Bull, papal, 254, 377
Bunche, Ralph, 784
Bundesrat, 608
Burbage, Cuthbert, 428
Burbage, James, 428
Burbage, Richard, 428
Burgesses, 251
Burghers, 224, 226, c263
Burgundians, 167–169, m168, m202, 203, 262
Burial mounds, 327
Burial ritual: prehistoric, 21; in ancient Egypt, 58–60, p59; of ancient China, 90, p91, p93; Viking, p212; Moche, 330, p331
Burma, 309–310, 580, 716
Bush, George, 772, 812, 818, 863, 865, 866, 867
Bushido, 293
Business, international, 835–836, c836
Buthelezi, Zulu chief, 795
Byblos, 39
Byron, Lord, 532–533, p532
Byzantine empire, 169, 178–197; geography of, 179–180, m179; rule from Constantinople, 179–185, m179; emperor's power in, 180; Christianity in, 180, 183–185; reconquering of Roman lands, 180–181, m181; trade of, 182; threats to, 185; Muslim attacks on, 186; Slavs and, 194–195; decline of, 195–197, m196; in Middle Ages, 210; Crusades and, 241–245
Byzantium. See Constantinople.

Cabinet, British, 472–473, c473
Cabot, John, m362, 365–366
Cabral, Pedro Alvares, m362, 363
Caesar, Julius, 144–146, p144
Cahokia, 328
Caillié, René, 572
Cairo, 314
Cajamarca, 395
Calais, 258, 261–262, 720
Calcutta, 577, 773, c837
Calendar: Chaldean, 45; Egyptian, 69; Julian, 146; Roman, 146; Maya, 333–334, p333; Russian, 449–450
Calico, 308
Calicut, India, 308
California, 563
Caligula, Roman emperor, 153, c156
Caliphs, 190–191
Calligraphy, p188
Calvin, John, 379, 382

Calvinism, 382, m383, c386, 402, 407, 411, 576
Calypso, 818
Cambodia, 309–311, 580, m776, 777, m779, m780, 780–781
Cambyses, Persian king, 47
Camp David Accords, 802
Canaan, 40–41. *See also* Palestine
Canada, 474, 477, 569, m823; in World War II, 720; since World War II, 745, 822; French-speaking, 865
Canals: Grand Canal of China, 277; Dutch, 404–405; British, 514; industrialization and, 514. *See also* Panama Canal; Suez Canal.
Canal Zone, 818
Candide (Voltaire), 463
Cannon, 259, p259, c263
Canon law, 229
Canossa, 229
Canton, 580, p581
Cape Colony, 576
Cape of Good Hope, 360
Capet, Hugh, 234
Capetian dynasty, 234, m235
Cape Verde, 359
Capital, 549
Capitalism, 403; democratic, c743
Cappers, 427
Caravel, 359
Cardinals, 228
Carib, m329
Caribbean Basin, m808, 813–819, m815
Carolingian dynasty, 207–211, m210, 234
Carranza, Venustiano, 671
Cartel, 809
Carter, Howard, 52, 68
Carter, Jimmy, 802
Carthage, 39, 137–140, m139, 181
Cartier, Jacques, m362, 365
Cartwright, Edmund, 512
Cash crop, 575–576, 688, 786
Cassius, 146
Caste system, 78
Castiglione, Baldassare, 348
Castile, 263, m264
Castro, Fidel, 552, 813–817, p814, 863
Çatal Hüyük, 27
Cataract (river), 54
Cathedral, p222, 231, p232
Cathedral of Florence, 351
Catherine II, Russian monarch. *See* Catherine the Great.
Catherine of Aragon, 379–380
Catherine the Great, 469–472, p470, m471
Catherine de Medici, 407
Catholicism: in Spain, 398–401; in France, 407–409; in Germany, 410–411; in Scotland, 422; in England, 422, 434–436; in Ireland, 433, 609, 752; in Mexico, 671. *See also* Roman Catholic Church.
Catholic League, 410
Catholic Reformation, 384–385
Cato, 140
Catt, Carrie Chapman, 603
Caudillos, 540
Cavaliers, 432

Cave paintings, 23–24, p23
Cavour, Camillo di, 555–556, p556
Ceauşescu, Nicolae, 856–857
Celebes, 716
Celsius, Anders, 389
Celts, 201, m202
Centennial Exposition, Philadelphia, 565
Central America: early culture of, m329, 330–335; Olmecs, 332, p333; Mayas, 333–334, p333, p334; Aztecs, 335; Spain in, 393–397, m397; independence of countries in, 535–540; nations of, 817–819. *See also* Latin America; Mesoamerica.
Central Powers, 626, m631
Cervantes, Miguel de, 400–401
Ceylon. *See* Sri Lanka.
Chaco Canyon, 327
Chad, 786
Chaeronea, Battle of, 123
Chaldeans, 44–46
Challenger (space shuttle), 831
Chamber of Deputies, France, 541–542, 607–608
Chamberlain, Neville, 702–703, 710
Chamorro, Joaquin, 818–819
Chamorro, Violeta, 819, p819
Champlain, Samuel de, 365
Champollion, Jean François, 69
Chandra Gupta I, 301
Chandra Gupta II, 302
Chandragupta Maurya, 80–81
Ch'Ang-an, 278–280, p280, 292
Chansons de geste, 238
Chaplin, Charlie, p686
Charlemagne, 206–211, m208, p208
Charles I, English king, 430–432
Charles II, English king, 367, 434–436
Charles VI, French king, 259–260
Charles VII, French king, 261–262
Charles VIII, French king, 352
Charles IX, French king, 407
Charles X, French king, 541
Charles VI, Hapsburg ruler, 453, 455
Charles V, Holy Roman Emperor, 372, 377, m378, 385–386, 397
Charles I, Spanish king. *See* Charles V, Holy Roman Emperor.
Charles II, Spanish king, 446
Charles XII, Swedish king, 450–451
Charles the Bald, 210–211
Charles the Dauphin, 260
Charles Martel, 188–189, 206
Charles the Simple, 214
Charles the Well-Served. *See* Charles VII.
Charlottetown Accord, 822
Charter, town, 227, c263
Chartres, 225
Chartres Cathedral, 222–223, 231, p232
Chaucer, Geoffrey, 347
Chavin civilization, 330
Checks and balances, 478
Chemistry, Islamic, 192
Cheng Ho, 289
Ch'eng-tsu, Chinese emperor, p288
Chernenko, Konstantin, 845
Chernobyl disaster, 838–839
Cherokee, m329

Chiang Ch'ing, p677
Chiang Kai-shek, 675–677, p675, 699, 764–765
Chichen Itza, p333
Child labor, 521–522, p521, 551, 601
Chile, 397, 537, 586, 672, 807, 811–813
China: prehistoric peoples of, 26; Confucianism in, 73, 87–88, 91–92; ancient, 82–93, m83; geography of, 82–84, m768; culture of, 84; Ch'in dynasty, 84, 89–93, m92; Chou dynasty, 84, 87–88, m87; Han dynasty, 84, 86, 89–93, m92, 277, 311; Shang dynasty, 84–86, m87; early cities in, 85; Taoism in, 88; Legalists in, 88, 91; Ming dynasty, p90, 287–290, m287; links with Persia, 92; Buddhism in, 93; Golden Age in, 276–290; Sui dynasty, 277, m278; invasion of Korea by, 277–278; T'ang dynasty, 277–280, m278, 292, 311; scholar-officials in, 278–279, p279, 289; Sung dynasty, 280–285, m281; Mongols, 283–287, m285; Yüan dynasty, 285; exploration by, 289; Manchu rule of, 290; Ch'ing dynasty, 290, 580–581, 674; influence on Japan, 291–292; rule of Vietnam, 311; industrialization of, c550, 768, 770; imperialism in, 580–583, m582, p583; Opium War, 580–582; Taiping Rebellion, 581; nationalism in, 583, 674; U.S. and, 583, 764–765, 770, 772; Japan and, 586; in World War I, 674; Soviet Union and, 674–675, 769; communism in, 675–677, m676, 764–772; civil war in, 676, 765; Japanese invasion of, 677, 699, 714; in World War II, 677, 714, 764–765; in U.N., 739; after World War II, 764–772; Korean War, 766–767, m766; agriculture in, 767–770; economy of, 767–770; under Mao, 767–700; cultural revolution in, 769–770; Second Revolution, 770; protests against communism in, 770–772, p771, p772; conflict with India, 774
"China's Sorrow". *See* Yellow River.
Ch'in dynasty, 84, 89–93, m92
Ch'ing dynasty, 290, 580–581, 674
Chinook, m329
Chintz, 308
Chivalry, 239–240
Chlorofluorocarbons, 838
Cholera, 520, 598, 600, 789
Chou dynasty, 84, 87–88, m87
Christendom, 205, 210
Christian Democrats, West German, 747
Christian humanist, 374–375
Christianity: in Roman empire, 160–164, m163, 166–167; in Byzantine empire, 180, 183–185; in Russia, 194–195; in Middle Ages, 200–205; spread of, 214; Crusades, 241–245, m243; in Japan, 295–296; in Africa, 318–319; in Middle East, 665; in Lebanon, 802; in Soviet Union, 849. *See also* Religion.

Franz Ferdinand, Austrian archduke, 620–621, p620, 624
Franz Josef, Austrian emperor, 620
Frederick I (Barbarossa), German emperor, 236, 242, 346
Frederick II, Holy Roman Emperor, 244
Frederick I, Prussian king, 455
Frederick II (the Great), Prussian king, 456, p457, p460, 469–472
Frederick William I, Prussian king, 455
Frederick William III, Prussian king, 526
Frederick William IV, Prussian king, 542
Frederick the Wise, 377
Free elections, 742
Free French, 710, p710, 720
Free trade, 467, 836
French and Indian War. *See* Seven Years' War.
French-Canadians, 822
French empire, 493–498
French Revolution, 482–491, p482
Fresco painting, 346–347, 352
Freud, Sigmund, 684–686
Friars, 230–231
Friedland, Battle of, 494
Friedrich, Caspar David, 535
The Friends of the People, 489
Frisians, m202
Fronde rebellion, 441–442
Fugue, 465
Fulton, Robert, 548
Fundamentalism, Muslim, 801–802
Fur trade, 365, 367

Gabelle, 262
Gagarin, Yuri, 831
Gaiseric the Hun, 169
Galba, Roman emperor, c156
Galen, 389
Galileo Galilei, 387–389, p388, 461
Gallipoli campaign, 630
Gama, Vasco da, 290
Gambetta, Léon, 560
Gandhi, Indira, 774–775
Gandhi, Mohandas K., 660–664, p664, 773
Gandhi, Rajiv, 775
Ganges River, 73
Gargantua and Pantagruel (Rabelais), 409
Garibaldi, Giuseppe, 556–557
Gasoline engine, 596
Gas warfare, 627, p629
Gaudalcanal, 717
Gaugamela, Battle of, 124
Gauguin, Paul, 604–605
Gauls, 137, 145
Gdansk, 757
General Agreement on Tariff and Trade (GATT), 836
General Assembly, 739
Genetics, c599, 600, 834–835
Geneva, 382
Genghis Khan, 284
Genoa, 528
Genocide, 724
Gentry, 279

Geoffrin, Marie Thérèse, 463–464, p463
Geometry, 126
George, David Lloyd, 609
George I, English king, 473
George II, English king, 473
George III, English king, 474–477
George V, English king, 609
Georgia (Soviet Union), 849, 852
Gepids, m202
German Confederation, 528, 532–533, 557, m558
German Democratic Republic. *See* East Germany.
Germanic tribes, 168, 201, 212
German-Italian empire, 236
Germany: prehistoric peoples of, 21; Charlemagne in, 208; Franks in, 211; in Middle Ages, 211, 228–229, 235–236; Renaissance in, 357; Reformation in, 372–377, 381; Schmalkaldic League in, 385; Thirty Years' War, 393, 409–411; religious wars in, 410–411; unification of, 447, 557–559, m558, 622; in American Revolution, 477; industrialization of, 518, 541, 559; nationalism in, 532–533, 555; revolutions of 1848, 542; First Reich, 559; Second Reich, 559; imperialism of, 570; in East Asia, m582, 583, 589; democracy in, 608; in World War I, 622–626, 628–634, 648–651; after World War I, 635–637, m636, 693–694; Jews in, 669; between the World Wars, 680–682, p680; Dawes Plan, 682; Weimar Republic, 682; economy of, 682, 694–695, c753; Great Depression, p689, 694; Nazism in, 693–696; communism in, 694; totalitarianism in, 694–695; defiance of Treaty of Versailles, 699–700; reoccupation of Rhineland, 700–701, m700; Rome-Berlin Axis, 700–701; takeover of Austria, 702; Munich Conference, 702–703; in World War II, 706–725; Cold War, 736–737, 741–742, 745–748; east-west split of, 741, 745–746, m746; in Common Market, 749–750; reunification of, 845, 855, 857; rebuilding eastern Germany, 858; economy of, 858; neo-Nazi violence in, 858, p859
Gestapo, 694
Ghana, 320–322, m321, 359, 574, 784–786, p784
Ghazis, 196
Ghazni, 303
Ghetto, 723–724, p723
Ghiberti, Lorenzo, 351
Gibraltar, Rock of, 446
Gildas the Wise, 201
Giotto di Bondone, 346, 352
Glacier, 25, 326, m327
Gladiator, p142, 150–151, p150
"Gladioli" (Monet), p605
Gladstone, William, 608
Glasgow, 519
Glasnost, 847
Glenn, John, 831
Global economy, 835–836, 863–864
Global unity, 830–841

Global warming, 25, 837–838
Globe Theater, p426, 428–429, p429
Glorious Revolution, 436, c436
Glyphs, 334
Goa, 308
"Goddess of Democracy" (statue), 771, p771
Godwinson, Harold, 233
Goebbels, Joseph, 694
Goethe, Johann Wolfgang von, 533
Golan Heights, 798
Gold, p33, 324, 359, 393–398, 401, 576, 786, 792–793, 811
Gold Coast. *See* Ghana.
Golden Horn, 180, 197
Golden Rule, 161
Goldman, Emma, 685
Gold-salt trade, 320–322
Gómez, Juan Vicente, 670, 673
Gomulka, Wladyslaw, 757
Good Neighbor Policy, 673
Gorbachev, Mikhail, 841, 844–851, 852, 853
Gospels, 161–162
Gothic architecture, 231, p232
Goths, 165
Gouges, Olympe de, 488
Goulart, João, 811
Government: Sumerian, 33–34; of Persian empire, 47–49; of ancient Egypt, 56–63; of India, 80–82; of China, 84, 89, 93, 278; of ancient Greece, 108–114; of Roman republic, 133–137, c136, 141–147; of Roman empire, 151–155, 166; of Byzantine empire, 180; of medieval Europe, 203; of Franks, 208–209; of Middle Ages, 233–236; of England, 251, 430–437, c433, 472–473, 511; of Japan, 292, 696, 761–763; of Florence, 350–351; of Netherlands, 403; separation of powers, 467–468; of U.S., 477–479; federal system, 478; laissez faire, 522–523; coalition, 681–682; authoritarian, 692; puppet, 699
Government of India Act, 662–664
Governor, Roman, 144
Goya, Francisco, p497
Gracchus, Gaius, 142–143
Gracchus, Tiberius, 142
Gramme, Zenobe, 594
Granada, 263–264, m264
Grand Alliance, 498–499
Grand Army, 498
Grand Canal, 277
Grand Fleet, 289
Granicus, Battle of, 123
Grasslands, of Africa, 316
Gravitas, 133
Gray, Martin, 706–707
Gray eminence. *See* Richelieu, Cardinal.
Great Britain: War of Spanish Succession, 446; War of Austrian Succession, 456; Seven Years' War, 456–457, 473; as limited democracy, 472–473; Hanoverian dynasty, 473; in India, 473, p568, 577–580, p577, m579, 660–665, p660, 741, 773; building of empire, 473–475; in North America, 473–475, m474,

Louis XV, French king, 447, 462, 464, 469
Louis XVI, French king, 477, 483–489
Louis XVIII, French king, 499, 528
Louis the German, 210–211
Louis Napoleon. *See* Napoleon III.
Louis Philippe, French king, 541–542
Louis the Pious, 210
Louis the Sluggard, 234
Louisiana, 365
Louisiana Purchase, 561–562, m562
Lowell, Francis, 517
Lower class, 484
Lower house, 608
Loyang, China, 87
Lucca, 555
Lucretia, 133
Lucy (fossil), 18, p18
Luftwaffe, 709, 712–713
Lully, Jean Baptiste. *See* Molière.
Lumumba, Patrice, 788
Lusitania (ship), 632
Luther, Martin, 372–379, p372, p376, c386
Lutherans, 377–378, 382, 410–411
Luxembourg, 710, 745, 750
Lycurgus, Code of, 110
Lyons, 518

Maat, 66
McAdam, John, 514
MacArthur, Douglas, 761, 766–767
Macbeth (Shakespeare), 428
Maccabee, Judas, 160
Macedon, 122–123
Macedonia, 860, c861, m861
Machiavelli, Niccolò, 352–353
Machine gun, 627
Machu Picchu, p395
McKay, Claude, 686
McKinley, William, 611
McLuhan, Marshall, 832
Macmillan, Harold, 785
Madeira, 359
Madison, James, 478
Madras (cloth), 577
Madras, India, 308
Magdalene, Mary, 162
Magellan, Ferdinand, m362, 363–364
"Magic" (decoding machine), 715
Maginot Line, 710, m721
Magna Carta, 250–251, p251
Magyars, 211, m213, 236
Maharajah, 577–578
Mahatma, 662
Mahmud of Ghazni, 303
Maine (ship), 588
Major, John, 752
Major domo, 206
Malacca, 308
Malaya, 714
Malay Peninsula, 311, 716
Malaysia, 309
Mali, 314, 320, m321, 322–324
Malindi, 319, m321
Manchester, 515, 519–523, 541
Manchuria, 586, 677, 696, 699, 769
Manchus, 290
Mandate, 636–637, 667
Mandate of Heaven, 84
Mandela, Nelson, 793–795, p794

Mandingo, 323, 574
Manet, Edouard, 604
Manganese, 576
Manifesto against Aggression, 756
Manila, 716
Manor, 217–219, p218
Mansa Musa, 313–314, 323
Mantua, 349
Manzikert, Battle of, 195
Mao Tse-tung, 552, 674–677, p675, 699, 764–700
Mao Zedong. *See* Mao Tse-tung.
Marat, Jean Paul, 489
Marathon, plain of, 112
Marconi, Guglielmo, 595–596
Marcos, Ferdinand E., 777
Marcus Aurelius, Roman emperor, 153–157, c156, 163–164
Marguerite of Navarre, 381, p381
Mariana Islands, 721
Maria Theresa, Austrian ruler, 443–444, p454, 455–457, 470–472
Marie Antoinette, French queen, 484, 486, p486, 489–490
Marie of Champagne, 240
Marina, Doña, 393–394
Marius, Roman commander, 143–144
Marketplace, in Constantinople, 182
Marne, Battle of the, 626, 633
Maronite Christians, 796, 802
Marquette, Jacques, m362, 365
Marriage, 216, 228–229
Mars (god), 130
Marshall Plan, 744–745, p744, 747
Martial law, 757, 771
Martin V, pope, 256, 354
Martyrs, Christian, 164
Marx, Karl, 551–552, 646–647, 675
Mary (Stuart), Scottish queen, 382
Mary I (Tudor), English queen, 421–422
Mary II, English queen, 436
Masaccio, 352, p352
Masada, 163
Massachusetts Bay Colony, 367
Mass culture, 606–607, 839–840
Mass production, 596
Mataco, m329
Materialism, 840
Mathematical Principles of Natural Philosophy (Newton), 462
Mathematics: in ancient Egypt, 69; Hellenistic, 126; Islamic, 192; Hindu, 302; French, 409
Matrilineal system, 324
Matthew, apostle, 161
Mau Mau, 786
Mauryan dynasty, 79–82, m80, 301
Maxwell, James C., 595
Maya, m329, 333–334, p333, p334
May Fourth protests, 674
Mazarin, Jules, 441–442
Mazowiecki, Tadeusz, 854
Mazzini, Giuseppe, 532, 555, 557
Mecca, 179, 186–188, p187
Meciar, Vladimir, 860
Medellin cartel, 809
Medes, 44
Medici, Catherine de. *See* Catherine de Medici.
Medici, Cosimo de, 350–351
Medici, Lorenzo de, 351–352, 354

Medici, Piero de, 352, 374
Medicine: in ancient Egypt, 69; Islamic, 192; medieval, 230, p230; in India, 302; Scientific Revolution and, 389; Enlightenment, 465, p465; vaccines, 465, p465, 598; anesthesia, 598, c599; of early 1900's, 598, c599; since World War II, 834–835, p835
Medieval period. *See* Middle Ages.
Medina, 187
Meditation, 296–297, p297
Meditations (Marcus Aurelius), 155–157
Meech Lake Accord, 822
Meerut, 578
Meiji era, 584–586, 762
Meitner, Lise, 721–722
Memphis, Egypt, 57
Mendel, Gregor, c599, 600
Mendeleev, Dmitri, c599, 600
Mendelssohn, Felix, 535
Menelik II, Ethiopian ruler, 574
Menem, Carlos, 810
Menes, Egyptian pharaoh, 57–58, p57
Menlo Park, 594–595
Mensheviks, 646–647, 649
Mercantilism, 442, 450, 467, 473–475
Mercenary, 138
Merchant guilds, 226–227
Meroë, 318
Merovingian dynasty, 206
Mesa Verde, p328, m329
Mesê, 182
Mesoamerica, 26
Mesolithic Age, 19
Mesopotamia. *See* Fertile Crescent.
Messenians, 110
Messiah, 162
Mestizos, 536–537, 809
Metalworking, 33, p33, 330. *See also names of metals.*
Metternich, Klemens von, 527–528, p527, 532–533, 543
Mexico, 326, 330, 672–673, 809; Olmecs, 332; Mayas, 333–334, p333, p334; Aztecs, 335; independence of, 539; war with U.S., 562–563; in World War I, 632; revolt of 1910, 670–672, p671; civil war in, 671; economy of, 812; modern, 812–813
Mexico City, p335, 397, 539, 562, 812–813, p813, c837
Miami, 816
Micah, 42
Michelangelo, 355–356, p355
Microscope, 389, 464, 834
Microtechnology, 832–833
Middle Ages: Christianity in, 200–205; early, 200–219; Frankish kingdoms in, 206–211; Vikings in, 211–214, m213; feudalism in, 214–219; agriculture in, 217–219, p219, 223–227; high, 222–245; religion in, 223, 228–231, 254–256; trade in, 223–227, 241–242, 245; growth of towns in, 224–227, p225; power of kings in, 233–236, 261–262; daily life in, 237; revival of learning in, 237–240; Crusades in, 241–245, m243; growth of European nations, 248–267; plague in, 257–258, p257

925

Middle class, 224, 253, 262, c263, 381, 401, 409, 452, 484, 522, 552, 681, 785, 820

Middle East: mandates after World War I, 636–637; nationalism in, 665–670, 795–803; after World War I, 665–666; economy of, 669, 799–801; border disputes in, 795–796; France in, 795–796; Cold War in, 798; Soviet Union in, 798; U.S. in, 798; cultural conflicts in, 799–802; oil, 799–801, p799, c800; today, m799; Persian Gulf War, 866–867. *See also names of countries.*

Midway, Battle of, 716–717, m717

Migration, rural to urban, 789, 809

Milan, 346, 353, 398, 518

Milan, Edict of, 166–167

Militarism: of ancient Egypt, 64–65; of ancient Greece, 109–111, p109; Macedonian, 123; Prussian, 455; industrialization and, 561; in Japan, 585–586, 696–697, 761; Europe before World War I, 624; in Germany, 636. *See also* Warfare; Weapons.

Mill girl, 517, p517

Milosevic, Slobodan, 860, 861

Milton, John, 434

Minamoto clan, 293

Minaret, p187, 300

Mines Act, 521

Ming dynasty, p90, 287–290, m287

Ming T'ai-tsu, Chinese emperor, 287, 289

Minoan civilization, 105, p105

Minorities, 726

Mir, 643

***The Misanthrope* (Molière),** 445

***The Miser* (Molière),** 445

Missi dominici, 209

Missionaries: Christian, 203, 205, 208; Catholic, 295–296; in Japan, 295–296; Buddhist, 310; Jesuit, 384; in Age of Imperialism, 570

Mississippian people, 328

Mississippi River, 326, 328, 365

Mitterand, François, 749–750

Mobutu, Joseph, 788

Moche, 330, p331

Model Parliament, 251–252, p252, c263

Modem, 833

Modena, 555

Moderate socialism, 751

Mogadishu, m321

Mohenjo-Daro, 75–76, p75

Moksha, 77

Moldavia, 849

Molière, 445

Moltke, Helmuth von, 561

Mombasa, 319, m321

***Mona Lisa* (Leonardo),** 356–357, p357, 445

Monarchy: limited, 251, 487–488; absolute, 437, 440–457, 529; constitutional, 472, 529; dual, 558

Monastery, 204, p204, 209, 228, 380

Monck, George, 434

Monet, Claude, 604, p605

Mongolia, 84

Mongols: invasion of Ottoman empire, 196; in Russia, 265–267,

m266; in China, 283–287, m285; in Japan, 285, 294; in India, 304–305; in Vietnam, 310

Monks, 204, p205, 228

Monnet, Jean, 749–750

Monopoly, 549

Monotheism, 40, 67, 160, 186–187, 324; ethical, 42

Monroe Doctrine, 540, 587–589, 672

Monsoon, 73

Montagu, Mary Wortley, 465

Montaigne, Michel de, 409

Monte Cassino, p204

Montenegrins, 611, 623

Montenegro, 860, c861, m861

Montesquieu, Baron de, 467–468

Montezuma, 392–394, p394

Montgomery, Bernard, 718

Monticello, p477

Montreal, 365

Moon landing, 831

More, Margaret, 381

More, Thomas, 374–375, p374, 380

Morelos, José María, 539

Morocco, 572, 611, 718, 785

Morse, Samuel F.B., 549

Mosaic, p180

Moscow, 265–267, p267, 451, 498, 652, 713–714, c837

Moses, 40–42

Mosque, 188, 193, p323

Mott, Lucretia, 602

Mount Olympus, 103, 108

Mount Sinai, 41

Mount Vesuvius, p159

Movies, 607, 686, p686, 839–840

Mozambique, 791, 793–794

Mozart, Wolfgang Amadeus, p456, 466

Mubarak, Hosni, 802

Muezzin, p187, 188

Mugabe, Robert, 793

Mughal empire, 304–308, m305, 577

Muhammad, prophet, 179, 185–187

Muhammad II, Ottoman sultan, 196–197

Muhammad Ghuri, Turkish sultan, 303

Mulattoes, 536

Multinational corporation, 820, 835–836

Mummy, 58

Munburucú, m329

Munch, Edvard, 605

Munich, 694

Munich Conference, 703–704, 707

Murrow, Edward R., 712

Muscat, m668

Muses (goddesses), 126

Museum, of Alexandria, 126

Music: polyrhythmic, 325; African, 325; French, 445; Enlightenment, 463–466, p466; romanticism in, 534–535; of early 1900's, 605–606; Russian, 644; American, 686; German, 695; Latin American, 818

Music hall, 606–607

Musket, 295

Muslim League, 579, 661, p663, 664–665, 773

Muslims: attacks on Byzantine empire, 186; in France, 188; at Battle

of Tours, 188, 191; in Spain, 188–191, 206, 263–264; in Egypt, 189; in Mesopotamia, 189; in Palestine, 189; in North Africa, 189–190; rule of caliphs, 190–191; religious divisions of, 191, c193; culture of, 192; in Italy, 211, m213; Crusades against, 241–245, m243; in China, 280; in India, 303, 306–307, 578, 660–665, 773, 865; in southeast Asia, 311; in sub-Saharan Africa, 319, 323–324, p323; in Middle East, 665; in Saudi Arabia, 667; in Pakistan, 773; in Lebanon, 796, 802; fundamentalism among, 801–802; in Soviet Union, 849; in Yugoslavia, 860–861, c861, m861; in Iraq, 866

Mussolini, Benito, 691–693, p692, 697, 699, 707, 710, 719–720

Mycenaeans, 105–106

Myth, Greek, 108

Nagasaki, 296, 584, 722, 740

Nagy, Imre, 755, 854

Nairobi, 788

Nalanda, university at, 302–303

Namibia, 794

Nampan, 295

Nanak, 307

Nanking, 287, 581, 699

Nanking, Treaty of, 581

Nantes, Edict of, 408–409, 443

Naples, 352–353, 398

Napoleon I (Bonaparte), 492–499, 561–562; rise to power, 492; as emperor, 493–498, p493, m495; exile of, 499, 527; return to power, 499, 528; conquest of Spain, 536

Napoleon III (Louis Napoleon), 543, 553, 555, 559

Napoleonic Code, 494

Nara, 292

Narodniki, 644

Nasser, Abdel, 797–798

Natal, 576

National Assembly, French, 484–487, 560

National Convention, French, 489, 491–492

National Covenant, Lebanese, 802

National debt, 689

Nationalism, 541; in Europe, 259–260; in Italy, 532, 555; in Germany, 532–533, 555; romanticism and, 533–535; in Latin America, 535–540; in France, 555; in India, 578–579, 661–665, 865; in China, 583, 674; in music, 605–606; in Ireland, 608–609, 611; in Balkans, 611, 623; in Middle East, 665–670, 795–803; Arab, 667–669; of Jews, 668; fascism and, 692; in Southeast Asia, 777; in Africa, 785–795; in Soviet Union, 849; in Eastern Europe, 853

Nationalist Republic of China, 675

Nationalists: Chinese, 674–677, 764–765; Spanish, 702

National Opposition Union, 819

National Salvation Front, 857

Nation-state, 253–254, 259, 261

Native Americans, m329, 393–397, 536–539, 809, 812
NATO. *See* North Atlantic Treaty Organization.
Natural gas, 594, 790
Natural selection, 598–599
Navarino, Battle of, 532
Navarre, 263–264, m264
Navigation Acts, 474
Nazis, c695; in Germany, 693–696; rise to power, 693–696, p693; persecution of Jews, 695–696; Nuremberg trials, 742
Nazi-Soviet Pact of 1939, 707–708, 849
Neanderthals, 21–22
Nebuchadnezzar, Babylonian king, 45–46, p45
Nefertiti, p67
Negotiation, 703
Nehru, Jawaharlal, p663, 664, 773–774
Nelson, Horatio, 494
Nepal, 73
Neolithic Age, 19, 24–27
Neo-Nazis, 858, p857
Nero, Roman emperor, 153, c156, 163
Nerva, Roman emperor, 153, c156
Netherlands, 398, 838; exploration by, m362; colonies in North America, 367; Reformation in, 373–375, 381–382; war with Spain, 399–403; republic established, 403; States General, 403; trade of, 403–404; War of Austrian Succession, 456; in French empire, 494; Congress of Vienna, 528; colonies in Americas, m538; imperialism of, 570; in Africa, 576, 792; in South Asia, m579; in World War II, 710, 715, 725; after World War II, 745, 750
Neumann, John von, 833
Neutrality, 625
Neutrality acts, 712
Neva River, 451
New Amsterdam, 367
Newcomen engine, 513
New Deal, 689–690
New Economic Policy, Soviet Union, 652
New England, 367
Newfoundland, 213, 366
New France, 365
New Harmony, Indiana, 551
New Model Army, 432
"New monarchs", 261
New Orleans, 365
New Spain, 393–397, m397
Newspapers, 450
New Stone Age. *See* Neolithic Age.
New Testament, 162
Newton, Isaac, 461–462, 684
New York, 367
New York City, 594, 739, c837
New York Stock Exchange, 687–690
New Zealand, 589, 604
Nez Perce, m329
Niami, 323
Nicaragua, 589, 672, 818–819, p819
Nice, 555–556
Nicholas I, Russian czar, 642–643
Nicholas II, Russian czar, 625, 641, 644–648, p645

Nietzsche, Friedrich, 599–600
Nigeria, 317, 324, 574, 786, 789–790
Niger River, 572
Nightingale, Florence, 601–602, p601
Night of the long knives, 694
The Night Watch (Rembrandt), p405
Nihilism, 644
Nile River, 26, 52–57, m55, 60, 126, 572
Nimitz, Chester W., 716
Ninety-five theses, 376, c386
Nineveh, 44, p44
Ninth Symphony (Beethoven), 534
Nippur, 34
Nirvana, 80
Nixon, Richard, 770, 779, 784, 846
Nkrumah, Kwame, 784–786, p784
Nobles: Egyptian, 63–65; Chinese, 85; Greek, 106, 109; Roman, 159; Frankish, 207–209; feudal, 219, 222–223, 226; of medieval Europe, 234; Japanese, 292, p292; Inca, 332; French, 408–409, 440–441, 444–445, 483–484; Russian, 470, 641, 643
Nobunaga, Oda, 295
Nok, 317
Nol, Lon, 780
Nomads, 283, 316
Nome, 56
Non-aligned nation, 774
Nonviolent protest, 662–663, 821
Noriega, Manuel, 818
Norman conquest, 233–234
Normandy, 213–215, 249, 720
Norsemen. *See* Vikings
North Africa: Muslims in, 189–190; Crusades in, 243; imperialism in, 572–574, m573; World War II in, 718, m720, 785; France in, 741, 749; nationalism in, 785. *See also* Africa.
North America: Anasazi, 327, p328, m329; Hopewell, 327–328, m329; Mississippian people, 328; France in, 365; England in, 365–367, 473–475, m474; Dutch in, 367; Spain in, 396–397, m397
North American Free Trade Association, 864
North American Woman Suffrage Association, 603
North Atlantic Treaty Organization (NATO), 745, m745, 747–749, 858
Northern Ireland, 752
Northern Renaissance, 354, 374
North German Confederation, m557, 558
North Korea, 765–767, m766
North Vietnam, 778–780
Northwest passage, 365
Norway, 382, 709–710, 745
Notre Dame, Cathedral of, 231
Novel, 554
Novgorod, 194
Nuclear family, 840
Nuclear power, 838–839
Nuclear waste, 838–839
Nuclear weapons, 740, 767, 865, 866
Number system, Hindu, 302
Nuns, 204, 228
Nuremberg laws, 696
Nuremberg trials, 742

Nur Jahan, Persian princess, 306
Nursing, p601, 602
The Nutcracker Suite, 644
Nyerere, Julius, 788, 790

Oasis, 316
Oba, 325
Obregón, Alvaro, 671
Obsidian, 27, 334
O'Connell, Daniel, 541
O'Connor, Sandra Day, 821
Octavian. *See* Augustus.
Odoacer, 169
Odo of Bayeux, 216
Odysseus, 107
Odyssey (Homer), 106–107
Oedipus (Sophocles), 117
Ohio River, 327–328
Oil, 594; in Middle East, 669, 799–801, p799, c800, 866; in Latin America, 672–673, 807, 812; North Sea, 751; in Indonesia, 777; in Nigeria, 790; crisis of 1973, 800
Oil industry, 549
Oil spill, 837
Okinawa, 721
Old Regime, 483–484, 488
Old Stone Age. *See* Paleolithic Age.
Olduvai Gorge, 19
Olga, Russian princess, 194
Olmec, m329, 332, p333
Olympia, Greece, 103, 107
Olympic games: ancient, 107–108; modern, 606, 696, 803
Oman, m668
Omar, caliph, 190
Open-Door Policy, 583
Opera, 466
Operation Desert Storm, 866
Operation Restore Hope, 867, p867
Operation Sea Lion, 712
Operation Vittles, 746
Operation Vulture, 778
Opium War, 580–582
Oprichniki, 267
Oracle bone, 86
Oral history, 325
Orange Free State, 576
Orb, p208
Ordeal, trials by, 200–201
Oregon Territory, 563
Organization of African Unity (OAU), 791
Organization of Petroleum Exporting Countries (OPEC), 800, c800
Organ transplants, 834
The Origin of Species (Darwin), 598–599
Orleans, 249, 260–261
Orozco, José, p671
Ortega, Daniel, 819
Orthodox caliphate, 190
Osaka, c837
Osiris (god), 66, 68
Oslo, p710
Osman, Ottoman sultan, 195–196
Ostpolitik, 748
Ostrogoths, 167, m168, 169, 181, 201, m202, 203, 205
Otho, Roman emperor, c156

927

Poetry: Greek, p118; Islamic, 192; medieval, 238–240; Chinese, 280; Japanese, 293; Southeast Asian, 310; Renaissance, 347; Aztec, 394; Elizabethan, 428–429; in Restoration, 434; British, 533; between the World Wars, 685–686
Pogroms, 611, 668
Poitiers, Battle of, 259
Poland, 528; kingdom of, 452, m453; partition of, 472; after World War I, 635–637; in World War II, 706–709, p709, 723–724; Cold War, 736–737; communism in, 742; protests against communism, 756–757; economy of, 757, 853, 859; collapse of communism in, 853–854; shock therapy in, 859
Polio vaccine, 834
Polis, 108
Polish corridor, 636, 707, p709
Politburo, 753, 845
Political liberty, 467–468
Politiques, 407
Pollution, 763, 830–831, 836–839
Polo, Marco, 285–286, 359
Poltava, Battle of, 451
Polytheism, 36, 67, 132, 160, 324
Pomeiock, p366
Pompeii, p159
Pompey, Roman general, 144–145
Pompidou, Georges, 749
Pope, 185; first, 164; power of, 204–205; Franks and, 207; in Middle Ages, 210, 228–231; decline of prestige of, 244; move to Avignon, 255; challenges to authority of, 256; Renaissance, 354, 373; Reformation, 372–386; Counter-Reformation, 384–385
Popular Front, 690
Population growth: agriculture and, 25–26; industrialization and, 510, 550; in India, 774; in Africa, 789–790; in Latin America, 809, 813; global, 837; pollution and, 837
Porcelain, 281
Port Arthur, 583
Porter, Edwin S., 607
Portrait painting, 347, p349
Port Said, 548
Portugal, 263, m264; exploration by, 289–290, 308, m362, 363–364; in Japan, 295; trade of, 308; in South Asia, 308, m309, m579; in Africa, 318, 320, 358–360, 572, m573, 786, 791; rule by Spain, 398; colonies in Americas, m538, 539; imperialism of, 570; in NATO, 745; in Common Market, 750; Cold War, 750–751
Pot, Pol, 780–781
Potatoes, 27, 331, 368, 450
Potsdam, 469
Pottery: prehistoric, 27; Athenian, 111–112, p112, 119; Anasazi, p328; Moche, 330
Po Valley, 518
Power loom, 512
Power vacuum, 452
Powhatan, 366
Praetorian Guard, 153, 166
Pragmatic Sanction, 455–456

Prague, 410, 454
Prague Spring, 756
In Praise of Folly **(Erasmus),** 374
Prayer rug, 190, p190
Predestination, 382
Prehistory, 17
Presbyterians, 382, c386, 422, 431
Priest: Sumerian, 34–36; Egyptian, 63, 67–68; Aryan, 76–77; Byzantine, 185; Roman, 185; marriage of, 228–229
Priestley, Joseph, 464
Primary Chronicle, 194
Prime Minister, British, 473, c473
The Prince **(Machiavelli),** 353
Princip, Gavrilo, 621
Printing, 282, 289, 375–376, p375, 606
Procopius, 180
Profit, 403
Proletariat, 141, 552, 651
Promontory Point, Utah, 548
Propaganda, p625, 628, p657, 695–696
Prophet, Jewish, 42
Protectorate, 572
Protestantism: Reformation, 372–386; in northern Europe, 379–383; spread in Europe, 382, m383; in France, 407–409, 494; in Germany, 410–411; in Scotland, 422; in England, 422, 431–432, 436; in Northern Ireland, 609, 752
Prussia: German unification, 447; Hohenzollern dynasty, 455–457; invasion by Frederick II, 456; Seven Years' War, 456; under Frederick the Great, 469; war with France, 489–490; in Third Coalition, 494; opposition to Napoleon, 498–499; Congress of Vienna, 526–528; German unification and, 557–559, m558; Seven Weeks' War, 557–559; Franco-Prussian War, 559
Ptolemaic dynasty, 139
Ptolemy, 126, 388
Public education, 601, 606, 666
Puccini, Giacomo, 605
Pueblo, 327
Puelche, m329
Puerto Rico, 362, 588, 817, p817
Pugachev, 470
Punic Wars, 137–140, 142
Punjab, 660
Puppet government, 699
Purdah, 307
Puritans, 367, 425, 430–434
Pyramid: Egyptian, 58–59, p59; Kushite, 317–318; in Peru, 330; Olmec, 332
Pyramid of the Sun, 334, p334
Pyrrhus, Greek king, 137

Quattrocento, 350
Quebec, 365, 822, 865
Quebecois, 822
Quetzalcoatl (god), 393–394
Quipu, 331

Rabelais, François, 409
Rabies, 598, c599
Rabin, Yitzhak, 803

Racine, Jean Baptiste, 445
Radar, 712
Radicalism, 529
Radio, 595–596, c599, 684, 712, 791, 832–833, 839–840
Radioactive element, archaeological dating using, 17
Radioactivity, c599, 600
Rafsanjani, Hasgemi, 802
Rag paper, 375
Ragtime, 606
Railroads, 547–548; British, 516, p516, 518; transcontinental, 548; in India, 578; Trans-Siberian, 645
Rain forest, 316, 811, 838, p838
Raj, 578–580
Rajputs, 303
Raleigh, Sir Walter, 365–366
Ramadan, 188
Ramos, Fidel, 777
Ramses, Egyptian pharaoh, 62, p62
Rao, P.V. Narasimha, 775
Raphael, 356
Rasputin, 648
Rationing, in World War I, 627–628, p627
Ravel, Maurice, 605–606
Reagan, Ronald, 819, 846
Realism, 553–554, p553
Realpolitik, 555
Recession, 822
Reconquista, 263
Red Army: Russian, 652–653; Chinese, 676–677, p677, 764–765
Red Cross, p563
Red Fort at Agra, 306
Red Fort at Delhi, p307
Red Guards, 651, 769, p769
Red Shirts, 556
Referendum, 822
Reformation, 256, 372–386, c386
Reformation Parliament, 380
Reform Bill of 1832, 541, 553
Refrigeration, 586
Refugees: displaced persons, 723, 740; Southeast Asian, 780–781, p781; in Africa, 789; Palestinian, 796, 802–803; Cuban, 816; in Germany, 858
Reggae, 818
Reichstag, 608, 694
Reign of Terror, 483, 490–491
Reims cathedral, 231
Reincarnation, 77
Relativity, theory of, 684–685
Relic, 225
Religion: prehistoric, 27; Sumerian, 34–36; in Persia, 49; in ancient Egypt, 54–60, p59, 66–68; in India, 76–78, p77; in China, 84, 87–88; in ancient Greece, 108, 133; in Roman republic, 132–133; in Roman empire, 160–167, m163; in Byzantine empire, 180, 183–185; of Slavs, 194; in Russia, 194–195; of Vikings, 212, 214; in Middle Ages, 223, 228–231, 254–256; in Japan, 291, 295–296; in sub-Saharan Africa, 323–324; Olmec, 332; Inca, 332, p332; Maya, 333; Reformation, 372–386; in England, 379–381, 422; in France, 407; in Soviet Union, 656–657, 847, 849. *See also specific religions.*

Religious toleration: in Netherlands, 402–403; in France, 407–408, 443, 493; in Virginia, 476
Rembrandt van Rijn, 405, p405
Remus, 130–131
Renaissance, 461; in Italy, 345–349, m346, 354; art and architecture of, 346–353; spread to northern Europe, 374
Renoir, Auguste, 604
Reparations, 636
Republic, 133
The Republic (Plato), 121
Republic of China, 765
Research science, p835
Restoration, 434–435
Revolution: American, 475–478; French, 482–491, p482
Revolution of 1905, 647–648
Revolutions of 1848, 555
On the Revolutions of the Heavenly Bodies (Copernicus), 387
Reza Pahlavi, Muhammad, 801
Reza Shah Pahlavi, 666, 801
Rhazes, 192
Rhineland, 636, 700–701, m700
Rhodes, Cecil, 570, 576
Rhodesia, 574, 786
Rice, 26
Richard I (the Lionheart), English king, 240, 242, 249
Richard III, English king, 262
Richelieu, Cardinal, 408–409, p408, 411, 441
Rig-Veda, 77–78
Rio de Janeiro, c837
The Rite of Spring (Stravinsky), 606
Roads: Inca, 331–332; industrialization and, 514; macadam, 514; Pan-American Highway, 806–807, p806. *See also* Transportation.
Roanoke colony, 366, p366
Robespierre, Maximilien, 490
Robotics, 834
Rock art, 23, p25
Rock church, 319, p319
Rockefeller, John D., 549
Rocky Mountains, 326
Rogers, Will, 684
Rollo, Viking leader, 214
Roman Catholic Church, 185, 210, 242–243; in Middle Ages, 203–207, 228–231; feudalism and, 254–256; popes in Avignon, 255; Great Schism, 255–256; Inquisition, 264; Reformation and, 372–386; Jesuits, 384; reforming popes of, 384–385; in France, 483, 487, 493; in Poland, 757. *See also* Catholicism.
Romance language, 202
Roman empire, 150–169, m154; government of, 151–155, 166; Pax Romana, 151–154, c156; Five Good Emperors, 153–154, m154, c156; culture of, 155–160; Greek influence on, 155–160; laws of, 158; daily life in, 159–160; religion in, 160–164, m163; decline and fall of, 164–169, c167; trade of, 164–165, m165; division of, 166; religion of, 166–167; barbarian invasions of, 167–169, m168, 201–203, m202

Romanesque architecture, 231, p232
Romania, 611, 623, 713, 840; communism in, 742, 745; collapse of communism in, 856–857
Romanovs, 267, 447–451, 648
Roman republic, 130–147; geography of, 131, m131; founding of, 131–134; religion of, 132–133; government of, 133–137, c136, 141–147; class structure of, 133–134; warfare of, 134; expansion of, 135–140; control of Italy, 137; war with Greeks, 137; war with Carthage, 137–140, m139; expansion to east, 139–140, m140; end of, 141–147; Triumvirates, 144–147; conquest of Gaul, 145; civil war in, 145–146
Romanticism, 533–535, 541, 553–554
Rome: sacking by Gauls, 137; Byzantine rule of, 181; Franks in, 211; Renaissance, 353–354; capital of Italy, 556–557
Rome-Berlin Axis, 700–701
Rommel, Erwin, 718
Romulus, 130–132
Romulus Augustulus, Roman emperor, 169
Roosevelt, Eleanor, 739
Roosevelt, Franklin D., 673, 712–715, 718, 720, 726–727, 736, p736, 738
Roosevelt, Theodore, 588–589, 672
Roosevelt Corollary, 589, 672
Rosetta Stone, p68, 69
Rotterdam, 710
Roundheads, 432
Rousseau, Jean Jacques, 467–468
Rowlatt Act, 662
Royal Air Force, 712
Royal estate, 209
Royal Road, 48
Royal Society of London, 465, 511
Royal vassal, 215
Rubáiyát, 193
Rubicon River, 145
Ruhr Valley, 518
Rumba, 818
Runnymede, 250
Rurik, Russian prince, 194
Russia: early kingdoms of, 194–195, m195; religion of, 194–195; geography of, 265, m266, 448; czarist, 265–267, 641–645; Mongol rule of, 265–267, m266, 284–285; under Peter thr Great, 447–451; under Romanov dynasty, 447–451; war with Turks, 450; expansion of empire, 450–452; Great Northern War, 450–451; Seven Years' War, 456; under Catherine the Great, 469–472, m471; constitution of, 470; war with Ottoman Turks, 470; in Second Coalition, 492; in Third Coalition, 494; invasion by Napoleon, 497–498, m498; Congress of Vienna, 526–528; industrialization of, c550; Crimean War, 560, 643; imperialism of, 570; in East Asia, 582–583, m582; Russo-Japanese War, 586, 647, p647; in World War I, 622–626, 629–633, m631, 640–641, 648, p649; Bolsheviks in , 632–633, 646–647, 650–654; after World

War I, m636, 637, 648–649; in 1800's, 641–645; Decembrists, 642, 646; economy of, 644–645, 862; revolutionaries in, 646–650; Bloody Sunday, 647; revolution of 1905, 647–648; under Romanovs, 648; provisional government, 648–650; power of soviets, 649; civil war in, 652; in Persia, 666. *See also* Soviet Union.
Russian Orthodox Church, 266, 450, 644
Russian Republic, 845, 849
Russo-Japanese War, 586, 647, p647
Rutherford, Ernest, 600
Rwanda, 790
Ryukyu Islands, 582, 721

Saar region, 635–636
Sadat, Anwar, 798, 802
Sahara, 315–316, m316, 573
Sahel, 316, 790
Saigon, 779
St. Augustine, Florida, p396
St. Bartholomew's Day massacre, 407
St. Basil's Cathedral, p267
St. Helena, 499
St. Lawrence River, 365
Saint Louis. *See* Louis IX
St. Petersburg, 451, p451, 640–641, 649–652
St. Simon, 551
Sakharov, Andrei, 754, 847, 848
Sakk, 191
Saladin, 242
Salamis, Battle of, 114
Salinas de Gortari, Carlos, 812
Sallust, 143
Salt, 320–322
SALT. *See* Strategic Arms Limitation Treaty.
Samudra Gupta, Indian king, 301–302
Samurai, 293–294, p294, p715
Sanchez, Oscar Arias, 819
Sand, George, 534, p534
Sandinistas, 819
Sandino, Augusto César, 819
San Francisco Conference, 739
Sanger, Margaret, 685
San Martín, José, 537–539, m538
San Salvador, 361
Sans-culottes, 484, 488
Sanskrit, 76, 310
Santiago, 397
São Paulo, 811, c837
Sappho, p118
Sarah, 40
Sarajevo, 620–621, 861
Sardinia, 492, 528, 555
Satellites, 831–832, 839–840
Satire, 157, 445
Satrap, 48
Satyagraha, 663
Saudi Arabia, 667, p667, m668, 669; conflicts with Israel, 796; oil in, 799–800; in Persian Gulf War, 866
Saul, Jewish king, 41
Savanna, of Africa, 316, 320
Savonarola, Girolamo, 374
Savoy, 447, 555–556

931

South Korea, 765–767, m765, p765, 781
South Vietnam, 778–779
Soviet, 649
Soviet satellite, 742
Soviet Union, under Lenin, 650–654; Kronstadt revolt, 652; economy of, 652–656, 752, c753, 846, 847, 849; communism in, 653–657, 752–757, 845; industrialization of, 654–657; under Stalin, 654–657, 698; agriculture in, 655–656; religion in, 656–657, 847, 849; totalitarianism in, 656–657; China and, 674–675, 769; in World War II, 707–709, 713–714, 718–729, 737; Cold War, 736–746, 752–757, 765; and Eastern Europe, 738; in U.N., 739; occupation zone in Germany, 741; in Warsaw Pact, 745; de-Stalinization of, 753; Cuban Missile Crisis, 753, 816; under Khrushchev, 753, p753; under Brezhnev, 753–754; in Middle East, 798; in space race, 831; under Gorbachev, 844–851; arms race, 845, 846, 865; war in Afghanistan, 846, 847; glasnost, 847, 853; perestroika, 847, 849, 853; demokratizatsiya, 848; ethnic unrest in, 849; nationalism in, 849; Union Treaty, 849; collapse of, 851, m851. See also Russia.
Soweto, 793
Soyinke, Wole, 791
Space Age, 831–832, p832
Spain: Byzantine rule of, 181; Muslims in, 188–191, 206, 263–264; Charlemagne in, 208; development as nation, 263–264, m264; Inquisition in, 264; in Italy, 353, 555; exploration by, 360–364, m362; colonies in Americas, 393–397, 536–539, m548; empire of, 393–397, m397; Catholicism in, 398–401; wars with Turks, 399; war with Netherlands, 399–403; Spanish Armada, 400, 420–424, m424; golden age of culture, 400–401; Thirty Years' War, 410–411; threatens England, 422–423; War of Spanish Succession, 446–447; War of Austrian Succession, 456; in American Revolution, 477; and Napoleonic Wars, 497, p497; Napoleon in, 536; trade of, 536; sale of Louisiana Territory, 561–562, m562; imperialism of, 570; in Africa, 572, m573; Spanish-American War, 587–588, 814; fascism in, 693, 701–702, p701; civil war in, 701–702, p701; in Common Market, 750; Cold War, 750–751; in Latin America, 814
Spanish-American War, 587–588, 814
Sparta, 103, 108–114, 119–120
Spartacus, 142
Special creation, 598
Spencer, Herbert, 599–600
Sphere of influence, 581, m582, 586
Spice trade, 359, 364, 404, 425
Spider King. See Louis XI.

Spinning jenny, 512
Spinning mule, 512
On the Spirit of Laws (Montesquieu), 467
Spiritual Exercises (Ignatius), 384
Sputnik I, 831
Squire, 239–240
Sri Lanka, p79, 82
SS, 694, 723
Stadtholder, 403
Stalin, Joseph, 653–657, p655, 698, 707–708, 713, 719, 726, p736, 737, 741–742, 746, 752, 769, 847
Stalingrad, Battle of, 719
Stamp Act, 474–475
Standard of living, 688
Standard Oil Company of Ohio, 549
Stanley, Henry, 571–572, 575
Starry Messenger (Galileo), 388
"Starry Night" (van Gogh), p605
Stasi, 756
States General, Netherlands, 403
Steam power, 509, 513–514, 520, 548, 596
Steel industry, 594, c599, 761
Stephen II, pope, 207
Stephenson, George, 515
Steppe, 283
Stirrup, 206, p206
Stock market, 687–688
Stocks, 549, 764
Stock ticker, 594
Stoicism, 155–157
Stolas, 134
Stone Age, 19–27. See also Neolithic Age; Paleolithic Age.
Stone tools, 19, 20, 22
Storm Troopers, 693
Strait of Magellan, 364
Strategic Arms Limitation Treaty (SALT), 846; (SALT II), 865
Stravinsky, Igor, 606
Stresemann, Gustav, 682
Stuart dynasty, 430–432, 434–435
Suarez, Ines, 397, m397
Subcontinent, 73
Submarine, 628, 632, 709, 713
Sub-Saharan Africa: Mali, 313–314, 322–324; geography of, 315–317, m316, m786; Kush, 317–318, m318; trade of, 317–318; Christianity in, 318–319; Axum, 318–319, m318; Muslims in, 319, 323–324, p323; kingdom of Zimbabwe, 319–320; trade in, 319–325, m321; Songhai empire, 320, 323–324; kingdom of Ghana, 321–322, m321; culture of, 324–325, 790–791; imperialism in, m573, 574; nationalism in, 785–795; agriculture in, 786, 790, 792; economy of, 786, 789–790; problems with independence, 786–788; industrialization of, 789–790
Subsidy, 442
Subsistence farming, 790
Succession, 153
Sudan, 572, 574, 790
Sudd, 53
Sudetenland, 637, 702–703, 707
Suez Canal, 548–549, p548, 572, m668, 718
Suez Crisis, 1956, 797–798

Suffrage. See also Voting rights.
Sugar trade, 474, 807, 814, 816
Suger, abbot, 231
Suharto, 777
Sui dynasty, 277, m278
Sukarno, 777
Sulieman the Magnificent, 452
Sulla, 143–144
Sultan, 195
Sumanguru, 323
Sumatra, 311, 716
Sumerian civilization, 31–37
Summa Theologiae (Aquinas), 238
Sundiata, 323
Sung dynasty, 280–285, m281
Sung T'ai-tsu, Chinese emperor, 280
Sun King. See Louis XIV, French king.
Sunni Ali, 323
Sunni Muslims, 191
Sun Yat-sen, 674–675
Superconductor, 839
Superpower, 736–740
Supply and demand, law of, 467
Supreme Spirit, 324
Surgery, 834
Surplus, 32
Surrealists, 686
Surveying, 69
Susa, 124
Suttee, 303
Swahili, 319, m321
Swaraj, 660, 664
Sweden: Reformation in, 382; Thirty Years' War, 410–411; Great Northern War, 450–451; opposition to Napoleon, 498–499; in World War II, 725
Switzerland, 382, 528
Syllogism, 122
Symphony, 465–466, 534–535
Syracuse, 120
Syria, 44, 161, 636–637, 667, m668, 795–796. See also Fertile Crescent.
Szechwan, 699

Tacitus, 157
Taghaza, 320
Tahiti, 589
Taille, 262
Taillefer, 233
Taiping Rebellion, 581
Taira clan, 293
T'ai-tsung, 277–278
Taiwan, 765, 781
Taj Mahal, 300–301, p300, 306
Takla Makan, 83
Talas, Battle of, 280
The Tale of Genji (Shikibu), 293
Tamerlane, 196, 304–305
T'ang dynasty, 277–280, m278, 292, 311
Tango, 818
Tank, armored, 627, p632, 709, 718–719, 726
Tannenberg, Battle of, 629
Tanzania, 16, 19, 319, 631, 786, 788, 790
Taoism, 88
Tariff, 442
Tartuffe (Molière), 445

932

Tatars, 281, m281, 283

Taxes: in ancient Egypt, 57, p57; in Islamic empire, 190; without representation, 250, 474–475; medieval England, 251–252; in feudal Europe, 261–262; in British colonies, 474–475; in France, 484; by colonial governments, 575

Tchaikovsky, Peter Ilyich, 644

Technology: prehistoric, 19, 21, 22–23, 27; Sumerian, 33; Chinese, 282; of early 1900's, 593–597; between the World Wars, 683–685; since World War II, 831–841; pollution and, 836–837; human impact of, 839–841. *See also* Science.

Tehaucán valley, 326

Tehran, 801

Tel-Aviv, p669

Telegraph, 549, c599

Telephone, 565, 593, 595, c599, 832

Telescope, 388, p388, 464

Television, 791, 832, 839–840, 864

Telstar, 832

Temple: Jewish, 42, p42; Egyptian, 62, p62; Athenian, 115–116, p115; Greek, 126; Roman, 133, 152; Muslim, 188; Inca, 332, p332

Temple of the Jaguar, p333

Temple Mount, 803

Temple of the Sun, 332

Temujin. *See* Genghis Khan.

Ten Commandments, 41, 161

Tenochtitlán, 335, 393–394

Ten Thousand Immortals, 47

Teotihuacán, 334, p334

Territorial integrity, 696

Terrorism, 752, 796, 802–803

Tetzel, Johann, 376

Textile industry, 308, 512–518, p513, p515, p517

Thackeray, William, 554

Thailand, 309–311, 580

Thames River, 426, p426

Thatcher, Margaret, 751–752, p751

Theater. *See* Drama.

Thebes, Egypt, 60, 123

Themistocles, 103, 114

Theocracy, 382

Theodora, Byzantine empress, 183, p183

Theodosius, Roman emperor, 167

Theotokopoulos, Kyriakos. *See* El Greco.

Thermidorian reaction, 491

Thermometer, 389

Thermopylae, 113–114

Third Estate, c263, 484–485, p485

Third Republic, 559–560

Third World, 774, 789

Thirty Years' War, 393, 409–411

Thomson, J.J., 600

Three-field system, 224, c224, 509

Three Fifths Compromise, 478

Three Principles of the People, 674

Thucydides, 119–120

Thuringians, m202

Thutmose III, Egyptian ruler, 61–62

Tiananmen Square, 770–772, p771, p772, 839–840

Tiberius, Roman ruler, 152, c156

Tiber River, 131–132

Tigris River, 31, 34, 44

Tikal, 333

Tillett, Ben, 610

Tilsit, Peace of, 494

Timbuktu, 320, 323, p323

Timisoara massacre, 840, 857

Tin, 42, 576

Tithe, 229

Tito, 742, 860

Titov, Gherman, 831

Titus, Roman emperor, 150

Tiv, 324

Tobacco, 366–367

Tocqueville, Alexis de, 523

Toga, 134, p134

Tokaido Corridor, 763

Tokugawa shogunate, 296, 584

Tokyo, 296, 584, 763–764, c837

Toledo, Spain, 238

Tolstoy, Leo, 554, 644–645

Tonkin Gulf, 778

Tontons Macoutes, 817

Tools: stone, 19, 22; metal, 33; iron, 42–43, 317–318

Topa Inca, 331

Torah, 41, p41

Tordesillas, Treaty of, 363

Torgau, 737–738, p738

Tories, 436

Torricelli, Evangelista, 389

Torrijos, Omar, 818

Totalitarianism, 656–657, 694–695, c695

Total war, 628

Touré, Samori, 574

Tournament, 240

Tours, Battle of, 188, 191, 206

Toussaint L'Ouverture, Pierre, 536, p536, 562

Town charter, 227, c263

Towns: prehistoric, 27; in Middle Ages, 224–227, p225

Townshend, Charles, 510

Tractor, 656, p656

Trade: of Sumer, 31–35; of Phoenicians, 39; of Persian empire, 49; of ancient Egypt, 56, 61; of ancient India, 75; of China, 86, 92–93, 279, 281, 289; of ancient Greece, 106, 109, 111; of Roman republic, 131; of Roman empire, 151–152, 164–165, m165, 202; of Constantinople, 179, m179; of Byzantine empire, 182, m182; of Islamic empire, 191; in Middle Ages, 202, 223–227, 241–242, 245, 263; of Vikings, 212; of Mongols, 285; of Portugal, 308; of Southeast Asia, 309–310; of sub-Saharan Africa, 317–325, m321; silent, 320–321; of Netherlands, 403–404; of Elizabethan England, 425; free, 467, 836; of Britain, 474, 496, 511–512, 518, 580, 690; of Spain, 536; global, 547–550, 835–836, c836; of Japan, 584, 762; of U.S., 687; Common Market, 750; of Europe, 857, 863–864

Trafalgar, Battle of, 494

Tragedy, 445; Greek, 117

Trajan, Roman emperor, 153–154, m154, c156

Transatlantic cable, 549

Transcontinental railroad, 548

Transistor, 833

Transjordan, 636–637, 665, 667, m668

Transportation: in Persian empire, 48; in ancient Egypt, 54, 60; in ancient China, 89–90; in ancient Greece, 103; in Roman empire, 151–152; in China, 277; in Elizabethan England, 426; in France, 442; industrialization and, 514–518, 547–549; in U.S., 565; increase between the World Wars, 683; in West Germany, 747; since World War II, 832. *See also specific modes of transportation.*

Trans-Siberian Railway, 645

Transvaal, 576

Treatises on Government (Locke), 437

Trench warfare, 627–630, p628, p629, p630

Trent, Council of, 384

Trevithick, Richard, 515

Trials by ordeal, 200–201

Tribune, Roman, 142–143

Tribute, 335

Trinidad, 362

Triple Alliance, 622–623, m623, 626

Triple Entente, 623, m623

"Triumphs" (holiday), 141, p143

Triumvirate, 144–145

Trojan War, 106

Trotsky, Leon, 651–654

Troubadour, 240

Troyes, Treaty of, 259–260

Trucial Coast, m668

Truman, Harry S, 720–722, 738, 743–746, 765–767

Truman Doctrine, 743–744

Tshombe, Moise, 788

Tsushima, Battle of, 586

Tswana, c795

Tuberculosis, 600

Tucano, m329

Tudor dynasty, 262, 379–380, 421–429, m424

Tu Fu, 280

Tulip trade, 404

Tull, Jethro, 509

Tumbledown Dick. *See* Cromwell, Richard.

Tunisia, 572, 718, 785

Tupi, m329

Turkestan, 285

Turkey: prehistoric, 27; in World War I, 626; becomes republic, 666; Cold War, 744; in NATO, 745

Turks, 283; invasion of Byzantine empire, 195; invasion of Islamic empire, 195; Seljuk, 195, 241; in India, 303–305, p304; war with Russia, 450. *See also* Ottoman empire.

Turner, Joseph, 535

Turpin of Reims, 216

Tuscany, 555

Tuscarora Indians, 366

Tutankhamon, pharaoh, 52–53, p52, 61–62, 68

Tutu, Desmond, 793

Twelve Tables, 135–136, 158

Two Sicilies, Kingdom of the, 528, 542, 555

Typewriter, 565

Typhus, 598
Tyrant, 109
Tyre, 39

U-boat, 628, 632
Uganda, 574, 786, 788
Uitlanders, 576
Ujamaa village, 790
Ukraine, 450, 713, 849, m851
Ulm, Battle of, 494
Ultimatum, 624
"Ultra" (decoding machine), 712, 719, p719
Ulyanov, Vladimir Ilyich. See Lenin.
Ulysses (Joyce), 686
Umayyad caliphate, 190–191
Umma, 31, 37
Unam Sanctam, 254
Unconscious mind, 685
Underconsumption, 688
Underground, French, 710, p710
Unemployment, p689
Union, labor, 523, 551–553, 601, 610, 645, 757, 794, 809
Union Treaty, 849
United Arab Emirates, 799–800
United Nations, 736, 738, 740; founding of, 739; in Korea, 766–767; creation of Israel, 796; Suez Crisis, 798; Declaration of Human Rights, 841; inspections of Iraq, 866
United Nations Educational, Scientific, and Cultural Organization (UNESCO), 739
United Provinces of the Netherlands, 402–403
United States, m823; European settlements in, 365–367; Spanish exploration of, 396, m397; Constitution of, 468, 477–479, c479; British colonies in, 473–475, m474; American Revolution, 475–478; slavery in, 478, 563–565; War of 1812, 497; industrialization of, 517, c550, 563, 565; Latin America and, 540, 587, 672–673, 809; Monroe Doctrine, 540, 587–589, 672; Civil War, 561–565, p563, p564; Louisiana Purchase, 561–562, m562; westward expansion of, 561–565, m562; war with Mexico, 562–563; economy of, 563, 565, 687–690, 738, 745, c753, 820–822, c820; imperialism of, 570, 586–589; in South Asia, m579; China and, 583, 764–765, 770, 772; trade with Japan, 584, p584; Spanish-American War, 587–588, 814; Panama Canal, 588–589; in Pacific islands, 589; in World War I, 632–634; after World War I, 635–637, 681; Treaty of Versailles and, 637; Good Neighbor Policy, 673; Dawes Plan, 682; isolationism in, 686–687, 701, 712; trade of, 687; Great Depression, 687–690; agriculture in, 688; New Deal, 689–690; in World War II, 701, 712–720, m717, 726–727, 737–738; Pearl Harbor, 715–716, p716, m717; Cold War, 736–746, 765; in U.N., 739; occupation zone in Germany, 741; Truman

Doctrine, 743–744; in NATO, 745; Berlin airlift, 745–746; Cuban missile crisis, 753, 816; occupation of Japan, 761–762; Korean War, 765–767, m765, p765; in Southeast Asia, 778; Vietnam War, 778–779, m779, p779, 821; in Middle East, 798; Iran and, 801–802; Cuba and, 814, 816; commonwealth of Puerto Rico, 817; Haiti and, 817; Panama and, 818; Nicaragua and, 818–819; civil rights movement in, 820–821, p821; after World War II, 820–822; space race, 831; Helsinki Accords, 841; arms race, 846, 865; in Gulf War, 866; in Operation Restore Hope, 867
University: at Constantinople, 184; medieval Europe, 237–238; at Timbuktu, 323; in Japan, 763; in China, 769
Untouchables, 78, 662, 773
Upanishads, 77
Upper class, 610
Upper house, 608
Ur, p30, 34, 37, 75
Ural Mountains, 265
Urban II, pope, 241
Urban VI, pope, 255
Urbanization, 809
Urbino, Duke of, p349
Uruguay, 670
Uruk, 31, 34, 37
Usury, 255
Uthman, caliph, 190
Utopia (More), 374–375
Utopian socialist, 551–552
Utrecht, Treaty of, 446–447, 455

Vaca, Cabeza de, 396
Vaccine, 834
Vaishyas, 78
Valdivia, Pedro de, 397, m397
Valerian, Roman emperor, 165
Valois dynasty, 406–407
Vandals, 167–169, m168, 181, 201, m202
Van Eyck, Jan, 357–358, p358
Van Gogh, Vincent, 604–605, p605
Van Leeuwenhoek, Anton, 389
Vassals, 215–217, 234, 261
Vatican, 355, 557
VCR, 839
Vedas, 77
Vedic Age, 76–77
Velázquez, Diego, 400
Vellum, 237
Venetia, 528, 532, 555–557
Venezuela, 362, 537, 670–673, 807
Venice, 346, 353
Verdi, Giuseppe, 605
Verdun, 629
Verdun, Treaty of, 210–211, m210
Vermeer, Jan, p403, 406, p406
Vernacular, 347
Verne, Jules, 548
Verrazano, Giovanni de, m362, 365
Versailles, 440, p440, 442–445, p444
Versailles, Treaty of, 633–637, p635, m636, 682, 687, 693, 699–701
Vesalius, Andreas, 389
Vespasian, Roman emperor, c156

Vespucci, Amerigo, 362–363, m362
Veto, 136
Veto power, 739
Viceroy, Spanish, 397
Vichy Regime, 711
Victor Emmanuel II, Sardinian king, 555–556
Victor Emmanuel III, Italian king, 692
Victoria, English queen, 547, p568, 580, 609
Vienna, p454, 526–528, p526, 533, 542, p542, 557, 693
Vienna Settlement, 527
Viet Cong, 778–779
Vietminh, 777–778
Vietnam, 309–311, 580, 749, 777–781, m779, p779
Vietnam War, 778–779, m779, p779, 821
Vietnam War Memorial, 821, p821
Vikings, 212–214
Villa, 160
Vindhya Mountains, 76
Virgil, 157
Virginia, 366–367, 474, 476
Virgin Islands, 362
Virgin Queen. See Elizabeth I.
Vishnu (god), 303
Visigoths, 167, m168, 169, 201, m202, 203
Vitellus, Roman emperor, c156
Vladimir, Russian ruler, 194
Vladivostok, 582
Vojvodina, 860, c861, m861
Volga River, 265
Volta, Alessandro, 594
Voltaire, 460–463, p460, 469
Voting rights, 552, 607; universal manhood suffrage, 553; of working class, 553; of women, 553, 602–604, p602, p603, 685, p685, 763
Voyager 2, 832
V-2 rockets, p713

Wagner, Richard, 605
Wake Island, 716
Waldseemüller, Martin, 363
Wales, 519
Walesa, Lech, 757, 853, 858
Wallace, Henry, 743
Wallenberg, Raoul, 725
Wallenstein, Albrecht von, 410–411
Wall Street, 687–690
Walpole, Robert, 473
The Waltz (Ravel), 605–606
Walvis Bay, 794
Warfare: in Sumer, 34, 36–37; of Assyrians, 44; of ancient Egypt, 55–56, 60–61; of ancient China, 89; of ancient Greece, 109, 119–120, 123; of Roman republic, p130, 134, 138, 143–145; of Roman empire, 165; of Byzantine empire, 186; of Ottoman Turks, 197; in Frankish kingdoms, 206; of Vikings, 212; medieval, 215, 261–262; of Mongols, 284; Japanese, 293, 295; Moche, 330; Elizabethan, 423–424; of Russia, 450; Prussian, 455; in American Revolution, 476; guerrilla, 497; scorched-earth policy,

934

934

Acknowledgments

Text Credits

p. 56 From James B. Pritchard, ed., *The Ancient Near East: An Anthology of Texts and Pictures.* Copyright © 1958 by Princeton University Press. Excerpts reprinted with permission of Princeton University Press. p. 81 From *The Teachings of the Compassionate Buddha,* edited by E. A. Burtt, © 1955, published by Mentor. p. 214 From *English Historical Documents,* II, edited by D. C. Douglas and G. E. Greenaway, © 1961, published by Eyre and Spottiswoode, London, pages 969–970. p. 253 From *Memoirs of the Crusades,* Geoffrion de Villehardouin and Jean de Joinville, translated by Sir Frank T. Marziolo, © 1958, published by Dutton. p. 369 From *The African Past,* Basil Davidson, © 1967, Grosset and Dunlap, New York. p. 394 From *The Broken Spears* by Miguel Leon-Portilla, copyright © 1962 by the Beacon Press. Reprinted by permission of Beacon Press. p. 630 From *All Quiet on the Western Front,* Erich Maria Remarque, copyright 1929, 1930 by Little, Brown, and Company, copyright renewed 1957, 1958 by Erich Maria Remarque. p. 614 From *Ten Days that Shook the World* by John Reed, © 1960, published by Random House. p. 685 From "The Waste Land" by T. S. Eliot from *Collected Poems 1900–1935.* © 1963 by T. S. Eliot, published by Faber and Faber, Ltd. p. 655 From *The Gulag Archipelago,* Aleksandr I. Solzhenitsyn, © 1973 by Harper and Row, New York. p. 686 From *Selected Poems* by Langston Hughes, © 1959, published by Alfred A. Knopf, Inc., New York. p. 697 From article by Francis H. Schott in *The New York Times,* November 9, 1988. pp. 706, 707 From *For Those I Loved,* Martin Gray, translated from the French by Anthony White, © 1972 by Little, Brown, and Company and the Bodley Head. p. 724 From *New Voices* by Primo Levi, translated from the Italian by Ruth Feldman, © 1986, Summit Books, a division of Simon and Schuster, Inc. p. 771 From *The San Francisco Examiner,* June 11, 1989. Reprinted by permission. p. 794 From speech by Nelson Mandela, quoted in *The New York Times,* February 12, 1990. p. 819 From speech by Violeta Chamorro, quoted in *The New York Times,* January 25, 1990.

Maps

p. 270 From *A History of Western Society,* Third Edition, by McKay, Hill, Buckler, © 1987, published by Houghton Mifflin Company, page 334. p. 502 From *The French Kings* by Frederic V. Greenfeld, © 1982, published by Stonehenge Press, Inc., pages 8–9. p. 338 From *Lost Empires, Living Tribes* and *Peoples of the Past: The Aztecs*

Tables and Graphs

p. 511 R. Davis, "English Foreign Trade, 1700–1774," *Economic History Review,* 2d series, 15 (1962): 302–303). p. 550 *P. Kennedy, The Rise and Fall of the Great Powers. Random House, New York, 1987, p. 149./W. Woodruff, Impact of Western Man: A Study of Europe's Role in the World Economy. St. Martin's Press, New York, 1967, p. 313 and references cited therein.* p. 613 P. Kennedy, *The Rise and Fall of the Great Powers,* page 202. p. 614 *Historical Statistics of the United States/E. J. Hobsbawm,* Age of Revolution, NAL. p. 689 *League of Nations, Statistical Yearbook for 1993–1934 and 1938–1939.* p. 750 *Organization for Economic Cooperation and Development.* p. 753 *Data Resources.* p. 800 *The American Petroleum Institute.* p. 820 *U.S. Statistical Abstracts, 1987.* p. 826 *D. Phillips and S. Levi, The Pacific Rim Region,* Enslow Publishers, Inc., 1988. p. 836 *International Monetary Fund,* Direction of Trade Statistics, Yearbook, 1987, *pages 2–7, 397; CIA, 1987 World Factbook, page 4. Compiled by World Eagle, February, 1988.*

Art Credits

Photo Research: Carole Frohlich
Art Editor: Penny Peters
Maps: pp. 872, 874–884, R. R. Donnelley & Sons; Locator globes, pp. 32, 55, 74, 83, 104, 163, 189, 235, 316, 329, 424, 471, 518, 538, 558, 579, 636, 676, 799, 815, atlas map, 873, Mapping Specialists Limited; all other maps, Richard D. Pusey/Charthouse
Illustrations: pp. 14–15, 35, 59, 100–101, 109, 116, 158, 176–177, 215, 218, 224, 232, 274–275, 288, 338, 342–343, 418–419, 429, 506–507, 618–619, 734–735, Tony Smith, Virgil Pomfret Agency

Graphs and charts: pp. 40, 68r, 352, 515, 519, James R. Hamilton; Graph p. 498, after Charles Joseph Minard, 1861; Graphs and charts pp. 511, 550, 614, 689, 750, 753, 800, 820, 826, 836, Fern Sandhouse; Charts pp. 85, 111, 136, 167, 193, 245, 263, 296, 386, 433, 436, 446, 473, 479, 496, 599, 633, 653, 695, 726, 743, 795, 837, Camille Venti
Time line illustrations: pp. 98*tl,* 99*tr,* 174*r,* 341*l,* 417*r,* 616*l,* Leslie Evans
Chapter review time lines: James R. Hamilton, Camille Venti, Claudia Abramson

Photo Credits

Cover: *l* An Keren PPS/Photo Researchers; *m* National Archaeological Museum, Athens; *r* Museum of Ife Antiquities.

Contents: iii*l* Scala/Art Resource **(AR)**; *tr* Wiltshire Archaeological & Natural History Society, Devizes, England; *br* Michael Holford. iv*tl* Dallas & Heaton/TSW-CLICK-Chicago; *bl, r* Courtesy of the Trustees of the British Museum **(BM)**. v*tl* Michael Holford; *bl* Biblioteca Apostolica Vaticana. vi*bl* Bibliotheque royale Albert 1ᵉʳ, Brussels; *r* Sonia Halliday. vii*bl* Bradley Smith Collection/Laurie Platt Winfrey, Inc.; *r* Eliot Elisofon Archives/Museum of African Art (Smithsonian Institution); viii*l* AR; *tr* Academia das Ciências, Lisbon. ix*bl* New York Public Library. x*tr* Ann Ronan Picture Library; *br* Don Hamilton, Photography. xi*tl* Compiègne Chateau/Bulloz; *bl* Brown Bros. xii*l* TASS Sovfoto; *tr* Trustees of the Imperial War Museum **(IWM)**; *br* Peter Menzel. xiii*tl* Bildarchiv Preussischer Kulturbesitz; *tr* Wide World Photos; *br* Bundesarchiv, Koblenz. xiv*l* © Margaret Courtney-Clarke; *tr* Gamma-Liaison; *br* P. Dale Ware/DDB Stock Photo. xv*l* Shepard Sherdell/Saba Press Photos; *r* National Aeronautics and Space Administration. xix*l* George Holton/Photo Researchers; *r* Michael Holford. xx © David Muench 1991.

Student Guide: 1 Anthony Suau/Black Star. 3 Bi/Gamma-Liaison. 6, 7*l* Robert Frerck/Odyssey Productions; 7*r* Anne Bolt. 8 Robert Frerck/Odyssey Productions. 9 GEOPIC™, Earth Satellite Corporation.

Unit I: 12*t* Sasaki Scanlon/Comstock; *l* Scala/AR; *m* Cultural Relics Bureau, Beijing, and Metropolitan Museum of Art **(MMA)**; *r* Jehangir Gazdar/Woodfin Camp & Associates. 13*l, br* Michael Holford; *m* © 1988 Dallas & Heaton/TSW-CLICK-Chicago; *tr* Courtesy of The Oriental Institute of the University of Chicago. 16 John Reader/Science Photo Library/Photo Researchers. 18 Reproduced with permission from *LUCY: The Beginnings of Humankind.* 19 John Reader/Science Photo Library/Photo Researchers. 20 Ralph S. Solecki. 23 Amplicaciones y Reproducciones "MAS." 25*l* Tassiti Fresco, n. Aijer, South Algeria; *r* Giraffe rock painting from Jabbaren. Henri Lhote, Montrichard, France. 26*l* Hank Morgan/Rainbow; *r* Musée de St. Germain-en-laye/Photo R.M.N. 27: D.R. Baston. 30 (detail) Standard of Ur, peace panel. Mosaic, ca 2500 B.C. BM. 33*t* Michael Holford; *b* Hirmer Verlag München. 36 Musee de Louvre. Scala/AR. 37 Statuette of seated couple, gypsum, ca 2500 B.C. Iraqi National Museum, Baghdad. Courtesy of The Oriental Institute of The University of Chicago. 39 Stele of Hammurabi, black basalt, h: 8'. Late Larsa period, 1930–1888 B.C. Hirmer Verlag München. 41 Jewish Museum of New York/AR. 42*l* A. Louis Goldman/Photo Researchers; *r* Silver calf and model shrine, on byre, ca 1600–1550 B.C. Courtesy of the Leon Levy Expedition to Ashkelon/Carl Andrews. 44 BM/Michael Holford. 45 Erich Lessing/Magnum. 46 Erich Lessing Culture and Fine Arts Archive. 48 George Holton/Photo Researchers; *r* Sassoon/Robert Harding Picture Library. 52 Lee Boltin Picture Library. 54 E. Streichan/Superstock. 56 BM/Michael Holford. 57*t* (detail) Harvest scene, Tomb of Menna. Dynasty XVII, Time of Tuthmosis IV-Amenhotpe III. (MMA); *b* The Narmer Palette, carved schist, h: 29¼", ca 3100 B.C. Jean Vertut. 59 Michael Holford. 61 Egyptian Museum, Cairo. John G. Ross/Mediterranean Archives. 62 George Holton/Photo Researchers. 64 BM/Michael Holford. 65*t* BM; *b* Reproduced by permission of the Syndics of the Fitzwilliam Museum, Cambridge. (Acc. no. E. 343-1954). 66 Egyptian Museum, Cairo. 67*l* Khafre

937

protected by the falcon Horus, diorite, H: 66-⅛". Dynasty IV. Egyptian Museum, Cairo; *m* Staatliche Museen, Berlin/Hirmer Verlag München; *r* John G. Ross/Newsweek Books Picture Collection/Laurie Platt Winfrey, Inc. 66 BM. 72 Roland & Sabrina Michaud/Woodfin Camp & Associates. 75*l* Paolo Koch/Photo Researchers; *r* Jehangir Gazdar/Woodfin Camp & Associates. 77 The British Library (**BL**)/Michael Holford. 79 C. M. Dixon Colour Photo Library. 81 Michael Holford. 82 © 1972 Raghubir Singh. 85 Cultural Relics Bureau, Beijing, and MMA. 86 The Seattle Art Museum, Eugene Fuller Memorial Collection. 88 Collection of The National Palace Museum, Taipei, Taiwan, Republic of China. 90 © 1988 Dallas & Heaton/TSW-CLICK-Chicago. 91 Pang Wei-liang/Xinhua News Agency. 93 Robert Harding Picture Library. 97*t* BM; *b* Michael Holford.

Unit II: 98*t* (detail) From the Villa of the Mysteries, Pompeii. Scala/AR; *b* Michael Holford. 99*bl* Giraudon/AR; *tr* Museo Nazionale, Naples/Fotografia Foglia. 102 R. Manley/Superstock. 105 Fresco, Palace of Knossos. Archaeologisches Museum Stierspringer/Hirmer Verlag München. 107*l*Diskobolos (Disk-thrower). Conjectural restoration of the statue, ca 450 B.C. by Miron. MMA, Dodge Fund, 1907 (07.96); *m*, *r* BM. 112 MMA, Rogers Fund, 1917 (17.230.14a). 115 National Archaeological Museum, Athens. 117*l* Robert Frerck/Odyssey Productions; *r* Archaeological Museum, Piraeus/Ekdotike Athenon. 118*l* Caecilia H. Krüger-Moessner; *m* BM; *r* Museo Nazionale Taranto. Giraudon/AR. 119 BM. 121 MMA, Catharine Lorillard Wolfe Fund, 1931 (31.45). 125 (detail) "La Battaglia di Alessandro." Museo Nazionale, Naples. Scala/AR. 127*l* Ekdotike Athenon; *m* Pergamum Museum, Berlin; *r* Lauros-Giraudon/AR. 130 (detail) Trajan's Column, Rome, 1st century AD. Josephine Powell, Rome. 132 Emmett Bright/Photo Researchers. 134 Giraudon/AR. 135 Stela of Lucius Erennius Praesens. Musée Calvet, Avignon. 142 (detail) Mosaic of Dar Bue Ammera, from Aliten. Musée des Antiquities, Tripoli. Pierre Belzeaux/Rapho/Photo Researchers. 143 (detail) Marcus Aurelius Column, Piazza Colonna, Rome, 1st century A.D. Josephine Powell, Rome. 144 Capitoline Museum, Rome. © Madeline Grimoldi. 147 BM. 150 Josephine Powell, Rome. 152 Robert Frerck/Odyssey Productions. 153 Museum of Roman Civilization, Rome. 154 Thomas B. Hollyman/Photo Researchers. 159*l* Roman wall painting from Boscoreale, Panel II. MMA, Rogers Fund, 1903 (03.14.13); *m*, *r* Museo Nazionale, Naples/Fotografia Foglia. 173*t* BM; *b* Emmett Bright/Photo Researchers.

Unit III: 174*t* "Les Très Riches Heures du Duc de Berry," May, 15th c. Private collection. The Bridgeman Art Library; *bl* Constantinople, *Notitia Dignatatum*, 1436. MS. Canon. Misc. 378, f. 84. Bodleian Library, Oxford; *bm* Saint Benedict in front of Monte Cassino, the monastery he founded. Ai. 1 Ai. 1202 f. 11². Biblioteca Apostolica Vaticana. 175*bl* Sonia Halliday; *bm* BL; *tr* Astrolabe, 1291. MMA, Bequest of Edward C. Moore, 1891. The Edward C. Moore Collection (91.1.535 a-h); *br* Robert Frerck/Odyssey Productions. 178 Alon Reininger/Contact Press Images. 180 Emperor Justinian and his court, A.D. 546–548, mosaic at San Vitale, Ravenna. Scala/AR. 183 (detail) Theodore, mosaic at San Vitale. Scala/AR. 184 K. Scholz/Superstock. 187 Camerapix, Nairobi. 188 Page from a Qur'an, late 11th c. Courtesy of The Harvard University Art Museums (Arthur M. Sackler Museum). Private collection. 190 MMA, The James F. Ballard Collection, Gift of James F. Ballard, 1922. Otto Nelson, photographer. 192 From an Ottoman illuminated manuscript, late 16th c. The Granger Collection. 200 C. M. Dixon Colour Photo Library. 204 Vittoriano Rastelli. 205 Lindisfarne Gospels, Northumbria, ca 1700. Initial age of the Gospel according to Saint John. Cotton MS. Nero D. IV. 51. 206 BM. 208 Metz Cathedral. Giraudon/AR. 212*l* Statens Historiska, Museet, Stockholm/Werner Forman Archive; *m* Viking Ship Museum, Bygdøy, Oslo/Werner Forman Archive; *r* © University Museum of National Antiquities, Oslo. Eirik Irgens Johnsen, photographer. 216 Add. MS 20698, f. 17. BL. 218 (detail) Luttrell Psalter, 1335–40 A.D. Add. MS 42130, f. 171. BL. 222 (detail) #E 2432-c, Cod 2549, fol. 164. Österreichische Nationalbibliothek, Vienna. 223 *Hours of the Virgin*, MS 399 (September). Courtesy of The Pierpont Morgan Library, NY. 225 (detail) *Ethiques politiques et économiques d'Aristote*. Ms. 927, fol. 145R. Musée Municipal, Rouen. Giraudon/AR. 227 (detail) *Chronique de Hainaut*, Ms. 9242, fol. 274 verso. Bibliothèque royale Albert 1ᵉʳ, Brussels. 230 (detail) *Livre de la vie active des réligieuses de l'Hôtel-Dieu*, 15th c. Musée

de l'Assistance Publique, Paris. 232*bl* Sonia Halliday; *br* Michael Holford. 234 (detail) Bayeux Tapestry, ca 1100 A.D., Bayeux, France; presumed to be the work of Matilda, queen of William the Conqueror. Michael Holford. 237 Pietro di Pavia illuminating an initial. From *Naturalis historia*, Pliny, 1389. Biblioteca Ambrosiana, Milan. 239*l* (detail) *Chronique de Hainaut*, Ms. 9242, fol. 48 verso. Bibliothèque royale Albert 1ᵉʳ, Brussels; *r* (detail) Siege of Antioch, Ms. Fr. 9084, f. 53r. Bibliothèque Nationale, Paris. 240 (detail) *Heures de la Bienheureuse Vierge Marie* (November). Dutuit B. 37, fol. 15r. Petit Palais, Paris/Bulloz. 244*l* Bildarchiv Foto Marburg/AR; *r* R. Manley/Superstock. 248 Equestrian statue of Joan of Arc by Pierre Juleo Roulleau. Place de l'Hotel de Ville, Chinon. Robert Descharnes, Paris. 251 Add. MS 4838, The Article of Barons, 1215. BL. 252 Windsor Castle, Royal Library © 1989 Her Majesty Queen Elizabeth II. 253 Cultural Service of the French Embassy. 255 (detail) Bishop Lendit blessing the fair, 15th c. Sonia Halliday. 257 MS 13076-77, fol. 24 verso. Bibliothèque royale Albert 1ᵉʳ, Brussels. 259 (detail) *Chronique d'Angleterre*, Jeane de Wavrin. Royal 14 EIV fol. 59. Flemish, late 15th c. BL. 267 TASS/Sovfoto. 271*t* Giraudon/AR; *b* BL.

Unit IV: 272*t* Robert Frerck/Odyssey Productions; *bl, bm* Lee Boltin Picture Library; *br* (detail) *The Tale of Genji*, Scroll, 12th c. Artist unknown. Tokugawa Art Museum, Nagoya. Bradley Smith Collection from Laurie Platt Whinfrey, Inc. 273*ml* The Board of Trustees of the Royal Armouries, London; *bl, m* Lee Boltin Picture Library; *tr* Bradley Smith Collection/Laurie Platt Winfrey, Inc. *br* Courtesy, Museum of New Mexico (neg. no. 14377). 276 Edimedia. 279 From a Ch'ing album. OE 5 a fol. p. 31/RcC 1486. Bibliothèque Nationale, Paris. 280 Wan-go H. C. Weng. 282*l* "Pine and Mountains in Spring," Mi Fei. National Palace Museum, Taipei, Taiwan, Republic of China; *r* Narcissus-bulb or flower pot stand; China, Chin (960–1234) to Yuan (1279–1368) dynasty. Courtesy of The Harvard University Art Museums (The Arthur M. Sackler Museum). Gift of Ernest B. Dane, 1892 and Helen P. Dane. 284 By courtesy of the Board of Trustees of the Victoria and Albert Museum. 286 Portrait of Kubilai Khan, Anonymous, 13th c., ink and color on silk. National Palace Museum, Taipei/Wan-go H. C. Weng. 288 National Palace Museum, Taipei/Wan-go H. C. Weng. 292 Benrido Company, Ltd., Kyoto. 294 The Board of Trustees of the Royal Armouries, London. 297*l* Burt Glinn/Magnum; *r* © 1988 Bob Brudd/TSW-CLICK/Chicago. 300 Ric Ergenbright. 303 Robert Ivey/Ric Ergenbright Photography. 304 Qutb Minār, begun by Qutb ad-Dīn Aybak about 588/1192 as a monument to the victory of the Turks over India. From THE ART OF INDIA, Calambus Sivaramurti (Harry N. Abrams, Inc.) Jean-Louis Nou, photographer. 307 Reproduced by permission of The India Office Library (BL). 308 (detail) India, Golconda or northern Madras. Painting on cotton, 1630–40 A.D. The Brooklyn Museum (14.719.2), Museum Collection Fund. 311 Superstock. 314 (detail) Catalan Atlas of 1375 by Abraham Cresques. Bibliothèque Nationale, Paris. 317 Nok terracotta head ca 500 B.C./ca 200 A.D.; h. 36 cm. From Rafin Kura, Nok. National Museum, Lagos, 79.R.1. 319 Kal Muller/Woodfin Camp & Associates. 320 Waugh/Peter Arnold, Inc. 322 Bibliothèque Nationale, Paris. 323 Aldona Sabalis/Photo Researchers. 325*l* Eliot Elisofon Archives/Museum of African Art (Smithsonian Institution); *r* Bronze plaque of mounted king and attendants. Court of Benin, Bini Tribe, ca 1550–1680. Metalworkbronze. MMA, The Michael C. Rockefeller Memorial Collection, Gift of Nelson A. Rockefeller, 1965. (1978.412.309). 328*l* © David Muench 1991; *r* Woman using metate, 0–500 A.D. Bradley Smith Collection/Laurie Platt Winfrey, Inc. 331*l* Martha Cooper © National Geographic Society; *r* Christopher B. Donnan. 332 George Holton/Photo Researchers. 333*l* Archeological Museum Jalapa, Veracruz, Mexico. Nathaniel Tarn/Photo Researchers; *tr* Maya sundish used to calculate day and year. Lee Boltin Picture Library; *mr* (detail) South Wall of the Upper Temple of Jaguars, Chichén-Itzá. Mural by Adela C. Breton. Peabody Museum, Harvard University. Photograph by Hillel Burger; *br* Maya ball player, from Jaina, Campeche, ca 700–900 A.D. Bradley Smith Collection/Laurie Platt Winfrey, Inc. 334 Robert Llewellyn/Superstock. 335 Stuart Cohen/Comstock. 339*t* Courtesy of The Harvard University Museums (The Arthur M. Sackler Museum), *b* Eliot Elisofon Archives/Museum of African Art (Smithsonian Institution).

Unit V: 340*t* Portuguese carracks in Lisbon Harbor, by Gregorio Lopes, 1521. National Maritime Museum/Michael Holford; *m* (detail) "Porto del Paradiso," Ghiberti. Florence. Scala/AR; *bl* (detail) "Crucifixion," Giotto, Padua. Capella Scrovegni. Scala/AR; *br* Engraving by Johannes Stradanus (Belgian, 1523–1605). Giraudon/AR. 341*m* Fotomas Index; *tr* Scala/AR; *br* (detail) "Flowers and Baluser, Motifs," 17th c. Philadelphia Museum of Art; 344 Copy of Map of Catena, Florence, 1490, S. Buonsignori. Museum of Florence. Scala/AR. 345 Bibliothèque de l'Institut de France. 348 "The School of Athens," 1509–11, Raphael. Stanza della Segnatura, Vatican. Scala/AR. 349*l* "Battista Sforza," Piero della Francesca. Uffizi. Scala/AR; *r* "Federico da Montelfeltro, Duke of Urbino," Piero della Francesca. Uffizi. Scala/AR. 352 "Story of St. Peter: Resurrection of Tabitha, and Healing of Cripple," ca 1425, Masaccio. Brancassi Chapel, S. Maria del Carmine, Florence. Scala/AR. 353 New York Public Library. 354 "Pieta," 1497–9, Michelangelo Buanarroti (1475–1564). St. Peter's, Rome. Scala/AR. 355*l* "David," 1501–4, Michelangelo Buanarroti. Accademia, Florence. Scala/AR; *r* Scala/AR. 357 "Mona Lisa," 1503, Leonardo da Vinci. Musée de Louvre. Scala/AR. 358 "The Marriage of Giovanni Arnolfini and Giovanna Cenami," Jan van Eyck (Flemish, 1422–1441). Cat. No. 186. Reproduced by courtesy of the Trustees, The National Gallery, London. 360*l* From *Chronicle of the Discovery and Conquest of Guinea*, 1453. Gomes Eanes de Zurara. Bibliothèque Nationale, Paris; *m* Magnetic compass by José da Costa Miranda. Whipple Museum of the History of Science, University of Cambridge; *r* Dundee Art Galleries & Museums. 361*m* Duke of Alba's Collection, Madrid; *r* Painting by Ridolfo Ghirlandaio (attr.). Museo Navale, Pegli. Scala/AR. 362 (detail) The Fleet of Vasco da Gama, in *Memoire of the Armadas that Journeyed from Portugal to India*, 16th c., Anonymous. Academia das Ciências, Lisbon. 363 (detail) Fleet of Pedro Álvares Cabral, in *O Sucesso dos Visoreis*, mid-16th c., Lizuarte de Abreu. The Pierpont Morgan Library, New York. M. 525, f. 17. 364 (detail) "Treatise of Pieto de Cresienzi," end 15th c. *Le Livre de Rustican des Prioffiz rurals*. BL. 366*l,r* Drawings, 1585, by John White, artist and later Governor of the 1587 English Colony at Roanoke. BM. 368 The Granger Collection, NY. 373 (detail) "Traum zu Schwinitz," Lucas Cranach the Elder (1472–1553). Courtesy, Dr. Henning Schleifenbaum, Siegen, Germany. 374 (detail) "Sir Thomas More," Hans Holbein. Copyright The Frick Collection, New York. 375 Engraving by Johannes Stradanus. Giraudon/AR. 376 "Martin Luther," 1526, Lucas Cranach the Elder. Nationalmuseum, Stockholm. 380 Painting from the studio of Hans Holbein. By kind permission of Warwick Castle, England. 381 Musée Condé, Chantilly. Giraudon/AR. 385*l* Bibliothèque publique et universitaire, Geneva; *r* Papal Coronation of Pius II, 3 Sept. 1458, Siena. Duomo, Libreria Piccolomini. Scala/AR. 388*l* Museo della Scienza, Florence. Scala/AR; *r* Gal. 48 c. 29v. Biblioteca Nazionale Centrale, Florence. Guido Sansoni, photographer. 392 Cat. #2183, Anonymous. Government Art Collection, London. Courtesy, Miss Lucie Strickland. 394 From *Lienzo de Tlaxcalla* Codex. The Granger Collection. 395 R. Manley/Superstock. 396 Oronoz Photo Archives, Madrid. 399*l* Reproduced by permission of Patrimonio Nacional. Amplicaciones y Reproducciones "MAS"; *r* Portrait by Alonson Sanchez. © Museo del Prado, Madrid. 400 "San Bernadino de Siena," El Greco. Museo-Casa Greco. Amplicaciones y Reproducciones, "MAS." 403 "The Little Street," Johannes Vermeer (Dutch, 1632–1675). Rijksmuseum-Stichting, Amsterdam. 404 (detail) "Flowers and Baluser, Motifs," 17th c. CAT #77. Philadelphia Museum of Art. Gift of Mrs. Francis P. Garvan. Eric Mitchell, photographer. 405 "The Nightwatch," Rembrandt van Rijn. Rijksmuseum-Stichting, Amsterdam. 406 (detail) "Young Woman with a Water Jug," Johannes Vermeer. MMA, Gift of Henry G. Marquand, 1889. Marquand Collection (89.15.21). 408 "Cardinal Richelieu Swearing the Order of the Holy Ghost," Philippe de Champaigne (French, 1602–1674). Musée de Louvre. Giraudon/AR. 415*tl* Scala/AR; *tr* Biblioteca Nazionale Centrale, Florence; *b* Scala/AR.

Unit VI: 416*t* George Holton/Photo Researchers; *ml* By kind permission of the Marquess of Tavistock, and the Trustees of the Bedford Estates; *mr* Painting by H. Rigaud. Musée de Louvre. Scala/AR; *br* "Self-portrait with first wife Isabella Brandt," Peter Paul Rubens. Alte Pinakothek Munchen. 417*l* New York Public Library, Slavonic Division; *m* (detail) "Die Tafelrunde," J. Tietze. Bildarchiv Preussischer Kulturbesitz; *tr* (detail) "Liberty," 1793–94, Nanine Vallain. Musée de la Révolution Francaise Vizille; *br* Musée Carnavalet, Paris/Jean-Loup Charmet. 420 "Armada Por-

trait," ca 1588, George Gover (attr.). By kind permission of the Marquess of Tavistock, and the Trustees of the Bedford Estates. 426–7 Visscher's View of London, MAP L85c no. 7 c.l. By permission of the Folger Shakespeare Library. 428 Portrait of William Shakespeare by Chardos. National Portrait Gallery, London. 431 Art Resource. 435 "Great Fire of London," Dutch School. Museum of London. 440 Giraudon/AR. 443 Painting by H. Rigaud. Musée de Louvre. Scala/AR. 444 Scala/AR. 448 "Peter the Great," Russian School. Rijksmuseum-Stichting, Amsterdam. 449 New York Public Library, Slavonic Division. 451 Bibliothèque Nationale, Paris/Bulloz. 454*l* Painting by Möller. Kunsthistorisches Museum, Vienna; *r* Schuster/Superstock. 456 (detail) "Mozart as a Child with his Father and his Sister," Louis Carmotelle. Musée Condé, Chantilly. Giraudon/AR. 457*l* AKG, Berlin; *tr* Colored engraving by Daniel Chodowiecki, 1777. AKG, Berlin; *br* Editions Peters, Leipzig. 460 "Die Tafelrunde," is a copy by Joachim Tietze, Berlin, of the painting, 1850, by Adolph von Menzel (destroyed in 1945). Bildarchiv Preussischer Kulturbesitz. 463 "Une Soirée chez Madame Geoffrin," Anicet-Charles-Gabriel Lemonnier (French, 1793–1824). Musée des Beaux-Arts, Rouen. Giraudon/AR. 465 Courtesy, Wellcome Institute, London. 466 Painting of a concert in a Venetian palace, 18th c., Anonymous. Casa di Goldoni, Venice. 468 From a medallion by Tassiel; engraved by W. Hott. The Bettmann Archive. 470 Painting by Groot, 1745. Leningrad Russian Museum/Novosti Press Agency. 477*l* Independence National Historical Park Collection; *r* Robert Llewellyn. 482 "Pillage des Invalides," J.-B. Lallemand fils. Musée Carnavalet, Paris/Bulloz. 485 "Le Serment du Jeu de Paume," d'après Jacques-Louis David. Musée Carnavalet, Paris/Bulloz. 486*l* "La Maraichère," Jacques-Louis David (French, 1748–1825). Musée des Beaux-Arts, Lyon; *r* Painting by Gautier d'Agoty. Bulloz. 488 (detail) "Liberty, 1793–4, Nanine Vallain. Oil on canvas. Musée de la Révolution Francaise Vizille. 490 "Execution of Louis XVI, January 21, 1793, Anon. Musée Carnavalet, Paris. Bradley Smith Collection/Laurie Platt Winfrey, Inc. 493 "Napoleon in His Study," Jacques Louis David. National Gallery of Art, Washington, D.C. Samuel H. Kress Collection. 497 "The Third of May, 1808," 1814–15, Francisco de Goya y Lucientes. Oil on canvas; 8'8" × 11' 3½". (c) Museo del Prado, Madrid. 503 Scala/AR.

Unit VII: 504*t* "The Docks of Cardiff," 1896, Lionel Walden (American, 1861–1933). Musée d'Orsay, Paris. Giraudon/AR; *ml* Kunsthistorisches Museum, Vienna; *bl* Michael Holford; *tr* Organization of American States; *br* (detail) "Wanderer über dem Nebelmeer," Caspar David Friedrich. Hamburger Kunsthalle. 505*ml* © Don Hamilton Photography; *bl* Culver Pictures; *tr* (detail) Historisches Museen der Stadt Wien; *mr* The Bettmann Archive; *br* (detail) "Lady with a Parasol and a Small Child on a Sunlit Hillside," Pierre Auguste Renoir (French, 1841–1919). Oil on canvas, 18½' × 22". Bequest of John R. Spaulding. Museum of Fine Arts, Boston. 508 Ann Ronan Picture Library, Somerset, England. 510 Henlow enclosure, from a map by John Goodman Maxwell, 1798. Bedfordshire County Record Office. 513*l,r* Mansell Collection. 516 Ann Ronan Picture Library, Somerset, England. 517 Museum of American Textile History. 521 Illustration appended to British Parliamentary Commission's report on work in mines, 1844. 522 Mansell Collection. 526 "Redoute paree am 10. November 1814," J. N. Hochle. Österreichische Nationalbibliothek, Vienna. 527 Copyright reserved to her Majesty Queen Elizabeth II. 530 (detail) Historisches Museen der Stadt Wien. 532 National Portrait Gallery, London. 533 "Henri de la Rochejacquelein," P. Guerin. Musée Municipal de Cholet/Studio Golder. 534*l* Bodleian Library, Oxford; *mt* Portrait of George Sand by Eugene Delacroix. Jean-Loup Charmet; *mb* Mansell Collection; *r* "Wanderer über dem Nebelmeer," Caspar David Friedrich. Hamburger Kunsthalle. 536 The Granger Collection, N.Y. 537 Organization of American States. 542 "Am 13. Marz 1848 vor dem Landeshause," J. Albert. Historisches Museen der Stadt Wien. 546 The Bridgeman Art Library. 548 "Inauguration of the Suez Canal," 1869, Edward Riou. Compiegne Chateau/Bulloz. 553 "The Third-Class Carriage," Honoré Daumier (French, 1808–1879). Oil on canvas. MMA, Bequest of Mrs. H. O. Havemeyer, 1929. The H. O. Havemeyer Collection (29.100.129). 554 Bettmann/Hulton. 556 Portrait by Francesco Hayez. Giraudon/AR. 558 The Bettmann Archive. 560 The Granger Collection, NY. 563 The Bettmann Archive. 564 Library of Congress. Alexander Gardner, photographer. 568 "Celebrations in India 1897," M. E. Caddy. The Bridgeman Art Library. 575*l* Slit drum, Barambo. Wood. Courtesy Department of Library Services, American Museum of Natural History. Photo by Lynton Gardiner. (Cat. no. 90.1/3670); *m* Bakota guardian figure from an ancestral shrine, Zaire. Wood covered with copper and brass. Friede Collection, New York/Werner Forman Archive; *r* Harp, Mangbetu. Wood, pangolin scales, plant fiber, pitch. Courtesy Department of Library Services, American Museum of Natural History. Photo by Lynton Gardiner. (Cat. no. 90.1/3969). 577 Lady Impey and her servants. Lawrence Impey, Hampshire, England. 578 (detail) "Scots Guards, attached to Guards Camel Corps, Nile Expedition, 1885," Lt. Frank Baden-Powell. National Army Museum, London. 581 Peabody Museum of Salem. 583 Jean-Loup Charmet. 584 "Commodore Perry Landing in Japan," Tsukioki Yoshitoshi. BM. 585 Exterior of the Tomioka silk reeling factory, ca 1870. Tsuneo Tamba Collection, Yokahama, Japan. Japan Information Bureau, London. 587 The Granger Collection, NY. 588 Wide World Photos. 592 Musée Toulouse-Lautrec, Albi. 593 Association des Amis de Jacques Henri Lartigue, Paris. 595 Science Museum, London/Michael Holford. 597 Science Museum, London. Reproduced by permission of George Weidenfeld & Nicolson Limited. 599 Brown Brothers. 601 Mary Evans Picture Library/Photo Researchers. 602*l* Library of Congress; *r* Museum of London. 603 © 1977, 1986 Organization for Equal Education of the Sexes. 605*l* (detail) "Gladioli," 1893, Claude Monet (French, 1840–1926). Oil on canvas, 22″ × 32½″. The Detroit Institute of Arts, City of Detroit (21.71); *r* "The Starry Night," 1889, Vincent van Gogh. Oil on canvas, 29″ × 36¼″. Collection, the Museum of Modern Art, NY. 606 National Baseball Hall of Fame and Museum, Inc. 609 Mary Evans Picture Library/Photo Researchers. 610 "Sirk-Ecke," 1900, Maxilian Lenz. Historisches Museen der Stadt Wien. 615*t* Michael Holford; *b* BM.

Unit VIII: 616*t* Hugo Jaeger, Life Magazine © Time Warner Inc.; *bm* "L'Après-midi d'un Faune: Portrait of Nijinsky as the Faun," 1912, Leon Bakst. Wadsworth Atheneum, Hartford. From the Serge Lifar Collection. The Ella Gallup Sumner and Mary Catlin Sumner Collection; *br* Robert Frerck/Odyssey Productions. 617*ml* (detail) TASS/Sovfoto; *bl* Jean-Loup Charmet; *m* Courtesy, Royal Air Force Museum, England; *tr* "The Spinner," 1946, Margaret Bourke-White, Life Magazine © Time Warner Inc.; *mr* Copyright 1945 Time Inc. Reprinted by permission; *br* United Nations/J. Isaac, photographer. 620 From *Le Petit Journal*, July 19, 1914. Jean-Loup Charmet. 621 © Librairie Larousse. 622 Robert Hunt Library. 625*l,m* ET Archive Ltd.; *r,* 627 IWM. 628 "Over the Top," John Nash. IWM. 629 "Gassed," John Singer Sargent. IWM. 630 AKG, Berlin. 632 IWM. 635 "Peace Conference," Orpen. IWM. 640 "Working People Arise" by V. Serov. S.D.R. Library. 642 "Volga's Barge Haulers," 1870–73, I. Repin. Novosti Press Agency. 645*l* Brown Brothers; *r* © The Forbes Magazine Collection, NY. Larry Stein, photographer. 647 Sovfoto. "The Bolshevik," 1920, oil on canvas. 649*l* Roger-Viollet; "The Russian and the German proletarians of all nations unite." Porcelain propaganda plate, 1921, after a design by Alexandra Shchekotikhina-Pototskaya. © Christies. 650 Painting by Axenov. TASS/Sovfoto. 655, 656 TASS/Sovfoto. 657 "By Force of Arms," 1921. From *Art of the October Revolution*, Mikhail Guerman (Aurora Publishers, Leningrad). Reproduced by permission of V/O Vneshtorgizdat. 660 The Bettmann Archive. 663 UPI/Bettmann. 664 "The Spinner," 1946, Margaret Bourke-White, Life Magazine © Time Warner Inc. 666 Courtesy of Andromeda (Oxford) Ltd. 667 Royal Geographical Society Picture Library, London. 669 By courtesy of Jewish National Fund Photo Archives, Jerusalem. 671 "Zapatistas," 1931, José Clemente Orozco. Oil on Canvas, 45″ × 55″. Collection, The Museum of Modern Art, NY. Given anonymously. 672 (detail) Mural by Diego Rivera. National Palace, Mexico City. Peter Menzel. 675 Jack Wilkes, Life Magazine © Time Warner Inc. 677 PRC/Sovfoto. 680 "KPA Versammlung, 1932," Hans Grundig. Staatliche Museen zu Berlin, Nationalgalerie. 683 Courtesy, Pan American World Airways, Inc. 684 Henry Ford Museum. 685 UPI/Bettmann. 686*t* "Langston Hughes," (1902–1967), Carl Van Vechten. Hand gravure print, 1939. The Studio Museum in Harlem. Courtesy, Eakins Press Foundation; *b* Photofest. 689, 690 Courtesy, Conservative Research Department, London. 692 Hugo Jaeger, Life Magazine © Time Warner Inc. 693 Wide World Photos. 697 Bildarchiv Preussischer Kulturbesitz. 700 Roger-Viollet. 701 "Guernica," 1937, Pablo Picasso. © Museo del Prado,

Madrid. (c) ARS, New York/SPADEM, Paris, 1987. 703 From *As I Saw It: A Review of Our Times with 311 Cartoons and Notes* by D. R. Fitzpatrick (New York: Simon and Schuster, 1953). 706 Painting by Junghaus. U.S. Air Force Art Collection. 709 Courtesy, *Richmond Times-Dispatch*. 710 "The Withdrawal from Dunkirk," Charles Cundall. IWM. 711 © 1987 Erich Lessing/Magnum. 713 The Hulton-Deutsch Collection. 715 Poster of Boccasile for Pearl Harbor, 1942. Giancarlo Costa, Milan, photographer. 716 National Archives. 717 National Archives/Imagefinders, Inc. 719 Polish Institute and Sikorski Museum/A. C. Cooper Ltd., photographer. 722 Painting by Takeichi Yamaguchi. Hiroshima-Nagasaki Publishing Company. 723 Roger-Viollet. 724 UPI/Bettmann. 725 "Buchenwald, 1945," Margaret Bourke-White, Life Magazine © Time Warner Inc. 727 "Bewilderment," Henry Sugimoto. Reproduced by permission of Madeleine S. Sugimoto.

Unit IX: 732*t* Steve Vidler/Superstock; *l* Bundesarchiv, Koblenz; *tm* UPI/Bettmann; *bm* "Haitian Landscape," Joseph-Jean Gilles. Museum of Modern Art of Latin America; *r* Harry Redl/Black Star. 733*l* T. Rannou/Gamma-Liaison; *m* Peter Jordan/Gamma-Liaison; *tr* Wide World Photos; *br* Eiji Miyazawa/Black Star. 736 Franklin D. Roosevelt Library, Hyde Park, NY. 738 Wide World Photos. 739 United Nations Photo Archive. 741 Wide World Photos. 744 Bundesarchiv, Koblenz. 749 Rothco Cartoons. 751 Peter Jordan/Gamma-Liaison. 753 Copyright 1960 Time Inc. Reprinted by permission. 754, 755 Wide World Photos. 756 Joseph Kovdelka/Magnum. 760 Rene Burri/Magnum. 762 Diego Goldberg/Sygma. 763 H. Yamagushi/Gamma-Liaison. 766 Suzanne Engelmann/Superstock. 769 Harry Redl/Black Star. 771 Gamma Liaison. 772 Wide World Photos. 775 Baldev Sygma. 777 Alberto Garcia/Gamma-Liaison. 779*t* Wide World Photos; *b* Larry Burrows, Life Magazine © Time Warner Inc. Reprinted with permission. 784 Mark Kauffman, Life Magazine © Time Warner Inc. 790 Camerapix/Gamma-Liaison. 791 © Margaret Courtney-Clarke. 792*l* Abbas/Magnum; *r* A. Tannenbaum/Sygma. 794 Jacques Witt/Sipa Press. 799 Alain Nogues/Sygma. 801 Simonet/Gamma-Liaison. 806 Betty Crowell. 813 Robert Frerck/Odyssey Productions. 814 Copyright 1959 Time Warner Inc.Reprinted by permission. 817 Les Stone/Sygma. 818 P. Dale-Ware/DDB Stock Photo. 819 Silvio/Gamma-Liaison. 821*bl* © 1967 Time Warner Inc. Reprinted by permission; *tr* Medford Taylor/Black Star. 827 Bill Strode/Woodfin Camp & Associates.

Unit X: 828*t* National Aeronautics and Space Administration *l* Charles Feil/Stock, Boston; *tm* World Wide Photos; *bm* Robert Trippett/Sipa Press; *r* Alberto Garcia/Gamma-Liaison. 829*l, m* Gamma-Liaison; *tr* K. Jettmar/Allstock/Picture Group; *br* Jacques Witt/Sipa Press. 830 Lisa Quinones/Black Star. 832 Greenwood/Gamma-Liaison. 833 Charles Feil/Stock, Boston. 834*l* Hank Morgan/Rainbow; *r* Rothco Cartoons. 835 Hemsey/Gamma-Liaison. 838*l* Kevin Horan/Picture Group; *r* K. Jettmar/Allstock/Picture Group. 840 Benson/Gamma-Liaison. 841 United Nations Photo Archive. 844 Shepard Sherdell/Saba Press Photos. 846 ITAR/TASS/Sovfoto. 848*l* Chris Niedenthal/Time Magazine; *r* Rogers/United Features Syndicate. 850 Alexandra Avakian/Contact Press Images. 852 Robert Arail. Courtesy Columbia State (S.C.). 854-5 Eric Bouvet/Gamma-Liaison. 856 Herman Kokojan/Black Star. 859 Adenis/Sipa Press. 862 Tom Stoddart/Katz Pictures. 864 Roger Sanoler/The Picture Group 865 Rama/Sipa Press. 867 Steve Lehman/Saba Press Photos.

Glossary: 899*l* R. Manley/Superstock; *m* (detail) Osterreichische Nationalbibliothek, Vienna; *r* Dundee Art Galleries & Museums. 900*l* Cultural Relics Bureau, Beijing, and MMA; *m* Courtesy of The Pierpont Morgan Library, New York. 901*m* Whipple Museum of the History of Science, University of Cambridge; *r* Bildarchiv Foto Marburg/AR. 902*l* Sovfoto; *m* Henri Lhote, Montrichard, France. 904*l* Lauros-Giraudon/AR; *r* (detail) "Lady with a Parasol," Pierre Auguste Renoir. Museum of Fine Arts, Boston. 905*tm* Culver Pictures; *bm* Michael Holford. 906*m* National Baseball Hall of Fame and Museum, Inc.; *tr* (detail) Ric Ergenbright; *br* Biblioteca Apostolica Vaticana. 907 K. Scholz/Superstock. 908 David Muench. 909*ml* Scala/AR; *bl* Historisches Museen der Stadt Wien; *m* The Board of Trustees of the Royal Armouries, London; *r* BL. 910*tl* Charles Feil/Stock, Boston; *bl* Gamma-Liaison; *r* Ekdotike Athenon. 911*m* (detail) Ann Ronan Picture Library, Somerset, England

General Books

Anderson, Bonnie, and Judith Zinsser. *A History of Their Own: Women in Europe from Prehistory to Present.* Harper Collins.

Brinton, Crane, et al. *A History of Civilization:* 6th ed. Prentice-Hall. (An illustrated survey from prehistoric times to 1715)

Charry, Elias, and Abraham Segal. *The Eternal People.* United Synagogue. (A history of the Jews)

Clark, Kenneth. *Civilisation.* Peter Smith. (World history through art, architecture, and literature)

Fage, J.D. *A History of Africa.* 2nd ed. Knopf. (History of the continent from earliest times to independence)

Goff, Richard, and Walter Moss. *The Twentieth Century.* Wiley. (A brief global history to 1983)

Grun, Bernard. *The Timetables of History.* 3rd ed. Simon & Schuster. (Comparative time charts of world history from prehistoric times to the present, including politics, literature, religion, philosophy, art, music, science, technology, and daily life)

Hourani, Albert. *A History of the Arab Peoples.* Balknap Press.

Keen, Benjamin, and Mark Wasserman. *A History of Latin America.* Houghton Mifflin.

Kennedy, Paul. *The Rise and Fall of the Great Powers.* Random. (Economic change and military history from 1500 to the present)

Langer, William L. *An Encyclopedia of World History.* Houghton Mifflin.

McKay, John P., et al. *A History of World Societies,* 2nd ed. (Vol I: To 1500; Vol II: Since 1500), Houghton Mifflin. (A comprehensive college text incorporating the most recent historical evidences and interpretations)

Mitchell, Brian. *European Historical Statistics.* Facts on File.

Palmer, R.R., and Joel Colton. *A History of the Modern World.* Knopf. (Includes analysis of factors that shaped the transition to modern society)

Smith, Vincent. *The Oxford History of India,* 4th ed. Oxford University Press.

Atlases

Baines, John, and Jaromir Maleh. *Atlas of Ancient Egypt.* Facts on File. (Includes topographical maps, photographs, and drawings)

Barraclough, Geoffrey. *The Times Concise Atlas of World History.* Hammond. (A classic reference)

Catchpole, Brian. *A Map History of Our Times.* Heinemann.

Matthew, David. *Atlas of Medieval Europe.* Facts on File.

McEvedy, Colin. *Atlas of African History.* Penguin. (African cultures, kingdoms, migrations, trade, wars, European contact; 59 maps)

Palmer, R.R. *Atlas of World History.* Rand McNally.

Robinson, Francis. *Atlas of the Islamic World since 1500.* Facts on File.

Book Series for the Student

Greenhaven World History Program. General editors: Malcolm Yapp, Margaret Killingray, and Edmund O'Connor. (Illustrated narratives of specific topics in world history, including biographies, profiles of civilizations, the great revolutions, great issues and ideas, and economic, political, social, and cultural transformations)

Religions on File. Facts on File. A collection of comparative religions with 650 charts or diagrams. Titles include, for example, *Ancient Religions, Hinduism, Asian Religions,* and *Christianity.*

Time-Life's The Emergence of Man, Great Ages of Man, and Treasures of the World. Titles include, for example, *Cradle of Civilization* (Samuel Noah Kramer on Mesopotamia), *Ancient China* (Edward H. Shafer), *Early Islam* (Desmond Stuart), *The First Americans* (Robert Claiborne), *The Israelis* (Time-Life editors), *Byzantium* (Phillip Sherrard), *Rise of Russia* (Robert Wallace), *Historic India* (Lucille Schulberg), and many others.

TimeFrame, a Time-Life series of books arranged chronologically and covering all main developments in world history. Titles for the periods from prehistoric times to A.D. 600 include, for example, *Age of God Kings, Barbarian Tides, A Soaring Spirit, Empires Ascendant,* and *Empires Beseiged.*

Video Series

The Ascent of Man, Jacob Bronowski/BBC/Time-Life Films. (13 episodes), Ambrose Video Publishing. (Two million years of human invention in technology, science, and philosophy)

Civilization, Sir Kenneth Clark/BBC. (13 episodes), Films, Inc. (Cultural history of human civilization)

The Greatest Thinkers, Edward de Bono/Blackbox. (13 programs), Social Studies School Service. (The thoughts of 13 thinkers whose ideas have shaped history, from Moses to Norbert Wiener)

A Walk through the 20th Century with Bill Moyers. (21 programs), PBS Video. (Narrated analysis of themes in twentieth century world history based on newsreel footage and historic photographs)

Technology Products

Listings and Reviews

Braun, Joseph A., Jr. *Microcomputers and Social Studies: A Resource Guide for the Middle and Secondary Teacher.* New York: Garland Pub., 1987. (Includes extensive software bibliography)

Ehman, Lee, and Allen Glenn. *Computer-Based Education in Social Studies.* ERIC Clearinghouse. (Trends in the use of computers in teaching social studies)

Software Reviews on File. New York: Facts on File. (Monthly reviews of new educational software, including social studies)

TESS: The Educational Software Selector. New York: EPIE Institute (Educational Products Information Exchange), 1989. (Reviews software for classroom use; extensive listings in world history)

Software

Balance of Power. Mindscape Educational Software/SVE. (Multi-level simulation with maps and database to teach global politics)

Code: EUROPE! Compu-Teach. (Game about European history, geography, trade, arts, and culture)

Culture 2.0: Guide to Western Civilization. Cultural Resources, Inc. (Multimedia guide to 3,700 years of history, art, literature, music, philosophy, and religion)

Global Recall 2.0. World Game Institute. (Interactive world atlas that covers economy, environment, food, energy, education, leaders, etc.; problem-solving feature)

MacTimeLiner/TimeLiner. Tom Snyder Productions, Inc. (Allows students to create time lines and merge data from the following data disks: A Day in the Life of . . . , Events of the 70's and 80's, Pre- and Ancient History, Women in History, World History)

The Other Side. Tom Snyder Productions, Inc. (Global conflict resolution)

Power of Nation States. International Society for Technology in Education. (Lessons, resource materials, and statistics for 167 nations of the modern world; contains databases and spreadsheets)

Revolutions: Past, Present, and Future. Focus Media, Inc. (Analysis of conditions leading to revolution)

Rise and Fall. Heizer Software. (Interactive maps of Europe that show Germany's expansion before and during World War II)

Seven Cities of Gold. Electronic Arts. (Simulation role play of the world of 16th-century Spanish conquistadors

The Stack of the Decades. Heizer Software. (HyperCard™ stack that includes a card with data about major events and people for each decade from 1650 to present)

SVE AutoGraph. Mindscape Educational Software/SVE. (Graph-making tool for pictographs, bar graphs, line graphs, and circle graphs)

TimeTreks. Earthquest, Inc. (Adventure game about world history from 3400 B.C. to present)

The Time Tunnel: European History Series. Focus Media, Inc. (Clues to help students apply historical knowledge to glimpse into the past)

Videodisc (Laserdisc)

Communism and the Cold War. Optical Data Corporation. (Level III; covers history and politics of the Cold War, and events that led to the collapse of communism; in English and Spanish)

Eagle and the Bear Series. Coronet/MTI. (Level I; covers historical events in the following years and places: *1943, Europe; 1954, Vietnam; 1961, Berlin; 1962, Cuba; 1968, Saigon; 1980, Gdansk; 1985, Moscow; 1989, Berlin; 1989, Prague; 1989, Romania; 1989, Tiananmen Square*

The First Emperor of China. The Voyager Company. (Level I; includes video footage of Qin Shi Huang Di excavation, Qin Museum, and Great Wall, still frame library, and commentary by excavation team and other scholars; in English and Mandarin)

Images of the French Revolution. G.K. Hall. (Level III; includes engravings, medals, maps, etc. with cross-reference capabilities)

In the Holy Land. Optical Data Corporation. (Level III; covers issues and events relevant to Israeli and Palestinian conflict)

The Middle East Series. Encyclopedia Britannica Educational Corporation. (Level I; 14 programs on 7 discs that cover Middle Eastern history, politics, culture, and economics)

Out of the Ashes (1945–1949). AIMS Media. (Level I; includes Nuremburg trials, the beginning of the Cold War, Mao Tse-Tung's establishment of communism on mainland China, etc.)

Policing the Peace (1948–1951). AIMS Media. (Level I; includes Israel's statehood, India's independence, the assassination of Ghandi, etc.)

Prelude to War (1935–1939). AIMS Media. (Level I; covers events prior to WWII in America, Germany, Japan, and Russia)

The Price of Peace (1917–1918). AIMS Media. (Level I; covers the final days of WWI)

Road to War Series Coronet/MTI. (Level I; events leading to WWII in various countries)

Seeds of Discord (1933–1936). AIMS Media. (Level I; events in Germany, Italy, India, Cuba, China, Japan, France, and Yugoslavia prior to WWII)

The Western Civilization Videodisc. Instructional Resources Corporation. (Levels I/III; 2,100 color and black-and-white historical images)

The World History Videodisc (Non-European History). Instructional Resources Corporation. (Levels I/III; narrated historical overviews, maps, and images)

CD-ROM

Countries of the World Encyclopedia. Bureau of Electronic Publishing. (Includes materials from foreign embassies, maps, photographs of historical figures, national anthems, etc.)

Great Cities of the World, Volumes I & II. InterOptica. (Data on ten cities in each volume)

Great Wonders of the World. InterOptica. (Includes Great Wall of China, Trans-Siberian Railway, Taj Mahal, etc.)

History of the World. Bureau of Electronic Publishing. (Covers history from cave dwellers to present)

Mediasource: Historical Library. Applied Optical Media Corporation. (Covers events and personalities from antiquity through World War II)

Middle East Diary. Quanta Press, Inc. (Includes a review of history, personalities, and conflicts; data to make decisions about Mid-East travel)

Picture Atlas of the World. National Geographic Society. (Interactive maps with political, topographic, regional, and continental data)

Time Traveler CD. Orange Cherry New Media. (Interactive exploration of all human history from 4000 B.C. to present)

Sources for Technology Products

AIMS Media
9710 DeSoto Avenue
Chatsworth, CA 91311-4409

Applied Optical Media Corporation
1450 Boot Road
Building 400
West Chester, PA 19380

Bureau of Electronic Publishing
141 New Road
Parsippany, NJ 07054

Compu-Teach
78 Olive Street
New Haven, CT 06511

Coronet/MTI Film & Video
108 Wilmot Road
Deerfield, IL 60015

Cultural Resources, Inc.
7 Little Falls Way
Scotch Plains, NJ 07076

Electronic Arts
1820 Gateway Drive
San Mateo, CA 94404

Encyclopedia Britannica
  Educational Corporation
310 South Michigan Avenue
Chicago, IL 60604-9839

Focus Media, Inc.
839 Stewart Avenue
P.O. Box 865
Garden City, NY 11530

G.K. Hall and Company
70 Lincoln Street
Boston, MA 02111

Heizer Software
1941 Oak Park Boulevard #30
Pleasant Hill, CA 94523

Instructional Resources
  Corporation
1819 Bay Ridge Avenue
Annapolis, MD 21403

International Society for
  Technology in Education
1787 Agate Street
University of Oregon
Eugene, OR 97403

InterOptica Publishing Limited
300 Montgomery Street
San Francisco, CA 94104

Mindscape Educational
  Software/SVE
Department E
1345 Diversey Parkway
Chicago, IL 60614-1299

National Geographic Society,
Educational Media Division
1145 17th Street NW
Washington, DC 20036

Optical Data Corporation
30 Technology Drive
Box 4919
Warren, NJ 07059

Orange Cherry New Media
P.O. Box 390
Westchester Avenue
Pound Ridge, NY 10576

Quanta Press, Inc.
1313 Fifth Street SE
Suite 208-C
Minneapolis, MN 55414

Tom Snyder Productions, Inc.
80 Coolidge Hill Road
Watertown, MA 02172-2817

The Voyager Company
1351 Pacific Coast Highway
Santa Monica, CA 90401

World Game Institute
3508 Market Street
Philadelphia, PA 19104

Unit I
The Beginnings of Civilization

Books for Teachers

Cotterell, Arthur, ed. *The Penguin Encyclopedia of Ancient Civilizations*. Viking Penguin. (Overview of the early cultures of Egypt, India, Asia, and Europe)

Fagan, Brian M. *World Prehistory*. Little, Brown. (A brief introduction describing patterns and trends in prehistoric societies that can be inferred from archaeological evidence)

Kramer, Samuel Noah. *History Begins at Sumer: Thirty-Nine Firsts in Man's Recorded History*. Doubleday. (Sumerian law, government, politics, agriculture, and daily life)

Mendelssohn, Kurt. *The Riddle of the Pyramids*. Thames Hudson.

Mertz, Barbara. *Red Land, Black Land: Daily Life in Ancient Egypt*. Peter Bedrick Books.

Starr, Chester G. *A History of the Ancient World*. Oxford University Press.

Trigger, Bruce G., et al. *Ancient Egypt: A Social History*. Cambridge University Press.

Books for Students

Ceram, C.W. *Gods, Graves, and Scholars: The Story of Archaeology*. Random House. (Popular account of archaeological digs in Babylonia, Sumeria, Assyria, and Egypt)

Coolidge, Olivia. *Egyptian Adventures*. Houghton Mifflin.

Johanson, Donald, and Kevin O'Farrell. *Journey from the Dawn: Life with the World's First Family*. Villard Books (Random)

Leroi-Gourhan, Andre. *The Hunters of Prehistory*. Macmillan. (Recreation of the life of prehistoric people)

Lewin, Roger. *In the Age of Mankind*. Smithsonian. (Study of the theory of human evolution and the controversies that have surrounded it)

Audiovisual Materials

Ancient River Civilizations. (3 cassettes/filmstrips or 1 video), Social Studies School Service. (Shows relationship between geography and history)

Iraq: Stairway to the Gods. (16 mm or video), Coronet/MTI. (Contributions of the Sumerians and the Assyrians to civilization)

Mysteries of Mankind. (Video), National Geographic. (Emmy award-winning series on human origins)

Pakistan: Mound of the Dead. (16 mm or video), Coronet/MTI. (The discovery of Mohnejo-Daro in the Indus River valley)

Rise of Civilization. (6 sound filmstrips), Encyclopaedia Britannica Educational Corporation. (Comparative overview of the Egyptian, Mesopotamian, Indian, and Chinese cultures)

Unit II
The Mediterranean World

Books for Teachers

Bowder, Diana, ed. *Who Was Who in the Greek World, 776 B.C.–30 B.C.* Cornell University Press. (Notable men and women; includes maps, bibliography, glossary, lineage charts; companion volume to *Who Was Who in the Roman World*)

Gibbon, Edward. *The Decline and Fall of the Roman Empire*. Penguin. (Abridged in one volume)

Grant, Michael. *Myths of the Greeks and Romans*. NAL/Dutton.

Hamilton, Edith. *The Greek Way*. Avon (Informal appreciation of Greek culture)

————. *The Roman Way*. Avon. (Roman customs, codes of conduct, and life-styles)

Kitto, H.D.F. *The Greeks*. Penguin. (Classic work on the Greek people, their way of life, and their lasting legacy)

The Oxford History of the Classical World. Oxford University Press. (Comprehensive survey of the Greek and Roman world)

Pomeroy, Sarah. *Women·in Classical Antiquity*. Schocken Books.

Stobart, J.C. *The Grandeur That Was Rome*. Merrimack. (Classic source on Roman history)

Books for Students

Asimov, Isaac. *The Greeks: A Great Adventure*. Houghton Mifflin. (Account of the development of Greek civilization)

Greece and Rome: Builders of Our World. National Geographic Society. (Illustrated text)

Levi, Peter. *Atlas of the Greek World*. Facts on File. (Includes 60 maps and 500 illustrations)

Nichols, Roger, and Kenneth McLeish. *Through Greek Eyes*. Cambridge. (Text with generous use of primary sources)

Payne, Robert. *The Horizon Book of Ancient Rome*. American Heritage.

Audiovisual Materials

Ancient Greek Civilization. (4 cassettes/filmstrips), Clearvue, Inc. (All aspects of Greek culture from Minoan Crete to classical times)

Greek and Roman Mythology. (3 cassettes/filmstrips or 3 videos), Clearvue, Inc. (Greek and Roman creation myths and stories of the Olympian gods)

Light of the Gods. (Video), Social Studies School Service. (Study of 500 years of Greek art)

Our Heritage from Ancient Greece. (Filmstrip-on-video), Guidance Associates. (Traces the Greek legacy)

Our Heritage from Ancient Rome. (Filmstrip-on-video), Guidance Associates. (Traces the Roman legacy)

The Roman Empire and Its Civilization. (4 cassettes/filmstrips or video), Clearvue, Inc. (Overview from the founding of Rome to the decline of the Roman Empire)

Turkey: Crossroads of the Ancient World. (16 mm or video), Coronet/MTI. (The geographic significance of the Anatolian peninsula from prehistoric times to the present, including the region's role in the histories of Assyria, Persia, Greece, Rome, and Byzantium)

Unit III
The Middle Ages

Books for Teachers

Hitti, Philip K. *The Arabs*. Regnery. (Culture history)

Kelly, Amy. *Eleanor of Aquitaine and the Four Kings*. Harvard University Press. (Out of print, but classic biography of Eleanor, queen of France and of England in the Middle Ages)

Maalouf, Amin. *The Crusades through Arab Eyes*. Schocken. (Based on early documents)

Power, Eileen. *Medieval People*. Harper. (An account of the lives of six individuals living in the Middle Ages)

Rorig, Fritz. *The Medieval Town*. University of California Press.

Tuchman, Barbara. *A Distant Mirror: The Calamitous 14th Century*. Knopf. (An account of the age of chivalry, the writings of Chaucer and Petrarch, and the Black Death)

Von Simson, Otto. *The Gothic Cathedral*. Harper. (Study of the meaning behind the art and architecture)

White, Lynn, Jr. *Medieval Technological and Social Change*. Oxford. (Examines the effects of technology on the rise of social groups in the Middle Ages)

Books for Students

Cosman, Madeline Pelner. *Fabulous Feasts: Medieval Cookery and Ceremony*. George Braziller.

Fremantle, Anne. *Age of Belief*. NAL/Dutton. (Introduction to medieval philosophy)

Gies, Frances. *The Knight in History*. Harper & Row.

Gies, Frances, and Joseph Gies. *Life in a Medieval City*. Harper & Row.

Gies, Joseph, and Frances Gies. *Life in a Medieval Castle*. Harper & Row.

————. *Women in the Middle Ages*. Harper & Row.

Lewis, Bernard. *Islam and the Arab World*. American Heritage.

Ross, James Bruce, and Mary Martin McLaughlin, eds. *The Portable Medieval Reader*. Viking. (Collection of primary sources)

Wernick, Robert. *The Vikings*. Time-Life series, The Seafarers.

Audiovisual Materials

The Crusades. (2 cassettes/ filmstrips or video), Clearvue, Inc. (Highlights cultural conflicts of first three Crusades)

The Great Thaw. (Video), Films, Inc. (Developments in Europe during the eleventh and twelfth centuries in education, architecture, religion, and the rise of nations. One of 13 programs in the television series *Civilization*)

Islam and the Sciences. (16 mm or video), Phoenix/BFA Films, Inc. (Seventh century Arab countributions in medicine, mathematics, and physics)

Medieval Art and Music. (2 cassettes/filmstrips or video), Clearvue, Inc. (Illuminated manuscripts, tapestries, paintings and sculpture, stained glass, architecture, and music)

The Middle Ages. (3 videos), BBC/Social Studies School Service. (Covers castles, cathedrals, revolts, and daily life.)

The Middle Ages: A Wanderer's Guide to Life and Letters. (Video), Coronet/MTI. (Includes narratives from period writings.)

Unit IV
An Age of Empires

Books for Teachers

Brundage, Burr C. *The Fifth Sun: Aztec Gods, Aztec World*. (Texas Pan American Series) University of Texas Press.

Cobo, Bernabe. *History of the Inca Empire*. (Roland Hamilton tr. from Spanish, Texas Pan American Series) University of Texas Press.

Cole, Wendell. *Kyoto in the Momoyama Period*. University of Michigan Press. (The social, political, and cultural changes in Japan between 1573 and 1615)

Cotterell, Arthur, et al. *China: A Concise Cultural History*. (Survey of history with emphasis on arts and technology)

Davidson, Basil. *A History of West Africa, 1000–1800*. Longman. (Includes in-depth description of the great kingdoms)

Fagan, Brian M. *The Great Journey*. Thames and Hudson. (Study of first human settlements in the Americas)

Frazier, Kendrick. *People of Chaco*. (Norton. (A look at one of the spectacular ancient cultures of North America)

Mazuri, Ali A., and Toby Kleban, eds. *The Africans: A Reader*. Greenwood.

Reischauer, Edwin O. *Japan: The Story of a Nation*. Knopf.

Sources of Chinese Tradition. Columbia University Press. (Scholarly work on the national, social, and political applications of Chinese philosophy)

Wolpert, Stanley. *A New History of India*, 2nd ed. Oxford University Press. (Culture history)

Books for Students

Addison, John, et al. *Traditional Africa*. Greenhaven. (Culture history survey)

Chu, Daniel, and Elliott Skinner. *A Glorious Age in Africa*. Doubleday. (Highly readable account of West African empires)

Humble, Richard. *Travels of Marco Polo*. Watts.

Statler, Oliver. *Japanese Inn*. Random House. (A glimpse at life in ancient Japan)

Stuart, Gene S. *The Mighty Aztecs*. National Geographic.

Audiovisual Materials

Caravans of Gold and Kings and Cities. (Video), RM Arts/Social Studies School Service. (Medieval gold trade and workings of ancient African kingdoms)

The Japanese: Yesterday and Today. (2 Videos), Social Studies School Service (Overview of Japan, past and present)

Mexico before Cortez. (Video), Social Studies School Service. (Overview of Toltec and Aztec)

The Mongol Empire: November 18, 1247. (Video), Social Studies School Service. (Descendants of Genghis Khan chart the future course of the empire.)

Unit V
The Spread of New Ideas

Books for Teachers

Bainton, Roland. *Here I Stand: A Life of Martin Luther*. NAL/Dutton.

Bernal, J.D. *Science in History*, Vol. 2. MIT Press. (Development of modern science and its impact on society)

Boorstin, Daniel. *The Discoverers*. Random House. (Breakthroughs that changed human perceptions of the world)

Butterfield, Herbert. *The Origins of Modern Science, 1300–1800*. Free Press. (Scholarly account of contributions to the development of modern scientific theory)

Morison, Samuel Eliot. *Christopher Columbus, Mariner*. New American Library. (Scholarly account of Columbus' voyages)

Warnicke, Retha M. *Women of the English Renaissance and Reformation*. Greenwood.

Books for Students

Bainton, Roland H. *Reformation of the Sixteenth Century*. Beacon.

Burckhardt, Jacob. *The Civilization of the Renaissance in Italy*. Penguin. (Discussion of Renaissance life and thought)

Davidson, Basil. *African Slave Trade*. Little, Brown.

George, Margaret. *Women in the First Capitalist Society: Experiences in Seventeenth Century England*. University of Illinois Press.

Goldstein, Thomas. *Dawn of Modern Science*. Houghton. (Development of science during the Renaissance)

Leon-Portilla, Miguel, ed. *The Broken Spears*. Beacon Press. (Aztec account of the Spanish conquest)

Miles, Dorathy. *Renaissance and Reformation Times*. (Out of print, but classic work on the rebirth of learning and efforts to reform the Church)

Audiovisual Materials

Age of Discovery: English, French, and Dutch Explorations. (16 mm or video), Coronet/MTI. (Follows explorers' routes using map animation.)

Martin Luther. (Video), Social Studies School Service. (Biography of Luther as reformer rather than as rebel)

The Protestant Reformation. (2 cassettes/filmstrips or video), Social Studies School Service. (Underlying causes of the Protestant Reformation and its relationship to the rise of capitalism)

Return to Glory: Michelangelo Revealed. (Video), Social Studies School Service. (History and restoration of the Sistine Chapel frescoes)

The Scientific Revolution. (3 cassettes/filmstrips or 1 video), Clearvue, Inc. (Development of modern science; documentary visuals)

Understanding the Art of the Renaissance: Ideas and Ideals. (Video), Social Studies School Service. (Makes clear the differences between medieval and Renaissance thought)

Unit VI
The Transition to Modern Times

Books for Teachers

Behrens, C.B.A. *The Ancien Regime*. Norton. (Clear explanation of prerevolutionary France's political system)

Durant, Will, and Ariel Durant. *The Age of Napoleon: A History of European Civilization from 1789 to 1815*. Simon & Schuster.

(Classic source focusing on the arts, sciences, politics, philosophy, and manners of the times)

————. *The Age of Voltaire: A History of Civilization in Western Europe from 1715 to 1756*. Simon & Schuster. (Classic source emphasizing the conflict between religion and philosophy)

Gay, Peter. *The Enlightenment: An Interpretation*. Knopf. (Classic account of the ideological development of the period)

Neale, J.E. *Queen Elizabeth I*. Doubleday. (Scholarly, award-winning biography)

Scarisbrick, J.J. *Henry VIII*. University of California. (Historically recognized study of Henry's personality and policies)

Books for Students

Brosse, Jacques. *Great Voyages of Discovery: Circumnavigators and Scientists*. Facts on File. (Explorers and voyaging scientists, 1764–1843)

Crankshaw, Edward. *Maria Teresa*. Macmillan.

Dartford, Gerald P. *The French Revolution*. Wayside. (Readable account of the revolution)

Fraser, Antonia. *Cromwell: The Lord Protector*. Donalid I. Fine, Inc.

George, Margaret. *The Autobiography of Henry VIII*. Ballantine. (Novel account of the English monarch)

Mattingly, Garrett. *The Armada*. Houghton

Palmer, Michael. *Elizabeth I*. Batsford. (Insightful study of Elizabeth's reign)

Audiovisual Materials

Age of Enlightenment in Europe. (16 mm or video), Coronet/MTI. (Leaders and ideas of the Scientific Revolution and of the Enlightenment and their effects on the American and French revolutions)

Elizabeth: The Queen Who Shaped an Age. (Video), Coronet/MTI. (Elizabeth's 40-year reign; original documents)

The French Revolution: 2nd Edition Revised. (2 cassettes/filmstrips or 1 video), Clearvue, Inc. (Focuses on causes and significance)

A Man for All Seasons. (Video), Columbia/Social Studies School Service. (Classic film on Thomas More's opposition to Henry VIII's divorce)

Shakespeare: A Mirror to Man. (Video), Coronet/MTI

Unit VII
The Age of European Dominance

Books for Teachers

Barzun, Jacques. *Darwin, Marx, Wagner: Critique of a Heritage*. University of Chicago Press.

Bowditch, John, and Clement Ramsland, eds. *Voices of the Industrial Revolution*. University of Michigan Press.

Farwell, Byron. *Queen Victoria's Little Wars*. Norton. (Military expeditions undertaken by Great Britain between 1837 and 1901 in Asia, Africa, and Canada)

Graham, Richard. *Independence in Latin America*. McGraw.

Heilbroner, Robert L. *The Worldly Philosophers*. Simon & Schuster. (Describes the lives of influential economists)

Robertson, Priscilla. *Revolutions of 1848*. Princeton University Press.

Rodney, Walter. *How Europe Underdeveloped Africa*. Harvard University Press. (A look at colonialism by a leading Guyanese scholar)

Smith, Page. *The Rise of Industrial America: A People's History of the Post-Reconstruction Era*. McGraw-Hill.

Taylor, Philip A. *The Industrial Revolution in Britain: Triumph or Disaster?* D.C. Heath. (Nineteenth-century essays give insight into workers' problems)

Books for Students

Achebe, Chinua. *Things Fall Apart*. Fawcett/Heinemann. (Novel about impact of imperialism on an African village by a noted Nigerian writer)

Barman, Roderick J. *Brazil: The Forging of a Nation, 1798–1852*. Stanford University Press.

Evans, Arthur N. *Railways*. Cambridge. (Highlights impact of the railroad boom on nations such as Britain, the United States, and Peru)

Hibbert, Christopher. *The Great Mutiny: India, Eighteen Fifty-seven*. Penguin.

Hsu, Immanuel C. *The Rise of Modern China*. Oxford University Press. (Four centuries of Chinese history)

Rose, Jonathan. *Otto von Bismarck*. Chelsea. (Introductory account of the life and times of the German leader)

Salisbury, Harrison E. *Black Night, White Snow: Russia's Revolutions*. Da Capo Press.

Vialls, Christine. *Iron and the Industrial Revolution*. Cambridge University Press. (Life in Great Britain before and during the Industrial Revolution)

Audiovisual Materials

American Lifestyle Series: Inventors. (4 Videos), AIMS Media. (Describes the lives of 4 key scientists and inventors)

Imperialism. (3 cassettes/filmstrips or 1 video), Clearvue, Inc. (Effects of imperialism: Spain in Latin America, Great Britain in India, the multinational division of Africa)

Nineteenth-Century Nationalism. (1 cassette/filmstrip or 1 video), Clearvue, Inc. (Defines the concept of nationalism; examples include Congress of Vienna and Revolutions of 1830 and 1848.)

Westward Expansion. (2 filmstrips-on-video), Guidance Associates. (Chronological survey of westward expansion of the United States)

Unit VIII
Years of Crisis

Books for Teachers

Conot, Robert E. *Justice at Nuremberg*. Carroll & Graf.

Elon, Amos. *Israelis: Founders and Sons*. Viking Penguin. (History of Zionism and the state of Israel)

Shirer, William L. *The Rise and Fall of the Third Reich*. Simon &

Schuster. (History of Nazi Germany)

Tuchman, Barbara. *The Guns of August*. Knopf. (Chronicle of the events that led up to World War I)

Books for Students

Corfe, Tom. *Russia's Revolution*. Cambridge University Press. (From Bloody Sunday in 1905 to *glasnost*)

Hershey, John. *Hiroshima*. Random. (Eyewitness accounts of the effects of the atom bomb; a classic)

Keylin, Arlene, ed. *The Depression Years: As Remembered by the New York Times*. Ayer. (Front pages of the *Times* on the Great Depression, 1929–1939)

Meltzer, Milton. *Rescue: The Story of How Gentiles Saved Jews in the Holocaust*. Harper & Row. (Eyewitness accounts of personal courage in the face of evil)

Audiovisual Materials

Courage to Care. (Video), United Way/Social Studies School Service. (The stories of non-Jewish rescuers who helped Jews during the Holocaust)

A Fragile Peace (1918–1929). (16 mm or video), Coronet/MTI. (World problems following the Treaty of Versailles)

Gandhi. (2 videos), Social Studies School Service. (Attenborough's award-winning film on the life of Gandhi)

Hiroshima and Nagasaki: Was Truman's Decision to Use the Bomb Justified? (Video), Zenger Video/Social Studies School Service.

The Longest Day. (Video), Social Studies School Service. (Acclaimed movie about D-Day from British, German, French, and American perspectives)

The Rise and Fall of the Third Reich. (Video), Social Studies School Service. (From the Weimar Republic to Hitler's death)

The Russian Revolution. (2 cassettes/filmstrips or video), Clearvue, Inc. (Focuses on causes and impact of the revolution through documentary footage)

Ten Days That Shook the World. (Video), Social Studies School Service. (Classic Eisenstein film on the 1917 Russian Revolution)

Warsaw Ghetto. (Video), Social Studies School Service. (Explicit scenes of the destruction of a Jewish community in Poland)

Unit IX
The Modern World

Books for Teachers

Davis, Stephen M. *Apartheid's Rebels*. Yale University Press. (Inside look at the growing strength of the African National Congress)

Hsu, Immanuel C.Y. *China without Mao: The Search for a New Order*. Oxford University Press. (Changes in China under Deng Xiaoping)

Lamb, David. *The Africans*. Random. (Political and social history from the time of independence)

McNaught, Kenneth. *Penguin History of Canada*. Penguin.

Books for Students

Clark, Leon E. *Through African Eyes*. Center for International Training and Education. (Primary accounts of the movement toward independence)

Collins, Larry, and Dominique Lapierre. *O Jerusalem!* Pocket Books. (The first Arab-Israeli war)

Dudley, William, ed. *Japan: Opposing Viewpoints*. Greenhaven Press. (Japanese viewpoints on the nation's role in world affairs)

Gibney, Frank. *Japan: The Fragile Superpower*. Revised edition. NAL/Dutton

Haskins, James. *The Life and Death of Martin Luther King, Jr.* William Morrow.

Paton, Alan. *Cry the Beloved Country*. Scribner. (Novel about apartheid in South Africa)

Skidmore, Thomas E., and Peter H. Smith. *Modern Latin America*. Oxford University Press. (Survey of modern Latin American social and political developments)

Audiovisual Materials
Americas in Transition. (16 mm or 1 video), First Run Icarus Films. (The political history of Chile, Cuba, Dominican Republic, El Salvador, Guatemala, and Nicaragua)
Central America Today. (Video), Social Studies School Service. (Survey of seven Central American nations)
Cold War. (2 cassettes/filmstrips or video), Social Studies School Service. (Topics include the Berlin airlift, Korean War, and Hungarian uprising)
Eastern Europe: The Curtain Rises. (Video), Social Studies School Service. (Report on recent democratization of Eastern European nations)
Pacific Horizons. (Video), Close-Up Foundation/Social Studies School Service. (Looks at the importance of the Pacific Rim)
South Africa: The White Laager. (Video), Coronet/MTI. (A balanced history of the philosophy and policies of apartheid)

Unit X
Perspectives on the Present

Books for Teachers
Cetron, Marvin, and Owen Davies. *American Renaissance: Our Life at the Turn of the 21st Century.* St. Martin's Press. (A look into the next century by two futurists)
De St. Jorre, John. *South Africa Update Series.* Foreign Policy Association. (Regularly updated series to keep readers advised of latest developments in South Africa, from 1990 to present)
Goldfarb, Theodore, ed. *Taking Sides: Clashing Views on Controversial Environmental Issues.* Duskin. (Leading experts debate environmental issues that affect life today and will affect it in the future.)

Gorbachev, Mikhail. *The August Coup: The Truth and the Lessons.* Harper.
———. *Perestroika: A New Thinking for Our Country and the World.* Perennial. (An explanation of *perestroika* by the Soviet leader who designed it)
Rourke, John T. *Taking Sides: Clashing Views on Controversial Issues in World Politics.* Duskin. (Balanced collection of pros and cons on recent issues)
Taubman, William, and Jane A. Taubman. *Moscow Spring.* Summit. (A look at Gorbachev's democratic revolution by two American specialists on Soviet policies)

Books for Students
Eisen, Jonathan. ed. *The Glasnost Reader.* NAL/Dutton. (A wide variety of Soviet views on recent changes under *perestroika* and *glasnost*; for advanced students)
Kaye, Tony. *Lech Walesa.* Chelsea House. (Profile of the founder of Poland's Solidarity)
McCuen, Gary, ed. *Our Endangered Atmosphere—Global Warming and the Ozone Layer.* GEM Publications. (An overview of the issue, with emphasis on how loss of tropical rain forests affects the environment)
Scheel, Randall L. *Introduction to the Future.* ETC. (Introduces students to the concept of future studies, focusing on the need for centralized global planning)

Audiovisual Materials
Communism Today: The Iron Curtain Rises. (Video), Guidance Associates. (First-hand look at former Soviet satellites in what was once called Eastern Europe)
The Effects of Glasnost *on Eastern Europe.* (Video), Close-Up Foundation. (Experts discuss how *glasnost* shattered the Soviet Communist system.)
Global Links. (7 videos), World Bank/Social Studies School Service. (Filmed on location, series highlights why global development of all nations is important to students' own lives.)
The Ozone Layer: How Important Is It? (Video), Social Studies

School Service. (Interrelates study of science and history in a two-part series)
Toward the Year 2000: Can We Survive the Future? (Video), Social Studies School Service. (A series of slides on video that shows positive and negative effects of technological change)

Audiovisual Sources
AIMS Media
9710 DeSoto Avenue
Chatsworth, CA 91311

Ambrose Video Publishing, Inc.
1290 Avenue of the Americas
Suite 2245
New York, NY 10014

Clearvue, Inc.
6465 Avondale Avenue
Chicago, IL 60631

Coronet/MTI Film and Video
108 Wilmot Road
Deerfield, IL 60015

Encyclopaedia Britannica Educational Corporation
310 South Michigan Avenue
Chicago, IL 60604-9839

Facts on File
460 Park Avenue South
New York, NY 10016

Films, Inc.
5547 N. Ravenswood Avenue
Chicago, IL 60640

First Run Icarus Films
153 Waverly Place
New York, NY 10014

Guidance Associates
90 South Bedford Road
Mount Kisco, NY 10549

National Geographic Society
Educational Services
P.O. Box 98019
Washington, DC 20090-8019

PBS Video
1320 Braddock Place
Alexandria, VA 22314

Phoenix/BFA Films, Inc.
2349 Chaffee Road
St. Louis, MO 63146

Social Studies School Service
10200 Jefferson Boulevard
P.O. Box 802
Culver City, CA 90232